A COMPREHENSIVE GRAMMAR OF THE ENGLISH LANGUAGE

A COMPREHENSIVE GRAMMAR OF THE ENGLISH LANGUAGE

Randolph Quirk
Sidney Greenbaum
Geoffrey Leech
Jan Svartvik

Index by David Crystal

Longman
London and New York

Longman Group UK Limited,
Longman House, Burnt Mill, Harlow,
Essex CM20 2JE, England
and Associated Companies throughout the world.

Published in the United States of America
by Longman Inc., New York

First published 1985
Standard edition ISBN 0 582 51734 6
De luxe edition ISBN 0 582 96502 0
Ninth impression 1991 (revised)

British Library Cataloguing in Publication Data
A comprehensive grammar of the English language.
1. English language—Grammar—1950–
I. Quirk, Randolph II. Crystal, David
428.2 PE1112

ISBN 0–582–51734–6

Library of Congress Cataloguing in Publication Data
A comprehensive grammar of the English language.
Bibliography: p.
Includes index.
1. English language—Grammar—195– . I. Quirk, Randolph.
PE1106.C65 1985 428.2 84–27848
ISBN 0–582–51734–6

Set in APS 4 Times and Univers.

Typeset, printed and bound in Great Britain
by William Clowes Limited, Beccles and London.

Designed by Arthur Lockwood

Preface

From the time when we started collaborating as a team in the 1960s, we envisaged not a grammar but a series of grammars. In 1972, there appeared the first volume in this series, *A Grammar of Contemporary English* (*GCE*). This was followed soon afterwards by two shorter works, *A Communicative Grammar of English* (*CGE*) and *A University Grammar of English* (*UGE*, published in the United States with the title *A Concise Grammar of Contemporary English*). These two were in part an abridgment of *GCE*, but what is more significant is that they were deliberately different both from the parent book and from each other. This is particularly obvious in the case of *CGE*, which looks at the whole grammar of the language from a semantic and communicative viewpoint. It is less obviously true of *UGE*, which follows the chapter divisions and in most cases the chapter titles of *GCE*, though in fact the abridgment was accompanied by a good deal of fresh thinking and radical revision.

With *A Comprehensive Grammar of the English Language*, we attempt something much more ambitious: a culmination of our joint work, which results in a grammar that is considerably larger and richer than *GCE* and hence superordinate to it. Yet, as with our other volumes since *GCE*, it is also a grammar that incorporates our own further research on grammatical structure as well as the research of scholars world-wide who have contributed to the description of English and to developments in linguistic theory.

It scarcely needs to be said that we take full collective responsibility for the contents of this book. But what does indeed need to be said is that it has been immeasurably improved as a result of the generous assistance that we have received, not least from our own students. We have benefited too from the perceptive attention that *GCE*, *UGE*, and *CGE* have received from reviewers throughout the world. But in addition to these scholars and writers, in addition also to the numerous scholars that we acknowledged in earlier prefaces, a further willing band of linguists put themselves generously at our disposal in giving detailed attention to earlier drafts of what has become *A Comprehensive Grammar of the English Language*.

Some few have even undertaken the heavy task of giving a detailed critique of the entire book in such an earlier draft. For their searching work to this degree, we are especially indebted to John Algeo, R A Close, and Robert de Beaugrande, who between them produced hundreds of pages of invaluable comments. But we are grateful also to W N Francis and Bengt Jacobsson, who gave comparably generous and skilled attention to large parts of the book.

Many other scholars have helped us with one or more individual chapters or with specific problems in the description of grammar. We list their names, but this can in no way convey our degree of gratitude or indicate the intellectual effort from which we have benefited: V Adams, B Altenberg, E Andersson, W-D Bald, D L Bolinger, J Coates, R Cureton, L Haegeman, R Ilson, S Johansson, H Kakehi (and his Kobe students), H Kinoshita, T

Lavelle, B Lott, C F Meyer, T Nevalainen, W J Pepicello, G Stein, J Taglicht, J Thompson, G Tottie, T Waida, K Wales. The fact that some of these friends are among the most eminent experts in the world on American, British, and other varieties of English has contributed beyond measure to the confidence with which we assign such descriptive labels as 'AmE' and 'BrE'.

Finally, we take great pleasure in making clear that David Crystal's role has extended far beyond what is indicated on the title page. He has not merely provided the detailed index which will make 'information retrieval' possible; in addition, in the course of this onerous and highly specialized task, he has contributed pervasively to the correction of error, the standardization of terminology, and the improvement of presentation.

But this Preface would be sadly incomplete if we did not also record our gratitude to the grant-giving bodies whose financial help (over and above the support we have received from University College London, Lund University, the University of Lancaster, and the University of Wisconsin) has made our research and writing possible: the Leverhulme Trust, the Gulbenkian Foundation, the Social Science Research Council, the British Academy, the Knut and Alice Wallenberg Foundation, the Bank of Sweden Tercentenary Foundation, and our publishers, the Longman Group.

RQ SG GL JS
February 1985

Contents

Pronunciation table

CONSONANTS				VOWELS	
VOICELESS		VOICED			
/p/	pig	/b/	big	/iː/	sheep
/t/	ten	/d/	den	/ɪ/	ship
/k/	cot	/g/	got	/e/	bed
/f/	fat	/v/	vat	/æ/	bad
/θ/	thin	/ð/	then	/ɑː/	calm
/s/	soon	/z/	zero	/ɒ/	pot
/ʃ/	fish	/ʒ/	pleasure	/ɔː/	caught
/tʃ/	cheap	/dʒ/	jeep	/ʊ/	put
/h/	hot	/m/	sum	/uː/	boot
		/n/	sun	/ʌ/	cut
		/ŋ/	sung	/ɜː^{r}/	bird
		/l/	led	/ə/	above
		/r/	red	/eɪ/	day
		/j/	yet	/əʊ/	coal
		/w/	wet	/aɪ/	lie
				/aʊ/	now
				/ɔɪ/	boy
				/ɪə^{r}/	here
				/eə^{r}/	there
				/ʊə^{r}/	poor
				/eɪə^{r}/	player
				/əʊə^{r}/	lower
				/aɪə^{r}/	tire
				/aʊə^{r}/	tower
				/ɔɪə^{r}/	employer

Syllabic consonants are indicated thus: n̩, l̩
/^{r}/ denotes the possibility (*eg* in AmE) of 'postvocalic r'.
For indications of stress, intonation, and other prosodic features see App II.

Abbreviations and symbols

A	adverbial	
A_o	object-related adverbial	
A_s	subject-related adverbial	
AmE	American English	
aux	auxiliary	
BrE	British English	
C	complement	
C_o	object complement	
C_s	subject complement	
comp	comparative	
E	end position of adverbial	
-ed	*-ed* participle form	
eM	end-medial position of adverbial	
I	initial position of adverbial	
iE	initial-end position of adverbial	
iM	initial-medial position of adverbial	
I/M	initial or medial position of adverbial	
-ing	*-ing* participle form	
LOB	Lancaster-Oslo/Bergen corpus	
M	medial position of adverbial	
mM	medial-medial position of adverbial	
NP	noun phrase	
O	object	
O_d	direct object	
O_i	indirect object	
oblig	obligatory	
op	operator	
opt	optional	
pass	passive	
ph	phrasal verb	
ph-pr	phrasal-prepositional verb	
pr	prepositional verb	
R	regular variant (in Ch. 3)	
-s	3rd person singular present tense form	
S	subject	
SEU	Survey of English Usage	
StE	Standard English	
SV	subject + verb	
SVA	subject + verb + adverbial	
SVC	subject + verb + complement	
SVO	subject + verb + object	basic structures
SVOO	subject + verb + 2 objects	
SVOC	subject + verb + object + complement	
SVOA	subject + verb + object + adverbial	

T_1 primary time-orientation (in Ch. 4)
T_2 secondary time-orientation (in Ch. 4)
T_3 tertiary time-orientation (in Ch. 4)
V verb
V-ed_1 past tense form of the verb (in Ch. 3)
V-ed_2 *-ed* participle form of the verb (in Ch. 3)
* unacceptable
?* tending to unacceptability, but not fully unacceptable
? native speakers unsure about acceptability
(*), (?) native speakers differ in their reactions
( ) optional constituent
[ ] comment (with examples); constituent boundaries; phonetic transcription
⟨ ⟩ style label (after examples); modified constituent (7.50); focused unit (8.116)
{ } free alternatives, as in:

$$\text{He came} \left\{\begin{array}{l}\text{to}\\ \text{from}\end{array}\right\} \left\{\begin{array}{l}\text{London}\\ \text{New York}\end{array}\right.$$

[ ] contingent alternatives, as in:

$$\left[\begin{array}{l}\text{He}\\ \text{She}\end{array}\right] \text{does} \left[\begin{array}{l}\text{his}\\ \text{her}\end{array}\right] \text{best}$$

/ alternatives (in examples)
/ / phonological transcription
~ systematic correspondence between structures
≁ no systematic correspondence between structures
△ ellipsis marker, indicating grammatical omission
▲ indicates possible semantic implication (in Ch. 19)
= semantically equivalent
≠ semantically nonequivalent
a 'better GRÀMmar |
Capitals in examples indicate *nuclear* syllables, accents indicate *intonation*, raised verticals *stress*, and long verticals *tone unit boundaries*; for all conventions relating to prosody, see App II.

1 The English language

The English language today

The importance of English

1.1 English is generally acknowledged to be the world's most important language. It is perhaps worth glancing briefly at the basis for that evaluation. There are, after all, thousands of different languages in the world, and each will seem uniquely important to those who speak it as their native language, the language they acquired at their mother's knee. But there are more objective standards of relative importance.

One criterion is the number of speakers of the language. A second is the extent to which a language is geographically dispersed: in how many continents and countries is it used or is a knowledge of it necessary? A third is its functional load: how extensive is the range of purposes for which it is used? In particular, to what extent is it the medium for highly valued cultural manifestations such as a science or a literature? A fourth is the economic and political influence of the native speakers of the language.

1.2 If we restrict the first criterion to native speakers of the language, the number of speakers of English is more than 300 million, and English ranks well below Chinese (which has over three times that number of speakers). The second criterion, the geographical dispersal of the language, invites comparison with (for example) Hebrew, Latin, and Arabic as languages used in major world religions, though only Arabic has a substantial number of speakers. But the spread of English over most of the world as an international language is a unique phenomenon in the world's history: about 1500 million people – over a third of the world's population – live in countries where English has some official status or is one of the native languages, if not the dominant native language. By the third criterion, the great literatures of the Orient spring to mind, not to mention the languages of Tolstoy, Goethe, Cervantes, and Racine. But in addition to being the language of the still more distinguished Shakespeare, English leads as the primary medium for twentieth-century science and technology. The fourth criterion invokes Japanese, Russian, and German, for example, as languages of powerful, productive, and influential nations. But English is the language of the United States, whose gross domestic product in 1980 was more than double that of its nearest competitor, Japan.

No claim has here been made for the importance of English on the grounds of its quality as a language (the size of its vocabulary, its relative lack of inflections, the alleged flexibility of its syntax). The choice of an international language, or lingua franca, is never based on linguistic or aesthetic criteria but always on political, economic, and demographic ones.

The use of English

1.3 English is the world's most widely used language. A distinction is often made that depends on how the language is learned: as a *native* language (or *mother tongue*), acquired when the speaker is a young child (generally in the home), or as a *nonnative* language, acquired at some subsequent period. Overlapping with this distinction is that between its use as a *first* language, the primary language of the speaker, and as an *additional* language. In some countries (particularly of course where it is the dominant native language), English is used principally for internal purposes as an *intranational* language, for speakers to communicate with other speakers of the same country; in others it serves chiefly as an *international* language, the medium of communication with speakers from other countries.

One well-established categorization makes a three-way distinction between a *native* language, a *second* language, and a *foreign* language. As a foreign language English is used for international communication, but as a second language it is used chiefly for intranational purposes. We can distinguish five types of function for which English characteristically serves as a medium when it is a second language: (1) *instrumental*, for formal education; (2) *regulative*, for government administration and the law courts; (3) *communicative*, for interpersonal communication between individuals speaking different native languages; (4) *occupational*, both intranationally and internationally for commerce and for science and technology; (5) *creative*, for nontechnical writings, such as fiction and political works.

Note [a] A bilingual child may have more than one native language, and a bilingual adult may be equally proficient in more than one first language. In some countries, English is one of two or more languages, and as a foreign language too it may be one of several that are known.

[b] Although one's native language is usually also one's first language, it need not be. People may migrate to a country where a language different from their native tongue is spoken. If they become proficient in the new language and use it extensively, that nonnative language may become their first language, displacing the native tongue. Such displacement has occurred, for example, among Pakistanis in the United Kingdom and among Vietnamese in the United States.

[c] Second-language writers in Southeast Asia and in East and West Africa are making important contributions to English literature. Their writings may incorporate features characteristic of their second-language variety, including rhetorical and stylistic features, but they are generally addressed to, and read by, an international English readership.

Native and second language

1.4 English is spoken as a *native* language by more than 300 million people, most of them living in North America, the British Isles, Australia, New Zealand, the Caribbean, and South Africa. In several of these countries, English is not the sole language: the Quebec province of Canada is French-speaking, most South Africans speak Afrikaans or Bantu languages, and many Irish and Welsh people speak Celtic languages. But those whose native language is not English will have English as their *second* language for certain governmental, commercial, social, or educational activities within their own country.

English is also a second language in many countries where only a small proportion of the people have English as their native language. In about twenty-five countries English has been legally designated as an official language: in about ten (such as Nigeria) it is the sole official language, and in some fifteen others (such as India) it shares that status with one or more other languages. Most of these countries are former British territories. Despite the association of the English language with the former colonial rulers, it has been retained for pragmatic reasons: where no one native language is generally acceptable, English is a neutral language that is politically acceptable, at least at the national level, for administrative and legal functions; and as an international language for science and technology it is desirable for higher education. English is an official language in countries of such divergent backgrounds as India, Nigeria, and Liberia, while in numerous other countries (Burma, Thailand, South Korea, and some Middle Eastern countries) it is used in some higher education. In Sri Lanka, English at one time lost its official status, while retaining its social, cultural, and economic importance, but it has been reestablished as an official language; indeed, as a result of the increase in secondary education more people today learn English there than at any time during the colonial period. It has been estimated that English is a second language for well over 300 million people: the number of second-language speakers may soon exceed the number of native speakers, if it has not done so already.

Note The significance of English for higher education in second language countries is reflected in statistics for book publishing and literacy in 1981/82 in India. India emerged as the world's third largest publisher of books in English and forty-one per cent of titles produced there were in English, although only 2.3 per cent of the population were literate in English. But that tiny percentage represented 15 million people.

Foreign language

1.5 By *foreign* language we mean a language used by persons for communication across frontiers or with others who are not from their country: listening to broadcasts, reading books or newspapers, engaging in commerce or travel, for example. No language is more widely studied or used as a foreign language than English. The desire to learn it is at the present time immense and apparently insatiable. American organizations such as the United States Information Agency (USIA) and the Voice of America have played a notable role in recent years, in close and amicable liaison with the British Council, which provides support for English teaching both in the Commonwealth and in other countries throughout the world. The BBC (British Broadcasting Corporation), like the USIA, has notable radio and television facilities devoted to this purpose. Other English-speaking countries such as Australia also assume heavy responsibilities for teaching English as a foreign language.

We shall look more closely in the next sections at the kind and degree of demand, but meantime the reasons for the demand have surely become clear. To put it bluntly, English is a top requirement of those seeking good jobs, and is often the language in which much of the business of good jobs is conducted. It is needed for access to at least half of the world's scientific literature, and the most important scientific journals are in English. It is thus intimately associated with technological and economic development and it is the principal language of international aid. The great manufacturing countries Germany and Japan use English as their principal advertising and sales medium; it is the language of automation and computer technology. Not only is it the universal language of international aviation, shipping, and sport, it is to a considerable degree the universal language of literacy and public communication. It is the major language of diplomacy, and is the most frequently used language both in the debates in the United Nations and in the general conduct of UN business.

Note [a] Some measure of the number and importance of publications in English is provided by the number of translations of English books. In 1977 out of a world total of 50 047 translations of books, 19 577 were from English. The nearest competitors were Russian (6771) and French (6054).

[b] The pervasive influence of English has induced language academies or other language-planning agencies in some countries to attempt to control the range of its functions and to prevent the acceptance of Englishisms (English loan words and loan translations) into their national languages, at least in official writing.

The demand for English

The teaching of English

1.6 The role of chief foreign language that French occupied for two centuries from about 1700 has been assumed by English – except of course in the English-speaking countries themselves, where French or (in the United States) Spanish is the foreign language most widely studied. Although patriotism obliges international organizations to devote far more resources to translation and interpreter services than reason would dictate, no senior post would be offered to a candidate deficient in English. The general equivalent of the nineteenth-century European 'finishing school' in French is perhaps the English-medium school organized through the state education system, and such institutions seem to be even more numerous in the Soviet Union and other East European countries than in countries to the West. There are also innumerable commercial institutions that teach English at all levels and to all ages, both in non-English-speaking countries and in English-speaking countries. Most language learning, of course, takes place in the ordinary schools of the state educational system.

The extent to which English is studied at the school level is shown in one analysis of the educational statistics for 112 countries where English is not a native language, but is either a foreign language or a second language. The study estimates that over 46 million primary school students and over 71 million secondary school students were in English classes in the early 1970s. These figures represent over 15 per cent of the primary school population and over 76 per cent of the secondary school population for those countries. It is significant that English was the medium of instruction for 30 per cent of the primary school students and for nearly 16 per cent of the secondary school students. Estimated figures would have been far higher if statistics for all non-English-speaking countries had been included. (A notable exclusion from the study was the People's Republic of China.) Since the secondary school population is increasing at a rapid rate in the developing countries, we can expect that the number of English learners at the secondary level has increased very considerably since the early 1970s.

Outside the primary and secondary schools, there are large numbers of students in institutions of higher and further education who are learning English for a variety of purposes: as the medium of the literature and culture of English-speaking countries; for access to scholarly and technological publications; to qualify as English teachers, translators, or interpreters; to improve their chances of employment or promotion in such areas as the tourist trade, international commerce, or international programmes for economic or military aid. In countries where it is a second language, English is commonly used as the medium for higher education, at least for scientific and technological subjects, even when it is not so used at the primary or secondary levels.

Many students come from abroad for their higher and further education to English-speaking countries, where English is of course the medium for their studies. In 1979, there were 286 340 foreign students enrolled at the post-secondary level of education in the United States, 56 877 in the United Kingdom, and 32 148 in Canada (where some will have studied in French-speaking institutions), apart from smaller numbers in other English-speaking countries. The country with the next highest figure after the United States was France, which had 112 042 foreign students in the same year.

School models of English

1.7 In countries where English is predominantly the native language, the form of written English taught in the schools is normally the STANDARD variety (*cf* 1.23), the variety associated with the educated users of the language in that country. However, it is now less usual than in the past for teachers to attempt to make the local spoken variety conform with some educated spoken norm.

In countries where English is a nonnative language, the major models for both writing and speech have generally been the standard varieties of British and American English. The choice between them has depended on various factors: whether the country was formerly a British or a US colony; its proximity to Britain or the United States; which of the two had most influenced its economic, cultural, or scientific development; and current commercial or political relations. In some countries both American and British standard varieties are taught, sometimes in different institutions, sometimes in the same institution.

The situation has been changing in those countries where English is a second language, used extensively for intranational purposes in the absence of a commonly accepted national language. In countries such as India and Nigeria indigenous educated varieties are becoming institutionalized and are acquiring social acceptability. In the meantime, teachers in those countries are uncertain, or vary, about the norms to which their teaching should be geared: to those of the evolving local standard or to those of some external standard. Such uncertainties are analogous to the uncertainties among teachers in native-English countries over divided usages or prescriptive norms that differ from their own usage (*cf* 1.17).

Where English is a foreign language, we may expect the American and British standard varieties to continue to be the major models, competing increasingly with the standard varieties of other countries such as Australia, in regions that are within the sphere of influence of those countries.

Note Countries where English is a foreign language may develop, to some extent, independent prescriptive norms that are enshrined in handbooks and textbooks and that are reflected in examination questions.

The international character of English

1.8 English is preeminently the most international of languages. Though the name of the language may at once remind us of England, or we may associate the language with the United States, one of the world's superpowers, English carries less implication of political or cultural specificity than any other living tongue (Spanish and French being also notable in this respect). At one and the same time, English serves the daily purposes of republics such as the United States and South Africa, sharply different in size, population, climate, economy, and national philosophy; and it serves an ancient realm such as the United Kingdom, as well as her widely scattered Commonwealth partners, themselves as different from each other as they are from Britain herself.

But the cultural neutrality of English must not be pressed too far. The literal or metaphorical use of such expressions as *case law* throughout the English-speaking world reflects a common heritage in the legal system; and allusions to or quotations from Shakespeare, the Authorized (or King James) Version of the Bible, Gray's *Elegy*, Mark Twain, a sea shanty, a Negro spiritual, or a pop song – wittingly or not – testify similarly to a shared culture. *The Continent* can have its British meaning of 'continental Europe' in the United States and even in Australia and New Zealand. At other times, English equally reflects the independent and distinct culture of one or other of the English-speaking communities. When an Australian speaks of *fossicking* something out ['searching for something'], the metaphor looks back to the desperate activity of reworking the diggings of someone else in the hope of finding gold that had been overlooked. When an American speaks of *not getting to first base* ['not achieving even initial success'], the metaphor concerns an equally culture-specific activity – the game of baseball. And when an Englishman says that something is *not cricket* ['unfair'], the allusion is also to a game that is by no means universal in the English-speaking countries.

The future of English

1.9 Predictions – often gloomy – have been made about the future of English. It is worth considering the bases for such predictions with respect to the various uses of English.

A single international language has long been thought to be the ideal for international communication. Artificially-constructed languages have never acquired sufficiently large numbers of adherents, although in principle such languages have the obvious advantage that they put all learners on the same footing (all are nonnative speakers), thereby not giving an advantage to speakers of any particular language. During the last few decades English has come closest to being the single international language, having achieved a greater world spread than any other language in recorded history. Yet in recent years doubts have arisen whether it will ever reach the ideal of the single international language or, indeed, whether its use as an international language will continue at the present level.

One reason for the doubts has been the fear that national varieties of English are rapidly growing further apart and will finally separate into mutually incomprehensible languages. Fears have also been expressed that justifiable sensitivity to the child's right to use his native dialect (regional, socioeconomic, or ethnic) within a national variety might lead to the abandonment of a national standard dialect and hence to the further disintegration of English. The diversity in English is greatest in countries where English is a second language and therefore has to be taught. Since in those countries students are usually taught by teachers who are themselves not native speakers of English and who have inevitably acquired the language to varying degrees of adequacy, it is not surprising that the standards of achievement are variable and subject to change. Some express concern about the excessive internal variability and the ill-acquired control of the language in such situations. Some fear the divisive effect of the emerging institutionalized varieties, which no longer look to native varieties for standards of acceptability.

1.10 While fears for the disintegration of English cannot be dismissed summarily, powerful forces are operating to preserve the unity of the language. Despite considerable dialectal differences within each national variety, the education systems have preserved the essential similarity of the national standards. The traditional spelling system generally ignores both the changes in pronunciation over time and the variations in pronunciation through space; despite its notorious vagaries, it is a unifying force in world English. Many factors are conducive to making differences in national varieties familiar and comprehensible: there is the influence of newspapers, magazines, and books on the written medium and of radio, television, and film on the spoken medium. Teachers and students can be made sensitive to, and tolerant of, language variation, and national examination systems can be made flexible enough to take account of variation. Despite a growing tolerance of nonstandard variation in speech, standard forms remain the norm for written English.

The future of English as an international language has also been said to rest on the practicability of teaching the language, especially on a mass scale, to the level required for international usefulness, given the enormous expenditures required for the purpose. It is possible that as developing countries become richer they will be able to increase their expenditure on the teaching of English and raise the levels of teacher and student proficiency. At all events, programmes have been devised to restrict the goals of language learning, thereby allowing a more realistic deployment of educational resources, as in the Teaching of English for Specific Purposes, for example for business or scientific communication. Following earlier attempts (such as 'Basic English') that were largely lexical, a proposal has also recently been made for constructing a simplified form of English (termed 'Nuclear English') that would contain a subset of the features of natural English; for example, modal auxiliaries such as *can* and *may* would be replaced by such paraphrases as *be able to* and *be allowed to*. The simplified form would be intelligible to speakers of any major national variety and could be expanded for specific purposes, for example for international maritime communication.

The long-range continuance of English as a second language is also questionable in some countries. The eagerness for rapid technological advancement conflicts with the demands for the establishment of authentic links with past native traditions: objections to an official status for English and calls for its replacement by native languages are expressions of national pride and independence. Since a good command of English is usually restricted to an elite, we may expect political resentment against a minority second language that brings benefits to those proficient in it. English is likely to be retained as an official language as long as no specific native language is politically acceptable to all, but we can expect that in at least some countries indigenous languages will become sufficiently dominant to acquire sole official status and eventually to displace English. In such cases English will gradually become recognized as a foreign language. However, irrespective of the degree of world influence exercised by the English-speaking countries themselves, English is likely to be retained generally as the medium for higher education as long as the major English-speaking countries retain their economic and political status.

Standards of English

1.11 Complaints by native speakers that English is deteriorating or being corrupted reflect in the main a conservative resistance to change. Some language changes result in the loss of distinctions, but if a distinction is needed the loss will be compensated for. For example, in some regional varieties the distinction between the singular and plural meanings of *you* has been retained by the use of such expressions as *you-all* or *you guys* for the plural meanings (*cf* 6.12 Notes [a, b]). The introduction of specific new words or expressions (such as *prioritize* or *interface*) sometimes provokes violent indignation, often conveyed in ethical terms. Usually the objections to the innovations (or supposed innovations) reflect objections to their typical users. Some of the complaints relate to variants that are in divided usage among speakers of the standard variety; for example, *graduated from* and *was graduated from* in American English, or *different from* and *different to* in British English. In yet other instances the forms are clearly recognized as unacceptable in the standard variety (such as the multiple negative in *I don't want no money from no one*; *cf* 10.63 Note), though they may be acceptable in some nonstandard varieties. Relatively few points are at issue. They do not justify generalizations about the state of the language as a whole.

Some native speakers claim that the *use* of the language is deteriorating. One charge is ethical: people are said to be abusing the language, more so than in the past, with intent to conceal, mislead, or deceive, generally through euphemism or obscure language. Usually, the accusation is directed principally against politicians, bureaucrats, and advertisers, but the abuse is felt to have an adverse effect on the language as such. Certainly, the contemporary mass media facilitate the rapid and widespread dissemination of such language abuses. The other charge is aesthetic or functional: people are said to be using the language less elegantly or less efficiently than in the recent past, a charge that is commonly directed against young people. The charge may or may not have some justification, but in any case is impossible to substantiate. Many variables inhibit the feasibility of making valid and reliable comparisons with earlier periods: for example, the phenomenal growth of the literate population and of the use of the written language.

Note On standard and nonstandard English, *cf* 1.22. On varieties of standard English, *cf* 1.23*ff*.

Grammar and the study of language

Types of linguistic organization

Sounds and spellings

1.12 We claim that on the one hand there is a single English language (the grammar of which is the concern of this book), and that on the other hand there are recognizable varieties. Since these varieties can have reflexes in any of the types of organization that the linguist distinguishes, this is the point at which we should outline the types, one of which is grammar. When people speak, they emit a stream of sounds. We hear the sounds not as indefinitely variable in acoustic quality (however much they may be so in actual physical fact). Rather, we hear them as each corresponding to one of the very small set of sound units (in English, /p/, /l/, /n/, /ɪ/, /ð/, /s/ . . .) which can combine in certain ways and not in others. For example, in English we have *spin* but not **psin*. (On the use of the asterisk and similar symbols, see 1.42.) We similarly observe patterns of stress and pitch. The rules for the organization of sound units (or phonemes) are studied in the branch of linguistics known as PHONOLOGY, while the physical properties of sounds and their manner of articulation are studied in PHONETICS.

The other major method of linguistic communication is by writing; and for English as for many other languages an alphabetic writing system has been developed, the symbols related in the main to the individual sounds used in the language. Here again there is a closely structured organization which regards certain differences in shape as irrelevant and others (for example capitals versus lower case, ascenders to the left or right of a circle, *eg*: *b* versus *d*) as significant. The study of ORTHOGRAPHY (or more inclusively, GRAPHOLOGY or GRAPHEMICS) thus parallels the study of phonology in several ways. Despite the notorious oddities of English spelling, there are general principles: *eg* combinations of letters that English permits (*tch*, *qu*, *ss*, *oo*) and others that are disallowed (**pfx*, **qo*) or have only restricted distribution (final *v* or *j* occurs only exceptionally as in *Raj*, *spiv*).

Lexicology, grammar, semantics, pragmatics

1.13 Just as the small set of arabic numerals can be combined to express in writing any natural numbers we like, however vast, so the small set of sounds and letters can be combined to express in speech and writing respectively an indefinitely large number of WORDS. These linguistic units enable people to refer to every object, action, and quality that members of a society wish to distinguish: in English, *door*, *soap*, *indignation*, *find*, *stupefy*, *good*, *uncontrollable*, and so on to a total exceeding the half million words listed in unabridged dictionaries. These units have a meaning and a structure (sometimes an obviously composite structure as in cases like *uncontrollable*) which relate them not only to the world outside language but to other words within the language (*happy* to *happiness*, *unhappy*, etc; *good* to *bad*, *kind*, etc; *door* to *room*, *key*, etc). The study of words is the business of LEXICOLOGY, but the regularities in their formation are similar in kind to the regularities of grammar and are closely connected to them (*cf* App I.1*ff*). It is GRAMMAR that is our primary concern in this book. Words must be combined into larger units, and grammar encompasses the complex set of rules specifying such combination. Meaning relations in the language system are the business of SEMANTICS, the study of meaning, and semantics therefore has relevance equally within lexicology and within grammar. Finally, the meaning of linguistic expressions when uttered within particular types of situation is dealt with in PRAGMATICS, which is concerned with the communicative force of linguistic utterances. Two terms are employed for the interconnection of grammar and the uses of grammar: TEXT LINGUISTICS and DISCOURSE ANALYSIS. All types of organization (but notably lexicology and grammar) enter into the structure of TEXTS, which constitute spoken and written discourse (*cf* Chapter 19).

The meanings of 'grammar'

Syntax and inflections

1.14 The word 'grammar' has various meanings, and since grammar is the subject matter of this book we should explore the most common meanings of the word. We shall be using 'grammar' to include both SYNTAX and that aspect of MORPHOLOGY (the internal structure of words) that deals with INFLECTIONS (or ACCIDENCE). The fact that the past tense of *buy* is *bought* [inflection] and the fact that the interrogative form of *He bought it* is *Did he buy it?* [syntax] are therefore both equally the province of grammar. There is nothing technical about our usage in this respect: it corresponds to one of the common lay uses of the word in the English-speaking world. A teacher may comment:

John uses good grammar but his spelling is awful.

The comment shows that spelling is excluded from grammar; and if John wrote *interloper* where the context demanded *interpreter*, the teacher would say that he had used the wrong word, not that he had made a mistake in grammar. But in the education systems of the English-speaking countries, it is possible also to use the term 'grammar' loosely so as to include both spelling and lexicology.

There is a further use of 'grammar' that derives from a period in which the teaching of Latin and Greek was widespread. Since the aspect of Latin grammar on which teaching has traditionally concentrated is the paradigms (or model sets) of inflections, it made sense for the learner to say:

Latin has a good deal of grammar, but English has hardly any.

This meaning of 'grammar' has continued to be used by lay native speakers. In effect, grammar is identified with inflections, so that nonspecialists may still speak of 'grammar and syntax', tacitly excluding the latter from the former.

Note The term *grammar school* (used in several English-speaking countries, though not always with reference to the same type of school) reflects the historical fact that certain schools concentrated at one time on the teaching of Latin and Greek. One sometimes comes upon the lay supposition that such schools do or should make a special effort to teach *English* grammar.

Rules and the native speaker

1.15 Nor have we completed the inventory of meanings. The same native speaker, turning his attention from Latin, may comment:

> French has a well-defined grammar, but in English we're free to speak as we like.

To begin with, it is clear that the speaker cannot now be intending to restrict 'grammar' to inflections: rather the converse; it would seem to be used as a virtual synonym of 'syntax'.

Secondly, the native speaker's comment probably owes a good deal to the fact that he does not feel the rules of his own language – rules that he has acquired unconsciously – to be at all constraining; and if ever he happens to be called on to explain one such rule to a foreigner he has very great difficulty. By contrast, the grammatical rules he learns for a foreign language seem much more rigid and they also seem clearer because they have been actually spelled out to him in the learning process.

But another important point is revealed in this sentence. The distinction refers to 'grammar' not as the observed patterns in the use of French but as a codification of rules compiled by the French (especially by the Académie Française) to show the French themselves how their language should be used. This is not grammar 'immanent' in a language (as our previous uses were, however much they differed in the types of pattern they referred to), but grammar as codified by grammarians: the Academy Grammar. There is no such Academy for the English language and so (our naive native speaker imagines) the English speaker has more 'freedom' in his usage.

The codification of rules

1.16 The 'codification' sense of grammar is readily identified with the specific codification by a specific grammarian:

> Jespersen wrote a good grammar, and so did Kruisinga.

And this sense naturally leads to the concrete use as in:

> Did you bring your grammars?

Naturally, too, the codification may refer to grammar in any of the senses already mentioned. The codification will also vary, however, according to the linguistic theory embraced by the authors, their idea of the nature of grammar rather than their statement of the grammar of a particular language:

> Chomsky developed a transformational grammar that differed considerably from earlier grammars.

In the usage of many leading linguists, this last sense of grammar has returned to the catholicity that it had in the Greek tradition more than 2000 years ago, covering the whole field of language structure. Thus, in the framework of formal linguistics, some grammarians speak of 'the grammar' as embracing rules not only for syntax but for phonological, lexical, and semantic specification as well.

Note Accidents of intellectual history in the nineteenth century result in the fact that an old-fashioned

Old High German grammar (or an Old English grammar) may well contain only inflections together with a detailed explanation of how the phonological system emerged.

Prescriptive grammar

1.17 Finally we come to the use of 'grammar' in statements such as:

It's bad grammar to end a sentence with a preposition.

Here the term refers to a way of speaking or writing that is to be either preferred or avoided. Such statements pertain to PRESCRIPTIVE GRAMMAR, a set of regulations that are based on what is evaluated as correct or incorrect in the standard varieties. Since we do not have an Academy of the English Language, there is no one set of regulations that could be considered 'authoritative'. Instead, evaluations are made by self-appointed authorities who, reflecting varying judgments of acceptability and appropriateness, often disagree.

Authorities on USAGE, in this restricted sense, primarily deal with DISPUTED usage, a relatively small number of syntactic and lexical items that are controversial within the standard varieties. Their objections may persuade some to avoid certain usages, at least in their formal writing. Over the last two centuries prescriptive rules have accumulated into a general prescriptive tradition for formal writing that is embodied (with some variation) in school textbooks and student reference handbooks, and in usage guides for the general public.

As an occasional consequence of prescriptive pressures, some speakers have mistakenly extended particular prescriptive rules in an attempt to avoid mistakes. A classic instance of such HYPERCORRECTION is the use of *whom* as subject (*cf* 6.35 Note [a]). Others are the pseudo-subjunctive *were* as in *I wonder if he were here* and the use of the subjective pronoun *I* in the phrase *between you and I*.

Our primary concern in this book is to describe the grammar of English. But we occasionally refer to the prescriptive tradition not only because it may lead to hypercorrection but also because it may affect attitudes towards particular uses that may in turn influence the preferences of some native speakers, at least in formal or more considered styles. It may lead some, for example, to replace their usual *was* by subjunctive *were* in *If I was strong enough, I would help you*, or to replace *who* by *whom* in *the teacher who I most admired*.

Grammar and other types of organization

1.18 Progress towards a more explicit type of grammatical description is inevitably slow and the whole field of grammar is likely to remain an area of interesting controversy. While theoretical problems are not the concern of this book, our treatment cannot be neutral on the issues that enliven current discussion. For example, we would not wish to assert the total independence of grammar from phonology on the one hand and lexicology or semantics on the other as was implied in the deliberate oversimplification of 1.12*f*. Phonology is seen to have a bearing on grammar even in small points such as the association of initial /ð/ with demonstrativeness and conjunctions (*this*, *then*, *though*, etc, *cf* 2.37). More important are the phonological conditions for the *-s* and *-ed* inflections in verbs and nouns (*cf* 3.5*f*, 5.80). It is seen to bear on lexicology, for example, in the fact that some nouns and verbs differ only in the position of the stress (*cf* App I.56):

That is an 'insult.
They may in'sult me.

But most obviously the interdependence of phonology and grammar is shown in focus processes (*cf* the connection between intonation and linear presentation: 18.2*ff*, 19.25*f*), and in the fact that by merely altering the phonology one can distinguish sets of sentences like those quoted in App II.21.

The interrelations of grammar, lexicology, and semantics are manifested in the semantic restrictions (*cf* 10.51) that permit [1] and [2], but not [1a] and [2a]:

Fear replaced indecision. [1]
*John replaced indecision. [1a]
John hated indecision. [2]
*Fear hated indecision. [2a]

The borderline between grammar and semantics is unclear, and linguists will draw the line variously. We shall not give guidance on such constraints in this book.

Similarly, the borderline between grammar and pragmatics (and even more so between semantics and pragmatics) is unclear. Although we shall have occasion to refer to the kinds of intended speech behaviour (such as request and invitation) that may be conveyed through certain sentence types (*cf* particularly Chapter 11), we shall not attempt a comprehensive account. But we shall attempt to give every indication of the meaning of the constructions we discuss.

Our general principle will be to regard grammar as accounting for constructions where greatest generalization is possible, assigning to lexicology (and hence beyond the scope of this book) constructions on which least generalization can be formulated. In applying this principle we will necessarily make arbitrary decisions along the gradient from greatest to least generalization.

Varieties of English

Types of variation

1.19 Having indicated how we may speak of different types of linguistic organization such as phonology, lexicology, and grammar, we may now return to the point we had reached at the beginning of 1.12. What are the varieties of English whose differing properties are realized through the several types of linguistic organization?

Formulating a theoretical basis on which the varieties of any language can be described, interrelated, and studied is one of the prime concerns of the branch of language study called SOCIOLINGUISTICS. This discipline is far from having achieved complete answers, and all attempts are in some degree oversimplifications.

We shall first consider five major types of variation. Any use of language necessarily involves variation within all five types, although for purposes of analysis we may abstract individual varieties (a related set of variation within one type).

(a) region (1.20*f*)
(b) social group (1.22*ff*)
(c) field of discourse (1.28)
(d) medium (1.29*f*)
(e) attitude (1.31*ff*)

The first two types of variation relate primarily to the language user. People use a regional variety because they live in a region or have once lived in that region. Similarly, people use a social variety because of their affiliation with a social group. These varieties are relatively permanent for the language user. At the same time, we should be aware that many people can communicate in more than one regional or social variety and can therefore (consciously or unconsciously) switch varieties according to the situation. And of course people move to other regions or change their social affiliations, and may then adopt a new regional or social variety.

The last three types of variation relate to language use. People select the varieties according to the situation and the purpose of the communication. The field of discourse relates to the activity in which they are engaged; the medium may be spoken or written, generally depending on the proximity of the participants in the communication; and the attitude expressed through language is conditioned by the relationship of the participants in the particular situation. A COMMON CORE or nucleus is present in all the varieties so that, however esoteric a variety may be, it has running through it a set of grammatical and other characteristics that are present in all the others. It is this fact that justifies the application of the name 'English' to all the varieties.

Note We have conspicuously omitted variation in time, since this book is solely concerned with the grammar of present-day English. Variation in the contemporary language, however, reflects in part historical change in progress. At any one period, older variants may coexist with newer variants, and some of the newer variants may eventually become the sole forms.

Regional variation

1.20 Varieties according to region have a well-established label both in popular and technical use: DIALECTS. Geographical dispersion is in fact the classic basis for linguistic variation, and in the course of time, with poor communications and relative remoteness, such dispersion results in dialects becoming so distinct that we regard them as different languages. This latter stage was long ago reached with the Germanic dialects that are now Dutch, English, German, Swedish, etc, but it has not been reached (and may not necessarily ever be reached, given the modern ease and range of communication) with the dialects of English that have resulted from the regional separation of communities within the British Isles and (since the voyages of exploration and settlement in Shakespeare's time) elsewhere in the world.

Regional variation seems to be realized predominantly in phonology. That is, we generally recognize a different dialect from a speaker's pronunciation or accent before we notice that the vocabulary (or LEXICON) is also distinctive. Grammatical variation tends to be less extensive and certainly less obtrusive. But all types of linguistic organization can readily enough be involved. A Lancashire man may be recognized by a Yorkshireman because he pronounces an /r/ after vowels as in *stir* or *hurt*. A *middy* is an Australian measure for beer – but it refers to a considerably bigger measure in Sydney than it does in Perth. Instead of *I saw it*, a New Englander might say *I see it*, a Pennsylvanian *I seen it*, and a Virginian either *I seen it* or *I seed it*, if they were speaking the rural nonstandard dialect of their locality, and the same forms characterize certain dialects within Britain too.

Note [**a**] The attitude of native speakers of one dialect towards the dialects of other native speakers varies greatly, but, in general, dialects of rural and agricultural communities are regarded as more pleasant than dialects of large urban communities such as New York or Birmingham. This is connected, of course, with social attitudes and the association of city dialects with variation according to education and social standing (*cf* 1.22) rather than according to region.
[**b**] Dialectologists and sociolinguists often use the term 'dialect' for social varieties.

1.21 It is pointless to ask how many dialects of English there are: there are indefinitely many, depending on how detailed we wish to be in our observations. But they are of course more obviously numerous in long-settled Britain than in areas more recently settled by Europeans, such as North America or, still more recently, Australia and New Zealand. The degree of generality in our observation depends crucially upon our standpoint as well as upon our experience. An Englishman will hear an American Southerner primarily as an American, and only as a Southerner in addition if further subclassification is called for and if his experience of American English dialects enables him to make it. To an American the same speaker will be heard first as a Southerner and then (subject to similar conditions) as, say, a Virginian, and then perhaps as a Piedmont Virginian. One might suggest some broad dialectal divisions which are rather generally recognized. Within North America, most people would be able to distinguish Canadian, Northern, Midland, and Southern varieties of English. Within the British Isles, Irish, Scots, Northern, Midland, Welsh, Southwestern, and London varieties would be recognized with similar generality. Some of these – the English of Ireland and Scotland for example – would be recognized as such by many Americans and Australians too, while in Britain many people could make subdivisions: Ulster and Southern might be distinguished within Irish English, for example, and Yorkshire picked out as an important subdivision of Northern speech. British people can also, of course, distinguish North Americans from all others (though not usually Canadians from Americans), South Africans from Australians and New Zealanders (though mistakes are frequent), but not usually Australians from New Zealanders.

Social variation

1.22 Within each of the dialects there is considerable variation in speech according to education, socioeconomic group, and ethnic group. Some differences correlate with age and sex. Much (if not most) of the variation does not involve categorical distinctions; rather it is a matter of the frequency with which certain linguistic features are found in the groups.

There is an important polarity between uneducated and educated speech in which the former can be identified with the nonstandard regional dialect most completely and the latter moves away from regional usage to a form of English that cuts across regional boundaries. To revert to an example given in a previous section, an outsider (who was not a skilled dialectologist) might not readily find a New Englander who said *see* for *saw*, a Pennsylvanian who said *seen*, and a Virginian who said *seed*. These are forms that tend to be replaced by *saw* with schooling, and in speaking to a stranger a dialect speaker would tend to use 'school' forms. On the other hand, there is no simple equation of regional and uneducated English. Just as educated English, *I saw*, cuts across regional boundaries, so do many features of uneducated use: a prominent example is the double negative as in *I don't want no cake*, which has been outlawed from all educated English by the prescriptive grammar tradition for over two hundred years but which continues to thrive as an emphatic form in uneducated speech wherever English is spoken.

Educated English naturally tends to be given the additional prestige of government agencies, the professions, the political parties, the press, the law court, and the pulpit – any institution which must attempt to address itself to a public beyond the smallest dialectal community. It is codified in dictionaries, grammars, and guides to usage, and it is taught in the school system at all levels. It is almost exclusively the language of printed matter. Because educated English is thus accorded implicit social and political sanction, it comes to be referred to as STANDARD ENGLISH, and provided we remember that this does not mean an English that has been formally standardized by official action, as weights and measures are standardized, the term is useful and appropriate. In contrast with standard English, forms that are especially associated with uneducated (rather than dialectal) use are generally called NONSTANDARD.

Note 'Substandard' is sometimes used in place of 'nonstandard', but less commonly now than in the past.

Standard English

1.23 The degree of acceptance of a single standard of English throughout the world, across a multiplicity of political and social systems, is a truly remarkable phenomenon: the more so since the extent of the uniformity involved has, if anything, increased in the present century. Uniformity is greatest in orthography, which is from most viewpoints the least important type of linguistic organization. Although printing houses in all English-speaking countries retain a tiny element of individual decision (*eg*: *realize*/*realise*, *judgment*/*judgement*), there is basically a single spelling and punctuation system throughout: with two minor subsystems. The one is the subsystem with British orientation (used in most English-speaking countries other than the United States), with distinctive forms in only a small class of words, *colour*, *centre*, *levelled*, etc. The other is the American subsystem, *color*, *center*, *leveled*, etc. Canadian spelling draws on both systems and is open to considerable variation. Learned or formal publications, such as academic journals and school textbooks, prefer British spellings, while popular publications, such as newspapers, prefer American spelling. Individuals may use both variants according to situation, but sometimes randomly. One difference between the American and British subsystems of punctuation is that the general American practice is to put a period or comma inside closing quotation marks, which are usually double in American usage for the primary set: *The sign said "No smoking."* A further orthographic point may cause Anglo-American misunderstanding: the numerical form of dates. In British (and European) practice 2/10/85 means '2 October 1985', but in American practice it means 'February 10, 1985' (*cf* 6.66).

In grammar and vocabulary, standard English presents somewhat less of a monolithic character, but even so the world-wide agreement is extraordinary and – as has been suggested earlier – seems actually to be increasing under the impact of closer world communication and the spread of identical material and nonmaterial culture. The uniformity is especially close in neutral or formal styles of written English on subject matter not of obviously localized interest: in such circumstances one can frequently go on for page after page without encountering a feature which would identify the English as belonging to one of the national standards (*cf* 1.28*ff*).

National standards of English

British and American English

1.24 What we are calling national standards should be seen as distinct from the standard English which we have been discussing and which we should think of as being supranational, embracing what is common to all. Again, as with orthography, there are two national standards that are overwhelmingly predominant both in the number of distinctive usages and in the degree to which these distinctions are institutionalized: American English ⟨AmE⟩ and British English ⟨BrE⟩. Grammatical differences are few and the most conspicuous are known to many users of both national standards: the fact that AmE has two past participles for *get* and BrE only one (*cf* 3.18), for example, and that in BrE either a singular or a plural verb may be used with a singular collective noun:

The government $\left\{\begin{array}{l}\text{is}\\ \text{are}\end{array}\right\}$ in favour of economic sanctions.

whereas in AmE a singular verb is required here. Some are less familiar, but are unlikely to hamper communication. For example, AmE may use the simple past in informal style in contexts where BrE normally requires the present perfective (*cf* 4.20 Note), as in:

$\left.\begin{array}{l}\text{Sue just}\\ \text{Sue's just}\end{array}\right\}$ finished her homework.

And BrE tends to use the construction with *should* where AmE generally uses the present subjunctive (*cf* 14.24):

I insisted that he $\left\{\begin{array}{l}\text{should take}\\ \text{take}\end{array}\right\}$ the documents with him.

Lexical examples are far more numerous, but many of these are familiar to users of both standards: for example, *railway* ⟨BrE⟩, *railroad* ⟨AmE⟩; *tin* ⟨BrE⟩, *can* ⟨AmE⟩; *petrol* ⟨BrE⟩, *gas(oline)* ⟨AmE⟩. Some items may confuse most speakers of the other standard because they are unfamiliar, at least in the relevant meaning: *boot* ⟨BrE⟩, *trunk* ⟨AmE⟩; *rubber* ⟨BrE⟩, *eraser* ⟨AmE⟩; *drawing pin* ⟨BrE⟩, *thumbtack* ⟨AmE⟩. *Public school* in AmE is a school maintained by public funds, but in BrE it applies to certain fee-paying schools. *Cider* (unless further specified, as in *hard cider*) is usually nonalcoholic in AmE, but (unless further specified as *sweet cider*) it is alcoholic in BrE. *School* in *I'm going to school* includes colleges and universities in AmE, but excludes them in BrE. Floors are numbered from ground level in AmE, so that *first floor* is generally level with the ground, but in BrE it is above the *ground floor*. In some instances an item that is normal in one standard is used in the other in restricted contexts: BrE *shop* (AmE *store*) is used in AmE for a small and specialized store, *eg: barber shop, shoe-repair shop*, and sometimes for a high-class establishment or one that has pretensions to be so considered, *eg: clothing shop/store, jewelry shop/store*; BrE *chips* (esp AmE *french fries*) now occurs in AmE, as a recent borrowing from BrE, in the combination *fish and chips*.

More recent innovations in either area tend to spread rapidly to the other. Thus while radio sets have had *valves* in BrE but *tubes* in AmE, television sets have *tubes* in both, and *transistors* and computer *software* are likewise used in both standards. Mass communication neutralizes differences; the pop music culture, in particular, uses a 'mid-Atlantic' dialect that levels differences even in pronunciation.

The United States and Britain have been separate political entities for two centuries; for generations, thousands of books have been appearing annually; there is a long tradition of publishing descriptions of both AmE and BrE. These are important factors in establishing and institutionalizing the two national standards, and in the relative absence of such conditions other national standards are both less distinct (being more open to the influence of either AmE or BrE) and less institutionalized.

One attitudinal phenomenon in the United States is of sociolinguistic interest. In affirming the students' right to their own varieties of language, many American educationalists have declared that Standard American English is a myth, some asserting the independent status (for example) of Black English. At the same time they have acknowledged the existence of a written standard dialect, sometimes termed 'Edited American English'.

Scotland, Ireland, Canada

1.25 Scots, with ancient national and educational institutions, is perhaps nearest to the self-confident independence of BrE and AmE, though the differences in grammar and vocabulary are rather few. There is the preposition *outwith* ['except'] and some other grammatical features, and such lexical items as *advocate* in the sense 'practising lawyer' or *bailie* ['municipal magistrate'] and several others which, like this last, refer to Scottish affairs. Orthography is identical with BrE, though *burgh* corresponds closely to 'borough' in meaning and might almost be regarded as a spelling variant. On the other hand, the

'Lallans' Scots, which has some currency for literary purposes, has a highly independent set of lexical, grammatical, phonological, and orthographical conventions, all of which make it seem more like a separate language than a regional dialect.

Hiberno-English, or Irish English, may also be considered as a national standard, for though we lack descriptions of this longstanding variety of English it is consciously and explicitly regarded as independent of BrE by educational and broadcasting services. The proximity of Great Britain, the easy movement of population, the pervasive influence of AmE, and like factors mean however that there is little room for the assertion and development of a separate grammar and vocabulary.

Canadian English is in a similar position in relation to AmE. Close economic, social, and intellectual links along a 4000-mile frontier have naturally caused the larger community to have an enormous influence on the smaller, not least in language. Though in many respects (*zed* instead of *zee*, for example, as the name of the letter 'z'), Canadian English follows British rather than United States practice, and has a modest area of independent lexical use, *eg*: *pogey* ['welfare payment'], *riding* ['parliamentary constituency'], *muskeg* ['kind of bog']; in many other respects it has approximated to AmE, and in the absence of strong institutionalizing forces it would continue in this direction. However, counteracting this tendency in language as in other matters is the tendency for Canadians to resist the influence of their powerful neighbour in their assertion of an independent national identity.

South Africa, Australia, New Zealand

1.26 South Africa, Australia, and New Zealand are in a very different position, remote from the direct day-to-day impact of either BrE or AmE. While in orthography and grammar the South African English in educated use is virtually identical with BrE, rather considerable differences in vocabulary have developed, largely under the influence of the other official language of the country, Afrikaans; for example, *veld* ['open country'], *kopje* or *koppie* ['hillock'], *dorp* ['village']. Because of the remoteness from Britain or America, few of these words have spread: an exception is *trek* ['journey'].

New Zealand English is more like BrE than any other non-European variety, though it has adopted quite a number of words from the indigenous Maoris (for example *whare* ['hut'] and of course *kiwi* and other names for fauna and flora) and over the past half century has come under the powerful influence of Australia and to a considerable extent of the United States.

Australian English is undoubtedly the dominant form of English in the Antipodes and by reason of Australia's increased wealth, population, and influence in world affairs, this national standard (though still by no means fully institutionalized) is exerting an influence in the northern hemisphere, particularly in Britain. Much of what is distinctive in Australian English is confined to familiar use. This is especially so of grammatical features like adverbial *but* or the use of the feminine pronoun both anaphorically for an inanimate noun (*job . . . her*) and also impersonally and nonreferentially for 'things in general':

The job's still not done; I'll finish her this arvo, but. ['. . . it this afternoon, however.']

A: Are you feeling better?

B: Too right, mate; she'll be jake. ['Absolutely . . .; everything will be fine.']

But there are many lexical items that are to be regarded as fully standard: not merely the special fauna and flora (such as *kangaroo*, *gumtree*, *wattle*), but special Australian uses of familiar words (for example *paddock* as a general word for 'field', *crook* ['ill'], *station* ['sheep farm'], *banker* ['river full to its banks'], *washer* ['face cloth']) and special Australian words (for example *bowyang* ['a trouser strap'], *waddy* ['a bludgeon']).

Pronunciation and standard English

1.27 The list in 1.25*f* does not exhaust the regional or national variants that approximate to the status of a standard. Beside the widespread Creole in the Caribbean, for example, there is the increasing recognition that the language of government and other agencies observes an indigenous standard that can be referred to as Caribbean English. Nor have we discussed the emerging standards in countries where English is spoken as a second language (*cf* 1.34). However, all the variants are remarkable primarily in the tiny extent to which even the most firmly established, BrE and AmE, differ from each other in vocabulary, grammar, and orthography. We have been careful, however, not to mention pronunciation in this connection. Pronunciation is a special case for several reasons. In the first place, it is the type of linguistic organization which distinguishes one national standard from another most immediately and completely and which links in a most obvious way the national standards to the regional varieties. Secondly (with an important exception to be noted), it is the least institutionalized aspect of standard English, in the sense that, provided our grammar and lexical items conform to the appropriate national standard, it matters less that our pronunciation follows closely our individual regional pattern. This is doubtless because pronunciation is essentially gradient, a matter of 'more or less' rather than the discrete 'this or that' features of grammar and lexicon. Thirdly, norms of pronunciation are subject less to educational and national constraints than to social ones: this means, in effect, that some regional accents are less acceptable than others (*cf* 1.20 Note [a]).

But there is an exception, noted above, to the generalization that regional pronunciation can be used without stigma. In BrE, one type of pronunciation comes close to enjoying the status of 'standard': it is the accent associated with the older schools and universities of England, 'Received Pronunciation' or 'RP'. Because this has traditionally been transmitted through a private education system based upon boarding schools insulated from the locality in which they happen to be situated, it is nonregional, and this – together with the obvious prestige that the social importance of its speakers has conferred on it – has been one of its strengths as a widely-favoured spoken form of the language. But RP no longer has the unique authority it had in the first half of the twentieth century. It is now only one among several accents commonly used on the BBC and takes its place along with others which carry the unmistakable mark of regional origin – not least, an Australian or North

American or Caribbean origin. Thus the rule that a specific type of pronunciation is relatively unimportant seems to be in the process of losing the notable exception that RP has constituted. Nevertheless, RP remains the standard for teaching the British variety of English as a foreign language, as can be easily seen from dictionaries and textbooks intended for countries that teach British English.

RP also shares a distinction with a variety of Midland American pronunciation known as 'network English'. BBC newsreaders are virtually all RP speakers, just as newsreaders on the national radio and television networks in the United States all speak with the 'network English' pronunciation.

In this book we do not attempt to represent the range of variation in pronunciation associated with different national standards. We do, however, record the major differences (using the system of symbols listed on page viii) between RP and network English.

Note The extreme variation that is tolerated in the pronunciation of English in various countries puts a great responsibility upon the largely uniform orthography (*cf* 1.23) in preserving the mutual comprehensibility of English throughout the world. A 'phonetic' spelling would probably allow existing differences to become greater whereas – through 'spelling pronunciation' with increased literacy – our conventional orthography not merely checks the divisiveness of pronunciation change but actually reduces it.

Varieties according to field of discourse

1.28 The field of discourse is the type of activity engaged in through language. A speaker of English has a repertoire of varieties according to field and switches to the appropriate one as occasion requires. The number of varieties that speakers command depends upon their profession, training, and interests.

Typically the switch involves nothing more than turning to the particular set of lexical items habitually used for handling the field in question. Thus, in connection with repairing a machine: *nut, bolt, wrench, thread, lever, finger-tight, balance, adjust, bearing, axle, pinion, split-pin,* and the like. But there are grammatical correlates to field variety as well. To take a simple example, the imperatives in cooking recipes: *Pour the liquid into a bowl,* not *You should* or *You might care to,* still less *The cook should* . . . Or the omission of direct objects that is common in instructional language in general: *Bake at 450°*; *Open (the box at) this end*; *Keep (this bottle) away from children.* More complex grammatical correlates are to be found in the language of technical and scientific description: the passive is common and clauses are often 'nominalized' (*cf* 17.51*ff*); thus not usually:

> You can rectify this fault if you insert a wedge . . .

but rather:

> Rectification of this fault is achieved by insertion of a wedge . . .

More radical grammatical differences are found in the language of legal documents:

> Provided that such payment as aforesaid shall be a condition precedent to the exercise of the option herein specified . . .

and in newspaper headlines:

Development Plan for Harlem Fought

The type of language required by choice of field is broadly independent from the variables (dialect, national standard) already discussed. Some obvious contingent constraints are however emerging: the use of a specific variety of one class frequently presupposes the use of a specific variety of another. The use of a well-formed legal sentence, for example, presupposes an educated variety of English.

We shall have occasion in this book to refer to variations in grammar according to the field of discourse with self-explanatory labels. Literature is of course a long-established field, but LITERARY English extends to other fields, for example nontechnical essays on humanistic topics and biographies. Some fields have certain characteristics in common; for example, LEGAL and RELIGIOUS English have numerous forms peculiar to their respective fields, but both may include usages that are otherwise ARCHAIC, though there is a trend away from such archaism in these fields. Poetry too has traditionally used archaic features. Indeed, poetry may deviate from the norms of the language in other respects, particularly in word order. Literary English is sometimes described as poetic if it displays features that are rare in prose.

As with dialects (*cf* 1.21), there are indefinitely many fields depending on how detailed we wish our discussion to be. LEARNED (or scholarly) language covers a wide range of subject matter (psychology, literary criticism, history, physics, medicine), each of which could be regarded as a separate field, though we shall need to distinguish only the field of SCIENTIFIC discourse. Applications of technology are reflected in INSTRUCTIONAL writing, itself included within TECHNICAL language. But instructional language may range from cooking recipes to instructions for playing games. When learned or technical language is used too obtrusively or (to all appearances) unnecessarily, it is often pejoratively referred to as JARGON.

Jargon may include obtrusive language from other discourse fields, for example JOURNALISTIC and (in particular) BUREAUCRATIC writing. Journalism in its widest sense includes reporting on radio and television, each of which may be distinguished from newspaper reporting. Some features of newspapers call for special consideration, in particular headlinese, the language of newspaper headlines.

We have by no means exhausted the fields that have developed their own linguistic expression. Among others we refer to, we may mention advertising and business.

Note Varieties according to field of discourse are sometimes called REGISTERS, though this term is applied in different ways.

Varieties according to medium

1.29 The only varieties according to medium that we need to consider are those conditioned by speaking and writing respectively. Since speech is the primary or natural medium for linguistic communication, it is reasonable to focus on the differences imposed on language when it has to be expressed in a graphic (and normally visual) medium instead. Most of these differences arise from two sources. One is situational: the use of a written medium normally presumes the absence of the person(s) to whom the piece of language is addressed. This imposes the necessity of a far greater explicitness: the careful and precise completion of a sentence, rather than the casual expression supported by gesture and terminating when speakers are assured by word or look that their hearers have understood. As a corollary, since the written sentence can be read and reread, slowly and critically (whereas the spoken sentence is evanescent), writers tend to anticipate criticism by writing more concisely as well as more carefully and elegantly than they may choose to speak.

The second source of difference is that many of the devices we use to transmit language by speech (stress, rhythm, intonation, tempo, for example) are impossible to represent with the relatively limited repertoire of conventional orthography. They are difficult enough to represent even with a special prosodic notation (*cf* App II). As a consequence writers often have to reformulate their sentences to convey fully and successfully what they want to express within the orthographic system. Thus instead of the spoken sentence with a particular intonation nucleus on *John* (*cf* App II.11*ff*), one might have to rephrase the sentence in writing to convey the intended focus:

> JǑHN didn't do it.
> It was not in fact John that did it.

The advantages are not all on one side, however; the written medium has the valuable distinctions of paragraphs, italics, quotation marks, etc, which have no clear analogue in speech.

1.30 As with varieties according to field, we are here dealing with two varieties that are in principle at the disposal of any users of English as occasion may demand, irrespective of the variety of English they use as a result of region and education. But again there are contingent constraints: we do not expect speakers with little formal education to compose in written English with the facility that educated speakers acquire. This indeed is what a great deal of education is about.

There are contingent constraints of another kind. Some field varieties of English (legal statutes especially) are difficult to compose except in writing and difficult to understand except by reading. Other varieties are comparably restricted to speech: a radio commentary on a football match will be phrased very differently from a newspaper report of the same game.

Varieties according to attitude

1.31 Varieties according to attitude constitute, like field and medium varieties, a range of English any section of which is in principle available at will to any individual speaker of English, irrespective of the regional variant or national standard he may habitually use. This present class of varieties is often called 'stylistic', but 'style' like 'register' is a term which is used with several different meanings. We are here concerned with the choice of linguistic form that proceeds from our attitude to the hearer (or reader), to the topic, and to the purpose of our communication. We recognize a gradient in attitude between FORMAL (relatively stiff, cold, polite, impersonal) on the one hand and INFORMAL (relatively relaxed, warm, rude, friendly) on the other. The corresponding linguistic contrasts involve both grammar and vocabulary. For example:

> Overtime emoluments are not available for employees who are non-resident . . .
>
> Staff members who don't live in can't get paid overtime . . .

While many sentences like the foregoing can be rated 'more formal' or 'more informal' in relation to each other, it is useful to pursue the notion of the common core (*cf* 1.19) here, so that we can acknowledge a median or unmarked variety of English, bearing no obvious colouring that has been induced by attitude. For example:

> This student's work is now much better and seems likely to go on improving.

On each side of this NEUTRAL (and normal) English, we may usefully distinguish sentences containing features that are markedly formal or informal. In the present work, we shall for the most part confine ourselves to this three-term distinction, leaving the middle one unlabelled and specifying only usages that are relatively formal or informal. It should be realized that the neutral term often covers items in one or the other extreme as well. For example, contractions such as *didn't* are appropriate in both informal and neutral English; they are excluded from formal English.

1.32 Mastery of such a range of attitudinal varieties seems a normal achievement for educated adults, but it is an acquisition that is not inevitable or even easy for either the native or the foreign learner of a language. It appears to require maturity, tact, sensitivity, and adaptability – personality features which enable the individual to observe and imitate what others do, and to search the language's resources to find an expression to suit his attitude. Young native speakers at the age of five or six have, broadly speaking, one form of English that is made to serve all purposes, whether they are talking to their mother, their pets, their friends, or an aged neighbour. And although this invariant language can cause parents twinges of embarrassment, it is generally recognized that it is a limitation that the child will grow out of.

Foreign learners are in a somewhat similar position. Until their skill in the language is really very advanced, it is attitudinally invariant, though the particular variety is much less predictable than that of the native child. If much of their practice in English has been obtained through textbooks specializing in commercial training, their habitual variety will be very different from that of the learner who has done vacation work helping on a farm. More usually, either an invariant literary (sometimes even an archaic) flavour or an invariant excessively informal flavour occurs in the speech of foreign students. But, in any case, just as the native child's youth inhibits criticism, so the foreign student's accent informs listeners that there are respectable reasons for occasional inappropriateness in the language variety.

1.33 The three-way contrast of formal–neutral–informal is not of course adequate to describe the full range of linguistic varieties that are evoked by differences of attitude. We should add at least one category at each end of the scale. On the one hand, we need to account for the extremely distant, rigid (or 'frozen') variety of English sometimes found in written instructions. For example:

Distinguished patrons are requested to ascend to the second floor.

But we must account also for the intimate, casual, or hearty – often slangy – language used between very close friends (especially of a similar age) or members of a family, or used when speakers feel for any other reason that they do not need to bother about what the listener (or reader) thinks of their choice of languge. We might thus match the foregoing example with:

(Get) upstairs, you lot!

We now have a potential five-term distinction:

very formal – FORMAL – neutral – INFORMAL – very informal

As we said above (1.31), we chiefly employ the labels 'formal' and 'informal', leaving unmarked the 'neutral' normal style; but we sometimes designate language as 'very formal' or 'very informal', occasionally replacing 'very informal' by 'casual' or 'familiar' as appropriate. The term COLLOQUIAL is also used for the very informal range, but particularly for the spoken language. A further term, SLANG, is needed to denote the frequently vivid or playful lexical usage typical of casual discourse, usually indicating membership in a particular social group.

One final point on attitude varieties. As with the English dictated by field and medium, there are contingency constraints in the normal selection of attitudinal variety. Just as statute drafting (field) normally presupposes writing (medium), so also it presupposes a particular attitude variety: in this case 'very formal'. Similarly it would be hard to imagine an appropriate football commentary on the radio being other than informal, or a radio commentary on the funeral of a head of state being other than formal, though both are in the same medium (speech).

Varieties according to interference

1.34 A very different type of variation applies to speakers of English as a second language or foreign language. The variation is caused by interference from another language. The Frenchman who says *I am here since Thursday* is imposing a French grammatical usage on English; the Russian who says *There are four assistants in our chair of mathematics* is imposing a Russian lexico-semantic usage on the English word 'chair'. Most obviously, we always tend to impose our native phonological pattern on any foreign language we learn. The practised linguist is able to detect the language background of students, and this has obvious implications for language teaching in that students can be helped with the problems that give them the greatest difficulty.

At the opposite extreme are interference varieties that are so widespread in a community and of such long standing that some believe them stable and adequate enough to be institutionalized and hence to be regarded as varieties of English in their own right rather than stages on the way to a more native-like English. There is active debate on these issues in India, Pakistan, and several African countries, where efficient and fairly stable varieties of English are prominent in educated use at the highest political and professional level and may possibly acquire the status of national standards. The new cultural settings for the use of English have produced considerable changes: different notions of appropriate style and rhetoric, and an influx of loan words, changes of meanings, and new expressions.

We can also recognize regional supranational varieties such as South Asian English (the English of the Indian subcontinent), East African English, and West African English, and these in turn may share characteristics. For example, in African English, and to some extent in South Asian English, *yes* is commonly used in a negative reply that confirms the speaker's assumption in a negative question:

A: Isn't she in bed?
B: Yes (, she isn't).

African and South Asian English very frequently use *isn't it?* as a universal tag, *They're late, isn't it?*, and often omit articles required in the major standard varieties, *They gave us hard time.*

Creole and pidgin

1.35 At an extreme of a different kind, there are the interference varieties known as creole and pidgin. It is a matter of debate, and to some extent politics, whether these should be regarded as falling within the orbit of the English language. Since, however, the expressions 'creole English' and 'pidgin English' are in common occurrence, we should say something about them, although they will not be described in this book. They have traditionally been used chiefly by the less prosperous and privileged sections of a community but have also been stable over several generations.

Pidgin is technically distinguished from creole by being essentially a second language used to replace a native language for restricted public (especially commercial) purposes rather than to conduct family affairs and talk to one's children. On the other hand, a creole is a native language. It is usually more varied than a pidgin, but it tends to be restricted to local, practical, and family matters. Political, educational, and sociolinguistic thought vacillates as to whether such creolized forms of English (as in Sierra Leone or the Caribbean) should be given official status or not. Would creole speakers benefit from the self-assurance this might give, or (since the elite in their society would still learn a more international English in addition) would the danger be that this would tend to perpetuate their underprivileged status? Here is a sample of Jamaican Creole in an orthography that already suggests partial institutionalization:

Hin sed den, 'Ma, a we in lib?' Hie sie, 'Mi no nuo, mi pikini, bot duon luk fi hin niem hahd, ohr eni wie in a di wohld an yu kal di niem, hin hie unu.' Hin sed, 'Wel Ma, mi want im hie mi a nuo mi.' 'Lahd nuo, masa! Duo no kal di niem, hin wi kom kil yu.' Hin sie, 'Wel Ma, hin wi haf fi kil mi.' (see Note [a])

Creole is normally the principal or sole language of its speakers, being transmitted from parent to child like any other native language. Moreover, for all its evidence of interference from other languages, a creolized form of English is usually more like ordinary English than a pidgin English is, and it gives less impression of being merely a drastic reduction of ordinary English.

Here are samples of Hawaiian Pidgin that are typical of three ethnic groups: Korean (a), Filipino (b), and Japanese (c):

(a) Aena tu macha churen, samawl churen. Haus mani pei. Mai churen go sakul, teiki haus mani pei, aeswai koria kim neim wan moa taim mi meri. (see Note [b])

(b) Ai go tel, 'Ae, mi no mo hapai klos oni diskain klos, da ispital-kain klos. Oni hia yu kaen hanapa, wahini-kain.' 'Orait, pau hana time, po klak, siks klak hi kam, hi go hapai yu klos.' (see Note [c])

(c) Samtaim gud rod get, samtaim, olsem ben get, enguru get, no? Olsem hyumen life, awl, enikain, stawmu get, nais dei get. Olsem, enibadi, mi olsem, smawl-taim. (see Note [d])

The definitions we have given may suggest an unjustified dichotomy between creoles and pidgins, and may also suggest that they are stable autonomous language systems. We should rather consider creoles and pidgins as not discrete stages in a changing process. On the one hand, through repidginization a creole comes to be used as a second language by neighbouring peoples who have little contact with the European language on which the creole is based. On the other hand, through decreolization a creole tends to merge with the European language when the creole speakers and the European language speakers are in frequent contact. Moreover, both creoles and pidgins may admit a very large amount of variation. A pidgin in its early stages of development, such as the English-based Hawaiian Pidgin, is highly unstable; we similarly find considerable instability in a repidginized creole, as in the second language use of the English-based Krio. When a creole is undergoing decreolization, as with the English-based Guyanese Creole, it can best be analysed as a continuum of varieties on a scale of least to most different from the European language. By contrast, Tok Pisin, which began as pidgin English in Papua New Guinea, has become highly institutionalized through use in education, government, and the media, and may already have some currency as a native language.

Note **[a]** He said then, 'Ma, and where does he live?' She says, 'I don't know, my child, but don't look hard for his name, or anywhere in all the world that you call the name, he will hear you.' He said, 'Well, Ma, I want him to hear me and know me.' 'Lord, no, master! Do not call the name, he will come and kill you.' He says, 'Well ma, he will have to kill me.'

[b] And I had too many children, small children. I had to pay for the house. My children were going to school, I had to take rent money to pay for them, that's why I married a second time a Korean named Kim.

[c] I said, 'Hey, I've no clothes to wear but those clothes, hospital clothes. You can only fasten them here, they're like women's clothes.' 'All right, after work, at four, six o'clock he'll come, he'll bring your clothes.'

[d] Sometimes there's a good road, sometimes, there's things like bends, angles, right? Human life is just the same, there's all sorts of things, storms, nice days. It's like that for everyone, for me too, when I was young.

Relationships among variety types

1.36 Varieties within each type of variation may be viewed in principle as independent from each other. Users of English may retain recognizable features of any regional variety in their use of a national standard; within that standard, they can discourse in English that is appropriate to their particular occupation or hobbies; they can handle these topics in English appropriate to either speech or writing; in either medium, they can adjust their discourse on any of the topics according to the respect, friendliness, or intimacy they feel for their hearers or readers. And all of this would apply equally if they are proficient in English as a foreign or second language and their use of English is affected by interference from their native tongue.

At the same time, the variation is to a large extent interdependent. We have drawn attention to several contingent constraints (for example, in 1.28), and we now consider the types of interdependence as they affect the varieties system as a whole.

Regional variation has been explicitly connected with the educational varieties: a person educated in Ohio will adopt standard AmE, not BrE. Similarly, for speakers of an interference variety: someone learning English in Europe or India is likely to approach a standard with BrE orientation; in Mexico or the Philippines, with an AmE orientation.

1.37 Next are varieties relating to fields of discourse. Certain fields of activity (farming and shipbuilding, for example) are associated with specific regions; clearly, it is in the dialect of these regions that the language of daily discourse on such activities is fully developed. In other fields (medicine, nuclear physics, philosophy) we expect to find little use of nonstandard English or of regionally distinctive English. On the other hand, we expect AmE to predominate in discussions of baseball and BrE in discussions of cricket.

Since writing is an educated art, we normally expect the educated English of one or other national standard in this medium. Indeed, when we occasionally try to represent uneducated English in writing, we realize acutely how narrowly geared to standard English are our graphic conventions. For the same reason there are subjects (for example, coaching a football team) that can scarcely be handled in writing and others (for example, legal statutes) that can scarcely be handled in speech.

Attitudinal varieties have a great deal of independence in relation to other varieties: it is possible to be formal or informal on biochemistry or politics in AmE or BrE, for example. But informal or casual language across an 'authority gap' or 'seniority gap' (a student talking to an archbishop) presents difficulties, and on certain topics (funerals) it would be considered distasteful. And very formal language when the subject is courtship or football would seem comic.

1.38 Finally, the interference varieties. At the extremes of creole and pidgin there is especial interdependence between the form of the language and its functions. Indeed, pidgins tend to be restricted to a few practical matters, though we have noted the expansion of functions in Tok Pisin (*cf* 1.35).

As to English taught at an advanced level as a second or foreign language, it is to be hoped that enough proficiency is achieved to allow the users the flexibility they need in handling (let us say) public administration, a learned profession such as medicine with its supporting medical journals, and informal conversation. Students are likely to be handicapped if they are taught English at the formal or informal levels only, or the spoken or written language only, or are restricted to the English necessary for a particular occupation ('English for engineers', for example).

Variation within a variety

1.39 We need to make two final points about variation in the use of English. First, the various conditioning factors (region, medium, attitude, for example) each constitute a continuum rather than a discrete category.

Secondly, we may not be able to account always for the choice of one rather than another linguistic form; we sometimes find DIVIDED USAGE, a choice between variants, the conditions for which cannot be attributed to the variety distinctions discussed in this chapter.

For example, we can say (or write) one or the other of each of these pairs:

He stayed a week. ~ He stayed for a week.
I consider her my friend. ~ I consider her as my friend.
I don't know whether I can be there. ~ I don't know if I can be there.

Neither member of such pairs is necessarily linked to any of the varieties that we have specified. Attempts have been made to find a basis for at least some of this seemingly random variation (often called 'free variation'). For example, it has been claimed that certain language varieties (termed 'randomly distributed dialects') define groups of speakers who are not associated regionally or sociologically, the groups being characterized by linguistic features that are related systematically.

1.40 It may help to see variation in terms of the relationships depicted in *Fig* 1.40, where both the verticals represent a 'more-or-less' opposition. The upper pole of the first vertical corresponds to the features of greatest uniformity, such as the invariable past tense of *bring* in the educated variety of English, or the many features characterizing the main stable common core

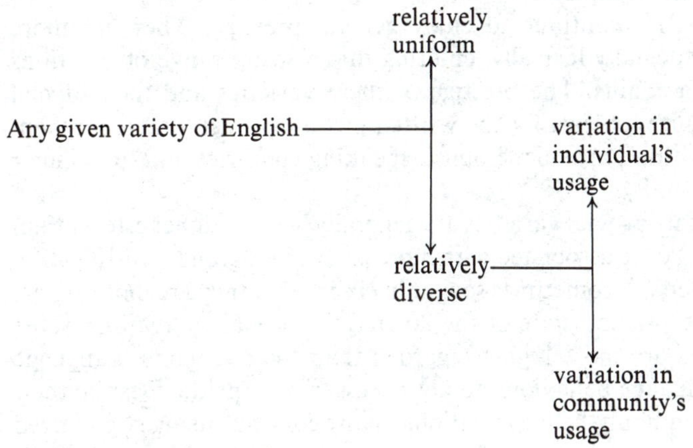

Fig 1.40 Variation within a variety

of the language, such as the position of the article in a noun phrase. The lower pole of the first vertical corresponds to the area of fluctuation illustrated in 1.39. The second vertical represents the situation in which, on the one hand, an individual may indulge in such a fluctuation (*I wonder whether* one moment and *I wonder if* a little later), and on the other hand, there may be fluctuation within the community as a whole (one member appearing to have a preference for *He didn't dare ask* and another a preference for *He didn't dare to ask*). This appears to be a natural state of affairs in language. Language change is constantly occurring in all languages and in all varieties of language with the result that older and newer variants always coexist; and some members of a society will be temperamentally disposed to use the new (perhaps by their youth) while others are comparably inclined to the old (perhaps by their age). But many will not be consistent either in their choice or in their temperamental disposition. Perhaps English may give rise to such fluctuation more than some other languages because of its patently mixed nature: a basic Germanic wordstock, stress pattern, word-formation, inflection, and syntax overlaid with a classical and Romance wordstock, stress pattern (*cf* App II.4), word-formation (*cf* App I.28*f*) – and even inflection and syntax.

Attitudes to variation

1.41 At various places in this chapter we have had occasion to refer to language attitudes; for example, the official acceptance of English as a neutral second language (1.4) and the views on the present state of the language expressed by native speakers (1.11). As we have indicated in 1.1, the current preeminence of English as an international language reflects its practical values, not some assumed aesthetic or linguistic qualities. The growing local acceptance of second-language educated varieties as standards derives from demands for national autonomy, an autonomy that was achieved long ago by transplanted varieties in native English-speaking countries, notably the United States of America. Increasing tolerance (by no means universal) for second-language varieties and for local nonstandard varieties reflects views that each speech community has a right to its own language and that no variety is intrinsically superior.

Standard varieties continue to enjoy general prestige. They are more differentiated, especially lexically, entering into a wider range of functions and situational domains. The prestige of these varieties and their official maintenance ensure, at least for the written medium, a neutral comprehensible language within particular English-speaking countries and (to a major extent) internationally.

Certain regional or social varieties are generally held in higher esteem than others because they are associated with more prestigious groups. Justification for the higher esteem is sometimes sought in claims that they are more logical or closer to some pristine state of the language. For similar reasons, some language features are more highly regarded than their variants. Language attitudes and language behaviour do not necessarily coincide. Despite their acceptance of commonly-held evaluations, many continue using stigmatized varieties or variants because they feel more comfortable with what they are used to, or because they want to retain their membership of a particular speech community. Those who are competent to do so may adjust their variety to suit their audience, particularly in the spoken medium, and are likely to monitor their language in the direction of standard varieties in the written medium, especially in formal style. On the other hand, some may retain stigmatized varieties or variants because they reject the evaluations of others.

Acceptability and frequency

1.42 The metaphor of the common core points to a distinction that applies to two other aspects of our description of English grammar. We distinguish between the central and the marginal also for acceptability and frequency.

Acceptability is a concept that does not apply exclusively to grammar. Native speakers may find a particular sentence unacceptable because (for example) they consider it logically absurd or because they cannot find a plausible context for its use or because it sounds clumsy or impolite. However, we are concerned only with the acceptability of forms or constructions on the grounds of their morphology or syntax.

In general, our examples are fully acceptable if they are left unmarked. But we sometimes contrast acceptable and unacceptable examples, marking the latter by placing an asterisk '*' before them. If they are tending to unacceptability but are not fully unacceptable, we put a query '?' before the asterisk. A query alone signifies that native speakers are unsure about the particular language feature. If native speakers differ in their reactions, we put the asterisk or query in parentheses. Our assessment of native speaker evaluations reflect in part our own research: elicitation experiments with informants in the United States and Britain.

Assessments by native speakers of relative acceptability largely correlate with their assessments of relative frequency; we have conducted experiments to elicit frequency judgments too. But we have also drawn on our research and that of others into the frequencies of language phenomena in several important corpora, preeminently:

(a) the corpus of the Survey of English Usage (SEU), covering spoken as well as written texts of British English
(b) the Brown University corpus, comprising samples of American printed English
(c) the parallel Lancaster-Oslo/Bergen corpus (LOB), comprising samples of British printed English

We leave unmarked those features of the language that occur frequently, drawing attention just to those that occur extremely frequently or only rarely.

Our approach in this book is to focus on the common core that is shared by standard British English and standard American English. We leave unmarked any features that the two standard varieties have in common, marking as ⟨BrE⟩ or ⟨AmE⟩ only the points at which they differ. But usually we find it necessary to say ⟨esp(ecially) BrE⟩ or ⟨esp(ecially) AmE⟩, for it is rare for a feature to be found exclusively in one variety. Similarly we do not mark features that are neutral with respect to medium and attitude. We distinguish where necessary spoken and written language, generally using 'speaker' and 'hearer' as unmarked forms for the participants in an act of communication, but drawing on the combinations 'speaker/writer' and 'hearer/reader' when we wish to emphasize that what is said applies across the media. We also frequently need to label features according to variation in attitude, drawing attention to those that are formal or informal.

In this book we offer a descriptive presentation of English morphology and syntax with a minimum of formalism. We make a direct connection between morphological and syntactic forms and their meaning, conducting excursions into lexicology, semantics, and pragmatics where these impinge closely on our grammatical description.

Note The terms 'grammatical' and 'ungrammatical' are commonly used by nonspecialists as synonyms of 'acceptable' and 'unacceptable'. We have avoided using the former terms in this book because of the various meanings which they have even among linguists.

Bibliographical note

On international varieties of English see Bailey and Görlach (1982); Kachru (1982); Quirk (1972), Chapters 1–7. Major works on regional varieties (including general bibliographies, dictionaries, and some accounts of social variation) are listed at the end of Bailey and Görlach (1982). Two series of books are in progress: *Varieties of English Around the World*, published by John Benjamins (Amsterdam and Philadelphia), and *English in the International Context*, published by Pergamon (Oxford). The journal *English World-Wide* is devoted to scholarly articles on English varieties world-wide.

On the international use of English, see Fishman et al (1977) and the data in the Statistical Yearbooks published by UNESCO and the United Nations.

On 'Nuclear English', see Quirk (1982), 37–53.

On variation in British and American English see Beaugrande (1983); Crystal and Davy (1969); Ferguson and Heath (1981), Parts I and IV; Hughes and Trudgill (1979); Joos (1962); Labov (1972); McDavid (1963). On random variation, see Carden (1973).

On creoles and pidgins see Valdman (1977). The samples of Hawaiian Pidgin came from Bickerton and Odo (1976).

On acceptability in general, see Greenbaum (1977b). On the relationship between syntactic frequency and acceptability, see Greenbaum (1976c). Evaluations of language attitudes and use appear in Bolinger (1980a); Daniels (1983); Greenbaum (1985); Michaels and Ricks (1980); Quirk (1982), esp Chapters 1, 2 and 4.

For a survey of attitudes to specific usage problems in British English, see Mittins et al (1970). The treatment of usage problems by American dictionaries and guides to usage is evaluated in Cresswell (1975). Opinions expressed in the leading American guides to usages are summarized in Copperud (1980). Popular guides to usage include Fowler (1965) and Partridge (1973) for British usage, and Bernstein (1965) and Follett (1966) for American usage.

2 A survey of English grammar

This chapter and its relation to later chapters

The plan of this grammar

2.1 Grammar is a complex system, the parts of which cannot be properly explained in abstraction from the whole. In this sense, all parts of a grammar are mutually defining, and there is no simple linear path we can take in explaining one part in terms of another. The method of presentation adopted in this book will be to order the description of English grammar so that features which are simpler (in the sense that their explanation presupposes less) come before those which are more complex (in the sense that their explanation presupposes more).

Our mode of progression can be best described as cyclic, rather than linear. In this way, a topic dealt with earlier in a cursory way can be taken up later for more extended treatment. There are three cycles: (a) Chapter 2; (b) Chapters 3 to 11; (c) Chapters 12 to 19.

The present chapter, which constitutes the first cycle, presents a general outline of English grammar and of its major concepts and categories, with particular reference to the simple sentence.

The second cycle, Chapters 3 to 11, is concerned with the basic constituents which make up the simple sentence. Thus Chapters 3 and 4 present the grammar and semantics of the verb phrase, and Chapters 5 and 6 the basic constituents of the noun phrase, in particular determiners, nouns, and pronouns. Chapter 7 deals with adjectives and adverbs, Chapter 8 with adverbials, and Chapter 9 with prepositions and prepositional phrases. In the light of these detailed studies, Chapters 10 and 11 then re-examine the simple sentence in all its structural variety.

The third cycle treats matters which involve more complex sentence structure. Chapters 12 and 13 move beyond the simple sentence, dealing with substitution, ellipsis, and coordination: three operations which may be carried out on simple sentences in order to produce structures of greater or less complexity. Chapters 14 and 15 introduce a further factor of complexity – the subordination of one clause to another – thereby leading to a more general study of the complex sentence. Chapter 16 follows up Chapters 3 and 4 in giving further attention to the verb phrase, with special reference to verb classification, together with issues relating to phrasal and prepositional verbs, and to verb and adjective complementation. Similarly, Chapter 17 resumes the topic of Chapters 5 and 6, exploring the full complexity of the noun phrase in terms of structures separately examined in earlier chapters. Chapter 18 also involves a knowledge of the whole grammar as described in preceding chapters, but this time with a view to presenting the various ways in which individual parts of a sentence can be arranged for focus, emphasis, and thematic presentation. Finally, Chapter 19 considers the ways in which sentence grammar relates to the formation of texts, including those comprising extended discourse in speech or writing.

The three Appendices summarize aspects of English which, though strictly peripheral to grammar, nevertheless impinge on it at many points, necessitating frequent reference in the body of the book to the topics concerned. They are word-formation (Appendix I); stress, rhythm, and intonation (Appendix II); and punctuation (Appendix III).

Each of the chapters and appendices ends with a bibliographical note giving guidance on further reading relevant to the material just presented. We concentrate in these notes on references to recent and germinal contributions, particularly in learned monographs and articles. We assume, normally without further recommendation, that the reader will consult the major grammarians of the past, whose works are of course cited in the general Bibliography at the end of this book: for example, the compendious studies by Curme, Jespersen, Kruisinga, Poutsma, Sweet, Visser, and others, to which (as well as to the bibliography by Scheurweghs and Vorlat) all succeeding grammarians are heavily indebted.

Note Word-formation is sometimes considered a part of grammar. See 1.14*ff* for a discussion of various uses of the term 'grammar', and the meaning of 'grammar' assumed in this book.

The purpose of this chapter

2.2 This chapter outlines the structure of the English sentence in such a way as to provide, as it were, a small-scale map of the territory to be explored in some detail in the main body of the book. As with all small-scale maps, most of the details have to be ignored, and complicated contours have to be smoothed out and simplified. But in compensation, it is intended that the details included in the chapter are more important for English grammar than those which are omitted. In particular, the chapter aims (a) to provide a general introduction to English grammar; and (b) to introduce important concepts and categories to which it will be necessary to make frequent reference in the larger-scale expositions of Chapters 3 to 19.

Parts of the sentence

Grammatical units

2.3 In order to state general rules about the construction of sentences, it is constantly necessary to refer to units smaller than the sentence itself: units such as those which are commonly referred to by the terms CLAUSE, PHRASE, WORD, and MORPHEME (*cf* 2.7). The relation between one unit and another unit of which it is a part is CONSTITUENCY. We may thus say that in [1], *the evenings*, *have turned*, *very cold*, and *just recently* are CONSTITUENTS of the whole sentence:

[The evenings] [have turned] [very cold] [just recently]. [1]

One way of indicating constituency is by bracketing, as in [1]; another is by a tree diagram:

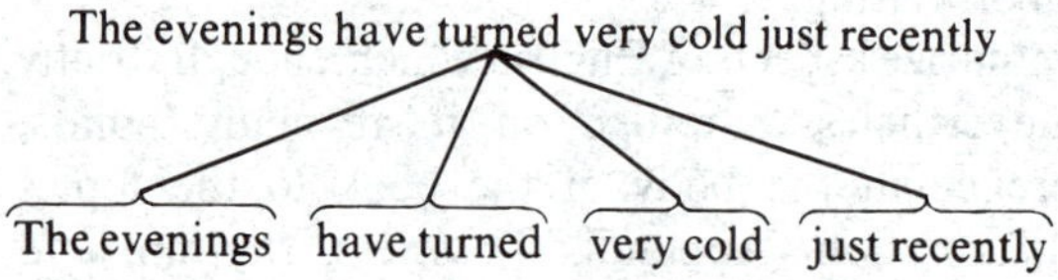

Fig 2.3a

Clearly the constituents of *Fig* 2.3a themselves contain units, namely the individual words of which they are composed; therefore, a fuller tree diagram would be:

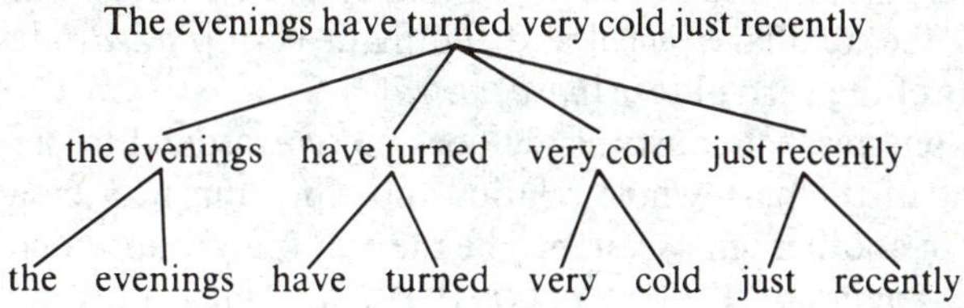

Fig 2.3b

This again may be presented more economically, if less clearly, in terms of bracketing:

[[The] [evenings]] [[have] [turned]] [[very] [cold]] [[just] [recently]]. [1a]

Furthermore, the words themselves in some cases consist of two or more units of smaller size: *evening* + *s*, *turn* + *ed*, *recent* + *ly*:

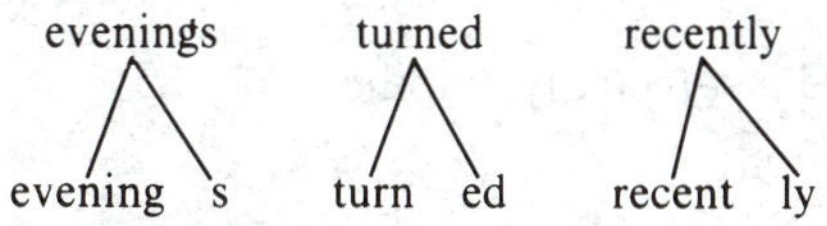

Fig 2.3c

A tree diagram is more informative if it labels the constituents as instances of particular units or classes of units; *Fig* 2.3b, for example, may be reconstituted as follows:

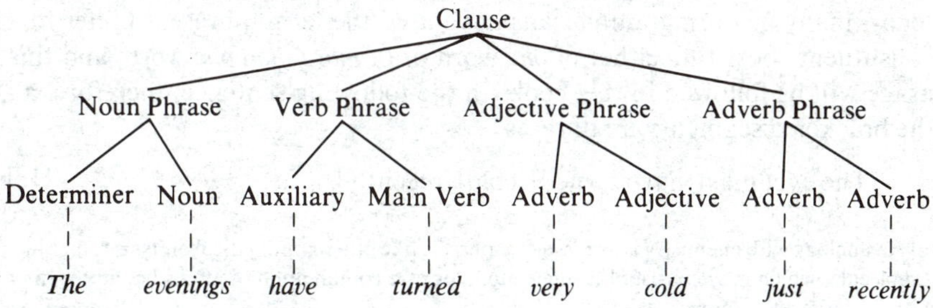

Fig 2.3d

Three 'sizes' of unit have here been distinguished: clause, phrase, and word. A further level would distinguish morphemes (*evening*, *-s*, *recent*, *-ly*) as constituents of words (*cf* 2.7). The terms for different phrases (noun phrase, adjective phrase, etc) obviously reflect the character of the words which are the main constituents of these units.

Constituents

2.4 *Figure* 2.3d shows constituents simply as the smaller parts into which a unit can be divided. We may extend this part–whole relation to include units which are only indirectly part of a larger unit: thus in *Fig* 2.3d not only [*the* *evenings*], but indirectly also [*the*] and [*evenings*], *evening* and *-s* are constituents of the whole clause. But it is useful to reserve the term IMMEDIATE CONSTITUENT for those units which are the parts into which another unit is immediately divisible: thus the verb phrase [*have turned*] is an immediate constituent of the whole clause, and the auxiliary [*have*] and the main verb [*turned*] are immediate constituents of the verb phrase [*have turned*].

More important, in one respect constituency does not correspond to our ordinary understanding of the part–whole relationship. One unit may be a UNITARY CONSTITUENT of another unit; *ie*, it may be the only 'part' into which another unit can be analysed. (UNITARY CONSTITUENCY may thus be distinguished from MULTIPLE CONSTITUENCY, where a unit is divided into two or more immediate constituents.) Traditional grammar has acknowledged this concept of unitary constituency in certain respects. For example, it has been normal to say that a SENTENCE may consist of a single clause, as in *Fig* 2.3d. Such sentences are called SIMPLE SENTENCES, and are distinguished from COMPLEX or COMPOUND SENTENCES, which include two or more clauses. (For further discussion of these distinctions, *cf* 10.1, 14.2*f*.) Thus while example [1] is a simple sentence, exhaustively analysed into a single clause, [1b] is a compound sentence:

> The evenings have turned very cold just recently, but the afternoons have been quite warm. [1b]

It has also been normal to say that a word may consist of just one morpheme, or of more than one: *night*, for example, consists of a STEM alone, while *nights* consists of the same stem followed by the inflectional SUFFIX *-s*.

On the other hand, the term PHRASE has traditionally been applied to a unit consisting of more than one word, and this has meant some inconsistency in the interpretation of grammatical constituency. Avoiding this inconsistency, many modern grammarians have used the term 'phrase' to refer to a constituent consisting either of *one* word or of *more than one* word, and this usage will be followed in this book. In the following sentence, therefore, all the bracketed segments are phrases:

> [The evenings] [have turned] [cold] [recently]. [1c]

Note **[a]** An analogy with chemistry is suggested: a phrase, like other grammatical units, is rather like a molecule, which may consist of a single atom, or of a combination of atoms bound together within a larger structure.

[b] Ideally, it would be convenient to make a terminological distinction between 'simple' units which have one constituent and 'complex' units or 'compound' units which have more than one. Unfortunately, however, this terminological convention might cause confusion, since grammatical tradition has preempted the terms 'complex' and 'compound' for purposes not entirely consistent with it. For example, the distinction between simple and compound sentences is different from the distinction between simple and compound nouns. Our use of the terms 'complex' and 'compound' will be made clear in later chapters; *cf* 10.1, 14.2*f*, and App I.57.

[c] Linguists differ on what are the immediate constituents of a clause. The above description represents the basis of our system of clause analysis, to be further developed in 2.13*ff*.

[d] Some linguists use the term 'sentence' for a clause which is part of a sentence.

Chain and choice relationships

2.5 The principle which allows both unitary and multiple constituents of a grammatical unit goes against the commonsense understanding of 'parts' and 'wholes', and therefore needs some justification. The justification lies in a distinction between CHAIN (*ie* syntagmatic) and CHOICE (*ie* paradigmatic) relationships among linguistic constituents. The chain relationship is an 'and' relationship, whereas the choice relationship is an 'or' relationship. Thus if two units *X* and *Y* occur one after the other in a larger unit, they are in a chain relationship, *X* + *Y*. But if *X* and *Y* can be substituted for one another in a larger unit, they are in a choice relationship, *X*/*Y*. (Substitution here means 'commutability', *ie* acceptable replacement in terms of the structure of the sentence, not necessarily in terms of meaning.) In examining a single sentence, we can observe only the chain relationships, and indeed, if we were interested only in chain relationships, we might be satisfied simply to represent a sentence as a sequence of morphemes as follows:

The + evening + s + have + turn + ed + very + cold + just + recent + ly.

Note It is worth observing, in passing, that choice relationships *are* made explicit in certain types of appositional self-correcting constructions; *eg*: *They were constantly quarrelling – well, arguing, anyway* (*cf* 17.80).

2.6 When, however, we consider what are the possibilities of English grammar (for example, what does and what does not make a grammatical sentence in English), we have to investigate choice relationships. Describing English grammar involves stating what choices exist in the construction of English sentences, and what the relations are between these choices. It is on this basis that it is necessary to distinguish units of different 'sizes', and to recognize the choices which exist at different levels of constituency. From here, consideration of examples like [1] and [2] leads to the recognition of unitary constituents:

$$\begin{matrix} \text{(a)} & \text{(b)} & \text{(c)} & \text{(d)} & \\ \left\{\begin{matrix}\text{The weather}\\ \text{It}\end{matrix}\right\} & \left\{\begin{matrix}\text{has been}\\ \text{was}\end{matrix}\right\} & \left\{\begin{matrix}\text{very cold}\\ \text{cold}\end{matrix}\right\} & \left\{\begin{matrix}\text{just recently}\\ \text{recently}\end{matrix}\right\} & \begin{matrix}[1]\\ [2]\end{matrix} \end{matrix}$$

(Braces { }, as well as the oblique stroke (or slash) /, are used in this grammar to indicate choice relations.)

In each of the structural positions (a–d) either a single word or a combination of words may be used. In this sense we may say that *the weather/it*, *very cold/cold*, etc in [1] and [2] are COMMUTABLE. We may also say that by virtue of this commutability, *very* and *just* in [1] are OPTIONAL constituents of the phrases in which they occur, and such optionality is indicated, in this grammar, by the use of parentheses ( ):

The weather has been (very) cold (just) recently. [3]

A typical English sentence will in fact contain a mixture of simple and complex units:

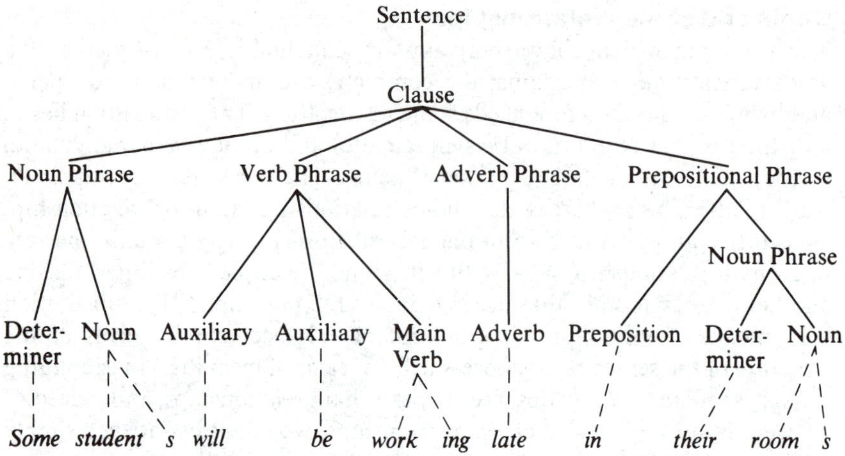

Fig 2.6

The occurrence of unitary constituents means that there is nothing contradictory in describing the same linguistic item on one occasion as a unit of one kind, and on another occasion as a unit of a different kind. For example, *late* in *Fig* 2.6 may be equally correctly described as an adverb phrase, as an adverb, or as a stem morpheme. When we say '*late* is an *X*', where *X* is the name for some grammatical unit or category, this identification means, more precisely, that *late* is a REALIZATION (or 'specimen') of *X*, and this does not rule out the possibility of its being at the same time a realization of some other unit or category *Y*. For this reason, any grammatical statement of the form '*i* is an *X*' (where *i* is an item, say a word or a sequence of words) is likely to be incomplete; but this form of words is so convenient that in spite of its incompleteness, we shall use it in this grammar when no confusion can arise.

The most extreme case of such multiple realization is that of a one-morpheme sentence such as the imperative *Hurry!* Here we may describe the same item as a sentence, a clause, a phrase, a word, or a morpheme.

The grammatical hierarchy

2.7 The existence of unitary constituents also leads to a superficial difficulty in talking of units of different 'size' or 'length'. As a particular unit may consist of one, or more than one, unit of a different kind, it follows that we cannot say, in a literal commonsense way, that 'a phrase is longer than a word', or 'a clause is larger than a phrase'. But at the same time, there is a hierarchical ranking of units in terms of their POTENTIAL size. Thus, although a given phrase (say *late* in *Fig* 2.6) may be no larger than a word, the choice category to which it belongs, that of adverb phrases, may have other realizations much longer than a single word, including such phrases as *quite late*, *quite late enough*, *very much later than I expected*. In this sense, units of grammar may be placed in a hierarchy of POTENTIAL SIZE or EXTENSIBILITY as follows:

HIGHEST UNIT: SENTENCES, which consist of one or more
CLAUSES, which consist of one or more

PHRASES, which consist of one or more
WORDS, which consist of one or more
LOWEST UNIT: MORPHEMES

By MORPHEME we understand a minimum unit of form and meaning which may be a whole word (*forget*), an inflection such as *-s* (*forget* + *s*) or a word-formation affix such as *un-*, *-ful* (*un* + *forget* + *ful*). On the sentence as the highest grammatical unit, *cf* 2.11.

In this hierarchy, the WORD is a unit of particular importance because it is the unit which primarily relates the grammar of a language to its lexicon (*cf* 2.34). Consequently the relation between words and their component morphemes is somewhat different from that which obtains between other units and their immediate constituents. The combination of morphemes in words is constrained not only by grammatical but by lexical considerations (*cf* App I.1*ff*), and the discrete segmentation of words into sequences of morphemes is not always possible – consider, for example, the relation between *crisis* and *crises*, between *sane* and *sanity*, or between *sing* and *sung*. It is because of these and other differences that grammar is generally divided (*cf* 1.14) into morphology (dealing with the internal form of words in so far as this is a grammatical matter; *cf* 2.35) and syntax (dealing with the way in which words are combined to form sentences).

Embedding

2.8 The above hierarchy still represents an oversimplified view of the relation between units. In *Fig* 2.6 it can be observed that one kind of phrase, the prepositional phrase *in their rooms*, contains as a constituent another phrase, the noun phrase *their rooms*. This is an example of the phenomenon of EMBEDDING which accounts for the indefinite extensibility of certain units of grammar. Both the noun phrase and the prepositional phrase may be immediate constituents of a clause, as are *some students* and *in their rooms* in the sentence of *Fig* 2.6:

Some students will be working late *in their rooms*.

Both units likewise can consist of more than one word (prepositional phrases, indeed, must normally consist of at least two words). There is therefore no reason to describe one unit as more extensible than the other; they are both, as phrases, placed at the same position in the hierarchy. But each unit can be a constituent of the other:

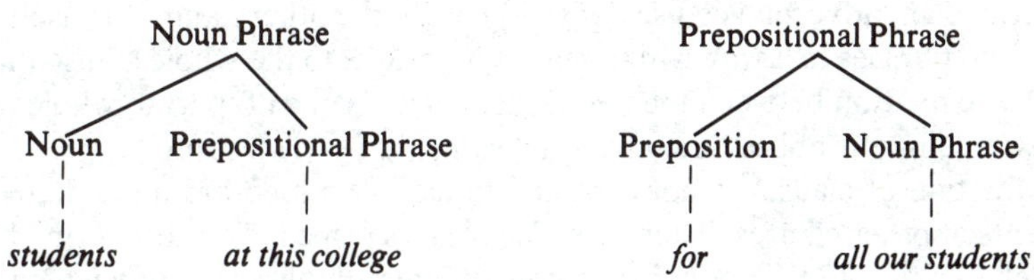

***Fig* 2.8**

This means that, by repeated embedding, both a noun phrase and a prepositional phrase can be indefinitely extended:

NOUN PHRASE: some students [at [the college [on [the other side [of [the park [at [the north end [of . . .]]]]]]]]]

PREPOSITIONAL PHRASE: on [the top floor [of [a house [in [the corner [of [the old square [behind [the church . . .]]]]]]]]]

In practice, of course, phrases of this degree of complexity rarely occur; but it is important to recognize that however long such a phrase may be, there is always the possibility of making it longer by further embedding. Moreover, the indefinite length of noun phrases and prepositional phrases does not affect their position in the grammatical hierarchy, since however long a phrase may be, the clause which contains it will always be (potentially) longer:

> I have been talking to *some students at the college on the other side of the park at the north end of . . .*
>
> They live *on the top floor of a house in the corner of the old square behind the church . . .*

Embedding, as we have illustrated it so far, can be defined as the occurrence of one unit as a constituent of another unit at the same rank in the grammatical hierarchy. (As we shall see in 2.9, the embedded unit need not be an *immediate* constituent of the equivalent unit in which it is embedded.)

Subordination

2.9 Another kind of embedding occurs when one clause is made a constituent of another clause: the case normally described as SUBORDINATION. The two clauses in [1] and [2] constitute simple sentences, but it is also possible to combine them into a single (complex) sentence, by subordinating one to the other, as in [3]:

> The weather has been remarkably warm. [1]
>
> We returned from Italy last week. [2]
>
> The weather has been remarkably warm since we returned from Italy last week. [3]

Clauses which are embedded in other clauses (*eg*: *since we returned from Italy last week* in [3]) are SUBORDINATE clauses, and they are often introduced by a subordinating CONJUNCTION (*since* in [3]). The subordinate clause in [3] is parallel in its function to the adverb phrase *just recently* in *Fig* 2.3d, and is indeed termed an 'adverbial clause' (*cf* 15.17*ff*). On the other hand, it is itself divisible into phrases in a way which makes it parallel to the whole clause in *Fig* 2.3d. The relation between the two clauses of [3] is one of 'part to whole', as is illustrated by the abbreviated tree diagram, *Fig* 2.9a, opposite.

Subordination of clauses is not confined to clauses which are immediate constituents of other clauses. There are also clauses (especially those termed relative clauses; *cf* 17.9*ff*) which are constituents of phrases, and which therefore are only indirectly embedded within a larger clause, *cf Fig* 2.9b opposite.

Once again, embedding gives rise to the theoretical possibility of grammatical units having indefinite length. The familiar nursery chant *The*

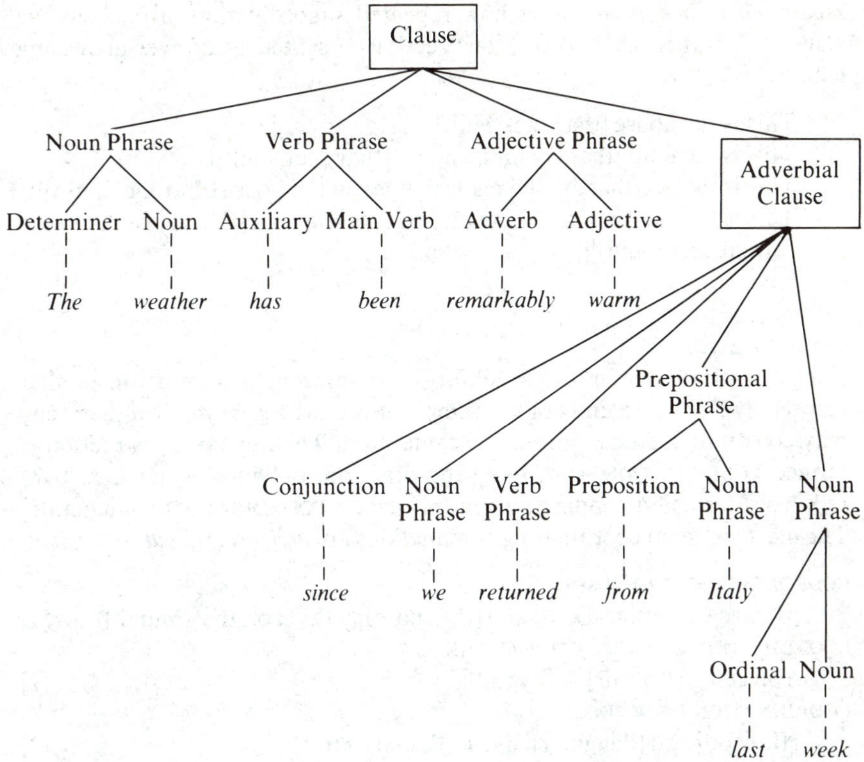

Fig 2.9a

Note Morphemes and unitary constituents (*eg* the Noun constituent above *Italy*) have not been included in this diagram.

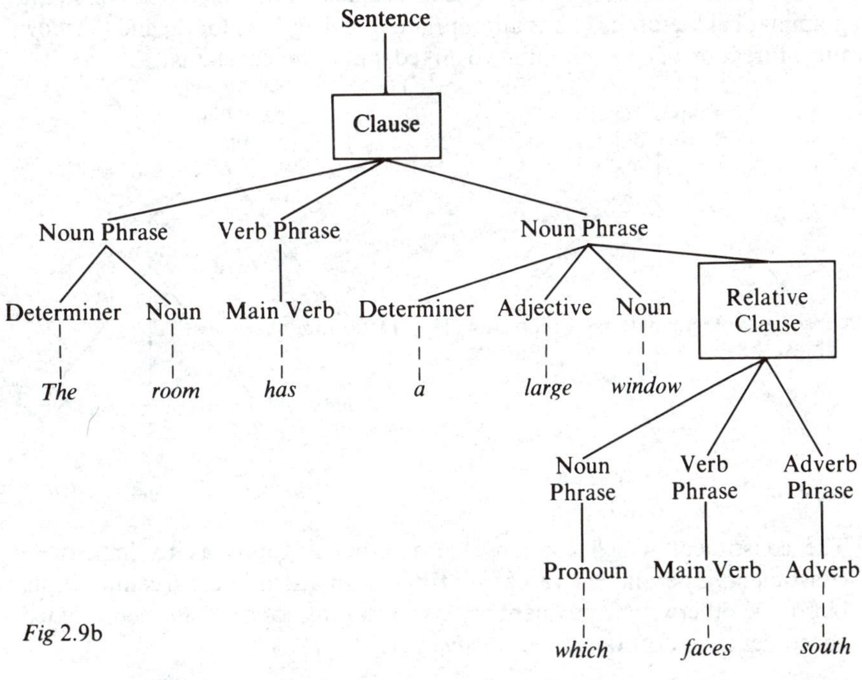

Fig 2.9b

House That Jack Built shows how repeated subordination of one relative clause to another leads to the construction of sentences of ever-increasing length:

This is the house [that Jack built].
This is the malt [that lay in the house [that Jack built]].
This is the rat [that ate the malt [that lay in the house [that Jack built]]].
This is the cat [that killed the rat [that ate the malt [that lay in the house [that Jack built]]]].
etc

Coordination

2.10 The principle of indefinite extensibility is also present in grammar in another respect: two or more units of the same status on the grammatical hierarchy may constitute a single unit of the same kind. This type of construction is termed COORDINATION, and, like subordination, is typically signalled by a link-word termed a conjunction: in this case a COORDINATING conjunction. The most common coordinating conjunctions are *and*, *or*, and *but*:

COORDINATION OF CLAUSES:
[[It was Christmas Day,] and [the snow lay thick on the ground]]. [1]
COORDINATION OF PREPOSITIONAL PHRASES:
You can go [[by air] or [by rail]]. [2]
COORDINATION OF NOUNS:
His [[son] and [daughter]] live in Buenos Aires. [3]

In these examples, the coordinated units are respectively clauses, phrases, and words. Coordination has many variations and complications which cannot be illustrated here (*cf* Chapter 13), but its essential principle is that units and structures may be duplicated without affecting their position in the grammatical hierarchy. Thus appropriate tree diagrams for [2] and [3] show the bifurcation of one unit into two linked units of equal status:

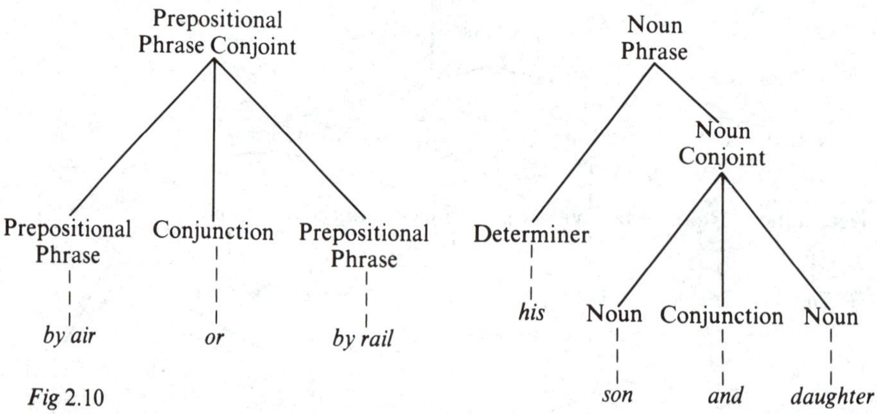

Fig 2.10

The constituent which contains the coordinated units as its immediate constituents is here labelled a 'conjoint' item, to mark its internal composition, but it is otherwise equivalent in its status to each of its coordinated constituents, or CONJOINS (*son*, *daughter*, etc).

These examples show the most common case, where the conjoint contains only two coordinated units; but the number of coordinated constituents is open-ended. We may compare the phrase *his son and daughter* in [3] with the treble coordination of *his wife, son, and daughter* (noting that the coordinating conjunction normally occurs before only the last conjoin), or with the more extended coordination of:

> The colours of the rainbow are *blue*, *green*, *yellow*, *orange*, *red*, *indigo*, *and violet*.

or with the theoretical extremity of an infinitely long coordination:

> The positive integers are *one*, *two*, *three*, *four*, *five*, *six*, *seven*, . . .

Note Conjoins are called 'conjuncts' by some grammarians, but in this grammar we use the latter term for linking adverbials (*cf* 8.134*ff*).

Sentences

2.11 It is usually assumed that the SENTENCE is the highest-ranking unit of grammar, and hence that the purpose of a grammatical description of English is to define, by means of whatever descriptive apparatus may be necessary (rules, categories, etc), what counts as a grammatical sentence in English. In this way, the terms 'grammar' and 'sentence' are mutually defining. In the past, grammarians have aimed to define 'sentence' as a prerequisite to defining 'grammar', or to define 'grammar' as a means of defining 'sentence'. But both approaches will be avoided here: indeed, neither of these terms can be given a clear-cut definition. The sentence is an indeterminate unit in the sense that it is often difficult to decide, particularly in spoken language, where one sentence ends and another begins (*cf* 19.29*ff*). The term 'grammar' is indeterminate in the sense that 'What counts as a grammatical English sentence?' is not always a question which permits a decisive answer; and this is not only because of the difficulty of segmenting a discourse into sentences but because questions of grammatical acceptability inevitably become involved with questions of meaning, with questions of good or bad style, with questions of lexical acceptability, with questions of acceptability in context, etc. To give a realistic presentation of English grammar, we therefore have to abandon neat boundaries, and to accept that grammar is a linguistic 'core' round which other aspects of linguistic organization and usage are integrated. Our intention, therefore, is to take a broad interpretation of grammar, which will enable us to give an account of other factors, especially meaning, which impinge on the discussion of grammatical rules and categories.

The CLAUSE, particularly the independent clause (*cf* 14.2), is in many ways a more clearly-defined unit than the sentence. It is for this reason that we shall concentrate, in this and the following nine chapters, on the SIMPLE SENTENCE (*ie* the sentence consisting of a single independent clause) as the most central part of grammar. We shall use the term MULTIPLE SENTENCE (subsuming complex and compound sentences) (*cf* 14.1*ff*) for all sentences which consist of more than one clause, either through subordination or through coordination. Thus the limits of the English sentence are defined, in practice, wherever grammatical relations (such as those of subordination and coordination) cannot be established between clauses. Such relations, and their limits, are explored in later chapters, particularly Chapters 13, 14, and 19.

Form and function

2.12 We have indicated how grammatical categories may be identified through relationships of choice (or substitution) between constituents. In the simple cases of examples 2.6 [1] and [2], repeated here as [1] and [2], we recognized four positions in the clause where different kinds of phrase can occur:

The weather	has been	very cold	just recently	[1]
It	was	cold	recently	[2]

But to describe more fully how clauses are composed of phrases, it is necessary to take account of other factors, *eg* whether a constituent may vary its position (MOBILITY), and whether a constituent can be omitted (OPTIONALITY). In both these respects, the adverb phrases of [1] and [2] are different from the other phrases:

The weather has been very cold *just recently*. [1]
Just recently, the weather has been very cold. [1a]
The weather has been very cold. [1b]

Another observation about the adverb phrase is that it may be replaced by a different kind of constituent, which is similarly optional and mobile. For example, a noun phrase such as *this month* or a prepositional phrase such as *during the past week* may be a substitute for *just recently* in [1] and [1a]:

The weather has been very cold	*just recently.*	[1]
	this month.	[1c]
	during the past week.	[1d]

On the other hand, we obviously cannot always replace a noun phrase by an adverb phrase or by a prepositional phrase:

This month has been very cold. [3]
**Just recently* has been very cold. [4]
**During the past week* has been very cold. [5]

That is, noun phrases are in a 'choice' relation to other kinds of phrase on some occasions, but not on others.

In order to state more complicated facts of constituency such as these, it is important to distinguish two ways of classifying constituents. We may classify a unit either on the basis of its FORM (*eg* its internal structure, as a noun phrase, or as a verb phrase), or on the basis of its FUNCTION (*eg* as a subject or an object of a clause). By function is meant a unit's 'privilege of occurrence', in terms of its position, mobility, optionality, etc, in the unit of which it is a constituent. Two units which have the same privilege of occurrence may be said to be FUNCTIONALLY EQUIVALENT. Thus the final phrases of [1], [1c], and [1d], although they belong to different formal categories (adverb phrase, noun phrase, prepositional phrase), may be said to belong to the same functional category of ADVERBIAL. Such categories define ELEMENTS OF STRUCTURE in the higher unit, which in this case is a clause. An adverbial, generally speaking, is distinguished from other elements by its variable position (for example, initial, medial, or final in the clause), by its optionality, and by the fact that the number of adverbials which can occur in a clause is not fixed.

The advantage of distinguishing functional from formal categories is that generalizations of two kinds can be made: those about a unit's status as a constituent of a higher unit, and those about its internal structure in terms of smaller or lower units. In some cases (*eg* prepositions; *cf* 2.29) the distinction is unimportant, but in other cases it is important and indeed necessary. For example, it is important to distinguish those prepositional phrases which act as adverbials from those which act as parts of noun phrases. It is also important to distinguish *adverbials* (a functional category) from *adverb phrases* (a formal category, whose members frequently function as adverbials). Here, as elsewhere, we trust that the advantage of using traditional and widely-understood terms outweighs any danger of confusion.

Note A FORMAL classification takes account of how a unit is composed of smaller units or components, including, in the case of words, stems and affixes. Since English often lacks formal indicators of word class, we often identify words by their function rather than their form.

Clause structure

Central and peripheral elements of the clause

2.13 The form–function distinction is particularly important in the case of clause structure, which we shall now discuss in some detail as the most familiar and important illustration of functional classification. To describe the constituency of clauses, we need to distinguish the following elements of clause structure:

SUBJECT (S), VERB (V), OBJECT (O), COMPLEMENT (C), and ADVERBIAL (A).

These are exemplified in the following simple declarative sentences:

Someone [S] was laughing [V] loudly [A] in the next room [A]. [1]
My mother [S] usually [A] enjoys [V] parties [O] very much [A]. [2]
In 1945 [A] the country [S] became [V] totally independent [C]. [3]
I [S] have been [V] in the garden [A] all the time [A] since lunch [A]. [4]
Mary [S] gave [V] the visitor [O] a glass of milk [O]. [5]
Most people [S] consider [V] these books [O] rather expensive [C], actually [A]. [6]
You [S] must put [V] all the toys [O] upstairs [A] immediately [A]. [7]

At the simplest level, we may make the following generalizations about clause structures from these examples. The verb element (V) is the most 'central' element, and in all the examples above it is preceded by the subject (S). Following the verb there may be one or two objects (O), or a complement (C), which follows the object if one is present. The most peripheral element is the adverbial, which can occur either initially (in front of the subject, as in [3]), or finally (after the verb, and after the object or complement if one is present, as in [1], [4], and [6]). Many adverbials, however, may also occur medially, as in [2]. A clause may contain a varied number of final adverbials; *eg* none [5], one [2], two [7], three [4]. These observations are summarized in the simplified formula:

(A) S (A) V (O) (O) (C) (A . . .)

(As elsewhere, parentheses signal elements which may or may not be present in any given clause.) As a first approximation, this indicates something of the variability of clause structures in declarative clauses, although it will need later modification (*cf* Notes [a] and [b]).

The distinction between 'centre' and 'periphery' is relative rather than absolute. The verb element is the most 'central' element in that (i) its position is normally medial rather than initial or final; (ii) it is normally obligatory; (iii) it cannot normally be moved to a different position in the clause; and (iv) it helps to determine what other elements must occur (*cf* 2.16*ff*). For the opposite reasons, adverbials are the most peripheral elements: (i) their position is most frequently final; (ii) they are usually optional; (iii) they are mostly mobile; and (iv) they do not determine what other elements occur. They may be regarded, from a structural point of view, largely as 'optional extras', which may be added at will, so that it is not possible to give an exact limit to the number of adverbials a clause may contain. The other elements, subject, object, and complement, are in various degrees more peripheral than the verb, and less peripheral than the adverbial.

Note **[a]** Although in [1–7] the subject is apparently just as indispensable to clause structure as the verb, it will be noted that in imperative and nonfinite clauses the subject is usually optional (*cf* 2.57, 11.24*f*, 14.6*ff*). There is also a category of clauses in which the verb is omitted (verbless clauses; *cf* 14.9), but this is a less significant category than those of imperative and nonfinite clauses.

[b] The above generalizations will, of course, be subject to modification when we consider a wider range of clauses, particularly subordinate and nondeclarative clauses. For example, elements other than adverbials have a limited mobility; on movement of subjects, *cf* 2.48; of verbs, 18.8*f*; of objects and complements, 18.20, 18.37, 18.38.

[c] It is unfortunate that traditionally the word *verb* does service both for a clause element, and for the class of word which occurs as a constituent of that element. For example, in the former sense *must put* in [7] is a verb, and in the latter sense, *must* and *put* are verbs individually (*cf* 2.27). The term 'predicator' has been sometimes used to replace 'verb' in the sense of 'verb element', but for lack of a familiar alternative, we shall continue to use *verb* in both senses, distinguishing between verbs as elements and verbs as words where there is some risk of confusion. In yet another sense (*cf* 2.35) *verb* designates a basic verb form, or LEXICAL ITEM, which is manifested in different morphemes or morpheme combinations; *eg*: *have*, *having*, and *had* are all forms of the lexical item HAVE. (A similar polysemy applies to other word classes, particularly nouns).

A 'fixed word-order language'

2.14 To illustrate the mobility of adverbials in contrast with other elements, we may observe that in example [2] *usually* can be moved to initial or final position:

My mother *usually* enjoys parties very much. [S A V O A] [2]
Usually my mother enjoys parties very much. [A S V O A] [2a]
My mother enjoys parties very much, *usually*. [S V O A A] [2b]

However, the other elements cannot be similarly moved from their S V O sequence:

*Usually enjoys parties my mother very much. [A V O S A]
*Enjoys usually my mother parties very much. [V A S O A]
*My mother parties usually enjoys very much. [S O A V A]

The fact that these orders, and many others of the same elements, do not readily occur, helps to explain why English is commonly described as a 'fixed word-order language'. In practice, discussion of word order in languages tends to revolve around the ordering of phrases which are clause elements, and it is notable, for instance, that in English the positions of subject, verb, and object are relatively fixed. In declarative clauses, they occur regularly in the order S V O, unless there are particular conditions (for example, the initial placing of the object pronoun in relative clauses) which lead to a disturbance of this order. Further conditions allow variations of this declarative order (for example, *Parties my mother usually enjoys very much* is a possible, though less usual, variant of [2]); these will be discussed in 2.59 and 18.20.

It is enough to state here that English does indeed have strict limitations on the ordering of clause elements, but that the more peripheral an element is, the more freedom of position it has. After V, S is the least mobile element, followed by O and C. Later we shall give attention to the various factors which lead to the displacement of an element from its regular position (*cf* esp 2.59, 11.5, 11.14, and 18.19*ff*).

Note [**a**] In [2], the restriction on movement even extends to the adverbial *very much*, which in comparison with other members of the adverbial category is relatively immobile:

*Very much my mother usually enjoys parties. [A S A V O] [2c]

[**b**] In terms of the present grammatical hierarchy (*cf* 2.7) the term *word order* ought to apply strictly to the ordering of words within phrases, rather than of phrases within clauses. This is not the normal interpretation of the expression, but it may be incidentally noted that in this more restricted sense, English has an even greater fixity of word order. Note, for example, beside [2a–2c], the still greater dislocation in:

**Mother my* usually enjoys parties *much very*.

Adverbials

2.15 It is worth pointing out that different degrees of centrality can be observed not only in different elements of clause structure, but also in different subcategories of the same element. Thus the adverbial category has been described as the most peripheral, but it is in fact a heterogeneous category, within which there are relatively central and relatively peripheral types of adverbial. In examples 2.13 [1–7], most of the adverbials are both mobile and optional: it is possible, for example, to omit the adverbial *usually* in [2] (*My mother enjoys parties very much*) as well as to change its position (as in examples 2.14 [2a] and [2b]). But there are, as we have just seen in [2c], some adverbials which cannot readily be moved from their position in a given clause, and there are even adverbials which are obligatory, such as the place adverbials *in the garden* in example 2.13 [4] and *upstairs* in 2.13 [7]:

I have been *in the garden* all the time since lunch. [4]
You must put all the toys *upstairs* immediately. [7]

Contrast:

*I have been all the time since lunch. [4a]
*You must put all the toys immediately. [7a]

Because they are essential to the 'completion' of the meaning of the verb, such elements are classified by some grammarians as complements (*cf* 2.17*f*, 10.11). Our position, however, is that adverbials represent a spectrum of types, the most central of which, because of their obligatoriness and relative immobility, resemble complements. In provisional support of this analysis, note that *in the garden* and *upstairs* are equivalent to adverbials in meaning, *eg* in answering the question *Where?*, even though they are similar to complements in acting as an obligatory element following the verb BE.

At the other end of the spectrum, there are elements which are frequently called SENTENCE ADVERBIALS, because they tend to qualify, by their meaning, a whole sentence or clause, rather than just part of a clause (such as a verb, or a verb and object):

To my regret, he refused the offer of help. [8]
He was, *however*, very interested in my other proposals. [9]

In Chapter 8, these adverbials are subdivided into DISJUNCTS (those which, like *to my regret* in [8], comment on the form or content of the clause) and CONJUNCTS (those which, like *however* in [9], have a connective function). Such sentence adverbials are distinguished from ADJUNCTS and SUBJUNCTS, adverbials which are more closely integrated with the rest of the clause, and which include such familiar categories as adverbials of manner, place, time, and degree (*cf* 8.39, 8.51, 8.79, 8.104).

Characteristic of disjuncts and conjuncts are such markers of peripherality as separation from the rest of the clause by intonation boundaries in speech (*cf* App II.11*ff*) or by commas in writing (*cf* App III.17*f*). The distinctions between these four major types of adverbial are significant enough to deserve careful analysis in a later chapter (8.24*ff*), and yet it must be concluded that there is no clear division between the more central and more peripheral adverbials. Here we anticipate a problem which will be confronted at the end of this chapter (2.60): that of the partial INDETERMINACY of grammatical categories.

Note Sentence [4a] is grammatical if *been* is interpreted as an auxiliary verb followed by ellipsis of the main verb, as in (*cf* 12.62):

A: You should have been waiting here when the taxi arrived.
B: I have been (waiting) all the time since lunch.

Clause types

2.16 By eliminating *optional* adverbials from the clause structures illustrated in 2.13, we arrive at a classification of the essential core of each clause structure. Of the obligatory elements, the main verb is the one that wholly or largely determines what form the rest of the structure will take. From examples [1–7] the following seven CLAUSE TYPES emerge:

Table 2.16 Clause types

	S(ubject)	V(erb)	O(bject(s))	C(omplement)	A(dverbial)	
Type *SV*	Someone	was laughing				[1a]
Type *SVO*	My mother	enjoys	parties			[2a]
Type *SVC*	The country	became		totally independent		[3a]
Type *SVA*	I	have been			in the garden	[4a]
Type *SVOO*	Mary	gave	the visitor			
			a glass of milk			[5a]
Type *SVOC*	Most people	consider	these books	rather expensive		[6a]
Type *SVOA*	You	must put	all the toys		upstairs	[7a]

This set of patterns is the most general classification that can be usefully applied to the whole range of English clauses whether main or subordinate. Each clause type is associated with a set of verbs, as will be shown in detail in 16.18–66.

The seven fall naturally into three main types. There are:

a two-element pattern: *SV*

three three-element patterns: $SV + \begin{Bmatrix} O \\ C \\ A \end{Bmatrix}$

three four-element patterns: $SVO + \begin{Bmatrix} O \\ C \\ A \end{Bmatrix}$

Cutting across this threefold classification are three main verb classes:

INTRANSITIVE VERBS (*eg*: *laugh* in [1a]), are followed by no obligatory element, and occur in type *SV*.

TRANSITIVE VERBS (*eg*: *enjoy* in [2a], *give* in [5a], *consider* in [6a], *put* in [7a]) are followed by an OBJECT (*cf* 2.17), and occur in types *SVO*, *SVOO*, *SVOC*, and *SVOA* respectively.

COPULAR VERBS (*eg*: *become* in [3a], *be* in [4a]) are followed by a SUBJECT COMPLEMENT (*cf* 2.17) or an ADVERBIAL, and occur in types *SVC* and *SVA*.

In a general sense, the term TRANSITIVE is often applied to all verbs which require an object, including those of clause types *SVOO*, *SVOC*, and *SVOA*. It is, however, convenient to make a further classification of the verbs in these patterns:

TRANSITIVE VERBS →
- MONOTRANSITIVE VERBS occur in type *SVO*
- DITRANSITIVE VERBS occur in type *SVOO*
- COMPLEX TRANSITIVE VERBS occur in types *SVOC* and *SVOA*.

The term 'verb' primarily refers not to the whole V element, but to the main verb (*cf* 2.29) of the verb phrase: in [7a], for example, it is the main verb *put* (or more strictly, the lexical item PUT; *cf* 2.35–36) which determines that an object and an adverbial must follow the verb element.

The term COPULA refers to the verb BE, and COPULAR verbs are those verbs (including BE and BECOME) which are functionally equivalent to the copula (*cf* 16.21*ff*). They are variously called 'copulative', 'equative', 'intensive', or 'linking' verbs.

Objects and complements

Before considering the verb further, however, it is important to notice differences between the various elements which have been labelled 'object' and 'complement'. The following distinctions will be made:

OBJECT →
- DIRECT OBJECT (O_d)
- INDIRECT OBJECT (O_i)

COMPLEMENT →
- SUBJECT COMPLEMENT (C_s)
- OBJECT COMPLEMENT (C_o)

An object such as *parties* in [2a] (*My mother enjoys parties*) clearly has a different semantic role in the clause from an object such as *the visitor* in [5a] (*Mary gave the visitor a glass of milk*), and this has been traditionally recognized by applying the term DIRECT OBJECT to the former, and INDIRECT OBJECT to the latter. Leaving the semantic distinction until 10.7, 10.18*ff*, we give priority here to the distributional fact that whenever there are two objects (in type *SVOO*), the former is normally the indirect object, and the latter the direct object. But although it is more central with regard to position (*cf* 2.13), in other respects the indirect object is more peripheral than the direct object: it is more likely to be optional, and may generally be paraphrased by a prepositional phrase functioning as adverbial (*cf* 2.23).

Similarly, we must distinguish between the type of complement found in the *SVC* pattern; *ie*: *totally independent* in:

The country became totally independent. [3a]

and the type of complement found in the *SVOC* pattern; *ie*: *rather expensive* in:

Most people consider these books rather expensive. [6a]

The distinction is effectively made by noting that in [3a] the country is understood to have become a *totally independent country*, while in [6a] the books are understood to be considered *rather expensive books*. In other words, in *SVC* clauses the complement applies some attribute or definition to the subject, whereas in *SVOC* clauses it applies an attribute or definition to the object. This distinction is usually denoted by the terms SUBJECT COMPLEMENT and OBJECT COMPLEMENT respectively. In these cases, the complement is an adjective phrase, but elsewhere, where the complement is a noun phrase, the same kind of distinction holds:

Type *SVC*: The country became *a separate nation*.
Type *SVOC*: Most people considered Picasso *a genius*.

In the *SVC* sentence, *a separate nation* is understood to be a definition of the subject, *the country*, while in the *SVOC* sentence, *a genius* is understood to be a definition of the object, *Picasso*.

Note [**a**] In place of 'subject complement', the term 'predicative noun' or 'predicative adjective' is sometimes used. Other alternatives are 'predicative nominal' and 'predicative adjectival', the choice between 'nominal' and 'adjectival' being determined by whether this element is a noun phrase or an adjective phrase.
[**b**] Also, some writers make use of a very broad sense of 'complement', subsuming complements, objects, and obligatory adverbials in the present grammar.

Obligatory adverbials

2.18 There is a parallel between complements and obligatory adverbials (*cf* 2.15). Obligatory adverbials are largely restricted to what in a broad sense we may term SPACE ADJUNCTS (*cf* 8.3, 8.39*ff*). Just as complements can be divided into subject complements and object complements, so can obligatory space adjuncts be divided into those occurring in the *SVA* pattern, in which a location is attributed to the referent of the subject, and those occurring in the *SVOA* pattern, in which a location is attributed to the referent of the object. The parallel may be brought out as follows:

He [S] stayed [V] *very quiet* [C_s]. [1]
He [S] stayed [V] *in bed* [A_s]. [2]

They [S] kept [V] him [O] *very quiet* [C_o]. [3]
They [S] kept [V] him [O] *in bed* [A_o]. [4]

The symbols A_s and A_o here indicate a subject-related adjunct and an object-related adjunct respectively. The parallel between the two sets of clause types is also evident in the verb classes, and we acknowledge this by calling the verb in both [1] and [2] COPULAR (since it is equivalent in function to the copula BE) and calling the verb in both [3] and [4] COMPLEX TRANSITIVE (*cf* 2.16).

Space adjuncts occurring in the *SVA* and *SVOA* patterns include not only those indicating position, such as *in bed* or *at the office*, but also those indicating direction, such as *down* in *She put the glass down* (*cf* 10.10, 16.24). By extension, they may also include adverbials which specify 'temporal location', as in:

The next meeting will be *on the 5th February*.

and by a more abstract and metaphorical interpretation of 'space' (*cf* 9.32):

The road [S] is [V] *under construction* [A_s].
We [S] kept [V] him [O] *off cigarettes* [A_o].

But there are still some obligatory adverbials to which a locational metaphor cannot be applied. Examples are the manner adjunct *kindly* in [5], and the prepositional phrase *without a job* in [6]:

They [S] treated [V] her [O] *kindly* [A]. [5]
He [S] is [V] *without a job* [A]. [6]

At the same time, the close relationship of the prepositional phrase in [6] to a subject complement is evident in its semantic equivalence to the adjective *unemployed*.

Note As the above examples suggest, the distinction between complement and adverbial is by no means clear-cut, and there are strong arguments for classifying prepositional phrases such as *without a job* in [6] as complements. For further discussion, *cf* 10.11. Another difficulty, in determining the function in a clause of some prepositional phrases, is that which arises over the status of prepositional verbs such as *consist of* (*cf* 16.5*ff*).

Clause elements subclassified

2.19 *Table* 2.19 Verb classes in relation to clause types

Type *SV*	S Prices	V (intransitive) rose			[1]
Type *SVO*	S Elizabeth	V (monotransitive) enjoys	O_d classical music		[2]
Type *SVC*	S Your face	V (copular) seems	C_s familiar		[3]
Type *SVA*	S My sister	V (copular) lives	A_s next door		[4]
Type *SVOO*	S We all	V (ditransitive) wish	O_i you	O_d a happy birthday	[5]
Type *SVOC*	S The president	V (complex transitive) declared	O_d the meeting	C_o open	[6]
Type *SVOA*	S The doorman	V (complex transitive) showed	O_d the guests	A_o into the drawing room	[7]

A_o object-related adverbial C_o object complement O_d direct object
A_s subject-related adverbial C_s subject complement O_i indirect object

We have now found it necessary not only to distinguish functional categories such as subject, verb, and object in the structure of the clause, but also to subclassify these into more specific categories, such as transitive verb, direct object, and subject complement. Such subclassification is typical of both formal and functional distinctions in grammar. Only through these finer distinctions can an adequate account be given of what combinations of constituents enter into the structure of the English clause. To clarify the terminology and its use, let us return to the seven clause types in *Table* 2.16, and specify the structures more precisely (again omitting optional adverbials) by means of subcategories of V, O, C, and A, in *Table* 2.19 opposite. The abbreviations used are those which will be current throughout this book (new examples are added for further illustration). Further variations on these clause types, including some exceptional patterns, are discussed in 16.18*ff*.

Systematic correspondences

2.20 The study of grammatical structure is aided by observing systematic CORRESPONDENCES between one structure and another. Such correspondences are sometimes described in terms of transformational rules, but we shall not make use of such theoretical formulations in this book. Instead, we shall use demonstrable correspondences as an informal way of showing similarities and contrasts between structures. They are important in explaining the relation between grammatical choice and meaning, and also in providing criteria for classification.

A systematic correspondence may be broadly defined as a relation or mapping between two structures X and Y, such that if the same lexical content occurs in X and in Y, there is a constant meaning relation between the two structures. (In using the term 'lexical content', we allow for the possibility that X and Y may contain different, though related, lexical items, such as *wise* and *wisely*.) This relation is often one of semantic equivalence, or paraphrase. In 2.21–24, we give three important examples of systematic correspondence, and show how they help in the identification of clause elements. Further types of correspondence will be examined in 2.45*ff*.

The symbol ~ is used in this book to represent such correspondences. Lack of systematic correspondence is symbolized by ≁.

We take the seven basic clause types of [1–7] as the point of departure for our description, but do not regard correspondences as unidirectional.

Active and passive structures

2.21 Clauses containing a noun phrase as object are distinguished by the fact that they are usually matched by passive clauses, in which the object noun phrase now appears as subject (V_{pass} = passive verb phrase), *cf Table* 2.21 on the next page. As type *SVOO* clauses have two objects, they can often have two passive forms – one in which the indirect object becomes the subject, and another in which the direct object becomes subject. Further discussion of the active–passive relationship is found in 3.63*ff*.

As the formulae show, this correspondence permits us to convert clauses of types with an object into equivalent types without objects (or, in the case of *SVOO*, with only one object). Thus the passive of *They considered him a genius* [*SVOC*] is closely parallel in meaning to the *SVC* pattern, except for the passive verb phrase:

He was considered a genius. [S V_{pass} C_s]
cf He seemed a genius. [S V C_s]

In all passive clause types, the agent *by*-phrase (*cf* 3.65*ff*, 9.50), which incorporates a noun phrase equivalent to the subject of the corresponding active clause, has the structural status of an optional adverbial (it is marked (A) in *Table* 2.21). Even when the agent *by*-phrase is absent, however, there is an implication of its presence at the level of meaning. In this sense, the agent *by*-phrase acts as complementation (*cf* 2.32) of the passive verb. Thus *He was considered a genius* carries the implication '. . . by someone or other'.

Table 2.21 Relations between active and passive clause types

	Type *SVO*
S V O_d ~	A number of people saw the accident
S V_{pass} (A)	~ The accident was seen (by a number of people)
	Type *SVOO*
S V O_i O_d ~	My father gave me this watch
{ S V_{pass} O_d (A)	{ (1) ~ I was given this watch (by my father)
{ S V_{pass} O_i (A)	{ (2) ~ This watch was given (to) me (by my father)
	Type *SVOC*
S V O_d C_o ~	Queen Victoria considered him a genius
S V_{pass} C_s (A)	~ He was considered a genius (by Queen Victoria)
	Type *SVOA*
S V O_d A_o ~	An intruder must have placed the ladder there
S V_{pass} A_s (A)	~ The ladder must have been placed there (by an intruder)

Note [**a**] There are some exceptions (*eg* the verbs *have, cost, resemble*; *cf* 10.14, 16.27) to the passive equivalence with type *SVO*; *eg*:

John had the book ~ *The book was had by John.

[**b**] The second passive corresponding to type *SVOO* in *Table* 2.21 above is unidiomatic in AmE. More acceptable, in both AmE and BrE, is the related *SVOA* ~ *SVA* passive with a prepositional phrase (*cf* 2.23); *eg*:

Some flowers had been brought *him*.

is less natural than:

Some flowers had been brought *for him*.

With some verbs the former type seems quite unacceptable (*cf* 16.55*ff*):

*Some fish had been caught/bought/cooked *us*.

Copular and complex transitive structures

2.22 Another correspondence often obtains between an *SVOC* clause and a clause with an infinitive or *that*-clause (*cf* 16.50*f*):

I considered *her beautiful*. ~ { I considered *her* to be *beautiful*. / I considered that *she* was *beautiful*. }

This correspondence indicates that the O and C of an *SVOC* clause are in the same relation to one another as the S and C of an *SVC* clause: *She was beautiful* (*cf* 16.43*ff*). This relation is expressed, wherever it is made explicit at all, by a copular verb, and we may therefore call it, for further reference, a COPULAR relationship. Copular relationships are important in other aspects of grammar apart from clause structure. They correspond, for example, to relations of apposition (*cf* 17.65*ff*) and many relations of modification (*cf* 2.31–33).

Further, we may extend the concept of 'copular relationship' to the relation between subject and adverbial in *SVA* clauses and the relation between object and adverbial in *SVOA* clauses (*cf* 10.10, 16.24, 16.48).

Indirect objects and prepositional phrases

2.23 There is a further correspondence by which *SVOO* clauses can be converted into *SVOA* clauses by the substitution of a prepositional phrase following the direct object for the indirect object preceding it:

She sent *Jim* a card ~ She sent a card *to Jim*.
She left *Jim* a card ~ She left a card *for Jim*.

To and *for*, indicating a recipient (*cf* 9.46), are the prepositions chiefly used, but others, such as *with* and *of*, are occasionally found (*cf* 16.57).

Note [**a**] There are however, some recipient *to*- and *for*-phrases which cannot be made into indirect objects: *He suggested the idea to Bill*; *She described her home to us*; etc. A borderline case is ?*He explained me his plan*, which is acceptable to some speakers, but not to others.

[**b**] We later (16.56*ff*) consider an alternative analysis in which the *to*-phrases and the *for*-phrases illustrated above are described as *prepositional objects*, and are regarded as grammatically equivalent to indirect objects.

The characterization of clause elements

2.24 For a fuller appreciation of the clause patterns outlined in 2.16, we need to know, of course, on what grounds the elements subject, verb, object, complement, and adverbial are identified. The identification of the verb element in general presents no problem, as this element can be realized only by a verb phrase (*cf* 2.27). For the other elements, it is necessary to use a variety of criteria. Although clause elements are functional categories (*cf* 2.12), their definitions are based on formal as well as on functional criteria. Thus it is an important part of the definition of both subjects and objects that they normally consist of noun phrases; it is an important part of the definition of complements that they are normally noun phrases or adjective phrases; and it is an important part of the definition of adverbials that they may be adverb phrases, prepositional phrases, or noun phrases. It is unnecessary to go into these definitions any further in this chapter, as they are elaborated systematically in 10.5*ff*.

Phrases

Phrases as clause elements

2.25 The constituents which function as elements of clause structure are either phrases or subordinate clauses (*cf* 2.9), and our next stage is to outline briefly how the phrases, in their turn, are constituted. The five formal categories of phrase we have mentioned in 2.24 are verb phrases, noun phrases, adjective phrases, adverb phrases, and prepositional phrases. In the following diagram, the upward-pointing arrows show how these phrase types (when not embedded in other structures) can function as clause elements:

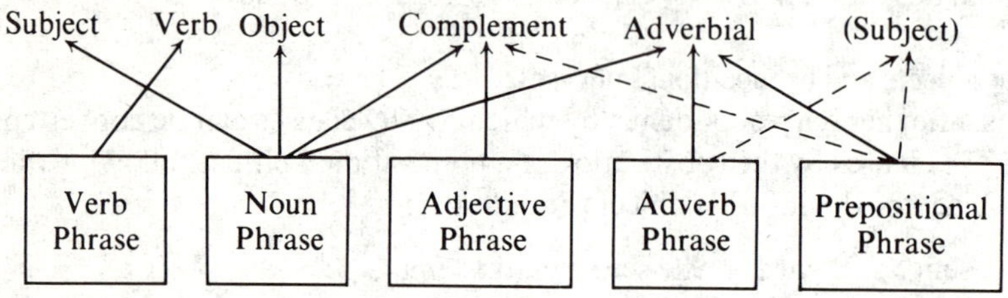

Fig 2.25 Phrases as clause elements

The broken arrows on the right indicate that adverb phrases and prepositional phrases can exceptionally function as subjects (*cf* 9.1 Note [a] and 10.15), and that prepositional phrases can exceptionally function as complements (*cf* 10.11).

Note [**a**] *Figure* 2.25 naturally omits reference to embedded phrases (*cf* 2.8), *eg* to prepositional phrases functioning as constituents of noun phrases.
[**b**] Phrases such as *the poor* and *the young* are only apparent exceptions to *Fig* 2.25: we shall argue (*cf* 7.23*ff*), that although they have an adjective as their main word (or head), such phrases are noun phrases.
[**c**] Only a limited range of adverbials can be realized as noun phrases (*cf* 8.39, 8.52).

General structural characteristics of phrases

2.26 Each phrase is named after a class of word which has a primary, and indeed obligatory function within it. This function, however, varies in different types of phrases, and we may usefully investigate it in terms of the distinction between optional and obligatory elements. One kind of construction is illustrated by prepositional phrases, which contain two normally obligatory elements: the preposition and the prepositional complement (*cf* 9.1). Another kind of construction is illustrated by adjective phrases, which have one obligatory element (an adjective), optionally preceded or followed by other elements. These two constructions will be called NONHEADED and HEADED respectively:

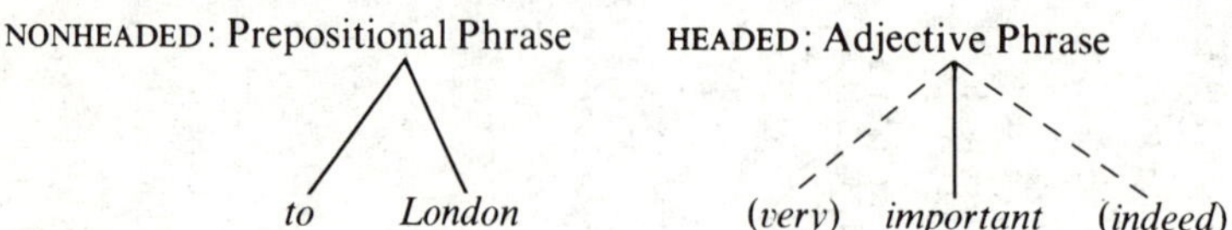

Fig 2.26

Thus in the sentence *I went to London*, neither *to* nor *London* could be omitted: **I went to*, **I went London*. But in the sentence *This is very important indeed*, the modifiers *very* and *indeed* can be omitted: *This is important*; while *important* is obligatory: **This is very indeed*. The obligatory element of a headed construction is called its HEAD; it may function in a manner equivalent to the whole construction of which it is a part. Adverb phrases resemble adjective phrases in that they have a head (an adverb) to which optional elements may be added; *eg*: (*rather*) *slowly*. But the two most important categories of phrase, verb phrases and noun phrases, do not entirely fit into either category: for them, the headed/nonheaded distinction is inadequate.

Note Technical terms for headed and nonheaded are 'endocentric' and 'exocentric'.

Verb phrases and noun phrases

2.27 The verb phrase and the noun phrase can be considered the most important phrasal categories for functional reasons. We note from *Fig* 2.25 that the verb phrase operates as the V element in a clause, *ie* as the most 'central' and indispensable part of the clause (*cf* 2.13). The noun phrase is important more because of its multiplicity of function: *Fig* 2.25 shows that a noun phrase can function as any of the clause constituents except V. A declarative sentence, indeed, normally contains a verb phrase and at least one noun phrase.

Verb phrases are headed to the extent that they are composed of two kinds of element, auxiliaries and main verbs, such that every unreduced verb phrase (*cf* 2.51) contains a main verb, but not necessarily an auxiliary. However, a nonfinite (3.53*ff*) main verb cannot normally stand on its own in independent clauses; the auxiliaries *can*, *have*, and *been* may not, therefore, be omitted in:

Jack *can play* the trombone. Our team *has been beaten*.

The relations between auxiliaries and main verbs are more complex than can be explained by the simple headed/nonheaded distinction; further consideration of this question will be given in 3.55.

Similar remarks apply to noun phrases. A noun phrase is headed to the extent that it has a central constituent or head, to which other elements can be optionally added. But if we change the plural noun phrase in [1] into a singular one in [2], the head can no longer stand alone:

The room contains { (some) (beautiful) (Flemish) vases. [1]
a (beautiful) (Flemish) vase. [2] }

For a large class of noun phrases, in fact, a DETERMINATIVE element such as *a* in [2] is obligatory. In another respect, too, noun phrases do not behave like headed constructions: members of one class of words, that of personal pronouns (*I*, *him*, *her*, etc), although they act as heads of noun phrases (in the sense that *I* can function alone as subject, *him* as object, etc), cannot normally have optional elements, such as articles and adjectives, added to them. Thus in some noun phrases the head must be accompanied, and in other noun phrases it cannot (normally) be accompanied, by another element. Such observations make it clear that phrases, like clauses, cannot be described by a single structural formula, and that various subclassifications have to be made of phrases and of the elements they contain.

Summary of phrase structures

2.28 In spite of the inevitable oversimplification, we give now a brief tabular summary of the main elements of each phrase class. Rather than label all elements with functional labels (as we did with S, V, O, C, and A), we shall merely illustrate certain general types of syntactic function within phrases. These types will receive further comment in 2.29–33.

VERB PHRASES (*cf* 3.52*ff*) consist of a main verb which either stands alone as the entire verb phrase, or is preceded by up to four verbs in an auxiliary function:

Table 2.28a Verb phrase

	auxiliary/auxiliaries				main verb	
The ship					sank	
				was	sinking	
			has	been	sunk	
		must	have	been	sinking	
	may	have	been	being	sunk	⟨rare; *cf* Note⟩

NOUN PHRASES (*cf* 5.1*ff*, 17.1*ff*) consist of a head, which is typically a noun, and of elements which (either obligatorily or optionally) determine the head and (optionally) modify the head, or complement another element in the phrase:

Table 2.28b Noun phrase

	determinative	premodification	head	postmodification	
					complementation
I remember			him		
			Peter		
	Alice's		wedding		
	that		girl	with the red hair	
	all those	fine warm	days	in the country last year	
	a	better	story		than that
	the	best	trip		that I ever had
	a	good	trip	that I once had	

ADJECTIVE PHRASES (*cf* 7.20*ff*) consist of an adjective as head, optionally preceded and followed by modifying elements:

Table 2.28c Adjective phrase

	premodification	head	postmodification	
				complementation
The weather was		pleasant		
	too	hot		to be enjoyable
	incredibly	cold		
		pleasant	enough	

Sometimes an obligatory or optional complementation (*cf* 2.32, 16.69) is added.

ADVERB PHRASES (*cf* 7.46*ff*) are similar to adjective phrases in their structure, except that they have an adverb, instead of an adjective, as their head:

Table 2.28d Adverb phrase

	premodification	head	postmodification	
				complementation
I spoke to him		yesterday		
	quite	often		
	very	severely	indeed	
	as	clearly		as I could

PREPOSITIONAL PHRASES (*cf* 9.1*ff*) consist of a preposition followed by a prepositional complement, which is normally a noun phrase:

Table 2.28e Prepositional phrase

	preposition	prepositional complement
I met her	for	lunch
	at	the corner of the street
	on	Saturday morning
	by	a strange coincidence

It is true of adjective and adverb phrases, as of noun phrases, that one-word elements tend to precede the head, whereas multi-word elements tend to follow it. But there are exceptions: *eg* the adverbs *indeed* and *enough* postmodify their head.

Note The verb phrase construction of *may have been being sunk* is so rare that an extended example is called for. The following dialogue could well occur during an interview for an appointment:

A: Has a candidate named Petersen been interviewed yet?

B: He wasn't in the waiting room two minutes ago. He may have been being interviewed then.

Form and function in phrase structure

2.29 We shall find it necessary to observe the distinction between form and function within phrases, as within clauses. It is true that there is a strong association between certain word classes and certain elements within the phrase. For example, in noun phrases the head is typically a noun, and the determinative function is typically performed by members of a relatively small class of words called, appropriately enough, DETERMINERS (*the*, *a*, *no*, *every*, etc). On the other hand, there is rarely a one-to-one match between formal and functional classifications. The head of a noun phrase may be a pronoun (as we have seen), or an adjective: *the poor*, *the unemployed*, etc. Similarly, the determinative function can be performed not only by a determiner, but by a genitive construction: *John's new bicycle*, etc (*cf* 5.121). In such cases, we need to make terminological distinctions between form and function, so that we can say, for example, that an adjective (formal term) can function either as modifier or as head (functional terms) in a noun phrase. It will be noted that a noun can be a premodifier as well as a head: contrast *the poor city* with *the city poor*.

In other cases, however, there is a one-to-one match, and it would be superfluous to introduce two terms for what is effectively the same category. A preposition nearly always functions as the 'preposed' element of a prepositional phrase, and no other word class shares this function. It might be equally claimed that there is no need to distinguish form from function in the verb phrase: that auxiliary verb and main verb will satisfy both requirements. But even here, we shall find good grounds for distinguishing 'auxiliary' and 'main', as functional terms, from the terms which define classes of verb word. Of these, there are three: MODAL verbs (*may*, *will*, *could*, etc) always function as auxiliaries; FULL verbs (*give*, *work*, *try*, etc) always function as main verbs; and PRIMARY verbs (the three most important verbs in the language: *be, have*, and *do*) can function either as auxiliaries or as main verbs.

There are three other terms designating broad functions which may be performed by various types of constituents, and we shall now explain their meaning. They are DETERMINATION, MODIFICATION, and COMPLEMENTATION.

Determination

2.30 This term may be used for the function of words and (sometimes) phrases which, in general, determine what *kind of reference* a noun phrase has: for example, whether it is definite (like *the*) or indefinite (like *a*/*an*), partitive (like *some*) or universal (like *all*). Semantically, all noun phrases are determined in some way or other; *eg* all noun phrases are either definite or indefinite in meaning. But some heads are by their very nature self-determining: proper nouns and personal pronouns, for example, are inherently definite, and in this sense incorporate their own determiner. In such cases, then, a noun phrase will not generally contain a separate word with a determinative function. When the head is a common noun, on the other hand, determination as a syntactic function is normal, if not obligatory: we cannot, for instance, omit the determiners *the* and *a* in *The driver was a man*.

Note It will be clear from the above that we treat the definite and indefinite articles as members of the larger class of determiners. There appears to be an exception to the generalization that common nouns are determined in the case of plural and noncount nouns like *women* and *water* respectively; but we shall prefer to say (*cf* 5.2) that the apparent absence of an article signals the presence of the ZERO article.

Modification

2.31 Modification, in contrast, is a largely optional function performed, for instance, by adjectives in the noun phrase, and by intensifying adverbs in the adjective or adverb phrase. Premodifiers precede the head, and postmodifiers follow it; in noun phrases, premodifiers follow determinatives. Semantically, modifiers add 'descriptive' information to the head, often restricting the reference of the head. Thus *a green table* has a more specific meaning than *a table*, and *very tall* has a more specific meaning than *tall* (*cf* however, 17.3*ff* for the distinction between restrictive and nonrestrictive modification). In this respect, modifiers in phrases parallel adverbials in the clause – a similarity brought out by:

He arrived (unexpectedly) (in Warsaw) yesterday. [1]
~ his (unexpected) arrival (in Warsaw) yesterday. [2]

In the clause [1] the parenthesized elements are adverbials, whereas in the noun phrase [2] the parenthesized elements are modifers.

Note **[a]** The particular correspondence between [1] and [2], whereby a clause-related meaning takes on the grammatical form of a noun phrase, is discussed under the heading of NOMINALIZATION (*cf* 17.51*ff*).
[b] The parallel between [1] and [2] also helps to explain a traditional characterization of adverbs as modifiers of verbs (a tradition enshrined in the term *adverb* itself). But as we shall see in Chapter 8, adverbs cannot be regarded in this light.

Complementation

2.32 We reserve the term COMPLEMENTATION (as distinct from *complement*) for the function of a part of a phrase or clause which follows a word, and completes the specification of a meaning relationship which that word implies. As such, complementation may be either obligatory or optional on the syntactic level. Complementation also overlaps with other functions, such as adverbials and modifiers.

We have already encountered complementation in clause structure: the clause types listed in *Table* 2.16 (*SVO*, *SVA*, *SVOA*, etc) were characterized by differences in the complementation (in terms of O, C, or A) required to complete the meaning of the verb. Thus the terms 'monotransitive' (as applied to the verb *deceive*) or 'ditransitive' (as applied to the verb *allow*) identify their complementations as O and O O respectively. In a similar way, certain adjectives require complementation by a postmodifier:

VERB COMPLEMENTATION

He deceived *his father*. BUT *He deceived.
He allowed me *a respite*. BUT *He allowed me.

ADJECTIVE COMPLEMENTATION

All sales are subject *to tax*. BUT *All sales are subject.
Mr Gould is likely *to resign*. BUT *Mr Gould is likely.

The verb *deceive* and the adjective *subject* are similar to the extent that their meaning requires not only a subject ('*X*') but some other element ('*Y*'): '*X* deceives *Y*', '*X* is subject to *Y*'. The meaning of a clause will be incomplete unless the '*Y*' is specified. In other cases, the complementation is optional:

VERB COMPLEMENTATION: Joan was eating (*her lunch*). [1]
ADJECTIVE COMPLEMENTATION: The boat was ready (*for departure*). [2]

The function of the optional elements here is still one of complementation because even when they are omitted, it is still implied that Joan was *eating something*, and that the boat was *ready for something*. In this connection, we may notice a contrast even between such semantically similar adjectives as *glad* and *cheerful*, in that the first implies that the emotion has a specific source, whereas the second does not. Thus *glad* will be typically followed by a complementing phrase or clause (*eg*: *glad about your prize*, *glad that you came*), and will occur without such complementation only if the context supplies the information which the clause fails to specify. On the other hand, *cheerful* may freely occur as both modifier and head in a way which is not possible with *glad*:

We always found him *cheerful*. BUT ?We always found him *glad*.
He was a *cheerful* person. BUT *He was a *glad* person.

Note Although we describe the complementation in [1] as 'optional', there is reason to claim that *her lunch* in *Joan was eating her lunch* is not optional in a strictly syntactic sense of the word. If, as we argue in 10.4, verbs like *eat* are dually classified as both transitive and intransitive, then the omission of the object involves a change in the classification of the verb element (*cf* App I.54).

Modification and complementation

2.33 Although complementing elements may be optional, such elements differ semantically from other optional elements (*eg* most modifiers) in that the omission of complementation, as in *The boat was ready* (2.32 [2]), implies that some element of meaning in a preceding word is 'unsatisfied', and therefore has to be provided through context. It must be admitted, however, that this criterion is not always clear-cut, since the need for semantic 'satisfaction' is a matter of degree.

Another difference between complementation and modification is a syntactic one. Whereas the modifying function always relates to the head of a phrase, the complementing function may relate to a premodifier which is separated from its complementation by the head:

Greek is a *more difficult language than French*. [1]
She was *too ill to travel*. [2]

In [1], the phrase *than French* complements the comparative adverb *more* rather than the head noun *language*; and in [2], *to travel* complements the adverb *too*, rather than the head adjective *ill*. To see this, we note that the omission of the relevant modifier results in an unacceptable sentence:

*Greek is a *difficult language than French.*
*She was *ill to travel.*
(But *cf*: She is (*rather*) *young to drive a car*; 16.76.)

It is clear, then, that there is not a straight choice between optional and obligatory elements of phrases. Determination, modification, and complementation all depend on the presence of some other element (usually the head) in the phrase. Heads are obligatory and modifiers are generally optional, but determination and complementation are functions whose conditions of occurrence cannot be defined so simply (*cf* 5.10*ff*, 16.18*ff*).

Note For completeness, it should be mentioned that modifiers may themselves contain modifiers (*cf* 17.118*ff*). For example, in *far more difficult*, *far* modifies *more*, and *far more* modifies *difficult*. Hence the unacceptability of **far difficult*.

Word classes

2.34 In dealing with phrases, we have already had occasion to refer to many of the general WORD CLASSES traditionally called 'parts of speech'. Members of the Indo-European group of languages have been analysed in terms of such categories since classical antiquity. It may be helpful now to list and exemplify the word classes that have been introduced:

(a) CLOSED CLASSES (*cf* 2.39)
preposition – *of, at, in, without, in spite of*
pronoun – *he, they, anybody, one, which*
determiner – *the, a, that, every, some*
conjunction – *and, that, when, although*
modal verb – *can, must, will, could*
primary verb – *be, have, do*

(b) OPEN CLASSES (*cf* 2.40)
noun – *John, room, answer, play*
adjective – *happy, steady, new, large, round*
full verb – *search, grow, play*
adverb – *steadily, completely, really*

To these may be added two lesser categories (*cf* 2.42):

(c) numerals – *one, two, three; first, second, third*

and the marginal and anomalous class of

(d) interjections – *oh, ah, ugh, phew*

and, finally, a small number of words of unique function (*eg* the negative particle *not* and the infinitive marker *to*) which do not easily fit into any of these classes.

Even so short a list of examples raises several important questions, to which we now turn.

Lexical items and grammatical words

2.35 First, we should notice that the examples are listed as *words* in their 'dictionary form', and not as they often appear in sentences when they function as constituents of phrases (but *cf* Note [a] on invariable words): thus the singular noun *room* is listed and not the plural noun *rooms*; the simple adjective *happy* and not the comparative adjective *happier*; the infinitive (or uninflected) verb *hope* and not the past form *hoped*; the subjective pronoun form *he* and not the objective form *him*. We cite these words in what may be called their BASE form (*cf* App I.2*ff*), *ie* the form to which, in regular cases, inflectional suffixes are added to make inflected forms (*rooms*, *happier*, etc). But such a manner of speaking reveals that we are using the term 'word' in two different senses. The ambiguity is more fully evident in:

'The word *works* occurs in the sentence *He works at home.*' [1]

'The word WORK occurs in the sentence *He works at home.*' [2]

Both sentences are acceptable in normal usage, but the ambiguity they show can be avoided if we adopt the term LEXICAL ITEM (*cf* App I.1) to replace 'word' in [2]. That is, a lexical item is a word as it occurs in a dictionary, where *work*, *works*, *working*, *worked* will all be counted as different grammatical forms, or variants, of the word WORK. We shall use a graphic convention (SMALL CAPITALS), where necessary (and particularly in Chapter 3), to distinguish lexical items from grammatical word-forms (*ie* words as units which are constituents of phrases). We shall not, however, in general distinguish lexical items by a separate terminology: following normal practice, class labels such as *verb*, *noun*, and *adjective* will be used to refer to words in both senses.

Like the distinction between forms and functions, that between words as forms and words as lexical items does not have to be made in all cases. Only certain parts of speech have inflections (*ie* endings or modifications which change one word-form into another): notably nouns (*answer*, *answers*), verbs (*give*, *gives*, *gave*, *giving*, *given*), pronouns (*they*, *them*, *their*, *theirs*), and adjectives (*large*, *larger*, *largest*). Moreover, not all words in these categories have more than one form. Other word classes, with a few exceptions (*cf* Note [a]), are invariable. In citing invariable words, we shall always use italics rather than small capitals.

Note **[a]** Apart from nouns, verbs, pronouns, and adjectives, a few adverbs (*soon*, *sooner*, *soonest*, etc) and determiners (*few*, *fewer*, *fewest*, etc) have inflected forms. Other parts of speech are invariable.

[b] On 'stem', as distinct from 'base', *cf* App I.2.

[c] When a grammatical or semantic distinction is realized morphologically by a contrast between the presence and the absence of an inflection, the word-form with the inflection is termed MARKED, and the form without it UNMARKED. Thus the plural forms of regular nouns, in contrast to their singular forms, are marked by the *-s* ending. The unmarked form is also frequently the term which is more neutral or general in use or meaning: the present tense, as opposed to the past, is thus not only unmarked in having (except in the third person singular) no inflection, but also in being able to refer to time in a general sense, including past, present, and future time (*cf* 4.3). From this concept, it is common to extend the use of 'marked' and 'unmarked' (as we do in this book) more generally to grammatical contrasts which are formally or semantically unequal in this way. It can be said, for example, that the progressive aspect (*eg*: *is living*) is marked in relation to the nonprogressive (*eg*: *lives*) both because it is realized by the additional syntactic MARKING of the BE + V*ing* construction (*cf* 3.54) and also because it is semantically more restricted than the nonprogressive. Further examples of a marked/unmarked distinction are mentioned in 3.58, 5.112, 6.10, and 7.88.

2.36 From even the few examples given in 2.34, it can be seen that a lexical item may consist of a sequence of more than one orthographic word (*cf* 2.37). This is especially common in the case of complex prepositions (*cf* 9.10*ff*) such as *in spite of*, *because of*, *away from*, and multi-word verbs (*cf* 16.2*ff*) such as *look at*, *set up*, and *stand out* (compare the related adjective *outstanding*, again one lexical item, but this time one word also). Equally, however, we can sometimes look upon a lexical item as being downgraded to become less than a word: for example, the adverbs *out* and *up* in *outstanding* and *upset* or (from this viewpoint) the noun *spite* and the prepositions *in* and *of* in *in spite of*.

The treatment of the subjective form (*I*, *he*, *she*, etc) of personal pronouns as the base or 'dictionary' form is conventional, but is not so clearly motivated as in the case of other word classes. We may note even here, however, a tendency to select the subjective form in derivational compounds: for example, *she-wolf* and *he-man* rather than **her-wolf* and **him-man*.

Morphological, phonological, and orthographic form

2.37 Secondly, some of the examples in 2.34 appear as more than one word class (*play* as a noun and verb, *that* as a demonstrative and conjunction) and more of them could have been given additional entries in this way (*round* can be a noun, verb, adjective, adverb, and preposition). In such cases we can say that the same MORPHOLOGICAL FORM is a realization of more than one lexical item. This is a highly important feature of English, and further attention will be drawn to it in App I.43*ff*. A morphological form may be simple (consisting of a stem only, as in the case of *play*) or complex (consisting of more than one morpheme, like *playful*). The morphological form of a word may therefore be defined as its composition in terms of morphemes (*cf* 2.7), *ie* stems and affixes.

While such morphological correspondences across parts of speech should be noted, we should also give attention to morphological characteristics which distinguish one part of speech from another, notably the occurrence of particular derivational affixes (*cf* App I.20*ff*) which mark a word as a member of a particular class. The suffix *-ness*, for example, marks an item as a noun (*kindness*, *happiness*, etc), while the suffix *-less* marks an item as an adjective (*helpless*, *careless*, etc). Such indicators enable a speaker of English to recognize implicitly the word class of an item, even if he has not met that item before, purely on the basis of its form.

When the need arises, therefore, we shall be able to distinguish a lexical item not only from the grammatical forms which it takes in various syntactic settings, but from the morphological forms which it may share entirely or in part with other lexical items of the same word class or of other word classes.

Thus the adjective LONG has precisely the same morphological forms as the adverb LONG (*long* ~ *longer* ~ *longest*); whereas the adjective GOOD shares the forms of the adverb WELL only in part: *ie* the comparative (*better*) and superlative (*best*) forms.

This morphological convergence may also occur at the level of grammatical forms, either between forms of different lexical items (*eg*: *meeting* as a singular noun and *meeting* as a verb participle) or between forms of the same lexical item (*worked* as a realization of both the past tense and the *-ed* participle forms of WORK). The latter is an example of the NEUTRALIZATION of inflectional forms which are distinct for other verbs (*cf* 3.2*ff*, 3.11*ff*) such as GIVE (*gave*, *given*).

For the sake of completeness, it should be added that a word also has a PHONOLOGICAL and an ORTHOGRAPHIC form, and that similarities and contrasts in pronunciation and spelling are not necessarily to be associated with those on the levels of lexicology and grammar. There is, for example, an important similarity between all words beginning /ð/ (*the*, *that*, *then*, for example), and likewise between many of those beginning *wh-* (*which*, *when*, for example): basically, the former are relater or indicator words, and the latter interrogative or relative words (*cf* 2.44*f*). But we should hesitate to attempt a morphological account of these similarities; rather, they are correspondences of pronunciation and spelling which reflect grammatical correspondences in the history of the language. Similarly, the variant spelling and pronunciation of the indefinite article *a*/*an* is not a case of inflectional variation, but of variation determined by phonology (*viz* by whether the following word begins with a consonant or not).

Homonyms and homomorphs

2.38 Words which share the same phonological or orthographic 'shape', but are morphologically unrelated, are termed HOMONYMS: for example, *rose* [noun] is a homonym of *rose* [past tense verb]. There is no standard term for words which also share the same morphological form (*eg*: *red* as a noun and *red* as an adjective, *meeting* as a noun and *meeting* as a verb), but it seems appropriate to adopt the term HOMOMORPH for this purpose. These and related distinctions such as 'homophone' and 'homograph' (*cf* Note) are explained in *Fig* 2.38 opposite.

To the set of equivalence relations between words, this diagram adds, for completeness, the relation of synonymy, or sameness of meaning. Strictly, synonymy (and its opposite, antonymy) holds between word senses, rather than between words. For example, *hard* is a synonym of *difficult* only in one sense; in another sense (that in which it contrasts with *soft*) it is not. Of the three major kinds of equivalence in *Fig* 2.38, homonymy is phonological and/or graphic, and synonymy is semantic. Only homomorphy is of primary concern to grammar.

Note There has been considerable disagreement and confusion over the use of the term 'homonym', which has often been extended to apply to cases we have referred to as homomorphs. Similarly, 'homonym' has often been used ambiguously, according to whether it denotes identity of pronunciation, of spelling, or of both. These distinctions can be made, where required, by the use of the terms HOMOPHONE and HOMOGRAPH. In practice, the distinction between homonymy and homomorphy is not always easy to draw. We judge *red* [noun] and *red* [adjective] to be

HOMONYM → HOMOPHONE, HOMOGRAPH

HOMONYM
same pronunciation/spelling
(morphologically unrelated)
eg: *saw* – *saw*
[noun] [past tense verb]
no – *know*
row/rəʊ/ – *row*/raʊ/

HOMOPHONE
same pronunciation
eg: *saw* – *saw*
[noun] [past tense verb]
no – *know*

HOMOGRAPH
same spelling
eg: *saw* – *saw*
[noun] [past tense verb]
row/rəʊ/ – *row*/raʊ/

HOMOMORPH
same morphological form
(different syntactic function)
eg: *fast* – *fast*
[adjective] [adverb]
down – *down*
[adverb] [preposition]

SYNONYM
same sense (different morphological form)
eg: *hard* – *difficult*
someone – *somebody*

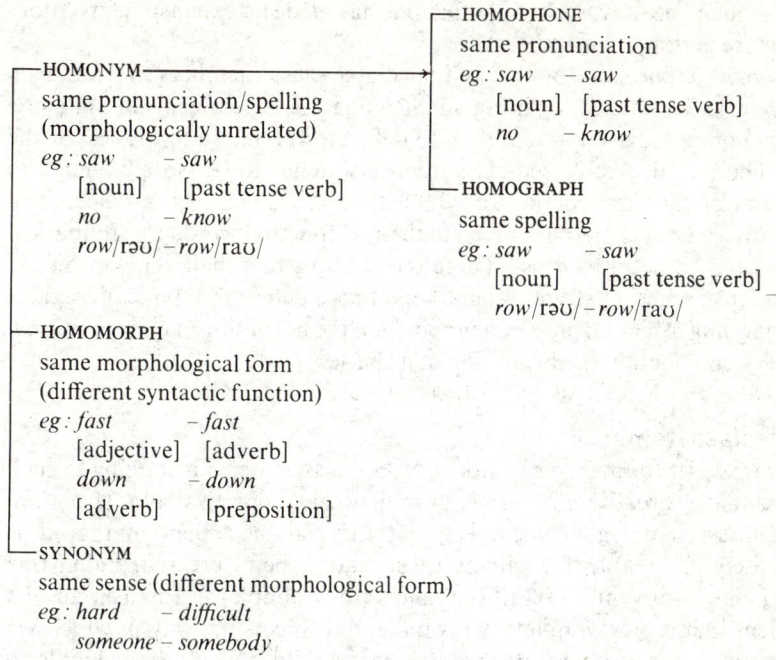

Fig 2.38 Types of equivalence between words

homomorphs only on the grounds that they share the same stem morpheme, and this in turn rests on the judgment that the two words are related through processes of word-formation, in a semantically systematic way (*cf* esp CONVERSION, App I.43*ff*). Thus to call two words such as *hard* [adjective] and *hard* [adverb] 'homomorphs' is to acknowledge their affinity in meaning. With other words (*eg*: *leave* [noun] and *leave* [verb]) this connection is less clear. Our use of 'homomorph' is also ambiguous (but harmlessly so) according to whether this relation of morphological identity exists between words *qua* grammatical forms (*eg* between *hidden* as an adjective and *hidden* as a verb participle) or between words *qua* lexical items (*eg* between WORK as a noun, comprising the word forms *work* and *works*, and WORK as a verb, comprising the forms *work*, *works*, *working*, and *worked*). And if we apply the term 'homomorphs' to WORK [noun] and WORK [verb], we must also apply it, where the occasion arises, to different secondary word classes (*cf* 2.41): *eg* WORK as an intransitive verb (as in *This watch doesn't work*) and WORK as a monotransitive verb (as in *She worked wonders*). By acknowledging in these ways the various senses in which words may be linguistically 'the same' or 'different', we do not imply any subordination of semantic to formal criteria, but merely recognize that grammatical and semantic criteria may be independent of one another. The conventional practices of lexicography, whereby different grammatical homomorphs are grouped under the same 'headword', should not necessarily be regarded, for grammatical purposes, as definitive.

Closed-class items

2.39 Thirdly, the parts of speech in 2.34 were listed in two main groups, (a) and (b), and this introduces a distinction of great significance. Set (a) comprises what are called CLOSED-CLASS items. That is, the sets of items are 'closed' in the sense that they are only exceptionally extended by the creation of additional members: a moment's reflection is enough for us to realize how rarely in a language we invent or adopt a new or additional pronoun. It requires no great effort to list all or most of the members of a closed class (even though one may not be sure that one has made an exhaustive inventory of its more peripheral members).

A semantic corollary of this is that closed-class members are mutually exclusive and mutually defining in meaning: it is less easy to state the meaning of an individual item than to define it in relation to the rest of the class. The meaning of closed-class items also tends to be closely bound up with that of the construction of which they are a part, as is reflected in alternative names sometimes given to them – 'function words', 'grammatical words', and 'structure words'. These terms also stress their function in the grammatical sense, as structural markers: thus a determiner typically signals the beginning of a noun phrase, a preposition the beginning of a prepositional phrase, a conjunction the beginning of a clause.

Open-class items

2.40 By contrast, set (b) in 2.34 comprises OPEN CLASSES. Items belonging to such a class have broadly the same grammatical properties and structural possibilities as its other members, but the class is 'open' in that it is indefinitely extendable. New items are constantly being created, and no one could make an inventory of all the nouns (for example) in English, and be confident that it was complete. This inevitably affects the way in which we attempt to define any item in an open class: while it would be valuable to relate the meaning of *room* to other nouns with which it has a semantic affinity (*chamber*, *hall*, *house*, etc) one could not define it as 'not house, not box, not plate, not indigestion, . . .' as one might define a closed-class item like *this* as 'not that'.

Of course, in any one phrase or sentence the decision to select a particular word at one place in the structure imposes great constraints on what can be selected at another. But in an arrangement like the following there is in principle a sharp difference between the number of possibilities in columns (i), (iii), and (iv) ('closed') and the number in (ii), (v), and (vi) ('open'):

	(i)	(ii)	(iii)	(iv)	(v)	(vi)
(John)	may	sit	by	the	fountain	sadly
	will	stare	at	this	tree	happily
	must	read	from	that	book	frequently
	⋮	hurry	along	⋮	window	⋮
		⋮	on		path	
			⋮		⋮	

The distinction between 'open' and 'closed' word classes must be treated with caution, however. On the one hand, we must not exaggerate the ease with which we create new words (*cf* App I.13*f*), and on the other we must not exaggerate the extent to which word classes in set (a) are 'closed': new prepositions (usually of the complex type 'preposition + noun + preposition' like *by way of*) continue to arise (*cf* 9.10*ff*).

The taxonomy of word classes

2.41 There is a yet more important caveat. Although they have deceptively specific labels, the word classes tend in fact to be rather heterogeneous, if not problematic categories. There is nothing sacrosanct about the traditional parts-of-speech classification, and we have indeed deviated from tradition to some extent in our list in 2.34. Thus the traditional category of article (*the* and *a/an*) has been subsumed under the larger heading of determiners (including, for instance, the demonstratives *this* and *that*); the traditional category of verb, on the other hand, has been divided into three categories, two closed (primary and modal verbs) and one open (full verbs). Both these adjustments are well-motivated for modern English. They do, however, raise questions about the justification for this or that classification.

The term 'word classes' (or more particularly the traditional term 'parts of speech') has been normally understood to refer to the most *general* categories to which lexical items can be appropriately assigned. There are, however, well-established subclassifications within these categories: nouns are subclassified into SECONDARY WORD CLASSES as common nouns, proper nouns, etc, and verbs as transitive verbs, intransitive verbs etc. But there is scope for considerable disagreement on the point at which we stop grouping subcategories into larger categories. The class of adverbs is notoriously heterogeneous, and may be separated into an open class consisting of adverbs with an adjectival base (especially those, like *completely*, which have an *-ly* suffix), and a closed class including adverbs such as *here, there, now*, etc. This closed class, however, will still be heterogeneous. An even better case can be made for splitting the conjunction class into subordinators (*cf* 14.11*ff*), which link a subordinate clause to a superordinate clause, and coordinators (*cf* 13.5*ff*), which link coordinate constructions. In the opposite direction, there are arguments, despite the clear criteria which separate modal, primary, and full verbs in modern English, for bringing these together, in the traditional way, within a global class of verbs. Indeed, the use of the term 'verb' itself in reference to these three categories reflects their overlap in terms of morphology, function, and meaning (*cf* 3.1*ff*).

Such arguments, however, have more to do with the labelling of categories than with the question of how we can best explain the grammatical behaviour of items on the basis of their various degrees of similarity and contrast. It is to this more substantial question that we shall address ourselves in the following chapters.

Additional classes

2.42 Some mention must be finally made of two categories, numerals and interjections, which are yoked together here only by virtue of the difficulty of classifying them as either closed or open classes.

(a) NUMERALS

Numerals, whether the cardinal numerals, *one, two, three*, . . . or the ordinal numerals *first, second, third*, . . . , must be placed somewhere between open-class and closed-class items: they resemble the former in that they make up a very large class – indeed, a class of infinite membership; but they resemble the latter in that the semantic relations among them are mutually exclusive and mutually defining. We do not create new numerals in the sense in which we create new nouns: in a way, numerals constitute a miniature syntax of their own, within the larger syntax of the English language (*cf* 6.63*ff*), combining a small number of morphemes according to regular rules.

(b) INTERJECTIONS
Interjections might be considered a closed class on the grounds that those that are fully institutionalized are few in number. But unlike the closed classes listed in 2.34(a), they are grammatically peripheral, in the sense that they do not enter into constructions with other word classes, and are only loosely connected to sentences with which they may be orthographically or phonologically associated. They are also peripheral to the language system itself, in that they frequently involve the use of sounds which do not otherwise occur in English words. Thus *ugh* is the spelling of an exclamation often pronounced something like [ʌx] or [əx] even though the 'achlaut' /x/ is not a phoneme in standard AmE or BrE (*cf* 11.55).

Note It can be argued that interjections form a relatively open class because they can be rather freely created by onomatopoeia. For example, comic-strip cartoons often contain such nonce interjections as *yucck*, *gr-r-r-r*, and *blaat*. These reflect a similar unstructured freedom to make use of expressive vocalizing in ordinary conversation.

Word classes in relation to meaning

2.43 It has already been implied that our characterization of parts of speech will depend on their grammatical form and function, rather than on their semantic properties. The 'notional' approach to word classes, manifested in its most naive form in schoolbook definitions such as 'a verb is a doing word', may be a useful pedagogical aid, but cannot in any way replace the definition of grammatical concepts in grammatical terms. At the same time, there are important generalizations to be made about the relation between word classes and their meaning, and the fact that these generalizations do not have complete reliability should not deter us from taking note of them. Broadly speaking, nouns can be characterized naturally as 'stative' (*cf* 4.4) in that they typically refer to entities that are regarded as stable, whether these are concrete (physical) like *house*, *table*, *paper*, or abstract (of the mind) like *hope*, *botany*, *length*. At the opposite pole, verbs can be more naturally characterized as 'dynamic': they are fitted (by their capacity to show tense and aspect, for example) to indicate action, activity, and temporary or changing conditions. Adjectives, in so far as they attribute stable properties to the referents of nouns, are to be associated with them in expressing stative meaning. Thus many adjectives contrast with verbs in their inability to be rendered 'temporary' by the progressive aspect (*cf* 4.28*ff*). Contrast:

John works hard.		John is working hard.
John is tall.	BUT	*John is being tall.

Again, adverbs (or more specifically, adjuncts), in so far as they add a particular condition of time, place, manner, etc to the dynamic implication of the verb, are also to be placed in the 'dynamic' category:

Marion is *beautiful*. Marion dances *beautifully*.

The contrast between these two sentences (where the adjective indicates a stable characteristic of a person and the adverb an evanescent characteristic of that person's behaviour) is one which has countless parallels in the language. On this basis, the relations between open classes can be crudely summarized thus:

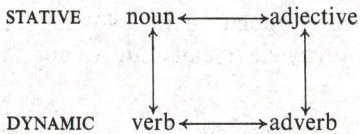

STATIVE noun ←——→ adjective
↕ ↕
DYNAMIC verb ←——→ adverb

But even the examples we have given show the weaknesses of this formulation: *John is a hard worker* and *Marion is a skilful dancer* show the adjective taking on some of the 'dynamic' implications of the adverb. Further, some verbs cannot normally be used with the progressive aspect (*eg*: **He is knowing English*) and therefore belong to the stative rather than the dynamic category (*cf* 4.29). There are also exceptions in the other direction among nouns and adjectives. For instance, a child may be well-behaved one minute and a nuisance or naughty the next. Although adjectives are primarily stative in meaning (*tall*, *red*, *old*), some, such as *naughty* or *insolent*, can resemble verbs in referring to transitory conditions of behaviour or activity. This is reflected in the possibility of their cooccurrence with the progressive aspect of the verb BE:

He is being {a nuisance / naughty} again.

Indeed, in spite of their associative connection with word classes, these semantic distinctions are not to be treated as criteria diagnostic of membership of those classes. Thus we can take a normally dynamic item (say the verb in *He wrote the book*) and 'nominalize' it (*the writing of the book*) pretending – as it were – to see the action as a static 'thing'. So also the verb *tax* beside the nouns *tax* and *taxation*. Again, the name *participle* reflects the fact that such a form 'participates' in the features both of the verb (*The car was approaching us*) and of the adjective (*the approaching car*). In later chapters (*cf* esp 4.27*ff*, 7.40*ff*, 17.51*ff*) these form–meaning relations will be explored further, but emphasis will be understandably placed on significant contrasts of meaning within word classes, rather than between them.

Pro-forms

2.44 The names of the parts of speech are traditional, and neither in themselves nor in relation to each other do these names give a safe guide to their meaning, which instead is best understood in terms of their grammatical properties. 'Adverb' is a classic instance (*cf* 7.46*ff*). We have seen some justification in the previous section for the term *participle*, and another exception is the term *pronoun* (*cf* 6.1*ff*) which is at least partially appropriate in suggesting that a pronoun can serve as a substitute for a noun:

John searched the big room and then the small {*room.* / *one.*} [1]

More generally, however, *pronoun* is a misnomer on two counts. First, a pronoun tends to be a surrogate for a whole noun phrase rather than a noun:

The man invited *the little Swedish girl* because *he* liked *her*. [2]

Secondly, the relationship which often obtains between a pronoun and its ANTECEDENT (an element to which it in some sense 'cross-refers') is not one which can be explained by the simple act of replacement. Notice, for example, that the following alternatives are by no means equivalent in meaning:

Many students did better than *many students* expected. [3]
Many students did better than *they* expected. [3a]

In [3a], *many students* and *they* are normally taken to refer to the same group of people. In [3], *many students* and *many students* are normally taken to refer to different groups. Hence it would be misleading to say that *they* 'replaces' *many students* in [3a]. It is none the less useful to apply a general term PRO-FORM to words and word-sequences which are essentially devices for recapitulating or anticipating the content of a neighbouring expression, often with the effect of reducing grammatical complexity.

Such devices are not limited to pronouns: the word *such* which begins this very paragraph may be described as a pro-modifier, and under appropriate circumstances there are also pro-forms for place, time, and other adverbials:

Mary is *in London* and John is *there* too.
Mary arrived *on Tuesday* and John arrived *then* too.
The police searched the big room *carefully*, but the small room less *so*.

In older English and still sometimes in very formal English, we find *thus* or *so* used more generally than in ordinary modern English as pro-forms for adverbials:

He often behaved *prudently*, but he did not always behave {*thus*. / *so*.} [4]

But *so* has a more important function in modern usage, namely to substitute – along with the 'pro-verb' DO – for a main verb and whatever follows it in the clause (*cf* 2.51):

She hoped that they would *clean the house carefully before her arrival*, but unfortunately they didn't *do so*. [5]

DO can also act as a pro-form on its own, as is shown in:

A: I *warned her about it*.
B: Yes, I *did*, too. [6]

It will be observed that the use of pro-forms greatly facilitates sentence connection, as in [6], and the combining of sentences to form more complex sentences, whether by coordination, as in [4] and [5], or by subordination, as in [2]. We shall examine the various pro-forms and their uses in 12.8*ff*.

Note The items *do* and *thing*, although they belong to the classes of verb and noun respectively, have semantic functions similar to pro-forms, in conveying a broad and undifferentiated meaning:

How do you *do* your laundry?

There's an important *thing* I'd like to discuss with you.

Wh-words

2.45 In pro-forms, we have identified a set of items which cuts across the standard classification of words into 'parts of speech'. This is true also for another set of items, the *wh*-words, including *what*, *which*, *who*, and *when* (*cf* Note). Indeed, *wh*-words may be regarded as a special set of pro-forms. To highlight both the similarity and the contrast between other pro-forms and *wh*-words, we may suggest that whereas other pro-forms have a general meaning roughly statable as 'We know what this item means/refers to, so I need not state it in full', the *wh*-words have a meaning something like 'It has not been known before what this item refers to, and so it needs to be stated in full'. This informal statement will account for the use of interrogative *wh*-words in questions:

WH-WORD	(FULL FORM)	OTHER PRO-FORM
Where is Mary?	Mary is *in London*.	John is *there* too.

But the paraphrase for *wh*-words is broad enough to help explain also their use in subordinate clauses such as:

The place *where Mary lives* is London.

I wonder *where Mary lives*.

Where Mary lives, the traffic is very noisy.

Initial position in the clause is a general characteristic of *wh*-words whether their role is interrogative (*cf* 6.36*ff*), relative (*cf* 6.32*ff*, 17.13*ff*), or subordinating (*cf* 14.12*ff*). Through the use of *wh*-words we can ask for the identification of the subject, object, complement, or an adverbial of a sentence. Thus in relation to a sentence consisting of S V O C A, like [1], we have:

They [S] make [V] him [O] the chairman [C] every year [A]. [1]
Who makes him the chairman every year? [*wh*-word as S] [2]
Who(m) do they make the chairman every year? [*wh*-word as O] [3]
What do they make him every year? [*wh*-word as C] [4]
When do they make him the chairman? [*wh*-word as A] [5]

It will be noticed from these examples that the *wh*-word assumes first position in the clause whatever the normal position of the corresponding element in declarative clauses such as [1], and that this shift of order is accompanied by other changes of structure in the last three examples, involving the placement of *do* in front of the subject – a topic to which we shall shortly return (2.49*f*). Our present point, however, is that what the *wh*-words have in common is independent of their word-class classification. Whereas *who*, *whom*, and *what* above are pronouns in their syntactic function, *when* in [5] is a time adverb, and further exemplification shows *wh*-words functioning as determiners (*Which cup is yours?*), as adjectives (*How do you feel?*), and as modifying adverbs (*How old are you?*).

Note The *wh*-words include not only *which*, *when*, *why*, *where*, etc but also, less obviously, a few items pronounced with initial /h/, some having the *wh*- in spelling (*who*, *whose*, *whom*), and one not (*how*). We are therefore using the term '*wh*-word' as a convenient mnemonic title for a group of words, most of which begin with the letters *wh*-, and which share certain grammatical properties.

Variations on the basic sentence patterns

Sentence processes

2.46 Having outlined the constituency of English simple sentences by working down the grammatical hierarchy from clauses through phrases to words, we may now resume consideration of systematic correspondences, some of which were illustrated in 2.20*ff*. Let us return to the simple declarative sentence seen as a whole, and consider what modifications of its basic constituency must be allowed for if we are to account for questions, negative sentences, and other types of simple sentence which go beyond the structures we have outlined. It is a widely accepted principle, which we acknowledge through this form of presentation, that the simple declarative sentence is in a sense the canonical form of sentence, in terms of which other types of sentence, including both those which are more complex ('complex' and 'compound' sentences) and those which are more simple ('reduced' sentences), may be explained by reference to such operations as conjunction, insertion, inversion, substitution, and transposition. Such operations can be called 'sentence processes', and to the extent that the relation between one structure and another can be more naturally elucidated by such means, we shall feel free to use the concept of process, as well as the concepts of pattern and structure, in describing systematic correspondences.

First, a terminological point. Terms such as DECLARATIVE, INTERROGATIVE, IMPERATIVE, and EXCLAMATIVE can be used (either as adjectives or nouns) in referring to grammatical categories, and will be applied, at this stage, to types of clause or types of simple sentence. The terms STATEMENT, QUESTION, DIRECTIVE, and EXCLAMATION on the other hand, will be applied to the logical or semantic status of an utterance – what it means, and what it is used for – and for our purposes will be regarded as defining categories of sentence (*cf*, however, the discussion of indirect speech in 14.30*ff*). Since we confine our attention here to simple sentences, the distinctions between these two sets of terms will not become important until later chapters (esp Chapter 10).

Note More careful consideration of the relation between grammar, semantics, and pragmatics will require further distinctions of terminology. Thus we may distinguish SENTENCE (a grammatically autonomous unit) from UTTERANCE (a unit which is autonomous in terms of its pragmatic or communicative function). Further, there is commonly a need to separate what a locution *is*, in terms of its logical status (*eg* 'statement') from what it *does* in terms of its force as a speech act (*eg* ASSERTION; *cf* 11.3). Similarly, a directive (viewed as a general semantic type) may have various communicative functions: not only giving orders (*Come here*), but making offers (*Have some chocolate*), etc (*cf* 11.29).

Subject and predicate

2.47 Simple sentences are traditionally divided into two major parts, a SUBJECT and a PREDICATE. This means that in terms of clause elements (*cf* 2.13), the subject (S) is distinguished from the other elements (V and combinations of O, C, and A) which follow it:

SUBJECT	PREDICATE
Julie	buys her vegetables in the market.
The train	arrived late today.
Tigers	are carnivorous.

This division, however, has more to do with the statement as a logical category than with the structural facts of grammar. Thus the subject is often described as the constituent defining the topic of the sentence – that which the sentence is 'about' and which it presupposes as its point of departure; whereas the predicate is that which is asserted about the subject. In general, we shall find little need to refer to the predicate as a separate structural unit in the description of English grammar.

Note One significant property of the predicate, however, is that it is the part of the clause which is typically affected by clause negation (*cf* 10.64*f*). Further, a predicate may be omitted through ellipsis (*cf* 12.61), or may be replaced by a pro-form (*cf* 2.44, 2.51, 12.21*ff*).

Operator and predication

2.48 A more important division, in accounting for the relation between different sentence types, is that between OPERATOR and PREDICATION as two subdivisions of the predicate. Not all simple statements have an operator, but when it occurs, it is normally the word which directly follows the subject. Provisionally defined as the *first or only auxiliary* (but *cf* 2.49), it has a crucial role in the formation of questions:

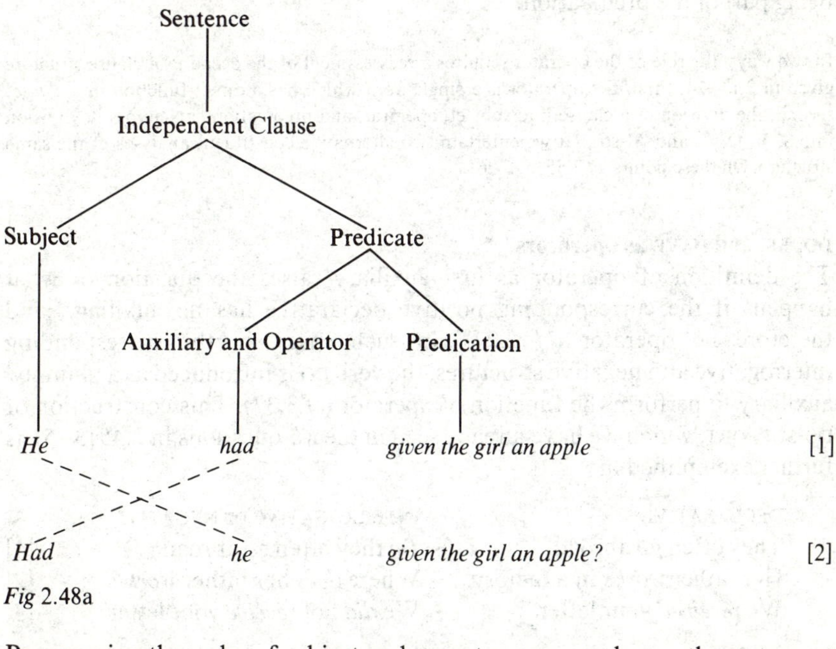

Fig 2.48a

By reversing the order of subject and operator, we can change the statement [1] into the *yes–no* question [2]. The operator has a similar role in the formation of most *wh*-questions. Compare, for example:

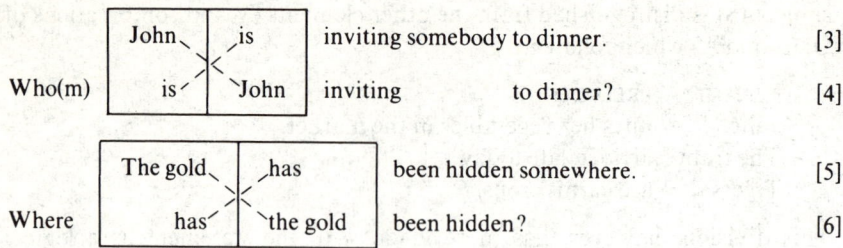

	John	is	inviting somebody to dinner.	[3]
Who(m)	is	John	inviting to dinner?	[4]

	The gold	has	been hidden somewhere.	[5]
Where	has	the gold	been hidden?	[6]

Fig 2.48b

Negation, also, makes crucial use of the operator: to make a positive statement negative, we insert *not* after the operator, or else add to the operator the informal enclitic *-n't* (*cf* 3.22*f*):

I	shall	not	be working this afternoon.	[7]
We	had	not	given the girl an apple.	[8]

Fig 2.48c

In all these and other ways, then, the operator, or first auxiliary, performs an 'operational' function in relating a positive declarative structure to another major structure in the language. That it is the first auxiliary, rather than a subsequent auxiliary, that takes on this role is clear from sentences like [6] and [7], where the second auxiliary (*been* and *be* respectively) is unaffected, being part of the predication.

Note In two ways, the role of the operator requires a reassessment of the account of clause structure given in 2.13–24. First, the operator is a single *word* which has a direct function in a *clause*; second, the division of a clause into subject, operator, and predication cuts across its division into S, V, O, C, and A, so that we entertain two alternative constituent analyses of the same structure. On these points, *cf* 2.55 and 2.61.

DO, BE, and HAVE as operators

2.49 The definition of operator as first auxiliary raises the question of what happens if the corresponding positive declarative has no auxiliary, and therefore no operator (*cf* 2.27). In such cases, in the corresponding interrogative and negative structures, the verb DO is introduced as a 'dummy' auxiliary to perform the function of operator (*cf* 3.37). This construction of DO-SUPPORT, which we have already seen in the *wh*-questions in 2.45 [3–5], is further exemplified in:

DECLARATIVE	INTERROGATIVE or NEGATIVE	
They often *go* abroad.	~ *Do* they often *go* abroad?	[1]
Her father *works* in a factory.	~ Where *does* her father *work*?	[2]
We *received* your letter.	~ We *did* not *receive* your letter.	[3]

Notice that DO as operator occurs in the variant forms of *do, does*, and *did*: as a finite verb (*cf* 3.2, 3.52), it realizes distinctions of number, person, and tense. Elsewhere however, DO may also, like BE and HAVE, function as a main verb: compare the positive sentence *He did it* with the negative *He did not do it*, where the two functions cooccur.

Unlike DO, BE functions as an operator even when it constitutes the whole verb phrase, and is thus a main verb:

Is everything ready? (~ Everything *is* ready) [4]
Was Titian a painter? (~ Titian *was* a painter) [5]
Are these books for sale? (~ These books *are* for sale) [6]

Thus in the questions [4–6], *is*, *was*, and *are*, which are here main verbs, are placed in front of the subject. The main verb HAVE, on the other hand, tends to resemble the main verb DO in not functioning as operator (*Do you have a box of matches?*), although there is also a traditional usage (chiefly BrE) in which it does so: *Have you a box of matches?* (*cf* 3.34*f*, 3.48). These usages are exceptions to our earlier definition of the operator as 'first auxiliary'.

Questions and negation

2.50 We can now venture process rules for forming questions and negative sentences in English, given that we know how to form simple statements:

(a) *YES–NO* QUESTIONS: Place the operator before the subject.
(b) *WH*-QUESTIONS: First, identify the *wh*-element, which is a phrase containing or consisting of the *wh*-word. Then:
   (i) If the *wh*-element is the subject, make no change in the statement order.
   (ii) If the *wh*-element is some other element (*eg* O, C, A), place it before the subject, and place the operator between the *wh*-element and the subject.
(c) NEGATION: Place *not* or *-n't* after the operator (*cf* 3.22*f*).
(d) In (a), (b), and (c), if there is no operator in the corresponding statement, introduce the operator DO.

The following examples may be compared with the statement *Someone (has) borrowed my pencil*:

(a′) Have you borrowed my pencil? [*yes–no* question]
(b′) (i) Who has borrowed my pencil?
(ii) Why have you borrowed my pencil? } [*wh*-question]
(c′) I haven't borrowed your pencil. [negation]
(d′) Did you borrow my pencil?
Why did you borrow my pencil?
I didn't borrow your pencil. } [with DO as operator]

Predications and pro-forms

2.51 The predication, like the operator, is a constituent of some importance in the English clause. One indication of this is the readiness with which two predications can be joined by coordination (*cf* 13.53):

You should *eat regularly* and *take more exercise*.
Someone has *broken into the house* and *stolen the money*.

English also has a composite pro-form *do so* which substitutes for a predicate or a predication (*cf* 12.23*ff*):

She hoped that he would *search the room carefully*,

and he {*searched the room carefully*. / *did so*.} [1]

but he didn't {*search the room carefully*. / *do so*.} [2]

Again, for sentences such as [1] and [2] there is the further alternative of omitting the predication altogether; the operator, left 'stranded' by this omission, thus shows its capability of standing as an independent unit:

She hoped that he would search the room carefully, {and he *did*. / but he *didn't*.}

The composite pro-form *do so* should be distinguished from the empty auxiliary DO used in DO-support. Like other auxiliaries, DO may constitute a residual operator in cases where the contents of the predication are implied and do not need to be expressed. We see a parallel, in this connection, between [3] and [4–6]:

A: *Do* they pay you for the work?

B: {Yes, they *do*. / No, they *don't*.} [3]

A: *Will* they pay you for the work?

B: {Yes, they *will*. / No, they *won't*.} [4]

A: *Are* they paying you for the work?

B: {Yes, they *are*. / No, they *aren't*.} [5]

A: *Have* they been paying you for the work?

B: {Yes, they *have*. / No, they *haven't*.} [6]

Ellipsis

2.52 The above response forms [3–6] illustrate another grammatical process, that of ELLIPSIS (*cf* 12.31*ff*), whereby elements of a sentence which are predictable from context can be omitted. Ellipsis obviously resembles the substitution of pro-forms in its abbreviatory function, and both processes will be considered in this grammar under the common heading of REDUCTION (*cf* 12.1*ff*) as means of avoiding redundancy of expression. There is thus a choice between unreduced forms, pro-forms, and ellipsis, as can be seen in the following equivalent answers to [5]:

Yes, they ÀRE {paying me for the work. [UNREDUCED] / doing so. [PRO-FORM] / . [ELLIPSIS]}

(On the position and function of the intonation nucleus on *are*, *cf* 18.15*f*, 2.56 Note.) Reduction is a particularly clear illustration of the advantage of explaining grammatical phenomena in terms of process: without postulating or 'reconstructing' an unreduced form, we should find it difficult to explain the meaning and grammatical status of reduced forms.

Note A more careful analysis will later require the recognition that one predication may be embedded in another (*cf* 3.21). This is already suggested by the optional presence of *been* in a reduced answer to [6]:

Yes, they have (been (paying me for the work)).

Here both the inner brackets and the outer brackets delimit an omissible predication. Thus there can be more than one predication in a clause, either by embedding, as in:

You must [have [been [working too hard]]].

or by coordination, as in:

You must [[eat regularly] and [get more exercise]].

One of the consequences of this use of the term 'predication' is that a predication may, unlike those predications exemplified in 2.48, be preceded by more than one auxiliary, of which only the first is to be considered an operator. Therefore in the following example, the coordinated elements are predications:

Someone must have [[broken into the house] and [stolen the money]].

Nonassertive forms

2.53 It is already clear that there is a close connection between questions and negation: both constructions involve an operator, and the question-and-answer sequences in 2.51 [3–6] show how a *yes–no* question elicits from its addressee a choice between a positive and negative statement. The term *YES–NO* QUESTION itself reinforces this point.

Yes–no questions are also related to negation through their association with a set of words which we may call NONASSERTIVE FORMS (*cf* 6.59*ff*): *any*, *anybody*, *anywhere*, *yet*, etc. These in turn contrast with corresponding ASSERTIVE FORMS (*some*, *somebody*, *somewhere*, *already*, etc) which are associated with positive statements:

Have you found *any* mistakes *yet*? [1]
Yes, I have found *some already*. [2]
No, I haven't found *any yet*. [3]

The contrast between assertiveness and nonassertiveness is basically a logical one: whereas a sentence like [2] asserts the truth of some proposition, the question [1] and the negative statement [3] do not claim the truth of the corresponding positive statement. We may thus represent the relations between [1–3] by the following diagram:

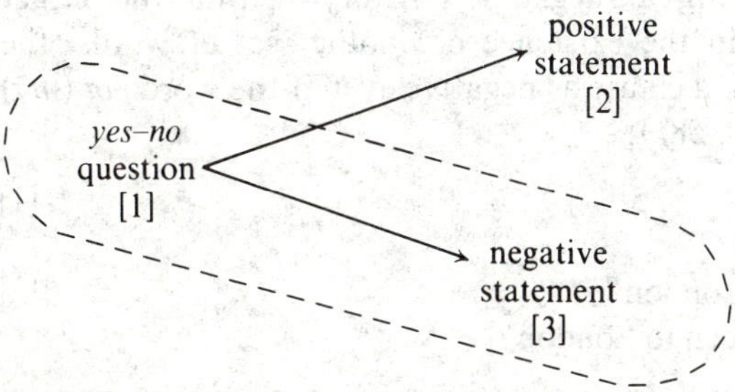

Fig 2.53 Nonassertive territory

The arrows represent relations between question and (unreduced) answer, and the area enclosed by the broken line ------ may be termed 'nonassertive territory'. However, the paradigm of [1–3] is not complete, in a grammatical sense, until we add a fourth category, that of the negative question:

Haven't you found *any* mistakes *yet*? [4]

This cannot be easily fitted into *Fig* 2.53, for there is a fundamental asymmetry between the relation of positive to negative statements, and that of positive to negative *yes–no* questions. Logically, negative *yes–no* questions are equivalent to positive ones, in that they elicit equivalent *yes* and *no* answers: they differ from the latter only in indicating that the corresponding negative statement has been implied (*cf* 11.7).

Note Whereas it is frequently impossible for a positive statement to contain nonassertive forms (**I have any ideas*), it is by no means unusual for assertive forms to occur in questions and negative clauses: *Do(n't) you have some ideas?* Our use of the term 'nonassertive territory' does not exclude, and indeed anticipates, a more delicate stage of analysis (*cf* 10.61*f*) at which we acknowledge that assertive forms can give an assertive 'bias' to constructions which are predominantly nonassertive.

Negative forms

2.54 The addition of negative questions therefore invites a reanalysis of *Fig* 2.53 as follows:

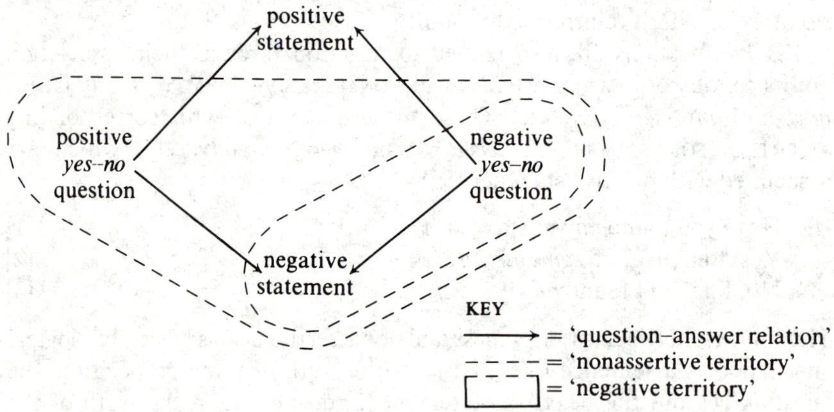

Fig 2.54 Nonassertive and negative territory

The justification for including a 'negative territory' within the larger 'nonassertive territory' lies in the existence of another set of words, the NEGATIVE FORMS, which mark a clause as negative even if the word *not* (*-n't*) does not occur in it (*cf* 6.62, 10.58*f*):

I saw *nobody*. [1]
[= I did*n't* see *anybody*.]
Have you *never* been to London? [2]
[= Have*n't* you *ever* been to London?]

We therefore have three parallel sets of words, as in the following:

ASSERTIVE FORMS:	*some*	*somebody*	*something*	*sometimes*
NONASSERTIVE FORMS:	*any*	*anybody*	*anything*	*ever*
NEGATIVE FORMS:	*no*	*nobody*	*nothing*	*never*

In [1] and [2] the negative forms are seen as equivalent in meaning to *not*, followed, not necessarily immediately, by a nonassertive form (*eg*: *never* = *not* ... *ever*); but since a negative clause normally contains only one mark of its negative status (*cf* 10.63), it is quite natural for a negative form to be followed by one or more nonassertive forms in the same clause or sentence:

John *never* invites *any* students to his parties.
No one *ever* gives her *any* encouragement.

It is this which justifies grammatically the treatment of negation as carrying the implication of nonassertion.

Note Like *wh*-words (*cf* 2.45), both nonassertive and negative forms tend to show a family likeness in their morphological form. But just as *wh*-words do not always begin with the spelling *wh*-, so nonassertive forms do not always begin with *any*-, nor negative forms with *no*-. Among exceptions are the negative words *few* and *rarely* (*cf* 10.59), and the nonassertive words *ever* and *yet* (*cf* 10.60).

Scope

2.55 In accounting for sentence processes, we have found it necessary to refer to a number of special classes of word – pro-forms (including *wh*-words), assertive forms, nonassertive forms, negative forms, operators – which intersect with the primary word-class categories. These classes may be described as having a *logical* function rather than a *structural* function in the sense of 2.12. In fact, all of them except operators are distributed across a range of word classes, and can have a number of different functions in clause structure; *eg* as S, O, C, A. Moreover, their contribution to the meaning of the sentence can stretch well beyond the particular phrase in which they occur. Their position, too, may bring particular significance: for example, a *wh*-word or an operator at the beginning of a sentence will mark the whole of what follows it as a question.

SCOPE is the general term that we shall use to describe the semantic 'influence' which such words have on neighbouring parts of a sentence. It deserves attention because of its close connection with the ordering of elements. The position of a negative form, for instance, is generally significant in defining whatever follows it as nonassertive:

Some people *never* send *any* Christmas cards.

In such a sentence, we may say that *any*, because it follows *never*, is within the scope of negation (*cf* 10.64) while *some* is not. It would therefore not be possible to reverse the positions of the assertive and nonassertive words:

**Any* people *never* send *some* Christmas cards.

This sentence may, however, be contrasted with an allowable sentence in which *any people* follows a negative:

I do*n't* know *any* people who *never* send Christmas cards.

In a similar way, the operator or *wh*-element which normally begins a question indicates that what follows is within the scope of interrogation. It is this which accounts in part for the difference of meaning between:

Does he *seriously* believe that? [1]
Seriously, does he believe that? [2]

or between:

Why doesn't he *also* take the children abroad? [3]
Also, why doesn't he take the children abroad? [4]

In [2] and [4] the adverb must be interpreted as a sentence adverbial (*cf* 2.15) which, because of its initial position, is not part of the matter being questioned.

Focus

2.56 The position of *also* in [3] above brings to notice another phenomenon of 'semantic influence'. We shall call certain adverbs, such as *also*, *only*, and *even*, FOCUSING SUBJUNCTS (*cf* 8.116*ff*), because they have the peculiarity of extending the application of their meaning to units of varying size and position. Thus [3] in different contexts could mean:

'Why doesn't *he* (in addition to his wife) take the children abroad?' [5]
'Why doesn't he take *the children* (in addition to his wife) abroad?' [6]
'Why doesn't he take the children *abroad* (in addition to taking them to places in this country)?' [7]
'Why doesn't he *take the children abroad* (in addition to, say, giving them presents)?' [8]

The italicized parts of these paraphrases identify the different focused elements which give rise to the ambiguities.

The ambiguities, however, are more apparent on paper than in speech. This is one aspect of grammar for which intonation plays a critical role, since the various meanings of [3] can be largely distinguished by different positions of the nucleus (*cf* App II.11). For example:

Why doesn't he ÀLso take the children abroad? [5a]
Why doesn't he also take the CHÌLDren abroad? [6a]
Why doesn't he also take the children aBRÒAD? [7a], [8a]

The term FOCUS, in fact, will be more generally applied to the varying placement of the nucleus so as to mark which parts of an utterance are meant to represent new or contrastive information (*cf* 18.8*ff*). The interaction between information focus in this sense, and scope in the sense of 2.55 is a somewhat difficult area of grammar (*cf* esp 10.65) which nevertheless has some obvious communicative effects. The nucleus can, for example, narrow down the negative or interrogative force of a sentence by giving contrastive prominence to a particular item:

I don't drink ǏNstant coffee.

carries the implication 'I drink some coffee, but not . . .', and similarly:

Have you read ÁLL her novels?

carries the implication 'I know you've read *some* of her novels, but what I want to know is . . .'.

Enough has been said to suggest that a full understanding of interrogation, negation, and other processes cannot be reached without a study of the phenomena of scope and focus. These illustrate particularly clearly the need for grammar to take account of other aspects of language, especially the semantic contrasts which are realized through grammar, and the phonological contrasts through which grammar itself is realized.

Note It is not surprising that the special grammatical functions of operators, *wh*-words, and negative words are associated with special meanings when the focus is placed on these items:

We HÀVE been working hard. (*cf* focus on the operator; 18.15*f*).
WHÉN are you leaving? (*cf* echo questions; 11.33*ff*).
I was NÒT telling lies. (*cf* denial negation; 10.65 Note [a]).

These are all, in a way, SECOND-INSTANCE SENTENCES, *ie* sentences about other sentences rather than sentences about the world outside language. Focus on the operator can involve the introduction of DO-support, showing that DO as operator can be found even in unreduced declarative sentences:

I DÒ believe you.

Other structural variations

Directives and exclamations

2.57 We finally take brief notice of grammatical processes other than those connected with questions and negation.

Apart from statements and questions, a classification of sentences in terms of communicative function (*cf* 2.46) must include DIRECTIVES (*cf* 11.24*ff*) and EXCLAMATIONS (*cf* 11.31*f*). The former, in their typical form, contain no subject or operator: they consist simply of a predication with an imperative verb, *ie* a verb in its base form:

Be quiet!
Search the room carefully!
Make yourself a cup of tea.

This is understandable; since an imperative normally refers to some future action which the hearer is urged to perform, its subject is semantically predictable, and therefore dispensable, while the verb phrase is required to make no distinctions of tense, number, and person. Imperatives can, however, be negative, and for this *do* is introduced as an imperative marker (*cf* 11.28):

Don't hurry!
Don't be frightened!
Don't wait for me.

Exclamatives, as a formal category, resemble *wh*-questions in beginning with a *wh*-word (*what* or *how*), but differ from them in generally retaining the regular declarative order of subject and verb:

What beautiful clothes she wears!
How well Philip plays the piano!

(Compare the *wh*-questions *What clothes does she wear?* and *How well does Philip play the piano?*) The exclamatory force of *what* and *how* resides in their function as an intensifying determiner and adverb respectively: the element in which they occur must be overtly or implicitly subject to modifications of degree (*cf* 7.42, 7.87*ff*). Like directives, therefore, they are grammatically restricted; but their restrictions are of a different kind.

For example they resemble *wh*-questions rather than directives in their general unsusceptibility to negation:

?How well Philip doesn't play the piano! [1]
?What beautiful clothes she doesn't wear! [2]

To explain this tendency we may again appeal to the notion of scope – the rest of the sentence being included in the scope of the initial intensifying phrase. Since negative states of affairs cannot be treated as matters of degree, negative exclamations are unusual.

Note Thus [1] can be given only an irregular or humorous interpretation such as 'I find Philip's behaviour perfectly delightful in that he, unlike so many other people I know, does not play the piano'.

Pragmatic considerations

2.58 The peculiarities of directives and exclamations have much to do with their pragmatic roles as utterances which relate specifically to the hearer's and the speaker's participation in the act of communication: a directive is 'hearer-oriented', whereas an exclamation is 'speaker-oriented'.

If we define PRAGMATICS as a study of language in relation to the communicative functions it may be used to perform, then there is a certain division of labour between grammar and pragmatics whereby the more the context contributes to the communicative force of an utterance, the less need there is for the utterance to be grammatically explicit. In this sense, directives and exclamations are towards the pragmatic end of the scale. They can take many forms other than the structures above, and are often reducible to formulaic utterances which make very limited use of grammatical structure: *Out with it! What a day! Perfect!* etc (*cf* 11.38*ff*). To the extent that the situation limits the need for full articulation of meaning, sentence grammar becomes otiose. Here again, attention must be given to the interaction between grammar and other factors in the totality of linguistic communication.

Note The contribution of grammar to the communicative process reaches its minimum in utterances which are merely interjections: *Ouch! Hush!* ([ʃ::]) etc. It is worth noting that these quasi-linguistic noises very frequently have either an exclamatory or an imperative force (*cf* 11.55). On the other hand, we must acknowledge that statements and questions, too, can occur as interjections or in markedly reduced forms: *Uh-huh, Yes, No, Eh?, Right?, Ready?*, etc.

Grammatical highlighting

2.59 Still thinking of grammar in a communicative context, we notice that many variations of grammatical structure relate to the speaker's or writer's need to present the message in a form readily adapted to the addressee's requirements as interpreter. Reduction (*cf* 2.52) and information focus (*cf* 2.56), in particular, enable users of language to suppress those elements of meaning which are informationally predictable, and to highlight those which are informationally important. In Chapter 18 we shall explore how such considerations interact with processes which involve varying the position of elements in the sentence.

The so-called CLEFT SENTENCE (*cf* 18.25*ff*), for example, is a grammatical device similar to, and associated with, information focus: it enables the user to select (within limits) which element of the sentence will be highlighted. The cleft sentence is divided into two main parts: an initial focal element, followed by a 'background' structure which resembles a relative clause. For the simple sentence [1] the alternative cleft sentences [2–4] are available:

Julie buys her vegetables in the market. [1]
It's *Julie* that/who buys her vegetables in the market. [2]
It's *her vegetables* that Julie buys in the market. [3]
It's *in the market* that Julie buys her vegetables. [4]

A less complex device with a similar function is FRONTING: the initial placing of an element such as an object or an adverbial (*cf* 18.20):

Her vegetables Julie buys in the market.
In the market Julie buys her vegetables.

The opposite device of postponing a normally nonfinal element to final position is shown by the EXTRAPOSITION of a subject clause (*cf* 18.33), as in [6]:

What you say doesn't matter. [5]
~ It doesn't matter *what you say*. [6]

The final position gives the element in question a different kind of prominence, which we shall discuss under the headings of end-focus and end-weight (*cf* 18.3*f*, 18.9).

The role of the anticipatory pronoun *it* in [6] is essentially a structural one in the sense that it carries virtually no information in itself, but merely supplies the structural requirement for an initial subject. (Its semantic function, in so far as it has one, is merely to signal that the content of the subject is expressed in a later position in the same sentence.) A somewhat parallel role is performed by the introductory word *there* in EXISTENTIAL sentences (*cf* 18.44*ff*), as in [8]:

Someone was knocking at the door. [7]
~ *There was someone* knocking at the door. [8]

The effect of the prelude *there was* in [8] is to postpone to a more 'focused' position the indefinite pronoun *someone*, which, because it ushers in new information, can only uneasily fill the unfocused position of subject (*cf* 2.55, 2.56).

We have merely hinted at the communicative value of these apparently unneeded constructions, and at the stylistic considerations which may lead users of English to select them. But they enable us to stress once again that the study of grammatical process, in all its variety and apparent arbitrariness, compels us to place grammar in its broader context of uses and users of language.

Gradience and multiple analysis

Gradience

2.60 Grammar is to some extent an indeterminate system. Categories and structures, for example, often do not have neat boundaries. Grammarians are tempted to overlook such uncertainties, or to pretend that they do not exist. Our guiding principle in this grammar, however, will be to acknowledge them, and where appropriate to explore them through the study of GRADIENCE. A gradient is a scale which relates two categories of description (for example two word classes) in terms of degrees of similarity and contrast. At the ends of the scale are items which belong clearly to one category or to another; intermediate positions on the scale are taken by 'in-between' cases – items which fail, in different degrees, to satisfy the criteria for one or the other category. At various points in the preceding survey we have hinted at gradience; in the contrast between central and peripheral elements of the clause (2.13), between adjuncts, subjuncts, disjuncts, and conjuncts (2.15), between complements and adverbials (2.17*f*), between modification and complementation (2.33).

The simplest cases of gradience to identify are those relating to word classes. We shall see, for example, in 13.18*f* that there is a scale relating coordinating and subordinating conjunctions, such that *and* and *if* represent clear cases of each category, whereas *for* is in an intermediate position:

COORDINATING SUBORDINATING

and←————*for*————→*if*

Nevertheless, *for* is closer to *if* in its syntactic behaviour than to *and* (*cf* 13.18*f*), and can reasonably be classed as a peripheral subordinator.

Multiple analysis

2.61 Another kind of indeterminacy is revealed through what may be called MULTIPLE ANALYSIS. It is one thing to analyse a sentence into a multiplicity of smaller units through progressive subdivision, as shown in the tree diagrams of 2.3–9; it is quite another thing to propose that two or more different analyses, each resulting in a different constituent structure, can be applied to the same sentence. There are occasions, however, when such alternative analyses seem to be needed, on the grounds that some of the generalizations that have to be made require one analysis, and some require another. It is for this reason that we have presented, in this chapter, two ways of analysing a clause: one analysis in terms of the elements S, V, O, C, and A, and the other in terms of subject and predicate, the predicate being subdivided into operator and predication (*cf* 2.48 Note). In other cases, there appears to be a gradient between two analyses, such that sentences may vary in the degree to which one analysis is more appropriate than another.

An important example of multiple analysis is that required for prepositional verbs such as *look at* and *approve of* (*cf* 16.13*ff*). In the terms of the present chapter, we regard the preposition as introducing a prepositional phrase which functions as an adverbial:

[They] [don't *approve*] [*of* noisy parties].

But there are also good reasons, such as the possibility of the (rather awkward) passive *Noisy parties are not approved of*, for an alternative analysis in which *noisy parties* is treated as an object of the multi-word verb *approve of*:

[They] [don't *approve of*] [noisy parties].

Such alternative analyses are further discussed in 16.5.

Conclusion

2.62 Both the complexities and indeterminacies of grammar place the prospect of writing a complete and definitive grammatical description of English beyond reasonable expectation. Given inevitable limitations, what we aim to achieve here is a description which combines breadth of coverage and depth of detail, and in which observation of particularities goes hand in hand with the search for general and systematic explanations.

Bibliographical note

For the general application of various models or theories to English grammar, see Akmajian and Heny (1975); Bloomfield (1933); Brown and Miller (1982); Dik (1978); Fillmore (1977b); Huddleston (1976b, 1984); Hudson (1976a); Newmeyer (1980); Pike and Pike (1977); Radford (1982); Stockwell et al (1973).

Descriptive and reference grammars of English include Curme (1931); Jespersen (1909–1949, 1933); Kruisinga (1931–32); Poutsma (1926–29); Quirk et al (1972); Svartvik and Sager (1980); Sweet (1891–98); Visser (1963–73); Zandvoort (1975).

On aspects of English sentence structure, see Crystal (1980); Firbas (1974); Greenbaum (1980); Halliday (1963); Huddleston (1965, 1971); Hudson (1971); Young (1980).

On elements of structure and their syntactic and semantic relations (both in English and in other languages), see Abraham (1978); Allerton (1980); Jacobson (1964); Li (1975, 1976); Mathesius (1975); Matthews (1980).

Studies relevant to the boundaries of grammar include the following: (a) relating to semantics and pragmatics: Austin (1962); Bolinger (1977a); Givón (1979); Searle (1969, 1979); (b) relating to lexical structures: Halliday (1966); Schopf (1969), esp Ch 3.

On topics related to gradience and multiple analysis, see Bolinger (1961a, 1961b); Givón (1984); Lakoff (1982); Mohan (1977); Quirk (1965); Ross (1973).

Among other works relevant to the general analysis of grammatical concepts and categories are Allerton (1979); Ellegård (1978); Gleason (1965), esp Pt 2; Greenbaum (1973a, 1977a); Hockett (1968); Lehmann (1978); Lyons (1966, 1977 esp Vol 2); Matthews (1974, 1981); Robins (1980, esp Chs 5 and 6); Sørensen (1958).

For further bibliographical information, consult Scheurweghs (1963–68), Vorlat (1979), and Yasui (1979, 1983).

3 Verbs and auxiliaries

Major verb classes

3.1 The function of the V element in English clause structure, as outlined in 2.13–24, is realized by the VERB PHRASE, which consists of one or more verb constituents, *eg*:

She *left* yesterday.	She *won't leave* tomorrow.
Has she *not left* yet?	She *will leave* tomorrow.
Did she *leave* yesterday?	She *might be leaving* next week.

Verbs, as a class of words, can be divided into three major categories, according to their function within the verb phrase; we distinguish the open class of FULL VERBS (or lexical verbs) such as LEAVE (*cf* 3.2*ff*) from the closed classes of PRIMARY VERBS (BE, HAVE, and DO; *cf* 3.31*ff*) and of MODAL AUXILIARY VERBS (*will*, *might*, etc; *cf* 3.39). Of these three classes, the full verbs can act only as main verbs (*cf* 2.28), the modal auxiliaries can act only as auxiliary verbs, and the primary verbs can act either as main verbs or as auxiliary verbs.

Note [**a**] Some verbs (variously termed marginal modals, semi-auxiliaries, catenative verbs, etc) have a status intermediate between that of main verbs and that of auxiliary verbs. (These are discussed in 3.40 – 3.51.)

[**b**] SMALL CAPITALS are generally used in this chapter in citing a verb as a lexical item (*cf* 2.35) instead of as a grammatical form. We will cite the modal auxiliaries, however, in *italics*, since it is often more appropriate to regard *can* and *could* (for example) as invariable words, than as forms of the same lexical item (*cf* 4.49*ff*, where special uses of the past modal forms *could*, *might*, *would*, and *should* are discussed).

Full verbs

The morphology of regular verbs

Verb forms and the verb phrase

3.2 Regular full verbs, *eg* CALL, have four morphological forms. Irregular full verbs vary in this respect; a verb like SPEAK has five, whereas CUT has only three forms (note, however, that the primary verb BE (*cf* 3.32) has as many as eight forms).

	REGULAR VERBS		IRREGULAR VERBS		
(1) BASE FORM	*call*	*want*	*speak*	*cut*	*win*
(2) -*S* FORM	*calls*	*wants*	*speaks*	*cuts*	*wins*
(3) -*ING* PARTICIPLE	*calling*	*wanting*	*speaking*	*cutting*	*winning*
(4) PAST FORM	*called*	*wanted*	*spoke*	*cut*	*won*
(5) -*ED* PARTICIPLE	*called*	*wanted*	*spoken*	*cut*	*won*

These verb forms have different functions in finite and nonfinite verb phrases (*cf* 3.52*ff*). On this basis, the -*s* form and the past form are called FINITE, whereas the -*ing* participle and the -*ed* participle are called NONFINITE. The

BASE form (the form which has no inflection) is sometimes finite, and sometimes nonfinite (see below). In a finite verb phrase (the kind of verb phrase which normally occurs in simple sentences), only the first verb word (in bold face below) is finite:

She ***calls*** him every day.
She ***is*** *calling* him now.
She ***has*** *called* twice today.

and the subsequent verbs, if any, are nonfinite. In a nonfinite verb phrase, on the other hand, all verbs are nonfinite; *eg*:

Calling early, she found him at home.
Called early, he ate a quick breakfast.
Having been called early, he felt sleepy all day.

The difference between finite and nonfinite phrases is discussed in greater detail in 3.52*ff*. Here we confine our attention to the syntactic deployment of the verb forms of which verb phrases are composed:

(1) The BASE FORM (*call*, *speak*, *cut*, etc) occurs as (a) a FINITE form in:
  (i) the present tense in all persons and numbers except 3rd person singular (which has the *-s* form): *I/you/we/they call regularly*. (*cf* 3.54, 4.3*ff*)
  (ii) the imperative: *Call at once!* (*cf* 3.54, 11.24*ff*)
  (iii) the present subjunctive: *They demanded that she call and see them*. (*cf* 3.59–61)

It also occurs as (b) a NONFINITE form in:
  (i) the bare infinitive: *He may call tonight*.
  (ii) the *to*-infinitive: *We want her to call*. (*cf* 3.53, 14.6*ff*)

(2) The *-S* FORM (*calls*, *speaks*, *cuts*, etc) occurs as a FINITE form in: 3rd person singular present tense: *He/She calls every day*.

(3) The *-ING* PARTICIPLE (*calling*, *speaking*, *cutting*, etc) occurs as a NONFINITE form in:
  (i) the progressive aspect following BE: *He's calling her now*. (*cf* 4.25*ff*)
  (ii) *-ing* participle clauses: *Calling early, I found her at home*. (*cf* 3.53, 14.6*ff*)

(4) The PAST FORM (*called*, *spoke*, *cut*, etc) occurs as a FINITE form in the past tense: *Someone called yesterday*. (*cf* 4.11*ff*)

(5) The *-ED* PARTICIPLE (*called*, *spoken*, *cut*, etc) occurs as a NONFINITE form in:
  (i) the perfective aspect following HAVE: *He has called twice today*. (*cf* 4.18*ff*)
  (ii) the passive voice following BE: *Her brother is called John*. (*cf* 3.63*ff*)
  (iii) *-ed* participle clauses: *Called early, he ate a quick breakfast*. (*cf* 3.53, 14.6*ff*)

As will become clearer when we discuss the structure of the verb phrase (3.52*ff*), the nonfinite forms of the verb occur not only in nonfinite verb phrases, but also in noninitial positions in finite verb phrases.

Note The *-ing* participle is sometimes called the 'present participle', and the *-ed* participle is sometimes called the 'past participle' or, with transitive verbs, the 'passive participle'. Since these terms are potentially misleading, we prefer to use terms which are descriptive only of morphological form. Note, however, that the *-ed* participle owes its name to the form this participle takes in regular verbs; some irregular verbs (*eg*: *taken*) have a more distinctive ending in *-en*, and some grammarians for this reason have preferred the term '*-en* participle'.

The morphology of regular full verbs

3.3 Morphologically, full verbs are considered under two heads: REGULAR verbs (such as CALL) and IRREGULAR verbs (such as DRINK). In both types, the *-s* form and the *-ing* participle form are almost invariably predictable from the base. Irregular verbs differ from the regular verbs, however, in that the past form and the *-ed* participle of irregular verbs cannot be predicted by general rule from the base.

3.4 Regular full verbs have only four different forms:

BASE	*call*	*like*	*try*
-ing PARTICIPLE	*calling*	*liking*	*trying*
-s FORM	*calls*	*likes*	*tries*
PAST FORM or *-ed* PARTICIPLE	*called*	*liked*	*tried*

These verbs are called regular because if we know the base form (*ie* the dictionary entry form; *cf* 2.35) of such a verb, we can predict all its other forms by rule. This is a very powerful generalization, since the vast majority of English verbs belong to the regular class. Furthermore, new verbs that are coined or borrowed from other languages adopt this pattern; *eg*: *xerox* ~ *xeroxing* ~ *xeroxes* ~ *xeroxed*. As the past form and the *-ed* participle form are identical for all regular verbs, it will be convenient to refer to them both as the *-ed* form, distinguishing where necessary between the V-ed_1 (past tense) and V-ed_2 (*-ed* participle) forms.

Note **[a]** The process of assimilating foreign words to the regular pattern is more marked in verbs than in nouns, where foreign plurals are often kept in English, sometimes with an alternative native ending (*cf* 5.82*ff*): *antenna* ~ *antennae*/*antennas*.

[b] Some archaic 2nd person and 3rd person singular present-tense verb forms survive in very restricted use: chiefly in traditional liturgical language. The 2nd person forms with *thou* as subject (*cf* 6.12 Note [c]) end in *-est* /ɪst/, /est/, whereas the even rarer 3rd person forms end in *-eth* /ɪθ/, /eθ/:

(thou)	*callest*	*givest*	*hearest*
(he/she)	*calleth*	*giveth*	*heareth*

Contracted nonsyllabic endings *-st* and *-th* occur with the primary verbs HAVE and DO: *hast*, *hath*; *dost* /dʌst/, *doth* /dʌθ/. (Similar forms *saist*, *saith* /seθ/ occur with the verb SAY, which also, however, has the regular forms *sayest* and *sayeth*.) The primary verb BE, here as elsewhere, is highly irregular: it has no *-st* or *-th* forms, but it has the archaic 2nd person form *art* and an analogous past tense form *wert*: *thou art*/*wert*. Other verbs have *-(e)st* '*thou*-forms' in the past tense: *hadst*, *didst*, *gavest*, *camest*, etc. The spelling of the *-est* forms of *see* and *lie* is irregular: *seest* /siː-ɪst/; *liest* /laɪ-ɪst/.

All the modal auxiliaries except those ending in *-t* have special '*thou*-forms': *will* ~ *wilt*, *shall* ~ *shalt*, *can* ~ *canst*, *may* ~ *mayst*, *would* ~ *wouldst*, *should* ~ *shouldst*, *could* ~ *couldst*.

The *-ing* participle and the *-s* form

3.5 The *-ing* form of both regular and irregular verbs is formed by adding *-ing* /ɪŋ/ to the base:

walk ~ *walking*	*agree* ~ *agreeing*	*push* ~ *pushing*
sing ~ *singing*	*pass* ~ *passing*	*weep* ~ *weeping*

(On the spelling of the *-ing* participle, *cf* 3.7*ff*.) The *-s* form of both regular and irregular verbs (sometimes spelled *-es*; *cf* 3.9) is also predictable from the base. It has three pronunciations /ɪz/, /z/, and /s/, which occur under the following phonological conditions:

(a) /ɪz/ after bases ending in voiced or voiceless sibilants; *eg*:

Table 3.5a

BASE			-S FORM		BASE			-S FORM	
/-s/	*pass*	~	*passes*	/-sɪz/	/-dʒ/	*budge*	~	*budges*	/-dʒɪz/
/-z/	*buzz*	~	*buzzes*	/-zɪz/	/-ʃ/	*push*	~	*pushes*	/-ʃɪz/
/-tʃ/	*catch*	~	*catches*	/-tʃɪz/	/-ʒ/	*camouflage*	~	*camouflages*	/-ʒɪz/

For these cases, the *-s* form always ends in *-es*.

(b) /z/ after bases ending in voiced sounds other than sibilants, including vowels; *eg*:

Table 3.5b

/-l/	*call*	~	*calls*	/-lz/	/-b/	*rob*	~	*robs*	/-bz/
/-iː/	*flee*	~	*flees*	/-iːz/	/-aɪ/	*try*	~	*tries*	/-aɪz/

(c) /s/ after bases ending in voiceless sounds other than sibilants, *eg*:

Table 3.5c

/-t/	*cut*	~	*cuts*	/-ts/	/-k/	*lock*	~	*locks*	/-ks/
/-p/	*hop*	~	*hops*	/-ps/	/-f/	*cough*	~	*coughs*	/-fs/

The rules on the spelling *-es* (*go*/*goes*), the changing of *-y* to *-i-* (*try*/*tries*), etc are the same as for the regular plural of nouns (*cf* 5.81).

Note [**a**] Apart from the three primary verbs BE, HAVE, and DO (*cf* 3.31*ff*), the only verbs which have an irregular *-s* form are *say* /seɪ/ ~ *says* /sez/, and derivatives of DO, *eg*: *outdo* /-duː/ ~ *outdoes* /-dʌz/; *overdo* /-duː/ *overdoes* /-dʌz/. In the *-s* form, SAY is irregular in pronunciation, but not in spelling. GAINSAY, historically a derivative of SAY, may have a regular or an irregular pronunciation in the *-s* form: *gainsays* /-seɪz/ or /-sez/.

[**b**] In some varieties of English (*eg* South African English and many varieties of AmE) the pronunciation of the syllabic ending of the *-s* form is /əz/ rather than /ɪz/. Similarly, the syllabic *-ed* form (*cf* 3.6) is pronounced in such varieties as /əd/ rather than /ɪd/.

[**c**] A common (especially nonstandard) pronunciation of the *-ing* inflection is /ɪn/, conventionally spelt *-in'*; *eg*: *gettin'* /ˈgetɪn/.

[**d**] The verb *lightning* ~ *lightnings* ~ *lightning* ~ *lightninged* is a sole exception to the rule for forming the *-ing* participle. Since the base form of the verb already ends in an *-ing* suffix, no further *-ing* is added: *It is lightning*/**lightninging*. The *-ing* participle of this verb is avoided probably because of the awkwardness of this irregularity.

The past form and the *-ed* participle

3.6 Like the *-s* form, the past and the *-ed* participle forms (both termed the *-ed* form) of regular verbs have three pronunciations:

(a) /ɪd/ after bases ending in /d/ and /t/, *eg*:

pad ~ *padded* /-dɪd/ *pat* ~ *patted* /-tɪd/

(b) /d/ after bases ending in voiced sounds other than /d/, including vowels, *eg*:

buzz ~ *buzzed* /-zd/ *budge* ~ *budged* /-dʒd/
call ~ *called* /-ld/ *tow* ~ *towed* /-əʊd/

(c) /t/ after bases ending in voiceless sounds other than /t/, *eg*:

pass ~ *passed* /-st/ *pack* ~ *packed* /-kt/

Note Some exceptions to the second rule above are verbs like *dwell* ~ *dwelled*/*dwelt*, which (esp in BrE) may end in /t/ rather than /d/. The devoicing may also be reflected in an irregular spelling: *dwelt*. These verbs are classed as irregular verbs (*cf* 3.13).

The spelling of regular verb inflections

3.7 The rules in 3.5 – 6 apply to pronunciation, but certain additional rules have to be stated to account for the spellings of verbs with regular verb inflections. First, however, we note the general spelling rules:

The *-s* form is written *-s*: *look* ~ *looks*
The *-ing* form is written *-ing*: *look* ~ *looking*
The *-ed* form is written *-ed*: *look* ~ *looked*

These rules apply except where one of the following additional changes applies: doubling of the final consonant of the base (*cf* 3.8); deletion or addition of a final *-e* (*cf* 3.9); substitution of *-i-* for a final *-y* or vice versa (*cf* 3.10).

These additional rules are necessary in order to account for such apparent anomalies as are illustrated in the following distinctions:

{*die* ~ *dying* ~ *died*
{*dye* ~ *dyeing* ~ *dyed*

{*bar* ~ *barring* ~ *barred*
{*bare* ~ *baring* ~ *bared*

{*sing* ~ *singing* ~ *sang*/*sung* (*cf* 3.19)
{*singe* ~ *singeing* ~ *singed*

{*hop* ~ *hopping* ~ *hopped*
{*hope* ~ *hoping* ~ *hoped*

{*stop* ~ *stopping* ~ *stopped*
{*stoop* ~ *stooping* ~ *stooped*

{*star* ~ *starring* ~ *starred*
{*stare* ~ *staring* ~ *stared*

As we see above, final *-e* can be preserved to avoid confusion in pairs like *dying* and *dyeing* (*cf* 3.9).

Doubling of consonant before *-ing* and *-ed*

3.8 A single consonant letter at the end of the base is doubled before *-ing* and *-ed* when the preceding vowel is stressed and spelt with a single letter:

bar ~ *'barring* ~ *barred*
beg ~ *'begging* ~ *begged*

ocˈcur ~ *ocˈcurring* ~ *ocˈcurred*
perˈmit ~ *perˈmitting* ~ *perˈmitted*
paˈtrol ~ *paˈtrolling* ~ *paˈtrolled*

There is normally no doubling when the preceding vowel is unstressed (*ˈenter* ~ *ˈentering* ~ *ˈentered*, *ˈvisit* ~ *ˈvisiting* ~ *ˈvisited*) or is written with two letters (*dread* ~ *dreading* ~ *dreaded*).

With some final consonants, however, doubling occurs even when the preceding vowel is unstressed. In the following cases (a – c), doubling is normal in BrE, whereas it is an alternative and less favoured practice in AmE:

(a) Verbs ending in an unstressed vowel followed by *-l*:

ˈtravel	{ *ˈtravelling*	*ˈtravelled*	⟨BrE and AmE⟩
	{ *ˈtraveling*	*ˈtraveled*	⟨AmE only⟩

Similarly: *ˈcancel*, *ˈcounsel*, *ˈdial*, *ˈmodel*, *ˈsignal*, etc.

(b) Verbs ending in an unstressed vowel followed by *-m*(*me*):

ˈprogram(me)	*ˈprogramming*	*ˈprogrammed*	⟨BrE and AmE⟩
ˈprogram	*ˈprograming*	*ˈprogramed*	⟨AmE only⟩

(c) Some verbs ending in an unstressed vowel followed by *-p*:

ˈworship	{ *ˈworshipping*	*ˈworshipped*	⟨BrE and AmE⟩
	{ *ˈworshiping*	*ˈworshiped*	⟨AmE only⟩

The verbs *handicap* and *kidnap* also follow the pattern of *worship*. But most verbs ending in *-p* after an unstressed vowel have no doubling either in BrE or in AmE: *deˈvelop* ~ *deˈveloping* ~ *deˈveloped*, *ˈgallop* ~ *ˈgalloping* ~ *ˈgalloped*, *ˈgossip* ~ *ˈgossiping* ~ *ˈgossiped*, etc.

(d) Verbs ending in an unstressed vowel followed by *-g*:

ˈhumbug	*ˈhumbugging*	*ˈhumbugged*

But note ⟨AmE⟩ *ˈcatalog* ~ *ˈcataloging* ~ *ˈcataloged*.

(e) In verbs ending with vowel + *-c*, the doubling of the final consonant is spelt *-ck-*:

ˈpanic	*ˈpanicking*	*ˈpanicked*
ˈtraffic	*ˈtrafficking*	*ˈtrafficked*

Similarly *ˈfrolic*, *ˈbivouac*, etc.

(f) In certain verbs whose base ends in a vowel followed by *-s*, there is variation between *-s-* and *-ss-* when the verb suffix is added:

ˈbias	*ˈbiasing/ˈbiassing*	*ˈbiased/ˈbiassed*
bus	*ˈbusing/ˈbussing*	*bused/bussed*
ˈfocus	*ˈfocusing/ˈfocussing*	*ˈfocused/ˈfocussed*

Note [**a**] With verbs like PLAY (~ *playing* ~ *played*) and ROW (~ *rowing* ~ *rowed*) there is no doubling, because the *-y* and *-w* do not count as consonants in these words, but as part of the spelling of the diphthong (*-ay*, *-ow*). (On LAY, PAY, *cf* 3.10.)

[**b**] There is, on the other hand, doubling in words such as E'QUIP (~ *e'quipping* ~ *e'quipped*) and AC'QUIT (~ *ac'quitting* ~ *ac'quitted*), because the *u* here counts as part of the consonantal spelling *-qu-*, rather than as a vowel.
[**c**] The letter *-x* is never doubled, since it represents the two consonant sounds /ks/: *fix* ~ *fixing* ~ *fixed*, etc.
[**d**] Final silent consonants are not doubled: *crochet* /-eɪ/ ~ *crocheting* ~ *crocheted*; *hurrah* /-ɑː/ ~ *hurrahing* ~ *hurrahed*.
[**e**] The rules given here for doubling are in general followed also in the addition of derivational suffixes (App I.32*ff*) beginning with a vowel.
[**f**] The spellings **catalogged* ~ **catalogging* do not occur (see (d) above), since the BrE spellings for AmE CATALOG are *catalogue* ~ *cataloguing* ~ *catalogued*.
[**g**] A rare exception to (e) above is *arc* ~ *arc(k)ing* ~ *arc(k)ed*, for which the spelling without *k* is also possible.
[**h**] The verb BENEFIT sometimes (esp in AmE) has forms with irregular consonant doubling (*'benefitting* ~ *'benefitted*) alongside the regular *benefiting* ~ *benefited*.

Deletion of and addition of *-e*

3.9 If the base ends in a mute (unpronounced) *-e*, this *-e* is regularly dropped before the *-ing* and *-ed* inflections:

create ~ *creating* ~ *created*   *shave* ~ *shaving* ~ *shaved*
bake ~ *baking* ~ *baked*   *type* ~ *typing* ~ *typed*

Verbs with monosyllabic bases in *-ye*, *-oe*, and *-nge*, pronounced /ndʒ/, are exceptions to this rule: they do not lose the *-e* before *-ing*, but they do lose it before *-ed*. So also *canoe*. For example:

dye ~ *dyeing* ~ *dyed*   *singe* ~ *singeing* ~ *singed*
hoe ~ *hoeing* ~ *hoed*   *tinge* ~ *tingeing* ~ *tinged*

Impinging and *infringing*, on the other hand, are regular. The final *-e* is also lost before *-ed* by verbs ending in *-ie* or *-ee*: *tie* ~ *tied*, *die* ~ *died*, *agree* ~ *agreed*.

Before the *-s* ending, on the other hand, an *-e* is added in the following cases:

(a) After the following letters, representing sibilant consonants:

-s	*pass* ~ *passes*	*-ch*	*watch* ~ *watches*
-z	*buzz* ~ *buzzes*	*-sh*	*wash* ~ *washes*
-x	*coax* ~ *coaxes*		

(b) after *-o* in GO (~ *goes*), DO (~ *does* /dʌz/), ECHO (~ *echoes*), VETO (~ *vetoes*).

Compare the spelling of regular *-s* plurals (*cf* 5.81).

Note [**a**] The loss of *-e* in *age* ~ *ag(e)ing* is optional.
[**b**] Where *-ch* represents a consonant other than the sibilant or affricate /tʃ/, the *-e* is omitted: *stomachs*.

Treatment of *-y*

3.10 In bases ending in a consonant followed by *-y*, the following changes take place:

(a) *-y* changes to *-ie-* before *-s*: *carry* ~ *carries*, *try* ~ *tries*
(b) *-y* changes to *-i* before *-ed*: *carry* ~ *carried*, *try* ~ *tried*

Similarly *dry*, *deny*, *fancy*, etc.

The *-y-* remains, however, where it follows a vowel letter: *stay* ~ *stayed*, *alloy* ~ *alloys*, etc; or where it precedes *-ing*: *carry* ~ *carrying*, *stay* ~ *staying*, etc. Two exceptions to these rules are: *pay* ~ *paid*, and *lay* ~ *laid*, in which the *y* changes to *i* after *-a-*. (On a third exception, *say* ~ *said*, *cf* 3.15.)

A different spelling change occurs in verbs whose bases end in *-ie*: DIE, LIE, TIE, VIE. In these cases, the *-ie* changes to *-y-* before *-ing* is added: *die* ~ *dying*, *lie* ~ *lying*, *tie* ~ *tying*, *vie* ~ *vying*.

Note [a] In verbs whose bases end in a vowel other than *-y* or mute *-e*, the addition of inflections involves no further change of spelling: *boo* ~ *boos* ~ *booing* ~ *booed*, *ski* ~ *skis* ~ *skiing* ~ *skied*, etc.

[b] LIE is a regular verb in the sense 'tell untruths'; on the irregular verb *lie* ~ *lay* ~ *lain*, *cf* 3.16.

[c] Like PAY and LAY are their derivatives REPAY (~ *repaid*), MISLAY (~ *mislaid*), WAYLAY (~ *waylaid*), and RE'LAY (~ *re'laid*). There is another verb 'RELAY, however, which is derived from the noun *'relay* and which has the regularly spelt *-ed* form *relayed*: thus *The floor was relaid*, but *The news was relayed far and wide*.

The morphology of irregular full verbs

3.11 Irregular full verbs are like regular verbs in that their *-s* forms and their *-ing* forms are predictable from the base (*cf* 3.2*f*). But they differ from regular verbs in that either the past inflection, or the *-ed* participle inflection, or both of these, are irregular. More precisely the major differences are:

(a) Irregular verbs either do not have the regular *-ed* inflection, or else have a variant of that inflection in which the /d/ is devoiced to /t/ (*eg*: *burn* ~ *burnt*, which occurs alongside the regular *burned*).
(b) Irregular verbs typically, but not invariably, have variation in their base vowel. The explanation of this phenomenon, called GRADATION or ABLAUT, is historical, and it is characteristic of Indo-European languages in general: *choose* ~ *chose* ~ *chosen*, *write* ~ *wrote* ~ *written*.
(c) Irregular verbs have a varying number of distinct forms. Since the *-s* form and the *-ing* form are predictable for regular and irregular verbs alike, the only forms that need be listed for irregular verbs are the base form (V), the past (V-ed_1), and the *-ed* participle (V-ed_2). These are traditionally known as the PRINCIPAL PARTS of the verb. Most irregular verbs have, like regular verbs, only one common form for the past and the *-ed* participle; but there is considerable variation in this respect, as the table shows:

	V	V-ed_1	V-ed_2
all three forms alike:	*cut*	*cut*	*cut*
V-ed_1 = V-ed_2:	*meet*	*met*	*met*
V = V-ed_1:	*beat*	*beat*	*beaten*
V = V-ed_2:	*come*	*came*	*come*
all three forms different:	*speak*	*spoke*	*spoken*

Note Where irregular verbs have regular inflections (as is normal in the *-s* and *-ing* forms), they follow the spelling rules for regular verbs (*cf* 3.7–10).

Irregular verb classes

3.12 The 250 or so irregular English verbs can be classified on the basis of criteria derived from the above similarities and differences. Since it is impractical to account for both pronunciation and spelling together, only pronunciation will be considered in setting up classes of irregular verbs, and for that matter in deciding whether a verb is irregular or not. The criteria of classification to be used are the following:

(a) Suffixation in V-ed_1 and/or V-ed_2, including not only the alveolar suffixes *-ed*/*-t* as in *dreamed*/*dreamt*, but also, for V-ed_2, nasal suffixes as in *shaken*, *torn*.
(b) V-*ed* identity: *ie* V-ed_1 = V-ed_2, as in *met* ~ *met*.
(c) Vowel identity, *ie* the various principal parts show no difference of base vowel.

Table 3.12 shows how these three criteria divide irregular full verbs into seven classes:

Table 3.12 Irregular verb classes

CLASS	USE OF SUFFIX	V-*ed* IDENTITY	VOWEL IDENTITY	*Example*		
				V	V-ed_1	V-ed_2
1	+	+	+	*burn*	*burned*/*burnt*	*burned*/*burnt*
2	+	±	+	*saw*	*sawed*	*sawed*/*sawn*
3	+	+	−	*bring*	*brought*	*brought*
4	+	−	−	*break*	*broke*	*broken*
5	−	+	+	*cut*	*cut*	*cut*
6	−	+	−	*strike*	*struck*	*struck*
7	−	−	−	*swim*	*swam*	*swum*

Class 1 has three pluses, which indicate that a verb like *burn* is very close to a regular verb. The only irregularity is that each verb has, or at least allows as a variant, a V-*ed* form with an irregular final consonant or consonant cluster; *eg*: *burned* has an irregular variant *burnt* /-nt/ with a voiceless suffix after a voiced sound (*cf* 3.6).

Class 2 has a past suffix in *-ed* and two alternative *-ed* participle suffixes, one alveolar (*sawed*) and the other nasal (*sawn*). All verbs have vowel identity, although some verbs also have alternative forms with vowel gradation.

Class 3 has no vowel identity; *eg*: *bring* ~ *brought*. Many of the verbs in Classes 1 and 3 manifest some differences between BrE and AmE. For instance, in a subclass of Class 1 which will be distinguished as Class 1A, AmE shows a stronger preference than BrE for the regular /d/ variants of *burned*/*burnt*, etc. But the frequency of each form varies from verb to verb, and there is no one-to-one correspondence between a spelling in *-t* and a pronunciation in /t/. Class 3 shows a similar pattern of preference for variant *-ed* forms such as *dreamed*/*dreamt* /driːmd/, /dremt/.

Class 4 has three different principal parts, usually with a nasal V-ed_2 suffix (*break* ~ *broke* ~ *broken*).

Class 5 has the same form for all principal parts (*cut* ~ *cut* ~ *cut*).

Class 6 has identity between V-ed_1 and V-ed_2, has no suffix, but does have a change of the base vowel (*strike* ~ *struck* ~ *struck*).

Class 7 is the most irregular major class of full verbs: V-ed_1 and V-ed_2 are different; there is no suffix, but there is change of the base vowel (*swim* ~ *swam* ~ *swum*). Particularly irregular is the exceptional verb *go* ~ *went* ~ *gone*, which has an entirely unconnected V-ed_1 form, *went*. The substitution of a different form in this way is termed SUPPLETION (*cf*: *was*/*were* as the past forms of BE, 3.32).

Although we will not further define the difference among the verbs of each class, for mnemonic reasons the verbs in the lists below will be grouped into subclasses as (A), (B), (C), etc. Parentheses, for example '(*dwelled*)' are used for less common forms, and decidedly uncommon verbs or verb forms are marked '⟨rare⟩'. '(R)' denotes the existence of a regular variant.

Note The following list contains most of the irregular verbs in present-day English, including those which are relatively rare, but is not meant to be exhaustive, particularly with regard to derivative verbs. For example, it does not include very unusual or archaic forms such as *girt* (a rare past form of *gird*); nor does it include less common derivatives such as *relend*. Some irregular *-ed* participle forms survive only in special contexts, especially in adjectival use (for example *sunken* in a *sunken road*; or *shaven* in a *recently shaven chin*). We do not note such forms where they are not used as verbs and where the verb from which they are derived is otherwise regular. Where the verb occurs in the list of irregular verbs for another reason, exceptional nonverbal forms are noted for comparison.

Irregular verbs listed in class order

Class 1

3.13 Characteristics:
The suffix is used but voicing is variable (contrast *spent* with *made*). V-ed_1 and V-ed_2 are identical (*burned*/*burnt* ~ *burned*/*burnt*) and there is vowel identity in all parts (*build* ~ *built* ~ *built*).

	V	V-*ed*		COMMENTS
1A	burn	burnt burned	(R)	
	dwell	dwelt (dwelled)	(R)	
	earn	earned	(R)	(*cf* Note [b])
	learn	learnt learned	(R)	Adj: *learned* /-ɪd/ ['scholarly']
	smell	smelt smelled	(R)	
	spell	spelt spelled	(R)	Also MISSPELL

	V	V-*ed*		COMMENTS
	spill	{ spilt		
		spilled	(R)	
	spoil	{ spoilt		
		spoiled	(R)	
1B	bend	bent		Also UNBEND. Adj: 'on *bended* knee'
	build	built		Also REBUILD
	lend	lent		
	rend	rent		⟨Rare; in restricted use⟩
	send	sent		
	spend	spent		Also MISSPEND
1C	have /hæv/	had		Primary verb: *cf* 3.33; -*s* form: *has* /hæz/
	make	made		Also REMAKE, UNMAKE

Note [**a**] For Class 1A verbs, the irregular -*t* spelling is generally rare in AmE. In BrE, the -*t* spelling is of varying frequency, but the /t/ pronunciation is widely current.

[**b**] EARN belongs marginally to Class 1A, since a pronunciation in /t/ has some BrE currency.

[**c**] There is a tendency to associate -*t* forms in Class 1A more with V-ed_2 than with V-ed_1, and with V-ed_1 when there is least implication of duration:

He *spelt*/*has spelt* it like this on only one occasion.

Contrast: *It smelled delicious.*

[**d**] The variation between /d/ and /t/ in Classes 1 and 3 applies to verbal uses but not to adjectival uses, for which /t/ is favoured. Both BrE and AmE have, for example, *burnt toast*, *burnt umber*. Even so, /d/ may occur attributively where the meaning emphasizes the process rather than the result of the process: *burnt wood* means 'wood which looks burnt', but *burned wood* might mean a quantity of wood which has been burned as fuel.

Class 2

3.14 Characteristics:

V-ed_2 has two suffixes, one alveolar which is R and identical with V-ed_1 (*mowed*), the other nasal (*mown*). There is no change of the base vowel for V-ed_1 (*saw* ~ *sawed*).

V	V-ed_1	V-ed_2		COMMENTS
hew	hewed	{ hewn		
		hewed	(R)	
mow /əʊ/	mowed	{ mown		Adj use: 'a *new-mown* lawn'
		mowed	(R)	
saw	sawed	{ sawn		⟨esp BrE⟩
		sawed	(R)	
sew /əʊ/	sewed	{ sewn		
		sewed	(R)	

V	V-ed_1	V-ed_2	COMMENTS
shear	sheared	shorn sheared (R)	
show	showed	shown (showed) (R)	Sometimes spelled *shew*, *shewed*, *shewn*
sow /əʊ/	sowed	sown sowed (R)	
strew /uː/	strewed	strewn strewed (R)	
swell	swelled	swollen swelled (R)	Adj use: 'a *swollen* ankle/head' Adj use: 'a *swelled* head' [metaphorical suggestion of conceit]

Note [a] As an adjective, *swollen* is generally accepted in both literal and metaphorical uses. *Swelled head* is metaphorical ⟨esp AmE⟩.
[b] To the Class 2 list may be added *prove* ~ *proved* ~ *proved*/*proven* and *shave* ~ *shaved* ~ *shaved*/*shaven*. Although these verbs are usually regular, the *-ed* participle ending in *-en* is quite common for *prove* and not unusual for *shave*. These *-en* forms are more current in AmE than in BrE. *Proven* also occurs in the Scottish legal phrase *not proven*.

Class 3

3.15 Characteristics:
The suffix is used but voicing is variable (contrast *meant*, *told*). V-ed_1 and V-ed_2 are identical (*left* ~ *left*), and there is change of base vowel (*think* ~ *thought*).

V	V-*ed*		COMMENTS
3A /iː/ ~	/e/		
bereave	bereft bereaved	 (R)	⟨Rare; restricted use⟩ Adj: '*bereft* of hope'; V-ed_2 *bereaved* usually = 'deprived of a close relative by death'
cleave	cleft cleaved	 (R)	Adj: *cleft palate*; also V-ed_1 = *clove*, V-ed_2 = *cloven*. Adj: *cloven hoof*
creep	crept		
deal	dealt /e/		Also MISDEAL
dream	dreamt /e/ dreamed	 (R)	⟨esp BrE⟩ ⟨esp AmE⟩
feel	felt		
flee	fled		
keep	kept		
kneel	knelt kneeled	 (R)	 ⟨esp AmE⟩
lean	leant /e/ leaned	 (R)	⟨esp BrE⟩ ⟨esp AmE⟩
leap	leapt /e/ leaped	 (R)	 ⟨esp AmE⟩
leave	left		

V	V-*ed*	COMMENTS
mean	meant /e/	
sleep	slept	Also OVERSLEEP
sweep	swept	
weep	wept	
3B: ~	/ɔː/	
beseech	besought	⟨Rare; in restricted use⟩
	beseeched (R)	⟨Rare; in restricted use⟩
bring	brought	
buy /aɪ/	bought	
catch	caught	
seek	sought	
teach	taught	
think	thought	Also RETHINK
3C: /uː/ ~	/ɒ/	
lose	lost	
3D: /e/ ~	/əʊ/	
sell	sold	
tell	told	Also FORETELL, RETELL
3E: /ɪə^{r}/ ~	/ɜː^{r}/	
hear	heard	Also MISHEAR
3F: /eɪ/ ~	/e/	
say	said	But -*s* form: *says* /e/. On GAINSAY, *cf* 3.5 Note [a].

Class 4

3.16 Characteristics:

V-ed_1 and V-ed_2 differ and, in practically all cases, the latter has a nasal suffix (*break* ~ *broke* ~ *broken*). There is no base vowel identity. There is a range of base vowel changes and the verbs have been ordered according to vowel patterning.

V	V-ed_1	V-ed_2	COMMENTS
4A: V-ed_1 and V-ed_2 have the same vowel.			
4Aa: V-*ed* = /əʊ/			
break /eɪ/	broke	broken	Adj: 'I'm *broke*' ['without money'] ⟨informal⟩
choose /uː/	chose	chosen	
freeze /iː/	froze	frozen	Also UNFREEZE, DEEPFREEZE (also R)
speak	spoke	spoken	
steal	stole	stolen	

V	V-ed_1	V-ed_2	COMMENTS
(a)wake(n)	(a)woke	(a)woken	*cf* R (A)WAKEN. But there is some tendency to produce blends of the regular and irregular verbs, as in 'You *waked* me too early.'
weave	wove weaved (R)	woven weaved (R)	
4Ab: /eə^{r}/ ~ /ɔː^{r}/			
bear	bore	borne	'She has *borne* six children' (but: 'She was *born* in 1955'); also FORBEAR, OVERBEAR
swear	swore	sworn	Also FORSWEAR
tear	tore	torn	
wear	wore	worn	
4Ac: /aɪ/ ~ /ɪ/			
bite	bit	bitten	V-ed_2 sometimes = *bit*
chide ⟨rare⟩	chid	chidden chid	Also R *chided*
hide	hid	hidden (hid)	
4Ad: /e/ ~ /ɒ/			
forget	forgot	forgotten	Sometimes ⟨esp AmE⟩ V-ed_2 = *forgot*; also BEGET, with *begat* as an ⟨archaic and scriptural⟩ alternative to *begot* (V-ed_1). See also GET, Class 6F, 3.18.
tread	trod	trodden (trod)	
4Ae: /aɪ/ ~ /eɪ/			
lie	lay	lain	['be horizontal']. Contrast LIE = 'tell a lie' (R). Sometimes confused with LAY 'put' (~ *laid* ~ *laid*)
4B: V and V-ed_2, but not V-ed_1, have the same vowel			
4Ba: V/V-ed_2 = /əʊ/			
blow	blew	blown	
grow	grew	grown	Also OUTGROW
know	knew	known	
throw	threw	thrown	Also OVERTHROW
4Bb: V/V-ed_2 = /eɪ/			
forsake	forsook	forsaken	⟨restricted use⟩
shake	shook	shaken	
take	took	taken	Also BETAKE ⟨restricted use⟩, MISTAKE, OVERTAKE, PARTAKE, UNDERTAKE

V	V-*ed*₁	V-*ed*₂	COMMENTS
4Bc: V/V-*ed*₂ = /ɪ/			
forbid	forbade /eɪ *or* æ/ forbad /æ/	forbidden (forbid)	*cf* BID, Class 5
give	gave	given	Also FORGIVE, MISGIVE
4Bd: V/V-*ed*₂ = /ɔː/			
draw	drew	drawn	Also WITHDRAW
4Be: V/V-*ed*₂ = /ɔː/			
fall	fell	fallen	Also BEFALL ⟨restricted use⟩
4Bf: V/V-*ed*₂ = /iː/			
eat	ate {BrE /e/ AmE /eɪ/}	eaten	Also OVEREAT
4Bg: V/V-*ed*₂ = /iː/			
see	saw	seen	Also FORESEE, OVERSEE
4Bh: V/V-*ed*₂ = /eɪ/			
slay	slew	slain	⟨restricted use, esp in BrE⟩
4C: all three parts have different vowels			
4Ca: /aɪ/ ~ /əʊ/ ~ /ɪ/			
drive	drove	driven	
ride	rode	ridden	Also OVERRIDE
rise	rose	risen	Also ARISE, which is ⟨rare⟩ except when metaphorical: 'The question *arose* . . .'
smite	smote	smitten	⟨Archaic⟩ except when metaphorical in V-*ed*₂, *eg*: '*smitten* with her charms'
stride	strode	strid stridden strode	Both *strid* and *stridden* are ⟨rare⟩; also BESTRIDE
strive	strove strived (R)	striven strived (R)	
write	wrote	written	Also REWRITE, UNDERWRITE
4Cb: /aɪ/ ~ /uː/ ~ /əʊ/			
fly	flew	flown	*cf*: *flee* ~ *fled* ~ *fled* (Class 3A)
4Cc: /uː/ ~ /ɪ/ ~ /ʌ/			
do	did	done	The -*s* form *does* has the irregular pronunciation /dʌz/. Also OUTDO, OVERDO, REDO, UNDO, etc (*cf* 3.36)

V	V-*ed*$_1$	V-*ed*$_2$	COMMENTS
4D: all three parts have the same vowel			
4D: /iː/			
beat	beat	beaten	*beat* is sometimes used as V-*ed*$_2$, esp in AmE
4E: V-*ed*$_1$ and V-*ed*$_2$ have different vowels in special alternative forms			
4E: /aɪ/			
dive	dived (R) (dove)	dived (R)	V-*ed*$_1$ *dove* is AmE only; the verb is R in standard BrE and often in AmE
shrive	shrived (R) shrove	shrived (R) shriven	⟨Rare⟩
thrive	thrived (R) (throve)	thrived (R) (thriven)	Normally R; *thriven* is ⟨archaic⟩

Note *Glide* is a regular verb in present-day English, but there are occasional occurrences of the archaic irregular past form *glode*.

Class 5

3.17 Characteristics:
All three parts V, V-*ed*$_1$, and V-*ed*$_2$ are identical. No suffix or change of the base vowel (*bet* ~ *bet* ~ *bet*).

V/V-*ed*	COMMENTS
bet	BrE also R: *betted*
bid	'make an offer (to buy)' etc. (But in the sense of 'say a greeting' or 'give an order', the forms *bid* ~ *bad(e)* ~ *bidden* may also be used in rather archaic style: 'Do as you are *bid(den)*.') Also OUTBID, UNDERBID.
burst	Also nonstandard BUST, with alternative R V-*ed* form *busted*
cast	Also BROADCAST, FORECAST, MISCAST, OVERCAST, RECAST, TELECAST (sometimes also R)
cost	COST = 'estimate the cost of' is R
cut	
fit	R ⟨in BrE⟩
hit	
hurt	
knit	Usually R: *knitted*
let	
put /ʊ/	But PUT(T) /pʌt/ in golf is R: *putted*
quit	Also R: *quitted*
rid	Also R: *ridded*
set	Also BESET, RESET, UPSET, OFFSET, INSET
shed	Also R ⟨rare⟩ = 'put in a shed'
shit	⟨Not in polite use⟩; V-*ed*$_1$ sometimes *shat*
shut	
slit	
split	
spread /e/	

V/V-*ed*	COMMENTS
sweat /e/	Also R: *sweated*
thrust	
wed	Also R: *wedded*
wet	Also R: *wetted*

Note The regular verb SHRED sometimes occurs with the Class 5 forms *shred* ~ *shred* ~ *shred*.

Class 6

3.18 Characteristics:

No suffix; V-ed_1 and V-ed_2 are identical; change of base vowel (*win* ~ *won* ~ *won*).

V	V-*ed*	COMMENTS
6A: Mainly /iː/ ~ /e/		
bleed	bled	
breed	bred	
feed	fed	Also OVERFEED, etc
hold	held	Also BEHOLD ⟨in restricted use⟩, UPHOLD, WITHHOLD, etc
lead /iː/	led	Also MISLEAD
meet	met	
read /iː/	read /e/	Also REREAD, etc
speed	sped	Also R: *speeded*, esp of mechanisms, and always R in the phrasal verb SPEED *up*
6B: Mainly /ɪ/ ~ /ʌ/		
cling	clung	
dig	dug	
fling	flung	
hang	hung	Also OVERHANG. But HANG is also R in the sense 'put to death by hanging'
sling	slung	
slink	slunk	
spin	spun	V-ed_1 = *span* is ⟨archaic⟩
stick	stuck	
sting	stung	
strike	struck	Literal use; in metaphorical, adjectival use V-ed_2 also *stricken*: '*stricken* (*struck*) by terror'
string	strung	Also RESTRING, HAMSTRING
swing	swung	
win	won	
wring	wrung	
6C: /aɪ/ ~ /aʊ/		
bind	bound	Also REBIND, UNBIND; Adj: 'one's *bounden* duty'
find	found	
grind	ground	
wind	wound	= 'turn round'; also REWIND, UNWIND; WIND/wɪnd/ = 'smell the presence of' etc is always R

V	V-*ed*	COMMENTS
6D: /aɪ/ ~ /ɪ/		
light	lit	Also R: *lighted*; ALIGHT and HIGHLIGHT are only R. Adj: 'a *lighted* candle'
slide	slid	
6E: /ɪ/ ~ /æ/		
sit	sat	
spit	spat	V-*ed* also = *spit* ⟨esp AmE⟩; SPIT = 'fix with a spit' is R
6F: ~ /ɒ/		
get	got	AmE also has *gotten* for V-ed_2 in certain senses of the word, *eg* 'acquire', 'cause', 'come'; thus AmE makes a distinction between *We've gotten tickets* = 'acquired' and *We've got tickets* = 'we possess'. On the related verbs FORGET and BEGET, *cf* Class 4Ad (3.16).
shine	shone {/ʃɒn/ ⟨BrE⟩ /ʃəʊn/ ⟨AmE⟩}	Also R when = 'polish' ⟨esp AmE⟩; also OUTSHINE
shoe /uː/	shod	Also R: *shoed*
shoot	shot	Also OVERSHOOT
6G: /aɪ/ ~ /ɔː/		
fight	fought	Also OUTFIGHT
6H: /æ/ ~ /ʊ/		
stand	stood	Also (MIS)UNDERSTAND, WITHSTAND, etc
6I: /aɪ/ ~ /əʊ/		
abide	abode	restricted use when = 'stay'; R when ABIDE *by* = 'obey', *eg*: 'He *abided by* our decision'.
6J: /iː/ ~ /əʊ/		
heave	hove	Usually R: *heaved*

Note In AmE, the normally regular verb PLEAD has an alternative Class 6A past form *pled*.

Class 7

3.19 Characteristics:
No suffix; V-ed_1 and V-ed_2 are different; change of base vowel (*began* ~ *begun*).

V	V-ed_1	V-ed_2	COMMENTS
7A: /ɪ/ ~ /æ/ ~ /ʌ/			
begin	began	begun	
drink	drank	drunk	*cf* Adj uses: 'He was *drunk*' but '*drunken* driving'
ring	rang (rung)	rung	Also R: *ringed* in the sense 'put a ring around'
shrink	shrank (shrunk)	shrunk	Adj: *shrunken*
sing	sang (sung)	sung	
sink	sank (sunk)	sunk	Adj: *sunken*
spring	sprang	sprung	V-ed_1 also *sprung* in AmE
stink	stank (stunk)	stunk	Has impolite connotations
swim	swam (swum)	swum	
7B			
come	came	come	Also BECOME, OVERCOME
run	ran	run	Also OUTRUN, OVERRUN, RERUN
7C			
go	went	gone	Also UNDERGO, FOR(E)GO (*cf* Note [b])

Note [**a**] In Class 7A, although the gradation series /ɪ/ ~ /æ/ ~ /ʌ/ is the one generally accepted as standard, V-ed_1 forms in /ʌ/ are commonly used (esp in AmE) and accepted. V-ed_2 forms in /æ/ also have some currency.
[**b**] On *been* in place of *gone*, *cf* 4.22 Note [b].

Irregular verbs (including derivatives) in alphabetical order

3.20 Since irregular verbs, if one includes prefixed and compound derivatives, make up to some extent an open and productive class, this list makes no claim to completeness. As before, rarer forms are enclosed in parentheses. Verbs in square brackets are those which are generally regular, but which have irregular spelling or irregular forms of limited currency.

In the right-hand column, reference is given to the typological classification above, which also includes relevant details of usage (AmE, BrE, archaic, pronunciation, etc).

Base (V)	Past tense (V-*ed*$_1$)	*-ed* participle (V-*ed*$_2$)	Reference
abide	abode, abided,	abode, abided	6I
arise	arose	arisen	4Ca
awake	awoke, awaked	awoken, awaked	4Aa
be	was, were	been	(*cf* 3.32)
bear	bore	borne	4Ab
beat	beat	beaten (beat)	4D
become	became	become	7B
befall	befell	befallen	4Be
beget	begot	begotten	6F
begin	began	begun	7A
behold	beheld	beheld	6A
bend	bent	bent	1B
bereave	bereft, bereaved	bereft, bereaved	3A
beseech	besought, beseeched	besought, beseeched	3B
beset	beset	beset	5
bestride	bestrode	bestridden, bestrid, bestrode	4Ca
bet	bet, betted	bet, betted	5
betake	betook	betaken	4Bb
bid	bad(e), bid	bade, bid, bidden	5
bind	bound	bound	6C
bite	bit	bitten, (bit)	4Ac
bleed	bled	bled	6A
blow	blew	blown	4Ba
break	broke	broken	4Aa
breed	bred	bred	6A
bring	brought	brought	3B
broadcast	broadcast	broadcast	5
build	built	built	1B
burn	burnt, burned	burnt, burned	1A
burst	burst	burst	5
bust ⟨non-standard⟩	bust, busted	bust, busted	5
buy	bought	bought	3B
cast	cast	cast	5
catch	caught	caught	3B
chide	chid, chided	chidden, chid, chided	4Ac
choose	chose	chosen	4Aa
cleave	cleft, clove, cleaved	cleft, cloven, cleaved	3A
cling	clung	clung	6B
come	came	come	7B
cost	cost	cost	5
creep	crept	crept	3A
cut	cut	cut	5
deal	dealt	dealt	3A
deepfreeze	deepfroze, -freezed	deepfrozen, -freezed	4Aa
dig	dug	dug	6B
dive	dived, ⟨AmE⟩ dove	dived	4E
do	did	done	4Cc; (*cf* 3.36)
draw	drew	drawn	4Bd
dream	dreamt, dreamed	dreamt, dreamed	3A
drink	drank	drunk	7A
drive	drove	driven	4Ca

Base (V)	Past tense (V-*ed*$_1$)	*-ed* participle (V-*ed*$_2$)	Reference
dwell	dwelt, dwelled	dwelt, dwelled	1A
[earn]	[earned]	[earned]	1A
eat	ate	eaten	4Bf
fall	fell	fallen	4Be
feed	fed	fed	6A
feel	felt	felt	3A
fight	fought	fought	6G
find	found	found	6C
[fit]	[fit]	[fit]	5
flee	fled	fled	3A
fling	flung	flung	6B
fly	flew	flown	4Cb
forbear	forbore	foreborne	4Ab
forbid	forbade, forbad	forbidden, (forbid)	4Bc
forecast	forecast	forecast	5
foresee	foresaw	foreseen	4Bg
foretell	foretold	foretold	3D
forget	forgot	forgotten, (forgot)	4Ad
forgive	forgave	forgiven	4Bc
forgo	forwent	forgone	7C
forsake	forsook	forsaken	4Bb
forswear	forswore	forsworn	4Ab
freeze	froze	frozen	4Aa
[gainsay]	[gainsaid]	[gainsaid]	3F
get	got	{got / gotten ⟨AmE⟩}	6F
give	gave	given	4Bc
go	went	gone	7C
grind	ground	ground	6C
grow	grew	grown	4Ba
hamstring	hamstrung	hamstrung	6B
hang	hung, (hanged)	hung, (hanged)	6B
have	had	had	1C; (*cf* 3.33)
hear	heard	heard	3E
heave	heaved, hove	heaved, hove	6J
hew	hewed	hewn, hewed	2
hide	hid	hidden, (hid)	4Ac
hit	hit	hit	5
hold	held	held	6A
hurt	hurt	hurt	5
inset	inset	inset	5
keep	kept	kept	3A
kneel	knelt, kneeled	knelt, kneeled	3A
knit	knitted, knit	knitted, knit	5
know	knew	known	4Ba
[lay]	[laid]	[laid]	(*cf* 3.10)
lead	led	led	6A
lean	leant, leaned	leant, leaned	3A
leap	leapt, leaped	leapt, leaped	3A
learn	learnt, learned	learnt, learned	1A
leave	left	left	3A

Base (V)	Past tense (V-ed_1)	*-ed* participle (V-ed_2)	Reference
lend	lent	lent	1B
let	let	let	5
lie	lay	lain	4Ae
light	lit, lighted	lit, lighted	6D
lose	lost	lost	3C
make	made	made	1C
mean	meant	meant	3A
meet	met	met	6A
miscast	miscast	miscast	5
misdeal	misdealt	misdealt	3A
misgive	misgave	misgiven	4Bc
mishear	misheard	misheard	3E
[mislay]	[mislaid]	[mislaid]	(*cf* 3.10 Note [c])
mislead	misled	misled	6A
misspell	misspelt, misspelled	misspelt, misspelled	1A
misspend	misspent	misspent	1B
mistake	mistook	mistaken	4Bb
misunderstand	misunderstood	misunderstood	6H
mow	mowed	mown, mowed	2
offset	offset	offset	5
outbid	outbid	outbid, (outbidden)	5
outdo	outdid	outdone	4Cc
outfight	outfought	outfought	6G
outgrow	outgrew	outgrown	4Ba
outrun	outran	outrun	7B
outshine	outshone	outshone	6F
overbear	overbore	overborne	4Ab
overcast	overcast	overcast	5
overcome	overcame	overcome	7B
overdo	overdid	overdone	4Cc
overeat	overate	overeaten	4Bf
overfeed	overfed	overfed	6A
overhang	overhung	overhung	6B
override	overrode	overridden	4CA
overrun	overran	overrun	7B
oversee	oversaw	overseen	4Bg
overshoot	overshot	overshot	6F
oversleep	overslept	overslept	3A
overtake	overtook	overtaken	4Bb
overthrow	overthrew	overthrown	4Ba
partake	partook	partaken	4Bb
[pay]	[paid]	[paid]	(*cf* 3.10)
[plead]	[pleaded, (pled)]	[pleaded, (pled)]	(*cf* 3.18 Note)
[prove]	[proved]	[proved, proven]	(*cf* 3.14 Note [b])
put	put	put	5
quit	quit, quitted	quit, quitted	5
read	read	read	6A
rebind	rebound	rebound	6C
rebuild	rebuilt	rebuilt	1B
recast	recast	recast	5

Base (V)	Past tense (V-ed_1)	*-ed* participle (V-ed_2)	Reference
redo	redid	redone	4Cc
[relay]	[relaid]	[relaid]	(*cf* 3.10 Note [c])
remake	remade	remade	1C
rend	rent	rent	1B
[repay]	[repaid]	[repaid]	(*cf* 3.10 Note [c])
reread	reread	reread	6A
rerun	reran	rerun	7B
reset	reset	reset	5
restring	restrung	restrung	6B
retell	retold	retold	3D
rethink	rethought	rethought	3B
rewind	rewound	rewound	6C
rewrite	rewrote	rewritten	4Ca
rid	rid, ridded	rid, ridded	5
ride	rode	ridden	4Ca
ring	rang, (rung)	rung	7A
rise	rose	risen	4Ca
run	ran	run	7B
saw	sawed	sawn, sawed	2
say	said	said	3F
see	saw	seen	4Bg
seek	sought	sought	3B
sell	sold	sold	3D
send	sent	sent	1B
set	set	set	5
sew	sewed	sewn, sewed	2
shake	shook	shaken	4Bb
[shave]	[shaved]	[shaved, shaven]	(*cf* 3.14 Note [b])
shear	sheared	shorn, sheared	2
shed	shed	shed	5
[shew]	[shewed]	[shewn]	2
shine	shone, shined	shone, shined	6F
shit	shit, shat	shit	5
shoe	shod, shoed	shod, shoed	6F
shoot	shot	shot	6F
show	showed	shown, (showed)	2
[shred]	[shredded, shred]	[shredded, shred]	(*cf* 3.17 Note)
shrink	shrank, (shrunk)	shrunk	7A
shrive	shrived, shrove	shrived, shriven	4E
shut	shut	shut	5
sing	sang, (sung)	sung	7A
sink	sank, (sunk)	sunk	7A
sit	sat	sat	6E
slay	slew	slain	4Bh
sleep	slept	slept	3A
slide	slid	slid	6D
sling	slung	slung	6B
slink	slunk	slunk	6B
slit	slit	slit	5
smell	smelt, smelled	smelt, smelled	1A
smite	smote	smitten	4Ca

Base (V)	Past tense (V-ed_1)	*-ed* participle (V-ed_2)	Reference
sow	sowed	sown, sowed	2
speak	spoke	spoken	4Aa
speed	sped, speeded	sped, speeded	6A
spell	spelt, spelled	spelt, spelled	1A
spend	spent	spent	1B
spill	spilt, spilled	spilt, spilled	1A
spin	spun, span	spun	6B
spit	spat, spit	spat, spit	6E
split	split	split	5
spoil	spoilt, spoiled	spoilt, spoiled	1A
spread	spread	spread	5
spring	sprang, (sprung)	sprung	7A
stand	stood	stood	6H
steal	stole	stolen	4Aa
stick	stuck	stuck	6B
sting	stung	stung	6B
stink	stank, (stunk)	stunk	7A
strew	strewed	strewn, strewed	2
stride	strode	stridden, strid, strode	4Ca
strike	struck	struck	6B
string	strung	strung	6B
strive	strove, strived	striven, strived	4Ca
swear	swore	sworn	4Ab
sweat	sweat, sweated	sweat, sweated	5
sweep	swept	swept	3A
swell	swelled	swollen, swelled	2
swim	swam, (swum)	swum	7A
swing	swung	swung	6B
take	took	taken	4Bb
teach	taught	taught	3B
tear	tore	torn	4Ab
telecast	telecast	telecast	5
tell	told	told	3D
think	thought	thought	3B
thrive	thrived, (throve)	thrived, (thriven)	4E
throw	threw	thrown	4Ba
thrust	thrust	thrust	5
tread	trod	trodden, (trod)	4Ad
unbend	unbent	unbent	1B
unbind	unbound	unbound	6C
underbid	underbid	underbid, (underbidden)	5
undergo	underwent	undergone	7C
understand	understood	understood	6H
undertake	undertook	undertaken	4Bb
underwrite	underwrote	underwritten	4Ca
undo	undid	undone	4Cc
unfreeze	unfroze	unfrozen	4Aa
unmake	unmade	unmade	1C
unwind	unwound	unwound	6C
uphold	upheld	upheld	6A
upset	upset	upset	5
wake	woke, waked	woken, waked	4Aa
[waylay]	[waylaid]	[waylaid]	(*cf* 3.10 Note [c])

Base (V)	Past tense (V-ed_1)	*-ed* participle (V-ed_2)	Reference
wear	wore	worn	4Ab
weave	wove	woven	4Aa
wed	wedded, wed	wedded, wed	5
weep	wept	wept	3A
wet	wetted, wet	wetted, wet	5
win	won	won	6B
wind	wound	wound	6C
withdraw	withdrew	withdrawn	4Bd
withhold	withheld	withheld	6A
withstand	withstood	withstood	6H
wring	wrung	wrung	6B
write	wrote	written	4Ca

Verbs in auxiliary function

3.21 In contrast to full verbs, the verbs we will consider in the next sections are capable of functioning as AUXILIARY or 'helping' verbs (*cf* 2.27*f*). These are the PRIMARY VERBS BE, HAVE, and DO, and the MODAL VERBS *can*, *may*, *will*, *shall*, *could*, *might*, *would*, *should*, and *must*. Since they can function only as auxiliaries, the modal verbs will generally be referred to as MODAL AUXILIARIES.

The auxiliaries make different contributions to the verb phrase (*cf* 3.55*f*). Of the three primary verbs, DO is only a semantically empty syntactic component in sentence processes such as negation and interrogation (*cf* DO-support; 3.37), whereas BE contributes to aspect and voice, and HAVE contributes to aspect. The modal auxiliaries are so called because of their contribution of meanings in the area known as MODALITY (including such concepts as volition, probability, and obligation); but such verbs have a broader semantic role than this label suggests (*cf* 4.49*ff*).

Although auxiliaries have different functions in the verb phrase, they have one important syntactic function in common, *viz* their ability to act as OPERATOR when they occur as the first verb of a finite verb phrase (*cf* 2.48); as such they are used, for example, in the formation of *yes–no* questions:

Is he *asking* any questions?
Has he *been asking* any questions?
Was he *asked* any questions?
Will he *be asked* any questions?
Has he *asked* any questions?
Does he *ask* any questions?

Here the operator, or first auxiliary of the verb phrase, is isolated from the rest of the predicate no matter how complex the verb phrase is. Since BE and (sometimes, esp in BrE) HAVE also have this function as main verbs, the term operator will also be used for them in sentences like:

Is she a tall girl? *Has* he any money? ⟨BrE⟩

(The variant constructions with HAVE are discussed in 3.33–35.) The complex verb phrase of *He might have been being questioned by the police* is thus analysed, within this sentence, as shown in *Fig* 3.21:

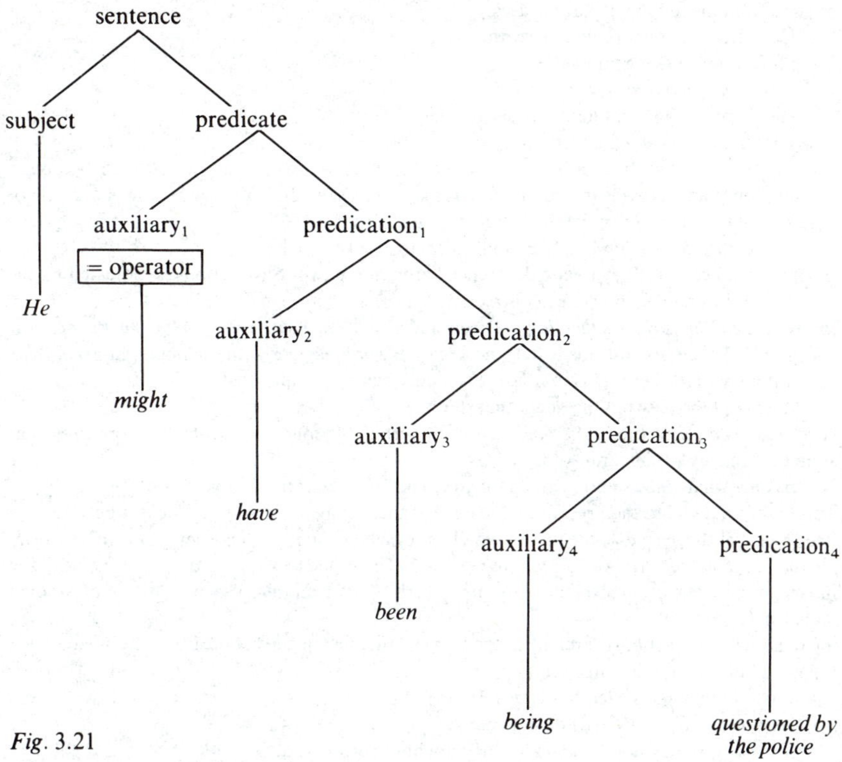

Fig. 3.21

(On the use of the terms predicate and predication in this diagram, *cf* 2.47–48.)

Many of the criteria for the syntactic function of auxiliaries have to do with their status as operators, and therefore apply also to BE and HAVE as main verbs. These are listed in (a), (c), (d), (e) below. Of the remaining criteria, (b) is morphological, (f) and (g) are syntactic and have to do with the ordering of elements in the verb phrase, and (h) is semantic.

Criteria for auxiliary verbs

(a) Operator in negation with *not*

3.22 In forming negative finite clauses, the first auxiliary is placed before the negative word *not*. Contrast:

She *can* do it.	She *can*not do it.
She *saw* the play.	*She *saw* not the play.

As the example shows, full verbs like SEE are distinguished from auxiliary verbs by their inability to form negation in this way.

Note [a] Whereas current English has no negative sentence such as **She saw not the play* (but *cf* Note [b]) we do have an acceptable negative sentence of the form:

He decided *not* to see the play.
I like *not* working on Fridays.

In these cases, however, negation is associated with the second, nonfinite verb phrases, *to see* and *working*, rather than with the initial finite verb phrases, *decided* and *like* (*cf* 14.7). This is obvious from the following paraphrases:

He decided that he would not see the play.
I like it not working on Fridays.

which are not synonymous with:

He did not decide that he would see the play.
I don't like it working on Fridays.

In these examples, the distinction between negation in the superordinate clause and negation in the nonfinite clause is clear; but in other cases, the semantic difference may be small or nonexistent (*cf* catenative verbs 3.49; transferred negation 14.36):

She seemed not to mind. = She didn't seem to mind.

Even here, however, the syntactic difference between the two constructions is indicated by the inability of the first negative to be contracted: **She seemn't to mind* (*cf* 3.23).

[b] Whereas **She saw not the play* was rejected above, *She saw not the play but the opera* is acceptable. The reason for this is that the negative word *not* goes with the noun phrase *the play* rather than with the verb (*cf* 13.42); *ie* the sentence can be paraphrased:

It was not the play but the opera that she saw.

A related example of the use of *not* after a full verb is the following quotation from President John F. Kennedy's Inaugural Address:

Ask not what your country can do for you; ask what you can do for your country.

This case is parallel to the preceding one, in that there is a contrastive parallelism between the two objects of the verb *ask*, the first of which is rejected by *not*: . . . *not what your country can do for you* . . . (*but*) *what you can do for your country*. The scope of *not* here therefore includes the interrogative clause, but excludes the main verb. This example also has an air of studied archaism (*cf* Note [c]).

[c] In archaic or facetiously archaic usage we can still meet negative constructions in which *not* follows a full verb and not an operator:

Whether they succeeded I *know not*. ['I do not know']
I *care not* who knows it. ['I do not care . . .']
If I *mistake not*, you were at Yale? ['If I am not in error . . .']

[d] *Not* also follows a full verb when it acts as a pro-form for a clause (*cf* 12.28):

Jean may be late, but I hope *not*. ['. . . hope that she won't be late']

[e] Negation in subjunctive and nonfinite verb phrases does not involve the occurrence of an operator (*cf* 3.58, 14.6).

(b) Negative and verb contractions

3.23 The negative word *not* following an operator can in most cases be contracted and attached, as an enclitic particle, to the auxiliary. The resulting negative auxiliary is spelled with a final *-n't*: *isn't, hadn't, didn't, won't, couldn't*, etc. The pronunciation of the contracted auxiliary and its conditions of use are given below in later sections (3.32*ff*, 3.39). Every auxiliary except the *am* form of BE has a contracted negative form (but *cf* 3.32 Note [c]), but two of these, *mayn't* and *shan't*, are now virtually nonexistent in AmE, while in BrE *shan't* is becoming rare and *mayn't* even more so.

In addition, many operators have contracted nonnegative forms:

BE:	*am* ~ *'m*; *is* ~ *'s*; *are* ~ *'re*;
HAVE:	*have* ~ *'ve*; *has* ~ *'s*; *had* ~ *'d*;
modals:	*will* ~ *'ll*; *would* ~ *'d*.

Notice that the contractions *'s* and *'d* are ambiguous, the former representing *is* or *has* (or, occasionally, *does*; *cf* 3.36 Note), and the latter *had* or *would*. Further information on individual contractions is given in 3.33, 3.36, 3.39.

The above verb contractions were called nonnegative because they cannot combine with negative contractions to form doubly-contracted forms:

(i) She *is not* studying. (ii) She *isn't* studying.
(iii) She'*s not* studying. (iv) *She'*sn't* studying.

There are, however, two constructions (ii) and (iii) corresponding to the uncontracted negative construction in (i). In the first contracted construction (ii), the contracted negative is attached to the uncontracted operator; in the second contracted form, the contracted operator is attached to the subject, the *not* being uncontracted. Generally speaking, the variant (ii) with contracted negation is more common than the variant (iii) with contracted verb and full negation. There are, however, exceptions to this generalization in Scotland and in Northern England, where forms such as *'ll not* seem to be preferred to forms such as *won't*.

Contractions are phonologically reduced or simplified forms which are institutionalized in both speech and writing. As such, they are to be distinguished from cases of PHONOLOGICAL REDUCTION only (*eg* the reduction of /ɑː^{r}/ to /ə^{r}/ in the pronunciation of *are*). A contracted form can undergo additional phonological reduction, and this is very commonly the case with the negative contractions, where the final /nt/ is reduced to /n/; *eg*: *haven't* /hævn/, *isn't* /ɪzn/.

Contracted forms, being enclitic to a preceding word, naturally do not occur initially, *eg* where the operator comes at the beginning of the clause, with inversion (*cf* 3.24). Further, being unstressed, they do not occur where the operator is the only verb in the verb phrase, and precedes an ellipsis (*cf* 3.26). These two circumstances are illustrated in:

{ *Will* you be in tonight?
{ *'*ll* you be in tonight?

{ No, but I *will* tomorrow night.
{ *No, but I'*ll* tomorrow night.

In other positions, the contraction is favoured in informal style. The choice between uncontracted *is* /ɪz/ and contracted *'s* /z/ in spoken English has been found to be conditioned by the following variables, listed in order of importance:

First, there is significant correlation of /z/ with a preceding pronoun, or with the preceding words *there* and *here*, *eg*:

It'*s* raining. There'*s* a car in the garage. Here'*s* my bus.

whereas the uncontracted form is associated with a preceding noun, *eg*:

The car *is* in the garage.

Second, but less important, /z/ is typical of informal and /ɪz/ of formal contexts.

Third, there is some tendency for the contracted form to be more common when functioning as an auxiliary than as a main verb.

When these three factors of preference are combined the choice of form is more predictable, *ie* /ɪz/ is most likely when it is a main verb and follows a noun in a formal context (*eg*: *Radiation is dangerous*), whereas /z/ is most likely when it is an auxiliary and follows a pronoun in an informal context (*eg*: *It's getting dark*). A similar pattern of choice is to be expected with other verb contractions.

Note [**a**] Although phonological reduction may result in pronunciations similar to those of orthodox contractions, such reductions are not represented in writing if they occur outside the normal conditions for contraction. For example, although the auxiliary at the beginning of *Have you eaten?* may be reduced, in speech, to /v/ (as in /vjuː ˈiːtn/), this will not be written in standard orthography ***'*Ve you eaten?*
[**b**] On the alternative constructions *usedn't to* and *didn't use(d) to*, *cf* 3.44.

(c) Inversion of subject and operator

3.24 Auxiliaries, as operators, admit inversion; *ie* the subject noun phrase and the auxiliary (the first auxiliary if there are two or more) change places, especially in interrogative clauses. Compare:

> She will come. ~ Will she come?
> She plans to come. ≁ *Plans she to come?

As with *not*-negation (*cf* 3.22) main verbs here require the use of DO (*cf* 3.37): *Does she plan to come?*

Inversion of subject and operator occurs not only in interrogatives but also in sentences with introductory negatives or semi-negatives (*cf* 18.24):

> At no time *was* the entrance *left* unguarded.

Note [**a**] In addition to subject–operator inversion, there is also inversion of subject and main verb, as in *Down came the rain* (*cf* 18.23).
[**b**] Subject–operator inversion is usual not only with *yes–no* questions, but with *wh*-questions. There are, however, one or two formulaic *wh*-questions in which the subject and main verb are inverted:

> How goes it? [a greeting: 'How are you doing?']
> How came you to miss the train? ['How did you come to . . .?']
> What say you, Peter? ['What is your opinion?']
> Where stands the Administration?

There tends to be a tone of archaism or mock-archaism in such questions.
[**c**] On *Used she to come?* and *Did she use(d) to come?* *cf* 3.44.

(d) Emphatic positive

3.25 Auxiliaries as operators can carry nuclear stress to mark a finite clause as positive rather than negative:

> Won't you try again? Yes, I WÌLL try again. [1]
>
> You must speak to the teacher. I HÀVE spoken to her. [2]

The function of this EMPHATIC POSITIVE use of the operator is to deny a negative which has been stated or implied. On the use of DO here in assertive contexts, *cf* 3.37, 18.16:

> You DÍD speak to her? ['I thought you didn't']
> You should listen to your mother. But I DÒ listen to her.

Sometimes the emphatic operator has no contrastive meaning, but is used purely for emotive force (*cf* 18.56):

I ÀM glad! I DÒ wish you would LǏsten. You HÀVE done well.

(e) Operator in reduced clauses

3.26 The reply to a question such as:

Won't you try again? Can you drive a car?

may be as indicated in [1] above:

Yes, I WÌLL try again. No. I CÀN'T drive a car.

On the other hand, a more likely reply would be the elliptical construction:

Yes, I WÌLL. No, I CÀN'T.

Auxiliaries can function as operators in a range of such reduced constructions (*cf* 12.21*f*, 12.60), where the main verb is omitted either by ellipsis or by pro-form substitution, and the clause is understood to repeat the content of an earlier clause. The nature of this type of operator function has been captured by various labels such as 'code' or 'stranding'.

Here we mention four types of reduced clause containing an operator without a main verb, of which the first two are the most important. DO is used as an 'empty' operator where the clause has no other auxiliary.

(i) *SO/NEITHER/NOR* + OPERATOR (*cf* 12.29)
Positive:
Ann will stay and so *will* BÀRbara.
Bill stayed and so *did* HÈNry.
Negative:
Ann won't stay and *neither* will BÀRbara.
Bill didn't stay, *nor* did HÈNry.

(ii) OPERATOR + *TOO/EITHER* (*cf* 12.59)
Positive:
Ann will stay late and Barbara *will* TÒO.
Bill broke his promise, and Henry *did* TÒO.
Negative:
Ann won't eat much and Barbara *won't* EÌTHer.
Bill didn't break his promise, and Henry *didn't* EÌTHer.

(iii) PREDICATION FRONTING (*cf* 18.20)
Ann SǍID she would be late, and late she *WÀS*.
Bill SǍID he would win the match, and win the match he *DÌD*.

(iv) RELATIVIZED PREDICATION (*cf* 6.34 Note [b])
Ann said she would be late, which she *was*.
Bill said he would win the match, which he *did*.

In these examples, the second auxiliary (unless it is DO) is the same as the first; but there are also reduced constructions in which the two auxiliaries may differ (*cf* 12.59, 19.45 Note):

Ann hoped that we *would* stay, but unfortunately we *couldn't*.
You *should* take a break whenever you *can*.

(f) Pre-adverb position

3.27 Frequency subjuncts, like *always* or *never*, and disjuncts, like *certainly* or *probably*, typically, but not necessarily, follow auxiliaries as operators, whereas they precede main verbs. Compare:

> She {*never* / *probably*} believed his story.
>
> She would {*never* / *probably*} believe that story.

If there is more than one auxiliary, the adverb will still generally occur after the first, *ie* after the operator:

> She would *probably never* have believed his story.

The position of an adverb, however, is often variable within the verb phrase (*cf* 8.14*ff*). Compare:

> She {would *probably never* have / *probably never* would have / would *probably* have *never*} believed that story.

The most important point is that such adverbs could not occur immediately after the main verb except where the main verb is BE (and therefore an operator):

> *She believed *never/probably* his story.

(*Cf*: She was *never/probably* a taxpayer.)

(g) Quantifier position

3.28 Quantifiers like *all*, *both*, and *each* which modify the subject of the clause may occur after the operator as an alternative, in many instances, to the predeterminer position (*cf* 5.15*f*):

> *All* the boys will be there. ~ The boys will *all* be there.
> *Both* my parents are working. ~ My parents are *both* working.

These quantifiers do not, however, occur after a main verb in the same type of construction:

> *All* our team played well. ≁ *Our team played *all* well.
> *Each* of us owns a bicycle. ≁ *We own *each* a bicycle.

But if the quantifier is placed before the main verb, these sentences become acceptable:

> Our team *all* played well. We *each* own a bicycle.

Note *All*, *both*, and *each* sometimes occur between subject and operator, but this is exceptional, and less acceptable than the post-operator position:

> ?We both were working late. ~ We were both working late.

(h) Independence of subject

3.29 Compared with most main verbs, auxiliaries are semantically independent of the subject. This is reflected in at least three ways.

First, there is a lack of semantic restrictions (*cf* 10.51) between the subject and the auxiliary verb. Contrast:

The man }
The bus } ought to be here at five.

The man }
*The bus } hopes to be here at five.

Second, there is the possibility of construction with existential *there*:

There *used* }
*There *hoped* } to be a school on the island.

Third, if other conditions are met for the active–passive correspondence (*eg* if the verb is transitive, *cf* 3.67*ff*), auxiliaries usually admit the change from one voice to the other without change of meaning:

Thousands of people will meet the president.
= The president will be met by thousands of people.

Compare the situation in which a full verb occurs as first (finite) verb:

Thousands of people hope to meet the president.
≠ The president hopes to be met by thousands of people.

These criteria for independence are, however, not infallible. For example, in some contexts some auxiliaries fail the active–passive test (*cf* 3.72), and there are also some verbs which by other criteria are not auxiliaries, but which pass this test. These verbs will be considered later (3.47*ff*) under the headings of semi-auxiliary and catenative verbs.

Additional features of modal auxiliary verbs

3.30 The criteria (a–h) discussed so far help to define auxiliaries as a functional class, but it must be remembered that all of them except (h) apply to operators in general, and therefore apply also to BE and (sometimes) HAVE as main verbs. Now we add the following morphological and syntactic criteria which apply specifically to modal auxiliary verbs, as distinct from the primary verbs BE, HAVE, and DO.

(j) Construction with the bare infinitive

Modal auxiliaries are normally followed by the infinitive, which is bare (*ie* the base form of the verb alone) except with *used* (*cf* 3.44) and (usually) *ought* (*cf* 3.43), verbs which for this reason, as well as for others, are somewhat marginal to the class of modals. Compare:

You *will* be asked questions. BUT: You *ought to* comb your hair.
They *might* have stolen it. BUT: He *used to* read for hours.

(On the marginal modal auxiliaries *dare* and *need*, *cf* 3.42.)

(k) Finite functions only

Modal auxiliaries can only occur as the first (operator) element of the verb phrase. They cannot occur in nonfinite functions, *ie* as infinitives or participles, and as a consequence of this can occur only as first verb in the verb phrase:

MODAL VERB	PRIMARY VERB	FULL VERB
**to may*	*to have*	*to eat*
*(is) *maying*	(is) *being*	(is) *eating*
*(has) *mayed*	(has) *been*	(has) *eaten*

The primary verbs have the full range of nonfinite forms, but not all of these forms can be used in auxiliary function. For BE, all three nonfinite forms can be auxiliaries: *be, being, been*; HAVE has no *-ed* participle in auxiliary function, but only *have* and *having*. 'Dummy' auxiliary DO, like the modal auxiliaries, can only occur as an operator, and the nonfinite forms of DO, *(to) do, doing*, and *done*, are constructed only as main verbs.

(l) No 3rd person inflection

Modal auxiliaries are not inflected in the 3rd person singular of the present tense; *ie*, they have no *-s* form:

You *must* } write. BUT: You *like* } to write.
She *must* }   She *likes* }

In contrast, the primary verbs do have an *-s* form, but it is irregular (*cf* 3.31*ff*).

(m) Abnormal time reference

Not only the present forms, but the past forms of the modal auxiliaries can be used to refer to present and future time (often with hypothetical or tentative meaning):

I think he *may/might* retire next May.
Will/would you phone him tomorrow?

Contrast:

*I think he *retired* next May.
**Did* you *phone* him tomorrow?

Also modal auxiliaries which do not have a distinct past form (*eg*: *must, need, ought*) can be used to refer to the past in indirect speech:

I told him he *must* be home early. ['. . . had to be . . .']

Note [**a**] The use of past forms to refer to present and future time is also possible with full verbs, but only in some special constructions: *eg* in hypothetical *if*-clauses (*cf* 14.23, 15.35*f*):

If you *phoned* ['were to phone'] me tomorrow, I could help you straight away.

[**b**] In dialectal use (*eg* Scots English, Tyneside English, and Southern AmE), there are varieties of popular speech in which one modal auxiliary can follow another: *He might could come* ['He might be able to come'] etc.

The primary verbs BE, HAVE, and DO

3.31 Having discussed auxiliary verb criteria, we can now consider the special morphological and syntactic characteristics of verbs which can function as auxiliaries: first the primary, and second the modal verbs.

Semantically, the primary verbs as auxiliaries share an association with the basic grammatical verb categories of tense, aspect, and voice (*cf* 3.63, 4.2, 4.17). In this they are broadly distinguished from the modal verbs, which are associated mainly with the expression of modal meanings such as possibility, obligation, and volition (*cf* 4.42*ff*). But first, we examine these primary verbs from a formal point of view.

BE

3.32 The verb BE is a main verb (with a copular function; *cf* 2.16) in:

> Ann *is* a happy girl. *Is* that building a hotel?

But BE also has two auxiliary functions: as an aspect auxiliary (Type C, 3.55):

> Ann *is* learning Spanish.
> The weather has *been* improving.

and as a passive auxiliary (Type D, 3.55):

> Ann *was* awarded a prize.
> Our team has never *been* beaten.

BE is unique in having a full set of both finite and nonfinite forms in auxiliary function; it is also unique among English verbs in having as many as eight different forms, *cf Table* 3.32 on the next page. In the nonnegative column of *Table* 3.32 the unstressed pronunciations (with vowel reduction) are given after the stressed pronunciation, where they differ.

Note [a] BE is the only verb in English to have a special form for the 1st person singular of the present (*am*) and two distinct forms of the past tense (*was, were*). In the subjunctive, however (*cf* 3.58*ff*), the form *was* does not occur.

[b] *Ain't* is a nonstandard contraction commonly used (esp in AmE) in place of *am not*, *is not*, *are not*, *has not*, and *have not*.

[c] There is no completely natural informal contraction of *am I not* (parallel to *isn't she* for *is she not*) in negative sentences. (On the position of *not* in negative questions, *cf* 11.7.) *Aren't I* is widely used, especially in BrE, whereas *ain't I*, usually considered nonstandard, is somewhat more current in AmE than in BrE. *Amn't I* is mainly Scottish and Irish.

[d] The following BrE example (of marginal acceptability) shows that it is possible for *aren't* to act as a contracted form of *am not* even in declarative contexts:

> HÈ WÁSn't and Ì probably *aren't* NÓRmally.

Here the substitution of *aren't* seems to have resulted from a desire for parallelism with the preceding occurrence of *wasn't*.

[e] Phonologically, the contracted *'s* ending /s/ or /z/ cannot occur after a sibilant consonant. Hence *Your place is over there* cannot become in writing **Your place's over there*. Compare the conditions for the pronunciation of the *-s* form of regular verbs (*cf* 3.5), and contrast the contraction following a nonsibilant:

> Your {place is /pleɪsɪz/ | seat's /siːts/} over there.

Other conditions on the use of the contraction *'s* in place of *is* are discussed in 3.23.

Table 3.32 Forms of BE

	NONNEGATIVE	UNCONTRACTED NEGATIVE	CONTRACTED NEGATIVE (*cf* Note)
base	*be* /biː/, /bɪ/		
present			
1st person singular present	*am* /æm/, /əm/ *'m* /m/	*am not,* *'m not*	(*aren't*)
3rd person singular present	*is* /ɪz/ *'s* /z/, /s/	*is not,* *'s not*	*isn't* /ˈɪzn̩t/
2nd person present, 1st and 3rd person plural present	*are* /ɑːʳ/ *'re* /əʳ/	*are not* *'re not*	*aren't* /ɑːʳnt/
past			
1st and 3rd person singular past	*was* /wɒz/, /w(ə)z/	*was not*	*wasn't* /ˈwɒzn̩t/
2nd person past 1st and 3rd person plural past	*were* /wɜːʳ/, /wəʳ/	*were not*	*weren't* /wɜːʳnt/
-ing form	*being* /ˈbiːɪŋ/	*not being*	
-ed participle	*been* /biːn/, /bɪn/	*not been*	

NOTE The final /t/ of the negative contraction is commonly not sounded.

HAVE

3.33 HAVE functions both as an auxiliary and as a main verb. As an auxiliary for perfective aspect (*cf* 4.18*ff*), HAVE combines with an *-ed* participle to form complex verb phrases:

> I *have* finished.
> What *has* she bought?
> They may *have* been eaten.

As a main verb, it normally takes a direct object, and has various meanings such as possession: *I have no money*; *They had two children*; etc (*cf* 3.34). The different forms of HAVE are shown in *Table* 3.33 opposite.

In negative constructions we have the following three variants:

I *have not* seen her.	(typical of written discourse)
I *haven't* seen her. I*'ve not* seen her.	(typical of spoken discourse)

Of the contracted forms, the *haven't* type is generally more common than the *'ve not* type. As an *-ed* participle, *had* is restricted to use as a main verb, as in

Have you had lunch?, or to use in the HAVE *to* construction, as in *They have had to sell their car.*

Note Phonologically, the *'d* contraction cannot occur after /t/ or /d/: if we encounter the written form *'d* in such contexts (*eg*: *It'd been damaged*), this must be understood to represent the syllabic reduced form /əd/. Compare a similar restriction in 3.32 Note [e].

Table 3.33 Forms of HAVE

	NONNEGATIVE	UNCONTRACTED NEGATIVE	CONTRACTED NEGATIVE (*cf* Note)
base	*have* /hæv/, /(h)əv/ *'ve* /v/	*have not* *'ve not*	 *haven't* /ˈhævn̩t/
-s form	*has* /hæz/, /(h)əz/ *'s* /z/, /s/	*has not* *'s not*	 *hasn't* /ˈhæzn̩t/
past	*had* /hæd/, /(h)əd/ *'d* /d/	*had not* *'d not*	 *hadn't* /ˈhædn̩t/
-ing form	*having* /ˈhævɪŋ/	*not having*	
-ed participle	*had* /hæd/, /(h)əd/		

NOTE The final /t/ of the negative contraction is commonly not sounded.

HAVE as main verb

3.34 When used as a main verb with stative meaning (*cf* 4.4), HAVE shows syntactic variation in that it not only combines with DO-support in forming constructions with an operator (*cf* 3.37):

We *don't have* any money. *Do* you *have* a lighter?

but also acts as an operator itself in constructions such as:

We *haven't* any money. *Have* you a lighter?

This latter construction, although it is the traditional construction in BrE, is now somewhat uncommon, particularly in the past tense: ?*Had she any news?*

There is also the informal HAVE *got* construction (*cf* 3.45), which although perfective in form is nonperfective in meaning, and is frequently preferred (esp in BrE) as an alternative to stative HAVE:

John *has* courage. = John *has got* courage.

It is particularly common in negative and interrogative clauses. To express some stative senses we can thus have three alternatives:

Possession: { (a) We *haven't* / (b) We *haven't got* / (c) We *don't have* } any butter.

Relationship: { (a) *Have* you / (b) *Have* you *got* / (c) *Do* you *have* } any brothers? { (a) No, I *haven't.* / (b) No, I *haven't.* / (c) No, I *don't.* }

Health: { (a) I *haven't* / (b) I *haven't got* / (c) I *don't have* } a headache any longer.

Of these alternatives, (a) is esp BrE ⟨more formal⟩; (b) is esp BrE ⟨informal⟩; (c) is AmE (and also common in BrE nowadays).

Note [**a**] A further alternative for expressing negation is of course a negative determiner or pronoun: *We have no butter* (*cf* 5.13, 6.62).
[**b**] On HAVE *to* compared with HAVE *got to*, *cf* 3.48.
[**c**] In informal English *has got*, *have got*, and *had got* may be reduced to *'s got*, *'ve got*, and *'d got*. In very informal English, *'ve got* may be further reduced to *got*:

What you *got* there? I *got* something nice for you.

In its written form, this omission of the auxiliary is nonstandard.

3.35 In dynamic senses (*cf* 4.4) such as 'receive', 'take', 'experience', and in idioms with an eventive object (*eg*: *have breakfast* = 'eat breakfast'), HAVE (in both AmE and BrE) normally has DO-support, and HAVE *got* is not possible:

A: *Does* she *have* coffee with her breakfast?
B: Yes, she *does*.
A: *Did* you *have* any difficulty getting here?
B: No, I *didn't*.
A: *Did* you *have* a good time in Japan?
B: Yes, we certainly *did*.

Other dynamic uses include HAVE in a causative sense followed by an *-ed* participle, or in a similar sense followed by a bare infinitive:

A: *Did* they *have* the house painted?
B: No, they *didn't*.
A: *Did* they *have* you paint the house?
B: Yes, they *did*.

Note [**a**] Note the following contrast between stative and dynamic meaning:

Had she *got* her baby at the clinic? ['Was her baby at the clinic with her?']
Did she *have* her baby at the clinic? ['Did she give birth to her baby at the clinic?']

Especially in AmE, the second sentence could have both of these meanings.
[**b**] Since HAVE with the DO construction is typically dynamic, in the present tense it tends to single out a habitual interpretation (*cf* 4.6). Compare:

Do you *have* bad headaches? [normally habitual: 'as a rule']
Have you *got* a bad headache? [nonhabitual: 'now, at this moment']
Have you *got* bad headaches? [This could only be addressed to more than one person in a nonhabitual sense.]

DO

3.36 DO, like BE and HAVE, can be both an auxiliary and a main verb. As an auxiliary, DO has no nonfinite forms, but only present and past forms, *cf Table* 3.36 opposite.

Note Occasionally *does* is contracted in informal style to *'s* /s/; *eg*: *What's it matter?* A more drastic kind of phonological reduction is indicated by the following (nonstandard) orthographic rendering of informal speech:

Whyncha do it yourself? ['Why don't you . . .?']

Table 3.36 Forms of DO

	NONNEGATIVE	UNCONTRACTED NEGATIVE	CONTRACTED NEGATIVE (*cf* Note)
base	*do* /du:/, /dʊ/, /də/	*do not*	*don't* /dəʊnt/
-s form	*does* /dʌz/, /dəz/	*does not*	*doesn't* /ˈdʌzn̩t/
past	*did* /dɪd/	*did not*	*didn't* /ˈdɪdn̩t/
-ing form (main verb only)	*doing* /ˈdu:ɪŋ/		
-ed participle (main verb only)	*done* /dʌn/		

NOTE The final /t/ of the negative contraction is commonly not sounded.

DO-support

3.37 The term DO-SUPPORT (or 'DO-periphrasis') applies to the use of DO as an 'empty' or 'dummy' operator (*cf* 2.49) in conditions where the construction requires an operator, but where there is no semantic reason for any other operator to be present. All uses of DO as an auxiliary come under this heading. The main ones are:

(a) In indicative clauses (*cf* 3.52) negated by *not*, where the verb is simple present or simple past:

She *doesn't* want to stay.
I *didn't* like mathematics at school.

Negative imperative clauses introduced by *Do not* or *Don't* may, with some reservation (*cf* 11.30, Note [a]), be placed in the same category.

(b) In questions and other constructions involving subject–operator inversion, where the verb is in the simple present or past tense:

Did he stay late? What *do* they say? *Does* it matter?

This category includes tag questions (*cf* 11.8*ff*) and other reduced questions where the dummy operator is not accompanied by a main verb:

He knows how to drive a car, *doesn't* he?
They didn't make any mistakes, *did* they?
I don't like him, *do* you?

It also includes inversion after an initial negative element:

Never *did* he think the book would be finished so soon.

(c) In emphatic constructions where the verb is simple present or simple past (*cf* emphatic positive constructions, 3.25):

They "*do* want you to come.
Michael "*did* say he would be here at nine, didn't he?

Here we may also include the 'persuasive imperative' introduced by *do*:

"*Do* sit down! "*Do* be quiet.
A: May I sit here? B: Yes, by all means DÒ.

(See, however, 11.30 Note [a] on the dubious status of DO as operator in this construction.)

(d) In reduced clauses, where DO acts as a dummy operator preceding ellipsis of a predication (12.60):

Mary reads books faster than I *do*. [do = 'read books']
Did you watch the game on television? No, but my brother *did*.
['. . . watch the game on television']

Note [**a**] There is no DO-support for negation in nonfinite clauses, where *not* precedes a full verb as main verb:

Not liking mathematics, he gave it up.
Not to go to the exhibition would be a pity.

There is also normally no DO-support for subjunctive verbs (*cf* 3.58):

It is important that this mission *not fail*.

[**b**] Negative words other than *not* do not require DO-support:

No one liked him.
They *never/seldom* go out.

[**c**] Nor is there any DO-support in questions without inversion, *ie* questions with the normal S V O/C/A order (*cf* 11.12, 11.15): *He said that? Who came first?*

[**d**] Auxiliaries have no DO-support, since they themselves perform the function of operators (*cf* 3.21). Thus DO does not precede other auxiliaries: **She does must come*. There is a rare exception, however, where *Do* or *Don't* precedes auxiliary BE in imperatives (*cf* 11.30 Note [a]): *Don't be drinking wine when he calls*; *Don't be frightened by that noise*.

[**e**] In some legal documents in archaic style, the auxiliary DO construction is used merely as an alternative to the simple present or past tense:

I, the undersigned, being of sound mind, *do* this day hereby *bequeath* . . .

DO as main verb

3.38 When used as a main verb, DO has the full range of forms, including the *-ing* participle *doing* and the *-ed* participle *done*:

What have you been *doing* today? I haven't *done* much, I'm afraid.

As a main verb, DO can combine with a pronoun object to act as a pro-predication referring to some unspecified action or actions. The pronoun object may be personal (*it*), demonstrative (*this/that*), interrogative (*what*), or indefinite (*nothing/anything*, etc):

I have been meaning to mend that radio, but I haven't *done it* yet. (*cf* 12.25)
A: I'm throwing these books away. B: Why are you *doing* THÀT?
A: *What* have they been *doing* to the road? B: Widening it.
A: *What* have you *done* with my pen? B: I've put it in the desk.
A: *What* did you *do* on holiday? B: We didn't *do anything*.
I didn't know *what* to *do*, so I *did nothing*.

See also the use of DO in pseudo-cleft sentences (18.29). DO is also used intransitively as a pro-predication (*cf* 12.22):

She didn't earn so much as she might have (*done*). ⟨esp BrE⟩

Apart from these uses as a pro-form, the main verb DO has a wide range of uses as a general-purpose agentive transitive verb, especially in informal speech:

Let's *do* the dishes – you wash and I'll dry. [1]
Who *does* your car? Fred Archer – and he *does* my neighbour's too. [2]
She's *done* some really good essays – and she always hands them in on time. [3]

DO in such sentences is often replaceable by a verb of more exact meaning; *eg* in [2] SERVICE or MAINTAIN, and in [3] WRITE. The meaning is narrowed down by the nature of the object: *eg* in *Will you do the potatoes?*, DO could mean 'peel' or 'cook', but scarcely 'polish', a meaning it might have in *Have you done the silver?*

Note There is also a resultative use of *done* meaning 'cooked': *Is the meat done?*

Modal auxiliaries

3.39 The criteria for identifying modal auxiliaries have been discussed in 3.22*ff*, and especially 3.30. Not all verbs respond to all criteria, however, and it is useful to make a distinction between central and marginal modals. We will discuss the marginal modals and other verbs of intermediate status in 3.40*ff*, and we will discuss the meanings of the modal auxiliaries later (4.49*ff*).

All that needs to be said about the form of the central modals is stated in *Table* 3.39 and the accompanying Notes. The Table gives the contracted

Table 3.39 Forms of the modal auxiliary verbs

NONNEGATIVE	UNCONTRACTED NEGATIVE	CONTRACTED NEGATIVE
can /kæn, kən/	*cannot,* (*can not*: *cf* Note [b])	*can't* /kɑːnt/ ⟨BrE⟩, /kænt/ ⟨AmE⟩
could /kʊd, kəd/	*could not*	*couldn't* /ˈkʊdn̩t/
may /meɪ/	*may not*	(*mayn't* /meɪnt/ *cf* 3.23)
might /maɪt/	*might not*	*mightn't* /ˈmaɪtn̩t/
shall /ʃæl, ʃ(ə)l/	*shall not*	(*shan't* /ʃɑːnt/ ⟨BrE⟩ *cf* 3.23)
should /ʃʊd, ʃ(ə)d/	*should not*	*shouldn't* /ˈʃʊdn̩t/, /ˈʃədn̩t/
will /wɪl/	*will not*	*won't* /wəʊnt/
'll /(ə)l/	*'ll not*	(*cf* Note [c])
would /wʊd/	*would not*	*wouldn't* /ˈwʊdn̩t/
'd /(ə)d/	*'d not*	(*cf* Note [c])
must /mʌst, məst/	*must not*	*mustn't* /ˈmʌsn̩t/

(Unstressed pronunciations with vowel reduction are placed after the stressed pronunciations. Rare forms are placed in parentheses.)

negative form, and also the pronunciation of both stressed and unstressed forms.

Semantic aspects of the negation of modal auxiliaries are examined in 10.67*f*.

Note [**a**] The words braced together can for some purposes be regarded as present and past forms of the same verb. But for other purposes, they behave as independent verbs (*cf* 4.59).

[**b**] The spelling of *can not* as two words is unusual: it occurs where main verb negation (*cf* 10.67*f*) is intended, or where special emphasis on or separation of the negative word is required; *eg*:

Can you *not* interrupt, please.
Can I *not* help you?
He says we *can* manage when we *can* certainly *not*.

[**c**] There are obviously no contracted forms of *'ll* and *'d* since they are themselves contractions. These forms are braced with *will* and *would* because *'ll* and *'d* can always be expanded to *will* and *would* (except, of course, when *'d* = *had*, *cf* 3.33).

[**d**] Regarding the frequency of the modal auxiliaries, the following findings, based on studies of the SEU, Brown and LOB corpora, are of significant interest:

(a) The frequency of individual modals varies greatly from *will* (four times per thousand in spoken BrE) to *shall* (three times per *ten* thousand words in written English). The marginal modals *ought to*, *need*, and *dare* are in their turn strikingly less frequent than *shall*.
(b) The modals as a whole are much more frequent in spoken than in written English.
(c) *Will*, *can*, and their past forms *would* and *could* are notably more frequent than other modals.
(d) Among less frequent modals, *should*, *shall*, and *ought to* are even less frequent in AmE than in BrE.

Verbs of intermediate function

3.40 In the following sections we examine verbs whose status is in some degree intermediate between auxiliaries and main verbs. These form a set of categories which may be roughly placed on a gradient between modal auxiliaries at one end, and full verbs, such as *hope*, which take a nonfinite clause as object, at the other. The extremes of the scale may therefore be represented by *I can go* and *I hope to go*, *cf Fig* 3.40a opposite.

The structural implication of this scale is that the construction (a) *I can go* contains one verb phrase, whereas the construction (f) *I hope to go* contains a finite verb phrase followed by a nonfinite one. This distinction will be further discussed in 3.57. Semantic aspects of the scale may also be noted (*cf* 4.66); many of the intermediate verbs, particularly those at the higher end of the scale, have meanings associated with aspect, tense, and modality: meanings which are primarily expressed through auxiliary verb constructions. Our principal task, however, is to distinguish these classes by formal criteria, while making any semantic observations that may be useful.

The criteria which will provide the framework for this analysis are those which were used in identifying the class of auxiliaries in 3.22*ff*. There are eight criteria for auxiliaries, and four criteria which more narrowly apply to the central modal auxiliaries. They are summarized in *Table* 3.40b opposite, together with illustratively contrasting examples.

(one verb phrase) ↑	(a) CENTRAL MODALS	*can, could, may, might, shall, should, will/'ll, would/'d, must*	(*cf* 3.39)
	(b) MARGINAL MODALS	*dare, need, ought to, used to*	(*cf* 3.41*ff*)
	(c) MODAL IDIOMS	*had better, would rather/sooner,* BE *to,* HAVE *got to,* etc	(*cf* 3.45*f*)
	(d) SEMI-AUXILIARIES	HAVE *to,* BE *about to,* BE *able to,* BE *bound to,* BE *going to,* BE *obliged to,* BE *supposed to,* BE *willing to,* etc	(*cf* 3.47*f*)
	(e) CATENATIVES	APPEAR *to,* HAPPEN *to,* SEEM *to,* GET + *-ed* participle, KEEP + *-ing* participle, etc	(*cf* 3.49)
(two verb phrases) ↓	(f) MAIN VERB + nonfinite clause	HOPE + *to*-infinitive, BEGIN + *-ing* participle, etc	(*cf* 16.38*f*)

Fig. 3.40a The auxiliary verb – main verb scale

Table 3.40b Criteria for auxiliary verbs

AUXILIARY CRITERIA (Op = operator)	AUXILIARY	MAIN VERB
(a) Op in negation	He *cannot* go.	*He *hopes not* to go. (*cf* Note)
(b) Negative contraction	*can't*	**hopen't*
(c) Op in inversion	*Can* we go?	**Hope* we to go?
(d) Emphatic positive	*Yes, I *DÒ can* come.	Yes, I *DÒ hope* to come.
(e) Op in reduced clause	I can come if you *can*.	*I hope to come if you *hope*.
(f) Position of adverb	We *can always* go early.	We *always hope* to go early.
(g) Postposition of quantifier	{ They *can all* come. / ?They *all can* come. }	{ ?They *hope all* to come. / They *all hope* to come. }
(h) Independence of subject	{ Ann can do it. ~ / It can be done by Ann. }	{ He hopes to do it. / *It hopes to be done by him. }
MODAL AUXILIARY CRITERIA	**MODAL AUXILIARY**	**MAIN VERB**
(j) Bare infinitive	I *can go*.	*I *hope go*.
(k) No nonfinite forms	**to can*/**canning*/**canned*	*to hope/hoping/hoped*
(l) No *-s* form	*She *cans* come.	She *hopes* to come.
(m) Abnormal time reference	You *could* leave this evening. [not past time]	You *hoped* to leave this evening. [past time]

NOTE *He hopes not to go* is acceptable in the sense 'He hopes that he will not go'; but this is then a case of the negation of *to go*, not of *hopes* (*cf* 3.22 Note [a]).

Marginal modals: *dare, need, ought to,* and *used to*

3.41 Given that in the above table modal auxiliaries are positive for all criteria, where main verbs like *hope* are negative, the marginal modals are verbs which closely resemble the central modal auxiliaries. It can be argued, indeed, for *dare* and *need* that these are proper modals, but that for each there is also a homomorphic verb (DARE, NEED) constructed as a main verb (*cf*, however, 3.42 Note [b]). *Ought*, too, may be treated as a central modal if speakers construct it with the bare infinitive (*cf* 3.43 Note [a]).

dare and *need*

3.42 *Dare* and *need* can be constructed either as main verbs (with *to*-infinitive and with inflected *-s*, *-ing* and past forms), or, under restricted conditions, as modal auxiliaries (with the bare infinitive and without the inflected forms).

Table 3.42

	MODAL AUXILIARY CONSTRUCTION	MAIN VERB CONSTRUCTION
Positive	—	He *needed/dared* to escape.
Negative	He *needn't/daren't* escape.	He *doesn't need/dare* to escape.
Interrogative	*Need/Dare* we escape?	*Do* we *need/dare* to escape?
Negative-interrogative	{ *Needn't* he escape after all? / *Dare* he *not* escape? }	{ *Doesn't* he *need* to escape after all? / *Doesn't* he *dare* to escape? }

The modal construction is restricted to nonassertive contexts (*cf* 2.53), *ie* mainly negative and interrogative sentences, whereas the main verb construction can almost always be used, and is in fact more common. The auxiliary construction with *dare* and *need* is rarer in AmE than in BrE, where it is also quite rare.

As a modal, *dare* exhibits abnormal time reference (*cf* 3.30) in that it can be used, without inflection, for past as well as present time:

The king was so hot-tempered that no one *dare* tell him the bad news.

The main verb form *dared* (*to*) might also occur here.

Note [a] 'Nonassertive contexts' are not confined to negative and interrogative clauses: they also include clauses containing semi-negative words such as *hardly* and *only*. The following examples illustrate sentences with negative import, but lacking *not*-negation:

No one dare predict the results. Standards are *lower than* they need be.

For further illustrations and discussion of this topic, *cf* 10.61.

[b] Blends between the auxiliary construction and the main verb construction occur and seem to be widely acceptable (more so in the case of *dare* than in that of *need*):

They *do* not *dare* ask for more. *Do* they *dare* ask for more?

These two examples combine the DO-support of the main verb construction with the bare infinitive of the auxiliary construction. On the hypothesis that there are two different verbs (the main verb DARE and the auxiliary verb *dare*), one would expect these to be ungrammatical; but they are not. The past tense form *dared* without DO-support may be regarded as another example of a blend, since the *-ed* past inflection is not characteristic of modal verbs:

They *dared not* carry out their threat.

Blends with *need* are usually of the type with *-s* inflection and bare infinitive: *?One needs only reflect for a second . . .*

[c] *Dare* occurs (with nuclear stress) in the following idiomatic constructions expressing a threatening rebuke:

How DÀRE you do such a thing? Don't you DÀRE speak to me like that.

The latter example, with DO-support and a bare infinitive *speak*, is another example of a blend.

[d] In another formulaic construction, *I dare say* followed by a *that*-clause, the two verbs are often written as a single word *daresay*:

I *daresay* she is right. ['I wouldn't be surprised if . . .']

The normal sense of *dare* is lost here.

[e] As main verbs, DARE and NEED can enter into a number of different constructions (*cf* 16.26, 16.39, 16.50). Thus, NEED can take a direct object:

You *need* a haircut.

As is to be expected, NEED and DARE as main verbs have to be replaced by DO in reduced clause constructions:

She *needs* to practise and so *do* I. They *didn't dare* to attack us, *did* they?

[f] As a modal auxiliary, *need* has no tense contrast. To express past time, however, we can place *need* before the perfective aspect (*cf* 4.18*ff*): *You need not have done it*. This is then approximately equivalent to the past tense of NEED as a main verb: *You did not need to do it*. But the NEED *to* construction does not have the counterfactual implication of the *need have* . . . construction. For instance, in the following the counterfactual meaning is inappropriate, and we could not therefore replace *did not need to say* by *need not have said*:

Anne was too nervous to reply, but fortunately she *did not need to say* anything.

[g] As an auxiliary, *dare* usually fails the independence of subject criterion (h) in 3.29. There is no semantic equivalence between the active *The boy daren't contact her* and the passive *She daren't be contacted by the boy*. One meets, however, exceptions such as *This is a problem which dare not be overlooked*.

[h] Further to Note [b] above, results of elicitation experiments indicate a higher acceptance rate for blends with AmE than with BrE speakers. This can be interpreted in two opposite ways: we can argue either that blends are more common in AmE, or that *dare* and *need* are such unusual verbs in AmE in these constructions, that speakers do not react critically to blends, but rather display passive acceptance of them. The latter interpretation (which has also been advanced for blends with another marginal auxiliary, *ought to*, *cf* 3.43) is supported by frequently introduced lexical changes such as the following:

Submitted sentence: *Needn't* he go?

Proposed lexical changes: { *Doesn't* he *have* to go? / *Does* he *have* to go? / *Shouldn't* he go? etc }

ought to

3.43 *Ought to* /ɔːt tuː/, /ɔːt (t)ə/, has the uncontracted negative *ought not to* and the contracted negative *oughtn't to*. It normally has the *to*-infinitive (although occasionally in familiar style the bare infinitive occurs in nonassertive contexts):

You *ought to* stop smoking.
You *oughtn't to* smoke so much.
Ought you *to* smoke so much?

The *to* is also optional following *ought* in ellipsis: *Yes, I think I ought (to)*. On the meaning of *ought to*, *cf* 4.56.

Note **[a]** Elicitation tests on young people have shown that, for both AmE and BrE, in nonassertive contexts the *to*-less *ought* construction is widely acceptable, and for some speakers even preferable to the construction with *to* in nonassertive contexts; *eg*:

They *ought not* (*to*) *do* that sort of thing. *Ought* we (*to*) *have done* it?
Oughtn't we (*to*) *send* for the police?

In assertive contexts, however, the *to*-less form is unacceptable:

> We { *ought to* / **ought* } give him another chance.

[**b**] Treating *ought* as a main verb with DO-support, which is usually described as a dialectal usage, proved to be the least popular alternative in a test with BrE teenage informants:

> They *didn't ought to* do that sort of thing.
> *Did* we *ought* to have done it?

However, the existence of this construction, even if it is not part of standard English, is an indicator of the marginal status of *ought to* which, like the other marginal modals, shows some tendency to pattern as a main verb. More generally, such results reflect change and uncertainty in the use of certain modals which, from a historical viewpoint, are in decline.

used to

3.44 *Used to* denotes a habit or a state that existed in the past (*cf* 4.15), and is therefore semantically not so much a modal auxiliary as an auxiliary of tense and aspect. In formal terms, however, it fits the marginal modal category.

It always takes the *to*-infinitive and only occurs in the past tense:

> She *used to* attend regularly. ['was in the habit of attending . . .']
> I *used to* be interested in bird-watching. ['I was formerly . . .']

It is typically pronounced /ˈjuːstuː/ or /ˈjuːstʊ/ before vowels or before an ellipsis, and /ˈjuːstə/ before consonants.

Used to occurs both as an operator and with DO-support. In the latter case the spellings *use to* and *used to* both occur, reflecting speakers' uncertainty of the status of this verb: an uncertainty, that is, as to whether it is to be treated as an invariable form, like a modal auxiliary, or as a form with an infinitive, like a full verb. The pronunciation of the verb does not allow discrimination between these possibilities. In the negative, the operator construction, which avoids this dilemma, is preferred by many in BrE:

> { He usen't to smoke. / He used not to smoke. } ⟨BrE⟩
>
> { He didn't use to smoke. / He didn't used to smoke. } ⟨BrE and AmE⟩

The construction *did . . . use to* is preferred to other constructions in both AmE and BrE. The spelling *did . . . used to*, however, is often regarded as nonstandard. The interrogative operator construction *used (he) to* is rare even in BrE. Tag questions also normally have DO-support; compare:

> Did he use to smoke? He used to smoke, didn't he?

Note [**a**] *Used to* + infinitive should be distinguished from *used to* + noun phrase or *-ing* participle clause:

> She is *used to* { *life* in the country. / *living* in the country. }

In this latter construction, although it has the same pronunciation as the marginal modal, *used to* is in fact a participial adjective followed by the preposition *to* ['accustomed to . . .'] (*cf* 16.69 Note [a]).

[**b**] A perfective form of *used to, had used to,* is occasionally attested.

[**c**] There is a tendency for speakers to avoid the problem of negating *used to* by employing the negative adverb *never*: *I never used to watch television.*

Modal idioms: *had better*, etc

3.45 This category contains the following four multi-word verbs, as well as some less common verbal constructions:

had better *would rather* HAVE *got to* BE *to*

They all begin with an auxiliary verb, and are followed by an infinitive (sometimes preceded by *to*):

We {*had* / *'d*} *better* leave soon. Yes, *we* {*had.* / *'d better.*} [1]
I'*d rather* not say anything. [2]
They'*ve got to* leave immediately. [3]
The conference *is to* take place in Athens. [4]

None of these idiomatic verbs has nonfinite forms; they cannot therefore follow other verbs in the verb phrase:

*I *will have got to* leave soon.
*The conference *has been to* take place in Athens.

In this respect they are not like main verbs. They are not, however, entirely like auxiliaries, since they do not behave as operators. It is normally the first word alone which acts as operator in (for example) negative and interrogative sentences:

Hadn't we *better* lock the door?
Would you *rather* eat in a hotel?
We *haven't got to* pay already, have we?
I *wasn't to* know that you were waiting.

However, *had better* and *would rather* have two kinds of negation. First, there is a negation in which *not* follows the whole expression:

I'*d rather not* stay here alone.
You'*d better not* lock the door.

A second type of negation, in which *not* follows the first word, is typically used in 'second instance' contexts (especially in negative questions) where an earlier statement or assumption is being challenged:

A: *Wouldn't* you *rather* live in the country?
B: No, I *would not*. I'd rather live here.

The two kinds of negation are sometimes associated with different meanings, the former being an instance of predication negation (*cf* 10.69):

Had we *better not* go? ['Would it be advisable if we didn't go?']
Hadn't we *better* go? ['I think we had better go; don't you agree?']

The contracted verb form followed by *not* is unacceptable with these two idioms:

*I'd not rather leave. *You'd not better resign.

Would rather differs from central modals and marginal modals in that it is incapable of showing active–passive synonymy:

I'd *rather rent* the cottage. *The cottage *would rather be rented* by me.

On the other hand, HAVE *got to* and BE *to* are more like main verbs in that they have an *-s* form and normal present/past tense contrast:

The committee { *is to* meet today. / *was to* meet yesterday. }

She { *has got to* leave by tomorrow. / *had got to* leave by the next day. ⟨BrE⟩ }

The past tense construction *had got to*, however, does not occur in AmE, and is rare in BrE, especially in questions.

Note [**a**] In addition to the four modal idioms illustrated above, the following sentences illustrate less common idioms which might be placed in the same category:

I *would sooner* leave the decision to you.
I *would (just) as soon* eat at home.
We *may/might (just) as well* pay at once. (*cf* 4.53 Note [e])
You *had best* forget this incident.

[**b**] Sometimes (particularly in AmE) the uncontracted form of *'d rather* is realized as *had rather* instead of *would rather*. Very occasionally the uncontracted form *should rather* is also encountered. These variations, and similar variations with *would sooner*, etc have presumably arisen because of the ambiguity of the contraction *'d*.

[**c**] *Would rather* and *would sooner* express preference ['. . . would prefer to . . .'] and may therefore be followed by a comparative construction beginning with *than*:

I'*d rather/sooner* live in the country *than* in the city.

[**d**] It is a sign of the 'in-between' status of modal idioms that either the whole idiom or just the first word of the idiom may be 'stranded' before ellipsis of the predication, as in [1] above, where the reply *Yes, we'd better* is an alternative to *Yes, we had*. (A third alternative is *Yes, we better had*.) With *would rather*, however, the *would* alone is usually stranded

A: *Would* you *rather* buy this one?
B: Yes, I { *would*. / *?would rather*. }

[**e**] In informal speech, the first word of HAVE *got to* and *had better* is often completely elided, so that the pronunciation of the whole idiom is reduced to /ˈgɒtə/, /ˈbetə^{r}/, thus making it resemble a single modal auxiliary. This reduction is represented in very informal written style (*eg* in fictional dialogue) by the omission of *'ve, 'd*, etc, and sometimes by the nonstandard spelling *gotta*:

You { *got to* / *gotta* } be careful these days. They *better* go home.

[**f**] HAVE *got to* is not to be confused with the perfective of the catenative verb GET *to*. The latter has, in AmE, the distinctive form HAVE *gotten to* (*cf* 3.18):

We'*ve gotten to* watch more TV this year than last. ⟨AmE⟩

The meanings of the modal idioms

3.46 All four of the modal idioms discussed above have meanings classifiable as 'modal'.

(a) *Had better* has a meaning of 'advisability', similar to the obligational meaning of *ought to* and *should* (*cf* 4.56).

(b) *Would rather* has the volitional meaning 'would prefer to'.

(c) HAVE *got to* has meanings of 'obligation' and 'logical necessity' (*cf*: *must* 4.54). From the semantic point of view, it is best considered a variant of the semi-auxiliary HAVE *to*. The respects in which its meaning differs from that of HAVE *to* are considered in 3.48 and 4.54*f*.

(d) BE *to* is an idiom expressing futurity, with varied connotations of 'compulsion', 'plan', 'destiny', etc, according to context. In the past, *was to* and *were to* express futurity from the standpoint of past time orientation; in conditional clauses, the subjunctive *were to* expresses hypothetical future meaning (*cf* 15.36). The meaning of BE *to* is further discussed in 4.47*f*.

Note [**a**] BE *to* must not be confused with an apparently identical construction in which the copula BE is followed by a nominal or adverbial infinitive clause (*cf* 15.10*f*, 15.48):

The committee is to find a solution. [1]
The problem is to find a solution. [2]

Whereas [1] illustrates the modal idiom BE *to*, in [2], *to find a solution* is a nominal infinitive clause acting as complement of *is* (*cf*: *The problem is how to find a solution*).

[**b**] The future meaning of BE *to* is particularly emphasized when it is accompanied by *still* or *yet*:

The most severe weather is *yet/still* to come.

The implication here is negative: 'has not yet come'. Compare a similar use of HAVE *to*, 3.48.

Semi-auxiliaries: *be going to*, etc

3.47 The semi-auxiliaries consist of a set of verb idioms which express modal or aspectual meaning and which are introduced by one of the primary verbs HAVE and BE; *eg*:

be able to	*be bound to*	*be likely to*	*be supposed to*
be about to	*be due to*	*be meant to*	*be willing to*
be apt to	*be going to*	*be obliged to*	*have to*

The boundaries of this category are not clear: they might be extended, for example, to include the negative *be unable to*, *be unwilling to*, etc (*cf* Note [a]). We will first of all deal with the semi-auxiliaries introduced by BE.

All these constructions satisfy the first seven criteria for auxiliary verbs (*cf* 3.22*ff*), in the sense that, for example, *be going to* has *be* as an operator in negation and inversion, rather than having DO-support:

{ Ada *isn't* going to win.
{ *Ada *doesn't be* going to win.

{ *Is* Ada *going* to win?
{ **Does* Ada *be* going to win?

However, this follows from the fact that the first word of the semi-auxiliary construction is the primary verb *be*. To be strictly comparable to an auxiliary in its entirety, *be going to* would have to form its negation by adding *not* to the second or third word: **is goingn't to* or **is going ton't*. It is therefore only by special interpretation of the operator criteria (a–e) that these semi-auxiliaries can be described as auxiliary-like. They do, however, resemble auxiliaries in permitting synonymous passives and *there*-constructions in accordance with the criterion of subject-independence (*cf* 3.29):

Brazil *is going to* win the World Cup.

~ The World Cup *is going to* be won by Brazil.
Several home teams are *going to* be beaten tomorrow.
~ There *are going to* be several home teams beaten tomorrow.

Moreover, such constructions as *be going to* and *be bound to* belie their appearance in not allowing contrasts of aspect and voice. There is, for example, no nonprogressive construction corresponding to *be going to*:

*Several home teams *go to* be beaten tomorrow.

And there is no active equivalent of the superficially passive *be bound to*:

He *was bound* to be a failure. ~ *Someone *bound* him to be a failure.

This is further evidence of a resemblance to auxiliaries rather than to main verb constructions.

These constructions are, however, in one respect much closer to main verbs than are the modal idioms. They have nonfinite forms such as *been going to* and *to be bound to*, and can therefore occur in combination with preceding auxiliaries:

James *will be obliged to* resign.
We *have* always *been willing to* help.

Two or more semi-auxiliaries may indeed occur in sequence:

Someone *is going to have to* complain.
No one *is likely to be able to* recognize her.

Although there are restrictions on this kind of combination (*cf* 3.57), the occurrence of nonfinite semi-auxiliaries means that these idioms can fill slots in a modal verb paradigm where modal auxiliaries of equivalent meaning cannot occur:

We haven't {*could / been able to} solve the problem. [*can* = 'ability']

To {*can / be allowed to} speak freely is a human right. [*can* = 'permission']

Other equivalences of this kind are between *must* and *have to* (*cf* 3.48), and between *will* and *be willing to*.

Note [**a**] There is a gradience between a semi-auxiliary such as *be bound to* and an occurrence of the copula BE followed by an adjectival or participial construction such as *happy to* or *compelled to*. One criterion of importance here is the ability of what follows BE to stand at the beginning of a supplementive clause (*cf* 15.60*ff*):

Compelled to take stern measures, the administration lost popularity. [1]
?*Bound* to take stern measures, the administration lost popularity. [2]

By this criterion, the combinations *able to* and *willing to* are less clearly independent than their negatives *unable to* and *unwilling to*:

Unable/*Unwilling* to resist, Matilda agreed to betray her country. [3]
?*Able*/?*Willing* to resist, Matilda declined to betray her country. [4]

Of these parallel sentences, [1] and [3] are clearly acceptable, whereas [2] and [4] are more marginal. But acceptability judgments tend to vary in this area.

[**b**] As semi-auxiliaries, *be meant to* and *be supposed to* have meanings similar to those of *ought to* (*cf* 4.56, 4.66) and are not to be confused with homomorphic passive constructions. In the case

of *be supposed to*, the semi-auxiliary is marked by a special pronunciation /. . . s(ə)ˈpəʊstʊ/ or /. . . s(ə)ˈpəʊstə/ (*cf* the special pronunciation of *used to*; 3.44).

have to

3.48 *Have to* is the only semi-auxiliary beginning with HAVE rather than BE, but its inclusion in this category is partly justified by its occurrence in the full range of nonfinite forms, a respect in which it differs from the semantically parallel *have got to* (*cf* 4.55):

> I *may have to* leave early. (*I *may have got to* leave early.)
> People *are having to* boil their drinking water during this emergency.
> The administration *has had to* make unpopular decisions.

As these examples show, *have to* can occur in modal, perfective, and progressive constructions. It would be impossible to substitute *have got to* for *have to* in these cases.

In meaning, *have to* is similar to *must* (*cf* 4.54), and can stand in for *must* in past constructions where *must* cannot occur:

> These days you *must* work hard if you want to succeed.
> In those days you *had to* work hard if you wanted to succeed.
> } [*have to* = 'obligation']
>
> There *must* be some solution to the problem.
> There *had to* be some solution to the problem.
> } [*have to* = 'logical necessity']

Have to patterns either as a main verb or as an auxiliary with respect to operator constructions:

> *Do* we *have to* get up early tomorrow? ⟨AmE and BrE⟩
> *Have* we *to* get up early tomorrow? ⟨BrE – somewhat old-fashioned⟩

In this, it resembles other uses of HAVE as a main verb (*cf* 3.34). DO-support, however, is the only construction in AmE and the dominant one in BrE (*cf* Note [c]).

Although *have got to* has the same meanings of 'obligation' and 'logical necessity' as are expressed by *have to*, *have got to* tends not to have habitual meaning, and when combined with a verb of dynamic meaning, tends to refer to the future. There is thus a potential difference between:

> Jim'*s got to check* the temperature every 12 hours. [1]
> Jim *has to check* the temperature every 12 hours. [2]

Whereas [1] is likely to have the force of a directive, stipulating what Jim's duties will be in the future, [2] is more likely to indicate a habitual action ['This is what Jim's present duties consist of'].

Note [**a**] Both *have to* and *have got to* occur with epistemic meaning like that of *must* (*cf* 4.54) in sentences such as:

> Someone {*has to* / *has got to*} be telling lies. You {*have to* / *'ve got to*} be joking.

This has until recently been regarded as an AmE usage, but is now also current in BrE.

[**b**] In other contexts *have to* and *have got to* express a stronger meaning of 'logical necessity' which cannot be matched by the use of *must*:

There *has* (*got*) *to be* a first time for everything.

[c] Studies in BrE usage show that over 85 per cent of instances of *have to* in negative and interrogative clauses are constructed with DO. Elicitation tests have further indicated that negative constructions without DO (of the kind *I hadn't to walk more than a mile*) are less acceptable than interrogative constructions without DO (such as *Has he to answer the letter this week?*).

Catenative verb constructions

3.49 The term CATENATIVE will in practice be used to denote verbs in such constructions as *appear to, come to, fail to, get to, happen to, manage to, seem to, tend to*, and *turn out to* followed by the infinitive:

Sam {appeared / came / failed / ?got / seemed} to realize the importance of the problem. [1]

Such constructions have meanings related to aspect or modality, but are nearer to main verb constructions than are semi-auxiliaries, patterning entirely like main verbs in taking DO-support:

Sam *didn't* {*appear* / *come*} to realize the importance of the problem. [2]

Most of them do, however, resemble auxiliary constructions in satisfying the 'independence of subject' criterion (*cf* 3.29). Thus [1] has the corresponding passive [3]:

The importance of the problem {appeared / came / ?failed / *got / seemed} to be realized by Sam. [3]

This criterion, however, applies somewhat marginally to agentive verbs like *fail* and *manage*, and does not apply at all to *get*.

Unlike main verb constructions such as *expect* (*to*), *want* (*to*), and *attempt* (*to*), catenative constructions are in no way syntactically related to transitive verb constructions in which the verb is followed by a direct object or prepositional object (*cf* 16.26*ff*, 16.38). Compare:

John {appeared / attempted} to attack the burglar. [4] [5]

But:

John {*appeared / attempted} an attack on the burglar. [6] [7]

We may also include among catenative verbs certain verbs which resemble the auxiliary BE in combining either with the *-ing* participle in progressive constructions, or with the *-ed* participle in passive constructions:

The girl { *started out* / *kept (on)* / *went on* } working.

Our team *got* beaten by the visitors.

(In BrE, *carried on* can be used as equivalent to *went on.*) These, again, should be distinguished from similar looking constructions in which a main verb is followed by a nominal *-ing* participle clause (*eg*: *The girl liked working*; *cf* 16.39) or by a participial adjective, as in the pseudo-passive (*cf* 3.77): *Our team looked beaten.*

Note [**a**] The term 'catenative' alludes to the ability of these verbs to be concatenated in sequences of nonfinite constructions, as in *Our team seems to manage to keep on getting beaten.* This propensity for forming chain-like structures is not, however, confined to catenative verbs, but is also characteristic of semi-auxiliaries and main verbs followed by nonfinite clauses as objects: Hence such improbable, but structurally possible sequences as:

We are going to have to enjoy seeming to like listening to his music.

[**b**] Some catenative verbs, like some semi-auxiliaries, are closely related to constructions with anticipatory *it* (*cf* 16.34, 16.72):

He seems to be rich. ~ It seems that he is rich.
She turned out to love horses. ~ It turned out that she loved horses.
Joan is likely to resign. ~ It is likely that Joan will resign.

Some further aspects of the gradience between modals and main verbs

3.50 Although they do not enter into the list of modal auxiliary criteria stated in 3.30*ff*, the following may be mentioned as additional characteristics of modal auxiliaries:

(a) They are either invariable, like *must*, or close to invariable, like *would*, which, although historically it is the past tense form of *will*, is from the standpoint of present-day English in many respects an independent form. Thus modals might without too much simplification be regarded as 'modal particles' which have lost their historical connection with the inflectional paradigm of verbs.

(b) From the semantic point of view, modal auxiliaries are often specialized towards the expression of certain speech acts; *eg* giving advice (*ought to*, *should*), making promises or threats (*will*), giving orders (*must*, *can*), etc (*cf* 4.49*ff*). In this respect, they give an utterance a force somewhat similar to that of a performative (*cf* 4.7) such as *I beg you . . .*, *I promise you . . .*, etc.

These characteristics of modals are also shared in various degrees by modal idioms, semi-auxiliaries, etc. For example, *had better* and *have got to* are more closely associated with speech acts such as giving advice and orders than is the semi-auxiliary *have to*, which is capable of undergoing variation of tense and aspect.

3.51 Adding points (a) and (b) together, we may go so far as to see in modals a tendency to develop into 'pragmatic particles'. This tendency is seen in its purest form in a construction such as *May you be happy!* (*cf* 3.60), where the modal *may* is placed at the beginning of the sentence, and marks it as an expression of wish. On a similar footing, *let* (*cf* 11.26) in sentences such as *Let them come here* or *Let the world take notice* may be regarded as a pragmatic particle of imperative or optative mood. In other respects, however, *let* is totally unlike auxiliary verbs. In being followed by a pronoun in the objective case (*Let them* . . ., *Let us* . . ., etc) it assimilates to the pattern of complex transitive verbs. Clearly, in terms of its syntactic affinities, it is a main verb rather than an auxiliary.

Another example of a verb which is syntactically a main verb, although it behaves rather like a pragmatic particle, is the verb *want* when followed by *to* + infinitive in utterances such as:

> You *want to* be careful with that saw. [1]
> I *want to* tell you how much we enjoyed last night. [2]

In [1], *You want to* expresses a warning or a piece of advice; in [2] *I want to* introduces an expression of wish, which, in effect, tones down a performative verb. This pragmatic device is particularly conventionalized in informal usage, where it is pronounced /ˈwɔnə/. (Especially in AmE, a nonstandard spelling *wanna* is also current.) What makes *want to* in [1] particularly similar to a pragmatic particle is the impossibility of obtaining an equivalent meaning when the sentence is changed into the past tense or into the progressive aspect:

> ?You *are wanting to* be careful with that saw. [3]
> You *wanted to* be careful with that saw. [4]

Sentences [3] and [4] no longer have a particular advice-giving function, and have to be interpreted simply as statements about the wishes of the hearer.

Note **[a]** On the other hand, the negative of *want to* can (in informal use) have a specialized advice-giving function even when combined with the progressive of the following verb:

> Come on: you *don't want to* keep them all waiting.
> You *don't want to* be sitting around doing nothing.

[b] A better candidate than *let* for quasi-modal status, in informal English, is the 1st person imperative marker *let's* regarded simply as an unanalysed particle pronounced /lets/ (*cf* 11.26). Here the relation to a transitive construction is no longer evident, and there is an interesting resemblance to marginal modals in the ability of *let's* to form a negation either by the postposition of *not*, or by DO-support:

> *Let's not* be late for the game.
> *Don't let's* be late for the game. 〈esp BrE〉

On *let's don't* 〈AmE〉, *cf* 11.28 (iv).

The particle-like status of *let's* is also supported by the existence, in familiar AmE, of the pleonastic variant *let's us* . . ., and of the construction *let's you* . . ., in which the addition of the 2nd person pronoun indicates that *'s* is no longer associated with *us*.

The structure of verb phrases

Finite verb phrases

3.52 We have seen that in one respect the structure of the verb phrase may be described in terms of auxiliaries and main verbs, the main verb normally being the sole verb in cases where the verb phrase consists of one verb only. In another way, the structure may be represented in terms of finite and nonfinite verb words. On this basis, a finite verb phrase is a verb phrase in which the first or only word is a finite verb, the rest of the verb phrase (if any) consisting of nonfinite verbs; on the other hand, a nonfinite verb phrase contains nonfinite verb forms only.

Using the description of finite and nonfinite verb forms in 3.2, we can now distinguish finite from nonfinite verb phrases as follows:

(a) Finite verb phrases can occur as the verb phrase of independent clauses (*cf* 14.6*ff*).

(b) Finite verb phrases have tense contrast, *ie* the distinction between present and past tenses (*cf* 4.3*ff*, 4.11*ff*):

> He *is* a journalist now.
> He *worked* as a travel agent last summer.

(c) There is person concord and number concord (*cf* 10.34*ff*) between the subject of a clause and the finite verb phrase. Concord is particularly clear with the present tense of BE:

> I *am* / You *are* } here. He/She/It *is* / We/They *are* } here.

But with most full verbs overt concord is restricted to a contrast between the 3rd person singular and other persons or plural number:

> He/She/Jim *reads* / I/We/You/They *read* } the paper every morning.

With modal auxiliaries there is no overt concord at all (*cf* 3.30):

> I/You/She/We/They *can* play the cello.

(d) Finite verb phrases contain, as their first or only word, a finite verb form (as described in 3.2) which may be either an operator (*cf* 3.21) or a simple present or past form. DO-support (*cf* 3.37) is used in forming (for example) negative and interrogative constructions.

(e) Finite verb phrases have mood, which indicates the factual, nonfactual, or counterfactual status of the predication. In contrast to the 'unmarked' INDICATIVE mood, we distinguish the 'marked' moods IMPERATIVE (used to express commands and other directive speech acts; *cf* 11.24*ff*), and SUBJUNCTIVE (used to express a wish, recommendation, etc; *cf* 3.58*ff*). Both the imperative and the present subjunctive consist of the base form of the verb:

> Please *come* here and *attend* to me.

The Council requires that every member *attend* at least one meeting per year.

The five criteria listed above lead to inconsistency, in that subjunctive and imperative verb phrases are according to criteria (a) and (e) finite, whereas according to criterion (c) they are nonfinite. This inconsistency is not, however, disturbing, but reflects the fact that the finite/nonfinite distinction may be better represented as a scale of 'FINITENESS' ranging from the indicative (or 'most finite') mood, on the one hand, to the infinitive (or 'least finite') verb phrase, on the other. The imperative and subjunctive have in some respects more in common with the infinitive (a nonfinite form which like them consists of the base form, and typically expresses nonfactual meaning). There is, indeed, a tradition of regarding the infinitive as a mood of the verb. On this basis, the gradience of 'finiteness' may be represented as follows (the symbols '+', '−', etc referring to the satisfaction or nonsatisfaction of each of the criteria listed above):

	(a)	(b)	(c)	(d)	(e)	
INDICATIVE	+	+	+	+	+	(Finite)
SUBJUNCTIVE	+	?	−	−	+	
IMPERATIVE	+	−	−	?	+	
INFINITIVE	−	−	−	−	−	(Nonfinite)

Fig. 3.52 A scale of finiteness

On the query in column (b), see the discussion of the *were*-subjunctive in 3.62. The query in column (d) reflects uncertainty as to whether DO-support occurs in imperative constructions (*cf* 3.58 on the position of *not* in the subjunctive construction, and 11.30 Note [a] on *do* with the imperative).

For the sake of clarity, we will continue to make a clear-cut distinction between finite verbs (including those in the indicative, imperative, and subjunctive moods) and nonfinite verbs (including the infinitive).

A clause with a finite verb phrase as its V element is called a 'finite verb clause' or, more tersely, a 'finite clause'. Similarly, a clause with a nonfinite verb as its V element is called a 'nonfinite (verb) clause' (*cf* 14.5*ff*).

Note Verb phrases introduced by modal auxiliaries are normally classified as indicative, but it is worth pointing out that not only semantically, but syntactically, they resemble imperatives and subjunctives. They lack person and number contrast and also (to some extent) tense contrast. It follows from the lack of person and number contrast that they have no overt concord with the subject.

Nonfinite verb phrases

3.53 The infinitive ((*to*) *call*), the *-ing* participle (*calling*), and the *-ed* participle (*called*) are the nonfinite forms of the verb. Hence any phrase in which one of these verb forms is the first or only word (disregarding the infinitive marker *to*) is a nonfinite verb phrase. Such phrases do not normally occur as the verb phrase of an independent clause. Compare:

FINITE VERB PHRASES	NONFINITE VERB PHRASES
He *smokes.*	*To smoke* like that must be dangerous.
Mary *is having* a smoke.	I regret having started *to smoke.*
He *must smoke* 40 a day.	The cigars *smoked* here tend to be expensive.
You *have been smoking* all day.	That was the last cigarette *to have been smoked* by me.

Simple and complex verb phrases

3.54 The finite verb phrase is SIMPLE when it consists of only one word, which may be present, past (*cf* 3.2), imperative (*cf* 11.24), or subjunctive (*cf* 3.58):

> He *works* hard. He *worked* hard. *Work* harder!
> It is important that he *work* hard.

Except in the 3rd person singular, the present tense of all verbs apart from BE is realized by the base form of the verb: *I/you/they work hard.*

The verb phrase is COMPLEX when it consists of two or more words, as in:

> John *has worked* hard. John *should be working* hard.
> *Don't let's upset* her. They *may have been sold.*

There are four basic types of construction in a complex verb phrase:

Type A (MODAL) consists of a modal auxiliary + the base of a verb: *eg*: *must examine.*

Type B (PERFECTIVE) consists of the auxiliary HAVE + the *-ed* participle of a verb: *eg*: *has examined.* (Traditionally the term PERFECT has been frequently used instead of PERFECTIVE.)

Type C (PROGRESSIVE) consists of the auxiliary BE + the *-ing* participle of a verb: *eg*: *is examining.*

Type D (PASSIVE) consists of the auxiliary BE + the *-ed* participle of a verb: *eg*: *is examined.*

These four basic constructions also enter into combination with each other:

> AB: *may have examined*
> AC: *may be examining*
> AD: *may be examined*
> BC: *has been examining*
> BD: *has been examined*
> CD: *is being examined*
> ABC: *may have been examining*
> ABD: *may have been examined*
> ACD: *may be being examined*
> BCD: *has been being examined*
> ABCD: *may have been being examined*

In these strings the different constructions are 'telescoped' into one another. This means that combinations of the basic types A, B, etc form structures in which the nonfinite verb of the first construction also functions as the auxiliary of the second, and so forth. For example, ABD (*may have been examined*) has the following structure, where *have* is shared by A and B, and *been* is shared by B and D:

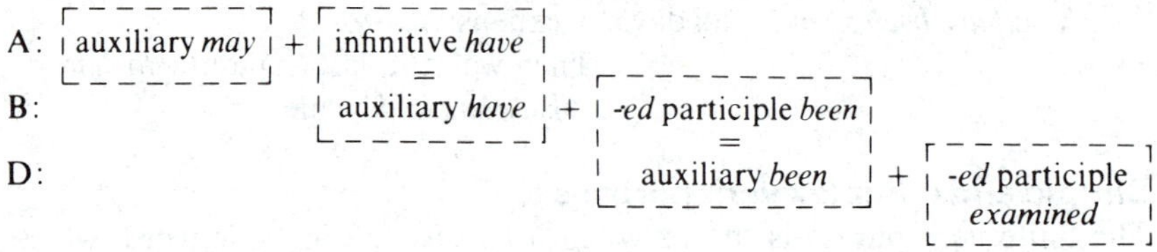

Fig. 3.54

Note *Beware* is used only in the imperative and in complex verb phrases with modal auxiliaries which have a quasi-imperative force:

> *Beware* (of) the dog.
> You must *beware* (of) what you say to her.

Simple and complex finite verb phrases

3.55 The order in which the four constructions can form combinations is indicated by the alphabetical symbols A, B, C, D, which label them. A cannot follow B, B cannot follow C or D, etc, but gaps are allowed: AC, AD, ACD, BD, etc. *Figure* 3.55 gives a graphic representation of how the finite indicative verb phrase (simple or complex) is built up in a left-to-right progression.

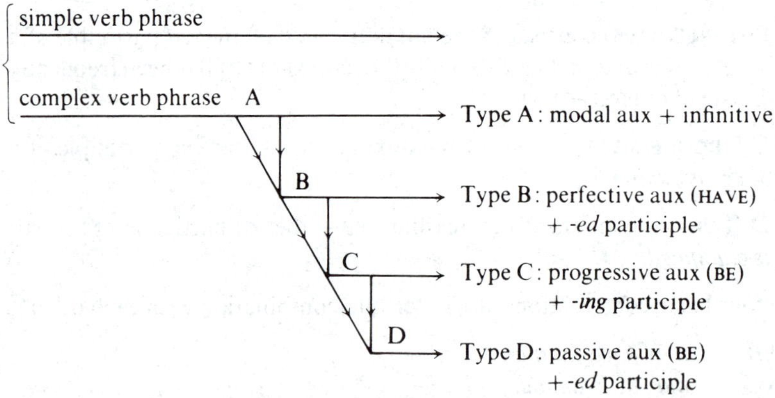

Fig. 3.55 The structure of the finite verb phrase

First comes the selection of the present or past tense of the finite verb, then the selection of none, one, two, three, or four of the complex phrase constructions as indicated by the direction of the arrows. On the whole, the more complex the verb phrase pattern is, the less commonly it occurs. Those complex phrases containing the combination CD (progressive + passive) are particularly uncommon (*cf* 3.73), but are undoubtedly acceptable as compared with sequences such as BCC (**have been being examining*) or CBD (**is having been examined*) which are not grammatical at all.

Note The rare ABCD pattern is illustrated in 2.28 Note. *Cf* also in A. N. Wilson, *The Sweets of Pimlico* (1977): '[She] must have been being pursued by [Price].'

Simple and complex nonfinite verb phrases

3.56 Unlike finite verb phrases, nonfinite verb phrases have no tense or mood distinctions (subject to the remarks on the gradience of finiteness in 3.52), and cannot occur in construction with a subject of a main clause. Contrast:

FINITE: He *was doing* it easily.
NONFINITE: *He *doing* it easily.

Since modal auxiliaries have no nonfinite forms (*cf* 3.30), they cannot occur in nonfinite verb phrases, and therefore the modal construction Type A is not available within such phrases. But the aspect and voice auxiliaries HAVE (Type B) and BE (Types C and D) suffer from no such restriction. If we relate the structure of the nonfinite verb phrase to that of the finite verb phrase, we can tabulate the eight possible combinations as in *Table* 3.56a:

Table 3.56a Nonfinite verb phrases

		INFINITIVES	PARTICIPLES
simple		*to examine*	*examining*
complex	B	*to have examined*	*having examined*
	C	*to be examining*	*[being] examining*
	D	*to be examined*	*[being] examined*
	BC	*to have been examining*	*having been examining*
	BD	*to have been examined*	*having been examined*
	CD	*to be being examined*	*[being] being examined*
	BCD	*to have been being examined* ⟨rare⟩	*having been being examined* ⟨rare⟩

Looking at the right-hand side of the *Table*, we may interpret the square brackets as follows. Whenever a phrase should theoretically begin with the auxiliary *being*, this participle is omitted. In this way, the *-ed* participle phrase *examined* is regarded as a special variant of the *-ing* participle phrase, *viz* the representative of the passive construction D. There does indeed occur a further construction *being examined*, but this is the one which combines progressive with passive meaning (CD), as in the contrast between:

the suspects *examined* by the police [not progressive]
the suspects *being examined* by the police [progressive]

(On progressive meaning in nonfinite phrases, *cf* 4.67.) Another result of the rule which omits the initial auxiliary *being* is that there are two types of nonfinite *-ing* participle phrase containing a main verb only (*examining*): one of these is progressive, and expresses the meaning characteristic of the progressive (*cf* 4.25), whereas the other is not. Contrast:

Smoking cigarettes is dangerous. [not progressive]
They caught him *smoking* cigarettes. [progressive: 'while he was smoking']

As with finite verb phrases, the combination CD is rare, and BCD is of marginal acceptability.

Note [a] The combination *being examining*, for phrase type C, is not quite impossible, as occasional examples such as the following have been attested in spontaneous conversation:

You can probably get an extension on the grounds of *being teaching*.

Being teaching here manages to draw particular attention to the progressive meaning 'on the grounds of being in the course of teaching', which the aspectually ambiguous *on the grounds of teaching* would fail to do.

[**b**] It may be helpful to illustrate various kinds of complex nonfinite verb phrase by means of the following sentences:

Table 3.56b

INFINITIVES	PARTICIPLES
We're glad *to have invited* you.	*Having invited* you, I expected you to come.
I'd like *to be working*.	*Being working* (*cf* Note [a])
I'd hate *to be questioned* about it.	When *questioned*, he denied everything.
I'm glad *to have been working*.	*Having been working* all day, I'm very tired.
He's said *to have been invited*.	*Having been invited*, he should have come.
I expected *to be being interviewed* then.	I saw her *being interviewed*.

Gradience between one and two verb phrases

3.57 In a single complex finite verb phrase, as already discussed, the order of constructions is limited to ABCD, and a similar restriction of nonfinite verb phrases to the order BCD has also been noted. If, however, a nonfinite verb phrase follows a finite one, as in certain types of verb complementation (*cf* 16.36*ff*), it is possible for the same construction to be repeated in each phrase:

We *had hoped*¦*to have finished* by then. [perfective + perfective]
I *am hoping*¦*to be seeing* her tomorrow. [progressive + progressive]

Moreover, it is possible for two constructions to occur outside their normal 'alphabetical' order so long as one construction occurs in a different verb phrase from the other:

I *was hoping*¦*to have finished* by then. (C + B)
Jackson *was believed*¦*to have been killed*. (D + BD)

In practice, however, most of the more complex possibilities, such as ABC + BCD, rarely if ever occur:

?They *must have been expecting*¦*to have been being paid* well.

The question arises as to what structures are possible when a semi-auxiliary or a catenative verb occurs in the string of verbs. For instance, should *will have to help* in *The children will have to help us* be analysed as one verb phrase, or as two? There is no clear answer to this question, since the gradient relating auxiliary to main verb functions implies a comparable gradient between a single verb phrase analysis and a multiple verb phrase analysis.

With semi-auxiliaries it is possible to repeat the same construction in such examples as:

Sarah and I *are going to be leaving* tonight. [1]
The walls *were supposed to be repainted*. [2]

But (as noted in 3.47) *are going to* in [1] is not truly progressive, and *were supposed to* in [2] is not truly passive, because these constructions do not contrast (in the relevant sense) with a nonprogressive and an active construction respectively. In other cases where the same construction is repeated, the meaning of the construction does not require this repetition:

If you'd done that, we *would have had to have arrested* you. [3]

Such verb sequences as *would have had to have arrested*, with its vacuous repetition of the past time meaning of the perfective construction, are not uncommon, but are felt to be 'illogical' or pleonastic, because their meaning is no different from that of the same sequence without the repetition: . . . *we would have had to arrest you*. The occurrence of such constructions, however, may be a mark of the intermediate status of semi-auxiliaries, which allow some syntactic duplication of constructions, but do not appear to allow for semantic duplications. It is reasonable to suggest that in [3] *would have had to have arrested* consists syntactically of two verb phrases *would have had* and *to have arrested*, but semantically of only one.

The subjunctive mood

3.58 The subjunctive in modern English is generally an optional and stylistically somewhat marked variant of other constructions, but it is not so unimportant as is sometimes suggested. There are two forms of the subjunctive, traditionally called the present and past subjunctive, although the use of these forms relates more to mood than to tense.

Terms for the two major categories of the present subjunctive are the MANDATIVE and the FORMULAIC subjunctive (*cf* 3.59*f*). These are realized, like the imperative, by the base form of the verb. Consequently, where the clause has a plural subject, there is normally no difference between the indicative and subjunctive forms. Except with BE, where the subjunctive form *be* is distinct from the indicative forms *am*, *is*, and *are*, the subjunctive is distinctive only in the third person singular:

I insist that we *reconsider* the Council's decisions. [indicative or subjunctive] [1]
I insist that the Council *reconsider* its decisions. [subjunctive] [2]
I insist that the Council's decision(s) *be* reconsidered. [subjunctive] [3]

The past subjunctive is conveniently called the *WERE*-SUBJUNCTIVE, since it survives as a distinguishable form only in the past tense of the verb BE.

Whereas the indicative form shows a contrast between *was* (1st and 3rd person singular) and *were* (plural and 2nd person singular), the subjunctive is invariably *were*, and hence is a form distinct from the indicative only in the 1st and 3rd persons singular:

> If I/he/she *was* leaving, you would have heard about it. [indicative]
> If I/he/she *were* leaving, you would have heard about it. [subjunctive]

Like the imperative verb phrase (*cf* 11.24*ff*), the subjunctive verb phrase allows few morphological or syntactic variations. As [3] above shows, a passive subjunctive is a possibility for the mandative subjunctive, as well as for the formulaic and *were*-subjunctive:

> God *be praised*! ⟨restricted use⟩
> It would be odd if she *were awarded* the first prize.

With all verbs except BE, the verb phrase is made negative by placing *not* before the subjunctive form. In the case of *be*, *not* may be placed either before or after the verb, whereas with *were* it follows it:

> It is essential that this mission *not fail*. [4]
> [Contrast the indicative variant '. . . *does not fail* . . .'; *cf* 16.72.]

> The Senate has decreed that such students {*be not* / *not be*} exempted from college dues.

> If I {*weren't* / *were not*} your best friend, you would regret that remark.

Uses of the subjunctive

The mandative subjunctive

3.59 This, the most common use of the subjunctive, occurs in subordinate *that*-clauses, and consists of the base form of the verb only. Thus there is a lack of the regular concord of the indicative mood between subject and finite verb, and there is no backshifting of tense (*cf* 14.33*f*); *ie* the present and past variants are formally indistinguishable:

> The committee {proposes / proposed} (that) Mr Day *be* elected.
> I demand(ed) that the committee *reconsider* its decision.
> His sole requirement is/was that the system *work*.

The mandative subjunctive is productive in that it can be used with any verb in a *that*-clause when the superordinate clause satisfies the requisite semantic condition, *viz* that the *that*-clause be introduced by an expression of demand, recommendation, proposal, resolution, intention, etc. This expression takes the form of a verb, an adjective, or a noun:

> They *recommend* / It is *appropriate* / We were faced with the *demand* } that this tax *be* abolished.

The following are among those expressions which commonly introduce a *that*-clause containing the mandative subjunctive:

VERBS: *decide, insist, move, order, prefer, request*
ADJECTIVES: *advisable, desirable, fitting, imperative*
NOUNS: *decision, decree, order, requirement, resolution*

Fuller lists of examples are given in 16.32, 16.72.

The mandative subjunctive is more characteristic of AmE than of BrE, where it is formal and rather legalistic in style. There are indications, however, that it is reestablishing itself in BrE, probably as a result of AmE influence. In 16.32 we present the patterns of preference in BrE and in AmE regarding the choice between the mandative subjunctive, putative *should*, and the indicative, in sentences such as:

The employees have demanded that the manager
{ *resign.* ⟨esp AmE⟩
{ *should resign.* } ⟨esp BrE⟩
{ *resigns.* }

Note [a] As example [2] suggests, the absence of DO-support, as well as the absence of an *-s* inflection, is a criterion distinguishing the present subjunctive from the present indicative:

{ Our decision is that the school *remain* closed. [subjunctive] [1]
{ Our decision is that the school *remains* closed. [indicative] [1a]
{ They insisted that we *not eat* meat. [subjunctive] [2]
{ They insisted that we *do not eat* meat. [indicative] [2a]

Thus the subjunctive can be marked as distinct from the indicative with either a singular subject, as in [1], or a plural subject, as in [2]. This makes it reasonable to say that where the base form can be analysed either as an indicative or as a subjunctive, there is a neutralization of the two moods:

Our decision is that the schools *remain* closed. [1b]

Such a view cannot be entertained, however, with the *were*-subjunctive (*cf* 3.62).

[b] The use of the subjunctive after *insist* depends on meaning. When this verb introduces an indirect statement, the indicative is used, but when it introduces an indirect directive, the subjunctive is more likely:

She *insists* that he *is* guilty of fraud. [3]
We *insist* that he *be* admitted to hospital immediately. [4]

[c] In addition to *should* and the indicative, there are other alternatives to the mandative subjunctive, notably (with some verbs) the object with infinitive construction (*cf* 16.63):

{ We ask *that the Government be circumspect.* [5]
{ We ask the Government *to be circumspect.* [6]

[d] There is a tendency in BrE to choose the subjunctive more especially when the finite verb is BE (*eg* in the passive voice), as in [4] and [5] above.

The formulaic subjunctive

3.60 Like the mandative subjunctive, the FORMULAIC SUBJUNCTIVE consists of the base form of the verb. It is used in certain set expressions chiefly in independent clauses:

Come what may, we will go ahead with our plan.
God *save* the Queen! ['May God save the Queen']
Suffice it to say that we won. ['Let it suffice . . .']
Heaven *forbid* that I should let my own parents suffer.

Be it noted that this offer was made in good faith. <formal, rather archaic>

Be that as it may, we have nothing to lose.

The force which the subjunctive conveys here, that of an expression of will, may also be conveyed by *let* or *may* (*cf* 3.51). The formulaic subjunctive tends to be formal and rather old-fashioned in style.

Other uses of the present subjunctive

3.61 Other contexts in which the present subjunctive can be used in subordinate clauses are noted in relevant sections of Chapters 14 and 15. They include:

(a) Clauses of condition and concession (*cf* 14.24):

(*Even*) *if* that *be* the official view, it cannot be accepted. <formal>

(b) Clauses of condition or negative purpose introduced by *lest* or *for fear that* (*cf* 15.48):

The President must reject this proposal, *lest* it *cause* strife and violence. <formal>

This *lest* construction is restricted to very formal usage in BrE, but is more current in AmE.

The *were*-subjunctive

3.62 The *were*-subjunctive (or past subjunctive) is hypothetical or unreal in meaning, being used in adverbial clauses introduced by such conjunctions as *if*, *as if*, *as though*, *though*, and in nominal clauses after verbs like *wish* and *suppose* (*cf* 14.24, 16.33). This subjunctive is limited to the one form *were*, and thus breaks the concord rule of the indicative verb BE in the 1st and 3rd person singular of the past tense. The indicative form *was* is substituted in less formal style:

If I *were/was* rich, I would buy you anything you wanted.

Tim always speaks quietly on the phone, *as though* he *were/was* telling a secret.

I *wish* the journey *were/was* over.

Just *suppose* everyone *were/was* to give up smoking and drinking.

The *were*-subjunctive may be regarded as something of a fossil. But it is still in common use, and particularly with clauses introduced by *as if* and *as though*, it is widely preferred to *was*. Indeed, with conditions formed by subject-operator inversion, *was* is not an acceptable alternative (cf 14.20).

Note [**a**] In the fixed phrase *as it were* ['so to speak'], however, *were* cannot be replaced by *was*; it is also normal in standard English to use *were* in the fixed phrase *If I were you*.

[**b**] As it is commonly supposed that the *were*-subjunctive always refers to circumstances contrary to fact, it is worth noting the occasional occurrence of a hypercorrect 'pseudo-subjunctive' *were* in contexts where the past time meaning of *was* seems to give the required interpretation:

The pilot appeared to deviate from his flight path to minimize the danger to people living in the town; but if this *were* his intention, he failed to communicate it to the control tower.

A similar anomalous use of *were* occasionally occurs in indirect questions:

It was difficult to tell whether the language *were* Semitic or Indo-European.

Active and passive voice

3.63 The term VOICE is used to describe the last major verb category to be considered in this chapter: that which distinguishes an active verb phrase (*eg*: *ate*) from a passive one (*eg*: *was eaten*). We have left this topic to the end of the chapter for two reasons: first, the passive construction, when it occurs, appears in final position in the verb phrase (*cf* Type D, 3.55), and second, voice is a category which, as we saw in 2.21, concerns not only verb phrases, but other constituents in the clause, and therefore points to connections between this chapter and sections in later chapters (esp 16.26*ff*, 18.32) where the contrast between active and passive must be reconsidered in a larger context.

Voice defined

3.64 Voice is a grammatical category which makes it possible to view the action of a sentence in either of two ways, without change in the facts reported:

The butler *murdered* the detective. [ACTIVE] [1]
~ The detective *was murdered* by the butler. [PASSIVE] [2]

As we see from [1] and [2], the active–passive relation involves two grammatical levels: the verb phrase, and the clause. In the former, a passive verb phrase (*ie* one containing a construction of Type D) contrasts with an active verb phrase, which is simply defined as one which does not contain that construction. For example:

Table 3.64

	ACTIVE		PASSIVE
present:	*kisses*	~	*is kissed*
past:	*kissed*	~	*was kissed*
modal:	*may kiss*	~	*may be kissed*
perfective:	*has kissed*	~	*has been kissed*
progressive:	*is kissing*	~	*is being kissed*
modal + perfective:	*may have kissed*	~	*may have been kissed*
modal + progressive:	*may be kissing*	~	*may be being kissed*
perfective + progressive:	*has been kissing*	~	*has been being kissed*
modal + perfective + progressive:	*may have been kissing*	~	*may have been being kissed*

In the verb phrase, the difference between the two voice categories is that the passive adds a form of the auxiliary BE followed by the past participle (*-ed* participle) of the main verb.

The active–passive correspondence

3.65 In addition, at the clause level, changing from the active to the passive involves rearrangement of two clause elements, and one addition (*cf* 2.21). (a) The active subject becomes the passive AGENT; (b) the active object becomes the passive subject; and (c) the preposition *by* is introduced before the agent. The prepositional phrase (AGENT *BY*-PHRASE) of passive sentences is generally an optional element (but *cf* 3.71). The active–passive correspondence for a monotransitive verb (*cf* 2.16) with an object (typically a noun phrase) can be seen diagrammatically as in *Fig*. 3.65:

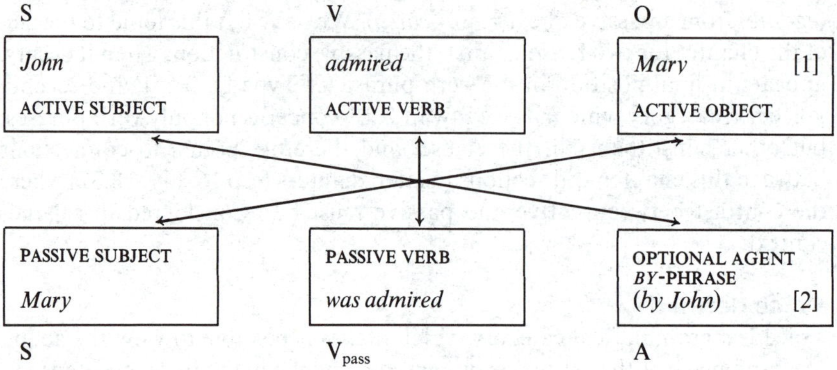

Fig 3.65 The active–passive correspondence

Alternatively, the active–passive correspondence can be expressed by this formula:

noun phrase_1 + active verb phrase + noun phrase_2
∼ noun phrase_2 + passive verb phrase + (*by* noun phrase_1)

The terms 'subject' and 'object' in *Fig* 3.65 are used here, as in 2.13 and 10.7, to refer to elements with a particular structural function in the clause: *eg* the subject has concord with the verb phrase, and contains a subjective rather than objective case pronoun. Thus certain changes apart from those represented in [1] and [2] may have to take place in changing a sentence from active to passive (*cf* 3.70):

The men *respect her*. [3]
∼ *She is* respected by the men. [4]

But although the corresponding active and passive sentences appear to be radically different, the relations of meaning between their elements remain the same: for example, [1] has the same truth value as [2], and [3] has the same truth value as [4]. In *John helped Mary* and *Mary was helped by John*, *John* is in both cases the 'performer of the action', even though structurally, *John* has a very different position and function in each.

Note [**a**] Corresponding active and passive sentences do not, however, always have the same truth value (*cf* 3.72).
[**b**] We distinguish terminologically the agent, as defined above (and in grammatical tradition), from the agentive, which is a semantic role (*cf* 10.19) often assumed by the subject of an active sentence or by the agent of a passive sentence (*cf* 9.50).

The passive auxiliaries: *be* and *get*

3.66 The passive auxiliary is normally *be*. Its only serious contender is *get*, which however is not, by most syntactic criteria, an auxiliary at all (*cf* 3.22*ff*).

Moreover, *get* tends to be limited to constructions without an expressed animate agent:

> The cat *got run over* (by a bus).   James *got beaten* last night.

Get with an animate agent is not, however, unknown:

> James *got caught* (by the police).

The *get*-passive is avoided in formal style, and even in informal English it is far less frequent than the *be*-passive. Further examples are:

> The house is *getting rebuilt*. [1]
> Such criticisms will *get treated* with the contempt they deserve. [2]
> This story eventually *got translated* into English. [3]

Get is much more common as a 'resulting copula' (*cf* 16.21*ff*) in sentences like *My mother is getting old*, and it may be best analysed as such in sentences which look superficially like passives, but which could not be expanded by an agent (*cf* 3.77):

> We are *getting bogged down* in all sorts of problems. ⟨informal⟩ [4]
> I have to *get dressed* before eight o'clock. [='dress'] [5]
> I don't want to *get mixed up* with the police again. ⟨informal⟩ [6]
> Your argument *gets* a bit *confused* here. [7]

Similarly *get bored*, *get tired*, *get* (*very*) *excited*, *get lost*, etc. *Get* is a dynamic conclusive verb (*cf* 4.33*ff*), and the participles in these sentences are stative (*eg*: *dressed* means 'in a state of wearing clothes', as in *Jane is already dressed*). Hence the meaning of such sentences is predictable if they are regarded as *SVC* sentences with *get* as main verb and the participle (with its modifiers if any) as complement, as suggested by this exchange:

> A: I [S] 'm [V] completely confused [C].
> B: Yes, I [S] 'm getting [V] confused [C], as well [A].

It is important, therefore, to draw a distinction between the passive sentences [1–3] and the copular sentences [4–7], which we may call PSEUDO-PASSIVE (*cf* 3.77). At the same time, there is an affinity between these sentence types, and this is evident when we consider the meaning of the *get*-passive, which, like the copular *get*, puts the emphasis on the subject rather than the agent, and on what happens to the subject as a result of the event. Compare *He got taught a lesson* ['it served him right'] with:

> He $\left\{ \begin{array}{c} \textit{was} \\ \textit{?got} \end{array} \right\}$ *taught* a lesson on the subjunctive (by our new teacher).

It is presumably because of the emphasis which *get* places on the subject referent's condition (usually an unfavourable condition) that the agent is less usual with a *get*-passive. This same emphasis may account in part for the fact that the *get*-passive often reflects an unfavourable attitude towards the action:

> How did that window *get opened*?

typically implies 'It should have been left shut!'

Note [**a**] The *get*-passive provides a convenient way of avoiding the passive with *be* in cases where there is a potential confusion between the normal passive interpretation and that of the 'statal passive' (*cf* 3.77). Thus the ambiguity between stative and dynamic meaning in *The chair was broken* is eliminated in *The chair got broken*.

[**b**] The idiomatic expression *get started* is anomalous, in that *start* cannot be treated as a transitive verb in this context:

How soon can we *get started* on the swimming pool?

This idiom appears to be closely related to the causative use of *get*, *eg* in:

How soon can we *get* $\left\{\begin{matrix}\text{work}\\ \text{ourselves}\end{matrix}\right\}$ started on the pool? (*cf* 16.54)

Compare a similar pseudo-passive construction with *be* (*cf* 3.77 Note [a]).

[**c**] Apart from *get*, verbs in pseudo-passive sentences include *become*, *grow*, and *seem* (*cf* 16.21, 16.23).

Voice constraints

3.67 Although it is a general rule that transitive verb sentences can be either active or passive, there are a number of exceptions where the active (transitive) and passive sentences are not in systematic correspondence. We will distinguish five kinds of 'voice constraint' associated respectively with the verb (3.68*f*), the object (3.70), the agent (3.71), meaning (3.72), and frequency of use (3.73).

Verb constraints

3.68 (a) ACTIVE ONLY

There are greater restrictions on verbs occurring in the passive than on verbs occurring in the active. In addition to copular and intransitive verbs, which having no object cannot take the passive, some transitive verbs, called 'middle' verbs, do not occur at least in some senses in the passive (*cf* 10.14); for example:

They *have* a nice house.
He *lacks* confidence.
The auditorium *holds* 5000 people.
The dress *becomes* her.
John *resembles* his father.
Will this *suit* you?

All these belong to the stative class of verbs of 'being' and 'having' (*cf* 4.31). But other stative verbs, such as those of volition or attitude, can easily occur in the passive. Contrast:

The coat does not fit you. ~ *You are not fitted by the coat.
The police want him. ~ He is wanted by the police.

(b) PASSIVE ONLY

Conversely, with some verbs and verb constructions only the passive is possible (*cf* 16.50):

John was $\left\{\begin{matrix}\text{said}\\ \text{reputed}\end{matrix}\right\}$ to be a good teacher.

~ *They $\left\{\begin{matrix}\text{said}\\ \text{reputed}\end{matrix}\right\}$ him to be a good teacher.

Other examples are *be born* (with an irregular past participle), and *be drowned* (in cases where no agent is implied):

He was born in Tübingen. ~ ?His mother bore him in Tübingen.

The wanted man fell into the water and was drowned. ≁ . . . and someone drowned him.

Prepositional verbs

3.69 In English, prepositional verbs (*cf* 16.5*ff*) can often occur in the passive, but not so freely as in the active. These prepositional verbs are verbal idioms consisting of a lexical verb followed by a preposition, such as *look at*. Compare the following sentences, in which [1a] and [2a] contain prepositional verbs, whereas [1b] and [2b] contain the same words in nonidiomatic use:

The engineers *went* very carefully *into* { the problem. [1a]
{ the tunnel. [1b]

~ { The problem / ?*The tunnel } *was* very carefully *gone into* by the engineers.

They eventually *arrived at* { the expected result. [2a]
{ the splendid stadium. [2b]

~ { The expected result / ?*The splendid stadium } was eventually *arrived at*.

In these sentences it is clear that the difference in acceptability can be stated in terms of concrete/abstract passive subjects. It is only in the abstract, figurative use that *go into*, *arrive at*, *look into*, and many other expressions accept the passive.

With some ingenuity, however, one may construct contexts where such verbal expressions will occur in the passive even where they are not used abstractly and idiomatically, especially in a coordinate construction:

This private drawer of mine has been *gone into* and rummaged so many times that it is totally disarranged.

Thus the distinction between prepositional verbs and nonidiomatic combinations of verb and preposition does not entirely determine the possibility of a passive. Rather, there is a scale of 'cohesion' between verb and preposition, which will be analysed later, in 16.12*ff*, when we come to examine prepositional verbs in more detail.

Object constraints

3.70 Transitive verbs can be followed either by phrasal or by clausal objects (*cf* 15.3*ff*, 16.30*ff*). With clauses as objects, however, the passive transformation is to a greater or lesser degree restricted in use:

(A) Noun phrase as object:

John loved *Mary*. ~ *Mary* was loved (by John).

(B) Clause as object:

(i) Finite clause:

John thought (*that*) *she was attractive*.

~ ?**That she was attractive* was thought (by John).

(ii) Nonfinite clause:

(a) infinitive:

John hoped *to meet her*. ~ **To meet her* was hoped (by John).

(b) participle:

John enjoyed *seeing her*.

~ *?*Seeing her* was enjoyed (by John).

The passive often becomes acceptable, however, particularly when the object is a finite clause, if the clausal object is extraposed and replaced by the anticipatory pronoun *it* (*cf* 16.34, 16.72*f*, 16.83, 18.33):

It was thought *that she was attractive*.
?*It* was hoped *to meet her*.

or if the subject of the object clause is made the subject of a passive superordinate clause (*cf* 16.50*f*, 18.36), as in:

She was thought *to be attractive*.

The construction with anticipatory *it* never occurs with participle clauses as subject, and is only sometimes acceptable with infinitive clauses (*cf* 16.38):

It was desired *to have the report delivered here*.

(Even then, the acceptability of this construction may be criticized on grounds of style.)

Coreference between a subject and a noun phrase object blocks the passive correspondence. This constraint occurs with (a) reflexive pronouns, (b) reciprocal pronouns, and (c) possessive pronouns when coreferential to the subject:

(a) John could see {Paul / *himself*} in the mirror.

~ {Paul / **Himself*} could be seen in the mirror.

(b) We could hardly see *each other* in the fog.

~ **Each other* could hardly be seen in the fog.

(c) The woman shook {my hand. / *her head*.}

~ {My hand / ?**Her head*} was shaken by the woman.

Note [**a**] The passive of the sentence with a reciprocal pronoun can be made acceptable if the pronoun is split into two parts as follows:

Each could hardly be seen by the other. (*cf* 6.31)

[**b**] Since reflexive and reciprocal pronouns are objective case replacements, we would in any case not expect them to take subject position in a passive sentence, or for that matter in any other sentence (*cf* 3.65).

[**c**] The passive is not possible for many idioms in which the verb and the object form a close unit:

The ship set sail. ~ *Sail was set.
We changed buses. ~ *Buses were changed.

Agent constraints

3.71 Unlike the active subject, the agent *by*-phrase is generally optional. In fact approximately four out of five English passive sentences have no expressed agent. This omission occurs especially when the agent is irrelevant or unknown, as in:

The Prime Minister has often *been criticized* recently.

or where the agent is left out as redundant:

Jack fought Michael last night, and Jack *was beaten*.

An agent phrase *by Michael* would clearly not be necessary or even fully acceptable in this context.

Since the agent phrase is usually left unexpressed, the identity of the agent may be irrecoverable, and it may be impossible to postulate a unique active clause corresponding to the passive one:

Order *had been restored* without bloodshed.

~ {Colonel Laval (?) / The administration (?) / The army (?)} *had restored* order without bloodshed.

Note In some sentences, the agent is not optional; *eg*:

{ The music *was followed* by a short interval. [1]
*The music *was followed*. [2] }

{ The rebels *were actuated* by both religious and political motives. [3]
*The rebels *were actuated*. [4] }

However, the nonoccurrence of the agentless sentences [2] and [4] may be due not so much to grammatical or lexical restriction, as to the fact that without the agent, the sentence becomes informationally vacuous. (In this connection, [2] may be contrasted with *We're being followed*.)

Meaning constraints

3.72 We cannot assume that matching active and passive sentences always have the same propositional meaning. The difference of order brought about by changing an active sentence into the passive or vice versa may well make a difference not only in emphasis (*cf* 18.3*ff*, 18.11*ff*), but also to the scope of negatives and quantifiers (*cf* 2.54*f*):

Every schoolboy *knows* one joke at least. [1]
~ One joke at least *is known* by every schoolboy. [2]

The most likely interpretation of [1] is quite different from the most likely interpretation of [2]: whereas [1] favours the reading 'Each schoolboy knows at least some joke or other', [2] favours the reading 'There is one particular joke which is known to every schoolboy'.

Moreover, a shift of modal meaning may accompany a shift of voice in verb phrases containing modal auxiliaries (*cf* 4.52):

John cannot do it.
~ It cannot be done (by John).

In the active, *can* here will normally be interpreted as expressing ability, whereas in the passive it is interpreted as expressing possibility. Even when it might be argued that *can* retains the same meaning of ability in both active and passive, a shift of meaning is detectable:

John can't be taught. ['It's impossible to teach him' OR 'He is unable to learn']
~ She can't teach John. ['She is unable to teach John']

Examples with other modal auxiliaries are:

{ Every one of them must be reprimanded.
['Every one of them is to blame']
~ You must reprimand every one of them.
['It's your duty to do so']

{ Why wouldn't Miranda ride the grey mare?
['Why did Miranda refuse?']
~ Why wouldn't the grey mare be ridden by Miranda?
['Why did the mare refuse?']

Note [**a**] The shift from active to passive may change the meaning not only of a modal construction, but also of the perfective aspect:

Winston Churchill has twice visited Harvard. [3]
Harvard has twice been visited by Winston Churchill. [4]

It has been claimed that the active sentence [3] can only be appropriately used in the lifetime of Churchill, since the subject of the sentence determines the interpretability of the perfective in terms of a period of time leading up to the present (*cf* 4.20). The passive sentence [4], according to this claim, could appropriately be said now, after Churchill's death, since Harvard University is still in existence. However, speakers have differing intuitions on this matter.

[**b**] Some difference between the meaning of an active sentence and its passive counterpart has also been noted in examples such as [5] and [6], where both subject and object of the active sentence are generic (*cf* 5.52*ff*):

Beavers build dams. ~ ?Dams are built by beavers. [5]
Excessive drinking causes high blood pressure. ~ ?High blood pressure is caused by excessive drinking. [6]

This difference, which is a difference of preferred interpretation only, arises from the fact that in subject position, a generic phrase tends to be interpreted universally, while in object or agent position, this universal meaning disappears. Thus the subject *beavers* in [5] is likely to mean approximately 'all beavers', while *dams* is likely to have a similarly generic meaning in the passive counterpart.

Frequency constraints

3.73 To the structural and semantic restrictions mentioned in the preceding sections, we may add 'frequency constraints'. There is a notable difference in the frequency with which the active and passive voices are used. The active is generally by far the more common, but there is considerable variation among individual text types. The passive has been found to be as much as ten times as frequent in one text as in another. The major stylistic factor determining frequency seems to be related to the distinction between informative and imaginative prose, rather than to a difference between spoken and written English. The passive is generally more commonly used in informative than in imaginative writing, and is notably more frequent in the objective, impersonal style of scientific articles and news reporting.

As might be expected, the passive becomes very much rarer in combinations with other complex verb constructions (*eg* Types AD, BD, CD, ACD in 3.54). This rarity is extreme in the combinations BCD or ABCD ('perfective progressive passive' and 'modal perfective progressive passive'), perhaps in part because of an avoidance of the awkwardness of the *be being* sequence:

The Conservatives *won* the election. [1]
~ The election *was won* by the Conservatives. [2]

But:

The Conservatives *have not been winning* seats lately. [3]
~ (?)Seats *have not been being won* by the Conservatives lately. ⟨rare⟩ [4]

As the passive paraphrase of [3], [4] offers no particular difficulties of interpretation. But it is likely to be replaced in actual use by the simpler construction *Seats have not been won by the Conservatives lately*, from which it differs little in meaning (*cf* 4.38, 4.40 Note [a]).

The passive gradient

3.74 The purely formal definition of the passive, *viz* that the clause contains the construction *be* (or *get*) + *-ed* participle, is very broad, and would include, for example, all the following sentences:

This violin *was made* by my father. [1]
This conclusion *is* hardly *justified* by the results. [2]
Coal *has been replaced* by oil. [3]
This difficulty *can be avoided* in several ways. [4]

- -

We *are encouraged* to go on with the project. [5]
Leonard *was interested* in linguistics. [6]
The building *is* already *demolished.* [7]
The modern world *is getting* ['becoming'] *more highly industrialized and mechanized.* [8]

But taking account of the verb's function and meaning, we prefer to consider only those above the broken line as passive. Those below the line, [5–8], do not have a clear correspondence with an active verb phrase or active clause, and are increasingly remote from the 'ideal' passive of [1], which can be placed in direct correspondence with a unique active counterpart. The variety of relationships displayed by [1–8] may well be regarded as points on a gradient or scale running from [1] to a sentence such as [9], which is clearly to be analysed as having an adjectival complement following a copular verb:

My uncle $\left\{\begin{array}{l}\text{was}\\ \text{got}\\ \text{seemed}\end{array}\right\}$ (very) tired. [9]

The possibility of inserting *very* confirms the adjectival status of *tired.*

Central passives

3.75 Examples [1–4] can be called 'central' or 'true' passives. Sentences [1] and [2] have a direct active–passive relation. The difference between the two is that the former has a personal, and the latter a nonpersonal agent (*cf* 9.50):

~ My father *made* this violin. [1a]
~ The results hardly *justify* this conclusion. [2a]

Sentence [3] brings some unclarity about the nature of the active counterpart. There are two possible active counterparts, depending on the interpretation of the *by*-phrase:

~ Oil *has replaced* coal. [3a′]
~ (People in many countries) *have replaced* coal by oil. [3a″]

(The supplied active subject, here and below, is given in parentheses.)

In the former case, the *by*-phrase has been interpreted as an agent phrase corresponding to the active subject, but in the latter case, the *by*-phrase has been given an instrumental interpretation (*by* = *with*). Similarly ambiguous expressions are *be confronted by/with* and *be impressed by/with*.

Sentence [4] exemplifies the most common type of passive, that which has no expressed agent ('agentless passive'), and so leaves the subject of the active counterpart undetermined.

Semi-passives

3.76 Sentences [5] and [6] represent a 'mixed' or semi-passive class whose members have both verbal and adjectival properties (*cf* 7.15*ff*). They are verb-like in having active analogues:

{ We are encouraged to go on with the project. [5]
{ ~ (The results) encourage us to go on with the project. [5a]

{ Leonard was interested in linguistics. [6]
{ ~ Linguistics interested Leonard. [6a]

On the other hand, their adjectival properties include the possibility of:

(a) coordinating the participle with an adjective;
(b) modifying the participle with *quite*, *rather*, *more*, etc;
(c) replacing *be* by a lexical copular verb such as *feel* or *seem*:

We *feel rather* encouraged *and content* . . .
Leonard *seemed very* interested in *and keen on* linguistics.

To these we may add the fact that [5] and [6] are stative rather than dynamic. This in itself does not exclude a passive analysis, for there are stative passives as well as dynamic passives, as is already illustrated by [2]: *This conclusion is hardly justified by the results.* It does, however, tilt the scales in favour of an adjectival analysis, since all participial adjectives have a stative meaning, whereas corresponding verbs usually do not.

In such adjectival uses of the past participle, it is rare to have a *by*-phrase expressing the agent, but blends such as the following do occur:

I feel rather let down *by his indifference.*
She seems extremely elated *by her success.*

Even *-ed* adjectives which have no corresponding active infinitive or finite verb forms may occasionally have agent *by*-phrases:

We were *unimpressed* by his attempts.
~ { *His attempts *unimpressed* us.
~ { His attempts did not impress us.

Evidently the ability to take an agent *by*-phrase cannot be regarded as diagnostic of the passive construction. (If further confirmation is needed, it will be found in noun phrases where the agent *by*-phrase occurs as postmodifier: *poems by Wordsworth.*)

There are, in fact, several prepositions which can introduce agent-like phrases; notably *about*, *at*, *over*, *to*, and *with* (*cf* 9.49*ff*, 16.69):

We were all worried *about the complication.* [10]
~ The complication worried us all. [10a]
I was a bit surprised *at her behaviour.* [11]
~ Her behaviour surprised me a bit. [11a]
You won't be bothered *with me* any more. [12]
~ I won't bother you any more. [12a]
This edition was not known *to earlier scholars.* [13]
~ Earlier scholars did not know (of) this edition. [13a]

But just as a *by*-phrase (as noted in 3.75) may cooccur, in an instrumental function, with an active subject, so these agent-like phrases may sometimes cooccur with an active subject, and so be interpreted ambiguously when in the passive:

Leonard was interested *in linguistics.*
~ (Someone) interested Leonard *in linguistics.*

There is thus no strong reason to treat such prepositional phrases, whether introduced by *by* or some other preposition, as diagnostic of the passive voice.

Note [**a**] Semi-passive constructions such as those of [10–13] can have a clause as complementation (*cf* 16.71):

I was surprised *that the food was so good.* [14]

In such cases, the clausal complementation can also be seen as analogous to an agent; *cf*:

~ *That the food was so good* surprised me. [14a]

[**b**] *Be known* (*to*) differs from other examples of the semi-passive in lacking the causative feature of *be worried* (*about*), *be surprised* (*at*), etc, and in not taking modifiers like *quite* and *rather*:

I was rather surprised at her methods.

but:

*Her methods are rather known to me.

(On the other hand, the *be known* (*to*) construction can be intensified by *well*; but the sequence *well known* can be hyphenated, and is perhaps a compound here.)

Pseudo-passives

3.77 Finally, [7] and [8] have neither an active transform nor a possibility of agent addition:

The building is already demolished. [7]
The modern world is getting more highly industrialized and mechanized. [8]

Such examples may be called 'pseudo-passives', since it is chiefly only their superficial form of verb + *-ed* participle that recommends them for consideration as passives. In terms of meaning, the active sentence corresponding to [7] is not [7a′], but [7a″]:

?*(Someone) already demolishes the building. [7a′]
(Someone) has already demolished the building. [7a″]

That is, *is demolished* denotes a resultant state: it refers, like the perfective, to a state resulting from the demolition, rather than to the act of demolition itself. Such a construction has been termed a 'statal passive'. In this connection, we note that an ambiguity is evident particularly in the past tense:

In 1972, the Democrats were defeated.

On the dynamic (central passive) reading, this means 'Someone defeated the Democrats'; on the statal (copular) reading, it means 'The Democrats were in a state of having been defeated'. The first reading can be singled out by adding the agent phrase:

In 1972, the Democrats were defeated by the Republicans.

The first (passive) reading can also be picked out if we change the verb to the progressive aspect:

In 1972, the Democrats were being defeated.

Neither of these tests apply to the statal passive construction because it is essentially copular, the verb *be* in this case being the copula rather than the passive auxiliary.

Similarly, the participles in [8] have adjectival values: compare *industrialized* with *industrial* and *mechanized* with *mechanical*, and note that these *-ed* words can be used adjectivally in phrases like *the industrialized world*. Moreover, no 'performer' can be conceived of: an *industrialized world* is simply a world that has reached a state of industrialization. Once we come to examples like this, we are firmly in the territory of *be* as a copula replaceable by other copular verbs such as *become*, *feel*, *seem*, *remain*, etc: *She became enraged*, *I felt cheated*, etc. Here the *-ed* word is a complement, and therefore adjectival.

Note **[a]** There is a pseudo-passive construction with intransitive verbs of motion or completion in which the participle is active rather than passive in meaning:

Why *are* all those cars *stopped* at the corner?
By the time she got there, her friend *was gone*.
I'*ll* soon *be finished* with this job.

With most intransitive verbs, this construction has been superseded by the perfective construction, which is almost synonymous. Compare *Mary has come* with the archaic *Mary is come*. The somewhat melodramatic imperative *Be gone* may be written as a single word *Begone*, and is sometimes, like *Beware* (*cf* 3.54 Note), treated as an infinitive: *I told them to begone from my sight*.

[b] A similar pseudo-passive is used with verbs of posture:

Grandfather *was sat* in the rocking chair.
I'*ve been stood* here for about ten minutes.

In this case, the construction is largely synonymous with, though less common than, the progressive construction: *was sitting*, *'ve been standing*, etc.

[c] The 'notional passive' with an intransitive active verb, as in *The clock winds up at the back* ['can be wound up'] is discussed under word-formation (App I.54).

Summary

3.78 Summarizing the passive gradient as exemplified in 3.74, we may set up the following classes:

I Central passives
  (a) With expressed agents: [1], [2], [3]
  (b) Without expressed agents: [4]

II Semi-passives: [5], [6]

III Pseudo-passives
  (a) With 'current' copular verbs *be*, *feel*, *look*, etc: [7]
  (b) With 'resulting' copular verbs *get*, *become*, *grow*, etc: [8]
  (*cf* 16.21–23 for the terms 'current' and 'resulting'.)

Bibliographical note

For general treatments of the English verb, see Palmer (1974); Allen (1966); Joos (1964); Huddleston (1976a).

On verb inflections, see Hidalgo (1967); Quirk (1970a).

On reduced and contracted forms, see Black (1977); Brown and Millar (1980); Cheshire (1981); Forsheden (1983); Jørgensen (1979); Zwicky (1970); Zwicky & Pullum (1983).

On tense and aspect, see Comrie (1976); Dušková (1974); Nehls (1975, 1980); Tedeschi and Zaenen (1981); also further references in the Bibliographical Note to Ch. 4.

On the progressive aspect in particular, see Adamczewski (1978); Dušková (1971b); Halliday (1980); Ljung (1980).

On auxiliaries in relation to main verbs, see Huddleston (1974, 1980); Langacker (1978); Ney (1981); Pullum and Wilson (1977); Reich (1968); Ross (1969); Twaddell (1965).

On specific verbs and special cases of auxiliary or main verb classification, see Chapin (1973); Collins (1978); Crowell (1959); Haegeman (1980); Jacobsson (1974, 1980); Quirk and Duckworth (1961); Seppänen (1977); Svartvik and Wright (1977); Tottie (1971, 1978).

On modal auxiliary verbs, see Greenbaum (1974); Kalogjera (1967); Lee (1978); Melchers (1980); Raynaud (1977); also further references in the Bibliographical Note to Ch. 4. The frequency data in 3.39 is derived from Coates (1983) and Hofland and Johansson (1982).

On the subjunctive, see Haegeman (forthcoming b); Jacobsson (1975); Turner (1980).

On the imperative, see Levin (1979); Stein (1976); also further references in the Bibliographical Note to Ch. 8.

On the passive voice, see Bennett (1980); Bolinger (1975b, 1978c); Buyssens (1979); Couper-Kuhlen (1979); Davidson (1980); Dušková (1971a, 1972); Granger (1981); Mihailovič (1967); Poldauf (1969); Stein (1979); Svartvik (1966). For frequency data, see Svartvik (1966) and Granger (1981).

Other relevant studies include Greenbaum (1977a); Jacobsson (1965); Wonder (1970).

For studies relating more particularly to meaning in the verb phrase, consult the Bibliographical Note to Ch. 4.

4 The semantics of the verb phrase

Introduction

4.1 In this chapter we examine the semantics of the verb phrase, and in particular of the finite verb phrase. We turn our attention to the meanings associated with tense, aspect, and the modal auxiliaries, having already dealt with the morphology and syntax of these categories in 3.52–7. The chapter will conclude with some observations on the meanings of verbs on the gradient between auxiliaries and main verbs, and of nonfinite verb phrases.

It is unfortunate that the terminology used in discussing the verb phrase often tempts us to confuse distinctions of grammatical form with distinctions of meaning. This applies to terms such as 'aspect', 'perfective', 'progressive', and 'modality', which, as names for grammatical categories, also reflect their typical meanings. But preeminently it applies to the terms 'present' and 'past' used in referring to tenses of the verb. The English present tense, for instance, usually, but by no means always, signifies present time (*cf* 4.5–10). The association between present tense and present time is strong enough to make the term 'present tense' plausibly appropriate, and at the same time, potentially misleading.

Time, tense, and the verb

4.2 It is therefore wise to begin by distinguishing three different levels on which the terms 'present' and 'past' can be interpreted. First, in abstraction from any given language, time can be thought of as a line (theoretically, of infinite length) on which is located, as a continuously moving point, the present moment. Anything ahead of the present moment is in the future, and anything behind it is in the past:

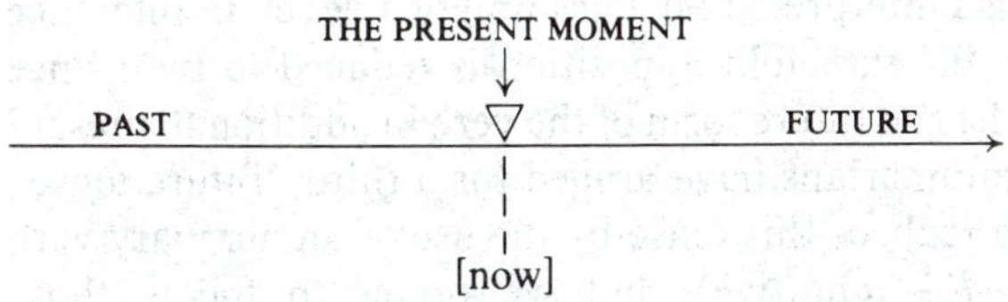

Fig 4.2a

This is an interpretation of past, present, and future on a REFERENTIAL level. But in relating this view of time to language and, more precisely, to the meaning of verbs, it is useful to reformulate the threefold distinction such that 'present' is defined in an inclusive rather than in an exclusive way: something is defined as 'present' if it has existence at the present moment, allowing for the possibility that its existence may also stretch into the past and into the future. Hence *Paris stands on the River Seine* may be correctly said to describe a 'present' state of affairs, even though this state of affairs has also obtained for numerous centuries in the past, and may well exist for an indefinite period in the future:

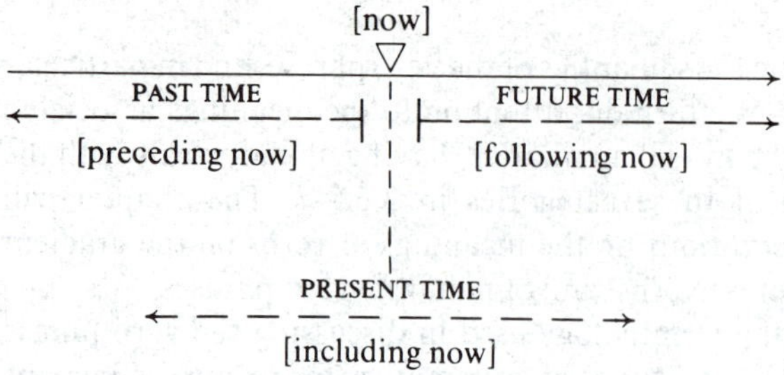

Fig 4.2b

On this second, or SEMANTIC level of interpretation, then, 'present' is the most general and unmarked category. In contrast to [1], which is a generic statement applicable to present, past, and future, [2] is a more limited statement, suggesting that the albatross, like the dodo, is extinct:

Albatrosses *are* large birds. [1]
Albatrosses *were* large birds. [2]

The author of [2] does not commit himself to the continuation of the past state of affairs it describes into the present. The same applies to sentences of more limited time span:

John spends a lot of money. [true for past, present, and future]
John spent a lot of money. [true for past only]

Note Nevertheless, a sentence like [2] does not exclude the possibility of such a continuation. It is possible to assert, without inconsistency: *Albatrosses were, are, and always will be large birds.*

The present tense as 'nonpast'

4.3 In 4.2 we distinguished past, present and future on a referential level, and also on a semantic level. It remains only to mention the familiar fact that 'present' and 'past' are also interpreted on a grammatical level, in reference to tense. Here, however, the threefold opposition is reduced to two, since morphologically English has no future form of the verb in addition to present and past forms. Some grammarians have argued for a third, 'future tense', maintaining that English realizes this tense by the use of an auxiliary verb construction (such as *will* + infinitive): but we prefer to follow those grammarians who have treated tense strictly as a category realized by verb inflection. In this grammar, then, we do not talk about the FUTURE as a formal category: what we do say is that certain grammatical constructions are capable of expressing the semantic category of FUTURE TIME (*cf* 4.41*ff*).

Some grammarians have gone further, avoiding the term 'present' in reference to tense, and preferring 'nonpast'. The terms PRESENT TENSE and PAST TENSE have this justification: that the tenses they name typically have reference to present and past time respectively:

She *is* quite well today. Yesterday she *was* sick.

But there is also some morphological justification for treating the present as the unmarked tense, since it is often realized by the base or uninflected form of the verb (compare the present tense *I need a rest* with the past tense *I needed a rest*). There is also a semantic justification, to the extent that the present tense may be used to express not only present but future time. Contrast:

Yesterday {*is / was} Sunday.	Today is Monday. Tomorrow is Tuesday.

Notice we can use the present tense in questioning someone about a future activity as well as about a present one:

*What are you doing yesterday?	{What are you doing today? What are you doing tomorrow?

And we can use the present form of the modal with future meaning, but not with past meaning:

*I can help you yesterday.	{I can help you today. I can help you tomorrow.

We have good reason for arguing, therefore, that the semantic triad of past, present, and future is unequally separated into past and nonpast categories for the purposes of tense. Tradition and familiarity favour the retention of the label 'present' in place of 'nonpast'. But this concession places upon us the responsibility of continually maintaining a clear distinction between present and past TENSE, on the one hand, and present and past TIME on the other.

Situation types: stative and dynamic verb senses

4.4 The semantic categories of past, present, and future apply, in fact, not so much to time, as to happenings which take place in time, and which are denoted by verbs. The point may be made in the following way:

Mary *hoped* for success.	REFERS TO	a *past hope* of Mary.
Peter *knows* a great deal.	REFERS TO	Peter's *present knowledge*.
The home team *will be defeated*.	REFERS TO	*a future defeat* of the home team.

Note that the same concept can be expressed both by a verb and by an abstract noun. Such words denote phenomena existing in time, variously called 'states', 'events', 'actions', 'processes', 'activities', etc. Regrettably there is no single generic term for such 'verb-denoted phenomena', but we shall distinguish different categories under the title of SITUATION TYPES (*cf* further 4.27*ff*).

Pursuing the analogy between nouns and verbs further, we observe that just as an abstract noun referring to an event can be singular or plural, so the corresponding verb can be 'pluralized' through the use of frequency adverbials:

A SINGLE EVENT	A PLURALITY OF EVENTS
Vesuvius *erupted* in 77 AD. = In 77 AD there was *an eruption* of Vesuvius.	The country *was invaded* many times. = There were *many invasions* of the country.

Such verbs as *erupt* and *invade* are therefore comparable to count nouns. One sign of this is that when such verbs are used with the present perfective, they cannot indicate a single unbroken state up to the present:

I *have driven* sports cars for years. [1]

This does not refer to an uninterrupted state of car-driving, but rather to a sequence of separate car-driving events. On the other hand, there are verbs like (usually) *be*, *have*, and *know* which refer to states, and which indicate an unbroken state in sentences otherwise similar to [1]:

I *have known* the Penfolds all my life. [2]

Such verbs also occur less readily with frequency adverbials:

?The chair *has* beautiful carved legs *quite frequently*. [3]

On this basis, we draw a broad distinction between DYNAMIC (count) meanings and STATIVE (noncount) meanings of verbs. It should be noted, though, that we talk of dynamic and stative *meanings*, rather than dynamic and stative *verbs*. This is because one verb may shift, in meaning, from one category to another. Contrast, for example, the stative meaning of *have* [= 'possess'] in [3] with a dynamic meaning of *have* ['eat'] in [4]:

We *have* dinner at Maxim's *quite frequently*. [4]

Having carved legs is a state, while having dinner is an event (*cf* 3.34*f*).

One of the characteristics of dynamic verb senses is that they often (but by no means always) imply agentivity (*cf* 10.19); *ie* they imply an active doer (initiator, performer) of the action concerned. Hence dynamic verb meanings can regularly occur with the imperative, but stative verb meanings cannot:

Learn how to swim. *Know how to swim.

Verbs with dynamic meanings moreover can generally occur following *do* in a pseudo-cleft sentence (*cf* 18.29*f*):

What she did was (to) *learn* Spanish.
*What she did was (to) *know* Spanish.

The dynamic/stative distinction is not clear-cut, however. When we come to study aspect (see esp 4.25*ff*) we shall need to look critically at this distinction, and to suggest various subdivisions of each category. But a coarse binary contrast is all that is required for the study of tense.

The distinction between stative and dynamic verb meanings is therefore a rough-and-ready one which will be refined later (*cf* 4.27*ff*). There are some verbs (*eg*: *stand, lie*; *cf* 4.32) whose meanings cannot be adequately described in terms of this dichotomy.

Note [**a**] In some cases, the same verb can be either dynamic (referring to an event) or stative (referring to the state resulting from that event). Hence the virtual equivalence, in some contexts, of *I've got the idea* and *I get the idea*; also of *I've forgotten* and *I forget*.

[**b**] *Know* can be used abnormally in the sense of 'make sure that you know' in imperatives such as:

Know this poem by heart by next week.

There is also an exceptional dynamic use of *know* in the archaic imperative *Know thyself!*

Meanings of the simple present tense with reference to present time

(a) State present

4.5 With stative verb senses, the present is used without reference to specific time: *ie*, there is no inherent limitation on the extension of the state into the past and future (unless such a limitation is indicated by adverbials or other elements of the clause). The STATE PRESENT, as we may call this category, includes general timeless statements, or so-called 'eternal truths':

Honesty *is* the best policy.
Water *consists* of hydrogen and oxygen.
Two and three *make* five.
The earth *moves* round the sun.

Whereas proverbial, scientific, or mathematical statements like these represent the extreme of temporal universality, geographical statements are equally likely to be examples of the 'timeless present':

The Nile *is* the longest river in Africa.
Peru *shares* a border with Chile.

We can also include with the state present examples such as the following, where our knowledge of the world tells us that the time span of the state is to a greater or lesser degree restricted:

Margaret *is* tall.
He *does not believe* in hard work.
She *knows* several languages.
Everyone *likes* Maurice.
This soup *tastes* delicious.
We *live* near Toronto.

Note [**a**] Authors often use a kind of 'timeless present' in addressing their readers about the contents of their book. In the present book, for example, we use such expressions as:

The last example *shows* that . . .

[**b**] Sentences such as **We live near Toronto since 1949*, in which the simple present is combined with an adverbial of duration, do not normally occur. This is because the adverbial is interpreted as defining a period of 'living' leading up to the present moment, and hence as referring to time before the present (*cf* 4.20*ff*). Therefore, even though the state referred to may well continue in the future, the present perfective rather than the present is used. Particularly in AmE, however, this requirement is sometimes relaxed, and sentences like *Since when do you read newspapers?* are quite often heard (*cf* further 14.26).

(b) Habitual present

4.6 When they are used with the simple present, dynamic verb meanings, like stative verb meanings, usually imply an inherently unrestricted time span. But in this case the verb refers to a whole sequence of events, repeated over the period in question:

We *go* to Brussels every year.
She *makes* her own dresses.
Bill *drinks* heavily.
Water *boils* at 100°C.

As the last example shows, the HABITUAL PRESENT also resembles the state present in being used for 'timeless' statements. It is a sign of the habitual present that one can easily add a frequency adverbial to specify the frequency of the repetition: *Bill drinks heavily every night*, etc. Some habitual statements, such as *We go to Brussels*, are contextually incomplete unless such an adverbial is added. Whereas the state present always refers to something which obtains at the time of speaking, this is not necessarily, or even usually, true of the habitual present.

Note [**a**] Verbs of stative meaning may sometimes be used in a habitual sense when accompanied by a frequency adverbial: *She is seldom alone*.

[**b**] A habitual use of the present tense occurs in a 'timeless' sense in authorial address to the reader on a book's content (*cf* 4.5 Note [a]): *We turn now to the question of* ... This may be alternatively viewed as a special case of the instantaneous present (*cf* the use of the present in demonstrations in 4.7 below).

(c) Instantaneous present

4.7 While the habitual present is the most common meaning of the simple present with a dynamic verb sense, a second possibility, the INSTANTANEOUS PRESENT, occurs where the verb refers to a single action begun and completed approximately at the moment of speech. We may thus add to the state present and habitual present, which respectively correspond to noncount and plural count nouns, a third meaning corresponding to that of singular count nouns. *Figure* 4.7 illustrates the three central uses of the simple present with reference to present time:

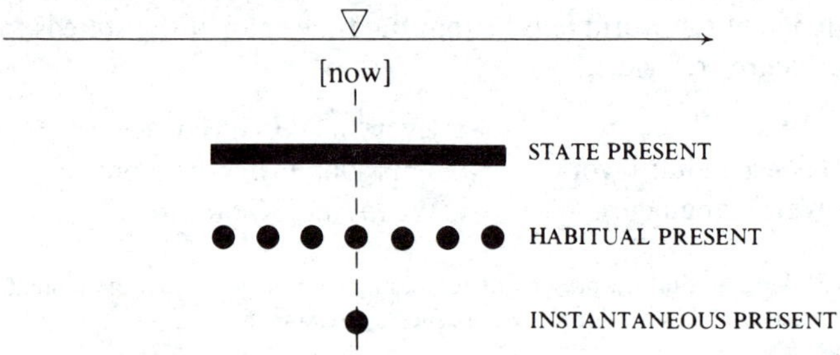

Fig 4.7

The instantaneous present, however, because it implies that the event has little or no duration, does not occur outside some rather restricted situations. Such situations include the following:

COMMENTARIES:

Black *passes* the ball to Fernandez ... Fernandez *shoots*!

DEMONSTRATIONS AND OTHER SELF-COMMENTARIES:

I *pick* up the fruit with a skewer, *dip* it into the batter, and *lower* it into the hot fat.

I *enclose* (herewith) a form of application.

SPECIAL EXCLAMATORY SENTENCES (with initial adverbials):

Here *comes* the winner! Up you *go*. (*cf* 18.23)

PERFORMATIVES:

I *advise* you to withdraw. I *apologize*. We *thank* you for your recent inquiry.

The verb in performatives (*cf* 11.3) is often a verb of speaking (such as *request*, *advise*, *predict*) describing the speech act of which it is a part. Other performatives such as *I resign* describe ritual acts and are accepted as the outward sign that such acts are taking place. In these cases, then, there is bound to be simultaneity between the event described and the speech event itself. In other cases, although such simultaneity does not obtain in any exact sense, there is an implication of simultaneity which gives the utterance with the instantaneous present a somewhat theatrical quality. Against the routine ordinariness of the present progressive in *Carlos is winning*, we may place the dramatic air of *Carlos wins!* which pinpoints the final and climactic moment of victory.

Note [**a**] In older English, the simple present was used more widely with reference to a present event which would now be described by use of the present progressive: Shakespeare's *I go, I go* may be contrasted with the present-day *I'm going*. Some relics of this archaic usage are found in one or two fixed expressions such as *How do you do?* and *How goes it?*
[**b**] On the closely related dramatic use of the present, *cf* 4.8, 4.10.

Special nonpresent uses of the present tense

(a) Simple present referring to the past

4.8 In the next three sections we bring together three additional uses of the simple present; these are best seen as transferred or extended interpretations of the basic meanings of 4.5–7.

The so-called historic present is characteristic of popular narrative style (*cf* also the fictional present, 4.10):

> I couldn't believe it! Just as we arrived, up *comes* Ben and *slaps* me on the back as if we'*re* life-long friends. 'Come on, old pal,' he *says*, 'Let me buy you a drink!' I'm telling you, I nearly fainted on the spot.

The historic present describes the past as if it is happening now: it conveys something of the dramatic immediacy of an eye-witness account.

A very different use of the present tense in reference to the past is that found with verbs of communication:

> The ten o'clock news *says* that there's going to be a bad storm.
> Martin *tells* me the Smiths are moving from No. 20.

Such verbs include also verbs like *understand*, *hear*, and *learn*, which refer to the receptive end of the communication process:

> I *hear* that poor Mr Simpson has gone into hospital.

These sentences would also be acceptable with the simple past or present perfective; but the implication of the present tense seems to be that although the communication event took place in the past, its result – the information communicated – is still operative. Thus:

> The Book of Genesis *speaks* of the terrible fate of Sodom and Gomorrah.

suggests that although the Book of Genesis was written thousands of years ago, it still 'speaks' to us at the present time.

The notion that the past can remain alive in the present also explains the optional use of the present tense in sentences referring to writers, composers, artists, etc and their extant works:

> In *The Brothers Karamazov*, Dostoevsky *draws/drew* his characters from sources deep in the Russian soil.
> Like Rubens, Watteau *is/was* able to convey an impression of warm, living flesh by the merest whiff of colour.

Again, it is something more than a figure of speech to suggest that the author is still able to speak to us through his works. The present can even be used, without respect to any particular work, for general artistic characterizations of the author:

> Brahms *is/was* the last great representative of German classicism.

But biographical details of the artist's life must normally be reported through the past tense (*cf* however Note [b]). Hence there is an interesting contrast between:

> Murasaki *writes/wrote* of life in 11th century Japan.
> Murasaki *wrote* in 11th century Japan.

Note [**a**] The simple present is usually used in newspaper headlines to report recent events: *Trade unions back merger*; *'No sell-out' says P.M.*; *Economic think-tank seeks assurances.* (On headlines, *cf* further 11.46).

[**b**] Two further minor uses of the historic present are (i) in photographic captions, for which, however, the *-ing* participle is an alternative form:

> The Queen *arrives/arriving* for the State Opening of Parliament.

and (ii) in historical summaries or tables of dates:

> 1876 – Brahms *completes* his first symphony.

[**c**] There is variation between past and present tenses in cross-references from one part of a book to the other: *This problem is/was discussed in Chapter 1.* The choice depends on whether the book is conceived of as existing at one time, like a static object; or whether it is imagined to progress in time, as it does for the reader who begins at Chapter 1 and moves from 'earlier' to 'later' parts of the book. Other verb constructions (*eg* the perfective construction or the modal construction with *will*) may also be used to imply progression in time: *This matter has been touched on in Chapter 2, but we will return to it in Chapter 5.*

(b) Simple present referring to the future

4.9 In main clauses, this typically occurs with time-position adverbials to suggest (*cf* 4.45) that the event is unalterably fixed in advance, and is as certain as it would be, were it taking place in the present:

> The plane *leaves* for Ankara at eight o'clock tonight.

In dependent clauses, the future use of the simple present is much more common, particularly in conditional and temporal clauses (*cf* 14.22):

> He'll do it if you *pay* him.
> I'll let you know as soon as I *hear* from her.

Note [**a**] The use of the simple present in directions with a 2nd person subject might be considered a case of the present tense referring to the future:

> You *test* an air leak by disconnecting the delivery pipe at the carburettor and pumping the fuel into a container.
> You *take* the first turning on the left past the police station, then you *cross* a bridge, and *bear* right until you *see* the Public Library.

However, these may more justly be taken as examples of the habitual present (*cf* 4.6), the *you* being interpreted impersonally, as equivalent to generic *one* (*cf* 6.21).
[b] The simple present may be used in reference to later parts of a book (*cf* 4.5 Note [a], 4.8 Note [c]) in examples such as the following:

In the next chapter we *examine* in the light of this theory recent economic developments in the Third World.

(c) Simple present in fictional narrative

4.10 There is a close connection between the historic present of (a) above, and the simple present as used in fictional narratives. The only difference is that whereas the events narrated by means of the historic present are real, those narrated by the fictional 'historic present' are imaginary:

The crowd *swarms* around the gateway, and *seethes* with delighted anticipation; excitement *grows*, as suddenly their hero *makes* his entrance . . .

This is stylistically marked in contrast to the normal convention of the past tense for story-telling. A special exception is the use of the present in stage directions:

Mallinson *enters*. The girls immediately *pretend* to be working hard. William *assumes* a businesslike air, *picks* up two folders at random, and *makes* for the door.

Here the present is used by convention, as if to represent the idea that the events of the play are being performed before our eyes as we read the script. A similar convention is used in summaries of narratives.

Meanings of the past tense with reference to past time

4.11 As most commonly used, the past tense combines two features of meaning:

(a) The event/state must have taken place in the past, with a gap between its completion and the present moment.
(b) The speaker or writer must have in mind a definite time at which the event/state took place.

The first of these conditions is most clearly exemplified by a sentence like *I stayed in Africa for several months*, where the usual implication is that I am no longer in Africa. The second condition is most explicitly shown in cooccurrence relations between the past tense and past time-position adverbials such as *last week*, *in 1932*, *several weeks ago*, *yesterday*, etc:

Freda started school {last year. [1] / in 1950. [2]}

Prices slumped {last winter. [3] / yesterday. [4]}

With such adverbials, the simple present or present perfective would be virtually ungrammatical (*cf*, however, 4.8 Note [b] and 4.23 Note [a]):

*Freda {starts / has started} school {last year. [1a] / in 1950. [2a]}

It is not necessary, however, for the past tense to be accompanied by an overt indicator of time. All that is required is that the speaker should be able to count on the hearer's assumption that he has a specific time in mind. In this respect, the past tense meaning of DEFINITE PAST time is an equivalent, in the verb phrase, of the definite article in the noun phrase. Just as with the definite article (*cf* 5.27–32), so with the verb phrase, an element of definite meaning may be recoverable from knowledge of (a) the immediate or local situation; (b) the larger situation of 'general knowledge'; (c) what has been said earlier in the same sentence or text; or (d) what comes later on in the same sentence or text.

Note A parallel may also be drawn, in terms of definite meaning, between the present and past tense, and the 'near' and 'far' reference of the demonstratives *this* and *that* (*cf* 6.40*ff*). Thus the present and past tenses can be added to other pairs of DEICTIC items (*cf* 6.43), such as *this/that*, *now/then*, and *here/there*.

Situational use of the past tense

4.12 The use of the past tense in relation to an immediate situation is illustrated by the sentence:

Did you *lock* the front door? [5]

in a domestic situation where it is known that the front door is locked at bedtime every night. In that case, [5] is more or less equivalent to *Did you lock the front door at bedtime?* (Incidentally, in [5], *the* in *the front door* is another case of situational definiteness; *cf* 5.28*ff*.)

Definiteness by virtue of the larger situation (or general knowledge; *cf* 5.29) may be invoked to explain the use of the simple past in historical or biographical statements which have specific people, places, or objects as their topics:

Byron *died* in Greece. [6]
I have a friend who *was* at school with Kissinger. [7]
This picture *was painted* by the owner's grandfather. [8]
Rome *was* not *built* in a day. [a proverb] [9]

It is a matter of general knowledge that Byron is a historical personage (and therefore that he must have died at some time or another). The past tense in [6] presupposes such common ground between speaker and hearer: it is as if the speaker had said: 'We all know that Byron died at some time or other; well, *when* he died, he died in Greece'. Similarly, [7] presupposes that most people spend a particular period at school, [8] presupposes that a picture one sees on the wall must have been painted at some time or another; and [9] presupposes that all cities (including Rome, the 'Eternal City') have to be built at some time or other.

Anaphoric and cataphoric use of the past tense

4.13 In line with the use of the term *anaphoric* with reference to the definite article (*cf* 5.30*f*), we may call the use of the past tense 'anaphoric' where the time in the past to which the reference is made is already indicated by a previous use of the past tense. In this sense, *was* is anaphoric in [10]:

Then we *entered* the city . . . the square *was* deserted . . . [10]

In other cases, a preceding use of the present perfective in the indefinite past sense (*cf* 4.20*f*) provides a peg, so to speak, on which to hang a subsequent occurrence of the past tense:

They *have decided* to close down the factory. It *took* us completely by surprise. [11]

There *have been* times when I *wished* myself safely home in bed. [12]

(In the latter sentence, the present perfective *have wished* would also be possible.) Again, this is similar to the case where the indefinite article (*cf* 5.30) prepares the way for a following coreferential definite article. In other cases, anaphoric reference is to an adverbial of time in the same clause:

Last Saturday, we *went* to the theatre.

When the adverbial follows the past tense, this may be called the *cataphoric* use of the definite past (*cf* 5.32):

We *went* to the theatre *last Saturday*.

Examples like [5–12] above show that for a verb phrase to be 'definite', the relevant time need not be specified: it matters only that the time should in principle be specifiable. This means that even very unspecific time adverbs such as *once* and *when* suffice to make the past tense appropriate:

When did she arrive? I was *once* a heavy smoker.

Finally, the use of a temporal conjunction such as *while* or *as soon as* with past reference is a sufficient condition for the use of the past tense in both main and subordinate clauses: *They left as soon as we arrived.*

Note **[a]** There are a few idiomatic constructions in which the element of definiteness seems to be absent from the meaning of the past tense: *eg* in comparative clauses containing the main verb *was/were*:

She's not so active *as she was.*

But here the past tense retains its other semantic feature: that the state no longer obtains; *ie*: *was* is equivalent to *used to be* (*cf* 4.15).

[b] In the following idiomatic examples, the past tense lacks both its implication of 'definiteness' and its implication of 'no longer obtaining':

I always *knew* you were my friend. [13]

Did you ever *hear* such nonsense? [14]

The past is here a colloquial alternative to the present perfective referring to a state or habit leading up to the present; *eg* [13] could be rephrased: *I've always known you to be my friend.* (In the ritual exclamation of astonishment *Well I never did!*, however, the perfective could not be substituted.) This usage is restricted to the occurrence of the past tense with *always*, *never*, or *ever*. Sentences such as [13] and [14] are to be distinguished from similar sentences containing a past time adverbial, such as: *In the past, I always thought you were my friend.* Here the regular interpretation of the past tense obtains, and so the implication is likely to be: '. . . but now I no longer think so'.

[c] On differences between AmE and BrE in the use of the simple past, *cf* 4.20 Note, 4.22 Note [a].

Event, state, and habit in the past

4.14 Having mentioned the pragmatic conditions for definiteness which are common to most examples of the past tense, we now have to distinguish three meanings of the past tense which match the three meanings of the present with reference to present time (4.5–7). For the past tense, however, it is better to place the three meanings in a different order. First we illustrate, as the most common sense, the EVENT PAST, which refers to a single definite event in the past:

The eruption of Vesuvius *destroyed* Pompeii. [1]

In [1], the dynamic verb sense of *destroyed* identifies a single event. But in [2], the verb *was* refers to a state, and is therefore an example of the STATE PAST:

Archery *was* a popular sport for the Victorians. [2]

In [3], we have an example of the HABITUAL PAST, since the verb *were held* refers to a sequence of four-yearly events:

In ancient times, the Olympic Games *were held* at Olympia in Southern Greece. [3]

We may present these three meanings, therefore, in a diagram corresponding to that used for the simple present (*Fig* 4.7):

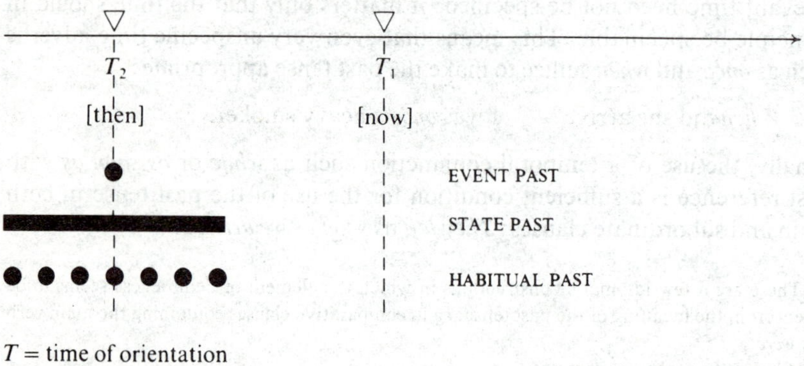

Fig 4.14

In *Fig* 4.14, the three meanings are located by reference to a definite time in the past (a SECONDARY TIME-ORIENTATION or T_2), and only indirectly by reference to the present moment (the PRIMARY TIME-ORIENTATION or T_1). The diagram shows T_2, like T_1, as a point of time having no duration; but it should be noted that T_2 can sometimes refer to an extended time period. Compare *The agreement was signed at 7 p.m.* (where T_2 is a momentary point of time) with *The agreement was signed in 1972* (where T_2 is a whole year and the actual signing is understood to take place at some unspecified point within that period).

4.15 It is easy to see why the event past is more common than the corresponding meaning of the present tense, *viz* the instantaneous present. From a vantage point in the present, we naturally see a happening in the past as a complete unit, with a beginning and an end; but it is more difficult to see a present event 'in close-up' in such a holistic way. With the past tense, there is a tendency to treat as holistic events even states of affairs persisting through an extended period, *eg*:

He *lived* and *died* in his native city of Padua.

It can thus be rather difficult, in practice, to distinguish the different meanings of the past tense. But one useful distinguishing mark is the fact that the habitual and state meanings can be paraphrased by means of *used to* (*cf* 3.44):

In those days we $\left\{\begin{array}{l}\textit{used to live}\\ \textit{lived}\end{array}\right\}$ in the country. [4]

We $\left\{\begin{array}{l}\textit{used to get}\\ \textit{got}\end{array}\right\}$ up at 5 a.m. every morning all through the summer. [5]

As it stands, the habitual past in [3] above in 4.14 is not formally distinguished from the event past: only general knowledge tells us that the Olympic Games were held more than once. If we wish to make sure that a sentence like [3] is given a habitual interpretation, we have to substitute the *used to* construction or else add an adverbial of frequency or duration, such as *every morning* and *all through the summer* in [5].

Another distinguishing feature is the tendency for dynamic verbs to have a sequential interpretation when they occur in textual sequence (especially in coordination):

She *addressed* and *posted* the letter. [6]
[≠ She *posted* and *addressed* the letter]
She *disliked* and *distrusted* her advisers. [7]
[= She *distrusted* and *disliked* her advisers]

In [6], the actions of addressing and posting are understood to take place in succession, while in [7] the emotions of dislike and distrust are understood to have existed side by side (*cf* 13.22*ff*).

Note Sometimes, however, two dynamic verbs in sequence are given a simultaneous interpretation, as in:

The explosion *wrecked* a car and *damaged* several shops.

Another relevant factor is that certain conjunctions, such as *before* and *after*, can overrule the normal order of temporal precedence:

Before the railroad gangs *arrived*, Dixon City $\left\{\begin{array}{l}\textit{was}\\ \textit{had been}\end{array}\right\}$ nothing but a sleepy cattle town.

(On the alternative use of *had been* here, *cf* 4.24.)

Meanings of the past tense with reference to present and future time

4.16 Just as the simple present does not always refer to present time, so the past tense is not always confined to past time reference. There are again three special meanings to mention:

(a) In INDIRECT SPEECH (or INDIRECT THOUGHT; *cf* 14.30*ff*), the past tense in the reporting verb tends to make the verb of the subordinate clause past tense as well. This phenomenon, known as backshift, is normally optional (*cf* 14.31), but can result in an apparently anachronistic use of the past tense for present time:

A: *Did* you *say* you have/*had* no money?
B: Yes, I'm completely broke.
A: How *did* you *know* that I am/*was* Max Wilson?
B: Well, I remembered that you are/*were* tall, and wear/*wore* glasses.

A different kind of backshift is observed when a sentence describing speech or thought in the future contains a reported speech clause referring retrospectively to the present:

My wife will be sorry that she *missed* seeing you this evening.

(b) The ATTITUDINAL PAST, used with verbs expressing volition or mental state, reflects the tentative attitude of the speaker, rather than past time. In the following pairs, both the present and past tenses refer to a present state of mind, but the latter is somewhat more polite:

Do/*Did* you want to see me now?
I wonder/*wondered* if you could help us.

(c) The HYPOTHETICAL PAST is used in certain subordinate clauses, especially *if*-clauses, and expresses what is contrary to the belief or expectation of the speaker (*cf* 14.23):

If you really *worked* hard, you would soon get promoted. [1]
It's time we all *took* a rest. [2]
I wish I *had* a memory like yours. [3]

The hypothetical past, as in [1–3], implies the nonoccurrence of some state or event in the present or future. The implication of [1], for example, is that the hearer does *not* work hard.

Note [**a**] The past subjunctive singular form *were* is often considered preferable to the past indicative form *was* in sentences such as:

He talks as if he *were*/*was* the most powerful politician in the country.

For further discussion, see 3.62 and 14.24.

[**b**] The past tense forms of modal auxiliaries (*could*, *would*, etc) frequently occur with special hypothetical force, and are somewhat restricted in their application to past time. These will be considered in some detail in 4.59–64.

Perfective and progressive aspects

4.17 The term ASPECT refers to a grammatical category which reflects the way in which the verb action is *regarded* or *experienced* with respect to time. Unlike tense, aspect is not deictic (*cf* 6.43), in the sense that it is not relative to the time of utterance. For some purposes, the two aspect constructions of English, the perfective and the progressive (*cf* 3.54), can be seen as realizing a basic contrast of aspect between the action viewed as complete (perfective), and the action viewed as incomplete, *ie* in progress (imperfective or progressive). But this is an oversimplified view, as is clear as soon as we observe that these two aspects may combine within a single verb phrase (*eg*: *I have been reading* is both perfective and progressive). In fact, aspect is so closely connected in meaning with tense, that the distinction in English grammar between tense and aspect is little more than a terminological convenience which helps us to separate in our minds two different kinds of realization: the morphological realization of tense and the syntactic realization of aspect.

We have seen (*cf* 3.54*ff*) that tense and aspect combine freely in the complex verb phrase, and so the following system of contrasts, with corresponding terminological distinctions, will form a useful starting point:

Table 4.17

SYMBOL	NAME	EXAMPLE
Type B	present perfective (simple) past perfective (simple)	*he has examined* *he had examined*
Type C	present progressive (simple) past progressive (simple)	*he is examining* *he was examining*
Type BC	present perfective progressive past perfective progressive	*he has been examining* *he had been examining*

We have already used the word 'simple' to describe a verb phrase totally unmarked for aspect (simple present, simple past). By extension, we may also, to avoid ambiguity, use the term 'simple' for verb phrases which are unmarked for one of the two aspects, as indicated in *Table* 4.17.

Note [**a**] It has been traditional for grammars to refer to the above set of oppositions of tense and aspect as 'compound tenses', in which they would include such categories as the 'past perfect' (or 'pluperfect') tense. This terminology, modelled on that used for inflectional languages such as Latin, can be misleading when applied to English, and for this reason we prefer to limit, as mentioned before, the term 'tense' to the morphological opposition between present and past forms of the finite verb.

[**b**] Because of the close connection between the perfective construction and time, the perfective is commonly termed the 'perfective tense' (or 'perfect tense').

Perfective aspect

4.18 The overlap of meaning between tense and aspect is most problematic in English in the choice that has to be made between simple past and present perfective:

simple past: John *lived* in Paris for ten years.
present perfective: John *has lived* in Paris for ten years.

Here both sentences indicate a state of affairs before the present moment, but the simple past indicates that the period of residence has come to a close, whereas the present perfective indicates that the residence has continued up to the present time (and may even continue into the future). This kind of difference, although by no means invariable, is often summarized in the statement that the present perfective signifies past time 'with current relevance'.

In order to appreciate why 'current relevance' is a common implication of the present perfective, it is as well to begin with the most general definition of the perfective aspect. In its broadest possible interpretation, the perfective indicates ANTERIOR TIME; *ie* time preceding whatever time orientation is signalled by tense or by other elements of the sentence or its context. To illustrate this definition, we take a preliminary look not only at the present perfective, but at cases where the perfective does not cooccur with the present tense:

I *have* already *met* your sister. [1]
The flight was cancelled after we *had paid* for the tickets. [2]
If you *had listened* to me, you would have avoided mistakes. [3]
By next week, they *will have completed* their contract. [4]
I *may have left* the key at the office (last night). [5]
I am/was sorry *to have missed* the concert. [6]
She regrets/regretted *having abandoned* the plan. [7]

The common factor of meaning which the perfective brings to all these examples is sketched in *Fig* 4.18:

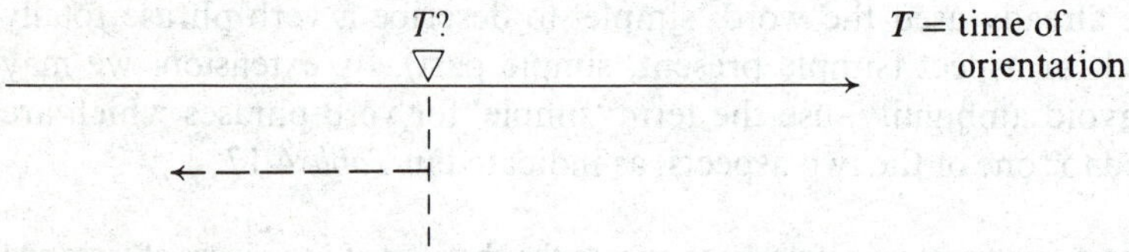

Fig 4.18 Anterior time zone

Note Perfective constructions are infrequent compared with nonperfective constructions. A corpus study of verb phrases has indicated that approximately ten per cent of finite verb phrases are perfective.

4.19 As the above figure shows, the perfective merely defines an anterior time zone (symbolized by the arrow ←—) within which the action of the verb takes place. The time of orientation (*T*?) is not fixed: with the present perfective [1], *T*? is equated with T_1, while with the past perfective, *T*? is equated with T_2 (a specifiable secondary time of orientation in the past). This is illustrated in [2] in 4.18 above, where *T*? (= T_2) refers to the time of cancelling the flight. In [3], however, the past perfective relates the event not to T_2, but to T_1, since the past tense indicates in this case not a past event, but a hypothetical event (*cf* the hypothetical past, 4.16). The conditional clause could be expanded:

If you had listened to me *before now* . . .

In [4] and [5], the infinitive perfective occurs after a modal auxiliary, and the time orientation derives not from the infinitive itself (which is tenseless), but from the modal. *Will* in [4] sets up an ancillary time orientation T_2 in the future, so that the meaning of the whole construction *will have completed* is 'past in future':

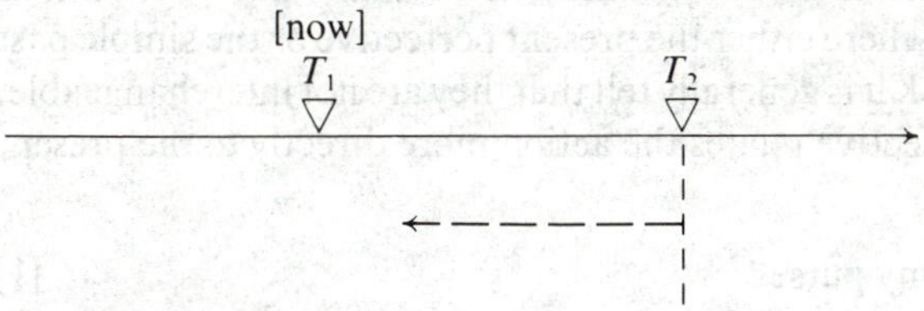

Fig 4.19 Past in future

In [5], on the other hand, the modal *may* has a present orientation, and T? is once again T_1. In the last two examples of 4.18, the perfective occurs in a nonfinite verb phrase, which, because it has no inherent time orientation, takes its orientation from the main verb. Hence the paraphrases below, in which the nonfinite clauses of [6] and [7] are replaced by finite subordinate clauses, require variation in the verb construction of the subordinate clause in correspondence with a similar variation in the main clause:

I ['m / was] sorry that I [*missed* / *(had) missed*] the concert. [6a]

She [regrets / regretted] that she [*abandoned* / *(had) abandoned*] the plan. [7a]

The past perfective is optional in the second variant of [6a] and [7a], for reasons explained in *Fig* 4.24b. These distinctions are neutralized when a nonfinite clause is used.

The overlap in the time-indicating functions of the past tense and the present perfective is clearly seen in the choice of paraphrasing [5] above either by the past tense [5a] or by the present perfective [5b]:

It is possible that I *left* the keys at the office (*last night*). [5a]
It is possible that I *have left* the keys at the office. [5b]

On the other hand, this example also shows that the present perfective is to some extent limited by the fact that it shares the same past time 'territory' as the simple past. If a time-position adverbial like *last night* is added to [5], then the finite verb paraphrase has to be the past tense [5a] rather than the perfective [5b]. In other words, [5c] is unacceptable:

*It is possible that I *have left* the keys at the office last night. [5c]

However, the rule of adverbial incompatibility which forbids [5c] is occasionally ignored; *cf* 4.23 Note [a] below.

Note The semantic overlap between the simple past and the present perfective gives rise to a further type of 'double marking' (*cf* 3.57, 4.24) where the perfective redundantly repeats the indication of anteriority present in the past tense: *We were glad to have seen you* can be used in a way which makes its meaning indistinguishable from that of *We were glad to see you*.

The present perfective

4.20 The examples in 4.18 have given evidence that 'past with current relevance' is not an adequate description of the meaning of the perfective aspect. Yet when we concentrate on the present perfective, there is indeed reason for such a description: the present perfective differs from the simple past in relating a past event/state to a present time orientation. Thus in situations (which are not unusual) where either the present perfective or the simple past can be appropriately used, it is generally felt that they are not interchangeable, but that the present perfective relates the action more directly to the present time. Compare:

Where did you put my purse? [1]
Where have you put my purse? [2]

The purpose of both of these questions may be to find the purse; but in [1] the speaker seems to ask the addressee to remember a past action; while in [2] the speaker apparently concentrates on the purse's present whereabouts. There are many such cases.

Leaving aside such virtual equivalences, we may now focus on the difference between the two constructions, contrasting the meanings of the simple past given in 4.14 with the following meanings of the simple present perfective:

(a) STATE LEADING UP TO THE PRESENT

That house *has been* empty for ages.
Have you *known* my sister for long?

(b) INDEFINITE EVENT(S) IN A PERIOD LEADING UP TO THE PRESENT

Have you (ever) *been* to Florence?
All our children *have had* measles.

(c) HABIT (*ie* recurrent event) IN A PERIOD LEADING UP TO THE PRESENT

Mr Terry *has sung* in this choir ever since he was a boy.
The province *has suffered* from disastrous floods throughout its history.

Of these meanings, (a) corresponds to the 'state past' use of the simple past, but differs from it in specifying that the state continues at least up to the present moment (*cf: That house was empty for ages – but now it's been sold*); (b) corresponds to the 'event past', but differs from it in that the past time in question is indefinite rather than definite (*cf: Did you go to Florence (last summer)?*); (c) corresponds to the 'habitual past', but, as with (a), the period identified must continue up to the present. Compare:

The journal *has been published* every month since 1850. [3]
The journal *was published* every month from 1850 to 1888. [4]

These three meanings may be represented in a diagram, *Fig* 4.20, which parallels that of *Figs* 4.7 and 4.14. It is normal for meanings (a) and (c) to be indicated by adverbials. A duration adverbial is virtually obligatory for both (a) and (c), and a frequency adverbial may also occur with (c), as in [3] above. Adverbials occurring with the indefinite past meaning will be mentioned in 4.22 below.

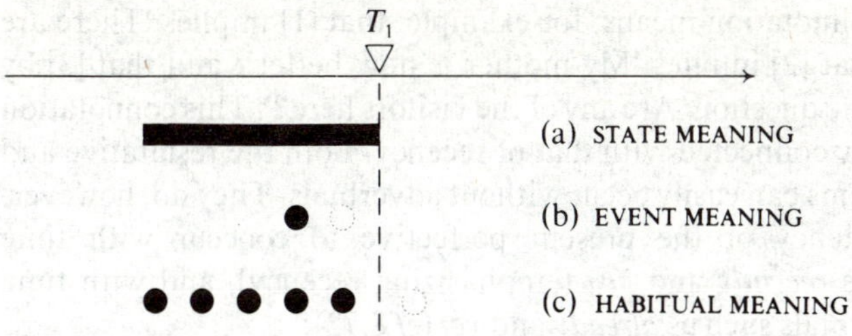

Fig 4.20 Meanings of the present perfective

Note In AmE there is a tendency to use the past tense in preference to the present perfective, especially for the indefinite past; *eg*: *Did you ever go to Florence?* (*cf* 4.13 Note [b], 4.22 Note [a]).

Variants of the indefinite past meaning

4.21 In reference to a single event in the past (meaning (b) above), the present perfective, particularly in BrE, is associated with three implications or connotations, each of which may or may not be applicable in a given instance. These implications are (i) that the relevant time zone leads up to the present; (ii) that the event is recent; and (iii) that the result of the action still obtains at the present time. The first of these implications is simply a restatement of what was said about the anterior time zone of the perfective in 4.18. The point to be made here is that the choice between the present perfective and the simple past is often determined by whether the speaker has in mind *an implicit time zone* which has not yet finished:

Have you seen the Javanese Art Exhibition? [yet]
Did you see the Javanese Art Exhibition? [when it was here]

The first of these implies that the Exhibition is still open; the second that the Exhibition has finished. From this concern with a period still existing at the present time, it is only a short step to the second implication often associated with the present perfective, *viz* that the event is recent. The simple present perfective is often used to report a piece of news:

Have you *heard* } the news? The president *has resigned*.
Did you *hear* }

Because of this connotation of recency, B's reply in the following exchange must be considered absurdly inappropriate:

A: Has the postman left any letters? B: Yes, he did six months ago.

Since postmen in general deliver letters daily, the implicit time zone in this case would be no longer than a day.

4.22 The third connotation, that the result of the action still obtains, applies to dynamic conclusive verbs (*cf* 4.33–5), *ie* verbs whose meaning implies the accomplishment of a change of state:

The apples have all been eaten. [1]
My mother has recovered from her illness. [2]
Have any of the visitors arrived? [3]

The resultative connotation means, for example, that [1] implies 'There are no apples left'; that [2] implies 'My mother is now better'; and that [3] by implication asks the question 'Are any of the visitors here?'. This connotation is obviously closely connected with that of recency. Both the resultative and recency connotations can easily occur without adverbials. They do, however, underlie the tendency of the present perfective to cooccur with time adverbials such as *recently* and *just* (emphasizing recency), and with time relationship adverbials such as *already* and *yet* (*cf* 8.72):

The plane has *just* landed. [4]
I've *already* told Gillian about the party. [5]
Have the children come home *yet*? [6]

Significantly, time relationship adverbs such as *already* and *yet* can occur *either* with resultative verbs and the perfective aspect, as in [5] or [6], *or* with stative verbs referring to the results of such actions: *eg* [5] could be placed alongside *Gillian already knows about the party*, and [6] alongside *Are the children home yet?*

Note [**a**] In AmE, the simple past is often preferred to the present perfective for the variants of the indefinite past discussed in this section. Compare [6], for example, with *Did the children come home yet?* ⟨esp AmE⟩. Other AmE examples are: *I just came back*; *You told me already*; and without an adverb: *I'm tired – I had a long day.*

[**b**] The two perfective constructions for the verb *go*, namely *have gone* and *have been*, differ in that the former is resultative:

My sister has gone to Rome. [She is there now]
My sister has been to Rome. [at least once]

Thus *have gone* cannot normally be used in a habitual sense:

?My sister has gone to Rome frequently.

The use of adverbials with the simple past and the present perfective

4.23 The choice between the simple past and the present perfective is associated with time orientation, and therefore with the choice and interpretation of time adverbials. (For the classification of the relevant types of adverbials, *cf* 8.4, 8.51*ff*, 8.97*f*.) Examples are:

(a) ADVERBIALS ASSOCIATED WITH THE PAST TENSE:

I saw her { yesterday (evening). / a week ago. / earlier this week. / last Monday. }

I saw her { the other day. / at four o'clock. / in the morning. / on Tuesday. }

(b) ADVERBIALS ASSOCIATED WITH THE PRESENT PERFECTIVE:

I haven't seen her { up to now. / since Monday. / since I met you. }

I haven't seen her { so far. / hitherto. ⟨formal⟩ }

(c) ADVERBIALS ASSOCIATED WITH BOTH:

I {saw / have seen} her {today. / this month. / this year. / recently.}

I {saw / have seen} her {before. / this June. / once. / already.}

Group (a) contains time position adverbials which indicate a specific point or period in the past, and therefore require the past tense. In Group (b) are adverbials which designate a period leading up to the present moment, and are therefore appropriate to the present perfective. Group (c) is a mixed group of adverbials, some of which, like *this month*, designate a period which includes the present moment, while others have meanings which vary according to whether a present or past time orientation is intended. For example, *I have seen him once* contains *once* in a frequency sense ('how often'), while *I saw him once* contains *once* in a time position sense ('when').

Note [**a**] One quite often meets (especially in BrE) sentences in which the present perfective cooccurs with time adverbials of Group (a); *eg*:

A: Have you ever seen *Macbeth* on the stage?
B: Yes, I've seen it *ages ago*, when I was a child.

Examples such as this may be explained as performance errors, induced by B's copying the form of A's question. Such explanations may not, however, be so readily available in other cases, such as *They asked me about something I've said years ago*.

[**b**] With phrases like *this week* and *this month* referring to a present period of time, the choice between the two verb constructions reflects merely a difference of focus or orientation:

Did you read *Punch* this week? Have you read *Punch* this week?

But expressions such as *this March* and *this morning* may refer to a past period of time ('the March of this year', 'the morning of today') rather than to a period containing the present moment. Some speakers feel that the present perfective with such expressions implies that the period referred to is not in the past; *eg* that *I have seen her this March* can be spoken appropriately only in March, and that *I have seen her this morning* can be spoken appropriately only in the morning. Other speakers, however, do not acknowledge this restriction.

The past perfective

4.24 The past perfective usually has the meaning of 'past-in-the-past', and can be regarded as an anterior version either of the present perfective or of the simple past. Consider the following examples:

No wonder Miss Matthews' French was excellent – she *had lived* in Paris since childhood. [1]
When we bought it, the house *had been* empty for several years. [2]

These can be diagrammed as in *Fig* 4.24a, which is a special case of the general perfective diagram *Fig* 4.18:

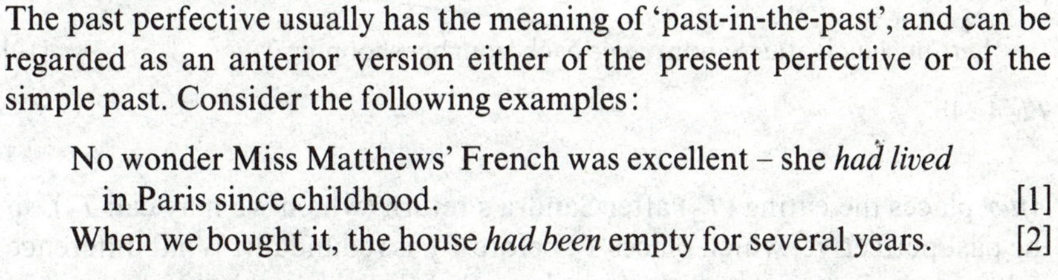

Fig 4.24a Meaning of the past perfective

More technically, the past perfective may be said to denote any event or state anterior to a time of orientation in the past. The three meanings of 'state', 'event' or 'habit' (as described in 4.14) can all occur. Whereas [1] and [2] have illustrated the 'state' meaning, [3] and [4] illustrate 'event' and 'habit' respectively:

The goalkeeper *had injured* his leg, and couldn't play. [3]
It was foolish to fire McCabe: in two seasons, he *had scored* more goals than any other player. [4]

When transposed into the 'past in the past' by means of the past perfective, the contrast between the simple past and the present perfective is neutralized:

My aunt *had lived* in Italy for four years. [5]
He *had died* in 1920, before his son was born. [6]

In [5], the four-year period could either be a period leading up to T_2, or a period which had ceased before T_2, as would be clear in:

In her youth, my aunt *had lived* in Italy for four years. That's why she spoke Italian so well.

Thus [5] could be a projection further into the past of either [7] or [8]:

My aunt *lived* in Italy for four years. [7]
My aunt *has lived* in Italy for four years. [8]

But of course, the past perfective does not have to refer to a more remote time than that referred to by the simple past. In some cases, particularly in a clause introduced by *after*, the two constructions can be more or less interchangeable:

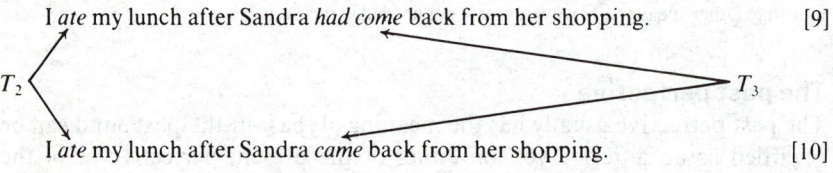

I *ate* my lunch after Sandra *had come* back from her shopping. [9]

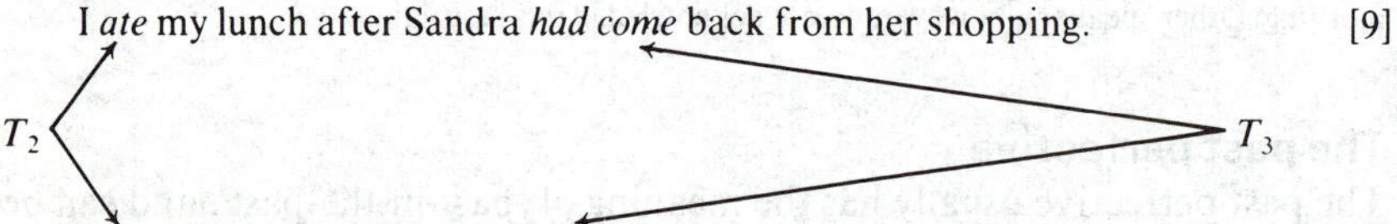

I *ate* my lunch after Sandra *came* back from her shopping. [10]

Fig 4.24b

After places the eating (T_2) after Sandra's return (which we may call T_3), so the past perfective, which places T_3 before T_2, is redundant. What difference it does make is a matter of the 'standpoint' of the speaker. In [9] the 'past in past' time T_3 is identified as being earlier than T_2 by the past perfective; but in [10] it is left to the conjunction *after* to signal this temporal relation.

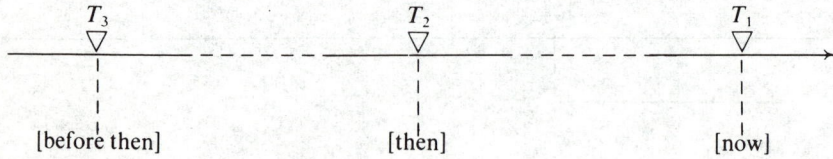

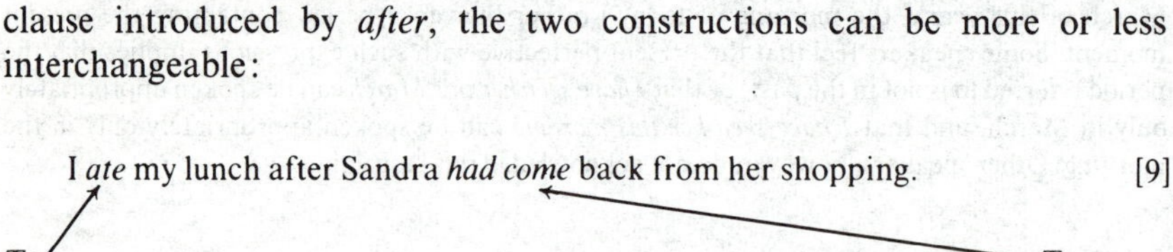

Fig 4.24c

Adverbials of time position, when used with the past perfective, can identify either T_2 or T_3. Placed initially, they often identify T_2:

When the police arrived, the thieves had run away. [11]

But in final position, the interpretation whereby the adverbial refers to T_3 is more likely:

The thieves had run away *when the police arrived*. [12]

Hence in [11], *when* is likely to be equivalent to *By the time that* . . ., but in [12] the *when* clause is likely to be an answer to the question: 'When had the thieves run away?'

Note [a] *When* in the sense of 'immediately after' behaves like *after* in sentences [9] and [10]. The following are therefore virtually synonymous:

I ate my lunch when Sandra *had come* back from her shopping.
I ate my lunch when Sandra *came* back from her shopping.

[b] There is one construction in which the past perfective clearly could not be replaced, as a means of referring to past time, by the simple past. This is an indirect speech construction, in which the past perfective indicates backshift (*cf* 14.31) into the more remote past: *I told her the parcel had not arrived.*

[c] The past perfective can also be a backshifted equivalent of the present perfective in expressions like *I hadn't noticed*; *I'm leaving – had you heard?* In these cases, a past time of orientation T_2 is implied by context.

[d] As well as past-in-past, the past perfective can be used to indicate hypothetical past (*cf* 4.19, 14.23, 15.35).

Progressive aspect

4.25 As its name suggests, the PROGRESSIVE ASPECT (also sometimes called the DURATIVE or CONTINUOUS aspect) indicates a happening IN PROGRESS at a given time. Compare:

SIMPLE PRESENT: Joan *sings* well. [1]
PRESENT PROGRESSIVE: Joan *is singing* well. [2]

These two sentences have the same tense, but different aspects. Notice the difference this makes to the meaning: *Joan sings well* refers to Joan's competence as a singer (that she has a good voice – a relatively permanent attribute); *Joan is singing well* refers to her performance on a particular occasion or during a particular season. The same formal contrast could be made for the past tense:

SIMPLE PAST: Joan *sang* well. [3]
PAST PROGRESSIVE: Joan *was singing* well. [4]

But in this case, the semantic contrast (assuming a 'past event' interpretation of [3]) is different: the simple past makes us see the event as a whole, while the past progressive makes us see it as an activity in progress. The different effect of the progressive in [1–2] and in [3–4] can be explained as follows.

The meaning of the progressive can be separated into three components, not all of which need be present in a given instance:

(a) the happening has DURATION
(b) the happening has LIMITED duration
(c) the happening is NOT NECESSARILY COMPLETE

The first two components add up to the concept of TEMPORARINESS. Thus in [2], the progressive signals that Joan's singing is a temporary rather than a permanent phenomenon; in [4], on the other hand, the progressive makes us see the event as enduring over a period, rather than as happening all at once. In [2], the progressive 'shrinks' the time span of *sings*; in [4] it 'stretches out' the time span of *sang*. This difference arises because component (a) is distinctive for single events; whereas component (b) is distinctive for states and habits. The component of incompletion (c) is distinctive chiefly in the case of certain types of dynamic verb meaning called CONCLUSIVE (*cf* 4.33–35):

I *read* a novel yesterday evening. [*ie* the whole novel]
I *was reading* a novel yesterday evening. [*ie* there is no implication that I finished the novel in the course of the evening]

Note [**a**] The progressive aspect is infrequent compared with the nonprogressive. A count of a large number of verb constructions has indicated that less than 5 per cent of verb phrases are progressive, whereas more than 95 per cent are nonprogressive. The same count shows that progressive forms are more frequent in conversation than in scientific discourse; also that they are marginally more frequent in conversational AmE than in conversational BrE.
[**b**] It may be argued that there is yet a fourth component in the meaning of the progressive: *viz* that the event described has an interrelationship or identity with another simultaneous event (*cf* 4.36 on 'temporal frames'):

Do you think he *was telling* the truth?

In this case, there is no suggestion of incompletion, but there does appear to be an unspoken implication '. . . when he said that'. This use of the progressive applies especially to verbs of speaking:

A: What did she mean by that?
B: I think she *was advising* you not to interfere.

State, event, and habit with the progressive

4.26 The three verb senses of state, event, and habit are differently interpreted with the progressive:

(a) STATE PROGRESSIVE
In many cases (*cf* 4.28–31) the progressive is unacceptable with stative verbs:

We *own* a house in the country.
*We *are owning* a house in the country.
*Sam's wife *was being* well-dressed.

This can be explained, in part, by the observation that stative verb meanings are inimical to the idea that some phenomenon is 'in progress'. States are 'like-parted' in that every segment of a state has the same character as any other segment: no progress is made. (Contrast *We are building a house in the country.*) Where the progressive does occur, it is felt to imply temporariness rather than permanence:

We *are living* in the country. [temporary residence]
We *live* in the country. [permanent residence]

(On the status of verbs such as *live*, *cf* 4.32).

(b) EVENT PROGRESSIVE

With event meanings (*cf* 4.33–5), the progressive conveys the idea that an event has duration, and has not yet come to an end. Contrast the instantaneous present (*cf* 4.7) meaning of [1] with the duration implied by [2] or [3]:

The referee *blows* his whistle. [1]
The referee *is blowing* his whistle. [2]
The train *was approaching*. [3]

Both [1] and [2] could be part of a radio commentary on a football match; but [1] would suggest a brief blast on the whistle, while [2] would tend to suggest a continuous or repeated blowing of the whistle. The present progressive is a more common way of referring to a present event than the simple present, because of the implication of duration that tends to accompany such events:

A: What {is Mary doing / *does Mary do} at this moment?
B: She {is watching / *watches} television.

(c) HABITUAL PROGRESSIVE

Combined with habitual meaning, the progressive implies that the repetition takes place over a limited period:

The professor *types* his own letters. [The habit is permanent.]
The professor *is typing* his own letters while his secretary is ill. [The habit is temporary.]
At that time she *was having* regular singing lessons.

Less frequently, the progressive combines with habitual meaning to suggest that every event in a sequence of events has duration/incompletion:

Whenever I see her, she*'s working* in the garden.
The Chief Secretary rises at 6.15 every morning. By 7 o'clock he has taken a light breakfast, and *is* already *reading* the morning newspapers.
Remember that when *you're taking* a rest, someone else *is* always *working*.

To have this interpretation, the clause must contain an adverbial of time position or of frequency.

Note [**a**] In combination with *always*, *continually*, or *forever*, the progressive loses its semantic component of 'temporariness':

Bill is {*continually* / *always* / *forever*} working late at the office. [4]

The progressive in such cases often imparts a subjective feeling of disapproval to the action described. Thus in [4], the speaker seems to suggest that working late at the office is an irritating or deplorable habit. This suggestion is stronger when the adverb *forever* is used. In other cases there may be no such derogatory implication: *A child is always learning*.

[**b**] With reference to the event progressive (b), a different kind of contrast with the instantaneous present is illustrated by certain verbs (*eg*: *write, enclose, send, hasten*) used with a 1st person subject in letter writing:

I {*write* / *am writing*} to inform you that. . . .

The simple present in such cases has a force similar to that of a performative (*cf* 4.7) such as *I (hereby) promise* . . ., and this analogy is indeed confirmed by the occurrence of *herewith* (an adverb similar to the *hereby* which can accompany performatives) in, *eg*: *I enclose herewith* . . . The simple present in this context is formal or official in tone, whereas the progressive is more informal, and more appropriate to a private letter.

Situation types

4.27 To explain the constraints on the use of the progressive, as well as for other purposes, it is useful to reconsider the stative/dynamic distinction of 4.4, and to subdivide verb meanings into a larger number of categories. One such subdivision is given in *Fig* 4.27, where 11 categories are recognized, and labelled *A–K*. It is important to note, also, that verb meanings can be separated only artificially, in this respect, from their complementations. For example, the verb *write* occurring *in vacuo* cannot be classified; for we may observe an important difference between *Jill is writing*, which designates an ongoing activity, and *Jill is writing a novel*, which designates an activity for which a goal or objective is implied (and for which the name 'accomplishment' will be used). More detailed explanation must now be given of the categories in *Fig* 4.27 opposite, and their relevance to the progressive.

Stative types *A* and *B*: qualities and states

4.28 Among stative situation types, a rough distinction may be drawn between QUALITIES (Type *A* in *Fig* 4.27) and STATES (Type *B* in *Fig* 4.27). Qualities are relatively permanent and inalienable properties of the subject referent. The primary verbs *be* and *have* are preeminently quality-introducing verbs; but they can also introduce the less permanent situation types called states. Contrast:

QUALITIES		STATES	
Mary is Canadian.	[1]	Mary is tired.	[3]
Mary has blue eyes.	[2]	Mary has a bad cold.	[4]

Normally such stative situation types do not occur with the progressive (this is especially true of qualities):

*Mary is being a Canadian.	[1a]	?*Mary is being tired.	[3a]
*Mary is having blue eyes.	[2a]	?Mary is having a bad cold.	[4a]

If sentences such as [1a–4a] do occur with the progressive, it is a sign that they have been in some sense reinterpreted as containing a dynamic predication. For example, *Peter is being awkward* signifies that 'awkwardness' is a form of behaviour or activity, not a permanent trait. If sentence [3a] were to occur, it would signify that Mary was *pretending* to be tired (*ie* indulging in a deceptive activity), rather than in a state of real lassitude.

Although verbs with stative meaning have sometimes been called 'nonprogressive', we should observe that the definition of stative verbs is not

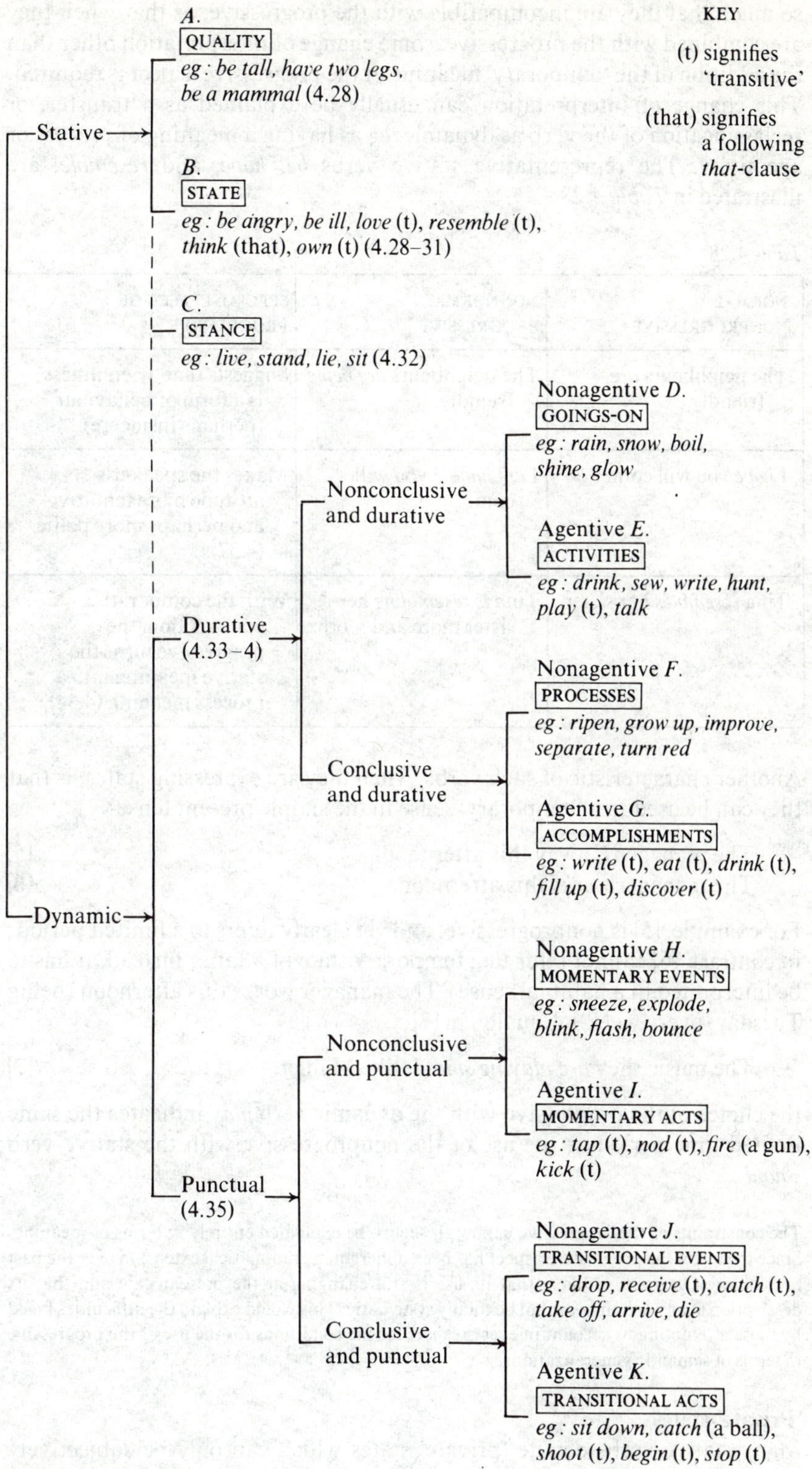
KEY
(t) signifies 'transitive'
(that) signifies a following *that*-clause
Stative
A. QUALITY
eg: be tall, have two legs, be a mammal (4.28)
B. STATE
eg: be angry, be ill, love (t), *resemble* (t), *think* (that), *own* (t) (4.28–31)
C. STANCE
eg: live, stand, lie, sit (4.32)
Dynamic
Durative (4.33–4)
Nonconclusive and durative
Nonagentive *D.* GOINGS-ON
eg: rain, snow, boil, shine, glow
Agentive *E.* ACTIVITIES
eg: drink, sew, write, hunt, play (t), *talk*
Conclusive and durative
Nonagentive *F.* PROCESSES
eg: ripen, grow up, improve, separate, turn red
Agentive *G.* ACCOMPLISHMENTS
eg: write (t), *eat* (t), *drink* (t), *fill up* (t), *discover* (t)
Punctual (4.35)
Nonconclusive and punctual
Nonagentive *H.* MOMENTARY EVENTS
eg: sneeze, explode, blink, flash, bounce
Agentive *I.* MOMENTARY ACTS
eg: tap (t), *nod* (t), *fire* (a gun), *kick* (t)
Conclusive and punctual
Nonagentive *J.* TRANSITIONAL EVENTS
eg: drop, receive (t), *catch* (t), *take off, arrive, die*
Agentive *K.* TRANSITIONAL ACTS
eg: sit down, catch (a ball), *shoot* (t), *begin* (t), *stop* (t)

Fig 4.27 Situation types

so much that they are incompatible with the progressive, as that when they are combined with the progressive, some change of interpretation other than the addition of the 'temporary' meaning of the progressive aspect is required. This change of interpretation can usually be explained as a transfer, or reclassification of the verb as dynamic, *eg* as having a meaning of process or agentivity. The representative stative verbs *be*, *hope*, and *resemble*, are illustrated in *Table* 4.28:

Table 4.28

NORMAL NONPROGRESSIVE	NONNORMAL PROGRESSIVE	SPECIAL EFFECT OF PROGRESSIVE
The neighbours *are* friendly.	The neighbours *are being* friendly.	Suggests that 'friendliness' is a form of behaviour (perhaps insincere).
I *hope* you will come.	I *am hoping* you will come.	Makes the speaker's attitude more tentative and perhaps more polite (4.37).
Tina *resembles* her sister.	Tina *is resembling* her sister more and more.	With the comparative construction, the progressive turns the stative meaning into a process meaning (4.34).

Another characteristic of such verbs, when they are expressing states, is that they can be used in a 'temporary' sense in the simple present tense:

The manager *is* away this afternoon. [5]
The manager *works* this afternoon. [6]

For example, [5] is nonprogressive, and yet clearly refers to a limited period; in contrast, [6] cannot refer to a temporary state of affairs; instead, it has to be interpreted in a habitual sense ['The manager works this afternoon (being Tuesday) every week']. Equally, in [7]:

The music they *are playing sounds* like Mahler. [7]

the choice of the progressive with the dynamic verb *play* indicates the same limited time period as the use of the nonprogressive with the stative verb *sound*.

Note The constraints of the progressive cannot, it seems, be explained entirely in terms of meaning. Since the use of the progressive aspect has been undergoing grammatical extension over the past few hundred years, it is likely that its use is still changing at the present day, and that its description at any one time cannot be totally systematic. This would explain the difficulties faced by those attempting to account in every respect for the conditions for the use of the progressive in terms of semantic generalizations.

'Private' states

4.29 Many stative verbs denote 'private' states which can only be subjectively verified: *ie* states of mind, volition, attitude, etc. We may distinguish:

(a) INTELLECTUAL STATES (*eg*: *know*, *believe*, *think*, *wonder*, *suppose*, *imagine*, *realize*, *understand*), especially when followed by a nominal clause as object:

I {*understand* / **am understanding*} that the offer has been accepted.

(b) STATES OF EMOTION OR ATTITUDE (*eg*: *intend*, *wish*, *want*, *like*, *dislike*, *disagree*, *pity*), especially when followed by clausal complementation:

She {likes / *is liking} to entertain the students.

Such verbs do, however, occur with the progressive when temporariness or tentativeness is being emphasized (*cf* 4.37), especially when the progressive is combined with the attitudinal past (*cf* 4.16):

What *were* you *wanting*?
I *was hoping* you would give me some advice.

The same applies to some verbs of Type (a) above (*eg think*).

(c) STATES OF PERCEPTION (*eg*: *see*, *hear*, *feel*, *smell*, *taste*), with which we may also place appearance as expressed by *seem* and *appear*. Perception verbs are more fully discussed in 4.30 below.

(d) STATES OF BODILY SENSATION (*eg*: *hurt*, *ache*, *tickle*, *itch*, *feel cold*). For predications belonging to this small but interesting category, the progressive and the nonprogressive are more or less interchangeable when referring to a temporary state:

My foot {*hurts.* / *is hurting.*} My back {*aches.* / *is aching.*}

Note The verb *feel* is versatile in that it can occur in all four categories above:

(a) I *feel* that the play will be a success. (c) The ground *feels* soft.
(b) We *felt* very angry. (d) She *feels* sick.

Feel can also occur as a dynamic perception verb (*cf* 4.30).

Verbs of perception

4.30 In the sphere of perception, stative meaning can be expressed in two ways: we can either place the perceiver in subject position, as in [1a–5a] below, or we can place the percept (or 'thing perceived') in subject position, as in [1b–5b]:

(i) PERCEIVER AT S

I *can see* the house. [1a]
We *could hear* singing. [2a]
I *could feel* vibrations. [3a]
Can you *smell* the soap? [4a]
I *could taste* the garlic in the soup. [5a]

(ii) PERCEPT AT S

The house *looks* empty. [1b]
The singing *sounded* far away. [2b]

The vibrations *felt* as if they could have been caused by an earthquake. [3b]
It *smells* of lavender. [4b]
The soup *tasted* strongly of garlic. [5b]

To express the state of perception with Type (i), we use the modal *can/could* followed by the verb of perception. The simple present or past would express dynamic meaning, so that the act of perception would be seen as an event with a defined beginning and endpoint. Compare:

I *heard* the bell ring. [event seen as a whole] [6]
I *could hear* the bells ringing. [perception continuing over a period] [7]

(A 'mixed-aspect' sentence *I heard the bells ringing* is also a possibility.) The present tense version of sentences like [6] is unusual:

I *hear* the bell ring! Aha, I *see* you!

Such sentences sound histrionic or playful because *hear* and *see* in this context exemplify the instantaneous present (*cf* 4.7). More acceptable examples with the simple present are sentences like *I smell something burning* and *Do you see anything moving outside?*, where emphasis is given to the suddenness of a perception.

Sentences such as [1a–5a] and [1b–5b] cannot normally occur with the progressive aspect, even though they are likely to refer to temporary rather than permanent states. This may be contrasted, however, with sentences containing the perception verbs *look* (*at*) and *listen* (*to*), which, being agentive and dynamic, describe an intentional activity, and occur quite commonly with the progressive:

A: What are you doing? B: { {*I'm *seeing* / I'm *looking at*} these photographs. / {?*I'm *hearing* / I'm *listening to*} a new record. }

The English language lacks special agentive perception verbs for the other three senses of touch, smell, and taste, so that the stative verbs *feel*, *smell*, and *taste* must do duty here, as well as for the two stative meanings:

What are you doing? { I'm *feeling* for the light switch. / I'm *smelling* the roses. / I'm *tasting* the wine, to see how sweet it is. }

In summary, then, we may display the four distinct uses of perception verbs as in *Table* 4.30.

Other verbs of similar behaviour to *see*, *hear*, etc are *perceive* and *detect*.

Note [a] *Look* in sense 'percept at S' is exceptional in occurring commonly with the progressive:

You {*look* / *are looking*} tired this evening.

There is little discernible difference between the progressive and nonprogressive variants here.

[b] Of course, there are nonperceptual uses of the verbs in *Table* 4.30. These include the use of *see* in the sense of 'meet': *I'm seeing the manager tomorrow*.

Table 4.30 Perception verbs

STATIVE		DYNAMIC	
PERCEPT AT S	PERCEIVER AT S	NONAGENTIVE	AGENTIVE
look	can/could *see*	*see*	*look (at)*
sound	can/could *hear*	*hear*	*listen (to)*
feel	can/could *feel*	*feel*	*feel*
smell	can/could *smell*	*smell*	*smell*
taste	can/could *taste*	*taste*	*taste*

[c] Note the exceptional use of *see* and *hear* with the progressive (focusing on the process of perception) in:

I need some spectacles. I'*m* not *seeing* things so well these days.

A: Did you hear a bell ring just then?

B: No. I can't hear a thing.

A: There it goes again! { I *am hearing* it now. / I *can hear* it now. }

In the following, too, the exceptional occurrence of the progressive seems to arise from perception being treated as an ongoing process: *Your soup's tasting better every day*; *My scarf is no longer smelling of lavender*. Such examples are very unusual, however.

Other states of 'being' and 'having'

4.31 The main verbs *be* and *have*, although they can both be used in dynamic senses, are the most central and characteristic of stative verbs, and can frequently be used in the paraphrasing of other stative verbs:

We *agree* with you. ~ We *are in agreement with* you.
The water *tasted* bitter. ~ The water *had* a bitter *taste*.

Apart from the 'private' verbs discussed in 4.29–30, there are other verbs which are paraphrasable in this way, and can be fittingly called 'verbs of being and having':

The box *contains* a necklace. [= 'A necklace is in the box']
The can *holds* two gallons. [= '. . . has a capacity of . . .']
Your age doesn't *matter*. [= '. . . is not important']
It *depends* on the weather. [= '. . . is dependent on . . .']
Jim *resembles* his sister. [= '. . . is like . . .']
She *belongs* to the tennis club. [= '. . . is a member of . . .']

These verbs also reveal their stative character in the above senses by their unacceptability with the progressive: **The box is containing a necklace*, etc.

Note Again, exceptional uses of these as 'process' verbs may be found; *eg*: *How much was the tank containing when you last inspected it?*

Type C: stance

4.32 In addition to the stative verbs noted above, there is a small but important class of verbs which express the situation type we will call STANCE, and which are intermediate between the stative and dynamic categories. The main stance verbs are *live*, *stand*, *sit* and *lie*, and they are characterized by their ability to be used both (a) with the nonprogressive to express a permanent state, and (b) with the progressive to express a temporary state:

James *lives* in Copenhagen. [permanent residence]
James *is living* in Copenhagen. [temporary residence]

The city *lies* on the coast. [permanent position]
People *were lying* on the beach. [temporary posture]

His statue *stands* in the city square. [permanent position]
He *is standing* over there. [temporary posture]

Similar possibilities exist with the perfective aspect: the perfective progressive, as well as the simple perfective, can be used to refer to a state leading up to the present:

I have *sat* here for over two hours. [1]
I have *been sitting* here for over two hours. [2]

Speakers differ, however, in judging how to choose between the constructions of [1] and [2]. Some speakers feel that [2] suggests a more temporary state, whereas others feel there is little to choose between the two variants. There is also sometimes a feeling that [1] is different from [2] in implying that the 'sitting' is concluded at the present moment, while [2] implies that the posture may well continue into the future.

Because of its intermediate status, the stance action type illustrates an element of gradience (*cf* 2.60) in the stative/dynamic contrast. At one end of the stative/dynamic scale, as *Fig* 4.27 shows, there are acts which lack appreciable duration, such as *nod* and *arrive*; at the other end, there are permanent qualities such as *be tall*. To some extent, the stative/dynamic dichotomy is an artificial division of this continuum. We move now to the bottom part of *Fig* 4.27, in order to consider the different varieties of dynamic meaning.

Dynamic types *D–K*

4.33 Among dynamic situation types in *Fig* 4.27, we have to distinguish eight types according to three binary oppositions:

Table 4.33 Dynamic situation types

	Durative		Punctual	
Non-conclusive	*D* GOINGS-ON	*E* ACTIVITIES	*H* MOMENTARY EVENTS	*I* MOMENTARY ACTS
Conclusive	*F* PROCESSES	*G* ACCOMPLISHMENTS	*J* TRANSITIONAL EVENTS	*K* TRANSITIONAL ACTS
	Nonagentive	Agentive	Nonagentive	Agentive

The DURATIVE/PUNCTUAL distinction separates happenings which are capable of having duration from those which are not. Since durative situation types take place over a (normally limited) period of time, they characteristically combine with the progressive. Punctual situation types, on the other hand, are theoretically incompatible with the progressive aspect: they can occur with the progressive, but only through a special interpretation (*cf* 4.35).

The CONCLUSIVE/NONCONCLUSIVE contrast draws a line between those situation types which result in a change of state and those which do not. For example, it is essential to the meaning of *opened* in *She opened the door* that the door ends up in a state of being open, which is different from the state in which it started. The notions of completion and incompletion apply to the conclusive situation types, but not to the nonconclusive ones. Conclusive situation types are those which allow a resultative interpretation of the perfective aspect (*cf* 4.22), *eg*: *The weather has improved* implies that 'the weather *is now better*'.

The AGENTIVE/NONAGENTIVE contrast is illustrated by *John was thinking* and *The sun was shining*. The first is agentive, in contrast to the second, because it implies that the subject refers to an agent or 'doer' of the action. The 'doer' is typically human, and is the deliberate or self-activating initiator of the action. To some extent, the agentive/nonagentive boundary is unclear; but agentive situation types are by definition dynamic rather than stative. The substitute verb *do* (*cf* 12.26) can substitute for an agentive situation type.

All dynamic situation types can combine with the progressive aspect, but they have various implications for the interpretation of the progressive, and it is to these that we now turn.

Durative situation types

4.34 Type *D*: GOINGS-ON

These are 'activities' carried out by inanimate forces; *eg*:

It *is raining*. The wind *is blowing* hard.
Is your watch *working*? The engine *was running* smoothly.

The difference between this type and Type *E* is that Type *E* is agentive.

Type *E*: ACTIVITIES

These (in contrast with Type *G*) are typically expressed by intransitive verbs with animate subjects:

Jill was writing/working/singing/dancing/eating/sewing/swimming/ etc.

But they also occur with some (normally noncount) direct objects:

The children are playing *chess*. Norman is reading *poetry*.

and occasionally with the passive: *The approaches to the city were being watched*.

Type *F*: PROCESSES

These denote a change of state taking place over a period:

The weather is *getting* warmer.
Our economic prospects *are* now *improving*.
The sun *is ripening* our tomatoes nicely.

As with Type *G*, the progressive with this type indicates the *incompleteness* of the change.

Type *G*: ACCOMPLISHMENTS
These denote an action or activity which takes place over a period and has a goal or endpoint. Intransitive verbs placed under Type *E* 'Activities' generally become accomplishments when a direct object or an adverbial of destination is added:

> Jill *is knitting* herself a sweater.
> The boys *were swimming* across the estuary.

By these additions, an activity becomes a task with a defined conclusion.

But the progressive indicates, with both processes and accomplishments, that the task was not necessarily completed:

> The boys *were swimming* across the estuary, but a giant wave made them turn back.
> One of the boys *was drowning*, but I dived in and saved him.

(*Cf*: **One of the boys drowned, but I dived in and saved him.*)

With accomplishments, there is a significant contrast between the constructions *finish V-ing* and *stop V-ing*:

> They have *finished* widening the road. [The task is complete.]
> They have *stopped* widening the road. [The task is not necessarily complete, but the activity has ceased.]

Punctual situation types

4.35 Types *H* and *I*: MOMENTARY EVENTS AND ACTS
The only difference between these two types is that *H* is nonagentive:

> The tops of the trees *were waving* in the wind, and the branches *were shaking* and *knocking* against the side of the house. Downstairs, a door *was banging*.

In this description, the verbs *knock* and *bang* can be said to describe momentary events (*ie* events effectively without duration) and when they are used with the progressive, we cannot make sense of them except by supposing that some repetition of the event took place. The same is true with momentary acts, expressed by verbs such as *nod* (when transitive), *fire*, and *jump*:

> John *was nodding* his head.
> Someone *was firing* at us.
> Kirov's horse *is jumping* well.

For example, *Someone was tapping on the window* would be inappropriate if there was only one tap. In this respect, momentary event verbs may be likened to count nouns such as *germ*, *pea*, *oat*, *hair*, *lentil*, which refer to small objects, and for which the singular count use (*a germ*, *a hair*, etc) is exceptional in comparison with the plural or noncount use. (On the analogy between noun and verb categories, *cf* 4.4.)

Types *J* and *K*: TRANSITIONAL EVENTS AND ACTS
These differ from Types *F* and *G* in that they have little or no duration, and

from Types *H* and *I* in that they involve a consequent change of state. Transitional events are nonagentive:

> The train *is arriving* at platform 4.
> The queen *was dying*.

Transitional acts are agentive:

> I'*m stopping* the car at this garage.
> It looks as if Juarez *is scoring* another goal.

Again, since the meaning of the predication effectively excludes duration, the progressive requires a special interpretation. In this case, the interpretation is likely to be anticipatory; *ie* that the progressive refers to a period LEADING UP TO the change of state: *eg*: *The Boeing 747 is taking off* refers to the accelerating of the plane preparatory to the actual take-off.

Note In other contexts, for example when the verb has a plural subject or object, a repetitive rather than anticipatory interpretation of such verb meanings is possible:

> At the airport, several freight aircraft *were taking off* noisily.

Progressive aspect in relation to tense

4.36 The progressive generally has the effect of surrounding a particular event or point of time with a 'temporal frame', which can be diagrammed:

That is, within the flow of time, there is some point of orientation from which the temporary event or state described by the verb can be seen to stretch into the future and into the past. With the present progressive, the time of orientation is normally 'now', although it can also be a recurrent time or an imaginary time, in accordance with the interpretation of the habitual progressive or the historic or fictional present:

> When the eight o'clock news comes on, I'*m* already *travelling* to work.
> The gunfire *is growing* louder ahead of us, as suddenly a fearful hush descends upon our company.

With the past tense, again the 'temporal frame' is often implied, this time by reference to a past time of orientation T_2 (*cf* 4.11–12):

> A moment later, we *were hurrying* for shelter beneath the trees.

Whereas the relationship between two simple past forms is normally one of TIME-SEQUENCE, the relationship between a past progressive and simple past form is one of TIME-INCLUSION:

> When we *arrived*, Jan *made* some fresh coffee.
> When we *arrived*, Jan *was making* some fresh coffee.

(*Cf* 14.27 Note [a] for exceptions.) The first example tells us that the coffee-making followed the arrival; the second, that the arrival took place during the coffee-making. The 'temporal frame', however, is not a necessary condition of the past progressive:

> We *were watching* the match all afternoon.

Since the adverbial *all afternoon* here refers to a longish period, there is no implication that the match forms a 'temporal frame' around the afternoon.

Note The idea of a 'temporal frame' is related to that of 'interrelationship or identity' discussed in 4.25 Note [b]; *cf*: *If he said that, he was lying.*

Other uses of the progressive aspect

4.37 In addition to its major function of indicating temporariness, the progressive also has the following special uses:

(a) It may be used to refer to the future or to the future in the past (*cf* 4.44, 4.48):

> *Are* you *going* to the meeting (tomorrow)?
> They *were getting* married the following spring.

On the future semi-auxiliary construction *be going to* + infinitive, *cf* 4.43.

(b) It may be used with the attitudinal past tense or the present tense, to refer tentatively to a present wish or attitude:

> I'*m hoping* to borrow some money.
> I *was wondering* if you could help me.

Contrast these sentences with the less tentative, and potentially less polite, use of the simple present:

> I *hope* to borrow some money.
> I *wonder* if you can help me.

Particularly when combined with the attitudinal past tense (*cf* 4.16), such forms enable us to avoid the impoliteness which might well result from expressing one's attitude too directly, *eg* in making a request.

(c) It may be used especially following the auxiliary *will* (or *shall*) with the special implication that the action will take place 'as a matter of course' in the future (*cf* 4.46):

> I'*ll be seeing* you next week.

Note The 'matter-of-course' implication of *will* (or *shall*) with the progressive is also found with other modal auxiliaries (*cf* 4.65 Note [a]), and possibly also with the past progressive in conversational contexts; *eg*: *I was talking to Ann, and she was telling me that the job is still vacant.* In contrast to the simple past *talked* and *told*, the progressive here suggests a casual chat rather than a purposeful discussion.

Perfective progressive

4.38 When the perfective and progressive aspects are combined in the same verb phrase (*eg*: *has been working*), the features of meaning associated with each of them are also combined. Nevertheless, the perfective progressive has a semantic range that is not entirely predictable from the meanings of its components.

Of the three features associated with the main meaning of the progressive (*cf* 4.25), DURATION, LIMITATION OF DURATION, and POSSIBLE INCOMPLETENESS, the first two give the perfective progressive a sense of 'temporariness', seen in these examples:

I'*ve been writing* a letter to my nephew.
How *have* you *been getting* on?
It'*s been snowing* again.

These sentences contain durative verbs which typically go with the progressive aspect, and the meaning of the construction is roughly that of TEMPORARY SITUATION LEADING UP TO THE PRESENT, comparable to the state-up-to-the-present use of the simple perfective (*cf* 4.18*ff*). With verbs such as *live, stand, lie*, etc, however, the limitation of duration is weak, and is not felt at all by some speakers:

We'*ve lived* in Europe all our lives. [1]
We'*ve been living* in Europe all our lives. [2]

Because of the lengthy time scale [2] is less likely than [1], but nevertheless [2] is by no means unacceptable.

The element of 'limited duration' makes it difficult to use the perfective progressive with punctual verbs:

He *has been starting* his car. [3]
?*He *has been starting* his book. [4]

Of these, [3] makes sense, although it reflects on the reliability of the car. On the other hand, [4] is nonsensical because it assigns duration to something which cannot have duration: the only way to make sense of it is to construe it as an ironical remark 'He has been trying/intending to start his book', in accordance with the anticipatory (*cf* 4.35) or future (*cf* 4.37) interpretation of the progressive.

4.39 The feature of possible incompleteness becomes evident when the perfective progressive is combined with accomplishment and process predications:

I've {cleaned / been cleaning} the windows.

The simple perfective here has a resultative meaning: 'The windows are now clean'. But the perfective progressive can be used even if the job is not finished:

{A: Have you cleaned the windows?
B: No, I haven't finished them yet.}

{A: Have you been cleaning the windows?
B: Yes, but I haven't finished them yet.}

{*I've written a novel, but I haven't finished it.
I've been writing a novel, but I haven't finished it.}

Because of its resultative meaning, the simple perfective cannot be used with accomplishment verbs when the clause contains an adverbial of duration:

They'*ve been repairing* the road *for months.*
*They'*ve repaired* the road *for months.*

An exception to this, however, occurs where the duration adverbial applies to the resultant state itself or where the clause is negative (*cf* 8.57*ff*):

They'*ve gone* to Spain *for two weeks.*
They *haven't repaired* the road *for years.*

If a conclusive verb is not accompanied by an adverbial of duration, the implication is often that the effects of the happening are still visible:

You've been fighting again. ['I can tell that from your black eye']
It's been snowing. ['Look, the ground is white']
Have you been crying? ['Your eyes are red']

In such cases, the activity indicated by the verb is assumed to have recently ceased. When accompanied by an adverbial of duration, however, the meaning of the verb is assumed to be still operative up to the present, and possibly to persist in the future:

He'*s been losing* money for years (and will probably continue to do so).

We may summarize the main use of the perfective progressive as follows:

The happening (a) has (limited) duration
(b) continues up to the present or recent past
(c) need not be complete
(d) may have effects which are still apparent.

4.40 As an additional possibility, the present perfective progressive may be used in the iterative sense of TEMPORARY HABIT UP TO THE PRESENT, comparable to the habitual use of the present perfective (*cf* 4.20):

Martin *has been scoring* plenty of goals (this season).
I've *been working* on the night shift for several weeks.

Again, it is implied that the repetition of the activity described may continue into the future.

The meaning of the perfective progressive may combine with those of the past tense and of the modal verbs:

The fire *had been raging* for over a week. [1]
You *should have been looking* after the baby. [2]
By Friday, we *will have been living here* for ten years. [3]

[1] and [3] require an appropriate shift of the time of orientation from 'now' (T_1) to a point (T_2) in the past or the future. As has already been explained with reference to the simple perfective (*cf* 4.19), the perfective progressive when combined with the past tense or a modal verb loses its restriction to a period of time leading up to the point of orientation. It may thus, unlike the

simple present perfective, be followed by an adverbial of time position. Contrast:

*I *have been talking* to him at the time of the murder.
I *had been talking* to him at the time of the murder.
I *must have been talking* to him at the time of the murder.

Note [a] The perfective progressive does not, however, combine freely with the passive voice. The following sentence is felt to be awkward (*cf* 3.55, 3.73):

The road *has been being repaired* for months.

The awkwardness of the perfective progressive passive is probably due in part to the juxtaposition of two forms of the verb *be* (*cf* 3.56). (*The road has been getting repaired for months*, for example, is more acceptable.)

[b] The perfective progressive can be ambiguous between habitual and nonhabitual readings. Such ambiguities, however, are unlikely to cause genuine misunderstanding:

I *have been cycling* to work for the last three weeks.

The nonhabitual reading, implying that the speaker has been cycling continuously for three weeks, in this case is factually absurd, but might provoke the comic response: *So why don't you get a job nearer home?*

Some means of expressing future time

4.41 Although according to the analysis we have adopted (*cf* 4.3) there is no future tense in English, it is useful at this point to consider the most important constructions for expressing future time, particularly in independent clauses (concerning dependent clauses, *cf* 14.22). Futurity, modality, and aspect are closely interrelated, and this is reflected in the fact that future time is rendered by means of modal auxiliaries, by semi-auxiliaries, or by the simple present or present progressive forms.

Will/shall + infinitive

4.42 The most common way of expressing futurity is the modal auxiliary construction with *will*, *shall*, or *'ll*:

He *will be* here in half an hour. [1]
Will you *need* any help? [2]
No doubt I*'ll see* you next week. [3]
If the crop fails there *will be* a famine. [4]

The modal verb *will* (or the contracted form *'ll*; *cf* 3.39–40) is used with future meaning with subjects of all three persons. The infrequent modal *shall* is used (especially in Southern Standard BrE) to indicate futurity, but only with a first person subject:

No doubt I *shall see* you next week. [3a]

Although *shall* and, particularly, *will* are the closest approximations to a colourless, neutral future, they do cover a range of meanings with modal colouring, from prediction to volition (*cf* 4.57*f*). A strong teaching tradition, especially in BrE, has upheld the use of *shall* as the correct form, in preference to *will*, with a first person subject in formal style.

Predictive *will* is particularly common in the clause superordinate to conditional or temporal clauses:

> You'*ll feel* better if/when you take this medicine. [5]

Even where no conditional clause is present, there is nevertheless frequently an implication that the future event or state of affairs will result from, or depend on, the fulfilment of certain future conditions which may not be specified:

> Take this medicine. You'*ll feel* better in an hour or so.
> How can you be sure that there *will be* a change of government at the next election?

Turning to the volitional examples, *will* and *shall* especially with the 1st and 2nd persons often express intention, *eg* in making agreements, promises, threats, etc:

> How soon *will* you *announce* your decision?
> We *shall ensure* that the repairs are carried out according to your wishes.

Other volitional and obligational uses are discussed in 4.57*f*.

Note With a 2nd or 3rd person subject, *will* can also express an abrupt and quasi-military command:

> You *will do* as I say.
> Officers *will report* for duty at 0600 hours.

Be going to **+ infinitive**

4.43 Another construction frequently used to express futurity, especially in informal speech, is *be going to* followed by the infinitive. Its general meaning is 'future fulfilment of the present'. Looked at more carefully, the construction has two more specific meanings, of which one, FUTURE FULFILMENT OF PRESENT INTENTION, is chiefly associated with personal subjects and agentive verbs:

> When *are* you *going to get* married?
> Leila *is going to lend* us her camera.
> I'*m going to complain* if things don't improve.

The other meaning, FUTURE RESULT OF PRESENT CAUSE, is found with both personal and nonpersonal subjects:

> It'*s going to rain.* She'*s going to have* a baby.
> There'*s going to be trouble.* You'*re going to get* soaked.

As these examples suggest, the association of *be going to* with the present often leads to the assumption that it indicates the proximity of the future event. Unlike *will* and *'ll*, *be going to* is not generally used in the clause superordinate to a conditional clause:

> If you leave now, you'*ll* never *regret* it.
> ?If you leave now, you *are* never *going to regret* it.

Note However, *be going to* does occur with conditional sentences like the following:

If you're expecting a first-class hotel, you*'re going to be* disappointed. [1]

Since the time of orientation for *be going to* is the present, it is used in conditional sentences only when the causal or contingent link between the meanings of the two clauses exists at the present time. In the more usual case, this link is placed in the future, and so *will* is used instead. The special import of *be going to* in [1] can be emphasized by adding before the subject of the main clause: 'I can already tell you that . . .'

Present progressive

4.44 The present progressive can refer to a future happening anticipated in the present. Its basic meaning is: FUTURE ARISING FROM PRESENT ARRANGEMENT, PLAN, OR PROGRAMME:

The orchestra *is playing* a Mozart symphony after this.
The match *is starting* at 2.30 (tomorrow).
I*'m taking* the children to the zoo (on Saturday).

We have seen that the progressive cannot normally be used with certain stative verb types (*eg* with the verb *be*) and this restriction also applies to the use of the progressive for future time:

*Strawberries are being more expensive next week.
(*cf*: Strawberries will be more expensive next week.)

Like *be going to*, the present progressive suggests that the future happening is imminent, unless this is contradicted by a more distant time mentioned in the context. Contrast:

That does it! I'm leaving. ['Soon' is understood]
I'm leaving the university *in two years' time*. [when I've finished my studies]

Note **[a]** It is easy to confuse this future use of the present progressive with the anticipatory use of the present progressive with transitional events or acts (*cf* 4.35). In principle, however, the distinction is clear between a future event which is planned and imminent, and a future event for which preparations are already taking place. *I'm leaving*, for example, could be understood in either of these ways, but *The old man was dying* can only be understood in the anticipatory sense.

[b] The future use of the present progressive is limited to actions brought about by human endeavour. Hence a sentence such as **The trees are losing their leaves soon* is inappropriate, implying that a tree has control over its future. Similarly, *He's dying next week* could only refer to a planned death, *eg* an execution.

Simple present

4.45 The simple present is, after the *will/shall* construction, the next most common means of referring to future actions in English (*cf* 4.9). This future use of the simple present is frequent, however, only in dependent clauses, where it is regularly used after conditional and temporal conjunctions such as *if* and *when*, as well as in some *that*-clauses (see further 14.22):

What will you say if I *marry* the boss?
At this rate, the guests will be drunk before they *leave*.

In main clauses, the future use of the simple present may be said to represent a marked future of unusual definiteness, attributing to the future the degree of certainty one normally associates with the present and the past. It is used, for example, for statements about the calendar:

Tomorrow *is* Thursday.   School *finishes* on 21st March.

Also to describe immutable events or 'fixtures', whether or not these are determined by human planning:

When *is* high tide?   What time *does* the match *begin*?

The simple present, like the progressive (*cf* 4.44), is used with dynamic transitional verbs *arrive*, *come*, *leave*, etc, both constructions having the meaning of 'plan' or 'programme':

The plane {takes off / is taking off} at 20:30 tonight. [1a] [1b]

The simple present, however, stresses the predetermined nature of the happening: while [1b] could well refer to a rescheduled take-off time (as a result, say, of a delay), this interpretation of [1a] would be unlikely.

Note [**a**] Although the simple present is the normal type of future construction to use in conditional clauses, the future use of *will* and *be going to* in such clauses is by no means impossible:

If the crops {*are* / *will be*} *ruined* by next month's drought, we'll have to buy in extra food.

If you'*re* (*going to be*) playing tennis against Jenny, you'd better borrow my racquet.

On the differences of meaning here, *cf* 14.22.

[**b**] Corresponding to the future use of the simple present in adverbial clauses is the following use of the present perfective referring to the past in the future:

The winner will be declared when every competitor *has finished* the course.

Will/shall + progressive infinitive

4.46 The modal verb construction discussed in 4.42 can be used with the progressive infinitive in a way which simply combines reference to a future time with the 'temporal frame' (*cf* 4.36) associated with the progressive:

When you reach the end of the bridge, I'*ll be waiting* there to show you the way.

This calls for no special comment. There is, however, a separate use of the *will/shall* + progressive construction to denote 'FUTURE AS A MATTER OF COURSE'. The use of this combination avoids the interpretation (to which *will*, *shall*, and *be going to* are liable) of volition, intention, promise, etc:

We'*ll be flying* at 30 000 feet.

This, spoken by the pilot of an aircraft to his passengers, means '30 000 feet is the normal and expected altitude for the flight'. If, on the other hand, the pilot said:

We'*ll fly* at 30 000 feet.

the impression might be quite different: it could well be that the pilot had just decided to fly at the specified height. Because of such differences, it is often an advantage to use this complex construction in situations where the nonprogressive with *will/shall* might be lacking in tact or consideration:

When *will* you {*pay* back / *be paying* back} the money? [1] [2]

Whereas [1] may seem like a rather abrupt demand for repayment, [2] seems more tactful, since it implies that the repayment is something which will happen 'as a matter of course'. In describing future happenings in which there is no direct human involvement, however, the choice between the progressive and nonprogressive alternatives is less important:

The next train to London *will* {*arrive* / *be arriving*} at platform four.

The only difference that need be mentioned here is that the progressive construction tends to be more informal than the ordinary nonprogressive construction.

Note Verbs that do not normally take the progressive can do so after future *will/shall* in this 'matter-of-course' sense: *He'll be owning his own house next.*

Concluding comments on constructions expressing future time

4.47 The foregoing five constructions are the most important methods of referring to future time. It has been found that in BrE the simple *will/shall* construction is much the most usual, followed by the simple present construction. (But by far the majority of simple present examples with future reference occur in dependent clauses, and are syntactically conditioned.) Of the remaining three constructions, *be going to* is the most common, followed by the present progressive, and finally by the *will/shall* + progressive construction. Although this last construction is least frequent, it is quite common in conversational contexts, and appears to be becoming more common.

Among other constructions referring to the future, reference must be made to the two quasi-auxiliary constructions *be to* + infinitive (*cf* 3.45*f*) and *be about to* + infinitive (*cf* 3.47). *Be to* is quite often used to refer to a future arrangement or plan:

Their daughter *is to be* married soon.
There'*s to be* an official inquiry.

In this use, *be to* + infinitive resembles the future use of the simple present (*cf* 4.45), except that the simple present cannot normally refer to the future unless accompanied by a time adverbial or some other future-referring expression.

Be about to, on the other hand, expresses near future:

The train *is about to* leave.
I'*m about to* read your essay.

The meaning of *be about to* could be alternatively expressed by *be on the point of* + *V-ing*, or by *be going to* together with the adverb *just* (meaning 'very soon'): *I'm just going to read your essay.*

This by no means exhausts the variety of verb constructions referring to future time. Futurity is often a secondary connotation of other modals than *will/shall*: *eg* with a dynamic verb, *may* or *must* usually locates the event in the future: *The weather may improve* (*tomorrow*); *You must have dinner with us* (*sometime soon*). The same secondary connotation of futurity is found with semi-auxiliaries such as *be sure to*, *be bound to* (*cf* 3.47), not to mention lexical verbs such as *hope* and *intend*.

While it is valuable to note differences of meaning between different future constructions, these differences should not be exaggerated. There are occasions where the choice of one construction (say *will* + infinitive) rather than another (say *be going to* + infinitive) has a scarcely perceptible effect on meaning. At the same time, there are differences of acceptability and usage which should not be ignored. Particularly, regarding the choice between *will* and *be going to*:

(a) *Will* is usually preferred to *be going to* in formal style.
(b) *Be going to* tends not to be repeated in a text referring pervasively to the future. Thus a weather forecast may run as follows:

> Tomorrow *is going to* be another cold day. There *will* be snow on high ground, and many mountain roads *will* be impassable. . . .

Note *Be to* + infinitive in referring to the future also conveys the connotations of 'requirement' and 'destiny' in examples such as:

> You *are to be* back by 10 o'clock. ['. . . required to be . . .']
> If he'*s to succeed* in his new profession, he must try harder.
> The prisoner *is to be* handed over to the civil authorities for trial.

Future time in the past

4.48 Most of the future constructions just discussed can be used in the past tense to describe something which is in the future when seen from a viewpoint in the past.

(a) MODAL VERB CONSTRUCTION with *would* ⟨rare; literary narrative style⟩

> The time was not far off when he *would* regret this decision.

(b) *BE GOING TO* + INFINITIVE (often with the sense of 'unfulfilled intention')

> You *were going to* give me your address. ['. . . but you didn't . . .']
> The police *were going to* charge her, but at last she persuaded them she was innocent.

(c) PAST PROGRESSIVE (arrangement predetermined in the past)

> I *was meeting* him in Bordeaux the next day.

(d) *BE TO* + INFINITIVE ⟨formal⟩; (i) = 'was destined to'; (ii) = 'arrangement'

> (i) He *was* eventually *to* end up in the bankruptcy court.
> (ii) The meeting *was to* be held the following week.

(e) *BE ABOUT TO* + INFINITIVE ('on the point of'; often with the sense of 'unfulfilled intention')

> He *was about to* hit me.

Of all these constructions, only (a) and (di) can be considered genuine expressions of future-in-the-past meaning, in that they alone can be understood to guarantee the fulfilment of the happening in question. For instance:

Few could have imagined at that time that this brave young officer {*was to be* / *would be*} the first President of the United States of America.

This sentence implies that the young officer (George Washington) *did* eventually become president of the United States. The other constructions, however (especially (b) and (e)), favour an interpretation of nonfulfilment.

Note These future-in-the-past interpretations, whether or not they imply fulfilment, should be distinguished from those of the same constructions used in indirect speech or free indirect speech (*cf* 14.31*ff*); *eg*:

I was convinced that no one *would* interfere.
Surely no one *would* object, she thought.
He told us he *was going to* resign.

In these cases, *would* and *was going to* report what was said or thought to be the case, according to some explicit or implicit 'speaker' or 'thinker'.

Meanings of the modal verbs

4.49 Like other terms used in analysing meaning in the complex verb phrase, such as *mood* and *aspect*, MODALITY has been used in various senses. At its most general, *modality* may be defined as the manner in which the meaning of a clause is qualified so as to reflect the speaker's judgment of the likelihood of the proposition it expresses being true. As with terms like *present* and *past*, this semantic definition makes only an imperfect match with the correspondingly-named formal category, that of modal auxiliary verbs. None the less, it will serve to indicate in general terms the function which these verbs perform in the language.

In the modal verbs, the constraining factors of meaning mentioned above may be divided into two types:

(a) Those such as 'permission', 'obligation', and 'volition' which involve some kind of intrinsic human control over events, and
(b) Those such as 'possibility', 'necessity', and 'prediction', which do not primarily involve human control of events, but do typically involve human judgment of what is or is not likely to happen.

These two kinds, between which there is a gradient, may be termed INTRINSIC and EXTRINSIC modality respectively. One important observation about the modals is that each one of them has both intrinsic and extrinsic uses: for example, *may* has the meaning of permission (intrinsic) and the meaning of possibility (extrinsic); *will* has the meaning of volition (intrinsic) and the meaning of prediction (extrinsic). However, there are areas of overlap and neutrality between the intrinsic and extrinsic senses of a modal: the *will* in a sentence such as *I'll see you tomorrow then* can be said to combine the meanings of volition and prediction. Another point of significance is that the modals themselves tend to have overlapping meanings, such that in some circumstances (but not in others), they can be more or less interchangeable. *Should* and *ought to*, for example, are more or less interchangeable with the meanings of 'obligation' and 'tentative inference'. *Can* and *may* overlap to a small extent in the areas of permission and possibility, but this overlap is almost entirely confined to written or formal English, and these modals are very far from being generally in free variation.

Note In place of *intrinsic* and *extrinsic* modality, other terminologies, such as *modulation* and *modality*, or *root* and *epistemic* modality, are widespread. An alternative practice, which we follow (*cf* 4.51, 4.53), is to regard the root/epistemic distinction as a subcategorization of extrinsic modality. Another term widely used for the modality of obligation and permission is *deontic*.

4.50 The above points help to show why the use of the modal verbs is one of the more problematic areas of English grammar, and one of the areas where many studies have been made. Other factors which impede easy generalization are the following:

(a) Certain modals such as *can* and *will* are extremely common, whereas others, such as *shall*, *ought to*, and *need* (*qua* auxiliary) are relatively rare (*cf* 3.39 Note).

(b) Although historically, most of the modals can be paired into past and nonpast forms (*can/could*, *may/might*, *will/would*, *shall/should*), the 'past tense' forms are only in some respects usefully classified as such from the point of view of meaning.

(c) The use of the modals varies significantly from one part of the English-speaking world to another. There are considerable differences in this respect between AmE and BrE: for example, the three verbs described as 'rare' above are in fact substantially rarer in AmE than in BrE; moreover, Scots, Irish, and Northern English varieties resemble AmE in some respects more than they resemble the 'standard' southern usage which tends to be treated as representative of BrE. Increasingly even in Southern Standard BrE the forms formerly associated with AmE are becoming the norm.

In view of such variations and complications, we can give only an outline of the semantics of the modals here. For the purposes of this outline, we consider the modal auxiliaries in groups with similar or overlapping meanings. We also relate the meanings of the central modals (*cf* 3.39), where useful, to the meanings of marginal auxiliaries such as *ought to*, *have* (*got*) *to*, and *need*. We shall give, where important, some idea of the frequency or stylistic range of a modal. We begin by treating the present and past forms (*eg*: *can* and *could*) together, and later (in 4.59–64) turn our attention to special aspects of the use of the past forms *could*, *might*, *should*, and *would*.

The modals are often associated with particular pragmatic uses, *eg* in requests, offers, etc, where the past forms tend to have implications of tentativeness or politeness. We deal with these aspects of modal usage mainly in the Notes, but *cf* also 4.63.

In the following sections (4.51–65) we concentrate primarily on the modals in declarative clauses. The negative and interrogative uses of the modals are dealt with in 10.67*f* and 11.13 respectively.

4.51

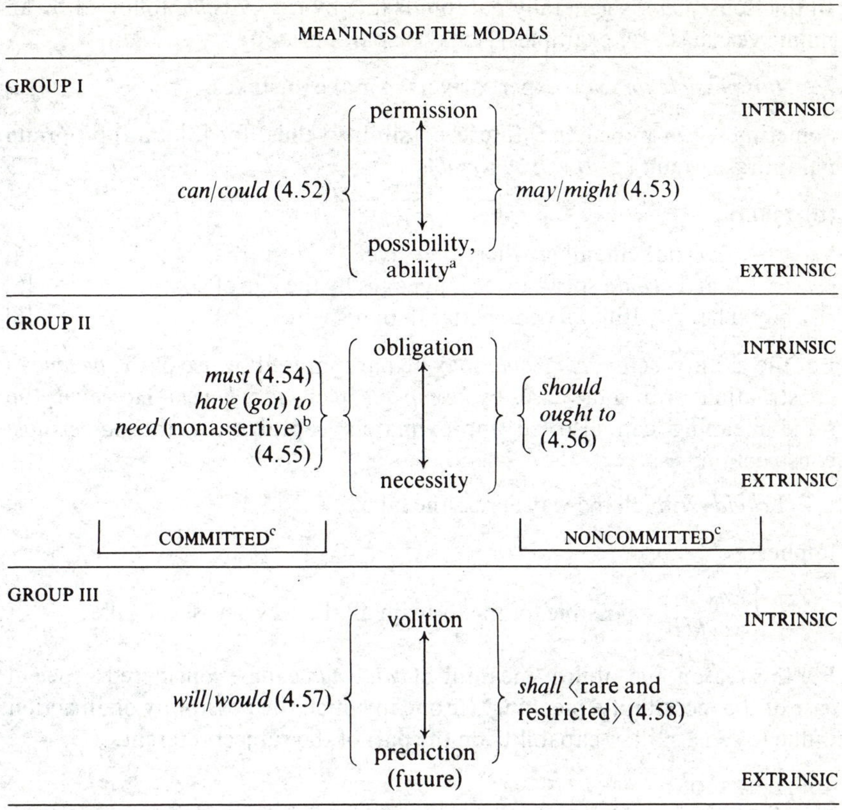

Fig 4.51

Notes to *Fig* 4.51:
[a] The 'ability' meaning of *can* is considered extrinsic, even though ability typically involves human control over an action. 'Ability' is best considered a special case of possibility (*cf* 4.52).
[b] On nonassertive restrictions in the use of *need* as an auxiliary, *cf* 3.42.
[c] The meaning of the labels 'committed' and 'noncommitted' with reference to *must*, *should*, etc is clarified in 4.54*ff* below, esp 4.56; *cf* also *Fig* 4.66.

Fig 4.51 gives a summary of the main modal meanings. The arrows separate intrinsic from corresponding extrinsic meanings, and are a reminder that the distinctions between these two are gradual rather than absolute. The *Figure* does not, however, distinguish the EPISTEMIC uses of *may*, *must* and *have* (*got*) *to* (*cf* 4.53–5); these form a clear-cut subcategory of the 'possibility' and 'necessity' meanings.

Can/could

4.52 Three major meanings of these modals may be distinguished:

(a) POSSIBILITY (especially in questions and negatives; *cf* 10.67*f*, 11.13)

Even expert drivers *can* make mistakes.	[1]
Her performance was the best that *could* be hoped for.	[2]
If it's raining tomorrow, the sports *can* take place indoors.	[3]

In this sense, *can* is generally paraphrasable by *it is possible* followed by an infinitive clause; for example, [1] may be paraphrased:

It is possible for even expert drivers *to* make mistakes. [1a]

Sometimes, *can* indicates a future possibility; thus, for [3] an appropriate paraphrase would be: *It will be possible . . .*

(b) ABILITY

Can you remember where they live? [4]
Magda *could* speak three languages by the age of six. [5]
They say Bill *can* cook better than his wife. [6]

For the 'ability' sense, *can/could* may be paraphrased by use of the *be able to* construction, or in some cases by *be capable of* or *know how to*. However, the same meaning can also be approximately captured by the *be possible* construction; *eg*:

I *could* swim all the way across the lake.

implies:

It {*was* / *would be*} possible for me to swim all the way across the lake.

For this reason, the 'ability' meaning of *can/could* can be considered a special case of the 'possibility' meaning, *viz* one in which the possibility of an action is due to some skill or capability on the part of the subject referent.

(c) PERMISSION

Can we borrow these books from the library? [7]
In those days only men *could* vote in elections. [8]

In this sense, *can/could* is less formal than *may*, which has been favoured by prescriptive tradition (*cf* 4.53). (However, *might* in the sense of past permission is so rare – *cf* 4.61 Note [a] – that not even traditionalists would favour its use in [8].) It is possible to paraphrase *can* in the sense of permission by *be allowed to*:

Are we *allowed to* borrow these books from the library? [7a]

Note [**a**] *Can/could* [= possibility] is often used in a quasi-imperative manner, to suggest a course of action to the addressee. The instruction can be made more polite by using *could* (*cf* 4.62*f*), or by adding a conditional clause such as *if you like*:

You *can* sit here until I get back (if you like).
You children *could* help me move these chairs.

By turning the statement into a question, the speaker changes the suggestion into a rather polite request:

Can/could you (please) check these figures?

[**b**] *Can* [= ability] occurs in certain informal negative verb phrases, such as *cannot/can't help*, *cannot/can't stand*, and *cannot/can't bear*. The negative orientation of these phrases means that their positive counterparts cannot be used, except in semantically negative contexts; *eg* in questions with a negative bias, or in 'second instance' contexts where a contrast with the negative is implied:

How *can* you bear that noise? [implies: 'It is unbearable']
A: I *can't help* singing out of tune.
B: Well, you CǑULD *help* it: you could simply be QUÌET.

[c] *Can* [= permission] is combinable with a future time adverbial (*eg*: *You can borrow my typewriter tomorrow*); but *can* [= ability] normally is not:

?You *can* pass your driving test next time you take it.

For future ability, the construction to use is *will be able to*:

You *will be able to* pass your driving test next time you take it.

except that *can* may be used in clauses, such as *if*-clauses, in which the present tense is normally used for future reference (*cf* 14.22):

If you *can* pass your driving test next month, you will be able to visit us more often during the summer.

[d] On the special stative use of *can/could* [= ability] with perception verbs (*eg*: *can see*), *cf* 4.30. There is a similar tendency to use this auxiliary with mental-state verbs such as *remember* and *understand*, as in [4] above, where *Can you remember . . .?* is scarcely distinguishable in meaning from *Do you remember . . .?*

May/might

4.53 (a) POSSIBILITY

We *may* never succeed. [It is possible that we'll never succeed] [1]
You *may* be right. [It is possible that you are right] [2]
There *might* be some complaints. [3]

As these examples suggest, the most common meaning of *may* [= possibility] is different from the possibility sense of *can*. To paraphrase *may*, we use *it is possible* followed by a *that*-clause, rather than an infinitive clause. *May* in this sense may also be paraphrased by *It may be that* . . ., or by the adverb *perhaps* or *possibly*. Thus [2] is equivalent to:

It may be that you are right. [2a]
Perhaps/possibly you are right. [2b]

This meaning of *may* is termed EPISTEMIC POSSIBILITY; *ie* it denotes the possibility of a given proposition's being or becoming true. *May* in the sense of epistemic possibility is normally stressed, and is often associated with fall-rise nuclear tone.

Might [= possibility] can be used as a (somewhat more tentative) alternative to *may* [= possibility], as in [3] (*cf* 4.63), and indeed is often preferred to *may* as a modal of epistemic possibility.

Less commonly, in formal English, *may/might* is used in the same possibility sense as *can/could*, a sense which may be distinguished by the label ROOT POSSIBILITY:

During the autumn, many rare birds *may* be observed on the rocky northern coasts of the island. [4]

May in [4] is a more formal substitute for *can*, and the whole sentence could be paraphrased *It is possible to observe* . . .

(b) PERMISSION

You *may* borrow my bicycle if you wish. [5]
Visitors *may* reclaim necessary travel expenses up to a limit of £50. [6]
Might I ask whether you are using the typewriter? [7]

As a permission auxiliary, *may* is more formal and less common than *can*, which (except in fixed phrases such as *if I may*) can be substituted for it.

However, *may* is particularly associated with permission given by the speaker. That is, a difference is sometimes felt between *You may leave when you like* [= 'I permit you . . .'] and *You can leave when you like* [= 'You are permitted . . .'], which can mean permission in a more general and impersonal sense. Not all English speakers acknowledge this distinction, however; and the prescriptive bias in favour of *may* leads to its use in official documents and notices, etc, as in [6] above, even where there is no restriction to 'speaker's permission'.

Again, *might* is used as a somewhat more tentative, and therefore polite, variant of *may* [= permission], as in [7] (*cf* 4.61). It is rare and apparently obsolescent in this usage.

Note [**a**] In interrogatives and in auxiliary negation, *may* in the sense of epistemic possibility is normally replaced by *can* (*cf* 10.67*f*, 11.13). Note the difference between:

She *may not* be serious. [It is possible that . . . not . . .]
She *can't* be serious. [It is not possible that . . .]

[**b**] There is a rare use of *may* with subject–operator inversion (*cf* 18.24) in volitional sentences which parallel the function of the formulaic subjunctive (*cf* 3.60):

May the best man win! [= Let the best man win!]
May he never set foot in this house again!
May God bless you! [= God bless you!]

[**c**] Another 'quasi-subjunctive' use of *may/might* is observed in subordinate clauses of concession or purpose:

Strange as/though it *may* seem . . . (*cf* 15.39)
Christ died, that we *might* live. (*cf* 15.48 Note [b])

Particularly in purpose clauses, this construction is formal and somewhat archaic.

[**d**] Related to the above use of *may* in concessive adverbial clauses, there is a tendency for main clauses containing *may* to have a concessive force preceding *but*:

We *may* have our differences from time to time, but basically we trust one another's judgment. [8]

The modal loses something of its 'possibility' sense here, as is shown by the paraphrase:

I admit that we have our differences . . . but . . .

ie the proposition expressed by the first clause of [8] is presumed to be true but (perhaps out of politeness) the modal construction is preferred to the alternative construction with the simple present.

[**e**] The idiomatic expression *may/might* (*just*) *as well* is typically used to make a somewhat reluctant or sardonic recommendation:

We *may as well* stay here the night (as look for a better place elsewhere). [9]
You *might as well* tell the truth (as continue to tell lies). [10]

The negative aspect of these recommendations is highlighted by the optional comparative clause, which is usually omitted. Their force could be expressed as follows:

'There's no point in looking elsewhere . . .'
'There's no point in your continuing to tell lies . . .'

Cf: *may/might/can/could well*, 8.103.

Must

4.54 (a) (LOGICAL) NECESSITY

There *must* be some mistake. [1]
You *must* be feeling tired. [2]
The Smiths *must* have a lot of money. [3]

The 'logical necessity' meaning of *must* is parallel to the use of *may* in the sense of epistemic possibility; it may, indeed, be called 'epistemic necessity', since it implies that the speaker judges the proposition expressed by the clause to be necessarily true, or at least to have a high likelihood of being true. *Must* in this sense means that the speaker has drawn a conclusion from things already known or observed. For example, the speaker of [3] has observed the Smiths living in a large house, travelling in an expensive car, etc, and therefore draws the conclusion that they 'must' be rich. *Must* [= logical necessity] cannot normally be used in interrogative or negative clauses. The negative of *can* [= possibility] fills the gap, so that *You must be joking* ['It is necessarily the case that you are joking'] is synonymous with *You can't be serious* ['It is impossible that you are serious']. Similarly:

She *must* be asleep = She *can't* be awake.

In addition to epistemic necessity, there is a ROOT NECESSITY meaning of *must* in examples like:

To be healthy, a plant *must* receive a good supply of both sunshine and moisture. [4]

Must here can be glossed 'It is essential for . . .' or 'It is necessary for . . .'. There is, however, no implication in [4] of human control, and this distinguishes the root necessity use of *must* from its other root sense of obligation, to which we now turn.

(b) OBLIGATION *or* COMPULSION

You *must* be back by ten o'clock. ['You are obliged to be back . . .'; 'I require you to be back . . .'] [5]
We *must* all share our skills and knowledge. [6]
Productivity *must* be improved, if the nation is to be prosperous. [7]

In these examples, there is the implication, to a greater or lesser extent, that the speaker is advocating a certain form of behaviour. Thus *must*, unlike *have (got) to*, typically suggests that the speaker is exercising his authority. An apparent exception to this occurs where the subject is in the first person:

I *must* remember to write to Aunt Anna. [8]
I'm afraid I *must* go now: I promised to be home at ten. [9]

But this, we can say, is perfectly consistent with *must* [= obligation], because the meaning is one of self-admonishment, *ie* the speaker in this case exercises authority over himself, appealing to his own sense of duty, expediency, etc.

Note [**a**] On the use of obligating *must* in negative and interrogative clauses, *cf* 10.67*f*; 11.13.

[**b**] Occasionally, *must* [= logical necessity] does occur with negations:

His absence *must not* have been noticed.

This has the same meaning as *His absence can't have been noticed.* Such sentences have been regarded by many commentators as impossible, but are increasingly accepted and used, especially in AmE.

[**c**] There is a similarly rare occurrence of *must* [= logical necessity] in questions:

Must there be some good reason for the delay?

This assumes a positive answer, and might be glossed: 'Does there have to be some good reason . . .?'

[**d**] *Must* [= root necessity] has a sarcastic use in some utterances with a 2nd person subject:

If you *must* smoke, at least you could use an ashtray.
Why *must* you always be finding fault with that girl?

Need, have (got) to

4.55 The close relationship between *must* and the quasi-modals *need, have got to,* and *have to* (*cf* 3.42, 3.45, 3.48) deserves comment at this point. *Need* (constructed as an auxiliary) is used (esp in BrE) as the negative and question form of *must* in root senses:

Need they make all that noise? [= '*Do* they *need*/*have to* make all that noise?'] ⟨esp BrE⟩
You *needn't* worry about the test. [= 'You *don't need*/*have to* worry about that test'.] ⟨esp BrE⟩

As the above glosses show, however, it is possible, and indeed, more common even in BrE, to replace auxiliary *need* by *need to* or *have to* accompanied by *do*-support (*cf* 3.37).

Have (*got*) *to* can also be substituted for *must* with little or no difference of meaning. Compare the following with the parallel sentences in 4.54:

(a) (LOGICAL) NECESSITY

There *has* (*got*) *to* be some mistake. ⟨esp AmE⟩ [1]
To be healthy, a plant *has to* receive a good supply of both sunshine and moisture. [4]

(b) OBLIGATION OR COMPULSION

You *have* (*got*) *to* be back by ten o'clock. [5]
We *have* all *got to* share our skills and knowledge. [6]
Productivity will *have to* be improved, if the nation is to be prosperous. [7]

In the logical necessity sense of [1], *have* (*got*) *to* is rather more emphatic than *must*, and is found chiefly in AmE. In the obligation sense of [5–7], *have* (*got*) *to* is often felt to be more impersonal than *must*, in that it tends to lack the implication that the speaker is in authority. This is particularly noticeable with a 1st person subject:

I'm afraid I *have* (*got*) *to* go now. [8]

Where *must* implies 'self-obligation', *have* (*got*) *to* implies 'obligation by external forces'. Thus [8] might be used where, for example, another appointment compels the speaker to leave at a particular time.

Since *must* has no past tense form and no nonfinite forms, *have to* is used in many contexts where *must* is impossible (*cf* 3.30, 3.48), *eg* following a modal verb: *We'll have to be patient.*

Note [**a**] *Have to* and *have got to* are used in sarcastic utterances like those illustrated for *must* in 4.54 Note [d]:

Do you *have to* make that noise when you eat?

There is an equivalent past tense use of *had to*:

The rain was bad enough – but then it *had to* snow!

The author of this sentence jokingly blames the weather's perverse behaviour.

[**b**] Some native speakers do not recognize the distinction between 'self-obligation' (*I*/*we must*) and 'obligation by external forces' (*I*/*we have to*).

Ought to and *should*

4.56 Here we turn to another marginal auxiliary, *ought to*, and a synonymous use of *should*. Although differing from *must* and *have (got) to*, these verbs express the same basic modalities of 'necessity' and 'obligation'. Where they contrast with *must* and *have (got) to* is in not expressing the speaker's confidence in the occurrence of the event or state described. Hence [1] is nonsensical, but [2] is not:

*Sarah {*must* / *has to*} be home by now, but she isn't. [1]

Sarah {*should* / *ought to*} be home by now, but she isn't. [2]

(a) TENTATIVE INFERENCE

The mountains {*should* / *ought to*} be visible from here. [3]

These plants {*should* / *ought to*} reach maturity after five years. [4]

The term which best seems to characterize the 'noncommitted necessity' meaning of *should* and *ought to* is 'tentative inference'. That is, the speaker does not know if his statement is true, but tentatively concludes that it is true, on the basis of whatever he knows. Apart from this tentativeness, *should* and *ought to* differ from *must* in that they frequently refer to the future; *eg*:

The job *should/ought to* be finished by next Monday.

(b) OBLIGATION

You {*should* / *ought to*} do as he says. [5]

The floor {*should* / *ought to*} be washed at least once a week. [6]

Like *must* [= obligation], *should* and *ought to* generally imply the speaker's authority; but unlike *must*, they do not imply that the speaker has confidence that the recommendation will be carried out. In fact, with the perfective aspect, *should* and *ought to* typically have the stronger implication that the recommendation has *not* been carried out:

They {*should* / *ought to*} have met her at the station. [7]

The likely implication of [7] is '. . . but they didn't'. In both senses (a) and (b) *should* is more frequent than *ought to*.

Note Another difference between *should* and *ought to* (in the sense of tentative inference) and *must* is that the former modals tend to carry over from their obligational sense the suggestion that the proposition within their scope is desirable. Contrast:

There *should* be another upturn in sales shortly.

?There *should* be another disaster shortly.

The second sentence is decidedly odd, suggesting that the speaker takes a favourable view of disasters.

Will/would ('ll/'d)

4.57 From the semantic point of view, as well as from the historical point of view, *'ll* and *'d* are to be regarded as contractions of *will* and *would* respectively, rather than of *shall* and *should*. To see this, we note that where *shall* and *should* are not interchangeable with *will* and *would*, the contraction does not substitute for *shall/should*, though it can for *will/would*. For instance, in [7] of 4.56 above, the contraction *They'd have met her at the station* is not possible in the sense of 'ought to'. Conversely, in:

You *will* feel better after this medicine. [1]

where *will* in the predictive sense could not be replaced by *shall*, the contraction to *'ll* is possible:

You*'ll* feel better after this medicine. [1a]

(a) PREDICTION

Under the heading of PREDICTION, three related uses of *will/would* are to be distinguished.

(a1) The common FUTURE predictive sense of *will* illustrated in [1] above has already been discussed in 4.42 and 4.46. The corresponding 'prediction in the past' sense of *would* (*cf* 4.48) is illustrated by:

I was told I *would* feel better after this medicine. [2]

(a2) The PRESENT predictive sense of *will*, which is comparatively rare, is similar in meaning to *must* in the 'logical necessity' sense:

She *will* have had her dinner by now. [3]
That*'ll* be the postman. [on hearing the doorbell ring] [4]

This meaning can be roughly paraphrased: 'It is (very) likely that . . .'

(a3) The HABITUAL predictive meaning often occurs in conditional sentences:

If litmus paper is dipped in acid, it *will* turn red.

or in timeless statements of 'predictability':

Oil *will* float on water.

In addition, it occurs in descriptions of personal habits or characteristic behaviour:

He*'ll* talk for hours, if you let him. [said of a chatterbox]
She*'ll* sit on the floor quietly all day. She*'ll* just play with her toys, and you *won't* hear a murmur from her. [of a good baby]
Every morning he *would* go for a long walk. [*ie* 'it was his custom to go . . .']

In past tense narratives, *would* in this sense is a popular means of describing habitual behaviour:

In the spring the birds *would* return to their old haunts, and the wood *would* be filled with their music . . .

This use of *would* is rather more formal than the equivalent use of *used to*, and unlike *used to*, needs to be associated with a time indicator, such as *In the spring* in the above example.

(b) VOLITION

Again, three different subsenses may be distinguished. The volitional range of *will* extends from the 'weak volition' of WILLINGNESS to the 'strong volition' of INSISTENCE. Between these two, there is the more usual volitional sense of INTENTION, which often combines with a sense of prediction (*cf* 4.42, 4.46):

(b1) INTENTION

> I'*ll* write as soon as I can.
> We *won't* stay longer than two hours.
> The manager said he *would* phone me after lunch.

(b2) WILLINGNESS

> *Will*/*Would* you help me to address these letters?
> I'*ll* do it, if you like.

This meaning is common in requests and offers. On the greater politeness of *would*, *cf* 4.63.

(b3) INSISTENCE

> If you '*will* go out without your overcoat, what can you expect?
> She '*would* keep interrupting me.

This somewhat rare use implies wilfulness on the part of the subject referent. The auxiliary is always stressed, and cannot be contracted to '*ll* or '*d*. In this case, the past form *would* expresses past time, rather than tentativeness or politeness.

Note [**a**] The predictive meaning of *will* is sometimes weakened, so that it resembles the ability meaning of *can*:

> That's a fine car. How fast *will* it go?
> The new grandstand *will* hold ten thousand spectators.

The negative of this 'potentiality' sense of *will* seems to have something of the personificatory force of 'refusal' (*ie* the negation of willingness):

> It's a good piano, but it just *won't* stay in tune.
> I tried to open the door, but the key *wouldn't* turn.

It is almost as if the piano or the key had a will of its own.

[**b**] In requests, the sense of willingness (b2) is often expressed more tentatively and politely by the use of the past tense form *would*:

> *Would* you please be quiet?

Cf the comparable use of *could*, 4.52 Note [a].

[**c**] There is an idiomatic use of *would* with nuclear stress conveying a certain feeling of exasperation at the behaviour of another:

> A: Of course, Ian spoiled the whole show with his feeble jokes.
> B: Oh, he WÒULD (spoil the whole show).

The force is that Ian's foolish behaviour was utterly typical and predictable. There is no equivalent use of *will*.

Shall

4.58 *Shall* is in present-day English (especially in AmE) a rather rare auxiliary and only two uses, both with a 1st person subject, are generally current:

(a) PREDICTION (with 1st person subjects)
Shall is a substitute for the future use of *will* in formal style:

According to the opinion polls, I {*will* / *shall*} win quite easily.

When {*will* / *shall*} we know the results of the election?

Especially in BrE, prescriptive tradition forbids *will* as a future auxiliary with *I* or *we*, but this prescription is old-fashioned and is nowadays widely ignored.

(b) VOLITION (with 1st person subjects)
In the intentional sense, *shall* is again a formal (and traditionally prescribed) alternative to *will* after *I* or *we*:

We {*will* / *shall*} uphold the wishes of the people.

In questions containing *shall I/we*, *shall* consults the wishes of the addressee, and thus moves from a volitional towards an obligational meaning. It is suitable for making offers:

Shall I/we deliver the goods to your home address? [= Do you want me/us to . . .?] [1]

and for making suggestions about shared activities:

What *shall* we do this evening? *Shall* we go to the theatre? [2]

It is only in such questions that *shall* cannot regularly be replaced by *will*. Note that [1] illustrates the exclusive use of *we* (*cf* 6.7), while [2] illustrates the inclusive use, *ie* the use of *we* which includes reference to the addressee(s).

Note [**a**] The inclusive *we* following *shall* is also found in tag questions following a 1st person imperative (*cf* 11.10, 11.26 Note [a]):

Let's have dinner out tonight, *shall* we?

[**b**] *Shall* is in very restricted use with 2nd and 3rd person subjects as a way of expressing the *speaker's* volition, either in granting a favour:

You *shall* do just as you wish.
She *shall* get her money as soon as she has earned it.

or in giving orders:

You *shall* do exactly as I say.
He *shall* be punished if he disobeys.

In these cases *shall* is archaic and 'authoritarian' in tone.

[**c**] A further restricted use of *shall* with a 3rd person subject occurs in legal or quasi-legal discourse, in stipulating regulations or legal requirements. Here *shall* is close in meaning to *must*:

The vendor *shall* maintain the equipment in good repair.

Note in this connection the archaic use of *shalt* in the Biblical Ten Commandments; *eg*: *Thou shalt not kill*. (On the archaic 2nd person form *shalt*, *cf* 3.4 Note [b].)

[**d**] Although *should* cannot normally be regarded as a past tense form of *shall*, there are occasions when it is appropriately interpreted as such. In [3] below, *should* is a past tense equivalent of *shall* in indirect speech, and in [4], it appears to be a tentative past tense equivalent of *shall* in offers:

I felt sure that we *should* meet again. [3]
Should I type these letters for you? [4]

The use of *should* illustrated in [3] can have a flavour of preciosity.

[**e**] Even in 1st person questions, where *shall* has generally been recognized as normal, it is

nowadays frequently replaced by more common verbal constructions. *Eg*: in [1] *shall I* could be replaced by *would you like us to* and in [2] *shall* could be replaced by *should*. Both these substitutes are typically AmE.

The past tense forms of the modals: *could, might, would,* and *should*

4.59 The uses of the past tense modals *could*, *might*, *would*, and *should* have already been illustrated in 4.52–8, but there is a need to examine the ways in which their uses differ from the corresponding nonpast modals *can*, *may*, *will*, and *shall*. Five particular uses of the past tense modals are noted in 4.60–4.

'Past time' in indirect speech

4.60 The past tense modals *could*, *might*, *would*, and *should* are used quite regularly as past tense equivalents of *can*, *may*, *will*, and *shall* in indirect speech constructions (*cf* 14.34):

You *can/may* do as you wish. [= permission]
~ She said we *could/might* do as we wished.
The king *can* do no wrong. [= ability]
~ It was seriously argued that the king *could* do no wrong.
It *may* rain later. [= possibility]
~ We were afraid that it *might* rain later.
What *can* be done? [= possibility]
~ Nobody knew what *could* be done.
The plan *will* succeed. [= prediction]
~ I felt sure that the plan *would* succeed.
Will you help me? [= volition]
~ I wondered if he *would* help me.
Shall I open the window? [in offers]
~ She asked me if she *should* open a window.

Must, together with *need* (as auxiliary), *ought to*, and *had better*, has no present/past distinction. These verbs are therefore unchanged in indirect speech constructions (*cf* 14.34), even where they refer to past time.

Note In free indirect speech (*cf* 14.35) the reporting clause is absent, so that the modal verb may occur backshifted to the past tense even in main clauses:
Could he be imagining things? (said Ahmed to himself.)

'Past time' in other constructions

4.61 Outside indirect speech contexts, the behaviour of the past tense modal forms is less predictable. *Could* and *would* act as the 'past time' equivalents of *can* and *will*; but on the whole, *might* and *should* do not act as the 'past time' equivalents of *may* and *shall* (*cf* however Note [a]).

(a) CAN ~ COULD

There were no rules: we *could* do just what we wanted. [= permission]
In those days, a transatlantic voyage *could* be dangerous. [= possibility]
Few of the tourists *could* speak English. [= ability]

(b) *WILL* ~ *WOULD*

Later, he *would* learn his error. [= prediction; *cf* 4.48, 4.57]
The old lady *would* sit in front of the television continuously. [= habitual prediction; *cf* 4.57 (a3)]
We tried to borrow a boat, but no one *would* lend us one. [= willingness]
He '*would* leave the house in a muddle. [= insistence]

Outside indirect speech, however, *would* is not used in the sense of intention; hence a sentence such as *He would meet me the next day* is almost inevitably interpreted as free indirect speech.

Note [a] There is a rare and archaic use of *might* outside indirect speech in the sense 'was/were permitted to':

We *might* leave the school only at weekends.

[b] Corresponding to *must*, which cannot normally be used in reference to past time outside indirect speech or indirect thought contexts, the past tense form *had to* can be used in main clauses. Compare:

I *must* confess her latest novels bore me. ~ I *had to* confess her latest novels bored me.

[c] In contrast to the past modals *could* [= ability] and *would* [= willingness], the constructions *was/were able to* and *was/were permitted to* (*cf* 4.66) emphasize not just the potentiality, but the fulfilment of an action. For instance, *We were able/permitted to leave the camp early* typically conveys the additional message: '. . . and, moreover, we *did* leave the camp early'. Hence *was able to*, but not *could*, is acceptable in contexts implying fulfilment:

I ran after the bus, and *was able to* catch it. [1]
*I ran after the bus, and *could* catch it. [2]

In the negative, however, this contrast between potential and fulfilled action is neutralized. Hence the following are both acceptable, and mean the same:

I ran after the bus, but *wasn't able* to catch it.
I ran after the bus, but *couldn't* catch it.

[d] On the other hand, *could* and *would* may refer to habitual fulfilment:

I *could* run after a bus and catch it twenty years ago, but I can't do that now.

Hypothetical meaning

4.62 The past tense modals can be used in the hypothetical (or unreal) sense of the past tense (*cf* 4.16) in both main and subordinate clauses. Compare:

If United *can* win this game, they *may* become league champions. [1]
If United *could* win this game, they *might* become league champions. [2]

Sentence [2], unlike [1], expresses an unreal condition; *ie* it conveys the speaker's expectation that United *will not* win the game, and therefore will *not* become league champions. For past hypothetical meaning (which normally has a contrary-to-fact interpretation), we have to add the perfective aspect:

If United *could have won* that game, they *might have become* league champions. [3]

The usual implication of this is that United did *not* win the game.

All past tense modals can be used in this way, to express the hypothetical version of meanings such as ability, possibility, permission, prediction, and volition. With the epistemic possibility of *might*, however, it is the meaning of the following predication, rather than of the modal itself, that is interpreted hypothetically. This will be evident from the following paraphrases:

They *might* have become champions.
[= It is possible that they would have become champions.]
We *could* have borrowed the money.
[= It would have been possible for us to borrow the money. (usually with the implication '. . . but we didn't')]

On the hypothetical use of *would* here, *cf* 4.64 below. In some contexts, especially when referring to the future, the 'unreal' meaning of past modals becomes weakened to something like improbability:

Not even a professional *could* do better than that.

From such instances, it is easy to understand how the hypothetical use of past modals has become adapted to express tentativeness (*cf* 4.63).

Note *Could/might* (+ perfective) are used in complaints or rebukes:
You *could/might* try to be more civilized!
You *could/might* have warned me she was coming.
The meaning here is close to the same construction with *should* [= 'ought to']: *eg*: *You should have warned us* . . . *Could* and *might* are interchangeable in this type of utterance.

Tentativeness or politeness: *could, might,* and *would*

4.63 Closely related to the hypothetical use above are specialized uses of *could, might,* and *would* in which the past tense form simply adds a note of tentativeness or politeness:

(a) TENTATIVE PERMISSION (in polite requests):

Could I see your driving licence?
I wonder if I *might* borrow some coffee?

(b) TENTATIVE VOLITION (in polite requests):

Would you lend me a dollar? [more polite than *will*, *cf* 4.57 (b2)]
I'd be grateful if someone *would* hold the door open.

(c) TENTATIVE POSSIBILITY

(I) in expressing a tentative opinion:

There *could* be something wrong with the light switch.
Of course, I *might* be wrong.

(II) in polite directives and requests (*cf* 4.52, Note [a]):

Could you (please) open the door?
You *could* answer these letters for me.

In these constructions, apart from the last-mentioned case of requests, *could* and *might* have the same meaning. In (cI), they both express the epistemic possibility associated with *may*. This is an exceptional case, in which *could* is the past tense equivalent of *may* instead of *can*.

Note There is a tendency for the difference between *may* and *might* (in a sense of tentative or hypothetical possibility) to become neutralized. Thus some speakers perceive little or no difference of meaning between *You may be wrong* and *You might be wrong*. This neutralization occasionally extends, analogically, to contexts in which only *might* would normally be considered appropriate:

?An earlier launch of the lifeboat *may* [= might] *have averted* the tragedy. [1]

The fact that sentences such as [1] occasionally occur is a symptom of a continuing tendency to erode the distinctions between real and unreal senses of the modals.

'Mood markers': *would* and *should*

4.64 Under this last heading of 'mood markers' we consider special uses of *would* and *should* in which these modals have nothing to do with the cognate modals *will* and *shall*, but are instead used to mark the MOOD of the clause.

(a) *WOULD/SHOULD* AS A MARKER OF HYPOTHETICAL MEANING

Would (and sometimes, with a 1st person subject, *should*) may express hypothetical meaning in main clauses:

If you pressed that button, the engine *would* stop. [1]
If there were an accident, we *would/should* have to report it. [2]

Would/should + infinitive contrasts in syntactic distribution, but not in meaning, with the past tense and the *were*-subjunctive, both of which express hypothetical meaning in many subordinate clauses. Hence the following cannot be interpreted as unreal conditions (although they might, with some difficulty, be interpreted in some other way; *cf* 15.35 on open and hypothetical conditions):

?If you *pressed* that button, the engine *stopped*. [3]
?If you *would press* that button, the engine *would stop*. [4]

In [3], the hypothetical past tense is wrongly used in the main clause, whereas in [4], the *would* construction is wrongly used in the subordinate clause.

Although the conditional sentence, as in [1] and [2], is the most typical context in which hypothetical *would/should* occurs, there are many other contexts in which hypothetical *would/should* is appropriately used:

I'*d* hate to lose this pen. [5]
It *would* be impossible to estimate how many crimes went undetected last year. [6]
Don't bother to read all these papers. It *would* take too long. [7]

In such sentences, there is often an implicit *if*. . .; for example, [7] could be expanded: *It would take too long if you did* (*try to read them all*).

(b) *SHOULD* AS A MARKER OF 'PUTATIVE' MEANING

In this use (*cf* 14.25), *should* + infinitive is often equivalent to the mandative subjunctive (*cf* 3.59). In using *should*, the speaker entertains, as it were, some 'putative' world, recognizing that it may well exist or come into existence:

She insisted that we *should* stay.
It's unfair that so many people *should* lose their jobs.
Let me know if you *should* hear some more news.
Why *should* anyone object to her enjoying herself?
I can't think why he *should* have been so angry.

Putative *should* is more common in BrE than in AmE (*cf* further 16.30*ff*, 16.59, 16.70).

Note [a] Hypothetical *would* as a 'mood marker' occurs in some types of subordinate clause; *eg* in nominal clauses (except some clauses which occur with the hypothetical past tense instead of *would*, *eg* clauses introduced by imperative *suppose* or by *wish*; *cf* 16.33) and in relative clauses:

I'm afraid the journey *would* be too expensive.

The journey was a disappointment to those who *would* have preferred to travel by road.

[b] An ironic or quasi-subjunctive use of *should* is current in certain Yiddishisms, especially in AmE:

I should talk. ['I shouldn't talk!']

I should worry. ['Why should I worry?']

I should be so lucky. ['I'm unlucky.']

[c] Hypothetical *would* when followed by a verb such as *like*, *love*, or *prefer* is used to indicate a tentative desire in polite requests, offers, or invitations:

A: *Would* you *mind* taking part? B: No, I'*d love* to.

A: *Would* you *like* some tea? B: Thanks; but I'*d prefer* coffee, if there is any.

Cf the use of *would* for tentative volition, 4.63 (b).

The modals with the perfective and progressive aspects

4.65 The perfective and progressive aspects are normally excluded when the modals express 'ability' or 'permission', and also when *shall* or *will* expresses 'volition'. These aspects are freely used, however, with extrinsic modal meanings other than ability; *eg*:

'possibility'	He *may/might have* missed the train.
	She *can't/couldn't be* swimm*ing* all day.
'necessity'	He *must have* lef*t* his umbrella on the bus.
	You *must be* dream*ing*.
'prediction' etc	The guests *will/would have* arriv*ed* by that time.
	Hussein *will/would* still *be* read*ing* his paper.

(On the meaning of the perfective aspect after a modal, and in particular the possibility of paraphrasing it by means of the simple past tense, *cf* 4.18*f*.)

'Obligation' can only be expressed with the perfective or progressive when combined with *should* or *ought to*:

'obligation'	I *ought to be* work*ing* now. ['. . . but I'm not']
	You *should have* finish*ed* it. ['. . . but you haven't']
	She *shouldn't have* left him. ['. . . but she did']

As the glosses indicate, these modals, in contrast to *must*, often imply nonfulfilment of the obligation. There are also examples which do not have this counterfactual implication; *eg*:

Have you heard from Maria? She *should have* started her job on Monday.

The combination of both perfective and progressive constructions with the modals is also possible, subject to the conditions already mentioned:

You *must have been* dream*ing*.

She *could*n't *have been* swimm*ing* all day.

The guests *would have been* arriv*ing* by now.

(On the meaning of the perfective and progressive in this combination, *cf* 4.38*f*.)

Note [**a**] The use of *will* + progressive in the sense of 'future as a matter of course' (*cf* 4.46) is paralleled by other modals in the same construction:

Jill says she *might be* call*ing* this afternoon. [1]

means approximately 'It is just possible that Jill will be calling...' In contrast to [1], *Jill says she might call this afternoon* implies that the visit will depend on Jill's decision.

[**b**] Note the use of *might/could* + perfective in certain colloquial speech acts:

They *could/might* have told me! [a complaint]

You *could/might* have been more careful. [a rebuke]

I *might* have *KNÒWN* someone would upset her. [an expression of irritation]

The meanings of marginal auxiliaries

4.66 We may use the expression 'marginal auxiliaries' to apply to all four categories (marginal modals, modal idioms, semi-auxiliaries, and catenative verbs) discussed in 3.40–51. Some of these have also claimed our attention in this chapter; *eg*: *used to* (4.15), *be going to* (4.43), *ought to* (4.56). But it is worth noting how closely these verbs tend to follow the pattern of the auxiliary verbs in the kinds of meaning they convey. On the one hand, we have aspectual or time-indicating verbs such as *used to*, *be going to*, and *be about to* (4.47). On the other hand, the largest group of marginal auxiliaries are modal in their semantic function, *eg*: *had better* (3.45) and *be able to*.

The semantic groups displayed in the right-hand part of *Table* 4.66 show a remarkable similarity to those of the modal auxiliaries, as indicated in *Fig* 4.51. We use the same terminology here, to make the comparison more evident:

Table 4.66 Meanings of marginal auxiliaries

Temporal and aspectual	Modal			
	Necessity	Obligation	Possibility, Ability	Permission
Past	(Committed)	(Committed)		
used to	*need (to)* *have to* *have got to* *be bound to* *be certain to* *be sure to*	*need (to)* *have to* *have got to* *be bound to* *be certain to* *be sure to*	*be able to*	*be allowed to* *be permitted to*
Future	(Non committed)	(Non committed)	Volition	Other
be going to *be to* *be about to* *be due to* *be destined to*	*ought to* *be likely to* *be supposed to*	*ought to* *had better* *be supposed to*	*be willing to* *would rather* *would sooner* *be going to*	*dare (to)* *tend to* *be liable to* *happen to*

In *Table* 4.66, several verbal constructions occur more than once, since, like the modal verbs, their semantic ranges tend to stretch across more than one category. This is particularly true of the extrinsic/intrinsic contrast which not only applies to all modals (*cf* 4.49), but also to many of the marginal and catenative constructions. Just as *must* and *should*, for example, have both 'necessity' and 'obligation' meanings, so do the semi-auxiliaries *be bound to* and *be supposed to*:

The plan *is bound to* fail. [= 'must inevitably fail'; necessity]
You *are bound* to pay your debts. [= 'are compelled to . . .'; obligation]

Their team *is supposed to* be the best. [= 'should be'; this is the recognized view]
You *were supposed to* be here at nine. [= 'ought to have been'; obligation]

The fact that semi-auxiliaries and catenatives have nonfinite verb forms (*cf* 3.47–9) means that two or even more modal concepts can be combined in a sequence of verb phrases:

We *may have to* play it again. [possibility + obligation]
You *should be able to* find enough food. [tentative inference + ability]
She *must have been willing to* help. [necessity + volition]
The students *are going to have to be able to play* three different instruments. [prediction + necessity + ability]

It is normal, in such combinations, for an extrinsic modality to precede an intrinsic one, as the examples show.

Note The quasi-adverbial status of many semi-auxiliary or catenative verbs can be shown by paraphrases such as the following:

She *appears to* like the show. = She *apparently* likes the show.
She *is certain to* enjoy the meal. = She will *certainly* enjoy the meal.

Meaning in the nonfinite verb phrase

4.67 Our discussion of meaning in this chapter has concentrated on finite verb phrases, and in conclusion we must give some attention to nonfinite verb phrases. The same semantic distinctions apply to both finite and nonfinite verb phrases, in so far as the structural possibilities of the nonfinite verb phrase permit. We have seen, however, in 3.56 that the modal construction and the distinction between present and past tense do not apply to the nonfinite verb phrase; and in 4.18*f* that the nonfinite perfective construction has the general meaning of anteriority. Distinctions of aspect are the only ones which are expressed within the constructional possibilities of a single nonfinite verb phrase. Even then, the full range is only possible within an infinitive phrase:

Sir Topaz appears {
to be winning his race. [simple progressive]
to have won his race. [simple perfective]
to have been winning his race. [perfective progressive]
}

In an *-ing* participle phrase in adverbial clauses, the perfective/nonperfective contrast is sometimes available:

Eating a hearty breakfast, } we prepared for our long journey. [1]
Having eaten a hearty breakfast, } we prepared for our long journey. [2]

From [1], we understand that the eating and the preparation took place together, while from [2], we understand that the breakfast preceded the preparation.

But the progressive/nonprogressive contrast is not normally applicable here, since *-ing* participle phrases are incapable of expressing this distinction formally (*cf* 3.56). Moreover, the *-ing* participle itself is not, in spite of its appearance, necessarily associated with the progressive:

Being an enemy of the Duke's,
Realizing he was in danger,
Having no news of his wife,
} he left the court immediately. [3]

(For further discussion of the semantics of such *-ing* participle constructions, see 16.40.)

To prove this point, the *-ing* participles in [3] are all stative and incompatible with the progressive:

*He was being an enemy of the Duke's.
?*He was realizing he was in danger.
*He was having no news of his wife.

Nevertheless, there are constructions in which the *-ing* participle construction has aspect contrast with the infinitive, and is progressive in meaning (*cf* 16.52*f*):

I {saw / heard} them {*shoot* at him. / *shooting* at him.}

Whereas the infinitive *shoot* suggests a single shot, the *-ing* participle suggests a repetitive action lasting over a period of time, in accordance with the interpretation of the progressive aspect in finite verb phrases referring to momentary events (*cf* 4.35). In:

I watched them {
climb the tower. [4]
climbing the tower. [5]
}

the infinitive *climb* suggests that they reached the top of the tower, whereas the participle *climbing* connotes the potential incompleteness of the progressive.

The *-ed* participle phrase has no formal contrasts of aspect, and is therefore the most restricted type of phrase in terms of semantic contrasts. Here again, however, there is a potential contrast with the passive *-ing* participle phrase:

I saw the tower { *climbed* by a student. [6]
I saw the tower { *being climbed* by a student. [7]

The participle *climbed* in [6] is the passive counterpart of the infinitive *climb* in [4]; it describes the climb as a completed event, whereas [7] describes it as in progress, and as possibly incomplete.

Note [**a**] The structural contrast between infinitive and *-ing* participle complementation occurs with categories of verb other than the perceptual verbs *see*, *hear*, etc illustrated above. In these other cases, however, there is almost no semantic contrast of aspect:

She started { to eat. / eating. } [8]

She likes { to talk. / talking. } [9]

Eating in [8] and *talking* in [9] are thus not to be classified as progressive (*cf* 16.40).

[**b**] With certain main verbs which imply anterior time in their complementation (*cf* 16.39), such as *admit*, *remember*, *regret*, there is no contrast of meaning between complementation by a perfective and by a nonperfective *-ing* participle phrase:

We { admitted / remembered / regretted } { *leaving* early. [10]
We { admitted / remembered / regretted } { *having left* early. [11]

In spite of the difference of construction, [10] and [11] are virtually synonymous with each other.

4.68 Although nonfinite verb phrases have no modal verbs, the meanings of the modals can be added to them through the use of semi-auxiliaries such as *have to*, *be (un)able to*, *be allowed to*, *be about to*, etc:

I am sorry to *have to* repeat this warning.
Being unable to free himself, he lay beneath the debris until rescued.
The suspects admitted *being about to* commit a crime.
Many inmates hate not *being allowed to* leave the premises.

Bibliographical note

General treatments of the meaning and use of verb constructions: Coates and Leech (1980); Edmondson et al (1977); Leech (1971); Palmer (1974).

On tense and aspect in general, see Crystal (1966); G. Lakoff (1970b); Lyons (1977), Vol 2; Schopf (1984); Zandvoort (1962).

On the perfective aspect, see McCoard (1978); Sørensen (1964).

On stative, agentive, and other classes of verb meaning, see Bache (1982); Cruse (1973); Ikegami (1973); Jacobson (1980a); Mańczac (1979); Mourelatos (1978); Quirk (1970b); Sag (1973); Vendler (1957).

On expression of future time, see Aarts (1969); Close (1977, 1980); Haegeman (forthcoming a); Haegeman and Wekker (1984); Tottie (1974); Wekker (1976).

On modal meanings in general, see Coates (1982); Halliday (1969); Hermerén (1978); Hofmann (1979); Johannesson (1976); R. Lakoff (1972); Leech and Coates (1980); Lyons (1977), Vol. 2; Matthews-Bresky (1975); Palmer (1977, 1979); Standwell (1979); Von Wright (1951); Wells (1979).

Studies of particular modal auxiliaries include: Coates (1980); Haegeman (1981a, 1981b, 1983); Jacobsson (1962, 1977b); Palmer (1980); Quirk (1981); Stubelius (1962); Zandvoort (1963).

5 Nouns and determiners

Types of noun phrase

5.1 The noun phrase typically functions as subject, object, and complement of clauses and as complement of prepositional phrases. Consider the different subjects in the following sentences:

The girl	is my sister.	[1]
The blonde girl		[2]
The blonde girl in blue jeans		[3]
The blonde girl wearing blue jeans		[4]
The blonde girl who is wearing blue jeans		[5]
She		[6]

Sentences [1–5] are alike in having the same noun (*girl*) as noun-phrase head (*cf* 2.28, 17.2). The noun phrase in [1] has the simplest structure, consisting of only the definite article and the head; in [2] it also has a premodifying adjective (*blonde*); in [3–5] the noun phrase has, in addition, postmodification: in [3] a prepositional phrase (*in blue jeans*); in [4] a nonfinite clause (*wearing blue jeans*); and in [5] a relative clause (*who is wearing blue jeans*). In [6] the noun phrase consists of only one word (*she*), which is one of a closed class of grammatical words called personal pronouns. Such pronouns can 'deputize' for noun phrases and hence cannot normally occur with determiners such as the definite article, premodification, or (normally) postmodification:

**the blonde she*   *?she in blue jeans*

Since noun phrases of the types illustrated in [2–5] include words and structures that will be dealt with in later chapters (adjectives, prepositional phrases, clauses), it will be convenient to reserve the treatment of 'complex' noun phrases incorporating such items until Chapter 17, which deals with the noun phrase as a whole. The present chapter will be restricted to the constituency of the 'basic' noun phrase, *ie* the classes of nouns together with articles or other closed-class determinative elements that can occur before the noun head, including predeterminers like *all*, central determiners like *these*, and postdeterminers like *last* and *few*:

all these last few days

The closed class of pronouns as in [6] is dealt with in Chapter 6.

Noun classes: count, noncount, and proper nouns

5.2 It is necessary, both for grammatical and semantic reasons, to see nouns as falling into different subclasses. That this is so can be demonstrated by taking the four nouns *Sid*, *book*, *furniture*, and *brick* and considering the extent to which it is possible for each to appear as head of the noun phrase functioning as object in the sentence *I saw* . . .: without any determiner (a); with the lightly stressed determiners *the* /ðə/ (b), *a* /ə/ (c), *some* /səm/ (d); and in the plural (e). The result of this test can be seen in *Table* 5.2:

Table 5.2 Test table for noun classes

	(1)	(2)	(3)	(2 + 3)
(a)	*Sid*	**book*	*furniture*	*brick*
(b)	**the Sid*	*the book*	*the furniture*	*the brick*
(c)	**a Sid*	*a book*	**a furniture*	*a brick*
(d)	**some Sid*	**some book*	*some furniture*	*some brick*
(e)	**Sids*	*books*	**furnitures*	*bricks*

The difference between column 1 (with only one possibility) and column 2 + 3 (with all possibilities) indicates the degree of variation between the noun classes. Nouns that behave like *Sid* in column 1 (*Confucius*, *Paris*, *Sierra Leone*, etc) are PROPER NOUNS, which will be further discussed in 5.60*ff*.

The nouns in the other columns are COMMON NOUNS, but there are important differences between them. Those which, like *book* in column 2 (*bottle*, *chair*, *forest*, *idea*, etc), must be seen as denoting individual countable entities and not as an undifferentiated mass, are called COUNT nouns. Nouns which, like *furniture*, conform to the pattern of column 3 (as do *bread*, *grass*, *warmth*, *music*, etc), must by contrast be seen as denoting an undifferentiated mass or continuum. These are called NONCOUNT nouns.

Finally we have nouns in column 2 + 3 which can be either count or noncount nouns (*eg*: *brick*, *cake*, *paper*, *stone*), in that we can view a noun like *brick* either as the noncount material [1], or as constituting the countable object [2]:

The house is built of *brick*. [1]
He used *bricks* to build the house. [2]

The type headed 2 + 3 may be classified grammatically in two ways: (a) either as a lexical class of noun which combines the characteristics of count nouns and noncount nouns, or (b) as two separate items, one count and the other noncount. The former mode of analysis is convenient for nouns like *brick* and *cake* with little difference in meaning between count and noncount uses. Therefore such nouns will be said to have 'dual class membership' (*cf* 5.4).

Although in sentences such as *I like music*, *I like Sid*, the two nouns look superficially alike in terms of article usage, we will say that *music* has ZERO ARTICLE but that *Sid* has NO ARTICLE. The label 'zero' is appropriate in the case of common nouns which have article contrast, *eg*: *music* as opposed to *the music* (*cf* 5.52*ff*) in:

I like *music* and dancing.
I think *the music* is too loud in here.

If, however, we disregard special grammatical environments like *the Sid I mean is tall* (*cf* 5.64), proper nouns have no article contrast (*Sid*/**the Sid*), and will therefore be said to have 'no article'.

Note COUNT nouns, as they are termed in this book, are by some grammarians called 'countable' nouns; similarly, our term NONCOUNT nouns corresponds to 'mass' nouns or 'uncountable' nouns in other grammars.

Concrete and abstract nouns

5.3 Cutting across the grammatical and semantic count/noncount distinction, there is a semantic division into nouns like *pig* which are CONCRETE (*ie* accessible to the senses, observable, measurable, etc) and nouns like *difficulty* which are ABSTRACT (typically nonobservable and nonmeasurable). But while abstract nouns may be count (like *remark/remarks*) or noncount (like *warmth/ *warmths*), there is a considerable degree of overlap between abstract and noncount (*cf* 5.58). *Figure* 5.3 shows the noun classes introduced so far.

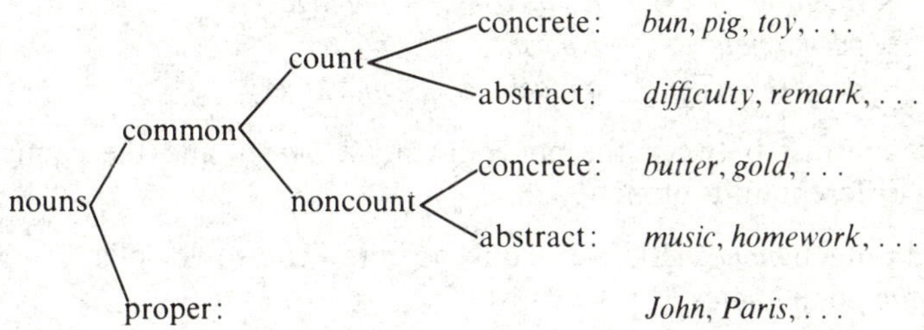

Fig 5.3 The most important noun classes

Nouns with dual class membership

5.4 The division of nouns according to countability into count nouns and noncount nouns is basic in English. Yet the language makes it possible to look upon some objects from the point of view of both count and noncount, as in the case of *cake*:

A: Would you like *a cake*? B: No, I don't like *cake*.

Such nouns may be said to have dual class membership. In other cases, *eg*: *paper*, there is no readily perceptible parallelism but a notable difference in meaning between the two nouns:

I want an evening *paper*. ['newspaper']	[1]
Wrap the parcel up in brown *paper*. ['wrapping paper']	[1a]

Note also the variation of quantifiers (*eg*: *much/many*) in some of the following examples of count and noncount nouns:

She was a *beauty* in her youth.	[COUNT]	[2]
She had great *beauty* in her youth.	[NONCOUNT]	[2a]
She's had many *difficulties*.	[COUNT]	[3]
She's not had much *difficulty*.	[NONCOUNT]	[3a]
He's had several odd *experiences*.	[COUNT]	[4]
He hasn't had much *experience*.	[NONCOUNT]	[4a]
There were bright *lights* and harsh *sounds*.	[COUNT]	[5]
Light travels faster than *sound*.	[NONCOUNT]	[5a]
She will give a *talk* on Chinese art.	[COUNT]	[6]
That's foolish *talk*.	[NONCOUNT]	[6a]
The *lambs* were eating quietly.	[COUNT]	[7]
There is *lamb* on the menu today.	[NONCOUNT]	[7a]

In many other cases, the type of distinction to be seen in the count noun *lamb* (the animal, as in [7]) and the noncount noun *lamb* (the meat from the animal, as in [7a]) is achieved by separate lexical items, as in:

They raise a great many *calves*, *pigs*, and *sheep*. [8]
We eat a great deal of *veal*, *pork*, and *mutton*. [8a]

Other count/noncount pairs realized by different lexical items are the following:

a garment ~ *clothing*	*a job, a task* ~ *work* (*cf* 5.9)
a laugh ~ *laughter*	*a suitcase* ~ *luggage*
a 'permit ~ *permission*	*a poem* ~ *poetry*
a weapon ~ *arms* (*cf* 5.77)	*a machine* ~ *machinery*

Note also the contrast between the noncount noun *money* and the count nouns naming different units of money:

We haven't much *money* left. We've only got a few *coins*/two dollar *bills*/some pound *notes*.

Note The distinction between count nouns and noncount nouns is not fully explainable as necessarily inherent in 'real world' denotata. This is clear when we compare the words of languages closely related to English (*cf* 5.9). Rather, the justification for the count/noncount distinction is based on the grammatical characteristics of the English noun.

Reclassification

5.5 Nouns may also be shifted from one class to another by means of conversion (*cf* App I.53). Thus a noncount noun like *cheese* can be 'reclassified' as a count noun involving a semantic shift so as to denote quality partition 'kind/type/form of', *eg*:

A: What *cheeses* have you got today?
B: Well, we have Cheddar, Gorgonzola, and Danish Blue.

Similarly, a noun like *coffee*, which is normally noncount, as in [1], can be reclassified as a count noun to mean an 'appropriate unit of' as in [1a] and [1b], or a 'kind/sort/brand of' as in [1c] and [1d]:

Do you want *tea* or *coffee*? [1]
Can I have *a coffee*, please. ['a cup of coffee'] [1a]
Two coffees, please. ['two cups of coffee'] [1b]
This is *a nice coffee*. [1c]
I like *Brazilian coffees* best. [1d]

Note There is a special case of reclassification in cases like the following:

Are you *cosmetics*?

Here there is no coreference relation between subject and complement as in *Are you a teacher?* The complement represents instead a compressed form of the predication; *eg*: *Are you* (*selling*) *cosmetics?* In this use of the noun there is an implied contrast: 'cosmetics as opposed to toys, jewellery, etc in a department store'. Similarly:

Are you *103*? ['the occupant of room number 103, as opposed to 104, etc']

The contrast may also be more explicit, as in:

Are you *church* or *chapel*? ['a member of the Church of England or a nonconformist']

In these last cases we may argue that the noun has been reclassified as an adjective (*cf* App I.51), as in *They're very Oxbridge*.

Partitive constructions

Partition in respect of quality

5.6 Both count and noncount nouns can enter partitive constructions, *ie* constructions denoting a part of a whole. Such constructions express both quality partition (*eg*: *a kind of paper*) and quantity partition (*eg*: *a piece of paper*). Quality partition is expressed by a partitive count noun like *kind*, *sort*, or *type* followed by an *of*-phrase, *eg*:

SINGULAR PARTITIVES	PLURAL PARTITIVES
a new *kind of* computer	new *kinds of* computers
a delicious *sort of* bread	delicious *sorts of* bread
another *type of* research	other *types of* research

Quality partition of noncount nouns may thus be expressed either by a partitive construction or by reclassification (*cf* 5.5):

a nice kind of coffee ~ *a nice coffee*
English types of cheese ~ *English cheeses*

Note Whether we are dealing with count or noncount nouns, we can express the quality partition in the form *a* + adjective + noun, such that a sentence like the following is superficially ambiguous:

We are importing *a new Italian shirt*.

It may mean either 'a new type of' or 'a new item' (the former interpretation naturally being more likely in this case).

Partition in respect of quantity

5.7 (a) Noncount nouns

Noncount nouns are seen, as we have said, as denoting an undifferentiated mass. However, the expression of quantity and thus countability may be achieved by means of certain GENERAL PARTITIVE NOUNS, in particular *piece*, *bit*, *item*, followed by an *of*-phrase:

SINGULAR PARTITIVES	PLURAL PARTITIVES
a *piece of* cake	two *pieces of* cake
a *bit of* chalk	some *bits of* chalk
an *item of* news	several *items of* news

Quantity of noncount nouns may thus often be expressed either by partitive nouns or by reclassification (*cf* 5.5): *two lumps of sugar* = *two sugars*.

The most widely used partitive expression is *a piece of*, which can be combined with both concrete and abstract nouns, *eg*:

Concrete: *a piece of bacon/chalk/coal/land/paper*
Abstract: *a piece of advice/information/news/research/work*

Bit generally implies a small quantity: *a bit of rice/news/fun/research*. With abstract nouns, *item* is used (besides *piece*):

an item of business/information/news ['a news item']

Item is not generally used with concrete nouns: **an item of oil/cake* (BUT *an item of clothing*).

In addition to these general partitives there are some more restricted and descriptive TYPICAL PARTITIVES which form expressions with specific concrete noncount nouns, such as the following:

an *atom/grain* of truth
a *bar* of chocolate/soap/gold/iron
a *blade* of grass
a *block* of ice/flats ⟨BrE⟩/seats [in a theatre]/shares [in a business]
a *cut* of lamb/meat; a *joint* of meat ⟨BrE⟩
a *drop* of water/oil/whisky
a *grain* of corn/rice/sand/salt
a *loaf* of bread
a *lump* of coal/lead/sugar
a *sheet* of paper/metal/ice
a *slice* of bacon/bread/cake/meat
a *speck* of dust/dirt
a *stick* of chalk/dynamite/celery/rock [a sweet] ⟨BrE⟩/candy ⟨AmE⟩
a *strip* of cloth/land/paper
a *suit* of clothing/clothes/armour

(b) Plural count nouns
Whereas the general partitive *a piece of* can be used with many of the noncount nouns (*a piece of paper/bacon/news*, etc), it cannot be used with plural count nouns (including invariably plural nouns like *cattle*; *cf* 5.76*ff*). Other partitives are used with them, *eg*:

a (large) *crowd* of people
a (huge) *flock* of birds/sheep
a (small) *herd* of cattle
a *packet* ⟨BrE⟩/*pack* ⟨esp AmE⟩ of cigarettes
a *series* of incidents/concerts/lectures
a *bunch* of flowers/keys [In informal style, *bunch* is also used about people, like 'group': *a bunch of teenagers*.]

(c) Singular count nouns
Partition can also be expressed in reference to singular count nouns, *eg*:

a *piece* of a loaf
a *branch* of a tree
a *page* of a book
a *section* of a newspaper
a *verse* of a poem

Fractional partition can also be expressed by such general quantitative items as *half*, *all*, *whole* + *of* + noun (*cf* 5.16*f*):

$$\text{I'd like}\left\{\begin{array}{l}\textit{half of}\\ \textit{a quarter of}\\ \textit{all of}\\ \textit{the whole of}\\ \textit{the rest of}\\ \textit{the remainder of}\end{array}\right\}\text{that piece (of meat).}$$

Note [**a**] When we modify a partitive noun sequence, the modification applies to the group as a whole: an expensive *cup of coffee* ['*The cup of coffee* cost a lot.']

But, of course, since in many cases the adjective modifying the whole group could equally apply to the second noun, we have some instances like the following where the meanings of the two phrases differ little, if at all:

a hot [*cup of tea*] = a cup of hot tea
a good [*stroke of luck*] = a stroke of good luck
a beautiful [*pair of legs*] = a pair of beautiful legs

The premodifiers (*hot*, etc) in such cases often apply more appropriately to the second noun than to the first; *ie* it is not the cup but the tea that is hot in *a hot cup of tea*. In *a nice glass of whisky*, *nice* is roughly equivalent to 'welcome' and offers only implicit comment on the quality of the liquor.

[b] Typical partitives sometimes have a negative intensifying force (*cf* 8.111):

A: Did you sleep well?
B: No, I didn't get *a wink* (of sleep).

[c] When the two partitive constructions combine, the quantity partitive is included in the scope of the quality partitive:

[*two kinds of* [*loaves of bread*]]
but not: **two loaves of kinds of bread*

Measure partitive nouns

5.8 The measure partitives relate to precise quantities denoting length, area, volume, and weight, for example (note the compulsory *of*):

Length:	a *foot* of copper wire	
	a *metre* ⟨BrE⟩/a *meter* ⟨AmE⟩/a *yard* of cloth	
	a *mile* of cable	
Area:	an *acre*/a *hectare* of land	
Volume:	a *litre* ⟨BrE⟩/a *liter* ⟨AmE⟩ of wine	
	a *pint*/a *quart* of milk	
Weight:	an *ounce* of tobacco	a *pound* of butter
	a *kilo* of apples	a *ton* of coal

Measure partitives can be either singular or plural:

{*a/one gallon* | *two/several gallons*} of water

If count, the second noun must be plural:

{*one kilo of* | *two kilos of*} {*apples* | **apple*}

Noncount nouns and their count equivalents

5.9 It may be noted that, apart from a tendency for concrete nouns to be count and for abstract nouns to be noncount, there is no necessary connection between the classes of nouns and the entities to which they refer. In some related languages, the nouns corresponding to *information*, *money*, *news*, and *work*, for example, are count nouns, but in English they are noncount:

He didn't give us *much information*.
Do you need *all this money*?
The news is rather bad today.
She doesn't like *hard work*.

Some noncount nouns with count equivalents are given below:

NONCOUNT NOUN	COUNT EQUIVALENT
This is important *information.*	a *piece/bit/word* of information
Have you any *news*?	a *piece*/a *bit*/an *item* of good news
a lot of *abuse*	a *term/word* of abuse
some good *advice*	a *piece/word* of good advice
warm *applause*	a *round* of applause
How's *business*?	a *piece/bit* of business
There is *evidence* that . . .	a *piece* of evidence
expensive *furniture*	a *piece*/an *article*/a *suite* of furniture
The *interest* is only 5 per cent.	a (low) *rate* of interest
What (bad/good) *luck*!	a *piece* of (bad/good) luck

Since such differences between languages can be adequately treated only in contrastive grammars, we will restrict the list below to a sample of some nouns (in addition to those mentioned earlier) which are noncount in English but correspond to count nouns in some other languages:

anger	*behaviour*	*cash*
chaos	*chess*	*'conduct*
courage	*dancing*	*education*
equipment	*fun*	*harm*
homework	*hospitality*	*leisure*
moonlight	*music*	*parking*
photography	*publicity*	*'refuse*
research	*resistance*	*safety*
scenery	*shopping*	*smoking*
sunshine	*traffic*	*violence*

Note **[a]** Some of the noncount nouns can be count nouns with special meanings, *eg*: *moneys* 'amounts of money', as can be seen in a dictionary.

[b] It can be argued that some nouns, like *weather*, are neither count (**a weather*) nor noncount (**a lot of weather*), but these nouns share features belonging to both classes. Noncount noun features include the premodified structures *a lot of good weather*, *some bad weather*, *what lovely weather*. On the other hand, count noun features include the plural *go out in all weathers*, *in the worst of weathers*.

[c] On the use of *fun* as adjective, *cf* 7.14 Note [c].

[d] Some noncount nouns accept the indefinite article when they are modified (*cf* 5.59), *eg*:

They are doing *a brisk business*. (NOT **a business*)

In some cases no modification seems to be required. In the following example, however, modification is in fact implied:

She has had *an education*. ['a good education']

[e] Names of languages are all noncount, *eg*:

She speaks *good English*. [~ 'a good English']

Occasionally, however, they are count, as in the partitive sense described in 5.6:

She speaks *a dialectal French*. ['a dialectal form of French']

Determinatives

5.10 When used in discourse, noun phrases refer to the linguistic or situational context. The kind of reference a particular noun phrase has depends on its DETERMINATIVE element, *ie* the item which 'determines' it. This function is typically realized by a set of closed-class items, or DETERMINERS, which occur before the noun acting as head of the noun phrase (or before its premodifiers) (*cf* 2.28*ff*). Thus we say that the noun phrase in [1] has indefinite reference, whereas the noun phrase in [2] has definite reference:

Have you seen { *a bicycle*? [1]
{ *the bicycle*? [2]

Indefinite reference is typically indicated by the indefinite article *a*/*an*, and definite reference is typically indicated by the definite article *the*, but, as we shall see, there are also other determiners with a similar function.

We distinguish three classes of determiners:

(I) PREDETERMINERS, *eg*: *half*, *all*, *double*;
(II) CENTRAL DETERMINERS, *eg*: the articles *the*, *a*/*an*;
(III) POSTDETERMINERS, *eg*: cardinal and ordinal numerals, *many*, *few*.

The three classes of determiners have been set up on the basis of their position in the noun phrase in relation to each other. Thus we do not find central determiner + predeterminer (**their all trouble*), or postdeterminer + central determiner + predeterminer (**five the all boys*), but only the order I + II + III given above: *all their trouble*, *all the five boys*.

We begin by discussing the articles and other central determiners (5.11–14), and then go on to predeterminers (5.15–19), and postdeterminers (5.20–25).

Central determiners

The articles

5.11 The most common and typical central determiners are the definite and indefinite articles, *the* and *a*/*an*, respectively. We have seen in 5.2 that different noun classes require different articles. For the two classes of common nouns, the count and noncount nouns, the distribution into number (singular/plural) and definiteness (definite/indefinite) can be stated as follows:

Table 5.11 Use of the articles with count and noncount nouns

		COUNT	NONCOUNT
SINGULAR	definite	*the book*	*the furniture*
	indefinite	*a book*	*furniture*
PLURAL	definite	*the books*	
	indefinite	*books*	

The forms of the articles depend on the initial sound of the following word.

In its unstressed (and normal) use, the definite article is always written *the* but pronounced /ðə/ before consonants and /ðɪ/ before vowels. The unstressed indefinite article is *a* /ə/ before consonants and *an* /ən/ before vowels. Note that it is the pronunciation, not the spelling, of the following word that determines their form:

the /ðə/ } *boy, usage, hole*　　*the* /ðɪ/ } *understanding, hour*
a /ə/ }　　　　　　　　　　　*an* /ən/ }

The use of the articles is discussed in 5.26*ff*.

Note [**a**] The indefinite article *a*/*an* can be regarded as an unstressed numeral, equivalent to stressed *one*. Compare:

a pound or two　　*one or two pounds*

A/*an* cannot cooccur with *one* (except, in limited cases, when *one* is the head of a noun phrase: *You are a one!*, *cf* 6.55 Note [b]), and may sometimes replace *one* (*cf* 5.38).

[**b**] There is fluctuation in the form of the indefinite article before some words that are written with initial *h*, depending on whether the *h* is pronounced or not:

a / *an* } { *hotel, herb*
historical novel　BUT: *a history*
habitual drunkard　BUT: *a habit*

[**c**] The initial *h* is not pronounced in *hour* (*hourly*), *honest*, *honour* (*honourable*), *heir* (*heiress*, *heirloom*). Thus: *an hour ago*, *an honours degree*.

[**d**] Note words which are spelled with an initial vowel but pronounced with a consonant: *a European car*, *a UNESCO official*; and, conversely, words which are spelled with an initial consonant but pronounced with a vowel: *an MP*, *an RP accent*.

[**e**] The articles are stressed only for very special emphasis. Here the distinction between the pre-vowel and pre-consonant form is neutralized for the definite article:

ˈ*the* /ðiː/ *boy, usage, understanding, hour*
ˈ*a* /eɪ/ *boy, usage*
ˈ*an* /æn/ *understanding, hour*

In writing, emphasis is often indicated by italics or underlining: '*the* man'.

The stressed definite article is often used to indicate excellence or superiority in some respect [1, 2], or the identity of somebody well-known [3] (*cf* 5.63):

He would be ˈ*the* /ðiː/ man for the job. [1]
The demonstration will be ˈ*the* /ðiː/ event this week. [2]
You don't mean ˈ*the* /ðiː/ Professor Hart? [3]

There is some criticism of the overuse of stressed articles for expected unstressed articles, especially on radio and TV (*cf* overuse of stressed prepositions, 9.9 Note, 18.14 Note [b]).

[**f**] The indefinite article means 'a certain', 'a person giving his name as' (*cf*: *one* 5.63 Note [b]), in such cases as:

A Mr Johnson came to see you last night.

[**g**] On *a*/*an* in distributive expressions of frequency like *twice a day*, *cf* 5.18.

Other central determiners

5.12 The use of the articles is not the only possibility for 'determining' nouns. Instead of *a* or *the* with *book* we may have *eg*: *this*/*that*/*every*/*each*/*no book*. Like the articles, these words, and some others, are called central determiners. They form a set of closed-class items that are mutually exclusive with each other, *ie* there cannot be more than one occurring before the noun head: **a the boy* and **a some boy*. Thus, the central determiners are in a 'choice relation', *ie* they occur one instead of another. In this respect they are unlike *eg*: *all*, *many*, and *white*, which are in a 'chain relation' (*cf* 2.5), *ie* they occur one after another in the noun phrase: *all the many white houses*.

The articles have no function independent of the noun they precede. Most other determiners have the additional function of pronouns, *eg*: *some*, *that*, and *either*:

DETERMINER FUNCTION	PRONOUN FUNCTION
A: I want *some ice*.	B: Here's *some* for you.
A: What's *that thing* over there?	B: *That*'s our computer.
Either book will do.	You can have *either* (of the books).

On pronouns like *either* with or without the alternative *of*-construction, *cf* 6.48.

No and *every* are exceptional: like the articles, they cannot function independently as pronouns. They can, however, form part of compound pronouns when followed by (-)*one*, -*body*, or -*thing* (*cf* 6.45*ff*):

no one	*nobody*	*nothing*
everyone	*everybody*	*everything*

Unlike other central determiners, the articles have no lexical meaning but solely contribute definite or indefinite status to the nouns they determine. Yet the dependence is not unilateral. For example, a count noun like *boy* is, on its own, only a lexical item. To assume grammatical status, it requires an 'overt' determiner of some kind. The use of the articles will be discussed in 5.26*ff*, and the use of other central determiners in Chapter 6.

Note [**a**] There are two exceptions to the rule that count nouns cannot occur without a determiner. One occurs in parallel structures (*cf* 5.50):

Man or *boy*, I don't like him.

The other exceptional case is that of vocatives (*cf* 10.52*f*):

Look here, *man*!

Man is also used generically without the article (*cf* 5.54 Note).

[**b**] Coordinated noun-phrase heads can share a determiner placed before the first head (*cf* 13.67):

the boys and (*the*) *girls*
the radios, (*the*) *tape recorders*, and (*the*) *television sets* in this store
a knife, (*a*) *fork*, and (*a*) *spoon*

Central determiners and noun classes

5.13 We have noted in 5.2 that there are certain cooccurrence restrictions between articles and common nouns. The definite article can occur with all three noun classes (singular count, plural count, and singular noncount), but the zero and indefinite articles cannot do so. When we consider determiners as a whole, we will find that there are many more restrictions. For *no*, for example, we have all three possibilities:

no pen	*no pens*	*no music*

But there are incomplete paradigms for *this*, *either*, and *enough*:

this pen	**this pens*	*this music*
either pen	**either pens*	**either music*
**enough pen*	*enough pens*	*enough music*

5.14 The central determiners can be divided into five types with respect to their cooccurrence with the noun classes singular count (*chair*, *problem*, etc), plural count (*chairs*, *problems*, etc), and noncount nouns (*furniture*, *information*, etc).

Type	SINGULAR COUNT	PLURAL COUNT	NONCOUNT
(a)	+	+	+
(b)	−	+	+
(c)	+	−	+
(d)	−	+	−
(e)	+	−	−

Fig 5.14 Cooccurrence of central determiners and noun classes

Type (a): Determiners of singular count, plural count, and noncount nouns.

(i) The definite article *the* (*cf* 5.27*ff*):

Where do you want me to put *the chair*/*the chairs*/*the furniture*?

(ii) The possessive pronouns as determiners: *my*, *our*, *your*, *his*, *her*, *its*, *their* (*cf* 6.29):

Have you seen *my suitcase*/*my suitcases*/*my luggage*?

(iii) The relative determiners *whose* (*cf* 6.34) and *which* (*cf* 6.35 Note [c]):

The lady *whose car* you hit was furious.
Call again at 11, by *which time* the meeting should be over.

(iv) The *wh*-determiners in *-ever* (*cf* 14.20):

Vote for *whichever proposal* you think most favourable.
For *whatever reason*, don't be late again.
Whosever idea this may be, I don't like it.

(v) The interrogative determiners *what*, *which*, *whose* (*cf* 6.36*ff*):

What colour?
Which information?
Whose ideas are these?

(vi) The negative determiner *no* (*cf* 6.62):

We have *no problem*/*problems* with violence here.
The sign said '*No parking*'.

Type (b): Determiners of plural count nouns and noncount nouns.

(i) Zero article (*cf* 5.39*ff*):

There were *people* everywhere.
Do you want to play *chess*?

(ii) The assertive determiner *some* (unstressed: /səm/) and the nonassertive determiner *any* (*cf* 6.59*ff*):

I want *some rolls*/*bread*, please.
Have we got *any rolls*/*bread* for breakfast tomorrow?

(iii) The quantitative determiner *enough* (*cf* 6.57):

I haven't got *enough equipment*/*tools* to do the job.

Type (c): Determiners of singular count nouns and singular noncount nouns. The demonstrative determiners *this* and *that* (*cf* 6.40*ff*):

Have you read *this*/*that book*?

Type (d): Determiners of plural count nouns. The demonstrative determiners *these* and *those* (*cf* 6.40*ff*):

Have you seen *these*/*those plays*?

Type (e): Determiners of singular count nouns.

(i) The indefinite article *a*/*an* (*cf* 5.36*ff*):

Have you got *a pen*?

(ii) The universal determiners *every* and *each* (*cf* 6.51):

I want to interview *every*/*each student* individually.

(iii) The nonassertive determiner *either* (*cf* 6.59*ff*):

You can park on *either side*.

(iv) The negative determiner *neither* (*cf* 6.62):

Neither party accepted the arbitration proposal.

Note [a] Strongly stressed *some* can occur also with certain singular count nouns, especially temporal nouns (*cf* 6.52):

"*Some* '*day* he will get his scholarship.

With the meaning 'a certain', etc, stressed *some* can also cooccur with other singular count nouns:

'*Some odd person* asked for you on the phone.

[b] Stressed *any* can occur also with singular count nouns under certain conditions (*cf* 6.61):

I will consider "*any offer*/*offers*. ['it doesn't matter which']

[c] *Every* is exceptional among central determiners in occasionally allowing a genitive or a possessive determiner to precede it:

His every action shows that he is a very determined young man. BUT NOT: **the*/*an every action*

Predeterminers

5.15 Predeterminers, which can occur before certain central determiners, include:

(i) *all*, *both*, and *half* (*cf* 5.16*f*):

all (*the*) girls, *both those* cars, *half an* hour

(ii) the multipliers *double*, *twice*, *three times*, etc (*cf* 5.18):

double the sum, *twice my* salary

(iii) the fractions *one-third*, *one-fifth*, etc (*cf* 5.19):

one-third the time

(iv) *such*, *what* (*cf* 7.63, 17.96):

Such a surprise!
What a fine day!

Predeterminers are mutually exclusive:

all girls, *both* girls BUT NOT: **all both* girls
half the sum, *double the* sum BUT NOT: **half double the* sum

Note The combination *all such*, as in [1], is an exception to the rule, just noted, that predeterminers are mutually exclusive:

Although every attempt is made to find suitable foster-homes for the children, it cannot be assumed that *all such* placements will be successful. [1]

The predeterminer *such*, used in this way as a pro-form (*cf* 2.44, 6.44 Note [b]), can also follow quantifiers such as *any*, *no*, and *many*, as well as cardinal numerals:

Outbreaks of small-arms fire along the frontier became more frequent in May,

{ but { *no* / hardly *any* } / and { *several* / *many* / *forty-one* } } *such* incidents were officially investigated. [2]

All, both, half

5.16 The predeterminers *all*, *both*, and *half* have restrictions on cooccurrence with determiners and noun heads. They can occur before the articles (*all the time*), possessive determiners (*all my time*, etc), demonstrative determiners (*all this time*). However, since they are themselves quantifiers, *all*, *both*, and *half* do not occur with the 'quantitative' determiners *every*, *(n)either*, *each*, *some*, *any*, *no*, *enough* (but *cf* 5.17 Note [a]). *Both* can occur only with plural nouns and has dual number (see below):

all (*the*) day	*all* (*the*) days	*all* (*the*) furniture
half a day	*half my* days	*half the* furniture
	both (*the*/*my*) eyes	

In addition to this predeterminer function, *all*, *both*, and *half* as pronouns can take partitive *of*-phrases, which are optional with nouns and obligatory with pronouns (*cf* '*of*-pronouns', 6.48):

all (*of*) *the* students	*all of them*/*whom*
both (*of*) *his* eyes	*both of them*/*which*
half (*of*) *the* time/cost	*half of it*/*this*

With a quantifier following, the *of*-phrase is preferred (esp in AmE):

all of the many boys

All three can be used as independent pronouns:

All/*both*/*half* passed their exams.

All and *both* (but not *half*) can occur after the head, either immediately or in the *M* adverb position (after the operator, *cf* 8.16). For *all* and *both* we have, then, the following possibilities:

All students were accepted. [1]
All the students were accepted. [2]
All of the students were accepted. [3]
The students were *all* accepted. [4]
All were accepted. [5]
All of them were accepted. [6]

They were *all* accepted. [7]
?*They all* were accepted. [8]

All is considered a pronoun in all these constructions except [1] and [2], where it is a predeterminer.

The predeterminer *both* and the central determiners *either* and *neither* are not plural proper but 'dual', *ie* they can refer to only two entities. Compared with the numeral *two*, *both* is emphatic:

{ *Both* (*the*) / *The two* } students were excellent.

For the use of these items as pronouns, *cf* 6.50 (*all*, *both*), 6.57 (*half*).

All and *whole*

5.17 The form *all* + noun with no article usually has generic reference (*cf* 5.26):

All men are created equal. [generic reference]

Contrast: *All the men* in the mine wore helmets. [specific reference]

But *all* + noun is not necessarily generic, *eg*:

I will see *all* (*the*) *students* at 11 a.m.
All (*the*) *men* must leave their coats here, but (the) women may take theirs with them.

The predeterminer *all* and the quantity partitive *whole* (*cf* 5.7) appear in parallel expressions. In *the whole of*, the definite article is obligatory. The use of *all* (*of*) (*the*) and *the whole* (*of*) is far from straightforward.

(i) *All*, *all the*, or *the whole* is used with temporal nouns, *eg*:

{ *all* (*the*) / *the whole* } day/morning/week

All of the + unit of time is rather uncommon:

?*all of the* day/hour/week

In the negated expression *I haven't seen him all day*, only the zero form is used. With indefinite reference, only *whole* can be used:

I spent { *a whole morning* / *the whole morning* } studying the script. ['full, entire']

(ii) *All the* or *the whole* is used with other count nouns that are understood to be divisible:

{ *all the* / *the whole* } family/way/story

All + noun occurs occasionally with concrete singular count nouns [1, 2], and it is less rare with contrastive stress [1a, 2a], where *book* and *banana* are treated as a divisible mass:

?I haven't read *all the BÒOK*. [1]

The monkey ate *all the baNÀna.* [2]
I haven't read *ǍLL the book.* [1a]
The monkey ate *ÀLL the banana.* [2a]

The normal constructions would be:

all of the / *the whole* } *book/banana*

Also with abstract nouns, *the whole* is often preferable to *all the*; *eg*:

the whole truth/distance/environment

(iii) With proper nouns and other nouns without the definite article, *all* (*of*) or *the whole of* is used:

all (of) / *the whole of* } Finland/London/next month/history

The use of *all* + a geographical name to denote the population is rather formal:

All Paris welcomed the General.

In less formal contexts, *The whole of Paris* . . . would be normal in denoting the population, or (more likely) referring to the city area.

(iv) With noncount nouns *all* (*of*) *the* is used:

Have you used up *all* (*of*) *the coffee*?
All (*of*) *the music* on the programme was modern.

The whole of is less preferred and *the whole* is unacceptable here.

Note [**a**] There is also an adverb *half* which can cooccur with noun heads, as in:

It is *half wine, half water.*

In the colloquial negation *n't half* ⟨esp BrE⟩, *half* can precede *enough* (*cf* 8.107 Note [b]):

He hasn't *half enough* money.

[**b**] *Both* and *half* with the *of*-construction are sometimes (especially dialectally) preceded by the definite article:

You don't know *the half of it.*
I've had enough of *the both of you.*

[**c**] The postposed pronoun *all* in *They were all hungry* must not be confused with *all* as an informal intensifying adverb in *He is all upset* (*cf* 7.57).

[**d**] For the following uses of *quite, rather, such,* and *what, cf* 7.56 Note [b], 7.63:

It was *quite a party.* It's *rather an odd story.*
Such a fine present! *What a stupid idea!*

[**e**] 'Restrictives' like *just, only, especially*, etc also occur before determiners:

Only the best cars are exported.

However, they have no special relation to noun phrase structure, since they can also modify verbs, adverbs, and adjectives (*cf* focusing subjuncts, 8.116*f*):

He's *just* { a boy. / feeling sick. / a little sick. / sleepy.

The multipliers *double, twice,* etc

5.18 The second type of predeterminer includes the multipliers which occur with nouns denoting quantity:

twice {his strength / her age} *double* {the amount / their salaries}

three times {this amount / the usual cost / the sum}

Once, *twice*, and *three*, *four*, etc *times* can cooccur with the determiners *a*, *every*, *each*, and (less commonly) *per* to form 'distributive' expressions of frequency with a temporal noun as head (*cf* 8.64):

once / *twice* / {*three* / *four*} *times* {*a* / *every* / *each* / *per*} {*day* / *week* / *month* / *year* / *decade*}

Such expressions can also occur with *every* + spatial nouns:

We stopped *once every mile.*

Both with temporal and spatial nouns, *every* can be followed by a numeral in such expressions as the above:

once every three months
twice every hundred miles

The fractions *one-third*, *two-fifths*, etc

5.19 The fractions can also be followed by determiners. Unlike the multipliers, the fractions have the alternative *of*-construction. The indefinite article can replace *one* (*cf* 5.38):

He did it in {*one-third* / *a third*} (*of*) *the time* it took me.

Postdeterminers

5.20 Postdeterminers follow predeterminers or central determiners (if such determiners are present). But they precede any adjectives and other premodifying items (*cf* 17.2). Postdeterminers include:

(a) Cardinal numerals (*cf* 5.21): *my three children*
(b) Ordinal numerals and 'general ordinals' (*cf* 5.22): *the first day*, *the last month*
(c) Closed-class quantifiers (*cf* 5.23*f*): *few people*
(d) Open-class quantifiers (*cf* 5.25): *a large number of people*

(a) Cardinal numerals

5.21 *One* cooccurs with singular count nouns (*one sister*), and the other cardinal numerals (*cf* 6.63) cooccur with plural count nouns (*two*, *three*, etc *brothers*). In many contexts, *one* may be regarded as a stressed form of the indefinite article and may sometimes replace it (*cf* 5.19, 5.38):

I would like {*a* / *one*} photocopy of this article.

Thus, the indefinite article normally cannot cooccur with *one*, but the definite article can:

$$\left.\begin{array}{l}\text{*}\textit{a one}\text{ book}\\ \textit{the one}\text{ ['only'] book}\\ \textit{the two}\text{ books}\end{array}\right\}\text{ I like best}$$

(b) Ordinal numerals and 'general ordinals'

5.22 The ordinal numerals have a one-for-one relation with the cardinals: *first/one*, *second/two*, *third/three*, *fourth/four*, *twentieth/twenty*, etc (*cf* 6.63*f*).

The 'general ordinals' include items like *next*, *last*, *past*, (*an*)*other*, *additional*, and *further* ['additional'], which resemble the ordinal numerals grammatically and semantically.

Ordinals cooccur with count nouns and usually precede any cardinal numbers in the noun phrase:

the *first two* days   *another three* weeks

Note [**a**] The general ordinals *last*, *past*, and *next* may precede or follow cardinals with a difference of meaning. For example: *the last two pages* would mean 'the last and penultimate page of a book', whereas *the two last pages* could mean 'the last page in each of two books'. On divided concord usage, *eg*: *The last two months is/are . . .*, *cf* 10.35 Note [b].

[**b**] *Another* has two functions. It can be the unstressed form of 'one other' in contrast with *the other* (definite; *cf* 6.58), as in [1]; or it can have the meaning of 'further', 'additional', 'second', in which case there is no definite form, as in [2]:

$$\text{I don't like this room. I'd prefer }\left\{\begin{array}{l}\textit{another}\\ \textit{the other}\end{array}\right\}\textit{one.}\qquad [1]$$

We need *another two rooms* for the meeting.
['two more rooms'; *cf*: *the other two rooms* 'the two different rooms'] [2]

Note that when it is followed by a plural cardinal number, *another* takes a plural noun as head.

(c) Closed-class quantifiers

5.23 There are two small groups of closed-class quantifiers which function as postdeterminers (*cf* 6.53*ff*).

(i) *Many*, (*a*) *few*, and *several* cooccur only with plural count nouns:

$$\text{There were }\left\{\begin{array}{l}\text{too }\textit{many}\\ \text{only }\textit{a few}\\ \text{very }\textit{few}\\ \textit{several}\end{array}\right\}\text{ mistakes in your essay.}$$

(ii) *Much* and (*a*) *little* cooccur only with noncount nouns:

She hasn't got *much* money.
She has only got (*a*) *little* money.

There are restrictions on the use of *much* with singular and *many* with plural nouns, and the corresponding open-class postdeterminers are widely used instead (*cf* 6.53). Thus *much* is typically used in a nonassertive sentence like [1]; but in an assertive sentence like [2], usually *a lot of* (chiefly in informal style), or a similar colloquial postdeterminer, is used:

We don't have *much* time. [1]

We have { *plenty of* / *a lot of* / *lots of* } time. [2]

In the case of (*a*) *few* ['a small number'] and (*a*) *little* ['a small quantity'], there is positive/negative contrast according to whether the indefinite article is used or not. When *a/an* does not precede, *few* and *little* are stressed:

He wrote { *a few* 'books. ['some, several'] / '*few* 'books. ['not many'] / *a little* 'poetry. ['some'] / '*little* 'poetry. ['not much'] }

The postdeterminers (*a*) *few* and (*a*) *little* (*cf* 6.53, 6.62), the determiners *any*, *no*, and *some* (*cf* 5.39*f*, 6.52), and the predeterminers *all* and *both* are all quantifiers although they belong to different syntactic classes.

Note [**a**] *Few* and *little* may be preceded by central determiners other than *a*, *eg*: *these few days*, *that little money*, but we shall refer only to *a few* versus *few*, *a little* versus *little* where the distinction is clearest.

[**b**] *Several* can be preceded by a possessive determiner in the sense of 'separate', 'respective': *their several opinions*.

[**c**] *Many* and *few* can also be used predicatively in formal style (*cf* 6.53 Note [b], 6.62):

His faults were *many*/*few*.

Many can also function as a predeterminer with singular count nouns preceded by the indefinite article:

many a good student ⟨rather formal⟩ ['*many good* students']

[**d**] The quantifier *enough* is used with both count and noncount nouns:

There are (not) *enough* students.

There is (not) *enough* money.

Occasionally it follows the noun (especially noncount: *money enough*). This use strikes many people as archaic or dialectal, but with *galore* (informal) it is obligatory ('money/students *galore*').

5.24 Since *a few* determines plural count nouns (*a few books*), and *a little* determines noncount nouns (*a little poetry*), neither of which noun classes cooccurs with the indefinite article, it will be clear that in these instances *a* belongs to the quantifier alone.

Few, *little*, *much*, and *many* are gradable, and also have comparative and superlative forms (*cf* 7.74*ff*):

few/fewer/fewest dollars	*many/more/most* dollars
little/less/least money	*much/more/most* money

There is a tendency to use *less* (instead of *fewer*) and *least* (instead of *fewest*) also with count nouns:

You've made *less* mistakes than last time.

This usage is however often condemned. *No less than* is more generally accepted:

No less than fifty people were killed in the accident.

Being gradable, *many*, *much*, *few*, and *little* can be modified by intensifying adverbs (*cf* 7.87*ff*): *too much*, *very few*, etc.

Note The quantifier *little* ['not much'] should be distinguished from the homonymous adjective *little* ['small'], which cooccurs with singular or plural count nouns: *a little girl, five little girls*. Thus *a little cake* is ambiguous according to whether it means 'a small cake' [*little* = adjective] or 'a small amount of cake' [*little* = postdeterminer].

(d) Open-class quantifiers

5.25 There is also a large open class of phrasal quantifiers which function semantically like the closed-class quantifiers, but most of which consist of a noun of quantity (*lot*, *deal*, *amount*, etc) followed by *of* and often preceded by the indefinite article. Some of these, including *plenty of*, can cooccur equally with noncount and plural count nouns:

The room contained { *plenty of* / *a lot of* / *lots of* } { students. / furniture. }

These quantifiers (especially *lots*) are chiefly used informally.

Others are restricted to quantifying only noncount nouns [1], or plural count nouns [2]:

The chest contained *a* { { *great* / *good* } *deal* / { *(large)* / *(small)* } { *quantity* / *amount* } } *of* money. [1]

The hall contained *a* { *(great)* / *(large)* / *(good)* } *number of* students. [2]

As the examples suggest, it is usual for these open-class quantifiers to be modified by a quantifying adjective, the latter being obligatory in Standard English with *deal*. (On concord with open-class quantifiers, *cf* 10.43.)

Although the quantity nouns *lot*, *deal*, etc look like the head of a noun phrase, there are grounds for arguing that the whole expression (*a lot of*, *a good deal of*, etc) functions as a determiner. Notably, the verb regularly has number concord with the second noun, rather than the first, as in:

{ *Lots of food was* on the table.
= There *was lots of food* on the table. }

Note **[a]** As with *less* and *least*, there is a tendency (esp in AmE) to use *amount* for the more generally acceptable *number* also with count nouns, despite objections to this usage:

There were *large amounts of tourists* on the ferry.
This hall can seat *a large amount of people*.

[b] In familiar spoken English we find a wide range of quantifiers roughly synonymous with *lots of*, *eg*:

We've got *bags of* time.
She's got { *stacks of* / *heaps of* / *loads of* } money.
They have *umpteen* jazz records.

The use of articles with common nouns

Specific and generic reference

5.26 In discussing the use of the articles, we must distinguish between specific and generic reference. Compare sentences [1] and [2]:

> *A lion* and *two tigers* are sleeping in the cage. [1]
> *Tigers* are dangerous animals. [2]

In [1] the reference is SPECIFIC, since we have in mind particular specimens of the class 'tiger'. But if we say [2], the reference is GENERIC, since we are thinking of the class 'tiger' without specific reference to particular tigers.

The distinctions between definite and indefinite, and between singular and plural, are important for specific reference. They tend to be less crucial for generic reference, because generic reference is used to denote the class or species generally. Consequently, the distinctions of number which apply to this or that member, or group of members, of the class are neutralized, being largely irrelevant to the generic concept. Singular or plural, definite or indefinite, can often be used without appreciable difference of meaning in generic contexts:

> *A German* is a good musician.
> { *Germans* / *The Germans* } are good musicians.

> { *A tiger* / *Tigers* / *The tiger* } can be dangerous.

A fourth possibility might even be included:

> *The German* is a good musician.

But the slight differences between these various forms, and the reasons for preferring one to another, will be considered in 5.52*ff*.

The use of articles with specific reference is summarized in *Table* 5.26:

Table 5.26 Use of the articles with specific reference

	DEFINITE		INDEFINITE	
	COUNT	NONCOUNT	COUNT	NONCOUNT
SINGULAR	*the tiger*	the furniture	*a tiger*	(some) *furniture*
PLURAL	the tigers		(some) *tigers*	

Only those choices italicized in this table are used for generic reference. At present we will concentrate on the specific use of the articles, which is much more frequent than the generic.

Specific reference: definite and indefinite

Uses of the definite article

5.27 The definite article *the* is used to mark the phrase it introduces as definite, *ie* as referring to something which can be identified uniquely in the contextual or general knowledge shared by speaker and hearer. The 'something' referred to may be any kind of noun phrase referent: a person (*the girl*), a group of people (*the firemen*), an object (*the lamp*), a group of objects (*the roses*), an abstraction (*the plan*), a group of abstractions (*the fears*), etc. Moreover, the noun determined by *the* may have pre- or postmodification, by which the 'something' identified by *the* may be more precisely specified, *eg*:

the *tall* lamp the lamp *on the table*

Given that the use of *the* relies on shared knowledge, there are several ways in which the identity of the referent may be determined or 'recovered' by the hearer, as we shall see in 5.28*ff*.

Note As elsewhere, when no distinction is necessary in this discussion of articles, 'speaker' subsumes 'writer', and 'hearer' subsumes 'reader'.

(a) Immediate situation

5.28 The term SITUATIONAL REFERENCE may be used to describe cases where the reference of *the* is derived from the extralinguistic situation. We first distinguish *the* used with reference to the IMMEDIATE situation:

The roses are very beautiful. [said in a garden]
Have you visited *the castle*? [said in a given town]
I missed both *the lectures* this morning. [said by one student to another]
Have you fed *the cat*? [said in a domestic context]
These are *the pistons*. [explaining the engine of a car]

It is, of course, possible for the speaker to misjudge the knowledge of the hearer, in which case the hearer may need to seek clarification through a *which-* or *what-*question (with the nucleus on the *wh*-item):

Have you fed *the cat*? WHÌCH cat?
Aren't *the red roses* lovely? WHÀT red roses?

Note In practice, since a speaker cannot always be sure of the hearer's state of knowledge, use of *the* involves a certain amount of guesswork. In fact, in some cases the assumption of shared knowledge is a palpable fiction. Notices such as *Mind the step* and *Beware of the dog*, for example, generally do not assume that the reader was previously aware of the hazards in question.

(b) Larger situation (general knowledge)

5.29 The identity of the referent may be evident from knowledge of the 'larger' situation which speaker and hearer share, *eg*:

the Prime Minister the airlines the last war

The larger situation may in fact be worldwide (*the Pope*), or be shared by all inhabitants of a country; *eg* in the United States, at a given time, virtually everyone will know which president is being referred to by the phrase *the President*. When it is as wide as this, the 'larger situation' is scarcely distinguishable from general knowledge and may extend, in extreme cases, to the whole planet or to the whole of human history. In the use of phrases like *the sun* there is the presupposition that, in our experience or fields of interest, there is only one such object. Similar examples are:

the North Pole	*the Equator*	*the earth*
the moon	*the sea*	*the sky*
the stars	*the universe*	*the cosmos*
the zenith	*the nadir*	*the Renaissance*
the Greek gods	*the Republic*	*the Church*

There is a tendency for some nominal expressions following *the* to be written with initial capitals. This is because such expressions in effect have UNIQUE DENOTATION, and in this respect resemble proper nouns (*cf* 5.60*ff*).

There is no clear dividing line between 'immediate' and 'larger' situations; instead, there is a scale of generality running from the most restricted to the least restricted sphere that can be envisaged: that of the whole universe of human knowledge.

Note [a] Singular noun phrases having unique denotation include phrases referring to classes, groups, etc of human beings such as the following (*cf* collective nouns, 5.108):

the working class *the proletariat*
the bourgeoisie *the aristocracy*

Similar plural phrases include those referring to clans, tribes, races, etc:

the Romans *the Gordon Highlanders*
the masses *the Italians*

The use of *the* in respect of the 'larger situation' overlaps with the generic use (*cf* 5.52*ff*).

[b] Both in idioms (such as *down to earth*) and in general usage, *earth* is often used with zero article (cf 5.41*ff*):

The space ship returned to *earth* this morning.

(c) Anaphoric reference: direct

5.30 The term ANAPHORIC REFERENCE is used where the uniqueness of reference of some phrase *the X* is supplied by information given earlier in the discourse (*cf* 12.6). We may distinguish two kinds of anaphora: direct and indirect. A definite noun phrase receives DIRECT anaphoric interpretation where the same noun head has already occurred in the text, and it is clear that a relation of coreference exists between the two noun phrases. (By COREFERENCE we understand a relation between the two noun phrases such that they have the same reference.) For example:

Felicity bought a TV and *a video recorder*, but she returned *the video recorder* because *it* was defective.

Here, as in other similar cases, there is a complementary role for the definite article and the indefinite article: the first reference to an object will ordinarily be indefinite; but once the object has been introduced into the discourse in this way, it can be treated as 'contextually known', and can thenceforward be referred to by means of the definite article.

(d) Anaphoric reference: indirect

5.31 INDIRECT ANAPHORA arises when a reference becomes part of the hearer's knowledge indirectly, not by direct mention, as in the example in 5.30, but by inference from what has already been mentioned:

John bought *a new bicycle*, but found that one of the wheels was defective. [1]

The wheels of the bicycle can be taken for granted in this sentence because (a) a bicycle has already been mentioned (ANAPHORA), and (b) we know that bicycles have wheels (GENERAL KNOWLEDGE). In this way, we can see that indirect anaphora combines two kinds of 'recoverability'. Another way to look at it is to say that indirect anaphora combines anaphoric reference with cataphoric reference (*cf* 5.32); *eg* we understand *the wheels* in [1] above to be an elliptical variant of *the wheels of the bicycle*. This latter explanation does not, as we shall see, apply to all such cases.

Some further examples of indirect anaphora are the following. Once we have introduced the topic of *a farm*, we can go on to talk about *the farmer*, *the farmhouse*, *the pigs*, *the barn*, etc; once we have introduced the topic of *an orchestral concert*, we can go on to talk about *the programme*, *the audience*, *the conductor*, *the second oboe*, etc.

Consider finally these examples:

> I lent Bill *a valuable book*, but when he returned it, *the cover* was filthy, and *the pages* were torn. [2]
>
> They *got married* in grand style. *The bride* wore a long brocade dress, and *the bridesmaids* wore pink taffeta. *The organist* played superb music, and *the choir* sang magnificently. [3]

In [3] the topic of 'a wedding' is introduced by means of the verb phrase *got married* (hence *the bride*, *the bridesmaids*); there is also the presumption of a church, and hence *the organist*, *the choir*. There is thus no easy way to explain the subsequent occurrences of *the* by means of ellipsis; to do so, it would be necessary to postulate such long-winded phrases as [3a]:

> the bridesmaids who accompanied the bride when she got married [3a]

(e) Cataphoric reference

5.32 By the CATAPHORIC use of *the* may be understood the use of the definite article in a context where what follows the head noun, rather than what precedes it, enables us to pinpoint the reference uniquely. 'Cataphoric' is therefore the opposite of 'anaphoric' reference. In practice, however, the cataphoric use of the definite article is limited to cases where the modification of the noun phrase restricts the reference of the noun, so that its referent is, for the purpose of the discourse, uniquely defined. Thus, the italicized postmodifiers of the following nouns justify the use of *the*:

> The President *of Mexico* is to visit China. [1]
>
> The girls *sitting over there* are my cousins. [2]
>
> The wines {*of France* / *that France produces*} are among the best in the world. [3]

In principle, however, there is no difference between postmodification and premodification as a means of specifying reference. Compare:

> the President *of Mexico* [1a]
>
> the *Mexican* President [1b]

Sometimes the definite noun phrase can be contrasted with an equivalent indefinite phrase. In such instances, the definite article is not in fact genuinely cataphoric but entails some degree of anaphoric reference. Compare [4] and [4a]:

The bicycle John bought has been stolen. [assumes unique reference; *cf*: *John's bicycle*] [4]

A bicycle John bought has been stolen. [*cf*: *a bicycle of John's*, *cf* 17.46] [4a]

At other times, there is no such indefinite alternative, because the whole phrase has unique denotation, like *the Equator* (*cf* 5.29):

{ the height *of Mont Blanc* / *a height *of Mont Blanc* }   { the parents *of Elvis Presley* / *(some) parents *of Elvis Presley* }

Note It is not necessary to postulate that the expression [5] presupposes some unspoken preamble such as [5a] but, rather, such as [5b]:

the mud on your coat [5]

There's *some mud* on your coat. [5a]

You know there's mud on your coat. [5b]

Contrast [6] with [6a]:

How did you get *the mud* on your coat? [6]

Did you know you have { *mud* / **the mud* } on your coat? [6a]

(f) Sporadic reference

5.33 *The* is sometimes used in reference to an institution of human society. For example, in [1] there are two possible interpretations of *the theatre*:

My sister goes to *the theatre* every month. [1]

By situational reference, it may mean a particular theatre, say the Criterion Theatre, which my sister attends regularly. But a more likely meaning is that my sister does not necessarily confine her theatre-going to one building: *the theatre* refers, rather, to the theatre as an institution, so that it would be inappropriate to ask, in response to [1]: *Which theatre?* We call this the SPORADIC use of *the*, because reference is made to an institution which may be observed recurrently at various places and times.

There is a similar use of *the news*, *the radio*, *the television*, *the paper(s)*, *the press*, etc, referring to aspects of mass communication:

Did you hear *the ten o'clock news*?

What's { *in the paper(s)* / *on the radio* / *on (the) TV* } this evening?

But with *television* or *TV*, there is also the possibility that the article will be omitted (*cf* 5.45).

The concept of sporadic reference also extends to expressions referring to modern transport and communication, such as *the bus*, *the train*, *the post* ⟨esp BrE⟩, *the mail* ⟨esp AmE⟩, *the telephone*:

Mary took *the bus*/*the train* to London. OR: *a bus*/*a train*

He promised that the letters would be in *the post*/*the mail* this evening.

In a temporal rather than spatial sense, sporadic reference may even be taken to apply to the optional use of *the* before words referring to seasons (*eg*: *the winter*, *cf* 5.47), and to festivals, etc (*the New Year*, *cf* 5.67).

Note [**a**] The sporadic use of *the* is in certain instances close to the generic use of *the* (*cf* 5.55*ff*). Compare the use of *the theatre* in [1] above with the generic sense of *the theatre* ['drama as an art form'] in [2]:

She's an expert on (*the*) (*Elizabethan*) *theatre*. [2]

Similarly: *the novel, the ballad*, (*the*) *drama*.

[**b**] The contrast between situational and sporadic use is manifest in this pair of examples:

There's a vase of flowers on { *the television* (*set*). / **television*. }

There's an interesting play on (*the*) *television*.

[**c**] On the sporadic use of *the* in cases like *the barber's*, *cf* 5.125.

(g) The 'logical' use of *the*

5.34 We may reserve the term LOGICAL for cases where the uniqueness of the referent is to be explained not so much by knowledge of the world, as by appeal to the logical interpretation of certain words. These words are postdeterminers and adjectives whose meaning is inalienably associated with uniqueness: ordinals such as *first*; 'general ordinals' such as *next* and *last* (*cf* 5.22); also *same, only, sole*; and superlative adjectives like *best* and *largest*:

When is *the first flight* to Chicago tomorrow? [1]
This is *the only remaining copy*. [2]
Of the three newspapers we have in this city, this is *the best*. [3]

In these cases the indefinite article or the zero article would generally be absurd:

Ada and I have { *the* / **a* } *same hobby*.

We must catch { *the* / **a* } *next bus*.

Note [**a**] The 'logical' use of *the* is closely related to cataphoric reference. Compare [1] with [1a]:

When is *the flight that leaves first* for Chicago tomorrow? [1a]

[**b**] The occurrence of fixed phrases such as *a best friend* is possible in special contexts: *eg* if a child is always changing his or her best friend, one may refer to the current favourite as *a new best friend*. More freely, zero article may be used in front of fixed phrases such as:

He was *best man* ['groomsman'] at the wedding. (*cf*: He was { *the best man* / **best man* } for the job.)

He won *first prize*.

(h) The use of *the* with reference to body parts

5.35 With reference to parts of the body and following a preposition, *the* is often used instead of possessive pronouns *my, your, her, their* (*cf* also the indefinite article, 5.36 Note), etc:

Mary banged herself on *the forehead*.
They pulled her by *the hair*.
Everyone gave us a pat on *the back*.
Don't keep digging me in *the ribs*.

In these examples, the personal pronoun or noun referring to the 'possessor' of the body part is the object, and the body part is a prepositional complement. There are virtually synonymous clauses in which the body part is preceded by a possessive pronoun, and functions as object:

I shook { *him by the hand.* [1]
his hand. [1a]

It is often possible, though sometimes unidiomatic, to use a possessive pronoun in place of *the*:

I shook *him by his hand.* [1b]
He kissed *her on her cheek.*
She patted *him on his shoulder.*

In other cases the 'possessor' phrase is subject of the clause:

My mother complains of a pain in *the/her hip.*
The wanted man has a scar on *the/his left cheek.*

Alternatively, the 'possessor' may be implied rather than stated:

The doctor diagnosed a fracture of *the collarbone.*
Many patients in the hospital suffered from a disease of *the liver.*

A similar use of *the* is acceptable in other rather impersonal contexts where the possessor is either irrelevant or already adequately clear:

It will improve your tennis if you keep *the back* straight when you serve.

By contrast:

Have you broken *your* arm? NOT: *Have you broken *the* arm?

A further restriction is that the possessive pronoun must be used if the body part does not refer to what is denoted by the direct object:

She throws the ball { *with her left hand.* [2]
?*with the left hand.* [2a]

One factor which could make [2a] acceptable, and indeed normal, is the interpretation 'she is left-handed'. Similarly:

She kicks the ball *with the left foot* (because she is *left-footed*).

With such an interpretation, *the* is normal, but the rule is not absolute.

Note [**a**] There can be a slight difference of meaning between the construction illustrated by [1] and by [1a]. The following appear to be synonymous:

They grabbed { *him by the arm.* [3]
his arm. [3a]

But one can imagine a grisly context in which [3a] refers to an arm severed from the body; this context could not apply to [3].

[**b**] It is difficult to generalize about cases of the above constructions. Some are purely idiomatic:

She *looked me in the eye* and told me the whole story. [but not here: *looked in my eye*, although this is what a doctor will do at an examination of the eye]

Further semantic factors are the following:

(i) The use of *the* is preferred when the reference is to unpleasant conditions of the body (*eg* aches, pains, wounds):

have a cold in the head *have spies on the brain*
be red in the face *be armed to the teeth*

(ii) This use applies only to parts of the body, and cannot usually be extended to things which are worn:

They seized him by *the throat/the beard/the collar/?the jacket.*

Moreover, only those verbs which can take the personal direct object without the prepositional phrase can occur in this construction:

He kicked/hit/tapped me on *the* shin. ['He kicked *etc* my shin.' But not: *He stepped me on *the* toes; *He stepped my toes.]

[**c**] Outside the above conditions, *the* is sometimes used instead of possessives in a masculine style of speech:

How's *the back*? [referring to an injury]

Let's have a look at *the arm.* [This is also what a doctor, of either sex, might say to a patient.]

Related to this usage is the habit of some men of referring to their wives, or children, by *the* ⟨informal⟩:

How's *the wife*? [normally: *your wife*]

Wait till I tell *the wife* about it! [normally: *my wife*]

How are *the children/kids*?

Note also ⟨familiar⟩:

How's *the old man*? ['your husband/father']

[**d**] On other uses of *the* (*eg*: *the more the merrier*; *40 miles to the gallon*), *cf* 11.43.

Uses of the indefinite article

5.36 The indefinite article is notionally the 'unmarked' article in the sense that it is used (for singular count nouns) where the conditions for the use of *the* do not obtain. That is, *a/an X* will be used where the reference of *X* is not uniquely identifiable in the shared knowledge of speaker and hearer. Hence *a/an* is typically used when the referent has not been mentioned before, and is assumed to be unfamiliar to the speaker or hearer:

An intruder has stolen *a vase*. *The intruder* stole *the vase* from *a locked case*. *The case* was smashed open.

As we see from this (unusually explicit) example, the indefinite article, in contrast to the definite article, makes no assumptions about an earlier mention. But in actual usage the distinction may be less overt. For example, a conversation may begin as [1] or as [1a]:

A house on the corner is for sale. [1]
The house on the corner is for sale. [1a]

The only difference in meaning is that, in [1a], the speaker presupposes that the hearer will know which house is meant (perhaps because there is only one such house), whereas, in [1], no such assumption is implied.

Unlike the definite article, the indefinite article does not signal coreference with a preceding indefinite noun phrase. In sentence [2], the speaker does not claim that the two watches are the same (although he may be obliquely suggesting that such is the case):

Bob lost *a gold watch* yesterday, and Bill was wearing *a gold watch* this morning. [2]

But if the second *a gold watch* is changed to *the gold watch*, the claim is made that the two watches are indeed identical, and that (probably) Bill is a thief.

Note The indefinite article, like the definite article (*cf* 5.35), is sometimes used with body parts:

Sally has sprained *an ankle.* [3]
He's broken *a leg.* [4]
BUT NOT: *Roger has hurt *a nose.* [5]

A/an cannot be used unless the body has more than one of the body parts mentioned; hence [5] is absurd in implying that Roger has more than one nose. Even when the body part is not unique, the possessive pronoun is the usual choice (*cf* 5.35):

Sally has sprained *her ankle.* [3a]
He's broken *his leg.* [4a]
I've cut *my finger.*

Nonreferring uses of the indefinite article

5.37 The indefinite article is strongly associated with the complement function in a clause, or more generally with noun phrases in a copular relationship (*cf* 2.22, 10.8). Here it has a descriptive role (similar to that of predicative adjectives), rather than a referring role:

Paganini was *a* great violinist.
My daughter is training as *a* radiologist.
We found Lisbon (to be) *a* delightful city.
What *a* miserable day (it is)! (*cf* 11.31)

Whereas the indefinite article is required in the previous examples, there is vacillation in the following cases (*cf* 'unique role', 5.42):

her duties *as* (*a*) *hostess*
my appointment *as* (*a*) *lecturer*
Jung *as* (*a*) *thinker*

Sometimes *a/an* is nonreferring in a stronger sense; it may not refer to anything in reality at all:

Leonard wants to marry *a* princess who speaks five languages.

From this sentence, we cannot tell whether Leonard knows a certain princess and wants to marry her, or whether he has simply laid down exceptionally stringent qualifications for his future wife. For all we know, there may be no princess who speaks five languages in existence.

Note Although *a/an* is used for descriptive exclamations such as *What a fool* (*he is*)*!*, there is also an exclamatory use of *the* in *The fool!*, *The silly boy!*, etc. Such expressions often accompany a declarative clause, and are added as a parenthesis (intonation remaining at a low pitch):

John is getting into *DÈBT*, *the idiot!*
My *DÀUGH*ter| *the little DÁR*ling| has broken the TV̀|<ironic>

There is a related type of descriptive exclamation in which a noun phrase with *the* or zero article is followed by *that* and a subject and verb (normally *be*):

(The) fool that he is!

On the exclamatory use of pronouns (*Silly me!*, *You fool!*, etc), *cf* 6.20.

The indefinite article and the numeral *one*

5.38 The indefinite article derives historically from the unstressed form of *one*, and in present-day English there are still many contexts in which this numerical function is uppermost. Thus *one* could be substituted as a slightly emphatic equivalent of *a* in the following coordinate constructions (*cf* 5.21):

a mile or two *cf*: *one or two miles* (10.41 Note [b])
The Wrights have *two daughters and a son.*
a foot and a half of water *cf*: *one and a half feet* (5.73 Note [b])

The following are other examples in which *one* could replace *a*/*an*, and where the adjective *single* can add an intensifying force to the indefinite article (or *one*):

Mungo can walk forty miles *in a* (*single*) *day.*
They didn't stop talking *for a* (*single*) *moment.*
There's *not a* (*single*) *pickled onion* in the house.

A/*an* often occurs in this quasi-numerical sense following a negative (*cf* 10.62).

Note [**a**] The use of the indefinite article in a numerical or quantifying function is perhaps most obvious in its occurrence in such expressions as (*cf* 6.65):

a hundred, a dozen, a score, a thousand, a million, a million and a half ['1,500,000'], *a quarter*/*a twelfth of* + noun

Other uses are seen in quantifiers (*cf* 5.23*ff*, 6.53) such as *a few, a little, a great many, a large number of*, etc; also in measure phrases (*cf* 5.18) such as:

half an hour, ten dollars a day, sixty miles an hour, three times a minute, etc

[**b**] In addition to being a numeral, *one* also has substitute and generic functions. But in the use of the indefinite article in a generic sense (*A tiger can be dangerous*), *a*/*an* cannot be replaced by *one* (*cf* 6.56).

Uses of the zero article

The zero article compared with unstressed *some*

5.39 With plural count nouns and with noncount nouns, the indefinite article does not occur (*cf* 5.13*f*). The zero article is used instead:

Have you ever eaten *roasted chestnuts*?
Milk is good for you.
Do you like *folk music*?

But the plural or noncount equivalent of *a*/*an* is sometimes the unstressed determiner *some* /səm/. Contrast referring [1] and descriptive [2] noun phrases:

Our guests included *some vegetarians.*

I've just bought { *a melon.* / *some melons.* / *some melon.* / *?melons.* } [1]

She has become *a vegetarian.*
They have become { *vegetarians.* / **some vegetarians.* } [2]

In the negative, unstressed *any* is the equivalent of *some* (but *cf* 10.59 Note [b]), so that a contrast may be observed between [3] and [4]:

I haven't bought { *any books.* / *?books.* } [3]

They haven't become { *vegetarians.* / **any vegetarians.* } [4]

The difference between the uses of zero and of *some* may be summarized as follows. Unstressed *some*, although it is sometimes considered a plural article, actually keeps its quantifying function, and indicates reference to a specifiable (though indefinite) quantity or amount. (Thus in [1], the speaker does not tell us the number of melons, but in principle the number could be found out.) The zero article, in contrast, indicates simply the category of the objects, etc referred to. So *vegetarians* in [4] names a category of persons, and the sentence simply indicates that the people referred to by *they* belong to that category.

Note The zero article may be used instead of *some*, particularly if a contrast is implied prosodically:

I've just bought *MĔLons* (but not grapes). [1a]

I haven't bought *BŎOKS* (but I've bought magazines). [3a]

5.40 Sometimes *some* and zero are both acceptable; in other cases one of them is less acceptable, or even quite unacceptable. In the following two examples, *some* would be unacceptable:

These shoes are made of *leather*. [1]

I've always preferred *coffee* to *tea*. [2]

In [1], the speaker is merely interested in the type of material of which the shoes are made: the quantity is irrelevant. In [2], the interest focuses on the two types of drink, and it is irrelevant to consider particular quantities.

In other cases, the introduction of *some* would necessitate a sharp difference in meaning, *eg*:

Joe's been chasing *women* ever since he was young. [3]

In [3], *some women* would produce the incongruous impression that Joe has been steadfastly chasing the same group of women, rather than that he is an incorrigible Don Juan.

The distinction we have to draw, then, is between the CATEGORIAL meaning of zero, and the QUANTITATIVE meaning of *some*. It can now be seen that the generic meaning of the zero article, as in *Tigers are fierce animals* (*cf* 5.26), is no more than a special variant of this categorial meaning. But it is still worth separating generic reference, where we could substitute *all tigers* with little change of effect, from the specific categorial reference of sentences like [3], where clearly there is no claim that all women have been chased by Joe (*cf* 5.56).

As has already been hinted, the choice between zero and *some* is sometimes more a matter of focus than of clear contrast of meaning. There are many situations in which either choice could be made, with only a minor alteration of the force. Compare:

Would you like (*some*) *coffee* or (*some*) *tea*? [4]

I've been writing (*some*) *letters* this morning. [5]

We have just received (*some*) *news* from Moscow. [6]

The variant without *some* will focus on the category as a whole; *eg* [4] is asking about two kinds of drink, and [5] is concerned with a kind of activity, *viz* the activity of writing letters. But when *some* is added, the focus changes to whatever quantities of tea and coffee, or of letters, that the speaker has in mind.

The zero article with definite meaning

5.41 Apart from proper nouns, nouns take the zero article with definite meaning only in rather special circumstances, as described in 5.42*ff*.

Noun phrases in a copular relation

5.42 Unlike many other languages, English normally requires an article with a singular count noun as complement (*cf* 5.37):

Bill is { *an engineer.* / **engineer.* }   Mary is { *the secretary.* / **secretary.* }

There is, however, one circumstance in which the zero article occurs in such constructions: this is where the complement (or an equivalent appositive noun phrase) names a UNIQUE ROLE or task. As the following examples show, in such cases the zero article alternates with *the*:

Maureen is (*the*) *captain of the team.* [1]
John F. Kennedy was (*the*) *President of the United States* in 1961. [2]
As (*the*) *chairman of the committee*, I declare this meeting closed. [3]
They've appointed Fred (*the*) *treasurer*, and no doubt he will soon become (*the*) *secretary*. [4]
Anne Martin, (*the*) *star of the TV series* and (*the*) *author of a well-known book on international cuisine*, has resigned from her post on the Consumer Council. [5]

The copular relation signalled by *as* (*cf* 9.48) is illustrated in [3], and the copular relation of apposition (*cf* 17.65*ff*) is illustrated in [5]. In each of these examples, it is implied that only one person holds the particular position mentioned.

Note [a] Here we may also place examples where the appositional noun phrase indicating a unique role or task is placed first:

FBI Chief J. Edgar Hoover [6]
Chelsea centre-forward Milton Smith [7]

With restrictive apposition [6, 7], the article is generally omitted, whereas in nonrestrictive apposition [7a] (*cf* 17.68), it is not:

the Chelsea centre-forward, Milton Smith [7a]

There is a gradient linking the former construction to the institutional use of titles, as in *King George*, *Chairman Mao*, *Doctor Smith*. But the use of more elaborate phrases of this kind preceding a name is characteristic of the journalistic style sometimes known as 'Timestyle', because of its association with *Time* magazine.

[b] The complement of *turn* (*cf* 16.22) is exceptional in having zero article even where there is no implication of uniqueness:

Jenny started out as a music student before she *turned linguist*. BUT: . . . before she *became a linguist*.

[c] Because a unique role is implied, the definite article is generally omitted following expressions such as *the post of*, *the position of*, and *the role of*:

After declining the post of *Secretary of State*, he nevertheless found himself taking on the role of *unofficial adviser to the President*.

[**d**] Determiners (*the*, *your*, etc) are frequently omitted in official forms, *eg*:

Please send the stipulated items, *viz*:
(i) *birth certificate*
(ii) *passport*
(iii) *correct fee*

Compare the omission of articles in headlines (11.45*f*).

Noun phrases with sporadic reference

5.43 We have already mentioned (*cf* 5.33) the use of *the* in noun phrases with 'sporadic' definite reference, as in *the radio*, *the theatre*. In other cases, however, the sporadic use has become so institutionalized that the article is not used. We distinguish, under this heading, a number of different categories of zero article usage which are 'frozen' as part of idiomatic usage.

(a) Some 'institutions' of human life and society

5.44 Certain nouns have the zero article, especially as complement of *at*, *in*, and *on* in quasi-locative phrases: thus someone may be *in church*, but not **in library*. We call them 'quasi-locative' because, although they appear to have locative meaning, their function is rather more abstract (*cf*: *the theatre*, 5.33). In such contexts, nouns such as *college*, *church*, etc do not refer to actual buildings or places, but to the institutions associated with them: to *be in prison*, for example, is to be a prisoner, not a casual visitor; to *go to sea* is to follow the occupation of a sailor; see the left-hand column below. In the right-hand column we illustrate the same nouns as used with *the* in situational or cataphoric reference:

		Compare:
be in / go to	*town*	*The* town/*the* city is very old.
	bed	lie down on *the* bed
	hospital ⟨BrE⟩	redecorate *the* hospital
	prison, *jail*	walk around *the* prison/*the* jail
	class ⟨esp AmE⟩	*The* class works hard.
be at / go to	*school* (*cf* 9.17)	visit *the* school
	sea	look out towards *the* sea
be in/be at *church*		admire *the* church
go to *college*		the gates of *the* college

Note [**a**] Other related phrases are the following, some of which show variation in the use of article:

get out of *bed*
during (the) *break*/*recess*
be in/return to *camp*
live on/off (the) *campus*
be on/off (the) *stage*
at (the) *court* [royal palace]; in (the) *court* [law court]; The case was settled out of *court*; take someone to *court*
come/go/leave *home*; be (at) *home*; feel at *home* (*cf* 5.51)

With *university*, the article is optional in BrE in the expressions *be at*/*go to* (*the*) *university*, whereas AmE requires the definite article (as also with *hospital* in AmE: 'He's in the hospital.').

[**b**] The article is sometimes left out also when the reference is to the building, not the institution:

I walked straight back *into*/*to school*.
She's *at church*, arranging flowers.

In AmE, and increasingly in BrE, the article is often omitted in expressions like:

in the center of *town*, the business part of *town*

(b) Means of transport and communication

5.45 This type is confined to zero article following *by*; but the same nouns can be used elsewhere with 'sporadic' *the* (*cf* 5.33):

			Compare:
travel / leave / come / go	by	*bicycle*	take *the* bicycle
		bus	be on *the* bus
		car	prefer *the* car
		boat	choose *the* boat
		train	take *a*/*the* train
		plane	be on *the* plane

communicate/communication by { *radio* / *telephone, telex* / *post* ⟨esp BrE⟩ / *mail* ⟨esp AmE⟩ / *satellite* }

Compare:

a talk on *the* radio
Jill is on *the* telephone.
put a letter in *the* post
send it through *the* mail
The satellite is replacing cable TV.

Also: *by hand* (*cf* 5.51, 9.49 Note [a]).

(c) Times of day and night

5.46 These take a zero article particularly after *at*, *by*, *after*, and *before*:

	Compare:
at dawn/*daybreak*	watch *the* dawn
when *day breaks*	during *the* day
at sunrise [AmE also: *at sunup*]	*The* sunrise was splendid.
at sunset [AmE also: *at sundown*]	We admired *the* sunset.
at/*around noon*/*midnight*	in *the* afternoon
at dusk/*twilight*	see nothing in *the* dusk
at/*by night*	wake up in *the* night
(*by*) *day and night*	in *the* daytime
before morning came	in/during *the* morning
Evening approached.	in *the* evening
after nightfall/*dark*	all through *the* night
Day/*Night came*; *day by day* (*cf* 5.50); *all day*/*night*/*week*/*year* (*long*) (*cf* 8.63 Note [b])	

(d) Seasons

5.47 The article is usually, but not always, omitted when referring to seasons generally, as distinct from referring to a particular part of a particular year (*cf* temporal names, 5.67):

(The) *winter* is coming.

in (the) *spring/summer*
in (the) *autumn* ⟨esp BrE⟩ [*Fall* in AmE has the article: *in the fall*]

But with reference to a particular season, the article is included:

The spring of last year was cold.
{ *The fall* ⟨AmE⟩ / *The autumn* ⟨esp BrE⟩ } *before last* was unusually busy.

Note the difference between [1] denoting calendar time and [2] denoting seasonal climate:

The winter of 1963 was an exciting time. [1]
Winter in 1963 was not like this last winter. [2]

(e) Meals

5.48 The zero article is in general use for meals as an institution [1], but *the* can be used for meals that need to be singled out [2]:

Where are we having *dinner* tonight? [1]
The dinner after his retirement party was quite lavish. [2]

Examples of the zero article for the meal as an institution which recurs day by day:

{ stay for / have / before / after / at/for } { *breakfast* / *brunch, cocktails* ⟨both esp in US⟩ / *tea* ⟨esp in UK⟩ / *lunch, dinner* / *supper* }

Often, however, *the* and the zero article are virtually interchangeable:

That day, (*the*) *lunch* was served on the terrace.

The indefinite article is used for a particular meal:

We had *a nice dinner*, just the two of us.

(f) Illnesses

5.49 The zero article is normally used for illnesses, *eg*: *anaemia*, *appendicitis*, *diabetes*, *influenza*, *pneumonia*. But *the* is often used, in a more traditional style of speech, for some well-known infectious diseases: (*the*) *flu*, (*the*) *measles*, (*the*) *mumps*, (*the*) *chicken pox*; also (*the*) *hiccups*. On the plural form of *mumps*, etc, *cf* 5.75.

Note [a] The article cannot normally be omitted with *the/a plague*, nor with some popular, nontechnical expressions such as *the bends*, *the jitters*, *the/a bellyache* ⟨familiar⟩. Except in the fixed expression *catch cold*, the indefinite article is required with *cold*, *fever*, and *temperature*:

Our daughter had *a terrible cold* last week.

I have { *a fever,* / *a temperature,* } so I'm staying in bed today.

[b] *Headache* is always a count noun:

I have *a splitting headache* this morning.

Other nouns formed from *ache* are treated as noncount when they denote a condition:

Nuts give me *toothache*.

When they denote a single attack or pain, they are usually count in AmE and noncount in BrE:

On and off she suffers from { *a stomachache.* ⟨esp AmE⟩ / *(the) stomachache.* ⟨esp BrE⟩ }

Parallel structures

5.50 There is a tendency to omit the article, even with singular count nouns, where two nouns are placed together in a parallel structure:

arm in arm	*face to face*	*day by day*
hand in hand	*eye to eye*	*teaspoonful by teaspoonful*
mile upon mile	*back to back*	*side by side*

Sometimes the same noun is repeated after a preposition, as in the above examples; at other times, one noun is balanced against another noun of contrasting meaning:

from father to son
husband and wife
from right to left OR: *from the right to the left*
from west to east OR: *from the west to the east*
from beginning to end OR: *from the beginning to the end*

Phrases with the noun repeated typically have an adverbial function:

They talked { *face to face.* / *man to man.* }   They stood { *toe to toe.* / *eyeball to eyeball.* }

It can be argued that the nouns have no article because they have largely lost their independent nominal status. We note, in support of this, that variation in the number, determination, or modification of these nouns is normally impossible:

*They talked *old man to young man.*
*They stood *toes to toes.*

Such parallel structures are, therefore, virtually idioms exemplifying 'frozen' article use.

There is one construction, however, in which the parallel structure with zero article is productive of new instances. This is where the two nouns are coordinated, and particularly where the coordination is emphasized by a correlative such as *both . . . and* or *neither . . . nor* (*cf* 13.35*ff*):

The birth took place this morning, and both (*the*) *mother* and (*the*) *child* are doing well.
They pitched camp between a small winding river and a ridge covered with brushwood; but neither (*the*) *river* nor (*the*) *brushwood* afforded the protection they needed in the event of attack.

Fixed phrases involving prepositions

5.51 In addition to adverbial phrase idioms such as *hand in hand*, *face to face*, there are other idioms in which nouns with a zero article occur before or after a preposition. Some of the prepositional phrases considered in 5.44*ff* (such as *at home*, *by hand*) fall into this category, and to them we may add further examples such as *on foot*, *in turn*, *out of step*.

Many complex prepositions (*cf* 9.11) also contain nouns without an article: *on top of*, *by way of*, etc; and there are also idioms in which a verb is followed by a noun with zero article and (often) by a preposition: *take advantage of*, *set fire to*, *get word of*, etc (*cf* 16.58). Such uses of nouns are fixed phrases, as can be seen in their lack of article and number contrast:

He took { *advantage* / **an advantage* / **advantages* } of the situation.

The articles in generic reference

5.52 Earlier (*cf* 5.26) it was noted that all three major forms of article (*the*, *a/an*, and zero) may be used generically to refer to the members of a class *in toto*:

The bull terrier makes an excellent watchdog. [1a]
A bull terrier makes an excellent watchdog. [1b]
Bull terriers make excellent watchdogs. [1c]

Of the possible combinations of the articles with singular and plural, the one which does not occur with count nouns – that of the zero article with the singular form – is the only possibility which occurs with noncount nouns:

Velvet makes an excellent curtain material. [2]

It should not, however, be assumed that the three options [1a], [1b], and [1c] are in free variation. One difference between them is that, whereas *the* [1a] keeps its generic function in nonsubject positions in the sentence, *a/an* [1b], and to a lesser extent zero [1c], tend to lose their generic function in these positions:

Nora has been studying { *the medieval mystery play.* [3a] / *a medieval mystery play.* [3b] / *medieval mystery plays.* [3c] }

Of these, only [3a] refers to mystery plays as a genre; [3b] refers to only one play; and [3c] is most likely to refer only to a subset of them. We consider other differences below.

Note *One* cannot replace *a* in the generic sense, as in [1b] (*cf* 5.38 Note [b]).

The generic use of the indefinite article

5.53 The generic use of *a/an* picks out ANY REPRESENTATIVE MEMBER OF THE CLASS. Thus *any* can be substituted for *a/an* in examples like:

The best way to learn *a language* is to live among its speakers.

Generic *a/an* is therefore restricted in that it cannot be used in attributing properties which belong to the class or species as a whole. Thus:

The tiger is } becoming almost extinct.
Tigers are }

BUT NOT: **A tiger* is becoming almost extinct.

The generic use of the zero article

5.54 The generic use of zero article with both plural nouns and noncount nouns identifies the class considered as an UNDIFFERENTIATED WHOLE (*cf* 5.39*f*):

Cigarettes are bad for your health.
Hydrogen is lighter than *oxygen*.
Necessity is the mother of *invention*.
Research shows that it is the elderly who are the prime victims of *inflation*.
Hunger and *violence* will continue to mark the future of *mankind/humanity*.

We consider the use of the zero article with noncount abstract nouns in 5.58*f*.

Note When it has the meaning of 'the human race' rather than 'a male human being', *man* and its synonym *mankind* are used generically without the article:

This book is an attempt to trace the history of { *man*. / *mankind*. }

Man meaning 'human being' (antonym: *beast*) and its plural *men* may also be used in the same way. Thus:

Man } is a social animal.
A man }
Men have been on this planet for over a million years.

Man and *woman* meaning 'the male/female part of the human race' are now less often used in a generic sense:

Woman is the glory of all created existence. (S. Richardson)

Because of objections to the generic use of *man*, other expressions are often preferred: *humankind*, *the human race*, etc.

Parallel structures make a special case (*cf* 5.50); note that *man and woman*, *man and wife* do not refer to the human race:

Man and rabbit display remarkably similar features in mating behaviour.

But the following is unacceptable except in technical, scientific use:

**Rabbit* displays similar features to *man*.

The generic use of the definite article

With singular noun phrases

5.55 *The* is rather limited in its generic function. With singular heads, it is often formal or literary in tone, indicating THE CLASS AS REPRESENTED BY ITS TYPICAL SPECIMEN:

A great deal of illness originates in *the mind*.
No one knows precisely when *the wheel* was invented.
My colleague has written a book on *the definite article in Spanish*.
Marianne plays *the harp* very well.

As the last example shows, names of musical instruments and also dances usually take the definite article:

play the violin [but: *play baseball*], *dancing the samba*

When the noun refers to a class of human beings, the typifying connotation of generic *the* can sound inappropriate:

?*The Welshman* is a good singer. [*cf*: *Welshmen* are good singers.]
?*The doctor* is well paid. [*cf*: *Doctors* are well paid.]
?As *the child* grows, it develops a wider range of vocabulary.

It is more appropriate when used to identify the typical characteristics of a class in terms of personality, appearance, etc:

He spoke with the consummate assurance and charm of *the successful Harley Street surgeon.*

Note [**a**] Another determinative word sometimes used with a typifying generic force is *your* (*cf* 5.63 Note [c]):

Your average football supporter is not interested in comfort.

In contrast to *the*, this use of *your* is associated with familiar speech; but it resembles *the* in its focus on the 'typical specimen' of the class.

[**b**] Ambiguity may occur over the generic/specific interpretation:

A: *The president* is too powerful.
B: Which president?
A: No, I mean presidents in general.

With plural noun phrases

5.56 Generic *the* occurs with plural noun phrases in two special cases:

(a) Nationality names, *ie* noun phrases referring to the people of a nationality, an ethnic group, etc, *eg*: *the Chinese*, *the English* (*cf* 7.25)
(b) Phrases with an adjective head referring to a group of people, *eg*: *the unemployed* ['people who are unemployed'], *the blind*, *the rich*, etc (*cf* 7.24)

In other cases, *the* + plural noun cannot be used for generic reference. Thus the following sentences are not acceptable in a generic sense:

**The wolves* are carnivorous. ~ *Wolves* are . . .
**The hydrogen* is lighter than *the oxygen*. ~ *Hydrogen* is . . .

In scientific descriptions, however, we may find expressions like *the rodents* (referring to the whole order Rodentia).

It is arguable, in fact, that instances of (a) and (b) are not truly generic, either. Rather, they are plural phrases with unique denotation because (like *the masses*, *the fairies*, *the clergy*, *the Saints*, etc) they designate a uniquely identifiable group of people. Hence there is a marked contrast between *the* (generic plural) in [1] and *the* (generic singular) in [1a]:

The Romans defeated *the Carthaginians* in 202 BC. [1]
?*The Roman* defeated *the Carthaginian* in 202 BC. [1a]

[1] is acceptable in comparison with [1a], because *the Romans* and *the Carthaginians* refer collectively to a group of people, rather than to a typical specimen. *The Romans* is thus a generalization (like *the mathematicians*, *the teenagers*, *the birds*, etc in similar use), whereas *the Roman* implies a generic statement. Nevertheless, it will be convenient to apply the term 'generic' to both the singular and plural uses.

With nationality nouns, there is a distinction to be drawn in many cases between the generic items (with invariable plural) ending in *-ish*, *-sh*, or *-ch*, and the nongeneric nouns ending in *-man* in the singular and *-men* in the plural (both forms pronounced /mən/). Compare:

The Welsh are fond of singing. [generic] [2a]
Welshmen are fond of singing. [generic] [2b]
The Welshmen are fond of singing. [specific] [2c]

The forms ending in *-men* are subject to the general tendency to disfavour words of masculine bias (*cf* 5.105), and if a sexually neutral expression is sought, *Welshmen* in [2b], for example, may be replaced by *Welsh people*. There is also the feminine term *Welshwomen*, etc but this type of word is rare or nonexistent in some cases, *eg*: **firewoman*, **freshwoman*.

With other nationalities, the distinction between generic and specific nationality nouns does not arise:

The Finns are fond of sport. [generic]
Finns are fond of sport. [generic]
The Finns I know are fond of sport. [specific]

In the following section, we give specimens of the various kinds of words for people and nationality.

5.57 Some nationality words

NAME OF COUNTRY, ETC	ADJECTIVE	SPECIFIC REFERENCE		GENERIC REFERENCE
		SINGULAR	PLURAL	PLURAL
(i)				
China	Chinese	a Chinese [a]	Chinese	the Chinese
Japan	Japanese	a Japanese	Japanese	the Japanese
Portugal	Portuguese	a Portuguese	Portuguese	the Portuguese
Switzerland	Swiss	a Swiss	Swiss	the Swiss
Vietnam	Vietnamese	a Vietnamese	Vietnamese	the Vietnamese
(ii)				
Iraq	Iraqi	an Iraqi	Iraqis	the Iraqis
Israel	Israeli	an Israeli	Israelis	the Israelis
Pakistan	Pakistani	a Pakistani	Pakistanis	the Pakistanis
(iii)				
Africa	African	an African	Africans	the Africans
America	American	an American	Americans	the Americans
Asia	Asian	an Asian	Asians	the Asians
Australia	Australian	an Australian	Australians	the Australians
Belgium	Belgian	a Belgian	Belgians	the Belgians
Brazil	Brazilian	a Brazilian	Brazilians	the Brazilians
Europe	European	a European	Europeans	the Europeans
Germany	German	a German [b]	Germans [b]	the Germans
Greece	Greek [c]	a Greek	Greeks	the Greeks
Hungary	Hungarian	a Hungarian	Hungarians	the Hungarians
India	Indian	an Indian	Indians	the Indians
Italy	Italian	an Italian	Italians	the Italians
Norway	Norwegian	a Norwegian	Norwegians	the Norwegians
Russia	Russian	a Russian	Russians	the Russians

NAME OF COUNTRY, ETC	ADJECTIVE	SPECIFIC REFERENCE		GENERIC REFERENCE
		SINGULAR	PLURAL	PLURAL
(iv)				
Argentina	Argentinian	an Argentinian	Argentinians	the Argentinians
(the) Argentine	Argentine	an Argentine	Argentines	the Argentines
(v)				
Denmark	Danish	a Dane	Danes	the Danes/Danish
Finland	Finnish	a Finn	Finns	the Finns/Finnish
Poland	Polish	a Pole	Poles	the Poles/Polish
Saudi Arabia	Saudi (Arabian)	a Saudi (Arabian)	Saudis/ Saudi Arabians	the Saudis/ Saudi Arabians
	Arab [d]	an Arab	Arabs	the Arabs
Spain	Spanish	a Spaniard	Spaniards	the Spaniards/ Spanish
Sweden	Swedish	a Swede	Swedes	the Swedes/ Swedish
(vi)		*cf* Note [e]		
England	English	an Englishman	Englishmen	the English
France	French	a Frenchman	Frenchmen	the French
Holland, the Netherlands	Dutch	a Dutchman	Dutchmen	the Dutch
Ireland	Irish	an Irishman	Irishmen	the Irish
Wales	Welsh	a Welshman	Welshmen	the Welsh
(vii)				
Britain	British	a Briton [f]	Britons	the British
(viii)				
Scotland	Scots [g]	a Scotsman [e]	Scotsmen	the Scots
	Scottish	a Scot	Scots	
	(Scotch)	(a Scotchman)	(Scotchmen)	(the Scotch)

Note **[a]** But items in (i) are normally followed by a noun: *some Chinese children, a Swiss lady.*

[b] The segment *-man* in *German* is not a gender suffix (as in *Englishman*); consequently there are no **Germen* or **Gerwomen.*

[c] *Grecian* is chiefly used of Ancient Greece, and tends to refer to objects or abstractions, rather than to people: *a Grecian urn.*

[d] *Arab* is the racial and political term (*the Arab nations*, etc). *Arabic* is used of language and literature, as well as in *Arabic numerals* (as opposed to Roman numerals). *Arabia(n)* is associated with the geographical area of the Arabian peninsula (*cf*: *Saudi Arabia*).

[e] Terms such as *Englishman/Englishmen* are included here because of their ability to be used generically for the inhabitants of the country (but *cf* 5.56); there are corresponding feminine terms *Englishwoman*, etc, but these are rarely used.

[f] *Britisher* and *Brit* are colloquial variants of *Briton.* The use of *Briton* is more restricted than *Englishman, Scot*, and *Welshman* with specific reference.

[g] The inhabitants of Scotland themselves prefer *Scots* and *Scottish* to *Scotch*, which however is commonly used in such phrases as *Scotch terrier, Scotch whisky, Scotch eggs, Scotch pancakes.* In contrast, *Scottish* denotes nationality and geographical area, rather than type: *the Scottish universities, the Scottish Highlands, a Scottish/Scots accent.*

[**h**] In cases where there is a language with a name related to a nationality word, the adjective form is used for the language (*cf* 5.58 Note):

She speaks *Chinese, Norwegian, Polish, Irish*, etc.

The articles with abstract noncount nouns

5.58 Abstract nouns tend to be count or noncount according to whether they refer to unitary phenomena (such as events) on the one hand, or to states, qualities, activities, etc on the other. The following illustrate typical count abstract nouns:

meeting ~ *meetings*
arrival ~ *arrivals*
discovery ~ *discoveries*

The following are typical noncount abstract nouns (*cf* also the list in 5.9):

employment, happiness, honesty, literature, sleep

But the same abstract nouns can often switch between count and noncount use (*cf* dual class membership, 5.4):

She showed me { *much kindness.* / *many kindnesses.* }

Society must be changed by { *revolution.* / *a revolution.* }

In English, noncount abstract nouns usually have no article when used generically:

My favourite subject is *history/French/mathematics/music* . . .
Happiness is often the product of *honesty* and hard *work*.
Theory must go hand in hand with *practice*.

Normally the zero article also occurs when the noncount abstract noun is premodified:

She's studying *European history*. [1]

But when the same noun is postmodified, especially by an *of*-phrase, the definite article normally precedes it:

She's studying { **history of Europe.* [1a] / *the history of Europe.* [1b] }

We thus find typical contrasts of the following kind:

human evolution ~ *the* evolution *of man*
medieval art ~ *the* art *of the Middle Ages*
Oriental philosophy ~ *the* philosophy *of the Orient*
18th century morality ~ *the* morality *of the 18th century*

It appears that the cataphoric *the* is added in examples like [1b] because the effect of the *of*-phrase is to single out a particular subclass of the phenomenon denoted by the noun, and thereby to change a generic meaning into a specific or partitive one. In this connection, we notice a slight difference between [1] and [1b]: whereas [1b] implies that she is studying the history of Europe as a whole, [1] allows the interpretation that she is studying only some aspects of European history or a particular college course.

The type of contrast illustrated above by [1] and [1b] can also be noted with concrete noncount nouns, and with plural nouns:

This museum specializes in {*18th century* furniture. [2]
{*the* furniture *of the 18th century*. [2a]

Alice is engaged in research on {*South American* butterflies. [3]
{*the* butterflies *of South America*. [3a]

But in these cases it is to a greater or lesser degree acceptable to omit *the*:

The museum specializes in *furniture of the 18th century*. [2b]
?Alice is engaged in research on *butterflies of South America*. [3b]

Note There are expressions in which the definite article is optional with the name of a language (*cf* 5.57 Note [h]), as in:

a word borrowed from (*the*) *French*/(*the*) *Italian*
examples from (*the*) *Sanskrit*/(*the*) *Hebrew*

The following expression is now archaic except in, for example, Irish English:

He has *the French*. [4]

The meaning of [4] is 'He knows French', to be contrasted with the regular curricular sense of [5]:

He has *French and English*. [5]

5.59 The partitive effect of the definite article in *the history of Europe* (example 5.58 [1b]) finds a parallel in the use of the indefinite article in such examples as these:

Mavis had *a good education*. [1]
My son suffers from *a strange dislike of mathematics*. ⟨ironic⟩ [2]
She played the oboe with (*a*) *remarkable sensitivity*. [3]

The indefinite article is used exceptionally here with nouns which are normally noncount. The conditions under which *a*/*an* occurs in such cases are unclear, but appear to include the following:

(i) the noun refers to a quality or other abstraction which is attributed to a person;
(ii) the noun is premodified and/or postmodified; and, generally speaking, the greater the amount of modification, the greater the acceptability of *a*/*an*.

In confirmation of (ii), notice that *a* would have to be omitted from [3] if the adjective were omitted:

She played the oboe with {**a sensitivity*. [3a]
{*sensitivity*. [3b]

However, *a* would become more acceptable than zero if the noun were modified:

She played the oboe with {(*a*) *charming sensitivity*.
{*a sensitivity that delighted the critics*.

Proper nouns

5.60 Proper nouns are basically names of specific people (*Shakespeare*), places (*Milwaukee*), months (*September*), days (*Thursday*), festivals (*Christmas*), magazines (*Vogue*), and so forth. As we saw in 5.2, proper nouns do not generally share the formal characteristics of common nouns. In particular, they lack articles, or rather article contrast:

Paris ~ **the Paris* ~ **a Paris* *The Hague* ~ **Hague* ~ **a Hague*

Within a given universe of discourse, proper nouns generally have unique denotation, and are usually written with initial capital letters (though not all nouns so written are proper nouns). Proper nouns often combine with descriptive words which we will call DESCRIPTORS, and which also begin with a capital letter, to make composite names like *Senator Morse*, *Dallas Road*. We may therefore draw a distinction between a PROPER NOUN, which is a single word, and a NAME, which may or may not consist of more than one word. A name normally functions as a single unit with respect to grammar. This means that, even if a composite name has an internal structure that is grammatically analysable (*eg* as *King's College* is analysable as genitive noun + head noun), that structure cannot normally be varied by the insertion of words, by change of inflection, etc. For example, *The Hague* has a built-in definite article, but *The* does not act as a variable determiner, nor is it capable of being followed by adjectives: **The beautiful Hague*. Equally unacceptable is **King's famous College*.

Note [**a**] Like other grammatical categories, the class of proper nouns has unclear boundaries. For example, a number of common nouns with unique denotation are close to proper nouns, and are sometimes spelled with a capital letter (*cf* 5.29), *eg*:

Fate, *Fortune*, *Heaven*, *Hell*, *Nature*, *Paradise*, *Earth*

Compare also, in their generic sense, *Man* and *Woman* (*cf* 5.54 Note). On another level, we might wonder whether *King's* in *King's College* is to be classed as a genitive common noun which is part of a composite name.

[**b**] In *The Hague Convention*, the article may be called 'conflated', since the definite article also occurs with premodifying names without built-in article: *The Paris Peace Talks*. As for loss of article in names, as in *my native Hague*, *cf* 5.72 (e).

Proper nouns behaving as common nouns

5.61 Having unique denotation, proper nouns may also be expected to lack number contrast, determination, and modification. In general they do, but there are also circumstances in which they take on the characteristics of common nouns.

(a) Number

5.62 Proper nouns normally lack number contrast. Most proper nouns are singular, and do not have a plural (*Indonesia* ~ ?*Indonesias*), or else they have a plural but no singular (*the West Indies* ~ **a West Indy*). There are, however, special circumstances in which proper nouns are reclassified as common nouns, so that they no longer have unique denotation (*cf* App I.53):

Shakespeares ['authors like Shakespeare']
Smiths ['people whose name is Smith']

Londons ['cities called or resembling London']

When a surname is made plural and preceded by the definite article, it takes on the meaning 'the family called X':

the Wilsons, the Joneses /-ɪz/, *the Prideaux* /-z/

The rules for making proper nouns plural are the same as for common nouns (*cf* 5.79*ff*: but note the rules for exceptional spellings in 5.81 III).

(b) Determination

5.63 Some types of proper nouns are customarily preceded by the definite article (*eg*: *the Andes*, *cf* 5.72), but they lack article contrast, since the article cannot normally be varied (**an Ande*, **some Andes*). If reclassified as common nouns, however, proper nouns can have their meaning varied by articles and other determiners:

a Shakespeare ['an author like Shakespeare']
his new Shakespeare ['his copy of the works of Shakespeare']

Other examples are:

I used to know *a Mary Roberts*, too. ['a person called Mary Roberts']
She is *the second Mrs White* – the first one died.
Lu Xun has been known as '*the Chinese Gorki*'.

The definite article with nuclear stress placed before a name has the special meaning of 'the well-known person/place named X' (*cf* 5.11 Note [e]):

A: I used to know John Lennon quite well.
B: Surely you can't mean *THÈ* /ðiː/ *John LÉNnon*?

By contrast, the indefinite article placed before a personal name can have the meaning 'a certain person called X but otherwise unknown':

A Mrs Robertson was trying to contact you this morning.

Note [a] There is a disparaging use of *that/those* in expressions like *that Mary, those Joneses*:

That Mr PHÌLlips has been on the phone again. Isn't he a *NÙI*sance!

But stressed *that* is not disparaging in:

Oh, you mean *THÀT Mr Phillips*. ['that particular person']

This has no such overtones in:

Who's *this Mrs RÒBertson* that phoned?

[b] The fact that the pronoun *one* can substitute for a name is strong evidence of its conversion to the status of a common noun in examples like this (*cf* 6.55):

I knew { *À John Lennon*, but not the FÀMous *one*. / *ǑNE* (person called) John Lennon. }

Note the nuclear stress on, and the pronunciation of, the indefinite article /eɪ/.

[c] Possessives and genitives can be used to denote close family relationships (*cf* 5.55 Note [a]):

Is *your Jennifer* still at SCHÓOL? ['your daughter Jennifer']
Did you know that *your Mrs WHÌTE* ['the one you know'] has been arrested for SHÓPlifting?
John and Mary are very anxious about *their Tom*. [*eg* their son or brother]
Granny is delighted with *Peter's Jane*. [*eg* Peter's girlfriend]

(c) Modification

5.64 When they have the normal unique denotation, proper nouns can only be modified by nonrestrictive modifiers, such as a nonrestrictive relative clause (*cf* 17.22*ff*) or nonrestrictive apposition (*cf* 17.68):

Dr Brown, *who lives next door*, comes from Australia.
Theseus, *a Greek hero*, killed the Minotaur.

Nonrestrictive premodifiers are limited to adjectives with emotive colouring, such as:

old Mrs Fletcher	*dear little* Eric	*poor* Charles
beautiful Spain	*historic* York	*sunny* July

In a more formal and rather stereotyped style, the adjective is placed between *the* and a personal name:

the *beautiful* Princess Diana ['Princess Diana, who is beautiful']
the *inimitable* Henry Higgins ['Henry Higgins, who is inimitable']

Proper nouns show that they can temporarily take on features of common nouns (*cf* 5.63), and accept restrictive modification of various kinds:

The Dr Brown I know comes from Australia.
The flower arrangement was done by *a Miss Phillips in Park Road*.
Do you mean *the Memphis which used to be the capital of Egypt*, or *the Memphis in Tennessee*?
I spoke to *the younger Mr Hamilton*, not *Mr Hamilton the manager*.

In such cases, a determiner (especially *the*) is usual. But in addition, cataphoric *the* with restrictive modification can have the effect of splitting up the unique referent of the proper noun into different parts or aspects. We may therefore classify this as a PARTITIVE meaning:

UNIQUE MEANING	PARTITIVE MEANING
during *Easter*	during *the Easter of that year*
in *England*	in *the England of Queen Elizabeth*
in *Denmark*	in *the Denmark of today*
Chicago	*the Chicago I like* ['the aspect of Chicago']
Shakespeare	*the young Shakespeare* ['Shakespeare when he was young']
Bradford	*the Bradford she grew up in*

Note [**a**] Compare the 'partitive' use of the genitive in *James Joyce's Dublin* ['the Dublin which James Joyce knew'], etc.
[**b**] In the names of monarchs, etc, an adjectival cognomen is placed after the proper noun, and is prefaced by *the*, *eg*: *Charles the Great, Ivan the Terrible*. This type of appellation is similar to an appositional type of name, in which the by-name is nominal: *William the Conqueror*. But in these latter cases, the article is sometimes omitted: *Richard* (*the*) *Lionheart, Richard Crookback*.
[**c**] On nonrestrictive premodification as in *an embarrassed Ben Miles*, etc, *cf* 17.3 Note.

Names with no article

5.65 We now turn to regular examples of names without an article. The following list summarizes the main classes of name that take no article, in accordance with the main rule (*cf* 5.60):

PERSONAL NAMES (with or without titles; *cf* 5.66)
TEMPORAL NAMES (*cf* 5.67):
(i) Festivals, religious periods, etc
(ii) Months, and days of the week
GEOGRAPHICAL NAMES (*cf* 5.68):
(i) Continents
(ii) Countries, counties, states, etc
(iii) Cities, towns, etc
(iv) Lakes
(v) Mountains
OTHER LOCATIVE NAMES consisting of proper noun + common noun descriptor (*cf* 5.69)

Personal names

5.66 Whether or not they are accompanied by titles, personal names normally have no article (*cf* apposition 17.88). The name itself may consist of:

given (first, or Christian) name alone: *Margaret, Jack*, etc
the surname (family name, or last name) alone: *Smith, Wilson*, etc
given name(s) and surname together: *Margaret Jane Smith, Jack Wilson*

In addition, one or more given names (in American usage normally the middle one) may be reduced to initials:

M. J. Smith; *J. Wilson*; *Charles R. Maguire*

Names such as these may be prefaced by the normal title of *Mr* for a man, or *Mrs*, *Miss*, *Ms* for a woman, or a courtesy title indicating the person's status. Among the titles ascribing status are those indicating royalty (*eg*: *Queen*), rank of nobility (*eg*: *Lord*), political, clerical, or judicial office (*eg*: *President*), military rank (*eg*: *Major*), or academic or professional status (*eg*: *Doctor*). Some examples:

Mr and Mrs Johnson	*General* MacArthur
Ms Waterhouse	*Professor* Smith
Dr Brown	*Cardinal* Spellman
Private Walker	*Inspector* Harris
Captain O'Connor	*Chancellor* Brandt
Lord Nelson	*Governor* Rockefeller
Lady Churchill	*Judge* Fox

Fuller details of appositional titles are given in 17.91. On the use of titles and names as vocatives without the article, *cf* 10.53.

Note **[a]** *Ms*, usually pronounced /mɪz/, is widely used as a female title which avoids making the distinction between married and unmarried (*Mrs* and *Miss*). On the plural of terms of address, *cf* 5.103.

[b] The title *Sir* is used for a knight or a baronet. It is exceptional in that it must be accompanied by the given name of the holder, but need not be accompanied by the surname. Thus *Sir Basil Spence* can be abbreviated as *Sir Basil*, but not as **Sir Spence*. With other titles, it is usually the given name that is omitted in an abbreviated version: *Ms (Julia) Waterhouse*.

[c] In naming monarchs and popes who have shared the same given name with others (*eg*: *King*

James I, Queen Elizabeth II), we normally write the appended numeral as a cardinal roman number; so too in some American families (Henry Ford II). In speech, this numeral is rendered as an ordinal (*cf* 6.63): *I* 'the first', *II* 'the second', *VII* 'the seventh', etc.

[**d**] The use of the article in the following is exceptional:

(i) imperial titles: *the Emperor Napoleon*; (*the*) *Emperor Haile Selassie*; (*the*) *Czar Alexander*; (*the*) *Archduke Ferdinand* [but: *Kaiser Wilhelm II*]

(ii) *the Lord* ['God']

(iii) (*the*) *Rev John Smith* [always *the Reverend John Smith* in the spoken form]

(iv) titles of peerage, when followed by an *of*-phrase: *the Duke of Wellington, the Countess of Derby*, etc

[**e**] In familiar style, kinship terms with unique reference behave like proper nouns in having no determiner, and often in beginning with a capital letter:

> Where's *mother*? [also: *Mummy, Mum* ⟨BrE familiar⟩; *Mommy, Mom* ⟨AmE familiar⟩]
> You'll see *Uncle* on Saturday.
> *Father* is here. [also: *Daddy, Dad, Pop* ⟨familiar⟩]
> Contrast: *My/The father* was the tallest of the family.

The following expressions are very informal, and used especially in a family environment by or to young children: (*my*) *Daddy*, (*your*) *Mom*, etc.

Temporal names

5.67 These have no article when they are used to refer to the period as a recurrent item in the calendar (*cf* sporadic reference, 5.43; seasons, 5.47):

(i) Names of festivals, religious periods, etc:

Christmas (*Day*)	*Independence Day*	*Easter* (*Sunday*)
Passover	*Good Friday*	*New Year*
New Year's Day	*New Year's Eve*	*Ramadan*

(ii) Names of months, and days of the week:

> *January, February, . . .*   *Monday, Tuesday, . . .*

However, these words behave more like common nouns when they refer to individual periods, or when they refer collectively to more than one occasion. Along with *next* and *last* + a noun, they have zero article when they are connected with a point of time implicit in the linguistic or situational context (on prepositional usage, *cf* 9.40). Contrast:

> We'll leave { *on Sunday.* / *next month.* }

> She left { *on the next Sunday.* / *the* { *next* / *following* } *day.* }

Days of the week also occur with the indefinite article, without reference to a particular Sunday:

> He left *on a Sunday*.

Days of the week have a plural, but months of the year normally do not:

> I hate *Mondays*.   ?I hate *Januaries*.

Note In rather popular BrE usage (felt by some to be nonstandard), the days of the week have the definite article in cases like the following:

And *on the Thursday* she got worse. So, *on the Friday* we called the doctor. ['the Thursday, etc of the week concerned']

Geographical names

5.68 The following categories of names normally have no article, even with a premodifying adjective:

(i) Names of continents:

(*North*) *America*	(*medieval*) *Europe*	(*equatorial*) *Africa*
(*Central*) *Australia*	(*East*) *Asia*	*Antarctica*

Note that *Antarctica* refers to the continent, while *the Antarctic* refers more generally to the polar region (*cf*: *the Arctic*).

(ii) Names of countries, counties, states, etc:

(*Elizabethan*) *England*	(*West*) *Scotland*	(*industrial*) *Staffordshire*
(*modern*) *Brazil*	(*French*) *Canada*	(*northern*) *Arkansas*

Note the exceptional use of *the* for certain countries and regions, *eg*: (*the*) *Argentine* (but *Argentina*, without the article, is more common; *cf* 5.57). Other examples:

the Crimea	*the Punjab*	*the Ruhr*
the Saar	*the Sahara*	(*the*) *Sinai*
(*the*) *Sudan*	(*the*) *Ukraine*	(*the*) *Yemen*

The is sometimes used with French names, *eg*: *the Auvergne*; it is also used with plural names such as *the Everglades* (*cf* 5.72), and for names ending with a compass point:

the Near/Middle/Far East, *the* (*Deep*) *South*, *the Midwest*

(iii) Names of cities, towns, etc:

(*downtown*) *Boston*	(*central*) *Brussels*
(*ancient*) *Rome*	(*suburban*) *New York*

Note the exceptional article in *The Hague*; also the use of the article in certain districts of large cities: *the Bronx*, *the City*, *the West/East End* (*of London*).

(iv) Names of lakes (*cf* 17.89):

(*Lake*) *Ladoga*	*Lake Michigan*	*Loch Ness*
Silver Lake	*Lake Nicaragua*	*Ullswater*

Note exceptions such as *the Great Salt Lake*.

(v) Names of mountains (*cf* 17.89):

Mount Everest	*Mont Blanc*	*Ben Nevis*
(*Mount*) *Snowdon*	*Vesuvius*	*Aconcagua*

Note As the examples above show, in the names of lakes and mountains, the descriptor usually precedes rather than follows the proper noun: *Lake Michigan*, not **Michigan Lake*. There are, however, some cases in which the descriptor follows: *Pikes Peak*, *Bassenthwaite Lake*.

Other locative names consisting of proper noun + common noun descriptor

5.69 The structure 'proper noun + common noun descriptor (or by-name)' is typical of the names of natural features (such as forests, woods, and hills) and man-made features (such as roads, streets, squares, buildings, airports, parks, and gardens). The article is normally omitted:

Epping Forest	*Park Lane*	*Paddington Station*
Clapham Common	*Madison Avenue*	*Kennedy Airport*
Hampstead Heath	*Times Square*	*Magdalen College*
Kew Gardens	*Portland Place*	*Canterbury Cathedral*
Hyde Park	*Scotland Yard*	*Windsor Castle*
Bredon Hill	*Westminster Bridge*	*Buckingham Palace*
Piccadilly Circus	*Hampton Court*	*Fountains Abbey*

There are, however, many exceptions. For example, in London, *the Albert Hall* and *the Mansion House* are buildings, and *the Mall* and *the Strand* are streets. More general exceptions are the names of theatres, museums, etc (*cf* 5.72).

Note [**a**] Names of British universities where one element is a place-name can usually have two forms: *the University of London* (which is the official name) and *London University*. In names of American universities, there is a fairly regular contrast between the two types, as in *the University of California* and *California State University*. Universities named after a person have only the latter form: *Yale University*, *Brown University*, etc.

[**b**] *The* can exceptionally occur with *Road* in the names of some urban thoroughfares:

(*the*) *Edgware Road*, (*the*) *Old Kent Road* [but only: *Oxford Street*, *Fifth Avenue*]

Large modern intercity highways also tend to have the article:

the San Diego Freeway, *the Merrit Parkway*, *the Pennsylvania Turnpike*, *the M1* (*Motorway*)

Names with the definite article

5.70 There is a gradient between names like *Sir Walter Scott* and noun phrases which are termed DEFINITE DESCRIPTIONS, such as *the author of Waverley*. Both names and definite descriptions have (situationally) unique denotation; but one of them is grammatically 'frozen', while the other is formed according to the normal productive rules for constructing definite noun phrases. The most obvious indicator of a name is its spelling with initial capitals; while the most obvious indicator of a definite description is its initial definite article. Expressions which combine both these features, such as *the Eiffel Tower*, are neither completely name-like nor completely description-like, but somewhere between the two. We may therefore illustrate the gradient between descriptions and names roughly as follows:

(i) *the Oxford road*	→	(ii) *the Oxford Road*	→	(iii) *Oxford Road*	→	(iv) *Oxford*

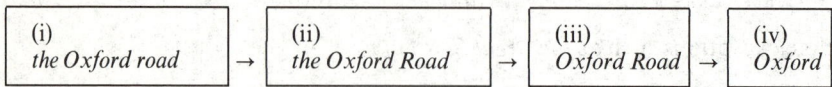

Fig 5.70 The gradient between descriptions and names

(i) is a definite description ('the road to Oxford'); in (ii) that description is conventionalized to the extent that *Road* is capitalized, so that the whole makes a composite name; in (iii) the loss of the article has taken this conventionalization further. The purest example of a name is perhaps (iv), the simple proper noun *Oxford*. Although native English speakers may be able to analyse this into two elements ('ford for oxen'), such an analysis plays no part in their understanding of *Oxford* as the name of a university city.

This 'scale of institutionalization' explains why there are many exceptions to the above categories of names which lack an article, and why there is sometimes vacillation between the use and omission of the definite article. It might be better, in fact, to regard names without articles as exceptions to the more general rule that definite noun phrases are introduced by the article *the*. But an even better way of looking at this problem is simply to acknowledge that what accounts for apparent exceptions is the absence of a clear-cut boundary between names and definite descriptions. Consider the following three cases:

In 1965–1968 she attended { *York University.* / *(the) Hatfield Polytechnic.* / *the Paris Conservatoire.* }

The reason for using the article in the one case, and omitting it optionally or obligatorily in the other two, seems to be largely a matter of how far the name is an institutionalized name among English-speaking (and in this case particularly British) people.

In the following sections we deal with the in-between area of names preceded by the definite article. They might, indeed, be called 'descriptive names', since not only do they take the article, but they can be analysed, in terms of noun-phrase structure, into head and modifiers.

Structure of names with *the*

5.71 (i) Without modification:

the Kremlin	*the Koran*	The Guardian
the Pentagon	*the Bible*	The Times
the Knesset	*the Parthenon*	*the Dáil*

(ii) With premodification:

the Suez Canal	*the* Washington Post
the National Gallery	*the American Civil War*
the Socialist Bookshop	*the Ohio State University Press*
The Ford Foundation	*the British Broadcasting Corporation (the BBC)*
the English Channel	

(iii) With postmodification:

the House of Commons	*the Institute of Psychiatry*
the District of Columbia	*the Bay of Fundy*

the Cambridgeshire College of Arts and Technology

Virtually all names with postmodification like those above are postmodified by an *of*-phrase, and have an obligatory *the*.

(iv) With ellipsis of elements:
The original structure of a name is sometimes unclear when one element has

been dropped and the elliptic form has become institutionalized as the full name:

the Tate (*Gallery*)	*the Mermaid* (*Theatre*)
the Atlantic (*Ocean*)	*the* (*River*) *Thames*
the Mediterranean (*Sea*)	*the Majestic* (*Hotel*)

Note When the article is written with a small *t*, it is not part of the name itself. Hence any modifier describing the referent follows, rather than precedes, the article: *the breathtaking Himalayas*, *the lower Mississippi*. In *The Hague*, however, *The* is part of the name (*cf* 5.72 e).

Classes of names typically preceded by *the*

5.72 **(a) Place names of plural form, *eg*: *the Netherlands*, *the Midlands*, *the Great Lakes*, particularly including the following two categories.**

(i) Groups of islands: *the Hebrides*, *the Shetlands*, *the Canaries* (or *the Canary Islands*), *the Bahamas*

(ii) Ranges of mountains or hills: *the Himalayas*, *the Alps*, *the Andes*, *the Rockies* (or *the Rocky Mountains*), *the Pyrenees*, *the Pennines*. Also nonplural names of ranges: *the Caucasus*, *the Sierra Nevada*. Exceptions: *Kensington Gardens*, *Burnham Beeches*

(b) Other geographical names:

(i) Rivers: *the Avon*, *the Danube*, *the Euphrates*, *the Potomac*, *the Rhine*. (The word *River* can sometimes be inserted after *the*: *the River Avon*, etc; but for some rivers it comes last: *the Potomac River*, etc; *cf* 17.89).

(ii) Seas and oceans: *the Pacific* (*Ocean*), *the Atlantic* (*Ocean*), *the Baltic* (*Sea*), *the Kattegat*

(iii) Canals: *the Panama Canal*, *the Suez Canal*, *the Erie Canal*

(iv) Other geographical features of coastline: *the Gulf of Mexico*, *the Cape of Good Hope*, *the Bay of Biscay*, *the Strait of Magellan*, *the Sound of Bute*, (*the*) *Bosphorus*, *the Isle of Man*, *the Isle of Wight*

Note that when there is premodification rather than postmodification in category (iv), *the* usually disappears. Thus:

the Isle of Wight BUT: *Long Island*
the Bay of Naples BUT: *Hudson Bay*

(c) Public institutions, facilities, etc:

(i) Hotels and restaurants: *the Grand* (*Hotel*), *the Waldorf Astoria*

(ii) Theatres, opera houses, cinemas, and clubs: *the Criterion* (*Theatre*), *the Globe* (*Theatre*), *the Athenaeum*

(iii) Museums, libraries, hospitals, etc: *the British Museum*, *the Bodleian* (*Library*), *the Middlesex Hospital*

Probably because of their origin as place-names, *Drury Lane* and *Covent Garden* are exceptions to the rule that theatres and opera houses take *the*, as in *the Metropolitan*. When the name of a public institution begins with a genitive, *the* is not used: *White's*, *Gaylord's* (*Restaurant*), *Brown's* (*Hotel*), *Guy's* (*Hospital*), *St John's* (*College*).

(d) Ships and planes, particularly when renowned in history, *eg*: *the Victory*, *the Spirit of St Louis*

(e) Newspapers and periodicals: *The Economist*, *The New York Times*, *The Observer*, *The Providence Journal*, *The London Review of Books*. *The* is generally spelt with a capital letter in names of newspapers.

Irrespective of whether or not the article is part of the name itself, it is not used after an indefinite article or other determiner or genitive:

Have you got a *Times*? [not: *a *The Times*]
She's a *Times* reporter.
Have you seen today's *New York Times*?
Malcolm lent me his *Guardian*.

Magazines and periodicals, on the other hand, often have a zero article: *Time*, *Punch*, *English Language Teaching Journal*, *New Scientist*, *Scientific American*.

Number

Number classes

5.73 The English number system constitutes a two-term contrast: SINGULAR, which denotes 'one', and PLURAL, which denotes 'more than one'. Each noun phrase is either singular or plural, and its number is determined in general by its head, which is typically a noun. In the following sections we will concentrate on number as a property of nouns, and as a basis for their classification.

Note [**a**] In addition to singular and plural number, we may distinguish dual number in the case of *both*, *either*, and *neither* (*cf* 5.16), since they can only be used with reference to two. *Both* has plural concord (*cf* 6.50); *either* and *neither* have singular concord (*cf* 6.59*ff*).
[**b**] Unlike some languages where plural implies 'two or more', English makes the division after 'more than one':

one half day, *one day* BUT: *one and a half days*, *two days*, *one or two days*

However, the following remain singular:

a pound and a half, *a day or two* (*cf* 5.38), *more than one day*

5.74 We distinguish three main number classes of nouns:

(A) SINGULAR INVARIABLE NOUNS, including noncount nouns (*eg*: *music*, *gold*), most proper nouns (*eg*: *Thomas*, *the Thames*). We may also consider here abstract adjective heads, *eg*: *the mystical* (*cf* 7.26).

(B) PLURAL INVARIABLE NOUNS, *ie* nouns occurring only in the plural, *eg*: *people*, *scissors*. We may also consider here personal adjective heads, *eg*: *the rich* (*cf* 7.23*f*).

(C/D) VARIABLE NOUNS, *ie* nouns occurring with either singular or plural number:

The *dog is* . . .
The *dogs are* . . .

We distinguish two subclasses: (C) REGULAR, with plurals predictable from the singular (like *dog*), and (D) IRREGULAR, where the plural is not predictable (*eg*: *foot* ~ *feet*, *child* ~ *children*). In this latter group we find a large number of nouns with foreign plurals, *eg*: *criterion* ~ *criteria*, *analysis* ~ *analyses*.

Figure 5.74 provides a summary of the classification with section references to the subsequent discussion.

	SINGULAR	PLURAL	NOUN CLASS	
(A) SINGULAR INVARIABLE				
noncount nouns	*gold*		(Aa)	(5.75)
abstract adjective heads	*the unreal*		(Ab)	(7.26)
most proper nouns	*Henry*		(Ac)	(5.60*ff*)
(B) PLURAL INVARIABLE				
summation plurals		*scissors*	(Ba)	(5.76)
pluralia tantum in *-s*		*thanks*	(Bb)	(5.77)
unmarked plural nouns		*people*	(Bc)	(5.78)
personal adjective heads		*the rich*	(Bd)	(7.23*f*)
some proper nouns		*the Alps*	(Be)	(5.62)
(C) NOUNS WITH REGULAR PLURAL	*dog*	~ *dogs*	(C)	(5.79*ff*)
(D) NOUNS WITH IRREGULAR PLURAL				
voicing and *-s* plural	*calf*	~ *calves*	(Da)	(5.83)
mutation plural	*foot*	~ *feet*	(Db)	(5.84)
-en plural	*child*	~ *children*	(Dc)	(5.85)
zero plural	*sheep*	~ *sheep*	(Dd)	(5.86*ff*)
foreign plurals	*stimulus*	~ *stimuli*	(De)	(5.93)
	larva	~ *larvae*	(Df)	(5.94)
	stratum	~ *strata*	(Dg)	(5.95)
	matrix	~ *matrices*	(Dh)	(5.96)
	thesis	~ *theses*	(Di)	(5.97)
	criterion	~ *criteria*	(Dj)	(5.98)
	bureau	~ *bureaux*	(Dk)	(5.99)
	tempo	~ *tempi*	(Dl)	(5.100)
	cherub	~ *cherubim*	(Dm)	(5.101)

Fig 5.74 Number classes

(A) Singular invariable nouns

5.75 Noncount nouns are singular and invariable, *ie* they have no plural. Some concrete noncount nouns can be reclassified as count nouns with specific meanings, for example *butters* ['kind(s) of butter'] and *a beer* ['a glass of beer'] (*cf* 5.5).

Abstract noncount nouns normally have no plural: *music*, *dirt*, *homework*, etc. But some can be reclassified as count nouns where they refer to an instance of a given abstract phenomenon: *injustices*, *regrets*, *kindnesses*, *pleasures*, etc. Many abstract nouns are equally at home in the count and noncount categories (*cf* 5.4).

Proper nouns are typically singular and invariable: *Henry*, *the Thames*, etc (*cf* 5.62).

Some noncount nouns, particularly those denoting natural phenomena, may be pluralized, *eg*:

walking through the *woods*	I have serious *doubts*/grave *fears*.
raise someone's *hopes*	Let's play on the *sands*.

Some plurals express intensity, great quantity or extent, and have a literary flavour, for example:

the *snows* of Kilimanjaro
the *sands* of the desert
sailing on the great *waters*

Note the following classes of invariable nouns ending in *-s* which take a singular verb, except where otherwise mentioned:

(i) *News* is always singular (*cf* 5.9):

Here is the *news* from the BBC. What's the *news* today?

(ii) Nouns ending in *-ics* denoting subjects, sciences, etc are usually invariable and treated as singular, *eg*:

Mathematics is the science of quantities.

Other such nouns include:

acoustics	*economics*	*linguistics*
athletics	*ethics*	*phonetics*
classics	*gymnastics*	*physics*

Some, however, can be singular or plural, in particular when such words can denote both one's knowledge of the subject and the practical application of results:

Politics is said to be the art of the impossible. [the science of government] [1]
His *politics* are rather conservative. [political views] [1a]

In some cases, there are forms without *-s* for special uses:

Statistics is a branch of mathematics. [2]
These *statistics* show that exports are still low. [2a]
There is a surprising *statistic* in your latest report. [2b]
A new *ethic* is needed in the world today. [3]
Has the new coach found a *tactic* that works? [4]

(iii) Names of certain diseases ending in *-s* are usually treated as singular (but some speakers also accept plural), *eg*: (*German*) *measles*, *mumps*, *rickets*, *shingles*:

A: Have you ever had *measles*?

B: Yes I had {*it* / *them*} when I was a child.

(iv) The names of some games ending in *-s* have singular concord, *eg*: *billiards* (but usually: *a billiard table*), *checkers* ⟨AmE⟩, *draughts* ⟨BrE⟩, *craps, darts* (but: *a dartboard*), *dominoes, fives, ninepins*:

Darts is becoming very popular as a spectator sport.

(B) Plural invariable nouns

(Ba) Summation plurals

5.76 Summation plurals denote tools, instruments, and articles of dress consisting of two equal parts which are joined together:

A: How much are *those binoculars*? B: *They are* £60.

The most common summation plurals are the following:

(i) Tools and instruments:

bellows; *glasses, spectacles, binoculars*; *scales* ['a balance']; *clippers, forceps, pincers, scissors, shears, tongs, tweezers*

(ii) Articles of dress:

braces ⟨BrE⟩, *breeches, britches* ⟨AmE⟩, *briefs, flannels, jeans, knickers, pants, pajamas* ⟨AmE⟩, *pyjamas* ⟨BrE⟩, *shorts, slacks, suspenders, tights, trousers, trunks*

Number contrast can be achieved by means of *a pair of*. Thus *a pair of trousers* refers to one item, but *two pairs of trousers* refers to two (*cf* 5.7 Note [a]):

That's a *nice pair of slacks*.
As I'm shortsighted I always carry *two pairs of glasses*.

Plural pronoun concord is usual even with a singular determiner + *pair*:

I like {*this* / **these*} *pair*. *How much* {*are they*? / *is it*?}

Although nouns that are summation plurals require plural concord, they differ from ordinary plural nouns in that they are not generally thought of as denoting plural number. Yet usage varies. For many speakers, it is as follows (*cf* 10.43 Note [c]):

{*Both pairs of scissors* / (?) *Both of the scissors* / (?) *Both scissors*} need sharpening.

I want {
two pairs of trousers.
(?) *two trousers*. ⟨informal⟩
a pair of trousers.
**one trouser*.
(?) *a scissors*. ⟨informal⟩
}

Many of the summation plurals can take the indefinite article, especially with premodification: (*a*) *new clippers*, (*a*) *garden shears*, (*an*) *old-fashioned curling tongs*. Forms are commonly singular when used attributively: *a spectacle case, a suspender belt, a trouser leg, a pajama/pyjama top* (*cf* 17.108).

Note *Compasses* can be used in the singular (*compass*) in the sense 'instrument for drawing circles':

She drew her circle with a *compass*.

In the sense of an instrument of navigation, it is a normal count noun:

A magnetic *compass* is } necessary for navigation.
Magnetic *compasses* are }

(Bb) Pluralia tantum ending in -*s*

5.77 Some 'pluralia tantum' (*ie* nouns that, in a given sense, occur only in the plural) end in -*s*, whereas others have no plural marking, *eg*: *people* (*cf* 5.78). They have plural concord, *eg*:

These damages have not yet been paid, *have they*? [*damages* = 'compensation in money imposed by law for causing loss or injury'] [1]

In many cases, pluralia tantum ending in -*s* also have singular forms, which however can be dissociated in meaning from the plural, *eg*:

That damage was repaired long ago. [*damage* = 'loss, harm'] [1a]

Other examples of pluralia tantum:

accommodations ⟨AmE⟩: living accommodations
amends: make every/all possible amends for something
annals ['a historical record of events']: in the annals of history
archives: The documents should be kept in the archives. (BUT: archive administration)
arms ['weapons']: arms aid; arms control; the arms race; take up arms; ALSO: *munitions*
arrears: He's in arrears with his payments; the arrears of work
ashes: burn to ashes; Her ashes were scattered; the ash(es) of a burned letter (BUT: cigarette ash; ashtray; Ash Wednesday)
auspices ['support']: under the auspices of
banns [of marriage]: publish the banns
bowels, entrails, intestines: the movement of the bowels; an infection of the intestines (BUT singular count: the large intestine)
brains ['the intellect']: You should use your brains. (BUT singular count is more common generally, and particularly so when the meaning is anatomical: 'The average human brain weighs 14 oz.')
clothes /kləʊ(ð)z/: warm clothes; a clothes basket (BUT: *cloths* /klɒθs/ as plural of *cloth*: a table cloth)
clubs, diamonds, hearts, spades [playing cards]: the ace of clubs; the jack of hearts; BUT: I've only one diamond in my hand. NOTE singular concord in: Spades is the suit. It was hearts last game.
the Commons/Lords [the House of Commons/Lords in the UK]: The Commons are discussing the new bill.
communications ['means of communicating']: communications gap; telecommunications network

congratulations: Many congratulations on your birthday!

contents: a table of contents (BUT: the silver content of a coin; the style and content of a book)

credentials: evaluate the credentials of students

customs: pay customs duty; go through customs at the airport; a customs officer

dregs: coffee dregs/grounds; the dregs of society

dues ['fee']: pay one's dues to a society; harbour dues

earnings: Her earnings are higher this year. (BUT: earning power); ALSO: *proceeds*, *returns*, *riches*

funds ['money']: for lack of funds; be short of funds (BUT: a fund ['a source of money'])

goods ['property, merchandise']: leather goods; a goods train ⟨BrE⟩ (AmE = a freight train)

grassroots ['the rank and file']: grassroots opinion/revolt/support (BUT: at grassroot level)

guts ['bowels'; ALSO 'courage' ⟨familiar⟩]: He's got the guts to do it. (BUT in premodification: a gut reaction; noncount: catgut)

heads ['front side of a coin']: Heads or tails?

heavens in the expression 'Good Heavens!' (BUT: go to heaven)

honours: an honours course/degree/list

humanities ['arts']: the humanities/arts faculty

letters ['literature']: a man of letters

lodgings: a lodgings bureau (BUT: a lodging house; a poor lodging); ALSO: *digs* ⟨BrE informal⟩: Many students move into digs instead of living on campus. ALSO: *quarters*: married quarters (BUT: the Latin quarter ['district'])

looks: He has good looks. (BUT: give somebody a hard look)

mains: turn the water off at the mains; NOTE in some phrases the *-s* is retained in premodification: mains adaptor; mains water supply

manners ['social behaviour']: Where are your manners?; manners and customs (BUT: Do it in this manner/way; I don't like his manner ['personal way of acting'])

minutes ['a record of proceedings']: the minutes of a meeting

odds: What are the odds?; be at odds with; odds and ends

outskirts: She lives on the outskirts of the city.

pains ['care, trouble']: take great pains with something; be at pains to do something

particulars ['details']: Take down the particulars of this event.

premises ['building' ⟨in official style⟩]: There is a suspect on the premises. (BUT in logic: a first premise)

regards ['good wishes']: Ann sends her regards. (BUT: win his regard ['respect'])

relations: an exercise in public relations

remains ['remainder']: the remains of the castle/the meal

savings ['money saved']: a savings bank; a savings account (BUT: a saving of £5)

spirits ['mood']: to be in good spirits (BUT: He showed a kindly spirit.)

stairs [inside a building]: a flight of stairs; downstairs (BUT: a staircase; a stairway)

steps [outside a building]: a flight of steps; on the church steps
surroundings ['environment']: These surroundings are not good for the child.
systems: a systems analyst; computer systems applications
thanks: Many thanks for . . .; All my thanks are due to you.
troops ['soldiers']: Many troops were sent overseas. (BUT: troop movement; a troop carrier; a troop of scouts)
tropics: living in the tropics (BUT: the Tropic of Cancer)
valuables: Are my valuables safe here?
wages ['weekly pay']: What are his wages? (BUT often also singular: a wage earner; a minimum wage; a good/poor/high wage; a wage freeze)
wits: live by one's wits (BUT: She has a keen wit. Her speech had wit.)
writings ['literary production' ⟨formal⟩]: His writings are not widely known.

(Bc) Unmarked plural nouns: *people, police*, etc

5.78 The following nouns have no plural marking but are used as plurals (*cf* also collective nouns like *clergy*, *staff*, etc, 5.108):

(i) *people*:

How *many people* are there in the world today?

People functions as the normal plural of *person*:

There was only *one person* } in the room.
There were *many people* }

Persons is often used instead of *people*, especially in official style: 'a person or persons unknown'. When *people* means 'nation', it is a regular count noun:

The Japanese are *an industrious people*.
They are *a great people*.
the English-speaking *peoples*

In this sense, however, the singular form *people* is normally constructed with plural concord:

The Portuguese *people have* chosen a new President.

(ii) *Folk* is more restricted in use than *people*: *country folk*, *fisher folk*, *island folk*, *folk art*, *folk music*. *Folks* is used in casual style (*That's all, folks!*) and often with a possessive determiner in the sense of 'family' (*my folks*).

(iii) *police*: 'The police have caught the burglar'.

To denote individual police officers we normally use *a police officer*, or *a policeman/policewoman* with the plurals *police officers*, *policemen*, *policewomen*:

Why don't you ask *a policeman*?

In a collective sense 'the police force', only *police* can be used:

He wants to join *the police*. [NOT, in this sense, *the policemen*]

(iv) *cattle*: 'All his *cattle* were grazing in the field.'

(v) *poultry* ['farmyard birds']: 'Where are your *poultry*?'

But it is treated as singular in the sense of 'meat': '*Poultry* is harder to come by nowadays than beef'.

(vi) *livestock* ['animals kept on a farm']: 'Our *livestock* are not as numerous as they used to be.'

(vii) *vermin*: 'These vermin cause disease.'

(C) Regular plurals

5.79 Variable nouns have two forms: singular and plural. The singular is the unmarked form that is listed in dictionaries. The vast majority of nouns are variable in this way and normally the plural is fully predictable both in pronunciation and spelling by the same rules as for the *-s* inflection of verbs (*cf* 3.5, 3.7), *ie* they form the regular plural. If the plural cannot be predicted from the singular, it is an irregular plural.

The pronunciation of the regular plural

5.80 The regular *-s* plural has three different pronunciations /ɪz/, /z/, /s/ depending on the final sound of the base.

(i) /ɪz/ after bases ending in sibilants:

/s/ in *horse* ~ *horses*; *box* ~ *boxes*	/tʃ/ in *church* ~ *churches*
/z/ in *size* ~ *sizes*	/ʒ/ in *mirage* ~ *mirages*
/ʃ/ in *rush* ~ *rushes*	/dʒ/ in *language* ~ *languages*

(ii) /z/ after bases ending in vowels and voiced consonants other than sibilants: *day* ~ *days*, *bed* ~ *beds*

(iii) /s/ after bases ending in voiceless consonants other than sibilants: *bet* ~ *bets*, *month* ~ *months*

The spelling of the regular plural

5.81 The plural suffix is written *-s* after most nouns: *hat* ~ *hats*, including nouns ending in silent *-e* (*college* ~ *colleges*). There are however several exceptions to this rule:

(I) Unless the noun is written with a silent *-e*, the plural suffix is spelled *-es* after nouns ending in sibilants which are spelled *-s* (*gas* ~ *gases*), *-z* (*buzz* ~ *buzzes*), *-x* (*box* ~ *boxes*), *-ch* (*church* ~ *churches*), *-sh* (*bush* ~ *bushes*).

(II) Nouns ending in *-o* have plurals in *-os* or *-oes*.

(i) *-OS*: When *-o* is preceded by a vowel (letter or sound), the spelling is *-os*: *bamboos*, *embryos*, *folios*, *kangaroos*, *radios*, *studios*, *zoos*.

When *-o* is preceded by a consonant, the spelling is also usually *-os*: *dynamos*, *pianos*, *quartos*, *solos*. Abbreviations are included in those nouns with *-os*: *kilos* (= *kilograms*), *memos* (= *memoranda*), *photos* (= *photographs*); and ethnic nouns: *Eskimos*, *Filipinos* (but also zero, *cf* 5.88).

(ii) *-OES*: The following are among those nouns which have plurals only in *-oes*: *domino* (plural: *dominoes*); also: *echo, embargo, hero, potato, tomato, torpedo, veto.*

(iii) *-OS* or *-OES*: In some cases there is variation between *-os* and *-oes* plurals, *eg*: *archipelago* (plural: *archipelagos* or *archipelagoes*); also *banjo, buffalo* (*cf* 5.87), *cargo, grotto, halo, innuendo, manifesto, motto, mulatto, tornado, volcano.*

(III) Nouns ending in *-y* preceded by a consonant change *-y* to *-i* and add *-es*: *sky* ~ *skies*; *-y* is kept after a vowel: *day* ~ *days*, except for nouns ending in *-quy* /kwiː/ (where *u* is only a spelling vowel required after *q*), which have the plural *-quies* (*soliloquy* ~ *soliloquies*). Proper nouns ending in *-y* have plurals in *-ys*: *the two Germanys, the little Marys.*

(IV) The final consonant is doubled in a few words, *eg*: *fez* ~ *fezzes*, *quiz* ~ *quizzes.*

(V) The apostrophe + *s* is used in some nouns of unusual form, *eg* letters: *dot your i's*; numerals: *in the 1890's* (or, increasingly, *1890s*); abbreviations: *three PhD's* (or, increasingly, *PhDs*).

Note In abbreviations, reduplication also occurs as a purely written convention, *eg*: *p* ~ *pp* [the plural = 'pages'], *l* ~ *ll* [= 'lines'], *MS* ~ *MSS* [= 'manuscripts'], *ex* ~ *exx* [= 'examples'], *c* ~ *cc* [= 'copies'], *f* ~ *ff* [= 'and following pages'].

(D) Irregular plurals

5.82 Irregular plurals are by definition unpredictable. Whereas the plural /ɪz/ in *horses*, /z/ in *dogs*, and /s/ in *cats* can be predicted from the final sound in the singular of the nouns, there is no indication in the written or spoken forms of, for example, *ox*, *sheep*, and *analysis* to suggest that their plurals are *oxen*, *sheep*, and *analyses*. The particular plurals of these nouns have to be learned as individual lexical units.

In many cases where foreign words are involved, it is of course helpful to know about pluralization in the relevant languages, particularly Latin and Greek. Thus, on the pattern of *analysis* ~ *analyses* we can construct the following plurals: *axis* ~ *axes*, *basis* ~ *bases*, *crisis* ~ *crises*, etc. But we cannot always rely on etymological criteria: unlike *larva* ~ *larvae*, for example, plurals like *areas* and *villas* do not conform to the Latin pattern (*cf* 5.94).

(Da) Voicing and *-s* plural

5.83 (i) Some nouns which, in the singular, end in the voiceless fricative /θ/ (spelled *-th*) form plurals with the corresponding voiced fricative /ð/ followed by /z/. The spelling of the plural is regular (*-ths*):

-th /θ/ ~ *-ths* /ðz/, *eg: path* ~ *paths*

There is considerable indeterminacy between voicing and nonvoicing in many nouns ending in *-th*. With a consonant letter before the *-th*, the pronunciation of the plural is regular /θs/:

berth ~ *berths, birth* ~ *births, length* ~ *lengths*

With a vowel before the *-th*, the plural has, again, often regular pronunciation /θs/, as with:

cloth, death, faith, heath, moth

In a few such cases, however, there are both regular and voiced plurals, *eg*:

truths /truːθs/ or /truːðz/; similarly: *oaths, sheaths, youths* (/juːθs/ ⟨esp AmE⟩), *wreaths*

(ii) Some nouns which, in the singular, end in the voiceless fricative /f/ (spelled *-f* or *-fe*) form plurals with the corresponding voiced fricative /v/ followed by /z/. The spelling of the plural is *-ves*:

-f /f/ ~ *-ves* /vz/, *eg*: *calf* ~ *calves*
-fe /f/ ~ *-ves* /vz/, *eg*: *knife* ~ *knives*

Voiced plurals, spelled *-ves* and pronounced /vz/, occur with:

calf ~ *calves*	*life* ~ *lives*	*shelf* ~ *shelves*
elf ~ *elves*	*loaf* ~ *loaves*	*thief* ~ *thieves*
half ~ *halves*	*self* ~ *selves* (*cf* 6.23)	*wife* ~ *wives*
knife ~ *knives*	*sheaf* ~ *sheaves*	*wolf* ~ *wolves*
leaf ~ *leaves*		

Both regular and voiced plurals are found with:

dwarf (plural: *dwarfs*/*dwarves*), *hoof, scarf, wharf*

Other nouns ending in *-f*(*e*) have regular plural *-f*(*e*)*s* /fs/, for example: *belief* (plural: *beliefs*), *chief, cliff, proof, roof, safe*.

(iii) One noun (*house*) ending in the voiceless fricative /s/ in the singular has the plural /zɪz/: *house* ~ *houses*.

Note [a] In BrE *bath* has the voiced plural /bɑːðz/ or /bɑːθs/ when it means 'swimming pools', but usually /bɑːθs/ when it means 'bathtubs'.
[b] *Cloverleaf* occurs with either *cloverleafs* or *cloverleaves* in the plural. Regular plurals occur in names, *eg* the Toronto icehockey team *Maple Leafs*.
[c] The painting term *still life* has a regular plural: *still lifes*.

(Db) Mutation

5.84 The plural is formed by MUTATION (a change of vowel) in the following seven nouns:

man /mæn/	~ *men* /men/	*woman* /ˈwʊmən/	~ *women* /ˈwɪmɪn/
foot /ʊ/	~ *feet* /iː/	*tooth* /uː/	~ *teeth* /iː/
goose /uː/	~ *geese* /iː/	*louse* /aʊ/	~ *lice* /aɪ/
mouse /aʊ/	~ *mice* /aɪ/		

Note [a] Compounds with unstressed *-man*, as in *Englishman* ~ *Englishmen* (*cf* App I.64), have no difference in pronunciation at all between singular and plural, since both are pronounced /mən/. Similarly: *fireman* ~ *firemen, postman* ~ *postmen*, etc.
[b] *German* and *mongoose* are not compounds with *man* and *goose*, and thus have regular plurals: *Germans, mongooses*. However, the irregular plural can be found also in nouns that are not 'true' compounds with *-man*; *eg*: *dragoman* ~ *dragomans* or *dragomen*.
[c] Regular plurals are normal in names, such as *Mother Gooses*, and may occur when otherwise mutational nouns have derived meanings, *eg*: *Those louses!, Silly gooses!* ⟨familiar use⟩.

(Dc) The *-en* plural

5.85 The *-en* /ən/ plural occurs in three nouns:

brother ~ *brethren* (with mutation as well as the *-en* ending) is limited to *brother* meaning 'fellow member of a religious society'; otherwise regular *brothers*
child ~ *children* (with vowel change /aɪ/ ~ /ɪ/ and *-r* added)
ox ~ *oxen* (In AmE, the plural *oxes* is also sometimes found.)

(Dd) Zero plural

5.86 Some nouns have the same spoken and written form in both singular and plural. Note the difference here between, on the one hand, invariable nouns, which either cannot be plural [1] or cannot be singular [2], and, on the other hand, zero plural nouns, which can be both singular and plural [3, 3a]:

This music is too loud. [1]
All the cattle are grazing in the field. [2]
This sheep seems to have something wrong with it. [3]
All those sheep are ours. [3a]

We distinguish the following types of nouns with zero plural: (I) animal names (*cf* 5.87), (II) nationality nouns (*cf* 5.88), (III) quantitative nouns (*cf* 5.89*f*), and (IV) nouns with equivocal number (*cf* 5.91).

(I) Animal names

5.87 Animal names normally have the regular plural:

cow ~ *cows, eagle* ~ *eagles, monkey* ~ *monkeys*, etc

However, many animal names have two plurals: *-s* and zero plurals, *eg*: *duck, herring*. Zero tends to be used partly by people who are especially concerned with the animals, partly when the animals are referred to in the mass as game:

Have you ever shot *duck*?
We caught only a few *fish*.

The regular plural is used to denote different individuals, species, etc:

Can you see the *ducks* on the pond?
the *fishes* of the Mediterranean

In some cases usage is variable, *eg*:

He caught five {*fish.* / *fishes.*}

The degree of variability with animal names is shown by the following examples:

(i) Regular plural, *eg*:
bird, cow, eagle, hen, hawk, monkey, rabbit
(ii) Usually regular plural:
elk, crab, duck (zero only with the wild bird)
(iii) Both regular and zero plurals:
antelope, reindeer, fish, flounder, herring, shrimp, woodcock

(iv) Usually zero plural:

bison, *grouse*, *quail*, *salmon*, *swine* (*cf* the normal word *pig* which always has regular plural)

(v) Always zero plural:

sheep, *deer*, *cod*

Note [a] *Swine* used as a word of abuse may also have a zero plural:

You swine! [about one or more persons]
He called them *swine*.

But it is occasionally used with a regular plural:

these *swines* with their big cars

[b] Some animal names, like *duck* and *goose*, refer to both game and food: *shoot/eat duck*. But in the latter case, the noun is noncount. For other animals there is a special word for the flesh of an animal considered as food, *ie*: *shoot deer* but *eat venison* (*cf* 5.4: *pig/pork*, etc).

(II) Nationality nouns

5.88 Nationality nouns ending in *-ese* also have zero plurals (*cf* 5.57):

one *Chinese* ~ five *Chinese*; similarly: *Japanese*, *Lebanese*, *Portuguese*, *Sinhalese*, *Vietnamese*, etc; also: *one Swiss* ~ *two Swiss*

Certain nationality and ethnic names are sometimes used without *-s*:

Apache(*s*), *Bantu*(*s*), *Bedouin*(*s*), *Eskimo*(*s*), *Navaho*(*s*)

Sioux has the same written form for singular and plural, but the pronunciation /suː/ in the singular corresponds to either /suː/ or /suːz/ in the plural.

(III) Quantitative nouns

5.89 (i) The nouns *dozen*, *hundred*, *thousand*, and *million* have zero plurals when they are premodified by another quantitative word (*cf* 6.65):

three *dozen* glasses	two *hundred* people
many *thousand* times	several *million* inhabitants

Million can take plural *-s* if no noun head follows:

They want { *a few hundred.* / *ten thousand.* / *several million*(*s*). }

The plural form is normally used with all four nouns when an *of*-phrase follows, with or without a preceding indefinite quantitative word:

(many) *dozens of* glasses
(many) *hundreds of* people
(several) *thousands of* spectators
(a few) *millions of* inhabitants

But the zero form is common enough:

a few *million of* us, several *hundred/thousand of* them

Note such combinations as:

tens of thousands of people
hundreds of millions of stars
hundreds (*and hundreds* (*and hundreds*)) *of* times

(ii) *Foot* denoting length and *pound* denoting weight often have zero plural, particularly when a numeral follows:

She's only *five foot two.*
She's only *five foot tall.* / *five feet tall.*
She's only *five feet.* ⟨usually⟩

(iii) Also *pound* denoting currency may have zero or regular plural when a numeral follows:

This ticket costs only *two pound(s) fifty.*
This ticket costs only *two pounds.*

Note The more general use of singular for plural with measure nouns is nonstandard but widely current:

It weighs *five pound.* He's nearly *six foot.*

More widely acceptable is:

Five pound of potatoes, please.

The singular is however standard in quantitative expressions of the following type (*cf* 17.108): *a three-foot ruler.*

5.90 Other quantitative nouns (some of them rather rare) with zero plurals include the following when used with definite numbers and measurements:

brace [= 2]: 'five brace of pheasants'
gross [= 12 dozen]: 'ten gross of nails'
head [= 1]: '400 head of cattle'
horsepower, *HP*: 'This engine has only fifty horsepower.'
hundredweight [British weight = 112 pounds]: 'five hundredweight (of coal)'
(*kilo*)*hertz*: 'Two kilohertz equals 2000 hertz.'
p /piː/ ['penny' ⟨informal BrE⟩]: 'The paper costs *25p* /piː/' ['25 *pence*' ⟨more formal⟩]. *Penny* is commonly used in BrE and AmE when referring to the actual coins as distinct from the value: 'Save your pennies and watch your dollars grow.'
quid ['pound' ⟨BrE slang⟩]: 'You owe me *five quid.*' [= *five pounds*; written: £5]
score [= 20]: 'four *score* and ten years ago'; BUT always: 'scores (and scores) of people'
stone [British weight = 14 pounds]: 'He weighs 18 stone(s).'
yen [Japanese currency]: 'one yen, 200 yen'
yoke [= 2]: 'two yoke(s) of oxen'

(IV) Nouns with equivocal number

5.91 The following nouns can be treated as singular or plural:

barracks: This barracks is new. / These barracks are new.

Also *s*-less form: 'a barrack square'; 'an enormous barrack of a place' [informal metaphorical use]

craft in the sense of 'ship(s)' with compounds: 'one/several (air)craft/hovercraft/spacecraft' (BUT: 'arts and crafts')

crossroads: { This is a busy crossroads.
There are several crossroads here. }

data ['information, especially information organized for analysis'] (from the Latin singular *datum*, plural *data*) is usually constructed as a plural [1]. But it is often constructed also as a singular, especially in scientific contexts [1a]:

Many of *these data are* inconclusive. [1]
Much of *this data is* inconclusive. [1a]

The regular English plural *datums* is used as a reference term in surveying.

dice: 'one/two dice' (or perhaps: 'one of the dice' for the singular). *Die* in the expression 'The die is cast' is no longer recognized as being the singular of *dice*. *Die* ['engraved stamp for coining, etc'] has the regular plural *dies*.

gallows: 'one/two gallows', 'gallows humour'

headquarters: 'a large headquarters', 'Where is/are the headquarters?'

innings [as a cricket term]: 'a long innings', 'two innings' [The corresponding baseball term is regular: 'an inning/two innings']

kennels (as well as being plural of regular *kennel*) ['a collection of kennels where dogs are kept']: 'a/some famous kennels'

links: 'a fine but difficult golf links', 'We have several links here.'

means: 'a means of communication', 'use every/all means available', 'a means test'

mews ⟨BrE⟩: { This mews is / These mews are } very fashionable.

oats: 'Is/Are oats grown here?'

offspring: { Is this / Are these } your offspring?

series: { This new series is / These new series are } beginning next month.

species: { This species is / These species are } now extinct.

works ['factory, plant'] with compounds (*steelworks*, *waterworks*):

a/two large works
{ An enormous steelworks was / A number of steelworks were } built here in the thirties.

But *works* ['the moving parts of a machine'] is a plurale tantum, and *work* ['job'] is noncount (*cf* 5.9).

Note [**a**] Most of the nouns in this group are count nouns and display a semantic difference between singular and plural (eg: *one/two mews*). The exceptions are *data* and *oats*.

[**b**] In BrE the singular form of collective nouns may also have either a singular or a plural verb (*cf* 5.108):

Our *team* { *has* / *have* } lost again. But not a plural determiner: { **these* / *this* } *team*

Foreign plurals

5.92 Foreign plurals often occur along with regular plurals. They are more common in technical usage, whereas the *-s* plural is the most natural in everyday language. Thus: *formulas* (general) ~ *formulae* (in mathematics, linguistics, etc), *antennas* (general and in electronics) ~ *antennae* (in biology).

Our aim here will be to survey systematically the main types of foreign plurals that are used in present-day English and to consider the extent to which a particular plural form is obligatory or optional. Most (but by no means all) words having a foreign plural originated in the language mentioned in the heading.

(De) Nouns from Latin ending in *-us* /əs/

5.93 The foreign plural in most cases is *-i* /aɪ/, as in *stimulus* ~ *stimuli* (also /'stɪmjəliː/). Other nouns with *-i* plural only: *alumnus, bacillus, locus.* The plural of *corpus* is *corpora* or *corpuses*, and the plural of *genus* /'dʒiːnəs/ is *genera* /'dʒenərə/.

Nouns with only the regular plural (*-uses*) include:

apparatus, bonus, campus, caucus, census, chorus, circus, impetus, minus, prospectus, sinus, status, virus

Nouns with both plurals include:

focus ~ *focuses* /'fəʊkəsɪz/, or *foci* /'fəʊkaɪ, 'fəʊsaɪ/
fungus ~ *funguses* /'fʌŋgəsɪz/, or *fungi* /'fʌŋdʒaɪ, 'fʌŋgaɪ, 'fʌŋdʒiː, 'fʌŋgiː/
also: *cactus, nucleus, radius, syllabus, terminus*

(Df) Nouns from Latin ending in *-a* /ə/

5.94 The foreign plural is *-ae* /iː/ as in *alumna* ~ *alumnae*. Other nouns with *-ae* plural only include: *alga, larva.*

Nouns with only regular plurals (*-as*) include: *area, arena, dilemma, diploma, drama, era,* etc.

Nouns with both plurals include: *antenna, formula, nebula, vertebra.*

(Dg) Nouns from Latin ending in *-um* /əm/

5.95 The foreign plural is *-a* /ə/ (in careful pronunciation, alternatively /ɑː/), as in *curriculum* ~ *curricula*. Other nouns with the *-a* plural only include: *addendum, bacterium, corrigendum, desideratum, erratum, ovum.*

Nouns with only the regular plural include: *album, chrysanthemum, museum, premium.*

Nouns which are usually regular: *forum, stadium.*

Nouns with both plurals: *aquarium, candelabrum, curriculum, maximum, medium, memorandum, millennium, minimum, moratorium, podium, referendum, spectrum, stratum, symposium, ultimatum.*

Note [**a**] *Media* is often used in the sense of 'news media' with reference to press, radio, and television, when it is sometimes treated as a singular with a regular plural *medias*:

The media is } wrong about this.
All the medias are }

Both of these uses however are widely condemned, especially the second.

[**b**] *Strata* is the common plural of *stratum*. With reference to society *strata* is also sometimes used as singular:

This is *an important strata* of education in society.

But again this usage is widely criticized.
[c] On *data*, *cf* 5.91.
[d] Besides singular *candelabrum* with the plural *candelabra*, there is also singular *candelabra* with the regular plural *candelabras*.
[e] *Agenda* and *insignia* (plurals of Latin *agendum* and *insignium*) are used in English as singulars with the regular plurals *agendas* and *insignias*.

(Dh) Nouns from Latin ending in *-ex*, *-ix*

5.96 The foreign plural is *-ices* /ɪsiːz/ as in *index* ~ *indices*. However, *index* and *appendix* have both regular and foreign plurals. The regular form *indexes* is used for reference to parts of a book or other publication; the plural *indices* is largely used for 'indicators'. *Appendix* has either plural for reference to parts of a book; it is regular for parts of the body. Other nouns that have both regular and foreign plurals are: *apex*, *vortex*, *matrix*. Only foreign plural: *codex*.

(Di) Nouns from Greek ending in *-is* /ɪs/

5.97 The foreign plural is *-es* /iːz/, as in singular *basis* /ˈbeɪsɪs/, plural *bases* /ˈbeɪsiːz/. Other nouns which take this plural are *eg*:

analysis, axis, crisis, diagnosis, ellipsis, hypothesis, oasis, paralysis, parenthèsis, synopsis, synthesis, thesis

Metropolis has the regular plural: *metropolises*.

Note *Bases* can be either the plural of *base*, *eg*: *naval bases* (pronounced /ˈbeɪsɪz/), or the plural of *basis*, *eg*: *bases of an opinion* (pronounced /ˈbeɪsiːz/). Similarly, *axes* can be the plural of *axe* or *axis*, and *ellipses* the plural of *ellipse* or *ellipsis*.

(Dj) Nouns from Greek ending in *-on*

5.98 The foreign plural is *-a*, as in *criterion* ~ *criteria*, *phenomenon* ~ *phenomena*, both of which regularly take the *-a* plural. Nouns with only regular plurals: *electron, neutron, proton*; chiefly regular: *ganglion*; both plurals: *automaton*.

Note Informally, *criteria* and *phenomena* are sometimes used as singulars, and *criterias* as plural. This usage is however widely condemned, and the objection to both these singular forms is stronger than to singular *data* (*cf* 5.91), *media* (*cf* 5.95 Note [a]), and *strata* (*cf* 5.95 Note [b]).

(Dk) Nouns from French: *bureau, corps*, etc

5.99 A few nouns ending in *-eau* and *-eu*, *eg*: *bureau* and *adieu*, may retain the French *-x* as the spelling of the plural (*bureaux*, *adieux*), beside the commoner *-s* (*bureaus*, *adieus*). In English, the plurals are however almost always pronounced as regular, *ie* /z/, irrespective of spelling. Similarly: *tableau*, *plateau*.

Some French nouns ending in *-s* or *-x* are pronounced without the final sibilant in the singular, *eg*: (*army*) *corps* /kɔːʳ/, and with a regular /z/ in the plural, with no spelling change (*corps* /kɔːʳz/): *chamois* (*leather*), *chassis*, (*faux*) *pas*, *patois*, *rendezvous*.

(Dl) Nouns from Italian ending in *-o* /əʊ/

5.100 The foreign plural is *-i* /ɪ/ as in *tempo* ~ *tempi*; only regular plural: *solo*, *soprano*; both regular and irregular plural: *virtuoso*, *libretto*, *tempo*.

Note *Confetti* (from Italian *confetto*, which is not used in English) and other Italian plurals like *macaroni, ravioli, spaghetti*, etc are usually treated as noncount nouns, and take a singular verb in English. *Graffiti* is usually treated as an invariable plural, but one also hears the singular *graffito*.

(Dm) Nouns from Hebrew: *kibbutz* ~ *kibbutzim*

5.101 The foreign plural is *-im*, as in *kibbutz* ~ *kibbutzim* beside the regular *kibbutzes*. Usually regular: *cherub*, *seraph*.

Compounds

5.102 Compound nouns, *ie* nouns which consist of more than one base (*cf* App I.57*ff*), form the plural in different ways. It is most common, particularly in informal usage, to consider the compound as a simple noun and pluralize the last element (even when it is not a noun, as in *sit-ins*).

(i) Plural in the last element (normal):

assistant director ~ assistant directors
babysitter ~ babysitters
breakdown ~ breakdowns
close-up ~ close-ups
ALSO: grown-up, take-over, sit-in, take-off (NOTE spelling in: stand-by ~ stand-bys)
gin-and-tonic ~ gin-and-tonics; SIMILARLY: forget-me-not ~ forget-me-nots, mouthful ~ mouthfuls (OR sometimes: mouthsful); SIMILARLY: bucketful, spoonful

(ii) Plural in the first element occurs especially when the compound includes a postmodifier or final particle:

notary public ~ notaries public
grant-in-aid ~ grants-in-aid
commander-in-chief ~ commanders-in-chief
man-of-war ~ men-of-war
coat-of-mail ~ coats-of-mail
passer-by ~ passers-by

The following occur with plural either in the first or last element:

attorney general ~ attorneys general (ALSO: attorney generals)
court martial ~ courts martial (ALSO: court martials)
mother-in-law ~ mothers-in-law (ALSO: mother-in-laws ⟨informal⟩)

(iii) Appositional compounds (*a woman doctor* ['The doctor is a woman']) whose first element is, or includes, *man* or *woman* pluralize both the first and the last element:

gentleman farmer ~ gentlemen farmers
manservant ~ menservants ⟨old-fashioned⟩
woman doctor ~ women doctors

But the plural is in the last element (type i) when the compound is not appositional: *woman-hater(s)* ['x hate(s) women']. Similarly: *man-eater* ~ *man-eaters*.

Forms of address

5.103 The plural of *Mr Smith*, to denote two people with that name, is *the two Mr Smiths*. *Messrs* /'mesə^{r}z/ ⟨BrE⟩ is chiefly used in the names of firms: *Messrs Smith and Brown Ltd*.

The plural of *Miss Smith* is *the Miss Smiths, eg*: *the two Miss Smiths. The Misses Smith* is rather formal and old-fashioned.

The plural of *Mrs* /'mɪsɪz/ *Smith* is *the two Mrs Smith(s)*; and, similarly, *Ms* /mɪz/ *Smith* (*cf* 5.66 Note [a]): *the two Ms Smith(s)*.

Gender

5.104 By GENDER is meant a grammatical classification of nouns, pronouns, or other words in the noun phrase, according to certain meaning-related distinctions, especially a distinction related to the sex of the referent.

In English, unlike many other related languages, nouns, determiners, and adjectives have no inflectionally-marked gender distinctions. Some 3rd person pronouns and *wh*-pronouns do, however, express natural gender distinctions:

it, which, etc	[NONPERSONAL] contrasts with the following:
who, whom, etc	[PERSONAL]
he, himself, etc	[MASCULINE, chiefly PERSONAL]
she, herself, etc	[FEMININE, chiefly PERSONAL]

Gender in English nouns may be described as 'notional' or 'covert' in contrast to the 'grammatical' or 'overt' gender of nouns in languages such as French, German, and Russian; that is, nouns are classified not grammatically, but semantically, according to their coreferential relations with personal, reflexive, and *wh*-pronouns. We use the terms MALE and FEMALE in reference to the 'covert' gender of nouns, as distinct from the 'overt' gender of pronouns.

The patterns of pronoun coreference for singular nouns give us a set of nine gender classes as illustrated in *Fig* 5.104:

		GENDER CLASS	EXAMPLE	PRONOUN COREFERENCE	
animate	personal	(a) male	*brother*	*who–he*	(5.105)
animate	personal	(b) female	*sister*	*who–she*	(5.105)
animate	personal	(c) dual	*doctor*	*who–he/she*	(5.106)
animate	personal / nonpersonal	(d) common	*baby*	*who–he/she/it*; *which–it*	(5.107)
animate	personal / nonpersonal	(e) collective	*family*	*which–it*; *who–they*	(5.108)
animate	nonpersonal	(f) higher male animal	*bull*	*which–he/it*; *(who)–he*	(5.109)
animate	nonpersonal	(g) higher female animal	*cow*	*which–she/it*; *(who)–she*	(5.109)
animate	nonpersonal	(h) lower animal	*ant*	*which–it*; *(he/she)*	(5.110)
inanimate		(i) inanimate	*box*	*which–it*	(5.110)

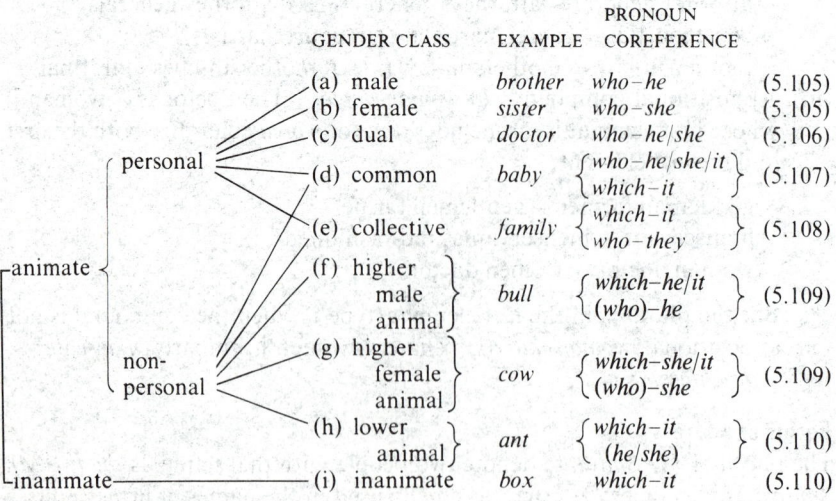

Fig 5.104 Gender classes

(a/b) Personal male/female nouns

5.105 Personal male nouns have pronoun coreference with *who–he* and female nouns with *who–she*. These nouns are of two types. Type (i) is morphologically unmarked between male and female, whereas in Type (ii) the two gender forms have a derivational relationship. The derivational suffixes are not productive, however. We cannot, except jocularly, for example, form *clerk* ~ **clerkess* on the *host* ~ *hostess* pattern (*cf* App I.33).

(i) Morphologically unmarked for gender, *eg*:

bachelor ~ *spinster*	*boy* ~ *girl*	*brother* ~ *sister*
father ~ *mother*	*king* ~ *queen*	*man* ~ *woman*
Mr ~ *Mrs, Miss, Ms*	*monk* ~ *nun*	*nephew* ~ *niece*
uncle ~ *aunt*		

(ii) Morphologically marked for gender, *eg*:

host ~ host*ess*	waiter ~ waitr*ess*
prince ~ princ*ess*	hero ~ hero*ine*
steward ~ steward*ess*	usher ~ usher*ette*
god ~ godd*ess*	emperor ~ empr*ess*

In the following two pairs, it is the male noun that is marked:

bride*groom* ~ bride   widow*er* ~ widow

Some male/female pairs denoting kinship have dual gender terms, for example *parent* for *father* ~ *mother* and *sibling* ⟨esp technical⟩ for *brother* ~ *sister*. Some optional female forms (*poetess*, *authoress*, etc) are no longer in normal use, being replaced by the dual gender forms (*poet*, *author*, etc).

In order to avoid sexual bias in language, attempts have been made (esp in AmE) to introduce sex-neutral forms, such as *s/he* for both *she* and *he*, *wo/man* for *woman* and *man*, *flight attendant* for *airline hostess*. The prospect of wider acceptance of *s/he* and *wo/man* is reduced by the fact that these are written forms only. Other such examples are:

supervisor *for* foreman	fisher *for* fisherman
firefighter *for* fireman	mail carrier *for* mailman
chair(person) *for* chairman	usher *for* usherette
spokesperson *for* spokesman	homemaker *for* housewife
Member of Congress *for* Congressman	

(c) Personal dual gender

5.106 This class of nouns, which has *who–he* or *she* pronoun coreference, includes, for example, the following:

artist	cook	doctor	enemy
foreigner	friend	guest	inhabitant
librarian	novelist	parent	person
professor	servant	singer	speaker
student	teacher	typist	writer

If it is felt desirable to give information on the sex of the person, a gender marker may be added, such as *male student/female student*. The dual class is on the increase, but the expectation that a given activity is largely male or female dictates the frequent use of gender markers: thus *a nurse*, but *a male nurse*; *an engineer*, but *a woman engineer*. No rational rules can be given for whether a noun should have dual gender distinction or not. It seems, for example, quite arbitrary that *guest* and *servant* should be dual in contrast to *host* ~ *hostess* and *waiter* ~ *waitress*.

(d) Common gender

5.107 Common gender nouns are intermediate between personal and nonpersonal. The wide selection of pronouns (*who*/*which*–*he*/*she*/*it*) should not be understood to mean that all these are possible for all nouns in all contexts. A mother is not likely to refer to her baby or child as *it*, but such nonpersonal reference may well be preferred by somebody who is emotionally unrelated to the child, or wishes to generalize across sex distinctions in scientific contexts:

> A *child* learns to speak the language of *its* environment.

Other nouns that belong here (chiefly when the animals are treated as pets or otherwise 'personified') include *blackbird*, *cat*, *monkey*, *rabbit*.

(e) Collective nouns

5.108 These differ from other nouns in taking as pronoun coreferents either singular *it* and relative *which* or plural *they* and relative *who* without change of number in the noun (*the army*: *it*/*which*–*they*/*who*; *cf* plural *the armies*: *they*–*which*). Consequently, the verb may be in the plural after a singular noun, though far less commonly in AmE than BrE (*cf* 10.36):

$$\text{The committee}\left\{\begin{array}{l}\textit{has}\text{ met and }\textit{it has}\\ \textit{have}\text{ met and }\textit{they have}\end{array}\right\}\text{rejected the proposal.}$$

The difference reflects a difference in point of view: the singular stresses the nonpersonal collectivity of the group, and the plural stresses the personal individuality within the group. Here are examples of collective nouns:

(i)

army	association	audience
board	cast	clan
class	club	college
commission	community	company
corporation	council	couple
crew	crowd	department
enemy	faculty ⟨AmE⟩	family
federation	firm	flock
gang	generation	government
group	herd	institute
jury	majority	minority
opposition	party	population
staff	team	university

(ii) The following usually occur in the singular only with the definite article:

the aristocracy	the bourgeoisie	the church
the clergy	the elite	the gentry

the intelligentsia	the laity	the press
the public	the rank and file	the youth (of today)

(iii) Collective proper names, *eg*:

the Commons (UK)	Parliament	the Vatican
(the) Congress (US)	the United Nations	the United States

Note [**a**] Just as *association*, *company*, *corporation*, *federation*, *firm*, *team*, etc are included among the collective nouns, names of commercial firms are treated in the same way:

ICI [*has* / *have* ⟨BrE⟩] increased [*its* / *their*] sales abroad.

[**b**] *Church* and *youth* in (ii) also occur of course as regular count nouns, the latter denoting a young male:

The police are looking for five *youths*. ['young men']

(f/g) Higher animals

5.109 Male/female gender distinctions in animal nouns are maintained by people with a special concern (for example with pets), *eg*: *cock* and *rooster* ⟨AmE⟩ for the male (with *which–he/it* or *who–he* coreference) and *hen* for the female (with *which–she/it* or *who–she* coreference). Other examples:

buck ~ doe	bull ~ cow	dog ~ bitch	gander ~ goose
lion ~ lioness	ram ~ ewe	stallion ~ mare	tiger ~ tigress

Note In general, in nonexpert contexts there is no need to make a gender distinction, such as *dog* ~ *bitch* and *stallion* ~ *mare*. We can then use one term to cover both sexes, as in the case of *dog* and *lion*, or use a different term, *eg*: *horse* to cover both *stallion* and *mare*.

(h/i) Lower animals and inanimate nouns

5.110 Both lower animals (*eg*: *beetle*, *butterfly*, *snake*, *toad*, *tadpole*) and inanimate nouns (*eg*: *box*, *car*, *idea*) have *which* and *it* as pronouns. However, lower animals may also be viewed as higher animals. Thus we may speak of 'goldfish who swim around', 'bees who are busy', etc.

Sex differences can be indicated by a range of gender markers for any animate noun where they are felt to be relevant, *eg*: *male* ~ *female frog*. Other examples:

buck-rabbit ~ doe-rabbit	cock-pheasant ~ hen-pheasant
dog-fox ~ bitch-fox	he-goat ~ she-goat
roe-buck ~ roe-doe	

We make no claim for the categories 'higher/lower animals' to parallel the biological classification. Some animals require finer gender distinctions in the language than others. This can be attributed to a number of factors. The layman normally has no knowledge about the sex of animals like *ant*, *herring*, *snake*, *spider*; or, even if he does, it may not be a fact that he wants or needs to indicate. *He* and *she* are only likely to be used for animals with which man, 'the speaking animal', has the closest connections (in particular the domesticated animals).

Names of countries

5.111 Names of countries have different gender depending on their use.

(i) As geographical units, they are treated as class (i), *ie* inanimate:

Here is a map of France. *It* is one of the largest countries of Europe.

(ii) As political/economic units, the names of countries are often feminine, *ie* class (b) or (g):

France *has* been able to increase *her* exports by 10 per cent over the last six months.
England *is* proud of *her* poets.

(iii) In sports, the teams representing their countries can be referred to by the name of the country used as a personal collective noun, *ie* class (e) ⟨esp BrE⟩:

France {*has* / *have* ⟨BrE⟩} improved {*its* / *their* ⟨esp BrE⟩} chances of winning the cup.

In AmE there may be number variation in the pronoun (but not in the verb, which is singular) in this construction.

Note Inanimate entities, such as ships, towards which we have an intense and close personal relationship, may be referred to by personal pronouns, *eg*:

That's a lovely ship. What is *she/it* called?

In nonstandard and Australian English, there is extension of *she* references to include those of antipathy as well as affection, *eg*:

She's an absolute bastard, this truck.

Case

Common case and genitive case

5.112 We shall distinguish between two cases of nouns: the unmarked COMMON CASE (*eg*: *boy* in the singular, *boys* in the plural) and the marked GENITIVE CASE (*eg*: *boy's* in the singular, *boys'* in the plural). Case in pronouns will be discussed in 6.2*ff*; on the genitive in relation to the *of*-construction, *cf* 5.115.

Distinctions of case mark the structural and semantic function of noun phrases within sentences. It is arguable, as we shall see, that even the common/genitive distinction in present-day English is not really a case distinction, although it is a relic of a former case system comparable to that of Latin or of modern Russian (*cf* 5.123). We adhere to established terminology in this respect, but since the common case is simply the form used when the genitive is not used, our attention in the following sections will be devoted to the genitive.

The 'central', but far from the only use of the genitive, is to express possession: to this extent the term 'possessive' is fittingly applied to genitive pronouns like *his*. We may compare:

The children's toys are new. ['the toys belonging to the children']
Their toys are new. ['the toys belonging to them']

But it should be borne in mind that the label 'possessive' does not adequately apply to all uses (*cf* 5.116).

The forms of the genitive inflection

5.113 The genitive of regular nouns is realized in speech only in the singular, where it takes one of the forms /ɪz/, /z/, or /s/, following the rules for the *-s* inflection of nouns (*cf* 5.80) and verbs (*cf* 3.5). In writing, the inflection of regular nouns is realized in the singular by apostrophe + *s* (*boy's*), and in the regular plural by the apostrophe following the plural *-s* (*boys'*).

As a result, the spoken form /spaɪz/ may realize three forms of the noun *spy* as follows:

The *spies* were arrested.	[plural, common case]
The *spy's* companion was a woman.	[singular, genitive case]
The *spies'* companions were women.	[plural, genitive case]

Since the genitive adds nothing to a regular plural noun in speech, and nothing except the final apostrophe in writing, this plural genitive may be called the ZERO GENITIVE.

By contrast, some nouns with irregular plural like *child* preserve a number distinction independently of the genitive singular and genitive plural distinctions:

child ~ *child's*, *children* ~ *children's*

With such irregular plurals, as *Fig* 5.113 shows, the same genitive ending (spelled *'s*) occurs with both singular and plural nouns.

<table>
<tr><th></th><th colspan="2">REGULAR -S PLURAL</th><th colspan="2">IRREGULAR PLURAL</th></tr>
<tr><td>SPOKEN</td><td>singular</td><td>plural</td><td>singular</td><td>plural</td></tr>
<tr><td>common</td><td>/bɒɪ/</td><td rowspan="2">/bɒɪz/</td><td>/tʃaɪld/</td><td>/ˈtʃɪldrən/</td></tr>
<tr><td>genitive</td><td></td><td>/tʃaɪldz/</td><td>/ˈtʃɪldrənz/</td></tr>
<tr><td>WRITTEN</td><td>singular</td><td>plural</td><td>singular</td><td>plural</td></tr>
<tr><td>common</td><td>boy</td><td>boys</td><td>child</td><td>children</td></tr>
<tr><td>genitive</td><td>boy's</td><td>boys'</td><td>child's</td><td>children's</td></tr>
</table>

Fig 5.113 The genitive inflection with regular and irregular plurals

Note [**a**] In addition to representing different case or number forms of the noun *spy* (*spies, spy's, spies'*), the pronunciation /spaɪz/ could of course also be the *-s* form of the verb, as in [1], or the noun with the contracted form of *is* [2], or *has* [3] (*cf* 3.32*f*):

He *spies* on behalf of an industrial firm. [1]
The *spy's* here. [2]
The *spy's* been cycling along the coast. [3]

[**b**] In postmodified noun phrases, there is a difference between the plural and the genitive endings, because the genitive ending is added to the end of the phrase, not to the end of the head noun (*cf* 'group genitives', 5.123):

The palace was *the King of Denmark's*.
They praised *the Kings of Denmark*.

The 'zero genitive'

5.114 In addition to its normal use with regular plurals such as *boys'*, the 'zero genitive' is used to avoid repetitive or awkward combinations of sounds in the following cases (*cf Fig* 5.114):

(i) with Greek names of more than one syllable which end in *-s*, as in:

Euripides' /diːz/ plays, *Xerxes'* army, *Socrates'* wife

(ii) with many other names ending in /z/ where, in speech, zero is a variant of the regular /ɪz/ genitive. There is vacillation both in the pronunciation and in the spelling of these names, but most commonly the pronunciation is /ɪz/, and the spelling is an apostrophe only. (In the following examples, the minority forms are given in parentheses.)

WRITTEN FORMS	SPOKEN FORMS
Burns' (*Burns's*) poem	/ˈbɜːʳnzɪz (bɜːʳnz)/
Dickens' (*Dickens's*) novels	/ˈdɪkɪnzɪz (ˈdɪkɪnz)/
Jones' (*Jones's*) car	/ˈdʒəʊnzɪz (dʒəʊnz)/

Names ending in other sibilants than /z/ have the regular /ɪz/ genitive: *Ross's*

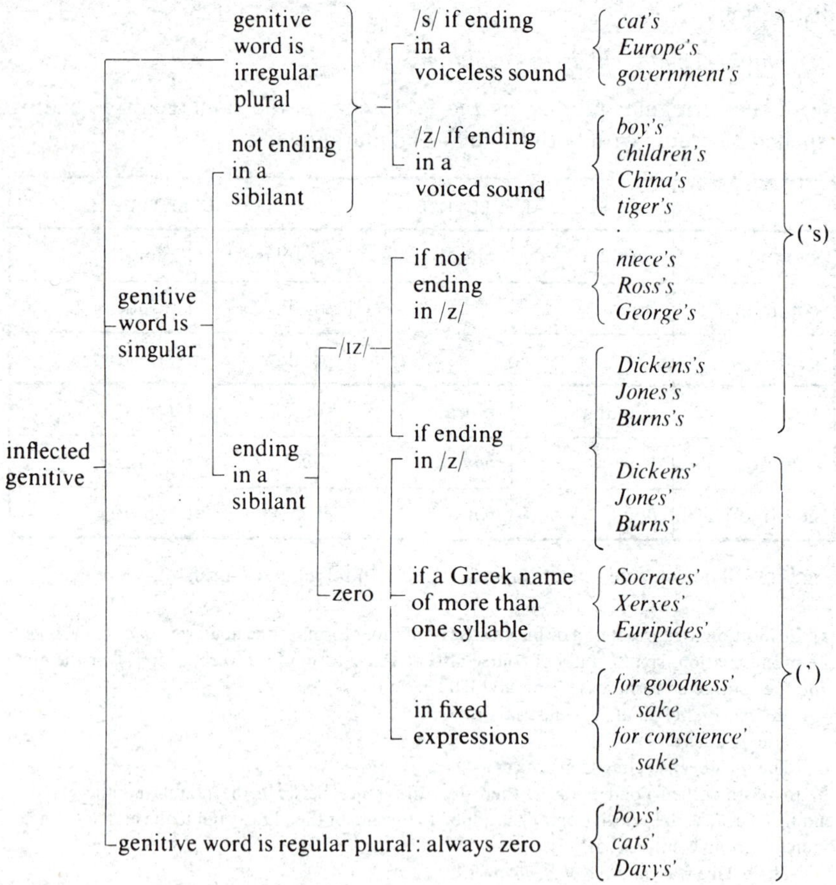

Fig 5.114 The forms of the inflected genitive

/SIZ/ *theories*. However, the genitive of *Jesus* is normally zero in speech, through written *Jesus*' or *Jesus's*; so too *Moses*.

(iii) with fixed expressions of the form *for . . . sake*, as in *for goodness' sake*, *for conscience' sake*, where the noun ends in /s/ (*cf* 5.120).

The genitive and the *of*-construction

5.115 In many instances there is a similarity of function and meaning between a noun in the genitive case and the same noun as head of a prepositional phrase with *of* (sometimes called the '*of*-genitive'). The genitive inflection of [1], where *ship's* precedes and determines the head noun *name*, corresponds to the OF-CONSTRUCTION of the prepositional phrase in [1a], where *of the ship* postmodifies the head *name*:

What is { *the ship's* name? [1]
What is { the name *of the ship*? [1a]

In many cases, like [1] and [1a], the two forms are equivalent in meaning and are both perfectly acceptable. In other cases, either the genitive or the *of*-construction is the only appropriate choice:

John's school BUT NOT: ?the school *of John*
the front *of the house* BUT NOT: **the house's* front

For further discussion of the *of*-construction, and its relation to the genitive, *cf* 5.116*ff* and, in particular, 17.38*ff*, where the *of*-construction is also compared with other types of postmodification. Our purpose in this chapter is to examine the genitive as a construction in its own right, and to indicate the semantic as well as the syntactic restrictions on its use.

The use of the genitive is determined by a combination of structural and semantic conditions. We will look in turn at

(i) the meanings expressed by the relation between the genitive noun and its head noun (*cf* 5.116)
(ii) the type of noun taking the genitive (*cf* 5.117–119)
(iii) the type of noun acting as head (*cf* 5.120)

Genitive meanings

5.116 The meaning expressed by the genitive can best be shown by sentential or phrasal analogues such as we present below. For comparison, a corresponding use of the *of*-construction is given where this is acceptable.

(a) POSSESSIVE GENITIVE

Mrs Johnson's passport	Mrs Johnson has a passport.
the earth's gravity	The earth has (a certain) gravity.
cf the gravity *of the earth*	

(b) SUBJECTIVE GENITIVE

the boy's application	The boy applied for . . .
her parents' consent	Her parents consented.
cf the decline *of trade*	Trade declined.

(c) OBJECTIVE GENITIVE

the family's support	(. . .) supports the family.
the boy's release	(. . .) released the boy.
cf a statement *of the facts*	(. . .) stated the facts.

(d) GENITIVE OF ORIGIN

the girl's story	The girl told a story.
the general's letter	The general wrote a letter.
?*France's* wines	France produces wines.
cf the wines *of France*	

(e) DESCRIPTIVE GENITIVE (*cf* 5.122)

a *women's* college	a college for women
a *summer's* day	a summer day, a day in the summer
a *doctor's* degree	a doctoral degree, a doctorate
cf the degree of *doctor*	

(f) GENITIVE OF MEASURE

ten days' absence	The absence lasted ten days.
cf an absence of *ten days*	

(g) GENITIVE OF ATTRIBUTE

the victim's courage	{ The victim had courage. The victim was courageous.
the party's policy	The party has a (certain) policy.
cf the policy *of the party*	

(h) PARTITIVE GENITIVE

the baby's eyes	The baby has (blue) eyes.
the earth's surface	The earth has a (rough) surface.
cf the surface *of the earth*	

Note [**a**] There is a tendency for genitives to be taken as subjective, and for *of*-constructions to be taken as objective. Thus, with inadequate context, a phrase like [1] is likely to be interpreted as 'The family supports . . .', but [2] as '. . . examined the fire department' (*cf* 17.41*ff*):

the family's support [1]

the examination *of the fire department* [2]

[**b**] A marginal additional category, the genitive of apposition, may be mentioned: *Dublin's fair city* (*cf*: *Dublin, a fair city*). In today's usage, however, this is normally replaced by an appositive *of*-construction (*cf* 17.47, 17.89): *the city of Dublin.*

[**c**] On the use of the genitive to denote close family relationships (*Peter's Jane*), *cf* 5.63 Note [c].

Gender of the genitive noun

5.117 The semantic classification in 5.116 is in part arbitrary. For example, one could claim that *cow's milk* is not a genitive of origin ['milk from a cow'] but a descriptive genitive ['the kind of milk obtained from a cow'], or even a subjective genitive ['The cow provided the milk']. For this reason, meanings and sentential analogues can give only inconclusive help in choosing between the genitive and the *of*-construction.

The choice can be more securely related to the gender class of the genitive noun. Generally speaking, the genitive is favoured for classes which are highest on the gender scale (*cf Fig* 5.104), *ie* 'personal' nouns (particularly those referring to human beings and higher animals) and collective nouns with personal gender characteristics. Relating this to 5.104, we may infer that the possessive use is especially associated with the genitive because we think of 'possession' chiefly in terms of our own species. It is possible to see the partitive genitive at the opposite pole on comparable grounds: the marginal acceptability of ?*the house's roof* matches the irrelevance of personal gender to a noun denoting something which is merely being measured or dissected.

Further factors influencing the choice of genitive are the principles of end-focus and end-weight (*cf* 17.45, 18.3*f*), which encourage the placing of more complex and communicatively more important units towards the end of the noun phrase. According to the principle of end-focus, the genitive tends to give information focus to the head noun, whereas the *of*-construction tends to give focus to the prepositional complement:

The explosion damaged *the ship's funnel*. [*funnel* in focus]
Having looked at all the funnels, she considered that the most handsome was *the funnel of the Orion*. [*the Orion* in focus]

This principle is congruent again with the preference for the *of*-construction with partitive and appositive meaning, where the genitive would result in undesirable or absurd final prominence:

**the problem's part*, **his resignation's shock*

The preference for placing complex constructions after the head accounts for the oddity of [1] (*cf* 5.123) in comparison with [1a]:

?She is *a man I met in the army's* daughter. [1]
She is the daughter *of a man I met in the army*. [1a]

And conversely, it accounts for the oddity of the *of*-construction with simple form, *eg* [2a], as compared to [2], which shows the normal preference for a possessive pronoun:

She is *his* daughter. [2]
?She is the daughter *of him*. [2a]

(On the 'post-genitive' in *a daughter of his*, *cf* 5.126.)

Note [**a**] The relevance of personal gender is shown also in the fact that indefinite pronouns with personal reference (*cf* 6.9), such as *someone* and *anybody*, admit the genitive inflection, while equivalent pronouns with nonpersonal reference do not: *someone's shadow*, but not **something's shadow*.

[**b**] Some idioms, in spite of end-focus, require a construction in which the personal pronoun is complement in a postmodifying *of*-phrase:

It will be the death *of me*.
the impudence *of him*
the cheek *of her* ['her rude behaviour'; BUT: 'I kissed her cheek.']
I don't like the taste/look/feel, etc *of it*.
For the life *of me*, I cannot remember her name, and yet my memory *of her* is still vivid.

The last example also illustrates the tendency (mentioned in 5.116 Note [a]) to use such a construction where the *of*-phrase has an objective meaning (compare: *my memory of her* 'I remember her').

The genitive in relation to noun classes

5.118 The noun classes (a–c) frequently take the genitive (*cf* 17.38*ff*):

(a) PERSONAL NAMES (*cf* 5.66):

Segovia's pupil, *George Washington's* statue

(b) PERSONAL NOUNS (*cf* 5.105):

the boy's new bicycle, *my sister-in-law's* problems

(c) ANIMAL NOUNS, in particular those denoting 'higher animals' (*cf* 5.109):

the horse's tail, *the dog's* collar

(d) COLLECTIVE NOUNS. The genitive is also used with collective nouns (*cf* 5.108) which emphasize the aspect of 'organized individuals', in particular those denoting authoritative and other organizational bodies, *eg*:

the government's economic plans *the nation's* resources
the committee's decision *the Company's* directors

The genitive is further used with certain kinds of inanimate nouns (e–h):

(e) GEOGRAPHICAL NAMES (*cf* 5.68), *eg*:
continents: *Europe's* future, *Australasia's* natural resources
countries: *China's* development, *the United States'* attitude
states: *Maryland's* Democratic Senator, *Rhode Island's* colonial period
cities and towns: *Hollywood's* studios, *London's* water supply
universities: *Harvard's* Department of Linguistics

(f) 'LOCATIVE NOUNS' denoting regions, institutions, heavenly bodies, etc. They can be very similar to geographical names, and are often written with initial capital letter, *eg*:

the earth's interior *the Church's* mission
the world's economy *the hotel's* entrance
the nation's waterways *a country's* population
the Club's pianist *the city's* atmosphere
the Gallery's rotunda *the school's* history

(g) TEMPORAL NOUNS, *eg*:

the decade's events *this year's* sales
a day's work *today's* paper
a moment's thought *the hockey season's* first event

(h) OTHER NOUNS 'OF SPECIAL RELEVANCE TO HUMAN ACTIVITY', *eg*:

the brain's total weight *the game's* history
the mind's development *science's* influence
the body's needs *love's* spirit
my life's aim *the play's* philosophy
in *freedom's* name *the book's* true importance
the treaty's ratification *the novel's* structure
duty's call *a word's* function
the poll's results *television's* future

Note [**a**] It seems that semantic relations other than possession (*cf* 5.117) place stronger restrictions on the 'personal' quality of the genitive noun than does possession itself. For example:

Table 5.118 Possessive and objective genitive with personal and nonpersonal nouns

	POSSESSIVE GENITIVE	OBJECTIVE GENITIVE
PERSONAL	*the man's* collar	*the man's* release from prison
NONPERSONAL	*the dog's* collar	?*the dog's* release from quarantine

In combination with the objective genitive, a nonpersonal noun results in a less acceptable noun phrase than does a personal noun.

[**b**] With temporal nouns in the plural, the apostrophe is sometimes omitted (*cf* 17.108):

several {*weeks'* / *weeks*} vacation

The genitive with superlatives and ordinals

5.119 The genitive is particularly common with locative nouns of Class (f) above when it is followed by a superlative adjective or a 'general ordinal' (*cf* 5.22) such as *only*, *first*, and *last*. The corresponding prepositional phrase in these cases is introduced by *in* rather than by *of*:

the world's best universities ~ the best universities *in the world*
this country's only university ~ the only university *in this country*
Africa's first arts festival ~ the first arts festival *in Africa*

More generally, the genitive combines with superlatives, ordinals, and 'general ordinals' to express a meaning which is independent of all the meanings listed in 5.116 above, and which can best be paraphrased by a relative clause:

Paganini's last performance
~ the last performance *that Paganini gave*
the Cabinet's greatest mistake
~ the greatest mistake *that the Cabinet made*

Noun heads with the genitive

5.120 So far, genitive constructions have been identified by reference to certain classes of the genitive noun (personal, collective, temporal, etc). There are, however, some constructions with the genitive which can best be described in terms of specific lexical noun heads.

Expressions with *edge*, *end*, *surface*, *for . . . sake* permit the alternative *of*-construction (*cf* 9.12 Note [c]):

She stood at {*the water's edge.* / *the edge of the water.*} He did it {*for charity's sake.* / *for the sake of charity.*}

Similarly: *at the river's edge, at his journey's end, for art's sake, the water's surface, for heaven's sake.*

The following expression does not permit the *of*-construction:

People don't get { *their money's worth.* / **the worth of their money.* }

Similarly: *at one's wits' end, at arm's length, within arm's reach.*

Note the stress typical of compounds (*cf* 17.104), which indicates that the following are compounds: *our* 'money's ˌworth, *a* 'stone's ˌthrow. Compare the relatively free syntactic constructions of, *eg*: *within/beyond/out of (her) reach.*

The grammatical status of the genitive

Genitive as determinative

5.121 Most commonly the genitive functions as a determinative (*cf* 5.10*ff*): it fills a slot in the noun phrase equivalent to a central determiner such as *the* [1]. This is so whether the genitive is a possessive pronoun (such as *her* [1a]), a single noun (such as *Jenny's* [1b]), or a noun accompanied by its own determiners and/or modifiers (such as *my daughter's* [1c]), as shown in *Fig* 5.121a:

DETERMINATIVE		HEAD	
the	(new)	desk	[1]
her	(new)	desk	[1a]
Jenny's	(new)	desk	[1b]
my daughter's	(new)	desk	[1c]

Fig 5.121a The genitive as determinative

It is obvious that in [1c], the genitive noun *daughter's* has its own determinative, *viz* the possessive pronoun *my*, which does not apply to *desk*, but to *daughter*. In other words, the genitive in this instance is not a single word, but a noun phrase in its own right. Such an analysis is even more compelling for phrases such as *many people's ambition*; *many*, requiring plural concord, must determine the plural noun *people*, rather than the singular noun *ambition*:

Many people's *ambition is* to own a house.

We therefore see the genitive construction as a noun phrase embedded as a definite determinative within another noun phrase (*cf* 2.8, 17.38 and *Fig* 5.121b):

SUPERORDINATE NOUN PHRASE		
GENITIVE NOUN PHRASE		
a horse's	hind leg	[2]
some people's	opinions	[3]
the older boys'	books	[4]
every teacher's	guide to child psychology	[5]
the Italian government's	recent decision	[6]

Fig 5.121b The structure of the superordinate noun phrase with a genitive noun phrase as determinative

That the genitive can be expanded into a phrase in this way is not surprising when we recall its equivalence to a prepositional phrase, in which *of* is followed by a noun phrase complement:

the hind leg *of* [*a horse*] [2a]
the opinions *of* [*some people*] [3a]
the recent decision *of* [*the Italian government*] [6a]

One implication of the determinative function of the genitive is that the genitive phrase is normally in initial position in the superordinate noun phrase, so that any words occurring in front of the genitive noun in the phrase belong to that noun rather than to the noun which is head of the superordinate noun phrase, as in [2–6].

One exception to this, however, arises when the genitive construction follows a predeterminer such as *all*, *both*, or *half* (*cf* 5.16). Since the genitive fills a position equivalent to that of a central determiner, these words preceding the genitive noun may apply either to that noun or to the superordinate head noun. In [7], the predeterminer *both* applies to *parents*, but in [8] *both* can only apply to *girls*':

both [the girl's] parents [= both parents of the girl] [7]
[both the girls'] success [= the success of both the girls] [8]

Note The construction with genitive or possessive pronoun with determinative function will have definite reference, *eg*:
(i) *Susan's* son (ii) *her* son
If we want the indefinite interpretation, we have to resort to the *of*-construction (*cf* 5.115):

(i) {a son *of Susan* / a son *of Susan's* (*cf* the 'post-genitive', 5.126)} (ii) a son *of hers*

Genitive as modifier

5.122 There are occasional examples where the genitive acts as a modifier rather than as a determinative. These are of the kind listed as 'descriptive genitive' in Class (e) of 5.116. They have a classifying role similar to that of noun modifiers and some adjective modifiers (*cf* 17.110):

There are several *women's universities* in Tokyo.
['several universities for women']
He wants to become a *ship's doctor* when he grows up.
['a doctor working on a ship']
There were ten {*farmer's* / *farmers'*} wives at the meeting.

Notice, in connection with the last example, that the expression *farmer's wives* does not imply polygamy: if this is a descriptive genitive, it is simply the plural of *farmer's wife*. The change to the plural genitive *farmers' wives* may, however, be preferred.

Another distinguishing mark of the descriptive genitive is the fact that any modifiers and/or determiners preceding it generally belong to the head noun, rather than to the genitive noun. The speaker who refers to *a quaint old shepherd's cottage* is passing a comment on the age and quaintness of the cottage, not of the shepherd. Nevertheless, there are cases where the modifying genitive itself contains a modifier:

How much do *those* [*farm workers'*] *cottages* cost?
It was meant to be a PhD thesis, but to me it read like *a* [*first-year undergraduate's*] *essay*.
This china used to be regarded as [*poor man's*] *Worcester porcelain*. ['the sort of porcelain which resembled Worcester, but which a poor man could afford']

Note [**a**] As the examples above suggest, the descriptive genitive tends to have an idiomatic connection with the head noun. The fullest stage of lexical assimilation to the head is observed in expressions where the genitive and the head form a compound (*cf* App I.57*ff*), as in *bull's-eye* and *cat's paw* (where the meaning is metaphorical). Between these and more freely constructed expressions such as *women's college* should be placed combinations where the two words are written separately, but where the stress is placed in the first (genitive) element, as in compounds:

'girl's ,school *'bird's ,nest* *'cow's ,milk* *'calves' ,liver*

Thus *bird's nest* resembles compounds both in meaning and in stress pattern (*cf*: *foxhole*, *rabbit warren*). In many cases the first noun ends with an *s*, which can be written in three ways:

a girl's school [genitive singular]
a girls' school [genitive plural]
a girls school [common case plural]

The second variant is favoured in *an all girls' school* ['a school entirely for girls'].

[**b**] Modifying genitives may occasionally contain their own determiners:

my this year's examination questions ['my examination questions for this year']

By this means, the strange cooccurrence of two central determiners *my this* may take place, as in the above example.

The group genitive

5.123 The modifying genitive, however, is rare in comparison with the genitive in determinative function; and since we observed in 5.121 that the genitive construction in this latter function can be a noun phrase, not merely a single noun, it is necessary to revise the idea (with which we introduced the genitive in 5.112) that the genitive is a noun inflection. The *-s* ending is not a case ending in the sense which applies to languages such as Latin, Russian, and German. It can be more appropriately described as an 'enclitic postposition': *ie*, its function is parallel to that of a preposition, except that it is placed after the noun phrase. This view is inescapable if we take into account the so-called GROUP GENITIVE (or 'embedded genitive'), in which the genitive ending is affixed to a postmodifier:

the teacher of music's room ['the room *of the teacher of music*']

Obviously the 'possessor' in this example is the teacher, not the music; but the *'s* cannot be added to the head, as one would expect if *'s* could only be a noun inflection. Instead, it is regularly added to a prepositional postmodification which is part of a name or a compound noun phrase:

[[*the University of Minnesota*]*'s*] President
[[*the Museum of Modern Art*]*'s*] Director
[[*my son-in-law*]*'s*] prospects

Since the group genitive fits most naturally into patterns of postmodification of the noun phrase, we defer further treatment of it until 17.119.

The independent genitive

5.124 The head of the superordinate noun phrase in a genitive construction may be omitted if the context makes its identity clear. The result is the so-called INDEPENDENT GENITIVE:

My car is faster than *John's*. [= John's car] [1]
Her memory is like *an elephant's*. [= an elephant's memory] [2]
This year's mixed doubles final was much better than *last year's*. [= last year's mixed doubles final] [3]
If you can't afford a sleeping bag, why not borrow *somebody else's*? [= somebody else's sleeping bag] [4]
Mary's was the prettiest dress. [= Mary's dress] [5]
Don't touch those cards – they're *my partner's*. [= my partner's cards] [6]

As the examples show, this genitive is frequently an elliptical variant of a noun phrase in which the genitive has its usual determinative function. But note that a possessive pronoun used in this genitive construction requires the independent form (*cf* 6.29):

Hers was the prettiest dress. [5a]

Strictly, the pronoun illustrates quasi-ellipsis rather than ellipsis (for this distinction *cf* 12.40).

Note With the *of*-construction in comparable environments, a demonstrative pronoun *that*/*those* is normally required (*cf* 12.19):

The population of New York is greater than {*that of Chicago.* / *Chicago's.*}

The 'local genitive'

5.125 The genitive is less clearly ellipted in expressions relating to premises or establishments (sometimes called the 'LOCAL GENITIVE'):

We'll meet *at Bill's*.

Here *at Bill's* normally means 'where Bill lives', but the hearer might not know whether the appropriate head would be *house*, *apartment*, *place*, etc. It is for this reason that the term 'ellipsis' is strictly not applicable (*cf* 12.32*ff*). The reference of a genitive proper noun could also be to a restaurant, a bar, etc, as in [1]:

Let's have dinner *at Tiffany's*. [1]

By contrast, where the genitive noun is a common noun, it would only refer to the dentist's professional establishment [2], and the same applies to proper nouns referring to commercial firms [3]:

I'm going to *the dentist's*. [2]
Wendy has just been shopping in *Harrod's*/*Foyle's*/*Macy's*. [3]

This usage is normal also in relation to 'one-person' businesses, as in [4]:

I buy my meat *at* (*Mr*) *Johnson's*. [4]

The 'local genitive' is used in the following three cases:

(i) For normal residences:

She is staying *at* { *my aunt's.* / *the Johnsons'*. [BUT: *with the Johnsons*] }

(ii) For institutions such as public buildings (where the genitive is usually a saint's name):

St Paul's (Cathedral), *St James's* (Palace), *Queen's* (College)

(iii) For places where business is conducted:

the barber's, the hairdresser's, the butcher's, the grocer's, W. H. Smith's, the chemist's ⟨BrE⟩, *the druggist's* ⟨AmE; usually *the drugstore*⟩

(On the 'sporadic' use of *the* here, *cf* 5.33.) The *'s* is often dropped:

at/to *the chemist* ⟨BrE⟩, *the druggist* ⟨AmE⟩, *the hairdresser, the greengrocer*

With large businesses, their complexity and in some sense plurality causes reinterpretation of the *-s* ending as a plural rather than genitive inflection (*Barclays, Harrods, Selfridges, Woolworths*). The genitive meaning – if it survives – is expressed by moving the apostrophe: *at Macys'*. This uncertainty over the status of the *-s* ending is matched by a vacillation in concord, reflecting the conflict between plurality and the idea of a business as a collective unity:

Harrods is/are very good for clothes.

In some cases, where the *-s* form cooccurs with the indefinite article, a genitive interpretation is unavoidable:

They have taken the rug to { *a cleaner's.* / *a cleaners'.* / **a cleaners.* }

Note In relation to commercial firms, all three forms (*Harrod's, Harrods, Harrod*) may be found and constructed as either singular or plural (plural is esp BrE, *cf* 10.36). Thus the following variants are used in the same document:

Liberty's are the wholesalers for this country.
Liberty's is probably best known for its beautiful printed silk.
This silk, for which *Liberty are* the wholesalers in this country, . . .

It can be noted, however, that the *Harrod's* form is more likely than the *Harrods* form to be followed by a singular verb. The *Harrod* form, which has become fashionable relatively recently and still strikes many people as odd or pretentious, tends to be used only for very large enterprises. With titles of firms involving multiple names, however, the forms without *-s* are more current, especially in AmE, *eg*: *Sears Roebuck*.

The 'post-genitive'

5.126 An *of*-construction can be combined with a genitive to produce a construction known as the POST-GENITIVE (or 'double genitive'). In this construction, the independent genitive acts as prepositional complement following *of*:

some friends *of Jim's* ['some of Jim's friends']

that irritating habit *of her father's*
an invention *of Gutenberg's*
several pupils *of his*

But the independent genitive is not in this case elliptical. Rather, the post-genitive contrasts in terms of indefiniteness or unfamiliarity with the normal determinative genitive. Whereas [1] and [2] presuppose definiteness, the presupposition in [1a] and [2a] is one of indefiniteness:

Jim's friend	[1]	*a friend of Jim's*	[1a]
Joseph Haydn's pupil	[2]	*a pupil of Joseph Haydn's*	[2a]

Like the group genitive, the post-genitive belongs more closely to the subject matter of Chapter 17 than to that of this chapter. We accordingly postpone further discussion until 17.46.

Bibliographical note

On noun classes, see Algeo (1973); Bolinger (1969); Quirk (1978); Seppänen (1974); Sloat (1969).

On reference and determiners, see Van der Auwera (1980); Behre (1967); Bolinger (1980b); Burton-Roberts (1976, 1977); Christophersen (1939); Hawkins (1978); Hewson (1972); Kałuża (1981); Kramsky (1972); Perlmutter (1970); Powell (1967); Robbins (1968); Rydén (1975); Sloat (1969); H. S. Sørensen (1959); K. Sørensen (1981).

On number, see Ball (1927/28); Hirtle (1982); Juul (1975); Seppänen (forthcoming a); Sussex (1979).

On gender, see Jacobsson (1968b); Kanekiyo (1965).

On case, see Altenberg (1982); Dahl (1971); Jahr Sørheim (1980); Svartengren (1949).

6 Pronouns and numerals

Pronouns

Introduction

6.1 Pronouns share several characteristics, most of which are absent from nouns. Their name implies that they 'replace' nouns, but we have already seen (2.44) that this is to a great extent a misnomer. It is best to see pronouns as comprising a varied class of closed-class words with nominal function. By 'nominal' here we mean 'noun-like' or, more frequently, 'like a noun phrase'. Semantically, a pronoun may be a 'pro-form' in any of the three senses illustrated in the following example:

Margot longed for a bicycle, and at last (C) *somebody* gave (B) *her* (A) *a brand new one*.

(A) It may substitute for some word or phrase (as *one* may substitute for a noun, and therefore be a 'pronoun' in a quite literal sense).
(B) It may signal, as personal pronouns like *her* do, that reference is being made to something which is given or known within the linguistic or situational context (*cf* 19.33*f*).
(C) It may stand for a very general concept, so that its reference includes the reference of untold more specific noun phrases: *somebody*, for example, indicates a broad class of people including *a girl*, *a man*, *a secretary*, etc.

All three pronouns in italics in the example have this in common: their meaning in itself is general and undetermined; their interpretation therefore depends to an unusual extent on what information is supplied by context.

Syntactically, most pronouns function like noun phrases rather than nouns (*cf* 5.1). They combine in only a limited way with determiners and modifiers. We can say, indeed, that most pronouns, being intrinsically either definite or indefinite, incorporate their own determiner (*cf* 5.10*ff*). Contrast:

{ *the men* / **the they* }   { *a tall man* / **a tall he* }

In addition, some pronouns have morphological characteristics that nouns do not have:

(a) CASE: There is a contrast between subjective and objective cases: *I/me*, *she/her*, *who/whom*, etc (*cf* 6.2*ff*).
(b) PERSON: There is a contrast between 1st, 2nd, and 3rd persons: *I/you/she*, etc (*cf* 6.6).
(c) GENDER: There are overt grammatical contrasts between (i) personal and nonpersonal gender; and between (ii) masculine and feminine gender: *he/she/it*, etc (*cf* 6.8*ff*).
(d) NUMBER: There are morphologically unrelated number forms, as in *I/we*, *he/they*, as opposed to the typical regular formation of noun plurals: *girl/girls*, etc (*cf* 6.11*f*).

These special distinctions associated with pronouns are found most notably in the class of PERSONAL PRONOUNS, which may be regarded, by reason of their frequency and their grammatical characteristics, as the most important and central class of pronouns. Accordingly, it is to personal pronouns above all that we turn in exemplifying these characteristics. In the following sections we examine the categories of case, person, gender, and number in more detail, before proceeding to a consideration of the various classes of pronouns.

Case

Case forms

6.2 Nouns and most pronouns in English have only two case forms: COMMON case (*children*, *someone*) and GENITIVE case (*children's*, *someone's*). However, the five personal pronouns *I*, *we*, *he*, *she*, *they* and the *wh*-pronoun *who* have a further distinction between SUBJECTIVE and OBJECTIVE cases.

Table 6.2 Personal pronouns with subjective, objective, and genitive case forms

<table>
<tr><td>SUBJECTIVE</td><td>I</td><td>we</td><td rowspan="2">you</td><td>he</td><td>she</td><td rowspan="2">it</td><td>they</td><td>who</td></tr>
<tr><td>OBJECTIVE</td><td>me</td><td>us</td><td>him</td><td>her</td><td>them</td><td>who(m)</td></tr>
<tr><td>GENITIVE
determinative
independent</td><td>my
mine</td><td>our
ours</td><td>your
yours</td><td>his</td><td>her
hers</td><td>its</td><td>their
theirs</td><td>whose</td></tr>
</table>

As *Table* 6.2 shows, there are additionally two genitive forms, a determinative and an independent form (*cf* 6.29), for five of the pronouns.

There is a merger (syncretism) of case forms in the following pronouns: the determinative genitive and objective forms of *she* are identical, and the subjective/objective distinction between *who* and *whom* is not always maintained (*cf* 6.35, 6.38). The personal pronouns *you* and *it* do not have distinct subjective and objective case forms (*cf* 6.14).

The genitive forms of the personal pronouns are, in accordance with grammatical tradition, called POSSESSIVE pronouns.

The use of case forms

6.3 The use of the possessive pronoun forms corresponds largely to that of the genitive of nouns (*cf* 5.112*ff*), except that the two different possessive forms, where they exist, function as determinative and independent genitives (*cf* 6.29). The latter are, in effect, 'true pronouns'.

The choice between subjective and objective cases is made on the basis of a pronoun's function in the clause. As their name implies, subjective personal pronouns function as subject and sometimes as subject complement; objective personal pronouns function as object, prepositional complement, and sometimes as subject complement.

Table 6.3 opposite shows that both subjective and objective case forms can be used as subject complement. Although the prescriptive grammar tradition stipulates the subjective case form, the objective form is normally felt to be the natural one, particularly in informal style. We shall now examine this overlapping use of case forms more carefully.

Table 6.3 Case functions of personal pronouns

FUNCTION	SUBJECTIVE CASE	OBJECTIVE CASE
subject	*He* was late.	
subject complement	It was *he*. ⟨formal⟩	It was *him*. ⟨informal⟩
object		I saw *him*.
prepositional complement		I gave it to *him*.

Subjective and objective cases

6.4 We have noticed in *Table* 6.3 a discrepancy between the use of case in formal and informal English. In the main, formal English follows the normative grammatical tradition which associates the subjective pronouns with the nominative case of pronouns in inflectional languages such as Latin, and the objective case with the oblique cases (especially accusative and dative cases) in such languages. Hence the subjective form appears not only in subject position, but in that of subject complement, and also in constructions where it can be postulated that the predicate has been ellipted, leaving a 'stranded' subject. This last, however, may have different realizations in the short response:

A: *Who* is there? B: { It's *I*/*me*. | (Only) *me*. | *Me* – John. } [1]

He is { more intelligent than | as intelligent as } *she* (is). [2]

But in response forms and comparative constructions, the subjective pronoun on its own, such as *she* in [2], sometimes gives a stilted impression, and it is preferable to add the operator after it: *she is*.

In contrast to the traditionally 'correct' use of the subjective form *It's I* in [1] and . . . *than*/*as she* in [2], informal usage favours the objective form:

A: Who's there? B: *Me*. [1a]

He is { more intelligent than | as intelligent as } *her*. [2a]

We may say that, in informal English, *as* and *than* count as prepositions (and are therefore followed by an objective pronoun as prepositional complement) instead of counting as subordinating conjunctions (*cf* 9.4, 14.12).

6.5 This purely structural explanation, however, is not the whole story. To account for the general pattern of pronoun usage in informal style, it is reasonable to say that the traditional case distinctions do not operate here any more than they do with the genitive (*cf* 5.112*ff*). Instead, there is a broad division of the finite clause into 'SUBJECT TERRITORY' (the preverbal subject position) and 'OBJECT TERRITORY' (which includes all noun-phrase positions apart from that immediately preceding the verb). In informal English, that is, the objective pronoun is the unmarked case form, used in the absence of positive reasons for using the subjective form. It is this which accounts for the use of *me, him, them,* etc in subject complement function in conversational contexts (*It's only me, That'll be them,* etc), and for the use of *me* informally in 'absolute' functions such as those of [1a] above. Pressing the point a little further, we may say that the same idea of 'object territory' explains an often condemned tendency for speakers to use the objective case even in the subject function where a pronoun is coordinated, and therefore is separated to some extent from the following verb, either by position or by failure of concord, as in the nonstandard:

{*Him and Mary* / *Mary and him*} are going abroad for a holiday. [3]

The nonstandard usage of [3] may become even more 'reprehensible', though not the less common, if the offending pronoun also violates the rule of politeness which stipulates that 1st person pronouns should occur at the end of the coordinate construction:

Me and Mary are going abroad for a holiday. [4]

The prescriptive bias in favour of subjective forms appears to account for their hypercorrect use in coordinate noun phrases in 'object territory': *between you and I, as for John and I,* etc. Another reason is that *x and I* is felt to be a polite sequence which can remain unchanged, particularly in view of the distance between the preposition and *I*. Compare also:

Let('s) *you and I* do it!
He says he saw *John and I* last night.

These are examples of a type which is not uncommon in informal conversation.

In cleft sentences there is often felt to be unclarity about the grammatical function of a pronoun acting as 'focus' (*cf* 18.25*ff*):

It was *she* who came. [5]

It was {?*she* / ?*her* ⟨informal⟩} (that) John criticized. [6]

It was *her that* came. ⟨informal⟩ [7]

It's not *me who*'s proud. ⟨informal⟩ [8]

The focal pronoun has a Janus-like status, being a subject complement with respect to the preceding verb *be,* and an element of variable function with respect to the following verb.

In [5], where *she* is a complement with respect to *was* and a subject with respect to *came,* there is no conflict in formal usage, since the subjective pronoun is favoured for both functions. But in [6] there is a conflict of functions, and neither pronoun form is felt to be completely satisfactory. Since *her* is the object of *criticize,* however, the objective form is superficially more acceptable, and is preferred in informal usage. In familiar usage, the objective form is often used even where the pronoun is a subject with respect to the following verb, as in [7] and [8].

After indefinite pronouns (*nobody*, *everyone*, *all*, etc) + *but* or *except*, usage is again divided between subjective and objective case forms (depending on whether *but* and *except* are considered conjunctions or prepositions):

nobody / everyone } { but / except } { *she* / *her*

There seems to be a tendency (at least among prescriptivists) to favour the subjective case after *but* in subject territory [9], and the objective case in object territory [10]; in [11], *I* would be considered a hypercorrect form:

Nobody but *she* can solve our problems. [9]
Nobody can solve our problems but *her*. [10]
Nobody said anything but *me*. [11]

To avoid the issue, the alternative construction with *myself* can be used (*cf* 6.27):

Nobody said anything but *myself*. [11a]

The objective form is the generally accepted form when the pronoun is in an object relation to the verb:

I want nobody but *him*. ['I want him and nobody else'] [12]

Note [**a**] See 10.44 Note [b] on the question of concord, as in:
{ It is *I who am* to blame.
{ It is *me who's* to blame. ⟨informal⟩

[**b**] The theory of 'subject territory' and 'object territory' can also be extended to deal with the peculiar distribution of *who* and *whom* (*cf* 6.35, 17.13*f*).

[**c**] In familiar speech, *us* may occur instead of *we* (*cf* 6.18) in expressions like:
Us girls can always take a joke.

Person

6.6 Personal, possessive, and reflexive pronouns have (unlike nouns) distinctions of person. The three persons may be defined as follows:

1ST PERSON PRONOUNS:
I, me, my, mine, myself
we, us, our, ours, ourselves

The reference of these pronouns includes the speaker(s)/writer(s) of the message.

2ND PERSON PRONOUNS:
you, your, yours, yourself, yourselves

The reference of these pronouns includes the addressee(s), but excludes the speaker(s)/writer(s).

3RD PERSON PRONOUNS:
he, him, his, himself
she, her, hers, herself
it, its, itself
they, them, their, theirs, themselves

The reference of these pronouns excludes both speaker(s)/writer(s) and addressee(s); *ie* 3rd person pronouns refer to 'third parties' not directly involved in the origination or reception of the utterance in which they occur.

All noun phrases (except those having 1st and 2nd person pronouns as heads) are 3rd person for purposes of concord:

> The man/*He* } has just arrived.
> The car/*It* }

To clarify the implications of person, we use the symbols *s*, *h*, and *o* (mnemonic aids: '*s*peaker', '*h*earer', '*o*ther') as follows:

- *s*: the originator(s) of the message, whether speaker or writer, and whether singular or plural
- *h*: the addressee(s) of the message, whether hearer or reader, and whether singular or plural
- *o*: any other referent(s) excluded from the definitions of *s* and *h*

Then the meanings of the three persons can be summarized as in *Fig* 6.6:

1st person	+*s*	±*h*	±*o*
2nd person	−*s*	+*h*	±*o*
3rd person	−*s*	−*h*	+*o*

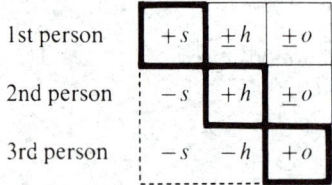

Fig 6.6 Meanings of 1st, 2nd, and 3rd person

The meanings of the singular pronouns are limited to the boxes with thick borders, while the meanings of the plural pronouns may include also the boxes with thin borders. These various possibilities are illustrated with reflexive pronouns in *Table* 6.6:

Table 6.6 1st, 2nd, and 3rd person pronouns

	s	*h*	*o*	PERSON	EXAMPLES WITH REFLEXIVE PRONOUNS
SINGULAR	+	−	−	1st	I gave *myself* up.
	−	+	−	2nd	You should be ashamed of *yourself*, Richard!
	−	−	+	3rd	Mary has hurt *herself*. / John has hurt *himself*. / The spider has hurt *itself*.
PLURAL	+	−	−	1st	We, the undersigned, pledge *ourselves* to . . .
	+	+	−	1st	We complimented *ourselves* too soon, John. ['inclusive *we*']
	+	−	+	1st	The children and I can look after *ourselves*. ['exclusive *we*']
	+	+	+	1st	You, Ann, and I are working *ourselves* to death.
	−	+	−	2nd	You ought to be ashamed of *yourselves*, children!
	−	+	+	2nd	You and John will have to cook for *yourselves*.
	−	−	+	3rd	They helped *themselves* to coffee and cakes.

6.7 The terms INCLUSIVE *we* and EXCLUSIVE *we* are sometimes used for 1st person plural pronouns which respectively include and exclude reference to the addressee. We should in addition distinguish a special type of exclusive *we* called COLLECTIVE *we* which indicates a plurality of speakers/writers, *eg* in petitions (*We, the undersigned, . . .*) or in prayers (*We thank Thee, O God, . . .*).

Unlike some languages, however, English does not make any formal distinction between 'inclusive' and 'exclusive' reference. The only circumstance in which inclusive *we* is grammatically distinct is in the 1st person imperative *Let's . . .* (*cf* 3.51 Note [b], 11.26). This contraction of *us* to *'s* (*cf* App II.9) is only possible where *us* has inclusive reference (*cf* 6.18). There is a corresponding question *shall we . . .?* in which *we* also has inclusive reference, and which may be added to the imperative as a tag question:

> *Let's* enjoy ourselves, shall *we*?

Gender

6.8 Gender distinctions are largely restricted to 3rd person singular pronouns of the categories of personal, possessive, and reflexive pronouns, as shown in *Table* 6.8:

Table 6.8 Gender distinctions in pronouns

<table>
<tr><td rowspan="2">PERSONAL GENDER</td><td>masculine</td><td>he</td><td>him</td><td>his</td><td>himself</td></tr>
<tr><td>feminine</td><td>she</td><td>her</td><td>her hers</td><td>herself</td></tr>
<tr><td colspan="2">NONPERSONAL GENDER</td><td colspan="2">it</td><td>its</td><td>itself</td></tr>
</table>

These gender distinctions are neutralized in the plural: *they*, *them*, etc. No pronouns other than those in *Table* 6.8 manifest a masculine/feminine contrast, but the personal/nonpersonal contrast is also found in relative pronouns (*who/whom* contrasted with *which*) and in indefinite pronouns (*somebody* contrasted with *something*, etc). The 1st and 2nd person pronouns are inevitably of personal rather than nonpersonal gender.

The choice between personal and nonpersonal gender is determined primarily by whether the reference is to a 'person', *ie* to a being felt to possess characteristics associated with a member of the human race. So defined, 'persons' are not only human beings, but may also include supernatural beings (the Deity, gods, angels, fairies, etc), and higher animals (*cf* 5.109). Exceptional uses such as *it* referring to babies and *she* referring to ships have already been noted (*cf* 5.107, 5.111 Note). The occurrence of *he* and *she* in cases of outright personification is common in informal use: *he* may refer to a computer; *she* (or, for some women, *he*) to a car. In poetry and fiction (especially children's fiction) there are virtually no limits to the kinds of object which can be personified in this way.

In the use of 3rd person singular pronouns, the absence of a pronoun of personal gender which is neutral between *he* and *she* influences the boundary between *he/she*, on the one hand, and *it* on the other. Just as a baby may be designated *it*, so a member of a nonhuman species may be designated *he* or *she* (*cf* 5.109*f*):

The robin builds *its* nest in a well-chosen position . . . and, after the eggs have hatched, the mother bird feeds *her* young there for several weeks.

As this example shows, the pronoun usage can vacillate within a single paragraph or even a single sentence.

Masculine and feminine gender

6.9 The choice between masculine and feminine pronouns is primarily based on the sex of the person (or animal) referred to:

Fred looked at *himself* in the mirror.
Freda looked at *herself* in the mirror.

Difficulties of usage arise, however, because English has no sex-neutral 3rd person singular pronoun. Consequently, the plural pronoun *they* is often used informally in defiance of strict number concord, in coreference with the indefinite pronouns *everyone, everybody*; *someone, somebody*; *anyone, anybody*; *no one, nobody* (*cf* 10.50):

Everyone thinks *they* have a right to be here. [1]
Has *anybody* brought *their* racket? [2]
No one should *pride themselves* on this result. [3]

The plural is a convenient means of avoiding the traditional use of *he* as the unmarked form when the sex is not determined (*cf*: *man*, 5.54 Note), as in the formal:

Everyone thinks *he* has a right to be here. ⟨formal⟩ [1a]

The use of the plural is also a means of avoiding the cumbersome device of coordinating masculine and feminine:

Has *anybody* brought *his or her* racket? [2a]

And the same choice may be made in referring back to a singular noun phrase with a personal noun of indeterminate gender as head:

Every student has to make up *his* own mind.
The applicant is required to sign *his* name clearly on page four of this form.

The dilemma of concord also arises with coordinate subjects and with subjects of common gender, but here resort to the evasive tactic of the plural pronoun, though common in everyday speech, is less acceptable:

Either *he or his wife* is going to have to change *their* attitude.
Not *every drug addict* can solve *their* problem so easily.

They is particularly difficult to avoid in cases like [4], and in tag questions [5] (*cf* 10.50 Note [a]):

Everybody came to the party, but *they*'ve left now. [4]
Someone died here yesterday, didn't *they*? [5]

Sexual bias in the use of pronouns

6.10 In recent decades, the use of *he*, *him*, etc as an 'unmarked' pronoun when the sex of the referent is undetermined has been opposed, particularly in the United States, by those campaigning against sexual bias in language. Some of the methods proposed for avoiding the unmarked masculine are illustrated in the following examples and suggested revisions (quoted from the *TESOL Quarterly* Style Sheet, Vol 13):

(a) The speaker must constantly monitor *his* listener to check that assumptions *he* is making are shared assumptions.
SUGGESTED REVISION (change to *the* and rephrase):
The speaker must constantly monitor *the* listener and check that the assumptions *the speaker is making are shared.*

(b) Very often the writer does not monitor *his* arguments very well or get *his* narrative in the right order.
SUGGESTED REVISION (change to plural):
Very often writers do not monitor *their* arguments very well or get *their* narratives in the right order.

(c) The students do almost all the interacting, the teacher taking a back seat. That is to say, *he* is not under the pressure of acting as *chairman or host.*
SUGGESTED REVISION (change to *s/he* and rephrase):
. . . That is to say, s/he is not under the pressure of acting as classroom director.

The last example illustrates the use of an invented sex-neutral pronoun *s/he*. It is uncertain how far such experimental forms as this will come into general use, especially when *s/he* is only a written form with no corresponding spoken form (unlike *Ms*; *cf* 5.66 Note [a]); and, still more seriously, there is no objective or possessive form. Generally, it is not certain how far the advocacy of nonsexist language will succeed in discouraging such usages as the unmarked masculine pronoun. What is clear is that the feminist movement in language has made many language users aware of problems of sexual bias which were overlooked by earlier generations.

Number

6.11 As already indicated (6.1 and 6.6), the personal, reflexive, and possessive pronouns have singular and plural forms which are morphologically unrelated. It is also worth noting that the plurals of the 1st and 2nd person have a more specific meaning than do those of nouns. Except when it refers to, for example, collective authorship (*cf* 6.18), *we* means 'I plus one or more other persons'; and, similarly, *you* with plural reference normally means 'you (singular) and one or more other persons, but not me'. But contrast of number is neutralized with *you*: in current standard English, only the reflexive forms *yourself* and *yourselves* preserve a distinction between singular and plural:

Harry, behave *yourself*!
Harry and Susan, behave *yourselves*!

(On archaic and nonstandard forms of the 2nd person singular and plural pronouns, *cf* 6.12 Notes [b] and [c].)

Reflexive pronouns in general show number contrast in the manner of nouns. The suffix *-self* in the singular changes, by the addition of a sibilant suffix, to *-selves* in the plural (*cf* such nouns in *-f* as *calf* ~ *calves*, 5.83):

singular	*myself*	*yourself*	*himself/herself/itself*
plural	*ourselves*	*yourselves*	*themselves*

Fig 6.11 Reflexive pronouns

There is also the rare (royal) singular form *ourself* (*cf* 6.18 Note [a]).

Pronouns belonging to other classes, such as interrogative, relative, and indefinite pronouns, do not in general have number contrast. Exceptions are the demonstratives *this/these* and *that/those*, and the indefinite pronoun *one* when used as a substitute. Other pronouns, like the corresponding determiners (*cf* 5.12), are invariable for number. The pronoun *both*, like the predeterminer *both*, has dual meaning, but is plural for purposes of concord.

6.12 There are formal grounds for saying that, just as the traditionally unmarked gender category is masculine, so the unmarked number category is singular. The compound indefinite pronouns *someone*, *everybody*, *nothing*, etc are singular, and have no plural counterparts (**someones*, **everybodies*, **nothings*); yet they themselves can refer to more than one entity, and be notionally plural:

A: Did you see *anyone* in the library?

B: { Yes, several people.
   { *No, several people.

Similarly, the substitute pronouns *any* and *none* are notionally often associated with plural number; but, according to prescriptive grammatical tradition, they are singular, and hence in formal English they are generally required to agree with a singular verb (*cf* 10.42).

The interrogative pronouns *who* and *what* are similar to *any* and *none* in that they are treated as singular for subject–verb concord, even though they may imply a plural answer:

A: *Who's* coming to the party? B: Most of our neighbours.
A: *What's* on the menu today? B: Lots of things.

Note [**a**] In the absence of a singular/plural distinction in the 2nd person pronoun, plural reference is sometimes indicated by lexical additions, *eg*: *you people*, *you boys*, and ⟨esp AmE⟩ *you guys*.

[**b**] The low-prestige plural form *youse* /juːz/ is current in Northern AmE and certain areas of Britain such as Liverpool and Glasgow. In Southern AmE, by contrast, the singular/plural distinction has been re-formed through suffixation of the originally plural form: *You-all* (*y'all* /jɔːl/) is widely used on all social levels in Southern AmE (always with a plural meaning by those to whom the form is native, although often misunderstood as a singular by outlanders). There is also a colloquial genitive *y'all's* /jɔːlz/, as in:

I really like *y'all's* new car. ['your family's new car']

[**c**] *You* in earlier English was a plural pronoun only, and was restricted to oblique cases. Although *you* has gained universal currency as a 2nd person pronoun which is neutral in case

and number, there is an archaic system of pronouns where other 2nd person pronouns survive in restricted situations, especially in religious language, as shown in *Table* 6.12:

Table 6.12 Archaic system of pronouns

	SUBJECTIVE	OBJECTIVE	REFLEXIVE	POSSESSIVE	
SINGULAR (*th*-forms)	*thou* /ðaʊ/	*thee* /ðiː/	*thyself*	*thy*	*thine*
PLURAL (*y*-forms)	*ye* /jiː/	*you*/(*ye*)	*yourselves*	*your*	*yours*

While we present this system of religious usage, it should be pointed out that there is a great deal of variation in current religious practice. There is a trend towards the adoption of present-day pronoun forms (*cf* verb forms, 3.4 Note [b]). For example, the traditional use of *th*-forms in Quaker usage seems to be no longer current. In some dialects of BrE, particularly in the north of England, forms deriving from the earlier singular *thou*/*thee* are still current also in nonreligious contexts.

Subclasses of pronouns

6.13 The class of pronouns includes a number of heterogeneous items, many of which, as we have already seen, do not share all of the above contrasts. For example, *somebody* (being 3rd person) has no corresponding 1st and 2nd person distinction, no subjective/objective contrast, and no masculine/feminine contrast. Yet it is included among our pronouns, as it incorporates its own determiner, is a closed-class item, and has the kind of generalized meaning we associate with pronouns. The point we want to make here is that the characteristics which single out the pronoun class from the noun class are not shared by all its members. *Figure* 6.13 shows the different subclasses of pronouns and gives references to sections where they are discussed:

- CENTRAL
  - personal: *I*/*me*, *we*/*us*, . . . — 6.15–22
  - reflexive: *myself*, *ourselves*, . . . — 6.23–28
  - possessive: *my*/*mine*, *our*/*ours*, . . . — 6.29–30
- RECIPROCAL: *each other*, *one another* — 6.31
- RELATIVE: the *wh*-series, *that* — 6.32–35
- INTERROGATIVE: the *wh*-series — 6.36–39
- DEMONSTRATIVE: *this*, *these*, *that*, *those* — 6.40–44
- INDEFINITE
  - positive
    - universal
      - *all* and *both* — 6.50
      - *each* and *every* — 6.51
    - assertive
      - the *some* series — 6.52
      - multal and paucal — 6.53
      - *one* — 6.54–56
      - *half*, *several*, *enough* — 6.57
      - *other* and *another* — 6.58
    - nonassertive: the *any* series and *either* — 6.59–61
  - negative: the *no* series and *neither* — 6.62

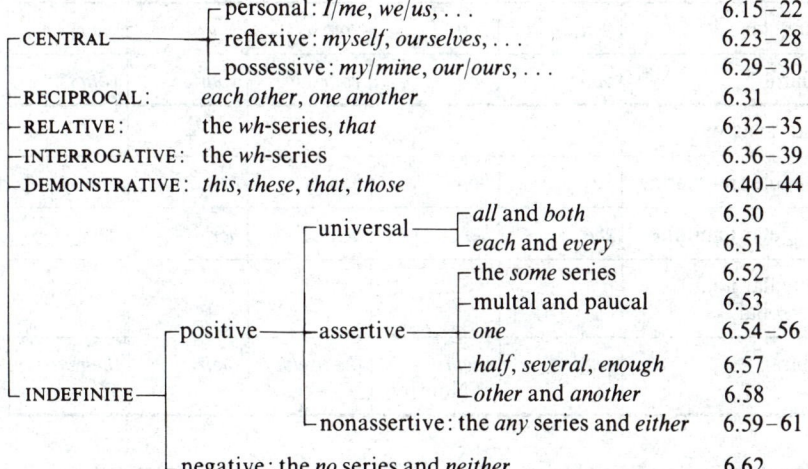

Fig 6.13 Pronoun subclasses

Personal, possessive, and reflexive pronouns may be called the CENTRAL PRONOUNS, since they share those features we have mentioned as being particularly characteristic of pronouns, *viz* contrast of person, gender, and subjective/objective case. Although these central pronouns fulfil different syntactic functions, they have obvious morphological resemblances. This is also the reason why the possessives *my*, *your*, etc have been grouped with central pronouns, although such possessives, being determinative in function, cannot function alone instead of nouns, but only together with nouns (*cf* 6.29).

Central pronouns

6.14 The central pronouns have in common the distinctions of person (1st, 2nd, and 3rd), gender (masculine, feminine, and nonpersonal), and number (singular and plural) that have already been discussed. In addition, most personal pronouns have distinctions of case. The various forms of the central pronouns are displayed in *Table* 6.14:

Table 6.14 Personal, reflexive, and possessive pronouns

	PERSONAL PRONOUNS		REFLEXIVE PRONOUNS	POSSESSIVE PRONOUNS	
	subjective case	objective case		determinative function	independent function
1ST PERSON					
singular	*I*	*me*	*myself*	*my*	*mine*
plural	*we* *cf* Note [a]	*us*	*ourselves*	*our*	*ours*
2ND PERSON *cf* Note [b]					
singular	*you*	*you*	*yourself*	*your*	*yours*
plural	*you*	*you*	*yourselves*	*your*	*yours*
3RD PERSON					
singular masculine	*he*	*him*	*himself*	*his*	*his*
singular feminine	*she*	*her*	*herself*	*her*	*hers*
singular non-personal	*it*	*it*	*itself*	*its*	
plural	*they*	*them* *cf* Note [c]	*themselves*	*their*	*theirs*

Note [a] On the 'editorial *we*' and other special uses of the 1st person plural pronoun, *cf* 6.18.

[b] Apart from *you*, there are the rare and/or restricted 2nd person pronouns *thou*, *you-all*, etc (*cf* 6.12 Notes [b] and [c]).

[c] *Them* is sometimes replaced by *'em* /əm/ in familiar use, as in *Kick 'em out!*

[d] *Us* is the only pronoun that has a contracted form (*'s*) in standard English (*cf* App II.9): *Let's go.*

Personal pronouns

With specific reference

6.15 The personal pronouns usually have definite meaning, and resemble the noun phrases introduced by the definite article in that they may have situational, anaphoric, or cataphoric reference (*cf* 5.28*ff*).

The 1st person and 2nd person pronouns, when they have specific reference, are used to refer to those directly involved in the discourse situation: *viz* the speaker(s)/writer(s) and the addressee(s) (*cf* 6.6).

The 3rd person pronouns may also be used situationally, to refer to some person(s) or thing(s) whose identity can be inferred from the extralinguistic context:

> Are *they* asleep? [spoken to his wife by a husband nodding his head towards the children's bedroom]
>
> Oh, how kind of you! May I open *it* now? [said by someone receiving a present from a guest]

Much more frequently, however, the identity of the referents of 3rd person pronouns is supplied by the linguistic context. As with the definite article, we distinguish between the ANAPHORIC and the CATAPHORIC uses of a 3rd person pronoun, according to whether the element with which it corefers (the ANTECEDENT) precedes or follows it (*cf* 5.30*ff*). The more common type of textual reference is anaphoric reference:

> We have *an excellent museum* here. Would you like to visit *it*? [= the museum] [1]
>
> *My brother* is afraid that *he* will fail the test. [2]
>
> *The young girl* stared at *Dan* and said nothing: *she* seemed offended by *his* manner, as if *he* had had the intention of hurting *her*. [3]
>
> *Dr Solway* took *the student's* blood pressure that day. *He* also examined *his* lungs and heart. [4]

It will be noticed that in [4] *he* and *Dr Solway* are coreferential, and *his* and *the student's* are coreferential. We recover the appropriate antecedent by means of the content of the sentence. For example, the second sentence of [4] can be changed so as to enforce a different interpretation of the pronouns:

> *Dr Solway* took *the student's* blood pressure that day. *He* had felt sick during the night and came for *his* help as soon as the clinic opened. [4a]

Now the content of the sentence suggests that *he* refers to *the student* and *his* to *Dr Solway*. If the use of the pronoun is felt to be ambiguous or confusing, the antecedent can be used again, or a lexical equivalent can be found:

> . . . *The student* had felt sick during the night, and came for {*Dr Solway's* / *the doctor's*} help as soon as the clinic opened. [4b]

'Referring *it*'

6.16 The neuter or nonpersonal pronoun *it* ('REFERRING *it*') is used to refer not only to inanimate objects as in example 6.15 [1] above, but also to noncount substances (such as *some soup* in [1] below), to singular abstractions (such as *the sack of Rome* in [2]), and even to singular collections of people, such as *Parliament* in [3]:

She made *some soup* and gave *it* to the children. [1]
The sack of Rome shook the whole of the Western World: in a sense, *it* was the end of the Roman Empire. [2]
Parliament's answer to all awkward problems is to establish a Royal Commission whose findings *it* can then ignore. [3]

In fact, in the personal/nonpersonal opposition, the nonpersonal gender is 'unmarked', in that for any antecedent for which *he* or *she* is inappropriate, *it* will be used instead. Hence, *it* can corefer to a whole clause or sentence, as in [4] and [5]:

A: Who said *that I was crazy*?
B: I said *it*. ['that you were crazy'] [4]
Rome was sacked by the Visigoths in 410 AD. It ['the sack of Rome'] was the end of civilization as the West had known it. [5]
Many students never improve. They get no advice and therefore keep repeating the same mistakes. It's a terrible shame. [6]

As is illustrated by [6], *it* can even corefer to a sequence of sentences.

It is the only personal pronoun which is almost always unstressed. *He* and *she*, for example, can be contrasted with one another by nuclear stress:

SHĚ earns more than HÈ does.

It, on the other hand, can only very rarely receive stress, for example when it is used as a citation form:

Is this word ÍT? [looking at a manuscript]

One reason why *it* is rarely stressed is that when a stressed nonpersonal pronoun is needed, *it* is supplanted by *this* or *that* (*cf* 6.40*ff*, 12.10*ff*). Thus [5a] is identical to [5], except that *this*, a stressed and slightly more emphatic proform, replaces *it*:

Rome was sacked by the Visigoths in 410 AD. ˈ*This* was the end of civilization as the West had known it. [5a]

Note There are several restricted usages with nuclear stress on *it*. For example:

Is that ÍT? ['Is that all you wanted me for?']

Also, with the sense of 'sex appeal', 'charisma', etc, *it* is stressed in:

She's got ÌT.

In children's games, stressed *it* is used to indicate whoever is next to play, in expressions like the following:

You're ÌT. She's ÌT.

'Prop *it*'

6.17 Since it is the most neutral and semantically unmarked of the personal pronouns, *it* is used as an 'empty' or 'prop' subject, especially in expressions denoting time, distance, or atmospheric conditions:

What time is *it*?	*It*'s half past five.
How far is *it* to York?	*It*'s a long way from here to Cairo.
It's warm today.	*It*'s been fine weather recently.
It's getting dark.	What day is *it* today?

This 'PROP *it*', if it has any meaning at all, refers quite generally to the time or place of the event or state in question (*cf* 10.26).

Even less meaning can be claimed for the *it* which occurs as an anticipatory subject in cleft sentences (*cf* 18.25*ff*) or in clauses with extraposition (*cf* 18.33*ff*), as in [1–3]:

Isn't *it* a shame *that they lost the game*? [1]
It must have been here *that I first met her*. [2]
I take *it* then *that you're resigning*. [3]

But here, too, it can be maintained that the pronoun is not quite void of meaning, since it arguably has cataphoric reference (forward coreference) to a clause (italicized in [1–3]) in the later part of the same sentence. One justification of this is the feeling of ellipsis in sentences such as [1a] and [2a], which are like [1] and [2] except that the antecedent of *it* has to be supplied from the linguistic context:

A: They lost the game.
B: Yes, so I hear. *Isn't it a shame?* [1a]
A: Where did you first meet her?
B: *It must have been here.* [2a]

In some cases, it is necessary to add words which do not precisely replicate those in the text, *eg*:

The bell rang, and I went to the door. *It* was Dr Long. [4]

To make full sense of sentences like [4], we have to supply, for example:

It was Dr Long (*who had rung the bell*).

Note **[a]** Perhaps the best case for a completely empty or 'nonreferring' *it* can be made with idioms in which *it* follows a verb and has vague implications of 'life in general', etc:

At last we've made *it*. ['achieved success']
have a hard time of *it* ['to find life difficult']
make a go of *it* ['to make a success of something']
stick *it* out ['to hold out, to persevere']
How's *it* going?
Go *it* alone.
You're in for *it*. ['You're going to be in trouble.']

[b] *It* can be used as a substitute for a predication, and especially for a characterizing complement (*cf* 10.20):

She was {*a rich woman* / *rich*} and she LÒOKED *it*. ['a rich woman', 'rich']
If there could ever be such a thing as a modest Roman, Augustus was not *ÌT*.
['not a modest Roman']

This last example is exceptional in that *it* is stressed (*cf* 6.16). Other uses of *it* as a substitute form are discussed in 12.13, 12.24*ff*.

Special uses of *we*

6.18 The 1st person plural pronoun has a number of special uses:

(a) One common use is the 'INCLUSIVE AUTHORIAL *we*' in serious writing, as in:

As *we* saw in Chapter 3, . . .

Here *we* seeks to involve the reader in a joint enterprise. Besides not having this 'intimate' appeal, *you* here would also be felt to be too informal or authoritative for discursive or scholarly writing. Compare also [1] with the more informal *let's* in [2]:

{ *We* now turn to a different problem. [1]
{ *Let's* turn now to a different problem. [2]

(b) The so-called 'EDITORIAL *we*' is still common enough in formal (especially scientific) writing by a single individual, and is prompted by a desire to avoid *I*, which may be felt to be somewhat egotistical. For instance, the writer of a scholarly article may prefer [3] to [4]:

{ As *we* showed a moment ago, . . . [3]
{ As *I* showed a moment ago, . . . [4]

('Editorial' here is not applied to the fully justified use of *we* with reference to the consensus of an editorial board or other collective body.)

(c) The 'RHETORICAL *we*' is used in the collective sense of 'the nation', 'the party', as in:

In the 19th century *we* neglected *our* poor as *we* amassed wealth. Today *we* are much more concerned with the welfare of the people as a whole.

This may be viewed as a special case of the generic use of *we* (*cf* 6.21).

(d) There is also a use of *we* in reference to the hearer (=*you*) which may occur for example when a doctor is talking to a patient:

How are *we* feeling today?

In the context, this use of *we* may be understood to be condescending, but it also has an implication of sharing the problem with 'you' in the situational context of a doctor/patient or teacher/student relation, for example. A teacher wishing to instruct without overtly claiming authority may use the 'inclusive' 1st person plural (*cf* 6.7):

Now then, let'*s* have a look at that project, shall *we*?

This can be an evasively polite equivalent of:

Now then, let *me* have a look at that project, will *you*?

(e) *We* may occasionally be used also in reference to a 3rd person (=*he, she*). For example one secretary might say to another with reference to their boss:

We're in a bad mood today.

Note [**a**] The virtually obsolete 'royal *we*' (=*I*) is traditionally used by a monarch, as in the following examples, both famous dicta by Queen Victoria:

We are not interested in the possibilities of defeat. *We* are not amused.

[**b**] In nonstandard use, plural *us* is commonly used for the singular *me*, as in:

Lend *us* a fiver.

[**c**] On the generic use of *we* and other personal pronouns, *cf* 6.21.

Anaphoric and cataphoric reference

6.19 Examples already given in 6.15–16 have illustrated the anaphoric use of personal pronouns. Cataphoric reference occurs less frequently, and under limited conditions. Where it does occur, anaphoric reference is also possible, so that we can equate two synonymous sentences such as [1] and [1a] in which the positions of pronoun and antecedent are reversed:

Before *he* joined the Navy, *Gerald* made peace with his family. [1]
= Before *Gerald* joined the Navy, *he* made peace with his family. [1a]

On the whole, cataphoric reference such as that in [1] is associated with formal written English. Also, it generally occurs only where the pronoun is at a lower level of structure than its antecedent (where 'level' is understood by reference to levels of branching on a tree diagram, as in 2.7 *ff*). Thus, in [2] and [3] the pronoun is a constituent in a relative clause:

Those who most deserve *it* rarely seem *to suffer defeat.* [2]
Melville well knew that to the men who sailed in *her, a whaler* was anything but a pleasure boat. [3]

And in [4], the cataphoric pronoun appears as part of the complement of an initial prepositional phrase:

On *his* arrival in the capital, *the Secretary of State* declared support for the government. [4]

When this condition of subordination is not fulfilled, there is no equivalent of the kind illustrated in [1] and [1a]:

Jacqueline thinks *she* understands me. [5]
≠ *She* thinks *Jacqueline* understands me. [5a]

While *she* can easily corefer to *Jacqueline* in [5], such coreference is impossible in [5a], so that here *she* and *Jacqueline* must be understood to refer to two different people.

The conditions under which a pronoun can have coreference to another constituent can be summarized as follows. The constituent to which coreference is made must have precedence over the pronoun in one of two senses:

(i) It must precede the pronoun, or

(ii) it must have a higher position in the constituent structure (*cf* 2.7) of the sentence than the pronoun.

With cataphoric pronouns, the first condition fails, and so the second condition must obtain.

Note [**a**] The above summary is not without exceptions. In journalistic writing, in particular, there is occasional use of cataphoric pronouns which appear in noninferior positions:

Failure of *his* latest attempt on the world record has caused heavy financial loss to the backers of daredevil balloonist *Felix Champ*.

[**b**] Personal pronouns cannot make cataphoric reference to part or all of a subsequent sentence, except for debatable cases such as:

It should never have happened. *She went out and left the baby unattended.*

Here, it appears that *it* refers to the whole content of the succeeding sentence. But perhaps this is not true cataphoric reference, but a special rhetorical device, found in popular narrative, whereby the writer assumes the reader is already 'in the know' at the beginning of the story.

Modification and determination of personal pronouns

6.20 Another use of pronouns which may be called cataphoric is illustrated in:

He who hesitates is lost. ['The person who . . .'; a proverb]
She who must be obeyed. ['The woman who . . .']

Here *he* and *she* are cataphoric in that their meaning is defined by the following postmodifier, which is a restrictive relative clause (*cf* 17.13). Their function is hence parallel to that of the cataphoric definite article (*cf* 5.32). *He* or *she* followed by a relative clause belongs to a literary and somewhat archaic style. Present-day English prefers the use of the plural demonstrative in such contexts (*cf* 12.19). *They* cannot be used:

{*Those* / **They*} *who* work hard deserve some reward.

There is no similar use of cataphoric *it* for nonpersonal reference; a nominal relative clause (*cf* 15.8*f*) is used instead:

{*What* / **It that*} stands over there is a church.

In modern English, restrictive modification with personal pronouns is extremely limited. There are, however, a few types of nonrestrictive modifiers and determiners which can precede or follow a personal pronoun. These mostly accompany a 1st or 2nd person pronoun, and tend to have an emotive or rhetorical flavour:

(a) Adjectives:

Silly me!, Good old you!, Poor us! <informal>

(b) Apposition:

we doctors, you people, us foreigners <familiar>

(c) Relative clauses:

we who have pledged allegiance to the flag, . . . <formal>
you, to whom I owe all my happiness, . . . <formal>

(d) Adverbs:

you there, we here

(e) Prepositional phrases:

we of the modern age
us over here ⟨familiar⟩
you in the raincoat ⟨impolite⟩

(f) Emphatic reflexive pronouns (*cf* 6.28):

you yourself, we ourselves, he himself

Personal pronouns do not occur with determiners (**the she*, **both they*), but the universal pronouns *all*, *both*, or *each* may occur after the pronoun head (*cf* 5.16, 6.50):

We all have our loyalties.
They each took a candle.
You both need help.

Note [**a**] The *he who* . . . and *she who* . . . constructions can in principle be varied by the substitution of other forms of personal and relative pronouns. But such variations strike the modern reader as decidedly unidiomatic:

?I dedicate this work *to him to whom it owes its conception*.

[**b**] Informally, *he* and *she* are converted to nouns when *he* = *male* and *she* = *female*. This accounts for the cooccurrence of the article with *he* and *she* in:

What a darling puppy! Is it *a he* or *a she*?

Generic uses of personal pronouns

6.21 Apart from the stylistically limited construction *he/she who* . . . in 6.20, a number of generic uses of personal pronouns need to be discussed and illustrated.

First, 3rd person pronouns can be used in anaphoric and cataphoric reference to generic noun phrases, in the normal way. The following example shows the generic use of *he* in coreference with a singular generic noun phrase (*cf* 5.54 Note, 6.9*f*):

Ever since *he* found a need to communicate, *man* has been the 'speaking animal'.

It is the pronoun which is used if we want to corefer to a singular generic noun phrase with zero article, whereas *they* is used if the zero article accompanies a plural:

A: Do you like *caviar*? B: I've never tasted *it*.
Music is my favourite subject. Is *it* yours?
Truffles are delicious, but *they*'re very expensive.

Second, apart from the special generic pronoun *one* (*cf* 6.56), plural pronouns of all persons can function generically with reference to 'people in general':

Science tells *us* that the earth goes round the sun. [1]
We live in an age of immense changes. [2]
You can never tell what will happen. [3]

These days *you* have to be careful with *your* money. [4]
They say it's going to snow today. [5]

Although used generically, these personal pronouns *we*, *you*, and *they* retain something of the specific meaning associated with the 1st, 2nd, and 3rd persons respectively. They are therefore not wholly interchangeable. Potentially, *we* and *us* in [1] and [2] have the widest meaning, because they may include reference to speaker, addressee, and 'third parties' (*cf* 6.6). The reference of 'inclusive *we*' can be progressively enlarged (as already illustrated by the 'rhetorical *we*' discussed in 6.18(c)) from those involved in the immediate speech situation to the whole human race. In this fully generic sense, a sentence with *we* as subject can be replaced by a passive sentence with unspecified agent (*cf* 3.71):

{ *We* now know that the earth is round.
{ = It is now known that the earth is round.

Generic *you*, on the other hand, is typically an informal equivalent of *one*:

{*You* / *One*} can always tell what she's thinking.

But *you* again retains something of its 2nd person meaning: it can suggest that the speaker is appealing to the hearer's experience of life in general, or else of some specific situation, as in:

This wine makes *you* feel drowsy, doesn't it?

Sometimes, the reference is to the speaker's rather than the hearer's life or experiences:

It wasn't a bad life. *You* got up at seven, had breakfast, went for a walk . . .

Like generic *you*, generic *they* is informal, and retains something of its specific quality as a personal pronoun. Being a 3rd person pronoun, it excludes reference to the speaker and the addressee. Consequently, it tends to designate, in a sometimes disparaging way, the mysterious forces which appear to control the ordinary citizen's life: 'the authorities', 'the media', 'the government', etc:

I see *they*'re raising the bus fares again. Whatever will *they* be doing next?
They don't make decent furniture nowadays.
(*cf*: *You* can't get decent furniture nowadays.)

Note The ordinary citizen's awareness of this use of *they/them* as a denial of personal responsibility can be seen in expressions like:
The members took up a *them* and *us* attitude to the Union.

Pronouns with coordinated antecedents

6.22 When a pronoun has as its antecedent two or more noun phrases coordinated by *and*, the pronoun itself must be plural, even if each of the noun phrases is singular:

John and Mary stole a toy from my son. *Their* mother told *them* to return *it* to *him*, but *they* said it was *theirs*.

The conditions of concord here, in fact, are the same as those which govern subject–verb concord (*cf* 10.34*ff*).

If the antecedent phrases governed by *and* contain noun phrases or pronouns of different persons, the choice of pronoun is determined by the criteria discussed in 6.6*f*. This means that there is an order of precedence whereby the 1st person outweighs the 2nd person, which in turn outweighs the 3rd person:

PERSONS IN ANTECEDENT		PERSON OF PRONOUN
1 + 2	----------→	1
1 + 3	----------→	1
2 + 3	----------→	2
1 + 2 + 3	----------→	1

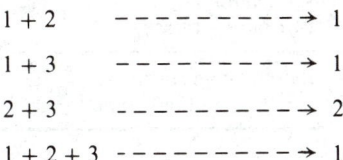

Fig 6.22 Pronouns with coordinated antecedents

Examples:

We have a lot to talk about, *you and I*. [2 + 1 → 1]
Freda and I have finished *our* work. Can *we* start lunch now? [3 + 1 → 1]
You and John can stop *your* work now, if *you* like. *You* can both eat *your* lunch in the kitchen. [2 + 3 → 2]

The same order of precedence applies where three or more noun phrases are combined in the antecedent:

If *you, Mary, and I* have already finished, *we* can have lunch. [2 + 3 + 1 → 1]
You, Mary, and John will meet at the station. *You* can then go together to the party. [2 + 3 + 3 → 2]

Note [**a**] A somewhat different situation arises when the antecedent noun phrases do not include the person appearing in the pronoun:

If *you and John* have already finished, *we* can have lunch. [1]
Mary and John will be at the station. *You* can then go together to the party. [2]

In spite of appearances, the italicized phrases and pronouns in these examples can be understood to be partly coreferential. But this interpretation requires the implication of a third omitted conjoin; *eg*: *we* in [1] is understood to mean 'you, John, and I'.

[**b**] In addition to a coordinated antecedent, the 3rd person plural pronoun may also have multiple antecedents, such as *She* and *an Indian* in:

She married *an Indian*, and *they* went to live in Delhi.

Reflexive pronouns

6.23 Reflexive pronouns end with *-self* (singular) and *-selves* (plural). These suffixes are added to the determinative possessive forms for the 1st and 2nd person (a), and to the objective form for the 3rd person (b) (*cf Table* 6.14):

(a) *myself* *yourself* *ourselves* *yourselves*
(b) *himself* *herself* *itself* *themselves*

There is also an indefinite generic reflexive pronoun *oneself* (*cf* 6.56), and a very rare 'royal *we*' singular reflexive pronoun *ourself* (*cf* 6.18 Note [a]).

As the name implies, reflexive pronouns 'reflect' another nominal element of the clause or sentence, usually the subject, with which it is in a coreferential relation:

Table 6.23 Functions of reflexive pronouns

ANTECEDENT	REFLEXIVE PRONOUN	EXAMPLE	
subject	direct object	*They* helped *themselves.*	[1]
subject	indirect object	*She* allowed *herself* a rest.	[2]
subject	subject complement	*He* is not *himself* today.	[3]
subject	prep. complement	*The café* pays for *itself.*	[4]
subject	appositional phrase	{ *We* couldn't come *ourselves.*	[5]
		{ *We ourselves* couldn't come.	[5a]

The reflexive pronoun has two distinct uses: basic and emphatic. The basic use is illustrated by [1–4] above: here, the reflexive pronoun functions as object or complement and has the subject of its clause as its antecedent. In the emphatic use, illustrated by [5] and [5a], the pronoun is in an appositional relation to its antecedent.

Note [**a**] As subject complement (but not normally as object) the reflexive pronoun receives nuclear stress:

He is not himsÈLF. ['He does not feel well.']

There is consequently an ambiguity only in writing between the object and complement interpretations when a reflexive pronoun comes after the verb:

He FÈLT himself. [S V C] He felt himsÈLF. [S V C_s]

[**b**] Very occasionally a reflexive pronoun precedes the subject with which it has coreference (*cf* fronting, 18.20*ff*):

For *yourselves you* have done a great deal, but for others nothing.

It was understood that getting *herself* married to an aristocrat was *Henrietta's* first duty to her family.

In emphatic use (*cf* 6.28), front position of *myself* is common:

Myself, I feel quite happy about the plan.

Basic use

6.24 The basic reflexive pronoun takes the function of a noun phrase in the structure of the clause or phrase: it may be an object, a complement, or a prepositional complement. Since it corefers to the subject, however, the reflexive pronoun cannot itself be a subject. In this, it shows that it belongs to 'object territory' (*cf* 6.5), and has affinities with the objective personal pronoun. But it contrasts with the objective pronoun in meaning in examples such as this:

He saw {*himself* / *him*} in the mirror. [1]

In [1], *himself* is necessarily coreferential to the subject *he*, while *him* necessarily refers to some other person. We have to use the reflexive rather than the ordinary objective pronoun. The reflexive pronoun must agree with the subject in terms of gender, number, and person:

She saw { *herself* / **himself* } in the mirror.

For an object, complement, or prepositional object which is coreferential with the subject, the reflexive pronoun is obligatory.

The basic reflexive pronoun always corefers to the subject of its own clause, even though that subject may be 'understood'. For example, the implied subject of the *-ing* participle clause in [2] is *Vincent*, and *himself* is therefore the appropriate reflexive pronoun:

Freeing *himself* with a sharp knife, *Vincent* lurched towards the door. [2]

In [3], it is *John* who is understood to be the subject of the infinitive clause, and the appropriate reflexive is therefore *himself*, even though the subject of the main clause is *she*:

She asked *John* to invite { *himself.* / **herself.* } [3]

Similarly, as the implied subject of a normal 2nd person imperative is *you* (*cf* 11.25), it would be ungrammatical for such an imperative clause to contain as its object any other reflexive than a 2nd person pronoun:

Help { *yourselves*! / **ourselves*! / **themselves*! }

Note [**a**] In a noun phrase which is a nominalization of a clause (*cf* 17.51), the antecedent of the reflexive will be an embedded noun phrase which functions as 'subject' of the nominalization:

{ *Philip's* boundless admiration of *himself* / *Your* confidence in *yourself* } is well known.

As in these examples, the antecedent is normally a subjective genitive (*cf* 5.116).

[**b**] When a nonfinite clause or a nominalization has an implied human subject of the most indefinite kind ('someone or other'), the reflexive *oneself* (or its informal equivalent *yourself*) may be used:

Voting for { *oneself* / *yourself* } is unethical.

Pride in { *oneself* / *yourself* } was considered a deadly sin.

[**c**] In informal AmE we can find uses of a personal instead of a reflexive pronoun as indirect object which is coreferential with the subject, *eg*:

He got *him* ['himself'] a new car. We're going to elect *us* a new president next year.

Obligatory reflexive pronoun as object

6.25 We may distinguish the following types of construction in which the reflexive pronoun, when coreferential with the subject, is always used in preference to the objective case pronoun:

(a) With REFLEXIVE VERBS, *ie* verbs which always require a reflexive object, such as *pride oneself on*:

She always { *prides herself* / **prides* } on her academic background.

Examples of other reflexive verbs:

absent oneself (*from*) *avail oneself* (*of*)
demean oneself ⟨formal⟩ *ingratiate oneself* (*with*)
perjure oneself

(b) With SEMI-REFLEXIVE VERBS, *ie* verbs where the reflexive pronoun may be omitted with little or no change of meaning, such as *behave* (*oneself*), *shave* (*oneself*):

{*Behave yourself* / *Behave*} now!

He has to {*shave himself* / *shave*} twice a day.

Other semi-reflexive verbs are:

adjust (*oneself*) *to* *dress* (*oneself*)
hide (*oneself*) *identify* (*oneself*) *with*
prepare (*oneself*) *for* *prove* (*oneself*) (*to be*)
wash (*oneself*) *worry* (*oneself*)

(c) With NONREFLEXIVE VERBS, *ie* verbs which are transitive, but are not particularly associated with the reflexive pronoun. Compare [1] and [1a]:

Williams publicly blamed *himself* for the accident. [1]
Nobody *blamed* him for the accident. [1a]

Other such nonreflexive verbs are, for example:

accuse, admire, amuse, dislike, feed, get, hurt, persuade

It is with reflexive verbs (type a) and nonreflexive verbs (type c) that the choice between reflexive and objective pronoun, as in 6.24 [1] may be made. Compare also *dress* (semi-reflexive verb) in [2] with *get up* (nonreflexive verb) in [3] (*herself* = the mother, *her* = Jane):

Jane's mother dresses {*her* / (*herself*)} before 8 a.m. [2]

Jane's mother gets {*her* / (*herself*)} up before 8 a.m. [3]

Note [**a**] Many verbs can have different constructions, *eg*: *enjoy*:

I enjoyed {*myself*. ['had a good time'] / *the party*. ['took pleasure in'] / *the guests*. ['liked'] ⟨esp AmE⟩}

In AmE this verb is also used intransitively as an imperative: *Enjoy!*, equivalent to 'Bon appétit'.

[**b**] *Feel* is semi-reflexive in a complex-transitive construction [4], but nonreflexive in copular use [5]:

She always *felt* (*herself*) {a stranger in their house. / wounded by his remarks.} [4]
She *felt* cold. [5]

[**c**] In complex-transitive complementation (*cf* 16.46*ff*), the coreferential item is the noun phrase that is object of the finite verb clause and subject of the nonfinite verb clause:

The hosts really want *us* to enjoy *ourselves*.
Nobody insisted on *your* sacrificing *yourself*.

Obligatory reflexive pronoun after a preposition

6.26 The following types of construction require a reflexive pronoun after the preposition, if the subject is the intended antecedent:

(a) With prepositional objects, *ie* prepositional complements which have a close connection with the preceding verb (*cf* 16.5):

Mary stood *looking at herself* in the mirror.
Do *look after yourselves*!
We did not know what to *do with ourselves*.
He *thinks* too much *of himself*.
They *take* too much *upon themselves*.

(b) With prepositional phrases following a noun which refers to a work of art, a story, etc:

Every writer's first novel is basically *a story about himself*.
Rembrandt painted *many remarkable portraits of himself*.
Do you have *a recent photograph of yourself*?

Optional reflexive pronoun

6.27 The basic reflexive pronoun is sometimes optional, in the sense that it may acceptably be replaced by the more usual ordinary objective pronoun. The *self*-forms are chosen to supply special emphasis:

(a) In some spatial prepositional phrases:

She's building a wall of Russian BÒOKS *about her(self)*.
Holding her new yellow bathrobe *around her(self)* with both arms, she walked up to him.
Mason stepped back, gently closed the door *behind him(self)*, and walked down the corridor.
They left the apartment, pulling the spring lock shut *behind them(selves)*.

(b) In 'semi-emphatic' use. Here the reflexive pronoun normally receives nuclear stress. It does not have the subject as its antecedent, but is commonly used as a more emphatic equivalent of the 1st and 2nd person personal pronouns. Especially, however, when it replaces *I* and *me*, *myself* is felt by many to be a hyperurbanism, a genteel evasion of the normal personal pronoun. The reflexive pronoun in these contexts can be reasonably called 'semi-emphatic' because it can be regarded as an abbreviated version of a sequence of the personal pronoun followed by the emphatic reflexive pronoun (*you yourself*, *him himself*, etc). Thus there are three possibilities in:

Anyone but { *YÓU* / *yourSÉLF* / *you yourSÉLF* } would have noticed the change.

The latter repetition of the pronoun (*you yourself*) is avoided, however, outside the subject position (*cf* 6.4*f*).

The constructions in which the 'semi-emphatic' reflexive occurs are the following:

(i) After the prepositions *like*, *than*, (*as* . . .) *as*, *but* (*for*), *except* (*for*), and *as for* (*cf* 9.7*ff*):

For someone *like me/myself*, this is a big surprise.
Except for us/ourselves, the whole village was asleep.
According to the manager, no one works *as* hard *as him(self)*.
Sandra's sister is even taller *than her(self)*.
No composer enjoyed a better family background than Mozart. *Like him(self)*, both his father and sister were remarkable musicians.
Guerrero's friends made their peace with the gang. *As for him(self)*, there was little he could do but await the inevitable bullet in his back.

(ii) When a reflexive pronoun (particularly a 1st person pronoun) is coordinated with another phrase:

They have never invited *Margaret and me/myself* to dinner.
This is a great tribute *to the Scout Movement, and to you/yourself* as its leader.

In this construction, the reflexive pronoun is not limited to 'object territory' (*cf* 6.5); it can replace a subjective pronoun:

My sister and I/myself went sailing yesterday.

Note [**a**] Unlike the prepositional phrases of (a) above, many prepositional phrases expressing a spatial (or temporal) relationship require the objective personal pronoun rather than the reflexive pronoun, in spite of coreference with the subject:

He looked *about him*.
She liked having her grandchildren *around her*.
Have you any money *on you*?
She had her fiancé *beside her*.
She pushed the cart *in front of her*.
They carried some food *with them*.
We have the whole day *before us*.

A possible explanation of this (historically older) use of the personal pronoun instead of the compound form in *-self* is that the personal pronoun is not normally in semantic contrast with any other pronoun, and therefore needs no emphasis:

*Have you any money *on me*?

The objective form is normally unstressed, so that the stress is thrown onto the preposition. In some cases the pronoun may in fact be omitted altogether:

Pat felt a sinking sensation *inside* (*her*).

The reflexive pronoun, on the other hand, will usually (except in the case of inherently reflexive verbs like *pride oneself*; *cf* 6.25(a)) imply a contrast between coreference to the subject and reference to something else.

[**b**] In the following metaphorical use of the preposition, the reflexive pronoun is required:

She was *beside* { *herself* / **her* } with rage.

(*cf*: 'She placed the attaché case *beside her*'.)

[**c**] For phonological reasons, sequences like *her herself* would be avoided by many speakers. Compare restrictions on verb sequences such as *be being* (3.73).

[**d**] In some dialects of English, especially Irish English, reflexive pronouns are common in expressions like:

Is *herself* in? ['Is the lady of the house in?']

Also in more general use we find, *eg*:

I went to see Mary and John but there was only *himself* at home.
She was, he knew, a very good secretary and always loyal to *himself*.

Emphatic use

6.28 Reflexive pronouns in emphatic use occur in apposition and have heavy (nuclear) stress. Unlike basic reflexive pronouns, they may have positional mobility:

{ *I mySE̊LF* wouldn't take any NÒTice.
I wouldn't take any NÒTice *mySÉLF*.
MySE̊LF, I wouldn't take any NÒTice of her.

Here the meaning of the pronoun is 'speaking personally'. In other contexts, the pronoun has a meaning better captured by the paraphrase 'X and nobody else':

Do you mean that you spoke to *the Pope himSÉLF*?
A: Who told you that Jill was leaving? B: *She herSÈLF* told me.

Sometimes there is an explicit contrast between the referent and some other thing or person:

I'd prefer *you* to do the job *yourSÈLF*, rather than to leave it to Tony.

On the positioning of the emphatic reflexive pronoun, *cf* 18.39*f*.

Note [**a**] Emphatic reflexives with cataphoric reference are generally literary in tone:
Himself a fervent believer, Newman was nonetheless able to sympathize with those who . . .
[**b**] Emphatic reflexives sometimes occur sentence-initially in rather mannered or literary uses:
Myself is thus and so, and will continue thus and so. (Bellow)
Oneself did not die; that, like the very quiddity of otherness, was for others. (Burgess)

Possessive pronouns

Determinative and independent possessives

6.29 Possessive pronouns consist traditionally of two series: the first, 'weak' set of possessive pronouns has a determinative function (*cf* 5.12*ff*), while the second, 'strong' set has an independent function as a noun phrase (*cf* 5.124):

DETERMINATIVE:	*my*	*our*	*your*	*his*	*her*	*its*	*their*
INDEPENDENT:	*mine*	*ours*	*yours*	*his*	*hers*	(*its*)	*theirs*

As the genitive forms of personal pronouns (*cf* 6.2), the possessive pronouns behave very much like the corresponding genitive noun constructions, and they have already been illustrated in that connection (*cf* 5.117*ff*).

But whereas the genitive noun does not change its form in moving from determinative to independent function, five of the possessive pronouns change by the addition of a consonant (either /n/ or /z/) to the determinative form:

my /maɪ/ → *mine* /maɪn/
your /jɔːʳ/ → *yours* /jɔːʳz/, *our* → *ours*, *her* → *hers*, *their* → *theirs*

His already ends in /z/ and therefore does not add a further sibilant; compare [1] and [1a]:

This is *MY̌* bike and that is *HÌS* bike. [1]
This bike is *MǏNE* and that is *HÌS*. [1a]

Its is extremely rare in independent function (but *cf* Note [a]):

*The collar is *its*.

One reason for this gap is that the pronoun *it* is very rarely stressed (*cf* 6.16), and this conflicts with the phonological status of the independent possessive, which is always stressed. Another and related reason seems to be that there is rarely semantic motivation for an independent nonpersonal possessive pronoun.

Parallel to the independent genitive, the independent possessive can occur as any of the following nominal elements: subject, object, complement, or prepositional complement. But it is particularly common in complement function. Compare:

DETERMINATIVE	INDEPENDENT
{*Mary's* / *my daughter's* / *her*} book	The book is {*Mary's.* / *my daughter's.* / *hers.*}

The independent possessive in other functions generally has a quasi-elliptical role, replacing a noun phrase with a determinative possessive:

If you need a bicycle, I'll lend you {*mine.* / *my bicycle.*}

It also occurs regularly as prepositional complement in the 'post-genitive' construction described in 5.126:

I have been talking to *a friend of yours*. ['one of your friends']
A: Do you know Wagner's operas?
B: No, the only *opera of his* I've seen is 'Lohengrin'.

Note [**a**] Independent *its* may occasionally be found in parallel constructions, such as:
History has *ÌTS* lessons and fiction has *ÌTS*.
She knew the accident was either her husband's fault or the car's: it turned out to be not *HÌS* but *ÌTS*.

[**b**] Like genitives and *of*-constructions (*cf* 5.115), constructions with possessive pronouns can be ambiguous, *eg*: *my* in *Give me back my photograph* may have at least three interpretations:
the one {I own / I took / taken of me}

[**c**] Note the following expressions where the *of*-construction, rather than the possessive, is used:
I can't understand it {*for the life of me.* / **for my life.*}
{*On the face of it,* / **On its face,*} it seems a good idea.
I don't trust *the likes of him*.
This will be *the death of me*.

Possessives and the 'emphatic determinative *own*'

6.30 The possessive cannot be accompanied by any modifiers or determiners, except for the 'emphatic determinative *own*'. Just as the emphatic reflexive pronoun (*cf* 6.28) intensifies the meaning of a personal pronoun, so *own* intensifies the meaning of a possessive pronoun. For example, *my own* carries the force of 'mine and nobody else's' in:

This book doesn't belong to the library – it's *my own copy*.

Elsewhere *own* emphasizes coreference between the possessive and the subject of the clause:

Sam cooks *his own dinner* every evening. ['cooks dinner for himself'] [1]

But whereas the reflexive pronoun is often obligatory where coreference with the subject is intended, the addition of *own* to the possessive is optional. Thus, in [1a], *his* could corefer to Sam, but it could also refer to someone quite different:

Sam cooks *his dinner* every evening. [1a]

Similarly, [2] is ambiguous according to whether *their* corefers to *the Housing Associations* or to *people*:

The Housing Associations are encouraging *people* to buy *their* houses. [2]

But only the second interpretation, the 'reflexive' one, is possible with:

The Housing Associations are encouraging people to buy *their own* houses. [2a]

In its turn, *own* can be intensified by the adverb *very*:

Do you like this cake? It's *my very own* recipe. ['a recipe I made up myself'] [3]

The independent genitive cannot combine with *own*: **yours own*, **mine own*; instead, *own* added to the determinative possessive can serve as an independent noun phrase:

The recipe is *my* (*very*) *own*. [3a]

Floyd sometimes plays other musicians' arrangements, but *his own* are much better.

In a similar way, the combination *your own*, *her own*, etc can follow *of* in a 'post-genitive':

I'd love to have *a home of my* (*very*) *own*. ['a home which belongs to me and nobody else']

We're resigning from the firm, and starting *a business of our* (*very*) *own*.

Note [**a**] *Own* can also occur with a genitive noun:

You must try these cookies: it's *Jill's* (*very*) *own* recipe.

Own cannot cooccur, however, with an indefinite determiner. Compare:

Have you got { *your own* car? / a car *of your own*? / **an own* car? }

[**b**] Unlike many other languages, English uses possessives to refer to parts of the body and personal belongings, as well as in a number of related expressions:

He stood at the door with *his* hat in *his* hand.

Mary has broken *her* leg.

Don't lose *your* balance.

They have changed *their* minds again!

The definite article is, however, required in:

She took me by *the* hand.

For a discussion of this use of *the*, *cf* 5.35.

Reciprocal pronouns

6.31 The RECIPROCAL PRONOUNS *each other* and *one another* are related to the reflexive pronouns in that they can be said to express a 'two-way reflexive relationship' (*cf* 13.46, 13.60). Yet there are important differences between reflexive and reciprocal pronouns. Compare:

REFLEXIVE PRONOUN	RECIPROCAL PRONOUN
Adam and Eve blamed *themselves.*	Adam and Eve blamed *each other.*
['Adam blamed himself, and Eve blamed herself.']	['Adam blamed Eve, and Eve blamed Adam.']

Other examples of typical functions of reciprocal pronouns:

> All the children trust *one another.*
> The party leaders promised to give *each other* their support.
> Meg and Bill are very fond of *each other.*

Each other and *one another* are both written as word sequences, but it is better to treat them as compound pronouns rather than as combinations of two pronouns. At the same time, they correspond to the correlative use of *each . . . other* and *one . . . another* (*cf* 6.58) in sentences such as:

> They *each* blamed *the other.*
> The passengers disembarked *one* after *another.*

The reciprocal pronouns have the genitive forms *each other's* and *one another's*:

> The students can borrow { *each other's* / *one another's* } *books.*

There is no difference in the use of the two pronouns *each other* and *one another.* Although in prescriptive tradition, *each other* is sometimes preferred for reference to two and *one another* to more than two, this distinction seems to have little foundation in usage. There is, however, a stylistic difference between the two reciprocals in that *each other* is more common in informal style and *one another* in more formal contexts.

Unlike the reflexive pronouns, the reciprocals can corefer only to plural noun phrases (or noun phrases that have a plural quality), since reciprocity presupposes more than one participant:

> Bill shaved { *himself.* / **each other.* }

With verbs like *embrace*, *meet*, and *kiss*, which are reciprocal and symmetrical in character (*cf* 13.60), the reciprocal pronoun is optional:

> { Anna and Bob met *each other* in Cairo.
> = Anna and Bob met in Cairo. }

With verbs which are not necessarily symmetrical, the reciprocal pronoun is required in order to express reciprocity:

> { Anna and Bob wrote letters to *each other.*
> ≠ Anna and Bob wrote letters. }

Each other and *one another* resemble reflexive pronouns in that they cannot be used naturally in subject position. Instead of [1], [1a] is preferred:

?The twins wanted to know what *each other* were/was doing. [1]
Each of the twins wanted to know what *the other* was doing. [1a]

There appears to be no such constraint on reciprocals as subject in nonfinite verb clauses:

The twins wanted *each other* to be present at all times.

However, the rule which excludes occurrence in subject position holds not only for independent pronominal use but also for genitival reciprocals in subject noun phrases. The reciprocals must have coreference with antecedent phrases which have some other genitive or possessive modification. Compare:

**Each other's letters*
?The letters to each other } were delivered by a servant.
Their letters to each other

Note [**a**] The plural genitive forms **each others'* and **one anothers'* are not used (although these forms sometimes occur as erroneous spellings of *each other's* and *one another's*).
[**b**] The reciprocal pronouns are rather infrequent items. In the million-word Brown corpus of printed AmE, for example, there are only 114 instances of *each other* and 45 instances of *one another*.

Relative pronouns

6.32 Relative pronouns introduce relative clauses, *eg*:

The book *which* you ordered last month has arrived. [1]

In [1], the relative pronoun *which* introduces the relative clause *which you ordered last month*. Relative pronouns differ from personal pronouns in that the element which contains or comprises the relative pronoun is always placed at the beginning of the clause, whether it is subject, complement, adverbial, postmodifier, prepositional complement, or object (as in [1]). Compare the position of *it* as object:

The book has arrived. You ordered *it* last month. [1a]

Relative pronouns resemble personal pronouns in that they have coreference to an antecedent (*cf* 6.15). In [1], the antecedent of *which* is *book*. Here, as in most relative clauses, the antecedent is the preceding part of the noun phrase in which the relative clause functions as postmodifier:

[the book [which you ordered last month]]

Relative pronouns have the double role of referring to the antecedent (which determines gender selection, *eg*: *who/which*) and of functioning as all of, or part of, an element in the relative clause (which determines the case form for those items that have case distinction, *eg*: *who/whom*). Further details of relative clause formation are given in 17.10*ff*.

Restrictive and nonrestrictive

6.33 The semantic relation between the clause and its antecedent may be either restrictive or nonrestrictive, and this is the basis of an important distinction between RESTRICTIVE and NONRESTRICTIVE relative clauses.

Restrictive relative clauses are closely connected to their antecedent or head prosodically, and denote a limitation on the reference of the antecedent, *eg*:

> This is not something *that would disturb me ÀNYway.*

Nonrestrictive clauses are parenthetic comments which usually describe, but do not further define, the antecedent, *eg*:

> They operated like poliTÌcians| *who notoriously have no sense of humour at ÀLL*|.

The differences between restrictive and nonrestrictive relative clauses will be further discussed in 17.13*ff*. For the present, we only need to mention this difference in order to indicate how it affects the choice of relative pronoun, as appears in *Table* 6.33:

Table 6.33 Relative pronouns

	RESTRICTIVE		NONRESTRICTIVE	
	personal	nonpersonal	personal	nonpersonal
SUBJECTIVE CASE	*who* *that*	*which* *that*	*who*	*which*
OBJECTIVE CASE	*whom* *that* zero	*which* *that* zero	*whom*	
GENITIVE CASE	*whose*			

***Wh*-pronouns, *that*, and zero**

6.34 Relative pronouns include two series:

(a) *wh*-pronouns: *who, whom, whose, which*
(b) *that* and zero

Compare:

> I'd like to see the car $\left\{\begin{matrix} \textit{which} \\ \textit{that} \\ (\quad) \end{matrix}\right\}$ you bought last week.

(Zero is indicated by '(   )'.) Neither series has number or person contrast. However, the *wh*-series has gender contrast between personal *who* and nonpersonal *which*, and case contrast between subjective *who*, objective *whom*, and genitive *whose*.

As *Table* 6.33 shows, *whose* – unlike *who* and *whom* – can have personal reference (*cf* 5.117), as in [1], and also nonpersonal reference, as in [2], although there is a certain reluctance to use *whose* for nonpersonal antecedents:

The lady whose daughter you met is Mrs Brown. [1]
The house whose roof was damaged has now been repaired. [2]

Nevertheless relative clauses such as that of [2] are quite frequently attested. If a speaker or writer wishes to avoid the use of *whose* with nonpersonal reference, this can be done, often with some awkwardness, by using *of which* (*cf* 17.14):

The house {*of which* the roof / the roof *of which*} was damaged . . . [2a]

Note [**a**] *Whose* cannot always be substituted for *of which* or *of whom*. When the *of*-phrase functions as an adverbial, there is no parallel with the genitive [3], but other constructions are available, *eg* [3a]:

*The poem *whose I am speaking* . . . [3]
The poem *of which I am speaking* . . . [3a]

[**b**] *Which* can have a personal noun phrase as its antecedent when the head is a complement with the role of characterization (*cf* 10.20 and the parallel use of *it*, 6.17 Note [b]):

They accused him of being a traitor, {*which* / **who*} *he was.*

In restrictive relative clauses, *that* is used in a similar function:

She's not the brilliant dancer {*that* / ( ) / **who*} *she used to be.*

Compare the exclamatory construction with identificatory *that*:

Fool *that* I was! ['I was such a fool']

In none of these sentences could *who* be used.

[**c**] If the antecedent contains a mixture of personal and nonpersonal elements, *that* can be used as a pronoun which is 'neutral' with respect to *who* and *which*:

The generals complained that the Defence Department had not sent the extra men and equipment *that they needed.*

Who and *whom*

6.35 In many ways the opposition between *who* and *whom* does not parallel the subjective/objective distinction in the personal pronouns. *Whom* is largely restricted to formal style, and can be avoided altogether in informal style, through the use of *who*, *that*, or zero.

It seems odd that the pronoun *whom* is decidedly 'marked' in relation to *who*, while elsewhere, with *I*/*me*, *she*/*her*, etc, the objective form is the 'unmarked' choice (*cf* 6.4). The best way of accounting for this seems to be to return to the concept of 'subject territory' (*cf* 6.5), which was defined, for colloquial English, simply as the position preceding the verb, *ie* the customary position of the subject. In relative clauses, because of the fronting of the *wh*-element, this is the only position of the relative pronoun, whether it is functioning as subject, object, or some other element. Hence, in informal English, there is a tendency to avoid *whom* altogether, and to replace it by the subjective form *who*. In formal style, on the other hand, the tendency is to use *whom* in accordance with the traditional prescriptive rule that *who* is the form for subject and subject complement functions, and *whom* is the form for other functions. When the relative pronoun is object, we meet all the following possibilities:

This is a person { *whom* / *who* / *that* / ( ) } you should know.

If the relative pronoun is a prepositional complement, we meet yet a further possibility, that of the preposition followed by *whom*:

This is the person { *to whom* you spoke. / { *whom* / *who* / *that* / ( ) } you spoke *to*. }

However, the further theoretical possibility does not occur, namely *who* following the preposition:

*This is the *person to who* you spoke.

The reason is that there is a stylistic incompatibility between the preposition + relative pronoun construction (*to whom*), which is rather formal, and the use of *who* rather than *whom* as prepositional complement (*who . . . to*), which is informal.

Thus the behaviour of *who* and *whom*, which would otherwise appear irregular and puzzling, can be explained in terms of the different notions of case operating in formal and in informal usage.

Note [**a**] The hypercorrect use of *whom* is common in examples of pushdown relative clauses (*cf* 17.63) such as this:

*The Ambassador, *whom* we hope will arrive at 10 a.m., . . .

Here the relative pronoun is the subject of *will arrive* but is felt to be in object territory in relation to *we hope* embedded in the relative clause (*cf*: *We hope that she will arrive at 10 a.m.*). On the other hand, no hypercorrection is involved in the following:

The Ambassador, *whom* we expect to arrive at 10 a.m., . . .

This is evident, again, if we compare the relative clause with a corresponding construction with a personal pronoun (*cf* 6.38 Note [b]):

We expect her to arrive at 10 a.m.

The following example represents a case where the hypercorrection has been institutionalized, and where in fact there is no alternative relative pronoun:

Here is Captain Morse than *whom* there is no braver soldier.

[**b**] The relative pronouns discussed above have been those used in adnominal relative clauses (*cf* 17.9). We should briefly mention here also the pronouns *what*, *whatever*, *whichever*, and *whoever*, which are used to introduce nominal relative clauses (*cf* 15.8*f*, 17.12), *eg*:

You can do *whatever you like*. ['that which you like']

[**c**] Very occasionally nonrestrictive relative clauses are introduced by the relative determiner *which*, rather than by a relative pronoun (*cf* 17.24):

We arrived at noon, *by which time* the demonstration was over.

Again, nominal relative clauses permit a different set of determiners: *which*, *whichever*, *whatever* (*cf* 15.8*f*), *eg*:

You should wear *whichever dress suits you best*.

Interrogative pronouns

6.36 These are formally identical with the *wh*-series of relative pronouns, but have a different function. They correspond closely to interrogative determiners (*cf*

5.14), and we shall discuss the use of both types of interrogative word together, *ie* the following items:

PRONOUN FUNCTION:	*who*	*whom*	*whose*	*what*	*which*
DETERMINATIVE FUNCTION:			*whose*	*what*	*which*

Who, *whom*, and *whose* are subjective, objective, and genitive case forms respectively, and have personal gender. The other interrogatives are not distinctive for case or gender. Note in particular that, unlike relative *which*, interrogative *which* can be used not only with nonpersonal but also with personal reference:

RELATIVE: The author {*who* / **which*} is my favourite is . . .

INTERROGATIVE: {*Which* / *Who*} is your favourite author?

In meaning, however, interrogative *who* and *which* differ, *who* being indefinite and *which* definite, as explained in 6.37.

Indefinite and definite interrogatives

6.37 There are two groups of interrogatives: those with INDEFINITE and those with DEFINITE reference.

(a) Interrogative pronouns referring to persons:

INDEFINITE: *Who* is your favourite conductor?
DEFINITE: *Which* is your favourite conductor? (Von Karajan or Stokowsky?)

(b) Interrogative pronouns not referring to persons:

INDEFINITE: *What*'s the name of this tune?
DEFINITE: *Which* do you prefer? (Classical or popular music?)

(c) Interrogative determiners with personal nouns:

INDEFINITE: *What* conductor do you like best?
DEFINITE: *Which* conductor do you like best? (Von Karajan or Stokowsky?)

(d) Interrogative determiners with nonpersonal nouns:

INDEFINITE: *What* newspaper do you read?
DEFINITE: *Which* newspaper do you read? (*The Times* or *The Guardian*?)

In these pairs, *which* implies that the choice is made from a limited number of alternatives which exist in the context of discussion. The alternatives may be made explicit (as they are by the words in parentheses in the above examples), or they may be implicit. Thus a speaker who asks the question [1] assumes that there is a definite set of dictionaries from which a choice can be made:

Which is the best English dictionary? [1]

A person looking at an old photograph may say *Which is you?*, asking for the identification of one member of the definite set of persons in the picture. Sometimes the relevant definite set is indicated by a following *of*-phrase, as in [2]:

Which of the three girls is the oldest? [2]

Note [**a**] The definite meaning of *which* is reflected in the fact that the definite article could not be omitted from [2] above:

* *Which of three girls . . .?*

[**b**] In this and in the following sections, we illustrate the interrogative pronouns by their use in direct questions. However, they can equally well occur in subordinate *wh*-interrogative clauses. Compare [3] and [3a]:

What was she wearing? I don't remember. [3]
I don't remember *what she was wearing.* [3a]

[**c**] The indefinite interrogatives *what, who,* and *whose* can be postmodified by *else* (*cf* 7.69):

What else? *Who else?*

[**d**] We can select *who* or *what* rather than *which* even in cases where the number of alternatives is strictly limited by the context:

Who/*Which* do you like best – your father or your mother?
What/*Which* will it be – tea or coffee?

Conversely, *which* can be used when there is no limited set of alternatives from which a choice is made:

After all, *which* American has not heard of someone who, a few days after his or her annual check-up, suffered a heart attack?

Who, whom, and *whose*

6.38 The interrogative determiners *what* and *which* can be personal or nonpersonal:

{*What* / *Which*} {*candidate* will you vote for? / *party* are you in favour of?}

But the interrogative pronouns *who* and *whom* are personal only:

Who told you where I was? *Who(m)* do you admire most?

In objective use, *who* is informal and *whom* is formal. The distinction is parallel to that between *who* and *whom* as relative pronouns (*cf* 6.35). Similarly, interrogative *whom* functions like relative *whom*, except that interrogative *whom* strikes most people as even more formal than relative *whom*.

As a prepositional complement, only *whom* can normally follow the preposition, as in [1], whereas both *who* and *whom* can take initial position, as in [1a], leaving the preposition deferred at the end of the clause (*cf* 9.6):

For whom is she working? (BUT NOT: **For who* is she working?) [1]
Who(m) is she working *for*? [1a]

As the possessive form of *who*, *whose* can occur in either a determinative function, as in [2], or an independent function, as in [2a] (*cf* 5.124):

Whose jacket is this? [2]
Whose is this jacket? [2a]

But, unlike relative *whose*, interrogative *whose* cannot have nonpersonal reference. For example, we can say *That ship's funnel was damaged*, but we cannot ask a question with *whose* for which *That ship's* would be an appropriate answer (even though ships are typically referred to as *she*; *cf* 5.111 Note):

A: *Whose* funnel was damaged? B: **That ship's*.

Note [a] *Who* has both singular and plural reference, but when neither is explicit in the linguistic context, singular concord is the unmarked term. Thus, even though several voices are heard outside, the natural question will be *Who's there?* rather than ?* *Who're there?*
[b] When *who* occurs in noninitial position in clause structure (*cf* 11.19), the objective use of *who* is acceptable colloquially even after a preposition:

History is written *about who*? Who sleeps *with who*?

In contrast to these, there is a tendency towards hypercorrection in the replacement of *who* by *whom* in noninitial position:

A: Janet was at the party. B: (?)Janet *whom*?

What and *which*

6.39 *What* and *which* can also occur in prepositional complements with the preposition either in initial or in final (deferred) position; but with an initial preposition, the construction is formal and rather rare:

What are you talking *about*? [1]
On what is he lecturing? ⟨formal⟩ [1a]
Which (girl) are you talking *about*? [2]
On which of the topics is he lecturing? ⟨formal⟩ [2a]

What has a wide range of use, either as a determiner or as a pronoun, and either with personal or with nonpersonal reference:

A: *What's* your address? B: (It's) 18 Reynolds Close.
A: { *What* nationality is she? / *What* is her nationality? } B: (She's) Finnish.
A: *What* date is it? B: (It's) the 15th of March.
A: *What*'s the time? B: (It's) five o'clock.
A: *What* is he doing? B: (He's) mending the phone.
A: *What* was the concert like? B: (It was) excellent.

When it refers to a person, however, *what* as a pronoun is limited to questions about profession, role, status, etc. Contrast:

A: *What*'s her husband?
B: He's a film director. [3]
A: *Which* is her husband?
B: He's the man on the right smoking a pipe. [3a]
A: *Who* is her husband?
B: He's Paul Jones, the famous art critic. [3b]

In this last function in [3], *what* elicits an identificatory noun phrase as complement, and so it is the interrogative counterpart of relative *which* (*cf* 6.34 Note [b]) and of the personal pronoun *it* (*cf* 6.17 Note [b]) in corresponding contexts.

Note Interrogative pronouns do not accept modification or determination, except for the occurrence of intensifying postmodifiers *What ever . . .?*, *Who on earth . . .?* (*cf* 11.14 Note [b]).

Demonstrative pronouns

6.40 The demonstrative pronouns *this, that, these,* and *those* exactly match the form of the four demonstrative determiners (*cf* 5.14). With the demonstratives, as with the interrogatives, we shall find it convenient to consider together the uses of the determiners and of the pronouns.

The demonstratives have number contrast in both determiners and pronouns. They also have a contrast between 'near' and 'distant' reference:

Table 6.40 Demonstrative pronouns

	SINGULAR	PLURAL
'NEAR' REFERENCE	*this* (student)	*these* (students)
'DISTANT' REFERENCE	*that* (student)	*those* (students)

Like the definite article and the personal pronouns, demonstratives have definite meaning, and therefore their reference depends on the context shared by speaker/writer and hearer/reader. Also, in the same way, their use may be considered under the headings of SITUATIONAL reference (reference to the extralinguistic situation), ANAPHORIC reference (coreference to an earlier part of the discourse), and CATAPHORIC reference (coreference to a later part of the discourse). As before, we will call the part of the text to which coreference is made the ANTECEDENT.

First, however, let us consider the purely grammatical aspects of the demonstratives.

Number and gender

6.41 The singular demonstratives *this* and *that* are used for both count and noncount meaning:

$$\textit{This}\left\{\begin{matrix}\textit{room}\\ \textit{water}\end{matrix}\right\}\text{ is too cold.}\quad \textit{That}\left\{\begin{matrix}\textit{loaf}\\ \textit{bread}\end{matrix}\right\}\text{ is stale.}$$

Both the singular and the plural pronouns can be used as pro-forms as substitutes for a noun phrase (*cf* 12.19):

This chair is more comfortable than *that.* [= *that chair*] [1]
Those apples are sweeter than *these.* [= *these apples*] [2]

The same meaning is conveyed by the demonstrative followed by *one*(*s*) (*cf* 6.55):

This chair is more comfortable than *that one.* [1a]
Those apples are sweeter than *these ones.* [2a]

In addition, the pronouns can refer to some unspecified object(s):

Come and have a look at *this.* ['this thing, this substance', etc]
Have you heard *this*? ['this piece of news, this joke', etc]
Leave *that* alone! ['that thing, that machine', etc]
Can I borrow *these*? ['these books, these screwdrivers', etc]

But especially in this use, the pronouns are nonpersonal. Thus instead of [3], which would be an insult (as if the person indicated is not human), we would have to say [3a]:

?Is she going to marry *THÁT*? [3]
Is she going to marry *THÁT man*? [3a]

Instead of [4] we would have to say [4a]:

*Come and meet *these* over here. [4]
Come and meet *these people* over here. [4a]

An exception to this is the introductory use of a demonstrative pronoun as subject of a clause; in this position the pronoun can have both personal and nonpersonal reference:

This is Mrs Jones. [introducing an acquaintance]
That's my stepmother. [pointing to a photograph]
Are *these* the students who have registered? [pointing to a list of names]
This is Sid. Is *that* Geoff? [on the telephone]

Note *That* refers to degree or measurement in contexts such as:

My brother is six feet tall, but yours must be even taller than *that*. ['taller than six feet']

In spite of appearances, therefore, such examples are not exceptions to the rule that, as a pronoun, *that* does not have personal reference (except in subject position; *cf* 12.19).

Modification and determination

6.42 The demonstrative pronouns are limited as to determination and modification. Like the demonstrative determiners (*cf* 5.14), they can be preceded by predeterminers, but the *of*-construction is often preferred:

All (*of*) *this* is mine.
Could you give me *half* (*of*) *that*?
Would you like *both* (*of*) *these*?
All (*of*) *those* are sold.

They are sometimes postmodified by place adverbials: *these over here*, etc. They can also be postmodified by restrictive relative clauses and other restrictive modifiers:

Those who try hard deserve to succeed. [1]

These watches are more expensive than *those* {*which* / *that* / ( )} *we saw in New York.* [2]

{*That which* / *What*} *upsets me most* is his manner. [3]

Of these, *those* is personal ['the people'] in [1], and nonpersonal in [2], like *that* in [3]. In fact, *that which* . . . is rare and formal, and is generally replaced by *what*.

There is no personal singular **that who* . . ., but other constructions are used instead, *eg*: *anyone who* . . ., *the person who* . . . ; *he who* . . . and *she who* . . . are archaic (*cf* 6.20).

Note [**a**] On the use of *that* and *those* as substitute forms ('the one, the ones'), as in the following example, *cf* 12.19:

The song by Schubert is more tuneful than *that* by Britten.

[**b**] The determiner *those* loses its deictic quality (*cf* 6.43) in cases like [4] where it is an emphatic equivalent of cataphoric *the* (*cf* 5.32):

Those memories which we acquire in early childhood rarely lose their vividness. [4]

Situational reference

6.43 When the demonstratives refer to the extralinguistic situation, they are often compared with other DEICTIC or 'pointing' items, which also contrast in terms of 'near' and 'distant' reference:

here ~ *there*, *now* ~ *then*, *today* ~ *yesterday*/*tomorrow*, etc

In the simplest cases, *this* and *that* contrast in terms of the nearness of the referent to the speaker:

This is my friend Charlie Brown. [introducing someone]
That is my friend Charlie Brown. [pointing out someone in a crowd]

The measurement of spatial proximity is a matter of psychological rather than real distance. It can easily be extended to the more abstract sphere of time:

this morning ['the morning of today']
that morning ['the morning of a day some time ago']

It can be extended to an even more abstract and subjective level of interpretation:

Have you seen *this report* on smoking?
['the one I have recently been thinking about'] [1]
Have you seen *that report* on smoking?
['the one I was looking at some time ago'] [2]

In practice, however, [1] and [2] could occur in the same situation, the only difference being the speaker's subjective concept of 'nearness'.

In reference to time, *this* is typically associated with 'what is before us', and *that* with 'what is behind us'. Hence with reference to days and months, *this Friday* or *this September* means 'the Friday/September to come' (*cf* 9.40). Also, a person about to demonstrate some skill, such as using a can opener, could say [3], but after the demonstration is finished, [4] would be more appropriate:

This is how you do it. [3]
That's how you do it. [4]

Another extension of the near/distant polarity is for *that* to imply dislike or disapproval:

Janet is coming. I hope she doesn't bring *that* husband of hers.
She's awful, *that* Mabel.

Note [**a**] In this connection, notice a familiar use (considered nonstandard by some speakers) of *this*/*these* to introduce some new thing or person into a narrative:

There were *these* three men . . .

Then I saw *this* girl . . .

I was walking home when *this* man came up to me and said . . .

Uncharacteristically *this* introduces new information here, instead of referring back to shared information, as is usual. One sign is the occurrence of *this* as a focus of a clause with existential *there* (*cf* 18.44*ff*) in a typical beginning of a joke, *eg*:

There was *this* man/place . . .

[**b**] On the other hand, *that/those* are used informally to 'point back' in a vague way to some shared experience:

I used to enjoy *those* enormous hotel breakfasts.

It gives you *that* great feeling of clean air and open spaces. ['the feeling we all know about']

Anaphoric and cataphoric reference

6.44 The anaphoric and cataphoric uses of the demonstratives are extensions of their situational use.

ANAPHORIC:

I hear you disliked his latest novel. I read his first novel, and *that* was boring, too.

He asked for his brown raincoat, insisting that *this* was his usual coat during the winter months.

CATAPHORIC

He told the story like *this*: 'Once upon a time . . .' [1]

The 'near' demonstratives *this/these* can have both anaphoric and cataphoric reference, while the 'distant' demonstratives *that/those* can have only anaphoric reference. The following is therefore decidedly odd (but *cf* Note [a]):

?He told the story like *that*: 'Once upon a time . . .' [1a]

The antecedent of a demonstrative may be either a noun phrase or a larger segment of discourse, *viz* a clause, sentence, or sequence of sentences. We call this larger segment a 'sentential antecedent':

They will probably win the match. *That* will please my mother.

Many years ago their wives quarrelled over some trivial matter, long forgotten. But one word led to another, and the quarrel developed into a permanent rupture between them. *That*'s why the two men never visit each other's houses.

This should interest you, if you're keen on boxing. The world heavyweight championship is going to be held in Chicago next June, so you should be able to watch it there live.

Anaphoric and cataphoric reference can also be illustrated with demonstrative determiners:

I longed to play the piano when I was a child; but in *those days* my parents could not afford an instrument.

These language options are open to our students: Spanish, French, and German.

Note [**a**] In very limited contexts, *eg* in expressions of indignation, *that* can be used cataphorically:

What do you think of THÀT! Bob smashes up my car, and then expects me to pay for the repairs.

[b] *Such* as a pro-form is similar to the demonstratives. It can have anaphoric reference both as a pronoun and as a predeterminer:

No one in his senses would dream of taking an innocent maiden aunt (if *such* exist) to Seneca's *Medea*. It is doubtful, indeed, if *such* plays should be performed at all on the modern stage. ['... if *innocent maiden aunts* exist'], ['... if plays *such as Seneca's Medea* ...'.] [1]

In [1], *such* occurs first as a pronoun and second as a predeterminer. In [2], *such* has a whole sentence as its antecedent, and could be replaced by *this* or *that* with virtually no change of meaning:

If officialdom makes mistakes, officialdom deserves to suffer. *Such*, at least, was Mr Boyd's opinion. [2]

The anaphoric pronoun *such* can also occur after indefinite determiners such as *all*, *few*, and *many* (*cf* 5.15 Note) in rather rare and restricted use:

Some reactions to the proposal may be hostile, but { there will surely not be *many such*. / ?we can afford to ignore *any such*. / **no such* have yet been reported. } [3]

As [3] shows, the acceptability of this construction varies according to the determiner which precedes *such*. For the unacceptable **no such*, postmodification of *none* by *such* is an acceptable alternative:

... but *none such* { has / have } yet been reported.

Indefinite pronouns

6.45 The remaining classes of pronouns are termed INDEFINITE: they lack the element of definiteness which is found in the personal, reflexive, possessive, and demonstrative pronouns, and to some extent also in the *wh*-pronouns. Although they are themselves indefinite, however, these pronouns can sometimes combine with elements of definite meaning, such as the definite article: *the ones*, *the few*, *the other*, etc. The indefinite pronouns are, in a logical sense, QUANTITATIVE: they have universal or partitive meaning, and correspond closely to determiners of the same or of similar form (*cf* 5.14). See *Table* 6.45 opposite for a list of the main ones.

Compound pronouns

6.46 The indefinite pronouns divide into two main categories according to their morphology and their syntactic behaviour. The COMPOUND PRONOUNS are those which are composed of two morphemes, *viz* a determiner morpheme *every-*, *some-*, *any-*, or *no-*, and a nominal morpheme *-one*, *-body*, or *-thing*. The remaining indefinite pronouns belong to a category which we shall call *OF*-PRONOUNS, because they can be followed by a partitive *of*-phrase: *many* (*of*), *some* (*of*), etc.

The compound pronouns in *Table* 6.46a opposite are divided into four classes (universal, assertive, nonassertive, and negative) corresponding to the four classes in *Table* 6.45.

The twelve compound pronouns are perfectly regular in their formation, the only anomalies being the spelling of *no one* as two words, and the pronunciation of *nothing* with the vowel /ʌ/ rather than /əʊ/.

The pairs of pronouns with personal reference (*eg*: *everybody*, *everyone*) are equivalent in function and meaning but the pronouns in *-one* are regarded

Table 6.45 Major indefinite pronouns and determiners

	NUMBER	FUNCTION	COUNT		NONCOUNT
			personal	nonpersonal	
UNIVERSAL	singular	pronoun	*everyone* *everybody*	*everything*	(it (. . .)) *all*
			each		
		determiner	*every* *each*		*all*
	plural	pronoun	(they (. . .)) *all/both*		
		determiner	*all/both*		
ASSERTIVE	singular	pronoun	*someone* *somebody*	*something*	*some*
		determiner	*a*(*n*)		
	plural	pronoun and determiner	*some*		
NONASSERTIVE	singular	pronoun	*anyone* *anybody*	*anything*	*any*
		determiner	*either* *any*		
	plural	pronoun and determiner	*any*		
NEGATIVE	singular	pronoun	*no one* *nobody*	*nothing*	*none*
			none		
		pronoun and determiner	*neither*		
	plural	pronoun	*none*		
	singular or plural	determiner	*no*		

Table 6.46a Compound pronouns

	PERSONAL REFERENCE		NONPERSONAL REFERENCE
UNIVERSAL	*everybody*	*everyone*	*everything*
ASSERTIVE	*somebody*	*someone*	*something*
NONASSERTIVE	*anybody*	*anyone*	*anything*
NEGATIVE	*nobody*	*no one*	*nothing*

as more elegant than those in *-body*. All the compound pronouns are singular, and have concord with a singular verb even though notionally they may denote more than one thing or person:

> {*Everybody* / *Everyone*} over eighteen now has a vote.
>
> I tried *everything* but *nothing* works.
>
> {*Somebody* / *Someone*} was telling me you've been to America.
>
> Has {*anybody* / *anyone*} got anything to say?
>
> There was {*nobody* / *no one*} at the office.

On the use of the plural in coreference to compound pronouns (*eg*: *Everybody has their off days*), *cf* 10.43.

Note [**a**] The frequencies of compound pronouns with *any-*, *every-*, and *some-* that have personal reference are as follows in the LOB and Brown corpora of printed BrE and AmE, respectively:

Table 6.46b Frequencies of compound pronouns with *any-*, *every-*, and *some-*

	BrE	AmE
anybody	32	42
anyone	141	140
everybody	33	72
everyone	106	94
somebody	27	57
someone	117	94

The table shows that, in both corpora, the compounds in *-one* are consistently more frequent than the corresponding compounds in *-body*; but also that compounds in *-body* are more frequent, and compounds in *-one* are less frequent, in AmE than in BrE.

[**b**] The compound pronouns are pronounced with initial stress, and are thereby minimally distinct in speech from combinations of a determiner and an independent word *body*, *one*, or *thing*. We must be careful, therefore, to distinguish pronouns from the superficially similar sequences of determiner + head: the pronoun *ˈno one* from *no ˈone*, as in *no ˈone answer* ['no single answer']; the pronoun *ˈeveryone* from *every ˈone*, as in *every ˈone of the students*; and the pronoun *ˈeverybody* ['any person'] from *every ˈbody*, as in *Every (human) body needs vitamins*.

6.47 The compound pronouns are the least problematic of the indefinite pronouns, since they behave in general like noun phrases of very general meaning:

> *everybody*, *everyone* ['all people']
> *everything* ['all things', 'all matter']

There is no pronoun corresponding to the universal singular determiner *every*. In nominal functions, the determiner combines with the pronoun *one* (with the stress pattern *every ˈone* or *ˈevery ˈone*):

Every '*one* of us will be present.
We played several matches against the visitors, but unfortunately lost *every* '*one*.

To emphasize the all-inclusive meaning, *single* is inserted: '(We lost) *every single one*'.

Unlike *every* '*one*, which has both personal and nonpersonal reference, the compound pronoun '*everyone* (with stress on the first syllable) can refer only to persons:

I want {'*everyone* / '*everybody*} to feel at home.

To the compound pronouns of personal gender we can add the singular genitive ending *'s*:

This will put *everyone's* mind at rest.
Could you borrow *anybody's* overcoat?
There's *somebody's* glove on the floor.
It was absolutely *nobody's* fault.

A postmodifier *else* can be added to the compound pronouns. Its meaning is illustrated by these paraphrases (*cf* 7.69):

everyone '*else* ['every other person']
nobody '*else* ['no other person']
anything '*else* ['any other thing']

The genitive ending is added to *else*, and not to the pronoun itself (*cf* 'group genitive', 5.123):

I must be drinking *someone else's* coffee.
(NOT: **someone's else* coffee)
His hair is longer than *anybody else's*.
(NOT: **anybody's else*)

In addition, the compound pronoun can be postmodified freely by normal restrictive noun-phrase postmodifiers (*cf* 17.9*ff*), such as prepositional phrases and relative clauses:

somebody *I know*	something *for dinner*
everyone (*that*) *you meet*	anything *made of silver*

The compound pronouns cannot be premodified by adjectives (**new nothing*), but instead, adjectival modification is added after the pronoun (*cf* 17.57):

somebody *very tall*
nothing *new*
something *nice for dinner*
anyone *kinder and more considerate than Janice*

Of-pronouns

6.48 The remaining indefinite pronouns, here called OF-PRONOUNS (*cf Table* 6.48 over page) are distinguished by the following characteristics:

(a) They can be followed by a partitive *of*-phrase:

Some *of us* were tired and hungry.

(b) They can be used as substitutes for noun phrases or other nominal constructions:

Many children learn to read quite quickly, but *some* [= *some children*] need special instruction.

On the classification of pronouns as substitutes, *cf* 12.10*ff*.

(c) They are all (with the exception of *none*) identical in form to the corresponding determiner (*cf* 5.14).

Table 6.48 Indefinite pronouns which take the partitive *of*-construction

	COUNT		NONCOUNT
	singular	plural	singular
UNIVERSAL (6.49–51)	*all (of)* *each (of)*	*all (of)* *both (of)*	*all (of)*
ASSERTIVE (i) *some* (6.52)	*some (of)*	*some (of)*	*some (of)*
(ii) multal (6.53)		*many (of)* *more (of)* *most (of)*	*much (of)* *more (of)* *most (of)*
(iii) paucal (6.53)		*a few (of)* *fewer/less (of)* *fewest/least (of)*	*a little (of)* *less (of)* *least (of)*
(iv) *one* (6.54–56)	*one (of)*	(*ones*)	
NONASSERTIVE (6.59–61)	*any (of)* *either (of)*	*any (of)*	*any (of)*
NEGATIVE (6.62)	*none (of)* *neither (of)*	*none (of)* *few (of)*	*none (of)* *little (of)*

Note All the *of*-pronouns can be interpreted as substitutes; but in addition, some of them can be used without the *of*-construction to refer to people in general. The following famous quotations from earlier English illustrate this use, which today is somewhat literary and archaic:

Many are called, but *few* are chosen. [*St Matthew's Gospel*]

Some are born great, *some* achieve greatness, and *some* have greatness thrust upon them. [Shakespeare, *Twelfth Night*]

In each case the meaning can be elucidated by inserting *people*: *some* = 'some people', etc.

Universal pronouns

6.49 Our plan now is to look at each of the categories of compound pronouns and *of*-pronouns in turn, beginning with the UNIVERSAL pronouns. With each category, we shall draw attention to parallels between pronouns and determiners.

The relation of universal pronouns to their determiners is shown in *Table* 6.49. The compound pronouns *everyone*, *everybody*, and *everything* have already been discussed (*cf* 6.46*f*).

Table 6.49 Universal pronouns

<table>
<tr><td colspan="2"></td><td colspan="2">COUNT</td><td>NONCOUNT</td></tr>
<tr><td colspan="2"></td><td>personal</td><td>nonpersonal</td><td>nonpersonal</td></tr>
<tr><td rowspan="3">SINGULAR</td><td rowspan="2">pronoun</td><td>everyone
everybody</td><td>everything</td><td rowspan="2">all
(?everything)</td></tr>
<tr><td colspan="2">all
each</td></tr>
<tr><td>determiner</td><td colspan="2">every } boy/pen
each</td><td rowspan="2">all ((of) the furniture)</td></tr>
<tr><td>PLURAL</td><td>pronoun and determiner</td><td colspan="2">all } ((of) the boys/pens)
both</td></tr>
</table>

All and *both*

6.50 *All* is used with plural nouns for quantities of more than two, and *both* is used with plural nouns for quantities of two only (dual number):

The club is open to people of *both sexes* and *all nationalities*.
Both (*of*) *his parents* died young.
All (*of*) *the children* were working hard.

When *all* and *both* are followed by a determiner such as *the* (but not by the zero article: **all of boys*), there is a choice between the insertion of *of* and its omission:

All (*of*) } *the boys* want to become football players.
Both (*of*) }

Technically, *all* or *both* is a pronoun when followed by *of*, and a predeterminer when followed by another determiner (*cf* 5.15*ff*).

All, unlike *both*, can also be followed by a singular count noun, as in [1], or by a noncount noun, as in [2]:

His action was condemned by *all* (*of*) *the civilized world*. [1]
All (*of*) *that money* you gave them has been spent. [2]

Before a singular count noun, however, *all* is somewhat formal, and is frequently replaced by a construction with *whole* as an adjective or noun:

The whole (*of the*) *civilized world* denounced the invasion.

Similarly, *both the boys* can be replaced by *the two boys* or *both boys*.

Unless followed by the *of*-phrase, *all* and *both* follow a personal pronoun rather than precede it:

{*All of us* / *We all*} like Peter.

I've met {*both of them* / *them both*} before.

When *all*, *both*, and *each* (*cf* 5.16) are postposed in this way, and apply to the subject, they appear in the position of a medial adverb (*cf* 8.16). According to the rules for adverb placement, this means that they occur immediately after the subject if there is no operator [3], otherwise after the operator [4, 5]:

They {*all* / *both*} *won* their matches. [3]

We were {*all* / *both*} {fast asleep. / working.} [4]

The villages have {*all* / *both*} *been* destroyed. [5]

As [5] shows, the postposed universal pronoun may also occur after a nonpronominal noun phrase as subject. In other positions in the sentence, however, the postposed pronoun occurs immediately after its head, and the head can only be a personal pronoun:

They told {*us* / **the men*} {*all* / *both* / *each*} to wait.

Note [a] Used alone, *all* can be equivalent to *everything*:

{*All* / *Everything*} is not lost.

In this sense, *all* can be preceded by a possessive pronoun:

He gave *his all*. ['everything he had']

[b] *All* can be premodified by degree adverbials and by modifiers of negative implication: *nearly all*, (*not*) *quite all*, *not all*, *by no means all*, etc.

[c] *Both* is intrinsically definite, and in this differs from the cardinal numeral *two*, even when it is not followed by the definite article:

{*Both* / ?*Two of*} *her eyes* were closed. {*Both* / ?*Two*} *eyes* were closed.

The statements containing *two* do not make sense when applied to an individual person, because they imply that there are more than two eyes in question. But determiner + unstressed *two* + noun can be used in:

Her two eyes were like saucers.

Compare also:

the/my/these two boys It was just *the two of us*.

Each and *every*

6.51 Words like *each*, *every*, and the compounds with *every-* can be termed DISTRIBUTIVE, because they pick out the members of a set singly, rather than considering them in the mass. They are therefore singular in number. Apart from this difference, *each* and *every* as determiners are often equivalent to *all*:

All good teachers study *their* subject carefully. [1]

Every / *Each* } good teacher studies *his* subject carefully. [1a]

(On the use of *his* in [1a], *cf* 6.9.)

All, *each*, and *every one* can also be equivalent in a pronominal function, except that *each* (unlike *every one* and *all*) can refer to just two people or things:

Several cars arrived.

{ *Each* (*one*) *of them* was mud-stained. [2]
Every one of them was mud-stained. [2a]
All of them were mud-stained. [2b]

There is also a noticeable difference between [3] and [3a, 3b]:

All (*of*) *the girls* } received a magnificent prize. [3]
Each one of the girls } received a magnificent prize. [3a]
Every one of the girls } received a magnificent prize. [3b]

While [3] might mean that the girls shared a single prize, [3a] and [3b] both mean that there were as many prizes as girls. Note that *each* as a pronoun [4] is equivalent to *each* as a determiner followed by *one* [4a], and to *each* as a determiner followed by a noun [4b]:

Each of the states } has its own flag. [4]
Each one of the states } has its own flag. [4a]
Each state } has its own flag. [4b]

Note [**a**] The distributive use of *each* is further discussed in reference to coordination in 13.61. On concord with *each*, *cf* 10.37 Note [b].

[**b**] All of the quantitative pronouns have a distributive use (*cf* 10.47), as in [5]; usually the plural has the same meaning and is preferred to the singular, as in [5a]:

All the children have *their own bicycle*. [5]
All the children have *their own bicycles*. ['one bicycle for each'] [5a]

Assertive pronouns

The *some* series

6.52 The term ASSERTIVE applies to pronouns and determiners which are associated with 'assertive territory' rather than 'nonassertive territory' (*cf* 2.53*ff*). The clearest case of this distinction is to be found in the contrast between *some* and *any*, and between their corresponding compound pronouns *somebody*, *anybody*, etc (*cf* 6.46).

Some as a determiner [1, 2] and as a pronoun [1a, 2a] occurs most typically with plural and noncount nouns:

Some rolls have been eaten. [1]
Some bread has been eaten. [2]
Some (of the *rolls*) have been eaten. [1a]
Some (of the *bread*) has been eaten. [2a]

In these examples, *some* as a plural form contrasts with *one*, which is singular (*cf* 6.54*ff*):

One } of the rolls has been eaten.
**Some*

But as a determiner, *some* also occurs with singular count nouns, especially temporal nouns:

"*Some* '*day*, I'll tell you a great secret. ['one day']
They've been staying in the village for '*some* "*time*.

With other singular nouns, *some* is less usual, and has the meaning 'a certain' or 'some . . . or other':

Did you see *some strange man* (or other) looking over the hedge?
I hear that *some rare animal* (or other) has escaped from the zoo.

The addition of *or other* underlines the indefinite or 'unknown' quality of the referent.

Some of followed by a singular count noun is used in a partitive sense:

Some of the loaf has been eaten. ['part of the loaf']

Note [a] On *some* as a substitute pronoun, *cf* 12.17*f*.
[b] *Or other* can also be added to compounds beginning with *some-*:
It's time you got *somebody or other* to help you.
[c] Especially in AmE, *some* is strongly stressed with a singular count noun in exclamatory sentences such as:
That was "*some* '*meal*! ['a very good meal'] ⟨very informal⟩
[d] On unstressed *some* in comparison with zero article, *cf* 5.39*f*.

Multal and paucal quantifiers

6.53 The multal and paucal group of pronouns, with their matching postdeterminers (*cf* 5.23), are antonyms with a similar distribution. *Many* ['a large number'] contrasts with *a few* ['a small number'], and *much* ['a large amount'] contrasts with *a little* ['a small amount']:

I know { *many* / *a few* } people in Boston.

Many / *A few* } (of my friends) were there.

I have eaten { too *much* / *a little* } (of the food).

Much has been said about the cost of medicine.

Much and, to a lesser extent, *many* have acquired some nonassertive force (*cf* 10.61 Note [b]), with the result that they are rarely used, at least in informal English, without some negative or interrogative implication. Sentences like [1] are uncharacteristic of modern idiomatic English, and there is a preference for open-class quantifiers such as *a great deal* (*of*), as in [1a]:

We have endured { ?*much*. [1]
{ *a great deal*. [1a]

Similarly, rather than [2] with *many*, informal English shows a preference for [2a] with *plenty of* and *a lot of* (*cf* 5.25):

She has {*many* good ideas. [2]
She has {*plenty of* / *a lot of*} good ideas. [2a]

As postdeterminer and substitute pronoun, *many* can be preceded by the definite article:

the many dangers we face

The quantifier is followed in this construction by a restrictive relative clause; the quantifier itself, however, has the meaning of a nonrestrictive modifier, so that [3] can be paraphrased as [3a]:

I am well aware of *the many dangers (that) we face.* [3]
I am well aware of the dangers we face – and there are many of them. [3a]

These quantifiers are gradable, and can be accompanied by degree adverbs such as *very, too, so, as, enough.* Notice that *quite* precedes the indefinite article in *quite a few* ['a considerable number'], but that *very* follows it in *a very few*:

A: Have you seen (*very*) *many* houses for sale?

B: {Yes, I've seen *quite a few.*
(BUT NOT: **quite many*, **quite several*)
No, I've seen *only a very few.*

There are also comparative and superlative forms as shown in *Table* 6.53. As

Table 6.53 Comparative and superlative forms of multal and paucal quantifiers

	MULTAL		PAUCAL	
	count	noncount	count	noncount
ABSOLUTE	*many*	*much*	*a few*	*a little*
COMPARATIVE	*more*		*fewer* (*less*)	*less*
SUPERLATIVE	*most*		*fewest* (*least*)	*least*

in the case of determiner function (*cf* 5.24), there are prescriptive objections against the use of *less* and *least* with plural nouns. Yet they are widely used in informal English. Hence alongside *fewer changes* and *less noise*, the table allows for the possibility of *less changes.* Examples:

There used to be *more* women than men in the country,
but now there are {*fewer.* / *less.*

Most of us enjoy reading.

The is optionally added to *most* in the sense 'the greatest number (of)' (*cf* 7.84):

> In this constituency, the Labour Party often polls (*the*) *most votes*, and the Tory Party (*the*) *fewest*/*least*. But this time, the Tories had *more success than usual*.

Note [**a**] We keep *a few* and *a little* distinct from *few* and *little*, which are dealt with in 6.62.

[**b**] *Many*, like *few* (*cf* 6.62), has a predicative use ['numerous'] in formal and literary English (*cf* 5.23 Note [c]):

> His sins were *many*, and his friends were *few*.

[**c**] The absolute forms *many*/*much* and *a few*/*a little* can precede the comparative forms *more*, *fewer*, and *less* in the comparison of different totals or amounts:

> We have had { *many* {*more* / *fewer*} (*apples*) / *a few more* (*plums*) / *much less* (*rain*) } this year than last year.

One

(a) Numerical *one*

6.54 *One* in its numerical sense fits into the list of indefinite pronouns at this point; but it is a versatile word with a number of different functions, which can conveniently be considered together. Three types of pronoun *one* can be distinguished morphologically:

(a) NUMERICAL *ONE*	(b) SUBSTITUTE *ONE*	(c) GENERIC *ONE*
one	*one, ones*	*one, one's, oneself*

Fig 6.54 Three types of the pronoun *one*

The cardinal numeral *one* is, naturally enough, singular and count. It is invariable, but can occur, like other cardinals, either as a determiner or as the head of a noun phrase:

DETERMINATIVE FUNCTION	HEAD FUNCTION
{(*the*) *one* / *a*} boy/pen	*one of the* boys/pens

One can be the stressed equivalent of the indefinite article (*cf* 5.38), and is also the singular equivalent of the indefinite pronoun *some* in a context like this:

> I've made some cakes. Would you LÍKE {*one* / *some*} (of them)?

One also occurs in contrast to *the other* or *another* in correlative constructions. *One* (or *the one*) . . . *the other* is used with reference to two:

> I saw two suspicious-looking men. (*The*) *one* went this way, *the other* that.
>
> *One* of his eyes is better than *the other*.

One . . . another or *one . . . the other* is used with reference to more than two:

We overtook *one* car after { *another.* / *the other.* }

I've been busy with *one* thing or *another*.

There is an adverbial use of these correlatives in the construction *one* + preposition + *another* [1] or, more usually, preposition + the reciprocal pronoun *one another* [1a], or *one* + preposition + *the other* [1b]:

They talked { *one with another.* ⟨literary⟩ [1] / *with one another.* [1a] }

She stacked the books *one on top of the other.* [1b]

Note On the use of *one* meaning 'a certain' before a name, *eg*: *one Charlie Brown*, *cf* 5.63 Note [b].

(b) Substitute *one*

6.55 The substitute pronoun *one* has the plural *ones*, and is used as a substitute for a count noun, or for an equivalent nominal expression (*cf* 12.15*f*):

A: I'm looking for a book on grammar.
B: Is this *the one* you mean? ['the book on grammar']
A: Yes, I'd like a drink, but just *a small one*. ['a small drink']
B: I thought you preferred *large ones*. ['large drinks']

Substitute *one* can be easily combined with determiners and modifiers:

those ones I like *the old one* in the kitchen

However, it is only exceptionally that *one* immediately follows the indefinite article: *a one*. *One* alone is used as a substitute for *a/an* + noun:

I'm having *a drink*. Would you like *one* too? ['a drink']

Note [**a**] *A one* as a numeral can occur when *one* is used as a noun:

I couldn't make out whether the number was a seven or *a one*. ['a number one']

[**b**] The indefinite article with *one* is also heard more widely in casual speech, as in [1], in the sense of exclamatory 'a single one'; and, as in [2], in coy nonstandard usage in the sense of 'an amusing person':

I had lots of pencils, and now I haven't got *a one*! [1]
You are *a one*! [2]

(c) Generic *one*

6.56 Generic *one* occurs chiefly in the singular and with personal gender. It has the genitive *one's* and the reflexive *oneself* (*cf* 6.23). The meaning of generic *one* is 'people in general', often with particular reference to the speaker, *eg*:

I like to dress nicely. It gives *one* confidence. [1]

The use of generic *one* is chiefly formal, and is often replaced colloquially by *you* (*cf* 6.21):

{ *One* would / *You*'d } think they would run a later bus than that! [2]

In AmE, the coreferential use of *one* (or genitive *one's* or reflexive *oneself*) is characteristically formal, *he/his/himself* being preferred in regular usage:

One must be careful about { *one's* investments. ⟨esp BrE⟩ / *his* investments. ⟨esp AmE⟩ }

However, concern over sexual bias (*cf* 6.10) has caused AmE in effect to move towards adoption of the BrE pattern. On the other hand, in both AmE and BrE the use of generic *one* has never occurred in natural informal use. In consequence, people who embark on sequences involving *one* mix the pronoun *one* with those more natural to informal use. Hence discourse in both AmE and BrE may show vacillation, *eg*:

It's difficult if *your* house gets burgled, when *one* is out late at work.

Note Generic *one* does not accept determiners or modifiers:

**The cautious one* can't be too careful, can *the one*?

Half, several, enough

6.57 A miscellaneous group of pronouns may be illustrated at this point. They all have corresponding determiners:

Half (of) *the class/children* were girls.
I've only read *half* (of) *the book*.
We had to wait for *half an hour*.
Several (of my friends) attended the conference.
I have *several books* on folklore.
I've had *enough* (of your tantrums/misbehaviour).
Tom is *enough of a sportsman* to accept defeat gladly.
There is *enough* (of the) *water* to last several weeks.

Several is always plural, and indicates a number slightly greater than *a few*. *Enough* contrasts with *too little* and *too few* (*cf* 15.73). As determiner, it usually occurs in front of the head noun, but can also (rarely) follow it:

There was { *enough* food / food *enough* } to last a whole year.

Note *Half*, normally a predeterminer, as in *half a loaf, half an hour* (*cf* 5.16), also occurs occasionally as a postdeterminer: *a half loaf, a half hour*.

Other and *another*

6.58 *Other* as a postdeterminer follows the other determiners, including quantifiers and (sometimes) numerals (*cf* 5.20*ff*):

all the *other* women	that *other* colour	several *other* trees
her *other* sister	many *other* ideas	two *other* letters

As a pronoun, it can follow the same wide range of determiners; it also occurs in a plural form *others*:

Some people complained, but *others* were more tolerant.
Where are *all the others*? ['people, books', etc]
I have one sock, but I've lost *the other* (one).

Others is used in an absolute sense in:

We should be considerate to *others*. ['other people generally']

Another, although spelt as a single word, is to be considered a fusion of the two words *an* and *other*, or alternatively as a reduced version of *one other*:

I've sold my bicycle and bought *another* (one).
I have a/one sister in New York, and *another* in Canberra.

Apart from its usual meaning, *another* also has an incremental meaning of 'a further' or 'one more':

May I borrow *another* piece of paper? ['an additional piece of paper']

In this sense, *another* can be followed by a numeral and a plural noun:

The farm already has ten cows, but they are buying *another* five (cows). ['five more cows']

Although comparatively rare with the *of*-construction, *other/others* and *another* may be classed with the *of*-pronouns. Examples of their use with this construction are:

Some members of our expedition wanted to climb to the summit, but *others of* us thought it too dangerous.
I saw *another of* those yellow butterflies yesterday.

The genitive of *another* and *other* is rare when the reference is general:

She has { **another's* / *another person's* / *somebody else's* } coat.

We are not interested in { ?*others'* / *other people's* } problems.

But with narrower reference:

Each looked after { *the other's bag*. [two people] / *the others' bags*. [several people] }

Note *Other* and *another* tend to occur as the second item in correlative combinations (*cf* 6.31, 6.54), *eg*:

some people . . . others, the one . . . the other, each . . . other, one . . . other, another.

Nonassertive pronouns

6.59 In addition to the compound pronouns *anybody*, *anyone*, and *anything*, there are two nonassertive *of*-pronouns *any* and *either*. With reference to the distinction (made in 2.53*ff*) between assertive and nonassertive forms, we can see that there is a parallel between assertive *some* and nonassertive *any*:

Assertive:
Pam bought *some* apples.
Nonassertive, interrogative, positive:
Did Pam buy *any* apples?

Nonassertive, interrogative, negative:
Didn't Pam buy *any* apples?
Nonassertive, negative:
Pam didn't buy *any* apples.

Besides *not*, the negative forms whose scope favours nonassertive forms include for example the following (*cf* 10.60*ff*):

(a) Words negative in form: *never, no, neither, nor*
(b) Words negative in meaning:
  (i) the adverbs and determiners *hardly, little, few, only, seldom*, etc
  (ii) the 'implied negatives' *just, before*; *fail, prevent*; *reluctant, hard, difficult*, etc; and comparisons with *too*

Compare the following assertive/nonassertive pairs of sentences:

{ Jean will *always* manage to do *something* useful.
{ Jean will *never* manage to do *anything* useful.

{ There was *a good* chance *somebody* would come.
{ There was *little* chance *anybody* would come.

{ John was *eager* to read *some* (of the) books.
{ John was { *reluctant* / *too lazy* } to read *any* (of the) books.

***Some* and *any* series**

6.60 The main 'superficial' markers of nonassertion are negative, interrogative, and conditional clauses, but it is the underlying or basic meaning of the whole sentence which ultimately conditions the choice of the *some* or the *any* series (*cf* 10.61). For example, in sentence [1], the basic meaning is negative and nonassertive, as appears in the paraphrase [1a]:

Freud contributed more than *anyone* to the understanding of dreams. [1]
Nobody contributed as much to the understanding of dreams as Freud. [1a]

Conversely, *some* is often used in negative, interrogative, and conditional sentences, when the basic meaning is assertive ('positive orientation', *cf* 11.6):

Did { *somebody* / *anybody* } telephone last night?

The difference between these last two can be explained in terms of different presuppositions: *somebody* rather suggests that the speaker expected a telephone call, whereas *anybody* does not. In making an invitation or an offer, it is for the same reason polite to presuppose an acceptance:

Would you like *some* wine?

The following sentences illustrate further the use of the *some* series in superficially nonassertive contexts:

If *someone* were to drop a match here, the house would be on fire in two minutes.
But what if *somebody* decides to break the rules?
Will *somebody* please open the door?
Why don't you ask *some* other question?

Note The primary difference between *some* and *any* is that *some* is specific, though unspecified, while *any* is nonspecific (*cf* 10.60).

Any and *either*

6.61 *Any* is distinguished from *either* in representing a choice between three or more, while *either* limits the choice to two; thus *either*, like *both* (*cf* 6.50) and *neither* (*cf* 6.62), has dual meaning. This difference obtains whether the determiner or the pronoun is used:

I haven't written to {*any of my relatives* / *either of my parents*} about the marriage.

Can you see {*any part* of the roof? / *either end* of the tunnel?}

Any is also used for plural and noncount phrases:

Have you seen *any* (*of the*) *men* working on this site?
Don't spill *any* ((*of the*) *wine*).

On concord of verbs and pronouns with *any*, *cf* 10.42.

Any in its stressed form occurs in 'assertive territory' with the meaning 'it doesn't matter which/who/what'. This is uncommon except (a) where the clause contains a modal auxiliary (especially *will*, *can*, or *may*), or (b) where the noun phrase introduced by *any* contains restrictive postmodification (especially a relative clause):

He *will* eat *any* kind of vegetables.
Any dog *might* bite a child if teased.
Any offer *would* be better than this.
I advise you to accept *any* offer *you receive*.

The compound pronouns *anybody*, *anyone*, and *anything* are similarly used:

He *will* eat *anything*.
Anyone who tells lies is punished.

And a parallel use of *either*, where the hearer is offered a choice between two, is exemplified in:

You *can* ask *either* of us to help you.
Either of the other offers *would* be preferable to this.

The following sentences illustrate yet another superficially assertive use of *any*:

Please return *any* overdue books to the library.
We are grateful for *any* aid the public can give.

The meaning of *any* is nonassertive here in that its force is conditional: 'overdue books, if there are any'; 'aid, if any can be given'.

Note *Any* and its compounds can be intensified by the postmodifier *at all*:

Any offer *at all* would be better than this.

Negative pronouns

6.62 Corresponding to the negative determiners *no* and *neither*, the negative pronouns are the *of*-pronouns *none* and *neither*, and the compound pronouns *nobody*, *no one*, and *nothing* (*cf* 6.46). In addition, *few* and *little*, although not morphologically negative, are negative in meaning and in syntactic behaviour. Examples are:

I have received *no* urgent message(s).

None (of the students) {has / have} failed.

Neither {of the accusations / accusation} is true.

That's *none* of your business!

I said *nothing* about it.

{*Nobody* / *No one*} has sent an apology so far.

Neither differs from *no* and *none* as *either* differs from *any*: it is restricted to a set of two people or things, while *none* applies to three or more entities, and *no* to any number.

Few and *little*, as distinct from *a few* and *a little* (*cf* 6.53), are negative quantifiers corresponding to *many* and *much*:

There were *few* visitors at the exhibition. ['not many visitors']
Few of the animals will survive the winter. ['not many of the animals']
They have many supporters, while we have *few*.
There was *little* enthusiasm for the project. ['not much enthusiasm']
Little of the original building remains today. ['not much']
They have plenty of money, but we have comparatively *little*.

Few and *little* may be used attributively following *the* and also predicatively:

What we have is but *little*.	the *little* money I have left
His faults are *few*.	the *few* friends he has

In the attributive construction, *few* follows a determiner such as *the*, *those*, and *what*. The predicative construction is rather literary.

Note **[a]** On the choice of singular and plural concord with *no*, *neither*, *none*, etc, *cf* 10.42.

[b] The relation between the negative and the nonassertive forms, *eg* the equivalence of *I have none* and *I haven't any*, is discussed in 10.58.

[c] The negative quantifiers *few* and *little* can be intensified by *very*, *extremely*, etc:

extremely few (visitors) *very little* (food)

No, *none*, and the compound negative pronouns, on the other hand, can be intensified by the postmodifiers *at all* and *what(so)ever* (*cf* also 10.62): *none at all*, *nothing at all*, etc:

A: Did she have an excuse for being late? B: *None at all*/*what(so)ever*.

Numerals

Cardinal and ordinal numerals

6.63 Numerals have both open-class and closed-class characteristics (*cf* 2.42). They can function either as determinatives or as heads in the noun phrase. The numeral system of cardinals (*one*, *two*, etc) and ordinals (*first*, *second*, etc) will be clear from Table 6.63 below:

0 **nought, zero**	
1 **one**	1st **first**
2 **two**	2nd **second**
3 **three**	3rd **third**
4 **four**	4th fourth
5 **five**	5th fifth
6 **six**	6th sixth
7 **seven**	7th seventh
8 **eight**	8th eighth
9 **nine**	9th ninth
10 **ten**	10th tenth
11 **eleven**	11th eleventh
12 **twelve**	12th twelfth
13 **thir**teen	13th thirteenth
14 fourteen	14th fourteenth
15 fifteen	15th fifteenth
16 sixteen	16th sixteenth
17 seventeen	17th seventeenth
18 eighteen	18th eighteenth
19 nineteen	19th nineteenth
20 **twenty**	20th twentieth
21 twenty-one	21st twenty-first
22 twenty-two	22nd twenty-second
23 twenty-three	23rd twenty-third
24 twenty-four	24th twenty-fourth
25 twenty-five	25th twenty-fifth
26 twenty-six	26th twenty-sixth
27 twenty-seven	27th twenty-seventh
28 twenty-eight	28th twenty-eighth
29 twenty-nine	29th twenty-ninth
30 **thirty**	30th thirtieth
40 forty	40th fortieth
50 fifty	50th fiftieth
60 sixty	60th sixtieth
70 seventy	70th seventieth
80 eighty	80th eightieth
90 ninety	90th ninetieth
100 a/one **hundred**	100th (one) hundredth
101 a/one hundred and one	101st (one) hundred and first
102 a/one hundred and two	102nd (one) hundred and second
1,000 a/one **thousand**	1,000th (one) thousandth
1,001 a/one thousand (and) one	1,001st (one) thousand and first
2,000 two thousand	2,000th two thousandth
10,000 ten thousand	10,000th ten thousandth
100,000 a/one hundred thousand	100,000th (one) hundred thousandth
1,000,000 a/one **million**	1,000,000th (one) millionth

Note [**a**] *One thousand million* (1,000,000,000) is called *one billion* in the American system of numeration. In the UK, *billion* has traditionally been used for 1,000,000,000,000 (10^{12}), corresponding to *one trillion* in the US. However, the American usage where *billion* = 10^9 is now often used also in the UK by people who are ignorant of the double meaning of the word. It is not used by scientists, engineers, and mathematicians according to the British Standards Institution, which recommends that the use of *billion*, together with the equally ambiguous *trillion* (10^{12} or 10^{15}) and *quadrillion* (10^{15} or 10^{18}), should be avoided.
[**b**] The convention for separating the thousands in writing varies. In finance it is still normal to use a comma in the UK, *eg*: *£50,000*. However, since the comma is used to indicate the decimal point in most non-English-speaking countries, the comma is often avoided also in English, as it would cause confusion. In science and engineering a space is used, *eg*: *50 000*, and there are signs that this practice (which accords with the recommendation of the International Organization for Standardization) is beginning to be accepted for money as well, *eg*: *£3 982*.

6.64 The typographical distinctions in the table draw attention to the fact that cardinal numerals for *1* to *13*, and *20*, *30*, *50*, *100*, *1000*, etc are unsystematic, and have to be learned as individual items. Cardinal numerals from *14* to *99* are largely systematic, since they are formed by adding endings to the other numbers. There are two sets of such derivative numerals: *14* to *19* are formed by the ending *-teen*; *40*, *50*, *60*, *70*, *80*, *90* are formed by the ending *-ty*. Compare the series:

six ~ six'*teen* ~ 'six*ty*
seven ~ seven'*teen* ~ 'seven*ty*

Note however the spelling shift in:

four ~ *four*'teen ~ 'forty

Note also the pronunciation and spelling changes in:
five /aɪ/ ~ *fif*'teen /ɪ/ ~ '*fif*ty /ɪ/

Ordinal numerals for 1 to 3 are unsystematic: *first*, *second*, *third*. The rest are formed by adding *-th* to the cardinal numerals. (But note the change in *five* ~ *fifth*.) Cardinal numerals ending in *-y* change to *-ie* before *-th*:

four ~ four*th*	fourteen ~ fourteen*th*	forty ~ fortie*th*
five ~ fif*th*	fifteen ~ fifteen*th*	fifty ~ fiftie*th*
six ~ six*th*	sixteen ~ sixteen*th*	sixty ~ sixtie*th*

Both cardinal and ordinal numerals can function like pronouns [1–4] or like postdeterminers [5–6]:

Five is an odd number. [1]
There are *nine* (of them). [2]
I was the *tenth* on the list. [3]
She was only *five*. ['five years old'] [4]
There are *57* people on board. [5]
He referred to the *Fifth* Amendment. [6]

On the appositive use in *number five*, *page nine*, etc, *cf* 17.88 Note.

The ordinals in pronominal use are usually preceded by the definite article [7], and thus resemble superlatives with ellipted heads [8]:

Today is *the fourteenth* (day) (of July). [7]
This is *the best* (runner) of them all. [8]

Note [**a**] Unlike the change of *-y* to *-ie(s)* in nouns (*cf* 5.81) and verbs (*cf* 3.10), the change from cardinals ending in *-y* to ordinals ending in *-ie(th)*, adds a syllable. Compare:

sixt*y* ~ the sixt*ies* /'sɪkstɪz/ ~ the sixt*ieth* /'sɪkstɪəθ/

[**b**] Numerals in word-form between 21 and 99 (except the multiples of ten) are hyphenated: *twenty-one*, *eighty-six*, etc (on written fractions, *cf* 6.67). Small numerals – variously taken as under 20 or under 100 – are usually spelled as words in connected writing. Even large numerals are spelled out at the beginnings of sentences.

[**c**] The sign *0* is frequently read as /nɔːt/, especially in BrE, where it is spelt *nought*. In AmE *zero* /'zɪərəʊ/ is more commonly used. In both varieties, *zero* is normal in scientific contexts and also for temperature:

It's five degrees below zero.

Oh /əʊ/ is most frequent in reading out large sequences such as telephone and house numbers:

Extension 5076 'five *oh* seven six'
(James Bond) 007 '*double oh* seven'

When one is not talking about number values but quantities, there is a wide range of expressions, *eg*:

Italy won 4–0. 'four *nil*', 'four (to) *nothing*' [football]
It's Georgia over Alabama, 7–0. 'seven *zip*' [AmE sports reporting]
The score is 30–0. 'thirty *love*' [racket sports]

Also expressions with the pronouns *no* and *none* are used (*cf* 6.62), *eg*:

We had five lectures last week but *none* this week.
There will be two lessons tomorrow but *no* lesson on Tuesday.

[**d**] Note the following informal ways of indicating approximate numbers:

some eighty people [*some* unstressed]
80-*odd* people [BUT NOT: *85-odd people]
80 people *or* {*so* / *thereabouts*}
80 *or so* people
a good eighty people ['at least 80']
} ['about eighty']

An example of approximate time:

I'll be there by eight*ish*. ['about eight o'clock']

Hundred, thousand, million

6.65 With *hundred, thousand*, and *million*, *one* has an unstressed variant *a* (*cf* 5.38):

$100 is read as 'one (*or* a) hundred dollars'

However, only *one* can be used after another numeral [1], and usually in the low year dates [2]:

1100 is read as {'one / 'a} thousand {one / *a} hundred' [1]

169 BC is read as 'one hundred (and) sixty-nine BC' [2]

Since *one* is a numeral, it can be preceded by a determiner:

the/a/that 100 ('one hundred') metre race

Hundred, *thousand*, and *million* are used both as numerals, as in [3], and as quantity nouns with plural *-s* and followed by *of* (*cf* 5.89), as in [4] and [5]:

Ten million viewers saw the title fight on TV. [3]
Millions (*of* people) are starving. [4]
Hundreds of thousands (*of* people) are homeless. [5]

In technical contexts, *thousand* is sometimes abbreviated *k* and *million m*:

That's a job which pays *$25k*.
$25m 'twenty-five million dollars'

Dates

6.66 We always read year dates as hundreds:

in 1985 { 'nineteen eighty-five'
'nineteen hundred and eighty-five' ⟨formal⟩
*'one thousand nine hundred and eighty-five' }

in the 1600s 'sixteen hundreds'

Other examples:

in the 17th century 'seventeenth century'
in the 1980s read (but rarely written) as: 'nineteen-eighties' (*cf*: *in the early eighties*; *a woman in her* (*early*/*mid*/*late*) *thirties*; *a girl in her early*/*mid*/*late teens*)

Day and month are usually indicated thus:

7(*th*) *February* or *February* 7(*th*) read as 'the seventh of February', 'February the seventh', also 'February seven', or 'February seventh'

In date abbreviations, numerals are normally separated by an oblique, or a period:

7/2/82 or *7.2.82*

Both could be used for '7(th) February 1982' ⟨BrE⟩ or 'July 2(nd), 1982' ⟨AmE⟩.

Numerals in abbreviations for times of day contain a colon ⟨esp AmE⟩ or a period ⟨BrE⟩, as in:

6:30 or *6.30* 'six-thirty' or 'half past six'

Fractions

6.67 Vulgar fractions are written and read thus:

$\frac{1}{2}$	'a/one half'	$\frac{2}{3}$	'two-thirds'
$\frac{1}{3}$	'a/one third'	$\frac{7}{8}$	'seven-eighths'
$\frac{1}{4}$	'a/one quarter'	$3\frac{3}{4}$	'three and three-quarters'
$\frac{1}{5}$	'a/one fifth'	$\frac{8}{76}$	{ 'eight over seventy-six' / 'eight seventy-sixths' }

Hyphens are often used, particularly in premodification:

a *three-quarter* mile; *three(-)quarters* of a mile [*fourths* is a less common alternative to *quarters* here]

Hyphens are not used with the indefinite article: thus *one-third* but *a third*. Note the different read forms for $\frac{3}{4}$ and $\frac{2}{3}$ in premodification:

a *three-quarter* majority a *two-thirds* majority

Compare:

He won the race by { *a/one hundredth* of a second. [$= \frac{1}{100}$] / *a/one two hundredth* of a second. [$= \frac{1}{200}$] }

He got *three hundredths* of the money. [$= \frac{3}{100}$]

The point at which integers cease and decimal fractions begin is indicated by a period (sometimes raised above the line in BrE). In decimal fractions, the whole numerals are read out in the usual way ('seventy-one', etc), but the numerals to the right of the decimal point are read out as single digits ('five three', etc):

71.53 'seventy-one point five three'

0.426 {'zero / 'nought} point four two six'

Note South African English follows the practice in most Continental European languages of writing decimal fractions with a comma (and reading it as 'comma') instead of a period:

1, 2% 'one comma two per cent'

Mathematical symbols

6.68 Small numerals are usually spelled out, as it is not usual to introduce mathematical symbols into ordinary writing; but such symbols as the following are normally flanked only by numerals, not words:

=	'equals'	+	'plus'
–	'minus'	×	'times' or 'multiplied by'
÷	'divided by'	√	'the (square) root of'

Thus:

$$(17 - \sqrt{9} + \tfrac{65}{5}) - (4 \times 3) = 15$$

would be read as 'seventeen minus the square root of nine, plus sixty-five over five, minus four times three, equals fifteen'. (Mathematical symbols make the relationships unambiguous.)

On concord in expressions like '2 and 2 is/are 4', *cf* 10.37 Note [e].

Currency statements

6.69 The dollar sign ($) and the pound sign (£) are written before the numeral but said after the numeral:

$475 'four hundred (and) seventy-five dollars'
£7.3m 'seven point three million pounds'

The abbreviations *p*, for both singular *penny* and plural *pence* (*cf* 5.90), and *¢*, for *cent(s)*, are written solid after the numeral:

87p 'eighty-seven pence' ⟨informal: /piː/⟩
75¢ 'seventy-five cents'

In currency statements, the period is usually ignored in reading. The combinations of *£* and *p* and of *$* and *¢* are pronounced as follows (from most to least formal):

£8.25
- 'eight pounds twenty-five pence'
- 'eight pounds twenty-five'
- 'eight twenty-five'

$3.40
- 'three dollars (and) forty cents'
- 'three dollars forty'
- 'three forty'

Bibliographical note

General on pronouns: Bolinger (1977b, 1979); Dušková (1965); Jackendoff (1968); Jacobsson (1970); Langacker (1969); Lees and Klima (1963); Storms (1964).

On personal, possessive, and reflexive pronouns, see Erdmann (1978); Helke (1979); Jacobsson (1968a); Seppänen (1980); Wales (1980); Wood (1955/6); on reciprocal pronouns, see Kjellmer (1982); on demonstrative pronouns, see R. Lakoff (1974).

On indefinite pronouns, see Bald (forthcoming); Bolinger (1976); Close (1976); Conrad (1979); Sahlin (1979).

On numerals, see Peters (1980); Seppänen (forthcoming b).

7 Adjectives and adverbs

ADJECTIVES

Characteristics of the adjective

7.1 We usually cannot tell whether a word is an adjective by looking at it in isolation, because the form of a word does not necessarily indicate its syntactic function. Some suffixes are indeed found only, or typically, with adjectives (*cf* App I.38*ff*), *eg*:

-able:	comfortable	*-al*:	seasonal
-ful:	playful	*-ic*:	scientific
-ish:	greyish	*-less*:	useless
-ous:	dangerous	*-y*:	dirty

However, many common adjectives have no identifying form, *eg*: *good*, *hot*, *little*, *young*, *fat*.

Nor can we identify a word as an adjective merely from its potentialities for inflection. It is true that many adjectives inflect for the comparative and superlative, *eg*:

great ~ *greater* ~ *greatest*

But many do not allow inflected forms (*cf* 7.81), *eg*:

disastrous ≁ **disastrouser* ≁ **disastrousest*

Moreover, a few adverbs can be similarly inflected (*cf* 7.83), *eg*:

(He worked) *hard* ~ *harder* ~ *hardest*

Many adjectives provide the base from which adverbs are derived by means of an *-ly* suffix (*cf* 7.46, App I.41), *eg*:

adjective *great* ~ adverb *greatly*

Nevertheless, some do not allow this derivational process; for example, there is no adverb **oldly* derived from the adjective *old*. And there are a few adjectives that are themselves derived from an adjective base in this way, *eg*: *kindly*, an item functioning also as an adverb.

Four criteria for adjectives

7.2 Four features are commonly considered to be characteristic of adjectives (but *cf* 7.4 Note):

(a) They can freely occur in ATTRIBUTIVE function (*cf* 7.20), *ie* they can premodify a noun, appearing between the determiner (including zero article) and the head of a noun phrase:

an *ugly* painting, the *round* table, *dirty* linen

(b) They can freely occur in PREDICATIVE function (*cf* 7.20), *ie* they can function as subject complement, as in [1], or as object complement, as in [2], *eg*:

The painting is *ugly*. [1]
He thought the painting *ugly*. [2]

(c) They can be premodified by the intensifier *very* (*cf* 7.56), *eg*:

The children are very *happy*.

(d) They can take COMPARATIVE and SUPERLATIVE forms (*cf* 7.75). The comparison may be by means of inflections (*-er* and *-est*), as in [3–4], or by the addition of the premodifiers *more* and *most* ('periphrastic comparison'), as in [5–6]:

The children are *happier* now. [3]
They are the *happiest* people I know. [4]
These students are *more intelligent*. [5]
They are the *most beautiful* paintings I have ever seen. [6]

Central and peripheral adjectives

7.3 However, not all words that are traditionally regarded as adjectives possess all of these four features. It is, for example, only in exceptional cases that *afraid* can occur attributively (feature (a) above) and *utter* can occur predicatively (feature (b)):

?**afraid* people ~ People are *afraid*.
utter nonsense ~ ?*That nonsense is *utter*.

Neither premodification by *very* (feature (c)), nor comparison (feature (d)), applies to, for example, *infinite* in:

God's infinite mercy ~ God's mercy is infinite.
BUT: *God's mercy is very infinite. *It's more infinite than . . .

We analyse adjectives with respect to these four features. To illustrate the types, we have selected eight words, including among them instances that are on the borderline between the adjective and adverb classes.

For testing predicative position, we use the following frame with *seem* as copular verb: '(*The*) noun *seemed*___'. Since words can belong to more than one class, we place them in the context of a sentence, so that it should be clear which use of the words is being tested (*cf Table* 7.3):

John is *hungry*. [1]
The universe is *infinite*. [2]
Susan is an *old* friend. [3]
The prisoners were *afraid*. [4]
Bob is an *utter* fool. [5]
The patient was *asleep*. [6]
The meeting is *soon*. [7]
Anna is *abroad*. [8]

Table 7.3 Criteria for establishing adjective classes

(a) = attributive use
(b) = predicative use after the copula *seem*
(c) = premodification by *very*
(d) = comparison

	(a)	(b)	(c)	(d)		
[1] *hungry*	+	+	+	+	CENTRAL	ADJECTIVES
[2] *infinite*	+	+	−	−		
[3] *old*	+	−	+	+	PERIPHERAL	
[4] *afraid*	?	+	+	+		
[5] *utter*	+	−	−	−		
[6] *asleep*	−	+	−	−		
[7] *soon*	−	−	+	+	ADVERBS	
[8] *abroad*	−	−	−	−		

7.4 If we examine *Table* 7.3, we see that [1] *hungry* alone satisfies all four criteria; [2] *infinite* accepts (a) and (b); [3] *old* accepts (a), (c), (d); [4] *afraid* accepts (b), (c), (d); [5] *utter* satisfies only (a), and [6] *asleep* only (b); [7] *soon* accepts (c) and (d); while [8], finally, satisfies none of the four criteria.

Criterion (c), acceptance of premodification by *very*, and criterion (d), the ability to take comparison, have no diagnostic value in distinguishing adjectives from adverbs. These two features generally coincide for a particular word, and are determined by a semantic feature, gradability, which cuts across word classes (*cf* 7.42). Thus, as we can see in the table, the adverb *soon* is gradable, just like the central adjective *hungry*. Many adverbs are gradable, just as many adjectives are gradable. And these two word classes use the same features to realize the gradability of an item, in particular premodification by *very* and comparison (*cf* 7.74*ff*). Hence, these two features neither distinguish adjectives from adverbs, nor are they found in all adjectives.

In this book the first six words in the table (*hungry*, *infinite*, *old*, *afraid*, *utter*, *asleep*) are regarded as ADJECTIVES, whereas *soon* and *abroad*, at the bottom of the table, are assigned to the ADVERB class.

We consider the ability of functioning both attributively and predicatively to be a central feature of adjectives. Words like *hungry* and *infinite*, which satisfy both these criteria (a *and* b), are therefore called CENTRAL adjectives.

Words like *old*, *afraid*, *utter*, and *asleep*, which satisfy at least one of these first two criteria (a *or* b), are called PERIPHERAL adjectives.

Note The use of the criteria for testing adjective status of words like *infinite* is complicated by the fact that there is a prescriptive tradition forbidding the use of *very* or the comparative with intensifying adjectives like *perfect*, *absolute*, *unique* (*cf* 7.33*f*), and also with the corresponding adverbs (*perfectly*, *absolutely*, *uniquely*) (*cf* 8.106).

The adjective in relation to other word classes

7.5 We now consider some other examples of overlapping between the adjective class and other word classes. The overlapping may be due to syntactic features that are characteristic of other classes but displayed by some adjectives, or to features characteristic of the adjective class but displayed by some members of other classes. The three relevant word classes are adverbs (7.6–11), nouns (7.12–14), and participles (7.15–19).

Adjectives and adverbs

Adjective and adverb homomorphs

7.6 There is a certain overlap between the adjective and adverb classes. Compare the adjective function of premodification in the left-hand column and the adverb function of adverbial in the right-hand column:

a *rapid* car ~ drive {*rapidly* / **rapid*} [1]

a *fast* car ~ drive {**fastly* / *fast*} [2]

a *slow* car ~ drive {*slowly* / *slow*} [3]

Example [1] represents the normal case, where there is regular variation between form and function of the adverb and adjective, and where the adverb is formed by the derivational suffix *-ly* (*cf* 7.46, Type (c)).

Fast in [2] has identical form in both adjective and adverb functions. Similarly, *long* and *short*, for example, can be used as both adjective and adverb:

Did you have to wait {a *long* time? / *long*? / **longly*?}

She stopped *short* when she saw him.

Whereas there is no adverb **longly*, there is an adverb *shortly*, but with a different meaning 'soon', as in *I'll be back shortly*. Adjective/adverb homomorphs are exceptional, and many such uses in adverb function occur chiefly in fixed expressions (*cf* 7.8).

7.7 In 7.6 [3], both *slow* and *slowly* function as adverb. Adjective forms like *slow* differ from the corresponding adverb forms in several ways. The adjective form, if admissible at all, is restricted to a position after the verb or (if present) the object:

He {*slowly* / **slow*} drove the car into the garage.

He drove the car {*slowly* / ?**slow*} into the garage.

In those cases where there is variation (*eg*: *drive slow* ~ *slowly*, *buy cheap* ~ *cheaply*), the adjective form and a corresponding *-ly* adverb form can be used interchangeably, with little or no semantic difference, except that some people prefer the adverb form, particularly in formal style.

In standard use, only a limited number of adverbs are formally identical to adjectives. Thus there are no acceptable sentences:

*He came back *sudden*.
*She buys her clothes *careful*.

By contrast, in nonstandard or very familiar English, the use of the adjective for the adverb form is widespread, *eg*:

Don't talk *daft*.
She pays her rent *regular*.
They played *real good*.
He spoke to John *sharp*.

However, unlike the absolute form, the comparative and superlative forms of some adjectives are common also in standard English. Compare:

?Speak *clear*. [1]
Speak *clearer*. ['more clearly'] [2]
This newsreader speaks *clearest* of all. ['most clearly'] [3]

Whereas *clear* in [1] is nonstandard for *clearly*, [2] and [3] are both acceptable standard English variants of *more clearly* and *most clearly*, respectively. Other examples:

It's *easier* said than done. ['more easily'] [4]
Ami ran (the) *slowest*. [5]
The car went *slower and slower*. [6]

(The warning 'Danger, go *slow*' is however fully acceptable also to speakers who reject 'Drive the car *slow*'.)

Example [6] with coordination illustrates a factor which helps to make the adjective form particularly acceptable. Whereas *speak clear* is nonstandard, *speak loud and clear* is fully acceptable in standard English. Other examples of coordination are the following:

lose *fair and square*
be brought up *short and sharp*
be tangled up *good and proper* ⟨nonstandard⟩

Note [**a**] *Cf* 7.20 for the use of adjectives expressing the result of the process denoted by the verb, *eg*: That powder washed the clothes *white*.

[**b**] *Cf* 7.27 for the use of adjectives as the sole realization of a verbless clause, *eg*: *Nervous*, the man opened the letter.

Adverbs without *-ly*

7.8 There are some other words which, like *fast* in 7.6, have the same form (without the *-ly* suffix) in adjective and adverb functions, *eg*:

She arrived in the *late* afternoon. [adjective]
She arrived *late* in the afternoon. [adverb]

Late also has an *-ly* form, *lately*, but with a different meaning:

Have you seen her *lately*? ['recently']

Other examples are the following (adjective uses are given first):

> *clean* clothes; play the game *clean*; The knife cut *cleanly*.
> a *close* friend; stay *close* together; He watched her *closely*.
> This ring must be *dear* [⟨esp BrE⟩ 'expensive']; I paid *dear*(*ly*) for my mistake; She loved him *dearly*.
> a *deep* breath; live *deep* in the woods; breathe *deep*(*ly*)
> a *direct* flight; We flew *direct*(*ly*) to Paris; Reply to me *direct*(*ly*) ['direct to me']; I'll see you *directly* ['immediately'] after lunch.
> a *fine* view; It works *fine*; The parsley was chopped *fine*(*ly*).
> a *flat* country; I'm *flat* broke ⟨informal⟩; He's *flatly* opposed to it.
> a *high* building; The plane flew *high* above; They were praised *highly*.
> *light* weapons; She travels *light*; They were *lightly* armed.
> a *sharp* turn; She turned *sharp*(*ly*) left; She turned the car *sharply*.
> The scar was an inch *wide*; The door was *wide* open; He seems to be *widely* known here.

Adjectives and adverbs in *-ly*

7.9 Some words in *-ly* can function both as adjectives and adverbs:

ADJECTIVE	ADVERB
an *early* train	We finished *early* today.
A *likely* story!	He'll very/most *likely* succeed. ⟨esp BrE⟩
a *monthly* visit	She visited him *monthly*.

Words in *-ly* like *monthly*, which denote time, can also function as time adverbs: *daily*, *fortnightly* ⟨esp BrE⟩, *hourly*, *nightly*, *quarterly*, *weekly*, and *yearly*.

When we require adverbs corresponding to *-ly* adjectives such as *friendly*, *grisly*, *kindly*, *kingly*, *lively*, *manly*, and *masterly*, we normally use an adjective construction, thus avoiding the double suffix *-lily*:

> She received us *in a friendly way*.
> She gave us a *friendly* welcome.
> [BUT NOT: *She received us *friendlily*.]

Verbs with percept as subject (*smell*, *feel*, *look*, *sound*) have an adjective phrase as complement (*cf* 4.29*f*). But there is some uncertainty in the use of adjective and related adverb forms:

> The flowers smell { *good*/**well*. | *sweet*/?*sweetly*. }

There are prescriptive objections to the adverb form for these items with *smell* in this use, and to *badly* with *feel*. With *feel* and *smell*, the adverb form is used to express intensity of feelings:

> He felt { *badly* [1] | *keenly* [2] | *strongly* [3] | *deeply* [4] } about it.
> It smells *strongly* of garlic.

Note [**a**] Note the difference in meaning between the adjective and adverb form in the following:

She feels { *bad* today. [health] [1a]
{ *bad*/*badly* about it. ['guilty', 'uneasy'] [1b]

The adjective *keen* has the different sense of 'enthusiastic':

He { felt / was } *keen* about/on it. [2a]

Contrast with the intensifying adverb *strongly* in [3] the physical sense of *strong* in [3a]:

He { felt / was } *strong*. [3a]

[**b**] The use of adverb forms after *taste* seems much less common and would be unacceptable to many speakers:

The food tastes { *good*/?*well*.
{ *marvellous*/?**marvellously*.

[**c**] Note the distinction in meaning between the adjectives *good* and *well* (*cf* 7.38) after *look*:

She looks *good*. [appearance]
She looks *well*. [health]

Adjectives and adverbs beginning with *a-*

7.10 Certain words beginning with *a-* (like *asleep* in 7.3*f*) have constituted a problem in classification for grammarians, some assigning them to the adjective class, and others to the adverb class. These *a*-words function predicatively, but only a few can be freely used attributively.

Only a relatively small number of adverbs can function predicatively, namely certain place adverbs, *eg*: *aboard*, *upstairs* (*cf* 8.41) and time adverbs, *eg*: *now*, *tonight* (*cf* 8.76). But even these adverbs are used predicatively only after *be*, while adjectives can be used with other copular verbs as well (*cf* 7.3*f*). Compare the different patterns with the copular *be* and *seem*:

The patient { was *asleep*/*hungry*/*abroad*/*there*.
{ seemed { *asleep*/*hungry*. [adjectives]
{ *abroad/*there*. [adverbs]

Another difference between *a*-adjectives and *a*-adverbs is that *a*-adjectives refer to temporary states and cannot be part of the predication after verbs of motion; *a*-adverbs, on the other hand, denote direction after such verbs. Contrast:

She went { *aboard*/*abroad*/*around*/*away*. [adverbs]
{ **afraid*/**alert*/**asleep*/**awake*. [adjectives]

The sentences with *a*-adjectives are acceptable only if the adjectives can be interpreted not as part of the predication but as supplementive adjective clauses (*cf* 7.27*f*). For example, we might be able to interpret *He went afraid* as 'He was afraid as he went'.

Examples of some other *a*-adjectives:

ablaze	*alike*	*ashamed*	*adrift*	*aghast*
alive	*afire*	*ajar*	*alone*	*averse*
afloat	*alert*	*aloof*	*awake*	*aware*

7.11 *A*-adjectives vary as to whether they can be attributive. Most *a*-adjectives are only marginally acceptable in attributive function, unless they are premodified:

?an *afraid* look ?an *alive* eye

Aloof and *alert*, however, are fully acceptable in attributive function, *eg*:

an *aloof* character an *alert* manner

Most *a*-adjectives can occur attributively when they are modified:

a *somewhat afraid* soldier
the *fast asleep* children
a *really alive/lively* student
the *wide awake* patient

Some *a*-adjectives have parallel *a*-less forms or synonyms in attributive function:

Their ambitions are *alike*. [*cf*: They have *similar* ambitions.]
The soldier was *alone*, patrolling. [*cf*: a *lone/solitary* soldier]
The animals are *alive*. [*cf*: They are *live/living* animals.]
The woman is *afraid*. [*cf*: a *frightened* woman]
The children were *asleep*. [*cf*: the *sleeping* children]
She was not *aware* of the consequences. [*cf*: a *conscious/deliberate* action]

Some *a*-adjectives freely take premodification by *very* and comparison, *eg*: *afraid*, *alert*, *alike*, *aloof*, *ashamed*, and *awake*. Others do so marginally, *eg*: *asleep* and *awake*. *Alive to* in the sense 'aware of' can be premodified by *very* and can be compared. Some of the *a*-adjectives can also be premodified by *very much* (particularly *afraid*, *alike*, *ashamed*, *aware*), and *aware* can be premodified by (*very*) *well*, too. There is vacillation between *so/too alike* and *so much/too much alike*. Since the modifiers *much* and *well* are characteristically taken by many adverbs (*cf* 7.16 Note), these *a*-words show themselves to be particularly marginal to the adjective class.

Note [**a**] Adverbs which cannot be used predicatively with *seem* can occur after *seem to be* (a construction which is also available for adjectives):

They seem to be { *aboard, abroad, around*. [adverbs] / *afraid, alert, asleep*. [adjectives] }

[**b**] Like the adverbs in *She was downstairs/outside*, *abroad* can be a response to a question introduced by the interrogative adverb *where*:

A: Where is he? B: *Abroad*.

Other *a*-adverbs, *eg*: *around* and *away*, are less likely to be the sole response to a *where*-question, though they can supply the information requested by *where*:

A: Where is he? B: He is *around/away*.

[**c**] Notice the contrast between the *a*-adjective in *They looked asleep* and the *a*-adverb in *They looked away*. With *asleep*, *looked* is a copular verb, synonymous with *seemed*. With *away*, it is an intransitive verb, similar in meaning and use to *glanced*.

[**d**] *Alike* requires reference to coordinated noun phrases or to a plural noun phrase, a constraint identical with that for reciprocal pronouns (*cf* 6.31). Compare:

{ John and Mary / The children } are { *alike*. / *like each other*. }

[**e**] *Alone* can refer either to a permanent characteristic 'solitary by nature', or to a temporary feature 'without companionship'. In the former sense, it is acceptable, at least to some speakers, in constructions with *seem* and *very*:

(?) She *seemed alone*. (?) She is *very alone*.
[BUT: ?*She *seemed very alone* in the house that morning.]

Adjectives and nouns

7.12 Nouns are commonly used attributively, and are thus superficially similar to peripheral adjectives in satisfying criterion (a) (7.3*f*), *eg*:

the *bus* station, a *business* friend, *lamb* chops

However, nouns do not satisfy any of the other criteria (b, c, d) for adjective status. Compare:

(a) the *large* station	the *bus* station
(b) The station seems *large*.	*The station seems *bus*.
(c) a very *large* station	*a very *bus* station
(d) a *larger* station	*a *busser* station

Furthermore, nouns have other features which distinguish them from adjectives. Compare, for example:

I saw a *bus*.	*I saw a *large*.
The *bus* is here.	*The *large* is here.
one *bus*/two *buses*	*one *large*/two *larges*

The relation of nouns to adjectives is further discussed in 7.13*f*, and premodification by nouns in 17.104*ff*.

7.13 Some items can be both adjectives and nouns. For example, *criminal* is an adjective in that it can be used both attributively and predicatively:

a *criminal* attack
The attack seemed *criminal* to us.

But the word *criminal* can also be a count noun, since it can:

(i) take determiners:

The criminal pleaded guilty.
He is probably *a criminal*.

(ii) be inflected for number:

one criminal ~ *several criminals*

(iii) be inflected for the genitive case:

the criminal's sentence, *the criminals'* views

(iv) be premodified by an adjective:

a *violent* criminal

Of course, the attributive use of an item such as *criminal* is not a sufficient criterion for calling it an adjective. As we have seen in 7.12, nouns, as well as adjectives, can be used as premodifiers of nouns. In [1], *criminal* is undoubtedly an adjective, since there is no article or number contrast [1a, 1b]:

His attack was { *criminal*. [1]
{ **a*/*the criminal*. [1a]
{ **criminals*. [1b]

Similarly, *criminal* in *a criminal attack* is also an adjective, since the phrase is equivalent to 'a brutal attack' and not to, say, 'an attack by a criminal' (*cf* 7.14). Moreover, *criminal* is gradable in that phrase:

a *very/rather* criminal attack

It is also an adjective in *criminal law* ('law relating to crime'; *cf*: *civil law*, *commercial law*) and in both senses of *criminal lawyer* ('a lawyer specializing in criminal law' and 'a lawyer who is criminal'; *cf* 7.37).

We will therefore say that *criminal* is a homomorph (*cf* 2.38), *ie* both an adjective and a noun, and that the relationship between the adjective *criminal* and the noun *criminal* is that of conversion (*cf* App I.43*ff*). Here are some other examples of conversions from adjective to noun:

ADJECTIVES	NOUNS
an *ancient* custom	She is investigating the *ancients'* conception of the universe.
a *black* student	There was only one *black* in my class.
a *classic* book	You won't find many *classics* in our library.
intellectual interests	She considers herself an *intellectual*.
a *noble* family	The king greeted his *nobles*.
a *natural* skier	He's a *natural* for the job.
a *six-year-old* boy	Our *six-year-old* is at school.

Note Items like *medical*, *physical*, and *oral* are also used without a noun head:

Have you had a *medical/physical* yet?

When is your French *oral*?

They differ, however, from the previous group in that speakers tend to feel that a noun like *examination* is implied, which is not the case with, say, *an intellectual*. On the other hand, *oral* has a plural *orals*, which is an indication of full conversion. *Medical* and *physical* do not have plurals (at least not in general use), and are therefore instances of partial conversion.

7.14 Nouns functioning attributively also possess other features which distinguish them from adjectives (*cf* 7.12). The basically nominal character of a premodifying noun, such as *garden* in *garden tools*, is shown by its correspondence to a prepositional phrase with the noun as complement: *tools for the garden*. Compare also:

the '*city* 'council ~ the council *for the city*
a '*stone* 'wall ~ a wall (made) *of stone*
'*August* 'weather ~ weather (usual) *in August*

Such a correspondence is not available for attributive adjectives:

a '*long* 'poem	a '*thick* 'wall
the '*urban* 'council	'*hot* 'weather

However, we can sometimes use a postmodifying prepositional phrase with a related noun as complement, *eg*:

a *long* poem ~ a poem *of considerable length*

As indicated, the normal (noncontrastive) stress for both groups is even stress. The stressing of noun + noun sequences and their relation to compounds and prepositional phrases are discussed in 17.104*ff*.

Like adjectives, nouns can function as subject complement after copular verbs, in particular after *be* (*cf* 2.17):

That man is *a fool.*
The noise you heard was *thunder.*
She became *a nurse.*

Some nouns can also be used within the subject complement after *seem* ⟨esp BrE⟩. These are indeed very close to adjectives:

He seems *a fool.* [= *foolish*]
Your remark seems (complete) *nonsense* to me. [= *nonsensical*]
My stay there seemed *sheer bliss.* [= *blissful*]
His friend seems very much *an Englishman.* [= very *English*]

Note however the change of premodifier in: *very much an Englishman* ~ *very English.*

The closeness is of course greatest for noncount nouns such as *nonsense* and *bliss*, since, like adjectives, they do not take number contrast. However, they can appear without an overt determiner (unlike adjectives functioning as heads of noun phrases, *cf* 7.23*ff*):

She doesn't like *nonsense.* [noncount noun]
She admires *the mystical.* [adjective as head of a noun phrase]

Some noun forms can function both attributively and predicatively, in which case we can perhaps regard them as adjectives (*cf* App I.51). They denote style or material from which things are made:

that *concrete* floor ~ That floor is *concrete.*
Worcester porcelain ~ This porcelain is *Worcester.*
those *apple* pies ~ Those pies are *apple.* ⟨informal⟩

Note [**a**] Attributive nouns can be coordinated with nongradable adjectives, *eg*: *weekly and morning newspapers*, *city and suburban houses*, but it seems that such conjoinings are normally possible only when there is an ellipted head, but not otherwise:

weekly newspapers and morning newspapers
city houses and suburban houses
*a city and pleasant house

Where both premodifiers are nouns, ellipsis need not be involved, *eg*:

a glass and concrete house ['a house made of glass and concrete']
a cheese and cucumber sandwich ['a sandwich containing cheese and cucumber']

These become ambiguous in the plural (*cf* 13.68), *eg*:

cheese and cucumber sandwiches ['each of the sandwiches contains cheese and cucumber' or 'cheese sandwiches and cucumber sandwiches']

[**b**] The nouns that can most easily appear as complement after *seem* are those that are gradable, that is to say the nouns that can be modified by intensifying adjectives (*cf* 7.33*f*). However, some speakers, while accepting in this function noncount nouns and singular count nouns, find plural nouns dubious:

?They seem *fools.* ?His friends seem very much *Englishmen.*

Material nouns, which are not gradable, are also dubious after *seem*:

?That floor seems *concrete.* ?Those pies seem *apple.*

[**c**] *Fun* is primarily a regular noncount noun: *a great deal of fun, great fun, some fun.* However, in informal usage ⟨esp AmE⟩, *fun* has been fully converted into an adjective:

The party was *fun*; *a fun person*; *a very fun party*

[**d**] On the use of nouns in cases like *Are you cosmetics?*, *cf* 5.5 Note.

Adjectives and participles

7.15 There are many adjectives that have the same suffixes as participles in *-ing* or *-ed* (including the variants of *-ed*). These will be called PARTICIPIAL ADJECTIVES:

PREDICATIVE USE	ATTRIBUTIVE USE
His views were very *surprising*.	~ his *surprising* views
The man seemed very *offended*.	~ the *offended* man

They include forms in *-ed* that have no corresponding verbs:

The results were *unexpected*.	~ the *unexpected* results
Her children must be *downhearted*.	~ her *downhearted* children
All his friends are *talented*.	~ his *talented* friends
His lung is *diseased*.	~ his *diseased* lung

When there are no corresponding verbs (**to unexpect*, **to downheart*, **to talent*, **to disease*), the forms are obviously not participles (*cf* Note below).

When there is a corresponding verb, attributively used *-ed* forms usually have a passive meaning (*cf* 17.29), *eg*:

lost property ~ property that *has been lost*

In some cases, however, the *-ed* participle is not interpreted as passive. The passive interpretation is excluded if the corresponding verb can be used only intransitively:

the *escaped* prisoner ['the prisoner who has escaped']
the *departed* guests ['the guests who have departed']

But even in other instances, the participle relates to the intransitive use of the verb; thus the passive interpretation is impossible in:

a *grown* boy ['a boy who has grown (up)']

It is unlikely in:

the *faded* curtains ['the curtains which have faded']
the *retired* manager ['the manager who has retired']

Predicative use occurs only with some of these participial adjectives:

The curtains are *faded*.
Her father is now *retired*.
Her son is *grown*. [dubious in BrE, but *full-grown* or *grown-up* is fully acceptable]
The guests are *departed*.

The last example is archaic, unlike the acceptable *the departed guests* (*cf* the reverse situation with *go*: *The guests are gone*, **the gone guests*). But contrast:

*The prisoner is *escaped*.

Sometimes there is a corresponding verb, but it has a different meaning. We can therefore have ambiguous sentences where the ambiguity depends on whether the word is a participle or a participial adjective:

{ ADJECTIVE: She is (very) *calculating* (but her husband is frank).
{ PARTICIPLE: She is *calculating* (our salaries). ['. . . so don't disturb her while she is doing the arithmetic.']

{ ADJECTIVE: They were (very) *relieved* (to find her at home).
{ PARTICIPLE: They were *relieved* (by the next group of sentries).

Notice that we can replace *be* by *seem* only with the adjectives (*cf* 3.77 on pseudo-passives):

She seems very calculating.
*She seems calculating our salaries.

Note [**a**] *Unexpected* corresponds to the *-ed* participle of *expect* plus the negative particle: *unexpected* ~ *not expected*. However, such *un-* + verb + *-ed* forms are not participles, since there is no verb *un-* + verb, *eg*: **unexpect* (unlike *undress*, etc). Unlike *expected*, *unexpected* can be premodified by *very*, so that the morphological change has been accompanied by a semantic/syntactic change. The situation is less clear for the morphologically negative forms *unwritten* (*eg*: *unwritten law*) and *unbroken* (*eg*: *unbroken succession*), which resemble the positive forms in not accepting *very* (but *cf* 7.16 Note and App I.21).

[**b**] Nouns can also have adjective derivatives in *-ed* (*cf* App I.38), *eg*: *hard-hearted*, *talented*, *four-legged*, *flat-bottomed*, *bearded*.

7.16 Often the difference between the adjective and the participle is not clear-cut (*cf* 17.98*ff*). The verbal force of the participle is explicit for the *-ing* form when a direct object is present. Hence, the following *-ing* forms are participles that constitute a verb phrase with the preceding auxiliary (*cf* 3.52*ff*):

Her views were *alarming* her audience.
You are *frightening* the children.
They are *insulting* us.

Similarly, the verbal force is explicit for the *-ed* form when a *by*-agent phrase with a personal agent (*cf* 3.63*ff*, 8.80*f*) is present, indicating the correspondence to the active form of the sentence:

The man was *offended* by the policeman.
He is *appreciated* by his students.
She was *misunderstood* by her parents.

For both participle forms, premodification by the intensifier *very* is an explicit indication that the forms have achieved adjective status:

Her views were very *alarming*.
You are very *frightening*.
The man was very *offended*.

BUT: He is { ?very / very much / highly } *appreciated*.

We might therefore expect that the presence of *very* together with an explicit indicator of verbal force would produce an unacceptable sentence. This is certainly so for the *-ing* participle form:

*His views were very *alarming* his audience.

However, with the *-ed* participle, there appears to be divided usage, with increasing acceptance of the cooccurrence of *very* with a *by*-agent phrase containing a personal agent:

?The man was very *offended* by the policeman.

In the absence of any explicit indicator, the status of the participle form is indeterminate:

The man was *offended*.

For the *-ed* form in this example, the participle interpretation focuses on the process, while the adjective interpretation focuses on the state resulting from the process. For the *-ing* form the difference is perhaps clearer. In the sentence *John is insulting*, with no object present, the participle interpretation is implausible because the verb is normally transitive. If, however, the participle interpretation is selected, then the sentence expresses that John is in the process of giving insults and we expect an object, while in the adjective interpretation, the sentence points to a characteristic of John (*cf*: *John is rude*). A participle interpretation is similarly unlikely for the following sentences:

She is *surprising*. ≁ ?She *surprises*.
He is *interesting*. ≁ ?He *interests*.
It is *exciting*. ≁ ?It *excites*.
It is *tempting*. ≁ ?It *tempts*.

Note Whereas gradable adjectives and adverbs are intensified by *very*, verbs are intensified by other intensifying adverbs such as *much* and *well* (*cf* 8.104*ff*), which themselves are often premodified by *very*, eg: *very much*, *very well*. The applicability of this criterion depends on whether the words are gradable, since (as we have seen in 7.3*f*) not all adjectives are gradable. Hence, if the corresponding verb allows (say) *very much* while the participle form disallows *very*, we have a good indication that the form in question is a participle rather than an adjective:

She loved him *very much*.
~ He was *very much* loved (by her).
~ He was loved *very much* (by her).
≁ (?*)He was *very* loved.

Generally, *-ed* participle forms accepting *very* can retain *very* when they cooccur with a *by*-phrase containing a nonpersonal semi-agent (*cf* 3.76):

I'm *very disturbed* by your attitude.
We were *very pleased* by his behaviour.

Also, as we have seen, personal agents sometimes occur in this construction, as in:

?I was *very influenced* by my college professors.

7.17 The participle sometimes reaches full adjective status when it is compounded with another element:

The eggs are *boiled* hard.	~ The eggs are (very) *hard-boiled*.
It is *breaking* my heart.	~ It is (very) *heart-breaking*.
He was *bitten* (by a snake).	[*cf*: He was *frost-bitten*.]

When an adjective or adverb is the first element of the compound, as in *hard-boiled*, an intensifier such as *very* can be interpreted as related to the first element rather than to the compound as a whole.

Note Sometimes the *-ed* participle cannot be used in environments where the adjective compound is admitted. For example, the verb *speak* does not allow a personal noun such as *man* as direct object, and hence we cannot have in the passive:

*That man is *spoken.*

But we can have *well-spoken* in place of *spoken.* Compare:

That man {*speaks well.* / is *well-spoken.*} ['has a good manner of speaking']

He {*dresses well.* / is *well-dressed.*}

Similarly, the verb *behave* does not take a direct object (except the reflexive), and therefore we cannot have a passive:

*The boy was *behaved.*

But we can have an adjective compound:

The boy was *well-behaved.*

7.18 Not only participial adjectives allowing the intensifier *very*, but also stative *-ing* and *-ed* participles can be attributive (*cf* 17.98*ff*), as the following examples show:

her *crying* children	a *married* couple
a *winning* team	his *published* work
boiling water	the *captured* prisoner

Note That the sense is stative can be seen in the meaning of, for example, *a winning team*: 'a team that has won (a lot of matches lately)', *ie* 'a strong team' rather than 'a team that is winning'; *a married couple* is 'a couple who are not single'.

7.19 Some verbs have different participle forms for verbal and adjectival use (*cf* 3.13*ff*):

You have *drunk too much.*	~ *drunk*(*en*) driving/driver
Have you *shaved*?	~ a *clean-shaven* young man
The shirt has *shrunk.*	~ a *shrunken* shirt

Note the pronunciation /ɪd/ of the ending *-ed* in some adjectives, *eg*: *beloved* /bɪˈlʌvɪd/. Other examples:

crooked	*dogged*	*jagged*	*learned*
naked	*ragged*	*wicked*	*wretched*

The suffix of *aged* is pronounced as a separate syllable /ɪd/ when the word is predicative or is attributive of a personal noun (*The man is aged*; *an aged man* 'old'), but not, for example, in *an aged wine* or *a man aged fifty.*

Syntactic functions of adjectives

Attributive and predicative

7.20 The adjective functions as the head of an adjective phrase, with or without modification (*cf* 2.28). For the sake of simplicity, we refer to the functions of the 'adjective' when, strictly speaking, we should refer to the functions of the 'adjective phrase'. For the same reason, we generally exemplify the functions of the adjective phrase with the adjective alone.

Adjectives are attributive when they premodify the head of a noun phrase (*cf* 17.96):

a *small* garden
popular ballads

Adjectives are predicative when they function as subject complement or object complement. There is a copular relationship between subject and subject complement (*cf* 10.8):

The children are *happy*.
He seems *careless*.

Adjectives are subject complement not only to noun phrases, but also to clauses, which may be finite clauses [1, 2] or nonfinite clauses [3, 4]:

That you need a car is *obvious*. [1]
Whether he will resign is *uncertain*. [2]
To drive a car is *dangerous*. [3]
Playing chess is *enjoyable*. [4]

There is a copular relationship between direct object and object complement (*cf* 10.8):

I find him *careless*.
He made the children *happy*.

Adjectives can also be object complement to clauses:

I consider {what he did / playing so hard} *foolish*.

The adjective functioning as object complement often expresses the result of the process denoted by the verb (*cf* 16.21):

He pulled his belt *tight*. [5]
He pushed the window *open*. [6]
He writes his letters *large*. [7]

The result can be stated for each sentence by using the verb *be*:

His belt is *tight*. [5a]
The window is *open*. [6a]
His letters are *large*. [7a]

Note The verbs in [5–7] have a causative meaning. For example, [5] can be paraphrased:

He caused his belt to be tight by pulling it.

Some verbs used in this type of construction primarily express cause:

She made him *happy*. ['She caused him to be happy.']
The news turned his hair *white*. ['The news caused his hair to be white.']

The analogy with adverbs can be seen in the resultative effect of an adverb such as *out*. Compare [6] with [8]:

He pushed the window {*open*. [6] / *out*. [8]}
['He caused the window to be open/out by pushing it.']

Postpositive

7.21 Adjectives can sometimes be postpositive, *ie* they can immediately follow the noun or pronoun they modify. We may thus have three positions of adjectives:

PREDICATIVE:	This information is *useful.*	[1]
ATTRIBUTIVE:	*useful* information	[2]
POSTPOSITIVE:	something *useful*	[3]

A postpositive adjective (together with any complementation it may have; *cf* 7.22) can usually be regarded as a reduced relative clause:

something *that is useful* [3a]

Compound indefinite pronouns and adverbs ending in *-body*, *-one*, *-thing*, *-where* (*cf* 6.46*f*, 17.57) can be modified only postpositively:

Anyone (who is) *intelligent* can do it.
I want to try on *something* (that is) *larger*.
We're not going *anywhere very exciting*.

Of course, adjectives that can occur only attributively (*cf* 7.32*ff*) are excluded:

*something (which is) *main* *somebody (who is) *mere*

Postposition is obligatory for *proper* meaning 'as strictly defined', *eg*:

the City of London *proper*

In several institutionalized expressions (mostly in official designations), the adjective is postpositive (*cf* 17.59), *eg*:

the president *elect* ['soon to take office']	vice-chancellor *designate*
	postmaster *general*
heir *apparent*	court *martial*
attorney *general*	notary *public*
from time *immemorial*	body *politic*

Note also:

the person *opposite* [BUT: the *opposite* direction]
all of us, me *included* [BUT: *including* me]
Monday to Friday *inclusive* ⟨AmE also: Monday *through* Friday; *cf* 9.37⟩
Longman Group *Limited*/*Ltd* ⟨UK⟩; Harcourt Brace Jovanovich, *Incorporated*/*Inc* ⟨US⟩

Asia *Minor*	Poet *Laureate*
devil *incarnate*	all things *English*
the best car *going*	B *flat*/*sharp*/*major*/*minor*

Adjectives ending in *-able* and *-ible* can have postposition when the noun is modified by another adjective in the superlative degree (*cf* 7.74*ff*), by *only*, or by the general ordinals *last*, *next*, etc (*cf* 5.22). We thus have either attributive position or postposition in:

the best *possible* use	~ the best use *possible*
the greatest *imaginable insult*	~ the greatest insult *imaginable*

the best *available* person ~ the best person *available*
the only *suitable* actor ~ the only actor *suitable*

The deverbal suffix *-able*/*-ible* combines with transitive verbs to produce gradable adjectives: 'of the kind that can be V-ed' (*cf* App I.40). Some postpositive adjectives, especially those ending in *-able* or *-ible*, retain the basic meaning they have in attributive position but convey the implication that what they are denoting has only a temporary application. Thus, *the stars visible* refers to stars that are visible at a time specified or implied, while *the visible stars* more aptly refers to a category of stars that can (at appropriate times) be seen. We have a similar distinction between the temporary and the permanent in *rivers navigable* and *navigable rivers*.

Appointed, *desired*, *required*; *following*, *past*, *preceding*; and *positive* also occur in either position:

at the *appointed* time ~ at the time *appointed*
in *past* years ~ in years *past*
the *preceding* years ~ the years *preceding*
positive proof ~ proof *positive*

Postposition is usual with the set phrase *pure and simple*, as in *the answer/truth pure and simple*.

Postposition (in preference to attributive position) is usual for a few *a*-adjectives (*cf* 7.10*f*) and for the four adjectives *absent*, *present*, *concerned*, *involved* when they designate 'temporary' as opposed to 'permanent' attributes (*cf* 17.7):

The house (which is) *ablaze* is next door to mine.
The boats (which were) *afloat* were not seen by the bandits.
The men (who were) *present* were his supporters.
The people (who were) *involved* were not found.
[*cf*: *the involved people*, which designates a permanent attribute, but *cf* Note [b]]

Postposition is used with *net* and *gross* when the precise amounts are stated:

He was paid a fee of *£12 gross*, on which he had to pay £4 tax, leaving the sum of *£8 net*. [BUT: *The gross sum* was £12. *The net sum* was £8.]

Compare *total*:

The {*sum total* / *total sum*} was £12.

Note [a] The postpositive adjective, as in *the president elect* and *vice-chancellor designate*, reflects a neoclassical style based on Latin participles and much in vogue in Elizabethan times. *Cf* the normal attributive position of English participles; 17.98*ff*:

the *elected* president, the *acting* professor

[b] Attributive *present* normally has temporal meaning (*eg*: *at the present time*); but it has the same sense as postpositive *present* (*ie* the antonym of *absent*) in the fixed expression *present company excluded* (where perhaps it has been transposed from its usual position because the participle has occupied that position) and in expressions that seem to be based on it, *eg*: *excluding present company* ('if we exclude present company').

In AmE, attributive and postpositive *involved* and *concerned* may have the same sense if the head of the noun phrase is *party* or *parties*:

the *involved* party, the *concerned* parties

Adjectives with complementation

7.22 Adjectives with complementation (*cf* 16.68*ff*) normally cannot have attributive position but require postposition. Compare:

a *suitable* actor BUT NOT: *a *suitable for the part* actor

The complementation can be a prepositional phrase or a *to*-infinitive clause:

I know an actor *suitable for the part.* [1]
They have a house *larger than yours.* [2]
The boys *easiest to teach* were in my class. [3]
Students *brave enough to attempt the course* deserve to succeed. [4]

The postpositive structures can of course be regarded as reduced relative clauses:

I know an actor *who is suitable for the part.* [1a]

If the adjective is alone or merely premodified by an intensifier, postposition is not normally allowed:

*They have a house (*much*) *larger*.
*The soldiers (*rather*) *timid* approached their officer.

However, if the noun phrase is generic and indefinite, coordinated adjectives, or adjectives with some clause element added, can be postposed, though such constructions are formal and rather infrequent:

Soldiers *timid or cowardly* don't fight well. [5]
Soldiers *normally timid* don't fight well. [6]
A man *usually honest* will sometimes cheat. [7]

The more usual constructions are premodification or a relative clause:

Timid or cowardly soldiers . . . [5a]
Soldiers *who are timid or cowardly* . . . [5b]
Soldiers *who are normally timid* . . . [6a]
A man *who is usually honest* . . . [7a]

Like relative clauses, postposed adjectives may be restrictive or nonrestrictive, *eg*:

Soldiers normally timid don't fight well.
['Soldiers who are . . .'] [generic and indefinite noun head] [6]
The soldiers, normally timid, fought bravely.
['The soldiers, who were . . .'] [specific and definite noun head] [6b]

The adjective of an adjective phrase can often be attributive, leaving its complementation in postposition. Thus, equivalent to sentences [2] and [3] are the somewhat more informal sentences [2a] and [3a]:

They have a *larger* house *than yours.* [2a]
The *easiest* boys *to teach* were in my class. [3a]

An adjective modified by *too* or *so* can be separated from its complementation if placed before the indefinite (or zero) article of the noun phrase; so too, beside the more usual 'a brave enough student to':

She is *brave enough* a student *to attempt the course*. [8]
It was *too boring* a book *to read*. [9]

With *enough*, the construction is more common if the adjective is premodified by *not*, as in [8a]:

She is *not brave enough* a student *to attempt the course*. [8a]

But with *enough* and *too*, this construction seems to be possible only if the adjective phrase is part of the subject complement or object complement (compare [8] and [8b]):

**Brave enough* a student *to attempt the course* deserves to succeed. [8b]

With *so*, the construction is also possible if the adjective phrase is part of the subject or object [10]:

A man *so difficult* } *to please* must be hard to work with. [10]
So difficult a man }

Exceptionally, certain short prepositional phrases may also premodify an adjective in attributive position:

a *by no means* irresponsible action
~ an action (which is) by no means irresponsible

Compound modifiers usually denoting measurements may have either attributive or postpositive position (note also the *foot* ~ *feet* shift):

a *5000-foot high* mountain ~ a mountain (which is) 5000 feet high

Note We find the postposition of adjectives in poetry in cases where attributive position is the norm elsewhere in the language, *eg*:

Ben Battle was *a soldier bold* . . . (Thomas Hood)

Adjectives as heads of noun phrases

7.23 Adjectives can function as heads of noun phrases, which (like all noun phrases) can be subject of the sentence, complement, object, and prepositional complement. Adjectives as noun-phrase heads, unlike nouns, do not inflect for number or for the genitive case and they usually require a definite determiner (*cf* 5.56, App I.45).

Adjectives are typically used as heads of noun phrases to refer to certain fairly well-established classes of persons, *eg*: *the brave*, *the weak*, *the maladjusted*, *the elderly*, *the underprivileged*.

There are three types of adjectives functioning as noun-phrase heads:

(a) *The innocent* are often deceived by *the unscrupulous*. (7.24)
(b) *The industrious Dutch* are admired by their neighbours. (7.25)
(c) She admires *the mystical*. (7.26)

Type (a): *the innocent*

7.24 Adjectives which can premodify personal nouns (*the young people*) can be noun-phrase heads (*the young*) with plural and generic reference denoting classes, categories, or types of people. The adjective can itself be premodified [3–5] or postmodified [6–7]:

The poor are causing the nation's leaders great concern. [1]
There is a lack of communication between *the young* and *the old.* [2]
The extremely old need a great deal of attention. [3]
The emotionally disturbed and *the physically and mentally handicapped* need the aid of society. [4]
The very wise avoid such temptations. [5]
The young in spirit enjoy life. [6]
The old who resist change can expect violence. [7]

Notice that these adjectives are restricted to generic reference and take plural concord. Hence, *the poor* cannot denote one person. (*The poor person, man, woman*, etc can have either specific or generic reference.) It is often possible to add a general word for human beings such as *people* and retain the generic reference, in which case the definite determiner is normally omitted (*eg*: *old people*), but the use of the adjective as head of the noun phrase (*eg*: *the old*) is also common. We must distinguish the noun phrases from cases of textual ellipsis (*cf* 12.33*ff*):

The young students found the course difficult, *the older* found it easy.

Here, *the older* is elliptical for *the older students.*

The adjective can itself be modified, usually by restrictive modification, *eg* [5]: *the very wise.* Inflected comparison forms of the adjective are also possible (*the wiser*). Comparative inflection and adverb modification are indications of the adjective status of these noun-phrase heads, while modification by adjectives is more typical of nouns, and modification by relative clauses is normally an indication of noun status. Avoidance of modification by adjectives is probably related to the fact that this type of adjective as noun-phrase head tends to accept only restrictive modification. Premodifying adjectives with this noun-phrase head are normally interpreted as nonrestrictive. For example, *the wretched poor* would not normally be taken as a subclass of poor people, whereas with its premodifying adverb *the wretchedly poor* would be so taken.

In *the young of London*, the prepositional phrase is postmodifying a general noun that has been ellipted:

[those who are young] [in London]

By contrast, in *the young in spirit* [6], it is clear that the adjective itself is postmodified by a prepositional phrase, since the general noun cannot be postmodified by *in spirit*: **the people in spirit who are young.* We then have the structure:

[those who are [young [in spirit]]]

Similarly, we can argue that the relative clause in [7]:

the old who resist change

is postmodifying an ellipted general noun:

the people who resist change and *who are old*

Since *people* is not the only noun we can supply (for example we could insert *persons* instead), such ellipsis must be weak ellipsis (*cf* 12.38).

The definite determiner is normally the generic definite article *the*. Note however the use of the possessive determiner in:

We will nurse *your sick*, clothe *your naked*, and feed *your hungry*.
It is the duty of the Government to care for *our poor, our unemployed*.

Other types are: *we rich, these dead*. On the other hand, the following examples with *those* are instances of postposition which can be analysed as reduced relative clauses (*cf* 7.21):

those *present* ~ those *who are present*
those *assembled* ~ those *who are assembled*

Those dead is ambiguous between 'those dead ones' (adjective as head of a noun phrase) and 'those who are dead'.

Although adjectives functioning as noun-phrase heads generally require a definite determiner, they can function as such without a determiner if they are conjoined (*cf* 5.50):

*He is acceptable to *old/young*.
He is acceptable to *both (the) old and (the) young*.

Also in some *of*-constructions:

The number of jobless/unemployed is rising.

Note [**a**] Adjectives functioning as heads of noun phrases should be distinguished from nouns that are converted from adjectives (*cf* 7.13), *eg*: *an editorial, two blacks*. There is a great deal of varying usage in this area, *eg*:

the world's greats — the party's faithful(s)
the undecided(s) — the retired(s)

[**b**] Adjectives which do not denote fairly well-established classes are less likely to be used as heads of noun phrases with generic reference, *eg*: *the agitated, the bored, the resentful, the sleepy, the dirty*. This is a norm, not a rule, as can be seen in sentences like the following:

The alert will notice my irony, *the sleepy* may not.

Type (b): *the Dutch*

7.25 Some adjectives denoting nationalities (*cf* 5.56*f*) can be noun-phrase heads:

The industrious Dutch are admired by their neighbours.
You French and we British ought to be allies.

The adjectives in question are virtually restricted to words ending in -(*i*)*sh*, -*ch*, and -*ese*; for example:

British, Cornish, English, Irish, Spanish, Welsh; *Dutch, French*; *Portuguese, Chinese*

As with type (a) in 7.24, these noun phrases normally have generic reference and take plural concord. Unlike type (a), type (b) cannot be modified by adverbs: *the very wise*, but not ?*the very English*, with generic plural reference. However, they can be modified by adjectives, which are normally nonrestrictive, *ie*:

the industrious Dutch ['the Dutch, who are industrious']

Postmodifying prepositional phrases and relative clauses can be either restrictive or nonrestrictive (*cf* 17.3*ff*):

The Irish (*who live*) *in America* retain sentimental links with Ireland.
The Dutch, for many of whom speaking English is second nature, have produced many of the greatest grammarians of the English language.

Note [**a**] Easily confused with adjectives denoting nationalities of type (b), but distinct from them, are ethnic names (*cf* 5.88), *eg*: *Eskimo, Navaho, Bantu*. These, however, show their nominal character by the possibility of being modified by determiners and numerals (*two Eskimo, several Navaho*) and, optionally, taking plural *-s*: *two Eskimo*(*s*).

[**b**] Nationality adjectives are sometimes used not to refer to the nation as a whole but to some part of it, for example, teams and troops representing their country (*cf* 5.111):

The English lost against *the Welsh* in the final.
In 1796 *the French* invaded northern Italy.

[**c**] *You British* and *you French* can also be analysed as having *you* as head and the names of the nationalities as noun phrases in restrictive apposition (*cf* 17.88).

[**d**] As stated above, adjectives denoting nationalities that can be noun-phrase heads normally have generic reference. There are, however, many exceptions, *eg*: *two Boston Irish* ['Irishmen/Irishwomen'] and *the other English*, as in

?Now tell me about *the other English* at the villa, especially the one who has disappeared.

Type (c): *the mystical*

7.26 Some adjectives can function as noun-phrase heads with abstract reference. They include, in particular, superlatives, in which case we can sometimes insert a general noun like *thing* in its abstract sense:

The latest (thing/news) is that he is going to run for re-election.

Unlike types (a) and (b), type (c) adjectives functioning as noun-phrase heads take singular concord:

They ventured into *the unknown*, which was . . .
The best is yet to come.

They can be modified by adverbs:

The very best (thing) is yet to come.
He went from *the extremely sublime* to *the extremely ridiculous*.

Type (c) is restricted chiefly to certain fixed expressions. Thus, for example, *the supernatural, the exotic, the unreal* are more likely to occur than *the lovely, the foreign, the exciting*, with abstract, generic reference.

Note There are a number of set expressions in which an adjective with abstract reference is complement of a preposition (*cf* 9.1 Note [c]), *eg*:

It's *for the good* of everyone.	He enjoyed it *to the full*.
He left *for good*.	*from bad to worse*
in public/private/secret	*out of the ordinary*
in the nude/in the wild	*in the extreme*
in short	*above* (*the*) *normal*
into the open	*on the loose*
on the sly	*in common*

In many of these examples, the word-class status of the word following the preposition (or *the*) is indeterminate between adjective and noun.

Supplementive adjective clauses

7.27 Adjectives can function as the sole realization of a verbless clause (*cf* 14.9) or as the head of an adjective phrase realizing the clause:

The man, *quietly assertive*, spoke to the assembled workers. [1]
Unhappy with the result, she returned to work. [2]
Glad to accept, the boy nodded his agreement. [3]
Anxious for a quick decision, the chairman called for a vote. [4]
Long and untidy, his hair played in the breeze. [5]

As the following examples demonstrate, the supplementive adjective clause (*cf* 15.60*ff*) is mobile, though (partly to avoid ambiguity) it usually precedes or (less usually) follows the subject of the superordinate clause:

Rather nervous, the man opened the letter. [6]
The man, *rather nervous*, opened the letter. [6a]
The man opened the letter, *rather nervous*. [6b]

When it follows the subject, as in [6a], it is in some respects like a nonrestrictive relative clause (*cf* 17.22*ff*):

The man, *who was nervous*, opened the letter.

But the adjective clause suggests that the man's nervousness is related to the content of the sentence, whereas the relative clause does not necessarily convey that implication. Another difference is that the adjective clause is related to the predication as well as to the subject. Furthermore, unlike the relative clause, the adjective clause is mobile and (with the exception discussed below) its implied subject is the subject of the sentence. Thus, while we have [7], we do not have as its equivalent [7a]:

The man restrained the woman, *who was aggressive*. [7]
*The man restrained the woman, *aggressive*. [7a]

However, if the supplementive adjective clause contains additional clause constituents, it can be related to a noun phrase other than the subject of the sentence:

She glanced with disgust at the cat, { *quiet* (*now*) *in her daughter's lap*. / *now quiet*. / **quiet*. }

Compare participle clauses, where the implied subject can also be other than the subject of the sentence (*cf* 15.62):

She glanced with disgust at the cat, { *stretched out on the rug*. / *mewing plaintively*. }

Under certain conditions, and with little change of meaning, an adjective functioning as a supplementive adjective clause may be replaced by an adverb. Thus, instead of [6] we might have

Nervously, the man opened the letter. [6c]

Like the adjective, an adverb with this function (*cf* 8.92*ff*) refers to an attribute or state of the subject, though it normally does so specifically in relation to the action that he is performing. This is typically expressed by adverbs in medial position (*cf* 8.16):

The man *nervously* opened the letter. [6d]

The adjective refers to the subject without explicit reference to the action, but unless otherwise stated, the characterization is only temporary.

Note [**a**] An adverb can (obviously) not be substituted if there is no corresponding adverb (*cf* 7.6), *eg*: *long* in [5]:

**Longly* / *Untidily* } his hair played in the breeze. [5a]

[**b**] Nor can replacement by an adverb take place if the complementation or modification of the adjective is disallowed for the adverb, *eg* [1a] **quietly assertively*, [3a] **gladly to accept*, [4a] **anxiously for a quick decision.* If *unhappy with the result* in [2] is replaced by *unhappily*, the likely meaning will be 'I'm sorry to say that . . .' (rather than 'She was unhappy'), *ie* a disjunct interpretation.

7.28 The implied subject of a supplementive adjective clause can be the whole of the superordinate clause:

Strange, it was she who initiated divorce proceedings. [1]
Most important, his report offered prospects of a great profit. [2]
More remarkable still, he is in charge of the project. [3]

For example, [1] is semantically equivalent to [1a]:

(*The fact*) *that* it was she who initiated divorce proceedings *is strange.* [1a]

These supplementive adjective clauses relate to the superordinate clause like comment clauses introduced by *what* (*cf* 15.53*ff*). For example, for [1] we have [1b]:

What is (even more) *strange*, it was she who initiated divorce proceedings. [1b]

The few adjectives that can be used for this purpose convey the attitude that what is being said is in some measure strange, *eg*: *curious*, *funny*, *odd*, *strange*, *surprising*. A few others seem possible if they are premodified by *more* or *most*, as in [2] and [3]. This type of adjective clause must precede its superordinate clause.

Note [**a**] A corresponding adverb can be substituted for the adjective with little or no difference in meaning, as with *strangely* for *strange* in [1] (*cf* content disjuncts in 8.127*ff*):

Strangely, it was she who initiated divorce proceedings. [1c]

The adjective, unlike the adverb, allows a *that*- or *how*-clause to follow:

Strange { that it turned out that way. [4]
{ how she still likes him. [5]

**Strangely*, { that it turned out that way. [4a]
{ how she still likes him. [5a]

This is because the adjective is elliptical for an extraposed construction (*cf* 18.33*ff*) [5b], or perhaps a pseudo-cleft construction (*cf* 18.29) [5c]:

It is strange how she still likes him. [5b]
What is strange is how she still likes him. [5c]

[**b**] Objections have been voiced against both *most important* (as in [2] above) and *most importantly*. Some usage books recommend the one construction, some the other.

Contingent adjective clauses

7.29 A special type of supplementive adjective clause is the contingent adjective clause, which expresses the circumstance or condition under which what is said in the superordinate clause applies. The contingent clause is elliptical (*cf* 12.31*ff*) with ellipsis of an appropriate form of *be*, and (sometimes) of the subordinator:

Whether right or wrong, he always comes off worst in an argument because of his inability to speak cogently. [1]
When fit, the Labrador is an excellent retriever. [2]
If wet, these shoes should never be placed too close to the heat. [3]

As with other supplementive adjective clauses (*cf* 7.27*f*), the implied subject of the contingent adjective clause is normally the subject of the superordinate clause, but the clause is not equivalent to a nonrestrictive relative clause. Unlike other supplementive adjective clauses, contingent adjective clauses often have a subordinator present. It is sometimes omitted, so that we can have [1a]:

Right or wrong, he always comes off worst . . . [1a]

When the implied subject is the subject of the superordinate clause, it is normal to put the adjective initially, as in [1–3], but it is not uncommon to put it finally in spoken English. If a subordinator is present, there is no problem in positioning the clause finally even in written English:

These shoes should never be placed too close to the heat *if wet*. [3a]

The contingent clause can also refer to the object of the superordinate clause, though only a few adjectives are available for this use:

He sells them *new*. [4]
I can't drink it *hot*. [5]
You must eat it *when fresh*. [6]

The adjective then usually comes finally and could be regarded as a complement in [4] and [5] (*cf* 10.16). A subordinator is also often present, as in [6]. As with all complements, the normal position of the adjective is final, whether it is in a copular relation to the object of an active clause [7] or to the subject of a passive clause [8]:

To make good tomato chutney, you should pick the tomatoes *green*. [7]
The tomatoes should be picked *green*. [8]
**Green* you should pick the tomatoes. [7a]
**Green* the tomatoes should be picked. [8a]

In informal spoken English, an adjective clause which refers to the object of the superordinate clause can occur initially, though the position would be avoided if ambiguity resulted, as in:

Hot, I can't drink coffee. ['When I'm hot . . .' or 'I can't drink coffee hot.'] [5a]

The adjective clause can also refer to the whole of the superordinate clause (which would be realized in the subordinate clause by the pro-form *it*). In such cases the subordinator cannot be omitted:

If (it is) *possible*, the puppy should be fed four times a day.

When (it is) *necessary*, he can be taken to the doctor.
You must come *as soon as* (it is) *possible*.

Note [**a**] *Cf* 14.9*ff* for further discussion of adjective clauses and other verbless clauses, as well as of nonfinite clauses that require similar treatment.
[**b**] Corresponding adverbs cannot replace adjectives in contingent adjective clauses. [1] is ambiguous between the more probable interpretation of the adjective clause as conditional ('Whether he is right or wrong . . .') and the other possibility that it is a noncontingent supplementive clause with the superordinate clause as its implied subject (*cf* 7.28) ('Whether it is right or wrong . . .'). In the latter interpretation, adverbs can replace the adjectives:

Whether rightly or wrongly, he always comes off worst in an argument . . . [1b]

Exclamatory adjective clauses

7.30 Adjectives (especially those that can be complement when the subject is eventive, *eg*: *That's excellent!*) can be exclamations, with or without an initial *wh*-element (*cf* 11.14*f*, 12.31*ff*):

Excellent! (How) *wonderful!* (How) *good of you!*

Such adjective phrases need not be dependent on any previous linguistic context, but may be a comment on some object or activity in the situational context.

Syntactic subclassification of adjectives

7.31 We turn now to consider the characteristics of the peripheral adjectives, those that are restricted to attributive or to predicative use (*cf* 7.3*f*). The restrictions are not always absolute, and sometimes vary with individual speakers.

Attributive only

7.32 In general, adjectives that are restricted to attributive position, or that occur predominantly in attributive position, do not characterize the referent of the noun directly. For example, *old* can be either a central adjective or an adjective restricted to attributive position. In *that old man* (the opposite of *that young man*), *old* is a central adjective, and can thus also be predicative: *That man is old*. On the other hand, in the usual sense of *an old friend of mine* ['a friend of old, a long-standing friend'], *old* is restricted to attributive position and cannot be related to *My friend is old*. In this case, *old* is the opposite of *new* ['recently acquired']. The person referred to is not being identified as old: it is his friendship that is old. Outside such well-established phrases as *old friend*, *new friend*, the contrast *old*/*new* requires the adjective to be stressed:

I'll take my '*old* car tonight.

Similarly, the attributive adjective in *the wrong candidate* does not refer to the wrongness of the person but to the mistake in identifying the person as a candidate. When adjectives characterise the referent of the noun directly (*that old man*; *my friend is rather old*), their use is called INHERENT. When they do not (*an old friend of mine*), it is called NONINHERENT (*cf* 7.43, 7.73).

Note Adjectives can also occur in a noninherent use in predicative position. In part, noninherent uses appear to be excluded from predicative position because of competition from inherent uses of the same adjectives associated with that position (as with *old*). But the reasons for the restriction are not always clear. For example, both *a new student* and *a new friend* are noninherent, yet only the former can be used predicatively:

That student is *new*. *My friend is *new*.

Some of the factors that are involved in the restriction will emerge in the course of an identification of the types of adjective that are restricted to attributive position.

A few adjective uses with strongly emotive value which will not be further discussed are restricted to attributive position, though the scope of the adjective clearly extends to the person referred to by the noun, *eg*: *you poor man, my dear lady, that wretched woman*. These all involve nonrestrictive modification (*cf* 17.3*ff*).

Intensifying adjectives

7.33 Some adjectives have a heightening effect on the noun they modify, or the reverse, a lowering effect. At least three semantic subclasses of intensifying adjectives can be distinguished (*cf* 8.99*ff*):

(a) emphasizers
(b) amplifiers
(c) downtoners

(a) EMPHASIZERS have a general heightening effect and are generally attributive only, *eg*:

a *true* scholar	[1]	*plain* nonsense	[7]
a *clear* failure	[2]	the *simple* truth	[8]
pure ['sheer'] fabrication	[3]	an *outright* lie	[9]
a *real* ['undoubted'] hero	[4]	*sheer* arrogance	[10]
a *certain* winner	[5]	a *sure* sign	[11]
a *definite* loss	[6]		

(b) AMPLIFIERS scale upwards from an assumed norm, and are central adjectives if they are inherent and denote a high or extreme degree:

a *complete* victory ~ The victory was *complete*.
great destruction ~ The destruction was *great*.

On the other hand, when they are noninherent, amplifiers are attributive only:

a *complete* fool ≁ *The fool is *complete*.
a *firm* friend ≁ *The friend is *firm*.

Complete refers to the completeness of the folly, and *firm* to the firmness of the friendship (in which sense it is asterisked here).

Amplifiers are only attributive also when they are used as emphasizers, conveying principally emphasis rather than degree. For example, *total* in *total nonsense* is an emphasizer, while in *total destruction* it is an amplifier and has a literal application ('the destruction of everything'). Hence the contrast:

total nonsense ≁ *The nonsense was *total*.
total destruction ~ The destruction was *total*.

Further examples of adjectives as amplifiers that are attributive only:

utter folly	the *absolute* limit
a *close* friend	a *complete* stranger
an *extreme* enemy	his *entire* salary
a *great* supporter	a *perfect* stranger
a *strong* opponent	*total* irresponsibility

(c) DOWNTONERS have a lowering effect, usually scaling downwards from an assumed norm. They are relatively few (*eg*: *slight* in *a slight effort*, *feeble* in *a feeble joke*) and can be ignored for our present purpose, since they are generally central adjectives.

7.34 Many of the intensifying adjectives in 7.33 can be related to intensifying adverbs (*cf* 8.104):

He is a *true* scholar.	~ He is *truly* a scholar.
It was a *clear* failure.	~ It was *clearly* a failure.
It is *utter* folly to do that.	~ It is *utterly* foolish to do that.

Notice that several intensifying adjectives have homonyms that can occur both attributively and predicatively. Compare:

I drank some *pure* ['clean'] water. [central adjective]
~ The water is *pure*.
That is *pure* ['sheer'] fabrication. [emphasizer]
≁ *The fabrication is *pure*.
Those are *real* flowers. [central adjective]
~ Those flowers are *real*, not artificial.
He's a *real* ['undoubted'] hero. [emphasizer]
≁ *The hero is *real*.

Examples of intensifying adjectives which can occur predicatively include:

His condemnation was *extreme*.	Their victory is *certain*.
His folly was *great*.	The earthquake was *strong*.

Note Many adjectives which can be used as intensifiers and are restricted to attributive position have severe restrictions on the nouns they modify, *eg*: *a great/big baby* ['very babyish'], *a big fool* ['very foolish']; also *a great friend* rather than *a big friend* in the sense of 'very friendly'.

Restrictive adjectives

7.35 Restrictive adjectives restrict the reference of the noun exclusively, particularly, or chiefly. Examples, within noun phrases, include:

a *certain* person	his *chief* excuse
the *principal* objection	the *exact* answer
the *same* student	the *sole* argument
the *only* occasion	the *specific* point
a *particular* child	the *very* man

Again, some of these have homonyms. For example, *certain* in *a certain person* is a restrictive (equivalent to 'a particular person'), while in *a certain winner* it is (as we saw in 7.33, example [5]) an intensifier (equivalent to 'a sure winner').

Some restrictive adjectives can be related to restrictive adverbs (*cf* 8.118):

It is the *main* reason.	~ It is *mainly* the reason.
That was the *precise* reason.	~ That was *precisely* the reason.

Note [**a**] Notice the use of *very* as a restrictive adjective rather than as an intensifying adverb (*cf* 7.89):

You are *the very man* I want.

The same meaning can be conveyed by restrictive adverbs outside the noun phrase (whereas *very* occurs within the noun phrase):

You are *precisely/exactly/just the man* I want.

[**b**] 'Universal' adjectives like *whole* (*cf* 5.17), *entire, full* are similar to restrictive adjectives:

The *whole* situation is ridiculous.
I'm in *entire/full* agreement with the committee.

Other adjectives related to adverbs

7.36 Some noninherent adjectives that are attributive only can be related to adverbs but do not always fall within the intensifying or restrictive types of adjectives. These noninherent adjectives (*cf* 7.43, 7.73) include:

my *former* friend	['formerly my friend']
an *old* friend	['a friend of old']
past students	['students in the past']
a *possible* friend	['possibly a friend']
the *present* king	['the king at present']
an *occasional* visitor	['occasionally a visitor']

The adverbial nature of these adjectives can be seen in their correspondences with a verb of general meaning and an adverb, *eg*:

rapid calculations	'make calculations *rapidly*'
occasional showers	'showers occur *occasionally*'

These verbs (*make, perform, act, occur, happen, take place*, etc) can be seen as lexical realizations of the predicational force that is inherent in the nouns. Even a noun like *friend* in *my former friend* signifies an activity, as appears in the correspondence of 'acting as a friend'. Some adjectives require implications additional to the adverbial:

the *late* president ['the person who was formerly the president (but is now dead)']

But compare:

the late bus ['the bus that leaves late (in the evening)' where *late* is a central adjective]
the *former* reason ['the reason stated formerly']

Many of these adjectives have a temporal meaning. We might include with them *acting* ['for the time being'], as in *the acting chairman*.

If the adjectives premodify agentive nouns, the latter also suggest a relationship to an associated verb (*cf* nominalization, 17.51*ff*):

a *big* eater ['someone who eats a lot']
a *clever* liar ['someone who lies cleverly']
a *hard* worker ['someone who works hard']
a *heavy* smoker ['someone who smokes heavily']
a *sound* sleeper ['someone who sleeps soundly']

Note Not all instances like *a clever liar* involve a restriction to attributive position. Possible conflict with homonyms seems a contributory factor. Thus *a clever liar* is analogous to *a clever writer*, *a clever student*, or *a clever detective*. In all four instances, *clever* refers to the ability of the person in respect of the reference of the noun – clever as a liar, clever as a writer, etc. However, these instances could be used predicatively, and so can antonyms of *clever*:

That writer is *clever*/*lazy*.
That student is *clever*/*weak*.
That detective is *clever*/*inefficient*.

Nevertheless, we normally cannot use these adjectives predicatively in the intended sense when the noun is both personal and pejorative:

a *clever* liar [≠ 'That liar is clever.']
a *clever* ruse [= 'That ruse is clever.']

On the other hand, one thief might well say of another *That thief is good*, but in that case he is not using *thief* pejoratively. *Cf*: *He is good at stealing, but bad at lying.*

Adjectives related to nouns

7.37 Some adjectives are derived from nouns by means of suffixes (*cf* App I.38*f*), *eg*:

-*ar*: *polar* bear	-*an*: *urban* population
-*en*: *earthen* pottery	-*al*: *tidal* wave
-*ic*: *atomic* scientist	-*ly*: *yearly* income

Many such denominal adjectives are nongradable and restricted to attributive position:

an *atomic* scientist ['a scientist specializing in the theory of atoms']
a *criminal* court ['a court dealing with crime']
a *criminal* lawyer ['a lawyer specializing in cases of crime']
a *polar* bear ['a bear living near the pole']
a *medical* school ['a school for students of medicine']
musical comedy ['comedy accompanied by music']
a *tidal* wave ['a wave produced by the tide']

The examples contain nouns with a denominal adjective referring to the activity of the agent or expressing an adverbial relation. In other uses, the same item may also be a central adjective, for example *criminal* in *a criminal lawyer* ['a lawyer who is criminal'] (*cf* 7.13).

Predicative only

7.38 Adjectives that are restricted, or virtually restricted, to predicative position (*cf* 7.3*f*) are most like verbs and adverbs. They tend to refer to a (possibly temporary) condition rather than to characterize. Perhaps the most common are those referring to the health (or lack of health) of an animate being:

He felt *ill*/*poorly* <both esp BrE>/*well*/*faint*/*unwell*.

However, many people use such adjectives as attributives too, for example:

A *well* person need see a doctor only for a periodic checkup.

Note *Sick* is the exception among these 'health' adjectives in that its attributive use is very common:

the *sick* woman ['The woman is sick.']

Be sick is especially AmE corresponding to *be ill* in BrE. *Be sick* can also mean 'vomit' in both AmE and BrE, especially with a verb in the progressive or an adverbial interpretable as a goal:

She is being *sick*.
The dog was *sick* on the new carpet.

This use of *sick* is euphemistic, and *ill* is occasionally used in the same way. For comparative forms of *ill*, *cf* 7.77.

7.39 A large group of adjectives that are restricted to predicative position comprises adjectives which can take complementation:

I'm *aware of that*.
She was *glad that everything was all right*.

Other adjectives which take complementation include (*cf* 16.68*ff*):

able (*to* + infinitive)	*fond* (*of*)
afraid (*that, of, about*)	*happy* (*that, to, with, about*)
answerable (*to*)	*loath* (*to*)
averse (*to, from*)	*subject* (*to*)
conscious (*that, of*)	*tantamount* (*to*)

Some of these adjectives must take complementation (*eg*: *subject to* and *tantamount to*), and many normally do.

Many of these adjectives closely resemble verbs semantically:

He *is afraid to* do it. ['He *fears to* do it.']
They *are fond of* her. ['They *like* her.']
That *is tantamount to* an ultimatum.
['That *amounts to* an ultimatum.']

Some constructions like *be willing to* and *be able to* function like modals where the modal auxiliary paradigm is defective (*cf* 3.39*ff*). Compare:

She *can* do it.	~	She *is able to* do it.
She *could* do it.	~	She *was able to* do it.
____________		She *has been able to* do it.
____________		She *might have been able to* do it.

Some of these adjectives that are restricted to predicative position have homonyms that can occur both predicatively and attributively, *eg*:

the *conscious* patient ~ The patient is *conscious*. [= 'awake']
Cf: He is *conscious* of his faults. [= 'aware']

With some adjectives that take complementation there appears to be no semantic distinction, and we must say that they can freely occur in both positions, *eg*: *eager, indignant, surprised*.

Note [**a**] Most of the adjectives beginning with *a-* are predicative only (*cf* 7.10*f*). As we have seen above, several of them can take complementation, *eg*: *afraid, averse*.

[**b**] It is not usually possible for the adjective to be complement if the subject is indefinite, and hence the oddness of [1] (*cf* 19.70*f*) compared with [2]. An exception occurs with the generic use of the indefinite article (*cf* 5.52*f*), as in [3]:

**A street* is wide. [1]
The street is wide. [2]
A tiger is dangerous. [3]

Semantic subclassification of adjectives

7.40 Some of the semantic distinctions that we are about to make have already been mentioned because they have syntactic correlates.

Three semantic scales are applicable to adjectives: STATIVE/DYNAMIC, GRADABLE/NONGRADABLE, and INHERENT/NONINHERENT. It is important to realize that we are dealing with scales rather than with a feature that is present or absent. That is to say, not all the realizations of a feature are available in each case. Furthermore, there may be idiolectal variations in the recognition of a feature or in the acceptability of its realizations.

Note Since adjectives can have more than one sense, it is rather the *uses* of adjectives than the adjectives as formal items that are characterised in these sections of the *Grammar*.

Stative/dynamic

7.41 Adjectives are characteristically stative. Many adjectives, however, can be seen as dynamic (*cf* 2.43). In particular, most adjectives that are susceptible to subjective measurement are capable of being dynamic. Stative and dynamic adjectives differ syntactically in a number of ways. For example, a stative adjective such as *tall* cannot be used with the progressive aspect or with the imperative:

*He's being *tall*. *Be *tall*.

On the other hand, we can use *careful* as a dynamic adjective:

He's being *careful*. Be *careful*.

(For other differences, *cf* 3.66.) A general semantic feature of dynamic adjectives seems to be that they denote qualities that are thought to be subject to control by the possessor and hence can be restricted temporally.

Adjectives that can be used dynamically include:

abusive	adorable	ambitious
awkward	brave	calm
careful	careless	cheerful
clever	complacent	conceited
cruel	disagreeable	dull
enthusiastic	extravagant	faithful
foolish	friendly	funny
generous	gentle	good
greedy	hasty	helpful
impatient	impudent	irritable

irritating	jealous	kind
lenient	loyal	mischievous
naughty	nice	noisy
obstinate	patient	playful
reasonable	rude	sensible
serious	shy	slow
spiteful	stubborn	stupid
suspicious	tactful	talkative
thoughtful	tidy	timid
troublesome	unfaithful	unscrupulous
untidy	vain	vicious
vulgar	wicked	witty

Gradable/nongradable

7.42 Most adjectives are gradable. Gradability is manifested through comparison (*cf* 7.74*ff*):

tall	~ tall*er*	~ tall*est*
beautiful	~ *more* beautiful	~ *most* beautiful

Gradability is also manifested through modification by intensifiers, *ie* adverbs which convey the degree of intensity of the adjective:

very tall   *so* beautiful   *extremely* useful

Gradability applies to adverbs as well as adjectives, and hence it is considered below in relation to both classes (*cf* 7.74*ff*).

All dynamic and most stative adjectives (*eg*: *tall*, *old*) are gradable; some stative adjectives are not, principally denominal adjectives like *atomic scientist* and *hydrochloric acid* (*cf* 7.37), and adjectives denoting provenance, *eg*: *British* (*cf* 7.45; but *cf* the qualitative use of nationality adjectives in 7.87).

Inherent/noninherent

7.43 The distinction between inherent and noninherent adjectives has been discussed in 7.32. Most adjectives are inherent, that is to say, they characterize the referent of the noun directly. For example, the inherent adjective in *a wooden cross* applies to the referent of the object directly: a wooden cross is also a wooden object. On the other hand, in *a wooden actor* the adjective is noninherent: a wooden actor is not (presumably) a wooden man. Some other examples:

INHERENT	NONINHERENT
a *firm* handshake	a *firm* friend
a *perfect* alibi	a *perfect* stranger
a *certain* result	a *certain* winner
a *true* report	a *true* scholar

Modification of a noun by means of a noninherent adjective can be seen as an extension of the basic sense of the noun. Thus *a firm friend* is 'a friend whose friendship is firm', and *a perfect stranger* is 'a stranger who is perfectly strange'.

If the adjective is inherent, it is often possible to derive a noun from it (*cf* 17.51*ff*):

her *soft* touch ~ the *softness* of her touch

However, with a noninherent adjective no such derivation is possible. Compare:

{a *firm* handshake ~ the *firmness* of the handshake
{a *firm* friend ≁ *the *firmness* of the friend

{a *true* report ~ the *truth* of the report
{a *true* scholar ≁ *the *truth* of the scholar

There are, however, exceptions to this generalization, since we find instances like:

a *wooden* actor ~ the *woodenness* of the actor

Patterns of semantic subclassification

7.44 Gradable adjectives are either inherent, as in *a black coat*, or noninherent, as in *a new friend*. Dynamic adjectives are generally inherent, though there are exceptions; for example, *wooden* in *The actor is being wooden* is both dynamic and noninherent.

Table 7.44 gives examples of adjectives that illustrate the various possibilities with respect to the three semantic distinctions that we have been discussing.

Table 7.44 Semantic subclassification of adjectives

GRADABLE	INHERENT	STATIVE	
+	+	+	That's a *big* boat; She is a *brave* woman. [central adjectives]
+	+	–	She is being very *brave*. [dynamic use of central adjective]
+	–	+	He is a *firm* friend; He is a *wooden* actor. [peripheral adjectives: noninherent]
+	–	–	This actor is being *wooden* tonight. [dynamic use of stative adjective]
–	–	+	She is a *medical* student. [peripheral adjective: nongradable and noninherent]

Note In *a dull teacher*, the adjective *dull* is noninherent, since a dull teacher is not necessarily a dull person. However, in the following sentence *dull* is being used dynamically and is now inherent:

The teacher is being *dull*.

In this case the process of being dull is ascribed to the teacher, but the same quality is ascribed to the referent of the subject if we replace *the teacher* by another designation for the person:

{That man / Mrs Jones} is being *dull*.

Ordering of adjectives in premodification

7.45 When there are two or more adjectives cooccurring in attributive position, the order of the adjectives is to a large extent determined by their semantic properties. The principles for the order of items in premodification are discussed in 17.113*ff*. Here we will only mention the major zones, or positional ranges, of adjectives in premodifying position in relation to the semantic and syntactic subclassification provided in this chapter.

In the premodification structure of the noun phrase, adjectives are placed between the determinatives (including predeterminers, central determiners, and postdeterminers) and the head of the noun phrase (*cf* 5.1*ff*). We distinguish four zones:

(I) PRECENTRAL
Here, after the determinatives, is where peripheral, nongradable adjectives are placed, in particular the intensifying adjectives (emphasizers, amplifiers, and downtoners; *cf* 7.33), *eg*: *certain*, *definite*, *sheer*, *complete*, *slight*.

(II) CENTRAL
This zone is the place of the central adjectives, *ie* the 'most adjectival items', which satisfy all four criteria for adjective status (*cf* 7.3*f*), *eg*: *hungry*, *ugly*, *funny*, *stupid*, *silent*, *rich*, *empty*.

(III) POSTCENTRAL
This zone includes participles, *eg*: *retired, sleeping*, and colour adjectives, *eg*: *red, pink*.

(IV) PREHEAD
This zone includes the 'least adjectival and the most nominal' items, such as denominal adjectives (*cf* 7.37) denoting nationality, ethnic background, *eg*: *Austrian, Midwestern*, and denominal adjectives with the meaning 'consisting of', 'involving', 'relating to', *eg*: *experimental*, *statistical*, *political*, *statutory*. In the prehead zone we also find nouns in attributive position (*cf* further 17.113*ff*).

On the basis of this classification, we can expect the following order:

I + II	*certain important* people
I + III	the *same restricted* income
I + IV	your *present annual* turnover
II + III	a *funny red* hat
II + IV	an *enormous tidal* wave
I + II + IV	*certain rich American* producers

ADVERBS

Characteristics of the adverb

7.46 The adverb functions as the head of an adverb phrase, with or without modification (*cf* 2.31). For the sake of simplicity, we refer to the functions of the 'adverb' when, strictly speaking, we should refer to the functions of the 'adverb phrase'. For the same reason, we generally exemplify the functions of the adverb phrase with the adverb alone.

Because of its great heterogeneity, the adverb class is the most nebulous and puzzling of the traditional word classes. Indeed, it is tempting to say simply that the adverb is an item that does not fit the definitions for other word classes. As a consequence, some grammarians have removed certain types of items from the class entirely, and established several additional classes rather than retain these as subsets within a single adverb class.

Morphologically, we can distinguish three types of adverb, of which two are closed classes (simple and compound), and one is an open class (derivational):

(a) SIMPLE adverbs, *eg*: *just*, *only*, *well*. Many simple adverbs denote position and direction, *eg*: *back*, *down*, *near*, *out*, *under* (*cf* further 8.39*ff*).

(b) COMPOUND adverbs, *eg*: *somehow*, *somewhere*, *therefore*; and ⟨the very formal⟩ *whereupon*, *hereby*, *herewith*, *whereto*

(c) DERIVATIONAL adverbs. The majority of derivational adverbs have the suffix *-ly*, by means of which new adverbs are created from adjectives (and participial adjectives):

odd ~ *oddly*
interesting ~ *interestingly*

Other, less common, derivational suffixes (*cf* App I.41) are:

-wise:	clockwise	*-ways*:	sideways
-ward(s):	northward(s)	*-style*:	cowboy-style
-fashion:	schoolboy-fashion		

Note [**a**] Corresponding to the prepositional phrase *towards the south* (*east*/*north*/*west*) there are the adverbs *south*, *southward*, and *southwards*, etc. The *s*-less form *southward*, etc is common, especially in printed AmE (*cf*: *towards*/*toward*, 9.17):

The window faces { *south* ⟨most common⟩ / *southwards* / *southward* ⟨esp printed AmE⟩ }

Compare other adverb expressions:

We walked { *home*/*up* ⟨most common⟩ / *homewards*/*upwards* / *homeward*/*upward* ⟨esp printed AmE⟩ }

[**b**] The creation of adverbs from adjectives by adding the *-ly* suffix is closely related to the dynamic quality in the adjective (*cf* 7.41). Thus we have, for example:

cheerful	~ *cheerfully*	*suspicious*	~ *suspiciously*
jealous	~ *jealously*	*reasonable*	~ *reasonably*

But we do not find *French* ≁ **Frenchly*, etc. It appears that *-ly* adverbs are not formed from typically stative adjective classes, such as adjectives denoting:

dimension:	*big*	≁ **bigly*	*tall*	≁ **tally*
colour:	*red*	≁ **redly*	*blonde*	≁ **blondely*
age:	*old*	≁ **oldly*	*young*	≁ **youngly*

7.47 Rules for forming open-class *-ly* adverbs from adjectives:

(a) Adjectives ending in consonant + *-le* form adverbs by replacing *-le* by *-ly*: simp*le* ~ simp*ly*. Exception: *whole* ~ *wholly*.

(b) In adjectives ending in consonant + *y*, *y* is usually replaced by *i* before *-ly*: *happy* ~ *happily*. In some cases there exist alternative spellings:

dry ~ dr*ily*/dr*yly* sly ~ sl*ily*/sl*yly*

In other cases, *-y* is kept in the adverb:

spry ~ spryly wry ~ wryly

Note the spellings: *coy* ~ *coyly* but *gay* ~ *gaily*; *due* ~ *duly*, *true* ~ *truly*.

(c) Adjectives ending in both *-ic* and *-ical* have corresponding adverbs in *-ically*:

economic / economical } ~ econom*ically* tragic / tragical } ~ trag*ically*

Exception: *public* ~ *publicly*

(d) *-ed* participles form adverbs in *-edly* with the pronunciation /ɪdlɪ/ (*cf* 7.19):

marked /mɑːʳkt/ ~ mark*edly* /ˈmɑːʳkɪdlɪ/
learned /ˈlɜːʳnɪd/ ~ learn*edly* /ˈlɜːʳnɪdlɪ/
assured /əˈʃʊəʳd/ ~ assur*edly* /əˈʃʊərɪdlɪ/

(e) Adjectives in *-ary* form adverbs in *-arily* with shift of stress, in AmE, to the antepenultimate syllable. This stress shift is now frequent also in BrE (*cf* App II.5 Note):

ˈseconˌdary { ~ ˌseconˈdarily ⟨esp AmE⟩ / ~ ˈsecondarily }

ˈprimary { ~ ˌpriˈmarily ⟨esp AmE⟩ / ~ ˈprimarily }

Adverb as clause element

7.48 There are two types of syntactic functions that characterize the traditional adverbs, but an adverb need have only one of these:

(a) clause element adverbial:

He *quite* forgot about it.

(b) premodifier of adjective and adverb:

They are *quite* {happy. / happily married.}

An adverb may function in the clause itself as adverbial, *ie* as an element distinct from subject, verb, object, and complement. As such it is usually an optional element and hence peripheral to the structure of the clause (*cf* 2.15):

Perhaps my suggestion will be accepted.
John *always* loses his pencils.
They may *well* complain about his appearance.
He has *nevertheless* refused to accept our excuse.
I spoke to her *outside*.

There are, of course, differences between the adverbials in the above sentences, most obviously the differences in their position and in their relationship to other elements of the sentence (*cf* Chapter 8).

Note [**a**] Certain adverbs may function as subject (*cf* 10.15 Notes [a] and [b]), *eg*:
Tomorrow will be fine. ['It will be fine tomorrow.']
[**b**] The adverb may itself be modified, in which case the adverb phrase as a whole functions as adverbial or premodifier:
John *nearly always* loses his pencils. *so very* helpful
They may *very well* complain about his appearance. *far too* often

Adjuncts, subjuncts, disjuncts, and conjuncts

7.49 The functions of the adverb as the clause element adverbial are examined in Chapter 8. For the present, we merely outline the four grammatical functions that are discussed in that chapter: adjuncts, subjuncts, disjuncts, and conjuncts.

ADJUNCTS and SUBJUNCTS are relatively integrated within the structure of the clause (*cf* 8.25*ff*, 8.88*ff*). Examples of adjuncts:

Slowly they walked back home.
He spoke to me about it *briefly*.

Examples of subjuncts:

We haven't *yet* finished.
Would you *kindly* wait for me.

By contrast, disjuncts and conjuncts have a more peripheral relation in the sentence. Semantically, DISJUNCTS (*cf* 8.121*ff*) express an evaluation of what is being said either with respect to the form of the communication or to its meaning. We identify disjuncts with the speaker's authority for, or comment on, the accompanying clause:

Frankly, I'm tired.
Fortunately, no one complained.
They are *probably* at home.
She *wisely* didn't attempt to apologize.

CONJUNCTS (*cf* 8.134*ff*) express the speaker's assessment of the relation between two linguistic units, *eg*:

She has bought a big house, *so* she must have a lot of money.
We have complained several times about the noise, and *yet* he does nothing about it.
All our friends are going to Paris this summer. We, *however*, are going to London.
If they open all the windows, *then* I'm leaving.
I didn't invite her. She wouldn't have come, *anyway*.

Adverb as modifier

7.50 An adverb may function as a modifier of an adjective or of another adverb. (In the examples, the modifier is indicated by italics and the modified constituent is indicated by angle brackets.) Examples of adverbs as modifiers of adjectives [1, 2, 6] and adverbs [3–5]:

They are *very* ⟨happy⟩. [1]
It was a *remarkably* ⟨good⟩ show. [2]
She drives *too* ⟨fast⟩. [3]
They play *so* ⟨very⟩ well. [4]
He gave a *far* ⟨more easily⟩ acceptable explanation. [5]
He is ⟨stupid⟩ *enough* to do it. [6]

In this function, the adverb generally *pre*modifies, except that *enough*, as in [6], can only *post*modify. The item being modified may itself function as a modifier. For example, the adjective *good* premodifies the noun *show* in [2], while *more easily* modifies *acceptable* in [5], and the adverb *very* premodifies the adverb *well* in [4]. In both [2] and [5], the adverb is within a noun phrase.

Adverbs functioning as modifiers of adjectives and adverbs will be further discussed in 7.56*ff*. However, not all adverbs that modify adjectives also modify adverbs (*cf* 7.60), and some adverbs may modify phrases, *viz* noun phrases and prepositional phrases. The most conspicuous example of an adverb that functions only as a modifier of adjectives and adverbs, and not as a clause element, is *very*. (For *very* as an adjective, *cf* 7.35 Note [a].)

The adverb and other word classes

7.51 We now briefly consider some examples of overlap between the adverb class and other word classes. Similarities between adverbs and adjectives have been discussed earlier (*cf* 7.6*ff*). The other relevant word classes are conjunctions, prepositions, and interjections. We also take into account certain words (other than conjunctions and some conjunct adverbs) that must be positioned initially, but these are not traditionally recognized as separate word classes.

Conjunct adverb and conjunction

7.52 A few conjunct adverbs, such as *so* and *yet*, resemble coordinators (coordinating conjunctions) both in being connectives and in having certain syntactic features (*cf* 13.11). In particular, these adverbs cannot be transposed with their clause in front of the preceding clause. Thus, the order of the following two clauses (with the conjunct adverb *so* in the second clause) is fixed:

> We paid him a very large sum. *So* he kept quiet about what he saw. [1]

If we invert the order of the clauses, the relationship between the two clauses is changed, and *so* must now refer to some preceding clause:

> *So* he kept quiet about what he saw. We paid him a very large sum. [2]

However, the conjunct adverbs differ from coordinators in that they can be preceded by a coordinator:

> We paid him a very large sum, *and so* he kept quiet about what he saw. [1a]

The restriction on the order of clauses also distinguishes the conjunct adverbs from subordinators, another type of connective. For example, a clause introduced by the subordinator *because* can follow or precede the matrix clause without disturbing the relationship between the two clauses (*cf* 14.4*ff*):

> { He will help us *because* we offered to pay him. [3]
> { *Because* we offered to pay him, he will help us. [3a]

Adjunct adverb and conjunction

7.53 A few subordinators can be seen to be a fusion of conjunction and pro-adjunct (*cf* 15.8), in particular *when* [time], *where* [place at or place to], *how* [manner], *why* [reason].

Where and *when* introduce adverbial clauses (*cf* 15.31):

> He saw them { *when* / *at the time(s) at which* } they were in Rome.
>
> I'll go { *where* / *to the place(s) to which* } they go.
>
> We'll go { *where* / *to the place(s) at which* } the food is good.
>
> He'll stay { *where* / *at the place(s) at which* } it is comfortable.

Where and *when*, and to a lesser extent *why*, are also used as relatives (*cf* 17.18*ff*):

> the place { *where* / *at which* } he is staying [1]
>
> the time { *when* / *at which* } she was here [2]

Where, *when*, *why*, and *how* are all used to introduce nominal clauses (*cf* 15.8*f*):

I know {*where* / *at which place*} he is staying. [1a]

I wonder {*when* / *at which time*} she was here. [2a]

I realize {*why* / *the reason for which*} he did it. [3]

That was {*how* / *the way in which*} they treated her. [4]

These four *wh*-words are also used as interrogative pro-forms (*cf* 11.14):

{*Where* / *At what place*} is he staying? [1b]

{*When* / *At what time*} was she here? [2b]

{*Why* / *For what reason*} did he do it? [3a]

{*How* / *In what way*} did they treat her? [4a]

The function of *where*, *when*, and *how* as pro-forms for adjuncts is clearly demonstrated in the few cases where a verb requires complementation by an obligatory predication (*cf* 8.27*ff*):

*She put it. [5]
*He lived. [6]
*They treated her. [unacceptable in the sense 'behaved towards her'] [7]

These sentences become acceptable if an adjunct of the appropriate type is added:

She put it *there*. [5a]
He lived *then*. [6a]
They treated her *well*. [7a]

But complementation can also be provided by the appropriate subordinators, evidence that they are functioning as pro-adjuncts:

He found it *where* she put it. [5b]
I wonder *when* he lived. [6b]
I saw *how* they treated her. [7b]

In a sentence such as [5c], one could argue that *where* is functioning as an adjunct in both clauses, which have been made to overlap by the subordinator:

She put it *where* he could find it. [5c]

= {She put it *there*.
There he could find it.}

On the other hand, it is equally possible to argue that the obligatory complementation of a place adjunct is satisfied by the whole clause of place rather than by *where*. The same reasoning applies to the obligatory complementation for *treat* provided by clauses of manner and comparison (*cf* 15.22):

She treated him { *as he deserved.* / *as though he were a stranger.* }

Note Most of the other *wh*-words are pro-forms for noun phrases and can clearly function as clause elements: *who, whom, which* (*cf* 10.6 Note [e]).

Reaction signal and initiator

7.54 Apart from conjunctions and some conjunct adverbs, certain other items must be positioned initially. They are important because of their high frequency in spoken English. Some are restricted to the spoken language. These can be assigned to two small classes (*cf* 11.54*f*):

(i) 'reaction signals', *eg*: *no, yes, yeah, yep, m, hm, mhm*
(ii) 'initiators', *eg*: *well, oh, ah*; *oh well, well then, why* ⟨esp AmE⟩

Here is an example from a conversation (*cf* App II for the prosodic notation):

|*ÔH*| |*WĒLL*| of |course he'll be working with overseas ↑STÙdents|. |*well* ↑ *YÈS*| |but ↑he's WÓRKing with ↑DÌBble| |*well NÔ*| he's in the de|partment of English LÌTerature|

Adjunct and preposition

7.55 There are several different types of combinations of verbs plus particles (*cf* 16.2*ff*). If the verb is intransitive, we can recognize the particle as a prepositional adverb (*cf* 9.65*f*) functioning as adjunct, *eg*:

The men looked *on*.
She is growing *up* quickly.
The airliner has taken *off*.
The prisoner broke *down* after many hours of interrogation.

When a noun phrase follows the particle, it sometimes appears as if we have a prepositional phrase, with the particle as preposition:

He took *in* the dog. [1]

However, the adverbial nature of the particle in such phrasal verbs (*cf* 16.3*ff*) is generally shown by its mobility, its ability to follow the noun phrase:

He took the dog *in*. [1a]

Similarly:

{ They turned *down* the suggestion. [2]
They turned the suggestion *down*. [2a] }

{ They turned *on* the light. [3]
They turned the light *on*. [3a] }

In contrast, a preposition must be directly followed by its complement:

{ They took *to* John quickly. [4]
{ *They took John *to* quickly. [4a]

The instances we have mentioned so far are not to be confused with examples like [5] and [6]. Compare:

{ He walked *past*. [prepositional adverb] [5]
{ He walked *past the car*. [preposition] [5a]
{ *He walked *the car past*. [5b]

{ He was moving *about*. [prepositional adverb] [6]
{ He was moving *about the town*. [preposition] [6a]
{ *He was moving *the town about*. [6b]

Past in [5] and *about* in [6] are prepositional adverbs, which can be regarded as prepositions with some generalized ellipsis of the noun phrase (*cf* 9.65*f*).

Syntactic functions of adverbs

Adverb as modifier

Modifier of adjective

7.56 An adverb may premodify an adjective. Most commonly, the modifying adverb is a scaling device called an intensifier, which cooccurs with a gradable adjective. We first distinguish two sets of intensifiers: amplifiers and downtoners (for further discussion and subclassification, *cf* 8.104*ff*).

(a) AMPLIFIERS scale upwards from an assumed norm, *eg* 'a *very* funny film', as compared with 'a funny film'. Other examples:

absurdly fussy	*amazingly* calm
awfully sorry	*deeply* concerned
downright ridiculous	*entirely* free
extremely dangerous	*highly* intelligent
irretrievably lost	*perfectly* reasonable
sharply critical	*strikingly* handsome
terribly nervous	*too* bright
totally anonymous	*unbelievably* smart

(b) DOWNTONERS have a generally lowering effect, usually scaling downwards from an assumed norm, *eg* 'It was *almost* dark', as compared with 'It was dark'. Other examples:

a bit dull	*a little* extravagant
almost impossible	*barely* intelligible
fairly small	*hardly* noticeable
nearly dark	*pretty* rare
quite normal	*rather* late
relatively small	*somewhat* uneasy

A similar set of intensifiers is used for both adjectives and adverbs (*cf* 7.87). For intensifiers which premodify comparatives and superlatives, *cf* 7.89*f*.

Note [**a**] *Quite* can have two different meanings (*cf* 8.111 Note [c]), as in:

She's *quite* right. ['absolutely', 'completely', *ie* an amplifier]

That's *quite* good. ['fairly', 'rather', *ie* a downtoner; in AmE *quite* here is also used in the sense of 'very', *ie* as an amplifier]

[**b**] *Fairly*, *pretty*, and *rather* can all be used as intensifiers of adjectives and adverbs, *eg*:

She is {*fairly* / *pretty* / *rather*} tall. She drives {*fairly* / *pretty* / *rather*} fast.

However, these downtoners have different uses. *Fairly* is typically used to modify an adjective or adverb which denotes a desirable quality. If we feel comfortable in a warm room, we can intensify the adjective by saying *It's fairly warm in here* ['warm enough'], whereas *rather warm* implies that the room is warmer than we desire ('too warm'). We would usually say *fairly clean* but *rather dirty* to denote, respectively, a desirable and an undesirable quality.

Pretty is the most informal and strongest of the three. Like *rather*, it can be used with both favourable and unfavourable import: *pretty clean/dirty*. Note that *pretty*, when used as an intensifier, is normally unstressed (or weakly stressed) – unlike the adjective *pretty*:

a ˌpretty ˈdark DRÈSS ['a rather dark dress']

a ˈpretty ˈdark DRÈSS ['The dress was pretty.']

Rather differs from *pretty* and *fairly* in that it alone can intensify:

(i) a comparative or *too*-construction (*cf* the implication 'too warm' above):

{*rather* / **fairly* / **pretty*} {better / too small / too quickly}

(ii) certain noun phrases denoting adjectival qualities (*cf* 7.63 Note [b]):

{*rather* / **fairly* / **pretty*} {a pity / a fool / a crowd} BUT: {*rather* / *fairly* / *pretty*} {pitiful / foolish / crowded}

(iii) certain verbs (*cf* 8.112):

It *rather*/**fairly*/**pretty* annoys me that . . .

(iv) With other nouns, *rather* alone has variable position in relation to the indefinite article (*cf* 7.63 Note [b]):

a {*rather* / *pretty* / *fairly*} difficult task {~ *rather* / ≁ **pretty* / ≁ **fairly*} a difficult task

[**c**] In informal speech, *kind of* and *sort of* are used as downtoners for adjectives and adverbs (*cf* 8.111):

He is *sort of* clever. She spoke *kind of* proudly.

[**d**] The following intensifiers are typical of informal speech ⟨esp AmE⟩:

real nice *awful* good

plain silly *mighty* helpful

Most people prefer *really* to *real*, and *awfully* to *awful*, particularly in formal style (*cf* 7.7):

She's *really* nice. That was *awfully* good.

Especially in informal AmE, *sure* is similarly used:

That's *sure* kind of you. ['certainly']

Surely, unlike *really*, is however a disjunct (*cf* 8.127), in which function *sure* is also used in informal AmE. Note also the use of *sure* in Irish English:

Surely, she's right. [persuasive: 'you surely agree']

Sure, she's right. [AmE = agreement: 'of course']

Sure, she's right. [Irish English = asseveration: 'I assure you']

Sure and *surely* (unlike *real*, *really*, and *truly*) cannot premodify another premodifier:

She's a {*real(ly)* / *truly* / **sure(ly)*} ⟨nice⟩ girl.

Sure cannot occur after other verbs than *be*:

She's *sure* nice. ⟨esp AmE⟩ — She *sure* is nice. ⟨esp AmE⟩
*She looks *sure* nice. — She *sure* looks nice. ⟨esp AmE⟩

But:

He'll *sure* fail. ⟨informal⟩ — He *sure* can play football. ⟨informal⟩

[e] Two informal intensifiers, *any* and *that*, are particularly associated with nonassertive contexts:

Is the team *any* different from last year? ['really very much different']
It's not (all) *that* unusual for women nowadays to join the police force, is it? ['so, very']

Outside nonassertive contexts, this usage of *that* is dialectal or nonstandard:

She's *that* clever! ['very'] — I was *that* tired I couldn't walk. ['so']

[f] As downtoners of adjectives in the absolute degree, *a bit* and *a little* can only occur in predicative position and with adjectives with 'unfavourable' meaning and an implication of 'more than wanted':

The weather's *a bit* (too) hot. — *The weather's *a bit* lovely.
**a bit* hot weather

[g] Some amplifiers are restricted to a small set of lexical items, *eg*:

dead tired [BUT NOT: *dead exhausted] — *fast* asleep
dead drunk [BUT NOT: *dead intoxicated] — *wide* awake

Nouns may also function as such restricted amplifiers:

stone cold   *rock* hard   *brand* new

[h] One difference between the set of downtoners *almost*, *nearly*, and *practically* (*cf* approximators, 8.111*ff*) is that only *nearly* can be used after *not*, *very*, *pretty* (*cf* 7.62):

It's {*nearly* / *almost* / *practically*} dark.   BUT: It's {not / very / pretty} {*nearly* / **almost* / **practically*} dark.

7.57 As in the treatment of adjectives, it may be possible to distinguish another class of adjective modifiers called EMPHASIZERS, which add to the force (as distinct from the degree) of the adjective:

She has a *really* ⟨beautiful⟩ face. — The play is ⟨very good⟩ *indeed*.
That's *just* ⟨impossible⟩. — He looked *all* ⟨confused⟩.

Unlike intensifiers, emphasizers cooccur with nongradable adjectives, but the effect is often similar to that of intensifiers:

You are *certainly* welcome. ['You are *very/most* welcome.']

Indeed can have either pre- or postposition (*cf* 8.103 Note [a]):

The play was {*indeed* ⟨excellent⟩. / ⟨excellent⟩ *indeed*.}

Compare:

Indeed, the play was excellent.

This example shows how the function of many emphasizers is similar to that of disjuncts (*cf* 8.121*ff*). Similarly *frankly*:

I'm *frankly* surprised at your behaviour. [emphasizer]
Frankly, I'm surprised at your behaviour. [disjunct]

Note *Too* can be a synonym of *extremely* in informal speech:

It's *too* ⟨kind⟩ of you.   That's *too* ⟨true⟩.

In informal style it is also commonly used (especially in AmE) as a synonym of *very* in negative sentences:

I'm not *too* ⟨sure⟩ about that.
I'm not *too* ⟨keen⟩ on his paintings.
I don't feel *too* ⟨good⟩. ['very well']

This use of *too* is given wide extension in Australian English, where *too* is common in the sense 'absolutely' in responses:

A: He's clever. B: *Too* right, he is. ['That is absolutely true.']

Compare informal AmE usage:

A: You can't do it. B: I can *too*. ['I certainly can.']

7.58 Adjunct adverbs (*cf* 7.49, 8.25*ff*) are sometimes converted into premodifiers of adjectives. In this position they tend to retain their general meaning of manner, means, etc, though they also acquire some intensifying effect:

an *easily* ⟨debatable⟩ proposition ['a proposition that can be easily debated']
an *openly* ⟨hostile⟩ attack
his *quietly* ⟨assertive⟩ manner
a *readily* ⟨available⟩ publication

On the other hand, disjunct adverbs (*cf* 7.121*ff*) tend to become intensifiers, *eg*:

surprisingly ⟨good⟩ *unnaturally* ⟨long⟩
incredibly ⟨beautiful⟩ *unusually* ⟨easy⟩

Thus *surprisingly good* in the following sentence can be paraphrased as 'He made a speech that was good to a surprising extent':

He made a *surprisingly* ⟨good⟩ speech.

Note We need to distinguish the adverb as premodifier of an adjective from the adjunct adverb constructed with a verb participle. For example, *a surprisingly worded letter* is 'a letter that is worded in a surprising manner', since *worded* is an *-ed* participle and not an adjective. Ambiguity arises when the form can be either a participle or an adjective. Thus, *a divinely inspired work* can be either 'a work that has been inspired in a divine manner (or by God)', in which case *inspired* is verbal and *divinely* an adjunct adverb, or 'a work that is inspired to a divine extent', in which case *inspired* is adjectival and *divinely* its intensifier. *Cf* the difference in aspect and implied 'permanence'; 17.28.

7.59 Apart from intensifiers, premodifying adverbs may be 'viewpoint' subjuncts (*cf* 8.88*ff*), *eg*:

politically ⟨expedient⟩ ['expedient from a political point of view']

Similarly:

artistically ⟨justifiable⟩ *economically* ⟨weak⟩
theoretically ⟨sound⟩ *technically* ⟨possible⟩
ethically ⟨wrong⟩

Modifier of adverb

7.60 An adverb may premodify another adverb. Similar sets of intensifiers are used for adverbs and adjectives (*cf* 7.56*ff*):

I expect them *pretty* ⟨soon⟩.
I have seen *so* ⟨very⟩ many letters like that one.

They didn't injure him *that* ⟨severely⟩. ⟨informal⟩
They are smoking *very* ⟨heavily⟩.
He spoke *extremely* ⟨quickly⟩.
He played *surprisingly* ⟨well⟩.

As with adjectives (*cf* 7.50, 7.57), the only postmodifiers are *enough* and *indeed*:

He spoke ⟨clearly⟩ *enough*. ['sufficiently clearly']

Indeed usually goes with *very*:

She spoke ⟨very clearly⟩ *indeed*.
?She spoke ⟨clearly⟩ *indeed*.

Adverbs modifying other adverbs can only be intensifiers. Thus, though we have the manner modification by *quietly* in *quietly assertive*, we cannot have it in:

*He spoke *quietly* ⟨assertively⟩.

And, similarly, the modification by a viewpoint adverb (*cf* 8.89) in *theoretically sound* does not have a corresponding

*He reasoned *theoretically* ⟨soundly⟩.

Notice that this is not merely a stylistic objection to the juxtaposition of two words ending in *-ly*, since the following sentence, where *extremely* is an intensifier, is acceptable:

He reasoned *extremely* ⟨soundly⟩.

Modifier of particle, prepositional adverb, and preposition

7.61 A few intensifying adverbs, particularly *right* and *well*, can premodify particles in phrasal verbs (*cf* 16.4), as well as prepositions, or (perhaps rather) prepositional phrases (*cf* 9.64):

He knocked the man *right* ⟨out⟩.
They left her *well* ⟨behind⟩.
The nail went *right* ⟨through⟩ the wall.
He made his application *well* ⟨within⟩ the time.
Her parents are *dead* ⟨against⟩ the trip. ⟨informal⟩

Modifier of pronoun, predeterminer, and numeral

7.62 Intensifying adverbs (including downtoners) can premodify:

(a) indefinite pronouns (6.45*ff*):

Nearly ⟨everybody⟩ came to our party.

(b) predeterminers (5.15*ff*):

They recovered *roughly* ⟨half⟩ their equipment.
He received *about* ⟨double⟩ the amount he expected.
Virtually ⟨all⟩ the students participated in the discussion.

(c) cardinal numerals (6.63):

They will stay *fully* ⟨ten⟩ weeks. ['for ten full weeks']
Over/under ⟨two hundred⟩ deaths were reported.
I paid *more/less than* ⟨ten⟩ pounds for it.
They will make a charge of *up to* ⟨as much as one million⟩ yen.
As many as ⟨fifty⟩ candidates had applied for the post.

(d) Noun phrases with the indefinite article can be intensified when *a(n)* is equivalent to the unstressed cardinal *one* (5.38):

I didn't have *more than* ⟨a dollar⟩ on me. ['I had no more than . . .']
They will stay for *about* ⟨a week⟩.
Nearly/almost ⟨a thousand demonstrators⟩ attended the meeting.

More than, *about*, etc are here not prepositions but intensifiers as part of the noun phrase, as can be seen by the occurrence of prepositions before such items:

There's a cover charge of *more than $3.*

(e) With the ordinals and superlatives, a definite determiner is obligatory for premodification:

We counted *approximately* ⟨the first⟩ thousand votes.
She gave me *almost* ⟨the largest⟩ piece of cake.

(f) Modification can also apply to larger units, *eg*:

The acceleration fell to *less than* ⟨ten metres per second⟩.

Note [**a**] We might add here the premodification of *the same* by *(very) much*:
They did it in *(very) much* ⟨the same⟩ way.
[**b**] Some of the items that are intensifying adverbs can also function as prepositions, *eg*: *over*, *about* (*cf* 9.7).
[**c**] Both the downtoners *almost* and *practically* can intensify all indefinite pronouns, whereas *nearly* can intensify only assertive pronouns (*cf* 8.113 on downtoners with verbs). Compare:

{*Almost* / *Practically* / *Nearly*} {everybody / all} came.

{*Almost* / *Practically* / **Nearly*} {nobody came. / any time will do. / no compensation was given.}

Modifier of noun phrase

7.63 A few intensifiers may premodify noun phrases and precede the determiner in doing so. The most common of these among adverbs are *quite* and *rather* ⟨esp BrE⟩:

We had *quite* ⟨a party⟩.
They will be here for *quite* ⟨some time⟩.
He was *quite* ⟨'some player⟩.

They were *quite* ⟨'some players⟩.
[*Quite* '*some* with count nouns is informal; note the stress on '*some*.]
It was *rather* ⟨a mess⟩. ⟨esp BrE⟩

Though not adverbs but predeterminers (*cf* 5.15), *such* and *what* have a similar function (*cf* 17.96):

He is *such* ⟨a fool⟩.	They are *such* ⟨fools⟩.
What ⟨a mess⟩ they made!	*What* ⟨babies⟩ they are!

Note [**a**] Other adverbs may be interpreted as not specifically modifying the noun phrase, since they are mobile. Compare the following two examples:

He was |*really* 'some PLÀYer| ⟨informal⟩ [1]
He |*really* was 'some PLÀYer| [2]

Transposition of *really* in [1] to pre-verb position in [2] does not seem to affect the meaning, provided that the appropriate intonation pattern is given. A similar transposition of *quite* is not possible.

[**b**] For many people, plural noun phrases cannot be premodified by *rather*:

He is *rather a fool*. ['rather foolish'; *cf* 7.56 Note [b]]
?*They are *rather* fools.

If the noun is nongradable, *rather* cannot be used unless a gradable adjective is present, in which case *rather* is intensifying the adjective. Positions before the adjective and before the determiner are both possible, with little or no semantic difference:

*It is rather a table. [not acceptable unless in the sense '. . . a table rather than . . .']
It is {*rather a* / *a rather*} big table.

[**c**] For the relationship between adverbs like *only* and *also* and noun phrases, *cf* focusing subjuncts, 8.116*ff*.

7.64 With *kind of* and *sort of* there are several possible constructions in informal style:

This must be
- *a sort of* joke.
- *sort of a* joke. ⟨informal⟩
- *a sort of a* joke. ⟨more informal⟩
- a joke, *sort of*. ⟨most informal⟩

Other *of*-phrases precede the determiner, if present:

I had *a bit of* ⟨a shock⟩.
They asked *a heck of* ⟨a lot⟩. ⟨familiar⟩
They gave me *a hell of* ⟨a time⟩. ⟨familiar⟩

In familiar style, the *wh*-words as interrogatives (*cf* 11.14 Note [a]) can be postmodified by certain set prepositional phrases, *eg*:

{⟨who⟩ / ⟨what⟩ / ⟨where⟩} {*on earth* / (*in*) *the heck* ⟨familiar⟩ / (*in*) *the hell* ⟨familiar⟩}

Omission of the preposition in the last two examples is preferred by some and obligatory for others.

Ever can be an intensifier. It normally occurs as a separate word and only with interrogative *wh*-words, for example:

⟨Why⟩ *ever* should she apply for such a post?

7.65 Some disjunct adverbs and conjunct adverbs occasionally appear within the noun phrase, not modifying the noun phrase but related to a modifying adjective phrase:

> A cure has now been found for this *fortunately* ⟨very rare⟩ disease. ['a disease that is fortunately very rare']
> He wrote an *otherwise* ⟨extremely good⟩ paper. ['a paper that was otherwise extremely good']

Similarly, subjunct adverbs expressing viewpoint (*cf* 8.89) appear after the noun phrase and relate to the premodifying adjective within the phrase:

> A ⟨good⟩ paper *editorially* can also be a ⟨good⟩ paper *commercially*.

The more usual form for the sentence is:

> An *editorially* ⟨good⟩ paper can also be a *commercially* ⟨good⟩ paper.

7.66 The gradable measure adjectives *deep*, *high*, *long*, *old*, *tall*, *thick*, and *wide* (*cf* 7.88) can take premodification by a noun phrase:

> Susan is *ten years* ⟨old⟩. ['of age']
> Peter is *five feet* ⟨tall⟩. ['in height']
> They stayed up *all night* ⟨long⟩.

In support of this analysis, *ie* that it is the noun phrase and not the adjective that is the modifier, we note that the question form with *how* evokes the noun phrase as the response:

> A: *How old* is Susan? B: *Ten* (*years*).
> A: *How tall* is Peter? B: *Five feet*.

Adverbs such as the following are also modified by noun phrases:

> The lake is *two miles* ⟨across⟩. ['wide']
> They live *five miles* ⟨apart⟩.
> We dug *ten feet* ⟨down⟩.
> The tree is *six feet* ⟨around⟩. ⟨esp AmE⟩
> I met her *a week* {⟨before⟩. / ⟨earlier⟩.} ['earlier by a week']

Compare:

> I met her *the week before*. ['the previous week']

In the following examples, the question is of the form '*How* + adverb + verb + noun':

> *How wide* is the lake? [NOT: *How across . . .?]
> *How far apart* do they live? [NOT: *How apart . . .?]
> *How deep* did they dig? [NOT: *How down . . .?]

Note [**a**] *All the year round* and *the whole year round* are fixed expressions. We cannot, for example, have **all the month round* or **the whole month round*. But note: *all* (*the*) *day* (*long*), *all the week* (*long*), *the whole night* (*through*).
[**b**] On *£8 net/gross*, *the sum total*, etc, *cf* 7.21.

Postmodifying adverbs

7.67 Postmodifying time adverbs appear to be limited to those denoting time position or time duration (*cf* 8.51*ff*, 17.55):

TIME:

the meeting *yesterday*	the day *before*
the meal *afterwards*	their stay *overnight*

PLACE:

the way *ahead*	your friend *here*
the direction *back*	that man *there*
his trip *abroad*	his return *home*
the sentence *below*	the players *offside*

There is no premodification possible with, for example, *home* in:

his return *home* ≁ *his *home* return

In other cases, both positions are available:

the *downstairs* hall	~	the hall *downstairs*
the *backstage* noise	~	the noise *backstage*
his *home* journey	~	his journey *home*
the *above* quotation	~	the quotation *above*
the *upstairs* neighbour	~	the neighbour *upstairs*

Note Many of these postmodifying adverbs can be used predicatively with *be*, *eg*:

The noise is *backstage*.	The sentence is *below*.
The meeting was *yesterday*.	The meal was *afterwards*.

Premodifying adverbs

7.68 Only a very few adverbs premodify nouns within the noun phrase. There is, for example, *an inside job* ['a robbery done by someone connected with the place which has been robbed'], which is not the same as *a job inside*. Other examples:

an *away* game	in *after* years
inside information	the *then* chairman
an *outside* door	an *outside* line

The occasional use of other adverbs as noun premodifiers, *eg*: *the now question*, is felt as very ad hoc, although specific expressions, such as *the now generation*, appear from time to time.

Despite their similarity to peripheral adjectives like *utter* (*cf* 7.3*f*), paraphrases of words like *away* show their essential adverb force:

an *away* game ~ a game that we play *away*
the *then* chairman ~ He was chairman *at the time*.

The situation for these adverbs is similar to that for premodifying nouns, as in *garden tools*, where we analyse *garden* as a noun, not as an adjective, in view of its nominal force, as shown for example by its correspondence to a prepositional phrase with the noun as complement (*cf* 7.14, 17.104):

garden tools ~ tools *for the garden*

Else

7.69 *Else* can postmodify:

(a) compound indefinite pronouns (*cf* 6.46*f*) and compound adverbs (*cf* 7.46) in *-body*, *-one*, *-place*, *-thing*, and *-where*:

> ⟨Somebody⟩ *else* must have done it. ['some other person']
> ⟨Anybody⟩ *else* for tennis?
> ⟨Nothing⟩ *else* happened.
> You must have left the keys {⟨somewhere⟩ *else*. / ⟨someplace⟩ *else*. ⟨esp AmE⟩}
> ['elsewhere']
>
> You'll have to borrow ⟨someone⟩ *else's* car. [on the genitive, *cf* 6.47]

(b) *wh*-pronouns and *wh*-adverbs in interrogative clauses (*cf* 11.14*ff*):

> ⟨Who⟩ *else* would do such a thing? ['which other person']
> ⟨Who⟩ *else* did you meet?
> ⟨What⟩ *else* can we do?
> ⟨Where⟩ *else* have you looked?
> ⟨How⟩ *else* could it have happened?
> ⟨When⟩ *else* can we meet?

The genitive *'s* is usually placed after *else* (*cf* the group genitive, 5.123):

> {*Who else's* / ?*Whose else*} fault could it be?

(c) singular *all* (= *everything*), *much*, *a great/good deal*, *a lot*, *little*:

> We will take this step only if *all else* fails.
> There's {*little* / *not much* / *not a great deal*} *else* we can do now.

Adverb as complement of preposition

7.70 A number of adverbs signifying place and time function as complement of a preposition. Of the place adverbs, *here* and *there* take the most prepositions, *eg*:

> Come *over here*!
> Do you live *near here*?
> Yes, I live *over there*.
> How do we get *out of here*?

Other prepositions that take *here* and *there* as complements are:

along	*around*	*down*	*from*	*in*
on	*round*	*through*	*under*	*up*

Home (which may alternatively be considered a noun; *cf* 5.51) can be the complement of *at*, (*away*) *from*, *close to*, *near*, *toward*(*s*), *eg*:

> I want to stay *at home* tonight.

The other place adverbs are restricted to the preposition *from*, *eg*:

You've got a letter *from abroad*.

Other adverbs that function as complement of *from* are:

behind	*above/below/beneath/underneath*
downstairs/upstairs	*indoors/outdoors*
inside/outside	*within/without*

The time adverbs that most commonly function as complement of a preposition are shown in the figure below.

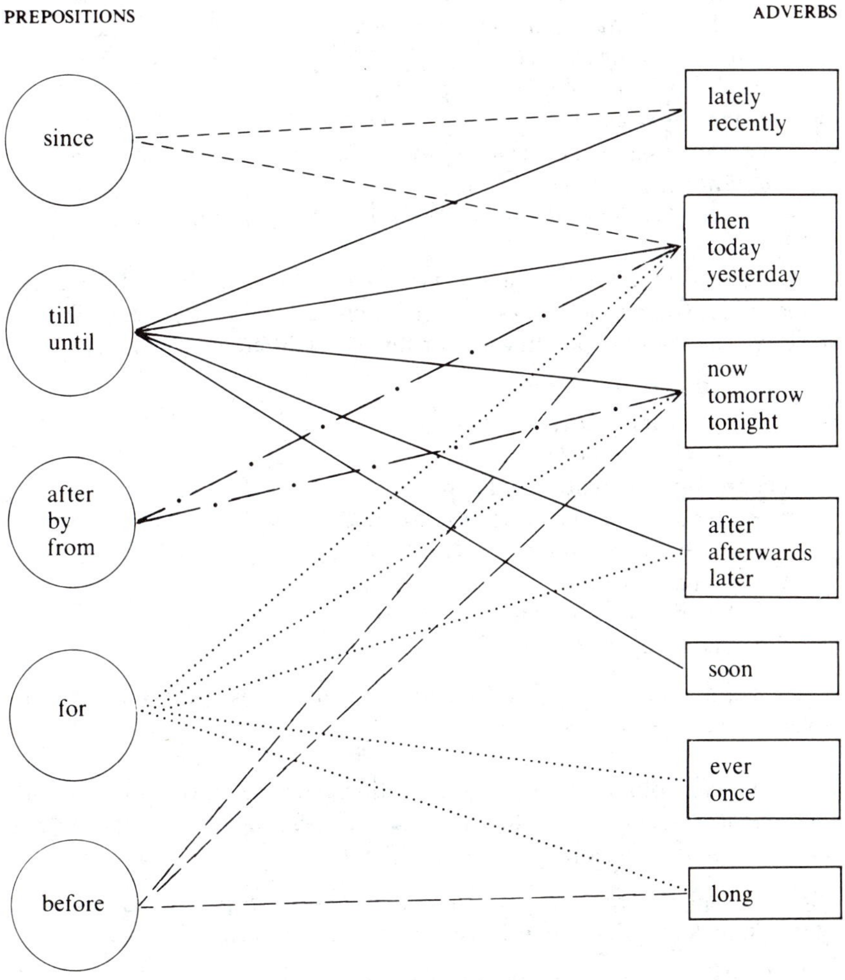

Fig 7.70 Time adverbs that most commonly function as complements of prepositions

Note [**a**] The preposition *of* also occurs in the phrase *of late* ['recently'].

[**b**] *Forever* is also written as two words: *for ever*. The expression *forever and ever* is typical of Biblical and liturgical styles of English. It is curious that analogous reduplicated phrases are virtually restricted to informal use: *for months and months*, *for years and years*.

Correspondence between adjective and adverb

7.71 We have earlier observed (7.46) that open-class adverbs are regularly, though not invariably, derived from adjectives by suffixation. There is another sense in which adjectives and adverbs are related, apart from this morphological relationship. A correspondence often exists between constructions containing adjectives and constructions containing the corresponding adverbs. The simplest illustration is with adverbs equivalent to prepositional phrases containing a noun or noun phrase that is a generic term and the corresponding adjective as premodifier:

He liked Mary *considerably*.
~ He liked Mary *to a considerable extent*.
He spoke to John *sharply*.
~ He spoke to John *in a sharp manner*.
He wrote *frequently*.
~ He wrote *on frequent occasions*.
Politically, it is a bad decision.
~ *From the political point of view*, it is a bad decision.

7.72 We have also noted some instances where either the adjective or the adverb forms appear, with little or no semantic difference (*cf* 7.6). But normally, the adjective and its corresponding adverb appear in different environments:

his *frequent* visits
~ His visits are *frequent*.
~ He visits *frequently*.
her *brilliant* explanation of the process
~ Her explanation of the process was *brilliant*.
~ She explained the process *brilliantly*.
her *incredible* beauty
~ Her beauty is *incredible*.
~ She is *incredibly* beautiful.

As the examples show, the adjective in nominalizations is equivalent to the adverb in a corresponding clause.

7.73 There are many other cases of nominalization where a construction with the adverb form seems basic to an understanding of the corresponding construction with the adjective form (*cf* 17.51*ff*):

(a) The adjective–noun sequence may imply a process or a time relationship, a corresponding clause containing an adverb:

a *hard* worker	~ somebody who works *hard*
an *eventual* loser	~ somebody who will *eventually* lose
a *frequent* visitor	~ somebody who visits *frequently*
a *heavy* eater	~ somebody who eats *heavily*
a *light* sleeper	~ somebody who sleeps *light*(*ly*)

We should include here cases where the agential noun lacks an agential suffix: *a former student, a clever liar*. Similarly, there are instances where the noun normally lacks a corresponding verb, but where the reference is to the process part of the noun's meaning:

a *poor* soldier ['one who acts poorly in his role as a soldier']
a *good* mother ['one who cares well for her children']
a *faithful* friend ['a friend who acts in a faithful way']

Many of these adjectives can occur only attributively in this use. They belong to the noninherent class of adjectives (*cf* 7.43).

(b) Analogous correspondences do not have this restriction to attributive position:

He loved her *deeply*.
~ his *deep* love for her
~ His love for her was *deep*.
He writes *legibly*.
~ his *legible* writing
~ His writing is *legible*.

She answered *quickly*.
~ her *quick* answer
~ Her answer was *quick*.
Surprisingly, he decided to leave.
~ his *surprising* decision to leave
~ His decision to leave was *surprising*.

(c) The adjective may refer to an implied process associated with a concrete object:

a *fast* car ['a car that can go *fast*']
a *slow* road ['a road on which one can only drive *slowly*']
a *neat* typewriter ['a typewriter which types *neatly*']

(d) Most intensifying adjectives (*cf* 7.33*f*) can be seen as related to adverbs:

total nonsense	~ It is *totally* nonsense.
a *clear* failure	~ It is *clearly* a failure.
a *true* scholar	~ He is *truly* a scholar.
a *real* idiot	~ He is *really* an idiot.

Many of these can occur only attributively in this use.

(e) Many restrictive adjectives (*cf* 7.35) can be seen as related to adverbs:

the *main* reason	~ The reason was *mainly* that . . .
the *precise* argument	{ ~ The argument was *precisely* that . . .
	{ ≁ The argument was *precise*.

Note [**a**] We can point to differences in grammar and meaning in the interpretation of *a beautiful dancer*:

a *beautiful* dancer
~ a dancer *who is beautiful*
~ a person *who dances beautifully* ['who does a beautiful dance' or 'beautiful dances']

In the second interpretation, the adjective refers to the process part of an agential noun.

[**b**] Note also the relations between adjectives and adverbs in the following examples:

an *apparent* enemy	~ He is *apparently* an enemy.
a *possible* meeting	~ They will *possibly* meet.
a *slight* disagreement	~ They disagreed *slightly*.
the *current* manager	~ She is *currently* the manager.

Comparison of adjectives and adverbs

7.74 With gradable adjectives and adverbs three types of COMPARISON are possible (*cf* 7.42), *ie* comparison in relation

(a) to a higher degree
(b) to the same degree
(c) to a lower degree

The three types of comparison are expressed by the following means:

(a) Comparison in relation to a higher degree is expressed by the inflected forms in *-er* and *-est* or their periphrastic equivalents with *more* and *most*:

Anna is {*cleverer* / *more clever*} than Susan.

Anna is the {*cleverest* / *most clever*} student in the class.

(b) Comparison in relation to the same degree is expressed by *as* (or sometimes *so*) . . . *as*:

Anna is *as tall as* Bill.

Anna is not {*as* / *so*} *tall as* John.

(c) Comparison in relation to a lower degree is expressed by *less* and *least*:

This problem is *less difficult* than the previous one.
This is the *least difficult* problem of all.

For higher degree comparisons, English has a three-term inflectional contrast between ABSOLUTE, COMPARATIVE, and SUPERLATIVE forms for many adjectives and for a few adverbs, the absolute being realized by the base form of the item. This can be seen in *Table* 7.74 which also gives the parallel periphrastic constructions (*cf* comparative clauses, 15.63*ff*):

Table 7.74 Comparison of adjectives and adverbs

	ABSOLUTE	COMPARATIVE	SUPERLATIVE
INFLECTION			
adjective	*high*	*higher*	*highest*
adverb	*soon*	*sooner*	*soonest*
PERIPHRASIS			
adjective	*complex*	*more complex*	*most complex*
adverb	*comfortably*	*more comfortably*	*most comfortably*

Comparison of adjectives

Irregular forms of comparison

7.75 A small group of highly frequent adjectives have comparative and superlative forms with stems which are different from the base:

good	~ *better*	~ *best*
bad	~ *worse*	~ *worst*
far	~ *further*	~ *furthest*
	~ *farther*	~ *farthest*

The two sets *farther/farthest* and *further/furthest*, which are both adjectives and adverbs, are used interchangeably by many speakers to express both physical and abstract relations. In fact, however, the use of *farther* and *farthest* is chiefly restricted to expressions of physical distance, and, in all senses, *further* and *furthest* are the usual forms found:

Nothing could be *further* from the truth.
My house is *furthest* from the station.

Note The most common uses of *further* are not as comparative form of *far* but in the sense of 'more', 'additional', 'later':

That's a *further* reason for deciding now. [BUT NOT: **a far reason*]
Any *further* questions?
The school will be closed until *further* notice.
We intend to stay for a *further* two months.

Comparison of *old*

7.76 *Old* is regularly inflected as *older* ~ *oldest*. In attributive position, particularly when referring to the order of birth of members of a family, the irregular forms *elder* ~ *eldest* are normally substituted (especially in BrE):

My *elder/older* sister is an artist.
His *eldest/oldest* son is still at school.

However, *elder* is not a true comparative in that it cannot be followed by *than*:

My brother is three years { *older* / **elder* } *than me.*

Note [**a**] There is a special use of *elder* in, for example, *William Pitt the elder, the elder Pitt*. In the honorific expression *elder statesman*, *elder* has no comparative meaning, and there is no corresponding use of *old* or *oldest*.
[**b**] *Elder* and *eldest* require personal reference:

This viola is the *older/*elder*.

Comparison of *good*, *well*, and *ill*

7.77 *Well* ['in good health'] and *ill* ['in bad health' ⟨esp BrE⟩, *cf* 7.38] are inflected like *good* and *bad*, respectively, for the comparative: *He feels better/worse*. *He is better* is ambiguous between (a) 'He is well again' and (b) 'He is less ill'. In the first use (a), we can have intensifiers expressing absolute degree:

He is *completely better*.

In the second use (b), we can have expressions with a comparative sense:

He is { *a little* / *a bit* / *somewhat* } *better*.

There is no superlative *best* in the health sense: **He is best. He is worse* corresponds to the second use (b), *ie* = 'less well'. There is no positive periphrastic comparison corresponding to the negative comparison *less well*:

*He is *more well* today. [= 'better' in its second use]

He is less well denotes that his state of health is not as bad as would be suggested by *worse*.

Compounds with *good*, *well*, and *ill* + participle can have either form of comparison (*cf* 7.83b):

good-looking { ~ *better-looking* ~ *best-looking* / ~ *more good-looking* ~ *most good-looking* }

Comparison of *little* and *small*

7.78 *Little* shares the comparative forms with *small*, *ie*: *smaller* and *smallest*, as an adjective modifying count nouns:

Anna is only a { *little* / *small* } child.

She is *smaller* than Susan.
She is the *smallest* child in her playgroup.

Lesser is used attributively in the sense of 'less important':

to *a lesser degree/extent*
lesser men than Churchill

Least in the sense of 'slightest' is common with abstract nouns in nonassertive contexts:

She did it without *the least/smallest hesitation.*
I haven't *the least idea.*

Least can also be the head of a noun phrase (*cf* 7.26):

That is *the least we can do.*

Note [**a**] *Littler* and *littlest* occur occasionally, typically in familiar use:
She is my *littlest* child.
Have you read the Christmas story called 'The *Littlest* Angel'?
The black dress was *littler* and subtler than volumes of *Vogue* could imply.
[**b**] *Lesser* also denotes 'of smaller size': *the Lesser Antilles* [in contrast to *the Greater Antilles*].

Changes in spelling

7.79 With adjectives taking the regular inflections, certain changes in spelling or pronunciation may be introduced in the base of the adjective when the suffixes are added.

(a) A single consonant at the end of the base is doubled before *-er* and *-est* when the preceding vowel is stressed and spelled with a single letter (*cf* the spelling of verb forms, 3.8):

big ~ *bigger* ~ *biggest*
sad ~ *sadder* ~ *saddest*

But contrast:

neat ~ *neater* ~ *neatest*
thick ~ *thicker* ~ *thickest*

There is a variant spelling in:

cruel { ~ *crueller* ~ *cruellest*
  ~ *crueler* ~ *cruelest* ⟨esp AmE⟩ }

(b) In bases ending in a consonant followed by *-y*, *y* changes to *-i* before *-er* and *-est*:

angry ~ *angrier* ~ *angriest*
early ~ *earlier* ~ *earliest*

(c) If the base ends in a mute (unpronounced) *-e*, this *e* is dropped before the inflection:

pure ~ *purer* ~ *purest*
brave ~ *braver* ~ *bravest*

The same applies if the base ends in *-ee*:

free ~ *freer* ~ *freest* /ˈfriːɪst/

Changes in pronunciation

7.80 (a) A disyllabic base ending in /l̩/ normally loses its second syllable before the inflection:

simple /sɪmpl̩/ ~ /ˈsɪmplə^{r}/ ~ /ˈsɪmplɪst/

humble /hʌmbl̩/ ~ /ˈhʌmblə^{r}/ ~ /ˈhʌmblɪst/

(b) Even for speakers that do not give consonantal value to a final *r* in spelling, the /r/ is pronounced before the inflection:

rare /reə^{r}/ ~ /ˈreərə^{r}/ ~ /ˈreərɪst/

(c) Final *ng* /ŋ/ in the absolute forms *long*, *strong*, and *young* is pronounced /ŋg/ before the inflection:

long /lɒŋ/ ~ /ˈlɒŋgə^{r}/ ~ /ˈlɒŋgɪst/

Choice between inflectional and periphrastic comparison

7.81 The choice between inflectional and periphrastic comparison is largely determined by the length of the adjective.

(a) Monosyllabic adjectives normally form their comparison by inflection:

low ~ *lower* ~ *lowest*

Real, *right*, *wrong*, and the preposition *like* (*cf* 9.4) take only periphrastic forms:

She is { *more like* / **liker* } her grandmother.

However, most other monosyllabic adjectives can take either inflectional or periphrastic comparison.

(b) Many disyllabic adjectives can also take inflections, though they have the alternative of the periphrastic forms:

Her children are { *politer/more polite.* / *(the) politest/(the) most polite.* }

Disyllabic adjectives that can most readily take inflected forms are those ending in an unstressed vowel, /l̩/ or /əʳ/, *eg*:

-y:	early, easy, funny, happy, noisy, wealthy, pretty
-ow:	mellow, narrow, shallow
-le:	able, feeble, gentle, noble, simple

(c) Trisyllabic or longer adjectives can only take periphrastic forms:

beautiful
~ *more beautiful* [BUT NOT: **beautifuller*]
~ *the most beautiful* [BUT NOT: **beautifullest*]

Adjectives with the negative *un*-prefix, such as *unhappy* and *untidy*, are exceptions:

~ *unhappier* ~ *unhappiest* ~ *untidier* ~ *untidiest*

(d) Participle forms which are used as adjectives regularly take only periphrastic forms:

interesting	~ *more interesting*	~ *most interesting*
wounded	~ *more wounded*	~ *most wounded*
worn	~ *more worn*	~ *most worn*

Note [**a**] Within the first group of (b), we may distinguish between adjectives ending in *-ly* and other adjectives ending only in *-y*. For *-ly* adjectives (*cf* 7.9), comparison with periphrasis is common, *eg* with *friendly*, *likely*, *lonely*, and *lively*:

lively { ~ *livelier* ~ *liveliest* / ~ *more lively* ~ *most lively* }

However, among other adjectives ending only in *-y*, inflectional comparison is favoured, *eg*:

easy ~ *easier* ~ *easiest*

[**b**] Among adjectives ending in *-er*, *eager* and *proper* can take only periphrastic comparison. In addition, the following disyllabic adjectives can occur with inflectional forms (as well as periphrastic forms, which seem to be gaining ground): *quiet*, *common*, *solid*, *cruel*, *wicked*, *polite*, *pleasant*, *handsome*.

7.82 Most adjectives that are inflected for comparison can also take the periphrastic forms with *more* and *most*. With *more*, they seem to do so more easily when they are predicative and are followed by a *than*-clause:

John is *more mad* than Bob is.
It would be difficult to find a man *more brave* than he is.
He is *more wealthy* than I thought.

Periphrastic forms are, however, uncommon with a number of monosyllabic adjectives (including those listed in 7.75 as forming their comparison irregularly):

bad	*big*	*black*	*clean*
fair [colour]	*far*	*fast*	*good*
great	*hard*	*high*	*low*
old	*quick*	*small*	*thick*
thin	*tight*	*wide*	*young*

Note [a] There seem to be fewer restrictions on using the periphrastic forms with adjectives in the comparative construction formed with the correlative *the . . . the* (*cf* 15.51):

The {*more old* / *older*} we are, the {*more wise* / *wiser*} we become. [BUT NOT: **a more old man*]

Good and *bad*, however, require nonperiphrastic forms (*better, worse*) even here.

[b] The suffix *-most* is used to express the highest degree in *her innermost feelings*. Also: *foremost, hindmost, outermost, uppermost*. These words are sometimes used also as adverbs: *They did their utmost*.

[c] A study of adjectives at the Survey of English Usage gives the following statistics:

(i) The comparative is, on average, more frequent than the superlative.

(ii) Only 25 per cent of the comparatives, as against 52 per cent of the superlatives, are accompanied by an explicit basis of comparison (*cf* 7.86).

(iii) *-er* is more frequent than *more*, which is more frequent than *less*; *-est* is more frequent than *most*, which is far more frequent than *least*.

(iv) Many of the occurrences of *-er*/*-est* adjectives represent a small number of relatively frequent adjectives. The following distribution is probably typical also for a larger corpus ('types' = different lexical items; 'tokens' = total number of instances):

Table 7.82 Frequencies of comparative forms

	-er/*-est*	*more*/*most*	*less*/*least*	TOTAL
TYPES	56	246	42	344
TOKENS	553	345	49	947

Comparison of adverbs

7.83 For a small number of adverbs, the inflected forms used for comparison are the same as those for adjectives. As with adjectives, there is a small group with comparatives and superlatives formed from different stems. The comparative and superlative inflections are identical with those for the corresponding adjectives *good*, *bad*, and *far* (*cf* 7.75), and the quantifiers *much* and *little* (*cf* 5.23):

badly	~ *worse*	~ *worst*
well	~ *better*	~ *best*
little	~ *less* (*lesser*)	~ *least*
far	~ *further*	~ *furthest*
	~ *farther*	~ *farthest*
much	~ *more*	~ *most*

(a) *Worse* as the comparative of *badly* is used in *eg*:

He behaves even *worse* than his brother.

With *need* and *want*, however, the periphrastic form is required in BrE:

I really need that job *more badly* than you. [AmE also: *worse*]

Here *badly* is not a process adverb, as also indicated by position:

I *badly* need that job. *He *badly* behaves.

In nonstandard use, one may find *iller/badder* ~ *baddest*. In very formal English, *ill* is synonymous with *badly* (*cf*: *ill-behaved*):

He behaved *ill* towards his parents.

(b) Compounds of *well* and *ill* + participle have both types of comparison (*cf* 7.77):

well-behaved	~ *better-behaved*	~ *best-behaved*
	~ *more well-behaved*	~ *most well-behaved*

The forms *better-* ~ *best-behaved* are more formal than *more* ~ *most well-behaved*. Compare *best-known* which is preferred to *most well-known*.

(c) *Lesser* is sometimes used in comparison to a lower degree: *lesser-known*, in the same way as *less well-known*. There is also a lower degree comparative *less well* [= *worse*], as in

He reads *less well* than she does.

Less well here indicates that his reading is not as bad as *worse* does (*cf* 7.77). There is no corresponding higher degree comparative **more well* = *better*.

(d) On the forms *farther/further* ~ *farthest/furthest*, *cf* 7.75, 8.48.

(e) Adverbs that are identical in form with adjectives (*cf* 7.9) take inflections: *fast, hard, late, long, quick*. They follow the same spelling and phonological rules as for adjectives, *eg*: *early* ~ *earlier* ~ *earliest*:

You have to work *harder/faster/longer*.

The *-er* ~ *-est* inflections cannot be added to open-class adverbs ending in *-ly*:

quickly	~ *more quickly*	~ *most quickly*
	≁ **quicklier*	≁ **quickliest*

When *earlier* is synonymous with *before* (*that*) or *previously*, and when *later* is synonymous with *after* (*that*), they are not comparatives of the adverbs *early* and *late* (*cf* 8.55 Note [a]).

(f) *Soon*, which has no corresponding adjective, is frequently used in the comparative (*sooner*). Some find the superlative (*soonest*) unacceptable, or at least very informal, but it seems perfectly acceptable as a premodifier of certain adjectives, *eg*:

the *soonest* possible date, the *soonest* available time

It is also used in the proverb 'Least said, *soonest* mended', and in telexes and telegrams:

Send prices *soonest*. ['as soon as possible']

(g) Similarly, *often* has the comparative forms *oftener* and *oftenest*, although they are less commonly used than the comparative *more often* and, in particular, the superlative *most often*.

(h) Sometimes the comparative *-er* form of the adjective can function as the comparative of the *-ly* adverb:

That's *easier* said than done. [= 'more easily']
Speak *clearer*! [= 'more clearly']

The use of the comparative is generally considered less objectionable than the use of the adjective instead of the adverb in the absolute form (*cf* 7.7):

?Speak *clear*! [= Speak *clearly*!]

(i) Comparative adverbs are involved in modal idioms (*cf* 3.45*f*):

I *had/'d better* go now.
You *had best* forget all about the whole thing.
I *would/'d sooner* stay at home tonight.
He *would/had/'d rather* not commit himself. [There is of course no absolute form of *rather* in present-day English.]

Article usage with comparatives and superlatives

7.84 In general, the comparative and the superlative express comparison between two sets. In the following examples [1, 2], the comparative is used to compare Jane with the others. There is no article with a *than*-construction, as in [1]:

Jane is *cleverer* than all the other girls in the class. [1]

With the superlative, Jane is included in the group and compared with all the others. The definite article is used with an *of*-phrase following, as in [2]:

Jane is *the cleverest* of all the students in the class. [2]

The superlative is often used for a comparison between two persons, items, etc [3], though this is avoided in careful usage where the comparative [3a] is preferred:

He is *the youngest* (of the two brothers). [3]
He is *the younger* (of the two brothers). [3a]

If the superlative is used attributively, the definite article (or other definite determiner) is required, as in [4] and [5]:

Anna is { {*the* / *their*} *youngest* child. / **youngest* child. } [4]

Della is { *the most efficient* publisher in the office. / *our most efficient* publisher. / **most efficient* publisher. } [5]

But if the adjective is not attributive, *the* is optional:

Anna is (*the*) *youngest* (of all). [4a]
Della is (*the*) *most efficient* (of all). [5a]

Without a definite determiner, the construction with *most* is always ambiguous between superlative and intensifier interpretation when the adjective is evaluative:

Della is *most efficient*. ['the most efficient of all' or 'extremely efficient'] [5b]

With the indefinite or zero article, *most* is always interpreted as an intensifier:

She is *a most efficient* publisher.
They are *most efficient* publishers. } ['extremely'] [5c]

When *most* functions as an intensifier, there is of course no parallel construction with the inflected form:

You are very helpful and { *most kind.* / **kindest.* }

I find this whole situation puzzling and { *most odd.* / **oddest.* }

There is a tendency to use *most* with a preceding definite article to express intensification:

Isn't she *the most beautiful woman*? ['an extremely beautiful woman', *ie* = *a most beautiful woman*]

The inflectional superlative is occasionally used in the same way, *eg*:

Lucille wears *the oddest clothes*, my dear.

Other expressions of comparison

7.85 In addition to the normal expression of comparison mentioned, there are some other, related expressions. Some Latin comparatives, *eg*: *senior* and *major*, retain their comparative force:

A is *senior* to B.

However, they are not true comparatives in English, since they cannot be used in comparative constructions with *than* as explicit basis of comparison (*cf* 7.86):

A is { *older* / **senior* } *than* B.

Such Latin comparatives may be called IMPLICIT. (Another term that occurs is 'absolute'.) Implicit comparatives include the following:

A is *senior* to B. ['of higher rank', 'older than'; *cf*: *a senior minister*; *senior citizens* 'old people', 'old age pensioners']
B is *junior* to A. ['of lower rank', 'younger than'; *cf*: *a junior minister*]
inferior management ['inadequate' rather than 'less good'; *cf*: X is *inferior* to Y.]

superior quality [a 'good' rather than 'better' quality; *cf*: Y is *superior* to X.]
a *prior* claim over X ['previous', 'more important'; *cf*: *prior to* 'earlier than']
the *major* political parties ['larger' or 'rather large']
a *minor* point ['less important' or 'quite unimportant']
anterior and *posterior* positions [technical terms in biology: 'near(er) the head' and 'near(er) the tail']

A more or less 'absolute' comparative may occasionally be found also with other adjectives, as in:

an *older* man ['rather old'], the *better* hotels, *finer* restaurants

Repeated and coordinated comparatives, as in the following examples, indicate gradual increase:

She is getting *better and better*. ['increasingly better']
They are becoming *more and more difficult*.

Too in the sense 'more than enough' might also be mentioned here:

It's *too long*. ['longer than it should be']
He speaks *too quickly*. ['more quickly than he should speak']

Enough (postpositive) and *sufficiently* (attributive) express sufficient degree:

The message is {clear *enough*. / *sufficiently* clear.} ['as clear as is necessary']

Note [a] Grading is a semantic process which may be expressed not only by means of comparison of adjectives and adverbs, but also by means of verbs that denote grading. We can distinguish three types of verb corresponding to the three types of comparison (*cf* 7.74):

(i) Verbs expressing comparison in relation to a higher degree, *eg*:
Demand *exceeds* supply. ['is greater than']

(ii) Verbs expressing comparison in relation to the same degree, *eg*:
The length of this boat *equals* the width of that boat. ['This boat *is as long as* that boat is wide.']

(iii) Verbs expressing comparison in relation to a lower degree, *eg*:
This action *diminishes* the possibilities of an early settlement of the dispute. ['makes the possibilities smaller']

Other such verbs containing a comparative element include the following:
increase, intensify, exaggerate, maximize, lengthen, enlarge, amplify; *lessen, curtail, lower, abridge, impair, minimize, decline*

[b] *More* and *most* have other uses in which they are not equivalent to the comparison inflections (*cf* 8.105). Notice the paraphrases in the following two uses of *more*:

He is *more than happy* about it. ['He is happy about it to a degree that is not adequately expressed by the word *happy*.']
He is *more good than bad*. ['It is more accurate to say that he is good than that he is bad.']
She is *more keen than wise*. ['She is keen rather than wise.']

The inflected form cannot be substituted in this function (*cf* 15.69*f*):

*He is *better* than bad. ?*She is *keener* than wise.

But compare:

It's *worse* than useless. He is *worse* than bad.

[c] *Upper* and *lower* have no comparative force in *upper case* ['capital letters'] and *the lower leg* ['the bottom part of the leg']. They are not comparatives of *up* and *low*, since we cannot say **up case*, **the low leg*, etc. A similar pair is *outer* and *inner*, *eg* in *an inner meaning*.

Basis of comparison

7.86 We can make the basis of comparison explicit. The most common ways of doing so include correlative constructions introduced by *than* (correlative to *-er*, *more*, *less*) and by *as* (correlative to *so*, *as*; on comparative clauses, *cf* further 15.63*ff*):

John is {*politer* / *more polite* / *less polite*} *than Bob* (*is*). [1]

John behaves {*more* / *less*} *politely than Bob* (*does*). [1a]

The basis of comparison to the same degree is *as* and, in nonassertive contexts, also *so* (both having the correlative *as*):

John is {*as polite* / *not* {*so* / *as*} *polite*} *as Bob* (*is*). [2]

John {behaves *as politely* / does *not* behave {*so* / *as*} *politely*} *as Bob* (*does*). [2a]

Bases of comparison to a higher or lower degree may also be expressed in other ways, as illustrated below in (a–e).

(a) A restrictive relative clause (full or ellipted):

John is the best player {(*I've ever seen*) / (*we have*) / (*they have*) / (*there is*) / (*that plays*)} *on the team.* [3]

(b) An *of*-phrase (not derivable from a relative clause):

{John is the more polite *of the* (*two*) *boys*. [4]
Of the (*two*) *boys*, John behaves the more politely. [4a]}

{John is the most polite *of the* (*three*) *boys*. [5]
Of the (*three*) *boys*, John behaves the most politely. [5a]}

The prepositional phrases can be either final, as in [4] and [5], or initial, as in [4a] and [5a]. Final position is more frequent, especially when the construction contains an adjective. Note the obligatory presence of *the* before *more* and *most* (*cf* 7.84).

(c) The noun (or its replacement *one*) which the adjective premodifies:

John is the more stupid {*boy.* / *one.*} ‹formal›

[more commonly: John is more stupid than the other boy.]

John is the most stupid {*boy.* / *one.*}

(d) A determiner with definite reference. With comparatives, either the definite article or demonstrative determiner (*cf* 5.14) is possible:

{*The* / *That*} taller boy is John.

Unlike comparatives, however, superlatives cannot normally cooccur with demonstrative determiners:

{*The* / *My* / **That*} youngest daughter is a dentist.

(e) A genitive construction or possessive determiner:

John is {*Mary's* / *her*} older/oldest brother.

Note Some basis of comparison may be implicit in the use of the absolute form of the adjective, and in such cases the basis of comparison can also be made explicit (*cf*: *for*, 9.62):

He is tall *for a child (of) his age*. [*ie* 'taller than normal']

Intensification

Restrictions on intensification

7.87 The types of intensifiers modifying adjectives and adverbs have been mentioned earlier (*cf* 7.56*ff*). Here we are concerned with restrictions on their use analogous to those for comparison. In general, amplifiers and comparatives are allowed by the same range of adjectives and adverbs, *ie* those that are gradable. The range for emphasizers and those downtoners not expressing degree (*eg*: *virtually*) is much wider, as we can see from their cooccurrence with a nongradable adjective such as *nonChristian*:

He is {*definitely* / *virtually* / **more* / **very*} nonChristian.

There are also restrictions on the use of particular intensifiers, and these can sometimes be stated in semantic terms:

most {*happy* [subjective; 'extremely happy'] / ?*tall* [objective]}

utterly {*wrong* [negative evaluation] / ?*right* [positive evaluation]}

perfectly {*natural* [positive evaluation] / ?*unnatural* [negative evaluation]}

Amplifiers and comparatives are available for adjectives that refer to a quality that is thought of as having values on a scale. Thus, in *John is English*, the adjective *English* does not allow amplifiers or comparatives if it refers to John's nationality, which is not a quality of John's. However, if the adjective refers qualitatively to the way he behaves or to his racial background, they are admitted:

> John is { *very English.* / *more English than* the English. }

> She is { *thoroughly* / *three quarters* } *Irish.*

Similarly, *original* in the sense of 'not copied' cannot normally be intensified or compared, as in *the original manuscript*, where it does not refer to a quality and there can be only one original manuscript. On the other hand, if *original* refers to the quality of the work, meaning 'of a new type', it may be intensified or compared: *a more original book*. We may compare the two uses with those of the corresponding adverb:

> She always writes { *originally*. ['in an original manner'] / *very originally.* }

> She came from Cleveland { *originally*. ['in the first place'] / **very originally.* }

In the last example, *originally* is a respect adjunct (*cf* 8.85) and cannot be intensified or compared.

Note [**a**] There are exceptions to the cooccurrence of a particular intensifier with a semantic class of adjective. For example, though *utterly* tends to cooccur with 'negative' adjectives, *utterly reliable* and *utterly delightful* are common.

[**b**] With reference to the use of *original*, we note that the following sentence has two possible meanings:

> This is *the more original* manuscript.

It can mean either 'This manuscript was written with more originality' or 'This manuscript is closer to the original'.

The unmarked term in 'measure' expressions

7.88 When we want to state the age of a person, we will normally use the expression *x years old*, for example:

> Mr Jespersen is 75 *years old.*

We will not say (except jokingly, as a compliment):

> *Mr Jespersen is 75 *years young.*

However, the choice of adjective here has nothing to do with the number of years, and we would use the same expression for somebody very young, *eg*:

> His granddaughter is two years { *old.* / **young.* }

Similarly:

> The water is two metres { *deep.* / **shallow.* }   Susan is only five feet { *tall.* / **short.* }

'Measure' adjectives like *old*, *deep*, and *tall* cover a scale of measurement. Such adjectives have two terms for the opposite ranges of the scale (*old/young*, *deep/shallow*, *tall/short*), but use the upper range as the 'unmarked' term in measure expressions (*old*, *deep*, *tall*). The 'measure' adjectives which are used in this way, preceded by a noun phrase of measure, include the following set with the marked term given in parenthesis:

deep (*shallow*)	*high* (*low*)	*long* (*short*)	*old* (*young*)
tall (*short*)	*thick* (*thin*)	*wide* (*narrow*)	

This set of 'measure' adjectives is used in the same way in *how*-questions and, again, the use of the unmarked term does not assume that only the upper range is applicable:

A: *How old* is your daughter? ['What is her age?']
B: She is *ten years old*. ['Her age is ten years.']

There are also adjectives outside the set listed above which are used in *how*-questions, in the same way as the 'measure' adjectives. Thus, if we want to know the size of something, we would normally use *big* or *large*, rather than *small* or *little*, *eg*:

How big is your computer?

Similarly, we use *bright* rather than *dim*, *strong* rather than *weak*, *heavy* rather than *light*, etc:

How strong is the engine of this car?
How accurate is your digital watch?

However, such adjectives are used in this way only in *how*-questions, not with noun phrases of measure:

A: *How heavy* is your suitcase? B: *It is only *20 kilos heavy*.

Some adverbs also use an unmarked term in *how*-questions. They include the italicized words in the following examples:

A: How *much* does she like him?	B: She likes him a lot.
A: How *often* did they complain?	B: Every day after school.
A: How *quickly* does he do his homework?	B: Usually in less than an hour.
A: How *far* did you drive today?	B: Over 200 miles.

Compare the following expressions of distance:

A: *How* {*far* / **near*} is it to the village?

B: {
The village is only *five miles* {**far*. / *away*.}
It's {*a long way* / **long*} to the village. [assertive]
It's {*not far* / *not a long way*} to the village. [nonassertive]
}

Compare time expressions:

> A: *How long* did the concert last?
>
> B: { Only 40 minutes. / It was only 40 minutes { *long.* / **short.* } }

Note [**a**] If we use the marked term, as in *How young is John?*, we are asking a question that presupposes that the relevant norm is towards the lower end of the scale, *ie* that John is young, whereas the unmarked term in *How old is John?* does not presuppose that John is old. Notice that neither term is neutral in exclamations:

> *How young* he is! ['He is extremely young!']
> *How old* he is! ['He is extremely old!']

[**b**] We use neither the marked nor the unmarked term of a measure adjective in:

> *He is *five pounds* { *heavy.* / *light.* }

The following constructions are however normal with the unmarked term:

> A: *How heavy* is he?
>
> B: He is { *five pounds too heavy.* / *too heavy by five pounds.* / *five pounds heavier than* John is. }

But, in specific contexts, either of two pairs of adjectives like *heavy/light*, *long/short* can be considered unmarked. The choice of term is determined by our point of orientation. When we want to relate a javelin throw to a specific purpose (to win, qualify, etc), we may say:

> His last javelin throw was *a few inches short.*

Short here is not the antonym of *long*, and there is no implication that it was a short throw. Compare an example like the following:

> How *high/low* is the water level now?

Here, the item selected (particularly the marked *high*) suggests the expectation that the level is getting higher and lower, respectively.

[**c**] In the case of 'nonliteral' measure items, *far* is also unmarked, as in:

> How *far* do you agree with the proposal?

[**d**] *Full* and *empty* can be used equally, although *How full?* is commoner than *How empty?*:

> *half full, half empty, three-quarters full, three-quarters empty*

Premodification of comparatives

7.89 Adjectives and adverbs in the absolute degree can be premodified by intensifiers like *very*, *quite*, *so*, etc (*cf* 7.56*ff*):

> The job was *very* { *easy.* / *difficult.* }
>
> She writes *very* { *well.* / *easily.* }

Comparatives of both adjectives and adverbs, whether inflected or periphrastic, can be premodified by amplifiers, such as *much* or *very much*:

> The job was (*very*) *much* { *easier* / *more difficult* } than I thought.
>
> She writes (*very*) *much* { *better* / *more easily* } than she used to.

Note the restriction on premodification of adjectives and adverbs in the absolute and comparative degrees:

That's {*very* / **much*} *good.* She works {*very* / **much*} *hard.*

That's {*much* / **very*} *better.* She works {*much* / **very*} *harder.*

Other intensifiers (and intensifying noun phrases) that are common with comparatives include the following:

somewhat easier
rather better

{*a lot* / *lots* ⟨informal⟩} shorter

{{*a great* / *a good*} *deal* / *a good bit* ⟨informal⟩} more/less difficult

{*a hell of a lot* / *a heck of a lot* / *a damn sight*} better ⟨very familiar⟩

Some intensifiers can be repeated for emphasis:

very very good ['extremely good']
very very . . . much sooner
much much . . . more careful
far far . . . more carefully
so so . . . much better [repeated *so* in BrE only]
so very very . . . much better

Generally, however, the repetition is permissible only if the repeated items come first or follow *so*:

so very very . . . much better
**very much much* . . . better

Repetition of intensifiers is a type of coordination that is always asyndetic (*cf* 13.102): **very and very good.*

Only *much* and *far* are used as intensifiers of premodifying adjectives. Compare:

That was a {*much* / *far* / **great deal*} *easier* job.

~ That job was {*much* / *far* / *a great deal*} *easier.*

Much can be premodified by *so*, *very*, and *that*:

{(*so*) (*very*) / *that*} *much* easier

Premodification of superlatives

7.90 The nonperiphrastic superlative may be premodified by the intensifier *very*:

> They arrived only at *the very last* moment.
> She put on *her very best* dress.

When *very* premodifies the superlative, a determiner is obligatory (*cf* 7.84):

Anna is { (*the*) *youngest.* / *the very youngest.* / **very youngest.* }

The periphrastic superlative is not premodified by the intensifier *very* (**the very most successful candidate*) but by other expressions, *eg*:

> the most successful candidate *of all*
> the most remarkable election *ever*
> { *far* (*and away*) / *by far* } the best solution

Note the different positions of intensifiers in:

It was { (*by*) *far* the best (film) / the best (film) { *by far* / **far* / **far and away* } } that I've seen for a long time.

Bibliographical note

On adjectives and adverbs, see Aarts and Calbert (1979); Bäcklund (1981); Bolinger (1967a); Dixon (1982a); Isitt (1983); Jacobsson (1961); Kjellmer (1984); Ljung (1970); Marchand (1966); Seppänen (1975); Teyssier (1968); Vendler (1968); Warren (1978, 1982, 1984). On adverbs, see further bibliographical note in Chapter 8.

On comparison and intensification, see Bolinger (1967b, 1972a); Bresnan (1973); Campbell and Wales (1969); Coates (1971); Fries (1977); Gnutzmann (1974); Gnutzmann et al (1973); Lees (1961); Rusiecki (1985); Wood (1959).

8 The semantics and grammar of adverbials

Introduction

8.1 The adverbial element (A) differs considerably from the other elements of clause structure (S, V, O, C), as we have already seen in 2.15. Differences in the following respects are especially notable:

(i) range of semantic roles;
(ii) propensity for multiple occurrence in the same clause;
(iii) range of realization forms;
(iv) range of possible positions in the clause;
(v) distinctive grammatical functions;
(vi) flexibility for use in information processing (*cf* 18.3*ff*) and in displaying textual connections (*cf* 19.53*ff*).

Since to some extent these variables are independent of each other, we shall outline each of (i) to (iv) separately. But since it is the grammatical aspects that concern us, we shall reserve most of the description and discussion of adverbials, in all their respects, for treatment under (v), 8.24*ff*. In any case, although the variables are indeed to some extent independent, they are also to a large extent interdependent. It is because there are different grammatical functions (v) as well as different semantic roles (i) that we can have more than one A-element in a clause (ii). It is because there is a range of possible positions for the A-element (iv) that this element lends itself to information processing (vi). Certain realization forms (iii) are especially associated with certain grammatical functions (v) and with certain positions in the clause (iv). We shall frequently be drawing attention to interactions like these. In particular, it must be stressed that a given semantic role (*eg* time) is not tied to a single grammatical function; time, for example, is expressed by both adjuncts and subjuncts.

We make a sharp and principled distinction in this book according as an adverb phrase, prepositional phrase, or other unit functions outside a clause element (*ie* is grammatically separate from it) or inside a clause element (*ie* is grammatically a part of it). Thus the units *very beautifully*, *in the garage*, and *really* are adverbials in [1], [2], and [3] respectively, but are not adverbials in [4], [5], and [6], where they operate grammatically as part of phrases which as a whole realize other elements, O in [4] and [5], C in [6]:

The girl was dressed *very beautifully*. [1]
I keep a spare bicycle *in the garage*. [2]
She *really* is an intelligent child. [3]
I saw a *very beautifully* dressed girl. [4]
I keep the bicycle *in the garage* well oiled. [5]
She is a *really* intelligent child. [6]

(See further 8.24.)

Note Of the clause elements S, V, O, C, A, the A-element is the next most frequent after S and V. The vast majority of clauses, dependent or independent, contain at least one adverbial, and in the Survey of English Usage corpus there are on average 15 adverbials in every 100 running words of material, spoken and written alike.

Outline of semantic roles

8.2 We shall distinguish seven main categories of semantic role, in most cases with further subdivisions as shown in the table below. We begin with the category SPACE, since the expression of other categories is often achieved in terms of figurative extension of spatial relations.

SPACE	*position* / *direction*	with interrelated subdivisions, *goal* ['to'] and *source* ['from']
	distance	
TIME	*position* / *duration*	with interrelated subdivisions *forward span* ['until'] and *backward span* ['since']
	frequency	
	relationship	
PROCESS	*manner*	
	means	
	instrument	
	agentive	
RESPECT		
CONTINGENCY	*cause*	
	reason	
	purpose	
	result	
	condition	
	concession	
MODALITY	*emphasis*	
	approximation	
	restriction	
DEGREE	*amplification*	
	diminution	
	measure	

Detailed discussion of these categories will be reserved for the sections dealing with the expression given them by the various classes of adverbials, 8.39*ff*. But since to some considerable extent the same semantic roles are performed by quite different grammatical classes of adverbial, we provide in 8.3–10 a preliminary discussion and illustration of the semantic categories listed above.

Space

8.3 We can readily distinguish five semantic relations expressed by adverbials in relation to physical SPACE, including the ordinary senses of 'place', a term we shall also use when this is convenient. First, there is POSITION, normally associated with verbs referring to stasis:

He lay *on his bed*.

But they can occur also with verbs referring to motion:

They are strolling *in the park*.

Secondly, we have DIRECTION, which may refer to directional path without locational specification, as in:

They drove *westwards*.

Or it can refer to direction along with a locational specification, as in:

She walked *down the hill*.
Their house faces *towards the sea*.

Thirdly, involving a positional aspect of direction, we can distinguish GOAL, as in:

She walked (down the hill) *to the bus stop*.

The interrelationship of the three is shown by the fact that, in particular contexts and with particular verbs, they can all be readily elicited by questions with *Where*:

Where was he lying? *On his bed.*	[position]
Where was she walking? *In the park.*	[position]
Where was she walking? *Down the hill.*	[direction]
Where was she walking? *To the bus stop.*	[goal]

But with the latter two, there are alternative question forms that are more role-specific:

Which way was she walking? [direction]
Where was she walking *to*? [goal]

A question with a more general verb as in 'Where was she going?' would be entirely open as to direction or goal use.

Fourthly, again involving direction and position, we have the obverse of goal in SOURCE; for example:

She walked (down the hill) *from the school.*

Questions concerning source would usually be expressed through a more general verb of motion than *walk*, especially one that is oriented to the speaker, and the 'source' preposition (*eg*: *from*) would have to be expressed:

Where was she coming *from*?

(On the grounds for seeing direction, goal, and source as involving the same basic *grammatical* category, see 8.46).

Finally, there is spatial measure, expressed as DISTANCE:

They had travelled *a long way*.
She had driven *(for) fifty kilometres*.
He hadn't gone *far*.

Such adverbials are elicited by *How far . . .?*

One further semantic factor should be mentioned. Sentences which superficially differ only in so far as one has a position adverbial and the other a direction, goal, or source adverbial are found on closer inspection to involve a considerable difference in the meaning of the verb concerned, triggered by the different prepositions:

He is travelling in Yorkshire. [1]
He is travelling to Leeds (*or* from Halifax). [2]

Sentence [1] seems to give equal weight to what he is doing (travelling) and where he is doing it (in Yorkshire), whereas sentence [2] seems to give weight only to the direction: 'Where is he travelling to/from?' 'Where is he going (to)?' 'Where is he coming from?' This is confirmed both by the plausibility of the paraphrases (*go*, *come*) and by the absence of an acceptable question:

*What is he doing from Halifax? Travelling?

beside:

What is he doing in Yorkshire? Travelling?

This suggests that, in addition to the semantic distinctions, the position adverbial is different from the others grammatically as well (*cf* 8.44*ff*).

Note In some very formal and stylistically mannered usage, we find the otherwise archaic *wh-* forms *whither* (direction and goal) and *whence* (source).

Time

8.4 Temporal relations are especially dependent for their expression upon figurative extension of locative items such as *in* and *at* (*cf* 9.34). As with space, several subroles can be distinguished, some of them closely analogous to those of space.

First, there is time seen as a fixed POSITION on a temporal scale: time as stasis – the time *when* an action took place or the time to which a state applies. For example:

She drove to Chicago *on Sunday*. He was there *last week*.

The relation is elicited by *when* and is often referred to as 'time *when*':

When did she drive to Chicago? *On Sunday*.

Secondly, DURATION. Since time is conceived as being linear and unidimensional, the analogy of spatial direction makes little impact on the conceptualization of time. But the concept of measure is as important to the consideration of time as it is to space, and temporal measure is seen as duration. Linking duration to specific positions on the linear time scale, we have the concept of SPAN, itself subdivided to correspond to the only rudimentary analogue to spatial direction that is conceptualized with respect to time, the FORWARD SPAN ['until, up to a specified point of time': *cf* spatial 'goal'] and the BACKWARD SPAN ['since, from a specified point of time': *cf* spatial 'source'].

FORWARD SPAN extends from the point of time to which the speaker and hearer are oriented, forward to some point which is 'future' in relation to the orientation point. For example:

I shall be staying here *till next week*.
Washington delayed his counter-attack *until the following spring*.

The converse of this, BACKWARD SPAN, indicates the stretch of time back from the speaker–hearer orientation point. For example:

I've been staying here *since last week.*
Washington's attack that spring was his first action *since the previous September.*

Then there are more general expressions of duration, without necessary relation to a particular point of orientation. For example:

I am staying (*for*) *three weeks.*

Here the reference of the adverbial may extend both into the past and into the future from the time point of utterance; equally, it may refer to a three-week period at some unspecified time in the future, just as in the following example it can refer to an unspecified period in the past:

I stayed (*for*) *three weeks.*

The elicitation of duration as well as forward and backward span is usually achieved by the same question form, *How long . . . ?* But for future and past extent, alternative forms are generally available, such as *Till when . . . ?* and *Since when . . . ?* respectively.

Thirdly, we have expressions of FREQUENCY, elicited by *How often . . . ?* For example:

A: *How often* do you go to the theatre?
B: Well, I like to go *frequently*, but in fact I've been only *three times* this year.

The two adverbials in the answer draw attention to the fact that frequency is a complex notion (as is 'direction' in its interaction with 'goal'), and we shall explore it in more detail in 8.64*ff* below.

Fourthly, there is the expression of RELATIONSHIP between one time and another, again a complex notion, and in this case with no role-specific question form. For example:

I was already writing my novel in 1980 and I'm afraid it is *still* in progress.
He had visited his mother *already* when I saw him yesterday.

Process

8.5 Here it is possible to distinguish four subclasses: MANNER (*casually, with deference, carefully, slowly, like John, just as John does*, etc); MEANS (*by bus, in mathematics, through insight*, etc); INSTRUMENT (*with a fork, using a dictionary, by means of interrogation*, etc); AGENTIVE (*by John*, with passive; corresponding to *John* as subject, with active). Since the last three subclasses seem to overlap, it is necessary to demonstrate their independence by a cooccurrence test (*cf* 8.11*f*), and it may well be that the distinction tends to be made in actual language use only when such cooccurrence obtains. Consider the four adverbials in each of the following sentences:

The student was *politely* [A_1] assessed *by the teacher* [A_2], *impressionistically* [A_3] *by means of an interview* [A_4].
The patient was *carefully* [A_1] treated *by the nurse* [A_2] *medically* [A_3] *with a well-tried drug* [A4].

In each sentence, A_1 is manner, A_2 agent, A_3 means, and A_4 instrument. But although the distinction may seem especially close only between means and instrument, it should be noted that manner is not necessarily always distinguished clearly from them. In principle, the distinction is clear enough: manner is relatively subjective and hence gradable (*cf* 7.4): *quite politely*, *very carefully*; means and instrument are objective and hence nongradable: **very surgically*. But consider the following sentence:

The teacher assessed the student *impressionistically*.

Here we may be unsure whether the adverbial means 'in a quite impressionistic manner', 'subjectively', or 'by means of an impression-forming technique'. And even if the means sense seemed to be endorsed by cooccurrence with an 'instrument' adverbial, cooccurrence with a manner adverbial like *casually* would interact semantically (*cf* 8.80) so as to make *impressionistically* equivocal between means and manner:

He *casually* [A_1] assessed the student *impressionistically* [A_2] *by interviewing him* [A_3].

Again, we are very dependent on the wider context in interpreting a sentence such as:

She did it *legally*.

The adverbial here may be manner (*quite legally*, *not illegally*), means (*by invoking the law*), instrument (*with legal arguments*), or – as in 8.6 – respect (*in respect of law*). See further 8.85.

Respect

8.6 This is a much broader and more abstract semantic category than time and place. We are here concerned with the use of an adverbial to identify a relevant point of reference in respect of which the clause concerned derives its truth value. For example:

So far as travelling facilities are concerned, we have obviously made a popular decision; but *with respect to the date*, many people are expressing dissatisfaction.
She helped him a little *with his book*.
She talked learnedly *about Kant*.
He has always been frightened *of earwigs*.
They are advising me *legally*. [where the adverbial does not mean 'lawfully, not illegally' (*cf* 8.5), but 'on points of law, with respect to law']

As we see from this last example, the respect role is often expressed by means of an adverbial form which could be used equally to express a different semantic relation. Moreover, the respect role may interact with another clause element such that it is expressed in the verb. Such interaction can be seen especially perhaps with adverbials basically relating to place. For example, the sentence:

He is working *in a* (*nearby*) *factory*.

seems concerned with *where* he is working, and the adverbial expresses the locative relation: there is a specific factory in mind. But equally, without the option of including an indication (such as *nearby*) that a specific factory is in mind, the adverbial in the following could rather serve to answer the question 'What is he doing?' than 'Where is he working?':

> He is working *in a factory*.

If the adverbial does indeed answer *What?* rather than *Where?* it is being predicated of a respect relationship: 'So far as his work is concerned, it is in a factory', 'He is a factory worker'.

There are analogous interactions with time, process, result, and degree adverbials as well as with the quasi-object (especially cognate object) that occurs with certain verbs. Compare:

> She died a peaceful death.
> [She died *peacefully*; *As for her death*, it was peaceful]
> They split their sides *laughing*.
> He's busy *writing*.

Contingency

8.7 The chief semantic relations in this important class of adverbials are:

(i) CAUSE	She died *of cancer*.
	She helped the stranger *out of a sense of duty*.
(ii) REASON	He bought the book *because of his interest in metaphysics*.
(iii) PURPOSE	He bought the book *so as to study metaphysics*.
(iv) RESULT	He read the book carefully, *so he acquired some knowledge of metaphysics*.
(v) CONDITION	*If he reads the book carefully*, he will acquire some knowledge of metaphysics.
(vi) CONCESSION	*Though he didn't read the book*, he acquired some knowledge of metaphysics.

In contrast to cause, which is concerned with causation and motivation seen as established with some objectivity, reason involves a relatively personal and subjective assessment. As well as between these and the means adverbials of 8.5 (the adverbial in 'She got the job *through her experience*' could be seen as means or as cause), it will be apparent that there are close ties between these six adverbial types. Whether we perceive an adverbial as reason or purpose depends in large measure upon point of view. Thus the adverbial in:

> He bought the book *(so as) to study metaphysics*.

can be seen as indicating his purpose in buying the book and equally his reason for buying it. So too, result is closely related to purpose in frequently (though not necessarily) indicating the fulfilment of a purpose (*cf* 8.86). Condition is linked to result in indicating the circumstances in which the result would be achieved. Concession, in turn, can be seen as an 'inverted' condition – indicating circumstances in which a result would ensue irrespective of the content of the concessive clause. But concession can also be seen as a 'blocked' or inoperative cause; compare:

Because of his enthusiasm, he won. [cause]
In spite of his enthusiasm, he didn't win. [concession]
Through his lack of enthusiasm, he didn't win. [cause]
Despite his lack of enthusiasm, he won. [concession]

Note There is a detailed consideration of contingency relationships including subcategories such as motivation in 15.30*ff*.

Modality

8.8 The truth value or force of a sentence such as:

She has been enthusiastic about her work.

can be enhanced or diminished by adverbials. On the one hand, there can be EMPHASIS on the positive or negative poles of the statement:

She has *certainly* been enthusiastic about her work.
She has*n't* been enthusiastic *at all* about her work.

On the other hand, the middle ground between these poles can be indicated by APPROXIMATION, which may take various guises:

She has *probably* been enthusiastic about her work.
She has *not* {*really* / *exactly*} been enthusiastic about her work.
She has *hardly* been enthusiastic about her work.
Cf also 'I've *almost* finished painting the bathroom.'

Approximation can include comment on the form of or authority for the statement:

She has *allegedly* been enthusiastic . . .
She has been, *if I may say so*, enthusiastic . . .
She has been, *as she puts it*, enthusiastic . . .

A third aspect of modality is RESTRICTION, especially with a view to directing focus upon a particular part of the statement:

She has been enthusiastic *only* about her WÒRK.
She ALÒNE has been enthusiastic . . .

The negative particle *not* (*n't*) serves the function of denying truth value and it must therefore be viewed as being central to the semantic role, modality. But although *not* (*n't*) has been traditionally regarded as an adverb, it does not realize an adverbial as defined in this book; rather, it is seen as a particle functioning in clause negation (*cf* 2.43, 10.54*ff*).

Degree

8.9 Though often similar to modality adverbials in their semantic effect, degree adverbials are concerned with the assessment of gradable constituents in relation to an imaginary scale. One of the subroles is AMPLIFICATION, which is concerned with asserting a generalized high degree; and another is its opposite, DIMINUTION. For example:

I *badly* want a drink.
She is *increasingly* adding to her work load. } [amplification]
He does*n't* like playing squash (*very*) *much.*
She helped him *a little* with his book. } [diminution]

Thirdly, there is the expression of MEASURE, without implication that the degree is notably high or low:

He likes playing squash *more than his sister does.*
She had worked *sufficiently* that day.

Degree is sometimes blended with time relations (frequency or duration); *eg* 'He doesn't play squash (*very*) *much*'.

Note Adverbial expressions of modality and degree, as well as the interrelation between them, will be examined in detail in the treatment of subjuncts, 8.99*ff*.

8.10 We have noted from time to time certain affinities between the semantic categories. It is doubtless because of these affinities that the same items such as prepositions, adverbs, and conjunctions can be used for different semantic relations. Thus *for* can indicate purpose (*He did it for money*), cause (*What did you do it for?*), and respect (*The doctor treated me for pleurisy*). Likewise *if* can be both conditional and concessive (*Come tomorrow if possible*; *He is lazy if intelligent*), and *still* often blends concessive with temporal implications:

Still, you should have visited them. [concession only]
There is *still* work to do. ['at the present time']
There is *still* work to do. ['despite the amount already done']

In 'He plays squash *a great deal*', degree and frequency are both involved (*cf* 8.9); again, *never* is both temporal (*cf* 8.4) and modal (*cf* 8.8). The interrelation of the semantic categories and the ease with which we see the same adverbial expressing one or another (or more than one simultaneously) is not, of course, a weakness but rather one of the great sources of the adverbial's communicative strength.

But although the same item can express different meanings, and although the different meanings shade one with another, there are good grounds for asserting the validity of the semantic distinctions we are making. We shall look presently (8.11, *cf* also 8.149) at the argument based upon cooccurrence, but we may note here that some semantic relations are so deeply entrenched, so well institutionalized, and so individually perceptible as to have special question forms to elicit them. Thus the *yes–no* question corresponds to the modality function:

A: (Are you going?) B: Yes/No/Probably/Never!

So too the question forms with *when*, (*for*) *how long, where, which way* (direction), *how*, *in which way* (process), *why* are directed to eliciting responses realizing some of the principal semantic relations that we have distinguished. (But *cf* 8.79*f*.)

Note **[a]** In pointing out the semantic overlap with certain conjunctions and prepositions, we must nonetheless note that prepositional phrases and (especially) finite clauses are considerably more explicit and consistent with respect to their *general* semantic functions than are adverbs, whose form (notably *-ly*) conveys little and whose semantic role is typically particular, being determined largely by the lexical meaning of the individual item.

[b] Adverbial semantics can be seen not only in respect of question forms but also with deictic pro-forms (*cf* 12.1*ff*). On this basis, one might conclude that space, time, and process are central, in that simplex pro-forms exist: *there, then, thus,* and *so* (*cf* 2.43*f*). The first two are fairly discrete and precise (*cf* also *here* and *now*). But *thus* and *so* are broader and more vague, overlapping, and subject to style restrictions (commoner expressions are *like this, like that*). For example:

He spoke *in the big hall* assuming that more people would hear him *there*.
He spoke *at 9.00 p.m.*, assuming that more people would be free *then*.
He spoke *in great detail* assuming that, if he explained matters *thus*, his words would have a more lasting effect.

Deictic pro-forms for other semantic relations are either morphologically complex words (*therefore, thereby*) or prepositional or noun phrases (*that way, by such means, for this purpose,* etc). All these forms reflect the fact that the relationships concerned are not as unequivocally discrete semantically as those that have been expressed by a single morpheme.

On the specific semantic functions of conjuncts, see 8.136*ff*.

Multiple occurrence

8.11 Despite the considerable overlapping of the semantic roles and the affinities we can see between them, those that we have distinguished can be given discrete grammatical expression. The basis of establishing separate categories of clause element is their potentiality for acceptable cooccurrence in the same clause. In consequence, our need to have two types of O-element is testified by the cooccurrence of direct and indirect object in such a sentence as:

They gave *their leader* [O_i] *strong support* [O_d]. [1]

In a directly comparable way, we must recognize several types of A-element and these different types clearly correspond in part to the various semantic roles that we have been considering. For example:

He *still* [A_1] *often* [A_2] works *on Sundays* [A_3] *for hours on end* [A_4]. [2]

where A_1 expresses time relationship, A_2 time frequency, A_3 time position, and A_4 time duration (*cf* 8.4).

Types of A-element are much more numerous than types of O and C, and they are much less dependent upon the clause concerned containing items of a specific class (such as ditransitive verbs). But in principle the grounds on which we establish the A types that we shall treat as grammatically distinct in 8.24*ff* are precisely analogous to those on which we distinguish O_i and O_d. That is, we note their propensity to cooccur in noncoordinate and nonappositive structures without tautology, contradiction, or unacceptability. This plainly applies to the cooccurrence of the four A-elements in example [2] above, though all of them concern *time*. Consider a further example, containing adverbials with a greater range of semantic roles:

Next Tuesday [A_1] I shall *probably* [A_2] visit her mother *in London* [A_3] *briefly* [A_4] *to see if she's feeling better* [A_5], *unless she telephones me before that* [A_6].

That these six adverbials are each expressing a different relation is shown not merely by their acceptable cooccurrence in the example sentence, but by testing the unacceptability of treating any pair as either coordinate or appositive:

> *I shall visit her mother *in London* [A_3] and *to see if she's feeling better* [A_5].
> *I shall *probably* [A_2] *ie briefly* [A_4] visit her mother.

While it is on such essentially *grammatical* grounds as cooccurrence and position in clause structure that we establish classes of adverbials, we shall give the classes so established the labels plausibly suggested by their *semantic* roles.

8.12 At the same time, it must be noted that the affinities that we have discussed (*cf* 8.10) between some of the semantic roles frequently allow adverbials to interact with each other and with the other clause elements in a way and to a degree that is fairly rare with the relatively discrete types of O (O_i, O_d) and C (C_s, C_o). Thus (*cf* 8.6):

> Martin is working *in the garden.*

This could be interpreted as indicating the place where Martin is working *or* indicating the type of work he is doing ('gardening'). Let us now add a further adverbial:

> Martin is working *in the garden* [A_1] *on his sermon* [A_2].
> Martin is working *in the garden* [A_1] *on his roses* [A_2].

We have now made clear the first and second interpretation respectively. Compare also the following pair of sentences:

> He spoke *about Shakespeare.*
> He spoke *about Shakespeare* [A_1] *sneeringly* [A_2].

Note that while the first might be paraphrased as 'The subject of his discourse was Shakespeare', a paraphrase of the second would be more like 'He had a contemptuous attitude to Shakespeare'. Consider now the sentence:

> Mr Ahmed *proudly* accepted the award.

This might imply something like 'Mr Ahmed was proud to receive the award', or equally that he gave the appearance of pride in his manner as he received it. On the other hand, compare:

> *Proudly*, Mr Ahmed accepted the award.
> Mr Ahmed accepted the award *proudly.*

The variant orders here will influence us in favour of the first and second interpretation respectively.

Finally, as an example of interaction, consider the two sentences:

> Frank *seldom* worked.
> Frank worked *in his bedroom.*

Each is very different from:

> Frank *seldom* worked *in his bedroom.*

In this connection, *cf* 2.54–5 on focus and scope.

Realization

8.13 The A-element can be realized by a great variety of linguistic structures:

Adverb phrase (*cf* 2.28) with closed-class (*cf* 2.36) adverb as head:
She telephoned (*just*) *then*.

Adverb phrase with open-class adverb (*cf* 7.47) as head:
She telephoned (*very*) *recently*.

Noun phrase (*cf* 17.1*ff*):
She telephoned *last week*.

Prepositional phrase (*cf* 9.1*ff*):
She telephoned *in the evening*.

Verbless clause (*cf* 14.10):
She telephoned *though obviously ill*.

Nonfinite clause (*cf* 14.7*ff*):
She telephoned *while waiting for the plane*.
She telephoned *hoping for a job*.
She telephoned *to ask for an interview*.
She telephoned *angered at the delay*.

Finite clause (*cf* 14.6):
She telephoned *after she had seen the announcement*.

We shall draw attention from time to time to the considerable degree of correspondence between the form of realization on the one hand, and semantic, positional, and grammatical properties on the other hand. Thus, for example, noun phrases as A chiefly realize A time position (*cf* 8.4); conditional adverbials are chiefly realized by finite clauses; an A occurring between S and V is likely to be one realized by an adverb phrase.

The different types of adverbial realization are textually distributed with widely different frequencies. In a fairly large sample of the Survey of English Usage corpus, where we examined approximately equal quantities of written material and impromptu spoken material, the distribution was found to be as presented in the table below. In the total of 75 000 words (40 000 words of transcribed impromptu speech and 35 000 words of written English), there were nearly 11 000 adverbials (*cf* 8.23):

Total number of adverbials	10981	
Realization types:		
Prepositional phrases		4414
Closed-class items		3948
Open-class adverbs and adverb phrases		1070
Finite clauses		980
Nonfinite and verbless clauses		346
Noun phrases		227

The distribution between the two broad categories of material, impromptu speech on the one hand and written English on the other, was as follows, expressing this distribution as an average per text of the SEU corpus, where a 'text' is a homogeneous stretch of material, 5000 running words in extent:

	Speech	*Writing*
Total number of adverbials	712	753
Realization types:		
Prepositional phrases	258	336
Closed-class items	278	246
Open-class adverbs and adverb phrases	76	66
Finite clauses	70	60
Nonfinite and verbless clauses	12	33
Noun phrases	18	12

It is worth drawing attention to some salient features in these figures:

(i) There are two forms in which the vast majority of A-elements are expressed: prepositional phrases on the one hand, and the (usually short) closed-class items such as *well*, *still*, *of course*, on the other hand.

(ii) Spoken and written materials do not greatly differ either in the gross occurrence of A-elements or in the distribution of realization types.

(iii) But while speech has a higher proportion of noun phrases as A (1:1.5), written material has a higher proportion of prepositional phrases (1:1.3) and nonfinite/verbless clauses (1:2.75). This last point is unsurprising, given the fact that the numerically strongest subtype is the *-ing* participle clause, as in:

Finishing her work early, Margaret decided to go for a swim.

(iv) Less expected perhaps is the higher proportion of finite clauses as A in spoken material (1:1.2). This runs counter to the widespread belief that the frequency of 'subordinate clauses' (typically adverbial clauses with finite verbs) is a good indication of relative 'syntactic complexity', and that impromptu speech is less complex syntactically than written English.

There are important differences between speech and writing that do not emerge from these broad statistics, and we shall explore these and other details of textual distribution at appropriate points below.

Position

8.14 There is a sharp difference between A and other elements in the relative freedom with which A can be put in different positions in a sentence. The following examples illustrate this freedom, and we add the positional notation which will be explored in 8.15*ff*:

By then the book must have been placed on the shelf.	*I*
The book *by then* must have been placed on the shelf.	*iM*
The book must *by then* have been placed on the shelf.	*M*
The book must have *by then* been placed on the shelf.	*mM*
The book must have been *by then* placed on the shelf.	*eM*
The book must have been placed *by then* on the shelf.	*iE*
The book must have been placed on the shelf *by then*.	*E*

Some of these positions are less likely than others for the A in this sentence, but none is unacceptable. Of course, the availability of different positions does not imply that the choice of position makes no difference to the meaning of the sentence. The selection of one position rather than another is influenced by several factors, but chief among them is the information structure of the sentence, and the relation of adverbials to information structure will require special attention both in this chapter and in Chapter 18. But not all A-elements have the same range of possible positions. The type of realization (*cf* 8.13) has a strong influence on where an adverbial is placed (in general, single-word adverb phrases are most mobile and finite clauses least), and of even greater influence are the semantic typology outlined in 8.2*ff* and the grammatical typology on which we shall concentrate in this chapter (8.24*ff*).

Initial

8.15 INITIAL position (symbol *I*) is that preceding any other clause element. In effect, this generally means the position immediately before S, as in:

Suddenly, the driver started the engine.

But in direct questions (*cf* 11.4*ff*), it is the position immediately before the operator or *wh*-element:

Seriously, do you believe in ghosts?
Anyhow, since when has she been ill?

On the other hand, in subordinate or coordinated clauses, it is the position following the conjunction:

(I had scarcely got into the taxi) when *suddenly* the driver started the engine.
(Are you afraid of the dark,) and, *to be blunt*, do you believe in ghosts?
(I know you are very charitable,) but, *seriously*, how can he be innocent?

If a clause has two *I* adverbials, it is of interest to note the order, I_1 and I_2 (*cf* 8.150*f*):

Anyhow [I_1], *by then* [I_2] she was very ill.

Most types of adverbial realization can occur at *I* and the same is broadly true of the different semantic roles as well. Among the exceptions, degree adverbials are unlikely at *I*. With respect to grammatical functions (*cf* 8.24*ff*), *I* is associated with those adverbials that can readily constitute the ground, theme (*cf* 18.8*ff*), or 'scene-setting' for what follows. It is thus particularly appropriate for sentence adverbials (*cf* 8.36), disjuncts (*cf* 8.121*ff*), and conjuncts (*cf* 8.134*ff*). Semantically, *I* has a strong association with expressions of time.

Note [**a**] In the Survey of English Usage sample (*cf* 8.13, 8.23), there was found to be a striking contrast within the dominant realization type, prepositional phrases. Twenty-six per cent of all *I*-placed prepositional phrases were temporal where only four per cent were spatial. By contrast, of all *E*-placed prepositional phrases fourteen per cent were temporal, thirty-one per cent spatial.
[**b**] On adverbials in nonfinite and subjectless finite clauses, *cf* 8.20 Note [b].

Medial

8.16 MEDIAL position (symbol *M*) can be preliminarily described as that between S and V:

The driver *suddenly* started the engine. [1]

The soprano *really* delighted her audience. [2]
They *seriously* considered him for the post. [3]

But when the V-element is realized by a verb phrase involving an operator, we see that this first approximation to a definition of *M* is inadequate. In the following variants of [1], [2], and [3], any native speaker would feel that the adverbials are still in the same position:

The driver has *suddenly* started the engine. [1a]
The soprano had *really* delighted her audience. [2a]
They are *seriously* considering him for the post. [3a]

In consequence, we must refine the definition and say that *M* is the position immediately after the subject *and (where there is one) the operator*. This formulation will provide for interrogative sentences:

Did the driver *suddenly* start the engine? [1b]
Had the soprano *really* delighted her audience? [2b]
Why are they *seriously* considering him for the post? [3b]

It will also provide for imperative sentences:

Don't *suddenly* start the engine!
Do *seriously* consider him for the post!

In view of these examples, we see that an 'initial' adverbial in an imperative such as:

{*Never* / *Carefully*} remove the cover.

must properly be regarded as 'medial'; *cf* 'We *never* remove the cover', *'*Never* we remove the cover'. One further complication can be seen in comparing the following examples with [2], [2a] and [2b]:

The soprano was *really* at her best tonight.
The soprano hasn't *really* been at her best for weeks.
Was the soprano *really* at her best tonight?
Has the soprano *really* been at her best recently?

We recognize that *really* seems to be in the 'same' position in all cases. The description of *M* must therefore be further clarified to accommodate the fact that, in this grammar, we treat BE as an operator even when it is the sole realization of V. So also HAVE, in those dialects of English that would not introduce *got* in [5] and [7]; *cf* 3.34*f*. Thus:

She has *really* a different approach to the subject. [4]
She has *really* (got) a different approach to the subject. [5]
She has *really* had a different approach to the subject. [6]
Has she *really* (got) a different approach to the subject? [7]

Note The claim that the position is the same (i) between operator and main verb as in [8], and (ii) between finite form of BE and complement as in [9] is strikingly confirmed by the fact that when the following was read aloud, it was perceived as [8] by some hearers, and as [9] by others:

The expression on her face was *seldom* {discussed. [main verb] [8] / disgust. [complement] [9]}

8.17 By reason of its being between two closely associated constituent elements, S and V, or between two constituent parts of the phrase realizing V (operator and main verb), the *M* position tends to determine the type of A realization. Only for a heavily special effect would a clause or lengthy prepositional phrase be placed at *M* (and it would then be clearly marked off by commas in writing, or by prosody in speech):

> You have, *though you may say it was accidental*, ruined this man's chances of a happy life.
> She had not, *despite years of anxious endeavour*, succeeded in living down that initial mistake.

In more general use, the adverbials at *M* are for the most part rather short adverb phrases, especially solitary adverbs – and for these (as the tables in 8.23 show) *M* is a numerically dominant position. Semantically, *M* is especially associated with modality and degree, such that adverbials tend to take on a tinge of these even when they purport to be expressing other relations ('time', 'space', 'respect', 'means', for instance). Thus:

> I have *at all times* indicated my willingness.
> He has *nowhere* stated this explicitly.
> I have not, *by word or deed*, betrayed your trust.

Grammatically, *M* is freely used for focusing and intensifying subjuncts (*cf* 8.88*ff*), and fairly freely for optional predication adjuncts (*cf* 8.24, 8.34), as well as for some disjuncts (*eg*: *obviously*; *cf* 8.121*ff*) and conjuncts (*eg*: *also*; *cf* 8.134*ff*).

Variants of medial

8.18 Consider again an example given earlier:

> The driver *suddenly* started the engine.

This sentence conceals the fact that *M* position is the one immediately after an operator (*cf* 8.16), just as it obscures the fact that there are three exceptional variants of *M*, each with its domain of contrast with *M* and with each other. Compare:

{ She *really* delighted her audience.	[1]
{ She *completely* delighted her audience.	[2]
{ She had *really* delighted her audience.	[1a]
{ She had *completely* delighted her audience.	[2a]
{ She *really* had delighted her audience.	[1b]
{ *She *completely* had delighted her audience.	[2b]

In running through this set, we recognize when we come to [2b] that *completely* was at *M* in [2], though this neutralized a distinction that emerges with [1b]. By contrast, we equally recognize that [1] is ambiguous as between *M*, distinguished in [1a], and a position in [1b] that we may regard as a fronted medial or INITIAL MEDIAL position, symbol *iM*. This may be defined as the position between the subject and the operator.

There are several possible paraphrases of [1b], but one of them might be stated thus: 'I wish to emphasize the fact that she had delighted her audience.' A comparable paraphrase of [1a] might be: 'I wish to emphasize the degree of delight she gave her audience'. There is not in fact much substantial difference *semantically* between these two, however much difference there may be *grammatically* between the intensifier (*cf* 8.104*ff*) in [1a], and the disjunct (*cf* 8.121*ff*) in [1b]. Where the predication is negative, however, the semantic distinction is clear:

She hadn't *really* delighted her audience. [*M*]
She *really* hadn't delighted her audience. [*iM*]

In consequence we find that while many disjuncts are freely placed at *M* (and less commonly at *iM*) in positive sentences, they must be at *iM* in negative ones:

{ They can *probably* find their way here. [*M*]
{ (?)They *probably* can find their way here. [*iM*]

{ *They can't *probably* find their way here. [*M*]
{ They *probably* can't find their way here. [*iM*]

{ He was *probably* unhappy. [*M*]
{ He *probably* wasn't unhappy. [*iM*]

We thus see that *iM* can be used when it is necessary to exclude the adverbial from the scope of negation (*cf* 10.64) and when there is prosodic focus on the following item:

I have *frankly* been seriously ìNterested.
I *frankly* haven't been seriously ìNterested.
I *frankly* HÀVE been seriously interested.

Note One notable use of *iM* occurs when the focused verb is BE; for example:

Well, you *never* WÈRE fond of work! That's where she *usually* ìs at this time of day.

8.19 Let us now consider the following example:

They *seriously* considered him for the post. [1]

Here we understand the meaning to be 'His suitability for the post was given serious consideration'. It is now clear that such an adverbial (apparently at *M*, but there is no operator) occupies a position that neutralizes both of what we have seen (*cf* 8.16) as the valid conditions of *M*. Thus it is not distinct from *M*:

They have *seriously* considered him for the post. [2]

Nor is it distinct from *iM*, which would be disallowed for *seriously* if the sentence had the meaning given above:

They *seriously* have considered him for the post. [3]

If, however, we expand the verb phrase to *will have considered*, we find that example [2] has also neutralized a contrast, since although *seriously* seems in [2] to be at *M*, the expanded form of [4] shows that the true *M* position will not yield the interpretation we have given to [1]:

They will *seriously* have considered him for the post. [4]

If, however, we place the adverbial immediately before *considered*, we have the required meaning:

They will have *seriously* considered him for the post. [5]

We now see that what is common to the sentences [1], [2], and [5] is that the adverbial is immediately before the main verb of the verb phrase in each case. This is the END MEDIAL position (symbol *eM*). It is associated with degree and manner adverbials (from a semantic viewpoint), with optional predication adjuncts (from a grammatical viewpoint), and with realizations by adverb phrases or prepositional phrases:

The room must have been *quite carefully* searched by the police.
My answer may have *to some extent* displeased them.

8.20 There is yet a further variant of *M*. It is to be found only rarely, and this is in part because it depends upon the occurrence of a verb phrase with three or more auxiliaries (*cf* 3.21*ff*):

They must have *often* been listening at the door.
The car may have *sometimes* been being used without permission.
The car may have been *indeed* being used without permission.

Adverbials that occur at the places occupied by *often*, *sometimes*, and *indeed* in these examples are said to be at MEDIAL MEDIAL position (symbol *mM*), and we see the validity of making this distinction by comparing the following:

*This bridge may have *badly* been designed by Brunel.

This bridge may have {*actually* / *partly*} been designed by Brunel.

But even the emphasizers and intensifiers that can, as we see, appear at *mM* would more usually be placed elsewhere, the emphasizer *actually* at *M* and the downtoner *partly* at *eM*:

This bridge may *actually* have been designed by Brunel.
This bridge may have been *partly* designed by Brunel.

It is unusual but not actually ungrammatical to have adverbials at *iM*, *M*, *mM*, and *eM* in the same clause, though the resultant sentence would be regarded as grossly unacceptable from a stylistic point of view, as in:

The new law *certainly* may *possibly* have *indeed* been *badly* formulated.
[= 'It is certainly true that what I say now is possible: the new law may indeed have been badly formulated']

Note [**a**] Since, as we have seen, a simple verb phrase neutralizes the distinction between *M* and *iM*, and a verb phrase consisting only of an operator and the main verb neutralizes the distinction between *M*, *mM*, and *eM*, the variants of *M* must be ignored in describing the position of most adverbials, reference usually being made only to *M*.

[**b**] With nonfinite clauses and finite clauses where the subject or the subject and an auxiliary are absent, it is still of course possible to distinguish *M* position and sometimes also variants of *M*. For example:

Being *often* in Paris, I enjoy . . . [*M*]
Having *carefully* studied the problem, he . . . [*M*]
To have been (*so*) *thoroughly* beaten by John was . . . [*eM*]
I had met her and may have *already* been influenced by her. [*mM*]

On the other hand, *iM* can be indistinguishable from *I*; consider:

I had met her and *already* had come to like her.

Here we cannot tell whether a fuller version of the second conjoin would have had the subject before or after the adverbial:

. . . and I *already* had come to like her.
. . . and *already* I had come to like her.

Indeed it is often impossible to distinguish *M* or any of its variants from *I*; for example:

I had been introduced to her and *already* influenced by her. [?*I*, ?*iM*, ?*M*, ?*eM*]
Already influenced by her, I had lost my former objectivity.

In such cases, it is best to acknowledge the neutralization of positional contrast by regarding the adverbials as at *I*/*M*, *ie* initial *or* medial position.

The 'split infinitive'

8.21 Quite strong stylistic objections are made to adverbials at (*e*)*M* when this position involves their being placed between *to* and the infinitive (the so-called 'split infinitive' construction), as in:

She ought to *seriously* consider her position. [1]
For me to *suddenly* resign my job is unthinkable. [2]
He wasn't able to *even* move his fingers. [3]

It should be noted that if the verb phrase is made perfective or if a modal not involving *to* is used in these examples, the adverbial remains immediately before the main verb:

She ought to have *seriously* considered her position. [1a]
She should *seriously* consider her position. [1b]
For me to have *suddenly* resigned . . . [2a]
He couldn't *even* move his fingers. [3a]

Since the position of the adverbials in [1a–3a] is perfectly acceptable and natural, it is easy to see why the closely parallel [1–3] should seem equally natural – however guiltily – despite generations of disapproval by teachers and stylists.

In comparing *ought to* in [1] and *should* in [1b], we might also note that there are several auxiliary sequences providing phonological evidence, matched by evidence from informal spellings, that the *to* has a closer link with the preceding than with the following word (*cf* 3.44*ff*):

used to	/ˈjuːstə/
have to	/ˈhæftə/
(have) got to, gotta	/ˈgɒtə, -də, -rə/
(be) going to, gonna	/ˈgənə/

In consequence, it would sound intolerably awkward to insert an adverbial before the *to*:

?*You have (got) *really* to be here early.

Again, where there is ellipsis of the predication, both with such sequences and more widely with verbs taking *to*-clause complementation (*cf* 16.38,

16.41, 16.50*ff*, 16.63), retention of *to* shows the leftward binding which encourages a split infinitive elsewhere:

A: Did you ever visit her after she had retired?
B: {I used to *sometimes*, but not recently.
{I intended to *often enough*, but seldom managed to.

(Compare: ?I used *sometimes* to, but . . .
?I intended *often enough* to, but . . .)

Nonetheless, the widespread prejudice against split infinitives must not be underestimated, especially with respect to formal writing, and indeed there is no feature of usage on which critical native reaction more frequently focuses. In consequence, it is by no means unusual to detect awkward and unidiomatic usage that clearly results from conscious avoidance:

They are *regularly* to attend all classes that have been arranged for the present semester.
Troops continue *heavily* to outnumber the normal residents in the area.
She was forced *apologetically* to interpose a question at this point.

In this last example, avoidance has produced ambiguity, since one cannot tell whether it was 'she' who was apologetic or those who 'forced' her. Consider similarly:

She has tried *consciously* to stop worrying about her career.

Here we cannot decide whether it was her trying that was conscious or whether she wished the stopping to be conscious. On the other hand, with an alternative avoidance:

She has tried to stop *consciously* worrying . . .

we do not know whether the sentence refers to 'a conscious stop' or to 'a conscious worry'. If the former were intended, defiance of the prejudice against the split infinitive would at least make the meaning clear:

She has tried to *consciously* stop worrying . . .

Compare also:

His hardest decision was to *not* allow the children to go to summer camp.

It will be noted that if the *not* had preceded the *to* in the last example it would have been difficult, even in speech, to prevent misinterpretation as 'To allow the children to go to summer camp was not his hardest decision.'

Split infinitives are commonest with subjuncts of 'narrow orientation' (*cf* 8.92*ff*) and hence perhaps especially where the infinitive is a 'gradable' verb. The subjuncts would not of course be those that most usually appear at *iM* or at *E* (*cf* 8.24) such as *too* or *as well*. Some further examples will illustrate these points:

Your task is to *really* understand your students' problems.
I do TRỲ to underSTÁND – to *TRÙly* understand.
We tended to *rather* sit back and wait for developments.

People who are in genuine need ought to have priority; but to *so* organize the service is administratively difficult.
To *further* prolong discussion beyond the present meeting would be very undesirable.
To *even* reprimand a member of staff, it is important to ensure that the agreed procedure is strictly followed.

Colloquially, the split infinitive is frequently associated with a following focus, as in:

Well, you ought to *at least* TRY̌.
As soon as I get the word, I'm going to *really* HÙRry.

Such preparation for focus may be expletive, as in:

I told them to *darned well* think for themSÈLVES.

Compare 8.100, App I.16 Note [d]. More generally the focus is intensified by superlatives or other expressions of real or implied comparison:

She was the first person to *ever* live in that house.
My grandson was the latest person to *either* discuss this with me or even allude to it.
She would be the last person to *even* THÌNK of plagiarizing.
No one invited me to *so much as* have a glass of water.
He is now reluctant to *so much as* SPÈAK to her.

Note In a Survey of English Usage text of circa 1980 involving four educated British adults (three women and one man) in a professional psychiatric discussion lasting three-quarters of an hour, there were nineteen 'split infinitives':

. . . to *actually* V . . .	7 ×	
. . . to *not* V . . .	3 ×	
. . . to *sort of* V . . .	2 ×	
. . . to *simply* V . . .	1 ×	
. . . to *openly* V . . .	1 ×	
. . . to *suddenly* V . . .	1 ×	
. . . to *emotionally* V . . .	1 ×	
. . . to *perhaps* V . . .	1 ×	
. . . to *always* V . . .	1 ×	
. . . to *all* V . . .	1 ×	['. . . it's going to *all* ruin things.']

End position

8.22 END POSITION (symbol *E*) is the position in the clause following all obligatory elements; it is also the position of the obligatory adverbial when this follows the other obligatory elements. For example:

The light was fading *rapidly*. [after *SV*]
Dr Blackett is *in Tokyo*. [A in *SVA*]
She was digging a trench *in the garden*. [after *SVO*]
He gives his car a wash *every week*. [after *SVOO*]
They became teachers *in the end*. [after *SVC*]
He put the vase in the cabinet *without a word*. [A in *SVOA*]

It is by no means rare to find more than one adverbial in this position:

She kept writing letters *feverishly* [A_1] *in her study* [A_2] *all afternoon* [A_3].

In such a case, all three of the adverbials are said to be at *E*, though of course their order relative to each other is of considerable significance (*cf* 8.150*f*).

The tendency for such *optional* adverbials to follow all *obligatory* elements can be readily ignored, however, in certain circumstances. Putting an adverbial at a subtype of *E* is found convenient when end-focus (especially associated with end-weight; *cf* 18.9) makes preferable an obligatory element in clause-final position despite the presence of an adverbial. This is called INITIAL END position (symbol *iE*); for example:

She kept writing *in feverish rage* long, violent letters of complaint. [S + V + A + O]

This position seems least disturbing of normal order when an adverbial comes between a direct object and obligatory adverbial, as in:

She placed the book *offhandedly* on the table.

In some cases *iE* is essential if clarity is to be achieved. Consider:

She herself interviewed *with hurtful disdain* the student I had turned down.

If we compare this with a version putting the same adverbial at *E*, we shall see that there is little chance that a reader would make the same interpretation:

She herself interviewed the student I had turned down *with hurtful disdain.*

As we might expect from these examples, *iE* is especially necessary when the last obligatory element is a clause, since otherwise the adverbial would seem to be an element in the subordinate clause. Compare:

He urged her dismissal *secretly.* [1]

Here it is clear that it was the urging that was done secretly.

He urged that she be dismissed *secretly.* [2]

But here, retention of *E* for the adverbial implies that it is the dismissing that is to be done secretly. To combine the meaning of [1] with the construction of [2], we must move the adverbial to *iE* or *M*:

He urged *secretly* that she be dismissed.
He *secretly* urged that she be dismissed.

Compare also:

He said *suddenly* that he had earlier lost his temper.
He hoped *fervently* to be applauded.

in contrast to:

He said that he had earlier lost his temper *suddenly.*
He hoped to be applauded *fervently.*

It should be noted, of course, that in these examples the choice is not merely between *E* and *iE*, but between either of these and *M*:

He *secretly* urged . . .
He *suddenly* said . . .
He *fervently* hoped . . .

But there is one important type of adverbial where the *M* option is not available. The adverbials in phrasal verbs (*cf* 16.3*f*, 16.16) may be placed at *iE* except when the O_d is a pronoun:

She waved *away* the offer of help.
She waved it *away*.
*She waved *away* it.

Most semantic roles can be expressed at *E*, though this is rarely true of modality; there is a particularly strong association of *E* with spatial expression: *cf* 8.15 Note [a]. Grammatically, *E* is the position for obligatory adjuncts unless there is an optional adjunct, in which case it would usually be this that appeared at *E*. As for realization, *E* is used for prepositional phrases and clauses rather than short adverb phrases.

Note With prepositional verbs, where we have the option (*cf* 16.13*ff*) of regarding them as transitive or intransitive (*cf* 8.24), as in:

He + looked at + the picture. [*SVO*]
He + looked + at the picture. [*SVA*]

it is best for present purposes to adopt the second of these but to regard the A-phrase as obligatory. This will account for native reaction to the apparent 'preposing' of an adverbial at *iE*, as well as accounting for the ease of tolerating discontinuity between the verb and its associated preposition. Hence:

He paid for the book *immediately*. [*E*]
She looked at the picture *in astonishment*. [*E*]
He paid *immediately* for the book. [*iE*]
She looked *in astonishment* at the picture. [*iE*]

Contrast with *SVO* interpretation the impossibility of *iE*:

*She looked at *in astonishment* the picture.

Positional norms

8.23 Although semantic and grammatical roles have a crucial influence on the position of A in a clause, the overwhelming majority of adverbials occur at *E*. There is however considerable variation, and there is a direct correlation in most cases between the semantic/grammatical category on the one hand and the realization form on the other. It is therefore of interest to study the distribution of some major realization types in relation to their position. We present below an analysis based on the Survey of English Usage corpus of which numerical data were given in 8.13, but now without the rather heterogeneous category of nonfinite and verbless clauses. In *Table* 8.23, the right-hand part of each line shows the *percentage* of each realization type at each of the positions distinguished in 8.14*ff*.

As with the general distribution of realization types (*cf* 8.13), so with the positions adopted, there is little difference between the norms of spoken and written English. The biggest difference is with noun phrases, and since this is numerically the smallest of the types, this difference is of little statistical importance. What is of greater moment is the difference between prepositional phrases and closed-class items which together constituted three-quarters of the many thousands of adverbials in the SEU sample. The lower proportion of closed-class (and open-class) adverbs at *E* doubtless reflects their relative lack of 'weight' (*cf* 18.9), while the higher proportion of closed-class items at *I* reflects the tendency to begin sentences with one of a small number of short conjuncts (*cf* 8.134*ff*) such as *then*, *now*, *yet*, and above all (in speech) *well*. The twenty-five per cent of closed-class items at *M* constitutes no less than nine per cent of all adverbials in the sample and this draws attention to the numerical importance of 'narrow orientation' subjuncts like *really* (*cf* 8.96*ff*).

Table 8.23

Whole SEU sample	10639	*I*	*iM*	*M*	*m/eM*	*iE*	*E*
Prep phrases	4414	9.5	1	1.5	0	9	79
Closed-class items	3948	25	1	25	1	6	42
Open-class adverbs	1070	16	3	42	2	6	31
Finite clauses	980	31	1	1	0	1	66
Noun phrases	227	16	0	5	1	4	74
Spoken material	5599						
Prep phrases	2063	6	0	1	0	8	85
Closed-class items	2226	29	1	22	1	4	43
Open-class adverbs	608	17.5	5	38	1.5	5	33
Finite clauses	559	30	1	1	0	2	66
Noun phrases	143	10	0	7	1	2	80
Written material	5040						
Prep phrases	2351	12	1	2	0	10	75
Closed-class items	1722	20	1	29	1	9	40
Open-class adverbs	462	15	1.5	47	1.5	7	28
Finite clauses	421	32	2	1	0	1	64
Noun phrases	84	26	0	2	0	6	66

Grammatical functions

8.24 Since the purpose of this book is to describe present-day English from the viewpoint of grammar, it is on the grammatical functions that we shall concentrate in our discussion of adverbials. There are four broad categories of grammatical function: ADJUNCT, SUBJUNCT, DISJUNCT, and CONJUNCT. We shall deal in turn with each of these and their subcategories, as set out in *Fig* 8.24 below.

When adverbs, prepositional phrases, and other structures are functioning as part of an element in the sentence structure, they cannot of course be regarded as 'adverbials' in terms of the sentence in question (*cf* 8.1):

Her *beautifully* manicured nails plucked at the harp strings. [1]
The man *in the corner* seems to be ill. [2]
She answered in a *quietly* assertive way. [3]

Though you may leave *when ready*, you are asked not to disturb other candidates. [4]

In [1], *beautifully* is functioning as part of the noun phrase realizing the subject; contrast [1a]:

She had manicured her nails *beautifully*. [1a]

where the same item is functioning as A. In [2], *in the corner* is likewise part of the noun phrase that is subject in the example; contrast [2a]:

The man was *in the corner*. [2a]

In [3], *quietly* is functioning within a prepositional phrase which as a whole constitutes the adverbial of the sentence; contrast [3a]:

She asserted her answer *quietly*. [3a]

In [4], *when ready* functions as an adverbial within a finite clause which itself constitutes the adverbial in the sentence as a whole; compare [4a]:

You may leave *when ready* if you wish. [4a]

Here, the same verbless clause is functioning as one of two adverbials within a sentence.

But although the structures operating within elements in [1–4] are functionally quite distinct from the same items functioning as A in [1a–4a], the distinction is not always so clear. Out of context, there may be ambiguity, as with *in the next house* in:

I could hear *the man in the next house*. [part of a noun phrase]
(perhaps continuing: 'singing to his children, as he often does')
I heard the man *in the next house*.[predication adjunct, *cf* 8.27]
(≁'*In the next house* I heard the man', but rather perhaps continuing: 'but he ran out at the back as I approached')
I heard the man *in the next house*. [sentence adjunct, *cf* 8.36]
(~'*In the next house*, I heard the man', and perhaps continuing: 'but I could no longer hear him when I left it and walked round outside')

In these examples, *in the next house* must be understood as one or other of the three possibilities; there is no grammatical or semantic blurring. With other examples, there may be multiple analyses. One can justify treating:

He approved of the idea.

as having a predication adjunct *of the idea* or as comprising a prepositional verb *approved of* with a noun phrase as object *the idea* (*cf* 16.13*ff*). Equally, one can justify treating alike the two sentences:

He couldn't bring the changes *into effect*.
He couldn't bring the changes *about*.

with the italicized portions regarded as obligatory predicational adjuncts. From other points of view, it is preferable to regard *bring about* as a phrasal verb (*cf* 16.3*f*, 16.13*ff*), since this analysis captures syntactic features that would otherwise be ignored.

But there are uses of adverbs and adverb phrases where the status depends on neither ambiguity nor multiple analysis. The adverb *today* in the following example seems to be part of the subject noun phrase:

The |pace of 'life toDÁY| is |proving 'too FÀST|

Yet on the one hand there seems to be little difference beyond the nuances of emphasis in versions of the sentence in which *today* is certainly functioning as the A-element:

ToDÁY the pace of 'life is 'proving 'too FÀST
The pace of 'life is toDǍY proving 'too FÀST
The pace of 'life is 'proving 'too FÀST toDÁY

And on the other hand the position of *today* in the original version is not one that excludes the occurrence of A; *cf*:

Mr Jones toDǍY must be heartbroken. [A at *iM*]

Consider also the following textual example:

A raw recruit to the police service at the beginning of this century was expected to be little more than physically fit and mindlessly obedient.

Thus punctuated, it appears as though the whole sequence before *was expected* is the subject; but it is perfectly possible that *at the beginning of this century* is an A at *iM*. Compare:

At the beginning of this century, a raw recruit to the police service was expected to be . . .

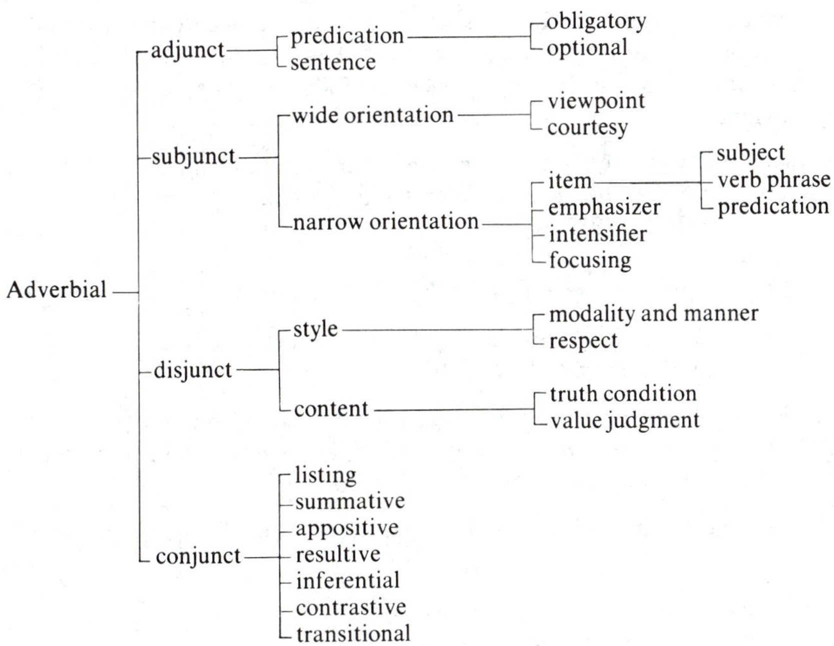

Fig 8.24

Adjuncts

8.25 Although in sentence schemata we designate as A realizations of adverbials in all four of the grammatical categories, it is only the adjuncts that closely resemble other sentence elements such as S, C, and O. Like them, for example, and unlike the other adverbials, an adjunct can be the focus of a cleft sentence (*cf* 18.26):

Hilda helped Tony because of his injury.
It was *Hilda* that helped Tony because of his injury. [S]
It was *Tony* that Hilda helped because of his injury. [O]
It was *because of his injury* that Hilda helped Tony. [A]

The parallels extend also to contrast in alternative interrogation or negation:

Did *Hilda* help Tony or did *Bill* help him? [S]
Hilda didn't help *Tony* but she helped *Wendy*. [O]
Did Hilda help Tony *because of his injury* or (did she help him) *to please her mother*?
Hilda didn't help Tony *because of his injury* but (she helped him) *to please her mother*. } [A]

The same applies to potentiality for being the focus of focusing subjuncts (*cf* 8.116):

Only *Hilda* helped Tony . . . [S]
Hilda only helped *Tony* . . . [= 'Hilda helped only *Tony* . . .'] [O]
Hilda only helped Tony *because of his injury*.
[= 'Hilda helped Tony only *because of his injury*'] [A]

Moreover, irrespective of their position in a clause, adjuncts come within the scope of predication ellipsis or pro-forms (*cf* 12.29*f*, 12.59*f*), exactly like other post-operator elements. In consequence, the following pairs of examples are synonymous:

{ *In 1981* [A], Grace *became a teacher* [C] and so did Hamish.
{ Grace *became a teacher* [C] *in 1981* [A] and Hamish *became a teacher* [C] *in 1981* [A].

{ Fred *carefully* [A] *cleaned his teeth* [O] but Jonathan { didn't. / not. }
{ Fred *carefully* [A] *cleaned his teeth* [O] but Jonathan didn't *carefully* [A] *clean his teeth*. [O]

{ Peter will *pay back the loan* [O] *when he gets paid* [A] and Bob may too.
{ Peter will *pay back the loan* [O] *when he gets paid* [A] and Bob may *pay back the loan* [O] *when he gets paid* [A] too.

Finally, like S, O, and C, adjuncts can be elicited by question forms. Compare:

Who became a teacher? (*Grace* [S])
What did Grace become? (*A teacher* [C])
Who(m) did Hilda help? (*Tony* [O])

Why did Hilda help Tony?(*Because of his injury* [A])

Cf also *When*, *Where*, *How*, and periphrastic question forms *How long*, *How well*, etc.

Note Some subjuncts (*cf* 8.89, 8.105) can also be elicited by periphrastic question forms; for example, *In what way* (viewpoint), *How much* or *To what extent* (amplifier). On the other hand, some process adverbials that are otherwise adjunct-like are resistant to being focus in a cleft sentence. Here as elsewhere in grammar, we recognize that a neat division is rare and gradience endemic.

Subcategories of adjunct

8.26 Although the characteristics outlined in 8.25 broadly hold for all adjuncts, there are three distinct types ranging in 'centrality' (*cf* 2.13) from the obligatory predication adjunct (which resembles an object both in the necessity of its presence for verb complementation (*cf* 16.1*ff*) and in its relative fixity of position) to the sentence adjunct, whose presence is never grammatically essential and which can be moved between *E* and *I* positions with relatively little consequence for its stylistic or semantic effect.

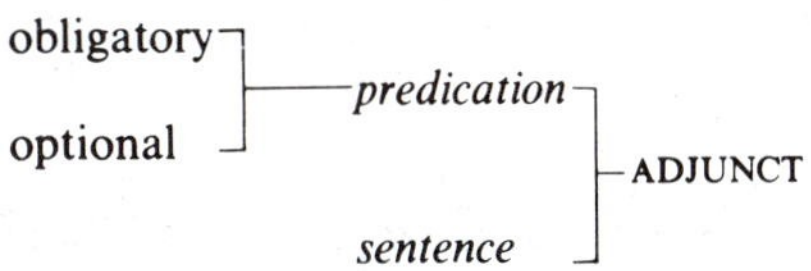

Fig 8.26

Obligatory predication adjuncts

8.27 If we compare sentences with *love* and *live* as V, we see that in each case a post-V element is required for complementation:

*He loved.
*He lived.

Beside:

He loved *Joan*. [O_d]
He lived *in Chicago*. [A_{oblig}]

The close and sequential relation of V O and V A in these sentences is demonstrated by their requiring similarly exceptional rhetorical circumstances for O and A fronting:

Joan he loved and *Joan* he always HÀD loved.
In Chicago he lived and *in Chicago* he always HÀD lived.

(*Cf* 18.20.) But the obligatory adjunct differs from the object in more readily permitting interruption between the V and itself:

?He loved at that time *Joan*.
He lived at that time *in Chicago*.

Such interruption is usually impossible where the A is a subjunct (*cf.* 8.97):

*She woke in bed *up*.

8.28 In fact, the number of verbs having sufficient semantic weight in themselves to require no further complementation is quite small. At one extreme, we have the class of copular verbs (*cf* 16.21*ff*) like BE and *turn* which, as their designation indicates, must link one element (the S) to another (the C or A_{oblig}):

She was *a teacher*. [C]
She was *in a hurry*. [A]
The chrysalis slowly turned *green*. [C]
The chrysalis slowly turned *into a butterfly*. [A]

At the other extreme, we have intransitive verbs like *disappear* or *apologize* which fairly freely occur without complementation:

The rabbit disappeared.
John apologized.

Even in these examples, however, there would be considerable dependence on a context which in fact provided the unexpressed adjunct:

The rabbit *suddenly* disappeared.
The rabbit disappeared *behind a bush*.
John apologized *to his host*.
John apologized *for being late*.

Still more so, between the extremes of BE and *apologize*, adjunct-less intransitive clauses are rare, and we must note that the addition of an adjunct reduces the semantic weight and 'communicative dynamism' (*cf* 18.3) of the verb. Compare:

The Queen arrived.	[*ie* the arrival is all important]
The Queen arrived *in a blue gown*.	[*ie* her dress is more important than the arrival]
The Queen arrived *in a blue car*.	

This is particularly noticeable in the case of certain verbs of broad meaning in respect of posture or motion: *sit, stand, come, go* (*cf* 16.24). These can take an obligatory adjunct of respect (*cf* 8.6) in the form of an *-ing* clause, with consequent weakening of the primary meaning of the main verb (*cf* 3.49):

He stood *waiting* (*patiently*).
She sat *reading* (*to the children*).
They went *hurrying* (*breathlessly*).
She came *running* (*in great haste*).

Such examples are, of course, superficially ambiguous. Prosodic adjustment can give fuller lexical meaning to the finite verb, at the same time transferring the *-ing* clauses from obligatory to optional adverbial status:

He STÒOD |waiting PÀTiently|
She sat with her CHÌLDren|RÈADing to them|

8.29 The nonfinite clause as obligatory adjunct in examples like 'He stood waiting' may be compared with the effect that perfective or progressive aspect has in conferring a plausible completeness of predication:

(?)He stood.
He stood waiting.
(?)She hitchhiked.
She was hitchhiking.
(?)They went.
They have gone.

Indeed, the progressive seems clearly able to combine the expression of a verbal inflection and of an obligatory adjunct of respect:

She was hitchhiking (to London).
She was (engaged in the activity of) hitchhiking.

Compare also:

She is teaching.

This last may refer either to current activity ('She is teaching in the next room at this moment') or to membership of a profession ('She is teaching for a living', 'She is in teaching', 'She is a teacher'), reminding us that historically the aspectual value seems to have been added to an original adverbial function (*cf* 'He's gone *a-hunting*', a dialectal or archaic form, derived historically from a prepositional phrase) which is still not entirely superseded.

8.30 A similar phenomenon to that observed with 'He stood waiting' is the obligatory adjunct with *come* and *go* in the form of an infinitive clause:

She'll come *to see you* (*about it*).
I went *to visit my mother*.

Again the lexical force of the main verb is reduced and the adjunct, while having the form common in the semantic role of purpose, is predominantly concerned with the respect role. This applies even more obviously to the obligatory adjunct following *try*:

He must try *to do better* (*next time*).
[≠ . . . 'so as to do better', 'in order to do better']

These adjuncts are noteworthy in that the semantic relation is alternatively realized by coordinated clauses, especially in rather informal usage (*cf* 13.98*f*, on pseudo-coordination):

She'll come *and see you* (*about it*).
I went *and visited my mother*.
He must try *and do better* (*next time*).

Note [**a**] When the coordinated clause is finite, the sense of the preceding verb is tilted towards its full lexical meaning. Compare:

I'll go *and visit my mother*.
I went and visited my mother.
I went and I visited my mother.

It is only in the first of these that the coordinated part has the resemblance to obligatory adjunct. With *try*, no finite verb coordination is possible:

Did he try *and see you*?
*Yes, he tried *and saw me*.

[**b**] Since *go*, *sit*, *try*, etc with infinitive clauses as obligatory adjunct seem to subordinate their lexical meaning to the verb in the adjunct, it is of interest to compare them with auxiliary verbs. *Cf* the treatment of *be going to* as a semi-auxiliary (3.47*f*).

8.31 Closely analogous to the obligatory adjunct, again frequently with the semantic role of respect (*cf* 8.6), are the structures in complementation of adjectives (*cf* 16.68*ff*). In some instances, without such complementation, the adjectives cannot constitute a predication:

*She is fond.	BESIDE	She is fond *of books*.
*This is tantamount.	BESIDE	This is tantamount *to an insult*.
?He is likely.	BESIDE	He is likely *to succeed*.

In others, the adjective has a different or at any rate much greater semantic weight when it is without complementation, serving more of an auxiliary role (*cf* 8.30 Note [b]) when complementation is present. Compare:

They are anxious. ~ They are anxious *to see you*. (*cf* 'They want to see you.')
They are (very) able. ~ They are able *to fly helicopters*. (*cf* 'They can fly helicopters.')
He is capable. ~ He is capable *of resigning over this*. (*cf* 'He may well resign.')
She is keen. ~ She is keen *on fishing*.
He is good. ~ He is good *at mathematics*.

Note As with the verbs with reduced meaning when accompanied by obligatory adjuncts (*cf* 8.28), some of the adjectives in informal usage take complementation in the form of a coordinate structure:

The room is good *and warm*.
He's nice *and generous*.

As with the verbs, too, the adjective requiring complementation can take on a subordinate role, as though it were a modification of what follows rather than being complemented by it. We may note that the following pairs are closely synonymous:

{The coffee is *nice and* hot.
{The coffee is *nicely* hot.

{He got *good and* angry. ⟨esp AmE⟩
{He got *very* angry.

(*Cf* pseudo-coordination, 13.98*f*)

8.32 In 8.27 obligatory adjuncts were compared with direct objects, and in 8.28 we considered intransitive verbs which appeared to have a different or somewhat weakened meaning when they were complemented by an adjunct. Both these factors come together in the consideration of prepositional verbs (*cf* 16.5*ff*, 16.13*ff*). Compare:

He went outside and *looked*; the evening sky was both radiant and peaceful. He came back in thoughtfully.

Here *looked* is fully intransitive and could be replaced by *gazed*. On the other hand, in:

He looked at the picture.

we seem to have as interdependent a tripartite sentence as we do in:

He lived *in Chicago*.

As with the latter, we may regard the prepositional phrase *at the picture* as an obligatory adjunct; *cf*:

It was *at the picture* that he looked.

But equally we may regard *look at* as a transitive verb, with *the picture* as O_d; *cf*:

It was the picture that he looked at.
The picture was looked at in admiration by him and several other visitors.

Note On the descriptive reasons for having multiple analyses for the same linguistic phenomenon, *cf* 2.61.

8.33 Just as prepositional verbs may be regarded either as transitive with obligatory O_d or as intransitive with obligatory adjunct, so sequences like *put away* can be regarded as potentially discontinuous transitive (phrasal) verbs:

She *put* the money *away*.
She *put away* the money.

or as simple transitive verbs requiring both an O_d and an obligatory adverbial (amplifier subjunct; *cf* 8.105). The former is convenient when we are considering the cooccurrence of closed-class particles (such as *away*) with verb items, as in 16.2*ff*. The latter is convenient when the verb item is accompanied by a wide range of phrases describable in terms suited to adverbial abstractions, as in this chapter. Thus we consider the italicized portion of the following sentences as obligatory predication adjuncts:

She put the money *into her purse*. (*cf* *She put the money.)
She put the money (*entirely*) *out of her mind*.
She placed *before me* a curiously ornate vase.

So also, while the adverb particle in the sentence:

He *stared* me *out*.

will be treated as part of a phrasal verb, the sentence:

He looked me (*straight*) *in the eye*.

is regarded as having an obligatory adjunct, susceptible of modification, as is shown by the parenthesized *straight*. The same verbs can occur, with a considerable difference in meaning according as they require or do not require an obligatory adjunct:

My father kept me.	['supported me financially']
My father kept me *in bed*.	['made me stay']
They have a cottage.	['own']
They have a cottage *for sale*.	['are selling']

(*Cf* the discussion of clause patterns, 10.1*ff*.)

Finally, just as we saw that copular verbs could have either C_s or an obligatory A (8.28), so there are a few verbs that can have either C_o or an obligatory A:

She made him *happy*. [C_o]
She made him *into a braver man*. [A]
He keeps his car *clean*. [C_o]
He keeps his car *in the street*. [A]

Optional predication adjuncts

8.34 Although it is often clear when an adjunct is obligatory, this is not always so. We noted in 8.28 that the mere addition of an adjunct after an intransitive verb reduced the verb's semantic weight. Nonetheless, it can be seen that the relation between S and V in:

The Queen arrived. [1]

is not radically altered when an A is added as in:

The Queen arrived *in a blue gown*. [2]

To the extent that [1] can obviously occur without the adjunct as in [2], or any other adjunct, while at the same time the relation between S and V in [2] is not at variance with the relation between the same S and V in [1], we can say that the adjunct in [2] is optional. Compare also further intransitive items where the optional status of A is indicated by parentheses:

The rabbit vanished (*behind a bush*).
She disappeared (*with the purse*).
The instrument has been tested { (*by a technician*). / (*electronically*). }
They are emigrating (*to South America*).
He protested (*vigorously*).

The optional status of adjuncts in *SVO* clauses can similarly be tested by observing that the relations (*eg* between V and O) remain constant irrespective of the presence or absence of the adjunct:

He defended his client (*with vigour*).
I found the letter (*in the kitchen*).
John forced open the door (*by means of a lever*).
They sent off the parcel (*to Australia*).
Grip the handle (*tightly*).
She kissed her mother (*on the cheek*).

Note Verbs that can be both monotransitive (16.25*ff*) and complex-transitive (16.43*ff*) enter into constructions of superficial similarity which are in fact very different. Compare:

She found him on the floor. [3]
[= 'He was on the floor when she found him.']
[≠ 'She found that he was on the floor.']
She found him of little help. [4]
[≠ 'He was of little help when she found him.']
[= 'She found that he was of little help.']

With *She found him in a coma*, the structure might parallel that in either [3] or [4].

Position of predication adjuncts

8.35 All predication adjuncts, obligatory and optional alike, are normally placed at *E*, as in most of the examples presented in 8.25–34. They may however be advanced to *iE* if an O or C is lengthy and complex or requires prosodic focus. Such positioning characterizes written rather than spoken usage, and it reflects some care in sentence planning.

With an obligatory adjunct at *iE*:

She keeps *in the garden* some of the most lovable little rabbits you ever saw.
They want to bring *into force* a new regulation about passengers in buses.
She made *into a braver man* the unfortunate and terrified victim of terrorism.

With an optional adjunct at *iE*:

I found *in the kitchen* the letter I thought I had burnt.
She kissed *on the cheek* her tearful and trembling mother.

We saw in 8.27 an example of exceptional fronting to *I* of an obligatory adjunct. Such fronting would be equally exceptional with most optional predication adjuncts, and although an accompanying subject–operator inversion is now largely confined to formal or emotive style, its continued existence demonstrates the severity of the dislocation. *Cf*:

By no properly qualified technician has this instrument ever been adequately tested.
In no circumstances must this door be left open.

With discontinuity:

So vigorously did he protest *that the authorities reconsidered his case*.

Note Negative adjuncts such as *in no circumstances* might be said to be obligatory since the meaning is different when they are omitted:

You should *in no circumstances* leave the door unlocked.
[≠ 'You should leave the door unlocked.']

Contrast:

You should not, *in any circumstances*, leave the door unlocked.

Here the adjunct can of course be omitted without serious change of meaning. Significantly in this connection, it is chiefly the negative adjuncts that can be fronted. Compare:

In no circumstances should you leave the door unlocked.
?*By several qualified technicians* was the instrument tested.

(*Cf* 10.65, 18.24.)

Sentence adjuncts

8.36 The most obvious way in which sentence adjuncts mark themselves off from predication adjuncts is by their relative freedom to occur at *I* position as well as *E*. In this way they demonstrate what we can intuitively feel: that they relate to the sentence as a whole rather than solely or predominantly to the V and post-V elements. Thus *on the cheek* and *on the platform* both possess the adjunct characteristics presented in 8.25:

She kissed her mother *on the cheek*. [1]
She kissed her mother *on the platform*. [2]

But the relative centrality (*cf* 2.13) of the adjunct in [1] as compared with the more peripheral orbit of that in [2] is shown by the awkwardness of:

?*On the cheek*, she kissed her mother. [1a]

as compared with:

On the platform, she kissed her mother. [2a]

If we combine fronting as in [1a] and [2a] with a truth-focusing paraphrase, the difference is brought out more sharply, though even [2b] is rather unidiomatic:

**On the cheek*, {it is a fact / the fact is} that she kissed her mother. [1b]

On the platform, {it is a fact / the fact is} that she kissed her mother. [2b]

If we combine the adjuncts of [1] and [2] at *E*, the adjunct in [1] would normally precede that in [2]; in other words, we expect the sentence adjunct *on the platform* to be located further from the centre of the clause (*cf* 2.13) than the predication adjunct *on the cheek*:

{She kissed her mother *on the cheek* [A_1] *on the platform* [A_2].
On the platform, she kissed her mother *on the cheek*.}

?*{She kissed her mother *on the platform* [A_2] *on the cheek* [A_1].
On the cheek, she kissed her mother *on the platform*.}

A further indication of the relatively peripheral status of the sentence adjunct is that it can be separated from the rest of the clause by a comma (and analogously occupy a separate tone unit in speech). Contrast the fronting of a predication adjunct (which requires a context of special motivation; *cf* 18.21) with a quite normally *I*-placed sentence adjunct:

In Chicago he LÍVED (and *in Chicago* . . .)
In ChiCĂGO| he studied metaPHỲsics|
**In Chicago*, he lived.
In Chicago, he studied metaphysics.

We should note also that an *I*-placed sentence adjunct has the potentiality to relate to the *whole* sentence, even where the sentence comprises two coordinate clauses, while the same *E*-placed adjunct will normally be interpreted as predicational and hence related only to the clause in which it is placed. Compare:

He travelled a great deal and eventually settled down *in Australia*.
In Australia, he travelled a great deal and eventually settled down.

(*Cf* 18.20–25).

Subject- and object-related

8.37 If we compare the identical adjuncts in the following sentences, we detect an obvious difference in their relations:

I found the letter *in the kitchen*. [1]
I typed the letter *in the kitchen*. [2]

Both [1] and [2] respond to the question 'Where did you . . . ?', just as both can be framed in a cleft sentence 'It was *in the kitchen* that I found/typed the letter'. Again, both can be paraphrased in terms of 'I was *in the kitchen* when I . . ..' But whereas [1] can be paraphrased as 'The letter was *in the kitchen* when I found it,' [2] cannot be paraphrased as 'The letter was *in the kitchen* when I typed it.' This test helps us to see that in [2] *in the kitchen* is a sentence adjunct, but it also helps us to see that example [1] is ambiguous as to whether the adjunct is more object-related ('The letter was in the kitchen') or more subject-related ('I was in the kitchen'). If we now reorder these examples:

In the kitchen, I found the letter. [1a]
In the kitchen, I typed the letter. [2a]

we seem to have done more than foreground the adjuncts to make them the informational point of departure for what follows (*cf* 18.21). We have in addition skewed the relations of the adjunct in [1a] to make the hearer predisposed to interpret it as subject-related ('I searched the kitchen and found the letter there') whereas in [1] the predisposition was to interpret it as object-related ('I went into the kitchen and there was the letter').

A strictly analogous skewing between a presumed object-related interpretation and a presumed subject-related one occurs on moving the adjuncts from *E* to *I* in such sentences as the following:

She saw my brother *in the garden*.
  [probably ~ 'My brother was in the garden']
In the garden, she saw my brother.
  [probably ~ 'She was in the garden']

I heard a noise *in the bathroom*.
  [probably ~ 'The noise was in the bathroom']
In the bathroom, I heard a noise.
  [probably ~ 'I was in the bathroom']

Compare subject orientation of space adjuncts (8.49), of time adjuncts (8.76), of process adjuncts (8.78), and the subjuncts of 8.92. Cases of subject–object skewing are clearly analogous to complex transitivity (*cf* 16.43*ff*). *Cf* also:

We foresaw a disaster *in June*.
  [probably ~ 'We foresaw that it was in June that there would be a disaster']
In June, we foresaw a disaster.
  [probably ~ 'It was in June that we foresaw that there would be a disaster']

8.38 We have noted that sentence adjuncts are more peripheral to the structure of the sentence in which they function than are predication adjuncts. The relatively peripheral character is shown positionally in the fact both that sentence adjuncts will normally follow predication adjuncts at *E* and that they can more readily be placed at *I*:

She had lived *in poverty* [A $_{\text{pred.oblig}}$] *for thirty years* [A $_{\text{sentence}}$].
I had found the letter *in the kitchen* [A $_{\text{pred.opt}}$] *by searching carefully* [A $_{\text{sentence}}$].

For thirty years, she had lived *in poverty*.
By searching carefully, I had found the letter *in the kitchen*.

By contrast, the predication adjuncts in these examples could be placed at *I* only with a striking disruption of normal expectations.

But a further indication of the greater mobility of sentence adjuncts is that – in contrast to predication adjuncts – they can usually appear at *M* without giving any impression of radical word-order dislocation:

She had *for thirty years* lived *in poverty*.
?*She had *in poverty* lived *for thirty years*.
I had *by searching carefully* found the letter *in the kitchen*.
(?)I had – *in the kitchen* – found the letter *by searching carefully*.

Where sentence adjuncts are moved from *E*, however, their 'scene-setting' role for the sentence is often pointed by punctuation and is in speech regularly marked by terminating the adjunct with a tone-unit break:

For thirty YÉARS| she had lived in PÒverty|
I HĀD| by searching CǍREfully| found the letter in the KÌTchen|

GRAMMATICAL REALIZATION OF SEMANTIC ROLES

Adjuncts of space

8.39 We saw in 8.2 that five semantic subroles were to be distinguished within the category of space. Where a verb (*eg*: *be*, *live*, *put*) takes an obligatory predication adjunct, this is in almost all cases concerned with POSITION or DIRECTION:

They are *on the Continent*.	He kept it *in the safe*.
She lives *in a cottage*.	He put it *on*(*to*) *the table*.

When a spatial predication adjunct is optional, on the other hand, it is less likely to express position than DIRECTION (including GOAL and SOURCE):

The children were running very fast { *towards the park*. / *to the swings*. / *from the school*. }

The DISTANCE relation is given two kinds of expression, SPECIFIC and GENERAL. The former is expressed solely by predication adjuncts, and these have only noun-phrase realization:

They ran *two miles* in ten minutes.
We climbed *a further thousand feet* before dusk.

General distance can also be realized by noun phrases, in which case the adjuncts are again predicational:

We hurried *a few miles* and then rested.
They had travelled *a long way* and were exhausted.

But prepositional phrases can also be used, and in this form the adjuncts can be predicational or sentential:

> We hurried *for a few miles* and then rested.
> *For the next two miles*, the road had a very poor surface, making speed impossible.

Distance phrases can be treated as singular despite their 'internal' plurality: '*another/a further* two miles'. But *cf* Note.

Position and source adjuncts readily assume a sentential role, especially when there is a direction or goal adjunct in the same clause:

> People move to a new house quite frequently *in America*.
> (*cf*: *In America*, people move to a new house quite frequently.)
> Mary went to Brussels *from London*.
> (*cf*: *From London*, Mary went to Brussels.
> ?*To Brussels, Mary went *from London*.)

To a limited extent, position adjuncts can be realized by noun phrases:

> *Which side of the street* does she live? She lives *this side*.
> *Whichever district* you live, try to do some walking every day.
> *We lived *this street* at one time.

Direction adjuncts involving a general reference item (especially *way*) are often realized as noun phrases introduced by *which*, *this*, *that*:

> He went *that way*.
> Come *this way* please.
> *Which direction* did she run?

Cf also ⟨informal, esp AmE⟩ 'My hair was blowing *every which way*' [*ie* 'in every direction'].

Note Noun phrases expressing specific distance are often treated as O_d rather than A, thus permitting passivization (*cf* 16.4*ff*, 16.27*ff*):

> They ran *the distance* in record time. *The distance* was run in record time.

There can be vacillation over concord: 'The remaining ten metres was/were completed in record time.'

Realization

8.40 Apart from the use of noun phrases for some predication adjuncts of distance (*cf* 8.39), space adjuncts are most commonly in the form of prepositional phrases, thus conveying with a given noun phrase (*the road*, *the house*, *the room*, . . .) the spatial discriminations set out in 9.16*ff* (*at*, *in*, *on*, . . .). Where the lexical form of the head noun is unimportant but where the location needs to be specified in detail, a postmodified noun phrase can be used, as in:

> I saw Joan at the {*office* / *place*} {*at which* / *where*} *her father works*.

But a head noun that is of little semantic weight (as *place* above) would more usually be omitted and the whole adjunct expressed with only the *where*-clause:

I saw Joan *where her father works.*

Clausal realization is especially convenient where the actual location is indefinite:

They must go {*where* / *wherever*} *we send them.*

So too with abbreviated clause forms:

Keep the keys {*where* / *wherever*} *convenient.*

Position in relation to animates (especially persons) may be expressed by prepositional phrases introduced by *with*:

A: Where is Mildred?

B: {She is (staying) *with her brother.* / She is *with the horse that was injured last week.* / She is *with the vet* but I don't know exactly where.}

Such answers to *where* are obviously relative to the position (known or unknown) of the entity mentioned; contrast 'She is *at her brother's*' (*cf* 5.124). In consequence, *with*-phrases establish little more than a conjunction with the person or animal named and they are often used as almost equivalent to conjoins with *and*:

Mildred is with her brother, discussing the horse's injury.
Mildred, with her brother, is discussing the . . .
Mildred along with her brother is/are discussing the . . . [*cf* 10.40]
Mildred and her brother are discussing the . . .

8.41 But in addition to the spatial pro-forms, *here* and *there* (*cf* 7.67), there are numerous common adverbs realizing spatial relations. Some of the following are atrophied prepositional phrases (*eg*: *overseas*), some can themselves be used prepositionally as well as adverbially (*cf* 9.5). Most can be used for both position and direction:

aboard, about, above, abroad, across, ahead, aloft, alongside, anywhere, around, ashore, astern, away, back, behind, below, beneath, between, beyond, down, downhill, downstairs, downstream, downwind, east, eastward(s) and other directions with the suffix *-ward* ⟨esp AmE⟩, *-wards* ⟨esp BrE⟩, *elsewhere, everywhere, far, here, hereabouts, home, in, indoors, inland, inshore, inside, locally, near, nearby, north, nowhere, off, offshore, on, opposite, out, outdoors, outside, overboard, overhead, overland, overseas, somewhere, south, there, thereabouts, through, throughout, under, underfoot, underground, underneath, up, uphill, upstairs, upstream, west, within*

Some items denote direction but not position:

after, along, aside, before, by, downward(s), forward(s), inward(s), left, outward(s), over, past, right, round, sideways, skyward(s), upward(s)

Note [**a**] The compass points used for both position and direction can be compounded; *eg*: *northwest, east-northeast.*

[b] There are some nautical terms used for both position and direction that are normally part of a technical vocabulary, but are found in literature dealing with the sea; *eg*: *aft*, *larboard* ⟨now rare⟩, *port*, *starboard*.
[c] For *here*, *above*, and *below* as signals in discourse reference, *cf* 19.46*f*.
[d] Several of the closed-class adverbs listed here can be regarded as abbreviated prepositional phrases. *Cf* 'He looked *outside* (*the house*)'.

Cooccurrence restrictions

8.42 Direction adjuncts of both goal and source can normally be used only with verbs of motion or with other verbs used dynamically (*cf* 4.33*ff*) that allow a directional meaning:

I think you should now turn *left*. ['to the left']
He jumped *over the fence*.
He kicked the ball *into the goal*.
She was whispering softly *into the microphone*.
He came *from America* last week.
It jumped *out of the cage*.

With very general directions, however, we find cooccurrence even with verbs used statively:

They {live / are living} *to the south of us*.
{My house faces / My car is facing} *toward(s) the park*.
This road is *to the north*.
Our course was *due south*.

Some direction adjuncts can also be used with the copular verb BE when they have a resultative meaning, indicating the state of having reached the goal (*cf* 9.7, 9.46):

They are *past* by now. ['have gone past']
The men will be *along* soon. ['will have arrived']
We will soon be *over the border*. ['have crossed over the border']
I've never been *to London*. ['never visited London']

On the other hand, position and distance adjuncts can be used with all verbs, including those in stative use (*cf* 4.27*ff*):

stative {
I heard about it *in London*.
I have the key *here*.
He lives *a long way from here*.
The ground seems very soft *locally*.
}

dynamic {
They're staying *in a nearby hotel*.
Was she swimming *near the boat*?
He's travelling *further* this year.
}

Position adjuncts can also be used with the copular verb BE:

It's much warmer {*inland*. / *where we now live*.}

Indeed, they frequently occur as the obligatory element with BE clauses, though not with copular verbs other than BE:

The birthday party is *in the next room.*
All our men are *abroad.*
The meeting will be *upstairs.*
The house you want is *on the other side of the street.*
*They will become *in Paris.*

The progressive is of course excluded:

*Charles is being *in the next room.*

Contrast (*cf* 3.76):

Charles is being boisterous (*in the next room*).

Spatial adjuncts can equally be obligatory adjuncts with verbs other than BE:

We don't live *here.*
I'll get *below.*
You should set that dish *in the middle.*
I'll put the kettle *on the stove.*
They keep their car *further from the house* now.

Note [**a**] Informally, *seem* and *appear* permit spatial adjuncts as sole complementation, especially those relating to distance or with general rather than specific reference:

They seem *further away* now.
?The children seem *upstairs*, to judge from the noise.

Note that 'She seems *at home*' could be freely used but only in the sense 'at ease', without spatial reference.

[**b**] Figurative use of basically spatial items is of course common with time adjuncts (*cf* 8.51*ff* below). On the nonspatial use of adverbial particles, as in 'The light is *on*', 'The car blew *up*', 'Drink *up* your milk, darling', *cf* 16.2*ff*.

Potential ambiguity

8.43 Given that the same items can be used in quite different semantic roles with the same verbs, it is easy for ambiguity to arise. *Cf*:

Did you drive the car *near the police station*?
The dog is not allowed to run *outside.*
The baby was crawling *upstairs.*

Each of the italicized adjuncts could be intended or interpreted as either directional ['towards the police station', etc] or positional ['in the vicinity of thc police station', etc]. In the former sense, the adjunct would be predicational, in the latter sentential and hence susceptible (in declarative sentences) of being placed at *I*, removing ambiguity; *eg*:

Outside, the dog is not allowed to run.

In speech, the sentential (*ie* positional) interpretation could also be conveyed prosodically, without moving the adjunct from *E*:

The dog is not allowed to RÙN| outsÍDE|

As predicational adjunct, however, the ambiguity can be removed only by rephrasing; *eg* (assuming that this is appropriate in the context):

The dog is not allowed to run *out* (*into the garden*).

Position and direction adjuncts in the same clause

8.44 Position and direction (or goal) adjuncts can cooccur, with the position adjunct normally following the other adjunct in *E*, for the reasons given in 8.39:

The children are running *around upstairs*.
He fell *overboard near the shore*.

With two prepositional phrases, there is often a superficial ambiguity in the status of the second phrase, which might be either an adverbial of the clause or a postmodifier of the noun head in the first phrase:

Some of the children are walking *to the lake in the park*.
['They are walking to the lake and are walking in the park' or 'They are walking to the lake which is in the park']
Middle-class people move *to a new house in the suburbs* every few years.
['They move to a new house every few years; they do this in the suburbs' or 'They move every few years to a new suburban house']

The position adjunct can be put in *I* position to avoid giving it end-focus (*cf* 18.3*f*): '*In the park*, the children are feeding the ducks.' Where the final phrase is a positional sentence adjunct, we can avoid ambiguity by placing it at *I*:

In the park some of the children are walking *to the lake*.
In the suburbs, middle-class people move *to a new house* every few years.

Depending on the structure of the sentence, there are other ways of avoiding such ambiguities; *eg*:

Some of the children are *in the park* and are walking *to the lake*.

Hierarchical relationship

8.45 It often happens that two spatial adjuncts enter into a contextual relation of hierarchy. This can occur where both adjuncts are of the same semantic class but of different grammatical functions (the one being a sentence adjunct, the other a predication adjunct). For example, with two position adjuncts:

Many people eat *in restaurants in London*.

The order here satisfies both the grammatical requirement (that the sentence adjunct be more peripheral than the predication one) and the logical requirement (that the smaller location be stated before the larger in which it is placed). But if the sentence adjunct is expressed with an adverb indicating that it is relatively 'given' (*cf* 18.8*ff*), the order may be reversed:

Many people eat {*here* / *there*} *in restaurants*.

Just as on grammatical grounds, it can only be the sentence adjunct that can appear at *I* ('*In London*, many people . . .'), so also on logical grounds, the lower member in the hierarchy cannot dominate the higher:

> **In restaurants*, many people eat *in London*.

Source adjuncts can also cooccur with goal or direction adjuncts in a hierarchical relationship:

> We came *to London from Rome*.
> We went *from Rome to London*.

These examples illustrate the normal order of the adjuncts, which is of course directly related to the semantics of the respective verbs, *come* (with orientation to goal) and *go* (with orientation to source, the point of departure). Nonetheless, in each case it is the source adjunct that alone is sentential and hence susceptible of positioning at *I*:

> *From Rome* we {came / went} *to London*.

Unless overridden by the pressure of orientation (as with *come*), the two adjuncts will be ordered with respect to the sequence of events referred to (thus source before goal), but if one is relatively 'given' (*cf* 18.8) and therefore expressed by a closed-class adverb, this will normally precede the other adjunct. Compare:

> They flew *over* (*the city*) *towards the border*.
> They flew *west over the city*.

Coordination

8.46 Two adjuncts can be coordinated if they are of the same grammatical function and semantic class; *eg* position adjuncts:

> Soldiers were on guard *inside* and *outside*.
> We can wait for you *here* or *in the car*.

Equally with direction adjuncts:

> They went *up the hill* and *towards the station*.
> They ran *across the field* and *past the farmhouse*.

But a position and a direction or goal adjunct normally cannot be coordinated. Hence in:

> The baby was crawling *upstairs* and *into his parents' bedroom*.

upstairs can be interpreted only as a direction adjunct (*cf* 8.43), since it is coordinated with a prepositional phrase that cannot have a positional function.

On the other hand, source and direction adjuncts admit coordination:

> They were hurrying *from the capital* and *towards the border*.

But directional path and specific goal cannot normally be coordinated without an additional adverbial such as *on* or *eventually*:

> We walked *up the hill* and so (*on*) *to the station*.

Contrast:

I drove *up Gower Street* and *into the College*.

Positions of space adjuncts

8.47 Irrespective of grammatical function or semantic role, space adjuncts favour *E* (but *cf* 8.87):

position	I'll meet you *downstairs*. We're eating *in the kitchen*. You'll find the sugar *where the coffee is*.
source	We moved the furniture *out of the room*. They travelled slowly *from Hong Kong*.
direction	I'll go *downstairs*. They shouldn't be going *south*.
goal	She hadn't yet moved *to Liverpool*. I'll go downstairs *to the kitchen*.
distance	By dawn, we had come *a long way*. Try to fly *the whole distance*.

Position adjuncts, particularly prepositional phrases, often appear in *I*. They may be put there to create a 'scene-setting' (*cf* 8.15), or to avoid end-focus (*cf* 18.11), or to avoid ambiguity (*cf* 8.43), or to avoid a clustering of adjuncts at *E*, though it is often impossible to isolate any one reason. *Cf*:

On the tree there were some very large oranges.
Outside children were jumping and skipping.
In the nursery the children were playing happily but noisily.
On the stage men were fighting, and *in the body of the hall* women were screaming.

The expressions *Here* . . . BE and *There* . . . BE with a personal pronoun as subject, and the verb in the simple present or (with *there*) past, are commonly used to draw attention to the presence of somebody or something:

Here it is, just where I left it.
There she is, by the phone box.
There they were, cold and miserable.

Source adjuncts can also be in *I* position and occasionally (though with more impression of disturbing the normal sequence of elements) in *M*:

From Liverpool, you can't often get international flights.
You could, *from Manchester*, get a plane to Amsterdam.

Speakers sometimes put position adjuncts in *M* and more rarely (and only with short items) in *iM*:

Life is *everywhere* so frustrating.
We are *here* enjoying a different kind of existence.
The poor had not *in this country* been left destitute.
As you proceed east along the side aisle, you *there* may notice a very curious statue.

Direction and goal adjuncts cannot usually be in *M*:

*They are { *(to) there* / *into the kitchen* } moving some new furniture.

But they can take the position between verb and object (*iE*), especially if the object phrase is long:

They moved *into the kitchen* every stick of furniture they possessed.

Occasionally, however, some direction adjuncts occupy *I*. As predication adjuncts, they have a dramatic impact and a rhetorical flavour in that position; normally the verb is in the simple present or simple past:

Down they flew.
Away he goes.
On they marched.

If the subject is not a personal pronoun but a noun phrase (with therefore a greater information value) or indefinite pronoun, subject–verb inversion is normal when a predication adjunct is in *I* (*cf* 18.23). This applies to intransitive verbs (**In the doorway saw me my brother*) without auxiliaries (**Up the hill has been climbing my brother*). Examples:

Down flew the jets.
Away goes my chance of winning!
Ah, *here* comes somebody – at last!
Along the road rolled the wagons.
Over the bridge marched the soldiers.
Ahead sat an old man.
Below is a restaurant.
In the doorway stood my brother.
On the very top of the hill lives a hermit.

On the presence of *there* (as in: 'Below, *there* is a restaurant'), *cf* 18.50.

Here . . . BE and *There* . . . BE with the verb in the simple present (or – with *there* – the past) are common in speech:

Here are the tools. ~ *Here* they are.
There's your brother, over by the bar. ~ *There* he is . . .
I turned the corner and *there* were my parents! ~ . . . *there* they were!

Direction adjuncts are put in *I* virtually only in literary English and in children's literature (stories, poems, and nursery rhymes). A few exceptions occur in informal speech, mainly with *go*, *come* and (more restrictedly) *get*; where the subject is *you*, such sentences often have imperative force:

{ *Up* (*the hill*) / *Down* (*the stairs*) / *In* (*the bath*) / *Out* (*of the water*) / *Off* (*the table*) / *Over* (*the fence*) / *On* (*the horse*) / *Under* (*the bridge*) } you { come. / go. }

<table><tr><td>On
Under
Round</td><td>you go.</td><td>There they</td><td>go.
come.</td><td>Here</td><td>I
we</td><td>go. Here he comes.</td></tr></table>

Note [**a**] Particles in phrasal verbs (*cf* 16.3*ff*) cannot be in *I*:

**Down* the car broke. **Up* cracked the soldier.

[**b**] There are some idiomatic expressions with *here* and *there*:

<table><tr><td>↑Here
↑There</td><td>you ÁRE [= 'This is for you']</td></tr></table>

HÈRE we ÁRE [= 'We've arrived at the expected goal']

↓There you ÁRE [= 'That supports or proves what I've said']

[**c**] For *here* as time indicator, *cf* 19.36. For the use of *here* in discourse reference, *cf* 19.47.

Syntactic features of space adjuncts

8.48 As predication adjuncts, direction and goal adverbials are normally the focus of negation in a negative sentence. They therefore normally do not precede clause negation:

Across the park he walked, hand in hand with his elder daughter.

but:

**Across the park* he didn't walk . . .
**Towards the fort* the soldiers did not march.

On the other hand, as sentence adjuncts, those of position can readily precede clausal negation:

Indoors, we could not hear ourselves speak.
Nearby, the farmyard animals hadn't even begun to stir.

Most space adjuncts, including prepositional phrases, accept intensification (*cf* 7.87*ff*, 9.5); this can involve combining measure indicators with adverbials in other semantic roles:

They drove (*due*) *east*.
They climbed (*straight*) *to the top*.
He went (*right*) *into the house*.
She was sitting (*right*) *at the door*.
He turned (*sharp*) *left*.
He went (*a long way*) *up* (*the mountain*).
They are staying (*far*) *inland*.

A type of clause comparison can be achieved by the use of {*further* / *farther*} . . . *than*:

<table><tr><td>They are</td><td>further
farther</td><td>ahead
downstream</td><td>than we are.</td></tr><tr><td>He went</td><td>further
farther</td><td>up the mountain
through the wood</td><td>than I did.</td></tr></table>

Many space adjuncts accept questioning with *How far*:

<table><tr><td>How far</td><td>across
away</td><td>are they?</td></tr></table>

while *here* and *there* accept questioning with *How near* instead:

> *How near* {*here* / *to us*} are they?

The following are among the space adverbs that do not allow premodification by *far*:

> *here, there*; the compounds in *-where*; *about, around, between, hereabouts, locally, opposite, throughout*

But *cf* the common expression *few and far between*, meaning 'rare': 'Trains on a Sunday are few and far between.'

Note Two space adjuncts are inflected for comparison, *near* (*nearer*, *-est*) and *far* (*further*, *-est*, *farther*, *-est*), and can be the focus of clause comparison. These can be premodified by *very* and by other premodifiers of degree. (But ?**very nearby*.)

Position adjuncts in relation to subject and object

8.49 Position adjuncts normally indicate the place of the referent of the subject and (if there is one) of the object; usually the place is the same for both referents:

> I met John *on a bus*. [This implies that John and I were on the bus]

But sometimes the places can be different, as we saw in 8.37; in such cases, the adjunct is predicational:

> I saw John *on a bus*. [This implies that John was on the bus but it does not imply equally that I was on the bus]

With certain verbs, the reference of an adjunct in *E* or *iE* is always to the place of the object, and normally that will differ from the place of the subject (*cf* 8.75 Note [a] for an analogous point with time adjuncts). These verbs denote 'owning' or 'placing':

> I {*have* / *keep* / *put* / *park* / *shelter*} my car *in a garage*.

With certain verbs, position adjuncts are resultative and are like object-related adjuncts (resembling indeed complex-transitive complementation; *cf* 16.43*ff*):

> I want *my car* [O] *in the garage* [A]. [*Cf* 'My car will be *in the garage*']
> I expect *a leak* [O] *in that pipe* [A]. [*Cf* 'A leak may occur *in that pipe*']

The verbs are verbs of arranging, saying, expecting, or wanting, where the predication has future reference. Not all such constructions allow an expansion simply by BE, but they usually have an analogue with a *that*-clause:

> I expected *a riot* [O] *in the city* [A]. ['there to be a riot *in the city*']
> They are threatening *a riot* [O] *somewhere* [A]. ['that there will be a riot *somewhere*']

He suggested *a picnic* [O] *on the island* [A]. ['that a picnic be arranged *on the island*']
They are planning *a meeting* [O] *at my house* [A]. ['that a meeting should be held *at my house*']

In some cases, another verb (such as *have*) rather than BE may be implied (as in the last example above: 'planning *to hold* a meeting'). *Cf*:

They offered *a barbecue* [O] *nearby* [A]. ['to have a barbecue *nearby*']
I like *my dinner* [O] *in the kitchen* [A]. ['to have my dinner *in the kitchen*']
She enjoys *tea* [O] *on the lawn* [A]. ['having tea . . .']
The doctor advised *a few days* [O] *off work* [A]. ['advised taking . . .']

In all such cases, the position adjunct is restricted to *E* and can sometimes be interpreted as a noun-phrase postmodifier:

He suggested a picnic *on the island*. ~ *A picnic on the island* was suggested.

The position adjunct may sometimes refer to the object in a contingency relationship:

We ought to condemn *such activities* [O] *here* [A].
I only like *barbecues* [O] *by the sea* [A]. [≠ 'By the sea, I only like barbecues'; *cf* 8.117]

These can be paraphrased by clauses with *if* or *when*: *such activities if they take place here*; *barbecues when they are held outdoors*. These adjuncts are also restricted to *E*, and again they can be interpreted as part of a noun phrase ('*Such activities here* ought to be condemned').

If any such adjunct is intended to be sentential, it has to be in *I* for the distinction to be clear:

At my house, they are planning a meeting.
Here we ought to condemn such activities.

Direction adjuncts as commands

8.50 Certain direction adjuncts can be used as brusque or very familiar directives, with an implied verb of motion (*cf* 11.42):

Waterloo, please. [for 'Drive me to Waterloo, please'], *Out*(*side*)*!*, *In*(*side*)*!*, (*Over*) *Here!*, (*Over*) *There!*, (*Right*) *Back!*, *Down!*, *Off!*, *Up!*, *Under!*, *Left!*, *Right!*, *Away with him!* ['Take him away'], *Upstairs with you!* ['Go upstairs'], *Out with it!* ['Tell me about it'], *Out of the house!*, *To bed!*

Note [**a**] Some other adjuncts can also be used as directives, *eg*: *Quickly!*, *Slowly!*, *Carefully!*
[**b**] Expressions like *Well, we'll to bed* and *I must away* are sometimes used in BrE with an implied verb of motion ('I must go away'); they have an archaic or dialectical flavour. But the following is wholly current:

After being treated at the hospital for shock, Mr Toyota was allowed *home*.

The adverbial here is equivalent to *to go home*; in the active, the verb of motion would be explicit:

They allowed Mr Toyota { *to go home.* / *?home.* }

Adjuncts of time

8.51 Obligatory predication adjuncts of time occur in BE clauses where the subject refers to an event (*cf* 10.10, 10.25):

> The wedding was *on Thursday*.
> The concert is *from seven till nine*.
> Guided tours are *twice a day*.

Just as *live* in the sense 'reside' has an obligatory space adjunct, so in the sense 'be alive' it has an obligatory time adjunct:

> Chaucer lived *in the fourteenth century*.

Verbs such as *last* take obligatory time adjuncts of duration:

> The concert lasts *two hours*.
> My mother-in-law is staying *for three weeks*.

Time adjuncts are readily predicational when a verb lacks other complementation:

> The guests arrived *in the early evening*.
> I waited *till 4.30*.
> She is coming *this afternoon*.

But when there is alternative complementation, most types of time adjunct just as readily assume a sentential function:

> I waited patiently enough for an interview *till 4.30*.
> *Till 4.30*, I waited patiently enough for an interview.
> She is coming for a tutorial *this afternoon*.

In many cases, moving a sentential adjunct from *E* to *I* has no effect on interpreting the scope of negation:

> She isn't coming for a tutorial *this afternoon*. [1]
> *This afternoon*, she isn't coming for a tutorial. [1a]
>
> We didn't speak to each other {*during the entire afternoon.* / *the whole day.*} [2]
>
> {*During the entire afternoon,* / *The whole day,*} we didn't speak to each other. [2a]

Realization

8.52 No other type of adjunct has such a wide range of grammatical realizations available as has the adjunct of time. Especially notable is the use of noun phrases and prepositional phrases. The noun phrase occurs for position, duration, and frequency:

> We were in France *last year*.
> They lived (*for*) *several years* in Italy.
> She writes an article or a review *every month*.

The conditions for noun-phrase realization, however, vary according to the semantic type. So far as time position is concerned, the noun phrases frequently have determiners:

She met him { *that afternoon.*
the following afternoon.
**the afternoon.*
in the afternoon. }

They put on the play { *last month.*
a month ago.
?**a month I well remember.* }

What time did he get there?

It is to be noted that, although a preposition can sometimes be inserted ('*At what time* did he get there?'), it often cannot; this is especially so before *next* or *last*. Compare:

We hoped to see Veronica { *on Monday.*
Monday. ⟨AmE⟩
next Monday.
last Monday.
on the following Monday.
on next*/on last Monday.*
on Monday next/last. }

A pinpointed time position cannot usually be realized by a noun phrase:

He arrived this morning *at ten-fifteen.*

But the prepositions are sometimes omitted, especially in AmE or informally:

?He arrived *ten-fifteen.*

It would seem that noun-phrase realizations typically imply a span and correspond to adjuncts introduced by *on*, *in the course of*, or *during*. Indeed it is with duration adjuncts that we have greatest freedom to use noun phrases, though for the most part they can be regarded as abbreviated prepositional phrases and can be made more explicit and rather more formal by the introduction of *for*:

They stayed *(for) a while.*
They lived (*for*) *several years* in Italy.

With or without *for*, time units can be postposed by *round* (with years) or *through*, especially when the reference is habitual:

The Stewarts now stay in Italy { *the whole summer through.*
the whole winter long.
the whole year round.
all the year round. }

Without a numeral or other quantifier, the *for* can often not be omitted:

?*He put up *the night* at a hotel.

But:

He stayed *the night* (at a hotel).
['He put up *that night* at a hotel' has a time position adjunct]

Nor can the prepositionless adjunct comfortably occur in *I*:

?*Some time,* / *For some time,* } he waited anxiously at the hospital.

[In '*Which afternoon* did he wait patiently?' the adjunct refers to time position]

As frequency adjuncts, noun phrases are virtually limited to '*every*/*each* + N', where N is a unit of time (*hour*, *day*, *year*, etc), or 'X + *times*' where X is a quantifier or numeral (*several*, *four*, etc):

He takes risks {
every day.
**in every day.*
**on every day.*
(*in*) *every period.*
(*in*) *every lecture.*
(*in*) *every game.*
}

She visited me {
four times.
**on four times.*
?**four occasions.*
on four occasions.
}

Note also the use of plurals without determiner:

She went to the theatre {
Saturdays. [= 'every Saturday']
?*Saturday.* ⟨BrE⟩ } [= 'on Saturday']
Saturday. ⟨AmE⟩ }
}

They work *nights*/*days*. [= 'they do night work/day work']
They worked *days* on the production before they were satisfied.
[= 'for several days']

8.53 As implied in discussing the limitations on noun-phrase realizations, time adjuncts much more usually take the form of prepositional phrases. The prepositions concerned have the values described in 9.33*ff*, and these are flexible and various enough to express all the semantic roles set out in 8.4. For example:

Time position:	He visited her { *on Monday.* / *in the evening.* / *at night.* }
Forward span:	She is staying *till Thursday.*
Backward span:	The house has been empty *since the war.*
Duration:	They worked steadily *for two hours.*
Frequency:	There are no lectures *on Saturdays.*
	He practises the piano *at every opportunity.*
Relationship:	I had confidence in her *up to that time.*

It should be noted, however, that this last semantic role is only inadequately expressed by prepositional phrases (*cf* 8.72 below).

Several of the prepositions used in the above examples can also function as conjunctions. We thus have a range of finite and nonfinite clause realizations of time adjuncts (*cf* 14.14):

She is staying *till she feels better.*
The house has been empty *since the war ended.*
The wall has been like this *since being damaged by a bomb.*

Above all, there are *when*-clauses. These express time position, as in:

I bought the car *when I received my first salary.*

but also other relations, such as duration:

She can write only *when the baby is asleep.* [= '*while*. . .']

Indefinite frequency is commonly realized by clauses introduced by *when(ever)*:

They come here *when(ever) they feel like it.*
Do your breathing exercises *when(ever) possible.*

Vaguer expression of time relation is often achieved by conjunctionless nonfinite and verbless clauses:

Travelling on the Continent, I get the impression of a greater affluence there. [frequency, 'whenever']
Travelling home last night, I suddenly had a bright idea. [position, 'when'; or duration, 'while']
I eventually had a chance to read her letter, *quietly alone at last.* [position, 'when']

8.54 But the shortest and frequently the most convenient realization of time adjuncts is the adverb. There is a wide range of these items, formally falling into two classes, closed-class adverbs and open-class adverbs. Semantically, the closed-class items can be subdivided into three sets. There are those like *then*, *before*, *since* which are essentially anaphoric, referring to a time contextually 'given' ('at that time', 'before that time', 'since that time'). Then there are those like *now*, *today*, *tomorrow*, *yesterday* that refer to very specific points of time. Finally there are those like *often*, *always*, *seldom* which are general and conveniently vague in their reference.

By contrast, the open-class adverbs are lexically specific and therefore idiosyncratic. They are for the most part *-ly* formations on adjective bases (*subsequently*, *eventually*, *immediately*, etc) or – to express frequency – on noun bases (*hourly*, *monthly*, etc). *Cf* App I.41.

We shall look at some of the commoner adverbs used as time adjuncts as we examine the expression of each major semantic role in turn.

Time-position adjuncts

8.55 Just as position in space may be as narrowly located as a pinpoint or as broadly as a continent, so position in time may be equally variable, and, in the case of prepositional-phrase adjuncts, the preposition's quasi-figurative use helps to distinguish the narrowness or broadness of the time 'location' (*cf* 9.34*ff*):

She arrived *at nine-fifteen.* He lived *in the fourteenth century.*

In these two examples, of course, the verbs also endorse the narrowness and broadness respectively. But a time position adjunct may be broad yet cooccur with a verb that rules out a broad time span:

He was born *in the fourteenth century.*
She arrived *on Monday.*

The adjuncts here refer to a span of time within which, at some *point* of time, the events took place.

But whether narrow or broad, position adjuncts typically serve as a response to a potential *when* question (and they can be referred to as 'time-*when*' adjuncts):

A: When did she arrive? B: { *Quite recently.* / *Last night.* / *At five o'clock.* / *While you were at the library.* }

When in its various uses (*cf* 7.53) is in effect partly a pro-form for the time adjuncts in this class. For *then* as a pro-form for these time adjuncts, *cf* 19.55. Note that *now* can also be used with reference to the past:

They had been courting for two years and he *now* felt she knew his worst faults.

Time-position adjuncts can be divided into two sets, largely determined by two modes of orientation (*cf* 4.18*ff*):

(a) those denoting a point or period of time, especially 'before';
(b) those which in addition imply attention to another period of time, especially 'after'.

Though the distinction is often negligible, it helps to explain cooccurrence as in 'She went there *again* (a) *afterwards* (b)'.

Common adverbs realizing adjuncts in these two groups include:

Group (a):

again ['on a subsequent occasion'], *early* ['at an early time'], *late* ['at a late time'], *now* ['at this time'], *sometime* ['at an unspecified time'], *nowadays* ['at the present time'], *presently* ['at the present time' ⟨esp AmE⟩], *simultaneously* ['at the same time'], *immediately*, *instantly*, *then* ['at that time']; *today*, *tomorrow*, *tonight*, *yesterday*.

For example:

They lived in London for the first few years of their marriage and were *then* very happy.
Come and see us *again*.
I was in New York *last year* and am *now* living in Baltimore.
Frank *immediately* hurried away to find a doctor.
Nowadays, Patricia cycles to work.

Does he want us to be here *early tonight*?
The meeting starts *tomorrow at eight o'clock, after we've had dinner.*
I was awarded my Bachelor of Arts degree *in 1980.*
I suggest that we see him *tomorrow night* or at the very latest *on Sunday.*
I'll tell you all the news *when I get back home.*

Note that the *when*-clause in:

Tell me *when you're ready.*

may be a noun-clause object or a time adjunct, the latter equivalent to:

Tell me *as soon as you're ready.*

By contrast, the *when*-clause in:

Tell me *when you'll be ready.*

can only be object ['Tell me *the time at which you'll be ready*'].

Group (b):
afterwards, before, earlier ['before'], *eventually* ['in the end'], *finally* ['in the end'], *first* ['before all else', 'before that', 'at first'], *formerly, initially* ['in the beginning', 'at first'], *last* ['after all else', 'in the end'], *lately* ['a short time ago'], *later* ['afterwards'], *momentarily* ['in a moment' ⟨AmE⟩], *next* ['after that'], *once* ['at some time in the past'], *originally* ['in the beginning', 'at first'], *previously* ['before'], *presently* ['soon'], *recently* ['a short time ago'], *shortly* ['soon'], *since* ['after that'], *soon, subsequently, then* ['after that'].

For example:

He's going to the barber but will be back here *later.*
I went into my room and *soon afterwards* started to work.
I haven't got any time at the moment but I'll see you *shortly.*
She *once* owned a dog.
Take a hot drink and *then* go to bed.
Originally, that building was a school.
He *recently* had an accident.
A preliminary investigation seemed to indicate that he was implicated in the fraud, but a fuller investigation has *since* proved beyond all doubt that he was innocent.
I left the factory *before the strike.*
Will you be there *after lunch*?
He owed me a lot of money and wouldn't pay me back until I got my lawyer to write to him. He has paid me back in full *since then.*
The appointment was made *a month ago.* } (*cf* 9.35, 9.66)
I wrote to him about it *a (good) while back.* }
She left him *after he struck her.*
The Prime Minister announced her resignation *before the votes were counted fully.*

There is a difference in the use of *once* according as the meaning is [1] 'on one single occasion' or [2] 'at a certain but unspecified time in the past'. Thus:

I *once* bought a fur hat. (*I *once* bought this fur hat) [1]
I *once* visited this city. [2]

If the reference is future, *sometime* is used instead of *once*:

I'll buy a fur hat *sometime*. [1a]
I'll visit this city (again) *sometime*. [2a]

The prepositional-phrase variant, *at some time*, is less vague and suggests a particular occasion; here *some 'time* (two words) is a noun phrase, in contrast to the adverb *'sometime* (**at 'sometime*) which is written and accented as a single word.

Most time-position adjuncts in Group (a) normally occur at *E*, but (as sentence adjuncts) *nowadays* and *presently* commonly occur at *I*; and *immediately* is common at *M*. Those in Group (b) commonly occur at *I* or *M*. The *iM* position is open to most of Group (b) and to *now*, *nowadays*, and *then* in Group (a).

Note [**a**] *Earlier* (*on*) and *later* (*on*) are synonymous with *before* (*that*), *beforehand*, and *after* (*that*), *afterwards* respectively:

He remembered the many insults that he had *earlier* experienced.
He handed in his resignation, and *later* (*on*) regretted his hasty action.

They are not the comparatives of *early* and *late* respectively and we cannot substitute (*more*) *early* and (*more*) *late* for them:

*He remembered the many insults that he had (*more*) *early* experienced.
*He handed in his resignation and (*more*) *late* regretted his hasty action.

The true comparatives of *early* and *late* (but only with *-er* forms) are exemplified in:

We are eating {*late* / *later*} today. Today we'll be leaving home {*early*. / *earlier*.}

[**b**] *Presently* is synonymous with *soon, in a short time* where there is a modal auxiliary or (for some) when the verb is in the past:

They {will *presently* call on him. [= 'in a short time from *now*'] / *presently* called on him. [= 'in a short time from *then*']}

Some find the latter use of *presently* unacceptable. On the other hand, when the verb is in the present, it is synonymous with *at present* and occurs especially in AmE:

They {are *presently* in London. / are *presently* calling on him.}

[**c**] *After*, *before*, and *since* are prepositions (*cf* 9.38) and conjunctions (*cf* 14.12) as well as adverbs. When used as adverbs, they could be regarded as prepositions in abbreviated prepositional phrases, though *after* as an adverb is not as common as its synonym *afterwards*, which cannot function as a preposition:

A preliminary investigation seemed to indicate . . ., but a fuller investigation has *since* (*that time*) proved . . .
He has been unhappy for a long time, but I've never seen him so unhappy *before* (*this time*).
The meeting is at six. I'm leaving now, but I'll see you *after* (*the meeting*)/*afterwards*.

[**d**] Some adjuncts seem to be a blend of time position with manner, reason, or space (*cf* 8.81):

He told them *secretly* of his intention to resign. ['in a covert manner', 'when they were by themselves']
They criticized him *publicly*. ['in a public place', 'when they were in public']

(In 'Mary hid it *secretly*' the adverb may connote both 'in a secret manner' and 'in a secret place').

They visited him *on their way to the country*. ['*where* they were going', '*when* they were going']
{*As soon as the light went off,* / *When the light didn't go off,*} he sounded the alarm. ['Because . . . he immediately . . .']

[**e**] For the use of many Group (b) adjuncts for time relationship, *cf* 8.72; on their correlative use as conjuncts, *cf* 8.145.

[f] Time position in the future can be expressed as in [3] by prepositional phrases introduced by *for*, or as in [4] by clauses or prepositional phrases introduced by *until* or *till* (*cf* 8.58); for example:

We have invited her *for 8 p.m.* [3]

She will not leave { *until 8 p.m.* / *till her brother gets there.* } [4]

8.56 Time-position adjuncts can be in a hierarchical relationship:

They were here *late* [A_1] *last night* [A_2].
I'll see you *at nine* [A_1] *on Monday* [A_2].
I spoke to her *earlier* [A_1] *today* [A_2].
We'll meet *tonight* [A_1] *after the show* [A_2].

The order of the adjuncts at *E* depends in part on information focus (*cf* 18.9*ff*), but the tendency is for the superordinate adjunct (the one denoting the more extended period) to come last. However, as in the last example above, the order may be reversed if the other adjunct is longer, nonetheless preserving the essential partitive relation between the two. Compare also:

I was in New York *last year* [A_1] *before the first snow fell* [A_2].
They became drunk *today* [A_1] *within a very short time* [A_2].

So far, however, we have looked at hierarchically related adjuncts which are both predication adjuncts. If the superordinate item is a sentence adjunct, it can appear in *I*, and the relation is no longer so essentially partitive, as can be seen from the parenthesized additions in the following:

Last night they were here *late* (again).
On Monday I'll see you *at nine* (as usual).

Adjuncts of span and duration

8.57 In contrast to the adjuncts which relate to time conceived as a fixed point or static span, there are three types of adjunct which relate to time as a linear dimension (*cf* 4.2*ff*, 4.23). Two of these have an orientation to the speaker's 'now' (that is, the time of primary concern to the speaker/writer within a given context), the one referring to a span in the past, the other to one in the future:

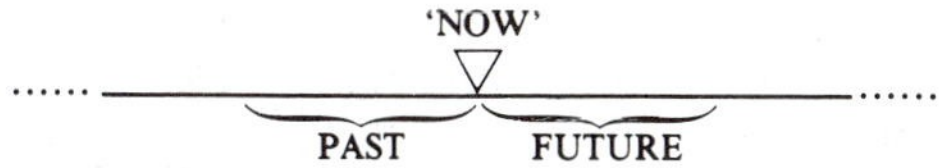

Fig 8.57

Thirdly, there are the adjuncts of more general temporal measure, requiring no orientation to a particular 'now'. In view of the similarity of purpose, it is not surprising that some of the same forms serve for all three types of adjunct.

Forward span

8.58 The key items in realizing adjuncts of forward span are *until* and *till* introducing either clauses or prepositional phrases. In the Survey of English

Usage corpus of (largely) British English, *until* occurs twice as often as *till*, and is used approximately equally as conjunction and as preposition, and equally too in spoken and written materials. On the other hand, *till* occurs chiefly in spoken texts, and is predominantly a preposition. For example:

They will live in Chicago *until William finishes his thesis.*
She will be working *till nine o'clock.*

Forward-span adjuncts are usually sentential, though they can be predicational especially in association with verbs which make their use virtually obligatory:

The performance lasted { *until the actors were exhausted.* / *until 2 a.m.* }

Phrases and clauses with *until/till* interact with verb semantics. A positive clause requires a verb of durative (*ie* nonmomentary) meaning and the span extends up to the reference of the time adjunct. Thus:

He waited *until I returned.*

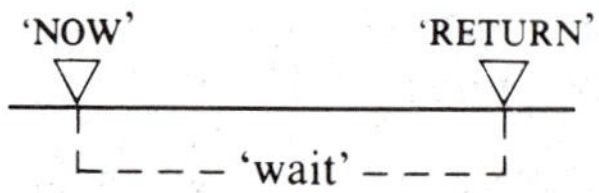

Fig 8.58a

With negative clauses and a verb of durative meaning, the span will also extend from the speaker's 'now', though not of course (by reason of the negative) up to the reference of the time adjunct:

He didn't wait *until I returned.*

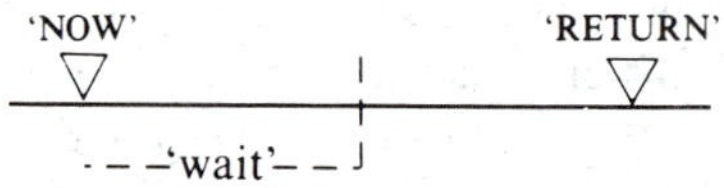

Fig 8.58b

On the other hand, with negative clauses and a verb of momentary meaning (*cf* 4.33, 4.35) the span denoted by the time adjunct marks the extent of the nonoccurrence of the momentary action:

He didn't arrive *until I returned.*

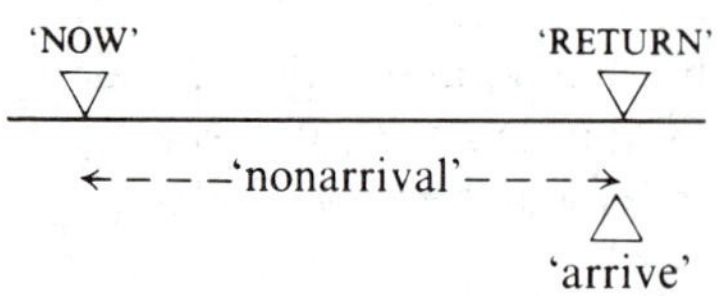

Fig 8.58c

The sentence can thus be referentially equivalent to 'He delayed his arrival until my return', though this of course implies a contingency relation and is thus not precisely a rhetorical equivalent. *Cf* also:

> He did not arrive *before I returned.*
> He arrived *when I returned.*

So also, 'She slept *till nine*' implies 'She *stopped* sleeping at nine', whereas 'She didn't sleep *till nine*' implies 'She *started* sleeping at nine'.

8.59 Other modes of realizing forward span involve the use of *up to*, *over*, *for*, *before*, *by*, *by the time* (*that*). For example:

> We'll be there *up to midday*; then we'll be out for lunch.
> Can you stay *over the weekend*?
> Can you stay *for a month*?
> I have to leave *before midday.*
> I have to leave *by midday.*
> I shall be away { *by the time* (*that*) *the clock strikes twelve.* / *by that time.* }

The phrase *in time* can be used both in the sense of 'by the due time' and also in the sense of 'eventually':

> He wants to leave at midday but he doesn't think I shall be ready *in time.* [= 'by that time']
> She's promised to finish the painting *in time* but she can't say when. [= 'in the course of time']

(Contrast *on time*, which refers to time position, '*at* the time required')

Prepositional phrases with *to* function like those with *until*/*till* provided they are correlated with *from*-phrases (expressed or implied: *cf* 9.37) marking the beginning of the time span:

> She will be working from May { *to September.* / *till September.* }

Neither phrase makes clear whether September is within or beyond the span, but in AmE we have complete clarification, as in:

> She will be working from May { *through August.* / *through September.* }
> [*ie* until the end of the month named]

where BrE achieves such precision only with more periphrastic expressions such as *to the beginning of*, *to the end of*. Noncorrelative phrases with *through* occur in both AmE and BrE:

> She will be working *through September.* [*ie* 'for the whole month of September' or 'from now until the end of September']

Noun-phrase realizations of forward-span adjuncts involve quantifiers as in:

> Would you like to stay with us { *a few days?* / *a day or so?* }

I shall be in Chicago { *all* (*next*) *week.* / *the whole month.* / (*part of*) *next year.* }

Consider, finally, the following dispositions of forward-span reference, taking the 'now' of speaker's concern as 6 o'clock:

I'm *not* ready *yet*; the work will take me { *another half hour.* / *till 6.30.* }

I think I'll be ready *by 6.30.*
I w*on't* keep you waiting *beyond 6.30.*

Note [**a**] Forward-span adjuncts can be evoked by means of questions with *Until when . . .*, *Till when . . .*, *How long . . .* (*for*). Postposition of *till* is awkward and of *until* almost unacceptable:

?*When* are you working *till*? ?* *When* are you working *until*?

[**b**] Noun phrases can be ambiguous between time position and forward span:

He'll be staying here *next month.* [EITHER 'he will arrive *next month* and stay for an unspecified time' OR 'he will be staying here *for* the whole of next month']

That is, the adjunct could be forward span but would normally be interpreted as time position. On the other hand, the prepositional-phrase variant can refer only to forward span:

He'll be staying here *for the next month.*

But phrases with *during* are ambiguous within the forward span itself:

He'll be staying here *during the next month.*

The adjunct here could either mean 'for some period falling within the month' or 'for the whole of the month'.

[**c**] For forward span, there are nonfinite *-ed* clauses with *until* and *till*, but not *-ing* clauses:

I shall stay here *until ordered to move.* ?I shall stay here *until getting further instructions.*

Cf also the idioms *until further notice* [= 'until you hear further'], where *notice* cannot be replaced by (for example) *information*; and *in future* [⟨BrE⟩ 'from now onwards'], as opposed to *in the future* which as well as being available for span [= 'in future'] is more usually used for time position ['at some time in the future'].

Backward span

8.60 The key item in realizing adjuncts of backward span is *since* introducing either a prepositional phrase or a clause, or used alone as an adverbial (by ellipsis):

She has not lived in America *since her graduation from high school.*
She has been trying to make a living as a writer *since her first novel was published.*
I spent some time in the National Gallery last year but I haven't been there *since.*

In the Survey of English Usage corpus, instances as conjunction (excluding causal use) and as preposition are roughly equal in number, but adverbial use accounts for only about 15 per cent of occurrences.

Backward span is elicited by such questions as *How long have you . . .*, *How long is it since you . . .*, *When . . .*, or *Since when . . .* (not **When . . . since*: *cf* 8.59 Note [a]). For example:

A: { *When* did you start giving the orders? / *Since when* have you been giving the orders? }

B: *Since I was made foreman.*

Regularly with perfective aspect in the clause of which the *since*-element is A, the span indicated by the adjunct reaches up to the 'now' of primary concern to the speaker (which may of course be 'then' if it is a past time that is of primary concern):

He has worked in the same office *since (he came here) in 1980.*

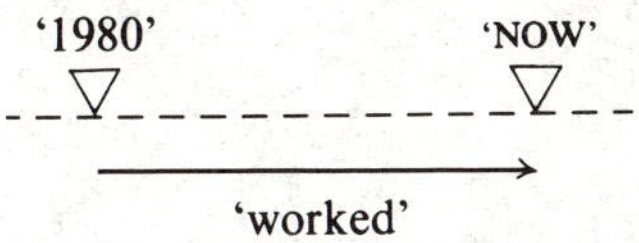

Fig 8.60a

When I came to know him in 1982, he had worked in the same office *since 1980.*

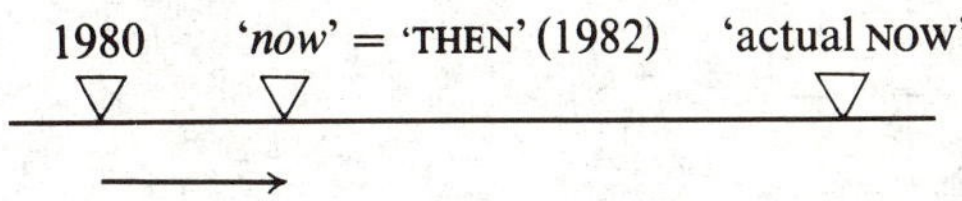

Fig 8.60b

The speaker can show that he thinks the span is long by using the intensifier *ever*: 'worked there *ever* since 1980', '. . . *ever* since he came here'.

Both *since*- and *for*-adjuncts specify a span of time, but *since* marks in addition the starting point. If the clause with a *for*-adjunct has its verb in the perfective, the span extends to the 'now', and the hearer is able to count back and calculate the initial point in the span:

He has worked in the same office *for two years.*

But, unlike adjuncts with *since* (*cf* 8.61), *for*-adjuncts do not require the perfective in the clause in which they function as A, and the time span may therefore be 'unlocated' in the past, the hearer knowing only that the span does not extend to 'now':

Mary was writing that play *for three years.*

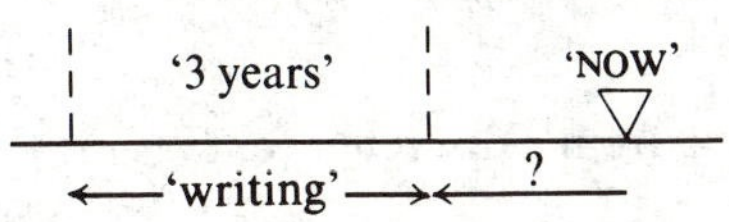

Fig 8.60c

Such backward-span adjuncts can be expressed without *for* if they are placed not at *E* but at *eM* and if the verb has progressive form:

Mary was *three years* writing that play.
Mary has been *three years* writing that play.
*He has *two years* worked in the same office.

Note [a] Noun phrases of the form *this/these* + *last/past* + N can express backward span:
A: How long have you worked here?

B: { *This past year.* / *Only this last month.* / *This/These past three years.* }

Without *past* or *last* such quantified noun phrases are somewhat archaic:

He has worked on the play *these two years.*

[b] A noun phrase that would indicate time position with past or perfective will indicate backward span with the progressive (*cf* 4.25*ff*):

I visited my mother *this morning.* [position]
I have visited my mother *this morning.* [position]
I have been visiting my mother *this morning.* [span]

8.61 The time span indicated by *during*-, *since*- and *while*-adjuncts may correspond either to a continuous state or activity, as in:

He has been sleeping *since two o'clock.*

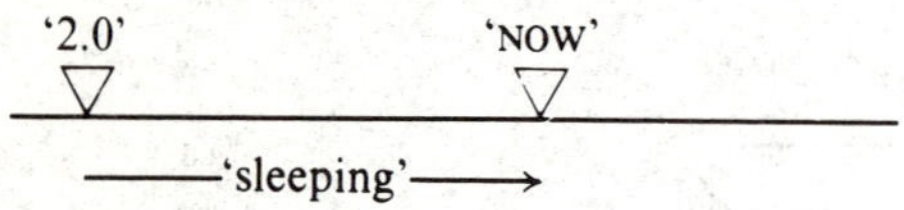

Fig 8.61a

or to a period within which one or more discrete actions took place, as in:

She has got married *since you saw her in June.*

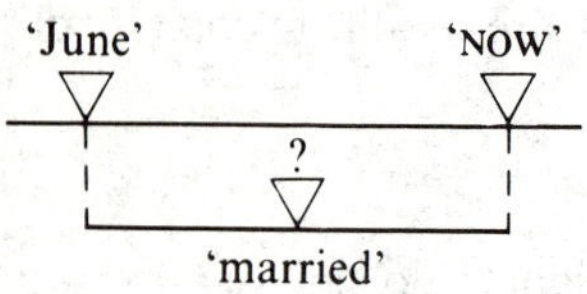

Fig 8.61b

Within the adjunct too it is possible to be specifying a continuous activity through the time span, as in:

Since they have lived in London, they have been increasingly happy. [='during that time'] [1]

Alternatively, we may refer to a period dating from a discrete event, as in:

Since they went to live in London, they have been increasingly happy. [='from that point in time'] [2]

There is thus a contrast between [1] and [3]:

Since they lived in London, they have been increasingly happy. [3]

This is because, while the span involved is the same, [1] defines their living in London as coterminous with that span (*ie* as still being true 'now', which is as far as the speaker can commit himself), but [3] makes no claim on how long they lived in London beyond the implication that they no longer live there 'now':

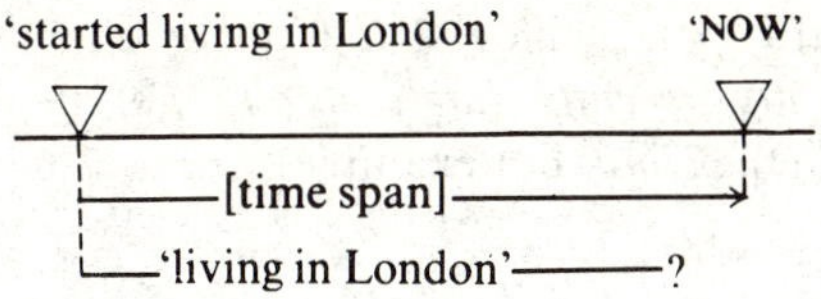

Fig 8.61c

On the other hand, if the verb in the *since* clause is not one of continuous activity (like *live*), a nonperfective carries no such implication as [3]. Consider the following set:

He's been getting bad headaches { *since he has been in the army.* [4]
since he joined the army. [5]
since he was in the army. [6] }

In [4] he must still be in the army 'now'; in [6] he cannot be still in the army; in [5] he may or may not be still in the army.

Note [**a**] Adjuncts with *since* are to be viewed as prepositional phrases with nonfinite *-ing* clauses as complement (*cf* 8.59 Note [c], 14.20):

He's been getting bad headaches { *since having been in the army.* [4a]
since joining the army. [5a]
since being in the army. [6a] }

In [4a], an unusual form, it would be implied that he was no longer in the army: contrast [4]. In [5a], it would be implied that he was still in the army: contrast [5]. In [6a], he might or might not be still in the army: contrast [6]. It should be noted that (despite its form) *having been* in [4a] is not an expression of aspect but of tense, *-ing* + *-ed* being the only means of expressing past with nonfinites (*cf* 4.55, 4.66). We therefore expect the *since*-clause in [4a] to mean 'Since he *was* in the army'. With nonfinite *-ed* clauses, the rare instances of *since*-adverbials would be causal, not temporal: 'I will not, *since so bitterly criticized*, continue in office any longer' (*cf* 8.124). Note that in 'The minister, *since returned*, has refused to comment', *since* is an adverb used here as a time adjunct in the nonfinite clause: 'who has returned *since*', *ie* 'subsequently'.

[**b**] Apparent exceptions to the requirement of a perfective verb occur when a phrase or clause introduced by *since* correlates with a superlative or ordinal:

Yesterday was the hottest day since I came to live here.
Joan came to work in her car last week for (only) the second time since October.

Such *since*-constructions are best regarded as postmodifications in noun-phrase structure and not as adjuncts. More substantial exceptions occur in AmE, especially where the clause in which the *since*-adjunct operates refers to the present; and increasingly, these exceptions apply to BrE as well (*cf* 14.26):

It *is* ages since she was (last) here. [NB '. . . since she's been here', '. . . *since she's been last here']
It *is* a long time since I saw him.
Since the accident { she *walks* with a limp. / she *can* no longer be left alone. }
I'*m* doing well since I bought those oil shares.
Things *are* much worse since you left.
Since I came to college, I *realize* how little I knew.

But in AmE we also have:

Since I last saw you, my mother *died*.
Since when *did* you own a word processor?
I *was* here since before 8 a.m.

[**c**] Indefinite or long backward span can be expressed by *for ages* or ⟨esp AmE⟩ *in ages*:

She hasn't been here { *for* / *in* } *ages*.

8.62 Other adverbials for indicating backward span include *up to* (date or time), *till/until* (date or time), *so far*, *subsequently*, *recently*, *lately*, *in all* (*N's*) *life*, *from*, correlatively *from* (time) . . . *to* (time), *before*. For example:

I worked in America {*up to 1979.* / *till/until 1979.*}

She has not finished her novel *so far*.
We moved to Chicago in 1980 and have lived there *subsequently*.

I have not been sleeping well {*recently.* / *lately.*}

He hadn't seen such a disaster *in all his life*.
He taught at Yale *from 1975*.
[contrast 'He *has* taught . . . *since* . . .']

They were on vacation {*from June to September.* / *from June through September.*} [⟨AmE⟩ *cf* 8.59]

I have never written a play *before*.

Adverbs such as *subsequently*, *recently*, *lately* would of course refer to time position if the V-element were not marked for perfective aspect. The same is true for *before*, though informally (and especially in AmE) this item can express backward span with the simple past in nonassertive clauses:

She never kissed a man *before*. Did you (ever) see her *before*?

In nonassertive clauses also, we have (*for*) *long* expressing backward span:

How long did you work there? They didn't wait (*for*) *long*.

Cf also forward span:

These shoes probably won't last {*long.* / *for long.*}

Duration

8.63 Just as several of the items discussed in 8.58*ff* can be used for both forward and backward span, so several of them can also be used to express measures of time that are not specifically confined to future or past. For example:

She writes *for an hour* every day.
It takes me *only ten minutes* to clean my car.
They spend *ages* just sitting in the garden.
Toshiko works *far into the night* at her thesis.
I have some time off *during the week*.

Certain adverbs are used for general measures of time: for example, *always*, *briefly*, *indefinitely*, *momentarily* ['for a moment'], *permanently*, *temporarily*. When used with the present perfective, the otherwise time-position adverbs *lately* and *recently* are used for duration:

His visits used to be rare, but {*lately* / *recently*} he has been here quite a lot.

Time-duration adjuncts are sometimes elicited by questions with *How long* . . . and are normally placed at *E* or *iE*. Single-word adverb realizations, however, would be unusual at *E* and are commonly at *M*:

She is *temporarily* working in a different building.

Note [a] With some verbs, noun phrases as expressions of time duration can be treated as direct objects (*cf* 8.39 Note). For example:

The committee {took (up) / spent} *an hour* on mere preliminaries.

An hour was {taken (up) / spent} on mere preliminaries.

[b] In expressions of duration, the intensified prepositional sequences *all through, all round* (but not the synonymous *right through, right round*) can be discontinuous:

He now sleeps *all night through*. [='right through the night']
She works there *all year round*. [='right round the year']

Cf also *all* (*day* etc) *long*; in BrE, *the* may precede the time noun: *all the day long, all the night through*, etc.

[c] Uninflected and unmodified *long* is normally a nonassertive form and positioned at *E*; this applies also to *very long*. Thus:

?The monsoon lasts *long*. [*cf* The monsoon lasts *a long time*]
The monsoon doesn't last *long*.
Does the monsoon last *long*?
?The journey took *very long*. [*cf* The journey took *a very long time*]

When inflected or modified other than by *very*, the item *long* can be either nonassertive or assertive and is also positioned at *E*:

The monsoon lasts {*longer*. / *too long*.}
The journey took *long enough for everyone to get to know each other*.

Uninflected *long* can be an assertive form when it cooccurs with the perfective and is then usually positioned at *M*. The verbs involved seem to be mainly verbs of belief or assumption, attitudinal verbs, and some verbs of speaking:

I have *long* thought of retiring at the age of 55. He has *long* admired my style of writing.
The merits of the scheme will be *long* discussed.

Long behaves like *much* and *far* in many respects (*cf* 8.104–7).

Time-frequency adjuncts

8.64 Frequency can sometimes be conceived in absolute terms without concern for the period of time over which the recurrence in question took place. For example:

A: *How many times* did you ring the bell? B: *Twice*.

More usually, however, we are concerned with frequency with respect to a specified or implied span of time. In other words, a frequency that responds to 'How often?'. Thus:

A: *How often* do you wash your car?
B: *Pretty rarely/Infrequently/Not very often.*
Monthly/Weekly.
Once a week.
Every Sunday.
From time to time.
As often as I can.
Whenever it gets very dirty.

Of course, even questions of the form 'How many times?' would not usually be satisfactorily answered with a simple numerical value that took no account of 'the rate of occurrences per unit of time'. That is, a question such as:

> *How many times* have you had a driving accident?

is likely to be answered with reference to a period:

> Four times, { over the past dozen years.
> { in the course of twenty years' driving experience.

That is, the respondent would reasonably conclude that the questioner was less interested in the absolute total than in that total related to the time span within which accidents could have occurred. Indeed the questioner might have framed his question as:

> *How often* { have you had / do you have } driving accidents?

Again, we may be concerned not with numerical indications of frequency but with more general or impressionistic frequency, as in [II] below. Here, the type of recurrence in which we are interested depends both on the semantics of the verb and also on its aspect. Compare:

> She *usually* smiles. [recurrent activity; *eg* 'When she sees me . . .']
> She is *usually* smiling. [continuous activity; *eg* 'Whenever one sees her . . .']

Apart from nonnumerical expressions of frequency (such as *whenever*-clauses) and some prepositional phrase patterns, time adjuncts of frequency are mostly realized by noun phrases or by adverbs. We can look in more detail at realizations in considering the semantic subclasses of frequency adjuncts. There are two major subclasses:

(I) those naming explicitly the times by which the frequency is measured: DEFINITE FREQUENCY;
(II) those not doing so: INDEFINITE FREQUENCY.

Each of these subclasses can in turn be subdivided:

(I) DEFINITE FREQUENCY

(A) PERIOD FREQUENCY
hourly, *daily*, *nightly*, *weekly*, *fortnightly* ⟨esp BrE⟩, *monthly*, *quarterly*, *annually*, *yearly*, *biannually* ['twice a year'], *biennially* ['every two years'], *semi-annually*, *twice a week/month*, etc, (n) *times a week/month*, etc, *every* (n) *week(s)/month(s)*, etc, *every other week/month*, etc ['on alternative weeks/months, etc']

For example:

> Committee meetings take place *weekly*. [=once a week]
> I shall be in my office *every other day*. [=on alternate days]
> *Each summer* I spend my vacation in Bermuda.
> Take three pills *twice a DÀY*.

Phrases of the form *per n* are occasionally used with reference to periodic money payments:

> If so desired, rent can be paid *per week* instead of *per month*.

(B) OCCASION FREQUENCY
once ['one time only'], *twice*; *thrice* ⟨archaic⟩; otherwise noun phrases or prepositional phrases, *eg*: *a time or two*, *three times*, *on five occasions*

For example:

> Veronica has been to Singapore (*only*) *ÒNCE*.
> Bob phoned *twice* today.
> I visit England *three times a year*.
> I perform operations *three days each week*.
> On (the) average, I see them *once every three weeks*.

8.65 (II) INDEFINITE FREQUENCY

(C) USUAL OCCURRENCE
commonly, *customarily*, *generally*, *habitually*, *invariably*, *normally*, *ordinarily*, *usually*

For example:

> He *generally* leaves home at seven.
> Does Jenny *usually* stay up so late?
> We *normally* go to bed before midnight.
> *As a rule* it's very quiet here during the day.
> *For the most part*, we play tennis on Sunday morning.

(D) CONTINUOUS/CONTINUAL/UNIVERSAL FREQUENCY
always, *constantly*, *continually*, *continuously*, *incessantly*, *permanently*, *perpetually*

For example:

> Does she *always* dress well?
> He is *continually* complaining about the noise.
> He *incessantly* asks for more money.
> They are *perpetually* in debt.

(E) HIGH FREQUENCY
frequently, *often*; *regularly*, *repeatedly*

For example:

> I have *often* told them to relax more.
> They *regularly* take their dog for a walk in the evening.
> Have you been drunk *many times*?
> He leaves the door unlocked *time after time*.
> They explained *again and again* that they couldn't help it, but she didn't believe them.

(F) LOW FREQUENCY
infrequently, *irregularly*, (*very*) *little*, *occasionally*, *periodically* ['from time to time'], *rarely*, *seldom*, *never*

For example:

> We are *occasionally* invited to their house for a party.
> We (*very*) *seldom* see our elder son these days.
> I have driven *a few times*.

She visits us *once in a while*.
You should phone them *now and again*. ['occasionally']
Do you visit your parents *from time to time*? ['occasionally']

We play cards {*on and off.* / *off and on.*} ['occasionally' ⟨informal⟩]
I have been in his office *on several occasions*.

Most time frequency adjuncts are normally positioned at *E*. However, those realized by adverbs and referring to indefinite frequency (Groups (C–F)) are normally positioned at *M*, while those realized by prepositional phrases and denoting usual occurrence (Group (C)) are normally positioned at *I*:

Mary has *sometimes/often* acted in Shakespeare plays.
On most days, I begin work at 8 a.m.

Adjuncts in some groups (especially in (C), (E), and (F)) can be inside or outside the scope of negation, and this coincides with their potentiality to appear at *iM*. Compare:

The students should {*normally* / *occasionally*} be given homework. [1]

The students should be given homework {*normally.* / *occasionally.*} [2]

The students {*normally* / *occasionally*} should not be given homework. [1a]

{*Normally,* / *Occasionally,*} the students should not be given homework. [2a]

(*Cf* 8.67*f*)

Note The adverb *once*, especially at *M*, also functions as a time position adjunct, 'at one time, on one occasion, at some time or other' (but *at once* means 'immediately'). Informally the corresponding noun phrase is likewise used for time position ('He came to see me one time and complained about his job'), as also when modified by *more*:

If you say that {*one more time* / *once more*}, I'm leaving.

8.66 Adjuncts of definite frequency in Group (A) denote the period of time by which the frequency is measured and are normally sentence adjuncts. Those in (B) express the measurement in number of times (*cf* 5.18) and are normally predication adjuncts. Items from each group can cooccur, normally with the item from (B) coming first:

You should take the medicine *twice* (B) *daily* (A). [= 'twice a day']

Those in (A) can also cooccur with each other in a hierarchical relationship:

She felt his pulse {*hourly* (A) *each day* (A). / *each hour* (A) *daily* (A). / *daily* (A) *every couple of hours* (A).}

The order of the adjuncts in *E* depends in part on information focus or end-weight (*cf* 18.9*ff*), but only the one denoting the longer period can occur in *I* (*cf* 8.45, 8.56):

[*Each day* / *Daily*] she felt his pulse [*hourly.* / *each hour.*]

*[*Hourly* / *Each hour*] she felt his pulse [*each day.* / *daily.*]

Cooccurrence of the adverb forms, however, is odd for stylistic reasons even if the one denoting the longer period is in *I*:

?*She felt his pulse *hourly daily.*
?*Daily* she felt his pulse *hourly.*

Those in (B) can likewise cooccur with each other in a hierarchical relationship, where the subordinate adjunct denotes the number of times for each of the times denoted by the superordinate adjunct, which assumes sentence-adjunct function. The verb must be one referring to a momentary event (*cf* 4.33, 4.35), such as *beat* 'to overcome (someone) in a contest'.

I beat him *twice on two occasions.* ['I won two contests on each of two occasions']

As in this example, the superordinate adjunct tends to follow the subordinate adjunct, but it can be in *I* position:

On two occasions I beat him *twice.*
?*Twice* I beat him *on two occasions.*

While the adverb and the noun phrases *X times* are ambiguous between superordinate and subordinate function in such a hierarchy, the prepositional phrases *on X occasions* are unambiguously superordinate. Adjuncts in (B) can often be the response to the question *How many times?* The question is used to elicit the adjunct when only one item from (B) is involved, but it can also elicit the subordinate or superordinate adjunct when two items from (B) are involved:

A: How many times did you beat him?
B: *Twice.*

A: How many times did you beat him on the two occasions?
B: *Twice.*

A: How many times did you beat him twice?
B: {*On two occasions.* / *Twice.*}

Adjuncts of definite frequency can also cooccur with items from each of the subclasses of adjuncts of indefinite frequency:

You should {*normally* (C) / *always* (D) / *regularly* (E) / *(only) occasionally* (F)} take the medicine *twice* (B) *daily* (A).

Note In the hierarchical relationship, repetition of the same adverb is avoided for stylistic reasons (*cf* 8.149):

?I beat him at chess *twice twice*. [*ie* there were two games on each of two occasions]
?*Twice* I beat him at chess *twice*.

8.67 Adjuncts of indefinite frequency in Group (C) denote usual occurrence. They differ from those of (especially) Group (D) in that they can precede the clausal negative, in which case they express that it is normal for something *not* to occur:

{*Generally,* / *Normally,* / *Usually,*} he doesn't take medicine.

They differ from those in (E) and (F) that can precede negation in that it is a contradiction to assert both that it is usual for something to occur and also that it is usual for it not to occur:

[**Generally,* / **Normally,* / **Usually,*] he doesn't take medicine, but [*generally,* / *normally,* / *usually,*] he does (take medicine).

On the other hand, those in (E) and (F) that precede negation express a high or low frequency. Here, we encounter a phenomenon that parallels multal and paucal items in noun-phrase quantifiers: 'Many arrows have hit the target but many have not' (*cf* 6.53, 8.71). Thus, it is not contradictory to assert that it is frequent (or infrequent) for something to occur and at the same time that it is frequent (or infrequent) for it not to occur:

[*Often* / *Occasionally*] he doesn't take medicine, but [*often* / *occasionally*] he does (take medicine).

We can see from this example that *often* does not necessarily imply the majority of times, and the same is true for *frequently*. However, those in (C), like *generally*, do imply the majority of times. Items in (C) not entailing exhaustiveness can obviously (unlike *invariably*, *habitually*) allow for exceptions. We can therefore say, for example:

{*Generally,* / *Normally,* / *Usually,*} he doesn't take medicine, but *sometimes* he does (take medicine).

Note **[a]** *Invariably* (commonly used in the sense 'usually') and *habitually* are the only ones in Group (C) that deny the possibility of exceptions:

**Invariably*, he doesn't take medicine, but *sometimes* he does (take medicine).

[b] *Generally speaking* and (occasionally) *normally speaking* are used as frequency disjuncts corresponding to the adjuncts *generally* and *normally* respectively (*cf* 8.125 Note [a]).

[c] The commonest frequency adverbials are in some ways more like time subjuncts (*cf* 8.98) than adjuncts:

She *usually* saw her patients in the mornings.
*It was *usually* that she saw her patients in the mornings.
It was *usually in the mornings* that she saw her patients.

Compare:

She used to see her patients *in the mornings*.
It was *in the mornings* that she used to see her patients.

8.68 Frequency adjuncts like *usually* in (C) as well as *often* and *frequently* in (E) can be the focus of negation:

He doesn't { *ǓSually* / *ǑFten* / *FRĚquently* } speak from notes.

But for those in (C), apart from 'exhaustive' items like *invariably*, there is as a general rule no logical difference resulting from whether the adjunct is within the scope of negation or not (*cf* 10.64*ff*). Somebody agreeing with a previous speaker could remove a frequency adjunct of (C) from the scope of negation:

A: He doesn't *ǓSually* speak from notes.
B: That's true. He *usually* DÒESn't (speak from notes).

To take the paraphrases of *usually*, there is no logical difference between the two sentences:

It's usual for him *not* to speak from notes.
It's not usual for him to speak from notes.

On the other hand, there is a logical difference between positioning *often* or *frequently* within the scope of negation and positioning them outside it. Where, as we saw in 8.67, we can say:

Often he doesn't take medicine, but *often* he does.

we cannot say:

*He doesn't *ǑFten* take medicine, but *often* he does (take medicine).

This is because, when *often* or *frequently* come within the scope of negation, we deny the frequency, and we obviously cannot then assert it.

If frequency adjuncts in (C) cooccur with duration adjuncts (*cf* 8.63), there can be a difference according to whether one of the adjuncts is or is not to be understood as within the scope of negation:

ǓSually he doesn't sleep for two days at a time.
['The usual thing is for him to go without sleep for two days at a time' or 'It is not usual for him to go to sleep for two days at a time']
He doesn't *ǓSually* sleep for two days at a time.
['It's rare for him to sleep for as long as two days at a time' or 'For two days at a time it is quite usual for him to go without sleep']

The same distinction applies for *often* and *frequently*.

Most frequency adjuncts can be the focus of a cleft sentence, particularly if they are modified or are in a negative or interrogative focal clause:

(?)It's *very frequently* that he loses money.
It's *not often* that I have a chance to speak to him.
Is it *often* that she drives alone?

For some speakers, the same is possible when the *that*-clause is negative:

It's *all too frequently* that people don't offer to help.
Is it *very often* that she doesn't speak to him?

It isn't *very often* that she doesn't speak to him.
It's *not often* that he doesn't help.

Rarely and *seldom* of Group (F) can sometimes be the focus of a cleft sentence, even unmodified, denoting negative frequency ('not often'):

It's {*rarely* / *seldom*} {that he loses any money. / that people don't offer to help.}

8.69 Indefinite-frequency adjuncts can cooccur in a hierarchical relationship (*cf* 8.45, 8.56, 8.66):

Normally (C), committee meetings are held *infrequently* (F).
Usually (C), he *constantly* (D) complains of headaches when he is assigned a responsible task.
They *seldom* (F) put on plays *again and again* (E).
I have *often* (E) telephoned him *a few times* (F) on the same day.

Some adjuncts even in the same group can cooccur where the verb is momentary (*cf* 4.33, 4.35) and we are thus able to distinguish between 'repeated action' and 'number of occasions' (*cf* 8.64):

They have *often* (E) pressed his bell *repeatedly* (E) without getting an answer.

Contrast:

?They have *often* (E) beaten him *frequently* (E).

Nonassertive *ever* ['at any time'] is sometimes used to intensify the negative forms *rarely, seldom* in (F), and it is especially common with the corresponding subjuncts (*cf* 8.98), though its use with *never* is considered nonstandard by some speakers:

(?)I *seldom ever* play squash now.

(Contrast the fully acceptable 'seldom if ever', which is not an intensified *seldom* but offers an alternative to it).

(?)I *never ever* go there.

Note Compare the following:

He {*always* / *never*} collects the groceries *on Tuesday*.

We could mean *either* that he collects (or never collects) them on Tuesday, *or* that whenever he collects them it is always (or never) on Tuesday.

8.70 Whereas frequency adjuncts in (C), such as *usually*, can precede negation (*cf* 8.67), those in (D) normally cannot:

?*He {*always* / *constantly*} doesn't pay his debts on time.

*He {*continually* / *incessantly*} didn't drink whisky.

Instead we use *never*, *not . . . ever*, or *not . . . at all*:

He {*never* pays / *doesn't ever* pay} his debts on time.

He *didn't* drink whisky *at all*.

Note, however, in ironic 'second instance' use:

A: Sorry; I haven't enough money.

B: You {*ÀLways* / *perPÈTually*} haven't enough money.

Adjuncts in (E), such as *frequently* and *repeatedly*, denote a high frequency and those in (F), such as *occasionally* and *never*, denote a low or zero frequency.

When the negative forms in (F), *rarely* and *seldom*, are in *I* position, they cause subject–operator inversion (*cf* 18.24), such usage being literary or oratorical in tone:

Seldom had I seen such confusion.

Note [**a**] The following items in (E) and (F) do not normally precede negation: (E) *regularly* (*cf* 'He *regularly* doesn't agree' beside the more usual 'He *regularly* disagrees'); (F) *infrequently*, *irregularly*, and other negative forms, including *seldom* and *rarely*.
[**b**] *Regularly* can denote high frequency as well as 'at regular intervals'.

Time-frequency adjuncts and quantifiers

8.71 If the subject is generic (*cf* 5.26*ff*), many adjuncts of indefinite frequency, particularly when positioned at *I* or *M*, are equivalent to quantitative determiners (*cf* 5.14, 5.16) or pronouns (*cf* 6.45*ff*) in the noun phrase realizing the subject. For example, in:

Students play squash *often*. ['on many occasions']

often is included in the predication and refers to the frequency of the games of squash. However, the effect of either of the versions with sentence adjuncts:

{*Often* students / Students *often*} play squash. ['it often happens that . . .']

is very similar to:

Many students play squash.

Other examples where there is often loose equivalence:

Good novels are *always* worth buying.
~ *All* good novels are worth buying.
Policemen are *usually* unarmed in Britain.
~ *Most* policemen are unarmed in Britain.
Universities *often* have linguistics departments.
~ *Many* universities have linguistics departments.
A dog is *sometimes* a dangerous animal.
~ *Some* dogs are dangerous animals.

Students *occasionally* fail this course.
~ *A few* students fail this course.
Englishmen *rarely* talk to strangers in trains.
~ *Few* Englishmen talk to strangers in trains.
Officers {*almost never* / *very seldom*} get drunk while on duty.
~ *Almost no* officers get drunk while on duty.

If the direct object is generic, the adjunct may be roughly equivalent to a predeterminer or quantifier in the noun phrase realizing this direct object:

Our university *always* welcomes well-motivated students.
~ Our university welcomes *all* well-motivated students.
The most highly trained soldiers *often* guard government buildings.
~ The most highly trained soldiers guard *many* government buildings.
A good listener *seldom* makes enemies.
~ A good listener makes *few* enemies.

Note At least two of the above sentences have alternative interpretations to those given above:
Policemen are *usually* unarmed in Britain.
~ It is usual for policemen to be unarmed in Britain, but they are sometimes armed.
Englishmen *rarely* talk to strangers in trains.
~ On rare occasions Englishmen talk to strangers in trains.

Time-relationship adjuncts

8.72 Time adjuncts expressing a relationship between two time positions that are both being considered in an utterance are realized by forms that serve more than one function. In consequence, most of them have already been considered under other headings. There are three chief subclasses:

Group (a):

Many of these denote temporal sequence and are also used for time position (*cf* 8.55):
afterwards, before, eventually, finally, first, later, next, originally, previously, subsequently, then

For example:

Did she *first* see him when he was a child?
I've been considering what to do since he *last* discussed his problems with me.
She broke her leg *for the first time* while she was skiing in Switzerland.
These techniques were *originally* used in the Second World War.
It wasn't until the end of the party that I was *finally* introduced to her.

Group (b):

Many of these imply something of the concessive relation (*cf* 8.7):
(*even*) *by that time*, (*even*) *before that time*, (*even*) *up to that time*

For example:

We hadn't eaten (*even*) *by that time*.

Even now, we don't know where we are going to live.
I have *so far* bought two shirts and a pair of shoes.
They have finished their work *by now*.

Group (c):

Here the tendency is to compare one time with another:
again, once more, afresh

For example:

I feel better *again*.
Millicent is revising her book *once more*.
The carpet is still dirty so you'd better scrub it *afresh*.

Note On *already*, *still*, and the time relationships (notably Groups (b) and (c)) that are chiefly expressed by subjuncts, *cf* 8.97.

Relative positions of time adjuncts

8.73 In the preceding sections we have specified, as the occasion arose, the normal positions of time adjuncts in the various subclasses. We now take a summary glance at the relative positions of adjuncts from the three major subclasses that can cooccur at *E* position: time position (*cf* 8.55), time duration (*cf* 8.63), and time frequency (*cf* 8.64). These tend to occur in the order:

time duration [d] – time frequency [f] – time position [p]

The following sentences exemplify the normal order (but *cf* 8.87):

I was there *for a short while* [d] *every day or so* [f] *in January* [p].
He played for us *very frequently* [f] *last year* [p].
I'm paying my rent *monthly* [f] *this year* [p].
Our electricity was cut off *briefly* [d] *today* [p].
We'll discuss the matter *during lunch* [d] *tomorrow afternoon* [p].
He'll be staying here *for the summer* [d] *every year* [f].
He does exercises *for several hours* [d] *every weekend* [f].

Coordination

8.74 Time adjuncts in the same subclass can be coordinated:

TIME POSITION
today and tomorrow
now or later
before or after
in 1990 and (in) 1991
when we were there and afterwards

eg I'll be working *today and tomorrow*.

TIME DURATION
permanently or temporarily
during the summer and (during the) winter
for the week or (for the) month
(for) three weeks or (for) longer

eg She'll be staying here *for three weeks or longer*.

TIME FREQUENCY
once or twice
often and regularly
each day and (each) night
every Tuesday and (every) Thursday
a few times or many (times)

eg You should take exercise *often and regularly*.

Note *Now and then* and *now and again* are common coordinated expressions used for time frequency ('from time to time', 'occasionally'). Similarly, *again and again* and *over and over* are used to denote frequent repetition and not just one or two repetitions.

Time adjuncts and time reference

8.75 Time adjuncts play a part in specifying the time reference of the verb. Thus, it is the adjuncts that determine that the time reference in:

He is playing *now*.

is present, whereas in:

He is playing *tomorrow*.

it is future. Because of their temporal significance, some time adjuncts cannot cooccur with particular forms of the verb. Thus, *tomorrow* does not cooccur with the simple past:

*He played *tomorrow*.

and *yesterday* does not cooccur with the modal auxiliaries (unless they refer to past time, including their occurrence in a dependent clause with back-shift; *cf* 14.31):

*He {may / will / should} play *yesterday*.

By contrast, *cf*:

We couldn't leave town yesterday. ['We *were* not able . . .']
He may have played *yesterday*.
I told him he should play *yesterday*.

(*Cf* 4.11*ff*)

Note [**a**] An apparent exception to the need for harmony between tense and adjunct is with verbs of saying, arranging, expecting, or wanting where the object is concerned with a future event (*cf* 8.49, 8.76). In such cases, though the expressed verb is in the past (*ie* the past for the speaker), there may be a time adjunct with future reference (though this may already be past for the hearer), since the adjunct's reference is the object:

He called for a meeting *next week*. ['He called for a meeting to be held next week', where *next week* referred to future at the time when 'He called']
She wanted the book *tomorrow*. ['She wanted to have the book tomorrow']
They predicted a crisis *next month*. ['They predicted that there would be a crisis next month']

There can also be an adjunct with past reference that relates to the verb in the past (*cf* 8.76):

As far back as March, they predicted a crisis *in a month's time*. [*ie* 'Their prediction of a crisis next month was made as far back as March'; but here the sentence is equivocal as to whether the crisis was to come a month after the prediction or a month after the speaker of the sentence tells us about it]

Cf also 'They predicted a crisis *last month*', which could mean 'They predicted a crisis in what is now "last month".'

[**b**] Where an adjunct is functioning within a dependent clause, it need not of course have any relation to the tense of the verb in the main clause, though where the dependent clause is nonfinite there may appear to be a time-reference contradiction:

We arranged (yesterday) to go *tomorrow*.

With *forget*, we can have complementation with *-ing* informally, provided (i) there is a time-position adjunct referring to the past, and (ii) the action of the dependent clause was fulfilled:

I forgot meeting her *in 1980*. [*ie* 'I met her, but the meeting subsequently escaped my memory']

Contrast:

I forgot to meet her *in 1980*. [*ie* 'I did not meet her because I forgot that I had arranged to do so']

Condition (i) may be relaxed if the nonfinite verb phrase is perfective. Thus 'I forgot having met her' need have no past-time adjunct (*cf* 16.38*ff*).

Time adjuncts as subject- and object-related

8.76 Time adjuncts can cooccur with all verbs including BE:

It's much warmer { *now.* / *when the wind drops.* }

Many of them can also be used as subject-related adjuncts with BE when the subject is an eventive noun (*cf* 10.25):

TIME POSITION

The meeting will be *tomorrow*. [*ie* 'will take place']
Lunch will be *in ten minutes*.
I hope coffee is *soon*.

TIME DURATION

I'm afraid the noise will be *for the whole summer*. ['it will last for . . .']
The show is *from nine till twelve*.

TIME FREQUENCY

Interviews are *every hour*.
Guided tours around the museum are *twice a day*.
The next appointments will be *when the doctor returns from vacation*.

The verb BE in such cases (rather informal) is often equivalent to *take place*, and so:

The opera will be *tonight*.

is interpreted as 'The performance of the opera will take place tonight'.

The progressive is of course excluded when time adjuncts are used as subject-related adjuncts with BE (*cf* 8.42):

*Interviews are being *every hour*.

Contrast:

Interviews are { *taking place* / *being held* } *every hour*.

Some adverbials of time cannot be subject-related adjuncts; this applies, for example, to frequency adjuncts in (C), *eg*: *as a rule*, and in (D), *eg*: *always* (*cf* 8.64*f*).

We saw that with certain verbs the reference of the space adjunct may be to the place of the object rather than to that of the subject (*cf* 8.49). Similarly, the reference of the time adjunct may also be concerned with the object. We can sometimes express the relationship by a sentence in which the object of the original sentence is subject and the time adjunct is subject-related with BE. The effect is that of the predication with complex-transitive verbs (*cf* 16.43*ff*). There are two types of such references to the object:

(i) Where the verbs denote the placing or movement of the object, and a cooccurring space adjunct indicates the relevant resulting place, a time adjunct denotes duration; for example:

> They threw him in prison *for life*. ['He will be in prison for life']
> He's moving the family into a hotel *temporarily*. ['The family will be in a hotel temporarily']
> We're sending her to London *for the summer*. ['She will be in London for the summer']
> They left the car in the street *for an hour*. ['The car was in the street for an hour']

(ii) Where the verbs refer to saying, arranging, expecting, or wanting and the object has future reference, the time adjunct denotes time position, time duration, or time frequency; for example:

TIME POSITION

> He expected the guests *next week*. ['that the guests would be here next week']
> They arranged the meeting *for later today*. ['that the meeting would be held later today']
> He set the alarm *for seven o'clock*. ['so that the alarm would go off at seven o'clock']

TIME DURATION

> He predicts a state of tension *for a long time*. ['that there will be a state of tension for a long time']
> They offered us the house *for the summer*. ['(their offer was) that we could use the house for the summer', 'the offer of the house was for the summer']

TIME FREQUENCY

> They promised her a party *every Saturday night*. ['that she would have a party every Saturday night']
> I suggest an informal discussion *occasionally*. ['that there should be an informal discussion occasionally']

Note Where the time adjunct can also refer to the action of the verb, there may be ambiguity. For example, the sentence:

> They promised her a party *every Saturday night*.

can also mean that the promise was made every Saturday night. If the adjunct is moved from *E* position, interpretation of it as such a sentence adjunct would be the natural one:

> *Every Saturday night* they promised her a party.

Syntactic features of time adjuncts

8.77 Most time adjuncts have syntactic characteristics that are general to adjuncts. However, time-frequency adjuncts in 8.65 (C), *eg*: *usually*, *as a rule*, allow only the following: they can be the focus of a question, they can be the focus of negation, and they can come within the scope of predication pro-forms or predication ellipsis.

Most time adverbs cannot be premodified by *very* or take analogous modification (such as *so* . . ., *however*. . ., *more* . . . *than*). Time adjuncts allowing such modifications are;

TIME POSITION: *early*, *late*, *recently*
TIME DURATION: *long*, *briefly*, *recently*
TIME FREQUENCY: *commonly* (C), *constantly* (D), *incessantly* (D), *often*, *frequently* (E); several in Group (F): *infrequently*, *irregularly*, *little*, *occasionally*, *rarely*, *seldom*

Some adverbs that cannot be premodified by *very* can be premodified by other intensifiers; for example:

(very) much
somewhat
a((very) long) while
a lot ⟨informal⟩
} { *later* ['afterwards'] / *before* / *earlier* ['before'] }

Others in the same semantic group do not easily allow at least some of these intensifiers:

*(very) much
?somewhat
?a lot
?a little
} *previously*

*(very) much
*somewhat
?*a lot
?*a little
} *subsequently*

*very
(?)quite
} *usually* [but fully acceptable: *very unusually*]

But *cf* time subjuncts, 8.97*f*.

Note [**a**] With respect to ability to be focused by a cleft sentence, by *only*, or by *also*, some general statements can be made for frequency adjuncts in 8.65 (D), *eg*: *constantly*, (E), *eg*: *often*, and (F), *eg*: *occasionally*. None of the three groups allow focusing by *also*, (D) and (E) cannot be focused by *only*, and (D) cannot be focused by a cleft sentence. There are also individual differences within the groups and acceptability in a cleft sentence is often improved if the item is modified or the focal clause is interrogative or negative.

[**b**] *Again*, *last*, and *instantly* cannot be the focus of *only* or of a cleft sentence, and except *again*, none of them can be the focus of *also*.

[**c**] Naturally, time adjuncts with past reference cannot cooccur with imperatives. It is less obvious that time frequency adjuncts in subclass (C) (*cf* 8.65) do not idiomatically cooccur with imperatives, especially at *E*; they are more acceptable at *I*. For example:

?Stay in this hotel *usually*, when you're in London!
Normally cut the grass every week, please.

Moreover, although imperatives cooccur with adjuncts meaning 'now, immediately', near paraphrases implying a longer extent of present time seem odd with imperatives, unless these are negative:

Buy new clothes { *now.* / *immediately.* / *this moment.* }   ?Buy new clothes *at the present time.*

[but fully acceptable: 'Don't buy new clothes *at the present time*']

Process adjuncts

Realization

8.78 All four semantic types of process adjunct (*cf* 8.5) can be realized by prepositional phrases:

> She uttered the words *with cold deliberation*. [manner]
> She spoke *from notes*. [means]
> The speech was made audible *with an amplifying system*. [instrument]
> It was heard *by millions*. [agentive]

Manner and means adjuncts can be realized by noun phrases though these are usually expandable to constitute prepositional phrases, so as to make it natural to regard the noun phrase as having an omitted preposition:

> They were walking *single file* through the wood. ['*in* single file']
> I'd like to send this parcel *air mail*. ['*by* air mail']

Manner adjuncts especially, and those of means and instrument to some extent, are also realized by adverb phrases:

> He glanced at her (*very*) *lovingly*. [manner]
> Some patients ask to be treated *homoeopathically*. [means, 'by homoeopathic medicine']
> She was examining a fossil *microscopically*. [instrument, 'with a microscope']

Finally, manner adjuncts can be expressed by clauses (*cf* 15.17*ff*), though the forms concerned strongly imply comparison as distinct from a direct reference to manner or mode of action:

> I try to cook vegetables *as the Chinese do*. ['in the Chinese way']

All process adjuncts are normally predicational. When fronted, the adverbial concerned tends to become a subject-oriented subjunct (*cf* 8.92), no longer corresponding to an inquiry 'How . . .?', 'In what way . . .?' Compare:

> She replied to the listeners' questions *obligingly*/*courteously*. ['in an obliging/courteous manner']
>
> {*Obligingly*, / *Courteously*,} she replied to the listeners' questions.
>
> ['She was obliging/courteous enough to reply . . .' Less claim is made that her *replies* were obliging or courteous]

Adjuncts of means or instrument, however, can be sentence adjuncts, especially when their reference is specific rather than generic and when there is adequate alternative complementation in the clause. Compare:

> He chopped the parsley *with a knife*. [predication adjunct]
> *With a knife like that*, you couldn't cut through this salami. [sentence adjunct]

Note [**a**] Although noun phrases as process adjuncts can be regarded as elliptical prepositional phrases (as with space adjuncts, 'jump (*over*) *a fence*'), they are apprehended in part as direct objects by virtue of their noun-phrase form. Hence, they may have a corresponding passive. Compare:

He's travelling *a different route* to Minneapolis ['*by* a different route', which is spatial ('along . . .') as well as process].

It is a route that has not been travelled before by car.

Has this particular route been travelled before?

[**b**] On common pro-forms for process adjuncts (*eg*: (*in*) *that way, like that, thus*, etc), *cf* 19.47. The form *thus* is largely formal, and as well as being a process adjunct pro-form it operates as a conjunct. In the latter role it tends to be at *M* and the reference is anaphoric; in the former it tends to be at *E*, especially if the reference is cataphoric:

She *thus* addressed herself to their problems. [='As you see from what has preceded': conjunct]

She addressed herself to their problems *thus*. [='in the following way': process adjunct]

(*Cf* 8.144).

Manner adjuncts

8.79 EXAMPLES OF THE USE OF MANNER ADJUNCTS:

She spoke to him *coldly*.

They sprayed tear gas *indiscriminately* on the protesters.

They were *categorically* told that no more oil would come from the wreck.

My little boy loves dressing up *cowboy-style*.

They are deluded if they think *otherwise*.

His influence showed itself *more obviously* in the choice of the furniture and curtains.

They began arguing *loudly*.

He failed to question the witness *thoroughly*.

She repaired the house *like an expert*.

He spoke *in a way that reminded me of his father*.

They played the game (*in*) *a different way*.

She dances (*in*) *the same way as I do*.

They cook ((*in*) *the*) *French style*.

He always writes *in a carefree manner*.

You should write *as I tell you to*.

Noun phrases with *way*, *manner*, and *style* as head tend to have the definite article:

She cooks chicken { *the way I like.* / *in* { *the* / *a* } *way I like.* }

An adverb manner adjunct can usually be paraphrased by *in a . . . manner* or *in a . . . way* with its adjective base in the vacant position. Where an adverb form exists, it is usually preferred over such a corresponding cognate prepositional phrase with *manner* or *way*. Hence:

He always writes *carelessly*.

is more usual than:

He always writes *in a careless* { *manner.* / *way.* }

But the latter, periphrastic form is preferred where the adjunct requires modification. Successive *-ly* adverbs are avoided, partly for stylistic reasons and partly because a sequence of adverbs leads one to expect the first to be a modifier of the second (as in 'He runs incredibly carelessly'). Thus, for the former reason, we would not say:

?He always writes *deliberately carelessly*. [but rather: 'in a deliberately careless way']

and for the latter reason, we would tend to avoid:

He spoke *stupidly frequently*. [but rather 'He *frequently* spoke *stupidly*'; if we meant 'He spoke *with stupid frequency*', this would again be preferable to the succession of adverbs]

Other examples of adverbs replaced by alternative forms of cognate adjunct:

He prayed { *fervently*. / *with profound but dignified fervour*. }

She spoke { *animatedly*. / *with (a) youthful animation*. }

(*Cf* 5.58).

In careful usage, clausal adjuncts with *as* are sharply distinguished from semantically equivalent phrasal adjuncts with *like*:

Please try to write { *as I do*. / *like me*. }

But informally (and especially in AmE), *like* is often used as a conjunction and one has:

Please try to write *like I do*.

Adverbs as manner adjuncts can sometimes serve as the response to a *How*-question:

A: *How* was your little boy dressed up that so amused the policeman?
B: Oh, *cowboy-style*.

But other units as manner adjuncts can more easily serve as responses:

A: *How* does she dance?	B: *The same way as I do*.
A: *How* should I write to him?	B: *As a friend would write*.
A: *How* do they prefer to cook?	B: *In the French style*.

It should be noted however that *How*-questions usually elicit means or instrument adjuncts (*cf* 8.80):

A: *How* did he clean his room? B: { ?**Carefully*. / *With a vacuum cleaner*. }

It is because *how* is only rarely expected to elicit a manner adjunct that we can have a joke like the following where the reply evades in supposed innocence a difficult question:

Teacher: Now, Henry, how does a quartz watch work?
Henry: Oh, marvellously!

Note On the formation of manner adverbs, *cf* App I.41.

Means, instrument, and agent adjuncts

8.80 EXAMPLES OF THE USE OF MEANS ADJUNCTS:

These linguistic units were separated *intonationally*.
He decided to treat the patient *surgically*.
I go to school *by car*.

(On the use of the zero article in such examples as the last, *cf* 5.45.)

He gained entry into the building *by means of a bribe to the guard*.
You can best influence them *by your own example*.
You can stop the machine *by pressing this button*.
We are travelling to Washington (*by*) *first class*.
Fly *Air India/by Air India/with Air India*.

EXAMPLES OF THE USE OF INSTRUMENT ADJUNCTS:

He examined the specimen *microscopically*. [='with a microscope']
You can cut the bread *with that knife/*by that knife*.
He was killed *with a bullet*.

EXAMPLES OF THE USE OF AGENTIVE ADJUNCTS:

He was killed *by a terrorist/*with a terrorist*.
The royal wedding was seen *by millions* on television.
Her speech could not be heard *by those sitting at the back*.

On the distinction between means and instrument, *cf* 8.5.

Most of the adverbs that can realize means and instrument adjuncts can also function as manner adjuncts; in consequence, there is some danger of misunderstanding, as with:

He examined the specimen *microscopically*.

Since the instrumental meaning ('with a microscope') would entail the manner meaning ('in great detail'), and since the latter might involve the former, it is not easy to ensure that the addressee understands the precisely intended adjunct. Unless it has been previously established in the context, it may be necessary to ensure clarity by expressing instrumentality by a prepositional phrase, and manner by implementing the gradability which manner (but not instrument) permits: '. . . quite microscopically'.

The examples of instrument and agent adjuncts illustrate the point of intersection between these categories. When accompanying the passive, instrument can often be expressed by *with* + NP or *by* + NP (the latter reflecting a corresponding active, as in *A bullet killed him*) but the agentive adjunct cannot be expressed by *with* + NP. See further 3.65f.

Means adjuncts are generally elicited by *how*-questions, instrument by *how* or *what . . . with*:

Means:

A: *How* are you flying to Europe?
B: (*By*) *British Airways*.

Instrument:

How shall we prop the door open?
What shall we prop the door open *with*?

Agent adjuncts can be elicited by *who/what* + active or (less usually, except in a context where the passive has already been used) by *who(m)/what* + passive + *by* or *by whom/what* + passive:

A: Who killed him?
B: He seems to have been killed *by a terrorist*.
A: You say she was cheated: { who (was she cheated) by? / by whom (was she cheated)? ⟨formal⟩ }
B: (*By*) *her own brother*, apparently.

Semantic blends

8.81 Some adjuncts express a blend of manner with some other relation:

(i) MANNER WITH RESULT, AND SOMETIMES INTENSIFICATION

She fixed it *perfectly*. ['in such a way that it was perfect' – manner and result]
He grows chrysanthemums *marvellously*. ['in such a way that the results are good' – manner and result]
The soldiers wounded him *badly*. ['in such a way and to such an extent that it resulted in his being in a bad condition' – manner, intensifier, and result]

(ii) MANNER WITH TIME DURATION

He's walking *slowly*. ['in a way that will prolong the time']

He stopped the car *suddenly*.
She gave me an answer *rapidly*. } ['in such a way that it took a very short time']

They broke the news to him *gradually*. ['in such a way that it was spread over a period of time']

Such items are likely to be solely time adjuncts when they appear in *I* or *M* positions:

Suddenly, he stopped the car.
Suddenly I felt free again.
Suddenly, it was night. } ['In an instant, . . .']

She *rapidly* gave me an answer. ['She soon . . .']
My brother *quickly* came to despise his school. ['soon']
We *gradually* appreciated his contribution to society. ['We gradually came to appreciate']

Noun phrases and prepositional phrases that seem at first sight to be equivalent to adverbs may be less flexible than the adverbs in this respect:

All of a sudden, I felt free again. ['it suddenly happened']
?He stopped the car *all of a sudden*. [queried in the sense 'in a way that took a very short time']
It is now going *at a fast rate*. ['very quickly']

**At a fast rate*,
Very quickly, } my brother came to despise his school.

We note that *very quickly* here means 'in a short space of time', a meaning that cannot be attributed to 'at a fast rate'.

(iii) AGENT WITH RESPECT OR SPACE

Their house was destroyed *by/in an earthquake*.
She couldn't be heard *by/in the back rows of the auditorium*.

The *in*-variant in each case makes possible a lack of direct agency: 'in floods consequent upon the earthquake', 'by a test microphone in the (empty) back rows' (*cf* also 8.80).

Note There are some adverbials with semantic blending where the 'process' admixture is rather vague but where manner, means, space, and respect seem to be involved:

He announced the agreement *publicly*. [in part = 'by means of a public statement', in part = 'openly'; *cf* also *secretly*, *privately*, and 8.55 Note [d]]
They approved the contract *generally* [or *in general*], but objected to a few clauses.
She directed the work *personally* [or *in person*].
'It's empty,' he announced *superfluously*.
These proposals come *strangely* from someone in his position.
He bought it *cheaply*.

In the last example, *cheaply* is regarded by some as a hypercorrection and is often replaced by the adjective form *cheap* (*cf* 7.9).

Cooccurrence restrictions on process adjuncts

8.82 Adverbials that function only as process adjuncts cannot cooccur with verbs in stative use:

He likes them } { **skilfully*.
He owns it } { **awkwardly*.

Nor can process adjuncts be used as adverbials with copular verbs:

He is a teacher }
They seem happy } { **skilfully*. / **awkwardly*.
She looks angry }

Of course, if the meaning is 'deliberate imitation', the verb's use is nonstative, and we then have fully acceptable sentences like 'She looks angry *skilfully*'.

The different types of process adjunct can cooccur with each other; for example:

He *frugally* travelled *economy* (*class*). [manner + means]
He travels *economy* (*class*) *by air* but *first* (*class*) *by train*. [means + instrument]
She was *accidentally* struck *with a racket by her partner*. [manner + instrument + agent]

Syntactic features of process adjuncts

8.83 Process adjuncts can be contrasted with one another in alternative interrogation and negation and can come within the scope of predication pro-forms or predication ellipsis. They can be the focus of *also* and of *only*. Normally, when manner adjuncts are realized by adverbs, they cannot be the focus of a cleft sentence (*cf* 8.25), but their acceptability is increased if they are modified or if the focal clause is interrogative or negative:

*It was *categorically* that they were told that no more oil would come from the wreck.

?Was it *categorically* that they were told that no more oil would come from the wreck?
?It's *in the French style* that they cook.
It isn't *in the French style* that they cook.
??It was {*violently* / *loudly*} that they argued.

(?)It was *so very* {*violently* / *loudly*} that they argued.

It was *with the utmost care/precision/caution* that the last girder was laid in place.

On the other hand, means, instrument, and agent adjuncts can readily become the focus of a cleft sentence, even as realized by single adverbs (though less idiomatically in these circumstances):

It was *with a bullet* that he was killed.
It was *by a terrorist* that he was killed.
It was *intonationally* that these linguistic units were separated.
It was *surgically* that he treated the patient.

Adverbs that are manner adjuncts can be the focus of clause comparison (as in 'She writes more clearly than I do') and can be premodified by *however*, *how*, and *so* (as in 'How cautiously he drives'). Adverbs expressing means or instrument do not allow these features, since they cannot of course be modified at all, derived as they are from nongradable adjectives (*cf* App I.41).

Positions of process adjuncts

8.84 Process adjuncts are usually placed at *E*, since they usually receive the information focus. Indeed, no other position is likely if the process adjunct is obligatory for the verb:

{ They live *frugally*.
{ *They *frugally* live.

{ They treated his friend *badly*.
{ *They *badly* treated his friend.

Since the passive is often used when the need is felt to focus attention on the verb, process adjuncts are commonly placed in *eM* rather than in *E* when the verb is in the passive:

Discussions have been *tentatively* begun (and it is hoped that they will be fruitful).
Tear gas was *indiscriminately* sprayed on the protesters.

Contrast also:

{ He put the point *well*.
{ *He *well* put the point. [but *cf* 'As he *well* knows']

{ The point was put *well*.
{ The point was *well* put.

However, *eM* is odd for means and instrument adverbials even in the passive, presumably because they have a higher priority for information focus than does the accompanying verb:

?These linguistic units should be *intonationally* separated.
?The specimen was *microscopically* examined. ['with a microscope']

The latter example would not of course be queried if the adjunct were manner [='meticulously'].

On process adverbials at *I*, *cf* 8.78.

Adjuncts of respect

8.85 Just as we saw that respect as a semantic category (*cf* 8.6) was parasitic on associated categories, so respect adjuncts show their parasitic character in being realized formally by expressions whose primary function is to realize other classes of adjunct. The point is illustrated by *formally* in the preceding sentence. Compare:

They are realized *formally*. [respect: 'so far as form is concerned']
He greeted the bishop *formally*. [manner: 'in a way that respected proprieties of form']

Not surprisingly in view of this, there is no category-specific question form that elicits adjuncts of respect. Besides nongradable adverbs, various types of prepositional phrase are used for respect adjuncts, some of them lexically specific (for example, *with reference to N*, *in/with respect to N*, *on the matter of N*), others based upon spatial phrases, especially those relating to 'position' and 'source':

She's advising them { *legally.* / *on legal issues.* / *with respect to law.* / *from a legal standpoint.* / *about matters of law.* }

Adjectives take complements of respect with phrases introduced by such common and polysemous prepositions as *of*, *at*, *on*:

They are { fond/frightened . . . *of cats.* / good/skilled . . . *at drawing.* / keen/adamant . . . *on moral standards.* }

(*Cf* 9.57, 16.68*ff*).

Adjuncts of respect are normally predicational (and hence tend to be placed at *E*), but it should be noted that respect is often expressed by means of subjuncts and disjuncts; *cf* 8.88, 8.124.

Note [**a**] Some verbs may take O_d or an adjunct of respect with little difference in meaning:

Having seen this sample, you may { judge / judge of } the remainder.

['assess or form an opinion about']

[**b**] Rather formal titles of essays and the like may comprise prepositional phrases relating to respect:

Of dreams and their significance. <archaic>
On (the question of) Disarmament.
In Pursuit of Happiness.

Adjuncts of contingency

8.86 Of the contingency relationships that are expressed by adjuncts (as distinct from disjuncts: *cf* 8.132), reason and the semantic correlate purpose are outstanding. Significantly, the same question forms are used to elicit either of these adjunct types:

A: { *Why* did he do it? / *What* did he do it *for*? B: { *Because he was angry*. [reason] / *To relieve his anger*. [purpose]

It is rare to find either reason or purpose adjuncts realized by adverbs (but see Note [a] below). Prepositional phrases introduced by *because of*, *on account of*, etc are common for cause adjuncts; for example:

She returned home early *because of his insistence*.
They want a better job *on account of their high mortgage payments*.
He did it *for his son*.
They've both stopped smoking *for fear of heart disease*.
She performed a recital *out of charity*.
There were several deaths *from malnutrition*.

Prepositional phrases expressing purpose adjuncts are chiefly introduced by *for*, indicating the relation not only to reason but to goal (*ie* space):

How many actors will you need *for this production*?
He set a trap *for the intruding fox*.
She's applying *for a better job*.
They attacked the police *as a protest*.

Clauses also realize these types of adjunct. For cause, there are finite clauses introduced by *because* (*cf* 15.21) and (especially informally) nonfinite clauses introduced by *with*:

She returned home early *because he insisted*.
With him being so bad-tempered, I was reluctant to tell him of the car accident.

The latter are resistant to adjunct criteria, and are more usually realized as disjuncts; *cf* 8.132. For purpose (*cf* 15.48), the commonest type of clause is the nonfinite (infinitive) type, as in:

They need a bigger apartment *to accommodate their elderly parents*.
She has gone alone to her room *so as to study for her exams*.
In order to stop the machine, press the red button.
The police stopped the traffic *for me to get across the street*.

Finite clauses are more formal:

The chairman hurried the meeting *in order that it might end before dark*.
One member had been suggesting an adjournment of the meeting *so that matters need not be hastened*.

But the finite purpose clause introduced by *so* alone is rather informal:

He's getting a new car *so he can impress his mother-in-law.*

By contrast, the clause introduced by *that* alone is exceptionally formal:

He died *that others might live.*

Equally formal (as well as rather archaic) is the negative purpose clause with *lest*:

The animals must be destroyed *lest the disease* (*should*) *spread.*

(*Cf* 3.61). In BrE, there is an informal alternative:

The animals must be destroyed *in case the disease spreads.*

On the mood in finite purpose clauses, *cf* 15.48. One further contingency relation is expressed by the adjunct, and that is concession when realized by prepositional phrases introduced by *in spite of* and *despite*. For example:

He won the race {*in spite of* / *despite*} *his injured leg.*

Except where they are obligatory (as in *He lived for his work*), adjuncts of cause, purpose, and concession tend to be sentential rather than predicational. Moreover, though more commonly at *E*, this is largely a matter of where information focus is required. They can equally well be placed at *I* and even (though less usually) at *M*:

On account of their high mortgage payments, they want a better job.
One member had, *so that matters need not be hastened,* been suggesting an adjournment of the meeting.

Note [**a**] In the following sentences the adverbs could be regarded as purpose adjuncts:

They were *symbolically* burying a new car in protest against pollution. ['for symbolic purposes']
The teacher addressed the students by their first names *experimentally*. ['for experimental purposes']

[**b**] Clauses of cause or reason introduced by *since* and *as* are disjuncts: *cf* 8.124, 8.132.

Relative positions of adjuncts

8.87 In the relevant sections, we have given indications of the norms of position in respect of each class of adjunct. We turn now to consider the positions of adjunct classes in respect of each other. Two general principles can be stated, applying to relative order whether within a class or between classes:

(i) The relative order, especially of sentence adjuncts, can be changed to suit the demands of information focus; *cf* 18.9*ff*.

(ii) Shorter adjuncts tend to precede longer ones, and in practice this often means that adverbs precede noun phrases, which precede prepositional phrases, which precede nonfinite clauses, which precede finite clauses.

Subject to these general principles, where adjuncts cluster in *E* position, the normal order is:

respect – process – space – time – contingency

It would be highly unusual to find all such five at *E* (or indeed all such five in the same clause), but for the purposes of exemplification we might offer the improbable and stylistically objectional (*cf* 8.20):

> John was working *on his hobby* [respect] *with the new shears* [process] *in the rose garden* [place] *for the whole of his day off* [time] *to complete the season's pruning* [contingency].

The same point could be made more acceptably (but at greater length) by forming a series of sentences, each with any two of these adjuncts.

Adjuncts that can occur at *I* are usually those that *either* have relatively little information value in the context (*eg* in reflecting what can be taken for granted) *or* are relatively inclusive or 'scene-setting' in their semantic role (*eg* an adjunct of time). Thus:

> *That whole morning*, he devoted himself to his roses.

Not only is the adjunct at *I* one of time, but the anaphoric *that* indicates that the period concerned has already been mentioned. It is unusual to have more than one adjunct at *I* except where one is realized by a pro-form (especially *then*), but they would tend to be in the reverse order to that observed at *E*. In practice, this usually means:

> space – time *or* process – time

For example:

> *In America* [A_1], *after the election* [A_2], trade began to improve.
> *Slowly* [A_1] *during this period* [A_2] people were becoming more prosperous.

Subjuncts

8.88 We apply the term SUBJUNCTS to adverbials which have, to a greater or lesser degree, a subordinate role (see below) in comparison with other clause elements. This is made manifest by the fact that they cannot usually be treated grammatically in any of the four ways stated in 8.25 as being applicable to adjuncts. Let us consider the matter in respect of two very different subjuncts, *visually* as in [1] and *fairly* as in [2]:

> This play presents *visually* a sharp challenge to a discerning audience. [1]
> He *fairly* SPRÀNG at her with his questions. ⟨esp BrE⟩ [2]

Notice that for the subjunct reading we must understand *visually* as operating in the semantic role of respect (*cf* 8.6), 'as a visual experience'. The same adverb in a different sentence might be grammatically an adjunct, operating in the semantic role of process (means, *cf* 8.5), 'with his eyes (alone)':

> He studied the play *visually* (but scarcely listened to a word). [3]

Likewise we must understand the subjunct *fairly* in [2] as having the semantic role of modality (*cf* 8.8), 'it is no exaggeration to say', though the same adverb can also be grammatically an adjunct in the semantic role of process (manner, *cf* 8.5), 'in a just and impartial way':

He questioned her (*quite*) *fairly*. [4]

If we now attempt the processes of 8.25 with [1] and [2], we either move away from the subjunct to the adjunct reading or produce an incomprehensible sequence:

It is *visually* that this play achieves a sharp challenge . . .
Does this play achieve a sharp challenge . . . *visually* or . . . ?
This play achieves *only visually* a sharp challenge . . .
How did this play achieve a sharp challenge . . . ?
[Perhaps, however, 'From what point of view . . . ?]
*It was *fairly* that he sprang at her . . .
*Did he spring at her *fairly* or . . . ?
*He *only fairly* sprang at her . . .
*[*How* did he spring at her . . . ?] **Fairly*.

The 'subordinate role' to which we referred at the beginning of this section may apply to the whole clause in which the subjunct operates: this is what appears as 'wide orientation' in *Fig* 8.88. Alternatively, the subjunct may be subordinated to an individual clause element (usually the S) or even to an item forming part of a clause element (the V): this is what appears as 'narrow orientation' in *Fig* 8.88, where the relationships of the subjunct class are shown in some detail.

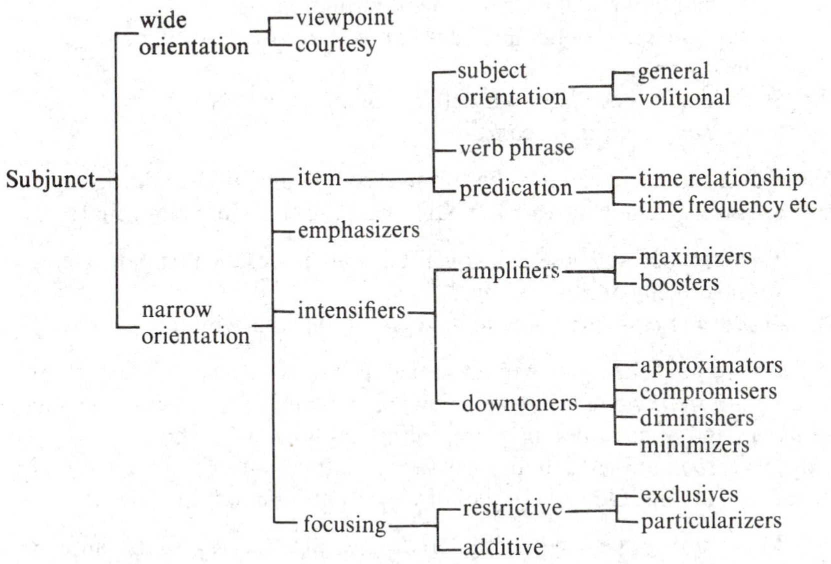

Fig 8.88

It is doubtless easier to appreciate the subordinateness of the role in relation to the subjuncts of narrow orientation. Some paraphrases for those of wide orientation (such as 'from a visual point of view') seem rather to raise the items so as to be superordinate to the other sentence elements; and they can even seem to have the scope of disjuncts (*cf* 8.121*ff*). In fact, however, even subjuncts of wide orientation typically relate specifically to an individual element or even to a constituent of an element, and alternative paraphrases can demonstrate this:

Visually, a film should present experience of a kind not assimilable by the ears alone.
~ A film should be a *visual* presentation of experience . . .
Economically, a nation can be bankrupt while still flourishing *intellectually*.
~ An *economically* bankrupt nation may still be an *intellectually* flourishing one.

Wide orientation

Viewpoint subjuncts

8.89 Viewpoint subjuncts can be roughly paraphrased by 'if we consider what we are saying from an [adjective] point of view' or 'if we consider what we are saying from the point of view of [noun phrase]'.

Adverbs realizing viewpoint subjuncts are most commonly derived from adjectives by the addition of an *-ly* suffix. Examples are:

Architecturally, it is a magnificent conception.
Morally, *politically*, and *economically*, it is urgent that the government should act more effectively on aid to developing countries.
Geographically, *ethnically*, and *linguistically*, these islands are closer to the mainland than to their neighbouring islands.
To tap a private telephone line is not *technically* a very difficult operation.
It could have been a serious defeat, not only *militarily* but *psychologically* and *politically*.

Viewpoint subjuncts can also be formed from nouns by the addition of the suffix *-wise* (especially in AmE), though these are considered informal:

Program-wise, the new thing on TV last night was the first part of a new Galsworthy dramatization.
Weatherwise, we are going to have a bad time this winter.

All *-ly* adverbs realizing viewpoint subjuncts have a corresponding participle clause with *speaking* that is also a viewpoint subjunct, *eg*: *visually* ~ *visually speaking*, and a corresponding prepositional phrase with the frame *from a* [adjective] *point of view* that also has the same function, *eg*: *morally* ~ *from a moral point of view*. Other examples of viewpoint subjuncts include:

Many of these people have suffered, *economically speaking*, because of their political affiliations.
He has done better *from a personal point of view* than any other executive in the firm.
They behave *with respect to their morals* as they always have done.

As far as mathematics is concerned, he was a complete failure.
Looked at politically, it was not an easy problem.
If we consider the financial position, the country is going to have a bad year.

Viewpoint subjuncts, whatever their structure, tend to be put in *I* position. As distinct from when they are used as process adjuncts, adverbs functioning as viewpoint subjuncts are nongradable. Hence they do not accept clause comparison or the modification possible for many adjuncts (*cf* 8.88):

**Very economically* (*speaking*), these people have suffered a great deal.

Note [**a**] The corresponding clause with *speaking* resembles one of the correspondences for speech-related disjuncts (*cf* 8.124). However, the other correspondences for such disjuncts do not constitute correspondences for viewpoint subjuncts. For example, *to speak morally* (*ie* 'not immorally') does not correspond to the viewpoint subjuncts *morally* and *morally speaking* (*ie* 'from the standpoint of morals').

[**b**] Most viewpoint subjuncts in *-wise* are written without hyphens as single words, unless they are in 'nonce' usage; *cf* App I.41.

Courtesy subjuncts

8.90 Courtesy subjuncts are chiefly realized by a small group of adverbs used in rather formulaic expressions of politeness and propriety. The most common are exemplified below:

He *kindly* offered me a ride.
We *cordially* invite you to our party.
She announced that she will *graciously* consent to our request.
Take a seat *please*.
Will you *kindly* address a few words to the new students? [*ie* 'be kind enough to . . .']

(On the comparably formulaic use of adjectives, *cf* 17.97.) This is clearly distinct from the normal adjunct of manner, as in:

She spoke *kindly* to the new students.
He offered me a ride *kindly*. ['He offered me a ride and he did so *kindly*']

Needless to say, however, it would be expected that if the subject was kind in undertaking an action he would perform the action in a kind manner as well. Greater distinction in role can be seen with such courtesy subjuncts in requests with question form:

Will you *kindly* take your seats?

Here the meaning can only be 'Will you be so kind (*ie* agreeable) as to take your seats?' (since one could hardly *sit* in a kind manner). So too in asking:

Will she *graciously* consent to his request?

one is asking if she will be gracious and not if she will do something in a gracious fashion.

The commonest courtesy subjunct, *please*, is irregular in form and irregular also in not having a corresponding adjunct function: no function, that is, other than this present formulaic one (*cf* 8.91).

Courtesy subjuncts differ from adjuncts having the same form in that they are restricted to (*e*)*M* position except in imperative clauses, where the two that are commonest in such utterances differ from each other. With *kindly*, *I* is then obligatory (but *cf* 8.20 Note [b]):

Kindly leave the room.
*Leave the room, *kindly*.

Kindly don't make a noise.
*Don't *kindly* make a noise.

With *please*, *I* is usual but *eM* is possible for some speakers; *iE* is by no means unusual, and *E* is quite common:

Please leave the room.
Leave the room, *please*.
Please don't make a noise.
(?)Don't *please* make a noise.
Write on this form, *please*, your full address.
Don't make a noise, *please*.

Courtesy subjuncts require the active subject or the passive agent (whether present or implied) to be of personal reference. When courtesy subjuncts appear in questions, the questions constitute a request. There are therefore restrictions on the person of the subject in questions; it is normally first for *cordially*, *humbly*; and second or third for *kindly* and *graciously*. Consider the following rather ceremonious examples:

May we *cordially* invite you to our party?
May I *humbly* offer my apologies?
Will you *kindly* take a seat?
Will you *graciously* consent to our request?
Will passengers *kindly* refrain from smoking?

Please, however, allows all persons:

May I *please* explain my reasons?

Could {you / Mr Brandt} *please* move to one side?

Both *kindly* and *cordially* (but not *please*) commonly cooccur with the passive in formally official usage:

Passengers are *kindly* requested to refrain from smoking.
Members of the public are *cordially* invited to submit their views on the project.

8.91 Courtesy subjuncts do not usually carry a nucleus or occupy a separate tone unit:

Kindly help yourSÈLF|
?*KÌNDly help yourself|
*KĬNDly| help yourSÈLF|

A form such as:

KÌNDly be quiet|

would suggest both irritation and a repetition of a more normally uttered request. Again, however, *please* is exceptional, and this subjunct frequently has a tone unit to itself, especially in final position with a rising tone. There is a discourse contrast between the following:

Help yourSÈLF please|
Help yourSÈLF|PLÉASE|

The former is more casual, the speaker taking for granted the courtesy subjunct; in the latter, the speaker seeks more deliberately (as perhaps with people he does not know so well) to emphasize the courtesy. But as the sole carrier of intonation nucleus, the courtesy subjunct conveys not merely emphasis but some urgency, insistence, or annoyance:

PLÈASE be quiet| Be quiet PLÈASE|

Kindly and *please* are the only courtesy subjuncts to appear freely with imperatives, though *graciously* occasionally does so too (in very ceremonious usage):

Graciously accept this gift from your admirers.

Indeed, unlike the other courtesy subjuncts, *please* is generally confined to imperatives or to sentences constituting a request or containing a reported one:

Will you *please* leave the room? ⟨rather coldly formal⟩
You will *please* leave the room. ⟨admonitory⟩
I wonder whether you would mind leaving the room *please*. ⟨polite⟩
I asked him whether he would *please* leave the room.
*He *please* left the room.
A box of matches, *please*.
May I *please* have my book back?

Please and (to a lesser extent) *kindly* are very commonly used to tone down the abruptness of a command.

With the exception of *please*, courtesy subjuncts can be modified by *very*. However, *kindly* cannot usually be so modified in questions and requests (whether or not these are grammatically imperatives). Compare:

He *very kindly* offered me a seat.
**Very kindly* take a seat.
?Will you *very kindly* take a seat?
Kindly take a seat.
?You will *very kindly* leave the room.

The queried examples above are perhaps possible when they are said in a tone of exasperation.

With *please* must be contrasted the courtesy formula *thank you* and its more informal variant *thanks* (the form with subject, *I must thank you for . . .*, *I thank you*, is capable of being a main clause but as such the latter is used as a courtesy marker only facetiously). These are normally at *E* (except as disjuncts of the form *thanks to X*, which can be at *I*, *M*, or *E*; *cf* 8.127*ff*), unless they are operating as verbless clauses (*cf* 15.58*ff*). In either case they normally carry a nucleus. For example:

A: Let me show you the WÀY|
B: Oh I can manage aLÒNE| { THÁNKS| / THÁNK you| }

Though normally opposites, *please* and *thank you* can be alternative ways of responding gratefully (normally to something that is being accepted):

A: Will you have another glass?

B: { (Oh) YÈS, { PLÉASE| / THÁNKS/THÁNK you| } [a falling tone on *please*, *thanks*, and *thank you* (often without *yes*) would show added enthusiasm]
(Oh) NÒ, { *please| / THÁNKS/THÁNK you| } [*No* THÀNKS or *No* THÀNK *you* would be so emphatic as to sound rude] }

But while the response *please* alone can pass for 'yes please', *thanks*/*thank you* cannot be used alone to mean 'no thank you'.

Note [a] The subjunct *please* is sharply different from the other items discussed above because of course it still retains some connection with the impersonal verb phrase ('it pleases N') from which it is historically derived and which is reflected in more formal expansions:

Come this way, *if you please*. [where *you* is historically the object]

I shall now call my last witness, *if it please your Lordship*. ⟨BrE: law court usage⟩

In this latter example, the third person 'your Lordship' is of course a very formal and largely archaic way of indicating respect for a person addressed. But true 3rd-person involvement with *please* still occurs as a brief prayer in fervent wishes:

The war will be over soon, *please God*. [= 'if it pleases God [to end the war]']

[b] English differs from several other languages (such as German and Russian) in not using the same courtesy subjunct to accompany both requests and acknowledgements of thanks. For the latter in English, we have *not at all*, *don't mention it*, *you're welcome* ⟨esp AmE⟩, (*it's*) *my pleasure*, and some variants of these. Thus:

A: Here is the book you lost.
B: Oh thank you very much.
A: { *Please. / Not at all. }

Again unlike many other languages, English lacks an institutionalized courtesy item for use in offering. It is difficult to make *HÈRE you ÁRE* sound courteous, and impossible to make it sound formal.

[c] Compare also the adverbs used in epistolary formulas:

Yours followed by *faithfully*, *sincerely*, *truly*, or *ever* ⟨esp BrE⟩

Cordially, *Sincerely*, *Truly* followed by *yours* ⟨esp AmE⟩

We also find *Yours* alone as well as (especially in informal use) *Sincerely* or *Affectionately* without *Yours*.

Narrow orientation

Item subjuncts

Subject-orientation

8.92 We saw in 8.88 that a subjunct might be in a sense subordinate to an element in clause structure or even to a constituent of the phrase or clause realizing an element. These subjuncts we call ITEM subjuncts.

If we move a sentence adjunct from *E* position to *I* or *M*, we can do more than allow another element to be highlighted by end-focus (*cf* 18.9). We may appear to narrow the application of the adverbial from the sentence as a whole so that it now seems to have a special relation with the subject. This is particularly true with process adverbials of the manner subclass (*cf* 8.5). Compare [1] where *casually* is such an adverbial, functioning as a sentence adjunct, with [2] where the function has been narrowed to subjunct status:

Leslie greeted the stranger *casually*. ['in a casual offhand manner', his *greeting* was casual] [1]

Casually, Leslie greeted the stranger. ['Leslie was casual, offhand, when he greeted the stranger'] [2]

That the relations of the adverbial in [1] and [2] are different is demonstrated not merely by the plausibility of the different glosses but by the fact that we can retain the item at *I* and also include a sentence adjunct of the same semantic value as that in [1] (though paraphrasing it, to avoid unwanted stylistic complications) without undue tautology:

Casually, Leslie greeted the stranger *in an offhand way*. [3]

Of course, such a combination as in [3] is unusual for the simple reason that to some extent [2] presupposes [1] and [1] presupposes [2]: it is natural for us to expect that in making a casual greeting the person doing so was casual. But it is by no means necessary for the two to go together.

A more convincing demonstration that the adverbials in [1] and [2] function differently, therefore, is provided if we polarize them semantically and show that we do so without seeming to be contradictory. If we imagine Leslie doing an action while studiously trying to show that he feels otherwise than his action implies, we have:

Carefully, Leslie greeted the stranger { *casually*. / *in an offhand way*. } [4]

To assume subject-orientation, an adverbial must be derived from an adjective that can be predicated of the subject concerned. Thus, there is subject-orientation in [2]:

Casually, Leslie greeted . . .

This is because it is possible to say:

Leslie was *casual*.

But consider the following, with adverbs such as *unintentionally* or *accidentally*:

Accidentally, Bernadette dropped the plate.

Here the adverbial remains a sentence adjunct and it is impossible to parallel [3] or [4], as in:

**Accidentally*, Bernadette dropped the plate *on purpose*. [5]

This is because it is impossible to say:

*Bernadette was *accidental*.

The apparent intention behind [5] is of course perfectly possible to express with a contingency adjunct:

As though accidentally, Bernadette dropped the plate *on purpose*.

There is, indeed, a stereotyped joke in which the two adverbs are juxtaposed: 'I suppose you did that *accidentally on purpose*.'

Note If we experiment in the manner of 8.25 with many subject-oriented subjuncts, we find that in doing so we have to understand them as adjuncts. For example:

It was *casually* that Leslie greeted the stranger.
Did Leslie greet the stranger *casually* or . . . ?

Furthermore some subjuncts, like *casually* in [2], can be outside the scope of negation while manner adjuncts cannot. Thus it makes perfectly good sense to say both of the following:

Casually, Leslie greeted the stranger.
Casually, Leslie didn't greet the stranger.

This last would not mean that he did not greet the stranger casually, but rather that he was so casual in his behaviour that he did not bother to make a greeting. But we cannot say both of the following, because *slowly* is an adjunct:

Slowly, the nun walked up the hill.
**Slowly*, the nun didn't walk up the hill.

8.93 Subject-orientation thus effects a characterization of the referent of the subject with respect to the process or state denoted by the verb. Most of the subjuncts concerned are manner adverbials, and all are either adverbs or prepositional phrases. Two groups can be distinguished: [A] a general group, and [B] a volitional group.

Group [A]: GENERAL GROUP

Group [A] appears to be an open class; for example:

Resentfully, the workers have stood by their leaders.
['The workers have stood by their leaders and were resentful about it' or – in context – '. . . but were nonetheless resentful']
With great pride, he accepted the award. ['He was very proud to accept . . .']
For once, they have *frankly* admitted their mistakes. ['For once they have been frank and admitted their mistakes']
Manfully, they insisted that the situation was not too bad. ['It was manful of them to insist . . .']
She has *consistently* overruled the lawyer's objections. ['She has been consistent in overruling . . .']
Bitterly, he buried his children. ['He was bitter when he . . .']
Sadly, she wandered through the library. ['She was sad when she . . .']
With great unease, they elected him as their leader. ['They were very uneasy when they . . .']

Group [B]: VOLITIONAL GROUP

Common volitional subject-oriented adverbials include:
deliberately, *(un)intentionally*, *purposely*, *reluctantly*, *voluntarily*, *wilfully*, *(un)willingly*, *without intention*, *on purpose*, *with reluctance*; for example:

Intentionally, they said nothing to him about the matter.
['It was their intention not to . . .']
On purpose, he left his proposals vague. ['It was his purpose to . . .']
With great reluctance, she called the police to arrest her guest.
['Though she was very reluctant to do so, she called the police . . .']

8.94 Many of these subjuncts, particularly those in Group [A], show their relationship to the subject by the paraphrase they allow, in which their adjective base is in predicative relationship to the subject (*cf* 8.92). For example, we must provide a different paraphrase for the subject subjunct *bitterly* as compared with the same item as manner adjunct or booster intensifier:

Bitterly, he buried his children. ['He was bitter when he . . .']
He spoke *bitterly* about the treatment he received. ['He spoke in a bitter way . . .']
He *bitterly* regretted their departue. ['He very much regretted . . .']

But similarly, with an example from Group [B]:

She refrained *deliberately* from joining the party. ['She was quite deliberate in refraining . . .']
She spoke slowly and *deliberately*. ['in a deliberate manner']

The volitional subjuncts differ from the others in several respects:

(I) Volitional subjuncts have in common that they express the subject's intention or willingness, or the reverse.

(II) Volitional subjuncts can often occur with copular verbs if (i) the adjective as complement is being used dynamically, or (ii) if the noun-phrase complement implies activity, or (iii) if there is a space adjunct:

He is being foolish *intentionally*.
He is being a nuisance *deliberately*.
He was in London *reluctantly* for his daughter's wedding.

Contrast:

*He is {wealthy / foolish} *intentionally*.

*He is an adult *deliberately*.

On the other hand, subjuncts in the general class, Group [A], cannot cooccur with intensive verbs:

*He was in London *proudly*.
**Sadly*, he is being foolish. [asterisked as subject-oriented subjunct: 'He is sad when he is . . .'; the sentence is fully acceptable if *sadly* is a content disjunct: *cf* 8.129]

(III) Volitional subjuncts can more easily appear before clause negation than the general subjuncts (*cf* 8.92 Note):

He *purposely* didn't write to me about it.

Deliberately, they didn't send him the money.
?*Proudly*, he didn't write to them about it.
?*Resentfully*, they didn't send him the money.

Subject subjuncts cannot cooccur with a nonpersonal subject in an intransitive or active-voice clause:

**Consistently*, the water kept boiling.
**Reluctantly*, the avalanche destroyed the chalet.

However, in the passive form it is the agent (whether present or not) that must not be nonpersonal:

The chalet was *reluctantly* destroyed { (by the developers). / *(by the avalanche). }

The lawyer's objections were *consistently* overruled.

The presence or implication of a personal agent does not in itself ensure acceptability of a subject subjunct. For example, the sentence:

?*The house was *resentfully* built last year.

is odd, presumably because building a house takes too long for resentment to be maintained. Contrast:

The house was *resentfully* sold last year.

Passive sentences with personal subject and agent leave an adverbial equivocal:

John was *willingly* sent to friends for the summer (by his mother).
[either 'John was willing' or 'his mother was willing']

Contrast:

The parcel of valuables was *willingly* sent to the charity organizers.
[only 'the sender was willing']

Nonetheless, even where a personal agent is well understood, subject subjuncts are often regarded as awkward with the passive. Although the following textual example in a recent book would be widely acceptable, it was criticized by a reviewer, presumably because with the agentless passive the adverbial could not easily be linked with a subject ('Someone *foolishly* destroyed the letters') and hence invited interpretation as an implausible manner adjunct:

The letters were *foolishly* destroyed.

Note [**a**] The analogy of regarding adjectives and clauses as restrictive or nonrestrictive (*cf* 17.3*ff*) provides another way of looking at the distinction between process adjuncts and subject subjuncts. The subjunct in, for example:

Bitterly, he buried his children.

can be paraphrased as in the italicized part below:

He buried his children *and I tell you that he was bitter when he did so.*

The nonrestrictive relative clause can similarly be paraphrased by a coordinate clause:

Alan, *who is my teacher*, has joined the army. ['Alan has joined the army and I tell you that he is my teacher'] [**b**] The volitional subject subjuncts are similar to purpose adverbials both semantically and in their grammar, resembling as they do purpose disjuncts (*cf* 8.121*ff*). *Cf* also the subject-oriented disjuncts such as *foolishly* and *wisely* (8.129).

8.95 Subjuncts in Group [A] of 8.93 tend not to precede clause negation:

> **Sadly*, she didn't wander through the library. [asterisked in the sense 'She was sad when she . . .']
> ?*With great unease*, they didn't elect him as leader.

Similarly, subject subjuncts in Group [A] tend for the most part not to precede a negative subject:

> **With great unease*, nobody elected him as leader.

However, if we can interpret the negated sentence as conveying the meaning of a volitional action, we can sometimes add a subject subjunct of Group [A]. For example, in comparing the following:

> ?**Proudly*, he didn't accept the award.
> *Proudly*, he wouldn't accept the award.

we note that, while the former is odd, the latter is acceptable, because 'wouldn't accept' means 'refused', and a refusal can be done with pride.

The volitional subjuncts allow alternative interrogation (*cf* 8.25), though with a decided shift towards adjunct interpretation (*cf* 8.92 Note):

> Did he leave his proposals vague *on purpose* or did he do so *unintentionally*?

Subjuncts from both groups can come within the scope of predication pro-forms or ellipsis:

> She has *consistently* overruled the lawyer's objections and *so has* her colleague (consistently overruled the lawyer's objections). [*ie* 'They were both consistent in overruling . . .']
> He *deliberately* misled us and *so did* she (deliberately mislead us).

Subject subjuncts often cannot cooccur with imperatives:

> **Uneasily* elect him as your leader. **Sadly* tell them about it.

It should be noted that, in such cases, it is equally odd to say:

> *Elect him as your leader *and be uneasy when you do so.*
> *Tell them about it *and be sad when you do so.*

(If *be* is interpreted as equivalent to *seem* or *pretend to be*, the sentences become acceptable, of course.)

On the other hand, we can have:

> *Gladly* reveal what you know.
> *With full confidence in your success*, make your views known to them.

just as we can have:

> Reveal what you know *and be glad when you do so.*

Make your views known to them *and have full confidence in your success when you do so.*

Subject subjuncts, like process adjuncts, do not seem to be acceptable before an emphatic auxiliary:

**Proudly* he DÌD accept the award.
**On purpose*, he DÌD leave the proposals vague.

In this respect they can be contrasted with the otherwise somewhat similar subject disjuncts such as *wisely* and *rightly* (*cf* 8.129, 8.94 Note [b]):

Wisely, he DÌD accept the award.
Rightly, he DÌD leave the proposals vague.

Subject subjuncts tend to occur in *I* and *M* positions, but can appear at *E* where an adjunct interpretation is excluded, as in:

He was in London *reluctantly*.

Verb-phrase and predication subjuncts

8.96 In 8.1, attention was drawn to the distinction between grammatical units functioning as clause element A and the same units functioning as a *part* of a clause element. The distinction is not, however, always self-evident. Between [1], where *really* is part of C, and both [2] and [3], where *really* is not, the distinction is clear enough; but it is not easy to establish whether [4] is more like [1] or more like [2] in this respect:

She is a *really* intelligent child. [1]
She is *really* an intelligent child. [2]
She *really* is intelligent. [3]
She is *really* intelligent. [4]

Semantically, there is little to choose between regarding *really* in [4] as part of C or as a separate subjunct; nor are there convincing grammatical grounds, since (for example) it is possible for some people to front a subjunct plus C just as it is possible for everyone to front an adverbially modified C:

Really intelligent, she is! *Really* an intelligent child, she is!

But while it is significant to see the relational similarities, we shall take the position here that if, as in [4], an adverb can be interpreted as part of a structure realizing a clause element, it is not to be regarded as falling within the purview of this chapter – any more than *very beautifully* in 'a very beautifully dressed girl' or *in the garage* in 'The car in the garage is Joan's'. By contrast, *really* in [2] is a predication subjunct.

The V-element has to be treated differently from S, O, C, and A in that subjuncts must be seen both as A and as simultaneously functioning within V. We can illustrate this by contrasting two sentences with a superficially similar beginning:

Freda is {able. / an able speaker.} [5]

SVC: 'Freda is (a) competent (speaker)'

Freda is able to address the meeting. [6]
SVO: 'Freda can address it'

In each case, we can introduce adverbs before *able*. But whereas in [5a] they relate to the regular accretion of phrase structure within an element, in [6a] they function as subjuncts, affecting the modality of the V-element. It will be noticed that some adverbs acceptable in the one are significantly disallowed in the other:

[Freda is / Freda is a] {very / really / quite / ?perfectly / *well / *totally} [able. / able speaker.] [5a]

Freda is {*very / really / quite / perfectly / well / totally} able to address the meeting. [6a]

Subjuncts in some verb phrases have become so institutionalized as to cause the whole sequence to be regarded as a separate unit. On modal idioms, *cf* 3.45*f*. Compare:

I would go ~ I would {*rather* / *sooner*} go.

I had *better* see a doctor.

This last example is especially clear because there is no '*I had see a doctor'.

Analogously, the subjuncts in phrasal verbs are sometimes thoroughly incorporated as part of an idiomatic whole. Contrast:

He drank (*up*) the rest of the milk.
He made *up* the rest of the story.

(*Cf* 16.3*f*)

Time-relationship subjuncts

8.97 The items to consider here are especially *already*, *still*, and *yet*, corresponding in semantic force to the time relationship adjuncts of Group (b) in 8.72. Positionally, *already* and *still* normally occur in *M*, and *yet* in *M* or *E*. These three adverbs differ from each other in usage with respect to negation and other sentence processes normally requiring nonassertives (*cf* 10.57*ff*). *Yet* is usually a nonassertive form, but it can occur in assertive verb phrases comprising modals or semi-auxiliaries (*cf* 3.21, 3.47*f*):

The first snowdrops are *yet* to appear.
I have *yet* to find out what he wants.
We may *yet* see her elected to the Senate.

Yet can be used as an assertive form also when it is closer in meaning to *still* ['even now']:

{I can see him *yet*.
{I can *still* see him.

{There's plenty of time *yet*.
{There's *still* plenty of time.

Still can precede negation, but normally cannot lie within the scope of clause negation (*cf* 10.54*ff*) except in questions. On the other hand, *already* cannot come within the scope of clause negation except in questions, and it normally cannot precede negation. The possibilities for the three adverbs in declarative, negative, and interrogative sentences are given below, where the paraphrases or suggestions for context indicate semantic similarities and differences between the adverbs. Note also the cooccurrence of perfective aspect in three of the five sets.

DECLARATIVE POSITIVE

I *already* like him. ['I have by this time come to like him']
*I *yet* like him.
I *still* like him. ['I continue to like him']

DECLARATIVE NEGATIVE (adverb preceding negation)

*I *already* haven't spoken to him.
*I *yet* haven't spoken to him.
I *still* haven't spoken to him. ['I haven't spoken to him so far', implying 'even after all this time']

DECLARATIVE NEGATIVE (adverb following negation)

*He can't *already* drive.
He can't {drive *yet* / *yet* drive}. ['He can't drive up to this time' implying 'even after all this time']
?He can't *still* drive. ['He can't continue to drive' or 'Surely it is not true that he can still drive?']

INTERROGATIVE POSITIVE

Have you *already* seen him? [expecting that you have or implying that you have done so earlier than expected]
Have you seen him *yet*? ['by now': *even yet* would imply 'after all this time', balancing *already* in the previous example; thus 'I've kept asking you to see him for weeks: have you seen him *even yet*?']
Do you *still* see him? ['Do you continue to see him?']

INTERROGATIVE NEGATIVE

Haven't you seen him *already*? ['Surely you have seen him by now?']
Haven't you seen him *yet*? ['Surely you should have seen him by now?']
Don't you *still* see him? ['Surely you continue to see him?' *ie* expecting that you do]

On the nonassertives *any more* and *any longer* and the negatives *no more*, *no longer* as time-relation subjuncts, consider the following examples:

Do you see him *any more*/*any longer*? }
Do you *any longer*/**any more* see him? } [expecting that you do not]

I see him *no more/no longer*. ⟨formal⟩
I do not see him *any more/any longer*.

Note [a] The difference between *already* and *yet* in questions is that *already* expects an affirmative answer whereas *yet* leaves open whether the answer is negative or positive (*cf* 11.6*ff*), except in 'conducive' (negative) questions such as 'Haven't you seen him *yet*?'

[b] *Yet* and *still* come close in meaning in modal verb phrases:

I have *yet* to meet him. [1]
We may *yet* see her elected to the Senate. [2]
I have *still* to meet him. [1a]
We may *still* see her elected to the Senate. [2a]

Both of the sentences [1] and [1a] mean 'It remains for me to meet him', but the examples with *still* both carry the implication of an objective that is likely to be fulfilled.

[c] *Still*, *yet*, and *already* often blend concessive and temporal meanings. For example, in:

It's 11.30 p.m. and he's { *still* at work. / at work *yet*. ⟨esp dialectal⟩ }
It's 5.30 a.m. but he's *already* at work.

The effect of *still* and *yet* is to express not only the continuance of the action but also to suggest that the continuance is surprising ('He's continuing even so to work'). So too, *already* expresses both the time relation ('by now') and some surprise at its realization. See also the concessive conjunct *still* (8.137).

[d] The subjunct *still* can be endorsed by *yet* at *E*, as in:

She's ˈ*still* there (even) YÈT. [but not the converse: '*She's *yet* there *still*']

Sometimes *as yet* is a more formal variant of *yet*:

I have not *as yet* decided to accept the appointment.

In other situations, *yet* and *as yet* have a quite distinct distribution:

I have { *yet* / ?**as yet* } to meet him.
Hasn't she arrived { *yet*? / ?**as yet*? }
As yet, he was only a minor official. [≠ 'Yet, he was . . .']

[e] Informally in AmE (especially in the Mid-West), *yet* at *E* can occur in assertive clauses, especially of an exclamatory kind and with *yet* having something of the function of a focusing subjunct; *cf* 8.116. For example:

Ah, so you've bought new SLÌPpers *yet*!
Everyone else turned discreetly away, but not John: John just had to turn and look *yet*!

Again in some varieties of AmE there is an exclamatory use of *any more*, with various meanings: '(even) yet; (even) now; more and more; would you believe it?' Frequently this usage amounts to little more than an expression of surprise:

Did you say 'encephalate'? What's that supposed to mean *any more*?' [approximately: 'What *on earth* does that mean?']
They're dancing in the street *any more*!
She's looking better and better *any more*!

Other time subjuncts

8.98 As well as being used for focusing and intensification (*cf* 8.116*ff*, 8.104*ff*) but in close relation to such uses, *just* (always at *M*) can express time position. With the perfective or progressive, it can mean either 'at this/that precise moment' or 'very recently':

He's *just* stopped talking.
I'm *just* finishing an article on the subject.
When I saw her, she had *just* come back.

In informal AmE, this is true also with the simple past ('Where's John?' 'He *just* went out'). More generally with the simple past, *just* means 'recently', and with the future or present progressive it means 'very soon', in both cases frequently in association with more specific time adverbials:

> She *just* spoke to me about it (a moment or so ago).
> He's *just* coming (in a moment or so).

On *just* as a downtoner (diminisher), *cf* 8.111.

The combination *just now* is used at *E* for either 'very recently' or 'very soon':

> I saw her *just now*. {I'm / I'll be} seeing her *just now*.

(Contrast *just* + *then*, *right* + *now*/*then*, 8.116.)

Time duration is expressed (by implication) in the use of some intensifiers such as *enough*:

> Have you talked to him *enough* now? ['sufficiently *long*']
> We played cards *a little* last night. ['for a *short* time']
> I hate having to wait *a lot* at the bank. ['a *long* time']

But it is time frequency that especially involves the use of subjuncts. For example:

> She {doesn't *ever* come / *never* comes / *hardly ever* comes} to see me.
> [*Cf* informally *never ever*: 'They *never ever* clean their windows'.]
> They are *forever* complaining.
> I am *ever* open to new ideas. ⟨formal⟩ [*always* would be more usual, and *ever* is normally nonassertive; *cf* 10.60]
> I have {*rarely* / *seldom*} reviewed a more dishonest book.
> They should *sometimes* give their dog a bath.

Several intensifiers (*cf* 8.104*ff*) are also used for time frequency, as in:

> I used to play squash *very often* but now I don't play *much*/*a lot*/*a great deal*.
> . . . but now I *barely*/*hardly*/*scarcely* play (*at all*).
> . . . but now I {*hardly* / *scarcely*} *ever* play.
> . . . and I *still* play *a little*/*a bit*.

Positional norms are as illustrated, but *sometimes* may also occur at *I* or *E*; *rarely* and *seldom* at *I* would usually require subject–operator inversion (*cf* 18.24) and at *E* would normally be rather heavily modified:

> I play squash *very seldom indeed*.

Note [**a**] Several of these subjuncts have some of the character of adjuncts, especially when premodified or focused:

> It is *very seldom* that I write poetry these days.
> It was *only just now* that I remembered our appointment.
> ?It is *only a little* that we play bridge.

[b] In very informal use, *hardly* can be at *E* without prosodic weight:

(She used to write a lot but now) she doesn't write at ÀLL *hardly*. [more usual: 'she *hardly* writes at all']

There is also an informal double negative as in: 'You *can't hardly* move in this office'. [more acceptably: 'You can *hardly* move . . .']

Emphasizers

8.99 There is a range of subjuncts concerned with expressing the semantic role of *modality* (*cf* 8.8) which have a reinforcing effect on the truth value of the clause or part of the clause to which they apply. In adding to the force (as distinct from the degree) of a constituent, emphasizers do not require that the constituent concerned should be gradable. When, however, the constituent emphasized is indeed gradable, the adverbial takes on the force of an intensifier (*cf* 8.104). Compare the use of *really* in the following:

He *really* may have injured innocent people. [1]
He may *really* have injured innocent people. [2]
He may have *really* injured innocent people. [3]

In [1] and [2] we have a pure emphasizer and we might paraphrase as follows:

It is *really* possible that he has injured . . . [1a]
It is possible that it is *really* true that he has injured . . . [2a]

With [3], however, the implication is of a high degree of injury as well as the assertion of certainty; *ie* both [3a] and [3b]:

It is possible that he has *really* [*ie* actually, indeed, certainly] injured . . . [3a]
It is possible that he has *really* [*ie* seriously, to a severe extent] injured innocent people. [3b]

Note The typical emphasizer *really* illustrates both the structural equivocation discussed in 8.96 and also the inherent nature of the subjunct in being subordinated semantically to another unit in the clause (*cf* 8.88, 8.25). Thus individual speakers will vacillate as to how the emphasis may be grammatically realized, as in:

He's in a real corner.	He's really in a corner.	(?) He's in really a corner.
He's in real difficulties.	He's really in difficulties.	

8.100 Common emphasizers include:

(a) *actually*, *certainly*, *clearly*, *definitely*, *indeed*, *obviously*, *plainly*, *really*, *surely*, *for certain*, *for sure*, *of course*
(b) *frankly*, *honestly*, *literally*, *simply*, *fairly* ⟨esp BrE⟩, *just*

Group (a) consists mainly of items that can also function as disjuncts expressing the comment that what is being said is true (*cf* 8.127). Group (b) consists mainly of items that can also function as disjuncts conveying the speaker's assertion that his words are the unvarnished truth (*cf* 8.124). Since it is normally expected that a person intends his hearer to accept what he says as true, the addition of the comment or assertion in no way alters but merely emphasizes the truth of the communication. When these emphasizers are positioned next to a part of the communication, without being separated intonationally or by punctuation, their effect is often to emphasize that part alone, though there may be ambivalence as to whether the emphasis is on the part or on the whole.

Examples of the use of emphasizers:

She *plainly* likes the dress.
I *honestly* don't know what he wanted.
I can't *really* believe him.
He *actually* sat next to her.
I *just* can't understand it.
They will *surely* object to his intervention.
They *literally* tore his argument to pieces. [*cf* 8.126]
They *obviously* don't want it.
He *fairly* jumped for joy. ⟨esp BrE⟩
I *simply* don't believe it.
They will warn us *for sure*.

With Group (a) should be considered responses to requests:

A: Please get me the file on Robert Schultz.
B: CÈRtainly
SÙRE ⟨esp AmE informal⟩
SÙREly ⟨esp AmE⟩
All RÍGHT
RÌGHT
ÒḰ
WÌLL DÓ ⟨BrE informal⟩
Very GÓOD

A: Are you willing to help her?
B: (Yes) CÈRtainly
SÙRE ⟨esp AmE informal⟩
SÙREly ⟨esp AmE⟩
Yes inDÈED
Yes YÉS
ÒḰ
RÌGHT ⟨esp AmE⟩
All RÍGHT [implies lack of enthusiasm]
HǍRDly
No inDÈED
Certainly NÒT
(No) NÒ

Only a few of these responses, of course, correspond directly to subjuncts in full clauses; *eg* 'I *certainly* will', 'I will *indeed*', 'I *sure* will'. It is especially with Group (a) that we should associate the asseveratives of very informal speech. Consider the following rather angry exchange:

A: You altered the clock.
B: I didn't! I *never even* touched it.
A: You DÌD.

As well as this last response we might find:

> You did *sò*. ⟨informal, esp by children⟩
> You *certainly* DĬD.
> You *darned well* DĬD. ⟨very informal⟩

Cf also the following, all very informal:

> {Who / What / Where / Why / How} {the hell / the blazes / on earth / in heaven / in (the) hell} [+ question +] {for goodness' sake / for pity's sake} ?

For example:

> *Why on earth* did you alter the CLÒCK *for goodness' sake*?

Other types of utterance with subjunct asseveratives include the very informal:

> I told them to *darned well* go. [*cf* 8.21]
> I told them to get their car {*the hell* / *to hell*} out of my drive.

Note [**a**] For some speakers, *plain* can informally function as a subjunct ('He's *plain* dishonest'), but more usually the informal version would be *just plain*, as in 'He's 'just 'plain disHÒNest' (*Cf* 8.96).
[**b**] The subjunct *sure* in 'I *sure* will' ⟨esp AmE⟩ is to be distinguished from the two adjectival uses:

> I am *sure* of winning. ['I feel confident that I shall win']
> I am *sure* to win. ['There is widespread confidence that I shall win']

[**c**] In Group (a), *for certain* and *for sure* cannot function as disjuncts of comment (among other things, they are only rarely positioned initially) but are obviously related to *certainly* and *surely* respectively in their emphasizer uses. In Group (b), *fairly* ⟨esp BrE⟩ and *just* cannot function as speaker's authority disjuncts. However, *fairly* can be related to the set of such disjuncts *to be fair*, *to put it fairly*, etc, for which there happens to be no corresponding adverb, while an association can be seen between *simply* in *Simply tell him he's wrong*, disjunct; *I am speaking simply*, process adjunct, 'in a simple manner'; *I simply say*, restrictive focusing subjunct (*cf* 8.116*ff*), 'merely', 'only', 'just'; and *just* in *I just say*, restrictive subjunct.
[**d**] On the use of *literally*, *cf* 8.126.

Cooccurrence restrictions on emphasizers

8.101 While emphasizers in Group (a) seem to be free to cooccur with any verb or predication, those in Group (b) tend to be limited. For example, *fairly* ⟨esp BrE⟩ and *absolutely* require some suggestion of exaggeration in the predication:

> In her anger, she {*fairly* ⟨esp BrE⟩ / *absolutely*} screamed at him.
> *In her anger, she {*fairly* ⟨esp BrE⟩ / *absolutely*} spoke to him.

On the other hand, *honestly* tends to cooccur with verbs expressing attitude or cognition:

> They *honestly* admire her courage.

He *honestly* believes their accusation.
?*In her anger, she *honestly* screamed at him. [≠ disjunct (*cf* Note) as in 'I am honestly telling you . . .']

When some emphasizers are used with gradable verbs they may also have a scaling effect akin to that of boosters (*cf* 8.105):

He *really* likes her. ['He likes her very much']
I *indeed* appreciate your help. ['I *greatly* appreciate your help']
He *definitely* impressed them. ['He impressed them *greatly*']

But unlike the boosters, these have of course a reinforcing and emphatic effect with nongradable verbs too:

He *really* was there. We *definitely* saw it.
She *indeed* sat next to them.

Other emphasizers tend to have a scaling effect more readily with gradable words that are adjectives and nouns (*cf* 7.4):

She is *certainly* intelligent. ['She is *very* intelligent']
I was *frankly* appalled at his attitude. ['I was *absolutely* appalled']
He's *obviously* a fool. ['He's a *big* fool']
He's *clearly* a dangerous man. ['He's a *very* dangerous man']

The scaling effect of *really* and *indeed* is more obvious with adjectives:

It was *really* funny.
He's dangerous *indeed*. [mannered without a correlating *very*: 'very dangerous *indeed*']

Speakers may vary in the extent to which they feel that all or some of these emphasizers have a scaling effect.

Note If *honestly* is used as in '*Honestly*, she screamed at him', the adverbial is a disjunct (*cf* 8.124), asserting the speaker's good faith in making the statement rather than emphasizing the particular choice of words in the predication. A move to *I* would likewise change the relationship in respect of several other items illustrated in the examples (*eg*: *frankly*); so too would a move to *E*, where the disjunct would require a separate intonation nucleus: 'She SCRÈAMED at him FRÁNKly', 'She SCRÈAMED at him| HÒNestly|.'

Syntactic features of emphasizers

8.102 Most emphasizers normally precede the item they emphasize (*iM*, *M*, *eM* positions in respect of verb phrases, *cf* 8.14*ff*), and *for certain* and *for sure* are exceptional in being at *E*. As subjuncts, emphasizers differ from adjuncts in several ways. They cannot be contrasted with one another in alternative interrogation or alternative negation; they cannot be the focus of focusing subjuncts or of a cleft sentence, nor (in the case of the adverbs) can they be the focus of clause comparison or be premodified by *however*, *how*, or *so*. Many can, however, come within the scope of predication pro-forms or ellipsis; for example:

Joan will {*certainly* / *surely*} object and so will Mary.
[= 'it is equally *certain*/*sure* that Mary will object']

As several of the examples in 8.100 show, most emphasizers can precede a negated verb phrase, except for *fairly* ⟨esp BrE⟩:

> They *fairly* danced for joy at the news. ⟨esp BrE⟩
> *They *fairly* didn't dance for joy at the news.

Several items tend to cooccur with clausal negation and precede the verb phrase in such a case, in particular *honestly, just, simply*.

Five emphasizers can lie within the scope of clause negation, and the last two listed are normally thus, since they are placed at *E*:

> *actually, definitely, really, for certain, for sure*

All of them can become the focus of negation:

> I don't *RĚALly* know him.
> He didn't *ǍCTually* sit next to her.
> They don't *DĚFinitely* want it.
> They don't know *for CĚRtain*.
> I can't tell you *for SǓRE*.

Since *actually*, *definitely*, and *really* can also lie outside the scope of clause negation, we have a contrast between the two possibilities, the scope of negation being marked by the horizontal bracket (*cf* 10.64):

> I really don't know him. ['The real truth is that I don't know him', *ie* 'I don't know him *at all*']
> I don't really know him. ['It's not the real truth that I know him', *ie* 'I don't know him *well*']
> He actually didn't sit next to her. ['The actual fact is that he didn't sit next to her']
> He didn't actually sit next to her. ['It's not an actual fact that he sat next to her']
> They definitely don't want it. ['It's definite that they don't want it']
> They don't definitely want it. ['It's not definite that they want it']

All the emphasizers except *certainly* and *surely* (and for most speakers *fairly* too) can appear in a question; compare:

> Do they { **certainly* / **surely* / *definitely* / *really* } want him to be elected?

In general, the emphasizers do not appear with imperatives, but some people use *actually*, *definitely*, and *really* with imperatives:

> Don't *actually* hate him for it – it wasn't really his fault.
> *Definitely* buy one now.
> Make an effort this time; but *really* make an effort.

Note The informal phrase *all right* can be a process adjunct (*cf* 8.79) as in 'Did she manage to find the place *all right*?'; a content disjunct (*cf* 8.127*ff*) as in 'All RÌGHT, she's a good STÙDent' (*ie* 'I grant you'); and also an emphasizer subjunct as in:

> She's a good STÙDent, all RÍGHT, ['She's certainly a good student']

The subjunct may relate to a specific element, as to the time adjunct in:

She won't worry unless you hurt yourself. THÈN she'll worry all RÍGHT.

[= 'Then {CÈRtainly / inDÈED} she'll worry']

8.103 The emphasizers either cannot be modified or are unlikely to be modified; an exception is *definitely*, which is sometimes premodified by *quite* or *very*.

Certain emphasizers not listed in 8.100 appear in restricted environments:

(i) *Always* when preceded by *can* or *could* must be in a positive declarative clause:

You can ″*always* sleep on the FLŎOR. ['You can certainly . . .']

The possibility of adding to this sentence an adverbial referring to a specific future time such as *tonight* or *just for one night* rules out the temporal meaning of *always*. By contrast, if the clause is negative, the temporal meaning alone is activated and the item is no longer a subjunct:

You can't *ÀLways* sleep on the FLÓOR.
[= 'You can't sleep on the floor *on all occasions*']

(ii) Unmodified *well* when preceded by *can, could, may*, or *might* must be in a positive declarative clause; the effect is to imply probability where the auxiliary alone connoted only possibility:

It {*may* / *might* / *can* / *could*} *well* be true that he beat her. [= 'It may indeed . . .' or even 'It is quite likely to be true . . .']

Note also with fronting (*cf* 18.20):

She hopes they will respond gratefully {{and / as} *well* they *may*. / which they *may well* do.}

This would imply 'should', and (especially with *as*) there would be little difference in meaning if the example ended '. . . as *well* they *ought/should*' – although, without fronting, *well* does not thus cooccur with *ought* or *should*:

*He {*should* / *ought*} *well* . . .

With some verbs, there are other restrictions on the auxiliaries admitted:

He {*may* / *might* / ?**can* / *could*} *well* attend the meeting instead of me.
['He may surely . . .', 'He can very easily . . .']

On the other hand, intensified by *very*, the subjunct usage has no such restriction to positive clauses or to certain verbs:

He {*can* / *can't*} *very well* attend the meeting.
['He surely can . . .', 'He surely can't . . .', 'He can't very easily . . .']

(iii) *Necessarily* is an emphasizer when preceded by *must*:

A school teacher who wishes to be honest *must necessarily* prepare her lessons. ['must inevitably']

Otherwise, *necessarily* is an adjunct of contingency which tends to cooccur with the clausal negative particle:

That doesn't {*necessarily* follow. / follow *necessarily*.} ['That doesn't follow inevitably']

(iv) *Needs* ⟨rare, literary⟩ has to be preceded or followed by *must* in a positive declarative or interrogative clause:

That *must needs* be their intention. ['must inevitably']

Note [**a**] *Indeed* can be postposed:
I appreciate your help *inDÈED*. ⟨rather formal or old-fashioned⟩
This is more common with adjectives (particularly if they are modified by another intensifier) and nouns with indefinite article:
He was very happy *inDÈED*.
It was a sacrifice *inDÈED*.
She became a much abler doctor *inDÈED*.
In some of these examples, *indeed* is functioning as an intensifier: 'very happy indeed'.
Contrast, with *indeed* as conjunct:
He was very HÀPpy, inDÉED. (*or* . . . HÀPpy, indeed.)
She became a much abler DÒCtor, inDÉED. (*or* . . ., indeed.)
It was a SÀCrifice, inDÉED. (*or* . . ., indeed.)

[**b**] *Readily*, *easily*, *with ease*, and *comfortably* (especially when in *M* position) come close to being emphasizers. *Easily* tends to cooccur with the modal auxiliaries. For example:
They *readily* admitted their guilt.
They might *easily* have been arrested. [*cf* 'might *well* . . .']
We will *comfortably* finish on time.
Contrast these with the manner adjunct *easily* and the manner/result adjunct *comfortably* in:
He answers questions *readily*. ['in a ready and cooperative way']
Are you sitting *comfortably*? ['in such a way that you are comfortable']

Intensifiers

8.104 The intensifier subjuncts are broadly concerned with the semantic category of DEGREE (*cf* 8.9). It should be noted that the term 'intensifier' does not refer only to means whereby an *increase* in intensification is expressed. Rather, an intensifying subjunct indicates a point on an abstractly conceived intensity scale; and the point indicated may be relatively low or relatively high. The scale is seen as applying to a predicate or to some part of a predicate, such as the predication, the verb phrase, or even an item within the verb phrase (*cf* 8.96). The verbs in question are largely expressive of attitude.

It is useful to distinguish two subsets of intensifiers:

(I) AMPLIFIERS {Maximizers (*eg*: *completely*) / Boosters (*eg*: *very much*)}

(II) DOWNTONERS
- Approximators (*eg*: *almost*)
- Compromisers (*eg*: *more or less*)
- Diminishers (*eg*: *partly*)
- Minimizers (*eg*: *hardly*)

Amplifiers scale upwards from an assumed norm; downtoners have a lowering effect, usually scaling downwards from an assumed norm. Such scaling requires that the item or unit to which the intensifier applies is gradable. The subtypes provide nothing more than a rough guide to semantic distinctions, because (i) the varying effects of intensifiers represent a semantic gradient, which is obscured by a clear-cut division into classes; (ii) some intensifiers are sometimes used for different effects; and (iii) speakers vary in their use of intensifiers.

Intensification is realized for the most part by adverbs, but occasionally also by noun phrases and prepositional phrases.

Note [**a**] On the relation between 'fully approve' and 'full approval' etc, *cf* App I.71 Note [b]. For intensifying adjectives, *cf* 7.33*f*. For modifying adverbs as intensifiers, *cf* 7.87*ff*.
[**b**] For gradability with reference to adjectives and adverbs, *cf* 7.4.

Amplifiers

8.105 Amplifiers scale upwards. They are divided into (a) MAXIMIZERS, which can denote the upper extreme of the scale, and (b) BOOSTERS, which denote a high degree, a high point on the scale. Both subsets, but especially boosters, form open classes, and new expressions are frequently created to replace older ones whose impact follows the trend of hyperbole in rapidly growing ineffectual.

Most amplifiers can be contrasted in alternative negation with *to some extent*, and this propensity is a semantic test for their inclusion in the class of amplifiers:

He didn't ignore my request *completely*, but he did ignore it *to some extent*.
They don't admire his music *greatly*, but they do admire it *to some extent*.

By contrast, emphasizers (*cf* 8.99*ff*) cannot be so used:

*He didn't *really* ignore my request, but he did ignore it *to some extent*.
*They don't *definitely* admire his music, but they do admire it to *some extent*.

Common amplifiers, within the two subclasses (*cf* 8.104), include:

(a) MAXIMIZERS
absolutely, *altogether*, *completely*, *entirely*, *extremely*, *fully*, *perfectly*, *quite* (contrast compromiser use, 8.111), *thoroughly*, *totally*, *utterly*; *in all respects*; the intensifying use of *most* (*cf* 7.87). For example:

They *fully* appreciate our problems.
They *thoroughly* disapprove of his methods.

They *totally* believed in the leader's integrity.
He has *completely* ignored my request.
I can *perfectly* see why you are anxious about it.
She *entirely* agrees with you.
We *utterly* deplore his tactics.
I enjoyed the play *extremely*.
I must *absolutely* refuse to listen to your grumbling.
She will *altogether* reject such views.
I *quite* forgot about her birthday.
He paid for the damage *fully*.
She hasn't closed the door *completely*.
I *most* appreciate your kindness.

(b) BOOSTERS
badly, *bitterly*, *deeply*, *enormously*, *far*, *greatly*, *heartily*, *highly*, *intensely*, *much*, *severely*, *so*, *strongly*, *terribly*, *violently*, *well*; *a great deal*, *a good deal*, *a lot*, *by far*; exclamatory *how*; the intensifying use of *more* (*cf* 7.85 Note [b])

Cf also *actively* (engaged in), *hard* (at work), 'working hard', where '(She's) at work' would connote spatial position.

For example:

They *greatly* admire his music.
I need a drink *badly*,
They like her *very much*.
They resent him *deeply*.
He must have *bitterly* regretted his mistake many times.
I *much* prefer the old methods.
I *so* wanted to see her. ['I wanted to see her very much']
His results will have *far* exceeded his expectations.
We all know him *well*.
They annoy me *a great deal*.
We miss our old friends *a lot*. ⟨informal⟩
How they suffered! ['How very much they suffered!']
I used to concentrate on Brahms but now I *more* enjoy Beethoven.

The distinction between maximizers and boosters is not a hard and fast one. In particular, when maximizers are in *M* position they often express a very high degree, whereas when they are in *E* position they are more likely to convey their absolute meaning of extreme degree. For example, many speakers may see very little difference in force between the maximizer *utterly* and the booster *violently* when these are in *M* position:

They {*utterly* / *violently*} detested him.

Speakers vary in the extent to which they give a seriously hyperbolic reading to the maximizer. The tendency to use the maximizer for merely a high degree is especially great for attitudinal verbs such as *detest*.

Note In somewhat old-fashioned informal BrE, *rather* functions as an exclamatory booster: 'Did you enjoy the party?' '*RĂther*!' (sometimes '*RaTHĔR*').

Modification and comparison of maximizers

8.106 If the maximizers are interpreted as expressing the absolute extreme on a scale, they cannot themselves be modified or compared for degree. Modification and comparison cannot apply to prepositional phrases or to most adverbs that do not end in *-ly* (*altogether*, *quite*, *most*). With the other adverbs there is considerable variation in usage, with the semantic class of verb as a further variable. We exemplify the variation by taking the first nine sentences in 8.105 that illustrate the use of maximizers as tested for modification and comparison. Let us consider four possibilities:

(i) premodification of the maximizer by *how*, introducing a question or exclamation, *eg*:

> *How thoroughly* do they disapprove of his methods?
> *How utterly* we deplore his tactics!

(ii) premodification of the maximizer by *however* to form the opening of a dependent adverbial clause, *eg*:

> *However totally* they believed in the leader's integrity, they were prepared to examine his actions dispassionately.

(iii) the maximizer as the focus of clause comparison, *eg*:

> He ignored my request *more completely than she did*.

(iv) premodification of the maximizer by *very*, *eg*:

> They *very fully* appreciate our problems.

Table 8.106a Modification and comparison of maximizers

	(i) *how*	(ii) *however*	(iii) *more than*	(iv) *very*
fully	+	+	+	+
thoroughly	+	+	+	+
totally	+	+	+	?
completely	+	+	+	?
perfectly	+	+	?	?
entirely	+	+	?	–
utterly	+	+	–	–
extremely	?	?	–	–
absolutely	–	–	–	–

Table 8.106a gives the results of the testing. As can be seen from the results, it is possible to use *fully* and *thoroughly* to denote a very high point on the scale, but only *absolutely* is felt to be absolute, marking the absolute extreme of intensification and hence not susceptible itself of modification. The queries in the *Table* indicate an area of divided usage. There is a prescriptive tradition forbidding the use of *very* or the comparative with *completely* and *perfectly*, as well as with their respective adjective forms.

Note Indeed, similar restrictions on modification and comparison apply to the adjective bases of these adverbs, though they are not identical. *Table* 8.106b lists these adjective bases and shows the results of tests on them for modification by *more* and by *very*. Modification by *how* and *however* coincides with that by *more*.

Table 8.106b Modification and comparison of adjective bases of maximizers

	more	*very*
full	+	+
thorough	+	+
total	?	–
complete	?	?
perfect	?	?
entire	–	–
utter	?	–
extreme	?	?
absolute	?	–

The queries represent in part divided usage. But the acceptability of the modifiers with these intensifying adjectives (*cf* 7.33*f*) also depends on the noun. If the noun is abstract and derived from a verb, it seems more acceptable to modify the adjective by *more* or *very*. Contrast:

I have never seen a more complete { *investigation.* / *?fool.* }

He has a very perfect { *?understanding* of the problem. / ?**right* to do what he likes. }

The item may also occur as other than an intensifying adjective and there need not then be any problem of modification:

She expressed *very extreme* views.
Her views on the subject are *more extreme* than mine. } [*extreme* = 'not moderate']

Cooccurrence restrictions on amplifiers

8.107 Certain amplifiers tend to cooccur predominantly with certain verbs; for example:

I *entirely* + agree
We *badly* + need, want
I *completely* + forget [*cf* also, informally, 'I *clean* forgot!']
They *greatly* + admire, enjoy

In some cases, the amplifiers cooccur with a semantic class of verbs, for example *greatly* with verbs having a favourable implication and *utterly* with verbs having an unfavourable implication. Some intensifiers, such as *deeply*, tend to occur with attitudinal verbs (*cf* 8.101):

They wounded him *deeply*. [would usually refer to emotional wounding]
They wounded him *badly*. [would usually refer to physical wounding]

Even when there is an item-class selectivity, the amplifier may not cooccur with all the items in the class. We have:

deeply + hate, dislike, admire, love, value, regret

but not:

**deeply* + like, prefer, favour

Further investigation may also show that semantically-definable classes of amplifiers tend to cooccur with semantically-definable classes of verbs.

But the situation can be even more complicated. Sometimes there are syntactic conditions for certain types of lexical cooccurrence. *Much* is largely used in nonassertives, unless premodified:

> *She likes him *much*.
>
> She likes him {*very* / *so* / *too*} *much*.
>
> I don't *much* care for Max Bruch.
>
> Do you like him *much*?
I don't like him *much*. } [though 'very much' would be more usual]

Yet with some verbs, unpremodified *much* can be used, but only in *M* position:

> We *much* {prefer his offer. / admire your technique. / appreciate your invitation. / regret the inconvenience.}
>
> *We {prefer his offer / admire your technique / appreciate your invitation / regret the inconvenience} *much*. [where 'very much' would be fully acceptable]

Note [**a**] *Very much* is another example of where it is possible to select the gradable sense of a verb. While:

> They missed her.

is ambiguous between the 'emotive' sense ('feel sorry or unhappy at the loss or absence of') and the sense of 'arriving too late for', the addition of *very much* allows only the emotive sense:

> They *very much* missed her.
>
> They missed her *very much*.

Where the emotive sense would not be normal, *very much* cannot be added:

> *They got up late, and so they {*very much* missed the bus. / missed the bus *very much*.}

Compare also:

> He *very much* expected trouble at the meeting.
>
> ?*He *very much* expected a 14 bus but it turned out to be a 73.
>
> She *very much* appears to be in trouble.
>
> ?*She *very much* appears in public.

[**b**] The colloquial *n't half* ⟨esp BrE⟩ tends to cooccur with predications already implying high or low intensification:

> She does*n't half* swear. ['She swears a great deal']
>
> It's *not half* cold today.
>
> It has*n't half* been cold today.

As well as being an amplifier, this phrase can be used (noncolloquially and more literally) as a downtoner; compare:

> I'm not HÀLF 'satisfied. ['I am only partially satisfied']
>
> I'm not ↑half SÀTisfied. ['I am highly satisfied']
Your new suit isn't half BÀD. ['I like it'] } ⟨informal, esp dialectal⟩

8.108 Amplifiers cooccur only with gradable verbs, and when adverbial items of the same form cooccur with nongradable verbs they do not function as amplifiers, but as quantifiers, duratives, or frequentatives (*cf* 8.115), or as process adjuncts (*cf* 8.78*ff*):

> She drinks milk *a lot*. ['often']
> He will judge us *severely*. ['in a severe manner']

However, a nongradable verb can become gradable when the focus is on the result of the process rather than on the process itself. For example, if the perfective particle *up* is added to *drink* or the perfective aspect of the verb is used, the focus is on the result, and an amplifier such as *completely* can cooccur with *drink*:

> He drank up his beer *completely*.
> He has *completely* drunk his beer.

Similarly, while *judge* is nongradable, *misjudge* is gradable, since *misjudge* is concerned with the result of the judging and is also susceptible of an evaluative meaning:

> *He {*very much* / *badly*} judged the situation.
>
> He {*very much* / *badly*} misjudged the situation.

And if *badly* is used with *judge*, it is interpreted as a process adjunct (perhaps expressing a blend of process with result) and must be put in *E* position:

> He judged the situation *badly*. ['in a way that was bad and with bad results']

Note [**a**] The perfective particles with certain verbs function as amplifying subjuncts (*cf* also 8.33):
He drank (*up*) his beer.

[**b**] The gradable/nongradable distinction (*cf* 7.4) between *judge* and *misjudge* is found in other morphologically-related verbs:

NONGRADABLE	GRADABLE
calculate	miscalculate
estimate	overestimate, underestimate
rate	overrate, underrate
represent	misrepresent
behave	misbehave
manage	mismanage

Positions of amplifiers

8.109 *M* and *E* positions are open to most adverbs that are amplifiers; noun phrases and prepositional phrases are restricted to *E* position. In positive declarative clauses, *M* position is favoured for both boosters and maximizers when we want to express a scaling upwards, but *E* position is preferred for maximizers when we want to denote the absolute upper extreme of the scale. Hence, the effect of the maximizer *completely* in *M* position in:

> He *completely* denied it.

is close to that of the booster *strongly* or the emphasizer *really*, which can have a scaling effect similar to that of boosters (*cf* 8.101):

He {*strongly* / *really*} denied it.

On the other hand, when *completely* is in *E* position:

He denied it *completely*.

the intention seems to be closer to:

He denied it *in every respect*.

Where the absolute meaning is expected, some people find only *E* position acceptable:

?He *completely* dissected the animal.
?They *completely* divided up the money.
He dissected the animal *completely*. ['into all the prescribed parts']
They divided up the money *completely*. ['the whole of the money']

We can also contrast the probable interpretations of *violently* in the two positions shown in:

They *violently* attacked him.
They attacked him *violently*.

In *M* position, *violently* is likely to be interpreted as a booster ['strongly'] and *attacked* will then be equivalent to 'condemned', a verbal assault. On the other hand, when *violently* is in *E* position, we are likely to interpret it literally ['with violence'] as a manner process adjunct (*cf* 8.79), with *attacked* now referring to physical assault.

In negative, interrogative, and imperative clauses, *E* position is normal in all cases.

Note [**a**] The subjuncts *extremely*, *most*, and (when no comparative clause follows) *more* are usually in *E* position. Exclamatory *how*, of course, appears only at *I*.

[**b**] Some boosters (including *well*) occasionally appear in *iM* position, usually (but not necessarily) when they are themselves intensified or before an emphatic auxiliary and especially when the utterances follow an associated statement; these subjuncts might thus be seen as subject-oriented (*cf* 8.92):

A: I'd prefer to see them tomorrow.
B: And Ĭ| very MÙCH| would prefer to see them tomorrow.

Cf also:

I *so* did want to meet them.
I *well* can understand your problem.

For some speakers, *iM* position is common for *very much* in *very much would like*, though others find it odd:

?I *very much* would like to speak to you sometime today.

In all these examples, *M* would be far more usual as in: 'I would *very much* prefer . . .', 'I did *so* want . . .' etc.

Syntactic features of amplifiers

8.110 Amplifiers can be contrasted with other intensifiers in alternative interrogation and negation, and they can come within the scope of predication proforms or ellipsis. On the other hand, they cannot be the focus of a cleft sentence:

*It was *completely* that he ignored your request.

But for some people, they can be the focus of a cleft sentence if they are modified or if the focal clause is interrogative or negative (*cf* 8.113, 8.83):

?Was it *completely* that he ignored your request?
?I know that it wasn't *entirely* that he agreed with us.
?I wonder how *fully* it was that they appreciated your problems.

Most boosters accept comparison and modification, but maximizers vary in this respect (*cf* 8.106).

Amplifiers do not usually serve as a response to a *How*-question, though they can if the verb in the question has to do with general evaluation:

*How do they admire his music? (They admire it) { *Very much.* / *Greatly.* }

How do you like it? (I like it) { *Very much.* / ?*Greatly.* }

They can often be evoked by *How much*:

How much do they admire his music? (They admire it) *Greatly.*

Note Other question forms eliciting amplifiers are *To what extent . . . ? How far* (*do you think . . .*)? *What do you think of . . . ?*

Downtoners

8.111 Downtoners have a generally lowering effect on the force of the verb or predication and many of them apply a scale to gradable verbs. They can be divided into four groups (*cf* 8.104):

(a) APPROXIMATORS serve to express an approximation to the force of the verb, while indicating that the verb concerned expresses more than is relevant.
(b) COMPROMISERS have only a slight lowering effect and tend, as with (a), to call in question the appropriateness of the verb concerned.
(c) DIMINISHERS scale downwards and roughly mean 'to a small extent'.
(d) MINIMIZERS are negative maximizers, '(not) to any extent'.

Groups (a) and (b) should be compared with disjuncts of metalinguistic comment, *cf* 8.126.

The four groups represent semantic distinctions among downtoners, both in the force of downtoning and in combining this aspect with questioning the expression in (a) and (b) as distinct from a simpler grading of intensity in (c) and (d). But the assignment of individual downtoners to particular groups would vary from speaker to speaker.

Common downtoners include:

(a) APPROXIMATORS
almost, nearly, practically ⟨informal⟩, *virtually, as good as* ⟨informal⟩, *all but*
For example:

I *almost* resigned.
He *virtually* dictated the terms of the settlement.
They *practically* forced him to resign.
They *as good as* ruined the school.
She *all but* kissed us.

(b) COMPROMISERS
kind of ⟨informal, esp AmE⟩
sort of ⟨informal⟩
quite [contrast maximizer use with nongradables, *cf* 8.105]
rather
enough, sufficiently, more or less

For example:
I *kind of* like him. ⟨informal, esp AmE⟩ [on positioning of *kind of*, *cf* 7.64]
As he was walking along, he *sort of* stumbled and seemed ill. ⟨informal⟩
I *quite* enjoyed the party, but I've been to better ones. ⟨esp BrE⟩
I'm sure you'll like her *enough* to invite her to your party.
He *more or less* resented their interference.

(c) DIMINISHERS
These may be divided as between (i) the EXPRESSION diminishers which seek to express only part of the potential force of the item concerned, and (ii) the ATTITUDE diminishers which seek to imply that the force of the item concerned is limited. With (ii) should be compared the restrictive subjuncts (*cf* 8.116).

(i) *mildly, partially, partly, quite, slightly, somewhat*; *in part, in some respects, to some extent*; *a bit, a little, least* (*of all*)

(ii) *only, merely, simply*; *just* ⟨informal⟩, *but* ⟨formal and rather archaic⟩

For example:

(i) The incident *somewhat* influenced his actions in later life.
We know them *slightly*.
I *partly* agree with you.
They have always *mildly* disliked him.
I can admire his courage *to some extent*.

(ii) I was *only* joking.
It was *merely* a matter of finance.
She'll *just* be out for a few minutes.
It seems *but* yesterday.

(d) MINIMIZERS
negatives: *barely, hardly, little, scarcely*;
nonassertives: *in the least, in the slightest, at all, a bit*

For example:
She *scarcely* knows me.
I didn't enjoy it *in the least*.
He *little* realizes what trouble he has caused.
They don't support her *at all*.

I don't like his attitude *a bit*.
We don't mind *in the slightest*.

There are several noun phrases that can be minimizers only in negative clauses *eg*:

I didn't sleep *a wink* last night.
I don't owe you *a thing*. } ⟨informal⟩

Cf 10.62 for other examples.

Note [**a**] For the distinction between *little* and *a little*, *cf* 5.23*f*.
[**b**] Some speakers use *kind of* and *sort of* as approximators with nongradable verbs:
He *sort of* smiled at us. ['You could almost say he smiled at us']
He *kind of* grunted. ['You could almost say he grunted']
When they are used as approximators, we can say (*cf* 8.112):
He *sort of* smiled at us, but in fact it was more like a sneer.
For other speakers, they are always nearer to *more or less* than to *almost*. Both uses are very informal and *kind of* is especially common in AmE. Somewhat more informally still, these items can be at *E*: 'I'm puzzled, *sort of*'.
[**c**] As well as being a maximizer (*cf* 8.105), especially with units that are either nongradable or are seen as being at the end of the scale (*quite perfect*), we see that *quite*, apparently contradictorily, has two further roles, whether used as a modifier (*cf* 7.56, 7.63) or as an adverbial. As compromiser, it is usually stressed only lightly; as diminisher, it is heavily stressed or actually made nuclear; with verbs, the usage is especially BrE. For example:
The book is quite GÒOD. [compromiser or amplifier]
It seems that they quite LÌKE her. [compromiser]
The book is QUÌTE GÓOD.
It seems that they QUÌTE LÍKE her. } [diminisher: *cf* 18.17]
There is however considerable variation idiolectically. Note that with negatives, only the maximizer use is found: 'She didn't *quite* approve'.

8.112 Approximators differ from most other downtoners in that they imply a denial of the truth value of what is denoted by the verb. Hence we can say, with the approximator *almost*:

I *almost* resigned (but in fact I didn't resign).

But we cannot deny in this way the truth value of what is said when we use most other downtoners:

*I *kind of* like him (but in fact I don't like him).
*We know them *slightly* (but in fact we don't know them).

The minimizers differ from other downtoners in providing a modification towards a version that is more strictly true rather than a denial of the truth value of what has been said:

She {*scarcely* / *hardly*} knows me (– in fact she doesn't know me).

I can *barely* understand him (– in fact I can't understand him).
He *little* realizes the trouble he has caused (– in fact he doesn't realize it).

In each case, the second clause turns the partial denial in the first clause into admitting a full denial.

Compromisers reach out towards an assumed norm but at the same time reduce the force of the verb. Consider the following:

> I *kind of* like him. ⟨informal, esp AmE⟩
> I *rather* like him. ⟨esp BrE⟩

In saying either of these, we do not deny liking him. But we seem to be rather deprecating and grudging: 'I might go as far as to say I like him'.

The difference between diminishers and minimizers is not the nearness to the bottom of the scale, though most minimizers are indeed near the bottom. They are distinguished in their behaviour with respect to negation. The effect of negation is to deny the truth value of what is denoted by the verb:

> They didn't praise him *in the SLÌGHTest*. ['They didn't praise him']
> We don't like it *a BÌT*. ['We don't like it']

Diminishers are not usually the focus of negation, but when they are, the effect is to push the scaling towards the top. For example, with fall-rise nuclei:

> They didn't praise him *SLǏGHTly*. ['They praised him a lot']
> We don't like it *a LǏTtle*. ['We like it a lot']

Four of the minimizers – *barely*, *hardly*, *little*, *scarcely* – form a subgroup. They are themselves negative (*cf* 10.59, 10.64) and cannot be negated. On the rare occasions when they are positioned initially, there is subject–operator inversion. Of these four, *hardly*, *scarcely*, and *barely* can cooccur with nonassertives or with minimizers like *a thing*:

> They { *scarcely* / *hardly* / *barely* } need { it *at all*. / *a thing*. }
> I *scarcely* slept *a wink*.

For some people, the cooccurrence of these nonassertives or minimizers is marginally acceptable with *barely*.

Certain minimizers not listed above appear in restricted environments (*cf* 8.103):

(i) *possibly* and *conceivably*, when they operate upon *can* or *could* in nonassertive clauses:

> They *can't possibly* leave now. ['They can't under any circumstances leave now']
> *Can* he *conceivably* want to see me? ['Is it possible to imagine that he wants . . . ?']

This use of *possibly* and *conceivably* is to be distinguished from their use as disjuncts (*cf* 8.127). Contrast:

> They can't *possibly* leave now. [minimizer]
> They *possibly* can't leave now. [disjunct – 'It's possible that they can't leave now']

(ii) *never* is a negative minimizer in:

You will *never* catch the train tonight. ['You will not under any circumstances catch the train tonight']

The presence of an adverbial referring to a specific future time such as *tonight* rules out the temporal meaning of *never* (*cf*: *always* in 8.103). In nonassertive clauses *ever* (with some retention of temporal meaning) can replace *never* as minimizer; this is common, for instance, in rhetorical questions:

Will they *(n)ever* stop talking? Won't they *ever* learn? (*Won't they *never* learn?)
I wondered if the train would *(n)ever* arrive.

Note Informally, in some AmE, we have *like to* as an approximator, especially in past-tense environments:

When he saw all the blood, he *like to* fainted. ['he nearly fainted']

Cf in more widespread informal use: 'They *damn near* killed themselves in that accident.'

Syntactic features of downtoners

8.113 Some downtoners can lie within the scope of clause interrogation and negation, but not the compromisers *kind of*, *sort of*, *rather*, *more or less*; the minimizer negatives; or most approximators. The focus of clause negation can be on the compromiser *quite*, the diminishers, and the approximators *almost* and *nearly*, but only when the negation is a denial of a previous assertion. For example:

A: He almost crashed his car.
B: He didn't ĂLmost crash| He CRÀSHED|

Contrast in alternative interrogation or negation seems possible only for the compromisers *enough* and *sufficiently*, for the diminishers, and for the approximators *almost* and *nearly*.

Downtoners come within the scope of predication pro-forms and of ellipsis. Some downtoners can be focused by *only*; these include all the diminishers of subset (ci) in 8.111 (excluding *least*), and the minimizers *barely* and *a bit*. The same downtoners can be the focus of a cleft sentence under the same conditions as for amplifiers (*cf* 8.110). None of the downtoners can be the focus of *also*. Only diminisher adverbs and the minimizer *little* can be the focus of clause comparison or be premodified.

A few downtoners can precede a negative verb phrase:

I *almost* didn't meet him.
She *kind of* wasn't listening. } ⟨informal, esp AmE⟩
He *sort of* didn't want to say anything about it. }

Many downtoners can serve as the response to a question introduced by *how much*, etc (*cf* 8.110 Note). These include *enough* (but only a few of the compromisers), the nonassertive minimizers (unless preceded by *not*), and none of the approximators.

On a use of *rather* as a booster, *cf* 8.105 Note.

Positions of downtoners

8.114 Most downtoners favour *eM* position and some are restricted to it:

quite, rather, as good as, all but

Thus:

He must have been *rather* in a difficulty.
She may have *as good as* finished the painting by now. ⟨informal⟩
She had *all but* finished the painting when the burglary took place.
*She may *all but* have finished . . .

Others tend to be restricted either to *M* or *iM*:

barely, hardly, scarcely, practically, virtually

For example:

He could *hardly* be described as an expert.
She will *virtually* have finished by the time they arrive.
She *scarcely* has had any sleep. [less usual than 'has *scarcely* had']

On the other hand, *iM* is unacceptable to many people:

?He *hardly* could be described as an expert.
?She *virtually* will have finished by the time they arrive.

A few downtoners are restricted to *M* in a positive clause, but can be at *iM* in a negative one (*cf* 8.113):

kind of, sort of, almost, nearly

A few others favour *E* position:

a bit, at all

or are largely restricted to *E*:

enough, a little, and the emphatic "*one bit*

For example:

She didn't like the play { "*one* / *a* } *BÌT*.
I will try and help them *a little*.

On the other hand, a few diminishers can be placed at *I*:

partly, in part, in some respects, to some extent

Intensifier items as quantifiers, frequentatives, duratives

8.115 Many items that are intensifiers are also used to denote a measure of quantity or of duration or of frequency in time (*cf* 8.98). These intensifiers include:

most of the minimizers;
the compromisers *enough, sufficiently*;
the boosters *much, a lot* ⟨informal⟩, *a good deal, a great deal*;
the diminishers *a bit* ⟨informal⟩, *a little, least, somewhat, to some extent*.

We can therefore contrast several uses of, for example, *a lot*:

I like them *a lot*. ['to a great extent' – booster intensifier]

I paid him *a lot* for his work. ['a large amount' – quantifier]
I see him *a lot*. ['often' – frequency]
I slept *a lot* last night. ['a long time' – duration]

In all of these uses, *a lot* can be evoked as an answer to the question *how much?* But in addition the frequency subjunct can be a response to a *how often* question ('How often do you see him?'), and the duration subjunct to a *how long* question ('How long did you sleep last night?').

There can be ambiguities as a result of more than one of these uses being allowed in a given instance:

He doesn't drink *very much*. ['a very large amount' – quantifier; or 'very often' – frequency]
She suffered *very little*. ['to a small extent' – diminisher intensifier; or 'rarely' – frequency]
They *scarcely* listened to him. ['to a minimal extent' – minimizer intensifier; or 'rarely' – frequency]
Did the singers please you *enough* last night? ['to a sufficient extent' – booster intensifier; or 'sufficiently often' – frequency; or 'for a sufficiently long time' – duration]

Some of the quantifiers must be regarded as direct objects rather than as subjuncts, because they can be made the subject of the passive form of the sentence:

The new owner paid him *a lot* for his work. ~ *A lot* was paid him (by the new owner) for his work.
The students have eaten *enough*. ~ *Enough* has been eaten (by the students).
An ex-mayor wrote *a bit* about conditions in the city. ~ *A bit* was written (by an ex-mayor) about conditions in the city.

Others cannot be made subject:

After their walk, the two friends ate and drank *somewhat*.
~ **After their walk, somewhat* was eaten and drunk (by the two friends).

Those that can be made subject can also be evoked by a *what* question and they can take the position normally occupied by the head of a noun phrase with postmodification by a prepositional phrase; they may be regarded as pronouns like *all* (*cf* 6.50):

In fact, { very little / enough / a lot / a bit / a good deal } of the work has been successfully completed.

Note [**a**] For the relationship between quantitatives and frequency subjuncts, *cf* 8.71.
[**b**] Many intensifiers, particularly boosters, can also function as process adjuncts (*cf* 8.78*ff*):
He *bitterly* regretted his mistake. [booster intensifier]
He spoke *bitterly* about the way he had been treated. ['in a bitter manner' – manner process adjunct]
Cf also 8.81 for the possibility of a blend of intensifier with process adjunct.

Focusing subjuncts

8.116 Focusing subjuncts can draw attention to a part of a sentence as wide as the predication or as narrow as a single constituent of an element (such as a premodifying adjective in a noun phrase as subject, or an auxiliary within a verb phrase). They are realized by a fairly limited set of items, mostly adverbs, but including also some prepositional phrases. Functionally, there are two main subdivisions, RESTRICTIVES and ADDITIVES.

RESTRICTIVE subjuncts indicate that the utterance concerned is true in respect of the part focused. There are two subsets:

(a) EXCLUSIVES restrict the application of the utterance *exclusively* to the part focused:

alone, *exactly*, *exclusively*, *just*, *merely*, *only*, *precisely*, *purely*, *simply*, *solely*

(b) PARTICULARIZERS restrict the application of the utterance *predominantly* to the part focused:

chiefly, *especially*, *largely*, *mainly*, *mostly*, *notably*, *particularly*, *primarily*, *principally*, *specifically*; *at least*, *in particular*

ADDITIVE subjuncts indicate that the utterance concerned is *additionally* true in respect of the part focused:

again, *also*, *either*, *equally*, *even*, *further*, *likewise*, *neither*, *nor*, *similarly*, *too*; *as well*, *in addition*

Examples of the use of focusing subjuncts (with the part that is focused placed in angle brackets):

I was *simply* ⟨taking my dog for a walk⟩.
We judge them *purely* ⟨on the final examination⟩.
You can get a B grade *just* ⟨for that answer⟩.
At least ⟨ten workers⟩ reported sick yesterday.
⟨The girls⟩ *especially* objected to his manners.
⟨The workers,⟩ *in particular*, are dissatisfied with the government.
Even ⟨Bob⟩ was there.
We bought ⟨some beer⟩ *as well*.
She *merely* forgot to give her husband ⟨a kiss⟩.
He favours *particularly* ⟨the young women⟩.
She is charming *only* to her ⟨wealthy⟩ clients.

Where a focusing subjunct precedes the item focused (immediately or otherwise), it is usually associated with an intonation nucleus on the item concerned. Where this item is lengthy (*eg* a predication), the intonation nucleus will be in the unmarked final position; *cf* 18.4*ff*. For example:

I was *simply* ⟨taking my dog for a WÀLK⟩.

Where the focused item is a prepositional or noun phrase, the intonation nucleus will be on the last stressed syllable of the phrase; *eg*:

Even ⟨some of her FRÌENDS⟩ criticized her.

Where the focused item is part of a phrase, the intonation nucleus will be on the stressed or only syllable of the phrase:

She is charming *only* to her ⟨WÈALTHy⟩ clients.

On the other hand, if the focusing subjunct follows the item focused, it is the subjunct that receives the associated intonation nucleus:

⟨The girls⟩ *esPÈCially* objected to his manners.

Contrast:

The girls *especially* objected to ⟨his MÀNners⟩.

The item selected for being focused is generally 'new' information (*cf* 18.8).

Note [**a**] The clausal negative particle *not* could be regarded as a negative restrictive subjunct, excluding the part of the clause that is focused. For clausal negation, *cf* 10.54*ff*. The phrasal use of *not* is frequently correlated (*cf* 13.33) with *but* when it is used as a focusing subjunct:

He had seen *not* her ⟨YǑUNGer⟩ brother *but* her ⟨ÈLDer⟩ one.

[**b**] Among the exclusive restrictive subjuncts, *but* has a minor role. As well as its archaic (but also current dialect) use for focusing an *E*-placed element (*?I saw but William*; *I saw William but once*), it appears at *M* after modal auxiliaries, especially *can*. For example:

When I asked if she thought she would win, she replied 'Well, I can *but* try.'

Position and focus

8.117 Whether restrictives or additives, focusing subjuncts are most frequently placed at *M* unless the item focused is the subject, a part of the subject, or an auxiliary verb. But with the subjunct at *M*, one has the choice of focusing the main verb, another part of the predication, or the whole predication. Compare the following, first with the restrictive *only*, second with the additive *also*:

John could *only* ⟨SÈE⟩ his wife from the doorway. [1]
[*eg* he could not talk to her]
John could *only* see ⟨his WÌFE⟩ from the doorway. [2]
[*eg* he could not see her brother]
John could *only* see his wife ⟨from the DÒORway⟩. [3]
[*eg* he could not see her from further inside the room]
John could *also* ⟨SÈE⟩ his wife from the doorway. [4]
[*eg* as well as being able to hear her]
John could *also* see ⟨his WÌFE⟩ from the doorway. [5]
[*eg* as well as her brother]
John could *also* see his wife ⟨from the DÒORway⟩. [6]
[*eg* as well as from further inside the room]

Perhaps because the clear discrimination made by intonation leaves no room for ambiguity, no objection is made on stylistic grounds to any of these examples in speech. When it comes to writing down such sentences within the normal conventions of English punctuation, however, we see at once that the identification of the focused item is quite uncertain:

John could only see his wife from the doorway. [1], [2], or [3]
John could also see his wife from the doorway. [4], [5], or [6]

Notice that if *not*, *never*, *hardly* were to replace *only* and *also*, the same degree of indeterminacy would obtain, though of course – given the norms of English sentence intonation – we would most naturally assume a reading like [3] or [6]; *cf* 18.3*ff*. In any event, written sentences do not occur in isolation any more than spoken sentences do, and if the context made a reading like [1], [4] or [2], [5] appropriate, we would unhesitatingly read the sentences accordingly. Nonetheless, the prescriptive grammatical tradition has left a strong prejudice against placing *only* at *M* for readings [2] and [3]; instead many would insist that the 'correct' form would be:

John could see only his wife from the doorway. [= 2]
John could see his wife only from the doorway. [= 3]

Illogically, no comparable objection is made to *also* at *M*; nor of course would it be conceivable to object to *hardly*, *never*, or *not* at *M*, since although precisely the same range of possibilities exists as to the item focused, these subjuncts and *not* do not have the range of possible positions to adopt.

Thus not only would the following sentence be most naturally understood as having the subjuncts focusing upon the final time adjunct, but in most cases the subjunct could not for this purpose be moved to a position immediately preceding or following the focused adverbial:

You could { *also* / *always* / *even* / *hardly* / *never* / *not* / *only* } leave her car at the airport for a month.

Cf You could leave her car at the airport *only* for a month.
You could leave her car at the airport for a month *only*.
but *You could leave her car at the airport *hardly* for a month.

The parallelism between *not* and *only*, both grammatical and semantic, is in fact endorsed by placing *only* at *M*, despite the continuing aversion. There are occasions when it has been found useful to express a kind of correlation between *not* and *only* as in the following regulatory example:

Students are advised that they can *only* attempt examinations after their full programme of study. They can*not* attempt examinations, for example, after completing two out of three prescribed courses.

At the same time, there are undoubtedly cases where the normal *M* position for *only* (and other subjuncts) leaves a sentence unnecessarily difficult to interpret, especially in writing:

The body of the church could *only* at that time be lit by candles.

This example in the Survey of English Usage corpus has the added complication of a time adjunct at *M* which seems on first reading to be the focus of *only*, though scrutiny of the context suggests that the writer's intention was in fact *only . . . by candles*.

Note [**a**] About half the examples of *only* in the Survey of English Usage corpus are at *M* with the focused item at *E*.

[**b**] When the focus of *only* is a time or space adjunct, two interpretations are possible, 'at [time/place] and nowhere else' or with the modality sense present in diminisher downtoners:

John *only* phoned Mary ⟨an hour ago⟩.
[either 'at no other time' or 'as recently as an hour ago']
John *only* lives ⟨in Islington⟩.
[either 'nowhere else' or 'as close as Islington' or 'in as humble a place as Islington']

[**c**] Consider the following sentence:

He's only thinking about marrying a fellow doctor.

This could conceivably express four different meanings:

He's *only* ⟨THÌNKing⟩ about . . . [7]
[*ie* nothing has yet been decided]
He's *only* thinking about ⟨marrying a fellow DÒCtor⟩. [8]
[*ie* he is thinking of nothing else these days]
He's *only* thinking about marrying ⟨a fellow DÒCtor⟩ [9]
[*ie* he would not consider a wife in any other profession]
The situation is *only* [*ie*: *merely*] that ⟨he's thinking about marrying a fellow DÒCtor⟩. [10]
[*ie* you musn't imagine, for example, that he is worried about a difficult patient]

In [10], we have as it were 'advanced' the subjunct from a 'preceding' (but unspoken) clause; *cf* informal utterances like 'Go on – you're *only* jealous', which can be glossed as 'It is *merely* the case that you're jealous'. Compare also the clause relations implied by disjuncts: 'He was *frankly* rude' ~ '*I tell you frankly* that he was rude' (*cf* 8.121*f*). In [9], by contrast, we have 'retracted' the subjunct from the clause in which it semantically operates and placed it in a preceding clause. This phenomenon commonly occurs also with *ever*, as in:

I can't *ever* recall that I told you about it.
[= I can't recall that I *ever* told you about it]
I don't *ever* remember seeing her here.
[= I don't remember *ever* seeing her here]

But *cf* also a newspaper example:

Hopes of finding the body were *virtually* said to be nil.

In this case, the context showed that this was intended to be understood as 'Hopes of finding the body were said to be *virtually* nil'. Such leftward movement of an item has a significant relation to transferred negation (*cf* 14.36). *Cf* also 'She didn't so much as say that she'd ever LÒVED him.'

Positions of restrictive subjuncts

8.118 Most restrictive subjuncts can either precede or follow the item on which they are focused, provided this is a complete clause element, though it is more usual for them to precede. *Just*, *merely*, *purely*, and *simply* must normally precede the focused part and precede it immediately; *ie* they can be at *M* only when the whole predication is focused, but they can also readily appear at *iE*. Thus:

You can {**just* / **merely* / **purely* / **simply*} get a B gradc ⟨for that answer⟩.

You can get a B grade {*just* / *merely* / *purely* / *simply*} ⟨for that answer⟩.

Compare:

I had {*just* / *merely* / *simply*} ⟨typed a letter to a friend on his typewriter⟩.

The subjunct *alone* normally must follow the focused item:

> You can get a B grade ⟨for that answer⟩ *alone*.

and hence *alone* as a restrictive subjunct does not occur in *I* position:

> **Alone* ⟨ten workers⟩ reported sick yesterday.

though the virtually synonymous *only* can take either position:

> *Only* ⟨ten workers⟩ / ⟨Ten workers⟩ *only* } reported sick yesterday.

When the item focused is part of a clause element, the restrictive subjunct must usually precede:

> He *only* ⟨MÀY⟩ come – I didn't say he would.
>
> I { *only* saw / saw *only* } his ⟨ÈLDer⟩ brother – not the younger one.

though in speech (not in writing) a part of a noun phrase like the foregoing could have the restrictive following:

> I saw his ⟨ELDer⟩ brother *only*.

Contrast:

> I saw ⟨his elder brother⟩ *ÒNly*.

where the whole noun phrase is focused.

Note [**a**] *In particular* favours a position after the focused part.

[**b**] *Exactly* commonly focuses on *wh*-items, and *precisely* does so too, but less commonly; this can mean that the focused part is discontinuous:

> *Exactly* ⟨who⟩ is asking for me?
> ⟨What⟩ *exactly* ⟨do you mean⟩?
> I know *exactly* ⟨where to find him⟩.

Otherwise, *exactly* does not precede the subject unless it focuses on a noun phrase with a quantifier, fraction, multiplier, or cardinal numeral:

> *Exactly* ⟨ten people⟩ were present.

Just also focuses on *wh*-interrogatives, but can only precede them:

> *Just* ⟨why do you want it⟩?

Just can also focus on *exactly* and *precisely*:

> *Just* ⟨*exactly*⟩ ⟨what do you expect⟩?

or on a *wh*-item also focused by *exactly* or *precisely*:

> *Just* ⟨⟨who⟩ *exactly*⟩ ⟨are you⟩?
> *Just* ⟨⟨where⟩ *precisely*⟩ ⟨do you want to go⟩?

It will be noticed that both discontinuity and embedding are involved in these examples.

[**c**] The restrictives *just*, *merely*, *simply* can freely appear in front of imperative sentences:

> You don't have to be present. { *Just* / *Merely* / *Simply* } ⟨send a letter of explanation⟩.

[**d**] When focusing noun phrases, *only* and *alone* are to some extent treated as though they formed part of the noun phrases concerned. *Cf*:

> *Only* two persons / Two persons *alone* } witnessed the accident.
>
> ~The accident was witnessed by { *only* two persons. / two persons *alone*. }

Positions of additive subjuncts

8.119 The following additives normally precede (either at *M* or immediately) a focused part if this is the whole or part of the predication; but they may follow the focused part, then carrying an intonation nucleus; and if the focused part is subject, they must follow it. *Even* is exceptional in possibly preceding the subject and in not taking a nucleus if it follows the focused part. The items are:

again, also, equally, even, similarly, in addition

Compare:

I've noticed the fox in my garden and

John has { *also* / *even* / *similarly* / *in addition* } seen it ⟨near his back DÒOR⟩.

John has seen it { *also* / *even* / *similarly* / *in addition* } ⟨near his back DÒOR⟩.

John has seen it ⟨near his back DǑOR⟩ { *ÀLSO.* / *SÌMilarly.* / *in adDÌTion.* }

John has seen it ⟨near his back DÒOR⟩ *even.* ⟨ informal⟩

⟨John⟩ { *ÀLSO* / *SÌMilarly* / *in adDÌTion* } has seen it.

even ⟨JÒHN⟩ has seen it.

The subjuncts *too* and *as well* normally follow the focused part and do not appear at *M*:

. . . John has seen it ⟨near his back DǑOR⟩ { *TÒO.* / *as WÈLL.* }

In rather 'prepared' usage, these may precede the focused part:

She has invited { *TǑO* / *as WĚLL* } ⟨some of her own FÀMily⟩.

In speech, especially informally, the additives can be at *E* and still focus even on the subject:

. . . ⟨JÒHN⟩ has seen it { *TÒO.* / *even.* ⟨informal⟩ / *in adDÌTion.* }

Neither and *nor* must precede the focused part, and when they are at *I*, there is subject–operator inversion (*cf* 18.24):

His father wouldn't give the money { {*and* / *but*} *neither* / *nor* / {*?and* / *?but*} *nor* } would he ⟨LÈND⟩ it.

For some speakers *nor* is treated as a coordinating conjunction, and it cannot therefore be preceded by a conjunction.

Neither and *nor* can also be correlative as additive subjuncts:

> He had *neither* seen ⟨the FÍLM⟩ *nor* (*even*) read ⟨the BÒOK⟩.
>
> She {had *neither* read / had read *neither*} ⟨the BÓOK⟩ *nor* ⟨the revÌEWS⟩.
>
> *Neither* ⟨SHÉ⟩ *nor* ⟨HÈ⟩ had read the book.

The subjunct *further* is placed at *M* whether it focuses upon the whole predication or only a part of it:

> She had studied metaphysics and she had *further* ⟨taken a degree in linguistics⟩.
>
> He has argued the case on behalf of John and has *further* argued it on behalf of John's ⟨BRÒTHer⟩.

Note [**a**] Additives are often positionally tied, such that 'As well as/along with X, Y admires Z' means 'X and Y admire Z'. If the order were switched (perhaps to achieve focus on X; *cf* 18.3), 'Y admires Z, as well as/along with X', this would be interpreted as 'Y admires Z and X'.

[**b**] The additive *also* can be used like *only* when focusing upon a part of a noun phrase (*cf* 8.118):

I *also* saw his ⟨ÈLDer⟩ brother. ~ I saw his ⟨ÈLDer⟩ brother *ÀLSO*.

[**c**] A further additive, *besides*, is less frequent:

. . . I saw his ⟨ÈLDer⟩ brother, *besÌDES*.

Syntactic features of focusing subjuncts

8.120 Focusing subjuncts cannot normally focus upon other focusing subjuncts (on *just*, however, *cf* 8.118 Note [b]). They cannot be the focus of a cleft sentence or of clause comparison, nor can they be premodified by *however*, *how*, or *so* (*cf* 8.25). While some focusing subjuncts can come within the scope of both interrogation and negation and be the focus of both question and negation, it is not usually possible to frame alternative interrogation or negation with focusing subjuncts.

Other syntactic features applying to focusing subjuncts include the fact that they cannot be modified (**very only*, **extremely also*). Moreover, most of them cannot be coordinated: **just and exactly*, **equally and likewise*. But we have one cliché coordination:

> He is making the suggestion *purely and simply* ⟨for your benefit⟩.

Focusing subjuncts are the focus of the question in:

> Did she see him *only* ⟨once⟩?
>
> Will they release ⟨the major⟩ *as well*?

and of negation in:

They won't punish *merely* ⟨John⟩.
They won't release ⟨the major⟩ *as well.*

But most additive subjuncts cannot be the focus of negation. Indeed, *too* cannot even be within the scope of negation, while *neither* and *nor* themselves effect the negation. An example of alternative interrogation with a restrictive subjunct:

Did she see him *only* ⟨once⟩ or did she see him *MÒRE than* ⟨once⟩?

And with a different type of contrastive interrogative:

Did she invite *merely* ⟨girls⟩ or did she invite *also* ⟨BÒYS⟩?

Alternative interrogation does not seem plausible with most additive subjuncts, and alternative negation seems implausible with both types of focusing subjuncts.

Certain restrictives can be the focus of an initial *not* with consequent subject–operator inversion. Besides the normal:

He *not only* ⟨protested⟩: he (*also*) ⟨refused to pay his taxes⟩.

we can also have:

Not only did he ⟨protest⟩: he (*also*) ⟨refused to pay his taxes⟩.

(On *not only . . . but*, *cf* 13.42.)

Restrictives allowing this subject–operator inversion are:

not + just, merely, only, simply

of which *not only* and *not merely* do so most commonly. The construction implies a correlative construction, with (*but*) *also* as common correlatives in the second clause. *Not only* can appear initially in such a sequence without subject–operator inversion when the focus is on the subject:

Not only ⟨HÈ⟩ protested: several others joined in.

Focusing subjuncts can appear in a construction resembling a cleft sentence:

It was {*only* / *particularly* / *also* / *even*}
{⟨John⟩ who protested.
⟨on Thursdays⟩ that he visited her.}

We should distinguish this construction from a similar one which is different in being correlative:

It was *not* that ⟨John proTÈSTed⟩; it was *rather* that ⟨he was RÙDE⟩.

In this example, the subjuncts are functioning within the superordinate clause to which the *that*-clause is complement. Restrictives, additives, and some disjuncts (*eg*: *possibly, probably*) commonly occur in such a correlative structure. Other examples:

It's *partly* that ⟨he's good-looking⟩; it's *partly* that ⟨he's clever⟩.

It's *not* that ⟨they object to him⟩; it's *more probably* that ⟨they have no interest in him⟩.

It's *not* just that ⟨she's young⟩; it's {*surely* / *more*} that ⟨she's inexperienced⟩.

Note [**a**] *Exactly* and *precisely* are used as comment utterances on a previous declarative sentence:

A: That was the day she was referring to.

B: {*Exactly.* / *Precisely.* / *Right.* ⟨esp AmE⟩}

But these seem to be related to some implied sentence such as 'That was *exactly/precisely* the day' or 'You are *exactly/precisely right*'. *Quite* ['I quite agree'] is used in the same way in BrE. *Right* is used, especially in AmE, to express agreement, and is more common than *exactly* or *precisely*; but it cannot be related like these to focusing subjunct use. Especially in BrE, *quite* ['I quite agree'] commonly expresses agreement with something said by another speaker, whether the preceding clause is positive or negative (*cf* 8.130 Note [c]):

A: She should (not) have told you!

B: *QUÌTE.*

[**b**] Like *not only*, but without a corresponding correlative, *not even* can focus upon the subject:

Not even ⟨HÈ⟩ protested.

Disjuncts

8.121 Like subjuncts, the adverbials that we call DISJUNCTS are grammatically distinct from adjuncts in terms of the features set out in 8.25. Consider in this connection the adverbials in the following sentences:

Sadly, the storm destroyed the entire tobacco crop. [1]
Your son is not, *in all frankness*, succeeding in his present job. [2]
Since she ran out of money, she had to defer buying a new car. [3]

We note, first of all, that it is not the *form* of these adverbials that makes them different from adjuncts or even from subjuncts:

Dr Fox sat *sadly* in her room. [4]
The arrested man answered *in all frankness* the rather awkward personal questions. [5]
She has been living in great hardship *since she ran out of money*. [6]

Nor yet is it the *positions* in which the adverbials are placed in [1], [2], and [3]. We could move the adverbials to *I* in [4] and [6]; we could move *in all frankness* to *M* in [5]; we would leave their grammatical relations broadly unchanged and still sharply different from the grammatical relations of the adverbials in [1], [2], and [3]. The adverbials in [4], [5], and [6] can be made the focus of a cleft sentence; can be the basis of contrast in alternative interrogation or negation; can be focused by focusing subjuncts; and can come within the scope of predication pro-forms or ellipsis. These propensities are those of their adjunct status (*cf* 8.25). But the adverbials in [1], [2], and [3] cannot, without producing absurdity or requiring a different interpretation, undergo any of these processes:

*Did the storm destroy the crop *sadly* or . . . ?
*It is *in all frankness* that your son is not succeeding . . .
*It is *since she ran out of money* that she had to defer buying a new car. [asterisked except as a time adjunct of backward span, whereas in [3] the adverbial concerns not time but *reason*]

Similar observations hold true for subjuncts, as we saw in 8.88, but it should not be thought on that account that disjuncts are especially akin to subjuncts. Rather, we have a three-fold distinction that can be set out informally as follows:

ADJUNCTS are similar in the weight and balance of their sentence role to other sentence elements such as subject and object.

SUBJUNCTS have in general a lesser role than the other sentence elements; they have for example less independence both semantically and grammatically and in some respects are subordinate to one or other of the sentence elements.

DISJUNCTS, by the same analogy, have a superior role as compared with the sentence elements; they are syntactically more detached and in some respects 'superordinate', in that they seem to have a scope that extends over the sentence as a whole.

We shall now scrutinize the general semantic roles of disjuncts in order to understand why they appear to have such a grammatical function in relation to the clauses in which they operate.

8.122 It is very difficult to make a wholly objective utterance, and almost everything we say or write conveys the impress of our attitude. Thus, a sentence such as

Mr Forster neglects his children. [1]

entails assumptions about the 'authority' on which the statement is made. It is unlikely that the speaker has heard Mr Forster say, 'I neglect my children', but if this were the source of authority, the speaker would have been more likely to make the sentence:

Mr Forster says (that) he neglects his children. [2]

This might well imply that the speaker cannot himself confirm it:

Mr Forster says (that) he neglects his children (*though I've seen no evidence of this*). [3]

If, indeed, he had such evidence, the sentence would be likely to be different again, both in the statement of the authority and the implication of the speaker's own view:

Mr Forster admits (that) he neglects his children (*as I myself have suspected*). [4]

By contrast with [2] and [4], the 'unattributed' sentence [1] is likely to mean and to be interpreted as meaning:

> From things I have heard and seen, I claim it to be a fair and true assessment that *Mr Forster neglects his children.* [5]

It need hardly be pointed out that such detailed specificity is rarely made explicit, though it is worth noting that in a court of law it would be by no means unusual for the speaker of [1] to be obliged either to expand it to [5] or at least to acknowledge that by his [1] he intended to mean neither more nor less than [5].

But even in ordinary speech and writing, it is not uncommon to find some overt indication of authority accompanying the bald statement [1], such as:

> I think / I gather / It seems } (that) Mr Forster neglects his children.
> I tell you . . .
> I tell you *frankly* . . .
> I tell you *privately* . . .
> I put it to you *crudely* . . .
> I say, *if you will allow me* (*to do so*), that . . . [6]

Each of the italicized sections in the various alternate forms of [6] is an adverbial in a clause which has the speaker as subject and *Mr Forster neglects his children* as its object. Thus:

I	tell	you	*frankly*	that Mr Forster neglects his children.	[7]
S	V	O_i	*A*	O_d	

But even the degree of overt authority in [7] can be abbreviated:

> *Frankly*, Mr Forster neglects his children. [8]

It is where sentences like [8] have the same meaning as [7], that we speak of the adverbials as disjuncts, and it can now be seen why such adverbials have in some sense a superordinate role in relation to the sentences in which they function.

Note [a] Not all disjuncts can be so straightforwardly related to adverbials in superordinate clauses. For example, the disjunct in:

> *Presumably*, Alison has bought a new car.

cannot be related to:

> *I tell you *presumably* that Alison . . .

But plausible paraphrases will nonetheless place 'Alison has bought a new car' as a clause functioning as an element in a superordinate clause, *eg*:

> *I presume* that Alison has bought a new car.
> That Alison has bought a new car *is widely presumed*.
> It *is widely presumed* that Alison has bought a new car.

It is a matter of interesting speculation to account for the processes by which we can express the meaning of these finite verb phrases in terms of verbless adverbials.

[b] Many conjuncts also correspond to a construction containing a verb of speaking; *cf* 8.138.

[c] Note the following examples of formal stereotyped expressions of authority:

> *I hereby declare that* I shall . . .
> Stop – *in the name of the law*.
> No flowers *by request*.

8.123 Disjuncts can be divided into two main classes: STYLE disjuncts (by far the smaller class) and CONTENT disjuncts. Style disjuncts convey the speaker's comment on the style and form of what he is saying, defining in some way under what conditions he is speaking as the 'authority' for the utterance. Content disjuncts (also known as attitudinal disjuncts) make observations on the actual content of the utterance and its truth conditions. These two classes and their subclasses are displayed in *Fig* 8.123.

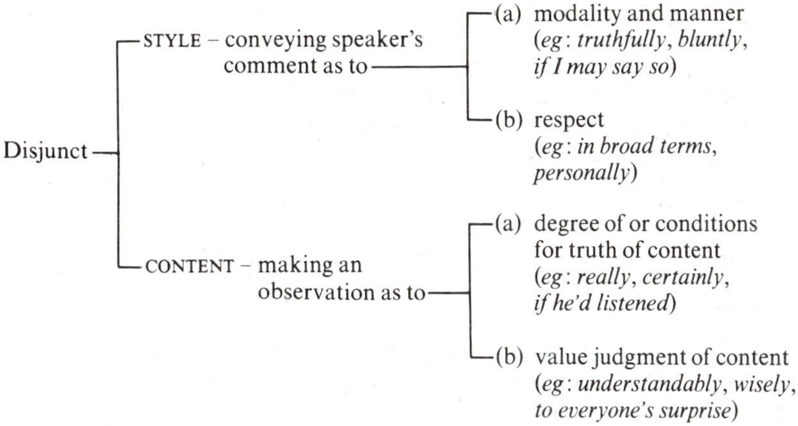

Fig 8.123

Style disjuncts

8.124 The relationship between a style disjunct and the clause to which it is attached can often be expressed (as we explained in 8.122) by a clause in which the same formal item as the style disjunct is a process adjunct (*cf* 8.78*ff*), with a verb of speaking, the subject of which is 'I'. Thus, *frankly* in:

Frankly, I am tired.

is equivalent to *I tell you frankly* or *I say frankly*. If the clause is a question, the disjunct may be ambiguous:

Frankly, is he tired?

In this example, the adverbial may correspond to *I ask you frankly* or to the more probable *Tell me frankly*. Often the disjunct is quite overt about the verb of speaking and the adverbial may take the form of a finite clause:

If I may say so without offence, your writing is immature.

In thus drawing attention not only to what is said but to how it is being said, the style disjunct is often an implicit comment on language itself (*cf* 8.126). Adverbs commonly used as style disjuncts include:

Type (a): Modality and Manner

candidly, *flatly*, *honestly*, *seriously*, *strictly*, *truly*, *truthfully*; *confidentially*, *privately*; *approximately*, *bluntly*, *briefly*, *broadly*, *crudely*, *frankly*, *generally*, *roughly*, *simply*

For example:

> *Briefly*, there is nothing more I can do about it.
> I don't want the money, *confidentially*.
> *Very seriously*, do you intend to resign?
> You ask me what he wants. *Quite simply*, he wants to move to a better climate.

Style disjuncts of Type (a) are also realized by prepositional phrases and by clauses. For example:

> *In short*, he is mad but happy.
> *Putting it bluntly*, he has little market value.
> *As a rough approximation*, you can expect a group of fifteen.
> There were twelve people present, *to be precise*.

Type (b): Respect

> *figuratively, generally, literally, metaphorically, personally, strictly*

For example:

> She was *strictly* out of order in adjourning the meeting at that point.
> *Generally*, the rainy season has already begun by September.
> *Personally*, I find the music too arid.

Frequently, however, respect disjuncts are realized by longer phrases or by clauses, thus making more explicit the respect in which a comment is being 'hedged':

> *Generally speaking*, the rainy season has already begun by September.
> *Strictly speaking* she was out of order.
> *Speaking purely* for myself, I find the music too arid.
> Mildred seemed to enjoy the concert, { *to judge from her remarks.* / *from what her brother told me.* / *since her brother told me himself.* }
> It was not a very difficult job to persuade him to go, *if you understand me*.
> { *If I may say so,* / *With respect,* } none of you are competent to make the legal judgment required.

Because-clauses can also be style disjuncts of this type (and as such they must be placed at *E*):

> He was drunk, *because he had to support himself on a friend's arm*.

In this type of usage (*cf* 15.21), *if* and *since*-clauses (normally *content* disjuncts) occur commonly as style disjuncts; these may occur at *I*, *M*, or *E*. Note, however, the prosody:

> *If you ask* MĚ, he was DRÙNK.
> He was DRÙNK, *if you ask* { *MĚ.* / *MÉ.* }
> *Since you* ˈ*want to* KNÓW, I saw him with your sìster.

I saw him with your SÌSter, *since you 'want to KNÓW*.

When a speaker wishes to emphasize that he or she alone is the authority, a style disjunct may be reinforced by another, even though a listener may find the cooccurrence objectionably tautologous (or obtrusively egotistical):

((*Speaking*) *for*) *mySÉLF*, I find the work here quite PLÈASant, PÉRsonally.

It will be noted that *-self* disjuncts in their truncated form can be identical with appositives (*cf* 17.65*ff*):

I mySÉLF find the work here quite PLÈASant.

(*Cf* 8.125 Note [b]).

Note [**a**] Informally, a somewhat indignant use of an *if*-disjunct not uncommonly occurs on its own, leaving the situational context to make obvious what the unspoken statement would have been. Note the exaggerated emphasis on *if*:

"*ÌF you don't MÍND* { (that is my seat). / (your umbrella is in my way). }

The *if*-clause is understood as short for something like 'If you don't mind my saying so/my pointing this out'.

Another stereotyped expression of indignation by means of an *if*-disjunct occurs when we call attention, for example, to the words used by someone else (*cf* 8.126):

She said I was ↑CHÌLDish, *if you please*.

[**b**] Use of the disjunct *personally* normally requires that the subject of the clause is the authority for it:

Personally I regard this music as boring.
Fred said that *personally he* found concentration increasingly difficult.
?**Personally*, *Fred* finds concentration increasingly difficult.

8.125 Corresponding to some adverbs as style disjuncts, a series of longer disjuncts may be used, often involving the same item or its lexical base. For example, in place of *frankly* in:

Frankly, he hasn't a chance.

we could have:

prepositional phrase: *in all frankness*
infinitive clause: *to be frank*, *to speak frankly*, *to put it frankly*
-ing clause: *frankly speaking*, *putting it frankly*
-ed clause: *put frankly*
finite clause: *if I may be frank*, *if I can speak frankly*, *if I can put it frankly*

Not every style disjunct will allow so full a range. Thus, we have *in all fairness* but not the disjunct *fairly*; *in short* but not *shortly*. Conversely, we have *flatly* but not *flatly speaking*.

But for almost all of the adverbs listed in 8.124, corresponding participle constructions with *speaking* are available as style disjuncts; *eg*: *frankly* ~ *frankly speaking*, *seriously* ~ *seriously speaking*. Many have infinitive clauses of the form *to be* plus the base adjective, *eg*: *bluntly* ~ *to be blunt*, *personally* ~ *to be personal*. Those allowing such infinitive clauses have a corresponding finite clause with *if*; for example: *if I may be blunt*, *if I may be personal*.

Note [**a**] The order of adjunct and verb in the disjunct participle construction with *speaking* is more or less stereotyped. *Speaking frankly* is far less likely than *frankly speaking*. On the other hand, *speaking generally* is the participle construction equivalent to the adverb style disjunct *generally*, as in:

The committee interviewed several writers and publishers. *Generally*, the writers were against censorship.

The style disjunct use of *generally* (with its corresponding prepositional phrase *in general*) is to be distinguished from the time adjunct use of the same word *generally*, synonymous with *normally* or *usually* (*cf* 8.66, 8.67 Note [b]). Perhaps because the time adjunct has an alternative form in the corresponding participle clause *generally speaking*, it is the inverted form *speaking generally* that is used as the expanded form of the disjunct.

[**b**] The style disjunct *personally* is to be distinguished from the intensifier *personally* that is synonymous with the appropriate reflexive form of the pronoun:

I {*personally* / *myself*} have never been to New York.

These are both to be distinguished from the adjunct *personally* that is synonymous with *in person*:

He signed the document *personally*.

[**c**] *Truly* has been included among style disjuncts. It corresponds to *I tell you truly* and also, in many environments, to *It is true* (*that*), the latter type of correspondence being common to many content disjuncts (*cf* 8.128). However, unlike such content disjuncts but like other style disjuncts, it can appear before a question:

I think he has no right to be there. *Truly*, what is your opinion?

Truly here can be replaced neither by *It is true* nor *Is it true*; it is perhaps to be seen as an abbreviation of *Tell me truly*.

Metalinguistic comment

8.126 Overt reference to the linguistic medium, such as in the selection or coining of an appropriate expression, is not of course peculiar to adverbials (*cf* App I.15):

Let us call this concept 'pre-impressionist'.
The only word for it is *banal*.
The look on his face was what I would call, not *baleful*, but *bileful*.

Nonetheless, adverbials lend themselves very conveniently to incorporating metalinguistic comment into a sentence whose purpose is not itself merely metalinguistic. There is, for instance, a subclass of conjuncts ('reformulatory', *cf* 8.141) whose chief function this is. But the style disjunct lends itself peculiarly well to such a role:

Hawkins was not, *strictly speaking*, a traitor.

In this sentence, we should notice that we are concerned both with the issue of whether or not Hawkins was a traitor and also with the issue of whether the word 'traitor' is a fitting term to express his behaviour.

Other disjuncts commonly used as 'hedges' in this way are illustrated by:

{They have not, *so to say*, 'combined' their resources; / They have not 'combined' their resources, *exactly*;} *rather* they have agreed to make some joint decisions.

(In this example, the reformulatory conjunct *rather* appears; *cf* above)

He has an idea, a hypothesis, *if you will*, that you may find interesting.
You ought to seize this opportunity, *if I may so put it*, with more grace than you are showing.

Cf also *so to speak*, *if you like*, *to quote X*, *as X puts it*, *in the immortal words of X*.

Frequently, however, metalinguistic comment is inextricably mixed up with expression of degree. The compromiser subjuncts *kind of* and *sort of* play a similar role; as do approximators (*cf* 8.104*ff*). Consider, for example, the subjunct usage in:

They have an idea, {*almost* a theory. / a theory, *almost*.}
She *just about* alienated her audience on that occasion.

It is not easy here to know whether we are to understand the latter as meaning *almost but not entirely alienated* or as *what I might almost call 'alienated'*, and we have no reason to believe that the originator of the sentence was making a distinction between these. So too when we are told that:

He {*almost* / *virtually* / *very nearly*} STÒLE the money.

we cannot be sure whether it means that he came close to stealing it or acted in such a way that it could almost be called 'stealing'. In consequence, some comment adverbials like *actually*, *frankly*, and others come to be used as subjuncts (emphasizers), *cf* 8.100*ff*. This is especially true of *literally*, as in:

The police *literally* left no square inch unexamined.
It was a tiny room – *literally* a 'one-man' office.
I could *literally* feel the earth shaking.
The car *literally* somersaulted off the road.

It would seem that the speaker wishes to emphasize the extraordinary nature of what he is describing – 'Believe it or not!' – , as well as to draw attention to the hyperbolic language used to describe it. The insertion of *literally* seems often to acknowledge that people tend to use the expression concerned (*somersault*, *earth shaking*) as merely figurative or exaggeratedly colourful whereas in the present instance the word is to be taken in its literal meaning. But in careless and informal speech, and even indeed in writing, the adverb comes to be used in ways that are 'literally' absurd:

She *literally* FLÈW out of the room.
I *literally* split my SÌDES laughing.

Note [**a**] On the same page of a recent novel, a policeman is described as parking his vehicle thus:

He literally threw his car into the last available space.

And in tackling a hoodlum:

He literally threw the man down from the stage.

A few pages further on, some criminals on motorcycles 'were, literally, using their machines as weapons'. In the second and third instance, the use of *literally* seems justified if hyperbolic; in the first it is absurd.

[**b**] With the comment adverbials, we can focus on individual items in the verb phrase (*cf* 8.96) as well as on the main verb or predication. Compare:

I *actually/frankly/literally* HÀD to crawl through the fence.
I had *actually/frankly/literally* to CRÀWL through the fence.
[. . . to *actually/frankly/literally* CRÀWL . . .; *cf* 8.21]

In the former, it is the obligation that has to be understood as literally and seriously expressed; in the latter, it is the act of crawling.

[c] In colloquial style, some predications are conventionally used in a nonliteral way, and this is frequently indicated by intonationally highlighting the verb:

> The boy was ÀSKing for trouble. ['. . . was *virtually* asking . . .']
> They went out of their WÀY to be helpful. ['went *as it were* out of . . .']

Content disjuncts

8.127 The speaker's comment on the content of what he is saying is of two principal kinds, which can in turn be subdivided.

Type (a): Degree of truth

These disjuncts present a comment on the truth value of what is said, expressing the extent to which, and the conditions under which, the speaker believes that what he is saying is true. Here belong the great classes of hypothetical clauses on which closely reasoned discourse depends. Disjuncts realized by concessive, conditional, reason, and other adverbial clauses will be given special attention in 15.32, and we shall concentrate here on shorter realizations, particularly by adverbs. Indeed, adverbs falling in Type (a) constitute what is virtually a closed class, and most items will be cited below. There are three main groups.

Group (i) These express conviction, either as a direct claim (*eg*: *undeniably*) or as an appeal to general perception (*eg*: *evidently*):

> *admittedly*, *assuredly* ⟨rare, formal⟩, *avowedly* ⟨formal⟩, *certainly*, *decidedly* ⟨rare, formal⟩, *definitely*, *incontestably* ⟨rare, formal⟩, *incontrovertibly* ⟨formal⟩, *indeed*, *indisputably* ⟨formal⟩, *indubitably* ⟨formal⟩, *surely*, *unarguably* ⟨formal⟩, *undeniably*, *undoubtedly*, *unquestionably*; *clearly*, *evidently*, *manifestly* ⟨formal⟩, *obviously*, *patently* ⟨formal⟩, *plainly*

Group (ii) These express some degree of doubt:

> *allegedly*, *arguably*, *apparently*, *conceivably*, *doubtless*, *likely* ⟨informal⟩, *maybe* ⟨informal⟩, *most likely*, *perhaps*, *possibly*, *presumably*, *purportedly* ⟨formal⟩, *quite likely*, *reportedly*, *reputedly* ⟨formal⟩, *seemingly* ⟨formal⟩, *supposedly*, *very likely*

Such items as *perhaps* and *by any chance* politely reduce the impact and urgency of questions and conditions, or convey an apologetic tone:

> Is Mary at home, { *perhaps*? / *by any chance*? }
> If Mary is (*perhaps*) at liberty, I could see her for a moment (*perhaps*).
> Mary is not free for a moment, *by any chance*?

Cf the similar effect by alternative means in:

> Is Mary at home, { I wonder? / would you (happen to) know? }
> Mary is not free for a moment, I suppose?

Group (iii) These state the sense in which the speaker judges what he says to be true or false. There is often a reference to the 'reality' or lack of 'reality' in what is said. Some assert the reality of what is said:

actually, really, factually ⟨rare, formal⟩

Several express a contrast with reality:

only apparently, formally, hypothetically, ideally, nominally, officially, ostensibly ⟨formal⟩, *outwardly, superficially, technically, theoretically*

A few claim that what is being said is true in principle:

basically, essentially, fundamentally

The distinction is often a fine one between content disjuncts and viewpoint subjuncts (*cf* 8.89), particularly when the same formal item is involved:

Technically, our task is to recycle the waste products. [disjunct]
Technically, recycling the waste products will be easy. [subjunct; *cf* 'Recycling . . . will be technically easy']

Some further examples of Type (a) disjuncts:

Mr Hasegawa seemed to enjoy the concert, *although Wagner is not one of his favourite composers.*
Since she had no time to have the car fixed, Mildred telephoned for a taxi.
The proposal would have been accepted *if the manager had been more tactful.*

Type (b): Value judgment

Disjuncts of this type convey some evaluation of or attitude towards what is said. As with Type (a), we concentrate on realization by adverbs and some of the more common items are listed below. Those with a participle base (*cf* App I.2) in *-ing* (*eg*: *surprisingly*) are the most productive class of adverbs as content disjuncts. There are two main groups.

Group (i) These express a judgment on what is being said as a whole and they normally apply the same judgment simultaneously to the subject of the clause. For example:

Rightly, Mrs Jensen consulted her lawyer. [She was right and her action was right]

With some, as in this example, judgment is passed on whether what is said is right or wrong:

correctly, incorrectly, justly, unjustly, rightly, wrongly

With others, judgment is passed on the wisdom or manner of what is described:

artfully, cleverly, cunningly, foolishly, prudently, reasonably, sensibly, shrewdly, unreasonably, wisely, unwisely

Group (ii) With these, the judgment carries no implication that it applies to the subject of the clause. For example:

Remarkably, Mrs Jensen consulted her lawyer. [Her action was remarkable; the speaker is not suggesting that Mrs Jensen was remarkable]

As with this example, some items judge what is said to be strange or unexpected (and items listed are frequently followed by *enough*):

amazingly, *astonishingly*, *curiously*, *funnily* ⟨BrE⟩, *incredibly*, *ironically*, *oddly*, *remarkably*, *strangely*, *suspiciously*, *unexpectedly*

With other adverbs, what is said is judged to be appropriate or expected:

appropriately, *inevitably*, *naturally*, *not unnaturally*, *predictably*, *understandably*

What is said is judged to cause satisfaction or the reverse:

annoyingly, *delightfully*, *disappointingly*, *disturbingly*, *pleasingly*, *refreshingly*, *regrettably*

What is said is judged to be fortunate or unfortunate:

fortunately, *unfortunately*, *happily* ⟨formal⟩, *unhappily* ⟨formal⟩, *luckily*, *unluckily*, *sadly* ⟨formal⟩, *tragically*

Other judgments:

amusingly, *conveniently*, *hopefully* (*cf* 8.129 Note [b]), *mercifully*, *preferably*, *significantly*, *thankfully*

Some examples of Type (b) disjuncts:

Certainly, he had very little reason to fear their competition.
Obviously, nobody expected us to be here today.
Really, the public does not have much choice in the matter.
Understandably, we were all extremely annoyed when we received the letter.
He is *wisely* staying at home today.

As well as by adverbs, content disjuncts of Type (b) are realized by prepositional phrases and clauses (*cf* 9.57*f*, 15.20*f*). For example:

To my regret, he did not accept our offer.
They arrived, *to our surprise*, before we did.
With justice, they have assumed their place among the nation's heroes.
To the great admiration of all the onlookers, he plunged into the water and rescued the struggling child.
On paper, she ought to have won, but *in fact* she lost.
Of course, nobody imagines that he will repay what he borrowed.
It was *no doubt* clever of him to offer his resignation at that point in the proceedings.
To be sure, we have heard many such promises before.
They are not going to buy the house, *which is not surprising in view of its exorbitant price*.
Even more important, she has control over the finances of the party.
What is even more remarkable, he manages to inspire confidence in the most suspicious people.

The use of *more* in the last two examples shows how content disjuncts can be adapted to conjunct use (*cf* 8.137).

Note [a] Several adverbs with *-ed* participle bases imply that the view not only of the speaker but of others is being quoted: *allegedly, reportedly, reputedly, supposedly*. Among common formulas by which the speaker identifies such an authority, however, the following two may be mentioned: *According to* (*Mary, the Government, the morning paper* . . .), and *By* (*their, her, his, Mary's, the Government's* . . .) *own admission*.

[b] *Doubtless* is not synonymous with 'without doubt'. Like *no doubt*, it in fact implies some doubt and is synonymous with 'very probably'. *Undoubtedly*, on the other hand, expresses conviction. *Apparently* is for most speakers equivalent to 'it appears' or 'it seems', and these do not express certainty. However, some speakers equate *apparently* with 'it is evident'. Prosody and phrasal form combine to make a distinction in the degree of commitment to a statement of authority:

The fire had already started, { to my KNŎWledge. [some doubt] / to my certain KNÒWledge. [no doubt] }

[c] *Admittedly* and *certainly* imply concession as well as certainty. Concession applies still more strongly to two disjuncts which take the form of nonfinite clauses:

That SĂID, / *Having SÀID THÁT,* } I have to agree that there are great difficulties.

Although the latter normally obeys the subject-attachment rule (*cf* 15.58*f*), the disjunct has become so stereotyped that one often finds examples like:

Having said that, the economy seems unlikely to show marked improvement for some time.

[d] Just as the verb *see* can be used for both visual and mental perception (*cf*: *I see* ['understand'] *what you mean*), so adverbs as disjuncts can be used for both types of perception. In:

Obviously, he doesn't want us to help him.

the speaker's conviction may well be based on what the person has said rather than anything that has been perceived visually. On the other hand, in:

Obviously, he is in very poor health.

it may be based largely on the person's appearance.

[e] Style disjuncts such as *truthfully* and *honestly* (*cf* 8.124) and content disjuncts such as *certainly* and *definitely* alike express conviction about what is said. But the style disjuncts assert that the speaker is saying something sincerely, while the content disjuncts assert the truth of what is said.

8.128 We have seen that adverbs as style disjuncts correspond to a clause with a verb of speaking (*cf* 8.122). Many adverbs as content disjuncts, though not all, also correspond to other structures. The set of correspondences presented below for adverbs of one or other type applies only to adverbs of the type concerned, and even so not necessarily to all the items of that particular type. For example, many adverbs of content Type (a), such as *evidently*, have the following correspondences:

Evidently, he doesn't object.
It is evident (*that*) he doesn't object.
That he doesn't object *is evident*.

But these correspondences do not apply, for example, to *perhaps*. To avoid repetition, we use only the variants with extraposition and anticipatory *it* (*cf* 18.33). Hence, we give the correspondence for *evidently* in Type (a) as simply:

It is evident that he doesn't object.

The semantic distinction between adverbs of Type (a) (*eg*: *admittedly, clearly*) and Type (b) (*eg*: *fortunately, wisely*) is reflected in the fact that it is possible to use putative *should* (*cf* 4.64, 14.25, 16.70*ff*) in the correspondences of Type (b). If *should* is inserted in correspondences of Type (a), it conveys obligation (*cf* 4.56*ff*) and alters the meaning of the sentence radically, since this group is concerned with the factual basis of what is asserted or questioned:

Type (a)

[*Certainly,* / *Clearly,*] she consults her lawyer regularly.

= It is [*certain* / *clear*] that she consults her lawyer regularly.

but:

≠ It is [*certain* / *clear*] *that* she *should* consult her lawyer regularly.

[this would mean 'She *ought to* consult her lawyer regularly']

By contrast, putative *should* enters the Type (b) correspondences, since here we are concerned with the expression of an opinion:

Type (b)

[*Fortunately,* / *Wisely,*] she consults her lawyer regularly.

= It is [*fortunate* / *wise*] that she {consult(s) / should consult} her lawyer regularly.

Most of the adverbs of Type (b) allow also a correspondence with an infinitive clause (commonly a replacement for a *that*-clause with putative *should*; *cf* 15.48*f*):

Foolishly, Bill declined the invitation.
= It was *foolish* of Bill to decline the invitation.

But this is not possible with adverbs of Type (a):

{*Certainly,* / *Admittedly,*} John declined the invitation.

*It was {*certain* / *admitted*} of John to decline the invitation.

Note [**a**] *Assuredly* and *decidedly* are roughly synonymous with *surely* and *undoubtedly* respectively. They do not correspond to such structures as:

It is {assured / decided} that . . .

{I am / One has} {assured / decided} that . . .

Surely is commonly used to challenge the addressee and implies disbelief or disagreement as to previously expressed assumptions, as well as the self-evident plausibility of what is being said.
[**b**] *Naturally* and the equivalent understatement, *not unnaturally*, are paraphrasable by 'as might have been expected' or 'of course'. They do not correspond to *it is natural* or *it is not unnatural.*

8.129 The semantic distinction between the groups (i) (*eg*: *rightly*, *wisely*) and (ii) (*eg*: *surprisingly*, *understandably*) of Type (b) in 8.127 is reflected in the fact that only in (i) is it normal to have a correspondence in which the judgment is predicated of the subject. Thus:

Group (bii)

$$\left[\begin{array}{l}\textit{Surprisingly,}\\ \textit{Understandably,}\end{array}\right] \text{John returned the money.}$$

$$\neq {}^{*}\text{John was} \left[\begin{array}{l}\textit{surprising}\\ \textit{understandable}\end{array}\right] \text{to return the money.}$$

But:

Group (bi)

$$\left[\begin{array}{l}\textit{Rightly,}\\ \textit{Wisely,}\end{array}\right] \text{John returned the money.}$$

$$= \text{John was} \left[\begin{array}{l}\textit{right}\\ \textit{wise}\end{array}\right] \text{to return the money.}$$

(Compare the discussion of subject orientation with subjuncts: especially 8.94.) The predication automatically applies to the subject in an active sentence and to the agent in a passive sentence, whether the latter is present or recoverable or indefinite (*cf* 3.63*ff*). Hence, we can still set up these correspondences for items in Group (bi) in the following instances:

$$\left[\begin{array}{l}\textit{Rightly,}\\ \textit{Wisely,}\end{array}\right] \text{the money was returned by John.}$$

$$= \text{John was} \left[\begin{array}{l}\textit{right}\\ \textit{wise}\end{array}\right] \text{to return the money.}$$

$$\left[\begin{array}{l}\textit{Rightly,}\\ \textit{Wisely,}\end{array}\right] \text{the money was returned.}$$

$$= \text{(Someone) was} \left[\begin{array}{l}\textit{right}\\ \textit{wise}\end{array}\right] \text{to return the money.}$$

These adverbs can be used wherever a personal agent is implied, though it may not always be possible to state the correspondences as systematically as in the above instances:

$$\left[\begin{array}{l}\textit{Rightly,}\\ \textit{Wisely,}\end{array}\right] \text{the meeting ended early today.}$$

$$= \text{X} \left\{\begin{array}{l}\text{was}\\ \text{were}\end{array}\right\} \left\{\begin{array}{l}\textit{right}\\ \textit{wise}\end{array}\right\} \text{to end the meeting early today.}$$

Here 'X' cannot be specified or identified but obviously cannot be the subject of the earlier sentence, *the meeting*.

$$\left[\begin{array}{l}\textit{Rightly,}\\ \textit{Wisely,}\end{array}\right] \text{the book costs only five dollars.}$$

$$= \text{X} \left\{\begin{array}{l}\text{was}\\ \text{were}\end{array}\right\} \left[\begin{array}{l}\textit{right}\\ \textit{wise}\end{array}\right] \text{to fix the price of the book at only five dollars.}$$

Again, the former sentence makes it impossible to identify a subject for the latter. Contrast:

[*Rightly*, / *Wisely*,] Bill's car is in a garage overnight throughout the winter.

= Bill is [*right* / *wise*] to keep his car in a garage overnight throughout the winter.

Since some adverbs in content Type (b) allow correspondence with a personal subject (usually, however, not the speaker as an individual but as a representative of what can be taken as a general view), it is useful to distinguish a FACTIVE type from a PERSONAL type:

FACTIVE:

Understandably, James refuses to speak.
That James refuses to speak is understandable.
It is understandable that James refuses to speak.
≠ {I understand / One understands} that James refuses to speak.
[but rather: 'One understands why James refuses to speak'; *cf*: '**Understandably*, the weather was appalling']

PERSONAL:

{*Regrettably*, / *Sadly*,} James refuses to speak.
That James refuses to speak is {regrettable. / sad.}
It is {regrettable / sad} that James refuses to speak.
= {I regret/One regrets / I am sad/One is sad} that James refuses to speak.
[*Cf*: *Regrettably*, the weather was appalling]

Within the personal type, however, there is a subset for which the first two of the above paraphrases cannot occur:

{*Happily* / *Thankfully*,} James refuses to speak.
≠ *That James refuses to speak is {happy. / thankful.}
*It is {happy / thankful} that James refuses to speak.

but rather:

= {I am / One is} {happy / thankful} that James refuses to speak.

With most of the personal type, it is possible to add *to say* in the paraphrases:

I regret (I am sad/happy, etc) *to say* that James . . .

We note, however, that beside 'Hopefully, the weather is improving', we have no '*I am hopeful to say that the weather is improving'.

Note [a] In '*Sadly*, I resigned the chairmanship', the adverbial may be close in meaning to a subject-oriented adjunct or subjunct (*cf* 8.78, 8.93); thus 'I was sad to resign', 'I was sad when I resigned'. But the meaning may be that corresponding to a style disjunct ('Sad to say, I resigned') or to a content disjunct: 'One is sad (People are sad, It is sad news *for you*) that I resigned'.

[b] Stylistic objections are raised to the use of the personal type of disjunct above, notably *thankfully* and above all *hopefully*. Strength of feeling concerning *hopefully* may be attributable in part to its lack of total fit with the others, as noted above ('*I am hopeful to say'). Since, however, the 'general view' in *hopefully* is usefully distinguished thereby from the purely individual viewpoint in *I hope*, the disjunct has considerable convenience, as can be seen in the following textual example from an administrator's note put before a committee:

> My assistant has arranged for the matter to be considered by an ad hoc working party, and *hopefully* a proposal will be ready in time for our next meeting. *I hope* this approach will be acceptable to members.

The two italicized parts are not identical in force and could not in fact be interchanged; the former ventures to express a general hope, attributed by the writer to the committee as a whole, or even a general assessment of probability ('It is likely that a proposal . . .'); the latter expresses the writer's personal hope that his action will be approved.

Syntactic features of disjuncts

8.130 Clausal realizations of content disjuncts occur fairly freely with questions:

> *If it stops raining*, may we go out and play in the wood?
> (*What is*) *even more interesting*, did you hear her reply to that second question?

When realized by adverbs, however, most content disjuncts cannot appear in any position in a direct or indirect question (*cf* Note [a]):

> *Does he *fortunately* know about it?
> *He asked whether, *fortunately*, they knew anything about it.

On the other hand, most style disjuncts can be freely used in direct and indirect questions, even initially:

> *Frankly*, does he know about it?
> They want to know whether, *strictly speaking*, they're trespassing.

But *cf*:

> **Personally*, is she very clever?

Most content disjuncts cannot appear with imperatives:

> **Fortunately*, don't tell him.

(But *cf*: '*Perhaps* tell him now.')

On the other hand, some style disjuncts (including most of 8.124 Type (a)) can do so, even in *I* position:

> *Seriously*, go and see her about it.
> *Frankly*, don't tell him.

While disjuncts can appear at almost any place in clause structure, the normal position for most disjuncts is *I*. However, some content disjuncts of

Type (ai), *eg*: *probably*, *possibly*, and all of Type (bi), *eg*: *rightly*, *wisely*, normally occur at *M*, and often at *iM*. Note also the potentiality of *eM*:

> You would have {*probably* / *certainly*} missed the plane.

If the clause is negative, *iM* would be more usual though *M* is perfectly possible with the same meaning:

> I *frankly* don't know.
> I don't *frankly* know.

If prosodic focus is on the operator, *iM* would be usual:

> I *frankly* WÀS annoyed.

Disjuncts can appear (though often with some awkwardness) in dependent finite clauses:

> He was a man who, *unaccountably*, had few friends.
> What, *interestingly enough*, pleased them most was her enthusiasm.
> Though he was *quite rightly* dismissed, he was given six months' salary.

Note [**a**] Certain content disjuncts of Type (ai) expressing some doubt (*eg*: *perhaps*, *possibly*, *conceivably*) are marginally acceptable in direct and indirect questions, but not at *I* position. *Cf* 'Can you *possibly*/*perhaps* see her now?' Some of Type (aiii) are acceptable in questions perhaps even initially, *eg*: *basically*, *essentially*, *fundamentally*, *ideally*.

[**b**] It seems that content disjuncts can appear within a clause that is loosely attached to a question:

> Did they refuse the first offer, expecting, *naturally*, a better offer?

[**c**] Some content disjuncts can be responses to questions or can be used as a comment on a previous utterance, usually accompanied by *yes* or *no*:

> A: They have returned to San Francisco.
> B: *Very wisely*. ['They were very wise to do so']
> A: They won't be coming back.
> B: *Unfortunately*, no. ['It's unfortunate that they won't]

A few style disjuncts (*honestly*, *literally*, *seriously*, *truly*, *truthfully*) are used as verbless questions:

> A: I'm going to resign.
> B: *Seriously*? ['Were you speaking seriously when you said that?']

The content disjunct *really* is commonly used in this way:

> A: I'm going to resign.
> B: *Really*? ['Is that so?']

A particular intonation contour is not obligatory, but certain adverbials have a characteristic intonation when used as responses; for example, following 'I hear you may soon be emigrating', someone might reply with one of the following (*cf* 8.120 Note [a]):

CÊRtainly	QUÌTE ⟨BrE⟩	Yes, inDÈED	AbsoLÙTEly
Well, PŎssibly	Quite sò ⟨BrE⟩	RĂTHer ⟨esp old-fashioned BrE⟩	HĂRDly

(*Cf* App II.11*ff*).

8.131 Most disjuncts can be modified. Common premodifiers are *very* and *quite*. For some content disjuncts of Type (bii), the postmodifier *enough* is common, particularly for those evaluating the communication as odd (*bizarrely*, *curiously*, *eerily*, *funnily*, *oddly*, *strangely*):

> *Oddly enough*, he hasn't said anything about it.

Several content disjuncts can be premodified by *not*, in particular *surprisingly*, and some with negative prefixes (*unexpectedly*, *unreasonably*, *unusually*, *unwisely*):

> *Not surprisingly*, he protested strongly about it.
> *Not unreasonably*, she refused him.

Other common premodifiers include (in intensifier use) *more*, *most*, *less*, *least*:

> *More personally*, I have to tell you that my wife is pregnant.
> *Less strangely*, he has been avoiding me lately; and (*even*) *less strangely still*, he has not given me a phone call.
> *More amusingly than wisely*, he kept on insisting on his right to speak.
> *Most unexpectedly*, Toshiko had to return to Japan before her studentship had expired.

Note [**a**] Content disjuncts with *-ed* participle bases (*eg*: *undoubtedly*, *allegedly*) cannot usually be modified; *cf* however *most assuredly*, *most decidedly*, *most unexpectedly*.
[**b**] *Enough* as a modifier of disjuncts does not so much intensify as draw attention to the meaning of the item. Thus, *oddly enough* is paraphrasable by 'odd though it may seem'.
[**c**] Negation of the disjunct can cooccur with clause negation:
Not surprisingly, they were *not* happy with their results.

8.132 When the semantic relations of condition, concession, reason, and result are realized by clauses, the adverbials concerned are normally content disjuncts. For example:

> *Unless you have a valid passport*, I cannot book your ticket.
> *Although John is so hard up*, he refuses to look for a better-paid job.
> *Since she remained adamant in her diagnosis*, her fellow doctors considered the case afresh.
> He went on arguing in a nasty tone, *so that in the end I lost my patience*.

Along with result disjuncts, we may consider the somewhat vaguer 'outcome' disjuncts, often realized by nonfinite (*to*) clauses (*cf* 15.25):

> Mary drove all the way to Maine, (*only*) *to find that her friends had moved to Florida*.

Contrast the superficially similar purpose adjunct:

> Mary drove all the way to Maine (*only*) *to visit some friends*.
> ~ It was (*only*) *to visit some friends* that Mary drove all the way to Maine.

As distinct from *because*-clauses, which indicate a cause or reason so essential that they are integrated into the sentence as adjuncts, nontemporal *since*-clauses have a looser relation, more resembling nonrestrictive relative clauses, and they function grammatically as disjuncts:

> It is *because you are lazy* that you lost your job.
> ~ *It is *since you are lazy* that you lost your job.

On *if*-, *since*-, and *because*-clauses as style disjuncts, *cf* 8.124.

A contingency relationship can be expressed by a content disjunct in the form of a verbless or nonfinite clause introduced by *with*(*out*):

With friends like that, who needs enemies?
With the audience making so much noise, I couldn't hear the opening of the concerto.
Without some indication of her approval, we shouldn't make up our minds on this occasion.

8.133 A specification of range can be added for content disjuncts of Type (bii) in 8.127, normally a prepositional phrase introduced by *for*:

Luckily for Herbert, the gun was not loaded. ['Herbert was lucky that . . .']

For Herbert specifies that *luckily* is not to be generalized, but applies specifically to Herbert. Specification can also be made by *from X's point of view*, or *from the point of view of X*:

Understandably enough from her point of view, Susan does not want the news to reach her family before she tells them herself.

An equivalent effect is obtained in prepositional phrases as content disjuncts, where the range is specified by the genitive or *of*-construction. Compare:

<table>
<tr><td>Annoyingly for Jack,</td><td rowspan="3">his brother was late arriving.</td></tr>
<tr><td>To Jack's annoyance,</td></tr>
<tr><td>To the annoyance of Jack,</td></tr>
</table>

Cf also: *to my regret, to her displeasure, to their disappointment, to John's surprise, to the delight of all present*. Adverbs of Type (bii) with participle base in *-ing* (*eg*: *annoyingly*) generally have a corresponding prepositional phrase in this form. The prepositional phrases are indeed more commonly used than the adverbs. We can achieve the same effect by sentential relative clauses (*cf* 15.57, 17.9), *eg*: *which annoyed Jack* or *which I regret*; or by comment clauses (*cf* 15.53*ff*), *eg*: *what delighted all present* or *what disappoints them*.

Note [**a**] *Surprisingly* and its synonyms can take a *for*-specification only if it refers to a noun or pronoun coreferential with a noun phrase later in the clause; even so, such examples as the following are unusual:

Surprisingly for him [*ie* for John], the altitude affected John adversely.
Surprisingly for him [*ie* for John], John failed the exam.
**Surprisingly for his father*, John failed the exam.

Contrast the last sentence with

Annoyingly for his father, John failed the exam.

Whereas *surprisingly for him* means others are surprised about him, *annoyingly for his father* means his father is annoyed.

This distinction does not apply to the corresponding prepositional phrases. *To my surprise* is equivalent to 'I am (or 'was') surprised'.

[**b**] Corresponding sentential relative clauses can be found for content disjuncts in all groups having corresponding clauses of the form '*it is* adj *that* . . .' except Type (ai):

<table>
<tr><td>Certainly,</td><td rowspan="4">Mrs Macdonald didn't want to have anything to do with them.</td></tr>
<tr><td>Obviously,</td></tr>
<tr><td>Understandably,</td></tr>
<tr><td>Wisely,</td></tr>
</table>

Mrs Macdonald didn't want to have anything to do with them,

<table>
<tr><td rowspan="4">which was</td><td>*certain.</td></tr>
<tr><td>(painfully) obvious.</td></tr>
<tr><td>understandable.</td></tr>
<tr><td>wise.</td></tr>
</table>

On the other hand, all have corresponding comment clauses, though often a modifier such as *very* or *more* is required. Hence, we can have:

What was even {*wiser*, / *more certain*, / *more obvious*,} he didn't speak at the meeting.

[c] Adverbs of content Type (bii) that express an opinion as to whether what is said is fortunate or not (*eg*: *fortunately*, *luckily*) allow the interpretation that the referent of the subject is fortunate or otherwise. But this is not an essential implication of their use. For example:

Fortunately, Bill keeps his car in a garage overnight during the winter.

does not necessarily mean that Bill is fortunate, though out of context this sentence conveys that implication strongly. But we can add to the sentence in such a way as to make it clear that it is someone else that is fortunate:

Fortunately, Bill keeps his car in a garage overnight during the winter. Susan was therefore able to start the car very easily when she needed to borrow it in a hurry early this morning.

From this context, it is clear that it is Susan who is fortunate. Compare also:

Fortunately for me, ['I am fortunate that'] Bill keeps his car in a garage overnight during the winter.

In contrast, adverbs of Type (bi), such as *rightly* or *wisely*, do not allow *for* prepositional phrases specifying the range of the adverb.

Conjuncts

8.134 Like subjuncts and disjuncts, the adverbials that we call CONJUNCTS are grammatically distinct from adjuncts in terms of the features set out in 8.25. Consider *nonetheless* in the following example:

She may be unable to attend the meeting. You should *nonetheless* send her the agenda.

The adverbial cannot be the focus of a cleft sentence; cannot be the basis of contrast in alternative interrogation or negation; cannot be focused by subjuncts; and cannot come within the scope of predication pro-forms or ellipsis. Compare:

... **It is nonetheless* that you should send her the agenda.
... *Should you send her the agenda *nonetheless* or *therefore*?
... *You should *only* ⟨*nonetheLÈSS*⟩ send her the agenda.

Conjuncts are more like disjuncts than adjuncts in having a relatively detached and 'superordinate' role as compared with other clause elements. But they are unlike disjuncts in not typically filling the semantic roles characteristic of adjuncts. Conjuncts, as part of their even greater distinctness from the closely interrelated clause elements such as S, C, and O, often have semantic roles that are conjunct-specific. That is, they have the function of conjoining independent units rather than one of contributing another facet of information to a single integrated unit (*cf* 8.136).

Thus, in considering conjuncts, we find it necessary to look beyond the particular grammatical unit in which they appear. Whereas, in the case of disjuncts, we related them to the speaker's 'authority' for (or the speaker's comment on) the accompanying clause, we relate conjuncts to the speaker's comment in one quite specific respect: his assessment of how he views the connection between two linguistic units. The units concerned may be very large or very small: sentences, paragraphs, or even larger parts of a text at one extreme (*cf* 19.86); at the other extreme, they may be constituents of a phrase realizing a single clause element. For example:

The candidate is a fine teacher, a broadcaster of some experience, and a respected drama critic. *In addition*, she has written a successful novel. [1]

The candidate has written a successful, lengthy, popular, and *in addition* highly original novel. [2]

As in [2], it is common for a conjunct to have a focusing role along with the conjoining one, especially when it is conjoining relatively small units. In this way, the extreme of conjoining words within a phrase can be taken one stage further: to conjoining constituents of a word:

The patient was carefully observed in the pre- and *likewise* ⟨PÒST⟩-operative phase of treatment.

Like disjuncts, such conjuncts can often be seen as equivalent to adverbials in clauses having the speaker as subject:

. . . a respected drama critic. I tell you *in addition* that she has written . . . [1a]

Some conjuncts include a pronominal reference to the unit which is to be related:

in addition to *this* (*ie* what I have mentioned)
first of *all* (*ie* of what I shall list)
best of *all* (*ie* of what I have listed)
for all *that* (*ie* what I have said)

In the case of the informal conjunct *though*, we seem to have an abbreviation of a concessive clause (*cf* 8.145). Thus with:

I'm afraid he doesn't eat much these days – but he looks pretty fit, *though*.

we are expected to understand something like the clausal disjunct (*cf* 8.143):

. . . pretty fit, *though I have said that he doesn't eat much.*

Note Disjuncts and conjuncts are sometimes called 'sentence adverbials' by grammarians on the double ground that they can concern a sentence as a whole (rather than a particular part of a sentence such as the predication) and – in the case of conjuncts – can relate one sentence to another. We do not follow this convention, partly because the double motivation involves two quite separate considerations; partly because other adverbials (our 'sentence adjuncts', *cf* 8.36) also relate to the sentence as a whole; partly because both disjuncts and conjuncts can also relate to quite specific units within sentences, as in:

I object to his hearty and, {*frankly,* / *above all,*} crude behaviour.

A further reason is that conjuncts can relate units much larger than sentences: *nonetheless* at the beginning of a paragraph or section of a text will indicate a conjoining contrast with the whole preceding paragraph or section.

8.135 Although we have said (*cf* 8.134) that conjuncts indicate how the speaker 'views the connection between two linguistic units', such an indication does not conversely entail the use of a conjunct. The semantic role of expressing a relation between two units can frequently be fulfilled by an adjunct. Compare the following (where a pronoun, as frequently, functions as a linking device):

> It was snowing, *and in spite of this* Mona went cycling.

The adverbial here which conjoins and indicates a concessive relation is an adjunct, as we see from its propensity to be focused in a cleft sentence:

> . . . and it was *in spite of this* that Mona went cycling.

By contrast, in:

> It was snowing, and *nonetheless* Mona went cycling.

the same conjoining function with the same concessive relation is fulfilled grammatically by a conjunct:

> *. . . and it was *nonetheless* that Mona went cycling.

Conjuncts thus *both* indicate the relation *and* are demonstrably outside the syntactically integrated clause structure which admits adjuncts.

Moreover, there is one significant respect in which we must relax the semantic characteristic concerning the conjoining of linguistic units. It is possible for conjuncts to be used as discourse-initial items. Thus speech may actually begin, in the following way, given a particular context of situation:

> *So* you're LÈAVing, *then*!

Both *so* and *then* are conjunctive comments of an inferential nature, but in this example the speaker's inference is based on extralinguistic evidence, which has been treated just as though the person addressed had been heard to say 'Well, I'll see you tomorrow' or even merely 'Now, where's my coat?'

Discourse-initiating items can be less easy to account for plausibly, but it seems significant that such items are usually those that have a well-established conjunctive role in mid-discourse use. Consider the following as each being the first words in a discourse; they would normally occupy a separate tone unit, with a falling nucleus, though solitary initial *well* may be exceptional in having a rising nucleus or none at all:

> *Well*, how are you this morning?
> *Why then* ⟨esp AmE⟩, how shall we spend the evening?
> *Well now*, I wonder if I could begin by asking you a few questions.
> *Right* (*then*), } how many of you know each other?
> *OK now* ⟨esp AmE, informal⟩, }
> *Now*, the subject of my talk is . . . [≠ 'The subject of my talk now, *ie* at this moment']

Compare some of the same expressions occurring *between* linguistic units:

> You didn't feel so good yesterday; *well*, how are you this morning?
> I've been looking forward to this meeting for months; *why then*, how shall we spend the evening?

Thank you for welcoming me here; *now* the subject of my talk is . . .

It would seem that, in discourse-initial use, these items seek to enforce by implication some continuity with what *might* have gone before. Silence is difficult to break without some such convention.

Note Items like *well, oh, ah* have conventional values in discourse that are related to subjuncts, disjuncts, and conjuncts. On *well cf* 19.54; this typically prefaces a part of discourse which, though having perhaps something in common with what has gone before, introduces a difference of some sort. In consequence, it is convenient as a frequent discourse initiator.

The semantics of conjuncts

8.136 Much more than with disjuncts, the conjunct function entails a conjunct-specific set of semantic relations. They are connected with, but are frequently rather remote from, the adverbial relation we must assume in the speaker-related clause to which they correspond. It is necessary, therefore, to set out the conjunctive meanings concerned, although we shall return to them in 19.53*ff* where they can be seen in the wider context of inter-sentence relations and discourse structure.

We can distinguish seven conjunctive roles, in some cases with fairly clear subdivisions; see *Fig* 8.136.

- (a) LISTING
  - (i) enumerative
  - (ii) additive
    - equative
    - reinforcing
- (b) SUMMATIVE
- (c) APPOSITIONAL
- (d) RESULTIVE
- (e) INFERENTIAL
- (f) CONTRASTIVE
  - (i) reformulatory
  - (ii) replacive
  - (iii) antithetic
  - (iv) concessive
- (g) TRANSITIONAL
  - (i) discoursal
  - (ii) temporal

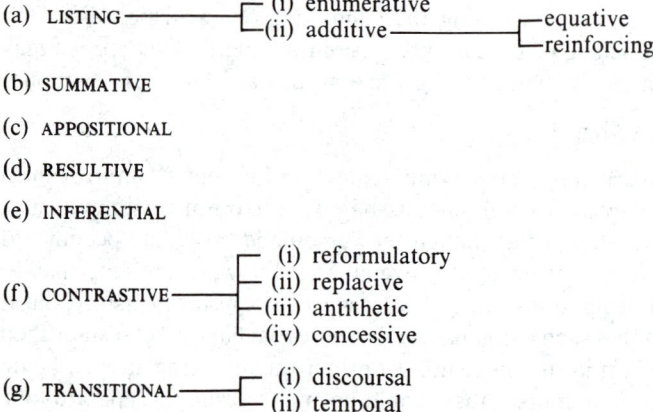

Fig 8.136

8.137 Some of the common conjuncts are listed below according to their role classes and subclasses. Except for enumerative conjuncts (which are an open class), all adverb realizations are given, as well as some frequently occurring prepositional phrases and noun phrases.

(a) LISTING

(i) ENUMERATIVE
first, second, third . . .
first(*ly*), *secondly, thirdly* . . .
one, two, three . . . ⟨esp in learned and technical use⟩
a, b, c . . . ⟨esp in learned and technical use⟩
in the first place, in the second place . . .

first of all
second of all ⟨AmE⟩
on the one hand . . . on the other hand [*cf* (fiii)]
for one thing . . . (*and*) *for another* (*thing*)
for a start ⟨informal⟩
to begin with, to start with
next, then
to conclude
finally, last, lastly, last of all

(ii) ADDITIVE

EQUATIVE
correspondingly ⟨formal⟩, *equally, likewise, similarly, in the same way, by the same token*

REINFORCING
again ⟨formal⟩, *also, besides, further* ⟨formal⟩, *furthermore* ⟨formal⟩, *more* ⟨rare, formal⟩, *moreover, in particular, then* ⟨informal, esp spoken⟩, *too* ⟨rare, AmE⟩, *what is more, in addition, above all*; and the following informal expressions: *on top of it all, to top it* (*all*), *to cap it* (*all*)

(b) SUMMATIVE
altogether, overall, then, therefore, thus ⟨formal⟩, (*all*) *in all*; and the following largely formal expressions: *in conclusion, in sum, to conclude, to sum up, to summarize*

(c) APPOSITIVE
namely (often abbreviated as *viz* in formal written English), *thus, in other words, for example* (often abbreviated to *eg* or *e.g.* in written English and sometimes spoken as /ˌiːˈdʒiː/), *for instance, that is* (often abbreviated to *ie* or *i.e.* in specialized written English and sometimes spoken as /ˌaɪˈiː/), *that is to say, specifically*; *cf* 17.73.

(d) RESULTIVE
accordingly, consequently, hence ⟨formal⟩, *now, so* ⟨informal⟩, *therefore, thus* ⟨formal⟩; *as a consequence, in consequence, as a result, of course*; *cf* also *somehow* ['for some reason or other']

(e) INFERENTIAL
else, otherwise, then;
in other words
in that case

(f) CONTRASTIVE

(i) REFORMULATORY
better, rather, more accurately, more precisely; *alias, alternatively, in other words*

(ii) REPLACIVE
again, alternatively, rather
better, worse;
on the other hand

(iii) ANTITHETIC
contrariwise ⟨formal⟩, *conversely* ⟨formal⟩
instead [blend of antithetic with replacive]
oppositely ⟨rare⟩, *then*;
on the contrary, in contrast, by contrast, by way of contrast, in comparison, by comparison, by way of comparison, (*on the one hand . . .*) *on the other hand*

(iv) CONCESSIVE
anyhow ⟨informal⟩, *anyway* ⟨informal⟩, *anyways* ⟨AmE informal⟩, *besides* [blend of reinforcing with concessive], *else, however, nevertheless, nonetheless* ⟨formal⟩ [also written *none the less*], *notwithstanding* ⟨formal⟩, *only* ⟨informal⟩, *still, though, yet, in 'any case, in 'any event* ⟨formal⟩, *at 'any rate, at 'all events, for 'all that, in spite of that, in spite of it all, after all, at the same 'time, on the other hand, all the same, admittedly, of course, still and all* ⟨informal AmE⟩; *that said*

(g) TRANSITIONAL

(i) DISCOURSAL
incidentally, now ⟨informal⟩
by the way
by the by(*e*) ⟨not commonly used⟩

(ii) TEMPORAL
meantime, meanwhile, in the meantime, in the meanwhile; note also the set: *originally, subsequently, eventually*

8.138 LISTING (role a) is of course a basic language function and we have structures of coordination for this purpose (*cf* 2.9), involving above all the conjunction *and*:

I did this *and* I did this *and* . . .   I saw John *and* Mary *and* . . .

Conjuncts are used to give a particular structure or orientation to a list. At its simplest, the structure shows order by having items performing an ENUMERATIVE function:

First the economy is beginning to recover, and *second*(*ly*) unemployment figures have not increased this month.

The relation of such items to adjuncts in the speaker's assessment of what he is saying can be seen in paraphrases:

I tell you first that the economy . . . and *I tell you secondly* that unemployment figures . . .

The enumerative function does more than merely assign numerical labels to the items listed: it connotes relative priority and endows the list with an integral structure, having a beginning and an end. The idea of an integral relation is especially conferred by the ADDITIVE conjuncts. By the use of the EQUATIVE subtype, we indicate that an item has a similar force to a preceding one:

She has high responsibilities and, *equally*, a high salary.

We might regard the conjunct here as a fragment of a speaker's comment in which the adverb functions as an adjunct: perhaps 'I assess (or rate) this *equally*'.

The REINFORCING subtype of additive conjunct typically assesses an item as adding greater weight to a preceding one:

> He has the opportunity, the motivation, and *above all* the courage to do it.

Here again we might postulate the conjunct as related to some such comment as 'I rate this *above all that I have said*.'

Note [**a**] The *-ly* forms of ordinal numerals are chiefly used as conjuncts. Contrast:

> He arrived *first* (**firstly*) and she arrived *second*. [adjuncts]
> *First*(*ly*), he is my friend, and *secondly* he is in desperate need. [conjuncts]

Ordinals as conjuncts occur with or without *-ly*, but for many people *firstly* is objectionable. Note that *first* (also *initially*, *originally*) can also have a subjunct use, especially when associated with such verbs as *invent* and *discover*. Thus:

> Hormones were *first* identified by Starling at University College London. [1]

The statement would be a different one if instead of the subjunct we had *first* as a conjunct:

> *First*, hormones were identified by Starling at University College London. [2]

Nor of course does [1] permit us either to replace *first* by *firstly* or to predict a further sentence:

> Hormones were *secondly* identified by . . .

[**b**] Conjuncts like *more* and *something else* must remind us that these truncated speaker-assessments are not necessarily related to adjuncts but (as in these instances) are more plausibly seen as objects: '(I will say) more'.

[**c**] The cardinal and ordinal numerals may be represented in writing by their symbols in the various systems:

> 1, 2, 3, . . . I, II, III, . . . i, ii, iii, . . .

Similarly, the alphabetic letters may be represented either as minuscules ('lower case', *a*, *b*, *c*, . . .) or as majuscules ('upper case' or 'capitals', *A*, *B*, *C*, . . .). These different systems allow the writer to choose a hierarchy of listings and sublistings. In general, no clear conventions have been established for which sets of symbols are to be subordinate to other sets, and the writer is therefore free to choose a hierarchy of sets for his own purpose. One would of course observe consistency and rationale; one would not subordinate capitals to lower-case letters, for example.

[**d**] *Too* as reinforcing conjunct 〈rare, AmE〉 occupies *I* position:

> She's had her novel published this year; but TŎO, she's written some interesting articles on acupuncture.

8.139 SUMMATIVE (role b) and APPOSITIVE (role c) conjuncts have this much in common: they precede an item which is to be looked at in relation to all the items that have gone before. SUMMATIVE conjuncts introduce an item that embraces the preceding ones:

> He lost his watch, his car broke down, and he got a letter of complaint from a customer: *all in all*, he had a bad day.

APPOSITIVE conjuncts are concerned rather to express the content of the preceding item or items in other terms (*cf* 17.65):

> She has some assistance – *for instance*, a secretary.

Where the apposition applies to more than one preceding item there is usually a summative implication:

> They took with them some chocolate, cans of beer and fruit juice, a flask of coffee, a pack of sandwiches: *in other words*, enough refreshments.

By contrast, when the apposition itself consists of several items, the conjunct has the effect of specifying a list:

> They took refreshments – *that is*, sandwiches, coffee, beer, fruit juice, and chocolate.

8.140 RESULTIVE (role d) and INFERENTIAL (role e) conjuncts again have something in common with each other, as well as with additive, summative, and appositional conjuncts. The more structured a list of items is, the more the final item will tend to be a conclusion in more ways than one: a mere termination, a reinforcement, a summary, a result, and a basis for further inference. This is reflected in the fact that the same conjuncts are listed under several heads. RESULTIVE *of course* and *so* are illustrated in:

> She arrived late, gave answers in an offhand manner, and *of course* displeased the interviewing panel.
>
> He was irritable, unjust, unreliable, and *so* became increasingly unpopular.

Result can be tentatively expressed by a coordinate clause with a vague reason item, *somehow* (*cf* Note):

> I argued that it wasn't my fault and *somehow* they let me go.

INFERENTIAL conjuncts indicate a conclusion based on logic and supposition:

> You haven't answered my question; *in other words*, you disapprove of my proposal.

Especially in formal usage, an *if*-clause can be followed by a correlating inferential *then* ('If this is agreed, *then* we may proceed . . .'). See further, 8.144*f*.

But the conjunct *then* is especially used in an inferential response to another speaker (*cf* also 8.135):

> A: Give my regards to John. B: *Then* you're not coming with me?

Note *Somehow* has been included among conjuncts because it fits the criteria for the class (*cf* 8.134), and it is mentioned in the context of resultive conjuncts because it is often close to them semantically: 'and so, in some way that I don't fully understand'. It differs from all other conjuncts in not indicating a relationship between its clause and what precedes; in this respect it resembles a reason disjunct:

> *Somehow* I don't trust him. ['for some reason or other']

Somehow is in fact used when the reason is not made explicit in the preceding context. In contrast, pure resultive conjuncts (*eg*: *therefore* ['for that reason']) require the reason or cause to be given in the preceding context. Hence the clause to which they are attached states the result or consequence.

8.141 CONTRASTIVE conjuncts (role f) present either contrastive words or contrastive matter in relation to what has preceded. The former type is obviously close to the appositive and differs in seeking less to add another formulation ('in other words') than to replace what has been said by a different formulation ('in other words'). Compare:

> He was exceedingly inebriated – hopelessly drunk, *in other words*. [appositive]

She has applied for a transfer – she is tired of her present job, *in other words*. [reformulatory]

Such REFORMULATORY conjuncts are, therefore, frequently preceded by *or*:

He invited several friends, or *better*, several people that he THÒUGHT were friends. [*ie* 'it would be better if I were to say']

Similarly, *rather* ['I should rather say'].

The item *alias* precedes proper nouns; for example:

He went to Constantinople, *alias* Istanbul.
She married Eric Blair, *alias* George Orwell.

With REPLACIVE conjuncts, contrastive matter may again be prefaced by *or*. The speaker withdraws an item, not to express it better but to replace it by a more important one. Examples of the REPLACIVE conjuncts:

He was opposed by his mother or, *rather*, by BÒTH his parents.
Please suit yourself. You can move in at once; (or) *again*, you may prefer to do so next week.

But an item may be contrasted with a preceding one by introducing a direct antithesis; this is effected by means of ANTITHETIC conjuncts, as in:

You promise to help me; *then* you let me down!
He expected to be happy but *instead* he felt miserable.

One item in this group is often used as part of a correlation: *on the one hand . . . on the other* (*hand*).

Where one unit is seen as unexpected in the light of the other, we have the use of CONCESSIVE conjuncts, as in:

She didn't get the award after all. *Still*, her results were very good.
He had worked hard but *all the same* he failed the exam.

Concessive *of course* makes a conjoin resemble a subordinate clause: '*Of course* he's a bit lazy; all the same I'd like to give him the job'. (*Cf* 'Although he's a bit lazy, I'd like to give him the job all the same.')

Note An example of the antithetic conjunct *oppositely* ⟨rare⟩:

Any normal person is depressed when given proper cause for depression. *Oppositely*, normal people become very excited when, for example, they have won a big prize.

8.142 TRANSITIONAL conjuncts (role g) serve to shift attention to another topic or to a temporally related event. We refer to the former as DISCOURSAL:

I want to tell you about my trip, but, *by the way*, how is your mother?

Among the other discoursal conjuncts, note that *now* has a function as discourse-initial; *cf* 8.135. Such conjuncts do not necessarily seek to change the subject of the discourse; they are frequently used merely to indicate a rather adventitious relation:

She is studying physics, astronomy, and, *incidentally*, meteorology.

This last is intended to mean not 'She is studying meteorology as a minor and incidental component of her work' but 'I regard it as an incidental fact worth passing on to you'. Often, however, *incidentally* is used as a polite way of changing the subject; in this usage, it resembles 'by the way' and is *incidental* to what has preceded only to the extent that something has been said that reminds the speaker of the other topic.

TEMPORAL transition similarly seeks to indicate a move away from the normal sequence in narrative:

> He saved a great deal of money but *in the meantime* his house deteriorated badly.

The speaker here is not, of course, concerned to report on two simultaneous happenings but to relate them (in this case, ironically: the money in the bank should have been used to repair the house).

Correspondences to other structures

8.143 We may now look more closely at the way conjuncts correspond to other structures. Almost all, indeed, are like style disjuncts in that the correspondence incorporates a verb of speaking and usually the subject is the speaker (*cf* 8.122). The conjunct is normally represented lexically in the correspondence by a cognate adverbial. We therefore consider the correspondences according to the class of the adjunct or other adverbial concerned.

(i) TIME AND SPACE ADJUNCTS AND SUBJUNCTS

The succession in time or space conveyed by the adverbial is converted into the logical succession of discourse when there is the implication of a verb of speaking. The corresponding clause has as its subject the speaker, but it is sometimes possible to envisage an indefinite pronoun instead (*eg* indefinite *one*, *we*, or *you*). The correspondence can usually be given the form:

> { *One* [etc] *can* / *I will* } *say* + adverbial

We can include here most listing conjuncts (role a in 8.136), the conjuncts *now* and *then* (whatever their subclass), and a few conjuncts scattered through other subclasses; *eg*: *by the way*, *yet*, *still*, *after all*, *at the same time*. Examples:

> There are two things that the Government can do: *First* ['I will say' + *first*], it can cut spending on defence; *second* ['I will say' + *second*], it can reduce the number of civil servants.
>
> If astronauts have landed on the moon, *then* ['one can say' + *then*] there is no reason why they can't land on Venus.

(ii) PROCESS ADJUNCTS

The same types of correspondence can be established here. The conjuncts involved are scattered through the various subclasses of conjuncts. Examples:

> *Incidentally* ['I tell you' + *incidentally*], he didn't want the book.
>
> *To conclude* ['I tell you' + (*in order*) *to conclude*], it was a great success.

(iii) ADDITIVE SUBJUNCTS

Here, too, the correspondence incorporates a verb of speaking and usually the subject is the speaker. We can include here the additive conjuncts (role a(ii) in 8.136). Examples:

> Most of us see no reason why capital punishment should not be abolished. *Further* ['I will *further* say'], the arguments in favour of corporal punishment seem trivial to most of us.
>
> The acts of a parish council must be confirmed by the parish meeting. *Likewise* ['I will *likewise* tell you'] decisions of a parish meeting must be confirmed by a referendum of all the electors in the parish.

The additive subjuncts (*cf* 8.116) can themselves often function also as time, space, or process adjuncts.

Miscellaneous correspondences that can be postulated for other conjuncts:

(iv) The enumerative conjuncts (role a(i) in 8.136) that are cardinal numerals and alphabetic letters:

$$\text{'I will say'} + \begin{cases} \textit{one, two, . . .} \\ \textit{a, b, . . .} \end{cases}$$

(v) The conjunct *only* ⟨informal⟩; role f(iv):

> I intended to read the book, *only* ['I would *only* say'] I felt too tired.

(vi) The conjunct *rather*, role f(ii):

> What unites the party is the absence of a policy. Or *rather* ['I should *rather* say'], there is a policy but it has not been properly formulated.

(vii) Reformulatory *better*, role f(i); in the example given for *rather* in (vi) above, *rather* could be replaced by *better* in the sense 'It would be *better* for me to say'.

(viii) Replacive conjuncts *better* and *worse*, role f(ii):

> You can write to him about it. *Better still* ['It would be *better still* to say'], write to his father.

(ix) Concessive conjunct *however*, role f(iv):

> He didn't like the food. *However* ['*However* true that may be'], he didn't complain about it.

(x) The conjunct *though* in role f(iv) is related to the conjunction *though* (*cf* 8.134). Often it is an informal equivalent to an abbreviated subordinate clause with the conjunction *though* as subordinator:

> His food is rather a problem. He looks fit, *though*.

The sentence is interpreted as:

> His food is rather a problem. He looks fit, *though* his food is rather a problem.

The implied subordinate clause need not be identical with the content of a previous clause:

> Singapore must now be one of the most enviably prosperous cities in

> the world. There is no reason, *though*, to suppose that the people of Singapore would want to spend as much money on defence as Britain used to spend.

The implied subordinate clause represented by the conjunct could be something like '*though* the people of Singapore might agree that it needed defending'.

Note [**a**] For some conjuncts, it is difficult to find a correspondence with a cognate adverbial homonymous adjunct; *eg*: *so*, *otherwise*, *at any rate*. With others, there is no direct correspondence at all; *eg*: *furthermore*, *moreover*, *namely*, *nevertheless*, *meanwhile*. But some of these are compounds with an element that functions as an additive or other subjunct; *eg*: *furthermore*, *moreover*, *nevertheless*.

[**b**] The concessive conjunct *though* is a marginal case. We have earlier pointed out that *though* is often equivalent to a subordinate clause with the subordinator *though* (*cf* 8.134). The problem arises when *though* is in *I* position (not to be interpreted as conjunct) and meaning is preserved if it is transposed elsewhere in the clause. In such cases, there is normally a major pause or punctuation mark between the two clauses. For example:

> He is poor – *though* he is satisfied with his condition.

is equivalent to:

> He is poor. He is satisfied with his condition, *though*. ⟨more informal⟩

In speech, a special kind of intonation is required for such a clause, normally a falling-rising nuclear tone:

> He is PÒOR| – *though* he is SǍTisfied with his condition|

Notice that the sentences are not equivalent to:

> *Though* he is satisfied with his condition, he is poor.

but to:

> *Though* he is poor, he is satisfied with his condition.

Compare replacements with although:

> He is poor. He is satisfied with his condition, *though*.
>
> = {He is PÒOR| – *although* he is SǍTisfied with his condition|
> {*Although* he is poor, he is satisfied with his condition.

But unlike *though*, *although* is not a conjunct, and it cannot be transposed elsewhere in the clause:

> He is poor. *He is satisfied with his condition, *although*.

Final *though*- and *although*-clauses can imply some claim of the speaker, *eg*:

> He is poor – [I maintain that this is true] {*although* / *though*} he is satisfied with his condition.

Cf end-placed *because*-clauses as disjuncts of reason (8.132).

Cooccurrence and position of conjuncts

8.144 As we have seen in the examples given in 8.138*ff*, conjuncts frequently cooccur with (and frequently immediately follow) conjunctions: *and so*, *or else*, *but instead*. The effect of the conjuncts is often, indeed, to give a more explicit orientation to such basic conjunctions as *and*, *or*, and *but*, and they can be thus used without tautology. What is more, conjuncts of different classes can cooccur without necessarily being tautologous, contradictory, or ungrammatical (though often, as in the following, at the cost of being stylistically objectionable):

> *And so* [resultive] *all in all* [summative] you think that despite her ill health she has *nonetheless* [concessive] made a good impression at the interview.
>
> *So* [resultive] you think *nonetheless* [concessive] she'll get the job *in other words* [inferential plus appositional].

We can even have a conjunct cooccur with one or more from the same class and achieve the effect of emphatic endorsement rather than of tautology; but again the following is stylistically very undesirable:

> But *yet, even so,* she has { *nevertheless* done well. / done well, *all the same.* }

While emphasis by such means is more characteristic of loose informal talk than formal writing, the converse holds for a related type of endorsement. This is the introduction of a conjunct in a main clause correlating with a conjunction introducing a preceding subordinate clause. For the most part, this belongs to a rather mannered and formal style of writing:

> *When* war actually came, *then* (and only then) the country started rearming.
> *Because* Jennifer foresaw this well in advance, she *therefore* had the necessary time to take preventive action.

But such correlation can freely occur in more ordinary discourse:

> *If* you knew this all along, *then* you could have told me.
> *Even though* you thought I knew, you could have told me *in any case.*
> *While* I'm out, you can *meantime* do the dishes.
> *Seeing that* he had no chance of winning, he *consequently* pretended he wasn't trying.

See further, 8.145.

Disregarding an introductory coordinating conjunction, *I* is the normal position for conjuncts and many are virtually restricted to it, notably *again, besides, yet, still,* (*what is*) *more, so, else, hence.* But as our examples have shown, *M* is quite normal for several of the conjuncts that could not be misinterpreted in this position: *however, nevertheless, in other words, on the contrary,* etc. At *E*, we often find *in other words,* the informal *anyhow, anyway,* and (especially) *though.* Conjuncts at *I* are often followed by a comma, and those at *E* are often preceded by one; such a comma is used especially when the conjunct would have a separate intonation nucleus in speech or when it might be misinterpreted as an adjunct. For example:

> Where did she GÒ| *THÉN*| [inferential conjunct: 'in that case'; 'So where did she go?']
> Where did she go *THÈN*| [time adjunct: 'after that']

At *M*, *thus* and *therefore* differ in that the former does not follow a negative, where there is no such constraint on *therefore*; *cf*:

> Rationalization will *thus* { not / never } be without difficulties.

> ?*Rationalization will { not / never } *thus* be without difficulties.

> Rationalization will { *therefore* { not / never } / { not / never } *therefore* } be without difficulties.

Note [a] Informally, *so* and *but* can be at *E* in Irish English, and *but* can be at *E* in Australian English: 'He has gone, *so*' (where *so* means roughly 'I gather'), 'I didn't do it, *but*' (where *but* means 'all the same').
[b] Despite their potentiality for cooccurrence, conjuncts cannot usually be coordinated. Enumerative conjuncts provide some stereotyped exceptions: *First and foremost*, *Last but not least*, *(Sixth)ly and finally*.
[c] *So*, *yet*, *only*, and *else* are distinguished by the punctuation convention that allows them to be separated from the previous clause by a comma where other conjuncts would require a more major mark of punctuation (*cf* App III.6*ff*, III.12*f*, III.17). However, *else* is normally preceded by the coordinator *or*.
So, *yet*, and *else* usually occur without intonation or punctuation separation from what follows. However, when *so* signals a general inference from the previous linguistic context and might be paraphrased by 'it follows from what we have said', it is often marked by punctuation and intonation:

So, you think you know best. ⟨informal⟩

For *so* and *yet* in relation to coordinators, *cf* 13.18*f*.

Conjuncts as correlatives

8.145 As we saw in 8.144, some conjuncts can correlate with the subordinator of a preceding clause to reinforce the logical relationship between the parts of a sentence. This is because a similar logical relationship is effected by both the subordinator and the conjunct. The difference is that whereas a subordinate clause may often either precede or follow its superordinate clause, a conjunct must always operate anaphorically (*cf* 5.30). For example, the following sentences are similar in meaning (*cf* 8.143):

Though (*he is*) *poor*, he is satisfied with his situation. [1]
He is poor, *yet* (he is) satisfied with his situation. [2]

The major difference is that [2] states his poverty as a fact, whereas in [1] his poverty is presupposed as a given assumption (*cf* 18.8). It is when we combine both subordinator and conjunct in one sentence that we have correlation:

Though he is poor, *yet* he is satisfied with his situation.

Indeed, with concessives we can endorse the concession by having more than one concessive conjunct in the second clause (*cf* 8.144, 13.20, 13.33*ff*), though this is stylistically undesirable:

Though he is poor, *yet* he is *nevertheless* satisfied with his situation.

The conjuncts that endorse particular subordinators by correlation are shown below. It should be noted, however, that it is less usual to endorse cause and time subordinators than condition and concession subordinators.

In sharp contrast to the objectionable redundancy to which attention was drawn in 8.144, formal correlation contributes both to stylistic elegance (through rhetorical balance; *cf* 19.18) and to textual clarity (especially where the two parts to be connected are long and complex).

Examples of correlatives:

CONDITION:	if	then
CONCESSION:	although (even) though while whilst ⟨esp BrE⟩ granted (that) even if	yet still however nevertheless nonetheless notwithstanding anyway ⟨esp informal⟩ anyhow ⟨esp informal⟩
CAUSE:	because seeing (that)	therefore hence ⟨unusual⟩ accordingly consequently
TIME:	while	meanwhile meantime

Note [a] The two instances of *while* listed above are different. *While* in the concessive list of subordinators is synonymous with the subordinator *though*, and the other *while* is equivalent to 'during the time that'. There is a further pair of time correlatives, sometimes used admonitorily: '*When* you've done your homework, *then* you'll get your pocket money.'

[b] Certain other expressions with concessive force may correlate with a concessive conjunct; for example, *true*, *clearly*, or *certainly*, *cf* 19.56.

Conjunctions with conjuncts

8.146 A clause containing a conjunct may be linked to a preceding clause by one of the coordinators (*and*, *or*, *but*; *cf* 8.144), but not all conjuncts cooccur with all coordinators. The following conjuncts seem to be limited to the coordinators indicated:

and so

but { *however* (?) / *then* [antithetic] / *though* }

or { *else* / *again* [replacive] }

and / *but* { *besides* / *then* (*again*) [antithetic] / *still* / *yet* / *nevertheless* }

One of these conjuncts – *though* – cannot follow the conjunction immediately (*cf* 8.143, Note [b]), and the same is true for *however* with many speakers. The reasons are different. When at *I*, *though* is used as a subordinator and the conjunct's nearest place to *I* is *M*. In the case of *however*, many people feel the sequence *but however* to be tautologous. Indeed, some speakers object to the cooccurrence of *but* and *however* even when they are not in immediate sequence. Compare:

John doesn't look very happy { *but* Mary seems all right, *though*. / *but* Mary, *though*, seems all right. }

(?)You can phone the doctor if you like, *but* I very much doubt, *however*, whether you will get him to come out on a Saturday night.

You can phone the doctor if you like. *However*, I very much doubt whether you will get him to come out on a Saturday night.

On the other hand, we cannot have:

*John doesn't look very happy, *but though* Mary seems all right.

For many speakers the following would also be unacceptable:

*You can phone the doctor if you like, *but however*, I very much doubt whether you will get him to come out on a Saturday night.

So, *only*, *yet*, replacive *again*, and antithetic *then* cannot be preceded by subordinators.

Note The concessive conjunct *only* ⟨informal⟩ is a marginal case. Some speakers allow the coordinator *but* to precede it:

?I intended to go, *but only* I didn't feel well.

For those who do not allow *but* to precede *only*, the latter item has a status similar to that of the subordinators causal *for* and resultive *so that* (*cf* 13.8*ff*). Some speakers can begin a question with *only*:

I'd like to come with you; *only*, would I be all right in these clothes?

Other syntactic features of conjuncts

8.147 Except chiefly for *only* and *somehow*, conjuncts can occur in questions. They can do so with similar range of position to that obtaining in declarative sentences:

Anyway, do you know the answer?
So will you be going?
Did he, *in other words*, cheat his employer?

The same is broadly true for indirect questions:

He asked whether they would *nonetheless* remain.

But conjuncts restricted to *I* are excluded:

*He asked whether *so* they would stay.

Unlike most disjuncts, most conjuncts occur freely in imperative sentences:

All the same, try to explain it.
Don't try, *what's more*, to justify yourself.

There are severe constraints on the gradability of conjuncts (as distinct again from disjuncts):

*Very incidentally, . . . *Accordingly enough, . . .

But we find *better still*, *even worse*, and several conjuncts can be intensified by *quite*:

I hoped he would go early but, *quite on the contrary*, he stayed till midnight.
And, *quite by the way*, how is your sister?

Conjuncts can indicate relations between two clauses even where one is subordinate to the other:

I will see him tonight because he will *otherwise* feel hurt. [*cf* I will see him tonight; *otherwise* he will feel hurt]

Where such a subordinate clause can be initial in the sentence, the conjunct – despite its normally anaphoric reference (*cf* 5.30) – may maintain its relating function:

Because he will *otherwise* feel hurt, I will see him tonight.

This is, however, exceptional. Normally, a conjunct in an *I*-placed subordinate clause will relate that clause not to the following matrix clause but to a clause in a preceding sentence:

I can explain it orally. If, *however*, you insist, I will put it in writing.

Transposing the *if*-clause here, we would put the conjunct into the matrix clause to show its constant relation to what has preceded:

I can explain it orally. I will, *however*, put it in writing, if you insist.

Adverbials in conspectus

8.148 We have seen repeatedly that the same item can operate in radically different grammatical functions. Normally, the semantic function is constant, as we may illustrate with the process (manner) adverb *frankly*:

He admitted his mistakes *frankly*. [1]
He *frankly* admitted his mistakes. [2]
Frankly, he was contemptuous of the pardon. [3]
His *frankly* admitted mistakes were pardoned. [4]
His *frankly* extraordinary attitude dismayed his friends. [5]

In [1] we have a sentence adjunct (*cf* 8.36), in [2] a subjunct with subject orientation (*cf* 8.92), in [3] a disjunct (*cf* 8.121). In [4] and [5] we have noun phrases incorporating adverbs that can be related to an adjunct and a disjunct respectively.

With some adverbials, notably the closed-class items, there can be a considerable range of meanings according as the grammatical function shifts: for example, *then* as an adjunct concerned with time, and as a conjunct concerned with enumeration, reinforcement, summation, inference, or antithesis; again, *so* can be an intensifying subjunct, a process adjunct proform, and a conjunct. But even with such items, a central core of meaning remains constant: 'in that event' is close enough to 'at that time' to justify the use of *then* for both; with *so*, we are never far from the meaning 'in that way'.

It is such facts as these that justified the basic separation of semantic roles (*cf* 8.22*ff*) and grammatical functions (*cf* 8.24*ff*), but they also have a bearing on cooccurrence and position.

Constraints on cooccurrence

8.149 It was argued in 8.11 that the grounds for distinguishing different classes of adverbial were basically the same as those for distinguishing two different types of object or complement. To this extent, therefore, we are committed to the principle that one (and only one) member of any one class of adverbial can cooccur in a clause with a member of any other class. But we have already drawn attention to infringement of this principle both ways. On the one hand, we have seen more than one member of the same class operating in a sentence without tautology or contradiction:

I'll meet you *downtown* [A-S1] *at the drugstore* [A-S2] *on Monday* [A-T1] *at five* [A-T2]. [where S and T refer to space and time respectively] [1]
We travelled *from Paris* [A1] *to Cologne* [A2] *via Liège* [A3]. [2]
Yet [A1] he succeeded *nevertheless* [A2]. [3]

In [1] we have two space (position) adjuncts and two time (position) adjuncts; in both cases we would account for the cooccurrence by invoking the principle of hierarchical relationship (*cf* 8.45). So also the source, goal, and path adjuncts of space in [2]. In [3] we have two conjuncts of the same concessive subclass and we may invoke the principle of semantic endorsement and reinforcement (*cf* 8.144).

On the other hand, we found that cooccurrence of quite distinct types of adverbial was often precluded: space–direction with space–position, for example, where the verb in the clause connoted stasis (*cf* 8.42). There are other grounds for the preclusion of cooccurrence. For example, although disjuncts and subjuncts with subject orientation are in sharply distinct classes, their cooccurrence in the same clause requires the hierarchically superior disjunct to be placed earlier than the subjunct.

Frankly, they have *deliberately* been keeping him without news.

With the converse order, they cannot cooccur:

**Deliberately*, they have *frankly* been keeping him without news.

Nor does it seem easy to have a style disjunct and a content disjunct in the same clause:

(?)*Wisely*, they have – *to be blunt* – kept him uninformed.

More generally, there are severe constraints on the same formal item appearing more than once in a clause, even when it is realizing distinct grammatical roles. This stylistic restriction is doubtless influenced by our unavoidable awareness of a common meaning despite the grammatical difference, and hence a correspondingly unavoidable feeling that there is tautology. Compare the following versions of the 'same' sentence:

> *Obviously* [disjunct], Ned can see *perfectly*. [predication adjunct]
> *Obviously*, Ned can see *clearly*.
> *Clearly*, Ned can see *perfectly*.
> ?*Clearly*, Ned can see *clearly*.

Note Avoiding double occurrence of the same formal item is of course general and has nothing specifically to do with adverbs or indeed with items having related meanings. One is embarrassed (or amused) to hear:

> I like most animals but I can't bear bears.

(*Cf* also 4.67, 13.78, 13.101, 17.61).

Relative positions of adverbials

8.150 Style affects also the positioning of adverbials, just as do other interacting factors: realizational, grammatical, and semantic.

Juxtaposition of *-ly* items is widely held to be stylistically objectionable. Thus, while the following is perfectly acceptable:

> In the end it is probable that John alone will be chosen.

a paraphrase like the following would not be:

> ?**Finally probably only* John will be chosen.

(There is little or no objection to *-ly* sequences if the first is an intensifier: 'She drove *extremely slowly*.') Similarity of form in other respects also militates against juxtaposition: thus while 'I kissed her *on the cheek*' [predication adjunct] and 'I kissed her *on the plane*' [sentence adjunct] are equally acceptable, 'I kissed her *on the cheek on the plane*' would be avoided.

It is partly on stylistic grounds that other realizational factors come into play. Since clause-final position is associated with prosodic and semantic 'weight' (*cf* 18.9), it is usually desirable to put adverbials realized by relatively long structures (such as clauses) at the end and have them preceded by adverbials whose realization is shorter (adverb or prepositional phrases); *cf* 8.87. Thus:

> He studied them *carefully* [A process] *that night* [A time].

but:

> He studied them *that night* [A time] *with the kind of care his wife had suggested* [A process].

In this instance, as frequently, such an order is determined in the interests not only of end-weight but of simple clarity: if *that night* were to follow the A process in the last example, it would seem to be functioning as an adjunct in the clause whose subject is *his wife*.

The notion of centre and periphery (*cf* 2.12) also has an important bearing on the relative position of adverbials. Thus if a predication adjunct and a sentence adjunct are required in one clause, the former would normally precede the latter in thus preempting a more central place:

He used to keep them *in his garage* [predication A] *in America* [sentence A]. [1]
He cut the string *with his penknife* [predication A] *with great care* [sentence A]. [2]

If as in [1] there is danger of ambiguity, or if there is stylistic objection to having two adverbials of similar structure in juxtaposition, then the more peripheral adverbial is moved to *I*:

In America, he used to keep them *in his garage*. [1a]
With great care he cut the string *with his penknife*. [2a]

Cooccurring adjuncts of the same grammatical class, subject to the stylistic and realizational factors already mentioned, will have their sequence determined by semantics and will normally appear in the order:

process – space – time

For example:

He worked *quietly* [process] *at home* [space].
He worked *at home* [space] *that day* [time].
The plane arrived *uneventfully* [process] *at Honolulu* [space] *by midnight* [time].

Thus within the same class of adjuncts, those concerned with time are seen to be relatively peripheral and this explains the ease with which they can be moved to *I*:

By midnight, the plane arrived *uneventfully at Honolulu*.

8.151 But if it is reasonable from one viewpoint to regard both *E* and *I* as appropriate locations for peripheral adverbials, it must be recognized

(i) that *E* and *I* are in no way to be equated in their communicative effect; and
(ii) that 'peripheral' implies different things for different types of adverbial.

On (i) we shall have more to say in Chapter 18, but for the present we should note that *E* and *I*, so far from being similar, are polarized in some respects – notably in that *E* usually indicates a climax to which all that has preceded contributes, while *I* usually indicates a general premise or background of which the hearer/reader needs to be aware as we proceed to communicate the real stuff of our message. This means that space as well as time adjuncts can be naturally placed at *I* when realized by pro-forms, since these reflect information that is 'given' (*cf* 18.8). Compare:

Hot and flustered, the two Congressmen anxiously arrived *at the airport*; *there* [space] they waited *all morning* [time].
The two Congressmen arrived *at midday*; *then* [time] they had been told the plane would be landing.

So far as (ii) is concerned, we need to note that for some adverbials peripheralness depends less on their grammatical relations than on their propensity (as we have noted with time adverbials in 8.150) to act as 'background', whereas with other adverbials – notably disjuncts and conjuncts – peripheralness depends on their grammatical relation to another clause whose subject is the speaker. On the face of it, we might expect the latter to be more peripheral than the former, and hence to be placed still closer to the sentential 'rim'. At *E* our expectations seem to be supported. This is not a position frequently occupied by disjuncts or conjuncts, and of course we would not normally want to cluster adverbials in a single position, preferring to put one at *I*, one at *M*, and a third at *E*. But if we had to juxtapose adverbials of different classes, we would be inclined to do so at *E* in the order:

adjunct – conjunct – disjunct

Awkward and implausible as are the following examples, they are comprehensible and unambiguous:

The old lady declined to see me *last night* [Ad], *however* [Con], *unfortunately* [Dis].
My assistant will be away again *tomorrow* [Ad], *what's more* [Con], *probably* [Dis].

At *I*, however, a corresponding attempt to move from 'rim' to 'centre' would be frustrated in more than one respect. A matching peripheralness order would give us:

Unfortunately [Dis], *however* [Con], *last night* [Ad] the old lady declined to see me.
Probably [Dis], *what's more* [Con], *tomorrow* [Ad] my assistant will be away again.

But first, the triple juxtaposition would be even more stylistically clumsy as well as being a little obscure from the viewpoint of information structuring. Secondly, there can be confusion as to whether both disjunct and conjunct are independently related to the following clause or whether the disjunct and conjunct are themselves related as though to mean 'There is the additional probability'. Thirdly, an adjunct at *I* has greater propensity to be the ground for the sentence that follows than has a speaker's comment, and it is thus liable to displace a disjunct or conjunct from *I*. Put differently, disjuncts and conjuncts easily preserve their *grammatical* peripheralness even when located at *M*:

Last night [Ad], she was *clearly* [Dis] unable to remember anything.
In America [Ad], he had *moreover* [Con] kept chickens in his garage.
Until recently [Ad], she was *in other words* [Con] obliged to fend entirely for herself.

8.152 Another factor conditioning the placement of adverbials is similar to the subject-attachment rule (*cf* 'unattached participle': 15.59) and hence affects especially those adverbials that have a close if elliptically expressed relation to a particular element of clause structure. Compare:

?In search of a new house, the evening papers turned out to be of little use to Patricia and her husband.

To Patricia and her husband, in search of a new house, the evening papers turned out to be of little use.

The misplacement of adverbials is particularly serious where the result happens to be a perfectly acceptable and comprehensible sentence, but not with the meaning that was intended. An example from an official letter:

Entirely in the spirit of protective support, could I suggest you pass on an appropriate comment to the personnel concerned?

Enquiry showed that the writer had not intended a suggestion that might protect and support either her or the addressee: she was suggesting that the addressee extend his 'protective support' to the 'personnel concerned'.

As in this example, misplacement often occurs where the originator is actually taking some care to achieve a certain balance in a fairly complicated sentence. The following example (from a newspaper review) is another illustration of this:

Along with Aristotle, Shaw, and William Golding, Bob Dixon finds it impossible to approve writers like Leon Garfield, in my view one of the best children's authors.

Although the syntax suggests quite otherwise, what the reviewer apparently intended was:

Bob Dixon finds it impossible to approve writers like Leon Garfield, along with Aristotle, Shaw, and William Golding. Yet in my view, Garfield is one of the best children's authors.

It is easy to understand why the writer would have found this version less satisfying than his own, which seeks to achieve a fine irony by fronting the list of great writers who are apparently dismissed by Dixon. By this fronting, moreover, it was apparently the writer's hope to append his own opinion neatly, economically, and even climactically after the first (and by this device, the only) mention of Garfield.

Realization and role

8.153 It was pointed out in 8.13 that adverbials could have widely differing types of realization, and we have seen that broadly speaking a particular semantic role or grammatical function does not determine a particular type of realization structure. This seems true of the sentence adjuncts relating to time (position) in the following:

He spoke to me {*then.* / *recently.* / *on a recent occasion.* / *when last Thursday's meeting was over.*}

In other words, for the most part, the choice of realization type is a direct function of the degree of specificity required, and the foregoing examples have ranged from a purely anaphoric reference (*then*), indicating a time which the speaker can assume has been adequately specified elsewhere, to a precise indication of a particular point on a particular day.

But we have seen evidence of a direct tie between realization and role such that (for instance) adjuncts of process (manner) are normally realized by an adverb phrase with an adjective-derived (*-ly*) adverb as head (*cf* 8.78), while adjuncts relating to space (position) are usually realized by prepositional phrases (*cf* 8.40).

There is a still more general relation between role and realization to which attention has been given only implicitly. We have noted that, the longer the adverbial, the more weight of information it rather obviously carries.

The corollary of this is that the adverb phrase (the more especially when this, in turn, is realized by an unmodified adverb) is relatively low in information content and that the adverbial roles that are most frequently so realized are presented to the hearer/reader as a rather minor contribution to the content of a sentence. This assessment we clearly endorse when we choose to place an adverbial at *M*:

John has *recently* been offered promotion.

Bibliographical note

There are major studies of adverbials as a whole by Buysschaert (1979, 1982); Greenbaum (1969b); Huang (1975); Nilsen (1972).

For some notable theoretical proposals, see Bartsch (1976); Dik (1975); Emons (1974); Haegeman (1985); Schlesinger (1979); Schreiber (1972).

On specific subsets of English adverbials, see Bolinger (1972a); Hartvigson (1969); Heny (1973); Hindle and Sag (1973); Jacobson (1978, 1981); Lewis (1975); Svartvik (1980); Swan (1982).

On adverbial collocations, see Bäcklund (1970); Crystal (1966); Greenbaum (1970).

For the positions of adverbials in sentence structure, see Greenbaum (1976b, 1977a); Jacobson (1964, 1975).

On intonational aspects of English adverbial usage, see Allerton and Cruttenden (1974, 1976, 1978); Halliday (1967); Taglicht (1983).

Other studies relevant to this Chapter include Anderson (1976); Crystal (1980); Halliday and Hasan (1976); Kolář (1975); G. Lakoff (1975); Menz (1981); Schreiber (1971).

9 Prepositions and prepositional phrases

Introduction

Syntactic functions of prepositional phrases

9.1 In the most general terms, a preposition expresses a relation between two entities, one being that represented by the prepositional complement, the other by another part of the sentence. The prepositional complement is characteristically a noun phrase, a nominal *wh*-clause, or a nominal *-ing* clause:

PREPOSITIONAL PHRASE	
PREPOSITION	COMPLEMENT
on	the table
from	what he said
by	signing a peace treaty
in terms of	money
at variance with	the official reports

Fig 9.1 Examples of prepositional phrases

Prepositional phrases have the following syntactic functions:

(I) POSTMODIFIER in a noun phrase (*cf* 17.37*ff*):
The people *on the bus* were singing.

(II) ADVERBIAL
(a) Adjunct (*cf* 8.24*ff*):
The people were singing *on the bus.*
In the afternoon, we went *to Boston.*
(b) Subjunct (*cf* 8.88*ff*):
From a personal point of view, I find this a good solution to the problem.
(c) Disjunct (*cf* 8.121*ff*):
In all fairness, she did try to phone the police.
(d) Conjunct (*cf* 8.134*ff*):
On the other hand, he made no attempt to help her.

(III) COMPLEMENTATION
(a) Complementation of a verb (*cf* 9.60*ff*; also prepositional verbs, 16.3*ff*):
We were looking *at his awful paintings.*
(b) Complementation of an adjective (*cf* 9.60*ff*, 16.68*ff*):
I'm sorry *for his parents.*

As complementation of a verb or an adjective, the preposition is more closely related to the preceding word (*look at*, *sorry for*), which determines its choice, than to the prepositional complement.

The positions and functions of prepositional phrases as adverbial are discussed in Chapter 8. The functions of prepositional phrases as modifiers in noun phrases are further dealt with in 17.37*ff*.

Note [**a**] Like adverbs (*cf* 7.46*ff*), prepositional phrases may occasionally take a nominal function, for example as subject of a clause (*cf* 10.15):

A: When are we going to have the next meeting?

B: { *On Tuesday* / *In March* / *During the vacation* / *Between 6 and 7* } { will be fine. / suits me. / is what we decided. / may be convenient. }

Such nominal uses can be viewed as related to sentences that have been restructured so as to leave only the adverbial prepositional phrase:

(The proposal that we meet) *on Tuesday* . . .
(To meet) *in March* . . .
(Meeting) *during the vacation* . . .

The preposition can be omitted under the same conditions as stated in 9.40*ff*:

{ *Tuesday* / **6 and 7* } suits me.

With the preposition omitted, however, there is ambiguity (*cf* 10.15 Note [b]), as in:

Tuesday will be fine. { 'Meeting on Tuesday / 'The weather on Tuesday } will be fine.'

[**b**] In addition to the functions of prepositional phrases mentioned in this chapter, we have a quasi-adjectival function as complement (*cf* 10.11), *eg*:

This machine is (very) *out of date*.
This dress seems *out of fashion*.

The adjectival nature of these prepositional phrases is evident from:

(i) their semantic similarity to adjectives, *eg*:
out-of-date ['obsolete'; *cf*: an *out-of-date* machine, 17.111]

(ii) their possibility of being coordinated with, or appositional to, adjectives, *eg*:
They're happy and *in good health*.
an old and *out-of-order* telephone

(iii) their use as complementation also for copular verbs other than *be* (*cf* 16.23), *eg*:
They seem *in good health*. ['healthy']

[**c**] Exceptionally (mainly in fixed phrases), an adverb or an adjective may function as prepositional complement (*cf* 7.26 Note):

at last	*at least*	*at once*	*at worst*	*before long*
by far	*in brief*	*in there*	*since when*	*until now*

[**d**] Prepositional phrases can themselves act as prepositional complements, so that two prepositions may occur in sequence:

He picked up the gun { *from under* the table. / *from behind* the counter. }
We didn't meet *until after* the show.
Food has been scarce *since before* the war.
The weather has been fine *except in* the north.

[**e**] Some prepositions form a correlative construction with a conjunction or another preposition, *eg*:

between Boston *and* New York   *from* six *to* seven

[**f**] The function of verb complementation (IIIa above) may alternatively be regarded as adverbial (*cf* 16.5).

A definition of 'preposition'

9.2 There are several points of similarity between prepositions and other word classes and constructions in English grammar, in particular conjunctions and adverbs, but also participles and adjectives. Before discussing the marginal cases, it will be useful to try to define central prepositions.

CENTRAL prepositions in English can be defined negatively with three criteria. They *cannot* have as a complement:

(i) a *that*-clause

(ii) an infinitive clause
(iii) a subjective case form of a personal pronoun:

He was surprised { *at (that) she noticed him. [1]
*at to see her. [2]
*at she. [3] }

That-clauses and infinitive clauses, although they frequently have a nominal function in other respects (*cf* 15.4), do not occur as prepositional complements in English. Alternations between the presence and absence of a preposition are observed in cases like the following:

He was surprised { *that she noticed him.* [1a]
to see her. [2a]
at her. [3a]
at her attitude.
at what he saw. }

They convinced him { *of the need for more troops.*
of how many troops they needed.
that / **of that* } *they needed more troops.*
to / **of to* } *send for more troops.* }

Such alternations show that the preposition that normally cooccurs with certain verbs and adjectives is omitted before a *that*-clause or infinitive clause. Further examples of verbs and adjectives which can have either prepositions or *that*-clauses are (*cf* 16.3*ff*, 16.68*ff*):

ask (*for*)	inform (*of*)	be bad (*at*)	be sorry (*about*)
decide (*on*)	tell (*of/about*)	be aware (*of*)	be interested (*in*)

When omission of the preposition is impossible, some construction other than a *that*-clause or infinitive clause must be used, *eg*:

I'm looking forward *to* { *the meeting with you.* [noun phrase]
meeting you. [-*ing* clause]
what you will say. [*wh*-clause] }

That-clauses can often become in effect prepositional complements through the use of an appositive construction with a 'general' noun such as *fact* (*cf* 17.26), often resulting in a rather clumsy expression:

They convinced him of *the fact that* they needed more troops.

Note The preposition preceding a *wh*-clause is optional in certain circumstances (*cf* 16.35, 16.73):
I wasn't certain (*of*) *what to do*.

Prepositions, conjunctions, and verbs

9.3 Both prepositions and conjunctions have a relating or connecting function. Compare:

the day { *when she arrived* [*when* = conjunction]
of her arrival [*of* = preposition] }

In certain cases, the same items can function both as prepositions and conjunctions, *eg*: *after, as, before, since, until*:

the day { *before she arrived* [*before* = conjunction]
before her arrival [*before* = preposition] }

One distinguishing criterion between the two word classes is that prepositions introduce complements which are nominal or nominalized, whereas the corresponding conjunctions (subordinators) introduce a subordinate clause (*cf* 14.11*ff*).

The situation is however complicated in the case of nonfinite clauses, since *-ing* clauses are permitted after a preposition in English (*cf* 14.6*ff*):

On arriving she took a taxi.

Compare *after*, which can be used either as a conjunction or a preposition, with on the one hand *when*, which can only be a conjunction, and on the other *by*, which can only be a preposition:

Table 9.3 Constructions after prepositions and conjunctions

	when = conjunction only	*after* = conjunction or preposition	*by* = preposition only
(a) + FINITE CLAUSE	*when she spoke*	*after she spoke*	**by she spoke*
(b) + NONFINITE CLAUSE	*when speaking*	*after speaking*	*by speaking*
(c) + NOUN PHRASE	**when her speech*	*after her speech*	*by her speech*

Some *-ing* and *-ed* participial forms can function both as marginal prepositions (*cf* 9.8), as nonfinite verb forms, and as conjunctions, *eg*: *considering* and *given*:

PREPOSITIONS:

Considering his age, he has made excellent progress in his studies. ['If one considers his age . . .', 'In view of his age . . .']

Given the present conditions, I think she's done rather well. ['If one takes into account . . .']

PARTICIPLES:

Considering the conditions in the office, she thought it wise not to apply for the job. ['When she considered the conditions . . .']

Given the chance, I'd do it again. ['If I were given the chance . . .']

CONJUNCTIONS:

Considering that he is rather young, his parents have advised him not to apply.

Given that this work was produced under particularly difficult circumstances, the result is better than could be expected.

Other *-ing* and *-ed* forms that can be used as conjunctions are *seeing* (*that*) and *provided* (*that*) (*cf* 14.12).

Note [a] *Instead of* may be classified as a marginal preposition. It fulfils the third criterion for a preposition (*cf* 9.2) in requiring the oblique case form:

I propose you *instead of* { *me.* / **I.* }

It fails the second criterion since it can have an infinitive clause as complement:

It must be so frightful to have to put things on in order to look better, *instead of to strip things off.* (Margaret Drabble, *A Summer Bird-Cage*)

Although *instead of* + infinitive has been attested in good written English, many would here prefer: '. . . *instead of stripping* . . .' (which, however, would spoil the parallelism with *to put* that may have motivated the use of *to strip* here).

Instead of may also have as complement a finite *as* clause:

He pictures people as he sees them *instead of as they are.*

[b] *On account of* is also used in familiar style as a conjunction, especially in AmE, violating the first condition in 9.2:

I was sitting over there wishing I could write, *on account of* I've thought up what I think's a pretty good spy story. (Kurt Vonnegut, Jr, *Mother Night*).

The directly corresponding standard English construction *on account of my having thought up* is generally clumsy and unidiomatic in the colloquial style here; *because* or *seeing* (*that*) would be the common alternative constructions.

[c] Combinations such as *except that, save that, but that* [= *except that*], and *in that*, which introduce finite clauses, are complex subordinators, not preposition + *that* (*cf* 14.12).

Functions of *than* and *like*

9.4 The gradience between prepositions and conjunctions also appears in comparative constructions (*cf* 15.63*ff*), such as:

He's bigger *than* { *I am.* [1a] / *I.* [1b] / *me.* [1c] }

With the definition of preposition given in 9.2, *than* is a conjunction in [1a] and [1b], and a preposition in [1c]. However, the choice between [1b] and [1c] is a well-known prescriptive issue in traditional grammar, and it may be argued that *than* is both a conjunction in [1a] and a preposition in [1c], and that *than I* in [1b] is not a reduction of [1a] *than I am* but a hypercorrect variant of [1c] *than me.*

As and *like* are two other items which have functions that are difficult to classify in terms of traditional word classes. The following examples with *like* illustrate the need for a gradient rather than a discrete form of classification:

She looks rather *like* { *me.* / **I.* } [2]

Like { *me,* / **I,* } she's a blonde. [3]

She's a teacher, just *like you and* { *me.* / ?**I.* } [4]

No one can write *like* { *her.* / **she.* } [5]

(?)She can't write *like she used to.* [6]

Like in [2] is adjective-like in accepting the intensifier *very* and comparison (*cf* 7.2):

She looks more *like me*. ['She resembles me more.'] [2a]

In [3], the prepositional use of *like* has a quasi-coordinative function (*cf*: *with, along with*; 10.40):

She's a blonde, and so am I. [3a]

In [4], the hypercorrect subjective form is avoided by many, although it occurs commonly enough when not immediately preceded by *like*. Compare:

She's a teacher { **like I and you.* / *?like you and I.* } [4a]

In [5], the meaning of *like* is similar to that in adverbial clauses 'in the same manner as (she does)', 'as well as (she does)', but the normal form is the objective *like her*; **like she* is generally considered unacceptable.

In [6], *like* introduces a finite clause with obligatory subjective pronoun form (*like she used to*), and thus functions as a conjunction. This use of *like* instead of *as* is widely criticized but common in informal style, especially in AmE. The situation is similar with *like* in clauses of comparison, such as [7]:

(?)He treats me *like I was his sister*. [7]

Here, many would prefer *as if* or *as though*, since *like* is widely regarded as nonstandard in this function. By contrast, out of hypercorrectness, *as* is sometimes used instead of *like* even as a preposition where a useful distinction should be kept between them (*cf* 9.48), as in:

He spoke { *as a leader of mankind*. ['in the capacity of'] / *like a leader of mankind*. ['in the manner of'] }

Note Another group of items with fuzzy borders between word classes includes *but*, *except*, and *besides* (*cf* 9.58).

Prepositions and adverbs

9.5 Prepositions are items which are often formally identical with and semantically similar to adverbs. Compare the following pairs:

She looked *up the hill*. [1]
She looked *up the word*. [1a]

She walked *across the street*. [2]
She walked *across*. [2a]

Both *up* in [1] and *across* in [2] are prepositions with prepositional complement (*up the hill, across the street*). However, in [1a], *up* is an ADVERB PARTICLE in a phrasal verb *look 'up* with, for example, positional mobility. Compare:

She *looked* the word *up*. [1b]
*She *walked* the street *across*. [2b]

Phrasal verbs are discussed in 16.3*f*. *Across* in [2a] with the complement omitted is called a PREPOSITIONAL ADVERB (*cf* 9.65*f*).

The distinction between preposition and adverb is not clear in expressions like the following:

He is *near to* (being) mad. ['nearly']
This seems *next to* impossible. ['almost']
Close to 200 people came. ['almost']
She is *far from* (being) weak. ['anything but']

The simple preposition *near* and the complex prepositions *near to* and *close to* (all locative; *cf* 9.20) satisfy all three criteria for prepositions. At the same time, they have certain affinities with adjectives and adverbs. *Near* (*to*) and *close to* are the only prepositions which have both comparison and intensification:

She sat {
(very) *near* (*to*)
(quite) *close to*
(much) { *nearer* (*to*) / *closer to* }
nearest (*to*)
next to
closest to
} me.

About is an adverb in the following use:

She is *about* forty. [3]

That the function is adverbial appears from the possibility of omission [3a], substitution by adverbs [3b], and postposition [3c]:

She is (*about*) forty. [3a]

She is { *about* / *roughly* / *approximately* } forty. [3b]

She is FǑRty { *about*. ⟨informal⟩ / *approximately*. } [3c]

Note Some phrases consisting of preposition + noun have become fixed and function as closed-class adverbs (*cf* 7.46), *eg*: *of course* ['naturally'], *in fact* ['actually']. Sometimes the combination is spelled as a single word: *indeed, instead*.

Deferred prepositions

9.6 Normally a preposition must be followed by its complement, but there are some circumstances in which this does not happen.

In the following three cases the DEFERMENT of the preposition is obligatory.

(a) Passive constructions with a prepositional verb where the subject corresponds to the prepositional complement in the active (*cf* 3.69, 16.14):

Has *the room* been paid *for*?
~ Has X paid *for the room*?
≁ *Has *for the room* been paid?

She was sought *after* by all the leading impresarios of the day. [also in premodification: 'a much *sought-after* singer']
He was not paid attention *to*.

(b) Infinitive clauses with thematization of the prepositional complement (*cf* 18.36):

He's impossible to work *with*.

(c) *-ing* clauses with thematization:

He's worth listening *to*.

With interrogative and relative pronouns as prepositional complement, there are often alternative positions available: one formal with the preposition in its normal place before the complement [1, 2], the other informal with the preposition deferred to final position [1a, 2a]:

WH-QUESTIONS (*cf* 11.14*ff*, 16.15):

{ *At which* house did you leave the car? ⟨formal⟩ [1]
{ *Which* house did you leave the car *at*? [1a]

Usually (*cf* 11.14 Note [e]):

Where did you leave your car? [1b]

RELATIVE CLAUSES (*cf* 17.16):

The old house { *about which* I was telling you is empty. ⟨formal⟩ [2]
The old house { (*which*) I was telling you *about* is empty. [2a]

A prejudice against such deferred (or 'stranded') prepositions [1a, 2a] remains in formal English which, for direct or indirect questions and for relative clauses, offers the alternative of an initial preposition [1, 2]. The alternative construction is often felt, however, to be stilted and awkward, especially in speech. In some cases, such as the following, the deferred preposition has no preposed alternative:

What did she look *like*?
What I'm convinced *of* is that the world's population will grow to an unforeseen extent.
All she could talk *about* was her dog.

In general, it is the most common and the short prepositions which can be deferred, in particular spatial prepositions (9.15*ff*), compare:

He left his coat *in the car*.
~ . . . the car { *in which* he left his coat / (*that*) he left his coat *in* } [3]

He left politics *because of the election results*.
~ . . . the election results { *because of which* he left politics / *(*that*) he left politics *because of* } [4]

The plane was destroyed *through the pilot's carelessness*.
~ . . . the pilot's carelessness { *through which* the plane was destroyed / *(*that*) the plane was destroyed *through* } [5]

Simple and complex prepositions

Simple prepositions

9.7 Most of the common English prepositions, such as *at*, *in*, and *for*, are SIMPLE, *ie* they consist of one word. Other prepositions, consisting of more than one word, are called COMPLEX (*cf* 9.10*ff*). The following is a list of the most common simple prepositions. In view of the different stress patterns (*cf* 9.9), they have been divided into mono- and polysyllabic. References are given to sections in this chapter where the uses of the prepositions are discussed.

(a) Monosyllabic prepositions

as	Basis of comparison 7.86; Role 9.4, 48
at	Space 9.15*ff*; Time position 9.34; Goal, target 9.46; Stimulus 9.51; Standard 9.62; Reaction 9.63
but	Exception 9.58
by	Space 9.20; Time 9.34, 39; Means and instrument 9.49; Agentive 9.50; Stimulus 9.51; Reaction 9.63
down	Movement 9.26, 32; Orientation 9.27
for	Duration 9.36, 38, 42; Cause, etc 9.44; Purpose, intended destination 9.45; Recipient 9.46; Support 9.53; Standard 9.62
from	Space 9.15*ff*; Orientation 9.27; Resultative 9.28; Originator 9.32; Duration 9.37; Cause, etc 9.44; Source, origin 9.47; Substance 9.61
in	Space 9.15*ff*, 32; Time position 9.34; Measurement into the future 9.35
like	Manner 9.4, 48
near (*to*)	(also comparative and superlative: *nearer* (*to*), *nearest* (*to*)) Space 9.20
of	Cause, means 9.49 Note [b]; various relations 9.54*f*; Subject matter 9.60; Material 9.61
off	Space 9.15*ff*
on	(*cf*: *upon*) Space 9.15*ff*, 32; Time position 9.34; Target 9.46 Note [b]; Means and instrument 9.49 Note [a]; Respect 9.57; Subject matter 9.60
out	⟨esp AmE⟩ Negative position 9.18 Note
past	Passage 9.25; Orientation 9.27; Resultative 9.28, 32
per	Distributive frequency 5.18, *cf* 8.64
pro	(see Note [a])
qua	(see Note [a])
re	Respect 9.57, (see Note [a])
round	⟨esp BrE⟩ Space 9.22; Movement 9.26; Orientation 9.27
sans	(see Note [a])
since	Time 9.38
than	Basis of comparison 9.4, 7.85
through	⟨in informal AmE also spelt *thru*⟩ Relative position 9.22; Passage 9.25; Orientation 9.27; Pervasive 9.29; Perseverance 9.32; Duration 9.36*f*; Intermediacy 9.50
till	(*cf*: *until*) Duration 9.37*f*
to	Space 9.15*ff*; Movement 9.26; Recipient 9.32; Duration 9.37; Reaction 9.63

up	Movement 9.26, 32; Orientation 9.27
via	(see Note [a])
with	Space 9.20; Pervasive 9.29; Manner 9.48; Means and instrument 9.49*f*; Accompaniment 9.52; Support and opposition 9.53; 'Having' 9.55; Ingredient 9.61

(b) Polysyllabic prepositions

aˈbout	Space 9.22; Respect 9.57; Subject matter 9.60
aˈbove	Relative position 9.19, 32
aˈcross	Relative position 9.22; Passage 9.25, 28; Movement 9.26; Orientation 9.27
ˈafter	Relative position 9.19; Time 9.38
aˈgainst	Position 9.17 Note [b]; Opposition 9.53
aˈlong	Movement 9.26; Orientation 9.27; Pervasive 9.29 (also *aˈlongside*)
aˈmid(st)	⟨formal⟩ Space 9.21, 32
aˈmong(st)	⟨*amongst* esp BrE⟩ Space 9.21; Relation 9.32
ˈanti	(see Note [a])
aˈround	⟨esp AmE for some uses⟩ Space 9.22; Movement 9.26; Orientation 9.27; Pervasive 9.29
aˈtop	⟨esp AmE; literary⟩ Relative position, *cf* 9.19
beˈfore	Relative position 9.19; Time 9.38
beˈhind	Relative position 9.19; Relative destination 9.23; Passage 9.24
beˈlow	Relative position 9.19, 32
beˈneath	⟨formal⟩ Relative position 9.19, 32
beˈside	Space 9.20
beˈsides	Addition 9.20, 58
beˈtween	Space 9.21; Relation 9.32; Time 9.39
beˈyond	Orientation 9.27, 32; Exception 9.58
ˈcirca	(see Note [a])
deˈspite	Concession 9.56
ˈduring	Time position 9.34; Duration 9.36
exˈcept	Exception 9.58
inˈside	Space 9.15 Note [a], 9.55 Note
ˈinto	Space 9.15*ff*; Movement 9.26, 32
ˌnotwithˈstanding	⟨formal⟩ Concession 9.56
ˈonto	Space 9.15*ff*
ˈopposite	Space 9.20
outˈside	Space 9.15 Note [a], 9.55 Note
ˈover	Survey of different senses 9.30; Relative position 9.19; Relative destination 9.23; Passage 9.24; Movement 9.26; Orientation 9.27; Resultative 9.28; Pervasive 9.29; 'more than' 9.32 Note [a]; Duration 9.36; Subject matter 9.60
ˈpace	(see Note [a])
ˈpending	Duration 9.38 Note [b]
throughˈout	Pervasive 9.29; Duration 9.36

to'ward(s)	⟨*to'ward* esp AmE⟩ Movement 9.17, 26
'under	Relative position 9.19; Relative destination 9.23; Passage 9.24; Subjection, etc 9.32; 'less than' 9.32 Note [a]
ˌunder'neath	⟨formal⟩ Relative position 9.19; Relative destination 9.23; Passage 9.24
un'like	Manner 9.48
un'til	Duration 9.37*f*
u'pon	⟨formal⟩ (see *on* above)
'versus	(see Note [a])
'vis-à-'vis	(see Note [a])
with'in	Space 9.15 Note [a], 9.55 Note
with'out	Means and instrument 9.49*f*; Accompaniment 9.52; 'Having' 9.55

Note [**a**] Some of the prepositions listed above are restricted in terms of frequency, style, or usage. The following are foreign borrowings that are restricted to certain contexts, usually formal or technical. Those that have not yet been fully anglicized are often italicized in print.

Latin origin: *anti, circa, pace, pro, qua, re, versus* [abbreviated *v* ⟨BrE⟩, *vs* ⟨AmE⟩], *via*
French origin: *sans, vis-à-vis*

[**b**] The prepositions *agin* and *anent* are rare and stylistically restricted; *agin* is common in Scots and so is *outwith* /'aʊtˌwɪθ/ ['except', 'outside']. Also ⟨BrE dialectal⟩: *while* ['till'].

[**c**] In poetic style, the reduced forms *'tween* and *'twixt* ['between'] may occur.

[**d**] '*Unto* ['to'] is archaic and biblical.

[**e**] As indicated in the lists above, there are differences between AmE and BrE in the use of some prepositions. One such example is *toward/towards* (*cf* 7.46 Note [a]).

Marginal prepositions

9.8 In addition to the prepositions listed in 9.7, there are some words which behave in many ways like prepositions, although they also have affinities with other word classes such as verbs or adjectives (*cf* 9.3*f*), *eg*:

Granted his obsequious manner, I still think he's ambitious enough to do the job.
He gave Mary all *bar* ['except'] three of the sketches.
Two gold-hilted swords, each *worth* £10,000, were sold at Sotheby's last Monday.

Here is a list of some marginal prepositions with verbal affinities:

bar, 'barring, ex'cepting, ex'cluding; save ⟨formal⟩ (Exception 9.58)
con'cerning ⟨formal⟩, *con'sidering* (*cf* 9.3, 57), *re'garding, re'specting, 'touching* ⟨formal or literary⟩ (Respect 9.57)
'failing, 'wanting
'following, 'pending ⟨formal⟩ (Time 9.38 Note [b])
'given, 'granted, in'cluding (*cf* 17.73)

Less, minus, plus, times, and *over* form a special group in their use with numerals (*cf* 6.68), *eg*:

6 + 2 is read as 'six plus two'.

In informal style, *minus* and *plus* can also occur in nonnumerical contexts:

I hope he comes *minus* his wife. ['without']
She's had mumps *plus* measles. ['and']

Plus can even be used as a conjunction (*cf* 13.5 Note [b]):

You can get what you want, *plus* you can save money. ⟨esp AmE⟩ ['and in addition', 'also']

Stressing of simple prepositions

9.9 As regards stress, simple prepositions can be divided into two groups:

(a) Prepositions which have no reduced form in their pronunciation (*cf* App II.9), *eg*: *like*, *round*, *since*, *through*. For example:
A: What's its SHÀPE *like* /laɪk/? B: It's *like* /laɪk/ a SÀUsage.

(b) Prepositions which have reduced forms, *eg*: *from* /frɒm, frəm, frm/ and where the choice of phonetic form varies according to function. For example:
A: Where's he *FRÒM* /frɒm/? B: He's *from* /frəm/ New JÈRsey.

Monosyllabic prepositions are normally unstressed; polysyllabic prepositions are normally stressed. However, stressed monosyllabic prepositions are by no means uncommon, especially in coordination:

Trains both '*to* and '*from* London are late this morning.
. . . government '*of* the people, '*by* the people, and '*for* the people

Stressing of prepositions also occurs in repeated patterns where the stress shifts from a 'given' item to a 'new' item (*cf* 19.25), as in:

A: Why don't you borrow the book from the LÌbrary?
B: It's not ÌN the library.

Yet stressing takes place not only in such contrastive use, but also in some other cases where the prepositional complement is unstressed or is the 'tail' of the tone unit (*cf* App II.15), *eg*:

Where are you *FRÒM*? He's *PÀST* it.
They took it *ÒFF* him. What's it *FÒR*?
What *ÒF* it?

The stress shift from the complement of the preposition, as in [1], to the preposition, as in [2], is clearly conditioned by the desire to avoid stressing the pronoun *it* (*cf* 6.16):

There's nothing { *to this STÒry.* [1]
There's nothing { *TÒ it.* [2]

Special stress patterns are used for special effects. Note the different meanings according to whether the preposition *by* is stressed or not in:

She wants to have a book { *BỲ her*. ['near herself'; place] ⟨esp BrE⟩
She wants to have a book { *by HÈR*. ['written by'; agentive; *cf* 9.50]

Note also the different meanings of *for* with varying stress in the following set:

Our vote is *FÒR* /'fɔːʳ/ *the students.* ['in favour of the students']
The exams are *for* /fəʳ/ *the STÙdents.* ['are designed for the students to take']

Note Stressing monosyllabic prepositions has become rather fashionable, although some people regard it as annoyingly affected. Public speakers and radio commentators tend to stress monosyllabic prepositions where weak forms are expected. Speakers may stress them when searching for the appropriate complement, *eg*:

FRÒM . . . /əhː/ . . . the Palace GÀTES . . . the Royal carriage proceeds . . .

However, some speakers do it when there is no such motivation, *eg*:

'ÒN this record| Benny plays beautiful VÌBES|

Complex prepositions

Two-word sequences

9.10 Complex prepositions may be subdivided into two- and three-word sequences.

In two-word sequences, the first word (which usually is relatively stressed) is an adverb, adjective, or conjunction, and the second word a simple preposition (usually *for*, *from*, *of*, *to*, or *with*). For example:

Except for Margaret, everybody was in favour of the idea.
We had to leave early *because of* the bad weather.
I sat *next to* an old lady on the train.

Here is a list of some two-word prepositions:

'up against	*'as per*
'as for (9.57) *ex'cept for* (9.58)	*'but for* (9.59)
a'part from (9.58) *a'way from* (9.15*ff*)	*a'side from* ⟨esp AmE⟩ (9.58) *'as from*
a'head of *'back of* ⟨informal AmE⟩ (9.11 Note) *ex'clusive of* *in'stead of* *'off of* ⟨informal AmE⟩ *out'side of* *'upwards of*	*'as of* *be'cause of* (9.44) *de'void of* *in'side of* *irre'spective of* (9.57 Note) *'out of* (9.15*ff*, 28, 32, 61) *re'gardless of* (9.57 Note) *'void of*
ac'cording to (9.57, 63) *'close to* (9.20) *'due to* *'next to* (9.20) *'owing to* *pre'paratory to* *'prior to* *'subsequent to* *'up to* (9.37)	*'as to* (9.57) *'contrary to* *'near(er)* (*to*) (9.20) *'on to* [*cf*: *'onto*] (9.7, 15 Note [b]) *pre'liminary to* *'previous to* *pur'suant to* ⟨formal⟩ *'thanks to*
a'long with	*to'gether with*

Note As with simple prepositions (*cf* 9.7 Note [a]), there are also complex prepositions of French origin which have not yet been fully anglicized and are often italicized in print, *eg*: *à la* (*cf* 17.60 Note) and *apropos* (*of*) ['with regard to'] (*cf* 9.57).

Three-word sequences

9.11 The most numerous category of complex prepositions is the type consisting of three words, as in:

Prep1 + Noun + Prep2: *in view of* the election [1]

Other examples:

In terms of money, her loss was small.
Two men were interviewed at Bow Street Police Station *in connection with* a theft from an Oxford Street store.
How many delegates are *in favour of* this motion?
His biography of Eisenhower is in many places *at variance with* the official reports.
In line with latest trends in fashion, many dress designers have been sacrificing elegance to audacity.

With three-word sequences we also include complex prepositions where the noun is preceded by a definite or indefinite article:

in the light of } the election [1a]
as a result of }

Complex prepositions may be subdivided according to which prepositions function as Prep1 and Prep2, *eg*:

in + noun + *of*:

in aid of | *in back of*
in behalf of ⟨AmE⟩ | *in case of*
in charge of | *in consequence of*
in (the) face of | *in favour of*
in front of (9.19) | *in (the) light of*
in lieu of | *in need of*
in place of | *in (the) process of*
in quest of | *in respect of*
in search of | *in spite of* (9.56)
in view of

---

in + noun + *with*:

in accordance with (9.63 Note) | *in common with*
in comparison with | *in compliance with*
in conformity with | *in contact with*
in line with

---

by + noun + *of*:

by dint of | *by means of*
by virtue of | *by way of*

---

on + noun + *of*:

on account of (9.44) | *on behalf of*

on (*the*) *ground*(*s*) *of*
on pain of
on the strength of
on the matter of (9.57)
on the part of
on top of (9.19)

Other types:
as far as (9.17)
at the expense of
for (*the*) *sake of*
in exchange for
in addition to (9.58)
with/in regard to (9.57)
with/in respect to (9.57)
at variance with
at the hands of
for/from want of
in return for
in relation to
with/in reference to (9.57)
with the exception of (9.58)

Note Some complex prepositions consisting of three-word sequences tend to be shortened to two-word sequences in casual speech, *eg*: (*in*) *back of*, (*by*) *way of*, (*by*) *means of*, (*on*) *pain of*, (*for*) *sake of*, (*in*) *spite of*:

Spite of this, I think we should go right ahead.
Let's do this *sake of* consistency.

Gradience between complex prepositions and free noun-phrase sequences

9.12 In the strictest definition, a complex preposition is a sequence that is indivisible both in terms of syntax and in terms of meaning. However, there is no absolute distinction between complex prepositions and constructions which can be varied, abbreviated, and extended according to the normal rules of syntax. Rather, there is a scale of 'cohesiveness' running from a sequence which behaves in every way like a simple preposition, *eg*: *in spite of* (*the weather*), to one which behaves in every way like a set of grammatically separate units, *eg*: *on the shelf by* (*the door*). Nine indicators of syntactic separateness are listed below.

(a) Prep2 can be varied:
on the shelf at (*the door*) [but not: **in spite for*, etc]

(b) The noun can be varied as between singular and plural:
on the shelves by (*the door*) [but not: **in spites of*]

(c) The noun can be varied in respect of determiners:
on a/the shelf by; *on shelves by* (*the door*) [but not: **in a/the spite of*]

(d) Prep1 can be varied:
under the shelf by (*the door*) [but not: **for spite of*]

(e) Prep + complement can be replaced by a possessive pronoun (*cf* Note [c] below):
on the surface of the table ~ *on its surface*
[but: *in spite of the result* ~ **in its spite*]

(f) Prep2 + complement can be omitted:
on the shelf [but not: **in spite*]

(g) Prep2 + complement can be replaced by a demonstrative:
on that shelf [but not: **in that spite*]

(h) The noun can be replaced by nouns of related meaning:
on the ledge by (*the door*) [but not: **in malice of*]

(i) The noun can be freely premodified by adjectives:
on the low shelf by (*the door*) [but not: **in evident spite of*]

In all these respects, *in spite of* 'qualifies' as a complex preposition, whereas *on the shelf by* does not. To these syntactic criteria of cohesiveness, a lexical criterion may be added: unlike syntactic constructions, the complex preposition *in spite of* has a synonymous simple preposition *despite*.

As examples of sequences which lie between these two poles, we may take *in quest of*, *in search of*, *in comparison with*, and *in defence of*, as showing progressively less of the character of a preposition and more of the character of a free syntactic construction.

In quest of is slightly less cohesive than *in spite of* in that it has property (h) (*cf*: *in search of*).

In comparison with goes further, in that it has property (d) (*cf*: *by/through comparison with*), as well as properties (f) (*cf*: *in comparison*) and (h) (*cf*: *in common with*). *In defence of* goes yet further, having four of the properties of a free construction, *viz* (c) *in the defence of*, (e) *in her defence*, (h) *in support of*, and (i) *in keen/stubborn/bold defence of*.

On the other hand, all these types might reasonably be considered 'complex prepositions', in that they have more in common with *in spite of* than with *on the shelf by*.

Note [**a**] The cohesiveness of complex prepositions (as compared with free constructions) should be related to complex subordinators like *in that*, *in order that*, *as long as* (*cf* 14.12*ff*), and to phrasal lexicalization (*cf* App I.9*ff*).

[**b**] Legal English is notable for complex prepositions, the following being among those found mainly in legalistic or bureaucratic usage: *in case of*, *in default of*, *in lieu of*, *in pursuance of*, *in respect of*, *on pain of*.

[**c**] Some complex prepositions ending in *of* have an alternative genitive construction (*cf* (e) above and 5.120), *eg*:

for the sake of the people ~ for the people's sake
on behalf of Jim ~ on Jim's behalf
at the expense of Susan ~ at Susan's expense

[**d**] Occasionally there appear variants of complex prepositional sequences, *eg*: *in light of* for the regularly used *in the light of*, and the rather idiosyncratic *for dint of* (obviously based on *by dint of*) in the following example from Norman Mailer, *Marilyn*:

. . . unable to put down a word *for dint of* listening to her . . . ['because he was listening']

Boundary between simple and complex prepositions

9.13 The boundary between simple and complex prepositions is also an uncertain one. Orthographic separation is the easiest test to apply, but anomalies such as writing *into* as one word but *out of* as two, and *instead of* as two words but *in lieu of* as three, merely emphasize the arbitrariness of the distinction between one and more than one word in writing.

A test that can be applied to many cases is that a preposition when simple is identical in form to its corresponding prepositional adverb (*cf* 9.65*f*), *eg*: *by* in:

{She stood *by the door*.
{She walked *by*.

A complex preposition, on the other hand, loses its final element when transferred to the function of adverb (*cf* 9.66):

She put the skis { *on top of the car.* / *on top.* }

Note In colloquial AmE use, *on top* occurs also as a preposition (*on top the car*), perhaps just by syncope of /ə/ to which *of* is reduced.

Prepositional meanings

9.14 As we said in 9.1, a preposition expresses a relation between two entities, one being that represented by the prepositional complement. Of the various types of relational meaning, those of SPACE and TIME are easiest to describe systematically. Other relationships such as INSTRUMENT and CAUSE may also be recognized, although it is difficult to describe prepositional meanings systematically in terms of such labels. Some prepositional uses may be elucidated best by seeing a preposition as related to a clause, *eg*:

the man *with the red beard* ['the man who has the red beard'; *cf* 9.55, 17.37]
my knowledge *of Hindi* ['I know Hindi'; *cf* 17.41]

We shall relate semantic categories to their most usual syntactic functions, but one semantic category often has more than one syntactic function (*cf* 9.1). For example, prepositional phrases of place can postmodify in nominalizations (*cf* 17.51*ff*), as in [1], as well as in their more usual adverbial function [2]:

his departure *from Paris* [1]
He departed *from Paris.* [2]

In the survey of prepositional meanings, to which most of this chapter is devoted, space and time relations will be dealt with first, and will be followed by a more cursory exemplification of other relations such as 'cause', 'goal', and 'origin'. So varied are prepositional meanings that no more than a presentation of the most notable semantic similarities and contrasts can be attempted here.

Prepositions denoting spatial relations

Dimension

9.15 When we use a preposition to indicate space, we do so in relation to the dimensional properties, whether subjectively or objectively conceived, of the location concerned. Consider *at* in example [1]:

My car is *at the cottage.* [1]

Here the use of *at* treats *cottage* as a dimensionless location, a mere POINT in relation to which the position of the car can be indicated. This is dimension-type 0. Compare *on* in [2]:

Our cottage is *on that road.* [2]

In [2], the road is viewed as a LINE ['along that road'], *ie* dimension-type 1. But *on* can also be used to denote an area, as in [3] and [4]:

There is some ice *on that road.* [3]
There is a new roof *on the cottage.* [4]

In [3] and [4], the road and the cottage are viewed as two-dimensional areas, *ie* as SURFACES.

Finally, compare *in*, as in [5]:

There are only two beds *in the cottage.* [5]

In [5], the cottage is viewed as the three-dimensional object which in reality it is. *In* is also capable of being used with objects which are essentially two-dimensional, as in [6]:

The cows are *in the field.* [6]

Here *field* is conceived of as an enclosed space (contrast: 'We walked on the beach'). *In* therefore belongs to dimension-type 2 or 3. *Figure* 9.15 below sets out the dimensional orientation of the chief prepositions of space:

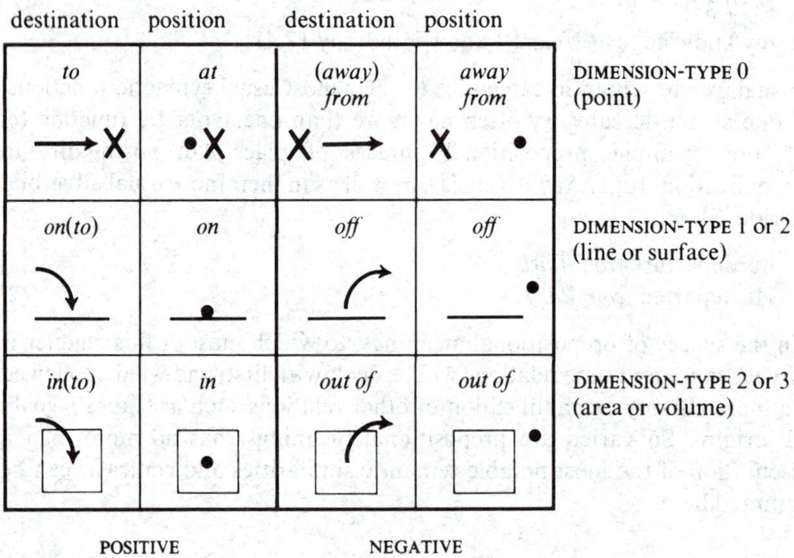

Fig 9.15 Space and dimension

Note [a] Some of the prepositions in the above figure can be replaced by other prepositions with the same meaning. *Upon* is a formal equivalent of *on* where a surface is referred to, or is the basis of, the metaphor concerned. When used metaphorically in archaic expressions, *upon* is obligatory: *upon/*on my word, upon/*on my soul*, etc. In some cases, *inside* and *within* can substitute for *in*, and *outside* for *out of*, but only *within* (not *in*) can be used in the following expressions: *within shooting distance, within these four walls.*

[**b**] *Onto* is sometimes spelled as two words, especially in BrE:

> She jumped {*onto* / *on to*} the horse.
>
> I think you're {*onto* / *on to*} something there. ⟨informal⟩

The particle *on* + the preposition *to* are always written as two words:

> From Lancaster we *went on to* York. ['continued to']

[**c**] *Into* is obligatory in fixed metaphorical expressions like *get into trouble*, *get into debt* (*cf* 9.32).

Positive position and destination: *at, to, on, onto, in, into*

9.16 Prepositional phrases of place are typically either adjuncts (relating an event or state of affairs to a location) or postmodifiers (relating some 'object' to a location).

Between the notions of simple position (or static location) and destination (movement with respect to an intended location) a cause-and-effect relationship obtains:

DESTINATION	POSITION
Ann went *to* Oxford.	AS A RESULT: Ann was *at* Oxford.
Ann climbed *onto* the roof.	AS A RESULT: Ann was *on* the roof.
Ann dived *into* the water.	AS A RESULT: Ann was *in* the water.

A prepositional phrase of 'position' can accompany most verbs, although this meaning is particularly associated with verbs of stative meaning (*cf* 2.43, 4.28*ff*), such as *be*, *stand*, *live*, etc. The meaning of 'destination' generally (but by no means always, *cf* 9.24*ff*) accompanies a verb of dynamic 'motional' meaning, such as *go*, *move*, *fly*, etc.

In many cases (especially in colloquial English), *on* and *in* may be used for both position and destination when *onto* and *into* make an unnecessary emphasis on the combination of destination + dimension:

> She fell *on* the floor.
>
> He put his hands *in* his pockets.

Note There are various restrictions, especially in BrE, on the interchangeability of *on* with *onto* and *in* with *into*: most verbs of motion such as *walk*, *slide*, *swim* require *onto* and *into* for destinational meaning. Note the difference between:

> Don't run *in the school*. ['when you are inside the building']
>
> Don't run *into the school*. [*ie* from outside it]

Causative verbs such as *place*, *stand*, *lay*, *sit*, on the other hand, usually permit combinations both with and without *to*, *onto*, and *into*:

> She put the typewriter case *on*(*to*) *the top shelf* and the key *in*(*to*) *the drawer*.

But there appear to be some restrictions:

> The mother sat the baby {*on* / ?*onto*} *the chair*.

9.17 Here are some more examples of each dimension-type.

Dimension-type 0:

at the bus stop
at the North Pole
at the end of the road

Dimension-type 1 and 2:

line: The city is situated { *on the River Thames.* / *on the boundary.* / *on the coast.* }

surface: A notice was pasted { *on the wall.* / *on the ceiling.* / *on my back.* }

Dimension-type 2 and 3:

area: *in the world*	volume: *in a box*
in the village	*in the bathroom*
in a park	*in the cathedral*

The contrast between *on* ['surface'] and *in* ['area'] has various implications according to context, as these examples show:

The frost made patterns *on the window*. [*window* = glass surface]
A face appeared *in the window/mirror*. [*window/mirror* = framed area]
The players were practising *on the field*. [*field* = surface for sports]
Cows were grazing *in the field*. [*field* = enclosed area of land]
She was sitting { *on the grass.* [surface, *ie* the grass is short] / *in the grass.* [volume, *ie* the grass is long] }

In is used for sizeable territories such as:

continents, countries:	*in Asia, in China*
provinces, counties:	*in British Columbia, in Cheshire*
city districts:	*in Brooklyn, in Hampstead*

But for towns, villages, etc, either *at* or *in* is appropriate, according to point of view: *at/in Stratford-upon-Avon.* A very large city (such as New York, London, or Tokyo) is generally treated as an area:

He works *in London*, but lives *in the country*.

But even a large city may be treated as a point on the map if global distances are in mind:

Our plane refuelled *at London* on its way from New York to Moscow.

Note the following difference between *at* and *in*:

She's { *at Oxford.* ['She's a student at Oxford University.'] / *in Oxford.* ['She's staying, etc in the City of Oxford.'] }

With buildings also, both *at* and *in* can be used. The difference here is that *at* refers to a building in its institutional or functional aspect, whereas *in* refers to it as a three-dimensional structure:

Ann works { *at* / *in* } *a publishing house.*

With *school*, we can find the following three constructions:

Sid is { *at school.* [1] / *in school.* [2] / *in the school.* [3] }

The meaning 'enrolled in' is expressed by [1] in BrE and by [2] in AmE; the meaning 'at the place, not at home' is expressed by [1] or [2] in BrE, and by [1] in AmE; the meaning 'within the building' is expressed by [3] in both BrE and AmE. On the zero article with *school*, *cf* 5.44.

To denotes completive movement in the direction of a place, as in:

The Smiths drove *to Edinburgh.* [suggests actual arrival]

Towards expresses movement without the idea of completion (*cf* 9.26; on the choice of the *-ward*/*-wards* forms, *cf* 7.46 Note [a]):

They drove *towards Edinburgh.*

Compare *to*, with progressive aspect, and *set out for*, neither of which express the idea of completion:

They were driving *to Edinburgh.*
They set out *for Edinburgh.*

As far as stresses the length of the journey (space only, not time):

They drove *as far as Edinburgh.*

With the perfective aspect, *to* may also be used in a way which appears to make it interchangeable with *at* or *in*:

Ann has been { *to*/*at Oxford.* ['as a student'] / *to*/*in Oxford.* ['as a visitor'] }

This occurrence of *been* followed by *to*, however, is a result of the substitution of the *-ed* participle of *be* for the *-ed* participle of *go* (*gone*) in order to convey the resultative sense of *go* (*cf* 4.22 Note [b]).

Note [**a**] When a place is being regarded as a destination rather than a position, it is more natural to see it vaguely as a geographical point than as an area. Hence the more frequent use of *to* than of *into* in reference to countries, etc:

The gypsies *came to England* in the fifteenth century. [Contrast: The gypsies *were in England.*]

[**b**] *Against* is commonly used as a preposition of simple position or destination in the sense 'touching the side surface of':

He's leaning *against the wall.*

[**c**] Additional uses of *on* as a preposition of position:

Humpty Dumpty sat *on the wall.* ['on top of']
There are still apples *on* the tree. ['hanging from']

We may see these as extending the basic meaning of *on* to include the most obvious static relationship of contiguity between a smaller and a larger object.

[**d**] Prepositions denoting position (not destination) are used with the verb *arrive* and the noun *arrival*:

{ She arrived / on her arrival } { *in London*/*Kenya*/*British Columbia* / *at the shop*/*bus stop*/*seaside* }

Source or negative position: *away from, off, out of*

9.18 There is a cause-and-effect relation with negative destination and position parallel to that of positive destination and position:

Ann *drove* (*away*) *from* home. ~ Ann *is away from* home.
The book *fell off* the shelf. ~ The book *is off* the shelf.
Tom *got out of* the water. ~ Tom *is out of* the water.

The negative prepositions *away from*, *off*, and *out of* may be defined simply by adding the word *not* to the corresponding positive preposition: *away from* ['not at'], *off* ['not on'], *out of* ['not in'].

Note In AmE, *out* is more commonly used than *out of* in such an expression as:

She looked { *out the window.* ⟨AmE and informal BrE⟩ / *out of the window.* ⟨BrE or AmE⟩ }

In this usage, there needs to be a reference to an opening or aperture:

The children gathered some bluebells before they went { *out of* / **out* } *the wood* and returned home.

Relative position: *over*, *under*, etc

9.19 Apart from simple position, prepositions may express the RELATIVE POSITION of two objects or groups of objects. *Above*, *over*, *on top of*, *under*, *underneath*, *beneath*, and *below* express relative position vertically, whereas *in front of*, *before*, *behind*, and *after* represent it horizontally. *Figure* 9.19 depicts the relations expressed by *above X*, *behind X*, etc.

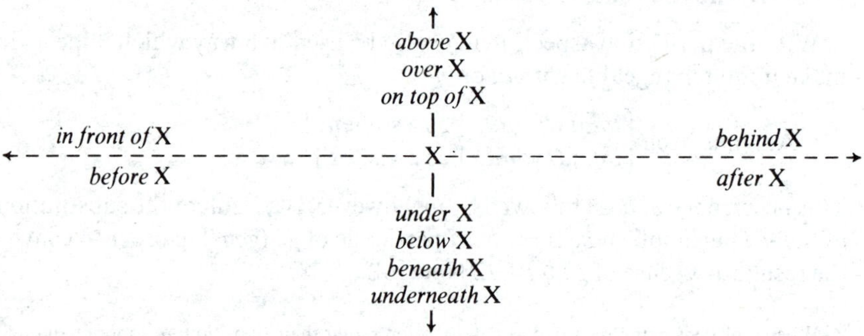

Fig 9.19 Vertical and horizontal direction

The antonyms *above* and *below*, *over* and *under*, *in front of* and *behind* are converse opposites:

{ The picture is *above* the mantelpiece.
= The mantelpiece is *below* the picture. }

{ The bus is *in front of* the car.
= The car is *behind* the bus. }

Over and *under* as place prepositions are roughly synonymous with *above* and *below*, respectively. The main differences are that *over* and *under* tend to indicate a direct vertical relationship or spatial proximity, while *above* and *below* may indicate simply 'on a higher/lower level than':

The castle stands on a hill { *above* / *?over* } *the valley.*

Keep this blanket { *over* / **above* } *you.*

The doctor and the policeman were leaning { *over* / **above* } the body when we arrived.

Underneath and *beneath* ⟨formal⟩ are less common substitutes for *under*. *Underneath*, like *on top of*, generally indicates a contiguous relation:

The police found the stolen money *under/underneath* the carpet.
We placed the skis *on top of* the car.

The following prepositional adverbs (*cf* 9.65*f*) or fixed phrases correspond to the prepositions of position:

PREPOSITIONAL ADVERBS	PREPOSITIONS
overhead	*over*
underneath ⟨formal⟩	*under, underneath* ⟨formal⟩
in front	*in front of*
on top	*on top of* (*cf* 9.13)
above	*above*
below	*below*
behind	*behind*
beneath ⟨formal⟩	*beneath* ⟨formal⟩

Example:

Would you like to sit { *in front?* [Prepositional adverb] / *in front of* us? [Preposition] }

Note [**a**] The actual use of the prepositions relating to relative position varies considerably. The frequencies for the bottom vertical set in *Fig* 9.19 are as follows in the LOB and Brown printed corpora (note the similar frequencies in BrE and AmE):

Table 9.19 Frequencies of *under, below, beneath,* and *underneath*

	Total	⟨BrE⟩	⟨AmE⟩
under	1352	645	707
below	295	150	145
beneath	117	60	57
underneath	22	11	11

[**b**] *Beneath* is obligatory in fixed metaphorical expressions like *beneath her dignity, beneath contempt* (*cf* 9.32).

Space: *by, beside, with, near (to), close to, opposite*

9.20 Other prepositions denoting space are *by, beside,* and *with*:

He was standing *by/beside the door.* ['at the side of']
I left the keys *with my wallet.* ['in the same place as']

Beside is usually a locative and *besides* a nonlocative preposition:

Beside Mary there stood a young man. ['at the side of']
Besides Mary there were several other students in the hall. ['in addition to']

However, the preposition *beside* is often used, especially in AmE, to mean 'in comparison with', 'apart from'. Unlike *beside*, *besides* may also be an adverb meaning 'in addition' (*cf* 8.137, 9.58):

She is intelligent. *Besides*, she is good-looking.

As a locative preposition, the simple preposition *near* meaning *close to* can be replaced by the complex preposition *near to*:

She was sitting { *near* (*to*) / *close to* } me.

Near (*to*) and *close to* are the only prepositions which inflect for comparison (*cf* 9.5). Unlike the absolute form, *nearer* and *nearest* usually require *to*. *Next* always does so:

She was sitting { *nearer* (*to*)/*nearest* (*to*)/*next to* me. / *closer to*/*closest to* me. }

Opposite means 'facing' and has optional *to*:

Her house is *opposite* (*to*) mine.

Space: *between, among, amongst, amid, amidst*

9.21 *Between* relates the position of an object to a definite or exclusive set of discrete objects, whereas *among* relates to nondiscrete objects. Thus:

The house stands { *between* two farms. / *among* farms. }

Switzerland lies { *between* / **among* } France, Germany, Austria, and Italy.

{ He likes getting *among* people. ['likes mixing with']
I saw Bill standing (*in*) *between* Mrs Bradbury and the hostess. }

Amid and *amidst* (which are both formal) mean 'in the midst of' and, like *among*, can apply to an indefinite number of entities:

The deserted house stood *amid* snow-covered fir trees. ⟨formal⟩

Note [**a**] The frequencies in the LOB and Brown corpora of printed English indicate that some of the prepositions in 9.21 are rare; in the case of *amongst* there is also a clear difference in usage between AmE and BrE. See *Table* 9.21, which, however, includes all uses, not just spatial.

Table 9.21 Frequencies of *between*, *among*(*st*), and *amid*(*st*)

	Total	⟨BrE⟩	⟨AmE⟩
between	1597	867	730
among	683	313	370
amongst	49	45	4
amid	23	9	14
amidst	8	5	3

[**b**] It is common, but not accepted by all speakers, to say *between each house* instead of *between each house and the next*.

Space: *around, round, about*

9.22 *Around* and *round* refer to surrounding position or to motion:

We were sitting *(a)round the campfire*.
The spaceship is travelling *(a)round the globe*.

About and *around* often have a vaguer meaning of 'in the area of' or 'in various positions in':

The guests were standing *about/around the room*.
There are very few taxis *about/around here*.

In AmE, *about* is rarer and more formal in this sense than *around*. In general, BrE often tends to use *about* or *round* where AmE uses *around*.

Relative position can also be expressed by prepositions which usually denote passage or path (*cf* 9.25*f*), *eg*:

The tree lay *across the road*.
The road runs *through the tunnel*.

Note The frequencies of *around* and *round* in the LOB and Brown corpora of printed English are as follows (all uses):

Table 9.22 Frequencies of *around* and *round*

	Total	⟨BrE⟩	⟨AmE⟩
around	806	245	561
round	410	336	74

Relative destination: *over, under, behind,* etc

9.23 As well as relative position, the prepositions listed in 9.19*ff* (but not, generally, *above* and *below*) can express RELATIVE DESTINATION:

He threw a blanket *over her*.
The bush was the only conceivable hiding place, so I dashed *behind it*.
When it started to rain, we all went *underneath the trees*.

This use is distinct from that denoting 'PASSAGE over, under, behind', etc (*cf* 9.24).

Passage: *over, under, behind,* etc

9.24 With verbs of motion, prepositions may express the idea of PASSAGE (*ie* movement towards and then away from a place), as well as destination. With the prepositions listed in 9.19*ff*, this occurs in sentences like [1–3]:

He jumped *over a ditch*. [1]
Someone ran *behind the goalposts*. [2]
The ball rolled *underneath the table*. [3]

In sentences such as [2] and [3], there is an ambiguity. In [3], we can supply either the meaning of 'passage' (= 'the ball passed under the table on the way to some other destination') or the meaning of 'destination' (= 'the ball rolled under the table and stayed there').

Note A triple ambiguity may in fact arise with the above sentences, or more clearly with:

A mouse scuttled *behind the curtain.*

This sentence may be interpreted not only in the senses of 'passage' and 'destination', but also (less plausibly) in the static sense, implying that the mouse stayed (scuttling back and forth) behind the curtain all the time.

Passage: *across, through, past*

9.25 The sense of 'passage' is the primary locative meaning attached to *across* (dimension-type 1 or 2), *through* (dimension-type 2 or 3) and *past* (the 'passage' equivalent to *by* which may also, however, be substituted for *past* in a 'passage' sense). Note the parallel between *across* and *on*, *through* and *in* in *Fig* 9.25:

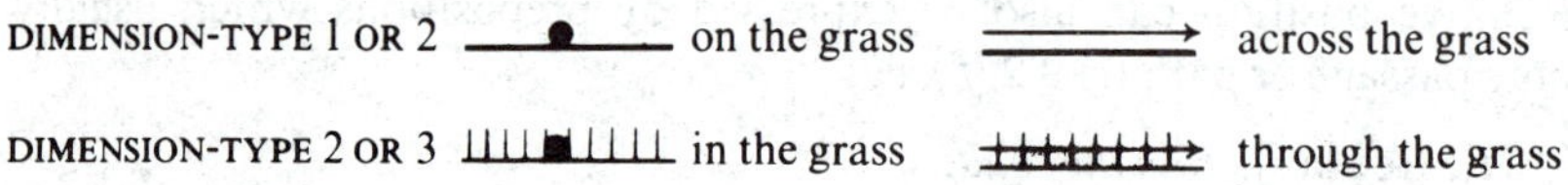

Fig 9.25 *On* and *across*, *in* and *through*

The upper pair treat the grass as a surface, and therefore suggest short grass; the lower pair, by treating the grass as a volume, suggest that it has height as well as length and breadth – that is, that the grass is long. There is a meaning of *over* corresponding to *across* in this sense:

The ball rolled {*over* / *across*} *the lawn.*

Movement with reference to a directional path: *up, down, along, across,* etc

9.26 *Up, down, along, across* (in a slightly different sense from that of 9.25) and *(a)round*, with verbs of motion, make up a group of prepositions expressing movement with reference to an axis or directional path, as illustrated in *Figs* 9.26a and 9.26b:

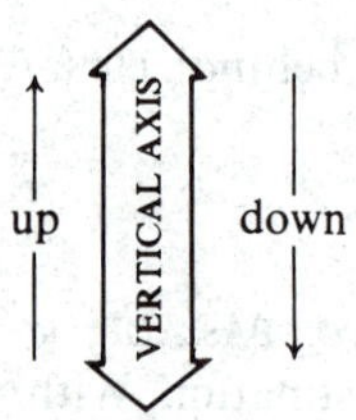

Fig 9.26a *up* and *down*

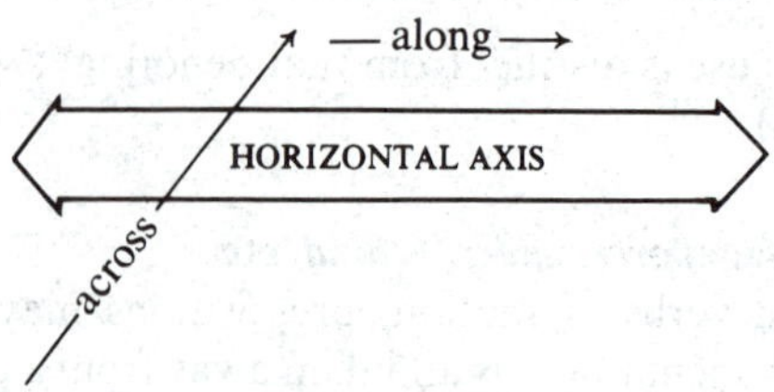

Fig 9.26b *along* and *across*

Up and *down* contrast in terms of vertical direction, *eg*:

We walked *up the hill* and *down the other side.*

But *up* and *down* are also used idiomatically in reference to a horizontal axis:

I walked *up and down the platform.*

She went { *up/down the road.* / *up/down the coast.* }

Up and *down* here express the notion of 'along', and need not have any vertical implications (*cf* 19.32).

Along denotes 'from one end towards the other' or 'in a line parallel with', *eg*:

We walked *along the streets,* just looking at people.
I took my dog for a walk *along the river.*

Along contrasts with *across* ['from one side to another'] in terms of a horizontal axis:

Be careful when you walk *across a street.*

With *(a)round*, the directional path is an angle or a curve:

We ran *(a)round the corner.*

Towards indicates both 'real' and 'implied' motion, 'in the direction of':

We walked *towards the old farmhouse.*
The window faces *towards the south.*

The concept of 'implied' motion also accounts for the use of other prepositions, *eg*: *to*, *over*, and *into*:

Is this the bus *to Oxford*?
She glanced *over her shoulder.*
He spoke *into the microphone.*

Note On the adverbs (*walk*) *home/homeward(s)*, etc corresponding to some prepositional phrases above, *cf* 7.46.

Orientation: *beyond, over, past, up, across,* etc

9.27 Most prepositions which express relative destination, passage, and movement with reference to a directional path (*cf* 9.26) can be used in a static sense of orientation. This brings in a third factor apart from the two things being spatially related: *viz* a POINT OF ORIENTATION, at which (in reality or imagination) the speaker is standing.

Beyond ['on the far side of'] is a preposition whose primary meaning is one of orientation. *Over*, *past*, *across*, and *through* combine the meaning of 'beyond' with more specific information about dimension, as described in 9.26:

They live *across the moors.* [*ie* 'from here']

The village is { *past the bus stop.* / *through the wood.* }

Up, *down*, *along*, *across*, and *(a)round* are used orientationally with reference to an axis in:

the shop *down the road* ['towards the bottom end of . . .']

Her office is { *up the stairs*. ['at (OR towards) the top of . . .'; = *upstairs*] / *down the stairs*. ['at (OR towards) the bottom of . . .'; = *downstairs*] }

There's a hotel *across/along* the road. ['on the other side/towards the other end of . . .']

We live just *(a)round the corner*.

We can, if we like, specify the viewpoint by using a *from*-phrase:

He lives up/down/along/across the road *from me*.

Resultative meaning: *from*, *out of*, *over*, *past*, etc

9.28 Prepositions which have the meaning of motion, as in [1], can usually have also a static resultative meaning when combined with *be*, indicating 'the state of having reached the destination', as in [2] (*cf* 8.42):

The horses *jumped over the fence*. [1]
The horses *are over the fence*. ['have now jumped over'] [2]

Out of context, resultative meaning is not always distinguishable from other static meanings. Its presence, however, is often signalled by certain adverbs (*already*, *just*, *at last*, (*not*) *yet*, etc). Resultative meaning is characteristically found with negative prepositions *from*, *out of*, etc, or with prepositions of 'passage' such as *across*, *through*, and *past*:

At last we are *out of the forest*. [3]
When you're *past the next obstacle*, you can relax. [4]

Pervasive meaning: *over*, *throughout*, *with*, etc

9.29 *Over* (dimension-type 1 or 2) and *through* (dimension-type 2 or 3), especially when preceded by *all*, have pervasive meaning (either static or motional):

That child was running (*all*) *over the flower borders*.

Throughout meaning (*all*) *through* is the only preposition whose primary meaning is 'pervasive':

Chaos reigned (*all*) *through the house*.
The epidemic has spread *throughout the country*.

Occasionally the 'axis' type prepositions of 9.26 are also used in a pervasive sense:

There were crowds (*all*) *along the route*.
They put flowers (*all*) *around the statue*.

With also has pervasive meaning in expressions such as the following:

The ground was *covered with* snow.
The garden was *buzzing with* bees.

Similarly: *loaded with*, *paved with*, *surrounded with*, *dotted with*, etc.

Eight senses of *over*

9.30 Let us now see how one preposition (*over*) may be used in some different senses:

POSITION (9.19):	A lamp hung *over the door*.
DESTINATION (9.23):	They threw a blanket *over her*.
PASSAGE (9.24):	They climbed *over the wall*.
ORIENTATION (9.27):	They live *over the road*. ['on the far side of']
RESULTATIVE (9.28):	At last we were *over the crest of the hill*.
PERVASIVE [STATIC] (9.29):	Leaves lay thick (all) *over the ground*.
PERVASIVE [MOTION] (9.29):	They splashed water (all) *over me*.
ACCOMPANYING CIRCUMSTANCES:	We discussed it *over a glass of wine*.

Verbs incorporating prepositional meaning

9.31 When a verb contains, within its own meaning, the meaning of a following preposition, it is often possible to omit the preposition. The verb then becomes transitive, and the prepositional complement becomes a direct, locative object (*cf* 10.27). The following examples have mainly spatial meaning, but other examples are included to show that this process is not restricted to spatial uses of prepositions:

roam (*about*/*around*) the city	*ponder* (*on*) a question
pass (*by*) a house	*turn* (*round*) a corner
flee (*from*) the country	*attain* (*to*) a position
cross (*over*) a street	*climb* (*up*) a mountain
jump/*leap* (*over*) a fence	*pierce* (*through*) the defences

In many cases there is a difference in meaning between the two constructions. The construction with preposition draws attention to the process, whereas the direct object construction has perfective meaning, indicating that the objective is achieved. Compare:

{ Let's *swim across the river*.
{ She was the first woman to *swim the Channel*.

Metaphorical or abstract use of place prepositions

9.32 Many place prepositions have abstract meanings which are clearly related, through metaphorical connection, to their locative uses. Very often prepositions so used keep the groupings (in terms of similarity or contrast of meaning) that they have when used in a literal reference to place. This is often true for example of temporal usage (*cf* 9.33*ff*).

One may perceive a stage-by-stage extension of metaphorical usage in such a series as (a) to (d):

(a) *in shallow water* [purely literal]
(b) *in deep water* [also metaphorical: 'in trouble']
(c) *in difficulties* [The noun is not metaphorical, but the preposition is.]
(d) *in a tough spot* ['in a difficult situation'; The preposition is analogous to that of (c), but another locative metaphor is introduced by the noun. The result is a phrase that could not occur in a literal sense, because *spot* would then require *at* or *on* (dimension-type 0).]

Examples in relation to the literal meanings are the following:

in/out of; *amid, amidst* ⟨both formal and rare⟩ (*cf* 9.21 Note [a])
position → state, condition:

to be *in/out of* danger
to be *in/out of* office
to be *in* difficulties
to keep *out of* trouble
to be *out of* a job
amidst many troubles

enclosure → abstract inclusion:

in books/plays
in a group/party
in/out of the race

into/out of
destination → abstract condition or circumstance:

He got *into* difficulties/trouble/debt/a fight.
Can you get me *out of* this mess?

in/on
position → membership, participation:

in the army
on the board/committee/project

above/below/beneath
vertical direction → abstract level:

to be *above/below* someone on a list
above/below [not: **beneath*] one's income
Such behaviour is *beneath* [not: **below*] him.
He's *above* [not: **over*] such behaviour.
above (the) average
above suspicion

under
vertical direction → subjection, subordination; process:

under suspicion/orders/compulsion
He has a hundred people working *under* him.
The bridge is *under* construction.

up/down
movement on vertical axis → movement on list or scale:

move *up/down* the scale
climb *up/down* the social ladder

from/to
starting point/destination → originator/recipient:

a letter/present *from* Browning *to* his wife (*cf* 9.46*f*)

beyond/past/over
resultative meaning; physical → abstract:

{*beyond* / *past*} {belief / endurance / hope / recovery}

We are *over* the worst.

between/among/amongst (*cf* 9.21 Note [a])
relative position → abstract relation between participants:

a fight/match *between* X and Y
We quarrel/agree *among* ourselves.
relationship/contrast/affinity *between* two things

through
passage → perseverance, endurance:

She came *through* the ordeal. We put him *through* his paces.
We are *through* the worst.

Note [a] *Over* and *under* act as 'intensifying prepositions' with the meanings 'more than' and 'less than' in expressions of measure (*cf* intensifiers in 7.87*ff*):

The car was travelling (*at*) {*over* / *under*} *sixty miles per hour.*

Cf: *overage*; *overconfident* ['overly confident']

For denoting temperature, *above* and *below* are also used:

The temperature is {*above/over* / *below/under*} 30°.

But with zero degrees only: *above/below zero.*

[b] A few prepositions (chiefly *in* and *out of*) can operate in an apparently converse relationship. For example:

The horse is *in foal.* ['There is a foal in the horse's womb.']
The office is *out of envelopes.* ['There are no envelopes in the office.']
We are *in luck/out of luck.*

[c] The infinitive marker *to* may be viewed as related to the spatial preposition *to* through metaphorical connection. Compare the series:

John went

to the pool.	[Direction: 'Where did he go?']
to the pool for a swim.	[Direction + purpose: 'Why did he go to the pool?']
for a swim in the pool.	[Purpose + location]
for a swim.	[Purpose: 'Why did he go there?']
to swim.	['Metaphorical connection' of infinitive marker (in *to*-infinitive clause)]
swimming.	[Nonfinite verb clause]

Prepositions denoting time

9.33 A prepositional phrase of time usually occurs as adjunct (*He came on Friday*), postmodifier (*the party on Friday*), or predication adjunct (*That was on Friday*); but it can occasionally be itself the complement of a temporal preposition (*cf* 9.1 Note [d]):

a voice *from out of the past*

The temporal uses of prepositions frequently suggest metaphorical extensions from the sphere of place similar to the metaphorical extensions discussed in 9.32.

Time position: *at, on, in, by*

9.34 *At*, *on*, and *in* as prepositions of 'time position' are to some extent parallel to the same items as positive prepositions of position (*cf* 9.16), although in the time sphere there are only two 'dimension-types', *viz* 'point of time' and 'period of time' (*cf* 8.51*ff*).

At is used for points of time (chiefly clock-time [1]) and also, idiomatically, for holiday periods [2]:

at ten o'clock, at 6.30 p.m., at noon [1]
at the weekend ⟨BrE; but in AmE: *on the weekend*⟩, *at Christmas, at Easter* [2]

The reference is to the season of Christmas/Easter, not the day itself. *At* can be used for periods when conceived of as points of time, as in:

at the/that time, at breakfast time, at night

On is used for referring to days as periods of time:

on Monday, on the following day, on May (the) first, on New Year's Day

Also in the expression:

Trains leave the station *on the hour*. ['hourly', *ie* 1 o'clock, 2 o'clock, etc]

In or, less commonly, *during* is used for periods longer or shorter than a day:

in the evening — *in summer*
in August — *during Holy Week*
in 1969 — *in the eighteenth century*
in the months that followed

On Monday morning, on Saturday afternoon, on the following evening, etc illustrate an exceptional use of *on* with a complement referring to a PART of a day, rather than a WHOLE day. This use also extends to other cases where the time segment is a part of a day which is actually mentioned: *on the morning of 1 June*, etc. But with phrases like *early morning* and *late afternoon* it is normal to use *in*: *in the late afternoon*.

When we want to refer to a period of the night we use *in*. Compare:

I woke up several times *in the night*.
At night I usually have the window open. ['during the night'; as opposed to *in the evening, in the day*]

By occurs in the idioms *by day* and *by night*, which replace *during the day/the night* with some activities such as travelling:

We preferred travelling { *by night.* / *during the night.* }

We stayed up *during the night*.

Measurement into the future: *in*

9.35 To denote measurement from the present time, the postposed adverb *ago* is used for a span back to a point of time in the past, and *in* for a similar span ahead into the future (*cf* 8.58*f*):

We met *three months ago*. [1]
We'll meet { *in three months' time.* [2] / *(in) three months from now.* [3] }

The construction in [2–3] is only acceptable with the meaning of 'at the end of a period of three months starting from now'. In measuring forwards from a point of time in the past, only the following construction is normal:

He finished the job { *in three months*. ['in the space of three months from when he started it'] [4]
?(*in*) *three months from then.* [5]
**in three months' time.* [6] }

Duration: *for, during, over, (all) through, throughout*

9.36 Phrases of duration answer the question *How long?* Duration is usually expressed by *for*. Compare duration and time-position:

A: How long did you camp in Scotland?
B: We camped there *for the summer*. ['all through, from the beginning to the end of the summer']
A: When did you camp in Scotland?
B: We camped there *in the summer*. ['at some time during the summer']

The duration phrase *for the summer* indicates that the stop lasted AS LONG AS the summer period; the time-*when* phrase *in the summer* indicates that the stop was INCLUDED in the summer period. *During the summer* could be used here with the same meaning as *in*, although *during* usually suggests duration:

We managed to stay awake *during the whole meeting*.

Without such durative markers as *stay* and *whole*, *during* refers to a point or period WITHIN DURATION rather than duration itself:

She spoke *during the meeting*.

During our { *stay* in / *visit* to } Japan we met several old friends.

For is also used in idiomatic phrases like *forever*, *for good* ['forever'], *for years* (*and years*).

Over, (*all*) *through*, and *throughout* have a durational meaning parallel to their pervasive meaning in reference to place (*cf* 9.29):

We camped there *over the holiday/over Christmas/over the weekend/over the Sabbath/over night*.
We camped there *through*(*out*) *the summer*.

Over normally accompanies noun phrases denoting special occasions (such as holidays and festivals), and so generally refers to a shorter period of time than *through*(*out*). Since Saturday and Sunday are 'special' compared with other days of the week, we have *over Saturday and Sunday* whereas ?*over Wednesday* is not generally used. Expressions like *over the last three years*, *over the last generation* seem to have become increasingly common.

Note *For* has different meanings in the following two sentences:

I've done that *for years*. [1]
I've *not* done that *for years*. [2]

In the positive [1], the action is included in the *for* time span, *ie* included duration. In the negative [2], on the other hand, the action is excluded from the *for* time span, *ie* excluded duration ('It's years since I've done that', 'I haven't done that in years'). Note that, here, *in* ⟨esp AmE⟩ can be used only in negative sentences:

I {*haven't* / **have*} done that *in years*.

Duration: *from . . . to, until, up to*

9.37 *From . . . to* (or *till*) is another pair of prepositions whose locative meaning is transferred to duration. The AmE alternative expression (*from*) . . . *through* avoids the ambiguity as to whether the period mentioned second is included in the total span of time (*cf*: *between . . . and*, 9.39; *cf* also 'forward span'; 8.58*f*):

We camped there (*from*) *June through September*. ⟨AmE⟩
['up to and including September']

We camped there *from June* {*to* / *till*} *September*.
['up to (?and including) September']

But with *from* absent, only *until*, *till*, *up to* (but not always simple *to*), and *through* ⟨AmE⟩ can be used:

We camped there {*until* / *till* / *up to* / *through* ⟨AmE⟩ / **to*} *September*.

On the other hand, *to* can be used alongside *till* in:

You can *stay to/till the end of September*.
The meeting can be *postponed to/till September*.
There are only *a few days to/till September*.
I have only *a few years to/till retirement*.

From and *up to* are used to denote, respectively, starting and ending points of a period. *Up to* normally specifies that the longer period does not include the period named in the prepositional complement:

From 1982 (onwards) the rules were changed.
We worked *up to Christmas* (but not over Christmas).

Informally, *until* and *till* are also sometimes preceded by *up*:

I worked (*up*) {*until* / *till* / *to*} *last week*.

Till and *until* can only cooccur with durative verbs, *ie* verbs that denote a period of time (such as *camp* and *work*). Contrast:

My girlfriend {worked / *arrived} there *till Christmas*.

The situation for *until* and *till* is thus the reverse of that for *by* denoting an end point, which cooccurs only with momentary verbs (*cf* 9.39):

She {*worked / arrived} *by Christmas.*

In negative contexts, *until* and *till* are acceptable with both durational and momentary verbs, as for example:

She didn't arrive there *till Christmas.*

The two meanings of *till* and *until* are, however, different with positive and negative predications. With positive predications, *till* and *until* specify a terminal point ('up to'), whereas, with negative predications, they specify a starting point ('before'):

We slept *until midnight.* ['We stopped sleeping then.']
We didn't sleep *until midnight.* ['We started sleeping then.']

Before, after, since, till, until

9.38 These words are conjunctions as well as prepositions (*cf* 14.12*ff*). As prepositions, they occur almost exclusively as prepositions of time, and are followed by either

(a) a temporal noun phrase (*after next week*);
(b) a subjectless *-ing* clause (*since leaving school*); or
(c) a noun phrase with a deverbal noun (*cf* App I.34*f*) or some other noun phrase interpreted as equivalent to a clause:

before the war ['before the war started or took place']
till/until the fall of Rome ['until Rome fell']
since electricity ['since electricity was invented']

To express the stretch of time (after the starting point denoted by *since*) we use *for* (*cf* 9.36):

We have lived in New York {*since 1980.* / *for 4 years.*}

We lived in Chicago *for 15 years.*

For verb forms with *since*-clauses, *cf* 14.26.

Before and *after* indicate relations between two times or events and have opposite meanings (*cf* 9.19, 9.35*ff*):

{*The meeting* will take place *after the ceremony.*
= *The ceremony* will take place *before the meeting.*}

Note [**a**] As a preposition, *until* is more frequent than *till* (*cf* 8.58).
[**b**] *Pending* is used in formal, especially legal style:
The decision must wait *pending his trial.* ['until']
Pending negotiations, the two parties should stop further action. ['during and till the end of']
Thus *pending* can also include a sense of 'during'.

Between . . . and, by

9.39 *Between . . . and* is used for periods identified by their starting and ending points but, in contrast to *from . . . to* (*cf* 9.37), does not refer to the whole time span:

We'll probably arrive some time *between 5 and 6 o'clock*.
I'll phone you *between lunch and dinner*.

Between X and Y can include *X* and *Y*, as in:

I'll ring *between Thursday and Saturday*.

This expression does not mean that the call will be on Friday, but could also be Thursday or Saturday. Thus *between . . . and* here means 'about', *ie* 'some time on Thursday, Friday, or Saturday'. *Between* is further required to indicate intervals between similar objects or events which occur repeatedly:

between meals/dances/acts/classes

By refers to the time at which the result of an event is in existence:

Your papers are to be handed in *by next week*. ['not later than']
She should be back *by now* (but I'm not sure).

By specifies an end point. *Already*, *still*, *yet*, and *any more* are related in meaning:

By the time we'd walked five miles, he was already exhausted.

Contrast:

By that time he was already exhausted. ['He was then exhausted.']
Until then he was not exhausted. ['Before then he was not exhausted.']

Thus *by*-phrases do not cooccur with durative verbs (*cf* 9.37):

The troops remained there {*until* / **by*} *midnight*.

Note As with prepositions of place (*cf* 9.32), prepositions and prepositional adverbs of time can have metaphorical uses, *eg* in viewing life as a journey:

At birth . . . *from* the age of two . . . reaching the age of 16, he left school days *behind*, and adulthood was *in front of* him . . . *all through* middle age . . . *up to* 1945.

Absence of preposition in point in time expressions

9.40 In many cases, a preposition of time is absent, so that the time adverbial takes the form of a noun phrase instead of a prepositional phrase.

Prepositions of time-*when* are always absent immediately before the deictic words *last*, *next*, *this*, *that*, and before the quantitative words *some* and *every*:

I saw her {*last Thursday*. / **on last Thursday*.}

I'll mention it *next time* I see her.
This year, plums are more plentiful than *last*.
Some day you'll regret this decision.
Every summer she returns to her childhood home.

Also nouns which have 'last', 'next', or 'this' as an element of their meaning lack prepositions:

I saw her {*today*. / *yesterday* (*morning*).} I'll see her *tomorrow* (*evening*).

The prepositions which are absent in point in time expressions seem to be restricted to *at*, *on*, *in*; *before* and *since*, for example, are obligatory:

I'll see you { *on Monday.* / *Monday.* } =
I'll see you { *before Monday.* / *Monday.* } ≠

I haven't seen her *since last week*.

The preposition is usually optional with deictic phrases referring to times at more than one remove from the present, such as:

(*on*) *Monday week*
(*on*) *the day before yesterday*
{ *in the January* before last ⟨BrE⟩
{ *the January* before last ⟨AmE and BrE⟩

The preposition is also optional in phrases which identify a time before or after a given time in the past or future:

(*in*) *the previous spring* ['the spring before the time in question']
{ (*at*) ⟨BrE⟩ / (*on*) ⟨AmE⟩ } *the following weekend*
(*on*) *the next day*

Thus, there are alternatives in cases like the following:

We met { *on the following day.* / *the following day.* } We met { *on that day.* / *that day.* }

On the whole, the sentence without the preposition tends to be more informal and more usual.

Postmodified nondeictic phrases containing *the* often have the preposition in BrE whereas it is optional in AmE:

We met { *on the day* / *the day* } *of the conference.*
We met { *in the spring* / *the spring* ⟨esp AmE⟩ } *of 1983.*

But without postmodification, the preposition is always obligatory:

We met *in the spring*. ≠ We met *the spring*.

The preposition is usually present in phrases like the following when the word order (*next Sunday*, *last January*) is inverted ⟨in BrE⟩:

(*on*) *Sunday next* (*in*) *January last*

Note Within a given week, if we refer to the name of the day that is yet to follow, the expression *next x-day* (*eg*: *next Friday*) will be used by some to mean 'x-day of the same week', by others 'x-day of the week to follow'. On the other hand, *this x-day* (*eg*: *this Friday*) will always mean 'x-day of the present week'. The same applies to months of the year, as in *next September* and *this September*.

Absence of preposition in frequency expressions

9.41 There is no preposition in frequency phrases like:

Every Sunday we usually go for a walk.

Without a frequency indication such as *every*, the preposition is optional, and nouns denoting weekdays may be either singular or plural. The construction without a preposition is informal in style ⟨esp AmE⟩:

On Sunday(s) / *Sunday(s)* / **On every Sunday* } we usually go for a walk.

Three times a week / **At three times a week* } we play darts.

But other frequency constructions always require the preposition:

with + adjective + *frequency*:	*with regular frequency*
at + adjective + *intervals*:	*at irregular intervals*
on + adjective + *occasions*:	*on specific occasions*
from time to time:	We saw each other *from time to time.*
at a/the rate of + noun:	*at the rate of $20 an hour*
between/at + *each* + singular noun, or *all* + plural noun:	He had dropped the habit of drinking coffee *at all hours.*

Absence of preposition in duration expressions

9.42 *For* refers to a stretch of time. The preposition is often absent in phrases of duration with a verb used with stative meaning:

We stayed there (*for*) *three months.*
The snowy weather lasted (*for*) *the whole time* we were there.
(*For*) *a lot of the time* we just lay on the beach.

The preposition is obligatorily absent in phrases which begin with *all*, such as *all* (*the*) *week, all day*. But compare the synonymous *whole* (*cf* 5.17):

We stayed there { *all* (*the*) *week.* / (*for*) *the whole week.* / **for all week.* }

I haven't seen her *all day.*

However, the preposition is obligatory with dynamic verbs where the action of the verb is clearly not continuously coextensive with the period specified. Compare:

I lived there { *for three years.* / *three years.* }

I taught her { *for three years.* / ?**three years.* }

Similarly:

I haven't spoken to her { *for three months.* / **three months.* }

The preposition is also required in initial position in the clause:

{ *For 600 years*, the cross lay undisturbed.
{ The cross lay undisturbed (*for*) *600 years*.

Similarly, when they occur initially, the preposition is usually required in *for*-phrases: *for ages, for days, for years*, etc. However, coordination in the time expression improves acceptability. Compare:

For years }
(?)*Years and years* } we have all been expecting this event.
?*Years* }

Ranges of meaning other than place and time

9.43 We now survey the more important prepositional usages apart from those of place and time. Fields of prepositional meaning are notoriously difficult to classify, and in some cases it is better to think of a range or spectrum of meaning, first as a single category, then as broken up into separate overlapping sections. First, therefore, we deal with two important spectra which may be referred to, for brevity, as CAUSE/PURPOSE and MEANS/AGENTIVE. In part, our reason for putting various meanings under a single heading is that some of them have, as a linking element, association with particular prepositions and *wh*-words: *for* and *why* and *how* in the case of cause/purpose, and *with* and *how* in the case of means/agentive. Here are the two ranges with an illustration of each meaning:

THE CAUSE/PURPOSE SPECTRUM (9.44–46)

Cause (9.44):	She lost her job *because of her age*.
Reason (9.44):	He was fined *for drunken driving*.
Motive (9.44):	She did it *out of kindness*.
Purpose (9.45):	Everyone ran *for shelter*.
Destination (9.45):	I'm leaving *for Seattle*.
Target (9.46):	This novel is aimed *at a young audience*.

THE MEANS/AGENTIVE SPECTRUM (9.48–51)

Manner (9.48):	She performed the operation *with great skill*.
Means (9.49):	They left *by plane*.
Instrument (9.49):	She tried to open the lock *with a knife*.
Agentive (9.50):	They were noticed *by no one*.
Stimulus (9.51):	I'm astonished *at your reaction*.

The cause/purpose spectrum

Cause, reason, motive: *because of, on account of, for, from*, etc

9.44 At one end of the cause/purpose spectrum, we have prepositions expressing either the material cause or the psychological cause (motive) for a happening. Phrases of cause, reason, and motive answer the question *Why . . . ?* Some examples:

We had to drive slowly *because of the heavy rain*.
On account of his wide experience, he was made chairman.

The survivors were weak *from exposure and lack of food.*
Some support charities *out of duty*, some *out of a sense of guilt.*
I hid the money, *for fear of what my parents would say.*
The plane was destroyed *through the pilot's carelessness.*

On account of is a more formal alternative to *because of* as an expression of cause or reason. *Out of* and *for* are mainly restricted to the expression of motive, *ie* psychological cause: *out of gratitude/kindness*, etc.

For is found with a relatively small number of expressions, *eg*:

for fear/love/joy/sorrow

He offered to fix my sink *for* { *nothing.* ⟨informal⟩
 free. ⟨informal, esp AmE⟩ }

Purpose, intended destination: *for*

9.45 *For* is used to express PURPOSE in the following examples:

He'll do anything *for money.*
Everyone ran *for shelter.*
For the journey, they packed three large picnic baskets of food.

In this use of *for*, there is a corresponding paraphrase with a clause (*in order*) *to* (*cf* 15.48):

for money = *in order to gain* money
for shelter = *in order to reach* shelter

To express INTENDED DESTINATION, *for* is used with verbs such as *run, start, head, leave*, and *set out*. For example:

He *set out for London.*

With *to*-phrases, the assumption is that the destination will be reached. Compare:

He { *went to* / *left for* } *London.* Is this *the train* { *to* / *for* } *London*?

Phrases of purpose or destination answer the questions *Why . . . ?*, *What . . . for?*, *Where . . . for?*, or *Who . . . for?* They occur as postmodifiers [1], as well as adjuncts [2], and complements in copular clauses [3–4]:

The scenery *for the play* is splendid. [1]
She came *for the play.* [2]
This present is *for you.* [3]
This machine is *for washing dishes.* [4]

Note Note the difference in meaning between *for fun* and *in fun*:
He did it *for fun.* ['with the object of getting amusement']
He said it *in fun.* ['jokingly', 'in jest']

Recipient, goal, target: *for, to, at*

9.46 When *for* is followed by noun phrases denoting persons or animals, the meaning is rather one of INTENDED RECIPIENT:

He laid a trap *for his enemies.* [1]
She made a beautiful doll *for her daughter.* [2]
He cooked a dinner *for her.* [3]

Denoting intended recipient (her daughter may or may not have actually received the doll), the *for*-phrase can often be equated with an indirect object (*cf* 10.7, 16.56):

She made *her daughter* a beautiful doll. [2a]
He cooked *her* a dinner. [3a]

In contrast to the notion of intended recipient expressed by *for*, the preposition *to* expresses ACTUAL RECIPIENT in sentences such as:

She gave a beautiful doll *to her daughter.*

Here again, there is often a relationship with the indirect object construction:

I {gave / lent / sold} the book *to my friend.* ~ I {gave / lent / sold} *my friend* the book.

But not, for example:

I delivered the book *to my friend.* ≁ *I delivered *my friend* the book.

At, in combinations such as *aim at* (where the prepositional phrase is complementary to the verb), expresses INTENDED GOAL or TARGET:

After *aiming* carefully *at* the bird, he missed it completely. [4]
A vicious dog was *snapping at* her ankles. [5]
She *smiled at* me. [6]

As sentence [4] shows, the intended goal need not be achieved. A contrast in many cases (*kick at, charge at, bite at, catch at, shoot at, chew at*) may be drawn between this use of *at*, in which some idea of 'aim' is implied, and the direct object construction, which indicates attainment of the goal or consummation of the action as planned. *She shot at him* means something very different from *She shot him*: to the first one could add 'but missed him', whereas one could not to the second. In other cases, where the verb is intransitive, *to* must be used if the attainment of the goal is to be stressed:

She ran *at me.* [denotes hostility: 'attacked']
She ran *to me.* [denotes movement to a goal]

Similarly: *point at/to, throw at/to*

Note [**a**] There is a comparable difference between *at* and *to* when combined with verbs of speaking such as *roar, bellow, shout, mutter, growl.* Sentence [7] suggests that I am being treated merely as a target (*eg* of abuse), while [8] implies that the shouter is communicating with me, *ie* that I am the recipient of the message:

He *shouted at me.* [7]
He *shouted to me.* [8]

At here usually suggests hostility. Similarly, *laugh at* indicates hostility [9], unless the object is something intended to provoke laughter, such as a joke [10]:

They *first laughed at us.* [9]
They *laughed heartily at* our jokes. [10]

[**b**] With *work* + target the preposition is *on* in AmE but either *on* or *at* in BrE:

She is *working* {*on* / *at* ⟨BrE only⟩} her new play.

Source, origin: *from*

9.47 The converse of *to* ['goal'] is *from* ['source'] (*cf* 18.31 Note):

Bill lent the book *to me*. ~ I borrowed the book *from Bill*.

From is also used with reference to 'place of origin':

He comes *from Scotland/Glasgow*. ['He is a Scot/a Glaswegian.']

This type of prepositional phrase occurs not only as an adjunct, but also as a complement in copular clauses [1] and as a postmodifier [2]:

I'm *from Madrid*. [1]
This is a friend of mine *from London*. [2]

The means/agentive spectrum

Manner: *in ... manner, like, with*

9.48 Manner can be expressed by *in . . . manner* and *with*. For example:

The job was done *in a workmanlike manner*.
We were received *with the utmost courtesy*.

With transitive or intransitive verbs, *like* can have the meaning of 'in a manner resembling'; with copular verbs, its meaning is purely that of 'resemblance':

The army swept through the city *like a pestilence*.
Life is *like a dream*.

This meaning of 'resemblance' is common with disjuncts (*cf* 8.121*ff*) in sentences whose main verb may be noncopular. Contrast:

Bill writes poetry *like his* BRÒTHer. ['in a manner resembling that of his brother's poetry']

Like his BRǑTHer, Bill writes PÒETry. }
Bill writes PǑETry, *like his* BRÒTHer. } [resemblance]

The last pair of examples show that the difference in meaning is not entirely a matter of ordering.

Unlike is used with the meaning of negative resemblance 'not like':

{ *Unlike his brother* (who writes poetry), Bill writes science fiction.
{ Bill writes science fiction, *unlike his brother* (who writes poetry).

As distinct from *like*, the preposition and conjunction *as* refers to actual role (*cf* 9.4):

She spoke { *like a LÀWyer*. ['in a manner resembling']
as a LÀWyer. ['in that capacity']
as a LÀWyer does. ['in that manner'] }

There is frequently commutability between manner phrases and manner adverbs: *with courtesy* ~ *courteously*. Manner phrases and manner adverbs can both sometimes be evoked by the question *How ... ?*, especially if the sense of 'means' is excluded by the context or the meaning of the verb:

A: How did she speak? B: She spoke { *competently*.
with great skill. }

BUT: A: How did you travel? B: { *By air*.
**Comfortably*. }

Means and instrument: *by, with, without*

9.49 Phrases of means and instrument answer the question *How ... ? By* can express the meaning 'by means of' (note the omission of the article; *cf* 5.45):

I usually go to work *by bus/train/car/boat*. [mode of transport]
Communication took place *by letter/telex/radio/post* ⟨BrE⟩/*mail* ⟨AmE⟩. [means of communication]
The thief must have entered and left the house *by* (= *through*) *the back door*.
By working the pumps, we kept the ship afloat for another 40 hours.

With, on the other hand, expresses instrumental meaning (*cf* 9.50):

Someone had broken the window *with a stone*. [1]
He caught the ball *with his left hand*. [2]

There is a correspondence between sentences [1–2] (which normally require a human subject and a direct object) and sentences [1a–2a] containing the verb *use* + a phrase with (*in order*) *to* + infinitive:

Someone had used *a stone* to break the window. [1a]
He used *his left hand* to catch the ball. [2a]

There is also an alternative construction in which the noun phrase denoting the instrument becomes the subject (on 'instrumental' subjects, *cf* 10.21):

A stone had broken the window. [1b]
His left hand caught the ball. [2b]

For most senses of *with*, including that of instrument, *without* expresses the equivalent negative meaning:

I drew it *without* (*using*) *a ruler*. ['I did not draw it with a ruler.']

Note [**a**] Mode of transport is expressed by *on* as well as *by*: *on the bus/the train/a ship/a plane*. These are not purely locative phrases – location in such cases would be expressed by *in* rather than *on* (*cf* 9.16*f*) – but rather indicate a condition of being 'in transit'. Compare sentences [3–6]:

I go to work *on the bus*. [3]
I go to work *by bus*. [4]
I met Peter *on the bus*. [5]
*I met Peter *by bus*. [6]

Sentence [3] is a less common alternative to [4]; but although one can say [5], one cannot say [6]. Absence of the article is normal with the unmodified noun phrase after *by*, but not obligatory:

It's easier to go to town *by the bus* (rather than *by the train*).

On is used instead of *by* in the phrases *on foot, on horseback*. Notice the absence of the article in these phrases, as well as in *by bus*, etc (*cf* 5.45). Modification of the noun phrase is not allowed after *by* unless a determiner is added:

by { *the last bus* / *the 2 o'clock bus* / **last bus* }

[**b**] *Of* is used with the verb *die* in *He died of hunger*, etc. This meaning is poised between 'cause' and 'means': on the one hand, one speaks of the 'cause of death' (*cf*: *He died from exposure*); on the other hand, this type of phrase would be evoked by the question *How did he die?* (or *What did he die of?*) rather than *Why did he die?*

Instrument and agentive: *with, by*

9.50 In 9.49 we had the following example [1], where *with* expresses the meaning of INSTRUMENT:

Someone had broken the window *with a stone*. [1]

We saw that [1] has correspondences with sentences [1a] and [1b]:

Someone used a stone to break the window. [1a]
A stone had broken the window. [1b]

Sentence [1] is also related to the passive sentence [1c]:

The window had been broken with a stone *by someone*. [1c]

In the passive sentence, the AGENTIVE is expressed with a *by*-phrase (*cf* 3.65): *by someone*. However, in most passive sentences, the agent *by*-phrase is actually omitted, as in [1d]:

The window had been broken *with a stone*. [1d]

In a passive sentence like [1c], the *by*-agent has the agentive role (*cf* 10.19), corresponding to the agentive role of the subject in an active sentence [1]. The agentive is the initiating cause and typically animate, usually personal, as also in:

{ *A passing stranger* observed us. [2]
We were observed *by a passing stranger*. [2a] }

However, we may also find inanimate *by*-phrases, as in [3a]:

{ *Frost* has ruined the crops. [3]
The crops have been ruined *by frost*. [3a] }

In cases like [1d], the instrument can also be expressed with a *by*-phrase:

The window had been broken *by a stone*. [1e]

Either of the sentences [1d] and [1e] could describe the same incident, but there can be a difference in meaning, as appears more clearly in the following two sentences:

My car had been damaged { *by the branch of a tree*. [4]
with the branch of a tree. [4a] }

By in [4] would exclude a human agency: a storm may have caused the branch to cause the damage. By contrast, *with* in [4a] would exclude the natural cause and would suggest that human agents had used the branch broken from a tree to inflict the damage.

We thus make a distinction between AGENTIVE, *ie* the animate being instigating or causing the happening denoted by the verb, and the INSTRUMENT, *ie* the entity (generally inanimate) which an agentive uses to perform or instigate a process. Both agentive and instrument may be said to denote the semantic role of AGENCY.

The *by*-phrase also occurs as a postmodifier to denote authorship (*cf* 17.46 Note [c]):

a picture *by Degas* ['painted by Degas'] [5]
a novel *by Tolstoy* ['written by Tolstoy'] [6]
a five-year-old horse *by Willwin out of Lady Barle* [parentage of a horse] [7]

Through implies intermediacy in:

They are related *through their grandmother*.
The presidents had to communicate *through an interpreter*.
through Jesus Christ Our Lord [used as a formula at the end of a prayer]

Note [**a**] One reason why we distinguish 'instrument' and 'agentive' is that they cannot be coordinated, or collapsed, by coordination, into a single prepositional phrase (*cf* 13.40):

*He was killed *by a man and* (*by*) *an arrow*.

If however different processes are involved, coordination is possible, though with an effect similar to that of zeugma (*cf* 13.87):

The area was ravaged *by floods and by guerilla forces*.

[**b**] Outside the passive clause proper, agentive and instrumental *by*-phrases can occur after *-ed* participial adjectives with passive meaning (*cf* 3.74*ff*):

I was very *alarmed by the news* he brought. [8]
The child was *unwanted by its parents*. [9]
His services to the community have not gone *unnoticed by those who have benefited*. [10]

The intensifier *very* in [8], the prefix *un-* in [9] and [10], and the copular use of *go* in [10] (*cf* 16.21) are indicators of the adjectival status of the participle (7.15*ff*).

[**c**] The *by*-phrase may indicate either 'means' or 'instrument' in a sentence such as:

The news was confirmed by a telegram. [either 'Someone confirmed it by means of a telegram' or 'A telegram confirmed it']

Since the instrumental sense is tied to a passive clause, only the 'means' interpretation is possible in an active clause:

The news came *by* (*a*) *telegram*.

Stimulus: *at*

9.51 The relation between an emotion and its stimulus (normally an abstract stimulus) can often be expressed by *at* or by the instrumental *by* (*cf* 9.50):

I was alarmed {*at* / *by*} *his behaviour*. [1]

Both of these can be treated as passive equivalents of:

His behaviour alarmed me. [1a]

The noun phrase following *at* may be treated as a semi-agent. Further exemplification of this use of *at* is given in 9.63 and 16.69.

The idea of 'stimulus' is sometimes expressed by other prepositions, in place of *at*, which function as semi-agents (*cf* 3.76):

I'm *worried about* this. ['This worries me.']
He's *interested in* history. ['History interests him.']
His plans were *known to* everyone. ['Everyone knew his plans.']

Note In BrE, *with* rather than *at* is used when the stimulus is a person or object rather than an event:
I was *furious with* John.
I was *delighted with* the present.
But in AmE, *at* is quite usual:
I was *furious/angry/livid/mad at* Christine.
With abstract nouns, *at* is equally acceptable in BrE and AmE:
I was *furious at* Christine's behaviour.
At has a common alternative in *about*: *annoyed at/about*, *pleased at/about*, etc. (*Cf* further examples in 16.69.)

Accompaniment: *with*

9.52 Especially when followed by an animate complement, *with* has the meaning 'in company with' or 'together with' (comitative function):

I'm so glad you're coming *with us*. [1]
Jack, (*together*) *with several of his noisy friends*, was drinking till after 2 in the morning. [2]

In [2], the *with*-phrase serves a function very close to coordination with *and*. Note however that, unlike *and*, *with* has a singular verb (*cf* 13.103):

Jack and several of his noisy friends *were* . . . [2a]

An example of a phrase of accompaniment occurring as postmodifier is:

Curry *with rice* is my favourite dish.

In this sense, as in most other senses (but *cf* 9.53), *without* is the negative of *with* (*ie* 'unaccompanied by'):

You never see him *without his dog*.
She was *without her children*.
Without you, I'm not going.

With is also used to express 'accompanying circumstances', as in [3], and to introduce a subject (*cf* 9.55, 14.15*ff*), as in [4]:

With all the noise, she was finding it hard to concentrate. [3]
It all started *with John('s) being late* for dinner. [4]

In both these uses, *with* implies cause: [3] 'Because of all the noise . . .'; [4] 'It all started as a result of John('s) being late . . .'.

Support and opposition: *for, with, against*

9.53 *For* conveys the idea of support ['in favour of'] and *with* that of solidarity or movement in sympathy:

Are you *for or against the plan*? ['Do you support or oppose the plan?']
Remember that every one of us is *with you*. ['on your side']

In this use, there is no negative *without* contrasting with *with*. The contrary idea of opposition is conveyed by *against*:

It is prudent to go *with* rather than *against the tide of public opinion*.
the movement *against nuclear arms* ['anti-nuclear'; *cf* prefixes of attitude, App I.25]

However, *with* conveys the idea of opposition between people in *fight with*, *quarrel with*, *argue with*, etc. Compare:

He's always *arguing* { *with* his sister. / *against* nuclear power. }

The verb *fight* is used with the preposition *with* to denote opposition in *fight with somebody*, which can mean *fight somebody* (*cf* 9.31) or *fight against somebody*; however, *with* in *fight with X against Y* denotes support ['on X's side']. But there is no prepositional form in: *fight a bad cause*, *fight an illness*. *Play* can be constructed in two ways, as in:

I played { *(a game of) chess with Sam.* / *Sam at chess.* }

Other prepositional meanings

Various relations indicated by *of*

9.54 The most common preposition, *of*, occurs chiefly as a postmodifier in noun phrases in a function similar to that of the genitive (*cf* 5.115*ff*), *eg*:

the gravity *of the earth* ~ *the earth's* gravity

The correspondence between the genitive and the *of*-construction is most conveniently discussed in the chapter dealing with the noun phrase (17.38*ff*).

However, postmodifying *of*-phrases also have a wide range of other uses (*cf* 5.6*ff*), *eg*:

(*a*) *part of* the city	[partition]
a kind of wood	[quality]
a lot of people	[quantity]

Here are some more examples with *of*-phrases:

the courage *of the man* ['the courage that the man shows']
a typewriter *of my father's* ['a typewriter that my father has']
the envy *of the world* ['the envy that the world feels']
the trial *of the conspirators* ['the trial that the conspirators face']
the virtue *of thrift* ['the virtue that consists in thrift']
a flock *of sheep* ['a flock that is made up of sheep']
a glass *of water* ['a glass that contains water']
seven *of my friends* ['seven from among my friends']
people *of the Middle Ages* ['people who lived in the Middle Ages']
the house *of my dreams* ['the house which I see in my dreams']
the College *of Surgeons* ['the college to which surgeons belong']
a boat *of fibreglass* ['a boat made of fibreglass']

'Having': *of, with, without*

9.55 The meaning of [1] is related to all the noun phrases [1a–d]:

The man has courage.	[1]
the man having courage	[1a]
the man's courage	[1b]
the courage of the man	[1c]
a man of courage	[1d]

Both [1c] and [1d] have postmodifying *of*-phrases. They differ in that the head of [1c] (*the courage*) is the notional object, whereas the head of [1d] (*the man*) is the notional subject. In the latter type of construction, *of* is limited to the expression of abstract attributes, as in:

a pianist *of great talent* ['a very talented pianist']
a performance *of distinction* ['a distinguished performance']

The notion of 'having' is more generally expressed by *with*, especially with concrete attributes:

a man *with a red nose* ['who has a red nose'; 'a red-nosed man']
an industrialist *with a house on the Costa Brava* ['who has a house . . .']
a woman *with a large family*
a box *with a carved lid*

Compare the following constructions: [2] can have either *of* or *with*, but only *with* is generally accepted in [3]:

a woman {*of* / *with*} *strong feelings* [abstract] [2]

a woman {*?of* / *with*} *strong hands* [concrete] [3]

The negative of *with* is *without* (*cf* 9.52):

a play *without any faults* ['a play with no faults']
women *without children* ['childless women']
the house *without a porch* ['. . . which has no porch']

The correspondence between phrases with *with* or *without* and relative clauses with *have* applies also to *have*-existential sentences (*cf* 18.54):

the girl *who has a boyfriend in the navy*
~ the girl *with a boyfriend in the navy*

With and *without* can also introduce a nonfinite or verbless clause as postmodifier in a noun phrase:

the factory *with its smoking chimney*
a room *with its door open*

Furthermore, they can introduce finite and verbless clauses as adverbial:

He wandered in *without shoes or socks on.*
With so many essays to write, I won't have time to go out tonight.

The fuller clausal equivalent is a participial adverbial clause expressing contingency (*cf* 15.46):

> *Having so many essays to write*, I won't have time to go out tonight.

Since *with* and *without* in these functions introduce clauses, they are subordinators, not prepositions. The nonfinite clause may also be a *to*-infinitive. Compare:

> { *With Mary being away* / *With no one to talk to* / *With Mary away* / *With the house empty* / *Without anyone to talk to* } John felt miserable.

In this construction, *with* and *without* require a noun phrase (not necessarily a subject):

> **With being away* . . .

This is a further indication that they function here not as prepositions but as subordinators (*cf* 14.15). Prepositions can have *-ing* clauses but not *to*-infinitive clauses as complement (*cf* 9.2):

> { *On arriving* / **On to arrive* } Mary took a taxi.

The clause-introducing function of *with* and *without* is similar to that of *for* in cases like the following (*cf* 14.6):

> I bought a car *for Mary to drive to work in.*

At the same time, we must recognize a relationship between their uses as conjunction and preposition. Compare:

> *With Mary* I always feel happy.
> *Without Mary* I always feel miserable.
> I bought a car *for Mary* (so that she could drive to work in it).

Note In this group, *without* has two meanings: (a) 'not with' and (b) 'outside':

(a) They work both *with and without assistance* from me.

(b) They operate both { *within and without* / *inside and outside* } *the organization.*

Note, however, that there is an imbalance in that *without* in the second sense can be used only when coordinated with *within*:

(a) They work { *with* / *without* } *assistance* from me.

(b) They operate { *within* / ?**without* } *the organization.*

Concession: *in spite of, despite, for all, with all,* etc

9.56 *In spite of* is a general-purpose preposition of concession; *despite* is rather more formal:

> I admire him, *in spite of his faults.*

Despite strong pressure from the government, the unions have refused to order a return to work.

With all and *for all* 'despite' are more colloquial and rather restricted in their use:

With / For *all his boasting and ostentatious training*, he was knocked out in the first round.

In concessive use, *all* must be present after both prepositions: *with all* and *for all.* In causal use, *all* is optional: *with* or *with all.* Compare:

With all / For all this noise I managed to get some sleep. [concessive: 'in spite of']

With all / With this noise, I couldn't sleep. [causal: 'because of']

Notwithstanding ['in spite of'] is formal and rather legalistic in style, particularly when postposed:

Thomas Carlyle, *notwithstanding his tedious rhetoric,* / *his tedious rhetoric notwithstanding,* is a master of the sublime in prose style.

Compare the adverbial use of *notwithstanding*, as in:

Notwithstanding, the case must be prosecuted. ['notwithstanding any conditions']

Respect: *with reference to, with regard to, as for,* etc

9.57 Some of the prepositions denoting respect are used in rather formal contexts, typically business letters, *eg*:

a particular aspect, point, or detail

With reference to [less usual: *In reference to*] *your letter/request/enquiry of April 29th*, I confirm my Directors' agreement to advance a further sum of £2000. ⟨formal⟩

With regard to the date of delivery . . . [less usual: *In regard to* or *Re* /riː/; typically introducing a secondary or tertiary topic in such a letter]

Re functions like *with regard to* but is more common in notes than in formal letters, *eg*:

Re your idea of extending the canteen . . .

Other prepositions within the same general area of meaning are *regarding, with respect to, in respect of, respecting, on the matter of, about, concerning, as to* (*cf* subject matter, 9.60).

As to functions like *with regard to, as regards*, etc:

As to the question you raise in your last letter, I think that . . .

As to is also used in the sense of *according to, eg*: *correct as to size and colour.*

As for, on the other hand, introduces a topic transition, so it cannot normally occur at the beginning of a discourse. It has the meaning of 'returning to the question of', and is less formal than the other complex prepositions denoting respect:

We had a delightful weekend in the country. *As for the traffic*, we had no difficulty.

There is a predisposition for initial *as for* to indicate a contemptuous attitude:

As for his book, I suppose you've read the reviews!

There are a number of marginal prepositions that have affinities with verbs which belong here: *concerning*, *regarding*, and *touching* ⟨formal⟩ (*cf* 9.8), *eg*:

Concerning the recent proposal by the chairperson, I suggest we . . .

Considering is used like *in view of* ['taking into consideration'], often 'if one takes into account the rather surprising fact that':

Considering the job situation, there were surprisingly few applications this year.

Prepositional phrases as adverbials denoting respect are chiefly used as disjuncts or conjuncts. Most of them can also function as postmodifiers in noun phrases:

Has the candidate expressed *an opinion* {*on* / *about* / *concerning* / *with regard to*} legal abortion?

We await *your decision as to whether* these repairs are to be carried out immediately.

Note The use of *irregardless* (*of*) for *regardless* (*of*) is widespread, especially in AmE, but is considered nonstandard by most people. It appears to be the result of a confusion between *regardless* and *irrespective*, or perhaps a choice of a double negative (*ir* + *less*) which is felt to be suitably emphatic.

Exception and addition

9.58 The most common prepositions denoting exception are: *except for*, *with the exception of*, *apart from*, *aside from* ⟨esp AmE⟩, *except*, *excepting*, *excluding*, *but*, and *save* ⟨formal⟩. When used in adverbials, prepositions denoting EXCEPTION function primarily as disjuncts (*cf* 8.121*ff*):

We had a pleasant time, *except for the weather*.
With the exception of James, none of us had any money.
The worst period of my life, {*apart from the war*, / *aside from the war* ⟨esp AmE⟩,} was when I was out of work.

Except and *excepting* function normally, and *but* exclusively, in postmodifying phrases:

All {*but* / *except*(*ing*)} *the captain* were rescued.

Finally we had packed everything {*but* / *except*} *the typewriter*.
Any time *but now*. ['any other time']

Thus *but* cannot occur initially as a preposition:

{**But* / *Except for*} me, everyone was tired.

The prepositional phrase, in such constructions, is often separated from its noun head, and postposed to the end of the clause (*cf* discontinuous noun phrases, 18.39):

Everyone but me was tired. ~ *Everyone* was tired *but me*.

Further, the noun phrase with *but*-modification must contain a determiner or indefinite pronoun of absolute meaning (positive or negative): *no*, *all*, *any*, *every*, *each*, *nobody*, *anywhere*, *everything*, etc or an interrogative *wh*-word (*who?*, *where?*, etc). Hence one may say *all but one*, but not, *eg*: **some but one*, or **many but one*. Other examples:

This car is *anything but* slow.
We've bought *everything but* milk.
Who should turn up *but* our old friend Tom.

Bar and *barring* are rarer substitutes for *except* and *excepting*:

This is the most versatile microcomputer on the market, *bar none*.
Barring accidents, we'll be there on time.

Beyond is sometimes used in nonassertive contexts in the sense of *except* (*for*):

Beyond the press release, there are no further comments.
He didn't help, *beyond showing a mild interest*.

ADDITION can be expressed by the prepositions *besides*, *as well as*, and *in addition to*. For example:

There were three people present {*besides* / *in addition to*} *the committee*.
As well as learning to swim he has been taking Spanish lessons this summer.

Compare the difference in meaning between *except* and *but* (both denoting exception), on the one hand, and *besides* (denoting addition), on the other, in the following examples:

Everyone passed {*except* / *but*} *Richard*. ['Richard did not pass but everyone else did.']
Everyone passed *besides Richard*. ['Everyone passed, in addition to Richard.']

In the negative, the difference is cancelled out, so that the following two sentences are synonymous:

No one passed {*except* / *besides*} *Richard*.

Note [**a**] *But* as a preposition has to be distinguished from *but* as a conjunction (*cf* 13.5*ff*). Both the resemblance and the contrast between the two functions are brought out in:

Everyone had a good time *but* John. [preposition = 'with the exception of', 'except for']

The students had a good time { *but not* John. / *but* John *did not*. } [conjunction]

However, there is often indeterminacy between the preposition and conjunction status of *except* and *but*, as can be seen in the variability of constructions such as:

He does everything in the house { *except* / *but* } { *put* / *putting* } *the children to bed.*

[**b**] As we have seen above, prepositions of exception and addition quite often have a prepositional phrase or clause as complement (*cf* 9.1 Note [d]):

except in the southeast
apart from when I last spoke to you
except for what I ordered
in addition to being a fine colleague

[**c**] The combination *all but* is used colloquially as an intensifier:

He *all but* ['very nearly'] strangled me.
Cf: She is *but* ['only'] a child. [where *but* is a restrictive subjunct, *cf* 8.116 Note [b]]

Negative condition: *but for*

9.59 *But for* is not used in the sense of exception, but rather that of 'negative condition':

But for Gordon, we would have lost the match. ['If it hadn't been for Gordon . . .', 'If Gordon hadn't played as he did . . .', etc]

Many people use *except for* in the same way as *but for* to denote negative condition. However, *except for* normally denotes exception (*cf* 9.58). Note the difference in meaning between the following two sentences:

Except for John they { would all have died. ['If it hadn't been for John . . .'] / all died. ['With the exception of John . . .'] }

Prepositional phrases used chiefly in complementation of verbs and adjectives

Subject matter: *about, on*

9.60 With the meaning 'on the subject of', 'concerning', *about* and *on* can combine with a considerable range of verbs and adjectives (*cf* 16.28, 16.69), *eg*:

She is *lecturing* { *about* / *on* } new techniques of management.

He *told me* { *about* / **on* } his adventures.

Other examples:

ABOUT/ON	ABOUT
argue about/on	*find out about*
be knowledgeable about/on	*hear about*
communicate about/on	*inform* (someone) *about*
confer about/on	*learn about*
hold forth about/on	*keep quiet about*
preach about/on	*quarrel about*
speak about/on	*read about*
write about/on	*teach* (someone) *about*

On is chiefly reserved for deliberate, formal linguistic communication (public speaking, lecturing, writing, etc), and is therefore inappropriate for verbs like *chat* or *quarrel*. Thus [1] would suggest she was making a formal speech ['gave a lecture on'], whereas [2] could refer equally to an informal conversation or casual allusion:

She *spoke* { *on butterflies.* [1]
{ *about butterflies.* [2]

This difference of meaning occurs also with postmodifying phrases where *on* and *about* mean 'on the subject of':

a book about/on butterflies	*a story about* a princess
a talk about/on antiques	*ignorance about* sex
a discussion about/on drugs	*the facts about* nuclear power
a word about/on the garden	*a fuss about* nothing

Prepositional phrases introduced by both *about* and *on* may function as obligatory predication adjuncts with the verb *be*:

This book *is* { *on* / *about* } *stamps.*

A less usual, and more formal, alternative to *about* and *on* is *concerning* (*cf* 9.57): *a dispute concerning land rights.*

Over is also used to denote 'on the subject of', 'in connection with':

They *quarrelled over money*.
It's no use *crying over spilt milk*.

Of is a somewhat rarer and more literary alternative to *about* in *tell, speak, talk, inform . . . of*, etc. Both *about* and *of* are frequently used with *think*, but with a difference of meaning:

He *thought* { *about the problem.* ['He pondered/considered the problem.']
{ *of the problem.* ['He brought the problem to his mind.']

Of can also be used in variation with *about* in noun phrases (*cf* above), as in:

a story of a princess   *ignorance of* sex   *the facts of* nuclear power

Material, ingredient: *with, of, out of*; substance: *from*

9.61 With verbs of 'making', *with* indicates an ingredient; *of* and *out of* signify the material or constituency of the whole thing; and *from* indicates a substance from which something is derived:

This cake is *made with* lots of eggs. ['Eggs are an important ingredient.']
He *made* the frame (*out*) *of* wood. ['Wood was the only material.']
Beer is *made from* hops.

With also enters into such pervasive expressions as *paved with brick*, *filled with water*, *loaded with hay* (*cf* 9.29).

Of (used with nouns denoting 'material') is found in a postmodifying function as well as in adverbials:

a bracelet of solid gold ['made out of', 'a solid gold bracelet']
a table of polished oak ['made/consisting of polished oak', 'a polished oak table']

It may also be used metaphorically:

a man of steel
a heart of stone [*cf* 'a woman of/with strong feelings', 9.55]

Standard: *for, at*

9.62 A comparative adjective must be related, explicitly or implicitly, to a basis of comparison (*cf* 7.86). Thus we cannot say [1], without some such implicit relation:

This boy is bigger. [1]

Similarly, a gradable adjective without the comparative form implies some standard or norm; *big* in [2] means something different from *big* in [3]:

This elephant is big. [2]
This cat is big. [3]

The reason is that 'big for an elephant' presupposes a larger scale, and a larger norm, than 'big for a cat'.

We can make the norm explicit by a *for*-phrase [4–5]:

He's not bad *for a youngster*. ['considering that he is a youngster'] [4]
That dog is long-legged *for a terrier*. [5]

A further way in which one may specify the meaning of a gradable adjective or noun is to use *at* to indicate the respect in which the adjective is appropriate to the subject (*cf* 16.69), as in [6–7]:

He's *good/clever/brilliant/an expert at organizing things*. [6]
He's *bad/better/terrible/no good at games*. [7]

The use of *for* and *at* is not restricted to adjectival complementation: these prepositions occur also in a number of other grammatical roles, as the following examples show:

I'm a complete dunce *at mathematics*.
She's getting on very well *at her job*.
For an Englishman, he speaks foreign languages remarkably well.
It's a dreadfully expensive toy *for what it is*.

Reaction: *at, to*

9.63 Consider these three sentences:

> Their rejection of the offer *surprised* me. [1]
> I was *surprised by* their rejection of the offer. [1a]
> I was *surprised at* their rejection of the offer. [1b]

Sentence [1] presents, by means of a straightforward subject–verb–object construction, the relationship between an event, an emotional reaction, and the person who undergoes the reaction. The same relationship can be expressed by the passive [1a] (*cf* 3.63*ff*), or, alternatively, by the passive with the preposition *at* replacing the agentive preposition *by* [1b]. Here *at* (as we saw in 9.51) signals the relation between the emotive reaction and its stimulus. *Surprised* in this context is a participial adjective (note that it can be preceded by *very*; *cf* 7.15), and it is with such adjectival forms that *at* ['stimulus'] characteristically combines (*cf* 3.76, 16.69):

> *alarmed at* *disgusted at*
> *amused at* *delighted at*

Less commonly, verbs and nonparticipial adjectives have this construction:

> *laugh/stare/gaze/glance/aim/rejoice . . . at*
> *be angry/glad . . . at*

Another way to state the same idea is to let the main clause represent the event acting as a 'stimulus', and to let the REACTION be expressed by the preposition *to* followed by an abstract noun of emotion, *eg*: *to my regret*, *to my annoyance*, *to my relief*, *to my surprise*, *to my horror*, *to my delight*:

> *To my regret*, they rejected the offer.

To my regret in this context is a content disjunct, comparable with adverbs such as *regrettably* (*cf* 8.127).

The reaction can also be expressed by *to* + personal pronoun or a phrase with *to* + possessive pronoun + *mind*, *in* + possessive pronoun + *opinion*, etc, to identify the person reacting:

> *To me*, } their rejection was a surprise.
> *To my mind*,
> *In my opinion*,

In this sense, *to* is not limited to emotive reactions but applies equally to intellectual or perceptual responses:

> *To a mind based in common sense*, his ideas are utterly absurd.
> It looked *to me* like a vast chasm.

However, in this last case the *to*-phrase is not a disjunct, but an adjunct.

According to is used to identify not so much a reaction to, as an interpretation of, events. It is used chiefly for a 3rd person (*cf* 8.127 Note [a]):

> *To* him/you/me } this is quite unexpected.
> *According to* him/?you/??me

Note This use of *according to* should be distinguished from the different sense of *in accordance/agreement/conformity with*:

> *in accordance with* } the new regulations
> *according to* }

Modification of prepositional phrases

9.64 Prepositional meanings (particularly of time and place) are subject to modification as regards degree and measure, and prepositions may therefore (like many adjectives and adverbs) be preceded by intensifiers (*cf* 7.61). For example:

> I left it *just* ⟨inside⟩ the garage. ['a little way']
> He had wandered *right* ⟨off⟩ the path. ['completely']
> Now their footsteps could be heard *directly* ⟨above⟩ my head.
> I got up *just/soon* ⟨after⟩ ten.
> There was rubbish *all* ⟨over⟩ the place.
> They followed *close* ⟨behind⟩ me.
> This cake mix comes *straight* ⟨out of⟩ the packet.
> The dog was lying *right* ⟨in the middle of⟩ the floor.

There is doubt in such cases as to whether the intensifier should be treated as applying to the whole prepositional phrase, or to the preposition alone. In the examples above, however, the intensifiers can modify the prepositional adverbs: *right in the middle*, etc.

Prepositions and prepositional adverbs

9.65 A prepositional adverb is a particle which is formally identical to or related to a preposition, and which often behaves like a preposition with ellipted complement:

> A car drove { *past the door*. [*past* is a preposition]
> A car drove { *past*. [*past* is a prepositional adverb]

Thus a prepositional adverb shares the form, but not the syntactic status, of a preposition. It is capable of standing alone as an adjunct, conjunct, postmodifer, etc without the addition of a prepositional complement:

> Despite the fine weather, we stayed *in* all day.
> *Besides*, I don't feel like a walk just now.
> The day *before*, I had spoken to her in the office.

Prepositional adverbs normally receive stress, whereas simple prepositions (especially monosyllables, *cf* 9.9) normally do not. In each of the following pairs, *in* is a stressed adverb in the first and an unstressed preposition in the second example:

She stayed *ÌN*. [1]
She stayed *in the HÒUSE*. [1a]

He thrust *ÍN* his HÀND. [2]
He swam *in the LÀKE*. [2a]

Which prisoner did they march *ÌN*? [3]
Which uniform did they MÀRCH *in*? [3a]

Both prepositions and adverbs commonly appear in idiomatic combinations with a preceding verb, *eg*: *make for*, *make up*, *make up for*. Here, however, we shall pay attention only to their meaning and syntactic behaviour as individual items, idiomatic usage being a concern of the dictionary rather than of the grammar. Phrasal verbs and prepositional verbs, *ie* combinations of verb + adverb and verb + preposition which behave syntactically or semantically as a single unit, are discussed in 16.2*ff*.

Note The relation between prepositional adverbs and prepositional phrases [4] may be compared to that between intransitive and transitive use of certain verbs [5] (*cf* 16.19):

She *stayed in* (the house). [4]
She *ate* (breakfast). [5]

9.66 (a) The following list includes some prepositional adverbs related to simple prepositions (*cf* 9.7), as in:

Why didn't you come { *before* 7 o'clock? / *before*? }

a'board	*a'bout*	*a'bove*
a'cross	*'after*	*a'long*
a'longside	*a'round*	*be'fore*
be'hind	*be'low*	*be'neath*
be'sides	*be'tween*	*be'yond*
by	*down*	*in*
in'side	*near* (*'nearer*, *'nearest*)	*off*
on	*'opposite*	*out'side*
'over	*past*	*round*
since	*through*	*through'out*
'under	*ˌunder'neath*	*up*
with'in	*with'out*	

All, with the exception of *without* and the conjunct *besides*, are primarily adjuncts of time or space.

(b) The following list includes some prepositional adverbs that are related to complex (two-word) prepositions (*cf* 9.10), as in:

Paul wants to go to the Zoo { *instead of* going to a museum. / *instead*. }

a'head	*a'way*	*back*
close	*east*, etc	*'eastward(s)*, etc
in'stead	*out*	*over'head*
to'gether		

(c) The following list includes some prepositional adverbs related to complex (three-word) prepositions (*cf* 9.11), as in:

Why don't you put the trunk { *on top of* the car? / *on top*? }

at variance	*in addition*	*in aid*
in case	*in charge*	*in common*
in comparison	*in context*	*in exchange*
in favour	*in front*	*in lieu*
in line	*in need*	*in relation*
in return	*on top*	

Most of the common prepositions listed in 9.7*ff* can also act as prepositional adverbs, for example:

Position (9.16):	Is your sister *in*? – No, she's *out/away*.
Destination (9.16):	She went *out/away/in*.
Passage (9.24):	The dog jumped *over/through*.
Path (9.26):	Move *along*.
	She came *round* to see me.
Orientation (9.27):	The man (who sat) *opposite* kept looking at her.
Resultative (9.28):	The price of oil is *up* again today.
Pervasive (9.29):	There were lots of people *around*.

Prepositional phrases and prepositional adverbs can be seen as the extremes on a scale with a stepwise reduction in explicitness as we proceed from [1] to [5]. In the sentence pattern 'They are all . . .' we can have:

in (great) *favour of the proposal* [1]
(greatly) *in favour of the proposal* [2]
(greatly) *in favour of it* [3]
(greatly) *in its favour* [4]
(greatly) *in favour* [5]

We have in [1] a free syntactic noun phrase with *favour* as head which admits adjectival premodification; in [2] a complex preposition *in favour of* with *the proposal* as complement; in [3] the pronominal substitute for the nominal complement in [2]; in [4] a possessive determiner *its*; and in [5] the prepositional adverb *in favour*, which relies for its interpretation on previous mention in the linguistic or situational context. The reduction in [4] (premodification) as compared with [2] and [3] (postmodification) is dealt with in connection with the noun phrase. The step from [4] to [5] is one step beyond premodification structure.

Note [a] *For* and *against* are used as prepositional adverbs only in phrases such as *votes for and against*.
[b] *To* is used as a prepositional adverb in *set 'to* (*and finish*), *turn 'to* (*and help*), and in a few idioms such as (*walk*) *to and fro*. Compare the prepositional phrase in *walk to and from work*.

[c] There is no prepositional adverb corresponding to *contrary to* (*cf* 9.10). But note the similar use of the reduced expression *to the contrary*.

His vote was { *contrary to mine.* / *to the contrary.* }

Compare also the conjunct adverbial (8.137):

On the contrary,
To the contrary ⟨AmE⟩, } what I said was this year, not next.

Bibliographical note

A general analytical bibliography of prepositions can be found in Guimier (1981).

Theoretical treatments of the roles of prepositions are provided by Bennett (1975); Bugarski (1969); Fillmore (1969); Rosenbaum (1967a); Vestergaard (1977).

Studies of other aspects of English prepositions can be found, for example, in Christophersen (1979); Hill (1968); Jacobsson (1977a); Lee (1969); Leech (1969a); Lindkvist (1950, 1972, 1976, 1978); Poutsma (1926–29), Part II.2; Quirk and Mulholland (1964); Sørensen (1979a, 1979b); Turner (1972); Zandvoort and Doodkorte (1962).

Frequencies have been taken from Hofland and Johansson (1982).

10 The simple sentence

Clause patterns

Simple and multiple sentences

10.1 Sentences are either SIMPLE or MULTIPLE. A simple sentence consists of a single independent clause. A multiple sentence contains one or more clauses as its immediate constituents. Multiple sentences are either COMPOUND or COMPLEX. In a compound sentence the immediate constituents are two or more COORDINATE clauses. In a complex sentence one or more of its elements, such as direct object or adverbial, are realized by a SUBORDINATE clause (*cf* further 14.1*ff*).

Elements such as subject and verb are constituents of sentences and also of clauses within sentences. We shall speak of CLAUSES and CLAUSE STRUCTURE whenever what we say applies both to sentences and to the clauses of which sentences are composed. Thus a complex sentence with one subordinate clause can be analysed twice over, once for the sentence as a whole and once for the subordinate clause included within the sentence:

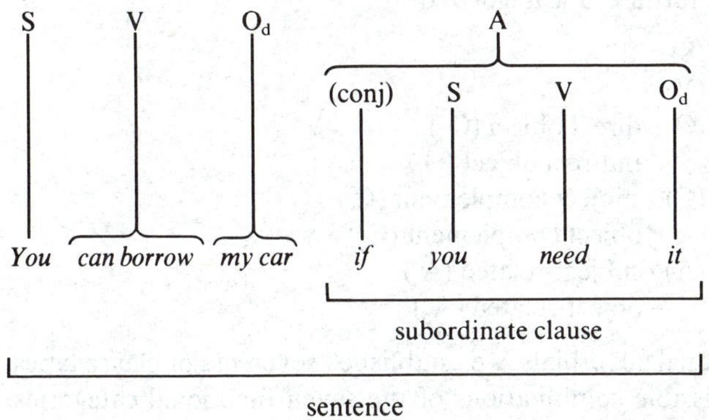

Fig 10.1 Sentence and clause elements

In the present chapter we are primarily concerned with simple sentences. Discussion of coordinate clauses is deferred to Chapter 13 and of subordinate clauses to Chapters 14 and 15. The present chapter is further restricted to aspects of the simple sentence chiefly involving the elements subject, verb, object, and complement. The adverbial, as a clause element that is generally more detachable and more mobile than the others, receives detailed consideration in Chapter 8.

Note **[a]** We use the term 'simple sentence' for an independent clause that does not have another clause functioning as one of its elements. Thus, [1] is a complex sentence in which *if you need it* functions as an adverbial:

You can borrow my car *if you need it*. [1]

However, a simple sentence may have a clause functioning within a phrase. In that case the complexity is at the level of the phrase, not at the level of the sentence or clause. Thus [2] is a simple sentence:

You can borrow the car *that belongs to my sister*. [2]

In [2] the relative clause *that belongs to my sister* is a postmodifier within the complex noun phrase constituting the object element *the car that belongs to my sister*. Clauses functioning as modification of noun phrases are discussed in Chapter 17. Clauses functioning in the complementation of adjective phrases are discussed in Chapter 16.

The term 'simple sentence' is frequently used elsewhere, but not in this book, for an independent clause that does not contain another clause, regardless of whether the contained clause is an immediate constituent of the sentence or not. In some grammars, nonfinite constructions (which have a nonfinite verb as their verb element) are considered phrases rather than clauses. We treat such constructions as clauses because they can be analysed into clause elements (*cf* 14.5). Nonfinite clauses themselves are intrinsically subordinate and therefore do not constitute simple sentences in the canonical forms (but *cf* 11.41).

[b] A simple sentence is not necessarily simple in a nontechnical sense. For example, a simple sentence may be very complicated because its phrases are complex:

> On the recommendation of the committee, the temporary chairman, who had previous experience of the medical issues concerned, made the decision that no further experiments on living animals should be conducted in circumstances that might lead to unfavourable press publicity.

Other factors apart from the complexity of phrases are mentioned in 14.2.

Clause structures

10.2 We now turn to a further consideration of the clause structures outlined in 2.13*ff*. We there distinguished five functional categories of clause constituents, three of which were further subcategorized.

subject	(S)	
verb	(V)	
object	(O)	– direct object (O_d)
		– indirect object (O_i)
complement	(C)	– subject complement (C_s)
		– object complement (C_o)
adverbial	(A)	– subject-related (A_s)
		– object-related (A_o)

By eliminating optional adverbials, we established seven major clause types, based on the permissible combinations of the seven functional categories, the clause elements. *Table* 10.2 opposite exemplifies the major clause types in their normal order in a simple declarative sentence, the canonical form of the sentence.

The clause types are determined by the verb class to which the full verbs within the verb constituent belong. Different verb classes require different complementation (O_d, O_i, C_s, C_o, A) to complete the meaning of the verb, or (in the case of *SV*, where the verb is intransitive) no complementation.

Multiple class membership of verbs

10.3 It must be borne in mind that a given verb can belong, in its various senses, to a number of different classes (*cf* App I.54), and hence enter into a number of different clause types. The verb *get* is a particularly versatile one, being excluded only from Type *SV* (and even then not universally; *cf* Note):

SVO	He'll get a surprise.
SVC	He's getting angry.
SVA	He got through the window.
SVOO	He got her a splendid present.
SVOC	He got his shoes and socks wet.
SVOA	He got himself into trouble.

Table 10.2 Major clause types

Type	S(ubject)	V(erb)	O(bject)(s)	C(omplement)	A(dverbial)
SV	*The sun*	intransitive *is shining*			
SVO	*That lecture*	monotransitive *bored*	direct object *me*		
SVC	*Your dinner*	copular *seems*		subject complement *ready*	
SVA	*My office*	copular *is*			subject-related adverbial *in the next building*
SVOO	*I*	ditransitive *must send*	indirect object *my parents* direct object *an anniversary card*		
SVOC	*Most students*	complex-transitive *have found*	direct object *her*	object complement *reasonably helpful*	
SVOA	*You*	complex-transitive *can put*	direct object *the dish*		object-related adverbial *on the table*

Note One minor clause type is the bare existential sentence (18.44*ff*): *There is no need for apologies; there must have been some misunderstanding.*

Through the multiple class membership of verbs, ambiguities can arise: *I found her an entertaining partner*, like *She called him her favourite waiter*, could be interpreted either as belonging to the *SVOC* or *SVOO* types.

The complementation of verbs receives detailed treatment in Chapter 16.

Note In informal (especially dialectal) AmE, *get* is used even as an intransitive verb (='leave at once') in Type *SV*: *She told him to get.*

Verb complementation

10.4 The elements, O_d, C_s, C_o, and A in the patterns exemplified in 10.2 and 10.3 are obligatory elements of clause structure in that they are required for the complementation of the verb. Given the use of a particular verb in a particular sentence, the sentence is incomplete if one of these elements is omitted, *eg*: **Your dinner seems* (type *SVC*) and **You can put the dish* (type *SVOA*) are unacceptable. In some cases, however, a direct object or an object complement could from one point of view be considered grammatically optional:

They're eating. [S V] ~ *cf* They're eating lunch. [S V O]
We elected her. [S V O] ~ *cf* We elected her our delegate. [S V O C]
He's teaching. [S V] ~ *cf* He's teaching chemistry. [S V O]
He's teaching them chemistry. [S V O O]

We regard these as cases of conversion, whereby a word such as *eat* is transferred from the transitive to the intransitive category. Thus, *They're eating* is an instance of type *SV* rather than of *SVO* (with optional deletion of the object). We adopt this approach because there is to a greater or lesser extent a shift in meaning.

To justify treating object omission as a matter of conversion, we may notice that it applies to some transitive verbs but not to others:

They're hunting deer. ~ They're hunting.
They're chasing cats. ~ *They're chasing.

Also, one can find nonce object omissions, which again points to a word-formation process rather than a syntactic process. Thus (*)*John is licking today* is a highly improbable sentence for which one could (as with all nonce-formations) find a plausible use if one tried hard enough (*eg* a situation in which two people are alternatively employed in licking and sticking stamps on letters). Conversions from one verb category to another, including from transitive to intransitive verbs, are exemplified in App I.54.

A similar approach may be made to instances where the indirect object is omissible:

She gives expensive presents. [S V O_d]
cf She gives her friends expensive presents. [S V O_i O_d]

But here the case for conversion is not so strong, and one may regard the indirect object with many verbs as an optional element similar in status to an optional adverbial.

We should in principle distinguish different types of omission of objects, though the distinction may be blurred in particular instances:

(1) A specific object is recoverable from the preceding linguistic context:

A: Show me your essay. B: I'll *show* you later.
Let's do the dishes. I'll *wash* and you *dry*.

In such instances the verb may be analysed as genuinely transitive with ellipsis of the direct object.

(2) A specific object is understood from the situational context:

Keep off [sign on grass] *Shake* well before use.
Watch! Don't *touch*.
The tie doesn't *fit*.

(3) A specific reflexive object is understood when the verb allows such an object (*cf* 6.25):

I'm *shaving*. They're *dressing*.

Some verbs allow omission of either a reflexive or a nonreflexive object: *She's washing* (*herself* or *the clothes*).

(4) A nonspecific object is semantically entailed (*cf* 16.19):

Are you *eating* again? Do you *drink*?
He *teaches*. I don't want to catch you *smoking* again.
They can't *spell*. I can't come now, because I'm *cleaning*.
I don't want to *read*.

The range of understood nonspecific objects is restricted with some verbs when they are used intransitively. For example, *Do you drink?* refers to the drinking of alcoholic drinks, *I'm cleaning* refers to domestic cleaning and not (say) to cleaning teeth or cleaning a pipe, and *to catch you smoking again* normally excludes (say) smoking fish. In other instances, the intransitive verb may lack the causative meaning of the transitive verb: Contrast *He walked* and *He walked the dog* (*cf* 10.22).

Note In some instances the omission of a sentence element radically changes the sense of the verb. Contrast the use of the verb *find* and *run* in these examples:

I have found her reasonably helpful. [S V O C] I have found her. [S V O]
He is running a business. [S V O] He is running. [S V]

Syntactic functions of clause elements

10.5 A partial characterization of the clause elements based on formal criteria is given in 2.24. Formal criteria usually suffice to identify the verb element within a clausal context, since the verb element is always realized by a verb phrase. We have also noted its syntactic importance in determining what other elements may or must occur in the clause (*cf* 10.3*f*). We now give further consideration to the other clause elements.

Distinctions between the elements – and between types within the elements – are based on (i) forms (noun phrase, verb phrase, adjective phrase, finite clause, etc), (ii) position, (iii) syntactic function other than positional potentialities, and (iv) semantic role. It is primarily on the basis of (iii) and (iv) that a distinction is made between O_d and O_i, C_s and C_o. The following sentences contain final phrases that are identical in form and position:

{They told the mayor. / They admired the mayor.} {They told his life story. / They admired his life story.}

But the identity stops there. While the process of admiring the mayor is parallel to that of admiring his life story, telling the mayor involves something very different from telling his life story. The difference is confirmed by coordination:

They admired the mayor and his life story.
*They told the mayor and his life story.

Equally, if we attempt to introduce apposition, we can contrast:

They admired the mayor, *ie* his life story.
*They told the mayor, *ie* his life story.

In other words, *the mayor* and *his life story* are realizations of the same type of O with *admire* but are realizations of different types of O with *tell*. Consequently, we cannot have:

*They admired the mayor his life story.

But we can have:

They told the mayor his life story.

Hence it is necessary (for this last sentence) to distinguish O_i (*the mayor*) from O_d (*his life story*).

Note If the verb is in the simple present, it may be indistinguishable from a noun in a sentence in block language (*cf* 11.45), where determiners are commonly omitted:

Mail leaves tomorrow. ['Mail the leaves tomorrow.' *or* 'The mail leaves tomorrow.']

Subject

10.6 Of the clause elements other than the verb, the subject is the most important in that (except for the verb) it is the element that is most often present. It is also the element for which we can find the greatest number of characteristic features. In characterizing the subject and the other clause elements, we identify the four types of distinction listed in 10.5. Because of its conspicuousness we treat position separately from other syntactic functions.

(a) FORM
The subject is normally a noun phrase (*cf* Chapters 5, 6, and 17) or a nominal clause (*cf* 15.3*ff*).

(b) POSITION
The subject normally occurs before the verb in declarative clauses, and after the operator in *yes–no* interrogative clauses (*cf* 11.5*ff*):

Everbody [S] *has left* [V] for the day.
Has [op] *everybody* [S] left for the day?

In *wh*-interrogative clauses, subject–operator inversion also occurs except where the *wh*-element is itself the subject:

What *have* [op] *you* [S] seen today?
What [S] *has* [op] kept you so long?

(c) SYNTACTIC FUNCTION

(i) A subject is obligatory in finite clauses except in imperative clauses, where it is normally absent but implied (*cf* 11.24*ff*).

(ii) In finite clauses the subject determines the number and person, where relevant, of the verb (*cf* 10.34*ff*):

Nancy [S] *knows* [V] my parents. [singular number concord]
Nancy and David [S] *know* [V] my parents. [plural number concord]
I [S] *am* [V] your new colleague. [singular number and 1st person concord]

(iii) The subject normally determines number of the subject complement when that is a noun phrase (*cf* 10.46):

Caroline [S] is *my sister* [C].
Caroline and Vanessa [S] are *my sisters* [C].

(iv) The subject determines the number and, where relevant, the person and gender of the reflexive pronoun as direct object, indirect object, subject complement, or prepositional complement (*cf* 6.23, 10.48, 10.50). The same concord relation generally applies when the emphatic genitive *my own*, etc is used (*cf* 6.30):

I [S] shaved *myself* [O] with *my own* razor.
He [S] shaved *himself* [O] with *his own* razor.

(v) The subject requires the subjective form for pronouns that have distinctive case forms (*cf* 6.4):

I [S] like him.
He [S] likes me.

(vi) There is a systematic correspondence between active and passive clauses in that the direct or indirect object of an active clause becomes the subject of a passive clause while the subject of the active clause is either omitted or made the complement in a *by*-agent phrase (*cf* 16.26):

My son [S] has prepared *lunch* [O] today. [active]
~ *Lunch* [S] has been prepared by *my son* today. [passive]

(vii) The subject is repeated in a tag question by a pronoun form (*cf* 11.8*ff*):

The milk is sour, isn't *it*?

(viii) The implied subject of a subjectless nonfinite or verbless clause is normally identical with the subject of the superordinate clause:

Susan telephoned *before coming over*. ['. . . before Susan came over']

(d) SEMANTIC PROPERTIES

(i) The subject is typically the theme (or topic) of the clause (*cf* 18.9*ff*).

(ii) It typically refers to information that is regarded by the speaker as given (*cf* 18.8*ff*).

(iii) In a clause that is not passive, the subject is agentive if the agentive role is expressed in the clause (*cf* 10.33).

Note [**a**] For adverbial forms functioning as subject, *cf* 10.15. On adjectives functioning as heads of noun phrases (*the young*), *cf* 7.23*ff*.

[**b**] For declarative clauses with subject–operator or subject–verb inversion, *cf* 10.58*f*, 15.36, 18.22*ff*.

[**c**] For the question of *there* as a subject in existential sentences, *cf* 18.46.

[**d**] The implied subject of a postmodifying participle clause is the head of the noun phrase:

I haven't yet seen *the friends staying with you.*
['The friends are staying with you.']
These are *the flowers given to us by our children.*
['The flowers were given to us by our children.']

[**e**] The identity of the subject can be tested in an independent declarative clause through a *wh*-question with *who* or *what*. The subject is the element that can be replaced in its normal position by the *wh*-item:

Joan [S] wants a piece of cake. ~ *Who* [S] wants a piece of cake?
The bright light [S] is disturbing Percy. ~ *What* [S] is disturbing Percy?

Other clause elements require fronting and subject–operator inversion:

Joan wants *a piece of cake* [O]. *What* [O] does Joan want?

Object: direct and indirect

10.7 Direct and indirect objects have some characteristics in common, and this fact justifies their sharing the term *object*:

(a) FORM

Like the subject, the object is normally a noun phrase or a nominal clause. There are constraints on the types of nominal clauses that can be indirect object: generally, only nominal relative clauses (*cf* 15.8*f*).

(b) POSITION

The object normally follows the subject and verb (but *cf* 10.58*f*, 11.14*f*, 18.20). If both objects are present, the indirect object normally comes before the direct object (but *cf* 18.38):

I gave *him* [O_i] *my address* [O_d].

(c) SYNTACTIC FUNCTION

(i) The object function requires the objective form for pronouns that have distinctive case forms:

They amuse *me* [O_d]. They gave *me* [O_i] some chocolate.
I amuse *them* [O_d]. I gave *them* [O_i] some chocolate.

(ii) If an object is coreferential with the subject, it usually requires a reflexive pronoun which agrees with the subject in person and, where relevant, in number and gender. Similar agreement is required for an emphatic genitive (*my own*, etc) within the object (*cf* 6.30):

You [S] can please *yourself* [O_d].
I [S] have given *myself* [O_i] a treat.
They [S] type *their own letters* [O_d].

(iii) The object of an active clause may generally become the subject of the corresponding passive clause (but *cf* Note [c] below, 16.27):

We have finished *the work* [O_d]. ~ *The work* [S] has been finished.

If both objects are present, it is often possible to make either the subject in a corresponding passive clause:

We sent *Jack* [O_i] *a copy of the letter* [O_d].
~ *Jack* [S] was sent *a copy of the letter* [O_d]. [1]
~ *A copy of the letter* [S] was sent *Jack* [O_i]. [2]

But [1] is far more common than [2]. Instead of the retained indirect object in [2], the prepositional paraphrase is more usual:

A copy of the letter was sent *to Jack*. [2a]

(iv) The indirect object generally corresponds to a prepositional phrase, which is generally placed after the direct object:

I'll send *Charles* another copy. ~ I'll send another copy *to Charles*.
Pour *me* a drink. ~ Pour a drink *for me*.

(v) The indirect object can generally be omitted without affecting the semantic relations between the other elements:

David saved *me* a seat. ~ David saved a seat. ≁ David saved me.

Hence, if there is only one object present, it is generally the direct object. But with a few verbs that are normally ditransitive, the indirect object may be retained while the direct object is omitted. In that case the only object present is the indirect object:

Bob is teaching *the older children*.
You can pay *me* instead.

(d) SEMANTIC PROPERTIES

(i) The direct object typically refers to an entity that is affected by the action denoted in the clause (*cf* 10.19, but *cf* also 10.27*ff*):

Norman smashed *a window in his father's car*.

(ii) The indirect object typically refers to an animate being that is the recipient of the action (*cf* 10.19, but *cf* also 10.32).

Note [a] We do not, as some do, apply the term 'indirect object' to the corresponding prepositional phrases (*eg*: *for me* in *Pour a drink for me*), though we use the term 'prepositional object' for the complement in such phrases (*cf* 16.56, 16.60). Some apply the term 'direct object' to an indirect object if it is the only object (*eg*: *you* in *I'll show you* or *his children* in *He's teaching his children*). Others again apply the term 'object' exclusively to the first (or only) object.

[**b**] Speakers vary in their acceptance of *wh*-questions in which the *wh*-interrogative pronoun replaces an indirect object. The corresponding prepositional phrase is fully acceptable:

?*Who* did the detective show his badge?

~ *Who* did the detective show his badge *to*?

~ *To whom* did the detective show his badge? ⟨formal⟩

Similar variation applies to relative clauses:

?The person I sent the book has not acknowledged receiving it.

~ The person I sent the book *to* has not acknowledged receiving it.

~ The person *to whom* I sent the book has not acknowledged receiving it. ⟨formal⟩

It also applies to retained indirect objects in passive clauses:

?No reply has been given *me*.

~ No reply has been given *to me*.

Retained indirect objects are generally restricted to pronouns.

All three constructions have been exemplified by indirect objects with corresponding prepositional phrases introduced by *to*. The constructions are less acceptable with other correspondences (*eg*: *for*-phrases) or no correspondences.

[**c**] In instances where the passive is inapplicable because the object is a clause, we can test for the presence of an object by adding a coordinate clause with a pro-form and making the second clause passive.

I asked whether he was there and his parents asked *that* too.

~ *That* was asked by his parents.

[**d**] The identity of the direct object can be tested in an independent declarative clause through a *wh*-question with *who* or *what*; fronting of the *wh*-item and subject–operator inversion are required:

The buzzer signals *the end of the game* [O_d].

~ *What* [O_d] *does* [op] *the buzzer* [S] signal?

On the difficulty of applying this test to the indirect object, *cf* Note [b] above.

Complement: subject and object

10.8 Both complements are in a copular relationship with another clause element. The subject complement relates to the subject, and the verb is copular (*cf* 16.21*ff*):

My glass is *empty*. [1]

Their daughter has become *an accountant*. [2]

The object complement relates to the direct object:

We find them *very pleasant*. [3]

Carol made Joshua and Peter *her assistants*. [4]

The implied relationship between the object and the object complement can be expressed by means of a corresponding *SVC* sentence with a copular verb, *be* if the object complement is a current attribute and *become* if it is a resulting attribute (*cf* 10.20):

They are *very pleasant*. [3a]

Joshua and Peter became *her assistants*. [4a]

(a) FORM

The complement is normally a noun phrase or an adjective phrase, but it may also be a nominal clause (*cf* 15.4*ff*). It is a defining characteristic of complements, in contrast to objects, that they may be adjective phrases.

(b) POSITION

The subject complement normally follows the subject and the verb. The object complement normally follows the direct object. (But *cf* 11.15, 11.31, 18.20*ff*, 18.37).

(c) SYNTACTIC FUNCTION

(i) If it is a noun phrase, the subject complement normally has concord of number with the subject, and the object complement normally has concord of number with the direct object (but *cf* 10.46). Contrast [2] and [4].

(ii) If it is a reflexive pronoun, the subject complement has concord of number, person and, where relevant, gender with the subject:

She is not *herself* today.

(iii) Unlike the object, the complement cannot become the subject of a corresponding passive clause. There is no corresponding passive clause for the *SVC* type. With the *SVOC* type, the direct object can of course be made the subject of a passive clause:

His friends call him *Ted*. [*Ted* is C_o] [5]
~He is called *Ted* by his friends. [*Ted* is C_s] [5a]

The object complement becomes the subject complement in the passive clause.

(iv) The complement can be questioned, but there is no one general way of doing so (*cf* 11.5 Note [e], 11.15 Note [i]).

(v) If the subject complement is a pronoun, there is a distinction between subjective and objective forms; the subjective form is more prevalent in formal use (especially in AmE):

This is *he*. ⟨formal⟩ That's *him*.

(d) SEMANTIC PROPERTIES

The complement typically identifies or characterizes the referent of the clause element to which it is related (*cf* 10.20).

Note [**a**] With some verbs, object complements can be omitted (*cf* 16.44*ff*):

We appointed her *our delegate to the convention*. ~We appointed her.
They have named their baby *Roger*. ~They have named their baby.

[**b**] The object complement cannot be the normal reflexive pronoun, but it can have a corresponding form with *self/selves*:

I prefer George *his normal self*. I did not find them *their usual selves*.

Adverbial

10.9 Adverbials are the most diverse of the clause elements, and we therefore distinguish several major types (*cf* Chapter 8, 15.17*ff*).

(a) FORM

The adverbial is normally an adverb phrase, prepositional phrase, or adverbial clause. It may also be a noun phrase (*cf* 8.13).

(b) POSITION

In general, the adverbial is capable of occurring in more than one position in the clause. Constraints on its mobility depend on the type and form of the adverbial. The adverbial in the *SVA* type normally follows the subject and verb, and the adverbial in the *SVOA* type normally follows the direct object (*cf* 10.10, also 8.27). Other predication adjuncts (*cf* 8.34*f*, 15.22) normally appear at the end of the clause.

(c) SYNTACTIC FUNCTION

(i) Except for the obligatory adverbial in the *SVA* and *SVOA* types (*cf* 10.10), adverbials are optional: they may be added to or removed from the clause without affecting its acceptability and without affecting the relations of structure and meaning in the rest of the clause.

(ii) Other syntactic potentialities depend crucially on the type of adverbial. At the most general level, the adverbial may be characterized negatively: it does not have the syntactic features listed for the other clause elements (*cf* 10.6*ff*).

(d) SEMANTIC PROPERTIES

The adverbial refers to the circumstances of the situation (adjunct and subjunct), comments on the form or content of the clause (disjunct), or provides a link between clauses (conjunct). A more specific semantic characterization relates to the semantic subtypes of adverbials (*cf* Chapter 8 and 15.24*ff*).

Note The term 'adjunct' is sometimes applied by others to all types of adverbial.

Obligatory adverbials: subject-related and object-related adverbials

10.10 Obligatory adverbials are a subclass of predication adjuncts (*cf* 8.27) that belong to the *SVA* and *SVOA* types. Inasmuch as they are obligatory, they are central elements of the clause (*cf* 2.13), part of the clause nucleus. They may be adverb phrases, prepositional phrases, or adverbial clauses. In 10.11 we suggest that some obligatory adverb phrases and prepositional phrases may be analysed as complements, belonging to the *SVC* and *SVOC* types.

Obligatory adverbials are commonly required as complementation for the verb BE in the *SVA* type, but they are also found as complementation for other verbs. The adverbials in this type are subject-related. Many are space adjuncts that designate the position of the referent of the subject:

Your children are *outside*.
Our car isn't *in the garage*.
We are now living *in a small village*.
The plane's *off the ground*.
Dorothy is remaining *at Oxford*.
Sam is staying *at a nearby motel*.
Your scarf is lying *on the floor*.
The road begins *in Denver*.

Some express other types of space relations:

We got *off the train*.
We all got *into my car*.
I stole *into her room*.
All roads lead *to Rome*.
The lawn goes *all the way around the house*.
The hills extend *from here into the next county*.

Others express metaphorical extensions of space relations:

They're *into yoga*. ['are keen on yoga'] ⟨informal⟩
We got *into a heated argument*.
He's *off cigarettes*.

Time adjuncts commonly cooccur with an eventive subject (*cf* 10.25):

Their holiday extended *through the summer*.
The next meeting is *on Monday*.
The last performance was *at eight o'clock*.
The play lasts *for three hours*.

On the conditions for omitting the prepositions in the last three examples, *cf* 9.40*ff*.

We briefly exemplify other semantic types of obligatory adverbials in the SVA_s type:

The two eggs are *for you*.	[recipient, 9.46]
The drinks are *for the journey*.	[purpose, 9.45]
If fruit prices are higher this year, it's *because of the bad harvest*.	[reason, 9.44]
Transport to the mainland is *by ferry*.	[means, 9.49]
Entrance was *by special invitation only*.	[means]
Payment is *by cash only*.	[means]
Melvin's main interest is *in sport*.	[stimulus, 9.51]
Jack and Nora are *with me*.	[accompaniment, 9.52]
The painting was *by an unknown artist*.	[agent, 9.50]
How much is this jacket? It's *£60*.	[measure, 8.9]

The connection of subject-related adverbial with subject is parallel to that of subject complement with subject:

Ronald is *off cigarettes*. [S V A_s]
Ann is *happy*. [S V C_s]

Similarly, the connection of object-related adverbial to direct object parallels that of object complement with direct object:

We kept Ronald *off cigarettes*. [S V O_d A_o]
We kept Ann *happy*. [S V O_d C_o]

Here are examples of object-related adverbials:

I put the kettle *on the stove*. ['The kettle is now on the stove.']
They are placing the blame *on us*.
I'm keeping most of my money *in the bank*.
I stuck the wallet *in the drawer*.
He set the typewriter *on the table*.
You should have your hands *on the wheel*.
He directed his speech *at the workers*.
She wants the payment *in dollars*.

Like optional adverbials of the same semantic types, most obligatory adverbials can be questioned with *wh*-interrogative adverbials such as *where*, *when, how long, why*. The exceptions include the metaphorical extensions of space relations, but also the semantic relations of recipient, means, agent, stimulus, and accompaniment.

Note [**a**] In certain instances, a verb of motion is implied before the obligatory adverbials:

She asked them *in*. Truth will *out*. I let the cat *out*.
I'll show you *out*. I want you *inside*.

The construction with the intransitive verb is common in some varieties of colloquial AmE and Scottish English, especially with *want*:

The dog wants *out*. I want *off* at Sixth Street.

[**b**] The obligatory manner adverbial with *behave* in *He's behaving badly* is related to the subject, though we do not have a corresponding sentence with the copula (**He is badly*) because of the adverb form. We similarly lack corresponding sentences when the prepositional phrase begins with directional *into*, as in *We all got into my car*, though we have the metaphorical informal *They're into yoga*. Compare also the metaphorical *They're on to his machinations* ['aware of'].

[**c**] The obligatory manner adverbial in *They treated him badly* seems to be related both to the subject ('They are behaving badly.') and to the object ('He is in a bad way.').

Gradience and multiple analysis

Prepositional phrases and adverbs as complement

10.11 Some clause structures and clause elements can be analysed in more than one way. In this and the following sections we examine instances that are best treated through gradience and multiple analysis (*cf* 2.60*f*).

The distinction between obligatory adjunct and complement is not clear-cut for all prepositional phrases. Some prepositional phrases are semantically similar to adjective or noun phrases functioning as complement:

They were *out of breath*. ~ They were breathless.
That is *of no importance*. ~ That is unimportant.
He is *under suspicion*. ~ He is a suspect.
She is *in good health*. ~ She is healthy.
They are not *at ease*. ~ They are not relaxed.

More importantly, such prepositional phrases can be coordinated with, or placed in apposition with, adjective phrases that undoubtedly function as complement:

She is young and *in good health*.
They were *out of breath* and extremely tired.
They are not *at ease*, *ie* not relaxed.

Furthermore, unlike clear instances of obligatory adjuncts, they can be used as complementation for copular verbs other than BE, a characteristic of adjective phrases functioning as subject complement:

They appear *out of breath*.
That seems *of no importance*.
She feels *in good health*.

Here are other examples of prepositional phrases functioning as subject complement:

They are *in love.*
We're *over the worst.*
The demonstration got *out of hand.*
He feels *at home.*
That child seems *in trouble.*
I don't feel *up to it.*
The house seems *in good condition.*
He sounds *in great danger.*

We similarly find prepositional phrases functioning as object complement:

They put me *at my ease.* ['I'm at my ease.']
I don't consider myself *at risk.*
He didn't feel himself *at home.*
She didn't want me *in any danger.*
He imagined himself *on the point of death.*
I found him *in trouble.*

Some adverbs can also be complements:

The milk seems *off.* ['sour'] ⟨informal⟩
The performance is *over.*
In technology we are *ahead.*
I am *behind* in my rent.
The television is still *on.*
He imagined himself *ahead.*
I declare this meeting *over.*
They let us *off.*

The adverbs and prepositional phrases that function as complement are metaphorically related to space adverbials. Unlike the latter, however, they cannot be questioned by adverbial *where.* Contrast in this respect:

A: Where are they? B: { They're *out of town.*
*They're *out of breath.* }

On the other hand, *how* may be used in some instances to question these complements, as it is for adjective phrases functioning as complement:

A: How does she feel? B: { She feels *very happy.*
She feels *in good health.* }

Note [**a**] Speakers may vary in particular instances as to whether a copular verb other than BE is acceptable; for example, in *I'm on time* (*cf: I'm early*) or *You're on your own* (*cf: You're alone*). Contrast: (?)*I seem on time* and, with *look* as a copular verb, (?)*You look on your own.*
[**b**] *Off* in *The milk is off* has moved into the adjective class for those who accept its premodification by *very.*
[**c**] There may be semantic differences between prepositional phrases and parallel adjective phrases. For example, *She is healthy* suggests a more permanent condition than *She is in good health.*

Particles and clause types

10.12 We have so far considered the verb element as realized only by a verb phrase.

That assumption requires us to analyse [1] as SVA, with *looked* as verb and *into the recent complaints* as adverbial:

The board looked into the recent complaints. [1]

But there are also grounds for analysing *looked into* as the verb, parallel to *investigated* in:

The board investigated the recent complaints. [2]

In that case *the recent complaints* would be direct object in both [1] and [2]. One of the reasons for the alternative analysis is the possibility of making *the recent complaints* the subject of a corresponding passive clause:

The recent complaints were looked into by the board. [1a]

Another is that *the recent complaints* can be questioned by a *what*-question, whereas *into the recent complaints* cannot be so questioned:

What did the board look into?
*What did the board look?

This alternative analysis views combinations of verbs and particles (whether the particles are prepositions or adverbs) as multi-word verbs. Examples can be found for six of the seven major clause types, the exception being type *SVOA*. We here give an example of each type, with the verb element (sometimes discontinuous) indicated in italics:

(1) *SV*	The soldiers *gave in*.
(2) *SVO*	Randolph is *paying for* the meal.
(3) *SVC*	It *turned out* a huge success.
(4) *SVA*	We are *putting up* at a motel.
(5) *SVOO*	They *spoke to* us *about* the problem.
	They *provided* her *with* everything she needed.
(6) *SVOC*	They *looked on* me *as* their role model.
	They *mistook* him *for* the new supervisor.

For this alternative analysis, *cf* 16.2*ff*.

Note [**a**] A similar multi-word analysis can be posited for verb-plus-adjective combinations (*make clear, cut short*) and for combinations of verb plus noun phrase plus preposition (*make fun of, put a stop to*) (*cf* 16.17, 16.58). Compare also *take a look at, give a jump* (10.30).

[**b**] Some particles provide obligatory complementation for the verb in the *SV* type, in that the verb otherwise cannot be used intransitively (*make up, give in*). Others are required for the *SVO* type (*look at, listen to*). Similarly, while *consider* can be used with or without the particle *as* in the *SVOC* type – *I consider them* (*as*) *acquaintances* – other verbs require a particle for this type, *eg*: *regard as, mistake for*. In a pattern with close analogies (*cf* 16.56*f*), a few verbs in the *SVOO* type have alternatives in which one of the objects requires a particle: *She blamed us for the failure, She blamed the failure on us*.

[**c**] In a sentence such as *I won't put up with such nonsense*, the multi-word verb is *put up with* and is monotransitive under this analysis, *such nonsense* being a direct object. In *They put the mistake down to my inexperience*, the analysis is less clear. We might consider the multi-word verb to be *put down to*, in which case the verb is ditransitive with two objects. We can support that analysis by noting that *wh*-pronominal questions apply for both noun phrases: *What do they put down to my inexperience?*; *What do they put the mistake down to?* On the other hand, only the first noun

phrase can be made subject of a corresponding passive: *The mistake was put down to my inexperience*. Furthermore, the indirect object in a ditransitive construction normally has personal reference, the exceptions occurring only when it takes an affected role (*cf* 10.32), but here neither noun phrase is personal. If we still wish to treat *put down to* as a multi-word verb, we must consider both noun phrases as direct objects; we should perhaps do the same for *They ascribed the mistake to my inexperience*, *ascribe to* being the multi-word verb, since both noun phrases here too may be questioned by *what*.

Extent and measure phrases: object or adverbial

10.13 Noun phrases of measure after certain verbs denoting measure and phrases of extent in space are indeterminate between direct object and adverbial:

EXTENT	MEASURE
He ran *a mile*.	It costs *ten dollars*.
I hobbled *a few feet*.	In length it measures *seven feet*.
She jumped *ten feet*.	It weighed *almost a ton*.

Both types do not generally permit the passive, but we occasionally find the extent phrase as passive subject in a generic sentence:

A mile can't be run in two minutes.

Both types allow adverbial questions:

How far did he run? *How much* does it cost?

But the measure phrases can also be questioned by *what*:

What does it cost?

The adverbial question indicates that the structure is SVA. On the other hand, the pronominal question and the possibility of passivization are indications that the structure is SVO. One further difference between the two types is that the measure phrases are obligatory complementation.

Note [**a**] If the phrases other than those of extent follow motion verbs, passivization is generally possible and the phrases can only be questioned by *what*; the structure is therefore SVO (*cf* 10.27):

The French team climbed *the mountain*. ~The mountain was climbed by the French team.

In some cases, passivization is possible only if the agentive *by*-phrase is absent:

Once that corner was turned, the road was easy to drive on.

[**b**] The indeterminacy applies also to some clauses in the *SVOO* pattern which allow both the *What* and *How much* questions, though they also allow the passive:

She charged me *twenty dollars*. I paid her *three pounds*.

In *I bet him a large sum that the horse would win*, we have either three objects (the first of which is O_i) or two objects and an adverbial (*a large sum*).

Middle verbs

10.14 A small group of apparently transitive verbs, the most common of which is *have*, normally occur only in the active. They are all stative relational verbs, and therefore normally do not occur in the progressive (but *cf* Note [c]):

Jack doesn't *possess* a life insurance policy. [*A life insurance policy isn't possessed by Jack.]

They *have* a small house.
Dennis *lacks* confidence.
Will this course *suit* them?
This dress doesn't *become* you.
The coat doesn't *fit* me.
Five times six *equals* thirty.

Because of their other characteristics (*cf* 10.7) these could be considered transitive verbs complemented by a direct object. Notice, for example, that the noun phrase following the verb requires the objective form in pronouns that have that form. On the other hand, the verbs are sometimes treated as a special class termed MIDDLE VERBS. The final element may then be assigned a general term such as VERB COMPLEMENT. The same analysis may be extended to clauses that contain obligatory measure phrases (*cf* 10.13).

Note [**a**] For most speakers, *resemble* is a middle verb; for some it can occur in the passive:

(?)Geoffrey is resembled by his eldest child.

[**b**] *Strike. . . as* in *She struck me as happy* and *consist of* in *The group consists of ten men and eight women* cannot occur in the passive, and therefore may also be considered middle verbs.

[**c**] *Marry* is a middle verb in the sense 'enter into a marriage', but it is dynamic and can therefore occur in the progressive:

My sister *is marrying* Ron.

Marry in the senses 'give in marriage' (more usually *marry off*) or 'perform the marriage ceremony for' is a transitive verb occurring in the passive:

David and Judith *are marrying off* their eldest son next week.
Father Brown *will be marrying* Ron and Joan.

Adverbial forms as subject

10.15 The subject is normally realized by a noun phrase or a nominal clause. In certain restricted contexts (all informal) prepositional phrases, adverbs, and adverbial clauses – all of which normally realize the adverbial element in the clause – function as subject. Two conditions allow this use of adverbials:

(i) the adverbial is a fragment of an understood clause (*cf* 15.16), or
(ii) the sentence can be related to one with prop *it* (*cf* 10.26):

Slowly is exactly how he speaks. ['Speaking slowly is exactly how . . .']
Out on the lake will be splendid. ['A trip out on the lake will be splendid']
Whenever you are ready will be fine. ['It will be fine whenever . . .'; *cf*: *Sunday will be fine*, 10.26]
Will *after the show* be soon enough?
Because Sally wants to leave doesn't mean that we have to.

Note [**a**] An adverb may be subject in the stereotyped construction with the predicate *does it*:

Carefully } *does it.*
Slowly }
Gently }

Easy may be subject in this construction too; although it has the same form as the adjective, it is presumably an adverb in this stereotyped construction. Compare *easy* in other stereotyped constructions: *Easy come, easy go*; *Take it easy*; *Go easy on . . .*

In this construction we cannot substitute a prepositional phrase (* *With great care does it*) or change the form of the verb (**Carefully did it*).

[**b**] *Today, yesterday*, etc regularly function as subject. But these are on the gradient from adverb to noun. Clauses such as *Today will be fine* illustrate blurring of nominal and adverbial functions.

The sentence is ambiguous between 'Today, the time you stipulated, will be a suitable time' and 'The weather will be fine today'.

Subject complement or verbless clause

10.16 There is a gradient relating the functional categories of complement and adverbial. The copula at its purest, *ie* a verb having merely a linking function, is the verb BE. Other copular verbs combine pure linking function with other meanings. For example, *become* has a resultative meaning, *grow* (*He grew angry*) usually adds a notion of gradual change, and *look* (*She looked happy*) adds a notion of inference from appearance.

The element following the verb is clearly a complement if the verb can acceptably be replaced by *be* with the final element retaining its sense and if the verb cannot be intransitive. Thus *very quiet* in *He became very quiet* is a complement because we can have *He was very quiet* and we cannot have **He became*. The final element is a complement also when the verb cannot be intransitive in the same sense. Thus *very quiet* in *He grew very quiet* is a complement, since we cannot have *He grew* in the same sense.

At the other extreme of the gradient, the final element is a verbless clause with adverbial status where the independence of the construction is marked by intonation or punctuation:

> He waited, *anxious for a reply*. ['He waited', 'He was anxious for a reply.']
> She was standing, *a picture of innocence*.

Here, we can substitute *be*, but the verb retains its full sense without the final element. The adverbial status of the final element is shown by the possibility of omitting it without affecting the acceptability of the sentence. Adverbial status is confirmed when the element can readily be fronted:

> *Anxious for a reply*, he waited.

Along the gradient from that extreme, we find similar instances without intonation or punctuation separation:

> He died *a poor man*. ['He was a poor man when he died.']
> They married *young*.
> He came in *drunk*.
> They parted *good friends*.

Further along the gradient we find greater collocational restrictions between the final element and the verb, *ie* fewer adjective or noun phrases can provide complementation for the verb, showing a closer connection between the final element and the verb. The first set readily allows omission of the final element without affecting the meaning of the verb:

> The fire is burning *low*.
> The sun shone *bright*.
> He blushed *scarlet*.
> The door banged *shut*.

In the second set, complementation of the verb is more usually required in the same sense:

The weather is continuing *mild*.
They are pleading *guilty*.
This detergent washes *whiter*.

We come next to instances where the verb cannot be intransitive, at least in the same sense. These are more clearly copular verbs, with the final element as subject complement. Some verbs are restricted in the complements they allow, restricted either syntactically (to adjective phrases only or to noun phrases only) or collocationally (to a relatively few lexical items) or in both respects:

Jane will make *a good doctor*.
The children are going *hungry*.
They turned *conservative*.
Bob's explanation doesn't ring *true*.
Your hands feel *cold*.
The room smells *musty*.
Mary fell *silent*.
Dan's hair is wearing *thin*.
The well ran *dry*.

Some verbs are somewhat less restricted, though noun phrases are less usual in AmE:

She seemed *the right choice*. [also: *She seemed to be the right choice*.]
Max appears *upset*. [also: *Max appears to be upset*.]
Nora looked *sober*.

The verbs *become* and *remain* are closest to the pure copula in that they impose no restrictions on the choice of the complement.

Note [**a**] In this section we are concerned with adjective and noun phrases functioning as complement or as adverbial. The distinction between adjective and adverb is discussed in 7.6*ff*.

[**b**] In some idiomatic collocations the final element may be considered a complement even though we cannot readily replace the verb with BE and retain a similar sense-relationship; for example, *His jokes fell flat*.

[**c**] Verbless adverbial clauses realized solely by adjective phrases can follow subject complements (type *SVC*):

They are happier *free*. He will be no use *dead*.

They can also follow other clause types:

We took a swim *naked*. She ran the business *single-handed*.	[type *SVO*]
She gave us our coffee *black*.	[type *SVOO*]
He came home *miserable*.	[type *SVA*]
They sent him home *sober*.	[type *SVOA*]

While the implied subject of the verbless clause is usually the subject of the superordinate clause, it can also be the direct object, as two of these sentences demonstrate ('Our coffee was black', 'He was sober').

[**d**] The verbless clause can often be preposed, a further indication of its adverbial status (*cf* further 15.58*ff*).

He drove the damaged car home *completely undismayed*.
~ *Completely undismayed*, he drove the damaged car home.

[**e**] In the rare pattern SVO_iC_s, we have a combination of optional indirect object with subject complement: *He made her a good husband* ['He was a good husband for her.'].

Order of clause elements

10.17 The order of the clause elements is relatively fixed, in general following the sequence in the designation of the clause types (*SVC*, *SVOO*, etc). But a number of factors may interfere with the order:

(a) Optional adverbials may intervene between the elements in the clause pattern. Although most multi-word adverbials occur finally, certain types of adverbials realized by adverbs or short prepositional phrases regularly occur medially (*cf* 8.23); and initial position is typical for conjuncts:

Does it *often* rain in London?
You have *perhaps* heard the story before.
They may *in fact* be at home now.
On the other hand, we aren't going either.
In any case, why should I make the first move?

(b) The basic order is that of the canonical declarative clause. But the order may be affected by variations in the syntactic form of the clause:

(i) In *yes–no* questions, the operator precedes the subject (*cf* 11.5):

Have [op] *you* [S] heard from Roger?

(*cf* 12.49*f* for elliptical questions such as *You seen Roger?*)

(ii) In *wh*-questions, the questioned part (the *wh*-interrogative or the whole phrase of which it is a constituent) and the operator precede the subject, if the questioned part is not identical with the subject (*cf* 11.14*ff*):

What [O_d] *did* [op] *they* [S] tell you?
Where [A] *are* [op] *you* [S] staying?

(iii) In relative clauses, the relative word or the whole phrase of which it is a constituent precedes the subject if it is not itself the subject (*cf* 17.10*ff*):

I know the food *that* [O_d] *they* [S] like.
Can you please show me the room *where* [A] *the lecture* [S] is being held?
This is the friend *about whom* [A] *you* [S] have heard so much.

Contrast, with the relative item as subject:

Let me introduce you to someone *who* [S] has been wanting to meet you for a long time.

(iv) In exclamative sentences, the *what*- or *how*-phrase precedes the subject, except in the rare instances where the *what*-phrase is identical with the subject (*cf* 11.31*f*):

What a good time [O_d] *we* [S] had!   *How polite* [C_s] *they* [S] are!

(v) Second-person imperative sentences normally have no expressed subject (*cf* 11.24*ff*):

Show [V] *me* [O_i] *your paper* [O_d] *now* [A].

(c) Considerations of informational highlighting and emphasis may prompt the movement of elements from their normal position, usually to initial or final position (*cf* 18.20*ff*):

That question [O_d] I won't answer. *In* [A] you go.
Sheila wants to leave, and so does *Henry* [S]. Here comes *Ethel* [S].

(d) A longer element in the predication, particularly if it is a clause, tends to be placed after a shorter element (*cf* 18.37*f*):

The discovery has made *possible* [C_o] *new techniques for brain surgery* [O_d].
She told *him* [O_i] *calmly* [A] *what she thought of him* [O_d].

(e) It is stylistically preferable for the part following the verb to be longer than the part preceding it (*cf* 18.39):

A petition [S] was circulated [V] *asking for a longer lunch break* [S].

In this example the subject is *a petition asking for a longer lunch break*, but the postmodifier of *a petition* is placed after the verb.

Note [**a**] A study of part of the Brown Corpus revealed that in 9 out of 10 cases the subject was immediately followed by the verb in clauses containing both S and V, and the verb was immediately followed by the direct object in clauses containing both V and O_d.
[**b**] For the alternative BrE order in which the direct object precedes the indirect object (*eg*: *She gave it me*), *cf* 18.38 Note [a].

Semantic roles of clause elements

Participants

10.18 In terms of meaning, every clause describes a situation in which a number of participants are involved. By PARTICIPANTS we understand entities realized by noun phrases, whether such entities are concrete or abstract. Thus, we have three participants in:

John found *a good spot* for *the magnolia tree*.

The sentence *The child tore my book* contains a verb describing the nature of the action, a subject denoting an agentive participant (the agent or doer of the action), and a direct object denoting an affected participant.

Clause elements denote semantic roles in the situation apart from the participants. Thus, the verb – or the copular verb in combination with a complement – is the primary device for distinguishing situation types as stative or dynamic and as subtypes of these two types (*cf* 4.27*ff* and the summary in *Fig* 4.27). The subject complement and the object complement denote attributes of the subject and direct object respectively. Adverbials denote such circumstances of the situation as time, place, and manner of action, express the speaker's evaluation of the situation, or provide logical connections across clauses or sentences.

Analysis of participant roles has not achieved a general consensus, nor has it fully explored all distinctions. Our description must therefore be considered tentative.

Note [a] The term CASE is often used for participant roles. This semantic use of the term is to be distinguished from its use as a grammatical category realized (usually through inflections) in varying forms of nouns and pronouns (*cf* 5.112*ff*, 6.1*ff*).
[b] We do not deal in this chapter with the semantics of adverbials or of subordinate clauses in general. See Chapter 9 for prepositional phrases, Chapter 8 for adverbials, and Chapters 14 and 15 for subordinate clauses.

Agentive, affected, and recipient roles

10.19 The most typical semantic role of a subject in a clause that has a direct object is that of the AGENTIVE participant: that is, the animate being instigating or causing the happening denoted by the verb:

Margaret is mowing the grass.

The most typical role of the direct object is that of the AFFECTED participant: a participant (animate or inanimate) which does not cause the happening denoted by the verb, but is directly involved in some other way:

Many MPs criticized *the Prime Minister*.
James sold *his digital watch* yesterday.

The most typical role of the indirect object is that of the RECIPIENT participant: *ie* of the animate being that is passively implicated by the happening or state:

I've found *you* a place. We paid *them* the money.

Note [a] Other terms used for AFFECTED are PATIENT and OBJECTIVE. Another term for RECIPIENT is DATIVE.
[b] Some distinguish a benefactive or beneficiary role ('intended recipient') from the recipient role:

I've found *you* a place. She made *her son* a scarf.

The benefactive indirect object is paraphrasable by a *for*-phrase:

I've found a place *for you*. She made a scarf *for her son*.

The two roles can cooccur in the same clause if the benefactive role is expressed by a *for*-phrase:

She gave *me* a scarf *for her son*.

[c] Although *I've found a place for the magnolia tree* and *I've found a place for Mrs Jones* appear to be equivalent utterances, only the second can be transformed into a clause with indirect object: *I've found Mrs Jones a place*, not ?*I've found the magnolia tree a place*. This is because the magnolia tree is not animate and therefore does not qualify for the recipient role (*cf* also 8.32).

Attribute

10.20 The typical semantic role of a subject complement and an object complement is that of ATTRIBUTE. We can distinguish two subtypes of role for the attribute: identification and characterization:

IDENTIFICATION:

Kevin is *my brother*.
Brenda became *their accountant*.
His response to the reprimand seemed *a major reason for his dismissal*.
Henry's room is *the one next to mine*.

CHARACTERIZATION:

Dwight is *an honest man*.
Martha was *a good student*.
The operation seemed *a success*.
The soup is *too hot*.
Daniel remains *helpful*.

Three syntactic features are associated with this semantic distinction:

(a) Only identification attributes normally allow reversal of subject and complement without affecting the semantic relations in the clause, if the copula is BE:

Kevin is *my brother*. ~ *My brother* is Kevin.

If the copula is other than BE we can test for reversal by substituting BE.

(b) Only characterization attributes can also be realized by adjective phrases.

(c) Identification attributes are normally associated with definite noun phrases. Noun phrases used as characterization attributes are normally indefinite.

The same semantic distinction applies to object complements. The subject–complement reversal cannot take place, but we can test for its possibility by forming a clause from the object and the complement.

I made Maurice *my assistant*.
~ Maurice is *my assistant*.
~ *My assistant* is Maurice.

IDENTIFICATION:

They called their daughter *Edna*.
She considers Susan *her role model*.
We made John *our representative*.

CHARACTERIZATION:

The teacher called their daughter *a good student*.
I consider the operation *a success*.
She made them *comfortable*.

We can further subdivide attributes into current or existing attributes (normally with verbs used statively) and resulting attributes, resulting from the event described by the verb (with verbs used dynamically) (*cf* 16.21*f*). Here are examples of the distinction for both subject and object complements:

CURRENT ATTRIBUTE:

He's *my brother*.
He seems *unhappy*.
We lay *quiet*.
We felt *cold*.
She remained *silent*.
I want my food *hot*.
I prefer my coffee *black*.
They consider me *their closest friend*.

RESULTING ATTRIBUTE:

We became *restless*.
He turned *traitor*.
He felt *ill*.
She'll make *a good worker*.
They elected him *president*.
The heat turned the milk *sour*.
He drives me *mad*.

Note [**a**] If the identification attribute is a noun phrase with an optionally omitted determiner, subject–complement reversal cannot occur:

Joan is *president of the company.*

Contrast:

Joan is *the president of the company.* ~ *The president of the company* is Joan.

[**b**] A subject complement may be realized by a genitive noun phrase:

That writing must be *Tom's.*	[subjective genitive]	[1]
That newspaper is *mine.*	[possessive genitive]	[2]
The idea was *Kathy's.*	[genitive of attribute]	[3]

The phrases express various genitive meanings (*cf* 5.116). In [1] the complement has the agentive role (*cf: That writing must be by Tom*), in [2] and [3] the role of recipient (*cf: That newspaper belongs to me*; *Kathy had that idea*).

[**c**] The notion of characterization extends to various measure and extent phrases:

Now she is *thirteen* (*years old*). The paperback is *three dollars.*
He is *six foot* (*tall*). The envelope is *one ounce.*

Similar to these are expressions that denote time or period:

It's *five o'clock.* I'm *your age.* The house is *seventeenth century.* ['seventeenth-century style']

Subject as external causer, instrument, and affected

10.21 We now turn to the roles of the subject, apart from its typical role as agentive (*cf* 10.19).

The subject sometimes has the role of EXTERNAL CAUSER; that is, it expresses the unwitting (generally inanimate) cause of an event:

The avalanche destroyed several houses. *The electric shock* killed him.

It may also have the role of INSTRUMENT; that is, the entity (generally inanimate) which an agent uses to perform an action or instigate a process:

A stone broke his glasses.
A car knocked them down.
The computer has solved the problem.

With intransitive verbs, the subject also frequently has the AFFECTED role elsewhere typical of the direct object:

Jack fell down (accidentally). *The pencil* was lying on the table.

The term 'affected' has been extended generally to subjects of copular verbs:

The pencil was on the table.

But we can make some further distinctions within the affected role for subjects according to whether the subject complement as attribute identifies or characterizes (*cf* 10.20). Thus, the subject is IDENTIFIED in [1] and CHARACTERIZED in [2]:

Kevin is my brother. [1]
Martha was a good student. [2]

The assignment of the affected role to the subject of an intransitive verb seems clearest when there is a corresponding transitive verb with which the same noun phrase is a direct object in the affected role:

I am frying *the fish.* [O_d as affected] [3]
The fish is frying. [S as affected] [3a]

We can also make [3] passive:

The fish is being fried. [S as affected] [3b]

But there is a difference between [3a] and [3b]: [3a] focuses on the process, without implying (as in the passive) human agency. In being given the subject function, *the fish* acquires a status that appears to assign it some responsibility for the process. Hence, there is greater constraint on what can appear as subject in the intransitive construction than in the corresponding passive construction. Contrast:

We raised *an alarm*.
~ *An alarm* was raised.
≁ **An alarm* rose.

In certain intransitive constructions, an adverbial is generally required:

Her books translate *well*.
The sentence reads *clearly*.
My shirts have dried *very quickly*.
The sheets washed *easily*.
My teapot pours *without spilling*.

The adverbial imputes a characteristic to the referent of the subject ('Her books are of the type that are good in translation'). The construction therefore does not correspond to a transitive construction. For example, *Tom translates her books well* imputes the characteristic to Tom and not to the books ('He is a good translator of her books'). The same imputation applies even when an adverbial, though usual, may be omitted. Thus *My books sell well* implies that the selling well is not being necessarily ascribed to the effect of an agent of the selling.

In some cases the *SV* clause may diverge from a corresponding SVO_d clause when an optional adverbial is added if an agent is required only for the initiation of the action:

The water is boiling *vigorously*.
≠ Someone is boiling the water *vigorously*.
The water has been boiling *for five minutes*.
≠ Someone has been boiling the water *for five minutes*.

The boundary between agentive and affected subjects depends on whether an element of causation or volition is present. Some verbs allow both interpretations: *Suddenly he jumped* might suggest an involuntary action (*eg* after being stung by a wasp) or a deliberate one. A purpose adverbial (*eg: in order to attract attention*) or a volitional adverbial (*eg: deliberately, on purpose*) can be added only to the agentive type. The subject must be agentive in, for example, *Jack fell down on purpose*.

One of the reasons for distinguishing the roles is that we generally cannot coordinate subjects with different roles. We can say *The gamekeeper wounded him* (agentive subject) and *A gun wounded him* (instrumental subject), but not **The gamekeeper and a gun wounded him*. Coordination is possible if two events are involved, as in the combination of external causer and agentive in *Hurricanes and marauding bands devastated the region* (*at different times*). On the other hand, when an instrument or external causer is the subject of a transitive verb it acquires metaphorically some notion of agency. We can therefore occasionally find combinations where the same event seems to be involved: *Clumsy musicians and poor instruments (together) spoiled the performance of the symphony.*

Note [a] The role of external causer has also been termed 'force'.

[b] The tendency towards a metaphorical perception of agentiveness in nonagentive subjects, as used in everyday language, is conspicuous in examples such as *Guns kill; Matches start fires; A car drove by; The door refused to open.*

[c] A different analysis allows more than one role for one element and allows for the repetition of the same role in one clause. In one such analysis, the external causer and affected roles can be combined with the agentive role. Here are examples of such an analysis:

Hurricanes [external causer] devastated the region [affected].
Marauding bands [agentive/external causer] devastated the region [affected].
The soldiers [agentive/external causer] paraded.
The warden [agentive/external causer] paraded the prisoners [agentive/affected].

Where two agentives cooccur in the same clause, the first has sometimes been distinguished as the 'initiator' of the action.

[d] The situation described with an agentive subject may be the result of an implied action: *She blew a fuse* ['She did something which caused a fuse to blow.'], *He burnt the food.*

[e] Animate subjects of copular verbs followed by an emotive complement might be assigned the role of 'experiencer':

The workers are angry. He is unhappy.

The same applies to animate subjects of certain transitive verbs used in nonvolitional sense:

I've hurt my knee. ['My knee is hurt.']

Here *I* is experiencer and *my knee* affected.

[f] In *The kettle's boiling*, the affected subject is related by metonymy to *The water's boiling.*

10.22 There is sometimes a regular relation, in terms of clause function, between transitive verbs expressing CAUSATIVE meaning and corresponding intransitive verbs or adjectives. In the first three groups below, the subject may be agent, external causer, or instrument; in the last group, it is agent.

(i) *SVO*	*SV*
Tom is cooking the dinner.	The dinner is cooking.
Geoffrey/The wind/My key opened the door.	The door opened.
Brenda is improving her writing.	Her writing is improving.
(ii) *SVO*	*SV*
Someone raised an arm.	An arm rose.
The frost has killed the flowers.	The flowers have died.
My axe has felled that tree.	That tree has fallen.
(iii) *SVO*	*SVC*
They have dimmed the lights.	The lights became dim.
The sun (almost) blinded him.	He (almost) went blind.
His manner angered me.	I got angry.
(iv) *SVO*	*SV*
The sergeant paraded the company.	The company paraded.
I am exercising my dog.	My dog is exercising.

While in many cases (Group (i)) the identical verb performs both transitive and intransitive roles without a change of form, in other cases (Group (ii)) the intransitive verb has to be replaced by another verb, which may resemble it in spelling and pronunciation. In Group (iii), an adjective X is matched by a causative verb (of the same, or slightly different, form) with the meaning to 'cause to be X'. Group (iv), on the other hand, shows that the subject of an intransitive verb may itself be agentive, in which case the switch to a causative construction may entail changing the role of the subject to affected. Thus, *He paraded the soldiers* does not necessarily imply any volition on the part of the soldiers; rather, it suggests the opposite.

In Groups (i–ii) the intransitive subject of the *SV* type generally has the affected role. In the sentence *The dinner is cooking*, however, *the dinner* is resultant, as in the object of *Tom is cooking the dinner* (*cf* 10.28). Other examples of resultant subject:

The cake is baking. *A new type of camera* is developing.

Note There are some triplets showing a combination of the relations in Groups (i) and (ii); *eg*: *open* (adjective); *open* (intransitive verb) [='become open']; *open* (transitive verb) [='cause to be open'].

Recipient subject

10.23 The subject may have a recipient role with verbs such as *have, own, possess, benefit* (*from*), as is indicated by the following relation:

Mr Smith has given his son a radio. [So now his son has a radio.]

The perceptual verbs *see* and *hear* also require a recipient subject, in contrast to *look at* and *listen to*, which are agentive. The other perceptual verbs *taste, smell*, and *feel* have both an agentive meaning corresponding to *look at* and a recipient meaning corresponding to *see*:

Foolishly, he tasted the soup. [1]
*Foolishly, he tasted the pepper in the soup. [1a]

The adverb *foolishly* requires the agentive; hence [1a], which can only be understood in a nonagentive manner, does not make sense. *The soup* in [2] has the affected role, just as in [1]:

The soup tasted good. [2]

Verbs indicating cognition or emotion may also require a recipient subject:

I thought you were mistaken. [*cf*: It seemed to me you were mistaken.]
I liked the play. [*cf*: The play pleased me/gave me pleasure.]

Normally, recipient subjects go with verbs used statively (*cf* 4.28*ff*). Some of them (notably *have* and *possess*) have no passive form (*cf* 10.14): *They have a beautiful house*, but not **A beautiful house is had by them.*

Note [a] A passive form of HAVE occasionally occurs in idioms: *A good time was had by all*; *Have you ever been had?* ⟨informal⟩ [=tricked; also with sexual meaning]. *Possess* has a passive in *He was possessed by the fear that she would leave him.*
[b] Alternatively, subjects with perceptual, cognitive, and emotive verbs might be assigned the role of 'experiencer' (*cf* 10.21 Note [e]).

Positioner subject

10.24 The subject may have the role of POSITIONER with intransitive stance verbs (*cf* 4.23) such as *sit, stand, lie, live* ['dwell'], *stay, remain*, and with transitive verbs related to stance verbs such as *carry*, *hold*, *keep*, *wear*. The transitive verbs are causative and the direct objects that follow them have an affected role. In this positioner role the participant is in control, but the situation is not resultative in that no change is indicated in the positioner during the period in which the situation lasts:

I have lived in London most of my life.
They are staying at a motel.
My friend is sitting in a chair near the door.
The hijacker was holding a revolver.
He kept himself upright.

Contrast the role of subjects in these two sentences:

Your sister [positioner] is lying on the bed. [stance]
Your book [affected] is lying on the bed. [state]

Note [**a**] As with the agentive type, a purpose adverbial (*to rest*) or a volitional adverbial (*reluctantly*) can be added to the positioner type.
[**b**] *Sit down* is a punctual verb. *Sit* may also be an action verb when it is used in the same sense as *sit down*, in which case the subject is agentive.
[**c**] Contrast the three uses of *hold* in these sentences:

Carol was holding a passenger's arm. [1]
They were holding the passengers against their will. [2]
Do *you* hold a British passport? [3]

In [1] *hold* ['keep in grasp'] is a transitive verb related to stance verbs and *Carol* is positioner; in [2], *hold* ['detain'] is an activity verb and *they* is agentive; and in [3] *hold* ['have'] is a verb denoting relation and *you* is recipient (*cf* 10.23). In *Mary held a New Zealand passport*, *hold* is ambiguous between the meanings in [1] and [3] and therefore *Mary* may be either positioner or recipient.

Locative, temporal, and eventive subjects

10.25 The subject may have the LOCATIVE role of designating the place of the state or action, or the TEMPORAL role of designating its time:

Los Angeles is foggy. ['It's foggy in Los Angeles.']
My tent sleeps four people. ['Four people can sleep in my tent.']
This path is swarming with ants. ['Ants are swarming all over this path.']
This jar contains coffee. ['There's coffee in this jar.']
Yesterday was a holiday. ['It was a holiday yesterday.']

Verbs following locative subjects normally have no passive or progressive form:

The bag holds seven pounds.
~ *Seven pounds are held by the bag.
~ *The bag is holding seven pounds.

An important role of the subject is EVENTIVE. The noun at the head of the noun phrase is commonly deverbal (*cf* App. I.47) or a nominalization (*cf* 17.51):

The match is tomorrow.
The Norman invasion took place in 1066.
The explosion caused many casualties.

The dispute over the inheritance lasted a decade.
There has been *an accident*.

Prop *it* subject

10.26 There are clauses in which no participant is required. In such cases, the subject function may be assumed by the 'prop' word *it* (*cf* 6.17), which has little or no semantic content.

Prop *it* mainly occurs in clauses signifying (a) time, (b) atmospheric conditions, and (c) distance:

(a) *time*

It's ten o'clock precisely.
It's very late.
It's our wedding anniversary next month.
It's already midnight.
It's Sunday tomorrow.

(b) *atmospheric conditions*

It's too windy in Chicago.
It's very hot in here.
Is it raining?
It's getting dark.
It was sunny yesterday.
It's freezing outside.

(c) *distance*

It's not very far to York.
It's a long way to Denver.
It's just one more stop to Toronto.
It's only a hundred miles from here to Philadelphia.

In many cases a clause with prop *it* subject corresponds to a clause in which a locative or temporal phrase is the subject (*cf* 10.25). The correspondence applies for the (a) set when the subject complement refers to a period of time and an adverbial is present that is a noun phrase:

It's Sunday tomorrow. [1]
~Tomorrow is Sunday. [1a]

Sentences [1] and [1a] differ from the seemingly analogous [2] and [2a]:

It's our wedding anniversary next month. [2]
~Next month is our wedding anniversary. [2a]

The difference is clearer for [1a] and [2a]. In [1a] *tomorrow* is identified as *Sunday*, the latter having the function of subject complement and the role of identifying attribute. In [2a], on the other hand, *next month* appears to be a fronted adverbial with consequent subject–verb inversion ('Our wedding anniversary takes place next month', *cf*: *Our wedding anniversary is in January*. ~ *In January is our wedding anniversary*.)

With one type of exception, the correspondence also applies for the (b) set when an adverbial is present that is a noun phrase or a prepositional phrase containing a noun phrase:

It's too windy in Chicago. ~ Chicago is too windy.
It was sunny yesterday. ~ Yesterday was sunny.

The exception is when the verb is not a copula (for example, *rain* or *snow*):

It's raining in Manchester. ≁ *Manchester is raining.

The correspondence generally applies for the (c) set:

It's not far to York.
~York is not far.
It's only a hundred miles from here to Philadelphia.
~Philadelphia is only a hundred miles from here.

The (c) set readily allows prepositional phrases as subject (*cf* 10.15):

To York is not very far.
From here to Philadelphia is only a hundred miles.

Note [**a**] Prop *it* has also been termed 'ambient' *it*, in accordance with the view that it has some generalized reference to the environment in a given context. Thus, we can use *it* for a more restricted environment in *It's too muddy to walk*. In clauses of time and weather the environment may be general and unspecified, but it may be specified by a locative or temporal phrase, as in *It was very chilly in my bedroom* or in some of the examples given above. Another term for prop *it* is 'expletive' *it*, the term indicating the view that this *it* merely fills a syntactic gap (that of subject) and is otherwise meaningless.
[**b**] On other uses of *it* as a personal pronoun, *cf* 6.15*f*. The prop subject *it* here should be distinguished from the anticipatory *it* of sentences like *It was a great pleasure to see you again* (*cf* 18.33*ff*), where *it* has cataphoric reference to a postponed clausal subject (*To see you again was a great pleasure*).

Locative object

10.27 We turn now to roles of the direct object. The most typical role of the direct object, that of the affected participant, has been mentioned in 10.19. The direct object may have a LOCATIVE role with such verbs as *walk*, *swim*, *pass*, *jump*, *turn*, *leave*, *reach*, *surround*, *cross*, *climb* (*cf* further examples in 9.31):

We walked *the streets*. ['We walked *through* the streets.']
She swam *the river*. ['She swam *across* the river.']
He passed *a cyclist*. ['He passed *by* a cyclist.']
The horse jumped *the fence*. ['The horse jumped *over* the fence.']

Superficially, these objects may seem to be adverbials with an omitted preposition (*cf*: *We stayed three days*, 9.40*ff*). In most cases their status as objects is clear, however, from their ability to assume subject role in a corresponding passive clause, *eg*: *The fence was jumped by the horse*.

Note [**a**] We should include here locative objects after such verbs as *occupy* and *inhabit*, where no preposition can be inserted:

We occupy *a spacious apartment*.
They had inhabited *the island* for over a century.

BrE may have a locative object after *visit*:

They are visiting *Amsterdam*.

AmE, on the other hand, restricts the direct object to personal reference, and requires *visit in* for places. In informal AmE, *visit with* is used in the meaning 'chat with':

I was *visiting with* Carol yesterday outside the bank.

[**b**] A related category of object consists of phrases of extent (*He ran a mile*; *cf* 10.13).

Resultant object

10.28 A RESULTANT object is an object whose referent exists only by virtue of the activity indicated by the verb:

Baird invented *television*.
John has painted *a new picture*.
I'm writing *a letter*.
They are designing *a new car*.
She made *a fire*.
I baked *a cake*.

With an agentive subject and an affected object, one may always capture part of the meaning of a clause (*eg*: *X destroyed Y*) by saying 'X did something to Y'; but this does not apply to a resultant object: *Baird invented television* does not imply 'Baird did something to television'. Contrast the affected object in *I'm digging the ground* with the resultant object in *I'm digging a hole*.

In one type of resultant object, the activity recreates the referent:

She acted *the part of Ophelia*. They are playing *the Egmont Overture*.

Note [a] Other terms for the resultant object are 'object of result' and 'effected object'.
[b] We should distinguish between *I baked a cake*, where *a cake* is resultant, and *I baked some potatoes*, where *some potatoes* is affected. Contrast similarly:
She cooked *a meal*. [resultant]
She cooked *some carrots*. [affected]
He's frying *an omelet*. [resultant]
He's frying *an egg*. [affected]
[c] In some cases it may be unclear whether the activity creates or recreates the referent:
Janet told me *a joke*.

Cognate object

10.29 A COGNATE object is similar to a resultant object in that it refers to an event indicated by the verb:

Chris will sing *a song* for us.
They fought *a clean fight*.
He died *a miserable death*.
She lived *a good life*.
He breathed *his last breath*.

In this type of object, the noun head is semantically and often morphologically related to the verb. The object can therefore not be considered a participant. Its semantic function is to repeat, wholly or partially, the meaning of the verb. Most cognate objects tend to convey a rather orotund style.

The noun is generally modified. The verb and the object are then equivalent to the verb and a corresponding adverbial:

They fought *a clean fight*. They fought *cleanly*.

Note [a] The object of *ran a race* might also be classed as a cognate object, although it is like a locative object in being replaceable by a prepositional phrase: *ran in a race*.
[b] There are rare cases in which it is the meaning of the subject that is presupposed by the verb: *The frost froze hard, Day dawned, The wind is blowing*.

Eventive object

10.30 A frequent type of object generally takes the form of a deverbal noun preceded by a common verb of general meaning, such as *do, give, have, make, take*. This EVENTIVE object (*cf* 10.25) is semantically an extension of the verb and bears the major part of the meaning. Compare:

They *are arguing*. [verb only]
They *are having an argument*. [verb + eventive object]

The more frequent eventive object can sometimes be related to a cognate object in that it substitutes for the major lexical meaning of the verb whereas the cognate object repeats the lexical meaning. Compare:

> They *fought for a long time*. [verb + adverbial]
> They *fought a long fight*. [verb + cognate object]
> They *had a long fight*. [verb + eventive object]

The construction with the eventive object provides greater weight than the corresponding *SV* type, especially if there are no optional adverbials, and is often preferred to the *SV* construction in informal English.

Some noun heads in eventive objects are not derived from verbs. For example there is no verb *effort*, although *an effort* is eventive in *I'm making an effort*, and whereas *work* in *He did some work* is deverbal, there is no related verb for *homework* in *He did some homework*; other examples: *have a game, have a haircut, make fun* (*of*), *make peace* (*with*), (*cf*: *make war* (*on*)).In some instances, the verb is not normally used intransitively: *I made a mistake/an attempt/a correction.* In other instances, the combination clearly does not have the same meaning as the verb alone, *eg*: *make love* (*to*), *take trouble* (*over*), *make a difference*. In a few instances, the combination has (or may have) a passive meaning, particularly with *have*:

> I had a fright. ['I was frightened.']
> The baby's having a bath. ['The baby is being bathed.']
> I'll have a shampoo, if I may. ['I want my hair to be shampooed.']
> He took offence at my remarks. ['He was offended by my remarks.']

Here are some common collocations of verb and eventive object where the noun heads in the object are derived from verbs:

DO	a dance	a left/right turn	a somersault
	a dive	a report	a translation
	a drawing	a sketch	some work

Verbal nouns are commonly used as objects, *eg*:

some cleaning	some repairing
some drawing	some sewing
some knitting	some thinking
some painting	some writing

GET a glance (at), a look (at), a shot at ⟨informal⟩, a view (of)

GIVE advice, an answer, a cheer, consideration (to), a cough, a cry, a definition, a description, encouragement, an explanation, help (to), a kick, a kiss, a laugh, a nod, permission, a push, a reply, a sigh, a smile, a wash, a wave

HAVE an argument, a bash ⟨informal⟩, a bath, a bite ⟨informal⟩, a chat ⟨informal⟩, a dream, a drink, an effect, a fight, a guess ⟨esp BrE⟩, a holiday ⟨esp BrE⟩, an influence (on/over), a lie down ⟨informal BrE⟩, a look (at), a meeting, a nap ⟨informal⟩, a quarrel, a rest, a seat, a shave, a shower, a sleep, a smoke, a swim, a talk, a taste, a walk, a wash

MAKE an accusation (against), an agreement (with), allowances (for), an attack (on), a bargain (with), a call (on), a choice, a comment, a contribution (to), a copy (of), a criticism (of), a decision, a discovery (that), an escape, a fuss, a guess, (an) inquiry (into/of), an impression (on), an improvement (on), an investigation (into/of), a note (of), an objection (to), an observation (that), an offer (that), a payment, a promise (that), a proposal (that), a recommendation (that), a reduction in, a reference to, a report (on), a request (that/for), a start, a suggestion, a turn, use of

OFFER an apology, one's resignation, a suggestion

PAY attention (to), a call (on), a visit (to)

PUT emphasis on, an end to, a question to, a stop to

TAKE a bath, a bite ⟨informal⟩, a breath, care (of), a dislike to, a dive, a drink, a glance (at), a guess, a look (at), a nap, (a) note (of), notice (of), offence (at), a photograph (of), pity (on), a rest, a risk, a seat, a shower, a shave, a sleep, a smoke, a swim, a vacation ⟨esp AmE⟩, a walk, a wash

It will be noticed that several noun phrases collocate with both *have* and *take*. In such cases, *have* is the typical British verb and *take* is the typical American verb.

Most of the subjects in clauses with an eventive object are agentive. But some are recipient (or experiencer, 10.21 Note [e]): *Bill got a view of the candidate*, *I had a wonderful dream*, *Sally took an instant dislike to the new tenant*. Others are affected: *Saul took a fall*, *The team has taken a beating*, *At the sudden noise Bob gave a jump*. The verbs *do*, *make*, *offer*, *pay*, and *put* always take agentive subjects.

Note [**a**] *Have* can more easily take an affected subject than *take*: *The baby's having a bath* (also in AmE), generally not ?**The baby's taking a bath*. *Do* and *make* overlap in the eventive objects they can take, but only *do* takes *-ing* verbal nouns.

[**b**] The verbs *vacation* ⟨esp AmE⟩ and *holiday* ⟨esp BrE⟩ are less usual than the expanded constructions.

[**c**] Contrast:

She gave a shriek. [an involuntary shriek]
She had a good shriek. [voluntary and for own enjoyment]
She did a (good) shriek. [a performance before an audience]

Instrumental object

10.31 The object may occasionally be instrumental (*cf* 10.21):

We employ *a computer* for our calculations.
She is playing *the piano*.
He nodded *his head*.

Note Occasionally the notion of instrument is incorporated into the verb:

He *headed* the ball into the goal. ['He hit the ball with his head . . .']
He *kicked* the ball into the goal. ['He hit the ball with his foot . . .']

This applies to *nod*, too: *his head* in the example in the text would be implied if omitted.

Affected indirect object

10.32 The indirect object normally takes the role of recipient (*cf* 10.19, and Note [c] below). It occasionally takes an affected role with a few of the verbs that combine with an eventive object (*cf* 10.30). The most common verb in the latter construction is *give*:

She gave *me* a push. ['She pushed me.']
I gave *Helen* a nudge. ['I nudged Helen.']
We gave *the baby* a bath. ['We bathed the baby.']
I should give *the car* a wash. ['I should wash the car.']
Give *the car* a push. ['Push the car.']
Judith paid *me* a visit. ['Judith visited me.']
Derek owes *us* a treat. ['It's Derek's turn to treat us.']

The indirect object has the same role as the affected direct object in the paraphrases. Unlike the recipient indirect object, the affected indirect object is not normally paraphrasable by a prepositional phrase:

I gave *Helen* a nudge.
~ ?I gave a nudge *to Helen*.

The reason is that this type of construction is intended to focus on the nominal equivalent of the verb (*nudge* in this example) and therefore the direct object should receive end-focus (*cf* 18.3*f*).

Note [**a**] In this use, *give* may be compared with *get, have*, and *receive* in a parallel passive sense: *I got a surprise, The car has had a polish, I received a shock*. There is also an interesting equivalence of *They gave* (or *shot*) *each other glances* and *They exchanged glances* ['They glanced at each other.'].
[**b**] We should include here metaphorical uses of other verbs, where paraphrases indicate that the indirect object has an affected role: *I taught him a lesson* [roughly 'I disciplined him.'].
[**c**] The indirect object has the role of 'comitative' ['together with'] or perhaps 'opposition' in this example:
I played *Sam* a game of chess. ['I played a game of chess with/against Sam.']

Summary

10.33 As a summary, we present in *Table* 10.33 over page the chief semantic functions for each clause type, with example sentences. Although, as the table shows, the semantic functions of the elements (particularly S and O_d) are quite varied, there are certain clear restrictions, such as that the object cannot be agentive; a subject (except in the passive) cannot be resultative; an indirect object normally has only two functions – those of affected and recipient. The following system of priorities generally obtains:

If there is an agentive, external causer, or positioner, it is S; if not,
If there is an instrument, it is S; if not,
If there is an affected, it is S; if not,
If there is a temporal, locative, or eventive, it may be S; if not,
The prop word *it* is S.

Naturally, in passive clauses the role of the direct or indirect object is assigned to the subject.

Table 10.33 Semantic roles

Type	*S*	O_i	O_d	C_s	C_o	*A*	*Example*
SVC	aff			attrib			*She's happy.*
	agent			attrib			*He turned traitor.*
	loc			attrib			*The Sahara is hot.*
	temp			attrib			*Last night was warm.*
	event			attrib			*The show was interesting.*
	it			attrib			*It's windy.*
SVA	aff					loc	*He was at school.*
	agent					loc	*She got into the car.*
	pos					loc	*He is lying on the floor.*
	event					temp	*The meeting is at eight.*
SV	agent						*He was working.*
	pos						*She is standing.*
	aff						*The curtains disappeared.*
	ext						*The wind is blowing.*
	it						*It's raining.*
SVO	agent		aff				*He threw the ball.*
	ext		aff				*Lightning struck the house.*
	pos		aff				*He is holding a knife.*
	instr		aff				*The stone broke the window.*
	recip		aff				*She has a car.*
	agent		recip				*We paid the bus driver.*
	instr		recip				*The will benefits us all.*
	agent		loc				*They climbed the mountain.*
	loc		aff				*The bus seats thirty.*
	agent		cog				*They fought a clean fight.*
	agent		result				*I wrote a letter.*
	agent		event				*They had an argument.*
	agent		instr				*He nodded his head.*
SVOC	agent		aff		attrib		*He declared her the winner.*
	ext		aff		attrib		*The sun turned it yellow.*
	instr		aff		attrib		*The revolver made him afraid.*
	recip		aff		attrib		*I found it strange.*
SVOA	agent		aff			loc	*He placed it on the shelf.*
	ext		aff			loc	*The storm drove the ship ashore.*
	instr		aff			loc	*A car knocked it down.*
	recip		aff			loc	*I prefer them on toast.*
SVOO	agent	recip	aff				*I bought her a gift.*
	agent	aff	event				*She gave the door a kick.*
	agent	recip	result				*She knitted me a sweater.*

KEY: aff(ected), agent(ive), attrib(ute), cog(nate), event(ive), ext(ernal causer), instr(ument), (prop) *it*, loc(ative), pos(itioner), recip(ient), result(ant), temp(oral)

Subject–verb concord

General rule

10.34 CONCORD (also termed 'agreement') can be defined as the relationship between two grammatical units such that one of them displays a particular feature (*eg* plurality) that accords with a displayed (or semantically implicit) feature in the other. The most important type of concord in English is concord of 3rd person number between subject and verb. The normally observed rule is very simple:

A singular subject requires a singular verb:

> My daughter *watches* television after supper. [singular subject + singular verb]

A plural subject requires a plural verb:

> My daughters *watch* television after supper. [plural subject + plural verb]

When the subject is realized by a noun phrase, the phrase counts as singular if its head is singular:

> *The* CHANGE *in male attitudes* is most obvious in industry.
> *The* CHANGES *in male attitude* are most obvious in industry.

Finite and nonfinite clauses generally count as singular:

> How you got there *does*n't concern me.
> To treat them as hostages *is* criminal.
> Smoking cigarettes *is* dangerous to your health.

Prepositional phrases and adverbs functioning as subject (*cf* 10.15) also count as singular:

> In the evenings *is* best for me. Slowly *does* it!

An apparent exception for clauses is the nominal relative clause. Nominal relative clauses are on the continuum from clause to noun phrase (*cf* 15.8*f*). For the purpose of concord, their number depends on the interpretation of the number of the *wh*-element. With the determiners *what* and *whatever*, the concord depends on the number of the determined noun. Contrast [3] and [4] below:

> What were supposed to be new proposals *were* in fact modifications of earlier ones. [1]
> What was once a palace *is* now a pile of rubble. [2]
> Whatever book a *Times* reviewer praises *sells* well. [3]
> What ideas he has *are* his wife's. [4]

A verb counts as singular if the first verb in a finite verb phrase has a singular form:

> My son *has* }
> My sons *have* } no intention of spending a vacation with me.

> A letter *has* }
> Two letters *have* } *been sent* to every applicant.

The application of the general rule is restricted in several general respects:

(1) Except for the verb BE, the verb shows a distinction of number only in the 3rd person present. Hence, the verb generally does not show concord in the past:

> My daughter } *watched* television after supper.
> My daughters }

The verb BE displays concord also in the 3rd person past:

> My daughter *was* watching television in my bedroom.
> My daughters *were* watching television in my bedroom.

(2) Number concord is displayed only in the indicative. Nonfinite verbs, imperatives, and subjunctives make no number distinctions.

(3) Modal auxiliaries (*cf* 3.39*ff*) make no number distinctions:

> My daughter } *may* watch television after supper.
> My daughters }

Note [**a**] It is possible to generalize the rule of concord to 'A subject which is not clearly semantically plural requires a singular verb'; that is, to treat singular as the unmarked form, to be used in neutral circumstances, where no positive indication of plurality is present. This would explain, in addition to clausal subjects, the tendency in informal speech for *is/was* to follow the pseudo-subject *there* in existential sentences such as *There's hundreds of people on the waiting list* (*cf* 18.44*ff*). Similarly, interrogative *who* and *what* as subjects normally take a singular verb even when the speaker has reason to believe that more than one person or entity is involved: *Who is making all that noise?* However, a plural verb may be used if other words in the sentence indicate that a plural subject is expected in the answer (*Who have not received their passes?*).

On the other hand, the principle of proximity (*cf* 10.35) effects a change from singular to plural more often than the reverse, perhaps because the plural is the form that is morphologically unmarked.

[**b**] Apparent exceptions to the concord rule arise with singular nouns ending with the *-s* of the plural inflection (*measles, billiards, mathematics*, etc, *cf* 5.75), or conversely plural nouns lacking the inflection (*cattle, people, clergy*, etc, *cf* 5.78):

> Measles *is* sometimes serious.   Our people *are* complaining.

[**c**] Plural phrases (including coordinate phrases) count as singular if they are used as names, titles, quotations, etc (*cf* further 17.90):

> *Crime and Punishment* is perhaps the best constructed of Dostoyevsky's novels, but *The Brothers Karamazov* is undoubtedly his masterpiece.
> 'The Cedars' has a huge garden.
> 'Senior citizens' means, in common parlance, people over sixty.

Such noun phrases can be regarded as appositive structures with an implied singular head: *the book 'Crime and Punishment', the expression 'senior citizens'*. The titles of some works that are collections of stories, etc, may be counted as either singular or plural:

> *The Canterbury Tales* { *exists* / *exist* } in many manuscripts.

[**d**] On the treatment of *data, media, criteria*, and *phenomena* as singular nouns, *cf* 5.91, 5.98 Note.

[**e**] Zero plural nouns (*cf* 5.86) do not display number. Hence, when they are subject and the verb is a modal or simple past, number differences manifest themselves only covertly through pronoun reference (*cf* covert gender, 5.104):

> The sheep jumped over the fence, didn't { *it?* / *they?* }

[**f**] It is a peculiarity of English that *-s* is the regular inflection for singular in the verb but for plural in the noun.

Principles of grammatical concord, notional concord, and proximity

10.35 The rule that the verb matches its subject in number may be called the principle of GRAMMATICAL CONCORD. Difficulties over concord arise through occasional conflict between this and two other principles: the principle of NOTIONAL CONCORD and the principle of PROXIMITY.

Notional concord is agreement of verb with subject according to the notion of number rather than with the actual presence of the grammatical marker for that notion. In British English, for example, collective nouns such as *government* are often treated as notionally plural:

The government *have* broken all *their* promises. ⟨BrE⟩

In this example, the plural notion is signalled not only by the plural verb *have*, but also by the pronoun *their*.

The principle of proximity, also termed 'attraction', denotes agreement of the verb with a closely preceding noun phrase in preference to agreement with the head of the noun phrase that functions as subject:

?*No one* except his own supporters *agree* with him.

The preceding plural noun *supporters* has influenced the choice of the plural verb *agree*, although the subject *No one except his own supporters* is grammatically singular, since the head *no one* is singular. On the other hand, the proximity principle is here reinforced by notional concord ('Only his own supporters agree with him'), making the sentence somewhat more acceptable than if the proximity principle alone applied. The choice of the verb may also be influenced by preceding coordinated noun phrases, even if they are singular:

?*A good *knowledge* of English, Russian, and French *are* required for this position.

Conflict between grammatical concord and attraction through proximity tends to increase with the distance between the noun phrase head of the subject and the verb, for example when the postmodifier is lengthy or when an adverbial or a parenthesis intervenes between the subject and the verb. Proximity concord occurs mainly in unplanned discourse. In writing it will be corrected to grammatical concord if it is noticed.

The three principles and their interaction will be illustrated below in three areas where concord causes some problems: where the subject contains (a) a collective noun head; (b) coordination; and (c) an indefinite expression.

English speakers are often uncertain about the rules of concord. Prescriptive teaching has insisted rather rigidly on grammatical concord, with the result that people often experience a conflict between this rule and the rule of notional concord, which tends to prevail over it. When the proximity principle is followed in defiance of the other principles, the result is likely to be condemned as an error.

Note [**a**] The principle of notional concord accounts for the common use of a singular with subjects that are plural noun phrases of quantity or measure. The entity expressed by the noun phrase is viewed as a single unit:

Ten dollars *is* all I have left. ['That amount is . . .']
Fifteen years *represents* a long period of his life. ['That period is . . .']
Two miles *is* as far as they can walk. ['That distance is . . .']
Two thirds of the area *is* under water. ['That area is . . .']
Cf: Sixty people means a huge party. ['That number of people means . . .']

[**b**] We also find a type of number concord at the phrase level in that certain determiners agree in number with their noun heads *that idea, those ideas*. There are apparent exceptions with measure noun phrases:

that five *dollars* (also: *those* five dollars)
this last two *weeks* (also: *these* last two weeks)
another two *days*
a happy three *months*
every few *miles*
each ten *ounces*
another five *per cent*

A few and *a good many* function as units:

a good many friends   a few days

[**c**] Grammatical concord is usually obeyed for *more than* and *many a*, though it may conflict with notional concord:

More than a thousand inhabitants *have* signed the petition. [1]
More than one member *has* protested against the proposal. [2]
Many a member *has* protested against the proposal. [3]

Although the subject is notionally plural in [2] and [3], the singular is preferred because *member* is analysed as head of the noun phrase. Contrast:

More members than one } *have* protested against the proposal.
Many members }

Collective nouns and notional concord

10.36 Singular collective nouns may be notionally plural. In BrE the verb may be either singular or plural:

The audience *were* enjoying every minute of it. [1]
The public *are* tired of demonstrations. [2]
England *have* won the cup. [3]
Our Planning Committee *have* considered your request. [4]

The choice between singular or plural verbs depends in BrE on whether the group is being considered as a single undivided body, or as a collection of individuals. Thus, in BrE plural is more likely in [1] than singular, because attention is directed at the individual reactions of members of the audience. On the other hand, the singular is more likely in these sentences:

The audience *was* enormous. [1a]
The public *consists* of you and me. [2a]
The crowd *has* been dispersed. [5]

In contrast to [1a], *The audience were enormous* might be interpreted to refer to an audience of enormous people. On the whole, the plural is more popular in speech, whereas in the more inhibited medium of writing the singular is probably preferred. It is generally safer in BrE to use the singular verb where there is doubt, in obedience to grammatical concord.

AmE generally treats singular collective nouns as singular. Terms for the government and for sports teams are nearly always treated as singular in AmE, but other terms may (less commonly than in BrE) take plural verbs:

The administration *has* announced its plans for stimulating the economy.
America *has* won the cup.
The public *has* a right to know. [also in AmE: The public *have* a right to know.]

But, as in BrE, plural pronouns are often used in AmE to refer to singular collective nouns:

The committee *has* not yet decided how *they* should react to the Governor's letter.

Note [a] If the collective noun subject occurs in the plural, the verb is of course plural in both BrE and AmE: *The various committees are now meeting to discuss your proposal.*

[b] When a noun referring to a collection of people has plural concord, the pronouns for which it is antecedent tend to be *who/whom/they/them* rather than *which/it*. Compare:

a family *who quarrel* amongst *themselves*

a family *which dates* back to the Norman Conquest

[c] *Couple* in the sense of two persons normally has a plural verb even in AmE: *The couple are happily married.* When it denotes a unit, the singular verb is used: *Each couple was asked to complete a form.*

Coordinated subject

Coordination with *and*

10.37 When a subject consists of two or more noun phrases (or clauses) coordinated by *and*, a distinction has to be made between coordination and coordinative apposition (*cf* 10.39).

Coordination comprises cases that correspond to fuller coordinate forms. A plural verb is used even if each conjoin is singular:

Tom and Alice *are* now ready. ['Tom is now ready and Alice is now ready.']

What I say and what I think *are* my own affair. ['What I say is my own affair and what I think is my own affair'; but *cf*: *What I say and do is my own affair*, 10.38]

A plural verb is similarly required in asyndetic coordination (without a coordinator):

His camera, his radio, his money *were* confiscated by the customs officials.

Conjoins expressing a mutual relationship (*cf* 13.60), even though they can only indirectly be treated as reductions of clauses in this way, also take a plural verb:

Your problem and mine *are* similar. ['Your problem is similar to mine and mine is similar to yours.']

What I say and do *are* two different things. ['What I say is one thing and what I do is another thing.']

Note [a] If a singular noun phrase is followed by *etc* and similar abbreviatory expressions (*and so on, and so forth*), a plural verb is normal:

The size etc *are* less important for our purposes.

[b] Preposed *each* or *every* has a distributive effect and requires a singular verb:

Every adult and every child *was* holding a flag.

Each senator and congressman *was* allocated two seats.

Contrast:

Each of them *has* signed the petition. They *have* each signed the petition.

[c] The coordination markers *respective* and *respectively* (*cf* 13.62*f*) occur in coordination, but not in coordinative apposition.

[d] The principle of notional concord explains:

The hammer and sickle *was* flying from the flagpole.

Danish bacon and eggs *makes* a good solid English breakfast.

The Bat and Ball *sells* good beer.

Despite the coordination, the subject names a single flag, a single meal, and a single pub respectively. Contrast:

Danish bacon and eggs *sell* very well in London.

[e] Arithmetical sums may be used with a singular or plural verb:

Two and two {*is* / *are*} four.

So also *Ten times five is* (or *are*) *fifty*; *Two fives make* (or *makes*) *ten*. But *Two fives are ten*; *Ten minus two is eight*; *Ten into fifty is five*.

Coordination within a singular subject

10.38 A singular noncount noun head may be premodified by phrases coordinated by *and*. As subject, the resulting noun phrase may imply two (or more) separate sentences, and may then be legitimately followed by a plural verb:

American and Dutch beer *are* (both) much lighter than British beer. ['American beer is . . . and Dutch beer is . . .']

White and brown sugar *are* (equally) acceptable for this recipe.

But a singular verb is often used in this context, and is required when the phrases are postmodifying:

Beer from America and Holland *is* much lighter than British beer.

When the subject is a nominal relative clause, coordination reduction allows some variation in number interpretation:

What I say and do *are* my own affair. ['What I say is . . . and what I do . . .'; *cf* 10.37]

What I say and do *is* my own affair. ['That which I say and do . . .']

A generic noun phrase with a singular count head requires a plural verb when the head is premodified and the premodification contains coordination by *and*:

The short-term and (the) long-term loan *are* handled very differently by the bank.

A first-language and (a) second-language learner *share* some strategies in their acquisition of the language.

These noun phrases are notionally plural ('short-term and long-term loans'; 'first-language and second-language learners').

Coordinative apposition

10.39 With the less common COORDINATIVE APPOSITION, no reduction is implied, since each of the coordinated units has the same reference. Hence, a singular verb is required if each noun phrase is singular:

This temple of ugliness and memorial to Victorian bad taste *was* erected in the main street of the city.

The two opening noun phrases here both refer to one entity (a statue). The following example, however, could have either a singular or plural verb, depending on the meaning:

> His aged servant and the subsequent editor of his collected papers {*was* / *were*} with him at his deathbed.

Singular *was* is used if the servant and the editor are the same person, and plural *were* if they are two different people.

Some latitude is allowed in the interpretation of abstract nouns:

> Your fairness and impartiality {*has* / *have*} been much appreciated.
>
> Her calmness and confidence {*is* / *are*} astonishing.
>
> Law and order {*has* / *have*} been established.

Invoking the principle of notional concord, we may use either singular or plural, depending on whether qualities are seen as separate or as a complex unity.

Note [**a**] The correlatives *both . . . and . . .* (*cf* 13.35) mark coordination in subject noun phrases: *Both her calmness and her confidence are astonishing*. With subject complements they mark coordinative apposition: *She is both secretary and treasurer*. Contrast:

> Both my wife and my secretary *were* there. [two persons]
> She *was* both my wife and my secretary. [one person]

[**b**] Noun phrases are usually apposed without a coordinator. If they are subject, a singular verb is of course required if the noun phrases themselves are singular:

> This temple of ugliness, a memorial to Victorian bad taste, *was* erected in the main street of the city.

[**c**] A repeated determiner biases the choice to plural:

> Your fairness and your impartiality *have* been much appreciated.

Quasi-coordination

10.40 Subject noun phrases may be linked by quasi-coordinators (*cf* 13.103), *ie* prepositions (such as *along with*, *rather than*, and *as well as*) that are semantically similar to coordinators. Grammatical concord requires a singular verb if the first noun phrase is singular:

> The captain, as well as the other players, *was* tired.
> One speaker after another *was* complaining about the lack of adequate sanitation.

Occasionally the principle of notional concord (sometimes combined with the proximity principle) prompts the plural, especially in loosely expressed speech:

> ?One man with his wife, both looking very anxious, *were* pleading with a guard to let them through.
> ?The President, together with his advisors, *are* preparing a statement on the crisis.

If an adverbial is attached to a second noun phrase linked to the first noun phrase by *and*, the construction is considered parenthetic, and grammatical concord similarly requires the verb to agree in number with the first noun phrase:

> A writer, and sometimes an artist, *is* invited to address the society.
> The ambassador – and perhaps his wife too – *is* likely to be present.

The same grammatical rule applies when the second phrase is negative, whether or not linked by *and*, though here the principle of notional concord reinforces the use of the singular:

> The Prime Minister, (and) not the monarch, *decides* government policy.

Coordination with *or* and *nor*

10.41 The rules are different for subject phrases or clauses which are coordinated with (*either . . .*) *or*:

> Either the Mayor or her deputy $\left\{\begin{matrix}\textit{is}\\ \textit{*are}\end{matrix}\right\}$ bound to come. [1]
>
> What I say or what I think $\left\{\begin{matrix}\textit{is}\\ \textit{*are}\end{matrix}\right\}$ no business of yours. [2]
>
> Either the strikers or the bosses $\left\{\begin{matrix}\textit{*has}\\ \textit{have}\end{matrix}\right\}$ misunderstood the claim. [3]
>
> Either your brakes or your eyesight $\left\{\begin{matrix}\textit{is}\\ \textit{?are}\end{matrix}\right\}$ at fault. [4]
>
> Either your eyesight or your brakes $\left\{\begin{matrix}\textit{are}\\ \textit{?is}\end{matrix}\right\}$ at fault. [5]

All these involve nonappositional coordination. Grammatical concord is clear when each member of the coordination has the same number: when they are both singular (as in [1] and [2]), the verb is singular; when they are both plural (as in [3]), the verb is plural. A dilemma arises when one member is singular and the other plural (as in [4] and [5]). Notionally, *or* is disjunctive, so that each member is separately related to the verb rather than the two members being considered one unit, as when the coordinator is additive *and*. Since the dilemma is not clearly resolvable by the principles of grammatical concord or notional concord, recourse is generally had to the principle of proximity: whichever phrase comes last determines the number of the verb, as in [4] and [5].

Where the disjunctive force is weak and *or* approaches the meaning of *and*, the plural verb is sometimes found with singular subject phrases, especially in informal usage:

> Jogging or swimming $\left\{\begin{matrix}\textit{is}\\ \textit{?are}\end{matrix}\right\}$ supposed to be good for the heart.

When *or* is used for coordinative apposition (*cf* 10.39), grammatical concord requires the number of the verb to agree with the first appositive if the two appositives differ in number:

The hero, or main protagonist, *is* Major Coleman.
The hawks, or bellicose officials, *are* in the ascendancy.
Gobbledygook, or the circumlocutions of bureaucratic language, *is* intentionally difficult to understand.
The circumlocutions of bureaucratic language, or gobbledygook, *are* intentionally difficult to understand.

The rules for the negative correlatives *neither . . . nor* are the same as for *either . . . or* in formal usage. In less formal usage, they are treated more like *and* for concord. Thus, [6] is more natural in speech than [7]:

Neither he nor his wife *have* arrived. [6]
Neither he nor his wife *has* arrived. [7]

This preference is probably connected with the use of the plural verb with *neither* as a determiner or pronoun (*cf* 10.42), but it may also reflect notional concord in that logically 'neither X nor Y' can be interpreted as a union of negatives: 'both (not-X) and (not-Y)'.

If the number alternatives for the verb are both felt to be awkward, speakers may avoid making a choice by postposing the second noun phrase or sometimes by substituting a modal auxiliary (*cf* 10.44):

Either your brakes are at fault *or your eyesight is.*
He hasn't arrived, *nor has his wife.*
Either your brakes or your eyesight *may* be at fault.

Note [**a**] The coordinating correlatives *not . . . but* and *not only/just/merely . . . but (also/even)* behave like *or* with respect to number concord:

Not only he but his wife *has* arrived.
Not (only) one but all of us *were* invited.
Not just the students but even their teacher *is* enjoying the film.

Where the noun phrases differ in number, the principle of proximity determines the concord.

[**b**] The mixed expressions *one or two* and *between one and two* follow the principle of proximity in having plural concord:

One or two reasons *were* suggested.

Similarly *one and* plus a fraction or percentage has plural concord, since the notion of plural applies not to at least two but to more than one:

One and a half years *have* passed since we last met.

The selection of the plural is reinforced also by the principle of proximity. But note:

A year and a half *has* passed.

The conjoint phrase is treated like 'a period of a year and a half', though the singular verb may be reinforced by the immediately preceding *a half.*

Indefinite expressions as subject

10.42 Another area of ambivalence for subject–verb number concord is that of indefinite expressions of amount or quantity, especially with the determiners and with the pronouns *no*, *none*, *all*, *some*, *any*, and fractions such as *half.* They have both count and noncount uses.

With noncount nouns (present or implied), the verb is of course singular:

So far no money *has* been spent on repairs.
None (of the money) *has* been spent on repairs.
Some cement *has* arrived.
Some (of the cement) *has* arrived.

With plural count nouns (present or implied) the verb is plural:

No people of that name *live* here.
Some books *have* been placed on the shelves.

{Some / Hardly any / All / Half} (of the books) *have* been placed on the shelves.

None with plural count nouns is in divided usage:

None (of the books) {*has* / *have*} been placed on the shelves.

Prescriptive grammars have tended to insist on the singular verb, but notional concord invites a plural verb, which tends to be more frequently used and is generally accepted even in formal usage. With *either* and *neither* the singular is generally used:

The two guests have arrived, {and either / but neither} *is* welcome.

But a plural verb sometimes occurs in informal usage when *either* or (particularly) *neither* is followed by a prepositional phrase with a plural complement, both because of notional concord and because of the proximity rule:

{*Either* / *Neither*} of them *are* welcome. ['Both are (not) welcome.'] ⟨informal⟩

The plural is even more favoured in such constructions with *none*:

None of them *have* been placed on the shelves.

10.43 The proximity principle may lead to plural concord even with indefinites such as *each*, *every*, *everybody*, *anybody*, and *nobody* (or indefinite phrases such as *every one*, *any one*), which are otherwise unambivalently singular:

Nobody, not even the teachers, {*was* / *?were*} listening.

Every member of the vast crowd of 50 000 people {*was* / *?were*} pleased to see him.

Although these sentences might well be uttered in casual speech, or inadvertently written down, most people would probably regard them as ungrammatical, because they flatly contradict grammatical concord.

Other, more acceptable, instances arise with expressions involving kind and number. The number choice in the verb is usually influenced by notional concord:

{These / Those} {sort / kind / type} of parties *are* dangerous. ⟨informal⟩ [1]

A (large) number of people *have* applied for the job. [2]
The majority *are* Moslems. [3]
Lots of the stuff *is* going to waste. ⟨informal⟩ [4]

[1] illustrates an idiomatic anomaly: there is a discrepancy in number between the noun and the determiner *those*, as well as with the verb. Rephrasing can avoid the anomaly:

Those kinds of parties *are*
That kind of party *is* } dangerous.
Parties of that kind *are*

[2] and [3] show seemingly singular phrases being treated as plural; notionally they are equivalent to *many* and *most*. Use of the singular in these sentences would be considered pedantic in [2], and unacceptable in [3] because of the plural complement (*cf* the pedantic but acceptable *The majority agrees with me*). The opposite phenomenon, attraction to the singular, is observed in [4] where *lots of* is treated as if equivalent to singular *plenty of* and *much of*; but the singular is also influenced by the proximity of singular *stuff*. Contrast:

Lots of people *are* coming to our party.

Notional concord ('many people') is reinforced by the proximity of plural *people*.

Note [**a**] For the analysis of quantifiers like *a number of*, *cf* 5.25.

[**b**] Determiners other than *those* or *these* are found in plural concord with the nouns in [1], *eg*: *some*, *any*. Like *a* (*large*) *number of* in [2] are locutions such as *a lot of*, *a* (*whole*) *set of*, *a spate of*, *plenty of*; analogous to *the* (or *a*) *majority* in [3] is *the* (or *a*) *minority*, and to *lots* in [4] are many other informal quantifiers, such as *loads of*, *heaps of*.

[**c**] The proximity principle may be extended to mean that concord is determined by whatever immediately precedes the verb, the position of the subject (which normally determines concord). The principle can then explain a singular verb in cases of inversion or of an adverbial quasi-subject: ?*Where's the scissors?*; ?*Here's John and Mary*; ?*There's several bags missing*. As what precedes the subject here is not marked for plural (*cf* 10.34 Note [a]), the singular verb follows by attraction. The occasional use of the singular verb in instances such as ?**Is the scissors on the table?* and ?**Has my glasses* ['spectacles'] *been found?* may be explained by a combination of two factors: these summation plurals (*cf* 5.76) are notionally singular, though morphologically and syntactically plural; since the verb precedes the subject, the influence of the subject on number is somewhat reduced. Compare the greater unacceptability of **My glasses has been found*. All these are colloquial examples; in formal English plural forms of the verb would be substituted.

[**d**] If a relative clause follows a noun phrase containing *one of* plus a plural noun phrase, there is often a choice as to whether the verb in the relative clause should agree in number with *one* or with the plural noun phrase:

He's one of those students who never *get*(*s*) a piece of work done on time.

The choice of singular or plural can depend on whether attention is directed to the generality or to the uniqueness. Compare:

Charlatanry is one of the many words in English that *are* of French origin.
[= Of the many words in English that *are* of French origin, *charlatanry* is one.]
Charlatanry is one of the common vices that *is* particularly contemptible.
[= Of the common vices, charlatanry is one that *is* particularly contemptible.]

Concord of person

10.44 In addition to 3rd person number concord with the subject, the verb in the present tense may have person concord (*cf* 3.2, 3.52) with the subject – 1st and 3rd person concord with BE and only 3rd person concord with other verbs:

I *am* your friend. [1st PERSON SINGULAR CONCORD]

He *is* your friend.
He *knows* you. } [3rd PERSON SINGULAR CONCORD]

Are is the unmarked form for the present of BE with persons other than 1st and 3rd singular; in all other verbs the base form is used in the present for persons other than the 3rd singular. Only the past of BE has further distinctions:

I *was* your friend.
He *was* your friend. } [1st and 3rd PERSON SINGULAR CONCORD]

The unmarked past form of BE – *were* – is used with the 2nd person singular and all the plural persons. Like number concord, person concord applies only to the indicative; the subjunctive has one form for all persons.

A coordinate subject with *and* as coordinator requires a plural verb. Person concord does not apply, since there are no person distinctions in the plural (*You and I know the answer*; *She and I are in charge*). If the coordinator is *or*, *either . . . or*, or *neither . . . nor*, in accordance with the principle of proximity the last noun phrase determines the person of the verb:

Neither you, nor I, nor anyone else *knows* the answer.
Either my wife or I *am* going.

Because of the awkwardness of this choice, a speaker may avoid it by using a modal auxiliary which is invariable for person (*eg*: *Either my wife or I will be going*) or by postposing the last noun phrase (*eg*: *Either my wife is going or I am*) (*cf* 10.41).

Note [**a**] In archaic English, there is also concord of 2nd person singular pronouns and verbs in the present and past (*cf* 6.14 Note [c]) *Thou, Lord, hast redeemed us*; *Thou didst hear my prayer*. (*Cf* 3.4 Note [b] for archaic 2nd and 3rd person forms of verbs.)

[**b**] In relative clauses and cleft sentences, a relative pronoun subject is usually followed by a verb in agreement with its antecedent: *It is I who am to blame*, *It is Kay who is in command*, *It is they who are complaining*. But 3rd person concord prevails in informal English where the objective case pronoun *me* is used: *It's me who's to blame*. Similarly, 3rd person singular may be used in informal English in these constructions when the pronoun *you* has singular reference: *It's you who's to blame*.

In the archaic *Our Father, which art in Heaven*, agreement is with the 2nd person status of the vocative *Our Father*, *ie*: *Our Father, thou which art in heaven*. Contrast a modern version *Our Father, who is in Heaven* ['he who is in Heaven'].

Summary

10.45 We suggest that the following generalizations apply to the system of subject–verb concord in English.

(a) The principle of GRAMMATICAL CONCORD tends to be followed in formal usage and has the sanction of teaching and editorial tradition.
(b) The principle of NOTIONAL CONCORD is most natural to colloquial English.
(c) The principle of PROXIMITY, despite its minor decisive role in cases where the other two provide no guidance, is generally felt to lack validity on its

own, and has more of an auxiliary role in supporting notional concord in colloquial speech.

Grammatical and notional concord generally work in harmony together. It is only occasionally that these principles are in conflict.

Other types of concord

Subject–complement and object–complement concord

10.46 Between subject and subject complement and between direct object and object complement, there is usually concord of number (but not of person):

My child is an angel.	I consider my child an angel.
My children are angels.	I consider my children angels.

This type of concord arises naturally from the semantic role of the two complements (*cf* 10.20). There are, however, exceptions:

My only hope for the future is my children. [also *are*] [1]
More nurses is the next item on the agenda. [also *are*] [2]
Their principal crop is potatoes. [3]
That man is nuts. ⟨slang⟩ ['insane'] [4]
Good manners are a rarity these days. [also *is*] [5]
The younger children are a problem. [6]
The next few bars are pure Tchaikovsky. [also *is*] [7]
Dogs are good company. [8]

The complement in [1] seems condensed, with perhaps an implied preposition: *My only hope for the future is in my children.* The subject of [2] may similarly be analysed as condensed (something like 'the question of more nurses') or may perhaps be treated as a title (*cf* 10.34 Note [c]). In [3] the subject complement is a generic noun phrase, which might equally be singular: *Their principal crop is the potato.* Sentences [4–8] contain a subject complement which, although nominal in form, has a characterizing function closer to that of an adjective. There is often no singular/plural contrast; for example, we do not have **The houses are bricks*, only *The houses are brick*.

Note [**a**] The complements in [1], [2], and [3] are identifying (*cf* 10.20), as is shown by the potentiality for subject–complement reversal: *My children are my only hope for the future*; *The next item on the agenda is more nurses*; *Potatoes are their principal crop.*

[**b**] Pseudo-cleft constructions with a fronted object *what* may have a plural subject complement (*cf* 10.34):

What we need most *is* books.

But *what* is ambivalent in number, often interpreted as equivalent to either 'the thing that' or 'the things that', so that we also find a plural verb in concord with the subject *what*-clause:

What we need most *are* books.

Some prescriptive teaching requires the singular both for the verb within the *what* clause and for the verb that is in concord with the clause:

What *is* needed most *is* books.

We also find a singular verb when the *what*-clause is subject complement, but there are objections to this infringement of the concord rule:

?*Books *is* { what we need most. / what is needed most. }

[c] If the subject is singular there is no subject–complement concord with the idioms *be all ears*, *be all elbows*, *be all fingers and thumbs*. For example: *I'm all ears* ['I'm listening with all my attention.'].

Distributive number

10.47 The distributive plural is used in a plural noun phrase to refer to a set of entities matched individually with individual entities in another set:

Have you all brought your *cameras*? ['Each has a camera.']
Hand in your *papers* next Monday. ['Each has to hand in one paper.']

While the distributive plural is the norm, the distributive singular may also be used to focus on individual instances. We therefore often have a number choice:

The students raised their *hand(s)*.
Some children have { understanding *fathers*. / *an* understanding *father*. }
We all have { good *appetites*. / *a* good *appetite*. }
Pronouns agree with their *antecedent(s)*.
Their { *noses need* / *nose needs* } to be wiped.
The exercise was not good for their *back(s)*.

The singular is sometimes obligatory or preferable with idioms and metaphors:

We are *keeping an open mind*. [?*open minds*]
They *vented their spleen on him*. [**their spleens*]
They can't *put their finger on* what's wrong. [**their fingers*]

The distributive singular is sometimes used to avoid ambiguity:

Students were asked to name their favourite *sport*.

The singular makes it clear that only one sport was to be named. Similarly:

Children must be accompanied by *a parent*.

Pronoun reference

10.48 Agreement between a pronoun and its antecedent (*cf* 12.8*ff*) should probably be considered coreference rather than grammatical concord, but it is appropriate to treat the phenomenon here.

Concord of number, person, and gender is necessary between subject on the one hand, and object or complement on the other hand, if the second element is a reflexive pronoun (*cf* 6.23*ff*):

He injured *himself* in both legs.
She bought *herself* a raincoat.
I haven't been *myself* for weeks. ['I haven't felt well.']

The same concord relation holds when the reflexive pronoun occurs in other functions (*eg* as prepositional complement), or when the emphatic genitive *his own*, etc is used:

She's making a sweater for *herself*.
I wrote to them about *myself*.
They're ruining *their own* chances.

For coreference relations of the type exemplified by *Everybody . . . their*, *cf* 10.50.

Note [a] In BrE, collective noun subjects permit, as one might expect, plural concord: *The navy congratulated themselves on, if not a victory, at least an avoidance of defeat*. In both BrE and AmE, plural reflexives often follow the indefinite pronouns (*cf* 10.50): *Everybody behaved themselves*; some, however, avoid the construction.
[b] The concord relation may be with an element other than the subject, notably an object:
I wrote to *my brother* about *himself*. I drove *them in their own car*.

10.49 This type of concord may extend beyond clause boundaries. Thus the relative pronouns *who*, *whom*, and *which* agree with their antecedent in the superordinate clause in gender, the first two being personal, and the last nonpersonal:

Here's the hammer *which* I borrowed yesterday.
That's the man *who(m)* I saw talking to your parents.

Whose is used with either personal or nonpersonal antecedents:

The man *whose* wallet he stole. The house *whose* rafters were burned.

There is a feeling, however, that *whose* is more appropriate to personal antecedents, presumably because of its morphological relationship to *who* and *whom*, and some speakers feel uneasy about its use with nonpersonal antecedents.

Personal and possessive pronouns in the 1st and 3rd persons agree with their antecedents in number. Those in the 3rd person singular (*he*, *she*, *it*) also agree with their antecedents in gender:

Tom hurt *his* foot. [1]
Beatrice knows that *she* is late. [2]
The books were too heavy, so I left *them*. [3]

The violation of concord in the case of nonreflexive pronouns does not lead (as it does in the case of reflexive pronouns) to an unacceptable sentence, but to a different interpretation. One may compare [1] with [4]:

Tom hurt *her* foot. [4]

In [4] the pronoun must refer to someone else, someone mentioned or known from the situational context. Of course, in both [1] and [2] the pronoun may also refer to somebody other than the subject.

Note In phrases denoting body parts and close personal belongings (*cf* 5.35), possessive pronouns refer back to the subject where some languages prefer the definite article:
John shook *his* head. *She* dirtied *her* shoes.
So also in [1], if the reference is to the subject.

10.50 The pronoun *they* is commonly used as a 3rd person singular pronoun that is neutral between masculine and feminine. It is a convenient means of avoiding the dilemma of whether to use the *he* or *she* form. At one time restricted to informal usage, it is now increasingly accepted even in formal usage, especially in AmE. (On sexual bias in pronoun usage, *cf* 6.10.)

Rather than use *he* in the unmarked sense or the clumsy *he or she*, many prefer to seek gender impartiality by using a plural form where possible in reference to the indefinite pronouns *everyone, everybody, someone, somebody, anyone, anybody, no one, nobody*:

Everyone thinks *they* have the answer. [1]
Has *anybody* brought *their* camera? [2]
No one could have blamed *themselves* for that. [3]

A similar use of the plural occurs with coordinate subjects referring to both sexes, as in [4], and with a singular noun phrase subject having a personal noun of indeterminate gender as head, as in [5]:

Either he or she is going to have to change *their* attitude. [4]
Every student has to hand in *their* paper today. [5]

In formal English, the tendency has been to use *he* as the unmarked form when the gender is not determined. The formal equivalent of [1], though increasingly ignored now, is therefore:

Everyone thinks *he* has the answer. [1a]

A more cumbersome alternative is the conjoining of both masculine and feminine pronouns:

Every student has to hand in *his or her* paper today. [5a]

This device is particularly clumsy if the pronouns have to be repeated:

If *a student* does not hand in *his or her* paper today, *he or she* will not be allowed to continue the course. [5b]

One way of avoiding the dilemma is to make the subject plural:

All students have to hand in *their* paper today. [5c]

Similar methods can usually be employed for the indefinite pronouns too:

All of them think *they* have the answer. [1b]
Have *any of you* brought *your* camera? [2a]

For [4] the only alternative in formal English is to rephrase the sentence:

Either he is going to have to change *his* attitude or *she hers*. [4a]

The indefinite pronoun *one* is followed in formal usage by the same pronoun for subsequent references:

One should choose *one's* friends carefully. [6]

But AmE may also use the masculine pronoun:

One should choose *his* friends carefully. [6a]

In accordance with the tendency to avoid the use of the masculine pronoun to subsume both male and female references we may expect that AmE will increasingly replace indefinite *one* with indefinite *we*, *you*, or *they*, as appropriate:

We should choose *our* friends carefully. [6b]

We have noted (*cf* 10.36) that, especially in BrE, singular collective nouns have plural subject–verb concord in cases where the speaker thinks of the group as made up of separate individuals. The same principle extends to pronoun concord:

The government *are* cutting *their* losses. ⟨BrE⟩ [7]
The government *is* cutting *its* losses. [8]

Although there is no number contrast in relative pronouns, the number distinction can be reflected in the choice of personal *who* (*ie* the group thought of as a set of individuals) as opposed to nonpersonal *which* (*ie* the group as an indivisible abstraction). Thus corresponding to [7] and [8], we may have:

the government, *who are* cutting *their* losses ⟨BrE⟩ [7a]
the government, *which is* cutting *its* losses [8a]

Hybrid forms are rare, and seem odd:

?the government, *who is* cutting its/their losses
?the government, *which are* cutting its/their losses

Note [**a**] Informally, with indefinite pronoun subjects, *they* is commonly used in subsequent tag questions: *Everybody is leaving, aren't they?*, *Nobody is leaving, are they?*
[**b**] For introductory *it*, *that*, and *this*, *cf* 6.17. Examples:
Somebody opened the door. *It* was David.
Hello! *This* is Susan. Is *that* Geoffrey? ⟨on phone⟩

Semantic restrictions

10.51 Apart from concord, there are other ways in which the choice of one clause element may affect the choice of another:

The *men* scattered.
not *The *man* scattered.
The police contingent dispersed the *rioters*.
not *The police contingent dispersed the *rioter*.
John and Mary collided.
not {*John / *The *car*} collided.
but John collided with Mary.
The *workers* assembled.
not *The *worker* assembled.

Each of the above pairs shows how a particular verb requires a particular type of subject or object: *collide* requires a plural subject, a collective singular subject (*The team collided*), or a prepositional phrase entailing notional plurality with the subject (*I collided with her*); *scatter*, *disperse*, and *assemble* require a plural affected participant – *ie* a plural subject or a collective singular subject (*The crowd scattered*) when used intransitively, or a plural or collective object when used transitively (*The police contingent dispersed the rioters/the mob*).

Rules of this kind differ from rules of concord in that they do not involve two elements sharing the same feature, but one element projecting on to another a feature which is necessary for its meaningful use. That it is 'plurality' as a semantic feature rather than as a strictly grammatical feature that is in question here is shown by the possibility of substituting a collective singular for the plural noun.

Other features commonly entering into such semantic restrictions include:

'concrete' vs 'abstract': { The glass contains water.
*The glass contains kindness.

'animate' vs 'inanimate': { A pedestrian saw me.
*A lampshade saw me.

'human' vs 'nonhuman': { Finally we got married.
*Finally the snakes got married.

These restrictions are frequently violated in poetry and in other imaginative uses of languages. The incongruity, in such cases, indicates that the speaker intends us to make sense of his words at some deeper level, *eg* by metaphorical interpretation. In poetry, *leaves* may *dance*, *stars* may *bless*, *fears* may *lurk* or *linger*, and *a look* may *contain kindness*.

Semantic restrictions apply not only to verbs, but also to other word classes, notably adjectives and prepositions. The oddity of **The music is too green* is explained by the requirement that *green* should be in a copular relationship with a concrete noun (unless the noun is a superordinate term as in *The colour* (*I like best*) *is green* or unless *green* has the metaphorical sense 'immature'). The oddity of **They ran until the town* is accounted for by a rule that *until* requires a prepositional complement or a clause with temporal meaning (*They ran until six*; *They ran until it was dark*).

Note [a] Semantic requirements of the types that have been exemplified have sometimes been called 'selectional restrictions'.

[b] Semantic restrictions apply of course within phrases and not just between clause elements: **those married snakes*, **the green music*.

[c] There are semantic restrictions that apply to particular lexical items. For example, the two verbs *eat* and *feed*, used intransitively, tend to require personal and nonpersonal subjects respectively; whereas *Janet and Joe are eating* implies that Janet and Joe are persons, *Janet and Joe are feeding* implies that they are animals. Similarly, *elder* (unlike *older*) requires a personal subject or head noun: *Carol is the elder*, but not **This building is the elder*. To take a very different example, many speakers do not accept that *unique* can be modified by an intensifier or comparative: ?*Her play is very unique*.

[d] There are also restrictions that hold between lexical items. Both *want* and *wish* may be intensified (for example, by *very much*), but we can say *I badly wanted to see them* and not **I badly wished to see them*. Such restrictions have been termed 'collocational restrictions'.

Vocatives

10.52 A vocative is an optional element, usually a noun phrase, denoting the one or more persons to whom the sentence is addressed. It is either a CALL, drawing the attention of the person or persons addressed, singling them out from others in hearing, as in [1], or an ADDRESS, expressing the speaker's relationship or attitude to the person or persons addressed, as in [2] and [3]:

JǑHN, DÌNner's ready. [voc S V C_s] [1]
And THÀT, my FRÍENDS, concludes my SPÈECH. [voc S V O_d] [2]
My BÀCK is aching, DÓCtor. [S V voc] [3]

Sentences [1–3] show that a vocative may take initial, medial, or final position in the sentence; in its optionality and freedom of position, it is more like an adverbial (or, more precisely, like a disjunct; *cf* 8.121*ff*) than any other element of clause structure.

Intonationally, the vocative is set off from the rest of the clause either by constituting a separate tone unit or by forming the tail of a tone unit (*cf* App II.15). The most characteristic intonations are shown above: fall–rise for an initial vocative functioning as a call, and otherwise rise; rise for a vocative functioning as an address (*cf* also Note [b]).

Note **[a]** When *you* precedes the vocative, the distinction between a vocative and an appositive may be neutralized in writing, though not in speech:

You, Robert, will have to work harder.
I have been looking for you, my friend.

[b] There are forms of address that are general in character and therefore have low informational value. They form the tail of a tone unit when they are medial as well as when they are final. Such addresses rarely occur initially:

I shall send you a CÁRD, sir, when the suit is RÈADY.
We mustn't be LÀTE, dear, MÙST we?
Don't be SÌLLY, darling.

Forms of vocatives

10.53 Vocatives may be:

(a) Names: first name, last name, full name, with or without a title, or a nickname or pet name: *David*, *Caldwell*, *Sarah Peterson*, *Mrs Johnson*, *Dr Turner*, *Ginger*

(b) Standard appellatives, usually without modification:

(i) terms for family relationships (sometimes with initial capitals): *mother*, *father*, *son*, *uncle*, *aunt*, *grandfather*, *grandmother*; or more familiar forms like *mom(my)* ⟨AmE⟩, *mum(my)* ⟨BrE⟩, *dad(dy)*, *auntie*, *granny*, *grandma*, *grandpa*.

(ii) titles of respect (sometimes with initial capitals for *your*): *madam*, *ma'am* ⟨esp AmE⟩, *sir*, *my Lord*, *your Honour*, *your Excellency*, *your Majesty*, *your Ladyship*.

(iii) markers of status (sometimes with initial capitals even for those not so marked here): *Mr President*, *Prime Minister*, *Father* [for priest], *Sister* [for a nun], *Bishop*, *professor*, *doctor*, *general*, *major*, *vicar*.

(c) Terms for occupations: *waiter, driver, cabbie* ⟨informal⟩, *barmaid* ⟨BrE⟩, *bartender* ⟨AmE⟩, *attendant, conductor, nurse, officer* [for a member of the police force].

(d) Epithets (noun or adjective phrases) expressing an evaluation:

(i) favourable (some also preceded by *my*): (*my*) *darling*, (*my*) *dear*, (*my*) *dearest*, (*my*) *love*, *honey* ⟨esp AmE⟩, (*my*) *friend*, *handsome*, *beautiful*, (*my*) *sweetie-pie* ⟨esp AmE⟩.

(ii) unfavourable (also preceded by *you* in noun phrases); *bastard*, *coward*, *fatty*, *idiot*, *imbecile*, *liar*, *pig*, *rotter* ⟨BrE⟩, *skinny*, *slowcoach* ⟨BrE⟩, *slowpoke* ⟨AmE⟩, *stupid*, *swine*.

(e) General nouns, but which are often used in more specialized senses: *brother*, *buddy* ⟨AmE⟩, *girl*, *guys*, *lady*, *ladies and gentlemen*; *man*, *mate* ⟨BrE⟩, *partner* ⟨AmE⟩, *son*. Except for *ladies and gentlemen*, these are usually familiar and considered impolite when addressed to persons with whom one is not familiar. *Boy* is avoided in the US because of its racial connotations.

(f) The personal pronoun *you* (*You, why haven't you finished yet?*); it is markedly impolite. An indefinite pronoun; *eg*: *Get me a pen, somebody* is abrupt.

(g) Nominal clauses (very occasionally): *Whoever said that*, (*come out here*). Other examples: *whoever you are, what's your name*.

(h) Items from (a), (d), (e), and (f) may be expanded by the addition of modifiers or appositive elements of various kinds:

(a) *my dear Mrs Johnson*; *young David*
(d) *my very dearest*; *my old friend*; *you silly bastard*; *you filthy liar*
(e) *old man, young man*; *old boy* ⟨BrE⟩; *old chap* ⟨BrE⟩; *old fellow* ⟨BrE⟩; *my dear fellow* ⟨BrE⟩
(f) *you over there*; *you with the red hair*. Less impolite and more jocular in tone are appositives like *you boys*, *you people*, *you chaps* ⟨BrE⟩, *you* (*young*) *fellows*. *You-all* ⟨Southern AmE⟩ and *you guys* ⟨esp AmE⟩ are not impolite.

Items in (bi) and (bii), unless the terms have unique reference (as in *mother* or *Mr President*), may be combined with names in (a): *Uncle David, grandma Peterson, Professor Johnson*.

Terms for occupations in (c) differ from markers of status (biii), which also denote occupations, in that occupation terms are normally used as vocatives only when the person addressed is functioning in that role, whereas status markers may be used at all times. For example, we may address a person as *professor* or *doctor* when we do not have a professional relationship with that person, but we only address a person as *waiter* or *nurse* in situations when we are interacting with the person in that particular role.

Some vocatives are listed in more than one set. For example, *son* in (bi) is used by a parent, but in (e) it is used by a superior who is not a parent. Similarly, *father* in (bi) is a kinship term, but in (biii) it is a status marker. Moreover, some items in (di) may express a varying degree of evaluation: *love* may be used between intimates, but in BrE it may be used generally for strangers by a female bus conductor; and *bastard* may also convey the speaker's admiration for the addressee's ingenuity.

In addressing somebody one knows by name, last name preceded by title (*Mr Jones*, *Miss Smith*, *Mrs Brown*, *Dr Robinson*) is a politely formal manner of address, while first name (*John*, *Mary*) indicates friendly familiarity. It is now much easier to be 'on Christian name terms' 〈BrE〉 or 'on a first name basis' 〈esp AmE〉 than formerly; address by family name alone (which used to indicate male comradeship, as in *Holmes* and *Watson*) is rarely heard today, except in special situations (armed forces, school).

Vocatives addressed to strangers are not neutral, since they always express some relationship or attitude. Their effect and frequency also vary considerably in AmE and BrE. For example, *miss*, *ma'am*, *mister*, and *sir* are used far more extensively in AmE as vocatives addressed to strangers; *mister* is considered nonstandard in BrE, and *miss* is unacceptable to some, while *sir* is much more formal in BrE than in AmE. Professional vocatives are also used sparingly nowadays, mainly *Doctor*, *Father*, *Vicar*, *Counsellor* 〈AmE〉. In most neutral interchange with strangers, no vocative is used, nor is one felt to be necessary. To gain the attention of strangers, speakers often rely on *Excuse me* or *I beg your pardon* 〈AmE〉 rather than a vocative. *Hey* is often used for the same purpose, but it is impolite when addressed to strangers.

Most vocatives that are realized by unmodified common nouns – except for the family relationship terms in (bi) – are syntactically different from the same nouns in other functions in that they do not require a determiner. Hence we can use *dear* as a vocative in *Come here, dear*. But we cannot of course say **Dear came here*. Adjectives such as *handsome*, and *stupid* cannot be used in such contexts either.

Note It is conventional to place a salutation above the body of the letter. The salutation, which is on a line of its own, is generally introduced by *Dear*;

Dear Ruth   Dear Dr Brown   Dear Madam   Dear Sir

When the sex of the addressee is unknown, it is customary in business letters to use *Dear Sir or Madam*. When the family name of a woman is known but her marital status is unknown or is considered to be irrelevant, many use *Ms* (*Dear Ms Wright*), but women differ strongly on whether they wish to be addressed, or referred to, by *Ms* (*cf* 5.66 Note [a]). When there is doubt over who should be the addressee, it is customary to write *To whom it may concern* 〈formal〉. *Dear* is often omitted in informal notes. Occasionally it is omitted in very formal letters addressed to a large number of people (*Friends*; *Gentlemen*).

Negation

Types of negation

10.54 We distinguish three types of negation:

(a) CLAUSE NEGATION, through which the whole clause is syntactically treated as negative (*cf* 10.55*ff*, 10.67*f*);

(b) LOCAL NEGATION, in which one constituent (not necessarily a clause element) is negated (*cf* 10.66);

(c) PREDICATION NEGATION, a minor type applying only after certain auxiliaries, in which the predication is negated (*cf* 10.69).

Note [a] This chapter deals only with negation as a syntactic process within the clause. On affixal negation, *cf* App I.21. In certain contexts, clauses with affixal negation are approximately synonymous with clauses negated by the clause negator *not* (*eg*: *That is not true* ~ *That is untrue*).
[b] For negative questions, *cf* 11.7*f*, 11.17; for negative directives, *cf* 11.28. Transferred negation is treated in 14.36.
[c] The difference between positive and negative has been termed a difference in POLARITY.

Clause negation

Clause negation through verb negation

10.55 A simple positive sentence (or a positive finite clause within a complex sentence) is negated by inserting the clause negator *not* between the operator and the predication (*cf* 2.48):

POSITIVE	NEGATIVE
I have finished.	I have not finished.
The children are playing.	The children are not playing.
They have been told.	They have not been told.
He may be working.	He may not be working.

The operator here (as for questions) is the first auxiliary verb of a complex verb phrase, or either BE or (especially in BrE) stative HAVE (*cf* Note [a]) as the verb in a simple verb phrase. Thus the negation of *They are noisy* is *They are not noisy*, and one negation (especially BrE) of *He has enough money* is *He has not enough money*.

If an operator is not present in the positive sentence, the dummy (or substitute) auxiliary DO is introduced. Like modal auxiliaries, it is followed by the bare infinitive:

She works hard.	She does not work hard.
They know you.	They do not know you.
I paid the porter.	I did not pay the porter.

Except in formal English, the negator more usually occurs also in the enclitic contracted form *n't*:

I haven't finished.	They don't know you.
The children aren't playing.	I didn't pay the porter.

Contracted negative forms of auxiliaries are listed in 3.32*f*, 3.36, 3.39.

The uncontracted form is of course required when the nucleus is on the negator for emphasis: *I did NÒT say that.*

Note [a] The dynamic main verb *have* requires DO as operator:

We didn't have a party last week.	~*We hadn't a party last week.
They don't have an argument every day.	~*They haven't an argument every day.
I didn't have a look at your material.	~*I hadn't a look at your material.

The stative main verb *have* usually has DO as operator, though (especially in BrE) it does not need to. In BrE especially, *got* is often added in informal style:

He has enough money { He doesn't have enough money. ⟨esp AmE⟩
He hasn't (got) enough money. ⟨esp BrE⟩

For the distinction between dynamic and stative verbs, *cf* 4.4, 4.27*ff*.
[b] For the restricted occurrence of certain negative forms, especially *mayn't*, *cf* 3.23.

[c] If the verb is subjunctive, the negator is positioned immediately before the verb, but without an operator:

It is important that he not stay beyond the end of the month.
I requested that they not interrupt me.

This use of the subjunctive is more common in AmE. In BrE putative *should* (*cf* 4.64, 14.25) or (to a lesser extent) the indicative are more likely with the consequent normal negation with the operator:

It is important that he {shouldn't / doesn't} stay beyond the end of the month.

I requested that they {shouldn't / (?)didn't} interrupt me.

[d] For examples such as *If I mistake not*, *cf* 3.22 Note [c].

[e] Some positive clauses are likely to be negated only in denials of previous statements:

A: He is {sure / bound} to succeed. B: No, he {ÌSn't / is NÒT} {sure / bound} to succeed.

Contracted forms of negator and auxiliaries

10.56 If the operator can be contracted to a form enclitic to the subject, there are two possibilities for contraction in negative clauses (though neither is used in formal English)—negator contraction and auxiliary contraction:

Jane isn't responsible.	Jane's not responsible.
We aren't ready.	We're not ready.
He wouldn't notice anything.	He'd not notice anything.
She won't object.	She'll not object.
They haven't caught him.	They've not caught him.

For the factors determining the choice between negator and auxiliary contraction, *cf* 3.23.

Note There is no standard negator contraction to parallel *I'm not ready*. For the status of *ain't*, *cf* 3.22 Note [b].

Syntactic features of clause negation

10.57 Certain syntactic features differentiate negative clauses from positive clauses:

(i) They are followed by positive checking tag questions (*cf* 11.8*ff*):

She doesn't work hard, *does* she?
[*cf*: She works hard, *doesn't* she?]

(ii) They are followed by negative tag clauses, with additive meaning:

I haven't finished, {and *neither* / *nor*} have you.
[*cf*: I've finished and *so* have you.]

Like positive clauses, however, they may be followed by positive tag clauses that do not have subject–operator inversion:

Ǐ haven't finished, but 'you HÀVE.
[*cf*: Ǐ've finished, and 'YÒU *have* TÒO.]

On *neither* and *nor*, *cf* 13.36.

(iii) In discourse, they are followed by negative agreement responses:

A: He doesn't know Russian. B: NÒ, he *DÒESn't*.
[*cf*: A: He knows Russian. B: YÈS, he DÒES.]

(iv) They are followed by nonassertive items (*cf* 10.60):

A: He won't notice *any* change in you.
B: She won't notice *any* change in you, *either*.
[*cf*: She'll notice *some* change in you, *too*.]

(v) They do not cooccur with items that have positive orientation (*cf* 10.62):

*It isn't *pretty* late. [*cf*: It's *pretty* late.]

Features (i–iii) apply only to independent declarative clauses, whereas features (iv–v) apply also to subordinate finite and nonfinite clauses. Features (iv–v) do not differentiate negative from positive clauses in other nonassertive contexts, particularly questions and conditionals (*cf* further 10.60 Note.):

Don't you want {*something* / *anything*} to eat?
Isn't it *pretty* late?
If you *ever* want my advice, don't hesitate to ask for it.
If you see her *at all*, give her my best wishes.

Note [a] Features (iv–v) do not apply to denials of positive statements previously stated or implied:

A: I understand she showed him {*some* / **any*} photographs.

B: No, she DÌDn't (show him {*some* / *any*} photographs).

[b] Like (ii) are tags with *either* or (in suitable contexts) *not even*:

I haven't finished, and you haven't *either*.
[*cf*: I have finished, and you have *too*.]
The baby couldn't walk, *not even* crawl.

[c] There are other features in discourse, apart from (iii), that differentiate negative from positive sentences; for example, disagreement responses:

He doesn't know Russian. – Oh yes, he DŎES.
He knows Russian. – Oh no, he DŎESn't.

Clause negation other than through verb negation

Words negative in form and meaning

10.58 Clausal negation may be accomplished by negating a clause element other than the verb with *no* or *not*, or by using a negative word such as *none* or *never*. We then sometimes have a choice between verb negation and negation of some other element (*cf* also 10.60):

VERB NEGATION	NEGATION OF OTHER ELEMENT
That was *not* an accident.	That was *no* accident.
He is *not* a friend of yours.	He is *no* friend of yours.
She is*n't* any different.	She is *no* different.

An honest man would *not* lie.	*No* honest man would lie.
Dogs are *not* permitted here.	*No* dogs are permitted here.
She is*n't* a fool.	She is *no* fool.
I do*n't* see any clouds.	I see *no* clouds.
He would*n't* say a word.	He would say *not* a word.
We did*n't* leave one bottle behind.	We left *not* one bottle behind.
They are *not* staying with us any longer.	They are *no* longer staying with us.
I wo*n't* make that mistake ever again.	I will *never* make that mistake again.

If the negated subject is not generic (in contrast to the subject in *No honest man would lie*), there is no corresponding negation with an operator:

Not one guest arrived late.	None of us were ready.
Neither of them wanted to stay.	Not many people came to the party.
No one listens to me.	

Where negation with an operator is also possible, it has a different meaning because the scope of negation (*cf* 10.64) is different. For example, *Many people did not come to the party* implies the absence of many people, whereas *Not many people came to the party* implies the presence of few people. In other instances, negation with an operator is not possible because a nonassertive form would be required to replace the negated subject, but it cannot precede *not* in the sentence *No one listens to me* ~ **Anyone doesn't listen to me*.

In formal style, the negative element may be moved out of its usual position to the initial position, in which case subject–operator inversion is often required (but *cf* 10.66 for some initial negative adverbials that do not require inversion):

Not a word would he say.
Not a moment did she waste.
Not one bottle did we leave behind.
No longer are they staying with us.
Never will I make that mistake again.
Under no circumstances will she return here.
Not until yesterday did he change his mind.
To no one will they admit their guilt.

All the examples in this section have clausal negation, as shown by their acceptance of the criteria listed in 10.57; for example they require the positive tag question:

No dogs are permitted here, *are they*?
Under no circumstances will she return here, *will she*?

They also require nonassertives:

Neither of us has *ever* had a university education.

Negation with *no* may have different implications than verb negation with *not*. While *He is not a teacher* denotes that his occupation is not teaching, *He is no teacher* indicates that he lacks the skills needed for teaching. The determiner *no* converts the usually nongradable noun into a gradable noun that characterizes the person. Contrast *I'm not a youngster* ['I'm not young.'] with *I'm no youngster* ['I'm quite old'; *cf* the idiom *I'm no chicken*], *She's not a fool* with *She's no fool* ['She's very intelligent.'], and *They didn't pay any tax this year* with *They paid no tax this year* ['They certainly should have done so.'], *He's not a diplomat* with *He's no diplomat* ['He's not diplomatic.']. A straightforward negation is *She isn't a politician*, but *She is no politician* evaluates her role and introduces gradability (*cf*: *She is no politician by any stretch of the imagination*).

Except for a few fixed phrases (*no good, no different*), the adverb *no* modifies adjectives only when they are comparatives (by inflection or by periphrasis): *no worse, no tastier, no better behaved, no more awkward, no less intelligent*. (Compare the positive with *the*: *He is the worse for it*.) For *no* as a modifier in local negation, *cf* 10.66.

Note **[a]** If an initial negative adverbial does not cause subject–operator inversion, the negation is not clausal but local (*cf* 10.66). Notice the negative tag question in such instances:

Not long ago, they lived in Montreal, didn't they?
Not surprisingly, he is on a diet, isn't he?

There is no inversion with negative conjuncts (*eg*: *nevertheless*; *no doubt*) and negative disjuncts (*eg*: *not unreasonably*; *not to my surprise*).

[b] *Not yet* does not occur initially in a finite clause: **Not yet have I seen him.* The combination can occur initially in nonfinite or verbless clauses, where there is a neutralization of *I* and *M* positions (*cf* 8.20 Note [b]):

Not yet having received her visa, she was unable to make arrangements for the tour.
Not yet sixteen, he has never been to an X-rated movie.

[c] Some speakers position *no more* initially, with subject–operator inversion, as a response in discourse following a negative sentence:

A: I don't play tennis.
B: *No more* do I. ['Indeed, I don't either.']

The usual equivalent responses are *Neither do I* or *Nor do I*. In a BrE construction that some find archaic or dialectal, *no more* also occurs initially without subject–operator inversion:

A: I thought you didn't play tennis.
B: *No more* I did, until this year.

Words negative in meaning but not in form

10.59 There are several adverbs and determiners which are negative in meaning but not in form. They include:

seldom, rarely
scarcely, hardly, barely
little, few (in contrast to the positive *a little* and *a few*)

These can effect clause negation: for example they are followed by nonassertive forms, and sentences in which they appear generally require a positive tag question:

I seldom get *any* sleep.
Hardly *anyone* wants the job.
Few changes have *ever* taken so many people by surprise.
I can barely speak to *any* of my colleagues.
They scarcely seem to care, *do they*?
They hardly have *any* friends, *do they*?

As with other initial negative adverbials (*cf* 10.58), the adverbs normally cause subject–operator inversion when they are positioned initially as adverbials or as modifiers within an adverbial in literary and oratorical style:

Rarely does crime pay so well as many people think.
Scarcely ever has the British nation suffered so much obloquy.
Little did I expect such enthusiasm from so many.

As well as the determiners, the adverbs *scarcely*, *hardly*, and *barely* function within a noun phrase subject, effecting clause negation:

Scarcely any wine has yet arrived, *has it*?
Barely any arms were accumulated before the war.
Little help can be expected from Peter.
Hardly fifty people were in the vast hall.

Only is to some extent negative. When it focuses on a subject noun phrase, the latter is followed by nonassertive items:

Only two of us had any experience in sailing.

And when it focuses on a fronted initial element other than the subject, it may occasionally (but need not) take subject–operator inversion:

Only his mother will he obey.
Only on Sundays do they eat with their children.

Contrast:

Only his mother he will obey. ['It's only his mother that he will obey.']

Verbs, adjectives, and prepositions with negative meaning may be followed by nonassertive items, particularly *any* and its compounds:

He *denies* I *ever* told him.
I *forgot* to ask for *any* change. [also: *some change*; The meaning would then be 'I wanted some change, but forgot to ask for it.']
She avoided *ever* speaking to us.
We are *unaware* of *any* hostility.
They were *unwilling ever* to accept our help.
I'm *against* going out *anywhere* tonight. [also: *somewhere*]
They decided to leave *without* telling *any* of their friends. [also: *some of their friends*]

Nonassertive items also follow implied negation:

Take it before he says *anything*. ['. . . so that he doesn't say anything'; also: *something*]

Note [**a**] *Rarely* may be positive when placed initially, in which case it does not cause subject–operator inversion:

Rarely, crime pays well. ['On rare occasions, crime pays well.']

[**b**] The noun phrase on which *only* focuses may contain an assertive item, but not a nonassertive item:

Only {*some* / **any*} *of us* had any experience in sailing.

Contrast:

{*Scarcely* / *Hardly* / ?*Barely*} {**some* / *any*} *of us* had any experience in sailing.

[c] Informally, *hardly* and (to a lesser extent) *scarcely* sometimes cooccur with the clause negator, although there are prescriptive objections to this usage on the grounds that these adverbs are negative in themselves. The most common combinations are *can't hardly* and *couldn't hardly*:

?I can't hardly see the words.

[d] Speakers vary in the extent to which they accept negative tag questions following these negative words. The tag questions seem most acceptable when positioned close to the end of the sentence:

He sees his parents rarely, *doesn't he*?

Hardly seems most resistant to a negative tag question:

?*He was hardly audible, *wasn't he*?

[e] *Just* is the positive adverb that is closest semantically to these negative adverbs. Compare *hardly* and *just* in these sentences:

{He *hardly* slept a wink.
He *just* slept a little.

{I could *hardly* see her.
I could *just* see her.

{She had *hardly* arrived when the orchestra started.
She had *just* arrived when the orchestra started.

Nonassertive items and negative items

10.60 As has already been pointed out (*cf* 10.57*ff*), clause negation is frequently followed (not necessarily directly) by one or more nonassertive items. Common nonassertives are listed below in the third column, and the corresponding assertive and negative items are given in parallel columns. (On nonassertive pronouns, *cf* further 6.59*ff*).

SYNTACTIC CLASS	ASSERTIVE	NONASSERTIVE	NEGATIVE
(1) determiner	*some*	*any*	*no*
(2) determiner	(*either one or the other*)	*either*	*neither*
(3) pronoun	*some*	*any*	*none*
(4) pronoun	(*one or the other*)	*either*	*neither*
(5) pronoun	*something*	*anything*	*nothing*
(6) pronoun	*somebody*	*anybody*	*nobody*
(7) pronoun	*someone*	*anyone*	*no one*
(8) process adverb	*somehow*	(*in any way*)	(*in no way*)
(9) place adverb	*somewhere*	*anywhere*	*nowhere*
	someplace ⟨informal AmE⟩	*anyplace* ⟨informal AmE⟩	*no place* ⟨informal AmE⟩
(10) time adverb	*sometime(s)*	*ever*	*never*
	always	*anytime* ⟨informal AmE⟩	
(11) time adverb	*already*	*yet*	—
(12) time adverb	*still*	*any more*	*no more*
		any longer	*no longer*
(13) degree adverbial	(*to some extent*)	*at all*	—
(14) degree adverbial	*somewhat*	*any* (*the*)	*no*, (*none the*) (*cf* [14] below)
(15) additive adverbial	*as well, too*	*either*	(*cf* Note [a])

The combination of *not* with a nonassertive form can be replaced, in most instances, by the negative word in the right-hand column; there are consequently two negative equivalents of each positive sentence:

[1] We've had some lunch. ~
- We haven't had any lunch.
- We've had no lunch.

[2] He saw one man or the other. ~
- He didn't see either man.
- He saw neither man. ⟨unusual⟩

[3] We've had some. ~
- We haven't had any.
- We've had none.

[4] He saw one or other of the men. ~
- He didn't see either of the men.
- He saw neither of the men.

[5] I've bought something for you. ~
- I haven't bought anything for you.
- I've bought nothing for you.

[6] I was speaking to somebody. ~
- I wasn't speaking to anybody.
- I was speaking to nobody.

[7] I was speaking to someone. ~
- I wasn't speaking to anyone.
- I was speaking to no one.

[8] They'll finish it somehow. ~
- They won't in any way finish it.
- They won't finish it at all.
- They will in no way finish it.

[9] He'll meet us somewhere. ~
- He won't meet us anywhere.
- He'll meet us nowhere. (*cf* Note [b])

[10] He sometimes [or *always*] visits us. ~
- He doesn't ever visit us.
- He never visits us.

[11] They've arrived already. ~ They haven't arrived yet.

[12] He's still at school. ~
- He's not at school any
  - longer.
  - more.
- He's no longer at school.

[13] I can help (to some extent). ~ I can't help at all.

[14] I'm (somewhat) wiser now. ~
- I'm not any (the) wiser now.
- I'm
  - no
  - none the

  wiser now.

[15] Her mother's coming, too. ~ Her mother's not coming either.

In all cases (except possibly that of *never*), the combination of *not* (*-n't*) and the nonassertive word is more colloquial and idiomatic than the negative variant. The absence of a negative word for *yet*, *at all*, and *either* means that there is only one negative version in examples 11, 13, and 15 (but *cf* Note [a]).

Assertive items may follow a negative if they fall outside the scope of negation (*cf* 10.64).

The primary difference between *some* and *any* (and between the *some-* and *any-* compounds) is that *some* is specific, though unspecified, while *any* is nonspecific. That is, *some* implies an amount or number that is known to the speaker. This difference tends to correlate with the difference between positive and negative contexts:

I have *some money* on me. [a specific, though unspecified amount of money]

I don't have *any money* on me. [an unspecified, and also nonspecific amount of money; no limit on the amount is assumed]

Note [a] It is not quite true to say that there is no negative word corresponding to the adverb *either*; *neither* and *nor* both occur as negative additive subjuncts, but only in an initial position with negative inversion:

He couldn't speak, (and) *neither* could he walk.
He couldn't speak, *nor* could he walk.
He couldn't speak, and he couldn't walk *either*.
He couldn't speak or walk *either*.

All these sentences mean the same, but the first two are somewhat literary in tone, while the last two are decidedly colloquial.

[b] *Nowhere* is more usual when a modal auxiliary is present. Compare *I can find it nowhere* with the unusual *I found it nowhere* and *I've found it nowhere*. But *cf* the usual *It's nowhere to be found* ['It can't be found anywhere.'].

Nonassertive contexts

10.61 Apart from negative contexts, nonassertive items appear in a number of other contexts. They include:

(i) *Yes–no* questions that expect a negative response or are neutral in expectation (11.6*f*):

Do you know any of the teachers here?

(ii) *wh*-questions (11.14*ff*):

Who has ever read the play?

(iii) putative *should*-clauses (14.25):

It's odd that he should ever notice it.

(iv) conditional clauses (15.33*ff*):

If anyone ever says that, pretend not to hear.

(v) comparative clauses (10.63*ff*):

I have more stamps than I've *yet* shown you.

(vi) restrictive relative clauses modifying generic noun phrases, where the clauses have conditional meaning:

Students who have any complaints should raise their hands.
['If students have any complaints, they should raise their hands.']

All that he has ever said confirms my suspicions of his motives.

(vii) after words that are morphologically negative or that have negative import:

It's *unlikely* that she has ever been to Scotland.

You still have time *before* you have any need to register.
['You don't have any need to register now.']

He's *too* old to play any rigorous games.
['He doesn't play any rigorous games.']

They can *prevent* any demonstrations.
I *fail* to see any force in your arguments.
I'm *reluctant* to give her any advice.
It's *hard* to do any work under these conditions.

Note [**a**] Some verbs (sometimes in combination with certain modal auxiliaries) tend to occur in negative or other nonassertive contexts:

I {*can't* / *couldn't*} {*bear* / *stand* / *abide*} that type of music. [*cf* ?*I can bear that type of music.*]
They do*n't mind* waiting. [*cf*: **They minded waiting.*]
I would*n't care* to be in his shoes.
My parents did*n't budge* from their first offer.
I wo*n't let on* what I saw.

On the other hand, *would rather* cannot be negated in a declarative sentence (*cf* 3.45):

I'd rather have an apple. [*cf*: ~*I wouldn't rather have an apple*; acceptable only as a denial sentence]
Would(n't) you rather have an apple?

The lexical verb can be negated: *I'd rather not tell you about it.*

When used as modal auxiliaries, *need* ⟨esp BrE as a modal⟩ and *dare* are restricted to nonassertive contexts. Stereotyped *I daresay* is an exception.

[**b**] *Much, many*, and *far* tend to be restricted to nonassertive contexts when unmodified:

I don't like them (very) *much*.
I don't have (very) *much* money.
We didn't see (very) *many* on our last visit.
They don't live (very) *far* from us.

On the other hand, other items that are semantically similar tend to be restricted to assertive contexts:

I like them {*a great deal.* / *a little.*} We saw {*a good many* / *a great many* / *a few*} on our last visit.

Contrast:

They {live / don't live} {*very far* / *too far* / *a long way*} from us.

Temporal *long* and *very long* tend to be restricted to assertive contexts:

I can't stay (*very*) *long*.

Contrast:

I can('t) stay {*longer.* / *a long time.*}

Negative intensification

10.62 There are various ways of giving emotive intensification to a negative, some examples of which are given here. Nonassertive expressions of extent besides *at all* include:

by any means *in any way*
in the slightest *a bit* ⟨informal⟩
in the least

Negative determiners and pronouns are given emphasis by *at all, whatever*, and *whatsoever*:

I found nothing at all the matter with him.
You have no excuse whatever.

Never is repeated for emphasis, or else combined with an intensifying phrase such as *in* (*all*) *my life*:

I'll never, never go there again.
I've never in all my life seen such a crowd.

Never itself may serve for some as an emphatic informal negative in denials:

(?)I never stayed there last night. ['I certainly didn't stay there last night.']

The combinations *not one* and *not a* (*single*) are emphatic alternatives to *no* as a countable determiner (*cf* 10.58):

Not a word came from her lips. We left not a single bottle behind.

Other emotively coloured expressions include:

He didn't give me *a thing*. ⟨informal⟩
I don't care *a damn* whether we win or lose. ⟨familiar⟩
She didn't say *a word* about it. ⟨informal⟩
No way will I accept such an offer. ⟨familiar⟩

Some expressions are formed in combination with specific verbs:

He won't *lift a finger* to help you.
I didn't *sleep a wink*.
She didn't *bat an eye*(*lid*).
They won't *budge an inch*.
I won't *drink a drop*.
He didn't *move a muscle*.
We didn't *see a soul*.

On the other hand, the intensifiers *quite*, *pretty*, and *rather* are assertive:

$$\text{They drive} \left\{ \begin{array}{l} \textit{quite} \\ \textit{pretty} \\ \textit{rather} \end{array} \right\} \text{fast.}$$

Contrast the unacceptability (except in denial sentences) of:

$$\text{*They do}\textit{n't}\text{ drive} \left\{ \begin{array}{l} \textit{quite} \\ \textit{pretty} \\ \textit{rather} \end{array} \right\} \text{fast.}$$

Similarly, *far* as intensifier of comparatives is assertive:

The food was *far* better than I expected.
*The food was*n't far* better than I expected.

Other assertive intensifiers include *no end* (*of*), which intensifies noun phrases as well as verbs:

She praised the play *no end*. It was *no end* of a mess.

For assertive *rather* in *would rather*, *cf* 10.61 Note [a], and for assertive *much*, *cf* 10.61 Note [b].

Note [a] *To speak of* is an informal nonassertive downtoner (8.111*ff*):

They haven't any money, *to speak of*.

[b] *Quite* is acceptable in a negative sentence when it modifies a phrase with the postmodifier *enough*:

They don't drive *quite* fast *enough*. It wasn't *quite* long *enough*.

[c] In informal style, *too* may be synonymous with *very*; hence, there may be a shift of meaning in negation or when *too* modifies words with negative meaning:

They drive *too* fast. ['They drive faster than they should'; 'They don't drive slowly enough.']

They don't drive *too* fast. ['They don't drive very fast'; the sentence can also be a denial of the positive statement.]

That's *too* bad. ['That's very bad.']

[d] *Could care less* <esp AmE> is sometimes used in the same sense as *couldn't care less*, but there are prescriptive objections to the locution.

[e] *Ever* is sometimes used as an intensifier in combination with *never*: *I'll never ever stay with them again.*

More than one nonassertive item

10.63 If a clause is negative, it is usually negative throughout, or at least until the beginning of a final adjunct (*cf* 10.64). Nonassertive items must normally be used after the negative element in place of *every* assertive item that would have occurred in the corresponding positive clause:

I've never travelled *anywhere* by air *yet*.
I haven't *ever* been on *any* of the big liners, *either*.
No one has *ever* said *anything* to *either* of us.
Not many of the refugees have *anywhere* to live *yet*.

Notice that negative items (normally only one) must always precede the nonassertive items, as in this series of corresponding clauses:

I *don't* give *any* pocket money to *any* of my children at *any* time.
I give *no* pocket money to *any* of my children at *any* time.
I give pocket money to *none* of my children at *any* time.
I give pocket money to my children at *no* time.

The further the negative word is postposted, the more questionable the sentence is, because the sentence is at first perceived as positive and then has to be reinterpreted as negative.

Note In nonstandard English, a negative item can be used wherever in standard English a nonassertive item follows a negative:

STANDARD: No one *ever* said *anything* to *anybody*.
NONSTANDARD: No one *never* said *nothing* to *nobody*.

Such double or multiple negatives are condemned by prescriptive grammatical tradition (*cf* further 10.70).

Scope of negation

10.64 A negative item may be said to govern (or determine the occurrence of) a nonassertive only if the latter is within the SCOPE of the negative, *ie* within the stretch of language over which the negative item has a semantic influence. The scope of the negation normally extends from the negative item itself to the end of the clause, but it need not include an end-placed adverbial. In a clause with the clause negator *not* or a negative word such as *never* or *hardly* in the same position after the operator, adverbials occurring before the negative normally lie outside the scope. There is thus a contrast between:

She definitely didn't speak to him.

['It's definite that she didn't speak to him.']

She didn't definitely speak to him.

['It's not definite that she spoke to him.']

(The scope is marked by the horizontal brackets.)

When an adjunct is final, it may or may not lie outside the scope:

I wasn't LǏstening all the TÌME. [1]

I wasn't listening all the TǏME. [2]

The difference of scope, which is here marked by intonation, reflects an important difference of meaning: [1] means 'For the whole time, I wasn't listening', whereas [2] means 'It is not true that I was listening all the time'. If an assertive form is used in the adjunct, the adjunct must lie outside the scope; therefore [3] and [4] below parallel [1] and [2]:

I didn't listen to some of the speakers. [3]

['There were some of the speakers that I didn't listen to.']

I didn't listen to any of the speakers. [4]

['There were not any speakers that I listened to.']

Disjuncts and conjuncts (*cf* 8.121*ff*) always lie outside the scope of clause negation, whatever their position:

She doesn't know him, unfortunately.

She doesn't know him, however.

The scope can sometimes extend into a subordinate clause:

She didn't know I would come to her *whenever she needed any advice*.

I wouldn't like you *to disturb anyone*.

Note When a negative adverbial is positioned initially, the subject and operator follow the negative item. In that case, the subject may have a nonassertive form:

Never have *any of them* been interested in music.

Very occasionally, the scope of negation may extend to an adjunct that has been fronted from its normal position, in which case a nonassertive may occur in the adjunct (without subject–operator inversion):

To any of those speakers I wouldn't listen. ⟨rare⟩

A more common fronting (with subject–operator inversion) is:

To none of those speakers would I listen.

The normal form is:

I wouldn't listen *to any of those speakers*.

Focus of negation

10.65 We need to identify not only the scope, but also the FOCUS of negation. A special or contrastive nuclear stress falling on a particular part of the clause indicates that the contrast of meaning implicit in the negation is located at that spot, and also that the rest of the clause can be understood in a positive sense. To distinguish the parts that are to be understood negatively and positively, we need to refine our notion of scope to allow for DISCONTINUOUS SCOPE and also to allow for the part preceding the negative item to come within the scope of negation. Different placements of the focus distinguish the following sentences. The parts that are not within the scope are understood positively:

I didn't take Joan to swim in the PÒOL today. – I forgot to do so.

I didn't take JǑAN to swim in the pool today. – It was Mary.

I didn't take Joan to SWǏM in the pool today – just to see it.

I didn't take Joan to swim in the PǑOL today. – I took her to the seaside.

I didn't take Joan to swim in the pool toDǍY. – It was last week that I did so.

Ǐ didn't take Joan to swim in the pool today. – It was my brother who took her.

The positive implications can be made explicit by alternative negation:

I don't like CǑFfee, but I do like TÈA.

I don't mind the NǑISE, but I do mind the HÈAT.

or by focused negation:

It's not CǑFfee that I like (, but tea).

It's not the NǑISE that I mind (, but the heat).

Scope and focus are interrelated such that the scope must include the focus. From this it follows that one way of signalling the extent of the scope is by the position of the focus. Indeed, since the scope of the negation is often not otherwise clearly signalled, we can indicate it by where we place the information focus. One example of this is when the scope of the negation is atypically extended to include a subordinate clause, with a contrastive fall-rise to emphasize this:

I didn't leave HÓME because I was afraid of my FÀTHer. [1]

[= Because I was afraid of my father, I didn't leave home.]

I didn't leave home because I was afraid of my FĂTHer. [2]

[= I left home, but it wasn't because I was afraid of my father.]

With more usual intonation, [1] allots a separate tone unit to each clause, and so places the *because*-clause outside the scope of the negative. (This interpretation can also be singled out by a comma in writing.) But [2] extends a single tone unit over both, and places a contrastive fall + rise on *father*. The effect of this is to place negative focus on the *because*-clause, so that the main clause is understood positively. Variable scope applies also to the *when*-clauses in [3] and [4]:

She didn't come to SÉE him when he ÀSKED. [3]

[= When he asked, she didn't come to see him.]

She didn't come to see him when he ĂSKED. [4]

[= She came to see him, but not at the time he asked her to come to see him.]

In [3] the *when*-clause is an adverbial of the sentence, whereas in [4] it is an adverbial of the preceding infinitive clause.

Intonation may be crucial also in marking whether or not the subject is the focus of negation, a distinction that may be needed in subjects containing one of the universal items *all* or *every*:

All the children didn't SLÈEP. ['All the children failed to sleep.'] [5]

ĂLL the children didn't sleep. ['Not all the children slept.'] [6]

[6] has contrastive (fall + rise) information focus. The construction of [5] is unusual; more common is the paraphrase with a negative subject: *None of the children slept*.

Note [a] In denial sentences the clause negator may have the focus, since the rest of the clause has already been asserted or implied:

I did NÒT offer her some chocolates. ['It is not true that I offered her some chocolates.']

The same effect is achieved by focus on a negative operator:

I DÌDn't offer her some chocolates.

or some other negative word:

I NÈVer offered her some chocolates.
NÒbody offered her some chocolates.

[b] When the focus is on a gradable item, the effect is usually to indicate less than the norm:

The room isn't LĂRGE, but it will do.

But the context may indicate the reverse:

The room isn't (just) LĂRGE, it's enormous.

Local negation

10.66 Local negation negates a word or phrase, without making the clause negative (*cf* 10.57). A common type is exemplified in [1]:

She's a not unattractive woman, { in some ways. / *in any respect. } [1]

In [1] *not* negates *unattractive* but not the whole clause, as we can see from the inadmissibility of the nonassertive item *any*. Contrast the clausal negation in [2], where the tag question is positive:

She's not an attractive woman / She isn't an attractive woman } in any respect, is she? [2]

The effect of *not* in [1] is merely to reverse the already negative force of the following expression. Such double negative phrases are devices of understatement, *She is a not entirely unintelligent woman* meaning 'She is a fairly intelligent woman'; similarly, *He's not a too sympathetic doctor* means 'He's a rather unsympathetic doctor'. The double negative phrases require a gradable adjective or adverb as head, the negation indicating a point between the two extremes of the gradable scale; for [1] the point is somewhere between *unattractive* and *attractive*. Here are other examples of double negative phrases:

They made some *not unintelligent observations*. [3]
They are paying a *not inconsiderable amount* in rent. [4]
The announcement was followed by a *not unexpected silence*. [5]
I visit them *not infrequently*. [6]
He writes *not inelegantly*. [7]

Each of these sentences corresponds to a positive sentence in which the double negative is replaced by a downtoner (*cf* 8.111*ff*). Thus, [3] may be paraphrased by *They made some fairly intelligent observations* and [4] by *They are paying a rather considerable amount in rent*. We may similarly paraphrase the double negative phrases in the other three sentences by positive phrases with downtoners: *a somewhat expected silence* [5], *fairly frequently* [6], *rather elegantly* [7].

Some content disjuncts (*cf* 8.127*ff*), those either having a negative prefix or conveying unexpectedness, may be negated:

Not unnaturally, we rejected their complaint. [8]
Not surprisingly, they missed the train. [9]

Not unnaturally in [8] is a double negative phrase, and the effect of the negation is to understate ('as was rather expected'), as in the double negative phrases in [1–7]. In [9], *not* simply negates *surprisingly* ('that's not surprising').

In another type of local negation, *not* modifies a degree adverb, which in turn modifies a positive gradable adjective or adverb:

They own two *not very fierce dogs*. ['rather docile'] [10]
I saw a *not too sympathetic report* about you. ['rather unsympathetic'] [11]
I visit them *not very often*. [12]
Janet arrived *not much earlier* than Bob. [13]
Derek drives *not as well* as expected. [14]

Sentences [12–14], with the gradable adverbs, correspond to negative sentences; for example, [12] corresponds to *I don't visit them very often*, though

[12] exhibits local negation, not clause negation. On the other hand, sentences [10] and [11] do not correspond to negative sentences, because the adjective phrases are not clause elements, but are embedded in noun phrases that are elements. The adjective phrases correspond to an antonymous adjective modified by a downtoner: 'rather tame dogs' [10], 'a somewhat unsympathetic report' [11].

Not may also modify adverbial expressions of extent in distance or time:

They live *not far* from us. [15]
I saw Dave *not long ago*. ['fairly recently'] [16]
We were there *not many years* after the war. ['just a few years'] [17]

Since the modified phrase is a clause element in [15], the sentence corresponds to a negative sentence ('They don't live far away from us.').

The quantifiers *a few* and *a little* may be negated by *not* and the quantifier *little* by *no*:

They have *not a few eccentrics* in their family.
I sensed *not a little hostility* in his manner.
They displayed *no little interest* in her progress. ⟨formal⟩

These negative quantifiers have the clear force of understatement. A similar effect is conveyed by the comparatives *more*, *less*, and *fewer* when they are negated by either *not* or *no*:

You may take *no more* than an hour's break for lunch.
They'll pay you *not less* than ten dollars an hour.
I have been able to collect *no fewer* than sixty signatures for the petition.

No is somewhat more emphatic and asseverative than *not* in these contexts.

Prepositional phrases may also be negated, whether as adjuncts or as postmodifiers in noun phrases, by a negative word within the complement:

He was decorated *by none other than the President*.
I'll give it to you *for nothing*.
We cleared the table *in no time*.
She replied *with not a moment's hesitation*.
[*cf*: *without a moment's hesitation*]
The brothers set out on their hike *with never a worry in the world*.
Our house has one wall *with no windows*.
It was a decision *of no consequence*.

An unusual type of local negation appears in noun phrases that express a compressed predication:

No news is good news.
['Receiving no news is good news.']
The company promised no victimization.
['The company promised that there would be no victimization.']
Something is better than nothing.
['Having something is better than having nothing.']
The children want nothing but television.
['The children want to do nothing but watch television.']

In local negation, an initial negative adverbial does not cause subject–operator inversion (*cf* 10.58*f*). We may therefore contrast local negation in the [a] sentences below with clause negation in the [b] sentences. The [a] sentences are distinctly less usual:

In no time we cleared the table.
['We cleared the table within a short time.'] [18a]
At no time was war as imminent as now.
['War wasn't as imminent as now at any previous time.'] [18b]

Not even ten years ago you could see such a film.
['You could see such a film as recently as ten years ago.'] [19a]
Not even ten years ago could you see such a film.
['You couldn't see such a film even ten years ago.'] [19b]

(Even) with no coaching he will pass the exam.
['He will pass the exam (even) without coaching.'] [20a]
With no coaching will he pass the exam.
['Whatever coaching is provided will not enable him to pass the exam.] [20b]

The paraphrases show that semantically the [a] sentences are positive and the [b] sentences are negative. The [a] sentences take a negative tag question (*In no time we cleared the table, didn't we*?) whereas the [b] sentences take a positive tag question (*At no time was war as imminent as now, was it*?)

It is convenient to refer briefly here to the uses of the negative response word *no*. The selection of *no* is determined by whether it negates the implied or given statement:

A: I didn't do too good a job today. B: No, you DÌDn't. [21]
A: I did a good job today. B: No you DǏDn't. [22]

Notice that the use of *no* is not determined by the speaker's disagreement with a previous speaker's statement, since in [21], unlike [22], speaker B agrees with speaker A. Contrast:

A: I didn't do too good a job today. B: Yes, you DǏD. [23]
A: I did a good job today. B: Yes, you DÌD. [24]

Yes is used in [23] even though speaker B disagrees with speaker A. The same principle applies to responses to *yes–no* questions:

A: Is it raining? B: { Yes (, it ǐs). / No (, it ìsn't). }

But since the *yes–no* question typically asks for a response on the truth value of the corresponding statement ('Is it or is it not true that it's raining?'), the responses coincide with an assertion (*yes*) or a denial (*no*) of its truth value.

Note [**a**] Local negation also occurs in correlation with *but* when *not* is positioned before a clause element (*cf* 13.42):

They want not your pity but your help.
[*cf* clause negation: They don't want your pity but your help.]

You should pay attention not to what they say but to what they do.
I saw not ǑNE official, but THRÈE.

A tone unit boundary is normal before *not*.

[**b**] *They argued about nothing* is ambiguous between clause and local negation: 'They didn't argue about anything' or 'They argued, but the argument was about nothing (of significance)'.

[**c**] For *not* as a pro-form for a negative direct object clause (as in *I believe not*, *I hope not*, *I guess not*), *cf* 12.28.

Negation of modal auxiliaries

Present forms of modals

10.67 The scope of negation may or may not include the meaning of the modal auxiliaries. We therefore distinguish between AUXILIARY NEGATION and MAIN VERB NEGATION. The contrast is shown in the two following sentences with *may not*, where the paraphrases indicate the scope of negation:

AUXILIARY NEGATION

You may not smoke in here. ['You are not allowed to smoke in here.']

MAIN VERB NEGATION

They may not like the party.

['It is possible that they do not like the party.']

We give examples below of the modal auxiliaries, according to whether the scope of negation usually includes the auxiliary or excludes it. The senses of the modal auxiliaries are discussed in 4.49*ff*.

AUXILIARY NEGATION

may not [= 'permission']

You may not go swimming. ['You are not allowed . . .']

cannot, *can't* [in all senses]

You can't be serious. ['It is not possible that . . .']

You can't go swimming. ['You are not allowed to . . .']

He can't ride a bicycle. ['He is not able to . . .']

need not, *needn't* ⟨both esp BrE⟩

You needn't pay that fine. ['You are not obliged to . . .']

It needn't always be my fault. ['It is not necessary that . . .']

dare not, *daren't*

I daren't quarrel with them.

['I haven't got the courage to quarrel with them.']

MAIN VERB NEGATION

may not [= 'possibility']

They may not bother to come if it's wet.

['It is possible that they will not bother to come . . .']

shall not, shan't ⟨all senses; esp BrE; *shan't* rare even in BrE⟩

Don't worry. You shan't lose your reward.

['I'll make sure that you don't lose your reward.']

I shan't know you when you return. ['I predict that I will not know . . .']

must not, mustn't ['obligation']

You mustn't keep us waiting.

['It is essential that you don't keep us waiting']

ought not, oughtn't [both senses; for *ought* with the bare infinitive, *cf* 3.43 Note [a]]

You oughtn't to keep us waiting. ['obligation']

He oughtn't to be long. ['tentative inference']

The distinction between auxiliary and main negation is neutralized for *will* in all its senses, as the paraphrases below indicate:

Don't worry. I won't interfere. ['I don't intend to interfere'; 'I intend not to interfere.']
He won't do what he's told. ['He refuses to do what he's told'; 'He insists on not doing what he's told.']
They won't have arrived yet. ['It's not probable that they've arrived yet'; 'I predict that they haven't arrived yet.']

The auxiliary negation of *must* in the logical necessity sense is usually achieved through *can't*:

They *must* be telling lies. ['It is certain that they are telling lies.']
~ They *can't* be telling lies. ['It's not possible that they are telling lies.']

But *must not* and *mustn't* occur in this sense occasionally in AmE and, still more occasionally, in BrE. This use (instead of *can't*) seems to be gaining favour. A less emphatic negation of *must* in the same sense may be achieved with *needn't* and *don't have to* ⟨esp AmE⟩, both of which have the epistemic meanings of 'not necessary' and 'not obliged to':

It must be hot now in Florida.

~ It {doesn't have to / needn't} be hot in Florida now.

['It's not certain that it is hot in Florida now' or 'It's not necessarily the case that it is hot in Florida now.']

The auxiliary negation of *must* in the obligation sense is *needn't* or *don't have to*:

A: Must we pack now?
B: No, we {don't have to / needn't} pack till tomorrow.
['It is not necessary for us to pack till tomorrow'; 'We are not obliged to pack till tomorrow.']

Because of the diametric opposition of meaning between 'permission' and 'obligation', an odd-seeming equivalence exists between *may not* ['not permitted to'] and *mustn't* ['obliged not to']:

You mustn't go swimming today.

= You may not go swimming today.

In the possibility sense, *cannot* and *can't*, which take auxiliary negation, contrast with *may not*, which takes main verb negation:

She can't be serious. ['It's not possible that she's serious.']

She may not be serious. ['It's possible that she's not serious.']

Past forms of modals

10.68 The past tense negative auxiliaries (*mightn't*, *couldn't*, *wouldn't*, *shouldn't*) follow the same negative pattern as their present tense equivalents (but *cf* 4.61*ff*):

AUXILIARY NEGATION

could not, *couldn't* [in all senses]

She couldn't be SĔRious. ['It is not possible . . . , is it?']

We couldn't smoke in the restaurant. ['We were not allowed to . . .']

He couldn't drive a car. ['He was not able to . . .']

MAIN VERB NEGATION

might not, *mightn't*

They might not be telling lies. ['It is possible that they are not . . .']

should not, *shouldn't* [all senses]

You shouldn't say anything. ['You are advised not to say anything.']

We shouldn't be long. ['According to my information, we won't be long'.]

They shouldn't be there yet. ['It is probable that they are not there yet.']

As is the case with *will* (*cf* 10.67), the distinction between auxiliary and main verb negation is neutralized for *would* in all senses:

> He wouldn't carry the baby. ['refused to carry' or 'insisted on not carrying']
> He usually wouldn't drive to work. ['was not in the habit of driving' or 'was in the habit of not driving']
> That wouldn't be the doorbell. ['It's not probable that it's the doorbell' or 'I predict that it's not the doorbell.']

The past tense negative auxiliaries display contrasts in the scope of negation similar to those for the present tense form. *Could not* and *couldn't* contrast with *might not* and *mightn't*:

> She couldn't be serious. ['It's not possible that she is serious' or 'She was not able to be serious.']
> She might not be serious. ['It's possible that she is not serious.']

Similar contrasts are found between *shouldn't*, on the one hand, and *couldn't*, *needn't*, and *don't have to*, on the other hand:

> It shouldn't be hot in Florida now. ['It's likely that it's not hot in Florida now.']
> It couldn't be hot in Florida now. ['It's not possible that it's hot in Florida now.']

$$\text{It}\left\{\begin{array}{l}\text{needn't}\\ \text{doesn't have to}\end{array}\right\}\text{be hot in Florida now.}$$

> ['It's not certain that it's hot in Florida now.']

Note [**a**] *Might* and *might not* in the permission sense are rare, occurring chiefly in polite questions:

> Might I (not) have a word with you?
> I wonder whether I might (not) have a word with you.

[**b**] The marginal modal auxiliary *need* forms its past equivalent with *have* ⟨esp BrE⟩:

> You needn't have paid that fine. ['You didn't need to pay . . . ⟨BrE and AmE⟩]

The marginal modal auxiliary *dare* has a past form *dared* ⟨esp BrE⟩:

> I dared not quarrel with them.

Negation with *do* and the bare infinitive is usual both for the present and the past:

$$\text{I}\left\{\begin{array}{l}\text{don't}\\ \text{didn't}\end{array}\right\}\text{dare quarrel with them.}$$

The lexical verbs are more commonly used: *didn't need to, didn't dare to* (*cf* 3.40*ff* for a more detailed discussion).

Predication negation

10.69 Very rarely, PREDICATION NEGATION occurs in the context of denials and permission. In predication negation, a modal auxiliary is used with a different scope of negation than is normal for that auxiliary. With a special emphatic pause before *not*, one might say:

> They may 'not go swimming. ['They are allowed not to go swimming.']

You can (simply) 'not obey the order. ['It's possible for you not to obey the order.']

In such instances of main verb negation, the clause is not negated (*cf* 10.57), since we can say (though it is unusual to do so):

A: They don't want to go swimming.
B: I suppose so. OK, let's agree that they may 'not go swimming.
A: YÈS, they MÀY.
You can 'not obey the order, can't you?

On the other hand, this predication negation differs from local negation (*cf* 10.66) in that it can extend over several clause elements beginning with the main verb.

Predication negation may also be followed by nonassertive forms:

You could 'not attend any of the meetings. ['It's possible for you not to attend any of the meetings.']

Because both kinds of negation may occur with the same auxiliary, acceptable instances of two negators in the same clause sometimes arise:

I can't 'not obey her. ['It's not possible for me not to obey her', 'I have to obey her.']
You can't 'not admire him. ['It's not possible for you not to admire him', 'You have to admire him.']

More natural ways of expressing a corresponding negation would be:

I can't help obeying her.
I can't help but obey her. ['The only thing I can do is to obey her.']

You can't help admiring him.
You can't (help) but admire him.

On the subjunct use of *but*, *cf* 8.111.

Occasionally, two negators may be used with auxiliaries other than modals:

She didn't 'not like them. ['She didn't dislike them.']
They don't often 'not remember her birthday.
['They don't often fail to remember her birthday.']
He hasn't ever 'not understood a lecture.
['He hasn't ever failed to understand a lecture.']

Double negation

10.70 As we have seen in 10.69, two negatives occasionally occur in the same clause. Our example there involved a combination of auxiliary and main verb negation, but other combinations occur:

Not many people have nowhere to live. ['Most people have somewhere to live.']
No one has nothing to offer to society. ['Everyone has something to offer to society.']
Nobody has nothing to eat. ['Everyone has something to eat.']

Not all imperatives have no subject. ['Some imperatives have a subject.']
Never before had none of the committee members supported the mayor.
['Some of the committee members had always supported the mayor before.']
None of us have never told lies. ['All of us have told lies at some time.']

These sentences are somewhat similar to the double negative of logic: each negative has its separate value, and it is possible to find paraphrases, like those just given, which cancel out each negative, leaving an entirely positive sentence in meaning. Syntactically, however, the sentences are negative; for example, they require positive tag questions (*cf* 11.8*ff*):

Not all imperatives have no subject, *do they*?

The double negation in standard English is very different from the double or multiple negation in nonstandard English, where the additional negatives are used in place of nonassertive words in standard English (*cf* 10.63 Note). The additional negatives in nonstandard English do not cancel out previous negatives.

Bibliographical note

On major theoretical discussions, see Chafe (1970); Chomsky (1957; 1965); Lyons (1977); Stockwell et al (1973).

On syntactic structures and functions, see Bach (1967); Dušková (1976); Ellegård (1978) for frequency data; Gleason (1965), esp Chapter 13; Halliday (1967–68); Keenan (1976); Matthews (1980); Mittwoch (1971); Smith (1978).

On semantic roles, see Anderson (1977); Chafe (1970), esp Chapters 9 & 12; Dik (1978), esp Chapters 3–5; Fillmore (1968; 1977b); Halliday (1967–68); Longacre (1976), Chapter 2; Lyons (1977), Chapter 12; Schlesinger (1979).

On *it* and *there*, see Bolinger (1977a), Chapters 4 & 5.

On cognate and eventive objects, see Baron (1971); Nickel (1968); Olsson (1961); Wierzbicka (1982).

On number concord, see Juul (1975).

On vocatives, see Whitcut (1980); Zwicky (1974).

On negation, see Bolinger (1977a), Chapters 2 & 3; Horn (1978a); Jackendoff (1969); Jespersen (1917); Klima (1964); Stockwell et al (1973), Chapter 5; Tottie (1977; 1980).

11 Sentence types and discourse functions

Sentence types

Formal classification

11.1 In Chapter 10 we described the simple sentence primarily in terms of declarative sentences. We now turn to the other major types of sentences. These are more easily described in relation to the declarative, since to describe them we require additional rules; for example, we need rules for the insertion of DO as operator in many *yes–no* interrogatives, for the initial positioning of the *wh*-element in *wh*-interrogatives and in exclamatives, and for the presence or (generally) absence of a normally obligatory subject in imperatives.

Simple sentences may be divided into four major syntactic types differentiated by their form. Their use correlates largely with different discourse functions (*cf* 11.2).

(I) DECLARATIVES are sentences in which the subject is present and generally precedes the verb:

Pauline gave Tom a digital watch for his birthday.

On exceptional declaratives not containing a subject *cf* 12.46*ff*.

(II) INTERROGATIVES are sentences which are formally marked in one of two ways:

(i) *yes–no* interrogatives: the operator is placed in front of the subject:

Did Pauline give Tom a digital watch for his birthday?

(ii) *wh*-interrogatives: the interrogative *wh*-element is positioned initially:

What did Pauline give Tom for his birthday?

(III) IMPERATIVES are sentences which normally have no overt grammatical subject, and whose verb has the base form (*cf* 3.2):

Give me a digital watch for my birthday.

(IV) EXCLAMATIVES are sentences which have an initial phrase introduced by *what* or *how*, usually with subject–verb order (*cf* 11.31*f*):

What a fine watch he received for his birthday!

There are also some minor sentence types, which will be considered in 11.38*ff*.

Note [**a**] For (II) above, the operator need not be placed immediately in front of the subject (*cf* 11.7).
[**b**] For dependent interrogatives, *cf* 15.5*f*; for dependent exclamatives, *cf* 15.7; for correspondences in indirect speech, *cf* 14.33.

Discourse functions

11.2 Associated with these four sentence types are four classes of discourse functions:

(a) STATEMENTS are primarily used to convey information.

(b) QUESTIONS are primarily used to seek information on a specific point (*cf* 11.4*ff*).
(c) DIRECTIVES are primarily used to instruct somebody to do something (*cf* 11.24*ff*).
(d) EXCLAMATIONS are primarily used for expressing the extent to which the speaker is impressed by something (*cf* 11.31*f*).

Direct association between syntactic class and semantic class is the norm, but the two classes do not always match, as the following sentences illustrate:

Pauline gave Tom a digital WÁTCH? [1]
What do ì care? [2]
I'd 'love a cup of TĚA. [3]
Isn't Christine CLÈver! [4]

[1] is a declarative question (*cf* 11.12); it is syntactically declarative but semantically a question. On the other hand, the rhetorical question (*cf* 11.23) in [2] is syntactically an interrogative but semantically a statement ('I certainly don't care'). In [3] the declarative is semantically a directive suggesting that the hearer bring the speaker a cup of tea. Finally, [4] is syntactically interrogative but semantically an exclamation; contrast *How clever Christine is!*, which is syntactically exclamative as well as semantically an exclamation.

Note A traditional term for directive is 'command', but that has a more restricted meaning in this book, *cf* 11.29.

Illocutionary acts

11.3 The four semantic classes of discourse functions constitute a closed class of sentence categories that distinguish discourse functions at the most general level. But we can make many more refined distinctions. For example, a statement can be used to make an assertion [1], to make a prediction [2], or to offer an apology [3]:

Engineers are building massive hydroelectric projects in China. [1]
It's going to rain any minute now. [2]
I'm sorry about the delay. [3]

Assertion, prediction, and apology are pragmatic categories that indicate how the semantic classes of sentences are used in actual utterances.

Utterances of sentences are SPEECH ACTS, *ie* acts of verbal behaviour (spoken or written). When a person performs a speech act, that person at one and the same time utters a particular utterance, namely a LOCUTIONARY ACT. We use ILLOCUTIONARY ACT to refer to a speech act identified with reference to the communication intention of the hearer. The intended effect of an illocutionary act is its ILLOCUTIONARY FORCE. Occasionally, the speaker explicitly refers to the illocutionary act being performed by using a PERFORMATIVE VERB:

I *apologize* for my remarks.
Your presence at the meeting is *requested*.

I *promise* you a bicycle for your birthday.
Smoking in this compartment is *forbidden*.

But generally, performative verbs are not present in speech acts.

Illocutionary acts are typically associated with particular semantic classes of sentences – for example, inquiry with questions; and requests, commands, and invitations with directives – though statements are related to a very large range of illocutionary acts. But semantic and pragmatic classes are not always directly associated, any more than semantic classes and syntactic types (*cf* 11.2). Sentences from one semantic class are very often used to express an illocutionary act typically associated with sentences from a different semantic class. In such instances, the sentence retains its normal semantic status but is at the same time indirectly used to perform another type of illocutionary act. Here are some examples of such INDIRECT SPEECH ACTS:

I think you'd better leave at once. [request by statement]
Dinner is ready. [request to come to eat by statement]
Could you please make less noise? [request by question]
Do you happen to have a pencil? [request to be given a pencil by question]
Tell me what you want. [inquiry by directive]
I'd like to know the name of your last employer. [inquiry by statement]
Do you want another cup? [offer by question]
Remember that I'm always ready to help. [offer by directive]
Why don't you take an aspirin? [advice by question]
I'd sell your car if I were you. [advice by statement]

The illocutionary force of an utterance is dependent on the context, and a particular utterance may have different illocutionary force in different contexts. For example, the sentence *My husband will be back soon* may be intended, among other possibilities, as a promise, a threat, or a warning. Furthermore, the categorization of illocutionary acts might suggest discrete distinctions that we often cannot make. Thus *Why don't you take an aspirin?* is indeterminate, in the same context, between advice and recommendation, and *Would you like to come outside and sit in the sun?* is poised between invitation and suggestion.

Note [**a**] Some performative verbs may be required or may be usual in ritual or legal situations:

I sentence you to one year's imprisonment. I name this ship Dreadnought.

The possible insertion of *hereby* is an indication of the performative use of the verb:

I hereby name this ship Dreadnought.

The same verb may be used in sentences which merely report the performative speech act:

She named that ship Dreadnought.

[**b**] One type of indirect speech act involves HEDGED PERFORMATIVES, which refer to the performance of a speech act indirectly, even though a performative verb is present:

I *must apologize* for my behaviour.
I *can swear* that I locked the door.
I *would like to thank* you for your hospitality.
I *am happy to inform* you that you have passed the examination.

For example, in *I must apologize for my behaviour* the sentence merely refers to an obligation to perform an apology, but the implication is that the acceptance of the obligation is equivalent to the performance.

[c] The indirectness of a speech act is commonly due to tact on the part of the speaker, who leaves it to the hearer to make the appropriate inferences. Thus, *It's cold in here* may indirectly convey a request to close a window or door or to turn on a heater, or it may indirectly convey a suggestion for those present to move elsewhere. The hearer is given a choice of responses. Similarly, *Your tie is not straight* allows the hearer to draw inferences, and is therefore more polite than *Straighten your tie.*

Questions

Major classes

11.4 Questions can be divided into three major classes according to the type of reply they expect:

(1) Those that expect affirmation or negation, as in *Have you finished the book?*, are *YES–NO* questions (*cf* 11.5*ff*);
(2) Those that typically expect a reply from an open range of replies, as in *What is your name?* or *How old are you?* are *WH-* questions (*cf* 11.14*ff*);
(3) Those that expect as the reply one of two or more options presented in the question, as in *Would you like to go for a WÁLK or stay at HÒME?*, are ALTERNATIVE questions (*cf* 11.20*f*).

Logically well-formed replies, responses that conform with expectations, are a subset of pragmatically appropriate answers. Many answers that are apparently irrelevant become relevant in terms of the implicatures they convey:

A: Have you seen my chocolates?
B: Well, the children were in your room this morning.

It is therefore possible for a question to be answered by another question:

A: Are you going to watch television again?
B: What else is there to do?
A: Is that your baby?
B: What do YÒU think? [sarcastic: 'Of course it's my baby.']

Any utterance of a question that has the illocutionary force of an inquiry may be answered by *I don't know* or *I'm not sure*, or by a refusal to answer, *eg*: *It's none of your business* ⟨impolite⟩, or by an evasion, *eg*: *Good question*, or by a challenge to a presupposition of the question, *eg*: *Do you like Joan Parker? – I don't know any Joan Parker.*

Questions primarily have the illocutionary force of inquiries. But they are often used as directives conveying requests, offers, invitations, and advice (*cf* 11.3, 11.16*f*). For exclamatory and rhetorical questions, *cf* 11.22*f*.

Note [a] Affirmation and negation may be conveyed by words or expressions other than *yes* or *no*, *eg*: *certainly*; *of course*; *not at all*; *never*. *Yes–no* questions may also be answered by replies that lie somewhere along the affirmation–negation scale, *eg*: *probably*; *perhaps*; *It appears so*; *to some extent*; *occasionally*; *very often*.

[b] An answer may be truthful and yet misleading:

A: Did you enjoy the play?

B: No.

B's answer is truthful even if B has not seen the play, but it is misleading in that both the question and the answer imply that B had seen the play.

[c] While questions generally imply that the speaker does not know the answer, they are also used in certain contexts where the speaker knows the answer but wants to know whether the hearer also knows it. Examples of such contexts are written examinations, exercises in textbooks, and questioning by teachers, parents, and interviewers to test the hearer's knowledge.

Yes–no questions

Form of *yes–no* questions

11.5 *Yes–no* questions are usually formed by placing the operator before the subject and giving the sentence a rising intonation:

The boat has LÈFT. ~ Has the boat LÉFT?
Ann is writing a PÀPer. ~ Is Ann writing a PÁPer?
Our team was BÈATen. ~ Was our team BÉATen?
He could have broken his LÈG. ~ Could he have broken his LÉG?
She'll be waiting outsÌDE. ~ Will she be waiting outsÍDE?

If there is no item in the verb phrase that can function as operator, DO is introduced, as with negation (*cf* 10.55):

They live in Sydney. ~ Do they live in Sydney?
Her efforts proved successful. ~ Did her efforts prove successful?
He likes driving. ~ Does he like driving?

Again as with negation, main verb BE functions as operator; in BrE main verb HAVE often acts as operator, but informally HAVE ... *got* is more common:

Patrick was late. ~ Was Patrick late?
She has a cold. ~ { Does she have a cold? ⟨esp AmE⟩
Has she (got) a cold? ⟨esp BrE⟩ }

Note [a] Obviously, 1st and 2nd person pronouns are exchanged for one another when a question is converted into an equivalent statement in a logically well-formed reply:

Have *I* met you before? ~ Yes, *you* have.
Do *you* like this climate? ~ Yes, *I* do.

[b] Declarative questions (*cf* 11.12) are exceptional in not requiring subject–operator inversion.

[c] Rising intonation is the norm for *yes–no* questions, but falling intonation occurs quite frequently. In a collection of *yes–no* questions taken from the files of the Survey of English Usage, chiefly in surreptitiously recorded unscripted spoken material, 430 questions ended in a rise and 290 in a fall. Further analysis showed that *yes–no* questions with the modal operators *can, could, may, might*, and *would* tended to have almost as many falling tones as rising tones.

[d] By placing the nuclear stress in a particular part of a *yes–no* question, we are able to focus the interrogation on a particular item of information which, unlike the rest of the sentence, is assumed to be unknown (*cf* focus of negation, 10.65). Thus the focus falls in different places in the following otherwise identical questions:

Was he a famous actor in THÓSE days?

['I know he was once a famous actor – but was it then or later?']

Was he a FÁMOUS actor in those days?
['I know he was an actor in those days – but was he a famous one?']

[e] *Yes–no* questions have also been called POLAR QUESTIONS (*cf* 10.54 Note [c]).

Positive *yes–no* questions

11.6 Like negative statements, *yes–no* questions may contain nonassertive forms such as *any* and *ever* (*cf* 10.60). The question containing such forms is generally neutral, with no bias in expectation towards a positive or negative response.

STATEMENT	QUESTION
Someone called last night.	Did *anyone* call last night?
The boat has left *already*.	Has the boat left *yet*?
I live *somewhere* near Dover.	Do you live *anywhere* near Dover?
I suppose *some* of the class will ask *some* boring questions.	Do you suppose *any* of the class will ask *any* boring questions?

But questions may be CONDUCIVE, *ie* they may indicate that the speaker is predisposed to the kind of answer he has wanted or expected. Thus, a positive question may be presented in a form which is biased towards a positive answer. It has positive orientation, for example, if it uses assertive forms rather than the usual nonassertive forms:

Did *someone* call last night? ['Is it true that someone called last night?']
Has the boat left *already*?
Do you live *somewhere* near Dover?

A positive question may also have negative orientation. Notice the effect of *really* in:

Do you *really* want to leave now? ['Surely you don't want to.']

A question that is not conducive, *ie* that has no bias for eliciting a positive or negative response, can be said to have NEUTRAL POLARITY.

Note Assertive forms in offers such as *Would you like some cake?* make the offer more polite, because of the assumption of a positive reply.

Negative *yes–no* questions

11.7 Negative questions are always conducive. Negative orientation is found in questions which contain a negative form of one kind or another:

Don't you believe me?
Aren't you joining us this evening?
Hasn't he told you what to do?
Have they never invited you home?
Has nobody called?

Negative orientation is complicated by an element of surprise or disbelief. The implication is that the speaker had originally hoped for a positive response, but new evidence now suggests that the response will be negative. Thus, *Hasn't he told you what to do?* means 'Surely he has told you what to do, hasn't he? I would have thought that he had told you.' Here there is a combining of a positive and a negative attitude, which one may distinguish as the OLD EXPECTATION (positive) and NEW EXPECTATION (negative). Because the old expectation tends to be identified with the speaker's hopes or wishes, negatively orientated questions often express disappointment or annoyance:

> Can't you drive straight? ['I'd have thought you'd be able to, but apparently you can't.']
> Aren't you ashamed of yourself? ['You ought to be, but it appears you're not.']

Notice the nonassertive items in the next two examples of negative orientation:

> Hasn't the boat left *yet*? ['I'd hoped it would have left by now, but it seems it hasn't.']
> Didn't he recognize you *either*? ['I'd thought he would, but it seems he didn't.']

If a negative question has assertive items, it is biased towards positive orientation:

> Didn't *someone* call last night? Didn't he recognize you *too*?
> Hasn't the boat left *already*?

Such questions are similar in effect to type (i) tag questions (*cf* 11.8), or alternatively to statements showing disbelief: 'Surely someone called last night!'

The position of the negative particle varies according to whether the full or enclitic negative particle is used; *n't* precedes the subject, whereas *not* generally follows it:

> Did*n't* they warn you? Have*n't* they left?
> Did they *not* warn you? Have they *not* left?

The construction with *not* after the subject is generally considered rather formal, and therefore the enclitic is usually preferred in spoken English. The formal alternative is particularly unlikely if the subject is lengthy. Both orders obey the general rule of subject–operator inversion, but since enclitic *n't* is fused with the operator into one grammatical word, it necessarily moves with the operator in subject–operator inversion.

Some speakers accept a third construction, also rather formal, in which the full particle is in the same position as the enclitic:

> Is *not* history a social science?

This construction is especially likely in formal contexts where the subject is lengthy:

> Does *not* everything we see about us testify to the power of Divine Providence?

The construction is an apparent exception to the regular placement of the subject immediately after the operator, but in print it may merely represent the printed equivalent of the attached enclitic. Focusing subjuncts (*cf* 8.116*ff*) can also appear between operator and subject, and their presence makes a preceding full particle more likely in formal contexts:

> Did *not* even a single student come to the lecture?

Note [**a**] If the subject is or contains a quantifier, there is a difference in meaning according to whether the negative particle precedes or follows the subject:

Does*n't* anyone know the answer? ['Surely someone knows the answer.']

Does anyone *not* know the answer? ['Is there anyone who does not know the answer?']

[**b**] Negative exclamatory questions are discussed in 11.22, and negative rhetorical questions in 11.23.

[**c**] Although a negative subject of a statement cannot be replaced by *not* + nonassertive form (*cf* 10.58), the same restriction does not apply to negative questions, where the subject follows the clause negator *not*. Two question forms therefore correspond to the single positive form *No one believes me*: *Does no one believe me?* and *Doesn't anyone believe me?*

[**d**] Negative questions sometimes occur as elliptical responses. The negative question affirms the speaker's agreement with what another speaker has just said:

A: Her performance in *Rigoletto* was outstanding. B: Yes, wÀsn't it?

Compare a fuller response in which the tag question might also have a falling tone:

Yes it was, wÀsn't it?

The positive question as response here (*wÀs* it?) would suggest that the speaker was not present at the performance and therefore cannot express an opinion. The positive question is also used to express disagreement, often ironically:

A: Isn't it a lovely day? B: ís it?

Tag questions

11.8 Maximum conduciveness is expressed by a further type of *yes–no* question which conveys positive or negative orientation – a tag question appended to a statement:

The boat hasn't left, *has it*?

Joan recognized you, *didn't she*?

The general rules for forming the most common types of tag question are:

(a) The tag question consists of operator and subject in that order (enclitic *n't*, if present, is attached to the operator, *cf* 11.7): *is he?*, *didn't she?*, *can't I?*, *will you?*. In formal English the negative particle is placed after the pronoun: *did they not?*, *is she not?* That position is usual in informal English in Northern BrE dialects.

(b) The operator is generally the same as the operator of the preceding statement (*cf* Note [c] below):

I *haven't* seen you before, *have* I?

If the statement has no operator, the dummy auxiliary DO is used, as for *yes–no* questions in general (*cf* 11.5):

She knows you, *doesn't* she?

(c) The subject of the tag must be a pronoun which either repeats, or is in coreference with, the subject of the statement, agreeing with it in number, person, and gender.

(d) If the statement is positive, the tag is generally negative, and vice versa (but *cf* 11.9).

(e) The nuclear tone of the tag occurs on the auxiliary, and is either rising or falling.

Four main types of tag question emerge from the observance of these rules. (The formula + S̀ – T́ represents a positive statement with falling nuclear tone followed by a negative tag with rising tone. The other formulae are similarly explicable.)

POSITIVE + NEGATIVE

RISING TONE	FALLING TONE
(i) + S̀ – T́	(iii) + S̀ – T̀
He likes his JÒB, DÓESn't he?	He likes his JÒB, DÒESn't he?

NEGATIVE + POSITIVE

RISING TONE	FALLING TONE
(ii) – S̀ + T́	(iv) – S̀ + T̀
He doesn't like his JÒB, DÓES he?	He doesn't like his JÒB, DÒES he?

The meanings of these sentences, like their forms, involve a statement and a question; each of them, that is, asserts something, then invites the listener's response to it. Sentence (i), for example, can be rendered 'I assume he likes his job; am I right?', (ii) means the opposite: 'I assume he doesn't like his job; am I right?' (*cf* also 11.11). Clearly these sentences have a positive and a negative orientation respectively. A similar contrast exists between (iii) and (iv). But it is important, again, to separate two factors: an ASSUMPTION (expressed by the statement) and an EXPECTATION (expressed by the question). On this principle, we may distinguish the four types as:

(i)	Positive assumption	+ neutral expectation	+ S̀ – T́
(ii)	Negative assumption	+ neutral expectation	– S̀ + T́
(iii)	Positive assumption	+ positive expectation	+ S̀ – T̀
(iv)	Negative assumption	+ negative expectation	– S̀ – T̀

The tag with a rising tone invites verification, expecting the hearer to decide the truth of the proposition in the statement. The tag with the falling tone, on the other hand, invites confirmation of the statement, and has the force of an exclamation rather than a genuine question. In this respect, types (iii) and (iv) are like (though not as emphatic as) exclamatory *yes–no* questions with a falling tone (*cf* 11.22). Compare, for example, *Isn't it wonderful WÈAther!* with *It's wonderful WÈAther, ÌSn't it?* and *Wasn't she ÀNgry!* with *She was ÀNgry, WÀSn't she?*

Note [a] The tag normally mirrors the subject and auxiliary of the main clause of a complex sentence. There are exceptions, however, with verbs like *suppose* when they are introduced by a 1st person subject and followed by a *that*-clause:

I suppose you're not serious, are you? [*not* *I suppose you're not serious, don't I?]

A further stage of irregularity is introduced in cases of transferred negation (*cf* 14.36): *I don't suppose he's serious, is he?* Here, the subject of the tag is taken from the *that*-clause, but the absence of negation from the tag is explained with reference to the negative particle of the main clause, which applies *semantically* to the *that*-clause, since *I don't suppose he's serious* is equivalent to *I suppose he isn't serious*.

[b] If the sentence is long, the tag question is occasionally inserted in the middle, but between constituents:

It's true, *isn't it*, that you're thinking of giving up your job?

[c] The negative tag question following a positive statement with modal auxiliary *may* poses a problem because the abbreviated form *mayn't* is rare (virtually not found in AmE). There is no obvious solution for the tag question, though some speakers will substitute *mightn't* or *can't*, or – when the reference is future – *won't*:

?I may inspect the books, {mightn't I? / can't I?}

?They may be here next week, {mightn't they? / won't they?}

The unabbreviated form is fully acceptable, but limited to formal usage:

I may inspect the books, may I not?
They may be here next week, may they not?

In a tag question following a statement with *used to*, the operator is *did*:

They used to write to you, {didn't they? / did they not?}

They {usedn't ⟨esp BrE⟩ (*cf* 3.44) / used not / didn't use ⟨esp AmE⟩} to write to you, did they?

Shouldn't is sometimes substituted for *oughtn't* as an abbreviated form:

We ought to go now, {shouldn't we? / oughtn't we?}

(On *aren't I*, *cf* 3.32).

[**d**] When the focus of a positive sentence is on a gradable unit, a negative tag question with a falling tone can be used as a response utterance to express agreement:

A: Their daughter is very clever.
B: (Yes,) ìsn't she? ['I agree']

Otherwise, the tag response with a rising tone expresses surprise, the tag being in constant polarity with the preceding statement:

A: Their daughter isn't very clever.
B: ísn't she? ['I thought she was.']
A: They're moving to New York.
B: ÁRE they? ['I didn't know that.']
A: They aren't moving to New York.
B: ÁREn't they? ['I thought they were.']

11.9 There is a further, less common, type of tag question in which both statement and question are positive:

Your car is outsÌDE, ÍS it?
You've had an ÀCcident, HÁVE you?

The tag typically has a rising tone, and the statement is characteristically preceded by *oh* or *so*, indicating the speaker's arrival at a conclusion by inference, or by recalling what has already been said. The tone may sometimes be one of sarcastic suspicion:

So THÀT's your little, game, ÍS it?

We may therefore add a fifth, less usual, type of tag question to the earlier four types:

POSITIVE + POSITIVE
RISING TONE
(v) + S̀ + T́
So he likes his JÒB, DÓES he?

The tag of this type sometimes has no nucleus, but is part of the preceding tone unit. Its effect may be scolding (*Oh, you've had another accident, have you?*), sarcastic (*So that's your game, is it?*), or sarcastically contradictory (*So your car is outside, is it?*).

Note Logically we should expect an equivalent sixth type in which both statement and tag are negative:

NEGATIVE + NEGATIVE

RISING TONE

(vi) – Ŝ – T́

So he doesn't like his JÒB, DÓESn't he?

This type, however, has not been clearly attested in actual use.

Tag questions with imperatives and exclamatives

11.10 Tag questions can be appended also to imperative sentences (*cf* 11.24*ff*), where they invite the listener's consent. For positive imperatives, types (i), (iii), and (v) are available. The auxiliary in the tag is usually *won't* for the negative and *will* for the positive, and the subject is usually *you*:

(i) Open the DÒOR, WÓN'T you?
(iii) Open the DÒOR, WÒN'T you?
(v) Open the DÒOR, WÍLL you?

Type (i) tag is least insistent, and type (v) tag is most insistent. Other auxiliaries and subjects also occur:

Open the door, can't you?
Hand me a knife, won't somebody?
Turn on the light, will somebody or other?
Save us a seat, can one of you?
Have another one, why don't you?

Negative imperatives are less commonly followed by tag questions. The only type that seems possible is *will you?* in type (iv), with a falling tone on the tag:

(iv) Don't make a NÒISE, WÌLL you?

The tag is a persuasive softener of the imperative. However, if the *will you?* is nonnuclear, it increases the peremptoriness of the directive.

First person plural imperatives (*cf* 11.26) may take *shall we?* as a tag question:

Let's play another game, } shall we?
Let's not discuss it now, }

Type (iii) tag and the (only occasionally used) type (i) tag are appended to exclamatives (*cf* 11.31*f*). The tag questions invite the hearer's agreement:

(iii) How THÌN she is, ìsn't she?
(i) What a beautiful PÀINTing it is, ísn't it? ['Or don't you agree?']

The tag may also be appended to abbreviated verbless exclamations:

What a beautiful painting, isn't it?
How odd, isn't it?

Note The imperatives and the tag may be positive and have falling tones, but the sentence is then very peremptory and is considered ill-mannered:

Open the DÒOR, WÌLL you?

Invariant tag questions

11.11 Several other tag questions inviting the listener's response may be appended to statements and exclamations. They have the same form whether the statement is positive or negative, and take a rising tone:

They {forgot / didn't forget} to attend the lecture, {*am I right?* / *isn't that so?* / *don't you think?* / *wouldn't you say?*}

She passed the exam, / She didn't pass the exam, } {right? ⟨informal⟩ / eh? /eɪ/ ⟨casual, may be impolite⟩}

Again the falling tone is more insistent than the rising tone.

Note Comment clauses (such as *you know* and *I hope*, *cf* 15.54) may in general be considered invariant tags, though they are usually not questions.

Declarative questions

11.12 Not all *yes–no* questions have subject–operator inversion. The declarative question is a type of question which is identical in form to a declarative, except for the final rising question intonation. It is rather casual in tone:

You've got the exPLÓsive?
They've spoken to the amBÁSsador, of course?
You realize what the RÍSKS are?
Boris will be THÉRE, I suppose?
He didn't finish the RÁCE?

Declarative questions are conducive (*cf* 11.6), and resemble tag questions with a rising tone in that they invite the hearer's verification. Positive questions have positive orientation (*cf* 11.6), and can therefore accept only assertive forms (*cf* 10.60*f*):

He wants something to eat?
Somebody is with you?

When followed by a comment clause, the declarative may have a fall:

You realize what the RÌSKS are, I {GÁther. / HÓPE. / TRÚST.}

Negative questions have negative orientation, and nonassertive forms may be used following the negative:

You didn't get anything to eat?
You want nothing to eat yet?
Nobody ever stays at your place?

Note [**a**] A second interrogative use of the statement construction is for echo questions (*cf* 11.34*ff*).
[**b**] A tag question may be added to a declarative question:
You've got the exPLÒsive, HÁVE you?
In that case the declarative usually has a falling tone.

Yes–no questions with modal auxiliaries

11.13 The formation of *yes–no* questions with modal auxiliaries is subject to certain limitations and shifts of meaning. (For the negation of modal auxiliaries, *cf* 10.67*f*). The modals of permission (*may* ⟨esp BrE⟩, and *can*) and of obligation (*must* ⟨esp BrE⟩, and *have to*) generally involve the speaker's authority in statements and the hearer's authority in questions:

A: {May / Can} I leave now? ['Will *you* permit me . . .']

B: Yes, you {may / can}. ['*I* will permit you . . .']

A: {Must I / Do I have to} leave now? ['Are *you* telling me . . .']

B: Yes, you {must / have to}. ['*I* am telling you . . .']

This means that the question form anticipates the form appropriate for the answer.

A similar switch from hearer to speaker takes place with *shall* [volition], which (esp in BrE) involves the speaker's will in statements, but the hearer's will in questions:

> You shall suffer for this! [rare; '*I* intend to make you suffer . . .!']
> Shall I switch off the television? ['Do *you* want me to . . .?']

Shall is rare with *you* as subject, and generally infrequent in AmE, except for inviting or requesting agreement (*Shall we eat now?*). It is unlike the other modals in two respects. First, its use in questions is virtually restricted to first person subjects. Secondly, its declarative use is not symmetrical with its interrogative use; hence, *shall* is not repeated in the response to a question with *shall*. The expected response after *shall I* and exclusive *shall we* is agreement, and may be a 2nd person imperative. After inclusive *shall we* it is a 1st person imperative:

> A: Shall we carry your suitcases? ['Would you like us to . . .?']
> B: Yes, please do (so).
> A: Shall we have dinner? ['Would you like us (including you) to . . .?']
> B: Yes, let's.

May in the possibility sense is not often used in questions:

> May we be doing him an injustice?

Can or (more commonly in AmE) *could* replaces it:

A: {Can / Could} they have missed the bus?

B: Yes, they {may have. / might have.}

The hypothetical uses (*cf* 4.62) of the auxiliaries *might* [permission], *would* [volition], and *could* [volition] require special treatment, since in *yes–no* questions these past forms are regularly used for politeness. If modal auxiliaries are retained, the present forms are generally substituted for *might* and *would* in responses, and the present form is usual for *could*:

A: Might I call you by your first name?
  B: Yes, you may. [1]
A: Would you pay for me?
  B: Yes, I will. [2]
A: Could I see you for a moment?
  B: Yes, you can. [Also *may* ⟨esp BrE⟩, and less usually, *could*] [3]

A more common response for [1–3] would be (*Yes,*) *of course*. Other responses might be (*Yes,*) *please do* for [1] and *I'll be glad to* for [2]. The questions have the polite past forms appropriate to their illocutionary force as requests.

Need (esp in BrE) is used as a nonassertive modal auxiliary, although (esp in AmE) the main verb *need* (*cf* 3.41*f*) and *do have to* are common substitutes:

Need they leave now? ⟨esp BrE⟩

Do they {need to / have to} leave now?

But the corresponding positive forms are *must*, *have to*, or the main verb *need*:

Yes, they {must. / have to. / need to.}

On the other hand, *must* in the necessity sense has positive orientation:

Why must it always rain when we want to have a picnic?

(On this last example, *cf* the discussion of rhetorical questions in 11.23.) Notice the assertive *always* after *must*, in contrast to the possible nonassertive *ever* after *need*:

Must it always happen this way?
Need it ever [*also*: always] happen this way?

Dare is occasionally used as a nonassertive modal auxiliary, especially in BrE. Common substitutes are the main verb *dare* and (esp in AmE) the blend construction with *dare* (DO and the bare infinitive, *cf* 3.42):

Do you dare to cast aspersions on my character?
Dare I suggest a compromise between your two positions? ⟨esp BrE⟩
Do we dare tell them the truth? ⟨esp AmE⟩

Negative responses may repeat the same verbs, but positive forms require the main verb *dare*:

Yes, they dared to complain.

Note As with the negative, *ought* may occur either with the *to*-infinitive or with the bare infinitive (*cf* 3.43).

Wh-questions

Form of *wh*-questions

11.14 *Wh*-questions are formed with the aid of one of the following simple interrogative words (or *wh*-words):

who/whom/whose, what, which, when, where, how, why

Unlike *yes–no* questions, *wh*-questions generally have falling intonation. As a rule,

(i) the *wh*-element (*ie* the clause element containing the *wh*-word) comes first in the sentence (apart from some conjuncts, such as *on the other hand*);

(ii) the *wh*-word itself takes first position in the *wh*-element.

The only exception to the second principle occurs when the *wh*-word is within a prepositional complement. Here English provides a choice between two constructions, one being formal. In formal style, the preposition precedes the complement, whereas otherwise the complement comes first and the preposition is deferred to the end of the sentence:

On what did you base your prediction? ⟨formal⟩
What did you base your prediction *on*?

We may perhaps express this difference more neatly by saying that neutral style generally requires that the *wh*-word comes first, but formal English requires that the *wh*-element as a whole comes first.

Note [a] *Wh*-questions are also called INFORMATION QUESTIONS.

[b] The *wh*-words are sometimes modified (except in formal style) by the intensifier *ever*, which emphasizes the bafflement or emotional involvement of the speaker. Usually they are spelled as two separate words, and *why ever* is invariably spelled so. They are thereby distinguished from the subordinating *wh*-words *whenever, whoever, however*, etc.

Why ever didn't he tell me? How ever did you find the key?
What ever are you doing? Who ever would want such a magazine?

Various other ways exist of intensifying the emotive effect of a *wh*-question:

Who *on earth* opened my letter? ⟨informal⟩
Who *the hell* are you? ⟨casual⟩
What *in heaven's name* do you think you're doing? ⟨casual⟩

[c] In a collection of 858 *wh*-questions from the files of the Survey of English Usage, chiefly in surreptitiously recorded spoken unscripted material, 775 had falling intonation.

[d] On factors affecting the choice between *who* and *whom*, *cf* 6.35, 6.38, 7.14*ff*.

[e] The construction with a preposition in final position (*cf* 9.6) is less desirable when the preposition is remote from its complement or when it is syntactically bound closer to the complement than to the verb. Awkward sentences like *What time did you tell him to meet us at?* are generally avoided. A sentence like that would be replaced by *At what time did you tell him to meet us?* in formal style or, more generally, by *When did you tell him to meet us?* or prepositionless *What time did you tell him to meet us?* The awkwardness reaches comic proportions when several final particles cooccur: *What did you bring this book to be read out of up for?*

The prepositions *since* and *during* occur only at the beginning of the question: *Since when do I have to explain my actions to you?, During which years were you living in Germany? Until* is also usually placed initially, although *till* can be regularly deferred: ?*When are you staying until?, When are you staying till?* (*cf* also 11.15 Note [a]).

[f] There are occasional declarative *wh*-questions, where the *wh*-element remains in the position normal in declaratives for that item. They are associated with interviews and interrogations:

A: So you boarded the train *where*? B: At Los Angeles.
A: And you got off *at what station*? B: At San Diego.

These declarative *wh*-questions are to be distinguished from echo questions (*cf* 11.34*ff*).

Functions of *wh*-element

11.15 The following sentences exemplify the various clause functions in which the *wh*-element operates:

Who ever opened my LÈTter? [*wh*-element: S] [1]
Which books have you LÈNT him? [*wh*-element: O_d] [2]
Whose beautiful anTÌQUES are these? [*wh*-element: C_s] [3]
How wide did they make the BÒOKcase? [*wh*-element: C_o] [4]
When will you be proMÒTed? [*wh*-element: A] [5]
Where shall I put the GLÀSses? [*wh*-element: A] [6]
Why are they always comPLÀINing? [*wh*-element: A] [7]
How did you MÈND it? [*wh*-element: A] [8]
How much does he CÀRE? [*wh*-element: A] [9]
How long have you been WÀITing? [*wh*-element: A] [10]
How often do you visit New YÒRK? [*wh*-element: A] [11]

We see above that normal statement order of elements is altered in *wh*-questions not only by the initial placing of the *wh*-element, but by the inversion of subject and operator in all cases except when the *wh*-element is subject, where the rule that the *wh*-element takes initial position applies, overriding the rule of inversion.

Subject–operator inversion is the same in its application to *wh*-questions as in its application to *yes–no* questions; if there is no operator in the equivalent statement, DO is introduced as operator in the question. The main verb BE and (occasionally, esp in BrE) HAVE act as operator: *Where is she?*, *What kind of car have they?*

Note [**a**] Adjuncts of instrument, reason, and purpose are normally questioned by the prepositional constructions:

What shall I mend it *with*? *What* did you do that *for*?

Although the latter could be replaced by *Why did you do that?*, it has no alternative with a preposed preposition: **For what did you do that?* In this respect it is like informal questions with BE followed by a final preposition: *What was it like?* (but not **Like what was it?*); *What was it in?* (but not **In what was it?*).

[**b**] Abbreviated questions consisting of a *wh*-word and a final preposition (which in this construction regularly bears nuclear stress), *eg*: *What FÒR?*, *Where FRÒM*|*TÒ?*, *What WÌTH?*, *Who WÌTH*|*BỲ?*, are as popular in informal speech as questions consisting of the *wh*-word only: *Where?*, *Why?*, *Who?* There is a common abbreviated negative question *Why NÒT?* (*cf* 11.17), and an informal abbreviated reason question (esp in AmE) *How CÒME?* (*cf* also 11.40 Note [a]).

[**c**] Although there is no *wh*-word for the verb, the content of the predication can be questioned by *what* as the object of the generalized agentive verb *do* or as subject of the generalized event verb *happen*:

A: What are you doing? B: I'm reading.
A: What have you done with my book? B: I've hidden it.
A: What's happening? B: It's snowing.

[**d**] Many speakers do not accept an indirect object as *wh*-element: ?*Who(m) did you give the present?* They use the equivalent prepositional complement construction instead: *Who(m) did you give the present to?* or (in formal style) *To whom did you give the present?* Some speakers, however, find the construction acceptable if there is no ambiguity as to which object is direct and which indirect. (There is ambiguity in **Who did you show your daughter?*)

[**e**] In *wh*-questions of the *SVC* pattern, it is possible to distinguish between noun phrases as S and C by signals of case and concord, where these apply: *Which is me?* (*wh*-element as S – said, for example, when looking at a photograph) contrasts with *Which am I?* (*wh*-element as C). *Whose* in the *SVC* sentence pattern must be C: *Whose is that book?*

The potential response may also indicate the clause elements:

A: Who was Hamlet? B: My brother was.
[*Who* is S, identifying a character in a play]

A: Who was Augustus? B: Augustus was a Roman Emperor.
[*Who* is C, referring to identity]

A: What was your brother? B: He was Hamlet.
[*What* is C, characterizing a role in a play, *cf* 6.39]

Notice the ambiguity of *Who* in the following:

A: Who is the captain?
{ B: My brother is. [*Who* is S]
{ B: The captain is my brother. [*Who* is C]

[f] *Why* ⟨esp AmE⟩ and *what* are used in informal speech as introductory words to express surprise, both with questions and with statements:

Why, what did she say? What, is the bus here already?
Why, they won't object. What, he couldn't have passed.

Why is also used informally after conditional clauses, especially in AmE. It is a more emphatic conjunct than *then* (*cf* 8.135):

If HÉ doesn't want to press charges, why YÒU should.

[g] For irregular *wh*-questions – such as those beginning with *how come*, *how about*, and *what about* – *cf* 11.40.

[h] *How goes it?* is a surviving common example of a *wh*-question that lacks the usual operator and inversion (*cf*: *How did it go?*).

[i] Interrogative *how* has various senses. Notice the ambiguity of *How does it work?*, where *how* may refer to process or effect. *How* is also used as a *wh*-word for a complement as current attribute (*cf* 10.20):

A: How is she? B: Fine. [evaluation of health or some other aspect]
A: How was the book? B: Excellent. [evaluative]

For *how* in the nonhealth evaluative sense, *What . . . like?* is available as an informal synonym (*cf* Note [a] above). *How*, *how much*, *how far*, and *to what extent* are used with gradable verbs as intensifying *wh*-elements: *How did you like her?*, *How much do you miss him?*, *How far do they agree with us?*, *To what extent would you trust them?*

Positive *wh*-questions

11.16 A *wh*-question may generally be matched with a statement called its presupposition. This is a statement which, in place of the *wh*-element, contains an indefinite expression such as *somebody*. The presupposed statement, which is assumed to be true by whoever uses the question, preserves of course normal statement ordering. Hence, if we list the presuppositions corresponding to some of questions [1–11] in 11.15, we can clarify the syntactic ordering of *wh*-questions in relation to statements:

PRESUPPOSITIONS

Someone opened my letter. [1a]
You have lent him *some of the books*. [2a]
You will be promoted *sometime*. [5a]
You mended it *somehow*. [8a]
You visit New York *sometimes*. [11a]

Modifying *what* and *which* (*cf* 6.39) have different presuppositions:

What composer(s) do you like best?
~ You like *some composer(s)* best.
Which composer(s) do you like best?
~ You like {*some* / *one*} *of the composers* best.

In some cases there is no sensible presupposition:

How does he feel? ~ *He feels somehow or other.
Where was she born? ~ She was born somewhere.
What time is it? ~ It's some time or other.
How should I know?
Why should I?

As the above examples indicate, a positive *wh*-question may generally be matched with a positive presupposition. There may, however, be no presupposition if nonassertive items (*cf* 10.60) are present:

When will we *ever* win *any* prizes?
What help have they *ever* given us?
Who has *any* money?

The questions are conducive, having a negative orientation. Questions introduced by *Why do you* have a positive presupposition, but a negative orientation when they have the illocutionary force of directives:

Why do you bother to reply? ['You are replying but shouldn't bother to reply.']
Why do you make so much fuss? ['You are making a lot of fuss but shouldn't make so much fuss.']

As a directive, it cannot have a past form. Thus *Why did you bother to reply?* is an inquiry, not a directive, though the overtone is still negative.

The abbreviated form with the bare infinitive is always a directive:

Why bother to reply?
Why make so much fuss?

Note On rhetorical *wh*-questions, *cf* 11.23.

Negative *wh*-questions

11.17 *Wh*-questions can also be negative:

Who hasn't had any coffee? [1]
Why didn't you tell me? [2]
When shouldn't I call? [3]
Which books don't you want? [4]
Where didn't you clean? [5]
How long haven't you heard from them? [6]
How often didn't he pay his rent? [7]

The presuppositions can be listed just as for positive questions (*cf* 11.16):

Somebody hasn't had any coffee. [1a]
You didn't tell me *for some reason.* [2a]
I shouldn't call *at some time.* [3a]
You don't want *some books.* [4a]
You didn't clean *in some place.* [5a]
You haven't heard from them *for some time.* [6a]
He didn't pay his rent *a number of times.* [7a]

In [1a–7a] the presupposed particular unknown is outside the scope of negation (*cf* 10.64). Thus [4a] may be paraphrased by 'There are some books that you don't want'.

Questions beginning with *Why don't you* and the abbreviated *Why not* are commonly used as directives (*cf* 11.16). The directives are invitations or (more commonly in AmE) suggestions or instructions:

Why don't you shave?
Why don't you clean your teeth?
Why don't you come for a meal one day next week?
Why don't you make yourself an egg?
Why don't you revise this paper?
Why not ignore their remarks?
Why not go by train?

Why don't you conveys advice, but it frequently has a critical and irritable tone, since it is used when the hearer has not performed or is not performing the recommended activity:

Why don't you take sleeping tablets? ['Anyone else would.']
Why don't you see a doctor?

Why don't you, unlike *Why not*, may also be used as an inquiry. Like the inquiry, the directive allows nonassertive items (*Why don't you ever write?*), but unlike the inquiry, the directive does not allow a past form of the verb (*Why didn't you write?*). On the other hand, the directive takes the operator *do* before *be*: *Why don't you be quieter?* (*cf* the inquiry *Why aren't you quieter?*). In these syntactic features, directives beginning with *Why don't you* and *Why not* resemble imperative sentences, which normally have the illocutionary force of directives.

Especially in AmE, *Why don't I* is used for offers (*Why don't I give you a hand?*), or *Why don't we* for offers (*Why don't we give you a hand?*) or suggestions (*Why don't we have a rest now?*).

Pushdown *wh*-element

11.18 In 11.15, the *wh*-element was shown to operate in various clause functions. But it can also operate indirectly in the main clause, as part of another clause element. We call the *wh*-element in such cases a PUSHDOWN element. Here are instances in which the *wh*-element is a pushdown element, the presuppositions being given in parentheses.

(I) *wh*-element as prepositional complement within a noun phrase:

(i) the prepositional phrase as adjunct:

{ *What side of the road* was he driving on?
{ On *what side of the road* was he driving? ⟨formal⟩
[He was driving on *one side of the road*.]

(ii) the prepositional phrase as modifier of a noun phrase:

{ *Which country* is Caracas the capital of? ⟨informal⟩
{ Of *which country* is Caracas the capital?
[Caracas is the capital of *some country*.]

(II) *wh*-element as element in a nominal *that*-clause or a *to*-infinitive or *-ing* clause; the clause functions as direct object in the main clause:

How long did he tell you (that) he waited?
[He told you (that) he waited *for some length of time*.]
What would you like me to buy?
[You would like me to buy *something*.]
What kinds of novels do you enjoy reading?
[You enjoy reading *some kinds of novels*.]

(III) *wh*-element as prepositional complement within a noun phrase, the noun phrase in turn functioning as element in a nominal clause – a combination of (I) and (II):

Who did the textbook say (that) Queen Elizabeth was the daughter of? ⟨informal⟩
[The textbook said that Queen Elizabeth was the daughter of some person]

(IV) *wh*-element as element (or part of an element) in a clause that is complementation to an adjective:

{ *What* is he ready to confess to?
{ To *what* is he ready to confess? ⟨formal⟩
[He is ready to confess to *something*.]
How much is she ready to pay? [She is ready to pay *something*.]

Note [**a**] There are limits to what can be a pushdown *wh*-element. Among the exclusions are:
(i) the complement of a prepositional phrase functioning as disjunct (*to my regret*) or conjunct (*on the contrary*), *cf* 8.121*ff*.
(ii) the complement of many prepositional phrases functioning as adjunct, when the complement refers to a specific time (*Monday*), place (*Denver*), or process (*great firmness*). The complement can, however, often be questioned by a *wh*-element with a general noun (*What day did you meet on?*, *What city did you go to?*, *In what manner did you speak to them?*)
(iii) an element in a relative clause or an adverbial clause.
(iv) an element in a nominal interrogative or nominal relative clause. This restriction is sometimes relaxed for nominal interrogative clauses in unscripted speech, particularly for *yes–no* interrogative clauses introduced by *whether* and functioning as direct object; a pronoun is inserted in the subordinate clause if the preposed *wh*-element functions as subject in the subordinate clause. These are felt to be deviant, but they are sometimes used because there is no obvious alternative:

?*Which exam* did you ask whether he would pass?
?*Who else* did you notice whether *they* passed the exam?

(v) an element in a coordinated phrase or clause.

[**b**] In complex sentences a pushdown *wh*-element may be ambiguous, functioning either in the main clause or in a subordinate clause:

When did she promise to meet him?

When may refer to the time of promising or to the time of meeting.

More than one *wh*-element

11.19 Ordinary questions can have more than one *wh*-element (for echo questions, *cf* 11.34*ff*):

I heard that Sylvia and Jane accused their husbands of various misdeeds, but *who* accused *whom* of *what*?
Which present did you give to *whom*?

If one of the *wh*-elements is subject, it must be initial:

Who said *what* to *whom*?

Otherwise, there is a choice as to which *wh*-element is fronted, so that the same question may be put in more than one way. Consider the presupposition:

You have hidden something somewhere.

We can move from it to either of these questions:

What have you hidden *where*? *Where* have you hidden *what*?

Generally, only one *wh*-element is fronted, but adverbial *wh*-elements may be coordinated:

When and where did they meet? *How and why* did it happen?

Alternatively, the second coordinated *wh*-element may be appended (*cf* 13.94):

When did they meet, and *where*?

If only one *wh*-element is adverbial and the other is direct object, only appended coordination is fully acceptable:

What does she teach, *and where*? *Who* did he hit, and *why*?
?*What and where* does she teach? ?*Who and why* did he hit?

Note Declarative *wh*-questions (*cf* 11.14 Note [f]) may rarely also have more than one *wh*-element:
Well now, you say your wife is a teacher. She teaches *what where*?

Alternative questions

11.20 There are two types of alternative questions. The first resembles a *yes–no* question, and the second a *wh*-question:

Would you like CHÓcolate, vaNÍLla, or STRÀWberry (ice cream)? [1]
Which ice cream would you LÌKE? CHÓcolate, vaNÍLla or STRÀWberry? [2]

The first type differs from a *yes–no* question only in intonation; instead of the final rising tone, it contains a separate nucleus for each alternative: a rise occurs on each item in the list, except the last, on which there is a fall, indicating that the list is complete. The difference of intonation between alternative and *yes–no* questions is important, in that ignoring it can lead to misunderstanding – as the contrast between these replies indicates:

alternative: A: Shall we go by BÚS or TRÀIN? B: By BÙS.
yes–no: A: Shall we go by bus or TRÁIN? B: No, let's take the CÀR.

The second type of alternative question is really a compound of two separate questions: a *wh*-question followed by an elliptical alternative question. Thus [2] might be taken as a reduced version of:

Which ice cream would you LÌKE? Would you like CHÓcolate, vaNÍLla, or STRÀWberry?

An alternative question presupposes the truth of only one of the propositions:

Are you a DÉMocrat or a REPÙBlican?
[You are either a Democrat or a Republican.]
Do you want SHÉRbet, YÓghurt, or FRÙIT?
[You are being given a choice of only one of the three.]

A *yes–no* question presupposes that one of two mutually exclusive possibilities is true:

Are you RÉADy?

Converting a *yes–no* question into an alternative question introduces this tautology into the presupposition:

ÁRE you ready or ÀREN't you ready?
[Either you are ready or you are not ready.]

The second conjoin may be reduced to *or not*:

ÁRE you ready or NÒT?

The tautology gives a petulant tone to the question and explains why such questions are not normal.

Note [**a**] An alternative question corresponding to a *yes–no* question is distinctly odd in certain sentences; for example, if the question has the illocutionary force of an invitation or a request:

?Would you have some more coffee or not?
?Will you open the door please or not?

There is no tautology if there is a nontrivial alternative:

Will you open the door please, or {should I? / would you rather not?}

[**b**] The second part of the *wh*-alternative question may be considered a kind of appositive to the *wh*-element:

{*Who* / *Which of them*} do you like best, *Tom or Derek*?

11.21 The structure of alternative *yes–no* questions follows the pattern of coordination (*cf* 13.43*ff*), the ellipted forms generally being preferred, where they are possible:

Did ÍTaly win the World Cup or did BRAZÌL win the World Cup?
Did ÍTaly win the World Cup or did BRAZÌL?
Did ÍTaly win the World Cup or BRAZÌL?

Often the remaining part of a second or subsequent alternative question is fronted to the appropriate position in the first question:

Did ÍTaly or BRAZÌL win the World Cup?

This type of fronting is also possible for the vacuous negative alternative:

Are you CÓMing or ÀREN'T you (coming)?
ÁRE you or ÀREN'T you coming?

There is no fronted version of *Are you coming or not?* (**Are you or not coming?*) because fronting would violate the requirement of structure equivalence of conjoins (*cf* 13.49).

Minor types of questions

Exclamatory questions

11.22 The exclamatory question is interrogative in structure, but has the illocutionary force of an exclamatory assertion. Typically it is a negative *yes–no* question with a final falling instead of rising tone:

Hasn't she GRÒWN!
Wasn't it a marvellous CÒNcert!

These invite the hearer's agreement to something on which the speaker has strong feelings. The meaning, contrary to the appearance of the literal wording, is vigorously positive.

A positive *yes–no* question, also with a falling tone, is another (but less common) way of expressing a strong positive conviction:

ˈAm ˈI HÙNGry! ˈDid ˈhe look anNÒYED! ˈHas ˈshe GRÒWN!

Both operator and subject usually receive emphatic stress. In written English an exclamation mark is usual at the end of the sentence for both kinds of exclamatory question.

The falling tone for negative and positive exclamatory questions has an effect similar to, but more emphatic than, the falling tone in tag questions (*cf* 11.8).

It seems odd that pairs of sentences which contrast in positive–negative polarity should have roughly the same effect: *Has she grown! Hasn't she grown!* There is, however, a slight difference: the negative question has, as a feature of its meaning, an appeal for the listener's confirmation; the positive question, on the other hand, implies that the positive response is self-evident, and would therefore be more appropriate where the listener's agreement would normally not be solicited, as in *Am I hungry!* (The experience reported here is of course not shared by the listener.) In situations where both the negative and the positive questions are possible, the difference is roughly represented by these paraphrases:

Wasn't it a marvellous CÒNcert! = 'What a marvellous CÒNcert it was!'
Has she GRÒWN! = 'She HÀS grown!'

Exclamatory questions do not admit nonassertives: *Hasn't she yet grown?* is an inquiry. Negative exclamatory questions must take enclitic *n't*; *Has she not grown?* is an inquiry, not an exclamation.

Note In AmE an exclamatory question can be pronounced with a rising tone:

Wasn't the concert terRÍfic?

But in this case, the expectation of a response is stronger.

Rhetorical questions

11.23 The rhetorical question is interrogative in structure, but has the force of a strong assertion. It generally does not expect an answer.

A positive rhetorical *yes–no* question is like a strong negative assertion, while a negative question is like a strong positive one.

POSITIVE:

Is that a reason for desPÁIR? ['Surely that is not a reason . . .']
Can anyone doubt the WÍSdom of this action? ['Surely no one can doubt . . .']

NEGATIVE:

Isn't the answer ÓBvious? ['Surely the answer is obvious.']
Haven't you got anything better to DÓ? ['Surely you have something better to do.']

Unlike exclamatory questions, these rhetorical questions have the normal rising intonation of a *yes–no* question, and are distinguished chiefly by the range of pitch movement.

There are also rhetorical *wh*-questions. The positive question is equivalent to a statement in which the *wh*-element is replaced by a negative element:

Who KNÔWS/CÂRES? ['Nobody knows/cares' *or* 'I don't know/care.']
What DÎFference does it make? ['It makes no difference.']
How should Î know? ['There is no reason why I should know.']
What SHÔULD I say? ['There is nothing that I should say.']
What makes YÔU think you can do better? ['Nothing should make you think you can do better.']
How can Î help it? ['There is no reason to suppose I can help it.']

Nonassertives may occur:

What has HÊ ever done for you?
Who has any MÔNey to spare these days?

The less common negative question is equivalent to a statement in which the *wh*-element is replaced by a positive element:

Who DÔESn't know? ['Everybody knows.']
How CÔULDn't you remember? ['You certainly should have remembered.']

Wh-questions generally have a rise–fall tone, less commonly a simple falling tone.

Rhetorical questions may also be responses to previous questions:

A: Do you want to eat? B: Do I look HÚNgry?

Note Some questions, termed RATIOCINATIVE QUESTIONS, are self-addressed. They are like rhetorical questions in not expecting an answer from others:

Let me see. Should I take the car or go by bus?

But the speaker may answer such a question:

What do I want to ÊAT? Well, a roll will do.

Directives

Directives without a subject

11.24 Directives typically take the form of an imperative sentence, which differs from a declarative sentence in that:

(i) it generally has no subject, but *cf* 11.25;

(ii) it has either a main verb in the base form or (less commonly) an auxiliary in the base form followed by the appropriate form of the main verb.

Otherwise, the clause patterns of imperative sentences show the same range and ordering of elements as declaratives (*cf* 10.2):

(*S*) *V*: Jump.
(*S*) *VO*: Open the door.
(*S*) *VC*: Be reasonable.
(*S*) *VA*: Get inside.
(*S*) *VOO*: Tell me the truth.
(*S*) *VOC*: Consider yourself lucky.
(*S*) *VOA*: Put the flowers on the table.

The imperative verb lacks tense distinction and does not allow modal auxiliaries. The progressive form is rare, and the perfective even rarer:

Be listening to this station the same time tomorrow night.
Be doing your homework when your parents arrive home.
Start the book and have finished it before you go to bed. (*cf* Note [a])

Passives with *be* occur chiefly in negative directives, where they generally have the meaning 'Don't allow yourself to be . . .':

Don't be deceived by his looks. Don't be made to look foolish.
Don't be bullied into signing. Don't be told what to do.

They are less common in positive directives:

Be guided by what I say.
Be reassured by me.
Hire a Rolls Royce and be driven around by a uniformed chauffeur.

What might be treated as passives occur with *get* (*cf* 3.66 on the *get*-passive):

Get washed. Get transferred. Get known.
Get dressed. Get weighed. Get introduced.
Don't get misled by their promises.
Get lost. ['go away' ⟨informal⟩]
Don't get dressed yet.

Imperatives are restricted to predications that allow a dynamic interpretation, hence the incongruity of **Need a car*, **Be old*, **Sound louder*. Many predications that are stative with respect to disallowing the progressive (*cf* 4.27*ff*) are easily available with a dynamic interpretation for imperatives: *Forgive us*, *Love your enemies*, *Owe nobody anything*, *Be early*, *Be glad that you* *escaped without injury, Don't be a stranger, Be a pilot, Know the poem by heart by the next lesson.*

Imperatives refer to a situation in the immediate or more remote future and are therefore incompatible with time adverbials that refer to a time period in the past or that have habitual reference: **Come yesterday*, **Usually drive your car*. Imperatives also do not cooccur with comment disjuncts (*cf* 8.127), since these disjuncts comment on propositions (*cf* the same constraint with questions): **Unfortunately, pay your rent now*. On tag questions with imperatives, *cf* 11.10.

Note [**a**] The rare perfective construction *Have finished it before you go to bed* is to be contrasted with the common causative complex-transitive *Have it finished before you go to bed*, where *have* is an active imperative and *finished* is a simple passive in the dependent clause; *cf*: *Get it finished before you go to bed*. The two sentences, however, are closely similar in meaning. The idiomatic *Have done with it* is presumably to be analysed as having a perfective imperative verb.

[**b**] The perfective passive may very occasionally be found with past time reference in a private prayer referring to information not yet known to the speaker: ?*Please, dad, don't have been in that plane*.

[**c**] For reported imperatives in indirect speech, *cf* 14.33.

[**d**] *Be seated* and *be prepared* are examples of pseudo-passives (*cf* 3.77).

Directives with a subject

11.25 It is intuitively clear that the meaning of a directive implies that the omitted subject is the 2nd person pronoun *you*. The implication can be demonstrated by the occurrence of *you* as subject of a following tag question (*Be quiet, will you?*), by the occurrence of only *yourself* or *yourselves* as the reflexive (*Behave yourself* or *Behave yourselves*, not **Behave myself*, etc), and by the occurrence of only the emphatic possessive *your own* (*Use your own comb*, not **Use her own comb*, etc).

There is, however, a type of directive in which the stressed subject *you* is added. *You* may be noncontrastive and admonitory:

ˈYou be QÙIet!
ˈYou ˈmind your own BÙSiness, and ˈleave this to MÈ!
ˈYou ˈshow me what to DÒ.
ˈYou ˈtake the BÒOK.

They frequently express strong irritation or (as in the last two examples) merely insistence. On the other hand, noncontrastive *you* may be persuasive:

I know you can do it if you try hard enough. ˈYou ˈshow me what you can DÒ.

You may also be contrastive in the sense of addressee-distinguishing, singling out one person or one set of persons. The identity of the persons may be made clear by a vocative or by some gesture such as pointing:

Don't tell MÊ to be quiet. YÒU be quiet!
Here! YÒU take the book!
ˈYou take THÍS chair, and I'll take THÀT one.

Vocative *you*, as opposed to imperative subject *you*, is very impolite:

YÒU| ˈcome HÈRE|

Third person subjects are also possible:

Somebody open this door.
Everybody shut their eyes.
Parents with children go to the front.
Nobody move.
Men in the front row take one step forward.

It is easy to confuse the subject, in these commands, with a vocative noun phrase (*cf* 10.52*f*). But whereas the subject always precedes the verb, the vocative is an element that can occur in final and medial, as well as initial, positions in the sentence. Another difference is that the vocative, when initially placed, has a separate tone unit (typically fall–rise); the subject merely receives ordinary word stress:

VOCATIVE: MǍRY, play on MỲ side.
Play on MỲ side, MǍRY.
SUBJECT: ˈMary play on MỲ side.

The distinctness of vocative and imperative subject is confirmed by the possibility of their cooccurrence:

JǑHN, ˈyou listen to MÈ!

Note [a] Apart from *will you?*, other tag questions heard with an imperative are *would you?*, *could you?*, *can you?*, *won't you?*, *can't you?*, *wouldn't you?*, *couldn't you?* Also the familiar *wh*-question *why don't you?* is sometimes appended: *Take a rest, why don't you?*

[b] Directives with 3rd person subjects take either 2nd or 3rd person pronouns in the tag question: *Somebody open this door, will you?/will they?*

[c] There is similar uncertainty about the person of a reflexive pronoun after a 3rd person subject: *Everyone behave yourselves* and *Everyone behave themselves* both seem acceptable. (On the use of a plural substitute pronoun for *everyone*, *cf* 10.43.) With a vocative, in contrast, only the 2nd person reflexive, in agreement with the understood subject, is allowable: *Behave yourselves, everybody.*

[d] Another confusion easily made is that between a directive with *you* as subject and a statement with *you* as subject as used, for example, in giving street directions: *You go up there until you reach the bridge, then you turn right* ... It is the unstressed subject of the statement that distinguishes it formally from the directive, since the subject of a directive is always stressed, even if a pronoun: *ˈYou go up there.* Needless to say, the admonitory tone of the directive would be quite unsuitable in giving street directions. (The negative *don't you* is less peremptory.)

Directives with *let*

11.26 First person imperatives can be formed by preposing the verb *let* followed by a subject in the objective case (*cf* 3.51):

Let us all work hard.
Let me think what to do next.
Let me see now. Do I have any money on me?

(*Cf* also ratiocinative questions, 11.23 Note). The same applies to 3rd person subjects:

Let no one think that a teacher's life is easy.
Let each man decide for himself.
If anyone shrinks from this action, *let him* speak now.

Except for the *let me* type, these are generally rather archaic and elevated in tone. A colloquial alternative to *let us*, however, is the common abbreviated form *let's*:

> *Let's* have a party.
> *Let's* enjoy ourselves.

In very colloquial English, *let's* is sometimes used for a 1st person singular imperative as well: *Let's give you a hand*. There are no 2nd person imperatives with *let*: **Let you have a look*.

Note [**a**] This type of imperative, in which *let* is no more than an introductory particle, should be kept separate from the ordinary 2nd person imperative of *let* as a transitive verb. That they are distinct is shown by the fact that *Let us go* in the sense 'Permit us to go' cannot be abbreviated to *Let's go*. Furthermore, the full verb *let* is followed by a tag question with *you* as subject (*Let us go, will you?*), whereas the 1st person imperative is followed by a tag question with *we* as subject (*Let's go, shall we?*). In *Let's don't forget* ⟨esp AmE⟩, the particle is institutionalized (*cf* 3.51 Note [b]).

[**b**] *Let's have a look* can refer to the speaker alone. Compare *Give us a hand to get the car started*, where *us* can also refer merely to the speaker.

Summary of forms of imperatives

11.27 We can now summarize the structural types of imperative:

		1st PERSON	2nd PERSON	3rd PERSON
without subject		—	(i) Open the door.	—
with subject	without *let*	—	(ii) You open the door.	(iii) Someone open the door.
	with *let*	(iv) Let me open the door. Let's open the door.	—	(v) Let someone open the door.

By far the most common type is the subjectless 2nd person imperative (class (i)).

Negative imperatives

11.28 To negate the first three classes of imperative, one simply adds an initial *Don't* or *Do not*, replacing assertive by nonassertive items where necessary:

(i) { Open the door.
Consider, my friends, that all is lost. }

~ { *Don't* open the door.
Do not, my friends, consider that all is lost. ⟨formal⟩ }

(ii) You open the door. ~ { *Don't you* open the door.
You don't open the door. ⟨less common⟩ }

(iii) Someone open the door. ~ { *Don't anyone* open the door.
No one open the door. }

First person imperatives, on the other hand, are generally negated by the insertion of *not* after the pronoun following *let*:

(iv) { *Let's not* say anything about it.
Let us not say anything about it.

(iv) *Let me not* believe such accusations. ⟨formal, rare⟩

Informally, however, the negation with *Don't* is frequently heard:

(iv) *Don't let's* say anything about it. ⟨esp BrE⟩
(iv) *Let's don't* say anything about it. ⟨esp AmE⟩
(iv) *Don't let me* disturb you. ⟨esp BrE⟩

Third person imperatives with *let* are negated by *not* after *let* or (more informally) by an initial *don't*:

(v) *Let not anyone* fool himself that he can get away with it. ⟨formal, rare⟩
[Also: *Let no one* fool himself that he can get away with it.]

(v) *Don't let anyone* fool himself that he can get away with it.

The distinction that we have noted (*cf* 11.25) between contrastive and noncontrastive *you* in positive directives applies also to negative directives:

Don't "YǑU say anything. [contrastive]
Don't 'you say ÀNYTHING. [noncontrastive]

Note [**a**] The more formal full particle *do not* cannot replace *don't* in classes (ii) and (iii), though it can in classes (i), (iv) and (v).

[**b**] Negative directives are seldom followed by tags. The only operators that seem possible are the positive auxiliaries *will* and *can*: *Don't make a noise, will you?/ can you?* The tag has a falling tone.

Illocutionary force of imperatives

11.29 Imperative sentences are used for a wide range of illocutionary acts. It is not, however, always possible to make precise distinctions because the illocutionary force depends on the relative authority of speaker and hearer and on the relative benefits of the action to each. Here are some examples of sentences that may be used for different illocutionary acts, but we should be aware that illocutionary force depends in most cases on the situational context. (For verbless directives, *cf* 11.42, 11.53.)

ORDER, COMMAND

Fire! [*fire* as verb] Make your bed at once.

PROHIBITION

Don't touch.

REQUEST

Shut the door, please.

PLEA

Help!

ADVICE, RECOMMENDATION

Take an aspirin for your headache.
Lock the door before you go to bed.

WARNING

Look out! Be careful! Mind your head!

SUGGESTION

Ask me about it again next month.
Let's have a party.

INSTRUCTION

Take the first street on the left.

INVITATION

Make yourself at home. Come in and sit down.

OFFER

Have a cigarette.

GRANTING PERMISSION

Help yourself.

GOOD WISHES

Enjoy your meal. Have a good time.

IMPRECATION

Go to hell!

INCREDULOUS REJECTION

Oh, come now. ['You don't really mean that.']

SELF-DELIBERATION

Let me see now. ('Should I go straight home?')

Note [a] Imperative clauses joined by *and* or *or* to a following clause may have a conditional implication (*cf* 13.25, 13.30). The illocutionary force of the construction varies:

REQUEST

Sit next to Joan and she'll explain what you have to do.

PROMISE

Finish your homework and I'll give you some ice cream.
Don't make any noise and I'll take you inside.

THREAT

Make a move and I'll shoot.
Don't make a move or I'll shoot.
[These two sentences convey the same meaning, but the positive imperative carries a stronger expectation of the hearer's readiness to move.]

WARNING

Join the committee and you'll regret the waste of time.
Don't eat so much or you'll be sorry.

In *Give him enough rope and he'll hang himself*, the sentence is close to being a pure conditional construction. For verbless directives of this type, *cf* 11.53 Note.

[b] Instructional imperatives are often used in writing:

Take one tablespoonful three times a day after meals.
Remove the bolt from the handle socket and slide the cord retainer into the slot at the back of the handle socket.

Written instructions are often in abbreviated form (*cf* 11.48).

[c] *Please* and (to a lesser extent) *kindly* (*cf* 8.90*f*) may be added to imperative sentences with the illocutionary force of a request to convey greater overt politeness: *Please eat up your dinner*; *Kindly move to the next seat*. Requests are often expressed by questions and statements, *eg*: *Will you shut the door, please?*, *Would you mind shutting the door?*, *Could you shut the door for me?*, *I wonder whether you would mind shutting the door*. Questions that convey indirect requests need not have a question mark (*cf* App III.23 Note [b]).

Do with positive imperatives

11.30 A positive imperative can be made more persuasive or insistent (esp in BrE) by adding *do* (with a nuclear tone) before the verb. *Do* reinforces the positive sense of the imperative. For many people this persuasive use of *do* seems more typical of female than male speech:

DÒ have some more tea. DÒ let's go for a walk.

This use of *do* applies only to classes (i) and (iv), and we therefore do not have **Do you have some more tea.*

Note [a] *Do*, like *don't* and *let's*, acts as an introductory imperative marker, and is not identical with the emphatic *do* of statements (*cf* 18.56). To see this, notice that neither *do* nor *don't* in imperatives fulfils the strict conditions of *do*-support (*cf* 3.37); they are not introduced to make good the lack of an operator, but indeed are added to the front of an operator if one is present: *Do be seated*; *Don't be silly*. (Contrast the unacceptability of **He does be silly*.) This peculiarity of imperative *do* is also found in the quasi-imperative *Why don't you* construction: *Why don't you be more careful?*

[b] *Do*, *don't*, *let's*, and *let's not* are used in isolation as elliptical directives:

A: Should I open the door? B: { Yes, do. / No, don't. }

A: Should we watch the game? B: { Yes, let's. / No, let's not. }

Exclamatives

11.31 Exclamatives as a formal category of sentence are restricted to the type of exclamatory utterance introduced by *what* or *how*. For exclamatory questions, *cf* 11.22.

Exclamatives resemble *wh*-questions in requiring the initial placement of an exclamatory *wh*-element. The syntactic order is therefore upset to the extent that the *wh*-element (which may be object, complement, or adverbial as well as subject) may be taken from its usual (statement) position and put into a position of initial prominence. On the other hand, in contrast to *wh*-questions, there is generally no subject–operator inversion:

wh-element as subject:
What an enormous crowd came! [S V – the rarest type] [1]

wh-element as object:
What a time we've had today! [O_d S V A] [2]

wh-element as complement:
How delightful her manners are! [C_s S V] [3]

wh-element as adverbial:

How I used to hate geography! [A S V O_d]	[4a]
What a long time we've been waiting! [A S V]	[4b]
How quickly you eat! [A S V]	[4c]

In addition, the *wh*-element, like the *wh*-element of the *wh*-question, can act as prepositional complement:

What a mess we're in!

It can occur even as a pushdown element of an indirect statement (again like the interrogative *wh*-element, *cf* 11.18):

How foolish you must have thought I was!

It is possible (but again rare) for the prepositional phrase as a whole to occur initially as *wh*-element:

In what poverty these people live!
For how many years did I live in that dreamworld of fantasies and false hopes!

This latter example and the following sentences illustrate the occasional inversion of subject and operator in literary English, particularly with a preposed adverbial, subject complement, or direct object:

How often have I bitterly regretted that day!
How strange is his appearance!
What magnificent characters does she present in her latest novel!

Inversion is preferred with negative *rarely*:

How rarely do I see you! ⟨rare and rhetorical⟩

For tag questions with exclamatives, *cf* 11.10.

11.32 Only two *wh*-words can be used to form the *wh*-element in exclamatory sentences: *what* as predeterminer in a noun phrase, *cf* [1], [2], and [4b] in 11.31; and *how* as intensifier of an adjective, adverb, or clause, *cf* [3], [4a], and [4c] respectively in 11.31. The limitation to these functions is not surprising when one realizes that the *wh*-word indicates an extreme position on some scale of value, and therefore can only appear at points in the sentence where an expression of degree is possible. Exactly the same functions are fulfilled (especially in some women's speech) by the emphatic degree items *such* (as a determiner) and *so* (as an intensifier) in statements and questions (*cf* 18.57):

We've had *such* a time. Why did they tease you *so*?
Her manners are *so* delightful.

Exclamatives are very frequently indeed reduced by ellipsis to the single *wh*-element: *What a terrible wind!*, *How encouraging!*

Note [**a**] *How* is like *so* (in exclamatory utterances) in that when it is an intensifier, it cannot modify an adjective which itself has a premodifying function. Instead of:

*a *how/so* noisy party

We must prepose *how noisy* or use *what* or *such* as intensifiers of the noun phrase:

how noisy a party
what/such a noisy party.

[**b**] The generalized exclamatory *and how* ⟨esp AmE⟩ is used informally to refer to a previous statement or question by the same or another speaker:

He can argue, and how! ['How he can argue!']
A: We had a cold winter last year. B: And how!

Echo utterances

11.33 Echo utterances are utterances which repeat as a whole or in part what has been said by another speaker. They may take the form of any utterance or partial utterance in the language, but in their discourse function they are either questions (*cf* 11.34*ff*) or exclamations (*cf* 11.37). Echo questions are either recapitulatory (*cf* 11.34*f*) or explicatory (*cf* 11.36).

Recapitulatory echo questions

11.34 A recapitulatory echo question is simply a question which repeats part or all of a message, as a way of having its content confirmed. The simplest type is a *yes–no* question which merely repeats, with rising intonation, what has just been said:

A: I didn't like that meal. B: You didn't LÍKE it?
A: The Browns are emigrating. B: ÉMigrating?
A: Switch the light off, please. B: Switch the LÍGHT off?

To make the meaning explicit, one could prefix to each of these questions the words 'Did you say ...?' Sometimes, indeed the invariant tag clause (*did*) *you say?* is added: *Switch the LÍGHT off, did you say?* (*cf* 11.11).

There is also a *wh*-echo question which indicates, by the *wh*-word, which part of the previous utterance the speaker did not hear or understand:

A: It cost five dollars. B: HÓW much did it cost?
A: He's a dermatologist. B: WHÁT is he?
A: We're leaving him here. B: WHÁT are you doing with him?

In this case '... *did you say?*' could be supplied immediately after the *wh*-element: *HÓW much did you say it cost?* These *wh*-echo questions, as we see above, have a characteristic intonation pattern: a rising intonation with the nucleus on the *wh*-word itself.

In the examples above, the *wh*-element is fronted as in normal *wh*-questions and inversion takes place according to the regular rule for *wh*-questions (*cf* 11.14*f*). In a variant type of *wh*-echo question, the statement order is retained:

A: I'll pay for it. B: You'll WHÁT?
A: I saw Ted Dawson today. B: You saw WHÓ?

The order where no fronting takes place is obligatory for directives:

A: Switch the light off. B: Switch WHÁT off?

What and *who* are not restricted in echo questions to their normal functions, but may replace a single noun or an adjective phrase. There is a declining acceptability the further one gets away from the normal functions of *who* and *what*:

A: His son is a macroengineer.
B: His son is a WHÁT?
A: She always wears a quizzical expression.
B: She always wears a WHÁT expression?

Furthermore, *what* may be made plural:

A: Astronomers have discovered some more black holes.
B: They've discovered some more WHÁTS?

It may even replace a verb:

A: She sat there and ratiocinated.
B: She sat there and WHÁTted?

Although recapitulatory echo questions are ostensibly requests for the repetition of information, they frequently have other functions, such as to express irony, incredulity, or merely to fill in a conversational gap. They are familiar, or even impolite, in implication unless accompanied by an apology:

Sorry, WHÁT was his job?

Note [**a**] The generalized recapitulatory *wh*-question *WHÁT did you say?* is sometimes truncated to the monosyllable *WHÁT*? (impolite except among friends), just as the alternative formula *I beg your pardon?* can be reduced simply to *Pardon?* Other abbreviated requests for repetition are *Pardon me?* ⟨AmE⟩, *Excuse me?* ⟨AmE⟩, and *Sorry?* ⟨BrE⟩.

[**b**] *What?* on its own can also express general incredulity:

A: I paid £1000 for that picture. B: WHÁT? You must be mad.

Questions about questions

11.35 Since an echo question can refer back to any type of utterance, a special case of it is a question about a question, sometimes called a question raised to the second power:

A: Have you borrowed my PÉN? B: (Have I) borrowed your PÉN?

This is a *yes–no* question about a *yes–no* question. In addition, there are three further types:

Yes–no question about *wh*-question:

A: What do you think of the picture?
B: What do I THÍNK of it? ['Did you say what do I think of it?']

Wh-question about *yes–no* question:

A: Have you ever been to Valladolid?
B: (Have I ever been) WHÉRE?

Wh-question about *wh*-question:

A: How did you enjoy the carnival?
B: How did I enjoy WHÁT?

Explicatory echo questions

11.36 The second main category of echo question is the explicatory echo question, which asks for the clarification, rather than the repetition, of something just said. It is always a *wh*-question, and is identical to the recapitulatory *wh*-question, except for the substitution of a falling tone for the rising tone on the *wh*-word:

A: Take a look at this! B: Take a look at WHÀT?
A: He's missed the bus again. B: WHÒ's missed the bus?
A: Oh dear, I've lost the letter. B: WHÌCH letter have you lost?

The last example could be paraphrased 'Which letter do you mean – [rather than 'did you say'] – you have lost?' The *wh*-word replaces some definite item of information meaning (*eg* a personal pronoun) that needs clarification in the context.

Note [**a**] There are abbreviated forms of these as of other *wh*-echo questions – A: *Look over there!* B: *WHÈRE?* The general explicatory echo question *WHÀT* may also be noted. Its meaning is roughly 'What do you want?' – A: *John!* B: *WHÀT?*
[**b**] An explicatory echo question may follow an incomplete question:
A: How did you enjoy the er er . . . ?
B: How did I enjoy the WHÀT?

Echo exclamations

11.37 The echo exclamation, like the echo question, repeats part or all of a preceding utterance; but in contrast to the rising tone of the echo question, it is characterized by a rise–fall (or high fall) tone. The form of the utterance to be repeated may be declarative, interrogative, imperative, or even exclamative:

A: I'm going to London for a holiday.
B: *To LÔNdon!* That's not my idea of a rest.
A: Have you been to Paris?
B: *Been to PÂris!* I'll say I have!
A: Open the door, please.
B: *Open the DÔOR*! Do you take me for a doorman?
A: What a beautiful day!
B: *What a beautiful DÂY*! You must be joking.
A: He must be the only applicant.
B: *Must be the ÔNLy applicant!* That can't be true.

Such exclamations, expressing astonishment at what has been said, are very similar in role to the incredulous type of echo question. Indeed, the repetitions italicized above could be spoken either with an exclamatory falling nucleus, or with the rising tone of the echo question.

Either in the echo question or the echo exclamation, one could repeat the earlier utterance with varying degrees of completeness. Thus, rather than *To*

London! in the first example, one could have said *You're going to London!*, *Going to London!*, or simply *London!* Some irregular subject–predicate constructions in which the finite verb is omitted are produced in these exchanges:

A: I hear you're a linguist.
{B: I a linguist! <formal>
{B: Me a linguist!
A: Ted's going to write the music.
B: Ted write the music? What a splendid idea!

Irregular sentences

11.38 Some sentences do not conform to the regular patterns of clause structures (*cf* 10.2) or to the variations of those structures in the major syntactic classes (*cf* 11.1). It is not possible to make precise distinctions, but we can mention several ways in which sentences are IRREGULAR:

(a) They contain forms not found in regular sentence structures, for example the subjunctive in the main clause of *Long live the Queen* (*cf* 11.39).

(b) They are marked as subordinate, for example by the subordinator *if* in *If only I had been there!* (*cf* 11.41).

(c) They are FRAGMENTARY, lacking constituents that are normally obligatory. The ellipsis may be recoverable from the linguistic form of the sentence (*cf* 12.46*ff*), for example the omission of the subject *I* and the verb *am* in:

Sorry to hear about your father.

Or it may be recoverable from the preceding linguistic context, as in B's reply in the following exchange:

A: When can I see you?
B: Tomorrow morning. ['*You can see me* tomorrow morning?']

On ellipsis, *cf* Chapter 12.

There are other instances where it is less convincing to postulate ellipsis and we shall not attempt to do so. We consider such instances to be NONSENTENCES, since we cannot analyse them with confidence in terms of clause elements. For example, we would not want to suggest that the sign *Exit* is elliptical for *This is the exit*, and that therefore *Exit* is a subject complement, though defective because it lacks a determiner such as *the*. We would not want to do so because it is equally possible to say that the sign stands for (among other possibilities) *The exit is here* (where *The exit* is subject). Other cases are more arguable; for example, *A good idea!* might reasonably be considered to be a subject complement, because of the tag question that we could add to it: *A good idea, isn't it?*

Irregular sentences may occur also as independent clauses in a compound sentence. For example:

Not BÀD, *that* JÓKE, but I've heard better.
A: Are you coming with us?
B: *Of course,* and so is Daniel.

Some irregular types are commonly used as parts of sentences, for example *Please God* as in:

Please God, there hasn't been an accident.

In the sections that follow we generally group irregular sentences by their form, but it is sometimes convenient to treat together certain features that are characteristic of a variety of the language. We deal separately (*cf* 11.54) with common formulae, most of them nonsentences, used for stereotyped communicative situations.

Sentences with optative subjunctive

11.39 One type of irregular sentence contains the optative subjunctive, used to express a wish (*cf* 3.51). The optative subjunctive survives in a few expressions of a fairly fixed type. It is combined with subject–verb inversion in:

Far ***be*** *it from me* to spoil the fun. *So* ***be*** *it*.
Suffice *it to say* we lost. *So* ***help*** *me God.*
Long ***live*** the Republic!

It is found without inversion in:

God ***save*** the Queen!

{God / The Lord / Heaven} {*bless* you! / *forbid*! / *help* us!}

The devil *take* you. ⟨archaic⟩

A less archaic formula (also with subject–verb inversion) for expressing wishes, usually blessings, is *may* + subject + predication:

May the best man win! May you always be happy!
May all your troubles be small! May you break your neck!

Another archaic formula is *would* (*to God*) followed by a *that*-clause with past forms of verbs:

Would (to God) that I'd never heard of him!

Irregular *wh*-questions

11.40 There are several types of irregular *wh*-questions, which occur mainly in conversation:

(i) *How about* and *what about* are generally followed by noun phrases or *-ing* clauses. They are principally used as directives:

How about another kiss?
What about following us in your car?

But they are also used as inquiries:

How about your parents? Are they well?

(ii) *How come* is used in informal speech (esp in AmE) to introduce reason questions:

How come you're so late? ['How does it come about (that) you're so late?']

The stereotyped *how come* is followed by a clause that follows the normal subject–verb order.

(iii) An irregular *why*-question is formed without subject or auxiliary: *why* (+ *not*) + predication, the verb being the base form. It is used as a directive (*cf* 11.16*f*):

Why (not) listen to him? ['Why should(n't)/do(n't)/did(n't) you listen to him?']

(iv) There is a verbless *why*-question, which is used as an inquiry. The questions correspond to existential sentences (*cf* 18.44*ff*):

Why no classes today? ~ Why are there no classes today?
Why all the noise? ~ Why is there all the noise?

(v) *Wh*-questions (except for *why*-questions) without a subject and with a *to*-infinitive as the verb are occasionally found as inquiries:

What to do next? ['What should I/we do next?']
Who to see?
Which way to go?

(vi) Dependent finite *wh*-interrogative clauses are used as directive headings in written English for suggestions:

How you can make your fortune
Where you should eat in Los Angeles

A dependent *why*-clause is used as a statement heading:

Why you should have a medical examination once a year

(vii) Dependent infinitive *wh*-clauses of the same form as those in (v) are more commonly used than the finite clauses in (vi) as directive headings:

What to do in an emergency ['What one should do in an emergency.']
Where to go for help ['Where one can go for help']
Who to phone after office hours
When to send in your application
How to mend a puncture
How to learn a foreign language

(viii) *What if* and *how if* introduce questions used as inquiries:

What if it rains? ['What happens if it rains?']

The questions are also used as directives:

What if you join us for lunch? [invitation]
What if you don't join us for lunch just this once? [suggestion]

What if and (occasionally, esp in BrE) *What though* may have the meaning 'What does it matter if . . .?':

What if they ÂRE illiterate? What though they ÂRE filthy?

Note [a] *What about it?*, *What of it?*, and *So what?* are used as responses to question the significance of what has been said by another speaker ('*What difference does it make?*'). *How about that?* is used (esp in AmE) to express surprise combined with approval or disapproval:

A: Fred and Pam have just got married. B: Well, how about that?

[b] On verbless exclamatory sentences such as *How very thoughtful!* and *What a good idea!* *cf* 7.30.

Subordinate clauses as irregular sentences

11.41 Apart from the subordinate *wh*-clauses discussed in 11.40, several other kinds of clauses that are subordinate in form are used as irregular sentences. They generally have the illocutionary force of exclamations, the omission of the matrix clause (*cf* 14.4) being mimetic of speechless amazement.

(i) *That*-clauses generally contain the putative *should* that may accompany expressions of surprise (*cf* 14.25). They typically convey disapproval or regret:

That he should have left without asking me!
That you could ever want to marry such a man!
That it should come to this!
That I should live to see such ingratitude!

But they may also convey approval or relief:

That all your friends should be so sympathetic!

These sentences are distinctly more formal than the infinitive sentences in (ii) below.

(ii) *To*-infinitive clauses convey kinds of illocutionary force similar to those for *that*-clauses. A common type begins with *To think* (*that*), and is very similar in its illocutionary force to the *that*-clauses in (i), though less formal:

To think that she could be so ruthless!
To think that I was once a millionaire!
To think that they would turn me down!
To think that he should be so mean!
To think that you might have been killed!

The implied subject in such sentences is the first person pronoun (*cf* Note [b] below). When the infinitive clause begins with some other verb than *think*, its subject is understood from an introductory subject (*cf* 18.58) or vocative, or it may be apparent from the previous context:

That brother of yours, to be so uncouth!
You fool, to forget your wedding anniversary!
You're going to be in trouble. To say something like that!

(iii) Infinitive clauses introduced by *oh* express an exclamatory wish. The style is poetic or archaic, except when jocular:

Oh to be in England! ['I wish I were in England.']
Oh to be free! ['I wish I were free.']

(iv) Negative *if*-clauses, usually preceded by *well* or *why*, are used to express surprise:

Well, if it isn't the manager himself! ['It is indeed the manager himself!']
Why, if it isn't Susan! ['It is indeed Susan!']

(v) Subordinate clauses beginning *if only* and containing the form of the verb appropriate to conditional clauses (*cf* 15.36) also express an exclamatory wish:

If only I'd listened to my parents! ['I wish I had listened to my parents.']
If only he were not so timid!
If only I could make them understand my point of view!

A similar construction has *only*, *just*, or *but* before the main verb:

If I'd *only* listened to my parents!
If I could *just* make them understand my point of view!
If I could *but* explain!

(vi) Subordinate clauses beginning with *supposing* may have the same force as *What if* (*cf* 11.40) or, indeed, of the imperative *suppose*:

Supposing I don't see her. [inquiry: 'What would happen if I . . .?']
Supposing you come with us. [invitation]
Supposing they ÂRE poor? ['What does it matter if they . . .?'] 〈impatience or scepticism〉

Note [**a**] Verbless clauses consisting of *Oh for* followed by a noun phrase also express an exclamatory wish. Like the analogous infinitive clauses, they are poetic or archaic unless used jocularly:

Oh for a drink! Oh for another glimpse of her!

On the other hand, the stereotyped exclamation *Oh for . . . 's sake* expresses impatience or anger:

Oh, for heaven's sake! 〈casual〉 Oh, for Christ's sake! 〈familiar〉

In AmE, *for heaven's sake* and *for goodness' sake* are used by some speakers to express surprise.

Exclamatory *Now for* . . . is used to express gratified anticipation that something wished for is indeed available immediately:

Now for a good hot bath!

[**b**] Infinitive clauses introduced by *To think* (*that*) may be interpreted as something like *It surprises me to think* . . . or *It surprises one to think* . . ., though the fuller forms are not exclamatory.

[**c**] Stereotyped *Not to worry!* is an informal friendly directive ('Don't worry!'). It is often self-addressed.

Adverbials as directives

11.42 Adverbials may have the illocutionary force of commands. Generally a verb of motion is implied:

Forward! On your feet! Faster!
Left, right! At the double! To the left!
At ease! Inside! That way!

Two adverbials may be combined:

Full speed ahead! Back to work!

Or a noun phrase subject and an adverbial:

Everybody inside! All aboard! Citizens to the left!

The implied verb of motion may be causative, the noun phrase being a direct object:

Backs to the wall! ['Put your backs to the wall!']
Hands up! Shoulders back!
Heads up! Eyes down!
Hands on heads! Thumbs up!

One kind of verbless command is constructed with an adverbial followed by a *with*-phrase:

On with the show! ['Begin or continue the show.']
Off with his head! ['Cut off his head!']
Off with your jacket! ['Take off your jacket!']
Out with it! [set expression: 'Tell me about it.']

Constructions with *up* and *down* are generally used to express approval and disapproval respectively:

Up with democracy! Down with racism!

Note [a] In two stereotyped verbless sentences a verb of motion is implied after the auxiliary:
Murder will out. ['Murder will come out'; 'Murder will become known']
Truth will out.

[b] Occasionally adjective phrases functioning as subject complement may be directives:
Careful! ['Be careful!'], Quiet!

Aphoristic sentences

11.43 The aphoristic sentence structure is found in many proverbs. The common structural feature is the balancing of two equivalent constructions against each other:

(i) The more, the merrier. The sooner, the better.
The less said, the better.

(ii) Least said, soonest mended. Easy come, easy go.
Nothing ventured, nothing gained. Here today, gone tomorrow.
Once bitten, twice shy. First come, first served.

(iii) Spare the rod, and spoil the child. Marry in haste, repent at leisure.
Love me, love my dog. Waste not, want not.

(iv) More haste, less speed. In for a penny, in for a pound.
No work, no money. Out of sight, out of mind.
Like father, like son. So far, so good.

All are to some extent anomalous. Items in set (i) appear to be elliptical. Thus, the first example may be considered elliptical (depending on the context) for something like *The more there are of us*, *the merrier we are*, a pattern which, although still on the aphoristic model, is more productive than those of any of the other sets. This pattern is dealt with under proportional clauses (*cf* 15.51).

In (ii) the verb is nonfinite; the first part is semantically subordinate (mostly conditional). In (iii) the verbs may be analysed as imperatives, the two clauses being in a conditional relationship similar to that in the regular structure exemplified in *Spare the rod, and you* (*will*) *spoil the child* (*cf* 13.25). In (iv) both parts are verbless.

Note [**a**] A single verbless comparative clause introduced by *the* may occur as a response:

A: I didn't call her. B: The more fool you!

It may be further reduced by the omission of *the*: *More fool you!* Similarly, *The more haste, the less speed* is equivalent to the form found in the saying *More haste, less speed*.

[**b**] Other sayings of anomalous form:

Better late than never.	First things first.
No sooner said than done.	Handsome is as handsome does.

In the last example, the adjective *handsome* is used in both positions as if it were a noun.

[**c**] New formations on the model of *No* . . . *no* . . . are occasionally produced:

No dinner, no dessert. ['If you don't eat your dinner, I won't give you any dessert.']
No homework, no TV.

Subject-plus-complement constructions

11.44 Several types of verbless sentences or clauses, most of them existential, have the basic structure of subject and subject complement, or of complement alone.

(i) In one colloquial type, the subject is appended like a noun-phrase tag (*cf* 18.59):

Not BÀD, that SÁLmon.
ÒDD sort, those NÉIGHbours of yours.
Just our LÙCK, SÙE finding out.

(ii) A verbless clause consisting of subject and subject complement (in that order) may be linked by *and* to a preceding clause with regular clause structure. Various logical relationships may be expressed:

How could you be so spiteful and her your best friend? ['. . . seeing that she is your best friend?']
You could have left before the speeches, and nobody the wiser. [conditional relationship: '. . . and if you had done so, nobody would have been the wiser.']

Less commonly, the subjective case is used for a subject pronoun:

They left without a word, and he so sensitive. ['. . . though he was so sensitive.']

(iii) A more colloquial pattern contains an existential verbless clause consisting of complement alone. The clause is a comment on the preceding clause, and is linked to it by *and*:

They are thick as thieves, and no mistake.
['They are thick as thieves, and that is no mistake.']
She left him, and a good thing too. ['. . ., and it's a good thing too']
He finally begged for help, and no wonder.

(iv) A literary and somewhat archaic type of verbless rhetorical *wh*-question (*cf* 11.23) is followed by *but* in the second clause. The *wh*-clause consists of subject followed by subject complement or of subject complement alone. The sentence, also existential, expresses a comparative relationship:

What belief so foolish but some will embrace it?
['There is no belief so foolish but that there will be some who will embrace it.']
Who so honest but some will doubt his integrity?
['There is none so honest but that there will be some who will doubt his integrity.']

(v) Another version of the rhetorical *wh*-question, but less formal, contains a comparative:

What better than a hot shower? Who more fitting than you?

Note A stereotyped subject–complement sentence occurs in *All clear*. Similar stereotyped sentences, but with an adverbial instead of a complement, are *All in good time* and *All over* ['It's finished'].

Block language

11.45 Block language appears in such functions as labels, titles, newspaper headlines, headings, notices, and advertisements. Simple block language messages are most often nonsentences, consisting of a noun or noun phrase or nominal clause in isolation; no verb is needed, because all else necessary to the understanding of the message is furnished by the context. Here are some examples:

Entrance	50 mph limit
No entry	No dogs without leash
National Forecast	Danger: falling rocks
English Department	The New York Times
Fresh Today	Pure Lemon Juice
For Sale	All the News That's Fit to Print

A Comprehensive Grammar of the English Language
The First Luxury Bound Collector's Edition of Agatha Christie's Work to be Available in This Country

Some forms of block language have recognizable clause structures. Those forms deviate from regular clause structures in omitting closed-class items of low information value, such as the finite forms of the verb BE and the articles, and other words that may be understood from the context.

Newspaper headlines

11.46 Newspaper headlines commonly contain block language because of pressure on space. They can generally be analysed in terms of clause structure, though frequently scrutiny of the text below a headline obliges us to reinterpret the structure.

> FILM STAR MARRIES EX-PRIEST [S V O_d]
> OIL SPILL THREAT DECREASING [S V]
> PRESIDENT CALLS FOR CALM [S V A]
> SHARE PRICES NOW HIGHER THAN EVER [S A C_s]
> STUDY LINKS DEATHS TO CROWDING IN PRISONS [S V O_d A]
> THREE JOCKEYS HURT [S V]
> CAMP HELPS ADULTS REDISCOVER WILDS [S V O_d C_o]

The regular structure of the last two examples, for instance, would be *Three jockeys are hurt* and *The camp helps adults rediscover the wilds.*

In addition to those mentioned for block language in 11.45, certain other syntactic features are characteristic of newspaper headlines:

(i) The simple present is used instead of the present perfective, which in other styles (for example in conversation) would be normal for recent news:

> MEAT PRICES RISE AGAIN ['Meat prices have risen again.']

(ii) *To* is commonly used to express the future or a predicted arrangement (*cf*: *be to*, 3.45*f*):

> SENATOR TO SEEK REELECTION ['The Senator is to seek reelection.']

(iii) Asyndeton (*cf* 13.1) is more common:

> WOMAN CLAIMS DRUG CAUSED CANCER, SUES ['A woman has claimed that a drug had caused her cancer, and she has sued somebody.']
> UTILITY POLE FALLS, KILLS PHONE COMPANY WORKER ['A utility pole has fallen and has killed a phone company worker.']

(iv) Verbs that are generally transitive are used intransitively:

> BRITISH VICTORY SURPRISES ['The British victory has surprised (?) experts.']

Note [**a**] The use of past *caused* in the headline *WOMAN CLAIMS DRUG CAUSED CANCER, SUES* follows the normal backshift rule in indirect speech (*cf* 14.31). Substitution of present *causes* changes the time reference of the verb to habitual.

[**b**] The example in (iv) is structurally ambiguous. In addition to the interpretation given above, which presupposes a noun phrase as subject with *surprises*, *surprises* may be a noun head of the noun phrase that comprises the whole of the title.

Personal letters, cables, diaries

11.47 Block language is common on postcards, where space is restricted, and is also often used in informal personal notes. The first person pronoun and perhaps also an obvious auxiliary are often omitted:

> Sorry about Jane. ['I'm sorry about the news about Jane.']
> Wish you were here. ['I wish you were here.']
> Having wonderful time. ['I'm having a wonderful time.']
> Weather marvellous. ['The weather is marvellous.']
> Know who I saw? ['Do you know who I saw?']

Elliptical sentences like the last example are also common in informal conversation (*cf* 11.49).

The language tends to be even more abbreviated in cables. The sender is likely to omit whatever can be understood by the receiver from a knowledge of the situation:

NO MONEY SEND HUNDRED ['I have no money. Send me a hundred dollars.']

NEGOTIATIONS PROGRESSING RETURNING END JULY STOP LETTER FOLLOWING ['The negotiations are progressing well. I am returning at the end of July. A letter will follow this cable.']

MANUSCRIPT RECEIVED CHANGES ACCEPTED PRINTING JANUARY ['Your manuscript has been received and your corrections have been accepted. Printing of the book will take place in January.']

The language used in diaries is also abbreviated:

Got up at 6, phoned Bill. Bill said he was ill, so had to cancel meeting. Went to office instead. Worked till 12 on government contract.

Note [**a**] *STOP* is used in cables in place of punctuation to indicate the ends of sentences if there is a danger of ambiguity.

[**b**] Notes taken from lectures, books, or articles are likely to be abbreviated, the form and extent of the abbreviation varying with the individual writer.

[**c**] The increasing use of telex instead of cable has rendered the extreme condensed form of cable language less common.

Abbreviated sentences in instructional writing

11.48 Abbreviated structures are typical of instructional writing, such as technical manuals, consumer leaflets on assembling or using products, instructional labels on products, and recipes. As in newspaper headlines, articles are often omitted. It is characteristic of this style to omit direct objects that can be understood from the context.

Tighten to hold bracket snugly against wall, but without excessive tightening of screws.
Disconnect cleaner from electrical outlet before replacing belt.
Add one can of cold water to the contents of this can. Heat to boiling point. Allow to simmer a few minutes and serve.
When mixing is finished, turn mixer off, unplug cord from outlet and eject beaters.
Cook to golden brown.
Beat egg lightly with fork.
Keep away from heat.
Just heat and serve.
Lay flat.

Occasionally the subject is omitted:

Makes four servings, $\frac{1}{2}$ cupful each
Contains whiteners and brighteners

Note [**a**] Ostensive identification indicates that a direct object has been omitted and that it refers to the article on which the sentence is written:

Refrigerate after opening [1]
Keep cool [2]
Keep out of reach of children [3]
Stand upright [4]

Out of context, sentences [1–4] would be interpreted to refer to the addressee's keeping cool, etc.

[b] Spoken demonstrations, for example of cooking, sometimes adopt these characteristics of instructional writing.

Abbreviated sentences in informal conversation

11.49 Initial words in a sentence are frequently omitted in informal conversation:

> Don't know where they are. ['*I* don't . . .']
> Want another cup? ['*Do you* . . .?']
> Lost something? ['*Have you* . . .?']
> Serves them right! ['*It* serves . . .']
> Good to see you again. ['*It's* good . . .']
> Anything wrong? ['*Is* anything . . .?']
> Hot? ['*Are you* (*feeling*) . . .?']

The pronouns and auxiliaries to be understood are partially cued by the words that begin the sentence and in case of ambiguity are dependent on the situational context. For example, *Hot?* could be interpreted as either *Are you hot?* or *Is it hot?*

For further discussion of such sentences in conversation, *cf* 12.46*ff*.

Abbreviated sentences in broadcast commentaries

11.50 Commentaries on radio and television often contain abbreviated sentences, usually with the omission of *there is*, *it is*, or a form of the verb BE:

> The first lap is over. Five more to come.
> Sport, and we have the latest from Wimbledon.
> Another batsman out.
> Two players wounded.
> And now a band of the marines.
> And again the sound of bugles.

Elliptical sentences in dialogue

11.51 In conversation and in written dialogue, it is common to find ellipsis in sentences that respond to, comment on, or question previous sentences spoken by another speaker. The ellipsis is interpreted from a preceding sentence; it avoids repetition so as to focus on the new material. The resultant fragmentary sentences can be analysed for clause functions through a reconstruction, based on preceding sentences, of the full forms:

> A: Is your daughter at home?
> B: Probably. [A – She is *probably* at home.]
> A: Who sent you?
> B: The manager. [S – *The manager* sent me.]
> A: I'm leaving.
> B: Why? [A – *Why* are you leaving?]
> A: I can't play baseball.
> B: I know. [S V – *I know* you can't play baseball.]

A: Nobody's here.
  B: Obviously. [A – *Obviously*, nobody's here.]
A: When will you leave?
  B: With luck, on Tuesday. [A A – *With luck* I'll leave *on Tuesday*.]

Elliptical sentences without change of speaker

11.52 Fragmentary elliptical sentences may also occur without change of speaker or writer. In writing, they appear especially in certain styles of fiction and advertising:

Two strange figures approached. *Martians!*
Janet felt uncomfortable. Yes, *very uncomfortable*.
It has a very distinctive taste. *Crisp and fresh*.
Designed in Sweden, this teak desk is a terrific buy. *Shown with our exceptionally priced desk chair*.

Note These fragmentary sentences are to be distinguished from the sentence fragments that are merely the result of a punctuation device to indicate a dramatic pause for emphasis. They are also common in fiction and advertising:

He was drunk. *And penniless*.
We have all kinds of contemporary furniture. *For every room in the house*.

Nonsentences

11.53 Nonsentences, usually but not exclusively noun phrases, occur frequently in speech, mostly in informal conversation. We can do no more than give some examples with their illocutionary force. (An optional vocative can frequently be added.)

(i) Exclamatory noun phrases modified by a restrictive relative clause (in most instances with the zero relative) generally express disapproval:

The clothes she wears! [*cf*: What clothes she wears!]
The things they get up to!
The way he complained about the food!
The fuss they made!

(ii) Also expressing scornful disapproval are exclamatory phrases consisting of a noun phrase, generally a pronoun, followed by *and* and another noun phrase with a matching possessive pronoun:

You and your statistics! ['I deplore the way you so frequently resort to statistics.']
Him and his malicious gossip!
Pat and her childish hobbies!

The subjective case is less commonly used for the first pronoun: *He and his malicious gossip!*

(iii) Exclamatory prepositional phrases beginning with *Of all* express strong disapproval:

Of all the impudence! Of all the stupid things to say!

(iv) Exclamatory noun or adjective phrases may express approval or disapproval:

Charming couple!	Dirty place!	Stupid!
Excellent meal!	Very interesting!	Poor thing!
(A) good idea!	Disgusting!	Big baby! ['What a helpless person you are!']

Notice that articles are often omitted.

If the phrase is directed at the person addressed, it may be prefaced by *you*; *eg*: *You angel!* ['You're an angel!'], *You poor thing!*, *You idiot!* To express a more familiar – and more affectionate – relationship *my* is used; *eg*: *My poor baby!*, *My silly boy!*

(v) Noun phrases may have the force of commands or requests. Where appropriate, an adverbial such as *please* may accompany the noun phrase:

Attention!	Patience!	A pound of butter, please.
Action stations!	Lights!	Another coffee, if you don't mind.
Taxi!	Phone!	
Your turn.	Just a drop more!	The letter, please.
Scalpel!	My hat, please!	The door!
Scissors, somebody!	Next slide, please.	

In some instances, the interpretation depends on the situational context. For example, *The door!* might mean 'Shut the door!', 'Watch the door!', 'Open the door!', or even 'Leave the room!' For other verbless commands, *cf* 11.42.

(vi) Noun phrases may have the force of offers or invitations, particularly when they are spoken with rising intonation:

Cigarette?	My apartment?
More coffee, anyone?	Another round?

Again the interpretation may depend on the situational context. Alternative questions may have the same force: *TÉA or CÒFfee?*, *My PLÁCE or YÒURS?*

(vii) Noun and adjective phrases with rising intonation may have the force of inquiries. They may function as *yes–no* questions:

New hat?	Good flight?	Boring?
Your book?	Any luck, Ron?	Tasty?
Next slide?	False alarm?	

In place of these questions, it is possible to use a noun phrase followed by a tag question, *eg*: *Too hot, are you?*, *New hat, is it?*, *Good flight, was it?*.

They may also function as alternative questions:

YÓUR car or your MÒTHer's? HÓT or CÒLD?

or as an inquiry having the force of *wh*-questions:

Your NÁME? ['Your name is . . .?'] Your ÁGE? Your RÁNK?
Your occuPÁtion?

These can be analysed as corresponding to (for example) *What is your name?*, *Tell me your name*, *Could you tell me your name?*

(viii) Noun phrases may make assertions, conveying information:

False alarm | No news
No luck | That way ['They went that way.']
Business call ['The phone call was a business call.']

(ix) Exclamatory noun phrases may convey a warning:

Fire! [noun] The police! Timber! Avalanche!

(x) Exclamatory negative noun phrases may convey a prohibition:

No smoking! No more noise! No pushing!

(xi) Noun phrases (with possible expansions) may merely convey sociability:

Nice day again. Good weather we're having. Lovely evening.

(xii) Exclamatory noun phrases may be self-addressed, expressing the hearer's alarm or frustration after a period of forgetfulness:

The cake! ['I should have taken the cake out of the oven.']
My husband's birthday! ['I've forgotten my husband's birthday.']
My interview!

(xiii) Vocatives (*cf* 10.52*f*) are used alone for a variety of purposes: for example, to summon, to rebuke, to question whether the person addressed is present, or to remind of an order or a request.

(xiv) Names or noun phrases referring to persons are used in verbless introductions, generally with a vocative:

Ladies and gentlemen, the next president of the United States of AmÈrica! ['I present the next president . . .!']
My mother and FÁther, SÙsan. ['These are my . . .']
DÁD – John TÒbin, a good friend of mine. ['Dad, let me introduce . . .']

Two or more persons may be introduced to each other, gestures perhaps indicating the different persons:

JÓAN, my SÍSter – JÒHN, a good FRÌEND of mine

Other examples of verbless sentences appear in the list of formulae (*cf* 11.54).

Note Verbless clauses appear as the first clause in coordinated constructions that express a conditional relationship (*cf* 11.29 Note [a], 13.25).

(a) The construction may have the force of a directive:

One more step and I'll shoot. [*cf*: Take one step more and I'll shoot.]
Twenty pounds and you can have the radio. [*cf*: Give me twenty pounds and you can have the radio.]
Another drink or I'll die of thirst. [*cf*: Give me another drink or I'll die of thirst.]

A stereotyped sentence has verbless clauses in both parts:

Your money or your life! [*cf*: Give me your money or I'll take your life.]

Trick or treat!⟨AmE⟩ ['Give me a treat or I'll play a trick on you.']

(b) The construction may have the force of a statement:

A minute more and we would have missed the train.

['If we had arrived a minute later, we would have missed the train']

Another such storm and the river would have overflowed its banks.

A few more feet and you would have gone over the cliff.

Notice the use of *would have*, typical in conditional sentences (*cf* 15.36).

Formulae

11.54 Most formulae used for stereotyped communication situations are grammatically irregular. Only in a very limited way can they be analysed into clause elements. In the following list, we give a few examples of the major types:

GREETINGS: Good morning, Good afternoon, Good evening ⟨all formal⟩; Hello; Hi ⟨familiar⟩

FAREWELLS: Goodbye, Good night, All the best ⟨informal⟩, Cheers, Cheerio ⟨BrE, familiar⟩, See you ⟨familiar⟩, Bye(-bye) ⟨familiar⟩, So long ⟨familiar⟩

INTRODUCTIONS: How do you do? ⟨formal⟩, How are you?, Glad to meet you, Hi ⟨familiar⟩

REACTION SIGNALS:

(a) *assent, agreement*: Yes, Yeah /je/; All right, OK ⟨informal⟩ Certainly, Absolutely, Right, Exactly, Quite ⟨BrE⟩, Sure ⟨esp AmE⟩

(b) *denial, disagreement*: No, Certainly not, Definitely not, Not at all, Not likely

THANKS: Thank you (very much), Thanks (very much), Many thanks, Ta ⟨BrE slang⟩, Thanks a lot, Cheers ⟨familiar BrE⟩

TOASTS: Good health ⟨formal⟩, Your good health ⟨formal⟩, Cheers ⟨familiar⟩, Here's to you, Here's to the future, Here's to your new job

SEASONAL GREETINGS: Merry Christmas, Happy New Year, Happy Birthday, Many happy returns (of your birthday), Happy Anniversary

ALARM CALLS: Help! Fire!

WARNINGS: Mind, (Be) careful!, Watch out!, Watch it! ⟨familiar⟩

APOLOGIES: (I'm) sorry, (I beg your) pardon ⟨formal⟩, My mistake

RESPONSES TO APOLOGIES: That's OK ⟨informal⟩, Don't mention it, No matter ⟨formal⟩, Never mind, No hard feelings ⟨informal⟩

CONGRATULATIONS: Congratulations, Well done, Right on ⟨AmE slang⟩

EXPRESSIONS OF ANGER OR DISMISSAL (familiar; graded in order from expressions of dismissal to taboo curses): Beat it ⟨esp AmE⟩, Get lost, Blast you ⟨BrE⟩, Damn you, Go to hell, Bugger off ⟨BrE⟩, Fuck off, Fuck you

EXPLETIVES (familiar; likewise graded in order of increasing strength): My Gosh, (By) Golly, (Good) Heavens, Doggone (it) ⟨AmE⟩, Darn (it), Heck, Blast (it) ⟨BrE⟩, Good Lord, (Good) God, Christ Almighty, Oh hell, Damn (it), Bugger (it) ⟨esp BrE⟩, Shit, Fuck (it)

MISCELLANEOUS EXCLAMATIONS: Shame ⟨familiar⟩, Encore, Hear, hear, Over my dead body ⟨familiar⟩, Nothing doing ⟨informal⟩, Big deal ⟨familiar, ironic⟩, Oh dear, Goal, Checkmate

Note *That's OK* ⟨informal⟩, *Don't mention it*, *You're welcome* ⟨esp AmE⟩, and *No problem* ⟨esp AmE⟩ are also used as responses to thanks.

Most of the formulae allow for little or no change in their form. The greeting formula (appropriate to a first meeting) *How do you do?* has a regular clause structure, but in the formulaic sense the verb cannot be made past (**How did you do?*), the subject cannot be changed from *you* (**How do they do?*), the sentence cannot be subordinated as an indirect question (**They asked him how he did.*) or answered in equivalent statement form (**I do very well*). The appropriate response to the greeting is the repetition *How do you do?*

Some imprecations are imperative in form, but they do not have the structural potentialities of imperatives. For instance, there are no negative forms **Don't blast you*, **Don't bugger it*, and an indefinite object, such as *some students*, is not possible: **Blast some students!* Similarly, the formulaic *Don't mention it* cannot be made positive (**Mention it*).

Interjections

11.55 Interjections are purely emotive words which do not enter into syntactic relations. Some of them have phonological features which lie outside the regular system of the language. *Whew*, for instance, contains a bilabial fricative [Φɪu], [Φː]; *tut-tut* consists of a series of alveolar clicks, [ɟɟ]. What we produce below are the spelling conventions for a wide range of sounds. Secondary pronunciations are derived from the spelling conventions (*cf* Note [c] below). In addition, many interjections may be associated with nonsystematic features such as extra lengthening and wide pitch range.

> *Ah* (satisfaction, recognition, etc); *Aha* (jubilant satisfaction, recognition); *Ahem*, [əʔəm] (mild call for attention); *Boo* (disapproval, usually for a speaker at gathering; also surprise noise); *Eh?* [eɪ] (impolite request for repetition, but *cf* 11.11); *Hey* (call for attention); *Mm* (casual 'yes'); *Oh* (surprise); *Oho* (jubilant surprise); *Ooh* (pleasure or pain); *Oops* (mild apology, shock, or dismay), *Ouch* [aʊtʃ], *Ow* [aʊ] (pain); *Pooh* (mild disapproval or impatience); *Sh* [ʃ] (request for silence or moderation of noise); *Tut-tut* [ɟɟ] (mild regret, disapproval); *Ugh* [ʌx] (disgust); *Uh-huh*, also *Uh-uh* (agreement or disagreement); *Wow* (great surprise)

Note **[a]** The above is not intended as a complete list. Some interjections are less frequent, *eg*: *Yippee* (excitement, delight), *Psst* [ps] (call for attention, with request for silence). The archaic interjection *Alas* (sorrow) may be encountered in literature.

[b] Interjections are sometimes used to initiate utterances: *Oh, what a nuisance*; *Ah, that's perfect.*

[c] There are also some spelling pronunciations: [ʌg] for *ugh*; [tʌt tʌt] for *tut-tut*, often with an ironic tone; [həʊ həʊ] and [hɑː hɑː], both representing laughter, are always ironic.

Bibliographical note

On speech acts see Austin (1962); Cole and Morgan (1975); Leech (1980), esp Chapter 4, and (1983); Lyons (1977); Searle (1969, 1979).

On questions see Huddleston (1971) Chapter 2; Hudson (1975b); Malone (1967); Pope (1976); Stockwell et al (1973) Chapter 9; on tag questions Bald (1979), Cattell (1973), Millar and Brown (1979); on alternative questions Bolinger (1957, 1978a); on more than one *wh*-element Bolinger (1978b); on negative questions Kontra (1980).

On directives see Bolinger (1967c), and (1977a) Chapters 8 & 9; Downes (1977); Stein (1976); Stockwell et al (1973), Chapter 10; Thorne (1966); on stative verbs in directives Mańczak (1979).

On anomalous utterances see Bowman (1966); Leech (1963); Morgan (1973); Straumann (1935); Yanofsky (1978).

12 Pro-forms and ellipsis

Introduction

12.1 The preceding chapters have been concerned with the basic structures of English sentences. We turn in this and the following chapters to the ways in which these basic constituent structures can undergo elaboration (or expansion) and reduction (or abbreviation). In 2.9–10 SUBORDINATION and COORDINATION were introduced as two principles whereby the structure of a simple sentence can enter into a more complex structure. In the case of subordination, one clause is embedded in another, while in the case of coordination, one clause, or part of a clause, is combined with another constituent of equivalent status in the structure of the sentence. In principle, both these processes, if they are used iteratively, allow a limitless complexity of grammatical structure.

In contrast to subordination and coordination, REDUCTION (*cf* 2.52) is a grammatical principle whereby the structure of a sentence is abbreviated, avoiding redundancy of expression. We have so far (*cf* 2.51–2) recognized two kinds of reduction, the use of PRO-FORMS, and ELLIPSIS:

MEANS OF STRUCTURE REDUCTION	MEANS OF STRUCTURE EXPANSION
Pro-forms (12.8–30)	Coordination (Chapter 13)
Ellipsis (12.31–70)	Subordination (Chapters 14 and 15)

These devices of expansion and abbreviation will now be more thoroughly investigated; but it will be convenient to divide the whole topic into three, concentrating in this chapter on reduction, turning in the next chapter to coordination, and leaving until Chapters 14 and 15 the detailed study of subordination.

Reduction and coordination

12.2 There is good reason, apart from convenience, for dealing with reduction and coordination in neighbouring chapters. When we coordinate two or more units, we duplicate the same kind of structure; for example, Clause + Clause; Noun Phrase + Noun Phrase + Noun Phrase. This kind of duplication does not normally occur without a parallelism of meaning or function between the conjoins. Such parallelism, in turn, implies an overlap of content and structure. For example, two clauses which apparently have no connection of meaning, like those of [1], are not likely to be juxtaposed or coordinated:

Pushkin was Russia's greatest poet.
Special terms are available for senior citizens. } [1]

But more commonly juxtaposed are sentences like [2], which share some common ground:

Pushkin was Russia's greatest poet.
Tolstoy was Russia's greatest novelist. } [2]

This common ground, moreover, often shows itself in the sharing of a common structure; *eg* each sentence of [2] has the structure *SVC*. It shows itself further in the repetition of the words themselves: thus both sentences of [2] contain the word sequence *was Russia's greatest*. This sharing of common lexical content is a typical condition under which the reduced alternative is chosen. Not only can [2] be expressed as a single unreduced sentence by the device of coordination:

Pushkin was Russia's greatest poet, and Tolstoy was Russia's greatest novelist. [2a]

It can also be reduced to a more compact form by, for example, the combination of ellipsis of the second verb with the pro-form *her*:

Pushkin was Russia's greatest poet, and Tolstoy her greatest novelist. [2b]

So close is the association between coordination and ellipsis that we cannot very well understand the one phenomenon without understanding the other (*cf* further 13.44*ff*).

Reduction as a syntactic phenomenon

12.3 Although reduction may in general be regarded in semantic or pragmatic terms as a means of avoiding redundancy of expression, what kinds of reduction are permitted is largely a matter of syntax. English permits, for example, no reduction of the form of [1], whereby the repetition of all three words *was Russia's greatest* is avoided:

*Pushkin was Russia's greatest poet, and Tolstoy novelist. [1]

One of the major tasks of this chapter will be to explain the conditions for ellipsis and the use of pro-forms, whereby, for instance, 12.2 [2b] is grammatical and [1] above is not. Such an explanation must give an account, also, of the different degrees and types of reduction which may be available to the language user as synonymous alternatives. For example, [2a–f] are reduced alternatives to [2]:

The girls swam faster than it was EXPÈCTed that the girls would swim. [2]
The girls swam faster than it was EXPÈCTed that they would swim. [2a]
The girls swam faster than it was EXPÈCTed that they would do. ⟨BrE⟩ [2b]
The girls swam faster than it was EXPÈCTed that they would. [2c]
The girls swam faster than it was EXPÈCTed they would. [2d]
The girls swam faster than was EXPÈCTed. [2e]
The girls swam faster than EXPÈCTed. [2f]

Motivation for reduction

12.4 Such synonymous possibilities as are illustrated in 12.3 [2a–f] are not equally acceptable. Whatever grounds there may be in any given case for expressing oneself with maximum explicitness, there are generally strong preferences for the most economical variant, *viz* the one which exhibits the greatest degree of reduction. Other things being equal, language users will follow the maxim 'reduce as much as possible'. This generally means preferring ellipsis to the use of pro-forms, where there is a choice between them. Thus [2c] is slightly more economical than, and to that extent preferable to, [2b]; similarly the ellipsis allowed in [1a] below is slightly more economical than the use of pro-forms in [1b]:

She might sing tonight, but I don't think she will (sing tonight). [1a]
She might sing tonight, but I don't think she will *do so*. [1b]

Such preference for reduction is not merely a preference for economy: it can also contribute to clarity, by reducing items which are shared as 'given information', so that attention will be focused on fresh material, or 'new information' (*cf* 18.8), as in the dialogue below:

A: Have you spoken to Bob? B: △ Not yet △. [2]

From here on we use, when convenient, the convention of marking ellipsis by the symbol △. Although the full, unreduced version of a sentence is often stylistically unfavoured, we shall also, from time to time, follow the practice, already introduced in [1a], of showing optionally ellipted words in parentheses:

A: Have you spoken to Bob? B: (I have) Not yet (spoken to Bob).

We have mentioned above a maxim 'reduce as much as possible'; but it should be added that reduction is avoided, at least in careful written style, where it would lead to ambiguity or some other kind of difficulty for the interpreter:

After Her Royal Highness had named the ship, *she* slid smoothly and gracefully down the slipway, hitting the water with barely a splash. [3]
In the course of the play, Atreus kills his wife Aerope, Aegisthus his uncle Atreus, and Pelopia herself. [4]
Only my cousin, the housekeeper, and Mrs Baldwin were in the house at the time of the burglary. [5]

Ill-advised reduction can have various effects; *eg* the amusement caused by [3], where *the ship* is clearly the intended antecedent of *she* (*cf* 5.111 Note); and the confusion or puzzlement which is likely to be a reader's first reaction to [4], where the double ellipsis of the verb *kills* adds to the comprehension problems caused by the Greek names. Further, sentence [5] exhibits ambiguity, since it is not clear whether *the housekeeper* is coordinated or appositive. This ambiguity could be avoided by using a relative clause instead of apposition (*my cousin, who is the housekeeper*), or by inserting an additional *and* (*my cousin and the housekeeper* . . .; *cf* 13.17).

Note Unreduced forms are used for rhetorical effect in cases of 'expressive repetition'; *cf* 19.23. In addition, repetition may sometimes be avoided by the substitution of coreferential expressions (*cf* 19.49), such as the coreferential noun phrase *the teacher* in:

Peter Sand denied he ever neglected his students: *the teacher* claimed that the school administration had a grudge against him.

Coordination and reduction as cohesive devices

12.5 There is a further reason, apart from the fact that coordination often involves ellipsis, for including reduction and coordination in neighbouring chapters. The two processes of reduction and coordination, although dissimilar in that one expands whereas the other contracts structure, actually have related functions, in that they provide cohesion in discourse (*cf* 19.11, 19.44*ff*, 19.57). When we examine how a sequence of sentences can be combined to form a spoken or written text, the two devices which most pervasively mark the connections between one idea and another are, on the one hand, the overt linkage of conjunctions and conjuncts, and, on the other hand, the covert linkage of coreference and substitution which exists by virtue of pro-forms and ellipsis. The phenomena we shall be discussing in this chapter can be illustrated not only through connections *within* sentences, but through connections *between* them, as in 12.4 [2]. Nevertheless, our treatment of coordination and reduction in this chapter will be largely confined to single sentences. The role of coordination and reduction in intersentence connection will be taken up in Chapter 19.

Recoverability

12.6 One aspect of reduction as a cohesive device in texts is the fact that the full form of what has been reduced is generally RECOVERABLE FROM CONTEXT. The relevant 'context' is often the linguistic context: *ie* a neighbouring part of the text; but (as noted in 5.28–31) there are other sources from which what has been reduced can be recovered. We shall first mention the most important type of recoverability from the grammatical point of view:

(i) TEXTUAL RECOVERABILITY: the full form is recoverable from a neighbouring part of the text.

To this we add two lesser kinds of recoverability, which do not contribute directly to cohesion of text:

(ii) SITUATIONAL RECOVERABILITY: the full form is recoverable from the extralinguistic situation.

(iii) STRUCTURAL RECOVERABILITY: the full form is recoverable not through knowledge of context, but simply through knowledge of grammatical structure.

A reduced form such as the pronoun *she* may be said to presuppose knowledge on the part of the hearer, as well as of the speaker, of its intended referent. We can recover the identity of the referent either from the situation outside language [1], or from the linguistic context [2–3], *ie* from information given in the discourse itself:

Is *she* badly hurt? [1]
The poor girl did not complain, although *she* was badly hurt. [2]
Although *she* was badly hurt, *the poor girl* did not complain. [3]

One can imagine someone saying [1] on arriving at the scene of an accident in which a girl has been struck by a car. It would be evident from the situation, without further elaboration, which person was meant by *she*. In [2] and [3], on the other hand, the identity of 'she' is given by the linguistic context. We recognize two kinds of textual recoverability: [2] is an example of the ANAPHORIC use of the pronoun and [3] is an example of the CATAPHORIC use (*cf* 6.19). We should, moreover, make the same point here as in Chapters 5 and 6: textual recoverability is best regarded as a special case of situational recoverability; *ie* the information given elsewhere in the text is, for the purpose of the discourse, the explicit part of the situational knowledge which is available to addresser and addressee. It is natural, then, that anaphoric reference (reference to some antecedent which has already been mentioned) should be much more common than cataphoric reference (reference to some 'antecedent' to be mentioned later). Although the term ANTECEDENT (*cf* 2.44) literally means 'going before', we apply it, as others have done, to items which follow the pro-form or ellipsis, as well as items which precede it.

The third kind of recoverability, structural recoverability, is illustrated by the optional omission of the conjunction *that* in:

It is strange (*that*) nobody heard the noise. [4]

Since the word *that* is uniquely recoverable in [4], it is reasonable to include it under the heading of ellipsis. But in this case, contextual information is irrelevant: the optionality of *that* is purely a matter of grammatical structure (*cf* 15.4).

12.7 Recoverability is crucial to the use of pro-forms. Pro-forms such as personal pronouns have very unspecific meanings; *eg*: *she* means simply 'the female person we know about', *it* 'the thing we know about', etc. Therefore it is necessary, for the interpretation of these words, to have information from which we can uniquely predict their intended referents. This information is usually found in a preceding or following part of the text, but it may also be found in the situation. The task of interpretation is the same for pronouns such as *he*, *she*, *it* as for definite noun phrases such as *the old lady* (*cf* 5.28*ff*), except that since the meaning of a 3rd person pronoun is less specific, there is consequently more dependence on context. In the case of 1st and 2nd person pronouns, on the other hand, the referents are usually easily recoverable from the situation.

Essentially the same distinctions apply to ellipsis. The normal understanding of the term ELLIPSIS is that words are omitted where understanding can be achieved without word repetition, as in:

She might *sing tonight*, but I don't think that she will (sing tonight). [1]

This is a case of textual recoverability, specifically of ANAPHORIC ELLIPSIS, since the antecedent occurs earlier in the text. The other possibility, that of CATAPHORIC ELLIPSIS, is illustrated in:

If you want (me to (buy the tickets)), I'll *buy the tickets*. [2]

(On the omission or retention of *to* in such cases, *cf* 12.64.) As with pro-forms, however, the redundancy need not relate to words implied by the linguistic context. The words may be obvious from the situation. For example, a host may invite a guest to eat a sandwich with the words: *Like one?* In this case, the sentence may be regarded as an elliptical variant of *Would you like one?* (*cf* 12.49).

Pro-form substitution

The difference between coreference and substitution

12.8 The bond between a pro-form and its antecedent may be of two different kinds: COREFERENCE and SUBSTITUTION. These relationships are in principle quite distinct, but in practice they overlap, as will be seen in 12.9.

Coreference, as the name implies, means the bond of 'cross-reference' between two items or expressions which refer to the same thing or set of things. It is, as we have seen, a typical function of personal pronouns such as *she* and *they*, as well as a common function of definite noun phrases containing *the*, *this*, *that*, *these*, and *those* (*cf* 5.30*f*, 6.44). In this chapter, however, we shall be more concerned with the relation of substitution than with that of coreference.

Substitution, as its name suggests, is a relation between pro-form and antecedent whereby the pro-form can be understood to have 'replaced' a repeated occurrence of the antecedent. A major test of substitution, therefore, is whether the antecedent can be copied, without change of meaning, into the position taken by its pro-form substitute. For example *one* substitutes for *a first prize* in [1], as the equivalence of [1], grammatically and semantically, with [1a] shows:

Bill got *a first prize* this year, and I got *one* last year. [1]
Bill got *a first prize* this year, and I got *a first prize* last year. [1a]

It is clear that the pronoun *one* is grammatically and semantically equivalent to *a first prize* in [1], but it is also clear that it does not refer to the same prize as does *a first prize*. In other words, the substitution relation between a pro-form and its antecedent is not necessarily a relation of coreference.

Conversely, a relation of coreference between two items is not necessarily a relation of replaceability:

Two players injured *themselves* during the match. [2]

In [2], the two phrases in italics are coreferential, in that the set of persons denoted by *two players* is the same set of persons as that denoted by *themselves*. We could not, however, replace *themselves* by *two players* without a change of meaning:

Two players injured *two players* during the match. [2a]

(In other cases of coreference, on the other hand, such replacement is possible; *cf* 12.9.)

Substitution does not imply an exact copying of an expression. When the repeated expression is restored in the position of the substitute, it may differ morphologically from the antecedent:

This *coat* is more expensive than the {*ones* / *coats*} I saw in the market.

In this respect, substitution is analogous to what we later call standard ellipsis (*cf* 12.38).

Note On the other hand, substitution brings with it the requirement that the repeated expression have the same meaning in both of its occurrences. Thus it would be impossible, except in joking, to substitute *one* for the repetitive occurrence of *a nail* in [3]:

$\neq$ { I hurt my *nail* while hammering *a nail* into the wall. [3]
I hurt my *nail* while hammering *one* into the wall. [3a] }

Characteristics of substitution

12.9 Although there are points at which coreference and substitution overlap, we should in general treat them as distinct kinds of cohesive relation. The main characteristics which distinguish substitution from coreference are:

(i) As already shown by examples 12.8 [1] and [1a], a substitute pro-form can be replaced by the antecedent without unacceptability on structural grounds and without change of meaning. This, of course, is subject to structurally predictable variation, as mentioned in 12.8.

(ii) A substitute pro-form (*eg*: *one*, *ones*, *some*) can be either definite or indefinite, while a coreferential pro-form (*eg*: *he*, *she*, *they*) is always definite.

(iii) Coreferential pro-forms are always pronouns or pronoun-related adverbs (*eg*: *there*, *then*; *cf* 12.10*f*), but substitute pro-forms may be outside the pronoun category (*eg* the substitute verb *do*).

(iv) A substitute pro-form is normally highly dependent on its linguistic context for interpretation; *eg* it is difficult to make sense out of context of:

I've never met *one*. Did you *do any*?
Agnes said *so*. I hope *not*.

Coreferential pro-forms, on the other hand, can be placed on a scale of text-dependence in this sense. Pronouns such as *he* and *she* tend to be highly dependent on linguistic context, whereas other words (such as *the*, *this*, and *that*) often point to something which is known or observed in the situational context.

While these distinctions will be illustrated in the following sections, it is as well to begin with a commonly arising example of the difficulty of distinguishing between these two relations:

George was the best runner in our school, and so everyone expected that *he* would win the prize. [1]

This is a straightforward case of coreference by personal pronouns: unless the context suggests another antecedent, it will generally be understood that *George* and *he* refer to the same person. But in this case, unlike 12.8 [2], the substitution of the antecedent for the pronoun will normally leave the meaning of the sentence unchanged:

George was the best runner in our school, and so everyone expected that *George* would win the prize. [1a]

In fact, the distinction between coreference and substitution as specified in criterion (i) above becomes indistinct wherever both the pro-form and the antecedent are definite. For this reason, it is important to consider the whole set of criteria (i–iv) above, rather than to rely on the first criterion only.

Note Even so, it is sometimes argued that the failure to reduce a noun phrase to a pronoun, as in [1a], invites a different interpretation from that of the reduced equivalent [1]. It is argued, that is, that the two *Johns* in *John thinks John will win* are not coreferential, and that therefore *John thinks John will win* and *John thinks he will win* have different meanings, only the latter involving coreference. More realistically, however, we can admit that both these sentences are ambiguous in that they may or may not be interpreted as containing coreference. For example, the two *Johns* in *John thinks John will win* may be coreferential, if the use of a pro-form is avoided for some special rhetorical effect, such as the irony of: *John's greatest admirer is John.*

Lists of pro-forms

12.10 In illustrating criteria (i–iv) in 12.9, we may take it that criterion (i) has been, and will continue to be, exemplified without the need for any further discussion. Criterion (ii), that of definiteness, can best be explained by a listing of the main pro-forms in each category:

LIST 1: PRO-FORMS USED FOR COREFERENCE

(a) PERSONAL PRONOUNS (6.15*ff*) such as *he, she, it, they*; *her, them*
(b) REFLEXIVE PRONOUNS (6.23*ff*) such as *myself, himself, themselves*
(c) POSSESSIVE PRONOUNS (6.29*f*) such as *my, his, her*; *mine, hers, theirs*
(d) DEMONSTRATIVE PRONOUNS (6.40*ff*) *this, that*; *these, those*
(e) DEFINITE ADVERBS of time (8.51*ff*) *then*; and of place (8.39*ff*) *here, there*
(f) the DEFINITE PRONOUN AND PREDETERMINER *such* (6.44 Note [b]).

LIST 2: PRO-FORMS USED FOR SUBSTITUTION

(a) INDEFINITE PRONOUNS (6.45*ff*) *one(s), some, any, none, either, neither, few/fewer/fewest, many/more/most, (a) little/less/least, much/more/most, several, enough, each, all, half, both, other(s), another*. These are indefinite (quantitative) pronouns of the kind which enters into the *of*-construction (6.48).
(b) DEMONSTRATIVE PRONOUNS (6.40*ff*) *that, those*
(c) PRO-PREDICATE and PRO-PREDICATION *do* (12.21*ff*)
(d) PRO-COMPLEMENT, PRO-PREDICATION, and PRO-CLAUSE *so* (12.27*ff*)
(e) PRONOUN and PRO-COMPLEMENT *the same, likewise, similarly* (12.20)
(f) ADVERBS of process (8.78*ff*) *so, thus*; and of degree or intensity (8.104*ff*) *so, that*.

From these lists, it is evident that pro-forms used in coreference are all items of definite, rather than of indefinite meaning. A large proportion of the items in the list of substitute forms, however, are indefinite.

Many of the pronouns which occur in List 1 are functionally parallel to noun phrases introduced by definite determiners, such as *the bag, this time, those new boots*. Coreference is a general feature of definite noun phrases, as has already been made clear in Chapters 5 and 6 (*cf* 5.30*f*, 6.19, 6.44), and as will be further discussed in 19.44*ff*.

List 2 includes *do* only as a main verb. The auxiliary *do*, and parallel 'stranded' modal auxiliaries, are sometimes analysed as substitute forms in examples such as:

A: [*Did* / *Will*] you leave early? [1]

B: Yes of CÒURSE we [*did* / *will*]. [2]

In fact, we will not analyse such auxiliaries in terms of substitution, but rather in terms of ellipsis; for further discussion of this point, *cf* 12.60.

The items in List 3 consist of more than one pro-form, in some cases bringing together aspects of coreference and substitution:

LIST 3: COMPLEX PRO-FORMS *which are substitutes for* PREDICATES *or* PREDICATIONS

do so, *do it*, *do (just) that*, *do the same*, *do likewise* (12.23*ff*)

Note *That* and *those* are exceptional in occurring in both List 1 and List 2. They can obviously be coreferential. On the use of these items as substitute forms, *cf* 12.19.

Adverbs with a coreferential or substitute function

12.11 Criterion (iii) in 12.9 makes the point that coreference is primarily a characteristic of pronouns. Yet in List 1, not only pronouns but adverbs occur. This apparent anomaly will now be explained. The concept of *reference* involves the naming of some object or set of objects in the world, and this referential function is characteristically performed by noun phrases. Pronouns, which have a noun-phrase-like character, are therefore the primary instruments of coreference. On the other hand, substitution can in principle apply to any type of constituent:

Please *sign your name* if you haven't already *done so*.

Here *done so* acts as a substitute for the predication *signed your name*.

However, the adverbs (e) and the predeterminer *such* (f) which appear in List 1 belong here because they contain definiteness as part of their meaning, and can be easily paraphrased by means of noun phrases: *then* can often be paraphrased by 'at/after that time', *here* and *there* by 'at this/that place', and the predeterminer *such* (as in *such a day*) can similarly be paraphrased by 'like this' or 'like that'. These items are typical of coreferential pro-forms in that they lend themselves to situational as well as to anaphoric or cataphoric interpretation.

The coreferential use of these items is illustrated in the following:

One morning the captain invited us to the bridge. He told us *then* about his secret orders. [1]

Between London and Oxford there is *a famous inn called the George and Dragon*. *Here* we stopped for lunch. [2]

With the above examples, as with previous examples of coreference, the pro-form cannot be replaced by the antecedent without some change of reference. For example, if we replace *then* by *one morning* in [1], it is not clear whether the morning mentioned in the first sentence is the same as the one mentioned in the second sentence. On the other hand, such replacement would be possible in [3], where both pro-form and antecedent are definite:

If you look *in the top drawer*, you'll probably find it *there*. [3]

The adverbs in List 2, however, are best classified as substitutes:

Professor Sands was *attending to one of the routine laboratory tasks*. While he was *thus/so* engaged, however, he observed that one of the rats was behaving oddly. ⟨formal⟩ [4]

To the Greeks, Pan was *a herdsman god, half-man, half-goat*; and he is *thus/so* represented in their sculpture. ⟨formal⟩ [5]

Though Bairstow designed the car to exceed *400 miles per hour*, few people believed that it would go {*so* fast. / *that* fast. ⟨formal⟩} [6]

(*cf* further 7.89, 19.50.)

Here, although paraphrase with such phrases as 'in that manner' or 'to that extent' is possible, the meaning is more abstract than in the case of *here*, *then*, etc. For example, [5] is paraphrased by:

To the Greeks, Pan was *a herdsman god, half-man, half-goat*; and he is represented *as a herdsman god, half-man, half-goat* in their sculpture. [5a]

Even though the repetition in [5a] maintains synonymy with [5], the italicized phrases in [5a] contain indefinite rather than definite noun phrases. We may therefore regard these adverbial uses of *so* and *thus* as instances of substitution rather than of coreference.

At the two poles of coreference and substitution the distinctiveness of these two cohesive relations is clear, but it is in the adverb category in particular that there tends to be a middle ground of overlap, as indicated in *Fig* 12.11.

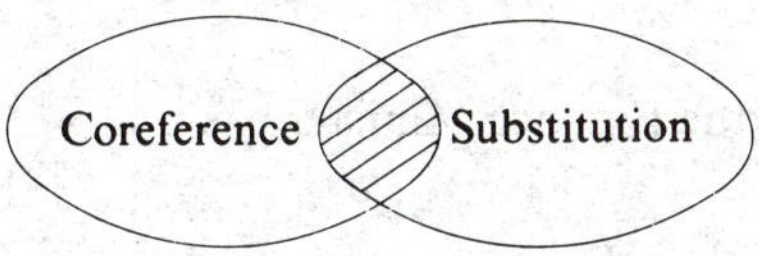

Fig 12.11 Pro-form–Antecedent Relations

Anaphoric, cataphoric, and situational use of substitution

12.12 Criterion (iv) of 12.9 is that the substitute pro-form almost always requires textual recoverability, whereas this is not generally true of coreferential pro-forms. For example, the forms *this* and *that* frequently have extralinguistic reference, as in *Is this/that my plate?* The same is true, less frequently, of 3rd person pronouns such as *he*, *she*, and *it* (*cf* 6.15, 12.6). On the other hand, substitutes such as the pronoun *one* and the pro-predication *do so* normally require an antecedent. The relation with the antecedent may be anaphoric, as in [1], or, occasionally, cataphoric, as in [2]:

There's *a clean towel* in the cupboard, if you need *one*. [1]

If you need *one*, there's *a clean towel* in the cupboard. [2]

Even with substitute forms, however, situational reference cannot be entirely excluded. Examples such as *Would you like one?* may be heard, where the meaning of *one* is only recoverable from the situation (*eg* where the speaker is carrying a bowl of peaches, so that *one* is interpreted as synonymous with *a peach*).

Note The conditions governing the cataphoric use of substitute forms are the same as those governing the cataphoric use of personal pronouns (*cf* 6.19) or of ellipsis (*cf* 12.45).

Cross-reference of *it*, *this*, *that*, and *so* to clauses and sentences

12.13 We turn now to a further respect in which coreference and substitution are sometimes difficult to distinguish. In both kinds of cross-reference, there can be a lack of correspondence in the grammatical status of the pro-form and its antecedent. This is clearly illustrated in the following examples, where the pronouns *it*, *this*, and *that* refer respectively to a clause, a sentence, and a sequence of sentences (*cf* further 19.44*ff*):

If you don't study for the examination, you'll regret *it*. [*ie*: you'll regret not studying for the examination] [1]

A: *She's expecting twins*. B: How do you know *THÀT*? [2]

After many weeks of rain the dam burst. Millions of gallons of water plunged into the valley, and villages were swept away in the flood. In a short time, thousands of square miles of low-lying ground were covered with water. This was a disaster on a scale which no one had foreseen. *It* led to loss of life, and widespread damage to livestock and crops. [3]

Similarly, *so* as a substitute pro-form can substitute for a whole clause or sentence:

A: *The Finance Minister has resigned.*
B: Who said *so*? [*ie*: Who said that the Finance Minister has resigned?] [4]

The difference between *it*/*this*/*that* and *so* in this connection is discussed in 12.28. For the kinds of cross-referential relation illustrated here, the term 'pro-clause' is appropriate.

The present section shows that, in the case of substitution, it is necessary to distinguish three different grammatical expressions: (i) the substitute item itself; (ii) the expression which it replaces, and which in turn could replace it; and (iii) the antecedent which supplies the textual recoverability condition for the substitution. This may be illustrated with reference to [4] above:

(i) The substitute pro-form: *so*
(ii) the expression it replaces (a clause): *that the Finance Minister has resigned*
(iii) the antecedent (a sentence): *The Finance Minister has resigned.*

When a substitute form is referred to as a 'pro-*X*', *X* identifies the item for which the pro-form substitutes, and not necessarily the antecedent.

Substitution for noun phrases and their constituents

12.14 Substitute pro-forms will be considered in the following order:

Pro-forms replacing noun phrases and their constituents (12.15–20)
Pro-forms replacing clauses and their constituents (12.21–30)

We begin with noun phrases. Parentheses will be used to indicate the possibility of ellipsis where both substitution and ellipsis are possible.

One as substitute form

12.15 There are two substitute pro-forms *one*: one has the plural *some*, and the other has the plural *ones*. Both are invariably unstressed, and are thereby distinguished from the numeral *one* (*cf* 6.54). Both types of *one* are restricted to substitution for phrases with count nouns as heads.

(i) *one/some* is a substitute for an indefinite noun phrase:

A: Can you give me *a few nails*? I need *one*.
B: I'll get you *some* soon.

Compare:

I need {*a nail.* / *one.*} I need {*some nails.* / *some.*}

The antecedent of *one*, however, may be definite:

The clean towels are in the drawer – if you need *one*. [= 'a clean towel']

Note Only stress distinguishes the numeral *one* from the substitute pronoun *one* in contexts such as the following:

Have you any postage stamps? I only want to {borrow ǑNE. [numeral] [1] / BǑRROW one. [pronoun] [2]}

In [1] *one* is a reduced version of *one stamp* (in contrast to *two*, *three*, etc). In [2], *one* is a reduced version of *a stamp*, and the nucleus on *borrow* implies the contrast 'I want you merely to lend me a stamp, not to give me one'.

12.16 (ii) *one/ones* has as its antecedent a noun phrase head with or without one or more modifiers. We call this unit a NOMINAL EXPRESSION: it acts as a single constituent for purposes of substitution and ellipsis (*cf* 13.75):

A: Have you any *knives*? I need a sharp *one*.
B: I can get you several very sharp *ones*, but this is the best (*one*) I have.

Unlike *he*, *it*, etc which stand for noun phrases, *one/ones* is more literally a 'pro-noun'.

In the above example, *one* substitutes twice for *knife*, and *ones* for *knives*. In all three instances *one/ones* is a substitute for a single word – the noun head. In other cases *one* may substitute for a nominal expression including premodification, as well as a head:

If you want to buy an *electric heater*, you may be interested

in this {*electric heater* / *one*} in the window. [1]

or for head + postmodifier:

I wish I'd bought a few *jars of honey*. Did you notice

the {*jars of honey* / *ones*} they were selling by the roadside? [2]

or for premodifier + head + postmodifier:

He goes about interviewing *retired sailors who served in the pre-1914 navy*. The *one* that he met in Devon last week was a fascinating storyteller.

One as a pro-form for a noun phrase is not accompanied by determiners or modification, whereas *one* as a pro-form for a nominal expression must have an overt determiner or modifier. The former *one* can be regarded as a merger of the latter *one* with a preceding indefinite article: *a* + *one*. This simplifying assumption has two advantages: (a) it explains why **a one* does not occur (but *cf* 6.55 Note); and (b) it reduces the two homomorphic forms *one* (i) and *one* (ii) to a single substitute form.

For noncount nouns, the noun phrase substitute is *some*:

Shall I pass the *butter*? Or have you got {**one* / *some*} already?

Note Ellipsis can be used instead of substitution both for count and noncount nouns:

Which mustard would you prefer? English or French △?

Which heater(s) do you use? Electric or gas △?

Some, none, etc as substitute forms

12.17 The indefinite or quantifier pronouns *some, none, any, few/fewer/fewest, many/more/most, little/less/least, much, several, enough, each, either, neither, all, both, half* can all act as substitutes for noun phrases introduced by the corresponding determiners (*cf* 5.10*ff*). For example:

Can you give me {a few *nails*? / a little *oil*?} I NÈED *some*. [= some nails/oil] [1]

When the *children* entered, *each* [= each child] was given a small present. [2]

Some *equipment* has been damaged, but *none* [= no equipment] has been lost. [3]

I'd like some *more coloured paper*, if you HǍVE *any*. [= any more coloured paper] [4]

Both the aircraft's *engines* had been hit, and *neither* [= neither engine] could be relied upon to bring us safely home. [5]

John and I went looking for *mushrooms*. He found *a few* [= a few mushrooms], I found *several* [= several mushrooms], and we soon had *enough* [= enough mushrooms] for breakfast. [6]

I asked for a dozen *tickets*, but they couldn't spare *many*. [= many tickets] [7]
This year we produced more *coal*, but we sold LÈSS. [= less coal] [8]
This year we produced more *coal*, but we didn't SÈLL SO MÚCH. [= so much coal] [9]
His sons go to the same school as he did, and *all* [= all his sons] want to become doctors. [10]

With some quantifiers, the substitute may be preceded by another word, which determines or modifies it:

I asked for a dozen tickets, but they couldn't

SPÀRE { *as*/*so* many as THÁT.
'*that* MÁny. ⟨rather informal⟩ }

John found a few mushrooms, and I found *several* MÒRE.

In *that many*, the adverb *that* modifies the pronoun *many*; and in *several more*, the determiner *several* determines the pronoun *more*. (*That many* is sometimes regarded as 'bad English', *so many* being preferred.)

With some other quantifiers, *neither*, *either*, and *both*, it is reasonable to regard the substitute pronoun as replacing a phrase beginning with a corresponding correlative conjunction:

Proust and James are great novelists, but I like Tolstoy better than ÈITHer. [= either Proust or James]
Proust and James are great novelists, but *neither* [= neither Proust nor James] is easy to read.

12.18 It is difficult to tell, in these cases, whether the pronoun is to be considered an example of substitution or ellipsis. *None* is the only quantifier pronoun whose form is different from that of its corresponding determiner (*no*). In all other cases, the pronoun and the determiner (or coordinator) are homomorphic (*cf* 2.38), and it seems reasonable to treat the construction as one of ellipsis rather than of substitution. For example:

I'd like *some more coloured paper*, if you HǍVE *any* △.

However, we shall propose to deal with cases like this as 'virtual ellipsis' (*cf* 12.40), *ie* as cases of a substitution of *X* for *Y*, where *Y* contains a homomorph of *X*. There is particular justification for this in the case of *some*, since *some* as a determiner can be reduced to an unstressed form /səm/ or /sm/, whereas the pronoun *some* cannot.

Note [**a**] Accepting this analysis will still, however, lead to uncertainty as to whether a reduction is to be treated as substitution or ellipsis. This is because many examples will accept a different type of analysis, if the antecedent is a definite noun phrase. Compare 12.17 [1–3], for example, with:

Can you give me a few of *these nails?* I NÈED *some* (of these nails). [1a]
When *the children* entered, *each* (of the children) was given a small present. [2a]
Some of *the equipment* has been damaged, but *none* (of the equipment) has been lost. [3a]

The problem of classification is highlighted by [3] and [3a]: it is clear that the sentence as analysed in [3] is a case of substitution, where *none* substitutes for *no equipment*, and it is equally clear that the sentence as analysed in [3a] is a case of ellipsis. These two types of reduction are so similar, however, that ellipsis has sometimes been considered a kind of substitution, *viz* 'substitution by zero'. In this light, the problem of distinguishing between substitution and ellipsis may seem a mere technicality. But it is a technicality which, as will be shown in this chapter, is important in enabling us to make generalizations about grammatical reduction.

[b] A further uncertain case is that of an antecedent consisting of coordinated proper names:

> *Manjit and Sherif* applied for a scholarship. *Each* was able to present excellent references.

Each here can be treated as an elliptical variant of *Each of Manjit and Sherif*, but in other cases such an analysis would mean postulating a source sentence of limited acceptability:

> *John, Bob, and Susan* were at the party last night.
> *All* (?of John, Bob, and Susan) are good dancers.

[c] There are restrictions of countability and number on the use of the indefinite pronouns we have been considering. Some are count, some noncount, some singular, etc. The details are given in 6.48.

[d] On problems of concord involving some of these pronouns, *cf* 10.42*f*.

***That* and *those* as substitute forms**

12.19 As demonstrative pronouns, *that* and *those* can function not only as coreferential pro-forms (*cf* 6.44) but as substitute pro-forms. In this latter function, they are always followed by restrictive postmodification, and are equivalent to *the one* and *the ones* respectively:

> Towards the end of his life, Schubert wrote two remarkable *trios*: *that* [= the trio] in B flat, and *that* [= the trio] in E flat. ⟨formal⟩
> The *paintings* of Gauguin's Tahiti period are more famous than *those* [= the ones] he painted in France.

That can also be used as a substitute with a noncount noun, where *the one* could not be used:

> The victim's own blood was of a different blood group from *that* [= the blood] found on the floor.

But whereas *that* is less restricted than *those* in this respect, it is more restricted in that it cannot have a personal antecedent:

> The blonde girl I saw was older than {the one / *that} you were dancing with.
>
> The blonde girls I saw were older than {the ones / those} you were dancing with.

It follows that the combination **that who* . . . is unacceptable, whereas *those who* is perfectly acceptable. Another restriction on *that* as a substitute is that it cannot normally precede a zero relative clause:

> The [problem / problems] confronting us today [is / are] not dissimilar from [that which / those (which)] the nation confronted in the 1930s.

Perhaps this restriction is due to a potential confusion of the demonstrative *that* with the relative *that*. This use of *that* is decidedly formal, and tends to be restricted to written English. *Those*, on the other hand, is only slightly formal.

Note [**a**] Once again, the distinction between substitution and ellipsis, while important in principle, is difficult to draw in practice. Although the above cases of *that* and *those* can only be analysed as substitutes (for insertion of the relevant head noun would not produce an appropriate noun phrase), there are other, similar instances for which the postulation of an ellipted noun or nominal expression would yield a reasonable analysis:

> The *topic* of cellular physiology is regrettably among *those* △ which lie outside the compass of this book.

The possibility of inserting *topics* after *those*, and thereby analysing this as an instance of ellipsis, has to be accepted in the stylistic context of formal written English, since in this variety of the language *that* and *those* are used as 'strengthened' equivalents of cataphoric *the* (*cf* 5.32). There is little difference between *the* and *those* in the following sentence, except that *those* is more emphatic:

> Cellular physiology is regrettably among *the/those* topics which lie outside the compass of this book.

[**b**] A further restriction on *that* as a substitute form is that it rarely combines with the relative pronoun *that*; the combination *those that*, on the other hand, is acceptable:

$$\begin{bmatrix}\text{More modern methods}\\ \text{A more modern method}\end{bmatrix} \text{ of horticulture } \begin{bmatrix}\text{have}\\ \text{has}\end{bmatrix} \text{ replaced } \left[\begin{matrix} \textit{those that} \\ \left\{\begin{matrix}\textit{?that that}\\ \textit{the one that}\end{matrix}\right\}\end{matrix}\right]$$

> prevailed at the time of the College's foundation.

Note, in this connection, other instances of avoiding repetition where one item fully or partially echoes a preceding one which has a different function (*cf* 3.5 Note [d], 4.40 Note [a]).

The same as substitute form

12.20 *The same* can be a substitute for a noun phrase:

> A: Can I have *a cup of black coffee with sugar*, please?
> B: Give me *the same*, please.

It can sometimes also be a substitute for an adjective phrase or prepositional phrase acting as a complement expressing a current attribute (*cf* 10.20):

> Yesterday I felt *under the weather*, and today I feel *the same*.
> The milk smells *sour* and this butter *the same*.

A further function of *the same* is as substitute for a nominal clause, especially after *say*:

> A: (I say) Oxford is likely to win the next boat race.
> B: I say *the same*. [= that Oxford is likely to win the next boat race, too]

In both these latter functions, *the same* partially overlaps with *so* (*cf* 12.29); in a similar way, *do the same* overlaps with *do so* (*cf* 12.23).

In all substitute uses, however, *the same* does not imply *identity* with but *similarity* to what is referred to by the antecedent, and we could not use *the same* in place of *so* in the following sentence:

> Tom *phoned for the doctor*, but didn't tell his mother he had *done so*.

But *the same* could replace *so* in the following:

> Tom *phoned for the doctor*, but didn't realize that his mother had just *done so*.

As illustrated in this example, there is an additive element of meaning in *the same*, which is not present in otherwise equivalent substitute forms.

Consequently, *Give me the same, please* can be roughly paraphrased *Give me one too please*; *Joan said the same* can be paraphrased *Joan said so too*, and *The same goes for me* can be paraphrased *That goes for me, too. The same* implies a comparison between two objects or events.

Note [**a**] But *the same* was formerly used coreferentially without any implication of comparison: *I invited Dr Jones to see me, and was visited by the same* [= him] *at 3 p.m.* This use is now rare and possibly nonstandard. It is associated with legal or bureaucratic jargon:

I recovered the weapon and delivered (*the*) *same* to the sergeant.

The variant in which *the* is omitted is felt to be especially objectionable.

[**b**] The use of *the same* as a noun phrase substitute should be distinguished from its use with a following ellipsis:

A: Is that a new bicycle?
B: No, it's *the same* (one) as (I had) before.

In such constructions, where identity of reference is implied, the addition of the pro-form *one* is preferred. Ellipsis is felt to be less acceptable particularly when a postmodifying clause follows:

A: We're staying at the Excelsior Hotel.
B: ?Is that the same *as/that you stayed in last summer*?

Substitution for clauses and clause constituents

The verb *do* in substitution and ellipsis

12.21 When we turn from the noun phrase to substitutive processes in the clause, the units to which primary attention must be given are the predicate and the predication. The two most important and versatile items to consider in this connection are the pro-predicate or pro-predication *do*, and the pro-clause, pro-complement, or pro-adverbial *so*.

A careful distinction must be made, however, between *do* as an auxiliary verb with the status of dummy operator, and *do* as a main verb (*cf* 3.36*ff*). It is in the latter function that *do* is a substitute form.

As an auxiliary, on the other hand, *do* is structurally parallel to other operators:

Martin drives a car, and his sìster does $_\triangle$, TÒO.
Martin can drive a car, and his sìster can $_\triangle$, TÒO.

In such cases, we will talk of ellipsis of the predication, rather than of substitution for the predicate. Further discussion and exemplification will be given in 12.60.

In the following sections 12.22–6, on the other hand, we examine the substitute role of *do* as a main verb. In this role, it is necessary to distinguish a transitive use of *do* from an intransitive one. There is also a problematic function of *do* in the expression *do so*: this is problematic in the sense that it is difficult to determine (partly because of variation between BrE and AmE) whether *do* is in this case transitive or intransitive (*cf* 12.26 Note).

Do as main verb

Do as intransitive verb

12.22 In BrE many allow the possibility of adding after the operator an optional *do* as an intransitive substitute verb. This can take place only rarely after *do* as an operator (a), but is more common after a modal (b), or after perfective *have* (c):

(a) Bob says he is going to join the Labour Party. It will be interesting to see whether he DÒES (*do*).

(b) The Americans are reducing their defence expenditure this year. I wonder if the RÙssians will (*do*) TÒO.

A: Will you be attending the meeting this evening?

B: I MǍY (*do*).

(c) I didn't touch the television set; but PĚRcy might have (*done*).

As the last example shows, this *do* form can also occur after a sequence of auxiliaries.

The intransitive substitute *do* must be distinguished both from the transitive substitute verb (*cf* 12.25) and from the general-purpose activity verb *do* (as in *Have you done the dishes? cf* 3.38).

Note [**a**] In some Northern varieties of BrE, it is also possible for the *-ing* form of the substitute verb *do* to be used after progressive *be*:

A: Why don't you sit quietly? B: I ÀM (*doing*). [= sitting quietly]

[**b**] This use of *do* does not occur in nonfinite clauses:

A: Peter hunts rabbits. B: *Yes, he wanted me *to do*, too.

Similarly, because this use of *do* is intransitive, it cannot occur in a passive construction.

The combination *do so*

12.23 The combination of pro-forms *do so*, seen as a unit, acts as a substitute for a predicate or predication, and contains the main verb *do*, rather than the operator *do*. We therefore find that the combination occurs not only in the finite form of *does so*, *do so*, and *did so*, but also in nonfinite forms following a modal, *be*, or *have*, or in infinitive and *-ing* participle clauses. (Unlike the intransitive *do* of 12.22, the *do* in *do so* is usually stressed, and the *so* is always unstressed.) Examples representative of these various contexts are:

They planned to reach the top of the mountain, but nobody knows if they *did* (*so*). [= reached the top of the mountain] [1]

You can take the train back to Madrid, but I shouldn't (*do* (*so*)) until tomorrow morning. [= take the train back to Madrid] [2]

The American team will have to think of some new tactics, and are probably *doing so* at this very minute. [= thinking of some new tactics] [3]

Would you mind feeding the dog, if you haven't already (*done* (*so*))? [= fed the dog] [4]

As no one else has succeeded in solving the mystery, I shall attempt to (*do so*) myself. [= solve the mystery] [5]

As no one else has succeeded in *doing so*, I shall attempt to solve the mystery myself. [= solving the mystery] [6]

The *do so* construction is somewhat formal, and in general there is an alternative ellipsis of the predication (*cf* 12.59) which is preferred in informal use, and which is indicated by the brackets in the above examples. In [2] and [4], also, the use of a main verb *do* without *so* is possible (as described in 12.22) in BrE.

There are some cases where the elliptical alternative is not possible (*eg* in the *-ing* participle clause of [6]), and other cases where the elliptical alternative is avoided, (*eg* in [3]), perhaps because ellipsis of the predication would leave the meaning unclear, especially when the ellipsis is medial (*cf* 12.62).

> ?The American team will have *to think of some new tactics*, and
> are probably △ at this very minute. [3a]

Note [**a**] There is one further major instance of the construction in which *do so* occurs: *do so* may follow another occurrence of *do*, this time as operator:

> They planned to reach the top of the mountain, but nobody knows if they DÌD ((do) so).
> [= reach the top of the mountain]

The repetition of *do* here, however, is felt to be awkward, and tends to be avoided. Again, the option with *do* but without *so* is associated with BrE.

[**b**] The combination *doing so*, whether in finite progressive constructions, or in *-ing* participle clauses, can be inverted to *so doing*:

> Roberts was rounding up the cattle. When asked why he was *so doing*, he replied: 'Orders are orders.'
>
> The rescue crew attempted to land a helicopter on the platform; but the fire and the fierce wind prevented them from *so doing*.

[**c**] There is a similar inversion (rare and formal) of *do* and *so* in a *to*-infinitive construction:

> Newspapers should not include editorial comment in their news columns.
>
> {*To* 'do *so* / '*So to* 'do} is to betray the confidence of their readers.

When it is fronted in this way, *so* receives stress. Another variant of the same construction involves placement of *so* between *to* and *do*: *to* '*so* '*do*. This is particularly rare, perhaps because of the prescriptive objection to a 'split infinitive' (*cf* 8.21).

Comparison of *do so* with *do it* and *do that*

12.24 The predication-substitute *do so* is similar to two other combinations, *do it* and *do that*. All three can be used in:

> A: Rover is *scratching the door*.
>
> B: Yes, he always {'*does so* / '*does it* / *does* '*that*} when he wants attention.
>
> Mr Brown goes to the hospital for treatment every week:
>
> in fact, he has been {'*doing so* / '*doing it* / '*doing* '*that*} ever since I have known him.

On more careful inspection, however, these expressions are used somewhat differently.

Do that and *do it* are combinations of the transitive main verb *do* (*cf* 3.38) with the demonstrative *that* and the pronoun *it*. As such, they combine the substitute function of *do* with the coreferential function of *it*/*that*.

In the following, a subtle difference between these and the *do so* construction is highlighted:

Martin is painting his house. I'm told he *does it* every four years. [1]
Martin is painting his house. I'm told this is merely because his neighbour *did so* last year. [2]

Although *do it* and *do so* could be interchanged in these examples, the use of *do it* is favoured in [1] because the same action (the painting of Martin's house) is being described on both occasions; while the use of *do so* is favoured in [2] because it is merely the same general *type* of action (painting of houses) that is being described.

Do it and *do that*, on the other hand, differ in that *do that* gives more prominence to the object (*that*), which often receives nuclear stress, and is treated to some extent as new or contrastive information (*cf* 18.8). The *it* of *do it*, on the other hand, is always unstressed:

Is Connie still trying to light the stove? She should have DÒNE *it* by NÓW. [3]
Are you trying to light the stove with a match? I wouldn't *do* *THǍT* [4]

In [3] the nature of the task described by *done it* is entirely given, and so the focus of information comes upon the completive implication of *done*. But in [4] the nature of the task itself is a cause of surprise, and so emphasis falls on *that*.

Note In addition, *do that* and *do it* differ for some speakers to some extent in meaning, in that *do it* substitutes for a narrower set of predications, those which convey volition on the part of the subject:

A: When you chop off a chicken's head and it's already dead, it still *kicks a few times*.
B: Why does it *do* THÀT? [B: *Why does it DÒ it?]

But *do it* is acceptable where the reason is not asked:

A: When you chop off a chicken's head and it's already dead, it still *kicks a few times*.
B: I wonder how it DÒES it.

The *do it* pro-forms appear to be acceptable only where *kick* implies agency on the part of the chicken. In the last example, B talks as if the chicken were still alive and had control over its movements.

12.25 Both *do it* and *do that* are straightforward verb + direct object constructions, and are parallel to other constructions in which a pro-form acts as object of the pro-verb *do*:

What is she *doing*? She's *making some coffee*.
What I *did* next was (*to*) *open the window*. (*cf* 18.29*f*)
She asked me to make some coffee, *which I did*. (*cf* 15.57)

It is possible for *it* or *that* to become the subject of the corresponding passive clause:

A: Have you noticed that the front wheel is buckled?
B: *That was done* ages ago.

For *do so*, however, there is no corresponding passive **So was done ages ago*. The *do it/that* constructions are also typical of the use of *do* as a transitive verb. In general, transitive *do* is (i) dynamic and (ii) agentive; *ie* it refers to some action that is performed or voluntarily initiated by the referent of the subject (*cf* 4.33*ff*, 4.4). It is hence abnormal (in spite of the case described in 12.24 Note) for *do* as a transitive main verb to be associated with stative predications, or with involuntary process predications, as in:

A: They think he is mad.
B: *WÈ *do it* TÒO. [1]

A: He owns a Cadillac.
B: *Yes, his BRÒTHer does {that / THÁT} TÒO. [2]

(Here as elsewhere, however, *do* as operator is acceptable: *Yes, his brother does, too.*)

With regard to *do so*, there is divided usage. Some speakers, particularly in AmE, treat the *do* in *do so* as agentive and therefore find replies such as those in [1] and [2] odd, even if *do so* is substituted for *do it/that*. Attitudinal verbs are doubtfully acceptable with *do so*:

?*A: Peter *likes work*.
B: I think BÒB *does* (*so*) TÒO.
?*A: She will hate the way he goes on about his prizes.
B: PÈTer will do (so) TÒO.
?*A: David might have wanted his food now.
B: MÀRy might have done (so) TÒO.

Again, *do* as operator or as an intransitive main verb (in BrE) is acceptable in these examples. Other verbs in this class seem to allow the substitutions in BrE, but they are odd to varying degrees in AmE:

A: They think he is mad.
B: WÈ {do / ?do so} TÒO.
A: I can smell perfume.
B: ?I can do so TÒO.
A: Bob might have heard the strange noises.
B: (?) He might WÈLL have *done so*.

However, even in the least acceptable of such examples, *do so* is more acceptable than *do it* and *do that* would be. Contrast:

All the children resemble their mother's relations more closely than they do their father's. They are thought to *do* {*so* / **it/that*} on account of the genetic effects of this curious kinship system.

Note *Do the same, do likewise, do similarly* are alternatives to *do that* when a comparison is involved. Just as *the same* cannot normally refer to the identical thing referred to by its antecedent (*cf* 12.20), so *do the same* cannot refer to the identical event. It not only is a substitute, but also has the additive meaning of *too*:

I'll contribute ten dollars, if you'll *do the same* [= do so, too].

The above observations on *do the same* also apply to *do likewise* and *do similarly*.

Do as substitute verb: a summary

12.26 By way of summary, we may now give the following list of uses of *do*. To avoid confusion, it is important to distinguish *do* functioning as an operator (where it is not a substitute, but a dummy operator) and *do* functioning as a main verb. The major criterion for distinguishing these two is that the main verb *do* has nonfinite forms (*doing* and *done*) as well as finite forms (*do*, *does*, *did*).

DO AS:	FOLLOWED BY:	SUBSTITUTING FOR:	RESTRICTIONS
operator *do*	–	–	not a substitute but used with quasi-ellipsis (12.60)
main verb *do* (intransitive)	–	predication	BrE only (12.22)
main verb *do* (transitive? *cf* Note)	+ *so*	predication	in AmE, and to some extent in BrE, dynamic meaning only (12.23*ff*)
main verb *do* (transitive)	+ *that*	predication	dynamic meaning only (12.24*f*)
main verb *do* (transitive)	+ *it*	predication	dynamic agentive meaning only (12.24*f*)

Note Whereas the *do* preceding *it*/*that* is clearly transitive, the status of *do* preceding *so* is not so clear. This reflects the uncertain nature of the *do so* construction both grammatically and to some extent semantically. What kind of word is *so*? If it is a pronoun, then it functions as direct object, like *it*/*that*, and the *do* preceding it is transitive, and has dynamic meaning. This analysis seems to accord with the facts of usage in AmE fairly well, but not with those in BrE, where there is, to complicate matters, an intransitive main verb (*cf* 12.22) pro-form which is not restricted to dynamic meaning. Perhaps it is association with this *do* which accounts for the less restricted use of *do so* in BrE. These observations suggest that *so* is more of an adverb than a pronoun, as would be supported by the paraphrase of *do so* as *behave in that way*. A similar conclusion is supported by the absence of a passive construction **so was done* . . . It seems safest, all in all, to treat this word as a unique substitute form which does not easily fit into any of the word classes. Further uses of this anomalous word will now be examined.

So as pro-form

So as complement substitute

12.27 *So* is a versatile pro-form. Apart from its use as an adverb (*cf* 7.89, 12.10), it can substitute for an adjective, an adjective phrase, or a noun phrase functioning as complement:

Prices at present are reasonably *stable*, and will probably remain *so*.
If he's *a criminal*, it's his parents who have made him *so*.
Brett's work is not yet *consistent in style and quality*, but will no doubt become *so*.

On the other hand, *so* cannot easily be retained following *be*, the usual form of reduction here being ellipsis, or (informally) the substitutes *like that* or *that way*. Compare:

The plants are healthy enough now, but I wonder how long they will {*be* (?*so*). / *remain so*.}

La Gioconda is *so called* because of her enigmatic smile.
Prices at present are *reasonably stable*, and will probably stay *that way*.

The combinations *more so* and *less so* substitute for a comparative adjective expression:

Although the poor girl was *exhausted*, she was less *so* than we feared.
The weather was *hot* in Cairo, but at Luxor it was even more *so*.

Other combinations of this kind are *too much so* and *so much so*:

The weather was *hot* in Cairo – so much *so*, that we stayed indoors all day.

Note [a] *So* as pro-complement can also appear in initial position in the clause:

We hoped that the programme would be a success, and *so* it turned out.

[b] Following the verb *be* in sentences such as *That is so*, *so* is not a substitute form, but a synonym for *true* or *the case*. Other comparable examples are:

It may be *so*. This must be *so*, because . . .

It is perhaps this construction that occurs with subject–verb inversion in the literary archaisms *So be it* and *Be it so*.

[c] *Otherwise* can be a negative counterpart of *so* as pro-complement:

They promised that the vessel would be in good condition [and / but] we found it [*so*. / *otherwise*.]

So and *not* as substitutes for *that*-clauses

12.28 A more frequent use of *so* is as a pro-clause substituting for a *that*-clause as direct object. The antecedent is often an entire sentence:

Oxford is likely to win the next boat race. All my friends say *so*. [= . . . that Oxford will win the next boat race]
Jack hasn't found a job yet. He told me *so* yesterday. [= . . . that he hasn't found a job yet]

This use of *so* applies both to reported speech (*cf* 14.30*ff*) and to reported beliefs or assumptions:

Many people believe that the international situation will deteriorate. My father thinks *so*, but I believe *not*.

As this example shows, the negative substitute equivalent to *so* in this construction is *not*. Unlike *so*, however, the substitute *not* usually receives nuclear stress:

A: *Has the news reached home yet*?
{B: I'm aFRǍID SO.
B: I'm afraid NǑT.}

Apart from the adjective *afraid*, this use of *not* is restricted mainly to verbs of belief or assumption, while the corresponding use of *so* is also found in some verbs of saying such as *say* and *tell*. Verbs that commonly allow both *so* and *not* (*cf* 16.31–2) include:

appear	expect	hope	presume	seem	suspect
believe	guess	imagine	reckon	suppose	think

In this list, *appear* and *seem* occur with an initial anticipatory *it* (*cf* 16.34, 18.33*ff*): *it appears so/not, it seems so/not*.

The pro-form *not* is occasionally used with the verbs *say* and *tell*, but the use of the positive pro-form *so* is much more frequent with such verbs of saying. With other verbs and adjectives, such as *know* and (*be*) *sure*, neither of these forms can normally be used, but the whole *that*-clause can be ellipted (*I know*; *I am sure*; *cf* 12.65), or else the pronoun *it* can be used: *I know it* ⟨AmE⟩; *I am sure of it*. For other examples of ellipsis in place of *so* (*eg*: *Who says? I agree*) *cf* 12.65.

So as a pro-clause occasionally occurs in initial position, with or without subject inversion:

A: Oxford will win the boat race; at least, *so* all my Oxford FRĬENDS say.

B: {And *so* say most of the SPÒRTS writers, TÒO.
So most of the SPÒRTS writers say, TÒO.}

When the subject is a pronoun, however, no inversion is possible:

A: Most people are backing the Oxford crew.
B: *So* I believe; but that doesn't mean they'll win. [**So* believe I]

The fronting of *so* does not occur with *afraid* (**So I'm afraid*), and occurs only marginally with certain verbs (?*So I guess*; ?*So we are hoping*). On the other hand, *So it appears* and *So it seems* are common expressions.

Note [**a**] The idiomatic clause *so they say* (where *they* refers to 'people in general'; *cf* 6.21) is often added to the end of a sentence, and has a status similar to that of a final comment clause (*cf* 15.55 Note [a]):

The town hall is going to be reBÙILT, so they SÁY.

[**b**] With verbs taking transferred negation (*eg*: *think*, *suppose*; *cf* 14.36), the use of *not* as a clause substitute is rather formal, and is often replaced by the use of *so* preceded by negation in the main clause:

I don't think so. (~ I think not.)
I don't suppose so. (~ I suppose not.)
I don't believe so. (~ I believe not.)

This construction with *so* is especially common when *I* is subject. With verbs not taking transferred negation, this alternative construction is not possible:

I don't hope so. ≁ I hope not.

[**c**] There is sometimes a contrast between *so* and *it/that* as pro-forms following verbs such as *believe* and *say*:

{I {can't / don't} believe {it / that}. [on receiving a piece of news; NOT *I can't believe so]
I really believe so. [confirming an opinion]}

(A: Come in!)
B: {Who 'says *so*? [= Who gives permission?]
Who said '*that*? [= Who said 'Come in'?]}

In such cases *it/that* refers to an actual utterance, while *so* refers to the content of an utterance. Compare the similar contrast between *do so* and *do it/that* (*cf* 12.24*f*).

[**d**] Exceptional combinations of a verb with the substitute *so* or *not* occasionally occur. For example, *I know so* is sometimes acceptable if it is used contrastively in a 'second instance' utterance:

A: Do you think Tom will succeed?
B: I don't THĬNK so, I KNÒW so!

Equally, a verb such as *claim* or *tell* may occur exceptionally with *not* as substitute when the context demands contrastive emphasis:

I thought they had agreed to write an indemnity into the contract. But THÈY CLÁIM NÒT.

Initial *so*

12.29 Three constructions with initial *so* have already been noted: the one in which *so* precedes *do* in nonfinite clauses (*eg*: *in so doing*, *cf* 12.23 Notes *b* and *c*), the one in which *so* is a pro-complement (*cf* 12.27), and the one in which *so* is a *that*-clause substitute (*cf* 12.28). But here we need to consider particularly two superficially similar constructions in which stressed '*so* precedes a subject and operator:

So + op + S CONSTRUCTION WITH SUBJECT–OPERATOR INVERSION

YǑU asked him to leave, and 'so did Ì. [= I asked him to leave, too]
The corn is ripening, and 'so are the ÀPPLES. [= the apples are ripening too]
You've spilled coffee on the table, and 'so have Ì. [= and I've spilled coffee on the table, too]

So + S + op CONSTRUCTION WITHOUT SUBJECT–OPERATOR INVERSION

You asked me to leave, and 'so I DÌD. [= and I DÌD leave]
A: It's starting to snow. B: 'So it ÌS!
A: You've spilled coffee on your dress. B: Oh dear, 'so I HÀVE.

In the former construction (*So* + op + S) *so* is not a pro-form at all, but an additive adverb, equivalent in meaning to *too* or *also* (*cf* 8.116). Notice, in confirmation of this, that the construction is elliptical, and that the missing predication can be supplied (*cf* 12.21):

YǑU asked him to leave, and 'so did WÈ (ask him to leave). [1]

In fact, the nonelliptical variant in [1] is rarely used, because it involves needless repetition. But the fact that it is possible implies that the connection between the clause *so did we* and its antecedent clause is made by ellipsis, rather than by a substitute form. A further pointer to this conclusion is that *so* in this construction is precisely parallel to the negative additive adverbs *neither* and *nor*, which similarly take subject–operator inversion (*cf* 13.36*ff*):

The corn isn't ripening, and *neither*/*nor* are the apples (ripening).

It is possible to apply a rule whereby *So* + op + S is changed into S + op, *too* (without change of meaning) for all clauses of this pattern.

Note [**a**] In spite of the parallel with the negative constructions *Neither*/*Nor* + op + S, *So* + op + S is occasionally used (in very informal style) with a negative operator, and in this case it refers back to a negative clause:

A: My sister can't drive a car.
B: *So can't a lot of other people*, but that doesn't prevent them from trying.
[= Neither can . . .]

The simpler construction of ?**So don't I* or ?**So can't she*, on the other hand, would be extremely unlikely as an alternative to *Neither do I* or *Neither can she*.

[**b**] Although we have described *so* in this construction as an additive adverb, it actually has the value of a conjunct, and may be compared with *so* as a resultive conjunct (*cf* 8.140).

So as pro-predication

12.30 For the second construction with initial *so*, that without subject–operator inversion, the possibility of supplying an ellipted predication is extremely doubtful:

A: You've spilled coffee on your dress.
B: ?*Oh dear, 'so I HÀVE spilled coffee on my dress.

and therefore it seems more reasonable to consider *so* in this construction to be not an adverb, but rather a predication substitute, equivalent to the *so* in *do so*. There is therefore little difference, except for the inversion, between:

I told Bob to eat up his dinner, and 'so he DÌD. [= indeed he DID]
I told Bob to eat up his dinner, and he DÌD so.

The only change of meaning brought about by the initial *so* here is an emphasis which might otherwise be conveyed by *indeed* or *in fact*. In replies, *So* + S + op expresses surprised confirmation of what the previous speaker has asserted:

A: It's past midnight. B: [looks at watch] 'So it ìs!

Note [**a**] In some varieties of popular speech, for example in dialects of Scotland and Northern England, *that* is used as a predication substitute rather like *so*, both in the initial and final positions:

A: He'll regret what he said. B: 'That he WÌLL.
A: Have you been working here long? B: I 'have THÀT.

When in final position, *that* carries the nucleus. The meaning of this construction is stronger than that of the *so* construction, and tends to be one of emphatic confirmation or agreement.

[**b**] In some regional varieties, particularly Irish English, a clause of the construction *so* + S + op (pronounced at a low pitch) can be added to a statement as a comment clause, by way of general emphasis:

He spoils those children to DÈATH, so he does.

[**c**] In another restricted variety of speech, the pro-form *so* is given nuclear emphasis:

A: They didn't hurt her. B: They did sò.

[**d**] Yet another regionally restricted variant is the use of *nor* as a negative pro-predicate with inversion (corresponding to the positive *so*) in:

A: I couldn't do anything for her.
B: *Nor* you CÒULD – but you might have got someone else to help.

[**e**] On the initial intensifier *so* in constructions like *So angry was she* . . ., *cf* 15.74 Note [b], 18.24 Note [a].

Ellipsis

The nature of ellipsis

12.31 Ellipsis may be more strictly described as 'grammatical omission', in contrast to other kinds of omission in language. There is, for example, the phonological loss (aphaeresis) of a syllable in the familiar form of *because* (often spelled *'cos*). In word formation (*cf* App I.74), the clipping of words (*eg*: *flu* from *influenza*) may well be regarded as a process of this kind: the omission is describable in terms of phonological units (syllables) rather than in terms of morphological units (morphemes) or grammatical units (words). There is also, arguably, semantic omission. In:

Frankly, he is very stupid.

The disjunct *frankly* implies a comment by the speaker on the way he is speaking (*cf* 8.124*f*). But there is no one set of missing words that can be supplied. We can expand *frankly* to (among many forms) *I am speaking frankly when I say* . . . or *If I may put it frankly I would tell you* . . . Similarly, in:

He's drunk, because I saw him staggering. [1]

there is an implicit meaning (*cf* 15.21) that might be expressed by:

He's drunk, *and I claim this* because I saw him staggering. [2]

But equally we can express this understood meaning in other forms, such as *and I know, and I am sure of it, and I am convinced of it, and the proof is that* . . . In such cases it is difficult to pin down in exact words what has been omitted, so it is more appropriate to describe this phenomenon as SEMANTIC IMPLICATION rather than as ellipsis.

Criteria for ellipsis

12.32 To distinguish ellipsis from other kinds of omission, it is important to emphasise the principle of VERBATIM RECOVERABILITY that applies to ellipsis; that is, the actual word(s) whose meaning is understood or implied must be recoverable. Even so, like those of so many other grammatical categories, the boundaries of ellipsis are unclear, and it is best to recognize different degrees of 'strength' in the identification of examples of ellipsis. To be ellipsis in the strictest sense, an example must satisfy all the criteria specified in 12.33–6.

(a) The ellipted words are precisely recoverable

12.33 This means that in a context where no ambiguity of reference arises, there is no doubt as to what words are to be supplied:

She can't *sing* tonight, so she won't $_\triangle$. [1]

Examples like this contain an ellipsis that presupposes words in a previous part of the same sentence. It is clear that in [1] it is the word *sing* that has been ellipted. But by 'precisely recoverable' we do not necessarily mean 'unambiguously recoverable'. Consider the following:

If he works hard, I won't have to $_\triangle$. [2]

In one context, the assumption will be made that *work hard* is ellipted at the end of the sentence; but in another context, this assumption can prove false:

A: You ought to speak to James about his laziness.
B: If he works hard, I won't have to (speak to James about his laziness).

There are also cases of simultaneous ambiguity, such as:

> The suspect admits stealing a car from a garage, but he can't remember which △.

where *which* could mean either 'which car' or 'which garage'.

This ambiguity of anaphora is parallel to the ambiguity of pronoun anaphora noted in 12.4 [3] above. In saying that with ellipsis the omitted words are precisely recoverable, we do not mean to exclude from ellipsis such cases of genuine ambiguity. Rather, we exclude indeterminate cases like 12.31 [1] above, where there is no clear-cut choice between one verbalization and another.

Note Verbatim recovery does not necessarily mean that the items replaced are morphologically identical to the items constituting the antecedent; *cf* 12.36 below.

(b) The elliptical construction is grammatically 'defective'

12.34 Typically, ellipsis is postulated in order to explain why some normally obligatory element of a grammatical sentence is lacking. If such 'gaps' did not occur, there would be no obvious grammatical motive for invoking the concept of ellipsis in the first place. For example, in 12.33 [1] above, the auxiliary *won't* occurs without a following main verb (*cf* 2.27). Similarly, in [2] the infinitive marker *to* occurs without the infinitive verb which it normally introduces. While we might agree that such cases involve some structural 'gap', however, there are many other cases for which this is less clear. Would we decide, *eg*, that [3] below is deficient if the optional infinitive clause is omitted?

> Visit me tomorrow, if you wish (to visit me tomorrow). [3]

This depends on whether we accept as 'normal' the occurrence of *wish* as an intransitive verb. Here, as in many other cases, the recognition of a structural 'deficiency' depends on a prior descriptive decision of grammar. The merits of each case must be argued on the basis of available evidence (*cf* for example 10.3 on intransitive and transitive verbs).

Some structures are clearly in some sense 'defective' but do not match the condition of precise recoverability. *Thanks*, for example, can act as a complete utterance, but lacking a clause structure, it does not fulfil the normal requirements of sentencehood (*cf* 11.38). It is not clear, however, what missing elements are left unexpressed. We could expand *Thanks* in various ways, for example:

> I owe you my *thanks*. I give you *thanks*.

Thanks is therefore not properly elliptical according to criterion (a) (12.33). Rather, it resembles examples like *Hello* in that it has a formulaic status, and cannot be readily analysed according to any productive grammatical pattern (for further examples *cf* 11.54). This suggests that the criterion of structural 'deficiency' cannot be usefully applied in isolation from that of precise recoverability.

Another kind of grammatical 'deficiency' which is not included in the category of ellipsis is illustrated by some postmodifying clauses:

Her hair is not so black *as it was*. [black] [4]
Mrs Trent is very charming *to speak to*. [Mrs Trent] [5]

For the completion both of the sense and of the grammatical complementation of the verb in the subordinate clauses of [4] and [5], it would be necessary to add the words in square brackets. But if we add these words, [4] and [5] become ungrammatical. This brings us to criterion (c).

(c) The insertion of the missing words results in a grammatical sentence (with the same meaning as the original sentence)

12.35 This third condition of ellipsis is met by all the examples we have so far considered except for [4] and [5] of 12.34. But it distinguishes between the following comparative constructions:

He always wakes up earlier than *I*. 〈formal〉 [1]
He always wakes up earlier than *me*. 〈informal〉 [2]

To [1] could be added the ellipted words *wake up*, but not to [2]:

He always wakes up earlier *than I wake up*. [3]
*He always wakes up earlier *than me wake up*. [4]

This difference means that [1] is a more definite example of ellipsis than [2], and indeed partly explains why prescriptive teaching has favoured [1] as the 'more correct' form (*cf* 15.67). Another contrast in terms of this criterion is provided by participial clauses (*cf* 4.67, 14.19, 15.58) such as:

While (I was) eating my lunch, I heard a loud noise. [5]
(*Since I was) Knowing no French, I could not express my thanks. [6]

The insertion is not possible in [6] because *know* belongs to a category of verbs of stative meaning which lack progressive forms: **I am knowing French* (*cf* 4.4). Thus while [5] can by this criterion be classified as ellipsis, [6] is not.

The bracketed part of criterion (c) above – '*with the same meaning as the original sentence*' – is needed because there is always the assumption that whatever is 'understood' through ellipsis is part of the meaning of the elliptical sentence. In fact, without the proviso of synonymy between the full and ellipted forms of the sentence, there would be no way of confining the concept of ellipsis within reasonable limits. This proviso excludes from ellipsis such cases as the following, in which the insertion leads to a grammatical sentence, but the meaning is slightly altered:

The poor (people) need more help. [7]

Noun phrases such as *the poor* presuppose, for their interpretation, some such general noun as *people*; but if we add such a noun, as in [7], the noun phrase changes its generic meaning into a specific meaning (*cf* 5.26, 5.52–9). Generic meaning requires that we delete the article: *Poor people need more help*.

Note The following observation lends some confirmation to the argument for not treating *the poor* as having an ellipted noun:

The poor in spirit need more help.
*The poor people in spirit need more help.
The people poor in spirit need more help.

Where *poor* is postmodified, but not otherwise, the noun *people* must be inserted before the adjective if the result is to be a grammatical sentence. A different form of ellipsis must therefore be posited according to whether a phrase like *in spirit* is added or not:

the poor △
The △ poor in spirit

But there is yet a further complication: with prepositional phrases that can be analysed as reduced relative clauses, the general noun can appear only after the adjective:

The poor (people) in the ghettos need more help.

While *in spirit* postmodifies *poor*, *in the ghettos* postmodifies *poor* (*people*).

Since no consistent account of ellipsis can be given for this construction, it is just as well that our analysis regards it as nonelliptical.

(d) The missing word(s) are textually recoverable, and
(e) are present in the text in exactly the same form

12.36 Of these two related criteria, the latter is dependent on the former. It may be held that textual recoverability is the surest guarantee of ellipsis, since without it, there is usually room for disagreement on what particular word or expression has been ellipted. To return to an example similar to that of *Like one?* in 12.7: it would be difficult to insist, for a situation in which a guest is offered peanuts with the words *Like some?* that it is *peanuts* that is ellipted after *some* rather than (say) *nuts* or *of these peanuts*. However, within the textually recoverable category there is an even stronger criterion, which distinguishes [1] from [2]:

She might *sing tonight*, but I don't think she will (sing tonight). [1]
She rarely *sings*, so I don't think she will (sing) tonight. [2]

The ellipted expression in [1] is an exact copy of the antecedent (*sing tonight*), while in [2] the ellipted verb is morphologically different from its antecedent. Criterion (e) might be trivially subsumed under that of (c) if we simply noted the ungrammaticality of the following:

*She rarely *sings*, so I don't think she will *sings* tonight. [2a]

But it is important to recognize that [1] and [2] illustrate what, for most grammatical purposes, is the same kind of ellipsis: it remains true, in particular, that the ellipsis of *sing* is 'precisely recoverable' in the sense of 12.33. It is only in some cases (*eg* some types of coordination; *cf* 12.68) that criterion (e) is significant. Compare these superficially similar cases of coordination:

The club always has *paid its way*, and always will (pay its way). [3]
?The club always has (paid its way) and always will *pay its way*. [4]

Both these sentences violate the 'exact match' criterion (e), in that different forms of the verb *pay* are required in the two clauses. But whereas the ellipsis of [3] is widely treated as quite acceptable, that of [4] is widely regarded as incorrect (*cf* 13.88). A similar pair of examples is:

This is one of the oldest buildings in town,
if not (actually) the oldest △. [5]
?This is one of the oldest △, if not the oldest, building(s) in town. [6]

Hence the technicalities of ellipsis, which we have been exploring in 12.33–6, are not *mere* technicalities, but have importance in enabling us to make different generalizations about what kinds of reduction are possible in English grammar.

Note [a] In [6], both the singular *building* and the plural *buildings* would be open to stylistic criticism, but *buildings* would be the more acceptable alternative.
[b] The disfavoured types of ellipsis illustrated in [4] and [6] are liable to occur, but will generally be avoided in careful spoken and written use.

Ellipsis defined in terms of gradience

12.37 In view of the variable application of the above criteria (a–e) for ellipsis, it is reasonable to use the term 'ellipsis' in a way which acknowledges different degrees of strictness in its interpretation. *Table* 12.37 illustrates that the kinds of omission discussed above show various kinds of family resemblance to one another, and may be loosely ranged on a gradient extending from the strictest form of ellipsis (1) to semantic implication (9):

Table 12.37 Criteria for ellipsis

(a)	(b)	(c)	(d)	(e)	
+	+	+	+	+	(1) I'm happy if you are (happy).
+	+	+	+	–	(2) She sings better than I can (sing).
+	?	–	+	(+)	(3) She works harder than him (*works).
+	+	+	–	0	(4) (I am) Glad to see you.
–	+	+	+	–	(5) {(Since he was) / (Being)} Angry, he stalked out.
+	?	+	–	0	(6) I believe (that) you are wrong.
–	+	+	–	0	(7) The man (that/who/whom) I saw was half asleep.
–	?	+	–	0	(8) Houses (that/which are) owned by Mr Smith . . .
–	–	+	–	0	(9) The door opened and (then/after that/. . .) Mary entered.

Criteria

(a) The missing expression is precisely recoverable.

(b) The elliptical construction is 'defective'.

(c) The insertion of the missing expression results in a grammatical sentence with the same meaning as the elliptical sentence.

(d) The missing expression is recoverable from the neighbouring text (rather than from the structural or situational context).

(e) The missing expression is an exact copy of the antecedent.

KEY

+	The criterion is satisfied.
–	The criterion is not satisfied.
?	There is doubt about the criterion's satisfaction.
(+)	With the required grammatical change, the criterion would apply.
0	The criterion is not applicable.

Types of ellipsis

12.38 To show how the criteria operate with respect to the specimen constructions (1–9), we add a few comments on each example, and also introduce the terms which will be used where necessary to describe the various subcategories or marginal categories of ellipsis.

(1) This is STRICT ELLIPSIS, to which all five criteria apply, and which is applicable mainly to coordination (*cf* 13.44*ff*).

(2) This is STANDARD ELLIPSIS, to which only the 'exact copy' criterion need not apply (we cannot expand the sentence to **She sings better than I can sings*, since only the infinitive may follow *can*). We shall use the term 'standard ellipsis' in cases where criterion (e), that the ellipted word(s) be an exact copy of the antecedent, is not required, but may well be incidentally satisfied as a result of constraints of constituent structure. For example, we may say that *She sings better than I can* (**sings*) and *She can sing better than I can* (*sing*) both exemplify standard ellipsis, and that the latter also happens to exemplify strict ellipsis. Standard ellipsis applies to those cases studied under the heading of 'general ellipsis' in 12.53–65.

(3) This is less strict than example (2), because the full form of the sentence cannot be recovered without changing the objective pronoun *him* to *he*. It is preferable to treat this as a case of substitution rather than ellipsis, and we shall call it QUASI-ELLIPSIS (*cf* 12.40).

(4) As an example of SITUATIONAL ELLIPSIS, this does not satisfy criteria (d) and (e) (*cf* 12.46*ff*).

(5) This example falls short of the criterion of unique recoverability (a), because various conjunctions, or alternatively a nonfinite verb, could be inserted: *Since he was angry*, *As he was angry*, *Being angry*, etc: (On verbless clauses such as (5), *cf* 14.9, 15.61.)

(6) Being structurally recoverable (*cf* 12.6), this may be termed STRUCTURAL ELLIPSIS.

(7) This might similarly be regarded as structural ellipsis; however, it does not quite match up to the 'precise recoverability' criterion, since an alternative relative pronoun, *who* or *whom*, could have been used.

(8) This is a nonfinite clause (*cf* 14.6*ff*) which can be analysed as a reduced version of a finite relative clause, with ellipsis of the relative pronoun and the verb *be*. Like (7), however, this example just falls short of standard ellipsis by criterion (a), since an alternative relative pronoun, *which*, could have been inserted.

(9) This example illustrates the endpoint of the ellipsis gradient, and indeed is more fittingly classified not as ellipsis at all, but as a case of SEMANTIC IMPLICATION (*cf* 12.31). Although the concept of sequence in time (expressed by *then*) is understood in the sentence *The door opened and Mary entered*, we cannot easily maintain that this is ellipsis, for there is no reasonable way of choosing between different adverbials conveying roughly the same concept: *then*, *after*, *afterwards*, *after that*, *thereupon*, etc.

Because the boundaries of ellipsis cannot be easily defined, we shall use the term quite generally for grammatical reduction through omission. For cases like (5), (7), and (8), where the choice of what to insert, although not unique, is restricted to a small number of grammatical alternatives, the term WEAK ELLIPSIS may be used.

Note The 'fuzziness' of the concept of ellipsis goes with an unclarity, in many cases, as to the acceptability of certain types of ellipsis (*cf* for example, 13.88–9).

Ellipsis and substitution

12.39 One consequence of the gradience of ellipsis is that it is sometimes difficult to distinguish between ellipsis and the use of pro-forms as substitutes. The phenomenon of pro-form substitution (*cf* 12.8–30) closely parallels ellipsis, in that a pro-form may be regarded as a replacement for a unique expression:

Our house is quite different from *theirs*. [*ie* their house] [1]
Many buildings were damaged, but *none* [*ie* no building] was destroyed. [2]

In these examples, however, the substitute pro-form is morphologically related to one of the replaced items. If we had chosen *his* rather than *theirs* in [1], and *few* rather than *none* in [2], the result would seem to fit the criteria of strict ellipsis:

Our house is quite different from *his* (*house*). [3]
Many buildings were damaged, but *few* (*buildings*) were destroyed. [4]

The reason for this technical difference between [1] and [3] is that *he* is exceptional as a personal pronoun in that it has the same genitive form in the determinative and head functions (*his*/*his*), in contrast to *my*/*mine*, *your*/*yours*, etc. Thus the choice between substitution and ellipsis seems to rest at this point merely on an irregularity of English pronoun morphology: the neutralization of *his* and *his*. (A similar point can be made about *few* and *few* in [4].) But there is another way of looking at this demarcation problem: a case can be made, despite appearances, for treating [3] as substitution.

The argument is that *his* [determinative] and *his* [head] are different words, in the sense that they are different grammatical forms which happen to be homomorphic (*cf* 2.38). On this basis, we may distinguish them as his_1 and his_2, and maintain that the contraction of [3] by the omission of *house* amounts to the substitution of his_2 for his_1 *house*, just as that of [1] amounts to a substitution of *theirs* for *their house*. A similar analysis may be made of [4], involving the substitution of few_2 [pronoun] for few_1 [determiner] *people*.

Quasi-ellipsis and virtual ellipsis

12.40 According to the argument in 12.39, we subsume under substitution:

(a) Examples such as *theirs* for *their house* [1] and *none* for *no person* [2], where the substitute form is a grammatical variant of the word or construction which appears in the replaced expression (we may call this QUASI-ELLIPSIS).

(b) Examples such as *his* for *his house* in [3] and *few* for *few people* in [4], where the substitute form is a homomorph of a grammatical form in the replaced expression (we may call this VIRTUAL ELLIPSIS).

Quasi-ellipsis may reasonably include not only cases such as *their/theirs*, in which there is a replacement by a different morphological form of the same lexical item, but also cases such as the DO-support construction, where the unstressed dummy operator fills the position of a 'stranded' operator (*cf* 3.26, 12.60):

SHĚ understands the problem better than HÈ does. [5]

Compare the modal auxiliary as operator in:

SHĚ would understand the problem better than HÈ would. [6]

It is possible to regard *understand the problem* as ellipted in [6], but it would not be possible to regard *understand(s) the problem* as ellipted in the parallel case of [5]:

SHĚ understands the problem better
than HÈ {*does understand / *does understands} the problem.

We may, however, view [5] as a case of quasi-ellipsis, in which the DO-support construction occurs as a regular variant of the present or past tense verb construction in circumstances (such as that of operator 'stranding') where the grammar of English requires an operator (*cf* further 12.60).

Whether quasi-ellipsis or virtual ellipsis are to be treated as cases of ellipsis or as cases of substitution is a matter of definition. We classify them technically as substitution, but at the same time, their labels are a reminder of the close interconnection between substitution and ellipsis.

Note [**a**] In other cases, the operator DO is followed by standard ellipsis (*cf* 12.60).

[**b**] Certain pronouns which exemplify quasi-ellipsis and virtual ellipsis in [1–4] above (*none, his, few*) would in other contexts provide instances of standard ellipsis. For example:

Many *of the buildings* were damaged, but *none/few* $_\triangle$ were destroyed.

Here we can postulate a straightforward ellipsis of the prepositional phrase *of the buildings*, since in both the elliptical and the antecedent constructions the quantifier is a pronoun. Such an explanation could not have worked for [2] and [4], however, because to match the antecedent, the noun phrase in its unreduced form would have to contain a pronoun in the determinative position, and would thereby become ungrammatical:

*Many buildings were damaged, but *none/few*$_2$ *buildings* were destroyed.

Hence for these sentences, explanation in terms of quasi- and virtual ellipsis is required.

An attempt to analyse [2] and [4] as standard ellipsis of *of the buildings* would come to grief because *of* would have to be added and *the* would add a meaning of definiteness not warranted by the antecedent. Once this addition of meaning were allowed, it would be impossible to adhere to the requirement of unique recoverability, since the ellipted expression could as easily be *of those buildings* or *of these buildings*, etc, instead of *of the buildings*.

The classification of ellipsis

12.41 In examining instances of ellipsis, we find it necessary to distinguish three major factors: (a) RECOVERABILITY TYPE; (b) FUNCTIONAL TYPE; and (c) FORMAL TYPE. Unless all three of these factors are taken into account, it is impossible to say exactly how and where ellipsis can take place.

Recoverability type

12.42 We have already made the relevant distinctions in 12.6*f*:

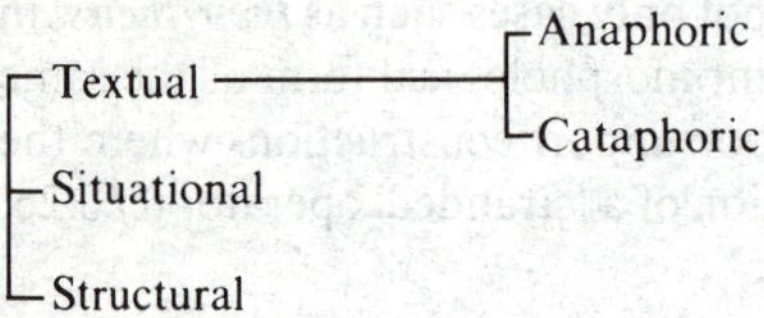

Fig 12.42

Functional type

12.43 When examining instances of textual ellipsis, whether anaphoric or cataphoric, it is often necessary to consider the relation of the antecedent construction to the elliptical construction within the larger construction of which they are both a part. For example, ellipsis in coordinate and comparative constructions is in some respects freer than in other kinds of construction, and merits separate treatment. Notice, in this connection, the difference between [1–2] and [3]:

Mary can beat Ann and △ Phyllis easily. [1]
[*ie* Mary can beat Ann easily and *Mary can beat* Phyllis easily.]
Mary can beat Ann more easily than △ Phyllis. [2]
[*ie* Mary can beat Ann more easily than *Mary can beat* Phyllis.]
*Mary can beat Ann if △ Phyllis easily. [3]
[*ie* Mary can beat Ann easily if *Mary can beat* Phyllis easily.]

In the second coordinate clause of [1] and the comparative clause of [2], it is possible to omit the subject and verb if these repeat the subject and verb of the other clause. But the parallel ellipsis cannot be carried out within the subordinate *if*-clause of [3].

Similarly, ellipsis is relatively free in response forms in dialogue (*cf* 11.51*ff*).

A: Whom can Mary beat most easily?
B: (Mary can beat) Phyllis (most easily).

Here, as in [1] and [2], the subject and verb *Mary can beat* may be ellipted.

The freer categories of ellipsis illustrated are possible only in certain constructions. On such grounds, we distinguish between GENERAL ELLIPSIS, where the functional relation between the elliptical and antecedent constructions is not important, and SPECIAL ELLIPSIS, where the possibilities of omission are closely determined by the relation (*eg* a coordinative or comparative relation) between these two constructions. In the present chapter we shall confine ourselves chiefly to general ellipsis, since special ellipsis is more appropriately handled in the chapters dealing with special relations such as coordination or comparison.

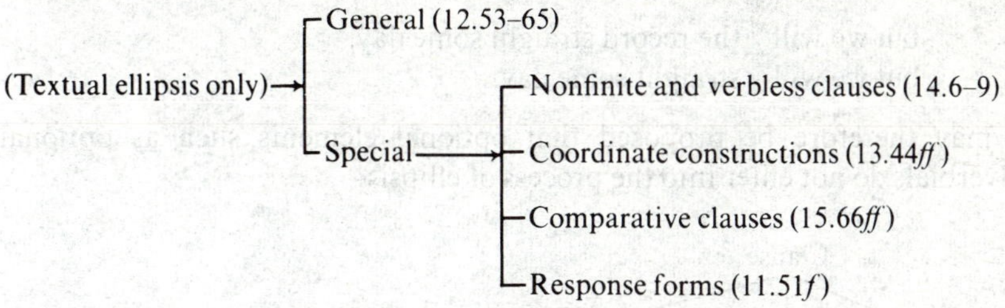

Fig 12.43 Functional types of ellipsis

Formal type

12.44 Formally speaking, elliptical constructions divide into three main categories. We shall distinguish INITIAL ellipsis, where initial elements are ellipted, from FINAL ELLIPSIS, where final elements are ellipted. For example, in [1] the *if*-clause is an example of initial ellipsis ('ellipsis on the left'), whereas in [2] the comparative clause is an example of final ellipsis ('ellipsis on the right'):

He will come later, if (*he comes*) *at all*. [1]
I have eaten more than *you* (*have eaten*). [2]

The conjunction *if*, because of its peripheral introductory role (*cf* 13.54), may be disregarded in judging an example like [1] as initial ellipsis. There is also a category of MEDIAL ellipsis, where only medial elements of a unit are omitted. But often it is better to argue that 'medial ellipsis' is a structural illusion which results from looking at too large a constituent in the sentence. If we examine conditions of ellipsis more carefully, medial ellipsis can often be treated as a special case of either initial or final ellipsis.

For example, within the clause it is often convenient to represent initial and final ellipsis as follows:

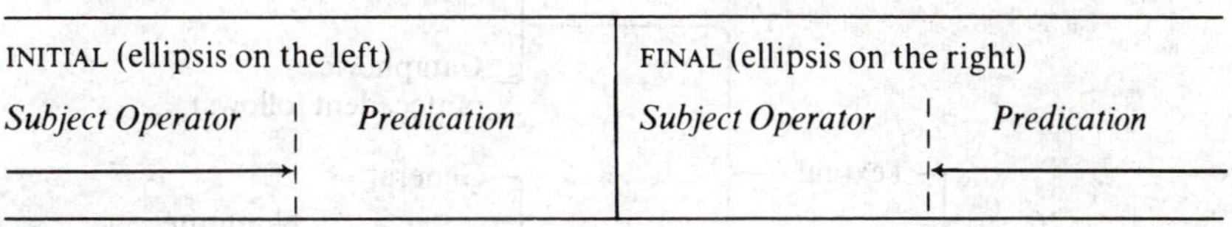

Fig 12.44a

That is, initial ellipsis applies to the subject and operator, and final ellipsis applies to the predication. But this scheme applies primarily to the more central elements of the clause. The more peripheral elements (*cf* 2.13) such as introductory conjunctions and optional adverbials are in general less essential features of the clause; and conversely, under ellipsis, it is these elements which are permitted to occur when others do not:

I know we have not yet *set the record straight*, but we will $_\triangle$ (some day). [3]

Just as in [1] the conjunction remains as a clause introducer, so in [3] the adverbial *some day* remains when the rest of the clause after the operator is omitted. Note that by contrast, the object or object complement in [3] could not be retained except as part of the whole predication:

*. . . but we will ▵ the record straight some day.
*. . . but we will ▵ straight some day.

It may therefore be proposed that optional elements such as optional adverbials do not enter into the process of ellipsis:

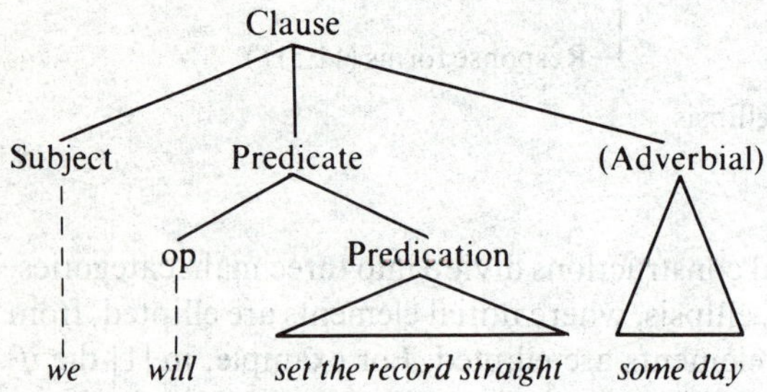

Fig 12.44b

On this basis, the ellipsis in [3] will be classified as final rather than medial.

Ellipsis which is definitely medial is also found, but in rather restricted circumstances (it will be discussed, with reference to coordination, under the heading of GAPPING in 13.92*f*). In general, final ellipsis predominates over both initial and medial ellipsis. It is a general condition that final optional elements (adverbials or postmodifiers) may be retained under conditions where final ellipsis operates. To conclude this general consideration of categories of ellipsis, we summarize the types mentioned in 12.41–4 in *Fig* 12.44c:

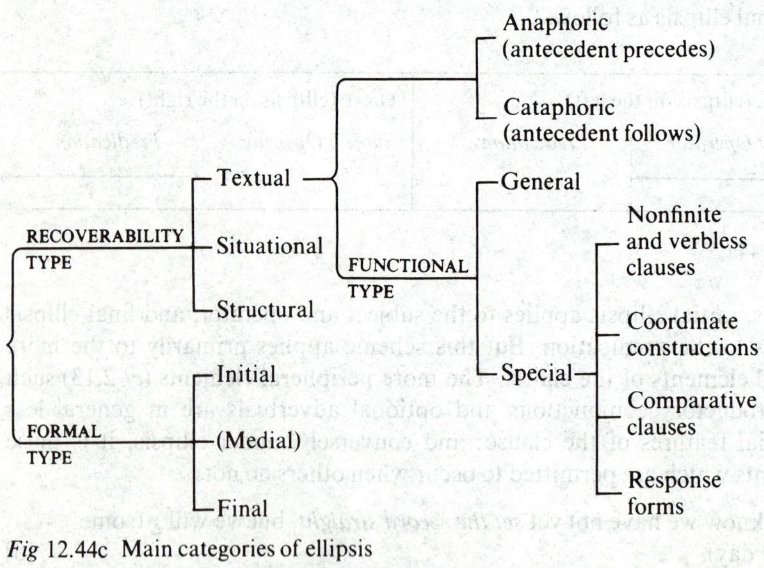

Fig 12.44c Main categories of ellipsis

Categories of ellipsis: recoverability

Anaphoric and cataphoric ellipsis

12.45 Returning to the recoverability types of ellipsis (*cf* 12.42), we begin with textual ellipsis, and the distinction between ANAPHORIC and CATAPHORIC reference (*cf* 12.6). Just as final ellipsis is the dominant formal type of ellipsis, so anaphoric ellipsis is the dominant type of textual ellipsis. In fact, ellipsis is governed in this respect by the same restrictions as pronoun reference (*cf* 6.19): the antecedent must normally have 'precedence' over the elliptical construction, by taking either an earlier position in the sentence, or a higher position (where 'higher' refers to a higher position in the tree diagram specifying the constituent structure of the sentence). Typically, cataphoric ellipsis occurs in a clause which is subordinate in relation to the clause in which the antecedent occurs.

If you want me to △, I'll *lend you my pen.*
We try, *whenever we can* △, to *leave a window open.*
Those *who prefer* (*to*) △ can *stay indoors.*
Don't ask me *why* △, but *the stone has been moved.*

(Both the elliptical clause and the antecedent expression are italicized in these examples.)

Note [**a**] It is difficult to specify the limits of acceptability for cataphoric ellipsis. Some kinds of ellipsis (including many cases of what we call general ellipsis) are acceptable if anaphoric, but only marginally so if cataphoric. For example, ellipsis of a noun head after an adjective:

I'll buy the red *wine* if you'll buy the white △.
?If you'll buy the white △, I'll buy the red *wine*.

The following valedictory sentence regularly used by a humorous broadcaster (John Ebdon, BBC Radio Four) illustrates the stylistically marked effect that often results from cataphoric ellipsis:

If you have been △, thanks for *listening*.

[**b**] However, when two noun phrases are in a parallel relationship similar to that of coordination, cataphoric ellipsis of the head (and postmodifiers) of the first phrase is quite usual: *I can't tell real* △ *from imitation jewellery*; *the change from a feudal* △ *to a democratic way of life*. This type of ellipsis appears to be modelled on a similar type of ellipsis in coordinated noun phrases; *eg*: *real or imitation jewellery* (*cf* 13.79).

Situational ellipsis

12.46 We have already seen that some types of ellipsis are not dependent on the linguistic context for their interpretation. In such cases, the interpretation may depend on knowledge of a precise extralinguistic context. For example, *Get it?* in one situation might be understood to mean the same as *Did you get it?* (*eg* 'Did you get the letter/shopping/etc?'), and in another situation *Do you get it?* (*ie* 'Do you understand?'). Similarly, *Told you so* might be expanded in one context to *I told you so*, and in another to *We told you so*. In still other contexts, the exact words ellipted might be unclear. The term SITUATIONAL ELLIPSIS can apply to such cases of weak ellipsis, and also to other cases where it happens to be quite clear what has been omitted; *eg* only *it* can be the ellipted subject in *Looks like rain*.

Situational ellipsis is sometimes final; for example, the weakly recoverable ellipsis *How could you* △*?* said as a rebuke to someone who has just committed some situationally known folly. But more typically, situational ellipsis is initial, especially taking the form of omission of subject and/or operator; *eg*: (*Do you*) *Want something?* In such cases, which are restricted to familiar (generally spoken) English, the ellipted words are those that normally occur before the onset of a tone unit (*cf* App II.11), and hence have weak stress and low pitch. It may therefore be more appropriate to ascribe the omission to subaudible utterance or some other reductive process on the phonological, rather than on the grammatical level (*cf* Note [b] below).

In what follows, declarative sentences are treated separately from *yes–no* questions, since the operator is obligatory in the full form of *yes–no* questions.

Note [**a**] Imperative sentences without a subject (*eg*: *Sit down*) cannot be considered comparable to declarative and interrogative sentences with initial ellipsis. The implied subject of the imperative verb is *you* (*cf* 11.24), but absence of the subject is the norm with imperatives, and where the imperative subject *you* does occur (*cf* 11.25), it receives stress; *eg*: '*You sit down.* These factors, together with the fact that it is not restricted to familiar style, distinguish the subjectless imperative from the types of situational ellipsis we are now considering.

[**b**] The explanation of situational ellipsis in terms of phonological reduction is favoured by the occurrence, in recorded speech, of 'phrasal aphaeresis' in such examples as:

'k you. /kjʊ/ [= Thank you]
's it matter? /ˌsɪt/ [= What does it matter?]
'd you rather . . . ? /djʊ/ [= Would you rather?]
's anyone there? /ˈzenɪ/ [= Is anyone there?]
's all right. /sɔːl/ [= It's all right]

It is difficult to say whether the missing syllables are lost because their utterance is subaudible, or because of more abstract phonological processes. In other cases, however, it is less realistic to talk in terms of subaudibility, since more than one syllable is lost:

△Your name?
△Two loaves of white bread, please.

Whatever the correct explanation of such initial ellipsis may be, it seems unquestionable (a) that the omissions are at least in part phonologically determined; and (b) that habits of rendering such omissions in writing (*eg* in popular fiction) have helped to conventionalize them in the form of omission of certain unstressed words.

Ellipsis in declarative sentences

(a) Ellipsis of subject alone

12.47 Either no auxiliary is available for ellipsis (*eg*: △*Serves you right*) or one is included in the sentence (*eg*: △*Can't see*). The element ellipted can be:

(i) the 1st person pronoun, normally *I*:

△Beg your pardon. △Told you so.
△Wonder what they're doing. △Hope he's there.
△Don't know what to say. △Think I'll go now.

Most of the verbs in such elliptical constructions can take a clause as object.

(ii) the 2nd person pronoun:

△Got back all right? △Had a good time, did you?
△Want a drink? △Want a drink, do you?

The 2nd person pronoun is ellipted, as the examples on the left show, in declarative questions (*cf* 11.12). It is ellipted in statements only if a tag question is added. (*Want a drink?* can also be interpreted as an ordinary *yes–no* question with *Do you* ellipted, *cf* 12.49).

(iii) the 3rd person pronouns *he, she, they*:

(*He/She*) Doesn't look too well.

(*He/She/They*) Can't play at all.

(iv) *it*:

△Serves you right. △Looks like rain.
△Doesn't matter. △Must be hot in Panama.

The *it* ellipted from the two examples on the left is related to the anticipatory *it* (*cf* 18.33) found in sentences with extraposition, as in *It serves you right that you fell*. In the sentences on the right, *it* is the 'prop' subject in sentences like *It is cold* (*cf* 10.26). These ellipted sentences could refer directly, however, to an action in the situational context; for example *Serves you right* might be said to a child immediately after a fall, if the child had been warned not to act in a dangerous way. On the other hand, *it* may be used in reference to something identified in the situation:

△Seems full. △Makes too much noise.

And some other expressions may be interpreted out of context as having ellipsis of either type of *it*:

△Sounds fine to me. △Won't be any use.

(v) *there*:

△ Ought to be some coffee in the pot.
△ Must be somebody waiting for you.
△ May be some children outside.
△ Appears to be a big crowd in the hall.

This is the existential subject *there* (*cf* 18.44*ff*), as distinct from the 'true subject' following the verb. The elliptical construction is unlikely to contain the modal *will*, but *won't* is common:

(There) Won't be anything left for supper.

Note In category (i) above, (*I*) *bet you* . . . is sometimes rendered nonstandardly in writing as *Betcha* . . .; *eg*: *Betcha don't know what this is!*

(b) Ellipsis of subject plus operator

12.48 If the main verb BE is ellipted, the elliptical sentence begins with what would be a subject complement in the full form:

(i) the 1st person pronoun (particularly *I*) plus BE:

(I'm) Sorry I couldn't be there.
(I'm/We're) Afraid not.

We alone cannot be ellipted, *eg*: **Are afraid not*. For many speakers, the same applies to the singular pronoun *I*: for them *Afraid not* is acceptable, but not **Am afraid not*.

(ii) *it* plus *is*:

△Good to see you.	△Odd he won't help us.
△No wonder she's late.	△(A) Shame he's late.
△No use worrying.	△Not that I mind.

The ellipted *it* here is generally the anticipatory *it* just mentioned in 12.47. The last example *Not that I mind*, however, exemplifies the empty 'prop word' *it*.

(iii) the 1st person pronoun followed by an operator other than *be*:

(I'll) See you later.	(We've) Got to go now.

Note [a] In familiar style the common elliptical phrases *(I've) got to* and *(I'm) going to* have acquired semi-institutionalized nonstandard spellings *gotta* and *gonna* respectively: *Gotta go now*; *Gonna go now* (*cf* 3.47*f*).
[b] *Had* is commonly ellipted in spoken English in the semi-auxiliary *had better* (*cf* 3.45*f*): *You better try it again.* It is also possible to ellipt the subject: *Better try it again.*
[c] There is also the possibility of medial omission of the operator alone in *You gotta be careful, I gonna do what I like*, where the nonstandard written form, including the omission, reflects phonological processes of reduction, as in Notes [a] and [b].

Ellipsis in interrogative sentences

(a) Ellipsis of subject plus operator

12.49 If the subject and a main verb BE are omitted in a *yes–no* question, the resulting elliptical sentence begins with a subject complement or an adjunct:

(Are you) Happy?	(Are you) In trouble?
(Are you) Afraid of him?	(Is it) Hot?
(Are you) Hot?	(Are they) Torn?

Why can't he get up? (Is he) Too weak?
(Is there) Anyone in?
(Is there) Any coffee left?

If the operator is auxiliary BE, HAVE, or DO, the elliptical sentence may begin with a nonfinite main verb, sometimes preceded by an adverbial:

(Do you) Want some?	(Are you) Looking for anybody?
(Have you) Got any chocolate?	(Have you) Ever seen one of these?

In such questions, the ellipted subject is generally *you*, but other interpretations would be possible in context; *eg*: *(Are they) Happy? (Is she) In trouble?*

Note [a] *Wanna*, as a nonstandard spelling of *want to* (especially in AmE), occurs in such sentences as *Wanna have a go?* with subject + operator ellipsis (*cf* 12.48 Note [c]).
[b] Some questions in category (a) above could alternatively be classified as declarative questions (*cf* 11.12) with ellipsis of the subject only. For example, *Want some?* could be a reduced version of *You want some?* rather than of *Do you want some?*

(b) Ellipsis of operator alone

12.50 There are also elliptical *yes–no* questions in which, although the operator is omitted, the subject is pronounced. This will be the case if, for any reason, the subject receives stress:

(Is) 'Anything the matter?	(Does) 'Anybody need a lift?
(Are) 'You hungry?	(Has) 'Joanna done her homework?
(Is) 'That you, Shirley?	(Is) 'Nothing coming?
	(Would) 'You rather I waited?

The examples on the left illustrate the omission of BE as main verb, while those on the right show the omission of an auxiliary.

Note [**a**] There are also comparable sentences in which the subject is partially ellipted:

Why isn't he here today? (Is his) 'Car still not working?

Here the determiner of the subject noun phrase is ellipted, while the head is realized.

[**b**] There is occasionally medial omission of the operator in *wh*-questions: *Where you going? What you want?* (*cf* 12.48 Notes [b] and [c]). This is characteristic of casual speech, but is often felt to be nonstandard in its written form. *You* in such questions is readily reduced to /jə/, and additional phonological simplification and assimilation following *What* can result in an affricated pronunciation represented in nonstandard spellings such as *Whatcha*; *Wotcher*.

Other cases of situational ellipsis

12.51 There are several other variants of the familiar initial type of situational ellipsis illustrated in 12.47–50. However, these further examples are less productive, and tend to occur only in idiomatic expressions:

(a) Ellipsis of an article:

(The) Trouble is there's nothing we can do about it.
(The) Fact is I don't know what to do.
(A) Friend of mine told me about it.

The omission of the indefinite article is common in the construction '*a*(*n*) + noun phrase + *of* prepositional phrase', as in *(a) friend of mine*. The omission of *a*/*an* or *the* may also combine with other ellipses:

(It is a) Pity he won't help.
(It is a) Shame they won't be there.
(Is the) Television not working?

(b) Ellipsis of a preposition:

(Of) Course he's there.

Such cases as these provide further evidence that initial situational ellipsis is a phonological, rather than a grammatical process. It is clear that in cases like *Pity he won't help* or *Car still not working?* (*cf* 12.50 Note [a]) the ellipsis cuts across the boundaries of grammatical constituents, and is terminated by the first stressed syllable of the fully-realized sentence. The truncation of *of course* to *course* is prevalent for the same reason. Such omissions relate to the fact that the ellipted syllables have a low information value within the situation.

Note There are also cases where the initial syllable of a word is omitted:

(I am a-)Fraid I won't be there.

The aphaeretic spelling *'Fraid*, in this particular case, is semi-institutionalized. A less common case is *'Deed* in *'Deed I do* (for *Indeed*). On the other hand, the analogous spelling of *because* as *'cause* or *'cos* ⟨BrE⟩ probably does not belong to the same category. This truncation, although also restricted to familiar style, is not necessarily found at the beginning of a sentence:

He did it 'cause he wanted to.

A parallel, though less common, example is the spelling of *except* as *'cept*. These cases of aphaeresis, together with the many examples of word clipping in English (*eg*: *(tele)phone*, *photo(graph)*, *(in)flu(enza)*), belong more to the lexical processes of word-formation than to grammar (*cf* App I.74).

Structural ellipsis

12.52 There is no clear dividing line between situational ellipsis and structural ellipsis (*cf* 12.6), where the ellipted word(s) can be identified purely on the basis of grammatical knowledge. Without entering into arguments on this score, we can illustrate structural ellipsis by citing the zero conjunction *that* (*cf* 15.4) in [1], and the ellipted prepositions (*cf* 9.40*ff*) in [2] and [3]:

I believe (that) you are mistaken. [1]
The Club meets (on) Monday evenings. 〈familiar〉 [2]
We're staying there (for) another three weeks. 〈informal〉 [3]

Further examples are provided by the common omission of determiners, pronouns, operators, and other closed-class words in block language (*cf* 11.45*ff*); *eg* in headlines, book titles, notices; also in lecture notes, diaries, telegrams, etc:

US heading for new slump. [*ie*: *The* US *is* heading for *a* new slump.]

Such structural ellipsis is confined to written style, and contrasts with the initial situational ellipsis characteristic of familiar spoken English, and discussed in 12.47*ff*. Both styles of ellipsis function as devices of economy, through the omission of items of little informational value. In the written elliptical styles known as 'headlinese' and 'telegraphese', however, closed-class items are often suppressed not only in initial position but also in the middle of sentences.

Categories of ellipsis: function

General ellipsis

12.53 General textual ellipsis is typically (i) final and (ii) anaphoric, and it is on such regular cases that we concentrate in the following sections. We find it convenient to distinguish three major formal categories: (a) elliptical noun phrases, (b) elliptical clauses, and (c) other elliptical constructions.

Elliptical noun phrases

12.54 Elliptical noun phrases (except in coordinate noun phrases) result from final ellipsis. This means that postmodifiers (if any) and heads tend to be ellipted:

My own camera, like *Peter's* △, is Japanese. [1]
He had to admit that *Sarah's drawings* were as good as *his own* △. [2]
You can't tax *one set of people* without taxing *the other* △. [3]
The first expedition to the Antarctic was quickly followed by *another two* △. [4]

Tomorrow's meeting will have to be *our first* △ and *our last* △. [5]
Although Helen is *the oldest girl in the class*, Julie is *the tallest* △. [6]

In these examples, the second noun phrase in italics is noteworthy in that its head is a word that elsewhere normally acts as a premodifier. In [1] the head is a genitive noun; in [2] and [3] it is a postdeterminer; in [4] it is a cardinal numeral; in [5] it is an ordinal numeral; and in [6] it is a superlative adjective.

Noun phrase ellipsis, like clause ellipsis (*cf* 12.59*ff*), involves some degree of parallelism between the elliptical construction and the antecedent. By virtue of this, some item(s) in the elliptical construction can be said to REPUDIATE, or semantically cancel out, some item(s) in the antecedent. Thus *the tallest* in [6] may be said to repudiate *the oldest*. This term is especially appropriate where the two constructions are in a contrastive relationship.

The shift of function from modifier to head in these examples is to be explained by the obvious fact that an 'understood' noun has been ellipted; *eg*: the noun *camera* in [1] and the noun *meeting* (twice) in [5]. In some examples, *viz* [3–6], postmodifiers are also ellipted; *eg*: *set of people* is ellipted in [3] and *girl in the class* in [6]. There is considerable variety in the structural relation between the elliptical noun phrase and its antecedent noun phrase. This variability is the hallmark of what we have termed *general ellipsis*.

Note [a] Although the reduced genitive constructions *Peter's* [1] and *his own* [2] are examples of ellipsis, similar constructions with a possessive pronoun as head (*eg*: *his*, *hers*) are treated as virtual ellipsis or quasi-ellipsis (*cf* 12.40), and therefore, strictly speaking, as substitution.

[b] Examples of genitives or possessive pronouns functioning as heads, but without an antecedent, may sometimes be treated as situational ellipsis. For example:

Let's go round to *Mona and Fred's* △ tonight.
It's about time you went to the *barber's* △. (*cf* 5.125)

[c] Cataphoric ellipsis of the head occurs somewhat exceptionally in examples such as: *Her first* △ *was bad enough, but this second husband is an absolute bore.*

Adjectives and nouns as heads

12.55 Not all premodifying elements can readily act as heads of elliptical noun phrases. Comparative adjectives, and (even more so) absolute adjectives (*cf* 7.74) are restricted in this function. The following, however, are acceptable:

Helen is *the older girl*, but Julie is *the taller* △.
This recipe requires *plain flour*, not *self-raising* △.
We've put *some chocolate* aside for you: six bars of *plain* △ and six △ of *fruit and nut* △.

For reasons which are not totally clear, these are much more acceptable than examples such as:

?**Those plastic containers* will last longer than *those wooden* △.
?*As the centuries went by, *the devout monks* were replaced by *more worldly* △.

Even less acceptable is ellipsis of the head of a noun phrase when preceded by the indefinite article and another modifier:

*We turned off *the* (*main*) *road* on to *a quieter* △. [1]
**This* (*previously unprotected*) *species* is now classified as *an endangered* △. [2]

As [1] and [2] show, the existence of a parallelism between the 'stranded' modifier and a modifier in the antecedent noun phrase plays little role in the acceptability of the ellipsis. In this, general ellipsis of the noun phrase differs from ellipsis associated with coordination (*cf* 13.64*ff*). Noun modifiers (*cf* 17.104*ff*), which are normally closely associated with the head noun, can rarely act as head of an elliptical phrase. Different degrees of acceptability are illustrated in:

Do you prefer *silver rings* to *gold* △? [3]
(?)The recipe requires *wine vinegar*, not *malt* △. [4]
*One tends to look after *personal books* better than *library* △. [5]

This limitation may be partly due to the ambiguity which arises, in the case of a noun head, as to whether the noun phrase is elliptical or not. Thus in [4], *malt* might be taken to refer simply to malt, rather than to malt vinegar. But more generally, there appears to be a principle that the closer a modifier is linked, by position and meaning, to its head, the less acceptable is the ellipsis of the head without the modifier.

Note **[a]** As observed in 12.35, we do not always regard noun phrases with adjectives as head as cases of ellipsis; *eg*: *the rich, the French, the absurd* are not elliptical.

[b] Similarly, we do not count cases like these as ellipsis:

I'd like a pint of *bitter*. [= *bitter beer*]
This apple is *my favourite*. [= *my favourite apple*]

In spite of appearances, *bitter* and *favourite* here are not adjectives, but nouns derived from adjectives by conversion (*cf* App I.48). We note, in support of this, that such words can be inflected for plural number, like count nouns: *Two bitters, please! These apples are my favourites.*

[c] Cataphoric ellipsis with adjectives (*eg*: *You should never mix old* △ *with new wine*) in contrast to anaphoric ellipsis, requires a parallelism between the adjectives:

?*Never mix *old* △ with *chilled* wine.

Such ellipsis (as already noted in 12.45 Note [b]) shows a close connection with coordination.

Ellipsis of modifiers

12.56 The dominance of final ellipsis in the noun phrase means that ellipsis will tend to take place according to the following order of precedence:

Determinative(s) | Premodifier(s) | Head | Postmodifier(s)
← ← ←

Thus we find:

(a) ellipsis of postmodifier(s) alone:

Stan spent PĂRT *of his winnings*, and *the rest* △ he saved.
If you need any *of that firewood*, I can give you *plenty* △.

Since postmodifiers are in general optional, it is difficult to recognize ellipsis in this position. The postmodifiers most readily omitted (as in the above examples) are partitive *of*-phrases.

(b) ellipsis of head + postmodifier(s) as in [3], [4], and [6] in 12.54 above:

The SĔcond *novel she wrote* was very different from the FÌRST △.

(c) ellipsis of premodifier(s) + head + postmodifier(s):

The SĔcond *historical novel she wrote* was very different from the FÌRST △.

Here it is understood that the whole expression *historical novel she wrote* is ellipted, including the premodifying adjective.

As postmodifiers are optional in any antecedent noun phrase, we may also find cases of final ellipsis which correspond to (b) and (c), except that no postmodifier is ellipted.

(d) ellipsis of head alone, as in [1], [2], and [5] in 12.54:

Her SĔcond *novel* was very different from her FÌRST △.

(e) ellipsis of premodifier(s) + head:

Liebknecht's *best pentathlon performance* is well ahead of *Lessing's* △.

Note [**a**] Although ellipsis of type (a) is limited because of potential ambiguity, the meaning of an elliptical rather than a nonelliptical construction can be singled out by the contrastive use of intonation, as already indicated in examples above. In the following case, the contrastive nucleus on *novel* is obligatory if the elliptical interpretation is intended:

Hardy's NŎvels *about Wessex* are better known than his PÒems △.

Compare the nonelliptical interpretation of:

Hardy's novels about WĔSSEX are better known than his PÒems.

[**b**] In appearance, type (b) above may be indistinguishable from type (c), and type (d) from type (e). The following are thus ambiguous, according to whether we read the italicized premodifier(s) as part of the meaning of the elliptical noun phrase or not:

The last *two* stanzas of the poem imitate *the first* ((*two*) stanza(s) of the poem).
My uncle built a *little wooden* house next to *my father's* (((*little*) *wooden*) house).

The nonoccurrence of initial general ellipsis

12.57 As one would expect with final ellipsis, it is possible to omit postmodifiers alone, as in type (a) above, but not (in general ellipsis) to omit premodifiers without omitting the head. If initial ellipsis of premodifiers were permitted, we should expect that the second occurrence of *Wessex* or *digital* could be ellipted in:

Hardy's *Wessex* novels are better known than his *Wessex* poems.
Digital wristwatches are as cheap as *digital* alarm clocks.

However, if *Wessex* or *digital* is omitted, the meaning of the sentence is different:

Hardy's Wessex novels are better known than *his poems*. [1]
Digital wristwatches are as cheap as *alarm clocks*. [2]

We may contrast this with the initial ellipsis of *Wessex* and *digital* which can occur in noun phrases in coordination (*cf* 13.67):

Hardy is best known for *his Wessex novels and poems*. [3]
This shop specializes in *digital wristwatches and alarm clocks*. [4]

Sentences [3] and [4] are ambiguous according to whether the adjective is understood to modify the second conjoin of the noun phrase. But no such ambiguity occurs in [1] and [2]. The contrast between general ellipsis, which is final, and the initial ellipsis which can occur in coordinate constructions is clearly illustrated by these two examples.

It also follows that ellipsis of every part of a noun phrase except for postmodifier(s) is impossible in general ellipsis:

*Joan prefers the trios of Mozart, while I prefer △ of Haydn.

(Contrast the acceptability of *Joan prefers Mozart's trios, while I prefer Haydn's △.*)

Here, as often elsewhere, ellipsis is in complementary distribution with substitute forms: the sentence above becomes grammatical if we insert the substitute head *those* before *of Haydn* (*cf* 12.19). In addition there is, of course, the option of replacing the final prepositional phrase by a genitive:

Joan prefers the trios of Mozart, while I prefer Haydn's.

Medial ellipsis

12.58 However, like clauses (*cf* 12.44), noun phrases can occur with medial ellipsis. This arises if an optional postmodifier is retained while the head of the phrase is ellipted:

They claim that *Danish butter* is *the finest* △ (*in the world*).
That letter was *the last* △ (*I ever received from her*).
A bird in the hand is worth *two* △ (*in the bush*). [a proverb]

In other cases of medial ellipsis, one or more modifiers, as well as the head, may be ellipted:

His recent *performance of Macbeth* is *the best* △ *he has ever done.* [1]
That *new thick plastic rope* that they sell is stronger than *any other* △ *you can get.* [2]

Once again, the elliptical phrase in [1] and [2] is ambiguous, according to whether the italicized modifiers are assumed to be an implicit part of the elliptical phrase. In fact, the ambiguity may be multiple. In [2], *any other you can get* might be regarded as an elliptical variant of any of the following:

any other rope you can get
any other plastic rope you can get
any other thick plastic rope you can get
any other new thick plastic rope you can get

To avoid such ambiguity, one has to repeat the words of the antecedent rather than ellipt them.

Elliptical clauses

Ellipsis of the predication in finite clauses

12.59 General ellipsis in the finite clause is similar to general ellipsis in the noun phrase, in that the dominant type of ellipsis is final. Typically, the clause is divided into two parts: subject and operator (which remain), and predication (which is ellipted). In terms of V, O, C, and A (*cf* 2.12*ff*), the constituency of the ellipted predication can be varied. For example:

SUBJECT COMPLEMENT only (the verb BE being the operator):

I'm *happy* if you are △.

SUBJECT COMPLEMENT + ADVERBIAL:

If they're not *ready by lunchtime*, they ought to be △.

ADVERBIAL only:

His father was *at Oxford* when Harold Wilson was △.

NONFINITE PART OF VERB only:

Tom will be *playing*, but I don't think Martin will (be) △.
I'll *do* what I can △.

NONFINITE PART OF VERB + ADVERBIAL:

When Shirley *resigns from the committee*, I'm sure that a number of other people will △.

NONFINITE PART OF VERB + OBJECT + ADVERBIAL:

Who is *cooking dinner today*? John is △.

All these, and many other possibilities, are summed up in the generalization that predications can be ellipted.

Note [a] Other possibilities, however, do not occur. Thus the lexical verb cannot remain 'stranded' preceding the ellipsis of an object, complement, or adverbial:

*I'll open *an account* if you'll open △.
*He always becomes *tired* faster than anyone else becomes △.
*As soon as the one aircraft had taken *off*, the other one took △.

Nor can an auxiliary alone be ellipted, nor an entire verb phrase:

*Susan *was* happy because Alice △ miserable.
*Tom *will* play the guitar if Mary △ sing.

[b] On the other hand, in special constructions such as the zero relative clause (*cf* 14.20, 17.14), the object can be ellipted: *the girl (whom) I met*. This, however, is structural rather than textual ellipsis.

[c] An auxiliary in its reduced form cannot precede ellipsis:

*Ned is as keen on boxing as {I am / *I'm} △ (on football).

DO as 'stranded' operator

12.60 Ellipsis of the predication is one of the constructions of English which require DO-support. That is, if the clause in its unreduced form has no operator, to create the conditions for omission of the predication it is necessary to introduce the dummy operator DO:

Sam kicked the ball harder than Dennis {*did.* / *kicked the ball.*}

This is strictly, however, not ellipsis, but quasi-ellipsis (*cf* 12.40), since the insertion of the omitted predication after *did* would result in an unacceptable sentence:

*Sam kicked the ball harder than Dennis *did kick the ball*. [1]

[1] is unacceptable because DO occurs in a context where the dummy operator cannot occur. But there are other constructions (*eg* clause negation, subject–

operator inversion, emphatic operator constructions) in which the operator would occur for independent reasons, and in these cases DO fulfils the conditions of standard ellipsis of the predication:

Rupert wanted to attend the bullfight, although his wife *didn't* (want to attend the bullfight). [2]
I don't like living in the country. *Do* you (like living in the country)? [3]
A: Does she like playing with dolls?
B: Yes, she *DÒES* (like playing with dolls). [4]

In [4], where DO has nuclear stress, the conditions for ellipsis are met even in a positive declarative sentence, since DO is used as an emphatic operator in the equivalent unreduced form.

Note It has been argued, contrary to the view presented here, that (like *do*) *can*, *would*, *have*, etc are substitute forms (*ie* pro-predicates) when they are 'stranded' operators.

Ellipsis of the predicate

12.61 Ellipsis of the predicate means in general that the only part of the clause to remain is the subject. This type of ellipsis is not widespread: it comes under the heading of special ellipsis, and occurs only in certain special constructions, such as comparative, coordinate, and response constructions:

Nigel *finished the exam* at the same time as George △. [1]
Nigel *finished the exam* first, then George △. [2]
A: Who *finished the exam first*? B: George △. [3]

The restricted distribution of this kind of ellipsis is evident if we compare [1] with [4]:

*I finished the exam when George △. [4]
I finished the exam when George *did*. [5]

In the comparative clause [1], the whole predicate can be ellipted, but this is not possible in the adverbial clause in [4]. To make [4] grammatical, we have to add the dummy operator *did*, as in [5].

Note [**a**] When the 'stranded' subject of the elliptical clause is a pronoun, in informal use an objective form of the pronoun is preferred (for further discussion *cf* 6.4). Thus *George* in [1–3] could be replaced by either *I* ⟨formal⟩ or *me* ⟨informal⟩. The use of the objective form is, however, traditionally regarded as an error. Structurally, *as me* replacing *as George* at the end of [1] would be classified as a prepositional phrase (*cf* 15.67).

[**b**] The statement that it is impossible to ellipt the whole predicate of an adverbial clause appears to be contradicted by the following:

Nigel finished the exam {after / before} George finished the exam. [6]

Nigel finished the exam {after / before} George. [7]

The acceptability of [7], in contrast to [4], appears to be due to the fact that unlike *when*, the words *after* and *before* are prepositions, as well as conjunctions (*cf* 9.38). Strictly, therefore, *after/before George* in [7] may be described not as an elliptical clause, but as a prepositional phrase with *George* as its complement. In support of this analysis, note that a subjective pronoun in the position of *George* is unacceptable:

*Nigel finished the exam {after / before} I.

It is striking, however, that despite this difference of analysis, [7] is interpreted as if it were an elliptical variant of [6].

Medial ellipsis

12.62 As noted earlier (*cf* 12.44), an optional adverbial can easily be added after an ellipted predication, so that the ellipsis becomes apparently medial rather than final:

When Shirley *resigns from the committee*, I'm sure that a number of other people will △, (too).

There are more *hungry people in the world* today than there were △ (in 1900).

This last example shows how an adverbial in the elliptical clause can REPUDIATE (*cf* 12.54), or cancel the meaning of, one in the antecedent clause. In this case, where one adverbial of time (*in 1900*) repudiates another (*today*), the ellipsis is genuinely medial. In the same category we may place the following, where only the lexical verb is omitted:

I'll gladly *pay* for the hotel, if you will △ for the food.

Since *for the hotel* is in this case repudiated by *for the food*, the only part of the antecedent clause that is recovered by ellipsis is the verb *pay*.

Medial quasi-ellipsis also occurs with auxiliary DO. The dummy operator can be followed by an adverbial (for example an adjunct of time or space) repudiating a similar adverbial in the antecedent clause:

We paid more for the tickets THĬS year than we
{did LÀST year.
have in PRÈvious years.}

A: Did Sato take the plane to TÓKyo today?
B: NÓ, I don't think he DÌD. But his WĬFE did to ŎSaka.

In the last example, *will* could replace *did*: there is no difference, in respect of such repudiatory constructions, between DO and other auxiliaries.

Unlike adjuncts, disjuncts and conjuncts (*cf* 8.121*ff*) are excluded from the antecedent when they occur after a 'stranded' operator. We can contrast in this respect the adjunct *usually* with the disjunct *wisely*:

A: Does Bob usually walk to work?
B: No, but his sĭster *does*. [= usually walks to work]
A: Bob wisely walks to work, doesn't he?
B: Well, at least he CLĂIMS he *does*. [= walks to work]

Similarly, a 'stranded' operator such as *do* or *have* excludes from the antecedent other, contrasting auxiliaries:

Not many people could have *enjoyed that trip* as much as your mother *did*.

In this example, *did* is interpreted to mean 'enjoyed that trip' rather than 'could have enjoyed that trip'.

Note There is also a less usual form of repudiatory medial ellipsis, in which the predication is omitted except for an object. Such ellipsis is of variable acceptability:

(?)I'll gladly *lend him* the clothing, if you will △ the money.
She was examining the pictures while I was △ the sculptures.

(*Cf* gapping, 13.92*f*).

Ellipsis in *wh*-clauses

12.63 A more thorough-going reduction of a clause by ellipsis involves ellipsis of the whole clause, or the whole clause except for an introductory word. One such clause is a *wh*-clause which is reduced, by ellipsis, to the *wh*-word alone. In such circumstances, the stranded *wh*-word normally receives nuclear stress:

Somebody had hidden my notebook, but I don't know WHÒ/WHỲ/WHÈRE △.
Have you ever wanted *to start a successful business*? This book tells you HÒW △.

This type of ellipsis is restricted to *wh*-interrogative clauses (*cf* 15.5). It does not apply to the relative type of nominal *wh*-clauses (*cf* 15.8*f*), nor to clauses introduced by *if* or *whether* (*cf* 15.6):

*Somebody *has hidden my notebook*, and I'll punish whoever △.
*They say *the treasure was buried*, but no one is sure whether △ or not.

The elliptical *wh*-question is found not only in dependent, but also in independent interrogative clauses (*cf* 11.14):

A: We're bound to *win the prize some day*.
B: Yes, but WHÈN △?

There is also a reduced negative *wh*-question, but this occurs only with *why* and with *wh*-infinitive clauses (*cf* 15.5):

Why NǑT? I don't KNÒW *why* not.
I don't want *to accept*, but I don't know *how not* (*to*).

Note **[a]** Elliptical *wh*-questions are discussed further in 11.15 Note [b].
[b] The following are idiomatic examples of informal elliptical *wh*-interrogative clauses, in which the ellipsis is situational: *I'll tell you what*; *Say when*. Their meanings, roughly, are: 'I'll tell you what we can/should do'; and 'Say when you have enough to drink in your glass' (said by the person serving a drink). *I'll tell you what* can be ellipted still further, by initial ellipsis (*cf* 12.44), to *Tell you what*:

(I'll) Tell you what – let's meet again when all the results are in.

Ellipsis in *to*-infinitive clauses

12.64 Like the elliptical *wh*-clause just described, the elliptical *to*-infinitive clause normally consists of just one word: in this case, the introductory unstressed particle *to*. Since *to* is unstressed, the nucleus of the tone unit normally falls on the preceding verb or noun:

You can *borrow my pen*, if you WÁNT to △. [1]
You will *speak to* who(m)ever I TÈLL you to △. [2]
Somebody ought to *help*. Shall I ask PÉter to △? [3]

A 'stranded' *to* also occurs as a result of ellipsis following the marginal modals *ought to* and *used to*, and following semi-auxiliary constructions such as *be able to*, *be going to*, *have to*, and *be supposed to* (*cf* 3.47):

> We don't *save* as much money these days as we { used to △. / ought (to) △. }
>
> I won't *disturb you again* unless I have to △.

As with *to*-infinitive clauses in general, these abbreviated clauses are made negative by placing *not* before *to*:

> She used my pen, although I told her NǑT to.

Both the elliptical dependent *wh*-clause and the elliptical *to*-infinitive clause are normally restricted to a function of complementation (*cf* 16.35*ff*). For example, in [1] *to* is the complementation of *like*; in [2], *to* is part of the complementation of *want*; and in [3] *to* is part of the complementation of *ask*. It is for this reason that it is rare to find ellipsis of these types in nonfinal position in the sentence. However, it is possible for *to* to be followed by medial ellipsis with a final optional adverbial:

> The committee did not *discuss your proposal*, but it hopes to △ (next month). [4]

Note Whether or not *to* is in a final position in the clause, if it is followed by an ellipsis it is normally pronounced in an unreduced form /tuː/ or /tʊ/ rather than as a fully reduced or weak form /tə/. In this respect it resembles auxiliary verbs, which also remain unreduced in these circumstances (*cf* 12.59 Note [c]). Compare the unacceptability of:

> *The committee did not discuss your proposal, but { they'*ll* next month. / they hope /tə/ next month. }

In very informal AmE, however, reduction of *to* to /tə/ occurs finally in examples like:

> Well, I don't *wanna*. So there!

Ellipsis of an entire clause

12.65 One stage further, in clause ellipsis, is the ellipsis of an entire clause, including introductory words, if any. This total clause ellipsis is limited, obviously enough, to dependent clauses, and mainly to *to*-infinitive clauses. It is also limited to clauses acting as complementation of other clauses. For example, the *to* in 12.64 [1] and [3] can be ellipted, so that no trace remains of the infinitive clause:

> You can borrow my pen, if you WÁNT △. [1a]
>
> Somebody ought to help. Shall I ask PÉter △? [3a]

Normally the word whose complementation clause is ellipted is either a verb of saying or thinking, such as *ask*, *know*, *wish*, or an adjective such as *eager*, *sure*, and *willing*. Contrast:

Whole *to*-infinitive clause omissible	*To* not omissible
I was *willing* (to (come)).	I would *hate* you to (see this).
She *begged* us (to (help)).	I would *love* you to (stay).
They *forced* him (to (recant)).	He *advised* us to (leave).

Other clauses which may be ellipted are some *-ing* clauses, some *that*-clauses, and some *wh*-clauses:

If *I am going too fast*, { please warn me (that I am going too fast). / please stop me (going too fast).

I asked *when she was leaving*, and she said she didn't know △.

It may be argued, however, that precise recovery of an ellipted clause cannot be insisted on here; and that therefore this is a case of weak ellipsis only.

Note [**a**] Certain subordinate clauses with an ellipted infinitive clause, such as *if you like*, are formulaic, and resemble comment clauses (*cf* 15.53). One sign of their idiomatic status is an inability to be expanded by the addition of *to*: instead of *if you like to*, speakers would say *If you'd like to*. Conversely, *if you'd like to* cannot normally be reduced to *if you'd like*.

[**b**] There is some variation between AmE and BrE in the use of ellipsis or a pro-form in colloquial sentences such as *I know* and *I suppose so* (*cf* 12.28). For example, possible variants in AmE, but not in BrE, are *I know it* and *I suppose*.

[**c**] There can be total clause ellipsis in comparative constructions (*eg*: *He's older than I thought*) and in dialogue (*eg*: *I know*; *Who told you?* and *Why do you ask?*) *cf* 15.65*f*.

Special types of ellipsis

12.66 We now turn from general ellipsis to the special types of ellipsis (*cf* 12.43) which are defined by a particular structural relation between the elliptical construction and the antecedent construction. Unlike general ellipsis, all cases of special ellipsis allow initial ellipsis.

In nonfinite and verbless clauses

12.67 Since these will be discussed fully in Chapter 14 (14.6–9), it is sufficient to note that typically nonfinite and verbless clauses lack both subject and operator, and that their relation to their main clause can be explained if we postulate, in many cases, an ellipsis of these elements, the identity of the subject being recoverable from the main clause. (The ellipsis may be either anaphoric or cataphoric.) The clearest cases of such ellipsis are adverbial clauses such as the following (*cf* 14.18*f*, 15.34, 15.39):

NONFINITE CLAUSES:

Although (he was) exhausted by the climb, he continued his journey.
Dogs will learn fast if (they are) working in reasonable conditions.

VERBLESS CLAUSES:

While (she was) *at Oxford*, she was active in the dramatic society.
Though (he was) *already middle-aged*, he took a swim every morning.
Whether (it is) *right or wrong*, the government always wins the argument.

In coordination

12.68 When clauses are coordinated by *and*, *or*, or *but*, a second clause or other noninitial clause is often reduced by general ellipsis, the antecedent being a parallel construction in the preceding clause:

I told him to *go home*, but he wouldn't △. [1]

But there is also a special kind of ellipsis associated with coordination. Coordination is essentially a relation between two or more structurally parallel units, which may be whole clauses or sentences, but which are often smaller units such as noun phrases or predications:

Margaret is [selling her bicycle] and △ [buying a car]. [2]
She has bought [a green dress] and △ [a silver necklace]. [3]

There is no structural reason for postulating ellipsis in such cases. Instead we recognize that units may be coordinated in conjoint units which function, as far as clause structure is concerned, in the same way as one of their conjoins (*cf* 2.10). However, from a semantic point of view, [2] and [3] are generally equivalent to [2a] and [3a] respectively:

Margaret is selling her bicycle and Margaret is buying a car. [2a]
She has bought a green dress and she has bought a silver necklace. [3a]

For this reason, it may be claimed that coordination allows both initial ellipsis, as in [2] and [3], and final ellipsis, as in [1]. In one respect, however, coordination is more restrictive than general ellipsis: coordination normally requires strict ellipsis rather than standard ellipsis (*cf* 12.37–8). Hence the following are usually regarded as ungrammatical (although they occur readily enough in the casual unconsidered use of language):

?*The city always has △ and will *be proud of its achievements.* [4]
?*The product is as good △ or even better *than its competitors.* [5]

For further discussion, *cf* 13.44*f*, 13.88.

In comparative clauses

12.69 Like coordinate constructions, comparative constructions show a parallelism between one structure and another, and hence lend themselves to ellipsis. Although comparative clauses will be described later (*cf* 15.63*ff*) it is to be noted here that, as in coordination, so in comparative clauses, both final and initial ellipsis is allowed. Hence the ambiguity illustrated by:

My uncle loved that dog more than his family (loved that dog).
My uncle loved that dog more than (my uncle loved) his family.

The resemblance between coordination and comparison accounts for the existence of quasi-coordinators such as *rather than*, which share in the characteristics of both (*cf* 13.103). There is, however, a major difference between coordination and comparison: in the latter case the ellipsis–antecedent relation obtains between a subordinate clause and a matrix clause, rather than between two constructions of the same level of constituent structure.

In appended clauses

12.70 An appended clause can be regarded as an elliptical clause (usually parenthetical or an afterthought) for which the whole or part of the preceding or interrupted clause constitutes the antecedent:

I caught the train – just. [1]
He told them (falsely, it transpired) how he came to be late. [2]

These two sentences presuppose that two separate assertions are being made. The usual form for [1] is *I (only) just caught the train*, so to explain the unusual word order of [1] we suppose it to be an elliptical version of:

I caught the train – I just caught the train.

Compare:

I caught the train, but △ only just △.

The same sort of analysis applies if the items added as an afterthought are in their normal order:

The train arrived – on time, for a change.

Whereas in these examples the whole of the initial clause acts as an antecedent for the elliptical parenthesis or afterthought, another kind of appended clause repudiates part of the original clause, so that only part (the part italicized below) acts as an antecedent:

They are meant to wound, perhaps △ to kill.
He is playful, △ even mischievous.
Her performance will be judged by her superiors – and even more importantly – △ by her colleagues.

On the related construction of appended coordination, *cf* 13.94.

Note [**a**] A clause involving quantifiers interestingly illustrates how the appended clause sometimes has to be interpreted as repudiating part of the preceding clause:

They visit many schools, sometimes in an official car.

This does not mean the same as:

They sometimes visit many schools in an official car.

Rather, it presupposes two assertions:

{They visit many schools. [3]
{They sometimes visit schools in an official car. [4]

The second assertion [4] does not imply that they visit many schools.

[**b**] Appended clauses consisting of an adverbial only are closely related to nonrestrictive adverbials (*cf* 15.23):

I only met him once – at your place. [5]

In [5], *at your place* is nonrestrictive ('I only met him once – and that was at your place'), in contrast to *I only met him once at your place* ('but I've met him many times elsewhere').

[**c**] An appended clause sometimes contains a repetition of some part of the antecedent clause:

I found their behaviour odd – very odd, in fact.

[**d**] Appended clauses resemble some types of apposition (*cf* 17.65*ff*), in which there is a duplication of an element structurally and semantically parallel to an element of the preceding clause:

We – that is to say, John and I – intend to resign.
You could have given them to a charity – to Oxfam, for example.
He tried to make treaties with the Indians: first with the Sioux, and then with the Cheyenne.

Bibliographical note

On reduction generally, see Allerton (1975); Halliday and Hasan (1976).

On pro-forms and substitutes, see Allen (1961); Bolinger (1977b); Bouton (1969); Crymes (1968); G. Lakoff (1970a).

On ellipsis, see Greenbaum and Meyer (1982); Gunter (1963); Karlsen (1959); Kypriotaki (1970).

For further references see the Bibliographical notes for Chs. 13 & 19.

13 Coordination

Syndetic and asyndetic coordination

13.1 The term COORDINATION is used by some grammarians for both syndetic (or linked) coordination, and asyndetic (or unlinked) coordination. The difference between the two constructions is that syndetic coordination is marked by overt signals of coordination (*and*, *or*, *but*), whereas asyndetic coordination is not overtly marked. Sentence [1a] exemplifies syndetic coordination, with *and* as explicit marker, while [1b] exemplifies asyndetic coordination, with *and* omitted:

Slowly and stealthily, he crept towards his victim. [1a]
Slowly, stealthily, he crept towards his victim. [1b]

Linking words which explicitly indicate coordination are termed COORDINATING CONJUNCTIONS, or (more simply) COORDINATORS. Not all juxtaposed words, phrases, or clauses are manifestations of asyndetic coordination. The possibility of inserting thc coordinator *and* with little alteration of meaning is evidence that a construction is one of asyndetic coordination. It is this that distinguishes [1b] from other types of construction, for example the appended clauses of 12.70.

Syndetic coordination is the more usual form, and we shall therefore generally exemplify coordination with a coordinator present. Asyndetic coordination is usually stylistically marked. It is used for dramatic intensification, as in [1b], or to suggest an open-ended list:

Mrs Varley sold sweets, chocolate, toffee apples – anything a child could desire.

In asyndetic coordination, the conjoins are generally separated by a tone-unit boundary in speech, or by a punctuation stop in writing. In the spoken form, the conjoins are typically marked by a parallelism in the tone of the nucleus; for example:

SLÒWly, STÈALTHily . . . *or*: SLÓWly, STÉALTHily . . .

Note In the present chapter we restrict our attention to coordination within the sentence. Coordination as a link between sentences is discussed in 19.57*ff*.

Coordination and subordination

13.2 Explicit indicators of subordination are termed SUBORDINATING CONJUNCTIONS or SUBORDINATORS. (They are more fully discussed in 14.11*ff*.) Both coordination and subordination (*cf* 14.1–4) involve the linking of units of the same rank; but in coordination the units are constituents at the same level of constituent structure, whereas in subordination they form a hierarchy, the subordinate unit being a constituent of the superordinate unit (*cf* 14.2*f* for the relevant tree diagrams). Coordination and subordination are special cases of two types of syntactic arrangement traditionally known as PARATAXIS ('equal arrangement') and HYPOTAXIS ('underneath arrangement'). Thus, to take an example within a phrase (*cf* 17.116), in *his first and best novel*, the coordinate adjective phrase *first and best* functions as a premodifier of *novel*, and in that phrase *first* and *best* are equal constituents. On the other hand, in *his first successful novel*, the adjective *first* does not modify *novel* directly; it modifies *successful novel*, and *successful* in turn modifies *novel*. Thus there is a hierarchy in relationships, and *first* and *successful* are in a hypotactic rather than a paratactic relation.

The opposition between coordination and subordination, and that between parataxis and hypotaxis, are often treated as equivalent. But we may distinguish them as follows. Parataxis applies not only to coordinate constructions, but to other cases where two units of equivalent status are juxtaposed: for example, an appended clause as discussed in 12.70 is in a paratactic relation to the clause preceding it; and a tag question is in a paratactic relation to the statement preceding it. But in neither of these cases could we insert an overt coordinator. Similarly, there are other hypotactic relations (such as the embedding of one phrase in another, *cf* 2.8), quite apart from the relation between a subordinate clause and the clause of which it is a part.

Semantic differences between coordination and subordination

13.3 A major difference between coordination and subordination of clauses is that the information in a subordinate clause is often placed in the background with respect to the superordinate clause (*cf* 19.60). Thus the syntactic inequality of subordination tends to bring with it a semantic inequality which is realized by syntactic hierarchization, as well as by position. This is particularly noticeable in the case of certain adverbial clauses, which present information as if it is presupposed as given (*cf* 18.8) rather than asserted as new:

{ He has quarrelled with the chairman *and* has resigned. [1a]
{ *Since* he quarrelled with the chairman, he has resigned. [1b]

{ He tried hard, *but* he failed. [2a]
{ *Although* he tried hard, he failed. [2b]
{ He tried hard, *although* he failed. [2c]

The cause–result relationship between the two events is expressed by a coordinator in [1a] and by a subordinator in [1b]; the semantic difference, however, is that in [1b] the hearer is assumed to know about the quarrel already. A similar observation applies to the concessive relationship expressed by *but* in [2a] and *although* in [2b] and [2c].

A third means of expressing the same relationship is a linking sentence adverbial, or conjunct (*cf* 8.134*ff*), such as *yet*:

He tried hard, *yet* he failed. [2d]

Unlike the other two words, however, *yet* can be preceded by a coordinator:

He tried hard, and *yet* he failed. [2e]

Despite its appearance, therefore, [2d], in contrast to [2e], illustrates asyndetic coordination (but *cf* further 13.11).

13.4 It is sometimes said that an important difference between coordination and subordination is that only in the former case can the relation between the two linguistic units be reversed without a change of meaning; *ie* (in symbolic terms):

A + conjunction + B = B + conjunction + A

This is no more than a half-truth. It is true that the order can be reversed in certain cases of coordination:

{ Mary studies at a university *and* John works at a factory.
{ = John works at a factory *and* Mary studies at a university.

But this potentiality is dependent on many factors, only one of which is the relationship of meaning between the coordinated units. Some of these factors are syntactic, others are a matter of semantic or pragmatic asymmetry (*cf* 13.22–7). For example, the following are obviously not synonymous:

He died *and* he was buried in the cemetery.
He was buried in the cemetery *and* he died.

Note When two coordinated units are placed in sequence, the second unit gains focal prominence from its position (*cf* 18.3*ff*). This prominence in terms of information focus also attaches to the final element in a subordination relation, but in the latter case the positional highlighting is combined with a highlighting based on the formal inequality of subordination.

Coordinators

Coordinators identified

13.5 We regard these conjunctions as clearly coordinators: *and*, *or*, and *but*. *And* and *or* are central coordinators, but *but* differs from them in some respects. On the gradient between 'pure' coordinators and 'pure' subordinators are *for* and *so that* (meaning in this chapter, unless otherwise stated, 'with the result that'). There is also a gradient relating coordinators to conjuncts: for example, *yet* and *so* are two words which we shall classify as conjuncts, but which nevertheless resemble coordinators in some respects. *Nor* is not a clear case of a coordinator, since for many speakers it can be preceded by another coordinator (a potentiality not available to the central cases *and*, *or*, and *but*, as we shall see). *Nor* also contains a negative feature, which introduces some syntactic differences (*cf* 13.36*ff*).

Both, *either*, and *neither* are used as the first item in a correlative pair with *and*, *or*, and *nor* respectively. These anticipatory words are optional endorsements of the coordination, and are obviously closely related to the corresponding determiners *both*, *either*, and *neither* (*cf* 5.12*ff*). Such ENDORSING ITEMS are not in themselves coordinators, since, like *nor*, they can be preceded by a central coordinator (*and* or *or*).

Note [**a**] We class the conjunctions *for* and *so that* as subordinators in this book; but *cf* below 13.8, 13.10.

[**b**] Another coordinator in marginal use is *plus*:

Mainframe computers are becoming less expensive, '*plus* the best software is available for desktops which of course are cheaper still.

Thus used, *plus* is normally stressed, and is an emphatic alternative to *and* in an additive sense (*cf* 13.27).

Syntactic features of coordinators

13.6 In 13.3 we showed how the same semantic linking function could be performed not only by coordinators, but by subordinators and conjuncts:

He tried hard, *but* he failed.
He tried hard, *although* he failed.
He tried hard, *yet* he failed.

Since all three of these word classes can in a general sense be termed LINKERS, it is important to understand the syntactic basis of the distinctions between them, and at the same time to appreciate that these distinctions are gradient (*cf* 2.60) rather than clear-cut.

We shall therefore examine six features which apply to the central coordinators, *and* and *or*. For each feature, we note whether it is applicable not only to *and* and *or*, but also to items which resemble them. At this stage we restrict ourselves mainly to central coordinators as CLAUSE LINKERS.

(a) Clause coordinators are restricted to clause-initial position

13.7 *And*, *or*, and *but* are restricted to initial position in the clause:

John plays the guitar, *and* his sister plays the piano.
*John plays the guitar; his sister *and* plays the piano.

This is generally true of both coordinators and subordinators, but it is not true of most conjuncts:

John plays the guitar; his sister, *moreover*, plays the piano.

Note [**a**] There are two or three subordinators which are exceptional in that they can occur noninitially (*cf* 15.39):

Though he is poor, he is happy. Poor *though* he is, he is happy.

[**b**] In colloquial Australian English (*cf* 1.26) *but* can occur in noninitial position; this indicates that in this variety, it resembles conjuncts (*cf* 8.134*ff*).

(b) Coordinated clauses are sequentially fixed

13.8 Clauses beginning with *and*, *or*, and *but* are sequentially fixed in relation to the previous clause, and therefore cannot be transposed without producing unacceptable sentences, or at least changing the relationship between the clauses:

They are living in England, *or* they are spending a vacation there.
**Or* they are spending a vacation there, they are living in England.

This is true for coordinators and conjuncts, but not for most subordinators. Contrast the unacceptability of [1a], containing the conjunct *nevertheless*, with the acceptability of [1b], containing the subordinator *although*:

***Nevertheless* John gave it away, Mary wanted it. [1a]
Although Mary wanted it, John gave it away. [1b]

In this respect, however, the subordinators *for* and *so that* resemble coordinators. Contrast:

***For* he was unhappy, he asked to be transferred.
Because he was unhappy, he asked to be transferred.

and the resultative *so that* in [2] with the purposive *so that* (*cf* 15.48*f*) in [3]:

***So that* we arrived home late, the rush hour traffic delayed us. [2]
So that he could buy a car, he sold his stamp collection. [3]

13.9 Related to the fixed position of the coordinate clause is the fact that when clauses are linked by the coordinators *and*, *or*, and *but* (also by *for* and *so that*), a pronoun in the first clause cannot normally have cataphoric reference to a noun phrase in the second clause. For example, *she* in [1a] and [1b] does not corefer to *my mother*:

She felt ill, and *my mother* said nothing. [1a]
She felt ill, but *my mother* said nothing. [1b]

On the other hand, a pronoun can (but need not) have cataphoric reference when it occurs in an initial subordinate clause (*cf* 6.19):

Although *she* felt ill, *my mother* said nothing. [1c]

But the most common position for a subordinate clause is final, in which case a coreferring pronoun will be anaphoric:

My mother said nothing, although *she* felt ill. [1d]

Again, as with cataphoric reference, the antecedent must be in the superordinate clause:

She said nothing, although *my mother* felt ill. [2]

In [2], *She* cannot cataphorically refer to *my mother*.

Note There are both apparent and real exceptions to the rule that a pronoun cannot have cataphoric reference to an element in a following coordinate clause. Consider:

No one who met *her* on social occasions could imagine a harsh word passing *her* lips – but *Liz Pettigrew* was notorious for speaking her mind on matters of business. [3]

The two occurrences of *her* in the first clause appear to corefer cataphorically to *Liz Pettigrew*; but this sentence would normally occur in a context in which Liz was already being discussed. These pronouns could then be explained as anaphorically coreferring to part of an earlier sentence. Exceptionally, however, a sentence such as [3] could occur without preceding anaphoric reference – *eg* at the beginning of a novel.

(c) Coordinators are not preceded by a conjunction

13.10 *And* and *or* do not allow another conjunction to precede them. This is also true for *but*, *for*, and *so that* (of which the latter two will be treated as subordinators; *cf* 13.18*f*). On the other hand, subordinators as well as conjuncts can usually be preceded by conjunctions:

He was unhappy about it, *and yet* he did as he was told.

In [1] and [2] two subordinate clauses are linked by *and*, which precedes the second subordinator *because* and the second subordinator *so that* (with purposive meaning):

He asked to be transferred, *because* he was unhappy *and because* he saw no prospect of promotion. [1]
She saved money *so that* she could buy a house, *and so that* her pension would be supplemented by a reasonable income after retirement. [2]

In contrast, the conjunctions *but*, *for*, and resultative *so that* (*cf* 15.49) cannot be preceded by *and* in this way:

*He was unhappy about it, *and but* he did what he was told.
*He asked to be transferred, *for* he was unhappy *and for* he saw no possibility of promotion.
*We paid her immediately, *so* (*that*) she left contented *and so* (*that*) everyone was satisfied.

Note A subordinate clause cannot normally be coordinated with a superordinate clause; but this is what appears to happen in the following case:

She wouldn't do it – *and* (*all*) *because I didn't ask her in person.*

The explanation of this example, however, is that the coordinated construction in italics is an elliptical appended clause (*cf* 12.70), the *because* clause being subordinated to this appended clause, rather than to the initial clause *She wouldn't do it.*

13.11 In initial position, some conjunct adverbs resemble coordinators in that they commonly occur with asyndetic coordination, and therefore provide a link similar to coordination:

I told her to go home, *yet* she refused to move. [*cf*: *but* she refused . . .]
The rain fell, *so* we all went home. [*cf*: *and* we all . . .]
Tom doesn't drink, *neither* does he use bad language.
The car turned suddenly, *then* screeched to a halt.

The ease with which the coordinator is omitted in these cases suggests that not only the possibility of adding a coordinator, but the probability of its being omitted should be considered a factor in comparing the behaviour of linkers. One way of explaining the unexpected likelihood of asyndeton in such cases is to postulate an optional merger of the coordinator *and* with the adverb; *eg*: *and* + *yet* merge into *yet*; *and* + *so* merge as *so*. This is a more convincing analysis where, as in all the examples except *then* above, the adverb is immobile in initial position. Other adverbs which behave similarly are *nor* (*cf* 13.18), *otherwise*, *neither*, *only* (as a conjunct), and *hence*.

On the use of comma punctuation with this set of adverbs, *cf* App III.6.

(d) Coordinators can link clause constituents

13.12 *And* and *or* may link constituents smaller than a clause; for example, they may link predicates, thus in effect allowing ellipsis of a second or subsequent subject (on the treatment of ellipsis in such cases, *cf* 13.44*ff*, 13.52*f*):

[I may see you tomorrow] *or* [I may phone later in the day].
I [may see you tomorrow] *or* $_{\triangle}$ [may phone later in the day].

Less frequently, this feature also applies to *but*:

> The Polish athletes [have succeeded today], *but* △ [may not repeat their success tomorrow].

However, it does not apply to *for* and *so that*:

> *He [did not want it], *for* △ [was obstinate].
> *He [did not spend very much], *so that* △ [could afford a trip abroad].

Nor does it apply to other conjunctions or to most conjuncts. But this construction seems to be acceptable with the conjunct *yet* and (to a lesser extent, at least in informal spoken English) with the conjunct *so* and the time adverb *then* (meaning 'after that'):

> They didn't like it, *yet* (they) said nothing.
> They were tired, *so* (they) left early.
> They went home, *then* (they) went straight to bed.

13.13 A subordinator, on the other hand, does not allow ellipsis of the subject even when its clause is linked by a coordinator:

> *She didn't say anything about it *because* he was new and *because* looked unwell. [1]

If the second subordinator of [1] is omitted, ellipsis is possible:

> She didn't say anything about it *because* he was new and (he) looked unwell. [1a]

This is allowed, being a regular case of coordination of predicates (*cf* 13.52), whereas that of [1] is an ungrammatical type of ellipsis (*cf* 12.44). For the same reason, ellipsis is possible preceding or following a conjunct (such as *nevertheless*) if the ellipted subject is itself preceded by a coordinator:

> He went to bed early, but { △ *nevertheless* / *nevertheless* △ } felt tired.

(e) Coordinators can link subordinate clauses

13.14 As well as linking two main clauses, *and* and *or*, as we saw in 13.10 [1] above, can link subordinate clauses:

> He asked to be transferred, *because* he was unhappy, (*because*) he saw no prospect of promotion, *and* (*because*) conditions were far better at the other office. [1]
> I wonder *whether* you should go and see her *or whether* it is better to write to her. [2]

Usually, as in [1], the second and any subsequent subordinators may be omitted. Such linking is not possible for conjuncts or for the other conjunctions except *but*. *But*, however, is restricted to linking a maximum of two clauses (*cf* 13.16):

> She said *that* John would take them by car *but* (*that*) they might be late. [3]

Even so, *but* can link only certain types of subordinate clauses:

(a) *That*-clauses (*cf* 15.4) as in [3] above; only with *that*-clauses can the second subordinator, the one following *but*, be omitted.
(b) Temporal adverbial clauses:

> I spoke to him *after* the conference was over, *but before* he started work.

(c) Clauses introduced by the same conjunctions, such as *in order that*, *so that*, and *because*, or by the same *wh*-words. In such cases the first part of the sentence has to be negative, so that it contrasts with the positive meaning of the part which follows *but* (*cf* 13.42):

> She didn't see who MĚT the ambassador, *but* who took him aWÀY.
> He didn't save in order to go to school, *but* in order to buy a car.

13.15 *But* cannot link most other subordinate clauses, because such clauses normally lie outside the scope of negation (*cf* 2.55, 10.64*f*), and so cannot contrast with the negative implication of the first conjoin:

> ?They won't help you *if* you pay them, *but if* you promise to help them in return.
> *They didn't stay *although* they were happy, *but although* they were bored.

An example with *if*-clauses, such as the one above, is marginally acceptable in a context which enables it to be interpreted as a reformulation of what someone has said or implied. Moreover, if the negation is outside the verb phrase, *but* can more easily link adjunct and subjunct clauses, including such *if*-clauses as:

> It might have turned out all right, *not if* he had been more forceful *but if* he had been more tactful.

On further aspects of the *not . . . but* construction, *cf* 13.42.

(f) Coordinators can link more than two clauses

13.16 *And* and *or* can link more than two clauses, and the construction may then be called one of MULTIPLE COORDINATION. All but the final instance of these two conjunctions can be omitted. Thus:

> The battery may be disconnected, the connection may be loose, *or* the bulb may be faulty. [1]

is interpreted as:

> The battery may be disconnected, *or* the connection may be loose, *or* the bulb may be faulty. [2]

In this respect, *and* and *or* differ from subordinators and conjuncts. They differ even from *but*, since *but* semantically speaking can only link two conjoins at the same level. While it is possible (though unusual) to construct a sentence such as:

> John played football, Mary played tennis, *but* Alice stayed at home. [3]

such a sentence is interpreted as if the first two clauses had been linked by *and*:

> John played football, *and* Mary played tennis, *but* Alice stayed at home. [4]

An indefinite number of clauses can be linked by *and* or *or*. But there is another way in which more than two elements can be combined by coordination: one set of coordinate clauses may become the conjoin of a higher-level coordinate construction. This is indeed what happens in [4], where the coordination by *but* is at a higher level than the coordination by *and*. The constituent structure can be conveniently shown by bracketing: [[A] *and* [B]] *but* [C]. When two different coordinators occur, like this, in the same complex construction, structural ambiguities are liable to arise. The ambiguity can be demonstrated by different bracketings. For example, in the following sentences, [A], [B], and [C] represent three clauses:

> [A] I'll pay for the meal *and* [B] you pay for the taxi, *or* [C] perhaps I'll pay for both. [5]

The relationship between the clauses can be represented as follows:

> [[A] *and* [B]] *or* [C].

On the other hand, the sentence:

> [A] His parents live in New York *and* [B] he writes to them from time to time *or* [C] (he) phones them. [6]

can be represented by a bracketing in which [B] and [C] make up a single conjoin of *and*:

> [A] *and* [[B] *or* [C]].

The contrast between [5] and [6] can be also represented by tree diagrams:

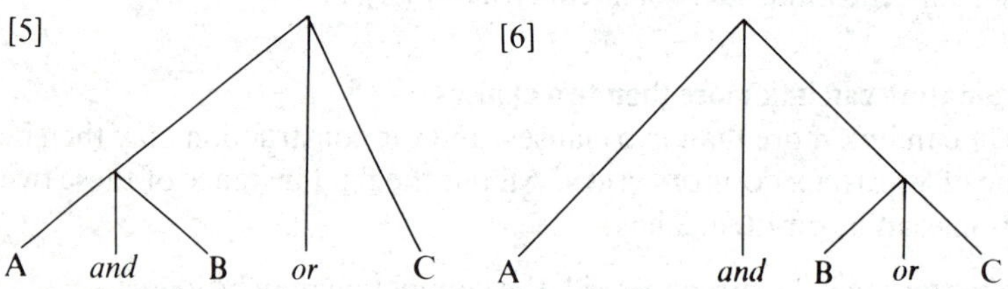

Fig 13.16

Note Punctuation is often used to make clear which is the major constituent structure boundary in mixed multiple coordinate constructions such as [5] and [6]. Thus, the potential ambiguity of the above two constructions can be eliminated by placing a comma before the main coordinator:

> [[A] *and* [B]], *or* [C]; [A], *and* [[B] *or* [C]].

A similar distinction can be made prosodically, by placing a tone-unit boundary before the major coordinator, and using additional forms of prosodic emphasis if required.

Polysyndetic coordination

13.17 When a construction with *and* or *or* has more than two conjoins, the ellipsis of all but the last coordinator is customary. Hence 13.16 [1] above, rather than [2], illustrates the usual pattern. In this way, the insertion of the coordinator between two conjoins signals that the last conjoin is about to be added. But where a coordinator occurs between each pair of conjoins, *eg* in [A] *and* [B] *and* [C], the construction is traditionally termed POLYSYNDETON:

> The wind roared, *and* the lightning flashed, *and* the sky was suddenly as dark as night. [7]

Polysyndetic coordination thus contrasts both with asyndetic coordination and with ordinary syndetic coordination (*cf* 13.1). Since it transgresses the principle 'reduce where possible' (*cf* 12.4), polysyndeton tends to be reserved for stylistically marked effects; for example, in [7] above it is used to emphasize a dramatic sequence of events, and in 13.16 [2] it suggests (in contrast to [1]) that the list of three possibilities may not be complete.

Note On the use of a punctuation mark as a separator of nonfinal conjoins of multiple coordinate constructions, *cf* App III.7–9.

Coordination–subordination gradient

13.18 *Table* 13.18 displays the gradient from the central coordinators *and* and *or* to subordinators like *if* and *because*, with *but*, *for*, and *so that* on the gradient. The conjuncts *yet*, *so*, and *nor* are added to the *Table*, because, as we have seen, they in some respects resemble coordinators. The six features of *and* and *or* noted in 13.7–17 have provided six criteria used in constructing the matrix. If an item satisfies a criterion, this is indicated by a '+' in the relevant cell. If it fails to satisfy the criterion, '–' is entered. The combination '±' takes care of cases, explained in the previous discussion, where the item satisfies the criterion only under certain conditions. The six criteria to be applied to each item are:

(a) It is immobile in front of its clause.
(b) A clause beginning with it is sequentially fixed in relation to the previous clause, and hence cannot be moved to a position in front of that clause.
(c) It does not allow a conjunction to precede it.
(d) It links not only clauses, but predicates and other clause constituents.
(e) It can link subordinate clauses.
(f) It can link more than two clauses, and when it does so all but the final instance of the linking item can be omitted.

Table 13.18 Coordination–conjunct–subordination gradients

		(a)	(b)	(c)	(d)	(e)	(f)
coordinators	*and, or*	+	+	+	+	+	+
	but	+	+	+	+	±	–
conjuncts	*yet, so, nor*	+	+	×	+	–	–
	however, therefore	–	+	–	–	–	–
subordinators	*for, so that*	+	+	+	–	–	–
	if, because	+	±	–	–	–	–

The cross '×' in column (c) records the fact, already noted in 13.11, that words like *yet*, *so*, and *nor*, although they allow a preceding coordinator, also allow the omission of the coordinator more readily than other conjuncts. In other words, they favour asyndeton, and to that extent resemble coordinators with respect to column (c) as much as they resemble conjuncts.

Note [**a**] When *because* introduces a disjunct clause (*cf* 8.124, 15.21), it resembles *for* and *so that*, in that the clause which it introduces cannot be moved to initial position in the sentence:

She PǍID for the book, *because* I SÀW her. ≠ *Because* I saw her, she paid for the book.

This explains the '±' in column (b).

[**b**] For many speakers, especially in AmE, *nor* cannot be preceded by a coordinator. In BrE, the combination *but nor* is somewhat more acceptable than *and nor*.

13.19 Although *Table* 13.18 demonstrates the absence of a clear divide between coordinators and other linking items, we can justify the traditional inclusion of *but* among the coordinators and the exclusion of *for* and *so that* or *yet* and *so* by pointing to two facts which distinguish *but* from these words: (i) it behaves like a coordinator with respect to subject ellipsis (*cf* 13.12 and criterion (d) above), and (ii) it resembles coordinators in its ability to link two clauses subordinate to the same main clause (criterion (e)). The latter potentiality, in particular, reflects its status as a coordinator, in that it links constituents at the same level. By the same criteria, *for* and *so that* are shown to be subordinators rather than coordinators; and yet they are more coordinator-like than the more typical subordinators *if* and *because*. Similarly, *yet*, *so*, *neither*, and *nor* are best treated as conjuncts which are nevertheless more coordinator-like than more typical conjuncts such as *however* and *therefore*. These words which share some of the distinguishing features of coordinators may be called SEMI-COORDINATORS (*cf* also QUASI-COORDINATORS, 13.103).

Coordination of clauses and of lesser constituents

13.20 In the above comparisons, we have assumed in general that the units to be linked are clauses. This has meant ignoring (except with reference to criterion (d)) an important distinguishing characteristic of coordinators: that they can be used to link elements which are parts of clauses, rather than whole clauses. Thus the conjoins in the following examples are adjectives acting respectively as subject complement and premodifier:

The weather will be *cold and cloudy*.
 ~ *cold and cloudy* weather
The weather will be *rainy or changeable*.
 ~ *rainy or changeable* weather
The weather will be *warm but windy*.
 ~ *warm but windy* weather

Here again, however, we note that linking words which are not coordinators nevertheless resemble coordinators. Certain concessive subordinators and conjuncts, in particular, are capable of replacing *but* in the above types of construction:

Tim's *squat yet ferocious* bulldog could be heard growling on the patio.
I immediately recognized Sarah's *bold if barely legible* handwriting.
Martin was inclined to boast about his *rich though disreputable* ancestors.

(On the concessive use of *if* here, *cf* 15.40.)

These concessive items can link not only adjectives, but other clause constituents, such as adverbials:

The admiral walked clumsily, { *yet* / *if* / *though* } with dignity.

Similarly, *nor*, in its capacity as a correlative conjunction after *neither* (*cf* 13.37), can link constituents such as adjectives or adverbials:

They were *neither able nor willing* to provide the necessary capital.

The gradience and overlap between coordinators, subordinators, and conjuncts has not, therefore, been exhausted by *Table* 13.18.

13.21 We shall note such in-between cases as they arise; but even with coordination, it is sensible to begin with the conjoining of clauses as the most basic construction. This is because in many cases (but by no means all; *cf* 13.45–6) the coordinating of smaller units may be elucidated as an elliptical reduction of clause coordination. For example, the coordinating of predications as in:

Sam has *trimmed the hedge* and *mowed the lawn.*

can be analysed as an elliptical coordination of clauses in which the initial subject and operator are repeated:

Sam has *trimmed the hedge*, and Sam has *mowed the lawn.*

Similarly, the following sentence with verb-phrase coordination:

I *washed and ironed* the clothes.

can be seen as a reduced version of:

I *washed* the clothes and I *ironed* the clothes.

In this analysis, we can treat ellipsis as a relation of SYSTEMATIC CORRESPONDENCE in the sense of 2.20, rather than attempting to explain it as a process of deriving the reduced construction from the fuller one. Nevertheless, it will be helpful to concentrate largely on clause coordination in the following sections, 13.22–32, therefore confining our attention to COMPOUND SENTENCES as defined in 14.2. It should be noted, however, that the semantic relations to be discussed apply to coordination of clause constituents, as well as of entire clauses.

The use of coordinators

The uses of *and*

13.22 *And* is the coordinator which has the most general meaning and use. The only restriction on the use of *and* as coordinator is the pragmatic one that the clauses should have sufficient in common to justify their combination. Thus the following is odd simply because it would be difficult to find any connection between the content of the clauses:

> The youngsters went off to a dance *and* the equator is equidistant from the two poles.

In logical terms, *and* merely conveys (for declarative clauses) that if the whole sentence is true, then each of its conjoined clauses is true. But the pragmatic implications of the combination vary, according to our presuppositions and knowledge of the world. The relation connoted by the link between the two or more conjoins can generally be made explicit by the addition of an adverbial. By using the term 'connotation', we intend to indicate that the relations of meaning between conjoins are not hard and fast: they vary in strength, and more than one can coexist in the same occurrence of *and*. For each connotation that we exemplify in the following sections, we insert (wherever possible) an adverbial that would make the relationship explicit (*cf* 19.20). For simplicity, we illustrate the connotation with sentences containing just two clauses.

Of the eight types of connotation, in only three – (c), (f), (g) – can the sequence of clauses perhaps be reversed without changing the relationship between the clauses. Even in these cases, the sequence is rarely random.

Note Thus the general principle of communicative dynamism (*cf* 18.3*ff*) determines that when two units are coordinated, the second is placed in focus against the background of the first.

13.23 (a) The second clause is a CONSEQUENCE or RESULT of the first; *ie*, the first conjoin presents the circumstances (frequently the circumstantial background) enabling the event described in the second conjoin to take place. This entails that the order of the clauses also reflects chronological sequence:

> He heard an explosion *and* he (*therefore*) phoned the police.

(b) The second clause is chronologically SEQUENT to the first, but without any implication of a cause–result relationship:

> I washed the dishes *and* (*then*) I dried them.

In (a) and (b), the verb of each clause is normally dynamic rather than stative.

Note [**a**] There can obviously be no implication of chronological sequence if the clauses are given in a sequence contrary to chronological order. Thus, if the second clause is tense-marked to indicate that its content is prior chronologically, coordination of the two clauses is unacceptable in the intended meaning:

> ?I dried the dishes *and* I had washed them.

This also applies when there is the additional implication of a cause–result relationship:

> ?He phoned the police *and* he had heard an explosion.

Such sequences, however, can be quite acceptable without linking by *and*:

He phoned the police; he had heard an explosion.

As such examples show, parataxis differs from coordination in allowing a relation between two clauses whereby the second gives the REASON or EXPLANATION for the event described in the first:

Bader's car dropped out of the race: the engine was overheating.

[b] The association of *and* with chronological sequence does not rule out the possibility that the two clauses linked by *and* refer to simultaneous events or states; *eg*:

Mother was reading *and* (at the same time) I was having a bath.

In this case, where the relation of meaning is ADDITIVE (*cf* 13.27), there would be no difference of meaning if the clauses were placed in the opposite order:

I was having a bath *and* mother was reading.

13.24 (c) The second clause introduces a CONTRAST:

Robert is secretive *and* (*in contrast*) David is candid.

(d) The second clause is felt to be surprising in view of the first, so that the first clause has a CONCESSIVE force:

She tried hard *and* (*yet*) she failed.

In both (c) and (d), *and* could be replaced by *but*.

13.25 (e) The first clause is a CONDITION of the second:

Give me some money *and* (*then*) I'll help you escape. [1]
Let's give him some money *and* (*then*) he won't tell anybody what we did. [2]

The implication of the first sentence is shown by the paraphrase:

Give me some money. If you give me some money (*then*) I'll help you escape.

This illustrates a pattern which is usual with the conditional use of *and*: the first clause is a directive and the second clause describes the consequence which will ensue if the directive is obeyed. It is not necessary, however, for the first clause to be in the imperative mood, or for the second clause to contain *will* or *shall*. One idiomatic pattern consists of two imperatives:

Go by air, *and* save time. [3]
Join the navy *and* see the world. [4]

Another pattern is illustrated by the following:

One more word from you, *and* I phone the police. [5]

Here the first clause is verbless, and the second illustrates the dramatically 'instantaneous' use of the present tense (*cf* 4.7).

Like the corresponding conditional use of *or* (*cf* 13.30), this use of *and* is associated with certain directive speech acts, such as promises (*eg* [1]) and threats (*eg* [5]).

Note **[a]** Since it is normal for the first clause to retain some directive force, there is no exact paraphrase relation between (say) [1] above and the following sentence with an *if*-clause:

If you give me some money, I'll help you escape.

On the other hand, there is a proverbial type of sentence in which the imperative clause lacks a directive meaning, and where the conditional sentence with *if* would offer a suitable paraphrase:

Ask me no questions, *and* I'll tell you no lies.
Give a dog a bad name, *and* he'll live up to it. [= 'If you give . . .']

[**b**] A quasi-conditional use of *and* in prohibitions is illustrated in the slogan: *Don't drink and drive* [= 'If you drink, don't drive']; *cf* 13.48.

13.26 (f) The second clause makes a point SIMILAR to the first:

A trade agreement should be no problem, *and* (*similarly*) a cultural exchange could be easily arranged.

13.27 (g) The second clause is a 'pure' ADDITION to the first, the only requirement being that the two statements are congruent in meaning:

He has long hair *and* (*also*) he often wears jeans.

(h) Similar to (g) is a sentence in which the second clause adds an appended COMMENT on or EXPLANATION of the first:

They disliked John – *and* that's not surprising in view of his behaviour.
There's only one thing to do now – *and* that's to apologize.

A sentential relative clause, *eg*: . . . *which is not surprising* . . . (*cf* 15.57), can replace the second clause here.

Note In type (h), if the first clause is long, the second is sometimes inserted parenthetically within it. Such parenthetical coordination gives the impression of being an *ad hoc* or unplanned interpolation:

Many students at our university – *and* it is difficult to explain this – reject the proposed reforms in university administration.

For a different kind of interpolated coordination, *cf* 13.95*ff*.

The uses of *or*

13.28 *Or* introduces an alternative. Logically, in contrast to *and* (*cf* 13.22) it conveys the meaning (with declarative clauses) that if one of the individual conjoins is true, then the whole sentence is true. But as with *and*, there is the pragmatic requirement that the contents of the two clauses should have sufficient in common to justify their juxtaposition as alternatives. Typically *or* is EXCLUSIVE; that is, it excludes the possibility that both conjoins are true, or are to be fulfilled:

You can sleep on the couch in the lounge *or* you can go to a hotel.

The person who makes the above suggestion does not expect the hearer to reply 'Thanks, I'll do both'. But even when both alternatives are clearly possible, as in:

You can boil yourself an egg *or* (*else*) you can make some sandwiches.

or is normally interpreted as exclusive. The meaning of *or* in such cases can be strengthened by the conjunct *else* or *alternatively*.

There can also occur, however, an INCLUSIVE interpretation of *or*, where it is implied that both conjoins may be true. This inclusive meaning is clearly signalled where a third clause is added to make it explicit, as in the following example:

You can boil an egg, (*or*) you can make some sandwiches, *or* you can do both.

In written varieties of the language where precision is required (*eg* in official instructions), the third possibility can be explicitly included by the combination of coordinators *and/or*:

If the appliance is defective, write directly to the manufacturer *and/or* complain to your local consumer protection service.

Note The exclusive meaning of *or* acquires a specialized use in alternative questions (*cf* 11.20*f*), in alternative interrogative clauses introduced by *whether* or *if* (*cf* 15.6), and in alternative conditional-concessive clauses (*cf* 15.41).

13.29 The alternative expressed by *or* may also be a restatement or a CORRECTIVE to what is said in the first conjoin:

They are enjoying themselves, *or* {(*at least*) / (*rather*)} they appĚAR to be enjoying themselves.

In such cases the second conjoin is, or purports to be, added as an afterthought. Such constructions are discussed under the heading of INTERPOLATED COORDINATION in 13.95*ff*.

13.30 In addition to introducing alternatives as indicated above, *or* may imply a NEGATIVE CONDITION. Thus in:

Give me some money *or* (*else*) I'll shoot.

the implication can be paraphrased by the negative conditional clause:

Give me some money. *If you don't give me some money* I'll shoot.

The conditional use of *or* is thus the negative analogue of the conditional use of *and* (*cf* 13.25). Unlike *and*, however, *or* typically follows a negative imperative clause:

Don't be too long, *or* you'll miss the bus.

In this case, the most appropriate paraphrase with an *if*-clause is positive instead of negative:

. . . if you are too long, you'll miss the bus.

Another difference between conditional *and* and conditional *or* is that the latter can readily occur after declarative, as well as imperative clauses:

They (must have) liked the apartment, *or* they wouldn't have stayed so long. [1]

Here *or* may be viewed as the negative counterpart of *because* used as an inferential disjunct (*cf* 15.21):

They (must have) liked the apartment, *because* they stayed there the whole summer. [1a]

The implication of *or* in [1] can be emphasized by adding the conjunct *else* (*cf* 8.137, 8.144, 8.146): . . . *or else they wouldn't have stayed so long. Or* can also be replaced by the conjunct *otherwise*: . . . *otherwise they wouldn't have stayed so long.*

The negative conditional *or* and the conditional *and* described in 13.25 are contrastingly related in meaning, as can be seen from the virtual synonymy of:

Make a move, *and* I'll shoot!
Don't make a move, *or* I'll shoot!

Note As with conditional *and*, the first conjoin with conditional *or* may be a verbless clause: *Your money or I shoot*. There is even the possibility that both conjoins are verbless: *Your money or your life* [='Give me your money, or I'll take your life'] (*cf* 11.53 Note).

And in relation to *or*

13.31 Because *and* and *or* contrast with one another in meaning, *or* following a negative is in some respects equivalent to *and*. Thus:

He doesn't have long hair *or* wear jeans. [1]

is logically equivalent to the combination of two negative statements '*He doesn't have long hair* AND *He doesn't wear jeans*'. Conversely:

He doesn't (*both*) have long hair *and* wear jeans. [2]

is logically equivalent to the inclusive disjunction of two negative statements: 'EITHER *He doesn't have long hair* OR *He doesn't wear jeans* (*or both*)'. The reversal of meaning arises because in [1] and [2], the coordinator is within the scope of negation (*cf* 10.64).

Hence *or* tends to replace *and* in contexts which we have called NONASSERTIVE (*cf* 2.53), and more generally in subordinate positions in the sentence:

Soldiers who mutinied *or* deserted were punished by death.
[= 'Soldiers who mutinied were punished by death, *and* soldiers who deserted were punished by death.']
If we complain *or* demand compensation, nothing happens.
[= 'If we complain nothing happens, *and* if we demand compensation nothing happens.']
He is good at painting with watercolours *or* with oil paints.

The same replacement takes place following *can*, *may*, and other expressions of permission or possibility:

You can go swimming *or* simply sit on the beach.
Permission has been granted for the play to be performed in public *or* private theatres.

In this last sentence, *and* could be substituted for *or* without effective change of meaning.

The use of *but*

13.32 *But* expresses a contrast which could usually be alternatively expressed by *and* followed by *yet*. The contrast may be in the unexpectedness of what is said in the second conjoin in view of the content of the first conjoin:

John is poor, *but* he is happy. ['. . . *and yet* he is happy']

This sentence implies that his happiness is unexpected in view of his poverty. The unexpectedness depends on our presuppositions and our experience of the world. It would be reasonable to say:

John is rich, *but* he is happy.

if we considered wealth a source of misery.

The contrast expressed by *but* may also be a repudiation in positive terms of what has been said or implied by negation in the first conjoin (*cf* 13.42):

Jane did *not* waste her time before the exam, *but* studied hard every evening. [1]

In such cases the force of *but* can be emphasized by the conjunct *rather* or *on the contrary* (*cf* 8.137):

I am *not* objecting to his morals, *but rather* to his manners. [2]

With this meaning, *but* normally does not link two clauses, but two smaller constituents; for example, the conjoins are two predicates in [1] and two prepositional phrases in [2]. The conjoins cannot be regarded as formed simply by ellipsis from two full clauses, since the *not* in the first clause conjoin is repudiated in the second. Thus the expansion of [2] into two full clauses must be as follows:

I am *not* objecting to his morals, *but* (*rather*) I am objecting to his manners.

Correlatives

13.33 To reinforce or clarify the conjoining function of *and*, it is frequently possible to place the word *both* in front of the first conjoin:

He has met (*both*) her mother *and* her father.

Similarly, *either* can be placed in front of the first conjoin to reinforce *or*, and there is a further correlative pair *neither . . . nor*:

He has met (*either*) her mother *or* her father.
He has met *neither* her mother *nor* her father.

This last construction is equivalent to:

He has*n't* met *either* her mother *or* her father.

where *either* and *or* are within the scope of negation (*cf* 13.31).

These pairs *both* . . . *and*, *either* . . . *or*, and *neither* . . . *nor* are termed CORRELATIVES, composed of an endorsing item (*cf* 13.5) and a coordinator. We may add to them two correlatives with *but*: *not* . . . *but* and *not only* . . . *but* (*cf* 13.42). Attention will first be given to *either* . . . *or* as the most straightforward correlative pair.

Note [**a**] On correlative subordinators such as *if* . . . *then*, *whether* . . . *or*, *cf* 14.13.
[**b**] On the 'misplacing' of the endorsing item, *cf* 13.40.

Either . . . or

13.34 *Either* . . . *or* emphasizes the EXCLUSIVE meaning of *or* (*cf* 13.28):

Either the room is too small *or* the piano is too large.

The conjoins may be complete clauses, as above, or else smaller constituents which are often related by ellipsis to complete clauses:

You may *either* [stand up] *or* [sit down].
Either [Sylvia] *or* [her sister] will be staying with us.

These sentences illustrate coordinated predications and coordinated subjects respectively.

Both . . . and

13.35 *Both* . . . *and* emphasizes the ADDITIVE meaning of *and* (*cf* 13.27). It separates the conjoins and puts them on the same footing, thereby dissociating the conjoins from the *consequential* or *sequent* relation (*cf* 13.23) that might otherwise be implied. Contrast:

David loves Joan *and* (therefore) wants to marry her.
David *both* loves Joan *and* wants to marry her.

Both . . . *and* also singles out the segregatory meaning of *and* (*cf* 13.59–63) rather than the combinatory use. Note the difference between:

David and Joan got divorced. [*ie* 'from each other']
Both David and Joan got divorced. ['so now they can get married']

At first sight, *both* . . . *and* appears to stand in the same relationship to *and* as *either* . . . *or* does to *or*. But in fact, *both* . . . *and* is not admissible where the conjoins are full finite clauses. There must be some kind of ellipsis. Hence, while we can have:

Mary washed the dishes *and* Peter dried them.

we cannot have:

**Both* Mary washed the dishes *and* Peter dried them.

On the other hand, *both* can be inserted if the conjoins are predicates or predications:

Mary *both* washed the dishes *and* dried them.
This new machine will *both* accelerate the copying process *and* improve the quality of reproduction.

or if the conjoins are phrases:

Both Mary *and* Peter washed the dishes.
The regulations are *both* very precise *and* very detailed.

Note *Both* . . . *and* can be awkward when they coordinate subordinate (finite or nonfinite) clauses, especially when those clauses have an overt subject:

We want someone *both* who is able *and* whom we can trust.
They have asked *both* for the floor to be repolished *and* for the lighting to be improved.

The second of these sentences is less objectionable than the first.

Nor, neither

13.36 *Nor* and *neither* can be used as negative additive adverbs (*cf* 8.116) without being a correlative pair. They generally presuppose that a previous clause is negative either explicitly, as in [1], or implicitly, as in [2] and [3]:

He did *not* receive any assistance from the authorities *nor* did he believe their assurance that action would soon be taken. ⟨rather formal⟩ [1]
Many people are *only* dimly aware of the ways in which the environment can be protected. *Nor* have governments made sufficient efforts to educate them. ⟨formal⟩ [2]
All the students were obviously very *miserable*. *Nor* were the teachers satisfied with the conditions at the school. ⟨formal⟩ [3]

Notice that *nor* in these examples is not the equivalent of *or* plus *not*, as might be thought from its morphological composition. Rather, it is nearer to being the equivalent of *and* plus *not* (*cf* 13.31). Thus:

They *never* forgave him for the insult, *nor* could he rid himself of feelings of guilt for having spoken that way. ⟨formal⟩ [4]

has much the same meaning as the more informal:

They *never* forgave him for the insult, *and* he could *not* rid himself of feelings of guilt for having spoken that way *either*. [4a]

In all the sentences [1–4], *neither* can replace *nor* without change of meaning. For many speakers (*cf* 13.18 Note [b]) both *neither* and *nor* can be linked to preceding sentences by *and* or *but*:

They never forgave him for the insult, $\left\{\begin{matrix}(\textit{and})\\(\textit{but})\end{matrix}\right\}\left\{\begin{matrix}\textit{neither}\\\textit{nor}\end{matrix}\right\}$ could he rid himself of the feelings of guilt for having spoken in that way. [4b]

This possibility excludes them from the class of central coordinators (*cf* 13.10, 13.19). Moreover, as the above examples show, *neither* and *nor* require subject–operator inversion when they introduce a clause, a feature which they share with negative adjuncts such as *never* and *nowhere* when they occur initially (*cf* 18.24).

On the other hand, by the criteria of meaning (*and* + *not*), of immobility, and susceptibility to asyndetic use (*cf* 13.11), *neither* and *nor* show themselves to be among that class of linking adverbs which most resemble coordinators.

Note In a formal and elevated style *nor* can be used where there is no negative implication at all in the first clause:

> This unique product carries a brand name that represents an entire country; *nor* is this an accident. [='and this is no accident']

The correlatives *neither . . . nor*

13.37 When *neither* . . . *nor* constitutes a correlative pair, on the other hand, *nor* functions as a central coordinator, like *and* and *or*, and *neither* as an endorsing item, like *both* and *either*. For example, the coordinated predicates of:

> David *loves Joan* and *wants to marry her.*

can be negated either by adding the negator *not* in each predicate:

> David does*n't* love Joan, *and* (*so*) does*n't* want to marry her. [1]

or by substituting the correlatives *neither* . . . *nor*:

> David *neither* loves Joan, *nor* wants to marry her. [2]

Whereas [1], however, tends to connote a consequential relation between the clauses, the correlatives in [2] emphasize that the negation applies to both conjoins. Correlative *neither* is mobile, its position reflecting the scope of negation (*cf* 10.63):

> Sam *neither* [has long hair], *nor* [wears jeans].
> Mary was *neither* [happy] *nor* [sad].
> *Neither* [Peter] *nor* [his wife] wanted the responsibility.

The same restriction applies to *neither* . . . *nor* as to *both* . . . *and* (*cf* 13.35); these correlatives cannot be used to negate whole clauses, as in:

> **Neither* Peter wanted the responsibility, *nor* his wife did.

Note The correlative *neither* . . . *nor*, being the negative counterpart of *both* . . . *and*, conveys a correspondingly additive meaning. Thus the use of *and* for other than additive purpose (*eg* to express a contrast or a condition; *cf* 13.24–5) has no parallel in *neither* . . . *nor*.

A 'mixed' construction with *neither . . . nor*

13.38 In 13.36–7 we have discussed *neither* and *nor* first as additive adverbs and second as correlative coordinators. These two grammatical roles are in principle quite distinct, but in practice are often superficially similar. It is not surprising that there exists a 'mixed' construction, in which *neither* and *nor* behave like additive adverbs, but are at the same time correlative, and have the 'segregatory' meaning associated with *both* . . . *and* (*cf* 13.59*ff*):

> Sam *neither* has long hair, *nor* does he wear jeans.
> Mary was *neither* happy, *nor* was she sad.
> ?Peter *neither* wanted the responsibility, *nor* did his wife.
> They have *neither* replied to my letters, *nor* have they answered my telephone calls.

Here, *neither* appears in a medial adverbial position in the first clause, and *nor* appears in initial position in the second clause, followed by subject–operator inversion. The meaning of this construction is the same as that of the corresponding construction with correlative coordination (*cf* 13.37). But the units which follow them in each clause are not equivalent, as one would expect them to be if this were a construction of coordination. This is clear when square brackets are inserted in the examples above, enclosing putative conjoins:

Sam *neither* [has long hair], *nor* [does he wear jeans].

Careful users of the language may indeed prefer to recast such a sentence in accordance with the principles outlined in 13.40:

Sam *neither* [has long hair], *nor* [wears jeans].

Restrictions on correlatives

13.39 According to a didactic tradition, the use of correlative coordinators is unacceptable when there are three or more conjoins:

?We are *both* willing, able, *and* ready to carry out the survey. [1]
?*Either* the Minister, *or* the Under-secretary, *or* the Permanent Secretary will attend the meeting. [2]
?Tompkins has *neither* the personality, the energy, *nor* the experience to win this election. [3]

(This restriction is felt especially strongly in the case of *both*.) *Both*, *either*, and *neither* (like *whether*; *cf* 15.6) are all historically associated with dual constructions, and these words have dual meaning when they occur as determiners in noun phrases (*cf* 6.50, 6.61, 6.62). The parallel between examples such as the following suggests that the initial word in [4] is in fact a determiner just as it is in [5]:

Both { her mother *and* her father [4] / her parents [5] } are alive.

But *both* cannot be classed as a determiner in sentences where the conjoins are not noun phrases:

He is a well-known writer *both* in Britain *and* on the Continent.

It is perhaps understandable, then, that the use of correlatives with more than two conjoins is judged if anything a more obvious stylistic 'fault' in [6], where the conjoins are noun phrases, than in [1], where they are not:

?**Both* her mother, her father, *and* her brother are still alive. [6]

Although commonly stigmatized, multiple correlatives such as [1–3] can add clarity to constructions whose complexity might otherwise cause confusion. For this reason, such constructions are sometimes used even in careful written English, *eg* in the rubric of an examination paper:

Candidates are required to answer *EITHER* Question 1 *OR* Question 2 *OR* Questions 3 and 4.

13.40 Grammatical tradition also holds that correlative coordinators should introduce constituents of equivalent function and status. (This reflects a general constraint that the conjoins of a coordinate construction must be equivalent; *cf* 13.88.) Hence in written English [1a] is preferred to [1b], and [2a] to [2b]:

?Evelyn is *either* [stupid], *or* [pretends that she is]. [1a]
Either [Evelyn is stupid], *or* [she pretends that she is]. [1b]

?I admire *both* [the drawings of Rembrandt] *and* [of Rubens]. [2a]
I admire *both* [the drawings of Rembrandt] *and* [those of Rubens]. [2b]

The bracketed portions of the above sentences are the conjoins which are marked off by the correlatives. The conjoins are comparable units in [1b] (where they are whole clauses) and [2b] (where they are noun phrases), but not in [1a] and [2a].

With *both* ... *and* and *either* ... *or*, the constraint that the conjoins delimited by the correlatives should be constituents of the same kind of status is frequently violated in speech, but is generally observed in careful written English. With *neither* ... *nor*, as we saw in 13.37*f*, the constraint is more frequently ignored, because there is a tendency to treat *nor* as an adverb (with subject–operator inversion; *cf* 18.24) rather than as a coordinator.

13.41 A further restriction on correlatives is that the first correlative word *both*, *either*, etc can occur only at a point which is the beginning of a phrase. Hence in the following examples, the [a] sentence is acceptable, whereas the [b] sentence is not:

The building is *both* [very old] *and* [very decrepit]. [1a]
*The building is very *both* [old] *and* [decrepit]. [1b]

The car's disappointing performance is due to *either* [faulty steering] *or* [faulty suspension]. [2a]
*The car's disappointing performance is due to faulty *either* [steering] *or* [suspension]. [2b]

(Again the conjoins are marked by square brackets.) The unacceptable feature of [1b] and [2b] is the placement of the initial coordinator between the modifier and the head, rather than at the beginning of the phrase. To avoid this, we can place (as in [1a] and [2a]) the coordinator in front of the modifier, and repeat the modifier in the second conjoin. This restriction means that the ambiguity of *old men and women* (*cf* 13.67) cannot occur with a correlative such as *both* ... *and*.

Not (only) ... but

13.42 The negator *not/n't* or the combination *not/n't only* may be correlative with a following *but*:

He did*n't* come to help, *but* to hinder us.
They *not only* broke into his office and stole his books, *but* (they) (*also*) tore up his manuscripts.

The repudiatory meaning of *not/n't . . . but* has already been noted (*cf* 13.32). The meaning of *not only . . . but* is essentially additive, like that of *both . . . and*: it distinguishes rather than equates the conjoins, forcing us to look at the first conjoin as 'given' ground. But with *not only . . . but* the emphasis is greater, suggesting that the content of the first clause is surprising, and that that of the second clause, often reinforced by an adverb such as *also* or *even*, is still more surprising. What particularly makes these combinations resemble correlatives is the option of moving the negative particle out of its normal position following the operator, so as to mark the parallelism between the two conjoins:

Not [Henry], *but* [his wife] is the owner. [1]
He came *not* [to help], *but* [to hinder us]. [2]
Not only [did they break into his office and steal his books], *but* [they also tore up his manuscripts]. [3]

The more dramatic effect achieved by positioning *not only* initially, with subject–operator inversion (*cf* 18.24), is illustrated by [3], where the two conjoins are entire clauses.

Note [a] The *not . . . but . . .* construction frequently occurs in a cleft sentence (*cf* 18.26*ff*): *It isn't the players, but the supporters, that are responsible for football hooliganism.*

[b] The correlatives (*just*) *as . . . so*, which have an emphatic effect similar to that of *not only . . . but* (*also*), are correlative subordinators rather than correlative coordinators (*cf* 14.13):

Just as they must put aside their prejudices, *so* we must be prepared to accept their good faith.

Cf also the correlatives *rather . . . than* and *not so much . . . as* (13.103, 15.52).

[c] Once *not* is moved out of its post-operator position, as in [1–3] above, it cannot of course occur in its enclitic form.

[d] There is a type of repudiatory coordination *and not . . .* in which the relation between the clauses is the reverse of that of *not . . . but* described above: *He came to help, and not to hinder us.* In this type, where the negative occurs in the second conjoin, a repudiatory force can also be expressed asyndetically, by omitting the coordinator: *He came to help, not to hinder us.*

Coordination of clause constituents

13.43 Although we regarded the clause as the most appropriate unit to start with in considering the use of coordinators (*cf* 13.20), the exemplification of correlatives in 13.33–42 has shown that the conjoins of a coordinate construction in many instances are, and in some instances have to be, smaller than a clause. In the following sections we deal in detail with single clauses or clause constituents which may be coordinated by means of *and*, *or*, or *but*. We will call this usual kind of coordination SIMPLE COORDINATION, and will distinguish it from less straightforward and less common types of coordination, *viz* COMPLEX COORDINATION or coordination of groups of constituents (*cf* 13.90–93), and APPENDED COORDINATION (*cf* 13.94). For the purpose of simple coordination, a conjoin may be any constituent such as a predicate, a predication, a phrase, or a word. The important point, however, is that the conjoins of each construction are parallel to one another in meaning, function, and also (generally) in form (*cf* 2.12).

Ellipsis and simple coordination

13.44 There are two different ways of examining simple coordination of clause constituents. On the one hand, we may examine a construction as an elliptical version of clause coordination, noting what elements are ellipted; and on the other hand, we may examine the construction in terms of the conjoins themselves – *viz* the elements which are left intact. These two different approaches are reflected in different principles of analysis. For example, the coordinate construction in:

They have already [finished their work] and △ [gone home]. [1]

can be viewed as a clause coordination in which a subject, operator, and adverbial have been ellipted; or it can be viewed as a single clause containing two coordinate predications. For simple coordination (though less so for other kinds of coordination) there are advantages in adopting the latter method as the major one (*cf* especially 13.47, 13.60). Thus in [1] we shall be interested in the fact that the conjoins (marked here, and in subsequent examples, by square brackets) are predications, and less interested in what elements have been omitted at the point marked by the symbol △.

Note We regard ellipsis as a relation of systematic correspondence (*cf* 2.20) between sentences. We therefore do not consider the explanations of [1] in terms of ellipsis and in terms of coordination of clause constituents as in competition with one another. Rather, they are complementary accounts: one focusing on sentence structure, and the other on intersentential relations (*cf* 2.20, 2.46).

Limits of ellipsis

13.45 Not all cases of coordination can be explained in terms of ellipsis. Although [1] in 13.44 could be expanded into:

They have already finished their work and *they have already gone home.* [1a]

a similar expansion could not be attempted for such cases as:

Many young wives [go to work] *and* [put their children in a playgroup]. [2]
I have never grown [apples] *or* [pears]. [3]
The national flag of Japan is [red] *and* [white]. [4]
[My sister] *and* [her husband] live in Texas. [5]
[Your house] *and* [mine] are similar (to each other). [6]

In the first place, [2] cannot be seen as an elliptical version of:

Many young wives go to work, and many young wives put their children in a playgroup. [7]

since [2] has a different meaning from [7]. The same applies if we try to expand [3] to:

I have never grown apples or I have never grown pears. [8]

The lack of synonymy, in these two examples, can be explained in terms of scope (*cf* 2.55*ff*): the scope of the quantifier *many* includes *and* in [2] but not in [7]; similarly, the scope of the negative word *never* includes *or* in [3] but not in [8].

It is for a semantic reason, too, that [4] cannot be regarded as a reduction of the self-contradictory sentence:

*The national flag of Japan is red, and the national flag of Japan is white. [9]

On the other hand, it is grammatical concord that prevents the expansion of [5] into:

*My sister live in Texas and her husband live in Texas. [10]

13.46 The last example in 13.45 is a reminder that two or more singular noun phrases, when coordinated by *and*, become plural, and therefore require concord with a plural verb (*cf* 10.37). With [6] in 13.45 above, the difficulty of the explanation of coordination by ellipsis is compounded: not only does grammatical concord fail in the unelliptical version [6a], but also the reciprocal pronoun *each other* cannot make sense in the absence of a plural noun phrase:

*Your house are similar (to each other), and mine are similar (to each other). [6a]

This nonsensical sentence also illustrates the more general point that, in addition to *each other*, there is a whole range of expressions (*be similar*, *be different*, *be the same*, *be in love*, *play chess*, *get married*, etc) which, when predicated of a noun phrase coordinated by *and*, can be interpreted in a reciprocal or symmetric manner (*cf* 13.60):

Margot and Dennis are in love. [11]

Thus in one obvious interpretation, [11] expresses a mutual relation ('. . . in love with each other') which is not suggested by the sentence:

Margot is in love and Dennis is in love. [12]

We return to such differences under the heading of combinatory and segregatory coordination (*cf* 13.59–63), but for the present we simply note the problems of concord, meaning, and scope that arise when a general attempt is made to interpret constituent coordination in terms of ellipsis.

Semantic implications of constituent coordination

13.47 These observations, and others, may be looked at from the opposite point of view – as evidence in favour of regarding simple coordination as what it appears to be on the surface – *viz* as a formation of a compound unit which is functionally analogous to each of its conjoined members. To understand the verb phrase coordination of *Peter washed and dried the dishes*, for example, we do not have to postulate a rather complex ellipsis of the object in the first clause and the subject in the second:

Peter washed (the dishes) *and* (Peter) dried the dishes.

but instead can treat *washed and dried* in [1] below as a verb element functionally comparable to *washed* in [2] and *dried* in [3]:

Subject	Verb	Object	
Peter	*washed and dried*	the dishes	[1]
Peter	*washed*	the dishes	[2]
Peter	*dried*	the dishes	[3]

This analysis is strengthened by the fact that in [1] *washed and dried* is typically interpreted as a single combined activity (*What are you doing to the dishes? I'm washing and drying them*), rather than as two separate activities.

A further example, this time of verb-words coordinated to form a single verb phrase of complex construction, shows the same principle at work at a lower level in the hierarchy of grammatical units:

Adam is *checking* and *revising* his manuscript. [4]

There is, in other words, a close correspondence between the structural aspect of coordination and the semantic aspect which accompanies it. This matching of meaning to form applies more strikingly in cases where the difference of meaning between clause coordination and constituent coordination is more obvious, as in questions with coordinated predications:

Did Peter [tell lies] *and* [hurt his friends]?

This is a single question about two events in combination; but:

[Did Peter tell lies], *and* [did he hurt his friends]?

is interpreted as two separate questions. Similarly:

Did John [break the window] *but* [refuse to pay for it]?

is a single question about John's past behaviour, which may be answered *yes* or *no*. But in this case a corresponding example of clause coordination would be impossible, because there is no intelligible way in which *but* can serve as a link between two questions:

*Did John break the window, *but* did he refuse to pay for it?

This difference may be explained in terms of the scope of interrogation (*cf* 2.55).

Note In similar questions containing *or*, there can be ambiguity, resolved by intonation, between interpretation as an ordinary *yes–no* question and as an alternative question (*cf* 11.20–21):

Did you [play football] *or* [go for a WÁLK]?

Did you [play FÓOTball] *or* [go for a WÀLK]?

Only in the latter case can the sentence be expanded into a coordination of two complete clauses:

[Did you play FÓOTball] *or* [did you go for a WÀLK]?

13.48 There is a similar implication of combined process when the two conjoined predications are within the scope of negation (*cf* 13.45). For example:

John DÌDn't [break the window] *but* [refuse to pay for it]. [1]

This is a denial of the statement:

John [broke the window] *but* [refused to pay for it]. [2]

As a negation of a combined process, [1] could evoke the retort *Yes, he did*. On the other hand, two separate processes are expressed by the clause and predicate coordinations of [3] and [4], and the scope of negation in the first conjoin does not extend to the second conjoin:

John did*n't* break the window, *but* he offered to pay for it. [3]
John did*n't* break the window, *but* he refused to pay for it. [4]
[= 'The claim is *not* that John broke the window, *but* that he refused to pay for its repair.']

Clearly [4] cannot be regarded as a semantically-equivalent unreduced version of [1].

There is a similar effect of negation in the slogan *Don't drink and drive*, the force of which is not to forbid either activity, but only to forbid both in combination. This directive therefore has a different meaning from the more severe prohibition: *Don't drink and don't drive*.

13.49 There is no doubt that ellipsis is important to the understanding of coordination, particularly with respect to meaning and style. But in the first instance, there is more to be gained from a purely structural view of coordination. This means that we regard coordination as a type of linkage whereby the resulting CONJOINT construction is equivalent, structurally speaking, to each of its members. For example, a noun phrase may act as subject of a clause; and likewise, a coordinated construction (or CONJOINT NOUN PHRASE) whose conjoins are noun phrases may also act as subject. Equally, if an adjective may act as head of an adjective phrase, then a coordinated construction whose conjoins are adjectives may also act as head of an adjective phrase. In more formulaic terms:

If [A], [B], . . . are conjoins of the conjoint construction X, then any structural function which may be taken individually by [A] or [B] or . . . may also be taken by X.

This generalization applies to all cases of simple coordination, and after slight extension will also apply to other cases of coordination.

Note [**a**] The generalization above should not be understood to deny that the privilege of occurrence of X may be different from those of [A], [B], . . . with regard to concord; *eg* [A] may be singular, and X may be plural, as in *[John] and [Mary] are friends* (*cf* 13.46).

[**b**] Apart from coordination, there are other types of construction for which the whole construction has the same privilege of occurrence as its members; *eg* some types of apposition (*cf* 17.65*f*):

We have been invited to meet *the Principal, Mrs Joyce*.

Types of simple coordination

Coordination of clauses

13.50 We have already illustrated the coordination of complete independent clauses:

[The winter had come at last], *and* [snow lay thick on the ground].
[Who are you], *and* [where do you live]?
[Have a look at the engine], *but* [don't take it to pieces].

Dependent clauses may also be coordinated, so long as they belong to the same function class:

If you pass the examination and (*if*) *no one else applies*, you are bound to get the job.
[COORDINATE ADVERBIAL CLAUSES] [1]

The Minister believes *that the economy is improving*, and (*that*) *unemployment will soon decrease*.
[COORDINATE NOMINAL *THAT*-CLAUSES] [2]

I didn't know *who she was*, or *what she wanted*.
[COORDINATE NOMINAL *WH*-CLAUSES] [3]

Someone *who knows the area*, but *whose home is outside it*, is more likely to be a successful representative.
[COORDINATE RELATIVE CLAUSES] [4]

In [1–2], the repetition of the introductory subordinator could be avoided by ellipsis of the second subordinator. However, against the principle of 'reduce where possible' must be set the opposite tendency to avoid ellipsis where it leads to ambiguity. It is more likely that the second *if* would be omitted in [1] than the second *that* in [2], because in [2] the sentence would be ambiguous, the second conjoin . . . *and unemployment will soon decrease* being interpretable as a main clause.

Nonfinite dependent clauses (*cf* 14.6–8) may also be coordinated:

I've asked him *to come this evening*, or (*to*) *phone us tomorrow*.
[COORDINATE *TO*-INFINITIVE CLAUSES] [5]

Samantha is fond of *working at night* and *getting up late in the morning*.
[COORDINATE *-ING* PARTICIPLE CLAUSES] [6]

All the villagers helped to rebuild the houses *damaged by the storm* or *washed away by the floods*.
[COORDINATE *-ED* PARTICIPLE CLAUSES] [7]

Again, if the initial subordinating word (such as the *to* in [5]) is common to both clauses, it may be omitted in the second and subsequent occurrences. A final category to be illustrated is that of coordinate verbless clauses (*cf* 14.9, 15.60):

With George ill and (*with*) *the children at home*, Jenny is finding life very difficult.

13.51 As noted earlier (*cf* 13.47, 13.49), the members of coordinate constructions tend to be parallel both in their structure and in their meaning. It is therefore quite usual for coordinate subordinate clauses to belong to the same semantic as well as functional category, or to share the same subordinator (as in [1–2]). Conversely, it is unusual for adverbial clauses to be coordinated if they belong to different categories, such as those of time and place (*cf* 8.2*ff*). The following are therefore unusual:

> *In order that you may submit a claim without delay* and *because you did not receive the form we sent earlier*, I suggest that you write again giving the fullest details.
>
> The book will be dispatched *as soon as the payment is received* and *unless the order is cancelled*.
>
> *When the pale sun rose briefly over the horizon*, and *wherever they looked*, the desert of ice seemed to stretch out to infinity.

A preferred construction in the last case would be one in which the two clauses functioned as adverbials of the same clause, but in different positions, and without being coordinated:

> *When the pale sun rose briefly over the horizon*, the desert of ice seemed to stretch out to infinity *wherever they looked*.

On the other hand *wh*-clauses introduced by different *wh*-words, such as those of 13.50 [3], can be coordinated with relative ease.

It is scarcely acceptable for different types of nonfinite clause to be coordinated, or for finite dependent clauses to be coordinated with nonfinite clauses, even where there is a strong semantic affinity between the two clauses. Occasional examples such as the following occur:

> The empress, *nearing her death* and *surrounded by doctors and necromancers*, was no longer in control of her ministers.
>
> The curfew bell rang at sunset every evening, *to warn the citizens that it was time for bed*, and *so that secret defensive measures could be taken by the army*.

But it seems impossible, for example, to coordinate a nominal infinitive with an *-ing* clause:

> *George likes *going to the races* and *to bet on the horses*.

Nor is it normal to coordinate a postmodifying relative clause with a postmodifying nonfinite clause:

> ?Charles was longing to talk to the girl *sitting in the corner* and *who had smiled at him*.

Instead of such hybrid coordinations, means have to be found to preserve equivalence of both the form and function of the conjoins:

> Charles was longing to talk to the girl *who was sitting in the corner* and *who had smiled at him*.

or else we have to juxtapose the modifiers without coordination, thus including the first modifier in the scope of the second:

Charles was longing to talk to the girl *sitting in the corner who had smiled at him*. (= [[the girl sitting in the corner] who had smiled at him])

Note [**a**] When clauses are conjoined, the noninitial conjoins often contain general ellipsis of the kinds dealt with in 12.59–65:

[Bob seemed angry], *and* [Eva certainly was △].

[Mary's parents did their best to protect her], *but* [[she wished that they wouldn't △], *and* [finally she asked them not to △]].

This does not affect the status of the conjoins as clauses (*cf* also appended coordination, 13.94).

[**b**] On the coordination of subordinators (*if and when, when and where*, etc) *cf* 13.83.

Coordination of predicates

13.52 In coordination of predicates (*cf* 2.47), which is very common, the conjoined predicates may be described as sharing the same subject:

Peter *ate the fruit* and *drank the beer*. [1]

I *send you my very best wishes* and *am looking forward to our next meeting*. [2]

Margaret *is ill*, but *will soon recover*. [3]

The predicates may, of course, have varied structures in terms of clause elements. For example, [1] and [2] have structures which can be represented as follows:

[1]: S [V O] and [V O] [2]: S [V O_i O_d] and [V A A]

Such sentences may be seen as elliptical alternatives to coordinated clauses, for example:

Peter ate the fruit, and *Peter/he drank the beer*. [1a]

But, on the whole, repetition of the subject is avoided where possible. In other cases (*cf* 13.45*f*), no elliptical explanation of the sentence is possible:

Two young men ate the fruit and (also) drank the beer. [4]

[≠ Two young men ate the fruit, and two young men drank the beer]

This is because for coordination of two predicates to take place, the subject of the one predicate must be coreferential with the subject of the other. Thus [4] is synonymous with the sentence which differs from it only in that a coreferential *they* is inserted before the second verb:

Two young men ate the fruit and *they* (also) drank the beer. [4a]

Note [**a**] It is common to insert a comma (or other punctuation) before the coordinator in conjoined clauses, but it is much less common to insert a comma before the coordinator in conjoined predicates. Hence [1] above is written with no comma, whereas in [1a] the comma is inserted. (The commas inserted in [2] and [3] are optional; *cf* App III.7.) This characteristic difference is one sign of the greater cohesiveness of the coordinated predicate: something which accords with the view that the major constituent boundary in such cases is between the subject and a conjoint predicate, rather than between the end of one clause and the beginning of another. Putting it more simply, we may say that in [1a] there are two clauses, while in [1] there is one clause with a conjoint predicate; this is shown in *Fig* 13.52 opposite. This constituent-structure account of predicate coordination does not, of course, prevent the postulation of ellipsis where criteria (*cf* 12.32–38) of ellipsis apply; *cf* 13.44 Note.

[**b**] The distinction between coordinate predicates and other coordinate constructions is sometimes neutralized. In the coordination of imperative clauses, *eg*: *Sit down and listen to this*,

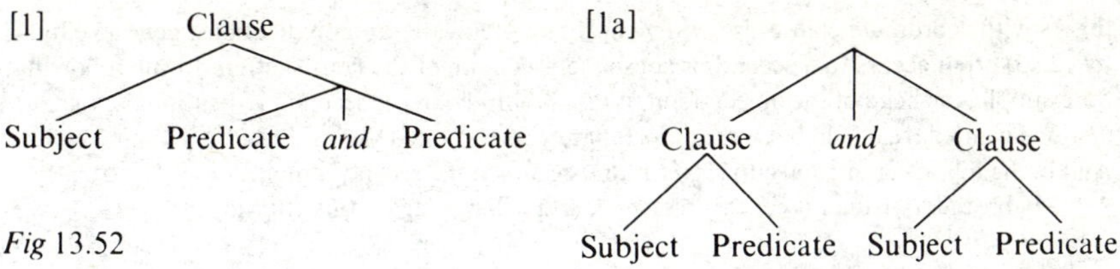

Fig 13.52

where there is no overt subject, this construction could be equally described as a coordination either of clauses or of predicates. (Contrast the imperative with a subject: *You sit down and listen* (*to this*) is likely to be one clause with coordinate predicates, whereas *Sit down and just you listen* (*to this*) has to be two coordinate clauses.) In *Mary skipped and jumped*, on the other hand, there is a different type of neutralization: this example could be analysed as containing two conjoined predicates, *skipped* and *jumped*, or alternatively as containing a single predicate (*skipped and jumped*) within which two verb phrases are conjoined. Yet a third possibility is that *skipped and jumped* is a single verb phrase, within which the main verbs are conjoined. Similar alternative analyses arise with coordination in relation to the scope of adverbials (*cf* 13.54–5).

Coordination of predications

13.53 Coordination of predications (*cf* 2.48), as of predicates, is very common, and often involves ellipsis. Consider the following examples:

Most people will have *read the book* or *seen the film*. [1]
They should have *washed the dishes*, *dried them*, and *put them in the cupboard*. [2]
You must *take the course* and *pass the examination*. [3]
They were *married in 1960*, but *divorced in 1970*. [4]
Are you *working* or *on holiday*? [5]
Why couldn't she *have finished work late* and *still be travelling home*? [6]

In all cases it is possible to regard the auxiliary or auxiliaries preceding the predication as ellipted. Thus [1], although we cannot regard it as equivalent to two coordinated clauses, can be regarded as an ellipted version of predicate coordination:

Most people will have read the book or ((will) have) seen the film. [1a]

As with predicate coordination itself, however, the most reduced form of the sentence will tend to be preferred; hence the omission of *will have* will be preferred in [1a]. As [2] shows, more than one auxiliary can be ellipted in the second and subsequent conjoins; and as [6] shows, it is also possible (though rare) for the coordinated predications to contain auxiliaries. What is not possible, however, is the omission of a repeated operator combined with the realization of a repeated or coreferential subject:

**You* must take the course and *you* △ pass the examination.
*Are *you* working or △ *you* on holiday?

This would no longer be a case of simple coordination, since the conjoins would consist of two separate constituents which are not coconstituents of a larger constituent: *viz* subject and predication (*cf* 13.90*f*).

Note [**a**] For the same reason, it is not possible for the second of two repeated auxiliaries to be ellipted without the ellipsis of the first:

*Most people will have read the book or will seen the film.

[b] As with coordinate clauses, so with coordinate predicates and predications, general ellipsis (*cf* 12.43) often occurs in a second or subsequent conjoin of the construction. In the following, for example, the head of the object noun phrase is ellipted in the second predication:

We wanted fried fish, but were unfortunately given boiled △.

And in the following, medial ellipsis (*cf* 12.62) occurs in the second conjoin:

My brother is using his car this morning, and will be △ again this afternoon.

Coordination and the scope of adverbials

13.54 In the types of coordination we have discussed, adverbials, as more peripheral elements of the clause (*cf* 2.13), often stand outside the structure of coordination:

Yesterday [the sun was very warm] and [the ice melted]. [1]

Although this example can reasonably be called coordination of clauses, the initial adverbial actually stands outside the two conjoins, and its meaning applies simultaneously to both of them. The structure of this sentence may be represented: A [S V C] + [S V]. Just as in 13.45 and 13.47 we noted that coordination could take place within the scope of interrogation and negation, so here we may say that the two conjoins are within the scope of the adverbial *yesterday*. The role of *yesterday* in [1] is therefore rather different from that which it has in the following:

[*Yesterday* the sun was very warm] and [*during the morning* the ice melted]. [2]

[*Yesterday* the sun was very warm] and [the ice has melted]. [3]

In [2], the appearance of an adverbial of the same semantic class in the second clause limits the scope of the first adverbial. In [3], for reasons of tense and aspect (*cf* 4.23), *yesterday* cannot apply to the second clause, and so it is restricted to the first conjoin. The formulae for these two examples are:

[2]: [A S V C] + [A S V]   [3]: [A S V C] + [S V]

There is good reason for saying that in a clause with an initial adverbial, as in *Yesterday the sun was very warm*, the whole of the clause including and following the subject is in the scope of the adverbial. This is partly on semantic grounds, and partly on grounds of punctuation and prosody: it is notable that if a prosodic or punctuation boundary occurs in such a clause, it will normally be located between the adverbial and the rest of the clause. The remainder of the clause, which thereby becomes a constituent in its own right (rather than a sequence of subject and predicate), may be termed the KERNEL of the clause. The type of coordination illustrated by [1] is classified as a coordination of two clause kernels. It is less common for a coordinate construction to come within the scope of a final adverbial; *eg* the analysis of:

The train arrived and we met our guests on time. [4]

would be [S V] + [S V O A] (where *on time* applies only to the second clause), rather than [S V] + [S V O] A.

Note The second interpretation of [4] could be obtained, however, if the sentence were a case of interpolated coordination (*cf* 13.95–7), with intonational or punctuational separation of the second conjoin:

The train arRÍVED, and we met our GÚESTS, on TÌME.

13.55 It is more usual, however, for a coordinate construction to be within the scope of adverbials where the conjoins are predicates or predications; *eg*:

Unfortunately we [missed the train] and [had to wait six hours]. [1]
The guests were [walking], [talking], and [drinking wine] *in the garden*. [2]

In [1], an example of predicate coordination, both the missing of the train and the long wait are regarded as *unfortunate*; and in [2], an example of predication coordination, all three activities are assumed to take place *in the garden*. (There is another possible interpretation of [2], however, whereby only the wine-drinking takes place in the garden.)

In the following more complex example of predicate coordination, the coordination takes place within the scope of three adverbials; one in initial, one in medial, and one in final position:

In those days they *often* used to [shoot the birds], [bring them home], [cook them] and [eat them] *on a single day*. [3]

Although the scope of the adverbial *on a single day* may be ambiguous here, by far the most likely interpretation is the one in which it applies to all four actions, as shown by the square brackets. But it is clear that the initial time adverbial has within its scope the whole of the rest of the sentence, and that *often* includes within its scope the whole of the predicate which follows it. Therefore a representation of the more likely interpretation of this sentence, with square brackets marking scope relations as well as the individual conjoins, is as follows:

In those days they [often used to [[shoot the birds,] [bring them home,] [cook them] and [eat them] on a single day]].

For an example of this complexity, it is obvious that no postulated elliptical conjoins could lead to a plausible correspondence with clause coordination:

?In those days they often used to shoot the birds on a single day,
in those days they often used to bring them home on a single day,
in those days they often used to cook them on a single day, *and*
in those days they often used to eat them on a single day.

Coordination of noun phrases and their constituents

Noun phrase coordination

13.56 In all positions where a noun phrase occurs (*eg* as subject, object, complement) there is also the possibility of a conjunction of two or more noun phrases, making up a CONJOINT noun phrase (*cf* 2.10, 13.49):

[Some of the staff], *and* [all of the students,] have voted for these changes. [SUBJECT]

On this farm, they keep [cows,] [sheep,] [pigs,] *and* [a few chickens.] [OBJECT]

Lucy Godwin is [a well-known broadcaster] *and* [winner of the Novelist of the Year Award for 1978]. [SUBJECT COMPLEMENT]

The plan was opposed by [Frederick,] [Mary,] *and* [me]. [PREPOSITIONAL COMPLEMENT]

Jane plays three instruments: [the piano,] [the viola,] *and* [the French horn]. [NOUN PHRASES IN APPOSITION]

These examples show how the conjoined noun phrases may be simple or complex, and may have a noun or a pronoun as their head. In fact, the structural possibilities of the conjoins are the same as for individual noun phrases (*cf* 2.25). One of the implications of this is that noun phrases in coordination may contain general ellipsis of the kinds discussed in 12.54–58. The first conjoin will often contain the antecedent for ellipsis in subsequent conjoins:

Which do you prefer: [the red *dress*,] [the green △,] *or* [the white △]?
It's [the longest *single-span bridge* in this country,] *and* [the second longest △ in the world].
That must be *either* [John's *writing*] *or* [Bridget's △].
There's little to choose between [that *method*] *and* [the other △].

Note [**a**] When one of the conjoins is a personal pronoun, it is considered polite to follow the order of placing 2nd person pronouns first, and (more importantly) 1st person pronouns last: *Jill and I* (not *I and Jill*); *you and Jill*, (not *Jill and you*), *you, Jill, or me* (not *me, you, or Jill*), etc.
[**b**] A complication arises if any of the coordinated noun phrases exemplified above is accompanied by one or more adverbials; *eg*:

Jane plays three instruments: the piano, the viola, and {*occasionally*, / *now and then*, / *last but not least*,} the French horn.

We can then no longer, strictly speaking, talk of noun phrase coordination; rather, this falls into a category of *complex coordination* to be discussed in 13.90*ff*.

But as a noun phrase coordinator

13.57 The use of *but* as a coordinator between noun phrases is restricted. *But* is seldom used in subject position, except where it has a repudiatory force following *not*, or an additive force following *not only*:

Not only [the students,] *but* [some of the staff] have voted for these changes.
We were disappointed to learn that *not* [a thousand,] *nor* [a hundred,] *but* [a mere twenty-three] had turned up for the inaugural meeting.

Even with these constructions, however, a nonsubject position is much more usual:

They applauded *not* the players *but* the referee.

Coordination of noun phrases by *but* in a nonsubject position is also liable to occur when *but* is followed by the adverb *only*, or by the clause substitute *not* (*cf* 12.28):

On this farm, they keep [[cows] and [sheep,]] *but* [*only* a few chickens]. [1]
[The plan was opposed by Frederick], *but* [*not* Maria]. [2]

Strictly, this last example is again a case of clause coordination, not noun phrase coordination. Elsewhere, *but* is frequently inappropriate as a phrase coordinator:

*On this farm, they keep cows *but* sheep, *and* only a few chickens.

When the conjoint noun phrase follows a preposition, as in [2], it is often stylistically preferable, for reasons of parallelism and clarity, to repeat the preposition, thereby replacing a conjoint noun phrase by a conjoint prepositional phrase, as in [3]:

The plan was opposed *not* [by Frederick] *but* [by Maria]. [3]

Note Another reason for repeating the preposition in [3] is the oddity of placing *not* between a preposition and its complement: ?*The plan was opposed by not Frederick but Maria.*

Multiple coordination of noun phrases

13.58 In noun phrase coordination, as in clause coordination (*cf* 13.16*f*), we have seen that it is possible to form constructions which are of more than two conjoins:

She asked me to buy [four oranges,] [a pound of plums,] *and* [a melon].

Asyndetic coordination (*cf* 13.1) of more than two noun phrases is also possible:

We had no friends, no family, no material resources.

and noun phrases may have polysyndetic coordination (with more than one coordinator; *cf* 13.17):

She asked me to buy [four oranges,] *and* [a pound of plums,] *and* [a melon].

There may also be, as in clause coordination, more than one level of coordination:

She asked me to buy [four oranges,] *and* [[one large melon] *or* [two small ones]].

Combinatory and segregatory coordination of noun phrases

13.59 When phrases linked by *and* function in the clause, they may express COMBINATORY or SEGREGATORY meaning. Combinatory coordination is coordination for which it is inappropriate to provide a paraphrase in terms of coordinated clauses; this is because the conjoins function 'in combination' with respect to the rest of the clause. When phrase coordination is segregatory, on the other hand, we can paraphrase it by clause coordination. The distinction applies to various kinds of coordinate construction, but is clearest with noun phrases. For example:

[John] *and* [Mary] make a pleasant couple.
[≠ *John makes a pleasant couple, and Mary makes a pleasant couple]
[John] *and* [Mary] know the answer.
[= John knows the answer, and Mary knows the answer]

Many conjoint noun phrases are ambiguous between a combinatory and a segregatory interpretation:

[John] *and* [Mary] won a prize.

This may mean either (a) that John and Mary each won a prize, or (b) that the prize was awarded jointly to them both. Reading (b), however, is preferred unless the insertion of *each* makes it clear that reading (a) is intended. (On the related topic of distributive number, *cf* 10.47.)

13.60 We may distinguish three kinds of combinatory meaning:

(a) JOINT PARTICIPATION
The conjoins are interpreted as jointly constituting a single participant (*cf* 10.18*ff*) in the process or relationship described by the clause. The sentence:

John and Mary played tennis against *Susan and Bill.* [1]

may refer to a single combined process, *viz* a game of doubles, as shown in *Fig* 13.60a; but the same sentence might also have a segregatory interpretation, referring to four games of singles as shown in *Fig* 13.60b.

A further segregatory interpretation involving two singles games, as represented in *Fig* 13.60c, is the one that would be selected if the adverb *respectively* were added to [1] (*cf* 13.63):

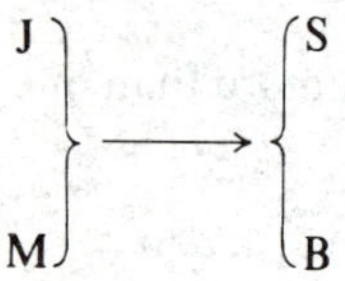

Fig 13.60a

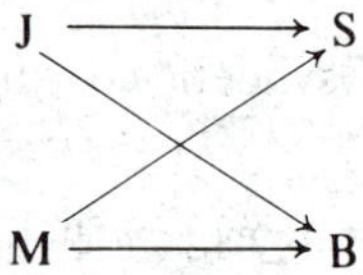

Fig 13.60b

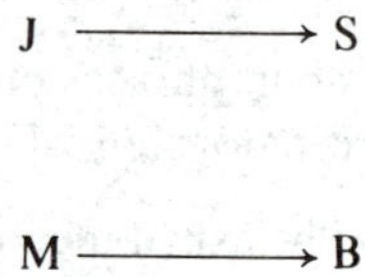

Fig 13.60c

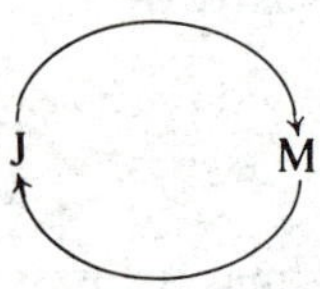

Fig 13.60d

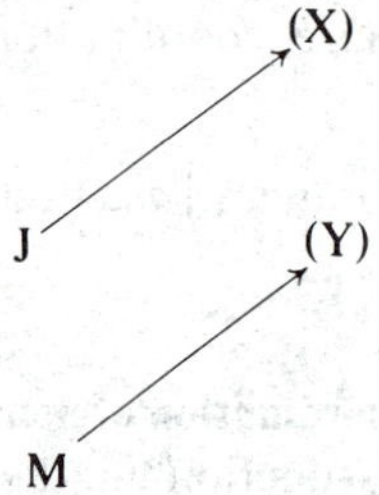

Fig 13.60e

KEY

J	John
M	Mary
S	Susan
B	Bill
X, Y	other players

(b) MUTUAL PARTICIPATION
The conjoins are interpreted as entering into a symmetric or reciprocal relation to each other, as indicated in *Fig* 13.60d. This is one interpretation of:

John and Mary played tennis.

But this sentence also allows a segregatory interpretation 'John and Mary each played tennis (with somebody)' as suggested by *Fig* 13.60e. The symmetric interpretation can be made explicit by adding or substituting some expression containing *each other* or *one another*.

Further examples of mutual participation are:

Peter and Bob separated.
Paula and her brother look alike.
Mary and Paul are just good friends.
John and Peter have different tastes.

Note the use of the plural nouns in complement position to indicate reciprocity:

Mary and Susan are sisters/cousins/colleagues (of each other).

The corresponding singular complement cannot be used with reciprocal meaning: ?*Mary is a cousin and Susan is a cousin.* But with the segregatory meaning of *Mary and Susan are teachers*, the corresponding conjoined singular constructions make an acceptable paraphrase: *Mary is a teacher and Susan is a teacher.* The same meaning of mutual participation occurs with three or more conjoins: *Smith, Brown, and Robinson became partners.*

(c) UNITARY PARTICIPATION
In some cases the conjoins are so closely linked in meaning that they participate in the meaning of the clause as if they referred to a single object. The whole phrase may behave as a singular noun phrase for purposes of concord (*cf* 10.37*ff*):

Law and order is a primary concern of the new administration.

Other examples are *fish and chips, a ball and chain, bread and butter, the Stars and Stripes*, and titles and names such as *Fathers and Sons* (a novel by Turgenev) and *the Fox and Hounds* (a public house). It is a characteristic of such unitary phrases that the order of the conjoins cannot be varied, and that no determiner precedes the second conjoin (*cf* 13.67).

Note [a] The distinction between combinatory and segregatory meaning applies not only to conjoint noun phrases, but to plural noun phrases in general. Thus the combinatory meanings of:

They are married. *The three girls* look alike.
We haven't met before. He painted the cars in *two colours.*

contrast with the segregatory meanings of *They are feverish*; *The three girls have a cold.*

[b] A special case of mutual participation is the use of *and* as a noun phrase coordinator following *between* (*cf* 9.39).

Indicators of segregatory meaning

13.61 Certain markers explicitly indicate that the coordination is segregatory:

both (. . . *and*)	*neither . . . nor*	*respectively* ⟨formal⟩
each	*respective* ⟨formal⟩	*apiece* ⟨rather rare⟩

While *John and Mary have won a prize* is ambiguous, we are left in no doubt that two prizes were won in:

John and Mary have *each* won a prize.
John and Mary have won a prize *each.*
Both John and Mary have won a prize.
John and Mary have *both* won a prize.

However, because of the distributive meaning of *each* (*cf* 6.51), there is a potential difference of meaning between [1] and [2]:

John and Mary have *each* won prizes. [1]
John and Mary have *both* won prizes. [2]

Both permits the distributive interpretation of *prizes* which occurs in [1] (= *John has won prizes and Mary has won prizes*), but also permits the nondistributive interpretation whereby *prizes* might refer to one prize won by John and another prize won by Mary.

Corresponding to the positive correlative *both . . . and* is the negative correlative *neither . . . nor*, which likewise has segregatory force:

John *and* Mary did*n't* win a prize. [3]
Neither John *nor* Mary won a prize. [4]

Whereas [3] is ambiguous, [4] is unambiguously segregatory, making it clear that two prize-winnings were involved. *Or* following a negative (*cf* 13.31) has a similar effect, seen in the contrast between the combinatory/segregatory ambiguity of [5] and the segregatory meaning of [6]:

He wouldn't lend his books to *Tom and Alice.* [5]
He wouldn't lend his books to *Tom or Alice.* [6]

Note [**a**] *Apiece*, a less common adverb which marks segregatory meaning, is normally placed finally after a direct object:

John and Mary have won a prize *apiece*.

It is restricted to clauses with an object, to which it gives the distributive interpretation of *each*.

[**b**] The ambiguity observed in [2] above remains when the coordinate subject is replaced by a plural noun phrase: *My children have both won prizes.* (*Cf* 13.66 Note [d] and 10.47 on distributive number.)

Respective

13.62 The adjective *respective* premodifies a plural noun phrase, *eg* as object, to indicate segregatory interpretation of a preceding conjoint noun phrase. In this function, it is normally preceded by a plural possessive pronoun:

Jill and Ben visited their uncles.

This could mean:

(a) Jill visited her uncle(s) and Ben visited his uncle(s).
(b) Jill and Ben together visited the uncles they have in common.
(c) Jill and Ben together visited Jill's uncle(s) and also Ben's.

On the other hand:

Jill and Ben visited their *respective* uncles.

can only mean (a). The use of *respective* does not, however, help us distinguish the number of uncles, since *respective* cannot be used with a singular noun-phrase head:

*Jill and Ben visited their respective uncle.

The related noun phrases do not have to be in a subject–object relationship:

We interviewed *the Director and the Producer* in their *respective* offices.
Mary and Susan went to their *respective* homes.

They can even be in different clauses or sentences:

Bob and his best friend have had some serious trouble at school lately. Their *respective* parents are going to see the principal about the complaints.

Note Like other markers of segregatory meaning, *respective* can be used analogously with preceding plural noun phrases: *The boys visited their respective uncles.*

Respectively

13.63 The adverb *respectively* is used to indicate segregatory meaning, and also tells us which constituents go with which when there are two parallel coordinate constructions. For example, if there are two sets of conjoins [A] *and* [B] . . . [C] *and* [D], *respectively* makes it clear that [A] goes with [C], and [B] goes with [D]. It can be added to the front or end of the second coordinate construction. Some illustrations follow:

John, Peter, *and* Robert play football, basketball, *and* baseball *respectively*.
[= John plays football, Peter plays basketball, and Robert plays baseball]
Arnold *and* his son were *respectively* the greatest educator *and* the greatest critic of the Victorian age.
[= Arnold was the greatest educator of the Victorian age, and his son was the greatest critic of the Victorian age]
Smith *and* Jones are going to Paris *and* to Amsterdam *respectively*.

The *respectively* construction is generally limited to formal discourse. In other contexts it smacks of pedantry.

Coordination of parts of noun phrases

13.64 When coordination takes place *within* a single noun phrase, it is often possible to postulate ellipsis from a full form in which coordination takes place *between* noun phrases:

They sell [manual] *and* [electric] typewriters. [1]
Your [son] *and* [daughter] look so much alike. [2]

These may be expanded respectively to:

They sell [manual typewriters] *and* [electric typewriters]. [1a]
[Your son] *and* [your daughter] look so much alike. [2a]

There is a further type of coordination within the noun phrase which allows no ellipsis at all. Thus [3] is not usually paraphrasable by [3a], or [4] by [4a]:

{They made [salmon] *and* [cucumber] sandwiches. [3]
{≠ They made [salmon sandwiches] *and* [cucumber sandwiches]. [3a]

{[Spacious] *and* [well-furnished] apartments to let. [4]
{≠ [Spacious apartments] *and* [well-furnished apartments] to let. [4a]

Here again, there is a distinction to be made, with *and*, between COMBINATORY and SEGREGATORY coordination. Combinatory coordination is associated with nonelliptical interpretation, and segregatory with ellipsis or quasi-ellipsis (*cf* 12.40). In the combinatory interpretation illustrated most clearly by [3], the conjoins act semantically 'in combination' with respect to the rest of the sentence. In the segregatory interpretation illustrated by [1], however, the parts of the noun phrase, and even of the clause, which are outside the conjoins can be regarded as the antecedents of an ellipsis or quasi-ellipsis, so that the noun phrase can be paraphrased by means of a coordination of noun phrases and ultimately of clauses. A test of segregatory coordination is whether the endorsing word *both* can be inserted before the first conjoin (*cf* 13.35): [1] means *They sell both manual and electric typewriters*, but [3] does not normally mean *They made both salmon and cucumber sandwiches*.

Note For some cases, it is possible to postulate yet a further stage of ellipsis, and to expand the conjoint noun phrase into a conjoint clause:

[They sell manual typewriters] *and* [they sell electric typewriters]. [1b]

But such an analysis leads to results which are both nonsensical and ungrammatical for other examples:

*[Their son look alike] *and* [their daughter look alike]. [2b]

13.65 As can be seen from the comparison of 13.64 [1] and [3] above, the combinatory/segregatory distinction may be made at various levels for the same construction. For example, the italicized phrase in:

Those are *the shelves for books on* [*skills,*] [*trades,*] *and* [*hobbies*].

permits a combinatory interpretation of *skills, trades, and hobbies* whereby each of the books in the whole set is assumed to deal with all three subjects; but if we assume a segregatory interpretation at this level (*ie*, 'books on skills, books on trades, and books on hobbies'), there is still another level at which the combinatory interpretation is possible: *viz* the shelves in question could each contain a mixture of the three types of book. In contrast, a segregatory interpretation on this level would mean that each shelf is reserved for one kind of book [= 'shelves for books on skills, shelves for books on trades, and shelves for books on hobbies']. In this way coordination creates possibilities of multiple ambiguity, and in general, the further down the tree of constituent structure the coordination occurs, the greater are the opportunities for ambiguity, in the manner indicated by *Fig* 13.65:

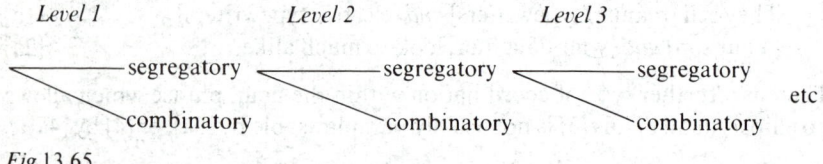

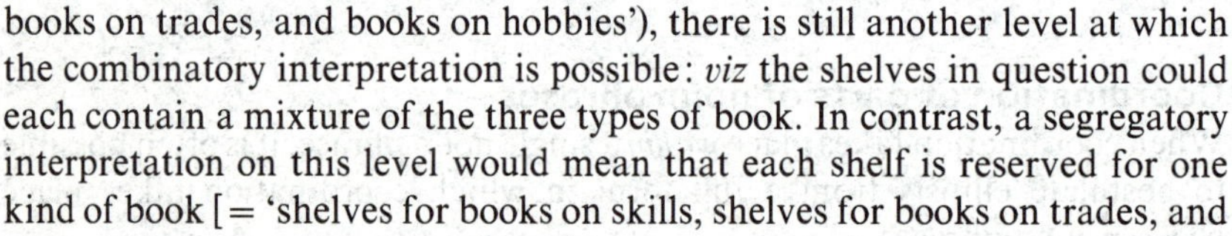

Fig 13.65

To avoid confusion, then, it is best to use the terms 'combinatory' and 'segregatory' in respect to a given contrast of interpretation, rather than with more general reference to a grammatical construction.

Coordination and number

13.66 Essentially the question of whether a given noun phrase (simple or conjoint) is singular or plural depends on whether it refers to one or more than one member of a class of denotata. (For special problems of concord, *cf* 10.37*ff*.) For instance, two noun phrases, even when both are singular, form a plural conjoint phrase when they are coordinated by *and*:

[Jane *is* well] *and* [Susan *is* well]. BUT: [Jane] *and* [Susan] *are* well.

Similarly with more complex noun phrases:

[The King of Denmark] *and* [the Queen of Denmark] *have* arrived. [1]

The plural *have* is appropriate in [1], because the subject refers to more than one person. The same is true when the determiner and modifier are ellipted, so that *King* and *Queen* are coordinated within a single noun phrase:

The [King] *and* [Queen] of Denmark *have* arrived. [1a]

If on the other hand the modifiers are coordinated, the noun head changes from singular to plural, thus indicating the plurality of the whole expression:

The Presidents [of Greece] *and* [of Austria] *were* present at the ceremony.
(= '[the President of Greece] *and* [the President of Austria]')

If the head, in such a case, is noncount, it cannot change to the plural, and there arises the oddity of a singular noun acting as head of a plural noun phrase (*cf* 10.38):

[Indian] *and* [Chinese] tea *smell* totally different from each other.

(The plural *teas* would also be possible here, but would have the slightly different meaning of 'kinds of tea'.) Another example is:

[Red] *and* [white] cabbage *are* (both) useful ingredients for a salad.

(Here the plural *cabbages* would be ludicrous, suggesting that each salad should contain whole cabbages; while the singular *is* would suggest that the variety of cabbage in question is particoloured red and white.)

Note **[a]** An apparent exception which proves the rule is the case of coordinative apposition (*cf* 10.39), where two singular count noun phrases are placed in apposition to form a *singular* noun phrase:

[Tom's father] *and* [Suzanne's uncle] is waiting for you.

The only possible interpretation of this is that Tom's father and Suzanne's uncle are the same person. A similar conclusion must be drawn when two singular nouns are coordinated as heads of a singular noun phrase:

The [owner] *and* [editor] of the *Daily Post* was a member of the club.

[b] On the singular or plural number of noun phrases containing coordination by *or*, *cf* 10.41.

[c] There is uncertainty over number where the *many a* construction (*cf* 5.23 Note [c]) is followed by singular heads conjoined by *and*:

Many a boy *and* girl {?*are* / ?*is*} left homeless.

[d] A further uncertainty arises when a noun is postmodified by a prepositional phrase, the complement of which contains coordinated nouns or noun phrases with segregatory meaning: *in the case*(*s*) *of France and Germany*; *at the back*(*s*) *of the stores and offices*. Normally the singular will indicate combinatory meaning (*eg*: *at the back of the stores and offices* will suggest that the stores and offices comprise a single building or block of buildings). But where the singular is to some degree a 'frozen' part of a complex preposition (*cf* 9.11), the plural would not be acceptable: **in cases of fire and theft*; **on the parts of all concerned.* Yet even in idioms of this kind the ability to pluralize is exercised in other constructions (*cf* 10.47):

We must all play { a part / our { part / parts } } in achieving victory.

Coordinated noun heads

13.67 It is evident from what has been said in 13.64*f* that various ambiguities arise when the constituents of noun phrases are coordinated.

When coordinated heads are preceded by a determiner, the usual interpretation is that the determiner applies to each of the conjoins:

a [knife] and [fork] (= *a* knife and *a* fork)
the [head] and [shoulders] (= *the* head and *the* shoulders)
his [wife] and [child] (= *his* wife and *his* child)

(On the interpretation of quantifiers such as *many* in *many girls and boys, cf* 13.76.)

A similar analysis in terms of segregatory coordination (*cf* 13.59) usually applies when the coordinated heads are preceded or followed by modifiers:

old [men] and [women] (= [old men] and [old women])
some [cows,] [pigs,] and [sheep] from our farm (= some cows from our farm, some pigs from our farm, and some sheep from our farm)

But then there is also the possibility of interpreting these phrases as conjoint noun phrases:

[Old men] and [women] were left to organize the community.
At the market were [some cows,] [pigs,] and [sheep from our farm].

If the determiner is not repeated in the noninitial conjoins, however, an ellipsis of the determiner is normally assumed:

the [boys] and [girls] staying at the hostel (= [the boys staying at the hostel] and [the girls staying at the hostel])

Coordinated premodifiers

13.68 If modifiers are coordinated, there may again be ambiguity according to whether the construction is understood to be segregatory. Thus:

He specializes in selling [old] and [valuable] books.

may mean 'books which are old and valuable' (combinatory meaning) or 'old books and valuable books' (segregatory meaning). Only the segregatory meaning is possible when the coordinated modifiers denote mutually exclusive properties:

old and *new* furniture *one-pound* and *two-pound* jars

Exceptions to this are colour adjectives (as in *red, white, and blue flags*), which allow the combinatory sense of 'partly one colour, partly another'. On the other hand, only the combinatory interpretation is available if the head is a singular count noun:

He is a *dishonest* and *lazy* student.

Another sign of combinatory meaning is the possibility of replacing *and* by asyndetic coordination:

He's a disHÓNest, LÁzy STÙdent.
They sell *old, battered* furniture.

This is not normally acceptable with segregatory meaning:

?*They sell *old, new* furniture.

In fact, for a combinatory interpretation of modifiers, asyndetic coordination is generally preferred to syndetic coordination. Again, however, colour adjectives are exceptional: *and* in such expressions as *a red and green uniform* cannot be omitted, even though the meaning is combinatory.

The endorsing item *both* placed at the beginning of a noun phrase identifies coordination of premodifiers as segregatory:

both young *and* old people [= *both* young people *and* old people]

But when the adjectives are placed in a predicative position, the converse applies, and the combinatory interpretation is selected:

*Men who were *both* young *and* old were invited.
Students who are *both* honest *and* clever always succeed.

Note [**a**] If the adjective phrase is postpositive (7.21), *both* . . . *and* is possible with either type of meaning, but the segregatory meaning is often marked by pitch movement, as indicated below:

Men *both* ↑ old *and* ↓ young were invited.
Students *both* honest *and* clever always succeed.

[**b**] With a series of adjectives, the final *and* is occasionally omitted even with segregatory meaning:

Old, young, wise, foolish, tall, (*and*) short men were invited without distinction.

[**c**] Occasionally a noun modifier is coordinated with an adjective modifier, as in *country and western music*.

[**d**] With *or* and *either* . . . *or*, the segregatory interpretation of premodifiers occurs even with singular heads; *eg*: *It's a Georgian or Regency sofa*.

Coordinated postmodifiers

13.69 Coordinated postmodifiers, like coordinated premodifiers, afford the possibility of either a segregatory or a combinatory interpretation of *and*. The following is likely to have a combinatory interpretation:

The bus for the Houses of Parliament *and* (for) Westminster Abbey leaves from this point.

But if the phrase is in the plural, an ambiguity results:

the buses for the Houses of Parliament *and* (for) Westminster Abbey

This could in theory mean either: 'the buses which go both to the Houses of Parliament and to Westminster Abbey' or 'the bus(es) for the Houses of Parliament and the bus(es) for Westminster Abbey'. The singular head *bus* does not allow the second segregatory interpretation with *and*.

The second preposition in examples such as these may be readily omitted, so that the coordination becomes one of prepositional complements rather than of prepositional phrases. But then a combinatory meaning is favoured; whereas if the preposition is repeated, a segregatory meaning is more probable. Hence these are likely to have different interpretations:

Elsa Graham's books on [reptiles] and [amphibians]
(probably combinatory)
Elsa Graham's books [on reptiles] and [on amphibians]
(almost certainly segregatory).

Note Here again (*cf* 13.68 Note [d]), the segregatory interpretation is possible with a singular head and with *or* as coordinator:

You have to take *a bus for the Houses of Parliament or for Westminster Abbey*.

Further ambiguities of coordination in the noun phrase

13.70 If a phrase containing modifiers coordinated by *and* has a singular count noun head, only one interpretation, the combinatory one, is possible. But if it has a plural head, there are four possible segregatory interpretations for a noun phrase containing two conjoins:

the meetings on Monday and on Tuesday
[= 'the meeting on Monday and the meeting on Tuesday'
OR 'the meetings on Monday and the meeting on Tuesday'
OR 'the meeting on Monday and the meetings on Tuesday'
OR 'the meetings on Monday and the meetings on Tuesday']

Every time an extra conjoin is added (as in *the meetings on Monday, Tuesday, and Wednesday*) the number of interpretations is doubled. The ambiguities can be avoided, if desired, by the use of the nonelliptical equivalents.

In addition, this phrase allows a combinatory interpretation: *viz* that the meetings, or some of the meetings, lasted for both days. The combinatory interpretation would, however, be more likely if the second preposition were ellipted: *the meetings on Monday and Tuesday*.

A similar set of readings is possible for:

bills for gas and (for) electricity
the taxes on earned and (on) unearned income

Since *tax* is sometimes a noncount noun, it is also possible to read the segregatory readings into the corresponding singular phrase: *the tax on earned and* (*on*) *unearned income*.

Note The following example shows how the segregatory reading of *tax on earned and unearned income* can be associated with the mutual participation (*cf* 13.60 Note [b]) of *between*:

There is no difference *between the tax on earned and* [= *'that on'*] *unearned income*.

Although the occurrence of a singular noun phrase as complement of *between* seems irregular, this sentence is in fact constructed regularly according to the principles outlined in preceding sections.

Coordination of determiners and numerals

13.71 The coordination of determiners is comparatively rare. The following are possible, but are unidiomatic: *this or other books, these and those chairs, a few* *or many students*, and there is a preference for a synonymous construction with conjoint noun phrases, such as *this book and that* (*one*), *a few students or many*, where the second conjoin is a noun phrase reduced by substitution or ellipsis. Comparative forms are more easily coordinated:

> Would you prefer MÓRE or LÈSS sugar?
> [= '. . . more sugar or less sugar?']

but even here the equivalent noun-phrase coordination, with reduction of the second conjoin by standard ellipsis, may be preferred:

> Would you prefer MÓRE sugar or LÈSS $_{\triangle}$?

There are some instances of idioms in which determiners are coordinated; *eg* the redundant and emphatic conjoining of *each* and *every* in:

> The secret was kept by *each and every* one of us.

Cardinal numerals are frequently coordinated with *or*, but here again there is an idiomatic function. *Five or six* means, for example, 'approximately in the range of five and six'; *ten or twenty* means 'a number in the region of 10 or 20'; and the most frequently-occurring coordination of this type, *one or two*, has the special idiomatic sense 'a small number'. This approximative use of numerals does not apply when the correlative *either . . . or* is used:

> I am inviting *one or two* students to a party.

does not mean the same as:

> I am inviting *either one or two* students to a party.

Note [**a**] Occasionally a postdeterminer such as *few* or *many* may be coordinated with an adjective: *his few but intelligent remarks*. Note also the idiom *few and far between*.

[**b**] The coordination of a singular with a plural determinative leads to an anomaly of concord: logically, the head of the noun phrase could be either singular or plural. The difficulty is resolved (*cf* 10.41) by making the head agree with the last conjoin: *one or two students* (NOT **one or two student*); *this and other arguments* (NOT **this and other argument*).

[**c**] Mention should be made of the rarity and *ad hoc* quality of coordinations of the definite and indefinite articles: *She is the* (*or a*) *professor in the department*; *He may be a, or even the, Vice-Chairman of the party*. Such coordination takes place only with *or*, and the unreduced pronunciations of the articles (/eɪ/ and /ðiː/) are normally required.

Coordination of genitives

13.72 Like determiners, genitives, when used in determinative function, are not often coordinated, and there is some uneasiness about the appropriate construction to use. A coordination of genitives such as *John's and Mary's children* resembles a coordination of modifiers in that it may be interpreted in either a combinatory or a segregatory fashion:

combinatory meaning:	'the children who are joint offspring of John and Mary'	(A)
segregatory meanings:	'John's child and Mary's child'	(B)
	OR 'John's children and Mary's child'	(C)
	OR 'John's child and Mary's children'	(D)
	OR 'John's children and Mary's children'	(E)

And as in the case of postmodifiers, a further ellipsis is common if the combinatory meaning is intended. The following can be given only reading (A) above:

[John] and [Mary]'s children (*cf* the children of John and Mary)

Here the *'s* is outside the coordinate construction, and is added to the whole conjoint noun phrase *John and Mary*. In this, it resembles the *'s* of group genitives (*cf* 5.123), which is a suffix to a phrase rather than to a single word.

Note The group genitive construction of *John and Mary's children* is characteristic of informal speech. In formal English, this construction is sometimes felt to be incorrect, and the construction of *the children of John and Mary* or (less commonly) *John's and Mary's children* might be preferred instead. The latter construction, however, is forced and awkward, especially if the conjoins are strongly associated with one another: *?Laurel's and Hardy's hilarious screen comedies.*

Coordination of possessive pronouns

13.73 Another problem of usage arises over the coordination of possessive pronouns. Two alternative constructions are the following:

(a) [POSSESSIVE] + [POSSESSIVE] + . . . HEAD
eg: *your and my problems*; *their and our students*
(b) [POSSESSIVE + . . . HEAD . . .] + [POSSESSIVE]
eg: *your problems and mine*; *their students and ours*

In (a) both possessives have a determinative function, while in (b) the second possessive pronoun has an independent function (*cf* 6.29*f*), so that strictly this is a conjoining of noun phrases rather than of possessives. Construction (b) is often preferred to construction (a), which can seem to be awkward. All these constructions, however, suggest a segregatory interpretation, and if a combinatory meaning is intended, a periphrasis may be preferred; *eg*: *her and my policy/policies* may be replaced by *the policy/policies which she and I share*. Yet another construction is sometimes encountered, but is not fully acceptable:

(c) [POSSESSIVE] + [POSSESSIVE + . . . HEAD . . .]
eg: *?yours and my problems*; *?theirs and our students*

This differs from (a) in that the first conjoin is an independent possessive pronoun such as *yours*, or *hers*, and differs from (b) in that the order of the conjoins is reversed. Of course, in many situations the awkwardness of this coordination of pronouns can be avoided by an inclusive use of *our* or *your*: *our problems*, etc.

Note **[a]** The polite order of conjoined personal pronouns (*cf* 13.56 Note [a]) may be applied to possessive pronouns, as well as to pronouns in the subjective or objective case: *your, his, and my reports*; *your and my books*; etc.
[b] The difference between constructions (b) and (c) above is neutralized in the case of *his*, since there is no contrast in this pronoun between the determinative and independent form of the possessive pronoun: *his and my favourite drink*.

Coordination of genitives with possessive pronouns

13.74 Three constructions corresponding to (a–c) above are also available when mixed coordinations of genitives and possessives are required. Here again, some uneasiness is felt in the choice of construction. For (a) and (b), there are variant orders: the possessive may precede the genitive, or vice versa:

(a) { [GENITIVE] + [POSSESSIVE] . . . + HEAD
[POSSESSIVE] + [GENITIVE] . . . + HEAD

eg: ?*my husband's and my names*; ?*your and your wife's bank account*

This construction is rarely used, and is felt to be awkward.

(b) { [GENITIVE + . . . HEAD . . .] + [POSSESSIVE]
[POSSESSIVE + . . . HEAD] . . . + [GENITIVE]

eg: *my husband's name and mine*; *your bank account and your husband's*

This construction is less awkward than (a), but is clearly associated with segregatory coordination. Thus *your bank account and your husband's* could not normally refer to a joint bank account shared by husband and wife. Also, since (b) is technically a coordination of noun phrases rather than of determinatives, this construction does not permit a 'segregatory singular' interpretation of a plural noun as head. For instance, *Jack's and my dogs* could mean 'Jack's dog and my dog'; but *Jack's dogs and mine* would tend to imply that Jack has more than one dog.

A construction corresponding to (c) in 13.73, where the independent possessive pronoun (*cf* 6.29) precedes the genitive, is a further possibility, which however has limited acceptability:

(c) [POSSESSIVE] + [GENITIVE] . . . + HEAD]
?*yours and your husband's bank account*

Note There is yet one further option, which corresponds to the construction of *John and Mary's children* (*cf* 13.72), and which resembles it in being associated with informal style and combinatory meaning: *you and your husband's bank account*. This will often be felt to be unacceptable where the first conjoin is a noun, or a phrase with a noun head, or a pronoun in the subjective case: ?*they and their friends' surprise*; ?*John and her book*. The use of an objective pronoun for the first conjoin is also possible, but is nonstandard: ?*me and my husband's bank account*.

Other elliptical coordinations within the noun phrase

13.75 We have already noted (*cf* 13.67) that when heads of noun phrases are conjoined, the determiner is often ellipted, resulting in a coordination at word level rather than at phrase level, with two nouns sharing a single determiner:

a [boy] or △ [girl]
that [butter] and △ [milk]
the [house] and △ [gardens]
my [father] and △ [mother]

The same kind of ellipsis may be observed when the determiner is accompanied by one or more modifiers:

those delicious [pies] and △ [pastries]

Yet another kind of ellipsis takes place when one or more modifiers are included in the conjoins. The units thus coordinated are neither words nor phrases, but the intermediate units we earlier called NOMINAL EXPRESSIONS (*cf* 12.16):

those [mince pies] and [Danish pastries]
those delicious [mince pies] and [Danish pastries]
those delicious [mince pies] and [Danish pastries] that you bought

In such constructions, the limits of the conjoins are variable, and this leads to ambiguity. *My elder brother and sister*, for example, may be interpreted as *my elder* [*brother*] *and* [*sister*] (= 'my elder brother and my elder sister'), or as *my* [*elder brother*] and [*sister*] (= 'my elder brother and my sister'). Of these two interpretations, the former is preferred, for the latter meaning would be singled out by the repetition of *my* before *sister*. The following illustrates a similar but more complex kind of ambiguity of construction:

The Municipal Art Gallery is famous for *its still life paintings and drawings by Van Gogh.*

Four interpretations are possible:

(a) its still life [paintings] and [drawings] by Van Gogh
(b) its [still life paintings] and [drawings] by Van Gogh
(c) its [still life paintings] and [drawings by Van Gogh]
(d) its still life [paintings] and [drawings by Van Gogh]

Other things being equal, an interpretation which preserves a parallelism between the conjoins will be preferred to one which does not. On this ground, (a) and (c) are more likely readings of the above example than (b) and (d); reading (b) is quite possible, however, because of the close association between *still life* and *paintings*.

Scope of quantifiers and numerals in the noun phrase

13.76 In 13.45 we studied the way in which quantifiers within the clause include coordinate constructions in their scope. A similar phenomenon occurs in the noun phrase, when quantifying determiners or numerals include within their scope the coordination of nominal expressions such as those discussed in 13.75 above. In such cases, the noun phrase cannot be expanded in the regular fashion, by repetition of the determinative item:

They have *no* books *or* magazines for sale.
[= *no* books *and no* magazines . . .]
[≠ *no* books *or no* magazines . . .] (*cf* 13.31)
They're going to plant several flowering trees or shrubs.
[≠ *several* flowering trees *or several* flowering shrubs]
There are ten boys and girls in the playgroup.

In the last example, *ten* may or may not include *boys and girls* in its scope. Hence it is possible that this phrase refers to a group of children adding up to a total of ten, rather than to a group of ten boys and ten girls. The former interpretation is not always selected, however, since *ten husbands and wives* or *ten knives and forks* would invite the contrary reading 'ten of the one and ten of the other'. This is because a husband and wife, or a knife and fork, form a unit in a way in which a boy and a girl do not.

Coordination of other constituents

13.77 All the main variations of construction we have noted in connection with clauses and noun phrases are also found in verb phrases, adjective phrases, adverb phrases, and prepositional phrases. The central coordinators *and* and *or*, and to a lesser extent *but*, are used as linkers. In the cases of *and* and *or*, there may be more than two conjoins in a given construction. Coordination is asyndetic, syndetic, or polysyndetic. When *and* is the coordinator, there is a further choice between combinatory and segregatory readings. Some representative examples of other phrases are given below.

Coordination of verbs and verb phrases

13.78 Verb phrase coordination is illustrated in:

Heinrich Schmidt [*was born*,] [*lived*,] *and* [*died*] in the city of Vienna. [1]
Good cooking [*can disguise*,] *but* [*cannot improve*,] the quality of the ingredients. [2]
Yesterday we [*bought*] *and* [*sold*] ten paintings. [3]

The implication of chronological sequence which is found in clause coordination (*cf* 13.23) is also found, if the main verb has dynamic meaning, in verb phrase coordination. We may contrast, in this respect, the stative verb meanings of *She knows and admires your work* and the dynamic verb meanings of *George repaired and sold the car*.

Coordination of main verbs, with shared auxiliary verb(s), is common:

I have *washed* and *dried* the dishes.
The guests were *sitting* or *lounging* around in the front room.
Quite a large number of people might have been *killed* or *injured* by the explosion.

Coordination of auxiliary verbs is less common and somewhat formal:

The country *can* and *must* recover from its present crisis.
Staffordshire pottery always *was*, *is*, and *will be* prized by collectors.

It is perhaps less rare when the auxiliaries are conjoined by *or*:

He *may*, or (certainly) *should*, resign.

But coordination then has the character of an interpolation (*cf* 13.95*ff*).

Note When two dynamic verbs of opposite meaning are conjoined, especially when combined with the progressive, the meaning of the construction is often iterative (*cf* 13.101): *He lay there opening and shutting his eyes* [*ie* repeatedly]; *Visitors came and went throughout the summer*.

Coordination of adjectives and adjective phrases

13.79 Adjective phrases are coordinated in:

The journey was *long* and *extremely arduous*.
Our team is *very fit*, *very keen*, and *ready to face the strongest competition in the world*.

In the following, there is a coordination of adjective heads:

I'm feeling *younger* and *healthier* than I have felt for years.

But in the following, there is an ambiguity, according to whether the premodifier belongs to the first conjoin or to both conjoins:

The souvenirs they bought were *very cheap and gaudy*.

It is unclear whether the analysis should be:

[*very cheap*] *and* [*gaudy*] OR *very* [*cheap*] *and* [*gaudy*]

But the second reading, in which the premodifier applies to the whole sequence, is preferred. A change in the order of the words will eliminate the ambiguity:

The souvenirs they bought were [*gaudy*] *and* [*very cheap*].

Adjectives can be coordinated either in predicative position, as above, or in attributive position:

His *clear and forceful* delivery impressed his audience. [1]

In attributive position (*cf* 13.68), the coordinator *and* is often omitted:

His *clear, forceful* delivery impressed his audience. [2]

The asyndetic construction in [2] is combinatory, and is associated with nonrestrictive modification (*cf* 17.95). It also suggests, more than the syndetic one, that the two epithets are meant to contribute to the same general effect: *ie* '. . . clear and, I may go so far as to say, forceful'. The syndetic construction of [1], on the other hand, has the additional possibility of a segregatory interpretation if the head noun is plural or noncount:

old and dilapidated buildings wet and windy weather

These phrases, in contrast to those of [1] and [2], are ambiguous.

Coordination of adverbs and adverb phrases

13.80 Coordinated adverbs and adverb phrases are normally of the same semantic class (*eg* of time, of place, of manner):

She made the announcement *quietly but quite confidently*.
The Governor never arrives *earlier or later* than the time of an appointment.
The piston moved *up and down* with increasing speed.
I have only spoken to her *once or twice*.

In this last example, *once or twice* is likely to have the vague meaning 'a few times', comparable to the use of *one or two* as discussed in 13.71. The rarer case of coordination, in which the adverbs or adverb phrases are of different semantic classes, is illustrated by:

He complained *strenuously and often*.
They met *somewhere and sometime*, but I have forgotten *how or why*.

Coordination of prepositions and prepositional phrases

13.81 The following illustrate coordination of prepositional phrases:

He spoke *for the first motion* but *against the second motion*.
John complained both *to Mary* and *to Peter*.
They are going *to France*, *to Germany*, or *to Switzerland*.
The talks held *in 1951*, *in 1952*, and *in 1955* met with only limited success.

If the two or more prepositions are identical, all but the first preposition can be ellipted; *eg*: *to Mary and Peter*; *in 1951 and 1952* (but a combinatory meaning is then allowed; *cf* 13.70). Further possibilities are the ellipsis of part of the prepositional complement in the first or subsequent conjoin (the former, cataphoric option being more formal):

He spoke *for the first* △ but *against the second motion*.
He spoke *for the first motion* but *against the second* △.

or the ellipsis of the prepositional complement altogether, in which case the construction is simply one of coordinated prepositions:

He climbed *up* and *over* the wall.
[= He climbed *up the wall* and *over the wall*]
Did you speak *for* or *against* the motion?
Do you like your coffee *with* or *without* milk?

Note Also possible is a construction synonymous with the above in which ellipsis occurs in the second conjoin:

Did you speak *for the motion* or *against* △?
Do you like your coffee *with milk* or *without* △?

These appear to resemble cases where a prepositional adverb replaces a prepositional phrase (*cf* 9.65–6); but in fact they belong to a different category, because they occur with words (*without* and *against*) which cannot normally be used as prepositional adverbs. We must therefore describe these as unusual cases of ellipsis in which a preposition appears without its prepositional complement. This analysis may be further extended to cases like *Asparagus is expensive out of season and in*, where, although *in* may be a prepositional adverb, in this instance it is obviously a preposition parallel to *out of*. The effect of placing *in* at the end, with ellipsis, in this way is to give it the emphasis associated with end focus (*cf* 18.9*ff*).

Mixed coordination of adverbials

13.82 The general principle governing the coordination of phrases and words is that the conjoins must belong to the same category, formally, functionally, and semantically. Sometimes, however, the normal formal parallelism is not maintained, so that there is coordination of different adverbial categories. In the following, adverb phrases are coordinated with prepositional phrases, and noun phrases with adverbial clauses. In each case, however, a close semantic parallel between the conjoins is maintained:

The enemy attacked *quickly* and *with great force*.
You can wash them *manually* or *by using a machine*.
They can call *this week* or *whenever you wish*.
I prefer the sentences *below* and *on the next page*.

Coordination of subordinators

13.83 If two subordinate clauses are identical except for their conjunctions, one of the clauses can be omitted, normally the first, so that coordination takes place between the conjunctions:

I am prepared to meet them *when* and *where* they like.
[= . . . *when* they like and *where* they like]
They will be arriving either *before* or *after* the show begins.

Note [**a**] On the formulaic coordination *if and only if*, *cf* 15.35 Note [i].
[**b**] *If and when* is a stereotyped expression weakening the expectation (conveyed by *when* alone) that the condition in the clause will be realized:

If and when he buys a car, I'll try to persuade him to buy the insurance from me.

With *if and when* ellipsis may be disregarded, since *if and when* has become a unit. Other institutionalized conjoinings of conjunctions are: *as and when*; *unless and until*.

Coordination of interrogative words and relative pronouns

13.84 Coordination can also take place between other clause-introducing words, such as interrogative words, whether they introduce an independent or a dependent clause (*cf* 11.14*f*):

I am determined to find out *who* or *what* caused this uproar.
How and *why* did you break into my room?

A coordination of *wh*-words is not possible if the *wh*-words function as different elements of structure. For example, it is impossible to coordinate a subject *who* with an adverbial *why*:

**Who* and *why* broke into my room?

But such a sentence becomes grammatical if the second *wh*-word is appended to the clause:

Who broke into my room, and *why*?

This is because the appended *why?* counts as an elliptical clause (*cf* 12.63) (= 'why did they break into my room?'), and so the structural equivalence between the first conjoin and the second is restored.

The same principle of structural and functional equivalence prevents coordination of relative pronouns, but the coordination of prepositional phrases containing a relative pronoun is quite common at the beginning of relative clauses:

I want to know *by whom* and *for whom* it was ordered.

Additional constraints on coordination

Restrictions on coordination of word-parts

13.85 The minimal unit which can normally be coordinated is the word. There are, however, occasional exceptions to this limitation. Some derivational prefixes which tend to be contrasted and which tend to be loosely attached to their base can be conjoined; *eg: ante-* (or *pre-*) *and post-natal*; *pro- and anti-establishment*; *sub- and super-human.* Tightly-attached prefixes do not permit such coordination: **im- and ex-ports.*

Similarly, constituents of a compound can sometimes be coordinated, with ellipsis of the other constituent; *eg*: *factory- and office-workers, sons- and daughters-in-law, hand-made and -packed, out- and in-patients, psycho- and sociolinguistics*. Once again, these constituents are loosely attached, and we do not find linking in more cohesive compounds such as *toothache* and *headache*: **tooth- and headaches*.

Order of conjoins in word and phrase coordination

13.86 Apart from semantic factors such as chronological sequence (*cf* 13.23) the order of conjoins in word and phrase coordination is relatively free. The order of conjoined words can, however, be influenced by a tendency for the longer word to come second (perhaps a variant of the end-weight principle; *cf* 18.9). This is particularly noticeable in so-called BINOMIALS, *ie* relatively fixed conjoint phrases having two members; *eg*: *big and ugly, cup and saucer*. One principle at work here appears to be a principle of rhythmic regularity: *eg* the dactylic rhythm of *'ladies and 'gentleman*, and the trochaic rhythm of *'men and 'women*, are preferable to the less balanced rhythm of **'gentlemen and 'ladies* and **'women and 'men*. It has also been argued that semantic factors play a role; *eg* that other things being equal, the first position is given to the semantically salient or culturally dominant member, as in *father and son, gold and silver, great and small, this and that*. Phonological constraints have also been suggested: that low vowels come after high ones; that back vowels come after front ones, etc. Whatever the constraints may be, they lead to stereotyped coordinations where the conjoins are virtually in an irreversible order; *eg*: *odds and ends, bread and butter, law and order, by hook or by crook, through thick and thin*; *knife, fork, and spoon*.

Note [**a**] Arguably 'cultural dominance' can be extended to include the traditional sexual bias (*cf* 6.10) shown in the tendency to place male terms before female ones in cases like *men and women, boys and girls*, (*if*) *he or she* (*wishes*). This tendency is reversed in *mother and father* (where cultural dominance works in the opposite direction) and in *ladies and gentlemen* (influenced by the courtesy convention of 'ladies first').
[**b**] On the ordering of *you and I*, etc, *cf* 13.56 Note [a].

'ill-assorted' coordination: (a) semantic

13.87 The requirement that the conjoins match one another in form, function, and meaning is observed with varying degrees of strictness. The following are apparently examples of a semantic violation of the constraint, but nevertheless such constructions can be used for humorous or rhetorical effect:

> She made up *her mind* and then *her face*.
> I drove home in *a hurry* and *a borrowed car*.

Such examples can be expanded, by supplying ellipted elements, into grammatical sentences; *eg*:

> She made up her mind and then she made up her face.

But it is clear from this that the ellipsis is based on an incongruous association of two homonymous idioms, *make up* (*one's mind*) and *make up* (*one's face*). It is to such examples of semantically ill-assorted coordination that the traditional term ZEUGMA is applied.

'ill-assorted' coordination: (b) grammatical

13.88 A different kind of 'ill-assorted' coordination is illustrated by the following:

We have washed, dried, and put the dishes away. [1]
By giving the police a pay rise, the Minister hopes to strengthen and make the force more efficient. [2]

There is no difficulty in understanding such sentences; this time the anomaly is a matter of structure. They contain a false parallel, in that *away* in [1] and *more efficient* [2] are structurally outside the coordinate construction, and yet semantically apply only to the last conjoin. Sentence [1] ought to be a reduced form of:

*We have washed the dishes away, we have dried the dishes away, and we have put the dishes away.

but clearly this does not make sense. Such sentences are likely to occur in the impromptu use of language, but will be 'corrected' in the more considered and especially in the written use of language; [1], for example, can be changed to:

We have [washed,] [dried,] and [put away] the dishes. [1a]

(On the ordering of the verb *put* and the adverb *away* here, *cf* 16.4*ff*.) The term 'corrected' above has been advisedly enclosed in quotation marks, since it is not clear how far such examples are to be regarded as sentences which are ungrammatical in a descriptive sense, or as acceptable sentences stigmatized merely because of prescriptive tradition. Other instances of a similar kind are:

The spy [was in his forties,] [of average build,] *and* [spoke with a slightly foreign accent]. [3]
Had the queen [lived five years longer] *or* [had given birth to an heir], the subsequent history of the nation would have been very different. [4]
Either [the children did not know what had happened], *or* [were trying to protect their parents]. [5]
?Our ancient city [has], *and* [always will], be proud of its achievements. [6]
I am fond *both* [of dogs] *and* [cats]. [7]

The anomalous structure of such sentences can be discovered by expanding each coordination construction to a postulated unreduced version, *ie* by repeating before or after each conjoin the parts of the sentence which lie outside the coordinate construction. The result will be an unacceptable sentence in each case. By way of illustration, the unreduced versions of [3] and [7] are:

*The spy was in his forties, the spy of average build, and the spy spoke with a slightly foreign accent. [3a]
*I am fond of dogs and I am fond cats. [7a]

The expansion in example [7a] is based on the principle that correlatives such as *both . . . and* mark the beginning of each conjoin. In fact, *both* cannot introduce clause coordination (*cf* 13.35), and would therefore be omitted from an unreduced sentence such as [7a].

Note Grammatically ill-assorted coordination can also occur at the morphological level:

The reader is invited to try the experiment for *his or herself* before reading on.

The problem with this example is revealed if we expand the first conjoin to *hisself* (which is not grammatical in standard English) by assuming, as the construction seems to require, an ellipsis of *-self*. Compare a related difficulty of coordinated possessive pronouns in 13.73.

'ill-assorted coordination': (c) lexical

13.89 A third type of 'ill-assorted' coordination is illustrated by the following:

He was *ashamed* and *alarmed at* the vengeful attitude of the War Cabinet.

Here the speaker confuses the prepositions of the two combinations *ashamed of* and *alarmed at*. The cause of the false parallel in this case is lexical, in the specific combinations of adjective and preposition (*cf* 16.69), rather than grammatical. Such confusions, which are not unusual, can be remedied by an insertion of the appropriate first preposition: *He was ashamed of and alarmed at . . .*

Less common types of coordination

Complex coordination

13.90 Up to this point we have been concerned with simple coordination: that is, the coordination of single grammatical constituents such as clauses, predications, phrases, and words. We turn now to three less regular and less common types of coordination, *viz* complex coordination, appended coordination, and interpolated coordination: these types of coordination may be seen as related, by ellipsis, to the coordination of clauses.

We apply the term COMPLEX COORDINATION to coordinate constructions of which the conjoins are combinations of units, rather than single units. In the clause, for example, it is possible not merely to coordinate objects or to coordinate complements; but also to coordinate one combination of object and complement with another combination of object and complement.

13.91 Our first examples illustrate coordination of contiguous combinations of elements in final position in the clause. (We reserve noncontiguous cases until 13.92.)

(i) INDIRECT OBJECT + DIRECT OBJECT
We gave [William a book on stamps], and [Mary a book on painting].

(ii) OBJECT + OBJECT COMPLEMENT
Jack painted [the kitchen white] and [the living room blue].

(iii) OBJECT + ADVERBIAL
You should serve [the coffee in a mug] and [the lemonade in a glass].

(iv) ADVERBIAL + ADVERBIAL
Paula is flying [to Madrid tonight] and [to Athens next week].

Such coordination usually establishes a strong parallelism between the conjoins, and for this reason it tends to be associated with a premeditated, written style of English, rather than with informal conversation.

But there is another type of complex coordination where there is no strong parallelism. In this type, the conjoins are unequal because one conjoin contains one or more adverbials where the other does not:

I found the music [unexciting] and – [frankly – discordant].
He wears [smart clothes], and [sometimes a yachting cap at weekends].

Such examples are more likely to occur in informal speech.

Gapping

13.92 The phenomenon known as GAPPING occurs when a second or subsequent conjoin of a complex coordination contains a medial ellipsis. This happens whenever the elements being coordinated are noncontiguous elements in the clause. For example:

(i) SUBJECT + OBJECT
[One girl has written a poem], and [the other ▵ a short story].

(ii) SUBJECT + ADVERBIAL(S)
[Smith completed the course in thirty-five minutes], and [Johnson ▵ in thirty-seven].

(iii) SUBJECT + COMPLEMENT
[Jane has looked more healthy], and [Maurice ▵ more relaxed], since their holiday.

There is normally prosodic separation of the conjoins, and in addition, the 'gap' or medial ellipsis is often marked by the end of a tone unit:

Maggie ordered a banana SPLÍT| *and* MY̌ra| an ice-cream SÙNdae.|

Coordination with gapping is apparently more difficult to decode and comprehend than coordination without gapping. An indication of this is that nongapped interpretations are preferred to gapped interpretations in cases where a sentence permits both kinds of interpretation. In a sentence such as [1], for example, the interpretation indicated by [1a] will be chosen in preference to that of [1b]:

Barbara gave Sue a magnolia and Ada a camellia. [1]
[= Barbara gave Sue a magnolia and Barbara gave Ada a camellia] [1a]
[≠ Barbara gave Sue a magnolia and Ada gave Sue a camellia] [1b]

Note [**a**] An additional, rather rare, kind of gapping is that in which the conjoins consist of a subject followed by a predication (the finite verb being ellipted):

John can clean the shed *and* Sidney ▵ feed the chickens.
The fortress had been attacked *and* its commander ▵ killed.

[**b**] The first element of a gapped coordination is normally the subject of the clause; but exceptions to this occur with fronting (*cf* 18.20), if the first element is an object or an adverbial, and the subject is ellipted:

The towns they attacked with tanks, *and* the villages △ with aeroplanes.

To God he committed his soul, *and* to the fire △ his body.

[**c**] Coordinations of nonfinal sequences of clause elements, *eg* subject + verb, will be viewed not as complex coordination, but as interpolated coordination (*cf* 13.95).

13.93 For a construction to count as an acceptable gapping, it is necessary that each conjoin consist of a sequence of units at the same level of structure: *viz* at the level of clause structure. It is not possible, for instance, for each conjoin to consist of a verb phrase together with the first word (a preposition) of a prepositional phrase. Thus:

Roberts won in 1979 and Dingwall in 1980.

is grammatical, but not:

*Roberts won in 1979 and Dingwall 1980.

Note This applies even to clauses where the verb and the preposition form a 'prepositional verb' (*cf* 16.5*ff*), and where the prepositional complement resembles a direct object. Although the preposition in such cases appears to be more closely related to the verb than to its complement, the ellipsis of the preposition is not permissible:

*I looked at Agnes, and she me.

Contrast:

I saw Agnes, and she me.

Appended coordination

13.94 There is a loose kind of coordination in which the second conjoin is appended to the clause in which the first conjoin occurs (*cf* appended clauses, 12.70). In fact, it is preferable to regard all such cases as clause coordination with ellipsis:

John writes extremely well – and SÀLly, TOÒ. [1]
My mother plays badminton, and sometimes even tennis. [2]
He got a bike for his birthday, and a book and a fountain pen. [3]
His left hook could fell the champion, and indeed any other boxer in his class. [4]

Unlike complex coordination, this type of coordination is characteristic of informal speech. We could argue that [1a] is a case of noun phrase coordination, and is a variant of [1] without a discontinuous subject:

John and Sally write extremely well. [1a]

But this does not account for the singular verb in [1], and it is more realistic to classify such a construction as a coordination of clauses in which the second conjoin, which is elliptical, is added as an afterthought. This latter description also accords better with examples like [2] in which the appended subject is accompanied by an adverbial. In [2] it is the object of an elliptical clause which is appended, rather than a subject.

With *and*, appended coordination has the air of a makeshift improvisation, sometimes accompanied by rhetorical emphasis (as in [4]). But with *or* and *but*, it is more likely to occur in careful and/or written types of language:

I am not sure whether JǍNE wrote the letter, or SÀLly. [5]
PĚTer plays football, but not JÒHN. [6]

In [5] the alternative interrogative clause (*cf* 15.6) allows the possibility of a postponed conjoin. The same applies to direct alternative questions, and alternative conditional–concessive clauses (*cf* 11.20*f*, 15.41). In [6] the repudiatory use of *but* (*cf* 13.32, 13.42 Note [d]) allows a postponed negative conjoin. These are special constructions in which appended coordination occurs freely.

Interpolated coordination

13.95 Another less regular type of coordination may be called INTERPOLATED, because one of the conjoins behaves as if it is inserted, as a parenthesis, in the middle of the clause. Once again, the coordination can be regarded as an elliptical reduction of clause coordination, and in some cases there is a direct parallel between interpolated coordination and clause coordination with general ellipsis in the second conjoin:

He is, {or WǍS at any rate, / or at least he WǍS,} a major composer. [1]

He is a major composer, or at least he WÀS △. [1a]

Similarly, appended coordination such as that of [1] of 13.94 can be reordered so as to produce an example of interpolated coordination:

John – and Sally, too – writes extremely well. [2]

If we attempt to analyse [2] as having a coordinated subject, we have to deal with the curiosity of a plural subject with a singular verb; but if we treat it as a case of interpolated coordination, we accept that the subject–verb concord will be unaffected by interpolated elements.

Note The coordination of the definite and indefinite articles (*cf* 13.71 Note [c]) may be treated as a case of interpolated coordination.

13.96 Two main distinguishing marks of interpolated coordination are these:

(a) The second conjoin is normally separated by prosody (in speech) or punctuation (in writing) from the rest of the clause, and thereby shows itself to be syntactically dislocated.
(b) There is no requirement that the interpolation acting as second or subsequent conjoin should constitute a grammatical unit, or even a sequence of grammatical units of the same rank. For example, the second conjoin in [1a] in 13.95 is *at least he was* [A S V], whereas in [3] below the second conjoin consists of an adverbial *at least*, a main verb *believes*, and the first part of a subordinate clause *that he is*:

He is, *or at least believes that he is*, a major composer. [3]
He may be, *and* (*certainly*) *believes that he is*, a major composer. [3a]

This sequence of words has no autonomy as a grammatical unit, and does not match the grammatical form of the first conjoin, *is*. But with interpolated coordination this does not matter: the only important requirement is that the second conjoin (or interpolation) be capable of replacing the first conjoin, so that the result of the substitution is a grammatical sentence. This condition, which is less exacting than that which applies to simple coordination (*cf* 13.43, 13.49, 13.88) is fulfilled in 13.95 [1a] and 13.96 [3]:

{*He is* a major composer.
At least he was a major composer.} (*cf* [1a])

{He *is* a major composer.
He *at least believes that he is* a major composer.} (*cf* [3])

Like complex coordination, interpolated coordination is a device of restricted use, normally associated with the premeditated, primarily written, use of English. Further examples are:

> The folk music of his native Romania [inspired], and [provided the thematic material for], his greatest work.
> She [can], and [probably will,] beat the world record.
> Sam [often thought about,] but [never revisited,] the haunts of his childhood.
> In these days, few people [learn,] or [indeed see any point in learning,] the languages of Homer and Virgil.

Stylistically, such interpolated coordination is often awkward, and is best avoided if a more straightforward construction can produce the same meaning and effect. Thus instead of the first sentence above one could write:

> The folk music of his native Romania inspired his greatest work, and provided the thematic material for it.

Note Interpolated coordination may be distinguished from PARENTHETICAL COORDINATION, where an unreduced coordinate clause is inserted parenthetically within another clause:

> They asked Bill Judd – and he's one of the best managers in the country – if he would take over the team next season.

Compare also PARENTHETICAL PARATAXIS, where the parenthetically included clause is completely independent of the other clause:

> Enterprising businessmen sell earthworms (they are one of the best soil conditioners) in hundreds of retail stores across the United States and Canada.

13.97 Some types of coordination which, on purely formal grounds, belong with complex coordination seem to belong with interpolated coordination in terms of prosody and style. These are coordinations where the conjoins consist of a sequence of nonfinal clause elements:

(i) SUBJECT + VERB

> [Richard admires], but [Margaret despises], the ballyhoo of modern advertising.

(ii) ADVERBIAL + VERB

> Gregory Peck [always was], and [always will be], her favourite Hollywood star.

(iii) VERB + OBJECT (when the object is not at the end of the clause)
Mrs Symes [gave a thousand dollars], and [promised several thousand more], to the fund for disabled athletes.

To see that these have the character of interpolated coordination, we note firstly the strength of the intonation boundaries enclosing the second conjoin:

Gregory Peck always WÁS| and always WĬLL be| her favourite Hollywood STÀR|

and secondly, the ease with which these examples could be changed by inserting or subtracting words from either conjoin. For example, if we add or subtract adverbials from one or the other conjoin in the above example, this is only a superficial variation within the basically versatile pattern of interpolated coordination:

Gregory Peck $\left\{\begin{array}{l}\text{was,}\\ \text{always was,}\end{array}\right\}$ and (no doubt) always will be,
her favourite Hollywood star.

Idiomatic and expressive uses of coordination

Pseudo-coordination: *try and come*, etc

13.98 When they precede *and*, members of a small class of verbs or predications have an idiomatic function which is similar to the function of catenative constructions (*cf* 3.49) and which will be termed PSEUDO-COORDINATION. The clearest example is *try*:

I'll try *and* come tomorrow.

This is roughly equivalent to *I'll try to come tomorrow*, but is more informal in style. Further:

They sat *and* talked about the good old times.

is similar in meaning to *They sat talking about the good old times*. Pseudo-coordination belongs to informal style, and many examples have a derogatory connotation:

Don't just stand there *and* grin. [= stand there grinning]
He went *and* complained about us.
They've gone *and* upset her again.
Run *and* tell him to come here at once.
Why did you go *and* do a silly thing like that?

Like *try* in being followed by a *to*-infinitive in the corresponding regular form are *stop*, *go*, *come*, *hurry up*, and *run*. Like *sit* are *stand* and (positional) *lie*.

This quasi-auxiliary use of *try* appears to be limited to the base form of the verb. Contrast the acceptability of:

> Try *and* see him tomorrow.
> He may try *and* see us tomorrow.
> They try *and* see us every day.

with the unacceptability of:

> *He tried *and* saw us yesterday.
> *She has tried *and* spoken to him.
> *He tries *and* sees us every day.

Instead of coordination, in such cases, we have to use the *to*-infinitive; *eg*:

> He tried to see us every day.

Note [**a**] Of the two *-ed* participle forms of *go* (*cf* 3.19 Note [b]) both *gone* and *been* occur in pseudo-coordination in BrE, but only *gone* occurs in pseudo-coordination in AmE:

> They've *gone* and spilled wine on the floor. ⟨BrE and AmE⟩
> They've *been* and spilled wine on the floor. ⟨BrE⟩

The normal meaning of *go* is lost in these sentences. There is no aspectual difference between them, of the kind normally associated with *gone* and *been* (*cf* 4.22 Note [b]), and both usages are informal and derogatory. BrE has a humorous usage in which both *been* and *gone* are conjoined with a third verb: *Look what you've been and gone and done.*

[**b**] In familiar speech we also find the idiom:

> He {*up* / *upped*} and hit me.   She {*up* / *upped*} and left him.

Pseudo-coordination: *nice and warm*, etc

13.99 Again in informal speech, there is a special use of some commendatory adjectives as first conjoin of a coordination by *and*. The most common adjective of this type is *nice*:

> This room is *nice and warm*. [= 'warm to just the right degree']

The semantic role of the first adjective is more like that of an intensifier than that of an adjective, hence this, too, may be regarded as *pseudo-coordination*. Other examples include:

> His speech was *nice and short*.
> It was *lovely and cool* in there. [= 'comfortably cool']

Some speakers (esp in AmE) use *good* in the same way:

> The road is *good and long*.

even where the adjectival form following *and* is used as an adverb:

> I hit him *good and hard*.   She drove *good and fast*.

Note [**a**] In attributive rather than predicative function, adjectives of the kind just illustrated commonly occur without *and* (*cf* 17.114):

> It's a *lovely warm* day.   He made a *nice short* speech.   It was a *good long* way to the corner.

[**b**] A comparable construction is the stereotyped use of the conjoined adverbs *well and truly* as in:

> Some of the guests were *well and truly* drunk.

The intensifying use of coordination

13.100 There are a number of circumstances in which a word or phrase is coordinated with itself. With comparative forms of adjectives, adverbs, and determiners, the effect is to express a continuing increase in degree. The comparative forms *more* and *less*, or else the inflected forms in *-er*, are often coordinated in this way:

She felt *more and more* angry.
She felt *angrier and angrier.* } [= She felt increasingly angry.]

The car went *more and more* slowly.
The car went *slower and slower.* } [= The car went increasingly slowly.]

Coordination of this kind with more than two conjoins also occasionally occurs:

The noise got *louder and louder and louder*, until it sounded as if a whirlwind had entered the house.

Asyndetic coordination is rare, but not impossible here: *The noise got louder, louder, louder . . .*

The iterative or continuative use of coordination

13.101 Another kind of expressive repetition with *and* conveys the idea of a repeated or continuing process. This iterative use of coordination may be found with verbs:

He *talked and talked and talked.* [= He talked for a very long time.]
They *knocked and knocked.* [= They knocked repeatedly.]

both with and without the conjunction:

They kept *talking, talking, talking* all night long.

It also occurs with adverbs, especially with *again* and the prepositional adverbs *over, on, around, up, down*, etc:

I've said it *again and again* [= repeatedly], but she still takes no notice.
He kept repeating the name *over and over.*
She talked *on and on and on.* [= continuously]
The balloon went *up and up* into the sky. [= continuously upwards]

Again, asyndetic coordination can be used for special dramatic emphasis:

The balloon went *up, up, up*, until it was a tiny speck in the sky.

A similar effect of iteration or alternating movement is sometimes achieved by coordinating contrasting prepositions or prepositional adverbs: *on and off, off and on, in and out, up and down, backwards and forwards*, etc:

Jill and Eric have been seeing one another *off and on* for the last five years. [= intermittently]
We watched the mother bird going *in and out* of the nest [= repeatedly in and out] trying to satisfy the appetite of the hungry fledglings.

The combination of this type of coordination with the repetitive coordination above produces a more vivid and emphatic effect:

> The soldiers marched *up and down, up and down* to the music of the band.

The repetitive types of coordination mentioned in this and the preceding sections, and especially the last type, are particularly characteristic of popular narrative style.

Other expressive uses of coordination

13.102 The coordination of identical items also occurs with nouns. The effect, if the noun is repeated once, may be to suggest that different types, especially good and bad, can be distinguished:

> There are *teachers and teachers*. [roughly: 'good and bad teachers']
> You can find *doctors and doctors*. [roughly: 'good and bad doctors']

But if the noun is repeated more than once, the effect is to suggest a large number or quantity:

> We saw *dogs and dogs and dogs* all over the place.
> There was nothing but *rain, rain, rain* from one week to the next.

Somewhat similar to these last examples is the intensifying effect of repetition of attributive adjectives and of degree intensifiers:

> an *old, old* man [= 'a very old man']
> *very, very, very* good [= 'extremely good']

But this type of coordination is always asyndetic.

In informal speech, the coordination of a noun phrase with . . . *or so* is used to express approximation. The noun phrase is normally a phrase of measurement. Compare the following with the coordination of numerals (*cf* 13.71):

> I liked { the year or { two / so } I spent there.
> I liked { *the man or { two / so } I saw there.

The limitations become clear with additional examples; thus although we can speak of:

> a dollar or so to spend
> a pound or so of butter
> a glass { of beer or so / or so of beer }

we cannot speak of **a chair or so*, **a child or so*, and still less of **the chair or so*, though '*another* chair or so' is acceptable. Hence the head nouns preceding the *or so* approximation must be units of measurement (*year, pound*) or items contextually rendered units of measurement (*another N*). It may be worth mentioning that 'a glass of beer or so' has the structure:

> a [glass [of beer]] or so.

Note [**a**] The stereotyped coordination in *out and out* has an intensifying effect in premodification of nouns:

He's an *out and out* liar. [= an utter, thoroughgoing liar]

Out-and-out is often hyphenated.

[**b**] In informal speech, expressions like *yes, no, well, OK, all right* are often repeated for emphasis (*cf* 18.58 on repetition).

Quasi-coordinators

13.103 In addition to the semi-coordinators *nor*, *so*, and *yet* mentioned in 13.19, there are several linking items which we may call QUASI-COORDINATORS, because they behave sometimes like coordinators, and at other times like subordinators or prepositions. The most prominent of them are clearly related to comparative forms (*cf* 15.63*ff*):

as well as, as much as, rather than, more than

Others are *if not*, *not to say*, and the correlative *not so much . . . as*.

In the following examples, the quasi-coordinators do not introduce clauses or noun phrases, and resemble coordinators in that they link 'conjoins' of varying grammatical constituency:

He [publishes] *as well as* [prints] his own books.
The speech was addressed [to the employers] *as much as* [to the strikers].
It was [how well] *more than* [how loud] she sang that impressed me.
He is [to be pitied] *rather than* [to be disliked].

Her manner was [unwelcoming] {*if not* / *not to say*} [downright rude].

His latest play is *not so much* [a farce] *as* [a burlesque tragedy].

In other sentences, however, they clearly have a prepositional or subordinating role, and have the mobility of adverbials, in that they can be placed in initial or final position (*cf* 15.52):

{*As well as printing the books*, he publishes them.
He publishes the books, *as well as printing them*.}

{*Rather than cause trouble*, I'm going to forget the whole affair.
I'm going to forget the whole affair, *rather than cause trouble*.}

Another reason for not treating these items as fully coordinative is that in subject position, they normally do not bring about plural concord if the first noun phrase is singular:

John, *as much as his brothers*, was responsible for the loss.

In this they resemble prepositions such as *with*, *in addition to*, and *after* more than coordinators like *and*; compare:

John, *with his brothers*, was responsible for the loss.
One senator *after another* has protested against the ban.

Compare, however, interpolated coordination (*cf* 13.95), where there can be a similar lack of plural concord, even with *and*. These observations remind us that coordination is related by gradience to subordination (*cf* 13.18*f*), and suggest that just as semi-coordinators such as *for* and *so that* are placed on the scale between coordinators and subordinators, so quasi-coordinators such as *as well as* may be regarded as taking their place on a scale between coordinators and prepositions.

Note [**a**] Nonrestrictive relative clauses have also been considered semantically equivalent to coordinated clauses. Such a classification seems particularly appropriate in the case of sentential relative clauses (*cf* 15.57), where the relative clause has the rest of the superordinate clause as its antecedent:

Pam didn't go to the show, *which is a pity*. ['. . . and that is a pity']

[**b**] Less common examples of quasi-coordinators are *still less* and its informal synonym *let alone*:

I've not even read the first chapter, {*still less* / *let alone*} finished the book.

To these may be added the infinitive construction *not to mention*, which is, however, more restricted in that it requires a following noun phrase:

He wrote twenty novels, *not to mention* six thick volumes of verse.

[**c**] The parallels between interpolated coordination ([1] *cf* 13.95*f*), quasi-coordination ([3]), prepositional phrases ([2]), and adverbial clauses ([4] *cf* 15.17*ff*) is illustrated in the following:

The next meeting, {*and* / *like*} *the one after it*, will be very important. [1] [2]
The next meeting, *as well as the one last month*, will be very important. [3]
The next meeting will be very important, *as was the one last month*. [4]

Whereas [5] is unacceptable because of the requirement that conjoins should be mutually substitutable, [6] is acceptable because of the status of *like* as a preposition:

*The next meeting, *and the one last month*, will be very important. [5]
The next meeting, *like the one last month*, will be very important. [6]

Abbreviations for coordination

13.104 The tags *and so on*, *and so forth*, and *et cetera* (Latin = 'and others', abbreviated in writing as *etc*) are abbreviatory devices which are added to a coordinated list, to indicate that the list has not been exhaustively given:

He packed his clothes, his books, his papers, *etc*.

And so on and *and so forth* (and their combination *and so on and so forth*) are used in the same way, but are restricted to informal use, and tend to occur after coordinated clauses rather than coordinated phrases. A less common phrase of the same kind is *and the like*.

Note [**a**] Another abbreviatory device used in a similar way to *etc* is the Latin *et al* (in full *et alii/aliae/alia* = 'and others'), which indicates incompletion of a list of names. It is most common in legal documents and in scholarly writing or lecturing, in the latter case to avoid repeating a list of coauthors:

J C Brown *et al.*

[**b**] Mention should also be made of the learned abbreviation *et seq* (Latin *et sequens*) meaning 'and the following (page)'. This sometimes has a plural form with letter reduplication *et seqq*, paralleling the use of reduplication of (final) letters to indicate plurality in other abbreviations such as *ff*, *MSS*, *pp* (*cf* 5.81 Note).

[**c**] The abbreviation *iff* in logical and mathematical discourse means '*if* and only if'.

Bibliographical note

General studies of coordination include: Dik (1968); Dougherty (1970–71); Gleitman (1965); Schachter (1977); Stockwell et al (1973), Ch. 6.

On coordination in relation to subordination and other kinds of connectivity, see Greenbaum (1969b, 1980); Halliday and Hasan (1976); Huddleston (1965); Talmy (1978).

On the coordinator *but*, see Greenbaum (1969a); R. Lakoff (1971).

On coordination in relation to ellipsis/reduction, see Greenbaum and Meyer (1982); Harries-Delisle (1978); Meyer (1979); Sanders (1977).

On gapping, see Hudson (1976b); Jackendoff (1971); Koutsoudas (1971); Kuno (1976a).

On ordering of coordinated elements, see Bolinger (1965); Malkiel (1959).

Among other studies of coordination are Ardery (1979); Hudson (1970); Lakoff and Peters (1969); Sørensen (1979a).

14 The complex sentence

Coordination and subordination

14.1 In Chapters 10 and 11 we studied the simple sentence, a sentence consisting of a single clause in which each of its elements (subject, object, adverbial, etc) is realized by a subclausal unit – a phrase. The multiple sentence, on the other hand, consists of more than one clause. One of the two major devices for linking clauses within the same sentence is coordination, which we discussed in Chapter 13. We there distinguished coordination from the other major device, subordination (*cf* 13.2*ff*). In this chapter we examine the complex sentence, a sentence in which one of the elements is realized by a subordinate clause. Here we discuss the structural types of subordinate clauses, the formal indicators of subordination, and the choices affecting the verb phrases of subordinate clauses.

Compound and complex sentences

14.2 The major types of multiple sentences are the compound and the complex sentence. A compound sentence consists of two or more coordinated main clauses; the clauses of a compound sentence provide classic instances of a paratactic relationship (*cf* 13.2), that is they have equivalent function, as diagrammatically indicated in *Fig* 14.2a overpage. The two main clauses in the Figure are equal constituents of the sentence, and are linked by the coordinator *but*.

A complex sentence is like a simple sentence in that it consists of only one main clause, but unlike a simple sentence it has one or more SUBORDINATE clauses functioning as an element of the sentence. Subordination is an asymmetrical relation: the sentence and its subordinate clauses are in a hypotactic relationship (*cf* 13.2), that is they form a hierarchy in which the subordinate clause is a constituent of the sentence as a whole – an adverbial in the example diagrammed in *Fig* 14.2b overpage.

Subordination is not the only factor that enters into either the length or the complexity of sentences, when 'complexity' is understood in a nontechnical sense. Phrases may be complex in the degree of their modification; the vocabulary may be obscure; because of their compression, nominalizations (*cf* 17.51*ff*) may be more difficult to understand than corresponding subordinate clauses; the coherence of the sentence as a whole may be difficult to understand; the content of the sentence may presuppose knowledge that is not generally available.

With respect to its function, a subordinate clause may be viewed as downgraded to a subclausal unit, such as a prepositional phrase:

Although I admire her reasoning, I reject her conclusions.
['Despite my admiration for her reasoning, I reject her conclusions']

Both the subordinate clause and the prepositional phrase in the paraphrase are functioning as adverbials within their sentence.

A clause that is not subordinate to another clause is an INDEPENDENT clause. Hence the two main clauses in *Fig* 14.2a and the main clause (identical with the sentence) in *Fig* 14.2b are independent clauses.

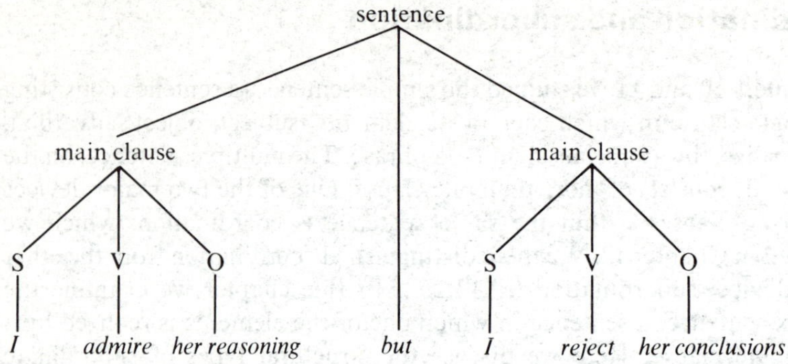

Fig 14.2a Compound sentence: coordination

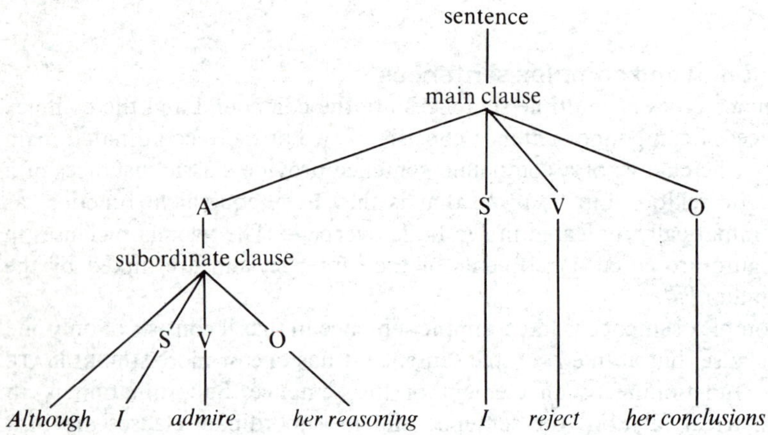

Fig 14.2b Complex sentence: subordination

Note [**a**] Main clauses have also been called 'principal clauses' or (less commonly) 'head clauses'.
[**b**] Subordinate clauses (sometimes abbreviated to 'sub-clauses') have also been called 'dependent', 'embedded', 'included', 'constituent', and 'syntactically bound' clauses.
[**c**] Some grammarians have extended the term *sentence* to cover what we have termed *clause*.
[**d**] Main clauses are generally also independent clauses. But if a coordinated main clause when it is isolated from the rest of the sentence is unacceptable as a simple sentence, it is not an independent clause. For example, the second clause below is structurally deficient as a simple sentence because of the ellipsis, the acceptability of the clause depending on its relationship to the first clause:

The plot was exciting and *the characterization plausible*.

Subordinate and superordinate clauses

14.3 *Figures* 14.2a and 14.2b present uncomplicated examples involving just two clauses. In *Fig* 14.2b the two clauses in the complex sentence are the subordinate clause and the SUPERORDINATE clause, of which the subordinate clause is a constituent; the superordinate clause is therefore also the main clause. But a clause may enter into more than one relationship; it may be subordinate to one clause and superordinate to another, as indicated in *Fig* 14.3a opposite.

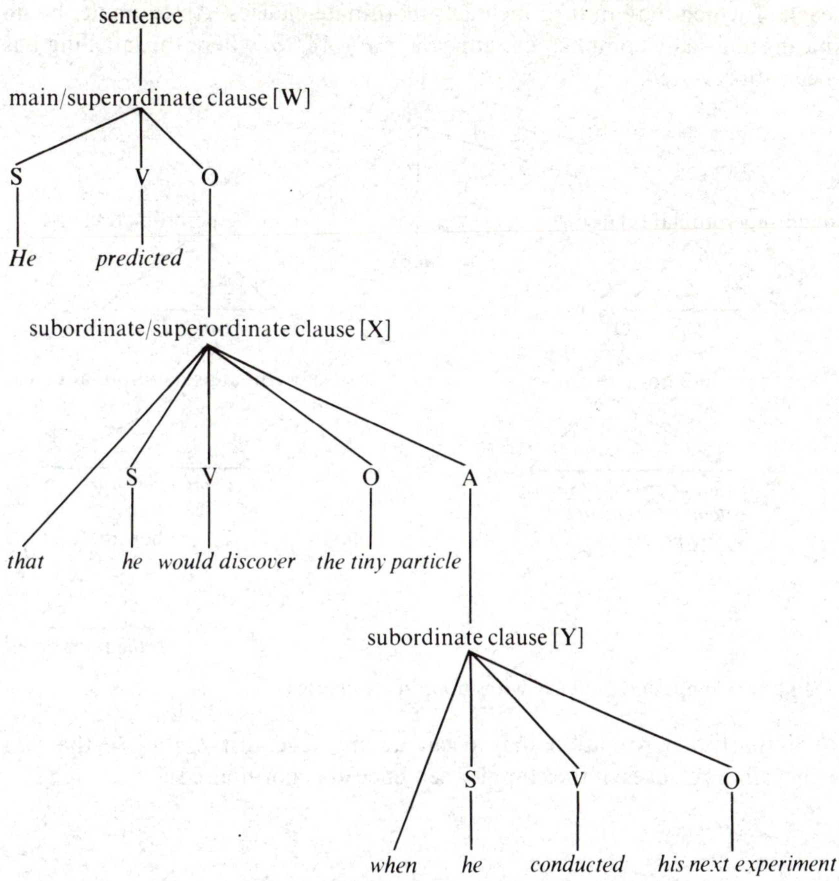

Fig 14.3a Superordinate and subordinate clauses

Clause [W] is superordinate to clause [X], which is in turn superordinate to clause [Y]. Conversely, clause [Y] is subordinate to clause [X], which is in turn subordinate to clause [W]. Clause [X] is therefore both superordinate to clause [Y] and subordinate to clause [W]. The relationships may be further clarified by labelled bracketing:

W- X-
(He predicted [that he would discover the tiny particle

Y- -Y-X-W
{when he conducted his next experiment}])

In each instance the subordinate clause is included in its superordinate clause: [X] functions as object in [W], while [Y] functions as adverbial in [X].

The device of subordination enables us to construct a multiple hierarchy of clauses, one within the other, sometimes resulting in extremely involved sentences (*cf* 14.37*ff*). Further complexity and structural variability are provided by the interrelation of subordination and coordination. Each main clause in a compound sentence may include one or more subordinate clauses, each of which may in turn include subordinate clauses. An example, by no means unusually complicated, appears in *Fig* 14.3b, where the labelling has been abbreviated:

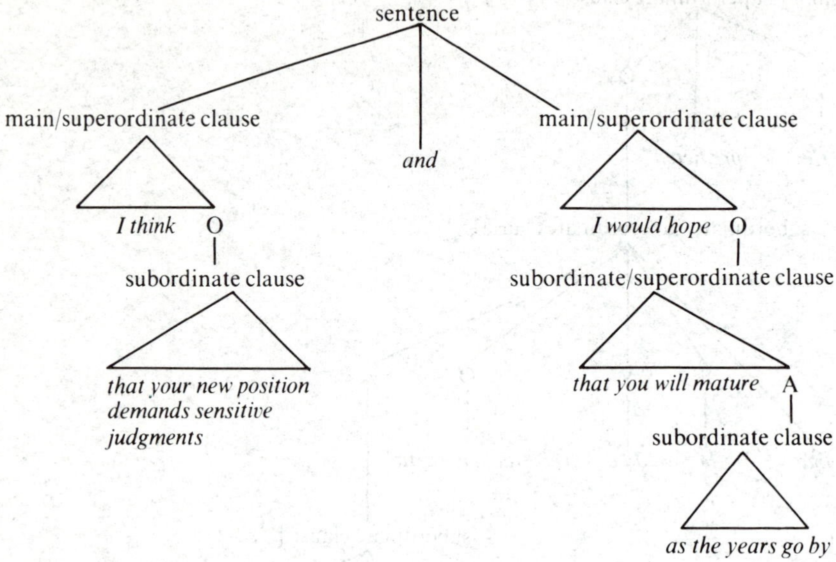

Fig 14.3b Compound sentence with subordinate clauses

Similarly, coordination may occur at any level. In *Fig* 14.3c the two subordinate clauses of the complex sentence are coordinated:

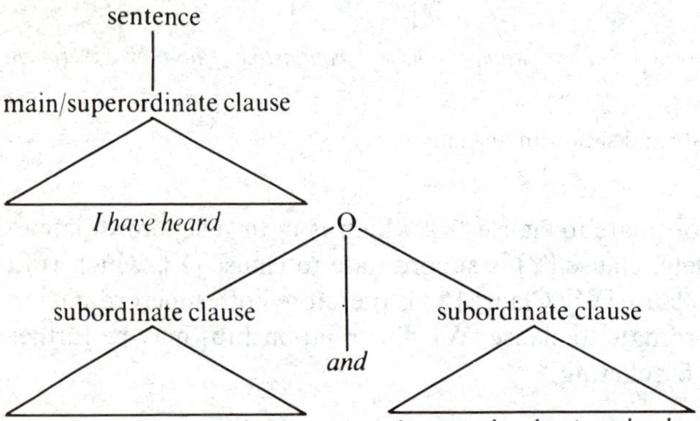

Fig 14.3c Complex sentence with coordinated clauses

A subordinate clause may function not only as a clause element of a superordinate clause but also as a constituent of a phrase, for example as a relative clause postmodifying a noun phrase:

The school *which my children attend* is within walking distance.

We consider such noun phrases to be complex, but we do not consider a sentence with a complex noun phrase to be a complex sentence merely on the grounds that it contains a complex phrase (*cf* 10.1 Note [a]).

Subordinate and matrix clauses

14.4 We have pointed out that a subordinate clause is a part of its superordinate clause, functioning as one of its elements. Thus, we can match clauses with phrases or words in the same function, direct object in [1] and adverbial in [2]:

We noticed { that they were nervous. / their nervousness. } [1]

One matures { as the years go by. / eventually. } [2]

We have no more reason to designate *We noticed* and *One matures* as clauses in their own right when they are followed by subordinate clauses than when they are followed by phrases or words. For both alternatives in [1] and [2] the clause that begins the sentence concludes the sentence.

Nevertheless, we find many occasions in this chapter, particularly in discussing adverbial clauses, when it is useful to distinguish between a subordinate clause and the rest of the superordinate clause of which it is part. When we have needed to do so, we have used the term MATRIX clause to designate the superordinate clause minus its subordinate clause. For example, we have referred to the situation described in the matrix clause as contingent on that of the subordinate conditional clause (*cf* 15.35):

I'll lend you some money if you don't have any money on you. [3]

The matrix clause *I'll lend you some money* conveys an offer that is consequent on the fulfilment of the condition expressed in the subordinate clause *if you don't have any money on you.* Similarly, we have referred to the matrix clause in discussing the time reference of adverbial clauses of time. For example, subordinators such as *before* and *until* indicate that the situation described in the matrix clause occurred before or led up to that in the subordinate clause (*cf* 15.27).

We illustrate in *Fig* 14.4 what we have termed a matrix clause.

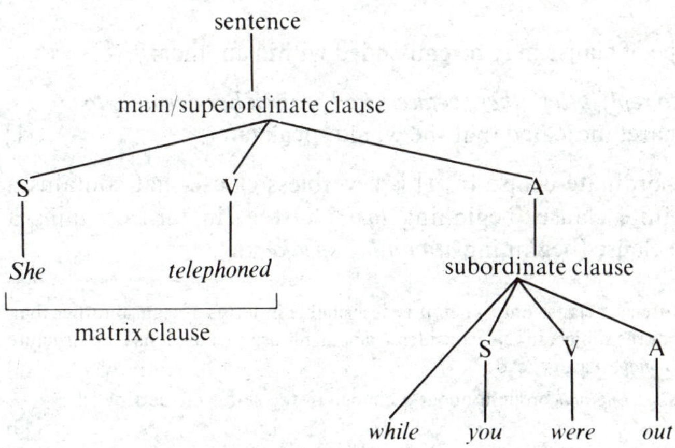

Fig 14.4 Matrix and subordinate clause

Note Some have used the term 'main clause' for what we term matrix clause.

Finite, nonfinite, and verbless clauses

14.5 We recognize three main structural types of clauses:

FINITE CLAUSE: a clause whose verb element is finite (such as *takes, took, can work, has worked, is writing, was written*; *cf* 3.52*ff*), *eg*:

I can't go out with you *because I am studying this evening.*

NONFINITE CLAUSE: a clause whose verb element is nonfinite (such as *to work, having worked, taken*; *cf* 3.53), *eg*:

Knowing my temper, I didn't reply.

VERBLESS CLAUSE: a clause that does not have a verb element, but is nevertheless capable of being analysed into clause elements, *eg*:

Although always helpful, he was not much liked.

We recognize nonfinite and verbless structures as clauses because we can analyse their internal structure into the same functional elements that we distinguish in finite clauses. Consider, for example, the analysis of the nonfinite clause in:

Knowing [V] *my temper* [O_d], I didn't reply.

The analysis depends on the analogy with the corresponding finite clause:

I [S] *know* [V] *my temper* [O_d].

Similarly, the verbless clause *although always helpful* in:

Although [conj] *always* [A] *helpful* [C_s], he was not much liked.

It is analysed as in the corresponding finite clause:

Although [conj] *he* [S] *was* [V] *always* [A] *helpful* [C_s], he was not much liked.

One structural type of clause may be embedded within another:

Too nervous to reply after other speakers had praised her devotion to duty, Margaret indicated that she would speak later. [1]

The italicized subordinate clause in [1] is a verbless clause that contains a subordinate nonfinite clause (beginning *to reply*) that in turn contains a subordinate finite clause (beginning *after other speakers*).

Note We recognize a structure as a clause only when it is describable in terms of clausal rather than phrasal structure. Hence the subject in [2] is considered a noun phrase because it has the structure of a noun phrase with *conquest* as its head:

William's conquest of England brought about a change in the status of the English language. [2]

Compare *William's conquests of other countries*, where the head of the phrase shows that it can take the number contrast that is characteristic of most nouns. On the other hand, the phrase structure of *William's conquest of England* is related to clause structure (*William conquered England*) through nominalization (*cf* 17.51*ff*). Both the clause and the phrase can be described semantically as a sequence of agentive, activity, and affected, but semantic grounds are not sufficient for syntactic analysis. Only the clause do we analyse syntactically as a sequence of subject, verb, and object. For example, consider *part-time teaching* in:

I enjoy *part-time teaching*.

It has the structure of a noun phrase with *teaching* as head and *part-time* as premodifier. Contrast *teaching undergraduates* in:

I enjoy *teaching undergraduates*.

It has the structure of a clause (as in *I teach undergraduates*) with *teaching* as verb and *undergraduates* as object. On the other hand, there is structural ambiguity in:

I enjoy *teaching*.

Teaching may be a noun phrase with only a head or a clause with only a verb (*cf* 15.13).

Nonfinite clauses

14.6 The nonfinite clause may be with or without a subject. The classes of nonfinite verb phrase (*cf* 3.53) serve to distinguish four structural classes of nonfinite verb clauses:

(i) TO-INFINITIVE

without subject: The best thing would be *to tell everybody*.
with subject: The best thing would be *for you to tell everybody*.

The infinitive clause with *to* plus a subject is found characteristically in constructions with anticipatory *it* (*cf* 18.33*ff*), *for* being used to introduce the subject: *It would be better for you to tell everybody*.

(ii) BARE INFINITIVE

without subject: All I did was *hit him on the head*.
with subject: *Rather than you do the job*, I'd prefer to finish it myself.

The bare infinitive is found characteristically in pseudo-cleft sentences (*cf* 18.29*f*), where the infinitival *to* is optional:

What they did was (*to*) *dig a shallow channel around the tent*.

(iii) -ING PARTICIPLE

without subject: *Leaving the room*, he tripped over the mat.
with subject: *Her aunt having left the room*, I asked Ann for some personal help.

When the subject of *-ing* clauses is expressed, it is often introduced by a preposition (*cf* 14.19 Note [b]):

With the audience turning restive, the chairman curtailed his long introduction.

On the question of genitive subjects, *cf* 15.12.

(iv) -ED PARTICIPLE

without subject: *Covered with confusion*, they apologized abjectly.
with subject: *The discussion completed*, the chairman adjourned the meeting for half an hour.

Categories (i) and (iii) are used most frequently; category (ii) is relatively rare.

Except for the *-ed* clause, which is inherently passive (*cf* 14.7), all types of nonfinite clauses have both active and passive forms, for example:

It would be possible *for my son to drive you to the airport.*
~It would be possible *for you to be driven to the airport by my son.*
Rather than *Michael guarantee the loan*, it can be done by his father.
~Rather than *the loan be guaranteed by Michael*, it can be done by his father.
The parents having paid for the damaged window, the police were not called.
~*The damaged window having been paid for by the parents*, the police were not called.

Progressive and perfective forms may function in the verb phrase of nonfinite clauses, though the nonfinite verb paradigm is somewhat defective (*cf* 3.56). But modal auxiliaries are excluded, since they have neither infinitives nor participles.

In negative nonfinite clauses, the negative particle is generally positioned before the verb or the *to* of the infinitive:

It's his fault for *not* doing anything about it.
The wisest policy is (for us) *not* to interfere.

Adverbs and brief prepositional phrases that intervene between *not* and the verb in finite clauses may also come between *not* and the verb:

It's his fault for *not ever* doing anything about it.

When *not* is inserted, there is often some aspectual marking:

The purse *not having* been found, } we went to the police.
The purse *not yet* found, }

On the split infinitive, *cf* 8.21.

14.7 The normal range of clause types (*cf* 10.2) is available for most nonfinite clauses, as in this set of *to*-infinitive clauses:

SV	I expect *them to come.*
SVO	They wanted *us to learn economics.*
SVC	Joe supposed *the stranger to be friendly.*
SVA	It's great *for everybody to be here.*
SVOO	It's best *for you to give him a call.*
SVOC	Paul prefers *me to make the difference clear.*
SVOA	He got *her to put the car in the garage.*

The subject of nonfinite clauses, however, is commonly absent.

Because it is generally both syntactically and semantically passive, the *-ed* participle clause is restricted to the four types of passive clauses. In [1] the subordinator *when* introduces the *-ed* clause:

$(S)V_{pass}$ ~ active *SVO*
When questioned, she denied being a member of the group. [1]

$(S)V_{pass}C$ ~ active *SVOC*
Considered works of art, they were admitted into the country without customs duties. [2]
$(S)V_{pass}A$ ~ active *SVOA*
Kept in the refrigerator, the drug should remain effective for at least three months. [3]
$(S)V_{pass}O$ ~ active *SVOO*
Allowed unusual privileges, the prisoner seemed to enjoy his captivity. [4]

14.8 Because nonfinite clauses lack tense markers and modal auxiliaries and frequently lack a subject and a subordinating conjunction, they are valuable as a means of syntactic compression. Certain kinds of nonfinite clause are particularly favoured in written prose, where the writer has the leisure to revise for compactness. We recover meanings associated with tense, aspect, and mood from the sentential context. We can also normally see a correspondence with a finite clause with a form of the verb BE and a pronoun subject having the same reference as a noun or pronoun in the same sentence (*cf* 15.58*ff*). For examples 14.7 [1–4], one might make the following insertions:

When (she was) *questioned*, she denied being a member of the group. [1a]
(Since/Because/As they were) *considered works of art*, they were admitted into the country without customs duties. [2a]
(If it is) *kept in the refrigerator*, the drug should remain effective for at least three months. [3a]
(Since/After he was) *allowed unusual privileges*, the prisoner seemed to enjoy his captivity. [4a]

On the other hand, [5] shows how the advantage of compactness must be balanced against the danger of ambiguity; for the absence of a subject leaves doubt as to which nearby nominal element is notionally the subject:

We met you (*when you?/we? were*) leaving the room. [5]

With infinitive clauses, a corresponding finite clause also enables one to identify an understood subject:

I asked *to go.* ~ I asked *if I could go.*
I asked *him to go.* ~ I asked *if he would go.*

When no referential link with a nominal can be discovered in the linguistic context, an indefinite subject may be inferred, or else the 'I' of the speaker:

To be an administrator is to have the worst job in the world. ['For a person to be . . .']
The prospects are not very good, *to be candid.* ['. . . if I am to be candid']

Contrast:

It's hard work *to be a student.* [indefinite subject; *cf* 10.42*f*]
It's hard work, *to be honest.* [*I* as subject; *cf* 8.125]

Verbless clauses

14.9 Verbless clauses take syntactic compression one stage further than nonfinite clauses and like them are also commonly subjectless. Once again (*cf* 14.8), we can usually postulate a missing form of the verb BE and to recover the subject, when omitted, from the context:

Whether right or wrong, he always comes off worst in argument. ['whether *he is* right or wrong']
One should avoid taking a trip abroad in August *where possible*. ['where *it is* possible']

Verbless clauses can also sometimes be treated as reductions of nonfinite clauses:

Too nervous to reply, he stared at the floor. ['*Being* too nervous to reply . . .']

(Here the verbless clause itself contains a subordinate nonfinite clause, *to reply*.)

When the subject is present, only the verb has to be recovered, though it is not always possible to insert it without juxtaposing the clause (*cf* [2] below):

73 people have been drowned in the area, *many of them children*. ['many of them being children'] [1]
There he stood, *a tray in each hand*. ['a tray was in each hand'] [2]

The subject is often introduced by *with* (*cf* 14.15):

With the children at school, we can't take our vacations when we want to. [3]

Since it is usually possible to interpret the clause as having an omitted BE, the verbless clause is limited to the two clause-types *SVC* and *SVA*, with or without a subordinator (*sub*):

She looked at him expectantly, *her eyes full of excitement and curiosity*. [S (V) C] [4]
I do not wish to describe his assertions, *some of them offensive*. [S (V) C] [5]
He looked remarkably well, *his skin clear and smooth*. [S (V) C] [6]
Though somewhat edgy, she said she would stay a little longer. sub [S (V) C] [7]
We can meet again tomorrow, *if necessary*. sub [S (V) C] [8]
Mavis sat in the front seat, *her hands in her lap*. [S (V) A] [9]
While at college, he was a prominent member of the dramatic society. sub [(S V) A] [10]

It is also possible in [9] to view the understood verb as HAVE ('having her hands in her lap', *cf* 'with her hands in her lap'), in which case the structure is [(S V) O A].

Optional adverbials may also be added, either initially or finally:

'Thank you very much,' said Raymond, *ever mindful of his manners*. [(S V) $A_{frequency}$ C_s]

Loath to reply for fear of offending her parents, she strode out of the room. [(S V) C_s A_{reason}]
Though now frail, they were quite capable of looking after themselves. sub [(S V) A_{time} C_s]

When the verbless clause is reduced to its minimum of a single complement or adverbial, it may not be easy to distinguish it from an appositive construction (*cf* 17.65*ff*), a nonrestrictive postmodifier (*cf* 17.48*f*), or an adverbial which is a direct constituent of the main clause. The initial prepositional phrase below is an adverbial of the sentence:

Of humble parentage, he began his working life in a shoe factory.

It might be regarded as an adverbial realized by a verbless clause consisting of just a complement, because its analysis is directly parallel to nominal or verbless clauses like:

A man of humble parentage, . . . ~ Born of humble parentage, . . .

Similarly, if the final noun phrase below had been placed next to the subject we would have recognized it as full apposition:

The river lay in its crescent loop entirely without movement, *an artifice of green-black liquescent marble*.

As it is, we could regard it as a verbless clause functioning as an adverbial. Indeed, many instances of partial apposition with noun phrases (*cf* 17.66) could be equally regarded as verbless clauses, *eg*:

Judge Clement Turpin, *now a federal appeals court judge*, is being considered for appointment to the US Supreme Court.

Formal indicators of subordination

14.10 Subordination is generally marked by a signal in the subordinate clause. The signal may be of various kinds:

(i) The clause is initiated by a subordinating conjunction (14.11*ff*).
(ii) The clause is initiated by a *wh*-element (14.20).
(iii) Initial elements in the clause are inverted (14.20).
(iv) The presence of certain verb forms in finite clauses is determined by the type of subordinate clause (14.21*ff*).
(v) The verb element of the clause is either nonfinite or absent (14.20).

More than one subordination signal may cooccur in the same subordinate clause. For example, a nonfinite or verbless clause may be introduced by a subordinating conjunction (*cf* 14.15*ff*).

Note [**a**] The verb form in the superordinate clause may also be affected by the type of subordinate clause. The clearest example is in the hypothetical condition relationship (*cf* 15.36).
[**b**] For nonfinite and verbless clauses that are not part of a superordinate clause, *cf* 11.40*f*.

Subordinators

14.11 SUBORDINATORS (or more fully SUBORDINATING CONJUNCTIONS) are the most important formal device of subordination, particularly for finite clauses. Like prepositions, which they resemble in having a relating function, subordinators forming the core of the class consist of a single word, but there is a larger range of complex subordinators which function, to varying degrees, like a single conjunction. In addition, there is a small class of correlative subordinators, which combine two markers of subordination, one being a subordinator.

Subordinators may be restricted to particular types of clauses, as the following sections show.

Subordinators for finite clauses

14.12 Most subordinators may introduce finite clauses. Here is a list of those subordinators. They are divided into simple, complex, and correlative subordinators. The correlative subordinators are listed and discussed in 14.13.

SIMPLE SUBORDINATORS

after, although, as, because, before, directly ⟨informal, esp BrE⟩, *if, immediately* ⟨informal, esp BrE⟩, *lest* ⟨esp AmE⟩, *like* ⟨informal, esp AmE⟩, *once, since, that, though, till, unless, until, when(ever), where(ver), whereas, whereupon, while, whilst* ⟨a minority alternative to *while*, esp BrE⟩

COMPLEX SUBORDINATORS

ending with *that*:

but that, in that, in order that, insofar that ⟨formal, rare⟩, *in the event that, save that* ⟨literary⟩, *such that*

ending with optional *that*:

(a) participle form:

assuming, considering, excepting, given, granted,
granting, provided, providing, seeing, supposing } *(that)*

(b) others:

except, for all,
now, so } *(that)*

ending with *as*:

according as, as far as, as long as, as soon as, forasmuch as ⟨formal⟩, *inasmuch as* ⟨formal⟩, *insofar as, insomuch as* ⟨formal⟩

Others:

as if, as though, in case

Note [**a**] The distinction in form between the simple and complex subordinators is in part orthographic, since some of the simple subordinators are internally (that is morphologically) complex. But their orthographical unity points to the central place of the simple subordinators in the system.

[**b**] In addition, the following archaic subordinators still have a limited currency: *albeit, whence, whereat, wherefore, whither*.

[**c**] Many of the subordinators indicate more than one logical relationship. The relationships are discussed in subsequent sections of this chapter.

[d] The omission of an optional *that* in the complex subordinators tends to lower the level of formality. On the other hand, the inclusion of *that* may avoid ambiguity (*cf* 14.41).

[e] *About* and *without* are used as subordinators for finite clauses in informal style, but are not generally considered acceptable:

?She explained to us *about there's nothing for teenagers to do in the village.*

?We can't even read in our bedroom *without one of the children comes barging in wanting something.*

They are among recent examples of a continuing trend to use prepositions also as subordinators. *On account* (*of*) ⟨esp AmE⟩, another recent example, has achieved somewhat greater acceptability in informal style:

I can't come now *on account* (*of*) *I have to look after my baby brother.*

[f] *But that* is a subordinator in the sense 'except (that)':

She would have ignored Edward *but that* she knew he would have complained to her sister.

Occasionally *that* is omitted:

It never rains *but* it pours.

Except is used without *that* in the sense 'unless' (*cf* 15.34):

I wouldn't be here *except* I had to.

But *that* is often added when *except* has the sense 'only' (*cf* 15.44):

I'd lend you my car *except* (*that*) I may need it later this afternoon.

[g] The temporal subordinators, interrogative *whether* and *if*, and conditional *if* can alone serve as truncated subordinate clauses functioning as exclamation tags:

A: Brian will attend the class {if / when} it suits him.

B: (Ah, yes) {*ÌF*! / *WHÈN*!}

Virtually any conjunction can function alone as an echo question:

A: I'll let you know *if* there are going to be refreshments.

B: ÍF? But surely you promised you would arrange it.

A: We're arriving in New York *after* you leave.

B: ÁFter? But I was hoping to see you there.

Correlative subordinators

14.13 The correlative subordinators are divided into five sets, listed below. The second correlative endorses the meaning of the first. For correlative coordinators, *cf* 13.33*ff*.

CORRELATIVE SUBORDINATORS

(a)	*as*	. . . *so*
(b)	{*as* / *so* / *such*}	. . . *as*
	{*so* / *such*}	. . . (*that*)
	{*less* / *more* (/-*er*)}	. . . *than*
	no sooner	. . . *than, when* ⟨informal⟩
	{*barely* / *hardly* / *scarcely*}	. . . *when, than* ⟨informal⟩
(c)	*the*	. . . *the*
(d)	{*whether* / *if*}	. . . *or*

(e) subordinator plus optional conjunct

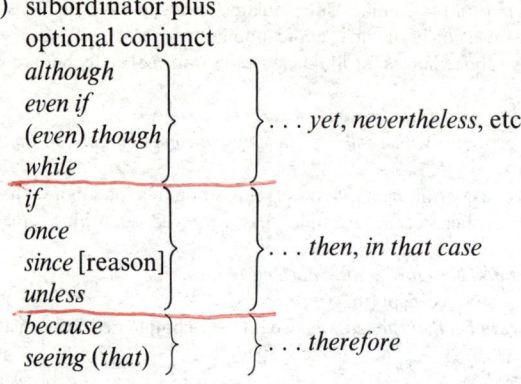

Concession
although / *even if* / (*even*) *though* / *while* } . . . *yet, nevertheless*, etc

Condition
if / *once* / *since* [reason] / *unless* } . . . *then, in that case*

Reason
because / *seeing* (*that*) } . . . *therefore*

The (a) set consists of the unique proportional correlative *as* . . . *so* (*cf* 15.51), also typical of formal and deliberative style. The conjunct emphasizes the relationship indicated by the initial subordinator:

> *As* the strength of the defenders failed, *so* the courage of the attackers grew.

The omission of *so* tends to give a temporal interpretation ('all the while that') to the subordinator *as*.

The (b) set contains comparative correlatives (*cf* 15.63*ff*). In this set the subordinate clause is positioned finally. The first element functions as degree modifier in the superordinate clause, while the second is a subordinator introducing the final subordinate clause:

> I was {*more* ashamed / angrier} *than* I have ever been.
> He had *no sooner* arrived *than* he asked for food.

The (c) set consists of the unique pair of proportional correlatives *the* . . . *the* (*cf* 15.51):

> *The* harder they worked, *the* hungrier they became.
> ['As they worked harder, so they became hungrier.']

If the order of the two clauses is reversed, the meaning relationship is changed (*cf* Note [d] below):

> *The* hungrier they became, *the* harder they worked.
> ['As they became hungrier, so they worked harder.']

The (d) set contains the *whether* . . . *or* correlatives used in two different types of subordinate clauses: alternative interrogative clauses (*cf* 15.6) and alternative conditional-concessive clauses (*cf* 15.41). In the interrogative construction the *or*-clause is optional:

> They didn't tell me *whether* I should write to the manager (*or whether* I should see him personally).

In the conditional-concessive construction, on the other hand, the *or*-clause is obligatory. In both instances, the correlative *or* coordinates two subordinate clauses (*cf* the *either* . . . *or* correlative, 13.33*f*), unlike the previous sets, where only one correlative is attached to the subordinate clause. *Or* is also an optional correlative in the alternative interrogative clause introduced by *if* (*cf* 15.6).

The (e) set combines a subordinator in an initial subordinate adverbial clause with an optional conjunct (*cf* 8.134*ff*) in the superordinate clause. The conjunct emphasizes the relationship indicated by the subordinator:

Though the workers were unhappy with some aspects of the proposed new contract, *nevertheless* they overwhelmingly voted in favour of it. [CONCESSIVE CLAUSE; *cf* 15.39*ff*]
If this year's harvest is good, *then* they will not need to import wheat. [CONDITIONAL CLAUSE; *cf* 15.33*ff*]
Because you have not replied to my formal letter of May 1, I am *therefore* withdrawing my offer.
[REASON CLAUSE; *cf* 15.45*ff*]

Some writers avoid the conjunct as redundant in these examples. Its insertion is more usual in an insistently persuasive argument or in a formal and deliberative style of writing, especially if the initial subordinate clause is lengthy and the relationship then needs to be recalled. The effect is to balance the two parts of the system, an effect akin to parallelism (*cf* 19.7), and to remind the reader or hearer of the force of the argument.

Note [**a**] The range of correlative subordinators can be extended somewhat in literary style to include, for example, *where . . . there* and *when . . . then*:

When her imagination was stirred, *then* there descended upon her a frenzy to inscribe her thoughts.

[**b**] The following occur with subject–operator inversion (*cf* 18.24) in the first clause:

no sooner . . . than *barely/hardly/scarcely . . when/before*

There is traditional objection to the use of *when* as correlative with *no sooner* and to the use of *than* as correlative with the three negative adverbs.

[**c**] Since subordinate adverbial clauses are usually in *E* position, the correlative in sets (a), (b), and (c) can be seen as providing the condition for the clause to be in *I* position and subsequently endorsing the force of the clause.

[**d**] *The* may be used in two ways to introduce a final subordinate clause without a preceding initial correlative *the*. In the first use, it correlates with a comparative in the superordinate clause, the construction then belonging to set (c):

They became (*the*) hungri*er* *the* harder they worked.

The construction is equivalent in meaning to the correlative *the . . . the* construction:

The harder they worked, *the* hungrier they became.
[*cf* *Harder they worked, hungrier they became.]

The equivalence provides an argument for suggesting that the first clause is semantically subordinate, as in sets (a) and (b).

In the second use, *the* is noncorrelative. It combines with a comparative, chiefly to introduce a final subordinate clause of purpose, especially a *to*-infinitive clause:

They moved to the front, *the* bett*er* to hear the speaker.

Less formally:

They moved to the front in order to hear the speaker better.

In formal style, the purpose clause may be initial:

The more easily to induce witnesses to testify, we are conducting our hearings in private.

Marginal subordinators

14.14 As with complex prepositions (*cf* 9.10*ff*), it is difficult to distinguish categorically between complex subordinators and free syntactic constructions. Several marginal types require discussion.

Type 1 consists of a habitual combination of a subordinator with a preceding or following adverb; for example *even if* and *if only*. We regard these as subordinators because the meaning of the subordinator is affected by the presence of the adverb. In contrast, combinations such as *only if* and *just as* consist of a premodifier preceding a subordinator.

Type 2 consists of noun phrases that commonly function as temporal adverbials; for example, *the moment* (*that*) and *every time* (*that*). We consider these to be more like free syntactic constructions than like complex subordinators. The relationship between *the moment* and the following clause, for example, can be explained as the head of a noun phrase modified by a restrictive relative clause, the noun phrase functioning as adverbial of time. Compare:

I recognized him *that moment*. I recognized him *the moment I saw him*.

The phrase permits the range of structural variations that one would expect from that analysis. For example:

$$\left.\begin{array}{l}\textit{at}\\ \textit{from}\end{array}\right\}\textit{(just) the}\left\{\begin{array}{l}\textit{first}\\ \textit{next}\\ \textit{last}\\ \textit{precise}\\ \textit{very}\end{array}\right\}\left\{\begin{array}{l}\textit{moment}\\ \textit{instant}\\ \textit{minute}\\ \textit{time}\end{array}\right\}\left\{\begin{array}{l}\textit{that}\\ \textit{when}\end{array}\right\}\text{ I saw him, I recognized him.}$$

Other examples of such free constructions include *during the period when*, *until such time as*, *since the days that*.

Type 3 consists of prepositional phrases ending in *the fact that*. They express relationships of reason or concession. Because they can be replaced more concisely by a simple conjunction, they are considered to be stylistically clumsy. Examples include:

$$\left.\begin{array}{l}\textit{because of the fact that}\\ \textit{due to the fact that}\\ \textit{on account of the fact that}\\ \textit{in (the) light of the fact that}\end{array}\right\}\text{['because']}$$

$$\left.\begin{array}{l}\textit{in spite of the fact that}\\ \textit{regardless of the fact that}\end{array}\right\}\text{['although']}$$

These allow some variation of the preposition and considerable variation of the head of the noun phrase. Compare:

$$\textit{In spite of}\left\{\begin{array}{l}\textit{the fact}\\ \textit{the news}\\ \textit{your report}\\ \textit{my belief}\end{array}\right\}\text{ that they were sick, I went to visit them.}$$

Only *in spite of the fact that* can be replaced by a simple conjunction (*eg*: *although*), yet it is clear that all the phrases have a similar function. We should therefore regard them as prepositional phrases followed by a clause in apposition to the noun-phrase complement.

Type 4 consists of participle forms such as *supposing* (*that*) and *provided* (*that*). The participles form a gradient. Some retain certain properties characteristic of verbs, while those that are most like simple conjunctions have lost all such properties. Thus, like other participles, *supposing* and *assuming* can be expanded by adverbials:

> supposing } { for the sake of argument } that
> assuming } { as a result of your advice }

But such expansion is not permitted for some of the other participle forms:

> *seeing } { for the sake of argument } that
> *provided } { as a result of your advice }

On the other hand, like many verbs, *seeing* and *considering* can be followed by conjunctions other than *that*:

> Seeing } *how* he reacted . . .
> Considering }

But most important of all, the conjunctional *seeing*, *provided*, *providing*, and *given* are now distinct from the participles in meaning and in not requiring subject identification (*cf* 15.58*f*), so that they cannot be viewed as the verb in a participle clause.

Note [**a**] The premodifier in the free constructions of type 1 may be focusing (*cf* 8.116), as in *even when* and *only if*; intensifying (*cf* 8.104), as in *ever since* and *just as* (in the similarity sense); or specifying further the time relationship, as in *just when* and *a few days before*.

[**b**] There are other conjunction-like prepositional phrases similar to those in type 3, but not ending in *the fact that*; for example, *in the event that*, *on the grounds that*, *in the sense that*.

Subordinators for nonfinite and verbless clauses

14.15 Nonfinite and verbless clauses are subordinate by virtue of the absence of a finite verb as the verb element of the clause. They are, however, sometimes introduced by a subordinator, which generally signals the clause to be adverbial.

The structural classes of clauses vary in the subordinators that they admit. However, all the classes except for that of the bare infinitive clauses may be introduced by the subordinators *with* and *without*. A noun phrase (not necessarily the subject) is required after the subordinator:

> *Without you to consult*, I would be completely lost.
> *With the mortgage paid*, they could afford to go abroad for their vacation.
> Don't walk around *with your shirt hanging out*.
> *With you as my friend*, I don't need enemies.

Note *Rather than* is found with all types of clauses, including finite clauses, but it is generally best treated as a quasi-coordinator (*cf* 13.103), with matching forms in the clauses (but *cf* 14.19 Note [c]):

> They were *screaming* rather than *singing*. She *telephoned* rather than *wrote*.
> He wanted *to sunbathe* rather than (*to*) *swim*.

The part after *rather than* refers to an earlier assumption that is rejected; *rather than* is here equivalent to 'and not'.

Subordinators for bare infinitive clauses

14.16 Bare infinitive clauses are limited to the two synonymous subordinators *rather than* and *sooner than* (*cf* 14.15 Note for the function of *rather than* as quasi-coordinator). The matrix clauses express the subject's preference (*cf* 15.52):

He paid the fine *rather than appeal to a higher court.*
Sooner than wait for a reply to your letter, I would telephone her.

The bare infinitive clause occasionally takes a subject:

Rather than RŎBert *drive in his present state*, I'd prefer to drive him home myself.

Note [**a**] In contrast to the constraints on the quasi-coordinator *rather than*, when clauses are introduced by the subordinators *rather than* and *sooner than* the verb forms do not need to match and the subordinate clause may be initial as well as final.
[**b**] If *would* or *should* is in the matrix clause, *rather* and *sooner* may be moved into that clause when the subordinate clause is final:

He would *rather* pay the fine *than appeal to a higher court.*

Such sentences have an obvious resemblance to comparative constructions and admit various comparative adverbs:

He would *more* {*readily* / *willingly* / *cheerfully*} pay the fine *than appeal to a higher court.*

Subordinators for *to*-infinitive clauses

14.17 *To*-infinitive clauses may be introduced by several subordinators: *as if*, *as though*, *for*, *in order*, *so as*, *whether* . . . (*or*), *with*, and *without*. *For* in this function is restricted to infinitive clauses with their own subject, and indeed is often obligatory (*cf* 15.10):

It would be an absurd idea *for them to move to another house at this stage of their careers.*

Since *for* may be combined with the subordinator *in order to*, it seems to be a device for introducing the subject rather than to be a true subordinator:

In order for you to be eligible for a student grant, your parents must receive less than a stipulated annual income.

Whether (with or without correlative *or*) introduces a subordinate interrogative clause:

I don't know *whether to put on the air-conditioning today.*

In the absence of a subject in the subordinate clause, the subject is understood as identical with that of the matrix clause.

Subordinators for *-ed* clauses and verbless clauses

14.18 Clauses with an *-ed* participle and verbless clauses may be introduced by some subordinators that are also used for finite clauses (*cf* 14.12):

although, *as* [manner], *as if*, *as soon as*, *as though*, *even if*, *if*, *once*, *though*, *unless*, *until* [only *-ed* participle clauses], *when*(*ever*), *where*(*ver*), *whether* . . . *or* [conditional-concessive], *while*, *whilst* ⟨esp BrE⟩

These clauses can be related to finite clauses for which the subject and the verb BE are supplied (*cf* 14.9):

When taken according to the directions, the drug has no side effects. ['When the drug is taken . . .'] [1]
Although not yet six months old, she was able to walk without support. ['Although she was not yet . . .'] [2]
Unless told otherwise, be here every night. ['Unless you are told . . .'; *you* is implied subject of the imperative superordinate clause] [3]
If necessary, he will take notes for you. ['If his taking notes is necessary, . . .'] [4]

The subject of the subordinate clause must generally be understood as identical with that of the matrix clause, but for verbless clauses such as *if necessary* and *where possible* it may refer to the matrix clause as a whole, as in example [4].

Note [**a**] The *if*-clauses may be used for hypothetical conditions (*cf* 14.19 Note [a], 15.35):
The milk would not turn sour *if boiled*. ['if it were boiled']
I would have typed your manuscript for you *if necessary*. ['if it had been necessary to do so']
[**b**] There is a stereotyped construction in which the *-ed* participle follows *no sooner than*:
(It was) no sooner said *than done*.

Subordinators for *-ing* clauses

14.19 Clauses with an *-ing* participle may be introduced by any of the subordinators for *-ed* participle clauses (*cf* 14.18), except that the subordinators *where*, *wherever*, *as* [manner], and *as soon as* are excluded (*cf* Note [a] below):

although, *as if*, *as though*, *even if*, *if*, *once*, *though*, *unless*, *until*, *when*(*ever*), *whether . . . or* [conditional-concessive], *while*, *whilst* ⟨esp BrE⟩

Unlike *-ed* participle and verbless clauses, however, these *-ing* participle clauses cannot be regarded as strictly elliptical clauses, since the *-ing* participle does not necessarily represent a progressive form in the equivalent finite clause. The *-ing* participle neutralizes that aspectual distinction:

When returning merchandise, be sure to bring your receipt. ['When you return . . .' *or* 'When you are returning . . .']

The nonequivalence of the *-ing* participle in these clauses with the finite progressive is most conspicuous when the progressive aspect is ruled out, as with the perfective or a verb used statively (*cf* 4.27*ff*):

Once having left the premises, you must buy another ticket to reenter. ['Once you have left . . .']
Though understanding no Spanish, she was able to communicate with the other students. ['Though she understood no Spanish, . . .']

Note [**a**] *-ing* clauses introduced by *if*, *even if*, and *unless* are restricted to open conditions (*cf* 15.35), in which they are roughly equivalent to 'in cases where'. Even so, *if* sounds somewhat stilted:
If coming by car, take the A10 and turn off at the A414.
Even if and *unless* are relatively more acceptable in such contexts:
{*Even if* / *Unless*} *receiving visitors*, patients must observe normal hospital rules.
[**b**] *After*, *before*, and *since* (subordinators with finite clauses) differ from subordinators such as *when* or *while* in that they are followed by *-ing* clauses but not by *-ed* clauses or verbless clauses:
He took a shower {*before* / *after*} *returning home*. [1]

Since moving here, I have felt more relaxed. [2]

These three also differ from the subordinators listed above in 14.19 in that they allow a subject in the *-ing* clause:

Since my coming here, life has become more comfortable for my parents. [3]

The differences suggest that *after*, *before*, and *since* are better classed with prepositions such as *on* and *through* (both of which permit a subject in the *-ing* clause) rather than with subordinators:

He took a shower *on returning home*. [1a]

Through my moving here, life has become more comfortable for my parents. [3a]

[**c**] Like *as well as* and *instead of*, *rather than* is a preposition, not a quasi-coordinator (*cf* 13.103), when it is followed by an *-ing* participle clause that does not match the verb in the matrix clause (*cf* 14.15 Note):

Their actions precipitated the war *rather than averting it*.
As well as visiting Niagara Falls, we spent a day in Toronto.
He intends to go as he is, *instead of changing into his best clothes*.

Other indicators of subordination

14.20 We now turn to other indicators of subordination apart from subordinators.

(i) *Wh*-elements are initial markers of subordination in subordinate interrogative clauses (*cf* 15.5*f*) and subordinate exclamative clauses (*cf* 15.7), in *wh*-relative clauses (*cf* 15.8*f*, 17.9*ff*), and in conditional-concessive clauses (*cf* 15.41*f*). The subordinating *wh*-words are:

who, *whom*, *whose*, *which*
when, *where*, *what*, *why*, *how*
whoever, *whomever* ⟨rare⟩, *whichever*
wherever, *whenever*, *whatever*, *however*
whosoever, *whomsoever*, *wheresoever*, *whatsoever*, *howsoever* ⟨all rare; legal and religious⟩

(ii) The relative pronoun *that*, which can often replace *wh*-pronouns, is a subordination marker in restrictive relative clauses (*cf* 17.9*ff*):

The style *that we are examining in this exhibition* was an unusual one.

The relative pronoun is to be distinguished from the subordinator *that*, which does not operate as an element in the subordinate clause.

(iii) Subject–operator inversion is a marker of subordination in some conditional, similarity, and comparative clauses (*cf* 15.36, 15.50 Note, 15.74). It is typical of a literary and elevated style of persuasion. The operators that permit the inversion are *had*, *were*, *should*, and (less commonly) *could* and *might*:

Had I been less forthright, I would have acquired more support.
Were she here, she would support the motion.

Inversion of a different kind – the fronting of the whole or part of the predication – may occur with the subordinators *as*, *though*, and *that* (*cf* 15.39, 15.47):

Eloquent though she was, she could not persuade them.

(iv) The absence of a finite verb is itself an indicator of subordination, since nonfinite and verbless clauses are necessarily subordinate:

Denying any interest in politics, she claimed that she wished to continue in forensic medicine.

There are only two types of subordinate clauses that have no clear indicator of subordination within them:

(a) Nominal *that*-clauses allow the omission of *that* in certain contexts (*cf* 15.4), but they may be said to be recognizable as subordinate through the potentiality for the insertion of *that*:

I suppose *I can use your phone.*
~ I suppose *that I can use your phone.*

Compare also the omissibility of relative *that*, 17.13*ff*.

(b) Some comment clauses (*cf* 15.54) have no overt mark of subordination, but – as with the zero relative clauses mentioned in (a) – they generally lack an obligatory verb complementation:

I have no alternative, *I suppose.*
It could be worse, *you know.*
= *You know*, it could be worse.
≠ *You know* (that) it could be worse.

The verb phrase in subordinate clauses

14.21 In general the rules for the uses of forms and categories of the verb phrase – such as tenses, aspects, and modal auxiliaries – apply both to subordinate and independent clauses. Nevertheless, there are cases in which choices affecting the verb phrase of a subordinate clause are determined by the particular type of subordinate clause it belongs to. With temporal *since*-clauses, on the other hand, it is the choice of verb phrase in the matrix clause that is more obviously affected.

Such determinations constitute a signal of subordination additional to other signals, such as initial subordinators. They are a particularly conspicuous signal when the verb phrase in the subordinate clause prevents that clause from constituting an independent sentence, even with the omission of the subordinator, as in (*Though*) *he be the President himself.* Less obviously, the meaning of the verb phrase would be different in an independent clause, as in (*When*) *the game ends.*

Note Dependency relations of this kind are not necessarily found in disjunct clauses, particularly style disjunct clauses (*cf* 15.21), where verb choices are primarily dependent on the circumstances of the speech act. Contrast, for example, the matching tenses in [1], where the *since*-clause is an adjunct, with the absence of matching in [2], where the *since*-clause is a style disjunct:

Since they really *wanted* to know, they *conducted* their own investigation. [1]
Since you really *want* to know, they *conducted* their own investigation. [2]

The present tense in adverbial and nominal clauses

14.22 The simple present is commonly used in certain types of adverbial clauses to express future meaning (*cf* also 14.26):

When / After / Before / As / If / As soon as / Once } he *arrives*, the band will play the National Anthem.

Even if tomorrow's match *is* cancelled, Lancashire will still be at the top of the league.
He'll come in case he'*s* wanted.
While I *am* away, the children will look after the house.
Whether or not they *win* this battle, they won't win the war.
Whatever they *say*, I won't pay.
Wherever she *goes*, I'll go.

The subordinators involved belong to the temporal, conditional, and conditional-concessive categories (*cf* 15.25, 15.34, 15.41*f*). Temporal *since*, however, is excluded (*cf* 15.26).

Clauses of similarity (*cf* 15.50) and proportion (*cf* 15.51) may also have the simple present to express future meaning:

Next time I'll do as he *says*.
The harder you *exercise*, the better you'll feel.

Nominal *that-* and *wh-*clauses tend to contain the simple present when the matrix clause (as well as the subordinate clause) refers to the future; but when the matrix clause refers to the present, *will* is likely to be used in the subordinate clause. Contrast:

In a few minutes I'll ask him what he *wants* tomorrow.
The question is what he *will want* tomorrow.

However, there are exceptional verb constructions like *hope*, *bet*, *see* (*to it*), *take care*, *be careful*, and (both in the imperative) *suppose* and *assume*, after which the simple present is often or (for *take care* and *be careful*) regularly used:

I hope that the parcel *comes* in time. [also *will come*]
Suppose he *loses* his way.
Let's assume our opponents *win* the election. [also *will win*]
I'll see that nobody *disturbs* you. [also *will disturb*]
Take care that she *doesn't* fall.

Will and *won't* occur in adverbial clauses, particularly in *if*-clauses, in certain uses. In general, the difference between the simple present and the modal is that the simple present refers to an assumed future actual situation whereas the modal refers to the assumed predictability of a situation or of situations. More specifically, *will* and *won't* are commonly used:

(i) where the modals have a volitional meaning:

If you'*ll help* us, we can finish early. ['are willing to'] [1]
If you *won't help* us, all our plans will be ruined. ['refuse to'] [2]
If he'*ll pay*, I'll go with him. [3]
If you'*ll use* it, you can have it. [4]

The use of the simple present in [1–4] would suppress the volitional meaning. In [5] the volitional meaning is metaphorically transferred to inanimate objects:

If your car *won't start*, call me any time and I'll help. ['refuses to'] [5]

(ii) where the modals express timeless and habitual prediction:

If drugs *will cure* him, this drug should do the job. [6]
If sugar *will dissolve* in a hot liquid, this chemical will do so too. [7]

Will can be replaced by *can* in [6] and [7]. In both sentences, the conditional clause does not refer to a specific actual situation.

(iii) where the modals express the present predictability of the occurrence or nonoccurrence of a future situation:

If you *won't arrive* before six, I can't meet you. ['If you won't be arriving before six'] [8]
If the game *won't be finished* until ten, I'll spend the night at your place. ['If the game is not going to be finished until ten'] [9]
If the water *will rise* above this level, then we must warn everybody in the neighbourhood. ['If the water is going to rise above this level, then we must now plan to warn everybody in the neighbourhood'] [10]
If she *won't be* here before midnight, there's no need to rush. [11]
If we definitely *won't win*, why should we bother to play? ['If we definitely aren't going to win, . . .'] [12]

The simple form is less usual in [8–12] than the progressive.

In [8–12] the matrix clause expresses the present consequence of the present predictability. In [8–9] the consequence is a present decision to take a future action, while in [10–12] it is a present decision that affects present action.

The modal can be replaced by the simple present in [8–9], but with a different implication. Contrast [8] with [8a]:

If you *don't* arrive before six, I can't meet you. ['in the event of your arrival after six'] [8a]

The situation in the conditional clause of [8a] is viewed as possibly occurring. In [10] replacement of the modal by the simple present yields the implausible sentence [10a]:

If the water *rises* above this level, then we must warn everybody. [*cf* 'when the water rises above this level, if it does so'] [10a]

Replacement of the modal by the simple present in [11] and [12] produces uninterpretable sentences.

Note [**a**] The simple present may be used for future reference in relative clauses that together with their antecedent express similar relationships to those expressed in the adverbial clauses:

I'll speak to her the first opportunity *I have.*

And similarly in appositive *that*-clauses modifying an appropriate noun phrase head:

We'll be there tomorrow on the assumption that it *doesn't rain.*

[**b**] The simple present in a conditional clause may refer to a state in present time:

If you *like* it, I'll give it to you.

For dynamic situation types, the present progressive is used to refer to present time:

If she'*s working*, I won't interrupt her.

The hypothetical past and past perfective

14.23 The verbs in hypothetical conditional clauses are backshifted, the past tense form being used for present and future time reference and the past perfective form for past time reference (*cf* 15.36). When these forms have such hypothetical implications we term them HYPOTHETICAL PAST and HYPOTHETICAL PAST PERFECTIVE. The general rule for verbs in both clauses of hypothetical conditions may be expressed thus:

Table 14.23 Verbs in hypothetical conditions

	conditional clause	matrix clause
present and future reference	HYPOTHETICAL PAST	PAST MODAL
past reference	HYPOTHETICAL PAST PERFECTIVE	PAST PERFECTIVE MODAL

The modal most commonly used in the matrix clause is *would*. It is used to express the hypothetical implication, without necessarily any other modal implications:

If she {*tried* / *were to try*} harder next time, she *would pass* the examination.

[future reference: 'but I expect she won't try harder']

If they *were* alive, they *would be* moving around.

[present reference: 'but I assume they are not alive']

If they *had invited* him to the conference, he *would have attended.*

[past reference: 'but they didn't invite him']

As the bracketed implications indicate, the hypothetical meaning is more absolute in the past, and amounts to an implied rejection of the condition; whereas with present and future reference the meaning may be merely one of negative expectation or assumption, the positive not being ruled out completely. Depending on the lexical verb, the progressive might be necessary to convey present reference, as is indeed the case for *try*:

If she *were trying* harder, her parents *would*n't be so anxious.

When modal auxiliaries are used in hypothetical conditional clauses they combine with past and past perfective. In the matrix clause they replace *would*, since two modal auxiliaries cannot cooccur. Modals in hypothetical conditions, apart from hypothetical *would*, are *would* in other uses, *could*, *might*, and *should*:

> If they *would help* us, we *could finish* early. [volitional *would*, 'would be willing to']
> If we had enough money, we *could* buy a typewriter.
> If you *could type*, you *might save* a lot of time.
> I *might have married* her if she *would have agreed*.
> If they had asked me, I *would have had to speak*. [*have to* as substitute for *must*, which lacks a past form]
> If he apologized, you *should have done* so too. [obligational *should*]

Some BrE speakers maintain a distinction between *would* and *should* in the matrix clause parallel to that between *will* and *shall* (*cf* 4.42):

> If I had been at home last night, I *should have heard* the noise.

Hypothetical past or past perfective are obligatory in certain other constructions that have hypothetical meaning:

> It's time you *were* in bed.
> I wish this bus *went* to the university.
> If only I *had listened* to my parents!

They are optional with other constructions that also have hypothetical meaning (on the subjunctive *were*, *cf* 14.24):

> He acts as if he *knew* you.
> It's not as though we *were* poor.
> Suppose we *told* her the truth.
> Imagine your child *played* truant.
> I'd rather we *had* dinner now.

Generally a negative inference can be drawn, which is more strongly negative with the hypothetical past perfective. Thus *If only I had listened to my parents* implies 'I did not listen to my parents', and *He acts as if he knew you* implies the expectation 'He doesn't know you'. In *I'd rather we had dinner now*, the hypothetical past may express tentative politeness rather than hypothetical meaning.

Note [**a**] The hypothetical past is also used after an archaic *Would that*, which expresses a wish:

> Would that everyone *treated* me as considerately.

[**b**] Restrictive relative clauses modifying generic noun phrases (*cf* 15.34 Note [i]) and their matrix clauses take the same forms as hypothetical conditionals if they refer to a hypothetical situation:

> Any person who *had behaved* in that way *would have been dismissed*.

[**c**] We have shown that the rules for past reference in a hypothetical condition require a past perfective in the conditional clause and a past perfective modal, generally *would have*, in the matrix clause:

> If I *had* seen her, I *would have* told her.

The operators are frequently contracted in informal style:

> If I'*d* seen her, I'*d have* told her.

In informal speech, the *have* in the second phrase is frequently reduced to /əv/ or /ə/, so that *I would have* may be rendered /aɪdə/. Informal AmE speech may have matching modals in both clauses:

> If I'*d have* seen her, I'*d have* told her.

The first part of both clauses may then be rendered /aɪdə/. The contraction for the operator in the conditional clause is sometimes misinterpreted as replacing *had* rather than *would*, giving rise to an error that is found in uneducated writing and its fictional representation:

If I *hadda* seen her, I *woulda* told her.

The nonstandard spelling *I'da* is similarly found as a representation of /aɪdə/, and *of* is a frequent misspelling of *have* when *have* follows a modal.

[d] In informal AmE the hypothetical past is sometimes used for past reference in place of the hypothetical past perfective:

If they *invited* her to the conference, she would have attended.

[e] Ambiguities are occasionally found between open and hypothetical conditions (*cf* 15.35), since open conditions take the full range of verb forms:

If he *found* a patient listener, he *would pour* out his troubles.

This sentence may be a hypothetical condition referring to the future ('I don't think he'll find a patient listener') or an open condition referring to the past (*would* having a habitual meaning).

[f] In subordinate clauses following *I wish* (*that*), the hypothetical past may be replaced by hypothetical *would* or by a *to*-infinitive:

I wish { she *visited* / she *would visit* / her *to visit* } me more often.

The present and past subjunctive

14.24 The present subjunctive (*cf* 3.58*ff*) is used very occasionally in formal style in open conditional clauses (*cf* 15.33 Note [d], 15.36) and in concessive clauses (*cf* 15.41 Notc [b], 15.42 Note [b]):

If any person *be* found guilty, he shall have the right of appeal.
Whatever *be* the reasons for their action, we cannot tolerate such disloyalty.
Whether she *be* right or wrong, she will have my unswerving support.

More usually, the simple present indicative is used.

Clauses of concession (*cf* 15.39*ff*) and purpose (*cf* 15.48) may also very occasionally in formal style contain a present subjunctive (esp in AmE) to express putative rather than factual meaning (*cf* 14.25):

Though he *be* the President himself, he shall hear us.
They removed the prisoner in order that he *not disturb* the proceedings any further.

The more usual verb forms for the *though*-clause are the simple present indicative or putative *should* followed by the infinitive. Clauses of purpose require modal auxiliaries, and therefore only the *should*-construction is a possible alternative.

The present subjunctive is also used in *that*-clauses (esp in AmE) after verbs, adjectives, or nouns that express a necessity, plan, or intention for the future:

Congress has voted that the present law *be* maintained. [1]

We insisted that { he / they } *leave* at once. [2]

They expressed the wish that { she / I } *accept* the award. [3]

It is essential that a meeting *be* convened this week. [4]

Notice that this mandative subjunctive (*cf* 3.59) is used even when the matrix verb is past (*cf* 14.25 Note [c]). If the matrix verb is present, the distinction between subjunctive and indicative is neutralized except in the third person singular or if the verb is *be*. In BrE, putative *should* with the infinitive is far more common. In both AmE and BrE, indicative forms are also occasionally used in this construction; for example, *left* in [2] and *is* in [4].

In general, the present subjunctive occurs more frequently in AmE than in BrE; in BrE it occurs chiefly in formal style.

The past (or *were*-) subjunctive (*cf* 3.62), which is a form distinct from the past indicative only in the first and third person singular forms of *be*, is used in formal style in hypothetical conditional clauses and in other constructions with hypothetical meaning exemplified in 14.23:

I wish she *were* not married. [5]
If only I *were* not so nervous. [6]
If she *were* here, she would speak on my behalf. [7]
The stuffed dog barked as if it *were* a real one. [8]
Suppose he *were* lost. [9]
I'd rather I *were* in bed. [10]

In nonformal styles, hypothetical past or indicative forms replace subjunctive *were*:

I wish she *was* not married. [5a]
If only I *was* not so nervous. [6a]
If she *was* here, she would speak on my behalf. [7a]
The stuffed dog barked as if it *was* a real one. [8a]
Suppose he {*was* / *is*} lost, what would you do? [9a]
I'd rather I *was* in bed. [10a]

The present indicative is a possible alternative after *as if* and *as though* when the reference is to present time (*eg*: 'The stuffed dog *barks* as if it *is* a real one') and after imperatives *suppose* and *imagine*.

Note [**a**] The use of the present subjunctive seems to be increasing in BrE in *that*-clauses. There is a greater use of the subjunctive than the indicative if the agentive (perhaps implied) in the *that*-clause is shown to be willing to perform the action. Contrast:

The committee was impressed by the candidate, but recommended that she *reapply* when she had been awarded her PhD.

He was *very reluctant* to leave, but I recommended that he *went*.

But in both instances the usual form for BrE is the *should*-construction, here *should go*.

[**b**] The *were*-subjunctive cannot replace the hypothetical past in constructions introduced by *It's time (that)*, *eg*: *It's time I was in bed*.

[**c**] *May* and *might* are alternatives, also in formal style, to the present subjunctive in purpose clauses (*cf* 15.48), in concessive clauses with *though*, *even though*, and *even if* (*cf* 15.39*ff*), and in conditional-concessive clauses (*cf* 15.41*f*):

Poor though you *might* be, you cannot live all your life on charity.

Let us fight on, that the light of justice and freedom *may* not die in our land.

Whatever *may* be the justification for their actions, we cannot tolerate such disloyalty.

But there may be a difference in meaning between the subjunctive and the modal auxiliaries. In the last example, the subjunctive does not cast doubt on the factuality of its clause; that is, *Whatever be the justification for their actions* presupposes that there is justification, whereas the sentence with *may* allows the possibility that there is no justification.

[**d**] Present subjunctive *come* is used in a temporal clause (generally initial) without a subordinator:

> *Come winter*, we'll have to pay a good deal more for vegetables and fruit. ['When winter comes, . . .']

Putative *should*

14.25 The modal auxiliary *should* is used extensively (esp in BrE, *cf* 14.24) in *that*-clauses to convey the notion of a 'putative' situation, which is recognized as possibly existing or coming into existence. Contrast:

> I'm surprised that he *should feel* lonely. [1]
> I'm surprised that he *feels* lonely. [2]

While [1] questions the loneliness, [2] accepts it as true. Here, as often, the difference is mainly one of nuance, since the factual bias of the matrix clause overrides the doubt otherwise implicit in the *should*-construction. On the other hand, the nonfactuality is clearer in these examples:

> It's unthinkable that they *should deny* my request.
> I prefer that she *should drive*.
> I'm anxious that I *shouldn't be* in the way.
> They've arranged that I *should absent* myself for part of the committee meeting.
> I can understand their eagerness that you *should be* the main speaker.
> It worries me that their children *should travel* alone.

The nonfactual bias of the *should*-construction emerges most clearly in instances where the construction is close in meaning to a conditional *if*-clause:

> It's a pity *that* they *should be* so obstinate.
> It's a pity *if* they *are* so obstinate.

In a further stage of remoteness, the conditional clause has putative *should*:

> It's a pity *if* they *should be* so obstinate. ['It would be a pity if they turned out to be so obstinate']

Putative *should* is used in *that*-clauses when the matrix clauses contain verbs, adjectives, or nouns that convey an emotional reaction or that express a necessity, plan, or intention for the future. In the latter case, a *that*-clause with *should* is frequently replaceable by an infinitive clause:

> I prefer *her to drive*.
> They've arranged *for me to absent myself for part of the committee meeting*.

It is also frequently replaced (esp in AmE) by a present subjunctive (*cf* 14.24):

> I prefer that she *drive*. [3]
> We insisted that the meeting *be* adjourned. [4]
> It was intended that you *be* the candidate. [5]

Indicative forms are occasionally used in BrE instead for [3] and [4].

A past verb in the matrix clause does not necessarily affect the form of *should* in the subordinate clause, even though the subordinate clause refers to a past situation:

I *was surprised* that *he should feel* lonely when he was in California.

But it is also possible to use a perfective form:

I *was surprised* that he *should have felt* lonely when he was in California.

Note [**a**] *Should* is also used in a subject *that*-clause when the matrix clause contains such verbs as *show*, *indicate*, *prove*, *demonstrate*, *require*, and *demand*:

That they *should refuse* to sign the petition required great courage.
It shows how considerate she is that she *should drive* you all the way to the airport.

[**b**] Putative *should* also occurs in some idiomatic questions and exclamations:

How *should* I know?
That he *should* dare speak in that tone of voice to me! [*cf* 11.41]
Who *should* come in but my youngest sister!

[**c**] The use of the present subjunctive or putative *should* in the subordinate clause evokes clearly the suasive meanings (*cf* 16.32) of the matrix verbs *insist* and *suggest*:

I *insisted* ['required'] that he {*change* / *should change*} his clothes. [6]

I *insisted* ['asserted'] that he *changed* his clothes. [7]

She *suggested* ['recommended'] that I {*be* / *should be*} responsible for the arrangements [8]

She *suggested* ['said tentatively'] that I *am* responsible for the arrangements. [9]

While [6] and [8] are unambiguously suasive, [7] and [9] may also be suasive for those who use the indicative even after suasive verbs.

The putative and obligational meanings of *should* sometimes merge:

The report recommended that education for the over-sixteens *should* be improved. ['. . . that education for the over-sixteens *be* improved' *or* '. . . that education for the over-sixteens *ought to be* improved']

[**d**] Similar to putative *should* is the tentative *should* used in open conditions with *if*-clauses (*cf* 15.36):

If she *should be* interested, I'll phone her.

It is also used in somewhat literary style, with inversion:

Should she *be* interested, I'll phone her.

The perfective with temporal clauses

The perfective with temporal *since*-clauses

14.26 A temporal *since*-clause generally requires the present perfective in the matrix clause when the whole construction refers to a stretch of time up to (and potentially including) the present:

I *have lost* ten pounds since I started swimming. [1]
Since leaving home, Larry *has written* to his parents just once. [2]

The perfective is also required when the clause contains a prepositional phrase introduced by *since* or the prepositional adverb *since*, just as it is required for certain other prepositional phrases and adverbs (*cf* 4.23):

Scholars *have been writing* English grammars since the sixteenth century.
They called to see us three years ago, but I *haven't seen* them since.

In informal AmE, and increasingly in informal BrE, nonperfective forms are commonly used in matrix clauses with *since*-clauses and in clauses with preposition or adverb *since*:

I *lost* ten pounds since I started swimming. ⟨informal⟩ [1a]
Since leaving home, Larry *wrote* to his parents just once. ⟨informal⟩ [2a]

There are some exceptions to the general rule for matrix clauses. In most cases, both perfective and nonperfective forms are possible.

(i) Verbs used statively (*cf* 4.28*ff*) – particularly *be* and *seem* – may take nonperfective forms when the predication is durative:

It'*s* OK since I had it fixed.
Things *are* different since you've gone.
Since Pat left, it *seems* dull here.
I'*m feeling* much better since I had an operation.

In all these instances, perfective forms may also be used, *eg*: *Things have been different since you've gone.*

The most common pattern that falls under this exception is *It* + BE + a time expression, in which the verb may be in the simple present or simple past, or have the *will*-future. Nonperfective forms are normal here:

It'*s* ten years since they were last here.
How long *is* it since you last spoke to them?
It *was* ages since they last paid their bills on time.
Next Tuesday it *will be* six years since I became an American citizen.

Other verbs, particularly *seem*, also fit into this pattern:

It *seems* a long time since we last met.
It *feels* like ages since I was last here.

Perfective forms may also be used here too, *eg*: *It's been ten years since they were last here*; *It had been ages since they last paid their bills on time*; *Next Tuesday it will have been six years since I became an American citizen.*

(ii) Modal auxiliaries, particularly *can* and *could*, or semi-auxiliaries occur in the matrix clause in nonperfective forms. *Ever* is usual here:

(Ever) since my teeth were pulled out I *can't* eat anything solid. [3]
I *have to* use crutches (ever) since I had a car accident. [4]
They *won't* smoke (ever) since they saw a film on lung cancer. [*won't* ≠ 'refuse to'] [5]

The modals cannot be used here in perfective forms, but perfective forms are available for semi-auxiliaries or equivalent lexical verbs:

(Ever) since my teeth were pulled out *I haven't been able to* eat anything solid. [3a]
I *have had to* use crutches (ever) since I had a car accident. [4a]
They *have* {refused to / decided not to} smoke (ever) since they saw a film on lung cancer. [5a]

Perfective modals may be used when the matrix clause refers to a situation in the past:

Since he *left* home, Larry *may have written* to his parents just once.

(iii) The simple present or the present progressive is sometimes used in the matrix clause when that clause has habitual reference:

(Ever) since we bought that car we *go* camping every weekend.
I'*m doing* well since I invested in the money market.

When the whole period under consideration is distanced in past time, the past perfective is generally used in the matrix clause:

Since the country had achieved independence, it *had revised* its constitution twice. [6]
Ever since they had joined the organization, they *must have had* little time for leisure activities. [7]

The past perfective may be replaced by the simple past, *eg*:

Since the country achieved independence, it *revised* its constitution twice. [6a]

When the period in the matrix clause refers to a future situation, a modal perfective (generally *will have*) is used in the matrix clause:

If the promotion is confirmed, you *will have been* promoted three times since you joined the company.
By tomorrow Daniel *will have been* in bed for a week since he caught the flu.
Their car *should* soon *have run* 100,000 miles since they bought it second-hand.

When the period in the matrix clause refers to a future time in the past, *ie* a future from the viewpoint of a past period (*cf* 4.48), a past modal perfective (generally *would have*) is used in the matrix clause. The construction is rare:

A: By next Sunday Harry will have completed 1200 miles since he started his walk.
B: At that rate, he *would have covered* 1000 miles by last Sunday.

We now consider the verb in the *since*-clause. When the whole construction refers to a stretch of time up to (and potentially including) the present, the general rule for the temporal *since*-clause is that the simple past is used when the clause refers to a point of time marking the beginning of the situation referred to in the matrix clause and the present perfective is used when the clause refers to a period of time lasting to the present:

POINT OF TIME

She has been talking since she *was* one year old.
Since I *started* swimming, I have lost five pounds.
Since I *saw* her last, she has dyed her hair.
Derek hasn't stopped talking since he *arrived*.

Similarly:

By tomorrow Daniel will have been in bed for a week since he *caught* the flu.

PERIOD OF TIME

> Max has been tense since he'*s been taking* drugs.
> Since I *have been* here, I haven't left my seat.
> Since I'*ve known* Caroline, she has been interested in athletics.
> I've had a dog ever since I'*ve owned* a house.
> I've gone to concerts ever since I'*ve lived* in Edinburgh.

Similarly:

> By next year Mary will have written her second book since she'*s been* at this university.

The present perfective may also be used in the pattern *It* + BE + time expression, when there is no explicit indication of point of time, such as *last*: *It's been a long time since I've seen Gerald* (*cf*: *I haven't seen Gerald for a long time*). The present perfective is similarly used occasionally for other *since*-clauses that refer to a point of time, *eg*: *I've been lonely since you've left*.

When the whole period is placed in past time, the past perfective or the simple past is used in the *since*-clause (*cf* backshift, 14.31). The past perfective corresponds to a past of the simple past or a past of the present perfective. It tends to be used more commonly for periods of time, corresponding to the use of the present perfective in the constructions previously discussed:

> Since the country (*had*) *achieved* independence, it (had) revised its constitution twice.
> Since he {*had known* / *knew*} her, she {had been / was} a journalist.

Similarly:

> By last Sunday he would have covered 1000 miles since he (*had*) *started* his walk.

Note [**a**] The nonperfective forms *can remember* and *could remember* are used in *since*-clauses to indicate the span over which personal memory extends:

> My parents have spent their summer vacations in France ever since I *can remember*.
> Ever since she *could remember*, the winters in her home town had been severe.

Ever is commonly used with this collocation.

[**b**] When we say that the construction refers to a stretch of time up to the present, we mean that the situation occurred within a period of time leading towards, but not necessarily up to, the moment of utterance:

> I've read ten books since I left college (but I haven't read any books in the last couple of months).
> Since we've owned a car we've gone camping every year except last year (and I'm afraid we're going to have to miss this year again).

On the anterior time zone, *cf* 4.18*f*.

The perfective with other temporal clauses

14.27 When an *after*-clause refers to a past event, the verb may be in the past perfective, though it is more commonly in the simple past:

> We ate our meal after we {*returned* / *had returned*} from the game. [1]

If a construction with a *when*-clause refers to a sequence of two past events, the clause allows the same choice:

> We ate our meal when we {*returned* / *had returned*} from the game. [2]

All four forms of these sentences are acceptable, and mean roughly the same. The only difference is that *when* and the simple past (probably the most popular choice) suggests that the one event follows immediately on the other in sequence.

There may, however, be a contrast if the subordinator is *when* and the predication in the subordinate clause is durative rather than punctual (*cf* 4.33*ff*):

> They walked out when I {*gave* / *had given*} the lecture. [3]

The variant with the simple past would normally mean 'as soon as I started giving the lecture' or 'during the time I was giving the lecture', whereas that with the past perfective means 'after the lecture was over'.

If the sequence of events is habitual, the verb in the *after-* or *when*-clause may be in the present perfective, though it is more commonly in the simple present:

> Every day we eat our main meal {after / when} we {*return* / *have returned*} from the game. [4]

Again, there may be a contrast when the predication is durative:

> The audience claps when she {*sings.* / *has sung.*} [5]

The differences in the interpretations of the *when*-clauses in [4] and [5] parallel those for the *when*-clauses in [2] and [3] respectively.

The present perfective is sometimes used in both clauses of a temporal construction to imply the repetitiveness of the situation:

> In the past, when(ever) I'*ve visited* London, I'*ve seen* them.
> My usual practice is that as soon as I'*ve taken* a shower, I'*ve eaten* breakfast.

The use of the present perfective rather than the simple present suggests that the situation may not apply in the future (for example, that I'm no longer going to visit London).

The present perfective is common in temporal as well as conditional clauses for a future event that precedes the future event referred to in the matrix clause (*cf* 14.22):

> When I'*ve read* the chapter, I'll put the kettle on. [6]
> When they'*ve scored* their next goal, we'll go home. [7]
> As soon as I'*ve retired*, I'll buy a cottage in the country. [8]
> After they *have left*, we can smoke. [9]
> If I'*ve written* the paper before Monday, I'll call you. [10]

A common alternative for [7–10] is the simple present, which is excluded from [6] because the *when*-clause is durative. A less common alternative, permitted also for [6], is *will* or (in BrE optionally with *I* or *we*) *shall* plus the perfective, *eg*: *When I'll have read the chapter, I'll put the kettle on.*

The use of the past perfective in *before*-constructions requires special consideration. These four sentences seem to be equivalent in meaning:

I *saw* him before he *saw* me. [11]
I *had seen* him before he *saw* me. [12]
I *saw* him before he *had seen* me. [13]
I *had seen* him before he *had seen* me. [14]

Sentence [13] appears to be paradoxical in that the second in the succession of events is marked with the past perfective, contrary to what we have noted above in *after*- and *when*-clauses. One explanation (*cf* 15.27) is that the *before*-clause in [13], and perhaps also in [14], may be nonfactual; that is to say, the event in the *before*-clause may not have taken place ('He did not get a chance to see me, because I evaded him').

Note [**a**] If the verb phrase in the matrix clause is progressive, or contains a verb used statively, *when* generally indicates simultaneity, rather than successivity, of the events:

When Paul returned home, his children *were using* the computer.
We *were* asleep when Norma telephoned.

However, *when* may sometimes have the meaning of 'after' even if the verb is used statively:

When I returned home, I *heard* my children playing in my bedroom.
I *didn't know* what to do when they left.

When always indicates simultaneity when the conditions apply to both clauses:

Pamela *was* always popular when she *was* at school.
The sun *was* shining when we *were playing*.
They *were working* when I *was* there.

[**b**] *Whenever* requires the verbs in the matrix and subordinate clauses to be matched in both tense and aspect. Hence if *whenever* replaced *when* in [2] and [3] above, both verbs would be in the simple past, and in [4] and [5] both would be in the simple present.

Reporting the language of others

14.28 There are several modes in which other people's language may be reported. The most explicit modes are introduced by a REPORTING CLAUSE referring to the speaker and the act of communication in speech or writing (*Caroline said*; *Caroline wrote*), and perhaps also to the person or persons spoken to (*Caroline told us*), to the manner of speaking (*Caroline said hesitantly*), or to the circumstances of the speech act (*Caroline replied*; *Caroline explained*; *Caroline said while washing her hair*).

If a reporting clause introduces the report of the communication, the REPORTED CLAUSE (which refers to the utterance itself) may take the form of

DIRECT SPEECH (*cf* 14.29) or INDIRECT SPEECH (*cf* 14.30*ff*). Direct speech purports to give the exact words that someone (who may be the reporter) utters or has uttered in speech or in writing. Indirect speech, on the other hand, conveys in the words of a subsequent reporter what has been said or written by the original speaker or writer (who again may be the same person as the reporter). Contrast the direct speech in [1] with the indirect speech in [1a]:

> David said to me after the meeting, 'In my opinion, the arguments in favour of radical changes in the curriculum are not convincing.' [1]
>
> David said to me after the meeting that in his opinion the arguments in favour of radical changes in the curriculum were not convincing. [1a]

Two secondary modes related to the primary modes of reporting are FREE INDIRECT SPEECH and FREE DIRECT SPEECH. In both these secondary modes there is no reporting clause; the act of communication is signalled by, for example, shifts in the tense forms of verbs (*cf* 14.35).

The report may be a representation of mental activity (internal communication), which by its nature is unspoken. Thus, [2] and [2a] contain direct speech and indirect speech respectively:

> 'Should I tell them now,' I thought to myself, 'or should I wait until they're in a better mood?' [2]
>
> He asked himself whether he should tell them then or wait until they were in a better mood. [2a]

Obviously, this type of direct or indirect speech normally involves a report of the supposed mental activity of the speaker of the reporting clause. The notable exception is in prose or verse fiction, where by convention the narrator is often assumed to have access to the thoughts and feelings of the characters.

Indirect speech frequently involves paraphrase or summary, and therefore the hearer or reader cannot uniquely recover the original speech or writing. The original utterance of [1] might well be reported as in [1b]:

> David told me after the meeting that he remained opposed to any radical changes in the curriculum. [1b]

Indeed, the act of communication may not be indicated at all:

> I saw David after the meeting. It's a pity that he remains opposed to any radical changes in the curriculum. [1c]

While [1b] is indirect speech, although a paraphrase of the original, [1c] does not have the recognizable form of a reported communication, and is irrelevant to the present discussion.

Note **[a]** Direct speech is also termed 'oratio recta', and indirect speech is also termed 'oratio obliqua' and 'reported speech'. Free indirect speech is also known by the German term *erlebte Rede* and by the French term *style indirect libre*.

[b] For the omission of reporting clauses with direct speech in certain written styles, *cf* 14.29.

Direct speech

14.29 Direct speech is usually signalled by being enclosed in quotation marks (*cf* App III.21):

> The President said, 'A failure by Congress to approve new taxes will lead to larger budget deficits, higher interest rates, and higher unemployment.' [1]

The reporting clause may occur before, within, or after the direct speech. Medial position is very frequent. When the reporting clause is positioned medially or finally, subject–verb inversion may occur if the verb is in the simple present or simple past:

> 'I wonder,' { *John said* / *he said* / *said John* }, 'whether I can borrow your bicycle.' [2]

> 'The radio is too loud,' { *Elizabeth complained.* / *she complained.* / *complained Elizabeth.* } [3]

Inversion is most common when the verb is *said*, the subject is not a pronoun, and the reporting clause is medial, as in [2]. It is unusual and archaic, however, when the subject of the reporting clause is a pronoun, even when the verb is *said* (*eg*: *said he*).

Direct speech may extend over many sentences. The reporting clause is then usually positioned within the first sentence.

Reporting clauses are often omitted, however, in the representation of conversation in fiction writing when the identity of the speakers is obvious from the context; quotation marks are sometimes omitted too. Reporting clauses and quotation marks are regularly omitted in written plays, in formal reports of meetings, and in some types of headlines; instead the name of the speaker (usually in capitals or italics and followed by a colon or period) prefaces the direct speech.

The structural relationship between the reporting clause and the direct speech poses some analytical problems. In some respects the direct speech functions as a subordinate clause:

> Dorothy said, '*My mother's on the phone.*' [4]

In [4] the direct speech seems to be a direct object. We can ask a *what*-question and elicit the direct speech as a response:

> A: What did Dorothy actually say?
> B: 'My mother's on the phone.' [5]

We can make it the subject complement in a pseudo-cleft construction (*cf* 18.29*f*):

> What Dorothy said was '*My mother's on the phone.*' [6]

Furthermore, in both [4] and [6] the structure is defective without the direct speech, which obligatorily complements *said* in [4] and *was* in [6]. Compare also:

The words that Dorothy actually used were 'My mother's on the phone.'

Here *were* requires complementation by a subject complement. Then, the direct speech may be appositive to a unit that is clearly a part or the whole of the direct object:

Dorothy used *the following* words: '*My mother's on the phone.*'

Finally, coordination with a following clause suggests that the reporting clause is an obligatory part of the first clause, in that coordination would otherwise not be possible:

'The radio is too loud,' *Elizabeth complained*, and she then stalked back to her room.

On the other hand, we can view the reporting clause as subordinate, functioning as an adverbial. Thus, like most adverbials it can be positioned variously and can – at least sometimes – be omitted. Both syntactically and semantically, it resembles the most important type of comment clause (*cf* 15.54). Compare the reporting clause in [7a] with the comment clause in [7b] and the adverb in [7c]:

'Generals,' *they alleged*, 'never retire; they merely fade away.' [7a]
Generals, *it is alleged*, never retire; they merely fade away. [7b]
Generals, *allegedly*, never retire; they merely fade away. [7c]

Moreover, the direct speech clause behaves like a main clause in that it can, for example, be a question or a directive:

Dorothy said, 'Is my mother on the phone?' [8]
Dorothy said, 'Tell my mother I'll be over soon.' [9]

But, of course, the reporting clause behaves likewise:

Did you really say to Ronald, 'You're my best friend'? [10]
Tell Richard, 'You're my best friend.' [11]

Finally, we may note the usual punctuation separation of the reporting clause (though this is not necessarily reflected intonationally), which suggests another parallel with comment clauses and many other adverbials. Indeed, if the direct speech clause is analysed as an object, this is the only construction where the subject and verb are separated from the object by a comma (*cf* App III.9, App III.21). Contrast the punctuation of [11] for direct speech with that of [11a] for indirect speech:

Tell Richard (that) he's my best friend. [11a]

It is best to recognize that there is a gradient from direct speech that is clearly independent to direct speech that is clearly integrated into the clause structure. At the most independent extreme we have direct speech without a reporting clause. Next along the gradient are instances where the reporting clause is medial or final and it exhibits subject–verb inversion:

'I wonder', *said John*, 'whether I can borrow your bicycle.'

Here there are severe restrictions on the form of the verb, and pronouns are generally excluded as subject. Further along the gradient are instances where the reporting clause is medial or final but without subject–verb inversion. Notice that the reporting clause is restricted also here to some extent in that it cannot readily be a question or a directive, a restriction that applies also when there is subject–verb inversion. There follow sentences like [4], where the reporting clause is initial and suffers from fewer restrictions. Most integrated are the partial quotations, as in this version of [1]:

> The President said that a failure by Congress to approve new taxes would lead to 'larger budget deficits, higher interest rates, and higher unemployment.' [1a]

Here we have a mixture of indirect and direct speech, the direct speech being only a part of a clause, and the reporting clause being implicit: '. . . would lead to what he said were larger budget deficits, higher interest rates, and higher unemployment'.

Here are some reporting verbs of speaking or thinking that are frequently used with direct speech, the most common of which is *say*:

add	*comment*	*object*	*say*
admit	*conclude*	*observe*	*shout* (*out*)
announce	*confess*	*order*	*state*
answer	*cry* (*out*)	*promise*	*tell*
argue	*declare*	*protest*	*think*
assert	*exclaim*	*recall*	*urge*
ask	*explain*	*remark*	*warn*
beg	*insist*	*repeat*	*whisper*
boast	*maintain*	*reply*	*wonder*
claim	*note*	*report*	*write*

In addition, there are numerous other verbs indicating the manner of speaking that are occasionally used with direct speech; for example, *falter*, *mumble*, *murmur*, *mutter*, *snap*, *sneer*, *sob*.

Note [**a**] Pronunciation and other speech features may be imitated in a spoken rendering of direct speech. In writing it may be indicated by irregular spelling or, to a limited extent, by italics or underlining. In both media, the reporting clause may have indications of the manner of speaking (*Tom lisped*, *Jacqueline whispered*, *Charles hinted darkly*, *John said casually*). Such indications are common in some fiction writing.

[**b**] In conversation, *says you*, *says he*, etc (with the invariant *-s*) are sometimes used in casual style as an impolite retort meaning 'That's what *you* say', 'That's what *he* says', etc:

> A: I'm going to win this game. B: *Says you!*

In old-fashioned speech, the nonstandard inversion *says I* sometimes occurs. The historic present (*cf* 4.8) is occasionally used in spoken narrative.

[**c**] In journalistic writing, a reporting clause with inversion sometimes occurs even in initial position: *Declared tall, nineteen-year-old Napier: 'The show will go on'.*

[**d**] Unlike indirect speech, direct speech may acceptably contain grammatical errors or even be in another language if it purports to give a record of the communication of another person:

> He said, 'I know not well English.'

[**e**] It is common in newspaper reporting to omit quotation marks in what appears to be direct speech, as exemplified in the first sentence in the following:

> New horses *will* strengthen the breed, Mr Steiner claimed. He said the newcomers *would* arrive after the epidemic was halted.

The second sentence switches to indirect speech, as indicated by the tense backshifts (*cf* 14.31).

Indirect speech

14.30 Typically, indirect speech is used to report statements, and takes the form of a nominal *that*-clause (*cf* 15.4):

Neighbours said *that as a teenager he had earned his pocket money by delivering newspapers.* [1]

In [1] the indirect speech is a direct object, but in [2] it is an extraposed subject and in [3] a subject complement:

It was said *that as a teenager Max had earned his pocket money by delivering newspapers.* [2]
What neighbours said was *that as a teenager he had earned his pocket money by delivering newspapers.* [3]

Reporting verbs that are used with indirect speech include those listed as frequently used with direct speech (*cf* 14.29). Lists of verbs of speaking and thinking used with indirect speech may be found in 16.31. Among the common verbs are *believe*, *feel*, *imagine*, *know*, *mention*, *realize*, *recognize*, *suppose*.

We have observed earlier (*cf* 14.28) that a reporter using indirect speech may paraphrase or summarize; changes may be made from the original wording without affecting the essential truth of the report. For example, the original wording may be as in [4]:

'My first task today,' said the teacher, 'will be to examine current views on the motivations for armed conflicts.' [4]

The indirect speech in [4a] approximates as closely as possible in that mode to the original wording:

The teacher said that his first task that day was to examine current views on the motivations for armed conflicts. [4a]

The hearer or reader, however, cannot be sure how close the indirect speech of [4a] is to the original wording, since [4a] could legitimately report the wording in [4b] instead:

'What I want to do now,' said the teacher, 'is to look at contemporary theories of the causes of wars.' [4b]

If, however, the report had been conveyed by [4c], there is no clear correspondence with the reported clause in direct speech:

The teacher announced his intention of discussing the causes of wars. [4c]

When the report is conveyed through indirect speech as in [4a], we can specify the changes in wording that are required because the situation of the utterance by the reporter may differ in certain respects from that of the utterance by the original speaker. The differences affect the use of deictic features of the language, those features that relate to the time and place of the utterance and to the persons referred to in the utterance. They include:

(i) tense forms of the verb
(ii) other time references, *eg*: *yesterday*, *now*, *last week*, *next Monday*

(iii) place references, *eg*: *here*, *there*
(iv) personal pronouns
(v) the demonstratives *this* and *these*

Changes in tense forms are discussed in 14.31 and the other changes in 14.32. Further changes may be required to identify references in the original utterance that may not be known to the person receiving the report, for example the identity of persons or things referred to by pronouns.

Note As with other *that*-clauses, the conjunction *that* is frequently omitted from the reported clause in less formal indirect speech.

Backshift in indirect speech

14.31 The reporting verb may be in the present tense for communications in recent past time, as in [1] and [2]:

Joan *tells* me she'*s* going to the airport in an hour's time. [1]
She *says* she *was* too busy to join us last night. [2]

The present tense is also used for reports attributed to famous works or authors which havc present validity, as in [3] and [4]:

The Bible says there's no end to the writing of books. [3]
Chaucer somewhere writes that love is blind. [4]

The choice of verb form in the reported clause depends on the time reference of the verb. Thus, the verbs in [1], [3], and [4] exemplify the state present (*cf* 4.5), while *was* in [2] refers to a time previous to the time of reporting as well as to the time of the original utterance.

Verbs of cognition may also be used in the reporting clause in the present tense:

I *know* they *don't* care.
Sylvia *thinks* Paul *went* to Lancaster last night.

When the time reference of the original utterance (or mental activity) no longer applies at the time that the utterance (or mental activity) is reported, it is often necessary to change the tense forms of the verbs. Such a change of verb forms in indirect speech is termed BACKSHIFT. The resulting relationship of verb forms in the reporting and reported clauses is known as the SEQUENCE OF TENSES (*cf* 19.39). The changes can be illustrated best if we postulate an exact correspondence for the reporting clauses of direct and indirect speech.

DIRECT SPEECH	BACKSHIFTED IN INDIRECT SPEECH
(i) present	~ past
(ii) past	~ past or past perfective
(iii) present perfective	~ past perfective
(iv) past perfective	~ past perfective

Thus, if the present deictic references in the direct speech become past deictic references in the indirect speech, there is a corresponding shift of verb forms into the past, or if necessary into the past perfective. Examples of each part of the rule are:

'I *am being paid* by the hour,' she said.
~ She said she *was being paid* by the hour. [5]

'The exhibition finished last week,' explained Ann.
~ Ann explained that the exhibition {*finished* / *had finished*} the preceding week. [6]

'I'*ve been waiting* over an hour for you,' she told him.
~ She told him that she *had been waiting* over an hour for him. [7]

'I *had studied* French for four years at school,' I said.
~ I said that I *had studied* French for four years at school. [8]

The choice in [6] represents the usual choice of a simple past in place of a past perfective when the context makes the relative time references clear, in this instance by the use of *the preceding week*. There is no change in [8] because the past perfective already expresses 'past in the past' and no further backshift to 'past in the past in the past' can be expressed. As [5] and [7] illustrate, the rule is not affected by combinations of the simple and perfective forms with progressive and passive forms.

Backshift is optional when the time-reference of the original utterance is valid at the time of the reported utterance, *cf* [5], [7], and [8]. Thus, the shift is obligatory in [9], but optional in [10]:

'I *am* a citizen, not of Athens, but of the world,' said Socrates.
~ Socrates said that he *was* a citizen, not of Athens, but of the world. [9]

'Nothing *can* harm a good man,' said Socrates.
~ Socrates said that nothing {*could* / *can*} harm a good man. [10]

Since the statement by Socrates in [9] deals with what is now past, it has to be reported by application of the backshift rule. The statement in [10], on the other hand, is a universal rule which, if it was true for Socrates' lifetime, should also be true today; the backshift rule is therefore optional.

Here are other examples where present forms may be retained in indirect speech:

Their teacher had told them that the earth *moves* around the sun. [11]
Sam told me last night that he *is* now an American citizen. [12]
I heard her say that she *is* studying Business Administration. [13]
A Yale professor has said that the Brooklyn Bridge *is* the most majestic embodiment of the American experience of the road. [14]
They thought that prison conditions *have* improved. [15]
I didn't know that our meeting *is* next Tuesday. [16]
She said that they *are* being discriminated against. [17]
The waiter told me that lunch *is* now being served. [18]

In all these sentences, past forms may also be used, by optional application of the backshift rule. Sentence [11] has the simple present in its timeless use, whereas the verbs in the subsequent sentences have a limited time-reference.

The appropriateness of the present forms in [12–18] therefore depends on their reference at the time of the reported utterance. For example, if at that time Sam had changed his citizenship, or if his citizenship was then in doubt, an appropriate form of [12] would be, for example:

Sam told me in 1970 that he *was then* an American citizen. [12a]

Similarly, if a long time had elapsed between the original utterance reported in [15] or if there was doubt as to its present validity, the past perfective would be used:

They thought that prison conditions *had* improved. [15a]

Again, if [18] were reporting what the waiter had said not five minutes ago but five days ago it would have read:

The waiter told me that lunch *was* then being served. [18a]

Note [**a**] If the indirect speech itself contains a subordinate clause, then the verb of that subordinate clause may be in the present tense because of current validity even though both the main verb of the sentence and the superordinate verb are in the past:

They *reminded* us that they *had* frequently *denied* that the drug *has* any therapeutic value.
She *thought* she *had told* me that breakfast *is served* between seven and ten.

[**b**] Backshift from simple past to past perfective is necessary when the simple past in the indirect speech may be misinterpreted as representing a simple present:

She said, 'I *was married* (, but my husband died last year).'
~ She said that she *had been married.*

Contrast, where there is no possibility of misinterpretation:

She said, 'I was married in church.'
~ She said that she {*was married* / *had been married*} in church.

[**c**] Backshift is normal if the proposition in the indirect speech is considered to be false:

The ancients *thought* that the sun *moved* around the earth, but from the time of Galileo it *was known* that the reverse *is* true.

[**d**] When *can't* or *couldn't* is combined with *say* or *tell* in a reporting clause, one meaning of the combination is roughly the same as *don't know* or *didn't know*:

I *can't* {say / tell you} where she *is*. ['I don't know']
They *couldn't* {say / tell me} who *called*. ['They didn't know']

[**e**] Since the simple past in indirect speech may represent either the simple past or the simple present of direct speech, it may give rise to ambiguity where both interpretations are plausible:

A: She told me the game *started* at seven.
B: {It *didn't.* / It *doesn't.*}

Other changes in indirect speech

14.32 If the identities of the person speaking and the person addressed are not identical in the situations of the original and reported utterances, the personal pronouns need to be changed. PRONOUN SHIFT requires the shift of 1st and 2nd person pronouns to 3rd person pronouns or to nouns, when the persons referred to in the original utterance are absent in the reported utterance:

'*I*'ll behave *myself*,' he promised.
~ He promised that *he*'d behave *himself*.

'*I* like *your* tie,' she told John.
~ She told John that *she* liked *his* tie.
'*You* know *my* family,' she said.
~ She told *him* [or *Tom*, for example] that *he* knew *her* family.
'*You* are too noisy,' Pamela told them.
~ Pamela told *them* that *they* were too noisy.

1st and 2nd person pronouns are used as appropriate to the reporting situation:

'*You* should be ashamed of *yourself*,' she told me.
~ She told me that *I* should be ashamed of *myself*.
'*I* am *your* friend, *Bob*,' he said to me.
~ He said to me that *he* was *my* friend.

Similarly, in reporting to Margaret a statement about herself:

'*Margaret* is very clever,' Tom said to *me*.
~ Tom told me that *you* are very clever.
'*Margaret* is in *my* class,' I said to him.
~ I told him that *you* were in *my* class.

We mention briefly other shifts that may be necessary. If the time relationship between time references in the indirect speech and the time of the utterance has changed between the original utterance and the reported utterance, it is necessary to make adjustments. Time references are changed variously according to the time of the reported utterance: for example, *yesterday* to *the day before yesterday*, *last Monday*, or *June 10*; *now* to *then*; *next Monday* to *last Monday* or *Monday two weeks ago*. If the places of the utterances are different, place references are changed accordingly: for example, *here* to *there*, or (if the reference is to the place of the reporting utterance) *there* to *here*, or the places may need to be specified by name. Demonstratives are also changed if the relative distancing has changed: *this* and *these* to *that* and *those*, but again the reverse if there is greater proximity at the time of the reported utterance.

Indirect statements, questions, exclamations, and directives

14.33 Our examples have so far been of indirect statements; but all the main sentence types (questions, exclamations, directives, as well as statements) may be converted into indirect speech. The constructions are as follows:

INDIRECT STATEMENT:	*that*-clause (15.4)
INDIRECT QUESTION:	dependent *wh*-clause (15.5*f*)
INDIRECT EXCLAMATION:	dependent *wh*-clause (15.7)
INDIRECT DIRECTIVE:	{ *that*-clause (15.10*f*) { *to*-infinitive clause (without subject) (15.10*f*)

Here are examples of the last three categories:

'Are you ready yet?' asked Joan. [*YES–NO* QUESTION]
~ Joan asked (me) *whether I was ready yet*.
'When will the plane leave?' I wondered. [*WH*-QUESTION]
~ I wondered *when the plane would leave*.

'Are you satisfied or not?' I asked her. [ALTERNATIVE QUESTION]
~ I asked her *whether or not she was satisfied.*
'What a brave boy you are!' Margaret told him. [EXCLAMATION]
~ Margaret told him *what a brave boy he was.*
'Tidy up the room at once,' I said to Tom. [DIRECTIVE]
~ I insisted *that Tom* {*tidy* ⟨esp AmE⟩ / *should tidy* ⟨esp BrE⟩} *up the room at once.*
~ I told Tom *to tidy up the room.*
'Have another apple,' Carol suggested (to me). [DIRECTIVE]
~ Carol suggested *that I* {*have* ⟨esp AmE⟩ / *should have* ⟨esp BrE⟩} *another apple.*
~ Carol asked me *to have another apple.*

All the types of changes outlined in 14.31*f* apply to questions and exclamations as well as statements. With directives, there is no tense backshift in the verb forms exemplified above: mandativc subjunctive, putative *should*, *to*-infinitive (*cf* 14.24*f*).

Directives in fact involve the summary type from which it is not possible to reconstruct the exact words of the direct speech.

If the *to*-infinitive construction is used for an indirect directive, the reporting clause normally requires an indirect object or a prepositional object:

'Eat your food up,' she begged him.
~ She begged him to eat his food up.
'Sit down,' I snapped at him.
~ I snapped at him to sit down.
'Don't say anything,' he whispered to her.
~ He whispered to her not to say anything.

Note [**a**] If the subject of the infinitive is not present in an indirect directive, it is understood to be identical with the indirect object or prepositional object when it is present:

She told me *to call again tomorrow.* ['that I should call again tomorrow']
I whispered to them *to be quiet.* ['that they should be quiet']

The subject may be introduced by *for*, especially in AmE, except when the reporting verb is ditransitive *tell*:

She said *for us to sit down.* I shouted *for them to clear the way.*

If the verb is *say* and the *for*-construction is not used, the subject is understood from the situational context:

She said *to sit down.*

[**b**] Echo questions occasionally occur in indirect speech:

A: Are you going home? B: Am I going home? A: Yes, that's what I asked.

The second sentence might appear in indirect speech as *I asked if you asked if I was going home.* There are, however, no indirect constructions for echo exclamations.

The subjunctive and modal auxiliaries in indirect speech

14.34 There is no indirect speech construction for the optative subjunctive (*cf* 11.39), but when it is used to express a wish the construction with *may* (with a possible backshift to *might*) is sometimes a near-equivalent:

'God *bless* America!' she said.
~ She expressed the wish that God *might bless* America.

There is no backshift for the mandative subjunctive (*cf* 3.59):

'We insisted that he *leave* at once,' she said.
~ She said that they (had) insisted that he *leave* at once.

The past subjunctive (*cf* 14.24) or hypothetical past (*cf* 14.23) is backshifted to hypothetical past perfective if there is a change in time reference:

'If he *were* here, he would vote for the motion,' she said.
~ She said that if he *had been* there, he would have voted for the motion.
'If she *stayed* another day, he would drive her home,' he said.
~ He told me the following week that if she *had stayed* another day, he would have driven her home.

Backshift is optional if the proposition in the indirect speech is still valid:

'If I *were* in New York, I *would* visit the current exhibition at the Metropolitan Museum,' he said.
~ He said that if he [*were* / *had been*] in New York, he [*would visit* / *would have visited*] the current exhibition at the Metropolitan Museum.

If there is a change in time-reference, a modal auxiliary is backshifted from present tense forms to past tense forms even if the past tense forms do not normally indicate past time in direct speech:

'You *may* be able to answer this question,' he told her.
~ He told her that she *might* be able to answer that question.
'I *won't* pay another penny,' I said.
~ I said that I *wouldn't* pay another penny.

If a modal auxiliary in the direct speech is already in the past tense form, then the same form remains in the indirect speech:

'You *shouldn't* smoke in the bedroom,' he told them.
~ He told them that they *shouldn't* smoke in the bedroom.
'We *could* be wrong,' I told them.
~ I told them that we *could* be wrong.
'I *could* speak Spanish when I was young,' I said.
~ I said that I *could* speak Spanish when I was young.
'When I was in college I *would* study till two or three in the morning,' she recalled.
~ She recalled that when she {*was* / *had been*} in college she *would* study till two or three in the morning.

In the last two examples (with *could* and *would*), the modal auxiliaries have past time reference in the direct speech, and therefore backshift entails changing to the perfective.

Several modal auxiliaries or marginal modals have only one form: *must*, *ought to*, *need*, and *had better*. That form remains in indirect speech:

'You *must be* hungry,' he said.
~ He said that they *must be* hungry.
'You *had better* not say anything about this,' he warned me.
~ He warned me that I *had better* not say anything about that.

In its obligational sense, however, the past of *must* may be replaced by *had to* in indirect speech:

'You *must* be in by ten tonight,' his parents told him.
~ His parents told him that he {*must* / *had to*} be in by ten that night.

As always, backshift (where possible) is optional if the proposition in the indirect speech is valid at the time of utterance:

'Persistence *can* overcome all obstacles,' she said.
~ She said that persistence {*can* / *could*} overcome all obstacles.

Note [**a**] If they are followed by a perfective infinitive, modal auxiliaries in the reporting clause are counted, for purposes of backshift, as past tense forms:

'What *are* you doing?' I ought to have asked.
~ I *ought to have asked* what he *was* doing.

[**b**] Backshift normally occurs in the subordinate clause after an attitudinal past used for politeness (*cf* 4.16):

What did you say your name {*is*? / *was*?}
I wondered if you *would* lend me some flour.
We were hoping you *would* stay with us.

There is no implication in these examples of past time reference.

Free indirect speech and free direct speech

14.35 FREE INDIRECT SPEECH is used extensively to report speech or (particularly in fiction) the stream of thought. It is basically a form of indirect speech, but (a) the reporting clause is omitted (except when retained as a parenthetical clause, as in direct speech), and (b) the potentialities of direct-speech sentence structure are retained (for example, direct questions and exclamations, vocatives, tag questions, and interjections). It is therefore only the backshift of the verb, together with equivalent shifts in personal pronouns, demonstratives, and time and place references, that signals the fact that the words are being reported, rather than being in direct speech. The italicized verbs below are backshifted to the past tense:

So that *was* their plan, *was* it? He well *knew* their tricks, and *would show* them a thing or two before he *was* finished. Thank goodness he *had* been alerted, and that there *were* still a few honest people in the world!

FREE DIRECT SPEECH is also used in fiction writing to represent a person's stream of thought. It is basically a form of direct speech, but it is merged with the narration without any overt indication by a reporting clause of a switch to speech. It is distinguished from the past time reference of the narration by its use of present-tense forms. In the following examples the parts in free direct speech are italicized:

I sat on the grass staring at the passers-by. Everybody seemed in a hurry. *Why can't I have something to rush to?*
A fly kept buzzing around, occasionally trying to settle on me. I brushed it off. It came back. *Keep calm! Wait until it feels safe. There! Got it.* On my hand was a disgusting flattened fly, oozing blood. I wiped my hand on the grass. *Now I can relax.*

We understand these as if there were quotation marks around the free direct speech.

Note For direct speech with a medial reporting clause but without quotation marks, *cf* 14.29 Note [e].

Transferred negation

14.36 TRANSFERRED NEGATION, particularly common in informal style, is the transfer of the negative from a subordinate clause (generally a *that*-clause), where semantically it belongs, to the matrix clause. For example, *I don't think it's a good idea* can have two meanings, one in which the negation applies to the matrix clause, and one in which it applies through transferred negation to the subordinate clause ('I think it isn't a good idea'). It is the difficulty of distinguishing the first meaning from the second that in part accounts for the transfer. Another explanatory factor is that generally the focus is on the content of the subordinate clause, which is pragmatically more important: the meaning of the sentence approximates to 'It's probably not a good idea'. The first meaning, however, becomes prominent if the focus is on *think*: *I don't THǏNK it's a good idea; I KNÒW it is.* In this context, transferred negation does not take place. Because of the presence of the two meanings of the matrix clause, the negative force of the transferred negation in *I don't think it's a good idea* is weaker for the subordinate clause than in the less common *I think it isn't a good idea*, where the negative is actually present in the clause.

The matrix verbs that allow transferred negation fall into several semantic groups:

(a) OPINION: *anticipate, be supposed to, believe, calculate, expect, figure* ⟨informal AmE⟩, *imagine, reckon* ⟨informal, esp AmE⟩, *suppose, think*

> I don't believe I've met you before. ['I believe I haven't met you before']
> She didn't imagine that we would say anything. ['She imagined we wouldn't say anything']
> He didn't expect to win. ['He expected not to win']

(b) PERCEPTION: *appear, seem; feel as if, look as if, sound as if* [these three verbs are also used informally, especially in AmE, with *like* in place of *as if*]

It doesn't seem that we can get our money back. ['It seems that we can't get our money back']
The baby doesn't appear to be awake. ['The baby appears not to be awake']
It doesn't look like it's going to rain. ['It looks like it isn't going to rain']

Transferred negation is an unclear phenomenon: intuitions may differ as to whether and to what degree two sentences with differently placed negatives are synonymous. Consider, for example, negative sentences with *likely* and *probable*:

It isn't {likely / probable} that oil prices will fall this year. [1]

It is not clear to what extent [1] is synonymous with [2]:

It's {likely / probable} that oil prices won't fall this year. [2]

A lack of synonymy becomes evident if the adjectives are intensified:

It isn't very {likely / probable} that oil prices will fall this year. [1a]
It's very {likely / probable} that oil prices won't fall this year. [2a]

Not all verbs in the same semantic field allow transferred negation. For example, *assume*, *presume*, and *surmise*, though similar to some of the verbs listed in (a) above, do not generally allow the transfer (*cf* Note [e]). The following two sentences, for example, are not equivalent in meaning:

I didn't assume that he knew me.
I assumed that he didn't know me.

The addition of modal auxiliaries or adverbials in the matrix clause may prevent transferred negation with verbs that otherwise allow it:

I can't believe that they are married.
You mustn't think he's stupid.
I wouldn't have imagined that Sandra would be here.
I didn't ever suppose they were happy.
It just didn't seem that it would rain.

Note **[a]** Transferred negation has also been termed 'negative raising' and 'negative transportation'.

[b] *Wish* allows transferred negation in infinitive clauses, but not in finite clauses:
I don't wish to be rude. ['I wish not to be rude']

[c] *Say* allows transferred negation if it is used with some modal auxiliaries (principally *wouldn't* and *couldn't*):
I wouldn't say I trust them. ['I would say that I don't trust them']

[d] In *can't seem* and *couldn't seem*, the meaning of the modal auxiliary is also transferred:
They can't seem to concentrate. ['They seem not to be able to concentrate']

[e] Verbs like *assume* sometimes allow transferred negation:
I don't assume it need happen under those circumstances.
I don't presume it would be in your best interest to acknowledge the insulting remarks.

[f] Many of the matrix verbs that allow transferred negation appear also in comment clauses (*cf* 15.54). In comment clauses they do not permit the transfer of negation:

My parents won't say anything about it, I think.
It won't rain today, I (don't) believe.
They don't care, I (don't) suppose.

But verbs not otherwise allowing the transfer also appear in comment clauses, *eg*: *know*, *see*.

[g] The subordinate clause is under the scope of negation (*cf* 10.64) and therefore accepts nonassertive items (*cf* 10.60*f*):

They didn't think I'd *ever* met you before.
I don't suppose you've paid for it *yet*.

But this feature applies to subordinate clauses when transferred negation does not apply:

They didn't know I'd *ever* met you before.

When the subject of the matrix clause is *I*, the tag question can correspond with the subordinate clause (*cf* 11.8 Note [a]):

I don't imagine he CÀRES, *DÒES he*? [~ I imagine he doesn't CÀRE, *DÒES he*?]
I don't think she knows FRÈNCH, DÒES *she*? [~ I think she doesn't know FRÈNCH, *DÒES she*?]

The use of the positive tag question with a falling tone is another indication that the subordinate clause is under the scope of negation. But again this feature is not limited to transferred negation:

I'm not sure he CÀRES, *DÒES he*?

Sentence complexity and comprehensibility

Combining subordination devices within a sentence

14.37 For simplicity of illustration, most of our examples in this chapter have been of sentences with just one subordinate clause. We now give some examples that illustrate how several devices of subordination can be combined in sentences. The sentences are fairly brief and not unduly complicated. All of them consist of one main clause, and none of the subordinate clauses are coordinated.

A B C
[They point out [that India has not had the luxury, [as the United States
C D E
did,] of [finding a fresh, virgin land at its disposal at the moment [when its
EDBA
modern development began.]]]]

(*The New York Times*, August 16, 1982, 1.4) [1]

AB B
[[To keep dirt roads even marginally useful,] barrier gates are swung shut
C C D
[when drops begin to fall,] [lest the roads become churned into
DA
impassability.]]

('Paraguay' by Gordon Young, *National Geographic*, August 1982, p. 259) [2]

A B C
[He was irritated at [Edwin taking [what seemed to him like an unfair
CB D E E
advantage]], [though [where the advantage lay] he could not have
DA
said.]]

(*Quartet in Autumn* by Barbara Pym, Perennial Library, 1980, Harper & Row, p. 95; first published 1977) [3]

A B B C
[In Kowloon he hired a car from the biggest outfit [he could find], [using
D E E
the escape passport and driving licence [because marginally [he thought]
F FDCA
the false name was safer [if only by an hour.]]]]

(*The Honourable Schoolboy* by John Le Carré, Bantam Books 1978, p. 462; first published 1977) [4]

A B
[A House-Senate conference committee agreed today [to preserve a feature
C D
of the tax code [that allows businesses [to deduct the cost of certain meals
DCB E F
]]] [as it moved toward final agreement on a bill [to raise taxes by $98.9
FEA
billion over three years.]]]

(*The New York Times*, August 16, 1982, 1.1) [5]

One of the factors which determine the order in which the constituent clauses of a sentence are arranged is the principle of RESOLUTION, the principle that states that the final clause should be the point of maximum emphasis (*cf* communicative dynamism, 18.3). In reading aloud, the resolutory effect of the final clause is often pointed by intonation. A typical reading of [1] would put rising or falling-rising tones on all points of information focus (18.9*ff*) except the last:

. . . ÓUT . . . LÚXury . . . STÀTES DÍD . . . disPÓSal . . . beGÀN

As rising and falling-rising tones have implications of nonfinality, the effect of this pattern is to build up a continuing sense of anticipation, which is at last resolved by the finality of the falling tone. This principle of resolution is the counterpart, on the sentence level, of the principle of end-focus (*cf* 18.3*f*) in the tone unit.

The principle of resolution is illustrated effectively in sentences [1–4]. It is infringed, however, in [5], since the *as*-clause is peripheral: *meals*, indeed, would probably receive a falling tone, although it is not the last point of information focus. This sentence was the first in this particular news item, and perhaps its arrangement accords with the journalistic practice (in contravention of the resolution principle) of presenting the most important information at the very beginning of the lead sentence. Nevertheless, the sentence would read more smoothly if the *as*-clause were positioned initially.

Note **[a]** The letters in sentences [1–5] serve to keep track of the bracketing. They do not always

indicate a superordinate–subordinate relationship. For example, in sentence [2], clauses [B], [C], and [D] are all adverbials that are immediately subordinate to the complex sentence [A].
[**b**] The principle of resolution, along with the intonation pattern associated with it, is generally applicable only to restrictive adjunct clauses (*cf* 15.23). It does not apply to other syntactic types of adverbial clauses.

Positions of subordinate clauses

14.38 Subordinate clauses may be positioned initially, medially, or at the end of their superordinate clause (*cf* 8.14*ff* for adverbial positions). Initial position and end position are here taken to be the very beginning and the very end of the superordinate clause, except that a subordinate clause cannot of course precede the conjunction (if present) of the superordinate clause. For example, the *if*-clause in the following sentence is in *I* position in the superordinate *that*-clause:

I suspect that *if it rains* we won't go.

We visually represent the three arrangements in *Fig* 14.38a. The triangle marked 'M' represents the matrix clause and the triangle marked 'S' represents the subordinate clause.

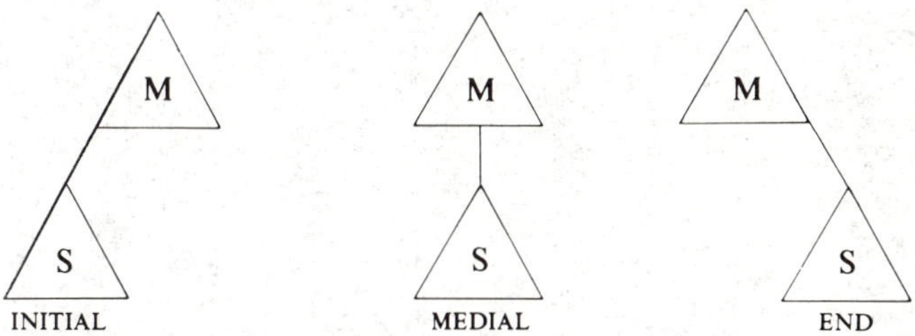

Fig 14.38a Placement of subordinate clauses

The lower clause is the subordinate clause, and its relative position in the superordinate clause (the combination of matrix and subordinate clauses) is indicated by the point from which the line leading to the lower triangle branches downward. Initial clauses are said to be LEFT-BRANCHING, medial clauses NESTING, and final clauses RIGHT-BRANCHING.

Examples of these three arrangements:

INITIAL: *When you're ready*, we'll go to my parents' place.
MEDIAL: We'll go, *when you're ready*, to my parents' place.
END: We'll go to my parents' place *when you're ready*.

We can now diagram in *Fig* 14.38b overpage the relative positions of the subordinate clauses in the five sentences in 14.37. If a subordinate clause is not an immediate constituent of its superordinate clause, we have inserted the triangle representing it within that for the superordinate clause; for example in [1], clause [D] is a complement of the preposition *of* and clause [E] is a postmodifier of *the moment*.

Clauses that are constituents of phrases almost always occur at the end of the phrases. If we consider the clauses that are immediate constituents of their superordinate clauses in [1–5], we see that most of the triangles in *Fig* 14.38b are right-branching. It is, in fact, a dominant tendency of syntactic

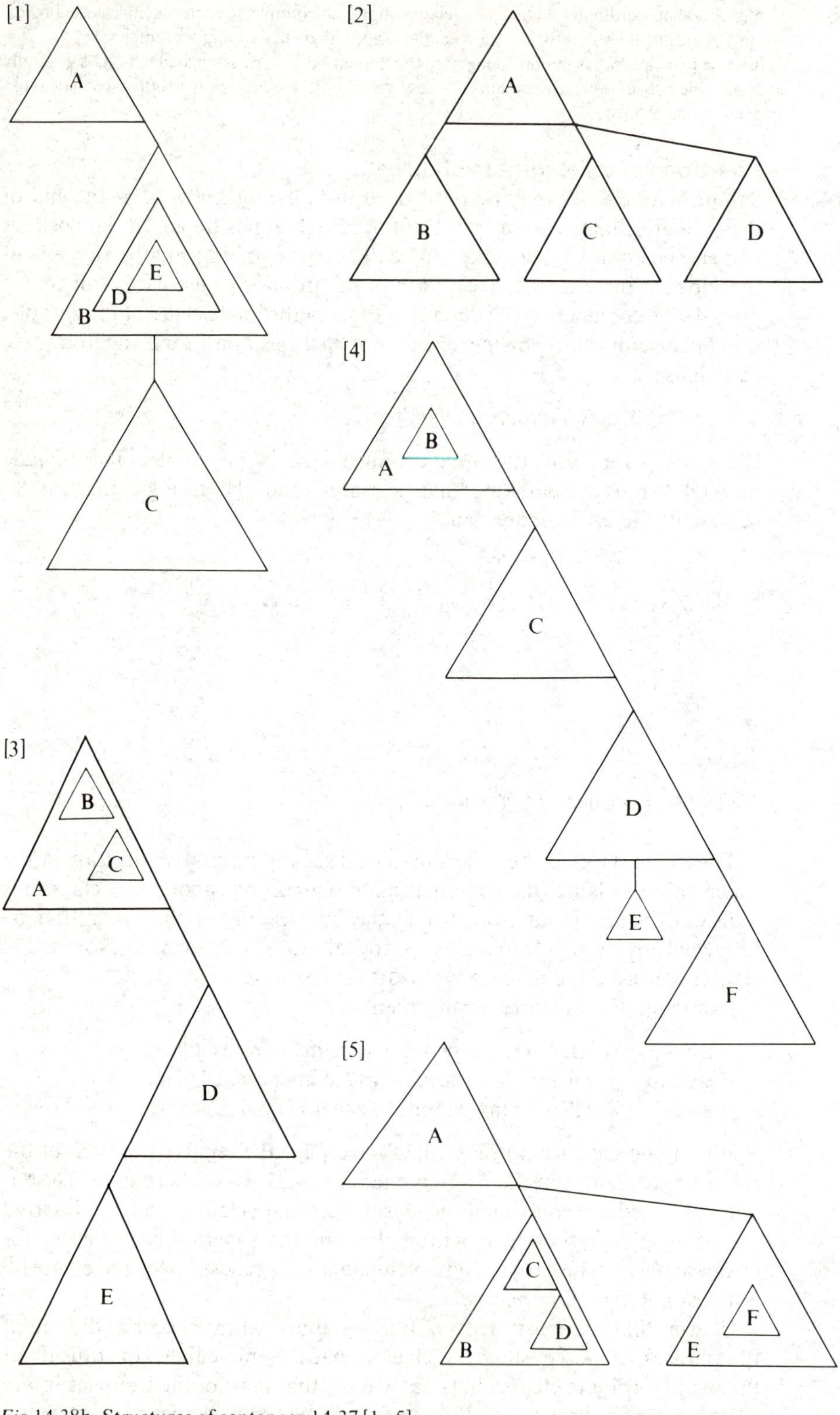

Fig 14.38b Structures of sentences 14.37 [1–5]

structure that the greatest depth of subordination is reached in the final part of the sentence.

14.39 Right-branching clauses are the easiest to comprehend. Considerable left-branching is possible in the noun phrase, as illustrated in the following genitive construction, although comprehension becomes more difficult as the complexity of left-branching increases:

12345 5 4 3 2 1
[[[[[Tom's] sister's] husband's] mother's] house]

But in clause structure, left-branching tends to be limited to two degrees of embedding:

1 2 3 4 4 3
[He said [that [if [when you've finished] you'd close the door] he'd be
21
very grateful.]] [1]

In [1] the *when*-clause is initial in the *if*-clause, and the *if*-clause in turn is initial in the *that*-clause. However this extent of embedding becomes extremely awkward and indeed incomprehensible if the clauses are positioned initially in the sentence, where the length and complexity of the clauses contravenes the principle of end-weight (*cf* 18.9):

* *That if when you've finished you'd close the door he'd be very grateful* was obvious to everyone present. [1a]

In initial position in the sentence, one degree of left-branching is possible, though still awkward:

12 3 3 2 1
[[That [if you could] you would help me] is of small comfort] [2]

We can reduce the awkwardness of [2] through extraposition of the subject (*cf* 18.33*ff*), thereby converting left-branching into right-branching:

1 2 3 321
[It is of small comfort [that you would help me [if you could]]] [2a]

Extraposition is usual, and the resulting sentence [2a] is much more acceptable than [2]. The change from [2] to [2a] brought about by extraposition is visually presented in *Fig* 14.39.

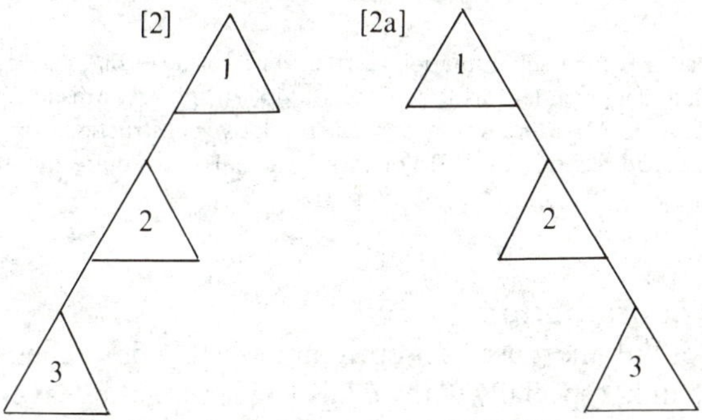

Fig 14.39 Structure of sentences [2] and [2a]

Nesting (medial branching) causes the most awkwardness, if the nested clause is long and is itself complex:

> Vanessa, whose brother Jim likes to tell at great length how he used to play tennis with famous movie stars when he lived in Los Angeles, is my best friend. [3]

Although the subordinate clauses within this nested relative clause are all right-branching, the nesting of just the one superordinate relative clause is sufficient to reduce the acceptability of the sentence. Contrast [3] with [3a], where by a switch of subject and subject complement the relative clause becomes right-branching, resulting in a much more acceptable sentence:

> My best friend is Vanessa, whose brother Jim likes to tell at great length how he used to play tennis with famous movie stars when he lived in Los Angeles. [3a]

There is a further factor contributing to the awkwardness of [3]: it violates the principle of end-weight. At the sentence level, this principle requires that the part of the sentence following the verb should be as long as, and preferably longer than, the part that precedes the verb.

Posing particular difficulties for comprehension is SELF-EMBEDDING, the medial subordination of one constituent within another constituent of the same kind. While the sentence (found in a well-known nursery story) *This is the . . . rat that ate the malt that lay in the house that Jack built* is tolerable and easily intelligible regardless of the number of relative clauses, the self-embedded alternative:

> ?*This is the house [^{1}that the malt [^{2}that the rat ate]^2 lay in]^1

is extremely awkward and not easy to understand, even though there is only one layer of self-embedding. We need add only a second layer of self-embedding to render the sentence completely baffling:

> *This is the house [^{1}that the malt [^{2}that the rat [^{3}that the cat killed]^3 ate]^2 lay in]^1

The various arrangements of subordinate clauses, therefore, do not just concern stylistic options and their relative merits, but also the more basic question of what constitutes a possible English sentence.

Note Despite the overall tendency towards final subordination, certain types of adverbial clauses favour initial position. They include conjuncts (*cf* 15.18), subjuncts (*cf* 15.19), most style disjuncts (*cf* 15.21), and sentence adjuncts (*cf* 15.22). Moreover, adverbial correlative constructions with a correlative adverbial in the second clause (*cf* 14.13) not merely favour but require initial placement of the subordinate clause.

Subordination versus coordination

14.40 Coordination is the kind of link most used for optimum ease of comprehension. At the same time the link, especially with *and*, is vague in that it leaves the specific logical relationships to the inference of the speaker (*cf* 13.22*ff*).

In the following examples we seek to demonstrate correspondences between coordination and subordination, while preserving the information ordering. This ordering, however, has the effect of suggesting an initial positioning of subordinate clauses that is more frequent than usual.

SUBORD: Reaching for the phone, he asked for the operator. [1]
COORD: He reached for the phone and (then) asked for the operator. [1a]

SUBORD: Although admission was free, few people attended the lecture. [2]
COORD: Admission was free, but (nevertheless) few people attended the lecture. [2a]

SUBORD: If you push the door hard, it will open. [3]
COORD: Push the door hard, and (then) it will open. [3a]

SUBORD: Unless you give it back to me, I'll tell your mother. [4]
COORD: Give it back to me or (else) I'll tell your mother. [4a]

SUBORD: Over fifty demonstrators were arrested, some of them women. [5]
COORD: Over fifty demonstrators were arrested, and some of them were women. [5a]

SUBORD: When the ship arrived at Naples, the sailors were given shore leave for twelve hours. [6]
COORD: The ship arrived at Naples, and the sailors were (then) given shore leave for twelve hours. [6a]

SUBORD: I lent my bicycle to Robert, who lent it to David. [7]
COORD: I lent my bicycle to Robert, and he (then) lent it to David. [7a]

SUBORD: Whereas the Northeast and the Midwest are rapidly losing population, the Sun Belt states are receiving more people than they can cope with. [8]
COORD: The Northeast and the Midwest are rapidly losing population, and/but (at the same time) the Sun Belt states are receiving more people than they can cope with. [8a]

SUBORD: Mortimer exploded a firecracker during the lesson, as a result of which he was suspended from school for a week. [9]
COORD: Mortimer exploded a firecracker during the lesson, and as a result of that he was suspended from school for a week. [9a]

SUBORD: Discovered almost by accident, this substance has revolutionized medicine. [10]
COORD: This substance was discovered almost by accident, and it has (since) revolutionized medicine. [10a]

SUBORD: As Jane was the eldest, she looked after the others. [11]
COORD: Jane was the eldest, and (so) she looked after the others. [11a]

The conditional uses of *and* and *or* exemplified in [3a] and [4a] are rarely encountered in written English. On the other hand, the adverbial participle clauses in [1] and [10] (*cf* 15.58*ff*) are rarely encountered in spoken English.

Parataxis without a coordinator (*cf* 13.2) is also a common substitute for subordination. The clauses may be punctuated as separate sentences or they may be separated by semicolons or (in restricted circumstances, *cf* App III.6) by commas within the same orthographic sentence. The three examples are based on the last three pairs above:

Mortimer exploded a firecracker during the lesson; as a result he was suspended from school for a week. [9b]
This substance was discovered almost by accident. It has since revolutionized medicine. [10b]
Jane was the eldest, so she looked after the others. [11b]

Structural ambiguity

14.41 Ambiguities may arise in complex sentences when two interpretations are plausible. If a complex sentence contains two final subordinate clauses, as in [1], the last subordinate clause may be interpreted as subordinate (a) to the sentence as a whole or (b) to the preceding subordinate clause. The two paraphrases are given in [1a] and [1b] respectively.

I'll let you know whether I'll need you here when the doctor arrives. [1]
When the doctor arrives, I'll let you know whether I'll need you here. [1a]
I'll let you know whether, when the doctor arrives, I'll need you here. [1b]

The two structures are shown in *Fig* 14.41a.

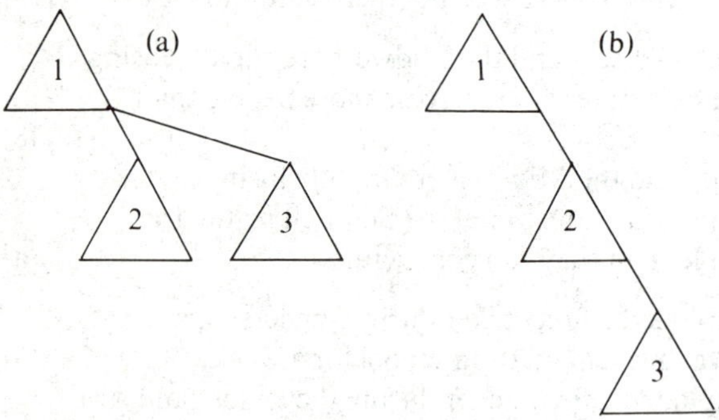

Fig 14.41a Structural ambiguity of [1]

If the (a) interpretation is intended, the last subordinate clause should be preposed, as in the paraphrase in [1a], since generally a final subordinate clause is interpreted as subordinate to the immediately preceding clause. But the final placement in [1] for the (a) interpretation is not uncommon. In conversation, any misinterpretation can be immediately corrected, but in writing the misplacement in [1] for the (a) interpretation is a stylistic error. The same ambiguities may occur with phrases as well as clauses:

Doris watched her children doing their homework *for a short time.*
I remembered having told Tom *soon afterwards.*

A similar ambiguity occasionally arises with two coordinated clauses followed or preceded by a subordinate clause:

> John reported to me and I informed Bob that everything was ready. [2]
>
> If Mary has recovered from the flu she is in the supermarket and the children are at a play centre. [3]

The interpretation of the sentences depends on whether the subordinate clause belongs (a) to both main clauses or (b) to only one of them. Punctuation (and in speech, intonation) can distinguish the two interpretations of [2]:

> John reported to me, and I informed Bob, that everything was ready. [2a]
>
> John reported to me, and I informed Bob that everything was ready. [2b]

For the [2a] interpretation of [3], separation by punctuation or intonation of only the subordinate clause may be sufficient:

> If Mary has recovered from the flu, she is in the supermarket and the children are at a play centre. [3a]

A clearer alternative is to subordinate the second clause:

> If Mary has recovered from the flu, she is in the supermarket while the children are at a play centre. [3a′]

For the (b) interpretation, the main clauses may be switched:

> The children are at a play centre and, if she has recovered from the flu, Mary is in the supermarket. [3b]

Alternatively, the subordinate clause may be placed at the end of the first main clause:

> Mary is in the supermarket, if she has recovered from the flu, and the children are at a play centre. [3b′]

Yet a further type of ambiguity involves a final coordinated clause which follows a subordinate clause. The ambiguity depends on whether the final clause (a) is a main clause or (b) is coordinated with the preceding subordinate clause:

> I know (that) he's cheating and I can't do anything about it. [4]

If a relation of coordination is represented as △△, then the two interpretations of [4] can be represented as in *Fig* 14.41b.

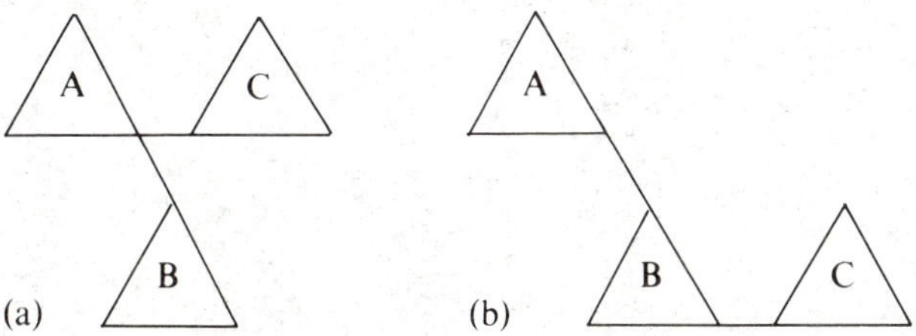

Fig 14.41b Structural ambiguity of [4]

To make it clear that interpretation (b) is intended, we could insert *that* at the beginning of the final clause as well as at the beginning of the first subordinate clause:

I know that he's cheating and that I can't do anything about it. [4b]

If we do not change the wording of [4] there is no sure way of insisting on interpretation (a), but the major syntactic break after *cheating* can be indicated at that point by a semicolon, or by a tone unit boundary and a pause. A clearer alternative requires in addition the omission of *and*:

I know that he's cheating; (however) I can't do anything about it. [4a]

In our discussion of structural ambiguity we have considered five devices that can be used to avoid ambiguity:

(1) changing the order of the clauses, as in [1a] [1b], [3b], [3b′]
(2) using punctuation to mark the major (*ie* least embedded) clause boundary, as in [2a], [2b], [3a]
(3) using intonation, if necessary endorsed by pause, to mark the major clause boundary, as in [2a], [2b], [3a]
(4) supplying ellipted elements, as in [4b]
(5) changing the structural relationship of the clause, *eg* from coordinate to subordinate, as in [3a′], or from coordinate to paratactic without a coordinator, as in [4a].

Bibliographical note

On the terminology for sentence and clause, see Greenbaum (1980).

On the complex sentence and subordination in general see Haegeman (1985); Hudson (1971); Nakajima (1982); Smaby (1974). On nonfinite and verbless clauses beginning with a subordinator, see Bäcklund (1984).

On the overlap of conjunction and preposition, see Jacobsson (1977a); Matthews (1981), esp 174–81.

On the choice of verb in subordinate clauses, see Palmer (1974; 1979), both *passim*. On more specialized topics, see Close (1980); Haegeman (forthcoming b); Johansson (1979); Quirk (1981). The last three cite evidence from elicitation experiments or from corpus analysis on the preferences for the mandative subjunctive, the *should*-construction, and the indicative.

On backshift in indirect speech, see Palmer (1974; 1979), both *passim*.

On transferred negation, see Cattell (1973); Horn (1978b); Lakoff (1969); Lindholm (1969).

On sentence complexity and comprehensibility, see Chomsky (1965), especially *pp* 10–14; Huddleston (1965); Rosenbaum (1967b); Williams (1979); Yngve (1961).

15 Syntactic and semantic functions of subordinate clauses

Syntactic functions of subordinate clauses

15.1 Subordinate clauses may function as subject, object, complement, or adverbial in a superordinate clause:

subject: *That we need a larger computer* has become obvious.

direct object: He doesn't know *whether to send a gift.*

indirect object: You can tell *whoever is waiting* that I'll be back in ten minutes.

subject complement: One likely result of the postponement is *that the cost of constructing the college will be very much higher.*

object complement: I know her *to be reliable.*

adverbial: *When you see them,* give them my best wishes.

In addition, subordinate clauses may function within these elements, *eg:*

postmodifier in noun phrase: (Few of the immigrants retained) the customs *that they had brought with them.*

prepositional complement: (It depends) on *what we decide.*

adjectival complementation: (We are) happy *to see you.*

Note There are constraints on the functioning of clauses as indirect objects or as object complements. Among the finite clauses, only nominal relative clauses function as indirect object (but *cf* 15.4 Note [a]) or as object complement.

Functional classes of subordinate clauses

15.2 On the basis of their potential functions, we distinguish several major categories of subordinate clauses: NOMINAL, ADVERBIAL, RELATIVE, and COMPARATIVE. The functional classification resembles to some extent that of subclausal units such as noun phrases and adverbs.

NOMINAL CLAUSES have functions that approximate to those of noun phrases: subject, object, complement, appositive, and prepositional complement. Every nominal clause may function in some or all of these functions. Unlike noun phrases, however, nominal clauses may also function as adjective complementation without a preposition (*cf* 16.70):

I'm not sure *that I can remember the exact details.*

The privilege of occurrence of nominal clauses is more limited than that of noun phrases because semantically the clauses are normally abstract; *ie* they refer to such abstractions as events, facts, dates, and ideas rather than to perceptible objects. The one exception to this generalization is the nominal relative clause (*cf* 15.8 *f*), which may refer to objects (including persons) and which has some of the properties of a noun phrase consisting of head and postmodifying relative clause, the head and relative pronoun coalescing to form a single *wh*-element. Compare the equivalent sentences:

What pleases one party infuriates the other.
That which pleases one party infuriates the other. ⟨formal⟩

Since indirect objects normally refer to persons, we can see why the nominal relative clause is the only type of clause that can normally function as an indirect object. Nominal clauses that are involved in the complementation of verbs and adjectives are examined in detail in Chapter 16.

ADVERBIAL CLAUSES (*cf* 15.17*ff*) function mainly as adjuncts or disjuncts (*cf* 15.20*f*). In those functions they are like adverb phrases, but in their potentiality for greater explicitness, they are more often like prepositional phrases:

> We left *after the speeches ended.*
> We left *after the end of the speeches.*
> We left *afterwards.*

RELATIVE CLAUSES generally function as restrictive or nonrestrictive modifiers of noun phrases and are therefore functionally parallel to attributive adjectives. Compare:

> a man *who is lonely* ~ a *lonely* man

But they are positioned like postmodifying prepositional phrases:

> tourists *who come from Italy* ~ tourists *from Italy*

These adnominal relative clauses are discussed in detail in Chapter 17, the chapter concerned with noun phrases. Two types of relative clauses, however, are discussed in this chapter: the nominal relative clause (15.8*f*) and the sentential relative clause (15.57). The status of the nominal relative clause is indeed equivocal between noun phrase and nominal clause, but its resemblance to nominal clauses proper is sufficient to justify its treatment together with them. The sentential relative clause does not function as a modifier of a noun phrase; its relative item refers anaphorically to a unit larger than a phrase, usually to a clause but sometimes even to a series of sentences. The inclusion of the sentential relative clause in this chapter is warranted by its resemblance in certain respects to adverbial clauses.

COMPARATIVE CLAUSES (*cf* 15.63*ff*) resemble adjectives and adverbs in their modifying functions:

> He's not *as* clever a man *as I thought.*
> I love you *more* deeply *than I can say.*

Semantically, the comparative clauses together with their correlative element (*eg*: *more, as, -er*) are equivalent to degree adverbs.

Nominal clauses

15.3 Nominal clauses (clauses approximating in function to noun phrases) fall into six major categories:

> *that*-clauses, or subordinate declarative clauses (15.4)
> subordinate interrogative clauses (15.5*f*)

subordinate exclamative clauses (15.7)
nominal relative clauses (15.8*f*)
to-infinitive clauses (15.10*f*)
-ing clauses (15.12*ff*)

Nominal clauses may take *it* or *that* as pro-forms:

> Ĭ know *that you mean well*, but THÈY don't know *it*.
> *How a book sells* depends on the author, but *it* also depends on the publisher.
> I hope *to see you tomorrow*, but *that* depends on the weather.
> *Collecting stamps* was her hobby, but she has given *that* up.

That-clauses

15.4 Nominal *that*-clauses may function as:

subject: *That the invading troops have been withdrawn* has not affected our government's trade sanctions.

direct object: I noticed *that he spoke English with an Australian accent*.

subject complement: My assumption is *that interest rates will soon fall*.

appositive: Your criticism, *that no account has been taken of psychological factors*, is fully justified.

adjectival complementation: We are glad *that you are able to join us on our wedding anniversary*.

They may not, however, function as object complement or (but *cf* 9.2) as prepositional complement.

When the *that*-clause is direct object or complement, the conjunction *that* is frequently omitted except in formal use, leaving a zero *that*-clause:

> I know *it's late*.

It is similarly omitted frequently when a subject *that*-clause (with anticipatory *it*) is extraposed (*cf* 18.33*ff*):

> *It*'s a pity *you don't know Russian*.

But otherwise *that* cannot be omitted in a subject clause, since without the subordinate marker the clause would be initially misinterpreted as a main clause:

> * *You don't know Russian* is a pity.

Subject *that*-clauses are usually extraposed. Extraposition is particularly preferred when the superordinate clause is interrogative or passive:

> Is *it* possible *that they can't afford to rent that apartment*?
> It was thought *that the cease-fire still held*.

If the superordinate clause is exclamatory, extraposition is obligatory:

> How strange *it* is *that the children are so quiet*!

Object *that*-clauses are normally extraposed when they cooccur with an object complement:

Their daughter's success makes *it* very likely *that she will return to California.*

Note [**a**] A nominal *that*-clause functioning as indirect object is marginally acceptable and rare:

They would not give *that she passed her examination with distinction* any consideration in determining her salary.

[**b**] The zero *that*-clause is particularly common when the clause is brief and uncomplicated. Retention of *that* is necessary under certain conditions other than when the clause is an unextraposed subject:

(i) to clarify whether an adverbial belongs to the matrix clause or the *that*-clause:

They told us once again *that the situation was serious.*

They told us *that once again the situation was serious.*

(ii) to prevent a coordinated *that*-clause from being misinterpreted as a coordinated main clause (*cf* 14.41):

I realise that I'm in charge and *that everybody accepts my leadership.*

~ I realize that I'm in charge, and everybody accepts my leadership.

(iii) when the object *that*-clause is fronted (as with an initial subject clause):

That she ever said such a thing I simply don't believe.

(iv) when a clause or a long phrase intervenes between the verb and the *that*-clause:

We decided, in view of his special circumstances, *that we would admit him for a probationary period.*

[**c**] Like most other nominal clauses, nominal *that*-clauses cannot be object complements, but alternative *to*-infinitive constructions are available with some verbs (*cf* 16.50*f*):

*I thought his argument *that we should pay.*

~ I thought his argument *to be that we should pay.*

Also a finite construction:

~ I thought (*that*) *his argument was* (*that*) *we should pay.*

[**d**] If the subject of the *that*-clause is a pushdown *wh*-element (*cf* 11.18) and is therefore moved to the front of the superordinate clause, the subordinator *that* must be omitted, perhaps to prevent *that* being initially misinterpreted as subject of the following verb:

Who did she hope would be the winner? [1]

* *Who* did she hope *that* would be the winner? [1a]

They pointed out the damage *which* they supposed had been done by last night's storm. [2]

*They pointed out the damage *which* they supposed *that* had been done by last night's storm. [2a]

Contrast [1b] with [1] and [1a]:

Who did she hope (*that*) *that* would be? [1b]

In [1b], the second *that* is indeed the subject of the *that*-clause; *who* is the subject complement and therefore the subordinator *that* may be optionally retained, the presence of a subject *that* before the verb preventing misinterpretation.

Here are several other examples of optional *that* when the *wh*-element is not the subject and hence a subject appears before the verb in the *that*-clause:

Who do you expect (*that*) *they* have chosen?

She told me *how* she thought (*that*) the machine worked.

They mentioned the name of the men (*who*) they knew (*that*) you had spoken to.

Wh-interrogative clauses

15.5 Subordinate *wh*-interrogative clauses occur in the whole range of functions available to the nominal *that*-clause (*cf* 15.4) and in addition may function as prepositional complement:

subject: *How the book will sell* depends on the reviewers.

direct object: I can't imagine *what they want with your address.*

subject complement: The problem is *who will water my plants when I am away*.

appositive: Your original question, *why he did not report it to the police earlier*, has not yet been answered.

adjectival complementation: I'm not sure *which she prefers*.

prepositional complement: They did not consult us on *whose names should be put forward*.

These subordinate clauses resemble *wh*-questions semantically (*cf* 11.14*ff*) in that they leave a gap of unknown information, represented by the *wh*-element. Contrast the known information expressed in the *that*-clause with the unknown information in the *wh*-clause:

I know (*that*) *Caroline* will be there.
Do you know *who* will be there?
I'm sure (*that*) *Ted* has paid.
I'm not sure *who* has paid.

The type of subordinate *wh*-interrogative clause that most closely resembles *wh*-questions is the indirect *wh*-question (*cf* 14.33):

She asked me *who would look after the baby*.

Compare the direct question:

She asked me, 'Who will look after the baby?'

But we can claim a chain of resemblance from the request for an answer to a question (as in the indirect question) through uncertainty about the answer (as in *I'm not sure who will look after the baby*), certainty about the answer (*It's obvious who will look after the baby*), expressions of other mental states or processes about the answer (*I found out who will look after the baby, It's irrelevant who will look after the baby*), and informing about the answer (*I told you who would look after the baby*). In all instances a question is explicitly or implicitly raised, a question focused on the *wh*-element.

There are also grammatical similarities to independent *wh*-questions:

(i) the *wh*-element is placed first in its clause, as in all the examples in this section. If the *wh*-element is a prepositional phrase, we have the same choices as for the *wh*-element in *wh*-questions (*cf* 11.14, and Note [a] below):

I asked them *on what* they based their predictions. ⟨formal⟩
I asked them *what* they based their predictions *on*.

(ii) The *wh*-elements have the same range of functions as the *wh*-elements in *wh*-questions (*cf* 11.15).

(iii) Although the subordinate clause usually does not have subject–operator inversion, such inversion may occur, particularly when the clause functions as complement and the superordinate verb is BE or when it functions as appositive:

The problem is *who can we get to replace her*.

Your original question, *why did he not report it to the police earlier*, has not yet been answered.

Furthermore, the superordinate predications that allow *wh*-clauses will generally also allow *yes–no* interrogative clauses:

Whether the book will sell depends on the reviewers.
I'm not sure *whether she prefers coffee.*
They did not consult us on *whether our names should be put forward.*

An infinitive *wh*-clause can be formed with all *wh*-words, though instances with *why* are rare:

I don't know *what to say*. ['. . . what I should say.']
You must explain to them *how to start the motor*.
['. . . how one/they should start the motor.']
I never know *who to speak to*. ['. . . who one/I should speak to.']
I'm wondering *where to put my coat*. ['. . . where I should put my coat.']
I'm wondering *why to go at all*. ['. . . why I should go at all.']

The infinitive clause has an obligational sense.

Note [**a**] As with *wh*-questions (*cf* 11.15 Note [a]), the final preposition following BE in certain informal questions must be deferred:

I can imagine *what it is like*. [**like what it is*]
I'm not sure *who it's for*. [**for whom it is*]

The preposition is generally deferred in:

I can't understand *what you did that for*. [**for what you did that*]

[**b**] In literary style, subject–verb inversion occasionally occurs when the *wh*-element is the subject complement or an obligatory adverbial, particularly if the subject is lengthy:

She told us *how strong was her motivation to engage in research.*
It took me some time to discover *in which village stood the memorial to our fallen comrades.*

In addition subject–operator inversion is common in Irish English and dialectally:

Whenever I see her, she asks *when will I be visiting her mother*.

[**c**] Prepositions are optionally omitted before *wh*-clauses:

We have solved the problem (*of*) *who was at fault*.
I'm not sure (*about*) *what to do*.

[**d**] There may be more than one *wh*-element in the clause:

I don't know *who* wants *what*.

Compare the multiple *wh*-elements in *wh*-questions (*cf* 11.19).

[**e**] The case distinction in formal contexts between subjective *who* and objective *whom* depends on the function of the *wh*-word in its clause:

I do not know *who wants you*.
I do not know { *who you want.* / *whom you want.* ⟨formal⟩ }

The distinction applies regardless of a governing preposition in the superordinate clause, since the complement of the preposition is the whole clause, not the *wh*-word:

It depends on *who wants you*.
It depends on { *who you want.* / *whom you want.* ⟨formal⟩ }

Nevertheless, the preceding preposition sometimes influences speakers to use objective *whom* as a hypercorrection even when it has the function of subject in the *wh*-clause. Except in formal contexts, *who* is used for all functions.

What we have said in this Note applies equally to the case distinction between subjective *whoever* and formal objective *whomever* in nominal relative clauses.

[**f**] Some noun phrases correspond semantically to subordinate *wh*-clauses, in contexts where such clauses are also appropriate:

He explained the way to the park. ['. . . how to get to the park.'] [1]
We found out the time it takes to get there. ['. . . how long it takes to get there.'] [2]

I don't know the { culprit. ['. . . who the culprit is'.] / person you want. } [3]

She asked the reason for the delay. ['. . . why there was a delay.'] [4]

Example [3] can also mean 'I am not acquainted with the culprit/the person you want'.

Yes–no and alternative interrogative clauses

15.6 Subordinate *yes–no* interrogative clauses (*cf* 11.5*ff*) and subordinate alternative interrogative clauses (*cf* 11.20*f*) occur in the whole range of functions available to subordinate *wh*-interrogative clauses (*cf* 15.5), and may include infinitive clauses. The *yes–no* clause is introduced by the subordinators *whether* or *if*:

Do you know *whether the banks are open*?
I wonder *if you can help me.*

The alternative clauses are formed with the correlatives *whether . . . or* or *if . . . or*:

I can't find out [*whether* / *if*] *the flight has been deLÁYED or* [*whether* / *if*] *it has been CÀNcelled.* [1]

If, as in [1], the second unit is a full clause, the subordinator is repeated. It is not repeated in [2–4], where the second unit is an abbreviated form:

They didn't say *whether it will RÁIN or be SÙNny.* [2]
I asked them *if they wanted MÉAT or FÌSH.* [3]
I don't care *if they JÓIN us or NÒT.* [4]

The abbreviated forms parallel those for independent alternative *yes–no* questions (*cf* 11.21). Repetition is optional with *to*-infinitive clauses:

He didn't tell us *whether to wait for him or* (*whether*) *to go on without him.*

But the subordinator is not repeated if the second clause is abbreviated by the omission of the infinitival *to*:

He didn't tell us *whether to wait for him or go on without him.*

Whether-clauses pose alternatives more obviously than *if*-clauses, which can be ambiguous between this construction and that of conditional clauses. *Whether*-clauses, unlike *if*-clauses, may be used where there is little resemblance to an indirect question:

It's irrelevant { *whether* / ?*if* } *she's under sixteen.*

You have to justify { *whether* / **if* } *your journey is really necessary.*

If tends to be more frequent than *whether* in informal style for *yes–no* clauses.

On the other hand, *if* is more restricted syntactically than *whether*. It must occur as complementation of verbs and adjectives, in consequence of which it is excluded from certain contexts:

(i) *If* cannot introduce a subject clause unless the clause is extraposed:

> { *Whether she likes the present* / **If she likes the present* } is not clear to me.
>
> It's not clear to me { *whether* / *if* } *she likes the present.*

(ii) *If* cannot introduce a subject complement clause:

> My main problem right now is *whether I should ask for another loan.*
> ?*My main problem right now is *if I should ask for another loan.*

(iii) The *if*-clause cannot be the complement of a preposition:

> It all depends on *whether they will support us.*
> ?*It all depends on *if they will support us.*

(iv) The *if*-clause cannot be an appositive:

> You have yet to answer my question, *whether I can count on your vote.*
> ?*You have yet to answer my question, *if I can count on your vote.*

In addition:

(v) *If* cannot introduce a *to*-infinitive clause:

> I don't know *whether to see my doctor today.*
> *I don't know *if to see my doctor today.*

(vi) *If* cannot be followed directly by *or not*:

> He didn't say *whether or not he'll be staying here.*
> *He didn't say *if or not he'll be staying here.*

But *or not* can be postposed:

> He didn't say *if he'll be staying here or not.*

Note [**a**] There is a close connection between conditional *if* and interrogative *if*; both convey doubt about the truth value of the clause. Compare:

> If she wants you, (then) she will say so.
> Does she want you? (Then) she will say so.

Where ambiguity may arise, intonation or punctuation separation may sometimes be necessary to distinguish the interrogative from the conditional clause:

interrogative [SVO_iO_d]:

> I'll tell you later *if I can find the time.* [*if* = *whether*]

conditional [SVO_iA]:

> I'll tell you later, *if I can find the time.* ['If I can find the time, I'll tell you later.']

[**b**] As with *either* (*cf* 13.39*ff*), *whether* or *if* can be used for more than two choices, despite a tradition of binary association (*cf* 15.41 Note [d]):

> I don't care *whether* you do your homework *or* play outside *or* go to bed.

[**c**] On *whether*- and *if*-clauses as complementation of verbs such as *doubt*, *cf* 16.73.

[**d**] There is some prescriptive objection to *or not* as redundant.

Exclamative clauses

15.7 Subordinate exclamative clauses generally function as extraposed subject, direct object, or prepositional complement:

extraposed subject: It's incredible *how fast she can run*. ['It's incredible that she can run so fast.']

direct object: I remember *what a good time I had at your party*. ['I remember that I had such a good time at your party.']

prepositional complement: I read an account of *what an impression you had made*. ['I read an account that you had made an excellent (*or* a terrible) impression.']

As in independent exclamative clauses (*cf* 11.31 *f*), the exclamative element is formed with *what* as predeterminer in a noun phrase and *how* as intensifier of an adjective, adverb, or clause; the exclamative element is positioned initially regardless of its normal position in a declarative clause.

Subordinate exclamative clauses generally have the same form as subordinate interrogative clauses introduced by *what* or *how* (*cf* 15.5). However, in exclamative clauses *what* is a predeterminer (preceding the indefinite article), while in interrogative clauses *what* is either a central determiner or a pronoun. Thus [1] with predeterminer *what* is unambiguously exclamative, while [2] with central determiner *what* and [3] with pronoun *what* are unambiguously interrogative:

They didn't know *what a crime he had committed*.
['. . . the terrible crime he had committed.'; *cf*: *What a crime he had committed!*] [1]

They didn't know *what crime he had committed*.
['. . . the identity of the crime he had committed.'; *cf*: *What crime had he committed?*] [2]

They didn't know *what the crime was*.
['. . . the identity of the crime'; *cf*: *What was the crime?*] [3]

The distinction between predeterminer and central determiner *what* is neutralized for noncount nouns (*what foolishness*) and plural nouns (*what crimes*).

If the superordinate clause has a predication appropriate for both types of clauses and the *wh*-words are *how* or *what* with a noncount or plural noun, the subordinate clause may be ambiguous:

You can't imagine *what difficulties I have with my children*.

exclamatory interpretation: You can't imagine the great difficulties I have with my children.

interrogative interpretation: You can't imagine the kinds of difficulty I have with my children.

I told her *how late she was*.

exclamatory interpretation: I told her she was very late.

interrogative interpretation: I told her the extent to which she was late.

We all saw *how strange a look she gave him.*

exclamatory interpretation: We all saw that she gave him an extremely strange look.

interrogative interpretation: We all saw the extent to which the look she gave him was strange.

Nominal relative clauses

15.8 Nominal relative clauses resemble *wh*-interrogative clauses (*cf* 15.5) in that they are also introduced by a *wh*-element. Indeed, a major reason for including nominal relative clauses in this chapter is that it is often difficult to distinguish them from the interrogative clauses.

On the other hand, in some respects nominal relative clauses are more like noun phrases, since they can be concrete as well as abstract and can refer even to persons. In fact, we can paraphrase them by noun phrases containing a noun head with general reference that is modified by a relative clause:

Whoever did that should admit it frankly.
['The person who did that . . .']
I took *what they offered me.*
['. . . the thing(s) that they offered me.']
Macy's is *where I buy my clothes.*
['. . . the place where I buy my clothes.']

Compare also the paraphrase when the *wh*-element is a determiner:

I took *what books she gave me.* ['. . . the books that she gave me.']

Furthermore, nominal relative clauses share with noun phrases a wider range of functions than are available to other nominal clauses (see below). In addition, like noun phrases, they may display number concord with the verb of the sentence (*cf* 10.34). Contrast for example:

Whatever book you see is yours to take.
Whatever books I have in the house are borrowed from the public library.

The nominal relative clause is basically a noun phrase modified by an adnominal relative clause (*cf* 17.9*ff*), except that its *wh*-element is merged with its antecedent (the phrase to which the *wh*-element refers). In that respect the nominal relative clause is more self-contained than the adnominal relative clause and can function as an element in a superordinate clause. Compare the nominal relative clause in [1] with the noun phrase in [1a]:

I eat *what I like.* [1]
I eat *that which I like.* 〈formal〉 [1a]

In [1a], which has approximately the same meaning as [1], the antecedent of the adnominal relative clause is *that.*

The *wh*-item may be a pronoun, such as *what* in [2], a determiner, such as *what* in [3], or an adverb, such as *where* in [4]:

She tasted *what* I bought. [2]
She saw *what food* I bought. [3]
Here is *where* I bought the food. [4]

On the *wh*-items that function as nominal relatives, *cf* 6.35 Note [b].

The *wh*-element may function within the nominal relative clause as subject, direct object, subject complement, object complement, adverbial, or prepositional complement:

subject: *What* happened (upset him).
(They welcomed) *whatever visitors* came their way.

direct object: *What* he saw (upset him).
(She took) *what* she needed.

subject complement: *What* she became in later life (distressed her friends).
(I'm happy with) *what* I am.

object complement: (That's) *what* she calls her sister.

adverbial: *Where* she went (was Manchester).
(Now is) *when* I need you.

prepositional complement: (I'll show you) *what* you can open the bottle with.

There are some restrictions on the use of the *wh*-element:

(a) The determiner *what* is only marginally acceptable when the *wh*-element is subject. Contrast [5] with [5a]:

?(They gladly accepted) *what money* came their way.
[*wh*-element as S] [5]
(They gladly accepted) *what money* people gave to them.
[*wh*-element as O_d] [5a]

Contrast [5] also with [5b], where the determiner *whatever* is fully acceptable:

(They gladly accepted) *whatever money* came their way. [5b]

(b) *Which, whom,* and *who* (in its nonspecific meaning, *cf* 15.9) are restricted to cooccurrence with a small semantic class of verbs (*choose, like, please, want, wish*):

She can marry { *whom(ever) she pleases.* ⟨formal⟩ / *who(ever) she pleases.* }
['. . . anyone that/who/whom she pleases.']
You can take *which(ever) you like.*
['. . . any (that) you like.']

In this environment, the three relatives have a nonspecific meaning (*cf* 15.9).

(c) *Who* in its specific meaning (*cf* 15.9) is most frequently found in a clause functioning as subject complement, particularly after *that's*:

You're not *who I thought you were.* ['. . . the person I thought you were.']
So that's *who he's working for.*
I'm *who you're looking for.*

How and *why* are generally restricted to the same environment (*cf* also Note [b] below):

That's *how she works*. ['. . . the way (that) she works.']
That's *how long it takes*. ['. . . the length of time (that) it takes.']
This is *how big it was*. ['. . . the size (that) it was.']
That's *why I don't go there anymore*. ['. . . the reason (that) I don't go there anymore.']

Nominal relative clauses have the same range of functions as noun phrases. In addition to the functions available generally to nominal clauses, they can function as indirect object and object complement:

subject: *What I want* is a cup of hot cocoa.

direct object: You should see *whoever deals with complaints*.

indirect object: He gave *whoever asked for it* a copy of his latest paper.

subject complement: April is *when the lilacs bloom*.

object complement: You can call me *what(ever) you like*.

appositive: I'll pay you the whole debt: *what I originally borrowed and what I owe you in interest*.

prepositional complement: You should vote for *which(ever) candidate you think best*.

Like noun phrases, nominal relative clauses require prepositions in adjective complementation:

He's aware *of* { *what I write.* / *the books I write.* }

Contrast the optionality of the preposition with *wh*-interrogative clauses (*cf* 15.5 Note [c]).

To-infinitive clauses may be nominal relative clauses, but they seem to be restricted to the functions of subject complement and prepositional complement:

subject complement: That's *where to go for your next vacation*. ['. . . the place to go . . .']

prepositional complement: The book is *on how to use a computer*. ['. . . the way to use . . .']

Excluded as relatives in *to*-infinitive clauses are all the *-ever* compounds and *which, why*, and the determiner *what*. The pronominal relatives *who(m)* and *what* do not function as subject within the infinitive clause, but otherwise have the same range of functions as in the finite clauses:

direct object: Here's *what to eat*. ['. . . the thing to eat.']

indirect object: That's *who(m) to ask*. ['. . . the person to ask.']

subject complement: That's *who to be*. ['. . . the role to be.']

object complement: Here's *what to call your dog*. ['. . . the name to call your dog.']

adverbial: This is *where to be*. ['. . . the place to be.']

prepositional complement: This is *what to season the rice with*. ['. . . the spice to season the rice with.']

Note [a] Nominal relative clauses have also been called 'independent' or 'free' relative clauses.

[b] *Why* is sometimes used in a pseudo-cleft sentence with a correlative *because* in the superordinate clause (*cf* 15.46 Note [h]):

Why we left early was because we were tired.

[c] There may be occasional ambiguity between a nominal relative clause and a universal conditional-concessive clause (*cf* 15.42):

Come here, *whoever you are.*

relative interpretation: Come here, you (I don't know your name).

concessive interpretation: Come here, no matter who you are.

[d] On the choice between subjective *whoever* and formal objective *whomever, cf* 15.5 Note [e].

[e] When a verb can be used transitively or intransitively, there may be ambiguity with time or place adverbials both with nominal relative clauses and corresponding noun phrases with relative clauses:

She remembered { *when she saw me.* / *the time she saw me.* } [direct object or time adverbial]

15.9 The *wh*-element may express either a SPECIFIC meaning (generally indicated by the absence of the *-ever* suffix) or a NONSPECIFIC meaning (generally indicated by the presence of the *-ever* suffix):

SPECIFIC:

I took *what was on the kitchen table.* ['. . . that which was on the kitchen table.'] [1]

May is *when she takes her last examination.* ['. . . the time when she takes her last examination.'] [2]

NONSPECIFIC:

Whoever breaks this law deserves a fine. ['Anyone who breaks this law . . .'] [3]

I'll send *whatever is necessary.* ['. . . anything that is necessary.'] [4]

As the paraphrases indicate, the *wh*-element in [1] and [2] is specific, while in [3] and [4] it is nonspecific. The contrast is highlighted in:

Quality is *what counts most.* ['. . . is that which counts most.']

Quality is *whatever counts most.* ['. . . is anything that counts most.']

The first sentence, with specific *what,* is a pseudo-cleft sentence (*cf* 18.29*f*) corresponding to *Quality counts most* ['Quality is supremely important.']; the second sentence, with nonspecific *whatever,* purports to define *quality.* The two meanings parallel those conveyed by specific *some* (and its compounds) and nonspecific *any* (and its compounds); *cf* 6.59*ff.*

There are problems in some instances in distinguishing nominal relative clauses from *wh*-interrogative clauses. They differ syntactically in several respects:

(a) While an interrogative clause as subject must take a singular verb, a nominal relative clause may take either a singular or a plural verb, depending on the meaning of the *wh*-element:

What money I have *is* yours. ['The money (that) I have is yours.']

What possessions I have *are* yours. ['The possessions (that) I have are yours.']

What were left behind *were* five empty bottles. ['The things (that) were left behind *were* five empty bottles.']

For the number choice, *cf* 10.34, 10.38. As we have suggested earlier (*cf* 15.8), the number variation is indicative of the gradience between the *wh*-element of a nominal relative clause and a noun phrase.

(b) While an interrogative clause allows a choice in the placement of the preposition in a *wh*-element (*cf* 15.5), a nominal relative clause requires the *wh*-word to be placed first and the preposition to be deferred:

> They ate *what they paid for.*
> ~ *They ate *for what they paid.*
> (*cf*: They ate the things *for which they paid.* [adnominal relative clause])
> *Whoever they lend the money to* must be trustworthy.
> (*cf*: *Anybody to whom they lend the money* must be trustworthy)
> Make sure you include in the examination paper *whatever questions they didn't know the answers to last time.*
> [pushdown nominal relative clause, *cf* 11.18]

(c) *Who, whom,* and *which* are common in interrogative clauses, but in nominal relative clauses they are restricted to cooccurrence with a small semantic class of verbs (*choose, like, please, want, wish*); *cf* 15.8.

(d) The compound forms in *-ever* are used in nominal relative clauses, but not in interrogative clauses. Thus while *They asked me what I didn't know* is ambiguous (see below), *They asked me whatever I didn't know* is unambiguously relative ('They asked me those things that I didn't know.') (*cf* Note [c]).

(e) Unlike in interrogative clauses, determiner *what* in nominal relative clauses has a paucal meaning:

> *What friends she has* are out of the country.
> ['The few friends she has are out of the country.']
> He collected *what information he could find.*
> ['He collected the little information he could find.']

In this function, *what* can be followed by only the paucal quantifiers *few* and *little* (*what few friends, what little information*) and not by the multal quantifiers *many* and *much* or by cardinal numerals. For some speakers the determiner *whatever* does not necessarily have a paucal meaning. Like *what* it cannot be followed by numerals or the multal quantifiers, but for some speakers it cannot be followed by the paucal quantifiers either.

The semantic distinction between the interrogative *wh*-clause and the nominal relative clause is easier to exemplify than to define. The interrogative clause contains a gap of unknown information, expressed by the *wh*-element, and its superordinate clause expresses some concern with the closing of that gap, with supplying the missing information. The nominal relative clause does not contain a gap in information, and therefore the superordinate clause is not concerned with the closing of that gap. The information may indeed be known to both speaker and hearer, as in *I took what was on the kitchen table.* Since only the nominal relative clause can be concrete, when semantic restrictions indicate that the clause is a physical object, the clause is unambiguously relative: *I sent them what they needed.* In other instances the clause may be ambiguous:

Do you remember *when we got lost*?

relative interpretation: Do you remember the occasion, the time we got lost?

interrogative interpretation: Do you remember when it was we got lost?
['When did we get lost? Do you remember?']

They asked me *what I knew*.

relative interpretation: They asked me things that I knew.

interrogative interpretation: They asked me, 'What do you know?'

What she wrote was a mystery.

relative interpretation: She wrote a mystery story.

interrogative interpretation: I don't know what she wrote.

Note [**a**] The nonspecific meaning of the *wh*-element often implies plurality of persons, things, or situations:

Write to *who(m)ever* you want. ['any persons']
Give me back *whatever* you took from my desk. ['the various objects']
He was happy with *whatever* she did. ['any actions']

The specific meaning leaves the number undetermined, except through context:

I took in *what* I found outside the door. ['the thing' or 'the things']

[**b**] Nonspecific *who* is occasionally found in nominal relative clauses that are not functioning as subject complement:

Who should run the business is me. [clause as S]
I've found *who you were looking for*. [clause as O_d]

[**c**] We distinguish the compound *wh*-words in *-ever* (*eg: whoever, whatever*) from the informal intensifying combinations that are normally spelled as two words (*eg*: *who ever, what ever*), which occasionally occur in subordinate interrogative clauses: *I can't imagine who ever would marry him* ['. . . who on earth . . .'] (*cf* 11.14 Note [b]).

To-infinitive clauses

15.10 Nominal *to*-infinitive clauses may function as:

subject: *To be neutral in this conflict* is out of the question.

direct object: He likes *to relax*.

subject complement: The best excuse is *to say that you have an examination tomorrow morning*.

appositive: Your ambition, *to become a farmer*, requires the energy and perseverance that you so obviously have.

adjectival complementation: I'm very eager *to meet her*.

The presence of a subject in a *to*-infinitive clause normally requires the presence of a preceding *for*. When the subject is a pronoun that distinguishes subjective and objective cases, it is in the objective case:

For your country to be neutral in this conflict is out of the question.
For us to take part in the discussion would be a conflict of interest.
I'm very eager *for them to meet her*.

When the clause is a direct object, however, *for* is generally absent before the subject:

He likes *everyone to relax*.

But, especially in AmE, certain verbs of wanting and their antonyms allow an optional *for* in the object clause (*cf* 16.41):

> He didn't like *me to be alone at night.*
> He didn't like *for me to be alone at night.* ⟨AmE only⟩

Prepositional verbs with *for* and adjectives complemented by a prepositional phrase with *for* allow *for* to have the additional function of introducing a *to*-infinitive clause with a subject:

> I am waiting *for her to say something.* (*cf*: I am waiting for her reply.)
> She must be impatient *for me to be appointed.* (*cf*: She must be impatient for my appointment.)

As with *that*-clauses (*cf* 15.4), extraposition is more usual for subject clauses:

> *It's* important (*for us*) *to agree on our position before the meeting.*

Object clauses are obligatorily extraposed when they cooccur with an object complement:

> I think *it* wiser (*for me*) *to leave at once.*
> They consider *it* their duty *to speak to his parents.*

For other types of nominal *to*-infinitive clauses, see also the sections dealing with *wh*-interrogative clauses (*cf* 15.5), *yes–no* and alternative interrogative clauses (*cf* 15.6), and nominal relative clauses (*cf* 15.8*f*).

Note [**a**] When the infinitive clause is not functioning as direct object, *for* is generally available. Contrast:

> Every employee in my company would prefer *for me to retire now.* ⟨AmE only⟩
> *For me to retire now* would be preferred by every employee in my company.

For is obligatorily omitted, however, in certain constructions where the focus is on the subject of the infinitive clause. Thus, *for* is optional in the sentence

> He didn't like *for me to be alone at night.* ⟨AmE only⟩

But the cleft sentence focusing on the subject of the clause is:

> It was *me* he didn't like to be alone at night.

And thematic fronting of the subject (*cf* 18.20*f*) produces:

> *Me* he didn't like to be alone at night.

Similarly, *for* is omitted in a question focusing on the subject:

> *Who(m)* didn't he like to be alone at night?

On the other hand, in a pseudo-cleft sentence that focuses on the whole infinitive clause *for* may be retained, and is indeed more usual even in BrE:

> What he didn't like was (*for*) *me to be alone at night.*

[**b**] Some AmE speakers also use *for* with the subject in an object clause following *want*:

> He wants *for me to go with him.*

[**c**] Where the subject of the infinitive clause can be made passive in the superordinate clause, the construction is complex transitive complementation of the superordinate verb (*cf* 16.50*f*):

> They considered *her to be the best candidate.*
> ~ She was considered *to be the best candidate.*

By analogy with *They considered her the best candidate, to be the best candidate* may be analysed as object complement of *her.*

[**d**] For sentences such as *It was clever of her to stay away, cf* 16.75*ff*. For *with* and *without, cf* 14.15.

15.11 The nominal *to*-infinitive clause often indicates that the proposition it expresses is viewed as a possibility or a proposal rather than something already fulfilled (*cf*: *-ing* clauses, 15.12). The infinitive clause is then closest semantically to a *that*-clause with putative *should* (*cf* 14.25):

It's natural *for them to be together*. [1]
It's natural *that they should be together*. [1a]

This putative feature of the infinitive clause may often be paraphrased by a conditional clause:

I prefer *them to stay with us*. [2]
I prefer it *if they stay with us*. [2a]
It would be unwise *for you to marry him*. [3]
It would be unwise *if you were to marry him*. [3a]

On the other hand, the infinitive clause may also refer to an actual fact. Thus [1] can also be paraphrased by [1b]:

It's natural *that they are together*. [1b]

Indeed, the infinitive clause may refer clearly to a proposition that is assumed to be true or (through the use of perfective *have*) to a situation that is assumed to have already occurred:

They found *him to be mentally competent to stand trial*.
I'm happy *to have met you*.

The subject and the subject complement may both be *to*-infinitive clauses, in which case the second clause expresses a characterization of the first:

To be human is *to err*. ['If one is human, one will err.']
To be a member of the Space Club is *to belong to one of the most exclusive clubs in the world*.

-ing clauses

15.12 Nominal *-ing* clauses (or more fully, nominal *-ing* participle clauses) may function as:

subject: *Watching television* keeps them out of mischief.

direct object: He enjoys *playing practical jokes*.

subject complement: Her first job had been *selling computers*.

appositive: His current research, *investigating attitudes to racial stereotypes*, takes up most of his time.

adjectival complementation: They are busy *preparing a barbecue*.

prepositional complement: I'm responsible for *drawing up the budget*.

If the *-ing* clause has a subject, the item realizing the subject may be in the genitive case or otherwise in the objective case (for pronouns having a distinctive objective case) or common case (for all other noun phrases). In general, the genitive is preferred if the item is a pronoun, the noun phrase has personal reference, and the style is formal (*cf* 16.42):

I intend to voice my objections to *their* receiving an invitation to our meeting. [1]

Contrast the preference for the common case in [2], where the item is a nonpersonal noun phrase and not a pronoun and the style is not formal:

I didn't know about *the weather* being so awful in this area. [2]

Traditional stipulation of the genitive case is based on the assumption that the *-ing* form in such clauses is a verbal noun (*cf* 17.52*ff*). That assumption is incorrect, as we can see from the direct object (*an invitation to our meeting*) that follows the *-ing* form in [1], which demonstrates that the *-ing* form has the force of a verb. On the other hand, the use in [1] of the genitive (which is a determiner in noun phrases) itself provides the *-ing* form with a nominal characteristic (*cf* also 15.13.)

The genitive is avoided when the noun phrase is lengthy and requires a group genitive (*cf* 17.119):

Do you remember *the students and teachers protesting against the new rule*?

On the other hand, the genitive case is preferred when the item is initial in the sentence:

My forgetting her name was embarrassing.

Some are troubled by the choice of case here. In some instances, an acceptable alternative is a *that*-clause, which is normally extraposed:

It was embarrassing *that I forgot her name*.

Unlike subject *that*-clauses (*cf* 15.4) and *to*-infinitive clauses (*cf* 15.10), subject *-ing* clauses are not normally extraposed. The superordinate clause can be interrogative or passive without the extraposition:

Will *our saving energy* reduce the budget deficit?
Postponing the proposed legislation is being considered by the subcommittee.

Note [**a**] Nominal *-ing* clauses are sometimes called 'gerundive' or 'gerundival clauses'. Their verb is commonly called a 'gerund'.

[**b**] For monotransitive and complex-transitive complementation with *-ing* clauses, *cf* 16.39, 16.42. For adjectives that allow complementation by an *-ing* clause, *cf* 16.83.

[**c**] The prepositional status of *worth* (*cf* 9.6) is confirmed by the fact that it can govern a noun phrase, a nominal *-ing* clause with a genitive subject, and a nominal relative clause (but not a *that*-clause or a *to*-infinitive clause):

San Francisco is worth {*frequent visits.* / *your visiting frequently.*}

The bicycle is not worth *what you paid for it.*

[**d**] The *-ing* form in the *-ing* clause occasionally takes determinatives other than the genitive:

I'm tired of *all that feeding the animals every day*.
This smoking your pipe on every possible occasion will ruin your health.

On *no* and *any* as determiners in this construction, *cf* 15.14.

15.13 A nominal *-ing* clause may refer to a fact or an action:

fact: *Your driving a car to New York in your condition* disturbs me greatly. [1]
action: *Your driving a car to New York* took longer than I expected. [2]

When an *-ing* form occurs alone or preceded just by a genitive noun phrase, the construction is syntactically ambiguous between an *-ing* clause and a noun phrase with a verbal noun in *-ing* as its head (*cf* 17.52*ff*):

My hobby is *swimming*. [3]
I hate *lying*. [4]
They liked *our singing*. [5]

Our singing in [5] can refer either to the action of singing or to the mode of singing. Without further expansion by an object or an adverbial, the genitive biases towards a mode interpretation. In contrast, the objective in [5a] allows only an action interpretation:

They liked us singing (while they worked). [5a]

Since the *-ing* clauses in [1] and [2] do not allow a mode interpretation, it appears that this interpretation belongs to the noun phrase structure rather than to the clause structure. Similarly, when we expand [5] by adding an object and thereby making the *-ing* construction unambiguously a clause, the mode interpretation is no longer available. In [5b] the *-ing* clause refers to an action:

They liked *our singing folk songs*. [5b]

Conversely, where only the mode interpretation is available, we may assume that the construction is a noun phrase:

Your driving has improved considerably since I last saw you. [6]

Contrast also [7] and [8], distinguished only by the position of *fast*:

I warned him against *fast driving*. [7]
I warned him against *driving fast*. [8]

In [7] *fast* is an adjective premodifying the noun *driving*, which is the head of the noun phrase. In [8] the adverb *fast* is an adverbial in the *-ing* clause *driving fast*. Compare the analogous contrasting pair in [7a] and [8a]:

I warned him against *careless driving*. [7a]
I warned him against *driving carelessly*. [8a]

When the *-ing* form is alone and is the direct object, as in [4], two interpretations of the implied subject are often possible. Thus, *I hate lying* may mean 'I hate it when I lie', linking the action specifically to the subject of the superordinate clause, or it may generalize ('I hate it when people lie'). When the *-ing* construction contains a direct object or an adverbial and is therefore unambiguously clausal, the usual interpretation is that there is an implicit link to the superordinate subject:

I hate telling lies. ['I hate it when I tell lies.']
They enjoy singing while playing the guitar. ['They enjoy it when they sing while playing the guitar.']

But this restriction is not absolute. It does not apply after verbs of speaking, where the generic interpretation holds:

She condemned *attacking defenceless citizens.*
['. . . that people attack defenceless citizens.']
They recommend *not paying taxes.* ['. . . that people not pay taxes.']

In other instances, the implied subject of the *-ing* clause may be taken from the context of the sentence:

Writing that letter was *his* downfall. [He wrote that letter]
Driving in heavy traffic makes *me* nervous. [I drive in heavy traffic]

But it may also be drawn from the previous linguistic context or even from the situational context:

Borrowing such a large sum was a big mistake.

And some sentences may allow a generic interpretation:

Borrowing large sums is a big mistake.

Note [**a**] An *-ing* form may also be a concrete noun (*cf* the discussion in 17.54).
[**b**] In *That was a plan of his friend's devising*, the *-ing* form is an *-ing* nominalization (*cf* 17.51*ff*). Compare *His friend devised the plan.*
[**c**] On the distinction between *They liked our singing* and *They liked us to sing*, *cf* 16.40, 16.42.

15.14 An *-ing* clause may be the subject of a bare existential clause (*cf* 18.47), in which case it normally appears in nonassertive contexts (*cf* 10.61). As with the *-ing* clause that has a genitive as its subject (*cf* 15.12), this construction is anomalous because the *-ing* form is preceded by a determiner, generally *no* but less commonly *any*:

There's *no mistaking that voice.* ['One could not mistake that voice.'] [1]
There was *no lighting fireworks that day.* ['One could not have lit fireworks that day.'] [2]
There isn't *any telling what they will do.* ['One could not tell what they will do.'] [3]
There must be *no standing beyond the yellow line.* ['One must not stand beyond the yellow line.'] [4]

If the *-ing* construction contains a direct object, it is generally paraphrasable with modal auxiliaries, as in [1–3]. In [4], where the construction lacks an object, a modal auxiliary is present in the sentence. Abbreviated forms with just the negative *-ing* clauses generally have the force of a prohibition:

No smoking. No parking here. No playing loud music.

The nonmodal interpretation is occasionally found, usually in certain fixed expressions:

There was *no turning the other cheek.* ['No one turned the other cheek.']

It is encouraged by the *-ing* nominalization (*cf* 17.51*ff*):

There was *no shooting of prisoners.* ['No one shot prisoners.']

If there is no direct object or *of*-construction, the *-ing* construction is ambiguous between the *-ing* clause and the *-ing* nominalization:

There was no smoking in the corridors.
(i) 'Smoking was not allowed in the corridors.'
(ii) 'No one smoked in the corridors.'

Note [**a**] Only the *-ing* nominalization occurs in the positive:
There was *shooting of prisoners*. ['They shot prisoners.']
There was *smoking in the corridors*. ['They smoked in the corridors.']

[**b**] The following sentence is triply ambiguous:
There's no writing on the blackboard today.
(i) *-ing* clause with modal interpretation:
'We can't write on the blackboard today (because we have no chalk).'
(ii) nominalization with nonmodal interpretation:
'We're not going to write on the blackboard today (because there's going to be an exam).'
(iii) deverbal noun:
'There's nothing written on the blackboard today.'

Bare infinitive clauses

15.15 The nominal bare infinitive clause (without *to*) is severely limited in its functions. It may be the subject complement or (rarely) subject in a pseudo-cleft sentence (*cf* 18.29*ff*):

subject complement: What the plan does is *ensure a fair pension for all*.
subject: *Mow the lawn* was what I did this afternoon. ⟨rare and informal⟩

It may also be the subject or subject complement of a variant of the pseudo-cleft sentence, where a noun phrase of general reference replaces *what*:

Turn off the tap was all I did.
The best thing you can do now is *write her an apology*.

The *to* of the infinitive is obligatorily absent when the infinitive clause is subject in these constructions, but it is optionally present when the clause is subject complement:

What they must do is (*to*) *propose an amendment to the resolution*.
The thing you should do is (*to*) *show them your diploma*.

The bare infinitive requires the substitute verb DO in the other subordinate clause. Contrast the obligatory *to* in [1] with the optional *to* in [2]:

All I wanted was *to help him*. [1]
All I wanted to *do* was (*to*) *help him*. [2]

A bare infinitive clause may function as object complement with a relatively few superordinate verbs (*cf* 16.52):

They made *her pay for the damage*.

Finally, the bare infinitive clause may follow prepositions of exception (*cf* 9.58):

She did everything but *make her bed*.

Verbless clauses

15.16 The nominal verbless clause is a more debatable category than the other nominal clauses. The category seems to be required to account for constructions which, although superficially noun phrases, have some of the semantic and structural characteristics of clauses:

A friend in need is *a friend indeed*. [proverb] [1]
Wall-to-wall carpets in every room is their dream. [2]
Are *bicycles* wise *in heavy traffic*? [3]

These may be paraphrased by nominal nonfinite existential clauses (*cf* 18.44*ff*):

To be a friend in need is *to be a friend indeed*. [1a]
Having wall-to-wall carpets in every room is their dream. [2a]
Is *it* wise *to have bicycles in heavy traffic*? [*or*: '. . . for there to be bicycles in heavy traffic?'] [3a]

Various syntactic features differentiate these constructions from noun phrases:

(i) The prepositional phrases in [1] and [2] are not of the kind that postmodify the head in a noun phrase. *A friend in need* as a noun phrase, for examplc, would mean 'a friend who is in need', whereas [1] means '(to be) a friend when another is in need' (*ie* 'Friendship in a time of need is indeed friendship').

(ii) The verb in [2] is singular, which would be difficult to explain if the subject were a plural noun phrase.

(iii) Semantic restrictions (*cf* 10.51) would make it anomalous to combine the noun-phrase head *bicycles* as subject with the attributive or predicative adjective *wise* (**wise bicycles*; **The bicycles are wise*). In the paraphrase [3a], *wise* complements the infinitive clause *to have bicycles in heavy traffic*. The proximity principle (*cf* 10.35) may account for the plural verb. The structure *SVC*, on the other hand, biases the syntax of the sentence towards clausal grammar and the consequent singular number concord (*cf* 10.15):

Bicycles in heavy traffic *is* sheer madness.

Syntactic functions of adverbial clauses

15.17 In Chapter 8 we distinguished four broad categories of syntactic functions for adverbials: adjuncts, subjuncts, disjuncts, and conjuncts. Adverbial clauses, however, function mainly as adjuncts and disjuncts.

In the next two sections we briefly consider adverbial clauses functioning as conjuncts and subjuncts. They will not be treated further in this chapter.

Conjuncts

15.18 The syntactic status of conjuncts is discussed in 8.134*ff*. They are peripheral to the clause to which they are attached. Only a few adverbial clauses function as conjuncts. They are stereotyped or virtually stereotyped, and can be comprehensively listed.

One finite clause type, the nominal relative clause (*cf* 15.8*ff*), functions as a reinforcing conjunct:

> What is more,
> What is most worrying, } . . .
> What interests me more,

In addition, *that is* (*to say*) is an apposition marker.

A number of *to*-infinitive clauses function as listing or summative conjuncts:

> *to begin* (*with*), *to cap it* (*all*) ⟨informal⟩, *to conclude*, *to continue*, *to recap* ⟨informal⟩, *to recapitulate*, *to start* (*with*), *to summarize*, *to sum up*

These allow a direct object or prepositional complement, *eg*: *to summarize the argument so far*; *to begin our discussion*. In addition, there are two *to*-infinitive clauses which require a prepositional complement:

> *to return to* [*eg*] my earlier discussion
> to turn to [*eg*] the next point

All of these *to*-infinitive clauses have corresponding *-ing* clauses, but most of them require complementation of the verb. Only a few can be used without complementation: *capping it all*, *continuing*, *recapitulating*, *recapping* ⟨informal⟩, *summarizing*, *summing up*.

Note The nonfinite conjuncts imply as subject the *I* (or authorial *we*) of the speaker. In this respect, they resemble style disjuncts (*cf* 8.124) such as *to put it bluntly* and *frankly speaking*. Indeed, they could alternatively be analysed as style disjuncts.

Subjuncts

15.19 The syntactic status of subjuncts is discussed in 8.116. Subjuncts are generally not realized by clauses, the exception being viewpoint subjuncts.

Both finite and nonfinite (participle) clauses function as viewpoint subjuncts. The verbs in the clauses constitute a restricted semantic set, principally *be concerned* and *go* (only in the finite clauses *as far as* . . . and *so far as* . . .), *consider*, *look at*, *view*:

> *As far as the economy* { *is concerned*, / *goes*, } the next six months are critical.

> *If we look at it from an historical point of view*, they have little claim on the territory.

> *Looking at it objectively*,
> *Viewed objectively*, } he is definitely at fault.

Note As with the conjunct clause (*cf* 15.18 Note), the *-ing* clause as viewpoint subjunct implies as subject the *I* of the speaker. On the other hand, the subject of the *-ed* clause is implicitly the matrix clause itself. Compare the anaphoric reference of the pronoun *it* in the corresponding *if*-clause: *If it is viewed objectively, he is definitely at fault.*

Adjuncts and disjuncts

15.20 Adjuncts and disjuncts tend to differ semantically in that adjuncts denote circumstances of the situation in the matrix clause, whereas disjuncts comment on the style or form of what is said in the matrix clause (style disjuncts) or on its content (content or attitudinal disjuncts). The primary difference is that they differ syntactically in that disjuncts are peripheral to the clause to which they are attached.

The syntactic difference does not manifest itself in differences in form or position. For example, finite clauses that function as adjuncts and disjuncts may share the same subordinator, and in both functions the clauses may be positioned initially or finally. The peripheral status of disjuncts is indicated mainly negatively: they do not allow a number of syntactic processes to apply to them that are allowed by adjuncts, processes that reflect a measure of integration within the superordinate clause.

In this section we consider the differences between adjunct and disjunct clauses. Below we exemplify the contrasts between adjunct clauses in the [a] sentences and content disjunct clauses in the [b] sentences:

temporal *since* [a] and reason *since* [b]:

I have been relaxing *since the children went away on vacation.* [a]
He took his coat, *since it was raining.* [b]

temporal *while* [a] and concessive *while* [b]:

He looked after my dog *while I was on vacation.* [a]
My brother lives in Manchester, *while my sister lives in Glasgow.* [b]

purpose *so that* [a] and result *so that* [b]:

They took a plane *so that they could get there early.* [a]
We know her well, *so that we can speak to her on your behalf.* [b]

conditional *if* [a] and conditional *unless* [b]:

They'll send it to you *if you ask them politely.* [a]
I'll get lost *unless I can find my compass.* [b]

temporal *as* [a] and reason *as* [b]:

The policeman stopped them *as they were about to enter.* [a]
I went to the bank, *as I had run out of cash.* [b]

The syntactic difference between adjunct and content disjunct clauses will be illustrated by two finite clauses, an adjunct *because*-clause and a disjunct *since*-clause. Both are incorporated within the same superordinate clause, and both are clauses of reason:

He likes them because they are always helpful. [1a]
He likes them, since they are always helpful. [1b]

Both can be positioned initially, although the adjunct clause is more usual finally:

Because they are always helpful, he (really) likes them. [2a]
Since they are always helpful, he (really) likes them. [2b]

The syntactic differences between the two types of clauses mainly involve focusing devices:

(i) Only the adjunct clause can be the focus of a cleft sentence:

It's because they are always helpful that he likes them. [3a]
*It's since they are always helpful that he likes them. [3b]

(ii) Only the adjunct clause can be the focus of a variant of the pseudo-cleft sentence:

The reason he likes them is because they are always helpful. [4a]
*The reason he likes them is since they are always helpful. [4b]

(iii) Only the adjunct clause can be the focus of a question, as we can test with alternative interrogation:

Does he like them because they are always helpful or because they never complain? [5a]
*Does he like them since they are always helpful or since they never complain? [5b]

(iv) Only the adjunct clause can be the focus of negation, as we can test with alternative negation:

He didn't like them because they are always helpful but because they never complain. [6a]
*He didn't like them since they are always helpful but since they never complain. [6b]

Contrast similarly:

He liked them, not because they are always helpful but because they never complain. [7a]
*He liked them, not since they are always helpful but since they never complain. [7b]

(v) Only the adjunct clause can be focused by focusing subjuncts (*cf* 8.116*ff*) such as *only*, *just*, *simply*, and *mainly*:

He likes them only because they are always helpful. [8a]
*He likes them, only since they are always helpful. [8b]

Contrast also:

Only because they are always helpful does he like them. [9a]
*Only since they are always helpful does he like them. [9b]

(vi) Only the adjunct clause can be the response to a *wh*-question formed from the matrix clause:

Why does he like them? Because they are always helpful. [10a]
*Why does he like them? Since they are always helpful. [10b]

Here are some further examples of content disjunct clauses (*cf* 8.127):

He brought me a cup of coffee *although I had asked for tea*.
William has poor eyesight, *whereas Sharon has poor hearing*.
You can return to a normal diet *now that you have lost enough weight*.

I'll take you for a ride *provided that your parents give you permission.*
He paid for a seat, *when he could have entered free.* [concessive *when*]
They ridiculed him *until she felt obliged to come to his aid.* [result *until*]
They will starve *before they will surrender unconditionally.* [negative result *before*]

In final position, content disjunct clauses tend more commonly than adjunct clauses to be separated from their matrix clauses by intonation or punctuation, though punctuation usage varies. Such separation is particularly common when the subordinator of a disjunct clause is frequently used as the subordinator of an adjunct clause, a condition that applies to reason *since* and *as*, concessive *while*, and result *so that*. In initial position, all adverbial clauses, regardless of form or function, are separated by intonation and (usually) by punctuation from their matrix clause.

Style disjuncts and content disjuncts

15.21 The syntactic differences enumerated in 15.20 apply equally to style disjuncts and content disjuncts. Style disjuncts are distinguished semantically in that they generally imply a verb of speaking and the subject *I*. The style disjuncts implicitly refer to the circumstances of the speech act, while the content disjuncts refer to the content of the matrix clause. The style disjuncts are therefore more peripheral to their superordinate clause than are the content disjuncts.

Here are some contrasts between either adjuncts or content disjuncts [a], and style disjuncts [b]:

adjunct *because* [a] and style disjunct *because* [b]:

We have no electricity, *because there's a power failure.* [a]
I have nothing in my bank account, *because I checked this morning.* [b]

adjunct *if* [a] and style disjunct *if* [b]:

We'll take along Sharon, *if she's ready.* [a]
We can do with some more butter, *if you're in the kitchen.* [b]

content disjunct *since* [a] and style disjunct *since* [b]:

Since you know Latin, you should be able to translate the inscription. [a]
What does the word mean, *since you're so clever*? [b]

content disjunct *though* [a] and style disjunct *though* [b]:

She enjoys driving, *though she doesn't like to drive in heavy traffic.* [a]
He deserved the promotion, *though it's not my place to say so.* [b]

We exemplify the semantic and syntactic differences by two finite clauses, a content disjunct *although*-clause and a style disjunct *since*-clause:

Elizabeth enjoyed last night's concert *although part of the programme included Wagner.* [1a]
Elizabeth enjoyed last night's concert, *since her brother told me so.* [1b]

The concession in [1a] refers to the content of the matrix clause, but the reason in [1b] refers to the speaker's motivation for the assertion ('I tell you this since her brother told me so'). The more peripheral status of the style disjunct is shown in its greater independence with respect to pro-forms. Thus, the style disjunct more readily allows the repetition of a noun phrase, whereas the content disjunct normally requires pronoun substitution:

> Elizabeth enjoyed last night's concert *although the programme was not entirely to* {*?Elizabeth's* / *her*} *taste*. [2a]
>
> Elizabeth enjoyed last night's concert, *since* {*Elizabeth's* / *her*} *brother told me so*. [2b]

Style disjuncts realized by clauses are always separated from the matrix clause by intonation and punctuation.

Here are some further examples of style disjuncts:

> *While we're on the subject*, why didn't you send your children to a public school?
> *If you will allow me to say so*, your attitude is equally racist.
> The latest unemployment figures are encouraging, *as it were*.
> *Before you leave*, where can I reach you?
> *Since you don't seem to know*, all further negotiations have been suspended.
> *Before you say anything*, you have the right to be silent.
> I'm in charge here, *in case you don't know*.
> *If you're so clever*, what's the answer?
> *Speaking of the devil*, here comes my nephew.
> *Stated bluntly*, I have legal control over their estate.

Note [**a**] The same form of clause can be a style disjunct in a statement and an adjunct when it is a response to a question. Style disjuncts can be the response to a question if the implied superordinate clause is made explicit. Compare the adjunct clause in [3], [3a], and [4a] with the style disjunct clause in [4]:

> We have no electricity, *because there was a power failure*. [3]
> ~A: *Why* do you have no electricity?
> B: *Because there was a power failure*. [3a]
> I have no money in my bank account, *because I checked this morning*. [4]
> ~A: *Why do you say that* you have no money in your bank account?
> B: *Because I checked this morning*. [4a]

The sentence relating to the question–response set in [5a] is [5], which (like [5a]) contains an adjunct *because*-clause; the question asks for some verification of the claim in the matrix clause in [5]:

> I know that I have no money in my bank account, *because I checked this morning*. [5]
> ~A: *How do you know that* you have no money in your bank account?
> B: *Because I checked this morning*. [5a]

Notice that the adjunct *because*-clauses in [3] and [5] can be positioned initially, but not the *because*-clause in [4], *cf* Note [c] below.

[**b**] In [6] the *because*-clause is an adjunct, while in [7] it is a style disjunct:

> He likes them because they are always helpful. [6]
> He likes them, because his wife told me so. [7]

Since two clauses with different syntactic functions cannot be coordinated, the two *because*-clauses cannot be coordinated:

> *He likes them because they are helpful and because his wife told me so.

They can cooccur in the same sentence, though the juxtaposition is stylistically clumsy in written

English. The disjunct clause is then positioned peripherally:

?He likes them because they are helpful, because his wife told me so.

[**c**] The style disjunct *because*-clause is exceptional in that it must follow the matrix clause:

I have nothing in my bank account, *because I checked this morning.*

**Because I checked this morning,* I have nothing in my bank account.

Contrast:

I'm up to my ears in debt, *since you ask me.*

Since you ask me, I'm up to my ears in debt.

[**d**] We have noted the analogies between clauses functioning as conjuncts (*cf* 15.18 Note) and viewpoint subjuncts (*cf* 15.19 Note), on the one hand, and style disjuncts, on the other hand. With respect to their integration within their superordinate clause, conjuncts are most like style disjuncts. Viewpoint subjuncts are closer to content disjuncts, as shown by the test involving repetition of a noun phrase:

As far as {*?Germany's* / *its*} economy is concerned, Germany shows signs of improvement.

[**e**] The style disjunct *as it were* ['as if it were so'] is roughly synonymous with *so to speak.*

Predication and sentence adjuncts

15.22 For adjunct clauses, a major distinction can be made between PREDICATION ADJUNCTS and SENTENCE ADJUNCTS. Predication adjuncts can in turn be divided into obligatory and optional adjuncts (*cf* 8.26*ff*). All obligatory adjuncts are predication adjuncts.

Predication adjunct clauses are normally positioned finally; fronting of a predication adjunct exceptionally occurs for rhetorical purposes. Obligatory adjunct clauses resemble direct objects and subject complements in providing complementation to the verb. Sentence adjunct clauses are more mobile than predication adjunct clauses: they may appear initially as well as finally, and occasionally even medially.

Obligatory adjunct clauses (*cf* 10.10) may provide complementation for the verb BE in the *SVA* type:

Your coat is *where you left it.*

Dinner will be *when everybody has arrived.*

The traffic jam was *because there was an accident.* ⟨informal⟩

The water is *in case you feel faint.* ⟨informal⟩

The purpose of the inquiry was *so that all complaints would be made public.*

And they may provide complementation for other verbs in the *SVA* type:

The water will last *until you return.*

My grandparents lived *before television was invented.*

He looks *as if he's tired.*

Jane looks *as if she doesn't know me.*

You may live *wherever you like.*

They are coming *to see us next week.*

They may also function as the adverbial in the *SVOA* type:

I put it *where I found it.*

He treated them *as if they were young children.* ['He behaved to them . . .']

They wanted the money *where it would earn the highest interest rates.*

Even when they are optional, direction adjuncts (*cf* 15.31) depend on the semantic category of verbs with which they cooccur – verbs denoting direction:

They moved *where the climate was milder.*
Throw it *where you wish.*

Similarity adjuncts (*cf* 15.50) are a blend of similarity with manner when they cooccur with verbs used dynamically:

She walks *exactly as her mother used to.*

Pronounce the word { *as I do.* / *like I do.* ⟨informal, esp AmE⟩ }

Likewise, comparison clauses (*cf* 15.50) are a blend of comparison with manner when they cooccur with verbs used dynamically:

He talks *as if he has a hot potato in his mouth.*
She is running *as if her life depended on it.*
Calvin laughed *as though he really understood the joke.*
They talk *like they know what they're doing.* ⟨informal, esp AmE⟩

Other optional predication adjuncts relate solely or predominantly to the verb complementation rather than to the matrix clause as a whole. The most common are position adjuncts:

I found the book *where you said it would be.* ['The book was where you said it would be.']
She hit him *where it hurts.* ['She hit him in that part of him where it hurts.']

Sentence adjunct clauses are not dependent on the predication and are therefore more mobile. The examples that follow are placed in initial position to show their ready acceptability in that position; these types of adjunct clauses could just as easily (and most would more usually) be at *E*.

Before I could sit down, she offered me a cup of tea.
When he saw us, he smiled.
To emphasize her point, she invited me to visit her village.
Because it is near Madrid, tourists come for the day.
If they achieve independence, conditions will improve.
As we ran toward the beach, it started to rain.
Whenever I come here, the hotels have new owners.
Where he stood, he could see sand dunes stretching for miles.
While she was in school, she became friendly with a boy whom she later married.

Note The subordinate clause in *He treated them as if they were young children* is an obligatory adjunct only if *treated* has the meaning 'behaved toward' in which case *treated* requires to be complemented by a manner adjunct. If *treated* is interpreted as 'gave medical treatment to' or 'gave a treat (*or* treats) to', the *as if*-clause is an optional predication adjunct.

Restrictive and nonrestrictive adverbial clauses

15.23 Some linguists have attempted to apply the distinction between restrictive and nonrestrictive modification in noun phrases (*cf* 17.3) to adverbials, thereby distinguishing between RESTRICTIVE and NONRESTRICTIVE adverbial clauses. The semantic analogy with modification in the noun phrase is that the restrictive adverbial restricts the situation in the matrix clause to the circumstances described by the adverbial. The nonrestrictive adverbial, on the other hand, makes a separate assertion, supplying additional information.

The restrictive/nonrestrictive distinction overlaps with some of the distinctions that we have made earlier. All disjunct clauses have been earlier characterized as peripheral because they do not give circumstantial information about the situation in the matrix clause (*cf* 15.20); they are therefore necessarily nonrestrictive. The same applies to the limited range of conjunct clauses (*cf* 15.18) and subjunct clauses (*cf* 15.19). On the other hand, obligatory adjunct clauses must be restrictive, since they are required to complete the description of the situation in the matrix clause. The restrictive/ nonrestrictive distinction therefore applies only to optional adjunct clauses.

Perhaps the clearest parallel to a nonrestrictive adjunct clause is the type that has been characterized as an appended clause, a type of clause that is usually parenthetic or an afterthought (*cf* 12.70):

Susan sees her father – *when her mother insists on it.* [1]

Utterance of the sentence in [1] conveys two separate assertions: Susan sees her father; she does so when her mother insists on it. On the other hand, the *when*-clause in [2] is normally interpreted as restricting the circumstances in which Susan sees her father (Susan sees her father only on those occasions):

Susan sees her father *when he comes to London.* [2]

The nonrestrictive clause is marked by intonation separation whether it follows or precedes its matrix clause. Punctuation practice is less consistent. In particular, punctuation may be omitted when the nonrestrictive clause is preposed. But, in fact, punctuation is a redundant signal when the nonrestrictive clause is preposed, since a preposed clause is always nonrestrictive. Thus, both [1a] and [2a] are nonrestrictive:

When her mother insists on it, Susan sees her father. [1a]
When her father comes to London, Susan sees him. [2a]

The semantic difference between restrictive and nonrestrictive adjunct clauses manifests itself when the matrix clause contains a focusing device. Nonrestrictive clauses cannot be the focus of such devices, and in this respect are syntactically similar to disjuncts (*cf* 15.20). For example, the focus of the negation can be on the restrictive *when*-clause in [2b], but not on the nonrestrictive clause in [1b]:

Susan doesn't see her father *when he comes to* LǑNdon.
['Susan sees her father, not when he comes to London, but at other times.'] [2b]
Susan doesn't see her FÀther – *when she can av*ÒID *it.*
['Susan doesn't see her father – the times she does are when she can't avoid it.'] [1b]

Notice that if the *when*-clause in [2b] is preposed, it is outside the scope of negation:

When her father comes to London, Susan doesn't see him. [2c]

The semantic difference is even sharper for *because*-clauses. Contrast the restrictive clause in [3a] with the nonrestrictive clauses in [3b] and [3c]:

Raven didn't leave the party early *because* CǍROL *was there*. [3a]
['Raven left the party early, not because Carol was there, but for some other reason.']

Raven didn't leave the party ÉARly, *because* CÀROL *was there*. [3b]
['Raven didn't leave the party early, and the reason he didn't was that Carol was there.']

Because CÁROL *was there*, Raven didn't leave the party EÀRly. [3c]
[= [3b]]

We can now distinguish three *because*-clauses: restrictive adjunct [4a], nonrestrictive adjunct [4b], and style disjunct [4c]:

Raven didn't leave the party early *because* CǍROL *was there*. [4a]
Raven didn't leave the party EÁRly, *because* CÀROL *was there*. [4b]
Raven didn't leave the party EÁRly, *because I* CHÈCKED. [4c]

Similarly, we can distinguish four *while*-clauses: predication (and restrictive) adjunct [5a], sentence (and nonrestrictive) adjunct [5b], content disjunct [5c], and style disjunct [5d]:

I didn't send my children to a boarding school *while I was in* ǏNDIA. [5a]
While I was in India, I didn't send my children to a boarding school. [5b]
My children enjoy jazz, *while I prefer classical music*. [5c]
While we're on the subject, I prefer classical music. [5d]

Semantic roles of adverbial clauses

15.24 We now turn to the semantic roles of adverbial clauses. The roles may be related to those for adverbials in general (*cf* Chapter 8) and for prepositional phrases in particular (*cf* 9.144*ff*).

For each semantic set, we first discuss finite clauses and then turn to nonfinite and verbless clauses introduced by a subordinator or (in some instances) a preposition (*cf* 15.25*ff*). We then consider separately nonfinite and verbless adverbial clauses that do not begin with a subordinator or preposition (*cf* 15.58*ff*). We conclude by discussing the verb phrase in those cases where the choice of form is linked to particular types of subordinate clauses.

Semantic analysis of adverbial clauses is complicated by the fact that many subordinators introduce clauses with different meanings; for example a *since*-clause may be temporal or causal. Furthermore, some clauses combine meanings, for example time with purpose or result (*cf* 15.48*f*); in such cases, we treat the clauses under sections that deal with what appears to be their primary meaning.

Clauses of time

Subordinators and structural types of clauses

15.25 Adverbial finite clauses of time are introduced by one of the following subordinators: *after, as, before, once, since, till, until, when, whenever, while, whilst* ⟨esp BrE⟩, *now* (*that*), *as long as, so long as, as soon as, immediately* ⟨informal, esp BrE⟩, *directly* ⟨informal, esp BrE⟩:

Buy your ticket *as soon as you reach the station.*
When I last saw you, you lived in Washington.
My family, *once they saw the mood I was in,* left me completely alone.
Drop by *whenever you get the chance.*
All applications, *when they are received before the deadline,* are dealt with promptly.
While I was asleep, I dreamed about you.
We came in *just as it started to rain.*
As I drove away, I saw them waving goodbye.
Wait *until you're called.*
Since I saw her last, she has dyed her hair.
I'll give you an answer *immediately I've finished reading your file.* ⟨esp BrE⟩

Adverbial *-ing* clauses of time are introduced by one of the following subordinators: *once, till, until, when, whenever, while, whilst* ⟨esp BrE⟩:

He wrote his greatest novel *while working on a freighter.*
Be careful *when crossing streets.*
Once having made a promise, you should keep it.

In addition, they are introduced by the prepositions *after, before, on,* and *since* (*cf* 14.19 Note [b]):

They washed their hands *before eating.*
Since coming here life has been much more pleasant.
I took a bath *after working in the garden all day.*
On becoming a member, you will receive a membership card and a badge. ['When you become a member, . . .']

Some speakers find *until* only marginally acceptable with *-ing* clauses:

?*Until meeting your parents,* I had no idea that you were annoyed with me.
?I'll wait here *until hearing from you again.*

Adverbial *-ed* clauses of time are introduced by one of the following subordinators that are also used with finite clauses: *as soon as, once, till, until, when, whenever, whilst* ⟨esp BrE⟩:

Spinach is delicious *when eaten raw.*
The dog stayed at the entrance *until told to come in.*
Once seen, that painting will never be forgotten.
He slept *while stretched out on the floor.*
Whenever known, such facts should be reported.

As soon as is only occasionally possible as a subordinator for *-ed* clauses:

The documents will be returned *as soon as* { *completed.* / *signed.* / *required.* }

Verbless clauses of time are introduced by the same subordinators as *-ed* clauses: *as soon as, once, till, until, when, whenever, while, whilst* ⟨esp BrE⟩:

When in difficulty, consult the manual.
Complete your work *as soon as possible.*
While in Rome, be sure to see the Colosseum.

Clauses with *as soon as* seem to be limited to a few adjectives that are used predicatively with nominal clauses and convey the modal meanings of possibility or necessity, principally *available, feasible, necessary, possible.* The implied subject of the verbless clause is *it*, referring to the matrix clause ('as soon as it is possible'). The same implication is common, though not required, for the other subordinators.

Some speakers find *until* and *till* only marginally acceptable with verbless clauses:

?Margaret stayed with her parents *until well.*
?Sam watched TV *until too tired to do so any more.*

They seem acceptable in instructional language:

Beat the mixture *until fluffy.*
File the edges *until smooth.*

To-infinitive clauses without a subordinator or a subject may have temporal function, expressing the outcome of the situation:

I rushed to the door, *only to discover that it was locked and barred.*
He left, *never to return.*
I awoke one morning *to find the house in an uproar.*
She turned around, *to find the car gone.*
The curtains parted, *to reveal a market scene.*
He survived the disgrace, *to become a respected citizen.*
Leech rose above the University College defence *to bullet the header a fraction over from a free kick.*

These clauses are restricted to final position, suggesting an analogy between them and result clauses (*cf* 15.49), which they resemble in meaning. The sentences can usually be paraphrased by reversing the relationship of subordination (*cf* 15.28 Note [a]), and using a *when-* or *after*-clause:

When I awoke one morning, I found the house in an uproar.
After he survived the disgrace, he became a respected citizen.

With durative verbs in the matrix clause, the construction expresses duration of time together with outcome:

She lived *to be 100.* ['She reached 100 years of age.']
You'll live *to regret it.* ['You'll eventually regret it.']
The show went on *to become a great success.* ['The show eventually became a great success.']
He lingered on *to see his daughter's wedding.*
She grew up *to be a successful actress.*

Some of the verbs in this type of construction have become catenatives (*cf* 3.49): *grow to, come to, turn out to.*

Finally, *-ing* clauses without a subordinator or a subject may also express time relationship:

> *Returning to my village after thirty years*, I met an old schoolteacher. ['When/After I returned . . .']
>
> The stranger, *having discarded his jacket*, moved threateningly toward me. [' . . . after he had discarded . . .']

Adverbial clauses of time are adjuncts. Since they are commonly sentence adjuncts (*cf* 15.22), they often appear initially and occasionally medially, as the examples in this section indicate.

Note [**a**] Noun phrases (sometimes introduced by a preposition) modified by a relative clause may have a semantic role similar to adverbial clauses of time (*cf* 14.14):

> *Every time* (*that*) *the telephone rings*, he gets nervous.
>
> Remain in your seats *until such time as you are told that you can leave.*
>
> *By the time the alarm went off*, I was awake.
>
> They made me feel at home *the moment I arrived.*
>
> Things have changed a great deal *since the last time you were here*. (*cf*: since you were here last time)
>
> *Throughout the period I was in London*, it rained heavily.

These noun phrases and prepositional phrases are adverbials of time, though not adverbial clauses.

[**b**] The correlatives *no sooner . . . than* (*cf* 14.13 Note [b]) express time relationship:

> The meeting had no sooner started } than there was an uproar.
> No sooner had the meeting started }

The meaning is similar to that of an *as soon as* clause, but it additionally expresses surprise. Syntactically, the *no sooner* clause is the matrix clause.

Time relationships

15.26 An adverbial clause of time relates the time of the situation denoted in its clause to the time of the situation denoted in the matrix clause. The time of the matrix clause may be previous to, subsequent to, or simultaneous with, the time of the adverbial clause. The situations in the clauses may be viewed as occurring once or as recurring. The time relationship may additionally convey duration and the relative proximity in time of the two situations.

Some of these time relationships are expressed not only by the choice of subordinator, but also by other devices in the two clauses: tense and aspect, the semantic category of the verbs, adverbs and prepositional phrases of time, and adjectives and nouns expressing time (*cf* 19.35). Temporal relationships between clauses may be implied by their semantic relationships in juxtaposed or coordinated clauses (*cf* 13.22*ff*). Here we are concerned mainly with the temporal subordinators.

Time before

15.27 *Until, till*, and *before* indicate that the situation in the matrix clause occurred before or leading up to the situation in the subordinate clause. *Till* is used in the same way as *until*, but is far less frequent as a subordinator. *Until* marks the time up to which the situation in the matrix clause applies:

I disliked Maurice *until I got to know him.*
The children were noisy *until told to be quiet.*

The matrix clause must be durative, the duration lasting to the time indicated by the *until*-clause. A negative clause is always durative, even though the corresponding positive clause is not durative (*cf* 8.58), since the absence of the event extends throughout the indicated period:

I didn't start my meal *until Adam arrived.*
*I started my meal *until Adam arrived.*

Before also marks the time from which the situation in the matrix clause applies, but the matrix clause need not be durative:

I started my meal *before Adam arrived.*

The situation in *until*-clauses is generally presupposed to be true, but that is not always so for *before*-clauses. Nonfactual *before*-clauses may imply preference, as in [1], or implausibility, as in [2]:

He'll beg for food *before he'll ask his parents for money*. ['He won't ask his parents for money'; 'He would rather beg for food than ask his parents for money.'] [1]
Pigs will fly *before he'll become a mathematician*. ['He'll never become a mathematician.'] [2]

Or the situation in the matrix clause may prevent that in the *before*-clause from taking place:

He died *before writing a will.*
Sally stopped Ted *before he had a chance to reply*. (*cf* 14.27)

Some *before*-clauses may be interpreted as either factual or nonfactual:

I sent a donation *before I was asked to.*

Before-clauses may imply purpose (*cf* 15.48) and result (*cf* 15.49) as well as time:

I had to put my complaint in writing *before they would take any action.* ['. . . so that they would take some action and with the result that they took action'; also 'They wouldn't take any action until I put my complaint in writing.']

Until-clauses may imply result as well as time:

She massaged her leg *until it stopped hurting*. ['. . .with the result that it stopped hurting.']

The *until*-clause expresses the result of the activity described in the matrix clause.

When the matrix clause is imperative, the sentence with a *before*-clause may imply a conditional relationship as well as time:

Go *before I call the police*. ['Go! If you don't go, I'll call the police.']

Compare the coordinate constructions implying the same relationship:

Go *or I'll call the police.* Go *and I won't call the police.*

Nonassertive items (*cf* 10.60) can appear in *before*-clauses, perhaps because *before*-clauses, like conditional clauses (*cf* 15.33*ff*), inherently relate to matters unfulfilled in respect of the matrix clause:

I spoke to them *before I ever heard any gossip about them.*
['At the time I spoke to them I had not heard any gossip about them']

Contrast:

*I spoke to them *after I had ever heard any gossip about them.*

Before may be modified to indicate relative proximity of time (*cf*: *after*, 15.29) by a range of modifiers, *eg*: *just*, *right*, *immediately*, *sometime*, *a long time*, *many days*:

I took the examination *a year before my brother did.*

Until is restricted to the modifiers *just* and *right.*

Note [**a**] Constructions with *before* and *after* are not necessarily converses. If we designate the first situation as 'X' and the second as 'Y', then in the factual use of *before*:

X *before* Y = X happened before Y happened.

On the other hand, the *after* construction has two interpretations:

Y *after* X = (i) Y happened after X happened. [converse]
(ii) Y continued to happen after X began to happen. [not converse]

If Y is nondurative, the two constructions are converses:

I shaved [X] *before* I went to the party [Y]. [3]
= I went to the party [Y] *after* I shaved [X]. [4]

However, if Y is durative, the two constructions need not mean the same:

I knew Cathy [X] *before* she practised medicine [Y]. [5]
≠ Cathy practised medicine [Y] *after* I knew her [X]. [6]

Sentence [6] allows the possibility that Cathy practised medicine even before I knew her.
Nonfactual *before*-clauses rule out an equivalent *after*-clause:

Sally stopped Ted [X] *before* he had a chance to reply [Y]. [7]
≠ Ted had a chance to reply [Y] *after* Sally stopped him [X]. [8]

Sentence [7] implies that Ted did not have a chance to reply.
When the *after*-clause implies cause, there is no equivalent *before*-clause:

After Norma spoke, she received a standing ovation.
≠ Norma spoke *before* she received a standing ovation.

[**b**] When both matrix and subordinate clause differ only in their subjects, a prepositional phrase corresponds to the *before*- or *after*-clause:

Janet left {*before* / *after*} I {*left.* / *did.*} [9]

= Janet left {*before* / *after*} *me.* [10]

Notice the use of the objective case in [10]. In some contexts there may be ambiguity between temporal and positional *before*:

They should stand up *before* me. ['before I do' *or* 'in front of me'] [11]

Positional *before* is used infrequently.

[**c**] Similar to the subordinators are prepositional phrases with *until*, *till*, and *before* followed by noun phrases modified by relative clauses, *eg*: *till the moment* (*that*), *before the time* (*that*), *cf* 15.25 Note [a]. But the *before*-phrases cannot be used in place of nonfactual *before*-clauses.

[**d**] *Until*-clauses, like *before*-clauses, may express a combination of time, purpose, and result. Contrast:

> Larry polished the table until {*he* / *you*} could see his face in it.

If the subject of the matrix clause and the *until*-clause are here coreferential (for example *Larry* and *he*), all three meanings are combined. If they are not coreferential, the *until*-clause conveys only time and result.

Same time

15.28 Several subordinators indicate the simultaneity of the situations in the matrix and subordinate clauses, or at least an overlap in time of the two situations: *as*, *as long as*, *so long as*, *while*, *whilst* ⟨esp BrE⟩. *When*, *whenever*, and *now* (*that*) may have the same function.

As, *as long as*, *so long as*, *while*, and *whilst* always denote simultaneity when they are used as temporal conjunctions. Temporal clauses introduced by the last four of these subordinators are duration adverbials.

As denotes merely simultaneity of two situations:

Matrix & S.C durative

> *Just as she was about to speak*, she was handed a note.
> *As it grew dark*, we could hear the hum of mosquitoes.

For *as long as* and *so long as*, both clauses must be durative. Generally, these subordinators imply that the situations begin and end at the same time:

> *As long as I live here*, I do it my way.
> He'll continue working *so long as he has the strength*.

They emphasize more strongly than the other subordinators both simultaneity and duration. *While* and the less frequent *whilst* require that their clause must be durative, but the matrix clause need not be:

S.C. durative, but matrix doesn't have to be

> They arrived *while I was sunbathing*.
> He cut himself *while shaving*.

Whenever is primarily used to introduce a frequency adverbial, denoting that the situation is repeated. It may also imply that the two situations overlap in time if at least one of the clauses is durative:

> It rains *whenever we're camping*. [' . . . at any time we're camping.']
> She visits her parents *whenever possible*.

Like *whenever*, *when* may imply simultaneity if one of the clauses is durative:

> *When I dream* I see angels running up and down a ladder.
> Be careful *when crossing streets*.

When may also imply repetitiveness, in which case it is synonymous with *whenever*:

> *When I read* I like to be alone.

As long as and *so long as* may imply condition ('provided that') as well as time:

> I'm happy *as long as my children are*.

Now that combines reason with temporal meaning, in present or past time. It may be used to indicate simultaneity:

We are happy *now that everybody is present.*
Now that she could drive, she felt independent.

Note [**a**] A type of *when*-clause, obligatory at *E* position, represents climactic information in narrative:

The last man was emerging from the escape tunnel *when a distant shout signalled its discovery by the guards.* [1]
I was playing the piano, *when there was a knock at the door.* [2]
I was watching the television, *when suddenly the lights went out.* [3]

The more important information is given in the subordinate clauses, which indicate that an event happened within a period referred to in the matrix clause. Notice that the matrix verb is in the progressive and that the *when*-clause is positioned finally. The effect is to provide a dramatic and emphatic climax. The *when*-clause is nonrestrictive (*cf* 15.23), and is usually separated by intonation and punctuation from the matrix clause.

[**b**] Certain noun and prepositional phrases combine with relative clauses to convey a meaning similar to that of these subordinators, *cf* 15.25 Note [a]. They include *every time* (*that*), *as often as*, *at the very moment* (*that*), *during the period* (*that*), *throughout the time* (*that*).

Time after

15.29 Several subordinators indicate a sequence in which the situation in the matrix clause occurs after that in the subordinate clause: *after*, *as soon as*, *directly* ⟨esp BrE⟩, *immediately* ⟨esp BrE⟩, *once*, *since*, *when*, *whenever*. *Now* (*that*) may have the same function.

As soon as, *immediately*, *directly*, and *once* add the notion of proximity in time of the two situations:

As soon as I left, I burst out laughing.
We'll eat *once I finish preparing the meal.*

Immediately and *directly* particularly emphasize proximity:

She returned *immediately she heard the good news.*

A similar effect is obtained by adding appropriate modifiers to *after* and *as soon as*, *eg*: *immediately after*, *just as soon as*.

After merely marks the sequence of the clauses. Modifications (*cf*: *before*, 15.27) may indicate relative proximity, *eg*: *just*, *right*, *immediately*, *moments*, *some time*, *a long time*, *soon*, *three days*, *a year*:

Come over *right after you've finished working.*
I went to sleep *soon after hearing the news.* [*after* as preposition]

Unlike the proximity subordinators, *after* allows the possibility that the situation in the matrix clause applied before the event:

He was still tired (*even*) *after he had had eight hours of sleep.*
*He was still tired *immediately he had had eight hours of sleep.*

Since marks the beginning of the period during which the situation in the matrix clause applies (*cf* 8.60*f*, 14.26):

He feels much more relaxed *since he left school.* [1]
Since returning home, Carol has been working in her parents' business. [*since* as preposition] [2]

Since I last saw you, I have given birth to a beautiful daughter. [3]
They had not read any books *since they left school*. [4]

The period marked by *since* may extend to the moment of utterance, as in examples [1–3], or to the past time of narration, as in [4]. But *since* does not rule out an extension beyond the period. The matrix clause may be durative, as in [1], [2], and [4], in which case we can premodify *since* by *ever* and ask a *How long?* question to elicit the *since*-clause. On the other hand, it may be nondurative, as in [3]. The matrix clause (*it* followed by BE) may merely specify the time period:

It has been two years *since I last saw you*. ['I last saw you two years ago.']

The period, however, may be left vague:

It's been {a long time / ages} *since you were here*.

When and *whenever* may indicate a sequence when the two clauses are nondurative:

She was shocked *when she heard his story*. [5]
When(ever) I cry, my eyes get puffy. [6]
I drink coke *when(ever) I feel sick*. [7]

Now (*that*) does not have that restriction, but it combines circumstantial (*cf* 15.45) with temporal meaning:

Now that they've moved, we won't see them very often.

The sequential meaning of *after*, *when*, and *whenever* may induce an implication of cause, as in [5] and the following:

He felt better *after he had a short nap*.
I hit him back *when he hit me*.
My heart leaps *whenever I see you*.

When, *whenever*, and *once* may combine time with condition, as in [7] and the following:

{*When* / *Whenever* / *Once*} *I make up my mind to do something*, I do it immediately.

When and *whenever* may also combine time, cause, and condition, as in [6].

When may imply concession as well as time. Like *whereas* (*cf* 15.43), it requires antithesis between two situations, but additionally has the meaning 'in that same situation' or 'in those same situations':

They were gossiping, *when they should have been working*.
['. . ., whereas they should have been working.']
She cleans the house by herself, *when she could easily have asked her children to help her*.

In this use, the *when*-clause is nonrestrictive and is usually in final position.

Note [**a**] The preposition *until* may introduce *after*-clauses:

Don't leave until *after I've spoken to you*.

[**b**] Several prepositions may combine with relative *when*, which is not to be confused with the subordinator: *by*, *since* ⟨esp BrE⟩, *till*, *until*:

Two years ago I bought a packet of your razor blades, *since when* I have used no others. ['since which time']

They settled in Seattle, *by when* she had obtained a master's degree in economics. ['by which time']

These constructions are sentential relative clauses (*cf* 15.57).

[**c**] Proximity may also be conveyed by phrases such as *the* (*very*) *moment that* and *from the minute* (*that*) followed by a relative clause, *cf* 15.25 Note [a]. Other phrases that combine with relative clauses to convey a meaning similar to that of subordinators in this section include *from the very first time* (*that*), *by the time* (*that*), *since the days* (*when*).

[**d**] See 15.25 for *to*-infinitive clauses that blend time with outcome.

Clauses of contingency

15.30 The meaning of several subordinators that primarily express time, place, or condition may be neutralized in certain contexts to convey a more abstract notion of recurrent or habitual contingency: *when*, *whenever*, *once*; *where*, *wherever*; *if*. The subordinators may then be paraphrased by such prepositional phrases as 'in cases when' or 'in circumstances where':

{*When*(*ever*) / *Where*(*ver*) / *If* / *Once*} {*there's smoke*, there's fire. / *children are involved*, divorces are particularly unpleasant. / *known*, such facts have been reported.} [1]

{*When*(*ever*) / *Where*(*ver*) / *If*} {*necessary*, send up a flare. / *in doubt*, see me. / *possible*, you should test all moving parts.} [2]

{*When*(*ever*) / *Where*(*ver*) / *Once* / *If*} *conscious of an infringement of his rights*, he always protested to the manager. [3]

She always wrote an encouraging remark, *even* {*when* / *where* / *if*} *the essay paper was poor*. [4]

Once, *whenever*, and *wherever* cannot be focused by focusing adverbs such as *even*, and are therefore excluded from [4].

Nonfinite and verbless clauses without a subordinator may also express recurrent contingency:

Driving at high speed, one may well miss direction signs.
The sentence is ambiguous, *taken out of context*.
Fresh from the oven, rolls are delicious.

We can supply the subordinator *when* for these clauses, and *if* for the -*ed* and verbless clauses.

The correlative construction with *the*-clauses (*cf* 15.51) sometimes expresses a meaning similar to that of a contingent relationship, the first *the*-clause roughly corresponding to a *when*-clause or an *if*-clause:

> *The harder he worked*, the happier he felt.
> *When he worked harder*, he felt happier.

Clauses of place

15.31 Adverbial clauses of place are introduced mainly by *where* or *wherever*. *Where* is specific and *wherever* nonspecific (*cf* 15.9). The clause may indicate position [1] or direction [2]:

> *Where the fire had been*, we saw nothing but blackened ruins. [1]
> They went *wherever they could find work*. ['to any place where'] [2]

The meaning of place merges with the general contingency meaning 'in cases where' (*cf* 15.30) in the following:

> He put colons *where(ver) he should have put semicolons*.

Where-clauses may combine the meanings of place and contrast:

> *Where I saw only wilderness*, they saw abundant signs of life.

Notice that the contrast subordinator *whereas*, which can replace *where* above, is a compound with *where* as one of its members.

Several temporal subordinators may have primarily a place meaning in descriptions of scenes, when the scenes are described dynamically in terms of movement from one place to another:

> Take the right fork *when the road splits into two*.
> The river continues winding *until it reaches a large lake*.
> The building becomes narrower *as it rises higher*.
> The road stops *just after it goes under a bridge*.
> *Once the mountains rise above the snow line*, vegetation is sparse.

Note [**a**] *Where* and *wherever* also introduce *-ed* and verbless clauses (*where grown*, *wherever necessary*), but the clauses then convey the general contingency meaning.
[**b**] The same place relationship may also be expressed by prepositional phrases with relative clause postmodification (*at the place that* . . ., *in the direction where* . . .) or with a *where*- or *wherever*-clause as complement (*toward(s) where* . . ., *to wherever* . . .).
[**c**] The archaic forms *whence* ['from where'] and *whither* ['to where'] are occasionally found, particularly in religious language.

Clauses of condition, concession, and contrast

Overlap of semantic roles

15.32 We have seen that some clauses of time and place may express a general notion of a contingency relationship between the situations described in the subordinate and matrix clauses, a relationship also conveyed by conditional *if*-clauses (*cf* 15.30). We have also noted that some temporal clauses may imply relationships of condition (*cf* 15.27*ff*) and concession (*cf* 15.29), and that some clauses of place may imply contrast (*cf* 15.31). We now further note that many subordinators and conjuncts expressing those three logical relationships of condition, concession, and contrast may otherwise convey meanings of time and place, as in the examples in *Fig* 15.32.

	subordinators	conjuncts
conditional	*as long as, in the event that*	*then, in that case*
concessive	*whereas, while*	*besides, yet*
contrastive	*whereas, while*	*on the other hand, instead*

Fig 15.32 Subordinators and conjuncts with overlapping roles

There is also considerable overlap in adverbial clauses that express condition, concession, and contrast. Conditional clauses (*cf* 15.33*ff*) convey that the situation in the matrix clause is contingent on that in the subordinate clause:

If the weather is fine, (*then*) we'll have a barbecue.

Clauses of contrast (*cf* 15.43) merely convey a contrast between two situations:

Whereas the US has immense mineral wealth, Japan (*in contrast*) has comparatively little.

Concessive clauses (*cf* 15.39*ff*) may also imply a contrast, but their main role is to imply that the situation in the matrix clause is unexpected in the light of that in the concessive clause:

Although admission was free, (*nevertheless*) few people attended the lecture.

The parenthesized items illustrate the different conjuncts that optionally correlate with the three clauses (*cf* 14.13).

The overlap between the three roles is highlighted by the overlapping use of subordinators: for example, *if* introduces all three types of clauses and *whereas* both contrast and concessive clauses. Furthermore, *even if* expresses both the contingent dependence of one situation upon another and the unexpected nature of this dependence:

Even if they offered to pay, I wouldn't accept any money from them.

All three types of clauses tend to assume initial position in the superordinate clause.

Conditional clauses

Direct and indirect condition

15.33 The central uses of conditional clauses express a DIRECT CONDITION: they convey that the situation in the matrix clause is directly contingent on that of the conditional clause. Put another way, the truth of the proposition in the matrix clause is a consequence of the fulfilment of the condition in the conditional clause. Here is an example:

If you put the baby down, she'll scream. [1]

In uttering [1] the speaker intends the hearer to understand that the truth of the prediction 'she'll scream' depends on the fulfilment of the condition of 'your putting the baby down'. The hearer also in practice infers the converse:

If you don't put the baby down, she won't scream.

However, the speaker may cancel this implication by hedging (expressing some uncertainty, *cf* 8.124, 8.126):

If you put the baby down, she'll scream. But she may scream anyway.

More peripheral uses of conditional clauses express an INDIRECT CONDITION. The condition is not related to the situation in the matrix clause. Consider [2]:

She's far too considerate, *if I may say so.* [2]

In uttering [2], the speaker does not intend the truth of the assertion 'She's far too considerate' to be dependent on obtaining permission from the hearer. Rather, the condition is dependent on the implicit speech act of the utterance: 'I'm telling you, if I may, that she's far too considerate'. In conventional politeness, the speaker is making the utterance of the assertion dependent on obtaining permission from the hearer, though the fulfilment of that condition is conventionally taken for granted. Here is another example:

She and I are just good friends, *if you understand me.*

The speaker warns the hearer that the correct interpretation of the utterance 'She and I are just good friends' depends on the hearer understanding what the speaker means by the utterance: 'I'm telling you that on the assumption that you understand me correctly'.

In direct conditions, the *if*-clause is an adjunct (*cf* 15.20*ff*); in indirect conditions, it is a style disjunct (*cf* 15.21).

Subordinators and structural types of clauses

15.34 The two simple subordinators for conditional clauses are *if* and *unless.* The most common and most versatile of the conditional subordinators is *if*; we therefore generally employ it in the sections that follow to illustrate the different uses of conditional clauses. The negative subordinator *unless* is the next most common. Other conditional subordinators are:

as long as, so long as, assuming (*that*), *given* (*that*) ⟨formal⟩, *in case, in the event that, just so* (*that*) ⟨informal⟩, *on condition* (*that*), *provided* (*that*), *providing* (*that*), *supposing* (*that*)

General recurrent contingency is expressed by *once, when, whenever, where,* and *wherever* (*cf* 15.30). In addition, several subordinators combine condition with time: *before* (*cf* 15.27), *as long as, so long as, when, whenever, once* (*cf* 15.28). *Except that* and conjunctive *only* combine exception with condition (*cf* 15.44).

All these subordinators are used with finite clauses:

If you want some more, you should ask me.
Unless the strike has been called off, there will be no trains tomorrow.

He doesn't mind inconveniencing others *just so he's comfortable.* ⟨informal⟩
She may go, *as long as he goes with her.*
You may leave the apartment at any time, *provided that you give a month's notice or pay an additional month's rent.*
In case you want me, I'll be in my office till lunchtime.
Given that $x = y$, then $n(x + a) = n(y + a)$ must also be true. ⟨in formal argumentation⟩
Assuming that the movie starts at eight, shouldn't we be leaving now?
Supposing they won the raffle, what would they do with an extra car?

Of the subordinators that are specifically conditional, only *if* and *unless* introduce nonfinite clauses (mainly *-ed* participle clauses) and verbless clauses. They are marginally acceptable in *-ing* participle clauses (*cf* 14.19 Note [a]):

The grass will grow more quickly *if watered regularly.*
Unless otherwise instructed, you should leave by the back exit.
If wet, the pipe won't give you a good smoke.
It has little taste, *unless hot.*

Here belong the positive and negative conditional pro-clauses *if so* and *if not.* The implied subject is the matrix clause itself (or part of it) in some verbless *if*-clauses, including the common *if possible* and *if necessary*:

Marion wants me to type the letter *if possible.*
['if it is possible for me to type the letter']
I can discuss the matter with you now, *if necessary.*
['if it is necessary to discuss the matter with you now']

Nonfinite and verbless clauses with *with* or *without* as subordinator may express a conditional relationship:

Without me to supplement your income, you wouldn't be able to manage.
With them on our side, we are secure.

Cf 15.36 for finite conditional clauses without a subordinator but with subject–operator inversion:

Had Mark been in charge, it wouldn't have happened.

Note [**a**] The traditional terms PROTASIS for subordinate clause and APODOSIS for matrix clause are especially used for conditional relationships.
[**b**] *Unless, except* ⟨informal AmE⟩, and archaic *save* also combine exception with condition, *cf* 15.35 Note [f]:

I'm not going {*unless* / *except*} *you go with me.*

[**c**] Conditional relationships are also implied in certain kinds of clauses coordinated by *and* and *or* (*cf* 13.25, 13.30) and in paratactic constructions such as *waste not, want not* (*cf* 11.43).
[**d**] Among some common stereotyped conditional expressions without subordinators are:
(a) absolute clauses (*cf* 15.58; and 9.58 for expressions such as *barring bad weather*):

{time / weather} permitting   God willing

Cf: for the time being

(b) subjectless clauses with a subjunctive verb:

come to that ['if it comes to that', 'if I may add to that']
please God ['if it pleases God']

[**e**] *Cf* 11.41 for *if*-clauses as sentences.

[**f**] Contingency relationships may also be expressed by various complex prepositions, *eg*:

on the {*assumption* / *supposition*} *that* *in case of* {fire / a fire breaking out}

on condition that

with the {*proviso* / *stipulation*} *that* *in the event of* {an accident / an accident occurring}

[**g**] Infinitive clauses sometimes combine condition with other contingency relations (*cf* 15.73) such as purpose or reason:

You must be STRÒNG *to lift that weight*. ['. . . in order to lift that weight', '. . . because you were able to lift that weight', '. . . if you were able to lift that weight']
You'd be a fool *not to take the scholarship*. ['if you didn't . . .']
To be considered for admission, you must make a formal application. ['If you are to be considered . . .', 'In order to be considered . . .']

[**h**] *Cf* 15.6 Note [a] for the relationship between conditional *if* and interrogative *if*.

[**i**] Restrictive relative clauses modifying generic noun phrases (*cf* 5.26) may be paraphrased by means of a conditional clause:

People who want security shouldn't take a job in commerce. ['*If people want security*, they shouldn't take a job in commerce']

The same sometimes applies to other restrictive modifiers with generic noun phrases:

Careless drivers cause accidents. ['*If drivers are careless*, they cause accidents']
Cars manufactured abroad are less expensive. ['*If cars are manufactured abroad*, they are less expensive']

Direct condition

Open and hypothetical condition

15.35 A direct condition may be either an OPEN CONDITION or a HYPOTHETICAL CONDITION. Open conditions are neutral: they leave unresolved the question of the fulfilment or nonfulfilment of the condition, and hence also the truth of the proposition expressed by the matrix clause:

If Colin is in London, he is undoubtedly staying at the Hilton.

The sentence leaves unresolved whether Colin is in London, and hence it leaves unresolved whether he is staying at the Hilton.

A hypothetical condition, on the other hand, conveys the speaker's belief that the condition will not be fulfilled (for future conditions), is not fulfilled (for present conditions), or was not fulfilled (for past conditions), and hence the probable or certain falsity of the proposition expressed by the matrix clause:

If he changed his opinions, he'd be a more likeable person. [1]
They would be here with us *if they had the time*. [2]
If you had listened to me, you wouldn't have made so many mistakes. [3]

The conditional clauses in these sentences convey the following implications:

He very probably won't change his opinions. [1a]
They presumably don't have the time. [2a]
You certainly didn't listen to me. [3a]

The precise formulation of the speaker's belief depends on the time reference of the conditional clause. For future reference as in [1], the condition is contrary to expectation; for present reference as in [2], it is contrary to assumption; for past reference as in [3], it is contrary to fact. *If* is the main subordinator used in hypothetical conditions.

The distinction between open and hypothetical conditions is important grammatically because the verbs in hypothetical conditions are backshifted (*cf* backshifting in indirect speech, 14.31).

	conditional clause	matrix clause
present and future reference	PAST *If I were younger,*	PAST MODAL *I would study Classical Greek.*
past reference	PAST PERFECTIVE *If I had seen you,*	PAST PERFECTIVE MODAL *I would have invited you home.*

Fig 15.35 Verb forms with hypothetical conditions

On the verb forms, *cf* further 14.23.

Conditional clauses – particularly clauses introduced by *if*, *in case*, and *in the event that* – are like questions in that questions are generally either neutral in their expectations of an answer or biased toward a negative response (*cf* 11.6*f*). Therefore, like questions, they tend to admit nonassertive forms (*cf* 10.60*f*):

> In the event that he is *at all* interested, I'll speak to him.
> If you *ever* touch me again, I'll scream.
> If you had *ever* listened to *any* of my lectures, you would have known the answer.
> She's taking a stick with her in case she has *any* trouble on the way.

Nonassertive items also appear in indirect conditions (*cf* 15.38):

> They're going steady, if it's of *any* interest to you. ['I don't know if it's of any interest to you.']
> I'll be in my office all DÀY, in case you have *any* PRÓBlem *at all*. ['I'm telling you this in case you have any problem at all.']

Most subordinators are not used, or rarely used, in hypothetical conditions. Their clauses tend to contain assertive forms:

> I won't phone you, unless *something* unforeseen happens.

Second-instance *if*-clauses may have assertive forms:

> A: I've got *something* to tell you later.
> B: Well, if you've got *something* to tell me, tell me now.

Note [**a**] Open conditions have also been termed 'real', 'factual', and 'neutral' conditions. Hypothetical conditions have also been termed 'closed', 'unreal', 'rejected', 'nonfactual', 'counterfactual', and 'marked' conditions.

[**b**] *If and when* is sometimes used for future open conditions.

[**c**] *If only* is an intensified equivalent of *if*, typically used in hypothetical clauses to express what the speaker wishes would happen, would be happening, or would have happened:

> *If only you would help me next week*, I would not be so nervous.

If only they were here now, we would be able to celebrate their wedding anniversary.
If only somebody had told us, we could have warned you.

When positive, the conditional clause generally contains assertive forms, and nearly always precedes the matrix clause. The clause is sometimes used on its own as a hypothetical wish (*cf* 11.41): *If only I hadn't lost it!* The combination *only if* is quite different: *if* is restricted by the focusing *only*.

[d] *Given* (*that*) and *assuming* (*that*) are used for open conditions which the speaker assumes were, are, or will be fulfilled, and from which a proposition is deduced. A clause introduced by *granted* (*that*) is also used as a premise for a deduction, but usually implies a previous statement on which the premise is based. *If* may be used in the same way: *If you were there* (*and you say you were*), *you must have seen her*; and so also in *if*-clauses with clausal pro-forms: *if so*, *if not*, *if that's true*, *if that's the case*, and (with nonassertives) *if anything*, *if at all*. *Given* (*that*) and *granted* (*that*) tend to be used in formal written style, particularly in argumentation.

[e] *As long as* and *so long as* are less formal than the semantically similar but formal *provided* (*that*) and *providing* (*that*). *Just so* (*that*) tends to appear in informal conversation. They all imply 'if and only if'.

[f] *Unless* introduces a negative condition; the *unless*-clause is usually roughly similar to a negative *if*-clause. With *unless* there is a greater focus on the conditions as an exception ('only if . . . not'). There are therefore contexts in which the *unless*-clause cannot occur:

I'll feel much happier { *if he doesn't come with us.* / **unless he comes with us.* }

{ *If you hadn't studied hard,* / **Unless you had studied hard,* } you'd have failed the exam.

[g] *In case* (*cf* also 15.46) is used for open conditions, normally with future reference ('if it should happen that'):

I'll let you know *in case they come by here*.

In formal AmE it also has the meaning 'on condition that':

The verb is plural (*only*/*just*) *in case the subject is plural*.

[h] *In the event* (*that*) can generally replace *if* in open conditions. Because of its greater length, it is regarded as stylistically clumsy.

[i] The form *if and only if* is used in mathematics and formal logic to introduce a necessary and sufficient condition on the truth of the matrix clause. It is sometimes abbreviated *iff*.

The verb phrase in the conditional clause

15.36 The present subjunctive is sometimes used for open conditions in conditional clauses, instead of the normal present tense:

If any vehicle *be* found parked on these premises without written permission, it shall be towed away at the expense of the vehicle's owner.

This use is mainly confined to very formal, legal, or quasi-legal contexts.

Two ways of expressing future hypothetical conditions are occasionally used in formal contexts. They have overtones of tentativeness:

(i) *was to* or *were to* followed by the infinitive:

If it { *was* / *were* } *to* rain, the ropes would snap. They're far too tight. [1]

(ii) *should* followed by the infinitive (*cf* putative *should* 14.25):

If a serious crisis *should* arise, the public would have to be informed of its full implications. [2]

In [1] *were* is the singular past subjunctive form of *be* and not the simple past form, *were* being used in the past subjunctive for the singular as well as the plural (*cf* 3.62). As [1] illustrates, both the past subjunctive and the past indicative forms are possible for hypothetical conditions, the subjunctive being preferred by many, especially in formal written English:

If John {*was* / *were*} here, we would soon learn the truth.

The idiom *if I . . . you* by convention usually contains the subjunctive *were*, though *was* also occurs frequently.

We may signal the conditional relationship, without using a subordinator, by subject–operator inversion. The most common use of this inversion in conditional clauses is with the operator *had*:

Had I known, I would have written before. ['If I had known, . . .']

For the negative, *not* is placed before the lexical verb, the enclitic *n't* not being possible:

Had I not seen it with my own eyes, I would not have believed it.

Inversion may also occur in a somewhat literary style with subjunctive *were* and tentative *should*:

Were it to reveal its secrets, that house would collapse in shame.
Were she in charge, she would do things differently.
Should you change your mind, no one would blame you.
Should she be interested, I'll phone her.

More rarely, the operator may be *could* or *might*:

{*Might* / *Could*} *I but see my native land*, I would die a happy man.

For this construction, these two operators require an adverb such as *but* or *just* before the lexical verb.

On the choice of verbs in both the conditional and the matrix clause, *cf* 14.23.

Rhetorical conditional clauses

15.37 Rhetorical conditional clauses give the appearance of expressing an open condition, but (like rhetorical questions, *cf* 11.23) they actually make a strong assertion. There are two types of rhetorical *if*-clauses, one in which the assertion is derived from the conditional clause and the other in which it is derived from the matrix clause.

(a) If the proposition in the matrix clause is patently absurd, the proposition in the conditional clause is shown to be false:

If they're Irish, I'm the Pope. ['Since I'm obviously not the Pope, they're certainly not Irish.']
If you believe that, you'll believe anything. ['You certainly can't believe that.']
If she doesn't get first prize, she's no daughter of yours. ['She certainly will get first prize.']

(b) If the proposition in the conditional clause is patently true, the proposition in the matrix clause is shown to be true. This type is used with measure expressions with the implication of at least the measure stated in the conditional clause. The *if*-clause is positioned finally:

> He's ninety *if he's a day*. ['If you'll agree that he's at least a day old, perhaps you'll take my word that he's ninety.']
> The package weighed ten pounds *if it weighed an ounce*. ['The package certainly weighed ten pounds.']
> The painting must be worth a thousand dollars *if it's worth a cent*. ['The painting must certainly be worth a thousand dollars.']

Note The matrix clause in type (a) has some fixed expressions which state patent falsehoods, with some variation in the person of the subject, such as *I'll eat my hat* and *He's a Dutchman*:

> If Dave's younger than me, I'll eat my hat. ['Dave's certainly not younger than me.']

More stereotyped, because restricted to an *I*-subject, are *I'll be* (or *I'm*) *damned* and *I'll be* (or *I'm*) *hanged*, both familiar in style:

> {I'll be / I'm} damned *if I apologize*. ['I'll certainly not apologize.']

As a result, these can stand alone as expressions of amazement, *eg*: *Well, I'll be damned*. Taboo expressions also occur in the matrix clause with rhetorical conditional clauses (*eg*: *Fuck me if I'm going to lift a finger to help them*).

Compare also the stereotyped patterns in *She's nothing if not tough* ['She's certainly tough.'] and *He's nothing if not cruel* ['He's certainly cruel.'].

Indirect condition

15.38 Indirect conditions are open conditions (*cf* 15.35) that are dependent on an implicit speech act of the utterance (*cf* 11.3), and are therefore style disjuncts (*cf* 15.21). They are mainly realized by *if*-clauses. We can distinguish several classes of style disjuncts:

(a) The conditional clause is a conventional expression of politeness which makes the speaker's utterance seemingly dependent on the permission of the hearer (*cf* 8.124*f*):

> *If you don't mind my saying so*, your slip is showing. ['If you don't mind my saying so, I'm telling you that . . .']
> *If I may be quite frank with you*, I don't approve of any concessions to ignorance.

Other examples include:

> *if I may say so (without contradiction), if I may put it bluntly, if I may be personal, if you can be serious for just this once, if you can keep a secret, if we can be practical for a moment, if I may put the matter as simply as possible, if I may interrupt, if I may change the subject*

(b) The conditional clause is a metalinguistic comment (*cf* 8.126) which hedges the wording of the utterance, either suggesting that the wording is not quite precise or that it should not be misunderstood in some sense not intended by the speaker. It explicitly or implicitly calls for the hearer's agreement:

His style is florid, *if that's the right word*. ['I'm not sure that *florid* is the right word.'] [1]

The Big Bang Theory of the origin of the universe bears a startling resemblance to the description of creation in Genesis, *if one may put it so*. ['I'm not sure that one may phrase the resemblance in that way.'] [2]

She is resigning, *if you know what I mean*. [Perhaps: 'You are to interpret that to mean that she has been asked to resign.'] [3]

In [1] and [2] the speaker is uncertain of the correctness of the wording. In [3] the speaker is uncertain whether the hearer will interpret the wording correctly and therefore warns the hearer to interpret it in the intended way. Other examples include:

if I may put it so, if that's the correct term, if that's the word for it, if you see what I mean, if I may phrase it delicately/loosely/crudely/figuratively, if you will ⟨formal⟩, *if you like*

Although the clauses with *I* indicate explicitly the speaker's uncertainty, clauses such as *if I may put it so* may be used to convey a warning more indirectly.

(c) The conditional clause expresses uncertainty about the extralinguistic knowledge required for a correct interpretation of the utterance. The uncertainty may be the speaker's or the hearer's:

I met your girl friend Caroline last night, *if Caroline ĭs your girl friend*. [4]

Chomsky's views cannot be reconciled with Piaget's, *if I understand both correctly*. [5]

The war was started by the other side, *if you remember your history lessons*. [6]

Einstein's theory of gravitation is based on a mathematical concept, *if you've not forgotten already*. ⟨ironical⟩ [7]

The conditional clauses in [4] and [5] hedge about the speaker's own knowledge, whereas those in [6] and [7] hedge about the hearer's knowledge. The possible clauses for this type are open-ended, particularly for those expressing the speaker's uncertainty. Other examples include:

if I'm correct, if I understand you correctly, if we can believe the experts, in case you don't remember, if you remember, if you know what I'm referring to, in case you don't know

(d) The conditional clause expresses the condition under which the speaker makes the utterance:

If you're going my way, I need a lift back. ['If you're going my way, will you please give me a lift back.'] [8]

In case he ever asks you, I don't know you. ['In case he ever asks you, tell him that I don't know you.'] [9]

If you want to borrow a shoebrush, there's one in the bathroom. ['If you want . . . use the one in the bathroom.'] [10]

Where did your parents go, *if you know*? ['If you know, tell me . . .'] [11]

Notice that the utterance of [8] and [9] has the illocutionary force of indirect requests, [10] of an indirect offer, and [11] of a direct question. The conditional clause expresses uncertainty. If the speaker is certain of the fulfilment of the condition, a *since*-clause is used instead:

Since you're going my way, I need a lift back. [8a]

For all four types the uncertainty of the condition provides a tentativeness which adds politeness to utterances.

Note Apart from *if*, other subordinators used to introduce indirect conditions are *in case* (*that*), *assuming* (*that*), *in the event* (*that*), and *supposing* (*that*).

Clauses of concession

Subordinators and structural types of clauses

15.39 Clauses of concession are introduced chiefly by *although* or its more informal variant *though*. Other subordinators used with concessive clauses are:

if, *even if*, *even though*, *when*, *whereas* ⟨formal⟩, *while*, and *whilst* ⟨esp BrE⟩.

Cf also below the exceptional concessive uses of *as* and *that* ⟨BrE⟩.

Although he had just joined the company, he was treated exactly like all the other employees.
No goals were scored, *though it was an exciting game*.
While I don't want to make a fuss, I feel I must protest at your interference.
Whereas the amendment is enthusiastically supported by a large majority in the Senate, its fate is doubtful in the House.
She paid *when she could have entered free*.
He used my mower *even though I told him not to*.

Except for *when* and *whereas*, the concessive subordinators may introduce *-ing*, *-ed*, and verbless clauses:

While not wanting to seem obstinate, I insisted on a definite reply.
Even though given every opportunity, they would not cooperate with us.
Though well over eighty, he can walk faster than I can.

The same types of clauses may also express concession without a subordinator though they then generally require a correlative conjunct to make the relationship clear:

Not wanting to give offence, they did so *all the same*.
Trained in karate, he *nevertheless* used a gun to defend himself.
Aware of the dangers to American citizens during the crisis, she *still* insisted on staying with the others.

Like conditional clauses (*cf* 15.36), concessive clauses sometimes have unusual syntactic orderings when the subordinator is *as* or *though*. In a rather formal style, the predication in the concessive clause may be fronted:

Genius though she was, she was quite unassuming.

Fail though I did, I would not abandon my goal.
Naked as I was, I braved the storm. ['Even though I was naked, . . .']
Change your mind as you will, you will gain no additional support. ['Even though you change your mind, . . .']

The ordering is optional for *though*, but obligatory for *as*, which would not be concessive if placed initially (but *cf* Note [d] below).

That is also used concessively with the same obligatory ordering as *as*, but in AmE only a noun phrase functioning as subject complement can be fronted:

Fool that he was, he managed to evade his pursuers. ['Even though he was a fool, . . .']

The noun phrase has the role of a characterizing attribute (*cf* 10.20). On the other hand, in BrE an adjective phrase functioning as subject complement can also be fronted:

Poor that they were, they gave money to charity. ⟨BrE⟩ ['Even though they were poor, . . .']

For a similar reordering of *as* and *that* in circumstantial clauses, *cf* 15.47.

Note [**a**] Concession may also be expressed by several prepositional phrases followed by a relative clause:

despite / in spite of / irrespective of / regardless of / notwithstanding } the fact (that)

Because of their greater length than the subordinators, they are considered stylistically clumsy.
[**b**] For *though* as a conjunct of concession, *cf* 8.137.
[**c**] In concessive clauses such as *greatly though I admire her* and *much as I would like to help*, only the adverb is in the obligatory initial position. This type is limited to the subordinators *though* and *as*.
[**d**] The noninitial placement of concessive *as* is perhaps to be related to *as . . . as* in the following example of an infrequent type of concessive clause:

As widespread as the effects may be, the Midwest still bears the brunt of the recession. ['Even though the effects may be widespread, . . .']

The noninitial *as* may therefore be regarded as a correlative to an omitted initial *as*. See also the similar omission of the initial comparative *as* (*cf* 15.71).

Concessive relationships

15.40 Concessive clauses indicate that the situation in the matrix clause is contrary to expectation in the light of what is said in the concessive clause. In consequence of the mutuality, it is often purely a matter of choice which clause is made subordinate:

No goals were scored, *although it was an exciting game*.
It was an exciting game, *although no goals were scored*.

Often they also imply contrast between the situations described by the two clauses.

Although and the more informal *though* are the most versatile of the subordinators, since they may in fact relate clauses in which the situations are similar:

Although Sam had told the children a bedtime story, June told them one too (*anyway*).

While and *whilst* ⟨esp BrE⟩, are more restricted, but they may relate clauses in which the contrast is muted, the concessive relationship arising from a contrary expectation:

While he has many friends, Peter is (*nevertheless*) often lonely.
While I admit I did it, (*nevertheless*) I didn't intend to.

Whereas is the most restricted of the four subordinators, requiring antithesis between two situations:

Whereas it would be naive to maintain that inflation is no longer of concern, (*nevertheless*) all the economic indicators suggest that the money supply can now be safely increased.

Even though and *even when* are more emphatic forms of *though* and *when*, the modifying *even* also expressing unexpectedness. *Even if*, on the other hand, combines the concessive force of *even* with the conditional force of *if*; hence the semantic contrast between [1] and [2]:

Even though you disLÌKE ancient monuments, Warwick Castle is worth a visit. [1]
Even if you dislike ancient monuments, Warwick Castle is worth a visit. [2]

Whereas the *even though* clause in [1] presupposes 'you dislike ancient monuments', the *even if* clause in [2] leaves open whether that is so or not. The presupposition of [1] can be cancelled by adding modal *may* or a hedging adverbial such as *perhaps*.

If by itself may be used concessively:

If he's poor, he's (*at least*) honest. ['He may be poor, yet he's at least honest.'] [3]
If he's poor, he's (*also*) honest. ['He is poor, yet he's also honest.'] [3a]

In [3] it is paraphrased as synonymous with *even if* and in [3a] with *even though*. These two different uses of concessive *if* are frequently realized in abbreviated verbless clauses:

It's possible, *if difficult*. ['It may be difficult.']
My car is as clean as yours, *if not cleaner*. ['It may be cleaner.']
He spoke ungraciously, *if not rudely*. ['He may have spoken rudely.']
They were in good health, *if somewhat fatter than desirable*. ['They were somewhat fatter than desirable.']
Her salary was good, *if not up to her expectations*. ['Her salary was not up to her expectations.']

Note On *when* with concessive implications, *cf* 15.29.

Alternative conditional-concessive clauses

15.41 The overlap between condition and concession, already noted with *even if* (*cf* 15.40), is particularly marked in the two types of adverbial clauses termed

ALTERNATIVE CONDITIONAL-CONCESSIVE and UNIVERSAL CONDITIONAL-CONCESSIVE.

The correlative sequence *whether . . . or* (*whether*) is an alternative condition in that logically it combines the conditional meaning of *if* with the disjunctive meaning of *either . . . or* (*cf* also Note [a]). It is thus a means of coordinating two subordinate clauses. If the second unit is a full clause, *whether* may be repeated, as in [1]; *cf* 15.6:

Whether Martin pays for the broken vase or (*whether*) *he replaces it with a new vase*, I'm not inviting HÌM again. [1]
You will have to face the publicity, *whether you want to or not.* [2]
Whether or not he finds a job, he's getting married. [3]

The concessive meaning emerges from the unexpected implication that the same situation applies under two contrasting conditions. Thus, [3] may be paraphrased 'Even if he finds a job or even if he doesn't find a job, he's getting married.' On alternative orderings for [2] and [3], *cf* Note [a].

The longer and more emphatic constructions *It doesn't matter whether* (initial only) and *No matter whether* can also be used to introduce clauses that are alternative conditional-concessive (*cf* 15.42).

You will have to face the publicity, *no matter whether you want to or not.* [2a]

It doesn't matter whether or not he finds a job, he's getting married. [3a]

The same subordinators also introduce nonfinite and verbless clauses:

Sarah is always intense, *whether working or playing.* [4]
Whether trained or not, Marilyn is doing an excellent job. [5]
No matter whether right or wrong, your son needs all the support you can give him right now. [6]

The subordinator may be omitted, but the clause is then normally initial:

Working or playing, Sarah is always intense. [4a]
Trained or not, Marilyn is doing an excellent job. [5a]

There are also verbless clauses introduced by *with*, which is then correlated with *without*:

We'll buy the house, *with a bank loan or without one.* [7]
With or without a bank loan, we'll buy the house. [7a]

The same meaning may be conveyed merely by the coordinated noun phrases if the second is negated by the determiner *no*:

We'll buy the house, *bank loan or no bank loan.* [8]

This construction is also available when the implied verb is *be* rather than *have*:

I have to go to work, *rain or no rain.* [9]
['. . . whether or not there *is* rain.']

A further reduction is possible, though less common, by the omission of the second noun phrase. The reduced clause is then usually placed initially:

Bank loan or no, we'll buy the house. [10]

In all the types exemplified by [7–10], the verbless clause may be either initial or final. In the types exemplified by [8–10], the indefinite article is omitted in the parallel structure before count nouns such as *bank loan*.

Note [**a**] We may see a relationship also with alternative interrogative clauses (*cf* 15.6). Compare [1] above with:

I don't know whether Martin will pay for the broken vase or whether he will replace it. I'm not inviting him again anyway.

The subordinate clause in [2] can be reordered as *whether or not you want to* and that in [3] as *whether he finds a job or not*. *Cf* alternative questions, 11.20*f*.

[**b**] Occasionally alternative conditional-concessive meaning is expressed by a finite clause without a subordinator, in which the verb is subjunctive (*cf* 15.34 Note [d], 15.42 Note [b]):

Rain or shine, we're having our party outside today. ['Whether it rains or shines, . . .']

Compare : (*Come*) *wind or rain* ['Whether wind or rain comes.']. A rarer and somewhat literary construction involves the use of subjunctive *be*:

(*Be he*) *friend or foe*, the law regards him as a criminal. ['Whether he is (*or* be) friend or foe, . . .']

[**c**] The alternative in the second clause may be parallel to only part of the first clause. Thus, the finite clause corresponding to [6] is:

No matter whether he's right or wrong, . . .

and a slightly amended version of [5] might be:

Whether trained as a nurse or as a radiologist . . .

[**d**] As with *either* (*cf* 13.39*ff*), some speakers allow more than two choices (*cf* 15.6 Note [b]):

Whether you do your homework *or* play *or* watch television, you must not disturb me.

[**e**] Like *no matter whether* are *regardless of whether* and *irrespective of whether* (*cf* 15.39 Note [a]):

Regardless of whether or not he finds a job, he's getting married.

Universal conditional-concessive clauses

15.42 The contrast between alternative clauses and universal clauses is parallel to that between alternative questions (*cf* 11.20*f*) and *wh*-questions (*cf* 11.14*ff*) or to that between their corresponding dependent clauses (*cf* 15.5*f*). The alternative conditional-concessive clause gives a choice between two (or occasionally more, *cf* 15.41 Note [d]) stated conditions, normally in sharp opposition, whereas the universal conditional-concessive clause indicates a free choice from any number of conditions. Compare:

Whether I shout at them or plead with them, I can't keep them quiet. [two stated alternatives] [1]

Whatever I say to them, I can't keep them quiet. [any number of choices] [2]

The concessive implication in [2] comes through the inference that, for example, I can't keep them quiet *even if* I promise them a treat.

The alternative clauses are introduced by the *wh*-words that are compounded with *-ever* and by the longer constructions *It doesn't matter* (initial only) and *No matter* (*cf* 15.41) followed by *wh*-elements. The clauses share with other *wh*-clauses the initial placement of the *wh*-element, and the consequent shift of that element (unless it is the subject) from its normal syntactic order:

Stand perfectly still, *wherever you are*. [A S V]

However much advice you give him, he does exactly what he wants. [O_dS V O_i]

Don't let them in, *whoever they are*. [C_s S V]

There is a subtle semantic difference between the universal clauses and the apparently identical time and place clauses beginning *whenever* and *wherever*. The contrast can be shown in a sentence such as:

Wherever you live, you can keep a horse.

The locative meaning is 'You can keep a horse at any place where you may live' (*cf* specific locative *where*: *You can keep a horse where you live*). The conditional-concessive meaning (more applicable to a city-dweller) is 'It doesn't matter where you live, you can keep a horse (and the horse need not be in the same place as you live)'.

Note [**a**] The verb *be* can be omitted from a universal clause if the subject of an *SVC* clause is an abstract noun phrase:

Whatever your problems (*are/may be*), they can't be worse than mine.
However great the pitfalls (*are/may be*), we must do our best to succeed.

[**b**] Occasionally the universal meaning is expressed by a finite clause without a subordinator, in which case the verb is subjunctive and is initial (*cf* 10.34 Note [d], 15.41 Note [b]): *Come what may* ['Whatever may happen.'], *Be that as it may* ['However that may be.'].

Clauses of contrast

15.43 Clauses of contrast are introduced by several of the subordinators that introduce concessive clauses (*cf* 15.39): *whereas*, *while*, and *whilst*. Indeed, there is often a mixture of contrast and concession. The contrastive meaning may be emphasized by correlative antithetic conjuncts such as *in contrast* and *by contrast* when the contrastive clause is initial:

Mr Larson teaches physics, *while Mr Corby teaches chemistry*.
I ignore them, *whereas my husband is always worried about what they think of us*.

The three subordinators are interchangeable, except that the less common *whilst* is found especially in BrE.

Clauses of contrast are very similar to clauses coordinated by *but*. This is particularly so when the contrastive clause is final. When the contrastive clause is initial, it is viewed as containing the subordinate information, the point of departure for the contrast.

Clauses of exception

15.44 Clauses of exception are introduced by several subordinators: *but that* ⟨formal⟩, *except* (*that*); less frequently *excepting* (*that*) and *save that* ⟨formal⟩. Several of the subordinators also blend exception with condition. *Except* (*that*), *excepting* (*that*), and *save that* have very similar uses, apart from the stylistic restriction on *save that*:

I would pay you now, *except I don't have any money on me*.
No memorial remains for the brave who fell on that battlefield, *save that they will leave their image for ever in the hearts and minds of their grateful countrymen*. ⟨formal⟩

But that, like the preposition *but*, requires that the matrix clause precede it and be negative:

> Nothing would satisfy the child *but that I place her on my lap.* ⟨formal⟩ [1]

More usually an infinitive clause would be used:

> Nothing would satisfy the child *but for me to place her on my lap.* [1a]

In stereotyped sentences, *but* alone may occur:

> It never rains *but it pours.*

Only, restricted to informal style, also expresses the meaning of exception (*cf* Note [a] below):

> I would've asked you, *only my mother told me not to.*

Unless combines condition with exception ('except if'), hence the negative meaning; *provided* (*that*) and its synonyms are the positive equivalent.

For prepositions of exception that introduce bare infinitive and *to*-infinitive clauses, *cf* 9.58.

Note [**a**] *Only* is a borderline case between conjunct and conjunction. It is unclear whether a coordinating conjunction (for example, *but*) can be inserted between the clauses; if it can, it has one of the defining characteristics of the class of conjuncts (*cf* 8.134*ff*), but if it cannot, its syntactic status is similar to *for*, which is on the gradient between coordinator and subordinator (*cf* 13.18*f*). It may be paraphrased 'The only thing is'.

[**b**] *Except* (*that*), *excepting* (*that*), and *save that* can usually be replaced by the coordinating conjunction *but*. They can also usually be replaced by longer, and hence stylistically clumsy, prepositional phrases followed by relative clauses, *eg*: *except for/apart from the fact* (*that*). Contexts excluding replacement by the conjunction and the prepositional phrases are where *but that* is admissible.

[**c**] AmE prefers the present subjunctive for the verb in the subordinate clause in [1], while BrE prefers putative *should* (*cf* 14.24*f*).

Reason clauses

Direct and indirect reason relationships

15.45 We subsume under clauses of REASON several types of subordinate clauses that convey basic similarities of relationship to their matrix clauses. For all types there is generally a temporal sequence such that the situation in the subordinate clause precedes in time that of the matrix clause. As the paraphrases indicate, the word *reason* is a superordinate term available for all types:

(a) Cause and effect: the construction expresses the perception of an inherent objective connection in the real world:

> The flowers are growing so well *because I sprayed them.* ['The cause for the flowers growing so well is that I sprayed them' *or* 'The reason that the flowers are growing so well is that I sprayed them.']
>
> He's thin *because he doesn't eat enough.*

(b) Reason and consequence: the construction expresses the speaker's inference of a connection:

> She watered the flowers *because they were dry*. ['The reason that she watered the flowers was that they were dry.']
> *Since she's my friend*, she must have put in a good word for me.

(c) Motivation and result: the construction expresses the intention of an animate being that has a subsequent result:

> I watered the flowers *because my parents told me to do so*. ['My motivation for watering the flowers was that my parents told me to do so' *or* 'The reason that I watered the flowers was that my parents told me to do so.']
> You'll help me *because you're my friend*.

Agency and intention are always involved in motivation.

(d) Circumstances and consequence: the circumstantial clause combines reason with a condition that is assumed to be fulfilled or about to be fulfilled, the construction expressing a relationship between a premise in the subordinate clause and the conclusion in the matrix clause:

> *Since the weather has improved*, the game will be held as planned. ['In view of the fact that the weather has improved, the game will be held as planned' *or* 'The reason that the game will be held as planned is that the weather has improved.']
> *Seeing that it is only three*, we should be able to finish this before we leave today.

The examples we have given so far express a DIRECT REASON relationship between the reason clause and the matrix clause. More peripheral uses of reason clauses express an INDIRECT REASON. The reason is not related to the situation in the matrix clause but is a motivation for the implicit speech act of the utterance:

> Percy is in Washington, *for he phoned me from there*. ['Since he phoned from there, I can tell you that Percy is in Washington.']
> *As you're in charge*, where are the files on the new project? ['As you're in charge, I'm asking you . . .?']
> Vanessa is your favourite aunt, *because your parents told me so*. ['Since your parents told me so, I can say that Vanessa is your favourite aunt.']
> *As long as we have this chance*, why don't we discuss our plans?
> *Since you seem to know them*, why don't you introduce me to them? ['Since you seem to know them, I ask you to introduce me to them.']

Since and *because* are the most common subordinators for indirect cause. Clauses expressing an indirect cause are style disjuncts, *cf* 15.21.

Subordinators and structural types of clauses

15.46 Reason clauses are most commonly introduced by the subordinators *because* (also *'cause*) and *since*. Other subordinators are *as* and (in somewhat formal style) *for*:

I lent him the money *because he needed it.*
As Jane was the eldest, she looked after the others.
Since we live near the sea, we often go sailing.
Much has been written about psychic phenomena, *for they pose fascinating problems that have yet to be resolved.*

In case combines reason with contingency ('because it may happen that'):

Take your umbrella *in case it rains*. ['Take your umbrella because it *may* rain', '. . . because of *the possibility* that it will rain.']
You should write a will *in case something happens to you abroad.*

Circumstantial clauses (*cf* 15.45) are introduced by the simple subordinators *because*, *since*, and *as* and by several complex subordinators: *seeing* (*that*); *as long as*; *inasmuch as* ⟨formal⟩:

Seeing that it seems as if it will rain soon, we had better leave now.
As long as you're here, we might as well talk about your last game.
It is doubtful whether research proposals by Freud himself would have been approved by reviewers, *inasmuch as he was not affiliated to any academic institution.* ⟨formal⟩

Clauses introduced by *with* may also be circumstantial:

With the exams coming next week, I have no time for a social life.
With so many children to support, they both have to work full time.

Cf also circumstantial *now* (*that*), 15.28.

In that ⟨formal⟩ combines reason with point of view:

The evidence is invalid *in that it was obtained through illegal means.* ['The evidence is invalid in this respect: it was obtained through illegal means.'] ⟨formal⟩

When *while* introduces a style disjunct, it blends time and reason:

While you're in the kitchen, bring me another drink.

Clauses without a subordinator may imply the meanings discussed in this section:

Knowing their tastes, she was able to bring a gift that they would like.
Constructed according to my specifications, the building was able to withstand the earthquake.
Assured of your support, he would not compromise.

It is a testimony of the close and obvious connection between reason and temporal sequence that *as* and *since* are conjunctions of time as well as of cause. This dual function can give rise to ambiguity:

As he was standing near the door, he could hear the conversation in the kitchen. ['Since he was standing near the door . . .' *or* 'While he was standing near the door . . .']

Note [**a**] A number of prepositional phrases are used to introduce reason relationships, but they are often considered to be stylistically clumsy because of their greater length:

because of
by virtue of
in (the) light of
in view of } the fact (that)
on account of
owing to
due to

For prescriptive objections to the use of *due to* as a preposition, *cf* 15.59 Note [d]. For the use of *on account of* as a subordinator in informal style (esp AmE), *cf* 14.12 Note [e].

[**b**] Infinitive clauses may convey a meaning similar to that of reason *in that*:

He's foolish *to make such a fuss*. ['. . . in that he makes such a fuss.']

They may also blend reason with condition, *cf* 15.34 Note [g].

[**c**] The stereotyped clause *come to think of it*, with no subordinator and with a verb in the base form is similar to *now that I come to think of it*:

Come to think of it, shouldn't you write to her?

[**d**] The reason/contingency meaning of *in case* easily merges into a negative purpose meaning (*cf* 15.35 Note [g], 15.48). Compare:

Write a will *in case you die*. ['. . . because you may die.']

Write a will *in case you die without providing for your family*. ['. . .because you may die without providing for your family', 'in order that you do not die without providing for your family']

[**e**] Circumstantial *what with* refers to one or more given circumstances of an unspecified set, whereas circumstantial *with* implies only one:

What with the prices (*being*) *so high*, (and (with) my wife being out of work), I can't afford a new refrigerator.

Notice that it is possible to add informal *and all* if a coordinated *and* (*with*) . . . is not present:

What with Carol (*being*) *out of work and all*, we didn't send any Christmas cards this year.

There is a stereotyped phrasal analogue:

What with one thing and another, I couldn't sleep last night.

[**f**] *As* followed by a noun phrase may correspond to a finite clause:

As I'm your mother,
As your mother, } I'll decide.

But the restriction to noun phrases suggests that *as* is here a preposition.

[**g**] An adjunct *because*-clause, but not a style disjunct *because*-clause, corresponds to a prepositional phrase introduced by *because of*:

The flowers are growing well { *because I fertilized them.*
because of my fertilizing them.

[**h**] A *because*-clause is sometimes used informally as equivalent to a *that*-clause:

(*Just*) *because I object to his promotion* doesn't mean that I'm vindictive. ['The (mere) fact that I object . . .'] [1]

There are prescriptive objections to this use. Alternatives are:

My objection
My objecting } to his promotion doesn't mean that I'm vindictive. [1a]

I can't be accused of being vindictive (just) because I object to his promotion. [1b]

There are also prescriptive objections against the alleged redundancy in the informal use of a *because*-clause that correlates with a previous *why* or *the reason* (*that*):

Why
The reason (*that*) } they didn't go to see the house is *because* they prefer to live in an apartment. [2]

Similar objections apply to the use of *the reason why* in place of *the reason* (*that*). The fully acceptable alternative to [2] would replace *because* by *that*.

15.47 Most subordinators used for direct cause introduce content disjuncts, but *because*, *in case*, and *in that* introduce adjuncts (*cf* 15.20).

Adjunct *because*-clauses tend to be in *I* position, while style disjunct *because*-clauses are always at *E*. *For*, which is close to coordinator status, is always at *E*. *Table* 15.47 draws on an analysis of British English based on a

100 000-word sample from both the London–Lund corpus (which contains most of the SEU spoken texts) and the LOB written corpus to provide figures for the positions of clauses introduced by the major reason subordinators.

Table 15.47 Distribution of reason clauses in samples from the written LOB corpus and the spoken London–Lund corpus

	LL	LOB	Total
as	7	19	26
initial	2	9	11
final	5	10	15
because (*cos*)	355	70	425
initial	4	8	12
medial	4	2	6
final	347	60	407
for (all final)	0	64	64
since	5	33	38
initial	2	12	14
medial	1	0	1
final	2	21	23

When *as* is a circumstantial subordinator, the predication may optionally be fronted:

> *Writing hurriedly as she was*, she didn't notice the spelling errors.
> *Tired as they were*, they went to bed as soon as they came back.

That may be a circumstantial subordinator, when the subject complement is obligatorily fronted:

> *Clumsy idiot that he was*, Michael completely ruined the dinner.

Cf 15.39 for a similar fronting with concessive clauses.

Clauses of purpose

15.48 Clauses of purpose, which are adjuncts, are more often infinitival than finite:

> *To open the carton*, pull this tab.
> I left early *to catch the train.*
> My publisher sent it *for me to comment on* (*it*).

More explicit subordinators of purpose are *in order to* ⟨formal⟩ and *so as to*:

> They left the door open (*in order*) *for me to hear the baby.*
> Students should take notes (*so as*) *to make revision easier.*
> The committee agreed to adjourn (*in order*) *to reconsider the matter when fuller information became available.*

Finite clauses of purpose are introduced by *so that* or (less commonly and more informally) by *so*, and (more formally) by *in order that*:

The school closes earlier *so* (*that*) *the children can get home before dark.*
The jury and the witnesses were removed from the court *in order that they might not hear the arguments of the lawyers on the prosecution's motion for an adjournment.*

These finite clauses, which are putative (*cf* 15.49), require one of these modal auxiliaries: *can, could, may, might, should, would.*

Negative purpose is expressed in the infinitive clauses by *so as not to* and *in order not to*:

Turn the volume down *so as not to wake the baby.*
I ignored the remark *in order not to prolong the dispute.*

In finite clauses it is expressed by *in order that . . . not*, but also by specific subordinators: *for fear* (*that*) ⟨formal⟩, *in case* ⟨BrE⟩, or the very formal *lest*:

They left early *for fear* (*that*) *they would meet him.* [1]
They evacuated the building *in case the wall collapsed.* [2]

For fear (*that*) conveys also the meaning of apprehension and requires a modal auxiliary, but *in case* need not have a modal auxiliary. In [2] there is an implicit negative purpose 'in order that, if the wall collapsed, they would not be affected.' Archaic *lest* tends to have a modal auxiliary or (esp in AmE) the present subjunctive:

Earthen mounds were being hastily erected *lest an attack*
{*should be* / *be* ⟨esp AmE⟩} *launched that night.*

Note [**a**] The implied subject of an infinitive clause may be the object (indirect or direct) of the superordinate clause:

I lent Paul a dollar *to get home.* ['. . . (for Paul) to get home.']

The purpose infinitive clause can be fronted when the implied subject is the subject of the superordinate clause:

To get home, I had to borrow money from Paul.

[**b**] As a subordinator for finite clauses of purpose, *that* is archaic:

The jury and witnesses were removed from the court *that they might not hear the arguments of the lawyers.*

Should not hear ⟨esp BrE⟩ and *not hear* ⟨esp AmE⟩ could also be used instead of *might not hear.*

[**c**] Purpose may be expressed by an *if*-clause containing the semi-auxiliaries *be to* or *be going to*:

If I'm to be there on time, I must leave at once.

Clauses of result

15.49 Clauses of result are introduced by the subordinators *so that* ⟨formal⟩ and *so.* These clauses overlap with those of purpose both in meaning and in subordinators. The chief semantic difference is that result clauses are factual rather than putative: both express result, but in the result clause the result is achieved, whereas in the purpose clause it is yet to be achieved – it is a desired or aimed-at result. Hence finite clauses of result do not require a modal auxiliary:

We paid him immediately, *so* (*that*) *he left contented.* [result] [1]
We paid him immediately *so* (*that*) *he would leave contented.* [purpose] [2]

As we see from these examples, *so* and *so that* express both purpose and result, but *so that* is more commonly used for purpose and *so* for result. When *that* is omitted in the result clause, the conjunction *so* is indistinguishable from the conjunct *so* in asyndetic coordination. If *and* is inserted, *so* is unambiguously the conjunct:

We paid him immediately, *and so* he left contented. [1a]

Result clauses differ syntactically from purpose clauses, in that result clauses are disjuncts whereas purpose clauses are adjuncts (*cf* 15.20). Furthermore, result clauses can only appear finally. Unlike the purpose clause, the result clause introduced by *so* (*that*) is separated by comma punctuation.

The result relation is the converse of that of motivation (*cf* 15.45). Consider the following sentence:

I took no notice of him, *so he flew into a rage.*

Its meaning can be expressed by reversing the matrix and subordinate clauses and using a conjunction such as *because*:

He flew into a rage *because I took no notice of him.*

That may introduce a final clause with resultative meaning in interrogative sentences:

What have I done, *that you should insult me*?

In one type of comparative clause, the clause expresses result. This type (*cf* 15.74) has the correlatives *so* . . . (*that*) or *such* . . . (*that*), in which *so* and *such* are intensifiers:

Her parents gave her *so* many toys (*that*) *she couldn't possibly play with them all.* [*cf* Note [b]] [3]
She is *such* a good lecturer (*that*) *all her courses are full.* [4]

Such that ⟨formal⟩ combines result with manner:

The two halves of the human brain behave independently, *such that each half can be taught opposite solutions to simple problems.* ['. . . in a way that has the result that . . .']

Note [**a**] *Cf* 15.25 for *to*-infinitive clauses that blend the meanings of time and outcome.

[**b**] If *that* is omitted in [3] and [4] above, an intonation break is normal at that place. If *so* intensifies a verb it may appear at the end of the clause, and an intonation break (or in writing, a comma) is normal after *so*:

They wanted it *so*, (*that*) *they agreed to pay more than the normal price.* [*so* = 'so much']

Compare the result clause with the complex subordinator *so that*:

They wanted it, *so* (*that*) *they agreed to pay more than the normal price.*

In formal style, *so* may be a manner adverb rather than an intensifier, in which case *that* must be retained:

They *so* arranged the seating *that all had a clear view of the stage.* [*so* = 'in such a way'] ⟨formal⟩

Again, *so* may be postposed:

They arranged the seating *so, that all had a clear view of the stage.* ⟨formal⟩

[**c**] In interrogative and negative sentences, *that* may introduce a result clause that is related to the correlative *so . . . that* comparative clause exemplified in [3] and [4] above, except that the intensifier *so* is omitted. The style is formal and archaic:

Do you know her intimately, *that you presume to address her in such a casual manner*?

(Compare: *Do you know her so intimately that . . .*)
They are not destitute *that they need your help.*
In the negative sentence, the result clause is counterfactual ('they do not need your help').

Clauses of similarity and comparison

15.50 Adjunct clauses of similarity are predication adjuncts (*cf* 15.22). They are introduced by *as* and *like* ⟨informal, esp AmE⟩. *As* and *like* are commonly premodified by *just* and *exactly*:

She cooks a turkey (*just*) *as her mother did.* ['. . . in a way that is similar to the way that . . .'] [1]
Please do it (*exactly*) *as I said.* [2]
?Say the word (*exactly*) *like I did.* ⟨esp informal AmE⟩ [*cf* Note [b]] [3]
It was (*just*) *as I imagined.* ['. . . similar to what I imagined.'] [4]

When the verb is dynamic, as in [1–3], similarity is combined with manner. The clause in [4], on the other hand, expresses pure similarity.

If the *as*-clause is placed initially, as in [5], correlative *so* introduces the matrix clause in formal literary style:

(*Just*) *as a moth is attracted by a light, so* he was fascinated by her. [5]

The clause then expresses an analogy.

Adjunct clauses of comparison are also predication adjuncts. They are introduced by *as if*, *as though*, and *like* ⟨informal, esp AmE⟩. As with similarity clauses, when the verb is dynamic they also convey a manner meaning. If the comparison is factual, the verb in the comparison follows the normal rules for temporal reference:

He looks *as if he's getting better.*

If the comparison is hypothetical (implying lack of reality), a subjunctive or hypothetical past may be used as an alternative (*cf* 14.23*f*):

She treats me *as if* {*I'm* / *I was* / *I were*} *a stranger.*

He talks *as if* {*he has* / *he had*} *a potato in his mouth.*

She treated me *as though* {*I was* / *I were* / *I had been*} *a stranger.*

The subordinators *as*, *as if*, and *as though* introduce nonfinite and verbless clauses:

Fill in the application form *as instructed.*
He bent down *as if tightening his shoe laces.*
You should discuss the company with him *as though unaware that you were being considered for a job.*

As if and *as though* may also introduce *to*-infinitive clauses:

She winked at me *as if to say that I shouldn't say anything.*

Note [a] An *as*-clause that blends manner with similarity may allow subject–operator inversion if the clause consists only of the subject and the operator:

His conducting of the third movement shows the subtlety of his interpretation, *as does his earlier recording of the Mass in C.*

The present owner is a keen art collector, *as were several of her ancestors.*

[b] There are prescriptive objections to the use of *like* as a subordinating manner or comparison conjunction, but it is commonly used as such in informal style, especially in AmE. It is more acceptable when it expresses pure similarity, as does the preposition *like*, though it still tends to be confined to informal style:

It was (*just*) *like I imagined.* 〈informal〉 [4a]

Compare the casual:

?It was (*just*) *like what I imagined.* 〈casual〉 [4b]

[c] Adverbial clauses of comparison are not to be confused with the comparative clauses in 15.63*ff*.

Clauses of proportion

15.51 Proportional clauses involve a kind of comparison. They express a proportionality or equivalence of tendency or degree between two situations. They may be introduced by *as*, with or without correlative *so* 〈formal〉, or by the fronted correlative *the* . . . *the* followed by comparative forms:

As he grew disheartened, (*so*) his work deteriorated.
As the lane got narrower, (*so*) the overhanging branches made it more difficult for us to keep sight of our quarry.
The more she thought about it, *the less* she liked it.
The harder he worked, *the happier* he felt.

The fronting of the comparative elements results in the kind of syntactic ordering found in relative and *wh*-interrogative clauses:

The later you arrive [A S V], the better the food is [C_s S V].
The more you tell him [O_d S V O_i], the less notice he takes [O_d S V].

On the correlative *the*-clauses, *cf* further 14.13 and (as expressing a contingency meaning) 15.30.

Note [a] Correlative clauses of proportion are found in some aphoristic sentences such as *The more, the merrier* (*cf* 11.43).

[b] The subordinators *insofar as, inasmuch as* 〈formal〉, and *insofar that* 〈formal, rare〉 introduce adjunct clauses of extent or degree:

We agreed with the lecturer *only insofar as she condemned the government's domestic policies.* ['. . . only to the extent that . . .']

Corresponding prepositions are *to the extent that* and *to the degree that.*

Clauses of preference

15.52 Clauses of preference are mainly introduced by the subordinators *rather than* and *sooner than*, with the bare infinitive as the verb of the clause:

Rather than go there by air, I'd take the slowest train. ['I'd prefer to take the slowest train.'] [1]
They'll fight to the finish *sooner than surrender*. ['They prefer to fight to the finish.'] [2]

The combination *'d rather* [= *would rather* or *had rather*] is a modal idiom (*cf* 3.45*f*). Corresponding to [1] is [1a]:

I'd rather take the slowest train *than go there by air*. [1a]

The subordinate clause may very occasionally have its own subject:

Rather than you say anything, I would speak to the manager myself. ['I'd prefer to speak to the manager myself.'] [3]

A rare and formal finite clause of preference occurs with putative *should* (*cf* 14.25):

Rather than she should feel lonely, her friends arranged to take her with them on the trip. [4]

The subordinate clause expresses the rejected alternative. That negative meaning allows it to contain nonassertive items (*cf* 10.60), as in [3] and [5]:

Rather than *ever* admit that he has *any* pain *at all*, he'll suffer for weeks. [5]

The matrix clause expresses an implied conditional meaning ('if there's a choice'), and therefore the matrix verb tends to contain a modal auxiliary.

Note [**a**] On *rather than* as a quasi-coordinator, *cf* 14.15 Note, and as a preposition with *-ing* clauses, *cf* 14.19 Note [c].

[**b**] The preference construction extends the notion of priority in time to the notion of priority in choice. It is therefore not surprising that temporal expressions other than *sooner* are used to convey preference: notably the subordinator *before*, but also such comparative adverbs as *quicker*, *faster*, *more readily*, plus *than*. Both clauses take modal auxiliaries:

He'd sit alone in the dark *before he'd watch television*. ['He prefers to sit alone in the dark.']
She'll use the telephone *before she'll put pen to paper*.
They would volunteer their own work *more readily than they would contribute money*.
I'd buy a typewriter *faster than I'd buy a television set*.

In earlier periods of English, *rather* also had temporal meaning.

Comment clauses

15.53 Comment clauses are parenthetical disjuncts. They may occur initially, finally, or medially, and thus generally have a separate tone unit:

KǏNGston, |*as you probably* KNÓW,| is the capital of JaMÀIca |

Comment clauses are either content disjuncts that express the speakers' comments on the content of the matrix clause, or style disjuncts that convey the speakers' views on the way they are speaking (*cf* 15.20*f*). Here we consider forms of these clauses that we have not discussed in the previous sections on the semantic roles of adverbial clauses.

We distinguish the following types:

(i) like the matrix clause of a main clause:

There were no other applicants, *I believe*, for that job.

(ii) like an adverbial finite clause (introduced by *as*):

I'm working the night shift, *as you know*.

(iii) like a nominal relative clause:

What was more upsetting, we lost all our luggage.

(iv) *to*-infinitive clause as style disjunct:

I'm not sure what to do, *to be honest.*

(v) *-ing* clause as style disjunct:

I doubt, *speaking as a layman*, whether television is the right medium for that story.

(vi) *-ed* clause as style disjunct:

Stated bluntly, he had no chance of winning.

In each category, there are idiomatic or cliché expressions: *you see*, *as I say*, *what's more to the point*, *to be fair*, *generally speaking*, *put bluntly*. Similarly, in each category there is at least some freedom to coin new expressions.

Comment clauses, many of which are characteristic of spoken English, are generally marked prosodically by increased speed and lowered volume.

15.54 Type (i) comment clauses, which are the most important, generally contain a transitive verb or adjective which elsewhere requires a nominal *that*-clause as object (*cf* 15.4). We can therefore see a correspondence between sentences containing such clauses and sentences containing indirect statements:

There were no other applicants, *I believe*, for that job. [1]
I believe that there were no other applicants for that job. [2]

To convert a sentence with a *that*-clause such as [2] into a sentence such as [1], we have to reverse the relationship of subordination between the two clauses, making the *that*-clause into the matrix clause, at the same time omitting the subordinator *that*, and making the matrix clause into the comment clause. Because of this reversal of syntactic roles, the two sentences [1] and [2] are not exact paraphrases; but the relationship between them illuminates the function of the comment clause. Furthermore, the verb in the comment clause may have only one of the meanings possible for the verb in the matrix clause. Verbs like *believe* and *think* may have a more definitive meaning or may merely hedge (express a tentative meaning); but only the hedging meaning is present in comment clauses. The possible difference is highlighted in the contrast between [3] and [4], and between [5] and [6]:

I believe that there is a God.
['I assert the belief that there is a God' or 'There may be a God.'] [3]
There is a God, *I believe*. ['There may be a God.'] [4]
You know that it belongs to me. ['You know that'] [5]
It belongs to me, *you know*. ['I want you to know that'] [6]

Since the *that* of an object *that*-clause is normally deletable (*cf* 15.4), only the intonation (reflected by comma separation in writing) distinguishes an initial comment clause from an initial matrix clause:

You KNÓW,| |I think you're WRÒNG|. } [*You know* is a comment clause]
You know, I |think you're WRÒNG|. }
You |know (that) I think you're WRÒNG|. [*You know* is a matrix clause]

Comment clauses resemble main clauses in that they contain at least a subject and a verb and are not introduced by a subordinator. However, they are not independent clauses, since they are defective syntactically: the verb or adjective lacks its normally obligatory complementation.

Many type (i) clauses are stereotyped, *eg*: *I believe, you know*. Outside this group, however, clauses can be fairly freely constructed, permitting variations of subject, tense, and aspect, or additions of adjuncts, etc:

> The Indian railways (*my uncle was telling me some time ago*) have always made a profit.

Type (i) comment clauses that are stereotyped may have various semantic functions:

(a) They hedge, *ie* they express the speaker's tentativeness over the truth value of the matrix clause. Commonly, the subject is *I* and the verb is in the simple present, but the subject may be an indefinite *one* or *they* or (usually with a passive verb) *it* and the verb may (for example) have a modal auxiliary or be in the present perfective. Here are some examples:

> *I believe, I guess, I think, I expect, I feel, I hear, I presume, I assume, I understand, I suppose, I consider, I suspect, I'm told, I have read, I have heard, I have heard tell, I can see, I may assume, I daresay, I venture to say, one hears, they tell me, they allege, they say, it is said, it is reported, it is claimed, it is rumoured, it has been claimed, it seems, it appears*

The comment clause may be negative (with *I* as subject) if the matrix clause is negative:

> They aren't at home, *I don't believe*.

The matched negative expresses greater tentativeness than the positive. The verbs that commonly allow the negative are *believe, expect, suppose, think*.

Some comment clauses are added to questions:

> What's he DÒing, *I WÓNder*?
> Are they to get aWÀY with it, *I ÁSK myself*?

(b) They express the speaker's certainty. Commonly, the subject is *I* and the verb is in the simple present. Here are some examples:

> *I know, I claim, I see, I remember, I agree, I admit, I'm sure, I'm convinced*; *I have no doubt*; *it's true, it transpires*; *there's no doubt*; *I must say, I must admit, I must tell you, I have to say*

Certainty may also be expressed by negation of a verb that expresses rejection or lack of certainty, *eg*: *I don't deny, I don't doubt*.

(c) They express the speaker's emotional attitude towards the content of the matrix clause. Again, usually the subject is *I* and the verb is in the simple present. Some are followed by a *to*-infinitive verb of speaking. Here are some examples:

> *I'm glad to say, I'm happy to say, I'm pleased to say, I'm delighted to say, I'm happy to tell you*; *I hope, I wish, I fear, I regret, I'm afraid*; *I regret to say, I'm sorry to say*; *it pains me to tell you, it grieves me to say*

Interjections such as *God knows* and *Heaven knows*, which express the speaker's lack of comprehension, perhaps belong here because they also imply an emotive attitude.

(d) They are used to claim the hearer's attention. Some also call for the hearer's agreement. At the same time, they express the speaker's informality and warmth toward the hearer. The subject is usually *you* or the implied *you* of the imperative. Here are some examples:

> *you know, you see, you realize; you can see, you may know, you may have heard, you must admit; mind you, mark you; it may interest you to know*

Negative questions generally call for the hearer's agreement, *eg*: *wouldn't you say?, don't you think?, don't you agree?, can't you see?, don't you know?* They are attached to declarative sentences:

> It's ethically wrong, *wouldn't you say*?

Positive questions generally call for the hearer's attention. They are attached to interrogative sentences:

> What's she doing, *do you think*?
> Is the heating on, *do you suppose*?

Note **[a]** The reporting clauses for direct speech (*cf* 14.29) are related to the semantic roles (a) and (b) of type (i) comment clauses, and may be considered an additional semantic category within type (i):

> 'It's time we went,' *I said*.

Like the other comment clauses, their verbs also normally require complementation.

[b] Tag questions (*cf* 11.8*ff*) are related to the semantic role (d) of type (i) comment clauses, and may also be considered comment clauses:

> They're in a great hurry, *aren't they*?

They may alternatively be analysed as related to the matrix clause by parataxis (*cf* 13.2) rather than by subordination, parataxis being a relationship that might be postulated for all type (i) comment clauses.

[c] Although comment clauses are syntactically dependent in that their verbs lack the required complementation, some clauses identical in form to comment clauses may be used as independent utterances in responses:

> A: Will you be leaving tonight? B: *I daresay*.
> A: Your tie is undone. B: *I know*.

Other such responses require a clausal pro-form as complementation, *eg*: *I think so*.

[d] Notice the difference between [7] and [8]:

> But is this RÍGHT, {*I WÓNder*? / *I wonder*?} [7]

> But is this RÍGHT, *I WÒNder*? [8]

Where [7] expresses reservation, [8] expresses decided disagreement. The falling tone, as with tag questions, invites confirmation.

[e] In an informal use, *I don't think* is attached to a positive sentence to indicate that the sentence is being used ironically:

> That's a MÀSterpiece, *I don't think*.

I don't think has tail intonation (*cf* App II.15).

[f] Notice that some comment clauses in subtype (b) may have a concessive force, *eg*: *It's true, I must say, I admit, I must admit*.

15.55 Type (ii) comment clauses, which are next in importance, are introduced by *as*. *As* serves one of two syntactic functions in these clauses: as a relative or as a subordinator.

In its relative function, *as* introduces a type of sentential relative clause that may precede or be inserted in its antecedent, in this case the clause or sentence to which it is attached. In its mobility, this *as*-clause is intermediate between the relative and adverbial constructions. Like the sentential relative *which* (*cf* 15.57), *as* may function as a relative pronoun:

> She is extremely popular among students, *as is common knowledge.* (*cf*: *which is common knowledge*)
> I live a long way from work, *as you know*. (*cf*: *which you know*)

Other examples of clauses with relative *as*: *as everybody knows, as you may remember, as you say, as I can see, as I have said, as I'm told, as you may have heard.*

As a subordinator, *as* introduces a clearly adverbial clause, and the sentential antecedent is replaced by *it*. It is roughly synonymous with *insofar as* ['to the extent that']:

> He is the best candidate, *as it seems*. ['. . . insofar as it seems that he is the best candidate.']

Other examples of clauses with subordinator *as*: *as it appears, as it happens, as it transpired, as it may interest you to know, as I see it, as I interpret it.*

The two types of construction often merge, providing a choice whether or not to insert *it*. Thus, some of the examples with subordinator *as* allow an optional *it* when they are extended: *as* (*it*) *seems likely, as* (*it*) *often happens.* Other examples with optional *it*: *as* (*it*) *was pointed out, as* (*it*) *was said earlier, as I remember* (*it*), *as I understand* (*it*).

> *As* (*it*) *appears from her essay*, she has read widely in Romantic literature.

Type (i) comment clauses can often be converted to type (ii) comment clauses by the addition of *as*:

> The Indian railways, ((*as*) *my uncle was telling me some time ago*), have always made a profit.

But the addition changes the meaning. The type (ii) clause is affirmative, implying the truth of the matrix clause, whereas the type (i) clause is neutral. The difference may be clearer with another pair of sentences:

> GĔORGE, *as you SÁID*, is a LÌar (*but I don't believe it).
> GĔORGE, *you said*, is a LÌar (but I don't believe it).

The affirmation of truth value is even more striking when the *as*-clause comes first:

> *As you said*, George is a liar.

Many of the stereotyped type (i) clauses become unacceptable if *as* is added (**as I see*, **as I daresay*) or change their meaning radically (*as you know*).

Note [**a**] The clausal pro-form *so* may be used in parenthetical clauses that correspond to type (i) in their meaning, although they resemble type (ii) in their form: *so he says, so I understand, so it* *seems, so I believe*. The semantic resemblance to type (i) comment clauses lies in their neutrality as to the truth value of the matrix clause.

[**b**] There are a few negative stereotyped comment clauses with *you* as subject, but they require a modal auxiliary, usually *may, might, will*, or *would*; *eg*: *as you may not remember, as you won't have heard, as you might not realize*.

[**c**] Relative *as* may have the function of subject in its clause, but only if the operator is *be* or another copular verb:

She has married again, *as* { *was/seemed natural.* / *was expected.* / **delighted us.* }

Contrast with the sentential relative:

She has married again, *which delighted us.*

This condition does not apply to the merged constructions where a subject *it* can sometimes be added:

She has married again, *as* (*it*) *often happens.*

There appears to be the additional requirement that the *as*-clause must be semantically congruent with its matrix clause:

She has married again, { **as was unexpected.* / *which was unexpected.* / **as was disgraceful.* / *which was disgraceful.* }

This requirement suggests that relative *as* retains some reason implication that is normal for *as* when it is a conjunction of reason.

15.56 The other types of comment clauses can be dealt with more briefly.

Type (iii) comment clauses are nominal relative clauses introduced by *what* (*cf* 15.8*f*):

What's more surprising, he didn't inform his parents. [1]

The *what*-clause must be initial. As with type (ii) (*cf* 15.55), sentences containing them correspond to sentences in which the relationship of subordination between the two clauses is reversed. For example, [1] corresponds to [2]:

It's more surprising (that) he didn't inform his parents. [2]

It also corresponds to a sentential relative clause (*cf* 15.57) as in [3], except that a sentential relative clause must be final:

He didn't inform his parents, *which is more surprising.* [3]

It further corresponds to a sentence in which the nominal relative clause is subject and linked to the subject complement by the verb *be*, as in [4]:

What's more surprising is (that) he didn't inform his parents. [4]

Other examples of type (iii) comment clauses: *what's more serious, what's most significant of all, what's very strange, what annoys me.*

Types (iv), (v), and (vi) of the comment clauses are style disjuncts (*cf* 15.21). They are nonfinite clauses, differentiated by form. We give some examples of stereotyped clauses for each type.

Examples of type (iv) comment clauses, which have a *to*-infinitive: *to be honest, to be fair, to be frank, to be precise, to be truthful, to be serious for a moment, to speak candidly, to put it briefly.*

Examples of type (v) comment clauses, which have an *-ing* clause: *broadly speaking, loosely speaking, roughly speaking, figuratively speaking, speaking frankly, speaking generally, speaking personally, putting it mildly, putting it crudely.*

Examples of type (vi) comment clauses, which have an *-ed* clause: *put in another way, rephrased, worded plainly, stated quite simply.*

Sentential relative clauses

15.57 Closely related to comment clauses of type (ii) (*as you know*, *cf* 15.55) and type (iii) (*what's more surprising*, *cf* 15.56) are SENTENTIAL RELATIVE CLAUSES. Unlike adnominal relative clauses, which have a noun phrase as antecedent, the sentential relative clause refers back to the predicate or predication of a clause, [1] and [2], or to a whole clause or sentence, [3] and [4], or even to a series of sentences [5]:

> They say he *plays truant, which he doesn't.* [1]
> He *walks for an hour each morning, which would bore me.* [2]

Relative clauses such as in [1] are used to affirm (if positive) or deny (if negative) an assertion or thought ascribed to others.

> Things then improved, *which surprises me.* [3]
> Colin married my sister and I married his brother, *which makes Colin and me double in-laws.* [4]

In [3] the antecedent matrix clause is a single clause and in [4] it is two conjoined clauses. But one might equally imagine a storyteller coming to the end of the story with the words:

> – *which is how the kangaroo came to have a pouch.* [5]

Here *which* could refer back to the whole length of the story.

Sentential relative clauses parallel nonrestrictive postmodifying clauses in noun phrases in that they are separated by intonation or punctuation from their antecedent. They are commonly introduced by the relative word *which.* In [1–5] *which* is a relative pronoun, but it may also be a relative determiner of general abstract nouns such as *fact, case, event*, or *situation*, or more specific verbal nouns such as *failure* or *claim.* The noun phrases, which may be prepositional complements, represent the antecedent:

> The plane may be several hours late, *in which case there's no point in our waiting.* [6]
> They are said to have taught chimpanzees to use human language, *which claim has been disputed by some scholars.* ⟨formal⟩ [7]

The rather formal construction in [7] is more commonly replaced by a noun phrase with a postmodifying relative clause, as in [8]:

They are said to have taught chimpanzees to use human language, *a claim which has been disputed by some scholars.* [8]
The prosecutor charged him with lying, *an allegation which he vehemently denied.* [9]

In [8] and [9] the noun phrase, including the postmodifier, is in apposition to the predication of the matrix clause. The determiner *which* may be found with prepositions other than *in* (exemplified in [6]):

They were under water for several hours, *from which experience they emerged unharmed.*
The last speaker assured the audience that the party would win the election, *on which optimistic note* the meeting ended.

Furthermore, the pronoun *which* may be a prepositional complement:

Mortimer exploded a firecracker during a lesson, *as a result of which he was suspended from school for a week.*
Her brother snatched the letter away, *at which she was furious.*

In a rather formal style, the pronoun *which* may be the object of a nonfinite verb:

There was a sudden increase in the readership of Sunday papers, *after noticing which several editors changed their policy.*
Profits had to be increased, *to achieve which object became the main occupation of business executives.*

Two special types of appositional clauses should be noted here, because they provide common alternatives to sentential relative clauses. Both types contain a noun head modified by an adnominal relative clause:

(a) RESUMPTIVE clauses repeat as the noun head a word or a morphological variant of a word:

She expressed her *belief* in the economic recovery of the country, *a belief that was well founded.*
The President *announced* that he would run for a second term, *an announcement that was acclaimed by most members of his party.*

(b) SUMMATIVE clauses provide as the noun head a word that summarizes the matrix clause:

Norman may be pretending to be sick to avoid going to school, *a possibility that we cannot ignore.*

Relative words other than *which* are used to introduce sentential relative clauses. *Whereupon* ['after which', 'in consequence of which'] and *whence* ['from which', 'in consequence of which'] are formal:

At the annual meeting, the parishioners severely criticized the minister, *whereupon he resigned.*
The army has been mobilized, *whence we may deduce that an invasion is imminent.*

The combinations *since when* ['since which time' 〈esp BrE〉], *until when*, *from when*, and *by when* are also used as sentential relatives:

> She joined the editorial staff of a local newspaper, *since when she has contributed to various monthlies.* ⟨esp BrE⟩

The status of the sentential relative clause is somewhat anomalous. Semantically it is similar to comment clauses that are content disjuncts; compare *which surprises me* in [3] above with the comment clause *what surprises me*. However, the *which*-clause cannot be initial, while the *what*-clause must be. On the other hand, it is similar to other nonrestrictive relative clauses in that it follows its antecedent and in that it can be most nearly paraphrased by a coordinate clause in which the *wh*-word is replaced by a demonstrative such as *that*; for example the relative clause in [4] can be replaced by *and that makes Colin and me double in-laws*, and the one in [6] by *and in that case there's no point in our waiting.*

Note [**a**] There are several archaic compounds with *where-* that introduce sentential relative clauses. They have the meaning 'in consequence of which' or 'after which': *whereafter, whereat, wherefore, wherewith.*

[**b**] The sentential relative clause is closest to the continuative nonrestrictive relative clause such as:

> Tom lent the book to Sue, who lent it to Pat, who returned it to Tom. ['. . . and she lent it to Pat, and she returned it to Tom.']

[**c**] Although the sentential relative clause is generally fixed in final position, it is occasionally found in medial position in informal conversation:

> Marvin and Terry – *which is something I'll never understand* – were quarrelling within a month of their marriage and were separated within three months.

Nonfinite and verbless adverbial clauses

The attachment rule for identifying the subject

15.58 In our discussion of the grammatical functions and semantic roles of adverbial clauses, we have frequently cited examples of nonfinite and verbless clauses. We conclude our discussion of adverbial clauses with a consideration of matters that particularly affect nonfinite and verbless clauses.

Nonfinite and verbless adverbial clauses that have an overt subject but are not introduced by a subordinator and are not the complement of a preposition are ABSOLUTE clauses, so termed because they are not explicitly bound to the matrix clause syntactically. Absolute clauses may be *-ing*, *-ed*, or verbless clauses, but not infinitive clauses:

> *No further discussion arising*, the meeting was brought to a close. [1]
> *Lunch finished*, the guests retired to the lounge. [2]
> *Christmas then only days away*, the family was pent up with excitement. [3]

Apart from a few stereotyped phrases (*cf* Note [b] below), absolute clauses are formal and infrequent.

When a subject is not present in a nonfinite or verbless clause, the normal ATTACHMENT RULE for identifying the subject is that it is assumed to be identical in reference to the subject of the superordinate clause:

The oranges, *when* (*they are*) *ripe*, are picked and sorted mechanically. [4]

In *-ed* and verbless clauses with a subordinator such as [4], an ellipsis of the subject and operator may be postulated. In other cases, a paraphrase by a finite clause reveals that the subordinate clause subject is identical with the superordinate clause subject. The attachment rule is commonly given for participle clauses, but it applies equally to infinitive and verbless clauses:

Persuaded by our optimism, he gladly contributed time and money to the scheme. ['Since he was persuaded . . .']
Driving home after work, I accidentally went through a red light. ['While I was driving home after work . . .']
Confident of the justice of their cause, they agreed to put their case before an arbitration panel. ['Since they were confident . . .']
To climb the rock face, we had to take various precautions. ['So that we could climb . . .']

Note [**a**] As we see from the examples above, tense, aspect, and mood are also inferred in nonfinite and verbless clauses from the sentential context, *cf* 14.8.
[**b**] Stereotyped absolute clauses include *present company excepted*, *all told*, *weather/time permitting*, *God willing*.

Unattached nonfinite and verbless clauses

15.59 It is considered to be an error when the understood subject of the clause is not identifiable with the subject of the matrix clause, and perhaps does not appear in the sentence at all:

?*Driving to Chicago that night*, a sudden thought struck me. [1]
?*Since leaving her*, life has seemed pointless. [2]
?*Walking down the boardwalk*, a tall building came into view. [3]

In these examples the implied subject of the clauses is presumably *I*, but *I* does not occur as the subject of the matrix clauses. If we wish to keep the nonfinite clauses as they are, we rephrase the matrix clauses to introduce *I* as subject; for example:

Driving to Chicago that night, I was struck by a sudden thought. [1a]
Since leaving her, I have felt that life seemed pointless. [2a]
Walking down the boardwalk, I saw a tall building. [3a]

Clauses involved in this type of error, as in [1–3], are UNATTACHED clauses. Here are some further examples of unattached clauses:

?*After serving on several committees*, the association elected her their secretary-treasurer.
?*Friend of statesmen and patron of the arts*, many honours were bestowed on him.
?*While in a hospital near the school*, her teachers visited her regularly.

?*To see the procession*, I put the child on my shoulders.
?*Being the eldest*, the responsibility fell particularly on my shoulders.
?*Although the latest model*, they didn't like the car.
?*Advised to study anthropology*, his choice was psychology instead.
?*An author of considerable distinction*, people flocked to her public lecture.

The same error may occur when an *-ing* clause is the complement of a preposition:

?*On reaching the summit*, the view delighted us all.

As with [1–3], we can interpret correctly the implied subject in these sentences, but these unattached clauses are frowned upon. Such clauses are totally unacceptable if the sentence provides no means for identifying the implied subject:

**Reading the evening paper*, a dog started barking.
**Using these techniques*, a wheel fell off.
**A result of the rise in prices*, our economy is suffering.

Sometimes the error suggests an absurd interpretation:

**Opening the cupboard*, a skeleton fell out.
**Grilled on charcoal*, everyone enjoyed the fish they caught.
**Having eaten our lunch*, the steamboat departed.

The attachment rule does not apply, or at least is relaxed, in certain cases:

(a) The clause is a style disjunct (*cf* 15.21), in which case the implied subject is the subject of the implied clause of speaking, normally *I*:

Putting it mildly, you have caused us some inconvenience.
His moral principles, *to be frank*, begin and end with his own interests.
To say the least, their techniques are old-fashioned.

(b) The implied subject is the whole of the matrix clause:

I'll help you *if necessary*. ['. . . if it is necessary.']
Unknown to his closest advisers, he had secretly negotiated with an enemy emissary. ['It was unknown to his closest advisers that . . .']
The siren sounded, *indicating that the air raid was over*. ['. . . which indicated that . . .']

(c) If the implied subject is an indefinite pronoun or prop *it* (*cf* 10.26), the construction is considered less objectionable:

When dining in the restaurant, a jacket and tie are required. ['When one dines . . .']
Being Christmas, the government offices were closed. ['Since it was . . .']

To-infinitive clauses are normal in this use:

To borrow books from this library, it is necessary to register as a member of the library. ['For one to borrow . . .']

(d) In formal scientific writing, the construction has become institutionalized where the implied subject is to be identified with the *I*, *we*, and *you* of the writer(s) or reader(s):

When treating patients with language retardation and deviation of language development, the therapy consists, in part, of discussions of the patient's problems with parents and teachers, with subsequent language teaching carried out by them.

To check on the reliability of the first experiment, the experiment was replicated with a second set of subjects.

Note [**a**] The error of unattached clauses has traditionally been discussed in connection with participle clauses, particularly *-ing* clauses. Other traditional terms for the error are 'unattached', 'unrelated', 'pendant', and 'dangling' participle.

[**b**] The acceptability of unattached clauses perhaps varies according to how easily the particular hearer or reader can perceive the implied subject. Participle forms that are lexicalized as conjunctions or prepositions are of course exempt from the attachment rule:

Provided that a film entertains, few people care about its merits.

Considering its cost, this machine is not worth buying.

[**c**] *As*-phrases are sometimes placed initially when they are related to an element in final position or to no element at all. They then resemble unattached clauses:

?*As a protection against inflation*, we must seek increasingly to diversify our investments.

?*As a professor of political science*, it has been interesting to spend a year in Germany.

[Presumably: '. . . I have found it interesting . . .']

[**d**] *Due to* is generally accepted as a complex preposition synonymous with *owing to*. Some speakers, however, consider that *due* functions as an adjective in that collocation and therefore object to its use in [4] as an infringement of the attachment rule for verbless clauses:

?*Due to bad weather*, classes have been cancelled today. [4]

For those who object to [4], [4a] provides an acceptable alternative:

Cancellation of classes today is *due to bad weather*. [4a]

Supplementive clauses

15.60 When adverbial participle clauses and adverbial verbless clauses are not introduced by a subordinator, there may be considerable indeterminacy as to the semantic relationship to be inferred. Infinitive clauses, although they exhibit a number of semantic relationships, present no particular problem in this respect, but *cf* 17.31*f*.

In their indeterminacy, adverbial participle and verbless clauses resemble the versatile relationships expressed by nonrestrictive relative clauses (*cf* 17.23) and the connective function of the coordinator *and* (*cf* 13.22*ff*). They are all capable of assuming, according to context, a more precise role:

Jason, *told of his son's accident*, immediately phoned the hospital. [1]

Jason, *who was told of his son's accident*, immediately phoned the hospital. [2]

Jason was told of his son's accident, *and he immediately phoned the hospital*. [3]

For all three sentences, although the mode of clause connection does not make this explicit, we infer a temporal sequence of events. On the other hand, in the next three sentences we infer that the logical connection between the clauses is primarily one of reason, although there is also a temporal sequence:

John, *knowing that his wife was expecting a baby*, started to take a course on baby care. [4]

John, *who knew that his wife was expecting a baby*, started to take a course on baby care. [5]
John knew that his wife was expecting a baby *and he started to take a course on baby care.* [6]

In [7] the connection is one of reason without temporal sequence:

Julia, *being a nun*, spent much of her life in prayer and meditation. [7]

Sentences [1], [2], [4], [5], and [7] all contain subordinate clauses, but only [1], [4], and [7] are adverbial clauses, since they can be positioned initially, medially, and (except for [1]) finally.

Adverbial participle and verbless clauses without a subordinator are SUPPLEMENTIVE CLAUSES; like nonrestrictive relative clauses and clauses in an *and*-coordination, they do not signal specific logical relationships, but such relationships are generally clear from the context. Subjectless supplementive clauses, *ie* those that (unlike supplementive absolute clauses, *cf* 15.58) do not have their own overt subject, resemble nonrestrictive relative clauses in another respect: the implied subject in the supplementive clause provides a link with the matrix clause rather as the relative pronoun provides a link in postmodifying relative clauses. The formal inexplicitness of supplementive clauses allows considerable flexibility in what we may wish them to convey. According to context, we may wish to imply temporal, conditional, causal, concessive, or circumstantial relationship. In short, the supplementive clause implies an accompanying circumstance to the situation described in the matrix clause. For the reader or hearer, the actual nature of the accompanying circumstance has to be inferred from the context. Here are some illustrations of process adverbials:

Using a sharp axe, Gilbert fought his way into the building. ['By using a sharp axe, . . .']
Marilyn crawled through the narrow tunnel, *hands in front.*
We spoke *face to face.*
They stood silently, *their eyes fixed on the horizon.*
Elizabeth dived in *head first.*
They strolled through the park *with their arms intertwined.*

Note [**a**] Clauses introduced by *with* and *without* often convey little more than a vague notion of accompanying circumstance:

With tears of joy in her eyes, she saw her daughter married.
Without anyone noticing, I slipped out of the room.

[**b**] In *-ing* clauses, verbs used dynamically tend to suggest a temporal link, and stative verbs a causal link:

Reaching the river, we pitched camp for the night. ['When we reached the river, . . .']
Being a farmer, he is suspicious of all governmental interference. ['Since he is a farmer, . . .']

Subjectless supplementive clauses

15.61 The formal characteristics of subjectless supplementive clauses are:

(a) They are participle or verbless clauses.

(b) Their most typical positions in the superordinate clause are initial, final, and immediately after their antecedent, *ie* the noun phrase in the superordinate clause which is identical with their implied subject.

The position immediately after the antecedent poses the most difficulties for analysis. When subjectless supplementive clauses occur in that position, they may be indistinguishable from postmodifying participle clauses or (in the case of verbless clauses) from noun phrases in apposition. Thus the two constructions may merge in that it is impossible (and semantically unimportant) to decide whether the participle clause in [1] is to be regarded as functionally equivalent to the nonrestrictive relative clause in [1a]:

This substance, *discovered almost by accident*, has revolutionized medicine. [1]
This substance, *which was discovered almost by accident*, has revolutionized medicine. [1a]

Alternatively, it may be equivalent to a subjectless supplementive clause:

Discovered almost by accident, this substance has revolutionized medicine.

There are, however, two types which in general may be unambiguously labelled supplementive:

(a) *-ing* clauses containing auxiliary verbs or the verb *be*:

The children, *having eaten their fill*, were allowed to leave the table.
The old man, *being of sane mind*, dictated and signed his will.

Such *-ing* clauses generally cannot be postmodifiers of noun phrases.

(b) verbless adjective clauses:

Lawson, *implacable*, contented himself with a glare of defiance.

Adjective clauses can, however, be nonrestrictive postmodifiers of noun phrases in certain circumstances:

(i) if the clause is lengthy and contains weighty information:

We took Joe, *unable to stand because of weakness*, to the nearest hospital.
I met Betty, *angry with me as always*, at the luncheon.

Contrast:

*We took Joe, *weak*, to the nearest hospital.
*I met Betty, *angry*, at the luncheon.

(ii) if the adjective can be object complement in the complementation of the superordinate verb:

I found George, *unconscious*, a few hours later.

Contrast:

*I treated George, *unconscious*, at the hospital.

In initial position, the clauses are unambiguously subjectless supplementive clauses. For supplementive clauses in final position, *cf* 15.62.

Supplementive clauses in final position

15.62 In spite of their resemblance to nonrestrictive relative clauses, supplementive clauses need not be separated from their matrix clause intonationally when they occur in final position. The following are therefore alternative renderings of the same sentence, differing only in that [1] has two focuses of information, whereas [2] has only one:

The manager apPRÒACHED us, SMÌLing. [1]
The manager approached us SMÌLing. [2]

One result of the alternative shown in [2] is the possible neutralization of the formal difference between nonfinite clauses functioning as supplementive clauses and those functioning as complementation of the verb. Thus [3] is ambiguous:

I saw Pam going home. [3]

On one interpretation (that of the supplementive clause), *I* is the implied subject of *going home*, whereas on the other (that of verb complementation), *Pam* is the overt subject.

Another result of the lack of intonation is illustrated in [4] and [5]. When the *-ing* participle immediately follows certain finite verbs with existential meaning, the latter seem close to being aspectual catenatives (*cf* 3.49):

Frank *sat reading* the newspaper. [4]
Edith *came running* towards us. [5]

Further, a sentence such as [6] is ambiguous in more than one way:

I caught the boy *waiting for my daughter.* [6]

In addition to the two possible structures of [3], this may be interpreted as having a third structure, in which the nonfinite clause is a postmodifying clause:

'I caught the boy while I was waiting for my daughter.' [supplementive clause]
'I caught the boy in the act of waiting for my daughter.' [verb complementation]
'I caught the boy who was waiting for my daughter.' [postmodification]

On the analogy of [2], we may identify the final adjective phrases of the following examples (where there is no intonational separation) as verbless supplementive clauses:

The manager approached us *full of apologies.* [7]
He drove the damaged car home *undismayed.* [8]

In each, the adjective phrase is in a copular relationship with the subject of the sentence, and is thus distinct from an object complement, which would be in a copular relationship with the direct object. Furthermore, an object complement could not normally be placed in initial position, whereas that position is perfectly natural for [7] and [8]:

Full of apologies, the manager approached us. [7a]
Undismayed, he drove the damaged car home. [8a]

Adjective phrases in final position that cannot be preposed are generally nonrestrictive postmodifiers of the preceding noun phrases (*cf* 15.61 for medial nonrestrictive postmodifiers), even though they are separated intonationally from the rest of the sentence:

The cows contentedly chewed the grass, *green and succulent after the rain*. ['which was green and succulent . . .']
The drill quickly penetrated the layer of rock, *loose and crumbly with years of weathering*.

Noun phrases in final position that cannot be preposed are generally appositives of the preceding noun phrases:

Shirley sent us a gift, *a box of chocolates*.

There is a gradient relating the functional categories of subject complement and restrictive adjunct (*cf* 15.23) realized by a verbless supplementive clause. We therefore find sentences in which the final phrases cannot be preposed (at least without changing the meaning), because they are on the gradient towards subject complement status:

They ended the season *bottom of the league*.
He came out of prison *a changed man*.
He began life *a Protestant*.
She emerged from the conflict *victorious*.

Note Prepositional phrases that may be construed as subject complement can also be viewed on the gradient between adverbial and complement (*cf* 10.11):

They ended the season *at the bottom of the league*.
He began life *as a Protestant*.
She emerged from the conflict *with a clear victory*.

Comparative clauses

15.63 In a comparative construction, a proposition expressed in the matrix clause is compared with a proposition expressed in the subordinate clause with respect to some STANDARD OF COMPARISON:

Jane is as healthy *as her sister* (*is*). [1]

The standard of comparison in [1] is health.

Broadly conceived, comparison includes comparisons of EQUIVALENCE (*cf* 15.71), as in [1], and comparisons of SUFFICIENCY and EXCESS (*cf* 15.72*ff*), as in [2] and [3]:

Don is *sensitive enough to understand your feelings*. [2]
Marilyn was *too polite to say anything about my clothes*. [3]

More narrowly considered, however, comparison concerns a standard measurable in terms of degree that is expressed by means of the correlative sequence *more*, *less*, or other comparative forms (*cf* 7.74*ff*) in the matrix clause, together with *than* in the subordinate clause. Such comparisons are COMPARISONS OF NONEQUIVALENCE:

Jane is {*more healthy* / *healthier* / *less healthy*} *than her sister* (*is*). [4]

The clause element in the matrix clause which specifies the standard of comparison (health in [1] and [4]) is the COMPARATIVE ELEMENT (abbreviated in our further discussion to 'comp-element'), in [1] and [4] *as healthy*, *more healthy*, *healthier*, *less healthy*. The BASIS OF COMPARISON is given in the COMPARATIVE CLAUSE, the correlative subordinate clause; it is Jane's sister in [1] and [4]. The basis of comparison need not be overtly expressed, but it is then implied from the context.

Comparative clauses of nonequivalence, equivalence, and excess may include nonassertive forms (*cf* 10.60):

They pleased me more than they can *in any way* imagine.
You have as much right to vote as you *ever* had.
I am too young to remember *any* of the events during the last war.

Note An alternative term for equivalence is 'equality'. Other terms for nonequivalence are 'inequality' and 'differentiation'.

The comp-element

15.64 We may imagine the semantics of the comparative construction arising from the answers [1a] and [1b], and [2a] and [2b] to the *how*-questions posed in [1] and [2]:

How old is Mary (compared with Jane)? [1]
How old is Jane (compared with Mary)? [2]
Mary is *older* than Jane (is). [1a]
Mary is *younger* than Jane (is). [1b]
Jane is *younger* than Mary (is). [2a]
Jane is *older* than Mary (is). [2b]

Of the four answers, [1a] and [2a] are synonymous, being converses of each other; and similarly [1b] and [2b]. Less frequently, comparison is expressed through *less*, which indicates a tendency to the negative pole of the standard of comparison:

Mary is *less old* than Jane (is). [1c]
Mary is *less young* than Jane (is). [1d]

Again, paraphrase relationships hold: [1c] is synonymous with [1b] and [2b], and [1d] with [1a] and [2a]. Sentences like [1d], in which the marked member of the pair of adjectives (*cf* 7.88) is combined with *less*, are rare. Sentences like [1c] are not common when the adjective is inflected for comparison rather than taking periphrastic *more*.

With other adjectives comparison with *less* is common enough when there is not an established pair of antonymous adjectives or when an available antonym sounds offensive:

Caroline is *less perceptive* than Rosemary (is). [3]
Violet is *less sophisticated* than Felice (is). [4]

Or a comparison of equivalence in the negative is substituted (*cf* 15.71):

Caroline is *not as/so perceptive* as Rosemary (is). [3a]
Violet is *not as/so sophisticated as* Felice (is). [4a]

Both types of comparison seem clearer than *more* with a negative adjective:

Caroline is *more imperceptive* than Rosemary (is). [3b]
Violet is *more unsophisticated* than Felice (is). [4b]

In the comparative constructions in [1a–1d], the comp-element (italicized) together with *than* forms a hinge by which the two *wh*-elements of the questions [1] and [2] could be said to be combined. This coalescence accounts for the appearance of defective structure in the comparative clause. For example, in [1a] the comparative clause *than Jane* (*is*) contains (optionally) a form of the verb *be*, but not a complement or adjunct such as the verb *be* normally requires for complementation. Some grammarians have postulated an omitted repetition of the standard of comparison in the comparative clause: *Mary is older than Jane is* (*old*). But we do not follow this analysis. In the first place, the full form suggests that Jane is old and Mary even older. And obviously this is not necessarily the case for the comparative construction: both Mary and Jane may be babies. The standard of comparison involves a scale without commitment to absolute values. Furthermore, a comparative clause element corresponding to the comp-element in the matrix clause can occur only when the standards of comparison in the two clauses are different, two scales then being compared: *Mary is cleverer than Jane is pretty*. Further structural gaps arise through the optional ellipsis of other elements in the comparative clause, as discussed in 15.66*ff*.

More and the inflectional variant in *-er* are the typical COMPARATIVE ITEMS within comp-elements. We therefore use them to exemplify comparative constructions in the sections that follow.

Note [**a**] Constructions with *more . . . than* and *less . . . than* do not necessarily introduce comparative clauses. There is a type of nonclausal comparison in which *than* is followed by an explicit standard or yardstick of comparison, normally a noun phrase of measure, or a noun phrase implying degree:

I weigh *more than 200 pounds*.
It goes *faster than 100 miles per hour*.
The strike was nothing *less than a national catastrophe*.

Here *than* is best considered a preposition, and the phrase which follows it a prepositional complement, since there is no possibility of expanding the *than*-phrase into a clause:

*It goes *faster than 100 miles per hour goes*.

[**b**] There is a second type of *more . . . than* construction not introducing a comparative clause. This is the quasi-coordinative type of construction illustrated by:

{I was *more* angry *than frightened*. / I was angry *more than frightened*.} ['It is more true to say that I was . . .']

A distinguishing characteristic of this construction is the nonoccurrence of the suffixal form of comparison:

*I was angrier than frightened.

[c] The negative comparative clauses *more often than not* and *more likely than not*, with the pro-clause *not*, are idioms that occur quite frequently:

He was found out *more often than not*. ['More often than he was not found out.']
She was satisfied with her job *more likely than not*.

It is sometimes preposed:

More likely than not, she was satisfied with her job.

Otherwise negative comparative clauses are rare, because we have little occasion to use them.

Clause functions of the comp-element

15.65 Like the *wh*-element of a *wh*-question (*cf* 11.15), the comp-element of a comparative construction can be any of the clause elements, apart from the verb:

S: *More people* use this brand than (use) any other window-cleaning fluid.
O_d: She knows *more history* than most people (know).
My grandparents gave me *more money* than my parents (did).
O_i: That toy has given *more children* happiness than any other (toy) (has).
C_s: Lionel is *more relaxed* than he used to be.
C_o: She thinks her children *more obedient* than (they were) last year.
A: You've been working *much harder* than I (have).
Ann treats the children *more harshly* than George (does).

The comp-element may also be a prepositional complement:

She's applied for *more jobs* than Joyce (has (applied for)).

Like *wh*-elements of various kinds (*cf* 11.18), the comp-element may represent a pushdown element within a nominal *that*-clause subordinate to the comparative clause:

Derek caught *more fish* than I expected ((that) he would (catch)).
She is *better* than she thinks ((that) she is).
I felt *more miserable* than I can say ((that) I felt).

or within a subordinate *to*-infinitive clause:

You arrived *earlier* than (it was) necessary (for you to arrive).

Ellipsis in comparative clauses

15.66 Ellipsis of a part of the comparative clause is likely to occur when that part is a repetition of something in the matrix clause. Since it is normal for the two clauses to be closely parallel both in structure and content, ellipsis is the rule rather than the exception in comparative constructions. However, there is no necessary parallelism between the matrix and comparative clauses; the comparative clause, so long as it overlaps with the content of the matrix clause in respect of the comp-element, can be of independent structure. Thus we may take two *how*-questions of disparate clause types (*SV* and *SVO*) in [1] and [2] and use them to construct the comparative construction in [3]:

How quickly does he speak? [1]

How quickly can his secretary take dictation? [2]
He speaks more quickly than his secretary can take dictation. [3]

The most characteristic type of comparative clause, on the other hand, is one which imitates the structure of the matrix clause, and repeats its whole content except for one element, the differing elements providing the contrast. This type of clause, as we see below, allows optional ellipsis and optional substitutions by pronouns and by pro-predication:

James and Susan often go to plays but
(i) James enjoys the theatre more than Susan enjoys the theatre.
(ii) James enjoys the theatre more than Susan enjoys it.
(iii) James enjoys the theatre more than Susan does.
(iv) James enjoys the theatre more than Susan.
(v) James enjoys the theatre more.

Ellipsis of the object generally cannot take place unless the main verb too is ellipted, as in (iii) and (iv), where there is a choice between the retention of an operator and its omission:

*James enjoys the theatre more than Susan enjoys.

But if the object is the comp-element itself, then in addition to (i–v) the verb alone may be retained:

James knows more about the theatre than Susan *knows*.

Compare also the corresponding pseudo-cleft construction:

What James knows about the theatre is more than Susan knows.

The subject is omitted in the comparative clause below:

You spent more money *than was intended to be spent*.

The omission suggests that *than* is functioning like a relative pronoun. Compare:

You spent the money *that was intended*.

Cf also *as is common knowledge*, 15.55.

Note [**a**] Infinitive clauses with a pushdown element (*cf* 11.18) can be ellipted fully or alternatively only the infinitive verb and what follows it can be ellipted, leaving a stranded *to* (*cf* 12.64):

She enjoyed it much more than I expected (her to (enjoy it)).
They did more than we made them (do).

The verb *be* alone, however, cannot be so easily ellipted in this context:

She was more beautiful than I imagined her *to be*.
[also: than I imagined *or* than I imagined her]
They wanted to be more playful than I let them *be*.

[**b**] *Different than* is a widely acceptable (esp AmE) sequence when a clause (particularly an elliptical clause) follows:

Schools are different than they used to be.
They are playing in a very different way than (they played) before.

There are, however, widespread objections to *different than* when only a noun phrase follows, on the grounds that *than* is inappropriate in contexts where it can be viewed as a preposition:

?Films are very different than plays.

Different from is the preferred form. *Cf* further 16.74.

Ambiguity through ellipsis

15.67 When normal ellipsis is taken to its fullest extent, we are often left with no more than the subject or object of the comparative clause:

> I speak Greek better than *you* (speak Greek).
> The photographs disappointed my parents more than (they disappointed) *me*.

Ambiguity can arise as to whether a remaining noun phrase is subject or object:

> He loves his dog more than his children.

The above example could mean either [1] '. . . than his children love his dog' or [2] '. . . than he loves his children'. If *his children* is replaced by a pronoun, formal English makes the distinction:

> He loves his dog more than *they*. [1]
> He loves his dog more than *them*. [2]

In other styles, however, the objective case *them* is used for both [1] and [2]. Prescriptive grammar requires the subjective case in [1], both on grammatical grounds (that *they* is the subject of the elliptical clause) and on grounds of clarity, since it preserves a useful distinction that can occasionally avoid potential ambiguity. On the other hand, we may account for the use of the objective pronoun for [1] in other styles by pointing out that as *than* in this construction may be considered a preposition (*cf* 15.64 Note [a]), the pronoun falls within object territory (*cf* 6.5). Since both forms can be criticized (on account of stiffness on the one hand, and 'bad grammar' on the other), and since in any event we cannot be sure that the objective case in [2] represents choice in formal style and is therefore unambiguous, we may wish to evade a choice by expanding the clause (*than they do*; *than he does them*).

Multiple and partial contrasts

15.68 If the two clauses in a comparison differed solely in the comp-element (**I hear it more clearly than I hear it*), the comparison would of course be nonsensical; therefore, a contrast of at least one variable is required between the two clauses. While the single-variable comparison is the most common type, more than one clause element can be contrasted. For example, there are two contrasts in:

> *James*[1] knows more about *films*[2] than *Susan*[1] does about *music*[2].

Even three-variable and four-variable comparisons are possible:

> *Walter*[1] *played*[2] *the piano*[3] more skilfully than *his brother*[1] *conducted*[2] *the orchestra*[3].

> *Walter*[1] *played*[2] *the piano*[3] more often in *Chicago*[4] than *his brother*[1] *conducted*[2] *concerts*[3] in *the rest of the States*[4].

On the other hand, the contrast may affect only part of a clause element. For example, the verbs may be lexically identical and differ only in tense or in the addition of a modal auxiliary. In such cases it is normal to omit the rest of the comparative clause after the auxiliary:

I hear it more clearly than I *did*. ['than I used to hear it']
I get up later than I *should*. ['than I should get up']

If the contrast lies only in tense, it may be expressed in the comparative clause solely by an adverbial:

She'll enjoy it more than (she enjoyed it) last year.

This provides the basis for the total ellipsis of the subordinate clause in examples like:

You are slimmer (than you were).
You're looking better (than you were (looking)).

The only contrast may be in the modality expressed in the main clause or through a pushdown comp-element in the comparative clause (*cf* 15.65):

He's a greater painter than people suppose (he is).
She thinks she's fatter than she (really) is.

The comp-element itself may contain a partial contrast without the pushdown device:

She is a *better psychologist* than ((she is) a) *pathologist*.
The house is *much taller* than it is *wide*.

When the contrast involves two points on the same scale, one higher than the other, the part following *than* cannot be expanded into a clause. *Than* is then functioning as a preposition in a nonclausal comparison (*cf* 15.64 Note [a]):

It's hotter than just warm. (*cf* It's hotter than 90°.)
He's taller than tall.
She's wiser than merely clever.
She became prettier than just middling pretty.
We drove farther than (beyond) Chicago.
They fought harder than that.
We have to build it stronger than this.

When the contrasts are not on precisely the same semantic scale, the construction is comparative and can be expanded:

He's more shrewd than (he is) clever.

(*He's more shrewd than clever* can also be the quasi-coordinative type, 'He's shrewd rather than clever', *cf* 15.64 Note [b]).

It is perhaps the existence of this nonclausal comparison of degree that makes it necessary to repeat the subject and verb in sentences such as *The house is much taller that it is wide*, since **The house is much taller than wide* would suggest the absurdity of a semantic overlap between *tall* and *wide*. The quasi-coordinative type, however, allows semantic disparity: *It's a big house, but more tall than wide* ['tall rather than wide'].

Note [**a**] There is a restriction on the partial contrast in the verb element. It is acceptable to say:

I stared at her more often than I { *should* (*have*). / *should have done*. ⟨BrE⟩ }

But it is odd to use the simple present or future *shall/will* alone as the partial contrast in the comparative clause:

*I liked her better than I *do*.

*Tom saw Betty more often than he *will*.

We need to add a temporal adverbial to point the contrast:

I liked her better than I *do now*.

Tom saw Betty more often than he *will in the future*.

[**b**] Analogous to the nonclausal comparison exemplified in *It's hotter than just warm* is another type of nonclausal comparison expressed by *more than* followed by one of a range of syntactic units:

I am *more than happy* to hear that.

He *more than complained*; he threw the whole book of rules at me.

They were *more than slightly wounded*.

She behaved *more than fairly* to him.

Semantically, *more than* expresses a higher degree, but it also conveys a comment on the inadequacy of the linguistic expression. For example, the last sentence could be rephrased '*Fairly* is an inadequate word to describe the way she behaved to him'.

[**c**] The contrast between the two clauses is, exceptionally, positive versus negative in the idioms *more often than not* and *more likely than not* (*cf* 15.64 Note [c]).

[**d**] There are two other contexts in which the comparative clause is omitted. One is where there is anaphoric reference to an implied or actual preceding clause or sentence:

I caught the bus from town; but Harry came home even *later*. [*ie* 'later than I came home']

The other is where the reference is to the extralinguistic situation:

You should have come home *earlier*. [*ie* 'earlier than you did']

Functions of comparative *more*

15.69 The comparative item (which, for present purposes, we identify with the word *more*) may have seven different functions within the comp-element:

(i) determinative (*cf* 5.10*ff*):
Isabelle has *more books* than her brother (has).

(ii) head of a noun phrase:
More (*of my friends*) are in New York than (are) here.

(iii) subjunct (*cf* 8.88*ff*):
I agree with you *more* than ((I agree) with) Robert.

(iv) modifier of an adjective head:
The article was *more objective* than I expected (it would be).

(v) modifier of a premodifying adjective:
It was a *more heated discussion* than we thought it would be.

(vi) modifier of an adverb:
The time passed *more quickly* than (it passed) last year.

(vii) modifier of a premodifying adverb:
I am *more severely handicapped* than you (are).

In each of the above examples, the whole comp-element is in italics. It will be noticed that in some cases *more* can constitute the whole of the comp-element. *More* is a determiner in (i), a pronoun in (ii), and an adverb in all the others.

In functions (i) and (ii), *more* refers to quantity and can be replaced in count contexts by *a greater number of*, as in the first two sentences above, and in noncount contexts by *a greater amount of*.

Function types (iv) and (v) have to be distinguished because of the semantic implications of (v). Consider:

There are more intelligent monkeys than Herbert. [1]

In [1] we normally imply that Herbert is a monkey of a certain level of intelligence (*cf*: *How intelligent a monkey is Herbert?*). That is, by placing the comparative adjective before the noun, we imply that the noun is part of the comp-element and therefore is also implied in the comparative clause. On the other hand, by placing the comparative adjective after the noun, we readily admit the more plausible interpretation that Herbert is a man:

There are monkeys more intelligent than Herbert.

This difference of meaning accounts for the insult implied in:

I've never met a more intelligent monkey than our Chairman.

The same distinction applies to the difference between (vi) and (vii):

I've never seen a dog more obviously friendly than your cat.
*I've never seen a more obviously friendly dog than your cat.

This last sentence is semantically unacceptable because it implies that the dog is a cat.

The normal position for the adjective phrase is shown in the example for (v), but it can also be preposed [2], or (less usually) postposed [2a]:

It was *more heated* a discussion than we thought it would be. [2]
It was a discussion *more lively* than we thought it would be. [2a]

The adverb phrase in (vii) can also be postposed:

I am handicapped *more severely* than you (are).

Note [**a**] In its determinative function in (i) or as modifier of an adjective in (iv), *more* is the comparative of the quantifiers *many* or *much*. Thus, *more expensive clothes* is ambiguous in:

Morton has more expensive clothes than I have.

In one interpretation *more* modifies *expensive*, the adjective phrase then being comparative; in the other interpretation *more* determines the noun phrase ('a greater quantity of expensive clothes').

[**b**] The modifying sequences *more of a* . . . and *less of a* . . . occur with gradable singular or noncount noun heads:

He's more of a fool than I thought (he was).
It was less of a success than I imagined (it would be).

Cf the *how*-question, *How much of a fool is he?* ['To what an extent is he (in your view) a fool?']

[**c**] The comparative items *more*, *-er*, and *less* cannot be used in a definite noun phrase in the comparative construction:

*Sally has *the* better radio than Daniel (has).

Contrast:

Sally has *the* better radio (of the two).

In certain contexts we can use *compared with* or *relative to* instead:

The superior reception of Sally's radio accounts for *its* higher price tag *compared with* that for Daniel's radio.

Contrast:

Sally's radio has a higher price tag than Daniel's (radio) (has).

[**d**] The determiner *other* is used as a comparative item:

I don't have any *other cups* than those ((that/which) I have) in the sink.

It can be (less usually) postposed:

I don't have *cups other* than those ((that/which) I have) in the sink.

15.70 When *more* is a determinative or a head of a noun phrase – functions (i) and (ii) in 15.69 – the unit *no more* (. . .) *than* is synonymous with *only as many* (. . .) *as* in countable contexts or with *only as much* (. . .) *as* in noncountable contexts:

Paul has no more friends than I have. [' . . . only as many as . . .']
I have no more money than you have. [' . . . only as much as . . .']
Ted got no more (of the votes) than he needed. [' . . . only as many as . . .']
She said no more than we expected. [' . . . only as much as . . .']

But when *more* is an adverb (or its inflectional variant *-er* is used), as in the other function types in 15.69, *no more . . . than* has special implications. Consider:

Rachel is no more courageous than Saul (is).

The sentence implies that both Rachel and Saul are not courageous ('Rachel is not courageous, any more than Saul is courageous'). Here are some further examples:

Tom is no more athletic than he ever was. ['Tom is not athletic, any more than he ever was athletic.']
I can no more apologize than I could kneel to them.
I would no more think of hitting a student than I would a policeman.

No more . . . than has the same meaning when *more* modifies a gradable noun:

She is no more a fool than you (are). ['She is not a fool, any more than you are', 'She is not more foolish . . .']
They are no more scholars than my baby (is). ['They are no more scholarly . . .']

The rhetorical effect of the construction is not so much to make a comparison as to intensify the negation. That effect is most obvious when the comparison is absurd (*cf* rhetorical *if*-clauses, 15.37):

He's no more your friend than I'm your mother.

Not any more (. . .) *than* is an emphatic variant of *no more . . . than*:

Paul hasn't any more friends than I have. ['only as many as . . .']
Rachel isn't any more courageous than Saul (is). ['Rachel isn't courageous, any more than . . .']

Not more . . . than, on the other hand, is different from both *no more . . . than* and *not any more . . . than* when *more* is an adverb or modifies a gradable noun:

Rachel is not more courageous than Saul (is).

This last sentence allows for the possibility that Rachel is less courageous than Saul. It may also be merely a denial sentence in response to *Rachel is more courageous than Saul* (*is*).

Similar distinctions apply to *no less* (. . .) *than, not any less* (. . .) *than*, and *not less* (. . .) *than*, except that the double negative is less common and as a consequence the distinctions are somewhat blurred.

Comparisons of equivalence: *as . . . as*

15.71 Broadening our discussion of comparison, we take into account not only comparisons of nonequivalence (lack of equivalence on some scale) such as those expressed by *more* and *less*, but also comparisons based on other relationships. One such relationship is that of equivalence, expressed principally by the correlatives *as . . . as*.

The *as . . . as* construction is grammatically parallel to the *more . . . than* construction, except that the *as*-paradigm lacks the determinative, pronoun, and subjunct functions of *more*; these gaps are filled by *as many* (count) and *as much* (noncount). We can therefore parallel the functions of *more* listed in 15.69, substituting *as many* and *as much* where necessary:

(i) determinative: Isabelle has *as many books* as her brother (has).
(ii) head of a noun phrase: *As many of my friends* are in New York as (are) here.
(iii) subjunct: I agree with you *as much* as ((I agree) with) Robert.
(iv) modifier of an adjective head: The article was *as objective* as I expected (it would be).
(v) modifier of a premodifying adjective: It was *as lively a discussion* as we thought it would be.
(vi) modifier of an adverb: The time passed *as quickly* as (it passed) last year.
(vii) modifier of a premodifying adverb: I am *as severely handicapped* as you (are).

The reason for differentiating (iv) and (v) and also (vi) and (vii) are the same as in the *more . . . than* construction (*cf* 15.69). Contrast *I've never seen a dog as friendly as your cat* with the unacceptable **I've never seen as friendly a dog as your cat*.

Notice that the adjective phrase precedes the determiner in (v). The phrase can also be postposed (*cf* 15.69):

It was a discussion *as lively as* we thought it would be.

The adverb phrase in (vii) can also be postposed:

I am handicapped *as severely as* you (are).

There are parallels between a positive *as . . . as* sentence and negative *more . . . than* and *less . . . than* sentences:

Caesar was *as* ruthless *as* Attila. [1]
Attila was *not more* ruthless *than* Caesar. [2]
Caesar was *not less* ruthless *than* Attila. [3]

But they are not exactly synonymous, since [2] allows the possibility that Attila was less ruthless and [3] that he was more ruthless. Similar parallels exist between a negative *as . . . as* sentence and positive *more . . . than* and *less . . . than* sentences, but the negative *as . . . as* sentence (*eg*: *Caesar was not as ruthless as Attila*) encourages the interpretation of *less . . . than*, though a heavy stress on the first *as* allows the interpretation of *more . . . than* (*eg*: *Caesar was not as ruthless as Attila*; *indeed, he was more ruthless*).

In negative superordinate clauses, *as . . . as* can be replaced by *so . . . as*, especially when there is total or considerable omission in the subordinate clause:

He's not as naughty as he was.
He's not so naughty as he was.
He's not so naughty (now).

Some prefer to use *so . . . as* with negative clauses. But for some people *so* tends to carry the absurd implication of a possibility that is then negated, and they therefore find it odd to say:

(?)Her baby is not so old as I thought.

The reason is that for them the sentence implies that a baby can be old. In other words, an unmarked term *old* (*cf* 7.88) cannot be used in this context to cover the whole scale.

The first *as* in the *as . . . as* construction is sometimes omitted in two contexts: (a) after a copular verb; (b) where a copular verb is implied.

(a) The omission of *as* tends to occur particularly in more informal style, especially if only a noun phrase follows. The single *as* provides a less emphatic comparison and is closer to *like* when *as* is followed by a noun phrase:

They were good *as* gold while you were away.
At the sight, she turned pale *as* a ghost.
You look pretty *as* ever.

In informal speech the subject complement may be fronted as in [4], or it may be initial because the subject and copula are ellipted, as in [5]:

White *as* snow, it was. [4]
Proud *as* ever, isn't he? [5]

(b) In a rather literary style, the first *as* may be omitted in verbless and subjectless supplementive clauses:

Lawson, *implacable as ever*, contented himself with a glare of defiance. [6]
Cautious as the rest of her family, she would not give an immediate reply to my question. [7]
He climbed over the wall and dropped onto the ground on the other side, *agile as a cat*. [8]

The addition of a verb (where that is possible) would convert the clause into a finite concessive or circumstantial clause with fronting of the subject complement (*cf* 15.39, 15.47):

Cautious as the rest of the family was, she seemed willing to give an immediate reply to my question.

Note [**a**] Count *as many* (. . .) *as* and noncount *as much* (. . .) *as* are equivalent to *more* (. . .) *than* when they are premodified by a *times*-phrase:

= { *Five times as many people* came to the demonstration *as* (did) last time.
Five times more people came to the demonstration *than* (did) last time. }

= { I paid *three times as much* for the meal *as* they did.
I paid *three times more* for the meal *than* they did. }

Other lexical comparatives can also be used:

= { The Gross National Product is *four times as much/high as* (it was) a decade ago.
The Gross National Product is *four times more/higher than* (it was) a decade ago. }

Twice is used with *as many as* or *as much as* rather than with *more*.

Fractions are also used in the *as many* (. . .) *as* and *as much* (. . .) *as* constructions:

We have *a third as many students* in our class *as* we had last term. ['a third of the number']
I paid *half as much* for the meal *as* they did. ['half the price']

When *again* is added, the meaning is equivalent to *more* (. . .) *than*:

= { Houses cost *a third as much again* this year *as* they did five years ago.
['The price is one third higher.']
Houses cost *one third more* this year *than* they did five years ago.
['Houses cost a third more.'] }

= { There were *a third as many arrests again* for assault this year *as* there were last year.
There were *a third more arrests* for assault this year *than* there were last year. }

But there is uncertainty and divided usage with the constructions when *again* is added. Some speakers find percentages odd in these constructions:

They cost { *50 per cent as much* / *?50 per cent as much again* } as last year.

[**b**] The construction analogous to *more of a . . . than* (*cf* 15.69 Note [b]) is *as much of . . . as*:

It was *as much of a success as* I had imagined it would be.
He's *as much of a fool as* I thought (he was).

Analogous to *less of a . . . than* is *as little of a . . . as*:

It was *as little of a success as* I had imagined it would be.

There are no such constructions for plural nouns.

[**c**] *As . . . as* is used like *more . . . than* and *less . . . than* in a nonclausal comparison containing an explicit standard of comparison after the second *as* (*cf* 15.64 Note [a]):

The car goes as fast as 100 miles an hour.
A reliable quartz watch can cost as little as ten dollars.
He drinks as many as three bottles of milk a day.
Our factory consumes as much as 500 tons of solid fuel per week.

Comparisons of sufficiency and excess

15.72 Comparative clauses of sufficiency and excess combine the notions of sufficiency or excess with the notions of purpose (*cf* 15.48) or result (*cf* 15.49). They differ from comparative clauses of nonequivalence and equivalence (*cf* 15.63*ff*) in that they do not match the matrix clause in terms of identical and contrasting elements, and therefore they do not lend themselves to ellipsis. Their structure is relatively independent of the structure of the matrix clause.

Enough* and *too

15.73 One type of comparative construction contains a word or phrase expressing the notion of sufficiency or excess followed by a *to*-infinitive clause of purpose, result, or condition (*cf* 15.34 Note [g]). The most common word for sufficiency is *enough* (as adverb, determiner, or pronoun) and the most common word for excess is the adverb *too*. Here are some examples of this type of comparison:

You're old *enough to look after yourself*. ['. . . so that you can look after yourself.']
I'm *much too* tired *to go out*. ['. . . with the result that I won't go out.']
Your teacher was *excessively* generous *to give you an A*. ['. . . if he gave you an A.']
They must be *pretty* cruel *to do that*. ['. . . if they do that.']
They worked *enough to be hungry*.
He protested *too much to be sincere*.
This coat is just the *right* length *to fit you*.
There was *enough* food *to feed an army*.
She knows *enough* about the topic *to explain it to you*.
Four thousand dollars is an *excessive* amount *to charge even for a luxury cruise like this*.
There isn't *sufficient* milk *to give everybody some*.

Paraphrase pairs may be constructed with antonymous items, in which one sentence is positive and the other negative; one sentence has *enough* or one of its synonyms, and the other *too* or one of its synonyms:

= { They're rich enough to own a car.
They're not too poor to own a car. }

= { The book is sufficiently simple to understand. <formal>
The book is not excessively difficult to understand. <formal> }

If the context allows, the infinitive clause may be omitted. *Sufficient*(*ly*) and *excessive*(*ly*) are more formal synonyms of *enough* and *too*.

The negative force of *too* is shown in the use of nonassertive forms (*cf* 10.60*f*). Contrast:

She's *old enough* to do *some* work. ['She is old enough so that she can do some work.']
She's *too old* to do *any* work. ['She is so old that she can't do any work.']

Here are further examples of *too* followed by nonassertive forms:

He's *too weak* to help you *at all*.
She's *too polite* to *ever* say *anything* like that.

The infinitive clause may also contain a subject:

It moves too quickly *for most people to see* (*it*).
The television in the apartment above was loud enough *for us to hear* (*it*).
My ambitions are modest enough *for me to fulfil* (*them*).
He was old enough *for us to talk to* (*him*) *seriously*.

Her parents are sufficiently generous *for her to take a long vacation abroad at their expense.*

As the first four of these examples indicate, a direct object or the object of a prepositional verb in a *to*-infinitive clause may be omitted or retained if it substitutes for the superordinate subject. When there is no subject in the infinitive clause, it is identified with the superordinate subject or with an indefinite subject:

She writes quickly enough *to finish the paper on time.* ['for her to finish the paper on time']
The knife is sharp enough *to carve the turkey.* ['for it to carve the turkey']

And there may be ambiguity as to which identification to make:

She was too young *to date.* ['. . . to date others' or 'for others to date her']

When the subject of the superordinate clause is agentive (*cf* 10.19), it may be redundantly repeated:

She writes quickly enough *for her to finish the paper on time.*
She's too polite *for her to ever say anything like that.*

A: Will John lend me money?
B: John's much too mean *for HǏM to lend you money.*

That optional redundancy (sometimes justifiable for emphasis) parallels the optional redundancy that we have just observed for a direct object or prepositional object. The infinitive may be passive in form:

The writing is too faint *to be read.*

In that case the implied subject is identical with the superordinate subject and it is either the implied agent known from the situational context or previous linguistic context or it is indefinite ('to be read by *anyone*'). But the infinitive may be active without a subject or object (*cf* Note [b]):

The writing is too faint *to read.* ['for anyone to read']
The food is good enough *to eat.*

When neither subject nor object is expressed in the infinitive clause, ambiguity is possible with verbs that may be used transitively.

She is friendly enough	[(for others) (for her)]	to help	[(her). (others).]
The lamb is too hot	[(for us) (for it)]	to eat	[(it). (anything).]
He is too good a person	[(for others) (for him)]	to swindle	[(him). (others).]

As we see from the last example, when an adjective phrase modified by *too* in turn modifies a singular count noun, the phrase precedes the indefinite article (*cf* 15.71: *as lively a discussion as . . .*). There is no plural or noncount equivalent for this construction. Instead, we have to postpose the adjective phrase: *It's food too good to throw away*; *They are persons too good to swindle.*

The same problem does not arise with *enough*, which is usually a postmodifier; but *enough* usually premodifies when it is a determinative: *We have enough money to last.*

Note [**a**] There is a threefold ambiguity in *It's too hot to eat*. Two of the meanings have been illustrated above: *The lamb is too hot* (*for it to eat* (*anything*)) and *The lamb is too hot* (*for us/me/anyone*) *to eat* (*it*). In the third meaning *it* is the prop-*it* used as a subject to refer to the weather. Both a subject and a direct object can then be supplied: *It is too hot* (*for anyone*) *to eat* (*anything*).

[**b**] Traditionally, grammarians have regarded the infinitive clause in *The writing is too faint to read* as having a passive meaning ('to be read'), but we analyse it as having an unexpressed subject and object ('for anyone to read the writing').

[**c**] The constructions *enough of a* . . . and *too much of a* . . . should be compared with those mentioned in 15.69 Note [b] and 15.71 Note [b] (*eg*: *more of a* . . . *than* and *as much of a* . . . *as*):

He's enough of a coward to do that.
That's too much of a bother to think about.

Cf also: *He was fool enough to go out without a coat.*

So . . . (that)* and *such . . . (that)

15.74 The pairs of correlatives *so* . . . (*that*) and *such* . . . (*that*) also introduce constructions that combine the notion of sufficiency or excess with the notion of result. The adverb *so* premodifies an adjective or adverb, whereas the predeterminer *such* precedes a noun phrase. The adjective premodified by *so* may itself premodify the head of a noun phrase. For both *so* and *such*, the noun phrase may have either the indefinite article or the zero article. *So* precedes the indefinite article together with the adjective it premodifies, but *such* (whose noun phrase need not have an adjective) does so alone.

I'm *so* happy to hear your good news *that* I could kiss you.
They walked *so* quickly *that* I couldn't catch up.
So few (people) came to the meeting *that* it was adjourned.
The children had *so* good a time *that* they wouldn't leave.
The soldiers encountered *such* (great) resistance *that* they retreated.
The apartment has *such* a (beautiful) view *that* I intend to rent it.

The correlative *that* is sometimes omitted in informal style:

He polished the floor *so hard you could see your face in it*.

There is a close correspondence between *so* . . . *that* and *such* . . . *that* constructions, when the *that*-clause is negative, and constructions with *too* and an infinitive clause:

It's *so* good a movie *that* we mustn't miss it.
~ It's *too* good a movie *to* miss.
It was *such* a pleasant day *that* I didn't want to go to school.
~ It was *too* pleasant a day *to* go to school.

There may also be a close correspondence between on the one hand *so* . . . *that* and *such* . . . *that* constructions, when the *that*-clause is positive, and on the other hand constructions with *enough* and an infinitive clause:

It flies *so* fast *that* it can beat the speed record.
~ It flies fast *enough to* beat the speed record.
I had *such* a bad headache *that* I needed two aspirins.
~ I had a bad *enough* headache *to* need two aspirins.

But the correspondence often does not obtain, since *so* and *such* are not used with adjectives and adverbs in their unmarked sense (*cf* 7.88); they indicate a high degree. Thus, the *enough*-construction cannot replace the *so . . . that* and *such . . . that* constructions in the following contexts:

The lion was *so tame that* the lionkeeper could enter its cage. [1]
The lion was *tame enough* for the lionkeeper *to* enter its cage. [2]
It was *such a clear* introductory lecture *that* we decided to take the course. [3]
It was a *clear enough* introductory lecture for us *to* decide to take the course. [4]

While [1] asserts that the lion was very tame, [2] does not; and similarly [3] asserts that the lecture was very clear but [4] does not.

So expresses a high degree when used alone with a verb, and *such* does the same when its noun phrase does not contain an adjective premodifier:

I *so* enjoyed it *that* I'm determined to go again.
['I so much enjoyed it . . .']
There was *such* a crowd *that* we couldn't see a thing.
['There was such a large crowd . . .']

Compare exclamatory *how* and *what*: *How I enjoyed it!*, *What a crowd there was!* In a more formal variant, *so* and *such* may be positioned before correlative *that*; an intonation break (or in writing, a comma) is normal before *that*:

I enjoyed it *so, that* I'm determined to go again.
The crowd was *such, that* we couldn't see a thing.

Such can be positioned here only if the sentence is rephrased to make it follow a copular verb. It also differs here from *so* in that it identifies ('of that type') and does not intensify (*cf* also 15.49 Note [b]).

In another variant, found in informal style, the *that*-clause is positioned first, but *that* is omitted:

I couldn't keep my eyes open, I was *so* tired. [5]

The first clause is semantically and intonationally subordinate, but it is preferable to regard the construction as paratactic. Compare:

I was *so* tired, *I couldn't keep my eyes open.* [5a]

In a more formal variation of [5] the element containing *so* is fronted; subject–operator inversion is usual:

He had no need to make speeches, *so impregnable was his position.* [6]
She was exhausted by four, *so hard had she worked.* [7]

Another informal variant (with regional restriction) of [5] substitutes intensifier *that* for *so*:

I was ˈ*that* tired *I couldn't keep my eyes open.* [5b]

But intensifier *that* is more common without the correlative clause:

Why should you be (all) *that* tired in the morning? [8]

Note [**a**] In a formal and somewhat archaic usage, the subordinate clause in a *such* . . . *as* construction is finite:

They were fed *such* sumptuous fare *as kings dream of.*

The paraphrase of *such* . . . *as* by 'of a kind which' suggests that these clauses are relative rather than comparative. Less restricted is *so* . . . *as* with the infinitive:

His temper was *so* violent *as to make even his closest companions fear him.*

[**b**] In formal (especially literary) style, the comp-element is sometimes fronted, accompanied by subject–operator inversion:

To such lengths did she go in rehearsal that two actors walked out.

[**c**] In philosophical exposition, *such that* is often used, *such* here being identifying:

If there is a four-sided figure *such that* three of its angles are 90°, the remaining angle will also be 90°.

Syntactic function of comparative clauses

15.75 There are two major analyses for the syntactic function of the comparative clause in comparisons of nonequivalence (*more*/*-er*/*less* (. . .) *than*) and of equivalence (*as* . . . *as*). One traditional analysis is presupposed in our use of the term comp-element – the comp-element on its own is a clause element and the comparative clause is an adverbial:

S V C_s A

John is [more intelligent] [than Bill is.]

One argument in favour of this analysis is that in inflected comparative adjectives or adverbs (*eg*: *longer*, *faster*) the comp-element is morphologically one word. But morphological and syntactic units do not necessarily coincide; otherwise, for example, we would need to give different syntactic analyses to *she's not* and *she isn't*. Closer parallels might be the syntactic function of the genitive inflection in the group genitive (*eg*: *the President of Mexico's daughter, cf* 17.119) and of the inflections in the structure of the verb phrase that exhibit morphological discontinuities to express aspectual and voice categories (*eg*: the discontinuous combination of *be* and *-ing* to express progressive aspect in *She's running*).

An alternative, and better, analysis is to regard the comparative clause together with the preceding comparative item (including instances where that item is the inflection *-er*) as a degree modifier, even though it is commonly a discontinuous modifier:

John is *more* intelligent *than Bill* (*is*).
Susan spoke long*er than I expected* (*she would* (*speak*)).
There was *less* noise *than* (*there was*) *yesterday*.
Helen is *as* energetic *as Tom* (*is*).

The comparative clause then provides complementation for the comparative *more* or the inflection *-er*. The modifier is sometimes postposed, and is then continuous:

John is intelligent, { *more* (*so*) *than* / *as much* (*so*) *as* } *Bill* (*is*).

This construction is possible even for an adjective or adverb that is normally inflected, but in that case *more* replaces the inflection:

John looks good, *more* (*so*) *than Ted* (*does*).

In this second analysis, neither the comp-element nor the comparative clause are clause elements. See *Figs* 15.75a and 15.75b:

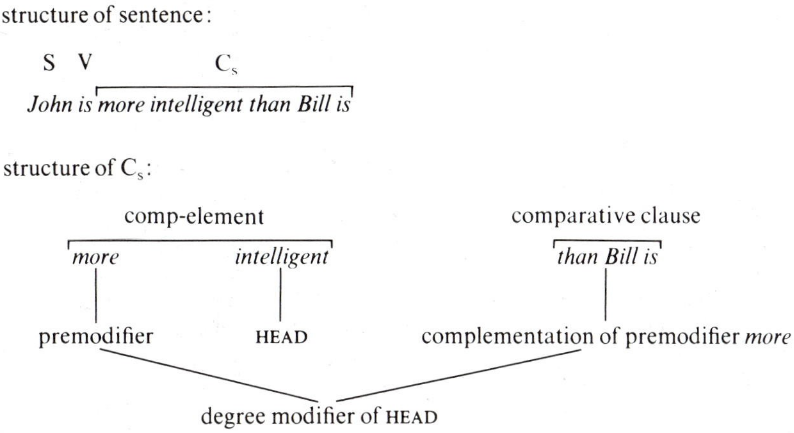

Fig 15.75a Comparative construction with *more*

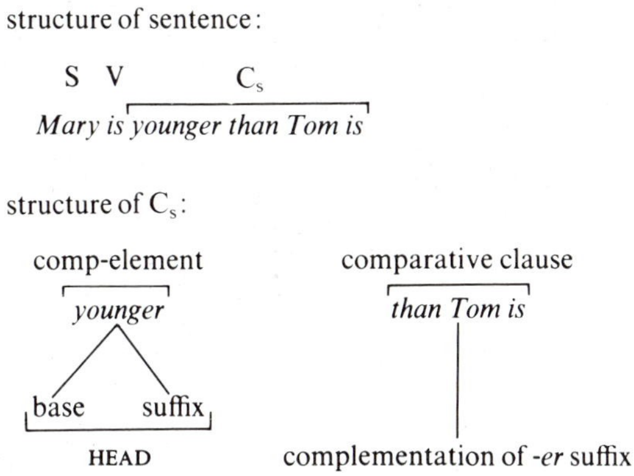

Fig 15.75b Comparative constructon with *-er* suffix

The comparative clause is usually separated from the comp-element when the comp-element is the subject:

> *More fatal accidents* occur in the home *than on the roads*.

But such a separation of premodification and noun head from postmodification is not unusual when a long noun phrase is subject (*cf* 18.39*f*):

> [*More* / *Many*] *difficult questions* were posed [*than* / *that*] *were convincingly answered by the panel of experts*.

On the other hand, in comparisons of sufficiency and excess (*cf* 15.72*ff*) the comparative clauses are more appropriately analysed as adverbials, since those clauses can properly be identified with adverbial clauses of purpose or result (*cf* 15.48*f*). Their restriction to final position is easily explained:

adverbial clauses of result are always positioned finally; adverbial clauses of purpose, though normally mobile, are restricted to final position in these comparative constructions because they are linked to a first correlative (*eg*: *as*, *too*).

Bibliographical note

On nominal clauses in general, see especially Aijmer (1972); Huddleston (1971), Chapters 4 and 5; Kiparsky and Kiparsky (1970); Lees (1960a); Stockwell et al (1973), Chapter 8; Vendler (1968). On *that*-clauses in particular, see Behre (1955); Elsness (1982); Hooper (1975); Storms (1966). On other specialized topics, see Jacobsson (1971); Kjellmer (1980); Luelsdorff and Norrick (1979); Thompson (1973).

On adverbial clauses of time in general, see especially Edgren (1971). On more specialized topics, see Aarts (1979); Declerck (1979); Heinämäki (1978); Karttunen (1974); Mittwoch (1980).

On adverbial clauses of condition and concession, see Geis (1973); Haegeman (1984; forthcoming a); Haegeman and Wekker (1984); Haiman (1974); Kjellmer (1975b); Morreall (1980); Yamanashi (1973).

On clauses of reason, see Altenberg (1984), which is the source of the data in *Table* 15.47, and Heinämäki (1975).

On comment clauses, see Emonds (1973); Lakoff, G. (1974); Mittwoch (1979).

On clauses introduced by *instead of* or *rather than*, see Dietrich and Napoli (1982); Jacobsson (1977a); Thompson (1972).

On adverbial *-ing* clauses, see Greenbaum (1973b).

On comparative clauses, see especially Huddleston (1971), Chapter 6. See also Hale (1970); Huddleston (1967); Jørgensen (1980); Lees (1961); Mittwoch (1974); Rivara (1975); Smith (1961).

16 Complementation of verbs and adjectives

Introduction

16.1 In 2.32 we defined COMPLEMENTATION as 'part of a phrase or clause which follows a word, and completes the specification of a meaning relationship which that word implies'. In this chapter, we examine the ways in which lexical verbs and adjectives determine, in this way, the grammatical patterns that follow them. We began this task in 2.19, where verbs were classified into various types (transitive, intransitive, copular, etc) according to their complementation. Now we must go further, and examine patterns of greater variety. But before doing so, we must analyse the phenomenon of multi-word verbs, a topic of peculiar importance in English. This study will occupy the first seventeen sections of the chapter, as a necessary prelude to the study of verb complementation.

Multi-word verbs

Verb–particle combinations

16.2 The main category of multi-word verbs consists of such combinations as *drink up*, *dispose of*, and *get away with*, which we will study under the headings of PHRASAL VERB, PREPOSITIONAL VERB, and PHRASAL-PREPOSITIONAL VERB respectively. However, these combinations are considered multi-word verbs only where they behave as a single unit.

Since the verb has been considered a class of word (*cf* 2.35), it may seem a contradiction to speak of 'multi-word verbs'. The term 'word' is frequently used, however, not only for a morphologically defined word class, but also for an item which acts as a single word lexically or syntactically (*cf* 9.10*ff* on complex prepositions). It is this extended sense of 'verb' as a 'unit which behaves to some extent either lexically or syntactically as a single verb' that we use in labels such as 'prepositional verb'. Thus in the sentence:

We *disposed of* the problem.

the word *disposed* remains morphologically a verb, being the item which has variable inflection (*dispose*/*disposes*/*disposed*, etc); but the sequence *disposed of* also functions in various ways as a single unit, such that for some purposes the sentence can be reasonably divided into:

[We] [disposed of] [the problem].

rather than into:

[We] [disposed] [of the problem].

The words which follow the lexical verb in expressions like *drink up*, *dispose of*, and *get away with* are morphologically invariable, and will be given the neutral designation PARTICLES. They actually belong to two distinct but overlapping categories, that of prepositions and that of spatial adverbs (though such adverbs are not necessarily used with spatial meaning). The term 'particle' will therefore apply to such words as these (see the fuller lists in 9.7 and 9.66), when they follow and are closely associated with verbs.

PARTICLES

(A) *against, among, as, at, beside, for, from, into, like, of, onto, upon, with,* etc.

(B) *about, above, across, after, along, around, by, down, in, off, on, out* <AmE>, *over, past, round, through, under, up,* etc.

(C) *aback, ahead, apart, aside, astray, away, back, forward(s), home, in front, on top, out* <BrE>, *together,* etc.

(On *out* as a preposition, *cf* 9.18 Note.)

Those grouped in list (A) are prepositions only; those in (C) are spatial adverbs only (unless they form part of a complex preposition, as in *out of*); and those in (B) can be either prepositions or spatial adverbs, and in the latter function are known as 'prepositional adverbs' (*cf* 9.65*f*). List (C) includes adverbs like *away* and *on top*, which correspond to complex prepositions such as *away from* and *on top of* and so are also known as prepositional adverbs (*cf* 9.66). Thus we include particles which form the first element of a complex preposition:

Come *along* (*with* us/me). They moved *out* (*of* the house).

The most obvious difference between the prepositions and the spatial adverbs is that where prepositions require a following noun phrase as a prepositional complement, there is no such requirement for adverbs (*cf*, however, the phenomenon of deferred prepositions, 9.6). Hence Classes (A), (B), and (C) can be distinguished as follows:

	PREPOSITIONAL CONSTRUCTION	ADVERBIAL CONSTRUCTION
(A)	The dog went *for me.*	*The dog went *for.*
(B)	Jack fell *down the hill.*	Jack fell *down.*
(C)	*We must not look *back the past.*	We must not look *back.*

Particles of Class (B) are the only ones which are acceptable in both constructions.

Not all multi-word verbs consist of lexical verbs followed by particles. We shall illustrate other types, such as those of *take pride in, cut short, see fit,* or *put paid to,* in 16.7–8 and 16.17.

Note [**a**] Although the inflection of a multi-word verb is regularly attached to the lexical verb, the occurrence of 'slips of the tongue' such as the following (noted during a radio interview) deserves attention:

*The editor must do precisely as he *see fits.*

This anomalous shift of the inflection from the verb to the adjective testifies to a tendency for speakers to perceive the multi-word verb as a single grammatical unit.

[**b**] On the exceptional use of some Class (A) words as adverbs (*eg*: *to*), *cf* 9.66 Notes [a] and [b].

[**c**] The lexical verbs occurring in multi-word verbs are frequently the most common lexical verbs, and are typically associated with physical movement or state: *eg*: *come, fall, get, give, go, keep, make, put,* and *take.* At the other extreme, however, are words which occur as verbs only when combined with particles, *eg*: *beaver* in *beaver away*, *egg* in *egg on*, and *eke* in *eke out*:

She *egged* him *on.* *She *egged* (him).

Note also that some normally intransitive verbs can become transitive when combined with a particle, and that conversely some normally transitive verbs can become intransitive when combined with a particle:

They are *living* it *down.* *They are *living* it.

The plane *took off.* *The plane *took.*

Phrasal, prepositional, and phrasal–prepositional verbs

Type I (intransitive) phrasal verbs

16.3 Our procedure in 16.3–9 will be to illustrate the main categories of multi-word verbs, before the criteria for certain distinctions are considered more carefully in 16.11–16. One common type of multi-word verb is the *Type I* or intransitive phrasal verb consisting of a verb plus an adverb particle, as exemplified in:

The plane has just *touched down.*	Did he *catch on*?
He is *playing around.*	The prisoner finally *broke down.*
I hope you'll *get by.*	She *turned up* unexpectedly.
How are you *getting on*?	When will they *give in*?
The plane has now *taken off.*	The tank *blew up.*

Such phrasal verbs are usually informal. The particles above come from Class (B) in 16.2, but similar examples can be given with particles from Class (C):

> One of my papers has *gone astray.*
> The news made him *reel back.*
> The favourite *romped home.*
> The two girls have *fallen out.* [= 'quarrelled']

The particle functions like a predication adjunct or subjunct (*cf* 8.26*ff*, 8.96), and usually cannot be separated from its lexical verb:

> ?*The news made him *reel* distractedly *back.*

Although some of these are more idiomatic and cohesive than others, we will draw a distinction between such phrasal verbs, on the one hand, and FREE COMBINATIONS in which the verb and the adverb have distinct meanings on the other. In phrasal verbs like *give in* ['surrender'], *catch on* ['understand'], and *blow up* ['explode'], the meaning of the combination manifestly cannot be predicted from the meanings of verb and particle in isolation. But in free combinations the verb acts as a normal intransitive verb, and the adverb has its own meaning. For example:

> He walked *past.* [= 'past the object/place']
> I waded *across.* [= 'across the river/water/etc']

Past and *across* here are adverbs (*cf* 9.65, 16.4 Note [d]), but their function is equivalent to that of a prepositional phrase of direction. The separability of verb and adverb in terms of meaning is shown by possible substitutions: for *wade* in *wade across*, for example, we could substitute *walk, run, swim, jump, fly*, etc; and for *across* we could substitute *in, through, over, up, down*, etc. In other cases, the particle may have an intensifying or aspectual force, as in *liven up, go on*, or *chatter away.*

There are also syntactic signs of cohesion. In free combinations, it is often possible to place a modifying adverb *right* (or sometimes *straight*) between the adverb particle and the verb:

> Go *right/straight* on. Drink *right* up. Walk *straight* in.

This insertion is to differing extents unacceptable with phrasal verbs:

?The prisoner broke *right* down.
*She turned *right* up at last.

Another sign of a free combination is the possibility of placing the adverb before the verb with subject–verb inversion (or without inversion where the subject is a pronoun):

Out came the sun.
Up you *come*.
On we *drove* into the night.

But with phrasal verbs this is not possible:

**Up blew* the tank.
**Up* it *blew*. ['exploded']
**Out* he *passed*. ['fainted']

However, in this as in other criteria, there is an unclear boundary between phrasal verbs and free combinations. With *They chattered away* the inversion is very marginally acceptable: ?**Away they chattered*. Some examples are more acceptable if the particle is reduplicated according to the pattern of iterative coordination (*cf* 13.101):

On and *on* he *went* about his wife and family.

And where the phrasal verb makes metaphorical use of spatial adverbs, inversion seems quite acceptable:

Down came the prices, and *up went* the sales.
There was a gust of wind, and *out went* the light.

We examine the boundary between multi-word verbs and free combinations more generally in 16.12.

Type II (transitive) phrasal verbs

16.4 Many phrasal verbs may take a direct object, and may therefore be described as transitive. However, to simplify comparison with prepositional verbs, we will call them *Type II* phrasal verbs, as contrasted with Type I (or intransitive) phrasal verbs. Examples are:

We will *set up* a new unit.
Shall I *put away* the dishes?
Find out if they are coming.
She's *bringing up* two children.
Someone *turned on* the light.
They have *called off* the strike.
He can't *live down* his past.
I can't *make out* what he means.
We *pushed home* our advantage.
She *looked up* her friends.
I've *handed in* my registration.
They may have *blown up* the bridge.

Examples here and in 16.3 show that some combinations, such as *give in* and *blow up*, can be either Type I or Type II. In some cases, *eg*: *give in*, there is a substantial difference in meaning, and in others, *eg*: *blow up*, there is not (*cf* App I.18).

With most Type II phrasal verbs, as with free combinations of the same pattern, the particle can either precede or follow the direct object:

They *turned on* the light. They *turned* the light *on*.

Bearing in mind the adverbial status of the particle, we would indeed expect the latter order (S V O A) to be the more usual, even though it means a separation of the particle from its verb. When the object is a personal pronoun, the S V O A order is in fact the only one allowable:

*They *switched on* it. They *switched* it *on*.

The particle tends to precede the object if the object is long, or if the intention is that the object should receive end-focus (*cf* 18.3*f*).

As before, phrasal verbs have to be distinguished lexically from free syntactic combinations of verb and prepositional adverb. Contrast:

She *took in* the box.	['brought inside']	[FREE COMBINATION]
She *took in* her parents.	['deceived']	[PHRASAL VERB]

The verb and particle in *put out the cat*, for instance, preserve their separate meanings in that combination, as well as in a wide range of comparable combinations: *put + down/outside/away/aside*; *take/turn/bring/push/send/drag + out*. A highly idiomatic expression like *put off* ['postpone'] has no such variants at all, for the two words *put* and *off* are fused into a unit which allows for no substitution for the individual elements. Once again, there are unclear cases between these two extremes: some substitutions, but a limited number only, can be made in a 'semi-idiomatic' example such as *Turn out the light*:

$$\text{Let's}\left\{\begin{array}{l}\textit{turn}\\ \textit{switch}\\ \textit{put}\end{array}\right\}\text{it}\left\{\begin{array}{l}\textit{on.}\\ \textit{off.}\\ \textit{down.}\\ \textit{up.}\end{array}\right.$$

With Type II phrasal verbs, there is no sensitive method of testing cohesion by placing the particle before the subject (*cf* 16.3), as this construction is scarcely possible even with free combinations: ?**Out he took a gun*. The other test of independence, insertion of an adverb before the particle, can however be used:

The pilot *jerked* the lever *right back*.
The dancer *threw* her hands *wildly about* above her head.

(Again, *right* is an intensifier of the particle, rather than an adverbial in itself.) Contrast the phrasal verb ?**They put the meeting hurriedly off*. Where there is an ambiguity between idiomatic and nonidiomatic interpretations of the same combination, insertion of an adverb will select the nonidiomatic one. Thus [1], unlike [2], can mean 'She reared the girls':

She *brought* the girls *up*. [1]
She *brought* the girls *right up*. [2]

But [2] can only have a spatial meaning 'She caused the girls to come up (the stairs, etc)'.

Like transitive verbs in general, Type II phrasal verbs can normally be turned into the passive without stylistic awkwardness (but *cf* Note [c]):

Aunt Ada *brought up* Roy. ~ Roy was *brought up* by Aunt Ada.

Note [**a**] Some Type II phrasal verbs do not easily allow the possibility of placing the particle after the object (unless the object is a pronoun):

They had *given up* hope. ~ ?They had *given* hope *up*.
They *laid down* their arms. ~ ?They *laid* their arms *down*.

This fixing of the S V A O order tends to occur, as the above examples illustrate, where there is a strong idiomatic bond (frequently matching a change from literal to metaphorical) between the phrasal verb and the object. In addition, the particle cannot normally be placed after a clausal object, such as an *-ing* clause, even when the clause is short:

She *gave up* trying. ~ *She *gave* trying *up*.

[**b**] Conversely, some phrasal verbs do not easily allow the placement of the particle before the object. In some cases the S V A O order is probably avoided because of ambiguity:

Get that parcel *off* right away! ≁ *Get off* that parcel right away!

Here the transitive phrasal verb *get . . . off* can be confused with the intransitive verb *get* followed by the preposition *off*. This latter construction occurs, for example, in *Get off that stool – it's just been painted!* but would suggest an inappropriate meaning in the above sentence. Other reasons for avoiding the S V A O order include coordination of particles:

I *switched* the light *on and off*. ~ ?I *switched on and off* the light.

Also, as in [a] above, the order tends to be fixed by idiomatic convention:

I was { *crying* my eyes *out*. / *laughing* my head *off*. / *sobbing* my heart *out*. } *I was { *crying out* my eyes. / *laughing off* my head. / *sobbing out* my heart. }

In these cases of conventionalized hyperbole, the S V A O order is impossible.

[**c**] Another restriction on phrasal verbs is that some of them do not have a passive. These are principally combinations for which the object is idiomatically limited to a particular noun or pronoun:

The train *picked up* speed. ~ *?Speed was *picked up* (by the train).
Jill and her boss don't *hit* it *off*. ~ *It is not *hit off* (by Jill and her boss).
['are not good friends']

[**d**] As in intransitive combinations, so in transitive verb–adverb combinations the adverb may be semantically equivalent to a reduced prepositional phrase, from which the complement has been omitted:

They *pulled* the cart *along*. ['*along* the road, etc']
Move the furniture *out*. ['*out* of the house, etc']

These are clearly free combinations, not phrasal verbs.

[**e**] Expressions like *be fed up*, *be run down* appear to be passive phrasal verbs without a corresponding active:

I *was fed up* with the noise. ≁ *The noise *fed me up*.

Yet these are not true passives, but rather 'pseudo-passives' (*cf* 3.77), as we see from their ability to combine with an intensifier such as *thoroughly*, and a copular verb such as *look*:

He *looked thoroughly* fed up.

and also by the impossibility of an agent *by*-phrase:

*I was fed up *by the noise*.

Type I prepositional verbs

16.5 Here, as in 16.3, we use *Type I* as a label for multi-word verbs without a direct object. A prepositional verb consists of a lexical verb followed by a preposition with which it is semantically and/or syntactically associated. The preposition, as is to be expected, precedes its complement:

Look at these pictures. Can you *cope with* the work?
I don't *care for* Jane's parties. I *approve of* their action.
We must *go into* the problem. His eyes *lighted upon* the jewel.

In these examples, the lexical verb is followed by a particle which is unequivocally a preposition (*ie* from Class (A) in 16.2).

In using the term PREPOSITIONAL VERB we indicate that we regard the second noun phrase in a sentence like [1] as the complement of the preposition *at* and not as the direct object of a verb *look at*:

Many people looked at *the pictures.* [1]

This is despite the fact that the passive is frequently possible (with some stylistic awkwardness) as in [1a]:

The picture was *looked at* by many people. [1a]

The intransitive interpretation, on the other hand, is justified (for example) by the potentiality of adverbial insertion:

Many people looked *disdainfully* at the picture.

where insertion between V and O_d is usually avoided:

*?Many people examined disdainfully the picture.

The noun phrase following the preposition in such constructions is termed a PREPOSITIONAL OBJECT.

There are therefore two complementary analyses of a sentence like *She looked after* ['tended'] *her son*:

ANALYSIS 1:	S	V	A	
	She	*looked*	*after*	*her son*
ANALYSIS 2:	S	V		O

The former analysis is the one we follow if we call this kind of construction intransitive. Analysis 2, on the other hand, highlights the resemblance between *She looked after her son* and *She tended her son.* By naming this category of prepositional verbs 'Type I', we avoid the unclarity which results from the use of 'intransitive' or 'transitive' in this connection. The above analyses are discussed further in 16.13–15.

Note Whereas a sequence of verb and preposition like *live at* is a purely nonidiomatic free combination, in prepositional verbs like *look at, look for*, etc the verb word has a literal use, but has a fixed association with the preposition. These cases may, in their turn, be distinguished from other prepositional verbs, *eg*: *go into* ['investigate'] where both words form a semantically idiomatic (often metaphorical) unit (*cf* 16.12 for a further exploration of these categories and their relation to a scale of idiomaticity).

Prepositional verbs contrasted with phrasal verbs

16.6 We must now briefly attend to another distinction between similar-looking constructions. The following exemplify Type I prepositional verbs which contain particles of Class (B) in 16.2, and are therefore capable of confusion with Type II phrasal verbs (*cf* 16.4):

She *called on* her friends.
We *saw through* his imposture.
I've *come across* a problem.
You should *invest in* property.
She *came by* a fortune.
The car *ran over* a bump.

These are distinguished from almost all Type II phrasal verbs by the inability of the particle to be moved to a position after the following noun phrase:

(1) She *called on* her friends. ~ *She *called* her friends *on.*
[*cf*: (2) She *switched on* the light. ~ She *switched* the light *on*.]
(1a) She *came by* a fortune. ~ *She *came* a fortune *by*. ['acquired']
[*cf*: (2a) She *put by* a fortune. ~ She *put* a fortune *by*. ['kept']]

Similarly, the order of particle and pronoun is different:

(1b) She *called on* them. NOT *She *called* them *on.*
(2b) She *switched* it *on.* NOT *She *switched on* it.

Another criterion is stress. Both constructions generally permit the corresponding passive, but in the Type II phrasal verb (2), a higher degree of stress (including nuclear stress when the particle is in final position) usually falls on the adverb particle. In the prepositional verb (1), on the other hand, the stress normally occurs on the lexical verb preceding the particle:

(1c) He '*called on* the dean. ~ The dean was *CÀLLED on.*
(2c) She *switched* '*on* the light. ~ The light was *switched ÒN.*

The same contrast of stress is observed in other constructions with a postponed particle, *eg* relative clauses:

(1d) the fortune (that) he *CÀME by.*
(2d) the fortune (that) he *put BỲ.*

Compare also:

(1e) This is a dangerous road to GÈT over. (*also* . . . to get òver)
(2e) It's a loss she will never get òver.

However, the 'stress test' is not entirely reliable, as polysyllabic prepositions like *across*, *over*, and *without* usually receive stress, and other factors such as contrastive focus may affect the positioning of the nucleus:

I could have done withÒUT that PRÉSent.
~ That's a present I could have done withÒUT.
She will never get òver it.
~ It is a loss that she will never get òver.

We shall return to these distinctions in 16.16.

Note [**a**] It is not unusual for the same sequence of verb + particle to function either as a phrasal verb or as a prepositional verb:

He '*turned* '*on* his supPÒRTers. [phrasal verb: 'He excited them'] [1]
He '*turned on* his supPÒRTers. [prepositional verb: 'He attacked them'] [2]

A reduced version of [1] would be *He* '*turned them* '*on*, while the correspondingly reduced version of [2] would be *He* '*turned on them.*

[**b**] A special case of the above homonymy occurs where the phrasal and prepositional verbs are not only identical in form, but similar in meaning. Examples are *run through*, *run over*, and *look over*. Thus:

The car *ran* him *over*. The car *ran over* him.

These have virtually the same meaning, but the former (the phrasal verb) is reserved for the description of driving accidents, in which the object refers to a casualty.

The car *ran* '*over* a BÙMP.

therefore has no corresponding phrasal verb construction:

*The car *ran* a 'bump *òver*.

Type II prepositional verbs

16.7 The Type I/Type II opposition applies not only to phrasal, but to prepositional verbs:

	TYPE I (without O_d)	TYPE II (with O_d)
PHRASAL VERB	Please *drink up.*	Please *drink* it *up.*
PREPOSITIONAL VERB	He *invested in* property.	He *invested* his money *in* property.

Type II prepositional verbs are followed by two noun phrases, normally separated by the preposition: the former is the direct object, the latter the prepositional object. Three subtypes may be distinguished; the italicized words indicate that the idiom has a different grammatical status in each case, as will be explained.

TYPE IIa

The gang *robbed* her *of* her necklace.
He *deprived* the peasants *of* their land.
They *plied* the young man *with* food.
Please *confine* your remarks *to* the matter under discussion.
This clothing will *protect* you *from* the worst weather.
Jenny *thanked* us *for* the present.
May I *remind* you *of* our agreement?
They have *provided* the child *with* a good education.

TYPE IIb

They have *made a* (terrible) *mess of* the house.
Did you *make* (any) *allowance for* inflation?
Mary *took* (good) *care of* the children.

TYPE IIc

Suddenly we *caught sight of* the lifeboat.
Give way to traffic on the major road.
I have *lost touch with* most of the family.

The first and most numerous type has a passive of the regular kind, the direct object becoming subject of the passive verb phrase:

She was *robbed of* her necklace (by the gang).
The peasants were *deprived of* their land.
The young man was *plied with* food.

With Type IIb, there are two possible passives: the regular passive in which the direct object becomes subject (labelled (1) below), and a less acceptable passive construction in which the prepositional object becomes subject (labelled (2) below):

{(1) *A* (terrible) *mess* has been *made of* the house.
{(2) (?)The house has been *made a* (terrible) *mess of.*

{(1) Has (any) *allowance* been *made for* inflation?
{(2) ?Has inflation been *made allowance for?*

{ (1) (Good) *care* was *taken of* the children.
{ (2) The children were *taken* (good) *care of*.

In Type IIc, on the other hand, the only acceptable passive is the irregular passive in which the prepositional object becomes subject:

The lifeboat was suddenly *caught sight of*.
?Traffic on the major road should always be *given way to*.
(?)Most of the family has been *lost touch with*.

Note **[a]** For completeness, mention must be made of a fourth type of transitive prepositional verb which has no passive whatsoever; an idiomatic type in which the direct object is a reflexive pronoun (*cf* 3.70):

He *prided himself on* his craftsmanship.
**Himself* was *prided on* his craftsmanship.

[b] In the interests of end-focus or end-weight (*cf* 18.9), it is sometimes acceptable to place an elaborate direct object after the prepositional object. Contrast:

He had been known to *reduce* movie-stars *to* tears.
He had been known to *reduce to* tears some of the most seasoned and idolized movie-stars in Hollywood.

16.8 To a great extent, membership of Types IIa–IIc above depends on the idiomatic status of the prepositional verb.

In *Type IIa* the lexical verb and the preposition, although normally separated by the object, form an idiomatic combination. Here as elsewhere, the idiomatic 'cohesion' of the two may be of variable strength. Verbs such as *accuse* N *of* and *thank* N *for* (where 'N' symbolizes the direct object noun phrase) are not idiomatic in the sense that applies to phrasal verbs like *put* N *off*, for the lexical verb is used in its primary literal meaning. We may nevertheless speak of the verb GOVERNING the preposition, in the sense that the preposition is selected by reason of the verb, rather than by independent semantic choice. Thus despite similarity of meaning, different prepositions are selected with *accuse* and *blame*, *viz*: *of* and *for* respectively.

I *accused* him { *of* the crime. / *for the crime. } I *blamed* him { *of the crime. / *for* the crime. }

In less idiomatic cases, the verbs group themselves into restricted sets such as *rob* N *of*, *cheat* N *of*, and *deprive* N *of*, where *of* to some extent carries its own privative force.

In a further subcategorization of Type IIa we need to recognize that the prepositional phrase is optional in some cases, but not in others:

They { *cheated* / *deprived* } the boy *of* his savings. They { *cheated* / **deprived* } the boy.

In yet another sub-type, the prepositional object forms part of the idiom: *lick* N *into shape* ⟨informal⟩; *lull* N *to sleep*; *put* N *to rights*; etc.

In *Type IIb* as well as the verb word and the preposition, the head noun of the direct object forms part of the idiom:

make a *mess* of	take *notice* of	lose *hope* of
pay *attention* to	take *advantage* of	make *mention* of

But the object is still variable to some extent: *eg* an open-class adjective or a determiner can be added:

make a *horrible* mess of	take *some* notice of
pay *careful* attention to	take *unfair* advantage of
lose *all* hope of	make *occasional* mention of

To this extent, the idiomatic bond is weakened, and it is easier, especially when the object contains a modifier or determiner, to separate the object from the rest of the construction by the regular passive transformation:

Some notice was taken . . . *Careful attention* was paid . . .

In *Type IIc* the direct object is more firmly welded in its idiomatic position, so that its separation by means of the regular passive construction is awkward if not impossible: ?**Sight was caught of the lifeboat.* The object is typically invariable, and cannot easily be augmented by an adjective or a determiner: *cross swords with, give rise to, keep pace with, keep tabs on*, etc. Hence the dubious acceptability of ?**cross violent swords with*, ?**keep fast pace with*, ?**keep watchful tabs on*, etc. Other combinations of this kind are far more acceptable, however: *keep close tabs on, give sudden rise to.*

Phrasal–prepositional verbs

16.9 There is a further major category of multi-word verbs which will be called PHRASAL–PREPOSITIONAL verbs, because they contain, in addition to the lexical verb, both an adverb and a preposition as particles. These combinations are largely restricted to informal English:

We are all *looking forward to* your party on Saturday.
He had to *put up with* a lot of teasing at school.
Why don't you *look in on* Mrs Johnson on your way back?
He thinks he can *get away with* everything.

A common sign of idiomatic status here, as with other categories, is the existence of a one-word paraphrase:

put up with = 'tolerate' *look in on* = 'visit'

The prepositional passive with such verbs is not too common, and is liable to sound cumbersome. Examples such as the following, however, are normal and acceptable:

These tantrums could not be *put up with* any longer.	['tolerated']
The death penalty has been recently *done away with.*	['abolished']
Such problems must be squarely *faced up to.*	['confronted']
They were *looked down on* by their neighbours.	['despised']

In addition to the Type I phrasal–prepositional verbs already illustrated, there are also Type II ones requiring a direct object:

fob N *off with* ⟨esp BrE⟩	*put* N *down to*	*take* N *out on*
fix N *up* (*with*)	*let* N *in on*	*put* N *up to*

(where 'N' again identifies the object noun phrase). Examples:

Don't *take* it *out on* me! ['vent your anger']
The manager *fobbed* me *off with* a cheap camera. ⟨esp BrE⟩
We *put* our success *down to* hard work. ['attribute to']
I'll *let* you *in on* a secret.

Only the regular passive occurs with these:

I was *fobbed off with* a cheap camera. ⟨esp BrE⟩
Our success can be *put down to* careful planning.
Are you *fixed up with* a job yet?

Note There are two equivalent phrasal–prepositional verbs in which the two noun phrases following the verb exchange roles:

= { He *fobbed* a cheap camera *off on* the unsuspecting tourist.
He *fobbed* the unsuspecting tourist *off with* a cheap camera. }

A summary of types of multi-word verb

16.10 We have now reached a point where it will be useful to summarize the various categories described in 16.3–9. The picture which emerges in *Table* 16.10 is a symmetrical one, with three binary contrasts, expressed in the formula:

verb ± direct object ± adverb ± preposition

Table 16.10 Principal types of multi-word verbs

		Lexical Verb	Direct Object	Particles: Adverb	Particles: Preposition	+ Prepositional Object
1 (free combination)	(A)	*come*	—	*in*	—	—
Type I PHRASAL VERB	(B)	*crop*	—	*up*	—	—
2 (free combination)	(A)	*send*	someone	*away*	—	—
Type II PHRASAL VERB	(B)	*turn*	someone	*down*	—	—
3 (free combination)	(A)	*come*	—	—	*with*	+ me
Type I PREPOSITIONAL VERB	(B)	*come*	—	—	*across*	+ a problem
4 (free combination)	(A)	*receive*	something	—	*from*	+ me
Type II PREPOSITIONAL VERB	(B)	*take*	someone	—	*for*	+ a fool
5 (free combination)	(A)	*run*	—	*away*	*with*	+ it
Type I PHRASAL-PREPOSITIONAL VERB	(B)	*come*	—	*up*	*with*	+ an answer
6 (free combination)	(A)	*send*	someone	*out*	*into*	+ the world
Type II PHRASAL-PREPOSITIONAL VERB	(B)	*put*	someone	*up*	*for*	+ election

[**a**] Examples (A) and (B) of each type illustrate respectively nonidiomatic and idiomatic variants. Thus (A) is a free combination, whereas (B) is a multi-word verb.
[**b**] The italicized words are those which make up the idiom or lexical unit.

Some semantic and syntactic distinctions

16.11 It will also be useful to analyse in a systematic manner three distinctions which underlie *Table* 16.10, and which have been found problematic by those dealing with this aspect of English grammar. The three distinctions, which have been touched on in preceding sections, are:

idiomatic versus *nonidiomatic* status (16.12)
prepositional verbs versus *free combinations of verb + prepositional phrase* (16.13–15)
phrasal versus *prepositional* verbs (16.16)

The first two of these are gradient rather than clear-cut.

Semantic criteria for idiomatic status

16.12 (A) The semantic unity of multi-word verbs can often be manifested in replacement by a single-word verb; *eg*: *visit* for *call for*, *summon* for *call up*, *omit* for *leave out*, *tolerate* for *put up with*. This criterion, however, is not always reliable. First, there are multi-word verbs, like *get away with* and *run out of*, which do not have one-word paraphrases. Second, there are nonidiomatic combinations, such as *go across* (= *cross*), *go past* (= *pass*), and *sail around* (= *circumnavigate*) which do have such paraphrases.

(B) The fact that the meaning of an idiom is not predictable from the meanings of its parts can be verified by noting that the meaning of the verb or particle in the combination does not remain constant when other parts of the idiom undergo substitution. This criterion leads us to recognize three main categories:

(i) Free, nonidiomatic constructions, where the individual meanings of the components are apparent from their constancy in possible substitutions:

bring	*in*	*walk*	*up*
take	*out*	*run*	*down*
. . .	. . .	. . .	. . .

(ii) 'Semi-idiomatic' constructions which are variable but in a more limited way. The relation between the verb and particle is similar to that between a stem and an affix in word formation (*cf* App I.5), in that the substitution of one verb for another, or one particle for another, is constrained by limited productivity. In phrasal verbs like *find out* ['discover'], *cut up* ['cut into pieces'] and *slacken off* ['reduce pace/energy'] the verb word keeps its meaning, whereas the meaning of the particle is less easy to isolate. In contrast, it is the particle which establishes a family resemblance in the following groups:

'persistent action'		'completion'	
chatter *away*	fire *away*	drink *up*	break *up*
work *away*	beaver *away* ⟨BrE⟩	finish *up*	use *up*

'aimless behaviour'		'endurance'	
play *around*	mess *around*	draw *out*	eke *out*
fool *around*	wait *around*	last *out*	hold *out*

Completion can also be signalled by *out*, as in *find out*, *point out*, *seek out*, *figure out*, *work out*, etc.

(iii) 'Highly idiomatic' constructions such as *bring up* ['rear'], *come by* ['acquire'], *turn up* ['make an appearance']. These are thoroughly idiomatic in that there is no possibility of contrastive substitution: *bring up/down*; *come by/past/through*; *turn up/down*; etc.

Putting a verb in the third category does not necessarily mean, however, that its meaning is completely opaque. We can see a metaphorical appropriateness in *bring up* for 'educate', and this is only one of many idiomatic verbs containing metaphors fairly clearly derived from their literal locative interpretations: *gloss over* (a difficulty); *hand down* (an heirloom), *piece together* (a story), etc. For our purposes it will be convenient in general to treat classes (II) and (III) as multi-word verbs.

Syntactic criteria for prepositional verbs

16.13 In distinguishing prepositional verbs such as *call on* ['visit'] in *He called on the dean* from other sequences of verb + preposition such as *called before* in *He called before lunch* (*cf* 16.5), the semantic criteria of idiomaticity must be supplemented by syntactic criteria.

We are chiefly concerned here with Type I verbs, whether these are prepositional verbs like *call on*, or phrasal–prepositional verbs such as *put up with*. How are we to choose between the two analyses of 16.5, that of SVO (with a prepositional object) and that of SVA (or in the case of phrasal–prepositional verbs, SVAA)? First, there are good reasons for arguing that even an idiomatic case like *He called on the dean* contains a phrase boundary between the verb and the particle:

(A) The whole prepositional phrase may be fronted, *eg* in questions:

On whom did he call?

(B) An adverb can be inserted between the verb and the particle:

He *called* unexpectedly *on the dean.*

(C) The prepositional phrase can be isolated in other constructions; *eg* (optionally) in responses, in coordinate constructions, or in comparative constructions:

A: {On whom did he call? / Who(m) did he call on?} *B*: (*On*) *his mother*.

Did he call on the dean or (*on*) *his friend*?

He calls on the dean more often than (*on*) *his friend*.

We do not reject the SVA analysis, therefore, but rather we offer the SVO analysis as, to varying degrees, a suitable alternative.

The prepositional passive

16.14 We will accept the possibility of turning the prepositional complement into the subject of a passive sentence (*cf* 3.64) as one criterion favouring the SVO analysis. This construction, which leaves the preposition DEFERRED ('stranded') in its post-verbal position, will be called the PREPOSITIONAL PASSIVE. Contrast:

The dean *was called on.*	*Lunch *was called after.*
The war *was put up with.*	*Andy *was gone out with.*

Notice that ambiguous combinations like *arrive at* take the passive only when the preposition is part of an idiom:

We arrived at a station.	~ *A station was arrived at.
We arrived at a conclusion.	~ A conclusion was arrived at.

Combinations of verb and prepositional phrase which are awkward in brief sentences can, however, become more tolerable with an enlarged context:

?*This office has *been called/phoned from.*
This office has *been called/phoned from* so many times that it was natural to assume that it was the source of the latest call.

Here are some more usual cases of the prepositional passive, where the passive verb is a Type I prepositional verb:

Though something very different from ordinary forest management *is called for*, the trees in the parks do need the forester's skilled consideration.
This matter will have to *be dealt with* immediately.
Other possibilities *are talked of* by many of our colleagues.
If a woman with a university degree rejects a career for marriage, her education is not to *be thought of* as thrown away unless we count the family arena of no importance.

Other prepositional passives are:

be asked for	*be done for*	*be shouted at*
be believed in	*be hoped for*	*be stared at*
be talked to	*be done away with*	*be sent away for*

However, the passive is also quite acceptable with prepositions which have a locative meaning, and which on other grounds (*eg* the *wh*-question criterion of 16.15) must be judged as introducing a prepositional phrase of place:

They must have *played on* this field last week. [1a]
~ This field must have *been played on* last week. [1b]
Visitors are not to *sit on* these Louis XV chairs. [2a]
~ These Louis XV chairs are not to *be sat on.* [2b]
Primitive men once *lived in* these caves. [3a]
~ These caves *were* once *lived in* by primitive men. [3b]

We cannot, therefore, invariably regard the prepositional passive as a marker of a prepositional verb. Rather, the passive is primarily an indicator of the fact that the prepositional complement is being treated as an *affected* participant in the clause (*cf* 10.19, 10.21). For example, in [1b] and [2b] above, the function of the passive is not merely to obtain end focus, but to imply that the subject of the passive clause refers to an object affected by the (unspecified) agent's action. The acceptability of the passive is thus accounted for in terms of clause participant roles (10.18*ff*), as well as in terms of convention or idiomatic status. Both factors play a role in making the passive select the abstract metaphorical meaning in:

They went into the tunnel. ~ *The tunnel was gone into.
They went into the problem. ~ The problem was gone into.

We may, in fact, recognize a strong association between these factors, and therefore between prepositional passives and prepositional verbs.

Note The prepositional passive is paralleled by a similar prepositional use in *-ed* participle clauses:

The shop *broken into* last week has now been reopened.

'Prepositional participles' can also be converted into adjectives: *the hoped-for arrival of the relief force*; *the much-talked-about visit of the Pope*. There are also 'pseudo-passive' (*cf* 3.77) occurrences of prepositional verbs, as in *I was feeling got at* ⟨informal⟩. The hyphen, in predicative position, is generally omitted.

The criterion of question forms

16.15 The second criterion for prepositional verbs is the formation of *wh*-questions with the pronouns *who(m)* and *what* (for personal and nonpersonal prepositional objects respectively), rather than with adverbial question forms such as *where*, *when*, *how*, or *why*:

John called on her. ~ *Who(m)* did John call on?
John looked for it. ~ *What* did John look for?

Contrast:

John called from the office. ~ *Where* did John call from?
John called after lunch. ~ *When* did John call?

Once again, the criterion is not clear-cut. There is firstly considerable overlap between the two question types: *She died of pneumonia* could be an answer either to the question *How did she die?* or (more usually) to the question *What did she die of?* Secondly, there are many types of prepositional phrases which are classified as adjuncts (*cf* 8.13, 9.14 – 53) but which regularly correspond with questions in *who(m)* or *what*. These are classes of adjunct for which English lacks an interrogative adverb, such as adjuncts of accompaniment:

A: { With whom did Peter go fishing? [1a]
Who(m) did Peter go fishing with? [1b]
B: ((He went fishing) with) his brother. [2]

The *with*-phrase in [2] can only be questioned by the interrogative pronoun *who(m)* in [1a] and [1b]; and yet the mobility and optionality of the *with*-phrase, as shown in [3], are signs of its adverbial status:

Peter (, with his brother,) went fishing. [3]

Since none of the criteria for prepositional or phrasal-prepositional verbs are compelling, it is best to think of the boundary of these categories as a scale, such as that depicted in *Fig* 16.15:

V_{pass}	Q_{pro}	No Q_{adv}		
+	+	+	The police have *asked for* details.	[4]
+	+	–	The queen *slept in* this bed.	[5]
–	+	+	White wine *goes with* poultry.	[6]
–	+	–	She *died of* pneumonia.	[7]
–	–	+	His job also *comes into* the picture.	[8]
–	–	–	She *left before* noon.	[9]

V_{pass} = passive Q_{pro} = pronoun *wh*-word Q_{adv} = adverb *wh*-word

Fig 16.15

Of these, [4] is a clear case of a prepositional verb, while [5] and [6] are marginally in that class. The matrix is so arranged that the larger the number of pluses, the stronger the characteristics of the prepositional verb. For this reason, the *wh*-adverb criterion is expressed in a negative form, *ie* a plus in this column means 'the prepositional verb canNOT be the answer to a *wh*-adverb'. *Ask for* in [4] is thus the combination which most clearly meets the requirements of the SVO analysis, and *left before* in [9], being least like a prepositional verb, is to be analysed with equal clarity as:

She [S] left [V] before noon [A].

It is perhaps surprising that [8], with its idiomatic character, scores so low on the prepositional verb scale. This is because in this sentence not only the verb and particle (*come into*) but also the object (*the picture*) is part of the idiom, a factor which inhibits the passive and interrogative transforms of the sentence.

An additional criterion for prepositional verbs is our unwillingness to have the preposition cut off from the lexical verb by fronting the whole prepositional phrase in (*eg*) *wh*-questions and relative clauses (*cf* 11.14*ff*, 17.9*ff*):

A: ?**After whom* did she look?
A: *Who*(*m*) did she look *after*? } B: She looked after Jim.

A: *With whom* did she agree?
A: *Who*(*m*) did she agree *with*? } B: She agreed with Jim.

Similarly *What did she wish for?* is fully acceptable, but not ?*For what did she wish?* By this test, *look after* and *wish for* come closer to the ideal prepositional verb than does *agree with*.

Note In addition to the mentioned *wh*-pronouns *who*(*m*) and *what*, there are other question forms with the determiners *what* and *which*; *eg* [5] could answer the question:

Which bed did the queen sleep in?

This alternative construction is ignored for the purposes of the above matrix.

Criteria for distinguishing phrasal and prepositional verbs

16.16 The question here is not one of gradience, but of how to distinguish two superficially like constructions, that of a Type I prepositional verb like *call*

on in *He called on the dean*, and that of a Type II phrasal verb such as *call up* in *He called up the dean* (*cf* 16.6).

The differences are both syntactic and phonological:

(a) The particle of a phrasal verb can stand either before or after the noun phrase following the verb, but that of the prepositional verb must (unless deferred) precede the noun phrase.
(b) When the noun phrase following the verb is a personal pronoun, the pronoun precedes the particle in the case of a phrasal verb, but follows the particle in the case of a prepositional verb.
(c) An adverb (functioning as adjunct) can often be inserted between verb and particle in prepositional verbs, but not in phrasal verbs.
(d) The particle of the phrasal verb cannot precede a relative pronoun at the beginning of a relative clause.
(e) Similarly, the particle of a phrasal verb cannot precede the interrogative word at the beginning of a *wh*-question.
(f) The particle of a phrasal verb is normally stressed (*cf* 16.6), and in final position normally bears the nuclear tone, whereas the particle of a prepositional verb is normally unstressed and has the 'tail' of the nuclear tone which falls on the lexical verb (*cf* App II.15).

These criteria are displayed in *Table* 16.16:

Table 16.16 Diagnostic frames for phrasal and prepositional verbs

	TYPE I PREPOSITIONAL VERB	TYPE II PHRASAL VERB
	call on = 'visit'	*call up* = 'summon'
(a)	They *called on* the dean. ≁ *They *called* the dean *on*.	They *called up* the dean. ~ They *called* the dean *up*.
(b)	They *called on* him. ≁ *They *called* him *on*.	They *called* him *up*. ≁ *They *called up* him.
(c)	They *called* angrily *on* the dean.	*They *called* angrily *up* the dean.
(d)	the man *on* whom they *called*	*the man *up* whom they *called*
(e)	*On* which man did they *call*?	**Up* which man did they *call*?
(f)	Which man did they CÀLL *on*?	Which man did they *call* ÙP?

Other multi-word verb constructions

16.17 Apart from the types of multi-word verb summarized in *Table* 16.10, some other idiomatic verb constructions may be briefly noted.

(a) VERB–ADJECTIVE COMBINATIONS

These are similar to phrasal verbs. Compare:

Meg *put* the cloth *straight*.   Meg *put* the cat *out*.

Like phrasal verbs, verb–adjective combinations form cohesive units; but unlike phrasal verbs, some of them allow comparative modification:

John didn't put { the cloth as straight / *the cat as out } as Meg.

They may be either copular (clause pattern *SVC*), or complex transitive (clause pattern *SVOC*):

SVC: *break even, plead guilty, lie low*
SVOC: *cut* N *short*, *work* N *loose*, *rub* N *dry*

Sometimes the idiom contains additional elements, such as an infinitive (*play hard to get*) or a preposition (*ride roughshod over . . .*).

(The 'N' above indicates a direct object in the case of transitive examples.)

(b) VERB–VERB COMBINATIONS
In these idiomatic constructions (*cf* 3.49–51, 16.52), the second verb is nonfinite, and may be either an infinitive:

make do with, *make* (N) *do*, *let* (N) *go*, *let* (N) *be*

or a participle, with or without a following preposition:

put paid to, *get rid of*, *have done with*
leave N *standing*, *send* N *packing*, *knock* N *flying*, *get going*

(c) VERBS GOVERNING TWO PREPOSITIONS
These are a further variant on prepositional verbs:

It *developed from* a small club *into* a mass organization in three years.

Similarly: *struggle with* N *for* N, *compete with* N *for* N, *apply to* N *for* N, *talk to* N *about* N. Normally either one or both prepositional phrases can be omitted; *eg*:

It *developed into* a mass organization in three years.

Note To end this survey of verb idioms and their grammatical characteristics, mention may be made of rare patterns such as *make sure/certain* followed by a *that*-clause; *see fit* followed by a *to*-infinitive; and verb + noun combinations such as *turn turtle* and *turn traitor*.

Verbs in relation to verb complementation

16.18 In 16.20–67 we survey types of verb complementation, before turning to adjective complementation (16.68–83), and (more briefly) to noun complementation (16.84–5). Many verbs are versatile enough to allow several complementation types (*cf* the discussion, for example, of *get* in 10.3). It is therefore likely to be misleading to talk of 'intransitive verbs', 'monotransitive verbs', 'complex transitive verbs', etc. Rather, it is often better to say that verbs have 'monotransitive use', 'monotransitive complementation', etc. Although one verb may belong to a number of different complementation types, it is usually possible to observe a common ground of meaning in the various uses.

For each type of complementation, we give a list of verbs belonging to that pattern. No claim of completeness is made for these lists: when the membership of a type is small, a fairly exhaustive list of verbs is given, whereas when the membership is very large (as in the case of intransitive verbs, or monotransitive verbs with a noun phrase object), we can give only a sample of common verbs. In any case, it should be borne in mind that the list of verbs conforming to a given pattern is difficult to specify exactly: there are many differences between one variety of English and another in respect of individual verbs, and many cases of marginal acceptability.

Note The term 'valency' (or 'valence') is sometimes used, instead of complementation, for the way in which a verb determines the kinds and number of elements that can accompany it in the clause. Valency, however, includes the subject of the clause, which is excluded (unless extraposed) from complementation.

Verbs in intransitive function

16.19 Where no complementation occurs, the verb is said to have an INTRANSITIVE use. Three types of verb may be mentioned in this category:

(I) 'PURE' INTRANSITIVE VERBS, which do not take an object at all (or at least do so only very rarely):

John has *arrived*. Your views do not *matter*.

Examples:

appear	*die*	*fall*	*happen*	*rise*
come	*digress*	*go*	*lie*	*wait*

(II) VERBS WHICH CAN ALSO BE TRANSITIVE WITH THE SAME MEANING, and without a change in the subject–verb relationship. Informally, such verbs can be described as having an 'understood object' (*cf* App I.54):

He *smokes* (a pipe). I am *reading* (a book).

But in some cases the intransitive verb acquires a more specific meaning, so that a particular kind of object is 'understood'; *eg*: *John drinks* (*heavily*) ['drinks alcohol'].

Examples:

approach	*drive*	*help*	*pass*	*win*
drink	*enter*	*leave*	*play*	*write*

(III) VERBS WHICH CAN ALSO BE TRANSITIVE, but where the semantic connection between subject and verb is different in the two cases; *eg* the intransitive use has an affected participant as subject (*cf* 10.21*f*), whereas the transitive use has an agentive as subject (*cf* App I.54):

The door *opened* slowly. *cf*: Mary *opened* the door.
The car *stopped*. *cf*: He *stopped* the car.

Examples:

begin	*close*	*increase*	*turn*	*walk*
change	*drop*	*move*	*unite*	*work*

Type (III) also includes intransitive verbs with MUTUAL PARTICIPATION (*cf* 13.60), as in:

I have *met* you. ~ We have *met*.
The bus *collided with* the car. ~ The bus and car *collided*.

Intransitive verbs are numerous, particularly in categories (II) and (III).

Note [**a**] The following are examples of intransitive (*ie* Type I) phrasal verbs (*cf* 16.3):

fall out ['quarrel']	*make off* ['escape']	*pass away* ['die']
blow over [of a storm, etc]	*fall back* ['retreat']	*catch on* ['understand']
come off ['succeed']	*make up* ['end a quarrel']	*pull up* ['stop']
look up ['improve']	*fall through* ['fail']	*crop up* ['occur']
come out ['bloom']	*pass out* ['faint']	*opt out* [of a choice]
come to ['become conscious']	*fall off* ['decline']	

Further examples are to be found in 16.3.

[**b**] Category (I) includes the intransitive verbs *lie* and *rise*, which are sometimes confused by native speakers with their transitive counterparts *lay* and *raise*, because of their formal similarity. A similar correspondence exists between *fall* (intransitive) and *fell* (transitive); *eg*: *They felled a tree.*

Types of verb complementation

16.20 There are four main types of complementation to consider:

[A] Copular, *eg*: *John is only a boy.*
[B] Monotransitive, *eg*: *I have caught a big fish.*
[C] Complex transitive, *eg*: *She called him a hero.*
[D] Ditransitive, *eg*: *He gave Mary a doll.*

Although these complementation types have already been generally discussed in 2.16 and elsewhere, it is necessary now to list the verbs of each type in more detail, paying particular attention to the active–passive relation (*cf* 3.69*ff*). In this survey, we shall also list variants on the above patterns; for example, cases where the verb is followed by a finite or nonfinite clause. Such variants will be distinguished by numbers: [A1], [B2], etc. The various subtypes of complementation under these headings are illustrated in *Table* 16.20.

In addition, we shall use where necessary the suffixes 'ph' (for phrasal verbs), 'pr' (for prepositional verbs), and 'ph-pr' (for phrasal–prepositional verbs). For example, [B4ph-pr] will refer to a class of phrasal–prepositional verbs taking a *wh*-clause as prepositional object (*eg*: *find out about whether* . . .). It is not always necessary to recognize such detailed classifications, but it is useful to be able to do so when the occasion arises. Two points may be noted about complementation of multi-word verbs. First, a phrasal verb cannot normally be interrupted by a clause as object:

He left off *driving a car*. ~ *He left *driving a car* off.

Second, a Type I prepositional or phrasal–prepositional verb is appropriately classified, for the purposes of complementation, as monotransitive, since the prepositional object is analogous (*eg* with respect to the active–passive relation) to a direct object (*cf* 16.14). In general, multi-word verbs behave like other verbs of the same general type, and we will make a point of mentioning them or listing them separately only when they are numerous or where there is something special to be noted about them.

(Note: in *Table* 16.20, +S = 'with subject'; −S = 'without subject'.)

Table 16.20 Verb complementation types

Variants	Example	Section
COPULAR (Types *SVC* and *SVA*)		
[A1] Adjectival C_s	*The girl seemed restless.*	(16.21)
[A2] Nominal C_s	*William is my friend.*	(16.22)
[A3] Adverbial complementation	*The kitchen is downstairs.*	(16.24)
MONOTRANSITIVE (Type *SVO*)		
[B1] Noun phrase as O (with passive)	*Tom caught the ball.*	(16.26)
[B2] Noun phrase as O (without passive)	*Paul lacks confidence.*	(16.27)
[B3] *That*-clause as O	*I think that we have met.*	(16.30)
[B4] *Wh*-clause as O	*Can you guess what she said?*	(16.35)
[B5] *Wh*-infinitive as O	*I learned how to sail a boat.*	(16.37)
[B6] *To*-infinitive (−S) as O	*We've decided to move house.*	(16.38)
[B7] *-Ing* clause (−S) as O	*She enjoys playing squash.*	(16.39)
[B8] *To*-infinitive (+S) as O	*They want us to help.*	(16.41)
[B9] *-Ing* clause (+S) as O	*I hate the children quarrelling.*	(16.42)
COMPLEX TRANSITIVE (Types *SVOC* and *SVOA*)		
[C1] Adjectival C_o	*That music drives me mad.*	(16.44)
[C2] Nominal C_o	*They named the ship 'Zeus'.*	(16.46)
[C3] O + adverbial	*I left the key at home.*	(16.48)
[C4] O + *to*-infinitive	*They knew him to be a spy.*	(16.50)
[C5] O + bare infinitive	*I saw her leave the room.*	(16.52)
[C6] O + *-ing* clause	*I heard someone shouting.*	(16.53)
[C7] O + *-ed* clause	*I got the watch repaired.*	(16.54)
DITRANSITIVE (Type *SVOO*)		
[D1] Noun phrases as O_i & O_d	*They offered her some food.*	(16.55)
[D2] With prepositional O	*Please say something to us.*	(16.56)
[D3] O_i + *that*-clause	*They told me that I was ill.*	(16.59)
[D4] O_i + *wh*-clause	*He asked me what time it was.*	(16.61)
[D5] O_i + *wh*-infinitive clause	*Mary showed us what to do.*	(16.62)
[D6] O_i + *to*-infinitive	*I advised Mark to see a doctor.*	(16.63)

Within the sub-types [A1], [A2], etc it is sometimes valuable to distinguish additional semantic sub-types, for which the roman numerals (i), (ii), etc will be used. Other distinguishing marks applied to verbs in the following sections will be explained where they occur.

Copular complementation

[A1] Adjective phrase as subject complement

16.21 A verb is said to have COPULAR complementation when it is followed by a subject complement (C_s) or a predication adjunct (*cf* 2.16, 2.22, 8.26*ff*), and when this element cannot be dropped without changing the meaning of the verb. The verb in such a clause is a COPULAR (or linking) verb, and is equivalent in function to the principal copula, the verb *be*. Copular verbs fall into two main classes, according to whether the subject complement has the role of CURRENT ATTRIBUTE or of RESULTING ATTRIBUTE (*cf* 10.20). This distinction corresponds to that between CURRENT copulas and RESULTING copulas (*cf* conclusive verbs, 4.35). Normally, current copulas are stative (*cf* 4.28*ff*), and cannot cooccur with the progressive aspect.

The distinction is illustrated below with an adjectival complement, the first kind of complementation we will consider:

CURRENT: The girl *seemed* very restless.
RESULTING: The girl *became* very restless.

The following is a fairly full list of verbs regularly used in this pattern, together with typical adjectival complements:

CURRENT

(i) *be* (friendly) [*N*]

(ii) *appear* (happy) [*N*]
feel (annoyed) [*N*]
look (pretty) [*N*]
seem (very restless) [*N*]
smell (sweet)
sound (surprised) [*N*]
taste (bitter)

(iii) *remain* (uncertain) [*N*]
keep (silent)
stay (motionless) [*N*]

RESULTING

(iv) *become* (older) [*N*]
come (true)
end up (happy) [*N*]
get (ready)
go (sour)
grow (tired)
prove (rather useful) [*N*]
turn (cold) [*N*]
turn out (fortunate) [*N*]
wind up (drunk) [*N*] ⟨informal⟩

End up, *turn out*, and *wind up* are copular phrasal verbs. The verbs marked [*N*] in the list also occur with a noun phrase complement (though not all with the same freedom or acceptability; *cf* 16.22). The roman numerals in the list identify semantic groups which are discussed in 16.24 below.

In addition to the copular verbs above, there are verbs which have this function with severe restrictions on the words occurring in the complement (*cf* 10.16). The restriction may be a lexical restriction to certain idiomatic verb–adjective sequences such as *rest assured* (*cf* 16.17), or it may be a semantic restriction (*eg* the meaning of *blush* restricts the adjective to a subset of colour words: *blush scarlet*, but not **blush green*). Some examples are given below, with typical adjective complements:

CURRENT

(v) *burn* (low)
lie (flat)
loom (large)
play (rough) [*N*]
plead (innocent)
rest (assured)
stand (firm) [*N*]
stand up (straight)

RESULTING

(vi) *blush* (bright red)
fall (silent)
fall down (dead)
freeze (solid)
run (wild)
slam (shut)
spring (open)
wax (eloquent) ⟨archaic⟩

Many of these verbs resemble intransitive verbs, the complement being added almost as an optional specifier.

Note [**a**] *Go* is current in *go hungry/naked*, but is normally resulting elsewhere, as in *go* [= 'become'] *sour/red/wild/mad*.

[**b**] *Die* as in *He died young/poor*, etc does not fit easily into either of the categories listed. The verb *die* itself is conclusive, but the complement which follows it refers to a current attribute. The meaning is: 'He was young/poor, etc at the time of his death'.

[A2] Noun phrase as subject complement

16.22 Again, the verb *be* is the principal copula used in this pattern:

William *is* my friend. Oslo *seems* a pleasant city.

The verbs marked [*N*] in 16.21 can be used with noun phrase complements, as well as with adjective phrase complements. The following list of such verbs is fairly full. However, it should be noted that especially in American English, there is a tendency to avoid this construction with certain verbs. Instead, both AmE and BrE prefer an infinitive construction (Type [B6] in 16.38 below) with *to be* following the finite verb:

It appears the only solution. ~ It appears *to be* the only solution.

There is also, especially in informal AmE, a tendency to prefer a construction in which a copular verb is followed by *like* (*cf* 16.24 Note [a]):

It seems *like* the only solution.

CURRENT	RESULTING
(i) *be* (my friend)	(iv) *become* (an expert)
(ii) *appear*[1] (the only solution)	*end up* (her slave)
feel[1] (a fool)	*prove*[1] (his equal)
look[1] (a fine day)	*turn* (traitor)
seem (a genius)	*turn out* (a success/disaster)
sound[1] (a reasonable idea)	*wind up* (a millionaire) ⟨informal⟩
(iii) *remain* (good friends)	

The classes (i–iv) match those in 16.21. (On the omission of the article in the complement in *become president*, etc, *cf* 5.42.) The superscript '1' indicates that such verbs do not often occur in this pattern but (particularly in AmE) are preferred in the construction with *to be* or *like* (see above).

Note [**a**] With a noun phrase complement, *feel* has the meaning 'have the sensation of being . . .'; but with an adjective complement, it has not only this meaning (as in *She felt ill*), but also the meaning of 'cause a sensation . . .', as in *The table felt rough* (*cf* 4.29*f*).

[**b**] The noun phrase following *act as, count as, pose as, pass for* and similar combinations is in a copular relation with the subject, and these combinations may be reasonably described as 'copular prepositional verbs' on the analogy of intransitive and transitive prepositional verbs (*cf* 16.5–7; also 16.47). Corresponding to these constructions with current meaning are resulting copular prepositional verbs such as *change into, grow into*, and *turn into*, with the general meaning of 'become'. Note the near-synonymy of *He turned traitor* and *He turned into a traitor*.

[**c**] Some verbs occur more marginally in the above patterns; *eg*: *stay* in *They stayed good friends*. *Turn* as in *turn traitor* is formulaic, and is more or less restricted to a small number of combinations.

[**d**] One or two verbs such as *make* and *part* can appear with a noun phrase complement, but not with an adjective phrase complement:

They *parted* the best of friends.
They *make* a charming couple.

(In a sentence like *They parted friendly once more, friendly once more* would be not a complement, but a verbless clause; *cf* 10.16, 14.9.)

Semantic notes on copular verbs

16.23 The main verb *be* is the most central copular verb, and the most neutral in meaning. It is also overwhelmingly the most common. Although it generally has current and stative meaning, notice should be taken of its use also in reference to events and activities:

> There *was* a roar as the ball bounced off the goalpost.
> You*'re being* very helpful. (*cf* 4.31)

In some cases, *be* is close in meaning to *become*:

> Ann will *be* a qualified nurse next year.
> Cora *was* angry when she heard about the accident.

As the lists in 16.21–2 show, copular verbs apart from *be* fall into three classes. First, there is the division between current and resulting verbs; then the current verbs divide further into 'verbs of *seeming*' (ii) (including *seem, appear*, and the perception verbs *look, sound*, etc), and 'verbs of *remaining*' (iii) such as *remain, stay*, and *keep*. The resulting verbs (iv) are in the main 'verbs of *becoming*', but their meanings differ in detail, as we shall now briefly show.

Become is a process verb (*cf* 4.34), placing emphasis on the duration of the change, whereas *get* places more emphasis on the agency behind the event or on the result of the change: *Get ready!* but not **Become ready! Go* and *turn* tend to refer to changes which happen in spite of human agency, and therefore are often used for deteriorations: *go mad*; *go wild*; *go sour*; *go stale*; *turn livid*; *turn white* [of hair]; *turn sour*. *Turn* more especially seems to apply to natural changes from one state to its opposite: *turn green/brown* [of leaves]; *turn fine/cold* [of weather]; *turn ripe* ⟨BrE⟩. *Grow* is also associated with natural changes, especially with gradual changes (*grow old, grow tall*), and is likely to occur with comparative adjectives as in *grow cooler, grow more content*. In many cases, more than one verb can occur with the same adjective, and it is difficult to give precise conditions for selecting one rather than another.

Note *Come* is very restricted as a copular verb, but it makes an interesting contrast with *go* in examples like *go wrong/come right*. The association of *go* with deterioration (*go rotten*, etc) is complemented by the association of *come* with improvement in *come true*, etc. These associations may be connected with the positive and negative direction (from the speaker's viewpoint) of *come* and *go* as verbs of motion.

[A3] Complementation by an adjunct

16.24 The principal copula that allows an adverbial as complementation is once again *be*. The complementing adverbials, termed predication adjuncts in this function, are mainly space adjuncts (*cf* 8.3, 8.39*ff*):

> The children are *at the zoo*. The kitchen is *downstairs*.

but time adjuncts too are common with an eventive subject (*cf* 8.76):

> The party will be *at nine*. The outing is *tomorrow*.

and other types of predication adjunct are grammatical (for further examples *cf* 10.10).

Get and *keep* are two more copular verbs which occur specifically with place adjuncts (or adjuncts metaphorically related to these):

At last we got *home*. Get *off that chair*!
They kept *out of trouble*. How did you get *here*?

Be, *get*, and *keep* are clearly copular verbs in this function because of their inability to occur without the adjunct: **The children are*; **At last we got*; **They kept*. More marginally, other verbs such as *live*, *come*, *go*, *remain*, *stay*, *stand*, *lie* belong to this category (*cf* 8.27). These also occur as intransitive verbs with roughly the same locative (or abstract locative) meaning, but are in many contexts felt to be incomplete unless some complementation is added:

My aunt *lives* in Shropshire.
?*My aunt *lives*.

The need for the verb to be followed by some complementation is perhaps strongest in pure locative statements such as *Cannes lies on the French Riviera*. Whereas verbs like *live* and *lie* show the resemblance of adverbial complementation to the 'zero complementation' of intransitive verbs, verbs like *remain*, *stay*, *come*, *go*, *turn*, and *grow* show its similarity to copular complementation by adjective phrases. The parallel is brought out by pairs such as:

{He turned *red*. / He turned *into a monster*.} {She grew *tall*. / She grew *into a fine woman*.}

However, for our purposes it will be preferable to treat sequences such as *turn into* and *grow into* as copular prepositional verbs (*cf* 16.22 Note [b]).

Note [**a**] The verbs of 'seeming' (*cf* 16.23) *seem*, *appear*, *look*, *sound*, *feel*, *smell*, and *taste* are complemented by an adverbial clause beginning *as if* (or less frequently *as though*) in sentences such as the following:

Jill *looked as if* she had seen a ghost.
It *seems as if* the weather is improving.

(In a similar meaning, *appear* and *seem* can also be followed by a *that*-clause; *cf* 16.34.) An alternative construction is one in which the *as if* clause is replaced by a phrase introduced by *like*:

That music *sounds like* Mozart. [*ie* 'like the music of Mozart']
Bill *looks* (just) *like* his father.

After the same verbs, one also frequently hears clauses introduced by *like*, but these are often regarded as nonstandard: *It seems like the weather is improving.*

[**b**] There is also a curious idiomatic use of *feel like* (*cf* 16.22 Note [a]) meaning 'want':

I *feel like* a cup of coffee.

Arguably, this is not copular; it belongs rather to the category of monotransitive prepositional verbs [B1pr] (*cf* 16.28).

[**c**] More exceptional cases of verbs with adverbial complementation are:

(i) *behave* followed by an adverbial of manner:

He *behaved* {well. / like a prisoner of conscience.}

(However, *behave* can also occur intransitively or reflexively as in: *Why don't you behave (yourself)?*)

(ii) *last* and *take* followed by an adverbial of measure (duration):

The haymaking {*took* / *lasted* (for)} a week.

In the case of *take* the duration adverbial is obligatory, since the verb entails the completion of the task. In the case of *last*, the adverbial is omissible in such examples as: *The hot weather won't last*.

Monotransitive complementation

16.25 Verbs used in monotransitive function require a direct object, which may be a noun phrase, a finite clause, or a nonfinite clause. In addition to these categories the verb may be a Type I prepositional verb (*cf* 16.5) or phrasal–prepositional verb (*cf* 16.9), which for our present purposes will be treated as analogous to a verb with a direct object. We will begin by considering the straightforward case of verbs with a noun phrase as direct object, and then continue with variants of this basic pattern.

Complementation by a noun phrase as direct object

[B1] With the passive

16.26 Direct objects are typically noun phrases which may become the subject of a corresponding passive clause:

Tom *caught* the ball. ~ The ball *was caught* (by Tom).

(On the limitations of the passive transformation, *cf* 3.67*ff*.) Common examples of monotransitive verbs allowing the passive are:

begin	*desire*	*get*	*love*	*pass*	*support*
believe	*do*	*hear*	*make*	*produce*	*take*
bite	*doubt*	*help*	*marry*	*receive*	*use*
bring	*end*	*hold*	*mean*	*remember*	*visit*
call	*enjoy*	*keep*	*meet*	*require*	*want*
carry	*expect*	*know*	*mind*	*say*	*wash*
close	*feel*	*lead*	*move*	*see*	*waste*
cut	*find*	*like*	*need*	*start*	*watch*
describe	*follow*	*lose*	*obtain*	*study*	*win*

Some of these verbs, such as *end* and *move*, belong to types which can be either intransitive or transitive (*cf* 16.19). Something of the range of monotransitive verbs can be seen by dividing them into semantic groups according to the kinds of subject and object that they take:

(i) Typically animate subject + typically concrete object:

Professor Dobbs *won* the prize.
~ The prize *was won* (by Professor Dobbs).

carry	*cover*	*examine*	*see*	*throw*	*win*
clean	*eat*	*lower*	*stop*	*watch*	*write*

(ii) Typically animate subject + either concrete or abstract object:

Everybody *understood* the problem.
~ The problem *was understood* (by everybody).

abolish	*define*	*explain*	*invent*	*report*	*utter*
cover	*discuss*	*forget*	*lose*	*rule*	*win*

(iii) Typically animate subject + typically animate object:

Mrs Wood *liked* the new neighbours.
~ The new neighbours *were liked* (by Mrs Wood).

admire	*despise*	*hug*	*kiss*	*reject*	*ridicule*
beat	*flatter*	*kill*	*meet*	*respect*	*support*

(iv) Typically concrete or abstract subject + animate object:

The news *shocked* our family.
~ Our family *was shocked* (by the news).

affect	*bother*	*fascinate*	*incense*	*satisfy*	*trouble*
appal	*deceive*	*grieve*	*please*	*surprise*	*upset*

Note The following is a sample of monotransitive (or Type II) phrasal verbs [B1ph] with typical objects. Further examples are illustrated in 16.4.

back up ['support' someone]	*let down* ['disappoint' someone]
blow down (a tree)	*make up* (a story)
break off (negotiations)	*pass over* (a question)
bring about (a change)	*put across* (an idea)
burn down (a house)	*put off* (an appointment)
draw up (a contract)	*tell off* ['rebuke' someone]
fill out (a form)	*turn off* (the light)
knock down (someone)	*win over* ['convince' someone]

These, like the verbs in (i–iv) above, can be used in the passive voice.

[B2] Without the passive

16.27 A few stative monotransitive verbs, the most common of which is *have*, normally do not allow a passive transformation:

They *have* a nice house. ~ *A nice house *is had* (by them).

These so-called MIDDLE VERBS, including *have*, *lack*, *fit*, *suit*, and *resemble*, are discussed in detail in 10.14.

Note A related type of verb is found in expressions of measure such as *cost ten dollars*; *weigh 20 kilos*; but these can equally well be analysed as having an obligatory adjunct as complementation, since *How much . . .?* is an alternative question to *What . . .?* in eliciting this kind of expression as a reply:

A: *What* } does it { cost? B: *Ten dollars.*
A: *How much* } does it { weigh? B: *Twenty kilos.*

Variants of monotransitive complementation

Complementation by noun phrase as prepositional object

[B1pr] Prepositional verbs

16.28 Although verbs such as *look at* have been classified as 'Type I prepositional verbs' (those without a direct object; *cf* 16.5), in the analysis of complementation they fit more happily with monotransitive rather than intransitive verbs. This is partly because of the resemblance of the prepositional object to a direct object, *eg* in accepting a passive voice (*cf* 16.14), though usually with some awkwardness of style:

The management *paid for* his air fares.
~ His air fares *were paid for* by the management.

But also when a prepositional verb is followed by a *that*-clause or a *to*-infinitive clause, the preposition disappears, and the prepositional object merges with the direct object of the monotransitive pattern. Compare the following two series, (A) with a prepositional verb and (B) with an ordinary monotransitive verb:

(A) They *agreed* {
on the meeting.
on it.
on meeting each other.
on when to meet.
(that) they would meet.
to meet each other.
}

(B) They *remembered* {
the meeting.
it.
meeting each other.
when to meet.
(that) they had met.
to meet each other.
}

Yet the preposition omitted before a *that*-clause can reappear in the corresponding passive: *That they should meet was agreed* (*on*), even in extraposition (*cf* 18.33*ff*), where the preposition immediately follows the passive verb phrase:

It was *agreed* (*on*) eventually that they should meet.

Examples of Type I prepositional verbs are:

account for	*concentrate on*	*look after/at/on/to*
add to	*conform to*	*object to*
adjust to	*consent to*	*part with*
admit to	*contribute to*	*pay for*
agree with/on/to	*deal with*	*pray for*
aim at/for	*decide on*	*preach about/on*
allow for	*dwell (up)on*	*provide for*
apply for	*enlarge (up)on*	*quarrel about/with*
argue about	*hear about/of*	*read about*
arrange for	*hint at*	*refer to*
ask for	*hope for*	*rejoice at*
attend to	*insist on*	*rely on*
believe in	*interfere with*	*resort to*
call for/(up)on	*learn about*	*run for*
care for	*lecture about/on*	*speak about/on*
comment on	*listen to*	*take to*
complain about	*live on*	*think about/of*
conceive of	*long for*	*wish for*

Note [**a**] When *to* precedes an infinitive, it is an infinitive marker (as in *forget to meet her*) and not a preposition; when it precedes an *-ing* participle, however, it is a preposition (as in *She consented to getting engaged*). Other examples of *to* in a prepositional verb preceding an *-ing* clause are:

He *admitted to* doing his bit.
This *amounts to* doing nothing.
I *confess to* telling a lie.
She *took to* playing golf.

[b] Prepositions may combine with *that* to form complex subordinators such as *in that*, *save that*, *except that* (*cf* 14.12).

[c] In general, choice of preposition is the same for morphologically related verbs and nouns: *refer to* ~ *reference to*; *believe in* ~ *belief in*, etc. There are exceptions, however: *hope* as a verb is followed by *for*, while the corresponding noun construction has *of*: *He hopes for success*, but *His hope of success*.

[B1ph-pr] Phrasal–prepositional verbs

16.29 Type I PHRASAL–PREPOSITIONAL VERBS also take a prepositional object. As we saw in 16.9, such verbs can, like prepositional verbs, occur in the passive (*eg*: *People look down on him* ~ *He is looked down on*); but many of them are awkward, in fact barely acceptable, in this construction: ?**The discussion was walked out on* (*by the principal negotiator*). In the sample list below, the verbs marked [P] are among those that can fairly readily occur in the passive:

break in on (someone's conversation)
catch up on (my reading)
catch up with ['overtake']
check up on ['investigate'] [P]
come down with (a cold)
cut down on (expenses)
do away with ['abolish'] [P]
face up to ['confront'] [P]
get away with (a crime)
get down to (serious talk)
keep away from ['avoid']
keep up with (the Joneses)
look down on ['despise'] [P]
look forward to ['anticipate with pleasure'] [P]
look out for ['watch for']
look up to ['respect'] [P]
put up with ['tolerate'] [P]
run away with
stand up for ['defend']
turn out for (a meeting)

Phrasal–prepositional verbs are rather informal, and many of them have idiomatic metaphorical meanings which are difficult or impossible to paraphrase (*eg*: *run away with*).

Complementation by a finite clause

[B3] *That*-clause as object

16.30 The conjunction in *that*-clauses which function as object may be zero, as in *I hope he arrives soon*; but when the clause is made passive, the *that* cannot be deleted, and thus obeys the same rules as other *that*-clauses as subject (*cf* 15.4). The normal passive analogue has *it* and extraposition, *that* being again optional:

Everybody hoped (that) she would sing.
~ { That she would sing was hoped by everybody. ⟨stilted⟩
*She would sing was hoped by everybody.
It was hoped by everybody (that) she would sing. }

That-clauses have one of three types of verb phrase, depending on the 'governing' verb in the matrix clause:

(A) indicative verb: I suppose that he { *is coming* alone. / *will be coming* alone. / *will come* alone. / *has come* alone. }

(B) putative *should*: I regret that he *should be* so stubborn.

(C) subjunctive verb: I request that she *go* alone.

(A) with the indicative is the most usual type. The putative *should* type (*cf* 14.25) (B) is more common in BrE than AmE, and (C) the mandative subjunctive (*cf* 3.58–9) is more common in AmE than in BrE. In BrE the subjunctive is felt to be formal, and is found typically in official styles of writing. Corresponding to these three constructions, it is necessary to recognize only two main categories of superordinate verbs. *Type (i)* may be called FACTUAL, since it goes with the indicative verb (A), and introduces what one might generally describe as factual or propositional information. *Type (ii)* may be described as SUASIVE; such verbs imply intentions to bring about some change in the future, whether or not these are verbally formulated as commands, suggestions, etc. Suasive verbs can be followed in the *that*-clause by all three constructions (A–C), but the indicative (A) construction is restricted, and is not generally accepted in AmE.

There are two minor categories, *Type (iii)* emotive verbs (*cf* 4.29, 10.23) and *Type (iv)* hypothesis verbs, which are dealt with in 16.33. These types are displayed in *Fig* 16.30:

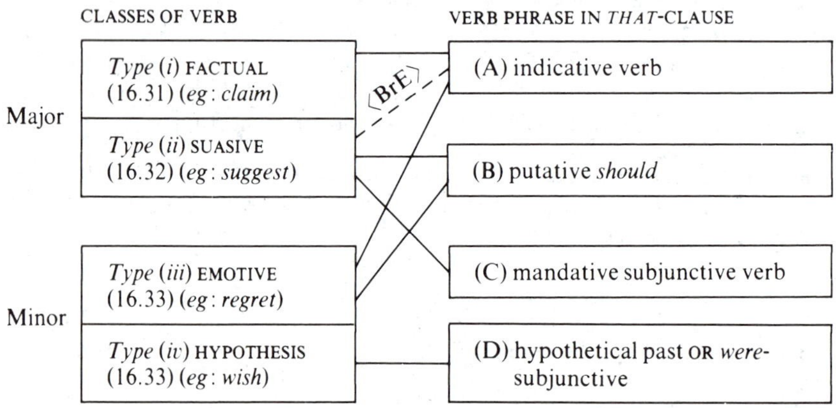

Fig 16.30 Monotransitive verbs with a *that*-clause as complementation (Class [B3])

Note In terms of the speech act classes of 11.2, *Type (i)* (factual) verbs are associated with the expression of speech acts concerned with STATEMENTS, while *Type (ii)* (suasive) verbs are associated with DIRECTIVES.

Type (i): Factual verbs

16.31 We may subdivide factual verbs into 'PUBLIC' and 'PRIVATE' types. The former consists of speech act verbs introducing indirect statements:

They *agree/admit/claim* that she was misled.

The superscripts 1–5 in the lists below are to be interpreted as follows:

1: The verb also occurs in the active with a *to*-infinitive directly following: *He promised to come* (*cf* 16.38).
2: The verb also occurs with a following noun phrase followed by a *to*-infinitive: *They supposed her to be dead* (*cf* 16.50).
3: The verb is also a member of the suasive group below, in 16.32.
4: The pro-form *so* can stand in place of the *that*-clause (*cf* 12.28); *eg*: *I think so.*
5: *Say* occurs with an infinitive, as in *She said to come before ten* in the directive sense of 'She told us to come before ten'.

Examples:

acknowledge[2]	*boast*	*declare*[2]	*mention*	*report*[2]
add	*certify*[2]	*deny*[2]	*object*	*retort*
admit[2]	*claim*[1]	*disclose*	*predict*[4]	*say*[2,4,5]
affirm[2]	*comment*	*exclaim*	*proclaim*[2]	*state*[2,4]
agree[1,3]	*complain*	*explain*[2]	*promise*[1,2,4]	*submit*
allege[2]	*concede*[3]	*forecast*	*pronounce*[2]	*suggest*[3]
announce[2]	*confess*[2]	*foretell*	*prophesy*	*swear*
argue	*confide*	*guarantee*[1,2]	*protest*	*testify*[2]
assert	*confirm*[2]	*hint*	*remark*	*vow*[1]
bet	*contend*	*insist*[3]	*repeat*	*warn*[2]
	convey	*maintain*[4]	*reply*	*write*

The 'PRIVATE' type of factual verb expresses intellectual states such as belief and intellectual acts such as discovery. These states and acts are 'private' in the sense that they are not observable: a person may be observed to *assert that God exists*, but not to *believe that God exists.* Belief is in this sense 'private'. Examples of such verbs are:

accept	*doubt*	*imagine*[2,4]	*realize*
anticipate	*dream*	*imply*	*reason*
ascertain	*ensure*[3]	*indicate*[4]	*recall*
assume[2,4]	*establish*	*infer*[4]	*reckon*[1,4]
believe[2,4]	*estimate*[2]	*insure*	*recognize*[2]
calculate	*expect*[1,2,4]	*judge*[2]	*reflect*
check	*fancy*[2]	*know*[2]	*remember*
conclude	*fear*[1,4]	*learn*[1]	*reveal*[2]
conjecture	*feel*[2]	*mean*[1,2]	*see*
consider[2]	*find*[2]	*note*[2]	*sense*
decide[1,3]	*foresee*	*notice*[2,4]	*show*[2]
deduce	*forget*[1]	*observe*[2]	*signify*
deem[2]	*gather*[4]	*perceive*[2,4]	*suppose*[2,4]
demonstrate	*guess*[4]	*presume*[2,4]	*suspect*[2,4]
determine[1,3]	*hear*[4]	*presuppose*[2]	*think*[2,4]
discern	*hold*	*pretend*[1]	*understand*[2,4]
discover[2]	*hope*[1,4]	*prove*[2]	

Many of these verbs, especially the 'public' verbs, are also used for introducing direct speech; *eg*:

'Perhaps it's time to leave', *suggested* Tim.

For detailed discussion of this use of verbs of speaking and thinking, *cf* 14.30*ff*.

Note [**a**] Not included in the first list above are verbs expressing manner of utterance, such as *mumble*, *mutter*, *shout*, *whimper*, *whisper*, and *yell*. These can introduce direct speech quotations (*eg*: 'I am ill', *she muttered*), but they can also introduce indirect or reported speech by means of a *that*-clause: *She muttered that she was ill.* The list of such verbs is large, and some verbs occur more easily with *that*-clauses than others do.

[**b**] All the following phrasal verbs belonging to this 'factual' category are 'public' verbs: *chime in*, *let on*, *let out*, *make out*, *point out*, *report back*:

> Tim *pointed out* that the train was often late.

In this construction, the particle has to precede the *that*-clause.

[**c**] Among the 'private verbs', *see*, *suppose*, and *assume* can be used with a *that*-clause in which the present tense refers to future time (*cf* 14.23):

> *See* (to it) that they get something to eat.

See here means 'make sure'.

[**d**] *Doubt*, being a verb of negative meaning, is typically followed by *whether*/*if* (*cf* 15.6, 16.35). But more especially when it is in a nonassertive context, *doubt* occurs with a *that*-clause:

> I don't doubt (*but*) *that* they'll accept at once.

Note that in this construction, *doubt* is sometimes followed by *but*. *Doubt* cannot be followed by an alternative *wh*-clause (*cf* 15.6):

> *I doubt whether or not they'll accept.

Type (ii): Suasive verbs

16.32 These verbs can be followed by a *that*-clause either with putative *should* (*cf* 14.25) or with the mandative subjunctive. A third possibility, a *that*-clause with an indicative verb, is largely restricted to BrE:

> People are demanding that she { *should leave* / *leave* / *leaves* ⟨esp BrE⟩ } the company. [1]

It is more difficult, in the case of suasive verbs, to make a subdivision between 'PUBLIC' and 'PRIVATE' verbs: for this reason, we present the verbs below in a single list. Nevertheless, generally it is useful to see a distinction between the 'public' verbs which describe indirect directives (such as *request*; *cf* 14.33), and the 'private' verbs which describe states of volition or desire, such as *intend*:

agree[1]	*demand*[1]	*intend*[1,2]	*recommend*[2]
allow[2]	*desire*[1,2]	*move*[4]	*request*[1,2]
arrange[1]	*determine*[1]	*ordain*[2,4]	*require*
ask[1,2]	*enjoin*[2]	*order*[2]	*resolve*[1]
beg[1,2]	*ensure*	*pledge*[1,2]	*rule*
command[2]	*entreat*[2]	*pray*[1,2,4]	*stipulate*
concede	*grant*	*prefer*[1,2,4]	*suggest*[2,4]
decide[1]	*insist*	*pronounce*[2]	*urge*[2]
decree[4]	*instruct*[2]	*propose*[1,2]	*vote*[1,2]

The superscripts 1, 2 and 4 have the same meaning as in 16.31 above. The choice between the three constructions in the *that*-clause in [1] above varies between AmE and BrE. For detailed discussion of these preferences, *cf* 14.25.

It will be noted that the noun phrase + infinitive construction (*cf* 16.50) is a common alternative to the *that*-clause for suasive verbs:

They intended { the news *to be* suppressed.
{ that the news (*should*) *be* suppressed. ⟨more formal⟩

With some verbs, such as *allow*, the infinitive construction is by far the more usual.

Other types of verb with *that*-clause complementation

Type (iii): Emotive verbs

16.33 This consists of a small group of verbs such as *regret*, *marvel*, *rejoice*, and *wonder*, which can occur with (A) the indicative or (B) the putative *should* construction, but not with the mandative subjunctive construction:

I regret that she { *worries* about it.
{ *should worry* about it.
{ **worry* about it.

Semantically, this group belongs with adjectival constructions such as *be sorry*, *be anxious* (*cf* 16.71).

Type (iv): Hypothesis verbs

The two verbs *wish* and (in the imperative) *suppose* may be followed by a *that*-clause containing a verb in the hypothetical past or the *were*-subjunctive: *I wish* (*that*) *she were here*; *She wished she hadn't spent the money*; *Suppose* (*that*) *one of us died*. *Cf* 14.24 on the use of tense and mood following these verbs, which may also occur in a number of other patterns. In particular, for other uses of *wish*, *cf* 16.38, 16.41, 16.44, 16.46, 16.57.

The modal idiom *would rather* (or its contraction *'d rather*) (*cf* 3.46) is a third example of a hypothesis verb:

I'*d rather* you didn't mention the price.
Many residents *would rather* that the bus service were subsidized.

Complementation by an extraposed subject *that*-clause

16.34 The *that*-clause in examples like *It seems that you are mistaken* is not an object of the verb, but rather an extraposed subject. Nevertheless, it resembles other *that*-clauses we have been examining (a) in having a deletable *that*, and (b) in being semantically associated with the preceding verb. Moreover, no nonextraposed *that*-clause is possible in this case (**That you are mistaken seems*), and so it seems appropriate to include this with *that*-clause complementation. The main verbs occurring in this pattern form two groups of synonyms: (i) *seem* and *appear*; and (ii) *chance*, *happen*, and *transpire*:

It *appears* that Frank lost his temper.
It *happened* that the weather was exceptionally cold.

The phrasal verbs *come about* [= 'happen'] and *turn out* [= 'transpire'] also belong here. *Appear* and *seem* can be followed by the pro-form *so*: *It seems/appears so*. The adverb *so* sometimes occurs before *happen* or one of its synonyms: *It so happens/happened that* . . . .

Note [a] A related construction with extraposed object (*cf* 18.35) occurs in the following transitive phrasal verbs:

let (*it*) *out*; *noise* (*it*) *about/abroad*; *put* (*it*) *about*; *rub* (*it*) *in*:
Jack *let* (*it*) *out* [= 'divulged'] that the animal had been stolen.

The *it* which occurs as preparatory object is in this case optional, although the omission is not usual. In the comparable construction *take it that*, the *it* is obligatory: *I take it that you are enjoying yourselves*.

[**b**] Compare the complementation of *seem, appear*, etc by an *as if* clause (*cf* 16.24 Note [a]).

[**c**] On the related constructions *It strikes me that . . . , It occurs/seems to me that . . . , cf* 16.59 Note, 16.60 Note.

[B4] *Wh*-clause as object

16.35 Many of the verbs which take a *that*-clause as object can also take a *wh*-interrogative clause (*cf* 15.5*ff*):

> I asked her to *confirm* whether the flight had been booked.
> Can you *confirm* which flight we are taking?
> They haven't yet *confirmed* how much the flight costs.

Notice that in all three illustrative sentences above, *confirm* occurs in what may be described as a nonassertive context (*cf* 2.53). The use of the *wh*-interrogative clause (which generally implies lack of knowledge on the part of the speaker) is particularly common where the superordinate clause is interrogative or negative. On the other hand, there are some verbs which themselves express uncertainty, such as *ask* and *wonder*: these occur with the *wh*-clause without this nonassertive constraint. Examples of verbs taking the *wh*-interrogative clause are:

anticipate [NA]
argue [NA][2]
arrange [NA][3]
ascertain[3]
ask[2,3]
beware[2]
calculate [NA][3]
care [NA][1,2]
check[2,3]
choose[3]
confirm [NA]
consider [NA][3]
decide[2,3]
demonstrate[3]
depend[2]
disclose
discover[3]
discuss[3]
doubt
enquire[2,3]
establish[3]
explain[3]
express
fathom [NA]
find out[2,3]
forget[3]
guess
hear [NA][2]
imagine [NA][3]
indicate [NA][3]
inquire[2,3]
judge[3]
know [NA][3]
learn [NA][3]
make out [NA]
mind [NA][1]
note [NA][3]
notice [NA][3]
observe [NA][3]
perceive [NA][3]
point out [NA]
ponder[3]
predict [NA]
prove
realize [NA]
record [NA]
reflect[2]
remember [NA][3]
say [NA][3]
see [NA][3]
show[3]
tell [NA][1,3]
think [NA][3]
wonder[3]

The symbol [NA] after a verb indicates that this complementation is particularly likely to occur in a nonassertive context. The superscripts 1–3 are interpreted as follows:

1: This verb is part of a negative or predominantly negative construction when combined with the *wh*-interrogative clause: *not care*; *not mind*; *can't fathom*; *can't tell*.

2: The verb is basically a prepositional verb, and has a preposition which may be optionally added (see below).

3: The verb can also occur with a following *wh*-infinitive clause (*cf* 16.37); *eg*: *I didn't know what to say.*

The preposition of a prepositional verb is optionally omitted before a *wh*-clause, and hence it is convenient to include in the above list verbs for which the *wh*-clause is basically a prepositional object. For example:

I *inquired* (*about*) whether the tickets were ready.
They haven't yet *decided* (*on*) which flight they will take.

For the corresponding passive, again, the preposition is optional, whether or not the nominal clause is in extraposition:

Which flight they will take has not yet been *decided* (*on*).
It has not yet been *decided* (*on*) which flight they will take.

Sometimes there is a slight difference of meaning if the preposition is included; contrast:

She *asked* what he wanted.
≠ She *asked about* what he wanted.

Whereas *ask* introduces the question which the speaker actually asked and for which she requires an answer, *ask about* does not indicate what the question might have been. Other prepositional verbs in this class are: *argue* (*about*); *beware* (*of*) (*cf* 3.54 Note); *not care* (*about*); *check* (*on*); *depend* (*on*); *hear* (*about*); *reflect* (*on*). There is also the phrasal–prepositional verb *find out* (*about*).

Note A few verbs are followed by a *wh*-exclamative clause (indirect exclamation; *cf* 10.104) beginning with *what* or *how*: *I realized what a fool I had been*; *I know how busy you are*. These clauses are difficult to distinguish from *wh*-interrogative clauses. Other verbs in the pattern include *exclaim, express, marvel, reflect, think*.

Complementation by a nonfinite clause

Nonfinite clauses in complementation

16.36 When a nonfinite clause follows the verb it is often difficult to separate three of the major types of complementation which we distinguished in 2.16. This is especially true if a noun phrase intervenes between the superordinate verb and the verb of the nonfinite construction:

They like *the children to visit them.* [1]
They supposed *the children to be guilty.* [2]
They asked *the children to bring some food.* [3]

On the face of it, all three of these sentences conform to the same pattern (verb + noun phrase + *to*-infinitive . . .). But there are reasons for classifying them differently:

[1] exemplifies MONOTRANSITIVE complementation (16.38*ff*)
(*cf*: *They like the children's visits – SVO*)
[2] exemplifies COMPLEX TRANSITIVE complementation (16.43*ff*)
(*cf*: *They supposed the children guilty – SVOC*)

[3] exemplifies DITRANSITIVE complementation (16.55*ff*)
(*cf*: *They asked the children a question* – *SVOO*)

We will return in 16.64*ff* to differences between examples such as these. At present, since we are dealing with monotransitive complementation, we are concerned only with the type illustrated by [1]. In nominal function, only two kinds of nonfinite clause normally occur: the *to*-infinitive clause and the *-ing* participle clause. Hence nonfinite clauses functioning as object can be distinguished, for the present purposes, in terms of the categories in *Table* 16.36:

Table 16.36 Nonfinite clauses as object

	Without subject	With subject
to-infinitive	[B6] Jack hates *to miss the train.*	[B8] Jack hates *her to miss the train.*
-ing participle	[B7] Jack hates *missing the train.*	[B9] Jack hates *her missing the train.*

In *Table* 16.36, the italicized parts are analysed as nonfinite clauses acting as direct object. The status of the infinitive clause and its subject in pattern [B8] is discussed in 16.41. Later, in 16.66, we consider the arguments for considering *her* an object in the [B8] and [B9] examples.

The following criteria confirm that the italicized portion of [B6–B9] is basically a nonfinite clause as direct object:

(A) The nonfinite clause can be replaced by a pronoun *it* coreferring to a clause, or by a noun phrase nominalizing the meaning of a clause: *Everyone likes it*; *He likes her frequent visits.*

(B) The nonfinite clause can be made the focus of a pseudo-cleft sentence (*cf* 18.29):

What everyone likes (best) is *to talk to her.* [B6]
What everyone likes (best) is *talking to her.* [B7]
What he likes (best) is *for her to call often.* [B8]

In this version of [B8], as the infinitive clause is now in complement position, the introductory *for* has to make its appearance.

(C) For [B8] the introductory *for* itself, where it appears, is a marker of the construction as a nonfinite clause.

(D) Correspondingly, for [B9], a subject pronoun in the objective case can often be replaced, in formal style, by a possessive pronoun (*cf* 14.6):

He doesn't like *me/my coming often.*

This is what one would expect (*cf* 15.12) given that *me* and *my* can both be subjects of an *-ing* clause.

Not all verbs that we consider direct objects satisfy all these criteria. Nevertheless, it is on this basis that the verbs listed below are included in the classes [B6–B9].

[B5] *Wh*-infinitive clause as object

16.37 It is as well to begin the survey of nonfinite clauses as objects with clauses which happen to be immediately related to those dealt with in 16.35. These are *wh*-infinitive clauses (*cf* 15.5):

> He learned *how to sail a boat* as a small boy.
> You must not forget *when to keep your mouth shut.*
> I couldn't decide (on) *which bicycle to buy.*

The last example illustrates the occurrence of the optional preposition with prepositional verbs, as already observed with finite clauses of the same type. The corresponding passive pattern also occurs:

> The Curies discovered *how to isolate radioactive elements.*
> ~ *How to isolate radioactive elements* was discovered by the Curies.

The passive with extraposition (*cf* 16.30, 16.35) is also sometimes possible:

> Early in the present century, it was discovered *how to isolate radioactive elements.*

The verbs marked '3' in the list in 16.35 above provide a sample of verbs occurring with the *wh*-infinitive clause as object.

Note Many verbs which introduce *wh*-infinitive clauses rarely if ever introduce *yes–no* interrogative clauses (introduced by *whether*) of the same type: *I have forgotten how to swim* but not **I have forgotten whether to swim.* Among such verbs are *demonstrate, discover*, and *explain.* Nevertheless in unusual contexts such sentences can be found:

> I have forgotten *whether to unfreeze this food before cooking it.*

[B6] Subjectless infinitive clause as direct object

16.38 When a subjectless infinitive clause is direct object, the 'understood' subject of the infinitive clause is always the same as the subject of the superordinate clause. Verbs taking this kind of complementation are listed below, subdivided into semantic categories:

(i) *dread* [B7, B8]
hate [B7, B8]
like [B7, B8]
loathe [B7, B8]
love [B7, B8]
prefer [B7, B8]

(ii) *begin* [B7]
cease [B7]
commence [B7]
continue [B7]
start [B7]

(iii) *forget* [B7]
remember [B7]
regret [B7]

(iv) *choose* [B7]
hope
intend [B7, B8]
mean [B7, B8]
need [B7]
plan [B7]
propose [B7]
want [B7, B8]
wish [B8]

(v) *deign*
disdain [B7]
help [B7, B8]
scorn [B7]
venture [B7]

(vi) *ask*
beg
decline
demand
offer
promise
refuse
swear
undertake
vow

(vii) *affect*
claim
profess [B7]

(viii) *afford* [B7]
attempt [B7]
contrive
endeavour
fail
learn
manage
neglect
omit
try [B7]

The symbols to the right of some verbs indicate that these verbs also occur with the subjectless *-ing* clause (Type [B7]) or with the infinitive clause with a subject (Type [B8]). From the latter group, however, verbs such as *ask* are excluded, because the construction of sentences like *He asked me to help* is ditransitive (*cf* 16.63) rather than monotransitive.

We now add a list of prepositional verbs belonging to the same pattern [B6pr]. The preposition is omitted before the infinitive clause object (*cf* 9.2), but is present where the prepositional object is a noun phrase or, for that matter, an *-ing* clause. Compare:

She didn't *bother*	*about* the baby.	[B1pr]
	about feeding the baby.	[B7pr]
	to feed the baby.	[B6pr]

In the following list, the verbs are placed in semantic groupings corresponding to some of those above (apart from an additional miscellaneous group (ix)), and the omitted preposition is placed in square brackets:

(i) *long* [*for*] [B8]
ache [*for*]
aim [*for*] [B8]
aspire [*to*]
burn [*for*]
burst [*for*]
(*not*) *care* [*for*]
clamour [*for*] [B8]
itch [*for*] [B8]
yearn [*for*] [B8]

(iii) *bother* [*about*] [B7, B8]
condescend [*to*]
delight [*in*] [B7]
hesitate [*about*] [B7]

(vi) *agree* [*to*/*on*/*about*]
consent [*to*]

(vii) *pretend* [*to*]

(viii) *strive* [*for*]
seek [*for*]

(ix) *arrange* [*for*] [B7, B8]
decide [*on*] [B7]
resolve [*on*] [B7]
prepare [*for*] [B7]
serve [*for*] [B7]

Examples:

Martin *longed* to leave home.
They *sought* to make amends.
I would *hesitate* to interfere.
We've *decided* to move to a new house.

Note [**a**] We distinguish the verbs of Type [B6] from catenative verbs (*cf* 3.49) of 'seeming' and 'occurrence' preceding infinitive clauses which are not direct objects, but which relate semantically to a *that*-clause as subject: *He appears to like the show* ~ *That he likes the show appears* [*true*]. The verbs in this class correlate closely with those occurring with obligatory extraposition of the subject (*cf* 16.34) *appear, seem, chance, happen, turn out*:

It *appeared*/*chanced* that the children were asleep.
~ The children *appeared*/*chanced* to be asleep.

[**b**] Another group of verbs which are closely associated with a following infinitive but which do not belong to Type [B6] includes *hasten, conspire,* and *set out*:

I hastened *to reassure her.*
They conspired *to murder Caesar.*
He set out *to conquer the world.*

The *to*-infinitive here, however, has a resultative meaning which makes the construction resemble on the one hand that of a catenative verb, and on the other hand that of an intransitive verb followed by an adjunct. With *pay* and (to a lesser extent) *wait*, the adjunct status is more obvious, as is clear from the possibility of fronting the infinitive clause:

> You have to pay *to go in*.
> ~ (*In order*) *to go in*, you have to pay.
> He waited *to see her*.
> ~ ?(*In order*) *to see her*, he waited.

Similarly, unlike *begin* + infinitive, the infinitive following *stop* is purposive; contrast:

> She [S] began [V] to eat lunch [O].
> BUT: She [S] stopped [V] to eat lunch [A].

On the other hand, these two verbs have matching uses in complementation Type [B7]:

> She {began / stopped} eating lunch.

[B7] Subjectless *-ing* participle clause as object

16.39 Again, with this type of complementation, the subject of the nonfinite verb is usually identical with the subject of the preceding verb:

> I love *listening to music*.
> The accused denied *having met the witness*.
> ['The accused denied *that he/she had met the witness*']

This rule accounts for the restriction that when the participle is followed by a reflexive pronoun, the pronoun normally has to agree (in number, person, and gender) with the subject of the superordinate clause:

> [She / He] enjoys singing to [*herself*. / *himself*.]

But with one small group of verbs (marked '2' in the list below) it is not the understood subject of the participle, but its understood object that is identified with the subject of the superordinate clause. In such cases, therefore, the participle construction matches in meaning the passive of the corresponding infinitive construction [B6]:

> Your shoes *need* {mending. / to be mended.}   That door *needs* {painting. / to be painted.}

(The above use of *need* is often replaced, in dialectally restricted usage, by an equivalent use of *want*.)

For an additional group of verbs (marked '3' in the list below), the subject of the participle is indefinite, and is independent of the subject of the preceding verb. For example, in *He recommended introducing a wealth tax*, it is clear that the person *recommending* the tax is likely to be different from the person(s) who would be responsible for *introducing* it. The meaning of this sentence is equivalent to that of *He recommended the introduction of a wealth tax*.

In the following list of verbs in the pattern of [B7], Types (i) and (ii) correspond to Type [B6(i)] ('emotive') and Type [B6(ii)] ('aspectual'). The verbs grouped under (iii) are however in this case a miscellany, since further semantic grouping is difficult.

(i) *(can't) bear*[1]
begrudge[1]
detest[1]
dislike[1]
dread[1]
enjoy
(not) fancy[1]
hate[1]
like[1]
loathe[1]
love[1]
(not) mind[1]
miss[1]
regret[1,4]
relish[1]
resent[1]
(can't) stand[1]

(ii) *cease*
commence
continue
quit
resume
start[1]
stop[1]

(iii) *admit*[4]
avoid
confess[4]
consider
deny[4]
deserve[2]
discourage[1,3]
envisage[1,3]
escape
forget[1,3,4]
(can't) help[1]
imagine[1]
involve[1,3]
justify[1,3]
need[1,2]
permit[1,3]
propose
recall[1,3,4]
recommend[1,3]
remember[1,3,4]
repent
require[2]
risk[1,3]
save[1,3]
try[5]
want[1], ⟨dialectal[2]⟩

The verbs of Type (i) preceded by a negative (such as *can't bear*) have a built-in negative bias, so that they cannot occur in straightforward assertive contexts:

Cora *doesn't mind* waiting. ?*Cora *minds* waiting.

They can, however, occur in nonassertive contexts:

Do you *mind* waiting?
How *can* anyone *bear* wearing clothes like that?

and also in 'second instance' contexts, *ie* where the construction refers back to a nonassertive occurrence of the same construction earlier in the discourse:

A: I [*can't stand* / *don't fancy*] working with that girl.

B: Well, I'm afraid you'll HÀVE to [*stand* it. / *fancy* working with her.]

Superscripts in the above lists are interpreted as follows:

1: The verb also occurs in pattern [B9], *ie* with a subject preceding the participle (*cf* 16.42).
2: The participle has a 'passive' interpretation (see above).
3: The participle has 'independent' interpretation; *ie* the subject of the participle clause is not necessarily coreferential with the subject of the preceding verb, and may have indefinite meaning.
4: The participle may occur with a perfective construction:

I admit *having seen* it. [1]

But with such verbs, the nonperfective construction can also be used with past meaning. Thus [1] is synonymous with [2]:

I admit *seeing* it. [2]

This paraphrase relation, however, exists mainly with verbs of dynamic meaning; contrast verbs of stative meaning:

I admit knowing him.
≠ I admit having known him.

5: On the construction with *try*, *cf* 16.40.

Examples of prepositional verbs belonging to this class ([B7pr]) are:

bank on[1]	*decide on*	*play at*	*see about*[1]
count on[1]	*delight in*[1]	*resort to*	*shrink from*

Examples of phrasal verbs ([B7ph]) are:

break off *give up* *leave off* *put off* *take up*

Examples of [B7ph-pr] are:

do away with *get around to* *go in for* *look forward to*

The following sentences illustrate these patterns:

We *counted on* getting there early. [B7pr]
I've *taken up* playing tennis. [B7ph]
Jim is *looking forward to* having the house to himself. [B7ph-pr]

It is important to notice that the *to* in *get around to*, *look forward to*, and *resort to* is not an infinitive marker, but a preposition. Hence *I am looking forward to seeing you* is grammatical, but not **I am looking forward to see you.*

Note [**a**] The superscript '1' in the above lists is not added to verbs like *stop*, although a noun phrase can be inserted between the participle and the preceding verb in such cases:

They stopped (her) working all night.

This is because the construction containing the extra noun phrase (*her* in the above example) is arguably complex transitive (*cf* 16.53) rather than monotransitive (as is evident from the marginally acceptable passive ?*She was stopped working all night*).

[**b**] Also we exclude from the above lists catenative verbs such as *go* in *We went running* and *get* in *Get moving!* (*cf* 3.49).

Choice between the infinitive and participle constructions ([B6] and [B7])

16.40 Where both constructions [B6] and [B7] are admitted, there is usually felt to be a difference of aspect or mood which influences the choice. As a rule, the infinitive gives a sense of mere 'potentiality' for action, as in *She hoped to learn French*, while the participle gives a sense of the actual 'performance' of the action itself, as in *She enjoyed learning French.* In the case of *try*, the double meaning is particularly clear:

Sheila tried { *to bribe* the jailor. [1]
Sheila tried { *bribing* the jailor. [2]

[1] implies that Sheila attempted an act of bribery, but did not manage it; [2] implies that she actually did bribe the jailor, but without (necessarily) achieving what she wanted. With other verbs, the difference is more subtle, and may be overruled or neutralized by the meaning of the verb of the main clause. For example, the negative meaning of *avoid* and *escape* cancels out the sense of 'performance' in *He escaped/avoided being branded as a traitor.*

Let us consider more carefully three classes of verb which take both constructions:

(i) EMOTIVE VERBS (see Type (i) in the lists in 16.38 and 16.39). With the verbs which take both constructions (*dread, hate, like, loathe, love,* and *prefer*) the bias of the infinitive towards 'potentiality' tends to favour its use in hypothetical and nonfactual contexts; *eg*:

$$\text{Would you } \textit{like} \left\{\begin{array}{c}\textit{to see}\\ ?{*}\textit{seeing}\end{array}\right\} \text{ my stamp collection?}$$

$$\text{I } \textit{hate} \left\{\begin{array}{c}\textit{to seem}\\ ?\textit{seeming}\end{array}\right\} \text{ rude, but you're blocking the view.}$$

On the other hand, the participial construction is favoured where the speaker is referring to something which definitely happens or has happened:

$$\text{Brian } \textit{loathed} \left\{\begin{array}{c}?\textit{to live}\\ \textit{living}\end{array}\right\} \text{ in the country.}$$

(But with *would loathe*, the infinitive is just as acceptable as the *-ing* participle.)

Here *to live* implies that Brian could exercise choice about where to live, whereas *living* presupposes that he actually did live in the country, and probably had no choice in the matter. But in other contexts there is little appreciable difference between the two constructions:

$$\text{Do you } \textit{prefer} \left[\begin{array}{c}\text{to cook}\\ \text{cooking}\end{array}\right] \text{ for yourself, or } \left[\begin{array}{c}\text{to eat}\\ \text{eating}\end{array}\right] \text{ in a restaurant?}$$

(ii) ASPECTUAL VERBS of beginning, continuing, and ending also in many cases take both constructions:

$$\text{Lucy } \textit{started/continued/ceased} \left\{\begin{array}{c}\textit{to write}\\ \textit{writing}\end{array}\right\} \text{ while in hospital.}$$

In such examples as this, there is no observable difference of meaning between the constructions. But in other cases, a contrast between 'potentiality' and 'performance' may influence the choice:

$$\text{He } \textit{started} \left\{\begin{array}{l}\textit{to speak}\text{, but stopped because she objected.}\\ \textit{speaking}\text{, and kept on for more than an hour.}\end{array}\right.$$

The association of the *-ing* participle with the progressive aspect may also influence a preference for the participle where multiple activities are involved:

$$\text{He } \textit{began} \left\{\begin{array}{l}\textit{to open}\text{ all the cupboards.}\\ \textit{opening}\text{ all the cupboards.}\end{array}\right.$$

Here *opening* is more appropriate than *to open*. While some verbs in this group (*begin, continue, cease, start*), allow both constructions, others (*finish, stop*) allow only the participle construction. (*Go on* and *keep* (*on*) may be classified as catenative verbs (*cf* 3.49); on *finish/stop* followed by the infinitive, *cf* 16.38 Note [b].)

(iii) RETROSPECTIVE VERBS. For three verbs *forget*, *remember*, and *regret*, the 'potentiality'/'performance' distinction becomes extended into the past so that there is a temporal (as well as in part modal) difference between the two constructions. The infinitive construction indicates that the action or event takes place after (and as a result of) the mental process denoted by the verb has begun, while the reverse is true for the participle construction, which refers to a preceding event or occasion coming to mind at the time indicated by the main verb:

> I *remembered* to fill out the form. ['I remembered that I was to fill out the form and then did so']
> I *remembered* filling out the form. ['I remembered that I had filled out the form']

> I *forgot* to go to the bank. ['I forgot that I was to go to the bank, and therefore did not do so']
> I *forgot* (*about*) going to the bank. [rare without *about*; 'I forgot that I went to the bank' or '. . . that I should have gone . . .']

> I *regret* to tell you that John stole it. ['I regret that I am about to tell you that John stole it']
> I *regret* telling you that John stole it. ['I regret that I told you that John stole it' or '. . . that I am now telling you . . .']

[B8] Complementation by *to*-infinitive clause (with subject)

16.41 The verbs in this group (as distinct from the apparently similar 'object + infinitive' construction; *cf* 16.50) are restricted to a small number chiefly denoting (not) liking or wanting: (*can't*) *bear*, *desire*, *hate*, *like*, *love*, *prefer*, *want*, and *wish*:

> They don't *like* the house to be left empty.
> I wouldn't *want* you to lose your way.

After these verbs, the noun phrase preceding the infinitive cannot be made the subject of a passive main clause: **The house isn't liked to be left empty* (*by them*).

There is moreover an alternative construction (chiefly restricted to AmE) in which the noun phrase is preceded by *for* which marks it as the subject of an infinitive clause, rather than as object of the main clause:

> Jack prefers *for* his wife to drive the truck. ⟨esp AmE⟩

These two observations point in the direction of a monotransitive analysis of such verbs.

In the following, however, *for* has a different status and must occur in both AmE and BrE:

> They arranged *for* Mary to come at once.

In this case the construction is that of a prepositional verb *arrange for* ([B8pr]), the infinitive clause acting as prepositional object. Other examples where *for* occurs as part of a prepositional verb are: *ask for, call for, ache for, aim for, burn for, burst for, care for, clamour for, crave for, hope for, itch for, long for, plan for, prepare for, wait for, yearn for*:

> We were all *aching/burning/bursting for* the performance to begin.
> They *planned for* the mayor to arrive on the following day.

For some of the verbs in these clauses, the *that*-clause with *should* ([B3(ii)]) is an alternative form of complementation:

> They planned that the mayor *should arrive* on the following day.

A further reason in favour of a monotransitive analysis of verbs of Type [B8pr] is the possibility (in some cases) of a passive, with or without extraposition:

> For the administration to resign so quickly was not called for.
> It had been arranged for the food to be served indoors.

Note [**a**] Some [B8pr] verbs, such as *arrange for, plan for*, and *prepare for*, also have a [B2] construction in which they are followed by a direct object. Compare: *Have you arranged the meeting? Have you arranged for the meeting?* Compare also *She asked for the children to leave* and *She asked the children to leave*.

[**b**] *Desire, expect*, and *intend*, although they fit into this category with respect to introductory *for* and the extraposed passive, also accept the passive of the 'raised object' which applies to [C4] (*cf* 16.50). Thus *expect*, for example, permits two associated passives:

> It was not expected for the administration to resign.
> The administration was not expected to resign.

The former of these, however, is felt to be awkward and of marginal acceptability. On such conflicts of classification *cf* 16.64*ff*.

[B9] Complementation by *-ing* participle clause (with subject)

16.42 Verbs which accept this pattern comprise a considerable subset of those verbs accepting the subjectless *-ing* clause as object: they include the verbs marked '1' in the list of 16.39. The genitive form of the subject is an option in formal English (*cf* 15.12), but is often felt to be awkward or stilted:

> I dislike *him/his driving my car*.
> We look forward to *you/your becoming our neighbour*.

In some cases, particularly when the subject of the participle is not a pronoun and does not have personal reference, the genitive option is rare:

> Peter stopped the {*vehicle* / ?*vehicle's*} crashing into the fence.

The genitive is also rare with a pronoun with nonpersonal reference:

> I look forward to {*it* / ?*its*} getting warmer in spring.

The verbs of negative meaning *stop, prevent*, and *prohibit* have a related ditransitive construction (*cf* 16.56*f*) in which the preposition *from* precedes the *-ing* clause as second object:

> They tried to *prevent* the plane *from* landing on the runway.

Thus the *from* is optional.

In the very few cases where we have a choice between an *-ing* participle and a *to*-infinitive construction there is usually felt to be a difference of aspect or mood such as that described in 16.40:

I *hate* the children *to quarrel* [. . . they're ordinarily such good friends]. [1]
I *hate* the children *quarrelling* [. . . all the time]. [2]

[1] focuses on the children's 'potential' for quarrelling; [2] emphasizes their 'performance' – the point being that they do quarrel, rather often in fact. An aspectual difference is uppermost in:

I *hate* the clock { *chiming* (. . . all night long). / *to chime* (. . . just when I'm going to sleep). }

The infinitive suggests a single chime, while the participle suggests continual chiming (*cf* 4.35, 4.67*f*).

Note Verbs of the 'observational' type, *eg*: *notice* in *I noticed him writing a letter*, do not belong in this group, and are dealt with in 16.53. For such verbs, the genitive is not a possible alternative: **I noticed his writing a letter*.

Complex transitive complementation

16.43 In 2.16 we applied the term COMPLEX TRANSITIVE to verbs in the patterns *SVOC* and *SVOA*. In this chapter we extend the term to other clause patterns in which an object is followed by another element which is not an object (*eg* a nonfinite clause). A distinguishing characteristic of complex transitive complementation is that the two elements following the verb (*eg* object and object complement) are notionally equated with the subject and predication respectively of a nominal clause. For example:

MONOTRANSITIVE:	She presumed *that her father was dead.*	[1]
COMPLEX TRANSITIVE:	She presumed *her father to be dead.*	[2]
	She presumed *her father dead.*	[3]

In [3], *her father* (O) and *dead* (C) are equivalent in meaning to a separate clause, *viz* the *that*-clause in [1]. This relationship remains where the object complement is expanded into an infinitive clause, as in [2]. Yet *her father to be dead*, in spite of its clause-like meaning and appearance, does not act syntactically as a single constituent, as is evident in the passive, where the O is separated from its complement:

Her father was presumed (by her) *to be dead.*

This divisibility into two elements of a semantically clausal construction following the verb is the defining property of complex transitive complementation.

We begin with three already familiar patterns of complex transitive complementation: those corresponding to [A1–A3] (*cf* 16.21–4).

Note On the similarities between complex transitive and ditransitive complementation, see 16.66*ff*.

[C1] Adjective phrase as object complement

16.44 The *SVOC* pattern (*cf* 2.16) in which the object complement is an adjective phrase is found with verbs which, like copular verbs, may be divided into CURRENT and RESULTING types:

You should *keep* the cabbage *fresh*. [1]
That music *drives* me *mad*. [2]

The verb *keep* in [1] introduces the current attribute *fresh*, while the verb *drive* in [2] introduces the resulting attribute *mad*. These two verbs therefore exemplify the two main categories of complex transitive complementation in this pattern. The current verbs (*cf* 16.21*ff*) are usually stative, and the resulting verbs are always dynamic. Further examples of each type are:

CURRENT

(i) *hold* [C2]
keep [C2]
leave [C2]

(ii) *call* [C2]
confess [B3, C2, C4]
profess [B3, C2, C4]
pronounce [B3, C2, C4]
report [B3, C4]

(iii) *like*
prefer [B3]
want
wish [B3, C2, C4]

(iv) *believe* [B3, C2, C4]
consider [B3, C2, C4]
deem [B3, C2, C4]
find [B3, C2, C4]
hold [B3, C4]
imagine [B3, C2, C4]
judge [B3, C2, C4]
presume [B3, C2, C4]
rate [C2, C4]
reckon [B3, C2, C4]
suppose [B3, C2, C4]
think [B3, C2, C4]

RESULTING

(v) *drive* [C4]
get [C4]
make [C2, C4]
prove [B3, C2, C4]
render [C4]
send
turn

(vi) *certify* [B3, C2, C4]
declare [B3, C2, C4]
proclaim [B3, C2, C4]

Type (i) is a category of current verbs of general meaning; Type (ii) consists of factual speech act verbs (*cf* 16.31); Type (iii) of volitional verbs; Type (iv) of verbs of intellectual state; Type (v) of general resulting verbs; and Type (vi) of resulting verbs referring to speech acts which have the performative force of declarations. (*Hold* occurs twice in the above list: as a general verb [Type (i), as in *She held her head high*]; and as an intellectual state verb [Type (iv), as in *I hold you responsible*]). The symbols added after some verbs indicate other related complementation types to which those verbs belong:

[B3] The verb can also be used monotransitively (*cf* Note [a]) with a *that*-clause.
[C2] The verb can also occur with a noun phrase as object complement.
[C4] The verb can also occur with an object + infinitive construction.

Examples:

The secretary *left* all the letters *unopened.* (i)
The doctors *pronounced* her condition *utterly hopeless.* (ii)
I *want* my coffee *stronger than this.* (iii)
We've always *found* the assistants *very friendly.* (iv)
The long walk *made* us all *hungry.* (v)
They have *declared* the house *unfit for habitation.* (vi)

Note that the adjectival complement may contain modifiers and adjectival complementation (*cf* 16.68–83). A passive construction in which the direct object becomes subject is also an important criterion:

All the letters *were left unopened* (by the secretary). (i)
Her condition *was pronounced utterly hopeless* (by the doctors). (ii)

Note [a] There is sometimes a meaning difference between the object complement construction and the corresponding *that*-clause [B3] or object + infinitive [C4] construction:

I imagined myself severely ill. [3]
≠ I imagined myself to be severely ill. [4]

Sentence [3] suggests that the speaker is indulging in a flight of fancy; sentence [4] suggests that the speaker is deluding himself (*eg* that he is a hypochondriac). A difference is also to be observed between [5] and [6]:

They *got* him angry. [5]
≠ They *got* him *to be* angry. [6]

where [5] suggests 'made him angry in spite of himself', and [6] suggests 'persuaded him to be angry'. (Yet a third meaning is represented by *Don't get me wrong* ['Don't misunderstand me'].) Two further contrasts are:

We *found* the children undernourished. ['We encountered them in that condition'] [7]
≠ We *found* the children *to be* undernourished. [8]
['Our examination revealed their condition']

and:

He *declared* the meeting official. [9]
He *declared* the meeting *to be* official. [10]

where [9] has a performative and resultative force ('The meeting became official as a result of his announcement') not regularly present in [10].

[b] *Have* in sentences such as *We have two employees sick* is not a member of the [C1] category, but belongs to a special *have*-existential construction to be discussed, with existential sentences in general, in 18.51. Since it has no passive, this clause construction lacks one criterial feature of complex transitive constructions: **Two employees are had sick.*

[c] There is a variant order in which the object complement precedes the object; *eg*: *He thought desirable most of the women in the room* (*cf* 18.37). This order tends to occur when the object is a long noun phrase.

16.45 In addition to the verbs listed in 16.44 above, there are many verbs which belong more peripherally to Type [C1]. Their membership is more peripheral in one or both of the following respects: (a) They occur only in restricted sequences such as *rub . . . dry* (*cf* 16.17); (b) They can occur in the [B1] monotransitive construction without appreciable change of meaning; *ie*, the object complement is optional, and resembles an optional adverbial. In the following typical collocations, the object noun phrase is symbolized by N:

CURRENT	RESULTING
bring (a child) *up healthy*[1]	*boil* (an egg) *soft*[1]
buy N *cheap*[1]	*crop* (hair) *short*[1]
return (a letter) *unopened*[1]	*freeze* N *hard*[1]
serve (food) *hot/cold*[1]	*paint* N *red/blue/ . . .*[1]
sell N *cheap/new*[1]	*roll* N *flat*
	sweep (the floor) *clean*[1]
	colour N *blue/yellow/ . . .*[1]
	dye N *pink/green/ . . .*[1]
	knock (someone) *senseless*
	polish N *smooth*[1]
	scrape N *clean*[1]
	swing (a door) *open*

For those combinations marked '1', the object complement could be easily omitted without a change in the basic sense of the verb.

Among resulting attributes, the adjectives *open*, *loose*, *free*, and *clean* are particularly common: *push* N *open*, *shake* N *loose*, *set* N *free*, *wipe* N *clean*.

The collocations *make sure* and *make certain* are peculiar in that the object is a *that*-clause and always follows the adjectival complement:

> Please *make sure/certain* that you enclose your birth certificate.

There is no passive **be made sure/certain* . . . With other collocations, the *that*-clause object is postponed by extraposition (*cf* 18.35):

> He *found* it *strange* that no one else had arrived.
> I *think* it *very odd* that she left without saying goodbye.
> The emperor *pronounced* it *illegal* for landlords to enfranchise their tenants.

Extraposition is optional with *make* N *clear*, and therefore the preparatory *it* may be omitted: *She made* (*it*) *clear that we were regarded as trespassers.*

Note [**a**] Some collocations require the object to be a reflexive pronoun: *I laughed myself sick*; *They roared themselves hoarse*. Here the object complement cannot be omitted: **I laughed myself.*

[**b**] The resultative pattern illustrated in this section is quite productive, and occurs with rare or newly-converted verbs such as *sellotape* and *scotchtape*: *sellotape* N *flat* 〈BrE〉; *scotchtape* N *flat* 〈AmE〉. Similarly:

> I've *deepfrozen* the bread solid.

[C2] Noun phrase as object complement

16.46 Most of the verbs listed in 16.44 can occur also with a noun phrase complement. In addition, there are a few verbs which occur with a noun phrase, but not with an adjective phrase, as complement, *eg*: *appoint*. These verbs, marked '1' in the list below, can also occur with the object + infinitive construction:

> The queen *appointed* William Cecil (to be) her personal secretary.

The list is subdivided into categories corresponding to those in 16.44:

(i) *hold*[2]
keep[2]
leave[2]

(ii) *call*
confess
profess
pronounce

(iii) *wish*

(iv) *believe*
consider[2]
deem
esteem[1,2,3]
find
imagine[2]
judge[2]
presume
rate[2]
reckon[2]
suppose
think

(v) *appoint*[1,2,3]
choose[1,2,3]
elect[1,2,3]
make
prove
vote[1]

(vi) *baptize*[2,3]
certify[2,3]
christen[2,3]
crown[2,3]
declare
proclaim
name[1,2,3]

The superscript '2' indicates that the *as*-construction (*cf* 16.47) is also possible. The superscript '3' indicates that the verb is also monotransitive, and that the verb retains the same meaning when the object complement is omitted. Hence *She appointed him secretary* implies that *she appointed him*. Examples of each sub-type follow. With *profess* and *wish*, which are used to illustrate sub-types (ii) and (iii) respectively, a reflexive pronoun as object is normal.

She *held* her niece (a) captive for several years. (i)
The prince *professed* himself a supporter of free speech. (ii)
I have often *wished* myself a millionaire. (iii)
Charles does not *esteem* him a trustworthy adviser. (iv)
The committee has *elected* you its chairman. (v)
Her parents *named* her Sophia after her grandmother. (vi)

Some verbs in this pattern are unlikely to occur in the active; *eg*: *think*, *believe*, *reckon*. The following are examples of the passive construction:

Her niece *was held* (a) captive for several years. (i)
She *was named* Sophia after her grandmother. (vi)

As with Type [C1], the object may be a clause postponed by extraposition:

We have made *it* a condition *that the new agreement be signed by all the original signatories*.
He has proved *it* a fallacy *that old age brings wisdom*.

Note [a] The zero article occurs optionally with *captive* and *prisoner* as object complements, as in (i) above: *She held her niece* (*a*) *captive*. *Hold . . . captive/prisoner* and *keep . . . captive/prisoner* are unusual in that the omitted article is indefinite rather than definite. Examples of the zero article with definite meaning (*cf* 5.42) are:

Edgar was judged overall *winner*.
They appointed Sue *captain* of the athletics team.

[b] The object + infinitive construction with *to be*, as with Type [C1], is not always equivalent to the pattern with a phrasal object complement. For example, *name* can be used with *to be* only if the following noun phrase designates a future role or status:

Her parents named her (**to be*) Gladys.
The selectors named her (*to be*) a member of the touring team.

As can be used with *name* only on the same condition as applies to *to be*: **Her parents named her as Gladys* (*cf* 16.47 below).

[c] The copular relation can obtain not only between the object and complement as in [1], but also between subject and complement as in [2]:

She made him a good husband. (SVO_dC_o) [1]

She made him a good wife. (SVO_iC_s) [2]

[1] has the passive analogue *He was made a good husband*; but in the entirely different construction of [2], where the copular relation is between *she* and *a good wife*, no passive is possible. The meaning is: 'She was a good wife to him'. A prepositional verb of this same unusual pattern is *strike . . . as* in, for example:

He *struck* me *as* a brilliant strategist.

where *a brilliant strategist* is subject complement.

[C1pr] and [C2pr] Object complement following prepositional verb

16.47 The preposition *as* designates a copular relation, particularly in specifying a role or status associated with the direct object: *The church condemned the relic as a fraud.* Following a complex transitive verb and a direct object, the prepositional complement of *as* functions semantically as an attribute, and may be termed a 'prepositional object complement' in the same way as the noun phrase following a transitive prepositional verb is called a prepositional object:

We considered him { a genius. [C2] / as a genius. [C2pr] / to be a genius. [C4] }

~ He was considered { (as) a genius. / to be a genius. }

Consider as, like *regard as*, *class as*, etc, therefore exemplifies yet another type of prepositional verb: one that is followed by a prepositional object complement rather than a prepositional object.

Occasionally the preposition *for* occurs in this copular function, instead of *as*:

He took these words *as* evidence. He took me *for* a fool.

In the following list, for verbs in column (i) the preposition is optional, where for verbs in column (ii) the preposition is obligatory:

(i)	(ii)
appoint (as)[1]	*accept as*
choose (as)	*acknowledge as*
consider (as)	*characterize as*
count (as)	*class as*
deem (as)	*define as*
esteem (as)[1]	*describe as*
rate (as)	*intend as*[1]
reckon (as)	*mistake for*
report (as)	*regard as*
elect (as)[1]	*see as*
certify (as)	*take as/for*
crown (as)[1]	*treat as*
make (into)[1]	*use as*
proclaim (as)	

Most verbs in [C1pr] and [C2pr] can also introduce an adjective phrase in the function of prepositional object complement:

The experts *rated* his paintings (*as*) *poor but representative of their class.*
They *classed* Jane *as partially sighted.*
The media *described* the situation *as hopeless.*
~ The situation was *described as hopeless.*

Verbs not allowing this construction are marked '1' in the above lists. The construction is exceptional in allowing an adjective phrase to occur after a preposition. A more orthodox construction is obtained by adding the word *being* before the adjective phrase, and thereby converting the prepositional complement into a nominal *-ing* clause:

The media described the situation *as being hopeless.*

Note [**a**] *Count as* and *rate as* can also occur in an analogous *as*-construction without the object, as 'prepositional' copular verbs; *eg*: *This counts/rates as a notable success* (*cf* 16.22 Note [b]).
[**b**] Although *as* is classed as a preposition in the above pattern, it in some ways resembles the conjunction *as* which introduces clauses of comparison (*cf* 15.71). Consider the following curious examples, in which *as* introduces on the one hand a clause and on the other hand a noun phrase in an appositional relation to the clause:
Report me *as I am – a superannuated don.*
He described her *as he found her, a liar.*

[C3] Complementation by object and adjunct

16.48 Our next category, Type [C3], consists of verbs which occur in the *SVOA* pattern (*cf* 2.16), *ie* verbs which have as their complementation an object followed by a predication adjunct. The most characteristic adjuncts to occur in this pattern are prepositional phrases of space, and more particularly of direction; *eg*:

I slipped the key *into the lock.* [1]
He stood my argument *on its head.* [2]
Take your hands *out of your pockets.* [3]

The passive is illustrated by:

The key was slipped *into the lock.* [1a]

Sentence [2] exemplifies the abstract or metaphorical use of such verbs and adjuncts. Many of the verbs which fit into this pattern are causative verbs of motion: *put*, *get*, *stand*, *set*, *sit*, *lay*, *place*, *send*, *bring*, *take*, *lead*, *drive*, etc. The class is open-ended, since verbs normally without causative meaning can be adapted to this function; *eg*: *show*, *see*, *elbow*, etc in:

The attendant *showed* us to our seats. ['conducted us . . .']
May I *see* you home? ['escort you . . .']
He *elbowed* and *bribed* his way to fame.
They *talked* me into it. ['persuaded me . . .']

Other verbs are associated with space position adjuncts rather than direction adjuncts:

They *left* the papers *at my office.*
Always *keep* your eyes *on the road* when driving.

The attackers *caught* us *off our guard*.
He *wished* them *at the bottom of the sea*.

Again, the spatial meaning of the adjunct may be understood in some abstract or metaphorical sense, as in the third example above.

Adjuncts of other semantic types are less common, but instances are the adjunct of manner following *treat*:

Her parents *treated* her { *badly*. / *as if she were a baby*. / *as/like a small child*. }

and the optional adjunct of duration following *last*:

This money will have to *last* you ((*for*) *six months*).

Note [**a**] *Treat* has a different meaning when the adjunct is omitted:
Her parents *treated* her. [= 'did something pleasant for her']

[**b**] Superficially similar to the above pattern is that illustrated by *remind* and *furnish* followed by an object and a prepositional phrase:
She *reminds* me *of my sister*.
They *furnished* all the passengers *with life jackets*.

These however are classed as transitive prepositional verbs (*cf* 16.7–8), and will be dealt with in 16.56*f* below. The difference between these prepositional verbs and verbs of complementation Type [C3] is that in the former case the lexical verb governs a particular preposition, *remind . . . of*, *furnish . . . with*. (Alternative prepositional constructions are sometimes available, however: *provide . . . with*, *provide . . . for*.)

Variants of complex transitive complementation

16.49 We now examine variants of complex transitive complementation in which the direct object is followed by a nonfinite clause acting as predication adjunct. All four kinds of nonfinite construction (*cf* 14.6–8) are possible:

[C4] *to*-infinitive: They knew him *to be a spy*.	[C6] *-ing* participle: I caught Ann *reading my diary*.
[C5] bare infinitive: I heard someone *slam the door*.	[C7] *-ed* participle: We saw him *beaten by the World Heavyweight Champion*.

The nonfinite clause in these patterns (in italics in the above table) has no subject itself, but its implied subject is always the preceding noun phrase, which is object of the superordinate clause. This noun phrase, which if a personal pronoun is in the objective case, is commonly termed a RAISED OBJECT (*cf* further 16.64*ff*): semantically, it has the role of subject of the nonfinite verb; but syntactically it is 'raised' from the nonfinite clause to function as object of the superordinate verb. Hence in general, this noun phrase (in italics in the table below) can become subject of the corresponding passive. (The passive of [C5] normally requires substitution of a *to*-infinitive for a bare infinitive; the passive of [C7] is of marginal currency; *cf* 16.54 Note [a].)

[C4] *He* was known to be a spy.	[C6] *Ann* was caught reading my diary.
[C5] *Someone* was heard to slam the door.	[C7] *He* was seen executed by a firing squad.

On the face of it, the patterns [C4] and [C6] are indistinguishable from the monotransitive patterns [B8] (*eg*: *She hates the train to be late*) and [B9] (*eg*: *She hates the train being late*), in which the nonfinite clause has a subject of its own. The ability of the noun phrase preceding the nonfinite verb to become subject of a passive is, however, an important distinction between them (see further 16.51 and 16.53).

Note These patterns [C4] and [C6] are distinguished from corresponding patterns in which the nonfinite clause is an adverbial by the fact that the implied subject of the nonfinite verb is O rather than S. Note the ambiguity of:

She left him *to finish the job*. She left him *holding the baby*.

[C4] Object + *to*-infinitive complementation

16.50 The verbs in this group are rather numerous, and may be subdivided, semantically, into the following categories:

(i) *announce*, *declare*, *proclaim*, *pronounce*, *report*, *repute* [esp P], *rumour* [P only], *say* [P only], *tip* ⟨esp BrE⟩

(ii) *assume*, *believe*, *conceive* ⟨formal⟩, *consider*, *expect*, *feel*, *find*, *imagine*, *know*, *presume*, *reckon*, *see* [P only], *suppose*, *take*, *think* [esp P], *understand*

(iii) *intend*, *mean*

(iv) *appoint*, *elect*, *name*, *vote*

(v) *cause*, *drive*, *force*, *get* [no P], *lead*, *prompt*

(vi) *allow*, *authorize*, *compel*, *constrain*, *enable*, *entitle*, *equip*, *fit*, *oblige*, *permit*, *require*

(vii) *assist*, *bother*, *bribe*, *condemn*, *dare*, *defy*, *encourage*, *help*, *induce*, *inspire*, *press*, *summon*

[P = Passive]

Types (i) and (ii) correspond to the factual verbs of category [B3] discussed in 16.31: the nonfinite construction following these verbs can often be replaced by a *that*-clause with an indicative verb. Compare:

{The police reported that the traffic was heavy. [B3]
= The police reported the traffic to be heavy. ⟨formal⟩ [C4]

{John believed that the stranger was a policeman. [B3]
= John believed the stranger to be a policeman. ⟨formal⟩ [C4]

With factual verbs such as these, the nonfinite clause normally contains the verb *be* or some other verb of stative meaning. Especially when the nonfinite main verb is other than *be*, the finite clause (of pattern [B3]) is preferred to the infinitive one, except that the infinitive construction provides a convenient passive form:

The traffic was reported to be heavy.
The stranger was believed to be a policeman.

Some verbs in this construction have no *that*-clause equivalent:

They tipped him to be the next president. ⟨esp BrE⟩
~ He was tipped to be the next president.
(*They tipped that he would be the next president.)

Some verbs (marked [P only] in the list above) occur only in the passive version of this construction:

The field marshal *was said* to be planning a new strategy.
(*Someone *said* the field marshal to be planning a new strategy.)

Other verbs (marked [esp P]) occur chiefly in the passive:

The Broadway production *was thought* to have made Max's fortune.
(?Newsmen *thought* the Broadway production to have made Max's fortune.)

Of the two classes of factual verbs, Type (i) consists of public verbs (*cf* 16.31) referring to a speech act, and Type (ii) consists of private verbs expressing belief, etc.

16.51 Of the remaining semantic types, Type (iii) consists of verbs of intention (on *intend* itself *cf* 16.41 Note [b]); Types (iv) and (v) consist of causative verbs, where the infinitive clause identifies the resultant state (Type (iv) verbs also belong to class [C1]); Type (vi) consists of verbs with a modal character, expressing such concepts as enablement, permission, and compulsion; and Type (vii) consists of a variety of verbs of 'influencing' between which a common factor appears to be that the nonfinite clause has a purposive meaning. Examples are:

(iii) They *intended* Mary to sing an aria.
(~ Mary *was intended* to sing an aria.)
(iv) The meeting *elected* Mr Martin to be the next treasurer.
(~ Mr Martin *was elected* to be the next treasurer.)

(v) This optimistic forecast *led* the administration to promise tax cuts.
(~ The administration was *led* (by this optimistic forecast) to promise tax cuts.)
(vi) My contract *allows* me to take one month's leave.
(~ I *am allowed* to take one month's leave.)
(vii) Our teachers *encouraged* us to think for ourselves.
(~ We *were encouraged* to think for ourselves.)

In Type (iv), the infinitive main verb is normally *be*, and can be omitted: *They appointed her* (*to be*) *the social secretary*. This type overlaps with Type (v), 16.46.

Note [**a**] There are a number of multi-word verbs in this category: [C4pr]: *count on . . . to . . .*; *depend on . . . to . . .*; *rely on . . . to . . .*; [C4ph]: *make . . . out to . . .*; [C4ph-pr]: *keep on at . . . to . . .* (which has no passive). Examples are:

I am *depending on* you to give us your full support.
They *made* him *out* to be a monster of depravity.
Why do you *keep on at* me to work harder?

[**b**] Some passives of pattern [C4] (*eg*: *be allowed*, *be supposed*) have a semi-auxiliary (*cf* 3.47*f*) interpretation in which they lose their connection with the corresponding active construction, especially as regards agency.

[C5] Object + bare infinitive complementation

16.52 This pattern occurs with a relatively small number of verbs:

(i)	(ii)		(iii)
have	*feel*	*overhear* [P?]	*help* [P?]
let	*hear* [P]	*see* [P]	*know* [P]
make [P]	*notice* [P?]	*watch*	
	observe [P]		

Type (i) consists of verbs of coercive meaning; Type (ii) has perceptual verbs of seeing and hearing; and Type (iii) is a residual class of two verbs which are optionally followed by a *to*-infinitive. The marker [P] indicates that the passive (normally with a *to*-infinitive) is possible; [P?] indicates that the passive is of doubtful or limited acceptability.

(i) You shouldn't *let* your family *interfere with our plans*.
We must *make* the public *take notice of us*.
(~ The public must *be made to take notice of us*.)
(ii) Did you *notice* anyone *leave the house*?
The crowd *saw* Gray *score two magnificent goals*.
(~ Gray was *seen to score two magnificent goals*.)
(iii) Sarah *helped* us (to) *edit the script*.
I have *known* John (to) *give better speeches than that*.
(~ John has been *known to give better speeches than that*.)

Know followed by the bare infinitive is confined mainly to BrE, and to the perfective aspect: *have known*. *Let* in group (i) is in other constructions classified as similar to an auxiliary (*cf* 3.51). *Let* has an apparent passive in combination with such verbs as *let go* and *let fall*, but these are best regarded as fixed expressions, in which *let* has an auxiliary or particle-like function:

They *let* the prisoner *go home*. ~ ?The prisoner was *let go home*.

Note that this apparent passive has the bare infinitive, in contrast, for example, to *make*, which has to have the *to*-infinitive in the passive:

They *made* him *understand*. ~ He was *made to understand*.

A third verb in group (i) is *have*, which (like *have* in monotransitive constructions) does not occur in the passive:

They *had* me *repeat the message*. ~ *I was *had* (to) *repeat the message*.

Note [**a**] The formulaic nature of *let him go* and similar expressions is illustrated by variants such as [1–3], which cannot be fitted into any regular complementation pattern:

They *let* { *go* the rope. [1]
the rope *go*. [2]
go of the rope. } [3]

[**b**] Of the two constructions with *help*, that with *to* is more common in BrE, and that without *to* is more common in AmE.

[**c**] A rare verb in category (i) is the now rather archaic *bid*, with a *to*-infinitive complementation in the passive.

They *bid*/*bade* me *sit down*. ~ I was *bidden to sit down*.

[C6] Object + *-ing* participle complementation

16.53 The verbs in category [C6] consist of verbs of perception (Type (i)), verbs of encounter (Type (ii)), and two verbs of coercive meaning (Type (iii)):

(i)		(ii)	(iii)
feel [C5]	*see* [C5]	*catch*	*have*
hear [C5]	*smell*	*discover*	*get*
notice [C5]	*spot*	*find*	
observe [C5]	*spy*	*leave*	
overhear [C5]	*watch* [C5]		
perceive			

Perception verbs marked [C5] occur also with the bare infinitive pattern [C5]. With such verbs there is an aspect difference between [C5] and [C6], as described in 4.61*f*:

Tim watched Bill *mend*/*mending* the lamp.

The bare infinitive, having nonprogressive meaning, implies that Bill did the whole job while Tim was watching; the *-ing* clause, with progressive meaning, has no such implication.

This complementation pattern differs from that of [B9], not only in its progressive aspect, but also in that the noun phrase following the superordinate verb cannot take the genitive (or possessive) form (*cf* 16.42):

I saw *him* lying on the beach ~ *I saw *his* lying on the beach.

Another difference from pattern [B9] is that the *-ing* predication can normally be omitted without radically altering the meaning:

I saw him lying on the beach. [entails: *I saw him*]

Contrast:

I hate my friends leaving early. [does not entail: *I hate my friends*]

The passive with this pattern is regular:

We could *hear* the rain *splashing on the roof.*
~ The rain could *be heard splashing on the roof.*
A teacher *caught* them *smoking in the playground.*
~ They *were caught smoking in the playground* (by a teacher).

Prepositional verbs with this type of complementation ([C6pr]) include *come across*, *come upon*, *listen to*, and *look at*: *Look at those children climbing the wall.* But these [C6pr] prepositional verbs have no prepositional passive:

The guards had been {*seen* / *spotted* / ?*watched* / **looked at*} searching the building.

Have in this construction (*cf* 18.51*ff*) also has no passive, in keeping with its use in other constructions:

She *had* us working day after day.
*We *were had* working day after day.

Note *Feel* occurs especially with a reflexive pronoun object: *She felt herself falling in love.*

[C7] Object + *-ed* participle complementation

16.54 We can distinguish three small groups of verbs complemented by a raised object followed by an *-ed* participle clause:

(i) CAUSATIVE verbs: *get*, *have*
She *got/had* the watch repaired immediately.
(ii) VOLITIONAL verbs: *want*, *need*, *like*
I *want/need* this watch repaired immediately.
(iii) PERCEPTUAL verbs: *see*, *hear*, *feel* (oneself), *watch*
Someone must have *seen/heard* the car stolen.

A fourth group is peripheral to this construction:

(iv) Verbs for which the *-ed* participle describes a resulting state: *find*, *discover*, *leave*
They *found/discovered/left* him worn out by travel and exertion.

In this construction, as in that of [C6], *have* can have either an agentive causative meaning, or a stative meaning. Hence *The guard patrol had two men shot* is ambiguous, meaning either 'The patrol caused two men to be shot', or 'The patrol suffered the loss of two men by shooting'. The latter meaning is that of the *have*-existential construction (*cf* 18.51*ff*). In general, this complementation type is semantically equivalent to one with an infinitive form of the verb *be*. Thus in Type (ii), *I would like my room cleaned* is synonymous with *I would like my room to be cleaned*; in Type (iii), *He saw the team beaten* is synonymous with *He saw the team be beaten.*

Note [**a**] There is no passive for most verbs in pattern [C7], and at best the passive is dubious: ?*The car must have been seen stolen.* The acceptability of the passive with Type (iv) is exceptional:

The car was found abandoned. This is, indeed, an indication that Type (iv) may not belong here so much as with the object complement construction [C1], the participle construction being adjectival (*cf*: *an abandoned car*).
[**b**] In addition to the two meanings of *have* + object + *-ed* participle above, a third meaning results if the *-ed* clause is analysed as a postmodifier of the object; *eg*: *She had a book* (*which was*) *stolen from the library*.

Ditransitive complementation

[D1] Noun phrases as both indirect and direct object

16.55 Ditransitive complementation in its basic form involves two object noun phrases: an indirect object, which is normally animate and positioned first, and a direct object, which is normally inanimate. The two noun phrases differ from those of [C2] in not being in a copular relationship:

He *gave* the girl a doll
S V O_i O_d

The difference between this and complex transitive complementation is seen in:

SVOC: He found her a loyal friend.
(~ She was a loyal friend)
SVOO: He found her an apartment.
(~ The apartment was for her)

The characteristics of indirect objects in contrast to direct objects are fully discussed in 10.7.

Some ditransitive verbs have two passive analogues, which we shall distinguish as 'first' and 'second':

The girl was given a doll. [FIRST PASSIVE]
A doll was given the girl. [SECOND PASSIVE]

Of these two, the first passive, in which the indirect object becomes subject, is the more common. The prepositional paraphrase is more usual, as an alternative, than the second passive: *A doll was given to the girl.* (For a list of verbs of Type [D1], *cf* 16.57 below.)

[D2] Object and prepositional object

16.56 In the ditransitive category, prepositional verbs form an important group with its own sub-divisions, and may therefore be given a separate category number [D2]. These verbs are those we have called Type II prepositional verbs (*cf* 16.7–8). Alongside the ordinary indirect object pattern, two main prepositional patterns may be distinguished:

Indirect object + direct object. [D1]
Direct object + prepositional object. [D2a]
Indirect object + prepositional object. [D2b]

The indirect object is normally animate, and is the recipient or beneficiary of the process described by the verb (*cf* 10.19). Unlike ditransitive verbs of category [D1] (*eg*: *give*), ditransitive verbs with prepositional objects normally have only one passive:

We addressed our remarks to the children. [D2a]
~ Our remarks were addressed to the children.
(*The children were addressed our remarks (to))

We reminded him of the agreement. [D2b]
~ He was reminded of the agreement.
(*The agreement was reminded him (of))

Some verbs have all three possibilities of construction in the active; many have two; for others there is only one possibility (in some cases the alternatives are not identical but very similar in meaning):

tell [D1 + 2a + 2b]	Mary *told* only John the secret. Mary *told* the secret only *to* John. Mary *told* only John *about* the secret.	[D1] [D2a] [D2b]
offer [D1 + 2a]	John *offered* Mary some help. John *offered* some help *to* Mary	[D1] [D2a]
envy [D1 + 2b]	She *envied* John his success. She *envied* John *for* his success.	[D1] [D2b]
wish [D1]	They *wished* him good luck.	[D1]
blame [D2a + 2b]	Helen *blamed* the divorce *on* John. Helen *blamed* John *for* the divorce.	[D2a] [D2b]
say [D2a]	Why didn't anybody *say* this *to* me?	[D2a]
warn [D2b]	Mary *warned* John *of* the dangers.	[D2b]

The different constructional possibilities of certain verbs provide a means of achieving different focus (*cf* 18.37*f*). Compare the following pairs of sentences as pronounced with unmarked (end) focus:

{ Mary blamed the broken vase on JÒHN.
{ Mary blamed John for the broken VÀSE.
(*Cf*: John was blamed . . . by MÀRY.)

{ The government supplied blankets for the HÒMEless.
{ The government supplied the homeless with BLÀNKets.
(*Cf*: Blankets were supplied . . . by the GÒvernment.)

Note [**a**] The above constructions are presented in the most typical syntactic ordering, but postponement of the direct or indirect object may take place in contexts where end-focus or end-weight is required (*cf* 18.37); *eg*: *John offered to Mary the help that she needed.*

[**b**] Additional prepositional verb patterns should be briefly mentioned. There is, for example, the double-prepositional-verb pattern noted in 16.17(c):

I am *applying to* the hospital *for* a job.

There is a further possibility that two prepositional objects may follow a direct object:

We are *paying* $100 *to* the garage *for* the repairs.

Verbs of complementation types [D1] and [D2]

16.57 The following list gives some of the verbs that occur in Types [D1], [D2a], [D2b], organized according to the cross-classifications of 16.56 above. We are interested here only in synonymous or nearly synonymous constructions, in which the same participant roles (*cf* 10.18*ff*) occur. Hence many possible prepositional verbs are ignored. *Pay for*, for example, is ignored because it introduces a further participant (the commodity bought) not included in *pay* (*with*) and *pay* (*to*).

Table 16.57

		Type [D1]	Type [D2a]	Type [D2b]
EXAMPLE		*serve* (Jack scampi)	*serve* (scampi) *to* (Jack)	*serve* (Jack) *with* (scampi)
[D1 + 2a + 2b]		*pay*	*pay to*	*pay with*
		provide ⟨AmE⟩	*provide for*	*provide with*
		serve	*serve to*	*serve with*
		tell	*tell to*	*tell about*
[D1 + 2a]	(i)	*bring*	*bring to*	
		deny	*deny to*	
		give	*give to*	
		grant	*grant to*	
		hand	*hand to*	
		leave	*leave to/for*	
		lend	*lend to*	
		offer	*offer to*	
		owe	*owe to*	
		promise	*promise to*	
		read	*read to*	
		send	*send to*	
		show	*show to*	
		teach	*teach to*	
		throw	*throw to*	
	(ii)	*do*	*do for*	
		find	*find for*	
		make	*make for*	
		order	*order for*	
		reserve	*reserve for*	
		save	*save for*	
		spare	*spare for*	
	(iii)	*ask*	*ask of*	

[D1 + 2b]	*envy* *excuse* *forgive*		*envy for* *excuse for* *forgive for*
[D1]	*allow* *charge* *fine* *refuse* *wish*		
[D2a + 2b]		*blame on* *supply for/to*	*blame for* *supply with*
[D2a]		*address to* *announce to* *communicate to* *explain to* *say to*	
[D2b]			*advise about* *punish for* etc

The membership of [D2b] is numerous. Here are further examples, arranged by prepositions:

thank for	*convince of*	*rob of*	*refer to*
prevent from	*deprive of*	*suspect of*	*sentence to*
protect from	*inform of*	*warn of*	*subject to*
interest in	*persuade of*	*congratulate on*	*treat to*
accuse of	*relieve of*	*confine to*	*charge with*
convict of	*remind of*	*introduce to*	*compare with*

Note that reflexive verbs (*cf* 6.25) sometimes occur with a prepositional object; *eg*: *We pride ourselves on the service we offer*. Some of the verbs above (such as *compare with*) can have two inanimate objects.

In *Table* 16.57, we have distinguished, under [D1 + 2a], verbs taking *to* as their preposition from those taking *for*; *eg*:

(i) She sent Paul a present. ~ She sent a present *to* Paul.
(ii) She made Paul a meal. ~ She made a meal *for* Paul.

Occasionally, a preposition other than *to* and *for* occurs in this function:

(iii) She asked Paul a favour. ~ She asked a favour *of* Paul.

16.58 Distinct from [D2a] and [D2b] above is a kind of prepositional verb which has already been discussed in 16.7–8; a verb for which the direct object forms part of an idiomatic unit with the verb and the preposition. The syntactic properties of this type, which we label [D2c], have already been dealt with, and it is enough here to list a further sample of such idioms:

catch sight of	*make allowance for*[1]	*put a stop to*
give place to	*make fun of*	*set fire to*
give way to	*make a fuss over/about*[1]	*take account of*[1]
keep pace with	*make room for*	*take advantage of*[1]
lose sight of	*make use of*[1]	*take care of*[1]
lose touch with	*pay attention to*[1]	*take note of*[1]
lose track of	*put an end to*	*take notice of*[1]

Those marked with a raised '1' can take not only a prepositional passive (*cf* 16.7–8) but also can easily take a passive for which the idiomatically-fixed direct object becomes subject; *eg*: (*Some*) *allowance was made for loss of earnings*; (*Little*) *notice was taken of this event*. Other verbs can take the passive, but with greater difficulty; with these examples, as with prepositional verbs in general, idiomatic cohesion is a matter of gradience.

Variants of ditransitive complementation

[D3] Indirect object + *that*-clause object

16.59 Corresponding to monotransitive verbs of Type [B3] (*cf* 16.30) are ditransitive verbs for which the direct object is a *that*-clause:

John *convinced* me (that) he was right.
~ I *was convinced* (by John) (that) he was right.

The second passive is unacceptable when the direct object is a clause: **That he was right was convinced me*. Thus the first passive (*cf* 16.55) above is the only passive that can occur with this pattern. With some verbs, such as *convince* above, it is impossible to delete the noun phrase object:

*John convinced (that) he was right.

With other verbs, such as *show*, the indirect object is optional:

The professor of mathematics showed me that Pythagoras was mistaken.
~ The professor of mathematics showed that Pythagoras was mistaken.

Ditransitive verbs followed by a *that*-clause may be divided into a subtype introducing an indirect statement, and a subtype introducing an indirect directive (*cf* 14.33). In the indirect statement, the *that*-clause contains an indicative verb; in the indirect directive the verb may be indicative or subjunctive, and often contains putative *should* or another modal verb (*cf* 16.32 for the distribution of these options):

INDIRECT STATEMENT:

May I *inform* you *that your order is ready for collection*?

INDIRECT DIRECTIVE:

She *petitioned* the king *that her father* {*might be* / *should be* / *be*} *pardoned*.

In the following list, Type (i) verbs introduce indirect statements, and Type (ii) verbs introduce indirect directives. The indirect directive construction is rare and formal in comparison with the similar infinitive construction (*cf* 16.63):

?I begged her that she {would / should} help. ⟨formal⟩

I begged her to help. ⟨more usual⟩

For those verbs marked 'O' the indirect object is obligatory; for those marked '(O)', the indirect object is optional; for those marked '((O))' the indirect object is not only optional, but unusual:

(i) *advise* (O)	*remind* O	(ii) *ask*[3] ((O))
assure O	*satisfy* O	*beg*[3] (O)
bet (O)	*show*[3] (O)	*charge* (O)
convince O	*teach*[3] (O)	*command* ((O))
forewarn (O)	*tell* O	*instruct* ((O))
inform O	*wager* (O)	*order* ((O))
notify[3] O	*warn* (O)	*petition*[3] (O)
persuade[1] O	*write*[2,3] (O)	*tell* O
promise[3] (O)		

The superscripts are interpreted as follows:

1: *Persuade* in the sense of 'convince' belongs to Type (i); but it may also be used in a Type (ii) sense of 'persuade someone to do something'.
2: *Write* is found with an indirect object + *that*-clause especially in AmE.
3: With verbs so marked, the indirect object can be replaced by a prepositional object (*cf* 16.60).

Note Superficially similar to the [D3] pattern is the 'impersonal' construction *it strikes/struck me* (*that*) . . . , as in:

It strikes me this work is for his own amusement.

But here the *that*-clause (as in 16.34) is the extraposed subject of the verb. Compare: *He strikes me as* . . . (*cf* 16.46 Note [c]) and *It occurs to me that* . . . (*cf* 16.34 Note [c]).

[D3pr] Prepositional object + *that*-clause object

16.60 The verbs marked '3' in the above list can be optionally followed by a preposition, thus forming a category similar to [D2a] in 16.56:

He *promised* ((*to*) *me*) that the debt would be repaid.

For most verbs of [D3] which permit a prepositional object, the preposition is *to*:

He *wrote to* me . . . He *reported to me* that . . . etc

Exceptions are *ask* and *beg*, which (in somewhat formal usage) are followed by the preposition *of*:

I *ask/beg* of you that you will keep this secret. ⟨formal⟩

There is, in addition, a group of verbs which were classified in 16.31–32 as monotransitive, but which optionally allow the preposition *to* preceding a prepositional object. These may be distinguished as Type [D3pr], and subdivided into sub-types (i) and (ii), as in the parallel description of [B3] verbs:

Joan *mentioned* (*to* me) that her father was sick. [Type (i)]
Dr Day *recommended* (*to* her) that the treatment be continued. [Type (ii)]

For example:

(i) *acknowledge*	*declare*	*remark*	(ii) *propose*
admit	*explain*	*report*	*recommend*
announce	*mention*	*say*	*suggest*
complain	*point out*	*signal*	
confess	*prove*	*state*	

As before, Type (i) verbs introduce indirect statements, and the less numerous Type (ii) verbs introduce indirect directives. As before, too, some exceptional verbs take a preposition other than *to*:

She demanded *of* me that . . . She agreed *with* me that . . . etc

Unlike the nonprepositional verbs of [D3], these prepositional verbs allow the *that*-clause to become subject of a corresponding passive clause, an option which is more acceptable with extraposition:

That several ministers are resigning has been *admitted to* our correspondent.
~ It has been *admitted to* our correspondent that several ministers are resigning.
It has been *shown to* us all that Miss Jones was innocent.

Without the preposition, *ie* with an ordinary indirect object, such sentences are at best marginally grammatical: ?**It has been shown us all that Miss Jones was innocent.*

Note The constructions of *It appears/happens/occurs/seems to me that* . . . superficially appear to belong to the pattern [D3pr], but in fact these contain monotransitive verbs with an extraposed *that*-clause as subject:

It *occurred/seemed to me* that he was lying.

Cf similar patterns with extraposition in 16.34, 16.59 Note.

[D4] Indirect object + finite *wh*-clause object

16.61 This pattern of complementation is primarily found with the verb *ask*, which introduces a reported question:

John *asked* me what time the meeting would end.
~ I was *asked* (by John) what time the meeting would end.

Also used with this pattern are verbs which take an indirect object followed by a *that*-clause (Type (i) of [D3]), but for these the *wh*-clause tends to be limited to nonassertive contexts (*cf* 16.35). Compare:

George didn't *tell* them that the train was late. [1]
George didn't *tell* them whether the train was late. [2]

The difference of meaning between the *that*- and *whether*-constructions can be stated in terms of presupposition. Sentence [1] typically implies that the train was late, while [2] is noncommittal on the matter. [D4] verbs can also introduce other question words such as *where* and *how*:

Jim was reluctant to *inform* us (*of*) where he got the money.
Would you *remind* me (*about*) how we start the engine?

A preposition may always be placed before the *wh*-clause. In the above cases, the preposition is optional, but in the case of verbs like *remind of* the preposition is obligatory: *she reminded me of what I had promised to do*. The complex preposition *as to* can be rather generally used for introducing the *wh*-clause; for example, *They advised us as to where the documents might be found*.

[D5] Indirect object + *wh*-infinitive clause object

16.62 This is yet another complementation pattern (comparable with [B5], 16.37) which may be taken by some verbs listed under [D3] in 16.59:

advise ask instruct remind show teach tell warn

The instructor *taught* us *how to land safely*.
~ We were *taught* (by the instructor) *how to land safely*.
They *advised* him *what to wear in the tropics*.
Please *remind* me *where to meet you after lunch*.

The equivalent prepositional verb pattern [D5pr] is illustrated by *suggest to*, *recommend to*:

Could you please *suggest to* the visitors *which museums to visit*?

Here, as in the [D4] type, a prepositional phrase introduced by *as to* can be used:

Helen *advised us* (*as to*) how to maintain the machine.

[D6] Indirect object + *to*-infinitive clause object

16.63 We have seen that the [D3] pattern may be used to introduce indirect statements, and that the [D4] pattern may be used to introduce indirect questions. Now we turn to the verbs of class [D6], which introduce indirect directives (*cf* 14.33):

I *told/advised/persuaded* Mark to see a doctor. [1]
~ Mark was *told/advised/persuaded* to see a doctor. [2]

This complementation category looks like those of [B8] and [C5], in that the verb is followed by a noun phrase and an infinitive construction. But the [D6] pattern differs from these in that the noun phrase following the verb is an indirect object, as will be clarified in 16.66 below. As with other verbs introducing indirect speech, the subject refers to the speaker of some speech act, and the indirect object refers to the addressee. Like [D3] verbs, [D6] verbs form only the first passive exemplified in [2] above: we do not find **To see a doctor was told Mark*. The following verbs belong to this class:

advise	*command*	*entreat*	*instruct*	*remind*	*teach*
ask	*counsel*	*exhort*	*invite*[1]	*request*[1]	*tell*
beg	*detail*[1]	*forbid*	*order*	*recommend*	*urge*
beseech	*direct*	*implore*	*persuade*		
challenge[1]	*enjoin*[1]	*incite*[1]	*pray*[1]		

Those verbs marked with a raised '1' do not have the equivalent construction with a *that*-clause containing a modal or a subjunctive verb (Types [B3(ii)], [D3(ii)]). Contrast:

They {*begged* / *invited*} her to stay another week.

They {*begged* / **invited*} (her) that she would stay another week.

The alternative *that*-clause construction, however, is more formal, especially when the indirect object is present.

Note [**a**] The verb *promise*, when it occurs with this kind of complementation, is exceptional in that the understood subject of the infinitive is identified with the subject rather than with the object of the main clause:

Sam promised me to get some food.

{= Sam promised me that *he* would get some food.
≠ Sam promised me that *I* would get some food.}

The present pattern [D6] is, however, less common with *promise* than the [B6] pattern without the indirect object: *Sam promised to get some food.*

[**b**] Only *order* can be followed by a passive infinitive: *He ordered them to be imprisoned/released.*

Multiple analysis and gradience in verb complementation

16.64 Before we leave verb classification, it is important to reflect on the problems of dividing verbs into complementation types. The major division of complementation patterns into copular [A], monotransitive [B], complex transitive [C], and ditransitive [D] categories (introduced in 2.16) has been extended with little difficulty to include patterns in which the verb's complementation includes finite and nonfinite clauses. This is the basis for the classification of verbs into types in 16.20–63 above. But unavoidably, our aim of presenting a clear classification has obscured some problems of gradience and multiple analysis (*cf* 2.60*ff*), and to illustrate these we return to three superficially identical structures already discussed in 16.36. These are now illustrated with three new examples, each of which conforms to the pattern N_1 V N_2 *to* V N_3, (where N = noun phrase, and V = verb phrase):

Table 16.64a

	N_1	V	N_2	*to V*	N_3	
[B8]	S	V	O			
	We	*like*	all parents	to visit	the school	[1]
[C4]	S	V	O	C_o		
	They	*expected*	James	to win	the race	[2]
[D6]	S	V	O_i	O_d		
	We	*asked*	the students	to attend	a lecture	[3]

Each of these sentences consists of the sequence N_1 *V* N_2 *to V* N_3, and yet we have analysed them respectively as monotransitive (S V O), complex transitive (S V O C_o), and ditransitive (S V O_i O_d). A different analysis, in some ways more revealing, would recognize an overlap between two competing descriptions of the intermediate noun phrase N_2. There is little doubt that in [1] this is to be analysed as subject of the infinitive clause (*cf* 16.36); whereas in [3] there are equally strong reasons for regarding N_2 as (indirect) object of the main clause (*cf* 16.66):

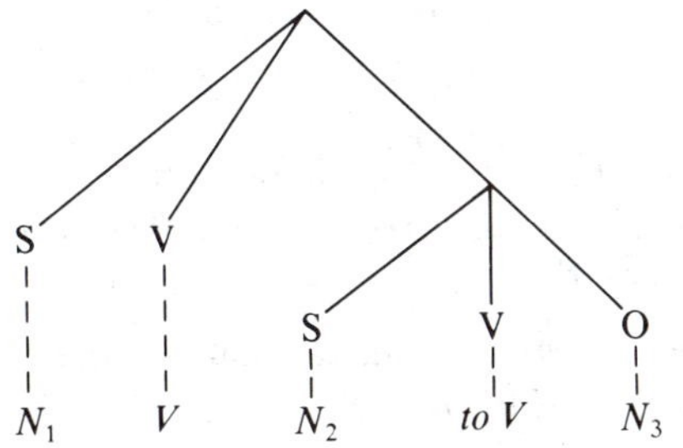

Fig 16.64b Sentence [1]

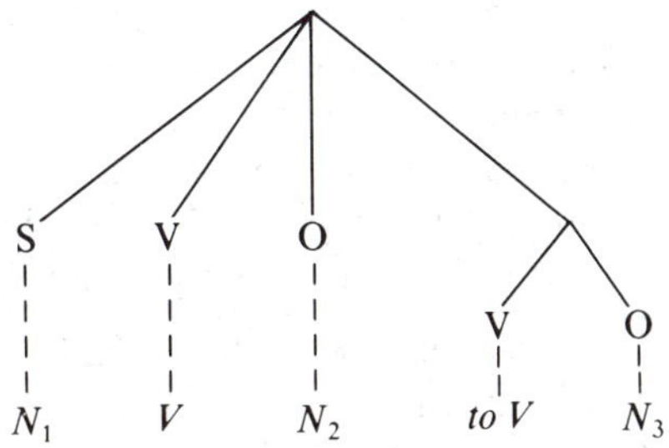

Fig 16.64c Sentence [3]

Sentence [2], however, partakes of both these descriptions. From the semantic point of view, it requires the analysis of *Fig* 16.64b (*cf*: *They expected* [*that James would win the race*]). But from the structural point of view, the analysis in *Fig* 16.64c is more appropriate, reflecting N_2's ability to become subject of the passive sentence: *James was expected to win the race*. We might reasonably say that in [2], N_2 behaves like an object (O_d rather than O_i) in relation to the first verb, but like a subject in relation to the second, infinitive verb. The term RAISED OBJECT, applied in 16.49*ff* to the intermediate noun phrase of patterns [C4 – C7], incorporates yet another way of recognizing this double analysis, by envisaging a process whereby the subject of the infinitive becomes the object of the preceding finite verb. This raised object will be symbolized, in what follows, S/O.

16.65 Given that the double analysis above provides some insight into clauses containing nonfinite complementation, we could take such an analysis further, and apply it to all complex transitive patterns, including the more straightforward *SVOC* and *SVOA* patterns of [C1 – C3]:

I consider	that John is a good driver.	[B3]
	John to be a good driver.	[C4]
	John a good driver.	[C2]

The parallelism of meaning and phrasal relations demonstrated in these three sentences recommends an analysis in which the complementation of pattern [C2], *John a good driver*, would be regarded as a clause in its own right: *ie* as a verbless clause consisting of S = *John* and C_s = *a good driver*, without an intervening V. This description would not, however, displace the by now familiar S V O_d C_o analysis, but would rather be seen as an alternative way of looking at the same construction.

Gradience

16.66 The technique of multiple analysis still leaves some subtleties unexposed. What this technique has suggested is that there are the following three categories corresponding to [1–3] in 16.64:

N_2 = S: We like *all parents* to visit the school. [1]
N_2 = S/O: They expected *James* to win the race. [2]
N_2 = O: We asked *the students* to attend a lecture. [3]

But more than three categories can be appropriately distinguished if we recognize [1] and [3] as end-points of a gradient, with [2] at some point on the scale between them. This area of grammar affords a good example of gradience.

At the monotransitive end of the scale, [1] can be characterized by a number of criteria which suggest that N_2 *to* $V N_3$ (*all parents to visit the school*) constitutes the direct object of an *SVO* pattern:

(a) It can be replaced by a pronoun referring to the clause or noun phrase nominalizing it: *We like it*; *We like all parents' visits.*

(b) It can be an answer to a *what*-question:
A: What do you like best?
B: We like all parents to visit the school.

(c) In some dialects, it can be preceded by the infinitive clause introducer *for*: *We like (it) for all parents to visit the school.*

(d) It can easily (when preceded by *for*) be the focus of a pseudo-cleft sentence: *What we like (best) is for all parents to visit the school.*

(e) When the sequence N_2 *to* $V N_3$ is turned into the passive form N_3 *to be* Ved_2 *by* N_2, there is no change of meaning:
We like all parents to visit the school.
= We like the school to be visited by all parents.

(f) In a reduced construction the infinitive marker *to* remains: *We like them* does not have the same meaning as *We like them to.*

At the other, ditransitive end of the scale, a contrasting set of criteria characterize [3], and support the analysis of N_2 (*the students*) as an indirect object and *to* $V N_3$, (*to attend a lecture*) as a clausal direct object:

(a′) *to* $V N_3$ can be replaced by a pronoun, a noun phrase, or a finite clause, with N_2 still functioning as indirect object:

We asked the students { *something.* / *a question.* / *what they wanted.* }

(b′) *to* $V N_3$ can be the answer to a *wh*-question, while N_2 functions as indirect object:
A: What did you ask the students?
B: We asked them to attend a lecture.

(c′) When the sequence N_2 *to* $V N_3$ is turned into the passive sequence N_3 *to be* Ved_2 *by* N_2, the meaning is always changed:
They asked the students to attend a lecture.
≠ *They asked a lecture to be attended by the students.
(In this case, indeed, the passive transform results in an absurdity.)

(d′) *to* VN_3 can marginally become the focus of a pseudo-cleft sentence: ?*What they asked the students was to attend a lecture.* (Contrast the decidedly unacceptable **What we like the parents is to visit the school.*)

(e′) N_2, which like O_i in general is usually 'personal', can be detached from its place after the first V to become subject of a corresponding passive sentence: *The students were asked to attend a lecture.*

(f′) In a reduced construction, the infinitive marker *to* can be omitted: *We asked them*; *We persuaded them*; etc.

Note [**a**] With some ditransitive verbs, criterion (a′) has to be interpreted as the replacement of the infinitive clause by a preposition and prepositional object (*cf* 16.56–8):

They *reminded* him *of his responsibilities.*
One man *challenged* the other *to a duel.*

[**b**] Criterion (d′) is less reliable than the others, since the pseudo-cleft sentence is unacceptable for many verbs. But a pseudo-cleft sentence in which the indirect object is replaced by a prepositional object tends to be more grammatical: *What they asked of the students was to attend a lecture.* (The alternative construction with the substitute verb *do*, which also occurs with [1], is always more acceptable: *What they asked the students to do was to attend a lecture.*)

16.67 To give a simplified illustration of the analysis of gradience in the sequence $N_1\ VN_2$ *to* VN_3, we now take a subset of the criteria listed above, and apply them to a range of verbs on the gradient connecting [1] and [3] of 16.66.

CRITERIA ↓ / VERB CLASSES →	(1) *ask, tell,* etc	(2) *elect, allow,* etc	(3) *intend, expect,* etc	(4) *want, like,* etc
(a′) *to* VN_3 can be replaced by a finite clause	+	–	–	–
(c′) change of meaning in passive of N_2 *to* VN_3	+	+	–	–
(e′) N_2 can become subject of passive	+	+	+	–

Fig 16.67 A complementation gradient

The matrix uses only three criteria, and thereby distinguishes only four categories. This is sufficient to indicate the principle, however, that the three categories [B8], [C4], and [D6] of our taxonomy could be broken down into a finer spectrum of categories between which the differences are small. In effect, *Fig* 16.67 distinguishes two subcategories of [C4]: one (including *elect* and *allow*) which is closer to the ditransitive type, and one (including *intend* and *expect*) closer to the monotransitive type. *Elect* and *allow* respond to criterion (c′):

They *elected* Miss Coe to succeed the present secretary.
≠ *They *elected* the present secretary to be succeeded by Miss Coe.
We don't *allow* residents to entertain visitors.
≠ We don't *allow* visitors to be entertained by residents.

while *intend* and *expect* do not:

They *intended* the students to see the professor.
= They *intended* the professor to be seen by the students.
They *expect* the students to enjoy the classes.
= They *expect* the classes to be enjoyed by the students.

Note For verbs in group (3), the voice of the infinitive clause and the voice of the main clause may be independently varied, with the result that a sentence like *They expected the students to enjoy the classes* has three corresponding passives with the same meaning:

= { They expected the classes *to be enjoyed* by the students.
The students *were expected* to enjoy the classes.
The classes *were expected to be enjoyed* by the students. }

The last example has a passive verb phrase in both the superordinate clause and the infinitive clause.

Adjective complementation

16.68 Categories of complementation in adjective phrases (*cf* 2.28, 7.21–2) are similar in variety to those of verb complementation. We distinguish [E1–E6] as follows:

[E1] Complementation by a prepositional phrase
[E2] Complementation by a *that*-clause
[E3] Complementation by a *wh*-clause
[E4] Complementation by a *than*-clause
[E5] Complementation by a *to*-infinitive clause
[E6] Complementation by an *-ing* participle clause

These complementation patterns can occur after an adjective (and its modifiers, if any) in various syntactic functions. For example:

The violin is (*rather*) *difficult to play*.
(adjective phrase as C_s)
Mary found the violin (*rather*) *difficult to play*.
(adjective phrase as C_o)
The violin is an instrument (*rather*) *difficult to play*.
(adjective phrase as postmodifier)

The only position in which an adjective cannot normally be followed by its complementation is the premodifying position in a noun phrase: **a keen child on chess*. But here, too, with certain constructions (Types [E5(i)] and [E5(v)]) the complementation can follow discontinuously after the head noun: *The violin is a difficult instrument to play* (*cf* discontinuity with comparative constructions, 15.75). For illustrative purposes, we will confine examples in the following sections to the subject complement function. The lists, like the verb lists in 16.20–63, will be selective.

Note There is a considerable parallel, as the categories [E1–E5] above demonstrate, between patterns associated with adjectives and those associated with monotransitive verbs. The chief difference is that adjectives cannot be followed by a noun phrase object. To bring out the parallel further, we could describe adjectives exemplified in 16.69 below (*averse to*, *conscious of*, etc) as 'prepositional adjectives' comparable with prepositional verbs. We could moreover identify 'phrasal adjectives' (derived from participial forms of phrasal verbs) such as *run down* ('exhausted, depressed') and 'phrasal–prepositional adjectives' such as *fed up* (*with*). These latter variants, however, are rare enough to be disregarded in the following lists.

[E1] Adjective complementation by a prepositional phrase

16.69 Like prepositional verbs, adjectives often form a lexical unit with a following preposition: *good at*, *fond of*, *opposed to*, etc. The lexical bond is strongest with adjectives for which, in a given sense, the complementation is obligatory: *Max is averse to games* ~ **Max is averse*. Such adjectives are marked '1' in the following lists.

The lists make a distinction between participial (*cf* 7.15–19) and nonparticipial adjectives. The difference between participial adjectives and the *-ed* participle of the passive construction is discussed in 3.75–77. These lists provide only a small sample of the adjectives accompanying the prepositions concerned. In particular, it is often possible for the same adjective to go with two or more prepositions, as in *angry about*, *angry at* and *angry with*.

ABOUT: He was very *worried about* her reaction. (*cf* 9.60)

NONPARTICIPIAL		PARTICIPIAL	
angry	*knowledgeable*	*aggrieved*	*frightened*
glad	*mad*	*annoyed*	*pleased*
happy	*reasonable*	*delighted*	*worried*

AT: She was *bad at* mathematics. (*cf* 9.62)

NONPARTICIPIAL		PARTICIPIAL	
angry	*good*	*alarmed*	*disgusted*
brilliant	*hopeless*	*amused*	*pleased*
clever	*terrible*	*delighted*	*puzzled*

FROM: The village is *remote from* the bustle of city life. (*cf* 9.18, 9.47)

different *distant* *distinct* *free* *remote*

OF: She was *aware of* his difficulties.

NONPARTICIPIAL			PARTICIPIAL
afraid	*conscious*[1]	*glad*	*convinced*
ashamed	*empty*	*proud*[1]	*scared*
capable	*fond*[1]	*short*[1]	*tired*
certain	*full*	*worthy*	

ON/UPON: Their plan was *based on* cooperation.

NONPARTICIPIAL			PARTICIPIAL	
contingent[1]	*intent*[1]	*reliant*[1]	*based*[1]	*set*[1]
dependent	*keen*	*severe*	*bent*[1]	

TO: All capital gains are *subject to* taxation.

NONPARTICIPIAL			PARTICIPIAL	
answerable	*close*	*liable*[1]	*accustomed*[1]	*inclined*[1]
averse[1]	*due*[1]	*similar*	*allied*[1]	*opposed*[1]

WITH: This plan is not *compatible with* our principles.

NONPARTICIPIAL		PARTICIPIAL	
angry	*happy*	*annoyed*	*drunk*
busy	*impatient*	*bored*	*enchanted*
comfortable	*incompatible*[1]	*concerned*	*obsessed*
compatible[1]	*sick*	*delighted*	*occupied*
content	*uneasy*	*depressed*	*overcome*
familiar		*disappointed*	*pleased*
friendly		*disgusted*	*satisfied*
furious		*dismayed*	*taken*[1]
		distressed	

Note [**a**] In general, choice of preposition remains the same after morphologically related verbs, adjectives, and nouns: *different from, differ from, difference from.* But this correspondence is not always to be relied on: contrast *full of* with *filled with*; *proud of* with *pride in.*

[**b**] Other prepositions which less commonly enter into *adjective + preposition* idioms include *for* and *towards*: *grateful for, sorry for, inclined towards.*

[**c**] *Used* followed by the preposition *to*, a more informal synonym of *accustomed* (*to*), is participial in spelling, but has the special pronunciation /'juːstə/. Unlike *accustomed*, however, *used* does not occur with a following infinitive (*cf* 16.79). This adjectival *used to*, in spite of identity of spelling and pronunciation, is quite distinct from *used to* as a marginal modal (*cf* 3.44). Contrast:

I'm *used to* hard work.   I *used to* work hard.

[**d**] In the past, prescriptive objections have been made to the use of *to* rather than *from* after *averse* and *different.* However, *to* is the normal preposition to follow *averse*, and *different to* is quite widely used (esp in BrE) as an alternative to *different from.* On *different than*, *cf* 15.66 Note, 16.74.

[**e**] *With* can be omitted after (*in*)*compatible* if the subject is plural, *cf* 'mutual participation', 13.60:

*Carl is incompatible.   BUT: Carl and Eva are incompatible.

[E2] Adjective complementation by a *that*-clause

16.70 Like *that*-clauses following a verb, *that*-clauses following an adjective may have:

(A) indicative verb: I am *sure* (that) he *is* here now.
(B) subjunctive verb: They were *insistent* (that) we *be* ready. ⟨formal⟩
(C) putative *should*: I'm *sorry* (that) he *should have* left. ⟨formal⟩

The uses of the mandative subjunctive and of putative *should* have been discussed in 3.59 and 14.25 respectively. Putative *should* often occurs after expressions of emotion (sorrow, joy, displeasure, surprise, wonder, etc), and is often accompanied by intensifying expressions such as *so, such, like this/that, ever*, or *at all.* The indicative *that*-clause, on the other hand, refers to an established fact. The following pairs illustrate choices of construction:

I am *sorry* { (that) I *have* to leave so early.
(that) you *should have* been (so) inconvenienced. }

I am *surprised* { (that) you *didn't call* the doctor before. / (that) anyone of your intelligence *should swallow* a lie like that. }

With some adjectives (those in category [E2b(ii)], 16.72) the *should*-clause can be paraphrased by an infinitive clause with a subject:

It was *natural* for him to go to London after the war.
= It was *natural* that he should go to London after the war.

That-clauses cannot be preceded by prepositions. Hence adjectives which are constructed with prepositions before noun phrases ([E1]) drop the preposition before a *that*-clause (*cf* 16.28). Compare the following:

I am *convinced* { *of* his innocence. [E1] / (*that*) he is innocent. [E2] }

Many *that*-clauses following an adjective are actually subjects postponed by extraposition (*cf* 18.33):

It is lucky (*that*) *you came*. ~ *That you came* is lucky.

These are listed separately in 16.72.

[E2a] Adjectives with experiencer (*cf* 10.23 Note) **as subject**

16.71 (i) *THAT*-CLAUSE HAS INDICATIVE VERB ONLY (*cf* Note [a] below)

These adjectives express degrees of certainty or confidence: *aware*, *certain*, *confident*, *sure*:

We were *confident* that Karen *was* still alive.

(ii) *THAT*-CLAUSE HAS PUTATIVE *SHOULD*, OR SUBJUNCTIVE VERB (or marginally also an indicative verb)

The three principal adjectives in this class are *anxious*, *eager*, and *willing*:

Are you *willing* that { he *should be* permitted to resign? / he *be* permitted to resign? / ?he *is* permitted to resign? }

(On the distribution of these three alternatives, *cf* 16.30.)

(iii) *THAT*-CLAUSE HAS INDICATIVE VERB OR PUTATIVE *SHOULD*

These adjectives express emotions:

I'm so *thankful* that nobody *was* hurt.
Were you *surprised* that Ray *should win* the prize?

NONPARTICIPIAL		PARTICIPIAL		
afraid	*hopeful*	*alarmed*	*depressed*	*horrified*
angry	*proud*	*amazed*	*disappointed*	*irritated*
glad	*sad*	*amused*	*distressed*	*pleased*
grateful	*sorry*	*annoyed*	*disturbed*	*shocked*
happy	*thankful*	*astonished*	*frightened*	*upset*

There is a tendency to prefer the putative *should* construction in nonassertive contexts, or where the adjective has negative or unfavourable associations.

Note [a] The restriction of Type (i) above to 'indicative verbs only' is meant to allow for the use of modal auxiliaries, including *should* in a nonputative sense; *eg*: *I am aware that I should* [= 'ought to'] *have joined long ago*.
[b] *Afraid* is unique among adjectives in that it accepts the pronoun *so* (and its negative equivalent *not*) as a *that*-clause substitute (*cf* 16.31): *I'm afraid so/not*.

[E2b] Adjectives with anticipatory *it* as subject

16.72 The *that*-clause in this construction is an extraposed subject. Three types are again distinguished, matching those in 16.71.

(i) *THAT*-CLAUSE HAS INDICATIVE VERB ONLY (*cf* 16.71 Note [a])
These adjectives have to do with truth or knowledge:

It is *true* that she never *comes* on time.

apparent	*evident*	*likely*	*possible*	*untrue*
certain	*implicit*	*obvious*	*true*	*well-known*
clear	*indubitable*	*plain*	*unlikely*	

(ii) *THAT*-CLAUSE HAS PUTATIVE *SHOULD*, OR SUBJUNCTIVE VERB (or marginally, also, an indicative verb)
These adjectives express concepts concerned with modality or volition:

It is essential that the ban { *should be* lifted tomorrow. / *be* lifted tomorrow. / (?) *is* lifted tomorrow. }

appropriate	*essential*	*important*	*necessary*	*vital*
compulsory	*fitting*	*impossible*	*obligatory*	
crucial	*imperative*	*improper*	*proper*	

Various deverbal adjectives ending in *-able* also belong to this group, *eg*: *advisable*, *desirable*, *preferable*.

(iii) *THAT*-CLAUSE HAS INDICATIVE VERB OR PUTATIVE *SHOULD*
This group consists mainly of emotive adjectives, and includes a large number of participial adjectives ending in *-ing*:

It is { *strange* / *upsetting* } that { she *is* so late. / she *should be* so late. }

NONPARTICIPIAL		PARTICIPIAL	
awkward	*logical*	*alarming*	*perplexing*
curious	*odd*	*annoying*	*pleasing*
disastrous	*peculiar*	*depressing*	*shocking*
dreadful	*sad*	*disappointing*	*surprising*
extraordinary	*silly*	*embarrassing*	
fortunate	*tragic*	*frightening*	
irrational	*unfortunate*	*irritating*	

Various *-able/-ible* adjectives also belong to this group: *admirable*, *commendable*, *deplorable*, *despicable*, *incomprehensible*, *inconceivable*, *lamentable*, *remarkable*, *understandable*, *unjustifiable*, etc.

Note [**a**] Although the pro-forms *so* and *not* cannot be used after these [E2b] adjectives (*cf* 16.71 Note [b]), there is a possibility of replacing the adjective + *so*/*not* by a related adverb + *so*/*not*:

A: It is *apparent* that she lives/doesn't live here. {B: Yes, *obviously*/*fortunately* so. / B: No, *evidently*/*sadly* not.}

[**b**] When an adjective of Type (iii) above occurs after a modal verb construction, the *that*-clause is commonly replaced by an *if*-clause. If the modal verb in the main clause is hypothetical (*eg*: *would*), the verb in the *if*-clause is placed in the hypothetical past. Compare:

It *is* sad *that* you *have* to leave.
It *will be* sad *if* you *have* to leave.
It *would be* sad *if* you *had* to leave.

[E3] Adjective complementation by a *wh*-clause

16.73 As with *that*-clauses, we have to distinguish those adjectives ([E3a]) which are predicated of an experiencer (normally a person) as subject, and those ([E3b]) which go with anticipatory *it*. In the latter case, the *wh*-clause is an extraposed subject. Examples are:

[E3a] I was *unsure* {(of) / (about)} {what I should say. [1] / whether the problem was solved. [2]}

[E3b] It was *unclear* what they would do. [3]

Type [E3a] consists of adjectives which are constructed with prepositions, and which therefore belong also to Type [E1]. The preposition is sometimes omitted before the *wh*-clause (*cf* 15.5 Note [c]). In Type [E3b], on the other hand, no preposition can be inserted: **It was unclear of*/*about what they would do*. Also no infinitive *wh*-clause is possible (*cf* 16.37): *It is unsure where to go* is unacceptable unless *it* refers to some animate being (such as a mouse), and is consequently not interpreted in terms of extraposition.

Returning to Type [E3a], we note that in some cases the adjective takes a *wh*-clause in assertive contexts: *eg*: *careful* (*about*), *doubtful* (*as to*), *fussy* (*about*), *puzzled* (*as to*), *unclear* (*about*), *uncertain* (*of*), *undecided* (*about*), *unsure* (*of*), *unaware* (*of*):

John is *careful* (*about*) what he does with his money.

Most of these adjectives are intrinsically negative in meaning. In other cases, although elsewhere it is associated with an indicative *that*-clause [E2a(i)], the adjective tends to occur with a *wh*-clause in nonassertive contexts (*cf* 16.35), *eg*: *aware*, *certain*, *clear*, *sure*:

Are you *sure* (*of*) how much the machine costs?
I wasn't altogether *clear* (*about*) what we had to do.

A similar division may be made among adjectives of the anticipatory-*it* type ([E3b]). Those which intrinsically express doubt, and therefore take this structure even in assertive contexts, include *doubtful*, *uncertain*, *unclear*, *unsure*, and *unknown*. Those normally occurring with an indicative *that*-clause (*ie* Type [E2b(i)]) include *apparent*, *certain*, *obvious*, and *plain*. They can take a *wh*-clause in nonassertive contexts. Each type is illustrated in:

It was *unclear* whether an amendment would be accepted.
It was not *obvious* how far the westernization process would go.

After adjectives of Type [E3a] there may also occur an infinitive *wh*-clause: *I was uncertain* (*of*) *what to do*. This is preferable to the finite clause in cases illustrated by [1–3] above, since the subject can remain unexpressed in the reduced nonfinite version.

[E4] Adjective complementation by a *than*-clause

16.74 There is an unusual construction in which a noncomparative adjective is followed by a comparative *than*-clause as complementation. *Different* is the only adjective which fits into this pattern, and even then there is a tradition which regards the use of *than* here as improper. There is, however, no felicitous alternative to the *different than* construction in examples such as:

> She's quite a *different* girl *than she was five years ago*. [1]

The various stylistic variants of, and alternatives to, the *than*-clause after *different* are examined in 15.66 Note [b]. When the clause is reduced to a noun phrase, it becomes possible to use *from* as an alternative to *than*:

> The unions are taking a very different attitude {*than* / *from*} the employers.

When the noun phrase following *than*/*from* cannot be derived by ellipsis from a clause, *than* is decidedly less acceptable than *from*:

> The main languages of southern India are totally different in origin {*from* / ?**than*} those of the northern part of the country.

Note [**a**] On *different from* and *different to*, *cf* 16.69 Note [d].

[**b**] It is also possible for a *than*-clause to be used after the adverb *differently*:

> In the west of the country, they pronounce their vowels quite *differently than* (*they do*) *in the east*.

The same prescriptive objections are made to *differently than* as to *different than*.

[E5] Adjective complementation by a *to*-infinitive clause

16.75 We distinguish seven kinds of construction in which an adjective is followed by a *to*-infinitive clause. They are exemplified in the following sentences, which are superficially alike:

(i) Bob is *splendid* to wait.
(ii) Bob is *slow* to react.
(iii) Bob is *sorry* to hear it.
(iv) Bob is *hesitant* to agree with you.
(v) Bob is *hard* to convince.
(vi) The food is *ready* to eat.
(vii) It is *important* to be accurate.

In Types (i–iv) the subject of the main clause (*Bob*) is also the subject of the infinitive clause. We can therefore always have a direct object in the infinitive clause if its verb is transitive. For example, if we replace intransitive *wait* by transitive *build* in (i), we can have: *Bob is splendid to build this house*.

For Types (v–vii), on the other hand, the subject of the infinitive is unspecified, although the context often makes clear which subject is intended.

In these types it is possible to insert a subject preceded by *for*; *eg* in Type (vi): *The food is ready* (*for the children*) *to eat.*

Note Infinitive complementation following adjectives modified by *too* and *enough* is discussed elsewhere, in 15.73.

[E5(i)] *Bob is splendid to wait*

16.76 Type (i) has an analogue in a construction involving extraposition (*cf* 18.33): *It is splendid of Bob to wait.* This type of construction also permits a head noun between the adjective and the infinitive:

> Bob must be *a splendid craftsman* {to build / to have built} this house.

As this example shows, the infinitive may be perfective. We may also compare constructions in which an evaluative noun with its determiner replaces the adjective:

> You're {*foolish* / *a fool*} to spend so much.
>
> You're {*wonderful* / *an angel*} to wait for me.

Adjectives in this group are evaluative of human behaviour. They include:

careful	*crazy*	*mad*	*silly*	*wise*
careless	*greedy*	*nice*	*unwise*	*wrong*

These adjectives can also occur with anticipatory *it* and an *of*-phrase as additional complementation (*cf* 16.82):

> It was *foolish* of you to spend so much.

[E5(ii)] *Bob is slow to react*

16.77 In Type (ii), the sentence corresponds to one in which the adjective becomes an adverb, while the infinitive becomes the finite verb:

> Bob is *slow* to react. ~ Bob reacts *slowly*.

In another analogue, the adjective is followed by *in* and an *-ing* participle: *Bob is slow in reacting*. The infinitive verb phrase must be simple: for example, unlike the infinitive phrase in [E5(i)], it cannot be perfective: **Bob is slow to have reacted.* Other adjectives in this small group are *quick* and *prompt*.

Note There is also a partial adverbial analogue (*cf* 8.127*ff*) for Type (i), but in Type (i), unlike Type (ii), the perfective infinitive, and even the *get*-passive (*cf* 3.66) can be used:

> Joan was wise to resign. ~ Joan wisely resigned.
>
> {Joan was careless to get beaten. ~ Joan carelessly got beaten. / Joan is careless to have got beaten.}

[E5(iii)] *Bob is sorry to hear it*

16.78 In Type (iii), the head of the adjective phrase is an emotive adjective (commonly a participial adjective), and the infinitive clause expresses causation:

I'm sorry to have kept you waiting. ['I'm sorry because I have kept you waiting']
I was *excited* to be there. [~ 'To be there *excited* me']

Adjectives in this group correspond closely to the adjectives followed by a *that*-clause in 16.71 (Type [E2a(iii)]):

NONPARTICIPIAL		PARTICIPIAL		
afraid	*happy*	*annoyed*	*disgusted*	*overwhelmed*
angry	*impatient*	*astonished*	*dissatisfied*	*perturbed*
ashamed	*indignant*	*bored*	*embarrassed*	*puzzled*
content	*jubilant*	*concerned*	*fascinated*	*relieved*
furious	*thankful*	*delighted*	*frightened*	*surprised*
glad		*depressed*	*interested*	*worried*
		disappointed	*overjoyed*	

[E5(iv)] ***Bob is hesitant to agree with you***

16.79 In Type (iv), the head of the adjective phrase expresses volitional meaning, or a modal meaning such as ability, possibility, or liability. Examples are:

NONPARTICIPIAL		PARTICIPIAL
able	*keen*	*determined*
anxious	*liable*	*disposed*
apt	*likely* [E2b]	*fated* [E2b]
certain [E2b]	*loath*	*inclined*
curious	*powerless*	*poised*
due	*prone*	*prepared*
eager	*ready* [E5]	(*all*) *set*
eligible	*reluctant*	*unqualified*
fit [E5]	*sure* [E2b]	
free [E5]	*unable*	
greedy	*welcome*	
hesitant	*willing*	
impotent	*worthy*	

The adjectives marked [E2b] occur with a corresponding construction with extraposition of a *that*-clause:

Jill is *likely* to attend.
~ It is *likely* that Jill will attend.

Those marked [E5] are capable of occurring with an infinitive construction of 'passive' meaning, *ie* with an indefinite implied subject and a coreferential implied object:

They are not fit *to eat*. = They are not fit *to be eaten*.

Some of the most common adjectives in this list have a tendency to coalesce with the preceding copula to form a semi-auxiliary verb (*cf* 3.47): *be able to*, *be willing to*, *be sure to*. In addition to modal and volitional adjectives, some adjectives of aspectual meaning, such as *accustomed* and *wont* may be placed here:

We are *accustomed* to take tea on the terrace. ⟨formal⟩
He was *wont* to leave the office at 5 p.m. ⟨formal, archaic⟩

[E5(v)] ***Bob is hard to convince***

16.80 In Type (v), the subject of the sentence is identified with the unexpressed object of the infinitive clause, which must therefore have a transitive verb; hence the unacceptable **Bob is hard to arrive*. There is an analogous construction in which the adjective is complement to an infinitive clause acting as (extraposed) subject (*cf* 18.36):

Bob is *hard* to convince. { ~ To convince Bob is *hard*. / ~ It is *hard* to convince Bob. }

Adjectives so used refer to degrees of ease or comfort, and include:

awkward	*hard*	*tough* ⟨informal⟩
convenient	*impossible*	*tricky* ⟨informal⟩
difficult	*nice* ⟨informal⟩	*unpleasant*
easy	*pleasant*	

Unless there is ellipsis, we cannot omit the infinitive clause, and so there is no semantic implication between (say) *The bread was hard to bake* and *The bread was hard*. Unlike the preceding types, Type (v) permits *for* + subject to be inserted at the beginning of the infinitive clause: *Those darts are tricky* (*for a beginner*) *to use*. Where the infinitive has no overt subject, its implicit subject is understood to have an indefinite meaning:

Jack is easy to fool. = Jack is easy *for anyone* to fool.

Note With some adjectives in this group, such as *nice* or *unpleasant*, the entailment relation between *be* + adjective *to* V and *be* + adjective is less easy to avoid; *eg*: *Jenny is nice to know* implies that *Jenny is nice*.

[E5(vi)] ***The food is ready to eat***

16.81 Again, in this type the subject of the main clause is identified with the object of the infinitive clause. But unlike Type (v), Type (vi) has no analogous construction with an infinitive clause subject:

The food is ready to eat. ≁ *To eat the food is ready.

Also, we can generally (a) omit the infinitive clause, or (b) substitute a passive infinitive clause without change of meaning:

Are these cups available (to use)?
= Are these cups available (to be used)?

Some adjectives of this type, such as *available*, *fit*, *free*, *ready*, and *sufficient*, belong additionally to Type (iv), so that a sentence like *The lamb is ready to eat* is ambiguous, in one sense (the most accessible) being equivalent to the passive *The lamb is ready to be eaten*. Then there is a wider set of adjectives which often occur without complementation at all:

The air is *frosty* (to breathe).
Its fur is *soft* (to touch).

In both Type (v) and Type (vi), the subject of the main clause can be equated with the prepositional object of the infinitive clause, so that the infinitive clause ends with a deferred preposition:

She is pleasant *to talk to.* (~ It is pleasant to talk to her.)
This paper is terribly flimsy *to write on.*
Is the cloth sufficient *to make a dress out of*?

In Type (vi), as well as in Type (v), *for* + subject may be inserted before the infinitive verb: *Are these books free* (*for visitors*) *to borrow?* [= 'Are these books available . . . to borrow?'].

[E5(vii)] *It is important to be accurate*

16.82 We saw in 16.72 that a *that*-clause following an adjective may prove to be a subject postponed by extraposition (*cf* 18.33). A *to*-infinitive clause following an adjective may have the same source:

It is *essential* to spray the trees every year.
~ To spray the trees every year is *essential.*

The infinitive clause can also be introduced by *for* + subject:

It is *vital* (for the children) to be properly clad.
It will be *strange* (for us) to be living alone.

Adjectives of Types (ii) and (iii) in 16.72 ([E2b]) may have this construction: *important, fortunate, lucky, surprising*, etc. *Possible* also belongs to this group.
An additional group of adjectives occurring after anticipatory *it* are those adjectives (chiefly naming evaluative attributes of persons) which occur in pattern [E5(i)] (*cf* 16.76). The adjective in this group is often followed by an *of*-phrase identifying the person(s) being discussed:

It was *wrong* (of him) to tell lies. It is *nice* of you to phone.

[E6] Adjective complementation by an *-ing* participle clause

16.83 A number of sub-types of this pattern may be mentioned.

(i) *Busy* is followed by an *-ing* participle clause without subject:

Margery is *busy* writing letters.

(ii) *Worth* and *worthwhile*, on the other hand, occur both with and without subject:

It is scarcely *worth*(*while*) (*you*/*your*) going home.

Here *worth*(*while*) follows preparatory *it*, and the participle clause is an extraposed subject (*cf* 18.34). Other adjectives of this pattern are *pointless* and *useless* (*It's pointless buying so much food*), and adjectives of Type [E2b(iii)] (*cf* 16.72) also sometimes have this complementation: *absurd, awkward, fortunate, annoying*, etc.

(iii) Elsewhere *worth* and *worthwhile* accompany an *-ing* participle clause without subject, but with a passive meaning, comparable to that of the infinitive clause in pattern [E5(v)] (*cf* 16.80):

The cartons are *worth(while)* saving.
(~ It's *worth(while)* saving the cartons).

(iv) There is a variant construction in which a preposition occurs between the adjective and the participle clause. In some cases the preposition is optional (*cf* (i) above):

I'm *busy* (*with*) getting the house redecorated.
We're *fortunate* (*in*) having Aunt Mary as a baby-sitter.

In other cases, the preposition is obligatory:

We are *used to* not having a car (*cf* 16.69 Note [c]).
I'm *hopeless at* keeping the garden tidy.
She's not *capable of* looking after herself.

Note [**a**] The adjectival constructions in (ii) above may be compared, in some cases, with nominal constructions of equivalent meaning:

It's *no good*/*use* telling him anything.
There's *no point* (in) telling him anything.

Such constructions are introduced either by anticipatory *it* (*cf* 18.33) or by existential *there* (*cf* 18.45). AmE also has *There's no use telling him anything.*

[**b**] *Worthwhile* is sometimes spelled as two words. The vacillation between the spellings *worthwhile* and *worth while* reflects an unclarity about the status of this sequence, which may alternatively be regarded as the preposition *worth* (*cf* 9.6) followed by a noun. Compare:

It's not *worth* your *while* staying. It's not {*worth while* / *worthwhile*} (your) staying.

Complementation of abstract nouns

16.84 In this concluding section we will show, as a connecting link between this chapter and the next, how the patterns of complementation described for verbs and adjectives in 16.20–83 are also to be found with abstract nouns which are morphologically related to those verbs and adjectives. (*Cf* nominalization, 17.51*ff*, and appositional constructions, 17.26, 17.35.) For example, the noun *likelihood* is derived from, and semantically related to, the adjective *likely*. It is therefore not surprising that a construction associated with the adjective is found with the corresponding noun:

It is *likely* that Joan will get married. [1]

~ { The *likelihood* is that Joan will get married. [2]
the *likelihood* that Joan will get married [3] }

But the assumption of correspondence cannot be automatic, for it may fail in both directions:

Joan is *likely* to get married.
≁ *Joan's *likelihood* to get married
*It is *likely* of Joan's getting married.
≁ the *likelihood* of Joan's getting married

In the following section, we illustrate how many of these patterns can be matched with corresponding patterns of noun complementation. Some fairly regular changes, it will be observed, take place in the conversion from the verb or adjective patterns to their nominalizations (*cf* 17.51*ff*). For instance, a preposition must be inserted between a head noun and an immediately following noun phrase or adjective. The list begins with monotransitive patterns, because there are no nominalized forms of copular verb complementation. (Many of the noun complementation patterns, particularly in categories [C] and [D], are stylistically awkward.)

16.85 *Table* 16.85 Verb/adjective and noun complementation compared

	VERB/ADJECTIVE COMPLEMENTATION	NOUN COMPLEMENTATION
[B1]	He *examined* the room.	his *examination* of the room
[B2]	Paul *lacks* confidence.	Paul's *lack* of confidence
[B2pr]	They *rely* on her.	their *reliance* on her
[B3]	I *predict* that it'll rain.	my *prediction* that it'll rain
[B4]	I *doubt* whether he will win.	my *doubt* (about) whether he will win
[B5]	We *enquired* (about) where to go.	our *enquiry* (about) where to go
[B6]	She *refused* to answer.	her *refusal* to answer
[B7]	He *denied* having taken it.	?his *denial* of having taken it (*cf*: his denial of the theft)
[B8]	X *needs* us to work harder.	the *need* for us to work harder
[B9]	She *resented* his/him losing.	her *resentment* of his/him losing
[C1pr]	They *elected* Joe (as) leader.	their *election* of Joe as leader
[C2pr]	X *certified* Max (as) insane.	the *certification* of Max as insane
[C3]	X *expelled* Sue from school.	the *expulsion* of Sue from school
[C4]	They *chose* Jim to be boss.	their *choice* of Jim to be boss
[C7]	We *got* her elected.	*our *getting* of her elected
[D1]	I *paid* him five pounds.	my *payment* to him of five pounds
[D2]	It *protected* Rio from attack.	the *protection* of Rio from attack
[D3]	X *warned* us that it would snow.	the *warning* to us that it would snow
[D3pr]	He *admitted* to me that he told lies.	his *admission* to me that he told lies
[D4]	X *reminded* us (of) who he was.	X's *reminder* to us of who he was
[D5]	X *advised us* (on) what to do.	the *advice* to us on what to do
[D6]	She *invited* me to stay.	her *invitation* to me to stay
[E1]	I was *impatient* with Freda.	my *impatience* with Freda
[E2]	It was *certain* that we would lose.	the *certainty* that we would lose
[E3]	I was *careful* (*over*) what to say.	my *care over* what to say
[E5]	Sam was *quick* to reply.	Sam's *quickness* to reply
[E6]	I was *lucky* meeting you.	my *luck* in meeting you

These structures with abstract nouns will be studied further in the next chapter.

Bibliographical note

On phrasal verbs and other types of multi-word verbs, see Akimoto (1983); Bolinger (1971a); Carvell and Svartvik (1969); Cowie and Mackin (1975); Dixon (1982b); Fraser (1976); Kennedy (1920); Lipka (1972); Live (1965); Makkai (1972); Sroka (1972); Witton (1979).

On general aspects of verb classification and complementation, see Alexander and Kunz (1964); Allerton (1982); Bresnan (1970); Chomsky (1965, Ch. 2); Fillmore (1968, 1977a, 1977b); Halliday (1967–1968); Jain (1978); Lyons (1977, Ch. 12); Rosenbaum (1967a, 1967b); Ureland (1973).

Some basic patterns of complementation are discussed in Bald (1972); Dušková (1976); Fillmore (1965); Huddleston (1969).

On verb complementation by finite clauses (especially by *that*-clauses), see Behre (1955); Greenbaum (1976a, 1977a); G. M. Horn (1978); Kiparsky and Kiparsky (1970); Quirk (1981); Storms (1966).

On verb complementation by nonfinite constructions, see Andersson (1985); Bladon (1968); Dušková (1979); Eagleson (1972); van Ek (1966); Freed (1979); Macháček (1965).

On the properties of specific verbs with regard to meaning and complementation, see Bald and Quirk (1970); Behre (1973); Bolinger (1971b); Fodor (1970); Kempson and Quirk (1971); Pittman (1970); Poldauf (1967); Postal (1971); Zandvoort (1961).

On adjective complementation, see Alexander and Matthews (1964); Bolinger (1961a); Herbst (1983, 1984); Lees (1960b).

Other studies relevant to complementation include Bridgeman (1965); Emonds (1976); Nickel (1968); Norrick (1979); Nosek (1965); Postal (1974).

17 The noun phrase

Introduction

The indefinitely complex noun phrase

17.1 Just as the sentence may be indefinitely complex, so may the noun phrase. This must be so, since sentences themselves can be reshaped so as to come within noun-phrase structure. For example, the following sentences [1a–e], simple and complex, can become one simple sentence [2] with a very complex noun phrase as subject:

The girl is Mary Smith. [1a]
The girl is tall. [1b]
The girl was standing in the corner. [1c]
You waved to the girl when you entered. [1d]
The girl became angry because you knocked over her glass. [1e]
The tall girl standing in the corner who became angry because you knocked over her glass after you waved to her when you entered is Mary Smith. [2]

Moreover, starting from [2], we could reconstruct any of the sentences listed in [1a–e] – and in fact we could not understand the noun-phrase subject (printed in italics) of [2], unless we recognized its constituent parts as they are set out in [1a–e].

Yet [2] has introduced many changes. We have, for example, suppressed all or part of the verbs in [1c] and [1d]; we have put *tall*, which is complement in [1b], as a modifier before the noun *girl*; we have replaced *the girl* of [1e] by *who*.

After describing determinatives and nouns in Chapter 5, the purpose of the present chapter is to state the conditions governing the making of noun phrases by processes such as those indicated above.

Noun-phrase constituents

17.2 In describing noun phrases we need to distinguish the following constituent parts:

(A) The HEAD, around which (for the most part) the other constituents cluster and which dictates concord with other parts of the sentence:

[The tall *girl* standing in the corner] is my sister.
[The tall *girls* standing in the corner] are my sisters.
[The tall *girl* in the corner $\left\{\begin{matrix} \textit{who} \\ \textit{*which} \end{matrix}\right\}$ has a blue sweater] is my sister.
I saw the tall girl in [the *corner* $\left\{\begin{matrix} \textit{which} \\ \textit{*who} \end{matrix}\right\}$ was full of people].

(B) The DETERMINATIVE, which includes

(a) predeterminers, *ie* all items which can precede any central determiner (including zero article) in a noun phrase, *eg*: *all, both, double* (*cf* 5.15*ff*):

all the furniture   *both* those musicians

(b) central determiners, including those items listed in 5.11*ff*, *eg* the articles, *this, some*:

some new office furniture   all *those* fine musicians

(c) postdeterminers, which follow central determiners but precede premodifiers, *eg* adjectives. Postdeterminers include *eg* numerals, *many, few, several* (*cf* 5.20*ff*):

the *many* new offices   the *few* survivors

(C) The PREMODIFICATION, which comprises all the items placed before the head other than determinatives, notably adjectives (or, rather, adjective phrases, *cf* 7.20) and nouns:

some furniture
some *expensive* furniture
some *very expensive* furniture
some *very expensive office* furniture
some *very very expensive office* furniture

(D) The POSTMODIFICATION, comprising all the items placed after the head, notably:

prepositional phrases:	the car *outside the station*
nonfinite clauses:	the car *standing outside the station*
relative clauses:	the car *that stood outside the station*
complementation (*cf* 15.63*ff*):	a bigger car *than that*

Restrictive and nonrestrictive modification

17.3 Modification can be restrictive or nonrestrictive. The modification is RESTRICTIVE when the reference of the head is a member of a class which can be identified only through the modification that has been supplied. The girl in example [2] in 17.1 is only identifiable as Mary Smith provided we understand that it is the particular girl who is tall, who was standing in the corner, and who became angry. Such modification would not have been actually necessary unless there had been other girls present, tall but not in the corner, or in the corner but not tall, or who had not become angry. Restrictiveness, then, indicates a limitation on the possible reference of the head.

Alternatively, the referent of a noun phrase may be viewed as unique or as a member of a class that has been independently identified (for example in the preceding context). Any modification given to such a head is additional information which is not essential for identification, and we call it NONRESTRICTIVE. For example, the relative clause *who is in the corner* in [1] is nonrestrictive:

Mary Smith, *who is in the corner*, wants to meet you. [1]

By reason of being designated by a proper name, Mary Smith's identity is independent of whether or not she is in the corner (though the information on her present location may be useful enough). If a man says [2], the daughter is identified as being one out of two daughters in the family and also as younger than the other daughter:

Come and meet my *younger* daughter. [2]

[2] is thus an example of restrictive premodification. If, on the other hand, a

man (in a monogamous society) says [3], the premodifier *beautiful* is understood as nonrestrictive:

Come and meet my *beautiful* wife. [3]

Another example:

I don't want him to put his *ugly* nose into my house again. [4]

Sentences [1], [3], and [4] are inevitably nonrestrictive since – being treated as unique – *Mary Smith, wife,* and *nose,* in these sentences will not admit restriction. But almost any head that can be restrictively modified is also susceptible of nonrestrictive modification, *eg*:

The tall girl, *who is a dentist*, is Mary Smith. [5]

Here the only information offered to identify the girl as Mary Smith is the allusion to her tallness; the mention of her work as a dentist is not offered as an aid to identification but for additional interest.

Other nouns which have nonrestrictive postmodification include those with generic reference:

The giant panda, *which is to be found in the remote parts of China*, lives exclusively on bamboo shoots.

Note In popular narrative style, there is a nonrestrictive use of premodifying adjective in cases like the following (*cf* cleft sentences, 18.26 Note [b]):

Reporters hounded an *embarrassed* Ben Miles over his TV gaffe last week and in reply to one questioner the *unhappy* Miles made things still worse by . . .

17.4 The fact that nonrestrictive relative clauses are not essential for identification enables us in [1] and [1a] to make different parts of the sentence into a relative clause:

My brother, *who is an engineer*, lives in America. [1]
My brother, *who lives in America*, is an engineer. [1a]

Semantic equivalence is still preserved in [1] and [1a] (although there is a difference in focus). A nonrestrictive relative clause may resemble an adverbial clause (*cf* simultaneous meaning, 15.28), *eg*:

My brother, *who has lived in America for over 30 years*, can still speak Italian. [2]

In [2], the relative clause is grammatically optional, like any other nonrestrictive item, but semantically obligatory as the correlate of *still* in the superordinate clause. The relative clause here can be paraphrased as an adverbial clause [2a], with initial position (unlike the relative clause) [2b], or as an adverbial prepositional phrase [2c]:

My brother can still speak Italian, *although he has lived in America for over 30 years.* [2a]
Although he has lived in America for over 30 years, my brother can still speak Italian. [2b]
After over 30 years in America, my brother can still speak Italian. [2c]

The predications of the two clauses [2a] and [2b] are contrastive.

Nonrestrictive relative clauses may also imply other adverbial functions, such as cause ('because he had been very helpful', 'for being very helpful') in [3]:

> Ann thanked her teacher, *who had been very helpful.* [3]

By contrast, restrictive relative clauses with general antecedents (*cf* 17.12) express conditional relationship, *eg*:

> Students *who work hard* pass their exams. ['If students work hard, they pass their exams.']

17.5 Proper nouns cannot have restrictive modification when they have the normal unique denotation. However, when the proper noun temporarily takes on features of a common noun, restrictive modification is possible (*cf* 5.64):

> *the Springfield* that is in Illinois [1]
> *the Johnson* who wrote the dictionary [2]

Nor are restrictive relative clauses possible with nonnominal antecedents (*cf* 'sentential relative clauses', 17.9):

> *He likes dogs*, which surprises me. [3]

Nonassertive heads cannot have nonrestrictive modification:

> *I won't see {*any person,* / *anyone,*} who has not made an appointment. [4]

By contrast, nonrestrictive modification is possible with assertive heads:

> *Someone*, who sounded like your mother, called to say she wanted to see you. [5]

Nonspecific determiners like *any, all*, and *every* usually have only restrictive modification:

> **Every book*, which is written to deceive the reader, should be banned. [6]
> **All the students*, who had failed the test, wanted to try again. [7]

However we may occasionally find nonrestrictive as well as restrictive modification, as in:

> *All the students*, who had returned from their vacation, wanted to take the exam. [8]

But positional variation of *all* is possible only with a nonrestrictive clause (*cf* 5.16, 6.50):

> *The students, who had all* (*of them*) returned from their vacation, failed the test. [7a]
> **The students who had all* (*of them*) failed the test wanted to try again. [8a]

17.6 We shall draw attention to the distinction between restrictive and nonrestrictive in the description of the modification types later on, but two general points may be of value now.

First, modification at its 'most restrictive' tends to come after the head:

Any person *who wishes to see me* must make an appointment.

By contrast, our decision to use an item as a premodifier (such as nonrestrictive *silly* in *a silly fool*) often reflects our wish that it be taken for granted and not be interpreted as a specific identifier.

Secondly, restrictive modification tends to be given more prosodic emphasis than the head, since there is a built-in contrast, as in (*cf* examples in 17.3):

Susan is my *ÈLDer* daughter.
John is my *LÀzy* son.

Nonrestrictive modification, on the other hand, tends to be unstressed in prehead position:

my *beautiful* WÌFE

In post-head position, its 'parenthetic' relation is endorsed by being given a separate tone unit (frequently with reduced prominence and narrow pitch range); or, in writing, by being enclosed by commas (*cf* 17.22).

Temporary and permanent modification

17.7 There is a second dichotomy that has some affinities with the distinction between restrictive and nonrestrictive but rather more with the contrast of nonprogressive and progressive in predication (*cf* 4.25*ff*), or permanent and temporary in agential nouns (*cf* App I.34*f*). Modification in noun-phrase structure may also be seen as permanent or temporary (*cf* 7.21), such that items placed in premodification position are typically given the status of PERMANENT or, at any rate, characteristic features. Although this does not mean that postmodification position is committed to either temporariness or permanence, those adjectives which have to be predicative have a notably TEMPORARY reference. Thus [1] would be understood as [1a]:

the *courteous* man [1]
the man *who is courteous*
[*ie* 'normally and not merely at this moment'] [1a]

In contrast, [2] would be understood as having reference only to a specific time, and this corresponds to the nonoccurrence of [2a]:

The man is *ready*. [2]
*the *ready* man [2a]

(On the relevance of the distinction in determiners between indefinite and definite, *cf* 5.26*ff*.) On this basis, we see that timidity and fear are contrasted in part according as the first is seen as permanent [3], the second as temporary [4]:

a man *who is timid* ∼ a *timid* man [3]
a man *who is afraid* ≁ *an *afraid* man [4]

Just as some modifiers are too strongly identified with temporary status to appear in prehead position, so there can be modification constrained to prehead position because it indicates permanent status. Thus the toe which is characteristically (and permanently) big in relation to the rest is called *the big toe*, and we cannot say of it **The toe is big* without destroying this permanent characteristic and making the expression seem to refer only (for example) to a temporary swelling. Compare also *the original* ['first, earliest'] *version* beside *His work is quite original* ['of a new type'], which would permit adverbial indication of time span (*now, always*, etc; *cf* 7.87).

The explicitness of postmodification

17.8 In general, premodification is to be interpreted (and, most frequently, can only be interpreted) in terms of postmodification and its greater explicitness. That is, *some tall college girls* will be interpreted as 'some girls who are tall and who are (studying) at a college'. The premodified noun phrase [1] may include, for example, all of the relations which are explicit in the postmodified noun phrases [1a–e]:

an *oil* man [1]
a man *who sells oil* [1a]
a man *who delivers oil* [1b]
a man *who produces oil* [1c]
a man *who investigates oil* [1d]
a man *who advocates the use of oil* [1e]

What normally happens, as in the case of *big toe* (in 17.7) and *oil man* [1], is that ambiguity does not arise since one sense is selected in a specific context (*cf* lexicalization, App I.9*ff*). Thus, for example, the question 'Will the oil man call today?' will normally carry only one interpretation in any given context.

Explicitness in postmodification varies considerably, however. It is greater in the finite relative clause [2] than in the nonfinite *-ing* clause [2a], from which the explicit tense (*is*?/*was*?) is absent, though this in turn is more explicit than the prepositional phrase [2b], from which the verb indicating a specific posture is absent:

the girl *who was standing in the corner* [2]
the girl *standing in the corner* [2a]
the girl *in the corner* [2b]

Reduction in explicitness in the noun phrase is closely related to the linguistic and situational context. There is, typically, a progression from 'more explicit' to 'less explicit' in a discourse. One instance of such sequential and gradual reduction from sentence [3], via relative clause [3a], via prepositional phrase [3b], to pro-form [3c], can be seen in Anthony Burgess's novel *Inside Mr Enderby*. When flying to Rome, the main character of the novel is warned by an American passenger:

'Your ticket does not entitle you to undisputed monopolization of the john.' [*ie* the lavatory] [3]

The fellow passenger who issued this warning is subsequently referred to as:

the American who had ousted Enderby from the john [3a]

to be further reduced to:

the American from the john [3b]

and finally:

an American, not *the john one*, poised his camera to shoot [3c]

The order of presentation in this chapter will be from most explicit to least explicit. We therefore start with the most explicit type of noun-phrase modification, *ie* postmodification by finite clause.

Postmodification by finite clauses

Types of postmodifying finite clauses

17.9 We distinguish two major types of finite clauses as noun-phrase postmodifiers, RELATIVE clauses [1] and APPOSITIVE clauses [2]:

The news *that appeared in the papers this morning* was well received. [1]
The news *that the team had won* calls for a celebration. [2]

Although superficially similar, the difference between these two types of finite clause becomes apparent, for example if we try to replace *that* by *which* in the two examples:

The news *which appeared in the papers this morning* was well received. [1a]
*The news *which the team had won* calls for a celebration. [2a]

Thus *that* is not replaceable by a *wh*-pronoun in appositive clauses, as it is in relative clauses. More significantly from a general point of view, *that* in [2] has no function as clause element within the *that*-clause, as it has in relative clause structure. Thus in [1], the relative pronoun is subject; in [1b] it is object:

The news *which we saw in the papers this morning* was well received. [1b]

Appositive clauses will be further discussed in 17.26*f*. The type of relative clause represented by [1] is called an ADNOMINAL relative clause, and will be discussed below.

In addition to adnominal relative clauses, we distinguish NOMINAL relative clauses, as in [3], and SENTENTIAL relative clauses, as in [4]:

What surprises me is that they are fond of snakes and lizards. [3]
They are fond of snakes and lizards, *which surprises me*. [4]

Nominal relative clauses are unique among relative clauses in that they 'contain' their antecedents. They are discussed, with other nominal dependent clauses, in 15.8*f*.

In sentential relative clauses, the antecedent is not nominal but clausal, *ie* in [4] the whole clause *They are fond of snakes and lizards* is postmodified by *which surprises me*. That this is so can be seen in the choice of singular verb concord (*surprises*). The sentential relative clause has affinities with, on the one hand, nominal relative clauses, and, on the other hand, with coordinate clauses (*cf* 13.50*f*):

They are fond of snakes and lizards, *and that surprises me*. [4a]

The adnominal relative clause is the central type of relative clause, and, unless indicated otherwise, 'relative clause' here means 'adnominal relative clause'. Within such relative clauses we make a distinction between restrictive [5] and nonrestrictive [6] (*cf* 17.3*ff*):

Snakes *which are poisonous* should be avoided. [5]
Rattlesnakes, *which are poisonous*, should be avoided. [6]

Among those two types, the restrictive is the more common, and will be treated before the nonrestrictive.

Characteristics of relative clauses

17.10 Part of the explicitness of relative clauses lies in the specifying power of the relative pronoun. It may be capable of

(i) showing concord with its antecedent, *ie* the preceding part of the noun phrase of which the relative clause is a postmodifier [external relation];

and

(ii) indicating its function within the relative clause either as an element of clause structure (S, O, C, A), or as a constituent of an element in the relative clause [internal relation].

Gender concord

17.11 Concord is on the basis of a two-term 'gender' system, personal and nonpersonal (*cf* 5.105*ff*, 6.8*f*), and applies only to the *wh*-series:

Joan, *who* . . .	London, *which* . . .
the boy/people *who* . . .	the fox/animals *which* . . .
the human being *who* . . .	the human body *which* . . .
the fairy *who* . . .	the unicorn *which* . . .

It will be seen from these examples that 'personality' is ascribed basically to human beings but extends to creatures in the supernatural world (angels, elves, etc) which are thought of as having human characteristics such as speech. Pet animals can be regarded as 'personal' (at least by their owners; *cf* 5.109*f*):

Rover, *who* was barking, frightened the children.

On the other hand, human babies can be regarded (though rarely perhaps by their parents) as not having developed personality:

This is the baby *which* needs inoculation.

Though ships may take the personal pronoun *she*, the relative pronoun is regularly nonpersonal (*cf* 5.111 Note):

Is {*it* / *she*} *the ship which* is due to leave for a Caribbean cruise tomorrow?

Collective nouns (*cf* 5.108) are normally treated as personal when they have plural concord (esp in BrE), and as nonpersonal when they have singular concord:

The committee {*who were* / *which was*} responsible for this decision . . .

The gender contrast is neutralized when the *wh*-series is replaced by *that* or a zero relative:

She must be *the nicest person that* ever lived.
That must be *the nicest thing that* ever happened.

With coordinated antecedents of mixed gender, the choice of relative pronoun may create a problem. It does not arise when zero relative is possible or when *that* is chosen, *eg*:

the people and things {she likes most / *that* amuse her most}

With *wh*-pronouns, the principle of proximity seems to be favoured (*cf* 10.35):

{the people and things *which* / the things and people *who*} amuse her most

Which can have a personal noun as its antecedent when the relative is a complement with the semantic role of characterization attribute (*cf* 10.20):

He imagined himself to be an artist, *which* he was not.

Note [**a**] Other nonhuman creatures besides pets may take *who* even in sentences where this involves an apparent clash with the neuter pronoun *it*; thus, from a recent work of nonfiction:

the chameleon *who* changes *its* colours

This is less likely however when the relative pronoun is object in its clause, as we see from the following examples on two successive pages of a work on zoology:

the black rhinoceroses *who* live in the park
the white rhinoceros *which* we saw in the wilds outside the park

On the factors involved in this difference, *cf* 17.16.

[**b**] It so happens that, in familiar speech, the word *character* can be used in the sense of 'person', and the word *personality* can be used for somebody who has achieved notoriety. In consequence, we may have not only [1] and [2] but also [1a] and [2a]:

Charles has a fine character *which* he inherits from his father. [1]
Smith has a strange personality *which* repels many people. [2]
Charles is a strange character *who* dislikes parties. ⟨familiar⟩ [1a]
Smith is now a famous personality *who* is often interviewed on television. [2a]

17.12 The nominal relative clause is common with definite nonpersonal reference (though with a different pronoun from that used in adnominal relative clauses; *cf* 15.8*f*, 6.35 Note [b]): *what, whatever, whichever.*

What is most highly valued in the tribe is valour. [1]

This is *what I can't understand.* [2]
She'll do *whatever you say.* [3]
Choose *whichever you like best.* [4]

In the case of definite personal reference, the only pronoun is *whoever*:

{ **Who* / *Whoever* } helped me has gone. [5]

A personal pronoun + a relative pronoun, on the other hand, is possible only in archaic or very formal contexts:

He who made this possible deserves our gratitude. [6]

It is more acceptable if *he* has generic reference, as in [7], which however also sounds archaic:

He who helps the handicapped deserves our support. [7]

The normal expressions are [7a] and [7b]:

{ *Anyone* / *Anybody* } *who* helps the handicapped deserves our support. [7a]
Those who help the handicapped deserve our support. [7b]

Replacement is impossible with plural **they who/which*, and also with singular **it which*:

{ *What* / **It which* } I can't understand is this: . . . [2a]

That is acceptable with *which* only in very formal style:

That which is most highly valued in the tribe is valour. [1a]

Note In relation to **it which* . . ., there is a similar constraint on postmodification by some other structures:

?*He in the corner* is my new boss. [8]
**It in the corner* is an antique. [8a]

Postmodification following *you* is possible in informal and peremptory vocatives (*cf* 10.53):

You in the corner, stop chattering! [8b]

Restrictive relative clauses

17.13 The choice of relative pronoun is dependent, in particular, on the following three factors:

(a) the relation of the relative clause to its antecedent: restrictive [1] or nonrestrictive [2], *eg*:

The woman *who is approaching us* seems to be somebody I know. [1]
The Bible, *which has been retranslated*, remains a bestseller. [2]

(b) the gender type of the antecedent: personal [3] or nonpersonal [4] (*cf* 17.11*f*), *eg*:

the person *who* I was visiting [3]
the book *which* I was reading [4]

(c) the function of the relative pronoun as subject, object, complement, or adverbial (including its role as prepositional complement) or as a constituent of an element in the relative clause, *ie* as a determiner (*in whose house*; *cf* 17.14).

In the following discussion of choice of relative pronoun, we will first make a division into restrictive and nonrestrictive relative clauses, and then consider other factors, such as medial or final position of the relative clause in relation to the superordinate clause, and length of the relative clause.

The set of relative pronouns has been given in 6.32*ff*. It is in the nonrestrictive relative clauses that the most explicit forms of relative pronoun, *ie* the *wh*-series (*who, whom, which, whose*) are typically used (*cf* 17.22). In restrictive clauses, frequent use is made of the *wh*-pronouns and also *that* or 'zero' relative. *That* differs from the *wh*-series:

(a) in not having gender marking and thus being independent of the personal or nonpersonal character of the antecedent;
(b) in not having an objective form (like *who/whom*);
(c) in not having a genitive (like *whose* of *who* and *which*), thus not being able to function as a constituent of an element in the relative clause.

17.14 In restrictive relative clauses, the pronouns given in the survey below are used. When we indicate a parenthesized relative pronoun, it means that there is the option between *that*-relative and 'zero':

This is the book (*that*) I bought at the sale.

When we use parentheses only '( )', this is to indicate 'zero':

This is the book ( ) I bought at the sale.

S, O, C, A in the survey below means that the relative pronoun functions respectively as subject, object, complement, and adverbial (or complement in a prepositional phrase functioning as adverbial) in the relative clause with personal and nonpersonal antecedents:

S: They are delighted with
- the person { *who* / *that* / *( ) } has been appointed.
- the book { *which* / *that* / *( ) } has just appeared.

O: They are delighted with
- the person { *who(m)* / *that* / ( ) } we have appointed.
- the book { *which* / *that* / ( ) } she has written.

C: She is the perfect accountant { *which* / **who* / **that* } her predecessor was not.

C: This is not the type of modern house { *which* / **that* / *( ) } my own is.

A: He is the policeman { *at whom* the burglar fired the gun. / { *who(m)* / *that* / ( ) } the burglar fired the gun *at*. }

A: She arrived the day { *on which* I was ill. / { *that* / ( ) } I was ill (*on*). }

A: I make cakes the way { *in which* / *that* / ( ) } my mother made them.

With a personal antecedent, the relative pronoun can show the distinction between *who* and *whom*, depending on its role as subject of the relative clause, or as object, or as prepositional complement:

the person	*who* spoke to him	[subject]	[1]
	to whom he spoke	[prepositional complement]	[2]
	who(m) he spoke *to*	[prepositional complement]	[2a]
	who(m) he met	[object]	[3]

When the governing preposition precedes its complement, as in the rather formal [2], the choice of *whom* is obligatory. When it does not, as in [2a], or when the relative pronoun is the object of the verb, as in [3], there is some choice between *who* or *whom*: the latter is preferred in formal English, the former is preferred in informal use, where however the zero form is by far the most common.

If the pronoun is a possessive determiner of the noun phrase, the form is *whose*:

The woman *whose daughter* you met is Mrs Brown. ['The woman is Mrs Brown; you met her daughter.'] [4]
The house *whose roof* was damaged has now been repaired. ['The house has now been repaired; its roof was damaged.'] [5]

In cases like [5] where the antecedent is nonpersonal, there is some tendency to avoid the use of *whose* (presumably because many regard it as the genitive only of the personal *who*), but avoidance involves stylistic difficulty. There is the stiffly formal and cumbersome *of which*:

The house *the roof of which* was damaged . . . [5a]

Other variants are clumsy or unacceptable in standard English:

?The house *that* they damaged *the roof of* . . . [5b]
*The house *that the roof* was damaged *of* . . . [5c]

Satisfactory alternatives can however be found, such as [5d], or even [5e]:

The house *that had its roof damaged* . . . [5d]
The house *with the damaged roof* . . . [5e]

In any case, in some fields of discourse such as mathematics, no evasion is felt to be necessary:

Let ABC be a triangle *whose sides* are of unequal length. [6]

The *of which* construction is sometimes placed before its head (like *whose*). Thus we have [7] besides the more usual [7a] and [7b]:

The investigation { *of which the results* will soon be published . . . [7]
{ *the results of which* will soon be published . . . [7a]
{ *whose results* will soon be published . . . [7b]

Relative pronoun as subject and object

17.15 When the antecedent is personal and the pronoun is the subject of the relative clause, *who* is favoured, irrespective of the style and the occasion; thus [1] rather than [1a], though there is nothing wrong or odd about the latter:

People *who* live in new houses . . . [1]
People *that* live in new houses . . . [1a]

Zero cannot replace the subject in a relative clause such as [2] and [3]:

*The table ( ) stands in the corner has a broken leg. [2]
*The man ( ) stands over there I know. [3]

However, constructions are encountered that are arguably exceptions; for example, in very informal speech where the antecedent is an indefinite pronoun:

?Anybody ( ) does that ought to be locked up. [4]

The reason for putting a question mark in [4] is, first, that it is of doubtful acceptability; secondly, that many speakers would condemn it as slovenly; thirdly, that it may result from the subaudibility of a relative pronoun *who* or *that* and thus not strictly be zero at all.

A commoner type of example is to be found in existential and cleft sentences (*cf* 18.44*ff*, 18.25*ff*):

There's a table ( ) stands in the corner. [5]
It's Simon ( ) did it. [6]

Sentences [5] and [6] would again be very colloquial, and the use of *that* or a *wh*-item would be regarded as more acceptable:

There's a table {*that* / *which*} stands in the corner. [5a]

It was Simon {*that* / *who*} did it. [6a]

However, there are good reasons for distinguishing such *that*/*which*-clauses from adnominal relative clauses. The obligatory nature of such portions of existential or cleft sentences would argue against our equating them with postmodifications in noun-phrase structure (*cf* 18.48).

That as subject and *that* or zero as object are preferred to *which* when the antecedent is nonpersonal *all, anything, everything, nothing, little*, or *much*:

All / Anything / Everything { *that* strikes you as odd . . . / (*that*) you find odd . . . }

There was *little that* ['not much that'] interested him at the motor show.

Much that ['much of what'] has been said tonight will soon be forgotten.

When the antecedent is modified by a superlative or by one of the postdeterminers *first, last, next, only,* the relative pronoun as subject is usually *that*, and, as object, *that* or zero rather than *which* or *who*(*m*) (*cf* 5.22):

She must be one of the most remarkable women *that ever* lived.

They eat the finest food { *that* is available. / (*that*) money can buy. }

In such sentences, an alternative to a postmodifying copular relative clause with an adjective as complement is pre- or postposition of the adjective (*cf* 7.21):

They eat the finest { *available food.* / *food available.* }

Note [**a**] The pronunciation of *that* as a relative pronoun is generally reduced to /ðət/, whereas the demonstrative *that* (*cf* 6.40) has the full form /ðæt/.

[**b**] One reason why zero relative subject is unacceptable may be related to perception. In example [2], it is only when encountering the verb *has* (the seventh word in the sentence) that the reader/hearer can interpret this sequence as a relative construction, instead of an expected *SVA* structure ending with *corner*, as in [2a]:

The table stands in the corner. [2a]

Compare the situation with the acceptable zero construction of nonsubject function in [2b], where it is clear on reaching *you* (the third word) that *you* begins a new construction:

The table you see standing in the corner has a broken leg. [2b]

Relative pronoun as object and prepositional complement

17.16 With the antecedent still personal but with the pronoun now object of a verb or prepositional complement, there is a much stronger preference for *that* or zero, perhaps to avoid the choice between *who* and *whom.* Thus [1] rather than [1a]:

People (*that*) I { visit . . . / speak to . . . } [1]

People *who*(*m*) I { visit . . . / speak to . . . } [1a]

Again, there is nothing actually wrong about [1a]; but *whom* here would seem pedantic to many people, while *who* as object in relative clauses is informal and tends to be regarded as incorrect. Since, therefore, neither *who* nor *whom* is wholly satisfactory, *that* (and particularly zero) is frequently used despite a personal antecedent.

Avoidance of *whom* may not be the only factor influencing *that* as object with personal antecedent. Grammatical objects are more likely to be nonpersonal, or to carry nonpersonal implication, than subjects.

There are several other factors influencing the selection of a pronoun that is object or prepositional complement in the relative clause, especially when the antecedent is nonpersonal. One is the proximity of the relative clause to the head of the antecedent phrase; another is the degree of complexity of the subject of the antecedent phrase.

When complex phrases or clauses intervene between the antecedent head and the relative pronoun, *which* is generally preferable to *that* and very much preferable to zero:

> I have [[*interests* outside my immediate work and its problems] *which* I find satisfying].

When the antecedent of the relative clause is no more complex than determiner + head, *that* is by many preferred to *which* and zero:

> I'll take you to [the building [*that* all elderly university teachers prefer]].

On the other hand, when the subject of the relative clause is a personal pronoun, zero is preferred to either *which* or *that*, especially if the relative clause itself is fairly short and simple:

> Who's drunk [the milk [( ) I bought]]?

Finally, other things being equal, more informal discourse will tend to have a preference for zero. In the following example from an informal conversation, the zero construction could not appropriately have been replaced by any of the other relative pronouns that are available in the system (*who, whom, that*):

> You learn a lot about [authors [you didn't know too much about to start with]].

Relative pronoun as adverbial

17.17 When the relative pronoun is the complement of a preposition (and, together with the preposition functioning as A), some choice exists in placing a preposition which has a *wh*-pronoun as its complement. No such choice exists with *that*, where postposition with deferred preposition represents the sole pattern:

<table>
<tr><td rowspan="2">the lady</td><td colspan="2">towards whom the dog ran</td></tr>
<tr><td>who(m)
that
( )</td><td>the dog ran towards</td></tr>
<tr><td rowspan="2">the table</td><td colspan="2">under which the boy crawled</td></tr>
<tr><td>which
that
( )</td><td>the boy crawled under</td></tr>
</table>

The choice of relative clause structure involves stylistic distinctions. In general, it is certainly true that *wh*-pronouns with initial preposition are used predominantly in formal English:

The person *to whom* any complaints should be addressed is . . . [1]

Initial prepositions are normally avoided in more informal use, where they would be felt to be stilted or pompous. A deferred preposition is more generally used with prepositional verbs:

That's the book ( ) he's been looking *for*. [2]

But many prepositions (especially those dealing with temporal and other abstract relations) cannot easily be deferred (*cf* 9.6):

?That was the meeting (*that*) I kept falling asleep *during*. [3]

One might find [3a], but in familiar speech an adverbial relative with *when* or *where* (*cf* 17.18) would be preferred to *during which*:

That was the meeting *during which* I kept falling asleep. [3a]

Prepositions expressing spatial relations allow a deferred preposition even when the preposition is complex:

This is the house he stood *in front of*. [4]

However, clarity of expression would often influence us in the direction of a construction otherwise regarded as formal if a final preposition leads to clumsiness. Consider the following sentence:

It was in a book that a former teacher of mine thought of at one time presenting me with some quotations from. [5]

Hearing or reading it, we may successively have to reject the interpretations, first, that the former teacher thought of the book; second, that the teacher thought of presenting me with the book, before the belated *from* enables us to achieve the correct interpretation ('. . . *from which* a former teacher . . .').

A deferred preposition may be the only natural choice when there is coordination of one prepositional and one nonprepositional construction in the relative clause. Thus instead of the clumsy [6], zero relative and a deferred preposition would be far more natural, as in [6a]:

You should restrict yourself to words *with which* you are familiar and *which* you can use confidently. [6]

You should restrict yourself to words ( ) you are familiar *with* and can use confidently. [6a]

But note that [6a] requires subject ellipsis, since coordination with zero relatives is not fully acceptable:

?You should restrict yourself to words ( ) you are familiar *with* and ( ) you can use confidently. [6b]

17.18 In adverbial expressions of place, time, and cause, there is a wide range of choice in addition to what was stated in 17.17 for the relative pronoun as adverbial. The preposition + pronoun can be replaced by special adverbs (*cf* 7.53), *eg*:

That's *the place* {*in which* / *where*} she was born. [1]

That was *the period* {*during which* / *when*} she lived here. [2]

That's *the reason* {*?for which* / *why*} she spoke. [3]

Note that *for which* in [3] has limited acceptability.

However, there are considerable and complicated restrictions on these *wh*-forms which operate in relative clauses expressing place, time, and cause. Many speakers find their use along with the corresponding antecedent somewhat tautologous – especially the type *the reason why* – and prefer the *wh*-clause without antecedent, *ie* a nominal relative clause (*cf* 15.8*f*):

Is this *where* she was born? [1a]
That was *when* she lived here. [2a]
That's *why* she spoke. [3a]

There is no relative *how* parallel to *where, when*, and *why* to express manner with an antecedent noun [4], but only [4a]:

*That's *the way how* she spoke. [4]

That's {*how* / *the way (that)*} she spoke. [4a]

The following patterns can be distinguished for time expressions in a sentence such as '. . . was Thursday'.

Pattern 1: antecedent + preposition + *wh*-pronoun:

the day on which she arrived

Pattern 2: antecedent + *wh*-pronoun + deferred preposition:

the day which she arrived *on*

Pattern 3: antecedent + *that* + deferred preposition:

the day that she arrived *on*

Pattern 4: antecedent + zero relative + deferred preposition:

the day she arrived *on*

Pattern 5: antecedent + *wh*-adverb:

the day when she arrived

Pattern 6: antecedent + zero relative + zero preposition:

the day she arrived

Pattern 7: antecedent + *that* + zero preposition:

the day that she arrived

Pattern 8: *wh*-clause without antecedent (*ie* a nominal relative clause, *cf* 15.8*f*):

when she arrived

17.19 There are also restrictions on the antecedent nouns. With relative clauses where the antecedent denotes cause or reason, *reason* is virtually the only possible antecedent; where the antecedents denote place and time, the most generic nouns (*place, period, time*, etc) also seem to be preferred. Thus pattern 5 is acceptable:

the office *where* he works

However, many would prefer alternative expressions (patterns 1, 2, 3, 4, where pattern 1 is most formal and pattern 4 least formal):

the office	*at which* he works	[pattern 1]
	which he works *at*	[pattern 2]
	that he works *at*	[pattern 3]
	( ) *he works at*	[pattern 4]

the day	*on which* she was born	[pattern 1]
	which she was born *on*	[pattern 2]
	that she was born *on*	[pattern 3]
	( ) *she was born on*	[pattern 4]

Place adjuncts in relative clauses admit of two further patterns: one with *where* and omission of the preposition (pattern 5), the other with the deferred preposition *at* (pattern 9):

the place	*where* she works	[pattern 5]
	?*where* she works *at*	[pattern 9]

Pattern 5 is acceptable, whereas pattern 9 is of doubtful acceptability. It requires a fairly specific antecedent, *eg*:

the government building where she works *at*

With a general antecedent, such as *place*, we may find the following patterns, which however are not acceptable to all speakers:

(?)That's *the place*	*she stays* when she's in London.	[1]
	she works.	[2]
	she studies.	[3]

However, a final *at* (pattern 4) would be fully acceptable, at least in familiar usage:

That's *the place*	*she stays at* when she's in London.	[1a]
	she works at.	[2a]
	she studies at.	[3a]

With a generalized antecedent such as *way*, expressing direction, we usually have zero rather than *that*:

Was that *the way she went*? ['Was that where she went?']

17.20 In expressions of time, omission of the preposition is usual whether the pronoun is *that* or zero:

What's *the time* { (*that*) she normally arrives (*at*)? / *when* she normally arrives? / **when* she normally arrives *at*? }

What was *the day* (*that*) she left (*on*)?

When (less frequently and more formally) the pronoun is *which*, however, the preposition must be expressed in all three instances, and it would be usual to make it precede the pronoun (pattern 1):

5.30 is *the time at which* she normally arrives.
I don't remember *the day on which* she left.
He worked for the whole three months *during which* he lived there.

With expressions of manner and reason, the zero construction is usual (occasionally *that*), and there is no preposition (patterns 6 and 7):

That's *the way* (*that*) he did it. ['That's how he did it.'] [4]
Is this *the reason* (*that*) they came? ['Is this why they came?'] [5]

In more formal style, we might find pattern 1:

That's *the way in which* he did it. [4a]

The rare use of *for which* after *reason* strikes most people as clumsy and unnatural, while *the reason why* seems tautologous; there is general preference for zero [5a] or a nominal relative clause [5b]:

Is that { *the reason* they came? [5a] / *why* they came? [5b] }

However, after other nouns which express adverbial-related meanings similar to *reason* and *way*, no *that* or zero construction without preposition is possible. Thus not [6] and [7] but only [6a] and [7a]:

{ *This is *the style* he wrote it. [6]
This is *the style* he wrote it *in*. [6a] }

{ *Is this *the* { *cause* / *motive* } she came? [7]
Is this { *the cause of* / *motive for* } her coming? [7a] }

There is a tendency to favour *when* or *where* if the antecedent is already the complement of a prepositional phrase, *ie* [8] rather than [8a] (to avoid repetition of the preposition):

He died *on the day* { *when* his son arrived. [8] / *on which* his son arrived. [8a] }

Occasionally plural antecedents can be met with, as in:

It would be wise to leave doctors *ways* ( ) they could add personal touches to their treatment.

Note Constructions with time nouns + zero relative clause (*eg*: *The moment you do something* . . .) may be ambiguous up to a certain point in the sentence, in that the noun phrase can be either adverbial, as in [9], or subject, as in [10]:

The moment ( ) *you do something they disagree with* they are at your throat . . . [9]

The moment ( ) *you realize the importance of animal psychology* will be embarrassing to you. [10]

Type [9] is normal; type [10] seems to be rare when, as here, the subject is 'heavy', but compare [11]:

The day she arrived at the congress was sunny. [11]

Telescoped relative clauses

17.21 The distinction between restrictive and nonrestrictive is valuable, but we should be prepared to view it as a gradient rather than as a dichotomy between two homogeneous categories. One type of relative construction which demonstrates the need for this approach can be illustrated by the following example of TELESCOPED relative construction:

All this I gave up for *the mother who needed me*. [1]

In [1], *mother* may be seen as having an appositional relation to a noun phrase whose head is a general noun such as *person*, accompanied by a relative clause as postmodifier:

All this I gave up for *a person who needed me*, ie *my mother*. [1a]

Another example:

This book is about *a Bloomsbury I simply don't recognize*. ['about a place I simply don't recognize; but I ought to recognize because I know Bloomsbury and the book says it is Bloomsbury'] [2]

Nonrestrictive relative clauses

17.22 In nonrestrictive relative clauses, the most explicit forms of relative pronouns, *ie* the *wh*-series, are typically used. The relative pronoun can be subject, object, complement, or adverbial. Here is a survey of the different forms for personal and nonpersonal antecedents:

S: I spoke to Dr Spolsky, { *who* / **that* / *( ) } was unwilling to give further details.

S: This excellent book, { *which* / ?**that* / *( ) } has only just been reviewed, was published a year ago.

O: I spoke to Dr Spolsky, { *whom* / ?*who* / **that* / *( ) } I met after the inquest.

O: This excellent book, { *which* / ?**that* / *( ) } Freda has only just received for review, was published a year ago.

C: Anna is a vegetarian, { *which* / **who* / **that* / *( ) } no one else is in our family.

C: She wants low-calorie food, { *which* / **that* / *( ) } this vegetable curry certainly is.

A: This is a new type of word processor,
{ *about which* there has been so much publicity.
{ *which* / **that* / *( ) } there has been so much publicity *about*. }

As can be seen, the choice of pronouns is restricted to *who(m)* and *which*. Nonsubject *who* is thought by many to be more objectionable in nonrestrictive than in restrictive clauses (*cf* 17.14). Zero cannot occur, and *that* is very rare.

With nonrestrictive relative clauses, we usually have a tone unit boundary, often accompanied by a pause, before the relative clause; and, often, a repetition at the end of the relative clause of the nuclear tone of the tone unit preceding the relative clause. In writing, nonrestrictive relationship is usually marked off by commas (*cf* App III.19). Compare:

WRITTEN: Then he met Mary, *who invited him to a party.*
SPOKEN: Then he |met MÀRy| – *who in|vited him to a PÀRty*|

By contrast, with restrictive relative clauses, there is usually no tone unit boundary or pause before the relative clause; nor in writing is the relative clause separated by a comma from what precedes. Compare:

WRITTEN: That's the girl (*that*) *he met at the party.*
SPOKEN: |That's the girl (*that*) *he met at the PÀRty*|

It must be emphasized that these are typical rather than obligatory prosodic features. The following example is exceptional in having a prosodic boundary before the relative clause though it is unquestionably restrictive:

but in the |LÒNG RÚN| – |these are FÒRces| that will |ÙLtimately| – |win supPÒRT| from the ma|jority of the people in this CÒUNtry|

17.23 Nonrestrictive relationship is often semantically very similar to coordination, with or without conjunction (*cf* 13.1*ff*), or adverbial subordination (*cf* 15.17*ff*). Both types are indicated by paraphrases in the following examples:

Then he met Mary { , *who* invited him to a party. [1]
, *and she* invited him to a party. [1a]
; she invited *him* to a party. } [1b]

Here is John Smith { , *who(m)* I mentioned the other day. [2]
; I mentioned *him* the other day. [2a]
, *who(m)* I talked *about* the other day. [2b]
; I talked about *him* the other day. } [2c]

He got lost on Snowdon {
, *which* was enveloped in fog. [3]
; *it* was enveloped in fog. [3a]
, *when it* was enveloped in fog. [3b]

She read a paper on lampreys {
, *which* she has studied. [4]
; she has studied *them*. [4a]
, *which* she has done research *on*. [4b]
, *on which* she has done research. [4c]
; she has done research on *them*. [4d]

My brother, *who* has lived in America since boyhood, can still speak fluent Italian. [5]

My brother can still speak fluent Italian, *and he* has lived in America since boyhood. [5a]

My brother can still speak Italian *although he* has lived in America since boyhood. [5b]

Note A nonrestrictive interpretation is occasionally introduced by *that* when a premodifier or determiner would make a restrictive clause absurd, but when *which*, on the other hand, might imply too parenthetic a relation:

I looked at *Mary's sad face, that* I had once so passionately loved. [6]

In [6] we seem to have an elliptical form of an appositive expression:

I looked at *Mary's sad face, a face that* I had once so passionately loved. [6a]

Here the appositive *a face* justifies the restrictive clause that follows.

Usually the use of nonrestrictive *that* shows that a writer has muddled what he has wanted to set down, as in the following example from a serious article:

One of the most important recent developments in neutral hydrogen studies of our Galaxy has been the discovery of high velocities in the centre and in regions away from the plane, *that* I have mentioned.

Despite the comma – and the corresponding prosodic separation if this is read aloud (a separation that is essential if *plane* were not to be thought the antecedent head) – it seems likely that the writer originally wanted the relative clause to be restrictive, as it could readily have been if placed earlier:

. . . has been *the discovery that* I have mentioned of high velocities . . .

However, this position of the relative clause violates the rule that prepositional phrases precede relative clauses as postmodifiers, producing a rhetorically unacceptable sentence (*cf* 18.39*f*).

17.24 Where the relative pronoun is a determinative in a noun phrase, there is again less choice than in restrictive clauses. Expressions with *which* tend to be uncommon except in formally precise writing. The preposition usually precedes *which*, and explicitness often extends to completion of the prepositional phrase by a general noun, locative or temporal, as the case may be (making *which* a relative determiner, *cf* 5.14):

In 1960 he came to London, *in which city* he has lived ever since. [1]

He came in 1960, { *at which time* / *in which year* } there was . . . [2]

More commonly, we find *where* or *when* instead of the *which* expression:

. . . to London, *where* . . . [1a]
. . . in 1960, *when* . . . [2a]

This is a point at which there is little distinction between adnominal relative clauses and adverbial clauses of place and time in complex sentence structure (*cf* 15.25*ff*).

Note the possible variations in word order with *of*-pronouns (*some, each, all, both,* etc; *cf* 6.48*ff*):

> There are two schools here, { *both of which* / *of which both* } are good.
>
> There are several schools here, { *all/some of which* I can recommend. / *of which* I can recommend *all/some*. }

For *both* there is also the possibility of the order *which are both good* (but hardly ?**which I can all recommend*).

Note also the use of the construction with *of*-pronouns when they modify the complement of a preposition:

> The hospital admitted several patients that month,
> { *for all of whom* chemotherapy was the appropriate treatment.
> **of whom* chemotherapy was the appropriate treatment *for all.*
> **whom* chemotherapy was the appropriate treatment *for all of.* }

Relative pronoun as complement

17.25 When the relative pronoun functions as nonprepositional complement in the relative clause, the choice is limited to *which* for both personal and nonpersonal antecedents, in both restrictive clauses (*cf* 17.14) and nonrestrictive clauses (*cf* 17.22):

> He is a teetotaller, *which* I am not.
> This is a powerful car, *which* my last car was not.

Appositive clauses

17.26 The remaining type of finite verb clause that plays a part in postmodification is the appositive (*cf* 17.35, 17.65*ff*). This resembles the restrictive relative clause in being capable of introduction by the unstressed *that* /ðət/:

> She objected to *the fact that a reply had not been sent earlier*. [restrictive appositive clause]

The appositive clause differs from the relative clause in that

(i) the particle *that* is not an element in the clause structure (functioning as subject, object, etc, as it must in a relative clause) but a conjunction, as is the case in nominal *that*-clauses generally;

(ii) the nonrestrictive appositive clause has the same introductory item as the restrictive, *ie*: *that* (*cf* 17.33):

> She rejected *their excuses*, even this last one, *that* investigations had taken several weeks. [nonrestrictive]

(iii) the head of the noun phrase must be a general abstract noun such as *fact, idea, proposition, reply, remark, answer*, and the like (*cf* 16.84):

> *The fact that he wrote a letter to her* suggests that he knew her. [1]
> *The belief that no one is infallible* is well-founded. [2]

I agree with *the old saying that absence makes the heart grow fonder.* [3]
He heard *the news that his team had won.* [4]

As with apposition generally (*cf* 17.65*ff*), we can link the apposed units with *be* (where the copula typically has nuclear prominence):

The |fact *ís*| that he |wrote a LÈTter to her| [1a]
The belief *is* that no one is infallible. [2a]
The old saying *is* that absence makes the heart grow fonder. [3a]
The news *was* that his team had won. [4a]

We should also note that nouns like *belief* with *that*-clauses correspond to verbs with object clauses (*cf* 16.30*ff*):

He *believes that no one is infallible.* [2b]

With both restrictive and nonrestrictive appositive clauses, an antecedent noun is often a nominalization (*cf* 17.51*ff*):

The police reported that the drugs had been found. [5]
The police report that the drugs had been found (appeared in the press yesterday). [5a]

These restrictive examples have the definite article before the head noun. This is normal, but by no means invariable (except with a few nouns referring to certainty, especially *fact*):

A message that he would be late arrived by special delivery. [6]
The union will resist *any proposal that Mr Johnson should be dismissed.* [7]
Stories that the house was haunted angered the owner. [8]

Plural heads, as in [8], are also rare with appositive postmodification, and are usually regarded as unacceptable with *belief, fact, possibility,* etc. We may contrast [9] with the perfectly acceptable plural head with relative clause postmodification [9a]:

?Her mother was worried at *the possibilities that her daughter was lazy and* (*that she*) *disliked school.* [9]
The possibilities that she was now offered seemed very attractive. [9a]

However, we occasionally find examples of plural nouns with appositive postmodification, such as *facts* in the following:

The reason probably lies in *the facts that* the Intelligence Service is rather despised, *that* the individual members change rapidly and are therefore inexperienced, and *that* they feel bound to put their own special interests first.

We have seen in 16.70 that certain verbs with *that*-clauses have a construction with putative *should* or with a mandative subjunctive, *eg*:

They *recommended that she* (*should*) *be promoted.* [10]

When such verbs are nominalized (*cf* 17.51*ff*), the object clause becomes an appositive clause, retaining the putative *should* or the mandative subjunctive:

There was *a recommendation that she* (*should*) *be promoted.* [10a]

The nominalized verb may be separated from the appositive clause under the conditions for discontinuous noun phrases (*cf* 17.122, 18.39):

The suggestion that the new rule (*should*) *be adopted* came from the chairman. [11]
The suggestion came from the chairman *that the new rule* (*should*) *be adopted.* [11a]

17.27 Despite the limited number of noun head types that may be postmodified by an appositive clause, the superficial similarity to relative clause postmodification can sometimes cause momentary difficulty. Total ambiguity, however, is rare since so many factors of selection have to be involved before anything like [1] can occur:

A report *that he stole* was ultimately sent to the police. [1]

The two interpretations ('he stole a report' or 'the report was that he stole') depend upon the possibility that *a report* can be a physical object or an abstraction (that is, nominalizing the verb *report*); upon *steal* being permissibly transitive or intransitive; and several other factors: *made* in place of *sent*, for example, would prevent the ambiguity (though it might not prevent the hearer or reader from having temporary difficulty).

Nonrestrictive appositive clauses like [2] can less easily resemble relative clauses since, irrespective of nonrestrictiveness, they still involve the particle *that*, in sharp contrast with nonrestrictive relative clauses:

This last fact, (namely) that *that* is obligatory, should be easy to remember. [2]

In illustrating the previous point, example [2] also illustrates the next point, (namely) that appositive indicators *namely* or *viz* can be optionally introduced in the nonrestrictive appositions, as can *that is* (*to say*) or *ie* (*cf* 17.73). It also illustrates the fact that with this type of clause, the antecedent head noun may be freely premodified by adjectives and with a choice of determiners. It will be recalled that, with restrictive appositives, *the* was obligatory before *fact*, and it may now be added that the only adjectives admissible would be nonrestrictive in scope (*cf* 17.3*ff*). Contrast [3], where the restrictive clause permits only the nonrestrictive adjective, with [3a], where the nonrestrictive clause permits a restrictive adjective:

The ugly fact that he was holding a gun indicated his guilt. [3]
The more relevant fact, that the gun had not been fired, was curiously ignored. [3a]

Note The nonrestrictive apposition may be closely related to a nonrestrictive relative clause (*cf* appositive *wh*-interrogative clauses, 15.5). Compare:

His last request, { *which was* / (*ie*) / (*viz*) } that his wife should come and visit him, was never granted.

Postmodification by nonfinite clauses

Postmodification by *-ing* participle clauses

17.28 Postmodification of the noun phrase is possible with all three of the nonfinite clause types: *-ing* participle, *-ed* participle, and infinitive clauses. The correspondence between *-ing* clauses and relative clauses is limited to those relative clauses in which the relative pronoun is subject:

The person *who* { *will write* / *will be writing* / *writes* / *is writing* / *wrote* / *was writing* } *reports* is my colleague. [1]

The person *writing reports* is my colleague. [1a]

The nonfinite clause *writing reports* in [1a] may be interpreted, according to the context, as equivalent to one of the more explicit versions in [1]. Other examples of postmodifying *-ing* clauses:

The dog *barking next door* sounded like a terrier. ['which *was barking* next door']
A tile *falling from a roof* shattered into fragments at his feet. ['which *fell* from a roof']
You should look for a man *carrying a large umbrella*. ['who *will be carrying* a large umbrella']

It must be emphasized that *-ing* forms in postmodifying clauses should not be seen as abbreviated progressive forms in relative clauses. Stative verbs, for instance, which cannot have the progressive in the finite verb phrase, can appear in participial form (*cf* 4.4, 14.19):

This is a liquid with a taste *resembling* that of soapy water. ['which resembles'; *not*: '*which is resembling'] [2]
It was a mixture *consisting* of oil and vinegar. ['that consisted of'; *not*: '*that was consisting of'] [3]

In all instances, the antecedent head corresponds to the implicit subject of the nonfinite clause. There is no nonfinite postmodifier, therefore, corresponding directly to the relative clause in [1b], without recourse to the passive [1c]:

Reports *that my colleague is writing* will be discussed tomorrow. [1b]
Reports *being written by my colleague* will be discussed tomorrow. [1c]

There are sharp constraints upon aspect expression in the participle clauses used in postmodification. We have just noted that *resembling* in [2] (*a taste resembling that of soapy water*) obviously could not represent the progressive, and the neutralization of the aspectual contrast can further be seen in [4] in contrast with [4a]:

the man { *who works* / *who is working* } behind the desk [4] the man { *working* / **being working* } behind the desk [4a]

On the loss of this aspectual distinction in nonfinite verb phrases, *cf* 3.56. Similarly the perfective aspect cannot usually be expressed in the nonfinite clause. Compare [5] and [5a]:

The man *who has won the race* is my brother. [5]
?*The man *having won the race* is my brother. [5a]

However, in a structure with an indefinite noun phrase as head, as in [6], perfective aspect is more acceptable:

?Any person or persons *having witnessed the attack* is under suspicion. [6]

The tense to be attributed to the *-ing* clause will usually be that of the finite clause in which the noun phrase occurs, especially if the noun phrase is object:

Do you know *the man talking to my sister*? ['who is talking to my sister']
Did you know *the man talking to my sister*? ['who was talking to my sister']

The tense of the nonfinite clause can also be inferred from the context:

The man sitting next to her (now) was speaking on the radio (last night). ['who is sitting'] [7]

In a sentence like [7], the tense of the *-ing* clause would be assumed to be the present tense [8], unless the context suggests otherwise, as in [8a]:

the man sitting next { *to her* ['who is sitting'] [8] / *to her* on that occasion ['who was sitting'] [8a] }

In [9], the past tense *was* indicates the tense of *being questioned* and does not mean that he was no longer my brother, *ie* [9] = [9a]:

The man *being questioned* by the police *was* my brother. [9]
The man *that was* (*being*) *questioned* by the police *is* my brother. [9a]

Note In some cases, *-ing* participles occur in frozen expressions with no relative clause alternative, *eg*: *for the time being* (*not*: '*for the time that is').

Postmodification by *-ed* participle clauses

17.29 As with *-ing* clauses, there is correspondence only with relative clauses that have the relative pronoun as subject. The nonfinite *-ed* participle clause in [1] can be related to the finite relative clauses in [1a]:

The car (*being*) *repaired* by that mechanic . . . [1]

The car *that* { *will be repaired* / *is* (*being*) *repaired* / *was* (*being*) *repaired* } by that mechanic . . . [1a]

The *-ed* participle clause [1] will be interpreted, according to the context, as equivalent to one of the finite clauses in [1a]. Thus:

The car { *being repaired* by that mechanic now . . . / *repaired* by that mechanic when it breaks down . . . / *repaired* by that mechanic before he left . . . }

Other examples:

A report *written by my colleague* appeared last week. ['that *was/has been* written . . .'] [2]

Any coins *found on this site* must be handed to the police. ['that *are found* . . .' or, more precisely, 'that *may be found* . . .'] [3]

The antecedent is always identical with the implied subject of the *-ed* postmodifying clause, as it is with the *-ing* construction. Also, postmodifying *-ed* and *-ing* participle clauses are both usually restrictive (but *cf* 17.34*f*). However, in the case of the *-ed* construction, the participle concerned is as firmly linked with the passive voice as that in the *-ing* construction is linked with the active. Since *-ed* participles can never be passive with intransitive verbs, there is no *-ed* postmodifier [4a] corresponding exactly to the relative clause in [4]:

The train *which has arrived at platform 1* is from York. [4]

?*The train *arrived at platform 1* is from York. [4a]

Exceptions occur where the *-ed* participle is preceded by certain adverbs, as in:

The train *recently arrived at platform 1* is from York. [4b]

A man *just* { *gone to India* / *come from the meeting* } told me about it. [5]

This phenomenon is related to our ability also to premodify nouns with participles which, unless themselves premodified, can only postmodify.

There are constraints on aspectual expression in *-ed* postmodifying clauses, though they are not identical with those for *-ing* clauses. Unlike *-ing* clauses, *-ed* clauses can indicate progressive aspect. A progressive contrast is possible, as in [6a], which reflects the aspectual contrast in [6]:

The food *which* { *was/has been eaten* / *is being eaten* } was meant for tomorrow. [6]

The food { *eaten* / *being eaten* } was meant for tomorrow. [6a]

As with *-ing* clauses, there is usually no perfective aspect in *-ed* clauses:

{ The food *which has been eaten* / ?*The food *having been eaten* } was meant for tomorrow. [6b]

Postmodification by infinitive clauses

17.30 Unlike *-ing* and *-ed* clauses, infinitive clauses as postmodifiers in noun phrases allow correspondences with relative clauses where the relative pronoun can be not only subject, but also object or adverbial and, to a limited extent, complement:

S: The man *to help you* is Mr Johnson. ['who can help you'] [1]
O: The man *(for you) to see* is Mr Johnson. ['who(m) you should see'] [2]
C: The thing *(for you) to be* these days is a systems analyst. ['the thing that people will try to be these days is a systems analyst'; *cf* pseudo-cleft sentences 18.29*ff*] [3]
A: The time *(for you) to go* is July. ['at which you should go'] [4]
A: The place *(for you) to stay* is the university guest house. ['where you should stay'] [5]

Unlike [1], [2] can have an optional subject of the infinitive clause introduced by *for* (*cf* 14.6*f*). Without such a subject, the infinitive clause in [2] could be understood, according to context, as '(The man) that *you/he/everyone,* etc should see'.

Similarly, in [3–5] the subject of the infinitive may also be omitted. A less common and more formal alternative is then to introduce the relative pronoun and retain the infinitive clause:

The time *at which to go* is . . . [4a]
The place *at which to stay* is . . . [5a]
A good place *at which to eat* is the pub round the corner. [6]

Compare also the formal [7] beside the informal [7b] (note that the preposition cannot be deferred in [7a]; nor can *in* be kept in [7c]):

the way {
in which to do it [7]
*which to do it in [7a]
to do it [7b]
*to do it in [7c]
}

Alternatively, we might have fully explicit relative clause constructions with preposition + relative pronoun, or adverbial relative (without preposition; *cf* 17.18*f*):

The time {*at which* / *when*} *everyone should go* is July. [4b]

The place {*at which* / *where*} *you should stay* is the university guest house. [5b]

A good place {*at which* / *where*} *anyone can eat* is the pub round the corner. [6a]

As stated above, there is no *-ing* or *-ed* clause as postmodifier which allows correspondences with relative clauses where the pronoun is adverbial. Compare the syntactic flexibility and the possibility of different degrees of reduction in infinitive clauses compared with *-ing* clauses:

the place {
at which {*staying / *to stay* / *you should stay*}
(for you) *to stay* (at)
}

She is not a person { *on whom* { **relying.* / *to rely.* / *one can rely.* } / (for one) *to rely on.* }

This is a good instrument { *with which* { **measuring* / *to measure* / *they measure* } vibration. / (for them) *to measure* vibration *with.* }

17.31 Under certain conditions, functional ambiguity may arise, as when the subject is not expressed by *for* . . . *to* and the verb can be used both intransitively and transitively. In the latter case there are no semantic restrictions to exclude the antecedent from being interpreted as either subject or object. Consider sentence [1]:

He is the best man *to choose.* [1]

It can then mean either [1a], *ie* subject interpretation and no equivalent finite relative clause possible, or [1b], *ie* object interpretation and with a corresponding finite relative clause alternative:

He is the best man {
to do the choosing. / *to make the choice.* } [1a]
that we (etc) *can choose.* / *for us* (etc) *to choose.* / *to be chosen* (*by us*, etc). } [1b]
}

As the examples have now shown, it is by no means only tense that has to be inferred in the infinitive clause. Mood is a far more variable factor, and the range accounted for in the adverbial infinitive clause is available also for noun-phrase postmodification (*cf* also [2–4] below and 17.32), *eg*:

The time *to arrive* is . . . ['at which you *should* arrive']

With infinitive clauses, aspect is also less restrained than with other nonfinite clauses:

The man { *to meet* / *to be meeting* / *to have met* } is Wilson.

The postmodifying infinitive clause can be active or passive:

He is the best man { *to choose.* / *to be chosen.* }

Beside the active examples already given, we may consider the following passives, which also further illustrate the variety of implicit tense and modality:

The case *to be investigated tomorrow* . . . ['that will, *or* is to, be investigated'] [2]
The animals *to be found in Kenya* . . . ['that can be, *or* are, found'] [3]

The procedure *to be followed* . . . ['that must, *or* should, *or* will, be followed'] [4]

In some cases, only active infinitives postmodifying clauses are natural, *eg* [5]; in some, only passive [6]:

I've got letters *to write* tonight.
?I've got letters *to be written* tonight. [5]

The animals *to be found* in Kenya . . .
?The animals *to find* in Kenya . . . [6]

In other cases, either active or passive infinitives seem equally possible with no or little change of meaning:

Give me a list of the people { *to invite.* / *to be invited.* } [7]

The procedure { *to follow* / *to be followed* } is this: . . . [8]

The best thing { *to do* / *to be done* } is as follows: . . . [9]

This is true also for the existential sentence pattern *there* + *be* + noun phrase + *to*-infinitive clause which is allied to relative clauses (*cf* 18.44*ff*):

There are letters { *to write.* / *to be written.* } [10]

There is no time { *to lose.* / *to be lost.* } [11]

There is no passive equivalent if *for* is used to introduce a subject:

The man { *to consult* / *to be consulted* } is Mr Johnson. [12]

The man { *for you to consult* / **for you to be consulted* } is Mr Johnson. [13]

Nor does a passive always sound plausible when the head is a quantifier:

We have { *a lot to do.* / ?*a lot to be done.* } [14]

We have { *plenty to eat.* / ?*plenty to be eaten.* } [15]

We have *a large number of pages* { *to write.* / (?)*to be written.* } [16]

With a *there*-construction there is no voice restriction:

There is a lot { (*for everybody*) *to do.* / *to be done* (*by everybody*). }

There is plenty { *to do.* / *to be done.* }

17.32 Postmodifying *to*-infinitive clauses can have either a modal or a nonmodal sense, but the modal interpretation seems to be normal, as indicated by most of the examples given so far. If the antecedent corresponds to the object of the infinitive, the modal interpretation is the only possible one:

> The thing *to do* is . . . ['The thing we should do is . . .'; *not* = 'The thing we do is . . .' *or* 'The thing we are going to do is . . .']

If the antecedent corresponds to the subject of the infinitive, the interpretation may be nonmodal, particularly if the antecedent has a 'restrictive' marker such as *last* and the infinitive is equivalent to a relative clause:

> They were the *last* guests *to arrive*. ['They were the last guests who arrived.']

Such 'restrictive' markers include adjectives in the superlative degree, general ordinals (*next, last, only*), *first*, or other ordinal numeral (*cf* 5.22).

Blurred relationships in postmodification

17.33 The sharply reduced explicitness in the *-ing, -ed*, and infinitive clauses allows us to blur or neutralize the distinction between noun-phrase postmodification and certain other types of construction. It is interesting, for example, that native English speakers confronted by sentence [1] are likely to agree that they see little or no difference in meaning between [1] and either of [1a–b]:

> I noticed { *a man hidden* behind the bushes. [1]
> *a man who was hidden* behind the bushes. [1a]
> *that a man was hidden* behind the bushes. } [1b]

So also with two other sentences of obviously different structure:

> He was warned by { *the fact that a light flashed repeatedly*. [2]
> *a light that flashed repeatedly*. } [3]

Grammatical rules for nominalization (*cf* 17.51*ff*) can readily provide for the relation of [2] to [4] and for the relation of both [2] and [3] to [5]:

> He was warned by { *the repeated flashing of a light*. [4]
> *a light flashing repeatedly*. } [5]

Sentence [5] can be a variant of the rarer form with genitive noun (*a light's*) corresponding to the subject of [2] (*cf* 15.12). The fact that [4] and [5] are virtually indistinguishable semantically means that, despite our ability to relate [4] grammatically to [2] rather than to [3], it is pointless to speculate on whether [5] is to be grammatically related primarily to [2] or to [3].

The infinitive clause occurs in similar merged constructions, but with additional possibilities. Example [6] is broadly unambiguous:

> She expects somebody *to repair the TV set*. [6]

However, it can be related to more than merely noun-phrase postmodification [7]:

> She expects somebody *who will repair the TV set*. [7]

It can also be related to a complementation type described in 16.30*ff*, the nonfinite clause corresponding to a finite clause:

She expects *that somebody will repair the TV set.* [8]

There are relations also with two possible adverbial purpose clauses [9] and [10]:

She expects somebody *in order that he will repair the TV set.* [9]
She expects somebody *in order that she can repair the TV set* (*with his help*). [10]

However, both [9] and [10] should be seen as rather cumbersome circumlocutions of the natural expression in [6]. Another and more natural alternative to [10] would be [11]:

She expects somebody *to help her repair the TV set.* [11]

It is doubtless convenient to have a structural type like [6] that has such flexibility. For example, the possibility of postmodifying the head (*somebody*) is crucially important if we wish to expand such a sentence into the more explicit form [7] rather than [9]. Example [6a], with a proper noun as head, rules out a nonrestrictive clause [7a] as an analogue to [7]:

She expects *Jonathan to repair the TV set.* [6a]
*She expects *Jonathan who will repair the TV set.* [7a]

So also, we can reduce [12] to the nonfinite form [12a] without perceptible change or loss of meaning:

She has somebody { *who checks the TV set regularly.* [12]
{ (*to*) *check the TV set regularly.* [12a]

However, we must not assume that any sentence of the form [13], and still less of the form [14], can have the nonfinite clause expanded as a relative:

She has *X to do Y.* [13]
She has *X do Y.* [14]

Nonrestrictive postmodification by nonfinite clauses

17.34 Nonrestrictive postmodification can also be achieved with nonfinite clauses:

The apple tree, *swaying gently in the breeze*, was a reminder of old times. ['which was swaying gently in the breeze . . .'] [1]
The substance, *discovered almost by accident*, has revolutionized medicine. ['which was discovered almost by accident . . .'] [2]
This scholar, *to be found daily in the British Museum*, has devoted his life to the history of science. ['who can be found daily in the British Museum . . .'] [3]

As with restrictive nonfinite clauses (*cf* 17.28*ff*), nonrestrictive *-ing* and *-ed* clauses only correspond to relative clauses where the relative pronoun is subject. But also infinitive clauses have this constraint when they are nonrestrictive:

*This scholar, *to find* . . .
*This place, *to stay* . . .

Nonrestrictive nonfinite clauses can be moved to initial position without change of meaning:

> *Discovered almost by accident*, the substance has revolutionized medicine. [2a]

But this mobility in fact implies that nonfinite nonrestrictive clauses are equivocal between adnominal and adverbial role. Thus, the nonfinite clause in sentence [4] could be a reduction of a relative clause [4a], but equally of a causal clause [4b], or a temporal one [4c]:

> The man, *wearing such dark glasses*, obviously could not see clearly. [4]
>
> The man, { *who was wearing . . .* [4a] / *because he was wearing . . .* [4b] / *whenever he wore . . .* [4c] }

So too, we can make the relative clause in [5] nonfinite:

> The cost, *which includes meals*, is 290 francs. [5]

However, we must then recognize that the result, *including meals*, may be regarded by a reader or hearer as a reduction of a conditional clause, 'if we include meals', or *including* may be regarded as a preposition (*cf* 9.8).

Note [**a**] The range of semantic possibilities and the mobility to initial position (before the noun phrase) of nonrestrictive nonfinite clauses make such clauses equivocal between noun modifiers and adverbials (*cf* 8.150*ff*).

[**b**] Compare the discussion in this section with that of finite nonrestrictive clauses in 17.22*ff* and supplementive clauses in 15.60*ff*.

Appositive postmodification by infinitive and *-ing* clauses

17.35 Appositive postmodification by nonfinite clause occurs with infinitive and *-ing* clauses; *-ed* clauses cannot enter into appositive postmodification. Appositive postmodification is fairly common by means of infinitive clauses. A restrictive example like [1] would correspond to the finite *that people* (*should*) *give blood*, though such a use of the subjunctive or of putative *should* (*cf* 4.64, 16.70*ff*) is uncommon:

> The appeal *to give blood* received strong support. [1]

There are also nonrestrictive examples, *eg* [2]:

> This last appeal, *to come and visit him*, was never sent. [2]

A common feature of infinitive clauses, applying to restrictive and nonrestrictive alike, is that they leave the subject of the infinitive clause to be inferred from the context (as in [1] and [2]), unless there is a prepositionally introduced subject, as in [1a] and [2a]:

> The appeal { *to us* / *for us* } to give blood received strong support. [1a]
>
> This last appeal { *to us,* / *, for us* } to come and visit him, was never sent. [2a]

The *-ing* clause functions as appositive postmodification in examples like [3–5]:

I'm looking for a job *driving cars*. ['a job as a driver'] [3]
We can offer you a career *counselling delinquents*. [4]
There is plenty of work (for us) *shovelling snow*. [5]

The typical postmodifying function of *-ing* clauses is as complement of a preposition (*the job of driving cars, the problem of learning English*; 17.37*ff*).

In appositive structures, *-ing* clauses have prepositions which are absent in the corresponding finite clauses:

the hope {*of winning* / *that X will win*} ~ X hopes *that X will win*.

Constructions with *to*-infinitive or *of*-phrase

17.36 Appositive postmodification by means of an infinitive clause [1] may have no corresponding finite clause as apposition [1b], but instead an alternative construction with a prepositional phrase [1a]:

He lost *the ability* {
to use his hands. [1]
of using his hands. [1a]
**that he could use his hands.* [1b]
}

Similarly:

Any attempt {*to leave early* / *at leaving early* / **that one should leave early*} is against regulations.

However, the choice between *to* + infinitive clause and preposition (usually *of*) + *-ing* clause as noun postmodification is also strictly limited. We may distinguish three main types of construction:

(a) *To*-infinitive only:

Anna has *the will* {*to win.* / **of winning.*}

(b) Either *to*-infinitive or *of* + *-ing*:

Their chance {*to go* / *of going*} abroad was lost.

(c) *Of* + *ing* only:

She found *the risk* {**to lose* / *of losing*} money too great.

Type (a) with *to*-infinitive is found chiefly after nouns which have intrinsic uses (*cf* 4.49), *ie* those nouns which express modal meanings that involve human control over events, *eg*:

agreement	*decision*	*determination*
disinclination	*inclination*	*invitation*
proposal	*readiness*	*refusal*
resolution	*(un)willingness*	*will*

We may distinguish two types: one where the constituent expressing modality and the following verb share the implied subject. Compare:

$$\text{Anna}\left\{\begin{array}{l}\text{wants to}\\ \text{'will [stressed]}\\ \text{is willing to}\end{array}\right\}\text{do the job.}$$

$$\sim \text{Anna's } \textit{willingness}\left\{\begin{array}{c}\textit{to do}\\ \textit{*of doing}\end{array}\right\}\text{the job}$$

A second type is found after nouns where the constituent expressing modality and the following verb have different subjects (irrespective of whether or not the infinitive has an expressed subject), as in:

Her father permitted her to do the job.

$$\sim \text{her father's } \textit{permission (for her)}\left\{\begin{array}{c}\textit{to do}\\ \textit{*of doing}\end{array}\right\}\text{the job}$$

The subject may be implicit or explicit (introduced by *for*) in cases like the following (where there is an open choice of subject):

$$\text{Here's } \textit{an invitation}\left\{\begin{array}{c}\textit{(for me)}\\ \textit{(for her)}\end{array}\right\}\textit{to visit}\text{ the motor show.}$$

Type (c) with *of* + *-ing* clause seems to occur chiefly after nouns expressing extrinsic modality, *ie* after nouns whose meanings do not primarily involve human control of the action itself, but typically involve human judgment, *eg*: *hope, possibility, prospect, risk*. Compare (on the choice of genitive *Anna's*, *cf* 15.12):

It is probable that Anna will do the job.

$$\sim \textit{the probability}\left\{\begin{array}{l}\textit{of (Anna('s)) doing}\\ \textit{*for Anna to do}\end{array}\right\}\text{the job}$$

Other examples:

The team is running *the risk of* (*us*/*our*) *losing* another game.
There is actually no *hope of* (*them*/*their*) *winning* the war.

In type (b) there is variation between the two kinds of construction, but certain nouns tend to have predominantly postmodification by *to*-infinitive, such as:

chance	*freedom*	*need*
obligation	*opportunity*	*plan*
power		

The following are examples of nouns that have predominantly *of* + *-ing* construction:

aim	*impossibility*	*intention*
necessity	*possibility*	*responsibility*

One reason for the choice among the two alternatives may be found in the contrast between root and epistemic possibility (*cf* 4.49), as in:

The possibility for man to coexist with man is slight.
[*cf*: 'It is possible for man to coexist . . .' with subject introduced by *for*; root possibility]

The possibility of (*them*/*their*) *coexisting* is slight.
[*cf*: 'It is possible that . . .'; epistemic possibility]

The construction with *to*-infinitive is especially suitable for cases where the subject of the infinitive is expressed:

Such schemes leave {*the worker some freedom* / *some freedom for the worker*} *to regulate* the relationship between effort and reward.

The construction with *of* + *-ing* clause is especially convenient when no expressed subject is present or implicit (generalizing function):

The freedom of holding an opinion and expressing it is a human right.

Postmodification by prepositional phrases

Relation to more explicit modifiers

17.37 In addition to reduction of sentences into noun phrases (*cf* 17.1) by means of postmodification by finite and nonfinite clauses, we have the further possibility of reduction of postmodification by prepositional phrases, as in the last item of the following series:

The car was standing outside the station.
the car *which was standing outside the station*
the car *standing outside the station*
the car *outside the station*

A prepositional phrase (*cf* 9.1*ff*) is by far the commonest type of postmodification in English: it is three or four times more frequent than either finite or nonfinite clausal postmodification. The full range of prepositions is involved, including complex prepositions (*eg*: *on board* in [4] and *in case of* in [5]; *cf* 9.10*ff*):

the road *to Lincoln* [1]
this book *on grammar* [2]
a man *from the electricity company* [3]
passengers *on board the ship* [4]
action *in case of fire* [5]
the meaning *of this sentence* [6]
the house *beyond the church* [7]
two years *before the war* [8]
a delay *pending further inquiry* [9]
a tree *by a stream* [10]

It is natural to relate such prepositional postmodifiers as (*the car*) *outside the station* to *be*-sentences ('The car is outside the station'), though in some instances the phrase seems to correspond with more than merely the finite verb *be*. For example, we presumably need to regard [11] as related to a somewhat fuller predication [11a]:

the university *as a political forum* [11]
The university is acting/regarded as a political forum. [11a]

Again, although there is no problem with [12], the interpretation is not so straightforward for [13], where an additional component has to be understood [13a]:

The present *for John* costs a great deal. ['The present is for John.'] [12]
The man *for the job* is John. [13]
The man is right/best for the job. [13a]

This is seen still more clearly in [14], which is a more explicit form of sentence [13]:

The *right* man *for the job* is John. [14]

Just as we do not wish to postulate [13b] in relation to [13], so we do not wish to postulate [14a] in relation to [14]:

*The man is for the job. [13b]
*The right man is for the job. [14a]

This problem will be seen in its more general context when we discuss discontinuous modification (*cf* 17.122).

The preposition *with* is another that we cannot fully account for unless we consider more than *be*-sentences; that is to say, these are adequate to explain [15], and even the idiomatic (and old-fashioned) [16]:

The woman *with the child* is Joan. ['The woman *is* with the child.'] [15]
The woman *with child* is Joan. ['The woman is with child, *ie* pregnant.'] [16]

But, in general, this is true only where *with* can be glossed as 'accompanied by'. No such gloss is possible in [17–18]:

the man *with a red beard* [17]
the girl *with a funny hat* [18]

Here we need to connect the prepositional phrase with a *have*-sentence: 'The man *has a red beard*', and hence with a relative clause: 'the man *who has a red beard*' (*cf* 9.55). The commonest preposition in noun-phrase postmodification, *of*, has a close correspondence to *have*-sentences (*cf* 17.38).

Note Among the prepositions used in postmodification, we should mention *like* (*cf* 9.4) which has the two senses of 'resembling in appearance' in [19] and 'resemblance in character' in [20]:

The man *like John* is over there. [19]
A man *like John* would never do that. [20]

The choice between the *of*-construction and the genitive construction

17.38 In many cases there is a regular correspondence between an *of*-phrase and the genitive (*cf* 5.115). Compare:

The ship has a funnel. It is red.
~The ship has a red funnel.
~*The ship's funnel* is red. [genitive construction]
~*The funnel of the ship* is red. [*of*-construction]

The GENITIVE CONSTRUCTION consists of two noun phrases: one a noun phrase marked for the genitive case by inflection; the other a succeeding and superordinate noun phrase unmarked for case in which the genitive noun phrase is embedded with a determinative function (*cf* 5.121). 'Determinative' function means that the genitive noun phrase functions like a definite determiner: it plays a role in the superordinate noun phrase equivalent to that of a determiner such as *the* or *our* (*cf* 5.11*ff*):

$\left.\begin{array}{l}\textit{the}\\\textit{our}\\\textit{the city's}\end{array}\right\}$ population

In the *OF*-CONSTRUCTION, which is often equivalent in meaning to the genitive construction, the superordinate noun phrase precedes a noun phrase introduced by *of*. The genitive phrase and the *of*-phrase thus occur in different order in the two constructions:

{[[*the city's*] population] [N1'*s* N2]
{[the population [*of the city*]] [N2 *of* N1]

In each construction, the two noun phrases may be expanded by modifiers, *eg*:

{[[the large city's] growing population]
{[the growing population [of the large city]]

However, the grammatical status of the genitive noun phrase is different from that of the *of*-phrase in that the former has the function of a definite determinative, whereas the second has the function of a postmodifier with the superordinate noun phrase either definite or indefinite. Thus, [1] shows direct correspondence with [1a]; [2] corresponds to [2a]; [3] has no correspondence with a genitive construction:

the funnel of the ship	[1]	~the ship's funnel	[1a]
the funnel of a ship	[2]	~a ship's funnel	[2a]
a funnel of the ship	[3]		

More distinctions can be made in post- than premodification generally, and this, as we can see here, is true also for the *of*-construction.

The only type of genitive where indefinite reference is permitted is the 'post-genitive', where the genitive and *of*-constructions are combined (*cf* 17.46):

a friend *of my brother's*

Note that the function of the genitive is not determinative in two uses: descriptive genitive, *eg*: *a girl's school* (*cf* 5.122, 17.110) and genitive of measure, *eg*: *an hour's delay* (*cf* 5.116).

We will now discuss other factors which influence the choice of construction:

(a) Lexical factors (17.39)
(b) Relational factors (17.40)
(c) Objective and subjective relation (17.41–43)
(d) Syntactic factors (17.44)
(e) Communicative factors (17.45)

(a) Lexical factors

17.39 As we have seen in 5.117, the genitive is favoured by those gender classes which are highest on the gender scale, in particular where N1 is a personal name, a personal noun, and a noun with personal characteristics, *ie* animal nouns and collective nouns:

Ann's car ≁ *the car *of Ann*
the lady's car ≁ *?the car *of the lady*
the dog's collar ≁ ?the collar *of the dog*
the family's car ≁ ?the car *of the family*

With inanimate, in particular concrete, nouns, the *of*-construction is normally required:

the roof *of this house* ≁ ?**this house's* roof

There is, however, a group of inanimate nouns which permit the genitive, especially geographical nouns and nouns denoting location and time (*cf* 5.118), *eg*:

China's population ~ the population *of China*
the world's economy ~ the economy *of the world*
last year's profit ~ the profit *for last year*

What has been said so far about lexical factors relates to gender in the determinative noun (N1). Specific lexical noun heads (N2) like *edge, length,* etc also influence the choice of construction (*cf* 5.120). The 'personal connection' of the genitive can be seen in a scale like the following where, without previous mention, N2 nouns that have the closest relation to the people of the country are most likely to be acceptable in the genitive:

*China's *map* — the *map* of China
?China's *climate* — the *climate* of China
(?)China's *roads* — the *roads* of China
China's *economy* — *the economy* of China

Note Whereas *the car of the lady* is unacceptable when unmodified, it becomes acceptable when there is postmodification of the whole noun phrase, or part of it (*cf* 17.44). Compare:

He crashed into { *?*the car of the lady.* / *the car of the lady in front of him.* / *the car of the girl he hoped to marry.* }

(b) Relational factors

17.40 The relation between the two nouns, as described by means of sentential and phrasal analogues in 5.116, is a powerful conditioning factor in the choice of construction. In particular, partitive constructions of the quantitative and qualitative types never have a genitive variant:

a glass *of water*	≁ *a *water's* glass
this kind *of research*	≁ *this *research's* kind

(c) Objective and subjective relation

17.41 The variable 'direction' of predications which correspond to noun phrases postmodified by *of* contributes greatly to the complexity of these expressions and has a bearing on the correspondence with the genitive. If we look at it in this way, we have left-to-right predication in the following:

the imprisonment of the murderer
~ (Someone) imprisoned the murderer. [1]
a woman of courage
~ The woman has courage. [2]

We have right-to-left predication in:

the arrival of the train
the train's arrival } ~ The train arrived. [3]
the funnel of the ship ~ The ship has a funnel. [4]

With the left-to-right examples [1] and [2], it seems reasonable to assume a verb–object relationship; similarly, the right-to-left examples [3] and [4] show a subject–verb relationship. These relations are more obvious in [1] and [3], where the heads are deverbal nouns, than in [2] and [4], where the predicational relationship is covert or implicit. When the genitive or *of*-construction has the relation in [1], we shall call it OBJECTIVE; when the relationship is like that in [3], we shall call it SUBJECTIVE.

With the objective relation, use of a premodifying genitive 'object' is rather uncommon and unnatural, as compared with the *of*-phrase, except where the head is a deverbal noun. Thus:

the imprisonment of the murderer ~ *the murderer's imprisonment*

But there is no *'s* genitive corresponding to the following:

a woman of courage [but not: **courage's woman*]
~ The woman has courage.
the love of power [but not: **power's love*]
~ (Someone) loves power.
reminiscences of the war [but not: **the war's reminiscences*]
~ *(Someone) remembers the war.*
men of science [but not: **science's men*]
~ Men (study) science.

17.42 By contrast, full correspondence between the subjective *of*-phrase and the genitive is common with most types of head, irrespective of whether the subject–predicate relation is overt or not:

the arrival of the train
~ the train's arrival [1]

the activity of the students
~ the students' activity ['The students are active.'] [2]
the *War Requiem* of/by Britten
~ Britten's *War Requiem* ['Britten composed the *War Requiem*.'] [3]

This is easy enough to understand in relation to [2] and [3], where the 'subject' is the type of noun ('animate, especially personal') that readily admits the genitive (*cf* 5.117*f*). For [1] and other such examples, the *of*-phrase may acquire, by implication, some properties of animateness through the very fact that the noun in question has a subject function.

Nevertheless, there are some subject constructions where replacement by genitive is impossible. For example:

the joy of his return [*but not*: *his return's joy] ['His return gives joy.'] [4]
an angel of a girl [*but not*: *the/*a girl's angel] ['The girl is an angel.'; *cf* 17.47] [5]

This constraint is marked by other restricted and special features in these examples, not least the property 'indefiniteness' in respect of the head noun, which is relevant also in:

an opera of Verdi's ['Verdi composed this opera – and others'] [6]

Here, however, there is no blocking of a direct correspondence with the genitive (*one of Verdi's operas*). We shall return to this example in 17.46.

17.43 Broadly speaking, the objective relation is usually expressed with the *of*-construction, and the subjective relation with either the *of*-construction or the genitive. Where the implicit verb is intransitive, *eg*: *arrive* in *the arrival of the train*, there can be no difficulty in interpreting the *of*-phrase as subjective. But problems can arise where the verb is one that can be used either transitively or intransitively, *eg*: *shoot*, as in *the shooting of the rebels*. The ambiguity in such phrases ('X shoots the rebels' or 'The rebels were shooting') is usually resolved by the context. The following sentence in a newspaper, however, is ambiguous:

The reminiscences of the Prime Minister were very amusing. [1]

The report did not explain whether it was the Prime Minister who had been reminiscing or whether someone had been reminiscing *about* the Prime Minister.

But in general it seems that, where an *of*-phrase can be interpreted as objective, it will be so interpreted unless there is a counter-indication. Thus [2] and [3] will tend primarily to suggest that someone is examining the fireman or scrutinizing the tenants:

the examination of the fireman [2]
the scrutiny of the tenants [3]

However, the converse would be perfectly reasonable, and indeed preferable with certain lexical items, as in [4]:

the examination of the experts [4]

Correspondingly, the genitive construction will probably be interpreted as subjective in the absence of a counter-indication, as in [2a] and [3a]:

the fireman's examination [2a]
the tenants' scrutiny [3a]

But a lexical counter-indication very easily swings interpretation in the other direction, as in [5]:

the student's examination [5]

A clear indication of the relationships in the genitive construction is achieved by adding a prepositional phrase beginning with *of* (after a construction of subjective relationship) and one beginning with *by* (after a construction of objective relationship). Such postmodifiers overrule any lexical pressure in the direction of a particular interpretation:

the man's examination of the student	[S V O]	[6]
the man's examination by the doctor	[O V S]	[6a]
the tenants' scrutiny of the landlord	[S V O]	[7]
the tenants' scrutiny by the landlord	[O V S]	[7a]

Here, we are dealing with transitive 'verbs' which can tolerate deletion of their objects more easily than other verbs. The verb *possess* would scarcely yield a noun phrase in which the subject could be expressed without the object:

?*The man's possession* worried me. [8]
?*The possession of the man* worried me. [8a]

If we knew (from the context) that *the man* was subject, we would be inclined to ask 'What does he possess?' as a condition of trying to assimilate either of these sentences. Contrast:

The pills came into *the possession of some children*. ['Some children possess pills.'] [9]
Some children came into *possession of the pills*. [9a]

English speakers would be inclined not to interpret the italicized portion of [9] as a noun phrase because there would not be a sentence having it as subject and preserving the subject-relation in the *of*-phrase:

*The possession of some children would be dangerous.

The analogous portion of [9a] would be more readily regarded as a unit with noun-phrase structure:

Possession of the pills would be dangerous.

In both [9] and [9a], however, (*the*) *possession* seems to enter into construction with *came* (*into*) rather than with the subsequent part of each sentence: compare the construction *take a rest* and the phrasal verb type *take advantage of* (*cf* 16.58).

The subjective relation is indicated by the article (*the charge/control of*) in the following *of*-construction [10], which has a genitive alternative [10a]:

$$\text{The children are in} \left\{ \begin{array}{l} \textit{the} \left\{ \begin{array}{l} \textit{charge} \\ \textit{control} \end{array} \right\} \textit{of John.} \qquad [10] \\ \textit{John's} \left\{ \begin{array}{l} \textit{charge.} \\ \textit{control.} \end{array} \right\} \qquad [10a] \end{array} \right.$$

The objective relation, however, cannot be expressed by the genitive without change of word order [11a], and the *of*-construction requires the complex preposition *in charge of* without article [11]:

$$\text{The children are } \textit{in} \left\{ \begin{array}{l} \textit{charge} \\ \textit{control} \end{array} \right\} \textit{of John.} \qquad [11]$$

$$\sim \text{John is in the } \textit{children's} \left\{ \begin{array}{l} \textit{charge.} \\ \textit{control.} \end{array} \right\} \qquad [11a]$$

Note In nouns with regular plural, the formal distinction in writing between the genitive plural (*boys'*), the genitive singular (*boy's*), and also the common gender plural (*boys*) does not exist in the pronunciation /bɔɪz/ (*cf* 5.113). In order to preclude ambiguity, the use of the genitive of nouns with regular plural tends to be avoided in speech, unless the number appears from the context (*the two boys' teacher*, etc). However, there is no problem with irregular plurals: *the children's teacher*.

(d) Syntactic factors

17.44 We have said that noun phrases may be indefinitely complex (*cf* 17.1). Since both the genitive and *of*-construction consist of two noun phrases each of which, at least theoretically, admits indefinite expansion, the minimal structures [1] and [1a] may be expanded to, for example, [2] and [2a]:

his daughter's arrival [1]
~ the arrival of his daughter [1a]
his 19-year-old daughter's arrival from Hamburg [2]
~ the arrival from Hamburg of his 19-year-old daughter [2a]

There are some types of expansion of noun-phrase heads that are of particular interest to the present discussion: left-branching structure by premodification, and right-branching structure by postmodification, apposition, and coordination (*cf* 17.121*f*).

Heavy restrictive postmodification of the head of the noun phrase constrains the choice of the *of*-construction, *eg*:

the arrival of a friend which had been expected for several weeks [3]

In such cases, the postmodification of the head is likely to be understood as nonrestrictive:

the arrival of a friend, which . . .

With restrictive modification, the genitive is compulsory or greatly preferred, in order to avoid awkwardness, discontinuity, or ambiguity:

a friend's arrival which had been expected for several weeks [3a]

The choice of construction is the converse when the other noun phrase is postmodified, in which case the *of*-construction is the natural choice:

the arrival of a friend who had been studying for a year at a German university [4]

*a friend's arrival who had been studying for a year at a German university [4a]

Such 'split genitives' as in [4a] are not acceptable. In some cases, the 'group genitive' can be used, in which the genitive marker is affixed to the last item of the postmodification, in particular prepositional phrases (*cf* 17.119), as in [5]:

the King of Spain's armada [5]

*the King's of Spain armada [5a]

Genitives after postmodification by finite clause, as in [6], would not be normally acceptable, but could well occur and be understood in a colloquial context:

*?the lady I met in the shop's hat [6]

The same principles that have been illustrated for postmodification also hold for other heavy right-branching structures like apposition and coordination. Thus, when the determinative noun head is coordinate [7] or has appositive expansion [8], the genitive construction is often impossible:

the arrival of his daughter and his German friend
?*his daughter's and his German friend's arrival } [7]

the arrival of his daughter, a student of German
*his daughter's, a student of German, arrival } [8]

(e) Communicative factors

17.45 The choice between the genitive and the *of*-construction is also conditioned by the linear organization of utterances in discourse, in particular factors (such as end-focus and end-weight, *cf* 18.3*f*) that encourage the placing of more complex and communicatively more important constituents towards the end of the superordinate noun phrase. The genitive (N1*'s* N2) is generally favoured when N2 has a higher communicative value than does N1 (example [1]), whereas the *of*-construction (N2 *of* N1) is preferred when the thematic distribution is the reverse (example [2]):

The speaker said that, among the global problems that face us now, the chief one is *the world's economy*. [*economy* is in focus] [1]

He went on to say, however, that in order to succeed we must first tackle *the economy of the industrialized nations*, which is the basis for *the sound economy of the world*. [*world* is in focus] [2]

We have seen that there are a number of factors which, singly or in combination, influence the choice of the *of*-construction. The most severe constraints on variation seem to be (i) the lexical constraint imposed by the choice of inanimate, especially concrete, noun (N1); and (ii) the use of the construction to express an objective relation. In both these cases, the *of*-construction is obligatory or widely preferred.

The 'post-genitive'

17.46 We may return now to example [6] in 17.42 and consider the peculiarities of this 'post-genitive' usage (*cf* 5.126). It will be observed that the postmodifier must be definite and human:

an opera *of Verdi's* BUT NOT: *an opera *of a composer's*
an opera *of my friend's* BUT NOT: *a funnel *of the ship's*

There are conditions that also affect the head of the whole noun phrase. The head must be essentially indefinite: that is, the head must be seen as one of an unspecified number of items attributed to the postmodifier. Thus [1–3] but not [4]:

A friend of the doctor's has arrived. [1]
A daughter of Mrs Brown's has arrived. [2]
Any daughter of Mrs Brown's is welcome. [3]
**The daughter* of Mrs Brown's has arrived. [4]

As a consequence of the condition that the head must be indefinite, the head cannot be a proper noun (*cf* 5.60*ff*). Thus while we have [5], we cannot have [6] and [7]:

Mrs Brown's Mary [5]
*Mary of Mrs Brown [6]
*Mary of Mrs Brown's [7]

The post-genitive thus involves a partitive as one of its components. The two constructions *a friend of his father's* and *one of his father's friends* are usually identical in meaning. One difference, however, is that the former construction may be used whether *his father* had one or more friends, whereas the latter necessarily entails more than one friend. Thus:

Mrs Brown's daughter [8]
Mrs Brown's daughter Mary [9]
Mary, (the) daughter of Mrs Brown [10]
Mary, a daughter of Mrs Brown's [11]

[8] implies 'sole daughter', whereas [9] and [10] carry no such implication; [11] entails 'not sole daughter'.

Since there is only one composition called the *War Requiem* by Britten, we have [12] but not [13] or [14]:

The *War Requiem* of/by Britten (is a splendid work.) [12]
*The *War Requiem* of Britten's [13]
*One of Britten's *War Requiems* [14]

Yet, we are able, in apparent defiance of this statement, to use demonstratives as follows:

that wife of mine [15]
this *War Requiem* of Britten's [16]

In these instances, which always presuppose familiarity, the demonstratives are not being used in a directly defining role; rather, one might think of them as allowing us to see *wife* and *War Requiem* as appositional, as members of a class of objects: 'This instance of Britten's works, namely, *War Requiem*'. Even where more than one object exists corresponding to the noun, the post-genitive phrase preceded by *this* should be regarded as having a generic partitive, *eg*:

this hand of mine [17]

Example [17] should be interpreted not as 'this one of my (two) hands' but rather as 'this part of my body that I call "hand"'.

Note [**a**] So too, when *a daughter of Mrs Brown's* [11] is already established in the linguistic context, we could refer to *the/that daughter of Mrs Brown's (that I mentioned)*.

[**b**] The use of *this* and *that* in such constructions parallels their use elsewhere, the former directing immediate and often sympathetic attention, the latter often having a negative or even contemptuous ring: *that son of yours* (*cf* 6.41).

[**c**] Note the different meanings in the following set (*cf* 9.50, 17.54):

a painting *of my sister's* ['done by my sister' *or* 'belonging to my sister']
a painting *of my sister* ['representing my sister']
a painting *by my sister* ['done by my sister']
a painting *of my sister by my brother* ['representing my sister and done by my brother']

Compare also:

He's *a student of Jespersen*. ['one who studies Jespersen's writings']
He was *a student of Jespersen's*. ['one who studied under Jespersen']

[**d**] In earlier English, an appositional structure was obvious in such a variant of *this hand of mine* as *this my hand*. It is a variant still occasionally used with oratorical tone:

Today, sadly, there is no room for humour in *this our country*. ['this country of ours']

Apposition with *of*-phrases

17.47 Some noun phrases have a prepositional phrase component, *eg*: *the city of Rome*, which is not a regular postmodifier, as in *the people of Rome* (*cf* 17.37). Such expressions are relatable to *be*-sentences whose subjects are put into *of*-phrases, when an indefinite complement is made definite:

Rome is a city.
~ The city (that I mean) is Rome.
~ the city *of Rome*

Similarly we might postulate such a relation as the following (*cf* 17.26*f*):

The team's victory was (announced as) news.
~ The news was the team's victory.
~ the news *of the team's victory*

We have here a basis for the prepositional postmodification which corresponds directly to the clausal appositive (on *the team* versus the *team's*, *cf* 15.12):

the news { that the team had won / *of the team('s) having won* }

Because of the obvious relation between, for example, *The city is Rome* and *the city of Rome*, it is common to regard such noun phrases as simply nominalizations of *be*-sentences in which the implied subject has become the head of the noun phrase.

A special case of prepositional apposition is offered by singular count nouns where the *of*-phrase is subjective (*cf* 17.41*ff*), *eg*:

the fool of a policeman [1]
an angel of a girl [2]
this jewel of an island [3]

This structure consisting of determiner + noun (N2) + *of* + indefinite article + noun (N1) is not a regular prepositional postmodification, since N1 is notionally the head, as can be seen in the paraphrases:

The policeman is a fool. [note the AmE informal variant *some fool policeman*] [1a]
The girl is an angel. [2a]
This island is a jewel. [3a]

The whole part N2 + *of* + *a* corresponds to an adjective:

the *foolish* policeman [1b]
an *angelic* girl [2b]
this *jewel-like* island [3b]

The natural segmentation is reflected in variant spellings, as in the familiar AmE expression *a hell of a guy* (nonstandard spelling: *a helluva guy*).

In this construction, the determiner of N1 must be the indefinite article, but there is no such constraint on the determiner of N2:

$$\left.\begin{array}{l}\textit{a}\\ \textit{the}\\ \textit{this}\\ \textit{that}\end{array}\right\}\ \textit{fool of}\left\{\begin{array}{l}\textit{a policeman}\\ {}^{*}\textit{the policeman}\\ {}^{*}\textit{policeman}\end{array}\right.$$

Also, N2 must be singular:

?**those fools* of policemen

The possessive determiner actually notionally determines N1, not N2:

her brute of a *brother* ['Her brother was a brute.']

Both N2 and N1 can be premodified:

a *little mothy wisp* of a man
this *gigantic earthquake* of a piece of music
a *dreadful ragbag* of *a British musical*
this *crescent-shaped jewel* of *a South Sea island*

Restrictive and nonrestrictive prepositional postmodification

17.48 Prepositional phrases may be restrictive or nonrestrictive in both appositional and nonappositional functions:

The course on English grammar starts tomorrow.
[nonappositional, restrictive] [1]
This course, on English grammar, starts tomorrow.
[nonappositional, nonrestrictive] [1a]
The question of student grants was discussed yesterday.
[appositional, restrictive] [2]
This question, of student grants, was discussed yesterday.
[appositional, nonrestrictive] [2a]

But we must mention some limitations: [1a] and [2a] are rare and rather awkward. Nonrestrictive appositives could equally have no preposition, as with:

This question, student grants, was discussed yesterday. [2b]

On the other hand, the noun phrase in [3] is ambiguous:

the issue of student grants [3]

It can either have appositional or nonappositional meaning. In the latter sense [objective *of*: 'Someone issued student grants'], nonrestrictive function would be rare and unnatural, plainly suggesting a parenthetic afterthought:

?*The issue, of student grants*, was slow because there were so many applicants.

Similarly:

One man, of around forty years, was convicted of bigamy.
?*A party, of children*, entered the theatre.
?*The end, of the world*, is at hand.

An appositional interpretation is impossible when the postmodification is clearly restrictive:

**The man, of property*, was Soames Forsyte.

Nonrestrictive, nonappositive modification is more usual with other prepositions than *of*:

This textbook, by a colleague of mine, will be out shortly.
The passage, from a famous speech by Churchill, has become proverbial.

By contrast, complex prepositions (*cf* 9.10*f*) seem to lend themselves less readily to restrictive postmodification:

His resignation, *on account of a bribery scandal*, was deeply regretted.
?His resignation *on account of a bribery scandal* was deeply regretted.

Position and varied functional relationship

17.49 As with nonfinite postmodifiers when nonrestrictive, so with prepositional phrases: the nonrestrictive function merges with adverbial expressions (*cf* 8.44). Compare [1] and [1a]:

The children {*behind the fence* / *on the bus*} jeered at the soldiers. [1]

The children, {*behind the fence* / *on the bus*}, jeered at the soldiers. [1a]

Example [1] means 'Those children who were . . .'; example [1a] may mean 'The children, who (by the way) were . . .' or 'The children, now that they were (safely . . .)' (*cf* similar vacillation in nonfinite clauses, 17.34*f*). It is rather this latter implication that becomes uppermost if the prepositional phrase is moved into initial position, as in [1b]:

Behind the fence,
On the bus, } the children jeered at the soldiers. [1b]

Again, the prepositional phrase in [2] is poised between interpretation as nonrestrictive postmodifier and as adverbial:

Money, *in aid of the refugees*, was collected from the students and staff. [2]

In the former interpretation, the money collected was in aid of the refugees, and in the latter, the act of collecting money was in aid of the refugees, since in this case the adverbial modifies the whole predication just as it would in initial position:

In aid of the refugees, money was collected . . . [2a]

Despite the similarity in meaning in the examples discussed here, we do indeed have different constructions and not merely the additional possibility of placing a prepositional postmodifier in front of the noun-phrase head. This becomes clear when it is shown that, unless a given phrase can be an adjunct, it cannot be moved from its postmodifying position. For example, the restrictive postmodification in *this leap right across the fissure* can be made nonrestrictive:

This leap, *right across the fissure*, was shown on television. [3]

But as the phrase cannot be adjunct in this sentence, it cannot be made initial [3a]:

**Right across the fissure*, this leap was shown on television. [3a]

17.50 The restriction on initial position naturally applies also to the *of*-postmodifiers that are almost solely restrictive:

**Of children*, a party entered the theatre. [1]

But there is an apparent exception with partitive expressions. Thus beside [2] we may thematically prepose the *of*-phrase with no obvious difference in meaning [2a]:

Only a few *of the ten reviewers* praised his play. [2]
Of the ten reviewers, only a few praised his play. [2a]

This example is misleading, however, in giving the impression that the initially placed phrase of [2a] is identical with the postmodifying phrase of [2]. They are not identical, as can be seen when we substitute zero article; this is acceptable when the phrase is in initial position, as in [3] and [4], but not in postmodification, as in [3a] and [4a]:

Of ten reviewers, only a few praised his play. [3]
Of fourteen women, ten were highly critical of the proposal. [4]
?*Only a few *of ten reviewers* praised his play. [3a]
?*Ten *of fourteen women* were single. [4a]

The fact that [4a] becomes acceptable if the postmodifying phrase is introduced by *out of* (as in *Ten out of fourteen women*, where the phrase can also be initial) confirms that the initially placed *of*-phrase is functionally different, although semantically similar to the postmodifying phrase.

In other words, we should regard the initial prepositional phrase in such examples as [3] and [4] as adverbial and not as displaced postmodification; indeed, *as for* and *as to* phrases, when denoting respect (*cf* 9.57), must always be initial. Perhaps better, we should see the initial phrase in [3] as directly related to an existential statement [3b] (*cf* 18.44*ff*):

Of ten reviewers that there were, } only a few praised his play. [3b]
There were ten reviewers, but }

Nominalization

17.51 We should not exaggerate the difference between (a) the prepositional phrase as adverbial and (b) the prepositional phrase as postmodifier (*cf* 17.37*ff*). The second of these should rather be regarded as a special instance of the first, depending for its interpretation on our ability to relate it to a sentence in which it is adjunct. In [1], for instance, both the prepositional phrases are introduced as adjuncts:

In the morning, a quarrel broke out *over pay*. [1]

If now we wish to refer again to the quarrel, we may do so in relation to either of these adjuncts, which now become postmodifiers:

The quarrel *in the morning* ruined their friendship. [1a]
The quarrel *over pay* was the reason for his resignation. [1b]

The relation of postmodifier to adjunct may be even clearer if, instead of [1], we take a sentence like [1c]:

In the morning, they quarrelled *over pay*. [1c]

In [1c], *quarrel* does not occur as a noun but as a verb, to which we also relate [1a] and [1b], but in this case through the process of word formation called conversion (*cf* App I.43*ff*). Conversion should be distinguished from nominalization.

A noun phrase such as *the quarrel over pay* in [1b] which has a systematic correspondence with a clause structure will be termed a NOMINALIZATION. The noun head of such a phrase is normally related morphologically to a verb [2], or to an adjective [3] (*ie* a deverbal or deadjectival noun, *cf* App I.34*ff*):

his *refusal* to help ~ He *refuses* to help. [2]
the *truth* of her statement ~ Her statement is *true*. [3]

But the correspondence may also sometimes be based on a concrete noun and a denominal abstract noun:

her *friendship* for Chopin ~ She was a *friend* of Chopin. [4]

By describing such phrases as having a systematic correspondence with a clause structure, we do not wish to imply that for every clause there is a corresponding noun phrase; the correspondence is best seen as obtaining in a less regular fashion, and as depending on whether, for example, there is a suitable nominal lexicalization of the verb's meaning (*cf* App I.8*ff*). The claim is, however, that we can match elements of the noun phrase (head, modifiers, determinatives) with elements of clause structure, considered semantically in terms of the verb and its associated participant roles (*cf* 10.18*ff*) of agentive, affected, etc.

We can also distinguish, in the case of deverbal noun heads, between active and passive nominalization patterns:

the critics' hostile *reception* of the play
~ The critics *received* the play in a hostile manner.
[subjective, *cf* 17.41*ff*] [5]

the play's hostile *reception* by the critics
~ The play *was received* in a hostile manner by the critics.
[objective, *cf* 17.41*ff*] [6]

17.52 The term nominalization may apply not only to noun phrases with an abstract noun head, as in [5] and [6] in 17.51, but also to concrete noun phrases with an agential noun head (*cf* 7.73), as in:

She is a good *writer*. ~ She *writes* well. [1]
He is a clever *liar*. ~ He *lies* cleverly. [2]

The relation between a nominalization and a corresponding clause structure can be more or less explicit, according to how far the nominalization specifies, through modifiers and determinatives, the nominal or adverbial elements of a corresponding clause. In this respect we may compare [3] with [3a–f]:

The reviewers criticized his play in a hostile manner. [3]
the reviewers' hostile criticizing of his play [3a]
the reviewers' hostile criticism of his play [3b]
the reviewers' criticism of his play [3c]
the reviewers' criticism [3d]
their criticism [3e]
the criticism [3f]

These noun phrases are ordered from most explicit [3a] to least explicit [3f], but each of them could occupy the function of a nominalization as prepositional complement in the following:

Lanzarotti was disappointed by . . .

The extreme of inexplicitness is reached with an abstract or agential noun standing on its own as a noun phrase:

Criticism is always helpful. [3g]

Some verbs have no corresponding deverbal noun: for example, corresponding to *lie* ['tell untruths'] there is no deverbal abstract noun, although there is the agential noun *liar*. In such cases, however, we can usually make use of a verbal noun ending with *-ing* (*cf* App I.35):

> *Lying* is all too common.
> *His firing* of William was a mistake.
> (Contrast: *His dismissal* of William was a mistake.)

Some such *-ing* nouns can also be used in the plural:

> The number of reported *sightings* of UFOs since 1980 is relatively small.

17.53 Verbal and deverbal nouns differ in their acceptance of modification by prepositional phrases. Compare the following:

their arriving *for a month*	[1a]
?the(ir) arrival *for a month*	[1b]
their behaving *with courtesy*	[2a]
?the(ir) behaviour *with courtesy*	[2b]
their acting *in a nasty manner*	[3a]
*the(ir) action *in a nasty manner*	[3b]
their contributing *out of kindness*	[4a]
*the(ir) contribution *out of kindness*	[4b]

It appears that adjuncts relating to duration, manner, or cause are awkward or inadmissible as postmodifiers. Deverbal nouns (especially from punctual verbs like *arrive*; *cf* 4.33) might be described as mere records of an action having taken place rather than as descriptions of the action itself. Thus the postmodifiers are the adjuncts that can occur in sentences like the following:

They arrived *on Thursday*.	[5]
The arrival took place *on Thursday*.	[6]

Contrast:

They arrived for *a month*.	[5a]
*The arrival took place *for a month*.	[6a]

The gradience from deverbal nouns via verbal nouns to participles

17.54 As well as distinguishing between deverbal nouns like *quarrel, arrival, behaviour, action,* and *contribution* (*cf* App I.35) and the corresponding verbal nouns in *-ing* (*quarrelling, arriving*, etc), we need to recognize a complex gradience, as in the following example, from the pure count noun in [1], *some paintings of Brown's*, to the purely participial form in a finite verb phrase in [14], 'Brown *is painting* his daughter':

some paintings of Brown's [[a] 'some paintings that Brown owns'; or [b] 'some paintings painted by Brown']	[1]
Brown's paintings of his daughter [[a] 'paintings depicting his daughter and painted by him'; or [b] 'paintings depicting his daughter and painted by someone else but owned by him']	[2]

The painting of Brown is as skilful as that of Gainsborough. [[a] 'Brown's mode of painting'; or [b] 'Brown's action of painting'] [3]

Brown's deft painting of his daughter is a delight to watch. ['It is a delight to watch while Brown deftly paints his daughter.'] [4]

Brown's deftly painting his daughter is a delight to watch. [= [3b] or [4] in meaning] [5]

I dislike *Brown's painting his daughter*. ['I dislike either [a] the fact or [b] the way that Brown does it.'] [6]

I dislike *Brown painting his daughter* (when she ought to be at school). [= [6a]] [7]

I watched *Brown painting his daughter*. [[a] 'I watched Brown as he painted'; or [b] 'I watched the process of Brown('s) painting his daughter.'] [8]

Brown deftly painting his daughter is a delight to watch. [= [3b] or [4]; *cf* 14.6*ff*] [9]

Painting his daughter, Brown noticed that his hand was shaking. ['while he was painting'; *cf* 5.12*ff*] [10]

Brown painting his daughter that day, I decided to go for a walk. ['since Brown was painting'; *cf* 5.12*ff*] [11]

The man painting the girl is Brown. ['who is painting'; *cf* 17.28] [12]

The silently painting man is Brown. ['who is silently painting'; *cf* 17.98*f*] [13]

Brown *is painting* his daughter. [*cf* 4.25*ff*] [14]

In [1] and [2] we have the DEVERBAL NOUN *paintings* with a plural ending. It could be replaced by *pictures* or *photos*; it is thus a perfectly regular concrete count noun, related only to the verb *paint* by word formation.

In [3] and [4] *painting* is also a noun, as can be seen by the definite article in [3], and in [4] not only by the genitive construction but also by the adjective premodifier *deft* (as compared with the adverb *deftly* in [5]). Yet *painting* here could not be replaced by *picture* or *photo*, but only by abstract nouns like *representation, portrayal, portraiture, depiction*, etc. Thus *painting* in [3] and [4] is an abstract noncount noun of the kind that can be formed from verbs by adding *-ing* and inserting *of* before the noun phrase that corresponds to the subject if the object is not expressed (*cf* 17.41):

the painting of Brown ~ Brown paints.
the writing of Smith ~ Smith writes.

This construction can also occur before the noun phrase that corresponds to the object, if this is expressed:

their polishing of the furniture ~ They polish the furniture.
the writing of novels (by Smith) ~ Smith writes novels.

Forms like *painting* in [3] and [4] are VERBAL NOUNS (*cf* 17.51, App I.3 Note).

In [5] and [6], the genitive *Brown's* is used, but in place of the adjective *deft* in [4] we have the adverb *deftly* in [5]; in place of the *of*-phrase *of his daughter* (in [4]), we have in [5] and [6] the noun phrase *his daughter* directly following *painting*, exactly as does the object of a finite verb phrase in [14]. Traditionally this mixture of nominal and verbal characteristics in the *-ing* form has been given the name 'gerund', while the uses of *painting* in [7–14] have been distinguished as those of the '(present) participle'.

Note **[a]** Where no premodifier appears, genitive or otherwise, the traditional view held *painting* to be 'gerund', as in [15], where the item is in a structure functioning nominally (in this case as subject); but it was considered a participle if the same structure functioned adverbially, as in [16]:

Painting a child is difficult. [15]

Painting a child that morning, I quite forgot the time. [16]

However, no analogous categorial distinction was made between *to paint* in [17] and [18]:

To paint a child is difficult. [17]

To paint a child, I bought a new canvas. [18]

Here the tradition was content to regard *to paint* as an 'infinitive' in both.

For reasons that will now be plain, we do not find it useful to distinguish a gerund from a participle, but terminologically class all the *-ing* items in [5–14] as PARTICIPLES. In [5–12], the participle is in each case the nonfinite verb of a nonfinite clause, in [13] a premodifier, and in [14] the head of a finite verb phrase. By avoiding the binary distinction of gerund and participle, we seek to represent more satisfactorily the complexity of the different participial expressions as we move along the gradient to the 'most verbal' end at [14].

One indication of the complexity of the *-ing* form is that what others have called the gerund carries in English both nonmodal meanings, as in [19], and modal meanings, as in [20]:

There was *no shouting, no merry-making, no waving of flags*. ['No shouting, merry-making, or waving of flags took place.'] [19]

There was *no mistaking that scream*. ['No one could mistake that scream.'] [20]

Thus in [19] the *-ing* form corresponds to the Latin gerund, but in [20] to the Latin gerundive which, unlike the gerund, typically manifests a modal meaning such as possibility or contingency. This lack of correspondence between the English gerund and the traditional use of the term can be advanced as a further reason for rejecting the term gerund in English.

Furthermore, there is potential ambiguity not only along the modal/nonmodal dimension but also along the (traditional) gerund/deverbal-noun dimension (*cf* 15.14 Note [b]). For example, sentence [21] can be interpreted in three ways [21a, b, c]:

There's *no writing* on the blackboard today. [21]

as a modal 'gerund' [21a]:

'We can't write on the blackboard today (because we have no chalk).' [21a]

as a nonmodal 'gerund' [21b]:

'We are not going to write on the blackboard today (since all our work is going to be oral).' [21b]

as a nonmodal deverbal noun [21c]:

'There's nothing written on the blackboard today (because we haven't used this classroom).' [21c]

The sense of [21c] is doubtless more expected than either [21a] or [21b].

[b] One expects the name in [3] to be that of an artist of some reputation if the *of*-construction is to be used; otherwise the genitive would be more natural to convey this meaning:

Jack's painting is nearly as good as his wife's.

[c] There is an aspectual difference between verbal nouns, which tend to denote activity that is in process, and abstract deverbal nouns, which denote completed activity (*cf* App I.35 Note).

Minor types of postmodification

Postmodification by adverb phrase

17.55 Some typical examples of postmodification by adverb phrases (*cf* 7.67) are the following:

The road back is dense with traffic. [1]
The way out was hard to find. [2]
The people behind were talking all the time. [3]

In [1], we recognize some such paraphrase as '*The road* which leads *back* to London' from which everything except an important adjunct has to be understood from the context. Similarly, for [2]: '*The way* which leads *out* of the auditorium'; and for [3]: '*The people* who were sitting *behind*'. In some cases, the postmodifying item could be regarded alternatively as a preposition with omitted complement: '*The people* who were sitting *behind* us'.

There are indeed a few cases where a prepositional interpretation is forced on us (*cf* 9.53), *eg*:

The votes for far outnumber those *against*. [4]

In [4], the related explicit structure has no alternative to the prepositional phrase:

The votes are *for the motion*.

But since most examples can be explained as adverbial and few as prepositional, it seems best to regard the few that must be prepositional as being modelled upon the adverbial ones.

As indicated in 7.67 (where more examples are given), adverbs which postmodify nouns signify time or place. In some phrases, the adverb can be used either as a pre- or postmodifier:

his *homeward* journey ~ his journey *homeward*

Some noun phrases of measure, denoting size, age, etc, can also be postposed:

A man *the size of a giant* came up to me.
Somebody *her age* shouldn't do such strenuous exercises.

Note *O'clock* is an adverb optionally added after numbers from 1 to 12 to denote time of day:
What time was the accident?
– At 10 (o'clock) in the morning/at night.
– At 12 (o'clock) noon/midnight.

O'clock is not used together with *a.m.* ['before midday'] or *p.m.* ['after midday']:
9 o'clock in the morning [= 9 a.m.]
9 o'clock in the evening [= 9 p.m.]

O'clock is used only in mentioning the exact hour, not the hour and a particular number of minutes:
at 7 o'clock, at 7 a.m./p.m.; at 7.15 a.m./p.m. BUT NOT: *at 7.15 o'clock, *at 15 past 7 o'clock

Postposed adjectives

17.56 Postposed adjectives (*cf* 7.21) can be divided into three main types, depending on whether the postposition is required by:

(a) the head of the noun phrase (*cf* 17.57), *eg*:

I want to try *something different* [as opposed to *a different approach*] [1]

(b) the postmodification or complementation of the adjective (*cf* 17.58), *eg*:

a play popular in the 1890s [as opposed to *a popular play*] [2]

(c) the particular noun–adjective combination (*cf* 17.59), *eg*:

the heir apparent [as opposed to *the apparent reason, the rich heir*] [3]

Types (a) and (b) are central constructions and can be seen as reductions of relative clauses:

something (*that is*) *different* [1a]
a play (*that was*) *popular in the 1890s* [2a]

Type (c) is restricted to idiomatic phrases.

Type (a): *somebody bigger*

17.57 This type includes noun-phrase heads consisting of indefinite pronouns in *-body, -one, -thing*, and the adverb *-where*, plus one or two *wh*-forms (*what else, who next,* etc), which can only be modified postpositively (*cf* 7.69):

Anybody younger would have done better.

However, we cannot postpose with indefinites every modifying item that can be preposed with ordinary noun heads. While we have both *a tall girl* and *an office girl*, we have *somebody tall* but not **somebody office* (*cf* 7.12).

Even adjectives need generally to be 'permanent' and hence eligible for attributive use (*cf* 17.7); thus *somebody timid* rather than ?*somebody afraid*.

Note [**a**] We not infrequently come upon noun phrases which defy the conditions described; for example, beside the regular *something nasty* we have:

That nasty something has reappeared.

In such instances (which are almost always familiar, playful, or ironic), the head items are not being used as compound indefinite pronouns (*cf* 6.45*ff*) but as nouns. The motivation for the deviation will vary from one example to another, but a possible explanation for the example just provided would find ready parallels. We might paraphrase it thus: 'You mentioned seeing *something nasty*; well, the thing you called "something" has reappeared'.

[**b**] The type of postmodification consisting of pronoun in *-thing* + adjective has an alternative construction with *a* + adjective + *thing* as head:

{*Something nasty* / *A nasty thing*} happened to me on the way to work this morning.

Some nasty things has the somewhat different sense of 'certain nasty things'. There is no **some things nasty*.

There is a possibility of using *one* (but not *body*) as a head in this way:

I'd like {*someone young* / *a young one* / *somebody young* / **a young body*} for the job.

Any young body ['anybody young'] is dialectal.

Type (b): *a mistake typical of beginners*

17.58 This type includes adjective phrases which are heavy in relation to the head, usually by having a prepositional phrase or a nonfinite verb phrase as complement. Whereas we have only the normal order in [1], postposition is required in [2]:

a *typical* mistake [1]
a mistake *typical of beginners* [2]

Thus English accepts neither [2a] (unless used ad hoc and specially marked by hyphens: 'That could be described as *a typical-of-beginners mistake*') nor [2b]:

*a typical of beginners mistake [2a]
*an of beginners typical mistake [2b]

With coordinated adjectives, either pre- or postposition is possible:

{a *both typical and common* mistake [3]
{a mistake *both typical and common* [3a]

When a head is nonrestrictively modified by a coordinate string of adjectives, it is common to postpose them:

A man, *timid and hesitant*, approached the official. [4]

However, the potential mobility of the string allows it to be detached from the noun phrase altogether (*cf* 7.27, 17.49) and shows it to be an adverbial rather than part of the noun phrase:

{*Timid and hesitant*, a man approached the official. [4a]
{A man approached the official, *timid and hesitant*. [4b]

Even a restrictively modifying adjective can be postposed if it is itself modified (by an adjunct, not by the intensifier *very*; *cf* 7.87*ff*):

A man always timid is unfit for this task. [but not: **A man very timid* . . .] [4c]

This construction is particularly common where the modification expresses a 'temporary' attribute (*cf* 17.7). Thus beside the dubiousness of ?*somebody afraid* (*cf* 17.49), complementation of the adjective (*somebody afraid of the dark*) results in complete acceptability. Comparison involving nouns of different gender classes requires postposition of the adjective as in [5]:

a man *taller than Mary*
≁ *a *taller* man *than Mary* } [5]

Where the nouns are of the same class, postposition is optional (*cf* 17.122):

a man *taller than John*
~ a *taller* man *than John* } [6]

Type (c): *the president elect*

17.59 This type of postposed adjective consists chiefly of the sprinkling of fixed noun-plus-adjective phrases (modelled on French) like *the president elect, heir apparent, blood royal* (*cf* further examples in 7.21). These are of little importance in themselves, being infrequently used (though our ability to form names like *Hotel Majestic* suggests that they are more than mere fossils), and it is likely that native speakers feel them to be very similar to compound nouns. Unlike the adjectives in free combinations, these postposed adjectives cannot be modified:

**The president newly elect*
The president newly elected } will take office next Monday.
The newly elected president

**The heir still apparent* was being well educated.
?She had *blood wholly royal* in her veins.

With a quantifier we can say 'A lot of royal blood flowed in the French revolution', but not '*A lot of blood royal . . .'. In some cases, a sequence has obviously been reanalysed as premodifier plus head; this can be seen in the plural *court-martials* (alongside *courts-martial*; *cf* 5.102):

No *court-martials* are held on Christmas Day.

Postposed 'mode' qualifier: *Lobster Newburg*

17.60 There is another French model of postposition in English that we may call postposed 'mode' qualifier, as in *Lobster Newburg*. Though virtually confined to cuisine (rather than mere cooking), it is moderately productive within these limits, perhaps especially in AmE. In BrE one finds *veal paprika* and many others, but there is some resistance to this type of postposition with other than French lexical items, as in *pâté maison, sole bonne femme*. Nevertheless (perhaps partly because, in examples like the latter, the French and English head nouns are identical), the language has become receptive to hybrids like *poached salmon mayonnaise, English scallops provencal*.

Note The prepositional phrase involving *à la* (*cf* 9.10 Note) is a related phenomenon. It appears in culinary formations like *chicken à la king*, but is very general in informal or facetious use to designate style, 'in the manner of':

Another play à la Stoppard has appeared, though I forget who wrote it.

Multiple postmodification

17.61 Multiple modification arises through any or all of the following three conditions (a, b, c):

(a) More than one modification is applicable to a single head. Thus the two sentences [1] and [2] can be brought together as [3]:

the man *in the corner* [1]
the man *talking to John* [2]
the man *in the corner* { *talking to John* / (?) *and talking to John* } [3]

The second postmodifier (*talking to John*) modifies the whole of the preceding complex noun phrase:

[[the man [in the corner]] talking to John]

The usual type of construction is with no conjunction. But, without a conjunction, there is ambiguity (though often with little difference in meaning in practice) between a coordinated relation of the postmodifiers as in *Fig* 17.61a and a hierarchical relation as in *Fig* 17.61b.

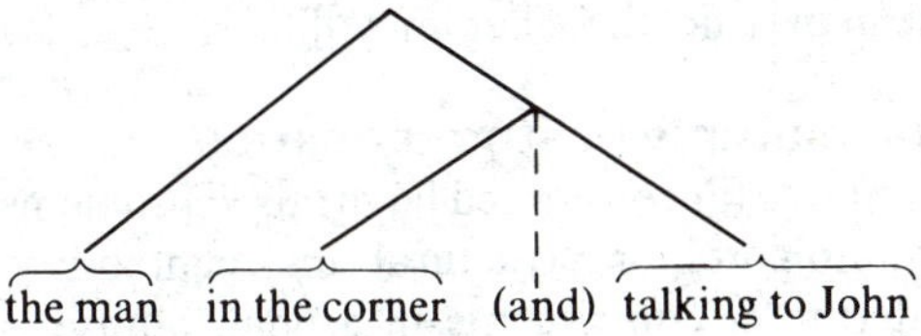

Fig 17.61a

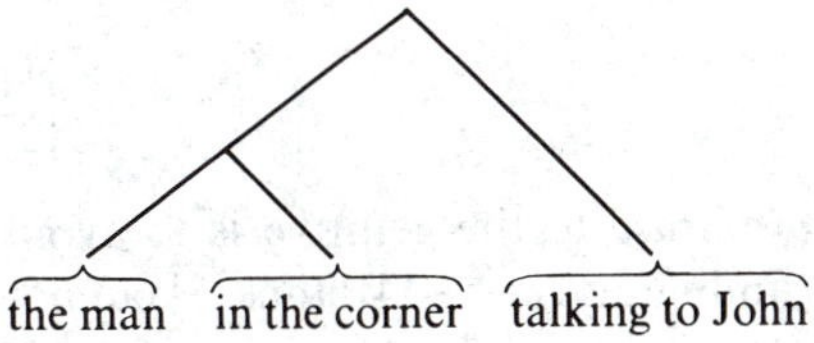

Fig 17.61b

(b) A modification is applicable to more than one head. Thus [4] can be brought together by multiple-head rules which permit the determiner to apply to both heads (*cf* 13.67) as [5]:

the man in the corner *and* the woman in the corner [4]
[the [man and woman] [in [the corner]]] [5]

(c) By bringing together the types of structure elucidated in (a) and (b), we can produce complexes such as [6]:

the man and woman in the corner talking to John [6]

The head of a modifying phrase may itself be further modified. We have already seen numerous examples of where such further modification is achieved by means of an adverb; we are here concerned with catenations like [9] from the linking of [7] and [8]:

the man in the corner [7]
the corner nearest the door [8]
[the man [in [the corner [nearest the door]]]] [9]

By bringing (a), (b), and (c) together, we form [10]:

[the [man and woman] [in [the corner [nearest the door]]] [talking to John]] [10]

Although the last postmodifier in this example (the nonfinite clause *talking to John*) is rather far removed from the head, ambiguity is impossible: the door could not be talking to John. Nevertheless, many users of English would prefer to use a finite relative clause here (. . . *who are talking to John*), no doubt in response to a desire for maximal explicitness at a point which is relatively distant from the head.

Probably more is involved than a need for explicitness: repetition of identical items (*eg* a sequence of prepositional phrases or relative clauses) is perhaps as objectionable in a lengthy postmodification as is the danger of losing the thread. Objections to the following sentence are obvious:

?He was [the man [who wrote the letter [which Mary found in the house [which she rented from the man [who knew her uncle]]]]].

Ambiguity and constraints on multiple postmodification

17.62 The instances of multiple modification so far considered have raised problems of style but hardly of actual ambiguity or structural unacceptability. Frequently, however, careful ordering of constituents in a noun phrase is essential to communicate one's intention. To take an example, the following pair [1] and [2] differ in meaning and are not mere stylistic variants:

the man *in black talking to the girl* [1]
the man *talking to the girl in black* [2]

One of the reasons for preferring the *of*-phrase to the genitive is to avoid discontinuity (with unwanted grotesque ambiguity, *cf* 17.44); thus [3] but not [4]:

the ears of the man in the deckchair [3]
**the man's ears* in the deckchair [4]

Pushdown elements

17.63 A special type of multiple postmodification that requires careful ordering occurs when the modifying clause becomes itself embedded in a clause ('pushdown relative clause'; *cf* 11.18, 15.4 Note [d]). Consider the following series:

John will send you a memo. [1]
Pat hopes (that) John will send you a memo. [2]
I will read the memo (which) Pat hopes (that) John will send you. [3]

In [3], the relative pronoun *which* is object in the relative clause *which . . . John will send you.* When, however, a relative pronoun is subject under analogous conditions, the conjunction *that*, which remained optional in [3], is obligatorily absent in [3a]:

A memo will be sent to you. [1a]
Pat hopes (that) a memo will be sent to you. [2a]

I will read the memo (which) Pat { hopes will / *hopes that will } be sent to you. [3a]

Since verbs in nominal clauses may be nonfinite or absent, variations in structure can be very considerable. Related to [4–6] we have the noun phrases [4a–6a]:

We thought {
(*that*) the boy was honest. [4]
the boy to be honest. ⟨rather rare⟩ [5]
the boy honest. [6]
}

the boy (*that*) we thought {
was honest [4a]
to be honest [5a]
honest [6a]
}

Nonfinite and verbless postmodification is less acceptable when the adjective is 'temporary' (*cf* 17.7):

The boy (*that*) we thought { *was ready* [4b] / ?*to be ready* [5b] / ?*ready* [6b] } is not, after all.

Clause embedding in postmodification can sometimes result in anacoluthon through the insertion of the personal pronoun, especially in speech (*cf* 11.14*ff* on *wh*-questions):

?*I'm going to a party *that* I don't know when *it* will end. [7]
?*The computer *which* you said you would teach me how *it* works has now arrived. [8]
?*There is in this country a trend *which* I don't know how strong *it* is towards a disintegration of the traditional party system. [9]

The relative clauses in [7–9] are deviant since they introduce a double pronominalization of the antecedent (*that* or *which, it*), but avoidance of the deviance involves rather radical reorganization, *eg*:

I'm going to a party { which will end I don't know when. [7a] / and I don't know when it will end. [7b] }

The computer { which you said you would teach me how to use has now arrived. [8a] / the operation of which you said you would teach me has now arrived. [8b] }

There is in this country a trend { which I don't know the strength of . . . [9a] / of which I don't know the strength . . . [9b] / whose strength I don't know . . . [9c] }

Note [**a**] There is no problem, of course, if the clauses concerned are made paratactic:

I'm going to a party; I don't know when it will end. [7c]
The computer has arrived; you said you would teach me how it works. [8c]
There is in this country a trend towards a disintegration of the traditional party system; I don't know how strong it is. [9d]

[**b**] Confusion of the finite with the nonfinite forms of embedded clause produces hypercorrect deviant sentences (*cf* 6.35 Note [a]) like [10]:

*That is the man *whom we thought was not coming*. (*Cf*: That is the man *whom we thought to be difficult*.) [10]

Relative clauses may be complicated more than we have illustrated so far, though one tends to avoid multiple embeddings with successive 'pushdown' clauses:

?I have read *the book which you thought I had asked John whether he would lend me*. [11]

In [12], the use of *whom* may seem odd:

. . . this Lady Macbeth is lumbered with such an alarming husband whom Harold Carter plays . . . on the brink of madness. [12]

The reason may be that the actor actually plays the *part* of the husband. However, the following construction [12a] may have been consciously avoided as being awkward and too heavy (and hardly necessary anyway):

. . . an alarming husband { *whose part* / *which part* } *Harold Carter plays* . . . [12a]

[**c**] There are also signs that relative clauses, by involving transposition of lexical items, weaken the ties between lexical items and their appropriate complement-forming prepositions. Even reputable newspapers will occasionally print sentences like [13]:

The authorities, against whom increasing numbers of refugees are fleeing across the sea, have not changed their policy. [13]

Although the oddity of the construction may well pass unnoticed by journalist and reader alike, neither would have accepted the verb + preposition sequence in [13a]:

*The refugees are fleeing against the authorities. [13a]

17.64 Even with simpler examples and more careful ordering, we may find clarity and acceptable grammar difficult to maintain in multiple modification. An example:

She recalled the smiles of delight on all the faces. [1]

A noun phrase based on sentence [1] and having *smiles* as its head may be ambiguous in one ordering (Was it the smiles or the faces that she recalled?):

the smiles of delight on all the faces that she recalled [1a]

Another ordering [1b] may be grammatically awkward, since it introduces discontinuity (*cf* 17.122) to avoid ambiguity:

?the smiles that she recalled of delight on all the faces [1b]

When we go on from this same sentence to attempt a noun phrase which has *faces* or *delight* as head, the problems increase:

?all the faces that she recalled the smiles of delight on [1c]

One solution to this problem is to replace the relative clause by a construction with preposition + *-ing* participle clause (although the subject then has to be merely implicit):

On recalling the smiles of delight on all the faces (she was reminded of birthday parties in her own childhood). [1d]

Note The objection in [1c] is not merely to the final preposition (*cf* 17.16), as is shown by the awkwardness also of [1e]:

?all the faces on which she recalled the smiles of delight [1e]

Noun phrases with *delight* as head are no less problematic:

?the delight that she recalled the smiles of on all the faces [1f]

*the delight of which she recalled the smiles on all the faces [1g]

*the delight on all the faces that she recalled the smiles of [1h]

*delight on all the faces {of which she recalled the smiles / whose smiles she recalled} [1i]

All these examples, however, involve discontinuous structures, which will be discussed in 17.122 and 18.39.

Apposition

The nature of apposition

17.65 In 17.26 we looked at appositive postmodification by *that*-clauses, in 17.35 at appositive nonfinite clauses, and in 17.47 at appositive prepositional phrases. We now consider the nature of apposition itself. Apposition is primarily, and typically, a relation between noun phrases, and this is the reason for treating apposition in this chapter.

For linguistic units to be APPOSITIVES, *ie* in apposition, they must normally be identical in reference. Thus in [1], *Anna* and *my best friend* are coreferential, and similarly, in [2], *Paul Jones* and *the distinguished art critic* refer to the same person:

Anna, my best friend, was here last night. [1]
Paul Jones, the distinguished art critic, died in his sleep last night. [2]

Alternatively, the reference of one must be included in the reference of the other, *eg* [3], where *a neighbour* is identified as *Fred Brick*:

A neighbour, Fred Brick, is on the telephone. [3]

The relationship denoted by apposition is therefore analogous to a copular relationship (*cf* 2.16):

Paul Jones was *the distinguished art critic*. [2a]
Fred Brick is *a neighbour*. [3a]

Such examples of apposition may be compared with nonrestrictive postmodification, in particular nonrestrictive relative clauses:

Anna, *who is my best friend*, was here last night. [1a]

The noun phrase *my best friend* in [1] may be considered to be a reduction of the relative clause in [1a]. Indeed, some grammarians have included nonrestrictive relative clauses among appositives. Presumably this assignment is motivated

(a) by the frequent possibility of expanding a second appositive into a relative clause;

(b) by the loose attachment of the nonrestrictive relative clause to the sentence; and

(c) by the requirement for coreference between the *wh*-word in the clause and an antecedent noun phrase.

However, in this grammar we make a distinction between a noun phrase with its relative clause and apposition, the latter being primarily a relation between two noun phrases. One reason for this is that, unlike relative clauses where a relative pronoun is an element or constituent in the clause (*cf* 17.10), apposition has no such item. The similarity between nonrestrictive relative clauses and apposition is in fact limited to relative clauses of the *SVC* type that have a noun phrase as complement, as in [1a]. There is no appositional construction [4a] parallel to clauses like [4] (*cf* 17.22):

Here is a letter from John, *who wants a job in London*. [4]
*Here is a letter from John, *a job in London*. [4a]

Thus, apposition differs from relative clauses in that it involves the linking of units of the same rank.

Apposition resembles coordination (*cf* 13.1*ff*) in that not only do coordinate constructions also involve the linking of units of the same rank, but the central coordinators *and* and *or* may themselves occasionally be used as explicit markers of apposition (*cf* 13.22*ff*).

Full and partial apposition

17.66 Grammarians vary in the freedom with which they apply the term 'apposition' even in the quite specific sense adopted here. Some have restricted it more narrowly to cases where the following conditions are met:

(i) Each of the appositives can be separately omitted without affecting the acceptability of the sentence.
(ii) Each fulfils the same syntactic function in the resultant sentences.
(iii) It can be assumed that there is no difference between the original sentence and either of the resultant sentences in extralinguistic reference.

For example, by omitting each appositive in turn from [1] we obtain the two sentences [1a] and [1b]:

A neighbour, Fred Brick, is on the telephone. [1]
A neighbour is on the telephone. [1a]
Fred Brick is on the telephone. [1b]

The apposition in [1] meets the three conditions:

(i) The resultant sentences are acceptable.
(ii) Both noun phrases are subject of their sentence.
(iii) Since *Fred Brick* and *a neighbour* are coreferential in [1], we can assume the reference of the two resultant sentences to be the same.

Apposition meeting these three conditions we term FULL APPOSITION.

On the other hand, we cannot exclude consideration of sequences which resemble such full apposition but nonetheless do not meet these three conditions entirely. If condition (i) alone is unfulfilled, the difference from full apposition is comparatively trivial. For example, from [2] only the second appositive can be omitted, as in [2a]:

An unusual present was given to him for his birthday, *a book on ethics.* [2]
An unusual present was given to him for his birthday. [2a]

Omission of the first appositive results in an unacceptable sentence [2b], unless we reposition it initially [2c]:

*Was given to him for his birthday, *a book on ethics.* [2b]
A book on ethics was given to him for his birthday. [2c]

The type of partial apposition where the position of the appositive is the sole difference might be considered 'discontinuous full apposition'.

Condition (ii) is not met in [3]:

Norman Jones, at one time a law student, wrote several best-sellers. [3]

Norman Jones is subject in [3a], but *at one time a law student* cannot be subject in [3b]:

Norman Jones wrote several best-sellers. [3a]

≁ *At one time a law student* wrote several best-sellers. [3b]

However, the prepositional phrase may precede the subject in adverbial function with the same meaning as [3]:

At one time a law student, Jones/he wrote . . . [3c]

The pair [3] and [3c] illustrate the general feature of grammar that a paraphrase relation often obtains between structures that are viewed as grammatically different.

Finally, condition (iii) is not met in [4]:

The reason he gave, that he didn't notice the car till too late, is unsatisfactory. [4]

We can omit each of the appositives in turn, and each fulfils the function of subject in the resultant sentences:

The reason he gave is unsatisfactory. [4a]

That he didn't notice the car till too late is unsatisfactory. [4b]

However, [4b] is different from both [4] and [4a] since it does not assert that a particular reason is unsatisfactory but that a particular fact is unsatisfactory:

(*The fact*) *that he didn't notice the car till too late* is unsatisfactory.

To designate the structures in [2], [3], and [4], we use the general term PARTIAL APPOSITION.

Note Coreferential relationships where the units fulfil distinctly different syntactic functions are not considered to be appositional, *eg*:

John washed *himself*. [subject + object of pronoun, *cf* 6.23*ff*]

Jane likes *her* own car best. [subject + determiner, *cf* 5.10*ff*]

Susan does whatever *she* wants. [subject + subject of embedded clause, *cf* 14.4*ff*]

Strict and weak apposition

17.67 The appositives may belong to the same general syntactic class (*eg* the central type noun phrase + noun phrase), as in [1]:

Football, his only interest in life, has brought him many friends. [1]

In such a case we term the construction STRICT APPOSITION.

On the other hand, appositives from different syntactic classes are said to be in WEAK APPOSITION (*cf* 17.92), for example, noun phrase + *-ing*-clause in [2]:

His only interest in life, playing football, has brought him many friends. [2]

Nonrestrictive and restrictive apposition

17.68 Apposition may be NONRESTRICTIVE or RESTRICTIVE (*cf* 17.3*ff*). So far, all our examples have shown nonrestrictive apposition. The appositives in nonrestrictive apposition are in separate information units (*cf* 18.3*ff*). This fact is indicated, in speech, by their inclusion in separate tone units (*cf* App II.16*ff*);

in writing, by their separation by commas or heavier punctuation. For example, the apposition is nonrestrictive in [1] but restrictive in [1a]:

Mr Campbell, a lawyer, was here last night. [1]
Mr Campbell the lawyer was here last night. [*ie* Mr Campbell the lawyer as opposed to any other Mr Campbell we know] [1a]

In nonrestrictive apposition, the two appositive units contribute relatively independent information, with the first appositive acting as the DEFINED expression, and the second appositive having a DEFINING role ('the definer'). The defining role is reflected in the fact that the second appositive is marked as parenthetic by punctuation [2] or intonation [2a]:

The President of the company, Mrs Louise Parsons, gave a press conference after the board meeting. [2]
The |PRĚSident of the company| |Mrs Louise PĂRsons| |gave a press conference after the BÒARD meeting| [2a]

In [2] and [2a], *the President of the company* is the defined and *Mrs Louise Parsons* the defining expression. On the other hand, in [2b], the roles are reversed:

Mrs Louise Parsons, the President of the company, gave a press conference after the board meeting. [2b]

In [2b], *Mrs Louise Parsons* is the defined expression, and *the President of the company* the defining expression, the latter constituting a separate information unit.

Note [**a**] The first (*ie* defined) appositive determines concord:

Land, brains, wealth, technology – in other words *everything we need* – {*are* / **is*} plentiful in our country.

Everything we need – *land, brains, wealth, technology* – {*is* / **are*} plentiful in our country.

[**b**] A defining appositive is not the same as a tag exclamation (*cf* 18.59 Note [a]). An aside such as *the utter fool* in [3] is an irregular insertion and can come anywhere in the sentence:

John (*the utter fool*) insisted on staying with them. [3]

Compare an interpolation such as in [3a]:

John (*can you believe it?*) insisted on staying with them. [3a]

The difference between the two constructions is highlighted in the ambiguity of [4]:

Richard (*the villain*) forced his sister into marriage. [4]

In one interpretation, *the villain* is intended as a critical term, 'the bad character in the play', and is appositive to *Richard*; in the other interpretation, it is an evaluative comment synonymous with 'the wicked man', and is an exclamatory aside. The two interpretations can be distinguished intonationally:

Apposition:

|RĬCHard| the |VĬLlain| |forced his sister into MÀRriage| [4a]

Exclamatory aside:

|RÌCHard the VÍLlain| |forced his sister into MÀRriage| [4b]

The aside in [4b], as well as being in the same tone unit as *Richard*, is also marked by a lowering of its pitch relative to that of the rest of the sentence.

[**c**] The most common type of separator used in delimiting a nonrestrictive apposition in writing is the comma; but dashes or parentheses are also used (as they are for other types of parenthetic items, *cf* App III.16*ff*):

Only *one person* {*, Susan Long,* / – *Susan Long* – / (*Susan Long*)} voted against me.

Defined/defining relationships

17.69 When apposition is full apposition (*cf* 17.66), it may not be clear which of the appositives is the defining one:

> *My friend Anna* was here last night. [full + strict] [1]
> *The question whether to confess or not* troubled the girl. [full + weak] [2]

In partial restrictive apposition, on the other hand, one of the appositives is definer of the other. In [3], the definer is *financial expert*:

> Next Saturday, *financial expert Tom Timber* will begin writing a weekly column on the national economy. [partial + strict] [3]

(On the stylistic aspect of this example, *cf* 17.88.) Similarly, in [4], the definer is *that he couldn't see the car*:

> *The explanation that he couldn't see the car* is unsatisfactory. [partial + weak] [4]

The syntactically subordinate role of one of the appositives is clear with partial apposition, since only the definer can be omitted (*cf* 17.66).

Combinations of appositional types

17.70 The three types of distinction we have made apply in combination, as illustrated below:

APPOSITION	*full*	[either omissible]
	partial	[only one omissible]
	strict	[same syntactic class]
	weak	[different syntactic class]
	nonrestrictive	[different information unit]
	restrictive	[same information unit]

(i) FULL, STRICT, NONRESTRICTIVE
Paul Jones, the distinguished art critic, died in his sleep last night.

(ii) FULL, WEAK, NONRESTRICTIVE
Playing football, his only interest in life, has brought him many friends.

(iii) FULL, STRICT, RESTRICTIVE
My friend Anna was here last night.

(iv) FULL, WEAK, RESTRICTIVE
The question whether to confess or not troubled the girl.

(v) PARTIAL, STRICT, NONRESTRICTIVE
An unusual present was given to him for his birthday, *a book on ethics*.

(vi) PARTIAL, WEAK, NONRESTRICTIVE
His explanation, that he couldn't see the car, is unsatisfactory.

(vii) PARTIAL, STRICT, RESTRICTIVE
Next Saturday, *financial expert Tom Timber* will begin writing a weekly column on the national economy. [typical of journalistic style]

(viii) PARTIAL, WEAK, RESTRICTIVE

His claim that he couldn't see the car was unconvincing.

More than two units in apposition

17.71 Though we have found it convenient to exemplify apposition with merely two appositives, there may occasionally be more than two units in apposition at the same level, as in [1]:

They returned to *their birthplace, their place of residence, the country of which they were citizens.* [1]

In [1], there seems to be no reason for combining any two of the noun phrases as one unit in the appositional relationship. On the other hand, we often find cases in which two or more noun phrases function as one appositive:

She had *a splendid vacation*: *a Mediterranean cruise and a trip to the Bahamas.* [2]

In this case, the coordinated noun phrases are together appositional to the general term *a splendid vacation* in relation to which *a Mediterranean cruise* and *a trip to the Bahamas* are the particulars. But the units functioning as a single appositive need not be coordinated by *and*:

We have *everything we need*: *land, brains, wealth,* (and) *technology*. [3]

In [3], the second appositive is an asyndetic series of juxtaposed units which, taken together, are included under the general first appositional unit *everything we need*. There is yet another possibility: a hierarchy of appositional relationships, as indicated here by bracketing:

We now find [*a new type of student*: [*the revolutionary* – [*the radical bent on changing the system and the anarchist bent on destroying it*]]]. [4]

A new type of student is the first appositive, while all that follows it in the sentence constitutes the second appositive. But within the second appositive there is further apposition: *the revolutionary* is the first appositive, while what follows in the sentence is appositive to it.

Ambiguity between apposition and other constructions

17.72 In 17.68 we noted the use of intonation and punctuation separation for the appositive in nonrestrictive apposition. Where the lexical items and syntactic construction allow for potential ambiguity, intonation or punctuation separation may or may not resolve the ambiguity. The pair of noun phrases in [1] is interpreted as indirect object and direct object, respectively, synonymous with [1a]:

They sent *Joan a waitress from the hotel.* [1]
They sent *a waitress from the hotel to Joan.* [1a]

On the other hand, the pair in [2] is interpreted as direct object and object complement, respectively, synonymous with [2a]:

They considered *Miss Hartley a very good teacher.* [2]
They considered *Miss Hartley to be a very good teacher.* [2a]

However, if the second noun phrase in each sentence is separated from what precedes by a tone unit boundary in spoken English or by a comma in written English, then the interpretation is weighted in favour of taking the first noun phrase as direct object with the second noun phrase in apposition to it:

They sent *Joan, a waitress from the hotel.*
['They sent Joan (who was a waitress from the hotel).'] [1b]
They considered *Miss Hartley, a very good teacher.*
['They considered Miss Hartley (who was a very good teacher).'] [2b]

Explicit indicators of apposition

17.73 Numerous expressions are available for explicitly indicating nonrestrictive apposition. They can be inserted between appositives, for example *namely* in [1]:

How can a solution be found to the current disease of contemporary society, *namely* the international economic crisis? [1]

If we add an explicit indicator of apposition such as *namely, that is, ie,* we do not regard this as changing full apposition into partial apposition, even though the presence of the indicator may affect the ability of the construction to meet the conditions for full apposition (*cf* 17.66).

The indicators express certain semantic relationships between the appositives, and therefore cannot be used for all cases of apposition. Some, however, have the same semantic function, though they may be associated with different varieties of the language. Common indicators are listed below, those marking the same, or similar, relationship being grouped together (*cf* 8.137):

that is to say, *that is*, *ie* ⟨formal and written⟩
namely, viz ⟨formal and written⟩
to wit ⟨formal, esp legal⟩
in other words
or, or rather, or better
and
as follows
for example, *for instance*, *eg* ⟨formal and written⟩, *say*, *including*, *included*, *such as*
especially, *particularly*, *in particular*, *notably*, *chiefly*, *mainly*, *mostly*
of

Some of these indicators either precede or (less commonly) follow the second a positive: *that is, that is to say, for example, for instance, in particular, in other words*:

Dickens's most productive period, {*that is* (*to say*) the 1840s, / the 1840s, *that is* (*to say*),} was a time when public demand for fiction was growing at a tremendous rate.

But other indicators can only precede the second appositive: *namely*, *and*, *or*, *or rather*, *or better*, *as follows*, *including*, *such as*, *of*; and the abbreviated forms *ie*, *viz*, *eg*. *Included* can only follow the second appositive (*cf* 9.8):

Many people, { *including* my sister, / my sister *included*, } won't forgive him for that.

The scale of strict nonrestrictive apposition

17.74 In addition to the relationships we have subsumed so far under our definition of apposition, we recognize a semantic scale running from equivalence (*ie* 'most appositive') to loose and unequal relationship ('least appositive'), such as exemplification. These semantic relationships are illustrated in *Fig* 17.74:

'most appositive' ↑
(A) EQUIVALENCE (17.75–80)
(Ai) appellation: *that is* (*to say*) (17.76)
(Aii) identification: *namely* (17.77–78)
(Aiii) designation: *that is to say* (17.79)
(Aiv) reformulation: *in other words* (17.80)
(B) ATTRIBUTION [= nonrestrictive relative clause] (17.81–84)
(C) INCLUSION (17.85–87)
(Ci) exemplification: *for example, say* (17.86)
(Cii) particularization: *especially* (17.87)
'least appositive' ↓

Fig 17.74 A scale of semantic relationships in strict nonrestrictive noun-phrase apposition

Of the three major semantic types (equivalence, attribution, and inclusion), inclusion is the most peripheral to the concept of apposition, in that this construction alone requires an indicator, such as *particularly* in [3]. Compare:

My best friend, (that is to say) *Anna*, was here last night. [1]
The house, (which is) *an imposing building*, dominates the street. [2]
The children liked *the animals*, particularly *the monkeys*. [3]

On the other hand, equivalence is the only type that allows either order of the appositives, as in [1] and [1a]:

Anna, that is to say *my best friend*, . . . [1a]
**An imposing building*, which is *the house*, dominates the street. [2a]
*The children liked *the monkeys*, particularly *the animals*. [3a]

Thus, in terms of these two criteria, the scale from 'most to least appositive' is in the order equivalence → attribution → inclusion.

Appositive-like relations exist also between other units than noun phrases, such as clauses [4], predications [5], and adjectives [6]:

Although she was reluctant, although she felt an understandable hesitation, she eventually agreed. [4]
They had *summoned help – called the police and fire brigade*. [5]
She is *better, very much better*, than she used to be. [6]

However, to talk about apposition of units other than noun phrases makes the concept of apposition too weak. Such apposition-like constructions will be treated as exceptional.

(A) Equivalence

17.75 Appositives in an equivalence relationship allow the insertion of *that is* (*to say*) and, less commonly, of *in other words*. As *Fig* 17.74 shows, there are four types of equivalence relationship: appellation, identification, designation, and reformulation. The types can be partly differentiated by the different optional indicators they admit.

(Ai) Appellation

17.76 With APPELLATION, *ie* a 'naming relation', both appositional noun phrases are definite, and the second is typically a proper noun. The second appositive is more specific than the first, and hence the use of *namely*, an indicator that introduces a more specific appositive. *Or* is less commonly used than the other indicators, *that is* (*to say*) and *in other words*:

The company commander, that is to say *Captain Madison*, assembled his men and announced their mission. [1]
My best friend, in other words *Anna*, was here last night. [2]
My best friend was here last night – *Anna*. [3]

Sentence [3] is an example of partial apposition.

There is a one-to-one correspondence between the references of the two appositives with appellation. The second appositive can be replaced by a corresponding relative clause:

The *company commander, who is Captain Madison*, assembled his men and announced their mission. [1a]

(Aii) Identification

17.77 With IDENTIFICATION, the first appositive is typically an indefinite noun phrase and the second appositive is more specific. Hence the optional relator *namely* may be inserted. If we make the first appositive of [1] in 17.76 indefinite, we now have identification:

A company commander, (namely) *Captain Madison*, assembled his men and announced their mission. [1b]

In [1b] there is no longer a one-to-one correspondence, as there was with [1]. The second appositive identifies what is referred to in the first appositive. A similar relationship obtains if the first appositive is, or contains, a pro-form coreferring to the second appositive:

We – that is to say *John and I* – intend to resign. [2]
She still enjoys *such books*: *science fiction, detective stories, historical novels*. [3]
We have *everything we need*: *land, brains, wealth, technology*. [4]

In partial apposition, the second appositive may be preceded by a colon as a graphological indicator of identification, as in [3], [4], and [5]:

An unusual present was given to him for his birthday: *a book on ethics*. [5]

Note There are other grammatical constructions which are somewhat similar to apposition in meaning. Compare examples [3] and [4] with, respectively, the correlative *such* . . . *as* in [3a] and the complex preposition in [4a]:

She still enjoys *such* books *as* science fiction . . . [3a]
We have everything we need *in the way of* land, brains, . . . [4a]

Postponed and anticipated identification

17.78 As a special subtype of identification, we might consider the phenomenon of 'postponed' and 'anticipated' identification.

Postponed identification involves placing a pro-form earlier in the sentence while the noun phrase to which it refers is placed finally as an amplificatory tag (*cf* 18.59). This construction, which is sometimes termed 'right dislocation', is restricted to informal spoken English, where it is very common:

He's a complete idiot, *that brother of yours*. [1]

Such utterances are usually spoken with divided focus (*cf* 18.17), with a rise on the 'tag' confirming its 'given' status:

It |went on far too LÒNG| |*your GÁME*| [2]

In informal spoken English we also have the reverse process, 'anticipated identification' (also called 'left dislocation'), where a noun phrase is positioned initially and a reinforcing pronoun stands 'proxy' for it in the relevant position in the sentence:

Your friend John, I saw *him* here last night. [3]
That play, *it* was terrible. [4]

Note [**a**] In even more informal style, the operator is sometimes included with postponed identification (*cf* 18.58):

It went on far too long, *your game did*. [2a]

In some dialects, there may be inversion when the verb is *be*:

He's a complete idiot, {*John is.* / *is John.*} [1a]

[**b**] In the following sentences, postponed identification in [5] contrasts in intonation and article usage with apposition in [6], where the definite article may be zero:

He's |had a lot of bad LÙCK| the |new meCHÁNic| [5]
He's |had a lot of bad LÙCK (the) poor man| [6]

(Aiii) Designation

17.79 DESIGNATION is the converse of appellation and identification. The second appositive is less specific than the first, and hence the optional insertions cannot include the indicator *namely*. Both appositives are commonly definite noun phrases:

Captain Madison, (that is to say) *the company commander*, assembled his men and announced their mission. [1]
Anna, (that is to say) *my best friend*, was here last night. [2]
Land, brains, wealth, technology – in other words *everything we need* – are plentiful in our country. [3]
He sent ahead *the sergeant*, in other words *the most experienced scout in the company*. [4]

Replacement of the second appositive by a corresponding relative clause is possible:

He sent ahead *the sergeant, who was the most experienced scout in the company*. [4a]

Designation may also include matching indefinite noun phrases:

We are using *Sirius* – *a new microcomputer with a large memory*. [5]

Examples of partial apposition:

Anna was here last night, *my best friend*. [2a]
Have *some Harveys* with your Christmas – *the most distinguished sherries you can buy*. [6]

(Aiv) Reformulation

17.80 REFORMULATION is a rewording in the second (defining) appositive of the lexical content of the first (defined) appositive. Four groups of reformulation may be distinguished:

(a) Reformulation based on linguistic knowledge
(b) Reformulation based on factual knowledge
(c) More precise formulation
(d) Revision

(a) Reformulation based on linguistic knowledge
In reformulation based on linguistic knowledge, the defining appositive is a synonymous expression:

This is what is sometimes referred to as *an intentional terminological inexactitude*, in other words *a lie*. [1]
Sound units of the language, technically *phonemes*, are usually surrounded by slant lines: /p/. [2]
You should have consulted *an ophthalmologist*, that is (to say) *an eye doctor*. [3]

A synonymous word or phrase may replace the first formulation in order to avoid misinterpretation or provide a more familiar or a more technical term. In addition to the markers it shares with other types of reformulation (in particular *or*), this type admits a large range of expressions that specifically mark linguistic reformulation (*cf* 8.89, 8.137), *eg*:

(*more*) *simply*	*in more difficult language*
in simple(*r*) *words*	*in scientific terminology*
in simple(*r*) *terms*	*in more technical terms*
put (*more*) *simply*	*technically* (*speaking*)
to put it (*more*) *simply*	*in words of one syllable*

Partial apposition involving linguistic reformulation includes translations from foreign languages: "*savoir* ('know' in English)".

(b) Reformulation based on factual knowledge
In this group, the reformulation is based less on linguistic knowledge than on knowledge about the external world:

Fred – or *Ginger* as he is usually called – . . . [4]
The Nordic countries, or *Denmark, Finland, Iceland, Norway, Sweden*, . . . [5]
The United States of America, or *America* for short, . . . [6]

The distinction between linguistic and factual knowledge is not absolute as, for example, in:

Alligator pears, or *avocados* as they are usually called, . . . [7]

It can be argued that it is our knowledge of the external world that is responsible for our awareness of the greater frequency of the synonymous *avocados* in [7].

Reformulation can also be negative, *ie* the modifying appositive is not a synonymous expression:

You should have consulted *an ophthalmologist, not* (that is) *an optician*, for your eyes. [3a]

Without context, such a sentence as the following is potentially ambiguous in writing:

Anna Wilson, not my best friend, voted against me. [8]

It either has a negative appositive meaning, 'Anna Wilson, who happens not to be my best friend, . . .' or a denial sense (*cf* 10.66): 'It was Anna Wilson who voted against me, not the other person'.

(c) More precise formulation
This type conveys a more precise reformulation, or a correction in the defining appositive of what was said in the first appositive:

They started going to *the church, the Catholic Church*. [9]

But the intention may be rhetorical (as indeed in [9]) to provide a climactic effect by repetition and expansion of the first noun phrase:

You could cut the atmosphere with *a knife, a blunt knife* at that. [10]

At that attached to the end of the modifying appositive in [10] is an explicit marker of rhetorical intention. When it is present, *and* can be inserted (*cf* appended coordination, 13.94; coordinative apposition, 10.39):

You could cut the atmosphere with *a knife*, and *a blunt knife* at that. [10a]

Perhaps under this type of reformulation we should include other instances of more precise formulation, some of which do not involve repetition but which have a constraining and antithetical force:

this and *just this*	*these* and *these alone*
the women and *only the women*	*those* and *no others*
then and *not before*	

(d) Revision
Under this heading we may include the form of 'editing' or 'self-correction' that is typical of impromptu spoken English where execution and planning, at least to some extent, take place simultaneously. Such editing is of course not limited to noun phrases. We may distinguish some different types:

'Reference editing' by the use of *that is* (*to say*) as in:

His party controls *London, Greater London* that is to say. [11]

This type is very similar to the previous one in [9], in providing more precise information. It is used when the speaker wants to achieve greater accuracy and precision.

'Nuance editing' by the use of *or rather* before a substituted expression, as in:

She puts such *vitality* (or rather *virility*) into her play. [12]

'Mistake editing' by the use of *I mean* in order to correct a phonological or semantic mistake (which is common enough in impromptu speech), *eg*:

The thirst thing, I mean *the first thing* to remember is that . . . [13]
Then you add *the peaches* – I mean, *the apricots* . . . [14]

'Claim editing' by the use of *well* when a speaker wants to modify a claim he finds excessive, *eg*:

All families, well (at least) *those who can afford to*, will be going away for their holiday. [15]

(B) Attribution

17.81 Attribution involves predication rather than equivalence, and the equivalence indicators *that is* (*to say*) and *in other words* are not admitted. On the other hand, we can replace the defining appositive by a corresponding nonrestrictive relative clause. The defining appositive is commonly an indefinite noun phrase:

Captain Madison, a company commander, assembled his men and announced their mission.
The house, an imposing building, dominates the street.
Ron Pall, a blatant liar, claimed that he had won first prize.

But the defining appositive can also be definite, with cataphoric *the* introducing a definite description (*cf* 5.32):

He introduced me to *the young woman, the heir to a fortune*.
Many students, the cream of the school, died in the war.
'I don't know what I would have done if I had seen him', exclaimed *Mary, the prey of violent and obscure emotions*.

Defining appositive with article omitted

17.82 In a type of partial apposition expressing attribution (particularly a unique role), an article (definite or indefinite) is absent from the defining appositive (*cf* 5.42):

Mary Cordwell, 25-year-old singer on television shows, is being invited to the reception. [1]

The omission of the article is optional in the defining appositive which may be seen as a reduced relative clause:

Robinson, (who is) (*the*) *leader of the Democratic group on the committee*, refused to answer questions. [2]

Note [**a**] The omission of the article is one of the devices used in headlines, where a sentence such as [2a] would not be unusual:

Democratic leader refuses to answer questions. [2a]

[b] If the defining appositive is short enough, it can be preposed in restrictive apposition (*cf* 17.68, 17.88):

Democratic leader Robinson refused to answer questions. [2b]
25-year-old television singer Mary Cordwell is being invited to the reception. [1a]

This usage is generally associated with the journalistic style of magazines, especially in AmE. It is to be distinguished from cases where the first element is an official title, *eg*: *Vice-President Durney*, though, here too, their use is commoner in AmE than BrE; thus *Secretary of State Smith* (but hardly *Foreign Secretary Brown*).

The relation of apposition to verbless adverbial clause

17.83 An adverbial (*then*, *obviously*, *also*, *normally*, etc) that is an element in a verbless clause may occur with the defining appositive:

Norman Jones, *then a student*, wrote several best-sellers.
Your brother, *obviously an expert on English grammar*, is highly praised in the book I'm reading.
They elected as chairman Edna Jones, *also a Cambridge graduate*.
Jones and Peters, *both of unknown address*, were charged with the murder of Williamson.
At the entrance there are two pillars, *one on each side*.

A somewhat different construction is where the defining appositive is a verbless clause comprising the structure subject + complement:

The two men, *one a Norwegian and the other a Dane*, were awarded medals. [1]

In each case, the participle *being* can be inserted between the two internal constituents of the defining appositive:

The two men, *one* (*being*) *a Norwegian and the other* (*being*) *a Dane* . . . [1a]

They can also be seen as reduced relative clauses:

The two men, *one* (*of whom was*) *a Norwegian and the other* (*of whom was*) *a Dane*, . . . [1b]

Defining appositive with adverbial

17.84 An attribution appositive is to be distinguished from a verbless adverbial clause. Verbless adverbial clauses (*cf* 14.9) often occur initially and are characteristically interpreted as concessive or causal:

An even-tempered man, Paul nevertheless became extremely angry when he heard what had happened. [1]
The heir to a fortune, her friend did not care about passing examinations. [2]

The verbless clause in [1] is interpreted as concessive: 'Though he was an even-tempered man'. (Notice that *nevertheless* refers back to the content of the initial clause: 'in spite of his being an even-tempered man'.) The verbless clause in [2], on the other hand, is interpreted as causal: 'Since she was the heir to a fortune'. These constructions differ from identification apposition (*cf* 17.77) in that, when they occur initially, the second noun phrase is the subject of the sentence, and is not marked off from the predicate by intonation or punctuation separation.

However, the verbless adverbial clause can occur after the subject and is then, like apposition, marked off by intonation or punctuation:

Her friend, the heir to a fortune, did not care about passing examinations. [2a]
Bob Rand, a notorious burglar, found it easy to force open the lock. [3]

In such cases, the lexical content of the sentence suggests the more probable interpretation. For example in [4], *a blatant liar* can be interpreted as a (verbless) adverbial causal clause, since it is reasonable to ascribe the expulsion to Pall's being a blatant liar:

Ron Pall, a blatant liar, was expelled from the group. [4]

In [4a], on the other hand, *a blatant liar* would normally be understood as a case of apposition:

Ron Pall, a blatant liar, used to be in my class at school. [4a]

In [4a], there is no motivation for assuming that Pall's presence in the class had anything to do with his being a blatant liar. If, however, the order of the appositives were reversed [4b], one would assume that there is such a causal or explanatory intention:

A blatant liar, Ron Pall, used to be in my class at school. [4b]

(C) Inclusion

17.85 Inclusion applies to cases of apposition where the reference of the first (defined) appositive is not identical with that of the second (defining), but rather includes it. The inclusion relationship applies only to partial apposition since the omission of the first appositive brings about a radical semantic change.

There are two types of inclusion: (i) exemplification, and (ii) particularization. Exemplification need not be indicated by explicit relators, while particularization must have them (*cf* 8.116).

(Ci) Exemplification

17.86 In EXEMPLIFICATION, the second appositive exemplifies the reference of the more general term in the first appositive:

They visited *several cities*, for example *Rome and Athens*.
His excuses, such as *the breakdown of his car*, never seemed plausible.
Many people, including *my sister*, won't forgive him for that.

The explicit indicators of exemplification apposition are those in the group headed by *for example* in 17.73.

Sometimes there may be ambiguity between exemplification and identification (*cf* 17.77) if no indicator is present:

Famous men – Henry James, Gandhi, Saul Bellow – have visited this university.

Presumably the men referred to in the second appositive are not the only famous men to visit the university, but are mentioned as examples of such visitors (*ie* the list of names is open-ended, and is usually marked as such in speech by rising intonation; *cf* asyndetic coordination, 13.1). On the other hand, it is not impossible for the relationship to be interpreted as one of identification (*ie* the list is closed, which is indicated by falling tone). If one of the indicators for identification – *namely, that is* (*to say*), *in other words*, all of which are optional – is inserted, the apposition must be an instance of identification; if the indicators *for example*, *for instance*, *eg*, *say*, or *including* are inserted (which is the norm), then we have an unambiguous case of exemplification.

Note We should perhaps include here instances like the following, where a numeral or quantifier in the second appositive indicates the inclusion:

The two men, one a Dane, were awarded medals.
The soldiers, some drunk, started fighting each other.
Several sailors, one looking like someone I know, stepped up to the bar.

(Cii) Particularization

17.87 PARTICULARIZATION is the marked form of inclusion and requires an explicit indicator which shows that the particularization has been chosen because it is in some way prominent:

The book contains *some fascinating passages*, notably *an account of their trip to North Africa*.
The children liked *the animals*, particularly *the monkeys*.
We want to invite *a number of friends*, especially *Joan and Betty*.

Other indicators of particularization are *in particular*, *chiefly*, *mainly*, and *mostly*.

Strict restrictive apposition

17.88 There are three types of strict restrictive apposition of noun phrases.

In type (a), the first appositive is preceded by a definite determiner (and possibly premodifier) and is more general than the second appositive:

that famous critic Paul Jones	the number three
the soprano Janet Baker	the year 2000
the novel 'Great Expectations'	your brother George

The type *friend Anna* usually implies criticism:

Our friend Anna here doesn't think so, however.

Type (b) is the reverse of (a), *ie* the second appositive is preceded by the determiner *the*, and is more general than the first:

Paul Jones the critic	Thompson the plumber
Janet Baker the soprano	Wright the lawyer

Type (c) is like (a) but with omission of the determiner (*cf* 17.76, 17.82 Note [b]); the examples in the right-hand column are especially AmE:

Brother George	Soprano Janet Baker ⟨esp AmE⟩
Farmer Brown	Lawyer Wright ⟨esp AmE⟩

Type (a) is the most common. Type (c), with omission of the determiner, produces partial apposition, with the first appositive becoming premodifier and resembling a title (*Lord Nelson, Mrs Johnson*, etc; *cf* 5.66). Generally, such reduction of the first appositive occurs only when the second is the name of a person. Hence we do not find **novel* '*Great Expectations*' or **year 2000*.

Pronouns followed by noun phrases, such as *you girls* (*cf* 10.53), *you British* (*cf* 7.25 Note [c]), and *we men*, can also be analysed as restrictive apposition.

Note Determiners are regularly omitted in proper noun use, as is observed not only in personal and geographical names, but also in, *eg*:

Operation Abolition, Hurricane Edna, Mission Impossible

Postposed numerals and letters perhaps imply the ellipsis of the words *number* or *letter*:

line (number) 12	room (number) 10A
equation (number) 4	Ward (letter) C

If that is so, the phrases contain appositional constructions, with the number or letter being in apposition to the ellipted word *number* or *letter*, *eg*: *number 10A* ~ *The number is 10A*. We also find premodifying numbers and letters, particularly on signs like *No 2 Platform, G Block*. The following constructions are fully acceptable in onomastic use:

Number 3, No 3, ⟨esp AmE⟩ # 3

Ch(apter) 6, Class 2b, Fig(ure) B, Section 10, Table 8, Type A

There is no type (a) with a definite determiner possible in the following use:

Are you in { *Number 103*? [NOT: *the number 103]
Room 103? [NOT: *the room 103] }

Geographical names

17.89 Geographical names (*cf* 5.68) merit separate treatment because the proper noun is often preceded or followed by a descriptor (*cf* 5.60) which has an appositive function. Certain names of individual mountains and lakes take *Mount* and *Lake*, respectively, as a title, *ie* type (c) (*cf* 17.88):

Mount Everest	Lake Michigan
Mount Vesuvius	Lake Windermere

We do not prefix them with a determiner. Most other geographical names take a determiner, the general term being preceded by the proper noun as premodifier:

the Atlantic Ocean	the Rocky Mountains
the Mediterranean Sea	the Nile Valley

Some rivers allow either strict apposition type (a) or premodification (*cf* 5.72):

the (River) Rhine/Thames/Seine/Rhône/Nile

New-world rivers have the proper noun before the descriptor:

the { Ohio
Mississippi
Potomac } (River)

In names of some districts and a few cities and villages, there is no article and the descriptor comes second. These examples of the 'name first' construction are especially common and in North America have a restrictive implication, *ie*: *New York City* is distinguished from, for example, *New York State*:

New York City	Milwaukee County
Quebec Province	Dulwich Village

In a name like *Kansas City*, *City* is in fact part of the name and can hardly be omitted. In other cases both orders are possible: *County Cork* or *Cork County* (and other Irish counties).

Instead of type (a) of strict restrictive apposition, the two appositives are more commonly linked by *of*, in which case there is no implication of restrictiveness, for the names of months and for the names of villages, cities, districts, counties, and regions:

the Borough of Camden	the State of Guatemala
the City of Westminster	the Island of Cyprus
the State of Washington	the Continent of Australia

In some cases we have a choice between the forms exemplified in *Washington State* (as distinct from *Washington, D.C.*) and *the State of Washington*. But, in many cases, the former option is not available:

the City of London [*not* *London City]
the District of Columbia [*not*: *Columbia District]
the month of December [*not*: *December month]
the Continent of Africa *or* the African Continent [*not*: *Africa Continent]
the Republic of France *or* the French Republic [*not*: *France Republic]

Note Books of the Bible normally have the *of*-construction:

the book of Genesis   the book of Job

For other uses of the appositive indicator *of*, *cf* 17.47*ff*.

Citations

17.90 An important use of type (a) of restrictive apposition (*cf* 17.68) is found with citations and titles of books, films, etc:

the term 'heavy water'
the expression 'do your own thing'

The first appositive is often absent:

(The word) *if* is a conjunction.
(The noun) *men* is an irregular plural in English.
I'm reading (the novel) *Crime and Punishment*.
(The verb) *hiss* expresses by its very sound the meaning it conveys.
The book and the papers is a coordinated noun phrase.

We may assume a weak form of ellipsis (*cf* 12.38) in such cases, an ellipsis of some general phrase such as *the expression* or *the citation form*, or of an appropriate term in the case of titles, such as *the book*, *the film*, *the play*. Notice the singular number concord with *men* and *the book and the papers* (*cf* 10.34 Note [c]), which can be explained if we assume the ellipsis of a singular first appositive.

Appositives with names of persons

17.91 With names, type (b) of restrictive apposition (*cf* 17.88) is restricted to cases where the first appositive is the name of a person and the second is the designation of an occupation, relationship, etc: *Bill Johnston the architect*.

In type (c) of restrictive apposition, the first appositive is used as if it were a title in *Architect Johnston* ⟨esp journalistic AmE⟩. This use should be compared with institutionalized titles (*cf* 5.66):

President Kennedy	Judge Harris ⟨esp AmE⟩
Dr Smith	Vice-president Johnson ⟨esp AmE⟩

With appositives, a preposed determiner is normal (type a), along with type (c):

the critic Paul Jones   the architect Bill Johnston

But a determiner is not used with titles like *queen* and *professor* unless the noun phrases are modified:

(the present) Queen Elizabeth
(the sprightly) Professor Brown
(the) Mr Porter (who lives next door to you)

With appositives, postposition with *the* (type b), as in *Paul Jones the critic*, is more common than pre-position without *the* (type c), as in *critic Paul Jones* (*cf* 17.88).

Brown the farmer is perhaps on the borderline in this respect. Since we have *my brother George*, and hence *George my brother*, *the* in **George the brother* and analogous constructions with family relationships are ruled out, unless *the* is cataphoric: *George, the brother of James*.

Pre-position is normal for titles, and those phrases that are nearest to being exclusively titles do not allow postposition at all: *Sir John Cartwright*, *Mr Porter*.

We can now show the gradience from apposition in *critic Paul Jones* to full title in *Mr Porter* with the following examples:

(1)	(2)	(3)
critic Paul Jones ⟨esp journalistic AmE⟩	Farmer Brown	Brother George
	the farmer Brown	my brother George
the critic Paul Jones	Brown the farmer	?the brother George
Paul Jones the critic	the farmer	*George the brother
the critic	*farmer [vocative]	the brother
*critic [vocative]		brother [vocative]

(4)	(5)	(6)
Professor Brown	Dr Smith [nonmedical]	Mr Porter
*the professor Brown	*the doctor Smith	*the Mr Porter
?Brown the professor	*Smith the doctor	*Porter the mister
the professor	*the doctor	*the mister
Professor [vocative]	Doctor [vocative]	mister [vocative; in nonstandard usage]

Note [**a**] Most appositive descriptors and titles can be used with a determiner and without the proper noun:

the farmer, the judge, the President, the doctor [when used for a medical practitioner]

But *sir* and *mister* are not used in this way: **the sir*. *The mister* occurs as nonstandard use = 'my husband'; *cf the missus* ['my (or your) wife']. *The Lord* (with a capital *L*) refers to God. On the use of initial capital letter for appositive titles, *cf* App III.29.

[**b**] Most titles can be used as vocatives (*cf* 10.52*f*) and so can some appositives such as *Farmer* and *Brother*. The title *Miss* is used in the vocative ⟨esp AmE and familiar or nonstandard BrE⟩, but otherwise is generally followed by a name. The accompanying name must be the last name (*eg*: *Miss Jones* and not *Miss Alice*), except in archaic or minority use ⟨especially southern AmE and old-fashioned BrE⟩.

On the other hand, *sir* when used as a title is followed by the first or full name: *Sir John* (*Spencer*) and not **Sir Spencer* (*cf* 5.66 Note [b]). The vocative *sir* (*This way, sir!*) is not an abbreviated form of the title found in *Sir John* but the general polite vocative for address to all adult males. The vocative *mister* occurs only in nonstandard use: *You come here, mister.*

The appositive *Esq* ['Esquire'] is used in BrE, but virtually only in writing (chiefly in addressing letters), and is postposed to a name consisting of a family name with either a first name or initials:

John Porter, Esq *or* J. Porter, Esq

This is a more formal alternative to:

Mr John Porter *or* Mr J. Porter *or* Mr Porter

Mr and *Esq* are not combined: **Mr J. Porter, Esq*. *Esq* cannot occur with surname alone (**Smith, Esq*) nor can it cooccur with other titles (**Sir Sidney Marx, Esq*).

[**c**] In certain titles, the proper noun is followed by an article and adjective (*cf* 5.64 Note [b]): *Catherine* (*the Great*); or numeral: *Henry VIII* ['the eighth']. In such designations there is occasionally a reordering with the modification preposed:

Pitt the Younger *or* the Younger Pitt

Weak apposition

17.92 In weak apposition, the appositives come from different syntactic classes (*cf* 17.67). The optional indicator *namely* may be used if the second appositive is more specific, which is the case when the second appositive is a clause (finite or nonfinite). Normally the noun phrase comes first, as in these instances of full apposition:

She has *a problem*: namely *should she charge them for the damage or should she forget about it*?

Their solution, namely *to appoint a committee*, is deplorable.

But the clause, particularly if it is a nonfinite clause, can come first:

For them to pay him a commission – *his own suggestion* – seemed an acceptable idea.

However, it would be more natural to have a relative clause: 'a commission, which was his suggestion . . .'. The second appositive, whether a noun phrase or a clause, can indeed be regarded as a reduced relative clause:

She enjoyed { *her job*, (which was) *teaching English*.
{ *teaching English*, (which was) *her job*.

Again, when the first appositive is a nonfinite clause, the relative clause construction would be preferable: '. . . teaching English, which was her job'.

In partial weak apposition between noun phrase and clause, the noun phrase appears first:

His explanation, that is to say *that he couldn't see the car*, is unsatisfactory.

He gave them *the news*: namely *that the troops would be leaving*.

The first appositive cannot be omitted without producing an unacceptable sentence (*cf* 17.66). *That is* (*to say*) and *namely* are the (optional) indicators for this type of apposition. The clause can be regarded as a reduced relative clause.

The first appositive may be part of the clause:

If the government had known what was going to happen, *it* would not *have increased credit facilities – a move that accelerated inflation.*

Apposition with general nouns

17.93 Restrictive apposition is common with such general nouns as *the fact*, *the view*, *the question*, *your duty*:

The fact that she wouldn't betray her friends is very much to her credit. [1]
I don't agree with *the view that there is no advantage in being patient*. [2]
The question whether to confess or not troubled her. [3]
Your duty to report the accident takes precedence over everything else. [4]

Finite appositive clauses like [1–2] are further discussed in 17.26*f*, infinitive clauses like [3–4] in 17.35.

With participle clauses, and sometimes with *wh*-clauses, *of* is used as an indicator (*cf* 17.47):

The thought of playing against them arouses all my aggressive instincts.
He didn't accept *the idea of working while he was studying*.
Her account of what she had done that year did not satisfy her colleagues.

Premodification

Types of premodifying item

17.94 In addition to determinatives that cooccur with the head of a noun phrase (*cf* 5.10*ff*), lexical and grammatical items of a wide range and indefinite complexity and interrelationship can precede a noun head to form a noun phrase whose modification is generally less explicit than that of postmodification (*cf* 17.8). A relationship has already been inferred between the predicative adjective (*The girl is tall*) and premodification (*the tall girl*), and in 17.3*ff* it was shown that such premodification can be restrictive or nonrestrictive.

The major types of premodifying items are the following (the head indicated by angle brackets):

(a) ADJECTIVE (17.96–97):

We also met her *delightful* ⟨family⟩. ['Her family is delightful.']

(b) PARTICIPLE (17.98–103):

They never found the *missing* ⟨report⟩. ['The report was missing.']
Have you reported the *stolen* ⟨car⟩? ['The car has been stolen.']

(c) NOUN (17.104–109):

I hate *city* ⟨traffic⟩. ['traffic in the city']

In addition, there are some minor, *ie* less frequent and less productive, types of premodification:

(d) GENITIVE (17.110):

I visited his *fisherman's* ⟨cottage⟩. ['The cottage belongs to a fisherman' or 'belonged to a fisherman' or 'resembles the cottage of a fisherman.']

(e) ADVERB AND OTHER PHRASES (17.111):

We have *round-the-clock* ⟨service⟩. ['The service is round the clock, *ie* all day and night.']

(f) SENTENCE (17.112):

She has asked *I don't know how many* ⟨people⟩ to the party. ['I don't know how many people she has asked to the party.']

Restrictive and nonrestrictive premodification

17.95 Before looking in more detail at the major types of premodification, there are two generalizations to be made about the restrictive/nonrestrictive and temporary/permanent distinctions.

Although there are few formal cues as to whether a premodification is restrictive or not, it may be noted that, by their improvised nature itself, types (e) and (f) tend to be restrictive and to be given more prosodic prominence (*cf* App II.2*ff*) than the head of the noun phrase. Now, it is a general rule that, where there is no postmodification, it is the head of a noun phrase that is given prosodic prominence. Although restrictive premodifiers need not affect this rule, it is interesting to note that where prominence is given to a premodifier (as it normally is to a postmodifier), the item concerned must be restrictive. Compare [1] and [2]:

my ugly NÒSE [1]
*my ÙGly nose [2]

The noun phrase [1] is not nonsensical, but [2] normally is, unless in the special context of, for example, drawing attention to someone else's unkind allusion. In this connection it should be noted that, although proper names do not normally need restrictive modification (*cf* 17.3*ff*), they can have it when a distinction is being made between entities bearing the same name:

Do you mean *the KenTÚCKy Richmond or the VirGÌNia* { *Richmond*? / *one*? }

Typically, nouns and adjectives are stative, and verbs are dynamic (*cf* 2.43).

It follows that, as modifiers, most adjectives and nouns describe permanent characteristics while most participles describe temporary ones. Since, as we saw in 17.7, prehead position in the noun phrase is strongly associated with relatively permanent characteristics, it further follows that premodification by participles is frequently subject to constraint but that premodification by adjectives and nouns is rarely so.

Premodification by adjectives

17.96 A premodifying adjective (or, more strictly, a premodifying adjective phrase; *cf* 7.20), especially when it is the first item after the determinative, can itself be premodified, as in [1], in the same way as it can in predicative position, as in [1a]:

Her family is [*really* [*quite* [*unbelievably*]]] ⟨delightful⟩. [1]
her [*really* [*quite* [*unbelievably*]]] ⟨delightful⟩ family [1a]

Some intensifiers tend however to be avoided with premodifying adjectives. Thus the predicative phrase in [2] would seem a little gushy in premodification [2a]:

her daughter who is *so beautiful* [2]
her *so beautiful* daughter [2a]

With indefinite determiners, including zero, *so* would be replaced by *such*. Thus, in place of *so* in postmodification, as in [3] and [4], we can have *such* in premodification [3a] and [4a]:

{ a daughter who is *so beautiful* [3]
{ BUT: *such a beautiful* daughter [3a]

{ daughters who are *so beautiful* [4]
{ BUT: *such beautiful* daughters [4a]

However, in rather formal contexts, *so* plus adjective can be placed before the indefinite article [3b]:

so beautiful a daughter [3b]

There is resistance also to transferring clause negation to a structure of premodification, which is possible only in limited circumstances (usually *not* plus intensifier or negative affix); thus [5] and [6] allow the formation of [5a] and [6a]:

His behaviour was *not* { *very courteous*. [5]
{ *unpleasant*. [6]

~ his *not* { *very courteous* behaviour [5a]
{ *unpleasant* behaviour [6a]

This gives a slight impression of improvisation (note that replacing *his* by *the* in [5a] and [6a] makes the noun phrase slightly less acceptable). Thus many might prefer to reformulate by lexicalization (*cf* App I.8*ff*), *ie* replacing the free, analytic negation *not* by an affixal negation (*cf* App I.21), as in [5b], or by selecting a positive instead of two negatives [6b]:

his *rather discourteous* behaviour [5b]
his *quite pleasant* behaviour [6b]

However, we have now changed the meaning in the direction of making the behaviour less courteous and more pleasant, respectively.

Nonpredicative adjectives

17.97 There are a few peripheral adjectives that cannot be used in premodification, and, conversely, some that cannot be predicative. Both types are discussed in 7.20*ff*, and here we will only give some further illustrations of adjectives which are restricted to attributive position.

First, consider the small group (*cf* 7.33 *ff*) exemplified as follows:

the *mere* mention BUT NOT: *The mention is *mere*.
the *only* trouble BUT NOT: *The trouble is *only*.

These adjectives behave irregularly also in not allowing intensification by *very*, though some will allow superlative use:

The *merest* word was enough to upset him.

Most of them are clearly related to adverb intensifiers:

The mention was *merely* of . . .
It was *utterly* disgraceful.

Some items in this class, however, have homonyms that are central adjectives (*cf* 7.3). Compare:

This is *pure* nonsense. [peripheral adjective]
The air is (very) *pure*. [central adjective]

Secondly, there is a group posing a special problem in that they are related to nouns (*cf* 7.12*ff*). While adjectives normally refer to quality or to resemblance with substance, some refer to the possessing of substance (*cf* 7.37). Thus *poetic* can mean 'having the qualities of poetry' or 'consisting of poetry'; in the latter sense, it cannot be predicative or be intensified or graded:

this very *poetic* image ~ This image is very poetic.

his *poetic* output { ~ his output of *poetry*
≁ *His output is (very) *poetic*.

Another example:

her rather *nasal* pronunciation ~ Her pronunciation is rather *nasal*.

the *nasal* cavity { ~ the cavity *of the nose*
≁ *The cavity is (rather) *nasal*.

Predicative usage with *nasal*, *oral*, *poetic*, etc is however possible in specialized contexts:

His output is exclusively *poetic*. ['consists . . . of poetry']

Other conditions of nonpredicability (at any rate, without introducing some difference of connotation) are to be seen in formulaic expressions, *eg*:

'*grateful* thanks' [but not: *'His thanks are *grateful*'; *cf* 8.90*f* on courtesy subjuncts]. Similarly: *humble* (*apologies*), *kind* (*regards*).

We should also mention items which fall both outside the closed-class postdeterminers discussed in 5.20*ff* and also outside the class of adjectives as normally understood. Numerals, for example, cannot be freely predicated: beside *the twenty men*, the predicative *The men are twenty* would normally mean that they were *aged* twenty. (However, 'How many are you?' – 'We are three', 'We are five', etc is a possible, if unusual, sequence for the normal 'There are three of us.') Again, absolute comparatives (*cf* 7.85) like *latter* (*the latter question*) and *upper* (*the upper storeys*) must be in premodification position.

Predication of the adjective is blocked when the noun head is agential and the adjective refers to the activity (*cf* 7.36; 'noninherent adjectives', 7.43):

He works *hard*. { ~ He is a *hard* worker. / ≁ The worker is *hard*. }

Where the noun can only refer to activity, there is of course no difficulty:

his *good* writing ~ His writing is *good*.

Compare also *an old friend*: 'He has been a friend for a long time' cannot be turned into *that friend of mine is old*, which only refers to the friend's age.

Note Special contexts create their own usage where the general rules of the language may be waived. Someone addicted to the game of bridge, for example, may well say: 'Good, now we are four, so let's start' without running the risk of being understood as referring to age.

Premodification by *-ing* participles

17.98 The possibility of modification by a present participle depends on the potentiality of the participle to indicate a permanent or characteristic feature. To a lesser extent, gradability (especially as indicated through intensification by *very*) is involved. Sentence [1] shows *interesting* as fully adjectival (*cf* 7.2, 7.15*ff*), despite the direct relation to the verb *interest* [2]:

She has a very *interesting* mind. [1]
Her mind *interests* me very much. [2]

But an item can be a premodifier and yet disallow *very*:

a *roaring* bull [BUT NOT: *very roaring]

And the converse can be true, *viz* a participle will have limited acceptability unless accompanied by an intensifier such as *very*:

He was a very { *reassuring* / *shocked* / *surprised* } person.

?He was a { *reassuring* / *shocked* / *surprised* } person.

This last example will illustrate the crucial significance of the 'permanence' characteristic; such participles can freely premodify nouns such as *look* and *smile*:

He greeted me with a very {*reassuring* / *shocked* / *surprised*} expression.

The man himself cannot have shock or surprise attributed permanently to him (though *cf*: *shell-shocked*), but a particular look can of course be permanently associated with such a value. So too we may speak of *a smiling face* more often than of *a smiling person*. It is thus necessary to realize that we are not here concerned with particular participles so much as with their contextual meaning. *A wandering minstrel* is one habitually given to wandering, but if we saw a man wandering down the street, we could not say [3] but only [4]:

*Who is the *wandering* man? [3]
Who is the man *wandering* down the street? [4]

Again, someone who told good stories could be *a (very) entertaining person* but one would not say this of someone who happened at the moment of speaking to be entertaining his friends with a good story.

Note The tendency towards permanence in the interpretation of premodifying participles is also seen in the nonprogressive interpretation of the participle in *eg*: *a working man*, *ie* 'one who does especially manual work', or 'one who works, especially manually'.

17.99 The indefinite article favours the habitual or permanent, the definite article the specific or temporary (*cf* 5.26). Thus some people find [1] strange, especially in BrE:

?The *approaching* train is from Liverpool. [1]

On the other hand, [2] is fully acceptable:

He was frightened by an *approaching* train. [2]

Here, we are concerned perhaps with what is characteristic in 'approaching trains'. Similarly, some find [3] odd, compared with [4]:

?The *barking* dog is my neighbour's. [3]
I was wakened by a *barking* dog. [4]

On the other hand, after an indefinite head has been postmodified by an *-ing* clause, the *-ing* participle can premodify the same head with the definite article (*cf* the similar conditions for noun premodification, 17.104):

a proposal *offending* many members
the *offending* proposal

In addition, the definite article may be used generically and hence evoke the same generality and permanence as the indefinite article:

The *beginning* student should be given every encouragement.
['beginners in general', not = 'a particular beginner']

This last example represents what may be a current trend in journalism and in technical writing (especially in the social sciences) to admit *-ing* participles rather more freely in premodification: *the developing countries, the (partially) hearing child, a continuing commitment, an ongoing concern, a voting member.*

Premodification by *-ed* participles

17.100 Much of what has been said of *-ing* participles (*cf* 17.98*f*) applies to *-ed* participles also, but there are additional issues. In the first place, the *-ed* participle can be active or passive but, as with postmodification (*cf* 17.29), the active is rarely used in premodification. Contrast:

the immigrant who has *arrived*
  BUT NOT: *the *arrived* immigrant

The following are exceptional:

the *vanished* treasure ['the treasure which has vanished']
a *retired* teacher
reduced/fallen/increased prices; *risen* costs 〈in the technical language of economics〉

Premodification is somewhat more common when an active participle is modified by an adverb:

the *newly-arrived* immigrant ['the immigrant who has arrived recently']
our *recently-departed* friend ['our friend who has departed recently']
a *well-read* woman ['a woman who has read a lot']
a *soft-spoken* person ['a person who speaks softly']
?a *recently-arisen* problem ['a problem which has arisen recently']

Within the passive, we must distinguish the passive which refers to process from the passive which refers to state (*cf* 'statal passive', 3.77). A statal example:

some *complicated* machinery
  ~ The machinery is *complicated.*
  ≁ The machinery was *complicated* by the designer.

With the statal type belong also *born* and some uses of *hidden, married, troubled, darkened,* etc, but in premodification they must either have 'permanent' reference or be modified by an adverb:

a *born* musician ['a natural musician'], a *newly-born* child
a *married* man, *married* life

The carefully hidden spy illustrates the general contrast between *-ing* and *-ed* participles. They are similar in postmodification:

The spy, carefully *hidden* in the bushes, } kept watch on the house.
The spy, carefully *hiding* in the bushes, }

But the *-ing* participle, unlike the *-ed* participle, resists premodification: **the carefully-hiding spy.*

Note With the acceptability of *a recently-arrived plane* beside **an arrived plane*, compare *a brown-eyed girl* beside **an eyed girl* (*cf* 17.102).

17.101 Most *-ed* participles have passive meaning, and only a few will easily admit the permanent reference that will permit premodifying use. We may contrast the participle of the stative verb in [1] with that of the dynamic verb in [2]:

The wanted man was last seen in Cambridge.
[the man goes on being wanted by the police] [1]
**The found purse* was returned to its owner.
[the purse was found at a particular moment] [2]

But *a lost purse* is acceptable, because, although a purse is no longer regarded as 'found' after it has been retrieved, a purse will be regarded as 'lost' throughout the period of its disappearance. This aspectual relation corresponds to that of the perfective of conclusive verbs (*cf* 4.33), as can be seen in the possible paraphrase: *a lost purse* ['a purse that has been lost']. Other examples:

the *defeated* army, a *damaged* car, a *broken* vase

Contrast:

a *wanted* man ['a man who is wanted by the police']

But not, except in special contexts, such as second instances (*cf* 17.109), which we must ignore here:

*a *sold* car	*a *built* house
*the *mentioned* article	*a *described* man

Exceptions to the general rule suggest that the semantic and aspectual factors are more complicated than we have indicated. For example, although a sum of money can go on being needed, one does not normally say ?*the needed money*; although a car is stolen at a moment of time, one can speak of *the stolen car* ['the car that has been stolen'].

The premodifying participle usually characterizes a type rather than an instance: *a muttered reply* is a type of reply, and *a drawn sword* describes a typical posture. With *an organized tour* we may perhaps explain the premodification through the continuing and professional nature of the organization (*ie* 'a package tour', as distinct from a tour privately organized on a specific occasion); or perhaps we should supply an omitted adverb 'an (officially *or* specially) organized tour', since we must remember that all of the starred participial phrases become acceptable when modified by adverbs (on the tendency, esp in BrE, to hyphenate such premodifiers, *cf* App III.4*f*):

a *recently* sold car	a *well-built* house
the *above-mentioned* article	a *carefully described* man

17.102 Modifiers in *-ed* may be directly denominal and not participles at all (*cf* App I.38):

a *bearded* man ['a man with a beard', 'a man who has a beard']
the *vaulted* roof ['a roof with vaults']
a *wooded* hillside ['a hillside covered with woods']

But constraints occur: while we have *a powerful engine*, and *a leggy spider*, we do not have

*a *powered* engine BUT: a *diesel-powered* engine
*a *legged* spider BUT: a *long-legged* spider

These constraints on unmodified *-ed* forms can be explained by the simple but communicatively relevant principle that what one says should carry useful, nontrivial information. Thus all engines will produce power and all spiders have legs. However, *-ed* denominals which provide new information, *an engine powered by diesel*, *a spider with long legs*, etc, become fully acceptable.

By the same principle, both the unmodified *a bearded man* and the modified *a white-bearded man* are acceptable, since not all men have beards and even fewer have white ones. A common feature of acceptable *-ed* adjectives is that they express the notion of 'inalienable possession', *ie* they are normally thought to be permanent attributes (*cf*: *I've lost my car*, but not normally: **I've lost my beard*). Those which express alienable possession, *eg*: **a carred man* ['a man with a car'], **a two-carred man* ['a man with two cars'], are not acceptable and productive formations.

It finally remains to explain the acceptability of adjectives not ending in *-ed*, but in *eg*: *-ful*, *-y*, *-ous*, *-ic*, *-ish*. Such formations express an unusual degree, amount, etc:

a *powerful* engine ['an engine with unusual power']
a *hairy* caterpillar ['a caterpillar with an unusual amount of hair']
a *leggy* spider ['a spider with unusually long legs']
a *pimply* face ['a face with an unusually large number of pimples']

Thus this type obeys the same principle that we invoked for *a bearded man* as well as *a diesel-powered engine*: to carry useful, nontrivial information.

Intransitive verbs rarely yield premodifying *-ed* participles (*cf*: **an arrived plane*, 17.100 Note).

17.103 If the *-ed* participle has a *by*-agent or other prepositional construction, only postmodification is possible (*cf* adjective complementation, 16.69). Thus we have 'the *defeated* army', but:

the army *defeated by the enemy* [NOT: *the by the enemy defeated army]
the army *defeated for lack of ammunition* [NOT: *the for lack of ammunition defeated army]

However, some unmodified *-ed* participles in fixed expressions have postposition (*cf* 7.21):

the amount *demanded/asked*	the earliest inventions *known*
for services *rendered*	money well *spent*

Prepositional verbs normally follow the head:

the sum *agreed upon*
the pages *referred to*
an event *unheard of* [but also: 'an *unheard-of* event']

Some *-ed* participles have pre- or postmodifying position with different meanings, *eg*:

the people *concerned* ['the people in question']	a *concerned* expression ['worried, anxious']
the students *involved* ['the students in question']	an *involved* question ['complicated']
jobs *wanted* ['jobs wanted by individuals']	*wanted* persons ['persons wanted by the police']

Premodification by nouns

17.104 Noun premodifiers are often so closely associated with the head as to be regarded as compounded with it, as indicated by the stress on the premodifying noun instead of the head:

his ˈ*life* story   a ˈ*dish* cloth   a ˈ*Sussex* man

On the other hand, we say:

an ˌ*iron* ˈrod   ˌ*life* imˈprisonment   a ˌ*Sussex* ˈvillage

The conditions under which the different stress patterns are adopted are by no means wholly clear, but are connected with the degree to which a sequence is 'institutionalized' as a lexical item, *ie* a compound (*cf* App I.57*ff*).

In most cases, premodifying nouns correspond to postmodification with prepositional phrases:

his *life* story	~ the story *of his life*
a *dish* cloth [NB singular]	~ a cloth *for dishes*
a *Sussex* man	~ a man *from Sussex*
an *iron* rod	~ a rod *of iron*
life imprisonment	~ imprisonment *for life*
a *Sussex* village	~ a village *in Sussex*
a *gift* tax [NB singular]	~ a tax *on gifts*

In accordance with the general tendency noted earlier (*cf* 17.8), the premodifying structure has reduced explicitness in relation to the postmodifying structure, and if the relationships between the nouns become unclear or unpredictable, premodification is unacceptable. This becomes apparent if examples [1–10] in 17.37 with the range of prepositions involved in prepositional phrase postmodification are tested for noun premodification:

the road *to Lincoln*	[1]	~	the *Lincoln* road	[1a]
this book *on grammar*	[2]	~	this *grammar* book	[2a]
a man *from the electricity company*	[3]	~	?an *electricity company man*	[3a]
passengers *on board the ship*	[4]	~	?*ship* passengers	[4a]
action *in case of fire*	[5]	~	?*fire* action	[5a]
the meaning of this *sentence*	[6]	~	?this *sentence* meaning	[6a]

the house *beyond the church*	[7]	~	the *church* house	[7a]
two years *before the war*	[8]	~	two *war* years	[8a]
a delay *pending further inquiry*	[9]	~	a *further inquiry* delay	[9a]
a tree *by a stream*	[10]	~	*a *stream* tree	[10a]

In this set, only [1a] and [2a] are fully possible premodification alternatives to postmodification by prepositional phrase; [3a], [4a], [5a], and [6a] have an unusual ring about them as equivalents of [3], [4], [5], and [6] respectively; [7a], [8a], and [9a] do not carry the respective meanings of [7], [8], and [9]; [10a] is unacceptable.

As observed in connection with premodifying nouns in the plural (*cf* 17.109), a phrase like [3a] is somewhat more likely to be used in second instances, *ie* after the explicit relationship has been fully clarified:

A: Today *a man from the electricity company* called.
B: Oh, so what did *the electricity company man* say?

Also, [3a] might conceivably be used in technical jargon where explicit relations need not be indicated or in headline language where the explanation follows.

Note An example similar to [7a] whose interpretation was indeed tried legally is the following:

Dock work is arduous.

It should be interpreted as 'work in or on the docks', not as 'work near the docks'. A British Court of Appeal upheld the above linguistic statement, and *The Times* law report had the following headline in consequence:

Work near docks is not dock work.

17.105 One noteworthy constraint against using nouns from postmodifying phrases as premodifiers is the relative impermanence of the modification in question. Thus [1] will readily yield [1a]:

The table in the corner was laid for dinner. [1]
The corner table . . . [1a]

But we cannot do the same with [2]:

The man in the corner spoke to me. [2]
**The corner man* . . . [2a]

However, this is not a property of the lexical item (in this instance, *corner*) but of the semantic relation. Premodification confers relative permanence, and because a table is not free to move of itself, we can premodify *table* but not *man* by *corner*.

Conversely, not all noun premodifiers have prepositional phrase analogues, *eg*:

consumer goods ~ goods *of the consumer*
a *welfare* state ~ a state *of welfare*

There is also an analogous relation between some types of premodification and coordination:

The plane is *both a fighter and a bomber*.
~ *a fighter-'bomber*

Bernard Miles was *both actor and producer*.
~ *the actor-producer* Bernard Miles

Similarly between premodification and apposition:

Smith is *a sergeant*.	~ *Sergeant* 'Smith
My friend is *a girl*.	~ my *girl*friend

However, the kind of apposition found in titles is severely restricted by convention and style (*cf* 5.66, 17.91).

In some cases, both constructions are acceptable but have different meaning, *eg*:

a glass *of wine*	['a glass containing wine']
a *wine* glass	['a glass for wine']
a box *of matches*	['a box containing matches']
a *matchbox*	['a box made to hold matches']

17.106 The main types of prepositional paraphrase of noun + noun combinations, including both free syntactic phrases and compounds, are the following, arranged according to semantic relations.

Source–result:	a ˌ*metal* 'sheet	~ a sheet *of metal*
Part–whole:	ˌ*clay* 'soil	~ soil *with clay*
Place:	a ˌ*top* 'drawer	'a drawer *at the top*'
	a ˌ*garden* 'fence	~ a fence *round the garden*
Time:	a ˌ*morning* 'train	~ a train *in the morning*
	a ˌ*night* 'sky	~ a sky *at night*
Whole–part:	a ˌ*board* 'member	~ a member *of the board*

With the following class we are closer to lexical compounds, thus the main stress on the first element. (The combinations above could equally occur with the main stress on the first element in other semantic relations.):

'*seafood*	['food from the sea']
a '*fireplace*	['a place for fire']
a '*bullet head*	['a head like a bullet']

It should be emphasized that the semantic relations illustrated in this section indicate no clear boundary between noun phrases and noun + noun compounds (*cf* App I.57*ff*). Stress on the first element is usually indicative of compounding, *eg*: '*fireplace* but ˌ*top* '*drawer*. Conversely, the possibility of substituting *one* for the second constituent indicates that the first is a premodifier in a noun phrase:

She wants an oak table but I'd prefer *a teak one*.
BUT NOT: *That's not an oak tree but *an elm one*.

17.107 In most cases, the constructions with both prepositional postmodification and with premodification are available, but the change from postmodification to premodification may have consequences other than a possible loss in explicitness. One such consequence is loss of the definite article, as in:

officials *in the Pentagon* ~ *Pentagon* officials

The use of articles is identical in the following:

a sheet *of metal* ~ a *metal* sheet

But it differs in:

life in *a* village ~ village life
the shooting of tigers ~ tiger shooting

Another consequence is the use of a prefix in premodification corresponding to the preposition in postmodification (*cf* App I.21*ff*):

demonstrations *against the war* ~ *anti-war* demonstrations
the period *after the war* ~ the *postwar* period

Plural attributive nouns

17.108 Attributive nouns are normally number-neutral. As a further illustration of the principle that postmodification is relatively explicit as compared with premodification, nouns which are plural in postmodification are singular (number-neutral) in premodification:

a chair with *arms* ~ an *arm*chair
decay of *teeth* ~ *tooth* decay
the picking of *hops* ~ *hop*-picking

A hyphen before the singular form is normal in expressions denoting age, time, weight, size, etc of the following type:

a girl (who is) ten *years* old ~ a ten-*year*-old girl
a pause lasting three *seconds* ~ a three-*second* pause
inflation amounting to two *digits* ~ two-*digit* inflation
an agreement between *four* powers ~ a four-*power* agreement
a bill worth ten *dollars* ~ a ten-*dollar* bill

However, in quantitative expressions of the following type there is possible variation (*cf* 5.118 Note [b]):

a ten *day* absence [singular]
a ten-*day* absence [hyphen + singular]
a ten *days* absence [plural]
a ten *days'* absence [genitive plural]

The use of singular holds even for some nouns that otherwise have no singular form (*cf* 5.76):

a sharpener *for scissors* ~ a '*scissor* sharpener
a press *for trousers* ~ a '*trouser* press

However, the plural attributive construction is on the increase, particularly in BrE where it is more common than in AmE, *eg*:

careers guidance
a *grants* committee

a new *systems* analyst
an *appointments* officer
the policy and *resources* working party

The choice of premodifying nouns in the plural rather than the singular may be attributed to a number of factors, but predominantly to the fact that an entity has been institutionalized in plural form. Since the plural attributive construction is relatively rare in AmE, the statements in the following section apply, for the most, only to BrE.

17.109 (i) 'Exclusive plurals'
One difference between *branch supervisor* and *branches supervisor* is that the singular is more vague and may be interpreted as 'supervisor of a branch or branches', whereas the plural can be interpreted only as 'supervisor of several branches' and thus excludes the ambiguity of number. The semantic distinction seems to be institutionalized in *career girl* 'a girl who puts advancement in her profession before other things' and *careers girl* 'a girl who has had several careers' or (more usually) 'a girl who deals with careers'. Such 'exclusive plurals' tend to occur with collective nouns and names of institutions as heads, and the stress tends to be on the premodifying plural:

parks department
courses committee
examinations board
the heavy *chemicals* industry
Scotland Yard's Obscene *Publications* Squad
Chesterfield *Hospitals* Management Committee
the British Museum *Prints* and *Drawings* Gallery

Highly institutionalized plurals are always retained, in particular when the singular form might lead to ambiguity:

an *Arts* degree ['a degree in the humanities', as opposed to *an art degree* 'a degree in fine art']

Pluralia tantum (*cf* 5.77) retain their plural since they have no singular:

a *customs* officer ~ a *custom* officer
a *goods* train ~ a *good* train

(ii) Plural denoting variety
There is a tendency for more generic terms to be plural and more specific terms to be singular:

soft ˈ*drinks* manuˌfacturer [*drinks* = 'kinds of drink';
BUT: ˈcar manuˌfacturer]
enterˈtainments ˌguide [*entertainments* = 'kinds of entertainment';
BUT: ˈtheatre ˌguide]
surgical *appˈliances* manuˌfacturer [*appliances* = 'kinds of appliance';
BUT: ˈbaby ˌcarriage manuˌfacturer]

(iii) 'Temporary institutionalization'
As we have seen, in most cases there is variation available between

premodification by noun and postmodification by prepositional phrase, with certain syntactic and semantic constraints. When such variation is freely available, the choice may be seen as conditioned by the explicit/inexplicit distinction or simply by a desire for stylistic variation. However, it should also be seen in terms of communicative factors, as in the case of the variation between the genitive and the *of*-construction (*cf* 17.38*ff*). In a book on linguistics we may find the italicized part of [1] resumed later, as a 'second instance', in the discussion by [1a] (*cf* 17.8):

The idea of levels has been a major issue for a long time. [1]
the levels idea [1a]

A special instance of 'temporary institutionalization' is the use of plurals in headlines. A topical issue will cause the plural to be retained in premodification when it is associated with a widely discussed public issue. If there is controversy over the wearing of crash helmets by motorcyclists, this can become referred to in the media as *the helmets issue.* In this way, during the internationally discussed crisis of President Nixon's administration concerning tape-recordings, we became habituated to read expressions such as:

the *tapes* issue	the Watergate *tapes* affair
the *tapes* compromise	the White House *tapes* mystery

The frequent use of attributive structure in newspaper headlines, *eg*: *jobs cut* for 'cut in jobs', would seem to contradict the given/new principle (*cf* 18.8). Other examples:

PHONES ORDER	HEADACHE PROBLEM
PRIORITY PROJECT	NUMEROUS WAR OFFICE STAFF RESIGNATIONS

The flouting of the given/new principle may be explained not only as a striving for brevity in a headline with limited space but also as 'premeditated inversion' of the given/new sequence in order to arouse the reader's interest in going on to read the fully explicit text of the news item.

Premodification by genitive

17.110 The illustration of the genitive as premodifier with restrictive function in 17.94 was the following example:

I visited *his fisherman's cottage.* [1]

The meaning is 'The cottage belongs/belonged to a fisherman' or 'resembles/resembled the cottage of a fisherman'. It should be noticed that if we had used another noun in the genitive, *eg*: *his friend's cottage*, we would have moved from nonrestrictive to restrictive function and, above all, changed the relationship of the constituents from premodification to determinative. The difference in structure is clearly brought out if further premodifying items are added:

I visited { *his old fisherman's cottage.* [1a]
{ *his old friend's cottage.* [1b]

The structures can be seen in a tree diagram (*Fig* 17.110):

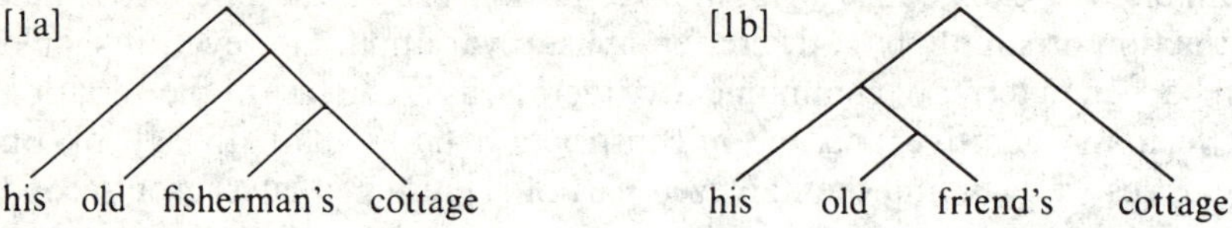

Fig 17.110

Thus, in [1a], *old* modifies *fisherman's cottage*, whereas, in [1b], *old* modifies the determinative genitive head *friend's*. In [1a], no item can intervene between *fisherman's* and *cottage* and the premodifying genitive may be replaced by, for example, a noun (*cf* 17.104*ff*): *his old country cottage*. In [1b], the head of the superordinate noun phrase (*cf* 5.121*f*) can be further modified in the usual way:

his old friend's *delightful but crumbling* cottage

Example [1b] is, then, a fully syntactic structure of the type discussed in 5.112*ff* and 17.38*ff* where the genitive has a determinative function; in [1a], on the other hand, the genitive acts as a descriptive premodifier (*cf* 5.122), and is related to the use of the genitive in compounds, such as *bull's-eye*.

Premodification by adverb and other phrases

17.111 Another minor type of premodification is the adverb phrase (*cf* 7.68), as in:

She travelled to many *far-away* places. ['The places are far away.']
I have this strange *under-the-weather* feeling. ['I feel under the weather.']

There is a medley of other premodifying phrases, some of which are common expressions, *eg*:

round-the-clock service
an *up-to-date* timetable
a *tongue-in-cheek* remark

Apart from a few institutionalized examples such as *an away match* ['the match is being played away from the home ground', in contrast with *a home match*], the flexibility of this type of premodification tends to be exploited only colloquially, and most examples have (and seem deliberately to have) a flavour of originality, convention-flouting, and provisional or nonce awkwardness:

their *day-after-day* complaints
her *too-simple-to-be-true* dress
a *come-and-fight-me* attitude

Examples like the following are more fully lexicalized, and may be regarded as cases of conversion (*cf* App I.43*ff*):

She's wearing a *with-it* dress.
That is the *in* thing at present.

Premodification by sentence

17.112 What was said of adverb phrases applies at least equally to premodification by a sentence:

(?)I visited his *what-do-you-call-it* cottage [*cf*: What do you call it when a cottage has walls made from overlapping pieces of timber? Clapboard.]

A few institutionalized examples retain a colloquial or slang flavour: *a whodunit story* is one about crime, and the nonstandard grammar and spelling are preserved as part of the ironic slang. *Do-it-yourself* as in *a do-it-yourself job* has become so often used as to pass out of the area of slang (and sometimes be reduced ⟨esp in BrE⟩ to *DIY*).

Somewhat more widely acceptable are noun phrases which can be interpreted either as having a sentence as premodifier or as being object (usually of *know*) in an embedded nominal clause:

He asked {*I don't know HÒW many* people. [1]
He asked {*I don't KNÒW how many* people. [1a]

With either intonation, the meaning is 'He asked a relatively large number of people, though I don't know precisely how many'. The meaning is somewhat different if the sentence is reordered, enforcing a different grammatical structure:

I don't know *how many people he asked*. ['I don't know the number of people he asked.']

For the most part, however, sentence premodifiers have an air of the outrageous and improvised. Part of a political leader's election campaign was described by a journalist as

today's meet the people (*if they can find you*) tour

Far more remarkable is the following quotation from a literary comment in which the sentence premodification itself has highly irregular and sophisticated punctuation to convey highly irregular coordination devices:

His other comments ignore . . . the obvious fallacies inherent in the '*But the poem* (*play, novel*) *was meant to be tedious/pretentious/ pointless*' line of critical argument.

Relative sequence of premodifiers

17.113 When a head has more than one premodifier, there arises the question of relative order; why either [1] or [1a]?:

a *thin dark* face [1]
a *dark thin* face [1a]

But why only [2] and not [2a]?:

a *cardboard detergent* carton [2]
*a *detergent cardboard* carton [2a]

The problem becomes even more acute with longer strings of premodifiers.

Although there is, theoretically, no grammatical upper limit to the number of premodifiers, it is unusual to find more than three or four. Premodification is an area of English grammar where there is considerable variation among the varieties of the language. To a large extent, such variation, as well as the existence of an upper limit, can be given a psycholinguistic explanation. For example, a technical manual, written exclusively for space research scientists, may have very long and complex structures of premodification, as in:

Apollo Block II fuel cell voltage current VI characteristics

Nothing comparable is likely to be used by the same scientist in a casual coffee-break chat where new topics will turn up unexpectedly and where concentration and perhaps audibility are low. There is indeed evidence of a higher proportion of three-or-more item sequences in written than in spoken English.

A sequence such as [3] may be unlikely. Yet, unlike [3a], it will be recognized as acceptable by a native speaker:

all the many other small inconspicuous carved jade idols [3]
*other the all jade carved inconspicuous small many idols [3a]

In order to describe the rules for the relative order of premodifiers, it will be helpful to divide the territory between DET (the determinative) and HEAD (the head) into four premodification zones (I, II, III, IV), for example:

DET	I	II	III	IV	HEAD
a	*major*	*new*	*customized*	*financial*	*service*

Precentral, central, postcentral, and prehead position

17.114 The four zones are largely correlated with the semantic classes discussed in 7.45.

(I) Zone I: PRECENTRAL

In the precentral zone we find peripheral nongradable adjectives (*cf* 7.42), in particular intensifying adjectives (*cf* 7.33*f*):

(i) emphasizers, *eg*: *certain, definite, plain, pure, sheer*
(ii) amplifiers, *eg*: *absolute, entire, extreme, perfect, total*
(iii) downtoners, *eg*: *feeble, slight*

(II) Zone II: CENTRAL

The central zone includes the central, gradable adjectives, *ie* the 'most adjectival items', which satisfy all four criteria of adjectival status (*cf* 7.3*f*), *eg*: *big, funny, intelligent, keen, powerful, slow, thick*. Central adjectives admit intensifiers (*a very cold day*), comparison (*It's colder than yesterday*), and alternative predicative position (*Last summer was very cold*). Their function is to describe or characterize and, consequently, they often form contrastive pairs like *big/small, good/bad, hot/cold*. They are typically inherent (*cf* 7.43) and include both nonderived adjectives (like those just mentioned) and derived adjectives, which are either deverbal (like *interesting, interested, hesitant*) or denominal (like *angry, rainy, peaceful*).

This morphological classification has a bearing on the internal structure of the zone of central adjectives in that the usual order is NONDERIVED + DEVERBAL + DENOMINAL:

a *tall attractive* woman
this *green hilly* slope
a *quiet satisfied sleepy* look

Within the class of nonderived adjectives, the order is largely arbitrary, but adjectives denoting SIZE, LENGTH, and HEIGHT normally precede other nonderived adjectives. Thus we usually prefer:

a small round table to *a round small table*;
long straight hair to *straight long hair*; and
a tall angry man to *an angry tall man*

Among adjectives in zone II, we may further distinguish a group of emotive, evaluative, or subjective adjectives (*lovely*, *nice*, *wonderful*, *terrible*, *horrible*, *nasty*, etc), which usually precede other central adjectives. Thus we prefer *beautiful long hair* to *long beautiful hair*. Such emotionally tinged adjectives often have an adverbial, subordinated relation as indicated by their notional similarity with adverbs:

beautiful warm weather ~ *beautifully warm* weather

The statements made about the relative order of zone II premodifiers should however be understood to be tendencies rather than absolute rules.

The relation of premodifiers in 'unbroken' sequences, *ie* without commas or coordinators, tends to be one of hypotaxis (*cf* 17.116).

(III) Zone III: POSTCENTRAL
This zone includes, in particular, participles and colour adjectives (with variable order), *eg*:

a *retired* colonel	a *working* theory
a *deserted* village	*blue* skies
his *thinning grey* hair	their *dark frowning* brows

(IV) Zone IV: PREHEAD
This zone includes the 'least adjectival and most nominal' premodifiers:

(i) Adjectives with a proper noun basis denoting nationality (*cf* 5.57), provenance, and style: *American*, *Gothic*

(ii) Other adjectives with a morphological or semantic relation to nouns (*cf* 7.37), often with the meaning 'consisting of', 'involving', or 'relating to': *annual*, *economic*, *medical*, *social*, *political*, *rural*

(iii) Nouns: *tourist* (attraction), *Yorkshire* (women), *college* (student)

Adjectives in zone IV are normally not central but peripheral adjectives, *ie* they do not generally admit intensifiers, comparison, or predicative position:

all those *medical* examinations for military service
*all those *very medical* examinations
*The examinations are *more medical than* . . .

Similarly, *political* and *rural* in the following uses will normally be interpreted as nongradable adjectives (*cf* 7.42):

all the *political* parties of this country
the backward *rural* areas in the north

When items from the same group cooccur, there is a tendency for those modifiers which denote place and time to take precedence:

local economic interests
the *annual linguistic* meeting

Premodifiers in the prehead zone cannot usually be coordinated:

the *local waterboard* authorities
*the *local and waterboard* authorities

Premodifying nouns, which are normally placed immediately before the head of the noun phrase, may form a compound or quasi-compound with the head, as is suggested in the compound stress pattern on the first item as in *'telephone call*, *'fireplace*. This is where noun-phrase structure impinges upon compounding (*cf* 17.104*ff*, App I.57*ff*), with two nouns forming a new conceptual unit.

In some cases there is little or no difference in meaning between denominal adjectives and nouns as premodifiers:

a *Liverpudlian* accent ~ a *Liverpool* accent
an *icy* patch ~ an *ice* patch
a *glamorous* girl ~ a *glamour* girl
a *beautiful* spot ~ a *beauty* spot
a *grassy* strip ~ a *grass* strip

One general distinctive feature is that the information provided by the adjective is felt to be temporary or subjective, whereas that provided by the noun premodifier is permanent, or objective, *ie* has a 'classifying' function.

Some examples of sequences of premodifiers are given in *Table* 17.114.

Table 17.114 Examples of sequences of premodifiers

	PREMODIFIERS				
DETERMINATIVE	Zone I: PRECENTRAL	Zone II: CENTRAL	Zone III: POSTCENTRAL	Zone IV: PREHEAD	HEAD
					attractions
				tourist	attractions
				London tourist	attractions
		splendid		African tourist	attractions
our	numerous	splendid		African tourist	attractions
all this			costly	social	security
a	certain		grey	church	tower
these			crumbling grey	Gothic church	towers
some		intricate	old interlocking	Chinese	designs
all the		small	carved	Chinese jade	idols
both the	major			Danish political	parties

General principle for the order of premodifiers

17.115 In part, the preferences seem clearly to correspond to the 'natural' order of recursive qualification. Thus [1] would be more usual than [1a]:

the two *typical large* country houses [1]
the two *large typical* country houses [1a]

In order to be typical, country houses must be large; but it would scarcely be true that, in order to be large, they must be typical. This is factual, not linguistic, information. The preferred order in the two noun phrases in [1] and [1a] thus reflects reality in showing that the speaker had been obliged to specify the houses as country houses and the country houses as large, before it became meaningful to specify the large country houses as typical. Again, the preferred orders *beautiful long hair* and *long straight hair* perhaps reflect the nonlinguistic world: length of hair may be a condition of its being adjudged beautiful, and the straightness of hair would tend to be a condition of its seeming long.

Attempts to explain preferences of premodifier ordering have invoked rhythm (*eg* short items before longer ones); common items before rare ones; restrictive before nonrestrictive. We suggest one principle accounting for all premodifiers: a subjective/objective polarity. That is, modifiers relating to properties which are (relatively) inherent in the head of the noun phrase, visually observable, and objectively recognizable or assessible, will tend to be placed nearer to the head and be preceded by modifiers concerned with what is relatively a matter of opinion, imposed on the head by the observer, not visually observed, and only subjectively assessible.

One need hardly add that, with criteria that are themselves so subjective, there is plenty of room for difference of opinion. The writers and speakers will naturally arrange premodification semantically, *ie* according to their communicative intentions. However, there is no total freedom.

Note Though there are many exceptions and few firm constraints, it seems that, to some extent, the order of premodifying adjectives is the inverse of predicative order:

beautiful long hair ~ hair that is *long and beautiful*
long straight hair ~ hair that is *straight and long*

With this we may compare the adverbial + object + head order in premodification with the inverse order of clause elements:

a *gas cigarette* lighter ~ It lights *cigarettes by gas*.

Also adjunct + subject + head:

Euston train arrivals ~ The *trains* arrive *at Euston*.

Similarly, the sequence of modifiers with subjective and objective genitive (*cf* 17.41*ff*) where, although inversion is not always involved, the same principle of ordered clustering in relation to the head is maintained:

the men's examination of the student ~ The men examined the student.
the men's examination by the doctor ~ The men were examined by the doctor.
the examination of them by him ~ They were examined by him.

Hypotactic relations and order of premodifiers

17.116 Different hypotactic relations of premodifiers will upset the normal order described in 17.113*ff*. Thus while *dirty British books* could be understood as books that had become grimy, *British dirty books* could only mean books that 'consisted of' or 'were characterized by' dirt (*ie* obscenity).

When two nouns premodify, one which corresponds to the head as object to verb will follow one relating to material, means, instrument, space, or any comparable adverbial relation:

a *detergent carton and a cardboard* carton
~ *a cardboard detergent* carton ['The carton contains detergent.']
≁ *a *detergent cardboard* carton [*'The carton contains cardboard.']

my *ciga'rette* lighter and my '*gas* lighter
~ my ˌ*gas ciga'rette* lighter
≁ *my *cigarette gas* lighter

a *city bread* delivery
≁ *a *bread city* delivery

a *diesel passenger* train
≁ ?a *passenger diesel* train

a *jet freight* aircraft
≁ ?a *freight jet* aircraft

Where an adverbial + verb sequence has prior institutionalized status, as with *pressure cooker*, this unit may be premodified by an object such as *vegetable*:

a vegetable pressure cooker ['which cooks vegetables by pressure']

Multiple adjective/noun premodification

17.117 The noun premodifier can be itself premodified by either an adjective or a noun and, if the latter, this can in turn be recursively premodified:

office furniture → { *expensive office* furniture / *tax office* furniture }
→ *income tax office* furniture
→ *overseas income tax office* furniture

Fig 17.117a

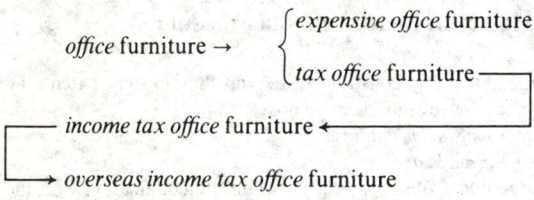

It should be noted, however, that if we introduce an adjective in this last noun phrase, already clumsy and improbable, the adjective has to come immediately after the determiner and would normally be interpreted as relating directly to the head *furniture*:

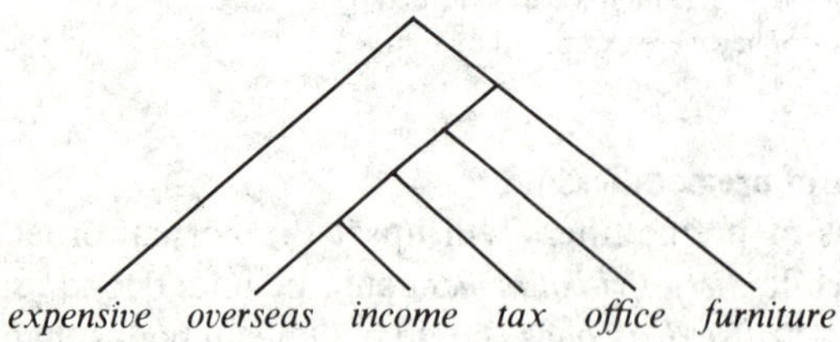

Fig 17.117b

However, such straightforward left-to-right ordering of premodifiers is not common. Compare the structure of the following two examples from a newspaper:

the [[[*food price*] *rise*] [*warning system*]] 'a system for warning against rises in the price of food'
the [*voluntary* [[*price rise*] [*warning system*]]] 'a system which is voluntary for warning against rises in prices'

The two examples look superficially alike but are in fact radically different in noun-phrase structure. The identical positioning of *food* and *voluntary* must not obscure the fact that the former modifies *price* and the latter *system*.

However, there is potential ambiguity with multiple noun modification. Consider:

a new giant size cardboard detergent carton

where size does not premodify *cardboard* and *cardboard* does not premodify *detergent* but where the linear structure is rather as in:

a [new [giant size] [cardboard [detergent carton]]]

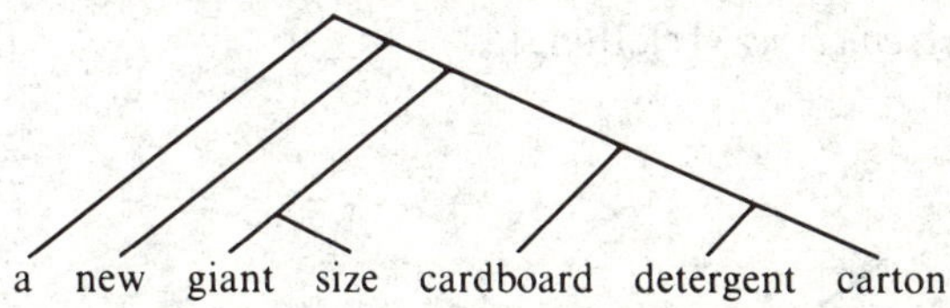

Fig 17.117c

Such an example is not, of course, obscure. Indeed, it is generally the case that obscurity in premodification exists only for the hearer or reader who is unfamiliar with the subject concerned and who is not therefore equipped to tolerate the radical reduction in explicitness that premodification entails.

Take even a fairly simple example like the following:

He had *some French onion soup.*

If we are unfamiliar with this type of soup, there is nothing about the grammatical, orthographic, or prosodic form that will tell us whether it is soup made from French onions, or French soup made from onions, or onion soup made in the French manner.

17.118 There are other special types of multiple premodification that should be mentioned. A friendship between a boy and a girl becomes:

a *boy and girl* friendship

A committee dealing with appointments and promotions can readily be described as (on the plural, *cf* 17.108*f*):

the *appointments and promotions* committee

A committee whose business is the allocation of finance can be:

the *allocation of finance* committee

A noun phrase in which there is noun premodification can be given the denominal affix which puts it into the 'consisting of' class of adjectives (*cf* 7.37, 17.114) while retaining the noun premodifier; hence, from *party politics* we have:

a *party political* broadcast

Similarly, a noun phrase having a denominal adjective may itself take a denominal affix to become a premodifier in a noun phrase. For example, beside *cerebral palsy* ['palsy of the cerebrum'], we have *cerebral palsied children* which has the following structure:

[[[*cerebral palsi*]*ed*] *children*] NOT: *[cerebral [palsied children]]

We see two types of modification with modified modifier in [1] and [2]. The premodifying adjective *delightful* is itself premodified by the adverb phrase *really quite unbelievably*:

his *really quite unbelievably delightful* cottage [1]

In [2], the genitive premodifier *women's* is itself premodified by *these chic*, and the whole genitive phrase could premodify another genitive:

[[[these [*chic women's*]] *employer's*] clothing] [2]

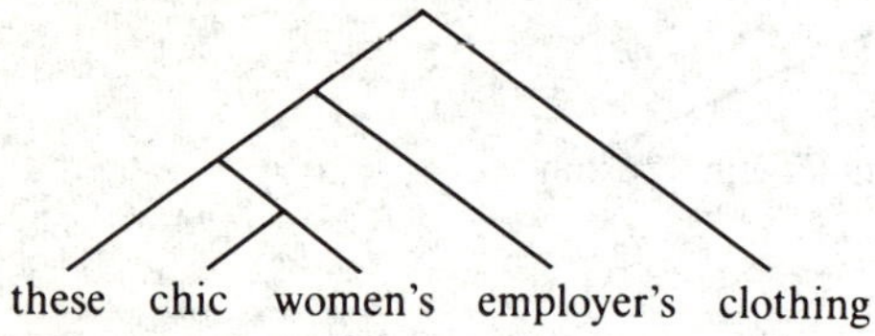

Fig 17.118

Although there is no theoretical limit to such sequences of genitives, there seems to be a practical limit of two – anything more being stylistically objectionable, comic, and difficult to comprehend:

?these *chic women's employer's wife's* clothing

Note With a singular genitive there may be ambiguity, in that *chic* may modify *woman's* [3] or *clothing* [3a]:

this [[*chic woman's*] *clothing*] [3]
this [*chic* [*woman's clothing*]] [3a]

The 'group genitive'

17.119 One important type of multiple premodification is the 'group genitive' (*cf* 5.123):

someone else's car	*The Wife of Bath's* Tale
Elizabeth the Second's heir	*a man of distinction's* influence

While the affixing to a noun of the genitive inflection and the plural inflection follows similar rules for regular nouns in general, the rules for the two inflections are different if the noun is postmodified (*cf Fig* 17.119):

singular	*the teacher*	*the teacher's* (*room*)
	the teacher of music	*the teacher of music's* (*room*)
plural	*the teachers*	*the teachers'* (*room*)
	the teachers of music	*the teachers of music's* (*room*)

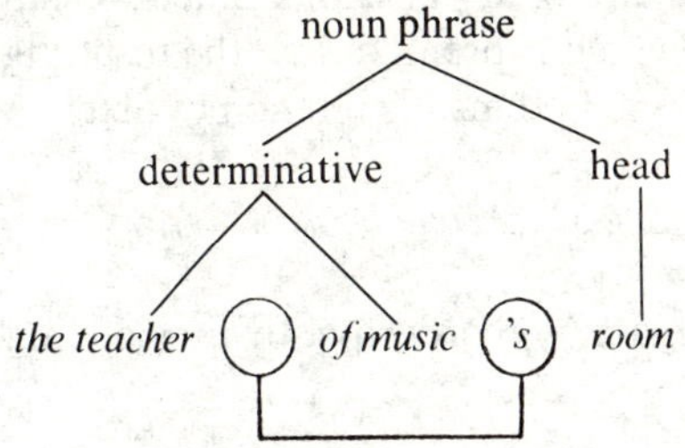

Fig 17.119

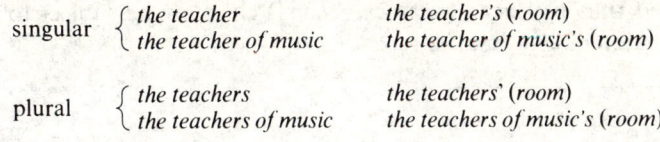

Other examples involve coordinations:

an *hour and a half's* discussion
a *week or so's* sunshine

The group genitive is not normally acceptable when the postmodification is a clause, though in colloquial use one sometimes hears examples like:

Old man what-do-you-call-him's house has just been sold.
?Have you seen *that man standing at the corner's hat*?
?Someone has stolen *a man I know's car*.

In normal use, especially in writing, such genitives would be replaced by *of*-constructions:

Have you seen *the hat of that man standing at the corner*?
Someone has stolen *the car of a man I know*.

The group genitive is tolerable even with prepositional phrases provided it encourages no unwanted interpretation. Thus [1] might pass muster:

the *man in the car's* ears [1]

But [2] would obviously be avoided if the meaning 'the ears of the man with the cat' was intended:

the *man with the cat's* ears [2]

Multiple heads

17.120 Modification may apply to more than one head (*cf* 13.68):

the new table } ~ *the new table and chairs*
the new chairs }

The multiple head thus produced (*table and chairs*) can now be subject to recursive modification or coordination:

the beautiful new table and chairs
the new (but) ugly table and chairs

The reduced explicitness naturally makes ambiguity possible. Since we can coordinate two noun phrases only one of which is premodified, the resulting string will suggest that the modifier applies to both heads if it comes first:

He writes *long papers.* }
He writes *books.* } ~ He writes *long papers and books.*

In these circumstances, we may disambiguate by reordering, by introducing separate determiners, etc:

He writes *books and long papers.*
He writes *some long papers and some books.*
He writes *long papers* {*as well as* / *and also*} *books.*

Noun phrases with separate premodification can however be jointly premodified, as in:

books and long papers ~ *excellent books and long papers*

Spoken with one tone unit, this noun phrase can be interpreted as having the structure of *Fig* 17.120:

[excellent [[books] and [long PÀPers]]]

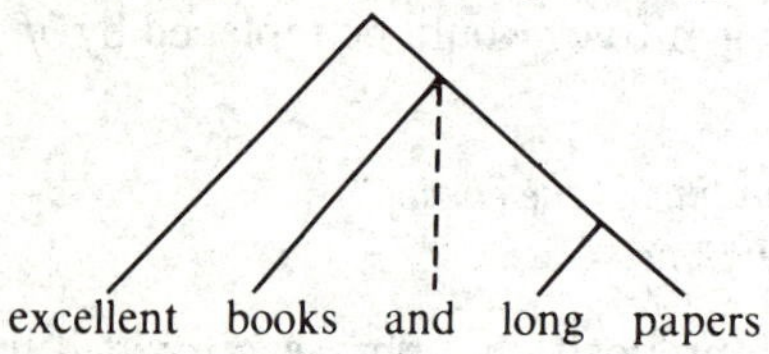

Fig 17.120

This interpretation would be almost inescapable if a determiner such as *some* preceded *excellent*. It follows that if we wish to coordinate noun phrases both of which are premodified, we must introduce either prosodic or punctuation separators, or separate determiners, if maximal clarity is required:

excellent books, and long papers
some excellent books and some long papers

Alternatively, the order can be reversed:

long papers and excellent books

Special relations between heads and modifiers

Some problems of coordination

17.121 Coordination provides some points of interest in relation to multiple modification. Consider the phrase [1]:

children *who have speech that is impaired* [1]

This can be reduced to [1a] or [1b]:

children *who have impaired speech* [1a]
children *with impaired speech* [1b]

The normal premodified form (*cf* App I.38) is then [1c]:

speech-impaired children [1c]

But if the impairment is in *speech and language* (a conventional conjoining recognized in speech therapy), the premodification form becomes:

speech and language impaired children [1d]

The hyphen is omitted after *language* since this would entail one after *speech* as well, a type of ellipsis indication reserved for rather stiff and technical writing (*cf* App III.5 Note [b]):

speech- and language-impaired children [1e]

Ellipsis provides difficulties in noun phrases involving comparison also. The following is unobjectionable:

an *equally serious or more serious* situation [2]

The sequence becomes objectionable when postmodifying complementation is added [2a]:

?an *equally serious or more serious* situation *than before* [2a]

The phrase [2a] wrongly suggests that we have a possible sequence (*cf* 17.122):

* an *equally serious* situation *than before* [2b]

A somewhat similar difficulty arises through coordination and rather careless ellipsis, as in [3]:

?the similarity of his houses in New York and Connecticut [3]

A more fully explicit form without ellipsis will help to show what has gone wrong:

the similarity of his house[1] in New York *to his house*[2] *in* Connecticut [3a]

The rules for ellipsis (*cf* 12.31*ff*) have to distinguish between identity of lexical item and identity of reference: if we have only the first without the second, there are constraints on ellipsis. Such constraints are not sufficient, however, to block ellipses like the following which retain complete acceptability:

more than one lecturer *some* book *or other* *one or two* books

Discontinuity between head and modifier

17.122 It is not uncommon for the noun phrase to be interrupted by other items of clause structure. Note, for instance, the placing of the time adjunct between the head and postmodifier in the following noun phrase:

I met *a man* this morning *carrying a heavy parcel.*

Although there is nothing wrong with this structure, to avoid discontinuity, the adverbial can be moved to initial position:

This morning I met *a man carrying a heavy parcel.*

Further examples of discontinuities in noun-phrase structure are presented in 18.39*f*, together with some discussion of the consequences for information processing.

Noun-phrase modifiers which have their own complementation can often occupy alternative positions. The structure is either continuous (noun head + adjective with complement) or discontinuous (adjective + noun head + adjective complement). We can distinguish the following types of complement:

(a) Adjective with a prepositional phrase as complement (*cf* 17.58):

facilities *comparable* } *to ours*
comparable facilities }

(b) Adjective with an infinitive clause as complement (*cf* 16.75*ff*):

a plan *difficult* } *to carry out*
a *difficult* plan }

(c) Adjective in comparative degree with a comparative clause as complement (*cf* 15.63*ff*):

a person *more qualified* } *than anybody else*
a *more* qualified person }

a plan *better* } *than the previous one*
a *better* plan }

in a time *shorter* } *than five microseconds*
in a *shorter* time }

With the following types it should be noted that alternative adjective position also entails change, compared with types (a–c), in the position of the indefinite article, such that it always immediately precedes the noun head.

(d) *As* + adjective + *as* with comparative clause:

a fact *as strange as* } anything you've ever heard of
as strange a fact *as* }

(e) *So* + adjective + *that*- or *as to*-clause:

an idea *so odd* } { that you won't believe it
so odd an idea } { as to be unbelievable

(f) *Too* + adjective + infinitive clause:

an accusation *too serious* } to be left unanswered
too serious an accusation }

In some of these examples, the variation is not stylistically free; for example, in relation to (a), many would prefer (at least in a more formal context) the continuous order [1] to the discontinuous [1a]:

{ facilities *comparable to ours* [1]
{ *comparable* facilities *to ours* [1a]

The prepositional phrases and other structures function here as complements to adjectives, not as modifiers of noun-phrase heads, as in *new roads to London*. Thus we have *roads to London* but not **facilities to ours*.

Compare now the following pairs:

{ the *handsome* man that she kissed [2]
{ the *first* man that she kissed [2a]

{ an *extraordinary* discovery that I made [3]
{ an *early* discovery that I made [3a]

{ The *most recent* play I know well is *Bedroom Farce*. [4]
{ The *most recent* play I've seen is *Hamlet*. [4a]

The superficial resemblance within each pair must not prevent us from seeing that, in each case, the second member has an adverbial relation in what is a plausible corresponding sentence:

the man was the { *first* / **handsome* } that she kissed

a discovery that I made { *early* / **extraordinary* }

The play I { 've seen / *know } *most recently* is *Hamlet*.

Note Comparatives of adjectives with comparative clause complements like [5] and [6] can have as ad hoc 'compounds' the normally postponed comparative constructions in [5a] and [6a] (*cf* 17.111; regarding the use of hyphenation, *cf* App I.17):

Her salary is *higher than average*. [5]
His car looks *worse than ever*. [6]
her *higher-than-average* salary [5a]
his *worse-than-ever-looking* car [6a]

Note that with a copular verb other than *be* [6a], the verb is included in the premodification. But:

*her *higher-than-average-being* salary [6b]

Conclusion

Reduced explicitness and increased economy structure

17.123 The noun phrase, then, is potentially very complex indeed. It is hoped that by now enough has been said to give some clear indication of the relationship that exists between types of noun-phrase structure and the forms of predication to which they appear to have an essential if often indirect correspondence. By means of the structures that have been developed in the noun phrase, we can take an indefinitely wide range of grammatical and semantic data which have either been previously established in the discourse or which can be assumed as knowledge held in common between speaker/writer and hearer/reader, and then express them, or refer to them, with greatly reduced explicitness, and consequently increased economy. To illustrate the degree of complexity that occurs quite readily in English prose, here are three examples:

> At the mouth of the respiratory tube is *a series of velar tentacles, corresponding exactly in position to those of amphioxus, and serving to separate the mouth and oesophagus from the respiratory tube while the lamprey is feeding.* [1]
>
> It was *the beginning of an operation in which the power of the Holy Spirit was fulfilled in the person and words and actions of a human character, Jesus of Nazareth.* [2]
>
> *Subsequent work by Huisgen (1951) and Hey, Stuart-Webb and Williams (1951, 1952) on the dependence of the rate of rearrangement on both the aryl and acyl groups of the acylarylnitrosamine, and on the catalysis of the reaction by bases such as piperidine,* has led to *the formulation of the rearrangement as an intramolecular process, as indicated in equation (6), involving nucleophilic attack, by an internal* S_N2 *mechanicism, of the oxygen of the . . . nitrosyl group on the carbonyl carbon atom.* [3]

In the italicized noun phrase of [1], we are expected to understand that the tentacles form a series and that they correspond to the tentacles found in the species amphioxus. More interestingly, we are expected to relate the tentacles to the velum without prejudice as to whether they are appended to it (a partitive relationship) or actually constitute it (an appositive relationship), on which distinction some biologists would not wish to commit themselves.

Types of noun-phrase structure in relation to variety

17.124 It must be emphasized that anything approaching full exploitation of the potentiality existing in noun-phrase structure is relatively rare and relatively confined to specific fields of discourse. A sample of some 17 000 noun phrases in the Survey of English Usage files yielded the striking contrasts that are summarized in *Table* 17.124.

'Simple' is here defined as nouns without modification, *ie* simple noun phrases (*eg*: *John, she, the man*). In view of their numerical and distributional importance, pronouns and names are distinguished as a subclass of 'simple'. 'Complex' embraces all other noun phrases, but a subclass is distinguished comprising those having multiple modification (more than merely a single adjective premodifier or prepositional phrase postmodifier). *Table* 17.124 shows that:

(a) Less than one-third of the 17 000 noun phrases in the sample are 'complex', even within these modest limits of 'complexity'.

Table 17.124 Noun-phrase structure and distribution

		TOTAL	SIMPLE NOUN PHRASES		COMPLEX NOUN PHRASES	
			All	Names and pronouns	All	Multiple modi-fication
Whole sample	subject	7898 46.6%	6749 39.8%	5821 34.3%	1149 6.8%	456 2.7%
	not subject	9063 53.4%	4753 28.0%	2193 13.0%	4310 25.4%	1777 10.5%
	total	16961 100%	11502 67.8%	8014 47.2%	5459 32.2%	2233 13.2%
Informal speech	subject	2212	2064	1941	148	62
	not subject	1980	1169	677	811	327
Fiction	subject	2431	2220	1943	211	92
	not subject	2803	1682	754	1121	434
Serious talk	subject	2088	1745	1478	343	127
	not subject	2511	1273	599	1238	492
Scientific writing	subject	1167	720	459	447	175
	not subject	1769	629	163	1140	524

(b) Only about one-eighth have multiple modification.

(c) Nearly one-half of the sample consists of pronouns or names.

(d) The majority of simple noun phrases – and the overwhelming majority of names and pronouns – are subjects of clauses or sentences, but only rather less than a quarter of complex noun phrases are subjects.

(e) When the whole sample is broken down into four types of text, one such type ('serious talk and writing') very closely follows the pattern of distribution for the sample as a whole.

(f) In respect of these particular noun-phrase parameters, prose fiction and informal spoken English agree closely and are sharply distinct from the other two varieties represented in the sample; they have a much higher proportion of simple to complex and a much stronger association of simple with subject, and complex with nonsubject, than the other varieties.

(g) Scientific writing differs greatly from the other varieties in having a distinctly higher proportion of noun phrases with complexity (and multiple complexity); a distinctly lower proportion of names and pronouns among its simple noun phrases; and the weakest association of simple with subject and complex with nonsubject.

A survey of prepositional phrases highlighted a difference between speech and writing. In a corpus of half a million words, prepositional phrases were found to be considerably more frequent in written than in spoken material, respectively about 140 and 100 phrases per 1000 words. Also, in written texts, 40 per cent of the prepositional phrases functioned as postmodification in noun phrases, as compared with only 33 per cent in speech.

Even such coarse-grained comparisons as these make clear how sensitive is the noun phrase as an index of style and how responsive it can be to the basic purpose and subject matter in varying types of discourse.

Bibliographical note

On relative clauses and other types of postmodification, see Aissen (1972); Bresnan and Grimshaw (1978); Downing (1978); Elsness (1982); Hartvigson (1979); Huddleston (1971); Jacobson (1983); Jacobsson (1963, 1970); Karlsen (1965); Kjellmer (1975a); Michiels (1975, 1977), Olofsson (1981); van Roey (1969); Roggero (1967); Romaine (1980); Rydén (1970, 1974); Schachter (1973); Sears (1972); Taglicht (1972, 1977); Weisler (1980); Young (1980).

On premodification, see Abberton (1977); Bache (1978); Bolinger (1967a); Coates (1977); Dierickx (1970); Fries (1970); Johansson (1980); Levi (1978); Martin and Ferb (1973); Mutt (1967); Pennanen (1980); Sampson (1980); Sørensen (1980); Warren (1978); Wyler (1979).

On modification in relation to function, see Aarts (1971); Fries (1972); Williams (1979); on special relations between heads and modifiers, see Aarts and Aarts (1982); Christophersen (1974), Seppänen (1978).

On nominalization, see Chomsky (1972); Colen (1984); Downing (1977); Fraser (1970); Kjellmer (1980); Lees (1960a); Vendler (1968); Webster (1977); Wonder (1970).

On the genitive and *of*-construction, see Altenberg (1980, 1982); Dahl (1971); Jahr Sørheim (1980).

On apposition, see Austin (1980); Du Bois (1974); Haugen (1953); Hockett (1955); Lee (1952).

18 Theme, focus, and information processing

Introduction

18.1 In earlier chapters, we have examined the construction of sentences in terms of the way in which units (such as subject, verb, and predication) are brought together to form grammatical sequences, and we have treated the order of such units in terms of positional norms. We shall now look upon the construction of a sentence from the viewpoint of constructing a message: segmenting the material into effective prosodic units and ordering the parts so as to achieve the desired result. This means studying the devices by which we lead our hearer/reader to recognize unmistakably the piece of information that we see as the highpoint of our message, at the same time providing enough additional material to ensure that the message is complete. If the message is heard, the highpoint will be marked in utterance by prosodic prominence; but even if the message is written and is silently read by the recipient, the writer must still ensure that the reader will identify the highpoint by being able to give it an internal or 'imagined' prosodic prominence. Intonation and other prosodic features are therefore essential in the processing and receiving of information, whether written or spoken, and we shall be constantly referring to the phonological distinctions described in Appendix II.

But lexical choice and grammatical organization have an important role. Consider these examples:

Will the new law help old people? [1]
The road will ultimately be repaired. [2]
I'll visit them occasionally. [3]
The honeymoon couple returned to Edinburgh in bright sunshine today. [4]

In the following variants, the truth value is unchanged, but the presentation is very different:

In your view, will the new law give old people the help they need? [1a]
It will be some time before the road is repaired. [2a]
I don't think I can do more than pay them an occasional visit. [3a]
It was bright sunny weather that welcomed the honeymoon couple back to Edinburgh today. [4a]

It is not merely that the variants are more verbose. In each case, an introduction has been provided which puts the utterance in a communicative context, as in [1a] and [3a], or which highlights an aspect of the utterance that is communicatively effective, as in [2a] and the journalistic [4a]. Moreover, care has been taken in [1a], [3a], and [4a] to make the ending an appropriate climax. But before we consider other modes of information processing we must look closely at the fundamental role of intonation and other aspects of prosody.

Prosodic aspects

18.2 Let us imagine that we know the answer to the question 'When shall we know what Mary is going to do?' Our reply might take the form:

She will de|cide 'next WÈEK|

The theme (*cf* 18.9), which in this sentence is the subject *she*, would be uttered without emphasis, since it functions as a mere cue that the speaker is cooperating in making a reply which has the expected subject with a known identity. The verb phrase *will decide* is given somewhat more prominence, since although it is semantically congruent with the form of the question, it is by no means wholly predictable in deflecting attention from 'our' knowledge to Mary's decision. If, for example, the question had been 'When will Mary decide?', the reply might have been:

She will do so |next WÈEK|

The verb phrase in this case would have little more prominence than the subject. But the main prominence is given to the time adjunct, *next week*, and this prominence is conveyed by the intonation nucleus on the head noun *week*.

Such prosodic data do not concern speech alone. If we had received the inquiry in writing and had scribbled the reply on paper also, 'She will decide next week' would have been given the prosodic values of our spoken response as the receiver glanced at the written message. And if the receiver were to read it aloud to a friend, it would normally be read with these prosodic values. If this were not so, our message might be distorted or replaced by some other that we had not intended, such as:

She will de|CÌDE next week|

Information and communicative dynamism

18.3 COMMUNICATIVE DYNAMISM refers to the variation in communicative value as between different parts of an utterance. The subject, verb, and adjunct in:

She will de|cide 'next WÈEK|

were described in 18.2 as being uttered with sequentially increasing prominence, with the S conveying least information, the V rather more (for the reasons stated), and the A conveying most – as is natural since it conveys (or implies that it conveys) the information sought by the *wh*-element of the question 'When (shall we know what Mary is going to do)?' A TONE UNIT is defined in Appendix II.13 as a stretch of speech containing one intonation nucleus, and since each such nucleus serves to highlight a piece of information, it follows that a tone unit is coextensive with an INFORMATION UNIT.

But although an information unit highlights one item, this does not mean that the rest of the unit is devoid of information. As in the present example, the 'communicative dynamism' can range from very low (corresponding to weak stress, as with the subject *she*), through medium (corresponding to nonnuclear stress, as with the verb phrase, *will decide*), to very strong stress (corresponding to intonation nucleus, as with the adverbial, *next week*). And, again as in this example, it is common – though by no means necessary – for the range of such communicative dynamism to increase from low to high in accordance with the linear progression of the information unit. To put it another (and better) way, it is common to process the information in a message so as to achieve a linear presentation from low to high information value (*cf* 19.12). We shall refer to this as the principle of END-FOCUS.

18.4 Though there is a one-for-one correspondence between tone unit and information unit, the correspondence is less direct between prosodic prominence and information value. Prominence by stress or intonation is realized on a *syllable*, a unit that has no necessary correlation with meaning, let alone information value. This is the case with the stress on *-cide* in:

She will de|cide 'next WÈEK|

The effect of prosodic prominence is to draw attention to the semantic unit within which the prominent syllable occurs (in this case the verb phrase *will decide*) and hence to give that unit information prominence. So also with the information climax in this example. The noun phrase, *next week*, which realizes the adverbial, would have the main stress on the head, *week*. It is therefore this syllable which carries the nuclear tone, though of course it is not the item *week* itself which is informationally prominent but the whole adverbial *next week*. Compare the parallel distribution of information in the following examples, noting the relation between the prosodically prominent *syllables* and the informationally prominent *semantic units*:

He will de|liver it on TÙEsday|
He should have re|plied to my LÈTter|

If, on the other hand, *my letter* had already been established in the context, it would no longer be appropriate to make the prepositional phrase informationally prominent. Instead, the nucleus would probably occur on *replied* and the adverbial might be lightened and abbreviated by pronominalization:

He should have re|PLÌED { to my 'letter| / to it| }

It is such circumstances that lead some to define end focus in terms of the (stressed syllable of the) last open-class lexical item of the last clause element (but *cf* 18.12 Note [a]).

Note In all the examples so far, the 'semantic units' identified by prosodically prominent syllables have also been grammatical units (V, A), but the broader term 'semantic unit' is necessary as a reminder that the informationally prominent unit need not be a syntactic element:

It was |neither an AŬTocratic| nor en|tirely a DÈMocratic government|

(See further 18.15.)

Tone units and grammar

18.5 Every sentence has at least one tone/information unit, and it is usual for such a unit to be coextensive with a grammatical unit. Sometimes this is the sentence itself, as in the example we have been considering:

She will de|cide 'next WÈEK|

But far more commonly, the tone unit corresponds to a grammatical unit within a sentence. This may be:

(a) An initially placed optional adjunct (*cf* 8.36), other than closed-class items:

|After my ÍLLness| I |went to FRÀNCE|

contrast:

|Then I went to FRÀNCE|

(b) An initially or finally placed disjunct or conjunct, especially when realized by a polysyllabic item:

|FRǍNKly| it has been dis|GRÀCEful|
More|ǒver| the |chairman may not be WÌLLing|
It was dis|GRÀCEful| |FRÁNKly|

(c) An initially placed vocative:

|JÓHN| are you |all RÍGHT|
|DÒCtor| I'm |very ÀNXious|

A vocative in end position will also occupy a separate tone unit if it is given a rising nucleus, whether for politeness or to single out the addressee more specifically (*cf* App II.15), following a different type of nucleus:

I'm |much BÈTTer| |DÓCtor|
But I |don't think you're RÎGHT| |MÁRy|

Contrast:

Are you |all RÍGHT 'John|
I'm |very ÀNXious 'Doctor|

(d) The subject, if this element is realized by a clause or a long noun phrase, especially one with postmodification (*cf* 17.1*ff*, 17.61):

|What we WÁNT| is |plenty of RÀIN|
The |tall 'lady by the DÓOR| |spoke to JÒHN|

Contrast:

|John 'spoke to the 'tall 'lady by the DÒOR|

(e) A fronted object or complement (*cf* 18.20*ff*):

Her |WRǏTing| I |find unintTÈLligible|

(f) The coordinate clauses in a compound sentence, especially when the clauses have different subjects:

She |won the RÁCE| and he was de|LÌGHTed|
They |WÁLKED| they |SWÁM| they |played GÒLF|

Contrast coordinated predicates and predications (*cf* 13.52*f*):

He |went out and 'slammed the DÒOR|
I have |seen them and 'offered my HÈLP|

On the segmentation of tone units, *cf* App II.18.

18.6 It will be noticed that, in each of the cases mentioned in 18.5, the remainder of the sentence is both a tone unit and a grammatical unit: the predicate in (d), a well-formed clause in (a), (b), (c), and (f). An untidier situation, with no one-to-one relation between tone units and major grammatical units, occurs when such items as those specified in (a), (b), and (c) are placed medially. The items concerned may then continue to be given prominence by an intonation nucleus, but – especially in conversational English – the resultant division of the sentence into tone units will not correspond to the grammatical units that we find it useful to distinguish in this book. Thus:

(a′) A sentence with medially placed optional adjunct:

You |should by NŎW| be |earning your LÌving|

(b′) A sentence with medially placed disjunct or conjunct:

It has |FRĂNKly| been dis|GRÀCEful|
The |chairman 'may moreóver| |not be WÌLLing|

(c′) A sentence with medially placed vocative:

You |should 'really JÓHN| be |earning your LÌving|

A further common circumstance in which tone units and sentence constituents do not completely coincide is where a noun-phrase postmodification takes the form of a nonrestrictive clause or appositional structure. For example:

The |JapaNĔSE| whose |industry is THRĬving| are de|servedly PRÒsperous|
I ad|mire the JapaNÈSE| whose |industry is THRÌVing|
|Harriet SMĬTH| our |new RepresĔNtative| |comes from AlaBÀma|
|Let me 'introduce you to 'Harriet SMÌTH| our |new RepresÈNtative|

Contrast (*cf* 18.5 (d)):

The |Japa'nese who 'live in TŎkyo| can |see Ka'buki 'theatre RÈGularly|

18.7 The generalizations made in18.5–6 provide only guidelines: no rigid rule can be made about the relation of grammatical to tone units or about the precise points at which tone units will form their divisions. Since tone units constitute information units, they are by their very nature variable stretches of language, readily adjustable to the demands of emphasis, grammatical complexity, speed of utterance, and other factors. For example, a sentence having a clausal object will generally form one tone unit, so long as all the elements are relatively short and simple. But if (i) we wish to highlight certain parts, or (ii) the length of the constituents goes beyond a certain point (very roughly, five or six words), the sentence will be split into two or more tone/information units:

The |man 'said we could 'park HÈRE|
The |man SĂID| we could |park HÈRE|
The |man assÙRED us| that we could |park our CÁR| |here 'opposite the hoTÈL|

There are extreme cases where every single word can constitute a tone unit; thus, in emphatic irritation, we might say:

|HÉ| |SÁID| |WÉ| |CÒULD|

Note In a corpus of speech, it has been found that 80 per cent of all tone units had between one and seven words, with a median of five words.

Given and new information

18.8 When we construct a message, it is a courtesy to the receiver, as well as a convenience for ourselves, to provide the point of the message with enough context for this point to be both clearly identified and unambiguously understood, as well as being placed in a normal linguistic framework. To return to the question at the beginning of 18.2:

When shall we know what Mary is going to do?

The answer might have been:

We'll know *next week.*

Here the unitalicized portion replicates material from the question; so far as the receiver is concerned, it is entirely GIVEN. But as well as providing assurance that the answer is indeed attending to the question, it serves as a convenient introduction to the actual point of the message, the NEW information conveyed by *next week*. Of course, in this instance, the message would have been adequately comprehensible if it had been confined to the new information alone:

Next week.

But in 18.2, the answer we considered was:

She will decide *next week.*

The italicized portion again presents the main point of the message and the entirely new information, but the introduction is less obviously and directly 'given'. Nonetheless, it serves as the necessary background and by contrast with the 'new' information it is relatively 'given'. The subject *she* and the futurity expressed by *will* are indeed entirely given, and in replacing *we* and *know* by *she* and *decide* (with consequently increased communicative dynamism; *cf* 18.3) we oblige the receiver to infer that if, as we might expect, we learn of her decision when it is made, the new information – in the context of this specific given information – constitutes an adequate answer to the question.

Note **[a]** The subsidiary half of the complex fall-plus-rise nucleus (*cf* 18.17, App II.15) represents 'semi-given' information: *eg: Pass me my CÒAT, FRÉD* (where Fred is assumed to be present, although he has not been actually mentioned). Compare also *I went to FRǍNCE in nineteen FÌFty* with *I went to FRÀNCE last WÉEK* ⟨esp BrE⟩ where 'last week' is not far from our minds, being recent history, and therefore need not bear the whole weight of new information. In AmE, *last week* in this sentence is likely to be treated as given information, and to receive no nuclear prominence at all:

I went to FRÀNCE last week.

[b] The notion of 'given' and 'new' isolates the two poles of least and most communicative dynamism (*cf* 18.3), such as *Joan* and *indigestible* in:

Joan finds seafood indigestible.

The item *seafood* is intermediate, but for the hearer who knows that Joan avoids seafood, it is towards the 'given' pole, while for the hearer who knows that Joan suffers from indigestion, it may be nearer the 'new' pole. If the hearer, on the other hand, is obliged to ask 'Who is Joan?', the speaker knows that he has misjudged even what he assumed to be 'most given'.

Compare also:

Have you |been to the BÀcon exhibition| or |don't you LÌKE that kind of painting|

In the second clause *that kind of painting* is presented as 'given', the speaker assuming that it will be known both which Bacon is meant and also the kind of work he did. Needless to say, a hearer is often in the position of needing to absorb the hint that has been presented as though it were unnecessary.

Theme and focus

18.9 There is commonly a one-to-one relation between 'given' in contrast to 'new' information on the one hand, and theme in contrast to focus on the other. THEME is the name we give to the initial part of any structure when we consider it from an informational point of view. When it occurs in its expected or 'unmarked' form (but *cf* 18.19), its direct relation to given information can be seen informally as announcing that the starting point of the message is established and agreed. In this sense, the definite article is thematic in relation to a noun phrase such as *the lecturer* in announcing that the identity has been established; but, comparably, in the noun phrase *the lecturer's name*, it is the genitive premodifier *the lecturer's* that is thematic. More usually, however, we apply the term 'theme' to the first element of a clause, such as the subject in *The lecturer's name wasn't announced*. Consider now these three examples as 'messages' in isolation:

The lecturer.
The lecturer's name.
The lecturer's name wasn't announced.

We should note a significant prosodic similarity between the italicized theme and the remainder of each structure. The theme's relative lack of stress mimes its status as 'given' and therefore in no need of emphasis. By contrast, the unitalicized portions are given greater prosodic prominence and it would be on these that the intonation nucleus would be placed if they were uttered as messages:

(Who led the discussion?) The |LÈCTurer|
(What did she want to know?) The |lecturer's NÀME|
(Didn't she know who was lecturing?) The |lecturer's 'name wasn't anNÒUNCED|

In other words, the new information in each case is the 'focus' of the message, and just as we saw in 18.8 that it seemed natural to place the new information after providing a context of given information, so we can regard focus (identified prosodically as we have explained in 18.4) as most neutrally and normally placed at the end of the information unit.

Since the new information often needs to be stated more fully than the given (that is, with a longer, 'heavier' structure), it is not unexpected that an organization principle which may be called END-WEIGHT comes into operation along with the principle of end-focus. The principle of end-weight can be seen operating in the following examples:

She visited him that very day.
She visited her best friend that very day.
She visited that very day an elderly and much beloved friend.

Even had the speaker/writer preferred to put the focus on the time adjunct and to locate this adjunct in its unmarked final position, the weight of the object noun phrase in the last example makes it preferable to have the adjunct at *iE* (*cf* 8.22). An even more preferred position might have been *I*: '*That very day*, she visited . . .'

Note In contrast to 'given' and 'new', which are *contextually* established and to that extent 'extralinguistic', 'theme' and 'focus' are linguistically defined, in terms of position and prosody respectively. With 'theme' there is an inviting alternative contrast, 'rheme', and the latter term (favoured by many linguists) will be used from time to time, especially in its adjectival form, 'rhematic', since it provides a convenient way of referring to degrees of communicative dynamism. Some linguists use the distinction 'topic'/'comment' for our 'theme'/'focus' or 'theme'/'rheme' (and sometimes for our 'given'/'new'). Others speak of given information as 'old', 'shared', or 'presupposed' information.

18.10 Although it is easy to see that the focus is in some obvious sense the most relevant part of a message, we must not underrate the theme, which is certainly the next most relevant. In clause structure, initial position is important for thematic presentation, and in this way it may be chosen for a wide range of items:

(a) Subject in a statement:

He and I have studied the instructions.

(b) Subject in a directive:

You study the instructions!

(c) Operator in a *yes–no* question:

Is she studying the instructions?

(d) *Wh*-element in a *wh*-question:

What is she studying?

(e) A verb item in a directive:

Study the instructions!
Let's study the instructions!
Do study the instructions!

(f) Adverbial (but *cf* 18.19) in a statement or directive:

Yet she studied the instructions.
Usually she studies the instructions.
Please study the instructions!

(g) Conjunction:

. . . *although* she studied the instructions.

All the examples are concerned with a single issue, 'studying the instructions', with the focus on the object phrase prosodically identified by an intonation nucleus on the stressed syllable of the noun head in this phrase, which we leave unmarked as to nucleus so that it may be clear that no specific type of nuclear tone is demanded:

. . . the inSTRUCTions|

But the theme varies widely from example to example and in each case plays a semantically crucial part in stipulating, from the outset, a governing condition for the entire clause that follows. This may be an indication of the clause's structure (*eg* interrogative); or its structural relationship (*eg* subordinate); or it may indicate a semantic relation (*eg* concession).

The theme type (a), however, differs from the others in being given significantly less prosodic prominence. This reflects the fact that the subject of a clause or sentence (and especially a pronominal subject) is likely to be contextually 'given' information and hence to carry least communicative dynamism. It is doubtless also an acknowledgment that the declarative sentence with initial subject is grammatically the least 'marked' type of clause.

The noticeably greater prominence given to the thematic items in (b–g), therefore, appropriately gives notice that a clause is *not* beginning in the least marked form. The necessity for such a distinction can readily be seen with (b):

|You 'study the inSTRÙCTions|

If we removed from *you* the stress implied by the 'onset' (*cf* App II.13), the utterance would be interpreted as a straightforward declarative, just as it would be in the following:

I notice that every time you set the alarm, you study the instructions. Is this because you keep forgetting them?

Where, as in (b–g), themes are significant enough to be given prominence at the tone unit's 'onset', they can be referred to as ONSET THEMES.

Note Onset theme should not be confused with 'marked theme', *cf* 18.19, though the distinction is ultimately gradient rather than absolute.

The relation between focus and new information

18.11 The focus indicates where the new information lies, and the intonation nucleus (which in turn signals the focus) occurs on the last appropriate syllable as determined by the prosodic rule outlined in 18.4.

It is necessary to state the correspondence in this rather broad and general way, since the new information can be anything from a syllable to a whole clause. If the nucleus falls on the last stressed syllable of the clause (according to the unmarked end-focus principle), the new element could, for example, be the entire clause, or the last element (*eg* complement) of the clause, or the predication of the clause. In the following sentence, we mark the extent of the new information for three possible uses of the same sentence:

Whole clause is 'new':

NEW

(What's on today?) We're going to the RÀCes. [1]

Predication is 'new':

NEW

(What are we doing today?) We're going to the RÀCes. [2]

Final adverbial is 'new':

NEW

(Where are we going today?) We're going to the RÀCes. [3]

The sentence as heard (and the same would of course apply to writing: *cf* 18.2) is neutral as to the three possible stretches of new information indicated by our marking, since the focus is at the same point in each case. Only the parenthesized questions (more broadly put, our knowledge of the context) provide the clue as to how much of the information is assumed as 'given' and how much is thus new.

When the nucleus occurs on a syllable earlier than that predicted by the principle of end-focus, however, no such openness of interpretation is possible:

NEW

(Who's going to the races?) WÈ'RE going to the races. [4]

(Have you decided whether you're going to the races?)

NEW

Yes, we ÀRE going to the races. [5]

This is an instance of 'marked' focus, to which we now turn.

Note [**a**] In conversation, where the sentences [2–5] were replies to the corresponding questions, it would be common of course for ellipsis (*cf* 19.44*f*) to permit only the new information to be uttered; *cf* 18.8. For example, in place of [2], [3], [4], and [5] we could have:

Going to the RÀCes. [2a]
To the RÀCes. [3a]
WÈ are. [4a]
We ÀRE. [5a]

[**b**] The contrast in the following is worth remarking:

Among those present were the Mayor and { MÌS(IZ) Martin. [6]
{ MIS(IZ) MÀRtin. [7]

In [7] the Mayor is accompanied by a woman having a different surname from his; in [6] the woman – his wife or daughter, perhaps – has the same surname as the Mayor and the speaker implies that the hearer knows already what this is.

[**c**] In examples like the following (especially with respect to items of personal wear), the final phrase is normally treated as given, being added only for informal clarification:

She's buying a SCÀRF for herself.

Contrast:

She's buying her mother a birthday present but she's also buying a SCÁRF for herSÈLF.

Marked focus

18.12 The principle of end-focus entails that we can confidently predict that a reader will interpret *blue* as the focal item in the written sentence:

I am painting my living room blue.

In other words, we are confident that he would read it aloud as:

I am |painting my 'living room BLÙE| [1]

with an increasing degree of communicative dynamism from *painting* to *blue*. But as we have just seen in 18.11, *all* of the information in this sentence may be new, and when we reflect upon the sentence we must realize that in fact no part is necessarily more obvious or predictable than another. This means that it is perfectly possible to make the sentence informationally appropriate with the intonation nucleus (and hence the information focus) elsewhere:

I am |painting my LÌving room 'blue| [2]
I am |painting MỲ 'living room 'blue| [3]
I am |PÀINting my 'living room 'blue| [4]
I |ÀM 'painting my 'living room 'blue| [5]
|Ì am 'painting my 'living room 'blue| [6]

It is when we move the focus from its predictable position as in [1] to another position as in [2–6] that we speak of MARKED FOCUS.

The condition for marked focus arises when special emphasis is required. Frequently this special emphasis is needed for the purposes of contrast or correction. Thus it would be easy to imagine [2] as following someone else's remark:

I am |painting my 'bathroom BLÙE|

or question:

|Are you 'painting your 'kitchen BLÚE|

Equally, [3] might follow on from:

|John is 'painting his 'living room BLÙE|

or:

|Are you 'painting 'John's 'living room BLÚE|

Again, [4] might follow on from:

I've |changed my 'mind about PǍPering|

So, too, [5] might be a response to:

|Weren't you in'tending to 'paint your 'living room BLÚE|

And [6] might follow on from:

|So 'John is 'painting your 'living room BLÙE|

But contrast, in the sense of replacing one presumed item by another, is not the only occasion for the special emphasis of marked focus. More generally, it is a matter of adjusting the focus according to what is presupposed in a given utterance; *cf* 18.8 Note [a]. The simple supply of required information may call for marked focus if the item supplying the information does not occur in the unmarked end position. This was the case with example [4] in 18.11:

|WÈ'RE going to the 'races|

It could also be the case in [6] above if this was in response to a *wh*-question:

|Who's 'painting your 'living room BLÙE|

Note [**a**] Not all apparently open-class items at *E* are in end-focus. With the written version of the following sentence, we could not be confident about the assigning of the rhematic nucleus:

I am painting my living room at present.

Despite the fact that *present* can be an open-class lexical item (*cf* 18.4), there are good grounds for seeing unmarked focus as follows:

I am |painting my LÌVing room at present|

This is because the adverbial *at present* need have little more role than merely to endorse the present tense of the verb phrase.

[**b**] Since in reading we assign end-focus unless the context makes it unambiguously clear that the focus should be elsewhere, other devices than prosody are usefully invoked where end-focus would produce a misreading. For example, the cleft-sentence structure; *cf* 18.26. But for some instances of marked focus, as in [3], [4], and [5], considerable reworking is required. Thus in place of [3], we might have a written version:

The living room I am painting blue is {my own. / mine.} [3a]

[**c**] Examples [3], [5], and [6] above illustrate the fact that, although focus is normally expected to fall on an open-class lexical item, exceptions can readily be made where a closed-class item requires special emphasis for contrastive or other purposes (*cf* 18.14). Even the articles may be thus focused:

Are you |talking about THÉ 'Mrs 'Reagan| (or only someone else of the same name)?

A: Did you |see the po'liceman conCÉRNED|

B: Well I |saw Ǎ po'liceman| [pronounced /eɪ/]

Compare also:

|YÒU should worry| [=This shouldn't worry YǑU|]

18.13 In certain circumstances, it is quite normal to have the focus on a noun phrase as subject of a clause, in violation of the end-focus principle. This is frequently because, with the subject concerned, the predicate is relatively predictable and thus has lower communicative dynamism. More broadly, it reflects the fact that nouns generally convey more information than verbs. It is significant that the phenomenon in question is especially associated with intransitives, where (if English structure permitted it freely) we might expect the element order *VS*. Compare:

The |TÈLephone's 'ringing|
The |SÙN is 'shining|
The |KÈTtle's 'boiling|
A |VÌsitor called|
|Has your SÍSter 'come 'home|

Predictability is easy to see with the first two examples, but it is arguable analogously that, in a domestic context, the most obvious thing to announce about kettles is that they are boiling; a visitor cannot visit without 'calling' at one's house; and what more predictable for a caller, interested in a person, than to ask whether she is at home? Contrast:

|Has your 'sister 'gone ÓUT|

But it is not only this extreme degree of predictability that makes a predicate carry less communicative dynamism. Consider the following sentences:

The |KÈTtle is 'missing|
The |TÈLephone is 'out of 'order|

There seem in fact to be several possible factors that lead us to identify by focus a subject as more important than the predicate. First, the subject must be a known and named individual (*John, The President*) or else an entity or activity that has great generality or whose existence is well known (*A visitor, The kettle*). Second, the predicate denotes typically a very general or commonly associated activity (especially one that presents a starkly positive/negative choice), such as the act of appearing/disappearing; or it denotes demise or other misfortune, again of a general nature. Some examples:

The |BÈLL is 'ringing|	*contrast*:	The |bell is GLÌTtering|
		My |ears are RÌNGing|
|JÒHN has ar'rived|	*contrast*:	|John has FÌNished|
The |PRÈsident has 'died|	*contrast*:	|Someone has DÌED|
My |CÒAT is 'torn|	*contrast*:	My |coat is FÀWN|
|MÀRy is 'ill a'gain|	*contrast*:	|Mary is PRÈGnant again|
A |WÀSP has 'settled on you|	*contrast*:	A |wasp has 'settled on your BÀCK|
The |BÀby's 'crying|	*contrast*:	The |baby's SMÌLing|

Emphasis may be given to an initial noun phrase (or indeed to any nonfinal item) by interposing a parenthesis with its own tone unit:

|This in SHÓRT| is |why I reFÙSED|

The device is comparably valuable in writing, where this conjunct would be separately punctuated and thus allow *This* to have more weight than it otherwise would:

This, in short, is why I refused.

Although we have associated this phenomenon with noun phrases as *subject*, it arises more broadly with noun phrases in construction with succeeding verb phrases:

Joan has a PLÀNE to 'catch|
We have various PRÒBlems to 'solve|
. . . STÙDents to 'teach|
. . . QUÈSTions to 'answer|
. . . FÌGures to 'add 'up|

By contrast, where it is less congruent with or less predictably associated with the noun phrase, it is the verb phrase that might be focused:

. . . students to repriMÀND|
. . . texts to comPÙTerize|

Similarly, within a noun phrase, if the head is more general and carries less semantic weight and specificity than the premodifier, it is the latter that may sometimes be focused:

> She's a |BRÌLliant 'person|
> (*contrast*: She's a |brilliant DÒctor|)

Again, where the noun-phrase object is of general reference, focus may be moved forward on to the head of the verb phrase:

> You should |always 'try to HÈLP { a 'chap| / a 'fellow| / a 'guy| }
>
> (*contrast:* You should |always 'try to 'help a poLÌCEman|)

Compare also noun phrases of mere expletive or evaluative force:

> I've been CHÈATed by the dirty scoundrel.
> She's given me a new TÌE, the 'little 'darling.

18.14 The instances of marked focus in 18.12 involved putting the focus earlier than where it would occur in unmarked focus. But there are two further types, (a) and (b), to be considered:

(a) First, the focus can be moved to a point subsequent to its expected position. This is sometimes because the unmarked focus is misleading, as it might be in:

> |What 'firm is your BRÒTHer with|
> |Who's the NÒvel by|
> I re|fused to GÒ with him|

If there were any danger that the hearer might take these as emphatic (for example, *your brother* in contrast to *your sister* or *your father*; *the novel* in contrast to *the review*; *go* in contrast to *stay talking*), the questions would be put with marked focus upon the prepositions:

> |What 'firm is your 'brother WÌTH|
> |Who's the 'novel BỲ|
> I re|fused to go WÌTH him|

Similarly, we may have:

> I |saw your 'sister WÌTH him|

In an exchange like the following:

> A: So what did you SÀY?
> B: There was nothing TÒ say.

it may seem vacuous to highlight the mere infinitive marker (*cf* 9.9). But on the one hand, *say* is given and would thus be an inappropriate bearer of a nucleus; on the other hand, there is a positive reason for placing the nucleus on the only part of this verb phrase which represents the modality. Compare an alternative version of B's response:

There was nothing that I CÒULD say.

Similarly, an example from a broadcast interview:

We must make clear our position TÒ the government.

The placing of the nucleus on *to* was doubtless motivated by the fact that, in the linguistic context, *our position*, *the government*, and *make clear* were already given.

Marked focus on such closed-class items may alternatively occur when we want them to have special contrastive emphasis:

|Who are you 'working FÒR| [*ie* not *with*]

Something similar can occur with the particle in phrasal verbs, since, although such items normally carry a degree of stress not associated with prepositions, they may constitute either an unmarked focus or a contrastive one. Beside:

I |think it's time to 'go ÌN|

we may have:

|Don't stand outsÍDE| |Please 'go ÌN|

Some further examples of marked focus:

He was |speaking to MÈ| (*not you*)
So we |bought THÌS 'house| (*instead of that one*)
I |told you to put them ÒN the 'bed| (*not under it*)
|Put your 'hat ÒN| (*it's raining*)
|Hand your 'ticket ÌN| (*you're not allowed to keep it*)

In view of what was said in 18.12 Note [a], it would similarly be a case of marked focus if we gave special emphasis to the adverbial in:

I am |painting my 'living room at PRÈsent|

(b) Secondly, we can have contrastive focus at precisely the point of unmarked focus. Thus:

I am |painting my 'living room BLÙE| (*or* . . . "↑ BLÙE|)

may connote in the context special emphasis ('Of all colours', 'Though it's the one I dislike most', or 'You are wrong in thinking that I'm painting it yellow'). In speech, such marked focus may be realized with additional stress or wider range of nucleus (*cf* App II.20). In writing, the comparable effect can often be conveyed only by expansion or rather elaborate paraphrase, but sometimes typographical devices are invoked, especially italics. In S J Perelman's *Last Laugh* (1981), we find the following piece of dialogue:

'Was that how you became a rustler?'
'A rustler?' I repeated. 'Not a rustler, Miss Cronjager – a *wrestler*.'

The word that requires marked contrastive focus for corrective purposes comes at the point where unmarked focus would occur. Perelman presumably expects the reader to imagine a realization in which the first repetition is uttered with a wider pitch range than where it occurs in Miss Cronjager's question, with special prosodic marking also of the second repetition and of the word that is to replace it:

> Was |that how you became a RÚstler|
> A |RÚstler| . . . |Not a RŬstler| . . . a "|WRÈstler|

Note [**a**] Radio and television announcers in both America and Britain are often accused of overusing marked focus on closed-class items (*cf* 19.34 Note).

[**b**] Where marked focus is required on a preposition, it is sometimes possible to achieve the required meaning with end focus by using a paraphrase. Thus beside:

> . . . apart from his LÀZiness|

we may have:

> . . . aPÀRT from his 'laziness|

or:

> . . . his 'laziness aPÀRT|

Compare also (in formal use, *cf* 9.56):

> . . . notwithSTÀNDing his 'laziness| . . . his 'laziness notwithSTÀNDing|

With the adverbial particle in phrasal verbs the same result is achieved merely by movement:

> He's |bringing 'in the CÀSes| He's |bringing the 'cases ÌN|

This helps to explain why such particles are in final position when the object is a personal pronoun (*cf* 16.2*ff*) or is a noun phrase of very general meaning:

> He's |bringing them ÌN|
> He's |bringing the thing ÌN|
> (?*He's |bringing 'in the THÌNG|)
> (*cf* *She's |bringing 'up the MÀTter|)

Compare also:

> They've |found a 'nice aPÀRTment to 'live in|
> They've |found a 'nice 'place to LÌVE|

18.15 Just as marked focus frequently involves putting emphasis on an unexpected part of a phrase ('. . . ÒN the bed'), so also it may involve unexpected emphasis on part of a proper noun, a compound, or even an ordinary word. Whereas normally we put the main stress on a person's family name and not the first name:

> Dylan THÒMas

marked focus may reverse this, often but not exclusively with a view to making a correction:

> But I |said DỲLan 'Thomas was 'born in 1914| – |not ÉDward Thomas|
> |Some 'readers pre'fer ÈMily 'Brontë| while |others 'favour CHÀRlotte ('Brontë)| but is there |anyone who 'still 'reads ÁNNE ('Brontë)|

Conversely, compound nouns with normal first-element stress (*cf* App II.7) can switch to second-element stress with marked focus:

> I |just 'wanted a 'couple of PÌCTure hooks| and he |started 'showing me some 'picture BÒOKS|

So also beside the normal:

> He's an in|SÙRance 'agent|

we may find ourselves needing to say, 'Oh no, I'm sorry' and to correct ourselves with:

He's |not an in'surance ÁGent| He's an in|surance BRÒker|

Equally, beside the normal:

It's a |chicken SÀNDwich|

we could have:

This is a |CHÌCKen 'sandwich| and I'd pre|fer a CHÈESE 'sandwich|

As for marked focus altering the accentuation within a word, we had an example in 18.4 Note (*cf* also App II.10 on contrastive stress). This phenomenon is perhaps most familiar with negative prefixes, but it occurs with other word elements also:

(Happy?) I |thought she 'looked ÙNhappy|
(Agreeable?) I |thought he 'seemed DÌSagreeable|
It |didn't disCÓURage me| I |actually 'felt ÈNcouraged|
She |suddenly changed the subject from ĔMigration| to |ÌMmigration|

Focus on the operator

18.16 One type of marked focus that deserves separate treatment is focusing on the operator, which often has the particular function of signalling contrast between positive and negative meaning:

(A: Why haven't you had a bath?) B: I |HÀVE had a 'bath|
(A: Look for your shoes.) B: I |AM̀ looking for them|
She |PRŎMised| so she| MÙST 'take him 'with her|
They've ac|cepted the ÒFFer| they |really HÀVE|

When the operator is positive, the meaning is 'Yes in contrast to No'; when the operator is negative, the meaning is contrastive in the opposite direction:

So you |HÀVEn't lost it| ['You thought you had']

It is not surprising that focus on the operator has this function, when we consider that the operator (in *yes–no* questions and in negatives) is the item most concerned in signalling the positive/negative polarity. Also, we may notice that the operator emphasizes positiveness or negativeness when it bears the focus (as it normally does) in elliptical replies:

(A: Have you seen my books?) B: |No, I HÀVEn't|
(A: Would you like black coffee?) B: |Yes, I WÒULD|
(A: Does this bell work?) B: |Yes, it DÒES|

This last example leads us on to the most significant point about focus on the operator, which is that when the finite verb phrase is in the simple present or past tense, and so would not otherwise have an auxiliary verb to function as operator, the 'dummy' operator DO is introduced to bear the nuclear stress. This, then, is a further example of DO-support (*cf* 3.37):

So you |DÌD go to the concert this 'evening|
[*ie* 'I thought you might, but . . .']
But I |DÒ think you're a 'good 'cook| [*ie* '. . . even if you imagine I don't']

With a rise or fall-rise as intonation nucleus, focus on auxiliaries indicating past or future often draws contrastive attention to the tense or aspect rather than to the positive/negative polarity:

He |owns – or DǏD own| – a |Rolls RÒYCE|
We've |sold ÒUT| but we |WǏLL be 'getting 'some|
It |HǍS been| and |still ÌS| a |difficult TÌME|

Similarly, the nucleus on auxiliaries such as *may, ought to,* and *could* often signals a contrast between the supposed real state of affairs, and a state of affairs thought desirable or likely:

The o|pinion 'polls MǍY be 'right| [*ie* 'but I suspect they're not']
My |purse ǑUGHT to be 'here| [*ie* 'but it probably isn't']
She |CǑULD drive you there| [*ie* 'but I don't think she has time']

But in courtesy enquiries about health and wellbeing, where there are in effect no information-bearing lexical items, focus on the operator carries no special emphasis:

How |ÀRE you 'these 'days|
Well, how |ÀRE you 'now, 'Mr 'Brown|

With focus on the subject or the adverbial, some emphasis (as, for example, contrast) can be implied:

|How are YÒU 'these 'days| |How are you NÒW|

Thus we would not find:

. . . *'these DÀYS   . . . *THÈSE 'days

If normally unstressed operators receive stress (especially nuclear stress), the effect is often to add exclamatory emphasis to the whole sentence:

That WÌLL be nice!
What ÁRE you DÒing?
We HÀVE enjoyed ourselves!

As noted above, DO-support is introduced where there would otherwise be no operator to bear the emphatic stress:

|You DÒ look a 'wreck|

Note On emotive emphasis, *cf* further 18.55*f*; on marked theme, with focus on the operator (as in *Stupid though he is*), *cf* 18.19.

Divided focus

18.17 It sometimes happens that we want to put nuclear focus upon two items in an information unit. An intonation pattern particularly associated with this in BrE is the fall-plus-rise contour (*cf* App II.17; see also 8.111 Note [c]). Compare the following:

He's |fairly CLÈver| [1]
He's |FÀIRly CLÉver| [2]

The implications differ in two ways. Semantically, [1] implies a positive estimate, though cautiously worded, while [2] is relatively grudging and disparaging, calling in question the estimate of cleverness. Informationally, [1] is compatible with answering a general inquiry about the person ('What do you think of Alec?'), while [2] implies that the question of his cleverness has already been raised ('Alec is clever, isn't he?'). Where such DIVIDED FOCUS is realized by fall-plus-rise, therefore, the item carrying the rise is made subsidiary to the other focused item, accepts that it represents information that is to some extent 'given', but (compatible with the rise) calls its status in question. Again, compare the following possible responses to the same inquiry, 'Alec is clever, isn't he?'

I |THÌNK so| [3]

I |THÌNK {só| / he ís|} [4]

Compare also:

I'm |SÙRE he is|

In [4] we have a strong note of reservation as compared with the relative confidence of [3]. The subsidiary item need not however carry such a reservation. Often it acts as merely confirmatory of 'given' status or confers a 'given' status where there happens to be no contextual warrant:

|William WÒRDSworth is my 'favourite 'English PÓet|

(which may be replying to the question 'Who is your favourite English poet?' or correcting a contrary statement 'I understand that John Keats is your favourite . . .').

|MÀNy 'people are disbe'lievers at the 'present TÍME|

In this example, the final adjunct is merely confirmatory of the tense in *are* and has no necessary connotation that the present time has been referred to; treating it with divided focus seems especially BrE; in AmE it would often be unmarked intonationally. Frequently indeed, the second focus conveys little more than courtesy, especially to one who has not been recently addressed in a particular discourse. Thus it is used with final vocatives and formulaic disjuncts:

|What's the TÌME, JÓHN| At|TÈNtion, PLÉASE|

In contrast to the fall-plus-rise, the rise-plus-fall contour is used to mark a divided focus where the first of the two focused items is made subsidiary to the second:

|HÉ is 'happy when SHÈ 'is| |She is HÁPpy but 'he ÌSN'T|

We can compare the two types of divided focus:

I |went to FRÀNCE in 'nineteen ÉIGHTy| [5]
I |went to FRÁNCE in 'nineteen ÈIGHTy| [6]

[5] suggests a context in which there is discussion of what I had done in 1980, this part therefore being relatively given; [6] suggests one in which the

discussion concerns when I went to France, the rise again coinciding with the relatively given, but this time preceding the relatively new instead of following it. It might be said that À B́ is informationally equivalent to B́ À (or B̌ À). Thus, in corrective response to 'I bet you enjoyed yourself in Spain in 1980', we might find either [5] or:

In |nineteen ÉIGHTy I went to FRÀNCE|

Note The prepositional highlighting mentioned in 18.14 frequently occurs with the pattern of divided focus discussed above:

. . . but ÌN the NÓRTH |there'll be |further SNÒW|

Sometimes the first of the two focused items seems to be focused for no better reason than to slow up delivery, perhaps while the speaker is deciding exactly what to say:

. . . and the 'attitude TÒ (er) 'these PÉOPle| is ap|PÀLLing|

But more generally the fall in such divided focus serves the purpose of making the whole phrase (and not of course merely the closed-class item) emphatic:

(He has written a book on African folklore, and he will be reading) 'extracts FRÒM his BÓOK (in the broadcast this evening).

(She hoped profoundly that they could enjoy a quiet dinner) and in'deed BỲ the Évening (the quarrel had been forgotten).

The emphasis may, of course, be actually contrastive:

(They thought the weather would be better in the south) but 'actually ÌN the SÓUTH (the snow and ice were more severe).

Compare also:

Thc |flight is 'now ex'pected TÒ dePÁRT| in |one HÒUR|

An alternative ('. . . 'now EXPÈCTed to dePÁRT') would tend to call in question the likelihood, where the relatively irregular prosodic focus on the preposition makes the departure seem more certain (*cf* 19.34 Note).

Concatenated focus

18.18 We saw in 18.17 that the rise in a rise-plus-fall divided focus sequence prepares us (with relatively 'given' material) for the fall that is to follow – on new material. It is in fact very common for a rise to function as preparatory for a climactic falling nucleus:

They |came 'last SÚNday| and they are |staying for a MÒNTH|

The phenomenon is particularly common with divided focus of the fall-plus-rise type:

I'm |not seeking BÙRGlary insÚRance| but |FÌRE insurance|

Compare also the following pairs:

{ They |captured 'three of our SÒLDiers|
{ They |captured THRÈE of ÓUR 'soldiers| and |we 'captured 'four of THÈIRS|

{ She ar|rived with her HÙsband|
{ She ar|rived WÌTH her HÚsband| but with|out the CHÌLDren|

Where a rise or fall-rise gives a general indication that a relevant fall is to follow, a fall-rise draws particular attention to an item that is actually to be contrasted:

Al|though 'G-'minor is a 'common 'key for MǑzart| in |BĚETHoven| it's |rather RÀRE|

Such anticipatory contrast may involve several focused items:

|DY̌Lan 'Thomas| was |born in 'nineteen-fourTĚEN| in |SWÀNsea| but
|HŬGH 'Thomas| was |born in 'eighteen-'eighty THRĚE| in |ÀNglesey|

But the contrast in such a concatenation may be anaphoric rather than anticipatory. This is the case with the fall-rise focus on *it* in the following playful exchange recorded between two friends. Notice also the repetition of the cliché 'one of God's little creatures', but without information focus when it is 'given', the point forcefully conveyed by the focus on *also*:

A: |Stop at'tacking that WÀSP| It's |one of 'God's 'little CRÈAtures|
B: But |I am ÀLSO 'one of 'God's 'little 'creatures| and |ǏT |was at|tacking MÈ|

Marked theme

18.19 The two communicatively significant parts of an information unit, the theme and the focus, are typically as distinct as they can be: one is the point of initiation, and the other the point of completion. The theme of an information unit, coming first, is more often 'given' information than any other part of it. Yet the two can coincide; for instance, when, as marked focus, the nucleus falls on the subject of a statement:

(Who gave you that magazine?) |BÌLL gave it to me| [1]

This is the extreme form of MARKED THEME, and we can compare [2] which has an unmarked theme (*He*) and minimum prosodic prominence:

He |gave me a magaZÌNE| [2]

We use the term 'marked theme' to designate a theme which is given at least as much prosodic marking as that entailed by being at the point of 'onset' (*cf* App II.11) in a tone unit.

Clearly, theme and focus will always coincide in one-word utterances, whether these are replies, questions, or military commands. For example:

|CÓFFee| |THÀNKS|

Even so, many such short units have an initial portion that can be used as thematic preparation. A striking instance of this is found in the military order, 'Attention!' The word is typically uttered with considerable drawl on the first two syllables, and while the onset appears at the point of normal stress, in military use it is the final syllable that is given word stress and the climactic nuclear focus:

at|ten – TÌON|

But between the extremes of a theme carrying no stress, as in:

She's |coming toNÌGHT|

and a theme coinciding with marked focus, as in:

|SHÈ'S 'coming to'night|

there is a wide range of prosodic weight that can be assigned to the theme. One such point in this range we have referred to as 'onset theme' in 18.10 (*cf* also App II.13):

. . . al|though she's 'coming toNÌGHT|
|Yet she's coming toNÌGHT|
The |doctor is 'coming toNÌGHT|

We perceive the theme as carrying greater prosodic weight when it is an item that is not (like subject or conjunction, for example) normally at initial position in a clause (*cf* 8.14*f*). Consider the following exchange:

A: Are you |going to in'vite JÓHN| B: Oh |John I've al'ready invÌTed|

In B's response, *John* is a marked theme and the term will be used for any such fronted item whether or not it carries (as such items commonly do) a marked focus (*cf* further 18.20; on fronting with amplificatory tags, see 18.59 Note [c]).

The value of marked theme in information processing can be seen in comparing the following, where [3–5] have *SVC* order but [6] has *CSV*:

|John is LÀZy| (but I think he will help me) [3]
Al|though 'John is LǍZy| (I think he will help me) [4]
Al|though 'John is LÁZy| . . . [5]
|Lazy though John ÍS| . . . [6]

In [3], *lazy* is new information; there is no assumption on the speaker's part that the listener knows. In [4], the fall-rise on *lazy* also implies that the information is new; the rise part of the complex nucleus is conditioned by the dependent status of the clause of which this is the focus. In [5] however, the simple rise on *lazy* is compatible both with the dependence of the clause concerned and the implication that the hearer already shares the speaker's view of John. In [6], making *lazy* a marked theme entirely implies the givenness of the information and additionally enables the speaker to focus upon the operator (*cf* 18.16) with consequent emphasis on its positive polarity (*cf* 15.39*ff*). A further example: 'Serious as has become the food shortage, worse news is to follow'; this embodies inversion of subject and verb (*cf* 18.22*f*).

Common short adverbials in initial position are often given the minimum (onset) thematic marking:

|Then he LÈFT|

Longer and semantically weightier adverbials at *I* will be somewhat more heavily marked themes:

"|Suddenly he LÈFT|

or they may actually be raised to the status of bearing a nuclear focus:

|SǓDdenly| he |LÈFT|

Finally, we should note that marked theme can be used to draw attention to contrasting pairs, and this often involves separate tone units:

|VĚRdi| [1] is |splendid in his WǍY| [2] but |MǑZart's operas| [3] I re|gard as 'pure perFÈCTion| [4]

Notice the prosodic concord of the fall-rises at [1] and [3]; the one at [2] is anticipatory of the fall at [4] (*cf* 18.18).

Note [**a**] We are concerned, here as elsewhere, with the subjective perception of prosodic weight rather than what might be measured instrumentally. In the two following examples, the theme *Miami* would probably be given the same prosodic weight objectively:

(Have you considered a holiday in Miami?)
|Miami BÒRES me| [7]
|Miami I've BÈEN to| [8]

In recognizing *Miami* in [8] as marked theme, therefore, we are noting not only its prosodic prominence but its prominence by reason of its unusual position in the clause concerned (*cf* 18.20).

[**b**] Fronting of a relatively given predication in concessive clauses can be further seen in structures that have no directly corresponding form without fronting:

Criticize him as we may, he has some excellent qualities.
Genius as you may be, you have no right to be rude to your teachers.

A similar analysis might apply to:

Say what you will of them, . . .

(See 15.39*ff.*) Further examples of marked theme: 'French he's quite good at', 'Now he tells me!', 'Tea I can drink at any time of day', 'Hope is all I CAN do'.

Grammatical aspects

Fronting

18.20 Fronting is the term we apply to the achievement of marked theme by moving into initial position an item which is otherwise unusual there. As we saw in 18.19, such a fronted item is frequently an entire sentence element. The reason for fronting may be to echo thematically what has been contextually given:

(You should take up swimming for relaxation)
|RelaxÀtion you 'call it|

Alternatively, the item fronted may be the one contextually most demanded:

|WÌLson his NÁME is|
An |utter FÒOL she 'made me 'feel|
|Really 'good MÈALS they 'serve at that hoTÉL|

It is as if the thematic element is the first thing that strikes the speaker, and the rest is added as an afterthought. The possible insertion of a comma in written English suggests that the nonthematic part is almost an amplificatory tag in status (*cf* 18.59): *Wilson, his name is.*

The foregoing have a distinctly informal flavour, but fronting is in no way confined to colloquial speech. It is very common both in speech and in conventional written material, often serving the function of so arranging clause order that end-focus falls on the most important part of the message as well as providing direct linkage with what has preceded:

That much the jury had thoroughly appreciated.
Most of these problems a computer could take in its stride.
This latter topic we have examined in Chapter 3 and need not reconsider.
To this list may be added ten further items of importance.

The definite items *that*, *this*, and *these* in these examples suggest that the marked theme in such cases most often expresses given information. It is common to find *-ing* participles fronted in similar information-processing circumstances:

> *Sitting at her desk in deep concentration* was my sister Flora. She looked as though she had spent a sleepless night.

(*Cf* subject-verb and subject-operator inversion, 18.23*f*.)

Note [**a**] A fronted item, like a fronted pushdown *wh*-element (*cf* 11.14*ff*), is sometimes an element from a subordinate clause:

> *Everything – or nearly everything – that the Labour movement exists to stop the Tories from doing* Labour will be asked to support the Cabinet in doing.

The whole of the italicized part of this example is the object of a nonfinite clause, itself a prepositional object within an infinitive clause within the main clause.

[**b**] Exceptionally, a part rather than the whole of a clause element may be fronted. *Yes–no* questions, for instance (as we have seen in 18.10), have part of the verb phrase only as their thematic component. In the following case, a prepositional phrase equivalent to a postmodifier of the subject complement (but *cf* 17.49*f*) acts as theme: '*Of all the early examples of science fiction*, the fantastic stories of Jules Verne are the most remarkable.'

[**c**] Sentences containing direct speech quotations seem to provide an example of a construction in which thematic fronting of the direct object is exceptionally easy (*cf* 18.23):

> I said: 'That's a pity.' ~ 'That's a pity', I said.

But one may propose an alternative analysis, in which the reporting subject and verb (here *I said*) constitute a dependent comment clause (*cf* 15.53*ff*) rather than the subject and verb of the sentence. This analysis is urged by the possibility of placing them in the middle of the direct speech, as a parenthesis: '*That,' I said, 'is a pity.*'

18.21 A more striking type of fronting is found in the heightened language of rather mannered rhetoric, including the strenuous colourfulness of journalistic writing. It is frequently employed to point a parallelism between two parts of a clause or between two related but contrasting parts of neighbouring clauses. The fronted parts may be prosodically marked as marked theme or marked focus, the latter typically with divided focus (*cf* 18.17), and they may be grammatically any of a wide range of units:

(a) Direct object or prepositional complement:

> *His face* not many {admired, / were enamoured of,} while *his character* still fewer could praise.

(b) Subject complement or object complement:

> *Traitor* he has become and *traitor* we shall call him.

(c) Predication adjunct:

> *Defiantly* they have spoken but *submissively* they will accept my terms.
> He might agree under pressure: *willingly* he never would.
> *In London* I was born and *in London* I shall die.

(d) Predication:

> They have promised to finish the work, and *finish it* they will.

With predications and predication adjuncts in front position, we often find subject–verb inversion (*cf* 18.23) if the subject is other than a personal pronoun:

> *Into the stifling smoke* we plunged. [A S V]
> *Into the stifling smoke* plunged the desperate mother. [A V S]

In examples like the following, common in journalism, the fronting of the predication seems largely determined in fact by the desire to give end-focus to the subject, at the same time using (as is normal) the early part of the sentence to 'set the scene':

> *Addressing the demonstration* was a quite elderly woman.
> *Shot by nationalist guerrillas* were two entirely innocent tourists.

Even the cleft sentence, itself a grammatical focus device (*cf* 18.25*ff*), is subject to fronting:

> They hoped that Herbert Frost would be elected and *Frost* indeed it was that topped the poll.

Note Parallelism in fronting often corresponds to contrastive focus in speech. For example:
I was BÓRN in London and I shall DÌE in London.

Inversion

18.22 As we have just seen, the fronting of an element is often associated with INVERSION. We distinguish two types, consisting respectively in the reversal of SUBJECT and VERB and the reversal of SUBJECT and OPERATOR.

Since the verb BE as a copula can be simultaneously regarded as verb and operator, we have a choice of regarding its placement before the subject as an instance either of subject–verb or subject–operator inversion. As the examples in 18.23 and 18.24 show, the decision is made according to whether BE, in the given construction, is commutable with another main verb or with another operator.

Subject–verb inversion

18.23 The clause patterns *SVC* and *SVA* (*cf* 10.1*ff*) have their obligatory third element in large measure because the V is commonly of itself so lacking in communicative dynamism:

> *SVC*: Her oval face was especially remarkable. [1]
> *SVC*: The sound of the bell grew faint. [2]
> *SVA*: His beloved body lies in a distant grave. [3]

In consequence, where information processing makes it desirable to front the third element concerned, the result would tend to be bathetic or misleading if normal order were preserved with the SV, suggesting that a nuclear focus be placed, inappropriately, on the verb (*cf* 18.13):

> CSV: ? Especially remarkable her oval face was. [1a]
> CSV: ? Faint the sound of the bell grew. [2a]
> ASV: (?)In a distant grave his beloved body lies. [3a]

If these were not to be dismissed as merely bad style, we would tend to read [1a] as equivalent to '. . . certainly was'; [2a] as 'growing louder, though nonetheless faint'; [3a] as 'being in prone posture' (rather than, say, foetally curved). In consequence, such fronting naturally carries with it the inversion that puts S in final position, and indeed it is to achieve end focus on the S that the fronting is generally undertaken:

CVS: Especially remarkable was her oval face. [1b]
CVS: Faint grew the sound of the bell. [2b]
AVS: In a distant grave lies his beloved body. [3b]

These particular examples have a rather mannered tone (poetic in the case of [2b] and [3b]), but the phenomenon is common enough in ordinary informal speech:

Here's the milkman.
Here comes my brother.
And there at last was the book I'd been looking for.
(The jets caused a great gust of wind and) off flew their hats.
Down came the rain.
Up went the flag.

In these instances with *here/there* + *be*, indeed, it is not simply a matter of stylistic choice: there is a sharp difference of meaning from the alternatives with SVA order. Although we must distinguish these from existential *there* (*cf* 18.45), there is in fact a close similarity. In contrast to ASV, the SVA order invites us not merely to put the nuclear focus upon the A but to see these adjuncts as referring to specific places. Compare:

{ Here's the milkman – he's come at last.
{ The milkman is here – at the door: shall I get two pints?
{ There's the book I want – I've been looking for it all week.
{ The book is there – by the typewriter.

Further examples which are less common in ordinary speech but yet which equally seem less rhetorically unnatural than [1b], [2b], and [3b]:

There at the summit stood the castle in all its medieval splendour.
By 'strategy' is meant the basic planning of the whole operation.
Away ran the terrified boy.
Slowly out of its hangar rolled the gigantic aircraft.
Equally inexplicable was his behaviour to close friends.

Subject–verb inversion (as distinct from subject–operator inversion; *cf* 18.24) with fronted object is chiefly limited to the reporting clauses where the object represents direct speech (including speech that is 'thought') and usually where the subject is not a personal pronoun:

'Please go away' said one child. 'And don't come back', pleaded another.
'Whatever shall I do now?' wondered Fred, remembering – too late – the appointment he had missed.

This is something of a literary convention, and in ordinary speech, VS would usually be replaced by SV (*cf* also 18.20 Note [c] and 14.20, 14.29). With the verb *say*, it is possible to have OSV where the O is the substitute *so*, though this is felt by some to be archaic:

So say the rest of us.

More important are CVS, AVS, where the C and A make comparative reference to something that has preceded:

His answer was a disgrace; *equally regrettable* was his departure immediately afterwards.
Her face was stony and *even stonier* was the tone of her voice.
A year ago, two crashes occurred at the corner, and *more recently* has come the news of a third.

Note [**a**] Subject–verb inversions occur with simple present and past tense verbs (contrast *Here comes my brother* with **Here is coming my brother*), and with certain verbs of stance (*be, stand, lie*, etc) or with very general verbs of motion (*come, go, fall*, etc).
[**b**] Subject–verb inversion does not usually take place in a clause with a personal pronoun alone as subject; hence corresponding to some of the examples above we would have *Here he is, Here he comes, Away he ran*, rather than **Here is he*, etc. But with contrast of subject, note:

There was *she*, on the tennis court, while *I* had to work.
Here am *I*, ill in bed, and *you* don't seem to care.

[**c**] There is inversion with a pronoun subject followed by post-modification in archaic English: *Happy is he who is reconciled with his lot*. There is an analogous inversion with verbless clauses: *Unlucky the man who hates his work*.

Subject–operator inversion

18.24 In addition to the inversion in questions, there are four common circumstances in which the operator precedes the subject.

(a) First we have elliptical clauses with initial *so* or the corresponding negatives *neither* or *nor* (*cf* 12.10, 12.17, 12.29):

John saw the accident and so did Mary. [*cf*. . . and Mary did (so), too.]

John didn't see the accident and {neither / ?nor} did Mary. [*cf*: . . . and Mary didn't, either]

She was angry and so was I.
She wasn't angry and neither was I.
He would love to go and so would she.
She must come and so must you.
He might fail and so might she.

But inversion is less common with certain modal auxiliaries (notably *may, might, ought*), and alternative substitute expressions with normal order are preferred:

She might be ill and he might (be) too.

Initial *so* in elliptical clauses may be followed by normal order when focus is required on the operator rather than the subject, though *so* is then liable to be mistaken for a conjunct (*cf* 8.134*ff*):

(You asked me to leave) and |so I DÌD| [undoubtedly conjunct in: 'and so I |DÌD|']

Compare also the subjunct *so* in:

(He wanted to leave) and |so did Ì|

More formally '(He wanted to leave,) as did I'; *cf* (c) below.

(b) Secondly, we have S-op inversion where a phrase of negative form or meaning is fronted (*cf* 10.58*f*):

Least of all is it in our interest to open negotiations now.
At no time must this door be left unlocked.

Contrast:

At certain times this door may be left unlocked.
*At certain times may this door be left unlocked.

Further examples:

He refused to apologize. Nor would he offer any explanation.
Scarcely had he started speaking when heckling broke out.
(*contrast*: He had scarcely started speaking when heckling broke out.)
Only in this way } is it possible to explain their actions.
In this way alone }

As well as with adverbials, we may have inversion also with object phrases of negative form or meaning:

Not a single book had he read that month.
Only one more point will I make.

(c) Thirdly, we have S-op inversion in comparative clauses when the S is not a personal pronoun:

Oil costs less than would atomic energy.
(*cf*: Oil costs less than it did ~ *. . . did it)
I spend more than do my friends.
She looks forward, as does her secretary, to the completion of the building.

With *as*, inversion is possible with a pronoun subject, especially if there is no correlative *as*:

(?) She was as delighted with the suggestion as was he.
They go to concerts frequently, as do I.

(d) Finally, S-op inversion occurs in subordinate clauses of condition and concession (*cf* 15.33*ff*), especially in rather formal usage:

Were she alive today, she would grieve at the changes.
Were we to withdraw our support, they would be justifiably indignant.
Had I known, I would have gone to her.
Should you change your plans, please let me know.
Even had the building been open, we would not have entered.

It is to be noted that with negative clauses of this form we do not find contraction:

Were she not so handicapped, we would take her to the Alps.
(*Cf*: *Weren't she so handicapped . . .)

Note [**a**] With examples like the following, the inversion involves the main verb rather than the operator:

So absurd was his manner that everyone stared.

This is shown by the fact that a whole verb phrase could replace *was*:

So absurd *had been* his manner that everyone stared.

Yet S-op inversion can also occur here: 'So absurd *did* his manner *seem* . . .'. In older English in any event, S-op inversion occurred without a preceding negative and some instances continue to be used in very formal style:

He invested the money – and bitterly did he come to regret it.
Often had she intended to speak of this.

In addition, there are a few examples in more common use but where the inverted expression is frozen and idiomatic:

Far be it from me to condemn him in any way.

This example of course has a negative implication, as is shown by the nonassertive form of the final adverbial.

[**b**] If an initial negative item is the vehicle for only a local negation (*cf* 10.66), no S-op inversion is possible. Thus, with the sentence adjunct (*cf* 8.36) in:

Not without reason, Charles had flown into a rage.
[= 'He had flown into a rage and it was not without reason']

Contrast, with predication adjunct (*cf* 8.27):

Not without reason had Charles flown into a rage.
[= 'He hadn't flown into a rage without reason']

Analogously:

Very rarely, Mary received letters from her brother.
[= 'She received letters, but very rarely']
Very rarely did Mary receive letters from her brother.
[= 'She didn't receive letters very often']

[**c**] For many speakers (especially in AmE), the subjunct *nor* cannot follow *and* or *but*, though fewer object to its following the latter:

(?) We could not hear the soprano, but nor could some friends who were nearer the front.

The item *nor* (*cf* 13.40) usually follows a clause that is negative in form or meaning, but in very formal usage this restriction does not obtain:

Veronica Taubman's oration was magnificent. Nor could anyone fail to be impressed by both her learning and her wit.

Cleft and pseudo-cleft sentences

18.25 In 18.20, we looked at examples of fronting where no other grammatical change was involved beyond the movement of the fronted item. For example, the direct object in:

His callousness I shall ignore. [1]

This might occur in a discussion of the bases on which the speaker proposes to criticize an opponent.

We now turn to devices for giving prominence to such an item as in [1] by more elaborate grammatical means, involving the division of the sentence into two clauses, each with its own verb:

It is his callousness that I shall ignore. [2]
What I shall ignore is his callousness. [3]
The thing I shall ignore is his callousness. [4]
His callousness is something I shall ignore. [5]

By reason of the division, these constructions have been called 'cleft sentences', though we shall distinguish the CLEFT SENTENCE proper, as in [2], from the PSEUDO-CLEFT sentence represented most typically by [3]. Although they are syntactically more complex than sentences with mere fronting, cleft sentences are in general less rhetorically obtrusive. It should not be thought, however, that they are merely stylistic variants. Each of the five examples, [1–5], carries distinct implications, especially in relation to given and new.

Cleft sentences

18.26 Of the four construction types [2–5] in 18.25, it is [2] that is the most flexible in what it will permit to be fronted. Moreover, its form, comprising the subject pronoun *it* as an empty theme, followed by the verb *be*, makes it natural to achieve focus on the item that follows: in effect, end-focus within an *SVC* clause:

It is his CÀLlousness.

For this reason, while very common in spoken English, the construction is particularly convenient in writing, since it provides unerring guidance to the reader in silently assigning appropriate prosody. But the cleft sentence does not of itself indicate what the appropriate prosody is. Essentially, the cleft sentence indicates divided focus (*cf* 18.17), and which of the two focused items is dominant (*ie* new) will depend on the context.

A: You should |criticize his CÀLlousness|
B: |No, it is his CǍLlousness| that I shall ig|NÒRE|
[*callousness* given, *ignore* new]
A: You should ig|nore his disHÒNesty|
B: |No, it is his CÀLlousness that I shall igNÓRE|
[*callousness* new, *ignore* given]

Note [**a**] Despite the obvious similarities between the *that*-clauses in cleft sentences and the nominal *that*-clauses of 15.3*ff*, the two are quite distinct (*cf* 18.28).

[**b**] Objection is sometimes made to the habit (especially perhaps in BrE radio and television news) of using the cleft sentence structure with an item that might be less obtrusive with simple fronting. Thus, in place of the following, where a time adjunct is made thematic, not because it is given, but merely as scene-setting to the weightier information that is to come:

Late last night a group of terrorists attacked an army post.

we might hear in a news broadcast:

It was late last NÍGHT that a group of terrorists . . .

This conveys unwarrantably the impression that the fact of the attack was known to the hearer but not the time at which it had taken place. The habit can be defended in that an adjunct (especially of time or place) is a fitting scene-setting and that it is this function that the cleft structure emphasizes. There is a comparable stylistic cliché to be found in conventional narrative. In place of a straightforward sentence such as:

When Harry returned that night, he found that his wife was very troubled.

a rather mannered form of writing might have (*cf* 17.3 Note):

It was a very troubled wife that greeted Harry on his return that night.

[**c**] Subject pronouns other than *it* sometimes occur:

(No,) *that* was the DÒctor I was speaking to.
Those are my FÈET you're treading on.
He was a real GÈNius that invented this.

In each of these, we could find divided focus (*cf* 18.17), with a rising tone on *speaking, treading,* and *this*.

18.27 The flexibility of the cleft sentence device can be seen in the ease with which different parts can be highlighted. Consider the sentence:

John wore a white suit at the dance last night.

From this, four cleft sentences can be derived. In the following, we shall assume that the aim in each case is to make the second focus subsidiary as relatively 'given':

S as focus:

It was |JÒHN {who / that} wore a 'white 'suit at the DÁNCE 'last 'night|

O_d as focus:

It was a |white SÙIT (that) 'John 'wore at the DÁNCE 'last 'night|

A_{time} as focus:

It was |last NÌGHT (that) 'John 'wore a 'white 'suit at the DÁNCE|

$A_{position}$ as focus:

{It was at the |DÀNCE that 'John 'wore a 'white SÚIT 'last 'night|
{It was the |DÀNCE (that) 'John 'wore a 'white SÚIT at 'last 'night|
⟨informal⟩

Two other clause elements can marginally act as the initial focus of a cleft sentence:

O_i as focus:

?It's *me* (that) he gave the book.

But more usually O_i would be replaced by a prepositional phrase:

It's *me* he gave the book *to*.
It's *to me* that he gave the book.

C_o as focus:

It's *dark green* that we've painted the kitchen.

There are severe restrictions (except informally in Irish English) on the use of C_s in this function, especially with the verb *be* at the end of the second clause and especially when C_s is realized by an adjective phrase:

?It's a *genius* that he is.
?It's *a lecturer* that I am now.
?It's *very tall* you are.

But, without these restrictions, C_s can be acceptable:

It was *a doctor* that he eventually became.

The V element does not occur at all as focus, just as it does not occur as a *wh*-element (*cf* 2.50):

*It's *wore* that John a white suit at the dance.

Informally, we sometimes find a predication fronted in a cleft sentence, the

V element made nonfinite and then subsequently replaced by *do* in the second clause; examples like the following are regarded, however, as stylistically awkward (again except in informal Irish English):

?It was *teach English in a school* that he did at that time.
?It was *teaching English in a school* that he was doing at that time.
?Is it *spying on us* he is?

Note [**a**] If the initial focal item is a personal pronoun, it may informally be in the objective case even though it is in fact a subject (of the *that*-clause) and the usage is hence widely condemned:

It was {they / she / ?her / ?them} that gave the signal.

Compare with fronting within the matrix clause: 'She it was that gave the signal'.

[**b**] Though the verb form in the first clause of a cleft sentence is usually simple present or past, forms with modals are perfectly possible:

It *may be* his father that you're thinking of.
It *would have been* at that time that he went to live in Wisconsin.

Decision between present and past, however, is somewhat complicated. Where the verb of the second clause is present, that of the first will be present:

It is novels that Miss Williams enjoys reading.
*It was novels that Miss Williams enjoys reading.
Cf: Was it novels that you said Miss Williams enjoys reading?

Where the second verb is past, the first can always be past:

It was novels that Miss Williams enjoyed as a pastime.
It was as a pastime that Miss Williams enjoyed reading novels.

But the first verb may be in the present where the persons concerned are still living or the objects concerned still familiar in the participants' experience:

It is Miss Williams that enjoyed reading novels as a pastime.
It is these very novels that Miss Williams enjoyed reading as a pasttime.
*It is as a pastime that Miss Williams enjoyed reading novels.

[**c**] The cleft sentence structure can be used in questions, exclamations, and subordinate clauses; we italicize the first focal item:

Was it *for this* that we suffered and toiled?
Who was it who interviewed you?
What a glorious bonfire it was you made!
He told me that it was *because he was ill* that they decided to return.

[**d**] It should be clear that in singling out an item for highlighting in the cleft sentence, strong presuppositions are entailed. Thus beside 'Bill didn't come to the party', we can have:

It was Bill that didn't come to the party. [1]
It wasn't Bill that came to the party. [2]

In [1], it is suggested that a memory search is trying to identify a missing guest, while [2] is concerned with converse reflections on who had in fact been present.

18.28 The second clause in a cleft sentence is obviously similar in structure to a restrictive relative clause; and yet (as we shall see below) there are considerable differences. Examples above show that pronouns used in relative clauses (*who, that,* 'zero' pronoun) are also used to introduce cleft sentences. Also suggestive of the relative clause is the fronting of the pronoun; moreover, as in relative clauses, the pronoun can be fronted from a position in a prepositional phrase, or from a pushdown (*cf* 11.18) position in a noun clause as object:

It's *the girl* that I was complaining about. [*ie* not the boy]

It's *next week's match* that he's hoping to attend. [*ie* not this week's]
It's *this watch* I said I would let you have. [*ie* not that]

There are differences from relative clauses, however, in that the *wh*-forms are rare in cleft sentences in comparison with *that* and zero. Although *whose* is allowed in cleft sentences (*It's Uncle Bill whose address I lost*), *whom* and *which* are only marginally possible, and it is virtually impossible to use *whom* or *which* preceded by a preposition. Thus:

It was the dog to which I gave the water.

can be read only as a sentence containing a postmodifying relative clause (compare *She was the woman to whom I gave the water*), and not as a cleft sentence. Characteristic intonation is also different:

It was the DÒG I gave the WÁTer to| [cleft sentence]

It / That } was *the dog I gave the WÀTer to*| [*SVC* sentence, the C being the italicized noun phrase incorporating a relative clause]

A further difference between the postmodifying relative clause and the clause following the first focused element in cleft sentences is the ability of the latter to have as its antecedent (*ie* the first focused element) not only an element realized by a noun phrase but an adjunct realized by a clause or prepositional phrase:

It was *because he was ill* (that) we decided to return.
It was *in September* (that) I first noticed it.

Indeed, such a construction, where there is no noun-phrase antecedent, makes inappropriate the use of the term 'pronoun' for the linking word *that*. It is noteworthy that a *wh*-relative pronoun cannot be used in cleft sentences where the focused element is an adjunct, and where consequently *that* does not have a strict 'pronominal' status:

*It was because he was ill *which* we decided to return.

Note Mention might be made of two further contrasts between relative clauses and the type of 'annex' clause that occurs in cleft sentences. One is the possibility, in familiar English, of omitting *that* as subject in a cleft sentence, but not as subject of a relative clause:

It was the President himself *spoke to me*.

The other is that cleft sentences may have a proper noun as a focus element, whereas restrictive relative clauses cannot have a proper noun as an antecedent. Thus *It's Chelsea (that) he lives in* is unambiguously a cleft sentence.

Pseudo-cleft sentences

18.29 The pseudo-cleft sentence is another device whereby, like the cleft sentence proper, the construction can make explicit the division between given and new parts of the communication. It is essentially an *SVC* sentence with a nominal relative clause as subject or complement (*cf* 15.8*f*). It thus differs from the ordinary cleft sentence in being completely accountable in terms of the categories of main clause and subordinate clause discussed in Chapter 10 (and *cf* 18.26, Note [a]). The following are virtually synonymous, assuming focus upon *rest*:

It's a good rest that you need most.
A good rest is what you need most.

The pseudo-cleft sentence occurs more typically, however, with the *wh*-clause as subject, since it can thus present a climax in the complement:

What you need most is a good rest.

It is less restricted than the cleft sentence (but *cf* 18.30) in one respect, since, through use of the substitute verb *do*, it more freely permits marked focus to fall on the predication:

What he's done is (to) spoil the whole thing.
What John did to his suit was (to) ruin it.
What I'm going to do to him is (to) teach him a lesson.

In each of these, we would have an anticipatory focus on the *do* item, the main focus coming at normal end-focus position. Thus: '. . . DÓNE . . . THÌNG'. The complement of these sentences is normally in the form of an infinitive clause (with or without *to*). When the verb in the *wh*-clause has progressive aspect, however, the complement (except in the case of *be going to*) matches it with an *-ing* clause (*cf* 18.27):

What *I'm doing* is *teaching him a lesson.*

The constraints are the same as for the pro-predicational *do*; *cf* 12.21. Occasionally, such matching of the two verbs is extended to verbs in the perfective aspect, which can have as their counterpart an *-ed* clause:

(?) What he'*s done* is *spoilt the whole thing*.

This last type is, however, of doubtful acceptability, and instances of it may indeed be interpreted as ellipted forms of an alternative construction involving apposition:

What he's done is ((this): he's) spoilt the whole thing.

18.30 In some respects, the pseudo-cleft sentence is more limited than the cleft sentence proper. It is indeed only with *what*-clauses that we can make a direct comparison (or choice) between the two constructions. Clauses with *who, where,* and *when* are sometimes acceptable, but mainly when the *wh*-clause is subject complement:

Here is *where the accident took place.*
(In) Autumn is *when the countryside is most beautiful.*
(?) The police chief was *who I meant.*

Clauses introduced by *whose, why,* and *how* do not easily enter into the pseudo-cleft sentence construction at all:

*With a Scottish accent is how he talked.
?*Why we decided to return was because he was ill.

To compensate for these restrictions, there are numerous 'paraphrases' of the pseudo-cleft construction involving noun phrases of general reference in place of the *wh*-item. Thus beside the cleft:

It must have been *the manager* that *spoke to you.*

we have a noun phrase in place of the pseudo-cleft:

The person who spoke to you must have been the manager.

So also:

Somebody I particularly like is John.
The way you should go is via Cheltenham.
The way we make a cake is by following mother's recipe.
The reason we decided to return was {that / because ⟨informal⟩} he was ill.
The place (where) the accident happened is here.
The time when the countryside is most beautiful is (in) autumn.
The hour at which she must make her decision was fast approaching.

Compare:

The hour was fast approaching *at which she must make her decision.*

See further 18.39.

Note [**a**] The device of general antecedent is also found where a corresponding pseudo-cleft is fully available:

{The thing / What} I like about Joan is her sense of humour.

[**b**] The cleft and pseudo-cleft types can cooccur. For example:

What it was you asked for was a ticket to Brighton. Did you mean Birmingham?

Postponement

18.31 It will be clear from the examples in the foregoing sections that one important communicative difference between the two types of cleft construction is that while the cleft sentence with *it* is often used to put the main focus near the front of the sentence, the pseudo-cleft is chiefly used to postpone the focus to end position. In this respect it is often in competition with the passive (*cf* 18.32):

The manufacturers tested the device.

Focus is placed on the noun phrase *the manufacturers* by means of the passive in [1] and by means of the pseudo-cleft in [2]:

The device was tested by the manufacturers. [1]
The people who tested the device were the manufacturers. [2]

It should be noted that [2] presupposes that the hearer knows that testing has taken place; with [1] this is not so.

Given the importance of end focus (*cf* 18.3), it is not surprising that English has numerous resources to enable us to phrase a sentence in such a way as to ensure the distribution of information according to our wishes. There are, for example, lexical and grammatical devices which reverse the order of roles:

{ An uncle, three cousins, and two brothers *benefited from* the will.
{ The will *benefited* an uncle, three cousins, and two brothers.

{ An unidentified blue liquid *was in* the bottle.
{ The bottle *contained* an unidentified blue liquid.

{ A red sports car was *behind* the bus.
{ The bus was *in front of* a red sports car.

The items or sequences in italics are converses; *ie* they express the same meaning, but with a reversal of the order of participants. The second sentence in each pair will be generally preferable, since the element with the 'definite' meaning, containing given information, would normally not take end-focus.

Note A special case of converseness is the relation of reciprocity expressed by certain terms such as *similar to, different from, near (to), far from, opposite, married to,* where reversing the order of the participants preserves the essential meaning without any other change in the construction:

My house is opposite the hotel. = The hotel is opposite my house.

A more complex relation of converseness is illustrated by:

{ The dealer *sold* the car *to* my friend.
{ My friend *bought* the car *from* the dealer.

Compare also *rent to/rent from, lend (to)/borrow from, give (to)/receive from.*

Voice and postponement

18.32 With transitive clauses, the passive voice provides a convenient way of postponing the agentive subject by turning it into the agent in a passive construction (*cf* 3.63*ff*). We thus reverse the active order of the agentive and affected elements (*cf* 10.19) where the agentive requires end focus:

A: Who makes these tablemats?

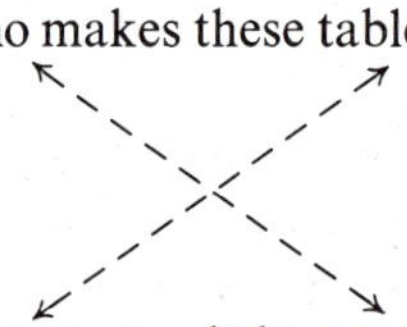

B: They are made by my sister-in-law.

A preference for end-focus (in this instance, coinciding with end-weight) can even override an aversion to passive constructions that are in themselves rather awkward (*cf* 16.14):

The regulations *were taken advantage of* by all the tramps and down-and-outs in the country.

A finite clause as subject is also readily avoided by switching from the active to the passive voice:

{ *That he was prepared to go to such lengths* astounded me.
{ I was astounded *that he was prepared to go to such lengths.*

It was pointed out in 18.27 that the V element cannot be focused in the cleft-sentence construction. Where such focus is desirable with an intransitive verb, end-focus is easily achieved; with a transitive verb, it can be achieved by the use of the passive, provided that the agent can be ignored as either given or otherwise dispensable (*cf* 3.71). Thus in place of:

But our |scientists 'finally SÒLVED 'all 'these 'problems|

we can have, ignoring the noun phrase *our scientists*:

But |all 'these 'problems were 'finally SÒLVED|

The passive can also ensure a smooth crescendo of communicative dynamism with ditransitive verbs by making the indirect object thematic. Thus, after 'Marion performed well for the judges', we might hear:

They a|warded her the PRÌZE|

But both *they* and *her* are obviously 'given' and there is thus a break in the crescendo of new information between the subsidiary *awarded* and the focal *prize*. Such a break is avoided in the alternative passive, now ignoring the active subject *they*:

She was a|warded the PRÌZE|

Note [**a**] It should be noted that the principle of end-focus applies just as much to the ordering of clauses within a sentence as to the ordering of elements within a clause. The principle of end-focus also has its analogue at sentence level in the principle of RESOLUTION (*cf* 14.37).

[**b**] The passive of *have* is rarely used, but when it occurs, the verb has a transitive meaning usually absent from the active. Compare:

(People) have little satisfaction from pop music.

with the following examples which combine existential *there* (*cf* 18.45) with the passive:

There's little satisfaction to be had from pop music.

I wanted to buy sherry but there was none to be had.

[**c**] Together with the phenomenon of discontinuous noun phrases (*cf* 18.39), the following textual example uses the passive to enable *no mention* to be thematized and *the police* to be focused (at some cost in possible misunderstanding of the written form of the sentence):

No mention is made in the report *of the police*.

[= They make no mention of the police in the report.]

Extraposition

Extraposition of a clausal subject

18.33 Postponement which involves the replacement of the postponed element by a substitute form is termed EXTRAPOSITION. It operates almost exclusively on subordinate nominal clauses. The most important type of extraposition is that of a clausal subject – *ie* a subject realized by a finite or nonfinite clause. The subject is moved to the end of the sentence, and the normal subject position is filled by the anticipatory pronoun *it*. The resulting sentence thus contains two subjects, which we may identify as the POSTPONED SUBJECT (the one which is notionally the subject of the sentence) and the ANTICIPATORY SUBJECT (*it*). A simple rule for deriving a sentence with subject extraposition from one of more orthodox ordering is:

subject + predicate ~ *it* + predicate + subject

Thus:

> To hear him say that + surprised me ~ It + surprised me + to hear him say that

But it is worth emphasizing that for clausal subjects (though *cf* 18.34) the postponed position is more usual than the canonical position before the verb (*cf* 10.26). Examples are:

Type *SVC*: It is a pleasure *to teach her.*
Type *SVA*: It was on the news *that income tax is to be lowered.*
Type *SV*: It doesn't matter *what you do.*
Type *SVO*: It surprised me *to hear him say that.*
Type *SVOC*: It makes her happy *to see others enjoying themselves.*
Type SV_{pass}: It is said *that she slipped arsenic into his tea.* [*cf* Note [a]]
Type SV_{pass} *C*: It was considered impossible *for anyone to escape.*

Note [**a**] For certain constructions which have all the appearance of clausal extraposition (*It seems/appears/happened/chanced/*etc), the corresponding nonextraposed version does not occur. For example, there is no sentence * *That everything is fine seems* to correspond with *It seems that everything is fine*, nor do we find * *That she slipped arsenic into his tea is said.* In such cases, we may say that the extraposition is obligatory. With *be*, this type of extraposition is used for expressions of possibility and (especially) for reflective questions:

> It may be that she no longer trusts you.
> Could it be that you left the keys in your office?

Other characteristics of the verbs entering into this category are presented in 18.36.

[**b**] Clauses with extraposed subject must be distinguished from superficially similar clauses in which *it* is a personal pronoun or empty 'prop' subject: *It's good to eat* (*ie* 'This (fish, etc) is good to eat'); *It's lovely weather to go fishing* (*cf* 10.32*f*).

[**c**] *If-* and *when*-clauses behave very much like extraposed subjects in sentences like:

> It would be a pity if we missed the show.
> [*cf* It is a pity that we missed the show]
> It'll be a great day when you win the sweepstake.

It is doubtful in each case, however, whether the clause could act as subject, although it could act as initial adverbial clause: *If we missed the show, it would be a pity* (*cf* 10.9*ff*). On balance, therefore, these appear to be adverbials rather than extraposed subjects. Contrast: *For us to miss the show would be a pity* ~ *It would be a pity for us to miss the show.*

[**d**] Another marginal case is the 'phrasal extraposition' of *It's two hundred miles from Boston to New York*, where the prepositional phrase sequence, if fronted, could act either as subject or as adverbial: *From Boston to New York (it) is two hundred miles.*

Compare also: *It's Wednesday today; Today (it) is Wednesday* (*cf* 10.15).

[**e**] While the extraposed clause can only rarely be a nominal relative in type *SV*, it is even rarer with *SVC*: *Whoever said that was wrong* but * *It was wrong whoever said that.* In examples like *It's a mystery why she did it/how he does it*, the *wh*-clauses are best regarded as indirect interrogatives; *cf* 14.33.

[**f**] The *it* used in extraposition is called 'anticipatory *it*' because of its pronominal correspondence to a later item. But informationally, this *it* is similar in effect to prop *it* (*cf* 6.17), as in '*It* started to rain' which likewise enables us to end the clause at a focal point. Contrast *Rain was starting.* Compare also *It was snowing* beside *Snow was falling.*

Extraposition of *-ing* clauses

18.34 Although we mentioned (18.33) that extraposition is usual for clausal subjects, there is an exception with *-ing* clauses which occur very naturally in ordinary subject position:

Teaching her to drive turned out to be quite enjoyable.
Getting the equipment loaded was easy.

Extraposition of *-ing* clauses is in fact uncommon outside informal speech. Compare:

It was easy *getting the equipment loaded.*

Some common informal examples are:

It's no use *telling him that.*
It wouldn't be any good *trying to catch the bus.*

The *-ing* clause often shows itself incompletely adapted to the extraposition construction, notably by being resistant to bearing the main information focus. Rather than:

It's |fun being a HÒSTess|

we hear:

It's |FÙN being a HÓSTess|

with main focus on the first element of the predicate. In writing, this example could well be punctuated as:

It's fun, being a hostess.

We might conclude from this that the participial clause has just as much affinity with a noun-phrase tag (*cf* 18.59; *eg: He's a friend of mine, that man*) as with a genuine extraposed subject.

Extraposition of a clausal object

18.35 When the object is an *-ing* clause in *SVOC* and *SVOA* clause types, it can undergo extraposition; when it is a *to*-infinitive clause or a *that*-clause, it must do so:

SVOC:
You must find *it* exciting *working here.*
Cf: You must find *working here* exciting.
Working here is exciting.
I made *it* my objective *to settle the matter.*
Cf: *I made *to settle the matter* my prime objective.
To settle the matter was my prime objective.

Contrast: I made *settling the matter* my prime objective.
*I made *it* my prime objective *settling the matter.*

SVOA:
I owe *it* to you *that the jury acquitted me.*
Cf: *I owe *that the jury acquitted me* to you.
Contrast: I owe *my acquittal* to you. [with corresponding nominalization]
Something put *it* into his head *that she was a spy.*
Cf: *Something put *that she was a spy* into his head.
Something put *the idea of her being a spy* into his head.

The construction type *She's a pleasure to teach*

18.36 Where the extraposed clause of 18.33 is of type *SVC* and contains an object or prepositional complement, the noun phrase concerned can sometimes be fronted to become the theme in place of *it*. For example:

To teach Elizabeth is a pleasure.
~ It is a pleasure to teach Elizabeth. (*cf* 18.33)
~ Elizabeth is a pleasure to teach.

Compare also:

It's impossible to deal with him. ~ He's impossible to deal with.
It's easy/difficult to beat them. ~ They're easy/difficult to beat.
It's fun (for us) to be with Margaret. ~ Margaret is fun (for us) to be with.

This thematic fronting does not apply to all constructions of the same kind. For instance, with:

$$\text{It's} \begin{Bmatrix} \text{rare} \\ \text{odd} \end{Bmatrix} \text{to} \begin{Bmatrix} \text{find} \\ \text{lose} \end{Bmatrix} \text{them.}$$

there is no corresponding:

$$\text{*They are} \begin{Bmatrix} \text{rare} \\ \text{odd} \end{Bmatrix} \text{to} \begin{Bmatrix} \text{find} \\ \text{lose} \end{Bmatrix}.$$

(See further 16.72*f*)

There is a similar construction with *be sure*, *be certain*, *seem*, *appear*, *be said*, *be known*, etc, except that in these cases the corresponding construction with anticipatory *it* requires a *that*-clause, not a *to*-infinitive clause, and except also that it is the *subject* of the extraposed clause that is fronted:

It's certain that we'll forget the address. ~ We're certain to forget the address.
It seems that you've made a mistake. ~ You seem to have made a mistake.
It is known that he's a coward. ~ He's known to be a coward.

Note [a] A combination of the movement explained in 18.33–34 permits a valuable range of sentence forms adjusting the development of communicative dynamism and the assignment of end-focus as desired. Thus along with the canonical *SVC* sentence:

To |play 'Mozart on 'this vio'lin is deLÌGHTful|

we have three further possibilities. First, with ordinary *it* extraposition:

It is de|lightful to 'play 'Mozart on 'this vioLÌN|

Secondly, with thematization of the object *Mozart* in the extraposed clause, we emphasize even more the properties of the violin:

|Mozart is de'lightful to 'play on 'this vioLÌN|

Thirdly, with thematization of the prepositional complement, we switch attention to the properties of Mozart's music:

|This vio'lin is de'lightful to 'play MÒzart 'on|

The shifting relations of the adjective can perhaps be seen more clearly in the following:

This |jug is DÌFficult to pour CRÉAM out of|
|Cream is DÌFficult to pour out of this JÚG|

The former implies difficulties with the jug (perhaps its spout is too narrow); the latter implies difficulties with cream (perhaps it is too thick).

[**b**] We must make a clear distinction between the type of thematic fronting discussed here (where the item assumes maximally 'given' status) and the fronting discussed in 18.20*f*, where the item retains its nonsubject status grammatically and is given greater rhetorical emphasis. Contrast the following pairs:

{ |Mozart is de'lightful to play on this vioLÌN|
{ |MŎZart| it is de|lightful to play on this vioLÌN|

{ E|lizabeth is a 'pleasure to TÈACH|
{ E|LĬZabeth| it is a |pleasure to TÈACH|

A slighter but somewhat corresponding difference occurs between:

In the garden there is a sundial. In the garden is a sundial.

See 18.23, 18.45*ff*.

[**c**] With *be certain, be sure,* a personal subject can be followed by either a *to*-infinitive clause or an *-ing* clause, but there is a crucial difference in meaning:

Janet is {certain / sure} {to be put on the committee. [The speaker is confident] / of being put on the committee. [Janet is confident]}

[**d**] The construction type 'She is a pleasure to teach' has been called 'Tough Movement' by reason of canonical (if rather informal) examples involving the adjective *tough*, as in *He's a tough man to argue with.*

Postponement of object in *SVOC* and *SVOA* clauses

18.37 When the object is a long and complex phrase, final placement for end-focus or end-weight is possible in *SVOC* and *SVOA* clause types. This does not involve an *it*-substitution.

(a) Shift from SVO_dC_o order to SVC_oO_d order:

They pronounced guilty *every one of the accused.*
He had called an idiot *the man on whose judgment he now had to rely.*

(b) Shift from SVO_dA to $SVAO_d$:

I confessed to him *all my worst defects.*
We heard from his own lips *the story of how he had been stranded for days without food.*
She dragged (right) in(side) *the two heavy boxes of chemicals.*
We cannot set (totally) aside *a whole system of rules devised by Congress itself.*

The fact that we are disturbing the normal order in such clauses is indicated by a tendency to adopt a different intonation pattern. Thus the movement forward of the C or A is usually accompanied by the assignment to it of a marked (subsidiary) focus (*cf* 18.17):

He had |called an ÍDiot his 'best FRÌEND|
She |pulled to 'one SÍDE the 'heavy CÙRtain|

Compare:

He had |called his 'best 'friend an ÌDiot|
She |pulled the 'heavy 'curtain to 'one SÌDE|

Note The sentence *He had called an idiot his best friend* need not of course involve movement; with unaltered SVOC we would understand that an idiot was his best friend.

Objects and paraphrases

18.38 In ditransitive complementation (*cf* 16.55*ff*), the indirect object precedes the direct object:

She |gave {her 'brother / him} a sìGnet 'ring| [1]

Thus whether or not the O_i is pronominalized, the implication is that it carries less communicative dynamism (is relatively 'given') as compared with the O_d. Where the converse is true, the O_i is replaced by a prepositional phrase and placed after O_d:

She |gave a 'signet ring to her BRÒTHer| [2]

But there is a third possibility; the prepositional paraphrase of the O_i can itself precede the O_d:

She |gave to her BRÓTHer a sìGnet 'ring| [3]

Note that we cannot have: **She gave (to) her brother it* (*cf* 10.7). The O_d in [3] has the same rhematic force as in [1] but the O_i has been replaced by a form that raises its communicative dynamism above that of the O_i in [1] though still below that of the paraphrase in [2].

Consider now the special type of ditransitive construction we find with eventive objects (*cf* 10.30):

We paid them a vìsit. [4]
He gave Helen a NÙDGE. [5]

Here we have a device which is convenient when our communicative requirement is to put focal emphasis on the activity rather than on a human participant. Contrast:

We paid a visit to some old FRÌENDS. [4a]
?He gave a nudge to HÈLen. [5a]

But as we can see from the doubtful acceptability of [5a], it may be preferable not to use the eventive object construction at all when it is a human participant that is needed in end-focus:

We visited some old FRÌENDS. [4b]
He nudged HÈLen. [5b]

(See further 18.43).

Note [a] Where both O_d and O_i are pronouns, it would be usual to replace the latter by a *to*-phrase:

She GÀVE it to him.
She gave it to HÌM.

Alternatively, we could have:

She GÀVE him it.
She GÀVE it him. } ⟨only BrE⟩
She gave it HÌM. }

but not:

*She gave HÌM it.
*She gave ÌT him.

[b] On the divided focus in example [3], compare the similar phenomenon in 18.37 accompanied by unusual positioning.

Discontinuous noun phrases

18.39 Sometimes only part of an element is postponed. The most commonly affected part is the postmodification of a noun phrase, and the units most readily postponed are nominal (in this case appositive) clauses (*cf* 17.122 and also 18.33*f*):

> *A rumour* circulated widely *that he was secretly engaged to the Marchioness*. (*Cf*: '*A rumour that he was secretly engaged to the Marchioness* circulated widely.')
> *The problem* then arose *(of) what contribution the public should pay*. (*Cf*: '*The problem (of) what contribution the public should pay* then arose.')

However, other postmodifying clauses, and even phrases, can be so postponed:

> *The time* had come *to decorate the house for Christmas*.
> *That loaf* was stale *that you sold me*.
> *A steering committee* had been formed, *consisting of Messrs Ogawa, Schultz, and Robinson*.

The postponement in each case results in a 'discontinuous' noun phrase (*cf* 17.122) which is italicized in the examples. Discontinuity often results, too, from the postponement of postmodifying phrases of exception (*cf* 9.58):

> *All of us* were frightened {*but* / *except*} *the captain*.

As well as subject, the discontinuous noun phrase can be a complement or object:

> *What business* is it *of yours*? (*Cf* 'It's no business of yours')
> We heard *the story* from his own lips *of how he was stranded for days without food*.
> I met *a man* this morning *carrying an injured child*.

But we may speak analogously of internal discontinuities: that is, where there is movement of parts of a noun phrase to achieve end-focus, without actual insertion of elements that do not form part of the noun phrase as a whole. Compare the following 'normal' example:

> *The discovery of new building materials in the course of this century* (has revolutionized architecture).

Compare SVOA: 'They discovered the new materials this century'. In fact, the unedited example was as follows:

> Architecture has been revolutionized by *the discovery in the course of this century of new building materials*.

This corresponds to SVAO: 'They discovered this century the new materials'. In 18.37, an agential phrase of our own was internally discontinuous:

> . . . is usually accompanied by *the assignment* to it *of a marked . . . focus*.

In such cases, as with the illustrative examples of 18.37–38, the item which has in effect been fronted (*to it* in this example) is frequently given marked focus:

. . . by the as|signment TǑ it| of a |marked . . . FÒCUS|

Let us take one final example to illustrate the flexibility offered by nominalization in providing, through 'internal discontinuities', a varied ordering of constituents to suit specific informational goals. Bearing in mind the constraints on permuting the sequence of sentence elements, we indicate the greater freedom within the noun phrase by putting in quotation marks the analogies between sentence elements and the noun-phrase constituents. It will be seen that we can give end focus to constituents corresponding to all four of the elements in an *SVOA* sentence:

Lovell discovered the new star in 1960.		SVOA
Lovell's discovery of the new star in 1960 . . .	~	'SVOA'
The discovery by Lovell in 1960 of the new star . . .	~	'VSAO'
The discovery of the new star in 1960 by Lovell . . .	~	'VOAS'
(?)Lovell's 1960 new star discovery . . .	~	'SAOV'

18.40 Whether we are reordering the constituents within a noun phrase or interrupting them to insert another sentence element, there appear to be two major motivations:

(a) The one is to achieve a stylistically well-balanced sentence in accordance with the norms of English structure; in particular to achieve END-WEIGHT. For example, it would be usual to avoid forming a sentence with a long subject and a short predicate. Thus we would prefer [1], with discontinuity, to [2], without discontinuity:

The story is told *of her phenomenal success in Australia*. [1]
(?) *The story of her phenomenal success in Australia* is told. [2]

(b) The other is to achieve an information climax with END-FOCUS. For example:

She rapidly spotted *the book* right on my desk *that I had been desperately searching for all morning*. [3]

Not merely would the adjunct be more interruptive of the syntax if it followed the verb immediately (. . . *spotted right on my desk the book* . . .), but the ordering found in [3] matches in a highly satisfying way the mounting communicative flow:

She rapidly spotted the book.
It was right there on my desk.
Yet I had been desperately searching for it all morning.

At the thematic end we have the rapidity of finding the book; at the rhematic end the long duration of the search; in the transition – the point of noun-phrase discontinuity – we have the ironic juxtaposition of the book and the desk.

In most of the examples given in 18.39, of course, the two factors (a) and (b) coincide, as indeed they do in [1] and [3] above. With another type of noun phrase, however, it is clearly to give end-focus rather than end-weight that the postponement takes place. This is the noun phrase with an emphatic reflexive pronoun (*himself*, etc) in apposition:

The driver himsÈLF told me. ~ The driver told me himsÈLF.
Did you yoursÉLF paint the portrait? ~ Did you paint the portrait yoursÉLF?

As the emphatic reflexive pronoun frequently bears nuclear stress, the postponement is necessary if the sentence is to have end-focus. Such postponement is possible, however, only if the noun phrase in apposition with the pronoun is the subject:

I showed Ian the letter *myself*.
*I showed *Ian* the letter *himself*.
(But *cf*: 'I showed *Ian himself* the letter')

Note With some other cases of pronominal apposition, we may prefer to postpone the second element to a position immediately following the operator rather than to the end of the sentence. This is especially true with *all, both, each* (*cf* 6.50). For example:

The advisers had *all* been carefully selected.

We also find:

My sisters don't *either of them* eat enough. ⟩ ⟨informal⟩
They are *none of them* very enthusiastic. ⟩ ⟨informal⟩

Correlative items in comparative sentences

18.41 Some degree of discontinuity is the rule rather than the exception in sentences containing comparative clauses, though where the comp-element (*cf* 15.63*ff*) is a degree adverbial, examples without discontinuity are fairly easy to find. For example:

He has worked for the handicapped *more than any other politician* (*has*).
He has worked *more* for the handicapped *than any other politician* (*has*).

Comparisons involving noun phrases as heads are rare without discontinuity and are frequently punctuated to indicate that they are regarded as ad hoc compounds (*cf* App I.59):

He is earning higher-than-average wages.

In such cases, verb ellipsis is obligatory; compare:

He is earning higher wages than (are) average.

There is thus a minimum 'discontinuity' that we should take as the norm, with the correlative item following the head of the comp-element phrase (though we regard these as complementation structures: *cf* 2.32):

She had *more* money *than her father (had)* by the time she was thirty.
He is *more* skilled *than his brother (is)* in matters of finance.
They visit her *more* frequently *than they used to* now that she's ill.
He was *too* hot *to do his work* despite the air-conditioner.

But if nuclear focus were required on the correlative item, it could be moved to final position in each case even though the discontinuity would now normally require separation into different tone units:

She had |more 'money by the 'time she was THÍRTy| than her |FÀTHer (had)|
He is |more 'skilled in 'matters of FÍNance| than his |BRÒTHer (is)|
They |visit her 'more 'frequently 'now that she's ǏLL| than they |ÙSED to|
He was |too 'hot desPÌTE the AÍR-con'ditioner| to |do his WÒRK|

Other discontinuities

18.42 Some adjectives that take complementation (*cf* 7.22, 16.68*ff*) can simultaneously function as premodifiers. Compare:

This result is { *different from yours.* / *similar to hers.* }

This is a { *different* result *from yours.* / *similar* result *to hers.* }

In cases like these last, discontinuity is felt to be quite normal and the position is similar to that of the correlative item in comparative sentences (*cf* 18.41). So also:

She works in the *opposite* room *to this.*
It is a *timid* dog *with strangers.*

Despite superficial similarity with prepositional phrases postmodifying a head, there is rarely danger of ambiguity:

I was told by a man in the office.

The possible difference here ('*A man* told me *in the office*' or '*A man in the office* told me') is unlikely to give rise to communicational difficulties, but the following example is more seriously ambiguous:

They made an embarrassing protest to the authorities.

In such instances, revision is essential to make it clear which of the two possible meanings is intended:

They made a protest that was embarrassing to the authorities. [1]
[*ie* 'Their protest embarrassed the authorities']
They made a protest to the authorities that was embarrassing. [2]
[*ie* 'They protested to the authorities in a way that was (generally) embarrassing']

If the meaning of [2] is intended but with the end focus on *the authorities* as in [1], further revision is necessary. Perhaps:

They embarrassed everyone by making a protest to the authorities. [2a]

Within the adjective complementation itself, discontinuity is possible, especially by the insertion of degree adverbials:

They were *fond* to some extent *of Brecht's early work.*
It was *different* in many respects *from what she had expected.*

A similar type of discontinuity can occur within prepositional phrases:

He worked hard, *without* for the most part *any reward*.

Note In addition, of course, we have the prepositional phrase discontinuities of the type:

Which group shall we put him *in*?

Although we do not speak of discontinuity in the verb phrase, there is often comparable informational motivation in the insertion of adverbials at *M*; *cf* 8.16. Doubtless the wish to avoid a 'split infinitive' (*cf* 8.21) is a wish to avoid a perceived discontinuity. Yet in writing, it is often convenient to use an adverbial along with the emphatic operator. For example:

They *did* indeed *find* a solution.

The interposing of *indeed* here justifies the emphatic *did* (*cf* the discussion of inserting *in short*, 18.13), achieving an effect comparable to the use of prosody alone in speech:

They |DÌD find a solution|

Structural compensation

18.43 A major preoccupation in the phenomena we have been considering in 18.31*ff* has been the achievement of end-weight – whether phrasal, clausal, or sentential. The very nature of theme and focus, given and new information, leads to the expectation that the thematic item (typically the subject) will be shorter than the focal item (typically a part of the predicate). Given, moreover, that the V element is not normally expected to carry the maximum communicative dynamism in a sentence (*cf* 18.3), we develop the expectation that V will be at a transition point between a thematic low communicative dynamism and a focal high:

|Jill will de'cide next WÈEK|
The |boy 'broke the WÌNdow|
My |friend be'came ÀNgry|

All this has the effect of making the simplest realization of the *SV* clause type sound oddly incomplete:

|Mary SÀNG| My |friend CÒOKED|

In consequence, this type of *SV* realization is rather rare and it would be more usual to find an optional predication adjunct (*cf* 8.34):

Mary sang for hours. My friend cooked enthusiastically.

At the very least, we would make intransitive verbs bipartite, an auxiliary serving as a transition between theme and focus:

|Mary was SÌNGing| My |friend would CÒOK|

Such rephrasing is obviously context-dependent; it is not often, for example, that a verb phrase might equally well be progressive or nonprogressive. Other means have therefore had to be devised for 'stretching' the predicate into a multi-word structure. One of the most generally serviceable (though it tends to be rather informal in tone) is to replace the intransitive verb by a transitive one of very general meaning, taking as its eventive object a nominalization of the intransitive item (*cf* 10.30, 17.51*ff*). The general verbs *do, make, give, have, take* are widely used in this construction, though the choice is strictly limited in any individual case (**She took a shriek*, **She did a shriek* – unless the latter is in the sense 'She *acted/*

performed a shriek', as on the request of the producer). Consider the following pairs:

{My friend {cooks. / cooked.} / My friend {does some cooking. / did the cooking.}}

{He ate. / He had a meal.}

{She replied. / She made a reply.}

{Mary shrieked. / Mary gave a shriek.}

{They strolled. / They took a stroll.}

{I bathed. / I had a bath. ['I took a bath' ⟨esp AmE⟩]}

So also *solve* ~ *find a solution, agree* ~ *reach* (or *come to*) *an agreement, apply* ~ *submit an application, suggest* ~ *offer* (or *make*) *a suggestion, permit* ~ *grant* (or *give*) *permission, attend* ~ *pay attention*, etc (*cf* also 10.28, 18.38).

Existential sentences

18.44 We have seen in 18.8–9 that the organization of sentences in terms of theme and focus generally presumes that a sentence begins with reference to 'given' information and proceeds to provide 'new' information. But there are many occasions when we must make statements whose content does not fall neatly into these two categories:

A |car is 'blocking my WÀY| [1]
|Many 'students are in fi'nancial TRÒUBle| [2]
|Quite a 'few 'species of 'animals are in 'danger of exTÌNCtion| [3]

Let us assume that the originator of these sentences has in each case put the focus where it was wanted. Nonetheless a certain awkwardness is sensed where the recipient is expected to interpret a theme as entirely new and unconnected with anything previously introduced. It is in these circumstances that it is convenient to have devices for providing some kind of dummy theme which will enable the originator to indicate the 'new' status of a whole clause, including its subject. Thus in place of [1], we might have:

{There is / I have} {a |car blocking / a |CǍR| |blocking} my WÀY| [1a]

Likewise, in place of [2] and [3]:

{There are / We have / One finds} {|many STǓdents| in fi|nancial TRÒUBle| [2a] / |quite a 'few 'species of ÁNimals| in |danger of exTÌNCtion| [3a]}

In serving to bring the existence of an entire proposition (such as those in [1], [2], and [3] to the attention of the hearer, the resultant constructions are known as 'existential sentences', by far the commonest being the type introduced by unstressed *there*, accompanied by the simple present or past of *be*.

Note [**a**] Many other constructions than those illustrated above are invoked to serve the same purpose; for example, *it* with the proposition as extraposed subject (*cf* 18.33):

It is a fact that } many students are in financial trouble.
It has to be said that }

Alternatively again, the proposition can be made a clausal object:

One finds that }
We must recognize that } many students are in financial trouble.
I have to say that }

[**b**] Block language (*cf* 11.45*ff*) often consists of verbless sentences that can be regarded as existential:

DANGER!
MEN AT WORK OVERHEAD

Note that there are two types of negative directives and slogans:

No way out }
No exit } = 'There *is* . . .'
No through way }
No arrest without warrant }
No reduction in wages } = 'There *must be* . . .'
No discrimination }

[**c**] Sentences with entirely 'new' themes seem to be less awkward if combined with discontinuous postmodification of the noun phrase (*cf* 18.39), thus placing the focus of new information at the end. Compare:

{ ?*A bird* is in that tree.
{ *A bird* is in that tree *which I've never seen around here before.*

{ ?*An idea* is in his head.
{ *An idea* is in his head *that the rest of us are against him.*

Existential *there*

Correspondence with basic clause patterns

18.45 There is a regular correspondence between existential sentences with *there* + *be* and clauses of equivalent meaning as specified in terms of the basic clause patterns (*cf* 10.1*ff*), provided that the clause concerned

(i) has an indefinite subject (but *cf* Note [a]); and
(ii) has a form of the verb *be* in its verb phrase.

Allowing for these two requirements, we may relate basic clauses to existential forms by means of a general rule:

subject + (auxiliaries) + *be* + predication
~ *there* + (auxiliaries) + *be* + subject + predication

The subject of the original clause may be called the 'notional' subject of the *there*-sentence, so as to distinguish it from *there* itself, which for most purposes is the 'grammatical' subject (*cf* 18.46). Examples of the seven clause types along with the existential correspondences are given below:

Type *SVC*
Something must be wrong. ~ There must be something wrong.

Type *SVA*
Was anyone in the vicinity? ~ Was there anyone in the vicinity?

Type *SV*
No one was waiting. ~ There was no one waiting.

Type *SVO*
Plenty of people are getting promotion.
~ There are plenty of people getting promotion.

Type *SVOC*
Two bulldozers have been knocking the place flat.
~ There have been two bulldozers knocking the place flat.

Type *SVOA*
A girl is putting the kettle on. ~ There's a girl putting the kettle on.

Type *SVOO*
Something is causing my friend distress.
~ There's something causing my friend distress.

Passive versions of the correspondences are also to be noted:

Type SV_{pass}
A whole box has been stolen. ~ There has been a whole box stolen.

Type $SV_{pass}\ C$
No shops will be left open. ~ There'll be no shops left open.

The notional subject can be postponed (*cf* 18.31) if it is required to have focal prominence:

There was in the vicinity a helpful doctor.
There'll be left open no single well-stocked shop.

Especially in informal usage, there is an existential sentence with an *-ed* clause following the noun phrase:

There's a parcel come for you.
There's a book gone from my desk.
There's a tree fallen across our driveway.
There's a new history of Indonesia published.

Note [**a**] The rule that existential sentences should have an indefinite noun phrase as 'notional subject' prevents us from constructing sentences like **There's the money in the box* from *The money is in the box*. This limitation can be waived, however, where the definite noun phrase conveys new information, in answers to existential questions (actual or implied), such that the answer provides a specific (and hence definite) instance:

A: Have we any loose cash in the house?
B: Well, there's the money in the box over there.
A: Is there anyone coming to dinner?
B: Yes, there's Harry and there's also Mrs Jones.

Compare also: 'There are *several animals* commonly depicted in heraldry; for instance, there is *the lion*'.

Also acceptable is the definite *the* which is determined by the absolute superlative (*cf* 7.84), as in:

There's the oddest-looking man standing at the front door.

This corresponds to an indefinite article in the following alternative sentence:

There's *a* man of *the oddest appearance* standing at the front door.

[**b**] Where *be* is part of a semi-auxiliary construction, there are restrictions with existential *there*:

A man is to fix it tomorrow. ≁ There is a man to fix it tomorrow.
A man is bound to arrive soon. ~ *There is a man bound to arrive soon.
A man is going to help me. ~ ?There is a man going to help me.

But:

A man is bound to be here soon. ~ There *is bound to be* a man here soon.
A man is going to be with her. ~ There *is going to be* a man with her.

[**c**] Noun phrases introduced by the 'universal' terms *all* or *every* are not so easily made 'notional subjects' of existential sentences (?* *There was everyone in the room*) as other types of indefinite expression. They act as such mostly in 'second instance' answers to existential questions:

A: What is there to be afraid of?
B: There's Èverything to be afraid of!

Negative universals are fully acceptable: 'There's nothing to worry about.'

[**d**] Existential *there* occurs freely in dependent clauses:

Let me know if there's anyone waiting.

[**e**] In *SVC*-related sentences, the C cannot usually denote a permanent property:

There were several students ill.

But:

?*There were several students tall.

[**f**] Some frozen existential clauses exist without *there*; for example ⟨informal⟩:

Time WǍS when I'd have tackled it. [= 'There was (once) a time . . .']

The status of existential *there* as subject

18.46 The *there* of existential sentences differs from *there* as an introductory adverb in lacking stress, in carrying none of the locative meaning of the place-adjunct *there*, and in behaving in most ways like the subject of the clause, doubtless reflecting the structural dislocation from the basic clause types:

(i) It often determines concord, governing a singular form of the verb (*cf* 10.34*ff*) even when the following 'notional subject' is plural:

There's some people in the waiting room. ⟨informal⟩

occurs alongside:

There are some people in the waiting room.

(ii) It can act as subject in *yes–no* and tag questions:

Is there any more soup? There's nothing wrong, *is there*?

(iii) It can act as subject in infinitive and *-ing* clauses:

I don't want *there to be any misunderstanding*.
He was disappointed at *there being so little to do*.
There having been trouble over this in the past, I want to treat the matter cautiously.

Note [**a**] The absence of locative meaning is indicated by the acceptability of existential sentences in which *here* cooccurs with introductory *there*:

There's a screwdriver here.

By contrast, adjunct *there* with inversion (*cf* 18.23), as in 'There's the girl', would be contradictory with an added *here*:

*There's the screwdriver here! (*But cf* |"THÈRE's the SCRÉWdriver| – |Right "HÈRE|

[**b**] Existential *there* can be fronted in association with the type of *to*-clause discussed in 18.36:

It {appears / is certain} that there is something wrong with the engine.

~ There {appears / is certain} to be something wrong with the engine.

In such sentences, the catenative verb (*cf* 3.49) often agrees with the notional subject in number:

There [happens / happen] to be [only one apple / only two apples] left.

But often informally, 'There happens to be only two apples left.'

'Bare' existential sentences

18.47 Apart from sentences related to basic clause types in the manner described in 18.45, we have to consider various other types of sentence introduced by existential *there*. Among them is the 'bare' existential (sometimes called 'ontological') sentence, which simply postulates the existence of some entity or entities. It has a simple clause structure *there* + *be* + indefinite noun phrase:

> There was a moment's silence.
> There's nothing to do.
> There was a sudden noise.
> There are numerous species of edible fungi.
> Undoubtedly, there is a God. ['God exists']
> Is there any other business? [as spoken by the chairman at the end of a meeting]
> There must be a more direct route.

Such sentences are perhaps to be explained as cases in which the final element is omitted as understood:

> There is a God (in the Universe). [*ie* now as always]
> Is there any other business (for the committee at this meeting)?
> There must be a more direct route (than the one we're discussing).

Other sentences superficially like these are certainly to be so explained. For example, the sentence *There'll be trouble*, occurring on its own, implies a definite context: 'There'll be trouble at the match/at the party', etc. Alternatively, it seems significant that many textual examples of 'bare' existentials comprise complexities that provide for the required double prominence. Compare such paraphrases of foregoing examples as:

> Edible fungi exist in numerous species.
> There was |sɪLence for a 'moment|

In 'There have always been wars', we have an *SVA* existential, though the A-element (*always*) is at *M* (*cf* 8.16); compare 'There have been wars *in all periods of history*'.

Existential sentences with relative and infinitive clauses

18.48 A more important additional type of existential sentence is that which consists of *there* + *be* + noun phrase + relative clause, and which resembles the cleft sentence (*cf* 18.25, example [2]) in its rhetorical motivation. Such sentences can be related to sentences of orthodox clause types without the two restrictions mentioned in 18.45: the verb need not be a form of the verb *be*, and although there must be an indefinite element, it need not be subject:

Something keeps upsetting him. (*Cf* 'Something is repeatedly upsetting him')
~ There's something (that) keeps upsetting him. [1]
I'd like you to meet some people.
~ There's some people (that) I'd like you to meet. [2]

It is interesting that the relative pronoun *that* in the 'annex' clause of [1] can be omitted (especially in informal usage) even when it is subject of the relative clause; something not permissible according to the normal rule for relative clause formation (*cf* 17.15):

There's a man lives in China. ~ *I know a man lives in China.

This omissibility is a sign of the special status within the main clause of the annex clause here, as in cleft sentences (*cf* 18.28 Note).

As with cleft sentences, we can have different tenses in the two parts of the sentence. Compare:

There were some paintings that were admired by everyone.
There are some planets that were discovered by the ancients.

The existential-with-relative construction is particularly common as a means of emphasizing a negative (*cf* Note below):

There's *nothing* I can do about it. (~ nothing *that/which* I can do)
There was *no way* they could persuade her to try again. (~ no way *in which* they . . .)

Compare, without this construction, 'They could persuade her *in no way* to try again.'

Again, as with cleft sentences, we can negate either part:

There was a student who didn't pass the exam. [= one failed]
There wasn't a student who passed the exam. [= all failed]

But we can also negate both parts:

There wasn't a student who didn't pass the exam. [= all passed]

One may also mention a common existential sentence pattern *there* + *be* + noun phrase + *to* + infinitive clause, which is problematic to the extent that it cannot be directly related to the basic clause types of 10.1*ff*:

There was no one for us to talk to.
There's (always) plenty of housework to do.

Such infinitive clauses are allied to relative clauses (*cf* 17.9*ff*), as we see on comparing:

At last there was something to write home about.

with the ⟨stiffly formal⟩ relative clause construction:

At last there was something about which to write home.

This type of existential sentence sometimes has a definite noun phrase as notional subject (*cf* 18.45, Note [a]):

There's the man next door to consider.

Note Also there is a restricted idiomatic construction consisting of *there* + *be* + negative + *-ing* clause:

There's no telling what he'll do. There isn't any getting away from it.

On the peculiarities of this construction, *cf* 15.14.

Existential sentences with verbs other than *be*

18.49 The existential sentence has been described as 'presentative', in serving to bring something on to the discoursal stage deserving our attention. This seems especially true of a rather less common, more literary type of existential clause in which *there* is followed by a verb other than *be*:

There rose in his imagination grand visions of a world empire.
There exist a number of similar medieval crosses in different parts of the country.
There may come a time when the Western Nations will be less fortunate.
Not long after this, there occurred a sudden revolution in public taste.

This construction, which may be related to other sentence forms by the simple correspondence S + V ~ *there* + V + S (where S is usually indefinite), is equivalent in effect and style to subject–verb inversion after an initial adverbial (*cf* 18.23). Indeed, in all *there*-existential sentences, *there* can be regarded as a 'dummy element', which, placed before the subject and verb, provides the necessary condition for inversion to take place. Grammatically, *there* is a subject, as we saw in 18.46 above and as we see again here with the operator inversion that takes place when the statement pattern is turned into a question, *eg*: *Will there come a time . . .? Did there occur a sudden revolution . . .?*

But the present construction requires some expansion of the rule given above. In the first place, the verb must be intransitive (exceptions are idiomatic or dubious; *cf* Note [a]), and of fairly general presentative meaning: verbs of motion (*arrive, enter, pass, come*, etc), of inception (*emerge, spring up*, etc), and of stance (*live, remain, stand, lie*, etc); but *cf* 18.50. In the second place, while 'ontological' or 'bare' existentials are commoner with these verbs than with *be* (*eg*: *There sprang up a wild gale*), the normal sentence pattern concerned is *SVA* and the existential rule might be restated as follows (treating *sprang up* as a single verb unit and not as V + A):

$$S + V + A \sim \begin{cases} \textit{there} + V + S + A & [1] \\ \textit{there} + V + A + S & [2] \\ A + \textit{there} + V + S & [3] \end{cases}$$

For example:

There sprang up a wild gale that night. [1]
There sprang up that night a wild gale. [2]
That night there sprang up a wild gale. [3]

Where the S is postponed (*cf* 18.31) as in [2], there is less constraint for the S to be indefinite, doubtless because the postponement itself implies the 'newness' of the item concerned:

There came to his mind her beautiful and intelligent face.

If however the transitive verb is one that forms a V + N multi-word verb (*cf* 16.58), such sequences are fully acceptable:

There *took place* an elaborate ceremony in honour of the visiting dignitaries.

Note [**a**] Transitive verbs in existential sentences are rare but would follow pattern [2] above in having the S in end position:

?There struck me a sudden idea. (*Cf* *There struck me a tall man.)
(?) There then addressed the meeting the new leader of the party.

In view of the constraints upon transitive verbs, it is perhaps better to regard examples with passives as being special cases of *be* existentials (*cf* 18.45). Thus with the passive of:

The mayor presented a gold medal (to the winner).

we can have:

There was a gold medal presented (to the winner) by the mayor.

Less commonly:

There was presented (to the winner) by the mayor a gold medal.

So also with progressive forms:

A dozen hungry people were standing in the rain.
There were a dozen hungry people standing in the rain.

Less commonly:

There were standing in the rain a dozen hungry people.

[**b**] Examples like 'There's a parcel come' and 'There's a new history of Indonesia published' (*cf* 18.45) should not be regarded as an existential division of the verb phrase as in 18.49 Note, since without the *there*-construction we would have 'A parcel *has* come' (not '*is* come') and 'A new history *has been* published' (rather than '*is* published'). *There* can provide further anomalies with perfectives, both passive and active:

There's a new grammar been written. [*A new grammar is been written.]
There's a visitor been waiting to see you. [*A visitor is been waiting to see you.]

Although we cannot expand *is* to *has* (?*'There has a visitor been waiting'), examples like these are doubtless facilitated by the fact that *'s* is a contraction for *has* as well as *is* (and occasionally *does*: 'What's it matter?'; *cf* 3.36). Acceptability is reduced when *'s* is replaced by *are* and (still more) by *was* or *were*:

There are three visitors (?been) waiting to see you.
There was a new grammar (*been) published recently.

Existential sentences with initial space adjuncts

18.50 We should now consider the type [3] ordering of 18.49:

A + *there* + V + S

For example:

That night there sprang up a wild gale.

Let us look at an example that pairs a verb of stance with the usual existential verb *be*:

In the garden there {was / stood} a sundial. [1]

Since the place adverbial, *In the garden*, provides in itself the condition enabling us to position the subject after the verb (*cf* 18.23), there is no grammatical requirement for *there* to be present:

In the garden {was / stood} a sundial. [2]

It should be noted that the range of verb-phrase forms with this type of ordering is considerably wider than was specified in 18.49. Compare:

Into the room (there) had staggered a total stranger.
?There had staggered into the room a total stranger.
?*There had staggered a total stranger into the room.

We see from these examples that the wider choice of verb coincides with the choice between the presence or absence of *there*. In considering examples [1] and [2] above, we find that, despite the close similarity in meaning, the absence of *there* as in [2] is preferred when the final noun phrase is relatively concrete and specific, its occurrence relatively expected. We may say that the verb in [1] tends to connote '*chanced* (to be)', '*happened* (to stand)', while the noun phrase in [2] tends to connote 'a *certain* (sundial)'. Significantly, indeed, there is much less constraint upon indefiniteness in [2]:

In the garden lay {*Joan* / *his father* / *the old lady*} (fast asleep).

Table 18.50 shows the distribution of existential sentences in a large sample of SEU material. They are all of the type under consideration here; that is:

A + (*there*) + V + S

and they are analysed in terms of three variables:

(i) whether the verb is *be* or not *be* (*ie: stand, lie, appear*, etc);
(ii) whether *there* is present as in example [1] or absent as in example [2];
(iii) whether the subject noun phrase is indefinite or definite.

Table 18.50

	Indefinite		Definite	
	be	not *be*	*be*	not *be*
+ *there*	160	23	28	7
– *there*	137	56	179	29

Among the interesting facts revealed by the figures, the most striking is doubtless the converse distribution (160:137, but 28:179) as between indefinite and definite with *be*, showing the greater tendency to omit *there* where the noun phrase is definite. It would seem that whereas the *AVS* construction without *there* is motivated by the wish to achieve end-focus, the *there*-construction has the more general 'presentative' function; *cf* 18.49.

The *have*-existential device

18.51 Corresponding to the type of existential sentence introduced in 18.45 (*there* + *be* + S + predication), there is a type in which the thematic position is not occupied by a mere 'dummy' element but is filled by a noun-phrase subject preceding the verb *have* (or, especially in BrE, *have got*):

> The porter has a taxi ready.
> [*Cf: There is a taxi ready*; *A taxi is ready*. – Type *SVC*]
> He had several friends in China.
> [*Cf: There were several friends (of his) in China*; *Several friends (of his) were in China*. – Type *SVA*]
> I have two buttons missing (on my jacket).
> My jacket has two buttons missing.
> [*Cf*: *There are two buttons missing*; *Two buttons are missing*. – Type *SV*]
> They had a few supporters helping them.
> [*Cf*: *There were a few supporters helping them*; *A few supporters were helping them*. – Type *SVO*]

As we show above, these clauses can be related to (and imply) some of the basic clause types; thus, for example, *The porter has a taxi ready* implies *A taxi is ready* [*SVC*].

But the correspondence with basic clause types is by no means as straightforward as it is with *there*-existentials. In the first place, an extra participant is introduced as theme (*The porter, He, I, They*, in the examples above). This is not merely absent from the corresponding basic clause but cannot usually be inferred from it. Consequently, in formulating the correspondence between *have*-existentials and the basic *SVC* type, we might postulate:

$$NP^1 + \textit{be} + C\,(NP^1) \sim NP^2 + \textit{have} + NP^1 + C\,(NP^1)$$

But while we are able to predict the tense of *have* (since it must correspond to that of *be*), we have no way of precisely predicting the NP^2 and usually no way of even imprecisely doing so:

$$\text{A taxi} \begin{bmatrix} \text{is} \\ \text{was} \end{bmatrix} \text{ready.} \sim NP^2 \begin{bmatrix} \begin{Bmatrix} \text{have} \\ \text{has} \end{Bmatrix} \\ \text{had} \end{bmatrix} \text{a taxi ready.}$$

Indeed, beyond saying that NP^2 will refer to a subject having considerable involvement in the existential proposition, we cannot specify what that involvement will be. Thus in:

> *The porter* has a taxi ready.

there is a strong implication that the NP^2 has an *agentive* role, whereas in:

> *You* have a taxi ready.

it is just as strongly implied that the NP^2 has a *recipient* or at any rate an *affected* role (*cf* 10.19). Calling it 'affected' seems to state the involvement with a degree of generality that satisfactorily accounts for most cases. Compare:

> A valuable watch was stolen. [SV_{pass}]
> *My friend* had a valuable watch stolen.

Note the possibility of other relationships:

> There are several oak trees in the garden.
> *They* have several oak trees in the garden.

Note [**a**] With a passive basic clause type, the verb generally has dynamic rather than stative (perfective) meaning: *My friend had his watch stolen* relates to *His watch was stolen* in the sense of 'Someone stole his watch' rather than of 'Someone had stolen his watch'.

[**b**] In a further *have*-construction (especially, but not necessarily, with the passive: *cf*: *He had us all addressing envelopes*), the subject of *have* gives up its 'recipient' role for one of indirect agency: *He had all his enemies imprisoned* is most likely to mean 'He caused all his enemies to be imprisoned'. In thus involving specification of agency, this *have*-construction is more remote from the corresponding basic clause (*His enemies were imprisoned*) than the other examples we have been considering. Compare analogous causatives and agentives:

> John is in prison.
> (They) put John in prison.

> The engine was repaired.
> (They) got the engine repaired.

18.52 But although we cannot in general predict from the basic clause the reference of the NP^2 in *have*-existentials (and still less its form – *John, He, My brother*, etc), the reference is often implied by nonexistential variants. For example:

> Two of *my* buttons are missing. [*SV*]
> *I* have two buttons missing.

> A brother of *his* was working in Chicago.
> *He* had a brother working in Chicago.

In some cases, reference (though not of course form) is not merely implied but actually specified in the nonexistential variant:

> A few supporters were helping {*Mary and Alice.* / *the three boys.* / *them.*} [*SVO*]
>
> {*Mary and Alice* / *The three boys* / *They*} had a few supporters helping *them*.

> John was working for *Mary*. [*SVA*]
> *Mary* had John working for *her*.

> Many apples were still on *the trees*.
> *The trees* still had many apples on *them*.

Again, where a basic clause type is extended to indicate recipient or other participant role, the reference concerned may then be anticipated in the subject of *have*. For example:

A taxi is ready *for you.* [*SVC*]
A valuable watch was stolen *from him.* [SV_{pass}]

beside:

You have a taxi ready for *you.*
{*John* / *He*} had a valuable watch stolen from *him.*

But the reference to a participant may be misleading, since the subject of *have* may be agentive:

They have a taxi ready for *you.*

Where the reference is the same, of course, pronoun identification works in the usual direction (*cf* 10.48*ff*); thus:

John had a valuable watch stolen from *him.*
≠ *He* had a valuable watch stolen from *John.*

Finally, it should be noted that in *have*-existentials, the 'notional subject' (*ie* the subject of the corresponding basic clause type) can freely be definite:

John's eldest son is helping him.
John has *his eldest son* helping him. [assuming *has* as existential and not causative: *cf* 16.52*ff*]

By contrast:

*There is {*John's* / *his*} *eldest son* helping him.

This would require a special context, such as 18.45 Note [a], to make it acceptable.

***Have*-existential sentences with relative and nonfinite clauses**

18.53 Corresponding to *there*-sentences of the same character (*cf* 18.48), the following illustrate *have*-sentences containing relative and infinitive clauses:

I've something I've been meaning to say to you.
He has a great deal to be thankful for.
(*Cf* There is a great deal for him to be thankful for.)
(?) They have a visitor come to see them. [= A visitor has come to see them]
She has a guest staying with her. [= A guest is staying with her]

Compare also with passive nonfinite clauses (*cf* 18.52):

He had a book stolen. [= A book was stolen from him]
She has had some poems published. [= Some poems (of hers) have been published]

In all these instances, the subject of *have* could be 'affected', but in some it could equally be agentive (*cf* 16.54, 18.51):

She has had some poems published. [= She has caused some poems (of her own *or* by someone else) to be published]

As with *have*-existentials in general, the subject of *have* may be totally unpredictable from the corresponding basic clause type or *there*-existential:

{There is a great deal for John to do.
Mary has a great deal for John to do.

Nonfinite and verbless existential clauses

18.54 Consider again finite-verb clauses of basic type and their corresponding existentials:

A taxi was soon available and Dr Lowe was able to catch the train.
There was soon a taxi available and Dr Lowe was able to catch the train.
Dr Lowe soon had a taxi available and was able to catch the train.

Corresponding to these finite clauses, nonfinite clauses can be formed, again existential as well as nonexistential:

A taxi being soon available,
There soon being a taxi available,
Soon having a taxi available,
} Dr Lowe was able to catch the train.

In this last case, the subject of the nonfinite clause would be identical with that of the main clause; if the subject is different, it can be supplied – at least in rather formal English:

The porter soon having a taxi available, Dr Lowe was able to catch the train.

There are also corresponding verbless clauses, especially introduced by *with* or its corresponding negative *without* (*cf* 9.49), and these prepositions may also occur in nonfinite clauses:

With a taxi soon available, Dr Lowe was able to catch the train.
Without a taxi soon enough available, Dr Lowe was unable to catch the train.
With a taxi speedily summoned, . . .
With a taxi already waiting, . . .

A further type of verbless existential clause is illustrated in 18.44 Note [b].

Emotive emphasis

18.55 Apart from the emphasis given by information focusing, the language provides means of giving a unit purely emotive emphasis. We have noted, in various sections of the grammar, a number of features of this type. They include exclamations (*cf* 11.31*f*), the persuasive *do* in imperatives (*cf* 11.30), interjections (*cf* 11.55), expletives and intensifiers (*cf* 7.87*ff*, 8.104*ff*), including the general clause emphasizers such as *actually, really,* and *indeed.* A thorough study of emotive expressions would involve examining figures of speech such as simile, hyperbole, and irony. Here we confine ourselves to two devices which fall squarely within the province of grammar.

Emphatic operators

18.56 We are here concerned with the difference between pairs like the following:

{ I'm |SÒRry| / I |ÀM 'sorry| } [1]
{ You |look PÀLE this 'morning| / You |DÒ 'look 'pale this 'morning| } [2]
{ |Mary will be PLÈASED| / |Mary WÌLL be 'pleased| } [3]
{ He |PRŎMised to 'go| / He |did PRŎMise to 'go| } [4]
{ I |TÒLD you| / I |did TĚLL you| } [5]

The second utterance in each case resembles prosodically the operator-stressed items discussed in 18.16. But as we see with [4] and [5], the operator, though emphasized, need not carry the nuclear force. More importantly, they all differ from the majority of those in 18.16 in not necessarily being contrastive. For example, in:

|Mary WÌLL be 'pleased|

the speaker is not here implying that someone has suggested that she will *not* be pleased. Rather, the speaker (in a style that is sometimes felt to be rather gushing and extravagant) is conveying enthusiasm: a personal conviction about the truth of what is predicated. But the emotion conveyed need not be enthusiasm: in [1] it is concern, in [2] sympathy, in [5] something like reproach or petulance. It is in this last connection that the *will/would* of 'insistence' (*cf* 4.57) is regularly stressed:

|John WĬLL 'keep| inter|RÙPting|
I |WÒULD go and make a 'MÉSS of it|

Note [**a**] While it is obviously necessary to stress the difference between emotive and contrastive emphasis, we saw in 18.16 that not all operator-focusing was contrastive. Moreover, some similarity in principle needs to be seen between emotive emphasis and the distribution of given and new information. For example, in [3] above, the emotive emphasis on *will* implies that *pleased* is relatively given: we can take the fact of her being pleased for granted and attend instead to expressing a degree of enthusiasm about it.

[**b**] Further intensification, if desired, can be achieved by placing an emphasizer such as *really* or *certainly* in front of the operator, or *indeed* after it: *It really does taste nice, It does indeed taste nice.* Such adverbials are especially helpful in writing since they draw attention to the need to supply operator-stress; *cf* 18.42 Note.

[**c**] Despite its similar emotive connotations, the 'persuasive' *do* in imperatives (*cf* 11.30) is again distinct from the above use of *do.* The imperative *do* does not obey the rule of *do*-support: one can say *Do be quiet!* in imperatives, but there is no corresponding statement **He DÒES be quiet!*

Noncorrelative *so* and *such*

18.57 In familiar speech of a style that strikes many people as extravagantly emphatic, the determiner *such* and the adverb *so* are stressed so as to give exclamatory force to a statement, question, or directive. In this usage, there is no accompanying correlative clause or phrase (*cf* 15.49):

She was |wearing 'such a lovely DRÈSS|
I'm |so afraid they'll get LÒST|
|Why are you 'such a BÀby|
|Don't upSÈT yourself 'so|

In consequence, *so* and *such* become equivalent to *how* and *what* in exclamations (*cf* 11.31*f*):

{They were so cross!
{How cross they were!
{They're such delightful children!
{What delightful children they are!

But *so* and *such* can also occur, as the earlier examples show, in questions and directives. Additional emotive emphasis is achieved by assigning a nucleus to *so* or *such*:

I'm |SÒ PLÉASED|

Note Other words of strong emotive import may take a nuclear tone for special emotive force:

I |WÌSH you'd LÍsten|
I |love that MŬSic| *or* I |LÒVE| that |MŬSic|
I'm |TÈRribly SÓRry|

Reinforcement

Repetition and 'proxy' pronouns

18.58 Reinforcement is a feature of colloquial style whereby some item is repeated (either completely or by pronoun substitution) for purposes of emphasis, focus, or thematic arrangement. Its simplest form is merely the reiteration (with heavy stressing) of a word or phrase for emphasis or clarity:

It's *far, far* too expensive. (*Cf* 7.89)
I agree with *every word* you've said – *every single word*.

In very loose and informal speech, a reinforcing or recapitulatory pronoun is sometimes inserted within a clause where it stands 'proxy' for an initial noun phrase:

This man I was telling you about – well, *he* used to live next door to me.
The book I lent you – have you finished *it* yet?

It will be noticed that in each case a complete noun phrase is disjoined from the grammar of the sentence, its role (as subject and object respectively) being grammatically performed by subsequent pronouns. But in being thus fronted, as marked themes (*cf* 18.19), the disjoined noun phrases clearly set out the 'point of departure' for the utterance as a whole. It is not uncommon for long noun phrases which are nonfocal to be thus treated in familiar speech, a convenience alike to hearer (in receiving an early statement of a complex item) and speaker (in not having to incorporate such an item in the grammatical organization of his utterance).

Note This phenomenon, along with that in 18.59, is sometimes termed 'left- and right-dislocation'; *cf* 17.78.

Amplificatory tags

18.59 In contrast to the fronting of items to be subsequently reinforced pronominally (as in 18.58), an amplificatory phrase may be informally added after the completion of a clause structure which contains a coreferential pronoun:

They're all the same, *these politicians.*
I wouldn't trust *him* for a moment, *your brother-in-law.*

Such utterances are usually spoken with divided focus (*cf* 18.17), with a rise on the 'tag' confirming its relatively 'given' status:

They're |all the SÀME, these poliTÍcians|
I |wouldn't trust him for a MÒment, your BRÓTHer-in-law|

The tag can be inserted parenthetically, as well as placed finally:

He's got a good future, your brother, if he perseveres.

An even more informal type of tag comprises a subject and operator:

That was a lark, *that was*!
He likes a drink now and then, *Jim does.*

In some dialects of English (especially Northern BrE), the operator may precede the subject:

She's a lovely girl, *is Ann.*

Postposed nonfinite clauses, of the kind discussed in 18.35, sometimes closely resemble amplificatory tags; contrast:

It was tough getting the job finished on time.
[|tough. . . . . .TÌME|]
It was tough, getting beaten in the last match.
[|TÒUGH|/. . . . . .MÁTCH|]

Note [**a**] The amplificatory tag should not be confused with either vocatives (*cf* 10.52*f*) or what may be called 'tag exclamations', such as *He ran away from* SCHÒOL, *the idiot* (*cf* 17.68 Note [b]). Both these constructions are distinguished from it intonationally, in that they may form the 'tail' of a preceding nucleus, instead of having their own (usually rising) nucleus. The intonation marks the following as usually tag and vocative respectively:

He's a |good CHÀP JÓHN|
He's a |good CHÀP 'John|

The exclamatory tag is further distinguished by being capable of (i) referring back to a noun phrase other than a pronoun:

That brother of mine ran away from school, the idiot.

and (ii) occurring initially as well as finally:

The idiot, he ran away from school.

The exclamatory tag is usually evaluative and the noun is very general in meaning; when premodified by an adjective, there may be zero article. We may thus contrast:

He's had a lot of bad LÙCK, { (the) poor man| / { the new / *new } CÁREtaker| }

[**b**] Expletives (in the broadest sense) provide a common mode of amplification in extremely informal speech, serving as a rhetorical transition between theme and an emotionally coloured focus:

He's a |silly ÌDiot|
They |lost their 'darned WÀY|
His |work is 'bloody ÀWful|
I |told them to 'darned 'well LÌsten|

Compare tmesis (App I.76 Note [c]) where the inserted amplification is usually made just prior to the point of main emphasis:

fan'tastic ~ fan-'flaming-"tastic

In 'She lost her darned way', it is not of course the final noun phrase as such that calls for expletive comment. The whole utterance is emotionally coloured, and in extreme cases such colouring (especially in exasperation) is expressed at additional points in the sentence structure:

These *blasted* people have *darned well* lost their *stupid* way!

Alternatively the 'scope' of the colouring as well as the colouring itself can be expressed by prosodic means, 'She's lost her way' being uttered with an exceptional intensity or other marking (*cf* App II.1*ff*).

Expletives also amplify the theme in *wh*-questions:

Who	on earth	+ op, etc
What	in heaven	
Where	(in) the hell	
When	the blazes	
Why	in the world	
How	in God's name	

[**c**] In responses of a rejoinder kind, we find a combination of fronting (*cf* 18.20*f*) with amplificatory tagging:

A: Have I arranged to see anyone this afternoon?
B: Well, Mrs BLÀKE, you HÁVE. [~'You have arranged to see Mrs Blake']
A: Do you write poetry?
B: SÒMEtimes I DÓ. [~'I write poetry sometimes']

Where such replies are negative, both parts are negated, though responses in this form are then restricted to rather informal usage:

A: Have I made this clear to you all?
B: Not to MÈ, you HÁVEn't. [~'To the others perhaps, but not to me']
A: May I go in?
B: Not YÈT, you CÁN'T. [~'You can't go in yet']

It will be noticed that the use of fall-plus-rise, putting the fall on the most salient part, the rise on the partly 'given', corresponds to the general use described in 18.17.

Bibliographical note

On information processing in relation to given and new, see Allerton (1978); Allerton and Cruttenden (1979); Chafe (1976); Dahl (1974); Firbas (1975, 1980); Halliday (1967–68); Kuno (1976b); Li (1976); Taglicht (1982, 1984); Waida (1979).

On Functional Sentence Perspective, see Daneš (1974); Firbas (1970, 1971); Hajičová and Sgall (1982); Hajičová and Vrbová (1981); Kuno (1972); Mathesius (1929).

On Communicative Dynamism, see Firbas (1971, 1975, 1980); Svoboda (1968).

On existential constructions, see Breivik (1979, 1983); Erdmann (1976); Jenkins (1975); Kimball (1973a); Milsark (1979); Rando and Napoli (1978).

On stylistic aspects of intonation, see Bald (1979/80); Bolinger (1972c); Charleston (1960); Crystal (1975).

On intonation and grammar, see André (1974); Crystal (1969, 1980); Halliday (1967).

On contrastive accentuation, see Allerton and Cruttenden (1979); Bolinger (1961c); Chafe (1976); Enkvist (1980).

On extraposition and other aspects of item ordering, see Erdmann (1981); Hartvigson and Jakobsen (1974); Rosenbaum (1967a); Rudanko (1982).

Other relevant studies include Bolinger (1975b, 1977a); Brazil et al (1980); Huddleston (1971); Leech (1981b); Lyons (1977); Mathesius (1975); O'Connor and Arnold (1973); Schmerling (1976).

19 From sentence to text

General: the notion of 'text'

19.1 Throughout this book, two interrelated acts of imagination have been demanded of the reader.

First, we have expected that examples, though inevitably appearing before the reader only in print, would be not only read but 'heard'. We have constantly stressed the primacy of speech, both in *mass* terms (the fact that far more language occurs in speech than in writing) and – much more significantly – in *linguistic* terms (the fact that the written form must evoke the oral form, just as though we heard the words read aloud). And we have sought to bring this home to the user of the book by repeated if clumsy reference to 'speaker/writer' and 'reader/hearer'.

Second, we have expected that examples would be placed in a suitable context. Thus, although we have presented forms and constructions as though they were fully explicated within isolated sentences, we have been aware that it would not have been possible to understand the presentation unless every structure and every exemplificatory sentence had been placed by or for the reader in an imagined context. Indeed we have made our awareness explicit in a large number of cases by providing cues to the type of context in which a given form was to be appropriately used and plausibly understood.

19.2 In the present chapter, we work in a converse way. We take TEXTS as our starting point and examine the language comprising them. In other words, we bring together all the grammatical processes already described but we do so now with a view to discussing their role in both the interpretation of a text and in the construction of a text. And we shall pay considerable attention to lexical and other features of textual structure in order to show that, important as is the role of grammar, many factors other than grammar are involved.

Moreover, as we are using the term, a text – unlike a sentence – is not a grammatical unit but rather a semantic and even a pragmatic one. A text is a stretch of language which seems appropriately coherent in actual use. That is, the text 'coheres' in its real-world context, semantically and pragmatically, and it is also internally or linguistically coherent. For this latter facet, the term 'cohesive' has been applied, referring to the actual forms of linguistic linkage.

A text may be spoken (as are the vast majority) or it may be in writing. It may be the product of a single speaker (as with an announcement on an airport public-address system) or of several speakers engaged in conversation. Textual structure relates to the concerns of this book – the grammar of English – by virtue of the fact that texts are realized in grammatical units. But the grammatical units occurring in a text are often very different from the corresponding grammatical units as they are described in terms of the English grammatical system. Consider for example, as part of a text, the response:

Me, too!

Among the possible texts in which this might occur, we could suggest:

'This noise is giving me a headache'
'Me, too!' [1]

'I wish I had a drink'
'Me, too!' [2]

'My feet are aching'
?'Me, too!' [3]

but not:

'Would you like a drink?'
*'Me, too!' [4]

or:

'It's starting to rain'
*'Me, too!' [5]

In [1] the second speaker makes his response on the basis of a relatively straightforward elliptical form of what he has just heard (*cf* 12.1*ff*, 12.31*ff*, 12.46*ff*, 13.44*ff*):

(This noise is giving) *me* (a headache), *too*!

With [2], what is superficially the same response involves pronoun-replacement (*cf* 6.14*ff*, 10.48*ff*, 12.8*ff*):

I (wish I had a drink), *too*!

Only the respective *textual* structure as a whole can determine the *grammatical* structure in terms of which *Me, too* is being used. The role of the response in [3] is clear enough semantically ('My feet are also aching'), but grammatically its relation to what has preceded is vague and uncertain; though it might occur in familiar speech, many people would find it textually ill-formed.

But by contrast with [1], [2], and [3], the response 'Me, too' in [4] and [5] is a non sequitur textually and equally impossible to relate to a plausible structure in the grammatical system.

Context and the one-sentence text

19.3 It is natural to think of a text as being realized in a string of several sentences: that it is connected sentences that constitute a text. But in fact a text may be wholly realized in a single sentence, and if we consider such an example we shall see the significance of the point made in 19.2 that a text was not so much a grammatical as a semantic or pragmatic unit. Even a single word can be a text that is 'appropriately coherent in actual use' (*cf* 19.2): a road sign bearing the word DANGER, for example, as compared with one that read SINCERITY.

Imagine receiving a note bearing only the words:

Roger's finished the thesis!

The same text might of course be spoken: someone comes into the room and withdraws again having said only:

|Roger's finished the THÈSis|

The grammatical properties of the sentence realizing this text and necessary for our understanding of it have been described in earlier chapters. The perfective *has finished* is understood (in contrast, for example, with *will finish*); the determiner *the* (in contrast to *a* or *his*); the singular *thesis*; the intonation nucleus on *thesis* (and not, for example, on *Roger*); the whole being declarative (and not interrogative, *Has Roger . . .?*), etc. But as realizing a text, there is much more here. The text depends upon our knowing Roger (and knowing him as *Roger* and not as *Mr Taylor*), on knowing what a thesis is, on knowing about this particular thesis (a different text might have had *a thesis on aeronautics*). Less obviously, perhaps, the text depends on our knowing what *finishing* involves: Roger may have been writing his own thesis, typing (or binding) one for someone else, or completing his work as an examiner of the thesis. As well as conveying all this, the text will mean more to us. It is another instance of Roger's speedy efficiency, perhaps (as though the text had included the adverbial *already*). Or it conveys relief after an intolerably lengthy period (as though the text had included the adverbial *at last*). Or it may be a signal that Roger is now free to indulge (let us say) in a game of tennis.

These are all covert connections (that is, they are given no actual expression), but according as the situation determines, the piece of text could be expanded by some such comment as one of the following:

> That's Roger TÀYLor, I suppose.
> Aha – so aeronautics takes a big step forward!
> Gosh – that was quick!
> And about time too!
> Oh, good: he can take on Frieda at the end of this set.

19.4 All of these additions have one thing in common: they each show a plausible interpretation of the original short text. They also form a close connection with it and with the wider context which determines the satisfactory coherence of the text. Clearly, not all of the interpretations involve grammar: the lexical meaning of *thesis*, for example, or the use of the text as an announcement that a game of tennis can start. But in the connections that texts manifest, it is equally clear that grammar plays a considerable role and it is on this connective potential of grammar that we shall be concentrating in this chapter. And 'potential' is a key word, since (as we have already seen) connection may be covert as well as overt.

Asyndetic connection

19.5 Just as a text realized by a single sentence has a complex of covert connections with its context, so any two neighbouring sentences will be perceived as being connected. Mere juxtaposition (parataxis rather than asyndeton) is an icon of connectedness, even where the juxtaposed parts have no grammatical or lexical feature in common:

> Go and visit your father; it's New Year's Day.
> It's New Year's Day. Go and visit your father.

The perceived connection here is the same, whichever sentence comes first, just as we will connect a child seen in the park with an adult, whether the child is running ahead or trailing behind. So too, the text in 19.3 might have been expanded as:

Roger's finished the thesis! Caroline arrived from New York last week.

These two sentences are grammatically asyndetic and quite unrelated. But as a text or as part of a text, they are connected, and – if the text is successful – the connection will be clear to the reader/hearer: Caroline's relation to Roger will already be known and doubtless also the connection between the thesis work and Caroline's arrival. Even if we are merely 'eavesdroppers' on this text, we find ourselves speculating on possible connections. Perhaps Caroline brought with her the last piece of material that Roger required for completing the thesis; perhaps Caroline's arrival spurred him on to completion; perhaps the connection with Caroline's arrival is merely that she brought the news. Any of these connections is fully compatible with the grammar of the two sentences but none is made linguistically overt. This would remain true if the two sentences were in converse order:

Caroline arrived from New York last week. Roger's finished the thesis!

Such sentences in text can be said to be truly asyndetic (*cf* 13.1), in allowing connection by *and*, should we so wish.

Note [**a**] It is tempting to draw an analogy between asyndetic connection and our familiarity with a situation such that overt expression can be curtailed. In 19.3, we noted that 'Roger's finished the thesis' might have covertly conveyed *at last*. If this interpretation is the correct one, then:

Roger's finished the thesis! [1]
Roger's finished the thesis at last! [2]
After ten long years, Roger's finished the thesis at last! [3]

can be seen as synonymous but with decreasing degrees of 'asyndeton' with the context. In [1], the reference to duration is totally covert; in [2] it is overt but imprecise; in [3] it is still more overt with the specification of the length of time that is held to justify *at last*. We shall have occasion to use this extended sense of asyndeton in examining the grammatical potential of sentences in texts (for example, in relation to the absence of necessarily invoked performatives; *cf* 19.64).

[**b**] Some scholars use the term 'parataxis' for clauses without formal linkage; others would call this '*asyndetic* parataxis', applying the unrestricted term to all clause relations that are not *hypotactic* (*ie* involving subordination). On our own use of these terms, *cf* 13.1*f*.

19.6 Consider now a variation on the two-sentence text given in 19.5:

Roger's finished the thesis! Caroline has gone out to the supermarket.

Although these sentences are asyndetic in the sense of 13.1, there is a slight but significant grammatical relation. The verb phrase is perfective in each case and while this does not enjoin a particular interpretation, it certainly helps to suggest a range of possible close connections: what Caroline has done seems to match in some way what Roger has done. The completion of the thesis has perhaps released her to go out on an errand; or it has caused her to go and buy celebratory wine.

Structural parallelism

19.7 Indeed, although they might formally be regarded as asyndetic (and they are certainly paratactic), neighbouring sentences that share grammatical features of tense, aspect, clause structure, or word order give a strong impression of being connected thereby. Such grammatical parallelism is often endorsed lexically. Consider the relatively abstract frame, now illustrating both coordination and subordination:

The __ was Ved in __ {and/while | but/whereas} the __ was Ved in __

and compare the following where the blanks are filled:

The baseball game was cancelled in New Haven
{and/while the hockey match was postponed in Hartford. [1]
{but/whereas the hockey match was (duly) played in Hartford. [2]

(where New Haven and Hartford are related as well-known cities in Connecticut).

The parallelism between sentences is more transparent, and hence the connection between the sentences is more strongly indicated, if the word order is not the normal one. The effect of fronting an element in such cases is to point to a contrast between the sentences. Indeed, in [3] the unusual order of the first sentence makes us expect a similar and related one to follow (*cf* 18.20):

My paintings the visitors admired. *My sculptures* they disliked. [3]
In New York it is hot and humid during the summer. *In Los Angeles* it is hot and dry. [4]
From the ceiling hung a huge lamp. *Along the wall* were pikes. [5]

The direct objects and the space adjuncts in [3] and [4] respectively are in initial position instead of their normal final position. In [5] the nonnormal position is accompanied by subject–verb inversion. When constituents are fronted, then we can infer a connection between the sentences even where there is little or no other structural similarity:

Proudly, the captain hoisted the flag. *Softly*, a bugle sounded. [6]

Moreover, only an apparent similarity in structure is sufficient to suggest parallelism between sentences:

My paintings the visitors admired. *My sculptures* irritated them. [7]

Our impression of a link between the two initial noun phrases in [7] is given impetus by the fronted position of the direct object *my paintings* in the first sentence and the expectation that we are encountering a similar inversion when we reach *my sculptures*, though in fact the former is direct object and the latter is subject, in its normal position. The impression of a link between the two initial noun phrases is reinforced by the internal structure of the two phrases and the lexical set to which both *painting* and *sculpture* belong. The two sentences are further linked by a semantic parallelism, realized syntactically in two ways: a person has a feeling towards an object, an object arouses a feeling in a person. They are also linked, of course, by the use of the pro-form *them* in the second sentence which replaces *the visitors* in the first sentence.

Connection by sequence

19.8 Sentences with grammatical features in common, such as the same subject or the same tense, often imply temporal and causal connection. In other words, where we saw juxtaposition in 19.5 as iconic of mere connection, we now see it as iconic of connected sequence. As the two real-world events, a policeman holding up his hand and a car coming to a standstill, follow each other in time, so asyndetic narration of these events will preserve this sequence:

> The policeman held up his hand. The car stopped.
> [≠ The car stopped. The policeman held up his hand.]

This is well illustrated in the text attributed to Julius Caesar after his Pontic triumph:

> I came. I saw. I conquered.

Even without the lexical meanings of the verbs, the sequence suggests:

> I did something.
> And then (in consequence; *cf* 13.23) I did something else.
> And then (in further consequence) I did something else.

Moreover, given that (as we shall see) triadic sequences have special implications, the third of the above suggests not merely 'in further consequence' but 'as a still further and climactic consequence'. Yet the text could not work as a text unless the lexical meanings of the verbs were known; these not merely confirm the consequential structure but make the particular sequence of paratactic sentences obligatory. Compare the relative difficulty of seeing the following as a coherent text:

> I conquered. I came. I saw.

On the other hand, even with formal asyndeton, if we alter grammatical features such as tense, we can then switch the order of sentences so that it is no longer iconic and no longer asyndetic in the sense of 13.1 (since *and*-connection is impossible). They are now merely paratactic:

> The car stopped. The policeman *had held* up his hand.

We here achieve paratactically the sequence freedom that is readily possible syndetically:

> The car stopped $\left\{\begin{array}{l}\text{after}\\ \text{because}\end{array}\right\}$ the policeman held up his hand.

19.9 We have spoken of texts realized by one or more *sentences*. But just as we saw that it made no necessary substantial and inherent difference to a text when it was expanded by an adverbial (*cf* 19.5 Note [a]), so it makes little difference whether a text is punctuated as three sentences or one:

> I came, I saw, I conquered.

Of course, a close relation between the parts is still more clearly implied when commas separate the first two and a period appears only after the third, and it is worth noting that a spoken form of this text (irrespective of punctuation) would normally show the 'dependent' status of the first two by rising nuclei in contrast to a fall on the third:

I CÁME| I SÁW| I CÒNquered.

(*Cf* further 19.25)

19.10 We have seen (*cf* 19.5, 19.7) that asyndetic connection has the effect of making the structure of a text extremely dependent upon the sequence of sentences realizing it. There are obviously no grammatical constraints upon the order of:

Roger's finished the thesis! Caroline arrived from New York last week.

as compared with:

Caroline arrived from New York last week. Roger's finished the thesis!

This being so, we must scrutinize the actual sequence all the more carefully to find a textual reason for the particular juxtaposition we encounter. In fact, the absence of grammatical constraints seems quite rare, to judge from both the spoken and written material of the Survey of English Usage. More commonly, the order necessary for the presentation of the text is enjoined by grammatical factors such as the sequence of pronouns in relation to antecedents:

Roger's finished the thesis. *His* wife arrived from New York last week.

The appearance of *his* here doubly provides a formal link between the two sentences in showing that Roger has a relation to both, and in confirming their particular sequence. (Contrast *Roger's wife arrived from New York last week. He's finished the thesis.* Here the pronominalization is again in the second sentence but the two sentences are reversed in sequence.)

Syndetic connection

19.11 Another way of indicating both the relevance of sequence and the closeness of textual connection is to introduce an overt connecting item, most frequently the coordinator *and* (*cf* 13.5*ff*):

Roger's finished the thesis and Caroline arrived from New York last week.

But although *and* is the most neutral and semantically uncommitted of connecting items, it will be noticed that some of the options for interpreting the text (*cf* 19.5) are now precluded. Even the 'eavesdropper' who knows nothing of Roger and Caroline may now interpret the two parts as having a temporal sequence matching the textual sequence: perhaps Caroline has waited for the thesis to be completed before leaving New York. This may be brought out more clearly with an alternative set of examples:

The rain has stopped. She's gone for a walk. [1]
The rain has stopped and she's gone for a walk. [2]
She's gone for a walk. The rain has stopped. [3]

?She's gone for a walk and the rain has stopped. [4]

The dubious textual coherence of the [4] version makes clear that, with syndetic connection, sequence is likely to be crucial. In contrast, the coherence of [1], [2], and [3] is beyond question and in interpretation they are closely similar, even though [3] reverses the sequence (concluding with a reason, where [1] and [2] conclude with a consequence). Compare also:

The student was late for the lecture. He missed his train.
The student missed his train and he was late for the lecture.

Note [**a**] With *and* connecting two sentences, the relation is made to seem less close. Thus, if [4] above were punctuated as two separate sentences, we could delete the query since the effect would be more like [3]. The *and* in [4] could perhaps connote 'by the way' (*cf* 19.29), though in this case we might expect something to follow the second sentence:

She's gone for a walk. And the rain has stopped (so she'll really enjoy being out).

[**b**] Clauses with reciprocal pronouns (*cf* 6.31) as objects are very similar in meaning to coordinate clauses, but where the former suggest simultaneous actions, the latter is conducive to an interpretation involving sequence. Compare:

Geoff and Sue {greeted / spoke to / saw / kissed} each other.

Geoff [greeted / spoke to / saw / kissed] Sue and Sue [greeted / spokc to / saw / kissed] Geoff.

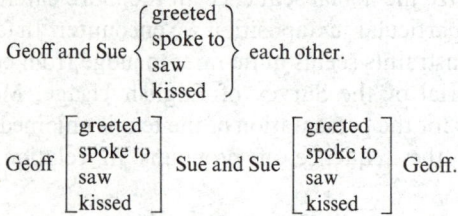

Thematic connection

19.12 In 19.3 we examined a text where the connections were extra-textual: our knowledge of Roger and the thesis in which he was involved. But although all texts necessarily have extra-textual connections (none would otherwise be understood), it is normal for them to generate internal connections as well. The basic way of doing this is by proceeding sequentially from the known ('given') to the unknown ('new'), thus forming a chain in which what was unknown becomes the known as a point of departure towards a further unknown item. We have already seen this process in Chapter 18, in relation to end focus. Consider now the following four-part text (truncated and idealized), which we may imagine being spoken over the public address system of a big organization:

|*Here* is an 'urgent MÈSSage| *It* is for |visiting salesman Herbert BLÀCK|
Will |*Mr Black* please contact the third floor SÙPervisor| *She* will be |waiting for him at the inQUÌRy desk|

A further example:

|*Mary* invited me to her BÌRTHday party| *It* was |held in a West End HOTÈL| *where I* |*met her* PÀRents| The |*father* is a retired DÈNtist|

It will be noticed that each part ends with a prosodic climax (as do the vast majority of clauses in the SEU spoken corpus), and begins with a thematic unit, shown in italics, the whole text having in consequence a rhythmic prosodic pattern that can be diagrammed thus to represent the sequence of crescendi:

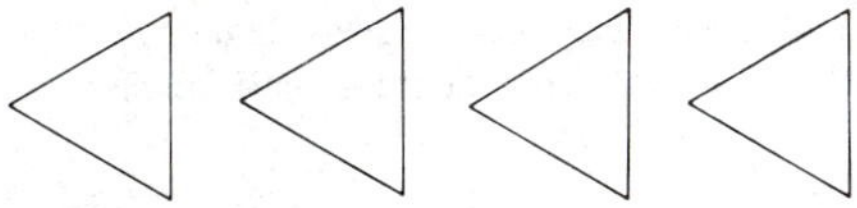

Fig 19.12

It is easy to see how this mirrors the increase in what is sometimes called the 'communicative dynamism' (*cf* 18.3) of each successive part. Irrespective of whether or not they are explicitly linked, the parts are linked thematically in that the 'rheme' (*cf* 18.9 Note) introduced in the first part, *an urgent message*, is pronominalized as *it* (*cf* 6.14*ff*) to become the 'theme' (*cf* 18.9) of the second. Compare also *Herbert Black* and *him* (via *Mr Black*), *the supervisor* and *She*.

19.13 But thematic connection is often by no means as linearly straightforward as it is in these examples. The interpretation of text depends upon the recipient's common sense and his knowledge acquired independently of the text, as we saw in 19.3. Grammar has potential in establishing plausible interpretations, but it is not required to provide unequivocal cues. Compare the two following texts in both of which there is thematic connection by pronominalization but where the pairing of pronouns and referents is sharply different:

> Mr Fraser^{1} sent for the doctor^{2}; he^{1} listened anxiously for his^{2} arrival; he^{1} asked him^{2} to examine his^{1} throat. [1]
>
> Mr Fraser^{1} sent for the doctor^{2}; he^{2} diagnosed his^{1} complaint; he^{1} soon felt better. [2]

The thematic connections are linked inextricably with the lexical items that are in turn linked to the situational context. Thus *he* and *his* in the second part of [1], while following one of the grammatical patterns of pronoun coreference, are identified with their respective referents through our knowing that the person that sends for someone will be the one to listen for his arrival. Again, in [2] the order of antecedent-pronoun sequence is one of those grammatically permissible: *he* in the second part refers to the last-mentioned noun phrase in the first part. But the actual interpretation relates this grammatical possibility to the extra-linguistic probability that the diagnosis will be carried out by the doctor and not by Mr Fraser.

In the following example, *they* is thematic in both the alternative concluding parts, but identification depends on lexical congruence with the verb of which *they* is subject:

> The police^{1} prohibited the strikers^{2} from demonstrating because
>
> {they^{1} anticipated / they^{2} advocated} violence.

Other types of thematic connection involve the fronting of adverbials or other elements more normally associated with end position:

> After rejecting the advice of the specialist at the hospital, Mr Fraser sent for the local doctor. *In him* he had the deepest confidence.
>
> Mr Fraser sent for a different doctor. *His usual one* he no longer trusted.

Note Commonly, a plural pronoun will refer back to antecedents each introduced as singular:

Mr Fraser[1] sent for the doctor[2] and *they*[1+2] discussed *his*[1] complaint for nearly an hour.

Rhematic connection

19.14 Compare the two following texts:

Jan lives in Holland and he writes poetry. [1]

Caroline arrived on Tuesday and Roger finished the thesis on Friday. [2]

In both there is syndetic linkage, giving a superficial similarity to the cohesion in the two examples, but informationally the types of connection are very different. In [1] there is the thematic connection that we have considered in 19.12; we need see no connection between the rhemes here (*in Holland* and *poetry*): it is enough that Jan has a relation to both. In [2] on the other hand there is no *textual* connection between the two themes, Caroline and Roger: the parts are firmly connected through the rhemes. This is achieved syntactically (two adjuncts, *on Tuesday* and *on Friday*), in form (both adjuncts involving items from the lexical *x-day* series), and in meaning (both indicating time *when*). There is also a more generally pervading cohesion through parallelism of form; *cf* 19.7. In speech, the connection would be endorsed by prosodic contrast or parallelism through the nuclei on *Tues-* and *Fri-* with perhaps a wider pitch range (*cf* App II.20) on the latter:

|Caroline arrived on TÚESday| and |Roger finished the thesis on ↑FRÌday|
. . . TŬESday . . .
. . . TÙESday . . .

An example of rhematic connection with pronominalization:

|Experts admire THÌS picture| but the |general public prefer THÀT (one)|

Textual orientation

19.15 In 19.1 we spoke of the need for every text to have a context. In particular we need an orientation in respect of *place*, *time*, *factuality*, and *participant relations*. Let us assume that a lecturer's opening words to an audience were as follows:

In this week's talk, I would like us to examine why some people allege a decline in religious faith.

The basic place and time orientation of the decline in religious faith is entirely covert, but the lecturer knows that his listeners will automatically relate this unlocated, undated decline to their own *here* and *now*. Individuals will naturally vary as to the broadness or narrowness with which they conceive *here* and *now*: this city, this part of the country, this country, here in the world as a whole; now in this present year, this decade, this century. But they will not normally exclude their narrowest concept of 'here' while embracing a wider one, and they will not exclude the present year while embracing the present century.

The same opening sentence could have begun a lecture that was part of a series on eighteenth-century France. In that case, the covert orientation would have been equally automatic and equally essential, but with a *there* and *then* which would have located and dated the alleged decline, while at the same time giving this location and dating an orientation with respect to the (similar or contrasting) *here* and *now* of the audience.

19.16 The example in 19.15 has a bearing upon participant relations in two respects. First, the speaker's personal and functional relation to his audience: he calls his activity a *talk* rather than a *lecture* or *address*, and with polite diffidence (*I would like*) invites his listeners to join him in an inquiry (*I would like us to examine*: *cf* 6.7, 6.18). A more distant lecturer–audience relation would have been set up with:

In this week's lecture, I shall explain why . . .

In either case he feels it relevant to specify the function of his text; *cf* 'Here is an urgent message', 19.12. Secondly, we have the speaker's relation to the rhematic *a decline in religious faith*: he does not commit himself to claiming a decline ('some people' might, but certainly need not, include the speaker) and indeed he hints at the insecurity of the claim by using the verb *allege*. Note the different relation he would have communicated between himself and his subject if he had said he would:

. . . examine why it is believed that there is a decline in religious faith.
or: . . . examine why there is, as we all believe, a decline . . .
or: . . . examine why there is a decline . . .

Basic relational structures

19.17 A text may have one (or more) of an indefinitely large number of purposes: description, persuasion, narrative, etc. Some of these correlate closely with particular connective devices and presentational styles, as we note throughout this book from time to time. Textual functions are too numerous, too fluid, and too interlocking for us to attempt separate treatment in terms of textual form. But irrespective of the various purposes and general intentions of a text, there are a few relationships within texts that constantly recur, which involve particular connective devices, and which are therefore useful to bear in mind as we consider the devices themselves. They can be seen as basic relational structures:

(a) general and particular
(b) progression
(c) compatibility

(a) It is common for a text to proceed from a general point to a particular:

Working in wood calls for great manual skill. The ordinary saw itself is not easy to handle. [1]

But we may equally proceed in the reverse direction:

The ordinary household saw is not easy to use. In fact, any sort of woodwork calls for great manual skill. [1a]

In conversational texts, the second part will often be supplied by another speaker who thus 'cooperates' in forming the text:

A: I must go and do some shopping.
B: Well, don't forget to buy a newspaper. } [general to particular] [2]

A: This chair is a bit wobbly.
B: Well, none of the furniture is very good. } [particular to general] [3]

(b) Whether we are giving instructions, telling a story, or conducting an argument, we are concerned to present the parts of our text so as to show the temporal or inferential relation of one to another:

Get ready: set: go. [4]
While Oscar was asleep, Mrs Pugh was sewing. [5]
This must be the way. I remember that house on the corner. [6]

Some dialogue examples:

A: My shoes are leaking.
B: So you'll be getting them repaired, I suppose. [7]
A: I spoke to Veronica on the phone last night.
B: And? [8]

Conversational explanations often include verbal encouragement such as *you see*, or *if you follow me*, or the like.

(c) Again, irrespective of the type of text, interpretation depends on recognizing whether or not parts are compatible with each other. The relation may be one of *matching*, as in:

The ordinary saw is not easy to use; a plane demands years of practice. [1b]
A: That climb up the mountain was marvellous.
B: The view from the top was glorious, too. [9]

Or the relation may be one of *contrast*:

The ordinary hand drill is not easy to use; this electric type is something any novice can handle. [1c]

Reluctance or inability to recognize compatibility is often expressed by another speaker's interjection beginning 'Sorry, what about . . .' or 'Well, I'm not sure . . .'. We may distinguish 'Sorry!' and 'Sorry?':

SǑRry|

'Sorry!' indicates as here conviction about counter-compatibility. By contrast, 'Sorry?' as in:

SÓRry|

is a request for repetition or explanation, perhaps implying serious doubts about the compatibility between the parts of a text, or merely indicating that something was inaudible.

Likewise, a speaker may help to demonstrate compatibility between one part and another by an explanation or example beginning:

You KNÓW|

or by urging a hearer to acknowledge the compatibility with such an explanation or example preceded by:

YÒU KNÓW|

Discourse strategies

19.18 Relational structures can be realized by a number of discourse designs or strategies that have been well described within the rhetorical tradition since ancient times. Some of the most outstanding may be seen in terms of the following metaphors:

(i) step
(ii) chain
(iii) stack
(iv) balance

(i) The simplest type of exposition is a 'step by step' procedure. It is one that has an obvious appropriateness for instructional material but it is normal also in description, narrative, or argument. The strategy is adequately illustrated by many of the short examples of text already given, but compare also:

The 100-metre race was run immediately after lunch. This was followed by the 400-metre relay. After a brief interlude with an acrobatic display, spectators spread around the track to watch the first cycling event.

Informal spoken narrative of 'step' design often involves repetitious coordination with conjuncts such as *then* or *next*: 'and then . . . and then . . . next there was . . .'

(ii) The chain resembles the step procedure in going from point to point, but whereas in a stepped text it is part of the technique to assure the hearer/reader in advance that the course is unidirectional and the goal planned, with the chain it is equally part of the technique to let it appear that though there are definite links (*cf* 19.11), the direction may curve, the course double back, and the ultimate point be unpredictable. The chain strategy is thus well suited to reflective or exploratory discourse:

Hamlet poignantly represents the indecisions that plague us all. Not that indecision is the worst of our ills. In some ways decisiveness can be more damaging. Many people have decided on their courses of action too rapidly, with disastrous results. Othello is a representative of this tendency, though here we have other factors to consider such as jealousy and the evil influence of a supposed friend. Friendship in itself, of course . . .

Like the step format, the chain is often characteristic of informal speech, where the varied and uncertain progression is acknowledged by sections beginning 'But of course', 'By the way', and the like.

The 'chain' type of structure, while technically well-formed (*eg* in thematic connection) characterizes desultory informal talk where one topic leads aimlessly to another. It is ridiculed in the following passage from Gilbert Sorrentino's *Mulligan Stew* (1980) where a character is musing on the reason for the late arrival of the police. He imagines their route blocked by a landslide so that they are forced to take the old road running beside the river:

> The narrow bridges, slats missing, are considered by the natives hereabouts to be dangerous, fit only for carefree boys to fish off. They rarely catch any fish, according to Old Cash at the general store. What crackers he has!

While each transition is linguistically explicable, the text wanders helplessly away from the central question of the journey by the police.

(iii) As with the step technique, the stack has a predetermined unity, but instead of a linear progression we have something more like a vertical structure, with a sound foundation (often called the *topic* sentence), an accumulation of 'layers', finally capped by a neat 'roof', securely 'roped down' to the foundations. For example:

> There is something very unsatisfactory about the maxim 'Honesty is the best policy'. It seems to equate virtue with profit, yet our common experience denies this. We could all cite instances of where an honest and virtuous action has brought disappointment and even ruin. We could equally point to people who have behaved with gross dishonesty and have become successful, powerful, wealthy. In any case it is surely rather immoral to incite people to honourable behaviour by seeming to promise reward. Honesty, if it requires a motive, must be valued for reasons other than 'policy'.

Carefully constructed stacks are frequently recommended for *paragraphing* and they cannot be expected in informal conversation, though we often try to impose such a structure by ending a description or argument with a part beginning with a summative conjunct (*cf* 8.137) such as *All in all* . . . or *In short* . . . Alternatively, the conclusion may be an exclamation like:

> What fun it all was!   So that's JÒHN for you!

(iv) Like the chain, the balance strategy is particularly suited to reflective and exploratory discourse, but it resembles the stack in the care with which the parts are put together. Plus and minus, hot and cold, are set one beside the other so that the text seems to anticipate objections and crosscurrents raised in the mind of the reader/hearer. In the following example, the balance technique is used within a dominant stack procedure:

> For a spring break, Cumbria is hard to beat. There is of course a strong risk of bad weather during the early months of the year. On the other hand, the early tourist is rewarded by empty roads and the feeling that he has the countryside to himself. Not all the hotels are open, it is true, and you may be obliged to drive on to the next village. But this is well offset by the welcome that awaits you in a guest house

where you may turn out to be the only resident. Early visitors to Cumbria rarely regret their initiative.

Balancing is common enough in ordinary conversation, using pointers like 'on the one hand ... but on the other hand', but ambitious attempts at balance often seem over-formal or even pompous. Informally, a balancing reservation is often introduced by 'Mind you':

I love Cumbria {. Mind YǑU, I don't like the weather!
{– not the weather, mind YÓU!

Connective devices

19.19 The relation between parts of a text is achieved by connective features that fall into four categories:

(a) pragmatic and semantic implication
(b) lexical linkage
(c) prosody and punctuation
(d) grammatical devices

Naturally, in a book on grammar, we shall be concentrating on (d), but grammatical devices need to be seen in the context of (a–c) from which they can never in practice be entirely separated. All four types of connective device not merely interact intimately but operate simultaneously. In principle, however, they can usefully be distinguished and we proceed here to examine each in isolation.

(a) Pragmatic and semantic implication

19.20 Consider the following sequence as constituting the beginning of a discourse:

Have you seen the paper? There's been a plane crash.

Interpretation depends on the institution of the (daily) *newspaper*, on the assumption that most of us regularly see some newspaper or other, and on our referring to it – irrespective of the particular newspaper we may have – as 'the paper' (*cf* 5.28). The connection between the two sentences depends in turn (i) on the convention that a question implies that there is something of special interest to which the speaker wants to draw attention, and (ii) on the plausibility that the following statement summarizes a news item that the speaker has read in the paper. On the other hand, if the second part had continued as:

... which has been completely ignored.

the implication would have been quite different: the speaker's announcement of the plane crash was not derived from the newspaper at all.

We may see the chain-like process of implication more clearly in a further example:

Mr Costello drove to London to take part in an antinuclear demonstration. [1]

As a complete text, this implies of course that Mr Costello did in fact take part in the demonstration and we would be unsurprised if the text continued:

He felt he had done something for peace. [2]

But in fact the continuation might well have been:

On the way, his wife suggested they go to the flower show instead. [2a]

This does not in itself frustrate our interpretation of [1]: it remains plausible, but we now recognize that whereas the direction adjunct (*to London*) in association with the past tense (*drove*) combine to entail in themselves actual arrival (contrast *was driving to London* or *set out for London*), the purpose adjunct in [1] (*to take part in . . .*) merely opens a possibility. He *intended* to take part in the demonstration and the fulfilment of this intention is implied only if nothing is said to the contrary.

Equally, [2a] merely opens an alternative possibility, and in view of this being given expression we are more cautious about assuming the fulfilment of either possibility now before us. With such a further continuation as the following, we conclude that the second possibility was fulfilled, the first tacitly excluded:

There were some of the loveliest chrysanthemums they had ever seen. [3]

But if, instead, [2a] were followed by:

But Mr Costello insisted. [3a]

there would be the implication (but nothing more) that our first interpretation of [1] was sustained. On the other hand, if the continuation were:

In the end, they went window shopping in Regent Street. [3b]

we would know, that neither of the possibilities that had been opened up was actually fulfilled, though both had been equally justified by the grammar and our knowledge of the language. With [3b], furthermore, we find an implication of the discussion and vacillation which led the couple to reject both the original intention [1] and the counter-proposal [2a] – a lengthy process of debate implied by the conjunct *in the end* [3b], at once enumerative, temporal, and summative (*cf* 8.136*f*).

(b) Lexical linkage

19.21 Contrast the following pairs of sentences:

Steve and Deborah are both doctors. She is a New Zealander. [1]
Steve and Deborah are both doctors. She is a surgeon. [2]

In both texts there is thematic connection (*she*; *cf* 19.12), but in [2] there is rhematic connection as well (*cf* 19.14), and this is achieved lexically. The lexical items *doctor* and *surgeon* belong to the same semantic set, the former being a superordinate term (hypernym) embracing *surgeon*, *pediatrician*, *gynecologist*, etc. Sometimes, lexical linkage is formally overt, as in:

Bill is an old *friend* of mine, but he shouldn't assume that *friendship* excuses rudeness. [3]

But more usually it involves, as in [2], semantic and pragmatic knowledge, not least a familiarity with words and allusions only covertly connected. Consider the relation in the following between *oven* and *baking* on the one hand, and between *fruit*, *Bramley's Seedlings*, and *apple* on the other:

Of all common fruit, Bramley's Seedlings are particularly suitable for baking. After only a short time in the oven, this apple becomes a light fluffy mass. [4]

As always (*cf* 19.19), there are relevant grammatical features as well: the demonstrative *this* links the generic singular *apple* with *Bramley's Seedlings* as though the latter were a singular generic noun phrase, *the* (or *a*) *Bramley's Seedling*.

In the following programme note heard on the radio, pragmatic and lexical linkage are combined in a tactful use of elegant variation which prompts interpretation while avoiding insult to the hearer's assumed knowledge and interpretive skill:

The zoological sequence is called *Cortège d'Orphée*, the music of Orpheus being so attractive that wild animals would follow him. [5]

The adjective *zoological* is related to the noun phrase (*wild*) *animals* in the next clause, while Poulenc's title *Cortège d'Orphée* is 'explained' by linking *sequence*, *attractive*, and *follow* as helpful glosses (like *Orpheus* beside the less familiar *Orphée*) on the French word *cortège*.

Note Lexical linkage involving the shared knowledge of allusion is illustrated in the following piece of dialogue from William Ash's novel *Incorporated* (1980):

'But life itself is like that. No man is an –'

'That's right,' interrupting her while he filled her wine glass. 'We're all isthmuses, and since I can still say "isthmuses", you obviously need a drink'.

The word *island* is so well known in the John Donne quotation that it is left unspoken, but we depend on it for the modified image involving the narrow connection between people expressed by the word *isthmus*. (The repetition of *isthmuses* does not in this case have lexical but phonological relevance, the wittiness of the switch in reference being further endorsed by the switch from the speaker's evident sobriety to the unsupported evidence that his woman companion is equivalently sober.)

Lexicon, shared knowledge, and grammar

19.22 We see, then, that discourse makes considerable use of words having quite general reference in relation to words denoting particularity (*cf* 19.17):

Some *animals* can be trained to use *tableware*. We have probably all seen a *chimpanzee* eating with a *spoon* or drinking from a *cup*. [1]

My *spaniel* was once a keen helper when I went *rabbit shooting*, but I suppose all *dogs* lose their *hunting* ardour as they get older. [2]

But lexical linkage can work through opposition and exclusion as well as through similarity and inclusion. Contrasts may be lexically realized by reference to *waking* and *sleeping*, *requesting* (*eg*: *beg*) and *granting* (*eg*: *allow*), and in the context of childhood an important opposition exists between *school* and *home*. In the following example, *discrimination* is hypernymic with reference to sex, race, and religion, but the particular items included are related through mutual exclusion:

> There has come to be increasing awareness of discrimination as a worldwide problem. Women have protested that they continue to have fewer rights than men. Blacks are conscious that their white neighbours get better jobs. Protestants in one community feel the odds are against them, while Catholics have a comparable feeling in another, as do Jews in yet another. [3]

As we also saw in 19.21, lexical links may be established not by our knowledge of the language but by additional information fed in by the speaker/writer. Such linkage can provide a chain-like course through a text (*cf* 19.18):

> The Senate last week refused to confirm the nomination of *Judge Robert Palmer*. The *Judge* is a *Californian* with a sound reputation and enjoying state-wide support. The defeat of the *Californian*, well remembered in *Hollywood studios*, is seen as a rebuke to the President. He is known to have given the *ex-actor* a good deal of personal encouragement. [4]

Linkage of a superficially similar kind may depend on the general knowledge of the hearer/reader to fulfil its role:

> In the 1960s the *Beatles* seemed a tightly knit group. The *quartet* developed a style of popular music that was not merely original but which was a product of their close relationship. Yet within a few years, the *Liverpool lads* had gone their separate ways. [5]

If the author had felt less confident about his audience's previously acquired knowledge, he could have prepared for the italicized links in the second and third sentences with an alternative opening such as:

> In the 1960s, the *four Merseyside* Beatles seemed . . . [5a]

Compare also:

> His opening remarks were directed to *flattering his audience by telling them how honoured he was to address such a distinguished gathering*. As he had expected, *this flattery* guaranteed him an attentive and appreciative hearing. [6]

The nominalization *this flattery* not only links with the same lexical base *flatter(ing)* in the preceding sentence: it provides a thematic connection (*cf* 19.12) by acting as a substitute for the whole nonfinite clause that is italicized in the preceding sentence. As such, it in fact requires no specific lexical linkage at all, as we see in the following alternative version:

> In his opening remarks, he *told his audience how honoured he was to address such a distinguished gathering*. As he had expected, *this flattery* . . . [6a]

A combination of lexical meaning, word-formation, and such syntactic processes as nominalization is a valuable resource in textual structure and we return to it in 19.72*ff*.

Lexical recurrence

19.23 Lexical linkage by recurrence of form is generally avoided since lexical items can easily seem obtrusive. The second speaker's remark in the following draws ironic attention to the overuse of one word:

> A: There was a delightful party at my office for the boss's fiftieth birthday. What I found particularly delightful were the speeches. They were delightfully witty.
> B: It all sounds a bit *too* delightful for my taste. [1]

On the other hand, a great deal of lexical recurrence is tolerated in legal language where misinterpretation is of more serious concern than adverse stylistic criticism. The following is from a current domestic insurance policy:

> If at the time of any loss, destruction, or damage arising under this Policy there is any other insurance covering such loss, destruction, or damage, the Company shall not be liable for more than its ratable proportion of such loss, destruction, or damage. [2]

In ordinary language, we would expect the second use of *loss, destruction, or damage* to be replaced by some such hypernym as *misfortunes* (*cf* 19.21) and the third to be pronominalized (*them*). But even in language that is being used in a less specialized way, repetition is common enough to convey emphasis. A tone of impatience in rejecting an accusation is noticeable in the following exchange:

> A: |Why weren't you kinder to your sìster|
> B: |But I WÀS kind to my sister| I |gave PRÈSents to my sister| I |introduced FRÌENDS to my sister| I |washed CLÒTHES for my sister| [3]

This example is presented in prosodic form to show the way in which the four repetitions of *my sister* have no nucleus, being treated as 'given' (*cf* 18.8), just as it would be if it had been replaced pronominally, *(to) her*. Repetition in ordinary discourse also occurs to indicate the repetition, extent, or confirmation of a phenomenon (*cf* 13.78, 13.101):

> The only remedy is work, work, work. [4]
> Everywhere I looked, there were children, children. [5]
> She screamed and screamed for hours. [6]
> She is very, very intelligent. [7]
> A lovely, lovely chrysanthemum. [8]

Note Not only do we tend to avoid lexical repetition in dialogue but an attempt is often made to replace an item by one of heightened meaning, rather than by a mere synonym. This again illustrates 'cooperation' in dialogue texts. For example, note the way emphatic agreement and assertion are expressed in [9] and [10] respectively:

> A: Isn't it a *lovely* day? B: *Gorgeous*! [9]
> A: Are you *sure* you've got the key? B: *Positive*! [10]

General hypernyms

19.24 Many lexical items are used hypernymically rather in the manner of pronouns and other substitutes. They thus have a quasi-grammatical function, as can be seen in the italicized examples in the following:

> The mayor's procession is very colourful and attracts many tourists and other spectators. The *event* always *occurs* on a Saturday. [1]
>
> Thousands were out of work; there was hunger, anger, and unrest. The *situation* required careful handling. [2]
>
> The *thing* that amused me most was her remark about her brother's swimming. [3]
>
> The candidate decided to support the building of another atomic power station. This is what the party leader had *done* at the previous election. But it turned out to be an unpopular *issue*. [4]

Compare also *field*, *set-up*, *problem*, *subject*, *matter*, and such verbs as *happen*, *take place*.

Note Being more obtrusive than closed-class items such as pronouns, demonstratives, and the pro-verb *do* etc, such hypernyms are liable to attract criticism when overused. This is particularly so of nouns like *issue*, *position*, *situation*, when premodified. Critics often feel (with some justification) that 'the weather situation', 'a strike situation', 'the women's lib issue', 'the Northern Ireland problem' mean little more than *the weather*, *a strike*, *women's lib*, and *Northern Ireland*. But if we consider the following comment in a radio broadcast:

> In view *of the weather situation*, many flights are being postponed. [5]

we see that the italicized phrase means much more than 'the weather' (*ie* what the weather actually is). It includes far more general allusion to the probabilities, the forecasts, the implications that have been set forth in an earlier part of the text.

Nonetheless, some uses of common hypernyms are avoidable clichés and are justified – if at all – only as a form of hackneyed 'elegant variation':

> Mabel told me with evident pride that she was pregnant again. *The happy event* will take place in March. [6]

(c) Prosody and punctuation

19.25 Consider the written sequence:

> I smiled at the supervisor and she greeted me. [1]

It would be possible to utter this with two sharply different prosodic realizations reflecting different interpretations and different bases of linkage:

> . . . and she GRÈETed me [1a]
>
> . . . and SHĚ greeted MÈ [1b]

In [1a], there is lexical contrast between the two parts; a verbal greeting is indicated: something actually heard in contrast to the silent smile in the first part of the text. In [1b], *greeted* is merely a lexical variant of *smiled*: the smile was a greeting and there was a similar silent greeting in response. This is prosodically indicated by *greeted* having no intonational prominence; it is 'given' informationally (*cf* 18.8), whereas in [1a] *greeted* is contrastive and 'new', as is indicated by the intonational nucleus. In [1b] what is new is neither the participants nor the verbal action but only the reciprocation; the roles are reversed and hence the subject and object pronouns are intonationally highlighted. But the endings of both [1a] and [1b] are equally dependent in their different ways on the preceding parts to which they are linked.

While there is a direct relation between speech and writing, as also (broadly) between prosodic features of speech and the punctuation devices of writing, the former must be given precedence in each case. In fact, as we see from [1] above, it is impossible to understand a written text until we assign to it a prosody – whether we take it in silently or read it aloud.

Since such prosodic features as stress, rhythm, and intonation have to do with information processing (*cf* 18.2–19, App II), and since the linkage between the parts of a text reflects the buildup of information (*cf* 19.12), it follows that prosody is a vitally important factor in textual coherence.

Note An example follows which shows the interaction of prosody with lexical linkage and which also demonstrates implication of a connection between meaning and linguistic form (alliteration and prosodic as well as grammatical shape: *grandest, greatest*):

It has been said that Schubert's Ninth Symphony is his Eroica. As in Beethoven's master work, we seem to hear the artist at his grandest if not greatest. [2]

The text depends of course on our knowing that the Eroica is a composition by Beethoven, and it consequently requires us to recognize a relation that may be represented as follows:

as Ninth *is to* Schubert *so is* Eroica *to* Beethoven

The phrase *master work* is thus 'given' (*cf* 18.8) and is a replacement for *Eroica* (elegant variation and hypernymic; *cf* 19.24); as such, this phrase must be downgraded prosodically, the premodifier (*Beethoven's*) taking a nucleus to show the link with Eroica and the contrast with Schubert:

. . . is his ERÒica. As in BĚETHoven's master work . . . [2a]

The lexical independence of prosody

19.26 The central place of prosodic features is emphasized throughout this book, and in the present chapter they are best illustrated along with the grammatical features they accompany. But we should note that prosodic variables are to some extent quite independent of the particular words used – and indeed no actual words need be used.

It is a characteristic of even the most one-sided dialogue that the speaker expects a prosodic response, even if it is realized with oral support that does not include institutional 'words':

A: So I told him that it was none of his business and that I would do as I pleased.
B: |M̀| [1]
A: After all, it's not as if I still owed him money.
B: |Ḿ| [2]
A: I repaid him that money I borrowed – well, nearly all of it, so I'm no longer under any obligation to him.
B: |M̌| [3]

In [1], B is assuring A with his falling tone that he follows (and perhaps agrees with) what A is saying. In [2], however, the rising tone indicates surprise or a question or some form of challenge; it is apparently enough to divert A from his thread of discourse to tell B about the loan repayment. In [3], B's fall-rise indicates understanding, but with only qualified assent, and A's next utterance might well go further into the morality of the position as he sees it. All three of B's contributions are textually important and in some circumstances their absence would bring the discourse to a halt: A would be puzzled, or he might be offended, at B's silence. On the telephone, he would have interrupted himself to ask 'Are you still there?' or 'Can you hear me all right?'

19.27 Irrespective of response-dependence (and in radio discourse, no response is usually possible), a speaker prosodically empathizes with the hearer in numerous ways. Pauses are helpfully introduced after completing a significant information unit; this indicates the end of what may be called a prosodic 'paragraph', and such a termination will be marked by being given a specially long curve to an intonation nucleus (usually a fall). Or a pause may be introduced immediately before a lexical item which the speaker feels may be unfamiliar or which he wishes to be heard clearly:

> The library has hundreds of extremely valuable books including several [*pause*] incuNÀBula. [1]

By contrast he may tactfully increase the tempo over parts of his discourse that he expects will be particularly familiar or which he modestly wishes to be treated as rather unimportant. As with B in [3] of 19.26, a speaker will use a fall-rise to hint at reservation and uncertainty, so that a contrast would be heard with the all-embracing summative conjunct (*cf* 8.139) in:

> On the WHÓLE| my childhood was a happy one. [2]
> On the WHǑLE| my childhood was a happy one. [3]

In [2] we have a confident statement, in [3] it is hedged with some doubt. A rising tone will especially be heard however to indicate clearly that something is to follow: a main clause, a further item in a list, and the like. It will also be used in direct appeals for the listener's cooperation and understanding, in such cases the rise being rather narrow (*cf* App II.15) and each appeal having lower prominence (*cf* App II.9) than the surrounding text.

For example:

> I had no idea where she had gone, you |SÉE| – and I could hardly wait there all night, |Ḿ| [4]

One final general point may be made. We saw in 19.26 that prosodic features could be used without actual words. In a similar way, prosody enables us to dispense with words that would be necessary for clarity in a written version of the same text. The two following utterances are obviously very different:

> And so it's just possible that she's ill. [5]
> And so she may be actually ill. [6]

A single string of fewer words could convey the difference by assigning different prosody:

> And so she MǍY be ill| [5a]
> And so she may be ÌLL| [6a]

Punctuation

The paragraph

19.28 Although in this book we repeatedly emphasize the primacy of speech over writing, and of prosody over punctuation, we have to recognize that many types of text take shape first on paper and have their normal realization in graphic form. Punctuation thus has a greater interest for the study of texts than for linguistics as a whole, where it can be generally looked upon as a surrogate and a rather inadequate substitute for the range of phonologically realized prosodic features at our disposal.

In considering the grammatical system of English, we think in terms of such units as sentence, clause, and phrase. We noted earlier (*cf* 19.9) that from a textual viewpoint, however, such distinctions are not particularly relevant: the difference between sentence and clause, for example. What is more significant is that there are textual units that cannot be recognized at all in grammar, and only the smallest of them can be recognized prosodically as units. Written texts may be in volumes, parts, chapters, sections; and few are so short as not to comprise more than one paragraph (itself a unit only uncertainly matched in prosodic terms). And this is to ignore such well-established genres of literary texts as the epic poem, the lyric, the play, the short story, the novel. Anthony Powell's novel, *Dance to the Music of Time*, comprises twelve volumes, each of which can itself be read as a complete novel.

We shall shortly come to consider sub-paragraph textual units, but first we should note that the decision as to where to impose paragraph boundaries is by no means self-evident or unequivocal. Yet a paragraph has on the one hand a relatively strong sense of internal coherence and on the other a relatively loose linkage with the textual material before and after it. Consider the following fragment of text:

> . . . and that was how I came to have some weeks observing the behaviour of their eight-year-old son. He broke eggs on the carpet. He twisted his kitten's tail till it mewed in anguish. He put garbage in his parents' bed and burned holes in his sister's clothes. (i) He was extraordinarily [*adjective*]. (ii) His parents intended to send him to a special school . . .

According to the adjective we supply at the bracketed segment, we can see that either (i) or (ii) could be a fitting place to begin a new paragraph.

If the adjective is *wicked*, *naughty*, *ill-behaved*, we might well start a new paragraph at (ii). The preceding part would have had a stack-like structure (*cf* 19.18) and the sentence 'He was extraordinarily ill-behaved' would fittingly round it off with a rather self-evident conclusion.

If, on the other hand, the adjective is *intelligent*, *gifted*, *musical*, or some other item not suggested by the account of his behaviour, then (i) would be a fitting – one might say essential – point at which to begin a new paragraph. This would reveal a totally different aspect of the boy and the text might go on to describe the special school at which his intelligence or other positive gifts could be suitably developed.

The sentence

19.29 In an analogous way, the decision to divide a paragraph into orthographic sentences depends on how the writer wishes these smaller sections of his text to be seen in relation to each other: intimately linked as though naturally indissociable (no punctuation); closely associated but separate (comma or semicolon, according to degree); relatively separate (pointed as independent sentences). Compare the different implications of the following:

I saw Miriam and Walter. [1]
I saw Miriam, and Walter. [2]
I saw Miriam – and Walter! [3]
I saw Miriam. And Walter. [4]

In [1], the normal and expected form, it seems to be suggested that Miriam and Walter are a couple who regularly appear together. This is not so in [2–4], where the punctuation may carry various implications according to the larger context. In [2], the two persons are being listed; in [3], the sight of Walter in addition to Miriam is given special and dramatic significance; in [4], the second person seems to be mentioned as an afterthought. But the suggested motivations for [3] and [4] might be expressed by either of the punctuation forms according to the taste of the writer or his belief in their communicative impact on the reader. Since (as we see in App III) punctuation is subject to fairly rigorous convention, many writers hesitate to show individuality, originality, or rhetorical effects by this means. Instead they will select grammatical constructions and carefully selected lexical items which they hope may achieve effects that in speech would be without difficulty indicated by prosodic features. In any event, aural realization cannot be disregarded. Even the silent reading of a typically paper-originating text (such as a legal document) demands the assignment of speech prosodies as an aid to understanding. The careful writer does not forget this, and punctuation choices are made (along with grammatical and lexical ones) in the hope of providing the reader with the cues necessary for assigning the prosody that the writer would himself have used in uttering his text aloud.

But as readers we have an obligation too. In listening to a spoken text, we automatically respond to the prosodic features that help to mould its structure. When we read, we have to create those prosodic features from the visual print. Stumbling as we read is a common experience: the further context then tells us of an earlier misinterpretation and we have to go back and reread a portion of the text, redistributing our imagined internal stresses and nuclei. Sometimes the fault is in the ineptness of the writer, but often it lies in our lack of sympathetic alertness to the textual structure in front of us.

Note Novelists and poets are more often prepared than other writers to be unconventional in their punctuation and hence to make their text easier to interpret prosodically. Consider the following passage from Peter Straub's *Ghost Story* (1979). A woman is announcing to a lover that she is returning to her husband (Ricky):

I think it is time I retired into respectability. And. If you cannot see that Ricky has four or five times your significance, then you are deluding yourself. [5]

The one-word sentence *And* functions as a heavy additive conjunct (*cf* 8.138; perhaps equivalent to *moreover* in a formal style). It is only by making it a sentence that the writer is able to ensure that we read it in the way it would have sounded in speech:

. . . into respectaBÌLity| |ĂND| If |you 'cannot SĔE| . . . [5a]

(d) Grammatical devices

19.30 We shall deal with some of the many relevant aspects of grammar in textual structure under the following main heads:

(i) Place and time relators
(ii) Tense, aspect, and narrative structure
(iii) Determiners, pro-forms, and ellipsis
(iv) Discourse reference
(v) The textual role of adverbials
(vi) Coordination and subordination
(vii) The part played by questions
(viii) Participant involvement
(ix) Information processing

Place and time relators

19.31 In 19.15 we stressed that textual structure requires firm orientation in respect to place and time. Let us assume that an acquaintance tells us:

> Long ago, I lived in the Far East. My father worked at a naval base. I went back to look at our old home soon after the Navy had withdrawn. [1]

In addition to the *here* and *now* of the speaker and hearer, one other location in space and two other 'locations' in time are mentioned; and the speech participants relate themselves to these locations:

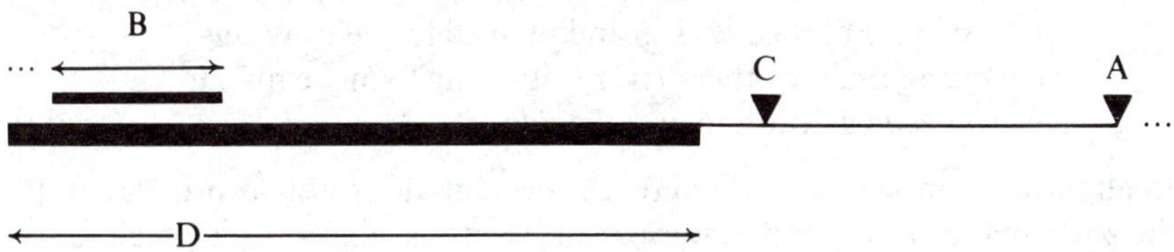

Fig 19.31

Taking A as 'here and now', this involves imagining a remote place where, for a relatively long time span in the past 'D', there had existed a naval base. Within that period, for a shorter but equally unspecified stretch of time 'B', the speaker had lived there. And between the times B and A, there is a time 'C' (narratively represented as without duration) when the speaker went back to the Far East but when the naval base no longer functioned.

In even so simple a narrative text, we should note the adequacy of the space and time references in providing the orientation, and yet the imprecision of these references: no actual locations that one could point to on a map, no actual dates. Note also the implicit relation to *here* and *now*: the 'Far East' is *far* only from (say) Britain, and is *east* only in relation to somewhere in the west; the time is 'long ago' only in relation to 'now' – it was itself 'now' when the speaker lived in the Far East.

Place relators

19.32 It is from the linguistic signs for spatial reference that we derive expressions for the most abstract relations such as time (*cf* 4.2*ff*, 8.75). Yet although physical location is essential for orientation in discourse, grammatical correlates to physical location are relatively meagre. Shifts or distinctions within space tend to be expressed by location-specific lexical items or even proper nouns (place-names, for example). Note the heavy dependence on lexical items in the following familiar spatial distinctions, where the relatively grammatical (*ie* generalizable) items are italicized:

> *within* my apartment – *through* the hall – *into* the kitchen – *inside* the bedroom – *part of* the bedroom ceiling
>
> Hampstead – *out of* the underground station – *up* Heath Street – *beyond* White Stone Pond – *to* Jack Straw's Castle
>
> New York – going *upstate* – *along* the Hudson – *near* the Catskills – *from* Poughkeepsie – *all the way past* Kingston

Nonetheless, as we saw in 8.39*ff*, certain spatial relations are firmly linked to grammatical expressions which are heavily exploited in textual structure. Thus an opening question or statement will normally involve reference to location in space (as well as in time):

> *Where* are you going tonight? [1]
>
> It's ages since I was *over there*. [2]
>
> On Tuesday evening, I was *at the front door* talking to a caller. Suddenly we heard a crash and two cars collided *just opposite*. We hurried *across* to see if we could help. One driver was scrambling *out*, bleeding profusely, and my visitor helped him *over* to the pavement. Then *along* came some people, running *up the street*. I dashed *back in* and phoned for help. When I went *out* again, the other driver was trying to move his car *down the road* a little and *in to the side*. [3]

In all three examples, spatial reference is essential, as well as orientation to the participants' *here* (*cf* 19.31): *where* in [1] entails a *here* from which to set out; *over there* in [2] entails 'in contrast to here'. But let us look more closely at the part played by spatial reference in [3], both in respect to orientation and to the structure of the narrative.

Even totally out of context, the institutionalized phrase *at the front door* would be understood as referring to the main entrance of the speaker's home, whether this was a house or a small apartment. Likewise, *just opposite* is at once understood as *just opposite* to where the speaker and his visitor were standing. A road is implied by the car crash and in this context *across* means 'across the intervening space (of footpath and street)'. The *back in* signifies a return across this intervening space and *into* the speaker's home. The two instances of *out* are of sharply different reference: the first refers implicitly to emergence from the car, the second to re-emergence from the speaker's home (thus correlating with the earlier *back in*). The contrasting phrases *up (the street)* and *down (the road)* are interesting in making spatial reference not necessarily in terms of relative elevation (though this is not excluded). The immediate contrast is in terms of orientation again: *up* indicating an approach towards the speaker (and his home), *down* indicating the converse (*cf* 9.24). The cluster of spatial references provides a continuous set of coordinates in relation to a base (the speaker's home, though this is merely a pragmatic implication) as well as a coherent account of the movements involved in the narrative.

Note In a text where it was known that a physical slope was involved, *up/down (the street)* would be used with respect to this absolute and objective physical feature, and it would outweigh personal orientation. The latter could then be expressed by alternative means: 'She *went (away)* up the street'; 'They *came* down the street'. Contrast also: 'They hurried *up* Fifth Avenue' (*ie* away from 'downtown' Manhattan); 'They sauntered *down* Fifth Avenue' (*ie* towards downtown Manhattan); 'They walked *along* Fifth Avenue' (neutral as to direction).

Elliptical, lexical, and grammatical indicators

19.33 Where place relators operate in text structure, ellipsis is often involved (*cf* 12.47*ff*):

He examined the car. The *front* was slightly damaged. [1]
The building was heavily guarded by police. The windows {on the *top storey* / at the *top*} were covered with boards. [2]

The ellipted items in [1] and [2] are *of the car* and *of the building* respectively. Often the ellipted items are not in the previous context, but are understood from the situational context (either accompanying the communication or established by the communication):

The traffic lights eventually changed. He walked *across* quickly. [3]

Across here implies *the road* or some similar noun phrase (*cf* 9.66, 19.32).

A few place adverbs do not involve ellipsis: *here*, *there*, *elsewhere*, the relative *where*, and (in formal contexts) *hence*, *thence*, *hither*, and *thither*. They are pro-forms:

The school laboratory reeked of ammonia. *Here*, during the first week of the term, an unusual experiment was conducted. [4]
All my friends have been to Paris at least once. I am going *there* next summer for the first time. [5]

Here in [4] is a substitute for *in the school laboratory* and *there* in [5] for *to Paris*.

Note **[a]** *Elsewhere* differs from the other substitutes in indicating that the places under consideration are other than those previously mentioned.
[b] In sentences like *Stand there* and *Here it is*, the pro-forms may refer directly to the situational contexts without any linguistic mention of location; *cf* 19.34.

19.34 Place relators often comprise two components. Most commonly these are a dimension or direction indicator plus a location indicator (*cf* 9.13*ff*). The latter is usually an open-class noun (or proper noun), but its locational use is often institutionalized, making the whole expression quasi-grammatical. Examples:

at the window	in town
on the ceiling	off work
in the air	on board
at the seaside	on the way

Another common type of pairing is a distance indicator plus a dimension indicator; for example:

$$\left.\begin{matrix}\text{(not) far}\\ \text{further}\\ \text{farther}\end{matrix}\right\} + \left\{\begin{matrix}\text{in}\\ \text{out}\\ \text{off}\\ \text{away}\\ \text{from}\end{matrix}\right.$$

$$\begin{matrix}\text{nearer} & + \left\{\begin{matrix}\text{in}\\ \text{to + Noun Phrase}\end{matrix}\right.\\ \text{high(er)} & + \text{ up}\\ \text{low(er)} & + \text{ down}\\ \text{close} & + \left\{\begin{matrix}\text{by}\\ \text{to + Noun Phrase}\end{matrix}\right.\end{matrix}$$

But note, in relation to the last example listed, that marine usage permits the absence of the noun phrase complement:

I shouted to attract her attention and she brought the boat *close to* so that I was able to jump on. [1]

Also in marine usage are *on board*, *aboard*, and *ashore* (though the first is also used of aircraft):

Are you coming $\left\{\begin{matrix}\textit{on board}\\ \textit{aboard}\end{matrix}\right\}$ or are you staying *ashore*? [2]

The partially antonymous *home* and *abroad* are exceptional (with *ashore* for example) in combining the dimension and locational factors:

After being *out* for a couple of hours, I'm now $\left\{\begin{matrix}\text{going}\\ \text{staying}\end{matrix}\right\}$ *home* for the evening. [reference to personal residence] [3]

After $\left\{\begin{matrix}\text{living}\\ \text{being}\\ \text{going}\end{matrix}\right\}$ *abroad*, I like to $\left\{\begin{matrix}\text{come}\\ \text{be}\end{matrix}\right\}$ *home* for a year or so. [reference to native *country*] [4]

In addition to their use as pro-forms, *here* and *there* can have purely situational reference, with orientation to the speaker:

I'm glad to welcome you *here* and I'd like to introduce two friends who are sitting (over) *there*. [5]

Note Locational connections in relation to coherence are not merely a necessary feature of individual texts. It is customary in newspapers to group the otherwise separate news-item texts on a regional basis. So too in radio broadcasts, a place relator may serve to give some kind of coherence to otherwise unrelated stories. There has developed a curious (and to many an objectionable) practice of drawing attention to the connection by giving prominence to a normally unstressed preposition. For example:

I |put it TÒ the 'President| [6]

There'll be some |black 'ice ÒN 'some 'roads| [7]

The practice is criticized in such instances for being vacuous at best, misleading at worst (in suggesting a contrastive denial: 'not just NĚAR some roads but ÒN some roads'), but it is sometimes defended as conferring a liveliness and informality. What seems to be true, at any rate, is that where a prepositional phrase has to carry the information focus, a focus on the prepositional complement may often imply unwanted emphasis or contrast. The complement may for example be contextually 'given' (*cf* an infinitive example, 9.9). In such instances, movement of the focus to the preposition may be preferable, especially if – as in the instances above – no contrast is plausible. Furthermore, we should compare:

The car was at the corner. [8]
The car was at or near the corner. [8a]
Trains to the city are delayed. [9]
Trains to and from the city are delayed. [9a]

Here in [8a] and [9a] both the prepositions carry some emphasis.

An example from broadcast news:

They are worried that another strike could break out in the United States similar to the one that affected Canada's economy so seriously two years ago.
ÌN CÁNada news is coming in of a plane accident near Toronto. The aircraft, a privately owned four-seater . . . [10]

The textual justification is that a main focus on *Canada* would be misleading since *Canada* is in some sense already 'given'. As explained above, this accounts for the prosodic highlighting of minor (especially closed-class) grammatical items more generally. For example:

Marion wants to read the book, so you should give it TÒ Marion. [11]

Here the speaker has chosen not to pronominalize the second use of *Marion*, but the focus cannot be placed on the name since it has already been given. At the same time, the speaker has chosen wisely not to move the focus to the next preceding lexical item *give* since emphasis on this word might be understood as conferring the literal sense of 'make a gift'. A focus is needed, and we are left with no other option than *to* (*cf* also 18.14).

Time relators

19.35 Like space, time has its lexically specific and labelled 'areas' and 'locations'. Along with open-class nouns, some of them – like places – are treated as proper nouns: *century*, *decade*, *year*, *1985*, *January*, *week*, *day*, *Thursday*, *evening*, etc. Again like units of space, these nouns have an institutionalized and hence quasi-grammatical use. Specifically, in addition to being used as subjects and objects in clause structure, they are used in (and indeed as) adverbials and they thus lend themselves to the connections and transitions of textual structure:

I've been working on this problem *all year* and I must find a solution *before January* when I'm due to go abroad *for a month or so*. [1]

Nouns of more general meaning are still more firmly harnessed for grammatical use:

I've been working *a long time*. [2]
I'm going abroad *for a while*. [3]
She hasn't visited me *for ages*. [4]

In addition, therefore, to closed-class items like *afterwards*, we take account here of numerous open-class words which, though with clear lexical meaning, are largely used in the constant process of keeping track of the many and complex references that are necessary in coherent text. Since time passes irrespective of location (which need not change), temporal cues to periods, and to references *before*, *after*, *within*, and *during* these periods, are more inherently essential than locational cues.

Once a time reference has been established, certain temporal adjectives and adverbs may order subsequent information in relation to the time reference. Three major divisions of time relationship may be set up, and examples will be given of adjectives and adverbials that signal the relationships:

(i) Temporal ordering previous to (ii) Temporal ordering simultaneous with (iii) Temporal ordering subsequent to	} a given time reference

On all three, *cf* further 8.51*ff*, 8.97*f*, 8.134*ff*.

Temporal ordering

19.36 (i) Temporal ordering previous to a given time reference:

ADJECTIVES

earlier, former, preceding, previous, prior

For example:

He handed in a good essay. His *previous* essays were all poor. [1]

The implication of *previous* is 'previous to the good essay just mentioned'.

ADVERBIALS

already, as yet, before, beforehand, earlier, first, formerly, hitherto ⟨formal⟩, *previously, so far, yet*; and phrases with pro-forms: *before that, before this, before now, before then, by now, by then, until now, until then, up to now, up to then*

For example:

I shall explain to you what happened. But *first* I must give you a cup of tea. [2]

First is to be interpreted here as 'before I explain to you what happened'. Compare also '*On the eve* (of the celebration)' [= 'on the day before'].

(ii) Temporal ordering simultaneous with a given time reference;

ADJECTIVES

coexisting ⟨formal⟩, *coinciding* ⟨formal⟩, *concurrent* ⟨formal⟩, *contemporary, contemporaneous* ⟨formal⟩, *simultaneous*

For example:

The death of the President was reported this afternoon on Cairo radio. A *simultaneous* announcement was broadcast from Baghdad. [3]

Simultaneous means 'simultaneous with the report of the death of the President on Cairo radio'.

ADVERBIALS

at this point, concurrently ⟨formal⟩, *contemporaneously* ⟨formal⟩, *here, in the interim* ⟨formal⟩, *meantime, meanwhile, in the meantime, in the meanwhile, now, presently, simultaneously, then, throughout*, and the relative *when*

For example:

> Several of the conspirators have been arrested but their leader is as yet unknown. *Meanwhile* the police are continuing their investigation into the political sympathies of the group. [4]

Meanwhile means 'from the time of the arrests up to the present'.

Note [**a**] The use of *presently* for time relationship (ii), with the meaning 'now', 'at present', is very common in AmE. In BrE, *presently* is more commonly synonymous with *soon*.
[**b**] An example of *here* as time indicator:

> I've now been lecturing for over an hour. I'll stop *here* since you all look tired. [5]

19.37 (iii) Temporal ordering subsequent to a given time reference:

ADJECTIVES

ensuing ⟨formal⟩, *following*, *later*, *next*, *subsequent* ⟨formal⟩, *succeeding* ⟨formal⟩, *supervening* ⟨formal⟩

For example:

> I left him at 10 p.m. and he was almost asleep. But at some *later* hour he must have lit a cigarette. [1]

Here *later* might mean 11 p.m., but equally 4 a.m., a time otherwise called 'the *early* hours of the morning'.

ADVERBIALS

after, *afterwards*, *(all) at once*, *finally*, *immediately*, *last*, *later*, *next*, *since*, *subsequently* ⟨formal⟩, *suddenly*, *then*; and the phrases *after that*, *after this*, *on the morrow* ['the day after']

For example:

> The manager went to a board meeting this morning. He was *then* due to catch a train to London. [2]

Then here means 'after the board meeting'. The temporal adverb *again* could be accommodated in this category. It is equivalent to 'another time', *ie* a time additional to one previously mentioned:

> He told her what he thought of her. He didn't speak to her *again*. [3]

Words with temporal significance do not always have a connective function. Often the time reference is not explicitly mentioned in preceding sentences. Thus, if somebody says:

> Mr Johnson's *previous* wife died last year. [4]

there need not have been any prior mention of the subsequent or present wife. The fact that Mr Johnson had been married before may be assumed as known to the hearer.

Note [**a**] *Anew* and *afresh* are synonyms of *again* and *once more*, but are rare and formal.
[**b**] Several compound adverbs that can be classed in (iii) are found only in certain formal varieties of contemporary English: *henceforth, henceforward, hereupon, thenceforward, thereafter, thereupon, whereupon.*

19.38 The ordinals constitute a temporal series of adjectives *first, second, third . . .* with *next* as a substitute for any of the middle terms when moving up the series, and *final* or *last* as a substitute for the term marking the end of the series. There is a corresponding series of conjuncts with *first* (also *at first* and, less commonly, *firstly*) as the beginning of the set; *secondly*, etc; *next, then, later, afterwards*, as interchangeable middle terms: and *finally, lastly*, or *eventually* as markers of the end of the set (*cf* general ordinals, 5.22).

Tense, aspect, and narrative structure

19.39 The many lexical and grammatical items we have been considering in 19.35*ff* provide fine distinctions in time relationships. But, as a further indication of the importance of time in language, all finite clauses (and many nonfinite ones) carry a discrete indication of tense and aspect. Although the contrasts involved are severely limited in comparison with adverbial distinctions, they contribute to the textual cohesion and progression, and of course they cannot be absent. Compare the different implications in the second part of what follows:

> She told me all about the operation on her hip.
> It seemed to have been a success. [1]
> It seems to have been a success. [2]

In [1], in accordance with our expectations with respect to sequence of tenses and backshift (*cf* 14.31), the past ties the second part to the first, as though both parts derive their authority from the woman concerned: 'It seemed *to her* . . .'; that is, '*She* was of the opinion that the operation had been successful'. The possibility of repudiation is therefore open: 'Unfortunately, this is not so'. In [2], by contrast, the present disjoins the second part and implies an orientation to the 'I' narrator: 'It seems *to me* . . .', '*I* am of the opinion . . .'

Alternation of past and present in this way is a regular mode of switching reference from the 'then' of the narrative reference to the 'now' of both the narrator and the hearer or reader (some items like parenthetic *you see* being confined to this 'now'):

> As a child, I lived in Singapore. It'*s* very hot there, you *know*, and I never owned an overcoat. I *remember* being puzzled at picture books showing European children wrapped up in heavy coats and scarves. I *believe* I thought it all as exotic as children here *think* about spacemen's clothing, you *see*. [3]

Consider now the instances of past tense in this text: *lived, owned, thought*. Not merely are these verbs morphologically identical: the text actually represents the past as being referentially identical. All the verbs refer back to a stretch of time during which these things were true:

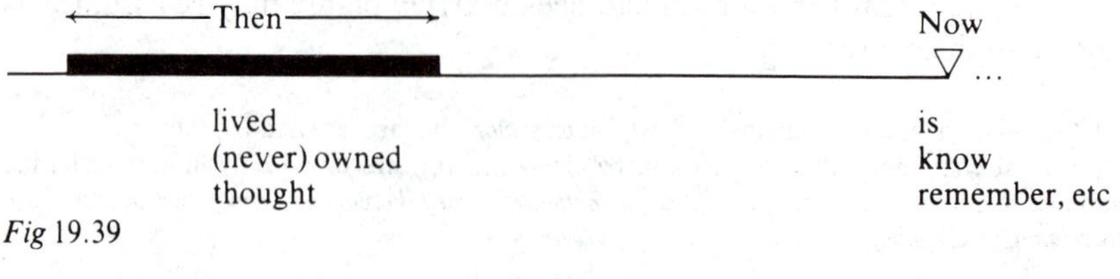

Fig 19.39

19.40 But past tenses need refer neither to the same time nor to stretches of time. With verbs which connote discrete actions, a narrative string of past tenses will be interpreted as referring to a sequence of events iconically represented by the sequence of verbs. For example:

> Do you want to hear about my adventures last Thursday? I *got up* at six, *had* some coffee, *kissed* my wife goodbye, and *set off* for Rome. I *took* a taxi and then the underground, *arrived* at Heathrow, *started* to check in my case, *patted* my pocket and *found* – no ticket, no passport. *Picked up* my case, *caught* the underground, *got* another taxi, *arrived* at my front door, *rushed in*, and of course *gave* my poor wife the shock of her life. [1]

We now have a very different diagram:

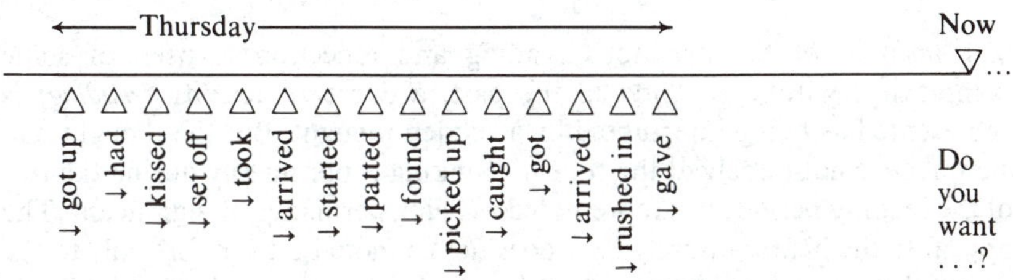

Fig 19.40

Note [**a**] While a sequence of past tenses implies sequential events if the lexical meaning of the verb makes this plausible as in [2], a sequence of past verbs with progressive aspect (*cf* 4.25*ff*) can imply simultaneity, as in [3]:

> René raged with anger. Janet went out for the evening. [2]
>
> René was raging with anger. Janet was going out for the evening. [3]

[**b**] Use of the past perfective can enable us to reverse the order of sentences in a text (*cf* 4.24). Note the way in which 'Time One' [T_1] precedes T_2 in [4] where T_2 precedes T_1 in [5]:

> There was a sudden violent noise outside [T_1]. John telephoned the police [T_2]. [4]
>
> John telephoned the police [T_2]. There had been a sudden violent noise outside [T_1]. [5]

Tense complexity in narrative

19.41 More usually, however, texts comprise much greater time-reference complexity than the examples in 19.39*f* show. They will have a mixture of state verbs and discrete-action verbs; the narrative will weave backwards and forwards, a mixture of tenses and aspects, of finite and nonfinite clauses enabling the narrator to depart from the linear sequence of historical order so as both to vary the presentation and to achieve different (*eg* dramatic) effects:

> I was reading Chaucer's *Troilus* the other night, and it suddenly occurred to me to wonder what Chaucer {expects / expected} us to make of the fact that Criseyde {has / had} been widowed whereas Troilus {has / had} never even been in love. Surely this is significant, yet I had never thought of it before. [1]

Here we have the additional complication of a narrative about a narrative within a narrative:

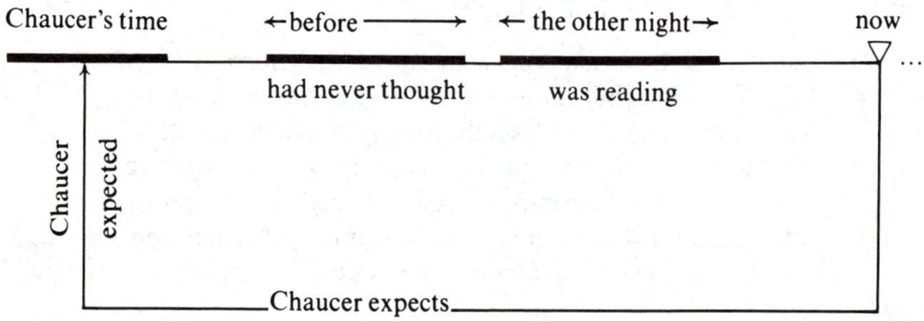

Fig 19.41a

The account of the narrator's reading and reflection is itself of some complexity: within a period in the past, a durative activity (*reading*) is represented as being interrupted by a sudden thought. But the thought had significance not merely at the time of thinking it nor merely during the rest of the reading period; it is represented as being permanently significant. The appeal to the hearer ('Surely . . .') does not connote that *is* refers only to the *now* of the speaker and hearer; there is no room for some such adverbial as *at present*:

*Surely this is *at present* significant.

The narrator is here using the present tense of timeless reference (*cf* 4.2*ff*). It is the potentiality for such a use of the present that made us give the two possibilities, 'Chaucer expects' and 'Chaucer expected'. The latter takes the historical view: a comment on the poet as he wrote in the fourteenth century. The former treats the Chaucer canon as timeless, permanently existing.

An analogous choice exists in referring to the fictional narrative of Chaucer's poem:

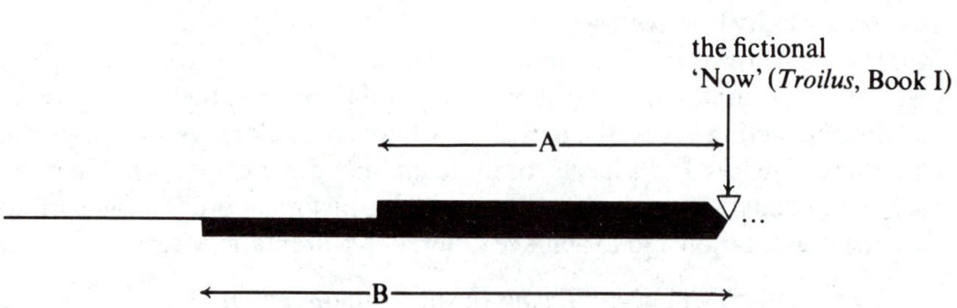

Fig 19.41b

'A' represents the (unknown) period during which Criseyde has been a widow when the poem begins; 'B' represents the longer period (in effect, Troilus's whole life) during which Troilus has never been in love. It will be noticed that in this commentary we have adopted the 'timeless' view of the fiction ('when the poem *begins*, Criseyde *has been* a widow for some time'). In the original example [1], the past variant was also given, implying a retelling of the story ('When Troilus first *saw* Criseyde, she *had been* a widow for some time').

Special uses of present and past

19.42 We have seen that the present tense can cooccur in textual structure with two distinct types of time references: ordinary 'state present' and universal 'state present' ('timeless'; *cf* 4.5):

> I *think* she had undergone an operation before I met her. [1]
> Troilus *is* totally fancy-free until he *sees* Criseyde. [2]

A third type of present, 'habitual' (*cf* 4.6), is common in ordinary narrative, and it can readily cooccur with past tenses:

> I had forgotten that they *dine* very early and I arrived at an awkward moment for both them and me. [3]

But there is a further use of the present tense: the so-called 'historic present' (*cf* 4.8). As well as occurring in rather mannered and formal prose of an old-fashioned tone, it is common in colloquial spoken narrative, especially at points of particular excitement. The time reference is unequivocally past. For example:

> It was on the Merritt Parkway just south of New Haven. I was driving along, half asleep, my mind miles away, and suddenly there was a screeching of brakes and I catch sight of a car that had been overtaking me apparently. Well, he doesn't. He pulls in behind me instead, and it's then that I notice a police car parked on the side. [4]

Note In nonstandard speech, the reporting verb in narrative is often in the historic present:

> 'Where did you put my coat?' he says. 'I never touched it,' I says. [5]

19.43 As well as being able to use the present tense to refer to the past, we can conversely use the past to refer to a narrator's 'now', exploiting that form of backshift that is referred to as free direct and indirect speech (*cf* 14.28, 14.35). Textual cohesion and congruity of reference are maintained by careful consistency of tense and aspect usage, present replaced by past, past by past perfective, even in the prolonged absence of reminders to the hearer/reader in the form of reporting verbs ('He reflected . . .', 'She said . . .'). In the following example, an entire paragraph coheres in this way, but the end of the preceding paragraph is quoted with the reporting verb (*recalled*) as a cue. The past with this verb is the normal past used by any narrator for the story that is being told and which is necessarily in the past for both narrator and hearer/reader. From this point onwards, however, the past refers to the recreated 'present' of the character whose reflections are recalled: they are reasonably referred to as occurring 'now' (the final word of the introductory paragraph), in a sentence which we reconstruct for ourselves as 'Well, what *does* it work out to *now*?'

> . . . He recalled vaguely that they had talked at one point in terms of debits and credits. Well, what did it work out to now?
>
> Credits? Well, there was all that money in Switzerland. And Devon, of course, but he felt he was wearing her down with his moping. Would she stick it out with him? Debits? He was an accomplice to one murder; the near victim of an assassination; indirectly responsible, probably, for other deaths. Worse still, it had all turned out exactly opposite to the way he had expected. The crooks and fools were in solider than ever. Which meant that he had in a way betrayed his country, if – as he most surely had done – helping to perpetuate the very monsters he had sought to extinguish was a betrayal. Not that he'd be tried or convicted for it; the country was fat and happy. The payment of the check had only been postponed; nothing had really changed. So much for deep thinking; so much for crusades.
>
> (M. M. Thomas, *Green Monday*, 1980) [1]

It will be noticed that the novelist emphasizes the impression of actual present-tense self-communion by colloquial style, as for instance in the one-word questions which serve to provide a continuity to the reflections.

Now let us consider this text rewritten as *current* rather than *reported* self-communion:

> I *recall* vaguely that we *talked* at one point in terms of debits and credits. Well, what *does* it *work* out to now?
>
> Credits? Well, there'*s* . . . Devon, of course, but I *feel* I'*m wearing* her down with my moping. *Will* she *stick* it out with me? Debits? I'*m* an accomplice to one murder . . . Worse still, it *has* all *turned* out exactly opposite to the way I *expected*. The crooks and fools *are* in solider than ever. Which *means* that I *have* . . . *betrayed* my country, if – as I most surely *have done* – helping to perpetuate the very monsters I (*have*) *sought* to extinguish *is* a betrayal. Not that I'*ll be tried* or *convicted* for it; the country *is* fat and happy. The payment . . . *has* only *been postponed*; nothing *has* really *changed* . . . [1a]

We notice that, while simple past becomes simple present, and past progressive becomes present progressive (line 3 of [1a]), the past perfective corresponds in two cases to the past, in five to the present perfective. In one further instance, line 9 of [1a], the correspondence is debatable. The text is, in fact, typical in showing the tendency of present perfective to cooccur in discourse with present rather than past tense forms.

Determiners, pro-forms, and ellipsis

19.44 Let us consider the following independent sentences:

> An argument over unilateral disarmament broke out between them. [1]
>
> An argument over unilateral disarmament finally put an end to their friendship. [2]

If we wished to make these sentences into a textual whole, there would be numerous possibilities, even keeping the first part unchanged:

. . . between them. {The / This / That} argument finally put an end to their friendship. [3]

. . . between them. {The / This / That} {dispute / controversy} finally put . . . [4]

. . . between them. {The / This / That} {issue / matter / affair} finally put . . . [5]

. . . between them – an argument that finally put . . . [6]

. . . between them, which finally put . . . [7]

. . . between them, and {this / that} finally put . . . [8]

. . . between them, and it finally put . . . [9]

. . . between them and finally put an end to their friendship. [10]

All these versions have two things in common. They abbreviate the second part and they connect it with the first part. These two features are in principle independent. Abbreviation need not be connective: we can use ellipsis merely to suppress what can be taken for granted, as for instance in greetings (*cf* 12.46*ff*):

Nice day! [*cf* It's a nice day, isn't it!] [11]

Off to work? [*cf* Are you going off to work?] [12]

Nor need connection involve abbreviation:

The argument was long and the argument was bitter.

Nonetheless, connection is commonly accompanied by abbreviation, and we can even say that it is in part actually *achieved* by abbreviation. In [3–10], for example, the coherence of the two parts is indicated by the fact that all the devices serve to show identity of reference between the subjects of the two verbs: *broke* (*out*) and *put*.

In some ways the most straightforward is [6], where a simple and direct shortening of the first subject phrase is used appositively; *cf* 17.65*ff*. There is something similar in [3], where reduction retains the original head-word of the noun phrase *argument*, but here the coreference with the preceding subject is indicated not by apposition but by the anaphoric determiners *the*, *this*, or *that*; *cf* 6.13. In [4] and [5] coreference is again carried by deixis, but in [4] the original noun phrase is not merely abbreviated but its head-word is replaced by a semantic paraphrase; *cf* 19.21*f* on lexical linkage. In [5], on the other hand, the head-word is replaced not by a semantic paraphrase but by a quasi-pronominal noun of very general meaning; *cf* 19.22. In [8], anaphoric deixis again points to the coreference, as in [4] and [5], but this time with the head-word replaced by zero; the demonstrative *this* or *that* is used pronominally; *cf* 6.40*ff*. In [9], the vaguest possible pronoun (*it*) is used, while in [7] a relative pronoun replaces the earlier noun-phrase subject (*cf* 17.15). Finally, in [10], there is total omission of the second subject (*cf* 13.12*f*).

All eight of [3–10] provide satisfactory coherence of the two parts. It is perhaps closest in [10], but only at the cost of muting the separate significance of the second part – in contrast to [3] and [4], for example, which insist on our considering the *beginning* of the argument on the one hand as well as its *result* on the other hand.

As we have indicated above by means of the cross-references, all of these devices are described elsewhere in the book in terms of grammatical rule. Here we have needed to add only some notes from a textual point of view.

Note Neither pronouns nor appositive noun phrases are restricted to referring back to preceding noun phrases. Consider the possibility that the first of the original sentences had been:

> They argued bitterly over unilateral disarmament. [1a]

In this event, the determiners and pronouns in the latter part of the combined text variants would have had sentential reference, and all would have been acceptable with the exception of version [10].

Limitations on pro-forms

19.45 What is grammatically tolerable has to be mediated by what is textually tolerable. Consider the following use of *do so* as a pro-form (*cf* 12.23*ff*):

> There was a certain beautiful girl who occasionally walked past our house. Whenever she *did so*, my brother would tease me. [1]

If we expand upon the first sentence, *did so* is less appropriate:

> There was a certain beautiful girl who occasionally walked past our house. Nothing particularly surprising in itself. We lived on a pretty lane, lined with rather attractive gardens. Yet whenever she *did so* . . . [1a]

Such relative remoteness of the relevant predication requires that we find a weightier substitute than *do so* and one that can more readily establish the backward link, even if our alternative is no more precise semantically than:

> . . . [Yet whenever] *this occurred* . . . [1a′]

(*Cf* 19.24). Again, where textual material puts identification of an antecedent even momentarily in doubt, a pro-form will be avoided – however 'grammatical' – and an alternative means of expression found. Consider the vagueness of the following hyperbole, contrasting one who is always very late for a flight with one who is always very early:

> YǑU chase the plane down the RÚNway. ″Ǐ get to the airport while it is being BÙILT. [2]

In place of *it* (which might refer to *the plane*, *the runway*, or *the airport*), a fuller anaphoric expression would have been clearer if less satisfactory in reducing the wit:

> . . . while $\left\{\begin{array}{l}\textit{the machine}\\ \textit{the place}\end{array}\right\}$ is being BÙILT. [2a]

It is often indeed a desire for witty brevity that leads to the use of over-economical reductions. In a printed book review, after commenting on Swift's saying about 'the nation's representers' that 'I would hang them if I could', the writer went on:

> The thing is said because he knows he can't: Swift doesn't 'mean it', though he doesn't not mean it either. The old bards apparently both meant it and *could.* [3]

The ellipsis after *can't* is clear: 'hang them'. The writer intends to echo this in the final *could* which he italicizes in the hope of taking us back to the quotation from Swift. But at that distance the ellipsis is unsatisfactorily vague.

Note In the following anecdote, the impact and wit are primarily achieved by the ellipsis, but in part also by the satisfying order adopted (*cf* 19.68) in the achievement of climax by means of a triadic structure (*cf* 19.8):

Prisoner: As God is my judge, I am not guilty.
Judge: He ̆isn't; I ̆AM; you ̀ARE!

It is not uncommon to find rhetorical effectiveness resting on such manipulation of the most ordinary grammatical items. Note the way in which *one* and *no* are contrasted in a speech by a British politician:

We have to learn to be ̆ONE nation or we shall become ǸO nation.

Discourse reference

19.46 There are numerous signals marking the identity between what is being said and what has been said before. The grammar of anaphoric and cataphoric substitution has been presented in 12.13*ff*. We concentrate here on devices that have a special value in referring less to concrete entities than to constituents or aspects of discourse itself. The signals can be divided into two groups, distinguished by the type of unit they refer to:

(a) sentence or clause reference signals
(b) noun-phrase reference signals

Many of them are adapted from their primary function of denoting temporal or spatial succession, *eg*: *former, above, here, the following*. Some signal both sentence/clause reference and noun-phrase reference.

Clausal reference

19.47 Common signals for sentence or clause reference include:

anaphoric and cataphoric: *here, it, this*
anaphoric only: *that, the foregoing* ⟨formal⟩
cataphoric only: *as follows, the following, thus*

Anaphoric examples:

> Many years ago their wives quarrelled over some trivial matter, now long forgotten. But one word led to another and the quarrel developed into a permanent rupture between them. *That's* why the two men never visit each other's houses. [1]
>
> Many students never improve. They get no advice and therefore they keep repeating the same mistakes. *It's* a terrible shame. [2]

Students want to be shown connections between facts instead of spending their time memorizing dates and formulas. Reflecting *this*, the university is moving away from large survey courses and breaking down academic fences in order to show subjects relating to one another. [3]

Cataphoric examples:

This should interest you, if you're still keen on boxing. The world heavyweight championship is going to be held in Chicago next June, so you should be able to watch it live. [4]

Here is the news. A diplomat was kidnapped last night in London . . . [radio announcement] [5]

It never should have happened. He went out and left the baby unattended. [6]

My arguments are *as follows* . . . [7]

In some instances, we can replace the reference signal by a corresponding *that*-clause. For example, *that* in [1] could be said to refer to a *that*-clause which corresponds to the immediately preceding clause:

. . . That the quarrel developed into a permanent rupture between them is why the two men . . . [1a]

In [2], on the other hand, *it* could be said to stand for the whole of the two preceding sentences. With cataphoric signals, the substitution might be inordinately long in practice. Certainly, *here* in [5] could refer forward to a following discourse of indeterminate length.

The pro-form may refer back to most, rather than all, of the sentence or clause:

They will probably win the match. *That* will please my brother. [8]

The more likely interpretation of *that* is *their winning the match* with the omission of auxiliary and disjunct but *that they will probably win the match* is also a possible interpretation.

Above and *below* are used for discourse reference to refer to units of varying length, and even to illustrations:

. . . the arguments given *below* [perhaps referring to several sentences]
. . . the question mentioned *above*
. . . the picture *above*
The diagrams *below* illustrate . . .

They need not refer to a unit of discourse which precedes immediately or which follows immediately. The furthest possible distance in the discourse between the unit referred to, on the one hand, and *above* or *below*, on the other hand, cannot be determined.

The above but not **the below* can be used as a noun phrase:

The above illustrates what we mean by . . .

Note [**a**] The nonrestrictive relative clause with a previous clause or sentence as the antecedent of introductory *which* (*cf* 17.9) is sometimes made into a separate orthographic sentence in some self-consciously 'lively' forms of writing. *Which* is then an anaphoric signal equivalent to *and that*:

She's borrowed a history book. Which suggests her teacher is having some influence on her. [9]

[**b**] In some (especially disapproving or ironic) contexts, *that* can be used cataphorically:

I like *THÀT*. Bob smashes up my car and then expects me to pay for the repairs. [10]

That's a thing I dislike – people whispering during a concert. [11]

THÀT'S what I like to SÉE: a chap who enjoys his work. [12]

Otherwise, *that* is used anaphorically. It could of course be argued that [10–12] are illustrative of anaphoric use: *that* referring 'back' to something situationally presented as well as 'forward' to a linguistic description of it.

[**c**] In informal spoken English, *what* can have cataphoric reference when it is the direct object of *know* in a question, or *guess* in a directive, or *tell* in a statement:

(Do you) Know WHÁT? }
Guess WHÀT. } He won't pay up. [13]

(I'll) Tell you WHÁT: I've forgotten the keys! [14]

[**d**] In written texts, discourse reference can be made to page numbers, section numbers, or chapters. In some texts, provision is made to take note of line numbers. Such reference may be to preceding or following material, and although we are writing, we usually use verbs of speaking:

As was *said* in Chapter Four, . . .

We will *speak* of this in Chapter Nine . . .

Less specific reference is made in terms of *above* (or *earlier*) and *below* (or *later* in the text), and some spoken material of a formal kind, such as lectures, make similar use of *above* and *below*.

[**e**] In legal English *the said*, *the* (*a*)*fore*ˈ*mentioned*, and *the a*ˈ*foresaid* are used for anaphoric reference, the last two both as a premodifier ('the aforementioned provisions') and as a noun phrase. In the latter function, they would normally refer to a previous noun phrase with personal reference.

Formulaic utterance

19.48 While deictic reference and ellipted matter must, from a grammatical viewpoint, be recoverable (*cf* 12.6*f*), discourse permits a good deal of vagueness. This seems to be actively cultivated in propaganda and other persuasive material, but it is especially common in informal conversation, not least in the semi-formulaic responses to expressions of thanks, apology, inquiry, and the like. Consider how difficult it would be to specify the precise reference or the exact ellipsis in the following responses:

A: Thank you very much.
B: Not at all. }
Not a bit. }
Don't mention it. }
You're WÉLcome. ⟨esp AmE⟩ } [1]

A: I'm terribly sorry.
B: Not at all. }
Not a bit. }
It's nothing. } [2]

A: I wonder if you'd mind coming and taking some dictation?
B: { Of course
Surely ⟨esp AmE⟩
ÒK } ⟨informal⟩
RÌGHT Ó } ⟨esp BrE⟩
WÌLL DÓ } }, Mrs Stewart. [3]

A: Would you mind my asking if you've ever taken drugs, Mr Hoover?
B: Absolutely NÒT. [4]

A: You wouldn't know a fortune-teller around here, I suppose?
B: { TRỲ me. [5]
Try MÈ. } [6]

In [5] the implication is that B knows one ('Try asking if I know one'); in [6], B is saying that he himself can tell fortunes. In [4], only the context could clarify whether B is saying that he 'absolutely (does) not (mind)', or that it is 'absolutely not' true that he has taken drugs. In [3], the formulaic response *Will do!* is a conventional way of saying 'I *will do* as you request', and B has interpreted (correctly, of course) A's polite inquiry as a request. In [1] and [2], the reference of *it*, in *Don't mention it*, *It's nothing*, is doubtless anaphoric in some way. But in the first line of [7], *it* is cataphoric if almost equally vague in its reference; the initial imperative is little more than an informal attention-requesting signal, a more severe form of which includes a cataphoric *here*:

A: By the way, Cynthia. It's awful of me, I know. But would you be able to look after my dog while I'm away next week?
B: (Now look) (Here), this is the third time you've left me with your dog. [7]

Within sentence sequences that are strictly alike from a grammatical point of view, a discourse pronoun can have sharply different reference:

She hoped he would not mention her unfortunate marriage.

{It / This / That} would be very { CÒURTeous of him. [8]
CÒURTeous of him in a WÁY, of course. } [8a]

In [8], the reference is to the predication including the negative ('His not mentioning the marriage would be courteous'). In [8a], the reference excludes the negative ('His mentioning the marriage would be courteous'). It is only the pragmatic implications of the hedging adverbial *in a way* and the concessive *of course* that lead us to this interpretation.

Note An interesting use of cataphoric *it* in textual structure is in the cleft sentence device (*cf* 18.26*ff*):

It was at 9.15 this morning that the government proclaimed a state of emergency. [9]

It was on their way from the airport that Gillian dropped the bombshell. In carefully casual tones, she asked him if he would agree to a divorce. [10]

In [9], it is unlikely that the narrator wishes to highlight the time adjunct: rather, the textual device is pointing to the climax at the end of the sentence. In [10], the same applies, but with a double cataphora: *the bombshell* which ends the first sentence is climactically explained in the sentence that follows.

Noun-phrase reference

19.49 Certain determiners are used to signal that a noun phrase is referentially equivalent to a previous noun phrase (*cf* 5.27*ff*, 12.14*ff*):

the this – these that – those

Such noun phrases may be discourse abstractions, and the heads may either be identical as in [1] or nominalizations that add lexical variation (*cf* 19.22), as in [2]:

> She set up a hypothesis that chemotherapy destroyed the will to live as well as the unwanted cells. *This hypothesis* attracted the attention of . . . [1]
>
> Deconstructionism holds that knowledge about literature is strictly unattainable . . . *This doctrine* is puzzling in several respects. [2]

It is not always certain, however, when such a reference is to a previous noun phrase or is a nominalization of a wider, clausally expressed proposition. The text from which [2] is quoted is a case in point. As presented in the abbreviated form of [2], *doctrine* seems to refer back unambiguously to *deconstructionism* and be a lexical variant of it. But in the original, there are several lines where we have indicated the curtailment, and these include the following:

> We must therefore abandon the old-fashioned quest to discover what a given author was trying to communicate. [2a]

The reference of *this doctrine* must therefore include, not merely the specific abstract *deconstructionism*, but the speculated consequence which the author went on to state. A fuller version might therefore read:

> This doctrine *of deconstructionism and the need to abandon the old-fashioned quest* . . . is puzzling in several respects. [2b]

When *such* is used, the intention is often to indicate disapproval (which may be sympathetic):

> We visited the Browns yesterday and heard their complaints about the condition of the house they live in. I never heard such a sorry tale. [3]
>
> . . . such a rigmarole. [3a]
>
> . . . of such wretchedness. [3b]

In [3] and [3a], the reference is primarily to the *complaints*, [3a] lexically indicating impatience rather than sympathy; in [3b] the reference is rather to the *condition*, with an implication of the speaker's sympathy.

Use of *the former* and *the latter* is largely confined to (rather formal) noun-phrase reference:

> We heard their complaints that no one came to visit them and also that their roof was leaking. I helped them over *the latter* [*ie* the complaint about the roof] and promised to let some friends know about *the former* [*ie* the complaint about loneliness]. [4]

For broader reference, both phrases might be expanded to include a noun head:

> They were upset that no one came to visit them and also that their roof was leaking. I helped them over *the latter problem* and promised to let some friends know about *the former complaint*. [5]

19.50 *So* and *that* can have anaphoric reference when they are intensifiers premodifying an adjective (*that* so used is informal and often criticized):

> There were two thousand people in the theatre. I didn't expect it to be {*so* / *that*} full. [1]

> I had a terrible headache yesterday and had to take some aspirins. I'm not feeling {*so* / *that*} bad today. [2]

> We took them to a circus and then to a zoo and gave them lots of ice cream and chocolate. They haven't had {*so* / *that*} good a time for years. [3]

Such is used more commonly than *so* or *that* when (as in this last example) the adjective accompanies a noun phrase, but *such* is followed by normal noun-phrase order:

> . . . They haven't had *such a good time* for years. [3a]

Note the different implications when *this*, *that*, and *so* are used as intensifiers. Compare:

> I didn't expect it to be {
> *this full.* [= as full as it *is now*] } ⟨informal⟩
> *that full.* [= as full as it *was then*] }
> *so full.* [neutral in time implication] } [1a]

Personal pronouns

19.51 As explained in 6.7, 6.18, *we* has several possible noun-phrase references. In discourse, we are concerned chiefly with the 'inclusive' *we* (*cf* 4.58, as with the subject of the present sentence), and with the 'exclusive' *we* as in:

> Will you stay here while *we* go for a policeman? [1]

In formal writing, and frequently indeed in the present book, *we* 'inclusive' and *we* 'exclusive' can cooccur. The former is common with verbs implying shared knowledge (*understand*, *see*, *appreciate*, etc), the latter with verbs of communication (*say*, *state*, *write*, etc). It would be possible to use both in the same sentence, though this would usually be avoided:

> *We* see now why *we* expressed reservations earlier. [2]

In [2], the second *we* is exclusive, the first inclusive or even (as often) indefinite and roughly equivalent to the more formal *one* or the *reader*.

The indefinite use of *you* and the *you* of direct 2nd person address (*cf* 6.2*ff*) can also cooccur. In [3], the first *you* is indefinite, the second makes direct address:

> In fourteenth-century England, *you* had a very poor chance of being taught to read, *you* see. [3]

Unlike the two uses of *we*, however, *you* is rather rare in formal writing and the indefinite use is virtually excluded. The same applies to the indefinite use of *they*; in formal styles, *they* in [4] would refer only to the council authorities, where informally it is more plausible with indefinite reference:

I intend to ask the council authorities why *they* are digging up the road again. [4]

In place of the informal indefinite *you*, there is *one*, but it can be used only sparingly without making a piece of writing (or even more so a spoken utterance) sound intolerably pompous. This is perhaps especially constraining in BrE, which lacks in general the facility (now in any case frowned on for social reasons) of replacing *one* by *he* in second and subsequent use:

One cannot control *one*'s temper easily if *one* is discussing a matter over which *one* has feelings of guilt or great personal involvement. 〈esp BrE〉 [5]

Here, we could have in AmE: *One* . . . *his* . . . *he* . . . *he* . . . Other indefinite pronouns such as *anyone*, *everybody* can be followed by *he* in both AmE and BrE, but this is vulnerable to the objection of seeming to have a male orientation, while the use of *they* to refer back to these indefinites is open to the objection of seeming ungrammatical in the switch from singular to plural. It is therefore largely confined to spoken (especially informal) usage (*cf* also 19.64).

Note There is a further and rare use of *one*, perhaps to avoid the egocentricity of 'I':

A: Did you enjoy your school days?
B: Well, one can hardly remember; it's all so long ago. [6]

Comparison

19.52 Signals of comparison and contrast play a frequent part in providing textual coherence. Most can be regarded as involving ellipsis (*cf* 12.1*ff*, 12.31*ff*).

The most obvious comparison signal is found in adjectives and adverbs, whether in the inflected forms or in the periphrastic forms with *more*, *most*, *as*, *less*, *least* (*cf* 7.74*ff*). If the basis of comparison (*cf* 15.63) is not made explicit in the clause, it must be inferred from the previous context:

John took four hours to reach London. Bill, on the other hand, was driving *more slowly*. [1]
Mary used to listen to records most of the time. Sally was a *more enthusiastic* student. [2]
There were ten boys in the group. Bob was by far the *best*. [3]
Barbara dances beautifully. Jack dances *no less well*. [4]
Gwen always hands in a well-constructed and intelligent paper. I'm afraid Joan doesn't expend *as* much effort and time on her papers. [5]

We can demonstrate the anaphoric reference by supplying the basis of comparison:

. . . more slowly *than John* (*drove*). [1a]
. . . a more enthusiastic student *than Mary* (*was*). [2a]
. . . the best (*of the ten boys*) (*in the group*). [3a]

. . . no less well *than Barbara* (*dances*). [4a]
. . . as much effort and time on her papers *as Gwen* (*expends on her papers*). [5a]

On comparative clauses, *cf* 15.63*ff*.

So too with expressions of similarity or difference; these may involve the use of equative and antithetic conjuncts (*cf* 8.137*ff*). For example:

Mrs White was the victim of a confidence trick. Bill was tricked
{*very differently.* / *in the same way.*} [6]

Tom gets ten dollars a week for pocket money. Bob receives a *similar* amount. [7]
Mrs Hayakawa complained that the roof leaked and the windows fitted badly, so that the place was freezing cold. Her husband complained *likewise*. [8]
Tom behaved himself at the party. However, the *other* boy had to be sent home. [9]
John didn't like the car. He asked to see a *different* one. [10]

We can display the basis of similarity or difference:

{. . . very differently *from the way in which Mrs White was* (*tricked*). / . . . in the same way *as Mrs White* (*was* (*tricked*)).} [6a]
. . . an amount similar *to what Tom receives.* [7a]
. . . complained *about the same things as Mrs Hayakawa* (*complained about*). [8a]
. . . the boy other *than Tom* . . . [9a]
. . . see one different *from the car he didn't like.* [10a]

Certain lexical items are used in a quasi-grammatical way to express identity, similarity, dissimilarity, and difference. Expressions involving *respective*(*ly*), *mutual*(*ly*), *converse*(*ly*), *opposite* (*-ly* is rare), etc effect considerable neatness and economy in discourse:

Brahms and Verdi wrote orchestral and operatic music, *respectively*. [11]
The chairman and the guest speaker expressed their *mutual* admiration. [12]
Mary told Harry that she never wanted to see him again. He *reciprocated*, but with even greater bitterness. [13]
I thought that Oregon had a greater rainfall than British Columbia, but Caroline says *the opposite*. [14]

The textual role of adverbials

19.53 In 19.48 we saw in example [8a] the communicative impact of the inserted adverbials *in a way* and *of course*. While the basic functions of adverbials are fully expounded in Chapter 8, we need here to emphasize their dual role in textual structure: interpreting the text to the hearer/reader (*eg* in encouraging a particular attitude), and expressing the relevant connection between one part of a text and another. The former is achieved primarily by subjuncts and disjuncts (*cf* 8.88*ff*), the latter by conjuncts (*cf* 8.134*ff*). Consider the following:

> My dog is fourteen {months / years} old and ▲ he is very frisky. [1]

Given the appropriate general knowledge, the choice of *months* or *years* will determine the aptness of adverbials that might be inserted at the insertion sign: *of course* or *naturally* on the one hand; *yet*, *still*, *surprisingly enough* on the other. A further example:

> My next-door neighbour {is an entomologist. / is a travelling salesman. / works for an oil company.} ▲ He knows more about treating mosquito bites than anyone I've ever met. [2]

The second sentence of [2] might be preceded by *Not surprisingly*, but this would seem appropriate only if we knew what an entomologist was, or if we connected travelling salesmen or oil executives with experience of mosquito-ridden areas. Preceding the second sentence with *All the same* or *Nonetheless* would obviously have very different implications.

But the postulated insertions in [1] and [2] would serve not only to nudge the hearer in the direction of adopting a particular attitude or to let the hearer know something of the speaker's attitude: they would also indicate the nature of the connection between the two parts of each text. Without the adverbials, each text is presented as offering two pieces of information; in this spirit, the second parts might have read respectively:

> . . . and he sleeps in the kitchen. [1a]
> . . . He got married last week to a former girlfriend of mine. [2a]

In other words, the connection is thematic only, in the sense of 19.12. With the adverbials inserted, the second part of each text is shown to be (as the original versions might chance to be *interpreted* as being) specifically related to the preceding rheme, either as a natural consequence or as a surprising paradox.

Note Since *of course* can hint at incongruity (concession) instead of expressing congruity, [1] might still be a well-formed text as:

> My dog is fourteen years old and of course he is very frisky (still) (, though I think he's beginning to show his age). [1b]

This use of *of course* commonly expresses superficial agreement with what has preceded while at the same time hinting at a more fundamental disagreement. For example:

> The chairman is of course absolutely right to draw attention to the error in my presentation. On the other hand, I wonder whether he is not using this lapse of mine to prevent discussion of the serious issue involved. [3]

Other adverbials that can convey such implications include *admittedly*, *certainly*, *doubtless*, *undeniably*, *undoubtedly*. Of these, *doubtless* is particularly barbed.

19.54 Responses in dialogue often begin with an adverbial which indicates the direction of transition between what has just been said and what is about to be said. On transitional conjuncts, *cf* 8.137, 8.142.

A: That man speaks extremely good English.

B: {[1] Well, / [2] Yet,} he comes from a village in Mongolia.

In one sense, the content of B's response is identical whether it begins as [1] or [2]. It presents an additional fact about the man, and without the adverbial, B's response would have only a thematic link with A's statement. With either of the adverbials inserted, however, B is making a significant comment not merely on the man but on the propensity of villagers in Mongolia to speak good English. If he begins with *Well*, he implies that it is an established fact (*Well, of course!*) that Mongolian villages provide excellent bases for learning English. If he begins with *Yet*, he implies that the man's good command of English was *despite* his Mongolian upbringing.

Note [**a**] The use of *well* is itself context-dependent, however. It would be perfectly plausible to use *well* in [1] as a very different transition (*Well, now!*) so as to connote 'Well, I'll tell you something surprising: he actually comes from a village in Mongolia'. Such an antithetic-concessive transition (*cf* 8.141) is implicit in the frequent note of reservation struck by the use of *well*. Consider a converse exchange of remarks on the same subject:

A: That man is from Mongolia.

B: {[1a] Well, / [2a] Yet,} he speaks extremely good English.

Here, both [1a] and [2a] would connote 'Despite that . . .'. There is in fact no one-word adverbial to express the relationship of the original [1] at [1a]; we would have to resort to a fully clausal expression, as in:

{So that explains why / Now I understand why} he speaks . . .

[**b**] Elliptical responses (*cf* 19.48) often contain an obligatory connective; for example (where in [4] intonation enables us to dispense with the use of an adverbial):

A: {Have a good weekend! / How nice to see you again!}

B: You *TÒO*! [3]
   ÀND YÓU! [4]

Adverbials as structural indicators

19.55 The basic relational structures briefly outlined in 19.17 depend rather heavily on adverbial pointers, especially when any great degree of complexity is involved.

(a) *General to particular*: Any of the following would usefully assist the relationship at the insert mark in the accompanying example:

for example
thus
even
indeed

For example:

Many of the audience became openly hostile. ▲ My uncle wrote a letter to the management next day. [1]

(b) *Progression*: According as the progression is locational, temporal, or logical, adverbials both help to indicate the direction and mark the successive stages. For example:

> *First*, boil the rice in well-salted water; drain it *immediately*. *Next*, warm the lightly buttered base of a small pie dish. You may *now* put the rice in the dish. *Then* add the cheese, tomato and onion. The pie is *at last* ready to be put in the oven. [2]

(c) *Compatibility*: It is frequently important to mark the match or mismatch between two parts of a text. Consider the presence or absence of (for example) *so too* in the following:

> The ordinary saw is not easy to use. ▲ A plane demands years of careful practice. [3]

Similarly, a contrastive conjunct (*cf* 8.141) such as *on the other hand* in a variant of this example:

> The ordinary saw is not easy to use. ▲ A hammer is something that any novice can handle. [3a]

19.56 The different discourse strategies (*cf* 19.18) will likewise call for different adverbial indicators. The 'step' technique is simplest, following as it does a progressive relation (*cf* 19.17). With the 'chain', however, it is particularly helpful to point to the existence and direction of transitions in the structure. Thus the illustrative text of 19.18 (ii) might have begun (though using adverbial linkage more densely than is usual or desirable):

> Hamlet poignantly represents the indecisions that plague us all. *Admittedly*, indecision is not the worst of our ills. *Indeed*, in some ways decisiveness can be more damaging. *At any rate* many people have come to grief that way . . . [1]

In a text of 'stack'-like structure, the 'layers' may call for enumeration (*first, at the outset, fundamentally*: *secondly, next*, . . .; *still more importantly* . . .), but it is especially desirable to draw the hearer's attention to what is to be regarded as the most crucial point: *thus, all in all, finally, last but by no means least* (though this alliterative conjunct is too hackneyed for a resounding climax), *in conclusion*, and many others.

The balance strategy, like the chain, requires adverbial pointers both to assist the sense of rhetorical balance and to ensure that the author's presuppositions match those of his audience. For example, in place of the travel illustration in 19.18 (iv), we might begin another like this:

> I am always thrilled at the prospect of having a mid-winter break in Switzerland. ▲ Frequently, the weather is quite warm . . . [2]

It might not be at all clear whether the second sentence of [2] contributed to the pleasure (vision of deckchairs) or was a counterbalancing unwelcome aspect (poor weather for skiing); in other words, we have left inadequate indication of compatibility (*cf* 19.17). For the balance strategy, we need to insert at the marked place some such indicator as *granted, admittedly, true, of course*, *even so*, etc. Most frequently the balanced movement is indicated by the items *on the one hand*, *on the other (hand)*, but there is usually a goal resembling that of the stack and so demanding a final summative such as *all in all* (*cf* 8.139).

Coordination and subordination

19.57 In 19.5*ff*, we pointed out that two utterances gave the impression of being textually related, even when juxtaposed without any formal indicator of connection. Asyndetic relation of this kind, moreover, raises the expectation that the second utterance followed the first as an iconic representation of being sequential in time or consequential in reasoning – and often both, as in:

He ate too much for dinner. He was ill the next day. [1]

A simple coordination (*cf* 13.43*ff*) of the two not only links them more firmly (since more formally); it can also enable us to show that a third utterance in the sequence is less closely linked to the second than the second is to the first; and, further, that the first and second form a sub-unity which as a whole has a relation to the third:

He ate too much for dinner and he was ill the next day. He decided to be less greedy in future. [2]

But since a result or conclusion seems in some sense more important than the factors leading to the result or conclusion, it is natural to seek a linguistic emblem of this hierarchical relation by subordinating one part to the other instead of coordinating the one with the other:

Because he ate too much for dinner, he was ill the next day. [3]

In [3], we have not merely made the first part of [1] the explicit reason for the second (*Because*), we have grammatically expressed the connection by making a totally new unit where the second part is the main clause of a complex sentence in which the original first part is reduced to the role of adjunct (*cf* 8.25*ff*).

19.58 English has four monosyllabic connective items which semantically belong together as constituting a symmetry of two related subsystems:

and : what precedes is congruent (*cf* 13.22*ff*)
but : what precedes is incongruent (*cf* 13.32)
so : what follows is a consequence
for : what follows is a reason (*ie* what precedes is a consequence)

For example (*cf* 19.11):

The rain has stopped, *and* she's gone for a walk. [1]
The rain hasn't stopped, *but* she's gone for a walk. [2]
The rain has stopped, *so* she's gone for a walk. [3]
She's gone for a walk, *for* the rain has stopped. [4]

This last is rather unnatural where the conjoins are so short. In any case, the symmetry is imperfect in several respects. In [1], [2], and [4], we have conjunctions (**and but*, **and for*; but *cf* 13.8*ff* on *for*). In [3], we have a conjunct (*and so*); *cf* 13.18*f*, 8.137*ff*. Moreover, *and* and *but* are distributionally distinct, *and* demanding in some respects greater structural similarity between the coordinated parts. Compare:

> ?*The rain has stopped *and* let's go for a walk. [5]
> The rain hasn't stopped *but* let's go for a walk. [6]

In this respect, although we normally think of *and* and *but* as closely related converses, the converse of *but* is in fact *so*:

> The rain has stopped (and) *so* let's go for a walk.

Thirdly and (from the viewpoint of text cohesion) most significantly, the symmetry is imperfect in that *for* is a much less frequently used connective than the other three. In other words, textual structure is resistant to stating a consequence in advance of the condition. In the event of this order being desirable, it is more usual to make the condition structurally subordinate to (rather than coordinate with) the consequence:

> She's gone for a walk, { {because / since} the rain has stopped. [7]
> the rain having (at last) stopped. }

Even so, the prior condition would often be stated first:

> Since the rain has stopped, she's gone for a walk. [8]

Note [**a**] There is a further asymmetry in the fact that *and* can subsume the role of *but* (*cf* 13.24), though the converse does not hold:

> He's sixty-two *and* he plays squash like a twenty-year old.

[**b**] Whereas *and* and *or* can be used to conjoin a sequence of several clauses, *but* and *for* can conjoin only two (*cf* 13.8*f*, 13.18*f*).

Pairs and triads

19.59 One of the ways in which coordination is exploited in textual structure is to assist the desire for parallelism and balance (*cf* 19.7). For example:

> These terrorists have destroyed their own credibility. They resisted arrest and then they gave themselves up. They went on a hunger strike and then they started taking food. Some of them claim that they are all nationalists and some of them claim that they are all opposed to nationalism. [1]

We note that the last three sentences in [1], each with clauses coordinated by *and*, form a triad (*cf* 19.8), a rhetorical pattern that seems to be especially attractive. Coordination achieves the seemingly impossible task of giving three units equal status and yet of making the third climactic; for example:

> She cleaned the room, (she) made a birthday cake, and (she) finished preparing a lecture. [2]

But the climax of the third part may be expressing a point which is strongly counter-consequential and concessive:

She works ten hours a day in the clinic, she spends ages helping him with his thesis, and he calls her lazy! [3]

The balanced units, whether in pairs or threes, may of course be coordinated *subordinate* clauses:

Because you're tired, because you're lonely, and because you're depressed, I want to insist on your coming to stay with us for a week or so. [4]

Subordinate coordination, however, is especially associated with alternatives rather than accretions. For this reason, pairing is very common since this gives the convenient impression of a total or very general polarization:

He doesn't know whether his wife is unhappy because the baby died or whether she's just no longer in love with him. [5]
When you're lonely or when you're unhappy for other reasons, listening to music can be a great consolation. [6]

Questions too can be linked to form a satisfyingly coherent sequence:

Did he jump or was he pushed? [7]
Will they arrive on time, will they listen carefully, and will they enjoy our performance? [8]

Of course, in ordinary unambitious writing and in familiar speech, coordination is used without striving for the balanced effects on which we have been concentrating in this section. But the momentum and implications of sequence, the relative cohesion of explicit coordination, and the contrasting entailments of the chief coordinating conjunctions are inherent in even the least self-conscious discourse.

Note Informal conversation is characterized by an overtly uncompleted pairing, especially through unfinished *but*-coordinations. These often occur where one speaker is effectively inviting another participant to speak. It can give a pleasantly apologetic and self-effacing tone:

A: My wife's not been feeling too well. She's seen the doctor, though, and he's told her it's nothing serious. But (er) [*trails off into silence*]
B: I'm sorry to hear about this. [9]

A voiced hesitation ('er') frequently follows such a use of *but*. A's speech might equally have ended: 'But I don't know . . .' or 'But don't let's talk about our little problems' or 'But how's the book going?' These all have in common: '*But*: let's change the subject'.

Contrasting coordination and subordination

19.60 In several of the examples provided in 19.59, coordination has been used along with subordination. This is in fact textually representative. Although from the viewpoint of grammar these two types of clause relation are thought of as alternatives, and although coordination is a far more frequently occurring form of cohesive device, it is normal to find both types in any text of a few lines (or a few seconds) in extent. It is particularly rare to find a text with subordination but without coordination.

It is the flexible use of both devices that endows a text with variety of expression on the one hand and with a well-ordered presentation of information on the other. The combination also enables one to achieve a high degree of complexity within a single, unified whole. For example:

Although I know it's a bit late to call, seeing your light still on and needing to get your advice if you'd be willing to help me, I parked the car as soon as I could find a place and ventured to come straight up without ringing the bell because, believe me, I didn't want to add waking your baby to the other inconveniences I'm causing you. [1]

Taking nonfinite as well as finite clauses into account, there are nearly twenty clauses in this example, which, without any pretensions to elegance, is grammatically well-formed as well as being textually coherent. And although it is often thought that a single sentence of such complexity belongs only to the most formal styles of written English, the example [1] is in fact only slightly edited from the transcribed form of an actual spoken utterance in informal conversation. Again, it is sometimes put as a generalization that nonfinite clauses are characteristic of formal texts, finite clauses of less formal ones. There is some truth in this so far as *-ing* adverbial clauses are concerned, especially those with subject, and especially passive clauses with subject:

The rain having (at last) stopped, she's gone for a walk. [2]
The play now having been reviewed, no one can ignore it. [3]
Having now seen the play myself, I agree that it is rather weak. [4]

Contrast:

Since the rain has stopped, she's gone for a walk [2a]
Now that the play has been reviewed, no one can ignore it. [3a]
Now that I have seen the play myself, I agree that it is rather weak. [4a]

But it is not true for nominal *-ing* clauses, and the following:

Finding you at home is a great surprise. [5]
He didn't mind *waiting for them in the rain.* [6]

are decidedly less formal than:

That I (should) find you at home is a great surprise. [5a]
He didn't mind *that he waited [was waiting, had to wait] for them in the rain.* [6a]

Indeed, with *to*-infinitive clauses, the general statement could profitably be reversed: the finite verb correspondences (to the extent that they exist) are almost always more formal in tone. For example:

To close the doors, just press the green button. [7]
In order that you may close the doors, merely press the green button. [7a]

Note [**a**] There are exceptions to the exclusive formality even of nonfinite passive clauses with subject. In the most commonplace of discourse, a concessive disjunct like the following (*cf* 8.127 Note [c]) is frequent enough to be criticized as hackneyed:

We've got to help the poorer nations with their economic and health problems. But *that (having been) said*, it's reasonable to expect them to meet us half way – with military bases, for example. [8]

[**b**] The interaction of coordination and subordination is seen also in the fact that while it is the latter that contributes most to tight coherence of grammatical (and hence of textual) structure, as well as to verbal economy (particularly through the use of nonfinite clauses), it is coordination that permits far more drastic economies of ellipsis (*cf* 12.1*ff*, 12.31*ff*). Compare:

I had been getting hungry and my wife △ anxious.
*I had been getting anxious because my wife △ hungry. } [△ = had been getting]

She was ill the next day and △ had to call a doctor.
*She was ill the next day when △ was particularly busy. } [△ = she]

This is not of course to ignore elliptical forms of subordinate clauses such as *If any*, *When in doubt*, *Though anxious*, which can be used initially as well as later in a sentence; *cf* 14.18.

[c] Subordination usually (though by no means invariably) indicates grammatically the subordinate *informational* status of the part so expressed. Similarly, when *and* is replaced by *like* or *as well as* in conjoining phrases (*cf* 13.103), the effect is usually to downgrade the following item, implying that it has 'given' status. Among the clausal exceptions are the clauses expressing outcome or result (*cf* 15.25, 15.27): for example, the journalistic use of infinitive clauses:

Sunderland played an energetic game, to win four-two.
[= and they won . . .]

The part played by questions

19.61 There is a sense in which it is true to say 'I can't tell you anything till you've asked me something'. In other words, what we choose to talk about depends crucially on what we think our hearer does not know and wants to know. Even conversations in which a participant keenly wishes to talk and inform (rather than listen and be informed) will frequently begin with a question. For example, as a conversation-initial gambit:

Have you heard about Mr Malloy? [1]

The questioner will be alert to the reply in two quite separate respects: whether his companion has heard about Mr Malloy, and whether he seems to *want* to hear. Only if the questioner is satisfied on both counts, will he launch forth – and even so the tactful conversationalist will begin with a careful lack of dogmatism:

Well, apparently, if I got it right, Malloy was on his way home on Friday, when . . . [1a]

Moreover, without prompting by questions in the course of his account ('What was the weather like?' 'When did you hear this?' 'Why didn't Rita Malloy . . .?'), the speaker would soon falter – again, for fear that he had lost his companion's interest or in doubt as to which aspects of the narrative to develop and which to ignore.

Even in the absence of questions from a companion, a speaker will insert them for himself. In written materials, the author is naturally constrained to do so. This is partly in the interests of information processing (*cf* 19.66*ff* below), that is, providing a focus closely similar to that attained by the pseudo-cleft (*cf* 18.29*f*). Compare:

What was he doing? He was trying to change a fuse. [2]
What was he doing but trying to change a fuse. [2a]
What he was doing was trying to change a fuse. [2b]

But in part the inserted question is to enliven and dramatize a narrative by supplying a query which the speaker thinks must be in his companion's mind – or which he thinks ought to be:

And that son of hers continues to be a big worry. And how do I know? She was in tears the other day – with a photo of him in her hand. She didn't think I saw the photo but I did. [3]

A question in discourse is often directed less to the hearer than to the speaker, though in seeming to reflect the speaker's self-questioning as to how he should proceed, the question equally directs the hearer's mind both to this point and to the tentativeness and spontaneity with which it is being made. For example:

> The horses seemed strangely disturbed as we groomed them that morning. *How shall I put it?* It was as though they were aware that Mary and I had quarrelled. [4]

> The book will be out in a couple of months. There's been some problem over the binding and this has been aggravated by shipping difficulties in Hong Kong where they've had this acrimonious seamen's strike. What a lot of unrest there is in the world, when you come to think of it. *But where was I?* When the book is finally published, I'm going to have a little party to celebrate. *And what was the other thing I wanted to tell you?* Oh yes . . . [5]

Note [**a**] Consider the part played by questions in the representation of internal reflection quoted in 19.43.

[**b**] Questions in dialogue are frequently uttered merely to elicit matter that was imperfectly heard or understood (*cf* 19.17):

HÚH?
WHÁT? } ⟨very informal⟩

WHÁT'S that?
SÓRry? } ⟨informal⟩

I beg your PÁRdon?

Given the appropriate context, any of these question forms could equally express strong surprise at what has just been said; in effect, they are used to inquire both 'What did you say?' and 'What do you mean?' (By contrast, the question 'What's THÀT?' seeks elucidation about a specific item – and 'Who's THÀT?' about a specific person – just mentioned.)

Questions as directives

19.62 Questions, direct and indirect, have an important role in discourse as polite equivalents of requests. On entering someone's room, a visitor will begin with such a question even if he is a fairly close friend:

> Are you free for a minute or two?
> Is this an awkward moment to see you about something?
> Am I disturbing you?
> Got a second? ⟨informal⟩
> I wonder whether you could help me.

These opening gambits would preface discourse itself. But question forms may equally preface physical action by the speaker or seek it from the hearer:

> Would you mind if I closed the window?
> Would you excuse me a moment? I must find a telephone.
> Do you think you could lock the door when you leave?
> Why don't you come and have dinner with me tonight?

The fact that such questions are not semantically interrogative is shown by the fact that they can be coordinated (especially in AmE) with statements and combine a request with an expression of intention:

> Why don't I go on ahead and you (can) come when you're ready?
> Why don't you get a taxi and I'll be out in a minute?

In the conventional language of formal meetings, procedure is often couched in elaborately interrogative structures, each widely recognized as a formula disguising a statement:

> Could I ask through you, Mr Chairman, whether the Secretary is thinking of the occasion under discussion?
> [~ 'The Secretary has muddled the dates']
> But may we not ask ourselves whether this is an appropriate time to raise taxes?
> [~ 'I am opposed to raising taxes now']
> I wonder if we might now turn to the next item.
> [~ 'The present discussion is closed']
> Am I {alone / right} in thinking the motion is out of order?

Rhetorical questions

19.63 The rhetorical question has in common with the formulaic questions discussed in 19.62 the fact that the answer is a foregone conclusion:

> She said she had been too ill to come to work that day, and certainly she sounded pretty groggy on the phone. Anyway, who was I to argue? [1]
> [= 'I wasn't in a position to doubt her word']
> The prisoners were grumbling about their cold cells and several claimed they weren't getting enough to eat. But what could I do? [2]
> [= 'I could do nothing']
> Do I have to tell you everything? You're a fully qualified architect and these things should be at your fingertips! [3]

As we see from these examples, especially [3], the rhetorical question is by no means confined to the highly wrought prose of formal speeches of persuasion that we may think of in connection with 'rhetoric'. Rather, the tag question so common in the most informal speech is strictly similar to the rhetorical question in its communicative effect, since it essentially seeks confirmation of what the speaker has explicitly assumed (by the preceding declarative) to be agreed truth:

> It's a glorious day, *isn't it*? [4]
> Joan Sutherland was the best coloratura singer of her generation, *wasn't she*? [5]

Compare:

> When have we had a better coloratura singer than Joan Sutherland? [5a]

Such a use of tags occurs in very informal speech (especially BrE and chiefly nonstandard) where the hearer cannot possibly be expected to know the answer or to take it for granted, but where the speaker seeks by such use of the question form to imply that the answer ought to be self-evident. These tags have a falling tone on the operator:

Well, I couldn't hear the phone, could I? It's in the next room and the door was shut. Besides, I was fast asleep, wasn't I? But I can't expect you to think of things from my angle, can I? [6]

Note Although *yes–no* questions are theoretically open to either response, it is striking that they normally occur when the speaker plainly expects 'yes'.

Participant involvement

19.64 Whether this is made explicit or not, every text is addressed *by* someone ('I') *to* someone else ('you'). In many cases, the relation of both participants is indeed explicit:

I tell *you* it's true! [1]

But equally both can be merely implicit:

Good luck! [= '*I* wish *you* good luck'] [2]

In very formal communications, where the precise identity of the addressee is unknown and where the originator is making the communication on behalf of an organization, the participants may be referred to in the 3rd person:

The management regret(s) any inconvenience to *clients* during repair work to the premises. [3]

In a similar tone and often for similar reasons, mention of one or both of the participants is avoided altogether:

The management regrets any inconvenience during repair work to the premises. [3a]
Any inconvenience to *clients* is regretted during . . . [3b]
Any inconvenience is regretted during . . . [3c]

In some texts, both participants are referred to simultaneously by means of the inclusive *we* (*cf* 6.7):

So now *we* know why there was no traffic coming towards *us* on this road. Well, since the road is obviously blocked, *we*'ll have to turn back and find a side road somewhere. *We*'ll manage somehow. [4]

(*Cf* 19.51)

But in many texts, the addressee is unmentioned and the speaker or writer leaves it implicit as to who is the authority for the communication. This is natural enough in face-to-face speech where the source is obvious; so too in a personal letter or even in a printed text which is accompanied by the author's name:

Julian is going to Detroit next week. In fact, if he likes it and finds a job, he may decide to stay there. His wife, of course, comes from that part of Michigan. [5]

We notice, however, that in the use of the adverbial *of course* the speaker/writer is appealing to the addressee's shared knowledge (just as he might, with *clearly*, *obviously*, *of course*, etc, to the addressee's shared opinion). Nor would it be unusual in such a text for the author to make explicit his relation to the information conveyed:

Julian, *I gather*, is going to Detroit next week. In fact, if he likes it and finds a job, *he tells me* that he may decide . . . [5a]

Even in a signed letter, some amplification of identity may be necessary if the writer is unknown to (or may have been forgotten by) the addressee, or if it is otherwise necessary to specify his role:

As a Camden resident and also as a qualified accountant, I write to inform you of an error in the recently published expenditure figures of your Council . . . [6]

You may not remember me, but I hope you will allow me to congratulate you on your marriage. It must give all of your former colleagues like me great pleasure to know of your happiness . . . [7]

Not so much as your father, but as man to man, I do implore you to be more considerate . . . [8]

So too in speech (and *cf* 19.77 Note):

I am employed by a detective agency. I wonder if you could help me in some inquiries I am making about a person who used to be a neighbour of yours. [9]

On the telephone, identification of both speaker and addressee usually prefaces discourse:

Hello. Is that Peter? Marjorie here. What? Oh sorry! – Marjorie Wong, your wife's assistant. Is Valerie there? [10]

Hello. Am I speaking to the Controller? This is the Works Department. We are having to cut off your electricity supply for an hour or so, but if the interruption becomes very inconvenient will you please phone me, Ram Patel, on extension 2018. [11]

In this last example, personal identification is given only incidentally (at the end), since the caller is primarily phoning not as an individual but as an institution ('the Works Department').

The addressee may equally need to have his role specified in the particular context: *you* may be friend, wife, mother, doctor, neighbour, according to who is in communication and on what occasion:

I wonder if I can ask you – as a friend rather than as my doctor – if you think I ought to give up smoking. I know that you discourage your children – but is this as a mother or as a doctor or because you know it affects your husband's breathing? [12]

I am writing to you in your capacity as a volunteer helper at the South Boston Youth Center. You will have noticed . . . [13]

Note [**a**] Identification and authority are made heavily explicit in legal documents. For example:
I, the undersigned, being of sound mind, do this day hereby bequeath . . .
[**b**] Examples [10] and [11] illustrate the normal telephone use of *this/here* for the speaker, *that/there* for the hearer. Perhaps because of the unfavourable values associated with *that* (*cf* 5.63 Note [a]), there is some tendency to address the unseen hearer with the question 'Is this X?'

Speaker/hearer contact

19.65 But in addition to establishing identity of participants and to indicating authority for content, textual structure tends to be punctuated by periodic references to both participants. The hearer is addressed by name, not for clarity but out of courtesy and friendliness. The speaker may repeatedly refer to himself, often successfully giving thereby an impression of courtesy and modesty rather than of egocentricity:

I'd like you to know . . . I think . . . I hear . . . I seem to remember . . . it occurs to me . . . I mean . . . [1]

A communication from a body or organization may self-refer similarly:

Your union officials suggest . . . we acknowledge . . . we claim . . . we hope . . . [2]

Direct allusions and appeals to the addressee are especially characteristic of speech, informally with interspersed comment clauses *you see*, *you know*, *get it?*, *do you follow me?*, *yes? right?*; more formally *as you well know*, *as you may know*, *if I make myself clear* (*to you*), *if you will pardon the allusion*. In familiar speech, such asides may be excessive. For example:

I was just turning into Regent Street, *right*? And *you know* that Italian restaurant, Rachel. Well, *you see* I was trying to see if it was open, and *would you believe it*, coming out was Martha Goldberg. *You remember her*, Rachel, she used to work with me, *yes*? Well, *as you can imagine*, I pulled in and tried to attract her attention. She has remarried, *you know*. [3]

At this point, *if you will allow me*, I shall revert, ladies and gentlemen, to the aspect of the theory that I was explaining a few minutes ago. *As I am sure you will recall*, the central interest of the double helix . . . [4]

Addressee-involvement obviously serves two related functions, often distinguished by intonation. On the one hand, the speaker wants assurance that the addressee is following the communication in all its detail and allusion; in this spirit the involvement is essentially interrogative (*cf* 19.61) and the inserted items have a rising nucleus:

YÉS
you KNÓW } [5]
SÉE

On the other hand, they are assurances to the addressee that he is not being underestimated and that it is highly probable that he knows the facts already; the speaker is recalling them as much for the clarification of his own mind as anything else. In this spirit, the inserts have a falling nucleus or are uttered with low prominence carrying no nucleus at all:

|she has reMÀRried you know| [6]

Confidence in shared knowledge not uncommonly permits the total replacement of an item of information by a heavily prominent *you know* with fall-plus-rise (*cf* 19.59 Note, on uncompleted *but*-conjoins):

I'd like to help him in any way I could, but YÒU KNÓW – [7]
[*ie* '. . . but there are notorious reasons for my not doing so, and these you know well']

A notable use of the 'shared knowledge' indicator, *you know* or *you see*, is where a participant breaks into discourse with a response or possibly a contrasting viewpoint (note the use of *well*; and *cf* 19.54):

A: Are you going to Warburton's?
B: Well *you see* I no longer work there. [8]

Again:

A: I find his explanation of relativity absolutely baffling. Isn't he an incredibly bad lecturer?
B: Well, *you know*, you missed the lecture before last and I think it was pretty crucial. [9]

The emphatic use of *you know* can serve as a connective within a continuous text:

I just couldn't bear going all the way to that place yet again.
|YÒU KNÓW| my |LÉGS were aching| the |CRÓWDS were thicker than ever| and I had a |HÈADache| [10]

Individuals differ in the extent to which they intersperse terms of address in discourse. In letters, they are used almost solely in the initial salutation: *Dear Mr Robinson, Dear Fred*; though between intimates, items like *darling* commonly accompany sentences throughout, as they would do in the corresponding speech. Letters to strangers can freely begin *Dear Sir* (less freely *Dear Madam*), and in formal style they may end *I remain, Sir, yours faithfully*. A general letter may begin *Gentlemen* (rather than ?*Dear Gentlemen*) or *Dear Sirs*, or *Ladies and Gentlemen*. On differences between AmE and BrE, *cf* App III.11.

In speech, it is normal to address a group as *Ladies and Gentlemen*; a group of men as *Gentlemen* (or, in military and analogous usage, as *Men*, though this would hardly be text-initial). At a formally constituted meeting, it is equally normal for individuals to be addressed as *Sir*, to or from the chair, less comfortably as *Madam*. But in chance encounters with strangers, severe constraints are felt over terms of address, especially in BrE. A request such as *I wonder if you could direct me to Pitt Street?* would in AmE (and especially in Southern AmE) be accompanied very widely by *Sir* or *Ma'am*, irrespective of the speaker's sex or an adult addressee's age. In BrE, *Sir* would be rather rare, and would be used chiefly by younger men addressing older men; it would almost never be used by women. *Madam*, though the only fully acceptable form of address to a woman, is felt to be inappropriate in most informal circumstances (though it is used in addressing customers, clients, etc). In general, women can use neither *Sir* nor *Madam* except where the speaker is in a recognizably serving role, though women students occasionally so address a teacher.

A younger woman is sometimes addressed by men as *Miss*, but this is widely regarded as nonstandard or felt to be demeaning to the person addressed. In nonstandard use, *Lady*, *Mister*, and *Missus* occur freely in men's speech; and *lady* also has an ironic use which is not uneducated but informal (and addressed to a woman who is *not* a stranger):

Oh, you can't use that argument, lady. [11]

Man is also used to acquaintances (especially in AmE), but more familiarly than the foregoing use of *lady*. The use of *woman* in address is informal and usually impolite.

Note [**a**] Just as a speaker involves the addressee with insertions like *right*, *you know*, so the addressee reassures the speaker with similar short comments: *Oh I see*, *Yes I know*, *Right*.

[**b**] Although the inserts for involvement and authority are most frequently uttered with little prosodic prominence, *you know* is not alone in having a stressed variant. There is, for example, a triumphant or retributive *you see*, as in (uttered with a wide range of pitch, in contrast to that normal in comment clauses):

So I was RÌGHT| you ''SÉE|. [12]

Compare also:

She has reMÀRried {I think / I THǏNK} [13]

In [13] the first variant is little more than a conventional reluctance to seem dogmatic, but the second is meant to express serious reservations about the truth of what has preceded.

[**c**] Tag questions are much used to facilitate participant involvement, and it is notable that they are commonly placed well in advance of end position (*cf* 10.57*ff*, 11.7*ff*). For example:

She hadn't at that time, *had she*, been fully recognized as a serious writer?

Information processing

19.66 It is appropriate to treat this aspect of grammatical organization last since, being more centrally significant than any other, information processing has already to no small degree been seen as the motivation behind other specific features of grammar discussed elsewhere. It is paramount in the use of coordination and subordination (*cf* 19.57*ff*), and it was specifically mentioned in the treatment of questions (*cf* 19.61). Consider a sequence like the following:

Our economic troubles continue to resist solution. We have tried subsidizing our weaker industries. We have experimented with import controls. We have on occasion resorted to the drastic device of devaluation. To no avail. *How then are we to proceed?* The answer lies in higher productivity and better products. [1]

The italicized question is pivotal in this text. It contains the conjunct *then* with anaphoric reference: the remedies already tried, which have been of 'no avail', are put behind us. The question both points forward (and this is lexically matched by 'The answer' which follows) and prepares us for a climactic alternative strategy. A similar anticipation of the information focus would have been:

> ... To no avail. *The way forward* is to seek higher ... [1a]

The essence of such anticipation is to indicate in general terms what is to follow (we are going to 'proceed', there is a 'way forward') and hence both to prepare the hearer/reader and to arouse his interest. Note the comparable function of the italicized *where*-clause in the next example:

> Robert Adam was in many respects typical of British architects of the eighteenth century. Like Inigo Jones and Lord Burlington, he drew eagerly on the inspiration both of the Renaissance and of Antiquity. He shared the enthusiasm of his contemporaries for collecting classical marbles. He was far from being alone in undertaking venturesome travel in the Mediterranean and in gazing with wonder at vase fragments and at sundrenched monuments. He was quintessentially a member of the Neo-classical movement. *Where he stands apart* is in his refusal to regard Antiquity as inviolable. It was an inspiration for new work, not a model for imitation. [2]

The major part of the paragraph is illustrative of the claim that Adam was typical of his time. The writer has one piece of counter-evidence, and he could have expressed this by the mere use of adversative *but*:

> ... a member of the Neo-classical movement. But he refused to regard ... [2a]

This would have made the point for an alert reader, though the exceptional feature would have been expressed rather tamely. The fact that we had come to an exception could have been more insistently expressed for the less alert reader by a further alternative:

> ... a member of the Neo-classical movement. But there is one respect in which he stands apart: he refused to regard ... [2b]

The writer might, however, have arrived at a compromise between [2b] and [2], as follows:

> ... a member of the Neo-classical movement. But he stands apart in his refusal to regard ... [2c]

We should note that, informationally, this is a subtle improvement over [2b] in seeming to assume (by the nominalization, *his refusal*) a significant item of shared knowledge. The writer credits his reader with being aware that Adam had this degree of creative independence. In fact, the original version [2] shows the writer going one better than this. He not merely achieves the objective of warning the reader that we have come to one respect in which Adam 'stands apart'; use of the pseudo-cleft enables him also to imply that the reader was well-informed enough to know that there was such a standing apart (as well as that Adam did not 'regard Antiquity as inviolable'), and that in consequence we have now simply arrived at the point of restating it. In presenting what may well be new information as though it were given (*cf* 18.8), the writer treats his reader with flattering respect as well as enabling himself to make the main point with great force and economy.

19.67 The highlighting of the main information is associated with intonation nucleus. As explained in 18.2*ff*, speech enables us to do this independently of the grammatical structure. Guiding a reader to assign focus is more difficult, and Chapter 18 explores a range of grammatical devices that can be exploited. One such device is ellipsis. By omitting as much as is grammatically and semantically tolerable, the writer limits the reader's choice and thus guides his decision. Compare the following:

> She felt trapped and frustrated. Whatever she said might so easily be misinterpreted. An idea crossed her mind, only . . . [1]

In reading this text, one might plausibly assign a prosody as follows:

> An i|dea crossed her MÍND| only . . . [1a]

In other words, we have given ourselves the expectation (congruent with the preceding sentence) that the text might continue:

> . . . only to be rejected the next minute. [1b]

But let us suppose the writer had intended it to be read as:

> An i|DÈA crossed her mind| only . . . [1c]

with the text continuing:

> . . . only just in time. [1d]

The reader's momentary error could have been avoided in several ways. The risk that the third sentence of [1] was continuing the implication of the second would not have arisen if a thematic adverbial (*Suddenly* . . ., *Then* . . .) had implied a radical change. A nucleus would have been placed on *idea* if a rewording had placed this word at the end:

> She had an idea. [1e]

But it might still have been given the wrong nucleus by a reader expecting a continuation like [1b]. With a more radical rewriting, we might have had a successful but highly elliptical verbless sentence, imperfectly suggesting the syntax but infallibly both conveying the semantics and pointing to the information focus:

> She felt trapped and frustrated. Whatever she said might so easily be misinterpreted. Suddenly – an idea! Only just in time. [1′]

Not merely would a reader unhesitatingly reconstruct this prosodically as:

> . . . |Suddenly – an i↑DÈA| . . . [1″]

but he would react to the dramatic expression of the pivotal point between the woman's difficulties and the beginning of their possible resolution.

One further example. Imagine an argument conducted by correspondence.

A has written to B saying that a certain problem had nothing to do with her. B replies:

> Let me set out the case as I see it and try to show you that the problem has something to do with you. [2]

A will probably read the last phrase as:

> . . . the |problem has something to do with YÒU| [2a]

whereas the words are in fact a paraphrase of a remark in A's own letter: they are 'given' information; all that is new is the positive (assertion) in place of A's original negative (denial). B has thus meant it to be read as:

> . . . the |problem HÀS something to do with you| [2b]

The required shift away from the normal (but here unwanted) end focus could have been achieved in the first place by some such device as emphatic *do* or an inserted subjunct (or both), thus drawing attention to the new polarity:

> . . . the problem does (indeed) have something to do with you. [2′]

which A would promptly have read with the required prosody:

> . . . the |problem {does inDÈED / DÒES} have something to do with you| [2″]

Information and sequence

19.68 Much of what we have been saying about the processing of information, not only here but in Chapter 18 and elsewhere in this book, concerns sequence. The order of presentation is clearly vital, whether we are concerned with premodifying adjectives, a group of noun phrases, a pair of independent clauses, a sequence comprising a matrix clause and a subordinate clause, or of course the elements within a single clause. We have choices such as:

> {an intricate and arduous task [1a]
> an arduous and intricate task [1b]

> {the cold night and the difficult journey [2a]
> the difficult journey and the cold night [2b]

> {They cheered and they sang. [3a]
> They sang and they cheered. [3b]

> {I saw the broken window when I arrived home. [4a]
> When I arrived home, I saw the broken window. [4b]

> {Our memories of past crises were being added to our uncertainties for the future. [5a]
> To our uncertainties for the future were being added our memories of past crises. [5b]

More is involved here than sequence, of course. As well as deciding on a pair (or longer set) of units, we have to decide on the actual choice of lexical items. Are they to be near-synonyms or are they to be in sharp contrast? In either case, should they prosodically resemble each other (*eg* by alliterating, having the same number of syllables, the same stress pattern; *eg*: *arduous* and *intricate*), or should they differ in these respects (*eg*: *tough* and *intricate*)? Formal similarity often conveys a sense both of euphony and of a harmony between substance and meaning; formal dissimilarity, on the other hand, can convey a sense of richness and variety. Considerations of euphony enter also into the question of sequencing, but for the most part, both in the selection of items and in their placement, we are concerned with 'the right words in the right place'.

Whatever is placed first will seem relatively introductory and 'scene-setting'. Clearly, *preparing* our hearer or reader for what is to follow is of the greatest importance if the following part is to have the proper impact. The converse of this is that whatever is placed last will be expected to be relatively consequential, of greater importance, and possibly climactic. So in choosing between [1a] and [1b], our decision may depend on whether we wish to convey that the task was arduous *because* it was intricate; intricate and *above all* arduous; arduous in *being* intricate; arduous and *furthermore* intricate. In choosing between [3a] and [3b], we may wish to imply one or other chronological sequence: that they did one thing before the other. But if the two actions are but different aspects of the same celebratory behaviour, we have decisions to make on similar principles to those concerning us in [1a] and [1b], [2a] and [2b]. With [4a] and [4b], however, the order will probably be contextually determined: one or other, the arrival or the seeing, will be relatively 'given' (that is, the hearer/reader will already have been told or led to expect that the subject is going home or that a window has been broken), and whichever is in consequence the relatively 'new' item will be placed in final position if a feeble anticlimactic 'tail' is to be avoided. So again with [5a] and [5b]: the former will be preferred if the preceding part of the text has been dealing with 'past crises' and the intention is to go on to some discussion of the future; if the converse holds, [5b] will be selected.

We shall draw attention to sequencing and other modes of effectively presenting information in the annotated specimens that now follow.

Note Some matters of sequence are determined by courtesy, convention, or idiom. In formal circumstances, women are named in address before men, and the speaker is mentioned last:

Ladies and gentlemen! It gives me great pleasure . . .

Harry and I were dismayed.

In 3rd person mention, however, sequence can freely depend upon the speaker's decision:

Joan and Peter / Peter and Joan } will be coming.   I saw lots of { boys and girls. / girls and boys.

On the other hand, we have a conventional mention of males first in *(the) men and women*, *he and she*, *Mr and Mrs (Jones)*. Numerous other sequences are idiomatically fixed (as in *give and take*, *pots and pans*, *knife and fork*, *(Please pass the) salt and pepper*, *(Do you take) milk and sugar?*) Doubtless these have become fixed historically in response to the operation of prosodic or semantic pressures. Principles like 'Short before long' and 'General setting before specific object' combine happily in the journal title *Homes and Gardens* (*ie* private gardens – not public or zoological). *Cf* on binomials, 13.86.

The scrutiny of an example

19.69 We now present a fictional memoir, which will be analysed fairly closely in terms of textual structure as described in the earlier parts of this chapter.

As a child, one of my sisters was endlessly troubled by bad dreams and she could never be persuaded that they meant nothing. Boylike, of course, I was very scornful of this. On one occasion her screams awoke the whole house and so far as I can remember none of us had any more sleep that night. She sobbed; she was inconsolable; she could not be induced even to tell us what she had been dreaming. It had obviously been a nightmare. And a much worse one than the poor child usually suffered. By breakfast time, she seemed so ill that my parents decided she should stay home. Yet this upset her still more. It was then that she was coaxed into telling us what had frightened her.

A school friend had a little kitten and because this boy's parents were out at work all day, the teacher used to allow him to bring his pet to school and the caretaker used to look after it until the day's classes ended and the children went home again. In my sister's dream some Fearsome Creature with huge jaws was threatening the kitten's life and only she had the power to save it. So although as an added terror the Monster had some terrifying power over her too, she begged to be allowed to go to school as usual. Reluctantly my parents gave in but they insisted that since she was still scared and weepy I accompany her all the way.

I was very glad I did. Near the school we came upon another tearful youngster, her friend, frightened and harassed by a rather vicious dog that was jumping up and trying to molest the kitten in the lad's arms. I managed to chase it away with my sister's help and all was well. But, as you can imagine, she was more convinced than ever that dreams gave a dire glimpse of the future. And, secretly, I was no longer so sure she was wrong.

Text 19.69

The passage has both overall unity and a comprehensible 'natural' progression from part to part within it. Yet many of the parts are juxtaposed asyndetically (19.5); *cf* lines 5–6. Syndetic connection (19.11) is in fact less common, but *cf* lines 2 and 4. Thematic connection (19.12) occurs in lines 5, 6, 9, and elsewhere (in lines 5–6 with a triadic set; *cf* 19.8). There is a striking instance of rhematic connection (19.14) in line 17 where the rheme *threatening the kitten's life* is matched by *save it* in the next clause. Textual orientation (*cf* 19.15) is shown in the dating of the narrative as a whole ('*As a child*, one of my sisters . . .', line 1) in the early life of the narrator who is male (*boylike*, line 3) and its location in the family's home community; the narrator relates to his hearer/reader (*cf* 19.64) both through direct involvement (*as you can imagine*, line 26) and by drawing attention to his own fallible authority for the narrative (*so far as I can remember*, line 4). Not least, the example illustrates the extent to which the text depends on the knowledge of culture and language shared by narrator and hearer/reader (*cf* 19.20). The whole has the structure identified as progression (19.17); it is realized by the *step* strategy (19.18) but achieves a stack-like unity.

We shall now look at the passage in some detail, taking each of the four categories of 19.19 in turn. We shall try to show that every feature, whether minute or relatively extensive, quite local or quite pervasive, contributes to every other feature: endorsing and enhancing the textual structure.

Pragmatics and semantics

19.70 Consider first the implications in the clause sequence: *the teacher used to allow him to bring his pet to school and the caretaker used to look after it* (lines 13*f*). The definite determiner in *his pet* is of course anaphoric (*cf* 6.15), grammatically determined by *a little kitten* earlier in the sentence. But this is not true of the definite articles in *the teacher* and *the caretaker*, which are in turn different from each other. The latter depends on our 'knowledge of the world': that a school has a person (designated *caretaker* in BrE) performing duties that justify the situational *the* (*cf* 5.28) in the noun phrase *the caretaker*. If, in place of this, the clause had had *the lieutenant* or *the waiter*, our world view would not have sustained a situational interpretation of *the*, and we would probably have guessed at anaphora and scanned backward (in vain) for earlier mention of a person who might be so described. With *the teacher*, the case is different again, because we assume that any school has *several* teachers: situational interpretation in this case depends upon our knowledge that one particular teacher has special responsibility for a particular group of children, and for each member *the teacher* concerned is so designated.

Consider now the function of *even* in line 6. This is a focusing subjunct with additive-concessive meaning (*cf* 8.116*ff*), and in the present instance the item on which it focuses (the nonfinite clause *to tell us* . . .) is itself within the scope of the negative focusing item *not*. So much from grammar. But our interpretation depends on our judgment of what is implied by the asyndetic sequence in which *even* appears. The clauses *She sobbed; she was inconsolable; she could not be induced even to* . . . are not only thematically linked but also seem to form a series of statements closely similar semantically, and reaching a climax in the third. The *even* thus appropriately presents an added measure of the child's misery. But the series can be seen rather differently: a narrative sequence in temporal order. The child sobbed. Her parents tried to console her, but in vain. They then tried to persuade her to tell them about the dream – and *even* this less ambitious aim was frustrated. There are further possibilities, still fully compatible with our understanding of the grammar. The implication may be that they could not persuade her to talk *even though* she was normally very keen to tell the family what she had been dreaming.

19.71 One further part of the narrative is worth examining in the present connection. The adjunct *on one occasion* (line 3) is temporal but very elastic in reference. Compare:

> On one occasion as I was having breakfast . . .
> On one occasion when I was sunbathing . . .
> On one occasion as I was going to bed . . .

It carries no necessary reference to a particular time, yet in line 3 we immediately understand it *in part* as 'one night' because dreaming entails sleep and the normal time to be asleep is at night. So the further time adjunct *that night* in the coordinate clause (line 5) is purely confirmatory and *that* is anaphoric. But in fact our chain of pragmatic reasoning has enabled us to make a still more precise interpretation of the phrase *on one occasion*. Although a child may scream on any occasion (and surely more often during waking hours), in the present context we do not need to be told that her screams were occasioned by a dream. We have automatically interpreted the adjunct as 'On one occasion *when she was being troubled by just such a bad dream*', taking the phrase to be thematic with reference to the rheme of the very first finite clause of the narrative.

Lexical features

19.72 When we want to sustain a reference between one part of a text and another, we usually resort to pro-forms (*cf* 12.1*ff*), but this is not always possible. We find the noun phrase *my parents* in line 9 and again in line 20. Clearly, the second reference could not be achieved by *they*, since the pronoun's antecedent would be too remote for correct identification. In any case, replacing lexical items by pro-forms is not always desirable: it may often be better to repeat the lexical item or to use another that is semantically appropriate. This is one of the means by which a text can be given added unity and coherence. The text under consideration concerns family life, with special reference to childhood, and more especially to the dreaming to which one little girl is prone. These matters are reflected in lexical sets as follows:

> family: *parents, child, girl, boy, sister, home, house, breakfast* (perhaps also *coax, allow*)
> childhood: *child, girl, boy, lad, youngster, school, class, teacher, friend, kitten, pet* (perhaps also *sob, scream, beg, fear* etc; *monster*)
> dreaming: *dream* (four times), *nightmare, sleep, night*

But this is to consider subject matter; the plot connects childhood and dreaming in terms of horror, and again this is endorsed by clusters of lexical items:

> *scream, sob, inconsolable, suffer, ill, upset, bad, trouble; fearsome, frighten, terror, dire, vicious, monster, power, harass, molest*

Most of the items in these sets have the semantic complementarity that confers an enrichment by lexical linkage, since we have not repetition so much as a wide selection from associated sets. But a valuable aspect of lexical distribution in texts is that items may be hierarchic as well as linear. A nightmare is hyponymic to (*ie* included within) the class of dreams; conversely, *child* is hypernymic to *boy* and *girl*.

These words, with their modest degree of repetition, do not of course entail the particular subject matter, still less the course of the narrative. The same lexical distribution might occur in a text concerned with a murder trial or even mountaineering. As with the potentiality of grammatical devices (*cf* 19.5*f*), it is the *compatibility* of the lexical items that matters, not so much evoking or endowing as confirming a textual coherence.

In any event there are limitations on actual repetition. Although there are exceptions (see below), we normally avoid repeated use of the same lexical item within short spans of text, especially in writing, since the effect can be unpleasant and clumsy. The required lexical reference and linkage can be achieved by the use of words that have the requisite closeness in meaning. This not merely has the negative advantage of avoiding monotony: it can enrich the text by presenting additional semantic facets. In line 12, a new character is introduced, *a school friend*, who is referred to in the next clause as *this boy*. The lexical items are complementary in the information they give us: a boy need not be a school friend; a school friend need not be a boy. Again, the *kitten* of line 12 is called *his pet* in line 14: very little meaning is added here, but we find it appropriate that it is in recognizing that the kitten is the boy's pet animal that the teacher permits him to bring it to school. Compare also the complementarity of *persuaded* (line 2), *induced* (line 6), and *coaxed* (line 10). From the examples of lexical linkage that have been cited, it will have become clear that the linkage transcends the syntactic function of the lexical items concerned. The same lexical item is present in *bad dreams* and *had been dreaming* (lines 2 and 6), in *to school* and *school friend* (lines 14 and 12), in *child* and *children* (lines 1 and 15), in *bad* and *worse* (lines 1 and 7), indeed even in *terror* and *terrifying* (line 18), to cite only examples from *Text* 19.69. Further, given that linkage operates through items of related meaning, we have comparable links between *sobbed* (line 5), *weepy* (line 21), and *tearful* (line 22). It is on these grounds that we are able to adduce a lexical contrast between waking and sleeping, though in the text this is realized by the noun *sleep* and the past-tense verb *awoke* (lines 5 and 4).

The text contains the clause *she was inconsolable* (line 5). This might have been related to a preceding clause (which is indeed perhaps implied), thus involving such a cross-grammatical linkage:

> My parents tried to *console* her but she was inconsolable.

More indirectly, but with an overtness not present in the text:

> My parents *cuddled* her and put her favourite teddy bear in her arms to *comfort* her, but she was *inconsolable*.

Now, there is an obvious semantic connection between *cuddling*, *comforting*, and *consoling*, but the predication *inconsolable* does more than conform to the linkage of a particular semantic chain: we understand it as an abbreviation of and substitute for something like '(She was) not consoled by the parental cuddling or by the comforting presence of the teddy bear'.

From punctuation to prosody

19.73 Our text is divided into paragraphs which in turn are divided into orthographic sentences, normally coinciding with the grammatical units of the same name, but not necessarily so. Note the sentence in lines 7–8 which consists of only a noun phrase. Sentences are divided into parts that may be marked punctuationally in various ways – semicolons, colons, commas, dashes. Although the semicolon normally terminates a clause, the generalization is insecure and there are still fewer correlations between grammatical units and the textual units bounded by the other punctuation marks (*cf* App III.15).

The points at which a writer chooses to begin new paragraphs will vary from text to text and from writer to writer (*cf* 19.28). Each paragraph will have in some sense a self-contained unity, it is true. Thus the first paragraph of our sample text deals with the family commotion caused by the dream; the second with the content of the dream; the third with the event that parallels the dream. But the point at which a paragraph comes to an end has by no means a sense of finality; in our text, indeed, the first paragraph ends in a way that frustrates the reader's hopes and expectations. Equally, a new paragraph need in no way herald a new topic; in our text, the third paragraph begins with a sentence that has exceptionally close linkage with the final sentence of the preceding paragraph, and many writers might well have preferred to postpone the new paragraph accordingly:

> . . . insisted that since she was still scared and weepy I accompany her all the way, and I was very glad I did.
>
> Near the school we came upon another tearful youngster . . .

Nonetheless, the actual points chosen to terminate the paragraphs are by no means casual, still less arbitrary. The writer has doubtless felt that the first sentence of his second paragraph has more connection with the sentences that follow than with those that have preceded. Moreover, having to inject some background material, its textual discreteness is displayed more readily by beginning a new paragraph at that point. But even if no background material had been needed and the next sentence after line 11 had begun:

> Some Fearsome Creature with huge jaws was . . .

the writer might still have felt it appropriate to begin a new paragraph, as though enforcing an expected pause after lines 10–11.

So too, beginning the third paragraph with *I was very glad I did* is readily justifiable. Not only does the alternative version suggested above entail a very long and rather clumsy end to the preceding paragraph, but again the typographic break at the point made in the original is textually superior in several ways. The gladness belongs to the content of the third paragraph and not the second: contrast an alternative wording, *I was perfectly happy to agree* which would more readily have belonged to the second paragraph. Moreover, this third paragraph is to be concerned as much with a change in the narrator's views as with the dog episode; and as the paragraph is to end with *I* as subject, it is fitting that it should so begin also. In addition, as with the division between the first and second paragraphs, this is a suitable point for a suspense-enhancing break.

The sentence units

19.74 As with paragraphs, so with sentences: their limits are determined by the author in accordance with his idea of the text's shape. There are two fairly striking indications of this in the present text. Lines 5–6 (*She sobbed . . . had been dreaming*) could have been three sentences and the writer made it one. Lines 7–8 (*It had obviously . . . usually suffered*) could have been one sentence (as grammatically it has to be understood) and the writer made it two. But again as with the paragraphs, the decision made on the sentence division is readily interpreted as purposeful. In putting a period after *a nightmare* in line 7, the writer gives more weight to this noun phrase and obliges us to consider the full significance of the word 'nightmare': the reader will not pass over it lightly, treating it merely as a vague hyperbole. The effect on the *And*-sentence that follows is equally great: again the separation forces us to treat it separately and to read it as though in fuller form: '*Moreover*, it was a much worse nightmare than . . .'.

The converse process of punctuating three possible 'sentences' as one in lines 5–6 is justified on several grounds. The three parts constitute a single unit, developing the *screams* (line 4) and the reason for there being no more sleep that night. Grouping as a single sentence also brings out the triadic structure (*cf* 19.8) which would have been blurred if they had been punctuated as separate sentences, depending only on the common subject *she* to distinguish the triad from the next following sentence. On the other hand, if the three parts had been separated by commas instead of semicolons (*cf* App III.6*ff*), too great a homogeneity would have been imposed.

Consider now the two finite clauses in the text that are introduced by *but*. The first (line 20) runs straight on without even a comma; the second (line 26) begins a new sentence. In the first case, the two clauses have the same subject and this justifies a closer textual relation to some extent. But a probably stronger factor is the psychological one: the writer is able to imply that the 'giving in' is directly conditional upon the child being accompanied to school. By contrast, in the second case (line 26), not merely are the subjects of the two clauses different but the concessive link between them is more oblique (*cf* 19.80).

While only one sentence is divided into units with semicolons, the comma occurs rather frequently. In general, its use is unremarkable, indeed conventional (*cf* App III.6*ff*), but in one or two instances both its presence and its absence are of some interest. Despite their similarity in form, position, and function (in being subject-oriented), *Reluctantly* in line 19 and *secretly* in line 27 have different relations with their contexts (*cf* 19.80), and this is endorsed by the punctuation used. But it would be false to suggest that there must be convincing textual reasons behind every punctuational distinction: though possessing considerable discriminatory potential, the comma is especially prone to careless and inconsistent use. For example, there seems no good reason for the absence of a comma after some of the initial adverbials, such as the one in lines 15–16. But the same is not true for the commas after *But* (line 26) and *And* (line 27); justified by the parenthetic comment clauses, the commas conveniently emphasize the converse effect of these two conjunctions, encouraging a pause or even a nuclear focus in reading. *Cf* 19.29 Note.

One minor point that must undoubtedly be deliberate is the use of initial capitals for *Fearsome Creature* and *Monster* (lines 16 and 18). Bearing in mind the conventions in this respect (*cf* App III.29), we must suppose that the writer's intention is to imply the unique, extra-generic nature of the creature in the dream: unique enough to merit the capitals suggestive of proper names. There is also, no doubt, the ironic suggestion of the grotesque importance the creature assumed in the child's mind.

Prosodic realization

19.75 From time to time in this book and especially in this chapter, we have used such clumsy expressions as 'speaker/writer' for the originator and 'hearer/reader' for the receiver of a text. The inelegance is perhaps justified if it has helped to keep both oral and written realizations of language in mind. We shall later look at texts that originated (and had their sole existence) in speech, and at others that originated (and have their main existence) on paper. But regardless of their origin, it is vital to understand that aural reception is rarely if ever to be disregarded. We must insist afresh that even silent reading of a typically paper-originating text (such as an insurance document) demands the silent assignment of speech prosodies as an aid to understanding. It is only on rare occasions that a punctuational device has no spoken analogue; initial capitals, as with *Fearsome Creature*, are perhaps among the exceptions, though even these could doubtless be expressed by ironic emphasis in speech. The careful writer makes his punctuation choices in the hope of giving his reader the cues necessary to assign the prosody that the writer would himself have used. For example, the use of semicolons in line 5 will induce us to read this as a triad and yet with more staccato separation of the members than if commas had been used. In other words, we are expected to impose some such prosody as this:

She |SÓBbed| she was |inconSÓLable| she |could not be in'duced
'even to 'tell us 'what she had been DRÈAMing| [1]

But cues to the most appropriate realization come not only or even chiefly from punctuation. They come pervasively from all aspects of lexical and grammatical selection and disposition. It will be our recognition of the semantics that will cause us to assign a narrower range of intonation (*cf* App II.20) on *secretly* in line 27 than on *Reluctantly* in line 19, in some way ironically miming the confidentiality of the confession that follows. Consider also the role played by the selection of and position assigned to the focusing subjuncts *only* in line 17 and *too* in line 18 (*cf* 8.116*ff*). We unhesitatingly realize the units concerned thus:

{and |only SHĚ| had the |power to SÀVE it| [2]
{the |Monster had 'some 'terrifying 'power over HÈR| |TÒO| [3]

Without the focusing subjuncts, we would not expect either pronoun to have a nucleus; replacement of noun phrases by pronouns normally connotes, indeed, that these repeated references need little or no prominence:

{and she had the |power to SÀVE it| [2a]
{the |Monster had 'some 'terrifying PÒWer over her| [3a]

If the author had been telling the story orally instead of writing it, he could have dispensed with the focusing items, or positioned them differently, or selected different ones; he would nonetheless have achieved the desired effect by putting nuclear focus where he wanted it. Thus:

{and |SHĚ| had the |power to SÀVE it| [2b]
{and |she aLŎNE| had the |power to SÀVE it| [2c]
{the |Monster had 'some 'terrifying 'power over HÈR| [3b]
{the |Monster 'also had 'some 'terrifying 'power over HÈR| [3c]

Features of grammar

Determiners and connective reference

19.76 In our consideration of the text so far, it has been rather artificial to remain silent on grammatical devices, because it is so clear that they inescapably interact with all the other linkage features. To cite just one example: in 19.72, we noted the lexical relation between *a school friend* and *this boy* (line 12). But in fact the lexical link in this instance is significantly preceded by grammatical deixis (*this*) and the whole is embedded in the noun phrase *this boy's parents*. We see the relevance of these grammatical points when we note the relative prosodic weight assigned to the three constituents:

'this ˌboy's "parents

The noun-phrase structure assigns greatest prominence to the head, rightly, since this is the new information feature (*cf* 19.84); least is assigned to *boy*, which thus conveys the impression of being a lexical repetition, having the role of merely indicating the friend's sex; *this* is intermediate in weight as being the effective carrier both of connection between the two noun phrases and of contrast between the two sets of parents and between the two friends, 'my sister' and 'the boy'. Different grammatical choices with the same lexical items would achieve very different results:

the parents of this boy
the parents of the boy
the boy's parents
a boy's parents

In several instances, demonstratives, definite articles, and possessives have anaphoric reference to noun phrases previously introduced with indefinites. Thus *the poor child* of lines 7–8 links back to *a child* in line 1; *my sister* of line 15 and elsewhere links back to *one of my sisters* [= *a sister of mine*] in line 1. Other instances: *a little kitten* ~ *his pet* ~ *the kitten* ~ *the kitten* (lines 12–24); *a school friend* ~ *this boy* (line 12); *some Fearsome Creature* ~ *the Monster* (lines 16–18); *another tearful youngster* ~ *her friend* (lines 22–23). The treatment of *dream*(*s*) is different in a way that is interestingly significant for the structure of the whole text. The subject is introduced with a plural noun phrase but indefinite as one would expect: *bad dreams* (lines 1–2). From that indefinite plurality we focus upon one specific dream, first mentioned in nominal form in line 7, again indefinite as we would expect: *a nightmare*. The next time it is mentioned in nominal form, it is of course made definite: *my sister's dream* (lines 15–16). The narrative ends with placing this back again in the whole class of indefinite *dreams* (line 26), which forms an effective link back to lines 1–2, thus conveying the 'stacklike unity' to which we alluded in 19.70.

But there are other exceptions to the simple indefinite–definite progression. Reference has already been made (*cf* 19.70) to the situational use of *the* in *the teacher* and *the caretaker* (lines 13 and 14). Compare also *the day's classes*, line 15. A situational usage independent of a specific culture occurs with *the future* in line 27, and it is only through the semantic link with *never . . . meant nothing* (line 2) and *more convinced than ever* (line 26) that the phrase has a connective role.

Definiteness in several noun phrases is achieved by possessives, *eg*: *my parents* (line 9); *the kitten's life* (line 17); *the lad's arms* (line 24); and here again we are concerned with situational reference: we need look for no previous mention of *parents*, *life*, or *arms* since everyone can be expected to have them. But the possessives themselves of course perform a connective role: '*my* parents' with the '*I*' narrator; '*this boy's* parents' (line 12), '*the lad's* arms' with 'another tearful *youngster*' (line 23). In *her friend* (line 23), however, we have both types of connection: (*her*) *friend* ~ *a school friend* (line 12) and *her* (*friend*) ~ *my sister* (line 15).

With deverbal nouns, definiteness with possessives works in yet another way. The phrases *her screams* (line 4) and *my sister's help* (line 25) are not determined by earlier references to *screams* or *help*. We seem to be expected to understand covert existentials like '(There were screams from my sister and) *her screams* . . .', '(There was help from my sister and) *my sister's help* . . .' Alternatively, the definiteness may be interpreted as cataphoric with the nominalizations: '*the* screams *of my sister*', '*the* help *of my sister*'. There is an unquestionable cataphoric *the* in *the power to save it* (line 17). In two instances, definiteness is carried by demonstratives: *that night* (line 5) and *this boy* (line 12). Both are anaphoric and the latter is completely straightforward: *this boy* refers back to *a school friend*, and the use of *this* rather than *the* is merely to distinguish *this*, the more recently mentioned child, from the more central figure, *my sister*. The phrase *that night* (line 5) is more complicated. In the first place, the anaphoric reference is by no means explicit (*one occasion*, line 3); *cf* the discussion in 19.71. In the second place, the adjunct phrase admits no simple contrast (**the night*) and replacement of *that* would entail further alteration (*the whole night*, *for the night*). Yet the use of *that* as distinct from *the* is justified by the remoteness in time of the occasion in question from the 'now' of the narration.

Note Definiteness in *the whole house* (line 4) and *the children* (line 15) has clearly anaphoric effect, but through semantic implication: *cf* 19.71. Lines 1–4 imply a family household justifying *the . . . house*; *the children* are anticipated by *my sister* and *a school friend* as well as being implied by the school's existence.

Pro-forms and connective reference

19.77 First and second person pronouns differ from third in not normally having antecedent noun phrases (*cf* 12.47*ff*). *I* and *you* operate in most texts as they do in everyday conversation in being the most direct form of connection between speaker and hearer. But in the text being analysed the *I* is complicated in having a double reference – the adult narrator, overt only in the second sentence, and himself at an earlier period: himself as brother and son in a family (*my sister, my parents,* passim; *none of us,* line 4); himself as actor in the story he is narrating. Though for the most part the roles of narrator and actor are simply distinct, it is not always clear when reference is to the one rather than to the other, and inevitably, this equivocation is caught up in tense. Thus it never emerges (and is irrelevant to the story) whether *one of my sisters* in line 1 implies 'I *have* sisters' or 'I *had* sisters'. Nor is it entirely clear (*cf Fig* 19.78) whether the concluding 'I was no longer' applies only to the *I* actor (*ie* to the period HC) or whether it also applies to the *I* narrator (*ie* to the period HA). The use of *Boylike* in line 3 is partly to distinguish the two age-values of *I* (as well as to establish the sex). It should be noted in passing that a diachronic/synchronic complexity with *I* arises whether a text is fictional or factual.

Most of the other pronouns in the text are straightforwardly anaphoric, but the more striking are the *she/her* references which (from *one of my sisters,* line 1) form a strong thread that binds the entire text. Other anaphoric references:

bad dreams . . . they	(line 2)
this boy . . . him . . . his	(lines 12*ff*)
his pet . . . it	(line 14)
the kitten's life . . . it	(line 17)
my parents . . . they	(line 20)
a rather vicious dog . . . it	(lines 23–25)

With others the antecedent is less obvious. The *us* of line 4 connects with the singular noun phrase *the whole house* earlier in the sentence, where (as object of *awoke*) this is not the ordinary inanimate but a collective in which *house* means 'household', the semantic plurality being endorsed by *whole.* The 1st person involvement in the pronoun *us* is justified by *my* in line 1; its plurality by the implied conjunction of *I, one of my sisters,* and (a little later, as we expect) *my parents.*

The antecedent of *this* in line 9 is not a noun phrase at all but the clause *my parents decided she should stay home* (*cf* 19.47), while the *it* that begins the next sentence is that special cataphoric use that enables us to make an item (in this case the time adjunct *then*) rhematic in the first part of the cleft sentence (*cf* 18.26*ff*). Another instance of *it* is less clear: *It had obviously been a nightmare* (line 7). Superficially, it might be anaphoric to the interrogative *what* in the preceding indirect question. Compare:

A: *What* have you got there?
B: I don't know the proper name for *it,* but I think *it* is called an ammeter.

But that would imply the scarcely acceptable 'She had been dreaming a nightmare'. Perhaps we have something more like the prop *it* of 'It's snowing', 'Isn't it cold?' Alternatively, the antecedent might be the whole clause *what she had been dreaming,* covertly nominalized as *the dream,* and this is perhaps the best interpretation, though there is the more remote possibility that the reference of *it* is much more general: 'the cause of all her trouble, the screams and the sobbing'. In this interpretation, we would see *it* as cataphoric in an incomplete cleft sentence:

> *It* had obviously been a nightmare *that had upset her.*

There are three other types of pro-form to consider in this text. In line 7, *one* stands for and replaces the noun which is head of the preceding noun phrase *a nightmare*. Another instance of *one* (line 1), together with its negative *none* (line 4), is more complex. Both forms are equivocal between their numerical and partitive indefinite-pronominal functions. Compare:

> one of my sisters ~ two of my sisters
> none of us ~ one of us ~ two of us

beside:

> one of my sisters ~ a sister of mine
> none of us ~ some of us

But it is in their partitive function that they play a connective role in the text, *one* anticipating *she* in line 2, *none* in a parallel but inverse way connecting with the preceding reference to *the whole house* (line 4).

The second type to mention is the predication pro-form *did* in line 22, connecting with the end of the preceding paragraph by replacing the predication *accompany her all the way*.

Thirdly, there is a rather similar use of some correlative expressions. A comp-element (*cf* 15.63*ff*) is usually followed by complementation introduced by *as* or *than*; there is an example in lines 7–8: *a much worse one than the poor child usually suffered*. But the complementation may be left implicit (*cf* 19.52). For example, in lines 9–10 we have *this upset her still more*, and just as *this* is a pro-form for the preceding clause, so *still more* requires us to understand something like *than her nightmare had done*. Again, in the final sentence the *so* has a totally ellipted correlative (*as I had been*) which has its connections right at the beginning of the narrative where *I was very scornful* connotes 'I was sure that dreams had no significance'.

Note A striking instance of *I* being used with reference to an individual at different periods is essential to the structure of Dan Jacobson's novel *The Rape of Tamar* (1970) where *I* is both the narrator, aware of contemporary addressees (*you*), but necessarily aware also – as the ghost of King David's nephew thousands of years earlier – of a temporal, locational, and cultural gulf separating the *I* whose memoirs are the point of the novel. On the references to time, *cf* 19.78; note also '*this* part of the world' and *cf* 19.31. Addressing the present-day reader:

> ... allow me to introduce myself. My name is Yonadab.
> Not a common name nowadays; at least in this part of the world. But some of you, a few of you, will have heard of me ... As I was saying, I am (or was) Yonadab ...

Tense and narrative structure

19.78 The narrator is *I*, giving a ready-made orientation (*cf* 19.15) to the hearer/reader, and a presumed identity with the 'here' and 'now'. Note *so far as I can remember* in line 4 and *as you can imagine* in line 26, where the present tenses relate precisely to this here and now shared by the narrator and his hearer/reader. But the narrative as a whole of course relates temporally to the past and the narrative 'stage' is set for this in the opening sentence: *was, could, meant* are endorsed by the opening adverbial *as a child* which carries the implication that the sister is no longer a child; that the event is in the past but within living memory (at least the narrator's). Within this past, the narrative focuses upon a very short time span of perhaps nine hours and the general progression is straightforward: from the beginning of the period (*awoke*) to the end of the incident with the dog (*managed to chase it away*). But when we look at the text more closely we find considerable complexity, with several points and periods of time involved and some switches in the temporal order. The time structure can be represented as in *Fig* 19.78.

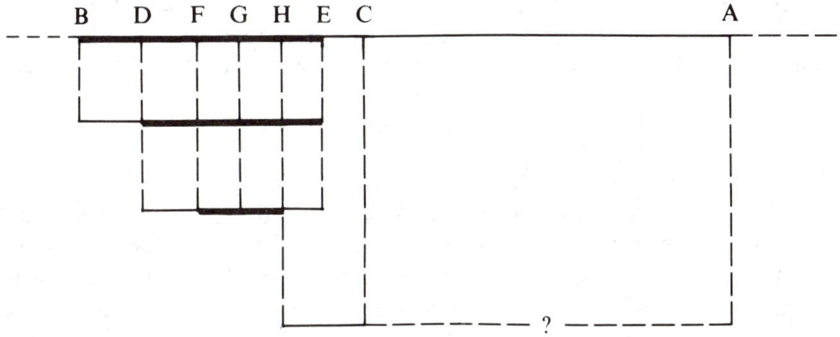

Fig 19.78

The *point A* is the 'now' shared by narrator and audience (*so far as I can remember*, line 4, applies to this point). The *period B* to *C* covers the sister's childhood and (so far as this text is concerned) is coterminous with her troubled dreams: the period of *was . . . troubled* and *could never be persuaded* (lines 1 and 2). The text implies at first that it was coterminous too with *I was very scornful* (line 3), but the point of the final sentence is to challenge this. Within *B* to *C*, another relevant stretch of time is involved: *D* to *E* covers the period when the school friend took his kitten with him every day (lines 12 to 15). It is within this sub-stretch *D* to *E* that the main events of the narrative take place, and we are predominantly involved in the *period* from *F* to *H*: from *F*, when the girl's screams awoke the family (line 4), to *H*, when the dog was chased off (line 25). And, unlike *BC* and *DE*, *FH* is less treated as a stretch of time than as a series of point-to-point events, with some emphasis upon *point G*, breakfast time.

Yet we manage to understand the different types of time reference in terms of largely undifferentiated past-tense verb forms. This applies even to the passage when the narrator interrupts events at *G* to supply background information (lines 12–15) relating to the *DE* period which will be essential to our understanding of the dream: *had* and *were* (lines 12, 13) refer to a span and *went* (line 15) to an iterative series, all sharply different from *upset* and *was coaxed* (lines 9 and 10).

Moreover, when the content of the dream is narrated, the past tenses in *was threatening*, *had* (lines 16*f*) relate not to *G* but to an earlier point, namely just before *F*. The only exceptions to the undifferentiated past are significant. The past perfective is used in line 6 (*had been dreaming*) and line 10 (*had frightened*). Both are in indirect questions and obey the rules for backshift (*cf* 14.31) to distinguish between the time reference of the superordinate verbs (post-*F* and *G* respectively) and that of the subordinate verbs (both pre-*F*). Replacing past perfectives by past tenses here would have made it seem that the girl *was dreaming* at the same time as she *could not be induced*, and that something *was frightening* her at the same time as she *was coaxed*.

One final point of interest. In the penultimate sentence, the past tenses refer clearly to point *H* in the narrative; but those in the final sentence refer to a span that begins at *H* and stretches to *C* or possibly even to *A*. It is perhaps significant that at the point where the time reference of the past tenses is switched, the narrator interposes the clause *as you can imagine* (line 26), not merely reestablishing the link with the here and now of *A* but helping to imply that the remaining past tenses connect the end of the adventure (*H*) with the present time.

The part played by marked aspect and voice

19.79 (a) ASPECT: The main uses of progressive aspect that form striking links relate to the dream ('what she *had been dreaming*', line 6); to the monster in the dream which '*was threatening* the kitten's life' (line 16); and to the corresponding dog next day which '*was jumping up and trying* to molest the kitten' (line 24). These progressive forms not merely link with each other but form a textual contrast with the accompanying punctual verbs which are aspectually unmarked; for example, *awoke* (line 4); *begged* (line 19); *gave in* and *insisted* (line 20); *came upon* (line 22); *managed* (line 25).

The occurrence of marked habitual aspect, though slighter, is also significant. At the point where the narrator has to interrupt the account of temporally sequential events to give necessary background information (lines 12–15), we have to be aware that the past tenses now have a different value; *cf* 19.78. The two verb phrases most relevant to the plot in this sentence are therefore marked for aspect and at the same time thus linked together: 'the teacher *used to allow her to bring* her pet to school and the caretaker *used to look after* it'.

(b) VOICE: Both morphologically and distributionally, the passive is the marked voice in relation to the active, and in consequence our attention is drawn to its use. There is a striking density of passives in this text. Their role in information processing in specific clauses and sentences will be the concern of 19.83. Our interest here is the part they play in the text as a whole. They are clearly associated with 'my sister' who is repeatedly the subject of passive verb phrases and indeed in almost no instance is she the subject of a transitive verb in the active voice. At the outset, we are told that she 'was troubled', that she 'could never be persuaded'. In the middle she was begging 'to be allowed'. At the end she 'was more convinced than ever', and the lowness of *convinced* on the passive gradient (towards adjectival status: *cf* 3.74*ff*; note also *scared*, line 20; *inconsolable*, line 5) does not diminish the strength of this final link in the continuous presentation of an 'affected' victim. Line 4 is interesting confirmation of this. If the narrator had said that

'She awoke the whole house with her screams', this might have implied an unwanted agentiveness: so it was *her screams* that awoke the house.

Note The adjective *inconsolable* is passive not only in meaning (*cf* App I.40) but in being juxtaposed and contrasted (*even*) with a formal passive in the next clause.

The cohesive role of adverbials

19.80 As we would expect in a narrative involving a sequence of events, time adverbials have a considerable role. In line 3, the sentence adjunct *on one occasion* (*cf* 8.36, 8.55) picks out the significant period for this text from the general time span (*BC* in *Fig* 19.78) in which this period is located; it is thus linked to but contrasted with *endlessly* and *never* in the preceding sentence. In turn it looks forward to the corresponding time-position adjunct, *that night* (line 5, *cf* 8.55). *By breakfast time* in line 8 takes us to the next temporal point to be distinguished, and in line 10 (still within the span (*cf* 8.57) covered by breakfast time) the adjunct *then* links back across an intervening sentence to the point at which the parents made the decision about staying home. For the rest, the progress of the narrative is managed without time adverbials, but it should be noted that the place adjunct *near the school* (line 22) is effectively temporal as well, marking the change of both place and time after the breakfast scene. In a similar way, within the background intermission of lines 12–15, the direction adjuncts (*cf* 8.39*ff*) *to school* and *home* look back to the time-duration adjunct *all day*, marking beginning and ending points (the *until* clauses of lines 14*f*) of the 'all day' span.

The course of the narrative depends in fact as much on place-sequences as on time-sequences. There are two polar locations, home and school, and references to these are frequent: (*stay*) *home* (line 9); (*bring* . . .) *to school* (line 14); (*went*) *home* (line 15); (*go*) *to school* (line 19); *Near the school* (line 22). Between these last two adjuncts, we find *all the way* (line 21), which elliptically links both: 'all the way (to school)' and '(on the way) near the school'.

Adverbial linkage is by no means limited to time and space. The second sentence begins with an adverbial verbless clause of respect (8.85; realized by the adjective *boylike*) which is obviously linked to the comparable item that begins the text, *As a child*, yet in balanced contrast to it: according to traditional stereotypes, a girl is easily frightened, a boy is not. The focusing subjunct (*cf* 8.116*ff*) *even* in line 6 links this clause with the previous one: 'not merely could she not be consoled, she could not *even* be induced . . .' Another focusing subjunct, *only* in line 17, both helps linkage with the preceding clause and also underlines the contrast between them. There is a further contrast with the following clause that is again pointed by a focusing subjunct, *too* in line 18. The concessive conjunct (*cf* 8.136*ff*) *Yet* in line 9 again provides a close link with what has immediately preceded, as does the inferential conjunct *So* in line 17. The additive conjunct *as an added terror* (line 18) links the *although*-clause back to the fearsome threat of line 16 as well as itself being lexically linked – rather obtrusively – to the object in the *although*-clause. The disjunct *obviously* (*cf* 8.121*ff*) in line 7 is interestingly equivocal in its relations (*cf* the discussion of the clause concerned; 19.77). It invites connection with the hearer/reader ('You will think it obvious'), as well as working as a disjunct with respect to the participants in the narrative ('we thought it obvious'). But it has an additional, textual function, in working as an inferential-summative conjunct with reference to the seriousness implied in the previous sequence of clauses: 'So, obviously, it must have been a nightmare'.

Although it is natural to think of adverbials at *I* position in a clause (*cf* 8.14*f*) as having a linking role with what has preceded, and thus being thematic (*cf*: *In my sister's dream* in line 15, *Near the school* in line 22), there are two interesting exceptions in this text. The two subject-oriented adverbials (*cf* 8.92*ff*), *Reluctantly* in line 19 and *secretly* in line 27, are in a sense counter-conjoining and they derive their adversative, concessive force in part through thus interrupting what would otherwise be a natural and logical sequence:

> The child begged to be allowed: the parents gave in.
> She was more convinced than ever: and I no longer disagreed.

But in each case where we have now entered colons, there is a caveat in the actual text. In the first case, *Reluctantly* (*ie*: '*although* with reluctance') constitutes a link, not with the preceding clause but with the reasons for parental anxiety which were presented in lines 4*ff* and which led to the decision of line 9, now to be reversed in the clause that follows *Reluctantly*. In the second case, *secretly* takes us right back to line 3: the reversal of the narrator's view of dreams has to be seen not only as a consequence of the sequence of events but as a reproach for his earlier scorn: *secretly* is an ironic parallel to *boylike* positionally, and invites us to see an (*although*) *secretly* as occasioned by a 'boylike' fear of losing face. The irony was in fact anticipated by the disjunct *of course* in line 3. This last example already illustrates the way in which adverbials can help shape a text's general structure. More directly in this connection, however, we have the adverbials relating to the consistency of the child's predicament throughout the whole *BC* period (*cf* 19.78) in which the narrative is placed. The text begins with the girl being '*endlessly* troubled' and '*never* . . . persuaded'. It ends with her being 'more convinced than *ever*', and it is the narrator who is *no longer* the same. Between these two points, several adverbials sustain the theme of continuity in addition to their immediate contextual role: *usually* (line 8), *still more* (line 10), *as an added terror* (line 18), *as usual* (line 19), *still scared* (line 20).

Coordinate and subordinate clauses

19.81 The text comprises nearly fifty finite clauses, approximately half of which are independent. We begin with such an independent clause, and – disregarding this one, since by definition it cannot be linked to a preceding one – thereafter a majority of the independent clauses follow other clauses paratactically. The minority of independent clauses formally linked to preceding clauses (seven by *and*, two by *but*) thus present some contrast with the general pattern, and it is worth considering this briefly. As we saw in 19.5, asyndeton is open and uncommitted: there may be a quite intimate connection, and the very openness can fuel our expectations of more to come; for example, lines 5–6:

> She sobbed; she was inconsolable; . . .

On the other hand, the following part may be merely paratactic, comprising what is virtually a new topic. Compare the clause that begins line 12, or the sequence in line 22:

> I was very glad I did. Near the school we came upon . . .

By contrast, coordination with *and* or *but* is relatively committed, implying a very close connection, consequential in the case of *and*, contrastive in the case of *but*. Moreover, especially with *and*, we have the converse of asyndeton's openness in that there is an implied *completeness* with the *and*-member; it is of some interest that in a list of three or more items, all but the last will usually be uttered asyndetically, whereas the last is preceded by *and* (*cf* 13.1, 13.22*ff*, App III.11). These considerations are relevant in a straightforward way to the coordinated units linked by *and* in lines 4, 12, 14, 17, 25, and with specially striking force in line 27. But we need go no further than the opening sentence in the text (lines 1–2). The parts are not merely made to seem relevantly connected: they seem to have a completeness and finality about them – and this is then borne out by the text as a whole. Equally rightly, the sentence beginning '*Boylike* . . .' (line 3) underscores the boy's detachment from his sister's troubles by being asyndetic.

The justification for the close but antithetic linkage in line 20 is obvious, but it is interesting to see how *but* endorses the *Reluctantly* with which the first member begins and is endorsed by the *since*-clause that follows. The need for *but* is just as clear in line 26. Despite the fact that *all was well* and the kitten was safe (which might have justified 'And therefore she was less afraid of dreams thereafter'), we are invited to reflect that the dog's attack has mirrored the attack by the dream monster so closely that the event has actually confirmed the child's fear of dreams. (It is to be noted that the initial *But* of line 26 is followed by significant address to the hearer/reader: *as you can imagine*.)

The fact that about half of the finite clauses in the text are subordinate might suggest that, unlike coordinate clauses, subordinate ones are so common as to call no attention to themselves. But we must distinguish subordination where the grammar gives us little or no choice from subordination available for deliberate selection. In the first category, we have clauses in verb complementation (*cf* 16.30*ff*), and there are more of these (seven) than of any other type of finite subordinate clause in the text: for example, *that they meant nothing* (line 2), *what she had been dreaming* (line 6). In the second category, we have primarily the five adverbial clauses, and we shall now look at some of these to note the effect that choice has had. In lines 8–9, there is the sequence:

> . . . she seemed so ill that my parents decided she should stay at home.

Several alternatives were available. The two clauses could have been independent and asyndetic:

> . . . she seemed (very) ill; my parents decided . . .

independent and coordinated:

> . . . she seemed (very) ill and my parents decided . . .

independent but with an explicit conjunct:

> ... she seemed (very) ill; in consequence, my parents decided ...

It requires very little consideration to conclude that all of these alternative versions cause an undesirable severance between the two parts which are interdependently connected, just as the original version makes them seem. Moreover, this original version has another advantage: it alone injects the correlation between the degree of the illness and the decision to keep the girl from school.

19.82 Let us now look at the concessive adverbial clause in lines 17–18:

> ... only she had the power to save it. So although as an added terror the Monster had some terrifying power over her too, she begged to be allowed to go to school as usual.

Alternatives avoiding subordination are possiblc:

(i) ... only she had the power to save it. So she begged to be allowed to go to school as usual. Yet as an added terror the Monster had some terrifying power over her too.

(ii) ... only she had the power to save it. Yet as an added terror the Monster had some terrifying power over her too. Nonetheless, she begged to be allowed to go to school as usual.

The (ii) alternative is multiply unsatisfactory; it necessarily involves two concessive conjuncts, though the second cannot escape seeming like a desperate evasion of the obvious repetition, *yet*; and this version loses the resultative conjunct *so* which formed a logical link in the original. The (i) alternative is somewhat better than (ii), but in postponing the clause that has concessive meaning, the decisiveness of the original is lost and there is perhaps even an implication that the girl had second thoughts after begging to go to school. The original not merely avoids the defects of both (i) and (ii), but by interrupting the *so*-constituent and interposing the *although*-clause, it manages to capture the balancing of pro and con that preceded the girl's decisive and brave request.

Similar arguments hold for the use and position of the *since*-clause in lines 20–21. If it had been placed after, instead of within, the *that*-clause, the reason for the parents' insistence might have seemed relatively incidental.

The choice of a nonfinite clause in line 23 is also of interest. A different version with an independent clause might have seemed attractive in making the sequence less lengthy and clumsy:

> Near the school we came upon another tearful youngster, her friend. He was being frightened and harassed by a rather vicious dog that was jumping up ...

But this has the disadvantage of forcing a separation between the encounter with the boy and an account of what was happening to him. The version in the text is superior in that the use of the nonfinite clause (as a nonrestrictive postmodifier in a noun phrase of which *youngster* is head) has the effect of the narrator and his sister seeing the friend and the dog's attack as a single complex unit.

Information structure

19.83 Many of the features that we have been considering seem to have been selected by the narrator in order to place the semantic and prosodic climax of clauses where they would be most effective. Usually this has meant end focus (*cf* 18.11) in clauses, in the manner outlined in 19.12. One interesting instance of this is in line 7:

It had |obviously been a NÌGHTmare|

Here, end focus on what is undoubtedly a rhetorically satisfying item has been achieved even at the expense of a rather vague use of the subject pronoun *it* (*cf* 19.77).

In 19.79, it was noted that the above-average use of the passive had the effect of drawing attention to the 'affected' status of the central character. But undoubtedly the passive has a much stronger role in information processing. In the opening sentence, there are two textually important noun phrases, both of them indefinite: *one of my sisters* and *bad dreams.* In principle, either could have been thematic and either rhematic: both are equally 'new' and both are very much the concern of the narrative as a whole in that the narrator wishes us to know more about the little girl as well as to consider the nature of dreams. But he rightly makes *one of my sisters* thematic (anyone may have sisters; bad dreams are more newsworthy), and his choice of phrasing, in contrast to *a sister of mine*, has the effect of implying that the hearer/reader already knew he had sisters. Though this choice of theme causes the selection of the relatively marked voice, the passive has the advantage not only of reaching an informational climax with *bad dreams* but of setting the tone from the outset in respect of the girl as 'affected'. In this instance, the passive has focused attention on the agent. Elsewhere, the passive has enabled the narrator to compress information by leaving the agency unspecified; *eg* lines 2, 6, 10. But although the narrator clearly finds the passive useful, there are equally noteworthy examples of its absence. In line 9, we have

Yet this upset her still more.

The subject of the immediately preceding clause is *she* and it would have been easy to have retained *she* as the next subject:

Yet she was still more upset by this.

But informationally this is inferior, ending as it does with a 'given' item (*this*) where the original ends with the degree adverbial, intensified by *still.*

19.84 Care in organizing information can also be seen in noun-phrase structures (*cf* 17.2*ff*). In several instances, we have genitive premodifiers which provide needed information but which allow prosodic focus upon the head:

this boy's parents (line 12)
the day's classes (line 15)
my sister's dream (line 15)
the kitten's life (line 17)
my sister's help (line 25)

Alternatives with postmodification (as in *the parents of this boy*; *classes for the day*; *the life of the kitten*) might have caused the focus to shift to the final item as in:

> the 'life of the "kitten

or – at best – have meant the focus being followed by anticlimactic afterthought:

> the "life of the 'kitten

A noteworthy resource in disposing information units is the use of initial 'scene-setting' adverbials (*cf* 8.15), as in:

> As a child . . . (line 1)
> On one occasion . . . (line 3)
> By breakfast time . . . (line 8)
> In my sister's dream . . . (line 15)
> Reluctantly . . . (line 19)
> Near the school . . . (line 22)

The information in such phrases is of sufficient weight to require an intonation nucleus, but as clause-initial the nucleus will normally be realized by a rise or fall-rise (*cf* App II.15*f*), thus both creating an expectation and forward-looking momentum, and also subordinating the information of these phrases to that of the clause rhemes that follow:

> |As a CHÍLD| . . . by 'bad DRÈAMS|

One sentence beginning with such an adverbial merits further attention. After *Near the school* in line 22, we have a verb phrase with notably low semantic content; (*we*) *came upon* is little more than a presentative device (*cf* 18.49) to introduce the focal point of the sentence: the friend in the course of being attacked. For reasons explored in 19.82, this focal point is presented as a single complex noun phrase with nonrestrictive postmodification. The postmodification itself makes use of a (nonfinite) passive, enabling rhematic weight to be given to the dog and at the same time structurally freeing this part of the nonfinite clause to accept its own postmodification in the form of a relative clause (*that was jumping* . . .).

Even our rather lengthy account of textual features (*cf* 19.70*ff*) has ignored several significant factors, such as modality (*should stay*, line 9; *accompany*, line 21; etc), and the connective role of adjectives such as *worse* in line 7, *added* in line 18. This very incompleteness of treatment, however, is a reminder of the indefinite complexity to be found in textual structure. We trust that the description offered and the points made will have demonstrated both this complexity and also the way in which grammatical features complement each other in conferring textual unity and in achieving a satisfying presentation.

Note The intensifier *still* functions in the text as a focusing subjunct ('even'). The part played in highlighting information by means of focusing items should be noted elsewhere in the text too: *even* (line 6); *only* (line 17); *too* (line 18).

Further illustrative texts

A personal letter

19.85 The following is the text of a handwritten letter from a middle-aged man to express thanks for hospitality. We reproduce the punctuation, capitalization etc, and we represent in italic what was underlined in the original.

> Dear Phyllis and Bob
>
> You really are the most marvellous of people. And the most charming of *hosts*. And the most enviable of *families*.
>
> Since of course envy is prominent among the Deadly Seven, you severely jeopardize my immortal soul every time you admit me to that unbelievably delightful family circle of yours. On the other hand, the Faust in me fully recognizes that your parties do wonders for my *body*!
>
> So, my sincerest thanks for yet another generous helping of good company, good talk, good drink, and good food. And may the New Year smile on your blessedly beautiful clan.
>
> Yours ever
>
> Jack

Note [**a**] The text depends upon two allusions: one to the Catholic Christian concept of there being Seven Deadly Sins, the other to the story of Faust who sold his soul to the Devil in return for temporal gain.

[**b**] The triadic structure of the first paragraph is made to seem spontaneous as well as weighty by the separate sentences and repeated coordinators, but the underlining of *hosts* and *families* as subsets of 'people' shows that the triad derives in fact from a bifurcation of the first part.

[**c**] There is a lexical link to the second paragraph, turning upon *enviable* (lightly used as a courteous compliment) and *envy* (ironically serious), the transition indicated by the concessive force of the conjunct *of course* in line 5; the second paragraph then moves from the joking mention of *soul* to *body*, ironically underlined as the more relevant in the context of good entertainment.

[**d**] The conjunct *so* (made weightier by the comma) links the second and third paragraph, returning to the main point of the first and of the letter as a whole. The expression 'generous helping' (line 13) is appropriate since it implies its normal use ('a generous helping of food'), justifying *food* being the last and climactic item in the coordinate string that follows.

[**e**] The phrase *your parties* (line 10) is a discourse reference (*cf* 19.46*ff*) to 'every time . . . circle of yours' (lines 7–9).

[**f**] The sequence in line 1 is conventional; *clan* in line 16 is a lexical variant on *family* (lines 3, 8), preceded by an alliterative premodifying phrase.

[**g**] The absence of punctuation at the opening and conclusion is informal and idiosyncratic.

Some paragraphs on food

19.86 This excerpt of a chapter on olives is from a book on cuisine written by a middle-aged woman for the nonspecialized family reader.

Before the war olives were imported in casks in the brine in which they were cured, and then packed on arrival into jars, which made them expensive. But the enormous increase during the last few years in the number of delicatessen shops throughout the country, and of delicatessen departments even in orthodox grocers' shops and supermarkets, means that nowadays we buy the larger part of our olive imports loose, which makes them much cheaper, usually about half the price.

You can buy olives of every shape and size like this – big green ones with a bite to them; little ones stuffed with pimento or anchovy, hazelnuts or onion; smooth, shiny, bitter black olives, and the crinkly, soft, fleshy ones; olives large and small, pointed or round, olives of every shade of green, brown, purple and black, and in flavour mild, sharp – or downright bitter like the special, and expensive, cracked olives from Cyprus.

In fact, the only olives you can't buy loose are the exquisite and expensive little *kalamata* olives from Greece, which are packed in oil and vinegar after curing, sharply incised down one side to allow this marinade to penetrate. These, considered by olive fanciers to be the finest of all, are only to be found in cans.

(Margaret Costa *Margaret Costa's Four Seasons Cookery Book* London: Sphere 1972)

Note [**a**] There is a three-fold temporal transition in the first paragraph: the thematic adjunct *Before the war* (line 1), the durational postmodifier *during . . . years* (line 3), and then – matching line 1 – an *I*-placed *nowadays* in line 6. The main contrast in time is indicated by the *But*-sentence.

[**b**] There are two relative clauses with discourse reference (*cf* 19.46*ff*), lines 1–2 and 7.

[**c**] Whereas the first sentence has a very short subject (*olives*, line 1), the second has an exceptionally long one, *the . . . increase . . . supermarkets* (lines 3–5).

[**d**] The second paragraph is linked to the first by *like this* (line 8) which relates to *loose* (line 6), the third to the second by the contrast between *you can't buy loose* (line 15) and *You can buy (loose)* in line 8.

[**e**] A number of passives occur, describing the fact but conveniently ignoring the agent: *cf* lines 1, 2, 9, 16, 17, 19; there is one instance where the agent is expressed (line 18) and where the passive allows this to be highlighted as well as permitting the clause to be nonfinite. Contrast 'These, which olive fanciers consider to be . . .'

[**f**] Participant involvement is expressed by the inclusive *we* (line 6) and rather informally by *you* (lines 8 and 15) which is probably addressed to the reader rather than being the still more informal indefinite (= 'one').

[**g**] Punctuation has an informal touch as well; the dash in line 8 heralds the long appositive list that takes up the rest of the paragraph, and another within this list preceding the climactic third of a triad of properties (line 13).

[**h**] The lexical item *olive* is used repeatedly, as a deliberate emblem of the profusion which is the subject matter of the second paragraph. Variety is provided (and indeed it is variety of olives that is being described), not only by the choice of lexical items describing the olives but by the varied syntax – notably the switch from premodifying triads of lines 10*f* to the postmodifying pairs in lines 11*f*.

[**i**] In lines 17–18, *this marinade* is interesting in being anaphoric, hypernymic (*cf* 19.24), yet tactfully informative: the reader is in effect told that 'oil and vinegar function as a marinade'.

From a formal speech

19.87 The remaining samples are from unscripted spoken texts filed in the Survey of English Usage archive. The transcription has been simplified and the material slightly abbreviated and edited (*eg* by omitting hesitation noises and syllable repetition) in order to make the excerpts more quickly and easily assimilable. We begin with the opening of an after-dinner speech (SEU S.11.2) to a large and distinguished gathering by the head of an institution (a man of about 60). Though prepared (in the sense that the content in general terms was thought out in advance), the speech was unscripted.

It's a |very CÚRious speech I've got to make|
I re|member last YÈAR| |when I SPÒKE on this
occÁSion| |SÀYing| that it was |really
a ↑very sig↑NǏFicant 'year this| because
it was the |year in which I didn't really have
to 'talk about "FÌNance| – we |had got
a de'velopment PRǑgramme| which had |come
aLÓNG| with the |whole idea of implementing
the Todd Report on medical eduCÁtion| and
de|velopments had occÚRRED| which |meant that
we were going to have a large scale BǓILDing
programme| in the |CÓLlege| – |which at that
TǏME| and |those PRÌCes| would have |been
five and a half MÍLlion| |to seven and a half
million PÒUNDS| – – |WÉLL| of |CÒURSE|
– |things have turned out very DÌFferently| it's
| been a CÙRious academic year up to date| – the
|first TÉRM| |that is to say in
MÍChaelmas| |ÓNwards| un|til NovÉMber| we |spent
our TÍME| |having CÀREfully prePÁRED| |all during
the SǓMmer| – – |in getting aGRÉEment| a|bout "↑how we
were going to "↑use the devÈLopment MÓNey| |which we'd
been GǏven| |by the GÒvernment| *m* |to ↑increase student
NÚMbers| to de"|velop in various di↑RĒCTions| – *m* |that was
what we did in the "↑FÌRST term| the |SÈCond TÉRM| of
|course we spent our ↑WHǑLE time| |making plans for
*q*con"↑TRÀCTion|*q* – be|cause of course the whole economic
CLÌmate| |had *f* totally ↑CHÀNGED| *f*

m . . . m: spoken with narrow pitch range
q . . . q: spoken breathily
f . . . f: spoken loudly

Note [**a**] Among the prosodic points of interest, attention might be drawn to the higher proportion of tone units ending with a rise (two dozen) than of those ending with a fall (one dozen). This is in sharp contrast to the two informal conversations of 19.88–9 (and to linguistic usage in general, where falling nuclei are more than twice as frequent as all other types added together; *cf* App II.17). The high ratio of rises is partly a function of personal style and partly a function of the style determined by the occasion: the need to make one's voice carry in a large company, the need to give the impression of inviting the audience's interest (*cf*: *well*, line 15) and of not seeming dogmatic. In part, however, the distribution reflects the general rhetorical structure of the 'prosodic paragraph'. Up to line 15, the speaker is talking about the assumptions on which past planning had been based; from line 16, we are told of the way in which the assumptions proved baseless; things have turned out *differently* (line 16) because the economy had *changed* (line 28), and the two quoted items significantly have falling nuclei. In this connection, note that the initial tone unit has a rising nucleus on *curious*; in line 17, we are reminded of this opening by the use again of *curious*, again carrying a nucleus despite its nonfinal and indeed premodifying status; but this time the nucleus is a fall. But even the second part, dealing with the change of fortunes, again postpones the critical conclusion by interposing a section on preparations (lines 18–24) that turned out to be wasted. And within the individual sections of each part, the pattern is to have a sequence of rises and fall-rises followed by a definitive fall. Note such falls at *finance* (line 6), *pounds* (15), *government* (23), *first* (25), *contraction* (27).

[b] We have mentioned in [a] that the prosody in part reflects the oratorical occasion. The style in question is commonly characterized by rather frequent and heavy nuclei, giving a distinctly deliberative impression to the succession of phrases; *cf* lines 19–20. The occasional unexpected nucleus is to be similarly explained; *spoke* (line 2), *saying* (3), *given* (23), above all *government* (23), for example. The level nucleus (on *directions*, line 24) is also characteristic of public speaking: it suggests an indefinitely long list, though in fact only one specific item is mentioned (the increase in student numbers).

[c] There is an interesting use of prosody to link and to contrast the three noun phrases with *term* as head (lines 18 and 25); in the formal reminder of the enumerative series, *cf* lines 23–26 in 19.90 where the prosodic contrast is similar. Note, however, the booster on *first* (25) and at other emotionally emphatic points (lines 4 and 26, for example).

[d] While the prosody is redolent of public speaking, the grammar seems to be almost self-consciously informal: the modal *got* (line 1) and perhaps especially the postposed appositive and identificatory *this* in line 4 (*cf* 18.59). The fact that the appositive is used offhandedly and not as genuinely emphatic, still less contrastive, is shown by its having less stress than the preceding noun head *year*. Compare:

He's an |odd CHÀP| |JÓHN| not a |bit like his BRŎTHer|

Informality is shown also by subjunct and conjunct usage (*really*, lines 3, 5; *well*, line 15; *of course*, lines 15, 25*f*, 27). A certain vagueness in syntactic relationship results from grammatical informality being used with the somewhat exaggerated prosody of oratory. Thus in line 6, *we had got* is merely existential, *come along* (lines 7*f*) is again existential (but also resultative), *the whole idea* (line 8) is an informal quantifier of purpose; in consequence, a short paraphrase of lines 6–9 might be 'The purpose of our development programme was to implement the Todd Report'; we might expect this to have two nuclei, one at *development programme*, the other at *Todd Report*, the only two informationally important points.

There is some vagueness too in the complementation of *we spent our time* (lines 19–20) by reason of two interposed tone units, though the prolonged silent hesitation (––) in line 21 warns us of the point at which complementation begins (*in getting agreement*).

Conversation among friends

19.88 A is a man, B a woman; both aged between 25 and 30 (SEU: S.2.13). The material is entirely unscripted and spontaneous.

A: |he's quite a good GÙY| and |I'm on quite good TÈRMS with him|
B: |YÊAH|
A: and I'm |sure I can DŎ him| for a |couple of weeks of unlicensed LÉAVE|
B: I |THÌNK| |most people coming back off CÓURSes| |CÀN|
A: |Ḿ| |SÓ| I |should be able to get at least THRĚE weeks|
B: |M̀| |M̀| – |WÊLL| we could |have aNÔTHer 'holiday|
A: |M̂|
B: because |Î shall have two weeks left| |TÔO|
A: I |rather fancy going down the LÒIRE| – |year after NÈXT|
B: |year after NÉXT|

A: |no NÈXT year| – |NÈXT year| – |YÈS| – for a |WÈEK|
B: [*speaking to a third person present*] |Kevin's a great PLÀNner|
he |has to have everything done in great DÈtail| be|fore
he'll emBÂRK on anything| |you SÉE| – – |hence his
absolute "↑HÒRror| when |we got ready to go to FRÁNCE|
and I |suddenly RÈALized| that in |all our great
PLÀNning| |I had taken down my little tin BÓX| to
my |MÙMmy| to |look ÂFTer| – and I'd |PÀCKED it|
|all full of all GÒodies| that |we couldn't leave
behind in the FLÀT| in|cluding the car ↑LÒGbook| –
so we |had to make a SPĚcial "|and the ÀUtoroute|
– so we |had to make a SPĚcial TRÌP| |down to
↑ÈPsom| to col|lect the bloody THÌNG| when we were |off
on our way to ↑FRÀNCE|

Note [**a**] In view of what was said in 19.64*f*, we draw attention to B's confirmatory *yeah* (line 3), *m* (9), A's *m* (11). By contrast, A's rise on *m* (7) is relatively interrogative ('Is that what you think?'), as is B's more sharply questioning repetition in line 14, answered by A correcting himself at once. A's third tone unit in line 15 (*yes*) is partly a final confirmation that B was right to question him, partly an indication that what follows can resume the interrupted statement: 'I rather fancy going down the Loire (next year) for a week'. In line 18, B involves a third participant with *you see*. Conveying excitement helps to involve another participant, and we note the boosters at *horror* (19), *Epsom* (27), *France* (28); this last being in ironic parallel to *Epsom*.

[**b**] Informality is shown by lexical items (*guy* in line 1, *do* in 4, *Mummy* in 22, *goodies* in 23, *bloody* in 27, etc), by grammatical features like omission of article (*year after next*, 13), zero subordinator in nominal clauses (4, 6 – but with *that* in line 20 where *realized . . . I had taken* is interrupted by an adverbial).

[**c**] Among other aspects of informality are the clear signs of unworried spontaneity. For example, the repeated *all* in line 23, resulting in a loose phrasing that the speaker might have intended to be 'all full of the goodies' or 'full of all the goodies'. Again, the anacoluthon in line 25 necessitated by B's remembering to mention the autoroute document which in turn makes her recapitulate the interrupted clause in line 26.

[**d**] The downtoners (*quite* twice in line 1, *rather* 13) and intensifying items (*great* 16, *absolute* 19, *bloody* 27) characterize conversation that is both informal and intimate. Note that *great* (*planner*) in 16 means 'enthusiastic' but *great* (*detail*) in 17 means 'minute'; *great planning* in 20*f* is an ironic lexical link with line 16 but this time uses *great* more in the sense of 'large-scale'. The expectation that an intimate companion sympathetically makes the semantic shifts enables a speaker to dispense with the search for the *mot juste*.

Telephone conversation

19.89 A and B are husband and wife respectively, both aged between 60 and 65 (SEU: S.7.2d). As in 19.88, the material is entirely unscripted and spontaneous.

B: |LÌsten| |Mother's CLÒCK| is |running ↑quarter
of an hour SLŎW| I've |slightly moved it to a faster
posĬTion| but |how do I move the HÀNDS| does
|that FĂCE| |spring ŎFF|
A: |NÒ| |NÒ| you |look on the BÂCK|
B: the |three little brown SCRĔW things|
A: |no NÒ| if |you just |which clock do you
MÈAN| the e|LÈCtric one|
B: the e|LÈCtric| |YÉAH|

A: |WÈLL| you |unHÓOK it|
B: |YÉS| I've |done THÁT| and I've |moved it to slightly to a ↑fast posÍTion|
A: to a ''|FÀST position|
B: |YÈS| because it's *q*''|LÒSing*q* a quarter of an HÓUR|
A: |YÈAH| |but ↑if you want to ''↑RĔGulate it|
B: |I've ↑↑RÈGulated it| *m* I |want to 'move the *q*''HÀNDS|*mq*
A: |well there's a ''↑KNÒB| I |can't sort of remember eXĂCTly| but it's
B: |Ǐs there a knob|
A: |WÈLL| there's |obviously ''↑SÒME means of DÓing it| you |don't have to take the FRŎNT off|
B: |ÔH| I |haven't been able to loCÀTE the KNÓB| |òk| I'll |have a closer LÒOK|

q . . . q: falsetto
m . . . m: spoken with 'spiky' rhythm

Note [**a**] Prosody is used to make *Mother's clock* in line 1 both new (as though it were predicative) and also the subject of a sentence. B uses a high booster in line 16 to justify the lexical repetition in the context of A's apparent obtuseness. Note also the boosters at *if* (15), *knob* (18), *some* (21). Excited emphasis is conveyed also by falsetto voice in lines 14 and 17, and by an impatiently 'spiky' rhythm in 16*f*. 'New' and 'given' are clearly polarized by prosody in lines 18 and 20: in the former *knob* has a nucleus, in the latter it has not.

[**b**] Informal approximations are expressed in *things* (6) ['things like screws'], *sort of . . . exactly* (18*f*), *just* (7). Other aspects of informality include the transitivity of *does that face spring off?* (3*f*), meaning 'Is one supposed to be able to make the face spring off?'; the anacoluthon in line 7 as A wonders if he has the right clock in mind; A's repetition of the prepositional phrase (13), with shift of nucleus to show his uncomprehending surprise; the equivocal use of *you* (5, 10, 22) between reference to B and indefinite reference (in line 7, the first *you* is equivocal, the second obviously refers to B). B's *How do I move the hands* exemplifies a use of *I* which is comparably equivocal between 1st person and indefinite (*cf* 6.2*ff*) as well as an informal obligational modality (*cf* 4.49). The question is equivalent to 'How is one to move the hands?'

[**c**] A begins with *well* three times: the first and second (lines 10 and 18) indicate that he has understood and is beginning a confident reply, but the former is made more deliberate and attention-seeking by occupying a tone unit; the third (21) is almost the converse, 'I don't care WHÀT you say' and its forceful dismissiveness is emphasized by its having a separate tone unit.

[**d**] B's peremptory-sounding imperative *Listen* (line 1) is used between friends as an indication that the speaker has something interesting or urgent to say; it is not accompanied by *please* in this usage.

Leaving a recorded message

19.90 A and B are conscious of being strangers to the person who will eventually listen to the recorded message; C seems to be very familiar with the office he is telephoning. All the speakers are men, ranging in age between 30 and 50 (SEU: S.9.3), and it is likely that their messages are prepared, perhaps with written notes on what they intend to say.

A: my |NÁME| is |GRÀNGE| |g r a n g É| |ÁND| I'm |speaking from ↑National GÀS Board| we've |got a de↑VÈLopment department| in |HÀRlow| the |telephone NŪMber| is |two four SĔVen| – |two

four double FÓUR| |and my enQUÌRy| con|cerns
the ↑Greek word for ↑SCÌENCE| – |this is a QÙESTion| that
|we have been asked HĚRE| – |none of us in this room
being Greek SCHÒlars| |know the ↑ÀNSwer|

B: my |name is WadDÉLL| |Wadash SCHÓOL| I |want to
contact Mister ↑VǏALing| – I will |phone a↑GÁIN| between
|two ↑TÉN| *m* and |two "↑TWĚNty|*m* – if I |fail to get him
THÉN| I'll |phone aGÁIN|*m*' |just after three forty "↑FÌVE|*m*'
|if it's unlikely that Mister Vialing will be "↑THĚRE| but could
|leave a MÉSSage| could |he "↑ÈIther| |PHÒNE| |WÁDash|
– |DÓUBle| |nine four one TWǑ| which is the |SCHǑOL
number| |or in the ↑ÉVEning| |double seven two nine
ĚIGHT| – a|GǍIN| a |Wadash NÚMber| which is my
|PĚRsonal number| and . . .

m . . . *m*: speaker uses a very precise articulation
m' . . . *m*': spoken in a regular rhythm

C: |this is SÌMon *m* Lessin SPÉAKing |*m* |good MÓRNing|
|TÓ you| I |have a number of QUÉRies| of |different KǏNDS|
to |which I would ↑very much like the ÁNSwer| |if you could
GǏVE it 'to me| |over the TĚLephone| |late this MÒRNing| –
|first of ÁLL| |some ↑small aca↑DÈMic QUÉRies| – –
| is the SPĚLLing| – |on the TǏTLE| |l u c i l ǐ| |or
is it l u ↑Ć |i |l DÒUBLE i| – |that is the FÌRST point|
– |NŌW| the |SĚcond one| |ĪS| |I would ↑like to have
the PÀGE RÉFerence| |from ↑LÀSky's| |History 'of
Greek LǏTerature| |where he ↑talks about a character
called *m*↑ǍRiston| *m* . . .

m . . . *m*: speaker articulates slowly

Note [**a**] The peculiar features of a medium in which there can be no reaction from the addressee are the main reason for the relative formality and careful articulation in these samples as compared with those in 19.87–89. This is less obvious in the case of C who apparently knows from experience the degree of clarity attained by the machine and who doubtless knows the actual person who will listen to the recording in due course. But even C seems to avoid using contracted forms (*I have* in 20, *I would* in 21 and 26, *that is* in 25), and we notice the uncolloquial syntax of line 21. A is especially cautious in speech, and it is doubtless this that leads him to make a tone unit of his introductory subject *my name*. With *my enquiry* (line 5), compare what was said about *Mother's clock* in 19.89 Note [a].

[**b**] In both A's and B's messages telephone numbers are given; the prosodic phrasing in the former is usual with the widespread seven-digit phone numbers. Both speakers follow the common British habit of reading a sequence like '22' as 'double 2', '222' as '2 double 2'.

[**c**] A's message ends with a syntactically muddled construction, involving a blend:

Not being Greek scholars, none of us know(s) . . .
None of us being Greek scholars, we do not know . . . } (*cf* 15.58*ff*)

There is confusion of a more pragmatic kind in B's recording. Presumably the *message* (line 14) is to the effect that Mr Vialing should telephone B (lines 15*ff*), but this is a message *for* Mr Vialing, not one that B wishes Vialing to 'leave' for B. Even C seems to find the medium uncongenial and one might suspect that there is some confusion in his prosody. For example, the treatment of *to you* in line 20 is odd both in occupying a separate tone unit and in having a nucleus (especially, perhaps, a rising one) on the preposition. Again, putting a nucleus on the first name (19), when the surname is also given, would normally suggest that there might be confusion with someone else of the same surname. Alternatively, we might suspect that 'Lessin' was added as an afterthought: perhaps it would turn out that it was not his usual colleague who would listen to the recording. (In fact, inspection of other recordings by the same speaker showed that it was a personal idiosyncrasy, frequently recurring.)

[d] The use of demonstratives and locative pro-forms is normal in telephoning: *this* and *here* referring to the speaker and his location (*cf* lines 7, 19), *that* and *there* to the addressee and his location (*cf* line 13, though it happens that our excerpts include no instance of *that*). But *cf* 19.64 Note [b].

Bibliographical note

For theoretical discussions of discourse see Cole and Morgan (1975); Davies (1979); Grice (1975); Haiman (1980); Halliday (1978); Hatcher (1956); Kempson (1977); Sinclair (1980); Winter (1979).

For treatments of textual structure as a whole, see de Beaugrande and Dressler (1981); D'Angelo (1975); van Dijk (1977); Grimes (1975); Halliday and Hasan (1976); Hoey (1983); Leech and Short (1981); Nash (1980); Winter (1982); Winterowd (1975); Young et al (1970).

On specific aspects of conversational discourse, see Arndt and Janney (1981); Bald (1980); Bublitz (1980); Crystal (1980); Edmondson (1981); Leech (1981b); Schenkein (1978); Svartvik (1980).

Other relevant studies: Allerton (1978); Bolinger (1965); Borkin (1980); Chafe (1976); Christophersen (1939); Enkvist (1980); Firbas (1971, 1975, 1979); Halliday (1967); Hawkins (1978); Li (1976); Schiffrin (1981); Svartvik and Törjas (1975); Waida (1979); Wales (1980); Widdowson (1979); Yee (1975).

I Appendix I Word-formation

Introduction

Grammar and lexicology

I.1 Both grammar and lexicology involve us in an indefinitely large number of superficially different units. In the case of grammar these are phrases, clauses, and sentences; in the case of lexicology the units are words, or more precisely (since some of the units comprise more than one word) *lexical items*. It is typical of grammar to make general and abstract statements about the units concerned, showing a common construction despite the formal differences. It is typical of lexicology to make specific statements about individual units. In consequence, while the grammar of a language is best handled in chapters devoted to different types of construction, it is normal to deal with the lexicon of a language in an alphabetic dictionary, each entry devoted to a different lexical item.

But there is an area in which grammar and lexicology share a common ground: where generalizations, as in grammar, are appropriate; but where the idiosyncrasies of individual units are also described. This area is word-formation. There are regularities of a similar nature in grammar and word-formation, and there are cases in which the two sets of regularities are directly connected. Consider the following (and *cf* 17.51*ff*):

[A]	[B]	
She *delegated* the work *speedily*.	Her *delegation* of the work was *speedy*.	[1]
He *communicated* the message *efficiently*.	His *communication* of the message was *efficient*.	[2]
They *fumigated* the house *thoroughly*.	Their *fumigation* of the house was *thorough*.	[3]

First the vertical dimension. The two columns exemplify the regularities of grammar, [A] with its three S V O A structures, [B] with its three S V C structures with S realized in each by a noun phrase having a genitive determiner and an *of*-phrase postmodifier. But the columns also illustrate the regularities of word-formation; in [A] the three verbs in *-ate* and the adverbs in *-ly*; in [B] the three nouns in *-ation*.

Next, the horizontal dimension. To grammar is referable the correspondence between *she* and *her* in [1], *he* and *his* in [2], *they* and *their* in [3], and the fact that we have adverbs in [A] but adjectives in [B]. But to word-formation are referable the form of the correspondence between the transitive *-ate* verbs in [A] and the abstract *-ation* nouns in [B], as well as the form of the correspondence between the adjectives in [B] and the adverbs in [A].

In proceeding to lengthen the columns, however, we would soon find that the regularities of word-formation are more limited in application than those of grammar:

She *used* the money *well*.	Her *use* of the money was *good*.
She *used up* the money *fast*.	Her *using up* of the money was *fast*.
He *rearranged* the furniture *with difficulty*.	His *rearrangement* of the furniture was *difficult*.

They *dismissed* his objections *in a hostile manner*.	Their *dismissal* of his objections was *hostile*.

These examples remind us that the products of word-formation are subject to the idiosyncrasies inherent in the lexicon, whereas the rules of grammar are far broader, transcending the individualities and unpredictabilities of the lexical items which the grammatical rules manipulate. Thus grammar can actually *predict* the basic synonymy of [4], [5], and [6]:

John gave Peter the money. [4]
John gave the money to Peter. [5]
The money was given to Peter by John. [6]

But only our knowledge of individual lexical items enables us to equate [7] and [8] with [4–6], as well as with each other:

John donated the money to Peter. [7]
Peter received the money from John. [8]

Again, grammar will predict the antonymy of [9] and [10] but not that of [9] and [11]:

Mary felt happy. [9]
Mary didn't feel happy. [10]
Mary felt miserable. [11]

In studying word-formation, we seek to transcend the individuality of items that is typical of the lexicon as a whole and set out the very widespread regularities that make the constitution and grammatical distribution of one word similar to those of another.

The constituents of word-formation

I.2 To the native speaker, many words have an obvious internal structure. With *blackbird* and *monkey-like*, we can see that each word comprises parts that occur elsewhere in the language with the same meaning (*blackboard* and *ladylike*, for example). We shall refer to such items as COMPLEX words, in contrast to those words – long or short – which to the native speaker have to be learnt as arbitrarily contrived units, with no recognizable parts: *cat* or *rhinoceros*.

Superficially, a complex word like *depolarization* looks like a simple linear string of items:

de + pol(e) + ar + iz(e) + ation

consisting of the WORD *pole* with AFFIXES which may precede (PREFIXES) or follow (SUFFIXES). But some complex words are not analysable into words plus affixes:

jealous = jeal- + -ous
pious = pi- + -ous
(*contrast* desirous = desire + -ous)

To capture what is common to *pole*, *desire*, *jeal-* and *pi-*, therefore, we obviously cannot use 'word' and we shall speak instead of STEM (*cf* 2.4). We can then say that the stems *desire* and *jeal-* combine with the affix *-ous* to yield the adjectives. But a further distinction is necessary, as this is inadequate when we want to describe *depolarization*, since if we said that the affixes *de-*, *-ar-*, *-ize*, and *-ation* are combined with the stem, this might imply that *de-* can combine with *pole* or *polar* to yield the words **depole*, **depolar*. In fact, it is with the verb *polarize* or the deverbal noun *polarization* that *de-* can combine. We need to distinguish a unit that may be neither STEM nor WORD but of which we can say that it is with this unit that a particular affix is combined. We shall call this unit the **BASE**.

We can now make analogous statements like the following:

jealous = base *jeal-* + affix *-ous*
[the base here is identical with the stem, but neither is a word in English]
polarize = base *polar* + affix *-ize*
depolarize = affix *de-* + base *polarize*
[the base here is not identical with the stem in either case, the stem being *pole*; but both the bases and the stem are English words]
(*be*)*spectacled* ['wearing spectacles'] = base *spectacle-* + affix *-ed*
[here the base is identical with the stem, but although the word *spectacle* exists in English it is only the stem of the plural *spectacles* that constitutes the base in *spectacled*.]

The STEM is thus the form of a word stripped of all affixes that are recognizable as such in English; *eg*: *man*, *person*, *apply*, *abattoir*, *rhinoceros*. But with a large number of words there can be debate as to what the stem is in this sense. If *abattoir* is a stem, despite the existence in English of *reservoir* (with an identical ending, both words referring to physical constructions), how should we regard *reservoir* itself? Should we regard it as having a stem identical with the word *reserve*? Again, should we relate *reserve*, *preserve*, *deserve* as having a common stem, perhaps seeing this as identical with the verb *serve*?

Various arguments come into play: etymological, semantic, even phonological. We note, for instance, that the *s* in *reserve* is pronounced /z/, where that in *serve* is pronounced /s/. The more indications there are of the remoteness of connection between one word and another, as perceived by the native speaker, the more we must be influenced to regard polysyllabic words like *reservoir* and *reserve*, *deceive* and *conceive* as individual stems. The obverse is actual productivity (*cf* App I.13): where, beside *depolarize*, we find new words being currently created such as *decompress* and *deregulate*, the *de-* element having a similar relation in each, we know that we are not dealing with isolated polysyllabic stems but with complex words.

Note [**a**] Reference has been made to 'the native speaker', but native speakers themselves vary widely in their apprehension of stems and affixes. To the layman, *rhinoplasty* ['plastic surgery of the nose'] is as unanalysable as *rhinoceros*, but not to the medical scientist. Recent coinages by philosophers (*illocutionary*, *perlocutionary*) show that, for some speakers of English, an affix like *per-* is readily enough seen as manipulable in a formation and that *locutionary* is a base in such words.

[**b**] As we saw in 2.3*ff*, in some linguistic descriptions the minimal unit in morphology and word-formation is called 'morpheme', with the further distinctions 'inflectional morpheme' (*eg* plural

-*s*), 'free morpheme' or 'minimal free form' (*eg*: *pole*), 'bound morpheme' (*eg*: *un-*, *jeal-*), with the latter necessarily further subdivided between 'affixal morpheme' (*eg*: *un-*) and 'stem morpheme' (or 'root' or 'lexical morpheme', *eg*: *jeal-*). What we are calling BASE might in this framework be termed 'base morpheme'. It should be noted that linguists differ in their terminology for these distinctions, some reversing our use of STEM and BASE, others using 'root' for what in this book is called 'stem'.

Word-formation processes

I.3 There are four main types of word-formation, the first two of which can be referred to as 'affixation':

[A] PREFIXATION: putting a prefix in front of the base, sometimes with, but more usually without, a change of word class; *eg*: *pre* + *determine* (*cf* App I.20*ff*).

[B] SUFFIXATION: putting a suffix after the base, sometimes without, but more usually with, a change of word class; *eg*: *friend* + *less* (*cf* App I.31*ff*).

[C] CONVERSION: assigning the base to a different word class with no change of form; *eg*: (*we shall*) *carpet* (*the room*) – verb from noun (*cf* App I.43*ff*).

[D] COMPOUNDING: adding one base to another, such that usually the one placed in front in some sense subcategorizes the one that follows; *eg*: *blackbird*, *armchair*, *bottle-feed* (*cf* App I.57*ff*); but contrast, for example, 'bahuvrihi' compounds (*cf* App I.67) such as *heavyweight*.

Showing some similarities with [A] and [D], but fitting neatly into neither, is derivation by COMBINING FORMS such as *psycho-*, *Anglo-*, *socio-*, *vice-*. These have the semantic characteristics of the first constituent in a compound but they resemble prefixes in mostly (*cf* App I.32, App I.66) being obligatorily initial, in having little or no currency as separate words, and in not normally being the stressed part of a COMPLEX WORD (*psycho-ˈtherapy*), by which we mean not merely polysyllabic words but words comprising constituents that are recognizable as such to native speakers.

Constituents in complex words are sometimes identical in form with bases but yet resemble affixes in certain respects so that it is not always easy to justify regarding the resultant words as compounds. For example, *input*, *output*, *sit-in* (n), *drop-out* (n), *childlike* have components formally and functionally resembling separate items in corresponding phrases ('they put the data in', 'he dropped out of college', 'he is like a child') that make them like compounds. On the other hand, the items *in-*, *-like*, etc, have the type of wide distribution and nonlexical character that is typical of affixes. Given the historical fact that *-like* is cognate with the indisputably affixal *-ly* and the synchronic fact that *-ful* (with spelling difference) is closer in function to the adjective *full* in *cupful* (*cf*: *a full cup*) than in *eventful* (different in sound as well), it seems clear that the distinction is gradient rather than absolute. A certain amount of arbitrary assignment is therefore inevitable in the descriptive tables that constitute the body of this Appendix.

This is borne out by another borderline example, *-man*, as in *policeman*. Though the spelling suggests identity with the base *man*, the pronunciation suggests otherwise: /mən/ (contrast /mæn/ in *ice-man*, *ape-man*, which seem more obviously to be compounds). Moreover, despite etymology, spelling, and inflection, *-man* (*-men*) in *woman* can no longer be regarded as even affixal: *woman* is itself a base. Yet, in response to sociopolitical pressures in recent years, we have come to recognize *-man* in *policeman*, *chairman*, etc (but not in *woman* itself) as effectively the base *man* and hence challenged for replacement by the sex-neutral *-person* (*cf* App I.64, 5.105).

Word-formation processes, as we saw already in App I.1, involve formal and semantic analogy. A pattern or paradigm of similar items becomes established, and to this pattern new coinings conform. On the basis of *psychotherapy* and *physiotherapy*, we could have a newly derived word *x-otherapy* which would mean 'treatment by means of *x*', where *x* would be filled by the name of the new treatment. DERIVATION, often used by linguists to mean only formation by the addition of affixes, is used in this book to embrace all the processes by which a new formation comes into existence, but clearly those that follow recognizable patterns are central to our concern as they are central to word-formation itself.

In numerous cases, word-formation rules (especially in suffixation) apply only to items of specific derivation. We shall find it convenient, therefore, to speak of DENOMINAL, DEVERBAL etc, so that DEVERBAL (nouns) will mean '(nouns) derived from verbs'. The term DEVERBAL applied to nouns is not synonymous with the term VERBAL NOUN which we use only for the 'gerund' class of nouns in *-ing* (*cf* further 17.52*ff*). On the distinction between inflectional and derivational suffixes, *cf* App I.31 Note.

I.4 We saw in 17.157 that the overt arrangement of a noun phrase having more than two constituents may express two quite different structures:

a local cookery class
either = a [[local cookery] class] [1]
or = a [local [cookery class]] [2]

In [1] we are concerned with teaching about regional cuisine; in [2] with a cookery class taking place nearby. Since it is bases and not stems that enter into word-formation, whether by affixation or compounding, and since the bases themselves may have been produced by affixation or compounding, the linear form of a complex word may conceal alternative structures similar to those in [1] and [2]. Contrast (*an*) *ex-film star* and (*a*) *silent-film star*:

[ex-[film star]] 'a former star in films'
[[silent-film] star] 'a star in silent films'

Again, in the sentence 'The robber was *unmasked*', the final word may have one of two quite different structures:

[un[[mask]ed]]

ie 'he was not wearing a mask', negative *un-* (*cf* App I.21), with noun *mask* + *-ed* (*cf* App I.38); or

[[unmask]ed]

ie 'someone removed his mask', privative *un-* (*cf* App I.22), in the verb *unmask*, with *-ed* participle.

Word-formation rules

I.5 A rule of word-formation usually differs from a syntactic rule in one important respect: it is of limited productivity, in the sense that not all words which result from the application of the rule are acceptable; they are freely acceptable only when they have gained an institutional currency in the language. Thus there is a line to be drawn between 'actual English words' (*eg*: *sandstone*, *unwise*) and 'potential English words' (*eg*: (*)*lemonstone*, (*)*unexcellent*), both of these being distinct from 'nonEnglish' words like **selfishless* which, because it shows the suffix *-less* added to an adjective rather than to a noun, does not even obey the rules of word-formation.

Rules of word-formation are therefore at the intersection of the historical and contemporary (synchronic) study of the language, providing a constant set of 'models' from which new words, ephemeral or permanent, are created from day to day. Yet on a larger scale, the rules themselves (like grammatical rules) undergo change: affixes and compounding processes can become productive or lose their productivity; can increase or decrease their range of meaning or grammatical applicability. In line with aims elsewhere in the book, we concentrate in this Appendix on productive or on marginally productive rules of word-formation, leaving aside 'dead' processes, even though they may have a fossilized existence in a number of words in the language. For example, the Old English affix *-th*, no longer used to form new words, survives in such nouns as *warmth*, *length*, *depth*, *width*, *breadth* (*cf*: *warm*, *long*, *deep*, *wide*, *broad*). A corollary of this approach is that the historical study of a word is irrelevant to its status as an illustration of present-day rules: the fact that the word *unripe* has existed in the English language since Anglo-Saxon times does not prevent us from using it as an example of a regular process of word-formation still available in the language.

Note [**a**] New formations, invented casually for a particular occasion (as in 'She needs guidance, and the poor child is as *guidanceless* as she is parentless') are normally comprehensible, but are used at a certain cost to acceptability. They are often referred to as NONCE FORMATIONS and are liable to be criticized if too many are used. *Cf* also the jocular *coolth* on the pattern of *warmth*.

[**b**] History provides quite a number of examples where a derived form has preceded the word from which (formally speaking) it is derived. Thus *editor* entered the language before *edit*, *lazy* before *laze*, and *television* before *televize*. The process by which the shorter word is created by the deletion of a supposed affix is known as BACK-FORMATION, since it reverses the normal trend of word-formation, which is to add rather than to subtract constituents. 'Back-formation' so described is a purely historical concept, however, of little relevance to the contemporary study of word-formation. To the present-day speaker of English, the relationship between *laze* and *lazy* need be no different from that between *sleep* and *sleepy*, *choose* and *choosy*, etc.

Borrowing and neo-classical formations

I.6 A second restriction of this account is that it takes only passing notice of word-formation according to Latin and Greek, rather than English models. From the Renaissance to the early twentieth century, English word-formation, like English (or for that matter European) architecture, was dominated by neo-classicism. The vocabulary was augmented by borrowing and adaptation of Latin and Greek words, or, as time went on, by the formation of words in English-speaking countries according to the Latin and Greek models. The habit of neo-classical formation still flourishes in certain learned areas of vocabulary, particularly in the natural sciences. However, English has adapted to her own purposes a large number of Latin and Greek word elements, and these, being productive in the 'common core' of the language, we must take into account. Moreover, some purely neo-classical affixes (*-ic*, *-ous*, etc) are so common that it would be perverse to exclude them from any account of English word-formation.

So great indeed has been the foreign or neo-classical influence on the English language, that the majority of prefixes (as distinct from suffixes) in the language are of Latin, Greek, or French origin. To give an illustration of the difference between native and neo-classical formation: *com-* (*col-/con-/cor-/co-*) is a Latin prefix in *collect*, *communication*, *conduct*, *coagulate*; but *co-*, one of its variants, has been appropriated by the English language and has developed a function of its own in such words as *co-author*, *co-chairman*, *co-education*. For our purposes, therefore, *co-* is an English rather than a classical or neo-classical prefix.

The 'ready-made' and the 'made to measure'

I.7 The words that we have just been considering come to us 'ready-made'. But this does not apply merely to words adopted from other languages: it is typical of the lexicon as a whole and underlines the distinction between lexicology and grammar to which attention was drawn in App I.1.

In principle, and to a large extent in practice, the language user works on the assumption that every sentence encountered is entirely new, created and assembled specially for the occasion. By contrast, we expect every *lexical item* we hear or read to be already 'institutionalized' (*cf* App I.5) and to have been selected from an existing stock of words, complete with its form and meaning.

We encounter widespread exceptions to both these generalizations. There are countless sentences that must have occurred before, even in the experience of a particular individual:

> I'm feeling tired this morning.
> How is your cold now?
> She's gone out to see a patient.

But no one would seriously suggest that the next time we want to say such things, we recall and re-use these sentences in the form previously heard. There are more convincing exceptions, however. There are formulaic utterances, 'pre-fabricated' in entirety ('How do you do?' 'Pleased to meet you!'), and proverbs ('Too many cooks spoil the broth'); *cf* 11.54. There are ready-made parts of utterances ('Many thanks for . . .', 'Far be it from me to . . .', 'How come . . .?', 'If only . . .', 'By no stretch of the imagination . . .'). Note also the many idiomatic phrases and collocations like 'eat . . . out of house and home' or '(They're) home and dry' (informal BrE, meaning 'They've achieved their goal'). We interlard our discourse with snatches of familiar texts: 'a foregone conclusion', 'seven days shalt thou labour' (*cf* App I.8 Note). In such cases, there is no question of our re-forming the phrases anew each time we use them. But numerous as these are, we must recognize that they are exceptional in a quite fundamental sense. In the lexicon, the converse is true. We encounter lexical items that we are content to believe the user has invented; for example, *sploopsing* in Jack Kerouac's 'I come sploopsing to a no-good end'. But we find this striking in large measure precisely because it is exceptional; we do not expect words to have been specially coined for the occasion. It is in fact a common occurrence for someone to apologize for having coined a word ('what I may be allowed to call . . .') or even for using a word that we cannot be expected to know ('what some people have called . . .').

At the same time there is a paradox. While we expect every sentence to be newly formed for the occasion, we expect to understand it without difficulty, in the sense of perfectly apprehending its structure. A question like 'What does this sentence mean?' is apt to be an ironic criticism of the person who spoke or wrote it. But although we correspondingly expect every lexical item to have been taken from an existing stock, we by no means expect automatically to understand it or even recognize it. A question like 'What does this word mean?' is therefore commonplace, implying no criticism of anyone. We go through life learning new words continually. Sometimes (and rather rarely) they are as lacking in general currency as Kerouac's *sploopsing* (and we depend on the context to guess its meaning) or as the word *googol* in the following:

> There are probably more than a googol germs on the outside of this one cherry.

With the former we may rely on the context to help us guess the meaning, but with the latter we must have recourse to a dictionary or a mathematician if we are to learn that it refers to the numerical value *ten* raised to the power of one hundred. But usually, the new lexical experience has something familiar about it. The word may be a metaphorical extension of an item we know in a different sense ('You're not on my *wavelength*') or it may be imported from another but familiar language ('She struck me as *soignée*') or it may be composed of familiar items. When Coleridge in 1820 used the word *mammonolatry*, he knew that this would be understood in relation to *mammon* in the same way as the already long-established *idolatry* was understood in relation to *idol*. Subsequent coinages like *bardolatry* are formed with the same confidence of being understood on this analogical basis:

> worship of mammon [=wealth] as though it were an idol
> worship of the bard [=Shakespeare] as though he were an idol

Note The word *idolatry* is a compression of *idol* and *-olatry*, not unlike the blends of App I.76.

I.8 It is in its dependence upon analogies of this kind that the formation of words like *mammonolatry* somewhat resembles grammar or at any rate constitutes a grey area between the full generalizations of grammar and the specific idiosyncrasies of the lexicon. The difference (and hence the idiosyncrasy of the lexicon) lies in two factors: first, the relatively rare and special circumstances in which vocabulary construction takes place ('lexicalization', *cf* App I.9); second, the range of formation devices available and the constraints upon our using them ('productivity', *cf* App I.13). Consideration of both these factors throws into relief a third factor: every word-formation (or any other mode of lexical change) is a step in the historical development of the language. Something has come into existence which did not exist before. Where the utterance of a new sentence (and we have argued that, for the purposes of grammatical description, we can regard virtually every sentence as newly formed) entails no change in the language, the utterance of a new word raises the possibility that an addition has been made to the total means of expression available in the language. Thus while a synchronic description of grammar or phonology is perfectly possible (even though historical allusions may be convenient in the description), a description of word-formation must of its nature be diachronic. The one is providing a blueprint as to how all new sentences will be freely constructed; the other providing a historical record (however short-term) of the formations that have taken place and venturing, on the basis of this, a tentative prediction of the lines along which further formations may take place in the future.

One indication of the diachronic orientation in word-formation can be seen in considering again the example *mammonolatry*. In grammar, a structural description is neutral as to the meanings that the structure can convey, whether or not the same words may be involved. Take the type *SVO*, for example, in:

> John worshipped mammon.
> John despised mammon.
> John lit the gas.

But every new formation of the form 'x-olatry', despite ability to paraphrase it as 'the worship of x', will carry with it the memory of similar constructions (such as *idolatry*), so that (for example) *wife-olatry* would mean 'having the same kind of misplaced devotion for one's wife as pagans are said to have for idols'.

Note As we have already shown in App I.7, phrases and sentences can also be stored up as additional expressive resources; *eg*:

> For only with such achievement could John expect the world to 'make a beaten path to his door', *as Emerson put it*.

Neither the quotation marks nor the authority need have been inserted, and many people's language is interlarded with re-used phrases and sentences in this way, where they have been found to be particularly memorable, effective, or merely a lazy convenience: 'Last but not least, and to make a long story short (if you'll pardon the clichés), it was Marjorie who helped me find my present job.'

Lexicalization

I.9 However new and unfamiliar it is, an entity, activity, or quality can be stated and described in sentences:

> Let us convert our railways from having steam-engines to using engines powered by $\left\{\begin{array}{l}\text{diesel oil.}\\ \text{electricity.}\end{array}\right\}$ [1]

The nub of this suggestion might then be expressed by means of nominalization such as:

> The use of $\left\{\begin{array}{l}\text{diesel-powered}\\ \text{electrically-powered}\end{array}\right\}$ engines (is being investigated). [2]

This already presupposes some discussion of and familiarization with the notion. But as the proposal becomes more widely accepted as viable, such a nominalization will seem too clumsy on the one hand and too under-committed on the other. At this stage, we will not be surprised to find the notion institutionalized by means of (as it happened) the word:

Dieselization }
Electrification } (is feasible). [3]

We can now conveniently marshal arguments for and against *dieselization* or *electrification*, discuss how much it will cost to *dieselize* or *electrify* suburban trains, and whether the new locomotives might co-exist for a time with *undieselized* or *unelectrified* services. We have now LEXICALIZED a notion that could previously be discussed only in sentences and periphrases which varied from person to person. In lay terms, we now 'have a *word* for it'.

But the precise form of the lexicalizations [3] could not have been predicted. When it became possible to split atomic nuclei (and the consequent lexicalization, *nuclear fission*, came into use), there was some vacillation and even public debate as to the most appropriate adjective to lexicalize the property of a substance in being capable of undergoing such fission. Competing forms included *fissible*, *fissile*, and *fissionable*. It turned out that two lexicalizations were necessary; one for the general capability, the other for the capability in consequence of slow neutron impact; physicists are apt to use *fissionable* for the former and *fissile* for the latter. In more extreme cases, the unpredictability of a lexicalization is even more obvious: for example, Kerouac's attempt to sum up the demise of a soft and flabby entity (for which the word *crash* was thus inappropriate) as *sploopse*; or the lexicalization by the mathematician Kasner of a particular numerical value as *googol*.

The other noteworthy point about such lexicalizations as [3] is that their meaning is not recoverable from the form. In this way, as in the unpredictability just discussed, it is sharply distinguished from the expressions in [1] and [2]. We can surmise that *dieselization* and *electrification* refer to inceptive action concerning diesel oil and electricity respectively, but there is nothing in the words as such that takes us much beyond that. With *fissile* and *fissionable*, it is inevitable from the discussion above that not merely do they not proclaim that they are inherently concerned with *nuclear* fission; it is impossible to tell from their form what their precise meaning may be, even when we are told that nuclear fission is involved.

This is no more than we should expect if we reflect upon the concentration of presupposition that is packed into a lexicalization by the time it is successfully institutionalized. The coinage *racism* (*cf* App I.32) reflects in two syllables the conscience and the agonized sensibilities of a whole generation.

Note Many coinages, however, seem on the face of it to be so transparent that – at least when we know their meaning – it would not occur to us to call their formation unpredictable. This is perhaps especially true of blends (*cf* App I.76). Yet when Wayne Oates coined *workaholic* around 1970, he apparently saw himself obliged to explain that the word was 'to describe those people so involved in their work that it interferes with their health, personal happiness, social functioning, and interpersonal relationships'. Oates felt it necessary to go further and hint at the reason for giving the coinage this particular form by referring to '*addiction* to work'.

I.10 Of the two negative points just made about lexicalization, unrecoverability is far more endemic than unpredictability. Given the finite resources for lexicalization and the fact that some resources are more productive than others (*cf* App I.13), there are various highly likely ways in which a lexicalization will be realized, and it is on these that we concentrate in this Appendix. Thus in the lexicalization of concepts that can be given nominal properties, it is very common to adopt a strategy based on noun-phrase structure. Compare:

Some paper is shiny.
Paper that is shiny is difficult to write on.
Please don't buy me *shiny paper*.

We may postulate the way this strategy works in lexicalization:

[A] Oil comes from various sources, including vegetable matter. Such oil has functions and properties important for us and not shared with oil from other sources (*eg* mineral or animal matter). It is therefore worth distinguishing:

This oil is from a vegetable source.
Oil from vegetable sources is healthy for cooking.
Vegetable oil . . . [1]

[B] The engines of cars require oil; it has to be a special oil (*eg* from mineral sources, and of particular viscosity etc); since cars are relevant to our daily lives, such oil is worth distinguishing:

This oil is for engines.
Oil for engines is expensive.
Engine oil . . . [2]

But if such noun-phrase type premodification is so common in lexicalization as to challenge our earlier statement about predictability, it can readily be seen by comparing [1] and [2] that our statement stands concerning unrecoverability. Both [1] and [2] are of similar semantic and formal structure, but it is only by learning each as an idiosyncratic item that we can know that [1] 'means' oil *from* vegetables, [2] oil *for* engines. There is nothing inherently absurd about oil *for* vegetables, or oil *from* engines.

The latter point gains force in considering the lexicalizations that have in BrE clustered round *lighter* 'that which lights things' (itself a straightforward *-er* agential noun, based on the verb *to light*, *cf* App I.34). On the one hand, we have *fire-lighter* 'something that helps one to light fires'; on the other hand, *petrol-lighter*, 'something that helps one to light (tobacco) by means of petrol'. But two independent lexicalizations give us *gas-lighter*: the one like *fire-lighter*, 'something that helps one to light the gas'; the other like *petrol-lighter*, 'something that helps one to light (tobacco) by means of gas'.

I.11 The idiosyncrasy of lexicalization needs to be borne in mind when one is considering, for example, conversion (*cf* App I.43*ff*). When beside the noun *paper* there comes into use a verb *paper*, this is sometimes loosely referred to as the conversion of the noun into a verb. But this is not so. What normally happens (as in this instance) is the lexicalization of an action that is related to *one specific sense* of the noun, the sense concerned being selected on purely pragmatic grounds. Consider four of the senses of *paper* as a noun:

material in thin sheets made from wood or cloth [1]
a newspaper [2]
a piece of writing for specialists [3]
wallpaper [4]

The transitive verb 'formed' from this noun by conversion (*cf* App I.49) relates only to [4]:

John has papered the bedroom.

There would be nothing inherently absurd in derivatives from other senses, such as [2]:

(*)The Hearst organization has papered most of the mid-West.
['has supplied most of the mid-West with its papers']

or [3]:

(*)I'm papering part of my research in a specialist journal.
['publishing a paper on part of my research']

The position is simply that the social need for derivatives from the other senses seems not to have been felt and in consequence no lexicalization of the actions concerned has taken place.

By contrast, beside the noun *paint* ['liquid colouring matter'], two verb senses have been separately lexicalized:

Frank paints other people's windows but ignores his own.
['decorates with paint'] [5]
Frank paints other people's children but ignores his own.
['makes pictures with paint'] [6]

To each of these lexicalized actions the agential noun *painter* could equally relate:

Frank is a painter.

This example illustrates further the idiosyncratic nature of the lexicon. *A painter* could be predicated of Frank in [6] even if his normal occupation was as a car salesman and he painted only in his spare time, as a hobby. It could not be predicated of Frank in [5] unless house-painting was his regular paid work. We must contrast with these institutionalized uses of *painter* the affixation of agential *-er* (*cf* App I.34) in the environment 'The X-er of Y' which is simply a regular nominalization of '(NP) X-ed Y': in other words, a grammatical correspondence with no necessary lexicalization. Compare:

Augustus John was a painter of portraits. He was a well-known London *painter*.
Augustus John was a flouter of conventions. He was a well-known London **flouter*.

Note [**a**] Like *a painter* in [6], *a golfer*, *an angler*, or *a tennis-player* could also earn a living as a baker or a cleaner. But a librarian who bakes her own cakes, cleans her own room, and plays the violin will not normally be called *a baker*, *a cleaner*, or *a violinist*.

[**b**] The words *paint* and *paper* can, as we have seen, function as both noun and verb. Since as nouns both are concrete, and the verbs could be glossed as 'apply N', it is likely that native speakers feel that the verb is derived from the noun. In actual fact, this is true for *paper*, but false for *paint*, which was a verb for centuries before a nominal sense was lexicalized from it. The extent to which awareness of the 'direction' of derivation is relevant in language use is a matter of dispute, though the notion of 'back-formation' (*cf* App I.5 Note [b]) appeals directly to directionality. What is beyond dispute is the relevance of recognizing that a lexical relation exists; *cf* App I.2, and also App I.14 on 'analysability'.

I.12 As we have seen, conversion shows lexicalization having specific sense-orientation, in that only a particular sense of a word may be converted to another word class. But lexicalization also shows considerable item-orientation. Thus a conversion will apply to a specific formal item and not to any otherwise relevant synonym:

> He offered her a { *cup* / *mug* } of coffee.
>
> { He *cupped* / (*)He *mugged* } his hands and drank from the stream.

Compare also:

> He has a { *carpet* / *rug* } in his bedroom.
>
> He has { *carpeted* / (*)*rugged* } his bedroom.

It is noteworthy that, in both these examples, it is the lexical item of more general meaning that has lent itself to conversion.

Again, while the verb *burst* can be replaced by *bust* ⟨nonstandard in BrE⟩, the converse is not true where *bust* is a (slang or very informal) lexicalization corresponding broadly to 'bankrupt':

> Don't keep *bursting* in!
> Don't keep *busting* in! ⟨nonstandard⟩
> The firm has gone *bust*. ⟨slang⟩
> *The firm has gone *burst*.

The point is further made by another slang lexicalization where *bust* refers to sudden intervention (especially by the police) and where the detachment from *burst* is additionally marked by regularization of the morphology:

> The police { *burst* / **bursted* } into the room.
>
> The police *busted* him for possessing drugs. ⟨slang⟩

Similarly, the verb *break* has two *-ed* participles, *broken*, and a largely nonstandard *broke*. But the latter is widely used adjectivally in the sense 'bankrupt', and though informal it is in educated use, even heard occasionally in broadcast news.

A comparable phenomenon of where two words are produced from one original is noticeable with 'back-formations' (*cf* App I.71). Despite the well-established correspondence between the verb *destroy* and the noun *destruction*, the lexicalization of the concept *self-destruction* has led to the emergence of a new corresponding verb, as in:

> The party is determined not to *self-destruct* on this issue.

Note that shortenings characteristically express in a specific form specific lexicalizations. Thus *lib* and *co-op* are not shortenings of *liberation* and *co-operative* respectively, as we see from

> He advocated the **lib* of the prisoners.
> She was very **co-op* and helpful.

but of (*women's/gay) liberation movement* and *co-operative* (*business organization*) respectively. Similarly, *exam* is a clipping of *examination* only in the sense of 'an (academic) test'.

Note Not all lexicalization falls within the tradition of 'word-formation' study that we follow here. It excludes, for example, lexicalization by adoption of items from other languages (such as *kung fu*). It also excludes metaphorical extension of meaning. Thus the compound *headache* is regarded as a word-formation phenomenon only in respect of its bringing together the two items *head* and *ache* to lexicalize a common type of physical pain. But when we find the same compound being used to lexicalize 'a nagging anxiety' (as in 'The financial situation is the President's biggest headache'), this is regarded as outside word-formation. Nor is the lexicalization of 'best method of access' as *key* regarded as a word-formation from the concrete instrument sense ('A good degree is the key to success'), though the use of one part of speech as another – without change of lexical meaning – does indeed fall within word-formation ('He cheats' – 'He is a cheat'). Equally, we shall follow here the tradition of ignoring what one might call *phrasal lexicalization*, as when the sentence:

> I was *on the carpet* again yesterday.

can be used in the literal sense and also in the sense 'My superior disciplined me' – though it is this latter sense (not permitting 'I was on the new brown carpet again yesterday'), that has led to the verb lexicalization as in:

> I was *carpeted* again yesterday. (*Cf* App I.49)

We should add one further word on the limits within which we are operating in this Appendix. The formation of complex prepositions (*in aid of*), complex subordinators (*in the event that*), and phrasal and prepositional verbs (*give up, see to*) is treated as a grammatical phenomenon (*cf* 9.10*ff*, 16.3*f*, 16.5*ff*), though without ignoring the lexicalization aspect. The decision to treat such phenomena thus and not in this Appendix is in part a result of taking the WORD (defined in terms of an integrity that resists interruption of its parts) as the unit of lexicology and hence the sole remit of Appendix I. Phrasal lexical items consist of more than one word and although they have the semantic and often the grammatical integrity of words (*cf*: 'She mustn't *lose sight of* them' ~ 'They mustn't be *lost sight of*'), some degree of separateness continues to be recognized ('They *lost* at one time *sight of* their main goals'). Such phrases show many signs, however, of COALESCENCE, both orthographic (*instead of* beside *in place of*, *indeed* beside *in fact*) and semantic; *cf* also *because*, *altogether*. This illustrates the gradience between grammar and lexicon, including a gradience in lexicalization; *cf* 2.35 and the distinction there made between lexical items and grammatical words. On the one hand, *lose sight of* can be viewed as a single lexical item; on the other hand, it comprises three grammatical words, one of them (*lose*) with some morphological variation.

Even without the inherent difficulties presented by gradience and even without the present unsatisfactory state of word-formation studies, it would be impossible in this Appendix to cover the entire field of lexical creativity. Rather, as is appropriate in a grammar, we concentrate on those aspects that most resemble the regularities of grammar and are most closely interrelated with them.

Productivity

I.13 Any description of word-formation in the context of present-day grammar should obviously be concerned with processes of word-formation that are productive at the present time. The fact that words have resulted from the past operation of word-formation processes is in itself irrelevant from a synchronic, monolingual point of view. Thus the word *gospel* cannot be seen as a modern English word-formation, though formed in earlier English from the words *good* and *spell* (in the obsolete sense 'news'). Nor, as an English word, can *abattoir*: though its constitution is clear enough in French, where the verb *abattre* exists as well as the common affix *-oir*. Nor, as an English word, can *karate* be seen as a 'formation', though in Japanese it is clearly a junction of *kara* 'empty' and *te* 'hand'. On the other hand, words like *ice-cream*, *conceptualize*, *psychosomatic*, *workaholic*, *motel*, and *bionic* have all been formed within English sufficiently recently as to be representative of currently productive processes. The native speaker operates daily in the implicit knowledge that the meaning of most adjectives can be negated by prefixing *un-* and that most adjectives will permit the formation of abstract nouns by suffixing *-ness*.

But the distinction between productive and nonproductive is by no means straightforward. In the first place, there are severe constraints of a sociolinguistic kind that inhibit any individual's freedom to make new words (*cf* App I.7*f*, I.15). Secondly, there are linguistic constraints. These may be phonological. When Kasner invited his child to invent a word for 10^{100}, it is unlikely that *sfoogol* would have been suggested in view of the rarity of /sf/ as an initial cluster; *mroogol* would have been unthinkable. Alternatively, linguistic constraint may be syntagmatic. A 'machine for transporting dodos' might be lexicalized as a *dodo-car* but not as a *car-dodo*; the absence of dodos might be lexicalized as *dodofree* or *dodoless* ('This part of Arkansas is . . .') but not as *freedodo* or *lessdodo*. Other linguistic constraints inhibit *untall* or *dishappy* or *thinkledge* (despite *knowledge*), or *carefreedom* (despite the existence of *carefree* and *freedom*). Thirdly, there are pragmatic constraints. We do not have *doorleg* (beside *doorknob*) because doors do not have legs. We do not have *legchair* (beside *armchair*) for the opposite reason: that it is normal for chairs to have legs (though many are designed without legs).

Obviously, pragmatic constraints are a primary bar to lexicalization, but even this statement is not as simple as it may seem. We have no word *snow-cream* (beside *ice-cream*), but that is hardly because there is 'no such thing'. Both from a linguistic and a pragmatic viewpoint, *snow-cream* is as possible and satisfactory as *ice-cream*; there are indeed fluffy varieties of ice-cream that resemble snow more than ice. Given the social urge to make a particular distinction, lexicalization can be seen as operating to some degree independently from the real-world constraints of pragmatics.

There is thus in word-formation no simple parallel to the use and non-use of the starred form in grammar. At best, we may assign a star to forms that are in some sense 'impossible':

*mroogol [on phonological grounds]
*fulgrace-dis [on syntagmatic grounds: *dis-* can only prefix]
*emptyless [on semantic and grammatical grounds: *-less* cannot be added to adjectives]
?*thinkledge [*-ledge* is obsolete]

We can then distinguish these from words which for one reason or another are very unlikely to be formed in the course of using processes that are both familiar and currently active:

(*)doorleg [pragmatically excluded in present world]
(*)meep [a possible but unused word]
(*)snow-cream [a possible but unused compound]
(*)untall [unused perhaps because alternatively lexicalized]
(*)psychophilatelic [unused because psychological aspects of stamp collecting have not called for lexicalization]

Finally, we have items that are in actual use like *motel*, *ice-cream*, *bionic*.

But the absence of an asterisk can only mean that the item concerned has been formed; it carries none of the implications of the unstarred sentence that we are invited to produce further items for ourselves on this pattern. Conversely, given the idiosyncrasies of lexicalization and the word-formation that may be used in response, the stars and parenthesized asterisks can do little more than assign degrees of improbability as to the form that new words may take.

Note [**a**] Certain processes and affixes have spurts of productivity at certain periods; *eg*: *mini-* in the 1960s, *-gate* (as in *cattlegate*, *oilgate*, *Muldergate*, but all modelled on *Watergate*), following the White House crisis in the 1970s; *cf* App I.76. Others are especially productive in certain activities: *eg* initialisms in civil administration, acronyms in computer science, etc. Even a dormant affix like *-hood* can come into restricted use, as in *sentencehood*.

[**b**] Word-formation was responsible for roughly half of the 6000 new words recorded by Merriam in the dozen years following the publication of the 1961 *Third International Dictionary*, about two-fifths of these by affixation, about three-fifths by compounding.

I.14 From the viewpoint of productivity, therefore, the ordinary user of English who is neither a poet nor an experimental scientist must be seen as having a fairly passive role in word-formation – whereas in grammar he has conversely a wholly active role. He *must* construct new sentences: he need not construct new words (and he lays himself open to criticism when he does so, neologism being an aspect of language use most open to prescriptive censure). But this does not mean that word-formation is of no practical concern or interest to the ordinary user of the language. If we are only rarely called on to construct words, we are prone to analyse them and are inclined to expect that complex items are composed of a relatively small number of basic ones. This is indeed one respect in which we seem to regard words somewhat analogously to the way we regard phrases and clauses. That is not to say that we expect complex words to be self-explanatory. We cannot from their names identify or define ice-cream or a blackbird, but once we have experience of the entities concerned, we understand why they are so called: the words seem well-motivated. So, too, when we know the meaning of *selfish* and *selfishness*, *lordly* and *lordliness*, they make sense in relation to *self* and *lord*, even though we might not have predicted the meanings of *selfish* and *lordly* from their composition. Indeed, it is likely that a sound general awareness of the specificity and idiosyncrasy of lexicalization helps to inhibit us from coining (for example) *doctorly* and *doctorliness* by analogy with *lordly* and *lordliness*. We note, however, that literary theory in the 1980s gave some currency to *writerly* and *readerly* (adjectives).

The phenomenon of 'popular' (or 'folk') etymology testifies to the ordinary person's concern for analysability. For example, *salt-cellar* seems a clear example of an attempt to make sense of the word *salier*, adopted from the French. Even though its meaning was known, the opaqueness of the form seems to have led to a reasoning something like this: 'The object is a container for salt; a cellar is a place for storing things, so this must be what people mean when they use this strange word "salier"; the thing is a *salt-cellar*.'

With the inevitable changes in language over time (*eg* the phonological change that now distinguishes *holy* from the first part of *holiday*), analysability of long-established words is reduced. If the language has adopted large numbers of words from other languages (as English has from French, Latin, and Greek), analysability is further impaired. Compare the English *rhinoceros* with German *Nashorn* 'nose-horn', or the English *rhododendron* with German *Alpenrose*. Nonetheless, our propensity to analyse enables us to recognize and interpret recurrent parts of words even where other parts are not in themselves recognizable as meaningful. Thus in:

*inter*mitt*ent*

we can link the first part with *international*, *interaction*, etc, and the *-ent* is recognizable as a possible adjective marker as in *different*, *innocent*, *prurient*, even if *-mit*(*t*)- remains totally opaque (since of course there is no reason why the ordinary user of English should connect this with the first syllable in *mission* or *missive*). So also with:

*dis*par*ity*

the negative force of *dis-* and the largely abstract noun marker *-ity* can be recognized even if *-par-* remains opaque. With:

*bishop*ric

we of course see a connection with *bishop* even though the suffix *-ric* is obsolete. In some instances like *knowledge* (the suffix of which again is obsolete), it is the spelling alone that permits partial analysis. The word *gumption* is marked as a probably abstract noun by its ending; *postpone* and *precede* link up with other *post-* and *pre-* words such that both their meaning and pattern of distribution are recognizable though *-pone* and *-cede* are isolates (divorced from *position* and *-cession* respectively).

We may conclude these considerations of lexicalization and productivity by recalling what we have said about the degree to which new formations are predictable in form, with meanings that are recoverable (*cf* App I.10*f*). It will have emerged from the examples discussed that, rather than speak of interpretability, it is more relevant to look at a formation from the viewpoint of motivatedness. When we become acquainted with a new word, we can often judge it, with hindsight as it were, as obviously well-motivated in its formation: *workaholic* is an example. But sometimes the motivation may seem entirely opaque, and *googol* is an example. There are more formations of the former kind than of the latter, no doubt fortunately, since they carry an in-built mnemonic as to their meaning.

Note The degree to which, independently of foreign language knowledge, the native speaker of English is able to analyse words and word-constituents of ultimately cognate form, is uncertain and a matter for psycholinguistic research. Some common examples are *people* and *popul(ar)*; *(trans)mit* and *(trans)mission*; *(pro)cede* and *(pro)cession*; *(con)demn* and *damn(ation)*; *col(laborate)* and *com(panion)*; *re(ject)*, *re(view)*, and *re(apply)*. Despite its spelling, a *cupboard* does not concern *cups* and *boards*, and it does not sound as if it does: /kʌbəd/. What is beyond question is that most of the affixes in productive use are ultimately from languages other than English, and that these adopted and neo-classical constituents can be regarded as fairly well assimilated by English speakers as a whole. This extends even to some evidence of an aversion to 'hybrid' formations like **workious* beside *laborious*. Compare our habit of adopting appropriate foreign-derived prosody (*ˈlegal*, *leˈgality* beside *ˈlawful*, *ˈlawfulness*), and this even where hybrids occur: *ˈMilton*, *ˈMiltonish*, but *Milˈtonic*, *cf* App II.3*ff*. Among the hybrids over which there was at one time strong protest, we may mention *amoral*, *bureaucracy*, *cablegram*, *pacifist*, and *speedometer*.

Individual creativity

I.15 It follows from what we have been saying that we must exercise caution when we speak of 'rules' in word-formation. The idiosyncrasies of lexicalization and the inherent restraint upon making up new words remove the predictive and permissive implications that the notion of 'rules' conveys. In word-formation study we are involved rather in describing an accretion of individual historical events and making generalizations about them to show the extent of recurrent patterning that exists.

But there are some exceptions to the largely passive role of the individual in the word-formation process. These are of two broad kinds.

[A] First, there are cases where no semantic lexicalization is required, but merely some formal reorganization which leaves the semantics of the base unchanged. This is preeminently true of nominalizations. Thus instead of saying 'We ought to be able to *punish* whoever *scribbled* this foul message', we might say:

> The *scribbler* of this foul message should be *punished*.
> The *scribbling* of this foul message should be *punishable*.

Again, instead of saying 'They borrowed my typewriter', one may venture upon a nonce-formation as in:

> They left me *typewriterless*.

(Contrast *penniless* which does not mean 'without pennies' but lexicalizes 'destitute, without money or other comparable resources'.) Other affixes (*cf* App I.13) that can also be used fairly freely include *un-*, *dis-*, *-ful*, *-ize*, *-able* ('Is this shirt *drippable-dry/drip-dryable*?' beside the simpler *drip-dry*), *pseudo-*, *mini-* ('I only want a *mini-loaf*'), *non-*, *-ness*, adjectival *-ish* and *-y* (both especially in the sense 'somewhat'), and several devices to form diminutives and the like, such as *-let*, *-y*, and ⟨esp AustralE⟩ *-o*; *cf* App I.77. We may convert one part of speech to another without affix with similar freedom, especially nouns to verbs ('You can *ˈenvelope* these letters now'), or verbs to nouns ('I'll have a *sit* for a few minutes'). We do not mean to imply that any given example would in actual historical fact be getting used for the first time, but rather that so far as the user is concerned the formation or conversion was his own.

[B] Secondly, as we saw in App I.7, there is the limited freedom to create new formations in order to satisfy by lexicalization a terminological need which may be as ad hoc and temporary as the formation concerned. Nonce-formations of this kind are often preceded by an explicit indication of the coinage to come (which may simultaneously function as an apology for thus interfering with the implicitly-held finite state of the lexicon): 'what one might call', 'and I shall refer to this as'. The commonest process of word-formation of this kind is compounding (*cf* App I.57*ff*). If we imagine a scientist describing a condition arising through weightlessness that may resemble the effect of alcohol, he may say 'I shall call this *space-inebriation*'. An international gathering discusses a special form of radio communication between ships or between ships and ports, and starts referring to this as *sea-speak*. Or compounding may coincide with abbreviation: a conference on communication between divers in off-shore oil exploration may speak of *subcom* (for 'submarine communication'), and the scientist who has coined *space-inebriation* may rapidly turn this into *SI* once he is assured that this will be understood by his audience. In the 1970s, *mediagenic* was used in a US journal to describe the qualities required of a presidential aide. It connoted broadly 'likely to promote good relations with press, radio, and TV', and it was obviously a blend involving the established *photogenic*. On the other hand, when a scientist at about the same time coined the term *supragenic*, the second part was the adjectival form of the noun *gene*, and the formation referred to heredity above the level of the gene. It hardly needs to be said that the vast majority of such new formations remain uninstitutionalized attempts at lexicalization.

Note Although commercial brand names (like the names of places and persons) are obviously beyond the scope of this Appendix (except where they achieve currency as common nouns; *cf* App I.53), it should be noted that they display vigorous creativity, involving several of the processes to be studied below (especially perhaps combining-forms, blending, and the use of neo-classical affixes). Inasmuch as these are aimed at international markets, they bear witness to the widespread use of these processes and affixes in other languages.

I.16 The two broad areas of individual creativity distinguished in App I.15 differ not only linguistically (in the forms and types of word-formation concerned) but in situational context. [B] implies a rather formal, serious, intellectual, or at any rate utilitarian setting. By contrast, [A] implies a rather informal, familiar, light-hearted setting. There seem indeed to be notable socio-linguistic correlates to the degrees of individual lexical creativity, such that on either side of a large conventional mass of people (on whom the constraints against creativity are most strongly felt), there are two areas in which such creativity is relatively frequent. On the one side, there is the world of new technology, learning, and research, where the coining of new terminology is almost endemic, and to a certain degree essential: *eg*: *maglev* (from 'magnetic levitation') in transport research; *paracharmonium* and *psi particle* in charm-theory physics. On the other side, there is the exuberance of slang talk between familiar (and especially young) friends: *lech* ['to lust after'], *knee-jerk* ['one who acts automatically'], *bird farm* ['aircraft carrier'], *mind-blowing* ['overwhelming'], *trendy* ['fashionable']. Many such lexicalizations are phrasal: *freak out* ['to undergo intense experience'], *do* (*one's*) *thing* ['to follow personal inclinations'], *get it together* ['to organize oneself'], *spaced out* ['drugged']. They include rather formal examples, such as *in the context of* ['as regards']. The willingness to be unconventional is sharply illustrated by the habit of splitting words in very familiar speech so as to insert (usually taboo) asseveratives: *absoballylutely*; *cf* App I.76 Note [c].

But in the last analysis, individual creativity depends less on the social context than on the particular individual. We vary enormously in our desire (and in our ability) to be lexically innovative.

Note [**a**] To a modest degree, creativity is going on continually, sometimes acknowledged, sometimes unnoticed. In a recent book on literary history, the author apologized for coining the word *canonical* in the sense of 'relating to the (authorial) canon'. It is noteworthy that he did not apologize (nor did he need to) for the ways in which he then proceeded to use it. These uses included: *canonical research* 'research towards identifying the canon', *canonical arguments* 'arguments about the extent of the canon', *canonical plays* 'plays that are recognized to be within the canon'.

[**b**] Though constraints on deviation from norms in phonology, grammar, and style are commonly acknowledged in the form of public rebuke and ridicule, this is nowhere more pointed than in cases of excessive lexical neologism. An American statesman was severely criticized in both the American and British press in 1981 for what was thought an unacceptable degree of conversion (*cf* App I.43*ff*), and *The Guardian* even devoted a leader to satirizing his usage. This included: 'He techniqued a new way to vocabulary his thoughts so as to uncertain anybody listening.'

[**c**] Our ability to operate correspondences between agential nouns in *-er* and abstract nouns in *-ing* from verbs, to make adverbs by adding *-ly* to adjectives (or, esp in AmE, *-wise* to nouns), to make ordinals by adding *-th* to cardinal numerals (even abstract ones as with 'to the *nth* degree') obviously resembles our comparable ability to make grammatical inflections like plural and past. For this reason, some theorists would regard such phenomena as being outside word-formation and as being rather a part of inflectional grammar. They would see a parallel between the 'formation' of the noun *driver* from *drive* and the 'formation' of the adjective *careful* from *carefully* in:

She *drives carefully*.
~ She is a *careful driver*.

Such a theoretical stance has far-reaching implications. For instance, just as *medical* in the phrase 'a medical student' is a nonpredicable adjective formed by derivation with the suffix *-al*, some would argue that *physics* in 'a physics student' is a nonpredicable adjective formed by conversion. One might adduce as parallels such informal adverbial uses of adjective forms as in 'Drive *slow*' (*cf* App I.46 Note). The controversial concept of a 'zero' suffix (*cf* App I.43 Note [a]) reflects just such an attempt to see conversion as parallel to the use of affixes such as *-al* and *-ly*.

[**d**] In connection with forms like *absoballylutely*, it is worth pointing out that the interposed intensifier in Eliza Doolittle's famous exclamation 'Not bloody likely' in Shaw's *Pygmalion* is in effect a similar phenomenon. It was not the *likeliness* that she was asseverating but the '*not-likeliness*'; *cf*: *not in any way likely*; the intensifier was inserted, however, before the stressed syllable in the same way as explained in App. I.76 Note [c]. The informal *Not likely!* is a further instance of a phrase having the status of a single lexical item; *cf* App I.12 Note.

Spelling and hyphenation

I.17 When suffixes are added to a base, spelling changes may occur, many of them parallel to those involved in inflection (*cf* 3.7*ff*, 5.11, 7.79). Thus:

y ~ *i*: *friendly* ~ *friendliness*, *happy* ~ *happily* (*cf* 7.46*f*, 7.80*f*, App I.41)
doubling: *red* ~ *reddish* (*cf* also *-c* ~ *-ck-*: *panic* ~ *panicky*)
-e loss: *cause* ~ *causation*
simplification: *full* ~ *fully* (=*full* + *ly*)

There are also foreign-derived assimilations *in-*/*im-*/*il-*/*ir-*, *con-*/*com-*/*col-*; *cf* App I.21. Although affixes are normally joined to bases without hyphens, hyphens may be used where the formation seems relatively unestablished;

where the affix (such as *-wise*, *non-*, *post-*) seems to be somewhat word-like (*construction-wise*, *ultra-reactionary*); in new formations with such prefixes as *co-*, *de-*, *re-*; or – especially in BrE – to prevent a double occurrence of a vowel (*re-emphasize*); *cf* App III.3*ff*.

With compounds, the constituents are often written as separate words when the collocation seems relatively unestablished:

(He has some) 'writing paper.

As the sequence of items becomes more established, it may be hyphenated (especially in BrE) as an intermediate stage before being written solid:

tax-exemption
bloodtest

Where the first constituent is a combining form, however (*cf* App I.66), hyphenation is the first step (again especially in BrE) rather than the second, since there is no stage at which the first component can be written as a separate word (but see Note):

(Her interests are more) lexico-semantic.

Hyphenation is used also to mark sequences as ad hoc 'compounds' for typographical clarity (*cf* App III.4). There was an example of this in App I.4, *a silent-film star*. So also, beside 'He collects foreign stamps':

He is a foreign-stamp collector.

to distinguish this from a foreign collector of stamps; again,

his higher-than-average wages

but 'His wages were higher than average'. Idioms are often hyphenated irrespective of their position in a sentence. Thus not only 'a *root-and-branch* revision', but 'The revision will be quite *root-and-branch*'. Hyphens are used for clarity where a sequence becomes the base for suffixation. Thus, while we may write without hyphens:

She has *short sight*.
He is *colour blind*.
They are both *old maids*.

hyphens are preferred in:

She is *short-sighted*.
He is affected by *colour-blindness*.
They are rather *old-maidish*.

Prefixation raises a different problem, since with new formations or ill-established ones the prefix would itself be hyphenated; and (except in premodifying phrases like *higher-than-average wages*) we avoid introducing more than one hyphen into a compound. Thus when we prefix *ex-* in:

He is an *army officer*.

we have, despite the implication of incorrect constitution,

He is an *ex-army officer*.

rather than a sequence of hyphens as in 'an *ex-army-officer*'. The elements *non-*, *vice-*, *mini-* and a few others are sometimes written as separate words: 'the new *vice consul*'.

Relations between phrase and complex word

I.18 We have noted earlier that we treat the formation of phrasal verbs, complex prepositions, and other types of word sequence, as a grammatical phenomenon, and therefore as falling outside word-formation (*cf* App I.12 Note). Informal spellings like *alright* for *all right*, *gonna* for *going to*, the uncertain division of *in so far* and *in as much*, the choice between *instead of him* and *in his stead* indicate the gradience that exists between words and phrases. When a phrasal verb is converted to another part of speech, the particle is sometimes treated like a prefix (*cf*: *income* 'earnings'):

{They *spread out* their arms.
{Their *outspread* arms . . .

{His behaviour *put* her *off*. ['disconcerted', ⟨informal⟩]
{She felt rather *offput* at his behaviour. ⟨BrE, very informal⟩
{She found his behaviour *offputting*.

{We are *taking in* more students this year.
{Our *intake* will be four thousand.

{Money is not *flowing in* fast enough;
{*inflow* was better last year.

{The rain *poured down* for hours,
{and this *downpour* delayed us.

In other cases, the particle is treated like a suffix:

{The plane *took off* at noon.
{*Take-off* was at noon.

Phrases also readily become complex words with suffixation:

{He could not *get at* the window.
{The window was *unget-at-able*. ⟨informal⟩

{The shirt will *drip dry*.
{The shirt is *drip-dryable*. ⟨BrE, informal⟩

In such cases the suffix can be used as though it were an infix:

{The window was unget*table*-at. }
{The shirt is dripp*able*-dry. ⟨BrE⟩} ⟨informal and 'nonce'⟩

{I was merely passing by.
{I was merely a pass*er*-by.

Note The 'infix' of *passer-by* is paralleled in grammar by such plurals as *consuls-general* (and indeed the plural of *passer-by* itself: *passers-by*) and the alternative pattern *unget-at-able* by 'group genitives' like *a man of honour's influence*, *Elizabeth the Second's heir*. The overlap of word and phrase can be further seen in ordinals like 'one hundred and sixty-seven*th*' and the pseudo-coordinations in *try and come*, *come and see* (*cf* 13.98), where there is resistance to separate inflection (**tried and came*; *?is coming and seeing*). Yet occasional (presumably accidental) utterances like 'He must do as he *see fits*' are heard in conversation. Unease and vacillation seem to lie behind the (jokingly nonstandard) agential nouns as in 'Will you wash up? I'm sure you're a good *washer-upper*'; *cf* also *usher-inner, walker-onner*.

Phonological consequences of word-formation

I.19 In the detailed description that follows, attention will be drawn to points of stress and pronunciation associated with particular affixes and processes. A series like:

'photograph /ˈfəʊtəgrɑːf/
photo'graphic /ˌfəʊtəˈgræfɪk/
pho'tography /fəˈtɒgrəfɪ/

illustrates the considerable stress variation (with consequent differences of vowel pronunciation) that accompanies the use of originally foreign affixes (*cf* App II.5). But vowel values can alter even where the stress remains constant:

'nation /neɪ-/
'national /næ-/

Prefixes and suffixes are usually unstressed in relation to the semantically weightier parts of words (*cf* App II.3*ff*), but:

[A] a few suffixes (*eg*: -'*ette*) assume primary stress; and

[B] prefixes have secondary stress if:
[i] they are disyllabic (*eg*: ˌ*inter*-), or
[ii] the base begins with an unstressed syllable (*eg*: ˌ*unat'tractive*), or
[iii] they are 'new' uses of 'old' items (*eg*: ˌ*pre*-, ˌ*re*-).

We shall draw attention to individual exceptions, but one general exception may be noted here. While many verbs have primary stress on the stem, as in:

She con'trasted her childhood with his.

the stress is moved on to the prefix when they are converted into nouns (*cf* App I.56, App II.6):

There is a 'contrast in meaning in the two uses of *painter*.

Moreover, noun compounds characteristically shift the stress to the first constituent where the corresponding phrase or clause has the primary stress on the second:

The ˌsun is 'rising.
The 'sunˌrise is . . .
This ˌblack 'bird [*phrase*] is a 'blackˌbird. [*compound*; *cf* App II.7]

Affixation

I.20 Although for ease of access to the information we shall present each set of affixes in alphabetical order, it should be noted that this obscures two important points. The first is that, within each set, it is usual that some affixes have far more frequent productive use than others. The second is that there are often significant relations between affixes: especially antonymy, as with *pre-* and *post-*, *-ful* and *-less*.

So that the relation between competing and contrasting affixes can be better understood, we shall use broad semantic categories as the basis of presentation, offsetting by means of cross-reference the inevitable disadvantages of this approach in oversimplifying the description. The semantic basis means, of course, that items having a single form (*eg*: *un-*, or *sub-*) but distinct semantic or grammatical functions will be given two or more separate entries. Only the chief affixes in productive use will be dealt with (subject to the words of caution in App I.13*ff*), but from time to time it will be convenient to make notes of comparison with rarer or nonproductive items. Where the item normally carries secondary or primary stress, the head form is marked accordingly (*eg*: ˌNON-, ˈMINI-), and exceptions are noted in the main body of the entry. Pronunciation is given where it is thought necessary.

Note Though most prefixes cannot occur as independent words, they can on occasion be detached to permit coordination, as in *pre- and post-hysterectomy*; *cf* 13.85.

Prefixation

Negative prefixes

I.21 ˌA- (/eɪ/ or /æ/), AN- (especially before vowels), 'lacking in', 'lack of', combines with adjectives, as in *amoral*, *asexual*, *anhydrous*, and is found in some nouns (*eg*: *anarchy*). Chiefly used in learned and scientific lexicon. Some items have the main stress on the prefix: *ˈanarchy*, *ˈatheist* /eɪ/, *ˈatrophied* /æ/.

DIS- (*cf* App I.22) 'not', 'the converse of', combines with open-class items including verbs: *eg*: *disobey*, *disloyal(ly)*, *disorder* (n), *disuse* (n), *disunity*, *discontent* (n).

IN- (and variants IL- before /l/, IM- before labials, IR- before /r/) 'not', 'the converse of', combines with adjectives of French and Latin origin, and is less common than *un-*; *eg*: *incomplete*. *Cf* also the noun *inattention*.

ˌNON- 'not', combines (usually hyphenated) with nouns, adjectives, and open-class adverbs: *eg*: *non-smoker*; *non-perishable*; *non-trivially*.

UN- 'not', 'the converse of' (but *cf* App I.22), combines fairly freely with adjectives and participles; *eg*: *unfair*, *unwise*, *unforgettable*; *unassuming*, *unexpected*.

Note [**a**] Of these prefixes, *un-* is by far the most productive, and it typically involves less lexicalization than the other prefixes. With adjectives, *un-* can usually replace *in-* or *dis-* for ad hoc use, but with semantic consequences. Thus *unrepairable, unreplaceable, unmovable*, etc are more absolute and more literally related to the respective bases than *irreparable, irreplaceable, immovable* etc. Converse replacement is not usually possible (**infaithful*, **dishappy*; *cf* App I.14 Note). It is noteworthy that several negative lexicalizations with *in-* and its variants have either no direct relation to the nonnegative base (*infirm* ~ *firm, infamous* ~ *famous*) or no nonnegative base at all (**ept*, **ert*). *Cf* also **couth*.

[**b**] *Non-* differs from *un-* in frequently expressing a binary contrast (without gradability) rather than the opposite end of a scale: *eg*: *non-scientific* (*?*rather non-scientific*) as distinct from (*rather*) *unscientific*; *non-American* beside *unAmerican*.

[c] Because of the possibility of confusion with negative *in-*, the nonproductive *in-* of *inflammable* (*cf*: *ingredient*) tends now to be avoided and this word is increasingly replaced by *flammable*, with a negative *non-flammable*. The following press report (*Observer*, 9 July 1978) illustrates how easily the terms are confounded: 'BR switched from highly *flammable* to *inflammable* but slow-smouldering material . . . They rightly discarded the highly *flammable* materials and went for those which were *non-flammable* with a low combustion point.' The writer appears to be using *non-flammable* and *inflammable* as synonymous.

[d] The assimilation variants of *in-* are to some extent paralleled with *un-* (*eg*:[ʌmˈplezənt]) and other affixes, but with *un-* and most others, these variants are not established in such a way as to be reflected in spelling.

[e] *Un-* often confers lexicalized acceptability on a participial or other deverbal adjective form: contrast **a heeded problem* with *an unheeded problem*, **a speakable condition* with *an unspeakable condition*. As compared with clausal negation, an *un-* item tends to connote 'frustrating the potential of the base'; *eg*:

The building { wasn't occupied. / was *unoccupied*. }

[f] *Non-person* illustrates a pejorative and ironic type of noun-formation which has shown some productivity in recent years. The meaning here is 'a person who is not (*ie* does not count as) a person', 'a person of no consequence'; *cf* also *non-event*.

[g] Other prefixes apart from those above have negative implications: notably, the reversative prefixes discussed below (*cf* App I.22), and the prefixes of opposition, *anti-* and *counter-*, discussed in App I.25.

Reversative or privative prefixes

I.22 DE- (/diː/) [i] 'reversing the action', combines fairly freely with (especially denominal) verbs and deverbal nouns; *eg*: *decentralize, defrost, desegregate, de-escalate, denationalization*;

[ii] 'depriving of', combines fairly freely with verbs and deverbal nouns (*eg*: *decapitate, deforestation*), including one or two items already connoting deprivation (*eg*: *denude, defraud*).

DIS- (*cf* App I.21) [i] 'reversing the action', combines fairly freely with verbs; *eg*: *disconnect, disinfect, disown*; in some cases with privative force, as in *dishearten, dispossess*;

[ii] 'lacking', combines limitedly with denominal adjectives; *eg*: *disinterested*; *discoloured* (also verb *discolour*) refers to unwelcome change of colour.

UN- (*cf* App I.21) [i] 'reversing the action', combines fairly freely with verbs; *eg*: *undo, untie, unzip, unpack, unwrap*;

[ii] 'depriving of', 'releasing from', 'degrading', combines limitedly with nouns, turning them into verbs; thus *unseat, unhorse, unmask, unman*.

Note Both *de-* (pronounced /dɪ/) and *dis-* occur also in words that already had the prefixes when adopted into English; in such cases they frequently have no meaning analysable by ordinary users of English. *Eg*: *depend, discern*.

Pejorative prefixes

I.23 ˌMAL- 'badly', 'bad', combines with verbs, participles, adjectives, and abstract nouns; *eg*: *maltreat, malformed, malodorous, malfunction, malnutrition*.

MIS- 'wrongly', 'astray', combines with verbs, participles, and abstract nouns; *eg*: *miscalculate, mishear, misfire, misinform, mislead(ing)*; *misconduct* (n).

ˌPSEUDO- 'false', 'imitation', combines freely with nouns and adjectives, *eg*: *pseudo-Christianity, pseudo-classicism, pseudo-intellectual* (n or adj); *pseudo-scientific*.

Note [**a**] Verbs prefixed by *mal-* and *mis-* tend to be gradable; *cf* 'He very much miscalculated the time required' beside '?He very much calculated . . .'

[**b**] Both in form and in degree of independent lexical meaning, *pseudo-* resembles the combining forms (*cf* App I.66), as is further suggested by the existence of the informal abbreviation *pseud* ⟨BrE⟩, *cf* App I.74.

[**c**] For other prefixes with pejorative overtones, see NON- (App I.21 Note [f]); ARCH-, OVER-, UNDER-, and HYPER- (App I.24).

Prefixes of degree or size

I.24 ˌARCH- 'supreme', 'most', combines freely with nouns, chiefly with human reference (*eg*: *archduke, archbishop*), and usually with pejorative effect (*eg*: *arch-enemy, arch-fascist, arch-hypocrite*): note the hyphens with these relatively ad hoc items; *archangel* is an isolated case, with pronunciation /ɑːk/ and normally with the prefix stressed.

ˌCO- 'joint(ly)', 'on equal footing', combines freely with nouns and verbs: *co-education, co-heir, co-pilot*; *co-religionist, cohabit, cooperate* ⟨also *co-operate* BrE⟩, *co-opt, coordinate, coexist.* In some nouns, the prefix is stressed: *ˈco-driver.*

ˌHYPER- 'extreme' (sometimes pejorative, 'too'), combines freely with adjectives: *hypersensitive, hypercritical, hyperactive.*

ˈMINI- 'little', combines freely (and especially informally) with nouns: *mini-market, mini-skirt, mini-cab*; a rather contrived contrast is possible with *ˈmaxi-* 'large' (*maxi-length*) and less commonly *ˈmidi-* 'medium'. In ad hoc collocations, the stress is often on the base: 'They started a *mini*(-)*ˈfactory.*'

ˌOUT- (*cf* App I.26) 'surpassing', combines freely with nouns and intransitive verbs to form transitive verbs: *outnumber, outclass, outdistance, outgrow, outrun, outlive.*

ˌOVER- 'excessive' (hence pejorative), combines freely with verbs and adjectives; *overeat, overestimate, overreact, overplay, oversimplify, overwork*; *overconfident, overdressed.* In more locative senses, 'from above', it combines fairly freely with verbs (*overflow, overshadow*); *cf* App I.26 Note [b].

ˌSUB- 'below' (but *cf* also App I.26 Notes [a] and [b]), combines with adjectives: *subconscious, subnormal.*

ˌSUPER- 'more than', 'very special' (but *cf* also App I.26), combines freely with adjectives (*eg*: *supernatural, supersensitive*) and nouns (with prefix stressed, *ˈsupermarket, ˈsuperman*, etc); 'on top', 'hierarchically superior', combines less freely with verbs (*super-impose*) and nouns (*ˈsuperstructure*).

ˈSUR- 'over and above', combines with nouns and takes the stress: *ˈsurcharge, ˈsurtax.*

ˌULTRA- 'extreme', 'beyond', combines freely with adjectives (hyperboles like *ultra-modern, ultra-conservative*; technical items like *ultrasonic, ultraviolet*); and with nouns in technical usage, sometimes with the prefix stressed (*ultramicroscopic, ˈultrasound, ultracentrifuge*).

ˌUNDER- (*cf* App I.26 Note [b]) 'too little', combines freely with verbs and *-ed* participles (*undercharge, underestimate, underplay*; *underprivileged, under-provided*), and corresponding nouns (*underprovision*); with the meaning 'subordinate', it combines less commonly with nouns (*eg*: *undermanager*).

Note [**a**] Several of these prefixes were already incorporated into words before they were adopted and in such cases they are frequently unanalysable semantically (*superficial*, *survey*, *subject*, *ultramarine*, etc), as is sometimes shown by stressing that ignores the structure of the prefix (*su'perfluous*, *hy'perbole*).

[b] *Supervisor* and *overseer* seem to reflect their respective origins (neo-classical and native) by acquiring associations with nonmanual and manual work respectively; like *overseer* is *foreman*.

[c] *Con-* (also *col-* and the original *com-*) has limited productivity in senses similar to those of *co-*: *conurbation*, *collateral*, *compatriot*; but it chiefly occurs in words already incorporating it before they were adopted into English.

[d] Implying 'minutely small', we have *'micro-* in *microcomputer*, *microchip*, *microparticle*, *microfilm* etc; the antonymous prefix *'macro-* is also used.

Prefixes of orientation and attitude

I.25 ˌANTI- (/æntɪ/ also /æntaɪ/ AmE) 'against', combines freely with denominal adjectives (*anti-social*, *anti-clerical*, *anti-clockwise*), and nouns (mainly to form premodifying adjectives; *the anti-war campaign*), as in *anti-missile*, *anti-war*.

ˌCONTRA- 'opposite', 'contrasting', combines with nouns, verbs, and denominal adjectives: *contradistinction*, *contraindicate*, *contrafactual*; with stress on the prefix, *'contraflow*, noun, used of traffic.

ˌCOUNTER- 'against', 'in opposition to', combines with verbs, abstract nouns, and denominal adjectives: *counter-espionage*, *counter-clockwise*; but often with main stress on the prefix: *'counteract* (also *counter'act*); *'counter-revolution*, *'countersink* (verb).

ˌPRO- (/prəʊ/) [i] 'for', 'on the side of', combines freely with denominal adjectives and nouns (mainly to form premodifying adjectives), *eg*: *pro-communist*, *pro-American*, *pro-student*.

[ii] 'on behalf of', 'deputizing for', combines fairly freely with nouns, *eg*: *pro-consul*, *pro-provost*.

Note [a] *Anti-* (antonym, *pro-*) suggests simply an attitude of opposition, while *counter-* suggests action in opposition to or in response to a previous action. A *counterattack* can take place only if there has already been an *attack*.

[b] In *'antibody* (exceptional in having initial stress), *cf* German *Antikörper*, *-body* does not have the ordinary sense of human or animate body, but rather the more technical sense of 'object' as in *foreign bodies*.

[c] Where (as in the many adopted words like *provide*) *pro-* is not analysed as a prefix, it is usually unstressed, /prə/.

Locative prefixes

I.26 These, like spatial prepositions (*cf* 9.14*ff*), may extend their meaning metaphorically to abstract spheres.

ˈFORE- (*cf* also App I.27) 'front part of', 'front', combines fairly freely with nouns such as *'forearm*, *'foreshore*, *'foreground*; *'foreleg*, *'forename*.

ˌINTER- 'between', 'among', combines freely with denominal adjectives, verbs, and nouns; *eg*: *international*, *interlinear*, *inter-continental*, *intertwine* (v), *intermarry*, *interweave*. With nouns, the product is chiefly used in premodification: (the) *inter-war* (years), (an) *inter-school* (event), but *cf* also (with initial stress) *'interplay* (n).

ˌSUB- (*cf* also App I.24) 'under', combines fairly freely with adjectives, verbs, and nouns; *eg*: *subnormal*; *sublet*, *subdivide*, *subcon'tract*, *subsection* (ˌ· ˈ· · or ˈ· ˌ· ·), *'subˌway*.

ˈSUPER- (*cf* also App I.24) 'above' combines rather infrequently with nouns *eg*: *ˈsuperstructure*, *ˈsuperscript*.

ˌTRANS- 'across', 'from one place to another', combines freely with denominal adjectives and with verbs. *Eg*: *transatlantic*, *trans-Siberian*; *transplant*, *transship*; with initial stress where it was already present in adopted nouns: *ˈtransport*.

[a] In limited use we have *ˈin-* and *ˈout-* as in *inhouse* (adverb), *outhouse* and *outstation* (nouns).

[b] In nominalization of verbs along with their accompanying particles, the locative particles are frequently prefixed and stressed: *ˈoverflow*, *ˈoverˌseer*, *ˈoutlook*, *ˈoutput*, *ˈoutset*, *ˈunderpass*, *ˈinput*, *ˈthroughput*.

[c] On the same prefixes already present in adopted words (*intermittent*, *translate*, etc), *cf* App I.24 Note [a].

[d] *Cf* also *ˌextra-* 'outside' and *ˌintra-* 'within' which combine with adjectives in rather formal and technical use: *extra-territorial*, *intra-uterine*; these prefixes are sometimes pronounced with second syllable /ɑː/. The former is more productive: *extramural*, *extraterrestrial*, *extrasolar*, *extralinguistic*. The meaning is 'outside/inside the *N* from which the adjective is derived'.

Prefixes of time and order

I.27 ˌEX- 'former', combines freely with (chiefly) human nouns, *eg*: *ex-president*, *ex-serviceman*, *ex-husband*. *Cf* the more general use of *ex-* in borrowed words with totally unstressed *ex-* (*expect*) and with voicing before a vowel (*examine* /gz/).

ˌFORE- 'before', combines fairly freely with verbs and nouns, *eg*: *foretell*, *forewarn*, *foreshadow*; *foreknowledge* (ˈ·ˌ·· for some speakers), *ˈforeplay*, *ˈforetaste*.

ˌPOST- (/pəʊst/) 'after', combines freely with nouns (mainly as premodifiers) and denominal adjectives; *eg*: *post-war*, *post-election*; *post-classical*. *Cf* borrowed words: *postpone*, etc. Attributively there is often a stress switch (as with *pre-*, below): *ˈpostˌwar* (euphoria).

ˌPRE- (/priː/) 'before', 'in advance', combines freely with nouns (mainly as premodifiers) and denominal adjectives, *eg*: *pre-war*, *pre-school* (children), *pre-19th century*, *pre-marital*. More rarely, it combines with verbs, such as *pre-heat*, *pre-cook*. The more learned competing prefix *ante-* 'before' is found almost entirely in borrowed and neo-classical words (*antediluvian*, *antenatal*, etc). *Cf* unstressed /prɪ/ in borrowed words: *prevent*, etc. When *pre*-items are attributive, there is often a stress switch, as in *ˈpre-ˌwar* (prices) (*cf* Note [a]).

ˌRE- (/riː/) 'again', 'back', combines freely with verbs and deverbal nouns such as *rebuild*, *reclaim*, *re-use*, *recycle*, *re-evaluate*; *re-analysis*. Occasionally, it combines with an adjective to yield a verb: *renew* (*cf* Note [b] below).

Note **[a]** Besides *pre-* there is, as we have seen, a more formal and rarer prefix *ante-* as in *antenatal*; even in technical use, its rarity is doubtless encouraged by the danger of confusion (in speech) with *anti-*.

[b] Several of these prefixes were already part of words in their adopted forms: *eg*: *prevent*, *postpone*, *expect*, *relieve*, etc; usually /ɪ/, but /e/ in *represent* (*cf* App I.24 Note [a]). In speech, the clearer enunciation of the productive prefixes (through secondary stress) usually makes them distinct, but in writing, ambiguity is possible between *recover* (/rɪ/) *my cushion* ['get it back again'] and *re(-)cover* (/riː/) *my cushion* ['put a new cover on it']. In writing, a hyphen is usefully introduced after the productive prefix to make the distinction clear.

Neo-classical items

Number prefixes

I.28 Items that are originally Greek or Latin are widely used as the first constituent in a range of expressions dealing with numerical values. It is arguable that at least some should be treated as combining forms, *ie* as the first constituent in the class of compounds dealt with in App I.66; *cf* the native analogues: *single-sex* (*schools*), *double-barrelled*, *three-sided*. But since some arbitrariness is involved in any case, we opt for treatment as prefixes, not least because – unlike constituents entering into compounds – they are a regularly recurring and relatively closed set, with semantic affinities between them. The following combine fairly freely, especially in specialized terminology, with nouns and denominal adjectives:

BI-, DI- 'two', as in *'bi,plane*, *'bicycle*, *'biped*, *,bi'lateral*, *,bi'focal*, *,bi'lingual*; *,di'chotomy*, *'diode*, *di'oxide*, *'digraph*, *di'valent*.

POLY-, MULTI- 'many', as in *'polyglot*, *'polygon*, *po'lygamy*, *,poly'andry*, *po'lysemy*, *,poly'technic*; *multi-* items are used chiefly in premodification: *,multi-'storey* (*building*), *'multi,form*, *,multi-'lateral*, *,multi'racial*, *,multi-'purpose*.

SEMI-, DEMI- (less productive, HEMI-: chiefly scientific), 'half' as in *'semi,circle*, *'semi,vowel*, *'semi,quaver* (music), *,semi-de'tached*, *,semi-'conscious*, *,semi-auto'matic*; *'demi,god*, *'demi,john*, *,demi'semiquaver*, *'demi,tasse*; *'hemi,sphere*, *,hemi'algia*, *,hemi'morphic*.

TRI- 'three', as in *'tripod*, *'tricycle*, *'trima,ran*, *,tri'mester*, *,tri'partite*, *,tri'nomial*.

UNI-, MONO- 'one', as in *'unisex*, *'univalve*, *,uni'lateral*, *,unidi'rectional*; *'monorail*, *'monoplane*, *mo'nogamy*, *'monolith*, *'monologue*, *,monosyl'labic*.

Note [a] *Mono-* is contracted in items like *,mo'noxide*; note also the insertion of *n* in *,bi'naural*. *Bi-* with units of time (*,bi'monthly*, *,bi'weekly*) can be used both to mean 'every two (units)' or 'twice each (unit)'. A somewhat arbitrary distinction exists between *,bi'ennial* 'every two years' and *,bi'annual* 'twice each year', but this is ill-established and many people recognize no such distinction. Not surprisingly, alternative expressions are often used: 'two-yearly conferences' *vs* 'twice-yearly conferences'.

[b] The -(*t*)*et* ending in *quartet* has a native analogue, *-some*, as in *'two,some*, *'four-,some*, 'a party of two, four'; *cf* also adjectival and adverbial *-fold*, as in *three-fold* ['three times'] etc.

[c] Higher numbers than three are less frequently involved: *,quadri'lateral*, *'pent,angle*, *,sex'agonal*, *,septuage'narian*, *,oc'tagonal*, etc. Note also sets like *,du'et*, (*'trio*), *,quar'tet*, *,quin'tet*, *,sex'tet* etc. *Du*(*o*)- occurs also in *,du'opoly*, *'duo,tone*, etc.

Miscellaneous neo-classical prefixes

I.29 As was noted in App I.28, it is possible to regard such items as combining-forms (*cf* App I.66), effecting compounds; compare *self* in *self-denial*, *deputy* in *deputy-director*, *under* in *under-secretary*, etc.

,AUTO- 'self', combines freely with nouns and adjectives; *eg*: *autosuggestion*, *autobiography*, *automation*, *'autocrat*.

,EXTRA- 'exceptionally', combines freely if informally with adjectives; sometimes written as a separate word: 'She was *extra affectionate* that day.'

,NEO- 'new', 'revived', combines with nouns and adjectives, especially with reference to political, artistic, etc movements: *neo-classicism*, *neo-Gothic*, *neo-Nazi*.

ˌPALEO- (also -ÆO-) 'old', chiefly in learned words like *paleography*, *paleolithic*.

ˌPAN- 'all', 'world-wide', combines especially with nouns and premodifying denominal adjectives with reference to world-wide or continent-wide activities; *eg*: *pan-African*, *pan-Anglican*, *pan-American*.

ˌPROTO- 'first', 'original', combines with nouns and adjectives such as *Proto-Germanic*, *ˈprotoˌtype*.

ˈTELE- 'distant', combines chiefly with classical bases to form nouns: *ˈtelescope*, *ˈtelegram*, *ˈtelephone*; new items are largely concerned with electronic communication: *ˌteleˈvision* (or ˈ· ·ˌ· ·), *ˌtelecommuniˈcations*; *cf* Blends, App I.76.

ˌVICE- 'deputy', combines freely with nouns, as in *vice-chairman*, *vice-admiral*, *vice-president*; *cf* also *ˈviceroy*.

Conversion prefixes

I.30 The following prefixes, with limited productivity in chiefly literary use, differ from those in other sections in having little discrete semantic value, their chief function being to effect a conversion (*cf* App I.43*ff*) of the base from one word class to another. In this respect they resemble suffixes, and, as the examples show, sometimes accompany suffixes in their conversion role. They are unstressed.

A- (/ə/) combines chiefly with verbs to yield predicative adjectives (*cf* 5.11); *asleep*, *astride*, *awash*, *atremble*, *aglow*, *aloud*. The meaning is similar to that of the progressive; *cf* 'Her cheeks were aglow' ~ 'Her cheeks were glowing'.

BE- [i] functions along with *-ed* (*cf* App I.38) to turn noun bases into adjectives with somewhat more intensified force ('wearing or surrounded by') than is suggested by *-ed* alone: *bewigged*, *bespectacled*, *befogged*, *bedewed*;
[ii] intensifies the force of verbs: *bedazzle*, *bestir*;
[iii] combines with nouns to yield transitive verbs: *bewitch*, *bedevil*, *befriend*. Most such *be-* items have a pejorative or facetious tone.

EN-, EM- before /p/, /b/, combines chiefly with nouns to yield verbs ('to put into', 'to provide with'): *enmesh*, *empower*, *endanger*, *enflame*, *entrain*; *embitter*.

Note In several *be-* words, change of meaning has made relations with the base obscure: *eg*: *belabour*, *beguile*, *benighted*; moreover, compared with *beleaguer* ['besiege'], the base *leaguer* ['encamp'] is a rarely used word.

Suffixation

General

I.31 As with prefixes, we shall concentrate on those suffixes that are in commonest productive use, but where our treatment of prefixes was on a generally *semantic* basis, our treatment of suffixes is on a generally *grammatical* basis. This is because, while prefixes primarily effect a semantic modification of the base (but *cf* App I.30), suffixes have by contrast only a small semantic role, their primary function being to change the grammatical function (for example the word class) of the base; but *cf* Note below.

Thus, although suffixes are by no means uniquely associated with a particular word class, it is convenient to group them according to the word class that results when they are added to a base. We therefore speak of NOUN SUFFIXES, VERB SUFFIXES, etc. But, in addition, since particular suffixes are frequently associated with attachment to bases of particular word classes, it is also convenient to speak of them as DENOMINAL SUFFIXES, DE-ADJECTIVAL SUFFIXES, etc. For example, *-ness* is a 'de-adjectival noun suffix' in that it forms nouns from adjectives such as *kind* or *gracious*. It is useful to extend this concept further and to speak of the derived words themselves as DENOMINAL, DEVERBAL, etc: *graciousness* is a 'de-adjectival' formation.

The complications that we noted with prefixes, especially in the mixture of native and foreign, productive and nonproductive, are paralleled with suffixes, but in some ways they are more serious. It is true that, while we cannot semantically link the *pre-* of unitary adoptions like *prefer* with the productive *pre-* in *pre-heat*, the grammatical function of (for example, -((*a*)*t*)*ion* is recognizable as a noun ending whether or not English possesses a separate base (*nation, duration, ovation, portion*). It is true also that, in contrast with the variability of stress in prefixation, a suffix is more often an unstressed addition to a base. But unlike prefixation, suffixation with originally foreign items is often accompanied by stress shifts and sound changes determined by the foreign language concerned. Thus even where the spelling of the base remains constant, the stress differences in sets like the following involve sharply different vowel sounds; for example, in BrE, the *graph* element in the following is pronounced /ɑː/, /ə/, and /æ/ respectively (*cf* App I.19):

'photograph ~ pho'tography ~ photo'graphic

Spelling as well as sound is affected in many sets; *eg*:

invade ~ invasion; persuade ~ persuasion, etc
permit ~ permission; admit ~ admission, etc
'drama ~ dra'matic, etc
able ~ a'bility, etc
in'fer ~ 'inference ~ infe'rential, etc

A further problem is that while productive prefixes can generally combine with bases of any origin, some of the originally foreign suffixes require originally foreign bases, and there has traditionally been some inhibition about forming 'hybrids'. This has resulted in pairs of (for example) nouns and denominal adjectives that are formally distinct:

mind ~ mental (*mindal)
nose ~ nasal (*nosal)
mouth ~ oral (*mouthal)

Note If suffixes had no more than a grammatical role, they would be like grammatical inflexions and have no place in word-formation. This indeed is how some linguists treat the adverb suffix *-ly*, and the line is not always clear. With *-ing*, it should be noted that, as well as appearing in lexicalized derivatives, it is also used in entirely predictable nominalizations; *cf* 17.51*ff*. Nouns in *-ing* are the 'verbal nouns' of 17.52*ff* (contrast 'deverbal' nouns):

He merely flouted the petty regulations.
~ His mere *flouting* of the petty regulations . . .

The situation is similar with agential *-er*, since for every verb (with a few exceptions such as copulas like *be, have, become*), a syntactic frame exists in which an *-er* form is predictable:

He merely flouted the petty regulations.

~ He was a mere *flouter* of petty regulations.

We have treated *-er* as a noun suffix because lexicalization is necessary before an *-er* formation (*cf* App I.34) can be used outside such a frame (**He is a flouter*). Although we have 'They *watch/see/look at* television a good deal', it is *view* that has become the base for the lexicalized *viewer* as in '*Viewers* will have noticed . . .'. Note that although *bird-watcher* is thoroughly institutionalized, we do not say '(*)*Watchers* may have noticed robins nesting in . . .'

It is significant that the fully and solely *grammatical* endings (like those for number, tense, comparison) always follow and cannot precede the *derivational* suffixes with which word-formation is concerned. This mirrors the way in which derivational affixes are part of the internal relations of a lexico-semantic unit, whereas inflections are concerned with the relations between this unit and the rest of the sentence or other grammatical construction. Exceptions ('two *spoonsful*', 'two *consuls-general*) attest to the general truth of this by their infrequency, by our tendency to move such 'infixed' inflexions ('two *spoonfuls*', 'two *consul-generals*', but **passer-bys*), and by the normal deletion of plural *-s* in the first element of compounds ('*a trouser-leg*', '*trouser-seam*'); but *cf* 17.108. Note also *(home)ward journey*, App I.41.

Noun suffixes

Denominal nouns: Abstract

I.32 Noun bases become largely noncount abstract, or aggregate nouns of status or activity, by means of the following suffixes:

-AGE (/ɪdʒ/) (*cf* App I.35) 'measure of', 'collection of', as in *baggage*, *frontage*, *mileage*.

-DOM, as in *officialdom*; this suffix, again not very productive, tends to convey pejorative overtones (though not perhaps in *stardom* and not in the old-established *kingdom*, which – in contrast to *kingship* – is concrete and countable).

-ERY, -RY (especially after /l/ and /t/):

[i] 'the condition or behaviour associated with', as in *drudgery*, *slavery*, *devilry* (also *deviltry*); often used in ironic nonce-formation: *nitwittery*, *take-over-biddery*, *day-trippery*, etc. There is some use of adjective bases: *bravery*;

[ii] 'location of', as in *nursery*, *rookery*, *refinery*, *bakery*, *nunnery*; these are used as concrete count aggregate nouns, and verb bases can be involved; there are occasional nonce-formations: *eatery* 'canteen';

[iii] noncount concrete aggregate nouns are rather freely formed, such as *machinery*, *rocketry*, *gadgetry*.

-FUL (/fʊl/, contrast App I.38), 'the amount contained in', as in *spoonful*, *glassful*, etc; such freely formed nouns approach concreteness in meaning and are count; *cf* App I.31.

-HOOD, as in *boyhood*, *brotherhood*, *widowhood*; only mildly productive, though items like *sentencehood* can achieve limited currency; the base is occasionally an adjective, as in *falsehood*, which is both count and noncount.

-ING (*cf* also App I.35): [i] noncount concrete aggregates are fairly freely formed, such as *tubing*, *panelling*, *matting*, *carpeting*, all with reference to the material of which the base is made;

[ii] 'activity connected with', as in *cricketing*, *farming*, *blackberrying*. Such nouns, abstract and noncount, are fairly freely made (*cf* 15.13*f*, 17.53*f*).

-ISM 'doctrine of', 'practice of', as in *Calvinism*, *idealism*, *impressionism*, *fanaticism*, *absenteeism*, *racism*. The items concerning religion, politics, philosophy, and art usually have a corresponding item in *-ist* to denote adherents or practitioners: *cf* App I.37.

-ˈOCRACY 'government by', as in *deˈmocracy*, *arisˈtocracy*, *meriˈtocracy*; they can be count and have corresponding personal nouns, *ˈdemocrat*, etc. They might be seen as combining-form compounds; *cf* App I.66.

-SHIP, as in *friendship*, *membership*, *dictatorship*, *professorship*; most items with this limitedly productive suffix can also be count and some have an adjective base (as in *hardship*); *lecturership* is less common than the irregular *lectureship*.

Note [**a**] With *-ery* [ii], compare the ultimate cognates *-teria* (largely in commercial coinages, such as *cafeteria*, *washeteria*), *-(at)orium* (as in *auditorium*, but also commercially used as in *lubritorium*), and *-(t)ory* (as in *dormitory*).

[**b**] The suffix *-er* can also effect abstract nouns in the sense of 'instance, process of V': 'The two firms are arranging a *merger*.'

Denominal nouns: Concrete

I.33 In contrast with those in App I.32, the following noun suffixes combine with noun bases to yield concrete and individualizing items over a rather wide semantic range. Only *-er* is freely productive. Note that some items (rarely for suffixes) become the stressed syllable in the derived word: *-eer*, *-ette* invariably.

-ˈEER 'skilled in', 'engaged in', as in *pamphleteer*, *profiteer*, *racketeer*; often pejorative (especially where this is suggested by the base), but not in *mountaineer*, *auctioneer*, *engineer*.

-ER (contrast App I.34), 'having as dominant characteristic', 'denizen of', as in *teenager*, *north-wester* (of wind), *three-wheeler*, *villager*, *Londoner*; in tone, this resembles the 'familiarity markers' of App I.77. In *cooker*, *roaster*, *boiler* ['cooking apple', 'boiling fowl' etc], the base seems to be a verb; but *cf*: *-ing* [ii] in App I.32.

-ESS as in *waitress*, *actress*, *lioness*, *manageress*, *stewardess*, *hostess* (the last four sometimes have stress on the suffix); adds feminine marking to animate nouns; sometimes the vowel of the preceding unstressed agential suffix is elided: *cf*: *wait* (at table) ~ *waiter*, *waitress*; *cf* also Note [a], and 5.105.

-ˈETTE [i] 'compact', fairly productive, as in *kitchenette*, *dinerette*;
[ii] 'imitation', as in *flannelette*, *leatherette*; formerly common in commercial coinages;
[iii] a feminine marker, as in *suffragette*, *usherette*; *cf* Note [a].

-LET 'small', 'unimportant', as in *booklet*, *leaflet*, *piglet*, *starlet*.

-LING 'minor', 'offspring of', as in *princeling*, *duckling*; other bases beside nouns are involved, as in *hireling*, *underling*. Where the referent is human, the formation is somewhat contemptuous.

-STER 'involved in', as in *trickster*, *gangster*, *gamester*; usually pejorative, but not in *roadster* (style of vehicle).

Note [**a**] Changing attitudes to women and to sex discrimination have much reduced the use of *-ess*, *-ette*, and compounds in *woman-*, *girl-*. Surviving usage would refer to the designation of an activity (*hostess, stewardess*) rather than to the sex of the person performing it; thus the same woman might say 'I am an actress' and 'I am a bad actor'. Since there are roles that must be filled by women, *actress* is tolerated where *authoress* and *poetess* have no such justification and are now in consequence rarely used. For other but related social reasons, *Jewess* and *negress* are little used. Note that in 'The *master/mistress* of the house' different roles are involved; teachers referred to as *form-master, form-mistress* ⟨chiefly BrE⟩ are however in the same role. The use of *master* for role irrespective of sex is to be found in:

She is giving *master*-classes (**mistress-*) in piano.
She is now a *master* in the art of dodging work.
She has now *mastered* the art of etching.
She now has *mastery* of the whole matter.

[**b**] Formations like *policeman, chairperson,* are treated as compounds; *cf* App I.13, I.61.
[**c**] With *-let, -ling, cf* familiarity markers, App I.77.

Deverbal nouns

I.34 The following suffixes combine with verb bases to produce concrete count nouns, largely of personal reference; *-er* is particularly productive.

-ANT, a chiefly formal agential, as in *inhabitant, contestant, informant*; it often corresponds to verbs in *-ate*: *participate* ~ *participant, lubricate* ~ *lubricant.* As the last example shows, reference may be nonpersonal.

-ˈEE 'one who is object of the verb', as in *appoinˈtee, paˈyee*; in some cases, as with *-ant*, it may replace the verb ending *-ate*: *nomiˈnee.* There are examples without verb base or 'object' meaning: *absenˈtee, refuˈgee.* Stressing is exceptional in *emˈployee.*

-ER, -OR (contrast App I.33), forms agential nouns (*cf* 17.51*ff* on nominalization), as in *singer* ['one who sings (especially) professionally'], *writer, driver, employer*, etc; used informally also with phrasal verbs (*washer-up, chucker-out*) and with object-verb compounds and some comparable compounds (*window-cleaner, high-flier*). Agentials may also be nonpersonal: *silencer, computer, thriller.* With neo-classical bases, the suffix is often spelled *-or* (*accelerator, incubator*; *supervisor, survivor*; *actor*); so too in cases where there is no free base (*author, doctor*, etc).

I.35 The following suffixes combine with verb bases to produce largely abstract nouns, nominalizations of the action expressed by the base:

-AGE (/ɪdʒ/) (*cf* App I.32), 'action of', 'instance of', abstract and usually noncount, as in *breakage, coverage, drainage, leverage, shrinkage, wastage.*

-AL 'the action or result of', chiefly count, as in *refusal, revival, dismissal, upheaval.*

-ˈATION [i] 'the process or state of', normally used as noncount, as in *exploˈration, starˈvation, ratifiˈcation, victimiˈzation*;
[ii] 'the product of', 'the institution produced by', aggregate count nouns, as in *founˈdation, organiˈzation.* This suffix freely combines with verb bases in *-ize, -ify, -ate*, with stress shift where necessary (*cf*: *ˈjustify, ˈeducate*). Pronunciation and stress suggest that analogous endings already present in adopted nouns (often paired with adopted verbs: *deˈcide* ~ *deˈcision*, etc) are analysed as related even though they are not productive.

-ING (contrast App I.32 and the verbal noun, 17.52*ff*), concrete count nouns referring to what results from the action of the base, as in *building, opening,* *filling* (in tooth); some are obligatory plurals: *earnings*, *savings*, *shavings*. Occasionally the formations are noncount: *stuffing*, *clothing*. The abstract count items *christening*, *wedding* refer rather to the occasion of the base verb's activity.

-MENT (/mənt/) 'the result of', as in *arrangement* (count), *amazement*, *puzzlement*, *embodiment*; in some cases the formation is concrete (*eg*: *equipment*, noncount), and *management* can be both abstract noncount and concrete aggregate count.

Note The glosses cannot capture the aspectual essence of the nominalizations in *-ation*, *-ment*, etc in contrast to those in the *-ing* verbal noun. Note the gradience presented in 17.54. The word-formations described in this section are relatively remote from the conduct of the action itself, and even at their 'most verbal' refer rather to the action as a whole event, including its completion. Compare:

His *exploring* of the mountain is taking a long time.
His *exploration* of the mountain took/will take three weeks.

De-adjectival nouns

I.36 There are two very common suffixes by means of which abstract (and normally noncount) nouns are formed from adjective bases:

-ITY, especially associated with adjectives of neo-classical or French origin, with stress shift wherever necessary, to place the stress on the last syllable before the suffix as in *e'lastic* ~ *ela'sticity*, *'rapid* ~ *ra'pidity*; further examples: *'sanity*, *'falsity*, *di'versity*, *ba'nality*. The vowel of the stressed syllable is often changed from long to short: *eg*: *ver'bose* /əʊ/ ~ *ver'bosity* /ɒ/. The suffix is freely productive, especially with adjectives in *-able* (*respecta'bility*), *-al* (*actu'ality*) and *-ar* (*regu'larity*). But there are examples in which the affix was already present when the word was adopted: *eg*: *eternity*, *humility*; these lack a direct adjective base in English (*cf* also App I.39 Note [a]).

-NESS, fairly freely added to any type of adjective, as in *meanness*, *happiness*, *usefulness*, *kindness*, *selfishness*, *unexpectedness*, *stoutheartedness*, *accurateness*, *falseness*. Items (including phrases) in common premodifying or predicative use can equally take the suffix: *up-to-dateness*.

Note [**a**] Both suffixes occur also in 'frozen' items in which no base is identifiable (*levity*, *business*, /'bɪznɪs/).

[**b**] These two suffixes resemble *in-* and *un-* both in their predominant association with foreign and native bases respectively, and in the tendency for *-ity* and *in-* to be especially associated with greater lexicalization, *-ness* and *un-* with direct reference to the adjective bases in ad hoc formations. Compare *pompousness* and *pomposity*; it is even possible to imagine an occasion when the ad hoc *unflexibleness* would be used rather than the institutionalized *inflexibility*. *Musicality* will tend to refer to technical properties in a piece of *music* (the base tending to be nongradable); *musicalness* to the degree to which the gradable quality *musical* obtains. Formations in *-ness* also exist beside other de-adjectival formations: *normalness* ~ *nor'mality* ~ *normalcy* ⟨esp AmE⟩; *(un)justness* ~ *(in)justice*; *accurateness* ~ *accuracy*; *ineptness* ~ *ineptitude*; *infiniteness* ~ *infinitude* ~ *infinity*. The need for a *-ness* formation is clearer where the lexicalized item has developed a meaning relatively remote from the ordinary meaning of the adjective base; *eg*: *sensible* ~ *sensibility* ~ *sensibleness*. In any event, the *-ness* items are less lexicalized and can be conveniently used to refer directly to the adjective:

There is nothing particularly odd about him; he's perfectly normal, and in fact it's his very *normalness* that makes him seem boring.

Noun/adjective suffixes

I.37 A number of suffixes yield items that can be used both as nouns and as (normally nongradable) adjectives. The formations basically relate to human beings, chiefly as members of a group, and may be both denominal and de-adjectival. On nationality names, *cf* also 5.56*f*.

-ˈESE (AmE usually -ˌESE) *cf* 5.88. [i] 'member of' (nationality or race), as in *Chiˈnese, Portuˈguese, Japaˈnese*;
[ii] '(in) the language of, the style of', as in *Chiˈnese, Cantoˈnese, Johnsoˈnese, journaˈlese*; both nouns and adjectives, except those relating to style (such as *officiaˈlese*) which are nouns only and are pejorative.

-(I)AN [i] 'adherent to', as in *Darˈwinian, reˈpublican*;
[ii] 'relating to', as in *Shakeˈspearian, Elizaˈbethan, ˈChomskyan, (sub)urban* (adjective only);
[iii] 'citizen of', as in *Paˈrisian, Indoˈnesian, Chiˈcagoan, Glasˈwegian* (of Glasgow);
[iv] '(in) the language of', *Indoˈnesian, ˈRussian* (where the base ends in *-a*).
The stress falls on the last syllable before the suffix. Most items can be used both as nouns and as adjectives, not gradable in [iv], variably in other instances: *The place is (awfully) urban*; *She is an (*awfully) urban guerilla.*

-IST 'skilled in', 'practising', as in *violinist, stylist, rac(ial)ist, masochist, Calvinist, socialist, loyalist.* Items relating to adherence as distinct from skill are normally paired with abstract nouns in *-ism* (*cf* App I.32) and may be adjectives or nouns, though adjectival endings, *-ic(al)*, may be added; *cf* App I.39. A final vowel in the base is often omitted: *cello* ~ *cellist*. Skill items may have verb bases, as with *typist*, and are nouns only.

-ITE [i] 'adherent to', 'member of (set)' as in *Benthamite, shamanite, Chomskyite, socialite*; these are primarily nouns but may be adjectives (*He is a Luddite*; *His views are rather Luddite*). The bases are chiefly personal names of those who have led movements;
[ii] 'denizen of', as in *Brooklynite, Hampsteadite*; these are nouns only.
Formations of both types tend to be used disparagingly unless long-established (*Israelite*) or where a movement excites little hostility (*Benthamite*).

Note [**a**] Some bases can take *-ist*, *-ian*, and *-ite*, equally. The first would suggest greatest commitment to the views or theory concerned: 'He is an out-and-out Darwinist'. It is used of ideas rather than of their proponents. The second would be more neutral and would lend itself in consequence to use more readily as a gradable adjective ('Isn't that approach rather Darwinian?'), but can also refer to the work of Darwin himself (as *Darwinist*, *Darwinite* cannot). The third tends to be disparaging and would be used chiefly by those who are not themselves adherents: 'He is a Darwinite', rather than 'Are you a Darwinite?' or 'I am a Darwinite'; a faction is implied.
[**b**] With *-ian* should be compared the more restricted use of *-ˈarian* to form personal nouns and adjectives as in *authoriˈtarian, vegeˈtarian, octogeˈnarian*.

Adjective suffixes

Denominal suffixes

I.38 A wide range of suffixes exists having the function of forming adjectives, especially from nouns. We begin with those that retain a native flavour:

-ED (*cf* participial *-ed*, 3.2, 17.29), 'having', forms largely nongradable adjectives from nouns and especially from noun phrases: *wooded*, *pointed*, *walled*; *simple-minded*, *blue-eyed*, *blonde-haired*, *fuller-flavoured*, *odd-shaped*, *giant-sized*. These formations are to be distinguished from compounds like *much-travelled*, *self-styled* (*cf* App I.68*f*), where the second part is a verb. In some cases (*eg*: *three-legged*), the suffix is syllabic /ɪd/ under phonological conditions where inflexional *-ed* would not be; several formations are gradable: *aged*, *crooked*, *ragged*.

-FUL (usually /fəl/; contrast App I.32), 'full of', 'providing', combines with chiefly abstract nouns to form gradable adjectives, as in *useful*, *delightful*, *pitiful*, *successful*, *helpful*; sometimes the base is a verb: *forgetful*.

-ISH [i] freely used with largely concrete nouns, 'somewhat like', as in *childish*, *monkeyish*, *foolish*, *roguish*, *snobbish*; with adjective bases, the meaning is 'somewhat', as in *coldish*, *brownish*; with people's ages, 'approximately', as in *sixtyish*; *cf* also 'She'll arrive about tenish';
[ii] with names of races, peoples, and languages, *-ish* forms nongradable adjectives and (with respect to languages) nouns: *Swedish*, *Cornish*, *Turkish*; *cf* *-(i)an* [iii], [iv], App I.37.

-LESS 'without', combines with both abstract and concrete nouns, formations with the latter being usually nongradable: *careless*, *restless*, *colourless*, *harmless*; *childless*, *homeless*. The suffix is often used as the antonym of *-ful* (*useful* ~ *useless*, *careful* ~ *careless*) but separate lexicalization makes some pairs nonantonymic (*pitiful* ~ *pitiless*, etc).

-LIKE 'like', freely used with largely concrete nouns, as in *childlike*, *statesmanlike*, *monkeylike*; such formations might be regarded as compounds, and the relation between base and suffix is very direct: *x-like* means 'like (an) *x*'.

-LY (*cf* App I.41) [i] with largely concrete nouns, 'having the qualities of', as in *(wo)manly*, *soldierly*, *motherly*, *brotherly*, *friendly*, *cowardly*, *deathly*; there is also some use of adjective bases: *deadly*. With *comely*, no relation to a base is semantically recognized;
[ii] with nouns that are units of time, 'every', as *daily*, *weekly*, etc.

-Y 'somewhat like', 'characterized by', freely used with largely concrete nouns to form gradable adjectives, often of colloquial tone, as in *sandy*, *meaty*, *creamy*, *hairy*, *wealthy*, *filthy*; *comfy* (*cf* App I.77); the bases may also be verbs as in *gushy*, *runny* (*nose*). In *sandy hair* we have the 'somewhat like' sense; in *sandy beach* the 'characterized by' sense.

Note [**a**] Among other denominal adjective suffixes, we may mention *-some* 'constituting', as in *burdensome*, *frolicsome*, *bothersome*; *-worthy* 'fit for', as in *praiseworthy*, *prizeworthy*, *seaworthy*.
[**b**] Where *-like* and *-ish* occur with the same base, the latter is relatively pejorative and more remote from literal comparison. In *manly*, *manlike*, *mannish*, the first refers to physical or heroic qualities (in a male), the second is a simile, usually applied to nonhumans, the third refers to unwelcome masculine attributes (usually in a woman).

I.39 The denominal adjective suffixes in our second group are of foreign origin and although some of them are among the commonest suffixes in use, they retain something of their foreign origin in relative formality and in being largely used with bases that have also been adopted. Correspondences both with bases and with further derivations often reflect patterns of Latin morphology. All the suffixes have the meaning roughly paraphrasable as 'having the properties of' or more generally 'having a relation to (the base)'; the adjectives formed are usually gradable.

-AL, also -IAL (especially after bases in *-or*), -ICAL (especially replacing the final *-y* of bases), as in *acciˈdental, diaˈlectal*; *ediˈtorial, profesˈsorial*; *psychoˈlogical, philoˈsophical*. It will be seen that stress is affected, usually coming on the last syllable before the suffix (*cf* App II.3*ff*); *ˈcultural*, *ˈcynical*, *ˈmusical* are among the exceptions.

-ˈESQUE, apart from its use in words of which it already formed a part when adopted (*burlesque, arabesque*), now chiefly used with names prominently associated with artistic individuality: *romanesque, Kafkaesque, Daliesque*.

-IC (*cf* Note [c] below), with the same stress rule as for *-al*; *eg*: *aˈtomic, heˈroic, oceˈanic, speˈcific*; with some bases in *-em*, the suffix is *-atic* (*probleˈmatic, phoneˈmatic* beside *phoˈnemic*). The suffix is also used for nongradable ethnic adjectives and for the names of the corresponding languages: *Celtic*, *ˈArabic* (contrast *Aˈrabian*; *cf* 5.57 Note [d]).

-OUS (also -IOUS, especially when replacing *-ion, -ity* in bases so ending), as in *deˈsirous, ˈvirtuous, ˈgrievous, amˈbitious, viˈvacious*, the stress usually placed on the last syllable before the suffix. Several formations are slightly irregular; *eg*: *courteous, erroneous* (*cf* 'courtesy', 'error').

Note **[a]** The noun suffix *-ity* (*cf* App I.36) can be attached to *-al*, *-ic*, and *-ous*, but its addition entails certain changes. The suffix *-al* receives the stressed pronunciation /ˈæl/ in place of /əl/ (*ˈneutral* ~ *neuˈtrality*); *-ic* changes its pronunciation from /ɪk/ to /ˈɪs/ (*eˈlectric* ~ *elecˈtricity*); *-ous* changes its spelling to *-os-*, and receives the stressed pronunciation /ˈɒs/ instead of /əs/ (*ˈcurious* ~ *curiˈosity*).

[b] Nouns in *-ite* (*cf* App I.37) do not accept adjective suffixes (except *-ish*), but those in *-ist* accept *-ic* and *-ical*; indeed with an *-ist* item as a nongradable adjective, we have an interesting series in rare cases:

He is an atheist/egotist.
His views are (solidly) atheist/egotist.
His views are (rather) atheistic/egotistic.
His views are (slightly) atheistical/egotistical.

A diminishing degree of the *-ism* is implied; *-istic, istical* also tend to be disparaging: *cf*: *casuistical*.

[c] In some adjectives, *-ic* alternates with *-ical*, with a difference of meaning:

a *classic* performance ['great', 'memorable']	~	*classical* languages ['Latin and Greek']
a *comic* masterpiece ['of comedy']	~	his *comical* behaviour ['funny']
an *economic* miracle ['in the economy']	~	the car is *economical* to run ['money-saving']
an *electric* light ['powered by electricity']	~	an *electrical* fault ['of electricity']
a *historic* building ['with a history']	~	*historical* research ['pertaining to history']
his *ˈpolitic* behaviour ['tactful'] ⟨unusual⟩	~	*poˈlitical* parties ['concerned with politics']

[d] There are several less common neo-classical affixes, among which *-ary*, *-ate*, and *-ory* are particularly notable: *revolutionary, affectionate, obligatory*. Adjectives in *-ory* alternate (with or without stress shift) with nouns in *-tion, oˈbligatory* ~ *obliˈgation, satisˈfactory* ~ *satisˈfaction*. Both *-ary* and *-ory* are reduced in BrE to /ərɪ/ or /rɪ/; in AmE they are often given a secondary stress, and are distinguished in pronunciation as /ˌeri/ and /ˌori/ or /ˌəʊri/.

Deverbal suffixes

I.40 Two common suffixes are used to form adjectives (largely gradable) from verbs and they are in polar contrast in respect of verbal voice: *-ive* is fundamentally related to the active, 'of the kind that can V'; *-able* is fundamentally related to the passive, 'of the kind that can be V-ed'. Thus 'The idea attracts me' ~ 'The idea is attractive'; 'The text cannot be translated' ~ 'The text is untranslatable'; *supportive* 'can support', *supportable* 'can be supported'.

-ABLE fairly freely combines with transitive verbs to produce gradable adjectives, 'of the kind that is subject to being V-ed', as in *debatable*, *washable*, *drinkable*, *manageable*. In many adopted words the suffix was already present, sometimes in the variant forms *-ible*, *-uble*, which are not productive in English, but where the passive relation can still be found: *inevitable* 'cannot be avoided', *visible* 'can be seen', *soluble* 'can be dissolved'. As with passive verb phrases, the agent can sometimes be expressed with a *by*-phrase (though chiefly a general agent rather than a specific one: 'The comet was observable by anyone owning a powerful telescope' but ?'. . . observable by John'). With *visible* the instrument is indicated with *to* ('The naked eye cannot see this' ~ 'This is not visible to the naked eye'). Passive adjectives in *-able* are chiefly used in negative clauses or with negation by affixation: 'His story is not refutable' ~ '. . . is irrefutable' ~ '. . . is unrefutable'; instead of 'His story is refutable', we would normally use 'His story can be refuted'.

In addition, however, *-able* yields no passive meaning but rather has a sense paraphrasable as 'apt to V': *changeable* (weather), *perishable*, *suitable*, etc. Bases may also be nouns, sometimes implying a modalized passive sense (*marriageable*, *saleable*), sometimes not (*peaceable*, *fashionable*, *seasonable*, etc).

-IVE, as in *attractive*, *effective*, *possessive*. In many cases the relation between the verb and adjective reflects Romance morphology: *produce* ~ *productive*, *explode* ~ *explosive*, *expand* ~ *expansive*, *presume* ~ *presumptive*, etc. In others, on the pattern of *decorate* ~ *decorative*, a longer affix, *-ative*, is used: *talkative*, *affirmative*, *causative*. Occasionally the base is a noun (*secret* ~ *secretive*) and sometimes the relation to the base is obscured (as in *sensitive*, *emotive*). The stress pattern of the base is not usually affected by the addition of *-ive*.

Note **[a]** Prefixal negation with adjectives in both *-ive* and *-able* treats the whole of what follows as the base: thus *untranslatable* has the structure *un*(*translatable*) and does not mean 'possible not to translate' but 'not possible to translate'. Contrast privative *un-* (*cf* App I.22): 'I found the equipment readily *unpackable* [to be understood as 'easy to unpack'] but certainly not *unbreakable*' [easily breakable].

[b] Prepositional and phrasal verbs usually form *-able* adjectives with omission of the particle: 'We can rely *on* John' ~ 'John is *reliable*'; *cf*: *unspeakable*. This has the effect of making *washable* capable of two interpretations: 'This shirt is *washable*' [='can (safely) be washed']; 'This ink is *washable*' [may = 'can be washed out/away', though in fact it may indicate a guarantee that water can be applied without the writing being washed out]. But *cf* also phrasal items ⟨informal⟩: *unget-at-able*, *unliveable with*. With *agreeable*, there are three uses: 'companionable', 'willing to agree', 'can be agreed *to*'; in this last sense it is predicative only:

I have *agreeable* friends.

Eventually, my friends were *agreeable*.

We must find a formulation that is *agreeable* to everyone.

[**c**] Sometimes a passive *-able* adjective can be predicated only of an inanimate, where no such restriction obtains in the corresponding transitive clause:

The error } is *forgivable/pardonable*.
*The man }

We can forgive/pardon { the error.
{ the man.

[**d**] Although the modality of most passive *-able* adjectives is usually potential ('can be'), with some it is intentional or obligational ('will be', 'must be'). Compare:

The deposit is *refundable*. ['will']
The money is *payable* on delivery. ['must']
The money is *payable* by cheque. ['can']

[**e**] Given that *-able* adjectives may be active (*changeable*) as well as passive, some items can be either:

The weather is *variable*. [must be *active*]
The date is *variable*. [may be *passive*]

[**f**] Some adjectives in *-able* have front-shifted stress:

ˈadmirable (*adˈmire*), *ˈpreferable*

[**g**] Since, like *-ly* (*cf* App I.41), *-able* can be fairly freely used in nonce-formation, an indication of spelling convention may be given. Bases in final *-y* have this replaced by *i* (as in *deniable*), but final *-e* is usually retained, especially where a misleading pronunciation might otherwise be suggested (thus *enticeable*, **enticable*; *expungeable*, **expungable*).

Adverb suffixes

I.41 -LY (*cf* 7.46*f*, App I.38) can be very generally added to an adjective in a grammatical environment requiring an adverb (gradable if the adjective concerned is gradable), so that it could almost be regarded as inflexional; *cf* App I.31 Note. The meaning can often be paraphrased as 'in a . . . manner', as in *calm* ~ *calmly*, or 'to a . . . degree', as in 'She looks *extremely* well', or 'in a . . . respect', as in '*Personally*, he would be suitable'. The range of meanings is related to the range of adverbial functions: *cf* 8.2*ff*, 8.24*ff*. With adjectives in *-ic*, *-al-* is usually added before the suffix (*eg*: *scenic* ~ *scenically*); *cf* App I.39 on the relation of adjectival *-ic* and *-ical*. No *-al-* is inserted in *publicly*, but in any case the insertion is inaudible since there is elision: *scenically* is pronounced /ˈsiːnɪklɪ/. The restrictions on the use of *-ly* may be summarized as follows: [i] there are some adjectives with no separate adverbial form (*eg*: *fast*, *hard*); (ii) *-ly* is not added to adjectives ending in *-ly* (*cf* 7.9, App I.38); **cowardlily*, though occasionally one finds *sillily*, *friendlily*; more usually, prepositional phrases or synonyms are used (*amicably*); (iii) there is avoidance of *-ly* also with adjectives ending in /l/, as with *hostile*, and it is usual to substitute a prepositional phrase such as 'with hostility'; exceptions include *wholly*, *solely*; (iv) *-ly* is not added to some miscellaneous adjectives (*eg*: *difficult*, but *cf* Note [a]). On the other hand, especially informally, *-ly* can be used with phrases, as in 'She spoke quite *matter-of-factly* on the subject'.

-WARD(S) forms nongradable directional adverbs where the base may be a noun as in *earthward*(*s*), a prepositional adverb as in *onward*(*s*), or a directional adverb as in *northward*(*s*). Nonce-formations like *theatreward*(*s*) or *Chicago-ward*(*s*) are common if jocular. The forms without *-s* are usual in printed AmE, those with *-s* are usual in BrE and are common in spoken AmE. This type of adverb lends itself to premodification in its form without *-s*: 'Homeward journeys are the happiest'.

-WISE is used to form nongradable adverbs from noun bases: [i] in relation to manner, as in *clockwise*, *crabwise*, it is limitedly productive; [ii] in relation to dimension, as in *crosswise*, *lengthwise*, it has a variant, *-ways* (*lengthways*), which is in fact more usual with the item *sideways*; [iii] in the sense 'so far as [the base] is concerned', as in *education-wise*, *moneywise*, it is more freely productive in AmE than in BrE, but many people object to these formations.

Note [**a**] Occasionally one hears (hardly reads) such forms as *difficultly*, sometimes as a slip of the tongue with subsequent correction, sometimes unconsciously and uncorrected; but sometimes the usage is quite deliberate, as in the following:

The doctor explained her diagnosis expertly enough but *difficultly* – I mean, the explanation was hard to understand.

The speaker's addition suggests awareness that the prepositional phrase *with difficulty* would have been inappropriate here in implying that the doctor herself found explanation difficult to formulate. *Cf* also 'The staff find themselves *difficultly* placed', meaning 'placed in a difficult situation', not 'placed with difficulty'.

[**b**] Since *-ly* can be used with a freedom akin to that with inflectional endings, it may be mentioned that there are some generally observed spelling conventions. Bases in *-y* have this replaced by *i* (as in *sloppily*). Bases with final *-e* usually retain it (as in *solely*; *wholly* is exceptional), except where syllabic *l* is involved; here as in *simple*, *probable* etc, *e* is dropped and only *y* added, the *l* ceasing to be syllabic (*simply*, *probably*). Thus:

/sɪmpl̩/ ~ /sɪmplɪ/

In the rare cases of final *-ll*, no additional *l* is added but the consonant is sometimes lengthened in pronunciation: *shrilly*; *cf* also *wholly* , *vilely*.

[**c**] Nongradable adverbs are also formed by adding *-style* or *-fashion* to chiefly noun bases: 'He dresses *bank-manager-style*', 'He swims *dog-fashion*'. Such formations resemble compounds based on noun-phrase structure, and where the base is itself equivocal (as in 'She eats *American-style*') they can be related to 'the style/fashion of N' or 'the Adj style/fashion'. Here might be mentioned *-fold* as in *three-fold*, *five-fold*, 'three (five) times as much'.

Verb suffixes

I.42 Only a few verb-forming suffixes occur with any great frequency in English, and only *-ize* is highly productive. All are concerned with forming transitive verbs of basically causative meaning.

ˌ-ATE (/eɪt/) combines with chiefly neo-classical noun bases, as in *orchestrate*, *hyphenate*: the suffix is especially productive in scientific English as in *chlorinate*, (*de*)*laminate*, etc.

-EN combines with adjectives as in *deafen*, *sadden*, *tauten*, *quicken*, *ripen*, *widen*, *harden*. As well as being causative, 'to make . . .', many of these can also be used intransitively, 'to become . . .': *The news saddened him* ~ *His face saddened*; this may be regarded as a conversion; *cf* App I.43*ff*.

-IFY, -FY (/(ɪ)ˌfaɪ/), combines with adjectives and nouns, as in *simplify* 'to make simple', *amplify* 'to express more fully', *codify* 'to put into code', *beautify* 'to endow with beauty'. It is most commonly found with neo-classical bases (*certify*, *identify*, etc, sometimes with a difference in stem as in *electrify*, *liquefy* ['to put into liquid form']), and formations outside this type of lexicon are often facetious or pejorative: *speechify*, *dandify*, etc.

-IZE (-ISE) combines freely with adjectives and nouns, as in *modernize* ['to make modern'], *legalize* ['to make legal'], *symbolize* ['to act as a symbol of'], *hospitalize* ['to put into hospital' (for treatment)], *publicize* ['to make well known'], *dieselize* ['to convert to diesel-engined power'], *burglarize* ⟨AmE⟩

['to subject to burglary']. Formations lend themselves readily to nominalization in *-ation*, as in *nominalization* itself. Over-use and new use of *-ize* items is often criticized on stylistic grounds. The dominant spelling is *-ize*. There is some confusion of *-ize* with the ending *-ise* in some verbs (*eg*: *advertise*).

Note Where there is a corresponding adjective, the ending *-ate* is usually unstressed /ət/, giving some contrasting pairs *ap'propri,ate* (verb) ~ *ap'propriate* (adjective).

Conversion

Conversion and suffixation

I.43 Conversion is the derivational process whereby an item is adapted or converted to a new word class without the addition of an affix. In this way, conversion is closely analogous to suffixation (as distinct from prefixation). For example, the verb *release* (as in *They released him*) corresponds to a noun *release* (as in *They ordered his release*), and this relationship may be seen as parallel to that between the verb *acquit* (as in *They acquitted him*) and the noun *acquittal* (as in *They ordered his acquittal*):

	VERB		DEVERBAL NOUN
SUFFIXATION:	acquit	→	acquittal
CONVERSION:	release	→	release

Conversion is unusually prominent as a word-formation process, through both the variety of conversion rules and their productivity.

Note [**a**] Other terms for conversion are 'functional conversion', 'functional shift', and 'zero derivation'. This last reflects the notion of a 'zero' suffix, analogous to the actual suffixes of App I.32*ff*.
[**b**] Conversion includes, in this treatment, cases where the base undergoes some slight phonological or orthographic change, *eg*: *shelf* ~ *shelve* (*cf* App I.56).

Direction of conversion

I.44 Certain difficulties arise in describing conversion, in that one does not have the addition of a suffix as a guide when deciding which item should be treated as the base and which as the derived form. Of course, as with other types of word-formation discussed in this Appendix, we treat conversion not as a historical process, but rather as a process now available for extending the lexical resources of the language. From this point of view, it is irrelevant whether the verb *release* preceded the noun *release* as an acquisition of English vocabulary (*cf* App I.11 Note [b]).

Nevertheless, it is convenient to attempt to state such a precedence, and often the semantic dependence of one item upon another is sufficient ground for arguing its derivational dependence. For example, the verb *net* can be paraphrased in terms of the noun as 'put into a net', but no comparable paraphrase could be constructed for the noun; that is, to define *net* in some such terms as 'an instrument for netting' would be to limit the meaning of the noun quite arbitrarily to exclude (for example) strawberry nets, mosquito nets, and hair nets.

This criterion cannot be easily applied to *release* above, but one may note that *release* as a noun is parallel to other nouns derived from verbs in dynamic use as regards semantic restrictions; that is, one may say *His release was sudden/on Tuesday*, etc just as one may say *His discovery/promotion etc was sudden/on Tuesday*, etc. Moreover, *release* behaves as a deverbal noun in structures of 'nominalization' (*cf* 17.51*ff*): *his release by the government*; *the government's release of the prisoners*. On these grounds, we treat abstract and agential nouns (*eg*: *love*, *'rebel*) as derived.

In the survey of types of conversion that follows, we resume the principle of classification that was adopted for suffixation: this means that we group words according to the class of the base and the class of the word derived. Thus *release* is to be classed as a deverbal noun in App I.47.

'Partial conversion'

I.45 Some grammars make a distinction between 'full conversion' (*ie* conversion as already discussed) and 'partial conversion', where a word of one class appears in a function which is characteristic of another word class. One may argue, for instance, that in such structures as *the wealthy* [= 'wealthy people'], *the ignorant*, *the wicked*, the adjective is 'partially converted' to noun status, in that it is syntactically in a position (head of noun phrase) characteristic of nouns rather than adjectives (*cf* 7.2*ff*). That there is not full conversion in such cases is demonstrated by the inability of *wealthy*, as it occurs in sentences like *The wealthy are always with us*, to behave inflectionally like a noun (that is, to vary in terms of number and case). One cannot say **I met a wealthy*; **Those wealthies are my friends*; etc.

Indeed, it is doubtful whether this rather restricted use of adjectives should be treated as a word-formation process at all; not only is there no inflectional evidence of the word's status as a noun, but there is inflectional evidence of its unchanged status as an adjective: *the wealthier*, *the poorest*, etc. Moreover, there does not appear to be any of the partial productivity, or the distinction between actual and potential English words, that we have seen as one of the hall-marks of a word-formation process (*cf* App I.13). Rather, we can claim that almost any adjective of a permitted class (*ie* applicable to human beings or to abstractions) might be used in such a structure, with no constraints on productivity:

The { wealthy / kind / well-dressed / foolish / ill-behaved / etc } are always with us.

The position adopted in this grammar, therefore, has been to treat such cases in purely syntactic terms, as 'adjective functioning as head of noun phrase', rather than to postulate that conversion, or the transfer of an item from one word class to another, has taken place.

I.46 The words produced by conversion are primarily nouns, adjectives, and verbs. It will be seen from the sets presented below that the most productive categories are the denominal verbs and the deverbal nouns. Only the major semantic types are noted under each heading, but one general point deserves special attention. A converted item typically does not carry with it the semantic range it had in the word class from which it was converted. This seems to be especially relevant in the case of denominal verbs which commonly relate to only one of the meanings possessed by the noun (*cf* App I.11, on *paper*).

Note In colloquial usage (firmly regarded as nonstandard in BrE, less so in AmE), recourse to conversion is especially common (*eg* 'He *upped* and left *on account of* that she laughed at him'), one of the products being de-adjectival adverbs: 'She writes *good/nice/careful/quick*' (*cf* 7.7). Some items of this kind occur in more general usage, as in official road signs, 'Drive *slow*!', and familiarly 'Come *quick*' and (especially with the comparative and superlative) 'He is reading *quicker*', 'She fought *strongest* for election'. In AmE, *sure* and *real* are widely used as intensifying adverbs: 'He's *sure* trying', 'She was *real* lucky'. *Cf* 8.100.

Conversion to noun

Deverbal

I.47 [A] 'State' [generally 'state of mind' or 'state of sensation'] (from verbs used statively to count or noncount nouns):

desire, dismay, doubt, love, smell, taste, want

[B] 'Event/activity' (from verbs used dynamically):

attempt, fall, hit, laugh, release, search, swim; *shut-down, walk-out, blow-out* (of a tyre)

[C] 'Object of V':

answer ['that which answers'], *bet, catch, find, hand-out*

[D] 'Subject of V':

bore ['someone who or that which bores/is boring'], *cheat, coach, show-off, stand-in*

[E] 'Instrument of V':

cover ['something with which to cover things'], *paper, wrap, wrench*

[F] 'Manner of V-*ing*':

walk ['manner of walking'], *throw, lie* (*eg*: in *the lie of the land*)

[G] 'Place of V':

divide, retreat, rise, turn, lay-by, drive-in

Note It will be noticed that the examples above include nouns formed from phrasal and prepositional verbs. The type of informal deverbal coinage represented by *teach-in* belongs to Type [B] rather than to any other, but unlike *shut-down* it cannot be derived from a phrasal verb (there is no **We taught-in last night*). The vogue for such formations produced *sit-in, love-in, swim-in*, and others. They signify an activity (that denoted by the verb) being carried on corporately (typically within an institution and with overtones of social protest).

De-adjectival

I.48 There is no very productive pattern of adjective → noun conversion (but *cf* 7.12*f*, 7.37, App I.45). Miscellaneous examples are:

I'd like two pints of *bitter*, please. [=type of beer] ⟨BrE⟩

As a football player, he's a *natural*. [=a naturally skilled player]
They're running in the *final*. [=the final race]

Also *daily* ['daily newspaper'], *weekly*, *monthly*, *annual*, *perennial*, *comic* ['comic actor'], *regulars* ['regular customers'], *roast* ['roast beef'], (*young*) *marrieds* ['young married people' ⟨informal⟩], *a wet*, *a red*. From these examples, it is seen that adjective → noun conversion can usually be explained in terms of a well-established adjective + noun phrase from which the noun has been ellipted. On conversions involving phrases containing adjectives, *cf* App I.52.

Conversion to verb

Denominal

I.49 [A] 'To put in/on N':

bottle ['to put into a bottle'], *carpet* (a subordinate ⟨BrE⟩), *corner*, *catalogue*, *floor*, *garage*, *position*, *shelve* (books: *cf* App I.56); common in nonce usages such as *rack* (the plates), *porch* (the newspaper).

[B] 'To give N, to provide with N':

butter (bread), *coat* ['to give a coat (of paint, etc) to'], *commission*, *grease*, *mask*, *muzzle*, *oil*, *plaster*.

[C] 'To deprive of N':

core ['remove the core from'], *gut*, *peel*, *skin*, *top-and-tail* ⟨BrE⟩

[D] 'To . . . with N' (more precisely, the meaning of the verb is 'to use the referent of the noun as an instrument for whatever activity is particularly associated with it'):

brake ['to stop by means of a brake'], *elbow*, *fiddle*, *hand*, *finger*, *glue*, *knife*

[E] 'To $\left\{\begin{matrix}\text{be}\\ \text{act}\end{matrix}\right\}$ as N with respect to . . .':

chaperon ['to act as chaperon to'], *father*, *nurse*, *parrot*, *pilot*, *referee*; occurs in nonce use such as 'He *Houdinied* himself out of the locked cell'.

[F] 'To $\left\{\begin{matrix}\text{make}\\ \text{change}\end{matrix}\right\}$ . . . into N':

cash ['to change into cash'], *cripple*, *group*

[G] 'To $\left\{\begin{matrix}\text{[i] send}\\ \text{[ii] go}\end{matrix}\right\}$ by N':

[i] *mail* ['to send by mail'], *ship*, *telegraph*
[ii] *bicycle* ['to go by bicycle'], *boat*, *canoe*, *motor*

Most of the verbs in this category are transitive, with the exception of Type G [ii], and a few members of Type D.

De-adjectival

I.50 [A] (transitive verbs) 'to make adj' or 'to make more adj':

calm ['to make calm'], *dirty*, *dry*, *humble*, *lower*, *soundproof*

[B] (intransitive verbs) 'to become adj'; generally adjectives in Type A can also have this function, and it may be seen as a secondary conversion (*cf* App I.54): *dry* ['to become dry'], *empty*, *narrow*, *weary* (*of*), *yellow*

Sometimes a phrasal verb is derived from an adjective by the addition of a particle: *smooth out* ['to make smooth'], *sober up* ['to become sober'], *calm down* ['to become calm'].

This category competes with *-en* suffixation (*cf* App I.42), and sometimes both derivations are available for the same adjective; *eg*: *black*(*en*), *quiet*(*en*):

He {blacked / blackened} his face with soot.

Conversion to adjective

Denominal

I.51 Membership of this category can be postulated only when the noun form occurs in predicative as well as in attributive position (*cf* 7.12*ff*) since the latter is freely available for nouns within the grammar of the noun phrase (*cf* 17.104*ff*). We may compare the discussion of adjectives and 'partial conversion' in App I.45 (*cf* also Note below and 7.14).

a *brick* garage ~ The garage is *brick*.
reproduction furniture ~ This furniture is *reproduction*. ⟨BrE⟩
Worcester porcelain ~ This porcelain is *Worcester*.

Cf also 'This dress is *cotton*, this one is *nylon*, but this one is *wool*.' Denominal adjectives are normally nongradable, but informally (and especially with reference to style) we find examples like:

His accent is very *Mayfair* (very *Harvard*).
It was a funny story but not quite *drawing-room*.

Note Although, for the reasons stated, we do not treat nouns as converted just because they are used prenominally, it should be noted that premodifying nouns are used in strictly parallel ways to denominal adjectives. Thus in the absence of denominal adjectives based on *city* or *physics* with senses parallel to *suburban* (based on *suburb*) or *medical* (based on *medicine*), we find the nouns being used. Compare:

He's taking a {*medical* course. ['course in medicine'] / *physics* course. ['course in physics']}

She dislikes {*suburban* life. ['life in a suburb'] / *city* life. ['life in a city']}

The parallelism is endorsed by the fact that, although predicative use of the denominal adjectives has been illustrated, such usage is in no case as firmly acceptable as attributive use. A further parallel can be seen in our ability to coordinate premodifying nouns and denominal adjectives:

She likes both *cotton* and *woollen* dresses.
They detest both *suburban* and *city* life.

Minor categories of conversion

I.52 There are several anomalous and miscellaneous types of conversion, chiefly used informally; among them the following are noteworthy:

[I] *Conversion to nouns*

[i] From closed-class words; there are some well-established examples:

His argument contains too many *ifs* and *buts*.
This book is a *must* for the student of aerodynamics.
It tells you about the *how* and the *why* of flight.

[ii] From affixes; very occasionally, an affix may be converted into a noun:

Patriotism, nationalism, and any other *isms* you'd like to name.

[iii] From phrases; sequences of more than one word are sometimes used as nouns, reduced to one-word status by conversion rather than by any of the normal patterns of compounding (*cf* App I.57*ff*):

Whenever I gamble, my horse is one of the *also-rans*. [*ie* one of the horses which did not win but merely 'also ran']

Cf also 'the *high-ups*', 'he is a *has-been*', 'a *been-to*' ⟨West African English⟩, 'a *free-for-all*', 'some *down-and-outs*', 'give me the *low-down*' ⟨slang⟩.

[II] *Conversion to verbs*

From closed-class and nonlexical items, chiefly informal:

They *downed* tools in protest.
She will *off* and do her own thing.
If you *uh-uh* again, I won't go on with my story.

[III] *Conversion to adjectives*

From phrases (such as that in 'The plane is up in the air'):

an *up-in-the-air* feeling ~ I feel very *up in the air*. [with reference to cheerful spirits]
an *upper-class* manner ~ His manner is very *upper-class*.

From closed-class items, we may cite examples like the following:

That's how the Fieldings next door do it, but it's not quite *us*. [=our style or standard]

Note [**a**] On adjectives used as adverbs, *cf* App I.46 Note, 7.6*ff*.

[**b**] Examples like 'There are too many *althoughs* in this paragraph', 'He has missed an *m* out of *accommodate*' might superficially suggest that *although*, *m*, and *accommodate* have been converted into nouns. Compare also the 'conversion' of proper nouns: 'There are two *Newcastles* in England'. Any item can, of course, be used nominally in this way, not by conversion but by an elliptical apposition ('the word *although*', 'letter *m*', 'towns called *Newcastle*'); *cf* 5.61, 5.64, 17.65*ff*. Contrast 'Men *are* mortal', '*Men is* plural', '*Scissors is* difficult to spell'; the different status would normally be indicated in writing with italic or quotation marks: '*Suspenders is* the AmE equivalent of BrE *braces*'.

Change of secondary word class: nouns

I.53 The notion of conversion may be extended to changes of secondary word class, within the same major word category: for example, when noncount nouns are used as count nouns or vice versa (*cf* 5.4). Such transfers are only partially productive, and yet can be explained systematically in terms of derivation. They are therefore parallel to the major conversion processes already discussed, though to the extent that they can be predicted as the regular products of grammatical processes, they might be considered as strictly lying outside the province of word-formation.

Types of conversion (or reclassification) within the noun category are:

[A] *Noncount noun → count noun*

[i] 'A unit of N':

two *coffees* ['cups of coffee']; two (huge) *cheeses*

[ii] 'A kind of N':

Some *paints* are more lasting than others.
This is a better *bread* than the one I bought last.

[iii] 'An instance of N' (with abstract nouns):

a *difficulty*; small *kindnesses*; a miserable *failure*;
home *truths*; a great *injustice*

[B] *Count noun → noncount noun*

'N viewed in terms of a measurable extent' (normally only when accompanied by expressions of amount):

An inch of *pencil*; a few square feet of *floor*

[C] *Proper noun → common noun*

[i] 'A member of the class typified by N' (*cf* 5.61*ff*):

a *Jeremiah* ['a gloomy prophet who denounces his age']
a latter-day *Plutarch* ['. . . chronicler of great men']
Edinburgh is the *Athens* of the north.

[ii] 'A product of N':

a *Rolls Royce* ['a car manufactured by Rolls Royce'], a pack of *Chesterfields* ['cigarettes with the brand name "Chesterfield"']
The museum has several *Renoirs*.

[D] *Stative noun → dynamic noun*

Nouns are characteristically stative (*cf* 2.43), but they can assume the dynamic meaning of 'temporary role or activity' as subject complement following the progressive of *be*:

He's being a { fool. / nuisance. / hero. / etc } ['He's behaving like a fool', etc]

Note The use of proper nouns as in [Ci] is to be contrasted with usages like 'An unhappy Susan was waiting for him' (*cf* 17.95) or 'There are two Susans in this office' [='persons called Susan'; *cf* App I.52 Note], though the latter type closely resembles our [Cii]. See further 5.60*ff*.

Change of secondary word class: verbs

I.54 [A] *Intransitive → transitive*

'Cause to V' (*cf* 10.22):

run the water ['cause the water to run']; *march* the prisoners; *slide* the bolt back.
Likewise: *budge, fly, slip, stop, turn, twist*

[B] *Transitive → intransitive*

[i] 'Be V-ed' (often with obligatory adverbial and with implied modality, 'can, must'), *cf* 10.21:

The clock *winds up* at the back ['is to be wound up'];
Your book *reads* well; The table *polishes* up badly;
The door *closed* behind him; You can close the door easily – it just *pulls*. ['you just pull it']

Likewise: *divide, drive, sail, sell, steer, undo, unlock, wash*; from causative verbs: *dry, harden* (*cf* App I.50)

[ii] 'To V oneself':

Have you *washed* yet? ['washed yourself']

Likewise: *bath* ⟨BrE⟩, *bathe* ⟨AmE⟩, *behave, dress, make up, shave*

[iii] 'To V someone/something/etc':

We have *eaten* already. ['eaten something, had a meal']

Likewise: *cook, drink, hunt, kill, knit, sew, write*. Contrast 'Please let me explain', where the object is understood from the context.

[C] *Intransitive → copular* (*cf* 16.21*ff*)

[i] Current meaning:

He *lay* flat; We *stood* motionless.

Likewise: *float* (free); *ride* (high); *arrive* (hungry)

[ii] Resulting meaning:

He *fell* flat; The sun was *sinking* low.

Likewise: *run* (cold); *boil* (dry); *wash* (clean)

[D] *Copular → intransitive*

What must *be*, must *be*. ['exist']

[E] *Monotransitive → complex transitive* (*cf* [C] and 16.44*ff*)

[i] Current meaning:

We *catch* them young. ['. . . when they are young']

Likewise: (*can't*) *bear, buy, find, hate, like, sell*

[ii] Resulting meaning:

I *wiped* it clean. ['made it clean by wiping it']

Likewise: *knock* (. . . unconscious); *lock* (. . . fast)
Note reflexive objects: *I laughed myself silly.*

Change of secondary word class: adjectives

I.55 [A] *Nongradable → gradable* (*cf* 7.86, App I.51)

He's more *English* than the English.
Some people's behaviour is rather *incredible*.
I have a very *legal* turn of mind.

[B] *Stative → dynamic* (*cf* 7.41)

As noted in App I.54 [D] above, dynamic meaning is signalled by the progressive aspect of *be*:

He's just being *friendly*. ['acting in a friendly manner']
Your uncle is being *bigoted*, as usual.
He's being *awkward* about it.
Martha is being *desirable* this evening.

Conversion with formal modifications

I.56 In some cases, conversion is accompanied by certain nonaffixal changes affecting pronunciation or spelling or stress distribution. The most important kinds of alteration are [A] voicing of final consonants, and [B] shift of stress. Both kinds (like most phenomena of word-formation) are idiosyncratic in respect of the particular instances that occur, though they follow certain clear patterns.

[A] VOICING OF FINAL CONSONANTS

The unvoiced fricative consonants /s/, /f/, and /θ/ in some nouns are voiced to /z/, /v/, and /ð/ respectively in the corresponding verb forms:

NOUN ~	VERB	NOUN ~	VERB
house /-s/	house /-z/	thief /-f/	thieve /-v/
advice /-s/	advise /-z/	belief /-f/	believe /-v/
use /-s/	use /-z/	relief /-f/	relieve /-v/
abuse /-s/	abuse /-z/	mouth /-θ/	mouth /-ð/
grief /-f/	grieve /-v/	sheath /-θ/	sheathe /-ð/
shelf /-f/	shelve /-v/	wreath /-θ/	wreathe /-ð/
half /-f/	halve /-v/		

It should be noted that, especially in BrE, the difference between *licence* (n) and *license* (v), like that between *practice* (n) and *practise* (v), is one of spelling only: both noun and verb are pronounced with a final /s/. In AmE, both noun and verb can have the same spellings (*license, practice*, respectively).

A substantial change of pronunciation, including modification of the final vowel, is observed in pairs such as: *breath* /e/ ~ *breathe* /iː/; *bath, glass* (/æ/ in AmE, /ɑː/ in RP BrE) ~ *bathe, glaze* /eɪ/; *cf* also *blood* ~ *bleed, food* ~ *feed.*

[B] SHIFT OF STRESS (*cf* App II.6)

When verbs of two syllables are converted into nouns, the stress is sometimes shifted from the second to the first syllable. The first syllable, typically a Latin prefix, often has a reduced vowel /ə/ in the verb but a full vowel in the noun:

He was *con'victed* (/kən/) of theft, and so became a *'convict* (/kɒn/)

The following is a fairly full list of words having end-stress as verbs but initial stress as nouns in BrE (in AmE, many have initial stress as verbs also):

abstract, accent, combine, compound, compress, concert, conduct, confine (the noun is plural only), *conflict, conscript, consort, construct, contest, contrast, convert, convict, decrease, dictate, digest, discard, discount, discourse, escort, export, extract, ferment, import, impress, incline, increase, insult, misprint, perfume, permit, pervert, present, produce, progress, protest, rebel, record, refill, refit, refund, regress, reject, resit, retail, segment, survey, suspect, torment, transfer, transform, transplant, transport, upset*

Occasionally, a word of more than two syllables varies in this way: *over'flow* (v) ~ *'overflow* (n). *Cf* also *en'velop* (v), *'envelope* (n).

There are many examples of disyllabic noun–verb pairs which do not differ in stress; for example, *de'bate* (v) and *de'bate* (n) both have end-stress, and *'contact* (v) and *'contact* (n) both have initial stress (as is usual where the verb is derived from the noun).

Note that *dis'count* means 'to disregard', *'discount* 'to give a discount'.

Compounds

I.57 A compound is a lexical unit consisting of more than one base (*cf* App I.2) and functioning both grammatically and semantically as a single word. In principle, any number of bases may be involved, but in English, except for a relatively minor class of items (normally abbreviated; *cf* App I.73), compounds usually comprise two bases only, however internally complex each may be.

Compounding can take place within any of the word classes, but – within the present framework – we shall in effect be dealing only with the productivity of compounds resulting above all in new nouns and, to a lesser extent, adjectives. These may involve the combination of the unchanged base (as in *taxfree*); or the first element may be in its special 'combining form' (as in the noun *trouserleg* or the adjective *socioeconomic*); or the second element may have a suffix required by the compound type (as in the noun *theatre-goer* or the adjective *blue-eyed*); or both elements may have a form that is compound-specific (as in the noun *laundromat*).

Before we consider the individual compound types, we shall give some attention to two issues: first, the conditions for lexicalization (*cf* App I.9) in respect of a particular collocation of bases; second, the formal characteristics of the composition thus made into an institutionalized whole.

Note [**a**] Compounds which belong to word classes other than the three major classes considered in this Appendix include prepositions such as *into, instead of, by dint of* (*cf* 9.6), pronouns such as *each other, anybody, himself* (*cf* 6.46), and adverbs such as *country-style, headlong, upside down, inside out* (*cf* 7.46). The latter are productive in terms of recurrent use of a second element, making them resemble the products of suffixation; *cf* App I.41.

[**b**] Compounding is readily recursive, one compound itself becoming a constituent in a larger one; *cf* the structure of [[*motor* + *cycle*] + *factory*].

Lexicalization conditions

I.58 In contrast to affixation, in which a base is typically altered in terms of certain very broad semantic or grammatical categories by the use of an effectively closed set of items, compounding associates bases drawn from the whole lexicon in a wide range of semantic relations. Nonetheless, although both bases in a compound are in principle equally open, they are normally in a relation whereby the first is modifying the second. In short, compounding can in general be viewed as prefixation with open-class items.

But this does not mean that a compound can be formed by placing any lexical item in front of another. Consider the following:

> Look at that dog in the street.
> She put the glass on the table.
> I heard an owl from my study last night.

Except on a 'nonce' basis, we cannot in response speak of 'another *street dog*' or 'another *table glass*' or 'Do you work much in your *owl study*?' Rather, given the general conditions for lexicalization discussed in App I.9*ff*, the relations between items brought together in compounding must be such that it is reasonable and useful to classify the second element in terms of the first. Thus a compound *XY* will be '*such a* Y *as* may have X essentially predicated of it', whereas the same *XY* sequence as a noun phrase is more likely to be '*a certain* Y that happens to have X predicated of it' (*cf* 17.104*ff*). In terms of theme and focus (*cf* 18.9), we therefore expect to find that the second constituent in a compound is thematic, with focus on the first constituent (as salient and categorizing), whereas the converse is true of premodifier and head in a noun phrase; *cf* App I.59. This distinction is endorsed by the widespread use of initial stress in compounds: *a 'blackbird* (contrast the phrase, *a ˌgrey 'bird*).

The relations consequently involved in compounding are frequently resemblance, function, or some other salient or defining characteristic. For example, *darkroom* is a lexicalization of something we might paraphrase as 'a room for [= purpose] photographic processing'. The item *dark* is used in the lexicalization not because such rooms happen to be dark, still less because one such room happens to be dark, but because the facility to make such rooms dark is a salient characteristic. For the reasons given in App I.10, we cannot expect the meaning of *darkroom* to be implicit in the meanings of the separate items (there are many 'dark rooms' which are not 'darkrooms' – nor need darkrooms always be in darkness): it is enough to make currency plausible that, when we know what it means, its constitution seems reasonable and mnemonic. Such reasonableness is somewhat more remote with *hothouse* (where the building concerned would not otherwise be called a 'house'), less so with *signature tune* (though even this equates music with writing for identification in only a very limited context); *cf* App I.12.

It is more remote still with *hot dog* where only the 'hot' can seem reasonable and where we use this as a subcategorization not within types of dog (alsatian, poodle, . . .) but within meanings of *dog*. The semantic atypicalness of *hot dog* significantly corresponds to its prosodic atypicalness; *cf* App I.59.

Formal characteristics

I.59 We have seen that the semantic structure of compounds tends to entail a focal first constituent. In consequence we have a contrast between the prosodic pattern of a noun phrase and that of a compound, the latter having primary stress (*cf* App II.4) on the first constituent:

a ˌdark 'room	a 'darkˌroom
a ˌhot 'house	a 'hotˌhouse
a ˌblack 'bird	a 'blackˌbird

a ˌbaby ˈgirl　　　a ˈbaby-ˌsitter
ˌmotor ˈtransport　　　ˈmotorˌcars

As we shall see in the sections that follow, almost all compounds have this accentual pattern, whether they are nouns, adjectives, or verbs. Exceptions (*cf* especially App I.70) are on the whole equally explicable in terms of thematization. In the compounds

ˌash-ˈblonde　　　ˌbottle-ˈgreen

we have the focus on *blonde* and *green* since the premodifiers merely denote degrees or shades. So too with 'combining-form' compounds like

ˌsocio-ecoˈnomic

or 'coordinate' compounds like

ˌSwedish-Aˈmerican

the prosody reflects the pragmatic facts: the referent of the 'head' is an admixture with that of the 'premodifier'. Given the pattern of such formations, however, only convention determines the selection, and pairs like *Anglo-French* and *Franco-British* are not necessarily in thematic contrast. Indeed, just as *Anglo-* corresponds to *-British* because there is no **Brito-*, so we find *American* as final item merely because ?**Americo-* is ill-established.

If prosody reflects the semantic structure, so too does orthography. The semantic unity of a compound is reflected in an orthographic unity:

a black bird　*but*　a blackbird

Spelling conventions are however less dependable than prosody. Practice varies in many words and some compounds may even occur in three different forms, 'solid', hyphenated, and 'open'; *eg*:

a flower pot　a flower-pot　a flowerpot

But in general there is a progression from open to solid as a given compound becomes established, and hence widely recognized and accepted as a 'permanent' lexical item.

In AmE, hyphenation is less common than in BrE, and instead we find the items open or solid (more usually the latter) where BrE may use a hyphen:

language retarded ⟨esp AmE⟩, *language-retarded* ⟨esp BrE⟩,
psychosomatic ⟨esp AmE⟩, *psycho-somatic* ⟨esp BrE⟩.

The open option does not normally occur with combining-forms (as in *psycho-somatic*, *psychosomatic*), and where these are in compounds of proper names the initial capital of the second constituent inhibits solid spelling; hence even in AmE we find a hyphen in examples like *Sino-Russian*, *Anglo-American* (though even these may appear solid, with lower case for the second element: *Angloamerican*, and always in *Amerindian*). In both AmE and BrE, hyphens are usual for ad hoc premodifying compounds as in *a much-needed rest*, *his higher-than-average wages*, *their come-and-fight-me attitude*, *nineteenth-century novels* (where the sequences concerned are not of course compounds outside this premodifying position: 'his wages were higher than average', 'novels of the nineteenth century', etc). Compare phrasal conversion, App I.52. For hyphen usage, see further App III.4*f*.

Note [**a**] It may be useful to conceive of 'partial' compounding (*cf* 'partial' conversion, App I.45) to account for the formal and semantic gradience between phrase and compound:

We need some furniture for the offices. [1]
We need some ˌoffice ˈfurniture. [2]
ˌOffice ˈfurniture is getting more expensive. [3]

In [2] we have an expression appropriate to phrase structure with no necessary lexicalization of 'office furniture' but merely referring to furniture that will be used in the office(s). In [3] however, the generic statement makes the beginning of lexicalization a more plausible interpretation: it is implied that there is furniture of a kind designed specifically for office use. 'Partial' compounding may be said to have taken place, though the stress pattern and spelling still lean in the phrasal direction.

[**b**] With coordinate compounds (*cf* App I.70), we sometimes find an oblique stroke used instead of a hyphen in rather technical (as well as in rather informal) writing: 'an *aural/oral* approach', 'the *in/out* motion'. *Cf* our use in this book of *speaker/writer, hearer/reader*.

The treatment of compounds

I.60 Although not all compounds are directly 'derived' from the clause-structure functions of the items concerned, we shall adopt a mode of presentation which (where possible) links compounds to sentential or clausal paraphrases. This is appropriate enough in the treatment of word-formation in the context of a general grammatical description, and it is in keeping with our policy in this Appendix of concentrating attention on the language's productive capacity.

As an example of this approach, we may take the two compounds *glow-worm* and *punch-card*, which are superficially similar, consisting of verb + noun. Yet the relations of their constituents, and hence the 'grammatical' meanings of the two compounds, are different:

glow-worm ~ *The worm glows, ie* verb + subject ['Some worms glow']
but
punch-card ~ *X punches the card, ie* verb + object

Similarly, *daydreaming* and *sightseeing* can be analysed in terms of their sentential analogues, thus capturing fundamental differences beside the superficial similarity:

X dreams during the day, ie verb + adverbial
but
X sees sights, ie verb + object

Within each of the major categories, therefore (notably Noun Compounds and Adjective Compounds), we shall distinguish subsets on the basis of a grammatical analysis of the elements involved in a canonical example, together with an informal indication of the relationship between them in terms of a syntactic paraphrase.

Noun compounds

Type 'subject and verb'

I.61 [A] ˈSUNˌRISE: subject + deverbal noun (*cf* 'The sun rises'). This is a very productive type. For example:

bee-sting	catcall	daybreak	earthquake
frostbite	headache	heartbeat	landslide
nightfall	rainfall	sound change	toothache

[B] ˈRATTLEˌSNAKE: verb + subject (*cf* 'The snake rattles'). This type is only weakly productive. For example:

crybaby	driftwood	drip coffee	flashlight
glowworm	hangman	playboy	popcorn
stinkweed	tugboat	turntable	watchdog

[C] ˈDANCINGˌGIRL: verbal noun in *-ing* + subject (*cf* 'The girl dances'); very productive. For example:

cleaning woman	firing squad	flying machine
investigating committee	wading bird	washing machine
working party		

Sequences with converse stress pattern (ˌ*flying* ˈ*saucer*, ˌ*working* ˈ*man*) show a lesser degree of institutionalization as compounds; contrast ˈ*workman*.

Type 'verb and object'

I.62 [A] ˈBLOODˌTEST: object + deverbal noun (*cf* 'X tests blood'). This is a moderately productive type. *Self* is a common first constituent. Some compounds denote an activity (*eg*: *handshake*), some the result of an activity (*eg*: *book review*), and some could be either (*meat delivery*). For example:

birth-control	book review	crime report
dress-design	haircut	handshake
meat delivery	office management	suicide attempt
self-control	self-destruction	tax cut
word-formation		

[B] ˈFAULT-ˌFINDING: object + verbal noun in *-ing* (*cf* 'X finds fault(s)'; *cf* also App I.68, *man-eating*). This type is very productive. For example:

air-conditioning	book-keeping	book-reviewing
brainwashing	dressmaking	housekeeping
letter-writing	oath-taking	sightseeing
story-telling	town-planning	

[C] ˈTAX-ˌPAYER: object + agential noun in *-er* (*cf* 'X pays tax(es)'). This is a very productive type, and designates concrete (usually human) agents; note however *dishwasher*, *lawn-mower*, *penholder*, *record-player* (*cf* App I.34, I.63 [C]). For example:

cigar smoker	computer-designer	crime reporter
gamekeeper	hair-splitter	language teacher
matchmaker	radio-operator	songwriter
stockholder	window-cleaner	

[D] ˈPUNCHˌCARD: verb + object (*cf* 'X punches the card'). For example:

call-girl	drawbridge	pin-up girl
punchball	push-button	scarecrow
treadmill		

[E] ˈCHEWINGˌGUM: verbal noun in *-ing* + object (*cf* 'X chews gum'); very productive. For example:

cooking apple	drinking-water	eating apple
boiling fowl ⟨BrE⟩	reading material	spending money
roasting joint	braising steak	

Note In [D] and [E], the syntactic paraphrase obscures the 'purpose' relationship (*cf* App I.58): 'The ball is *for* punching', 'The gum is *for* X to chew'.

Type 'verb and adverbial'

I.63 [A] ˈSWIMMINGˌPOOL: verbal noun in *-ing* + adverbial (consisting of a prepositional phrase; *cf* 'X swims in the pool'). This is a very productive type. Several adverbial relations are involved (but *cf* Note [b]). For example:

PLACE:	diving board	['dive from a board']
	drinking cup	['drink out of a cup']
	freezing point	['freeze at a point']
	frying pan ⟨BrE⟩	['fry in a pan']
	hiding-place	['hide in a place']
	living-room	['live in a room']
	typing paper	['type on paper']
	waiting room	['wait in a room']
	writing desk	['write at a desk']
INSTRUMENTAL:	adding machine	['add with a machine']
	baking powder	['bake with powder']
	carving knife	['carve with a knife']
	sewing machine	['sew with a machine']
	walking stick	['walk with a stick']
	washing machine	['wash with a machine']

[B] ˈDAYˌDREAMING: adverbial + verbal noun in *-ing* (*cf* 'X dreams during the day'). This is a moderately productive type (*cf* App I.69, *ocean-going*). For example:

PLACE:	churchgoing	['going to church']
	horse riding	['ride on a horse']
	tight-rope walking	['walk on a tight-rope']
	sun-bathing	['bathe in the sun']
TIME:	sleepwalking	['walk in one's sleep']
INSTRUMENTAL:	fly-fishing	['fish with a fly']
	handwriting	['write by hand']
OTHER:	shadow-boxing	['box against a shadow']

[C] ˈBABYˌSITTER: adverbial + agential noun in *-er* (*cf* 'X sits with the baby'). This is a moderately productive type (*cf* App I.62[C]). For example:

PLACE:	backswimmer	['swim on the back']
	city-dweller	['dwell in the city']
	factory-worker	['work in a factory']
	gate-crasher	['crashes through a gate', *ie* 'uninvited guest']

	housebreaker	['break into a house']
	playgoer	['go to a play']
	tight-rope walker	['walk on a tight rope']
	sun-bather	['bathe in the sun']
	theatre-goer	['go to the theatre']
TIME:	daydreamer	['dream during the day']

[D] ˈHOMEˌWORK: adverbial + deverbal noun (*cf* 'X works at home'). This is a moderately productive type. For example:

PLACE:	boat-ride	['ride in a boat']
	field-work	['work in the field']
	table talk	['talk at the table']
	moon walk	['walk on the moon']
TIME:	daydream	['dream during the day']
	night flight	['fly during the night']
INSTRUMENTAL:	gunfight	['fight with a gun']
OTHER:	smallpox vaccination	['vaccinate against smallpox']
	tax-exemption	['exempt from tax']
	telephone call	['message by the telephone']

So also *self-determination*.

[E] ˈSEARCHˌLIGHT: verb + adverbial (*cf* 'X searches with a light'). Several adverbial relations are involved (but *cf* Note [b]). For example:

PLACE:	dance hall	['dance in a hall']
	springboard	['spring from a board']
	workbench	['work at a bench']
INSTRUMENTAL:	grindstone	['grind with a stone']
	plaything	['play with a thing']

Some further examples: *cookbook* ⟨esp AmE⟩, *fry-pan* ⟨AmE⟩, *restroom* ⟨esp AmE⟩, *swimsuit* ⟨esp AmE⟩, *washroom* ⟨esp AmE⟩. The labels indicate the popularity of this pattern in AmE; in BrE there is a corresponding preference for the pattern in App I.63 [A].

Note [**a**] Somewhat like items in [B] is *dry-cleaning* (but note the phrasal accentuation in BrE, *ˌdry-ˈcleaning*), 'cleaning (the clothes) when/though dry'. *Cf*: *sleep-walking* 'walking when/though asleep'. For the adjective form *ˌdry-ˈcleaned*, *cf* App I.69 [D].

[**b**] In [A] and [E], the 'purpose' relationship is lost in this presentation; compare 'The pool is *for X* to swim in', 'The light is *for X* to search with'.

'Verbless' compounds: Type 'subject and object'

I.64 [A] ˈWINDˌMILL: noun$_1$ + noun$_2$ (*cf* 'noun$_1$ [powers/operates] noun$_2$', 'the wind powers the mill'). For example:

air-brake	air rifle	cable car	coal fire (ˌ·ˈ· in BrE)
motorcycle	steam engine	gas cooker (ˌ·ˈ·· in BrE)	
hydrogen bomb (ˌ···ˈ· in AmE)			

[B] ˈTOY ˌFACTORY: noun$_1$ + noun$_2$ (*cf* 'noun$_2$ [produces/yields] noun$_1$', 'the factory produces toys'). For example:

honey-bee	oil well	power plant	silkworm
tear gas	textile mill	water pistol	gold mine

[C] ˈBLOODˌSTAIN: noun$_1$ + noun$_2$ (*cf* 'noun$_1$ [produces/yields] noun$_2$', 'the blood produces stains'). For example:

bloodstain	cane sugar	eiderdown	food poisoning	gaslight
hay fever	sawdust	tortoise-shell	whalebone	

[D] ˈDOORˌKNOB: noun$_1$ + noun$_2$ (*cf* 'noun$_1$ [has] noun$_2$', 'the door has a knob'). This is a very productive type. Noun$_1$ is inanimate. With animate nouns, we use a noncompound genitive phrase: compare *the ˈtable ˌleg* with *the ˌboy's ˈleg*. For example:

arrowhead	bedpost	bottleneck ⟨metaphorical⟩
cartwheel	piano keys	shirt-sleeves
table leg	telephone receiver	television screen
window-pane		

[E] SEˈCURITY ˌOFFICER: noun$_1$ + noun$_2$ (*cf* 'noun$_2$ [controls/works in connection with] noun$_1$', *cf* 'The officer looks after security'). For example:

chairperson	deckhand	fireman	gasman
motorman ⟨AmE⟩	police-officer	postman	

This is a very productive type, with the second constituent always a human agent. Indeed, so commonly has *man* been thus used (in its unmarked gender role, 'human adult') that in some compounds it has a reduced vowel, /mən/, as in *postman*, *draughtsman*, *fireman*, *workman*, *businessman*. This item and its gender-free alternative *person* might in fact be viewed as a suffix (*cf* I.3). Contrast the unreduced form of *man* in *ˈhandyˌman* (*cf* App I.65), perhaps because in this case the compound does not refer to a regular occupational role.

Type 'subject and complement'

I.65 [A] ˈGIRLˌFRIEND: noun$_1$ + noun$_2$ (*cf* 'noun$_2$ [is] noun$_1$', 'the friend is a girl'). Noun$_1$ often refers to a subset of the class denoted by noun$_2$. For example:

blinker light	drummer boy	feeder bus	killer shark
manservant	oak tree	pine tree	tape-measure

Numerous sequences of this appositional type occur with phrasal prosody: *ˌwoman ˈwriter*, *ˌtoy ˈfactory* ['the factory is a toy'; contrast App I.64 [B] above]. *Cf* App I.59 and the question of 'partial' compounds.

[B] ˈDARKˌROOM: adjective + noun (*cf* 'noun [is] adjective', 'the room is dark'). For example:

blackboard	blackbird	blueprint	double-talk
dry dock (or ˌ·ˈ·)	greyhound	grey matter (= brain)	handyman
highchair	hothouse	longboat	madman

The initial constituents in *knitwear* and *mincemeat* were originally *-ed* participle adjectives.

Along with this type should be considered many sequences with phrasal prosody:

ˌfancy ˈdress ˌhot ˈdog (ˈ·ˌ· in AmE) ˌill ˈomen ˌill reˈpute
ˌill ˈwind ˌrisen ˈcosts

Despite the apparent parallelism of:

He suffers from { bad health. / poor health. / ill health. }

compounding is nonetheless suggested in the last by the fact that *ill* is not normally a premodifier in noun-phrase structures (*cf* 7.38), nor are past participles of intransitive verbs (*risen*). Semantically, moreover, some of these examples have a high degree of lexicalization; on *hot dog*, *cf* App I.58.

[C] ˈFROGˌMAN: $noun_1$ + $noun_2$ (*cf* '$noun_2$ [is like] $noun_1$', 'the man is like a frog'). This is a very productive type. For example:

butter-bean	catfish	dragonfly	goldfish
kettledrum	sandwich man	tissue paper	

[D] ˈSNOWˌFLAKE: $noun_1$ + $noun_2$ (*cf* '$noun_2$ [is of, consists of] $noun_1$', 'a flake of snow'). For example:

breadcrumb	chocolate bar	dustheap	raindrop
sand dune	soap flake		

[E] ˈASHˌTRAY: $noun_1$ + $noun_2$ (*cf* '$noun_2$ [is for] $noun_1$', 'the tray is for ash'). This is a highly productive type expressing purpose; *cf* Note [a]. For example:

birdcage	breakfast time	coffee time	cough drops
cowshed	doghouse	facecloth	fire engine
fish-pond	flowerbed	flypaper	safety belt
tearoom			

Note [**a**] The difference between *teacup* (~'cup for tea') [E] and *cup of tea* (~'cup containing tea') is paralleled in *flowerpot*, *matchbox*, *winebottle*, *soup plate*, etc. With the purpose factor in [E], and underlying some examples in [B], compare the Notes to App I. 62*f*.

[**b**] Like type [A] are the (largely colloquial) compounds of hypocoristic plus generic, as in *pussy-cat*, *puppy-dog*; *cf* App I.77.

Combining-form compounds

I.66 ˌPSYCHO-AˈNALYSIS: $noun_1$ (in its 'combining form') + $noun_2$ (= '$noun_2$ [in respect of] $noun_1$'), 'the analysis of the psyche'. This is a highly productive type and various relations can be involved. Typically, the first constituent is neo-classical (*cf* App I.6, I.28) and does not occur as a separate noun base in English, but the model has been widely imitated with common bases, with a vowel (usually *-o-* but often *-i-*) as a link between the two parts: *ˌcryptˈography*, *inˈsecticide*, etc. *Cf* also the use of combining-forms in adjective compounds, App I.70. Stress patterns are various and the primary stress often falls on the link vowel of the combining-form. Among common second constituents are *-meter*, *-graph(y)*, *-gram*, *-logy*, and the formations are especially in the fields of science and learning. In consequence, many are in international currency, adopted or adapted in numerous languages. Some miscellaneous examples:

ˈagriˌculture	baˈrometer	ˌbioˈphysics
ˌbiotechˈnology	ˈEuroˌdollar	ˈhortiˌculture
ˌmicroelecˈtronics	ˌporˈnography	ˌpsyˈchology
ˈstereo-ˌvision	ˌturbo-ˈjet	

Cf also *ˈdramaˌturgy*, *ˈmetalˌlurgy*. On *pseudo-*, *cf* App I.23. With *ˈstereoˌtyped* and *ˌstereoˈphonic*, we have adjectives that are more commonly used than the corresponding nouns.

Compounding may involve more than one combining-form; *eg nephrolithotomy*, *neurolymphomatosis*: *cf* App I.57 Note [b].

On the model of neo-classical combining-forms, we have compounds to whose initial base a connecting *-o-* is added; *eg*: *ˌspeeˈdometer*.

There is vacillation between *ˈkilometre* and *kiˈlometre*.

'Bahuvrihi' compounds

I.67 All of the compounds to be listed in this section are formed on one or other of the patterns already described. Most of them are like *ˈdarkˌroom*, others are like, for example, *ˈfrogˌman* or *ˈsnowˌflake* (*cf* App I.65 [B], [C], and [D] respectively). The term 'bahuvrihi' refers not to their pattern of formation but to the relation they have with their referents. Neither constituent of such a compound refers to the entity named but, with a semantic movement that may be thought of as 'lateral', the whole refers to a separate entity (usually a person) that is claimed to be characterized by the compound, in its literal or figurative meaning. Thus a *ˈhighˌbrow* means 'an intellectual', on the basis of the facetious claim that people of intellectual interest and cultivated tastes are likely to have a lofty expanse of forehead. Similarly *ˈheartˌthrob* (*cf* App I.61 [A] for its non-bahuvrihi use) is someone who causes the heart to throb in a person of the opposite sex; *ie* 'a sexually attractive person'. Many bahuvrihi compounds are (like *highbrow*) somewhat disparaging in tone and are used chiefly in informal style. Some further examples:

birdbrain	blockhead	bluebell	butterfingers
egghead	fathead	featherbrain	featherweight
hardback	hardtop	heavyweight	hunchback
loudmouth	paleface	paperback	pot-belly
redcap	scarecrow	shellback	

Cf also *hardhat* 'construction worker' ⟨esp AmE⟩.

Note The term *bahuvrihi* is from Sanskrit. Compounds of this type have also been called 'exocentric'.

Adjective compounds

Type 'verb and object'

I.68 ˈMAN-ˌEATING: object + *-ing* participle (*cf* 'X eats men'; also App I.62, *faultfinding*). This is a very productive type. *Self* is a frequent first constituent but takes secondary stress. For example:

breathtaking	fact-finding	heart-breaking	life-giving
record-breaking	ˌself-deˈfeating	ˌself-ˈjustifying	

In *mouth-watering*, there is a causative relation: 'X makes the mouth water'.

In informal AmE we have such a compound used to premodify an adjective in *finger-licking good*.

Type 'verb and adverbial'

I.69 [A] ˈOCEAN-ˌGOING: adverbial + *-ing* participle (*cf* 'X goes across oceans'. *Cf* App I.63, *daydreaming*). For example:

fist-fighting law-abiding lip-sucking

[B] ˈHEARTˌFELT: adverbial + *-ed* participle (*cf* 'X feels it in the heart'). The type is particularly productive when the noun has agential meaning and consists of *self*: *self-styled*, *self-appointed*, *self-employed*, *self-taught* (but a *self-addressed* envelope is one that is addressed *to* oneself). Examples are:

airborne	cost-led	custom-built	handmade
home-brewed	home-made	language-retarded	suntanned
typewritten	thunder-struck	town-bred	weather-beaten

Cf also *speech*(-) *and language*(-)*impaired*.

[C] ˌHARD-ˈWORKING: adverb/adjective + *-ing* participle (*cf* 'X works hard', 'X looks good'). For example:

easy-going	everlasting	far-reaching	good-looking
high-sounding	sweet-smelling	well-meaning	

[D] ˌQUICK-ˈFROZEN: adjective/adverb + *-ed* participle (*cf* 'X was frozen quickly'). For example:

dry-cleaned (*cf* App I.63)		far-fetched	fresh-baked
long-awaited	ˈnew-ˌlaid	true-born	well-meant
ˈwideˌspread			

Note [**a**] The idiomatic isolation of some compounds of this type is evident in the replacement of lexical items in sentential analogues, *eg*: *NEW*-laid (eggs) ~ *X has laid* (the eggs) *RECENTLY*. But like this, several have closer analogues in phrases: 'The eggs are *newly laid* and the loaves *freshly baked*.' The absence of *-ly* is normal in such compounds, but *cf* examples like *fully-fledged*, *newly wed*.

[**b**] The superficially similar adjective compounds *well-meant*, *well-spoken of* on the one hand and *well-behaved*, *well-spoken* on the other differ in respect of voice: *a well-meant remark* ~ *a remark that is meant well*, *She is well spoken of* ~ *People speak well of her* [passive], but *a well-behaved person* ~ *a person that behaves well*, *a well-spoken boy* ~ *a boy who speaks well* [active].

[**c**] It will be noted that compounds in [C] and [D] have phrasal stressing (though in [C] belongs also ˈ*off-putting*); *cf* App I.59.

[**d**] Fashionable ad hoc formations of type [B] include ˈ*export-ˌled* (*recovery*), (*a*) *weather-related* (*air-crash*).

Type 'verbless'

I.70 [A] ˈFOOTˌSORE: noun-based adverbial of respect (*cf* 8.6) + adjective (*cf* 'sore in respect to (one's) feet'). This is a very productive type, especially with certain adjectives that have prepositional complementation (*cf* 16.68*ff*), such as *free* (*from*), *proof* (*against*), *weary* (*of*). For example:

airsick	air-tight	camera-ready	carsick
dustproof	duty-free	fireproof	foolproof
homesick	oven-ready	tax-free	war-weary
watertight			

With some there is phrasal stress, as in ˌ*class-ˈconscious*, ˌ*cost-efˈfective*, ˌ*labour-inˈtensive* and (involving a combining form), ˌ*stereoˈphonic*.

[B] ˌGRASS-ˈGREEN: noun (denoting basis of comparison) + adjective (*cf* 'as green as grass'). This is a fairly productive type and the items formed can usually be used also as nouns: stress is variable, but phrasal stress is usual. Some examples:

age-old	ash-blonde	bottle-green	brick red
jet black	midnight blue	rock-hard	sea-green

[C] ˌGREY-ˈGREEN: adjective + adjective in a coordinating relation but where the phrasal stress pattern implies that the first is relatively thematic, the second focal and hence semantically dominant. *Cf* 'The colour is basically green but with a greyish tint'. Informally, this can be reflected in the first adjective having the suffix *-y* or *-ish* (*cf* App I.38), as in *reddish-brown*, *greeny-grey*. Coordinate compounds are, however, widely used with reference to international relations where (despite the phrasal stress) parity is theoretically fundamental: 'A *Japanese-American* trade pact is about to be signed'. In many coordinate compounds the first element assumes a combining form (*cf* App I.66). Some examples of various types:

Anglo-Polish	auditory-visual	aural-oral
deaf-mute	Franco-German	phonetic-syntactic
psychosomatic	Russo-Chinese	sensori-neural
Sino-Italian	socio-economic	Swedish-Brazilian
tragi-comic		

Note In compounds as premodifiers of *dictionary*, the first adjective indicates the language which is the basis or starting-point, hence again justifying the phrasal stressing in terms of thematization. For example, an ˌ*English-ˈFrench Dictionary* is one that translates English words into French, a ˌ*French-ˈEnglish* one translates from French to English; but an ˌ*Anglo-ˈFrench* dictionary would be one produced by a joint Anglo-French enterprise. Coordinating compounds are sometimes referred to by the Sanskrit term 'dvandva'.

Miscellaneous modes

Back-formation

I.71 Pairs of words like *advise* ~ *advisor*, *burgle* ~ *burglar*, *inspect* ~ *inspector*, *edit* ~ *editor*, suggest an identical relationship between the members which from the synchronic viewpoint of the ordinary language user is perfectly correct. But as a matter of historical fact, while *advisor* and *inspector* were indeed formed from *advise* and *inspect* by suffixation, we have derived *burgle* and *edit* from *burglar* and *editor*, analysing these on the analogy of other agential nouns. *Cf* App I.12, I.34. This is the process known as 'back-formation', and in addition to well-established items, whether from long ago (like *laze* from *lazy*) or more recently (like *televize* from *television*), new formations of this kind continue to be made. The process is particularly fruitful in creating denominal verbs. It should be noted that new formations tend to be used with some hesitation, especially in respect of the full range of verbal inflexions. For example, the textual instance cited in App I.12 was significantly in the base form, *self-destruct*, but although clearly used as a verb, there is less obvious clash with the well-established verb *destroy* than when (as occasionally) ordinary verb inflections are added: ?'The organization *self-destructed* in 1985'. So also we had the agential *baby-sitter* before the verb *baby-sit*, and the base form ('Will you *baby-sit* for me?') before inflected forms ('He *baby-sat* for them'). Other back-formations continue to display their lack of established acceptability: *(*They*) *sight-saw*, *(*She*) *housekept*.

A particularly productive type of back-formation relates to the noun compounds in *-ing* and *-er* (*cf* App I.62 [B], [C], App I.63 [B], [C]). For example, the verbs:

bottle-feed	brain-wash	chain-smoke	day-dream	dry-clean
fire-watch	house-hunt	house-keep	lip-read	sight-see
sleep-walk	spring-clean	window-shop		

Less commonly, we have nouns from adjectives by back-formation: *eg polymer* from *polymeric*.

Note [**a**] Compare also, from (*a*) *sing-song*, the nonce-formation *He sing-songed* (not **He sang-song*). It is likely that such regularizations of inflection result from that process of linguistic analogy known as *metanalysis* (word segmentation counter to etymology), of which back-formation may be seen as a special case. For example, from 'The fridge needs regular defreezing' we find 'They defreezed (*beside* defroze) the fridge that evening'. But regularization in such verbs can also indicate a synchronic failure to analyse in terms of their historical components; thus one occasionally hears 'This cannot be gainsayed' or 'I was overrided', and the like, a phenomenon of relexicalization which is again akin to back-formation.

[**b**] In connection with back-formation we might consider grammatically regular correspondences such as the following (*cf* 7.33*f*):

He *completely* refused . . .	~	His *complete* refusal
She *totally* rejected . . .	~	Her *total* rejection
They *utterly* despaired . . .	~	Their *utter* despair
I *fully* endorse . . .	~	My *full* endorsement
She *absolutely* disapproved . . .	~	Her *absolute* disapproval
They *entirely* agree . . .	~	Their *entire* agreement

It will be observed that the adjectives in the second column emerge only on nominalization of the clauses in the first column. The fact that they are to this extent derived from the corresponding adverbs is confirmed by their meaning, which directly reflects that of the respective subjunct.

Reduplicatives

I.72 Some compounds have two or more constituents which are either identical or only slightly different, *eg*: *goody-goody* (chiefly noun, 'a self-consciously virtuous person', informal). The difference between the two constituents may be in the initial consonants, as in *walkie-talkie*, or in the medial vowels, *eg*: *criss-cross*. Most of the reduplicatives are highly informal or familiar, and many belong to the sphere of child-parent talk, *eg*: *din-din* ['dinner']. The most common uses of reduplicatives (sometimes called 'jingles') are:

[i] to imitate sounds, *eg*: *rat-a-tat* [knocking on door], *tick-tock* [of clock], *ha ha* [of laughter], *bow-wow* [of dog];

[ii] to suggest alternating movements, *eg*: *seesaw*, *flip-flop*, *ping-pong*;

[iii] to disparage by suggesting instability, nonsense, insincerity, vacillation, etc: *higgledy-piggledy*, *hocus-pocus*, *wishy-washy*, *dilly-dally*, *shilly-shally*;
[iv] to intensify, *eg*: *teeny-weeny*, *tip-top*.

Note With [iii] above, we may compare informal AmE sequences of the type *Boston-Schmoston*, which tend to be used with ironic or playful dismissiveness of the first constituent.

Abbreviations

I.73 It is of the essence in lexicalization that, however lengthy and complex the formation of an item, it comes to be regarded as a single unit in relation to the meaning so lexicalized. In consequence, it is not the constituents of the word in combination that are seen as conveying this meaning but its individuality as a whole. Provided any part of the item is itself sufficiently individual to call up the whole, it can be shortened to a form which is linguistically convenient but need not reflect the morphological make-up of the full form. For example, *bus* (from *omnibus*), *ad* (from *advertisement*), *bit* (in information processing, from *binary digit*); *TV* (from *television*). We distinguish three highly productive ways in which abbreviation is involved in English word-formation, giving us CLIPPINGS, ACRONYMS, and BLENDS.

Note Compare the related use of abbreviation as a graphic device; App III.27*ff*.

Clippings

I.74 Especially in informal usage, we tend to show our familiarity with polysyllabic words (especially nouns), by shortening them, often to a single syllable. The 'clipping' seems often to start from the graphic form, since the surviving fragment is usually initial and need not constitute either prosodically or semantically the salient part of the original (but *cf* Note [a]):

ad ˈadvert ⟨BrE⟩ }	*from*	adˈvertisement (*also* adverˈtisement *in AmE*)
ˈcosec /ˈkəʊsek/	*from*	cosecant /kəʊˈsiːkənt/ (*in trigonometry*)
ˈdemo	*from*	demonˈstration (*but in BrE chiefly in the political sense*; *in AmE 'a demonstration car'*)
eˈxam	*from*	(academic) examiˈnation (*but not the verb* eˈxamine *or* examiˈnation *in the medical sense*)
French fries ⟨*esp AmE*⟩	*from*	French fried potatoes ⟨*esp AmE*⟩
gents	*from*	gentlemen's (*especially* = gentlemen's lavatory)
lab	*from*	laˈboratory ⟨*BrE*⟩, ˈlaboraˌtory ⟨*AmE*⟩
lib	*from*	libeˈration (*but only in lexicalizations like* Women's Liberation Movement)
ˈmemo	*from*	memoˈrandum
mike	*from*	ˈmicroˌphone
ˈphoto	*from*	ˈphotograph (*but not* phoˈtography)
prof	*from*	proˈfessor
pseud ⟨BrE⟩	*from*	ˌpseudo- (ˌintelˈlectual)
pub	*from*	ˌpublic ˈhouse

ˈstereo	*from*	ˌstereoˈphonic
telly ⟨BrE⟩	*from*	ˌteleˈvision

Less commonly, the clipped form has resulted from discarding the initial part of a word, as in:

phone	*from*	ˈtelephone (*but not*, *eg*, microphone)
plane	*from*	ˈairplane, ˈaeroplane

Occasionally, syllables have been discarded at both ends of a word, as in:

flu	*from*	ˌinfluˈenza
fridge ⟨esp BrE⟩	*from*	reˈfrigerator

Stress patterns have been indicated to show that the shortened form is not necessarily (indeed not usually) the stressed part of the word concerned and that it is given an independent stress pattern of its own (as in ˈ*demo*). Even stronger evidence for the acquisition by clipped forms of a quite specific lexicalization is indicated by the parenthesized restrictions we have shown where relevant. Thus *lib* is not an abbreviated form of the word *liberation* as such, still less of the verb *liberate*, but only of very specific uses of *liberation*. The examination of a patient by a doctor is not an *exam*. A further sign of the lexical independence of clipped forms is that *mono* (with a meaning that was unlexicalized, of course, when sound-recording could be nothing else) came into existence by analogy with *stereo*, and in specific contrast to it; hence its immediate use in a parallel abbreviated form, and the fuller form *monophonic* remains relatively rare.

Note **[a]** The informality that is typical of clipped forms is frequently reflected in informal spellings; for example, *showbiz*, *fridge*, *mike*, *telly* ⟨BrE⟩, *cos* or *'cos* ⟨both BrE: 'because'⟩, *praps* ['perhaps']. In these cases, the spelling has been adapted to suit the pronunciation of the original fragment. The converse holds for '(the student music) *soc*' ⟨esp BrE⟩, where the original spelling of *soc*(*iety*) remains but the final /s/ of the fragment comes to be pronounced /k/. In '(meat and two) *veg*' ⟨BrE⟩ neither spelling nor pronunciation (/vedʒ/) has been changed, while in *bike* ['bicycle'] both have been changed. In *hanky* ['handkerchief'], we find an additional familiarity marker in the suffix *-y* (*cf* App I.77); *cf* also *nighty*, *undies*, *comfy* ['comfortable'].

[b] Some clipped forms preserve a final *s*, as in *specs* ['spectacles'], *maths* ⟨BrE⟩ ['mathematics', but AmE *math*], *gents*, *French fries*; some add an *s*, as in BrE *turps* ['turpentine'] (*cf* App I.77).

[c] It is not uncommon to find clipped forms becoming so well-established as to lose their informal tone. This is true of *plane*, *stereo*, *taxi* (from *taxicab* – itself a clipping), *pram* ⟨BrE⟩ (note spelling, from 'perambulator'); and in many long-established cases the fuller form is rarely used (*eg*: *omnibus* for *bus*) or is not ordinarily known (*eg*: *mobile vulgus* for *mob*).

[d] *Ozalid* (in reprography) is basically a reverse spelling of *diazo*; *cf* App I.15 Note.

Acronyms

I.75 Acronyms are words formed from the initial letters of words that make up a name. New acronyms are freely produced, especially by scientists and administrators (*cf* App I.15), and particularly for names of organizations. There are two main types:

[A] Acronyms which are pronounced as sequences of letters (also called 'alphabetisms'), *eg C.O.D.*/ˌsiː əʊ ˈdiː/, are most like ordinary abbreviations and hence most peripheral to word-formation. In writing, the more institutionalized formations have no periods between the letters. The use of capitals is not determined solely by whether the items abbreviated are proper nouns.

[i] The letters represent full words:

c/o	(in) care of [used on envelopes]
C.O.D.	cash on delivery
DIY ⟨informal BrE⟩	do-it-yourself [used of self-help repairs, etc]
EEC	European Economic Community
eg	exempli gratia [Latin, 'for example']
ESP	extra-sensory perception
FBI	Federal Bureau of Investigation
ie	id est [Latin, 'that is']
KL	Kuala Lumpur
LA	Los Angeles
MIT	Massachusetts Institute of Technology
p.c. ⟨BrE⟩	postcard
UFO	unidentified flying object
UN	the United Nations
VIP	very important person

[ii] The letters represent constituents in a compound or just parts of a word:

GHQ	General Headquarters
ID	identification (card)
TB	tuberculosis
TV	television

Acronyms of Type [A] are sometimes given a quasi-phonetic written form. For example, *M.C.* ['Master of Ceremonies'] may be informally written as *Emcee*; DJ ['Disc Jockey'] as *Deejay*, *OK* as *Okay*. In AmE, *Jaycee* is used for *Junior Chamber of Commerce* (member).

[B] Acronyms which are pronounced as a word, *eg* NATO /ˈneɪtəʊ/, are often used without our knowing what the letters stand for:

laser	lightwave amplification by stimulated emission of radiation
NATO	the North Atlantic Treaty Organization
radar	radio detecting and ranging
UNESCO	the United Nations Educational, Scientific and Cultural Organization
WASP	White Anglo-Saxon Protestant ⟨AmE, informal⟩

Acronyms of this second type frequently derive from phrasal names specially devised for their acronymic convenience. For the same reason, initial syllables as well as initial letters may be involved, as in *binac* ('*bin*ary *a*utomatic *c*omputer').

Note Some abbreviations are read aloud in unabbreviated forms; *eg*: *c/o*, *p.c.* Others are normally (*eg*: *viz*) or sometimes (*eg*: *ie* and *eg*) read out as English phrases, 'namely', 'that is', and 'for example' respectively.

Blends

I.76 As the term suggests, blends are formations in which a compound is made by 'blending' one word with another. Enough of each is normally retained so that the complex whole remains fairly readily analysable (*cf* App I.14). To this end also, and preserving the normal attributes of the compound such that the end-part is the thematic base to which the new initial part is related, the blend tends to have as a whole the prosodic shape of the untruncated end-part. Thus on the basis of *hoˈtel* we preface enough of *motor* both to achieve the new contrast with *hotel* (a hotel specially equipped for the needs of motoring guests), and to achieve the dominance of the base pattern: *moˈtel.*

So too with a special kind of *lunch* which has some of the features of *breakfast*, we have coined *brunch*; if the meal had been primarily conceived as a kind of *breakfast*, we might have had instead (*)*ˈlunkfast*. Thus we may conclude that a *spork* (first recorded in 1976) is a fork like a spoon, rather than a spoon that looks like a fork (which might have given us (*)*foon*). Note the distinction between *tigon* (where the sire is a *tig*er) and *liger* (where the sire is a *li*on). In such formations, an attempt seems to be made at matching the pragmatic position with a linguistic form.

Blending is a very productive process, especially in commercial coinages, which suggests that its rather daring playfulness is popular. Where many types of neologism are criticized adversely (*eg* as 'unnecessary jargon'), blends seem rather to be enjoyed. Perhaps in consequence, many of them are short-lived or never achieve currency beyond the advertising copy in which they may originate. *Eg*: *swimˈsation* of a *swimsuit* that will cause a *sensation*; *lubriˈtection* of a new *lubricant* that will provide engine *protection.*

Others not merely become well-established but act as a highly productive model for new formations; *cf*: *ˈcheeseˌburger*, *ˈbeefˌburger*, *ˈshrimpˌburger*; *ˌwasheˈteria*, *ˌcandyˈteria*, *ˌlunchaˈteria*, etc (and we note again that a matching in prosodic shape is a determining factor in establishing the blended form). Others again achieve a brief surge of productivity in response to an outstanding event. In the years following the Washington Watergate scandals, the name *ˈWaterˌgate* became a model for such blends, being the thematic element in items like *ˈMulderˌgate*, *ˈBillieˌgate*, *ˈcattleˌgate*. All of these denoted specific cases of political crisis resulting from scandalous deception connoted by the underlying *Watergate*, the whole of which (with the associations) had to be understood in each alternative formation.

Some further and more general examples:

ˈbreathaˌlyser	[breath + ˈanalˌyser]
eˈlectroˌcute	[electro + ˈexeˌcute]
ˈEuroˌvision	[European + ˈteleˌvision]
ˈheliˌport	[helicopter + ˈairˌport]
ˈnewsˌcast	[news + ˈbroadˌcast]
ˈparaˌtroops	[ˈparaˌchute + troops]
smog	[smoke + fog]
ˌstagˈflation	[ˌstagˈnation + inˈflation]
ˈteleˌcast	[television + ˈbroadˌcast]
ˈtraveˌlogue	[travel + ˈcataˌlogue]

There is rather more radical abbreviation in *bi'onic* (*biological* + *electronic*). Items like *bit* ('binary digit'), *interpol* ('international police'), *moped* ('motor pedal-cycle'), *telex* ('teleprinter exchange'), are outside the general pattern outlined above, both in the way in which the word-fractions are made up and in the disregard for the prosody of a thematic starting-point. In some respects, they more resemble acronyms of the [B] type in App I.75.

Note [**a**] The ease with which word-fractions can be used in blends accounts for the way certain sounds and sound-sequences achieve a semi-morphological status; *cf* the many derogatory words in English beginning with /sn/ (*eg*: *sneer*, *snide*, *snoop*) or the frequentative verbs ending in a consonant plus syllabic /l/ (*eg*: *rattle*, *sizzle*, *tinkle*). In this connection, one notes that recurrent items in blends (*eg*: *tele-*, *Euro-*, *-teria*, *-burger*, *-gate*) come to be used like affixes.

[**b**] The feminist movement has produced several blends, notably *Ms* (/mɪz/: *Miss* + /mɪsɪz/), and including purely graphic items like the pronoun *s/he* (*she* + *he*), or in the striking title of a book by Mary Daly, *gyn/ecology* (*gyne* + *ecology*). On the use of the oblique stroke, *cf* App I.59, Note [b].

[**c**] It is a kind of blending that produces (especially in BrE) the very informal and usually scatological 'tmesis' or use of infixes in *ˌabsoˌbloody'lutely*, *ˌstonyˌgoddam'broke*, *ˌalˌruddy'mighty*. Semantically, these combine an already emotional hyperbole with an extreme intensifier, and as the indicated stressing shows, there is a common essential prosodic pattern such that the infixed intensifier comes immediately before the most emphasized syllable (*cf* 18.59 Note [b].).

Familiarity markers

I.77 We bring together here types of abbreviation with affixation that have in common a highly informal tone and a mode of referring that indicates close community with (together with familiar, and often affectionate, knowledge of) what is referred to. In many instances they characterize the type of slang developed in close social groups such as families, schools, military institutions, etc. Thus, in Oxford the examination known as 'Divinity Honour Moderations' came to be called 'Divvers', St Stephens Hall 'Staggers', and a Professor Lightfoot 'Lighters'. Among other affixes for diminutives and analogous 'pet' forms (also known as *hypocoristics*), we have *-let*, *-ette*, *mini-*, and a few others (*cf* App I.24, I.33).

Along with abbreviation (and frequently syllabic modification as in 'Staggers'), certain affixes are recurrent: *-y*, *-o*, *-er*, *-s*:

-Y, -IE: *hippy*, *Aussy*, *telly*, *chevie*, *baddy*, *goalie*, *hanky*, *weirdie*, *druggy* ⟨BrE⟩, *nudie*, *chappie* ⟨BrE⟩, *chippie* [⟨BrE⟩ 'carpenter']; particularly common in that type of intimate discourse called 'baby talk' (and note *baby* itself): *comfy*, *sweetie*, *drinky*, *auntie*, *daddy*, *mummy* ⟨BrE⟩, *mommy* ⟨AmE⟩. Familiar forms of personal names also frequently have *-y* or *-ie*: *Katie*, *Freddy*, *Charlie*, *Molly*, *Billy*, *Susie*

-O: *ammo* ['ammunition'], *aggro* [⟨BrE⟩ 'aggravation' in slang senses such as 'mob mischief'], *arvo* [⟨AustralE⟩ 'afternoon'], *doggo* [⟨BrE⟩ 'quiet'], *weirdo*

-ER: chiefly BrE, as in *rugger*, *soccer*, *footer*, *tucker* [⟨AustralE⟩ 'food'], *boner* ['blunder'], *fresher* ['freshman']

-S: *Babs*, *Debs*, *nuts*, *bananas* ['mad'], *Moms*

These and other such informal affixes often occur in combination: *fatso*; *tootsies*, *Momsie*; *the willies*, *falsies*; *-ers* ⟨BrE⟩ as in *starkers*, *bonkers*, *Daffers* ['Daphne'], *shampers* ['champagne'], *preggers* ['pregnant'].

Note [**a**] The above use of *-o* (unstressed) is to be distinguished from the equally informal but stressed *-o* after monosyllabic responses: *right'o, good'o* ⟨both BrE⟩.

[**b**] Other informal (and especially AustralE) suffixes include *-'oo* as in *shi'voo* ['party'], *ma'goo* ['important person'], *-eroo* as in '(It was a real) *'flope,roo*', though in AustralE the stress pattern would more usually be *,flope'roo, ,socke'roo*.

Bibliographical note

For general accounts of English word-formation, see Jespersen (1909–49), vol VI; Koziol (1972); Marchand (1969). Stein (1973) provides an extensive bibliography.

On broad theoretical issues, see Adams (1973); Aronoff (1976); Bauer (1983); Greenbaum (1976a); Hansen et al (1982); Jackendoff (1975); Kastovsky (1982a, 1982b); Lipka (1972); Lipka and Günther (1981); Pennanen (1972, 1982); Siegel (1979); Stein (1977).

On noun compounds, see Brekle (1970); Levi (1978); Warren (1978); Zimmer (1971).

On adjective formation, see Hirtle (1970); Hudson (1975a); Levi (1973); Ljung (1970, 1976); Meys (1975); Stein (1971).

On affixation, see R. W. Brown (1927); Colen (1984); Isitt (1983); Stein (1984); Tottie (1980); Zimmer (1964).

On other specific topics in word-formation, see Algeo (1975); Biese (1941); R. W. Brown (1954); Lindelöf (1938); McMillan (1980); Pennanen (1966); Praninskas (1968); Soudek (1967); Thun (1963).

Other relevant studies include Algeo (1978, 1980); Burgschmidt and Cornell (1981); Danielsson (1948); Górska (1982); Panagl (1982); Vendler (1968).

Among dictionaries and other reference works of interest for current word-formation study are Barnhart et al (1973, 1980); Burchfield (1972–86); McDavid (1963); Urdang (1978); Webster (1976); Wentworth and Flexner (1975).

II

Appendix II Stress, rhythm, and intonation

Introduction

II.1 The study of stress, rhythm, and intonation is an extremely complex area of linguistics to which it is impossible to give adequate attention within the space of this Appendix. Our aim must here be strictly limited to presenting an outline of the part these features play in English grammar, to explaining the allusions that have been made to them in this book, and to guiding the reader to the selective bibliographical note at the end of the Appendix.

Stress, rhythm, and intonation are all concerned with the perception of relative PROMINENCE. We speak of STRESS when we are considering the prominence, usually perceived as greater loudness by the listener, with which one part of a word or longer utterance is distinguished from other parts. Thus we will say that *indignant* has stress on the second syllable; and we may also indicate that the word *like* is normally stressed in *Does he like it?* In such cases, we can show the stress by a raised vertical mark (*cf* further App II.3):

in'dignant   Does he 'like it?

We speak of RHYTHM when we are considering the pattern formed by the stresses perceived as peaks of prominence or beats. These occur at somewhat regular intervals of time, the recurring beats being regarded as completing a cycle or 'measure'. Thus, as a language with a tendency for 'stress-timed' rhythm, English often shows an identity of rhythm in sentences like the following, provided that the number of syllables does not vary too widely:

'John is	'here	'now.
'John is at	'home	to'night.
The pro'fessor is in	'London this	'evening.

We speak of INTONATION when we associate relative prominence with PITCH, the aspect of sound which we perceive in terms of 'high' or 'low', 'falling' or 'rising', broadly as these terms are used with reference to a scale of musical notes. Thus we will say that the 'intonation nucleus' in the following utterance (using the notation explained in App II.12*ff*) has a 'falling tone', as is normal when a sentence is a statement:

The 'man has GÒNE

By contrast, if this nucleus had a rising tone, the sentence would usually have the value of a question:

The 'man has GÓNE

Finally, when we have occasion to indicate the PRONUNCIATION of vowels and consonants, we use the symbols listed in the pronunciation table (p. viii). By this means, we can show, for example, the different sounds that are represented by the letter *o* in forms of the verb DO (*cf* 3.36):

Do /duː/ they
Don't /dəʊnt/ they } read much?
Does /dʌz/ he

The symbols follow a tradition of 'broad transcription' so as to represent English pronunciation on as wide a basis as possible, but where there are differences between BrE (as represented by RP) and AmE (as represented by 'network English'; *cf* 1.27), our symbols seek to indicate these.

Physical properties

II.2 The physics of these phenomena cannot concern us here, though we must utter a warning against simple equations such as regarding stress as identical with loudness. Stress is closely associated with loudness or amplitude on the one hand and articulatory force on the other, but other factors are or can be involved–notably duration and pitch. Pitch seems to be the most important factor when a stress is final in a phrase (or when a word is spoken in isolation): the stress is then associated with (or realized by) pitch prominence and often with pitch movement. But what matters is that the hearer expects sharp contrasts of prominence and expects peaks of prominence at particular places in a word or a phrase. Understanding is severely handicapped if such expectations are frustrated.

Again, we can agree on discriminations between various kinds (and even degrees) of 'rhythmicality' without committing ourselves to a definitive view on the physical nature of English rhythm itself. The stresses are regarded by speaker and hearer as 'beats' at more or less regular intervals of time. We thus have an accentual sequence analogous to the quasi-isochronous 'feet' in poetic metre, each foot consisting of a stressed syllable, usually with one or more unstressed syllables. Perception of the rhythmic base may involve observing variations in loudness or pitch, or measuring intervals of time – or a combination of these. But these are matters of controversial debate, to which we will not turn our attention here.

So far as pitch is concerned, we should recognize that, although 'fundamental frequency' is doubtless a more prominent component than anything else in providing cues to our perception, nevertheless loudness or intensity is a significant cooccurrent factor and can readily, in fact, replace fundamental frequency. Evidence of our ability to dispense with fundamental frequency is that, largely through amplitude variation (though other factors are no doubt involved), whispered speech is perceived as having the same intonation as normal voiced speech.

We need also to distinguish intonation from musical melody. In contrast to music, there is, in speech, no absolute pitch and there are no fixed intervals to be observed in intonation. All pitch distinctions are acoustically relative, however absolute they may be linguistically.

Lastly, it should be noted that the three interrelated factors of stress, rhythm, and intonation are not the only distinctions that are observed in the stream of speech modifying an utterance while the grammar and vocabulary are held constant. Other 'prosodic systems', as they are called, include for example tempo, *ie* the relative speed of utterance. It is widely agreed, however, that stress, rhythm, and intonation are the most pervasively important, and we shall virtually exclude the others from consideration in this short description. They are however illustrated in the texts presented in 19.87*ff*, which depend on our recognizing some of these other distinctions.

Note The meaning attached by linguists to 'prosodic' is based on the use of this term in traditional rhetoric but with considerable difference in emphasis and specialization.

Stress within the word

Stress patterns in words

II.3 As soon as an utterance is longer than a single syllable, the syllables are arranged in rhythmic patterns comprising a succession of strong–weak–strong–weak, and so on. This is true whether the polysyllabic stretch is a sentence, a phrase, or a single word. It is possible to distinguish several degrees of stress in a sequence of syllables. But it would seem that what is most linguistically relevant is a simple binary opposition: stress versus no stress. We mark PRIMARY stress with a high vertical stroke before the syllable carrying the stress, leaving lack of stress unmarked:

ˈfriendship	ˈaperture
unˈhelpful	deˈparture

But it is often relevant to distinguish, from primary stress, an intermediate SECONDARY stress. When it is desirable to indicate secondary stress, this will be marked by a low vertical stroke before the syllable concerned:

ˈhouseˌkeeper ˌcontriˈbution

When it is necessary to distinguish a specially HEAVY stress, we can make use of a double high vertical mark. Heavy stress can be used to mark sharp contrasts or to indicate relative stress in phrases without recourse to indicating intonation (*cf* App II.11*ff*), *eg*:

ˈseveral ˈgenerous ˌcontriˈˈbutions

Although, as speakers, we have a good deal of freedom in assigning stresses in utterances longer than a word, the placing of the stress within English words is – save for relatively minor exceptions – so rigorously invariant that it is often difficult for the hearer to understand a word where the accentuation is deviant. Compare [1–3] with [1a–3a]:

imˈportant	[1]	*ˈimportant	[1a]
eˈmergency	[2]	*ˈemerˌgency	[2a]
ˈenergy	[3]	*eˈnergy	[3a]

Moving the primary stress from the second syllable to the first (as in [1a] and [2a]), or from the first to the second (as in [3a]), could be enough to make the word incomprehensible or misunderstood.

But although the stresses are normally in a fixed position in a word, their position is unpredictable in the sense that – in contrast with some languages – there is no single position where the primary stress of a word can be expected to fall in English. For example, to count from left to right, it may fall on the

1st syllable:	'family	*4th syllable*:	fa,mili'arity
2nd syllable:	fa'miliar	*5th syllable*:	,nationali'zation
3rd syllable:	,natio'nality	*6th syllable*:	in,dustriali'zation

Thus, to a large extent, the stress pattern of each polysyllabic word has to be learned separately, though we shall presently see that some valuable generalizations can be made. We shall also see that, with some classes of words, it is helpful and relevant to count syllables from the end rather than from the beginning.

II.4 The generalizations that can be made about the stress pattern of English are complicated by the mixed nature of English vocabulary: a basic core of Germanic words is surrounded by a much larger number of words from foreign languages (notably French, Latin, and Greek). Native words and early French adoptions tend to have the primary stress on the stem syllable and to keep it there, regardless of the affixes that word-formation may add (FIXED STRESS):

'kingly	'passion	stand
'kingliness	'passionately	under'stand
un'kingliness	dis'passionate	,misunder'stand

By contrast, with more recent adoptions, and with derivations based on foreign and classical elements (*cf* App. I.31), the place of the stress varies according to the affixation (MOVABLE STRESS):

	ANTEPENULTIMATE	PENULTIMATE
'telegraph	~ te'legraphy	~ tele'graphic
'photo(graph)	~ pho'tography	~ photo'graphic
'transport	~ trans'portable	~ transpor'tation
'argument	~ argu'mentative	~ argumen'tation

The items in the third column above exemplify two valuable generalizations.

The stress falls on the syllable before adjectival *-ic* (*cf* App I.39), *ie* on the penultimate syllable:

e'conomy	~ eco'nomic
'phoneme	~ pho'nemic
'problem	~ proble'matic
'sympathy	~ sympa'thetic

All abstract nouns ending in *-ion* are stressed on the syllable preceding this ending, *eg*:

counter'action   sus'picion   tabu'lation

This stress remains even after further affixes are added after *-ion*:

re'vision   ~ re'visional   ~ re'visionist

II.5 But there are numerous other comparable generalizations which help us to predict the placing of English stress. Thus the stress falls on the last syllable before nominal *-ity* (*cf* App I.36):

'curious ~ curi'osity
pro'miscuous ~ promis'cuity
u'nanimous ~ una'nimity

The stress also falls on the last syllable before the nominal and adjectival suffix *-ian*:

'Cromwell ~ Crom'wellian
'grammar ~ gram'marian
'library ~ li'brarian
u'tility ~ utili'tarian
Greek ~ 'Grecian
'Asia ~ 'Asian
'Croat ~ Cro'atian
'Alsace ~ Al'satian

By contrast, the affix *-ite* leaves the place of the stress unchanged (*cf* App I.37). Compare:

'Jefferson ~ { 'Jeffersonite / Jeffer'sonian }

A fairly numerous set of words that can operate without affixal change as noun or adjective on the one hand, and as verb on the other, have a stress difference in the two functions (*cf* App I.56), for example:

NOUN	ADJECTIVE	VERB
'attribute		at'tribute
'conduct		con'duct
'contrast		con'trast
'convict		con'vict
'present	'present	pre'sent
	'perfect	per'fect

In one of these (*contrast*) and in several of the other examples that might have been cited (*eg*: *export*), there is a tendency to discontinue a separate verb form and to use the form as stressed for the noun also in other functions.

Note In numerous words, interchange of primary and secondary stress would produce a comprehensible pronunciation. This is especially so with words where the native speakers themselves show variation, as in:

'abdomen *or* ab'domen fi'nance *or* 'finance
'controversy *or* con'troversy ⟨esp BrE⟩ ˌmaga'zine *or* 'magaˌzine

In some words there are different stress patterns in the two major standards of English, with a tendency for BrE, especially among younger speakers, to adopt the AmE pattern. The two nouns *adult* and *ally* are examples of varying usage where the stress is often on the first syllable in BrE but usually on the second in AmE (*cf* App II.6 Note for a contrary tendency in some words).

Stress in compounds

II.6 Compound nouns (*cf* App I.61*ff*) generally have a primary stress on the first element but with a secondary stress on the second constituent:

'earthˌquake 'lifeˌboat
'waitingˌroom 'fire-exˌtinguisher

Contrast here compounds with the corresponding noun phrases, *eg*:

> That sounds like a *'black,bird*. [compound]
> A carrion crow is a completely *,black 'bird*. [noun phrase]

Other examples:

COMPOUND		NOUN PHRASE
'black,board	*but*	,black 'board
'green,fly	*but*	,green 'fly
'hot,house	*but*	,hot 'house

When such a compound is made part of another compound, the primary stress and the secondary stress are redistributed to give the same rhythm:

> 'light,house *but* 'lighthouse-,keeper

A smaller number of compounds do not have the primary stress on the initial element:

> ,vice-'chancellor ,first-'rate

As well as nouns, these compounds include:

verbs:	,back-'fire
adverbs:	,hence'forth
adjectives:	,knee-'deep, ,flat-'footed

In some cases we may be in doubt as to whether we should regard sequences with this stress pattern as compounds or free syntactic phrases, and we vacillate between writing them with hyphens or as separate words (*cf* App I.59, App III.4*f*), for example:

> ,lawn(-)'tennis ,country(-)'house

On the other hand, we vacillate in our stressing of some examples which are apparently in the process of becoming recognized as compounds of the *'black,bird* type; for example:

,field 'marshal	*or* 'field ,marshal
,over'seas	*or* 'over,seas
,week'end	*or* 'week,end
,head'master	*or* 'head,master

In any case, the stress often shifts from the second to the first element when the compound is being used attributively in a noun phrase:

The room is ,down'stairs.	*but* a 'down,stairs 'room
His work is ,first 'class.	*but* his 'first, class 'work
The water is ,knee-'deep	*but* 'knee-deep in 'water

This is analogous to the redistribution that occurs in compounds like *lighthouse-keeper*.

Note In AmE, and quite often also in BrE, there is a strong tendency to give initial stress to many of these compounds, *eg* in:

> lawn(-)tennis, back-fire, country(-)house, apple-sauce

Stress in phrases and other syntactic units

II.7 The examples and the discussion have already taken us outside the limits of the word and into the distribution of stresses in phrases and other syntactic units. It is usual to emphasize the distinction between the word, where convention and semantic integration tend to produce a fixed stress and rhythm which the individual speaker cannot alter, and connected speech, where the disposition of stresses is subject to the speaker's will and the meaning he wishes to convey.

There is much validity in this but it must not be pressed too far, since it depends on a much sharper distinction between phrases and (compound) words than English grammar and lexicology in fact warrant. It will not do to say that initial stressing (as in *'black ˌbird*) indicates compounds, and final stressing (as in *eˌlectric 'clock*) the syntactic phrases of connected speech. We have seen compounds like *ˌdown'stairs* which (despite similarity with phrases like *'down the 'street*) we would not wish to analyse as phrases. And *ˌstill 'life* (in painting), which is usually stressed in BrE as though it were a phrase, shows that it is a compound in having a different plural (*still lifes*) from the noun *life* ~ *lives* (*cf* 5.83). So too there are initial-stressed phrases that linguists would not normally regard as compounds, since – as is not general in word-formation (*cf* App I.1*ff*) – we are as free to form such sequences as we are to form any other kind of syntactic unit, especially with 'general nouns':

I was talking to the *'turkey ˌman* about this *immuni'zation ˌbusiness.*

II.8 The stress distribution provides a firm basis for distinguishing not so much between compound and phrase as between different semantic relations:

{A *'bull-ˌfight* involves bulls. [1]
{A *ˌbull 'calf* is a young bull. [1a]
{A *'French ˌteacher* teaches French. [2]
{A *ˌFrench 'teacher* is French. [2a]
{A *'slate ˌquarry* yields slate. [3]
{A *ˌslate 'roof* is made of slate. [3a]
{A *'toy ˌfactory* produces toys. [4]
{A *ˌtoy 'factory* is a model of a factory used as a toy. [4a]

Thus the distribution of stresses in units higher than the word is subject to rule, just as it is within the word. Apart from 'object' premodifiers (as in *'French ˌteacher*), there is a heavier stress (indicated by a double vertical mark) on the head of a noun phrase where the head is the last item in the phrase:

a rea'listic ˌlittle ˌtoy "factory
'several 'stale ˌhalf-'eaten 'currant "buns

Postmodified noun-phrases normally have the primary stress on the last stressable item (*ie* generally an open-class lexical item) in the postmodification:

the ˌtoy 'factory he 'got for his "birthday
the 'currant 'buns that I 'tried to "eat

With equal regularity (and subject to the special factors explored in 18.1*ff*), a noncontrastive primary stress falls on the main verb, or on the subsequent particle if the head is a phrasal verb (such as *wash up*; *cf* 16.3), or on the operator in an elliptical verb phrase:

A: 'Will he have "gone? B: 'Yes, he "will.
A: He 'must be "working. B: Yes, he "must be.
She 'can't have been 'washing "up.

In these last examples, the verb phrases come at the end of sentences. End position is a point where, in any case, a climax of prominence is expected and normally occurs on the last word unless it is a pronoun or (frequently) a preposition (*cf* 9.6). Compare the regular, noncontrastive shift of stress placement in the following two sentences:

He 'saw his "mother. ~ He "saw her.

Compare also the following sentences:

It's the ad'dress he 'sent the "letter ˌto. [5]
He 'sent the 'letter to the ad'dress he'd been "given. [6]

Final position of the preposition in [5] gives it a secondary stress and an unreduced vowel /ʊ/, whereas in a syntactically analogous nonfinal use in [6], the preposition would be unstressed and the vowel reduced to /ə/.

Peaks of prominence in syntactic units of the kinds discussed in this and later sections would in actual speech be normally associated with pitch, and we shall shortly (*cf* App II.11*ff*) reinterpret these peaks in terms of intonation. For the present purpose, however, this fact may be ignored without undue distortion.

Note We have previously (*cf* App II.6) noted the stress shift that occurs in compounds when used attributively. The same phenomenon also occurs in syntactic phrases:

after'noon	*but* ˌafternoon 'tea
over'seas	*but* ˌoverseas 'student
ˌconti'nental	*but* a ˌcontinental 'climate
uni'versity	*but* the ˌuniversity 'library
ˌPicca'dilly	*but* ˌPiccadilly 'Circus
prin'cess ⟨esp BrE⟩	*but* ˌPrincess 'Anne

In the case of polysyllabic words, other situations than the attributive position may trigger off the stress shift:

The 'princess fell in "love.

Contrastive stress

II.9 Since the language determines stress location almost as rigidly in phrases and sentences as it does in individual words, we should not attempt to impose too sharp a distinction between 'words' and 'connected speech' on these grounds.

However, the individual speaker has the possibility of placing stress freely in units larger than the word by means of CONTRASTIVE STRESS which is capable of highlighting any word in a sentence. This is particularly striking in the case of some closed-class words (*cf* 2.39) which, when unstressed, make use of the 'schwa' vowel /ə/ or other form of phonological reduction. Under contrastive stress, they assume the form that they have as isolated dictionary items:

	UNSTRESSED	STRESSED
a	/ə/	/eɪ/
an	/ən, n/	/æn/
and	/ənd, ən, n̩/	/ænd/
but	/bət/	/bʌt/
not	/nt, n/	/nɒt/
he	/hɪ/	/hiː/
was	/wəz/	/wɒz/
would	/wəd, əd, d/	/wʊd/
does	/dəz, dz, s/	/dʌz/

The unstressed form /s/ of *does* occurs for example in:

What's he mean? ['What does he mean?']

Examples of stressed *and* and *he* in sentences:

ˈJohn ˈˈand his ˈmother ˈwent. ['It is not true that only one of them went.']

Will ˈˈhe have ˈgone? ['Granted that others have gone, is it true of him also?']

The focus device of contrastive stress (*cf* 18.12) involves pitch prominence and we shall therefore return to it when we are dealing with intonation. For the present we must observe, however, that contrastive stress is not limited to sequences longer than the word. The normal accentuation within the word can also be distorted at the speaker's will if he wants to make a contrastive point. Thus instead of *unˈhappy* one might say ˈˈ*unhappy* in a context such as:

A: She was looking very happy tonight.
B: You thought so? *She seemed ˈˈunhappy to me.* [1]

Unstressed (or weak) forms represent phonological REDUCTION where there may be a wide range of variants, *eg* /ənd/, /ən/, /n/ of a stressed (or strong) form /ænd/. CONTRACTION, on the other hand, is the term used for institutionalized written representations of reduction, *eg* /aɪm/ represented in writing as *I'm*. Since contraction is institutionalized, we do not find variation in writing corresponding to the range of reduced forms in speech. For example, there is only one contracted form *'d* of *would*, and there is no generally acceptable or widely used contraction of *and* in writing, compared with the range of reductions illustrated above.

The major types of contraction are the following:

(i) *Not*-contraction, *eg*: *don't, haven't, shouldn't* (*cf* 10.55*f*)
(ii) Auxiliary verb contraction, *eg*: *I'm, you've, they're*; *we'll, that'll*; *she's, one's, somebody's, there's*; *you'd, who'd* (*cf* 3.23)
(iii) Personal pronoun contraction of *us* in *let's* (*cf* 3.51 Note [b])

In combinations of two potential contractions, the writer has a choice between alternatives. In general, *have* and *will* favour *not*-contraction, whereas the auxiliary contraction predominates with *are*. Thus:

I haven't	rather than *I've not*
I won't	rather than *I'll not*
we're not	rather than *we aren't*

Double contractions are never allowed: **I'ven't.*

Note Contrastive stress can also override the distinction made in App II.8. Thus in the following sentence (*cf* example [2a] in App II.8), we could be making it clear that the teacher had been described as *French*, not *fresh*:

I 'said she was a "French ˌteacher, not a "fresh ˌteacher.

Rhythm

II.10 Broadly speaking, and disregarding the special case of contrastive stress, English connected speech has stresses on the open-class words, and absence of stress on the closed-class words accompanying them:

It's the ad'dress he 'sent the "letter ˌto.
She was 'looking "happy to'night.

Just as word stress in rapid or informal connected discourse differs from stress on words in isolation, so the pronunciation of words is influenced by their linguistic surroundings. This is true not only of closed-class items but also of open-class words. The processes affecting the edges of words and syllables are referred to as 'assimilation', 'coalescence', and 'elision'. Thus we may find the following reductions in connected discourse:

	IN ISOLATION	IN CONNECTED DISCOURSE
I'm going (to York)	/aɪm 'gəʊɪŋ/	/aɪŋ'gɜŋ/
actually	/'æktjʊəlɪ/	/'æktʃlɪ/

The natural rhythm of English is a regular beat. When unaffected by such factors as hesitation, which may slow down the speaker, or excitement, which may speed him up, English rhythm provides roughly equal intervals of time between the stresses. Compare examples [1] and [2]:

He told his mother. [1]
He sent it to his mother. [2]

If these two sentences were spoken by the same person under similar conditions, they would have the same basic rhythmic pattern, would occupy roughly the same amount of time, and would thus oblige the speaker to utter the sequence *sent it to his* more rapidly than the sequence *told his* which occupies the same rhythmic unit:

He 'told his "mother.
He 'sent it to his "mother.

Absolute regularity of rhythm is, however, the exception rather than the rule.

When the intervals between stresses cease to be merely 'roughly equal' and achieve something like metronomic equality, the stylistic effect is oppressive. One exception is counting. When we have to count a fairly large number of items, it seems easier to prevent ourselves from getting lost if we adopt a strictly timed rhythm:

'one, ... 'two, ... 'three
'seventeen, ... 'eighteen, ... 'nineteen
seventy-'four, ... seventy-'five, ... seventy-'six
a hundred-and-'three, . . a hundred-and-'four, . . a hundred-and-'five

A regular rhythm is also used when we are compiling an inventory, giving a list of names, or the like. An insistent regularity may also be introduced for emphasis, especially when one is implying repetition of something which ought to be accepted without argument or when the speaker is expressing irritation or sarcasm:

You should ' never . . . ' move the . ' files of . . . ' papers . . . ' on my . . . '' desk.

It is the requirements of rhythm rather than of the message, which here causes the normally unstressed *on* to be emphasized, and we commonly find that the special use of regular rhythm distorts the normal stress patterns in this way. An earlier example was *a hundred-and-'three* in counting rhythm where this number in isolation would have two stresses: *a 'hundred-and-'three*. So too the numerals in *-teen*, *eg*: *'seventeen*, but in isolation, *seven'teen*.

But, for the most part, approximations to strictly timed rhythm are rare, brief, and rhetorical; for example in public speaking, such as appeals, sermons, and political speeches. More prolonged use occurs with the listener's full sanction in the reading of poetry and in forms of religious discourse, especially prayer.

Intonation

Tone unit, nucleus, and onset

II.11 Spoken English is not produced in an undifferentiated stream, but is marked off into brief stretches, usually corresponding to units of information (*cf* 18.3*ff*). These stretches we shall refer to as TONE UNITS. Tone units, the terminal boundaries of which are here indicated by a thick vertical (**|**), consist of a sequence of stressed and unstressed syllables, in a broadly rhythmic alternation, and with each unit containing at least one syllable marked for pitch prominence. The peak of greatest prominence is called the NUCLEUS of the tone unit, and the syllable carrying the nucleus has been indicated in this book by being printed in small capitals. This practice will be followed from this point onwards in the present Appendix. Usually the tone unit consists of several words, *eg*:

Is she leaving toDAY**|**

But occasionally, a tone unit may consist of a single pitch-prominent syllable, *eg*:

YES|

The first prominent syllable in a tone unit is the ONSET, and it is commonly preceded by one or more syllables which are unstressed and pronounced on a low pitch. The position of the onset is indicated by a preceding thin vertical (|), *eg*:

He |told his MOTHer| [1]
It's the ad|dress he sent the LETter to| [2]
She was |looking HAPpy tonight| [3]
You |THOUGHT so| [4]
She |seemed UNhappy to ME| [5]

Concerning the two nuclei in [5], *cf* II.15.

The falling tone

II.12 Usually, pitch prominence is associated with pitch change, and the commonest change is a FALL in pitch (indicated by (\`) above the nuclear syllable). We would expect a fall on the nuclear syllable in, for example, both [1] and [2]:

He |told his MÒTHer| [1]
It's the ad|dress he sent the LÈTter to| [2]

Likewise, we expect a fall on the nuclear syllable in most questions beginning with a *wh*-word, as in [3] and [5], in one-word responses to questions on words or names [4], or even letters uttered in isolation, as in [6]:

|What's his NÀME| [3]
Phy|LÀKtis| [4]
|What's the first LÈTter| [5]
|P̀| [6]

The falling tone is by far the most frequent. It might be said that it communicates an impression of completeness and that a tone unit has a falling nuclear tone unless there is some specific reason why it should not.

The rising tone

II.13 When there is a reason for departing from the norm of a falling tone, the most frequently used tone is a RISING one (indicated by (´) above the nuclear syllable). Broadly speaking, this is when we wish to indicate that our utterance is nonfinal or that we are leaving it open and inconclusive. This may be because we are counting or listing and have not come to the last item:

|TWÉLVE| |THÍRteen| |FÓURteen| |FÌFteen|
There are |fifTÈEN|

(Notice again the difference between numerals in *-teen* in sequence and in isolation.)

It may also be because another clause is going to follow:

|When I CÁME| he |greeted me WÀRMly|
I |saw her this MÓRNing| and in|vited her to DÌNner|

Alternatively, we may be seeking a response from someone (but not by means of a *wh*-question):

|Have I kept you WÁITing|
You're |leaving alRÉADy|

Some of the examples in App II.11 might well have a rising nucleus, for example [3]:

She was |looking HÁPpy tonight|

This would make it not a question but a polite suggestion that a (confirmatory) comment would be welcome. This might be expanded by adding a tag question (*cf* 11.8*ff*) with a falling nucleus:

She was |looking HÁPpy tonight| |WÀSn't she|

Elsewhere, the absence of dogmatic finality in the rise may enable us to make an imperative more gentle and persuasive:

|Don't be unPLÉASant|
|Please sit DÓWN|

Fall-rise, level, and rise-fall

II.14 There are no nuclear tones anything like so common as the fall and the rise, but four other tones are nevertheless important. The FALL-RISE (ˇ) occurs in many 'contingency' environments, for example in doubtfully expressing a condition:

I'll |see her if she CǑMES|

The fall-rise is especially common with initial adverbials (*cf* 8.15):

|FǏNally| we de|cided not to GÒ|

The LEVEL tone (¯) may be viewed as a variant of the rise (*cf* App II.18 Note), and it is used to suggest (often somewhat pompously) the predictability of what is to follow:

He |DRĀNK| he |STŌLE| he was |soon desPÌSED|

The RISE-FALL (ˆ), on the other hand, is really a rather emotive variant of the falling tone, used to express, for example, a genuine or sarcastic warmth, as in:

|That's WÔNderful|

Equally it can express a feeling of surprise or shock:

He's a com|plete FÔOL|

Note We might also mention the rather rare rise-plus-fall pattern, in which the first nucleus draws attention to a (subordinate) point of information focus, and the second places a decisive fall on the main point of information focus, for example:

She re|fused both the BÓOK and the THÈatre tickets|

Fall-plus-rise

II.15 The remaining tone pattern is by no means rare, but we have left it till the end because, unlike the tones mentioned previously, this pattern has two nuclei. It is the FALL-PLUS-RISE, and (esp in BrE) it would be expected in an example such as the following:

She |seemed ÙNhappy to MÉ| [1]

The nucleus is always a peak of semantic or 'information' content in the tone unit; with the fall-plus-rise we have two such peaks of information interest, and they are related, the first being superordinate (*cf* 18.17). The subordinate nature of the rise in the fall-plus-rise tone pattern is indicated by a narrower pitch range (*cf* App II.18) than where a rise is sole nucleus in a tone unit. The fall-plus-rise pattern should be seen as related to contrastive stress (compare the example above with example [1] in App II.9).

Now, contrastive stress usually involves moving a tonal nucleus from its normal, unmarked position on to the contrasted item. But it does not require the tone unit concerned to have two nuclei:

A: Are you |HÁPpy| B: |No I'm ÙNhappy|

Compare also the contrast between first and second mention expressed by different position of the nucleus in the noun phrase in [2], as opposed to [3]:

|This book cost 'twenty |DÓLlars| and |this one THÌRty 'dollars|
[*. . . 'thirty DÒLlars|] [2]
|This book cost 'twenty |DÓLlars| and |this one 'ten PÒUNDS|
[*. . . TÈN 'pounds|] [3]

But in all these variants, there remains a single point of information focus. By contrast, the fall-plus-rise allows the speaker to draw attention to two focal information points, for example:

She |seemed ÙNhappy to MÉ|

Here the two nuclei enable us to say (a) that she seemed unhappy (contrary to the suggestion of someone else), and (b) that this is the speaker's personal view: of course there may be others.

In addition to its use in thus contradicting what a previous speaker has said, marked focus (*cf* 18.12*ff*) also commonly occurs with this intonation pattern in order to contrast two items within a single information unit. The fall is always on the marked focus and carries most prominence, the contrasting rise being relatively subordinate. Note the following example using the cleft sentence (*cf* 18.25*ff*):

It's his |WÌFE that I don't LÍKE| = The |one that I don't LÍKE| is his WÌFE|

Contrast the normal end-placed focus:

I |don't like his WÌFE|

A further pair of examples:

It's his |JÒB that's WÓRrying him|
His |job is WÒRrying him|

When, as in those two examples, the nucleus does not occur in the last word of the tone unit, the part of the tone unit after the nucleus is referred to as the TAIL.

Note The frequencies of the different tones will of course vary depending on a wide range of factors, such as the relation of the participants, the field of discourse, etc. In a BrE corpus of conversation, half the tone units had a single falling nuclear tone. The frequencies of occurrence for all intonation types were as follows:

Falling (̀)	51.2%
Rising (́)	20.8%
Fall-rise (̌)	8.5%
Fall-plus-rise (̀ + ́)	7.7%
Rise-fall (̂)	5.2%
Level (̄)	4.9%
Rise-plus-fall (́ + ̀)	1.7%

Prosodic segmentation

II.16 Tone units are produced by the speaker and processed by the hearer as units of information. Compared with the sentence, which is essentially a conventional unit characteristic of written language, the tone unit is more individually variable and psycholinguistically responsive to the communicative needs of the individual speaker. Such variation is particularly noticeable in spoken language, where the conditions of planning and processing are radically different from those obtaining in writing and reading.

In spontaneous conversation, the mean length of the tone unit is around five or six words, or two seconds. But the length of the tone unit, in the individual case, depends on a number of factors such as grammatical structure, lexical realization, discourse structure in terms of given/new and theme/focus (*cf* 18.3*ff*), speech situation, speed of utterance, and the speaker's personality. Thus no rigid rule can be made about the relation of tone to grammatical units. However, it has been found that there is a strong tendency for breaks between tone units to occur at grammatical junctures. Thus there is considerable correlation between the length of the tone unit and its grammatical content. In one study, the major grammatical segments corresponding to a tone unit were found to be as follows (*cf* 18.5*ff*):

Two clauses, one of which is a nominal *that*-clause as direct object (*c* 8 words), *eg*:

I really think that he'll come toMORrow|

One clause (5–6 words), *eg*:

He'll arrive by train toMORrow|

Verb phrase plus adverbial (4–5 words), *eg*:

will arrive at ten THIRty|

Noun phrase as subject (3–4 words), *eg*:

the train from LONdon|

Prepositional phrase as adverbial (3–4 words), *eg*:

at this PLATform|

Miscellaneous noun phrases (2–3 words), *eg*:

and the SOUTH|

Adverb (1 word), *eg*:

OBviously|

The interdependence of grammar and prosody can be seen for example in the following two sentences:

The |old man opened the elegant jewel case very SLÒWly| [1]
The |old man ÓPENED| |very SLÓWly| an |elegant JÈWel case| [2]

(Note that *the . . . case* in [1] makes the noun phrase sufficiently 'given' to justify the end position of the adverbial; *cf* 18.8.) The different segmentation with prosodic focus in [2] is a result of the placing of the adjunct *very slowly* at *iE* instead of *E* in [1] (*cf* 8.14).

The grammatical status of different types of adjunct may be reflected in prosodic segmentation. Thus the relatively peripheral status of the sentence adjunct [3] (as compared with the predication adjunct [4]) can be indicated by different tone unit segmentation (*cf* 8.36):

In Chi|CǍgo| he |studied ÀRchitecture| [3]
In Chicago he LÍVED| and |in Chicago he DÌED| [4]

Intonation in relation to other features

Tone of voice, pitch, and music

II.17 'Intonation' must be distinguished from 'tone of voice' on the one hand and from 'intoning' on the other. One's tone of voice may be warm or cold, kind or harsh, happy or sad – irrespective of the intonation pattern, the length of the tone unit, the location of the nucleus, or the direction of the pitch movement. Indeed, while there can be no doubt that intonation is linguistically relevant, there must be considerable doubt as to whether tone of voice involves linguistic parameters at all. True, on hearing someone say:

I've |bought a CÀR|

we can add to our understanding of this statement the inference that the speaker sounded happy or proud or perhaps nervous, but, merely because we deduced this from the way he spoke, we need not go to the lengths of regarding the deduction as springing from the linguistic form.

As to the distinction between intonation and intoning, something has already been said in App II.2. In sharp contrast to the specific intervals of a musical scale, the movements in linguistic pitch are purely relative. A person speaking with a high-pitched voice may end a fall at a point far higher than the point at which a fall began as uttered by a low-pitched voice: yet, despite total dissimilarity in fundamental frequency or acoustic quality, both falls would be instantly recognized as linguistically identical. Again, even where they begin at the same point in pitch, two speakers will differ very considerably in the amount of pitch movement that may constitute a rise, yet both rises may be received by hearers as in some sense identical, so far as a purely linguistic interpretation is concerned. Nor indeed is it necessary for a speaker to be consistent in this width of pitch movement (*cf* App II.18), even in consecutive tone units.

Note The part played by musical tone in English is very slight, but it may be of interest to mention that calls to attract attention make considerable use of descending minor thirds. A wife may call jocularly to her husband down the garden when supper is ready:

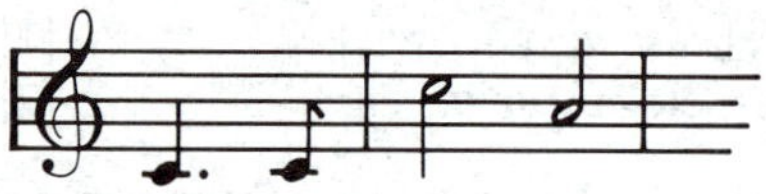

'Come and get it!'

Fig II.17a

The second bar would be the tune also in trying to attract the attention of a person some distance away: *Ro-bert!*, *Ma-ry!*. It appears also in the ending of the long-standing children's taunt, the words of course being freely varied:

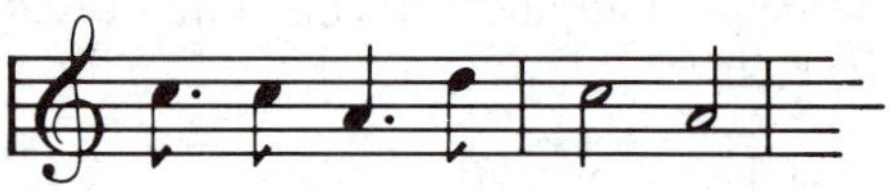

'Johnnie's torn his trousers!'

Fig II.17b

Pitch height and pitch range

II.18 In the previous section, reference was made to the fact that it is possible to make what is linguistically the same nuclear tone with considerable variety in actual pitch and pitch movement. Without diminishing the validity of this, and without suggesting further comparison with the specific tonal intervals of music, we must note the existence of other relative systems in intonation which will allow certain broad differences in pitch height and pitch range to assume linguistic significance.

By PITCH HEIGHT we are referring to the point on the pitch scale at which a stressed syllable occurs in relation to the previous syllable. Most commonly, there is a gentle stepping down in pitch level from syllable to syllable, and against this expected pattern (particularly in assertive statements), variations stand out clearly. A step upwards in pitch, called a 'booster' and symbolized as (↑), or a marked step downwards (↓), can add considerably to the feeling that is being conveyed. Thus:

His |wife is ↓always ↑NÀSty| [1]

Such a use of pitch contrast as in [1] would be one way of achieving emphasis on both the adverbial and the complement of this sentence, while at the same time indicating that the nastiness has not been mentioned by either speaker before or is perhaps alleged as a matter of potential dispute between the speakers. A variant form is [2]:

His |wife is always ↓NÀSty| [2]

Sentence [2] might suggest that while the nastiness needs emphasis, it is of a familiar kind. In conjunction with a pointedly regular rhythm, a regularly ascending or descending pitch height can be very effective in achieving climax, as in [3] and [4]:

And |all the ↑people of ↑this ↑great ↑CÓUNTry| . . . [3]
|Why on ↓earth don't you ↓do some ↓WÒRK| [4]

By PITCH RANGE we are referring to the amount of pitch movement on the nucleus or from stress to stress in the course of the tone unit, irrespective of whether the starting point is high or low. An ingratiating, warmly interested, or excited attitude can be indicated by a wide range, while a narrow range (as well as being used to indicate boredom, for example) is frequent on the nucleus of subordinate clauses. But these are by no means the only contrasts we can imply by altering our pitch range.

The following question, for example, can be given two interpretations depending on the pitch range of its nuclear syllable:

Was it |MÝ fault|

Uttered with a narrow pitch range, it is a regular open question; with a wide pitch range, it is a rhetorical, exclamatory question (*cf* 11.23): 'Surely you are not suggesting that the fault is mine!'

Note It is through the prosodic property of pitch range that we should relate the association of level nuclei to rising ones (*cf* App II.13). That is, level nuclei occur most frequently where rising ones might be expected, and we could thus regard level as a very narrow rise. We need to note, however, that the nuclei in pre-final subordinate syntactic units may be not only narrow rises or levels but not infrequently narrow falls.

Pauses

II.19 In the course of this Appendix, we have been gradually developing a notation for expressing on paper the more important linguistic distinctions that are made not by words but by sound patterns affecting syllables and syllable sequences. There is one further parameter that we must not ignore. The PAUSE in speech is by no means of random occurrence. Together with the tone unit, it tends to divide up the stream of speech into grammatically and lexically relevant chunks and, although it is by no means essential to pause at the end of tone units marking completed syntactic constructions, lengthy pauses are more usual at such points than elsewhere. Speech is however more flexible than writing in allowing us to introduce a 'space', *ie* momentary silence, to suit the speaker's or hearer's needs, before (or perhaps after) a difficult or specially significant lexical item, even if this occurs in the middle of a grammatical phrase. Pauses are most relevantly measured in terms of a speaker's own rhythm and tempo, and we take the unit of pausing (denoted by a dash '–'), as equivalent in time to one rhythmic measure or cycle (*cf* App II.1). A pause shorter than such a unit is indicated by a period (.):

She is . un|HÀPpy| – |VÈRy un'happy|

As for TEMPO, to which reference has just been made, we sometimes find it valuable to contrast, with a given speaker's normal speed of utterance, the relatively slow or fast stretches that occur from time to time, as he displays –

for example – special care or seriousness at one point, or an off-handed dismissal or cheerful levity at another point. Here, as with height and range or with tone of voice (*cf* App II.17*f*), we can easily slip beyond the normal bounds of linguistic description.

Prosodic marking compared with punctuation

II.20 Even ignoring, as we must, several other features of spoken English, we now have a system of conventions capable of expressing on paper for spoken English what the system of punctuation marks does (on the whole, much less well) for written English. There are numerous respects in which conventional punctuation is inadequate (*cf* App III.5), but we need mention here only a few such points to show how our prosodic notation both explains and transcends the difficulty.

Since the early nineteenth century, institutionalized usage has disallowed any punctuation (except correlative punctuation, *cf* App III.2) between subject and predicate. Yet (as student essays show), users of English are still strongly motivated to put a comma between a long noun-phrase subject and the verb, *eg*:

*The newspaper article on the recent conflict, was utterly misleading.

There is a very good reason for this. After a long noun phrase, the coherence of the structure just completed is regularly marked in speech by a prosodic break, usually realized by the end of a tone unit, often by a pause as well:

The |newspaper article on the recent CÓNflict| (–) was |utterly misLÈADing|

II.21 Again, although we can indicate emphasis in written English (usually by means of italics in print and underscoring in typescript or handwriting), we cannot distinguish emphases of radically different sound and value:

You shouldn't give her *any* flowers.
['You must give her no flowers at all.'] [1]
You shouldn't give her *any* flowers.
['You must give her only certain flowers.'] [2]

Our prosodic notation for spoken English, however, adequately represents the difference we hear:

You |shouldn't give her ↑ÀNy flowers| [1a]
You |shouldn't give her ǍNy flowers| [2a]

Unlike punctuation, prosody readily helps to identify focused items also in examples like the following (*cf* 8.117):

|John could only SÈE his wife from the doorway| [3]
|John could only see his WÌFE from the doorway| [3a]
|John could only see his wife from the DÒORway| [3b]

The position of the nucleus and the type of tone are decisive for the interpretation of the following expressions with *there* and *here* (*cf* 8.47 Note [b]):

|THÈRE you are| *or* |HÈRE you are| ['So I've found you!'] [4]

|THĚRE you are| *or* |HĚRE you are| ['This is for you.'] [4a]

|There you ÀRE| ['That supports or proves what I've said.'] [4b]

|Here we ÀRE| ['We've arrived at the expected place.'] [4c]

The item focused on by a focusing subjunct is identified by the location of the nucleus (*cf* 8.116) in:

The |girls ESPÈCially objected to his manners|
['It was especially the girls who objected to his manners.'] [5]

The |girls especially objected to his MÀNners|
['It was his manners that the girls especially objected to.'] [5a]

Compare also:

|Help yourSÈLF please| ⟨ informal⟩ [the speaker takes for granted the courtesy subjunct *please*; *cf* 8.91] [6]

|Help yourSÈLF PLÉASE| [the speaker seeks more deliberately to emphasize the courtesy] [6a]

Consider now some other prosodic realizations which give sharply different meanings to the various constituents within the following sets of sentences. In each case, we begin with the 'unmarked' and most neutral form the sentence might have.

I should |GÒ| [7]

I should |GÓ| ['Is that your advice?'] [7a]

|Ì should go| ['Not you!'] [7b]

I |SHÒULD go| ['. . . and I defy you to deny it.'] [7c]

I |SHŎULD go| ['. . . but I don't think I will.'] [7d]

|Somebody must have TÀKen it| [8]

|Somebody must have ↑TÀKen it| ['surprising as it may seem'] [8a]

|Somebody ↑MÙST have 'taken it| ['It's no use your arguing'] [8b]

|SŎMEbody must have 'taken it| ['even if you didn't'] [8c]

You |said he would CÒME| [9]

|You said he would CÒME| ['. . . but I was personally doubtful'] [9a]

You |said HĚ would come| ['You didn't say that his wife was coming as well.'] [9b]

You |SĂID he would come| ['. . . but that doesn't mean he really will'] [9c]

You |SÀID he would CÓME| ['. . . and, my goodness, there he is!'] [9d]

|I'm not ↑half SĂTisfied| ⟨informal⟩ ['I am highly satisfied.'; *ie*: *not half* is an amplifier; *cf* 8.107 Note [b]] [10]

|I'm not HÀLF 'satisfied| ['I am only partially satisfied.'; *ie*: *half* is a downtoner] [10a]

It |seems that they quite LÌKE her| ['rather, kind of'; *ie*: *quite* is a compromiser; *cf* 8.111 Note [c]] [11]

It |seems that they QUÌTE LÍKE her| ['moderately'; *ie*: *quite* is a diminisher; the contrast between [11] and [11a] is especially BrE] [11a]

We |don't like it a BÌT| ['We don't like it.'; *ie*: *a bit* is a minimizer; *cf* 8.112] [12]

We |don't like it a LǏTtle| ['We like it a lot.'; *ie*: *a little* is a diminisher] [12a]

Now |LÌSTen| [*now* is a transitional conjunct; *cf* 8.137] [13]

|NÒW listen| [*now* is *I*-placed time adjunct; *cf* 8.55] [13a]

She |didn't leave HÓME| be|cause I've been watching the house all DÀY| [*because*-clause as disjunct; *cf* 8.132] [14]

She |didn't leave 'home be'cause her father ↑TÒLD her to| [*because*-clause as adjunct; *cf* 8.86] [14a]

All the examples presented in this Appendix have been of isolated tone units or very short sequences. The system of stress, rhythm, and intonation operate significantly, however, over considerably longer stretches of speech, indicating degrees of connection and providing significant cues to interrelationship of grammatical, semantic, and pragmatic units as 'text'. Some aspects of speech in these respects are described in 19.87*ff* along with transcriptions of both formal and informal varieties of spoken discourse.

Note [**a**] Because of our inability to express prosodic nuances in writing, we frequently find (especially in fiction) the use of verbs such as *sneer*, *mutter*, *whisper*, *whine* to assist the reader in assigning the appropriate prosodic and paralinguistic features. So also adverbial expressions accompanying verbs of saying, such as *inquiringly*, *indignantly*, *sneeringly*, *in a haughty tone*. Thus the written sentence [15] might be intended to equate with [15a] in speech:

'But you're going to answer his letter, I suppose' she said *inquiringly*. [15]

But you are |going to answer his "letter I supPÓSE| [15a]

[**b**] We may also find instances of the opposite state of affairs, *ie* when speech lacks distinctions that can be made in writing. One such case is the use of 'quote – unquote', or even a gesture with the fingers, to signal quotation marks.

Bibliographical note

On stress, see Arnold (1957); Chomsky and Halle (1968); Gimson (1980).

On rhythm, see Abercrombie (1967); Chatman (1965); Leech (1969b); Uldall (1971).

On contraction, see Black (1977); Forsheden (1983); Zwicky (1970); Zwicky and Pullum (1983).

On various aspects of intonation and prosody, see Bald (1975); Bing (1980); Bolinger (1972c); Brazil et al (1980); Brown (1977); Brown et al (1980); Cruttenden (1981); Crystal and Quirk (1964); Halliday (1967, 1970); Kingdon (1958); Liberman (1978); O'Connor and Arnold (1973); Pike (1945); Quirk and Crystal (1966); Quirk et al (1964); Waugh and van Schooneveld (1980).

A detailed account of prosodic systems is given in Crystal (1969) and these are related to style in Crystal and Davy (1969, 1975).

III Appendix III Punctuation

Introduction

III.1 In Appendix II we surveyed a set of prosodic devices that help to communicate grammatical and other distinctions in spoken English. The purpose of the present Appendix is to examine the visual devices that perform a similar role for written English. Since prosodic devices are acquired naturally by native speakers, they do not have to be taught them formally, and educational tradition has largely ignored them. With punctuation, on the other hand, the array of devices is well recognized; there are established names for the individual items; and their use is (to a considerable extent) equally institutionalized, through education and the practice of the publishing and printing organizations.

There are three stretches of written language formally recognized by name whose bounds are indicated visually: the WORD, the SENTENCE (consisting of one or more words), and the PARAGRAPH (consisting of one or more sentences). Words are delimited as orthographic units (*cf* 1.12) by being preceded and followed either by a space or by one or more punctuation marks and a space, as illustrated for the italicized words in the following:

. . . the *grammar* of . . .	. . . the *reader's* aim . . .
. . . in *scorn*, when . . .	. . . line (*usually* indented . . .
. . . the *co-authors* are . . .	. . . (or 'upper *case*') . . .

Sentences begin with a CAPITAL letter and usually end with a PERIOD (*cf* App III.14). Less frequently, the termination point of a sentence is a QUESTION MARK or EXCLAMATION MARK, complex symbols that visually incorporate the period (*cf* App III.23). As we see later (*cf* App III.14), paragraphs are usually separated by spaces at their beginning and end. Apart from the termination points of sentences, the remaining punctuation marks – by far the majority – perform functions within the sentence (and a very few within the word) but do not mark off units as well-established as the sentence or the word. Their separating or specifying functions however are for the most part clear and readily describable.

III.2 The punctuation system serves two broad purposes, SEPARATION and SPECIFICATION, the former in turn inviting a twofold division.

SEPARATION

(a) *Successive units*

The punctuation mark separates units that are in a simple linear relation to each other (units in a series); for example, a space separates two successive words, or a period followed by a spacc scparates two successive sentences.

(b) *Included units*

The punctuation mark is CORRELATIVE. It indicates the beginning and end of an included unit, a unit which is inserted within some larger unit; for example, the commas mark off the parenthetic clause in:

He is, *I think*, a teacher.

SPECIFICATION

The punctuation mark specifies a grammatical, semantic, or pragmatic function, sometimes in addition to the marking of separation. Thus the apostrophe in *the reader's* specifies the ending as genitive in contrast to the phonologically identical plural in *the readers*.

In respect of these purposes, punctuation practice is governed primarily by grammatical considerations and is related to grammatical distinctions. Sometimes it is linked to intonation, stress, rhythm, pause, or any other of the prosodic features which convey distinctions in speech, but the link is neither simple nor systematic, and traditional attempts to relate punctuation directly to (in particular) pauses are misguided. Nor, except to a minor and peripheral extent, is punctuation concerned with expressing emotive or rhetorical overtones, as prosodic features frequently are (*cf* App II.17*ff* for example). It follows that there is less room in punctuation than in prosody for personal decision in the use of the various devices: understandably so, since in writing, the originator of the message is not usually present to clear up any difficulty that may arise. Punctuation marks tend, therefore, to be used according to fairly strict conventions and even in the peripheral areas where universal convention does not obtain, each individual publishing house imposes one for all materials that it puts forth in print.

There are two important qualifications to the foregoing generalizations. In the first place, there is, as we shall see, a great deal of flexibility possible in the use of the comma: in its presence or absence, or in its replacement by other marks. The comma in fact provides considerable opportunity for personal taste and for implying fine degrees of cohesion and separation. Secondly, the conventions as a whole are not followed as rigorously in manuscript use (especially personal material, such as private letters), where there may be inconsistencies in their application that would not be permitted in most printed material.

Separation

Separation of successive units

Hierarchy of punctuation marks

III.3 We have a well-defined hierarchy of signs reaching from the word to the paragraph. The hierarchy can be illustrated from the following passage:

> . . . and the chairman was careful to point out the help he had had from the secretary and from the members recently elected to the committee. He mentioned two other men, since co-opted: Smith and Fox; they had been very useful. Votes of thanks were proposed and unanimously carried.
>
> Before the meeting closed, some further business was transacted. A motion proposed by Johnson sought to raise money by . . .

Thus we have:

unseparated letters	. . . opted . . .
hyphen (-)	. . . co-opted . . .
word-space	. . . since co-opted . . .
comma (,)	. . . men, since co-opted . . .
colon (:)	. . . men, since co-opted: Smith . . .
semicolon (;)	. . . men, since co-opted: Smith and Fox; they . . .
period (.)	. . . men, since co-opted: Smith and Fox; they had been very useful. Votes of thanks . . .
paragraph	. . . had been very useful. Votes of thanks were proposed and unanimously carried. Before the meeting closed, some further business was transacted . . .

Two signs (which also have specifying function) not illustrated in the passage are generally (but *cf* App III.23) on the same level in the hierarchy as the period: the question mark (?) and the exclamation mark (!).

Parentheses and other types of bracketing, which are also not illustrated in the passage, are outside the hierarchy because their function is to represent a sharp interruption in the structure within which they are inserted (*cf* App III.16).

One other sign absent from the passage is the dash. The dash fits somewhat uneasily into the hierarchy, perhaps between the comma and the colon. It is often a substitute for the comma, but indicates a sharper separation:

> They knew many of the ills that continue to affect us – and many of the remedies that we still use.

In general, punctuation marks are followed by a space, but there are several exceptions:

(a) A space precedes (not follows) the opening quotation mark and the opening mark for parentheses and other bracketing.
(b) There is a space on either side of the dash.
(c) There is no space on either side of the hyphen.

The period, question mark, exclamation mark, and colon are generally followed (especially in printed material) by a longer space than that for other marks, notably the comma or semicolon. When closing quotation marks or closing parentheses cooccur with each other or with other marks, there is no space between the two marks. For example, a closing quotation mark may be immediately followed by a closing parenthesis, a comma or period by a closing quotation mark, or a closing parenthesis by a period. (For permissible and nonpermissible cooccurrences, *cf* App III.16.)

Our main concern in this Appendix is with punctuation marks in the hierarchy that are beyond the level of the word and up to the level of the sentence. In particular contexts, writers can choose whether to use one of these punctuation marks rather than another, whether to use (for example) a period or an exclamation mark, a period or a semicolon, a comma or a semicolon, a comma or a colon, a comma or a dash. But it is relevant to note that by far the most frequent marks are the period and the comma, which are almost identical in frequency of use.

Note In samples from the Brown corpus of about 72 000 words drawn in equal proportions from journalism, learned writing, and fiction, the figures for punctuation marks were:

commas	4054	semicolons	163
periods	3897	question marks	89
dashes	189	colons	78
pairs of parentheses	165	exclamation marks	26

The hyphen

III.4 The hyphen marks divisions within a word for two main purposes. First, it is used for word division between lines, to separate a word into two parts between the end of one line of text and the beginning of the next. Since printers can vary the space between words, they prefer to avoid dividing words in this way, especially in books. When division is unavoidable, it is made at a natural point in the structure of a word. That is, one would not leave *str-* at the end of a line and begin the next line with *ucture*. But there can of course be a difference of opinion as to what constitutes a 'natural' point. AmE practice is to respect the phonologically natural points – in other words, syllable division; this would divide *structure* at *struc-*. BrE practice is to give more weight to morphological and etymological considerations, being thus more inclined to make a break in the word at *struct-*. With many words the different criteria give the same result, however, so that the divergence in usage is slight.

Secondly, the hyphen is sometimes used to mark the parts of a word: to separate the bases of a compound (*cf* App I.57*ff*) or to separate the prefix of a word from its base (*cf* App I.21*ff*). The rules for this use of the hyphen are subject to considerable variation in the practice of publishing houses and individual writers as well as in the guidance of dictionaries and style manuals. AmE inclines to fewer hyphens than BrE, preferring words to be written either OPEN (separated by a space) or SOLID (without separation) rather than hyphenated.

Types of compounds that are commonly hyphenated include:

(1) noun compounds in which the second base is an adverb, *eg*: *runner-up*, *break-in*

(2) adjective compounds in *-ed* that are formed from noun phrases, *eg*: *cold-blooded*, *brown-eyed*

(3) adjective compounds in which the second base is a participle, *eg*: *far-fetched*, *habit-forming*

If the first base is an adverb, it is hyphenated when the participle is premodifying a noun (*well-established facts*) but not when the participle is a main verb (*The facts are well established*). In AmE (and often in BrE), however, hyphenation does not apply even when the participle is a premodifier if the adverb ends in *-ly*, *eg*: *carefully written* (report), *rapidly disappearing* (languages).

(4) other modifying phrases and modifying clauses (which are generally written open when not modifying), *eg*: *on-the-spot* (investigation), *face-to-face* (meeting), *ten-item* (test), *right-to-life* (movement), *up-to-date* (news), *take-it-or-leave-it* (attitude), *do-it-yourself* (job)

(5) coordination compounds (*cf* App I.70), *eg*: *Russian-English* (dictionary), *student-teacher* (relationships)
(6) compounds expressing numerals and fractions (*cf* 6.63*ff*), *eg*: *twenty-five*, *three-fifths*
(7) compounds in which the first base is a single capital letter *eg*: *U-turn*, *H-bomb*
(8) compounds ending in *-in-law*(*s*), *eg*: *mother-in-law*
(9) relationships in which the first base is *great*, *eg*: *great-uncle*, *great-grandchildren*

The hyphen is usual after a prefix if the base begins with a capital letter as in *un-French* or with a figure as in *post-1984*. It is also common after certain prefixes, particularly *ex-* ['former'], *half-*, *quasi-*, *self-*, *eg*: *ex-husband*, *half-caste*, *quasi-judicial*, *self-sacrifice*. BrE tends to use the hyphen after other prefixes, where AmE tends to write the words solid, notably after *non-*, *eg*: *non-standard* ⟨esp BrE⟩, *nonstandard* ⟨esp AmE⟩. BrE often uses the hyphen where juxtaposition would suggest a misleading pronunciation such as *co-ordinate* or *pre-eminent*, whereas AmE generally writes such words solid (but *co-worker*, for example, is hyphenated in AmE too); however, BrE is increasingly conforming to AmE practice.

The hyphen is used both in compounds and after a prefix to avoid misinterpretation, even if the misinterpretation is only momentary, *eg*: *small-claims court* ['court for small claims'], *re-cover* ['cover afresh', *cf*: *recover* 'regain control'], *re-form* ['form again', *cf*: *reform* 'change for the better'], *co-op* [informal clipping of noun *co-operative*, also *cooperative* ⟨esp AmE⟩].

Note [**a**] AmE occasionally favours the DIAERESIS in words such as *coöperate*. The diaeresis is also very occasionally used in both AmE and BrE to indicate separate syllables in words where juxtaposed vowels do not result from affixation and where the hyphen could not be used; for example, *naïve*. More commonly, however, such words are spelt without indication of the separate syllabification: *naive*.

[**b**] Despite a tendency to avoid the hyphen after prefixes, AmE prefers it to avoid doubling the vowel *i* (*anti-isolationist*) or tripling a consonant (*bell-like*).

[**c**] For two minor uses of the hyphen, *cf* App III.26 Note [b].

The word in speech and writing

III.5 There are numerous respects in which we cannot reproduce in writing the distinctions made prosodically in speech (*cf* App II.20). In the visual indicators of word limits we have the converse. In informal speech, we do not normally attempt to make a difference in pronunciation between *a nice drink* and *an ice*(*d*) *drink*. In writing, such distinctions are absolute and must be regularly made. Similarly, irrespective of the sound we make in speech, we must indicate in writing what counts as an orthographic word (*cf* App I.11*f*), sometimes deciding between total separation, hyphenation, and total juxtaposition: *tax payer*, *tax-payer*, and *taxpayer*. Examples like these are a reminder (a) that, while the rules of punctuation are related to grammar and lexicology, they are by no means necessarily so related through an intermediate connection with speech; (b) that there is an element of arbitrariness in punctuation, and it is particularly conspicuous in the use of the hyphen; and yet (c) that consistency and regularity assume an importance in punctuation (as in spelling) quite unparalleled in the analogous signalling function of prosodic systems in speech.

Note [**a**] Hyphens are used to link syntactically-related premodifiers of noun phrases as in *Mexican-Cuban negotiations*. If one of the modifiers is itself a phrase, the hyphen may seem to connect illogically: *Mexican-San Salvador negotiations, New York-Miami flight*. Indeed, for such cases some printers use the en dash (–), which is half the length of the em dash — the form most commonly used for the dash punctuation mark — and is slightly longer than the printed hyphen. But it is doubtful whether most readers notice that the en dash is different from the hyphen. Should the position of the hyphen feel troublesome, the phrase can be reworded to avoid the premodification; for example, *negotiations between Mexico and San Salvador*.

[**b**] Coordination of hyphenated items, especially in formal or technical writing, frequently involves ellipsis with word-space following a hyphen, as in *pro- and anti-government opinion* or *those who are speech- and language-impaired*. Hyphens are similarly used after prefixes, even though the prefixes are not hyphenated in isolation, in which case the final item is generally not hyphenated; for example, *mono- and polysyllabic syllables, inter- and intranational uses, homo- and heterosexual relations* (*cf* also 13.85).

The comma

The comma with coordinated clauses

III.6 Of all the punctuation marks the comma is the most flexible in the range of its use, and hence the most difficult to categorize.

One dominant use of the comma is to separate closely associated clauses within a sentence, a use that the comma shares with the colon and semicolon. But we cannot substitute a comma in either [1] or [2], because the comma is not normally used to separate independent clauses unless they are linked by a coordinator:

> I've just had some good news: I've been offered a job in a law firm. [1]
>
> Schoolchildren have adopted the fund as one of their favourite charities; their small contributions have enabled the fund to reach its target. [2]

In [1], where a coordinator would not be possible, the colon is serving its classic function of separating an independent clause that is in apposition to a previous unit, here *some good news*. In [2] we should need to insert *and* if we wished to replace the semicolon with a comma:

> Schoolchildren have adopted the fund as one of their favourite charities, and their small contributions have enabled the fund to reach its target. [3]

Sentence [3] illustrates the conditions favouring the use of the comma to separate independent clauses in compound sentences:

(a) the parts are closely related semantically (both dealing here with the children's contributions to the fund);

(b) they are linked by a coordinator (in this case by *and*).

If condition (a) did not apply, the two parts could scarcely be brought into one sentence at all. If condition (a) applied but not condition (b), a comma normally could not be used, though a semicolon would be appropriate, as in [2]. Punctuation marks are also usual if the clauses are linked by the conjunction *or* and the conjunction-like adverbs *nor*, *neither*, *so*, and *yet*.

If three or more clauses are coordinated but only the last is preceded by *and* or *or*, commas (or semicolons) are required between the clauses, including the last pair:

Prices fell, interest rates fell, and employment figures rose.

The comma in such instances is termed a SERIAL COMMA (*cf* App III.8).

Note Despite condition (b), coordinate clauses are occasionally separated asyndetically only by commas, especially when the clauses are short, parallel, and (often) three in number (*cf* 19.5*ff*):

I must, I can, I will.

Sometimes he would chuckle softly to himself, sometimes he would grunt to some invisible onlooker.

III.7 Two further related considerations influence our decision over the punctuation of a series of independent clauses. First, punctuation marks are frequently omitted if the clauses are relatively short, provided they are linked by a coordinator:

The work was pleasant and the hours were short. [1]

On the other hand, if despite close semantic connection there is a contrast prompting the use of *but* (or *and yet*) rather than *and* as the appropriate conjunction, there is a greater tendency to use a punctuation mark, particularly the comma:

We are thinking of buying a short-wave radio, but we haven't made up our minds. [2]

This latter tendency emerged from an analysis of materials in the Survey of English Usage. The materials comprised coordinate full clauses, as in [1] and [2], and instances in which the subject (and perhaps also operator) of the second clause was absent, resulting in coordinated predicates or predications, as in [3] and [4]:

The hotel boasts a gourmet restaurant and offers a range of sports facilities. [3]

You can sit at my desk and write your letters. [4]

Three-quarters of the clauses coordinated with *but* had a comma ('+' in *Fig* App III.7a), whereas only about a half of the clauses coordinated with *and* had a comma.

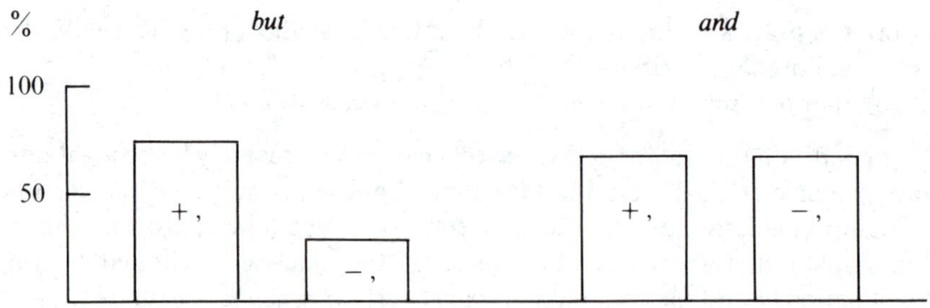

Fig App III.7a Comma punctuation with *but* and *and*

For coordination with *and*, however, it was relevant to distinguish further according to whether the subject of the second clause was present ('*and* + S' in *Fig* App III.7b) or absent ('*and* – S'). Where the subject was absent as in [3] and [4], the comma appeared in only a third of the sentences, while a comma was inserted in three-quarters of the sentences that had an expressed subject in both clauses.

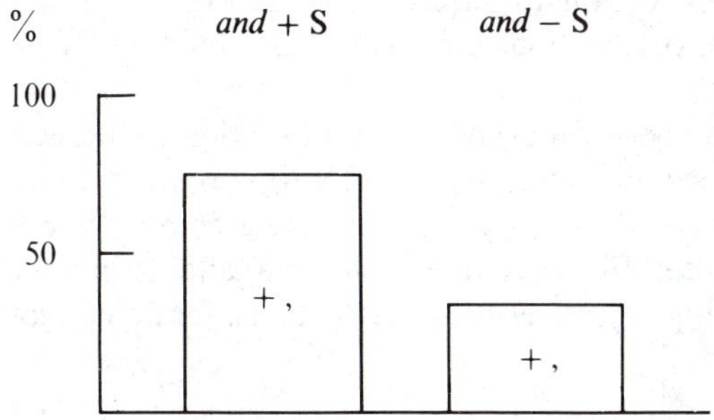

Fig App III.7b Comma punctuation with *and* according to presence or absence of subject in second clause

These results show that we are dealing with tendencies rather than rules. There are many sentences where despite coordination with *and* and despite subject ellipsis, a comma is nevertheless preferred. In such cases, it is probable that the generalization that punctuation conforms to grammatical rather than rhetorical considerations is in fact overridden. If we compare sentences [5] and [6] the extent to which we prefer a comma in [6] is a measure of our wish that the punctuation should endorse the meaning – the separation of the second clause matching the moment's pause that is mentioned:

He put on his spectacles and then picked up the phone. [5]
He paused for a moment, and then began to speak. [6]

The contrast between *and* and *but* is also shown in an analysis of samples from the Brown corpus (*cf* App III.3 Note), which counted coordinate clauses with an expressed subject in the second clause. Of 228 compound sentences with *and*, 72 (32 per cent) had no punctuation mark, and 147 (64 per cent) had commas, 5 (2 per cent) semicolons, and 4 (2 per cent) dashes. On the other hand, of 98 compound sentences with *but*, only 6 (6 per cent) had no punctuation mark while 74 (76 per cent) had commas and 18 (18 per cent) semicolons. In the same corpus, independent sentences were far more frequently introduced by *but* (87) than by *and* (47).

The comma with other coordinated units

III.8 We generally do not insert any punctuation mark if we coordinate two units within a sentence other than independent clauses:

The movie was long and boring.
The company may have branches in London or New York.
I argued for implementation of the report and against any further discussion.

All I know about them is that they work on a farm and that their parents live with them.
You can and must tell us.
She called me and invited me for dinner.
I enjoy tennis but don't play it often.
I'll read the book and then tell you whether it's worth reading.

In such instances a comma is occasionally inserted for rhetorical reasons, particularly when predicates or predications are coordinated (*cf* App III.7), as in the last three sentences.

We sometimes have a choice between asyndetic coordination (without a coordinator), in which case a serial comma (*cf* App III.6) is required, and syndetic coordination (with a coordinator), in which case a comma is not required. The most frequent occasions when this choice is available involve the coordination of premodifying adjectives or adverbs. Thus, for adjectives we may choose between [1] and [1a]:

He walked with long, slow strides. [1]
He walked with long and slow strides. [2]

If we wish to add further coordinated adjectives to [1], we need to place a comma after each adjective except the last:

He walked with long, slow, steady, deliberate strides. [1a]

If we wish to add further adjectives to the syndetic coordination in [2], we generally insert *and* before the last adjective in the series as in [2a]:

He walked with long, slow, steady(,) and deliberate strides. [2a]

(For the possible omission of the comma, see below.) There are analogues for adverbs to [1–2a]:

She slowly, carefully moved the box. [3]
She slowly and carefully moved the box. [4]
She slowly, carefully, deliberately moved the box. [3a]
She slowly, carefully(,) and deliberately moved the box. [4a]

The asyndetic coordination of [1] should be distinguished from the hypotactic relationship of adjectives in [5], *cf* 13.2:

I noticed a large rear hatch. ['a rear hatch that was large'] [5]

Since *large* and *rear* are not coordinated in [5], we cannot of course insert either *and* or a comma between the adjectives. Similarly, if we wish to indicate not that the strides were both long and slow as in [1] and [2], but that they were slow strides which were long, we omit punctuation and conjunctions, as in [6]:

He walked with long slow strides. [6]

An adverb analogue to [5] occurs with adverbs in a hierarchical relationship, *cf* 8.56:

She is expected later today. [7]

More stylistically-marked asyndetic coordination (in contrast to the more usual syndetic coordination) is found occasionally with noun phrases and prepositional phrases, particularly at the end of the clause:

The company provides pleasant working conditions, above-average salaries, numerous fringe benefits.
They have been criticized for their business dealings, for their political views.

These phrases occur usually in a series of three or more units.

If we coordinate a series of three or more units, we normally omit the conjunction *and* or *or* before all but the last unit. We of course insert serial commas before all the units, except that there is a choice as to whether to insert or omit the comma before the conjunction. AmE generally favours the insertion of the comma, while AmE journalistic style favours its omission; in BrE, usage is divided:

Dogs, cats(,) and other animals can recognize friends by smell alone.
Change in human biological history is slow, steady(,) and progressive.

In the next two sentences we see examples of the use of the serial comma in listing, irrespective of the linguistic status of the items listed. Again the comma before the last item is optional, provided that this is preceded by *and*:

She bought eggs, butter, cheese, bread, rice(,) and coffee.
He wrote down 73, 12, 41, 9, 7(,) and 13, and added them up.

Note What has been said of the inclusive conjunction *and* applies also to the exclusive conjunction *or* (as in *to or from town*; *by, with(,) or to a person*; *butter, eggs(,) or fruit*).

Where separation by comma is disallowed

III.9 With regard to the central clause elements S, V, O, and C (but not A), there is a strict rule that they cannot be interrupted by punctuation except where 'inclusion' (*cf* App III.16) or 'specification' (*cf* App III.23) is involved, and with one or two additional but minor exceptions that we shall outline shortly. Thus whether such a sentence element consists of a phrase or a clause, it cannot be separated from the verb by a comma:

*The man over there in the corner, is obviously drunk. [1]
*I know, that you are tired. [2]
*It is perfectly natural, that men should go bald. [3]
*He gave the leading lady, a bouquet. [4]

In speech, [1] and possibly [3] and [4] might have a tone unit break where the unacceptable comma has been inserted and we are sometimes tempted to match this with a comma in writing, an error particularly likely to arise with lengthy subjects as in [1] (*cf* also App III.16 Note). The rule, however, is clear enough and is strictly observed in print. Equally clear (and this time generally observed unhesitatingly even in manuscript) is the rule that phrases constituting any of the elements S, V, O, C, or A cannot be interrupted by noncorrelative commas, unless the commas are required for serial use (*cf* App III.8):

*The old, man died.
*He may, go there.
*They emigrated after, the war.

One exception to these rules is that a comma may come between S and V when there might otherwise be momentary confusion, as for instance through two occurrences of the same word:

What his name is, is of no interest to me.
Whatever she does, does not concern me.
What one person may think of, another may not.

Rarely, a comma may also come at the point of gapping (*cf* 13.92*f*) in an elliptical clause:

Rock aspires to recognition as art, and new classical music, to a larger following.

But more commonly no punctuation is used:

One bedroom was very large, and the other quite small.

Finally, a comma is placed between a subject-verb sequence and a direct object in direct speech (*cf* App III.21).

Note The need for easy recognition of structure determines the convention of using commas between thousands in numerals: 41,396,728. Spaces are sometimes used instead of commas for this purpose: 41 396 728 (*cf* 6.63 Note [b]).

The colon

III.10 The colon makes a sharper separation than the comma. It was placed between the comma and the semicolon in App III.3 because it indicates a closer interdependence between the units separated than does the semicolon. Indeed, it sometimes indicates as close a relation as the comma does, but it is a different relation. The functions of the colon, a rather infrequent punctuation mark, can be summed up as follows: what follows (as in this sentence) is an explication of what precedes it or a fulfilment of the expectation raised (even if raised only by its own use). Thus:

I've just had some good news: I've been offered a job in a law firm. [1]
Those who lead must be considerate: those who follow must be responsive. [2]

In [1] the explication is a clause which can be viewed as being in apposition to a noun phrase in the preceding clause, if the notion of apposition is extended beyond noun phrases (*cf* 17.65*ff*). Compare:

The good news is that *I've been offered a job in a law firm.*

Such a relationship is typical between units separated by a colon. A further example:

The man had been drinking heavily: this, not age, explained his unsteady walk. [3]

Here the pronoun *this* refers back to the whole of the preceding clause ('the fact that the man had been drinking heavily'). Sometimes the relationship is more indirect and subtle, however, as in:

> Joan and Mary were obviously weary: I got up to go. [4]

The colon in [4] helps to indicate that it was my observation of their weariness that made me decide to go.

In each of the examples, a semicolon could replace the colon, and with examples [2–4] a semicolon would be more usual. On the other hand, provided that a coordinating conjunction were introduced between the clauses, the colon could also be replaced in [2–4] by a comma or by no punctuation. In this respect, too, the [2–4] set is distinguished from [1], in which we have the more central use of the colon to imply 'as follows' or 'namely'. Related to that central use is the very frequent use of the colon (as in this book) to introduce examples, whether immediately following the colon or indented on the next line or lines.

Note The independent clause following a colon may begin with a capital letter, but generally not in BrE. A capital letter is in any case used if the part introduced by the colon consists of more than one sentence, or if it is a quoted sentence (*cf* App III.21):

> I asked myself: Where was it all leading?

III.11 So far, the illustrations have shown the colon separating only clauses. But it commonly separates smaller units such as phrases, and it was its potentiality to do so that justified its place between comma and semicolon in the hierarchy in App III.3. Notice that the semicolon in [1] marks the major division of the sentence:

> There remained one thing she wanted above all else: a room
> of her own; but she did not acquire her own room until she
> was eighteen. [1]

The use of the colon in examples like [1] resembles most closely the purpose it serves (especially in technical or specialized writing) when it precedes a formal list of items, often preceded by its verbal equivalents *for example*, *eg*, *namely* (sometimes written *viz*), *ie*, *as follows*, or the like (*cf* 17.73). For example:

> Please send the stipulated items (, namely):
> (i) birth certificate
> (ii) passport
> (iii) correct fee [2]

When it appears in such a formal or official use as [2] implies, it is sometimes followed in BrE by a short dash (:–), but this is generally regarded as rather heavy punctuation (*cf* App III.22). Certainly, when it introduces lists in nontechnical writing, as in the illustration of the hierarchy in App III.3, it is never followed by a dash.

Punctuation is generally omitted after the items in a formal vertical list as in [2], though sometimes all but the last item are followed by semicolons or commas and the last item (of course) by a period (but *cf* App III.23 Note [b]).

Contrast the required commas in the horizontal list in [2a]:

> Please send the stipulated items: your birth certificate, your passport, and the correct fee. [2a]

The colon may be replaced by a comma when what follows is one item as in [1], or if the following list itself does not contain separating commas, as in [2b]:

> Please send the stipulated items, namely your birth certificate and your passport. [2b]

In this connection – one of the few in which the colon and the comma seem to be interchangeable – it is of interest to note that, whereas the vocative formula at the beginning of letters is normally separated by a new line and sentence capitalization, it is additionally marked by a comma or (in AmE) by a colon:

> Dear Mr Wilson,
> Thank you . . . ⟨BrE and informal AmE⟩
> Dear Mr Wilson:
> Thank you . . . ⟨AmE⟩

The sentence following the vocative formula begins with a capital letter (*Thank you* . . . in the above examples); it is commonly indented as marking the beginning of the first paragraph in the body of the letter (*cf* App III.14).

Note If the horizontal list contains more than two items, unlike [2b], a colon is required if there is no apposition marker (*cf* 17.73), as in [2a]. If an apposition marker such as *namely* is inserted, it is usual to replace the colon by a semicolon (*cf* App III.13):

> Please send the stipulated items; namely(,) your birth certificate, your passport, and the correct fee.

The semicolon

III.12 The semicolon is next below the period in the hierarchy, but it is particularly associated with formal writing. It is best regarded as the coordinating mark of punctuation (*cf* asyndetic coordination, 13.1), corresponding most nearly in value to the linguistic coordinating conjunction *and*. That is, when two independent clauses are regarded as being sufficiently related to belong to one sentence, this may be shown by prosody in speech (*cf* App II.13) – for example, narrow pitch range or a rising nucleus at the end of the first clause, with or without a coordinating conjunction. In writing, it may be shown by a comma followed by a coordinating conjunction as in [1]:

> Taylor was, as always, a consummate actor, and with a few telling strokes he characterized King Lear magnificently. [1]

Or it may be shown asyndetically by a semicolon without a coordinating conjunction as in [2]:

> Taylor was, as always, a consummate actor; with a few telling strokes he characterized King Lear magnificently. [2]

Thus if we represent a clause as SVOA, we can compare the use of commas and semicolons connecting such clauses as follows:

[a] S V O A(,) and (then) (S) V O A
[b] S V O A; (and) (then) S V O A

In the formulas [a] and [b], *and* represents the coordinators *and*, *but*, and *or*, while *then* represents any appropriate way of additionally linking the clauses. The coordinator cannot be omitted in [a], and the subject cannot be ellipted in the second clause of [b].

We have noted earlier that, especially when the clauses are short and parallel, there are exceptional uses of commas without a coordinator (*cf* App III.6 Note) and that the conjunction-like *nor*, *neither*, *so*, and *yet* may be preceded by a comma when they alone link independent clauses (*cf* App III.7).

III.13 In App III.12 we noted that the semicolon is primarily a coordinating mark, but we indicated that it may also be followed by a coordinator, as we now illustrate in [1] below:

I had been aware that they sometimes disagreed violently, particularly over how to raise their children, and that there were also periods when they would not speak to each other; but I had not realized that they were seriously contemplating divorce. [1]

Such a use (in effect, replacing a comma) is chiefly found in rather formal writing and in sentences whose complexity already involves the use of one or more commas and whose major divisions call for a hierarchically superior punctuation mark if the reader is not to be momentarily puzzled or misled. A simple but convenient application of this principle occurs in lists, where it is often desirable to show subgroupings:

The breakfast menu consisted of fruit juice or cereal; a boiled, fried, or poached egg; toast and marmalade; and a pot of tea or coffee. [2]

Somewhat related is the chief point at which the semicolon shows affinity of use with the colon; namely, the convention (as in this sentence and in [3]), of preceding such apposition indicators as *namely* or *that is* by a semicolon. Without such an indicator, as in [3a], a colon would usually be appropriate:

In one respect, government policy has been firmly decided; that is, there will be no conscription. [3]

In one respect, government policy has been firmly decided: there will be no conscription. [3a]

But other forms of punctuation may occur in such cases. For example, the appositive may be in a separate sentence (as in this sentence), or it may be enclosed in parentheses, or if it is not a clause the apposition indicator may be preceded by a comma (*cf* App III.11).

Punctuating for sentence and paragraph

III.14 The two highest separators constitute combinations of symbols. We mark off one orthographic sentence from the next by terminating it with a period, question mark, or exclamation mark, and by beginning the next with a capital letter; between the period and the capital, there will usually be a somewhat wider space than we normally have between words. The paragraph (*cf* 19.28) is also marked off by a combination of symbols in most writing: leaving blank the remainder of the line in which it ends; indentation (also called 'indention') of the line beginning the new one; and (especially in typescript) a slightly larger space between lines at this point. At the beginning of a chapter or section, the first paragraph normally (as in this book) begins without indentation, and in some styles of writing this practice (called 'block style') is followed with all paragraphs; as a result, if the end of the previous paragraph happens to coincide with the end of a line, the new one may not in effect be marked at all, unless the convention is adopted of a larger space between lines.

Note [**a**] A period is usually called a 'full stop' in BrE. It is also called a 'full point' or (informally) a 'dot'.
[**b**] Numbered sections of a chapter, as in this book, are sometimes called 'paragraphs' even where they comprise more than one 'punctuation' paragraph.
[**c**] On capitals at the beginning of letters and direct speech, *cf* App III.11, App III.21.
[**d**] Reverse indentation (indentation of all lines back from the first) is common for entries in reference books, for example dictionaries and encyclopedias, for entries in glossaries and indices of books, and for indented examples that require more than one line (like sentences [1], [2], [3], and [3a] in App III.13).
[**e**] In official letters, paragraphs are often marked by a larger space without indentation.

III.15 It was stressed in App III.2 that punctuation was linked primarily to grammar rather than to prosody. This does not mean that the sentence and the paragraph, as punctuated, are obvious grammatical units. Although they are co-terminous with one or more grammatical units and hence no grammatical units extend beyond their limits, they do not necessarily consist in their entirety of a grammatical unit. The decision to coordinate several independent clauses within one sentence or to separate them as different sentences, with or without formal sign of their logical connection, is dependent largely upon the style of material one is handling or indeed upon the personal preference of the writer. Guidance on sentence limits which invokes criteria such as 'completeness', 'independence', 'intelligibility as a single whole' is essentially circular, since (a) the writer will necessarily have to decide for himself how 'complete' to make any part of his argument, and (b) punctuation of itself imposes the impression of completeness and independence on units marked off as sentences and conversely helps to show connection between units grouped within sentence limits.

Such points apply even more obviously in the case of paragraph limits. Rather than attempting to recommend an ideal size of paragraph or models for its ideal identity, we should note that the paragraph enables a writer to show that a particular set of sentences should be considered as more closely related to each other, and that those grouped within one paragraph are to be seen as a whole in relation to those that are grouped in the paragraphs preceding and following (*cf* 19.28).

Note Short paragraphs provide convenient resting places during reading and aesthetically pleasing contrasts between print and white space. Both considerations account for the shorter paragraphs in the columns of newspapers and magazines, the more popular publications tending to have the shortest paragraphs.

Separation of included units

Included units and correlative marks

III.16 A unit that is loosely attached to the rest of the sentence may be, and sometimes must be, marked off by punctuation, usually commas. The decision to mark off the adverbial in [1] requires not one comma but two:

Crocodiles, *in fact*, do not particularly like human flesh. [1]

The punctuation marks for inclusion are CORRELATIVE: the first sign indicates the beginning and the second the end of the included unit. But one of the correlative commas may be superseded by a punctuation mark above it in the hierarchy (*cf* App III.3), the punctuation system not permitting the cooccurrence of the comma with marks further up. Thus, one of the correlative commas is absent in [1a] and [1b]:

In fact, crocodiles do not particularly like human flesh.
[*, *In fact*, . . .] [1a]
Crocodiles do not particularly like human flesh, in fact.
[* . . . *in fact*,.] [1b]

Examples [1a] and [1b] exemplify the general rule that one of the correlative marks is omitted if it coincides with a higher mark. Thus, there would not be an initial correlative comma in [1a] if *in fact* were preceded by a dash, colon, or semicolon; and similarly there would not be a final correlative comma in [1b] if *in fact* were followed by a dash, colon, or semicolon. Correlative dashes obey the same rule:

To change the subject, if I may – where are we eating tonight?
[* – To change the subject, if I may – . . .] [2]
The universe is expanding – that is, the galaxies are receding
from each other at immense speeds. [*. . . at immense speeds –.] [3]
One theme represents the outer world – the world of battles and
banquets; it is seen from a distance, and is quite distinct from
the quieter spiritual life in the monastery. [*. . . battles and
banquets – ;] [4]

It will be noticed that the final correlative comma after *if I may* in [2] and the initial correlative comma before *that is* in [3] are superseded by a dash.

On the other hand, parentheses (and other types of bracketing), which are outside the hierarchy of punctuation marks, must always be present in pairs. They represent a sharp interruption and therefore appear medially or finally within the interrupted unit, but not initially. For those reasons, parentheses may cooccur with other punctuation marks that follow them:

You should see Ruth (my niece), when you are next in Washington.
I spoke about the incident to Ted Wilson (the manager of the factory) –
but he denied seeing anything unusual.

When the parentheses enclose one or more sentences, the final termination point is placed within the closing parenthesis (*cf* App III.20).

Any of the pairs of correlative marks may enclose any other pair, but different pairs tend to be used; otherwise it would be difficult to identify the pairs of commas, as in [5]:

?The operation, I was convinced, after some resistance, by my doctor, had now become essential. [5]

More understandable would be [5a] or [5b]:

The operation (I was convinced, after some resistance, by my doctor) had now become essential. [5a]

The operation, I was convinced (after some resistance) by my doctor, had now become essential. [5b]

One of the correlative marks, as we have also seen earlier in this section, may be superseded by a mark above it in the hierarchy:

Jason, during a hundred hours of testing – an hour a day, five days a week – expanded his powers of recall over ten times. [6a]

But the punctuation hierarchy would be clearer here if it corresponded with the grammatical hierarchy, thereby enabling the higher marks to be visible:

Jason – during a hundred hours of testing, an hour a day, five days a week – expanded his powers of recall over ten times. [6b]

Note A common error in manuscript punctuation by inexperienced writers is to omit the first correlative comma in a medial included unit, *eg*: *Crocodiles in fact, do not . . .* The error reflects the fact that in normal speech the medial included unit is not necessarily separated prosodically from the previous part of the sentence, though it may be so separated from the following part (*cf* App III.9).

Correlative commas

Commas with adverbials

III.17 Loose attachment of an adverbial to a sentence is linked to adverbial mobility: just as the least mobile are normally those with closest and most indispensable connection with the rest of the sentence, so the least mobile are those least requiring separation by commas:

He put the chair between you and me. [1]

?Between you and me he put the chair. [1a]

He failed the exam, between you and me. [2]

Between you and me, he failed the exam. [2a]

On the distinction between types of adverbials, *cf* 8.24.

Even those adverbial elements that are so closely related to the rest of the sentence as not to need commas in final position, however, often need to be thus separated when they are in initial or medial positions if they are clauses or phrases longer than two or three words:

Some scientists have succeeded in cloning human cells in experiments at Stanford University. [3]

In experiments at Stanford University(,) some scientists have succeeded in cloning human cells. [3a]

Some scientists, in experiments at Stanford University, have succeeded in cloning human cells. [3b]

You'll succeed if you try hard. [4]
If you try hard(,) you'll succeed. [4a]

Loosely attached adverbials are infrequent in medial positions, except for conjuncts (*cf* 8.134*ff*) such as *however*, or *moreover*.

As [3a] and [4a] show, the comma is often optional after many adverbials in *I* position, but it becomes obligatory with participle and verbless clauses, and is normal with infinitive clauses:

Knowing my views, they refrained from discussing the subject.
Out of breath, he slumped down in a chair.
To keep the star moving so quickly and in such a small orbit, its invisible travelling companion would have to be at least nine times more massive than the sun.

The comma is desirable on occasion where its absence might cause the reader to stumble. Thus, although the adverbial has identical function in [5] and [5a], it is necessary in the latter to avoid misleading the reader into thinking at first that the prepositional phrase is longer than it is:

After dark(,) I strolled around the square. [5]
After dark, men and women strolled around the square. [5a]

For a comparable reason, a comma would be preferable in

He tried in vain to find her, in his underclothes.

And although no ambiguity or comic overtones could affect the following example, the sequence 'in in' would seem less confusing with the separation provided by a comma (*cf* App III.9):

They hurried on in, in great excitement.

Note [**a**] Predication adjuncts (*cf* 8.26*ff*) are sometimes fronted. Since they are strongly integrated within clause structure, they cannot be followed by a comma (*cf* also App II.16):

*To the very top of the mountain, they climbed.

[**b**] Somewhat analogous to the use of the comma for preposed adverbials is its use in index entries to mark a surname moved from its normal end-position: *cf*: *John Quincy Adams*, but *Adams, John Quincy*.

III.18 In general, punctuation is determined less by the length of an adverbial or its structure (whether a single word, a phrase, or an entire clause) than by its function. Indeed, a finite clause may often need marking off to a lesser extent than a shorter nonfinite or verbless clause:

Though he was suffering great pain(,) he walked home alone.
Though suffering great pain, he walked home alone.
Weary and impatient, she left the meeting early.

Often, however, mere length of an adverbial will make it seem more loosely linked to the rest of the sentence than a short one and so seem to need marking off by a comma; and length may also make punctuation desirable for sheer clarity's sake:

If you prefer to wake up gradually with a cup of hot coffee rather than with fifty laps in a cool pool, you should set aside some time for swimming before lunch or after work.

Function, however, is usually more important than length. Thus even where an initial adjunct needs no comma, as in [1], the same adverb as conjunct (*cf* 8.134*ff*) requires one, as in [1a]:

Again he felt hesitant. [= 'Once more . . .'] [1]
Again, he felt hesitant. [= 'It should be added that . . .'] [1a]

Here is another case where punctuation somewhat mirrors the prosodic difference, since [1] would usually constitute one tone unit in speech (*cf* App II.11) while there would be two for [1a]:

A|GÀIN he felt 'hesitant| [1]
A|GĂIN|he|felt HÈsitant| [1a]

Nonrestrictive adjunct clauses (*cf* 15.23) are punctuated in final position, though not invariably in initial position:

Betty will help you, when she has finished her own work.

Disjuncts (*cf* 8.121*ff*, 15.20*f*) tend to be punctuated with a comma in final position, particularly when the subordinator can also introduce an adjunct clause. Contrast the disjunct clause in [2] with the adjunct clause in [3]:

He's at home, because I've just spoken to him. [2]
He's at home because he's not feeling well. [3]

Clauses introduced by *for* are always preceded by a comma or a mark above it in the hierarchy, partly to differentiate the conjunction from the preposition *for* and partly because the conjunction is close to being a coordinator (*cf* 13.18*f*):

I am convinced that you will find none better to advise you, for she has had much experience in industrial negotiations.

Commas with other units

III.19 Adverbials are not, however, the only common types of included units. Others are nonrestrictive modifiers (*cf* 17.3), including nonrestrictive relative clauses (*cf* 17.22) and nonrestrictive appositions (*cf* 17.68), interpolated coordinate constructions (*cf* 13.95*ff*), and analogous parallel structures:

Susan Fenton, who used to work with me, has moved to New York.
The other man, David Johnson, refused to make a statement.
The portrait, painted by a local artist, was unveiled before a large audience.
The person we need, the person we have been waiting for, is someone adequately trained in business management.
She is a close friend to, and supporter of, the Republican candidate.
He should, or rather must, attend better to his studies.

So also with vocatives (*cf* 10.52*ff*):

John, I think you would be wiser not to go.

But how, ladies and gentlemen, are we to proceed to a freer society?
Help yourself, Carol.

Dashes and parentheses

III.20 Although commas are the only items so far illustrated, two other common sets of correlative punctuation marks can be used to mark the separation of included units when the units are positioned medially or finally. They are dashes and parentheses, the latter known in BrE also as 'brackets' (*cf* Note [a] below):

The other man – David Johnson – refused to make a statement.
The other man (David Johnson) refused to make a statement.
I have not yet obtained a statement from the other woman – Ann Taylor.
I have not yet obtained a statement from the other woman (Ann Taylor).

The comma is the least obtrusive correlative mark and for that reason is preferred unless there is a disruption of the syntactic structure of the clause, or the danger of confusion with other neighbouring commas or of failure to mark adequately a rather lengthy inclusion. In these cases dashes or parentheses are preferable, except that dashes tend to give a somewhat more dramatic and informal impression, suggesting an impromptu aside, rather than a planned inclusion:

At that time, the students – goodness knows for what reason – reversed their earlier, more moderate decision, and a big demonstration was planned. [1]

In [1] the inclusion is sufficiently informal an interruption to justify dashes rather than parentheses.

Under certain circumstances, even short included items tend to be enclosed by parentheses. In formal writing, for example, they are used for cross-references and figures denoting life span:

We shall see below (*p* 63) that Eleanor's first love was William Bevan (1812–73).

and for figures or letters used in lists or for examples.

Dashes or parentheses are used if the unit included in the sentence is an independent clause:

Enterprising businessmen sell earthworms and their castings (they are one of the best soil conditioners) in hundreds of retail stores across the US and Canada. [2]

A period does not conclude a parenthetic sentence when that sentence is inserted within another sentence, as in [2], though a question or exclamation mark may do so (*cf* App III.23). If a sentence or set of sentences is included as a digression in a paragraph, parentheses are required and final punctuation marks precede the closing parenthesis, as in [3]:

They decided that it was impossible to recreate Vietnam battle scenes, since the war was still on and they felt that the Philippines were an unacceptable substitute. (*Apocalypse Now*, made in the Philippines, did not change their feeling.) So they set to work on a home front drama. [3]

Note [**a**] In BrE usage parentheses are generally called 'brackets', a term reserved in AmE for what in BrE are called 'square brackets'; they are sometimes used when inclusions have to be made within inclusions:

'. . . the other man (David Johnson [*alias* Wilson])'

[**b**] 'Square brackets' are used in serious writing also to include the author's or editor's comment upon the form rather than the content:

He said that *Thursday* was his normal visiting day [italics mine].

It was stated that the heir to the property was Jon [sic] Roberts.

They are also used for explanations of the reference of pronouns:

Martin Tutin claimed that she [the Prime Minister] was chiefly responsible for the crisis.

and to replace pronouns or other omitted items in quotations:

The author claims that '[Jonathan Swift] advocated the establishment of a Language Academy to purify the English language and prevent its further deterioration'.

[**c**] All forms of bracketing, including the braces used in mathematics and other technical writing, { }, differ from other inclusion marks except quotation marks (*cf* App III.21) in clearly distinguishing the opening (left-hand) and closing (right-hand) items in the correlative pair, and in requiring the presence of both items. The fact that each item thus indicates independently its correlative status and that both items must be present makes parentheses the clearest of the inclusion signs and especially appropriate for lengthy inclusions.

Quotation and quotation marks

III.21 There is one further correlative pair of inclusion marks that is of great importance and in frequent use: the 'quotation marks', informally 'quotes', or 'inverted commas' ⟨esp BrE⟩. Opening and closing quotation marks are generally distinguished in print, but not in typed material and sometimes not in handwritten material.

Quotation marks may be single '. . .' or double ". . .". The latter are more usual in handwritten and typed material and in American printing; the former are more usual in British printing, but the choice lies primarily with individual printing houses. Whichever form is not used for ordinary quotation is then used for quotation within quotation:

'I heard "Keep out" being shouted,' he said. ⟨esp BrE⟩

"I heard 'Keep out' being shouted," he said. ⟨esp AmE⟩

Like parentheses, quotation marks can cooccur with other marks of punctuation, but with some differences between AmE and BrE. AmE always puts a period or a comma inside the closing quotation marks.

She enjoyed the article "Cities Are for Walking." ⟨AmE⟩

She enjoyed the article 'Cities Are for Walking'. ⟨BrE⟩

He couldn't spell "mnemonic," and therefore failed to reach the finals. ⟨AmE⟩

He couldn't spell 'mnemonic', and therefore failed to reach the finals. ⟨BrE⟩

In BrE too the period and comma are inside the closing quotation marks for direct speech with reporting clauses (*cf* 14.29):

'You are just in time,' she said. [1]

She said, 'You are just in time.' [1a]

Although the quoted sentence in [1] begins with a capital letter, it does not end with a period because the including sentence is not complete.

Both [1] and [1a] infringe a rule given in App III.9. This exception to the rule is that when the direct object is a piece of direct speech it may be (and usually is) separated by punctuation from the verb and subject (but *cf* 14.29).

Quoted matter does not always require quotation marks. In dramatic dialogue and in newspaper reports of speeches or court proceedings, speakers' names are usually followed by a colon and the quotation:

Judge Harlan: If you do not answer frankly, the jury will draw its own conclusions.
I asked myself: Where was it all leading?

And in serious writing only short quotations from other writers are put in quotation marks; longer quotations are indented and given without quotation marks.

Note [a] On the punctuation of quoted questions and exclamations, *cf* App III.24.
[b] In some writing, a quotation extending over more than one paragraph will have opening quotation marks at the beginning of each new paragraph though closing marks will occur only at the end of the entire quotation.

Light and heavy punctuation and the grammatical hierarchy

III.22 It was shown in App III.17*f* that an initial adverbial is often separated from the rest of the sentence by a comma. Consider, however, the following:

?Slowly, he strolled over and she smiled at him. [1]

The punctuation in [1] suggests that *slowly* applies (almost nonsensically) to both clauses. If *slowly* is intended to apply to the first clause only, the punctuation seems illogical in making a break within the first clause where there is none between the two clauses. The principle that would here influence writers is that punctuation should not work against the hierarchy of grammatical units (*cf* 2.7*ff*). Given the constituents of [1], we may feel obliged to counteract the objections by adding more punctuation:

Slowly, he strolled over, and she smiled at him. [1a]

Or we may insert the comma at the higher constituent boundary:

Slowly he strolled over, and she smiled at him. [1b]

Or perhaps we will omit internal punctuation entirely:

Slowly he strolled over and she smiled at him. [1c]

Sentence [1a] is a simple example of how once a little punctuation is admitted, more is necessary in order to preserve a consistent and logical ordering of hierarchical relationships. In preference to the heavy punctuation of sentences like [1a], writers often move in the opposite direction towards a light punctuation, just sufficient to make their sentences quickly and easily understood.

A similar tendency towards light punctuation is exemplified for adverbials in the next four sentences, but the consequences are very different:

Marilyn was the most persuasive speaker in the society, and *for that reason* was chosen to represent the society in the regional competition. [2]

The researchers say that *although the drug was successful experimentally*, it must be tested over a long period to discuss its possible side-effects. [3]

Bushes and undergrowth had blotted out the old path that led to the town, and *without the direct light of the sun to act as a compass*, I could no longer be sure of my direction. [4]

We expected an immediate reply but *in fact*, it was several months before we heard from him. [5]

In all four sentences the choices made for the light punctuation reflect the prosody rather than the grammar. The punctuation treats the part of the sentence following the conjunction as if it began a new sentence, in which case the initial correlative comma would be necessarily omitted (*cf* App III.16). In [2] correlative commas have not been used to separate the included unit *for that reason*, which would normally be so separated; instead the comma is inserted at the end of the first clause, thereby separating the coordinated predicates. In [3–5] initial correlative commas have been omitted in violation of an important punctuation rule (*cf* App III.16). Furthermore, the retention of the final correlative comma obscures the grammatical hierarchical relationships in the sentence. In each instance a conjunction (a subordinator in [3] and a coordinator in [4] and [5]) is separated from most of its clause by the comma at the end of the initial adverbial. In [3] the comma makes the major grammatical division seem to be in the middle of the *that*-clause. In [4] the coordinator *and* is thereby made to appear as if coordinating a prepositional phrase. Finally, in [5] the division between the coordinated clauses is bypassed in favour of a final correlative comma after the phrase *in fact*; here the motivation is primarily rhetorical, to place the greatest emphasis on this emphatic adverbial.

Although the light punctuation of [2–5] is incongruous grammatically, the incongruity does not lead to misinterpretation or ambiguity and the punctuation is acceptable. Indeed, heavy punctuation in [2], [4], and [5] would have the odd effect of enclosing the coordinator in commas, one for separating successive units and the other for separating included units. On the other hand, consider the effect of including the participle clause *seeing this* in the following example:

He smiled at Joan and Mary was cross. [6]

*He smiled at Joan and Mary, seeing this, was cross. [6a]

The punctuation in [6a] is unacceptable in seriously misrepresenting the hierarchy of grammatical relations: it would make the reader think at first that *and* was coordinating the two names rather than the two clauses, and so we must have:

He smiled at Joan, and Mary, seeing this, was cross.

So also, although a comma is optional in [7], it is obligatory when *in short* has been included, as in [7a]:

If this is what he seems to want(,) he can have it. [7]
If this, in short, is what he seems to want, he can have it. [7a]

Specification

Question and exclamation marks

III.23 Although in App III.2, specification was exemplified with the use of the apostrophe to mark the genitive, in many ways a more obvious example is the question mark. This indicates that the sentence it terminates is a question, whether it is interrogative or (less frequently) declarative in form:

What can be done to help these people? [1]
You are leaving already? [2]

In [1], as with other *wh*-questions, there is no necessary prosodic distinction from declarative sentences to match the punctuation contrast between period and question mark, since unmarked *wh*-questions generally have falling tones (*cf* App II.12). In [2], on the other hand, the question mark matches in writing the prosodic contrast between this sentence as question and the same sentence as statement (*cf* App II.13).

The exclamation mark (in AmE, also 'exclamation point') is more rarely used and indeed its excessive use is often taken as a sign of frivolous or immature writing. It is however quite normal in representing a sentence uttered with great emotive force, whether or not this has exclamative form:

How silly they are!
What a perceptive article she wrote!
Aren't they tall! (*cf* Note [b])

Well done!
Fire!
You don't say!

Both the question mark and the exclamation mark generally exclude the use of other separation punctuation and have the value of a period inasmuch as what follows begins with the capitalization of a new sentence. But when they co-occur with the end of quotation, they come within the quotation marks and if more of the including sentence follows, no capital letter is used:

'How tall they are!' she thought.

Both here and when they end a parenthetic sentence included within another sentence (*cf* App III.20), they differ from periods:

She paid 40 000 dollars (Isn't that over 20 000 pounds?) for a new sports car.

In this respect they are not hierarchically on the same level as the period, which could not occur in those environments. When they end an included parenthetic sentence, as above, they have only a specifying function, not a separating function.

Note [**a**] Sentences with exclamative form (*cf* 11.31*f*) always end with an exclamation mark. The exclamation is used in environments where there is great urgency; it serves alone, for example, in road signs as a symbol of warning. Imperative sentences generally do not end with an exclamation mark unless they represent very peremptory and urgent commands:

> 'Get outside!' he shouted angrily.

Likewise, vocatives ordinarily do not take exclamation marks unless they are used alone as an urgent warning or command.

[**b**] For pragmatic reasons, not all sentences which are interrogative in form end in a question mark. A period is often preferred if the interrogative form is operating as a request:

> Would the gentleman who left a silk scarf on the manager's desk care to retrieve it from the porter's office.

On the other hand, an exclamation mark is used with exclamatory questions, such as *Aren't they tall!* (*cf* 11.22).

When a formal list of items appears at the end of a question, the question mark is omitted, since its position at the end of the list might be misinterpreted as a query on the final item:

> What would you like me to send to the following people:
> Sam and Mary Paton
> Julian and Kate Coleman
> Robert Fowler
> Susan Goodman

Specification of included units

III.24 The following illustrates the use of question and exclamation marks in relation to included material:

Did you see the words {'Are you happy?' / 'You fools!'} on the wall? [1]

I saw the words {'Are you happy?' / 'You fools!'} Did you see them? [1a]

Did you see the words {'Are you happy?' / 'You fools!'} [1b]

Did you see the words 'Are you happy'? [1c]
?Did you see the words 'Are you happy?'? [1d]
*I saw the words 'Are you happy?'. [1e]
These words ('Are you happy?') were on the wall. [1f]
?These words, 'Are you happy?', were on the wall. [1g]

Though logically correct, [1d] is less acceptable than either [1c] or [1b] as a means of handling the same problem. The general rule is that only one noncorrelative mark can occur at one place. The rule is infringed more severely in [1e] than in [1d] because two types of marks co-occur.

Although they are primarily used at the end of interrogative or exclamatory sentences, there is a consciously exceptional rhetorical use of question and exclamation marks to specify doubt or surprise about individual parts of a sentence; in such use, they are often enclosed in parentheses, following the relevant item:

> A further semantic (?) problem may be formulated as follows.
> The old woman insisted that her name was Shirley Temple (!) and muttered something about being born in what sounded like Abbis (?) Ababa.

The question mark may sometimes precede, our practice in this book when indicating doubtfully acceptable sentences, as in [1d] and [1g]:

I think she said (?)Abbis.

Note The use of more than one question mark or exclamation mark or combinations of the two to suggest extreme doubt or surprise is confined to very informal writing such as stories for children.

Quotation marks, italics, and underlining

III.25 Quotation marks are used far more widely in manuscript and typescript than is underlining, perhaps because underlining is firmly associated with emphasis. Only those involved in the writing and production of printed material are aware that underlining in manuscript and typescript is used to represent italics in print.

In print, italics are used for the titles of works such as books, magazines, journals, newspapers, films, musical compositions, and paintings; in typescript and manuscript these may be underlined or in quotation marks. Quotation marks are generally used in all written material for parts of larger works, for example articles in journals, chapters in books, short stories, and songs.

In print, italics represent cited words or expressions:

The plural of *woman* is *women*.

In other written material, underlining may be used for this purpose, but quotation marks are more common. We indicate that words are introduced from a different style by quotation marks, as with the colloquialism in [1]:

The stranded colonel was obliged to 'hitch' a ride from a passing motorist. [1]

Words from a foreign language are indicated by italics in print and by quotation marks (less frequently by underlining) in other written material:

His slightest *jeu d'esprit* was impressive. [2]

In all material, quotation marks are used to give the meaning of an expression, as in [3]:

The word *schadenfreude*, which means 'malicious enjoyment', is quite fashionable in English. [3]

Quotation marks, as in [1] above, may indicate a hesitant or apologetic introduction of a doubtful or discordant item. Or they may indicate a term that is not fully accepted. But elsewhere they may equally imply that the item is of doubtful validity because merely alleged; in this usage they may be sly or sarcastic and match a heavy prosodic marking in speech:

I told him that his 'wife' had come and let him know by the way I said it that I didn't think she really *was* his wife. [4]

As in [4], italics in print and underlining or wriggle underlining in manuscript and typescript can be used informally to indicate emphasis. Other devices occasionally used for emphasis are capitals and (in print) bold face and small capitals.

Dashes and other specifiers of breaks

III.26 A syntactic break or anacoluthon is indicated by a dash, but naturally this device belongs largely to informal writing:

They gave him a prize for getting top marks – and a certificate as well. [1]
'I hoped that you –' His voice broke. [2]
John wasn't altogether – I thought he seemed a little unhappy. [3]

An analogous use of the dash is made to suppress (now rarely) a name or obscenity ('Mr B–'; 'F– off').

Note [**a**] An unfinished sentence is also frequently expressed by means of ellipsis or suspension dots or periods (normally three), which could replace the dash in [2] above, though perhaps giving the impression of trailing away rather than an abrupt break. In formal writing, the dots can indicate 'that which it is unnecessary to specify':

Take a sequence of prime numbers (1, 2, 3, 5, 7, 11, 13, 17, . . .) and consider . . .

or the omission of parts of quoted material:

The review of the book stated, 'The author is enthusiastic at the prospect of systems by which you can call up information on your television screen . . . I can imagine governments of the future being worried about the use of such reference libraries and their influence on public opinion.'

In AmE an additional fourth period indicates that the ellipsis coincides with the end of a sentence.

[**b**] Stammering is sometimes informally indicated by hyphens and reduplication of letters:

'P-p-p-please t-t-try', his teeth chattered through fear and cold.

The same device is used to indicate prolongation of vowels:

'He-e-elp!' she cried.

The apostrophe

III.27 The apostrophe is most frequently used in serious writing to denote genitive singular and plural as in *the girl's* and *the girls'*; in speech these are indistinguishable from each other and from the nongenitive plural, *the girls*. In ordinary use, however, it also marks contractions in the verb phrase: *I'm*, *he's*, *we're*, *can't*, *won't*, etc. It is still very occasionally found marking the abbreviation at the beginning of such institutionalized clipped forms as *'cello* or *'flu* (*cf* App I.74). It is regularly used in *o'clock*, and it is found in such poetic contractions as *e'er* and *o'er*. In fiction or casual writing it is sometimes used to indicate nonstandard or casual pronunciation in such forms as *goin'*, *'cos* ⟨BrE⟩, and *'cause*. It is similarly used informally for contraction of year numbers, especially in figures; thus for *1984* we have *'84*.

The apostrophe is frequently used before the plural *s* with items which lack institutionalized spelling:

There are three i's in that word. [1]
the late 1990's [2]

But more often the *s* is affixed without an apostrophe (*1990s*) if there is no danger of misreading (as there would be in example [1]).

Note The apostrophe is occasionally used (especially in manuscript) for written abbreviations that do not represent abbreviations in speech, *eg*: *pron'n* [pronunciation].

Abbreviations and the use of special symbols

III.28 Abbreviation is marked most generally by a single period following an initial letter or shortened form of a word, as in *Gen. Bradley*, *U.K.*, *i.e.*, *e.g.*, *etc.* (but some printers, as in this book, conventionally italicize *ie* and *eg* without periods). When the abbreviation includes the final letter of the word abbreviated, there is a widespread convention in BrE of ignoring the need for a period: *Dr*, *Mr*, for example. Indeed, in much modern practice, abbreviation is carried out by means of word shortening without the use of periods: *etc* or *&c*, *cf*, *UN*, *USA*, *PTO*, for example (*cf* App I.73). Such abbreviations as *etc* are used sparingly in formal writing, though *RSVP* with or without periods is found almost only in formal use (on invitation cards).

The abbreviation period is never followed by a period, though it may be followed by another mark.

Note [**a**] For the use of numerical and mathematical expressions, *cf* 6.63*ff*.

[**b**] A dash (an en dash in print, *cf* App III.5 Note [a]) is an abbreviating device for a sequence:

pages 15–36 [read as 'pages fifteen to thirty-six'; in AmE, for inclusive numbering, as 'pages fifteen through thirty-six']

1985–1995 9 a.m.–5 p.m.

September 12–December 22 [also, BrE: September 12th–December 22nd]

Further abbreviation may be possible:

1985–95 pages 115–17

Cf also the following Note [c] and App III.30 for the use of the oblique stroke in abbreviation. *Cf* also 6.66*f*.

[**c**] In date abbreviations, numerals are separated by the oblique stroke (*cf* App III.30), dash (an en dash in print, *cf* App III.5 Note [a]), colon, or period. Thus:

7/2/84 7–2–84 7.2.84 7.ii.84 ⟨BrE⟩ 7:2:84 ⟨BrE, least frequently⟩

could all be used for '7th February 1984' ⟨BrE⟩ or 'July 2, 1984' ⟨AmE⟩. Numerals in abbreviations for time of day use colon ⟨esp AmE⟩ or period ⟨esp BrE⟩, as in:

6:30 6.30

[**d**] AmE has the alternatives *O.K.*, *o.k.*, *OK*, and *okay*, while BrE prefers *O.K.* and *OK* and does not use *o.k.*

Capitals

III.29 In addition to marking the beginning of a sentence, initial capitals are used for specifying proper nouns (*cf* 5.60*ff*); for example, persons, places, works of literature, days of the week, months of the year (but not usually the seasons), and the planets (but not the earth, the sun, or the moon). They are also used for accompanying appositional titles and descriptors and for status markers (*cf* 10.53) in vocatives:

John Mills is a colonel. BUT He is Colonel John Mills.
These are the forms you wanted, Principal.

So also (but in AmE with periods at the ends of the abbreviations):

Those present included Mr Jones, Miss Graham, Dr Rabin, Mrs Willis, Professor Maisky, and Mrs McDonald.

Initial capitals are commonly used for the names of organizations and institutions:

the Home Office the Social Security System
the Environmental Protection Agency British Airways

the Congressional Budget Office   the Mineworkers Union

They are occasionally used to mark key words in formal discourse, especially at the point where such words are introduced for the first time:

> The next problem, that of Ultraviolet Radiation, is one on which considerable progress has been made.

An alternative, used in this book, is for the whole word to be printed in SMALL CAPITALS. Initial capitals for key words are a particular feature of legal usage:

> The Company's Registrars must receive a copy of the Letter together with the Form of Renunciation.

At the opposite extreme, capitals are sometimes used in light or facetious writing to indicate spoken prominence for the words so specified:

> 'She Who Must Be Obeyed,' he growled ironically.
> 'I must certainly see the Man of the House,' she announced pompously.
> 'And what do YOU want?' he shouted.

Initial capitals are used as a sign of respect in *God* and very commonly in nouns (*Lord*, *Creator*, *Supreme Being*, *Almighty*) and 2nd and 3rd person pronouns referring to God.

Capital letters also appear in the specification of many abbreviations, as we saw in App III.28, whether the items abbreviated are proper nouns (where the use of initial capitals is normal) or not, as usually in *RSVP* or *PTO* ('Please turn over the page', ⟨BrE⟩).

Note [**a**] Initial capitals or capitals throughout the word are commonly used in block language (for example, telegrams, notices, headlines; *cf* 11.45*ff*).

[**b**] Initial capitals are used in personification, thereby indicating that the words are to be considered as names:

> Discretion fought with Valour and was triumphant.

[**c**] In the Middle Ages, the letters *i*, *j*, and *y* were used to some extent interchangeably and it is for complicated reasons of paleographical preference (rather than the egocentric immodesty it might suggest) that capital *I*, itself an alternant of *j*, emerged as the regular spelling of the 1st person singular pronoun.

[**d**] Publishing houses have a strong tradition for distinguishing capitals in titles, generally excluding short closed-class words (*cf* 2.39):

> To the End of Time

Miscellaneous minor conventions

III.30 Lesser punctuation conventions may be grouped as (a) chiefly technical, and (b) formulaic:

(a) 1. Parenthesized figures or letters commonly distinguish parts of an exposition, like the (a) and (b) in this section; *a*) and *b*), and *a*. and *b*., are common variants.

2. The oblique stroke (also called 'slant', 'slash', 'solidus', 'virgule') is used to indicate abbreviation and also to specify alternatives and subsectioning:

> the academic year 1985/6
> c/o [in postal addresses, read as 'care of']

students and/or staff
Rule A/32

Cf also App III.28 Note [c].

3. **Bold face** draws special attention to an item.

4. In manuscripts and typescripts a caret (⁁ or ∧) indicates the place where material in the margin or between the lines is to be inserted.

(b) A new line may specify the formulaic termination of a letter before the signature on a further new line. This convention requires a capital at the beginning of the formula and a comma at the end:

Yours sincerely, ⟨esp BrE⟩
Sincerely yours, ⟨esp AmE⟩

A new line (often indented) is also used to specify each major item in the structure of postal addresses, except that city and state appear as one line in AmE practice; again each line except the last may terminate with a comma, but a 'light punctuation' variant is also possible and is becoming more common:

26 Park Drive	53, Camden Gdns.,
Portsmouth, RI 02480	London, NW11 9HY,
USA	England.

Note [**a**] The symbol ✓ is a tick ⟨BrE⟩ or check ⟨AmE⟩ used to check that an item or point has been noted or accepted. It is also used in BrE to indicate that a point is correct (for example, by a teacher on a student's paper), whereas in AmE it normally indicates that the point is incorrect. In BrE, and sometimes in AmE, the symbol × is used to indicate an incorrect point (read as 'cross' in BrE and as the name of the letter *x* in AmE).
[**b**] Prefixing a name by a cross indicates a church dignitary. Suffixing a name by an obelisk (†) indicates that the person is dead.
[**c**] The word *number* is abbreviated as *No.* ⟨BrE⟩ and symbolized as # ⟨AmE⟩.

Bibliographical note

Accounts of AmE punctuation practice are given in Meyer (1983); Prentice-Hall (1974), pp 99–239; Summey (1949); University of Chicago Press (1982), pp 131–55; and US Government Printing Office (1973), pp 7–250; and of BrE practice in Carey (1957); Hart (1974); and Partridge (1977). AmE and BrE conventions are compared in a final chapter by John W. Clark in Partridge (1977). Frequency data for an AmE corpus is cited from Meyer (1983). Beaugrande (1983), pp 192–213, discusses the motives for punctuation.

Bibliography

Aarts, F. (1969) 'On the Use of the Progressive and Non-Progressive Present with Future Reference in Present-Day English', *English Studies* 50, 565–579

Aarts, F. (1971) 'On the Distribution of Noun-Phrase Types in English Clause Structure', *Lingua* 26, 252–264

Aarts, F. (1979) 'Time and Tense in English and Dutch: English Temporal *since* and its Dutch Equivalents', *English Studies* 60, 603–624

Aarts, F. and J. Aarts (1982) *English Syntactic Structures*, Oxford: Pergamon Press

Aarts, J. and J. P. Calbert (1979) *Metaphor and Non-Metaphor: The Semantics of Adjective-Noun Combinations*, Tübingen: Niemeyer

Abberton, E. (1977) 'Nominal Group Premodification Structures', in Bald and Ilson (1977), 29–72

Abercrombie, D. (1967) *Elements of General Phonetics*, Edinburgh: University Press

Abraham, W. (1978) (ed) *Valence, Semantic Case, and Grammatical Relations*, Amsterdam: Benjamins

Adamczewski, H. (1978) *BE + ING dans la Grammaire de l'Anglais Contemporain*, Lille: Atelier Reproduction des Thèses

Adams, V. (1973) *An Introduction to Modern English Word-Formation*, London: Longman

Aijmer, K. (1972) *Some Aspects of Psychological Predicates in English*, Stockholm Studies in English 24, Stockholm: Almqvist and Wiksell

Aissen, J. (1972) 'Where Do Relative Clauses Come From?', in *Syntax and Semantics*, ed J. P. Kimball, 187–198, New York: Seminar Press

Akimoto, M. (1983) *Idiomaticity*, Tokyo: Shinozaki Shorin

Akmajian, A. and F. Heny (1975) *An Introduction to the Principles of Transformational Syntax*, Cambridge, Mass.: M.I.T. Press

Alexander, D. and W. J. Kunz (1964) 'Some Classes of Verbs in English', Linguistic Research Project, Indiana University

Alexander, D. and P. H. Matthews (1964) 'Adjectives before *That*-Clauses in English', Linguistic Research Project, Indiana University

Algeo, J. (1973) *On Defining the Proper Name*, Gainesville: University of Florida Press

Algeo, J. (1975) 'The Acronym and its Congeners', in *The First LACUS Forum*, edd A. and V. Makkai, Columbia, S. C.: Hornbeam Press

Algeo, J. (1978) 'The Taxonomy of Word Making', *Word* 29, 122–131

Algeo, J. (1980) 'Where Do All the New Words Come From?', *American Speech* 55, 264–277

Allen, R. L. (1961) 'The Classification of English Substitute Words', *General Linguistics* 5, 7–20

Allen, R. L. (1966) *The Verb System of Present-Day American English*, The Hague: Mouton

Allerton, D. J. (1975) 'Deletion and Proform Reduction', *Journal of Linguistics* 11, 213–237

Allerton, D. J. (1978) 'The Notion of Givenness and its Relation to Presuppositions and to Theme', *Lingua* 44, 133–168

Allerton, D. J. (1979) *Essentials of Grammatical Theory*, London: Routledge

Allerton, D. J. (1980) 'Grammatical Subject as a Psycholinguistic Category', *Transactions of the Philological Society*, 62–80

Allerton, D. J. (1982) *Valency and the English Verb*, New York: Academic Press

Allerton, D. J. and A. Cruttenden (1974) 'English Sentence Adverbials: their Syntax and their Intonation in British English', *Lingua* 27, 1–29

Allerton, D. J. and A. Cruttenden (1976) 'The Intonation of Medial and Final Sentence Adverbials in British English', *Archivum Linguisticum* 7, 29–59

Allerton, D. J. and A. Cruttenden (1978) 'Syntactic, Illocutionary, Thematic and Attitudinal Factors in the Intonation of Adverbials', *Journal of Pragmatics* 2, 155–188
Allerton, D. J. and A. Cruttenden (1979) 'Three Reasons for Accenting a Definite Subject', *Journal of Linguistics* 15, 49–53
Altenberg, B. (1980) 'Binominal NP's in a Thematic Perspective: Genitive vs. *of*-Construction in 17th Century English', in Jacobson (1980b), 149–172
Altenberg, B. (1982) *The Genitive v. the* of-*Construction: A Study of Syntactic Variation in 17th Century English*, Lund Studies in English 62, Lund: Gleerup/Liber
Altenberg, B. (1984) 'Causal Linking in Spoken and Written English', *Studia Linguistica* 38, 20–69
Anderson, J. (1977) *On Case Grammar*, New York: Humanities Press
Anderson, S. R. (1976) 'Pro-Sentential Forms and Their Implications for English Sentence Structure', in McCawley (1976), 165–200
Andersson, E. (1985) *On Verb Complementation in Written English*, Lund Studies in English 71, Lund: Gleerup/Liber
André, E. (1974) *Studies in the Correspondence between English Intonation and the Noun Phrase in English Grammar*, Liège: Université
Ardery, G. (1979) 'The Development of Coordinations in Child Language', *Journal of Verbal Learning and Verbal Behavior* 18, 745–756
Arndt, H. and R. W. Janney (1981) 'An Interactional Linguistic Model of Everyday Conversational Behaviour', *Die Neueren Sprachen* 80, 435–454
Arnold, G. F. (1957) *Stress in English Words*, Amsterdam: North-Holland
Aronoff, M. (1976) *Word Formation in Generative Grammar*, Cambridge, Mass.: M.I.T. Press
Austin, F. (1980) '"A crescent-shaped jewel of an island", Appositive Nouns in Phrases Separated by *of*', *English Studies* 61, 357–366
Austin, J. L. (1962) *How to Do Things with Words*, Oxford: University Press
Auwera, J. Van der (1980) (ed) *The Semantics of Determiners*, London: Croom Helm
Bach, E. (1967) '*Have* and *Be* in English Syntax', *Language* 43, 462–485
Bach, E. (1968) 'Nouns and Noun Phrases', in *Universals in Linguistic Theory*, edd E. Bach and R. T. Harms, 91–122, New York: Holt, Rinehart and Winston
Bache, C. (1978) *The Order of Premodifying Adjectives in Present-Day English*, Odense: University Press
Bache, C. (1982) 'Aspect and Aktionsart: Towards a Semantic Distinction', *Journal of Linguistics* 18, 57–72
Bäcklund, I. (1984) *Conjunction-Headed Abbreviated Clauses in English*, Studia Anglistica Upsaliensia 50, Stockholm: Almqvist and Wiksell
Bäcklund, U. (1970) *The Collocation of Adverbs of Degree in English*, Uppsala English and American Theses 1
Bäcklund, U. (1981) *Restrictive Adjective–Noun Collocations in English*, Umeå Studies in the Humanities 23, Umeå: Acta Universitatis Umenis
Bailey, C.-J. N. and R. W. Shuy (1973) (edd) *New Ways of Analyzing Variation in English*, Washington, D.C.: Georgetown University Press
Bailey, R. W. and M. Görlach (1982) (edd) *English as a World Language*, Ann Arbor: University of Michigan Press
Bald, W.-D. (1972) *Studien zu den Kopulativen Verben des Englischen*, Munich: Hueber
Bald, W.-D. (1975) 'Englische Intonation in Forschung und Lehre: ein Überblick', *Forum Linguisticum: Contributions to Applied Linguistics*, 139–163, Frankfurt: Lang
Bald, W.-D. (1979) 'English Tag-Questions and Intonation', in *Anglistentag 1979*, ed K. Schuhmann, 263–291, Berlin: Technische Universität
Bald, W.-D. (1979/80) 'English Intonation and Politeness', *Studia Anglica Posnaniensia* 11, 93–101
Bald, W.-D. (1980) 'Some Functions of *yes* and *no* in Conversation', in Greenbaum, Leech, and Svartvik (1980), 178–191

Bald, W.-D. (forthcoming) *Which ONE* (mimeo)
Bald, W.-D. and R. Ilson (1977) (edd) *Studies in English Usage, The Resources of a Present-Day English Corpus for Linguistic Analysis*, Frankfurt: Lang
Bald, W.-D. and R. Quirk (1970) 'A Case Study of Multiple Meaning', *Essays and Studies* 23, 101–119
Ball, C. R. (1927/8) 'English or Latin Plurals for Anglicized Latin Nouns?', *American Speech* 3, 291–325
Ball, W. J. (1983) '*Might/May* as Well', *IATEFL Newsletter* 77, 14–16
Barnhart, C. L., S. Steinmetz, and R. K. Barnhart (1973) *The Barnhart Dictionary of New English Since 1963*, Bronxville: Barnhart
Barnhart, C. L., S. Steinmetz, and R. K. Barnhart (1980) *The Second Barnhart Dictionary of New English*, Bronxville: Barnhart
Baron, N. S. (1971) 'On Defining "Cognate Object"', *Glossa* 5, 71–98
Bartsch, R. (1976) *The Grammar of Adverbials. A Study in the Semantics and Syntax of Adverbial Constructions*, Amsterdam: North-Holland
Bauer, L. (1983) *English Word-Formation*, Cambridge: University Press
Bazell, C. E., J. C. Catford, M. A. K. Halliday, and R. H. Robins (1966) (edd) *In Memory of J. R. Firth*, London: Longman
Beaugrande, R. de (1983) *Text Production*, Norwood: Ablex
Beaugrande, R. de and W. Dressler (1981) *Introduction to Text Linguistics*, London: Longman
Behre, F. (1955) *Meditative-Polemic SHOULD in Modern English THAT-clauses*, Gothenburg Studies in English 4, Göteborg: Acta Universitatis Gothoburgensis
Behre, F. (1967) *Studies in Agatha Christie's Writings. The Behaviour of* 'A Good (Great) Deal, A Lot, Lots, Much, Plenty, Many, A Good (Great) Many', Gothenburg Studies in English 19, Göteborg: Acta Universitatis Gothoburgensis
Behre, F. (1973) *Get, Come and Go. Some Aspects of Situational Grammar*, Gothenburg Studies in English 28, Göteborg: Acta Universitatis Gothoburgensis
Bennett, D. C. (1975) *Spatial and Temporal Uses of English Prepositions. An Essay in Stratificational Semantics*, London: Longman
Bennett, P. A. (1980) 'English Passives: A Study in Syntactic Change and Relational Grammar', *Lingua* 51, 101–114
Bernstein, T. M. (1965) *The Careful Writer: A Modern Guide to English Usage*, New York: Atheneum
Bickerton, D. and C. Odo (1976) *Change and Variation in Hawaiian English* (Vol I, *General Phonology and Pidgin Syntax*), Final Report on NSF Grant GS-39748, University of Hawaii, mimeo
Bierwisch, M. and K. E. Heidolph (1970) (edd) *Progress in Linguistics*, The Hague: Mouton
Biese, Y. M. (1941) *Origin and Development of Conversions in English*, Helsinki: Academia Scientiarum Fennica
Bing, J. (1980) *Aspects of English Prosody*, Bloomington: Indiana University Linguistics Club
Black, M. (1977) 'An Investigation into Factors Influencing the Choice between the Syllabic and Contracted Forms of *Is*', in Bald and Ilson (1977), 171–182
Bladon, R. A. W. (1968) 'Selecting the *to*- or *-ing* Nominal after *like, love, hate, dislike* and *prefer*', *English Studies* 44, 203–214
Bloomfield, L. (1933) *Language*, New York: Holt, Rinehart and Winston
Bolinger, D. (1957) *Interrogative Structures of American English*, Birmingham, Alabama: University of Alabama Press
Bolinger, D. (1961a) 'Syntactic Blends and Other Matters', *Language* 37, 366–381
Bolinger, D. (1961b) *Generality, Gradience and the All-or-None*, The Hague: Mouton
Bolinger, D. (1961c) 'Contrastive Accent and Contrastive Stress', *Language* 37, 83–96
Bolinger, D. (1965) *Forms of English*, Cambridge, Mass.: Harvard University Press
Bolinger, D. (1967a) 'Adjectives in English: Attribution and Predication', *Lingua* 18, 1–34

Bolinger, D. (1967b) 'Adjective Comparison: A Semantic Scale,' *Journal of English Linguistics* 1, 2–10
Bolinger, D. (1967c) 'The Imperative in English', *To Honor Roman Jakobson* I, 335–363, The Hague: Mouton
Bolinger, D. (1969) 'Categories, Features, Attributes', *Brno Studies in English* 8, 37–41
Bolinger, D. (1971a) *The Phrasal Verb in English*, Cambridge, Mass.: Harvard University Press
Bolinger, D. (1971b) 'Semantic Overloading: A Restudy of the Verb *Remind*', *Language* 47, 522–547
Bolinger, D. (1972a) *Degree Words*, The Hague: Mouton
Bolinger, D. (1972b) 'Accent is Predictable (if you're a Mind-reader)', *Language* 48, 633–644
Bolinger, D. (1972c) (ed) *Intonation*, Harmondsworth: Penguin
Bolinger, D. (1975a) *Aspects of Language*, 2nd edn, New York: Harcourt Brace Jovanovich
Bolinger, D. (1975b) 'On the Passive in English', in *The First* LACUS *Forum*, edd A. Makkai and V. Becker, 57–80, Columbia, S. C.: Hornbeam Press
Bolinger, D. (1976) 'The in-group: *One* and its Compounds', *The Second* LACUS *Forum 1975*, ed P. A. Reich, 229–237, Columbia, S. C.: Hornbeam Press
Bolinger, D. (1977a) *Meaning and Form*, London: Longman
Bolinger, D. (1977b) 'Pronouns and Repeated Nouns', Bloomington: Indiana University Linguistics Club
Bolinger, D. (1977c) 'Neutrality, Norm and Bias', Bloomington: Indiana University Linguistics Club
Bolinger, D. (1978a) 'Yes-No Questions Are Not Alternative Questions', in *Questions*, ed H. Hiż, 87–105, Dordrecht: Reidel
Bolinger, D. (1978b) 'Asking More Than One Thing At A Time' in *Questions*, ed H. Hiż, 107–150, Dordrecht: Reidel
Bolinger, D. (1978c) 'Passive and Transitivity Again', *Forum Linguisticum* 3, 25–28
Bolinger, D. (1979) 'Pronouns in Discourse', *Syntax and Semantics* 12, 289–309
Bolinger, D. (1980a) *Language – The Loaded Weapon: The Use and Abuse of Language Today*, London: Longman
Bolinger, D. (1980b) 'Syntactic Diffusion and the Indefinite Article', Bloomington: Indiana University Linguistics Club
Borkin, A. (1980) 'On Some Conjuncts Signalling Dissonance in Written Expository English', *Studia Anglica Posnaniensia* 12, 47–59
Bouton, L. (1969) 'Identity Constraints on the *Do So* Rule', *Papers in Linguistics* 1, 231–247
Bowman, E. (1966) *The Minor and Fragmentary Sentences of a Corpus of Spoken English*, The Hague: Mouton
Brazil D., M. Coulthard, and C. Johns (1980) *Discourse Intonation and Language Teaching*, London: Longman
Breivik, L. E. (1979) 'A Note on the Use and Non-Use of "Existential *there*" in Present-Day English', *Nordlyd* 1, 4–29
Breivik, L. E. (1983) *Existential* There: *A Synchronic and Diachronic Study*, Studia Anglistica Norvegica 2, Bergen: Department of English
Brekle, H. E. (1970) *Generative Satzsemantik und transformationelle Syntax in System der englischen Nominalkomposition*, Munich: Fink
Bresnan, J. (1970) 'On Complementizers: Toward a Syntactic Theory of Complement Types', *Foundations of Language* 6, 297–321
Bresnan, J. (1973) 'Syntax of the Comparative Clause Construction, *Linguistic Inquiry* 4, 275–343
Bresnan, J. and J. Grimshaw (1978) 'The Syntax of Free Relatives in English, *Linguistic Inquiry* 9, 331–391
Bridgeman, L. I. (1965) 'Further Classes of Adjectives', Linguistics Research Project, Indiana University

Brown, E. K. and M. Millar (1980) 'Auxiliary Verbs in Edinburgh Speech', *Transactions of the Philological Society*, 81–133

Brown, E. K. and J. E. Miller (1982) *Syntax: Generative Grammar*, London: Hutchinson

Brown, G. (1977) *Listening to Spoken English*, London: Longman

Brown, G., K. L. Durrie, and J. Kenworthy (1980) *Questions of Intonation*, London: Croom Helm

Brown, R. W. (1927) *Materials for Word Study: a Manual of Roots, Prefixes, Suffixes, and Derivatives in the English Language*, New Haven: van Dyck

Brown, R. W. (1954) *Composition of Scientific Words*, Washington, D.C.: Brown

Bublitz, W. (1980) 'Höflichkeit im Englischen', *Linguistik und Didaktik* 41, 56–70

Bugarski, R. (1969) 'Symmetry and Asymmetry in Prepositional Systems', *Papers to Mark the Fortieth Anniversary of the Department of English, University of Belgrade*, 57–69

Burchfield, R. W. (1972–86) (ed) *A Supplement to the Oxford English Dictionary*, Oxford: University Press

Burgschmidt, E. and A. Cornell (1981) *Wortbildung*, Braunschweig: Burgschmidt

Burton-Roberts, N. C. (1976) 'On the Generic Indefinite Article', *Language* 52, 427–448

Burton-Roberts, N. C. (1977) 'Generic Sentences and Analyticity', *Studies in Language* 1, 155–196

Buysschaert, J. (1979) *An Examination of the Syntactic Status, Surface Position and Intonation of English Adverbials*, Mimeo, University of Ghent

Buysschaert, J. (1982) *Criteria for the Classification of English Adverbials*, Brussels: Koninklijke Academie

Buyssens, E. (1979) 'The Active Voice with Passive Meaning in Modern English', *English Studies* 60, 745–761

Campbell, R. N. and R. J. Wales (1969) 'Comparative Structures in English', *Journal of Linguistics* 5, 215–251

Carden, G. (1973) *English Quantifiers*, Tokyo: Taishukan

Carey, G. V. (1957) *Punctuation*, Cambridge: University Press

Carvell, H. T. and J. Svartvik (1969) *Computational Experiments in Grammatical Classification*, The Hague: Mouton

Cattell, R. (1973) 'Negative Transportation and Tag Questions', *Language* 49, 612–639

Chafe, W. (1970) *Meaning and the Structure of Language*, Chicago: University of Chicago Press

Chafe, W. (1976) 'Givenness, Contrastiveness, Definiteness, Subjects, Topics, and Point of View', in Li (1976), 25–55

Chapin, P. G. (1973) 'Quasi-Modals', *Journal of Linguistics* 9, 1–9

Charleston, B. M. (1960) *Studies on the Emotional and Affective Means of Expression in Modern English*, Bern: Francke

Chatman, S. (1965) *A Theory of Meter*, The Hague: Mouton

Cheshire, J. (1981) 'Variation in the Use of *ain't* in an Urban British English Dialect', *Language and Society* 10, 365–381

Chesnutt, M., C. Færch, T. Thrane, and G. D. Caie (1979) (edd) *Essays Presented to Knud Schibsbye*, Publications of the Department of English, University of Copenhagen 8, Copenhagen: Akademisk Forlag

Chomsky, N. (1957) *Syntactic Structures*, Mouton: The Hague

Chomsky, N. (1965) *Aspects of the Theory of Syntax*, Cambridge, Mass.: M.I.T. Press

Chomsky, N. (1972) 'Remarks on Nominalization', *Studies on Semantics in Generative Grammar*, 11–61, The Hague: Mouton

Chomsky, N. and M. Halle (1968) *The Sound Pattern of English*, New York: Harper and Row

Christophersen, P. (1939) *The Articles: A Study of their Theory and Use in English*, Copenhagen: Munksgaard

Christophersen, P. (1974) 'A Note on the Construction "Adjective + *A* + Noun"', *English Studies* 55: 538–541

Christophersen, P. (1979) 'Prepositions before Noun Clauses in Present-Day English', in Chesnutt et al (1979), 229–234
Close, R. A. (1976) *English Language Units: Unit 33, Determiners 3*, London: Longman for the British Council
Close, R. A. (1977) 'Some Observations on the Meaning and Function of Verb Phrases Having Future Reference', in Bald and Ilson (1977), 125–156
Close, R. A. (1980) '*Will* in *if*-clauses', in Greenbaum, Leech, and Svartvik (1980), 100–109
Coates, J. (1971) 'Denominal Adjectives: A Study in Syntactic Relationships between Modifier and Head', *Lingua* 27, 160–169
Coates, J. (1977) 'A Corpus Study of Modifiers in Sequence', in Bald and Ilson (1977), 9–27
Coates, J. (1980) 'On the Non-equivalence of MAY and CAN', *Lingua* 50, 209–220
Coates, J. (1983) *The Semantics of the Modal Auxiliaries*, London: Croom Helm
Coates, J. and G. Leech (1980) 'The Meanings of the Modals in Modern British and American English', *York Papers in Linguistics* 8, 23–33
Cole, P. and J. L. Morgan (1975) (edd) *Syntax and Semantics* 3: *Speech Acts*, New York: Academic Press
Cole, P. and J. M. Sadock (1977) (edd) *Syntax and Semantics* 8: *An Introduction to Grammatical Relations*, New York: Academic Press
Colen, A. (1984) *A Syntactic and Semantic Study of English Predicative Nominals*, Brussels: Koninklijke Academie
Collins, P. (1978) '"Dare" and "Need" in Australian English: a Study of Divided Usage', *English Studies* 59, 434–441
Comrie, B. (1976) *Aspect*, Cambridge: University Press
Comrie, B. (1981) *Language Universals and Language Typology*, Oxford: Blackwell
Conrad, B. (1979) '*One* and the Indefinite Article', in Chesnutt et al (1979), 264–286
Cook, W. A. (1969) *Introduction to Tagmemic Analysis*, New York: Holt, Rinehart and Winston
Couper-Kuhlen, E. (1979) *The Prepositional Passive in English*, Tübingen: Niemeyer
Copperud, R. H. (1980) *American Usage and Style: The Consensus*, New York: Van Nostrand Reinhold
Cowie, A. P. and R. Mackin (1975) *Oxford Dictionary of Current Idiomatic English* 1: *Verbs with Prepositions and Particles*, Oxford: University Press
Cresswell, T. J. (1975) *Usage in Dictionaries and Dictionaries of Usage*, Publication of the American Dialect Society 63–64, University, Alabama: University of Alabama Press
Crowell, T. L. (1959) '*Have Got*, A Pattern Preserver', *American Speech* 34, 280–286
Cruse, D. A. (1973) 'Some Thoughts on Agentivity', *Journal of Linguistics* 9, 11–23
Cruttenden, A. (1981) 'Falls and Rises: Meanings and Universals', *Journal of Linguistics* 17, 77–91
Crymes, R. (1968) *Some Systems of Substitution Correlations in Modern American English*, The Hague: Mouton
Crystal, D. (1966) 'Specification and English Tenses', *Journal of Linguistics* 2, 1–34
Crystal, D. (1969) *Prosodic Systems and Intonation in English*, Cambridge: University Press
Crystal, D. (1975) *The English Tone of Voice*, London: Arnold
Crystal, D. (1980) 'Neglected Grammatical Factors in Conversational English', in Greenbaum, Leech, and Svartvik (1980), 153–166
Crystal, D. and D. Davy (1969) *Investigating English Style*, London: Longman
Crystal, D. and D. Davy (1975) *Advanced Conversational English*, London: Longman
Crystal, D. and R. Quirk (1964) *Systems of Prosodic and Paralinguistic Features in English*, The Hague: Mouton
Curme, G. O. (1931) *Syntax*, *A Grammar of the English Language*, 3, Boston: Heath
Dahl, L. (1971) 'The *s*-Genitive with Non-Personal Nouns in Modern English Journalistic Style', *Neuphilologische Mitteilungen* 72, 140–172
Dahl, Ö. (1974) *Topic and Comment: Contextual Boundness and Focus*, Hamburg: Buske

Daneš, F. (1974) *Papers on Functional Sentence Perspective*, The Hague: Mouton
D'Angelo, F. (1975) *A Conceptual Theory of Rhetoric*, Cambridge, Mass.: Winthrop
Daniels, H. A. (1983) *Famous Last Words: The American Language Crisis Reconsidered*, Carbondale and Edwardsville: Southern Illinois University Press
Danielsson, B. (1948) *Studies on the Accentuation of Polysyllabic Latin, Greek, and Romance Loanwords in English*, Stockholm Studies in English 3, Stockholm: Almqvist and Wiksell
Davidson, A. (1980) 'Peculiar Passives', *Language* 56, 42–66
Davies, E. C. (1979) *On the Semantics of Syntax*, London: Croom Helm
Declerck, R. (1979) 'Tense and Modality in English *Before*-Clauses', *English Studies* 60, 720–744
Dierickx, J. (1970) 'Why are Plural Attributives Becoming More Frequent?', *Linguistique contemporaine, Hommage à E. Buyssens*, edd J. Dierickx and Y. Lebrun, 39–46, Bruxelles
Dietrich, T. G. and D. J. Napoli (1982) 'Comparative *rather*', *Journal of Linguistics* 18, 137–165
Dijk, T. A. van (1977) *Text and Context*, London: Longman
Dik, S. C. (1968) *Coordination: Its Implications for the Theory of General Linguistics*, Amsterdam: North-Holland
Dik, S. C. (1975) 'The Semantic Representation of Manner Adverbials', in *Linguistics in the Netherlands 1972–73*, ed A. Kraak, Amsterdam: Van Goreum
Dik, S. C. (1978) *Functional Grammar*, Amsterdam: North-Holland
Dixon, R. M. W. (1982a) *Where Have All the Adjectives Gone? and Other Essays in Semantics and Syntax*, Berlin: Mouton
Dixon, R. M. W. (1982b) 'The Grammar of English Phrasal Verbs', *Australian Journal of Linguistics* 2, 1–42
Dougherty, R. C. (1970–71) 'A Grammar of Coordinate Conjoined Structures', I, *Language* 46, 850–898; II, 47, 298–339
Downes, W. (1977) 'The Imperative and Pragmatics', *Journal of Linguistics* 13, 77–97
Downing, B. T. (1978) 'Some Universals of Relative Clause Structure', in Greenberg, Ferguson, and Moravcsik (1978), 375–418
Downing, P. (1977) 'On the Creation and Use of English Compound Nouns', *Language* 53, 810–842
Du Bois, J. (1974) 'Syntax in Mid-Sentence', *Berkeley Studies in Syntax and Semantics* 1, III: 1–25, Department of Linguistics and Institute of Human Learning, University of California, Berkeley
Dušková, L. (1965) 'On Some Disputed Points in the Use of Pronouns in Present-Day English', *Philologica Pragensia* 2–3, 163–170
Dušková, L. (1971a) 'On Some Functional and Stylistic Aspects of the Passive Voice in Present-Day English', *Philologica Pragensia* 14, 117–144
Dušková, L. (1971b) 'Some Quantitative Aspects of Continuous Forms in Present-Day English', *Prague Studies in English* 14, 7–39
Dušková, L. (1972) 'The Passive Voice in Czech and English', *Philologica Pragensia* 15, 93–118
Dušková, L. (1974) 'The Perfect Tenses in English vs. the Perfective Aspect in Czech', *Philologica Pragensia* 17, 67–91
Dušková, L. (1976) 'A Note on Intransitivity in the English Verb', *Philologica Pragensia* 19, 172–181
Dušková, L. (1979) 'A Note on the Object + Infinitive Construction in English', *Philologica Pragensia* 22, 73–84
Eagleson, R. D. (1972) 'Selecting the *to*- and *-ing* Nominal after *Prefer*', *English Studies* 53, 141–143
Edgren, E. (1971) *Temporal Clauses in English*, Uppsala: Almqvist and Wiksell
Edmondson, W. (1981) *Spoken Discourse*, London: Longman

Edmondson, W., J. House, G. Kasper, and J. McKeown (1977) *A Pedagogic Grammar of the English Verb*, Tübingen: Narr

Ek, J. A. van (1966) *Four Complementary Structures of Predication in Contemporary English*, Groningen: Wolters

Ellegård, A. (1978) *The Syntactic Structure of English Texts: A Computer-based Study of Four Kinds of Text in the Brown University Corpus*, Gothenburg Studies in English 43, Göteborg: Acta Universitatis Gothoburgensis

Elsness, J. (1982) '*That* v. Zero Connective in English Nominal Clauses', *ICAME News* 6, ed S. Johansson, 1–45, Bergen: Norwegian Computing Centre for the Humanities

Emonds, J. (1973) 'Parenthetical Clauses', in *You Take the High Node and I'll Take the Low Node*, 333–347, Chicago: University of Chicago Linguistic Society

Emonds, J. (1976) *A Transformational Approach to English Syntax*, New York: Academic Press

Emons, R. (1974) *Valenzen englischer Prädikatsverben*, Tübingen: Niemeyer

Enkvist, N. E. (1980) 'Marked Focus: Functions and Constraints', in Greenbaum, Leech, and Svartvik (1980), 134–152

Erdmann, P. (1976) *THERE-sentences in English*, Munich: Tuduv

Erdmann, P. (1978) '*It's I, it's me*: A Case for Syntax', *Studia Anglica Posnaniensia* 10, 67–80

Erdmann, P. (1981) 'Preposed *Ing*-Forms in English', *Folia Linguistica* 15, 363–386

Ferguson, C. A. and S. B. Heath (1981) (edd) *Language in the USA*, Cambridge: University Press

Fillmore, C. (1965) *Indirect Object Constructions in English*, The Hague: Mouton

Fillmore, C. (1968) 'The Case for Case', in *Universals in Linguistic Theory*, edd E. Bach and R. T. Harms, 1–90, New York: Holt, Rinehart, and Winston

Fillmore, C. (1969) 'Toward a Modern Theory of Case', in Reibel and Schane (1969), 361–375

Fillmore, C. (1977a) 'Topics in Lexical Semantics', in *Current Issues in Linguistic Theory*, ed R. W. Cole, 76–138, Bloomington, Indiana

Fillmore, C. (1977b) 'The Case for Case Reopened', in *Syntax and Semantics 8: Grammatical Relations*, edd P. Cole and J. Sadock, 59–82, New York: Academic Press

Fillmore, C. and D. T. Langendoen (1971) (edd) *Studies in Linguistic Semantics*, New York: Holt, Rinehart and Winston

Firbas, J. (1970) 'On the Interplay of Prosodic and Non-Prosodic Means of FSP', in *The Prague School of Linguistics and Language Teaching*, ed V. Fried, 77–94, Oxford: University Press

Firbas, J. (1971) 'The Concept of Communicative Dynamism in the Theory of Functional Sentence Perspective', *Sborník prací filozofické fakulty brněnskě univerzity*, A. 19, 135–144

Firbas, J. (1974) 'Some Aspects of the Czechoslovak Approach to Problems of Functional Sentence Perspective', in F. Daneš (1974), 11–37

Firbas, J. (1975) 'On the Thematic and the Non-Thematic Section of the Sentence', in Ringbom (1975), 317–334

Firbas, J. (1979) 'A Functional View of "Ordo Naturalis"', *Brno Studies in English* 13, 29–59

Firbas, J. (1980) 'Post-Intonation-Centre Prosodic Shade in the Modern English Clause', in Greenbaum, Leech, and Svartvik (1980), 125–133

Fishman, J. A., R. L. Cooper, and A. W. Conrad (1977) (edd) *The Spread of English: The Sociology of English as an Additional Language*, Rowley, Mass.: Newbury House

Fjelkestam-Nilsson, B. (1983) *ALSO and TOO: A Corpus-Based Study of their Frequency and Use in Modern English*, Stockholm Studies in English 58, Stockholm: Almqvist and Wiksell

Fodor, J. A. (1970) 'Three Reasons for not Deriving "Kill" from "Cause to Die"', *Linguistic Inquiry* 1, 429–438

Follett, W. (1966) *Modern American Usage*, ed and completed by J. Barzun, New York: Hill and Wang

Forsheden, O. (1983) 'Studies on Contraction in the London-Lund Corpus of Spoken English', ETOS Report 2, English Department, University of Lund
Fowler, H. W. (1965) *A Dictionary of Modern English Usage*, 2nd ed revised by E. Gowers, Oxford: University Press
Fraser, B. (1970) 'Some Remarks on the Action Nominalization in English', in *Readings in English Transformational Grammar*, edd R. A. Jacobs and P. S. Rosenbaum, Waltham, Mass.: Ginn
Fraser, B. (1976) *The Verb-Particle Combination in English*, New York: Academic Press
Freed, A. (1979) *The Semantics of English Aspectual Complementation*, Dordrecht: Reidel
Fries, P. H. (1970) *Tagmeme Sequences in the English Noun Phrase*, Dallas, Texas: Summer Institute of Linguistics
Fries, P. H. (1972) 'Problems in the Description of the English Noun Phrase', *Proceedings, 11th International Congress of Linguists*, ed L. Heilman, 222–229
Fries, P. H. (1977) 'English Predications of Comparison', *Studia Anglica Posnaniensia* 9, 95–103
Geis, M. L. (1973) '*If* and *Unless*', in *Issues in Linguistics: Papers in Honor of Henry and Renée Kahane*, ed B. B. Kachru, 231–253, Chicago: University of Illinois Press
Gimson, A. C. (1980) *An Introduction to the Pronunciation of English*, 3rd edn, London: Arnold
Givón, T. (1979) *Understanding Grammar*, New York: Academic Press
Givón, T. (1984) *Syntax: A Functional-Typological Introduction*, Vol I, Amsterdam: Benjamins
Gleason, H. A., Jr (1965) *Linguistics and English Grammar*, New York: Holt, Reinhart and Winston
Gleitman, L. R. (1965) 'Coordinating Conjunctions in English', *Language* 41, 260–293
Gnutzmann, C. (1974) 'Zur Graduierbarkeit von Adjektiven im Englischen', *Linguistische Berichte* 31, 1–12
Gnutzmann, C., R. Ilson and J. Webster (1973) 'Comparative Constructions in Contemporary English', *English Studies* 54, 417–438
Gorska, E. (1982) 'Formal and Functional Restrictions on the Productivity of Word-Formation Rules', *Folia Linguistica* 16, 149–162
Granger, S. (1983) *The* Be + *Past Participle Construction in Spoken English with Special Emphasis on the Passive*, Amsterdam: North-Holland
Greenbaum, S. (1969a) 'The Question of *But*', *Folia Linguistica* 3, 245–254
Greenbaum, S. (1969b) *Studies in English Adverbial Usage*, London: Longman
Greenbaum, S. (1970) *Verb-Intensifier Collocations in English: An Experimental Approach*, The Hague: Mouton
Greenbaum, S. (1973a) 'Informant Elicitation of Data on Syntactic Variation', *Lingua* 31, 201–212
Greenbaum, S. (1973b) 'Adverbial *-ing* Participle Constructions in English', *Anglia* 91, 1–10
Greenbaum, S. (1974) 'Problems in the Negation of Modals', *Moderna Språk* 68, 244–255
Greenbaum, S. (1976a) 'Current Usage and the Experimenter', *American Speech* 51, 161–175
Greenbaum, S. (1976b) 'Positional Norms of English Adverbs', *Studies in English Linguistics* 4, 1–16
Greenbaum, S. (1976c) 'Syntactic Frequency & Acceptability', *Lingua* 40, 99–113
Greenbaum, S. (1977a) 'Judgments of Syntactic Acceptability and Frequency', *Studia Linguistica* 31, 83–105
Greenbaum, S. (1977b) (ed) *Acceptability in Language*, The Hague: Mouton
Greenbaum, S. (1980) 'The Treatment of Clause and Sentence in *A Grammar of Contemporary English*', in Greenbaum, Leech, and Svartvik (1980), 17–29
Greenbaum, S. (1985) (ed) *The English Language Today*, Oxford: Pergamon Press
Greenbaum, S., G. Leech, and J. Svartvik (1980) (edd) *Studies in English Linguistics for Randolph Quirk*, London: Longman

Greenbaum, S. and C. F. Meyer (1982), 'Ellipsis and Coordination: Norms and Preferences', *Language and Communication* 2, 137–149

Greenberg, J. H., C. Ferguson, and E. Moravcsik (1978) (edd) *Universals of Human Language*, Stanford: University Press

Grice, H. P. (1975) 'Logic and Conversation', in Cole and Morgan (1975), 41–58

Grimes, J. E. (1975) *The Thread of Discourse*, The Hague: Mouton

Guimier, C. (1981) *Prepositions: An Analytical Bibliography*, Amsterdam Studies in the Theory and History of Linguistic Science 5, Amsterdam: Benjamins

Gunter, R. (1963) 'Elliptical Sentences in American English', *Lingua* 12, 137–150

Haegeman, L. (1980) '*Have to* and Progressive Aspect', *Journal of English Linguistics* 14, 1–5

Haegeman, L. (1981a) *The Use of* will *and the Expression of Futurity in Present-Day English*, Ph.D. diss., University of Ghent (mimeo)

Haegeman, L. (1981b) 'Modal *shall* and Speaker's Control', *Journal of English Linguistics* 15, 4–9

Haegeman, L. (1983) *The Semantics of* Will *in Present-Day British English: A Unified Account*, Brussels: Koninklijke Academie

Haegeman, L. (1984) 'Pragmatic Conditionals in English', *Folia Linguistica* 18, 485–502

Haegeman, L. (1985) 'Subordinating Conjunctions and X̄-Syntax', *Studia Germanica Gandensia*

Haegeman, L. (forthcoming a) 'Teaching the Expression of Future Time at Advanced Levels of TESOL' (mimeo)

Haegeman, L. (forthcoming b) 'The Present Subjunctive in Contemporary British English' (mimeo)

Haegeman, L. and H. Wekker (1984) 'The Syntax and Interpretation of Future Conditionals in English', *Journal of Linguistics* 20, 45–55

Haiman, J. (1974) 'Concessives, Conditionals, and Verbs of Volition', *Foundations of Language* 11, 341–359

Haiman, J. (1980) 'The Iconicity of Grammar', *Language* 56, 515–540

Hajičová, E., J. Panevová, P. Piťha, and P. Sgall (1980) 'Meaning, Sense and Valency', *Folia Linguistica* 14, 57–64

Hajičová, E. and P. Sgall (1982) 'Functional Sentence Perspective in the Slavonic Languages and in English', *Juznoslovenski filolog* 38, 19–34

Hajičová, E. and J. Vrbová (1981) 'On the Salience of the Elements of the Stock of Shared Knowledge', *Folia Linguistica* 15, 291–303

Hale, A. (1970) 'Conditions on English Comparative Clause Pairings', in *Readings in English Transformational Grammar*, edd R. Jacobs and P. S. Rosenbaum, 30–55, Waltham, Mass.: Ginn

Halliday, M. A. K. (1963) 'Class in Relation to the Axes of Chain and Choice in Language', *Linguistics* 2, 5–15

Halliday, M. A. K. (1966) 'Lexis as a Linguistic Level', in Bazell, Catford, Halliday, and Robins (1966), 148–162

Halliday, M. A. K. (1967) *Intonation and Grammar in British English*, The Hague: Mouton

Halliday, M. A. K. (1967–68) 'Notes on Transitivity and Theme in English', *Journal of Linguistics* 3, 37–81, 199–244; 4, 179–215

Halliday, M. A. K. (1969) 'Functional Diversity in Language, as seen from a Consideration of Modality and Mood in English', *Foundations of Language* 6, 322–361

Halliday, M. A. K. (1970) *A Course in Spoken English: Intonation*, Oxford: University Press

Halliday, M. A. K. (1978) *Language as Social Semiotic*, London: Arnold

Halliday, M. A. K. (1980) 'On Being Teaching', in Greenbaum, Leech, and Svartvik (1980), 61–64

Halliday, M. A. K. and R. Hasan (1976) *Cohesion in English*, London: Longman

Hansen, B., K. Hansen, A. Neubert, and M. Schenkte (1982) *Englische Lexikologie*, Leipzig: Enzyklopädie

Harries-Delisle, H. (1978) 'Coordination Reduction', in Greenberg, Ferguson, and Moravcsik (1978), 515–584

Hart, H. C. (1974) *Rules for Compositors and Readers*, Oxford: University Press

Hartvigson, H. H. (1969) *On the Intonation and Position of the So-called Sentence Modifiers in Present-day English*, Odense: University Press

Hartvigson, H. H. (1979) 'Adverbial Relative Clauses – and One More Type', in Chesnutt et al (1979), 235–246

Hartvigson, H. H. and L. K. Jakobsen (1974) *Inversion in Present-Day English*, Odense: University Press

Hatcher, A. G. (1956) 'Syntax and Sentence', *Word* 12, 234–250

Haugen, E. (1953) 'On Resolving the Close Apposition', *American Speech* 28, 165–170

Hawkins, J. A. (1978) *Definiteness and Indefiniteness*, London: Croom Helm

Heinämäki, O. (1975) '*Because* and *Since*', *Linguistica Silesiania* 1, 135–143

Heinämäki, O. (1978) 'Semantics of English Temporal Connectives', Bloomington: Indiana University Linguistics Club

Helke, M. (1979) *The Grammar of English Reflexives*, New York: Garland

Heny, F. W. (1973) 'Sentence and Predicate Modifiers in English', in Kimball (1973b), 217–245

Herbst, T. (1983) *Untersuchungen zur Valenz englischer Adjective und ihrer Nominalisierungen*, Tübingen: Narr

Herbst, T. (1984) 'Adjective Complementation: a Valency Approach to Making EFL Dictionaries', *Applied Linguistics* 5, 1–11

Hermerén, L. (1978) *On Modality in English*, Lund Studies in English 53, Lund: Gleerup/Liber

Hewson, J. (1972) *Article and Noun in English*, The Hague: Mouton

Hidalgo, C. A. (1967) 'English Verb Inflection', *Lingua* 18, 113–130

Hill, L. A. (1968) *Prepositions and Adverbial Particles: An Interim Classification Semantic, Structural, and Graded*, Oxford: University Press

Hindle, D. and I. Sag (1973) 'Some More on *anymore*', in *Analyzing Variation in Language*, edd R. W. Fasold and R. W. Shuy, Washington, D.C.: Georgetown University Press

Hirtle, W. H. (1970) '*-Ed* Adjectives like "verandahed" and "blue-eyed"', *Journal of Linguistics* 6, 19–36

Hirtle, W. H. (1982) *Number and Inner Space, A Study of Grammatical Number in English*, Québec: Presses de l'Université Laval

Hockett, C. F. (1955) 'Attribution and Apposition', *American Speech* 30, 99–102

Hockett, C. F. (1968) *The State of the Art*, The Hague: Mouton

Hoey, M. P. (1983) *On the Surface of Discourse*, London: Allen and Unwin

Hofland, K. and S. Johansson (1982) *Word Frequencies in British and American English*, London: Longman

Hofmann, T. R. (1979) 'On Modality in English and Other Languages', *Papers in Linguistics* 12, 1–31

Hooper, J. B. (1975) 'On Assertive Predicatives', in Kimball (1975), 91–124

Horn, G. M. (1978) 'Another Look at Complement Sentences', *Studia Anglica Posnaniensia* 10, 17–34

Horn, L. R. (1978a) 'Some Aspects of Negation', in Greenberg, Ferguson, and Moravcsik (1978), 127–210

Horn, L. R. (1978b) 'Remarks on Neg-Raising', in P. Cole (ed), *Syntax and Semantics* 9: *Pragmatics*, 129–220, New York: Academic Press

Huang, S. F. (1975) *A Study of Adverbs*, The Hague: Mouton

Huddleston, R. D. (1965) 'Rank and Depth', *Language* 41, 574–586

Huddleston, R. D. (1967) 'More on the English Comparative', *Journal of Linguistics* 3, 91–102

Huddleston, R. D. (1969) 'Predicate Complement Constructions in English', *Lingua* 23, 241–273

Huddleston, R. D. (1971) *The Sentence in Written English: A Syntactic Study Based on an Analysis of Scientific Texts*, Cambridge: University Press
Huddleston, R. D. (1974) 'Further Remarks on the Analysis of Auxiliaries as Main Verbs', *Foundations of Language* 11, 215–229
Huddleston, R. D. (1976a) 'Some Theoretical Issues in the Description of the English Verb', *Lingua* 40, 331–383
Huddleston, R. D. (1976b) *An Introduction to English Transformational Syntax*, London: Longman
Huddleston, R. D. (1980) 'Criteria for Auxiliaries and Modals', in Greenbaum, Leech, and Svartvik (1980), 65–78
Huddleston, R. D. (1984) *Introduction to the Grammar of English*, Cambridge: University Press
Hudson, R. A. (1970) 'On Clauses Containing Conjoined and Plural Noun Phrases in English', *Lingua* 24, 205–253
Hudson, R. A. (1971) *English Complex Sentences: An Introduction to Systemic Grammar*, Amsterdam: North-Holland
Hudson, R. A. (1975a) 'Problems in the Analysis of *Ed*-adjectives', *Journal of Linguistics* 11, 69–72
Hudson, R. A. (1975b) 'The Meaning of Questions', *Language* 51, 1–31
Hudson, R. A. (1976a) *Arguments for a Non-Transformational Grammar*, Chicago: University Press
Hudson, R. A. (1976b) 'Conjunction Reduction, Gapping and Right-Node Raising', *Language* 52, 555–561
Hughes, A. and P. Trudgill (1979) *English Accents and Dialects: An Introduction to Social and Regional Varieties of British English*, Baltimore: University Park Press
Ikegami, Y. (1973) 'A Set of Basic Patterns for the Semantic Structure of the Verb', *Linguistics* 117, 15–58
Isitt, D. (1983) Crazic, menty *and* idiotal: *An Inquiry into the Use of Suffixes* -al, -ic, -ly *and* -y *in Modern English*, Gothenburg Studies in English 52, Göteborg: Acta Universitatis Gothoburgensis
Jackendoff, R. (1968) 'Quantifiers in English', *Foundations of Language* 4, 422–442
Jackendoff, R. (1969) 'An Interpretive Theory of Negation', *Foundations of Language* 5, 218–241
Jackendoff, R. (1971) 'Gapping and Related Rules', *Linguistic Inquiry* 2, 21–35
Jackendoff, R. (1975) 'Morphological and Semantic Regularities in the Lexicon', *Language* 51, 639–671
Jacobson, S. (1964) *Adverbial Positions in English*, Stockholm: Studentbok
Jacobson, S. (1975) *Factors Influencing the Placement of English Adverbs in Relation to Auxiliaries. A Study in Variation*, Stockholm: Almqvist and Wiksell
Jacobson, S. (1978) *On the Use, Meaning, and Syntax of English Preverbal Adverbs*, Stockholm: Almqvist and Wiksell
Jacobson, S. (1980a) 'Some English Verbs and the Contrast Incompletion/Completion', in Greenbaum, Leech, and Svartvik (1980), 50–60
Jacobson, S. (1980b) (ed) *Papers from the Scandinavian Symposium on Syntactic Variation*, Stockholm Studies in English 52, Stockholm: Almqvist and Wiksell
Jacobson, S. (1981) *Preverbal Adverbs and Auxiliaries*, Stockholm: Almqvist and Wiksell
Jacobson, S. (1983) 'Modality Nouns and the Choice between *to* + infinitive and *of* + *ing*', *Studia Anglica Posnaniensia* 15, 61–71
Jacobsson, B. (1961) 'An Unexpected Usage: *ahead, alive*, and the like before Nouns', *Moderna Språk* 55, 240–246
Jacobsson, B. (1962) 'A Note on the Use of *Will* in Questions in the First Person', *Moderna Språk* 56, 17–21
Jacobsson, B. (1963) 'On the Use of *that* in Non-Restrictive Relative Clauses', *Moderna Språk* 57, 406–416

Jacobsson, B. (1965) 'Professor Joos and the English Verb', *Moderna Språk* 59, 305–316

Jacobsson, B. (1968a) 'Simple Personal Pronouns and Compound Pronouns in *-Self/-Selves*', *Moderna Språk* 62, 24–37

Jacobsson, B. (1968b) 'A Note on Common-Number *they/them/their* and *who*', *Studia Neophilologica* 40, 141–145

Jacobsson, B. (1970) 'English Pronouns and Feature Analysis', *Moderna Språk* 64, 346–359

Jacobsson, B. (1971) 'A Note on the Classification of Relative Nominal Clauses in English', *Moderna Språk* 65, 312–322

Jacobsson, B. (1974) 'The Auxiliary *Need*', *English Studies* 55, 56–63

Jacobsson, B. (1975) 'How Dead is the English Subjunctive?', *Moderna Språk* 69, 218–231

Jacobsson, B. (1977a) 'Adverbs, Prepositions, and Conjunctions in English: A Study in Gradience', *Studia Linguistica* 31, 38–64

Jacobsson, B. (1977b) 'Modality and the Modals of Necessity *Must* and *Have to*', *English Studies* 60, 296–312

Jacobsson, B. (1980) 'On the Syntax and Semantics of the Modal Auxiliary *Had Better*', *Studia Neophilologica* 52, 47–53

Jahr Sørheim, M.-C. (1980) *The* s-*Genitive in Present-Day English*, University of Oslo, Department of English

Jain, M. P. (1978) 'Longman Dictionary of Contemporary English', *Indian Journal of Applied Linguistics* 4, 86–104

Jenkins, L. (1975) *The English Existential*, Tübingen: Niemeyer

Jespersen, O. (1909–49) *A Modern English Grammar on Historical Principles* I–VII, Copenhagen: Munksgaard

Jespersen, O. (1917) *Negation in English and Other Languages*, Copenhagen; reprinted in *Selected Writings of Otto Jespersen*, London: Allen and Unwin

Jespersen, O. (1933) *Essentials of English Grammar*, London: Allen and Unwin

Johannesson, N.-L. (1976) *The English Modal Auxiliaries: A Stratificational Account*, Stockholm Studies in English 36, Stockholm: Almqvist and Wiksell

Johansson, S. (1979) 'American and British English Grammar: An Elicitation Experiment', *English Studies* 60, 195–215

Johansson, S. (1980) *Plural Attributive Nouns in Present-Day English*, Lund Studies in English 59, Lund: Gleerup/Liber

Joos, M. (1962) *The Five Clocks*, The Hague: Mouton

Joos, M. (1964) *The English Verb*, Madison: University of Wisconsin Press

Jørgensen, E. (1979) '"Aren't I?" and Alternative Patterns in Modern English', *English Studies* 60, 35–41

Jørgensen, E. (1980) 'Some Notes on Negated Comparatives (+*than*)', *English Studies* 61, 543–551

Juul, A. (1975) *On Concord of Number in Modern English*, Copenhagen: Nova

Kachru, B. B. (1982) (ed) *The Other Tongue: English Across Cultures*, Urbana, Ill.: University of Illinois Press

Kalogjera, D. (1967) 'Register Variation with Regard to the Use of the Auxiliary *Shall*', *Studia Romanica et Anglistica* 23, 75–80

Kałuża, H. (1981) *The Use of Articles in Contemporary English*, Heidelberg: Groos

Kanekiyo, T. (1965) 'Notes on Gender in English', *Philologica Pragensia* 8, 234–237

Karlsen, R. (1959) *Studies in the Connection of Clauses in Current English: Zero, Ellipsis, and Explicit Forms*, Bergen: Eides

Karlsen, R. (1965) *On 'Identifying', 'Classifying' and 'Specifying' Clauses in Current English*, Bergen/Oslo: Norwegian Universities Press

Karttunen, L. (1974) '*Until*', in *Papers from the Tenth Regional Meeting of the Chicago Linguistic Society*, 284–297, University of Chicago

Kastovsky, D. (1982a) *Wortbildung und Semantik*, Düsseldorf: Bagel

Kastovsky, D. (1982b) 'Word-Formation: A Functional View', *Folia Linguistica* 16, 181–198

Keenan, E. L. (1975) (ed) *Formal Semantics of Natural Language*, Cambridge: University Press

Keenan, E. L. (1976) 'Towards a Universal Definition of "Subject"', in Li (1976), 303–333

Kempson, R. M. (1977) *Semantic Theory*, Cambridge: University Press

Kempson, R. M. and R. Quirk (1971) 'Controlled Activation of Latent Contrast', *Language* 47, 548–572

Kennedy, A. G. (1920) *The Modern English Verb-Adverb Combination*, Stanford: University Publications, University Series, Language and Literature 1:1

Kimball, J. P. (1973a) 'The Grammar of Existence', *Papers from the Ninth Regional Meeting of the Chicago Linguistic Society*, 262–270, University of Chicago

Kimball, J. P. (1973b) (ed) *Syntax and Semantics* 2, New York: Seminar Press

Kimball, J. P. (1975) (ed) *Syntax and Semantics* 4, New York: Seminar Press

Kingdon, R. (1958) *Groundwork of English Intonation*, London: Longman

Kiparsky, P. and Kiparsky, C. (1970) 'Fact', in Bierwisch and Heidolph (1970), 143–173

Kjellmer, G. (1975a) 'Are Relative Infinitives Modal?', *Studia Neophilologica* 47, 323–332

Kjellmer, G. (1975b) '"The weather was fine, if not glorious": On the Ambiguity of Concessive *if not*', *English Studies* 56, 140–146

Kjellmer, G. (1980) '"There is no hiding you in the house": On a Modal Use of the English Gerund', *English Studies* 61, 47–60

Kjellmer, G. (1982) '*Each Other* and *One Another*: On the Use of the English Reciprocal Pronouns', *English Studies* 63, 231–254

Kjellmer, G. (1984) 'Why *great*: *greatly* but not *big*: **bigly*? On the Formation of English Adverbs in *-ly*', *Studia Linguistica* 38, 1–19

Klima, E. S. (1964) 'Negation in English', in *The Structure of Language: Readings in the Philosophy of Language*, edd J. A. Fodor and J. J. Katz, 246–323, Englewood Cliffs, N.J.: Prentice-Hall

Kolář, S. (1975) 'Aspects of Polyfunctionality in English Sentence Adverbs', *Philologica Pragensia* 18, 222–227

König, E. and P. Lutzeier (1973) 'Bedeutung und Verwendung der Progressivform im heutigen Englisch', *Lingua* 32, 277–308

Kontra, M. (1980) 'On English Negative Interrogatives', in *The Seventh LACUS Forum 1980*, edd J. E. Copeland and P. W. Davis, 412–431, Columbia, S.C.: Hornbeam Press

Koutsoudas, A. (1971) 'Gapping, Conjunction Reduction, and Coordinate Deletion', *Foundations of Language* 7, 337–386

Koziol, H. (1972) *Handbuch der Englischen Wortbildungslehre*, 2nd edn, Heidelberg: Winter

Krámský, J. (1972) *The Article and the Concept of Indefiniteness in Language*, The Hague: Mouton

Kruisinga, E. (1931–2) *A Handbook of Present-Day English*, Groningen: Noordhoff

Kuno, S. (1972) 'Functional Sentence Perspective', *Linguistic Inquiry* 3, 269–320

Kuno, S. (1976a) 'Gapping: a Functional Analysis', *Linguistic Inquiry* 8, 300–318

Kuno, S. (1976b) 'Subject, Theme, and the Speaker's Empathy – A Reexamination of Relativization Phenomena', in Li (1976), 417–444

Kypriotaki, L. (1970) 'Aphaeresis in Rapid Speech', *American Speech* 45, 69–77

Labov, W. (1972) *Sociolinguistic Patterns*, Philadelphia: University of Pennsylvania Press

Lakoff, G. (1970a) 'A Note on Ambiguity and Vagueness', *Linguistic Inquiry* 1, 357–359

Lakoff, G. (1970b) 'Tense and its Relations to Participants', *Language* 46, 838–849

Lakoff, G. (1974) 'Syntactic Amalgams', *Papers from the Tenth Regional Meeting of the Chicago Linguistic Society*, 321–344, University of Chicago

Lakoff, G. (1975) 'Hedges: A Study in Meaning Criteria and the Logic of Fuzzy Concepts', in *Contemporary Research in Philosophical Logic and Linguistic Semantics*, edd D. Hockney et al, 211–271, Dordrecht: Reidel

Lakoff, G. (1977) 'Linguistic Gestalts', *Papers from the Thirteenth Regional Meeting of the Chicago Linguistic Society*, 236–281, University of Chicago

Lakoff, G. (1982) 'Categories and Cognitive Models', Trier: Linguistics Agency University of Trier, Series A Paper 96

Lakoff, G. and S. Peters (1969) 'Phrasal Conjunction and Symmetric Predicates', in Reibel and Schane (1969), 113–142

Lakoff, R. (1969) 'A Syntactic Argument for Negative Transportation', *Papers from the Fifth Regional Meeting of the Chicago Linguistic Society*, 140–147, University of Chicago

Lakoff, R. (1971) 'If's, And's, and But's about Conjunction', in Fillmore and Langendoen (1971), 114–149

Lakoff, R. (1972) 'The Pragmatics of Modality', *Papers from the Eighth Regional Meeting of the Chicago Linguistic Society*, 247–258, University of Chicago

Lakoff, R. (1974) 'Remarks on *this* and *that*', *Berkeley Studies in Syntax and Semantics* 1, XVII: 1–12, Department of Linguistics and Institute of Human Learning, University of California, Berkeley

Langacker, R. W. (1969) 'On Pronominalization and the Chain of Command', in Reibel and Schane (1969), 160–186

Langacker, R. W. (1978), 'The Form and Meaning of the English Auxiliary', *Language* 54, 853–882

Lee, D. A. (1978) 'Modal "Auxiliaries" in Generative Grammar – Some Pedagogic Implications', in Nehls (1978), 33–62

Lee, D. W. (1952) 'Close Apposition: An Unresolved Pattern', *American Speech* 27, 268–275

Lee, W. R. (1969) 'A Point about *in* and *into*', *Brno Studies in English* 8, 121–122

Leech, G. (1963) 'Disjunctive Grammar in British Television Advertising', *Studia Neophilologica* 35, 256–264

Leech, G. (1969a) *Towards a Semantic Description of English*, London: Longman

Leech, G. (1969b) *A Linguistic Guide to English Poetry*, London: Longman

Leech, G. (1971) *Meaning and the English Verb*, London: Longman

Leech, G. (1980) *Explorations in Semantics and Pragmatics*, Amsterdam: Benjamins

Leech, G. (1981a) (2nd edn) *Semantics*, Harmondsworth: Penguin

Leech, G. (1981b) 'Pragmatics and Conversational Rhetoric', in *Possibilities and Limitations of Pragmatics*, edd H. Parret, M. Sbisà, and J. Verschueren, 413–441, Amsterdam: Benjamins

Leech, G. (1983) *Principles of Pragmatics*, London: Longman

Leech, G. and J. Coates (1980) 'Semantic Indeterminacy and the Modals', in Greenbaum, Leech, and Svartvik (1980), 79–90

Leech, G. and M. Short (1981) *Style in Fiction*, London: Longman

Lees, R. B. (1960a) *The Grammar of English Nominalizations*, Indiana University Center in Anthropology, Folklore, and Linguistics 12, Bloomington: Indiana University

Lees, R. B. (1960b) 'A Multiply Ambiguous Adjectival Construction in English', *Language* 36, 207–221

Lees, R. B. (1961) 'Grammatical Analysis of the English Comparative Construction', *Word* 17, 171–185

Lees, R. B. and E. S. Klima (1963), 'Rules for English Pronominalization', *Language* 39, 17–28

Lehmann, W. (1978) 'The Great Underlying Ground-Plans', in *Syntactic Typology*, ed W. Lehmann, 3–56, Austin, Texas: University of Texas Press

Levi, J. (1973) 'Where Do All those Other Adjectives Come From?', *Papers from the Ninth Regional Meeting of the Chicago Linguistic Society*, 332–345, University of Chicago

Levi, J. (1978) *The Syntax and Semantics of Complex Nominals*, New York: Academic Press

Levin, S. (1979) 'The Imperative in Relation to Other Verbal Forms or Functions', *The Sixth LACUS Forum 1979*, 162–169, Columbia, S.C.: Hornbeam Press

Lewis, D. (1975) 'Adverbs of Quantification', in Keenan (1975), 3–15

Li, C. N. (1975) (ed) *Word Order and Word Order Change*, Austin, Texas: Texas University Press
Li, C. N. (1976) (ed) *Subject and Topic*, New York: Academic Press
Liberman, M. Y. (1978) *The Intonational System of English*, Bloomington: Indiana University Linguistics Club
Lindelöf, U. (1938) *English Verb-Adverb Groups Converted into Nouns*, Helsingfors: Societas Scientiarum Fennica
Lindholm, J. (1969) 'Negative Raising and Sentence Pronominalization', in *Papers from the Fifth Regional Meeting of the Chicago Linguistic Society*, 148–158, University of Chicago
Lindkvist, K.-G. (1950) *Studies on the Local Sense of the Prepositions IN, AT, ON, and TO in Modern English*, Lund Studies in English 20, Lund: Gleerup/Liber
Lindkvist, K.-G. (1972) *The Local Sense of the Prepositions OVER, ABOVE, and ACROSS. Studies in Present-Day English*, Stockholm Studies in English 25, Stockholm: Almqvist and Wiksell
Lindkvist, K.-G. (1976) *A Comprehensive Study of Conceptions of Locality in which English Prepositions Occur*, Stockholm Studies in English 35, Stockholm: Almqvist and Wiksell
Lindkvist, K.-G. (1978) *AT versus ON, IN, BY: On the Early History of Spatial AT and Certain Primary Ideas Distinguishing AT from ON, IN, BY*, Stockholm Studies in English 49, Stockholm: Almqvist and Wiksell
Lipka, L. (1972) *Semantic Structure and Word-Formation*, Munich: Fink
Lipka, L. and H. Günter (1981) (edd) *Wortbildung*, Darmstadt: Wissenschaftliche Buchgesellschaft
Live, A. H. (1965) 'The Discontinuous Verb in English', *Word* 21, 428–451
Ljung, M. (1970). *English Denominal Adjectives, A Generative Study of the Semantics of a Group of High-Frequency Denominal Adjectives in English*, Gothenburg Studies in English 21, Göteborg: Acta Universitatis Gothoburgensis
Ljung, M. (1974) *A Frequency Dictionary of English Morphemes*, Stockholm: AWE/Gebers
Ljung, M. (1976) '*-Ed* Adjectives Revisited', *Journal of Linguistics* 12, 159–168
Ljung, M. (1980) *Reflections on the English Progressive*, Gothenburg Studies in English 46, Göteborg: Acta Universitatis Gothoburgensis
Longacre, R. E. (1976) *An Anatomy of Speech Notions*, Lisser: de Ridder
Longman Dictionary of Contemporary English (1978), London: Longman
Longman Dictionary of English Idioms (1979), London: Longman
Luelsdorff, P. A. and N. R. Norrick (1979) 'On *if* and *whether* Complementation', *Linguistische Berichte* 62, 25–47
Lyons, J. (1966) 'Towards a "Notional" Theory of "Parts of Speech"', *Journal of Linguistics* 2, 209–236
Lyons, J. (1977) *Semantics*, 2 vols, Cambridge: University Press
Macháček, J. (1965) *Complementation of the English Verb by the Accusative-with-Infinitive and the Content Clause*, Acta Universitatis Palackianae Olomucensis, Facultas Philosophica 11
Macháček, J. (1969) 'Historical Aspect of the Accusative with Infinitive and the Content Clause in English', *Brno Studies in English* 8, 123–132
Makkai, A. (1972) *Idiom Structure in English*, The Hague: Mouton
Malkiel, Y. (1959) 'Studies in Irreversible Binomials', *Lingua* 8, 113–160
Malone, J. H. (1967) 'A Transformational Re-examination of English Questions', *Language* 43, 686–702
Mańczac, E. (1979) 'Stative Verbs in Imperative Sentences', *Zeszty Naukowe Uniwersytetu Jagiellońskiego* 63, 43–47
Marchand, H. (1966) 'On Attributive and Predicative Derived Adjectives and Some Problems Related to the Distinction', *Anglia* 84, 131–149
Marchand, H. (1969) *The Categories and Types of Present-Day English Word-Formation*, 2nd edn, Munich: Beck

Martin, J. E. and T. E. Ferb (1973) 'Contextual Factors in Preferred Adjective Ordering', *Lingua* 32, 75–81
Mathesius, V. (1929) 'Zur Satzperspektive im Modernen Englisch', *Archiv für das Studium der Neueren Sprachen*, 155, 200–210
Mathesius, V. (1975) *A Functional Analysis of Present-Day English on a General Linguistic Basis*, ed J. Vachek, Prague: Academia
Matthews, P. H. (1974) *Morphology*, Cambridge: University Press
Matthews, P. H. (1980) 'Complex Intransitive Constructions', in Greenbaum, Leech, and Svartvik (1980), 41–49
Matthews, P. H. (1981) *Syntax*, Cambridge: University Press
Matthews-Bresky, R. J. H. (1975) 'Some Remarks on the Teaching of English Modals', *Zielsprache Englisch* 1, 20–24
McCawley, J. D. (1976) (ed) *Syntax and Semantics* 7: *Notes from the Linguistic Underground*, New York: Academic Press
McCoard, R. W. (1978) *The English Perfect*, Amsterdam: North-Holland
McDavid, R. I., Jr (1963) (ed) *The American Language by H. L. Mencken*, New York: Knopf
McMillan, J. B. (1980) 'Infixing and Interposing in English', *American Speech* 55, 163–183
Meier, H. H. (1975) 'The Placing of English Idioms in Lexis and Grammar', *English Studies* 56, 231–244
Melchers, G. (1980) 'Modal Auxiliaries in Regional Dialects', in Jacobson (1980b), 113–123
Menz, H.-P. (1981) 'Probleme der Grammatiktheorie: Adverbiale und Adverben', *Hamburger Phonetische Beiträge* 35, 75–82
Meyer, C. F. (1979) 'The Greater Acceptability of Certain English Elliptical Coordinations', *Studia Linguistica* 33, 130–137
Meyer, C. F. (1983) *A Theoretical and Descriptive Study of American Punctuation*, Unpublished PhD thesis, University of Wisconsin-Milwaukee
Meys, W. J. (1975) *Compound Adjectives in English and the Ideal Speaker-Listener*, Amsterdam: North-Holland
Michaels, L. and C. Ricks (1980) (edd) *The State of the Language*, Berkeley: University of California Press
Michiels, A. (1975) 'Relative Pronouns in Time, Place and Manner Adjuncts', *English Studies* 56, 504–512
Michiels, A. (1977) 'Relative Pronouns in Time Adjuncts', *English Studies* 58, 26–37
Michiels, A. (1978) 'A Note on the Relation between Agent and Stativity', *Neophilologus* 62, 172–177
Mihailovič, L. (1967) 'Passive and Pseudo-Passive Verbal Groups in English', *English Studies* 48, 316–326
Millar, M. and E. K. Brown (1979) 'Tags in Edinburgh Speech', *Linguistische Berichte* 60, 24–45
Milsark, G. L. (1979) *Existential Sentences in English*, New York: Garland
Mitchell, T. F. (1958) 'Syntagmatic Relations in Linguistic Analysis', *Transactions of the Philological Society*, 101–118
Mittins, W. H., M. Salu, M. Edminson, and S. Coyne (1970) *Attitudes to English Usage*, Oxford: University Press
Mittwoch, A. (1971) 'Optional and Obligatory Verbal Complements in English', unpublished University of London PhD diss.
Mittwoch, A. (1974) 'Is there an Underlying Negative Element in Comparative Clauses?', *Linguistics* 12, 39–45
Mittwoch, A. (1979) 'Final Parentheticals with English Questions – their Illocutionary Function and Grammar', *Journal of Pragmatics* 3, 401–412
Mittwoch, A. (1980) 'The Grammar of Duration', *Studies in Language* 4, 201–227
Mohan, B. A. (1977) 'Acceptability Testing and Fuzzy Grammar', in Greenbaum (1977b), 133–148

Morgan, J. L. (1973) 'Sentence Fragments and the Notion "Sentence"', in *Issues in Linguistics: Papers in Honor of Henry and Renée Kahane*, edd B. B. Kachru et al, 719–751, Urbana, Ill.: University of Illinois Press

Morreall, J. (1980) 'Austinian Ifs and Conditional Telling', *The Sixth LACUS Forum 1979*, edd W. C. Cormack and H. J. Izzo, 475–482, Columbia, S.C.: Hornbeam Press

Mourelatos, A. P. D. (1978) 'Events, Processes, States', *Linguistics and Philosophy* 2, 5–34

Mutt, O. (1967) 'Some Recent Developments in the Use of Nouns as Premodifiers in English', *Zeitschrift für Anglistik und Amerikanistik* 15, 401–408

Nakajima, H. (1982) 'The V4 System and Bounding Category', *Linguistic Analysis* 9, 341–378

Nash, W. (1980) *Designs in Prose*, London: Longman

Nehls, D. (1975) 'The System of Tense and Aspect in English', *IRAL* 13, 275–292

Nehls, D. (1978) (ed) *Studies in Descriptive English Grammar*, Heidelberg: Groos

Nehls, D. (1980) 'Zur Strukturierung des Englischen Verbalsystems', *Die Neueren Sprachen* 28, 43–59

Newmeyer, F. J. (1980) *Linguistic Theory in America*, New York: Academic Press

Ney, J. (1981) *Semantic Structures for the Syntax of Complements and Auxiliaries in English*, The Hague: Mouton

Nickel, G. (1968) 'Complex Verbal Structures in English', *IRAL* 6, 1–21

Nilsen, D. L. F. (1972) *English Adverbials*, The Hague: Mouton

Norrick, N. R. (1979), *Understood Complement Objects*, Linguistic Agency University of Trier, Series A, 61

Nosek, J. (1965) 'Overlapping Predications in Modern English', *Acta Universitatis Carolinae*, Philologica 3, *Prague Studies in English* 11, 33–51

O'Connor, J. D. and G. F. Arnold (1973) *Intonation of Colloquial English*, 2nd edn, London: Longman

Olofsson, A. (1981) *Relative Junctions in Written American English*, Gothenburg Studies in English 50, Göteborg: Acta Universitatis Gothoburgensis

Olsson, Y. (1961) *On the Syntax of the English Verb*, Gothenburg Studies in English 12, Göteborg: Acta Universitatis Gothoburgensis

Palmer, F. R. (1974) *The English Verb*. London: Longman

Palmer, F. R. (1977) 'Modals and Actuality', *Journal of Linguistics* 13, 1–23

Palmer, F. R. (1979) *Modality and the English Modals*, London: Longman

Palmer, F. R. (1980) '*Can, Will*, and Actuality', in Greenbaum, Leech, and Svartvik (1980), 91–99

Panagl, O. (1982) 'Produktivität in der Wortbildung von Corpussprachen: Möglichkeiten und Grenzen der Heuristik', *Folia Linguistica* 16, 225–239

Partridge, E. (1973) *Usage and Abusage: A Guide to Good English*, rev. edn, Harmondsworth: Penguin

Partridge, E. (1977) *You Have a Point There*, reprint of 1953 edn, London: Routledge

Pennanen, E. V. (1966) *Contributions to the Study of Back-Formation in English*, Acta Academiae Socialis 4: Tampere

Pennanen, E. V. (1972) 'Current Views of Word-Formation', *Neuphilologische Mitteilungen* 73, 292–308

Pennanen, E. V. (1980) 'On the Function and Behaviour of Stress in English Noun Compounds', *English Studies* 61, 252–263

Pennanen, E. V. (1982) 'Remarks on Syntagma and Word-Formation', *Folia Linguistica* 16, 241–261

Perlmutter, D. M. (1970) *On the Article in English*, The Hague: Mouton

Peters, F. J. J. (1980) 'Phrasing Rules for Complex Number Sequences in English', *Studia Linguistica* 34, 124–134

Pike, K. L. (1945) *Intonation of American English*, Ann Arbor: University of Michigan Press

Pike, K. and E. Pike (1977) *Grammatical Analysis*, SIL Publications in Linguistics

and Related Fields No. 53, Dallas, Texas: The University of Texas at Arlington
Pittman, G. A. (1970) 'Advanced Vocabulary Development: the *Bring-Come* Nexus', *English Language Teaching* 24, 147–154
Poldauf, I. (1967) 'The *Have* Construction', *Acta Universitatis Carolinae, Prague Studies in English* 12, 23–40
Poldauf, I. (1969) 'The So-Called Medio-Passive in English', *Acta Universitatis Carolinae, Prague Studies in English* 13, 15–34
Pope, E. N. (1976) *Questions and Answers in English*, The Hague: Mouton
Postal, P. (1971) 'On the Surface Verb "Remind"', in Fillmore and Langendoen (1971), 181–272
Postal, P. (1974) *On Raising*, Cambridge, Mass.: M.I.T. Press
Poutsma, H. (1926–29) *A Grammar of Late Modern English*, Groningen: Noordhoff
Powell, A. F. (1967) 'Forms and Uses of Nouns of Nationality', *English Language Teaching* 21, 159–165
Praninskas, J. (1968) *Trade Name Creation: Processes and Patterns*, The Hague: Mouton
Prentice-Hall (1974) *Words Into Type*, 3rd edn, Englewood Cliffs, N.J.: Prentice-Hall
Pullum, G. and D. Wilson (1977) 'Autonomous Syntax and the Analysis of Auxiliaries', *Language* 53, 741–788
Quirk, R. (1965) 'Descriptive Statement and Serial Relationship', *Language* 41, 205–217
Quirk, R. (1970a) 'Aspect and Variant Inflexion in English Verbs', *Language* 46, 300–311
Quirk, R. (1970b) 'Taking a Deep Smell', *Journal of Linguistics* 6, 119–124
Quirk, R. (1972) *The English Language and Images of Matter*, Oxford: University Press
Quirk, R. (1978) 'Grammatical and Pragmatic Aspects of Countability', *Die Neueren Sprachen* 78, 317–325
Quirk, R. (1981) 'A Problem of Modality', in *Forms and Functions*, edd J. Esser and A. Hübler, 93–96, Tübingen: Narr
Quirk, R. (1982) *Style and Communication in the English Language*, London: Arnold
Quirk, R. and D. Crystal (1966) 'On Scales of Contrast in Connected English Speech', in Bazell et al (1966), 359–369
Quirk, R. and A. P. Duckworth (1961) 'Co-existing Negative Preterite Forms of *Dare*', *Language and Society*, Copenhagen, 135–140: Det Berlingske Bogtrykkeri
Quirk, R., A. P. Duckworth, J. P. L. Rusiecki, J. Svartvik, and A. J. T. Colin (1964) 'Studies in the Correspondence of Prosodic to Grammatical Features in English', *Proceedings of the Ninth International Congress of Linguists*, 679–691, The Hague: Mouton
Quirk, R., S. Greenbaum, G. Leech, and J. Svartvik (1972) *A Grammar of Contemporary English*, London: Longman
Quirk, R. and J. Mulholland (1964) 'Complex Prepositions and Related Sequences', *English Studies* 45, 64–73
Radford, A. (1982) *Transformational Syntax: A Student's Guide to Chomsky's Extended Standard Theory*, Cambridge: University Press
Rando, E. and D. J. Napoli (1978) 'Definites in *there*-sentences', *Language* 54, 300–313
Raynaud, F. (1977) 'Noch einmal Modalverben!', *Deutsche Sprache* 5, 1–30
Reibel, D. A. and S. A. Schane (1969) (edd) *Modern Studies in English*, Englewood Cliffs, N.J.: Prentice-Hall
Reich, P. A. (1968) *The English Auxiliaries: A Relational Network Description*, Linguistic Automation Project, Yale University, New Haven, Conn.
Ringbom, H. (1975) (ed) *Style and Text*, Stockholm: Skriptor
Rivara, R. (1975) 'How Many Comparatives are There?', *Linguistics* 163, 35–51
Robbins, B. L. (1968) *The Definite Article in English Transformations*, The Hague: Mouton
Robins, R. H. (1980) *General Linguistics: An Introductory Survey*, 3rd edn, London: Longman
Roey, J. Van (1969) 'The Order of Post-Nominal Modifiers in Present-Day English', *English Studies* 50, 21–31

Roggero, J. (1967) '*Whose* et *of which*', *Les Langues Modernes* 61, 405–415
Romaine, S. (1980) 'The Relative Clause Marker in Scots English: Diffusion, Complexity, and Style as Dimensions of Syntactic Change', *Language in Society* 9, 221–247
Rosenbaum, P. S. (1967a) *The Grammar of English Predicate Complement Constructions*, Cambridge, Mass.: M.I.T. Press
Rosenbaum, P. S. (1967b) 'Phrase Structure Principles of English Complex Sentence Formation', *Journal of Linguistics* 3, 103–118
Ross, J. R. (1969) 'Auxiliaries as Main Verbs', in *Studies in Philosophical Linguistics* 1, ed W. Todd, 77–102, Evanston, Ill.: Great Expectations Press
Ross, J. R. (1973) 'A Fake NP Squish', in Bailey and Shuy (1973), 96–140
Rudanko, J. (1982) 'Towards a Description of Negatively Conditioned Subject Operator Inversion in English', *English Studies* 63, 348–359
Rusiecki, J. (1985) *Adjectives and Comparison in English: A Semantic Study*, London: Longman
Rydén, M. (1970) 'Determiners and Relative Clauses', *English Studies* 51, 1–6
Rydén, M. (1974) 'On Notional Relations in the Relative Clause Complex', *English Studies* 55, 542–545
Rydén, M. (1975) 'Noun-Name Collocations in British English Newspaper Language', *Studia Neophilologica* 47, 14–39
Sag, I. A. (1973) 'On the State of Progress on Progressives and Statives', in Bailey and Shuy (1973), 83–95
Sahlin, E. (1979) *'Some' and 'Any' in Spoken and Written English*, Studia Anglistica Upsaliensia 38, Stockholm: Almqvist and Wiksell
Sampson, R. (1980) 'Stress in English N + N Phrases', *English Studies* 61, 264–270
Sanders, G. A. (1977) 'A Functional Typology of Elliptical Coordinations', in *Current Themes in Linguistics*, ed F. Eckman, 241–270, Washington, D.C.: Hemisphere
Schachter, P. (1973) 'Focus and Relativization', *Language* 49, 19–46
Schachter, P. (1977) 'Constraints on Coordination', *Language* 53, 86–103
Scheffer, J. (1975) *The Progressive in English*, Amsterdam: North-Holland
Schenkein, J. (1978) (ed) *Studies in the Organization of Conversational Interaction*, New York: Academic Press
Scheurweghs, G. (1963–8) *Analytical Bibliography of Writings on Modern English Morphology and Syntax, 1877–1960*, 4 vols, Leuven: Nauwelaerts
Schiffrin, D. (1981) 'Tense Variation in Narrative', *Language* 57, 45–62
Schlesinger, I. M. (1979) 'Cognitive Structures and Semantic Deep Structures; the Case of the Instrumental', *Journal of Linguistics* 15, 307–324
Schmerling, S. F. (1976) *Aspects of English Sentence Stress*, Austin: University of Texas Press
Schopf, A. (1969) *Untersuchungen zur Wechselbeziehung zwischen Grammatik und Lexik im Englischen*, Berlin: de Gruyter
Schopf, A. (1984) *Das Verzeitungssystem des Englischen und seine Textfunktion*, Tübingen: Niemeyer
Schreiber, P. A. (1971) 'Some Constraints on the Formation of English Sentence Adverbs', *Linguistic Inquiry* 2, 83–101
Schreiber, P. A. (1972) 'Style Disjuncts and the Performative Analysis', *Linguistic Inquiry* 3, 321–347
Searle, J. R. (1969) *Speech Acts: An Essay in the Philosophy of Language*, Cambridge: University Press
Searle, J. R. (1979) *Expression and Meaning: Studies in the Theory of Speech Acts*, Cambridge: University Press
Sears, D. A. (1972) 'The Noun Adjuncts of Modern English', *Linguistics* 72, 31–60
Seppänen, A. (1974) *Proper Names in English: A Study in Semantics and Syntax*, Publications of the Department of English Philology 1, University of Tampere
Seppänen, A. (1975) 'On the Modern English "Adjective" *Own*', *Anglia* 93: 293–306

Seppänen, A. (1977) 'The Position of *Let* in the English Auxiliary System', *English Studies* 58, 515–529
Seppänen, A. (1978) 'Some Notes on the Construction "Adjective + *A* + Noun"', *English Studies* 59, 523–537
Seppänen, A. (1980) 'Possessive Pronouns in English?', *Studia Linguistica* 34, 7–22
Seppänen, A. (forthcoming a) 'The Dual and the Development of the Number System in English'
Seppänen, A. (forthcoming b) 'Cardinals and the Problem of Word-Classes in English', *Neuphilologische Mitteilungen*
Siegel, D. (1979) *Topics in English Morphology*, New York: Garland
Simon-Vandenbergen, A. M. (1981) *The Grammar of Headlines in the Times 1870–1970*, Turnhout: Brepols
Sinclair, J. McH. (1980) 'Discourse in Relation to Language Structure and Semiotics', in Greenbaum, Leech, and Svartvik (1980), 110–124
Sloat, C. (1969) 'Proper Nouns in English', *Language* 45, 26–30
Smaby, R. M. (1974) 'Subordinate Clauses and Assymetry in English', *Journal of Linguistics* 10, 235–269
Smith, C. S. (1961) 'A Class of Complex Modifiers in English', *Language* 37, 342–365
Smith, J. B. (1978) 'The Noun Phrase as Complement and as Adverbial Clause in Contemporary English', *English Studies* 59, 361–368
Sørensen, H. S. (1958) *Word-Classes in Modern English*, Copenhagen: Gad
Sørensen, H. S. (1959) 'The Function of the Definite Article in Modern English', *English Studies* 40, 401–420
Sørensen, H. S. (1964) 'On the Semantic Unity of the Perfect Tense', *English Studies* 45S, 74–83
Sørensen, K. (1979a) 'Co-ordinate Prepositions with a Single Complement', in Chesnutt et al (1979), 207–228
Sørensen, K. (1979b) 'Preposition + X + Complement', *English Studies* 60, 42–48
Sørensen, K. (1980) 'From Postmodification to Premodification', in Jacobson (1980b), 77–84
Sørensen, K. (1981) 'Determinative *that of* vs. Zero', in *Studies in English Language and Early Literature in Honour of Paul Christophersen*, ed P. M. Tilling, 137–146, Coleraine: The New University of Ulster
Soudek, L. (1967) *Structure of Substandard Words in British and American English*, Bratislava: SAV
Sroka, K. A. (1972) *The Syntax of English Phrasal Verbs*, The Hague: Mouton
Standwell, G. J. B. (1979) 'A Contrastive Study of the Modals of English and German', *IRAL* 17, 251–264
Stein, G. (1971) *Primäre und sekundäre Adjektive im Französischen und Englischen*, Tübingen: Narr
Stein, G. (1973) *English Word-Formation over Two Centuries*, Tübingen: Narr
Stein, G. (1976) 'The Imperative in English', *Anglo-American Forum* 5, 83–105
Stein, G. (1977) 'The Place of Word-formation in Linguistic Description', in *Perspektiven der Wortbildungsforschung*, edd H. E. Brekle and D. Kastovsky, 219–235, Bonn: Bouvier
Stein, G. (1979) *Studies in the Function of the Passive*, Tübingen: Narr
Stein, G. (1984) 'Champers, Preggers, Starkers: *-ers* in Present-Day English', *Navicular Tubigensis, Festschrift A. Tovar*, 353–357, Tübingen: Narr
Stockwell, R. P., P. Schachter, and B. Hall Partee (1973) *The Major Syntactic Structures of English*, New York: Holt, Rinehart and Winston
Storms, G. (1964) 'The Subjective and the Objective Form in Modern English', *English Studies* 45, 57–63
Storms, G. (1966) '*That*-Clauses in Modern English', *English Studies* 47, 249–270
Straumann, H. (1935) *Newspaper Headlines*, London: Allen and Unwin

Stubelius, S. (1962) 'The *You Will* Request; A Study on Intonation', in *Contributions to English Syntax and Philology*, Gothenburg Studies in English 14, Göteborg: Acta Universitatis Gothoburgensis
Summey, G. (1949) *American Punctuation*, New York: Ronald Press
Sussex, R. (1979) 'Deformed "Plural's" in English', *Papers in Linguistics* 12, 527–534
Svartengren, H. (1949) 'The -*'s*-Genitive of Non-Personal Nouns in Present-Day English', *Stockholm Studies in Modern Philology* 17, 139–180
Svartvik, J. (1966) *On Voice in the English Verb*, The Hague: Mouton
Svartvik, J. (1980) '*Well* in Conversation', in Greenbaum, Leech, and Svartvik (1980), 167–177
Svartvik, J. and O. Sager (1980) *Engelsk Universitetsgrammatik*, 2nd edn, Stockholm: Esselte Studium
Svartvik, J. and B. Törjas (1975) 'Rhythmic Variation in the Use of Time References', in Ringbom (1975), 416–432
Svartvik, J. and D. Wright (1977) 'The Use of *ought* in Teenage English', in Greenbaum (1977b), 179–202
Svoboda, A. (1968) 'The Hierarchy of Communicative Units and Fields as Illustrated by English Attributive Constructions', *Brno Studies in English* 7, 49–102
Swan, T. (1982) 'A Note on the Scope(s) of *Sadly*', *Studia Linguistica* 36, 131–140
Sweet, H. (1891–98) *A New English Grammar*, 2 Vols, Oxford: University Press
Taglicht, J. (1972) 'A New Look at English Relative Constructions', *Lingua* 29, 1–22
Taglicht, J. (1977) 'Relative Clauses as Postmodifiers: Meaning, Syntax and Intonation', in Bald and Ilson (1977), 73–108
Taglicht, J. (1982) 'Intonation and the Assessment of Information', *Journal of Linguistics* 18, 213–230
Taglicht, J. (1984) *Message and Emphasis: On Focus and Scope in English*, London: Longman
Talmy, L. (1978) 'Relations between Subordination and Coordination', in Greenberg, Ferguson, and Moravcsik (1978), 487–513
Tedeschi, P. and A. Zaenen (1981) (edd) *Syntax and Semantics* 14: *Tense and Aspect*, New York: Academic Press
Teyssier, J. (1968) 'Notes on the Syntax of the Adjective in Modern English', *Lingua* 20, 225–249
Thompson, S. A. (1972) '*Instead of* and *rather than* Clauses in English', *Journal of Linguistics* 8, 237–249
Thompson, S. A. (1973) 'On Subjectless Gerunds in English', *Foundations of Language* 10, 374–384
Thorne, J. P. (1966) 'English Imperative Sentences', *Journal of Linguistics* 2, 69–78
Thun, N. (1963) *Reduplicative Words in English. A Study of Formations of the Type* tick-tick, hurly-burly, *and* shilly-shally, Uppsala: Studentbok
Tottie, G. (1971) *HAVE TO. A Study of Usage and Acceptability in Present-Day British English*, Stockholm Theses in English 4
Tottie, G. (1974) 'On Promising in Swedish and English', *Papers from the First Scandinavian Conference of Linguistics*, University of Gothenburg: Department of Linguistics
Tottie, G. (1977) *Fuzzy Negation in English and Swedish*, Stockholm Studies in English 39, Stockholm: Almqvist and Wiksell
Tottie, G. (1978) 'Idioms with *have*? An Experimental Study of Negative Sentences with *have* in British and American English', in *Studies in English Philology, Linguistics and Literature Presented to Alarik Rynell*, 151–169, Stockholm Studies in English 46, Stockholm: Almqvist and Wiksell
Tottie, G. (1980) 'Affixal and Non-affixal Negation in English – Two Systems in (Almost) Complementary Distribution', *Studia Linguistica* 34, 101–123
Turner, G. W. (1972) 'The Grammar of Newspaper Headlines Containing the

Preposition *on* in the Sense "about"', *Linguistics* 87, 71–86
Turner, J. F. (1980) 'The Marked Subjunctive in Contemporary English', *Studia Neophilologica* 52, 271–277
Twaddell, W. F. (1965) *The English Verb Auxiliaries*, 2nd edn, Providence, R.I.: Brown University Press
Uldall, E. (1971) 'Isochronous Stresses in RP', in *Form and Substance. Phonetic and Linguistic Papers Presented to Eli Fischer-Jørgensen*, edd L. L. Hammerich, R. Jakobson, and E. Zwirner, Copenhagen: Akademisk Forlag
University of Chicago Press (1982) *A Manual of Style*, 13th edn, Chicago: University of Chicago Press
Urdang, L. (1978) (ed) *Verbatim* I and II, Essex, Conn.: Verbatim
Ureland, S. (1973) *Verb Complementation in Swedish and Other Germanic Languages. Studies in Comparative Syntax*, Stockholm: Skriptor
U.S. Government Printing Office (1973) *Style Manual*, revised edn, Washington, D.C.: U.S. Government Printing Office
Vachek, J., see Mathesius (1975)
Valdman, A. (1977) (ed) *Pidgin and Creole Linguistics,* Bloomington: Indiana University Press
Vendler, Z. (1957) 'Verbs and Times', *Philosophical Review* 56, 143–160
Vendler, Z. (1968) *Adjectives and Nominalizations*, The Hague: Mouton
Vestergaard, T. (1977) *Prepositional Phrases and Prepositional Verbs*, The Hague: Mouton
Visser, F. T. (1963–1973) *An Historical Syntax of the English Language*, Leiden: Brill
Von Wright, G. H. (1951) *An Essay on Modal Logic*, Amsterdam: North-Holland
Vorlat, E. (1979) (ed) *Analytical Bibliography of Writings on Modern English Morphology and Syntax* 5, Leuven: University Press Editions, Nauwelaerts
Waida, T. (1979) 'On Focusing: Information Focus at the Clause-Initial Subject', *Letters and Essays* 12, 23–50
Wales, K. (1980) 'Exophora Re-examined: the Uses of the Personal Pronoun *we* in Present-Day English', *UEA Papers in Linguistics* 12, 21–44, Norwich: University of East Anglia
Warren, B. (1978) *Semantic Patterns of Noun-Noun Compounds*, Gothenburg Studies in English 41, Göteborg: Acta Universitatis Gothoburgensis
Warren, B. (1982) 'New Ideas Concerning Adjectives', *Studia Neophilologica* 54, 169–178
Warren, B. (1984) *Classifying Adjectives*, Gothenburg Studies in English 56, Göteborg: Acta Universitatis Gothoburgensis
Waugh, L. R. and C. H. Van Schooneveld (1980) *The Melody of Language*, Baltimore: University Park Press
Webster, J. (1977) 'A Corpus-Based Exploration of Prepositional Phrases Post-Modifying Verbally-Related Heads', in Bald and Ilson (1977), 109–124
Webster (1976) *6000 Words, A Supplement to Webster's Third New International Dictionary*, Springfield: Merriam
Weisler, S. (1980) 'The Syntax of *That*-less Relatives', *Linguistic Inquiry* 11, 624–630
Wekker, H. C. (1976) *The Expression of Future Time in Contemporary British English*, Amsterdam: North-Holland
Wells, G. (1979) 'Learning and Using the Auxiliary Verb in English', in *Language Development*, ed V. J. Lee, 250–270, London: Croom Helm
Wentworth, H. and S. B. Flexner (1975) *Dictionary of American Slang*, 2nd supplemented edn, New York: Crowell
Whitcut, J. (1980) 'The Language of Address', in Michaels and Ricks (1980), 89–97
Widdowson, H. G. (1979) *Explorations in Applied Linguistics*, Oxford: University Press
Wierzbicka, A. (1982) 'Why can you *have a drink* when you can't **have an eat*?', *Language* 58, 753–799
Williams, J. M. (1979) 'Defining Complexity', *College English* 40, 595–690

Winter, E. O. (1979) 'Replacement as a Fundamental Function of the Sentence in Context', *Forum Linguisticum* 4, 95–133
Winter, E. O. (1982) *Towards a Contextual Grammar of English*, London: Allen and Unwin
Winterowd, W. Ross (1975) *Contemporary Rhetoric*, New York: Harcourt Brace Jovanovich
Witton, N. D. (1979) 'The Classification of English Phrasal and Prepositional Verbs', *Working Papers of the Speech and Language Research Centre Macquarie University* 2, 1–30, North Ryde, New South Wales: Macquarie University
Wonder, J. P. (1970) 'Ambiguity and the English Gerund', *Lingua* 25, 254–267
Wood, F. T. (1955/6) 'Further Thoughts on the Pronouns in *-self*', *English Language Teaching* 10, 97–108
Wood, F. T. (1959) '*Fairly*, *rather* and *pretty* as Adverbs of Degree', *Moderna Språk* 53, 372–381
Wyler, S. (1979) 'Some Remarks on the Nature of Left-Branching Structures', *English Studies* 60, 505–515
Yamanashi, M.-A. (1973) 'Where Do Conditional Expressions Qualify?', in *Analyzing Variation in Language*, edd R. W. Fasold and R. W. Shuy, 228–240, Washington, D.C.: Georgetown University Press
Yanofsky, N. M. (1978) 'NP Utterances', in *Papers from the 14th Regional Meeting of the Chicago Linguistic Society*, 491–502, University of Chicago
Yasui, M. (1979) *Current Bibliography of Linguistics and English Linguistics 1960–1978*, Tokyo: Kaitakusha
Yasui, M. (1983) *Current Bibliography of Linguistics and English Linguistics 1978–1982*, Tokyo: Kaitakusha
Yee, C. T. S. (1975) 'Sequence Signals in Technical English', *RELC Journal* 6, 63–101
Yngve, V. (1961) 'The Depth Hypothesis', in *Proceedings of the American Philosophical Society* 12, 130–138
Young, D. (1980) *The Structure of English Clauses*, London: Hutchinson
Young, R. E., A. L. Becker, and K. L. Pike (1970) *Rhetoric: Discovery and Change*, New York: Harcourt Brace Jovanovich
Zandvoort, R. W. (1961) '"I Found Myself Walking" (An Essay in Syntactic Substitution)', *English Language Teaching* 16, 19–24
Zandvoort, R. W. (1962) 'Is "Aspect" an English Verbal Category?' in *Contributions to English Syntax and Philology*, Gothenburg Studies in English 14, Göteborg: Acta Universitatis Gothoburgensis
Zandvoort, R. W. (1963) '"May have" for "might have"', *English Studies* 44, 447–448
Zandvoort, R. W. (1975) *A Handbook of English Grammar*, 7th edn, London: Longman
Zandvoort, R. W. and A. C. J. Doodkorte (1962), 'On the Stressing of Prepositions', *English Studies* 43, 1–7
Zimmer, K. E. (1964) *Affixal Negation in English and Other Languages*, Supplement to *Word* 20, Monograph 5, New York: Linguistic Circle
Zimmer, K. E. (1971) 'Some General Observations about Nominal Compounds', *Stanford Working Papers on Language Universals* 5, 1–24, Stanford University
Zwicky, A. M. (1970) 'Auxiliary Reduction in English', *Linguistic Inquiry* 1, 323–336
Zwicky, A. M. (1974) 'Hey, Whatsyourname!', *Papers from the Tenth Regional Meeting of the Chicago Linguistic Society*, 787–801, University of Chicago
Zwicky, A. M. and G. K. Pullum (1983) 'Cliticization vs. Inflection: English *n't*', *Language* 59, 502–513

Index

The alphabetical arrangement of the index is word-by-word. Three kinds of entry are included: abbreviations for grammatical categories used in the *Comprehensive*; lexical items which have been treated within classified lists, or which have been the focus of discussion; and general concepts. Where homonymy occurs, abbreviations precede lexical items, which precede general concepts. Head words are assigned word-class labels where necessary, to avoid ambiguity.

In all entries, references are to section numbers, not pages. A reference to a section implies reference to any Notes accompanying that section. Where n follows a section number, the reference is to the Note(s) alone. Major references are given in italics. Cross-reference to another entry is indicated by (→).

Within lexical entries, single word items are given first, sometimes followed by subheadings concerned with usage. Multi-word or inflectionally derived forms follow these in parentheses, the items being arranged alphabetically in run-on paragraphs. Parentheses within parentheses enclose optional elements.

In multi-word items, the symbol (~) is used to indicate the place of the head word or morpheme: for example, under *speak*, (~ *about*) should be read as *speak about*; (*so to* ~) should be read as *so to speak*; and (*to* ~ *of*) should be read as *to speak of*. The ~ symbol is also used before bound morphemes: for example, under *absolute*, (~*ly*) should be read as *absolutely*. (. . .) refers to an unspecified part of a construction: for example, under *though*, (~ . . .) refers to a construction beginning with the word *though* and followed by a wide range of possibilities; under *before*, (. . . ~) refers to a construction ending with the word *before* and preceded by a wide range of possibilities.

A

B

C

D

E

F

G

H

I

J

K

L

M

N

O

Q

R

S

U

V

W

X

Y

Z